ROGET'S
21ST CENTURY THESAURUS
Second Edition

ROGET'S
—21ST—
CENTURY
THESAURUS

Second Edition

IN DICTIONARY FORM

*The Essential Reference for Home,
School, or Office*

EDITED BY THE PRINCETON LANGUAGE INSTITUTE
BARBARA ANN KIPFER, PH.D., HEAD LEXICOGRAPHER

Produced by The Philip Lief Group, Inc.

A DELL BOOK

Published by
Dell Publishing
a division of
Random House, Inc.
1540 Broadway
New York, New York 10036

Published by arrangement with
The Philip Lief Group, Inc.

ISBN: 0-440-23513-8

Reprinted by arrangement with Delacorte Press

Printed in the United States of America

Published simultaneously in Canada

July 1999

10 9 8

OPM

CONTENTS

PREFACE

More than ever before, our language and our ideas about language are changing as rapidly as the world around us. Our Information Age has been made possible, of course, by the ever-expanding technology of computers and the extraordinary explosion of information from the Internet and World Wide Web. We are receiving more information than we had ever imagined possible.

But how do we process this information—and articulate it in speech and writing? With expanded research and development of artificial intelligence systems, we have been able to examine more closely the complex cognitive relationships human beings form between their ideas and the words they choose. We now know more about how this process works, and how it can be re-created. Learning from this, current lexicographical research must go beyond traditional methods and techniques to develop effective and contemporary reference materials for students, linguists, and writers.

Most people learn a new word by guessing, based on context, what that word means. Recent studies on students' ability to develop reference skills bear this out. Combining this proven pattern with the advanced theories of language gained through electronic media, we have arrived at an "onomasiological" approach to understanding American English. That is, we are capable of traveling successfully from a meaning to a word instead of the straightforward dictionary approach of going from word to meaning. Onomasiologically, readers move from the concepts of "yellow" and "flower" to a selection of words that describe the combination, or from the notion of a "positive state of mind" to its qualities, actions, and conditions.

We have searched for a method of presenting this lexical theory in a format that provides diversified access to words within one resource. In *Roget's 21st Century Thesaurus, Second Edition,* the text is designed to do just that: allowing users to search both from word to meaning and from meaning to word. The dictionary format is familiar to use, and the Concept Index provides helpful links between words as it illustrates the language's semantic structure. The A to Z listings further amplify the resonances between words with their parts of speech and different sense divisions.

This second edition of *Roget's 21st Century Thesaurus* has almost 3,000 new headwords reflecting the dynamic changes in our language and the fabric of our lives. It continues as the most complete and comprehensive selection of synonyms published in print media today.

BARBARA ANN KIPFER, PH.D.

INTRODUCTION

The history of *Roget's Thesaurus* is a long and fascinating one. It began in 1805, when P. M. Roget, a British surgeon and inventor, took up a peculiar hobby: the classification of words according to ideas. He hoped to create a kind of verbal catalogue that would assist writers and linguists in their search for the right expression. His work was perhaps inspired by two earlier texts: the ancient Sanskrit *Amarakosha,* arguably the first arrangement of words by subject, and the French *Pasigraphie* (published in 1797), which was an attempt to order words so they could be understood universally, without translation. Roget called his own work a "thesaurus"—a Latin word meaning "treasury" or "storehouse of knowledge."

Gradually, Roget's casual pastime became his lifelong passion. In 1852, some forty-seven years of work culminated in the publication of Roget's *Thesaurus of English Words and Phrases, Classified and Arranged so as to Facilitate the Expression of Ideas and Assist in Literary Composition.* This new reference book (published when Roget was seventy-three) became enormously popular, and a second edition was published only a year after the first. By the time of his death in 1869, there had been twenty-eight editions and printings. Today, his name is literally "synonymous" with the thesaurus.

RENOVATING THE ORIGINAL THESAURUS

Although Roget's original idea was brilliant, his thesaurus assumed that all users shared the compiler's ideas about language. Its classifications and indexes presented a labyrinth of possibilities in which each route could end in a disappointing or inappropriate selection of synonyms. The classification of terms made the text almost impenetrable and forced the reader to rely on the index, which did not even include every synonym. All too often, the right word remained elusive, or the thesaurus remained on the shelf. And today, Roget's nineteenth-century thesaurus is difficult for many twenty-first-century readers to use or even understand.

For over a century, thesaurus editors have strived to redefine the nature and function of the thesaurus. Essentially, their goal has been to present accurate information in a highly usable format. Attempts to improve Roget's thesaurus began with Roget's own son, John Lewis, who expanded the selection of synonyms. Later, Thomas Y. Crowell acquired publishing rights to the thesaurus. His 1886 edition of *Roget's* provided a clearer page design and format that enhanced the book's readability. Subsequent generations of Crowells have added Americanisms, foreign expressions, slang and nonstandard speech, prefixes, suffixes, and quotations. Although these changes were indeed improvements, *Roget's* original structure of categories, cross-references, and indexes actually became *more* complicated by the addition of an elaborately conceived type design, boldface entries, numbered paragraphs, and a decimal system that required an explanatory diagram.

One of the most important breakthroughs in the evolution of the thesaurus came in the early twentieth century when C. O. Sylvester Mawson attempted to simplify and reorganize

Roget's Thesaurus into a dictionary-like format. Roget's original work and the early revisions had not been arranged alphabetically. In 1911, Mawson radically changed the book's organization by issuing his alphabetical presentation of the famous Roget system. Twentieth-century editors quickly followed his lead, eager to find an easier method for frustrated thesaurus users.

Even with this improvement, the thesaurus still lacked something, for it did not suggest any relationships between words beyond the simple group of synonyms listed with a main entry. Although it did offer a more straightforward presentation than the index-reliant *Roget's*, it neither helped users organize thoughts nor provided broad conceptual links between ideas as expressed through language in words.

A THESAURUS FOR THE NEW MILLENNIUM

Roget's 21st Century Thesaurus achieved what no other thesaurus has been able to do: combine the simplicity of the dictionary format with the utility of arranging words according to ideas. This revolutionary design has become the new standard for thesaurus users. It is, simultaneously, a fast and efficient handbook for writers and a medium to facilitate the expression of ideas—both of Roget's original objectives brought forward and reinterpreted for the twenty-first-century user.

This second edition of *Roget's 21st Century Thesaurus* has been electronically compiled using state-of-the-art techniques. It lists approximately 20,000 main entries, or headwords, in alphabetical order. These generate over 500,000 synonyms—more than any other thesaurus in dictionary form.

Reflecting the most recent changes in language, *Roget's 21st Century Thesaurus, Second Edition* is the most contemporary and useful thesaurus in history. The final selection of main entry words and synonyms was derived with today's practices of speaking and writing in mind. Reflecting contemporary usage, obsolete terms have been replaced by timely words and phrases. You will find terms from all areas of our experience, particularly the high-tech world of computers (such as "hacker," "computerese," "on-line," and "artificial intelligence"), the Internet and World Wide Web ("cyberpunk," "chat room"), video and multimedia ("telecast," "digital library"), medicine ("AIDS," "attention deficit disorder"), political and civil spheres ("politically correct," "affirmative action," "out of the closet"), the environment ("ecosystem"), and money and business ("mutual fund," "desk jockey"). A nonsexist, nonracist approach to language replaces outmoded epithets. Foreign words and phrases that reflect our global consciousness have been included ("au pair," "schlemiel"), as well as hundreds of Americanisms ("psyched," "rubberneck"). Synonyms that represent colloquial or slang terms are marked with an asterisk.

Roget's 21st Century Thesaurus, Second Edition is not just ultra-contemporary but also eminently usable. Drawing upon computer technology and recent innovations in typesetting and design, the pages are printed in a highly readable and contemporary format so the reader can make quick and effective choices. The synonym lists are not littered with cross-references, usage labels, or abbreviations, all of which can come between the user and the words themselves. Like main entries, the synonym lists are arranged in alphabetical order, completely objective, and not prescriptive, leaving the user to choose from the wealth of synonym choices available.

USING *ROGET'S 21ST CENTURY THESAURUS, SECOND EDITION*

The book's sensible format ensures swift access to the right alternatives. For quick identification, each headword in the A to Z listing is printed in boldface; its part of speech follows in bracketed italics. Some headwords have more than one listing; separate entries are included for each different part of speech—adjectives, nouns, and verbs, as well as adverbs, conjunctions, and prepositions. "Pass," for example, has thirteen entries—four noun forms and nine verb forms. Each sense of the word "pass" is treated individually to help writers pinpoint the precise sense of the word desired.

Concise definitions accompany the headwords, supplying users with a basic reference point and helping them to evaluate synonym choices. Semicolons sometimes appear within definitions to denote fine points of sense for a word's particular usage when the differences are too subtle to warrant a separate entry.

Remember that no two words mean exactly the same thing. No two words are directly interchangeable. It is the subtle nuance and flavor of particular words that give the English language its rich and varied texture. We turn to a thesaurus to find different, more expressive ways of speaking and writing, but we must turn to a dictionary, a sophisticated semantic tool, to determine meaning. Always consider synonyms in their desired context and consult a dictionary if you have any doubt about the application of a word or phrase.

USING THE CONCEPT INDEX

The entries in *Roget's 21st Century Thesaurus, Second Edition* are enriched by directing users to related concepts in the Concept Index. This unique index offers users an up-to-the-minute language hierarchy that bridges the gap between thought and expression. The Concept Index actually helps writers organize their thoughts by generating possibilities for millions of word choices—far beyond the capabilities of a traditional thesaurus.

Each of the book's approximately 20,000 headwords is referenced to at least one of the 837 individually numbered concepts in the index. The words "SEE CONCEPT(S)" appear in small caps at the end of a main entry, followed by the numbers for all relevant concepts for that word. When an initial search does not yield the desired results, the Concept Index automatically provides users with alternative places to look.

For example, if none of the synonyms listed with the word "scintillating" seems appropriate, the Concept Index directs the writer to concepts #401, "attributes of behavior"; #529, "cognitive qualities"; and #617, "visual brightness." Each concept gathers together scores of headwords that share the same characteristics. Persistent writers or linguists can turn back to the A to Z listing to find the synonyms for any of these headwords, allowing them to locate even more word choices.

The Concept Index follows the alphabetical listing of headwords and begins with a reference key. The concepts appear in the index in numerical order and are divided into ten overarching categories of interest: Actions, Causes, Fields of Human Activity, Life Forms, Objects, The Planet, Qualities, Senses, States, and Weights and Measures. All headwords grouped under a specific concept are ordered alphabetically and by different parts of speech, if applicable.

The most advanced theories of communication and learning available have been used to determine concept names and classifications. The word hierarchies in *Roget's 21st Century Thesaurus, Second Edition* have been streamlined into categories that reflect contemporary ways of thinking. It is clear what concepts mean and how they are organized. Whether performing a speedy search through the concepts or entering the index with just a vague notion in mind, users will find the Concept Index to be a fast and reliable research tool.

A CLASSIC FOR TODAY AND TOMORROW

In the minds of writers and linguists, Roget has always been the trademark of a dependable thesaurus. As we enter an era unimagined by P. M. Roget two hundred years ago, *Roget's 21st Century Thesaurus, Second Edition* upholds that reputation. Adapting Roget's thesaurus to reflect today's concerns, this new text represents a fresh and vital reference of American English.

ROGET'S
21ST CENTURY THESAURUS
Second Edition

A

aback [*adv*] *taken unawares*
confused, surprised, thrown off, thrown off guard*; SEE CONCEPT *403*

abaft [*adj*] *to the rear*
astern, back, behind, rearward; SEE CONCEPTS *586,820*

abandon [*n*] *careless disregard for consequences*
disregard, freedom, impulse, licentiousness, recklessness, spontaneity, thoughtlessness, uninhibitedness, unrestraint, wantonness, wildness; SEE CONCEPTS *633,645*

abandon [*v1*] *leave behind, relinquish*
abdicate, back out, bail out*, bow out*, chicken out*, cop out*, cut loose*, desert, discard, discontinue, ditch*, drop, drop out, duck*, dump*, dust*, flake out*, fly the coop*, give up the ship*, kiss goodbye*, leave, leg it*, let go, opt out, pull out, quit, run out on, screw*, ship out, stop, storm out*, surrender, take a powder*, take a walk*, throw over*, vacate, walk out on, wash hands of*, withdraw, yield; SEE CONCEPT *195*

abandon [*v2*] *leave in troubled state*
back out, desert, disown, forsake, jilt, leave, leave behind, quit, reject, renounce, throw over*, walk out on; SEE CONCEPTS *7,19,195*

abandoned [*adj*] *left alone, deserted*
alone, cast aside, cast away, deserted, discarded, dissipated, dropped, dumped, eighty-sixed*, eliminated, empty, forgotten, forsaken, given up, godforsaken*, jilted, left, left in the cold*, left in the lurch*, neglected, on the rocks*, outcast, passed up*, pigeon-holed*, rejected, relinquished, shunned, sidelined*, side-tracked*, unoccupied, vacant, vacated; SEE CONCEPT *577*

abandoned [*adj2*] *free from moral restraint; uninhibited*
corrupt, depraved, dissolute, immoral, incontinent, incorrigible, licentious, profligate, shameless, sinful, uncontrolled, unprincipled, unrestrained, wanton, wicked; SEE CONCEPT *545*

abase [*v*] *deprive of self-esteem, confidence*
belittle, debase, degrade, demean, diminish, disgrace, dishonor, humble, humiliate, lower, mortify, reduce, shame; SEE CONCEPTS *7,19*

abasement [*n*] *disgrace*
degradation, dishonor, downgrade, humiliation, shame; SEE CONCEPT *388*

abashed [*adj*] *exhibiting mental discomfort, ill at ease*
ashamed, bewildered, bugged*, chagrined, confounded, confused, crushed, discombobulated*, disconcerted, embarrassed, fazed*, fuddled, humbled, humiliated, in a tizzy*, mortified, rattled, shamed, taken aback; SEE CONCEPT *403*

abate [*v*] *lessen, grow or cause to grow less*
allay, chill out*, coast*, cool, cool it*, decline, decrease, diminish, dull, dwindle, ebb, go with the flow*, hang easy*, hang loose*, lay back*, let go, let it all hang out*, let up, mellow out*, moderate, quell, recede, reduce, slacken, slow, subdue, subside, take it easy*, taper, taper off, unlax*, wane; SEE CONCEPTS *240,698*

abbey [*n*] *building that houses monks, nuns, or priests; church*
cloister, convent, friary, ministry, monastery, nunnery, priory, temple; SEE CONCEPTS *368,439*

abbreviate [*v1*] *shorten*
abridge, abstract, boil down*, clip, compress, condense, contract, cut, cut back, cut down, cut off, cut out, digest, encapsulate, get to the meat*, pare, prune, put in a nutshell*, reduce, summarize, take out, trim; SEE CONCEPTS *236,247*

abbreviate [*v2*] *cut short an activity*
abort, curtail, restrict, stop short, truncate; SEE CONCEPT *234*

abbreviation [*n*] *something shortened*
abridgement, abstract, abstraction, clipping, compendium, compression, condensation, contraction, digest, outline, precis, reduction, sketch, summary, syllabus, synopsis; SEE CONCEPTS *283,652*

abdicate [*v*] *give up a right, position, or power*
abandon, abjure, abnegate, bag it*, bail out*, cede, demit, drop, forgo, give up, leave, leave high and dry*, leave holding the bag*, leave in the lurch*, opt out*, quit, quitclaim, relinquish, renounce, resign, retire, sell out*, step down, surrender, vacate, waive, withdraw, yield; SEE CONCEPTS *133,298*

abdomen [*n*] *the stomach and area directly below in an animate being*
bay window*, belly, bowels, breadbasket*, corporation, gut*, guts, intestines, middle, midriff, midsection, paunch, pot*, potbelly*, spare tire*, tummy, venter, viscera; SEE CONCEPT *393*

abdominal [*adj*] *concerning the stomach and the area below it*
belly, duodenal, gastric, intestinal, stomachic, ventral, visceral; SEE CONCEPT *393*

abduct [*v*] *take by force and without permission*
carry off, dognap*, grab, kidnap, make off with, put the snatch on*, remove, seize, shanghai*, snatch, sneeze*, spirit away*; SEE CONCEPT *139*

abducted [*adj*] *taken away by force*
appropriated, kidnapped, seized, snatched, stolen; SEE CONCEPTS *90,139*

abduction [*n*] *taking away by force*
appropriation, kidnapping, rape, seizure, theft; SEE CONCEPTS *90,139*

abend [*n*] *abnormal end of task*
abort, crash, loss; SEE CONCEPTS *658,674*

aberrant [*adj*] *not normal; varying from the usual*
abnormal, atypical, bizarre, deviant, different, flaky*, mental*, nonstandard, odd, off-base, off-color, out of line*, peculiar, psycho*, strange, unusual, weird; SEE CONCEPT *547*

aberration [*n1*] *state of abnormality*
delusion, eccentricity, oddity, peculiarity, quirk, strangeness, weirdness; SEE CONCEPT *647*

aberration [*n2*] *different from that expected*
departure, deviation, difference, distortion, divergence, diversion, irregularity, lapse, straying, wandering; SEE CONCEPT *665*

abet [*v*] *assist, help in wrongdoing*
advocate, back, condone, egg on*, encourage, endorse, goad, incite, instigate, prod, promote, provoke, sanction, spur, support, urge; SEE CONCEPTS *14,110*

abettor [*n*] *assistant*
accessory, accomplice, co-conspirator, confederate, cooperator, helper, partner in crime*, second, supporter; SEE CONCEPT *348*

abeyance [*n*] *being inactive or suspended temporarily*
deferral, discontinuation, dormancy, inactivity,

intermission, latency, postponement, quiescence, recess, remission, suspension, waiting; SEE CONCEPTS *681,705*

abhor [*v*] *regard with contempt or disgust*
abominate, be allergic to*, be down on*, be grossed out by*, despise, detest, hate, have no use for*, loathe, scorn; SEE CONCEPT *29*

abhorrence [*n*] *disgust*
detestation, enmity, hate, hatred, horror, loathing, malice, odium, repugnance, revulsion; SEE CONCEPTS *485,548*

abhorrent [*adj*] *disgusting*
despicable, detestable, execrable, loathsome, offensive, repulsive, revolting; SEE CONCEPTS *485,548*

abide [*v1*] *submit to, put up with*
accept, acknowledge, bear, bear with*, be big about*, concede, consent, defer, endure, hang in*, hang in there*, hang tough*, live with*, put up with*, receive, sit tight*, stand, stand for, stomach, suffer, swallow, take, tolerate, withstand; SEE CONCEPTS *23,35*

abide [*v2*] *live in a certain place*
bide, bunk*, bunk out*, crash*, dwell, hang out*, inhabit, lodge, nest, perch, reside, room, roost, settle, squat, stay; SEE CONCEPT *226*

abide [*v3*] *remain or continue in a state*
continue, endure, keep on, last, persevere, persist, remain, survive; SEE CONCEPTS *23,239*

abide [*v4*] *stop temporarily and wait for*
anticipate, bide, expect, linger, pause, remain, rest, sojourn, stay, stick around*, stop, tarry, wait; SEE CONCEPTS *119,681*

abiding [*adj*] *continuing or existing for an indefinite time*
constant, continuing, enduring, eternal, everlasting, fast, indissoluble, lasting, permanent, perpetual, persistent, persisting, steadfast, steady; SEE CONCEPT *551*

ability [*n1*] *power to act, perform*
aptitude, capability, capacity, competence, competency, comprehension, dexterity, endowment, facility, faculty, intelligence, might, potentiality, qualification, resourcefulness, skill, strength, talent, understanding; SEE CONCEPT *630*

ability [*n2*] *natural or acquired power in a particular activity*
adeptness, adroitness, bent, capability, cleverness, command, craft, deftness, expertise, expertness, finesse, flair, genius, gift, handiness, ingenuity, knack, know-how, mastery, mind for, proficiency, savvy, skill, skillfulness, strength, talent, the goods*, the right stuff*, what it takes*; SEE CONCEPT *706*

abject [*adj*] *hopeless and downtrodden*
base, contemptible, degraded, dejected, deplorable, dishonorable, fawning, forlorn, groveling, hangdog, humiliated, low, miserable, outcast, pitiable, servile, submissive, worthless, wretched; SEE CONCEPT *571*

abjure [*v*] *give up*
abstain from, forswear, recant, renege, renounce, retract, take back, withdraw; SEE CONCEPTS *30,54,195*

ablate [*v*] *wear away*
erode, evaporate, melt, vaporize; SEE CONCEPTS *252,469*

ablaze [*adj1*] *on fire*
afire, aflame, alight, blazing, burning, confla-

grant, fiery, flaming, flaring, ignited, lighted; SEE CONCEPTS *485,605*

ablaze [*adj2*] *very excited*
afire, angry, aroused, enthusiastic, fervent, frenzied, fuming, furious, heated, impassioned, incensed, intense, on fire, passionate, raging, stimulated, vehement; SEE CONCEPT *550*

ablaze [*adj3*] *brightly illuminated*
aflame, aglow, brilliant, flashing, gleaming, glowing, incandescent, luminous, radiant, refulgent, sparkling; SEE CONCEPT *617*

able [*adj1*] *capable of performing; having an innate capacity*
adept, adequate, adroit, agile, alert, apt, bright, capable, competent, cunning, deft, dexterous, easy, effortless, endowed, equipped, facile, fitted, good, intelligent, knowing, powerful, ready, smart, strong, worthy; SEE CONCEPTS *402,527*

able [*adj2*] *able to perform well; having a proven capacity*
accomplished, adroit, agile, artful, au fait, brilliant, capable, clever, deft, dexterous, effective, effectual, efficient, equal to, experienced, expert, facile, gifted, ingenious, intelligent, keen, know backwards and forwards*, know one's onions*, know the ropes*, learned, masterful, masterly, powerful, practiced, prepared, proficient, qualified, responsible, savvy, sharp, skilled, skillful, smart, talented, there*, trained, up to it*, up to snuff*, up to speed*, with it*; SEE CONCEPTS *402,528*

able-bodied [*adj*] *physically strong and capable*
firm, fit, hale, hardy, healthy, hearty, lusty, powerful, robust, staunch, stout, strapping*, sturdy, vigorous; SEE CONCEPTS *314,489*

ablution [*n*] *washing*
bath, cleansing, decontamination, lavation, purification, shower, showering; SEE CONCEPTS *161,165*

ably [*adv*] *capably*
adroitly, capably, competently; SEE CONCEPT *527*

abnegate [*v*] *renounce*
abstain, decline, forbear, forgo, give up, refrain, reject; SEE CONCEPTS *30,54,195*

abnegation [*n*] *denial, renouncement of something*
abandonment, abstinence, eschewal, forbearance, giving up, nixing, refusal, rejection, relinquishment, renunciation, sacrifice, self-denial, stonewall*, surrender, temperance; SEE CONCEPTS *18,25*

abnormal [*adj*] *different from standard or norm*
aberrant, anomalistic, anomalous, atypical, bizarre, curious, deviant, deviate, deviating, divergent, eccentric, exceptional, extraordinary, fantastic, funny, grody*, gross, heteroclite, heterodox, heteromorphic, irregular, odd, off-base, off-color, out of line, peculiar, preternatural, queer, screwy*, spastic*, strange, uncommon, unexpected, unnatural, unorthodox, unusual, weird; SEE CONCEPT *547*

abnormality [*n*] *being different from standard or norm*
aberrancy, aberration, anomalism, anomaly, atypicalness, bizarreness, deformity, deviance, deviancy, deviation, eccentricity, exception, extraordinariness, flaw, irregularity, oddity, peculiarity, preternaturalness, singularity, strangeness, uncommonness, unnaturalness, unusualness, weirdness; SEE CONCEPT *647*

aboard [*adj*] *on or in a transportation object*
boarded, consigned, embarked, en route, in transit, loaded, on, on board, traveling; SEE CONCEPT 583

abode [*n*] *building or place where one resides*
address, apartment, base, casa, condo, co-op, crash pad*, crib*, den, digs*, domicile, dwelling, flat, flop*, habitat, haunt, headquarters, hearth, hole*, home, homestead, house, joint*, lodging, pad, quarters, residence, roost*, sanctuary, seat; SEE CONCEPT 515

abolish [*v*] *do away with or put an end to*
abate, abrogate, annihilate, annul, call off, cancel, destroy, disestablish, dissolve, end, eradicate, erase, expunge, extinguish, extirpate, finish, inhibit, invalidate, kill, negate, nix, nullify, obliterate, overthrow, overturn, prohibit, put an end to, put kibosh on*, put the kibosh on*, quash, repeal, repudiate, rescind, revoke, scrub*, set aside, squelch, stamp out, subvert, supersede, suppress, terminate, undo, vacate, vitiate, void, wipe out, zap*; SEE CONCEPTS 121,252,298

abolition [*n*] *formal act of putting an end to, annulling*
abolishment, abrogation, annihilation, annulment, cancellation, destruction, dissolution, elimination, end, ending, eradication, extirpation, invalidation, negation, nullification, obliteration, overthrow, overturning, quashing, repeal, repudiation, rescinding, rescindment, rescission, revocation, subversion, suppression, termination, voiding, wiping out, withdrawal; SEE CONCEPTS 121,252,298

abolitionist [*n*] *person wanting something ended*
activist, advocate, opponent, revolutionary; SEE CONCEPT 366

A-bomb [*n*] *atomic bomb*
nuclear bomb, nuclear weapon, physics package*, thermonuclear bomb; SEE CONCEPT 500

abominable [*adj*] *awful, detestable*
abhorrent, atrocious, awful, bad, base, beastly, contemptible, cursed, despicable, disgusting, foul, grim, grody*, gross*, hairy*, hateful, heinous, hellish, horrible, horrid, loathsome, lousy, nauseating, obnoxious, odious, offensive, repellent, reprehensible, repugnant, repulsive; revolting, rotten, sleazy*, stinking, terrible, vile, wretched; SEE CONCEPTS 29,544,571

abominate [*v*] *detest*
abhor, despise, dislike, hate, loathe; SEE CONCEPT 29

abomination [*n1*] *object of extreme dislike, hate*
anathema, aversion, bother, curse, detestation, evil, horror, nuisance, plague, shame, torment; SEE CONCEPTS 29,666

abomination [*n2*] *wrongdoing*
crime, offense, wrong; SEE CONCEPT 691

aboriginal [*adj*] *belonging to one, existing in a place since prehistory*
ancient, earliest, endemic, first, indigenous, native, original, primary, primeval, primitive, primordial; SEE CONCEPT 549

aborigine [*n*] *first inhabitant*
aboriginal, autochthon, bushman*, indigene, native, primitive; SEE CONCEPT 413

abort [*v1*] *stop or cancel something*
arrest, break off, call it quits*, call off, check, cut off, drop, end, fail, halt, interrupt, knock it off*, lay off*, nullify, scrap, scratch, scrub*, terminate; SEE CONCEPT 121

abort [*v2*] *terminate or fail to complete pregnancy*
miscarry; SEE CONCEPTS 121,304,308

abortion [*n1*] *expulsion of fetus*
aborticide, feticide, misbirth, miscarriage, termination; SEE CONCEPTS 230,699

abortion [*n2*] *failure*
disappointment, disaster, fiasco, misadventure, premature delivery; SEE CONCEPTS 304,308,674

abortive [*adj*] *failing to achieve a goal*
failed, failing, fruitless, futile, ineffective, ineffectual, miscarried, unavailing, unproductive, unsuccessful, useless, vain, worthless; SEE CONCEPT 528

abound [*v*] *exist in abundance*
be alive with, be all over the place*, be knee deep in*, be no end to*, be plentiful, be thick with*, be up to one's ears in*, crawl with*, crowd, flourish, flow, have a full plate*, infest, overflow, proliferate, swarm, swell, teem, thrive; SEE CONCEPT 141

abounding [*adj*] *plentiful*
abundant, bountiful, copious, filled, flush, plenteous, prodigal, profuse, prolific, replete, teeming; SEE CONCEPTS 762,781

about [*adv1*] *in an opposite direction*
around, back, backward, in reverse, round; SEE CONCEPT 581

about [*adv2*] *lying anywhere without order, arrangement*
anyhow, any which way*, around, here and there; SEE CONCEPT 583

about [*prep1*] *near an amount, quantity*
almost, approximately, in general, in the ball park*, in the neighborhood*, nearly, practically, pretty nearly, roughly; SEE CONCEPT 771

about [*prep2*] *concerning, relating to*
apropos, as concerns, as respects, dealing with, in connection with, in relation to, in respect to, referring to, regarding, relative to, touching, touching on; SEE CONCEPT 532

about [*prep3*] *near or close to in position*
adjacent, beside, nearby; SEE CONCEPTS 586,778

about [*prep4*] *on every side, in every direction*
around, encircling, round, surrounding, through, throughout; SEE CONCEPT 586

about-face [*n*] *change in direction*
changeabout, double, doubleback, reversal, reverse, turn, turnabout, volte-face; SEE CONCEPT 697

above [*prep1*] *higher in position*
aloft, atop, beyond, high, on high, on top of, over, overhead, raised, superior, upon; SEE CONCEPT 752

above [*prep2*] *more, higher in amount, degree*
beyond, exceeding, greater than, larger than, over; SEE CONCEPT 793

above [*prep3*] *superior to*
before, beyond, exceeding, prior to, superior to, surpassing; SEE CONCEPT 567

aboveboard [*adj*] *candid*
forthright, frank, honest, open, overt, right on*, square, straight, straightforward, straight from shoulder*, true, trustworthy, truthful, up front*, veracious; SEE CONCEPT 404

aboveboard [*adv*] *candidly*
frankly, honestly, on the up and up*, openly, overtly, truly, truthfully, veraciously; SEE CONCEPT 404

above suspicion [*adj*] *innocent*
above reproach, blameless, guiltless, having clean hands*, inculpable, irreproachable, scrupulous, sinless; SEE CONCEPT 545

abracadabra [*n*] *magic word*
hocus-pocus, incantation, invocation, mumbo jumbo, open sesame, spell; SEE CONCEPTS 370,673,689

abrade [*v*] *scrape*
chafe, erode, grate, rub, rub off, scuff, triturate, wear, wear down; SEE CONCEPTS 165,186,215

abrasion [*n1*] *scraped area*
chafe, injury, scrape, scratch, scuff; SEE CONCEPT 309

abrasion [*n2*] *scraping or wearing down by friction*
abrading, chafing, erosion, grating, rubbing, scratching, scuffing; SEE CONCEPT 186

abrasive [*adj1*] *irritating in manner*
annoying, biting, caustic, cutting, galling, hard to take*, hateful, hurtful, nasty, rough, rubbing the wrong way*, sharp, spiky*, unpleasant; SEE CONCEPT 404

abrasive [*adj2*] *scraping or wearing*
cutting, erosive, grinding, polishing, rough, scratching, scratchy, scuffing, sharpening, smoothing; SEE CONCEPT 606

abreast [*adv1*] *next to, alongside*
beside, equal, in alignment, in line, level, opposite, shoulder to shoulder, side by side; SEE CONCEPT 586

abreast [*adv2*] *up-to-date*
acquainted, au courant, au fait, contemporary, familiar, informed, in touch, knowledgeable, up*, versed; SEE CONCEPT 402

abridge [*v*] *shorten*
abbreviate, abstract, blue pencil*, chop, clip, compress, concentrate, condense, contract, curtail, cut, decrease, digest, diminish, downsize, lessen, limit, narrow, put in nutshell*, reduce, restrict, slash, snip*, summarize, trim, truncate; SEE CONCEPTS 236,247

abridgement [*n*] *shortening, summary*
abbreviation, abstract, brief, compendium, condensation, conspectus, contraction, curtailment, cutting, decrease, digest, diminishment, diminution, lessening, outline, precis, reducing, reduction, synopsis; SEE CONCEPTS 283,652

abroad [*adj*] *in a foreign country*
away, elsewhere, in foreign lands, in foreign parts, out of the country, overseas, touring, traveling; SEE CONCEPT 583

abrogate [*v*] *formally put an end to*
abate, abolish, annul, cancel, dissolve, do in*, end, finish off*, invalidate, knock out*, negate, nix, nullify, quash, reject, renege, repeal, retract, revoke, scrub*, torpedo*, undo, vacate, vitiate, void; SEE CONCEPT 121

abrogation [*n*] *cancellation*
annulment, discontinuation, ending, invalidation, quashing, repudiation, rescission, retraction, reversal, voiding, withdrawal; SEE CONCEPT 119

abrupt [*adj1*] *rude or brief in manner*
blunt, brusque, crude, crusty, curt, direct, discourteous, gruff, impetuous, impolite, matter-of-fact, rough, short, snappy, snippy, uncivil, ungracious; SEE CONCEPT 542

abrupt [*adj2*] *happening suddenly and unexpectedly*
hasty, hurried, jerky, precipitate, precipitous, quick, rushing, sudden, surprising, unanticipated, unceremonious, unexpected, unforeseen; SEE CONCEPT 820

abscess [*n*] *swelling*
boil, carbuncle, pustule, ulcer; SEE CONCEPTS 306,309

abscond [*v*] *run away, depart secretly*
beat it*, bolt*, break, clear out*, cut and run*, decamp, disappear, dog it*, duck out, escape, fade*, flee, fly the coop*, get, go AWOL*, go south*, hightail*, jump*, leave, make a break*, make off, make scarce*, pull out, quit, run off, scram*, skedaddle*, skip out*, slip, sneak away, split*, steal away, take off*, vamoose*, vanish; SEE CONCEPTS 102,195

absconder [*n*] *person who escapes*
absentee, bolter, escapee, quitter, truant; SEE CONCEPTS 403,583

absence [*n1*] *state of not being present*
absenteeism, AWOL*, cut*, French leave*, hooky*, nonappearance, nonattendance, no show*, truancy, vacancy; SEE CONCEPT 746

absence [*n2*] *state of lacking something needed or usual*
dearth, deficiency, drought, inadequacy, insufficiency, lack, need, omission, privation, unavailability, void, want; SEE CONCEPT 646

absent [*adj1*] *not present*
astray, away, AWOL*, elsewhere, ghost, gone, hooky*, missing, nobody home*, no-show*, removed, vanished; SEE CONCEPT 583

absent [*adj2*] *deficient in something needed or usual*
bare, blank, devoid, empty, hollow, lacking, minus, missing, nonexistent, omitted, unavailable, vacant, vacuous, wanting; SEE CONCEPT 546

absentee [*adj*] *not being present*
absent, distant, oblivious, remote; SEE CONCEPTS 403,583

absenteeism [*n*] *state of not being present*
absence, defection, desertion, skipping, truancy; SEE CONCEPT 746

absent-minded [*adj*] *unaware of events, surroundings*
absent, absorbed, abstracted, airheaded*, bemused, daydreaming, distracted, distrait, dreaming, dreamy, engrossed, faraway, forgetful, goofing off*, heedless, inattentive, inconscient, lost, mooning*, moony*, oblivious, out to lunch*, pipe dreaming*, preoccupied, remote, removed, space cadet*, spacey*, unconscious, unheeding, unmindful, unobservant, unthinking, withdrawn, woolgathering*; SEE CONCEPT 403

absent-mindedness [*n*] *preoccupation*
absorption, abstraction, distraction, dreaminess, forgetfulness, heedlessness, inattention; SEE CONCEPTS 293,410,532,690

absolute [*adj1*] *without limit*
complete, consummate, downright, entire, flat out*, free, full, infinite, no catch*, no fine print*, no holds barred*, no ifs ands or buts*, no joke*, no strings attached*, outright, plenary, pure, sheer, simple, straight out, supreme, thorough, total, unabridged, unadulterated, unconditional, unlimited, unqualified, unrestricted, utter; SEE CONCEPT 554

absolute [*adj2*] *in control or complete authority*
absolutist, arbitrary, authoritarian, autocratic, autonomous, despotic, dictatorial, full, monocratic,

preeminent, sovereign, supreme, totalitarian, tyrannical, tyrannous; SEE CONCEPT 536

absolute [*adj3*] *certain*
actual, categorical, conclusive, consummate, decided, decisive, definite, exact, factual, fixed, genuine, infallible, positive, precise, sure, unambiguous, undeniable, unequivocal, unmitigated, unquestionable; SEE CONCEPT 535

absolute [*adj4*] *excellent, perfect*
categorical, complete, faultless, flawless, ideal, impeccable, thorough, ultimate, unblemished, unflawed, untarnished; SEE CONCEPT 574

absolutely [*adv1*] *certainly, without question*
actually, categorically, come hell or high water*, conclusively, decidedly, decisively, definitely, doubtless, easily, exactly, for sure*, no ifs ands or buts*, no strings attached*, on the button*, on the money*, on the nose*, positively, precisely, really, right on*, straight out*, sure as can be*, sure as hell*, sure enough*, surely, sure thing*, the very thing*, truly, unambiguously, unconditionally, unquestionably; SEE CONCEPT 535

absolutely [*adv2*] *in a complete manner, degree*
completely, consummately, entirely, fully, thoroughly, utterly, wholly; SEE CONCEPT 531

absolution [*n*] *forgiveness*
acquittal, amnesty, compurgation, exculpation, forgiveness, mercy, pardon, release; SEE CONCEPTS 685,689

absolve [*v*] *free from responsibility, duty*
acquit, bleach, blink at, clear, discharge, exculpate, excuse, exempt, exonerate, forgive, free, go easy on, launder*, let off*, let off easy*, let off the hook*, let up on*, liberate, lifeboat*, loose, pardon, release, relieve, sanitize*, set free, spare, spring*, vindicate, whitewash, wink at*, wipe it off*, wipe the slate clean*, write off*; SEE CONCEPTS 83,317

absorb [*v1*] *physically take in a liquid*
blot, consume, devour, drink in, imbibe, ingest, ingurgitate, osmose, soak up, sop up*, sponge up*, suck in*, swallow, take in; SEE CONCEPT 256

absorb [*v2*] *mentally take in information*
assimilate, comprehend, digest, follow, get, get into*, grasp, incorporate, latch onto, learn, sense, soak up, take in, understand; SEE CONCEPT 31

absorb [*v3*] *occupy complete attention*
captivate, concern, consume, employ, engage, engross, fascinate, fill, hold, immerse, involve, monopolize, obsess, preoccupy, rivet; SEE CONCEPT 17

absorbed [*adj*] *being completely occupied mentally*
captivated, consumed, deep in thought, engaged, engrossed, fascinated, fixed, gone*, head over heels*, held, immersed, intent, involved, lost, preoccupied, rapt, really into*, up to here*, wrapped up*; SEE CONCEPT 403

absorbent [*adj*] *capable of physically taking in a liquid*
absorptive, bibulous, dry, imbibing, penetrable, permeable, porous, pregnable, retentive, spongy, thirsty; SEE CONCEPT 603

absorbing [*adj*] *holding one's attention*
arresting, captivating, consuming, engrossing, enthralling, exciting, fascinating, gripping, interesting, intriguing, monopolizing, preoccupying, riveting, spellbinding; SEE CONCEPT 403

absorption [*n1*] *assimilation, incorporation*
consumption, digestion, drinking in, exhaustion, fusion, imbibing, impregnation, ingestion, inhalation, intake, osmosis, penetration, reception, retention, saturation, soaking up, suction, taking in; SEE CONCEPTS 169,256

absorption [*n2*] *total attention toward something*
captivation, concentration, engagement, engrossment, enthrallment, fascination, hang-up*, holding, immersion, intentness, involvement, occupation, preoccupation, raptness; SEE CONCEPT 410

abstain [*v*] *hold back from doing*
abjure, abnegate, avoid, cease, constrain, curb, decline, deny oneself, do without, eschew, evade, fast, fence-sit*, forbear, forgo, give the go by*, give up, go on the wagon*, keep from, pass, pass up, quit, refrain, refuse, renounce, shun, sit on one's hands*, sit on the fence*, sit out, spurn, starve, stop, take the cure*, take the pledge*, withhold; SEE CONCEPTS 25,121

abstemious [*adj*] *restraining behavior or appetite*
abstinent, ascetic, austere, continent, frugal, moderate, moderating, restrained, self-denying, self-restrained, sober, sparing, temperate; SEE CONCEPT 401

abstention [*n*] *refraining*
abstaining, abstinence, avoidance, non-indulgence, self-control, self-denial, self-restraint, sobriety; SEE CONCEPT 633

abstinence [*n*] *restraint from desires, especially physical desires*
abnegation, abstaining, abstemiousness, asceticism, avoidance, chastity, continence, fasting, forbearance, frugality, moderation, refraining, renunciation, self-control, self-denial, self-restraint, soberness, sobriety, teetotalism, temperance; SEE CONCEPT 633

abstract [*adj*] *conceptual, theoretical*
abstruse, complex, deep, hypothetical, ideal, indefinite, intellectual, nonconcrete, philosophical, recondite, transcendent, transcendental, unreal; SEE CONCEPT 582

abstract [*n*] *short document prepared from a longer one*
abridgment, brief, compendium, condensation, conspectus, digest, outline, precis, résumé, summary, synopsis; SEE CONCEPT 283

abstract [*v1*] *take away from*
detach, disconnect, disengage, dissociate, extract, isolate, part, remove, separate, steal, take out, uncouple, withdraw; SEE CONCEPTS 135,211

abstract [*v2*] *prepare short document from longer one*
abbreviate, abridge, condense, digest, outline, review, shorten, summarize; SEE CONCEPTS 79,236,247

abstracted [*adj*] *preoccupied*
absent-minded, daydreaming, inattentive, lost in thought, out in space*, out to lunch*, remote, withdrawn; SEE CONCEPT 403

abstraction [*n*] *state of being lost in thought*
absorption, aloofness, brooding, cogitation, consideration, contemplation, daydreaming, detachment, engrossment, entrancement, musing, pensiveness, pondering, preoccupation, reflecting, reflection, remoteness, reverie, ruminating, thinking, trance; SEE CONCEPT 410

ab
ab

abstruse [adj] difficult to understand
abstract, clear as dishwater*, complex, complicated, deep, enigmatic, esoteric, Greek to me*, heavy*, hidden, incomprehensible, intricate, involved, muddy, obscure, perplexing, profound, puzzling, recondite, subtle, unfathomable, vague; SEE CONCEPTS 402,562

absurd [adj] ridiculous, senseless
batty, campy, crazy, daffy, dippy*, flaky*, fooling around, foolish, for grins*, freaky, gagged up*, goofy*, idiotic, illogical, inane, incongruous, irrational, jokey, joshing, laughable, loony, ludicrous, nonsensical, nutty, off the wall*, preposterous, sappy*, screwy*, silly, stupid, tomfool, unreasonable, wacky; SEE CONCEPTS 544,552,558

absurdity [n] ridiculous situation or behavior
applesauce*, BS*, bull*, crap*, craziness, farce, flapdoodle*, folly, foolishness, hot air*, idiocy, illogicality, illogicalness, improbability, inanity, incongruity, insanity, irrationality, jazz*, jive*, ludicrousness, ridiculousness, senselessness, silliness, stupidity, unreasonableness; SEE CONCEPTS 650,656

abundance [n] great amount or supply
affluence, ampleness, bounty, copiousness, fortune, myriad, opulence, plenitude, plenty, plethora, profusion, prosperity, prosperousness, riches, thriving, wealth; SEE CONCEPTS 710,767

abundant [adj] plentiful, large in number
abounding, ample, bounteous, bountiful, copious, crawling with*, cup runs over with*, eco-rich, exuberant, filled, full, generous, heavy, lavish, liberal, lousy with*, luxuriant, mucho*, no end of*, overflowing, plate is full of*, plenteous, plenty, profuse, rich, rolling in*, stinking with*, sufficient, teeming; SEE CONCEPT 781

abuse [n1] wrong use
corruption, crime, debasement, delinquency, desecration, exploitation, fault, injustice, misapplication, misconduct, misdeed, mishandling, mismanage, misuse, offense, perversion, prostitution, sin, wrong, wrongdoing; SEE CONCEPT 156

abuse [n2] physical hurting, injuring
crime, damage, defilement, harm, hurt, impairment, injury, malevolence, maltreatment, manhandling, misdeed, offense, pollution, violation, wrongdoing; SEE CONCEPT 246

abuse [n3] verbal attack
bad-mouthing*, blame, castigation, censure, curse, curses*, defamation, derision, hosing*, insults, invective, kicking around*, knifing*, libel, obloquy, opprobrium, pushing around*, put-down, quinine*, reproach, revilement, scolding, signifying, slander, swearing, tirade, upbraiding, vilification, vituperation; SEE CONCEPT 54

abuse [v1] physically hurt or injure
bang up*, beat up, bung up*, corrupt, cut up*, damage, defile, deprave, desecrate, harm, hose*, ill-treat, impair, maltreat, mar, mess up*, mishandle, mistreat, misuse, molest, oppress, persecute, pollute*, roughhouse, rough up, ruin, shake up*, spoil, taint, total*, victimize, violate, wax*; SEE CONCEPT 246

abuse [v2] use wrongly
dissipate, exhaust, misemploy, mishandle, misuse, overburden, overtax, overwork, prostitute, spoil, squander, taint, waste; SEE CONCEPT 156

abuse [v3] attack with words
backbite, bad-mouth, bash, belittle, berate, blow off*, calumniate, cap*, castigate, cuss out*, cut down*, cut to the quick*, decry, defame, derogate, discount, do a number on*, dump on*, give a black eye*, hurl brickbat*, insult, knock*, minimize, nag, offend, oppress, persecute, pick on, put down*, rag on*, reproach, revile, ride*, rip up*, run down*, scold, signify, slam*, slap*, sling mud*, smear*, sound*, swear at*, tear apart*, trash*, upbraid, vilify, vituperate, zing*; SEE CONCEPTS 52,54

abuse [v4] take advantage of
do an injustice to, exploit, impose on, use, wrong; SEE CONCEPTS 156,384

abusive [adj] exhibiting unkind behavior or words
calumniating, castigating, censorious, contumelious, defamatory, derisive, disparaging, insolent, insulting, invective, libelous, maligning, obloquious, offensive, opprobrious, reproachful, reviling, rude, sarcastic, scathing, scolding, scurrilous, sharp-tongued, slanderous, traducing, upbraiding, vilifying, vituperative; SEE CONCEPT 267

abut [v] touch or be next to something
adjoin, be adjacent to, border on, butt against, join, neighbor; SEE CONCEPT 749

abutment [n] masonry mass
arch end, bridge end, end piece, jutting piece, support, vault end; SEE CONCEPTS 745,827,833

abysmal [adj1] great extent; immeasurable
bottomless, boundless, complete, deep, endless, extreme, illimitable, incalculable, infinite, profound, thorough, unending, unfathomable, vast; SEE CONCEPTS 772,793

abysmal [adj2] extending deeply
bottomless, fathomless, plumbless, plummetless; SEE CONCEPT 777

abyss [n] something very deep, usually a feature of land
abysm, chasm, crevasse, depth, fissure, gorge, gulf, hole, pit, void; SEE CONCEPTS 509,514

academia [n] scholarly world
academe, academic community, academicians, college, savants, school; SEE CONCEPTS 287,288,289

academic [adj1] relating to schooling, learning
bookish, book-learned, college, collegiate, erudite, intellectual, learned, pedantic, scholarly, scholastic, studious, university; SEE CONCEPT 536

academic [adj2] relating to theories, philosophy
abstract, closet, conjectural, formalistic, hypothetical, notional, speculative, theoretical; SEE CONCEPTS 402,529

academic [n] scholar or university/college teacher
academician, lecturer, professor, pupil, scholar, scholastic, student, tutor; SEE CONCEPT 350

academy [n1] school, especially for higher education
boarding school, brainery*, finishing school, halls of ivy*, institute, military school, preparatory school, prep school, secondary school, seminary; SEE CONCEPT 289

academy [n2] society or institution interested in learning
alliance, association, circle, council, federation,

foundation, fraternity, institute, league; SEE CONCEPT 288

accede [v] *agree or consent*
accept, acquiesce, admit, allow, assent, be game for*, cave in*, comply, concede, concur, cooperate, cry uncle*, endorse, enter into, fold, give the go-ahead*, give the green light*, go along with, grant, let, okay, permit, play ball*, roll over and play dead*, subscribe, throw in the towel*, yield; SEE CONCEPTS 8,50,82,88

accelerate [v] *increase speed, timing*
advance, drive, dust*, expedite, fire up*, forward, further, gun*, hammer on*, hasten, hurry, impel, lay a patch*, lay rubber*, make tracks*, nail it*, open up*, peel rubber*, precipitate, put on afterburners*, put pedal to metal*, quicken, railroad*, rev, rev up, roll*, speed up, spur, step on gas*, step up, stimulate, tool*; SEE CONCEPTS 234,242

acceleration [n] *increasing speed, timing*
dispatch, expedition, hastening, hurrying, quickening, speeding up, spurring, stepping up, stimulation; SEE CONCEPT 234

accent [n1] *importance, emphasis*
significance, stress, weight; SEE CONCEPT 668

accent [n2] *stress or pitch in pronunciation*
accentuation, articulation, beat, cadence, emphasis, enunciation, force, inflection, intonation, meter, modulation, pronunciation, rhythm, stroke, timbre, tonality, tone; SEE CONCEPT 77

accent [v] *place emphasis, importance*
accentuate, draw attention to, emphasize, highlight, intensify, stress, underline, underscore; SEE CONCEPTS 69,243

accept [v1] *receive something given physically*
acquire, gain, get, obtain, secure, take, welcome; SEE CONCEPT 124

accept [v2] *allow into group*
admit, receive, welcome; SEE CONCEPT 384

accept [v3] *believe the goodness, realness of something*
acknowledge, affirm, approbate, approve, buy*, countenance, fancy, favor, go for*, hold, hold with, like, recognize, relish, swallow*, take as gospel truth*, take stock in*, trust; SEE CONCEPT 12

accept [v4] *put up with*
acknowledge, acquiesce, agree, assent, bear, bear with, bow, capitulate, defer to, don't make waves*, don't rock the boat*, endure, fit in, go along with, live with, play the game*, recognize, respect, sit still for*, stand, stand for, stomach, submit to, suffer, swallow, take, tolerate, yield to; SEE CONCEPT 23

accept [v5] *receive by agreeing; consenting*
accede, acknowledge, acquiesce, admit, adopt, affirm, agree to, approve, assent, assume, avow, bear, buy, check out*, comply, concur with, cooperate with, give stamp of approval*, give the go-ahead*, give the green light*, give the nod*, go for*, lap up*, okay, recognize, rubberstamp*, set store by*, sign, sign off on*, take on*, take one up on*, thumbs up*, undertake; SEE CONCEPTS 8,82

acceptable [adj] *satisfactory, agreeable*
adequate, admissible, all right, A-OK*, average, big*, common, cooking with gas*, cool*, copacetic, decent, delightful, fair, hep*, hip*, hunky-dory*, in the swim*, kosher*, large, okay, on the ball*, on the beam*, passable, peachy keen*, pleasant, pleasing, respectable, right on*, standard, sufficient, swell*, tolerable, trendy, unexceptional, unobjectionable, up to code*, up to snuff*, welcome; SEE CONCEPTS 533,558

acceptance [n1] *agreement, taking*
accepting, acknowledgment, acquiring, admission, approval, assent, compliance, consent, cooperation, gaining, getting, go-ahead*, green light*, nod*, obtaining, okay, permission, receipt, receiving, reception, recognition, securing, taking on, undertaking, yes; SEE CONCEPTS 8,124

acceptance [n2] *belief in goodness of something*
accedence, accession, acknowledgment, acquiescence, admission, adoption, affirmation, agreement, approbation, approval, assent, concession, concurrence, favor, recognition, seal of approval; SEE CONCEPTS 12,32

accepted [adj] *generally agreed upon*
accustomed, acknowledged, allowed, approved, arrived at, authorized, card-carrying*, chosen, confirmed, conventional, credited, current, customary, endorsed, established, fashionable, in vogue, kosher*, legit*, normal, okayed, orthodox, passed, popular, preferred, received, recognized, regular, sanctioned, standard, straight*, time-honored, touted, universal, unopposed, usual, welcomed; SEE CONCEPTS 547,558

access [n] *admission, means of entry, approach*
admittance, approach, avenue, connection, contact, course, door, entrance, entree, entry, in, ingress, introduction, key, open arms*, open door*, passage, path, road, route, way; SEE CONCEPTS 501,631

accessible [adj] *approachable; ready for use*
attainable, available, door's always open*, employable, exposed, getatable, handy, near, obtainable, open, operative, possible, practicable, public, reachable, susceptible, unrestricted, usable; SEE CONCEPT 576

accession [n1] *something that augments, adds to*
accretion, addition, augmentation, enlargement, extension, increase, increment, raise, rise; SEE CONCEPTS 700,775

accession [n2] *coming to power*
assumption, attainment, inauguration, induction, investment, succession, taking on, taking over; SEE CONCEPTS 133,298

accession [n3] *agreement*
accedence, acceptance, acquiescence, assent, concurrence, consent; SEE CONCEPTS 8,410

accessorize [v] *add ornament*
accent, add on, adorn, equip, supplement; SEE CONCEPTS 162,177

accessory [n1] *ornament; accompanying item; supplementary part*
accent, addition, adjunct, adornment, appendage, appendix, appliance, appurtenance, attachment, component, decoration, extension, extra, frill, help, supplement, trim, trimming; SEE CONCEPT 834

accessory [n2] *person peripherally involved in illegal activity*
abettor, accomplice, aid, aide, assistant, associate, co-conspirator, colleague, confederate, conspirator, helper, insider, partner, plant*, ringer*, shill*, stall*, subordinate; SEE CONCEPT 412

accident [n1] *unexpected, undesirable event; often physically injurious*
blow, calamity, casualty, collision, crack-up*, disaster, fender-bender*, fluke*, hazard, misad-

ab
ac

venture, misfortune, mishap, pileup*, rear ender*, setback, smash*, smashup*, stack-up*, total*, wrack-up*; SEE CONCEPT 674

accident [n2] *chance event*
adventure, circumstance, contingency, fate, fluke*, fortuity, fortune, happening, luck, occasion, occurrence, turn; SEE CONCEPT 679

accidental [adj] *happening unexpectedly*
adventitious, casual, chance, coincidental, contingent, fluky*, fortuitous, inadvertent, incidental, random, uncalculated, unexpected, unforeseen, unintended, unintentional, unplanned; SEE CONCEPTS 530,552

accidentally [adj] *by chance*
by mistake, fortuitously, haphazardly, unintentionally, unwittingly; SEE CONCEPTS 548,552

accident-prone [adj] *clumsy*
all thumbs*, bungling, inept, klutzy*, two left feet*; SEE CONCEPTS 401,402,584

acclaim [n] *expression of approval*
acclamation, acknowledgment, applause, approbation, celebration, cheering, clapping, commendation, eulogizing, exaltation, honor, kudos, pat on the back*, pat on the head*, plaudits, PR, praise, puff, pumping up*, rave, recognition, strokes*, stroking*; SEE CONCEPT 69

acclaim [v] *give approval*
applaud, approve, blow horn*, boost, celebrate, cheer, clap, commend, complement, eulogize, exalt, extol, give a bouquet*, give a posy*, give kudos*, hail, hand it to*, hear it for*, honor, laud, praise, puff up*, push*, rave, recommend, root, salute, stroke*; SEE CONCEPT 69

acclaimed [adj] *praised*
cheered, extolled, hailed, lauded, renowned; SEE CONCEPTS 568,574

acclamation [n] *enthusiastic expression of approval*
acclaim, adulation, applause, approbation, big hand*, cheer, cheering, cheers, hand, honor, jubilation, laudation, ovation, plaudits, salutation, standing O*, tribute; SEE CONCEPTS 69,377

acclimate [v] *make or become adjusted, adapted*
acclimatize, accommodate, acculture, accustom, climatize, conform, get used to, habituate, harden, season, toughen; SEE CONCEPTS 202,701

accolade [n] *strong praise, recognition of achievement*
approval, award, badge, decoration, distinction, honor, kudos*, laurels; SEE CONCEPT 69

accommodate [v1] *make room, lodging available*
board, contain, domicile, entertain, furnish, harbor, hold, house, put up*, quarter, receive, rent, shelter, supply, take in, welcome; SEE CONCEPT 226

accommodate [v2] *make, become suitable for something*
accord, accustom, adapt, adjust, agree, attune, bend over backwards*, comply, compose, conform, coordinate, correspond, don't make waves*, fit, go by the book*, go with the flow*, harmonize, integrate, make consistent, modify, play the game*, proportion, reconcile, settle, shape up, suit, tailor, tailor-make, tune; SEE CONCEPTS 23,126

accommodate [v3] *perform service*
afford, aid, arrange, assist, avail, benefit, bow, comfort, convenience, defer, favor, furnish, gratify, help, humor, indulge, obligé, pamper, please,

provide, serve, settle, submit, suit, supply, support, sustain, yield; SEE CONCEPT 136

accommodating [adj] *willing to help*
considerate, cooperative, friendly, generous, handy, helpful, hospitable, kind, neighborly, obliging, on deck*, on tap*, polite, unselfish, user friendly*; SEE CONCEPTS 542,555

accommodation [n] *adjustment for different situation, circumstances*
adaptation, compliance, composition, compromise, conformity, fifty-fifty deal*, fitting, modification, reconciliation, settlement; SEE CONCEPT 697

accommodations [n] *place of residence, usually temporary*
apartment, board, boardinghouse, crash pad*, crib*, digs*, hotel, house, housing, lodging, motel, pad*, quarters, roof, room and board, rooming house, rooms, shelter; SEE CONCEPT 516

accompaniment [n1] *necessary part or embellishment*
accessory, adjunct, appendage, appurtenance, attachment, attendant, attribute, augmentation, complement, concomitant, enhancement, enrichment, supplement; SEE CONCEPTS 834,835

accompaniment [n2] *music that supports a theme or performer in a composition*
back, background, backing, back-up, harmony, instrument, part; SEE CONCEPT 262

accompany [v1] *go or be with something*
associate with, attend, chaperon, come along, conduct, consort, convoy, date, dog*, draft*, drag*, escort, follow, go along, guard, guide, hang around with*, hang out*, keep company, lead, look after, shadow, shlep along*, show about, show around, spook, squire, stick to*, string along*, tag along*, tailgate*, take out, usher; SEE CONCEPTS 113,224

accompany [v2] *occur with something*
add, appear with, append, be connected, belong to, characterize, coexist, coincide with, come with, complete, co-occur, follow, go together, happen with, join with, occur with, supplement, take place with; SEE CONCEPT 643

accomplice [n] *helper, especially in committing a crime*
abettor, accessory, aid, aide, ally, assistant, associate, co-conspirator, collaborator, colleague, confederate, conspirator, insider, partner, plant*, stall*; SEE CONCEPT 412

accomplish [v] *succeed in doing*
achieve, arrive, attain, bring about, bring off, carry out, conclude, consummate, do, do a bang-up job*, do justice*, do one proud*, do the trick*, effect, finish, fulfill, gain, get someplace*, get there*, hit*, make hay*, make it, manage, nail it*, perform, produce, pull off*, put it over*, rack up*, reach, realize, score*, sew up*, take care of, win; SEE CONCEPTS 91,706

accomplished [adj] *skilled in activity*
able, adept, brainy, consummate, cool*, cultivated, expert, gifted, hep*, hip*, masterly, polished, practiced, proficient, savvy, sharp, skillful, talented, wised up*, with it*; SEE CONCEPTS 326,528

accomplishment [n] *something successfully done, completed*
ability, achievement, act, art, attainment, bringing about, capability, carrying out, completion, conclusion, consummation, coup, deed, effect-

ing, effort, execution, exploit, feat, finish, fulfillment, performance, production, proficiency, realization, skill, stroke, talent, triumph; SEE
CONCEPT 706

accord [n] *agreement, mutual understanding
(often written)*
10-4*, accordance, concert, concord, concurrence, conformity, congruence, correspondence,
deal, good vibes*, good vibrations*, harmony,
okay, pact, rapport, reconciliation, sympathy,
treaty, unanimity; SEE CONCEPT 684

accord [v1] *give approval, grant*
accede, acquiesce, admit, allow, award, bestow,
concede, confer, endow, give, present, render,
tender, vouchsafe; SEE CONCEPTS 50,83,88

accord [v2] *come to agreement*
affirm, agree, assent, be in tune, concur, conform, correspond, fit, harmonize, jibe, match,
square, suit, tally; SEE CONCEPTS 8,664

accordant [adj] *in agreement*
agreeing, conforming, congruous, harmonious,
in concert; SEE CONCEPTS 558,563

accordingly [adv] *in an appropriate, suitable
way*
appropriately, as a consequence, as a result, consequently, correspondingly, duly, equally, ergo,
fitly, hence, in consequence, in respect to, in that
event, properly, proportionately, respectively, re-
sultantly, so, subsequently, suitably, then, therefore, thus, under the circumstances; SEE CONCEPT
558

accordion [n] *musical instrument*
concertina, groanbox*, melodeon, squeezebox*,
stomach Steinway*, windbox*; SEE CONCEPTS
463,499

accost [v] *approach for conversation or solicitation*
address, annoy, bother, brace*, buttonhole*, call,
challenge, confront, cross, dare, entice, face,
flag, greet, hail, proposition, run into, salute,
welcome, whistle for*; SEE CONCEPTS 48,51

account [n1] *written description of past events*
ABCs*, annal, blow by blow*, bulletin, chronicle, detail, explanation, history, lowdown*,
make*, narration, narrative, play by play*,
recital, report, run-down, score, story, tab, take,
tale, the picture*, the whole picture*, version;
SEE CONCEPT 282

account [n2] *record of finances, fees, or charges*
bad news*, balance, bill, book, books, charge,
check, computation, cuff*, grunt*, inventory, invoice, IOU*, ledger, reckoning, record, register,
report, score, statement, tab, tally; SEE CONCEPTS
331,332

account [n3] *basis or consideration for action*
cause, ground, grounds, interest, justification,
motive, rationale, rationalization, reason, regard,
sake; SEE CONCEPT 229

accountability [n] *responsibility*
answerability, blameworthiness, liability; SEE
CONCEPT 645

accountable [adj] *responsible for having done*
answerable, charged with, culpable, liable, obligated, obliged, on the hook*; SEE CONCEPT 527

accountant [n] *person who maintains financial
accounts of a business*
actuary, analyst, auditor, bookkeeper, calculator,
cashier, clerk, comptroller, CPA, examiner, public accountant, reckoner, teller; SEE CONCEPTS
348,353

account for [v] *offer reason, explanation*
answer for, clarify, elucidate, explain, illuminate,
justify, rationalize, resolve; SEE CONCEPT 57

accounting [n] *keeping financial accounts*
auditing, balancing the books*, bookkeeping,
calculating, computing, reckoning; SEE CON-
CEPTS 28,764

accredit [v1] *attribute responsibility or achievement*
ascribe, assign, charge, credit, refer; SEE CON-
CEPTS 49,69

accredit [v2] *give authorization or control*
appoint, approve, authorize, certify, commission,
empower, enable, endorse, entrust, guarantee, license, okay, recognize, sanction, vouch for; SEE
CONCEPTS 50,88

accretion [n] *gradual growth, addition*
accession, accumulation, augmentation, buildup, increase, increment, raise, rise; SEE CONCEPT
780

accrual [n] *growth*
accumulation, amassing, amassment, buildup, increase; SEE CONCEPTS 432,780

accrue [v] *increase by addition or growth, often
financial*
accumulate, amass, build up, collect, enlarge,
flow, gather, grow, increase; SEE CONCEPTS
763,780

acculturation [n] *adjustment to culture*
acclimatization, assimilation, culture shock, na-
tionalization, naturalization; SEE CONCEPTS
202,701

accumulate [v] *gather or amass something*
accrue, acquire, add to, agglomerate, aggregate,
amalgamate, assemble, bring together, cache,
clean up*, collect, collocate, compile, concentrate, cumulate, draw together, expand, gain,
gather, grow, heap, heap together, hoard, incorporate, increase, load up*, lump*, make a bundle*, make a killing*, mass, pile*, pile up*,
procure, profit, rack up*, roll up*, round up*,
scare up*, stack up, stockpile, store, store up,
swell, unite; SEE CONCEPTS 236,245

accumulation [n] *gathering or amassing*
accession, accretion, addition, agglomeration,
aggrandizement, aggregation, amassment, augmentation, build-up, chunk, collecting, collection, conglomeration, enlargement, gob, growth,
heap, hoarding, hunk, increase, inflation, intensification, mass, multiplication, pile, quantity,
stack, stock, store, trove, up, upping; SEE CON-
CEPTS 432,780

accuracy [n] *precision or correctness*
accurateness, carefulness, certainty, closeness,
definiteness, definitiveness, definitude, efficiency, exactitude, exactness, faultlessness, incisiveness, mastery, meticulousness, preciseness,
sharpness, skill, skillfulness, strictness, sureness,
truthfulness, veracity, verity; SEE CONCEPTS
638,654

accurate [adj] *precise*
authentic, careful, close, concrete, correct, defined, definite, deft, detailed, discriminating, discriminative, distinct, exact, explicit, factual,
faithful, genuine, judicious, just, literal, matter-
of-fact, methodical, meticulous, on the button*,
on the money*, on the nose*, particular, proper,
punctilious, punctual, regular, right, rigid, rigorous, scientific, scrupulous, severe, sharp, skillful,
solid, specific, strict, systematic, true, ultrapre-

ac
ac

cise, unerring, unmistakable, veracious; SEE
CONCEPT 535

accurate [adj2] *correct, without error*
absolute, actual, authentic, authoritative, certain,
conclusive, definite, definitive, errorless, exact,
factual, faultless, final, flawless, genuine, infallible, irrefutable, official, perfect, right, straight,
strict, true, truthful, undeniable, undisputed,
unimpeachable, unquestionable, unrefuted, valid,
veracious; SEE CONCEPT 557

accurately [adv] *correctly*
exactly, flawlessly, meticulously, precisely,
scrupulously, veraciously; SEE CONCEPTS
535,557

accursed [adj] *cursed*
bedeviled, condemned, damned, done for*,
doomed, hexed, ill-fated, star-crossed, unfortunate; SEE CONCEPTS 548,571

accusation [n] *charge of wrongdoing, fault*
allegation, arraignment, attribution, beef*,
blast*, bum rap*, censure, citation, complaint,
denunciation, dido, exposé, gripe, impeachment,
imputation, incrimination, indictment, insinuation, recrimination, roar*, rumble*, slur,
squawk*, stink*; SEE CONCEPT 54

accuse [v] *place blame for wrongdoing, fault*
allege, apprehend, arraign, arrest, attack, attribute, betray, blame, blow the whistle*, brand,
bring charges, censure, charge, cite, complain,
criminate, denounce, file claim, finger*, frame,
hang something on*, hold accountable, impeach,
implicate, impute, incriminate, inculpate, indict,
lay at door*, let have it*, libel, litigate, lodge
complaint, name, pin on*, point finger at*, prosecute, recriminate, serve summons, slander, slur,
sue, summon, tax; SEE CONCEPT 44

accuser [n] *person laying blame*
indicter, informer, prosecutor, rat*, tattletale*;
SEE CONCEPTS 412,423

accustom [v] *get used to*
acclimatize, acculturate, acquaint, adapt, familiarize, habituate, season; SEE CONCEPTS 35,202

accustomed [adj1] *be or become prepared, used
to*
acclimatized, acquainted, adapted, addicted, confirmed, disciplined, familiar, familiarized, given
to, grooved*, habituated, habituated in, in the
habit, inured, seasoned, settled in, trained; SEE
CONCEPT 403

accustomed [adj2] *normal, usual*
accepted, chronic, common, conventional, customary, established, everyday, expected, general,
habitual, ordinary, orthodox, regular, routine, set,
traditional, typical; SEE CONCEPT 547

AC-DC [adj] *bisexual*
ambidextrous, androgynous, bi*, double-gaited,
epicene, gay, gynandrous, hermaphroditic, hits
both ways*, intersexual, monoclinous, swings
both ways*, switch-hitting*; SEE CONCEPT 372

ace [adj] *exhibiting expertise in some activity*
brilliant, champion, distinguished, excellent, expert, first-rate, great, master, outstanding, superb,
virtuoso; SEE CONCEPT 528

ace [n] *expert in some activity*
champion, genius, master, pro, star, virtuoso,
winner, wizard; SEE CONCEPT 416

ace in the hole [n] *secret weapon*
card up one's sleeve, reserve; SEE CONCEPTS
274,340

acerbate [v] *exasperate*
aggravate, annoy, disturb, perturb, provoke, rattle one's cage*; SEE CONCEPTS 7,19

acerbic [adj] *bitter, sharp, or sour*
acidic, acrid, astringent, caustic, harsh, sharp,
tart; SEE CONCEPT 613

acerbity [n1] *bitterness of taste*
acidity, asperity, astringency, mordancy, sourness, tartness; SEE CONCEPTS 462,613

acerbity [n2] *harsh speech, behavior*
acrimoniousness, causticity, ill temper, irritability, rancor, rudeness, sarcasm, sarcasticness, vit-
riolicism; SEE CONCEPTS 267,401

aces [adj] *great*
excellent, fabulous, peachy, wonderful; SEE CON-
CEPTS 527,528,574

ache [n] *sore feeling; dull pain*
anguish, hurt, misery, pang, pounding, smarting,
soreness, spasm, suffering, throb, throbbing,
throe, twinge; SEE CONCEPTS 316,410,728

ache [v] *feeling soreness or dull pain, often physical*
be sore, hurt, pain, pound, smart, suffer, throb,
twinge; SEE CONCEPTS 13,17,303,308,313

achievable [adj] *doable*
attainable, feasible, obtainable; SEE CONCEPTS
528,552,558

achieve [v] *bring to successful conclusion; reach
a goal*
accomplish, acquire, actualize, attain, bring
about, bring off*, bring to pass, cap, carry out,
carry through, close, complete, conclude, consummate, deliver, discharge, dispatch, do, earn,
earn wings*, effect, effectuate, enact, end, execute, finish, follow through, fulfill, gain, get, get
done, manage, negotiate, obtain, perfect, perform, procure, produce, rack up*, reach, realize,
resolve, score, seal, see through, settle, sign,
solve, win, wind up, work out; SEE CONCEPT 706

achievement [n] *something completed successfully; goal reached*
accomplishment, acquirement, acquisition, act,
actualization, attainment, completion, conquest,
consummation, contrivance, creation, deed, effectuation, effort, enactment, encompassment,
execution, exploit, feat, fulfillment, hit, masterpiece, performance, production, realization,
stroke, success, tour de force, triumph, victory;
SEE CONCEPT 706

Achilles' heel [n] *vulnerability*
chink in the armor*, deficiency, frailty, handicap, soft underbelly*, susceptibility, weakness;
SEE CONCEPTS 101,230,411,580

acid [adj1] *bitter, sour in taste*
acerbic, acidulous, biting, piquant, pungent,
sharp, tart, vinegarish, vinegary; SEE CONCEPT
613

acid [adj2] *having acidic, corrosive properties*
acerbic, acidulous, acrid, anti-alkaline, biting,
bleaching, corroding, disintegrative, dissolvent,
eating away, eroding, erosive, oxidizing, rusting;
SEE CONCEPT 485

acid [adj3] *bitter in words or behavior*
acerbic, biting, caustic, cutting, dry, harsh, hateful, hurtful, mordant, nasty, offensive, sarcastic,
sharp, stinging, trenchant, vitriolic; SEE CON-
CEPTS 267,401

acid [n] *lysergic acid diethylamide, LSD*
black tabs*, blotter*, blue acid*, blue dot*, blue
Owsley*, California sunshine*, candy*, cubes*,

dot*, electric Kool Aid*, green dragon*, hallucinogen, instant Zen*, Lucy in the sky with diamonds*, magic mushrooms, mescalin, microdots*, mushrooms, orange sunshine*, Owsley's acid*, peyote, purple haze*, strawberry fields*, sugar cubes*, yellow sunshine*; SEE CONCEPT 307

acidity [n] bitterness
acerbity, acridness, astringency, causticity, pungency, sourness, tartness; SEE CONCEPT 614

acid test [n] test of value, genuineness
proof, proving ground, substantiation, trial, verification; SEE CONCEPTS 87,290,291

aciduous [adj1] bitter, sour
acerb, acerbic, acetose, dry, piquant, sharp, tart; SEE CONCEPT 613

aciduous [adj2] bitter in speech
biting, cutting, ironical, mocking, sarcastic; SEE CONCEPT 267

acknowledge [v1] verbally recognize authority
accede, accept, acquiesce, agree, allow, approve, attest to, certify, defend, defer to, endorse, grant, own, ratify, recognize, subscribe to, support, take an oath, uphold, yield; SEE CONCEPTS 8,50,88

acknowledge [v2] admit truth or reality of something
accede, accept, acquiesce, allow, avow, come clean*, come out of closet*, concede, confess, cop a plea*, crack*, declare, fess up*, get off chest*, grant, let on*, open up*, own, profess, recognize, yield; SEE CONCEPTS 12,49

acknowledge [v3] verbally recognize receipt of something
address, answer, greet, hail, notice, react, remark, reply, respond, return, salute, thank; SEE CONCEPTS 38,45,51,60

acknowledgment [n1] act of recognizing authority or truth of something
acceptance, accession, acquiescence, admission, admitting, affirmation, allowance, allowing, assent, assertion, asseveration, avowal, compliance, conceding, concession, concurrence, confession, confirmation, corroboration, declaration, profession, ratification, realization, recognition, yielding; SEE CONCEPTS 8,50,88

acknowledgment [n2] physical symbol of recognition
acclamation, addressing, answer, apology, applause, appreciation, bestowal, bow, card, confession, contract, credit, gift, gratitude, greeting, guarantee, hail, hailing, letter, nod, notice, reaction, receipt, reply, response, return, salutation, salute, signature, statement, support, thanks, token; SEE CONCEPTS 595,628

acme [n] pinnacle of achievement or physical object
apogee, capstone, climax, culmination, height, highest point, high point, meridian, optimum, peak, summit, top, ultimate, vertex, zenith; SEE CONCEPTS 706,836

acne [n] blemishes
blackheads, pimples, pizza-face*, pustules, rosacea, skin inflammation, whiteheads, zits*; SEE CONCEPT 580

acolyte [n] attendant, usually in a church
aid, assistant, follower, helper; SEE CONCEPT 361

acoustic [adj] sound
audile, audio, auditory, aural, hearing, phonic; SEE CONCEPTS 591,594

acoustics [n] sound quality
echo, noise, sound, sound properties, sound transmission; SEE CONCEPT 595

acquaint [v] inform oneself or another about something new
accustom, advise, apprise, bring out, clue, come out with*, disclose, divulge, enlighten, familiarize, fill in, fix up*, get together*, habituate, inform, intro*, introduce, knock down*, let know, make familiar, notify, post, present, reveal, tell, warn; SEE CONCEPTS 31,60

acquaintance [n1] a person known informally
associate, association, colleague, companion, contact, friend, neighbor; SEE CONCEPT 423

acquaintance [n2] knowledge of something through experience
awareness, cognizance, conversance, familiarity, fellowship, grasp, intimacy, ken, relationship, understanding; SEE CONCEPT 409

acquainted [adj] aware
abreast, advised, apprised of, clued in*, conversant, enlightened, familiarized, familiar with, informed, in the know*, versed in; SEE CONCEPT 402

acquiesce [v] agree with some reluctance
accede, accept, accommodate, adapt, adjust, agree, allow, approve, bow to, buy, cave in*, come across, come around, comply, concur, conform, consent, cry uncle*, cut a deal*, ditto*, give in, give out, go along, jibe*, okay, pass, play ball*, reconcile, roll over and play dead*, say uncle*, set, shake on, submit, subscribe, yes, yield; SEE CONCEPTS 8,10,23,82

acquiescence [n] reluctant agreement
acceptance, accession, approval, assent, compliance, concurrence, conformity, consent, giving in, obedience, permission, resignation, submission, submissiveness, yielding; SEE CONCEPTS 8,10

acquire [v] obtain or receive
access, achieve, amass, annex, attain, bring in, buy, catch, collect, cop*, corral*, earn, gain, gather, get, get hands on, get hold of, grab, have, hustle, land, latch onto, lock up, pick up, procure, promote, rack up*, scare up*, secure, snag*, take, take possession of*, wangle*, win; SEE CONCEPTS 120,124,142

acquisition [n1] obtaining or receiving
accretion, achievement, acquirement, acquiring, addition, attainment, buy, gain, gaining, learning, obtainment, possession, prize, procuration, procurement, procuring, property, purchase, pursuit, recovery, redemption, retrieval, salvage, winning; SEE CONCEPTS 120,124,142

acquisition [n2] something obtained, received
accomplishment, achievement, allowance, annuity, award, benefit, bonus, commission, dividend, donation, earnings, fortune, gain, gift, grant, income, increment, inheritance, net, premium, prize, proceeds, profit, remuneration, return, reward, riches, salary, security, wages, wealth, winnings; SEE CONCEPTS 120,337,710

acquisitive [adj] eager to obtain knowledge or things
avaricious, avid, covetous, demanding, desirous, grabbing, grabby, grasping, greedy, predatory, prehensile, rapacious; SEE CONCEPT 542

acquit [v1] announce removal of blame
absolve, blink at*, clear, deliver, discharge, disculpate, exculpate, excuse, exonerate, free, let

go, let off, let off the hook*, liberate, release, relieve, vindicate, whitewash*, wink at*, wipe off*; SEE CONCEPTS 50,83,88,317

acquit [v2] behave some way

act, bear, carry, comport, conduct, deport, perform; SEE CONCEPT 633

acquittal [n] declaration removing blame

absolution, acquitting, amnesty, clearance, deliverance, discharge, discharging, dismissal, dismissing, exculpation, exemption, exoneration, freeing, letting off, liberation, pardon, release, releasing, relief from, reprieve, vindication; SEE CONCEPTS 127,317,318

acre [n] piece of land, unit of area

acreage, bit, estate, grounds, manor, plot, property; SEE CONCEPT 792

acreage [n] land

back forty*, expanse, holding, parcel, plot, property, real estate; SEE CONCEPTS 509,513

acrid [adj1] bitter, sour to taste

acid, amaroidal, astringent, biting, burning, caustic, harsh, irritating, pungent, sharp, stinging; SEE CONCEPT 613

acrid [adj2] nasty in behavior or words

acrimonious, austere, biting, bitter, caustic, cutting, harsh, mordant, sarcastic, sharp, trenchant, vitriolic; SEE CONCEPTS 267,401

acrimonious [adj] nasty in behavior, speech

acerbic, acid, angry, astringent, belligerent, biting, bitter, caustic, censorious, churlish, crabby, cranky, cross, cutting, indignant, irascible, irate, ireful, mad, mordant, peevish, petulant, rancorous, sarcastic, sharp, spiteful, splenetic, tart, testy, trenchant, wrathful; SEE CONCEPTS 267,401

acrimony [n] nasty behavior, speech

acerbity, animosity, antipathy, asperity, astringency, belligerence, bitterness, churlishness, crankiness, harshness, ill will, irascibility, malevolence, malice, mordancy, peevishness, rancor, rudeness, sarcasm, spite, tartness, unkindness, virulence; SEE CONCEPTS 633,657

acrobat [n] performer who does tricks, physical feats

aerialist, artist, athlete, balancer, clown, contortionist, dancer, funambulist, gymnast, performer, stunt person, trapezist, tumbler; SEE CONCEPT 352

acrobatics [n] athletic floor exercises

balancing, feats, gymnastics, somersaults, stunts, tumbling; SEE CONCEPT 363

across [prep] traversing a space, side to side

athwart, beyond, cross, crossed, crosswise, opposite, over, transversely; SEE CONCEPT 581

across-the-board [adj] all

all-inclusive, blanket, complete, comprehensive, everything, sweeping, total; SEE CONCEPTS 513,772

act [n1] something done

accomplishment, achievement, action, deed, doing, execution, exploit, feat, move, operation, performance, step, thing, undertaking; SEE CONCEPT 1

act [n2] legislative document

amendment, announcement, bill, clause, code, commitment, decree, edict, enactment, judgment, law, measure, order, ordinance, resolution, statute, subpoena, summons, verdict, warrant, writ; SEE CONCEPTS 271,318

act [n3] part of a performance

bit*, curtain, epilogue, gag*, introduction, number, piece, prologue, routine, scene, schtick*, show, sketch, spot, turn; SEE CONCEPT 264

act [n4] pretended behavior

affectation, attitude, bit*, chaser*, dissimulation, fake, false front*, feigning, front, performance, phony, pose, posture, pretense, put-on, sham, show, shuck and jive*, simulation, soft soap*, stall, stance, stunt, sweet talk*; SEE CONCEPT 633

act [v1] do something

accomplish, achieve, begin, carry on, carry out, consummate, cook, create, develop, do, do a number*, do one's thing*, enforce, execute, function, get in there*, go about, go for broke*, go for it*, go in for*, go that route*, go to town*, intrude, knock off*, labor, make progress, maneuver, move, officiate, operate, percolate*, perk*, perpetrate, persevere, persist, practice, preside, pursue, respond, serve, take effect, take part, take steps, take up, transort, undertake, work out; SEE CONCEPTS 1,4

act [v2] behave in a certain way

appear, behave, carry, carry oneself, carry out, comport, conduct, do, enact, execute, exert, function, give the appearance, go about, impress as, operate, perform, play part, react, represent oneself, seem, serve, strike, take on; SEE CONCEPT 633

act [v3] entertain by playing a role

be on*, bring down the house*, burlesque, characterize, do a turn*, dramatize, emote, enact, feign, go on, go over ham*, ham it up*, impersonate, lay an egg*, make debut, mime, mimic, mug, parody, perform, personate, play, play act, play gig, play part, play role, portray, pretend, put it over*, rehearse, represent, say one's piece*, simulate, star, stooge*, strut*, take part, tread the boards*; SEE CONCEPT 292

acting [adj] substituting in a role

ad interim, adjutant, alternate, assistant, delegated, deputy, interim, pro tem, pro tempore, provisional, surrogate, temporary; SEE CONCEPT 560

acting [n] entertaining, performing

assuming, characterization, depiction, dramatics, dramatizing, enacting, enactment, feigning, hamming*, histrionics, imitating, imitation, impersonation, improvisation, mime, mimicry, pantomime, performance, play acting, playing, portrayal, portraying, posing, posturing, pretending, pretense, putting, rendition, seeming, showing off, simulating, stagecraft, stooging*, theatre, theatricals; SEE CONCEPT 292

action [n1] something done

activity, agility, alacrity, alertness, animation, bag*, ballgame*, big idea*, bit*, business, bustle, commotion, dash, deal, energy, enterprise, flurry, force, functioning, game, going, happening, haste, hoopla*, hopper*, industry, in the works, life, liveliness, motion, movement, occupation, operation, plan, power, process, proposition, racket*, reaction, response, rush, scene, spirit, stir, stunt, trip, turmoil, vigor, vim, vitality, vivacity; SEE CONCEPT 1

action [n2] individual deed

accomplishment, achievement, act, blow, commission, dealings, doing, effort, enterprise, execution, exercise, exertion, exploit, feat, handiwork, maneuver, manipulation, move, operation, performance, procedure, step, stroke, thrust, transaction, undertaking; SEE CONCEPTS *91,706*

action [*n3*] *a legal process*
case, cause, a claim, lawsuit, litigation, proceeding, prosecution, suit; SEE CONCEPT *317*

action [*n4*] *an aggressive military deed*
battle, combat, conflict, contest, encounter, engagement, fight, fighting, fray, skirmish, warfare; SEE CONCEPT *320*

activate [*v*] *initiate something; start a function*
actify, actuate, arouse, call up, energize, impel, mobilize, motivate, move, prompt, propel, rouse, set in motion, start, stimulate, stir, switch on, take out of mothballs*, trigger, turn on; SEE CONCEPT *234*

active [*adj1*] *having movement*
alive, astir, at work, bustling, effective, efficacious, exertive, flowing, functioning, going, hasty, impelling, in force, in play, in process, mobile, movable, moving, operating, operative, progressive, pushing, rapid, restless, rolling, running, rushing, rustling, shifting, simmering, speeding, speedy, streaming, swarming, traveling, turning, walking, working; SEE CONCEPT *542*

active [*adj2*] *very involved in activity*
aggressive, agile, alert, alive, animated, assiduous, bold, brisk, bustling, busy, chipper, daring, dashing, determined, dexterous, diligent, dynamic, eager, energetic, engaged, enlivened, enterprising, enthusiastic, eventful, fireball*, forceful, forcible, fresh, frisky, hard-working, high-spirited, hyper*, industrious, intense, inventive, jumping, keen, lively, nimble, on the move, perky, persevering, purposeful, pushing, quick, rapid, ready, resolute, sharp, sprightly, spry, whiz*, zealous; SEE CONCEPTS *401,542*

activism [*n*] *action for change*
advocacy, boycotting, championing, effecting change, influence peddling, involvement, logrolling, militancy, moving and shaking*, picketing, striking; SEE CONCEPT *689*

activity [*n1*] *state of being active*
action, activeness, animation, bustle, enterprise, exercise, exertion, hustle, labor, life, liveliness, motion, movement; SEE CONCEPTS *1,748*

activity [*n2*] *special interest or pursuit*
act, avocation, bag*, ballgame*, bit*, deed, endeavor, enterprise, entertainment, game, hobby, job, labor, occupation, pastime, project, racket, scene*, scheme, stunt, task, trip, undertaking, venture, work, zoo*; SEE CONCEPT *32*

act of God [*n*] *natural disaster*
accident, earthquake, freak accident, hurricane, tornado, unforeseen event; SEE CONCEPTS *674,675*

actor [*n*] *person who performs, entertains by role-playing*
amateur, artist, barnstormer, bit player, character, clown, comedian, entertainer, extra, foil, ham*, hambone*, headliner, idol, impersonator, ingénue, lead, mime, mimic, pantomimist, performer, play-actor, player, soubrette, stand-in, star, stooge*, straight person, thesp*, thespian, trouper, understudy, ventriloquist, villain, walkon; SEE CONCEPT *352*

actress [*n*] *woman actor*
diva, ingenue, leading lady, prima donna, starlet, thespian; SEE CONCEPT *352*

actual [*adj*] *truly existing, real*
absolute, authentic, categorical, certain, concrete, confirmed, definite, factual, for real*, genuine, hard, honest injun*, honest to God*, indisputable, indubitable, kosher*, physical, positive, realistic, substantial, substantive, sure enough*, tangible, true, truthful, undeniable, unquestionable, verified; SEE CONCEPT *582*

actual [*adj2*] *existing at the present time*
current, exact, existent, extant, live, living, original, prevailing; SEE CONCEPT *799*

actuality [*n*] *something that truly exists, is real*
achievement, actualization, attainment, brass tacks*, fact, materiality, materialization, reality, real world*, straight stuff*, substance, substantiality, truth, what it is*; SEE CONCEPT *725*

actualize [*v*] *make real*
accomplish, bring about, engineer, produce, realize; SEE CONCEPT *91*

actually [*adj*] *truly real, existent*
absolutely, as a matter of fact, de facto, genuinely indeed, in fact, in point of fact, in reality, in truth, literally, really, veritably, very; SEE CONCEPT *582*

actuate [*v*] *start a function or action, motivate*
activate, animate, arouse, cause, drive, egg on*, energize, excite, fire up*, impel, incite, induce, influence, inspire, instigate, key up*, mobilize, motivate, move, prompt, propel, put up to*, quicken, rouse, spur, stimulate, turn on*, work into lather*, work up*; SEE CONCEPTS *221,234*

act up [*v*] *misbehave*
act out*, carry on, raise hell*, rebel, sow one's wild oats*; SEE CONCEPTS *106,633*

acumen [*n*] *ability to understand and reason*
acuity, acuteness, astuteness, awareness, brains, brilliance, cleverness, comprehension, cunning, discernment, discrimination, farsightedness, good taste, grasp, guile, ingenuity, insight, intellect, intelligence, intuition, judgment, keenness, perception, percipience, perspicacity, perspicuity, refinement, sagacity, sensitivity, sharpness, shrewdness, smartness, smarts*, understanding, vision, wisdom, wit; SEE CONCEPT *409*

acute [*adj1*] *deeply perceptive*
astute, canny, clever, discerning, discriminating, incisive, ingenious, insightful, intense, intuitive, judicious, keen, observant, penetrating, perspicacious, piercing, quick-witted, sensitive, sharp, smart, subtle; SEE CONCEPT *402*

acute [*adj2*] *very important*
afflictive, critical, crucial, dangerous, decisive, desperate, dire, essential, grave, serious, severe, sudden, urgent, vital; SEE CONCEPT *568*

acute [*adj3*] *severe, intense*
cutting, distressing, excruciating, exquisite, fierce, keen, overpowering, overwhelming, piercing, poignant, powerful, racking, severe, sharp, shooting, stabbing, sudden, violent; SEE CONCEPT *569*

acute [*adj4*] *having a sharp end or point*
acicular, aciculate, acuminate, acuminous, cuspate, cuspidate, knifelike, needle-shaped, peaked, piked, pointed, sharpened, spiked; SEE CONCEPT *485*

adage [*n*] *saying or proverb*
aphorism, apothegm, axiom, byword, dictum, maxim, motto, precept, saw; SEE CONCEPT *276*

adamant [*adj*] *unyielding*
determined, firm, fixed, hanging tough*, hardnosed, immovable, inexorable, inflexible, insistent, intransigent, obdurate, pat*, relentless,

ac
ad

resolute, rigid, set, set in stone*, standing pat*, stiff, stubborn, unbendable, unbending, uncompromising, unrelenting, unshakable, unswayable; SEE CONCEPT 401

adamant [adj2] *hard like rock*
adamantine, flinty, impenetrable, indestructible, rock-hard, tough, unbreakable; SEE CONCEPT 604

adapt [v] *adjust to a different situation or condition*
acclimate, accommodate, accustom, alter, change, come around, comply, conform, familiarize, fashion, fit, get act together*, get used to, grow used to, habituate, harmonize, make, match, modify, play the game*, prepare, qualify, readjust, reconcile, remodel, revise, roll with punches*, shape, shape up*, square, suit, tailor; SEE CONCEPTS 232,697

adaptable [adj] *able and usually willing to change*
AC-DC*, adjustable, all around, alterable, can-do*, changeable, compliant, conformable, convertible, ductile, easy-going, flexible, hanging loose*, malleable, modifiable, moldable, plastic, pliable, pliant, resilient, supple, switch-hitting, tractable, variable, versatile; SEE CONCEPTS 550,576

adaptation [n1] *act of adapting*
adjustment, adoption, alteration, conversion, modification, refitting, remodeling, reworking, shift, transformation, variation; SEE CONCEPT 697

adaptation [n2] *condition of something resulting from change*
acclimatization, accustomedness, agreement, compliance, correspondence, familiarization, habituation, naturalization; SEE CONCEPT 230

adaptive [adj] *adjusting*
flexible, modifying, robust; SEE CONCEPTS 314,489,613

add [v1] *simple arithmetical process of increase; accumulation*
calculate, cast, compute, figure, reckon, count up, do addition, enumerate, figure, reckon, reckon up, sum, summate, tally, tot*, total, tote*, tot up*; SEE CONCEPT 764

add [v2] *adjoin, increase; make further comment*
affix, annex, ante, append, augment, beef up*, boost, build up, charge up, continue, cue in*, figure in, flesh out*, heat up*, hike, hike up*, hitch on*, hook on*, hook up with*, include, jack up*, jazz up*, join together, pad, parlay, piggyback*, plug into*, pour it on*, reply, run up*, say further, slap on*, snowball*, soup up*, speed up, spike, step up, supplement, sweeten*, tack on*, tag; SEE CONCEPTS 51,113,236,245

addendum [n] *something conjoined, added*
addition, adjunct, appendage, appendix, attachment, augmentation, codicil, extension, extra, postscript, rider, supplement; SEE CONCEPTS 270,827

addict [n] *person who has compulsion toward activity, often injurious*
aficionado, buff, devotee, enthusiast, fan, fanatic, fiend, follower, freak*, habitué, hound*, junkie*, nut, practitioner, zealot; SEE CONCEPTS 412,423

addicted [adj] *dependent on something, compulsive*
absorbed, accustomed, attached, dependent, devoted, disposed, fanatic, fond, given over to, given to, habituated, hooked, hyped*, imbued, inclined, obsessed, predisposed, prone to, spaced

out*, strung out*, under the influence, used to, wedded to; SEE CONCEPT 542

addiction [n] *a habit of activity, often injurious*
bag*, bent, craving, dependence, enslavement, fixation, hang-up*, hook, inclination, jones*, kick*, monkey*, monkey on back*, obsession, shot*, sweet tooth*, thing*; SEE CONCEPTS 20,316,709

addictive [adj] *habit-forming*
enslaving, hooking, obsessive; SEE CONCEPTS 530,547

addition [n1] *process of conjoining, adding*
accession, adding, adjoining, affixing, annexation, attachment, augmentation, enlargement, extension, inclusion, increasing; SEE CONCEPTS 236,245

addition [n2] *something conjoined to or enlargement of something*
accession, accessory, accretion, accrual, addendum, additive, adjunct, aggrandizement, annex, appendage, appendix, attachment, augmentation, bonus, boost, commission, dividend, enhancement, enlargement, expansion, extension, extra, gain, hike, increase, increment, option, profit, raise, reinforcement, rise, supplement, wing; SEE CONCEPTS 640,835

addition [n3] *arithmetical process of augmentation*
accretion, accruing, adding, computing, counting, enlarging, expanding, increasing, reckoning, summation, summing, tabulating, totaling, toting*; SEE CONCEPT 764

additional [adj] *extra, supplementary*
added, affixed, appended, further, increased, more, new, on the side, option, other, over-and-above, padding, perk, spare, supplementary; SEE CONCEPT 771

addled [adj] *confused*
balled up*, befuddled, bewildered, fouled up*, gone*, mixed up, out of it, punchy, rattled, shaken, shook, shook up, slap-happy, thrown, unglued*, woozy*; SEE CONCEPT 403

address [n1] *place of residence or business where one can be contacted*
abode, box number, direction, domicile, dwelling, headquarters, home, house, living quarters, location, lodging, number, place of business, place of residence, street, whereabouts, zip code; SEE CONCEPT 516

address [n2] *speech given to formal gathering*
chalk talk*, discourse, dissertation, lecture, oration, pep talk*, pitch, sermon, soapbox*, spiel*, talk; SEE CONCEPT 278

address [v1] *write directions for delivery*
consign, dispatch, forward, inscribe, label, mark, postmark, remit, route, send, ship, superscribe, transmit; SEE CONCEPTS 60,79

address [v2] *speak to a formal gathering*
approach, bespeak, call, deliver speech, deliver talk, discourse, discuss, get on a soapbox*, give speech, give talk, greet, hail, lecture, memorialize, orate, pitch, pontificate, root for, sermonize, spiel*, spout, stump*, take the floor, talk; SEE CONCEPTS 60,266,285

address [v3] *devote effort to something*
apply oneself to, attend to, concentrate on, devote oneself to, dig, direct, engage in, focus on, give, go at*, go for*, hammer away*, have a go at*, have at*, knuckle down to*, peg away*, pitch into*, plug away at*, take care of, take up,

throw oneself into, try, turn, turn to, undertake; SEE CONCEPT *100*

adduce [v] *affirm*
cite, illustrate, point out, prove, show; SEE CONCEPTS *49,50,88*

adept [adj] *very able*
accomplished, ace*, adroit, brainy, capable, clean*, crack*, crackerjack*, deft, dexterous, expert, hot*, hotshot*, know stuff*, masterful, masterly, nobody's fool*, no dummy*, no slouch*, on the ball*, on the beam*, practiced, proficient, quick, savvy, sharp, sharp as a tack*, skilled, skillful, slick, smooth, there*, up to speed*, versed, whiz*, wizard; SEE CONCEPTS *402,527*

adequacy [n] *ability, competency in some action*
capability, capacity, commensurateness, competence, enough, fairness, plenty, requisiteness, satisfactoriness, sufficiency, suitableness, tolerableness; SEE CONCEPTS *636,656*

adequate [adj] *enough, able*
acceptable, all right, capable, comfortable, commensurate, competent, decent, equal, fair, passable, requisite, satisfactory, sufficient, sufficing, suitable, tolerable, unexceptional, unobjectionable; SEE CONCEPTS *533,558*

adequately [adv] *sufficiently*
abundantly, acceptably, appropriately, capably, competently, copiously, decently, fairly well, fittingly, modestly, pleasantly enough, presentably, satisfactorily, sufficiently, suitably, to an acceptable degree, tolerably, well enough; SEE CONCEPTS *558,560*

adhere [v1] *conform to or follow rules exactly*
abide by, be attached, be constant, be devoted, be devoted to, be faithful, be loyal, be true, cleave to, comply, follow, fulfill, heed, keep, maintain, mind, obey, observe, practice, respect, stand by, support; SEE CONCEPTS *87,636*

adhere [v2] *stick or become stuck to, either physically or mentally*
attach, cement, cleave, cling like ivy*, cohere, fasten, fix, freeze to*, glue, hold fast, hold on like bulldog*, paste, stay put, stick like a barnacle*, stick like glue*, unite; SEE CONCEPTS *85,113,160*

adherent [n] *supporter or follower*
advocate, aficionado, backer, believer, card-carrying member*, devotee, disciple, enthusiast, fan, hanger-on; SEE CONCEPTS *352,366,423*

adhesion [n] *holding fast*
adherence, adhesiveness, attachment, bond, cling, grip, stickiness, sticking; SEE CONCEPTS *85,160*

adhesive [adj] *sticking*
adherent, adhering, agglutinant, attaching, clinging, clingy, gelatinous, glutinous, gooey, gummed, gummy, holding, hugging, mucilaginous, pasty, resinous, sticky, tenacious, viscid, viscous, waxy; SEE CONCEPTS *488,606*

ad hoc [adj] *for a specific purpose*
impromptu, provisional, special, specific, specified; SEE CONCEPTS *535,557,564*

adieu [n] *parting remark or action*
adios*, congé, farewell, goodbye, leave-taking, parting, so long, valediction; SEE CONCEPT *276*

ad infinitum [adj] *neverending*
ceaselessly, endlessly, forever, perpetually; SEE CONCEPT *798*

adjacent [adj] *next to, abutting*
adjoining, alongside, beside, bordering, close, close by, contiguous, near, neighboring, next door, touching; SEE CONCEPT *586*

adjective [n] *word that modifies a noun*
accessory, additional, adjunct, adnoun, attribute, attributive, dependent, descriptive, identifier, modifier, qualifier; SEE CONCEPT *275*

adjoin [v1] *be next to*
abut, approximate, be adjacent to, border, butt, communicate, connect, join, lie, lie beside, link, neighbor, touch, verge; SEE CONCEPT *747*

adjoin [v2] *attach*
add, affix, annex, append, combine, connect, couple, interconnect, join, link, unite; SEE CONCEPTS *85,113,160*

adjoining [adj] *being next to*
abutting, adjacent, approximal, bordering on, connecting, conterminous, contiguous, coterminous, impinging, interconnecting, joined, joining, juxtaposed, near, neighboring, next door, touching, verging; SEE CONCEPT *586*

adjourn [v] *stop a proceeding*
curb, defer, delay, discontinue, hold off, hold over, hold up, postpone, prorogue, put off, recess, restrain, shelve, stay, suspend; SEE CONCEPTS *121,234*

adjournment [n] *discontinuation or delay of a proceeding*
break, deferment, deferral, intermission, interruption, pause, postponement, prorogation, putting off, recess, stay, suspension; SEE CONCEPTS *121,703*

adjudicate [v] *formally judge*
adjudge, arbitrate, decide, determine, mediate, referee, settle, umpire; SEE CONCEPTS *18,317*

adjudication [n] *judgment*
conclusion, decision, determination, finding, pronouncement, ruling, settlement, verdict; SEE CONCEPTS *103,689*

adjunct [n] *addition; help*
accessory, addendum, appendage, appendix, appurtenance, associate, auxiliary, complement, detail, partner, subordinate, supplement; SEE CONCEPTS *484,835*

adjure [v] *command*
beseech, charge, entreat, implore, obligate, order, require, supplicate; SEE CONCEPT *53*

adjust [v1] *become or make prepared, adapted*
acclimatize, accommodate, accustom, adapt, alter, arrange, compose, conform, dispose, do as Romans do*, doctor*, fiddle with*, fine-tune, fit, fix, fix up, get act together*, get it together*, grin and bear it*, habituate, harmonize, make conform, modify, order, quadrate, reconcile, rectify, redress, regulate, remodel, settle, suit, swim with the tide*, tailor, tailor-make, tune; SEE CONCEPTS *35,232,697*

adjust [v2] *mechanically alter, especially to improve*
accommodate, align, balance, bring into line, calibrate, connect, correct, fine-tune, fit, fix, focus, grind, improve, mend, overhaul, polish, put in working order, readjust, rectify, regulate, renovate, repair, service, set, sharpen, square, tighten, troubleshoot, tune up; SEE CONCEPTS *202,212*

adjust [v3] *bring into agreement or to a standard*
accord, allocate, arrange, clarify, conclude, conform, coordinate, doctor*, fiddle with*, fine-

tune, fix up, grade, methodize, modify, organize, reconcile, regulate, settle, sort, standardize, straighten, systematize, tally; SEE CONCEPTS 84,117

adjustable [*adj*] *alterable*

accommodating, adaptable, changeable, conformable, flexible, malleable, modifiable, pliable, tractable; SEE CONCEPT 534

adjustment [*n1*] *adaptation*

acclimation, acclimatization, alteration, arrangement, balancing, conformance, correcting, fitting, fixing, improvement, mending, modification, ordering, organization, organizing, orientation, readjustment, redress, regulating, regulation, repairing, setting, shaping, standardization, turning; SEE CONCEPT 697

adjustment [*n2*] *financial retribution, payment of claim*

agreement, allotment, apportionment, benefit, compensation, compromise, pay, reconciliation, reimbursement, remuneration, settlement, share, stake, stipulation; SEE CONCEPT 332

adjutant [*n*] *assistant*

aide, auxiliary, helper; SEE CONCEPT 348

ad-lib [*adj*] *improvised*

extemporaneous, extempore, extemporized, impromptu, made-up, off-the-cuff*, spontaneous, unprepared, unrehearsed; SEE CONCEPT 267

ad-lib [*adv*] *in an improvised manner*

extemporaneously, extempore, impromptu, off the cuff*, off the top of one's head*, spontaneously, without preparation, without rehearsal; SEE CONCEPT 267

ad-lib [*v*] *improvise speech*

extemporize, invent, make up, speak extemporaneously, speak impromptu, speak off the cuff*; SEE CONCEPT 266

administer [*v1*] *manage an organization or effort*

administrate, be in the driver's seat*, be in the saddle*, boss*, carry out, conduct, control, crack the whip*, direct, execute, govern, head, head up*, hold the reins*, oversee, pull the strings*, pull the wires*, render, ride herd on*, run, run the show*, sit on top of*, superintend, supervise; SEE CONCEPTS 117,298

administer [*v2*] *dispense something needed*

apply, apportion, authorize, bring, contribute, deal, deliver, disburse, distribute, dole out, execute, extend, furnish, give, impose, inflict, issue, measure out, mete out, offer, perform, portion, proffer, provide, regulate, serve, supply, tender; SEE CONCEPTS 108,136

administration [*n1*] *management of an organization or effort*

administering, agency, application, authority, charge, command, conduct, conducting, control, directing, direction, dispensation, disposition, distribution, enforcement, execution, governing, government, guidance, handling, jurisdiction, legislation, order, organization, overseeing, oversight, performance, policy, power, provision, regulation, rule, running, strategy, superintendence, supervision, surveillance; SEE CONCEPTS 117,298

administration [*n2*] *human or group who manages effort of an organization*

admiral, advisers, board, bureau, cabinet, chair, chairperson, chargé d'affaires, command, commander, committee, consulate, department, di-

rectors, embassy, executive, executives, feds*, front office*, general, governing body, headquarters, legislature, management, ministry, officers, officials, powers, presidency, president, presidium, stewards, superintendents, supervisors, top brass*, upstairs*; SEE CONCEPT 299

administration [*n3*] *period during which a particular human group is in power*

dynasty, incumbency, presidency, regime, reign, stay, tenure, term; SEE CONCEPTS 298,816

administrative [*adj*] *involved in managing or using power*

authoritative, bureaucratic, central, commanding, controlling, deciding, decisive, departmental, directing, directive, directorial, executive, governing, governmental, in charge, in control, jurisdictional, legislative, managerial, official, organizational, policy-making, presiding, regulative, regulatory, ruling, superintending, supervising, supervisory; SEE CONCEPTS 319,536

administrator [*n*] *person who manages organization*

ambassador, authority, boss, bureaucrat, captain, CEO, chair, chairperson, chief, commander, consul, controller, custodian, dean, director, exec*, executive, front office*, governor, head, head honcho*, head person*, inspector, judge, leader, manager, mayor, minister, officer, official, organizer, overseer, person upstairs*, premier, president, prez*, producer, superintendent, supervisor; SEE CONCEPTS 347,354

admirable [*adj*] *held in great respect*

A-1*, ace*, A-OK*, attractive, best ever, cat's pajamas*, choice, commendable, cool*, copacetic*, crackerjack*, deserving, dream*, estimable, excellent, exquisite, fine, good, great, greatest, hunky dory*, keen*, laudable, meritable, meritorious, neat*, out of sight*, out of this world*, peachy*, praiseworthy, rare, solid, super, super-duper*, superior, unreal*, valuable, wicked*, wonderful, worthy, zero cool*; SEE CONCEPTS 572,574

admiration [*n*] *great respect*

account, adoration, affection, applause, appreciation, approbation, approval, deference, delight, esteem, estimation, favor, fondness, glorification, homage, honor, idolatry, idolization, liking, love, marveling, obeisance, pleasure, praise, prizing, recognition, regard, reverence, valuing, veneration, wonder, wonderment, worship; SEE CONCEPT 32

admire [*v*] *hold in high regard*

adore, applaud, appreciate, approve, be crazy about*, be crazy for*, be crazy over*, be mad about*, be nuts about*, be stuck on*, be sweet on*, be wild about*, cherish, commend, credit, delight in, esteem, eulogize, extol, fall for*, get high on*, glorify, go for*, groove on*, hail, hold in respect, honor, idolize, laud, look up to, marvel at, moon over*, pay homage to, praise, prize, rate highly, respect, revere, take pleasure in, think highly of, treasure, value, venerate, wonder at, worship; SEE CONCEPT 32

admirer [*n*] *person who holds someone in high regard*

adherent, beau, believer, booster, boyfriend, buff, bug*, cat*, devotee, disciple, enthusiast, fan, fancier, fiend*, follower, freak*, girlfriend, groupie*, hound*, junkie*, lover, nut*, partisan, patron, rooter*, suitor, supporter, swain, sweetheart, wooer, worshiper; SEE CONCEPT 423

admissible [*adj*] *able or deserving of consideration; allowable*
acceptable, allowed, applicable, appropriate, concedable, fair, fitting, just, justifiable, lawful, legal, legitimate, licit, likely, logical, not impossible, not unlikely, okay, passable, permissible, permitted, pertinent, possible, probable, proper, rational, reasonable, relevant, right, suitable, tolerable, tolerated, warranted, worthy; SEE CONCEPT 533

admission [*n1*] *entering or allowing entry*
acceptance, access, admittance, certification, confirmation, designation, door, entrance, entree, ingress, initiation, introduction, permission, reception, recognition, way, welcome; SEE CONCEPTS 83,159

admission [*n2*] *confession or acknowledgment*
accession, admittance, affidavit, affirmation, allowance, assent, assertion, attestation, averment, avowal, concession, confirmation, declaration, deposition, disclosure, divulgence, profession, revelation, statement, testimonial, testimony; SEE CONCEPT 57

admit [*v1*] *allow entry or use*
accept, be big on*, bless, buy, concede, enter, entertain, give access, give the nod*, give thumbs up*, grant, harbor, house, initiate, introduce, let, let in, lodge, okay, permit, receive, shelter, sign*, sign off on*, suffer, take, take in; SEE CONCEPT 83

admit [*v2*] *confess, acknowledge*
accept, accord, acquiesce, adopt, affirm, agree, allow, approve, avow, bare, bring to light*, communicate, concede, concur, confide, confirm, consent, cop a plea*, credit, declare, disclose, divulge, enumerate, expose, go into details*, grant, indicate, let, let on, make known, narrate, number, open up, own, own up*, permit, proclaim, profess, recite, recognize, relate, reveal, spill*, subscribe to, talk, tell, tolerate, uncover, unveil, yield; SEE CONCEPTS 57,82

admittance [*n*] *permission to enter*
access, entrance, entry, ingress, pass, passage, reception; SEE CONCEPTS 388,685

admixture [*n*] *blending*
amalgamation, blend, combination, commixture, compound, fusion, melange, mingling, mixture; SEE CONCEPT 432

admonish [*v*] *warn, strongly criticize*
advise, berate, call down, call on the carpet*, censure, check, chide, come down hard on*, counsel, ding*, draw the line*, enjoin, exhort, forewarn, give a going over*, give a piece of one's mind*, glue*, growl*, hoist*, jack up*, notice, rap*, rap on knuckles*, rebuke, reprimand, reprove, scold, sit on, slap on wrist*, speak to, talk to, tell a thing or two*, tell off*, upbraid, warn; SEE CONCEPTS 52,78

admonition [*n1*] *caution*
advice, appraisal, counsel, forewarning, warning; SEE CONCEPTS 78,274

admonition [*n2*] *scolding*
berating, dressing down*, rebuke, reprimand, reproach, reproval, talking to*, upbraiding; SEE CONCEPTS 44,52

ad nauseum [*adv*] *to the point of illness*
more than one can stomach, to a sickening degree, too much; SEE CONCEPTS 529,571

ado [*n*] *fuss*
bother, confusion, excitement, flurry, hubbub, to-do*, travail, trouble, turmoil; SEE CONCEPTS 46,106,388,633

adolescence [*n*] *state of puberty, preadulthood*
boyhood, girlhood, greenness, juvenility, minority, pubescence, spring, teens, youth, youthfulness; SEE CONCEPT 817

adolescent [*adj*] *preadult or immature*
boyish, girlish, growing, juvenile, pubescent, puerile, teen, teenage, young, youthful; SEE CONCEPTS 401,578,797

adolescent [*n*] *person in puberty, preadulthood*
juvenile, minor, stripling, sweet sixteen*, teen, teenager, teenybopper*, youngster, youth; SEE CONCEPT 424

adopt [*v1*] *choose or take something as one's own*
accept, adapt, affiliate, affirm, appropriate, approve, assent, assume, borrow, embrace, endorse, espouse, follow, go down the line*, go in for*, imitate, maintain, mimic, opt, ratify, seize, select, support, take on, take over, take up, tap, use, utilize; SEE CONCEPT 18

adopt [*v2*] *legally care for another's child*
choose, foster, naturalize, pick, raise, select, take in; SEE CONCEPT 317

adoption [*n1*] *choosing or taking something as one's own*
acceptance, approbation, appropriation, approval, assumption, choice, confirmation, embracement, embracing, enactment, endorsement, espousal, following, maintenance, ratification, selection, support, taking on, taking over, taking up; SEE CONCEPT 18

adoption [*n2*] *legal taking of another's child*
adopting, fosterage, fostering, naturalizing, raising, taking in; SEE CONCEPT 317

adorable [*adj*] *cute, lovable*
ambrosial, appealing, attractive, captivating, charming, cute, darling, dear, delectable, delicious, delightful, dishy*, dreamy*, fetching, heavenly, hot*, luscious, pleasing, precious, sexy, suave; SEE CONCEPTS 579,589

adoration [*n*] *intense love*
admiration, amore, ardor, attachment, crush, devotion, esteem, estimation, exaltation, glorification, hankering, honor, idolatry, idolization, infatuation, pash*, passion, puppy love*, reverence, shine*, veneration, weakness*, worship, worshipping, yen*; SEE CONCEPT 32

adore [*v*] *love intensely*
admire, be crazy about*, be gone on*, be mad for*, be nuts about*, be serious about*, be smitten with*, be stuck on*, be sweet on*, be wild about*, cherish, delight in, dig*, dote on, esteem, exalt, fall for, flip over*, glorify, go for*, honor, idolize, prize, revere, reverence, treasure, venerate, worship; SEE CONCEPT 32

adorn [*v*] *decorate*
array, beautify, bedeck, deck, doll up*, dress up, embellish, enhance, enrich, fix up, furbish, garnish, grace, gussy up*, ornament, spruce up, trim; SEE CONCEPTS 162,177

adornment [*n1*] *decorating, enhancing*
beautification, decoration, embellishment, gilding, ornamentation, trimming; SEE CONCEPTS 162,177

adornment [*n2*] *a decoration*
accessory, dingbat, doodad, embellishment, fan-

dangle*, floss*, frill, frippery, furbelow*, gewgaw*, jazz*, ornament, thing, trimming; SEE
CONCEPTS *446,484*

adrift [*adv1*] *floating out of control*
afloat, drifting, loose, unanchored, unmoored;
SEE CONCEPT *488*

adrift [*adv2*] *without purpose*
aimless, directionless, goalless, purposeless; SEE
CONCEPT *542*

adrift [*adv3*] *off course*
amiss, astray, erring, wrong; SEE CONCEPT *581*

adroit [*adj*] *very able or skilled*
adept, apt, artful, clean, clever, crack*, crackerjack*, cunning, cute, deft, dexterous, expert,
foxy*, good, handy, hot tamale*, ingenious,
masterful, neat*, nifty*, nimble, on the ball*, on
the beam*, proficient, quick on the trigger*,
quick on the uptake*, quick-witted, savvy, sharp,
skillful, slick, smart, up*, up to speed*, whiz*,
wizard; SEE CONCEPT *527*

adulate [*v*] *flatter*
apple polish*, brown-nose*, fall all over*, fawn,
gush, kiss feet*, praise, worship; SEE CONCEPTS
59,69

adulation [*n*] *overenthusiastic praise*
applause, audation, blandishment, bootlicking*,
commendation, fawning, flattery, sycophancy,
worship; SEE CONCEPTS *32,69*

adult [*adj*] *being mature, fully grown*
developed, grown, grown-up, of age, ripe,
ripened; SEE CONCEPT *406*

adult [*n*] *a mature, fully grown person*
gentleperson, grownup, man, person, woman;
SEE CONCEPTS *394,424*

adulterate [*v*] *alter or debase, often for profit*
alloy, amalgamate, attenuate, blend, cheapen,
commingle, contaminate, cook, corrupt, cut*, defile, degrade, denature, depreciate, deteriorate,
devalue, dilute, dissolve, doctor*, doctor up*,
falsify, impair, infiltrate, intermix, irrigate, lace*,
make impure, mingle, mix, phony up*, plant*,
pollute, shave*, spike*, taint, thin, transfuse, vitiate, water down*, weaken; SEE CONCEPTS
240,254

adulterated [*adj*] *debased or dirty*
attenuated, blended, contaminated, corrupt, defiled, degraded, depreciated, deteriorated, devalued, diluted, dissolved, impaired, mixed,
polluted, tainted, thinned, vitiated, watered
down, weakened; SEE CONCEPT *485*

adulterous [*adj*] *unfaithful*
cheating, double-crossing*, extracurricular*, fast
and loose*, illicit, immoral, moonlighting*,
speedy*, two-faced*, two-timing*, unchaste; SEE
CONCEPT *372*

adultery [*n*] *extramarital affair*
affair, carrying on*, cheating, extracurricular activity*, fling, fornication, hanky-panky*, immorality, infidelity, matinee*, playing around*,
relationship, thing*, two-timing*; SEE CONCEPT
633

advance [*adj*] *ahead in position or time*
beforehand, earlier, early, first, foremost, forward, in front, in the forefront, in the lead,
leading, previously, prior; SEE CONCEPTS
583,585,799

advance [*n1*] *forward movement*
advancement, headway, impetus, motion,
progress, progression; SEE CONCEPTS *152,208*

advance [*n2*] *improvement, progress in development*
advancement, amelioration, betterment, boost,
break*, breakthrough, buildup, development, enrichment, furtherance, gain, go-ahead*, growth,
headway, increase, progress, promotion, rise,
step, up, upgrade, upping; SEE CONCEPTS
700,704

advance [*n3*] *money given beforehand*
accommodation, allowance, bite*, credit, deposit, down payment, floater*, front money*,
hike, increase, loan, prepayment, retainer, rise*,
score, stake, take*, touch*; SEE CONCEPTS
340,344

advance [*v1*] *move something forward, often
quickly*
accelerate, achieve, bring forward, come forward, conquer, continue ahead, continue on, dispatch, drive, elevate, forge ahead, gain ground,
get ahead, get green light*, get there*, get with
it*, go ahead, go forth, go forward, go great
guns*, go places*, go to town*, hasten, launch,
make headway, make the scene*, march, move
on, move onward, move up, press on, proceed,
progress, promote, propel, push ahead, push on,
quicken, send forward, skyrocket*, speed, step
forward, storm; SEE CONCEPTS *152,208,704*

advance [*v2*] *promote or propose an idea*
adduce, allege, ballyhoo, beat the drum for, benefit, boost, cite, encourage, foster, further, get ink
for*, hype*, introduce, lay forward, make a pitch
for*, offer, plug*, present, proffer, puff*, push,
put forward, put on the map*, serve, set forth,
splash, spot, submit, suggest, throw spotlight
on*, urge; SEE CONCEPTS *49,60,68*

advance [*v3*] *give money beforehand*
furnish, lend, loan, pay, provide; SEE CONCEPT
341

advance [*v4*] *increase in amount, number, or position*
boost, break the bank*, develop, elevate, enlarge,
get fat*, get rich*, grade, grow, hit pay dirt*, hit
the jackpot*, improve, magnify, make a killing*,
make out*, multiply, pan out*, prefer, prosper,
raise, strike gold*, strike it rich*, thrive, up, upgrade, uplift; SEE CONCEPTS *236,244,245*

advanced [*adj*] *ahead in position, time, manner*
avant-garde, breakthrough, cutting-edge*, excellent, exceptional, extreme, first, foremost, forward, higher, late, leading, leading-edge*,
liberal, precocious, progressive, radical, state-of-
the-art*, unconventional; SEE CONCEPTS
574,578,585,797

advancement [*n1*] *promotion, progress*
advance, amelioration, betterment, elevation,
gain, growth, headway, improvement, preference, preferment, prelation, rise, upgrading; SEE
CONCEPTS *700,704*

advancement [*n2*] *forward movement*
advance, anabasis, gain, headway, march,
progress, progression; SEE CONCEPTS *152,208*

advance(s) [*n4*] *desirous pursuit of someone*
approach, move, overture, proposal, proposition,
suggestion; SEE CONCEPTS *20,384*

advantage [*n*] *benefit, favored position or circumstance*
aid, ascendancy, asset, assistance, authority,
avail, blessing, boon, break, choice, comfort,
convenience, dominance, edge, eminence, expediency, favor, gain, good, gratification, help,

hold, improvement, influence, interest, lead, leeway, leg-up*, leverage, luck, mastery, odds, position, power, precedence, pre-eminence, preference, prestige, prevalence, profit, protection, recognition, resources, return, sanction, starting, superiority, support, supremacy, upper hand*, utility, wealth; SEE CONCEPT 574

advantageous [adj] *favorable*
auspicious, beneficial, expedient, for the best, fortunate, handy, helpful, opportune, profitable, propitious, worthwhile; SEE CONCEPTS 537,558,572

advent [n] *beginning or arrival of something anticipated*
appearance, approach, arrival, coming, entrance, occurrence, onset, visitation; SEE CONCEPTS 119,159

adventure [n] *risky or unexpected undertaking*
chance, contingency, emprise, endangerment, enterprise, experience, exploit, feat, happening, hazard, incident, jeopardy, occurrence, peril, scene, speculation, trip, undertaking, venture; SEE CONCEPTS 384,386

adventurer [n] *person who takes risks*
charlatan, daredevil, entrepreneur, explorer, fortune-hunter, gambler, globetrotter, hero, heroine, madcap, mercenary, opportunist, pioneer, pirate, romantic, speculator, stunt person, swashbuckler, traveler, venturer, voyager, wanderer; SEE CONCEPT 423

adventurous [adj] *daring, risk-taking*
adventuresome, audacious, bold, brave, courageous, dangerous, daredevil, enterprising, foolhardy, hazardous, headstrong, intrepid, rash, reckless, risky, temerarious, venturesome, venturous; SEE CONCEPTS 404,542

adverb [n] *word modifying a verb*
limiter, modifier, qualifier; SEE CONCEPT 275

adversary [n] *opponent*
antagonist, attacker, bad person, bandit, competitor, contestant, enemy, foe, match, opposer, opposite number*, oppugner, rival; SEE CONCEPT 412

adverse [adj] *unfavorable, antagonistic*
allergic to*, conflicting, contrary, detrimental, disadvantageous, down on*, down side*, have no use for*, inimical, injurious, inopportune, negative, opposed, opposing, opposite, oppugning, ornery*, reluctant, repugnant, stuffy*, unfortunate, unfriendly, unlucky, unpropitious, unwilling; SEE CONCEPT 570

adversity [n] *bad luck, situation*
affliction, bad break*, bummer*, calamity, can of worms*, catastrophe, clutch, contretemps, crunch*, difficulty, disaster, distress, downer*, drag*, evil eye*, hard knocks*, hardship, hard times, hurting, ill fortune, jam, jinx, kiss of death*, misery, misfortune, mishap, on the skids*, pain in the neck*, poison*, reverse, sorrow, suffering, the worst*, tough luck*, trial, trouble; SEE CONCEPT 674

advertise [v] *publicize for the purpose of selling or causing one to want*
acquaint, advance, advise, announce, apprise, ballyhoo*, beat the drum for*, bill, blazon, boost*, build up, circularize, communicate, declare, disclose, display, divulge, drum*, endorse, exhibit, expose, flaunt, get on soapbox for*, hard sell, herald, hype*, inform, make a pitch*, make known, notify, pitch, plug, press agent*, proclaim, promote, promulgate, puff*, push, put on

the map*, reveal, show, soft sell, splash*, sponsor, spot, tout, uncover, unmask; SEE CONCEPTS 60,324

advertisement [n] *public notice of sale*
ad, announcement, bill, blurb, broadcast, circular, classified ad, commercial, communication, declaration, display, endorsement, exhibit, exhibition, flyer, literature, notice, notification, placard, plug, poster, proclamation, promotion, promulgation, propaganda, publication, publicity, squib, throwaway, want ad; SEE CONCEPTS 270,277,278,280

advertising [n] *public notice of sale; notices to increase consumer desire*
announcement, announcing, ballyhoo*, billing, blasting*, broadcasting, buildup, displaying, exhibiting, exhibition, exposition, hard sell, hoopla*, hype*, pitch, plug, posting, PR, proclamation, promo*, promoting, promotion, publicity, puff*, screamer*, spread, squib; SEE CONCEPTS 97,138,324

advice [n] *recommendation*
admonition, advisement, advocacy, aid, bum steer*, caution, charge, consultation, counsel, directions, dissuasion, encouragement, exhortation, forewarning, guidance, help, information, injunction, input, instruction, judgment, lesson, news, opinion, persuasion, prescription, proposal, proposition, recommendation, steer, suggestion, teaching, telltale, tidings, tip, tip-off*, two cents' worth*, view, warning, word, word to the wise*; SEE CONCEPTS 75,274

advisable [adj] *recommended, wise*
appropriate, apt, commendable, desirable, expedient, fit, fitting, judicious, politic, prudent, seemly, sensible, sound, suggested, suitable, tactical; SEE CONCEPT 574

advise [v1] *offer recommendation*
admonish, advocate, caution, charge, commend, counsel, direct, dissuade, encourage, enjoin, exhort, forewarn, give a pointer*, give a tip*, guide, instruct, kibitz*, level with*, move, opine, point out, preach, prepare, prescribe, prompt, put bug in ear*, put in two cents*, recommend, steer, suggest, tout, update, urge, warn; SEE CONCEPT 75

advise [v2] *offer information*
acquaint, apprise, clue*, clue in*, fill in, give the word*, inform, keep posted*, lay it out*, let in on*, make known, notify, post*, put next to*, put on the line*, put on to*, report, show, tell, tip off*, update, warn; SEE CONCEPT 60

advisedly [adv] *with due consideration*
carefully, cautiously, consciously, deliberately, discreetly, intentionally, prudently, thoughtfully; SEE CONCEPT 544

adviser/advisor [n] *person who recommends, teaches, or otherwise helps*
aide, attorney, authority, backseat driver*, buttinski*, clubhouse lawyer*, coach, confidant, consultant, counsel, counselor, director, doctor, Dutch uncle*, expert, friend, guide, helper, instructor, judge, kibitzer*, lawyer, mentor, monitor, partner, priest, quarterback*, referee, righthand person, second-guesser, teacher, tutor; SEE CONCEPTS 348,350

advisory [adj] *able, authorized to recommend*
advising, consultative, consultive, counseling, helping, recommending; SEE CONCEPT 537

advocacy [*n*] *support for an idea or cause*
advancement, aid, assistance, backing, campaigning for, championing, defense, encouragement, justification, pleading for, promotion, promulgation, propagation, proposal, recommendation, upholding, urging; SEE CONCEPT **689**

advocate [*n*] *person supporting an idea or cause publicly*
apostle, attorney, backer, campaigner, champion, counsel, defender, exponent, expounder, lawyer, pleader, promoter, proponent, proposer, speaker, spokesperson, supporter, upholder; SEE CONCEPTS **359,423**

advocate [*v*] *support idea or cause publicly*
advance, advise, argue for, back, be in corner*, bless, bolster, boost*, brace up*, build up, campaign for, champion, countenance, defend, encourage, favor, further, get on bandwagon*, give a leg up*, give a lift*, go for, go to bat for*, go with, hold with, justify, plead for, plug*, plump for*, press for, promote, propose, push, recommend, ride shotgun for*, root for*, run interference for*, say so*, side, speak for, spread around*, stump for*, support, tout, uphold, urge, vindicate; SEE CONCEPTS **10,49,75**

aegis [*n*] *protection*
auspices, backing, patronage, shelter, sponsorship, wing*; SEE CONCEPTS **94,376**

aerial [*adj*] *occurring in the air*
aeriform, aeronautical, airy, atmospheric, birdlike, ethereal, flying, lofty, pneumatic, up above, vaporous; SEE CONCEPT **583**

aerobics/aerobic [*n/adj*] *exercise regime designed to increase heart and lung activity while toning muscles*
aquarobics, dance workout, drill, exercise, high impact, low impact, slimnastics, step, warm-up, workout; SEE CONCEPT **363**

aesthetic/esthetic [*adj*] *beautiful or artful*
artistic, creative, gorgeous, inventive; SEE CONCEPTS **485,579**

afar [*adv*] *a great distance away*
distant, far away, far off, remote; SEE CONCEPT **778**

affable [*adj*] *friendly*
amiable, amicable, approachable, benevolent, benign, breezy, civil, clubby*, congenial, cordial, courteous, genial, gentle, good-humored, good-natured, gracious, kindly, mild, nice, obliging, pleasant, polite, sociable, urbane, warm; SEE CONCEPT **401**

affair [*n1*] *matter or business to be taken care of; happening activity*
assignment, avocation, calling, case, circumstance, concern, duty, employment, episode, event, hap, happening, incident, interest, job, mission, obligation, occupation, occurrence, office function, proceeding, profession, project, province, pursuit, question, realm, responsibility, subject, task, thing*, topic, transaction, undertaking; SEE CONCEPTS **2,349,362**

affair [*n2*] *illicit sexual relationship*
affaire, amour, carrying on*, extracurricular activity*, fling, goings-on*, hanky-panky*, intimacy, intrigue, liaison, love, playing around*, relationship, rendezvous, romance, thing together*, two-timing*; SEE CONCEPTS **32,375**

affair [*n3*] *party or celebration*
do, entertainment, function, gathering, reception, shindig, soiree; SEE CONCEPTS **377,383**

affect [*v1*] *influence, affect emotionally*
act on, alter, change, disturb, impinge, impress, induce, influence, inspire, interest, involve, modify, move, overcome, perturb, prevail, regard, relate, stir, sway, touch, transform, upset; SEE CONCEPTS **7,19,22,228**

affect [*v2*] *pretend, imitate*
act, adopt, aspire to, assume, bluff, contrive, counterfeit, do a bit*, fake, feign, lay it on thick, make out like*, playact, put on, put up a front*, sham*, simulate, take on; SEE CONCEPT **59**

affectation [*n*] *pretended behavior to make an impression*
air, airs, appearance, artificiality, facade, false front*, front, going Hollywood*, imitation, insincerity, mannerism, pose, pretense, pretension, pretentiousness, put-on, putting on airs*, sham*, show, showing off, simulation; SEE CONCEPT **633**

affected [*adj1*] *deeply moved or hurt emotionally*
afflicted, altered, changed, compassionate, concerned, damaged, distressed, excited, grieved, impaired, impressed, influenced, injured, overwhelmed, overwrought, sorry, stimulated, stirred, sympathetic, tender, touched, troubled, upset; SEE CONCEPT **403**

affected [*adj2*] *changed in a bad or artificial way*
apish, artificial, assumed, awkward, campy*, chichi*, conceited, contrived, counterfeit, counterfeited, faked, false, feigned, fraud*, gone Hollywood*, ham*, hammy*, high falutin'*, hollow, imitated, insincere, melodramatic, ostentatious, overdone, pedantic, phony, playacting, pompous, precious, pretended, pretentious, put-on*, schmaltzy*, self-conscious, shallow, sham*, simulated, spurious, stiff, stilted, studied, superficial, theatrical, unnatural; SEE CONCEPTS **401,570**

affection [*n*] *strong fondness*
amore, ardor, attachment, care, case*, closeness, concern, crush, desire, devotion, emotion, endearment, feeling, friendliness, friendship, good will, hankering*, heart, inclination, itch*, kindness, liking, love, passion, predilection, propensity, puppy love*, regard, sentiment, shine*, soft spot*, solicitude, tenderness, warmth, weakness*, yen*; SEE CONCEPT **32**

affectionate [*adj*] *having or showing fondness*
all over*, attached, caring, crazy over*, dear, devoted, doting, fond, friendly, huggy*, kind, lovey-dovey*, loving, mushy*, nutty about*, partial, soft on*, sympathetic, tender, warm, warmhearted; SEE CONCEPTS **401,403**

affective [*adj*] *concerning feelings and intuition*
emotional, emotive, feeling, intuitive, noncognitive, perceptual, visceral; SEE CONCEPT **529**

affidavit [*n*] *written legal declaration*
affirmation, oath, sworn statement, testimony; SEE CONCEPTS **271,318**

affiliate [*n*] *organization that is associated with another*
affil*, associate, branch, offshoot, partner, sibling; SEE CONCEPT **381**

affiliate [*v*] *associate or be associated with a larger organization*
ally, amalgamate, annex, associate, band together, combine, come aboard, confederate, connect, form connection, go partners*, hook up*, incorporate, join, line up*, plug into*, relate*, team up, throw in with*, tie up, unite; SEE CONCEPTS **113,114**

affiliation [*n*] *association with an organization*
alliance, amalgamation, banding together, bunch, cahoots*, clan, coalition, combination, confederation, conjunction, connection, crew, crowd, gang, hookup*, incorporation, joining, league, merging, mob, outfit, partnership, relationship, ring, syndicate, tie-in, union; SEE CONCEPT 381

affinity [*n1*] *liking or inclination toward something*
affection, attraction, closeness, compatibility, cotton*, cup of tea*, druthers*, fondness, good vibrations*, leaning, partiality, rapport, same wavelength, simpatico, sympathy, thing*, weakness*; SEE CONCEPTS 20,32,709

affinity [*n2*] *similarity*
alikeness, alliance, analogy, association, closeness, connection, correspondence, kinship, likeness, relation, relationship, resemblance, semblance, similitude; SEE CONCEPT 670

affirm [*v*] *declare the truth of something*
assert, asseverate, attest, aver, avouch, avow, certify, cinch, clinch, confirm, cross heart, declare, guarantee, have a lock on*, ice*, insist, lock up*, maintain, nail down*, okay, predicate, profess, pronounce, put on ice*, ratify, repeat, rubber-stamp*, say so, set, state, swear, swear on bible*, swear up and down*, testify, vouch, witness; SEE CONCEPTS 49,50,88

affirmation [*n*] *declaration of the truth of something*
affidavit, assertion, asseveration, attestation, averment, avouchment, avowal, certification, confirmation, declaration, green light*, oath, okay, pronouncement, ratification, stamp of approval*, statement, sworn statement, testimonial, testimony; SEE CONCEPT 49

affirmative [*adj*] *being agreeable or assenting*
acknowledging, acquiescent, affirmatory, affirming, approving, complying, concurring, confirmative, confirmatory, confirming, consenting, corroborative, endorsing, favorable, positive, ratifying, supporting; SEE CONCEPTS 542,572

affirmative action [*n*] *equal rights policy*
anti-discrimination, equal opportunity, fair hiring, fair treatment, quota system, reverse discrimination; SEE CONCEPTS 388,645,667

affix [*v*] *attach or stick*
add, annex, append, bind, fasten, glue, hitch on*, join, paste, put on, rivet, slap on*, subjoin, tack, tack on*, tag, tag on*; SEE CONCEPTS 85,113,160

afflict [*v*] *cause or become hurt*
agonize, annoy, beset, bother, burden, crucify, distress, grieve, harass, harrow, harry, irk, lacerate, martyr, oppress, pain, pester, plague, press, rack, smite, strike, torment, torture, trouble, try, vex, worry, wound; SEE CONCEPTS 7,19,246,313

affliction [*n*] *hurt condition; something that causes hurt*
adversity, anguish, calamity, cross, crux, depression, difficulty, disease, disorder, distress, grief, hardship, illness, infirmity, misery, misfortune, ordeal, pain, plague, plight, scourge, sickness, sorrow, suffering, torment, trial, tribulation, trouble, woe; SEE CONCEPTS 306,309,674,728

affluence [*n*] *wealth*
abundance, fortune, luxury, opulence, plenty, prosperity, riches, wealthiness; SEE CONCEPTS 340,710

affluent [*adj1*] *wealthy*
flush*, loaded*, moneyed*, opulent, prosperous, rich, stinking rich*, upper class, upscale, well-off, well-to-do; SEE CONCEPT 334

affluent [*adj2*] *plentiful*
abundant, bountiful, copious, full, plenteous; SEE CONCEPT 771

afford [*v1*] *able to have or do; within financial means*
allow, be able to, bear, be disposed to, have enough for, have the means for, incur, manage, spare, stand, support, sustain; SEE CONCEPTS 335,713

afford [*v2*] *give, produce*
bestow, furnish, grant, impart, offer, provide, render, supply, yield; SEE CONCEPTS 108,143

affront [*n*] *an insult*
abuse, backhanded compliment*, brickbat*, dirty deed*, indignity, injury, left-handed compliment*, offense, outrage, provocation, put-down*, slap*, slap in the face*, slight, slur, vexation, wrong; SEE CONCEPTS 7,19,44,54

affront [*v*] *insult or involve in entanglement*
abuse, anger, annoy, confront, criticize, displease, dispraise, dump on*, encounter, face, give a zinger*, give the cold shoulder*, hit where one lives*, meet, offend, outrage, pique, provoke, put down*, slander, slight, taunt, vex; SEE CONCEPTS 7,19,44,54

aficionado [*n*] *fan*
connoisseur, devotee, enthusiast, fanatic; SEE CONCEPTS 352,366,423

afraid [*adj1*] *fearful*
abashed, aghast, alarmed, anxious, apprehensive, aroused, blanched, cowardly, cowed, daunted, discouraged, disheartened, dismayed, distressed, disturbed, faint-hearted, frightened, frozen, have cold feet*, horrified, in awe, intimidated, nervous, panic-stricken, perplexed, perturbed, petrified, rattled, run scared*, scared, scared stiff*, scared to death*, shocked, spooked, startled, stunned, suspicious, terrified, terror-stricken, timid, timorous, trembling, upset, worried; SEE CONCEPTS 403,690

afraid [*adj2*] *reluctant, regretful*
averse, backward, disinclined, hesitant, indisposed, loath, reluctant, sorry, uneager, unhappy, unwilling; SEE CONCEPT 529

afresh [*adj*] *new or repeated*
again, anew, de novo, lately, newly, of late, once again, once more, over, over again, recently; SEE CONCEPTS 578,797

Afro [*n*] *frizzy hairstyle*
curly hair, fro; SEE CONCEPT 718

after [*adj*] *following in position or time*
afterwards, back, back of, behind, below, ensuing, hind, hindmost, in the rear, later, next, posterior, postliminary, rear, subsequential, subsequently, succeeding, thereafter; SEE CONCEPTS 586,820

afterlife [*n*] *life after death*
eternity, heaven, hereafter, immortality, the great beyond*; SEE CONCEPTS 370,410,435

aftermath [*n*] *situation following an event, occurrence*
after-effects, causatum, chain reaction*, consequences, end, eventuality, flak*, impact, issue, outcome, payoff*, remainder, residual, residuum, results, upshot, waves*; SEE CONCEPT 230

ad
af

afternoon [n] *period after 12 noon and before sunset*
cocktail hour, P.M., post meridian, siesta, teatime; SEE CONCEPTS *801,806,810*

afterthought [n] *idea that occurs after it is timely*
reconsideration, review, second thought; SEE CONCEPT *529*

afterward/afterwards [adv] *following a time, event*
after, another time, at a later time, a while later, behind, by and by, ensuingly, eventually, in a while, intra, late, later, latterly, next, on the next day, soon, subsequently, then, thereafter, thereon, ultimately; SEE CONCEPT *799*

again [adv1] *another time; repeated*
afresh, anew, anon, bis, come again, encore, freshly, newly, once more, one more time, over, over and over, recurrently, reiteratively, repeatedly; SEE CONCEPTS *553,799*

again [adv2] *in addition*
additionally, also, besides, further, furthermore, moreover, on the contrary, on the other hand, then; SEE CONCEPT *577*

against [prep] *opposite to*
across, adjacent, contra, contrary to, counter to, facing, in contrast to, in opposition to, opposed to, opposing, versus; SEE CONCEPT *564*

age [n1] *period of animate existence*
adolescence, adulthood, boyhood, childhood, dotage, elderliness, girlhood, infancy, life, lifetime, majority, maturity, middle age, milestone, old age, senility, seniority, wear and tear*, youth; SEE CONCEPTS *816,817*

age [n2] *a period of time*
aeon, blue moon*, century, date, day, duration, epoch, era, generation, interim, interval, life, lifetime, millennium, span; SEE CONCEPT *807*

age [v] *become older*
decline, deteriorate, develop, get along, grow, grow feeble, grow old, grow up, mature, mellow, push, put mileage on*, ripen, wane; SEE CONCEPT *105*

aged [adj] *old*
age-old, ancient, antediluvian, antiquated, antique, been around*, creaky*, elderly, getting on*, gray, moth-eaten*, oldie*, over the hill*, passé*, rusty*, senescent, senior citizen, shot*, timeworn, venerable, worn, worse for wear*; SEE CONCEPTS *578,797*

ageism [n] *age-based discrimination*
age bias, generation gap; SEE CONCEPT *689*

agency [n1] *organization, often business-related*
bureau, company, department, firm, office; SEE CONCEPTS *325,381,441*

agency [n2] *power, instrumentality*
action, activity, auspices, channel, efficiency, force, influence, instrument, instrumentality, intercession, intervention, means, mechanism, mediation, medium, operation, organ, vehicle, work; SEE CONCEPTS *376,658*

agenda [n] *list of things to do*
calendar, card, diary, docket, lineup, plan, program, schedule, timetable; SEE CONCEPT *283*

agent [n1] *person representing an organization or person in business*
abettor, actor, advocate, ambassador, assignee, assistant, attorney, broker, commissioner, delegate, deputy, doer, emissary, envoy, executor, factor, factotum, functionary, go-between, handler, intermediary, lawyer, mediary, middleperson, minister, mover, negotiator, officer, operative, operator, principal, proctor, promoter, proxy, representative, salesperson, servant, steward, substitute, surrogate, ten percenter*, worker; SEE CONCEPT *348*

agent [n2] *power, instrument for achievement*
cause, channel, factor, force, means, medium, organ, power, vehicle; SEE CONCEPTS *376,658*

agent provocateur [n] *instigator*
agitator, goad, incendiary, rabble-rouser, troublemaker; SEE CONCEPT *412*

agglomeration [n] *collection*
cluster, heap, jumble, load, mass, pile; SEE CONCEPTS *432,786*

aggrandize [v] *cause something to seem or be greater, bigger*
acclaim, applaud, augment, beef up*, boost, commend, dignify, distinguish, enlarge, ennoble, expand, extend, glorify, heighten, hike, hike up*, honor, hype, increase, intensify, jack up*, jump, magnify, multiply, parlay, praise; SEE CONCEPTS *50,69,88,236,245*

aggravate [v1] *annoy*
be at*, be on the back of*, bother, bug, bum*, dog, drive up the wall*, exasperate, gall, get, get on one's nerves, get to, give a hard time, grate, hack, irk, irritate, nag, needle, nettle, peeve, pester, pick on, pique, provoke, tease, vex, wig*; SEE CONCEPTS *7,19*

aggravate [v2] *cause to become worse*
complicate, deepen, enhance, exacerbate, exaggerate, heighten, increase, inflame, intensify, magnify, mount, rise, rouse, worsen; SEE CONCEPT *240*

aggravation [n1] *annoyance*
affliction, aggro*, bother, botheration*, difficulty, distress, exasperation, hang-up*, headache*, irksomeness, irritation, pain, pain in the neck*, pet peeve*, provocation, teasing, vexation, worry; SEE CONCEPT *410*

aggravation [n2] *worsening of a situation, condition*
deepening, exacerbation, exaggeration, heightening, increase, inflaming, inflammation, intensification, magnification, sharpening, strengthening, worsening; SEE CONCEPT *240*

aggregate [adj] *forming a collection from separate parts*
accumulated, added, amassed, assembled, collected, collective, combined, composite, corporate, cumulative, heaped, mixed, piled, total; SEE CONCEPT *781*

aggregate [n] *collection*
accumulation, agglomerate, agglomeration, all, amount, assemblage, body, bulk, combination, conglomerate, conglomeration, gross, heap, lump, mass, mixture, pile, quantity, sum, the works*, total, totality, whole, whole ball of wax*, whole enchilada*, whole schmear*, whole shooting match*; SEE CONCEPT *432*

aggregate [v] *combine into a collection*
accumulate, add up, amass, amount, assemble, collect, combine, come, heap, mix, number, pile, sum, total; SEE CONCEPT *109*

aggression [n1] *attack, often military*
assailment, assault, blitz, blitzkrieg, encroachment, injury, invasion, offense, offensive, onset, onslaught, push, raid; SEE CONCEPTS *86,320*

aggression [*n2*] *hostile or forceful behavior, attitude*
aggressiveness, antagonism, belligerence, blitz, combativeness, destructiveness, fight, hostility, pugnacity, push; SEE CONCEPTS *29,411*

aggressive [*adj1*] *belligerent, hostile*
advancing, antipathetic, assailing, attacking, barbaric, bellicose, combative, contentious, destructive, disruptive, disturbing, encroaching, hawkish, intruding, intrusive, invading, martial, militant, offensive, pugnacious, quarrelsome, rapacious, threatening, warlike; SEE CONCEPT *550*

aggressive [*adj2*] *assertive*
assertory, bold, brassy*, cheeky*, cocky*, come on*, domineering, dynamic, energetic, enterprising, flip*, forceful, fresh*, get up and go*, go after, hard sell, imperious, masterful, militant, nervy*, pushing, pushy, sassy, shooting from the hip*, smart*, smart alecky*, strenuous, tough, vigorous, zealous; SEE CONCEPTS *404,542*

aggressor [*n*] *attacker*
assailant, initiator, instigator, intruder, invader, provoker, raider, trespasser; SEE CONCEPT *412*

aggrieved [*adj*] *very distressed*
afflicted, depressed, disturbed, grieving, harmed, hurt, injured, oppressed, pained, peeved, persecuted, saddened, unhappy, woeful, wronged; SEE CONCEPT *403*

aghast [*adj*] *horrified; very surprised*
afraid, agape, agog, alarmed, amazed, anxious, appalled, astonished, astounded, awestruck, confounded, dismayed, dumbfounded, frightened, horror-struck, overwhelmed, shocked, startled, stunned, terrified, thunderstruck; SEE CONCEPTS *403,690*

agile [*adj*] *physically or mentally nimble, deft*
active, acute, alert, athletic, brisk, buoyant, bustling, clever, dexterous, easy-moving, energetic, fleet, frisky, limber, lithe, lively, mercurial, prompt, quick, quick on the draw*, quick on the trigger*, quick-witted, rapid, ready, sharp, spirited, sportive, spright, sprightly, spry, stirring, supple, swift, twinkle toes*, vigorous, vivacious, winged, zippy; SEE CONCEPTS *485,527,588*

agility [*n*] *physical or mental nimbleness, deftness*
activity, acuteness, adroitness, alacrity, alertness, briskness, celerity, cleverness, dexterity, dispatch, expedition, fleetness, friskiness, litheness, liveliness, promptitude, promptness, quickness, quickwittedness, sharpness, sprightliness, spryness, suppleness, swiftness; SEE CONCEPTS *410,630,748*

aging [*n*] *becoming older*
crumbling, declining, developing, fading, fermenting, getting along*, getting on*, maturing, mellowing, senescent, slumping, stale, waning, wearing out*; SEE CONCEPT *701*

agitate [*v1*] *shake physically*
beat, churn, concuss, convulse, disturb, rock, rouse, stir, toss; SEE CONCEPT *152*

agitate [*v2*] *disturb, trouble someone*
alarm, argue, arouse, bug*, bug up*, burn up*, confuse, craze*, debate, discompose, disconcert, discuss, dispute, disquiet, distract, disturb, egg on*, examine, excite, ferment, flurry, fluster, get to*, incite, inflame, make flip*, move, perturb, psych*, push buttons*, rouse, ruffle, spook, stimulate, stir, trouble, turn on*, unhinge*, upset,

ventilate*, work up*, worry; SEE CONCEPTS *7,19,46*

agitation [*n*] *shaking, mixing*
churning, commotion, discomposure, disturbance, rocking, stirring, tizzy, tossing, turbulence, turmoil, unrest, upheaval; SEE CONCEPTS *158,170*

agitator [*n*] *person who disturbs, causes trouble*
adjy, advocate, agent, anarchist, champion, demagogue, disrupter, dissident, dogmatist, fighter, firebrand*, fomenter, heretic, incendiary, inciter, instigator, leftist, malcontent, mover, partisan, propagandist, provocateur, pusher, rabble-rouser, radical, reactionary, rebel, reformer, revisionist, revolutionary, ringleader, sparkplug*, troublemaker, wave maker*, zealot; SEE CONCEPT *412*

agnostic [*n*] *person unsure that God exists*
doubter, freethinker, materialist, skeptic, unbeliever; SEE CONCEPT *361*

ago [*adv*] *in the past*
ages ago, back, back when, before, from way back, from year one*, gone, since, since God knows when*, time was; SEE CONCEPT *820*

agog [*adj*] *enthralled*
anxious, avid, breathless, eager, enthusiastic, excited, expectant, impatient, in suspense, on tenterhooks; SEE CONCEPTS *401,542*

agonize [*v*] *suffer or cause another to suffer*
afflict, bleed, carry on, crucify, distress, disturb, eat heart out*, excruciate, harrow, hurt, labor, lament, martyr, pain, rack, sing the blues*, squirm, stew over, strain, strive, struggle, take it badly*, torment, torture, try, wince, worry, writhe; SEE CONCEPTS *7,19,410*

agonizing [*adj*] *difficult and painful, suffering*
disturbing, excruciating, extreme, fierce, harrowing, intense, racking, struggling, tearing, tormenting, tortuous, torturing, vehement, violent; SEE CONCEPTS *403,565*

agony [*n*] *suffering, pain*
affliction, anguish, distress, dolor, misery, pangs, passion, throes, torment, torture, woe; SEE CONCEPTS *410,728*

agrarian [*adj*] *concerning land, farming*
agricultural, natural, peasant, rural, rustic, uncultivated, undomesticated; SEE CONCEPT *536*

agree [*v1*] *be in unison, assent with another*
accede, acknowledge, acquiesce, admit, allow, be of the same mind*, bury the hatchet*, buy into*, check, clinch the deal*, come to terms, comply, concede, concur, consent, cut a deal*, engage, give blessing*, give carte blanche*, give green light*, give the go-ahead*, go along with, grant, make a deal*, okay, pass on, permit, play ball*, recognize, see eye to eye*, set, settle, shake on*, side with, sign*, subscribe, take one up on*, yes*; SEE CONCEPTS *8,10,45,235*

agree [*v2*] *be similar or consistent*
accord, answer, attune, be in harmony, blend, click, cohere, coincide, concert, concord, concur, conform, consort, correspond, equal, fall in with*, fit, get along with, go hand in hand*, go together, go well with, harmonize, jibe, match, parallel, square, suit, synchronize, tally; SEE CONCEPTS *118,656,670*

agreeable [*adj1*] *pleasing*
acceptable, dandy, delicious, delightful, enjoyable, fair, fine, gratifying, hunky-dory*, mild, nice, peach*, peachy*, pleasant, pleasurable, pleasureful, pussycat*, ready, satisfying, spiffy*,

af
ag

swell*, to one's liking, to one's taste, welcome;
SEE CONCEPT 572

agreeable [adj2] appropriate, in keeping
befitting, compatible, congruous, consistent, consonant, fitting, proper; SEE CONCEPT 558

agreeable [adj3] willing to be in unison, assent
acquiescent, amenable, approving, complying, concurring, congenial, consenting, favorable, grateful, in accord, responsive, sympathetic, well-disposed, willing; SEE CONCEPTS 401,542

agreeably [adv] willingly, assenting; pleasantly; in keeping
affably, affirmatively, amiably, amicably, appropriately, benevolently, charmingly, cheerfully, convivially, favorably, genially, good-humoredly, good-naturedly, graciously, happily, kindly, mutually, obligingly, peacefully, pleasingly, politely, satisfactorily, sympathetically, well, wonderfully; SEE CONCEPTS 401,572

agreement [n1] concurrence
acceding, accession, accommodation, accord, accordance, acknowledging, adjustment, affiliation, affinity, alliance, amity, approving, arbitration, arrangement, assenting, authorizing, bargaining, compatibility, compliance, complying, compromise, concert, concession, concord, concordance, concurring, conformity, congruity, consistency, correspondence, endorsing, granting, harmony, mediation, ratifying, reconciliation, similarity, suitableness, sympathy, understanding, union, unison, verification, verifying; SEE CONCEPT 684

agreement [n2] document of concurrence, contract
acknowledgment, adjudication, affidavit, approval, arrangement, assent, avowal, bargain, bond, cartel, charter, codicil, compact, compromise, confirmation, covenant, deal, indenture, lease, negotiation, note, oath, okay, pact, piece of paper*, protocol, recognition, settlement, stipulation, the nod*, transaction, treaty, understanding, writ; SEE CONCEPTS 271,331

agricultural [adj] concerning farming, land
aggie*, agronomical, arboricultural, floricultural, gardening, horticultural, ranch, rural, rustic; SEE CONCEPTS 536,583

agriculture [n] farming, crop production
agronomics, agronomy, cultivation, culture, horticulture, husbandry, tillage; SEE CONCEPTS 205,257

aground [adv] on the bottom of
ashore, beached, disabled, foundered, grounded, high and dry*, marooned, reefed, shipwrecked, stranded, stuck, swamped, wrecked; SEE CONCEPT 583

ahead [adv] in front or advance of
advanced, advancing, ahead, along, ante, antecedently, at an advantage, at the head, before, beforehand, earlier, first, fore, foremost, forward, forwards, in the foreground, in the lead, leading, on, onward, onwards, precedent, precedently, preceding, previous, progressing, to the fore; SEE CONCEPTS 586,632,820

aid [n1] help, support
advancement, advice, advocacy, alleviation, allowance, assist, assistance, attention, backing, backup, benefaction, benefit, benevolence, bounty, care, charity, comfort, compensation, cooperation, deliverance, encouragement, endowment, favor, furtherance, gift, giving, guidance,

hand, handout, leg up*, lift, ministration, ministry, patronage, promotion, reinforcement, relief, rescue, reward, salvation, service, shot in the arm*, subsidy, sustenance, treatment; SEE CONCEPT 110

aid [v] help, support
abet, alleviate, assist, bail out, befriend, benefact, encourage, favor, go to bat for*, go with*, lend a hand*, lighten, mitigate, open doors for*, promote, relieve, serve, stick up for*, straighten out*, subsidize, sustain; SEE CONCEPT 110

aid/aide [n2] person who helps
abettor, adjutant, aide-de-camp, assistant, attendant, coadjutant, coadjutor, crew, deputy, helper, lieutenant, second, supporter; SEE CONCEPT 348

AIDS [n] immunological disorder
acquired immune deficiency syndrome, HIV, HIV-positive, sexually transmitted disease, STD, virus; SEE CONCEPT 306

ail [v] hurt
afflict, annoy, bother, distress, pain, sicken, trouble, upset; SEE CONCEPTS 14,246

ailing [adj] not feeling well
below par, debilitated, diseased, down, down with, enfeebled, feeble, feeling awful, ill, indisposed, rocky*, run down*, sick, sick as a dog*, sickly, under the weather*, unwell, wasting, weak; SEE CONCEPT 314

ailment [n] mild sickness
ache, bug, complaint, condition, disease, disorder, dose*, flu, illness, indisposition, infirmity, malady, syndrome; SEE CONCEPTS 306,316

aim [n] goal
ambition, aspiration, course, desideratum, design, desire, direction, end, intent, intention, mark, object, objective, plan, purpose, scheme, target, where one is heading*, wish; SEE CONCEPT 659

aim [v] point or direct at a goal
address, angle, aspire, attempt, cast, concentrate, contemplate, contrive, design, direct, endeavor, essay, fix, focus, intend, level, mean, plan, propose, purpose, set one's sights on*, sight, slant, steer, strive, target, train, try, want, wish, zero in on, zoom in; SEE CONCEPTS 20,41,201

aimless [adj] having no goal
accidental, any which way*, bits-and-pieces*, blind, capricious, careless, casual, chance, desultory, directionless, drifting, erratic, fanciful, fickle, fits and starts*, flighty, fortuitous, frivolous, goalless, haphazard, heedless, hit-or-miss*, indecisive, indiscriminate, irresolute, objectless, pointless, purposeless, random, shiftless, stray, thoughtless, unavailing, undirected, unguided, unplanned, unpredictable, vagrant, wandering, wanton, wayward; SEE CONCEPTS 401,535,544

air [n1] gases forming the atmosphere
blast, breath, breeze, draft, heavens, ozone, puff, sky, stratosphere, troposphere, ventilation, waft, whiff, wind, zephyr; SEE CONCEPT 437

air [n2] distinctive quality or character; style
address, affectation, ambience, appearance, atmosphere, aura, bearing, comportment, demeanor, deportment, effect, feel, feeling, flavor, impression, look, manner, mannerism, mien, mood, pose, presence, property, quality, semblance, tone; SEE CONCEPTS 644,673

air [n3] musical tune
aria, descant, lay, melody, song, strain, theme; SEE CONCEPTS 77,595

air [*vl*] *put into the atmosphere; freshen*
aerate, aerify, air-condition, circulate, cool, eject, expel, expose, fan, open, oxygenate, purify, refresh, ventilate; SEE CONCEPT 255

air [*v2*] *express opinion publicly*
broadcast, circulate, communicate, declare, disclose, display, disseminate, divulge, exhibit, expose, make known, make public, proclaim, publicize, publish, put, reveal, speak, state, tell, utter, ventilate, voice; SEE CONCEPTS 51,52

aircraft [*n*] *airplane*
airliner, airship, balloon, blimp, chopper*, dirigible, flying machine, flying saucer, helicopter, jet, UFO, zeppelin; SEE CONCEPT 504

airplane [*n*] *vehicle that transports cargo or passengers through the air*
aeroplane, airbus, aircraft, airliner, airship, cab*, crate*, jet, kite*, plane, ramjet*, ship*; SEE CONCEPT 504

airport [*n*] *center for transportation by air*
aerodome, airdrome, airfield, airstrip, hangar, helipad, heliport, home plate*, installation, landing strip, runway, strip; SEE CONCEPTS 325,439

airs [*n*] *affectation; pretended behavior*
affectedness, arrogance, false front, front, haughtiness, hauteur, mannerism, ostentation, pomposity, pose, pretense, pretension, pretentiousness, put-on*, show, superciliousness; SEE CONCEPT 633

airtight [*adj1*] *sealed*
closed, impenetrable, impermeable, shut; SEE CONCEPTS 483,490

airtight [*adj2*] *certain*
incontestable, indisputable, invulnerable, irrefutable, unassailable; SEE CONCEPT 535

airy [*adj1*] *open to the atmosphere*
aerial, atmospheric, blowy, breezy, drafty, exposed, fluttering, fresh, gaseous, gusty, light, lofty, out-of-doors, uncluttered, vaporous, ventilated, well-ventilated, windy; SEE CONCEPT 583

airy [*adj2*] *delicate or ethereal*
dainty, diaphanous, flimsy, fragile, frail, frivolous, illusory, imaginary, immaterial, intangible, light, rare, rarefied, tenuous, thin, vaporous, visionary, volatile, weightless, wispy; SEE CONCEPTS 490,582

airy [*adj3*] *buoyant, light, or lively in nature*
animated, blithe, bouncy, cheerful, cheery, effervescent, elastic, fanciful, flippant, frolicsome, gay, graceful, happy, high-spirited, jaunty, light, light-hearted, merry, nonchalant, resilient, sprightly, volatile, whimsical; SEE CONCEPTS 404,550

aisle [*n*] *passageway dividing something*
alley, artery, avenue, clearing, corridor, course, egress, gangway, hallway, ingress, lane, opening, passage, path, walk, way; SEE CONCEPTS 440,513,830

ajar [*adj/adv*] *slightly open*
open, unclosed, unlatched, unshut; SEE CONCEPT 586

akin [*adj*] *related or connected*
affiliated, agnate, alike, allied, analogous, cognated, comparable, connate, consonant, corresponding, incident, kindred, like, parallel, similar; SEE CONCEPTS 487,563,573

alacrity [*n*] *liveliness; promptness*
alertness, avidity, briskness, cheerfulness, dispatch, eagerness, enthusiasm, expedition, fervor, gaiety, hilarity, joyousness, promptitude, quick-

ness, readiness, speed, sprightliness, willingness, zeal; SEE CONCEPTS 633,657

alarm [*n1*] *feeling of sudden fear*
anxiety, apprehension, cold feet*, consternation, dismay, distress, dread, fright, horror, nervousness, panic, scare, strain, stress, tension, terror, trepidation, unease, uneasiness; SEE CONCEPTS 410,690

alarm [*n2*] *warning, signaling device*
alert, bell, blast, buzzer, call, caution, clock, cry, drum, flap*, flash*, forewarning, gong, high sign*, horn, Mayday*, nod*, scramble*, scream, shout, sign, signal, siren, SOS, squeal, tip, tip off*, tocsin, trumpet, warning, whistle, wink*, yell; SEE CONCEPTS 269,463

alarm [*v*] *upset*
amaze, astonish, chill, daunt, dismay, distress, frighten, give a turn*, make jump*, panic, scare, scare silly*, scare stiff*, scare to death*, spook, startle, surprise, terrify, unnerve; SEE CONCEPTS 7,14,19,42

alarmist [*n*] *person who spreads alarm*
Cassandra, Chicken Little*, pessimist, scaremonger, voice of doom*; SEE CONCEPTS 412,423

albatross [*n*] *burden*
cross to bear, disgrace, load, millstone, misery, woe; SEE CONCEPTS 532,690

album [*n*] *blank book for collecting; holder*
anthology, collection, depository, index, memento, memory book, miscellany, notebook, portfolio, register, registry, scrapbook; SEE CONCEPTS 271,446

alchemy [*n*] *medieval science*
black arts, black magic, hermetics, magic, pseudo science, sorcery, thaumaturgy, witchcraft, wizardry; SEE CONCEPTS 367,370,689

alcohol [*n*] *intoxicating, flammable liquid*
alky*, booze*, canned heat*, cocktail, drink, ethanol, firewater*, hard stuff*, hootch*, intoxicant, liquor, methanol, moonshine*, palliative*, red-eye*, rotgut*, sauce*, smoke*, spirits, tipple*, toddy*; SEE CONCEPTS 454,467

alcoholic [*adj*] *intoxicating*
brewed, distilled, fermented, hard, inebriant, inebriating, sprituous, vinous; SEE CONCEPT 462

alcoholic [*n*] *drunk*
bar fly*, boozer*, dipsomaniac, hard drinker, inebriate, lush*, problem drinker, sot, souse, substance abuser, tipper, wino; SEE CONCEPT 423

alcoholism [*n*] *alcohol abuse*
addiction, alcohol addiction, alcohol dependence, crapulence, dipsomania, drunkenness, methomania, problem drinking, substance abuse, vinosity; SEE CONCEPTS 20,316,709

alcove [*n*] *nook, secluded spot*
anteroom, bay, bower, compartment, corner, cubbyhole, cubicle, niche, recess, study; SEE CONCEPTS 440,448,513

ale [*n*] *intoxicating, fermented beverage*
beer, brew, hops, malt, suds*; SEE CONCEPT 454

alert [*adj*] *attentive, lively*
active, all ears*, bright, cagey*, careful, circumspect, clever, fast on the draw*, good hands*, heads up*, heedful, hip, intelligent, jazzed*, observant, on guard*, on one's toes*, on the ball*, on the job*, on the lookout*, on the qui vive*, perceptive, psyched up*, quick, ready, sharp, spirited, switched on*, vigilant, wary, watchful, wide-awake, wired*, wise, with it*; SEE CONCEPTS 402,403

ag
al

alert [n] *warning*
admonition, alarm, flap*, high sign*, Mayday*, sign, signal, siren, SOS, tip off, wink*; SEE CONCEPTS 78,278,595,628

alert [v] *warn*
alarm, flag, forewarn, give the high sign*, inform, notify, put on guard, signal, tip, tip off, wave flag*; SEE CONCEPT 78

algae [n] *rootless, leafless plants living in water*
dulse, kelp, scum, seaweed; SEE CONCEPT 429

alias [adv] *otherwise known as*
also called, also known as, otherwise; SEE CONCEPT 582

alias [n] *false name*
AKA, anonym, assumed name, handle*, moniker, nickname, nom de guerre, nom de plume, pen name, pseudonym, stage name, summer name*; SEE CONCEPT 683

alibi [n] *defense against charges of wrongdoing; evidence of absence*
account, affirmation, airtight case*, allegation, answer, assertion, assurance, avowal, case, cop-out*, cover, declaration, excuse, explanation, fish story*, justification, plea, pretext, profession, proof, reason, reply, retort, song and dance*, stall, statement, vindication; SEE CONCEPT 661

alien [adj] *foreign*
conflicting, contrary, estranged, exotic, extraneous, extrinsic, inappropriate, incompatible, incongruous, opposed, remote, separate, unusual; SEE CONCEPT 564

alien [n] *foreign being*
blow in*, floater*, foreigner, greenhorn*, guest, immigrant, incomer*, interloper, intruder, invader, migrant, newcomer, noncitizen, outsider, refugee, settler, squatter, stranger, visitor, weed*; SEE CONCEPT 423

alienate [v] *cause unfriendliness, hostility*
break off, come between, disaffect, disunite, divide, divorce, estrange, make indifferent, part, separate, set against, turn away, turn off, wean, withdraw the affections of; SEE CONCEPTS 7,19,231

alienation [n] *unfriendliness*
breach, breaking off, coolness, disaffection, diverting, division, divorce, estrangement, indifference, remoteness, rupture, separation, setting against, turning away, variance, withdrawal; SEE CONCEPT 410

alight [v] *land*
come down, debark, descend, disembark, dismount, get off, light, perch, settle, touch down; SEE CONCEPTS 159,181

align [v1] *line up, arrange next to*
adjust, allineate, coordinate, even, even up, fix, make parallel, order, range, regulate, straighten; SEE CONCEPT 158

align [v2] *join; bring to agreement*
affiliate, agree, ally, associate, cooperate, enlist, follow, join sides, sympathize; SEE CONCEPTS 8,114

alignment [n] *lining up*
adjustment, arrangement, calibration, order, positioning, sequence, sighting; SEE CONCEPTS 721,727

alike [adj] *similar*
akin, allied, analogous, approximate, associated, carbon copy*, cognate, comparable, concurrent, correspondent, corresponding, dead ringer*, ditto*, double, duplicate, equal, equivalent, even, facsimile, identical, indistinguishable, kindred, like, look-alike, matched, matching, mated, parallel, proportionate, related, resembling, same, same difference*, similar, spitting image*, undifferentiated, uniform, Xerox*; SEE CONCEPTS 487,566,573

alike [adv] *similarly*
analogously, comparably, comparatively, consonantly, correspondingly, equally, equivalently, evenly, identically, in accordance with, in common, in the same degree, in the same manner, likewise, similarly, the same way, uniformly; SEE CONCEPTS 487,566,573

alimentary [adj] *digestive*
comestible, dietary, digestible, nourishing, nutrient, nutritional, nutritious, nutritive, peptic, salutary, sustaining, sustentative; SEE CONCEPTS 406,485

alimony [n] *money paid in support of a former spouse*
keep, livelihood, living, maintenance, provision, remittance, subsistence, sustenance, upkeep; SEE CONCEPT 344

alive [adj1] *being animately existent*
animate, around, awake, breathing, cognizant, conscious, dynamic, existing, extant, functioning, growing, knowing, live, living, mortal, operative, running, subsisting, viable, vital, working, zoetic; SEE CONCEPT 539

alive [adj2] *being active, full of life*
abounding, alert, animated, awake, brisk, bustling, cheerful, dynamic, eager, energetic, lively, overflowing, quick, ready, replete, rife, sharp, spirited, sprightly, spry, stirring, swarming, teeming, vigorous, vital, vivacious, zestful; SEE CONCEPTS 401,542

alkali [n] *soluble base; opposite of an acid*
antacid, caustic soda, salt; SEE CONCEPT 472

alkaline [adj] *being basic, not acid (chemically)*
acrid, alkalescent, alkali, antacid, bitter, caustic, neutralizing, salty, soluble; SEE CONCEPT 472

all [adj1] *whole quantity*
complete, entire, full, greatest, gross, outright, perfect, total, utter; SEE CONCEPT 771

all [adj2] *each; every one of a class*
any, bar none*, barring no one, complete, each and every, entire, every, every bit of, every single, sum, total, totality, whole; SEE CONCEPT 772

all [adj3] *exclusively*
alone, nothing but, only, solely; SEE CONCEPT 554

all [adv] *completely, without exception*
all in all, altogether, entirely, exactly, fully, just, purely, quite, totally, utterly, wholly; SEE CONCEPTS 771,772

all [n] *whole; totality*
accumulation, across the board, aggregate, aggregation, collection, ensemble, entirety, everyone, everything, gross, group, integer, jackpot*, lock stock and barrel*, mass, quantity, sum, sum total, total, unit, utmost, wall to wall*, whole ball of wax*, whole enchilada*, whole nine yards*, whole schmear*, whole shooting match*, whole show*, works; SEE CONCEPTS 787,837

all-around [adj] *multifaceted*
comprehensive, diverse, inclusive, versatile; SEE CONCEPTS 527,542

allay [v] *reduce something, usually a pain or a problem*
abate, alleviate, assuage, calm, compose, cool out*, decrease, ease, lessen, lighten, make nice*, mitigate, moderate, mollify, pacify, play up to*, pour oil on*, quiet, square, take the bite out*, take the sting out*; SEE CONCEPTS 7,22,244

allegation [n] *assertion placing blame*
accusation, affirmation, asseveration, avowal, charge, claim, declaration, deposition, overment, plea, profession, statement; SEE CONCEPT 49

allege [v] *assert; claim*
adduce, advance, affirm, asseverate, aver, avouch, avow, charge, cite, declare, depose, lay, maintain, offer, plead, present, profess, put forward, recite, recount, state, testify; SEE CONCEPT 49

alleged [adj] *asserted, often doubtful*
averred, declared, described, dubious, ostensible, pretended, professed, purported, questionable, so-called, stated, supposed, suspect, suspicious; SEE CONCEPT 552

allegiance [n] *loyalty*
adherence, ardor, consecration, constancy, dedication, deference, devotion, duty, faithfulness, fealty, fidelity, homage, honor, obedience, obligation, piety; SEE CONCEPT 689

allegorical [adj] *symbolic*
emblematic, figurative, illustrative, metaphorical, parabolic, symbolizing, typifying; SEE CONCEPT 582

allegory [n] *indirect representation, storytelling*
apologue, emblem, fable, figuration, moral, myth, parable, story, symbol, symbolism, symbolization, tale, typification; SEE CONCEPT 282

allergen [n] *irritant*
antigen, dander, dust mite, foreign substance, immune trigger, irritant, pollen, ragweed; SEE CONCEPT 478

allergic [adj] *having a reaction to food, material, etc.*
affected, averse to, dyspathetic, hypersensitive, immune sensitive, sensitive, sensitized, susceptible; SEE CONCEPTS 403,542

allergy [n] *reaction to certain food, material, etc.*
allergic reaction, aversion, hay fever, hypersensitivity, sensitivity, susceptibility, vulnerability; SEE CONCEPTS 405,410

alleviate [v] *relieve; lessen*
allay, assuage, ease, lighten, mitigate, mollify, pacify, pour oil on*, soft-pedal*, take the bite out*, take the edge off*, take the sting out*; SEE CONCEPTS 7,22,110,236,247

alley [n] *narrow passage*
alleyway, back street, lane, passageway, path, pathway, walk; SEE CONCEPT 501

alliance [n] *friendly association, agreement*
accord, affiliation, affinity, betrothal, bond, coalition, coherence, collaboration, collusion, combination, communion, compact, concord, concurrence, confederacy, confederation, congruity, conjunction, connection, consanguinity, cooperation, engagement, entente, federation, fraternization, friendship, interrelation, kinship, league, marriage, matrimony, membership, mutuality, pact, participation, partnership, relation, support, tie, treaty, union; SEE CONCEPTS 301,423,684

allied [adj] *friendly; united*
affiliated, agnate, akin, amalgamated, associated, bound, cognate, combined, confederate, connate,

connected, incident, in league, joined, joint, kindred, linked, married, related, unified, wed; SEE CONCEPTS 555,563

allocate [v] *assign; divide among*
admeasure, allot, apportion, appropriate, budget, cut, designate, dish out*, divvy*, earmark, give, mete, set aside, share, slice; SEE CONCEPTS 41,98,108,129

allocation [n] *distribution*
allotment, apportionment, appropriation, portion, quota, ration, share; SEE CONCEPT 835

allot [v] *assign; give portion*
admeasure, allocate, appoint, apportion, appropriate, assign, budget, cut, cut the pie*, designate, distribute, divvy*, dole, earmark, mete, set aside, share, shell out*, slice, split up; SEE CONCEPTS 41,108

allotment [n] *portion assigned or given*
allocation, allowance, apportionment, appropriation, bite, chunk, cut, cut of pie*, end, grant, lot, measure, part, piece, piece of the action*, quota, rake off*, ration, share, slice, split, stint*; SEE CONCEPT 835

all-out [adj] *complete*
absolute, determined, entire, exhaustive, full, full-blown, full-fledged, full-scale, maximum, optimum, resolute, supreme, thorough, total, undivided, unlimited, utmost, utter; SEE CONCEPTS 531,772

allow [v1] *admit; acknowledge*
acquiesce, avow, concede, confess, grant, let on, own; SEE CONCEPTS 60,82

allow [v2] *permit an action*
accord, accredit, admit, approve, authorize, bear, be big*, be game for*, brook, certify, commission, consent, empower, endure, favor, free up*, give a blank check*, give carte blanche, give leave, give permission, give the go-ahead, give the green light*, go along with, grant permission, hear of, hold with, indulge, let, license, live with*, oblige, okay, pass, pass on, put up with, recognize, release, sanction, sit still for*, stand, suffer, support, take kindly to, tolerate, warrant; SEE CONCEPTS 83,99

allow [v3] *set aside*
admeasure, allocate, allot, apportion, assign, deduct, give, grant, lot, mete, provide, remit, spare; SEE CONCEPTS 41,108

allowance [n1] *amount of money or other supply*
aid, alimony, allocation, allotment, annuity, apportionment, bequest, bite*, bounty, commission, contribution, cut, endowment, fee, fellowship, gift, grant, honorarium, inheritance, interest, legacy, lot, measure, part, pay, pension, piece, portion, prize, quantity, quota, ration, recompense, remittance, salary, scholarship, share, slice, stint, stipend, subsidy, taste, wage; SEE CONCEPTS 337,340

allowance [n2] *discount; concession*
accommodation, adaptation, adjustment, admission, advantage, cut, deduction, rebate, reduction, sanction, sufferance, toleration; SEE CONCEPT 775

alloy [n] *mixture, usually of two metals*
admixture, adulterant, adulteration, amalgam, amalgamation, blend, combination, composite, compound, debasement, denaturant, fusion, hybrid, intermixture, reduction; SEE CONCEPTS 260,476

al
al

alloy [*vl*] *mix metals*
admix, amalgamate, blend, combine, compound, fuse, intermix, mix; SEE CONCEPTS *109,113*

alloy [*v2*] *adulterate*
debase, denature, devalue, diminish, impair, reduce; SEE CONCEPT *240*

all right [*adj1*] *satisfactory*
acceptable, adequate, appropriate, average, decent, fair, fit, fitting, good, hunky-dory*, okay, okey-dokey*, passable, proper, satisfying, standard, sufficient, swell*, tolerable, unexceptional, unobjectionable; SEE CONCEPTS *547,558*

all right [*adj2*] *in good condition or health*
hale, healthy, safe, sound, unharmed, unhurt, unimpaired, well, whole; SEE CONCEPT *572*

all right [*adj3*] *correct; excellent*
accurate, exact, good, great, precise, right; SEE CONCEPTS *557,574*

all right [*adv1*] *satisfactorily*
acceptably, adequately, okay, passably, tolerably, unobjectionably, well enough; SEE CONCEPTS *547,558*

all right [*adv2*] *yes*
agreed, certainly, definitely, of course, okay, positively, surely, very well, without a doubt; SEE CONCEPT *572*

all-time [*adj*] *unsurpassed and permanent*
best, champion, enduring, everlasting, perpetual; SEE CONCEPTS *574,798*

allude [*v*] *hint at*
advert, bring up, imply, insinuate, intimate, point, refer, suggest; SEE CONCEPTS *60,66*

allure [*n*] *appeal*
attraction, bedroom eyes*, charisma, charm, come-hither look*, come-on*, enchantment, enticement, glamor, inveiglement, lure, magnetism, seductiveness, temptation, the jazz*; SEE CONCEPTS *673,720*

allure [*v*] *entice*
attract, bait, beguile, bewitch, cajole, captivate, charm, coax, come on*, decoy, draw, enchant, entrap, fascinate, hook*, inveigle, lead on, lure, magnetize, persuade, pull, seduce, suck in*, sweep off feet*, tempt, turn on*, wile, win over; SEE CONCEPTS *7,22*

alluring [*adj*] *attractive*
beguiling, bewitching, captivating, charming, enticing, magnetic, seductive, tempting, winning; SEE CONCEPTS *529,579*

allusion [*n*] *indirect reference; hint*
casual remark, charge, citation, connotation, denotation, figure of speech, implication, imputation, incidental mention, indication, inference, innuendo, insinuation, intimation, mention, play on words, quotation, remark, statement, suggestion; SEE CONCEPTS *60,274*

ally [*n*] *something united with another, especially by treaty*
accessory, accomplice, associate, coadjutor, collaborator, colleague, confederate, co-worker, friend, helper, partner; SEE CONCEPTS *299,322,354,359*

alma mater [*n*] *school from which one has graduated*
academy, college, institution, old school, place of graduation, place of matriculation, university; SEE CONCEPTS *288,289*

almanac [*n*] *document containing information for a year*
annual, calendar, chronicle, ephemeris, journal, record, register, registry, yearbook; SEE CONCEPTS *280,801,809,823*

almighty [*adj1*] *having complete power, control*
absolute, all-powerful, invincible, mighty, omnipotent, puissant, supreme, unlimited; SEE CONCEPT *540*

almighty [*adj2*] *godlike*
all-knowing, all-seeing, boundless, celestial, deathless, deific, divine, enduring, eternal, everlasting, godly, heavenly, illimitable, immortal, infinite, omnipotent, omnipresent, omniscient, pervading; SEE CONCEPT *539*

almighty [*adj3*] *severe*
awful, desperate, enormous, excessive, extreme, great, intense, loud, terrible; SEE CONCEPT *569*

almost [*adv*] *nearly, very nearly*
about, about to, all but, approximately, around, as good as, bordering on, close to, close upon, essentially, for all practical purposes, for the greatest part, in effect, in the neighborhood of, in the vicinity of, just about, most, much, near to, nigh, not far from, not quite, on the brink of, on the edge of, on the point of, on the verge of, practically, pretty near, relatively, roughly, substantially, virtually, well-nigh, within sight of; SEE CONCEPTS *531,586,799*

alms [*n*] *handout*
aid, assistance, benefaction, charity, contribution, dole, donation, offering; SEE CONCEPTS *337,657*

alone [*adj1*] *separate; apart*
abandoned, batching it*, by itself/oneself, companionless, deserted, desolate, detached, forlorn, forsaken, friendless, hermit, individual, in solitary*, isolated, lone, lonely, lonesome, me and my shadow*, me myself and I*, onliest*, only, on one's own, shag*, single, sole, solitary, solo, stag, traveling light*, unaccompanied, unaided, unassisted, unattached, unattended, unescorted, unmarried, widowed; SEE CONCEPTS *577,583*

alone [*adj2*] *to the exclusion of; unique*
incomparable, matchless, peerless, singly, singular, solely, unequalled, unique, unmatched, unparalleled, unrivaled, unsurpassed; SEE CONCEPTS *556,653*

along [*adv1*] *ahead*
forth, forward, on, onward; SEE CONCEPT *581*

along [*adv2*] *together with*
accompanying, additionally, also, as companion, as well, at same time, besides, coupled with, furthermore, in addition to, likewise, moreover, side by side, simultaneously, too, with; SEE CONCEPT *577*

along [*adv3*] *near*
adjacent, at, by; SEE CONCEPT *586*

alongside [*prep*] *close, near side of*
along the side of, apace with, at the side of, beside, by, by the side of, close at hand, close by, equal with, in company with, next to, parallel to, side by side; SEE CONCEPT *586*

aloof [*adj*] *remote*
above, apart, casual, chilly, cold, cold fish*, cool, detached, distant, forbidding, hard-boiled*, hardhearted, haughty, incurious, indifferent, laid back*, loner*, lone wolf*, offish*, on ice*, putting on airs*, reserved, secluded, solitary, standoffish*, stuck up*, supercilious, thick-skinned*, unapproachable, unconcerned, unfriendly, uninterested, unresponsive, unsociable,

unsympathetic, uppity*, withdrawn; SEE CONCEPTS **401,542**

aloud [adv] *in a spoken voice, usually not softly*
audibly, clearly, distinctly, intelligibly, loudly, lustily, noisily, out loud, plainly, vociferously; SEE CONCEPT **594**

alphabet [n] *letters of a writing system*
ABCs, characters, elements, fundamentals, graphic representation, hieroglyphs, ideograph, morphemes, phonemes, pictograph, rune, signs, syllabary, symbols; SEE CONCEPT **276**

alphabetical [adj] *in ascending order of a writing system*
A to Z, consecutive, graded, indexed, logical, ordered, progressive; SEE CONCEPT **585**

alphabetize [v] *place in order of a writing system*
index, order, systematize; SEE CONCEPT **84**

alpine [adj] *mountaintop; high altitude*
aerial, elevated, high, high-reaching, in the clouds, lofty, montane, mountainous, rangy, snowcapped, soaring, towering; SEE CONCEPTS **779,836**

already [adv] *before expected time*
as of now, at present, before, before now, but now, by now, by that time, by then, by the time mentioned, by this time, earlier, even now, formerly, heretofore, in the past, just now, now, once, previously, then, up to now; SEE CONCEPT **799**

also [adv] *in addition to*
additionally, again, along, along with, and, as well, as well as, besides, conjointly, further, furthermore, including, in conjunction with, in like manner, likewise, more, moreover, more than that, on top of, over and above, plus, still, to boot*, together with, too, withal; SEE CONCEPT **577**

altar [n] *church table, pedestal*
chantry, font, reredos, retable, shrine, tabernacle; SEE CONCEPT **443**

alter [v1] *change*
adapt, adjust, amend, change, convert, cook, correct mid-course*, develop, dial back*, diversify, doctor, fine tune*, make different, metamorphose, modify, mutate, phony up*, recalibrate, recast, reconstruct, refashion, reform, remodel, renovate, reshape, revamp, revise, shift, transform, transmute, turn, vary; SEE CONCEPT **232**

alter [v2] *sterilize animal*
caponize, castrate, change, desexualize, emasculate, fix, geld, mutilate, neuter, spay, unsex; SEE CONCEPTS **310,375**

alteration [n] *change*
about-face, accommodation, adaptation, adjustment, amendment, conversion, correction, difference, diversification, exchange, fixing, flip-flop*, metamorphosis, mid-course correction*, modification, mutation, reformation, remodeling, reshaping, revision, shift, switch, switch-over*, transformation, transmutation, turn, variance, variation; SEE CONCEPT **701**

altercation [n] *fight, often verbal*
argument, beef*, bickering, blowup*, bone of contention*, brawl*, brush*, combat, contest, controversy, dispute, embroilment, flap*, fracas*, fuss, go*, hassle, quarrel, row, rumble*, run-in*, set-to*, squabbling, tiff*, words*, wrangle; SEE CONCEPTS **46,106**

altered [adj] *changed*
adapted, adjusted, amended, converted, cooked, corrected, diversified, doctored, fitted, fixed, modified, qualified, redone, refitted, reformed, remade, remodeled, renovated, reshaped, retailored, revised, spiked, transformed, turned, updated; SEE CONCEPT **564**

alter ego [n1] *other side to personality*
doppelganger, evil twin*, second self; SEE CONCEPTS **410,423**

alter ego [n2] *companion*
buddy, chum, confidante, counterpart, doppelganger*, pal, soul mate; SEE CONCEPT **423**

alternate [adj1] *every other*
alternating, every second, intermittent, periodic, recurrent, recurring, rotating; SEE CONCEPT **553**

alternate [adj2] *substitute*
alternative, another, backup, different, interchanging, makeshift, second, surrogate, temporary; SEE CONCEPT **566**

alternate [n] *substitute*
backup, double, equivalent, fill-in, proxy, replacement, stand-in, sub*, surrogate; SEE CONCEPT **667**

alternate [v] *take turns, change back and forth*
act reciprocally, alter, blow hot and cold*, change, come and go, exchange, fill in for, fluctuate, follow, follow in turn, interchange, intersperse, oscillate, relieve, rotate, seesaw, shift, shilly-shally*, substitute, sway, vacillate, vary, waver, yo-yo*; SEE CONCEPTS **13,104,232,701**

alternative [adj] *other, alternate*
another, back-up, different, flipside, other side, second, substitute, surrogate; SEE CONCEPT **564**

alternative [n] *possible choice*
back-up, druthers*, opportunity, option, other, other fish in sea*, other fish to fry*, pick, preference, recourse, redundancy, selection, sub*, substitute, take it or leave it*; SEE CONCEPT **529**

although [conj] *even though*
admitting, albeit, despite, despite the fact, even if, even supposing, granting, granting all this, in spite of, much as, notwithstanding, still, supposing, though, when, whereas, while; SEE CONCEPT **544**

altitude [n] *height in the sky*
apex, distance, elevation, eminence, loftiness, peak, summit; SEE CONCEPTS **739,752,791**

altogether [adv1] *as a whole*
all, all in all, all things considered, all told, bodily, by and large, collectively, conjointly, en masse, everything considered, everything included, for the most part, generally, in all, in sum, in toto, on the whole, taken together; SEE CONCEPT **771**

altogether [adv2] *completely*
absolutely, fully, perfectly, quite, thoroughly, totally, utterly, well, wholly; SEE CONCEPT **531**

altruism [n] *unselfish concern*
benevolence, charity, humanitarianism, kindness, magnanimity, philanthropy, public spirit, selflessness, social conscience; SEE CONCEPT **633**

altruistic [adj] *unselfish*
all heart*, benevolent, big*, big-hearted*, bleeding heart*, charitable, considerate, generous, good, good scout, human, humane, humanitarian, kind, magnanimous, openhanded, philanthropic, Robin Hood*, self-sacrificing; SEE CONCEPT **404**

alumnus/alumna [n] *graduate*
alum, old grad*, postgraduate; SEE CONCEPT **350**

always [*adv*] *forever; continually*
consistently, constantly, eternally, ever, everlastingly, evermore, forevermore, for keeps, in perpetuum, invariably, perpetually, regularly, repeatedly, till blue in the face*, till cows come home*, till hell freezes over*, unceasingly, without exception; SEE CONCEPTS *551,798*

amalgam [*n*] *mixture*
admixture, alloy, amalgamation, blend, combination, combo*, composite, compound, fusion, mishmash*, soup; SEE CONCEPT *432*

amalgamate [*v*] *blend*
admix, alloy, ally, coalesce, combine, come together, compound, consolidate, fuse, hook up with*, incorporate, integrate, interface, intermix, join together, meld, merge, mingle, network, pool, team up*, tie in, tie up*, unite; SEE CONCEPT *113*

amass [*v*] *gather, accumulate*
aggregate, assemble, clean up*, collect, compile, corral*, garner, heap*, hoard, lay up*, make a killing*, make a pile*, pile, round up*, scare up*, stockpile, store; SEE CONCEPTS *109,120*

amateur [*n*] *casual participant*
abecedarian, apprentice, aspirant, beginner, bush leaguer*, dabbler, dilettante, greenhorn, ham*, hopeful, layperson, learner, neophyte, nonprofessional, novice, probationer, putterer, recruit, Sunday driver*, tenderfoot*, tyro; SEE CONCEPT *366*

amateurish [*adj*] *unprofessional*
bush-league*, incompetent, inept, inexperienced, inexpert, insipid, unskilled, untrained; SEE CONCEPTS *527,538*

amatory [*adj*] *affectionate, desirous*
admiring, amorous, aphrodisiac, ardent, attracted, devoted, doting, erotic, fervent, fond, languishing, lovesick, loving, passionate, rapturous, romantic, sentimental, tender, wooing, yearning; SEE CONCEPTS *372,403*

amaze [*v*] *surprise*
affect, alarm, astonish, astound, bewilder, blow away*, blow one's mind*, bowl over*, daze, dumbfound, electrify, flabbergast*, impress, move, perplex, put one away*, shock, stagger, startle, strike, stun, stupefy, touch*; SEE CONCEPT *42*

amazement [*n*] *state of surprise*
admiration, astonishment, awe, bewilderment, confoundment, confusion, marvel, one for the books*, perplexity, shock, something else*, stopper*, stunner*, stupefaction, wonder, wonderment; SEE CONCEPTS *230,410*

amazing [*adj*] *astonishing*
awesome, fascinating, incredible, marvelous, prodigious, shocking, stunning, surprising, unbelievable, wonderful; SEE CONCEPTS *547,572*

ambassador [*n*] *representative to a foreign country*
agent, consul, deputy, diplomat, emissary, envoy, minister, plenipotentiary; SEE CONCEPT *354*

amber [*n/adj*] *gold-colored*
brown, golden, tan, yellowish; SEE CONCEPT *618*

ambience [*n*] *environment*
ambient, atmosphere, climate, medium, surroundings; SEE CONCEPT *673*

ambiguity [*n*] *uncertainty of meaning*
double-entendre, double meaning, doubt, doubtfulness, dubiety, dubiousness, enigma, equivocacy, equivocality, equivocation, incertitude, inconclusiveness, indefiniteness, indeterminateness, obscurity, puzzle, tergiversation, uncertainty, unclearness, vagueness; SEE CONCEPTS *638,682*

ambiguous [*adj*] *having more than one meaning*
clear as dishwater*, cryptic, doubtful, dubious, enigmatic, enigmatical, equivocal, inconclusive, indefinite, indeterminate, inexplicit, muddy, obscure, opaque, puzzling, questionable, tenebrous, uncertain, unclear, unintelligible, vague; SEE CONCEPTS *267,535*

ambition [*n1*] *strong desire for success*
appetite, ardor, aspiration, avidity, craving, desire, drive, eagerness, earnestness, emulation, energy, enterprise, enthusiasm, fire in belly*, get up and go*, hankering*, hope, hunger, initiative, itch*, keenness, longing, love, lust, moxie*, passion, pretension, push, right stuff*, spirit, striving, thirst, vigor, yearning, zeal; SEE CONCEPT *20*

ambition [*n2*] *something desired*
aim, aspiration, desire, dream, end, enterprise, goal, hope, intent, mark, objective, purpose, target, wish; SEE CONCEPT *659*

ambitious [*adj*] *desiring success*
aggressive, anxious, ardent, aspiring, avid, ball of fire*, bent upon, climbing, come on, come on strong, designing, desirous, determined, driving, eager, eager beaver*, earnest, energetic, enterprising, enthusiastic, fireball*, get up and go*, goal-oriented, go-getter*, hard ball*, high-reaching, hopeful, hungry, industrious, inspired, intent, longing, power-loving, purposeful, pushing, pushy*, resourceful, self-starting, sharp, soaring, striving, thirsty, vaulting, zealous; SEE CONCEPTS *326,542*

ambitious [*adj2*] *requiring great effort, ability*
arduous, bold, challenging, demanding, difficult, elaborate, energetic, exacting, formidable, grandiose, hard, impressive, industrious, lofty, pretentious, severe, strenuous, visionary; SEE CONCEPT *538*

ambivalent [*adj*] *conflicting*
clashing, contradictory, debatable, doubtful, equivocal, fluctuating, hesitant, inconclusive, irresolute, mixed, opposed, uncertain, undecided, unresolved, unsure, vacillating, warring, wavering; SEE CONCEPTS *534,564*

amble [*v*] *walk casually*
ankle*, boogie*, dawdle, drift, gander*, hoof it*, loiter, meander, mosey*, percolate*, ramble, sashay*, saunter, stroll, toddle*, wander; SEE CONCEPT *151*

ambulance [*n*] *emergency vehicle*
EMS, hospital wagon, rescue, transport; SEE CONCEPT *505*

ambulatory [*adj*] *changing position; able to move under own power*
ambulant, itinerant, nomadic, perambulant, perambulatory, peripatetic, roving, vagabond, vagrant; SEE CONCEPT *584*

ambush [*n*] *lying in wait; concealed position*
ambuscade, ambushment, camouflage, concealment, deception, hiding, hiding place, lurking, pitfall, shelter, trap, trick*, waiting, waylaying; SEE CONCEPTS *86,188*

ambush [*v*] *lie in wait; attack*
ambuscade, assail, assault, box in*, bushwhack*, decoy, dry gulch*, ensnare, entrap, hem in*, hide, hook*, jap*, jump, lay for, lurk, net, set

trap, surprise, surround, trap, wait, waylay; SEE CONCEPTS 86,188

ameliorate [v] *make, become better*
alleviate, amend, help, improve, lighten, meliorate, mitigate, relieve, step up, upgrade; SEE CONCEPT 244

amenable [adj1] *willing, cooperative*
acquiescent, agreeable, biddable, docile, influenceable, manageable, obedient, open, persuadable, pliable, responsive, susceptible, tractable; SEE CONCEPT 404

amenable [adj2] *able to be judged; responsible*
accountable, answerable, chargeable, liable, subject; SEE CONCEPT 402

amend [v] *improve, correct*
alter, ameliorate, better, change, elevate, enhance, fix, help, lift, make up for, mend, modify, pay one's dues*, raise, rectify, reform, remedy, repair, revise, right, square*; SEE CONCEPTS 126,244

amendment [n1] *correction, improvement*
alteration, amelioration, betterment, change, correction, enhancement, improvement, mending, modification, rectification, reform, reformation, remedy, repair, revision; SEE CONCEPT 700

amendment [n2] *addition to a document*
act, addendum, adjunct, alteration, attachment, bill, clarification, clause, codicil, measure, modification, motion, revision, rider, suggestion, supplement; SEE CONCEPT 270

amends [n] *compensation*
apology, atonement, expiation, indemnification, indemnity, quittance, recompense, redress, reparation, reprisal, requital, restitution, restoration, satisfaction; SEE CONCEPTS 67,104,384

amenity [n1] *pleasant thing*
advantage, betterment, comfort, convenience, enhancement, enrichment, excellence, extravagance, facility, frill, improvement, luxury, merit, quality, service, superfluity, virtue; SEE CONCEPT 712

amenity [n2] *pleasing, agreeable behavior*
affability, agreeableness, amiability, attention, attractiveness, charity, charm, complaisance, cordiality, courtesy, delightfulness, enjoyableness, etiquette, gallantry, geniality, gentility, gratefulness, kindness, mildness, pleasantness, politeness, refinement, suavity, sweetness; SEE CONCEPT 633

amiable [adj] *friendly, agreeable*
affable, amicable, attractive, benign, breezy, buddy-buddy*, charming, cheerful, clubby*, complaisant, cool*, copacetic*, cordial, cozy, delightful, downright neighborly*, easy, engaging, friendly, genial, good-humored, good-natured, gracious, home cooking*, kind, kindly, lenient, lovable, mellow, mild, obliging, palsy-walsy*, pleasant, pleasing, princely*, pussycat*, responsive, right, righteous, sociable, sweet-tempered, swell*, tight*, warm, warmhearted, winning; SEE CONCEPT 401

amicable [adj] *friendly, especially regarding an agreement*
accordant, agreeing, amiable, civil, clubby*, concordant, cordial, courteous, cozy, empathic, good-humored, harmonious, kind, kindly, likeminded, mellow, neighborly, pacific, peaceable, peaceful, polite, regular, right nice*, sociable, square shooting*, sympathetic, understanding; SEE CONCEPTS 529,542

amid/amidst [prep] *in middle of; among*
amongst, between, during, in the midst of, in the thick of, mid, over, surrounded by, throughout; SEE CONCEPTS 586,820

amiss [adj] *wrong; defective*
awry, bad, confused, crooked, erring, erroneous, fallacious, false, faulty, flawed, foul, glitched up*, haywire, imperfect, improper, inaccurate, inappropriate, incorrect, mistaken, out of order, sick, unfair, unlawful, unsuitable, untoward; SEE CONCEPT 570

amiss [adv] *wrongly; defectively*
afield, afoul, badly, erringly, erroneously, faultily, improperly, inappropriately, incorrectly, mistakenly, out of turn, unfavorably, unsuitably; SEE CONCEPT 570

amity [n] *friendship*
amicableness, benevolence, comity, concord, cordiality, friendliness, good vibrations*, goodwill, harmony, hitting it off*, kindliness, neighborliness, same wavelength*, simpatico*, togetherness*; SEE CONCEPT 388

ammonia [n] *pungent gas, liquid*
alkali, salts, spirits, vapor; SEE CONCEPT 472

ammunition [n] *projectiles for weaponry*
ammo*, armament, ball, bomb, buckshot, bullet, cannonball, cartridge, charge, chemical, confetti*, explosive, fuse, grenade, gunpowder, iron rations*, materiel, missile, munition, napalm, powder, rocket, round, shell, shot, shrapnel, torpedo; SEE CONCEPTS 498,500

amnesty [n] *pardon, often by government*
absolution, condonation, dispensation, forgiveness, immunity, reprieve; SEE CONCEPTS 298,300

among [prep1] *in the middle of; between*
amid, amidst, betwixt, encompassed by, in dispersion through, in the midst of, in the thick of, mid, surrounded by, with; SEE CONCEPT 586

among [prep2] *in a group*
by all of, by the whole of, in association with, in connection with, in the class of, in the company of, mutually, out of, together with, with, with one another; SEE CONCEPT 785

amorous [adj] *loving, affectionate*
amative, amatory, aphrodisiac, ardent, attached, boy crazy*, doting, enamored, erotic, fond, girl crazy*, have a crush on*, horny*, hot, hot and heavy*, impassioned, infatuated, in love, lovesick, lovey dovey*, lustful, passionate, romantic, sexy, sweet for*, sweet on*, tender, turned on*; SEE CONCEPTS 372,403,555

amorphous [adj] *without definite shape, character*
baggy, blobby, characterless, formless, inchoate, indeterminate, irregular, nebulous, nondescript, shapeless, unformed, unshaped, unstructured, vague; SEE CONCEPTS 404,490

amount [n1] *quantity*
aplenty, bags*, bulk, bundle, chunk, expanse, extent, flock, gob*, heap, hunk, jillion*, load, lot, magnitude, mass, measure, mess*, mint*, mucho*, number, oodles*, pack, passle, peck, pile, scads*, score, slat*, slew*, supply, ton*, volume, whopper*; SEE CONCEPTS 787,837

amount [n2] *total*
addition, aggregate, all, bad news*, body, budget, cost, damage*, entirety, expense, extent, list, lot, net, outlay, output, price tag*, product, quantum, score, set-back*, sum, tab*, tidy sum*, whole; SEE CONCEPTS 329,784,787

amount [n3] *whole effect*
body, burden, core, full value, import, matter, purport, result, sense, significance, substance, thrust, upshot, value; SEE CONCEPT 676

amount [v] *equal, add up to*
aggregate, approach, approximate, become, be equivalent to, be tantamount to, check with, come to, correspond, develop into, effect, extend, grow, match, mean, number, purport, reach, rival, sum, tally, total, touch; SEE CONCEPT 667

amour [n] *romance*
affair, entanglement, liaison, love, love affair, passion, relationship; SEE CONCEPT 32

amphetamine [n] *hard drug*
analeptic, benny*, crank*, crystal, dexy*, pep pill*, speed*, stimulant, STP*, tab*, upper*; SEE CONCEPT 307

ample [adj] *more than necessary, sufficient*
abounding, abundant, big, bounteous, bountiful, broad, capacious, commodious, copious, enough, expansive, extensive, full, galore, generous, great, heavy, large, lavish, liberal, no end, plenteous, plentiful, plenty, profuse, rich, roomy, spacious, spare, substantial, unrestricted, voluminous, wide; SEE CONCEPTS 558,781

amplification [n] *increase in size or effect*
addition, augmentation, boost, boosting, buildup, deepening, development, elaboration, enlargement, exaggeration, expansion, expatiation, extension, fleshing out, heightening, intensification, lengthening, magnification, padding, raising, strengthening, stretching, supplementing, upping, widening; SEE CONCEPTS 236,245,780

amplify [v] *increase in size or effect*
add, augment, beef up*, boost, build up, deepen, develop, elaborate, enlarge, exaggerate, expand, expatiate, extend, flesh out*, heighten, hike up*, inflate, intensify, jack up*, lengthen, magnify, pad, pyramid, raise, soup up*, strengthen, stretch, supplement, swell, up, widen; SEE CONCEPTS 236,245

amply [adv] *fully, sufficiently*
abundantly, acceptably, adequately, appropriately, bountifully, capaciously, completely, copiously, enough, extensively, fittingly, generously, greatly, lavishly, liberally, plenteously, plentifully, profusely, properly, richly, rightly, satisfactorily, substantially, suitably, thoroughly, well; SEE CONCEPTS 558,771

amputate [v] *remove a limb*
cut away, cut off, dismember, eliminate, excise, lop, separate, sever, truncate; SEE CONCEPTS 176,211

amuck [adv] *crazily*
berserk, destructively, ferociously, frenziedly, in a frenzy, insanely, madly, maniacally, murderously, savagely, uncontrollably, violently, wildly; SEE CONCEPT 401

amulet [n] *charm*
fetish, lucky piece, ornament, talisman; SEE CONCEPTS 260,446

amuse [v] *entertain; make laugh*
break one up*, charm, cheer, crack up*, delight, divert, fracture*, gladden, grab*, gratify, interest, kill*, knock dead*, make roll in the aisles*, occupy, panic*, please, put away*, regale, slay*, tickle, wow*; SEE CONCEPTS 9,292,384

amusement [n1] *entertaining, making someone laugh*
action, ball*, beguilement, cheer, delight, diversion, enjoyment, entertainment, field day*, fun, fun and games*, gladdening, gratification, grins*, high time*, hilarity, hoopla*, laughs*, laughter, merriment, merry go round*, mirth, picnic*, play, pleasing, pleasure, regalement, whoopee*; SEE CONCEPT 292

amusement [n2] *game, pastime*
distraction, diversion, entertainment, hobby, interest, joke, lark, play, prank, recreation, sport; SEE CONCEPT 364

amusing [adj] *entertaining, funny*
agreeable, boffo*, camp, campy, charming, cheerful, cheering, comical, cut up*, delightful, diverting, droll, enchanting, engaging, enjoyable, entertaining, for grins*, fun, gladdening, gratifying, gut-busting*, humorous, interesting, jocular, jokey*, joshing*, laughable, lively, merry, pleasant, pleasing, priceless, screaming*, sidesplitting*, too funny for words*, witty; SEE CONCEPTS 267,548

anachronism [n] *error in time placement*
chronological error, metachronism, misdate, misplacement, postdate, prolepsis, solecism; SEE CONCEPT 818

analgesic [n] *pain remover*
anesthetic, anodyne, painkiller, soother; SEE CONCEPT 307

analogous [adj] *agreeing, similar*
akin, alike, comparable, consonant, convertible, correspondent, corresponding, equivalent, homologous, interchangeable, kindred, like, parallel, related, resembling, undifferentiated, uniform; SEE CONCEPTS 487,573

analogy [n] *agreement, similarity*
affinity, alikeness, comparison, correlation, correspondence, equivalence, homology, likeness, metaphor, parallel, relation, relationship, resemblance, semblance, simile, similitude; SEE CONCEPTS 278,670

analysis [n1] *examination and determination*
assay, breakdown, dissection, dissolution, division, inquiry, investigation, partition, reasoning, resolution, scrutiny, search, separation, study, subdivision, test; SEE CONCEPTS 24,103

analysis [n2] *statement of results from examination*
estimation, evaluation, finding, interpretation, judgment, opinion, outline, reasoning, report, study, summary; SEE CONCEPTS 271,274

analyst [n] *person who examines and determines; psychoanalyst*
accountant, couch doctor*, examiner, guru*, head shrinker*, inquisitor, investigator, number cruncher*, psychiatrist, psychotherapist, questioner, shrink*, therapist; SEE CONCEPTS 348,357

analytic/analytical [adj] *examining and determining*
cogent, conclusive, detailed, diagnostic, discrete, dissecting, explanatory, expository, inquiring, inquisitive, interpretive, investigative, judicious, logical, organized, penetrating, perceptive, perspicuous, precise, problem-solving, questioning, ratiocinative, rational, reasonable, scientific, searching, solid, sound, studious, subtle, systematic, testing, thorough, valid, well-grounded; SEE CONCEPT 402

analyze [v1] *examine and determine*
assay, beat a dead horse*, chew over*, confab*, consider, estimate, evaluate, figure, figure out, get down to brass tacks*, hash*, inspect, interpret, investigate, judge, kick around*, rehash, resolve, scrutinize, sort out, spell out, study, talk game*, test, think through; SEE CONCEPTS 24,37,103

analyze [v2] *break down to components*
anatomize, break up, cut up, decompose, decompound, determine, disintegrate, dissect, dissolve, divide, electrolyze, hydrolyze, lay bare, parse, part, resolve, separate, x-ray; SEE CONCEPTS 135,310

anarchist [n] *person who opposes the idea of government and laws*
agitator, insurgent, insurrectionist, malcontent, mutineer, nihilist, rebel, revolter, revolutionary, terrorist; SEE CONCEPTS 359,412

anarchy [n] *lawlessness; absence of government*
chaos, confusion, disorder, disorganization, disregard, hostility, misrule, mob rule, nihilism, nongovernment, rebellion, reign of terror, revolution, riot, turmoil, unrest; SEE CONCEPTS 29,674

anathema [n1] *something hated*
abomination, bane, bugbear, detestation, enemy, hate, pariah; SEE CONCEPT 529

anathema [n2] *denouncement*
ban, censure, commination, condemnation, curse, damnation, denunciation, excommunication, execration, imprecation, malediction, proscription, reprehension, reprobation, reproof, taboo; SEE CONCEPT 278

anatomy [n1] *study of animal, plant structure*
analysis, biology, cytology, diagnosis, dissection, division, embryology, etiology, examination, genetics, histology, inquiry, investigation, medicine, morphology, physiology, zoology; SEE CONCEPT 349

anatomy [n2] *physical structure of animals, plants*
build, composition, figure, form, frame, framework, makeup, physique, shape; SEE CONCEPT 733

ancestor [n] *predecessor in family*
antecedent, antecessor, ascendant, forebear, forefather, foregoer, foremother, forerunner, founder, precursor, primogenitor, progenitor; SEE CONCEPT 414

ancestral [adj] *related to previous family or family trait*
affiliated, born with, congenital, consanguine, consanguineous, familial, genealogical, inborn, inbred, inherited, innate, in the family, lineal, maternal, old, past, paternal, running in the family, totemic, tribal; SEE CONCEPT 549

ancestry [n] *family predecessors; family history*
ancestor, antecedent, antecessor, blood, breed, breeding, derivation, descent, extraction, forebear, forefather, foregoer, foremother, forerunner, genealogy, heritage, house, kindred, line, lineage, origin, parentage, pedigree, precursor, primogenitor, progenitor, race, source, stock; SEE CONCEPTS 414,648

anchor [n] *something used to hold another thing securely*
ballast, bower, comfort, defense, fastener, foothold, grapnel, grappling iron, grip, hold, hook, kedge, mainstay, mooring, mud hook, pillar, protection, safeguard, security, staff, stay, support; SEE CONCEPTS 464,502,731

anchor [v] *hold, be held securely*
attach, berth, catch, dock, drop, fasten, fix, imbed, make port, moor, plant, secure, stay, tie, tie up; SEE CONCEPTS 85,160,190

ancient [adj] *old, often very old*
aged, age-old, antediluvian, antiquated, antique, archaic, back number*, been around*, bygone, creaky*, early, elderly, few miles on*, fossil*, hoary, lot of mileage*, moth-eaten*, obsolete, older, old-fashioned, old goat*, oldie*, outmoded, out-of-date, primal, primeval, primordial, relic, remote, rusty, superannuated, timeworn, venerable, worse for wear*; SEE CONCEPTS 578,797

ancillary [adj] *extra; supplementary*
accessory, accompanying, additional, adjuvant, appurtenant, attendant, attending, coincident, collateral, concomitant, contributory, incident, satellite, secondary, subordinate, subservient, subsidary; SEE CONCEPT 835

and [conj] *in addition to; plus*
along with, also, as a consequence, as well as, furthermore, including, moreover, together with; SEE CONCEPT 577

androgynous [adj] *having male and female traits*
bisexual, cross-sexual, epicene, hermaphrodite, trans-sexual, unisexual; SEE CONCEPT 372

anecdote [n] *interesting or amusing story*
chestnut*, episode, fairy tale*, fish story*, gag*, incident, long and short of it*, narration, narrative, old chestnut*, recital, relation, reminiscence, short story, sketch, tale, tall story*, tall tale*, yarn; SEE CONCEPT 282

anemic [adj] *weak and pale*
bloodless, feeble, frail, infirm, pallid, sickly, wan, watery; SEE CONCEPTS 314,483,618

anesthesia/anaesthesia [n] *induced sleep; induced absence of feeling*
analgesia, insentience, numbness, stupor, unconsciousness; SEE CONCEPTS 313,315,728

anesthetic/anaesthetic [n] *sleep-inducing or numbing drug*
analgesic, anodyne, dope*, gas, hypnotic, inhalant, narcotic, opiate, pain-killer, shot, soporific, spinal; SEE CONCEPT 307

anew [adj/adv] *fresh; again*
afresh, another time, come again, de novo, from scratch, from the beginning, in a different way, in a new way, lately, new, newly, once again, once more, one more time, over, over again, recently; SEE CONCEPT 820

angel [n1] *attendant of God*
archangel, celestial being, cherub, divine messenger, God's messenger, guardian, heavenly being, holy being, seraph, spirit, spiritual being, sprite, supernatural being; SEE CONCEPTS 361,370

angel [n2] *sweet, kind person*
beauty, darling, dear, dream, gem, ideal, jewel, paragon, saint, treasure; SEE CONCEPT 416

angel dust [n] *phencyclidine; PCP*
angel hair*, angel mist*, aurora borealis*, black whack, crystal*, cyclones*, devil dust*, dummy dust*, embalming fluid*, hallucinogen, horse tranquilizer*, jet fuel*, magic dust*, rocket fuel*, star dust*; SEE CONCEPT 307

angelic [adj] *sweet, kind, and usually beautiful*
adorable, archangelic, beatific, beneficent, celes-

tial, cherubic, devout, divine, entrancing, ethereal, godly, good, heavenly, holy, humble, innocent, lovely, otherworldly, pure, radiant, rapturous, righteous, saintly, self-sacrificing, seraphic, virtuous; SEE CONCEPT 572

anger [n] state of being mad, annoyed
acrimony, animosity, annoyance, antagonism, blow up*, cat fit*, chagrin, choler, conniption, dander*, disapprobation, displeasure, distemper, enmity, exasperation, fury, gall, hatred, hissy fit*, huff, ill humor, ill temper, impatience, indignation, infuriation, irascibility, ire, irritability, irritation, mad, miff, outrage, passion, peevishness, petulance, pique, rage, rankling, resentment, slow burn*, soreness, stew, storm, tantrum, temper, tiff, umbrage, vexation, violence; SEE CONCEPTS 29,410

anger [v] make someone mad; become mad
acerbate, affront, aggravate, agitate, annoy, antagonize, arouse, bait, blow up*, boil*, boil over*, bristle, burn, burn up, chafe, craze*, cross, displease, egg on*, embitter, enrage, exacerbate, exasperate, excite, fret, gall, get mad, get on one's nerves*, goad, incense, inflame, infuriate, irritate, lose one's temper, madden, make sore*, miff, nettle, offend, outrage, pique, provoke, raise hell*, rankle, rant, rave, rile, ruffle, seethe, steam up*, stew, stir up*, tempt, umbrage, vex; SEE CONCEPTS 7,19

angle [n1] shape formed by two lines meeting at a point
bend, corner, crook, crotch, cusp, decline, divergence, dogleg, edge, elbow, flare, flection, flexure, fork, incline, intersection, knee, nook, notch, obliquity, point, slant, turn, turning, twist, V, Y; SEE CONCEPT 436

angle [n2] personal approach, purpose
aim, approach, aspect, direction, hand, intention, outlook, perspective, plan, point of view, position, side, slant, standpoint, viewpoint; SEE CONCEPTS 660,661

angle [v] fish
cast, dangle a line*, drop a line*; SEE CONCEPT 363

angle for [v] attempt to get
aim for, be after, cast about for, connive, conspire, contrive, fish for, hint, hunt, invite, look for, maneuver, plan, plot, scheme, seek, solicit, strive, try for; SEE CONCEPTS 20,87

angry [adj] being mad, often extremely mad
affronted, annoyed, antagonized, bitter, chafed, choleric, convulsed, cross, displeased, enraged, exacerbated, exasperated, ferocious, fierce, fiery, fuming, furious, galled, hateful, heated, hot, huffy, ill-tempered, impassioned, incensed, indignant, inflamed, infuriated, irascible, irate, ireful, irritable, irritated, maddened, nettled, offended, outraged, piqued, provoked, raging, resentful, riled, sore, splenetic, storming, sulky, sullen, tumultous/tumultuous, turbulent, uptight, vexed, wrathful; SEE CONCEPT 403

angst [n] feeling of anxiety
agony, apprehension, blues, depression, dread, mid-life crisis*, misgiving, nervousness, uneasiness, Weltschmerz; SEE CONCEPTS 410,532,690

anguish [n] severe upset or pain
affliction, agony, distress, dole, dolor, grief, heartache, heartbreak, hurting, misery, pang, rue, sorrow, suffering, throe, torment, torture, woe, wretchedness; SEE CONCEPT 410

angular [adj1] bent
akimbo, bifurcate, cornered, crooked, crossing, crotched, divaricate, forked, intersecting, jagged, oblique, sharp-cornered, skewed, slanted, staggered, V-shaped, Y-shaped, zigzag; SEE CONCEPT 486

angular [adj2] thin, especially referring to people
awkward, bony, gangling, gaunt, lank, lanky, lean, rangy, rawboned, scrawny, sharp, skinny, spare; SEE CONCEPT 773

animal [adj] beastlike; carnal
beastly, bestial, bodily, brute, brutish, corporeal, earthly, earthy, feral, fleshy, mammalian, muscular, natural, physical, sensual, untamed, wild, zoological; SEE CONCEPT 406

animal [n] animate being; mammal
beast, being, brute, bum*, creature, critter, invertebrate, living thing, mutt*, pet, stray, varmint*, vertebrate, wild thing; SEE CONCEPT 394

animate [adj1] alive
breathing, live, living, mortal, moving, viable, vital, zoetic; SEE CONCEPT 539

animate [adj2] lively
activated, active, alert, animated, dynamic, energized, gay, happy, spirited, vivacious; SEE CONCEPT 401

animate [v] bring to life
activate, arouse, cheer, embolden, encourage, energize, enliven, exalt, excite, fire, gladden, hearten, impel, incite, inform, inspire, inspirit, instigate, invigorate, kindle, liven, make alive, move, quicken, revive, revivify, rouse, spark, spur, stimulate, stir, urge, vitalize, vivify; SEE CONCEPTS 231,241

animated [adj] lively
activated, active, alert, animate, ardent, brisk, buoyant, dynamic, ebullient, elated, energetic, energized, enthusiastic, excited, fervent, gay, happy, passionate, peppy, quick, snappy, spirited, sprightly, vibrant, vigorous, vital, vitalized, vivacious, vivid, zealous, zestful, zingy, zippy; SEE CONCEPT 401

animation [n] liveliness; activity
action, ardor, bounce, brio, briskness, buoyancy, dash, dynamism, ebullience, élan, elation, energy, enthusiasm, esprit, excitement, exhilaration, fervor, gaiety, high spirits, life, oomph*, passion, pep*, sparkle, spirit, sprightliness, verve, vibrancy, vigor, vim, vitality, vivacity, zap*, zeal, zest, zing*, zip*; SEE CONCEPT 657

animosity [n] extreme dislike, hatred
acrimony, animus, antagonism, antipathy, bad blood, bitterness, displeasure, enmity, hate, hostility, ill will, malevolence, malice, malignity, rancor, resentment, virulence; SEE CONCEPT 29

ankle [n] joint between leg and foot
anklebone, astragalus, bone, talus, tarsus; SEE CONCEPTS 392,418

annal(s) [n] history, records
account, archive, chronicle, journal, memorial, record, register; SEE CONCEPTS 271,281

annex [n] something added; extension
addendum, addition, adjunct, affix, appendix, arm, attachment, ell, subsidiary, supplement, wing; SEE CONCEPTS 440,441,484

annex [v] join or add
adjoin, affix, append, appropriate, associate, attach, connect, fasten, hitch on*, hitch up*, hook on*, hook up*, link, slap on*, subjoin, tack on*,

tag, tag on*, take on, take over, unite; SEE CON-
CEPTS *85,113,160*

annexation [*n*] *adding, joining*
addition, annexing, appropriation, attachment,
grab, incorporation, increase, increment, merger,
takeover; SEE CONCEPTS *113,324*

Annie Oakley [*n*] *complimentary ticket*
Chinese ducket*, free admission, freebie*, free
pass, free seats, free ticket; SEE CONCEPTS
271,685

annihilate [*v*] *destroy completely*
abate, abolish, abrogate, annul, blot out*, crush*,
decimate, demolish, do in*, eradicate, erase, expunge, exterminate, extinguish, extirpate, finish
off, invalidate, liquidate, massacre, murder,
negate, nullify, obliterate, quash, quell, raze, root
out*, rub out*, ruin, slaughter, take out*, undo,
vitiate, wipe out*, wrack*, wreck; SEE CONCEPT
252

anniversary [*n*] *yearly observance, celebration*
ceremony, commemoration, feast day, festival,
holiday, jubilee, recurrence, red-letter day; SEE
CONCEPTS *800,801,815,823*

annotate [*v*] *write explanatory notes*
comment, commentate, construe, define, elucidate, explain, expound, footnote, gloss, illustrate,
interpret, note, remark; SEE CONCEPTS *51,57,79*

annotation [*n*] *explanatory note*
comment, commentary, definition, elucidation,
exegesis, explanation, explication, footnote;
gloss, glossary, illustration, interpretation, note,
observation; SEE CONCEPTS *274,283*

announce [*v1*] *make a proclamation*
advertise, annunciate, blast, blazon, broadcast,
call, communicate, declare, disclose, disseminate, divulge, drum*, give out, impart, intimate,
issue, make known, make public, pass the
word*, proclaim, promulgate, propound, publicize, publish, release, report, reveal, run off at
mouth*, sound off*, spread around*, state, tell,
trumpet; SEE CONCEPT *49*

announce [*v2*] *declare arrival*
augur, forebode, forecast, forerun, foreshow,
foretell, harbinger, herald, indicate, portend, predict, presage, signal, signify; SEE CONCEPTS
60,70

announcement [*n*] *proclamation, declaration*
advertisement, advice, briefing, broadcast,
broadcasting, bulletin, communication, communiqué, disclosure, dissemination, divulgence,
edict, exposing, exposition, expression, intimation, message, narration, news, notice, notification, prediction, promulgation, publication,
publishing, recitation, release, report, reporting,
revelation, statement; SEE CONCEPTS *49,274*

announcer [*n*] *media commentator*
anchorperson, broadcaster, communicator, deejay, disc jockey, DJ, leader of ceremonies, newscaster, reporter, rip and reader*, spieler*, talker,
telecaster, veejay*, VJ; SEE CONCEPT *348*

annoy [*v*] *irritate, upset*
abrade, agitate, ask for it*, badger, be at*, bedevil, beleaguer, be on the back of*, bore,
bother, break, bug, burn up, chafe, displease, distress, disturb, egg on*, exasperate, fire up*, gall,
get, gnaw, harass, harry, heat up*, henpeck, hit
where one lives*, irk, madden, make waves*,
miff, nag, needle, nettle, nudge, peeve, perturb,
pester, plague, provoke, push button*, ride, rile,

ruffle, tease, tick off*, T-off*, trouble, turn off*,
vex, work on*, worry; SEE CONCEPTS *7,19*

annual [*adj1*] *occurring, done yearly*
anniversary, each year, every year, once a year,
year end; SEE CONCEPTS *541,823*

annual [*adj2*] *lasting for a year*
a year's worth, yearlong; SEE CONCEPT *798*

annual [*n*] *book produced once a year*
annuary, report, summary, yearbook; SEE CON-
CEPT *271*

annually [*adv*] *occurring, done yearly*
by the year, each year, every year, once a year,
per annum, per year, year after year; SEE CON-
CEPTS *541,823*

annul [*v*] *void an agreement*
abate, abolish, abrogate, annihilate, blot out, call
off, cancel, countermand, declare, delete, discharge, dissolve, efface, erase, expunge, get off
the hook*, invalidate, kill, negate, neutralize,
nix, nullify, obliterate, quash, recall, render null
and void, repeal, rescind, retract, reverse, revoke,
scrub*, undo, vacate, vitiate, wipe out*; SEE
CONCEPTS *252,297,317*

annulment [*n*] *voiding an agreement*
abatement, abolition, abrogation, annihilation,
breakup, cancellation, countermanding, dedomiciling, deletion, discharge, dissolution, erasing,
going phfft*, invalidation, negation, neutralization, nullification, obliteration, recall, repeal, rescinding, rescindment, rescission, retraction,
reversal, revocation, split*, split up*, undoing*,
vitiation, voiding; SEE CONCEPTS *297,317,691*

anoint [*v*] *bless, usually with oil or water*
bless, consecrate, daub, embrocate, grease, hallow, rub, sanctify, smear; SEE CONCEPT *367*

anomalous [*adj*] *deviating from normal, usual*
aberrant, abnormal, atypical, bizarre, divergent,
eccentric, exceptional, foreign, heteroclite, incongruous, inconsistent, irregular, odd, peculiar,
preternatural, prodigious, rare, strange, unnatural,
unorthodox, unrepresentative, untypical, unusual; SEE CONCEPT *547*

anomaly [*n*] *deviation from normal, usual*
aberration, abnormality, departure, deviation, eccentricity, exception, incongruity, inconsistency,
irregularity, oddity, peculiarity, rarity, unconformity, unorthodoxy; SEE CONCEPT *647*

anonymous [*adj*] *unknown, usually by choice*
bearding*, incognito, innominate, Jane/John
Doe*, nameless, pseudo, pseudonymous, secret,
so and so*, such and such*, unacknowledged,
unattested, unavowed, unclaimed, uncredited,
undesignated, undisclosed, unidentified, unnamed, unsigned, unspecified, whatchamacallit*,
what's his/her name*, whatsis*, X*, you know
who*; SEE CONCEPT *683*

anorexic [*adj*] *starving*
bulimic, emaciated, malnourished, sickly looking, thin, without appetite; SEE CONCEPTS
490,491

another [*n*] *other person*
addition, a different person, one more, someone
else, something else; SEE CONCEPT *423*

another [*prep/det*] *additional, different*
added, a distinct, a further, a separate, else, farther, fresh, further, more, new, one more, other,
some other, that; SEE CONCEPT *564*

answer [*n*] *reply; reaction*
acknowledgment, antiphon, backcap*, back talk,

band-aid*, close, comeback, comment, cooler*, counterclaim, crack, defense, disclosure, echo, elucidation, explanation, feedback, guff*, interpretation, justification, key, lip*, observation, parting shot*, pay dirt*, plea, quick fix*, rebuttal, refutation, rejoinder, remark, repartee, report, resolution, response, result, retort, return, riposte, sign, solution, statement, thank-you note*, the ticket*, topper*, vindication, wisecrack; SEE CONCEPTS 274,278

answer [vi] *reply, react*
acknowledge, answer back, argue, back at you*, back talk, be in touch*, claim, comeback, contest, counterclaim, defend, deny, disprove, dispute, echo, explain, feedback, field the question*, get back at*, get back to*, give a snappy comeback*, parry, plead, rebut, refute, rejoin, remark, resolve, respond, retaliate, retort, return, sass*, say, settle, shoot back*, solve, squelch, talk back, top*; SEE CONCEPTS 45,266

answer [vi] *solve; fulfill*
clarify, conform, correlate, correspond, crack*, deal with*, do*, dope, dope out*, elucidate, fill, fit*, lick*, measure up, meet, pass, qualify, satisfy, serve, suffice, suit, unzip*, work, work through; SEE CONCEPTS 87,664

answerable [adj] *responsible*
accountable, amenable, bound, chargeable, compelled, constrained, liable, obligated, obliged, subject, to blame; SEE CONCEPT 545

antagonism [n] *causing problem; opposition*
animosity, animus, antipathy, antithesis, clashing, competition, conflict, contention, contradistinction, contrariety, difference, disagreement, discord, dissension, enmity, friction, hatred, hostility, incongruity, oppugnancy, rancor, resistance, rivalry; SEE CONCEPT 29

antagonist [n] *person causing problem*
adversary, angries*, bad person*, bandit*, competitor, contender, crip*, enemy, foe, match, opponent, opposer, opposite number*, oppugnant, rival; SEE CONCEPT 412

antagonize [v] *cause problem; oppose*
alienate, anger, annoy, counteract, estrange, insult, irritate, neutralize, offend, repel, struggle, work against; SEE CONCEPTS 7,19,231

antecedent [adj] *prior*
anterior, earlier, foregoing, former, past, precedent, preceding, precursory, preliminary, previous; SEE CONCEPT 820

antecedent(s) [n] *predecessor(s) in family*
ancestor, ancestry, antecessor, blood, descent, extraction, forebears, forefather/mother, genealogy, line, primogenitor, progenitor, stock; SEE CONCEPT 414

antedate [v] *occur or cause to occur earlier*
accelerate, anachronize, antecede, backdate, date back, forerun, misdate, pace, precede, predate; SEE CONCEPT 84

antediluvian [adj] *out-of-date; prehistoric*
age-old, ancient, antiquated, antique, archaic, hoary, obsolete, old, old-fashioned, passé, primeval, primitive, primordial, timeworn, venerable; SEE CONCEPTS 578,797,799

antenna [n] *appendages for sensing, usually on insects or electronics*
aerial, bird snapper*, bullwhip*, ears*, feelers*, rabbit ears, receiver, sky wire*, whip*, wire; SEE CONCEPT 464

anterior [adj] *beginning, prior*
antecedent, foregoing, former, past, precedent, preceding, previous; SEE CONCEPT 799

anthem [n] *song*
canticle, chant, chorus, hymn, melody, paean; SEE CONCEPTS 263,595

anthology [n] *literary collection*
album, analect, compendium, compilation, digest, garland, omnibus, selection, treasury; SEE CONCEPTS 280,432

anthropology [n] *study of humans and their culture*
folklore, sociology; SEE CONCEPT 349

antibiotic [n] *medicine*
amoxicillin, ampicillin, erythromycin, penicillin, streptomycin, sulfa drug, sulfonamide, tetracycline, wonder drug*; SEE CONCEPT 307

antic [n] *funny act*
caper, dido, frolic, joke, lark, romp, shenanigan, tomfoolery, trick; SEE CONCEPT 292

anticipate [vi] *expect; predict*
assume, await, bargain for*, be afraid*, conjecture, count chickens*, count on, cross the bridge*, divine, entertain*, figure, forecast, foresee, foretaste, foretell, have a hunch*, hope for, jump the gun*, look for, look forward to, plan on, prepare for, prevision, prognosticate, promise oneself, prophesy, see, see coming*, see in the cards*, suppose, visualize, wait, wait for; SEE CONCEPTS 26,70

anticipate [v2] *act in advance of*
apprehend, beat someone to it*, be early, be one step ahead of*, block, delay, forestall, hinder, hold back, intercept, precede, preclude, prepare for, prevent, provide against; SEE CONCEPTS 100,121

anticipation [n1] *expectation*
apprehension, awaiting, contemplation, expectancy, foresight, foretaste, high hopes, hope, impatience, joy, looking forward, outlook, preconception, premonition, preoccupation, prescience, presentiment, promise, prospect, trust; SEE CONCEPTS 26,689

anticipation [n2] *readiness; forethought*
apprehension, awareness, foreboding, forecast, foreseeing, foresight, foretaste, forethought, inkling, intuition, preconception, premonition, prescience, presentiment, prevision, prior knowledge, realization; SEE CONCEPTS 409,410

anticlimax [n] *ineffective conclusion*
bathos, comedown, decline, descent, disappointment, drop, letdown, slump; SEE CONCEPTS 230,674

antidote [n] *counteracting agent*
antitoxin, antivenin, corrective, counteractant, counteragent, countermeasure, counterstep, cure, medicine, negator, neutralizer, nullifier, preventive, remedy; SEE CONCEPT 307

antipathy [n] *strong dislike, disgust*
abhorrence, allergy, animosity, animus, antagonism, aversion, avoidance, bad blood*, contrariety, distaste, dyspathy, enmity, escape, eschewal, evasion, hate, hatred, hostility, ill will, incompatibility, loathing, opposition, rancor, repellency, repugnance, repulsion; SEE CONCEPT 29

antiquarian [adj] *old, ancient*
aged, antique, archaic, hoary, obsolete, primitive, timeworn, venerable; SEE CONCEPTS 578,797

antiquated [adj] *obsolete*
aged, ancient, antediluvian, antique, archaic,

dated, elderly, fusty*, hoary, moldy, obsolescent, old, old-fangled, old-fashioned, old hat*, outmoded, out-of-date, outworn, superannuated; SEE CONCEPTS 530,578,797

antique [adj1] *old*
aged, ancient, elderly, obsolescent, obsolete, outdated, out-of-date, prehistoric, superannuated; SEE CONCEPTS 578,797

antique [adj2] *old-fashioned*
antiquarian, archaic, classic, obsolete, olden, outdated, vintage; SEE CONCEPTS 530,578,797

antique [n] *old object, often of great value*
antiquity, artifact, bygone, heirloom, monument, objet d'art, rarity, relic, ruin, vestige; SEE CONCEPTS 259,443

antiquity [n1] *old object*
antique, relic, ruin; SEE CONCEPT 259

antiquity [n2] *oldness*
age, ancientness, antiqueness, archaicism, archaism, elderliness, hoariness, old age, venerableness; SEE CONCEPT 715

antiquity [n3] *distant past*
ancient time(s), classical times, days of old, days of yore, former age, old days, olden days, remote time, time immemorial; SEE CONCEPT 807

antiseptic [adj] *completely clean, uncontaminated; decontaminating*
antibacterial, antibiotic, aseptic, bactericidal, clean, disinfectant, germ-destroying, germ-free, germicidal, hygienic, medicated, prophylactic, pure, purifying, sanitary, sterile, sterilized, sterilizing, unpolluted; SEE CONCEPT 485

antiseptic [n] *decontaminating agent*
bactericide, detergent, disinfectant, germicide, preservative, preventative, preventive, prophylactic, purifier, sterilizer; SEE CONCEPTS 307,472,492

antisocial [adj] *nonparticipating; avoiding company*
alienated, ascetic, asocial, austere, cold, cynical, eremetic, hermitlike, introverted, misanthropic, reclusive, remote, reserved, retiring, solitary, standoffish, uncommunicative, unfriendly, unsociable, withdrawn; SEE CONCEPT 555

antithesis [n1] *exact opposite*
antipode, antipole, contra, contradictory, contrary, contrast, converse, counter, flip side*, inverse, other side, reverse; SEE CONCEPT 665

antithesis [n2] *contrast, opposition*
antagonism, contradiction, contradistinction, contraposition, contrariety, inversion, opposure, reversal; SEE CONCEPTS 633,665

antithetical [adj] *reverse*
contradictory, contrary, contrasted, converse, counter, inverse, opposed, opposite, polarized, poles apart*; SEE CONCEPT 542

antitoxin [n] *agent for negating the effect of an infection or poison*
antibiotic, antibody, antipoison, antiseptic, antiserum, antivenin, counteractant, counteragent, medicine, neutralizer, preventive, serum, vaccine; SEE CONCEPT 307

antonym [n] *word with opposite meaning to another word*
opposite, reverse; SEE CONCEPT 275

antsy [adj] *fidgety*
anxious, edgy, impatient, on pins and needles*, restless; SEE CONCEPT 401

anxiety [n] *worry, tension*
all-overs*, angst, ants in pants*, apprehension,

botheration*, butterflies*, care, cold sweat*, concern, creeps*, disquiet, disquietude, distress, doubt, downer*, drag*, dread, fidgets*, flap*, foreboding, fretfulness, fuss, goose bumps*, heebie-jeebies*, jitters, jumps*, misery, misgiving, mistrust, nail-biting*, needles*, nervousness, panic, pins and needles*, restlessness, shakes*, shivers*, solicitude, suffering, suspense, sweat*, trouble, uncertainty, unease, uneasiness, watchfulness, willies*, worriment; SEE CONCEPTS 410,532,690

anxious [adj] *worried, tense*
afraid, aghast, antsy*, apprehensive, basket case*, bugged*, butterflies*, careful, choked*, clutched*, concerned, disquieted, distressed, disturbed, dreading, fearful, fidgety, fretful, hacked*, hyper*, in a state*, in a tizzy*, in suspense*, jittery, jumpy, nervous, nervy, overwrought, restless, scared, shaking, shaky, shivery, shook up*, shot to pieces*, solicitous, spooked*, strung out*, sweating bullets*, taut, troubled, uneasy, unglued*, unquiet, uptight*, watchful, wired*, worried sick*, wreck*; SEE CONCEPTS 403,690

anxious [adj2] *eager*
agog, ardent, avid, breathless, desirous, enthusiastic, expectant, fervent, impatient, intent, itching*, keen, thirsty, yearning, zealous; SEE CONCEPTS 401,542

any [det] *one, some; unspecified, indiscriminate*
a bit, a little, all, each, each and every, either, in general, part of, several, whatever; SEE CONCEPT 762

anybody [n] *one, some unspecified person or people*
all, any of, anyone, anyone at all, any person, a person, each and every one, everybody, everyone, masses, one, public, whole world; SEE CONCEPT 417

anyhow [adv] *by any means*
about, anyway, any which way, around, at any rate, at random, haphazard, haphazardly, helter-skelter, however, in any case, in any respect, in any way, in either way, in one way or another, in whatever way, nevertheless, random, randomly, regardless, under any circumstances, whatever happens, willy-nilly; SEE CONCEPT 544

anyone [n] *one, some unspecified person*
all, anybody, anybody at all, any of, any person, a person, each and every one, everybody, everyone, masses, one, public, whole world; SEE CONCEPT 417

anyplace [n] *unspecified area*
all over, anywhere, everywhere, in any place, in whatever place, wherever; SEE CONCEPT 198

anything [n] *unspecified object or event*
all, any one thing, anything at all, everything, whatever; SEE CONCEPTS 2,433

anytime [n] *unspecified moment, period*
at all, at any moment, at one's convenience, every-time, no matter when, whenever, when one will; SEE CONCEPTS 807,819

anyway [adv] *by any means*
anyhow, at all, at any rate, ever, however, in any case, in any event, in any manner, nevertheless, once; SEE CONCEPT 544

anywhere [n] *unspecified area*
all over, anyplace, everywhere, in any place, in whatever place, wherever; SEE CONCEPT 198

apart [*adv*] *separate*
afar, alone, aloof, aside, away, by itself, cut off*, disassociated, disconnected, distant, distinct, divorced, excluded, exclusively, freely, independent, independently, individually, isolated, lone wolf*, separated, separately, singly, special, to itself, to one side; SEE CONCEPTS 586,785

apartheid [*n*] *racial segregation*
discrimination, racism, separation; SEE CONCEPT 689

apartment [*n*] *set of rooms for rent*
accommodation, cave*, chambers, cold-water*, condo, coop, cooperative, crash pad*, den*, digs*, dump*, flat, living quarters, lodging, pad*, penthouse, rental, residence, suite, walk-up; SEE CONCEPTS 448,516

apathetic [*adj*] *uncaring, disinterested*
blah*, callous, cold, cool, could care less*, couldn't care less*, don't give a damn*, draggy*, emotionless, flat, impassive, indifferent, insensible, laid-back*, languid, moony*, passive, stoic, stolid, unconcerned, unemotional, unfeeling, uninterested, unmoved, unresponsive, untouched, what the hell*, wimpy*; SEE CONCEPTS 401,403

apathy [*n*] *uncaring attitude, lack of interest*
aloofness, coldness, coolness, detachment, disinterest, dispassion, disregard, dullness, emotionlessness, halfheartedness, heedlessness, indifference, insensibility, insensitivity, insouciance, lassitude, lethargy, listlessness, passiveness, passivity, stoicism, unconcern, unresponsiveness; SEE CONCEPTS 410,633

ape [*v*] *mimic*
affect, caricature, copy, counterfeit, ditto*, do*, do like*, echo, emulate, go like*, imitate, impersonate, make like*, mirror, mock, parody, parrot, take off*, travesty; SEE CONCEPTS 111,171

aperture [*n*] *hole*
breach, break, chasm, chink, cleft, crack, cut, eye, fissure, gap, gash, interstice, opening, orifice, outlet, passage, perforation, pinhole, puncture, rift, rupture, slash, slit, slot, space, vent; SEE CONCEPT 757

apex [*n*] *top, high point*
acme, apogee, climax, crest, crown, culmination, cusp, greatest, height, max*, maximum, meridian, most*, ne plus ultra, peak, pinnacle, point, roof, spire, sublimity, summit, tip, tops, up there*, vertex, zenith; SEE CONCEPTS 706,836

aphorism [*n*] *saying expressing a belief, often true*
adage, apothegm, axiom, dictum, maxim, moral, precept, proverb, rule, saw, saying, truism; SEE CONCEPTS 275,278,689

aphrodisiac [*n/adj*] *seductive; inducing sex*
amative, amatory, amorous, erotic, love drug, popper*, Spanish fly*, turn-on*, wampole*; SEE CONCEPTS 372,537

apiece [*adv*] *each*
all, a pop*, aside, for each, from each, individually, one by one, per, respectively, separately, severally, singly, successively, to each; SEE CONCEPT 762

apocalypse [*n*] *mass destruction*
annihilation, Armageddon, cataclysm, catastrophe, decimation, devastation, end of the world, holocaust; SEE CONCEPT 674

apocryphal [*adj*] *questionable; fake*
counterfeit, doubtful, dubious, equivocal, false, fictitious, inaccurate, mythical, spurious, unauthenticated, ungenuine, unsubstantiated, untrue, unverified, wrong; SEE CONCEPTS 570,582

apologetic [*adj*] *expressing remorse, regret*
atoning, attritional, compunctious, conciliatory, contrite, expiatory, explanatory, on one's knees*, penitent, penitential, propitiatory, regretful, remorseful, repentant, rueful, self-effacing, self-incriminating, sorry, supplicating; SEE CONCEPT 267

apologize [*v*] *express remorse, regret*
admit guilt, ask forgiveness, ask pardon, atone, beg pardon, bow to*, clear oneself, confess, cop a plea*, cop out*, crawl*, excuse oneself, get down on knees*, give satisfaction*, make amends, make reparations, make up for, make up with, offer compensation, offer excuse, purge, retract, say one is sorry, square*, withdraw; SEE CONCEPTS 48,67

apology [*n*] *offering of remorse, regret*
acknowledgment, admission, amends, atonement, concession, confession, defense, excuse, explanation, extenuation, justification, mea culpa, mitigation, plea, redress, reparation, vindication; SEE CONCEPTS 48,67

apoplexy [*n*] *loss of consciousness from blockage in vein or artery*
occlusion, seizure, stroke, thrombosis; SEE CONCEPTS 316,720

apostate [*n*] *traitor*
backslider, defector, deserter, dissenter, heretic, nonconformist, rat*, recreant, renegade, turncoat; SEE CONCEPTS 359,412

apostle [*n*] *preacher; supporter*
advocate, champion, companion, converter, evangelist, follower, herald, messenger, missionary, pioneer, propagandist, proponent, proselytizer, witness; SEE CONCEPTS 359,361

apotheosis [*n*] *glorification*
deification, elevation, idolization, immortalization; SEE CONCEPTS 69,367

appall/appal [*v*] *horrify*
alarm, amaze, astound, awe, consternate, daunt, disconcert, dishearten, dismay, faze, frighten, get to*, gross out*, insult, intimidate, outrage, petrify, scare, shake, shock, terrify, throw, unnerve; SEE CONCEPTS 7,19,42

appalling [*adj*] *horrifying*
alarming, astounding, awful, bad, daunting, dire, disheartening, dismaying, dreadful, fearful, formidable, frightening, frightful, ghastly, grim, grody*, gross*, harrowing, heavy*, hideous, horrible, horrid, horrific, intimidating, mean, petrifying, scaring, shocking, terrible, terrifying, the end*, unnerving; SEE CONCEPT 529

apparatus [*n*] *equipment with a purpose*
accoutrement, appliance, black box*, contraption, device, dingbat, doodad*, doohickey*, furnishings, gaff*, gear, gimcrack*, gimmick, gizmo*, grabber*, habiliments, idiot box*, implement, jigger*, job*, machine, machinery, means, mechanism, outfit, paraphernalia, provisions, setup, stuff, supplies, tackle, thingamajig*, tools, utensils, whatchamacallit*, whatsis*, whosis*, widget*; SEE CONCEPTS 260,463,499

apparatus [*n2*] *organization or system*
bureaucracy, chain of command, hierarchy, network, setup, structure; SEE CONCEPTS 381,770

apparel [*n*] *clothing; covering*
accoutrement, array, attire, clothes, costume, drapery, dress, duds*, equipment, garb, garment,

gear*, getup*, habiliment, habit, outfit, raiment, rig*, robe, suit, threads*, trapping, vestment; SEE CONCEPTS *451,473*

apparent [*adj1*] *seeming, not proven real*
credible, illusive, illusory, likely, ostensible, outward, plausible, possible, probable, semblant, specious, superficial, supposed, suppositious; SEE CONCEPTS *552,582*

apparent [*adj2*] *obvious*
barefaced, big as life*, clear, clear cut, conspicuous, crystal clear, discernible, distinct, evident, glaring, indubitable, make no bones*, manifest, marked, noticeable, observable, open, open and shut*, out in the open*, overt, palpable, patent, perceivable, plain, self-evident, transparent, unambiguous, under one's nose*, understandable, unequivocal, unmistakable, visible; SEE CONCEPTS *535,582*

apparently [*adv1*] *seemingly*
allegedly, as if, as though, at a glance, at first sight, in all likelihood, intuitively, it appears that, it seems that, most likely, on the face of it, ostensibly, outwardly, plausibly, possibly, probably, professedly, reasonably, reputably, speciously, superficially, supposedly, tangibly, to all appearances; SEE CONCEPTS *552,582*

apparently [*adv2*] *obviously*
clearly, conspicuously, evidently, expressly, indubitably, in plain sight, manifestly, officially, openly, overtly, palpably, patently, perceptibly, plainly, transparently, unmistakably; SEE CONCEPT *535*

apparition [*n*] *ghost*
bogeyman, bump in the night*, chimera, delusion, hallucination, haunt, illusion, phantasm, phantom, revenant, specter, spirit, spook, visitant; SEE CONCEPTS *370,689*

appeal [*n1*] *request for help*
address, adjuration, application, bid, call, claim, demand, entreaty, imploration, importunity, invocation, overture, petition, plea, prayer, proposal, proposition, question, recourse, requisition, solicitation, submission, suit, supplication; SEE CONCEPT *48*

appeal [*n2*] *power to attract, interest*
allure, attraction, attractiveness, beauty, charm, charmingness, engagingness, fascination, glamor, interestingness, pleasingness, seductiveness; SEE CONCEPTS *655,673*

appeal [*v1*] *request*
address, adjure, advance, apply, ask, beg, beseech, bid, call, call upon, claim, contest, crave, demand, entreat, hit on, implore, importune, petition, plead, pray, propose, proposition, question, refer, require, resort to, solicit, strike, submit, sue, supplicate, urge; SEE CONCEPT *48*

appeal [*v2*] *attract, interest*
allure, beguile, captivate, catch the eye, charm, enchant, engage, entice, fascinate, intrigue, invite, please, tantalize, tempt; SEE CONCEPTS *7,19,22,384*

appear [*v1*] *come into sight*
arise, arrive, attend, be present, be within view, blow in*, bob up*, break through, breeze in*, check in*, clock in*, come, come forth, come into view, come out, come to light*, crop up*, develop, drop in*, emerge, expose, issue, loom, make the scene*, materialize, occur, pop in*, pop up*, present, punch in*, punch the clock*, recur, ring in*, rise, roll in*, show, show up,

spring, surface, time in*, turn out, turn up; SEE CONCEPTS *159,261*

appear [*v2*] *seem*
have the appearance, look as if, look like, occur, resemble, sound, strike one as; SEE CONCEPTS *543,716*

appear [*v3*] *be obvious, clear*
be apparent, be evident, be manifest, be patent, be plain; SEE CONCEPT *725*

appear [*v4*] *be published; perform*
become available, be created, be developed, be invented, come into being, come into existence, come on, come on stage*, come out, enter, make an appearance, oblige, perform, play, play a part, present oneself, take part; SEE CONCEPTS *292,324*

appearance [*n1*] *coming into sight*
actualization, advent, appearing, arrival, coming, debut, display, emergence, entrance, exhibition, introduction, manifestation, materialization, presence, presentation, representation, rise, showing up, turning up, unveiling; SEE CONCEPTS *159,261*

appearance [*n2*] *outward aspect, characteristic*
air, attitude, bearing, blind, carriage, cast, character, condition, countenance, demeanor, dress, expression, face, fashion, feature, figure, form, front, guise, image, look, looks, manner, mannerism, mien, mode, outline, pose, presence, presentation, screen, semblance, shape, stamp; SEE CONCEPTS *543,716*

appearance [*n3*] *outward show; pretense*
aura, beard*, blind, countenance, dream, facade, front, guise, idea, illusion, image, impression, mirage, phenomenon, reflection, screen, seeming, semblance, sound, specter, vision; SEE CONCEPT *673*

appease [*v*] *satisfy, pacify*
allay, alleviate, assuage, be enough, blunt, calm, compose, conciliate, content, diminish, do*, ease, gratify, lessen, lull, make matters up, meet halfway, mitigate, mollify, patch things up, placate, propitiate, quell, quench, quiet, serve, soften, soothe, subdue, sweeten, tranquilize; SEE CONCEPTS *7,22,126*

appeasement [*n*] *satisfaction; pacification*
abatement, acceding, accommodation, adjustment, alleviation, amends, assuagement, blunting, compromise, concession, conciliation, easing, grant, lessening, lulling, mitigation, moderation, mollification, peace offering, placation, propitiation, quelling, quenching, quieting, reconciliation, reparation, restoration, settlement, softening, solace, soothing, tranquilization; SEE CONCEPTS *7,22,126*

appellation [*n*] *name*
designation, epithet, handle*, label, moniker*, nickname, sobriquet, title; SEE CONCEPTS *268,683*

append [*v*] *add, join*
adjoin, affix, annex, attach, conjoin, fasten, fix, hang, subjoin, supplement, tack on*, tag on*; SEE CONCEPTS *85,113,160*

appendage [*n*] *limb; accessory*
addendum, addition, adjunct, ancillary, annex, appendix, appurtenance, attachment, auxiliary, extremity, member, projection, protuberance, supplement; SEE CONCEPT *835*

appendix [*n*] *added material at end of document*
addendum, addition, adjunct, appendage, appurtenance, attachment, codicil, excursus, index,

notes, postscript, rider, sample, supplement, table, verification; SEE CONCEPT 270

appertain [v] *belong, be connected*
apply, bear, be characteristic of, be part of, be pertinent, be proper, be relevant, have to do with, pertain, refer, relate, touch upon, vest; SEE CONCEPT 532

appetite [n] *desire for food, worldly goods*
appetence, appetency, appetition, big eyes*, craving, demand, fondness, gluttony, greed, hankering, hunger, inclination, itch*, liking, longing, lust, passion, penchant, proclivity, propensity, ravenousness, relish, soft spot*, stomach, sweet tooth*, taste, thirst, urge, voracity, weakness, willingness, yearning, yen, zeal, zest; SEE CONCEPTS 20,32 .

appetizer [n] *snack before meal*
antipasto, aperitif, canapé, cocktail, dip, finger food, hors d'oeuvre, munchies*, relish, sample, spread, taste, tidbit; SEE CONCEPTS 457,828

appetizing [adj] *tasting very good*
aperitive, appealing, delectable, delicious, delish*, divine*, flavorsome, heavenly, inviting, luscious, mouthwatering, palatable, saporous, savory, scrumptious, succulent, sugar-coated*, sweetened, tantalizing, tasty, tempting, toothsome, yummy*; SEE CONCEPT 613

applaud [v] *clap for; express approval*
acclaim, approve, boost, cheer, commend, compliment, encourage, eulogize, extol, give a hand*, give ovation, glorify, hail, hear it for*, kudize*, laud, magnify, plug, praise, rave, recommend, root*; SEE CONCEPTS 10,69,189

applause [n] *clapping; expression of approval*
acclaim, acclamation, accolade, approbation, big hand, bring down the house*, cheering, cheers, commendation, eulogizing, hand, hand-clapping, hurrahs, kudos, laudation, ovation, plaudits, praise, rooting, round, standing ovation; SEE CONCEPTS 69,189

appliance [n] *machine, usually with domestic purpose*
apparatus, device, gadget, implement, instrument, mechanism, tool; SEE CONCEPT 463

applicable [adj] *appropriate*
applicative, applicatory, apposite, apropos, apt, associable, befitting, felicitous, fit, fitting, germane, kosher, legit*, material, on target*, on the button*, on the nose*, pertinent, relevant, right on*, suitable, suited, that's the idea*, that's the ticket*, to the point, to the purpose, useful; SEE CONCEPTS 558,563

applicant [n] *person trying for position*
appellant, aspirant, candidate, claimant, hopeful, inquirer, petitioner, postulant, seeker, suitor, suppliant; SEE CONCEPTS 348,359

application [n1] *use*
appliance, appositeness, employment, exercise, exercising, function, germaneness, operation, pertinence, play, practice, purpose, relevance, usance, utilization, value; SEE CONCEPTS 680,694

application [n2] *request*
appeal, blank, claim, demand, draft, entreaty, form, inquiry, letter, paper, petition, requisition, solicitation, suit; SEE CONCEPT 48

application [n3] *hard work*
assiduity, attention, attentiveness, busyness, commitment, concentration, consideration, dedication, deliberation, diligence, effort, industry, perseverance, study, zeal; SEE CONCEPTS 91,410

application [n4] *putting substance on another*
administering, administration, applying, creaming, dosing, oiling, rubbing, treatment; SEE CONCEPT 200

applied [adj] *used*
activated, adapted, adjusted, brought to bear, correlated, devoted, enforced, exercised, practiced, related, tested, utilized; SEE CONCEPTS 538,546

apply [v1] *put into use*
administer, assign, bring into play, bring to bear, employ, engage, execute, exercise, exploit, handle, implement, practice, utilize; SEE CONCEPT 225

apply [v2] *be appropriate, relevant*
affect, allude, appertain, be applicable, bear upon, be pertinent, concern, connect, fit, involve, pertain, refer, regard, relate, suit, touch; SEE CONCEPT 532

apply [v3] *put substance on another*
administer, affix, anoint, bestow, cover, fasten, join, lay on, massage, paint, place, put on, rub, smear, spread, touch; SEE CONCEPT 200

apply [v4] *ask, request*
appeal, claim, demand, inquire, petition, put in, put in for, requisition, solicit, sue; SEE CONCEPT 48

apply [v5] *work hard*
address, bear down, be diligent, be industrious, bend, buckle down*, commit, concentrate, dedicate, devote, dig, direct, give, give all one's got*, give best shot*, give old college try*, grind, hammer away*, hit the ball*, hustle*, knuckle down*, make effort, peg away*, persevere, plug*, pour it on*, pull out all stops*, scratch, study, sweat*, throw, try, turn; SEE CONCEPTS 87,100

appoint [v1] *assign responsibility; decide*
accredit, allot, assign, choose, command, commission, decree, delegate, designate, determine, direct, elect, enjoin, establish, finger, fix, install, name, nominate, ordain, select, set, settle, tap; SEE CONCEPTS 41,50,88

appoint [v2] *furnish*
arm, equip, fit, fit out, gear, outfit, provide, rig, supply, turn out; SEE CONCEPT 140

appointment [n1] *arrangement for meeting; prearranged meeting*
assignation, assignment, blind date*, consultation, date, engagement, errand, gig, interview, invitation, meet, rendezvous, session, tryst, zero hour*; SEE CONCEPTS 324,384

appointment [n2] *assignment of responsibility*
allotment, approval, assigning, authorization, certification, choice, choosing, commissioning, delegation, deputation, designation, election, empowering, installation, naming, nomination, ordination, promotion, selection; SEE CONCEPTS 41,50,88

appointment [n3] *job, position of responsibility*
appointee, assignment, berth, candidate, delegate, employment, nominee, office, officeholder, place, post, representative, situation, station, work; SEE CONCEPT 349

appointment [n4] *furnishing(s)*
accoutrement, appurtenance, equipage, fitting, fixture, gear, outfit, paraphernalia, trappings; SEE CONCEPT 475

apportion [v] *divide into shares*
accord, admeasure, administer, allocate, allot, as-

sign, bestow, cut, cut up, deal, dispense, distribute, divvy, divvy up, dole out, give, lot, measure, mete, parcel, part, partition, piece up, prorate, ration, slice, split, split up; SEE CONCEPTS 98,108

appraisal [n] *judgment, estimation*
appraisement, assessment, estimate, evaluation, opinion, pricing, rating, reckoning, stock, survey, valuation; SEE CONCEPTS 18,328,766

appraise [v] *judge, estimate*
adjudge, assay, assess, audit, calculate, check, check out*, deem, evaluate, examine, eye*, figure, figure in, figure out, gauge, guesstimate*, have one's number*, inspect, look over, peg, price, rate, read, review, set at, size, survey, take account of, valuate, value; SEE CONCEPTS 18,764

appreciable [adj] *easily noticed; considerable*
apparent, ascertainable, clear-cut, definite, detectable, discernible, distinguishable, estimable, evident, goodly, good-sized, healthy, large, manifest, marked, material, measurable, noticeable, observable, obvious, perceivable, perceptible, plain, pronounced, recognizable, sensible, significant, sizable, substantial, tangible, visible; SEE CONCEPTS 619,781

appreciate [v1] *be grateful, thankful*
acknowledge, be appreciative, be indebted, be obliged, enjoy, flip over*, freak out on*, get high on*, give thanks, groove on*, welcome; SEE CONCEPTS 12,32,76

appreciate [v2] *increase in worth*
enhance, gain, grow, improve, inflate, raise the value of, rise; SEE CONCEPT 763

appreciate [v3] *recognize worth*
acknowledge, apprehend, be aware of, be cognizant of, be conscious of, catch the drift, comprehend, dig, fathom, grasp, know, perceive, read, realize, recognize, savvy, see daylight*, sympathize with, take account of, understand; SEE CONCEPT 15

appreciate [v4] *value highly*
admire, adore, applaud, apprise, cherish, enjoy, esteem, extol, honor, like, look up to, love, praise, prize, rate highly, regard, relish, respect, savor, treasure; SEE CONCEPTS 10,32

appreciation [n1] *thankfulness*
acknowledgment, gratefulness, gratitude, indebtedness, obligation, recognition, testimonial, thanks, tribute; SEE CONCEPTS 12,32

appreciation [n2] *increase in worth*
enhancement, gain, growth, improvement, inflation, rise; SEE CONCEPTS 346,763

appreciation [n3] *recognition of worth*
admiration, aesthetic sense, affection, appraisal, assessment, attraction, awareness, cognizance, commendation, comprehension, enjoyment, esteem, estimation, grasp, high regard, knowledge, liking, love, perception, realization, recognition, regard, relish, respect, responsiveness, sensibility, sensitiveness, sensitivity, sympathy, understanding, valuation; SEE CONCEPTS 15,409

appreciative [adj1] *thankful*
beholden, grateful, indebted, obliged, responsive; SEE CONCEPT 403

appreciative [adj2] *understanding, recognizing worth*
admiring, affectionate, alive, aware, cognizant, conscious, considerate, cooperative, cordial, enlightened, enthusiastic, favorable, friendly, generous, keen, kindly, knowledgeable, magnanimous, mindful, perceptive, pleased, receptive,

regardful, respectful, responsive, satisfied, sensitive, supportive, sympathetic, understanding; SEE CONCEPT 402

apprehend [v1] *catch and arrest*
bag*, bust*, capture, collar, cop*, grab, nab, nail*, place under arrest, run in, seize, take in, take into custody, take prisoner; SEE CONCEPTS 90,191,317

apprehend [v2] *understand*
absorb, accept, appreciate, believe, catch, comprehend, conceive, digest, fathom, get, get the picture*, grasp, have, imagine, know, perceive, read, realize, recognize, sense, think; SEE CONCEPT 15

apprehension [n1] *anxiety, fear*
alarm, apprehensiveness, concern, disquiet, doubt, dread, foreboding, misgiving, mistrust, premonition, presage, presentiment, suspicion, trepidation, uneasiness, worry; SEE CONCEPTS 27,690

apprehension [n2] *catching and arresting*
booking, capture, collaring, detention, seizure, taking; SEE CONCEPTS 90,317

apprehension [n3] *understanding*
awareness, comprehension, grasp, idea, intellect, intelligence, judgment, ken, knowledge, notion, perception, perspicacity, thought; SEE CONCEPT 409

apprehensive [adj] *anxious, fearful*
afraid, alarmed, biting nails*, butterflies*, concerned, disquieted, doubtful, feel in bones*, foreboding, frozen*, get vibes*, have a hunch*, have cold feet*, have funny feeling*, have stage fright*, hung up*, in a cold sweat*, in a dither*, in a sweat*, jellyfish*, jittery, jumpy, lily-livered*, mistrustful, running scared*, scaredy-cat*, shaky*, stiff, suspicious, troubled, uncertain, uneasy, uptight, weak, worried, worried sick*; SEE CONCEPT 403

apprentice [n] *novice/learner of a trade*
amateur, beginner, flunky*, greenhorn*, heel*, neophyte, newcomer, new kid on block*, novitiate, probationer, pupil, rook*, rookie*, starter, student, tenderfoot*, tyro; SEE CONCEPTS 348,423

apprise [v] *tell*
advise, brief, enlighten, fill in, inform, notify, tip off; SEE CONCEPTS 57,60,75

approach [n1] *way, means of arriving*
access, accession, advance, advent, avenue, coming, drawing near, entrance, gate, landing, nearing, passage, path, reaching, road, way; SEE CONCEPTS 159,501

approach [n2] *request, suggestion*
advance, appeal, application, offer, overture, proposal, proposition; SEE CONCEPT 278

approach [n3] *plan of attack, resolution*
attitude, concept, course, crack, fling, go*, idea, lick, manner, means, method, mode, modus operandi, new wrinkle*, offer, procedure, program, shot, stab, style, technique, way, whack*, wrinkle*; SEE CONCEPTS 655,660

approach [v] *come nearer*
advance, approximate, bear, be comparable to, be like, belly up to*, border, buzz*, catch up, close in, come, come at, come close, compare with, contact, converge, correspond to, creep up, draw near, equal, gain on, go toward, impend, loom up, match, meet, move in on, move toward, near, progress, reach, resemble, surround, take

after, threaten, verge upon; SEE CONCEPTS
159,198,701

approach [*v2*] *make request, suggestion*
accost, address, advise, appeal to, apply to, beseech, confer, consult, entreat, feel, feel one
out*, give a tumble*, greet, im-
plore, make advance, make overture, make up to,
plead, propose, sound out, speak to, supplicate,
take aside, talk to, thumb, tumble; SEE CONCEPTS
48,75

approach [*v3*] *begin*
commence, embark, set about, start, undertake;
SEE CONCEPT *234*

approachable [*adj*] *accessible*
attainable, come-at-able*, convenient, door's always open*, getable*, obtainable, reachable; SEE
CONCEPT *576*

approachable [*adj2*] *friendly*
affable, agreeable, congenial, cordial, open, receptive, sociable; SEE CONCEPT *404*

approbation [*n*] *praise*
admiration, approval, bells*, consent, endorsement, esteem, favor, go-ahead*, high regard,
okay, permission, recognition, sanction, support,
the nod*; SEE CONCEPTS *10,69*

appropriate [*adj*] *suitable*
adapted, applicable, appurtenant, apropos, apt,
becoming, befitting, belonging, congruous, convenient, correct, deserved, desired, due, felicitous, fit, fitting, germane, good, just, on the
button*, on the nose*, opportune, pertinent,
proper, relevant, right, rightful, seemly, tailor-
made, true, useful, well-suited, well-timed; SEE
CONCEPT *558*

appropriate [*v1*] *set aside; allocate*
allot, allow, appoint, apportion, assign, budget,
devote, disburse, earmark, reserve, set apart; SEE
CONCEPT *135*

appropriate [*v2*] *steal*
annex, borrow, clap*, confiscate, cop, embezzle,
filch, get fingers on*, get hands on*, glom on
to*, grab, grab hold of*, hijack, liberate, lift,
misappropriate, moonlight requisition*, pilfer,
pocket, secure, snatch, swipe*, take over, usurp;
SEE CONCEPT *139*

appropriation [*n1*] *allocation, setting aside*
allotment, allowance, apportionment, assignment, budgeting, concession, donation, earmark-
ing, endowing, funding, giving, grant, provision,
setting apart, sponsoring, stipend, stipulation,
subsidy; SEE CONCEPTS *135,340*

appropriation [*n2*] *stealing*
confiscation, embezzlement, expropriation, grab,
misappropriation, pilfering, seizure, takeover,
taking, usurpation; SEE CONCEPT *139*

approval [*n1*] *authorization*
acquiescence, assent, bells*, blessing, compliance, concurrence, confirmation, consent, countenance, endorsement, go-ahead*, green light*,
leave, license, mandate, okay, permission, ratification, recommendation, sanction, support, the
nod*, validation; SEE CONCEPTS *10,685*

approval [*n2*] *good opinion*
acclaim, admiration, applause, appreciation, approbation, commendation, esteem, favor, liking,
pat on the back*, pat on the head*, PR*, praise,
puff, pumping up, regard, respect, strokes,
stroking, wow*; SEE CONCEPT *32*

approve [*v1*] *agree something is good*
accept, acclaim, admire, applaud, appreciate, ap-

probate, be big on*, commend, countenance, esteem, face it, favor, go along with, grin and bear
it*, handle, like, live with*, praise, put up with,
regard highly, respect, roll with punches*, string
along with*, take up on*, think highly of; SEE
CONCEPT *10*

approve [*v2*] *allow, authorize*
accede, accept, accredit, acquiesce, advocate, affirm, agree, assent, authorize, back*, bless*,
boost, buy, buy into*, certify, charter, concur,
confirm, consent, dig*, empower, encourage, endorse, establish, get behind, give go-ahead*, go
along with, groove*, hats off to*, lap up*, license, maintain, make law, make valid, mandate,
okay, permit, pronounce, push for, ratify, recommend, sanction, seal, second, sign, sign off on,
stump for, subscribe to, support, thumbs up*, uphold, validate; SEE CONCEPTS *50,83,88*

approximate [*adj1*] *almost accurate, exact*
almost, close, comparative, near, proximate, relative, rough; SEE CONCEPT *557*

approximate [*adj2*] *inexact*
estimated, guessed, imperfect, imprecise, loose,
rough, surmised, uncertain, unprecise, unscientific; SEE CONCEPT *557*

approximate [*adj3*] *similar*
alike, analogous, close, comparable, like, matching, near, relative, resembling, verging on; SEE
CONCEPTS *487,573*

approximate [*adj4*] *near*
adjacent, bordering, close together, contiguous,
nearby, neighboring; SEE CONCEPT *586*

approximate [*v*] *come close*
approach, border on, come near, estimate, near,
reach, resemble, touch, verge on; SEE CONCEPT
664

approximately [*adv*] *nearly*
about, almost, around, ballpark figure*, bordering on, circa, closely, close to, comparatively,
generally, in the ballpark*, in the neighborhood
of, in the region of, in the vicinity of, just about,
loosely, more or less, most, much, not far from,
not quite, proximately, relatively, roughly, upwards of*, very close; SEE CONCEPT *566*

apropos [*adj*] *relevant, suitable*
applicable, apposite, appropriate, apt, befitting,
belonging, correct, fit, fitting, germane, kosher*,
legit*, material, on the button*, on the nose*, opportune, pertinent, proper, related, right, right
on*, seemly; SEE CONCEPT *558*

apropos [*adv*] *relevantly, suitably*
appropriately, aptly, opportunely, pertinently,
suitably, timely; SEE CONCEPT *558*

apropos [*prep*] *in respect of*
about, against, as for, as regards, as to, concerning, on the subject of, regarding, respecting,
touching, toward, with reference to, with respect
to; SEE CONCEPT *532*

apt [*adj1*] *suitable*
applicable, apposite, appropriate, apropos, befitting, correct, felicitous, fit, fitting, germane,
happy, just, pertinent, proper, relevant, seemly,
suitable, timely; SEE CONCEPT *558*

apt [*adj2*] *tending, inclined*
disposed, given, liable, likely, of a mind, prone,
ready; SEE CONCEPT *542*

apt [*adj3*] *quick to learn*
able, adept, astute, bright, clever, expert, gifted,
ingenious, intelligent, nobody's fool*, no
dummy*, not born yesterday*, prompt, quick on

the trigger*, quick on the uptake*, ready, savvy, sharp, skilled, skillful, smart, talented, teachable; SEE CONCEPT 402

aptitude [*n1*] *inclination*
bent, disposition, drift, leaning, predilection, proclivity, proneness, propensity, tendency; SEE CONCEPT 657

aptitude [*n2*] *quickness at learning*
ability, capability, capacity, cleverness, competence, faculty, flair, gift, giftedness, intelligence, knack, proficiency, savvy, smarts, stuff*, talent, what it takes*; SEE CONCEPT 409

aquarium [*n*] *fish tank*
aquatic museum, fishbowl, marine exhibit; SEE CONCEPTS 396,438,514

aquatic [*adj*] *occurring in water*
amphibian, amphibious, floating, marine, maritime, natatory, oceanic, of the sea, sea, swimming, watery; SEE CONCEPTS 396,536

aqueduct [*n*] *canal*
channel, conduit, course, duct, pipeline, water passage, waterworks; SEE CONCEPT 514

arbiter [*n*] *person who settles dispute*
adjudicator, arbitrator, fixer, go-between, holdout, judge, maven, mediator, middleperson, moderator, referee, umpire; SEE CONCEPT 354

arbitrary [*adj1*] *whimsical, chance*
approximate, capricious, discretionary, erratic, fanciful, frivolous, inconsistent, injudicious, irrational, irresponsible, offhand, optional, random, subjective, supercilious, superficial, unaccountable, unreasonable, unscientific, wayward, willful; SEE CONCEPTS 534,542

arbitrary [*adj2*] *dictatorial*
absolute, autocratic, bossy, despotic, dogmatic, domineering, downright, flat out*, high-handed, imperious, magisterial, monocratic, no ifs ands or buts*, no joke*, overbearing, peremptory, straight out*, summary, tyrannical, tyrannous; SEE CONCEPT 401

arbitrate [*v*] *achieve settlement*
adjudge, adjudicate, adjust, bring to terms, come to school, come to terms, conciliate, decide, determine, hammer out a deal*, interpose, intervene, judge, make a deal, mediate, meet halfway, negotiate, parley, pass judgment, placate, play ball*, reconcile, referee, settle, smooth, soothe, step in, straighten out, strike happy medium*, trade off, umpire, work out a deal; SEE CONCEPTS 126,300

arbitration [*n*] *settlement of dispute*
adjudication, adjustment, agreement, compromise, decision, determination, judgment, mediation; SEE CONCEPTS 126,300

arbitrator [*n*] *settler of a dispute*
adjudicator, arbiter, fixer, go-between, holdout, judge, maven, mediator, middleperson, referee, umpire; SEE CONCEPTS 348,359

arc [*n*] *curve*
arch, bend, bow, crescent, curvation, curvature, half-moon, round; SEE CONCEPT 436

arcade [*n*] *covered way*
cloister, colonnade, gallery, loggia, mall, passageway, piazza, portico, stoa, walkway; SEE CONCEPT 501

arcane [*adj*] *hidden, secret*
cabalistic, esoteric, impenetrable, mysterious, mystic, occult, recondite, unaccountable, unknowable; SEE CONCEPT 576

arch [*adj1*] *principal, superior*
accomplished, champion, chief, consummate, expert, finished, first, foremost, greatest, head, highest, leading, main, major, master, preeminent, premier, primary, top; SEE CONCEPT 574

arch [*adj2*] *knowing, coy*
artful, frolicsome, mischievous, pert, playful, roguish, saucy, sly, waggish, wily; SEE CONCEPT 401

arch [*n*] *curve, curved structure*
arc, archway, bend, bow, curvature, dome, semicircle, span, vault; SEE CONCEPT 436

arch [*v*] *curve*
arc, bend, bow, bridge, camber, extend, form, hook, hump, hunch, round, shape, span, stretch; SEE CONCEPT 184

archaeologist [*n*] *student of the physical remains of ancient cultures or eras*
archaeologian, classicist, excavator, paleologist, paleontologist, prehistorian; SEE CONCEPT 348

archaeology [*n*] *study of the physical remains of ancient cultures or eras*
antiquarianism, excavation, paleohistory, paleology, paleontology, prehistory; SEE CONCEPT 349

archaic [*adj*] *very old*
ancient, antiquated, antique, bygone, obsolete, olden, old-fashioned, outmoded, out of date, passé, primitive, superannuated; SEE CONCEPTS 578,797

archetype [*n*] *typical example*
classic exemplar, form, ideal, model, original, paradigm, pattern, perfect specimen, prime example, prototype, standard; SEE CONCEPTS 636,686

architect [*n*] *person who designs buildings*
artist, builder, creator, designer, draftsperson, engineer, inventor, maker, master builder, originator, planner, prime mover; SEE CONCEPT 348

architecture [*n1*] *design of buildings*
architectonics, building, construction, engineering, planning; SEE CONCEPTS 349,439

architecture [*n2*] *design, structure of something*
composition, constitution, construction, formation, framework, make-up, style; SEE CONCEPTS 660,733

archive [*n*] *collection, usually of records*
annals, chronicles, clippings, documents, excerpts, extracts, files, papers, registers, roll, scrolls, writings; SEE CONCEPTS 271,281,432

archives [*n*] *place where records are stored*
athenaeum, library, museum, office, registry, repository, storage, treasury, vault; SEE CONCEPT 439

archway [*n*] *curved opening*
entrance, passage; SEE CONCEPT 440

arctic [*adj*] *very cold*
chill, chilly, cool, freezing, frigid, frosty, frozen, gelid, glacial, icy, nippy, polar; SEE CONCEPT 605

ardent [*adj1*] *very enthusiastic*
agog, avid, blazing, burning, desirous, eager, fervent, fervid, fierce, fiery, horny*, hot*, hungry, impassioned, intense, keen, lovey-dovey*, lusty, passionate, spirited, thirsty, vehement, warm, zealous; SEE CONCEPTS 401,404

ardent [*adj2*] *loyal*
allegiant, constant, devoted, faithful, resolute, steadfast, true; SEE CONCEPT 404

ardor [*n*] *enthusiasm*
avidity, devotion, eagerness, earnestness, feeling, fervor, fierceness, fire, gusto, heat, intensity,

jazz*, keenness, oomph*, passion, pep talk*, spirit, turn on*, vehemence, verve, warmth, weakness*, zeal, zest, zing; SEE CONCEPT *411*

arduous [adj] *difficult, hard to endure*
backbreaking, burdensome, exhausting, fatiguing, formidable, grueling, harsh, heavy, labored, laborious, murder, no picnic*, onerous, painful, punishing, rigorous, rough, severe, strenuous, taxing, tiring, toilsome, tough, troublesome, trying, uphill; SEE CONCEPT *565*

area [n1] *extent, scope of a surface*
breadth, compass, distance, expanse, field, operation, range, size, space, sphere, stretch, width; SEE CONCEPTS *651,792*

area [n2] *region, district*
belt, block, city, county, division, domain, dominion, enclosure, field, kingdom, locality, neck of the woods*, neighborhood, parcel, patch, plot, precinct, principality, quarter, section, sector, sphere, square, state, stretch, territory, township, tract, turf, vicinity, ward, zone; SEE CONCEPT *508*

arena [n1] *building or enclosure for entertainment or sports*
amphitheatre, boards*, bowl*, circus, coliseum, course, diamond, field, gridiron, ground, gym, gymnasium, hippodrome, ice, park, pit, platform, ring, rink, square, stadium, stage; SEE CONCEPT *438*

arena [n2] *area of activity*
battlefield, battleground, domain, field, province, realm, scene, sector, sphere, territory, theatre; SEE CONCEPT *198*

argot [n] *jargon*
cant, dialect, idiom, lingo, parlance, patois, slang, terminology, vernacular, vocabulary; SEE CONCEPT *276*

argue [v1] *verbally fight*
altercate, bandy, battle, bicker, break with, buck, bump heads, contend, cross, cross swords, disagree, dispute, face down, face off, feud, gang up on, get in one's face*, go one on one, hammer, hammer away, hash, hash over, hassle, have at each other, have at it, jump, jump on, knock around, lock horns*, mix it up*, pettifog, pick an argument, put up a fight, put up a struggle, quarrel, quibble, rehash, row, sass, set to, sock it to*, squabble, stick it to, talk back, wrangle; SEE CONCEPT *46*

argue [v2] *try to convince; present support*
appeal, assert, attest, claim, contend, controvert, defend, demonstrate, denote, display, elucidate, establish, evince, exhibit, explain, hold, imply, indicate, justify, maintain, manifest, persuade, plead, present, prevail upon, reason, show, suggest, talk into, testify, vindicate, warrant, witness; SEE CONCEPT *68*

argue [v3] *discuss*
agitate, canvass, clarify, debate, dispute, expostulate, hold, maintain, question, reason, remonstrate, talk about; SEE CONCEPTS *46,56*

argument [n1] *verbal fight*
altercation, beef, bickering, blowup, bone, bone of contention, bone to pick*, brannigan*, brawl, brush, clash, controversy, debate, difference of opinion, disagreement, dispute, donnybrook, dustup*, exchange, face-off, falling, feud, finisher*, flap, fuss, gin*, go*, hassle, knockdown*, knock down and drag out*, out, quarrel, rhubarb*, romp, row, ruckus, ruction, rumpus, run-in, scene, scrap, set-to, shindy*,

spat, squabble, static*, stew*, talking heads*, tiff, words, wrangle; SEE CONCEPT *46*

argument [n2] *effort to convince; presentation of support*
argumentation, assertion, case, claim, contention, debate, defense, discussion, exchange, expostulation, grounds, line of reasoning, logic, plea, pleading, polemic, proof, questioning, reason, reasoning, remonstrance, remonstration; SEE CONCEPT *68*

argumentative [adj] *wanting to quarrel*
belligerent, combative, contentious, contrary, controversial, disputatious, factious, fire-eating, having a chip on one's shoulder*, litigious, opinionated, pugnacious, quarrelsome, salty, scrappy, spiky, touchy; SEE CONCEPT *401*

aria [n] *operatic solo*
descant, hymn, song; SEE CONCEPTS *263,595*

arid [adj1] *dry*
barren, bone-dry, desert, dry as a bone, dry as dust, dusty, moistureless, parched, thirsty, waterless; SEE CONCEPT *603*

arid [adj2] *uninterested, spiritless*
boring, colorless, drab, dreary, dry, dull, flat, insipid, lackluster, lifeless, tedious, unanimated, uninspired, vapid, wearisome; SEE CONCEPT *542*

arise [v1] *come into being; proceed*
appear, begin, come to light, commence, crop up, derive, emanate, emerge, ensue, flow, follow, happen, head, issue, occur, originate, result, rise, set in, spring, start, stem; SEE CONCEPT *105*

arise [v2] *get, stand, or go up*
ascend, climb, jump, mount, move upward, pile out*, rise, rise and shine*, roll out*, soar, stand, tower, turn out, wake up; SEE CONCEPTS *154,166*

aristocracy [n] *privileged class, government*
elite, gentility, gentry, haut monde, high society, nobility, noblesse, patricians, patriciate, peerage, society, upper class, upper crust*; SEE CONCEPTS *296,423*

aristocrat [n] *privileged person*
blueblood, gentleperson, lace curtain*, noble, patrician, peer, silk stocking, swell*, upper cruster*; SEE CONCEPT *423*

aristocratic [adj] *privileged, elegant*
aloof, blue-blooded, courtly, dignified, elegant, elite, fine, haughty, noble, patrician, polished, refined, snobbish, stylish, upper-class, well-born, well-bred; SEE CONCEPT *555*

arithmetic [n] *mathematics*
addition, calculation, computation, division, estimation, figuring, multiplication, reckoning, subtraction; SEE CONCEPTS *349,764*

arm [n1] *limb, appendage*
bender, bough, bow, branch, fin, flapper, flipper, handle, hook, member, offshoot, projection, prong, rod, stump, wing; SEE CONCEPTS *392,471*

arm [n2] *subdivision, annex*
affiliate, authority, block, branch, command, department, detachment, division, ell, extension, force, offshoot, power, projection, section, sector, wing; SEE CONCEPTS *824,835*

arm [n3] *narrow body of water*
branch, brook, channel, creek, estuary, firth, fjord, inlet, rivulet, sound, strait, stream, subdivision, tributary; SEE CONCEPT *514*

arm [v] *equip with weapon or power*
accouter, appoint, array, deck, equalize, fortify, furnish, gear, gird, guard, heel*, heel up*, issue, load, load up, lug iron*, make ready, mobilize,

outfit, pack, pack a rod*, prepare, prime, protect, provide, rig, rod up*, strengthen, supply, tote; SEE CONCEPTS *50,88,182*

armada [*n*] *group of ships or aircraft*
fleet, flotilla, force, navy, squadron; SEE CONCEPTS *432,504,506*

armament(s) [*n*] *weapon(s)*
ammunition, arms, defense, gun, hardware, heat*, material, materiel, munitions, ordnance, protection, security, weaponry; SEE CONCEPT *500*

armed [*adj*] *with weapon*
accoutered, equipped, fitted out, girded, loaded, outfitted, packing*, steeled, supplied; SEE CONCEPT *182*

armistice [*n*] *peace-establishing agreement*
ceasefire, suspension, treaty, truce; SEE CONCEPTS *230,684*

armor [*n*] *protective covering, often made of metal*
bulletproof vest, defense, guard, mail, plate, protection, security, sheath, shield; SEE CONCEPTS *451,476*

armory [*n*] *military building, usually for storing weapons*
arsenal, center, depot, dump, factory, headquarters, magazine, plant, range; SEE CONCEPTS *321,439*

arms [*n1*] *weaponry*
accoutrements, armaments, artillery, equipment, firearms, guns, munitions, ordnance, panoply, weapons; SEE CONCEPT *500*

arms [*n2*] *family crest*
blazonry, coat, emblazonry, emblem, ensign, escutcheon, heraldry, insignia, shield, signet; SEE CONCEPTS *284,625*

army [*n1*] *military force, usually for land*
armed force, artillery, battalion, brigade, cavalry, column, command, company, corps, detail, division, flight, formation, infantry, legion, outfit, patrol unit, platoon, regiment, soldiers, soldiery, squad, troops, wing; SEE CONCEPT *322*

army [*n2*] *group resembling military force*
array, cloud, company, crowd, division, flock, horde, host, legion, mob, multitude, outfit, pack, regiment, scores, swarm, throng, unit; SEE CONCEPT *417*

aroma [*n*] *distinctive smell*
balm, bouquet, fragrance, incense, odor, perfume, redolence, scent, spice; SEE CONCEPT *599*

aromatic [*adj*] *distinctive smelling*
ambrosial, balmy, fragrant, odoriferous, perfumed, pungent, redolent, savory, scented, spicy, sweet, sweet-smelling; SEE CONCEPT *598*

around [*adv1*] *situated on sides, circumference, or in general area*
about, all over, any which way, encompassing, everywhere, in the vicinity, in this area, neighboring, over, throughout; SEE CONCEPT *581*

around [*adv2*] *close to a place*
about, almost, approximately, close at hand; near, nearby; SEE CONCEPT *586*

arouse [*v*] *excite, entice*
agitate, alert, animate, awaken, call, challenge, electrify, enliven, fire up, foment, foster, goad, heat up, incite, inflame, instigate, kindle, move, provoke, rally, rouse, send, spark, spur, stimulate, stir, thrill, turn on, waken, wake up, warm, whet, whip up, work up; SEE CONCEPTS *7,19,22*

arraign [*v*] *accuse*
blame, charge, criminate, hang on, incriminate,

inculpate, indict, lay at one's door*, pin it on*, point the finger at*, summon; SEE CONCEPTS *44,317*

arrange [*v1*] *put in an order*
align, array, class, classify, clear the decks, dispose, file, fix up, form, group, line up, methodize, organize, police, police up, position, put in good shape*, put in order*, put to rights*, range, rank, regulate, sort, spruce, spruce up, systematize, tidy, whip into shape*; SEE CONCEPTS *84,158*

arrange [*v2*] *make plans, often involving agreement*
adapt, adjust, agree to, blueprint, chart, come to terms, compromise, concert, construct, contrive, decide, design, determine, devise, direct, draft, establish, frame*, get act together*, get ready, hammer out a deal*, harmonize, iron out*, lay out, line up, make a connection, make ready, manage, map out, negotiate, organize, prepare, project, promote, provide, pull a wire, pull things together, quarterback*, resolve, schedule, scheme, set stage, settle, shape up, tailor, work out, work out a deal; SEE CONCEPTS *36,84*

arrange [*v3*] *prepare musical composition differently*
adapt, instrument, orchestrate, score; SEE CONCEPT *292*

arrangement [*n1*] *an understanding*
adjustment, agreement, compact, compromise, deal, frame-up*, game plan*, layout*, organization, package*, package deal*, plan, preparation, provision, schedule, settlement, setup, terms; SEE CONCEPT *684*

arrangement [*n2*] *something that has been ordered*
alignment, array, classification, combination, composition, design, display, disposition, distribution, form, grouping, lineup, method, ordering, organization, pattern, pecking order*, ranging, rank, sequence, setup, structure, system; SEE CONCEPTS *84,727*

arrangement [*n3*] *musical adaptation*
chart, composition, instrumentation, interpretation, lead sheet, orchestration, score, version; SEE CONCEPTS *262,595*

arrant [*adj*] *flagrant*
absolute, blatant, glaring, notorious, out-and-out, unmitigated, unregenerate; SEE CONCEPTS *401,545,576*

array [*n1*] *collection, considerable group*
arrangement, batch, body, bunch, bundle, clump, cluster, design, display, disposition, exhibition, formation, host, lineup, lot, multitude, order, parade, pattern, set, show, supply, throng; SEE CONCEPTS *432,769,787*

array [*n2*] *fine clothes*
apparel, attire, drapes*, dress, duds*, finery, full dress, garb, garments, getup*, rig*, threads*; SEE CONCEPT *451*

array [*v1*] *arrange in collection or order*
align, display, exhibit, form, group, line up, methodize, organize, parade, range, set, show, systematize; SEE CONCEPT *84*

array [*v2*] *dress in fine clothes*
attire, bedeck, clothe, deck, deck out, decorate, dog out*, drape, dud, dude up*, fit, fit out, garb, outfit, suit up, tog, try on, turn out, wrap; SEE CONCEPT *167*

arrears [*n*] *debt*
back payment, balance due, claim, debit, deficiency, deficit, liability, obligation, unpaid bill; SEE CONCEPTS *332,335*

arrest [*n1*] *taking into custody*
accommodation, apprehension, appropriation, bag*, booby trap*, bust, captivity, capture, collar, commitment, confinement, constraint, crimp*, detention, drop*, fall*, gaff*, glom*, grab*, heat*, hook*, imprisonment, incarceration, jailing, mitt*, nab*, nail*, nick*, nip*, pickle*, pick up*, pinch*, preventive custody, protective custody, pull*, pull in*, restraining, run in*, sequestering, snare, sweep*; SEE CONCEPTS *90,317*

arrest [*n2*] *slowing or stopping*
blockage, cessation, check, checking, delay, end, halt, hindrance, inhibition, interruption, obstruction, prevention, restraining, restraint, stalling, stay, staying, stoppage, suppression, suspension; SEE CONCEPTS *121,234*

arrest [*v1*] *take into authorized custody*
apprehend, bag*, book, brace*, bust, capture, catch, collar, detain, drop*, gaff*, get*, glom*, grab*, hook*, imprison, incarcerate, jail, kick*, nab*, nail*, net*, nick*, pick up*, pinch*, pull*, pull in*, put the arm on*, put the cuffs on*, round up*, roust*, run in*, secure*, seize*, sidetrack*, snag*, tab*, tag*, take in, take prisoner, toss in jail*; SEE CONCEPTS *90,317*

arrest [*v2*] *stop or slow*
block, can, check, delay, drop, end, freeze, halt, hinder, hold, inhibit, interrupt, knock off, obstruct, prevent, restrain, restrict, retard, scrub*, shut down, stall, stay, suppress; SEE CONCEPTS *121,234*

arrest [*v3*] *get someone's attention*
absorb, catch, engage, engross, fascinate, grip; SEE CONCEPTS *7,19,22*

arrival [*n1*] *coming to a destination*
accession, advent, alighting, appearance, approach, arriving, debarkation, disembarkation, dismounting, entrance, happening, homecoming, influx, ingress, landing, meeting, occurrence, return; SEE CONCEPT *159*

arrival [*n2*] *something that makes it to a destination*
addition, arriver, caller, cargo, comer, conferee, delegate, delivery, entrant, envoy, freight, guest, mail, newcomer, package, parcel, passenger, representative, shipment, tourist, traveler, visitant, visitor; SEE CONCEPTS *337,423,712*

arrive [*v1*] *come to a destination*
access, alight, appear, attain, barge in, blow in, bob up*, breeze in*, bust in*, buzz*, check in*, clock in*, disembark, dismount, drop anchor, drop in, enter, fall by, fall in, get to, hit*, hit town*, land*, make it*, make the scene*, pop in*, pop up*, pull in*, punch the clock*, reach, report, roll in*, show, show up, sign in, sky in*, take place, turn up, visit, wind up at; SEE CONCEPT *159*

arrive [*v2*] *achieve recognition*
accomplish, become famous, flourish, make good, make it, make the grade, make the top, score, succeed, thrive; SEE CONCEPT *706*

arrogance [*n*] *exaggerated self-opinion*
airs, aloofness, audacity, bluster, braggadocio, brass*, cheek*, chutzpah*, conceit, conceitedness, contemptuousness, crust*, disdain, disdainfulness, ego, egotism, gall, haughtiness, hauteur, high-handedness, hubris, imperiousness, insolence, loftiness, nerve, ostentation, overbearance, pomposity, pompousness, presumption, pretension, pretentiousness, pride, priggishness, scornfulness, self-importance, self-love, smugness, superciliousness, swagger, vanity; SEE CONCEPTS *411,633*

arrogant [*adj*] *having exaggerated self-opinion*
aloof, assuming, audacious, autocratic, biggety*, bossy, bragging, cavalier, cheeky, cocky, cold-shoulder*, conceited, contemptuous, cool*, disdainful, domineering, egotistic, haughty, high and mighty*, high-handed, imperious, insolent, know-it-all*, lordly, on an ego trip*, overbearing, peremptory, pompous, presumptuous, pretentious, proud, puffed up*, scornful, self-important, smarty, smug, sniffy*, snippy*, snooty*, snotty*, stuck up*, supercilious, superior, swaggering, uppity*, vain, wise guy*; SEE CONCEPTS *401,404*

arrogate [*v*] *claim without justification*
accroach, appropriate, assume, commandeer, confiscate, demand, expropriate, preempt, presume, seize, take, usurp; SEE CONCEPTS *142,266*

arrow [*n*] *pointed weapon or symbol*
bolt, cursor, dart, indicator, missile, pointer, projectile, shaft; SEE CONCEPT *500*

arsenal [*n*] *storage of weapons*
armory, depository, depot, dump, factory, magazine, ordnance, plant, repository, stock, stockpile, store, storehouse, supply, warehouse; SEE CONCEPTS *432,439*

arson [*n*] *intentional burning*
firing, incendiarism, pyromania, setting fire, torching, touching off; SEE CONCEPT *249*

art [*n1*] *skill, creativity*
adroitness, aptitude, artistry, craft, craftsmanship, dexterity, expertise, facility, imagination, ingenuity, inventiveness, knack, know-how, knowledge, mastery, method, profession, trade, virtuosity; SEE CONCEPT *706*

art [*n2*] *cunning*
artfulness, artifice, astuteness, canniness, craftiness, deceit, duplicity, guile, slyness, trickery, wiliness; SEE CONCEPT *411*

art [*n3*] *creation meant to communicate or appeal to senses or mind*
abstraction, carving, description, design, illustration, imitation, modeling, molding, painting, pictorialization, portrayal, representation, sculpting, shaping, simulation, sketching, symbolization; SEE CONCEPT *349*

artery [*n*] *channel*
avenue, boulevard, canal, conduit, corridor, course, duct, highway, line, passage, pathway, road, route, sewer, thoroughfare, track, tube, way; SEE CONCEPT *501*

artful [*adj*] *skillful; cunning*
adept, adroit, clever, crafty, designing, dexterous, foxy*, ingenious, masterly, politic, proficient, resourceful, scheming, sharp, shrewd, slick*, sly, smart, smooth*, tricky, wily; SEE CONCEPTS *404,528*

article [*n1*] *item, object*
commodity, dojigger*, gizmo*, piece, substance, thing, thingamabob*, thingamajig*, unit; SEE CONCEPT *433*

article [*n2*] *piece of writing*
beat*, blurb*, column, commentary, composi-

tion, discourse, editorial, essay, exposition, feature, item, paper, piece, scoop*, spread, story, theme, think piece*, treatise, write-up; SEE CONCEPTS 270,271,280

article [n3] *section of document*
branch, chapter, clause, detail, division, element, head, heading, item, matter, paragraph, part, passage, piece, point, portion, provision; SEE CONCEPTS 270,318

articulate [adj] *clearly, coherently spoken*
clear, coherent, comprehensible, definite, distinct, eloquent, expressive, fluent, intelligible, lucid, meaningful, understandable, well-spoken; SEE CONCEPT 267

articulate [v1] *say clearly, coherently*
enunciate, express, mouth, pronounce, say, sound off*, speak, state, talk, utter, verbalize, vocalize, voice; SEE CONCEPTS 47,55

articulate [v2] *connect*
concatenate, couple, fit together, hinge, integrate, join, link; SEE CONCEPT 113

articulation [n1] *clear, coherent speech*
delivery, diction, enunciation, expression, pronunciation, saying, speaking, statement, talking, utterance, verbalization, vocalization, voicing; SEE CONCEPT 55

articulation [n2] *connection*
coupling, hinge, joining, joint, junction, juncture, unification, union; SEE CONCEPT 113

artifice [n1] *hoax; clever act*
con, contrivance, device, dodge, expedient, gambit, gimmick*, machination, maneuver, play, ploy, racket*, ruse, savvy, scam*, stratagem, subterfuge, tactic, wile; SEE CONCEPT 59

artifice [n2] *cunning; deception*
artfulness, chicanery, craftiness, dishonesty, duplicity, guile, scheming, slyness, trickery, wiliness; SEE CONCEPT 411

artifice [n3] *skill, cleverness*
ability, adroitness, deftness, facility, finesse, ingenuity, invention, inventiveness, know-how*, skill; SEE CONCEPT 630

artificial [adj1] *fake; imitation*
bogus, counterfeit, ersatz, fabricated, factitious, faked, false, falsie*, hyped up*, manufactured, mock, phony*, plastic, sham, simulated, specious, spurious, substitute, synthetic, unnatural, unreal; SEE CONCEPT 582

artificial [adj2] *pretended; affected*
assumed, contrived, false, feigned, forced, hollow, insincere, labored, mannered, meretricious, phony*, put-on, spurious, theatrical, unnatural; SEE CONCEPT 401

artificial intelligence [n] *development of "thinking" computer systems*
AI, expert system, natural language processing, neural network, robotics; SEE CONCEPTS 269,463

artillery [n] *weaponry or military unit*
arms, battery, bazooka, big guns*, cannon, cannonry, force, gunnery, heavy stuff*, munitions, ordnance, rainmakers*, stovepipe, weapons; SEE CONCEPTS 322,500

artist [n] *person skilled in creative activity*
artisan, artiste, authority, composer, craftsperson, creator, expert, handicrafter, inventor, painter, virtuoso, whiz*; SEE CONCEPT 352

artistic [adj1] *beautiful, satisfying to senses*
aesthetic, creative, cultivated, cultured, decorative, dramatic, elegant, exquisite, fine, graceful, grand, harmonious, ideal, imaginative, musical, ornamental, pictorial, picturesque, pleasing, poetic, refined, rhythmical, sensitive, stimulating, stylish, sublime, tasteful; SEE CONCEPT 579

artistic [adj2] *being skilled in creative activity*
accomplished, artful, artsy-craftsy*, arty, crafty, discriminating, gifted, imaginative, inventive, skillful, talented; SEE CONCEPT 527

artistry [n] *great skill in creative endeavors*
ability, accomplishment, artfulness, brilliance, craftship, creativity, finesse, flair, genius, mastery, proficiency, style, talent, taste, touch, virtuosity, workmanship; SEE CONCEPTS 630,655

artless [adj] *simple*
direct, genuine, guileless, honest, ingenuous, innocent, naive, natural, open, plain, pure, sincere, straight, straightforward, talking turkey*, true, unadorned, unaffected, uncontrived, unpretentious, unsophisticated, up front*; SEE CONCEPTS 267,562

arty [adj] *pretended expertise in art; affected interest*
affected, deceptive, ephemeral, false, flaunting, illusory, imitative, overblown, popular, popularized, pretentious, pseudo, tasteless; SEE CONCEPT 582

as [conj1] *while, when*
at the time that, during the time that, in the act of, in the process of, just as, on the point of; SEE CONCEPT 544

as [conj2] *in the way that; to a degree*
acting as, being, by its nature, comparatively, equally, essentially, for instance, functioning as, in the manner that, in the same manner with, just as, just for, like, serving as, similarly, such as; SEE CONCEPT 544

as [conj3] *because*
as long as, being, cause, considering, for, for the reason that, inasmuch as, now, seeing that, since, whereas; SEE CONCEPT 544

as [prep] *in the role of*
being, in the character of, under the name of; SEE CONCEPT 544

ascend [v] *go up*
arise, climb, escalate, float, fly, lift off, mount, move up, rise, scale, soar, sprout, take off, tower; SEE CONCEPTS 149,166

ascendancy/ascendency [n] *domination*
advantage, authority, command, control, dominance, dominion, edge, influence, jump*, leg up*, mastery, on top, power, predominance, preeminence, prepotence, prevalence, reign, rule, sovereignty, superiority, supremacy, sway, upper hand*, whip hand*; SEE CONCEPTS 376,671

ascension [n] *going up*
ascent, climbing, escalating, flying, mounting, rise, rising, scaling, soaring, towering; SEE CONCEPTS 149,166

ascent [n1] *upward movement*
ascendance, ascending, ascension, clambering, climb, climbing, lift, mounting, rise, rising, scaling, spring, take off; SEE CONCEPT 166

ascent [n2] *upward slope*
acclivity, grade, gradient, incline, ramp, rise; SEE CONCEPTS 738,757

ascertain [v] *make sure*
catch on, check, check out*, check up on*, confirm, determine, dig*, discover, divine, doublecheck*, establish, eye*, eyeball*, find out, fix, get down cold*, get down pat*, get hold of*, get it down*, get the hang of*, identify, learn, learn

the ropes*, look-see*, make certain, make sure, peg*, pick up*, pick up on*, read, see, settle, size, size up*, tell, verify; SEE CONCEPTS 31,34,38

ascetic [adj] *self-denying*
abstaining, abstemious, abstinent, austere, disciplined, puritanical, Spartan, strict; SEE CONCEPT 401

ascribe [v] *assign to source*
accredit, attribute, charge, credit, hang on, impute, lay, pin on*, put down, refer, reference, set down; SEE CONCEPTS 39,49

ashamed [adj] *regretting, remorseful*
abashed, apologetic, bashful, blushing, chagrined, compunctious, conscience-stricken, contrite, crestfallen, debased, demeaned, discomfited, disconcerted, distraught, distressed, embarrassed, flustered, guilty, hesitant, humble, humbled, humiliated, meek, mortified, muddled, penitent, regretful, reluctant, repentant, shamed, shamefaced, sheepish, shy, sorry, stammering, stuttering, submissive; SEE CONCEPT 550

ashen [adj] *gray*
anemic, blanched, cadaverous, colorless, ghastly, gray, leaden, pale, pallid, pasty, sallow, wan, white; SEE CONCEPT 618

ash(es) [n] *remains of burning*
charcoal, cinders, dust, embers, powder, relics, remains, ruins, slag, soot; SEE CONCEPT 260

ashore [adv] *toward, onto land from water*
aground, beached, on dry land, on land, on shore, shorewards; SEE CONCEPT 583

aside [adv] *away from; to the side*
abreast, afar, alone, alongside, apart, away, beside, by oneself, down, in isolation, in reserve, near, nearby, neck and neck, out, out of the way, privately, separately, sidewise; SEE CONCEPT 586

aside [n] *confidential statement*
departure, digression, discursion, interpolation, interposition, parenthesis, tangent, throwaway*; SEE CONCEPT 51

asinine [adj] *senseless*
absurd, cretinous, daft, foolish, half-witted, idiotic, inane, moronic, silly, sophomoric, stupid; SEE CONCEPTS 402,548

ask [v1] *question*
buzz*, canvass, catechize, challenge, cross-examine, demand, direct, enjoin, examine, give the third degree*, go over, grill*, hit*, hunt for*, inquire, institute, interrogate, investigate, needle*, pick one's brains*, pop the question*, pry into, pump, put the screws to*, put through the wringer*, query, quiz, request, roast*, sweat*; SEE CONCEPT 48

ask [v2] *request*
angle, appeal, apply, beg, beseech, bite*, bum*, call for, charge, claim, command, contend for, crave, demand, entreat, file for, hit*, hustle*, implore, impose, knock*, levy, mooch*, order, petition, plead, pray, promote*, request, requisition, seek, solicit, sue, supplicate, touch*, urge; SEE CONCEPT 53

ask [v3] *invite*
bid, call upon, propose, suggest, summon, urge; SEE CONCEPT 75

askance [adv] *sideways*
askew, disapprovingly, disdainfully, dubiously, obliquely, sidelong, sideways, skeptically, suspiciously; SEE CONCEPTS 581,583

askew [adj] *crooked*
askance, askant, aslant, awry, bent, buckled, catawampus*, cockeyed*, crookedly, curved, knotted, lopsided, oblique, obliquely, off-center, slanted, slanting, to one side, topsy-turvey*, turned, twisted, yaw ways*, zigzag*; SEE CONCEPT 586

asleep [adj] *unconscious*
catching some zzz's*, comatose, conked*, crashed*, dormant, dozing, dreaming, flaked out*, getting shut-eye*, hibernating, inactive, in dreamland*, inert, in repose, napping, on the kip*, out*, out cold*, out like a light*, out of it*, reposing, resting, sacked out*, sleeping, slumbering, snoozing, snoring, somnolent, taking forty winks*; SEE CONCEPTS 210,315,681

aspect [n1] *visible feature*
air, appearance, attitude, bearing, condition, countenance, demeanor, expression, face, facet, form, look, manner, mien; SEE CONCEPTS 434,628,673

aspect [n2] *element to consider*
angle, bearing, direction, facet, feature, gimmick, hand, outlook, perspective, phase, point of view, position, prospect, regard, scene, side, situation, slant, switch, twist, view, vista; SEE CONCEPT 668

asperity [n] *harshness; bad temper*
acerbity, acrimony, bitterness, churlishness, crabbiness, crossness, difficulty, disagreeableness, irascibility, irritability, meanness, moroseness, peevishness, regard, roughness, sharpness, sourness, sullenness, tartness; SEE CONCEPT 633

aspersion [n] *verbal exhibition of bad temper*
abuse, animadversion, backbiting, backhanded compliment, black eye*, calumny, defamation, detraction, dirty dig*, hit*, invective, knock*, libel, obloquy, put-down*, rap*, slam*, slander, smear*, vituperation; SEE CONCEPTS 52,54,58

asphyxiate [v] *cut off air*
choke, drown, smother, stifle, strangle, strangulate, suffocate; SEE CONCEPTS 121,246

aspirant [n] *person with wish, dream*
applicant, candidate, competitor, contestant, hopeful, postulant, striver, wannabe; SEE CONCEPTS 366,423

aspiration [n] *goal, hope*
aim, ambition, ambitiousness, craving, desire, direction, dream, eagerness, endeavor, fire in the belly*, hankering, inclination, longing, object, objective, passion, pursuit, push, right stuff*, urge, vocation, wish, work, yearning; SEE CONCEPTS 20,659

aspire [v] *aim, hope*
be ambitious, be eager, crave, desire, dream, hanker, long, pursue, seek, strive, struggle, try, want, wish, yearn; SEE CONCEPT 20

aspiring [adj] *hopeful*
ambitious, aspirant, eager, eager beaver*, endeavoring, enthusiastic, impassioned, longing, on the make*, striving, wishful, would-be, zealous; SEE CONCEPT 403

ass [n] *stupid person*
blockhead*, dolt, donkey*, dope, dunce, fool, idiot, imbecile, jackass*, jerk*, nitwit*, numbskull*, simpleton*, twit*; SEE CONCEPT 412

assail [v] *attack, usually with words*
abuse, assault, bash, berate, beset, blast, blister, bust, charge, come at, criticize, encounter, have at*, impugn, invade, lambaste, lay into*, malign,

maltreat, molest, revile, set upon*, trash*, vilify, work over; SEE CONCEPTS *52,86*

assailant [*n*] *attacker*
aggressor, antagonist, assaulter, bushwhacker*, enemy, foe, goon*, hit person, invader, mugger, opposite number*, trigger person; SEE CONCEPT *412*

assassin [*n*] *murderer of prominent or important person*
butcher*, clipper*, dropper*, eliminator, enforcer, executioner, guerrilla*, gun*, gun person, hatchet person, hit person, killer, liquidator, piece person*, plugger*, slayer, soldier, torpedo*, trigger person; SEE CONCEPT *412*

assassinate [*v*] *murder prominent or important person*
bump off*, do in*, eliminate, execute, gun down, hit, kill, knock off*, liquidate, slaughter, slay; SEE CONCEPT *252*

assault [*n*] *attack*
advance, aggression, charge, incursion, invasion, offensive, onset, onslaught, rape, storm, storming, strike, violation; SEE CONCEPT *86*

assault [*v*] *attack*
abuse, advance, assail, bash, beset, blast, blitz, bushwhack, charge, come down on*, go for, haul off on*, invade, jump, jump down one's throat*, jump on one's case*, lay into, let have it*, light into*, rape, ruin, set upon, shoot down, slam, slap around, storm, strike, trash, violate, work over, zap*; SEE CONCEPTS *52,86*

assay [*n*] *analysis*
appraisal, assessment, estimation, evaluation, examination, inspection, investigation, measurement, rating, survey, test, trial, valuation; SEE CONCEPTS *24,103,290*

assay [*v*] *analyze*
appraise, apprise, assess, check, check out, estimate, evaluate, examine, eyeball*, inspect, investigate, measure, peg*, prove, rate, read, see, size, size up*, survey, test, try, valuate, value, weigh; SEE CONCEPTS *24,103*

assemblage [*v*] *gathering of people*
aggregation, assembly, association, collection, company, congregation, convergence, crowd, group, throng; SEE CONCEPT *417*

assemble [*v1*] *congregate*
accumulate, agglomerate, amass, bring together, bunch, bunch up, call, call together, capture*, collect, come together, convene, convoke, corral*, flock, gang up*, gather, group, hang around*, hang out*, huddle, lump, make the scene*, meet, meet up, mobilize, muster, rally, reunite, round up, scare up*, summon, unite; SEE CONCEPT *114*

assemble [*v2*] *put together*
compile, connect, construct, contrive, erect, fabricate, fashion, fit, form, join, make, manufacture, model, mold, piece together, produce, set up, shape, unite, weld; SEE CONCEPT *113*

assembly [*n1*] *congregation*
accumulation, aggregation, assemblage, association, band, body, bunch, clambake*, cluster, coffee klatch*, collection, company, conclave, confab*, conference, convocation, council, crew, crowd, faction, flock, gathering, get-together*, group, huddle, mass, meet*, meeting, multitude, rally, sit-in*, throng, turnout*; SEE CONCEPTS *381,432*

assembly [*n2*] *putting together*
adjustment, attachment, building, collection, connecting, construction, erection, fabrication, fitting together, joining, manufacture, manufacturing, modeling, molding, piecing together, setting up, shaping, welding; SEE CONCEPT *113*

assent [*n*] *agreement*
acceptance, accession, accord, acknowledgment, acquiescence, admission, affirmation, approval, authorization, compliance, concurrence, consent, nod, permission, sanction; SEE CONCEPTS *8,684*

assent [*v*] *agree*
accede, accept, accord, acquiesce, adopt, allow, approve, buy, cave in*, comply, concur, conform, consent, cut a deal*, defer, ditto*, embrace, espouse, give five*, give in, go along with, grant, knuckle under*, okay*, pass on*, permit, recognize, sanction, say uncle*, shake on*, subscribe; SEE CONCEPT *8*

assert [*v*] *insist, declare, maintain*
advance, affirm, allege, argue, asserverate, attest, aver, avouch, avow, butt in*, cite, claim, contend, defend, horn in, justify, mouth off*, pop off*, predicate, press, proclaim, profess, pronounce, protest, put forward, say, shoot off one's mouth*, shoot one's wad*, stand up for, state, stress, swear, uphold, vindicate, warrant; SEE CONCEPT *49*

assertion [*n*] *declaration, positive statement*
affirmation, allegation, asseveration, attestation, avowal, contention, defense, insistence, maintenance, mouthful, okay, predication, profession, pronouncement, report, say so*, stamp of approval, stressing, two cents' worth*, vindication; SEE CONCEPTS *49,278*

assertive [*adj*] *aggressive*
absolute, assured, certain, confident, decided, decisive, demanding, dogmatic, domineering, emphatic, firm, forceful, forward, insistent, militant, overbearing, positive, pushy, self-assured, self-confident, strong-willed, sure; SEE CONCEPT *404*

assess [*v1*] *evaluate, determine*
appraise, apprise, assay, check*, check out*, compute, determine, dig it*, estimate, figure*, fix, gauge, guess, judge, nick*, peg*, rate, reckon, set, size*, size up, survey, take measure*, valuate, value, weigh; SEE CONCEPT *24*

assess [*v2*] *assign fee*
amount charge, demand, evaluate, exact, fix, impose, levy, rate, tax, value; SEE CONCEPT *330*

assessment [*n1*] *evaluation*
appraisal, computation, determination, estimate, estimation, judgment, rating, reckoning, valuation, value judgment; SEE CONCEPT *24*

assessment [*n2*] *assignment of fee, amount*
appraisal, charge, demand, duty, estimate, fee, levy, rate, rating, tariff, tax, taxation, toll, valuation; SEE CONCEPT *332*

asset [*n1*] *advantage*
aid, benefit, blessing, boon, credit, distinction, help, resource, service, treasure; SEE CONCEPT *661*

asset(s) [*n2*] *property or money possessed*
ace in the hole*, ace up sleeve*, backing, bankroll, budget, capital, credit, equity, estate, funds, goods, holdings, kitty*, mattress*, means, nest egg*, nut*, possessions, rainy day*, reserve(s), resources, riches, sock*, something put aside, something put away, stake, stash*, stuff, valuables, wealth; SEE CONCEPTS *332,340,710*

assiduous [*adj*] *hard-working*
active, attentive, busy, constant, diligent, eager beaver*, exacting, grinding, indefatigable, industrious, laborious, persevering, plugging, scrupulous, sedulous, steady, studious, unflagging, untiring, whiz, zealous; SEE CONCEPTS *538,542*

assign [*v1*] *select and give a responsibility*
accredit, allow, appoint, ascribe, attach, attribute, authorize, cast, charge, choice, commission, commit, credit, delegate, deputize, designate, downlink, download, draft, elect, empower, enroll, entrust, hang on*, hire, hold responsible, impute, name, nominate, ordain, pin on*, refer, reference, select, slot, tab, tag; SEE CONCEPTS *41,50,88*

assign [*v2*] *set apart for a reason*
allocate, allot, appoint, apportion, appropriate, consign, designate, detail, determine, dish out*, distribute, divide, earmark, fix, fork out*, give, grant, hand out*, hand over, indicate, mete, prescribe, relegate, shell out*, specify, stipulate; SEE CONCEPTS *129,135*

assignation [*n*] *clandestine meeting*
affair, appointment, date, engagement, heavy date*, illicit meeting, love nest*, one-night stand*, quickie*, rendezvous, secret meeting, tryst; SEE CONCEPTS *375,386*

assignment [*n1*] *responsibility, task*
appointment, beat, charge, chore, commission, drill, duty, homework, job, mission, position, post, practice, stint; SEE CONCEPT *362*

assignment [*n2*] *selecting or setting apart*
allocation, allotment, appointment, apportionment, appropriation, ascription, assignation, attribution, authorization, choice, consignment, delegation, designation, determination, distribution, giving, grant, nomination, selection, specification, stipulation; SEE CONCEPTS *41,129*

assimilate [*v1*] *absorb mentally*
comprehend, digest, grasp, incorporate, ingest, learn, osmose, sense, soak up, take in, take up, understand; SEE CONCEPT *15*

assimilate [*v2*] *become adjusted; adjust*
acclimatize, accommodate, acculturate, accustom, adapt, become like, become similar, blend in, conform, fit, go native*, homogenize, homologize, intermix, match, mingle, parallel, standardize; SEE CONCEPTS *232,701*

assist [*n*] *help*
abetment, aid, assistance, backing, benefit, boost, collaboration, comfort, compensation, cooperation, facilitation, furtherance, hand, helping hand, lift, reinforcement, relief, service, support; SEE CONCEPT *110*

assist [*v*] *help*
abet, aid, back, bail out, benefit, boost, collaborate, cooperate, do for*, expedite, facilitate, further, give a boost*, give a leg up*, give a lift*, go down the line for*, go for, go to bat for*, go with, grease the wheels*, hype*, lend a hand*, make a pitch for*, open doors*, plug*, puff*, push*, put on the map*, reinforce, relieve, ride shotgun*, root for*, run interference for*, serve, stand up for, stump*, support, sustain, take care of, thump*, work for, work with; SEE CONCEPT *110*

assistance [*n*] *help*
abetment, aid, assist, backing, benefit, boost, collaboration, comfort, compensation, cooperation, facilitation, furtherance, hand, help, helping hand, lift, reinforcement, relief, service, support, sustenance; SEE CONCEPT *110*

assistant [*n*] *helper*
abettor, accessory, accomplice, adherent, adjunct, aide, ally, appointee, apprentice, associate, attendant, auxiliary, backer, backup*, coadjutant, coadjutor, collaborator, colleague, companion, confederate, cooperator, deputy, fellow worker, flunky*, follower, friend, gofer*, help, helpmate, mate, partner, patron, peon*, representative, right-hand person, secretary, subordinate, supporter, temp*, temporary worker; SEE CONCEPTS *348,423*

associate [*n*] *colleague*
accessory, accomplice, affiliate, aid, ally, assistant, auxiliary, branch, buddy, chum, clubber*, cohort, collaborator, companion, compatriot, comrade, confederate, consort, cooperator, co-worker, crony, fellow, friend, helper, joiner, kissing cousin, mate, offshoot, one of the folks*, pal, pard*, partner, peer, playmate, sidekick; SEE CONCEPTS *348,423*

associate [*v1*] *connect in the mind*
affiliate, blend, bracket, combine, concord, conjoin, correlate, couple, group, identify, join, league, link, lump together, mix, pair, relate, think of together, unite, yoke; SEE CONCEPT *39*

associate [*v2*] *befriend*
accompany, amalgamate, be friends, be in cahoots*, buddy up, bunch up, come together, confederate, consort, fraternize, gang up, get in on, get into, get in with, get together, go along with, go partners*, hang around, hang out, hang out with*, hobnob, join, join up with, line up with, mingle, mix, pal up, play footsie with*, pool, run around with, run with, string along with, swing with, take up with, team up, throw in together, tie in, tie up, truck with, work with; SEE CONCEPTS *114,384*

association [*n1*] *group with common interest or pursuit*
affiliation, alliance, band, bunch, circle, clan, clique, club, coalition, combination, combo, company, confederacy, confederation, congress, cooperative, corporation, crew, crowd, family, federation, fellowship, fraternity, gang, guild, hookup*, league, mob, order, organization, outfit, partnership, pool, rat pack*, ring, society, sodality, sorority, syndicate, tie-in, tie-up, tribe, troops, troupe, union, zoo*; SEE CONCEPTS *323,325,387*

association [*n2*] *friendship*
acquaintance, acquaintanceship, affiliation, agreement, assistance, camaraderie, companionship, comradeship, conjunction, cooperation, familiarity, fellowship, fraternization, frequenting, friendliness, hookup*, intimacy, membership, participation, partnership, relation, relationship; SEE CONCEPTS *387,388*

association [*n3*] *mental connection*
bond, combination, concomitance, concordance, connotation, correlation, identification, impression, joining, juxtaposition, linkage, linking, lumping together, mixing, mixture, pairing, recollection, relation, remembrance, tie, train of thought, union; SEE CONCEPT *39*

assorted [*adj*] *various*
different, diverse, diversified, heterogeneous, hybrid, indiscriminate, miscellaneous, mixed, motley, sundry, varied, variegated; SEE CONCEPT *564*

assortment [n] *variety*
array, choice, collection, combination, combo, diversity, garbage, group, hodgepodge, jumble, kind, medley, mélange, miscellany, mishmash, mixed bag, mixture, potpourri, selection, sort; SEE CONCEPTS *432,665*

assuage [v] *soothe, relieve*
allay, alleviate, appease, calm, compose, conciliate, cool*, ease, fill, lessen, lighten, lull, make nice*, mitigate, moderate, mollify, pacify, palliate, placate, pour oil on*, propitiate, quench, quiet, sate, satisfy, soften, still, surfeit, sweeten, take the edge off*, take the sting out*, temper, tranquilize; SEE CONCEPTS *7,22,244*

assume [v1] *believe, take for granted*
accept, ascertain, be afraid, be inclined to think, conclude, conjecture, consider, count upon, deduce, deem, divine, estimate, expect, fall for, fancy, find, gather, get the idea*, guess, have a hunch*, have sneaking suspicion, hypothesize, imagine, infer, judge, posit, postulate, predicate, presume, presuppose, speculate, suppose, surmise, suspect, theorize, think, understand; SEE CONCEPTS *12,26*

assume [v2] *take, undertake*
accept, acquire, appropriate, arrogate, attend to, begin, confiscate, don, embark upon, embrace, enter upon, seize, set about, take on, take over, take up; SEE CONCEPTS *87,142*

assume [v3] *pretend*
act, adopt, affect, bluff, counterfeit, fake, feign, imitate, impersonate, mimic, pretend, put on, simulate; SEE CONCEPT *59*

assume [v4] *adopt, acquire*
annex, appropriate, arrogate, borrow, clap hands on*, commandeer, confiscate, expropriate, get fingers on*, get hands on*, glom onto*, grab, grab hold of*, hijack, kipe*, liberate, moonlight requisition*, preempt, seize, snatch, swipe, take over, usurp; SEE CONCEPTS *139,142*

assumed [adj1] *pretended*
affected, artificial, bogus, counterfeit, fake, false, feigned, fictitious, imitation, made-up, make-believe, phony, pretended, put-on, sham, simulated, spurious; SEE CONCEPT *582*

assumed [adj2] *expected*
accepted, conjectured, connoted, counted on, given, granted, hypothesized, hypothetical, inferred, postulated, presumed, presupposed, supposed, suppositional, surmised, tacit, taken as known, taken for granted, understood; SEE CONCEPTS *403,689*

assuming [adj] *presumptuous, arrogant*
bold, conceited, disdainful, domineering, egotistic, forward, haughty, imperious, overbearing, pushy, rude; SEE CONCEPT *404*

assumption [n1] *taking something for granted; something expected*
acceptance, accepting, assuming, belief, conjecture, expectation, fancy, guess, hunch, hypothesis, inference, posit, postulate, postulation, premise, presumption, presupposition, shot*, shot in the dark*, sneaking suspicion, stab, supposal, supposition, surmise, suspicion, theorization, theory; SEE CONCEPT *689*

assumption [n2] *assuming possession, power*
acceptance, accepting, acquisition, adoption, appropriation, arrogation, assuming, embracing, grab, seizure, shouldering, takeover, taking, tak-

ing on, taking up, undertaking, usurpation; SEE CONCEPTS *129,142*

assumption [n3] *arrogance*
brass*, chutzpah*, cockiness, conceit, imperiousness, insolence, nerve, presumption, pride, sass*, self-importance; SEE CONCEPT *411*

assurance [n1] *statement to relieve doubt*
affirmation, assertion, declaration, guarantee, insurance, lock*, lock on*, oath, pledge, profession, promise, rain or shine*, security, shoo-in*, support, sure thing*, vow, warrant, warranty, word, word of honor; SEE CONCEPTS *71,278*

assurance [n2] *confidence*
aggressiveness, aplomb, arrogance, assuredness, audacity, boldness, bravery, certainty, certitude, conviction, coolness, courage, effrontery, faith, firmness, impudence, nerve, poise, positiveness, presumption, security, self-confidence, self-reliance, sureness, surety, temerity, trust; SEE CONCEPT *410*

assure [v1] *convince, relieve doubt*
bag*, bet on*, comfort, encourage, hearten, inspire, persuade, reassure, satisfy, sell*, sell on*, soothe; SEE CONCEPT *68*

assure [v2] *promise*
affirm, attest, aver, brace up, buck up, certify, confirm, give one's word, guarantee, pledge, swear, vouch for, vow; SEE CONCEPT *71*

assure [v3] *make certain*
cinch, clinch, complete, confirm, ensure, guarantee, have a lock on*, ice*, insure, lock, lock on, lock up, make sure, nail down*, put on ice*, secure, set; SEE CONCEPTS *36,91*

assured [adj1] *absolutely certain*
beyond doubt, cinched, clear-cut, clinched, confirmed, decided, definite, dependable, ensured, fixed, guaranteed, indubitable, insured, in the bag*, irrefutable, made certain, nailed down*, on ice*, pronounced, racked*, sealed, secure, set, settled, sewed up*, sure, surefire, undoubted, unquestionable; SEE CONCEPT *535*

assured [adj2] *confident*
assertive, audacious, bold, brazen, certain, cocksure*, collected, complacent, composed, confident, cool, gung ho*, gutsy*, high*, imperturbable, overconfident, poised, positive, puffed up*, pumped up*, pushy, rosy*, sanguine, secure, self-assured, self-confident, self-possessed, sure, unflappable, unhesitating, upbeat*; SEE CONCEPTS *401,404*

astern [adv] *backward*
abaft, aft, rear, rearward; SEE CONCEPT *581*

astonish [v] *surprise*
amaze, astound, bewilder, blow away*, blow one's mind*, boggle, bowl over*, confound, daze, dumbfound, flabbergast, floor*, knock over*, overwhelm, put one away*, shock, spring on, stagger, startle, stun, stupefy, take aback, throw a curve*; SEE CONCEPT *42*

astonishing [adj] *surprising*
amazing, astounding, bewildering, breathtaking, extraordinary, impressive, marvelous, miraculous, spectacular, staggering, startling, striking, stunning, stupefying, stupendous, wonderful, wondrous; SEE CONCEPTS *547,572*

astonishment [n] *state of surprise*
amazement, astoundment, awe, bewilderment, confusion, consternation, dumbfoundment, one for the books*, shock, something else*, stunner,

stupefaction, wonder, wonderment; SEE CONCEPTS **230,410**

astound [v] *amaze*
astonish, bewilder, blow away, bowl over*, confound, confuse, daze, dumbfound, flabbergast, knock over with feather*, overwhelm, shock, stagger, startle, stun, stupefy, surprise, take aback; SEE CONCEPT **42**

astounding [adj] *amazing*
astonishing, breathtaking, confounding, eye-popping*, mind-blowing*, mind-boggling*, overwhelming, shocking, startling, stupefying, surprising, wondrous; SEE CONCEPTS **548,571**

astray [adj] *off the path or right direction*
adrift, afield, amiss, awry, gone, lost, off, off course, off the mark, roaming, straying, vanished, wandering, wrong; SEE CONCEPTS **545,581**

astride [adj] *with a leg on either side*
astraddle, athwart, on the back of, piggyback, sitting on, straddling; SEE CONCEPT **583**

astringent [adj] *harsh*
acetic, acrid, biting, bitter, cutting, sharp, tonic; SEE CONCEPTS **598,613**

astrology [n] *prophesy of the future by observation of stars and planets*
astrometry, horoscope; SEE CONCEPT **70**

astronaut [n] *space explorer*
cosmonaut, moonwalker, pilot, rocketeer, rocket scientist, space person, star person; SEE CONCEPT **348**

astronomy [n] *study of the stars and planets other than Earth*
astrochemistry, astrography, astrolithology, astrometry, astrophysics, selenology, sky-watching, stargazing, uranology; SEE CONCEPT **349**

astute [adj] *perceptive*
adroit, brainy, bright, calculating, canny, clever, crafty, discerning, foxy, insightful, intelligent, keen, knowing, not born yesterday*, on the ball*, perspicacious, quick on the uptake*, sagacious, savvy, sharp, sharp as a tack*, shrewd, sly; SEE CONCEPT **402**

asunder [adv] *apart; into pieces*
disconnected, disjoined, divided, in half, loose, separated, split, torn, to shreds; SEE CONCEPT **785**

asylum [n1] *refuge*
cover, den, harbor, haven, hideaway, hideout, hole, ivory tower*, port, preserve, refuge, retreat, safe house, safety, sanctuary, security, shelter; SEE CONCEPTS **435,515**

asylum [n2] *psychiatric hospital*
institution, loony bin*, madhouse*, mental hospital, mental institution, sanatorium; SEE CONCEPTS **312,439,516**

asymmetrical [adj] *uneven*
awry, crooked, disproportional, gibbous, lacking correspondence, not proportionate, not uniform, unbalanced, unequal, unsymmetrical; SEE CONCEPTS **480,566,606**

at [prep] *about; in the direction of*
appearing in, by, found in, in the vicinity of, near to, on, placed at, situated at, through, toward; SEE CONCEPTS **581,583,799**

atheism [n] *belief that no God exists*
disbelief, doubt, freethinking, godlessness, heresy, iconoclasm, impiety, infidelity, irreligion, irreverence, nihilism, nonbelief, paganism, skepticism, unbelief; SEE CONCEPT **689**

atheist [n] *nonbeliever*
agnostic, free thinker, heathen, infidel, irreligionist, pagan, skeptic; SEE CONCEPTS **361,423**

athlete [n] *person involved in sports*
amateur, animal, challenger, competitor, contender, contestant, games player, gorilla*, iron person*, jock, jockey, muscle person*, player professional, shoulders, sport, sportsperson, superjock*; SEE CONCEPT **366**

athletic [adj1] *agile; prepared to participate in sports*
able-bodied, active, brawny, energetic, fit, lusty muscular, powerful, robust, strapping, strong sturdy, vigorous; SEE CONCEPTS **406,489**

athletic [adj2] *relating to sports*
competitive, contesting, exercise-related, recreational, sporting, team; SEE CONCEPT **536**

athletics [n] *sports*
contest, drill, events, exercises, games, practice races, recreation, workout; SEE CONCEPT **363**

atmosphere [n1] *gases around the earth*
air, envelope, heavens, pressure, sky, substratosphere, troposphere; SEE CONCEPT **437**

atmosphere [n2] *general feeling or mood*
air, ambience, aura, background, character, climate, color, environment, feel, feeling, flavor impression, local color, medium, mood, place property, quality, scene, semblance, sense, space spirit, surroundings, taste, tone; SEE CONCEPT **673**

atom [n] *smallest part of something*
bit, crumb, dot, fragment, grain, iota, jot, minimum, mite, modicum, molecule, morsel, mote ounce, particle, scintilla, scrap, shred, smidgen speck, spot, tittle, trace, whit; SEE CONCEPT **831**

atom bomb [n] *nuclear weapon*
A-bomb, backpack nuke*, doomsday machine* fission bomb, H-bomb, hydrogen bomb, neutron bomb, nuclear bomb, nuke*, thermonuclear weapon; SEE CONCEPT **500**

atomic [adj1] *tiny*
diminutive, fragmentary, granular, microscopic, minute; SEE CONCEPT **773**

atomic [adj2] *nuclear*
atom-powered, fissionable, thermonuclear; SEE CONCEPT **485**

atone [v] *compensate; make amends for former misdoing*
absolve, answer, apologize, appease, balance correct, counterbalance, do penance, expiate, make amends, make redress, make reparation make up for, offset, outweigh, pay, pay one's dues*, propitiate, recompense, reconcile, redeem, redress, repair, set off, square, take one's medicine*; SEE CONCEPTS **108,126**

atonement [n] *compensation*
amends, expiation, indemnification, payment, penance, propitiation, recompense, redemption redress, reparation, restitution, satisfaction; SEE CONCEPTS **126,337**

atrocious [adj1] *outrageous; widely condemned*
awful, bad, barbaric, beastly, desperate, diabolical, fiendish, flagrant, godawful*, grody*, gross*, hairy*, heinous, lousy, monstrous, nefarious, rotten, scandalous, shocking, villainous wicked; SEE CONCEPTS **545,571**

atrocious [adj2] *offensive*
appalling, awful, bad, beastly, detestable, disgusting, dreadful, execrable, foul, godawful* grody*, gross*, horrible, horrid, horrifying,

icky*, loathsome, noisome, obscene, repulsive, rotten, sickening, terrible; SEE CONCEPTS 548,571

atrocity [n1] *outrageous behavior*
atrociousness, barbarity, barbarousness, enormity, fiendishness, heinousness, horror, monstrousness, nefariousness, shockingness, villianousness, wickedness; SEE CONCEPTS 411,657

atrocity [n2] *cruelness, offensiveness; widely condemned action*
abomination, barbarity, brutality, crime, enormity, evil, horror, infamy, inhumanity, iniquity, monstrosity, offense, outrage, ruthlessness, savagery, viciousness, wrong; SEE CONCEPTS 29,645

atrophy [n] *wasting away, disintegration*
decline, degeneracy, degeneration, deterioration, diminution, downfall, downgrade; SEE CONCEPTS 674,698

attach [v1] *join, fasten*
add, adhere, affix, annex, append, bind, connect, couple, fix, hitch on, hitch up, hook on, hook up, latch onto, link, make fast, prefix, rivet, secure, slap on*, stick, tag on*, tie, unite; SEE CONCEPTS 85,113,160

attach [v2] *socially join*
accompany, affiliate, associate, become associated with, combine, enlist, join forces with, latch onto*, sign on with, sign up with, unite with; SEE CONCEPT 114

attach [v3] *attribute, ascribe*
allocate, allot, appoint, assign, associate, connect, consign, designate, detail, earmark, impute, invest with, lay, name, place, put, second, send; SEE CONCEPTS 62,73

attachment [n1] *fastening*
adapter, bond, clamp, connection, connector, coupling, fastener, joint, junction, link, tie; SEE CONCEPT 471

attachment [n2] *something joined, fastened to another*
accessory, accoutrement, adapter, addition, adjunct, annex, appendage, appurtenance, auxiliary, extension, extra, fitting, fixture, part, supplement; SEE CONCEPT 824

attachment [n3] *affection, high regard*
affinity, amore, attraction, bond, case, crush, devotion, fidelity, fondness, friendship, hankering*, liking, love, loyalty, partiality, possessiveness, regard, shine*, tenderness, weakness, yen*; SEE CONCEPT 32

attack [n1] *physical assault*
advance, aggression, assailing, assailment, barrage, blitz, blitzkrieg, charge, defilement, dirty deed*, drive, encounter, encroachment, foray, incursion, initiative, inroad, intervention, intrusion, invasion, irruption, mugging, offense, offensive, onrush, onset, onslaught, outbreak, push, raid, rape, rush, skirmish, storming, strike, thrust, violation, volley; SEE CONCEPT 86

attack [n2] *verbal assault*
abuse, aggression, belligerence, blame, calumny, censure, combativeness, criticism, denigration, denunciation, impugnment, libel, pugnacity, slander, vilification; SEE CONCEPTS 52,54

attack [n3] *sudden dysfunction or disorder*
access, ailment, bout, breakdown, convulsion, disease, failure, fit, illness, paroxysm, relapse, seizure, spasm, spell, stroke, throe; SEE CONCEPT 308

attack [v1] *assault physically*
advance, aggress, ambush, assail, assault, bash, bat, bean*, beat, beset, besiege, biff*, blast, blister, boff*, bombard, boot*, bop*, brain*, bust, charge, chop down, clip, clock*, club, combat, cook*, harm, hit, hurt, infiltrate, invade, jump, kick, knock block off*, knock cold*, knock for a loop*, larrup*, lay siege to, light into*, molest, mug, overwhelm, pounce upon, punch, raid, rush, set upon, slog, soak, stab, storm, strike, take the offensive, turn on, wallop*, whop*; SEE CONCEPT 86

attack [v2] *assault verbally*
abuse, berate, blame, blitz, censure, criticize, impugn, jump down one's throat*, jump on one's case*, lay into, malign, refute, reprove, revile, shoot down*, stretch, vilify; SEE CONCEPTS 52,54

attack [v3] *set to work*
buckle down*, deal with, dive into, plunge into, set to, start in on, tackle, take up, tear into*; SEE CONCEPT 112

attacker [n] *aggressor*
assailant, assaulter, mugger, raider, traducer; SEE CONCEPT 412

attain [v] *achieve, accomplish*
accede to, acquire, arrive, arrive at, bring off, come through, complete, cop*, earn, effect, fulfill, gain, get*, get fat*, get hands on, get there, glom onto*, grasp, hit, latch onto, make it, obtain, procure, promote, pull off*, rack up, reach, realize, reap, score, secure, snag, succeed, unzip*, win; SEE CONCEPTS 120,706

attainable [adj] *within reach; achievable*
accessible, accomplishable, at hand, available, cherry pie*, duck soup*, easy, feasible, gettable, likely, no problem*, no sweat*, obtainable, piece of cake*, possible, potential, practicable, probable, procurable, reachable, realizable, securable; SEE CONCEPTS 528,552

attainment [n] *achievement, accomplishment*
acquirement, acquisition, arrival, completion, feat, finish, fulfillment, gaining, getting, obtaining, procurement, reaching, realization, reaping, securing, succeeding, winning; SEE CONCEPT 706

attempt [n] *try, effort*
all one's got*, attack, bid*, crack*, dry run*, endeavor, exertion, experiment, fling, go, header*, lick*, one's all, one's darnedest*, one's level best*, pursuit, shot, stab, striving, struggle, trial, try, tryout, undertaking, venture, whack*, workout; SEE CONCEPT 87

attempt [v] *try, make effort*
aim, attack, do level best*, endeavor, essay, exert oneself, experiment, give a fling*, give a whirl*, give best shot*, give it a go*, give it a try*, give old college try*, go the limit*, have a crack*, have a go at*, make a run at*, pursue, push, seek, shoot the works*, solicit, strive, tackle, take a stab at*, take best shot*, take on, try one's hand at*, undertake, venture; SEE CONCEPT 87

attend [v1] *be present at*
appear, be a guest, be at, be present, be there, bob up*, catch, check in, clock in*, come to light*, drop in, frequent, go to, haunt, make an appearance, make it*, make the scene*, pop up*, punch in*, punch the clock*, ring in*, show, show up, sit in on, time in, turn up, visit; SEE CONCEPT 114

attend [v2] *care for*
be in the service of, doctor, do for, look after,

mind, minister to, nurse, serve, take care of, tend, wait upon, watch, work for; SEE CONCEPT *110*

attend [*v3*] *pay attention; apply oneself*
catch, concentrate on, devote oneself, follow, get a load of*, hear, hearken, heed, keep one's eye on*, lend an ear*, listen, listen up*, look after, look on, mark, mind, note, notice, observe, occupy oneself with, pay heed, pick up, regard, see to, watch; SEE CONCEPTS *34,596,623*

attend [*v4*] *accompany*
bear, be associated with, be connected with, catch, follow, issue from, make the scene, occur with, result from; SEE CONCEPT *714*

attend [*v5*] *escort*
accompany, chaperon, companion, consort, convoy, escort, guard, squire, usher; SEE CONCEPTS *114,714*

attendance [*n1*] *being present*
appearance, attending, being in evidence, being there, participation, presence; SEE CONCEPT *388*

attendance [*v2*] *people present at event*
assemblage, assembly, audience, box office, company, congregation, crowd, draw, gate, gathering, gross, house, observers, onlookers, patrons, public, spectators, turnout, witnesses; SEE CONCEPT *417*

attendant [*adj*] *being present or related*
accessory, accompanying, ancillary, associated, attending, coincident, concomitant, consequent, incident; SEE CONCEPT *577*

attendant [*n*] *person who serves others*
aide, alarm clock*, assistant, auxiliary, baby sitter, bird dog, chaperon, companion, custodian, domestic, escort, follower, guide, helper, lackey, nurse, orderly, secretary, servant, understudy, usher, waitperson; SEE CONCEPT *348*

attention [*n1*] *concentration*
absorption, application, assiduity, consideration, contemplation, debate, deliberation, diligence, engrossment, heed, heedfulness, immersion, industry, intentness, mind, scrutiny, study, thinking, thought, thoughtfulness; SEE CONCEPT *409*

attention [*n2*] *consideration, care*
awareness, big rush*, brace, concern, consciousness, looking after, ministration, notice, observation, recognition, regard, spotlight, tender loving care, TLC*; treatment; SEE CONCEPTS *32,410*

attention deficit disorder [*n*] *learning disability*
ADD, ADHD, hyperactiveness, hyperactivity, short attention span; SEE CONCEPTS *403,542*

attention(s) [*n3*] *courtesy*
amenity, assiduities, care, civility, compliment, consideration, deference, gallantry, mindfulness, politeness, regard, respect, service; SEE CONCEPT *644*

attentive [*adj1*] *concentrating*
alert, all ears*, awake, aware, conscientious, enrapt, enthralled, fascinated, glued, hanging on every word*, heedful, hooked, immersed, intent, interested, listening, mindful, observant, on one's toes*, on the ball*, on the job*, on the lookout*, on the qui vive*, preoccupied, regardful, studious, vigilant, watchful; SEE CONCEPT *403*

attentive [*adj2*] *considerate*
accommodating, civil, courteous, devoted, gallant, gracious, kind, obliging, polite, respectful, solicitous, thoughtful; SEE CONCEPT *401*

attenuate [*v*] *weaken*
abate, constrict, contract, cripple, debilitate, deflate, disable, dissipate, enfeeble, extenuate, lessen, mitigate, sap, shrink, thin, undermine, vitiate; SEE CONCEPT *240*

attest [*v*] *affirm, vouch for*
adjure, announce, argue, assert, asservate, authenticate, aver, bear out, bear witness, certify, confirm, corroborate, countersign, declare, demonstrate, display, exhibit, give evidence, indicate, prove, ratify, seal, show, substantiate, support, sustain, swear, testify, uphold, verify, warrant, witness; SEE CONCEPT *49*

attic [*n*] *space under the roof of a house*
garret, loft, sky parlor*, top floor; SEE CONCEPTS *440,448*

attire [*n*] *clothing*
accoutrements, apparel, array, bib and tucker*, clothes, costume, drapes, dress, duds*, garb, garments, gear, getup, habiliments, habit, outfit, raiment, things, threads*, togs, uniform, vestment, wear; SEE CONCEPT *451*

attire [*v*] *clothe*
accoutre, array, clad, costume, deck, deck out*, doll up*, drape, dress, dud*, dude up*, equip, fit out, outfit, suit up, tog, turn out; SEE CONCEPT *167*

attitude [*n1*] *mental outlook*
air, angle, approach, belief, bent, bias, character, demeanor, disposition, frame of mind, headset*, inclination, leaning, like it is*, mental state, mindset*, mindtrip*, mood, notion of view, perspective, philosophy, point of view, position, posture, predilection, prejudice, proclivity, reaction, routine, say so*, sensibility, sentiment, set, slant, stance, stand, standing, standpoint, temper, temperament, twist, view, where one is at*; SEE CONCEPTS *410,689*

attitude [*n2*] *stance*
aspect, bearing, carriage, manner, mien, pose, position, posture, stand; SEE CONCEPT *757*

attorney [*n*] *lawyer*
advocate, ambulance chaser*, barrister, counsel, counselor, DA, eagle*, legal beagle*, legal eagle*, lip*, mouthpiece*, pleader*, proxy, spieler*; SEE CONCEPT *355*

attract [*v*] *draw attention*
allure, appeal to, bait, beckon, beguile, bewitch, bring, captivate, charm, come on*, court, drag, draw, enchant, endear, engage, enthrall, entice, entrance, exert influence, fascinate, freak out*, give the come-on*, go over big, grab, hook, induce, interest, intrigue, inveigle, invite, kill, knock dead*, knock out*, lure, magnetize, make a hit with*, mousetrap*, pull, rope in*, score, seduce, send*, slay*, solicit, spellbind, steer, suck in*, sweep off one's feet*, tempt, turn on, vamp, wile, wow*; SEE CONCEPTS *7,11,22*

attraction [*n*] *ability to draw attention; something that draws attention*
allure, allurement, appeal, attractiveness, bait, captivation, charm, chemistry, come-on*, courting, draw, drawing power, enchantment, endearment, enthrallment, enticement, fascination, gravitation, inclination, inducement, interest, invitation, it*, lure, magnetism, pull, seduction, solicitation, temptation, tendency; SEE CONCEPTS *14,676*

attractive [*adj*] *appealing, drawing attention*
adorable, agreeable, alluring, beautiful, beckoning, bewitching, captivating, charming, comely, enchanting, engaging, enthralling, enticing, fair,

fascinating, fetching, glamorous, good-looking, gorgeous, handsome, hunky*, interesting, inviting, looker*, lovely, luring, magnetic, mesmeric, pleasant, pleasing, prepossessing, pretty, provocative, seductive, stunning, taking, tantalizing, teasing, tempting, winning, winsome; SEE CONCEPTS *529,579*

attribute [*n*] *feature*
aspect, character, characteristic, facet, idiosyncrasy, indication, mark, note, particularity, peculiarity, point, property, quality, quirk, sign, speciality, symbol, trait, virtue; SEE CONCEPTS *411,673,834*

attribute [*v*] *ascribe, assign to source*
account for, accredit, apply, associate, blame, charge, connect, credit, fix upon, hang on, hold responsible, impute, lay, pin on, refer, reference, trace; SEE CONCEPT *73*

attrition [*n1*] *wearing down or away*
abrasion, attenuation, debilitation, depreciation, disintegration, erosion, grinding, rubbing, thinning, weakening, wear; SEE CONCEPTS *469,776*

attrition [*n2*] *regret*
contriteness, penance, penitence, remorse, remorsefulness, repentance; SEE CONCEPTS *410,689*

attune [*v*] *adjust*
acclimatize, accommodate, accord, accustom, adapt, balance, compensate, conform, coordinate, counterbalance, familiarize, harmonize, integrate, make agree, proportion, reconcile, regulate, tune; SEE CONCEPT *232*

atypical [*adj*] *nonconforming*
aberrant, abnormal, anomalous, deviant, different, divergent, exceptional, heteroclite, irregular, odd, peculiar, preternatural, strange, unnatural, unrepresentative; SEE CONCEPTS *547,564*

auburn [*n*] *reddish-brown color*
chestnut, copper, hazel, henna, nut, russet, rust, tawny, titian; SEE CONCEPT *622*

au courant [*adj*] *up-to-date*
aware, current, enlightened, hip*, informed, up to speed*, well-informed; SEE CONCEPTS *530,820*

auction [*n*] *competitive sale; sale by bid*
bargain, jam*, sell-off; SEE CONCEPTS *324,345*

audacious [*adj1*] *reckless, daring*
adventurous, aweless, bold, brassy, brave, cheeky*, courageous, daredevil, dauntless, enterprising, fearless, foolhardy, gutty*, intrepid, nervy, rash, resolute, risky, smart ass*, unafraid, uncurbed, undaunted, ungoverned, valiant, venturesome; SEE CONCEPT *401*

audacious [*adj2*] *arrogant, presumptuous*
assuming, bantam, bold, brash, brassy, brazen, cheeky*, defiant, disrespectful, forward, impertinent, impudent, insolent, nervy, rude, saucy, shameless; SEE CONCEPTS *401,404*

audacity [*n1*] *recklessness, daring*
adventurousness, audaciousness, boldness, bravery, courage, dauntlessness, enterprise, fearlessness, guts, intrepidity, nerve, rashness, valor, venturesomeness; SEE CONCEPT *633*

audacity [*n2*] *arrogance, presumptuousness*
assurance, audaciousness, brass, cheek*, chutzpah*, cockiness*, crust, defiance, disrespectfulness, effrontery, forwardness, gall, guts*, gutsiness, hardiness, impertinence, impudence, insolence, moxie, nerve, rudeness, shamelessness, spunk, stuff*; temerity; SEE CONCEPTS *411,633*

audible [*adj*] *able to be heard*
aural, auricular, clear, deafening, detectable, discernible, distinct, hearable, loud, loud enough, perceptible, plain, resounding, roaring, sounding, within earshot; SEE CONCEPTS *591,594*

audience [*n1*] *group observing an entertainment or sporting event*
admirers, assemblage, assembly, congregation, crowd, devotees, fans, following, gallery, gathering, hearers, house, listeners, market, moviegoers, onlookers, patrons, playgoers, public, showgoers, spectators, theatergoers, turnout, viewers, witnesses; SEE CONCEPT *417*

audience [*n2*] *hearing*
audition, conference, consideration, consultation, conversation, discussion, interview, meeting, reception; SEE CONCEPT *266*

audit [*n*] *inspection of financial records*
analysis, balancing, check, checking, examination, investigation, report, review, scrutiny, survey, verification, view; SEE CONCEPT *330*

audit [*v*] *inspect financial records*
analyze, balance, check, examine, go over, go through, investigate, report, review, scrutinize, sit in, survey, verify; SEE CONCEPTS *103,330*

audition [*n*] *test of ability*
audience, demo, hearing, reading, trial, try on, tryout; SEE CONCEPT *290*

auditor [*n*] *person who inspects financial records*
accountant, actuary, bookkeeper, cashier; SEE CONCEPT *348*

auditorium [*n*] *room, building for entertainment events*
amphitheater, assembly hall, barn*, concert hall, hall, movie house, music hall, opera house, playhouse, reception hall, theater; SEE CONCEPTS *293,439,448*

augment [*v*] *make greater; improve*
add to, aggrandize, amplify, beef up*, boost, build, build up, compound, develop, enhance, enlarge, expand, extend, grow, heighten, increase, inflate, intensify, magnify, mount, multiply, pad, piggyback*, progress, raise, reinforce, strengthen, sweeten, swell, tag on; SEE CONCEPTS *236,244,245*

augmentation [*n*] *making greater; improving*
accession, accretion, addition, amplification, beefing up*, boost, buildup, development, enhancement, enlargement, enrichment, expansion, extension, fleshing out, growth, heightening, hike, increase, increment, inflation, intensification, magnification, multiplication, raise, reinforcement, rise, strengthening, swelling, up, upping; SEE CONCEPTS *244,245*

augur [*n*] *predictor*
diviner, forecaster, harbinger, herald, oracle, prognosticator, prophet, seer, soothsayer; SEE CONCEPT *423*

augur [*v*] *predict; be an omen of*
adumbrate, bespeak, bode, call it*, call the shots*, crystal-ball, figure out, forecast, foreshadow, foretell, harbinger, have a hunch, herald, portend, presage, prognosticate, promise, prophesy, psych out*, read, signify, soothsay; SEE CONCEPT *70*

augury [*n1*] *omen*
auspice, boding, forerunner, foretoken, forewarning, harbinger, herald, portent, precursor, presage, prognostication, promise, prophecy, sign, token, warning; SEE CONCEPT *284*

augury [n2] *prediction*
divination, prediction, prophecy, soothsaying; SEE CONCEPT **70**

august [adj] *dignified, noble*
baronial, brilliant, eminent, exalted, glorious, grand, grandiose, highfalutin'*, high-minded, high-ranking, honorable, imposing, impressive, lofty, lordly, magnificent, majestic, monumental, pompous, regal, resplendent, stately, superb, venerable; SEE CONCEPTS **404,567**

au pair [n] *live-in nanny*
babysitter, caregiver, day care provider, domestic servant, governess, housekeeper, live-in; SEE CONCEPT **295**

aura [n] *air, character*
ambience, appearance, aspect, atmosphere, background, emanation, feel, feeling, mood, quality, scent, semblance, suggestion, tone; SEE CONCEPT **673**

auspices [n] *protection; support*
advocacy, aegis, authority, backing, care, charge, control, countenance, guidance, influence, patronage, sponsorship, supervision; SEE CONCEPTS **94,376**

auspicious [adj] *encouraging; favorable*
advantageous, bright, favorable, felicitous, fortunate, golden, halcyon, happy, hopeful, lucky, opportune, promising, propitious, prosperous, rosy, timely, well-timed; SEE CONCEPT **572**

austere [adj1] *severe in manner*
ascetic, astringent, cold, earnest, exacting, forbidding, formal, grave, grim, hard, harsh, inexorable, inflexible, obdurate, rigid, rigorous, serious, sober, solemn, somber, stern, stiff, strict, stringent, unfeeling, unrelenting; SEE CONCEPT **550**

austere [adj2] *refraining; abstinent*
abstemious, ascetic, chaste, continent, economical, puritanical, self-denying, self-disciplined, sober, straightlaced, strict, subdued, unrelenting; SEE CONCEPT **401**

austere [adj3] *grim, barren*
bald, bare, bare-bones, bleak, clean, dour, plain, primitive, rustic, severe, simple, spare, spartan, stark, subdued, unadorned, unembellished, vanilla*; SEE CONCEPT **485**

austerity [n1] *severity*
acerbity, asperity, astringence, coldness, exactingness, exactness, formality, formalness, gravity, grimness, hardness, harshness, inclemency, inflexibility, obduracy, rigidity, rigor, seriousness, solemnity, sternness, stiffness, strictness, stringency; SEE CONCEPT **644**

austerity [n2] *refraining; abstinence*
abstemiousness, asceticism, chasteness, chastity, continence, determination, economy, prudence, puritanism, self-denial, self-discipline, sobriety, stoicism, strictness, temperance; SEE CONCEPT **633**

austerity [n3] *grimness, barrenness*
baldness, bareness, dourness, economy, plainness, primitiveness, rusticism, severity, simplicity, spareness, spartanism, starkness, unadornment; SEE CONCEPT **723**

authentic [adj] *real, genuine*
accurate, actual, authoritative, bona fide, certain, convincing, credible, creditable, dependable, factual, faithful, for real*, legit*, legitimate, official, original, pure, reliable, sure, true, trustworthy, trusty, twenty-four carat*, valid, veritable; SEE CONCEPT **582**

authenticate [v] *establish as real, genuine*
accredit, attest, authorize, bear out, certify, confirm, corroborate, endorse, guarantee, justify, prove, substantiate, validate, verify, vouch, warrant; SEE CONCEPTS **12,103**

author [n] *composer of written work*
biographer, columnist, composer, creator, essayist, ghost, ghostwriter, ink slinger*, journalist, originator, playwright, poet, producer, prose writer, reporter, scribbler*, scribe, scripter, word slinger*, wordsmith, work-for-hire*, writer; SEE CONCEPT **348**

authoritarian [adj] *domineering*
absolute, authoritative, autocratic, despotic, dictatorial, disciplinarian, doctrinaire, dogmatic, harsh, imperious, magisterial, rigid, severe, strict, totalitarian, tyrannical, unyielding; SEE CONCEPTS **319,401**

authoritarian [n] *domineering person*
absolutist, autocrat, despot, dictator, disciplinarian, tyrant; SEE CONCEPTS **354,412**

authoritative [adj1] *recognized as true, valid*
accurate, attested, authentic, authenticated, circumstantiated, confirmed, definitive, dependable, documented, factual, faithful, learned, legit*, proven, reliable, righteous, scholarly, sound, straight from horse's mouth*, supported, trustworthy, truthful, validated, verified, veritable; SEE CONCEPT **582**

authoritative [adj2] *domineering*
assertive, authoritarian, autocratic, commanding, confident, decisive, dictatorial, doctrinaire, dogmatic, dominating, imperative, imperious, imposing, masterly, officious, peremptory, self-assured; SEE CONCEPT **550**

authoritative [adj3] *official, authorized*
administrative, approved, bureaucratic, canonical, departmental, ex cathedra, executive, ex officio, imperial, lawful, legal, legitimate, magisterial, mandatory, ruling, sanctioned, sovereign, supreme; SEE CONCEPTS **319,536**

authority [n1] *power, control*
ascendancy, authorization, beef*, charge, clout*, command, credit, domination, dominion, edge, esteem, force, goods*, government, guts*, influence, juice*, jump, jurisdiction, leg up*, license, mastery, might, might and main*, permission, permit, pizzazz*, pow*, powerhouse, prerogative, prestige, punch, right, ropes*, rule, say, say so*, steam, strength, strong arm*, stuff*, supremacy, sway, upper hand*, warrant, weight, what it takes*, whip hand*, word, zap*; SEE CONCEPTS **376,685,688**

authority [n2] *expert, animate or inanimate*
arbiter, aristocrat, bible, big cheese*, big shot*, big wig*, boss, brains*, brass*, buff*, CEO, city hall*, connoisseur, czar, egghead*, establishment*, exec*, executive, expert, feds*, front office*, governor, guru, ivory dome*, judge, kingfish*, kingpin*, law*, power elite, pro, professional, professor, pundit, scholar, specialist, textbook*, top brass*, top dog*, top hand*, upstairs*, veteran, virtuoso, whiz, wizard; SEE CONCEPTS **280,348,354**

authorize [v] *give power or control*
accredit, bless, commission, empower, enable, entitle, give authority, give the go-ahead*, give

au
av

the green light*, give the word*, invest, license, okay, rubber-stamp*, say the word*, vest; SEE CONCEPTS 50,88

authorize [v2] *permit, allow*
affirm, approve, confirm, countenance, endorse, give leave, let, license, qualify, ratify, sanction, suffer, tolerate, warrant; SEE CONCEPTS 10,83

autobiography [n] *written account of one's own life*
adventures, bio, biography, confession, diary, experience, journal, letter, letters, life, life story, memoir, personal history, reminiscences, self-portrayal; SEE CONCEPT 280

autocracy [n] *government by one*
absolutism, czarism, despotism, dictatorship, monarchy, monocracy, oppression, totalitarian government, tyranny; SEE CONCEPTS 354,691

autocrat [n] *dictator*
authoritarian, Caesar*, despot, Fascist, Hitler*, overlord, totalitarian, tyrant; SEE CONCEPT 354

autocratic [adj] *holding power exclusively*
absolute, all-powerful, arbitrary, bossy, czarlike, despotic, dictatorial, domineering, driving, imperious, monocratic, pushing, tyrannical, tyrannous; SEE CONCEPTS 319,536

autograph [n] *handwritten signature*
endorsement, handwriting, inscription, John Hancock*, seal, token, undersignature, writing; SEE CONCEPT 284

autograph [v] *write signature*
endorse, engross, handwrite, ink, inscribe, pen, sign, signature, subscribe, write by hand; SEE CONCEPT 79

automated [adj] *made or done by a machine*
automatic, computerized, electrical, electronic, mechanical, mechanized, motorized, programmed, robotic; SEE CONCEPTS 538,549

automatic [adj1] *done or made by machine*
automated, electric, electronic, mechanical, mechanized, motorized, robotic, self-moving, self-regulating, self-starting; SEE CONCEPTS 538,549

automatic [adj2] *done by habit*
autogenetic, habitual, impulsive, instinctive, instinctual, intuitive, involuntary, knee-jerk, mechanical, natural, perfunctory, reflex, routine, spontaneous, unconscious, unforced, unintentional, unmeditated, unthinking, unwilled; SEE CONCEPTS 403,538

automatic [adj3] *occurring as natural consequence*
assured, certain, inescapable, inevitable, necessary, routine, unavoidable; SEE CONCEPTS 530,535

automation [n] *machine control*
computerization, industrialization, mechanization; SEE CONCEPT 770

automobile [n] *land vehicle; car*
auto, bucket of bolts*, bug*, buggy*, bus, clunker*, compact, convertible, crate*, four-wheeler*, gas guzzler*, go-cart*, hardtop, hatchback, heap*, jalopy*, junker*, lemon*, limousine, motor car, oil burner*, passenger car, pickup truck, ride*, sedan, sports car, station wagon, subcompact, taxi, transportation, truck, tub*, van, wheels*, wreck*; SEE CONCEPT 505

autonomous [adj] *independent*
free, self-determining, self-governing, self-ruling, sovereign, uncontrolled; SEE CONCEPT 554

autonomy [n] *independence*
freedom, liberty, self-determination, self-government, self-rule, sovereignty; SEE CONCEPT 652

autopsy [n] *examination of dead body*
dissection, necropsy, pathological examination, postmortem; SEE CONCEPTS 103,310

autumn [n] *season between summer and winter*
autumnal equinox, fall, harvest; SEE CONCEPT 814

auxiliary [adj] *supplementary*
abetting, accessory, adjuvant, ancillary, appurtenant, backup, complementary, contributory, extra, reserve, secondary, spare, subordinate, subservient, subsidiary, supporting; SEE CONCEPTS 546,824

auxiliary [n] *helper*
accessory, accomplice, adjutant, ally, assistant, associate, companion, confederate, crutch*, partner, reserve, subordinate, supporter; SEE CONCEPT 423

avail [n] *use*
account, advantage, applicability, appropriateness, fitness, service, usefulness; SEE CONCEPT 680

avail [v] *be of use; use*
account, advantage, answer, be adequate, benefit, fill, fulfill, meet, profit, satisfy, serve, suffice, work; SEE CONCEPTS 91,225

available [adj] *ready for use*
accessible, achievable, applicable, at hand, at one's disposal*, attainable, come-at-able*, convenient, derivable from, feasible, free, getatable*, handy, obtainable, on deck*, on hand*, on tap*, open to, possible, prepared, procurable, purchasable, reachable, ready willing and able*, realizable, securable, serviceable, up for grabs*, usable, vacant; SEE CONCEPT 576

avalanche [n] *falling large mass; sudden rush of large quantity*
barrage, deluge, flood, inundation, landslide, landslip, snowslide, torrent; SEE CONCEPTS 509,524,787

avant-garde [adj] *unconventional, forward-looking*
beat*, experimental, head*, hip*, innovative, lead, leading-edge*, liberal, new, new wave, pioneering, progressive, radical, state-of-the-art, vanguard; SEE CONCEPTS 564,585

avarice [n] *extreme greed*
avidity, close-fistedness*, covetousness, cupidity, frugality, grabbiness, greediness, miserliness, niggardliness, parsimony, penny-pinching*, penuriousness, rapacity, stinginess, thrift; SEE CONCEPTS 335,410

avaricious [adj] *greedy*
covetous, gluttonous, hoarding, money-grubbing*, pleonectic, predatory, rapacious, selfish, tight*; SEE CONCEPTS 404,542

avenge [v] *retaliate*
chasten, chastise, come back at, even the score, get back at, get even, payback, punish, redress, repay, requite, retribute, revenge, stick it to, take satisfaction, take vengeance, venge, vindicate; SEE CONCEPTS 122,126

avenue [n] *street; path*
access, alley, approach, boulevard, channel, course, drive, entrance, entry, exit, outlet, parkway, passage, pathway, promenade, road, route, thoroughfare, way; SEE CONCEPT 501

average [*adj1*] *normal, typical*
boilerplate*, common, commonplace, customary, dime a dozen*, everyday, fair, fair to middling*, familiar, garden*, garden-variety*, general, humdrum*, intermediate, mainstream, mediocre, medium, middle of the road*, middling, moderate, nowhere*, ordinary, passable, plastic*, regular, run of the mill*, so-so*, standard, tolerable, undistinguished, unexceptional, usual; SEE CONCEPT 547

average [*adj2*] *numerical mean*
intermediate, median, medium, middle; SEE CONCEPT 762

average [*n*] *normal, typical amount*
mean, median, medium, middle, midpoint, norm, par, rule, standard, usual; SEE CONCEPTS 647,787

average [*v*] *obtain numerical mean*
balance, equate, even out; SEE CONCEPT 764

averse [*adj*] *opposing*
afraid, allergic, antagonistic, antipathetic, contrary, disinclined, disliking, having no use for*, hesitant, hostile, ill-disposed, indisposed, inimical, loath, nasty, perverse, reluctant, uneager, unfavorable, unfriendly, unwilling; SEE CONCEPTS 403,564

aversion [*n*] *dislike; opposition*
abhorrence, abomination, allergy, animosity, antagonism, antipathy, detestation, disfavor, disgust, disinclination, disliking, displeasure, dissatisfaction, distaste, dread, hate, hatred, having no use for*, horror, hostility, indisposition, loathing, odium, reluctance, repugnance, repulsion, revulsion, unwillingness; SEE CONCEPT 29

avert [*v*] *thwart; avoid by turning away*
avoid, deflect, deter, divert, fend off, foil, forestall, frustrate, halt, look away, preclude, prevent, rule out, shove aside, shunt, stave off, turn, turn aside, turn away, ward off; SEE CONCEPTS 121,623

aviation [*n*] *flying an aircraft; study of flying aircraft*
aerodynamics, aeronautics, flight, navigation, piloting; SEE CONCEPTS 148,187,324

aviator [*n*] *person who flies aircraft*
ace, aeronaut, airperson, barnstormer, bird legs*, eagle*, flier, hotshot*, jockey*, navigator, pilot; SEE CONCEPTS 348,366

avid [*adj*] *enthusiastic*
ardent, athirst, avaricious, breathless, covetous, desirous, devoted, dying to*, eager, fanatical, fervent, gotta have*, grasping, greedy, hungry, impatient, insatiable, intense, keen, passionate, rapacious, ravenous, thirsty, voracious, zealous; SEE CONCEPTS 20,401,403

avocation [*n*] *hobby*
amusement, diversion, kick*, occupation, pastime, recreation, schtick*, shot*, side interest, sideline, thing*; SEE CONCEPT 364

avoid [*v*] *refrain or stay away from; prevent*
abstain, avert, bypass, circumlocute, circumvent, deflect, desist, ditch, divert, dodge, duck, elude, escape, eschew, evade, fake out*, fend off, flee, give the slip*, hide, hold off, jump, keep clear, lay low*, obviate, recoil, run for cover*, shake, shake and bake*, shake off, shirk, shrink from, shuffle off, shun, shy, sidestep, skip*, skip out on*, skip town*, skirt*, stay away, stay out, steer clear of*, step aside, turn aside, ward off, weave, withdraw; SEE CONCEPTS 102,121

avoidance [*n*] *eluding; preventing*
absention, circumvention, delay, departure, dodge, dodging, elusion, escape, escapism, eschewal, evasion, flight, forbearance, nonparticipation, parry, passive resistance, prevention, recession, recoil, restraint, retreat, run-around, self-restraint, shirking, shunning, steering clear of*; SEE CONCEPTS 102,121

avow [*v*] *state; profess*
acknowledge, admit, affirm, allow, assert, aver, avouch, concede, confess, cross one's heart*, declare, grant, maintain, own up, proclaim, swear, swear on bible*, swear up and down*; SEE CONCEPTS 49,60,71

avowal [*n*] *acknowledgment*
admission, affirmation, announcement, assertion, confession, declaration, oath, proclamation, testimony; SEE CONCEPTS 8,50,88

await [*v*] *wait with expectation*
anticipate, attend, be prepared for, be ready for, cool one's heels*, count on, hang around*, hang in*, hang out*, hope, look for, look forward to, stay, sweat*, sweat it out*; SEE CONCEPT 26

awake [*adj*] *conscious; alert*
alive, aroused, attentive, awakened, aware, cognizant, excited, heedful, knowing, observant, on guard, roused, vigilant, wakeful, waking, watchful; SEE CONCEPTS 402,406

awake [*v1*] *become alert or cause to rise from sleep*
arise, awaken, call, gain consciousness, get up, roll out*, rouse, stir, wake, wake up; SEE CONCEPTS 250,315

awake [*v2*] *become or make aware*
activate, alert, animate, arouse, awaken, call forth, enliven, excite, incite, kindle, provoke, revive, stimulate, stir up, vivify; SEE CONCEPT 231

awaken [*v*] *make conscious or alert*
activate, animate, arouse, awake, call, enliven, excite, fan, incite, kindle, pile out*, provoke, rally, revive, rise and shine*, roll out*, rouse, show a leg*, stimulate, stir up, turn out*, vivify, wake; SEE CONCEPTS 7,19,22,105,231

awakening [*n*] *making conscious or alert*
activation, animating, arousal, awaking, birth, enlivening, incitement, kindling, provocation, rebirth, renewal, revival, rousing, stimulation, stirring up, vivication, waking, waking up; SEE CONCEPTS 13,105,231

award [*n*] *prize or reward*
accolade, adjudication, allotment, bestowal, citation, conferment, conferral, decision, decoration, decree, distinction, donation, endowment, feather in cap*, gift, gold, gold star*, grant, honor, order, presentation, scholarship, trophy, verdict; SEE CONCEPT 337

award [*v*] *give prize or reward*
accord, adjudge, allocate, allot, apportion, assign, bestow, concede, confer, decree, dish out*, distribute, donate, endow, fork out*, gift, grant, hand out, present, render, reward, shell out*, sweeten the kitty*; SEE CONCEPT 132

aware [*adj*] *knowledgeable*
acquainted, alert, alive, appraised, appreciative, apprehensive, apprised, attentive, au courant, awake, cognizant, conscious, cool*, enlightened, familiar, go-go*, groovy*, grounded*, heedful, hip*, informed, in the know*, in the picture*, into*, know-how, knowing, know the score*,

know what's what*, latched on*, mindful, on the beam*, on to*, perceptive, plugged in*, receptive, savvy, sensible, sentient, sharp, tuned in, up on, wise, wised up*, wise to*, with it*; SEE CONCEPT 402

awareness [n] *knowledge*
acquaintance, acquaintanceship, alertness, aliveness, appreciation, apprehension, attention, attentiveness, cognizance, comprehension, consciousness, discernment, enlightenment, experience, familiarity, information, keenness, mindfulness, perception, realization, recognition, sensibility, sentience, understanding; SEE CONCEPT 409

away [*adv1*] *in another direction; at a distance*
abroad, absent, afar, apart, aside, beyond, distant, elsewhere, far afield, far away, far off, far remote, forth, from here, hence, not present, off, out of, out of the way, over, to one side; SEE CONCEPTS 581,778

away [*adv2*] *continuously*
endlessly, forever, incessantly, interminably, on and on, relentlessly, repeatedly, tirelessly, unremittingly, without break, without end, without rest, without stopping; SEE CONCEPT 553

awe [n] *amazement*
admiration, apprehension, astonishment, consternation, dread, esteem, fear, fright, horror, regard, respect, reverence, shock, stupefaction, terror, veneration, wonder, wonderment, worship; SEE CONCEPTS 230,410

awe [v] *amaze*
alarm, appall, astonish, blow away*, cow*, daunt, dazzle, flabbergast, frighten, grandstand, horrify, hotdog*, impress, intimidate, knock socks off*, overawe, scare, showboat*, startle, strike, stun, stupefy, terrify; SEE CONCEPTS 7,19,22,42

awesome [adj] *amazing*
alarming, astonishing, awe-inspiring, awful, beautiful, breathtaking, daunting, dreadful, exalted, fearful, fearsome, formidable, frantic, frightening, grand, hairy*, horrible, horrifying, imposing, impressive, intimidating, magnificent, majestic, mean, mind-blowing*, moving, nervous, overwhelming, real gone*, shocking, something else*, striking, stunning, stupefying, terrible, terrifying, wonderful, wondrous, zero cool*; SEE CONCEPTS 537,572

awful [adj] *very bad; terrible*
abominable, alarming, appalling, atrocious, deplorable, depressing, dire, disgusting, distressing, dreadful, fearful, frightful, ghastly, grody*, gross*, gruesome, grungy*, harrowing, hideous, horrendous, horrible, horrific, horrifying, nasty, offensive, raunchy, repulsive, shocking, stinking, synthetic, tough, ugly, unpleasant, unsightly; SEE CONCEPTS 570,571

awfully [*adv1*] *badly*
clumsily, disgracefully, disreputably, dreadfully, inadequately, incompletely, poorly, reprehensibly, shoddily, unforgivably, unpleasantly, wickedly, wretchedly; SEE CONCEPTS 570,571

awfully [*adv2*] *very*
badly, dreadfully, excessively, extremely, greatly, hugely, immensely, indeed, much, quite, really, truly, very, very much; SEE CONCEPT 569

awhile [*adv*] *for a short period*
briefly, for a bit, for a little while, for a moment, for a spell, for a while, for the moment, momen-

tarily, not for long, temporarily, transiently; SEE CONCEPT 798

awkward [*adj1*] *clumsy, inelegant*
all thumbs*, amateurish, artless, blundering, bulky, bumbling, bungling, butterfingers*, coarse, floundering, gawky, graceless, green*, having two left feet*, having two left hands*, incompetent, inept, inexpert, klutzy*, lumbering, maladroit, oafish, rude, stiff, stumbling, uncoordinated, uncouth, unfit, ungainly, ungraceful, unhandy, unpolished, unrefined, unskilled, unskillful; SEE CONCEPTS 406,480,527

awkward [*adj2*] *difficult to handle*
annoying, bulky, chancy, cramped, cumbersome, dangerous, disagreeable, discommodious, hard to use, hazardous, incommodious, inconvenient, perilous, risky, troublesome, uncomfortable, unhandy, unmanageable, unwieldy; SEE CONCEPTS 558,565

awkward [*adj3*] *embarrassing*
compromising, delicate, difficult, embarrassed, ill at ease, inconvenient, inopportune, painful, perplexing, sticky*, thorny*, ticklish*, troublesome, trying, uncomfortable, unpleasant, untimely; SEE CONCEPT 555

awkwardness [*n1*] *clumsiness; inelegance*
amateurishness, artlessness, boorishness, cloddishness, coarseness, crudeness, gawkiness, gracelessness, greenness*, ignorance, inability, incompetence, ineptitude, ineptness, inexpertness, maladroitness, oafishness, rudeness, tactlessness, uncoordination, uncouthness, ungainliness, unskillfulness; SEE CONCEPTS 405,630,717

awkwardness [*n2*] *difficulty*
bulkiness, chanciness, cumbersomeness, danger, hazardousness, inconvenience, peril, perilousness, risk, troublesomeness, uncomfortableness, unhandiness, unmanageability, unwieldiness; SEE CONCEPTS 656,666

awkwardness [*n3*] *embarrassment*
delicacy, difficulty, discomfort, inconvenience, inopportuneness, painfulness, stickiness*, thorniness*, ticklishness*, trouble, uncomfortableness, unpleasantness, untimeliness; SEE CONCEPT 388

awning [n] *canopy*
covering, door cover, marquee, protection, shade, shelter, sunshade, tent; SEE CONCEPTS 440,473

awry [adj] *off course; amiss*
afield, askance, askew, aslant, astray, badly, bent, cockeyed, crooked, curved, slanting, turned, wrong, zigzag; SEE CONCEPTS 537,581

ax/axe [n] *large cutting tool*
adz, chopper, hatchet, tomahawk; SEE CONCEPT 499

ax/axe [*v1*] *cut with large blade*
chop, cut, cut down, fell, hew; SEE CONCEPT 176

ax/axe [*v2*] *dismiss from service*
boot*, bounce*, can*, cancel, cut back, discharge, dispense with, eliminate, fire, get rid of, give a pink slip*, give the boot*, kick out, lay off, remove, sack*, terminate, throw out; SEE CONCEPT 351

axiom [n] *principle*
adage, aphorism, apothegm, device, dictum, fundamental, law, maxim, moral, postulate, precept, proposition, proverb, saying, theorem, truism, truth; SEE CONCEPTS 278,688,689

av
ax

axiomatic [*adj*] *understood; aphoristic*
absolute, accepted, aphoristic, apothegmatic, assumed, certain, fundamental, given, indubitable, manifest, obvious, presupposed, proverbial, self-evident, unquestioned; SEE CONCEPT 529

axis [*n*] *point around which something revolves*
arbor, axle, hinge, pivot, pole, shaft, spindle, stalk, stem, support, turning point; SEE CONCEPT 830

axle [*n*] *shaft around which wheels rotate*
arbor, axis, gudgeon, mandrel, pin, pivot, pole, rod, shaft, spindle, stalk, stem, support; SEE CONCEPTS 464,830

ax to grind [*n*] *hidden motive*
agenda, driving force, hidden agenda, incentive, motivation, motive, reason, score to settle*; SEE CONCEPTS 20,661,689

B

babble [*n*] *trivial talk, often incessant*
blubbering, burble, chatter, clamor, drivel, gab, gabble, gibberish, gossip, gushing, idle talk, jabber, jabbering, jargon, murmur, muttering, prattle, ranting, tattling; SEE CONCEPTS 266,278

babble [*v*] *talk trivially, often incessantly*
blab, blubber, blurt, burble, cackle, chat, chatter, gibber, go on, gossip, gush, jabber, mumble, murmur, mutter, patter, prate, prattle, rant, rave, run off at the mouth*, run on, spill the beans*, squeal*, talk foolishly, talk incoherently, talk nonsensically, tattle, trivialize, yak*, yakkety yak*; SEE CONCEPTS 51,266

babe [*n*] *baby*
bairn, child, infant, little one, newborn, suckling; SEE CONCEPTS 414,424

baby [*adj*] *miniature*
babyish, diminutive, dwarf, little, midget, mini*, minute, petite, small, tiny, wee, youthful; SEE CONCEPT 773

baby [*n*] *infant*
angelface*, babe, bairn, bambino, bundle, buttercup*, button, cherub, chick, child, crawler*, deduction*, dividend*, dumpling*, kid, little angel*, little darling*, little doll*, little one*, newborn, nipper*, nursling, papoose, preemie*, suckling, tad*, toddler, tot, write-off*, youngster; SEE CONCEPTS 414,424

baby [*v*] *treat like a child*
cater to, cherish, coddle, cosset, cuddle, dandle, dote on, foster, humor, indulge, nurse, overindulge, pamper, pet, please, satisfy, serve, spoil; SEE CONCEPTS 110,295

babyhood [*n*] *period of infancy*
childhood, diaper days*, infanthood; SEE CONCEPT 817

babyish [*adj*] *acting like an infant*
baby, childish, foolish, immature, infantile, juvenile, kid stuff, puerile, silly, sissy, spoiled; SEE CONCEPTS 401,550

baby-sit [*v*] *care for a child*
guard, sit, take care, tend, watch; SEE CONCEPT 295

bachelor [*n*] *unmarried man or woman*
available*, celibate, single*, single person, stag*, unattached; SEE CONCEPTS 415,419,423

back [*adj1*] *end*
aback, abaft, aft, after, astern, back of, backward, behind, final, following, hind, hindmost, in the wake of, posterior, rear, rearmost, rearward, tail; SEE CONCEPTS 827,833

back [*adj2*] *from earlier time*
delayed, elapsed, former, overdue, past, previous; SEE CONCEPT 820

back [*n*] *end part*
aft, back end, backside, extremity, far end, hindpart, hindquarters, posterior, rear, reverse, stern, tail, tail end, tailpiece; SEE CONCEPTS 392,471,827,833

back [*v1*] *support*
abet, abide by, advocate, ally, angel*, assist, bankroll, boost, champion, countenance, encourage, endorse, favor, finance, give a boost, give a leg up*, give a lift*, go to bat for*, grubstake, sanction, second, side with, sponsor, stake, stand behind, stick by, stick up for, subsidize, sustain, underwrite, uphold; SEE CONCEPTS 8,50,88

back [*v2*] *put in reverse direction*
backtrack, drive back, fall back, recede, regress, repel, repulse, retire, retract, retreat, reverse, turn tail, withdraw; SEE CONCEPTS 195,208

backbiting [*n*] *hateful talk*
abuse, aspersion, backstabbing*, belittlement, calumniation, calumny, cattiness, defamation, denigration, depreciation, detraction, disparagement, gossip, invective, lie, malice, obloquy, scandal, slander, spite, spitefulness, tale, traducement, vilification, vituperation; SEE CONCEPTS 54,58,63

backbone [*n1*] *strength of character*
courage, determination, firmness, fortitude, grit, guts, hardihood, heart, intestinal fortitude*, mettle, moral fiber, nerve, pluck, resolution, resolve, spunk, stamina, steadfastness, tenacity, toughness, will, willpower; SEE CONCEPT 411

backbone [*n2*] *spinal column of vertebrate*
base, basis, foundation, spine, support, vertebrae, vertebral column; SEE CONCEPTS 420,442

backbreaking [*adj*] *strenuous*
arduous, exhausting, grueling, hard, laborious, punishing, taxing, toilsome, wearisome; SEE CONCEPT 538

back door [*n*] *secretive or illicit method*
back entrance, back way, indirect access, means of entry, trap door; SEE CONCEPTS 274,631

back down [*v*] *withdraw from agreement or statement*
abandon, accede, admit, back off, back out, back pedal*, backtrack, balk, beg off*, cancel, chicken out*, concede, cop out*, demur, give in, give up, go back on, hold back, recant, recoil, renege, resign, retreat, surrender, take back, withdraw, yield; SEE CONCEPTS 266,697

backer [*n*] *supporter*
advocate, ally, angel*, benefactor, champion, endorser, follower, grubstaker, meal ticket*, money, patron, promoter, protagonist, sponsor, staker, underwriter, well-wisher; SEE CONCEPT 359

backfire [*v*] *have an opposite effect*
backlash, boomerang, bounce back, disappoint, fail, flop, miscarry, rebound, recoil, ricochet, spring back; SEE CONCEPTS 42,701

background [n] *experience or circumstances*
accomplishments, acquirement, actions, atmosphere, attainment, aura, backdrop, breeding, capacity, credentials, cultivation, culture, deeds, education, environment, framework, grounding, history, practice, preparation, qualification, rearing, seasoning, tradition, training, upbringing; SEE CONCEPTS 673,678,706

backhanded [adj] *underhanded*
ambiguous, double-edged, equivocal, sarcastic, sardonic, two-edged; SEE CONCEPTS 401,544

backing [n] *support*
abetment, accompaniment, adherence, advocacy, aegis, aid, assistance, auspices, championing, championship, encouragement, endorsement, funds, grant, help, patronage, reinforcement, sanction, secondment, sponsorship, subsidy; SEE CONCEPTS 110,332

backlash [n] *adverse reaction*
backfire, boomerang, counteraction, kickback, reaction, recoil, repercussion, resentment, resistance, response, retaliation, retroaction, tangle; SEE CONCEPT 230

backlog [n] *uncompleted work; accumulation*
excess, hoard, inventory, quantity, reserve(s), reservoir, resources, stock, stockpile, store, supply; SEE CONCEPTS 432,787

back out [v] *withdraw*
avoid, back down, back pedal*, beg off*, blow it off*, cancel, chicken out*, cop out*, get cold feet*, give up, go back on, recant, renege, resign, scratch, shy from, surrender, throw in the towel*, weasel out, welsh, wiggle out, worm out*; SEE CONCEPTS 50,88,121,266,697

backpack [n] *sack carried on the back*
haversack, knapsack, pack, rucksack; SEE CONCEPT 446

backside [n] *rear end*
behind, bottom, butt*, buttocks, derrière, fanny*, posterior, rear, rump*, seat*, tail*, tush*; SEE CONCEPT 392

backslide [v] *go astray*
apostatize, deviate, fall from grace, lapse, leave the straight and narrow*, relapse, revert, sin, slip; SEE CONCEPTS 195,665,697

backstab [v] *attack indirectly*
backbite, betray, double-cross*, play Judas*, sell down the river*, slander, smear; SEE CONCEPTS 54,192

back talk [n] *nasty reply*
cheek, guff, lip, mouth, sass; SEE CONCEPTS 46,278

backup [n] *auxiliary*
alternate, extra, substitute; SEE CONCEPTS 546,824

backward [adj1] *toward the rear*
astern, behind, inverted, rearward, regressive, retrograde; SEE CONCEPT 581

backward [adj2] *bashful*
afraid, averse, demure, diffident, disinclined, hesitant, hesitating, humble, indisposed, late, loath, modest, reluctant, reserved, retiring, shy, sluggish, tardy, timid, uneager, unwilling, wavering; SEE CONCEPT 401

backward [adj3] *slow in growth*
arrested, behind, checked, delayed, dense, dull, feeble-minded, imbecile, late, moronic, stupid, subnormal, underdeveloped, underprivileged, undeveloped; SEE CONCEPTS 402,562

backward [adv] *toward the rear*
aback, abaft, about, astern, back, behind, in reverse, inverted, rearward, turned around; SEE CONCEPT 581

backwash [n] *repercussion*
aftermath, result, wake; SEE CONCEPTS 230,674

backwoods [n/adj] *forests; land distant from settled area*
backcountry, boondocks*, frontier, hinterland, interior, isolation, outback, rural area, sticks*, timberland, woodland; SEE CONCEPT 509

backyard [n] *expanse behind house*
courtyard, garden, grass, lawn, patio, play area, terrace, yard; SEE CONCEPT 513

bacteria [n] *microorganisms*
bacilli, germs, microbes, organisms, pathogens; SEE CONCEPTS 306,393

bad [adj1] *poor quality*
abominable, amiss, atrocious, awful, bad news*, beastly, blah*, bottom out, bummer*, careless, cheap, cheesy*, crappy*, cruddy*, crummy*, defective, deficient, diddly*, dissatisfactory, downer*, dreadful, erroneous, fallacious, faulty, garbage, godawful*, grody*, gross*, grungy*, icky*, imperfect, inadequate, incorrect, inferior, junky*, lousy*, not good, off, poor, raunchy*, rough, sad, slipshod, stinking, substandard, synthetic,* the pits*, unacceptable, unsatisfactory; SEE CONCEPT 571

bad [adj2] *harmful*
damaging, dangerous, deleterious, detrimental, hurtful, injurious, ruinous, unhealthy; SEE CONCEPTS 537,570

bad [adj3] *immoral*
base, corrupt, criminal, delinquent, evil, iniquitous, mean, reprobate, sinful, vicious, vile; villainous, wicked, wrong; SEE CONCEPT 545

bad [adj4] *mischievous*
disobedient, ill-behaved, misbehaving, naughty, unruly, wrong; SEE CONCEPT 401

bad [adj5] *decayed*
moldy, off, putrid, rancid, rotten, sour, spoiled; SEE CONCEPTS 485,613

bad [adj6] *severe*
disastrous, distressing, grave, harsh, intense, painful, serious, terrible; SEE CONCEPT 569

bad [adj7] *sick*
ailing, diseased, ill, in pain, unwell; SEE CONCEPT 314

bad [adj8] *sorry*
apologetic, conscience-stricken, contrite, crestfallen, dejected, depressed, disconsolate, down, downcast, downhearted, guilty, low, regretful, remorseful, sad, upset, woebegone; SEE CONCEPT 403

bad [adj9] *distressing*
adverse, disagreeable, discouraged, discouraging, displeasing, distressed, gloomy, grim, melancholy, troubled, troubling, unfavorable, unfortunate, unhappy, unpleasant; SEE CONCEPTS 403,529

bad blood [n] *ill will*
acrimony, anger, animosity, antagonism, bad feeling, bitterness, dislike, distrust, enmity, hard feelings, hatred, hostility, malevolence, malice, nastiness, odium, rancor, resentment, unfriendliness, venom; SEE CONCEPT 29

bad form [n] *bad style*
barbarism, impropriety, indecorum, inelegance, infelicity, solecism; SEE CONCEPTS 275,633

badge [*n*] *emblem worn*
brand, cordon, device, identification, insignia, mark, marker, medallion, motto, pin, ribbon, scepter, shield, sign, stamp, symbol, token; SEE CONCEPTS 260,284,476

badger [*v*] *nag, bother*
annoy, bait, bug, bully, eat*, give the business*, goad, harass, harry, hassle, heckle, hound, importune, insist on, needle, nudge, pester, plague, ride, tease, torment, work on; SEE CONCEPTS 14,51

bad luck [*n*] *adversity*
blow, hard luck, hard time, mischance, misfortune, reverse, setback; SEE CONCEPTS 388,674,679

badly [*adv1*] *inadequately*
abominably, awkwardly, blunderingly, carelessly, clumsily, crudely, defectively, erroneously, faultily, feebly, haphazardly, imperfectly, incompetently, ineffectively, ineptly, maladroitly, negligently, poorly, shoddily, stupidly, unfavorably, unfortunately, unsatisfactorily, unskillfully, unsuccessfully, weakly, wrong, wrongly; SEE CONCEPT 571

badly [*adv2*] *immorally*
criminally, evilly, improperly, naughtily, shamefully, unethically, wickedly; SEE CONCEPT 545

badly [*adv3*] *very much; desperately*
acutely, deeply, exceedingly, extremely, gravely, greatly, hard, intensely, painfully, roughly, seriously, severely; SEE CONCEPT 569

bad manners [*n*] *improper behavior*
boorishness, discourtesy, disrespect, impoliteness, inconsideration, unmannerliness; SEE CONCEPTS 29,633

bad-mouth [*v*] *to denigrate*
belittle, criticize, cut down to size*, dis*, disparage, dump on*, find fault, knock*, malign, mudsling*, pan, pooh pooh*, put down*, rap, rip, roast*, run down*, slam, slander, take a dig at*, take down a peg*, tear down*, tear to pieces*; SEE CONCEPTS 52,54

bad news [*n*] *trouble*
bind, bother, concern, danger, deep trouble, difficulty, dilemma, dire straits, disappointment, distress, grief, headache*, hindrance, hot water*, inconvenience, mess, misfortune, nuisance, pain, predicament, problem, struggle, torment, woe; SEE CONCEPTS 532,674,675,690,728

bad scene [*n*] *misfortunate event*
bad trip*, bummer*, bum trip*, depressing experience, disaster, downer*, drag*, raw deal, rotten hand, unhappy situation, unpleasant experience, unpleasant situation; SEE CONCEPTS 674,675

bad time [*n*] *agony*
going-over, grief, grilling, hard time, third degree, torture; SEE CONCEPTS 410,728

bad trip [*n*] *unpleasant experience*
bad scene, bummer*, bum trip*, disaster, downer*, drag*, freak-out*, unhappy situation, unpleasant drug experience, unpleasant situation; SEE CONCEPTS 674,675

baffle [*v1*] *perplex*
addle, amaze, astound, befuddle, bewilder, buffalo*, confound, confuse, daze, disconcert, dumbfound, elude, embarrass, faze, floor*, get, mix up, muddle, mystify, nonplus, puzzle, rattle, stick*, stump*, stun, throw; SEE CONCEPTS 7,19,42

baffle [*v2*] *hinder*
beat, block, check, circumvent, dash, defeat, disappoint, foil, frustrate, impede, obstruct, prevent, ruin, thwart, upset; SEE CONCEPT 121

bag [*n1*] *container for one's possesions*
attaché, backpack, briefcase, carryall, carry-on, case, duffel, gear, handbag, haversack, holdall, kit, knapsack, pack, packet, pocket, pocketbook, poke, pouch, purse, rucksack, sac, sack, saddlebag, satchel, suitcase, tote; SEE CONCEPTS 339,450,494

bag [*n2*] *special interest*
expertise, favorite activity, hobby, preference, speciality, thing*; SEE CONCEPTS 32,529

bag [*v1*] *catch*
acquire, apprehend, capture, collar, gain, get, hook, kill, land, nab, nail, net, seize, shoot, take, trap; SEE CONCEPT 90

bag [*v2*] *droop*
balloon, billow, bulge, flap, flop, hang, lop, sag, swell; SEE CONCEPTS 754,757

baggage [*n*] *gear*
accoutrements, bags, belongings, carry-on, effects, equipment, fortnighter, gear, impedimenta, luggage, overnighter*, paraphernalia, parcels, slough, suitcases, things, tote, tote bag, trappings, two-suiter; SEE CONCEPT 494

baggy [*adj*] *drooping*
billowing, bulging, droopy, flabby, floppy, ill-fitting, loose, oversize, roomy, sagging, slack, unshapely; SEE CONCEPTS 486,490

bail [*n*] *money for assurance*
bond, collateral, guarantee, pawn, pledge, recognizance, security, surety, warrant, warranty; SEE CONCEPTS 318,332

bail out [*v1*] *help*
aid, deliver, release, relieve, rescue, spring; SEE CONCEPT 110

bail out [*v2*] *escape*
flee, quit, retreat, withdraw; SEE CONCEPT 102

bait [*n*] *something for luring*
allurement, attraction, bribe, come-on*, drag, enticement, inducement, lure, seducement, shill, snare, temptation, trap; SEE CONCEPT 709

bait [*v1*] *lure*
allure, attract, bedevil, beguile, draw, entice, fascinate, lead on, seduce, tempt; SEE CONCEPTS 9,14

bait [*v2*] *needle*
anger, annoy, badger, bother, gall, harass, heckle, hound, irk, irritate, nag, persecute, provoke, tease, torment; SEE CONCEPTS 7,19

bake [*v*] *cook in oven*
heat, melt, scorch, simmer, stew, warm; SEE CONCEPT 170

baked [*adj*] *cooked in oven*
dried, heated, melted, scorched, simmered, stewed, warmed; SEE CONCEPT 462

baker [*n*] *person who cooks baked goods*
chef, cook, dough puncher*, pastry maker; SEE CONCEPT 348

bakery [*n*] *cooking business where baked goods are produced*
bake shop, confectionery, pastry shop, pâtisserie; SEE CONCEPTS 325,439,449

balance [*n1*] *equilibrium*
antithesis, correspondence, counterbalance, equity, equivalence, evenness, even-steven*, hang, harmony, parity, proportion, stasis, symmetry, tension; SEE CONCEPTS 664,667

balance [*n2*] *composure*
equanimity, poise, self-control, self-possession, stability, steadfastness; SEE CONCEPT *633*

balance [*n3*] *money remaining in account*
difference, dividend, excess, profit, remainder, residue, rest, surplus; SEE CONCEPT *332*

balance [*v1*] *make equal; cause to have equilibrium*
accord, adjust, attune, cancel, collate, come out, come out even, compensate, correspond, counteract, counterbalance, equalize, equate, even, harmonize, level, make up for, match, neutralize, nullify, offset, oppose, pair off, parallel, poise, readjust, redeem, set, square, stabilize, steady, tie, weigh; SEE CONCEPTS *197,697*

balance [*v2*] *compare*
assess, consider, deliberate, estimate, evaluate, weigh; SEE CONCEPT *17*

balance [*v3*] *make equal numerically*
adjust, audit, calculate, compute, count, enumerate, equate, estimate, figure, settle, square, sum up, tally, total; SEE CONCEPT *764*

balanced [*adj1*] *equalized*
counterbalanced, equitable, equivalent, evened, fair, just, offset, proportional, stabilized, symmetrical, uniform; SEE CONCEPT *566*

balanced [*adj2*] *settled financially*
certified, confirmed, validated; SEE CONCEPT *334*

balance sheet [*n*] *financial statement including gains and losses for a period*
account, annual report, assets and liabilities, budget, ledger, report; SEE CONCEPTS *271,332*

balcony [*n*] *porch or structure above the ground*
balustrade, box*, catwalk, gallery, mezzanine, piazza, platform, porch, portico, stoop, terrace, veranda; SEE CONCEPT *440*

bald [*adj1*] *having no covering*
baldheaded, bare, barren, depilated, exposed, glabrous, hairless, head*, naked, shaven, skin head*, smooth, stark, uncovered; SEE CONCEPT *485*

bald [*adj2*] *simple, unadorned*
austere, bare, blunt, direct, downright, forthright, outright, plain, severe, straight, straightforward, unembellished; SEE CONCEPTS *485,589*

bale [*n*] *bunch*
bundle, package, parcel; SEE CONCEPT *432*

baleful [*adj*] *menacing*
calamitous, deadly, dire, evil, foreboding, harmful, hurtful, injurious, malevolent, malignant, noxious, ominous, pernicious, ruinous, sinister, threatening, venomous, vindictive, woeful; SEE CONCEPTS *537,570*

balk [*v1*] *stop short*
cramp, crimp, demur, desist, dodge, evade, flinch, hesitate, recoil, refuse, resist, shirk, shrink from, shy, turn down, upset apple cart*; SEE CONCEPTS *119,121,188*

balk [*v2*] *thwart*
baffle, bar, beat, check, circumvent, counteract, cramp, cramp one's style*, dash, defeat, disappoint, disconcert, foil, forestall, frustrate, hinder, obstruct, prevent, ruin, stall, stop, throw a curve*, throw monkey wrench in*, upset the apple cart*; SEE CONCEPT *121*

balky [*adj*] *uncooperative*
averse, contrary, hesitant, immovable, indisposed, inflexible, intractable, loath, negative, negativistic, obstinate, ornery, perverse, reluctant, stubborn, unbending, unmanageable, unpredictable, unruly; SEE CONCEPT *401*

ball [*n1*] *dance party*
hoedown, hoodang, hop, jump, mingle, prom, promenade, reception, shindig; SEE CONCEPT *386*

ball [*n2*] *globe, sphere*
apple, balloon, drop, globule, orb, pellet, pill, round, spheroid; SEE CONCEPT *436*

ballad [*n*] *narrative song*
carol, chant, ditty, serenade; SEE CONCEPT *595*

ballast [*n*] *something giving balance*
balance, brace, bracket, counterbalance, counterweight, equilibrium, sandbag, stability, stabilizer, support, weight; SEE CONCEPT *712*

ballet [*n*] *graceful, expressive dancing*
choreography, dance, toe dancing; SEE CONCEPT *263*

ballet dancer [*n*] *person who performs graceful dance*
company, coryphee, dancer, danseur, danseuse, figurant, figurante, hoofer*, prima ballerina; SEE CONCEPT *352*

balloon [*n*] *inflated material or vehicle*
airship, bladder, blimp, dirigible, zeppelin; SEE CONCEPTS *293,504*

balloon [*v*] *billow out; bloat*
belly, blow up, bulge, dilate, distend, enlarge, expand, inflate, puff out, swell; SEE CONCEPTS *208,756*

ballot [*n1*] *voting; recording of vote*
election, franchise, plebiscite, poll, polling, referendum, slate, tally, ticket; SEE CONCEPTS *300,301*

ballot [*n2*] *candidates from political party*
choice, lineup, slate, ticket; SEE CONCEPT *301*

balm [*n1*] *oily substance*
analgesic, application, balsam, cerate, compound, cream, demulcent, dressing, embrocation, emollient, formula, lotion, medicine, ointment, potion, poultice, preparation, prescription, salve, soother, soothing agent, unction, unguent; SEE CONCEPTS *307,466*

balm [*n2*] *something soothing*
alleviation, anodyne, assuagement, comfort, consolation, curative, cure, easement, mitigation, palliative, refreshment, relief, remedy, restorative, solace, soother; SEE CONCEPTS *337,529*

balmy [*adj1*] *comfortable with respect to weather*
mild, moderate, moist, pleasant, refreshing, summerlike, summery, temperate, tropical; SEE CONCEPTS *603,605*

balmy [*adj2*] *insane*
absurd, bugged out*, cracked*, crazed, crazy, daft, deranged, dotty*, foolish, harebrained*, idiotic, loony, mentally incompetent, moronic, nuts*, nutty*, odd, potty*, preposterous, silly, stupid, wacky; SEE CONCEPT *403*

bamboozle [*v*] *fool; cheat*
baffle, befuddle, bilk, con, confound, confuse, deceive, defraud, delude, dupe, flimflam*, hoax, hoodwink*, hornswoggle*, mystify, perplex, puzzle, stump, swindle, trick; SEE CONCEPT *59*

ban [*n*] *official forbiddance*
a thou-shalt-not*, boycott, censorship, don't*, embargo, injunction, interdiction, limitation, no-no*, off limits*, out of bounds*, prohibition, proscription, refusal, restriction, stoppage, suppression, taboo; SEE CONCEPTS *50,88,121,688*

ban [v] *officially forbid*
banish, bar, blackball*, close down, close up, curse, declare illegal, disallow, enjoin, exclude, halt, ice out*, illegalize, inhibit, interdict, outlaw, pass by, pass up, prevent, prohibit, proscribe, restrict, shut out, suppress; SEE CONCEPTS 50,88,121

banal [adj] *commonplace*
blah*, bland, bromidic, clichéd, common, conventional, cornball*, cornfed*, corny, dull as dishwater*, dumb, everyday, flat, hackneyed, ho hum*, hokey*, humdrum*, insipid, mundane, noplace, nothing, nowhere, old hat*, ordinary, pabulum*, pedestrian, platitudinous, square, stale, stereotyped, stock, stupid, tired, tripe, trite, unimaginative, unoriginal, vapid, watery, wishywashy*, zero*; SEE CONCEPT 530

banality [n] *common saying*
adage, boiler*, buzzword, chestnut*, cliché, corn*, dullsville*, familiar tune*, high camp*, hokum*, old chestnut*, old saw*, plate*, platitude, prosaicism, prosaism, saw*, trite phrase, trivia, triviality, truism; SEE CONCEPT 275

band [n1] *something which encircles*
bandage, bandeau, belt, binding, bond, braid, cable, chain, circle, circuit, copula, cord, fillet, harness, hoop, ligature, line, link, manacle, ribbon, ring, rope, sash, scarf, shackle, snood, stay, strap, string, strip, tape, tie, truss; SEE CONCEPTS 470,751

band [n2] *group of people with same interest*
assembly, association, bevy, body, bunch, clique, club, cluster, collection, company, corps, coterie, covey, crew, gang, gathering, horde, menagerie, outfit, party, society, troop, troupe; SEE CONCEPTS 387,391,417

band [n3] *musical group*
combo, ensemble, orchestra, philharmonic, symphony, troupe; SEE CONCEPT 294

band [v] *group or join group*
affiliate, ally, amalgamate, belt, coadjute, combine, conjoin, consolidate, federate, gather, league, merge, team, unite; SEE CONCEPTS 113,114

bandage [n] *covering for wound*
cast, compress, dressing, gauze, plaster; SEE CONCEPT 311

bandage [v] *cover a wound*
bind, dress, swathe, truss, wrap; SEE CONCEPT 310

bandanna [n] *colorful scarf*
handkerchief, kerchief, neckerchief, silk; SEE CONCEPT 450

bandit [n] *thief*
brigand, criminal, crook, desperado, forager, gangster, gunperson, highwayperson, hijacker, holdup person, hooligan, marauder, mobster, outlaw, pillager, pirate, plunderer, racketeer, raider, ravager, robber, villain; SEE CONCEPT 412

bandwidth [n] *frequency range*
high frequency, low frequency, radio band, radio bandwidth, transmission capacity; SEE CONCEPT 279

bane [n] *cause of misery*
affliction, bête noir, blight, burden, calamity, curse, despair, destruction, disaster, downfall, fatal attraction, misery, nuisance, pest, plague, poison, ruin, ruination, scourge, torment, trial, trouble, undoing, venom, woe; SEE CONCEPTS 529,674

baneful [adj] *ruinous, injurious*
baleful, calamitous, deadly, deleterious, destructive, disastrous, evil, fatal, harmful, hurtful, malefic, noxious, pernicious, pestilent, pestilential, poisonous, venomous, wicked; SEE CONCEPTS 537,570

bang [adv] *suddenly, with force*
abruptly, hard, headlong, head on, noisily, precisely, smack, straight, suddenly; SEE CONCEPT 540

bang [n1] *explosive noise*
blast, boom, burst, clang, clap, clash, crack, detonation, discharge, howl, peal, pop, report, roar, roll, rumble, salvo, shot, slam, smash, sound, thud, thump, thunder, wham; SEE CONCEPT 595

bang [n2] *loud hit or knock*
bash, bat, belt, blow, box, bump, collide, crack, cuff, punch, slam, smack, smash, sock, stroke, wallop, whack, whop; SEE CONCEPT 189

bang [n3] *thrilling situation*
enjoyment, excitement, kick*, pleasant feeling, smash, wallop, wow*; SEE CONCEPT 230

bang [v1] *hit or knock loudly*
boom, burst, clang, clatter, crash, detonate, drum, echo, explode, make noise, peal, rattle, resound, sound, thump, thunder; SEE CONCEPTS 65,189

bang [v2] *moving by hitting hard*
bash, beat, bump, clatter, collide, crash, hammer, hit, knock, pound, pummel, rap, slam, smash, strike, thump, whack; SEE CONCEPT 189

banish [v] *expel from place or situation*
ban, cast out, deport, discard, discharge, dislodge, dismiss, dispel, drive away, eject, eliminate, eradicate, evict, exclude, excommunicate, exile, expatriate, expulse, extradict, get rid of, isolate, ostracize, oust, outlaw, proscribe, relegate, remove, rusticate, sequester, shake off, shut out, transport; SEE CONCEPTS 121,217

banister [n] *railing of stairs*
baluster, balustrade, handrail, rail, support; SEE CONCEPT 443

bank [n1] *financial institution*
coffer, countinghouse, credit union, depository, exchequer, fund, hoard, investment firm, repository, reserve, reservoir, safe, savings, stock, stockpile, store, storehouse, thrift, treasury, trust company, vault; SEE CONCEPTS 333,339,439

bank [n2] *ground bounding waters*
beach, cay, cliff, coast, edge, embankment, lakefront, lakeshore, lakeside, ledge, levee, oceanfront, reef, riverfront, riverside, seabank, seaboard, seafront, shore, strand, streamside, waterfront; SEE CONCEPT 509

bank [n3] *row or tier of objects*
array, dashboard, group, line, rank, row, sequence, series, succession; SEE CONCEPT 464

bank [v1] *collect money or advantage*
amass, deposit, heap, hill, hoard, invest, lay aside, lay away, mass, mound, pile, put by, salt away, save, sock away, speculate, squirrel, stash; SEE CONCEPTS 109,330

bank [v2] *lean or tilt*
bend, camber, cant, incline, pitch, slant, slope; SEE CONCEPTS 148,213

banker [n] *professional in financial institution*
broker, capitalist, croupier, dealer, financier, house, investor, manager, money-lender, officer, teller, treasurer, usurer; SEE CONCEPTS 347,348,353

bank on [*v*] *depend upon*
assume, believe in, be sure about, bet on, build on, count on, gamble on, lean on, look to, reckon on, rely on, stake, trust, venture, wager; SEE CONCEPT 12

bankrupt [*adj*] *unable to pay debts*
broke, depleted, destitute, exhausted, failed, impoverished, in Chapter 11*, insolvent, lacking, lost, out of business, ruined, spent, tapped out; SEE CONCEPT 334

bankruptcy [*n*] *inability to pay debts*
Chapter 11*, defalcation, default, destituteness, destitution, disaster, exhaustion, failure, indebtedness, indigence, insolvency, lack, liquidation, loss, nonpayment, overdraft, pauperism, privation, repudiation, ruin, ruination; SEE CONCEPT 335

banner [*adj*] *successful*
exceptional, foremost, leading, outstanding, red-letter; SEE CONCEPT 528

banner [*n1*] *flag, usually with message*
banderole, burgee, colors, emblem, ensign, gonfalon, heading, headline, pennant, pennon, standard, streamer; SEE CONCEPTS 270,277,278

banner [*n2*] *ad on Web/Internet page*
advertisement, burst page, headline, streamer; SEE CONCEPTS 270,277,278,280

banquet [*n*] *formal dinner, usually ceremonial*
feast, festivity, fete, meal, reception, regale, repast, spread, treat; SEE CONCEPTS 377,459

bantam [*adj*] *small*
diminutive, little, petite, tiny; SEE CONCEPTS 491,773

banter [*n*] *teasing*
badinage, chaff, chaffing, chitchat, derision, dissing*, exchange, fun, gossip, jeering, jesting, joking, joshing, kidding, mockery, persiflage, play, raillery, repartee, ribbing, ridicule, small talk; SEE CONCEPTS 59,278

banter [*v*] *tease*
chaff, deride, fool, fun, jeer, jest, jive*, joke, josh, kid, make fun of, mock, rag*, razz*, rib, ridicule, satirize, taunt; SEE CONCEPTS 59,273

baptism [*n*] *church rite; initiation*
ablution, baptismal, christening, debut, dedication, dunking, immersion, introduction, launching, lustration, purgation, purge, purification, rite of passage, ritual, sanctification, sprinkling; SEE CONCEPTS 367,377

baptize [*v*] *initiate in church rite*
admit, asperse, besprinkle, call, christen, cleanse, denominate, dip, dub, entitle, immerse, name, purify, regenerate, sprinkle, term, title; SEE CONCEPT 367

bar [*n1*] *rod; straight length of material*
batten, billet, boom, crossbar, crosspiece, ingot, lever, paling, pig, pole, rail, rib, rule, shaft, slab, spar, spoke, stake, stick, streak, strip, stripe, stroke; SEE CONCEPTS 470,471

bar [*n2*] *barrier; blockage*
barricade, blank wall, block, clog, deterrent, encumbrance, fence, hindrance, hurdle, impediment, obstacle, obstruction, pale, rail, railing, restraint, road block, snag, stop, stumbling block, traverse, wall; SEE CONCEPTS 470,652,680

bar [*n3*] *establishment serving alcohol*
alehouse, barroom, beer garden, bistro, canteen, cocktail lounge, drinkery, inn, lounge, pub, public house, rathskeller, saloon, tap, taproom, tavern, watering hole*; SEE CONCEPTS 325,439

bar [*n4*] *legal system*
attorneys, barristers, bench, counsel, counselors, court, courtroom, dock, judgment, judiciary, jurists, law, law court, law practice, lawyers, legal profession, solicitors, tribunal; SEE CONCEPTS 318,381

bar [*v1*] *secure, usually with a length of material*
barricade, block, blockade, bolt, caulk, clog, close, dam, deadbolt, dike, fasten, fence, jam, latch, lock, plug, seal, secure, trammel, wall; SEE CONCEPTS 121,130

bar [*v2*] *prohibit*
ban, boycott, circumvent, condemn, debar, deny, disallow, discountenance, discourage, eliminate, enjoin, except, exclude, exile, forbid, freeze out, frustrate, hinder, interdict, interfere, keep out, limit, obstruct, ostracize, outlaw, override, preclude, prevent, refuse, reject, restrain, rule out, segregate, shut out, stop, suspend; SEE CONCEPTS 50,61,88

barb [*n1*] *point*
arrow, bristle, dart, prickle, prong, quill, shaft, spike, spur, thistle, thorn; SEE CONCEPTS 434,836

barb [*n2*] *pointed comment*
affront, criticism, cut, dig, gibe, insult, rebuff, sarcasm, scoff, sneer; SEE CONCEPTS 52,54

barbarian [*adj*] *crude, savage*
barbaric, barbarous, boorish, brutal, coarse, cruel, inhuman, lowbrow, merciless, philistine, primitive, rough, rude, uncivil, uncivilized, uncouth, uncultivated, uncultured, unsophisticated, untamed, vicious, vulgar, wild; SEE CONCEPT 401

barbarian [*n*] *crude, savage person*
beast, bigot, boor, brute, cannibal, clod, hooligan, hun, ignoramus, lout, monster, philistine, rascal, ruffian, troglodyte, vandal; SEE CONCEPT 412

barbaric [*adj*] *crude, savage*
barbarian, barbarous, boorish, brutal, coarse, cruel, fierce, graceless, inhuman, lowbrow, primitive, rough, rude, tasteless, uncivilized, uncouth, vulgar, wild; SEE CONCEPT 401

barbarism [*n*] *crudity, savagery, especially in speech*
atrocity, barbarity, brutality, catachresis, coarseness, corruption, cruelty, impropriety, inhumanity, localism, malapropism, misusage, misuse, primitive culture, provincialism, solecism, uncivilizedness, vernacularism, vernacularity, vulgarism; SEE CONCEPTS 275,633

barbarity [*n*] *crudity, savagery*
boorishness, brutality, crudeness, cruelty, inhumanity, ruthlessness, savageness, viciousness, vulgarity; SEE CONCEPT 633

barbarous [*adj*] *crude, savage*
atrocious, barbarian, barbaric, brutal, brutish, coarse, cruel, ferocious, heartless, ignorant, inhuman, inhumane, monstrous, primitive, rough, rude, ruthless, sadistic, truculent, uncivil, uncivilized, uncouth, uncultured, unsophisticated, vicious, vulgar, wicked, wild, wolfish; SEE CONCEPT 401

barbecue [*n1*] *meal cooked on grill*
bake, clam bake, cookout, party, picnic, weinie roast; SEE CONCEPT 459

barbecue [*n2*] *grill for cookout*
broiler, charcoal grill, fireplace, gas grill, griddle, pit of coals, roaster, spit; SEE CONCEPT 493

ba
ba

barbecue [*v*] *cook outside, usually on a grill*
broil, charcoal, fry, grill, rotisserie, sear; SEE
CONCEPT *170*
barber [*n*] *hair cutter*
beautician, coiffeur, coiffeuse, cosmetologist,
hairdresser, hair stylist, shaver, tonsorial artist;
SEE CONCEPT *348*
bare [*adj 1*] *without clothing*
bald, bareskinned, denuded, disrobed, divested,
exposed, in one's birthday suit*, naked, nude,
peeled, shorn, stripped, unclad, unclothed, uncovered, undressed, unrobed; SEE CONCEPT *485*
bare [*adj2*] *without covering or content*
arid, barren, blank, bleak, clear, desert, desolate,
empty, lacking, mean, open, poor, scanty, scarce,
stark, unfurnished, vacant, vacuous, void, wanting; SEE CONCEPT *490*
bare [*adj3*] *simple, unadorned*
austere, bald, basic, blunt, chaste, cold, essential,
hard, literal, meager, mere, modest, scant, severe, sheer, simple, spare, stark, unembellished,
unornamented; SEE CONCEPT *562*
bare [*v*] *reveal*
disclose, divulge, exhibit, expose, publish, show,
uncover, unroll, unveil; SEE CONCEPTS *60,138*
barefaced [*adj*] *shameless; open*
apparent, arrant, audacious, blatant, blunt, bold,
brash, brassy, brazen, candid, clear, flagrant,
frank, glaring, immodest, impudent, insolent,
manifest, naked, obvious, palpable, temerarious,
transparent, unabashed, unconcealed; SEE CON-
CEPT *401*
barefoot [*adj*] *wearing no shoes*
barefooted, discalceate, discalced, shoeless, un-
shod; SEE CONCEPT *406*
barely [*adj*] *not quite*
almost, hardly, just, only just, scantily, scarcely;
SEE CONCEPT *772*
bareness [*n*] *state of being unclothed*
dishabille, nakedness, nudity, starkness, unadornment, undress; SEE CONCEPT *453*
bargain [*n1*] *agreement*
arrangement, bond, business, compact, contract,
convention, covenant, deal, engagement, negotiation, pact, pledge, promise, stipulation, transaction, treaty, understanding; SEE CONCEPT *684*
bargain [*n2*] *something bought at cheap price*
budget price, buy, closeout, deal, discount, giveaway, good buy, good deal, good value, low
price, markdown, nominal price, reduction, steal,
value; SEE CONCEPTS *332,338*
bargain [*v*] *negotiate terms of sale or agreement*
agree, arrange, barter, buy, compromise, confer,
contract, covenant, deal, dicker, do business,
haggle, make terms, palter, promise, sell, stipulate, trade, traffic, transact; SEE CONCEPTS *56,330*
bargain for [*v*] *expect*
aim for, anticipate, contemplate, count on, foresee, imagine, look for, plan on, reckon on; SEE
CONCEPT *26*
barge [*n*] *large work boat*
ark, canal boat, dory, flatboat, freight ship,
lighter, raft, scow; SEE CONCEPT *506*
barge in/barge into [*v*] *charge*
break in, burst in, collide, infringe, interrupt, intrude, muscle in, push, shove, stumble; SEE CON-
CEPTS *150,208*
bark [*n1*] *plant covering*
case, casing, coat, cortex, crust, husk, peeling,
rind, shell, skin; SEE CONCEPT *428*

bark [*n2*] *animal yelp*
bay, growl, grunt, howl, roar, snarl, woof, yap,
yip; SEE CONCEPT *64*
bark [*v1*] *yelp*
arf, bay, cry, gnarl, growl, howl, snap, snarl,
woof, yap, yip; SEE CONCEPT *64*
bark [*v2*] *shout*
bawl, bellow, clamor, cry, growl, grumble, mutter, roar, snap, snarl, yell; SEE CONCEPT *77*
barn [*n*] *animal shelter*
farm building, outbuilding, shed; SEE CONCEPTS
439,517
baroque [*adj*] *decorative, especially architecture*
bizarre, convoluted, elaborate, embellished, extravagant, flamboyant, florid, gilt, grotesque, ornamented, ornate, overdecorated, rich, rococo;
SEE CONCEPTS *562,589*
barracks [*n*] *shelter for military*
billet, bivouac, camp, cantonment, dormitory,
encampment, enclosure, garrison, headquarters,
hut, prefab, quarters, Quonset hut, tent; SEE CON-
CEPTS *321,516*
barrage [*n1*] *weapon fire*
battery, blast, bombardment, broadside, cannonade, crossfire, curtain of fire, discharge, enfilade,
fire, fusillade, gunfire, hail, salvo, shelling,
shower, storm, volley; SEE CONCEPT *320*
barrage [*n2*] *profusion of something*
assault, attack, blast, bombardment, burst, deluge, hail, mass, onslaught, plethora, rain,
shower, storm, stream, surge, torrent; SEE CON-
CEPT *787*
barrel [*n*] *cylindrical container*
butt, cask, cylinder, drum, firkin, hogshead, keg,
pipe, receptacle, tub, tun, vat, vessel; SEE CON-
CEPT *494*
barren [*adj1*] *unable to support growth*
arid, depleted, desert, desolate, dry, effete,
empty, fallow, fruitless, impotent, impoverished,
infecund, infertile, parched, sterile, unbearing,
uncultivable, unfertile, unfruitful, unproductive,
waste; SEE CONCEPTS *485,522*
barren [*adj2*] *unprofitable*
dull, flat, fruitless, futile, lackluster, profitless,
stale, uninspiring, unproductive, unrewarding,
useless, vain, vapid; SEE CONCEPT *560*
barricade [*n*] *blocking object*
bar, barrier, blank wall, block, blockade, bulwark, fence, obstruction, palisade, rampart, roadblock, stockade, stop, wall; SEE CONCEPT *470*
barricade [*v*] *block, usually to protect*
bar, blockade, defend, fortify, obstruct, shut in;
SEE CONCEPTS *130,201*
barrier [*n1*] *obstruction*
bar, barricade, blank wall, blockade, bound,
boundary, confines, curtain, ditch, enclosure,
fence, fortification, gully, hurdle, impediment,
limit, moat, obstacle, pale, palisade, railing, rampart, roadblock, stop, trench, wall; SEE CONCEPTS
435,470,513
barrier [*n2*] *obstruction to goal*
bar, check, difficulty, drawback, encumbrance,
handicap, hindrance, hurdle, impediment, limitation, obstacle, pale, preventive, restraint, restriction, stumbling block; SEE CONCEPT *532*
barter [*v*] *trade goods or services*
bargain, exchange, haggle, swap, trade, traffic,
truck; SEE CONCEPT *104*
base [*adj*] *vulgar, low*
abject, abominable, cheap, coarse, common, con-

temptible, corrupt, depraved, despicable, disgraceful, dishonorable, disreputable, foul, grovelling, humble, ignoble, immoral, indelicate, loathsome, lowly, mean, menial, offensive, paltry, pitiful, plebeian, poor, scandalous, servile, shameful, shoddy, sleazy, sordid, sorry, squalid, trashy, ugly, unworthy, vile, worthless, wretched; SEE CONCEPTS *542,570*

base [*n1*] *foundation*
basement, basis, bed, bedrock, bottom, foot, footing, ground, groundwork, infrastructure, pedestal, rest, root, seat, seating, stand, substratum, substructure, support, underpinning; SEE CONCEPT *442*

base [*n2*] *fundamental part*
authority, backbone, basis, chief constituent, core, essence, essential, evidence, foundation, fundamental, groundwork, heart, important part, infrastructure, key, origin, primary element, principal, principle, root, source, underpinning; SEE CONCEPT *826*

base [*n3*] *headquarters*
camp, center, depot, dock, field, garrison, hangar, harbor, home, port, post, settlement, site, starting point, station, strip, terminal; SEE CONCEPTS *435,449*

base [*v*] *build plan or opinion on*
construct, depend, derive, establish, found, ground, hinge, locate, plant, predicate, prop, rest, set up, station, stay; SEE CONCEPT *36*

baseless [*adj*] *without substantiation*
bottomless, flimsy, foundationless, gratuitous, groundless, reasonless, unconfirmed, uncorroborated, unfounded, ungrounded, unjustifiable, unjustified, unsubstantiated, unsupported, untenable, unwarranted; SEE CONCEPT *582*

basement [*n*] *room on lower floor of building*
bottom, cellar, crypt, excavation, furnace room, storage, substructure, subterranean room, underbuilding, understructure, vault; SEE CONCEPT *440*

bash [*n*] *party*
celebration, spree, wing-ding*; SEE CONCEPT *383*

bash [*v*] *hit*
clobber*, pop*, punch, slam, slug, smash, strike, whack; SEE CONCEPTS *189,200*

bashful [*adj*] *shy*
abashed, backward, blushful, blushing, chary, confused, constrained, coy, demure, diffident, embarrassed, humble, modest, nervous, overmodest, recoiling, reserved, reticent, retiring, self-conscious, self-effacing, shamefaced, sheepish, shrinking, silent, timid, timorous, unassertive; SEE CONCEPT *404*

bashing [*n*] *abuse against a group or individual based on identity or ideological beliefs*
assault, attack, beating, beating up, bias crime, censure, charge, condemnation, criticism, denigration, harassment, hate crime, hounding, jumping, offensive, persecution, strike, torment; SEE CONCEPT *86*

basic [*adj*] *elementary, fundamental*
basal, capital, central, chief, elemental, essential, indispensable, inherent, intrinsic, key, main, necessary, primary, primitive, principal, radical, substratal, underlying, vital; SEE CONCEPT *568*

basically [*adv*] *fundamentally*
at heart, at the bottom, firstly, in essence, inherently, in substance, intrinsically, mostly, primarily, radically; SEE CONCEPT *568*

basin [*n*] *container or area where water is held*
bay, bowl, concavity, depression, dip, ewer, gulf, hole, hollow, lagoon, pan, pool, pot, sag, sink, sinkage, sinkhole, tub, valley, vessel, watershed; SEE CONCEPTS *494,509,514*

basis [*n1*] *physical foundation*
base, bed, bottom, foot, footing, ground, groundwork, rest, resting place, seat, substructure, support; SEE CONCEPT *442*

basis [*n2*] *foundation for belief, action*
antecedent, assumption, authority, axiom, backbone, background, backing, base, bedrock, cause, center, chief ingredient, core, crux, data, dictum, essence, essential, evidence, explanation, footing, fundamental, hard fact, heart, infrastructure, justification, keynote, keystone, law, nexus, nucleus, postulate, premise, presumption, presupposition, principal element, principle, proof, reason, root, rudiment, sanction, security, source, substratum, support, theorem, theory, underpinning, warrant; SEE CONCEPTS *661,688,689*

bask [*v1*] *lie in sunlight*
laze, loll, lounge, relax, sun, sunbathe, swim in, toast oneself*, warm oneself; SEE CONCEPTS *162,210*

bask [*v2*] *lie in glory*
delight in, derive pleasure, enjoy, indulge, luxuriate, relish, revel, rollick, savor, take comfort, take pleasure, wallow, welter; SEE CONCEPT *32*

basket [*n*] *woven container*
bassinet, bin, box, bushel, cradle, crate, creel, hamper, nacelle, pannier; SEE CONCEPT *494*

basketball [*n*] *team sport*
ball, B-ball*, brownball*, hoops*; SEE CONCEPT *363*

bastard [*adj*] *illegitimate*
adulterated, baseborn, counterfeit, fake, false, imperfect, impure, inferior, irregular, misbegotten, misborn, mixed, mongrel, natural, phony, sham, spurious, supposititious, ungenuine; SEE CONCEPT *549*

bastardize [*v*] *debase*
adulterate, bestialize, brutalize, corrupt, debauch, declare illegitimate, degrade, demoralize, deprave, pervert, vitiate, warp; SEE CONCEPT *44*

baste [*v1*] *moisten during cooking*
brush with liquid, drip, grease, lard, season; SEE CONCEPT *170*

baste [*v2*] *sew temporarily*
catch, fasten, stitch, tack; SEE CONCEPT *218*

baste [*v3*] *pummel, thrash*
batter, beat, berate, blister, clobber, club, drub, lambaste, lash, maul, pelt, revile, scold, trounce, wallop, whip, whomp; SEE CONCEPTS *52,189*

bastion [*n*] *support; fortified place*
breastwork, bulwark, citadel, defense, fortification, fortress, mainstay, parapet, prop, protection, rock, stronghold, support, tower of strength; SEE CONCEPT *712*

bat [*n/v*] *a hit with a solid object*
bang, belt, blow, bop, crack, knock, rap, slam, smack, sock, strike, swat, thump, thwack, wallop, whack, whop; SEE CONCEPT *189*

batch [*n*] *group of same objects*
accumulation, aggregation, amount, array, assemblage, assortment, bunch, bundle, clump, cluster, clutch, collection, crowd, group, lot, pack, parcel, quantity, set, shipment, volume; SEE CONCEPTS *432,787*

bath [*n1*] *washing with water and, usually, soap*
ablution, cleansing, dip, douche, dousing, gargle, laving, scrubbing, shower, soak, soaking, soaping, sponging, tub, wash; SEE CONCEPTS *161,165*

bath [*n2*] *room for bathing*
bathroom, lavatory, powder room, restroom, sauna, shower, shower room, spa, steam room, toilet, washroom; SEE CONCEPT *448*

bathe [*v*] *wash with water and, usually, soap*
bath, clean, cleanse, dip, douse, dunk, flood, hose, imbathe, imbue, immerse, moisten, rinse, scour, scrub, shower, soak, soap, sponge, steep, submerge, suffuse, tub, water, wet; SEE CONCEPTS *161,165*

bathing suit [*n*] *clothing for swimming, sunning*
bathing costume, beach costume, bikini, maillot, one-piece, swimsuit, trunks, two-piece; SEE CONCEPT *451*

bathos [*n*] *sentimentality*
anticlimax, comedown, letdown, melodrama, mush, schmaltz*; SEE CONCEPTS *32,410,689*

bathroom [*n*] *room for bathing, toilet use*
bath, lavatory, powder room, restroom, sauna, shower, shower room, spa, steam room, toilet, washroom, water closet; SEE CONCEPT *448*

baton [*n*] *stick used for conducting or for protection*
billy, billy club, blackjack, club, cudgel, mace, nightstick, rod, staff, truncheon, wand; SEE CONCEPTS *262,470,500*

battalion [*n*] *military division*
army, brigade, company, contingent, corps, force, horde, host, legion, multitude, regiment, squadron, throng, unit; SEE CONCEPT *322*

batten [*v1*] *fasten securely*
board up, clamp down, cover up, fix, nail down, secure, tie, tighten; SEE CONCEPTS *85,160*

batten [*v2*] *grow fat*
burgeon, feed on, grow, prosper, thrive, wax; SEE CONCEPT *704*

batter [*n*] *mixture before baking*
concoction, dough, mix, mush*, paste, preparation, recipe; SEE CONCEPTS *457,466*

batter [*v*] *strike and damage*
assault, bash, beat, break, bruise, buffet, clobber, contuse, cripple, crush, dash, deface, demolish, destroy, disable, disfigure, drub, hurt, injure, lacerate, lambaste, lame, lash, mangle, mar, maul, mutilate, pelt, pommel, pound, pummel, punish, ruin, shatter, smash, thrash, wallop, wreck; SEE CONCEPTS *189,246,252*

battery [*n1*] *series of similar things*
array, batch, body, bunch, bundle, chain, clot, clump, cluster, group, lot, ring, sequence, set, suite; SEE CONCEPT *432*

battery [*n2*] *physical abuse*
assault, attack, beating, mayhem, mugging, onslaught, thumping, violence; SEE CONCEPTS *189,246*

battery [*n3*] *group of weapons*
artillery, cannon, cannonry, gunnery unit, guns; SEE CONCEPTS *321,500*

battle [*n1*] *military fight*
action, assault, attack, barrage, blitzkrieg, bloodshed, bombing, brush, campaign, carnage, clash, combat, conflict, contention, crusade, encounter, engagement, fighting, fray, havoc, hostility, onset, onslaught, press, ravage, scrimmage, significant contact, skirmish, sortie, strife, struggle, war, warfare; SEE CONCEPT *106*

battle [*n2*] *struggle*
agitation, campaign, clash, conflict, contest, controversy, crusade, debate, disagreement, dispute, strife; SEE CONCEPTS *46,106*

battle [*v*] *fight, struggle*
agitate, argue, clamor, combat, contend, contest, dispute, feud, oppugn, skirmish, strive, tug, war, wrestle; SEE CONCEPTS *46,106*

battlefield [*n*] *location of military fights*
arena, Armageddon, battleground, combat zone, field, front, front line, salient, theater of operations, theater of war; SEE CONCEPTS *198,321*

bawdy [*adj*] *vulgar, dirty*
blue, cheap, coarse, erotic, gross, indecent, indecorous, indelicate, lascivious, lecherous, lewd, libidinous, licentious, lustful, obscene, off-color, prurient, ribald, risqué, rude, salacious, suggestive; SEE CONCEPT *545*

bawl [*v1*] *yell*
bark, bellow, bluster, call, cheer, clamor, holler, howl, roar, rout, scream, screech, shout, shriek, vociferate; SEE CONCEPT *77*

bawl [*v2*] *cry*
blubber*, boohoo*, howl, shed tears, sob, squall, wail, weep, yowl; SEE CONCEPTS *77,185*

bay [*n1*] *shoreline indentation*
anchorage, arm, basin, bayou, bight, cove, estuary, fiord, firth, gulf, harbor, inlet, lagoon, loch, mouth, narrows, sound, strait; SEE CONCEPTS *509,514*

bay [*n2*] *alcove in wall*
bow window, compartment, niche, nook, opening, oriel, recess; SEE CONCEPT *440*

bay [*n3*] *howl*
bark, bellow, clamor, cry, growl, howl, ululation, wail, yelp; SEE CONCEPT *64*

bazaar [*n*] *fair; sale place*
exchange, exposition, fete, market, marketplace, mart; SEE CONCEPTS *345,438,449*

bboard [*n*] *electronic messaging system*
BBS, board, bulletin board, bulletin board system; SEE CONCEPTS *349,770*

• **be** [*v1*] *exist*
abide, act, be alive, breathe, continue, do, endure, go on, have being, have place, hold, inhabit, last, live, move, obtain, persist, prevail, remain, rest, stand, stay, subsist, survive; SEE CONCEPT *407*

be [*v2*] *happen*
befall, come about, come to pass, occur, take place, transpire; SEE CONCEPT *2*

beach [*n*] *sandy area by body of water*
bank, coast, lakeshore, lakeside, littoral, margin, oceanfront, seaboard, seafront, seashore, seaside, shingle, shore, strand, waterfront; SEE CONCEPTS *509,514*

beached [*adj*] *grounded*
abandoned, aground, ashore, deserted, high and dry, marooned, stranded, wrecked; SEE CONCEPT *583*

beacon [*n*] *light used as signal, guide*
alarm, alert, balefire, beam, bonfire, flare, guidepost, heliograph, lamp, lantern, lighthouse, lodestar, pharos, radar, rocket, sign, signal fire, smoke signal, warning signal, watchtower; SEE CONCEPT *628*

bead [*n*] *droplet, blob*
bean, bubble, dab, dot, driblet, drop, globule, grain, particle, pea, pellet, pill, shot, speck, spherule, stone; SEE CONCEPT *436*

beads [*n*] *string of small, often round, objects*
chaplet, choker, necklace, necklet, pearls, pendant, rosary, wampum; SEE CONCEPTS *368,446*

beak [*n*] *nose of animal*
bill, mandible, muzzle, neb, nib, nozzle, pecker, proboscis, projection, prow, snout; SEE CONCEPT *392*

beam [*n1*] *length of material used as support*
axle, bail, balk, bolster, boom, brace, cantilever, column, crossbar, crosspiece, girder, jamb, joist, lath, lintel, pile, piling, pillar, plank, pole, post, prop, rafter, reach, scaffolding, scantling, shaft, sill, spar, stanchion, stay, stringer, strip, strut, stud, timber, transverse, trestle, two-by-four; SEE CONCEPTS *471,479*

beam [*n2*] *ray of light*
bar, beacon, chink, column, dartle, emission, finger, flicker, glare, gleam, glimmer, glint, glitter, glow, laser, radiation, ray, shaft, shimmer, shoot, sparkle, streak, stream, twinkle; SEE CONCEPTS *624,628*

beam [*v1*] *broadcast on air waves*
emit, give off, give out, glare, glimmer, glow, radiate, send, shed, shine, throw off, transmit; SEE CONCEPTS *519,624*

beam [*v2*] *smile broadly*
gleam, glow, grin, laugh, radiate, shine, smirk; SEE CONCEPT *185*

beam [*v3*] *shine, as a light*
burn, emit, glare, gleam, glitter, glow, radiate, yield; SEE CONCEPT *624*

beam [*v4*] *make electronic transfer*
emit, radiate, send out, transfer file, transmit, transmit signal; SEE CONCEPT *266*

beaming [*adj*] *radiant; beautiful*
bright, brilliant, effulgent, flashing, fulgent, gleaming, glistening, glittering, glowing, incandescent, lambent, lucent, luminous, refulgent, scintillating, sparkling; SEE CONCEPT *617*

beaming [*adj2*] *very happy*
animated, cheerful, genial, grinning, joyful, radiant, shining, smiling, sparkling, sunny; SEE CONCEPT *401*

bean counter [*n*] *number cruncher*
accountant, actuary, analyst, auditor, bookkeeper, certified public accountant, comptroller, CPA, financial executive, statistician, treasurer; SEE CONCEPTS *348,353*

beanpole [*n*] *a tall, thin person*
beanstalk*, broomstick*, hatrack*, stick*, string bean*; SEE CONCEPT *417*

bear [*v1*] *bring*
buck, carry, convey, deliver, ferry, fetch, lug, move, pack, take, tote, transfer, transport; SEE CONCEPTS *108,143*

bear [*v2*] *support mentally*
cherish, entertain, exhibit, harbor, have, hold, hold up, maintain, possess, shoulder, sustain, uphold, weigh upon; SEE CONCEPTS *8,12*

bear [*v3*] *endure*
abide, admit, allow, brook, encounter, experience, permit, put up with, stomach, suffer, tolerate, undergo; SEE CONCEPTS *23,239*

bear [*v4*] *give birth*
be delivered of, beget, breed, bring forth, create, develop, engender, form, fructify, generate, invent, make, parturiate, produce, propagate, provide, reproduce, yield; SEE CONCEPTS *173,251,302,373*

bearable [*adj*] *endurable*
acceptable, admissible, allowable, livable, manageable, passable, satisfactory, sufferable, supportable, sustainable, tolerable; SEE CONCEPT *529*

beard [*n1*] *facial hair on human*
bristles, brush, five-o-clock shadow*, fuzz, goatee, imperial, muttonchops, Santa Claus*, stubble, Vandyke*; SEE CONCEPT *418*

beard [*n2*] *decoy*
false face, front, mask; SEE CONCEPT *716*

beard [*v*] *confront*
brave, face, oppose, stand up to; SEE CONCEPTS *46,96*

bearded [*adj*] *having facial hair*
barbate, beardy, bewhiskered, bristly, bushy, goateed, hairy, hirsute, shaggy, stubbled, stubbly, unshaven, whiskered; SEE CONCEPTS *406,485*

bear down [*v*] *close in on*
advance on, approach, converge on, near, press, weigh down; SEE CONCEPTS *152,208,704*

bearer [*n1*] *person who carries messages or deliveries*
agent, beast of burden*, carrier, conveyor, courier, drogher, emissary, envoy, internuncio, messenger, porter, runner, servant, shipper, transporter; SEE CONCEPT *348*

bearer [*n2*] *person who requests payment of bill*
beneficiary, casher, collector, consignee, payee; SEE CONCEPT *353*

bearing [*n1*] *person's conduct, posture*
address, air, aspect, attitude, behavior, carriage, comportment, demeanor, deportment, display, front, look, manner, mien, poise, port, pose, presence, set, stand; SEE CONCEPTS *411,633*

bearing [*n2*] *significance*
application, connection, import, meaning, pertinence, reference, relation, relevance, weight; SEE CONCEPT *668*

bearing/bearings [*n3*] *position, usually of water vehicle*
aim, course, direction, location, orientation, point of compass, position, situation, track, way, whereabouts; SEE CONCEPTS *739,746*

bear in mind [*v*] *be aware of*
be cognizant of, be mindful of, beware, consider, heed, mind, note, remember; SEE CONCEPTS *17,623*

bear on/bear upon [*v*] *concern*
affect, appertain to, apply, belong to, involve, pertain to, refer to, relate to, touch upon; SEE CONCEPT *532*

bear out [*v*] *substantiate*
authenticate, confirm, corroborate, endorse, justify, prove, substantiate, support, uphold, validate, verify, vindicate; SEE CONCEPTS *50,88,97*

bear up [*v*] *endure*
carry on, persevere, soldier on, suffer, withstand; SEE CONCEPT *23*

bear with [*v*] *tolerate*
be patient, endure, forbear, make allowance, put up with, suffer, wait; SEE CONCEPT *23*

bear witness [*v*] *vouch for*
attest, confirm, corroborate, demonstrate, depose, evidence, evince, prove, show, testify, testify to; SEE CONCEPTS *49,71,317*

beast [*n*] *large wild animal; brute*
barbarian, beastie*, creature, critter*, fiend, gargoyle, glutton, lower animal, monster, monstros-

.ity, pig, quadruped, swine, varmint*; SEE CON-
CEPT **394**

beastly [*adv1*] *savage; vulgar*
abominable, animal, barbarous, base, bestial,
boorish, brutal, brute, brutish, carnal, coarse,
cruel, degraded, depraved, disgusting, feral, ferine, foul, gluttonous, gross, inhuman, irrational,
loathsome, low, monstrous, obscene, piggish,
prurient, repulsive, sadistic, swinish, unclean,
vile; SEE CONCEPT **401**

beastly [*adv2*] *offensive*
awful, disagreeable, disgusting, foul, gross,
mean, nasty, revolting, rotten, terrible, unpleasant, vile; SEE CONCEPTS **537,542**

beat [*adj*] *very tired*
dog tired*, exhausted, fatigued, kaput*, wearied,
weary, worn out; SEE CONCEPTS **316,720**

beat [*n1*] *throbbing*
cadence, cadency, flow, flutter, measure, meter,
oscillation, palpitation, pound, pressure, pulsation, pulse, quake, quiver, rhyme, rhythm, ripple,
shake, surge, swell, swing, throb, thump, tick,
undulation, vibration; SEE CONCEPTS **150,185**

beat [*n2*] *blow, stroke*
hit, lash, punch, shake, slap, strike, swing,
thump; SEE CONCEPT **189**

beat [*n3*] *area of responsibility*
circuit, course, march, path, patrol, precinct,
rounds, route, walk, way; SEE CONCEPTS **513,532**

beat [*v1*] *injure by striking*
bang, bash, bat, batter, belt, box, break, bruise,
buffet, cane, castigate, clout, club, collide, crush,
cudgel, drub, flagellate, flail, flog, hammer, hit,
knock, lambaste*, lash, lick*, maltreat, mash,
maul, pelt, pound, pummel, punch, punish, ram,
rap, slap, slug, smack, spank, strike, swat, thrash,
thresh, thump, thwack, trounce, wallop, whale*,
whip; SEE CONCEPTS **189,246**

beat [*v2*] *defeat, surpass*
best, better, be victorious, conquer, exceed,
excel, outdo, outplay, outrival, outrun, outshine,
outstrip, overcome, overtake, overwhelm, shoot
ahead of, subdue, top, transcend, triumph, vanquish, whip; SEE CONCEPTS **95,141**

beat [*v3*] *forge*
fashion, form, hammer, malleate, model, pound,
shape, work; SEE CONCEPTS **137,175**

beat [*v4*] *throb*
agitate, alternate, bob, bounce, buffet, flap,
flicker, fluctuate, flutter, heave, jerk, jounce, oscillate, palpitate, pitch, pound, pulsate, pulse,
quake, quaver, quiver, ripple, shake, shiver,
swing, thrill, throb, thump, tremble, twitch, undulate, vibrate, writhe; SEE CONCEPTS **150,185**

beat [*v5*] *mix*
stir, whip; SEE CONCEPT **170**

beaten [*adj1*] *defeated*
baffled, bested, circumvented, conquered,
cowed, crushed, disappointed, discomfited, disheartened, frustrated, humbled, licked, mastered,
overcome, overpowered, overthrown, overwhelmed, routed, ruined, subjugated, sur-
mounted, thwarted, trounced, undone,
vanquished, worsted; SEE CONCEPTS **403,674**

beaten [*adj2*] *forged*
formed, hammered, milled, pounded, rolled,
shaped, stamped, tamped, tramped, tramped
down, trodden, worked; SEE CONCEPTS **486,490**

beaten [*adj3*] *mixed*
aerated, blended, bubbly, churned, creamy,

foamy, frothy, meringued, stirred, whipped,
whisked; SEE CONCEPTS **491,606**

beat it [*v*] *go away*
leave, scram, shoo, skedaddle, vamoose; SEE
CONCEPT **195**

beatitude [*n*] *blessedness*
bliss, ecstasy, felicity, happiness, peace, serenity;
SEE CONCEPT **410**

beatnik [*n*] *uncoventional, free-sprited person*
beat, Bohemian, demonstrator, dropout, flower
child*, hippie, iconoclast, maverick, nonconformist, peacenik*, protester, radical; SEE CON-
CEPT **423**

beat up [*v*] *assault*
attack, batter, do over, hammer, knock around,
pulverize, thrash; SEE CONCEPTS **52,86**

beau [*n*] *boyfriend*
admirer, beloved, cavalier, escort, fiancé, flame,
gentleman caller, gentleman friend, honey, inamorato, love, lover, paramour, squire, steady,
suitor, swain, sweetheart, true love; SEE CONCEPT
423

beautiful [*adj*] *physically attractive*
admirable, alluring, angelic, appealing, beauteous, bewitching, charming, classy, comely,
cute, dazzling, delicate, delightful, divine, elegant, enticing, excellent, exquisite, fair, fascinating, fine, foxy*, good-looking, gorgeous,
graceful, grand, handsome, ideal, lovely, magnificent, marvelous, nice, pleasing, pretty, pulchritudinous, radiant, ravishing, refined, resplendent,
shapely, sightly, splendid, statuesque, stunning,
sublime, superb, symmetrical, taking, well-
formed, wonderful; SEE CONCEPTS **485,579,589**

beautifully [*adv*] *in an attractive or pleasing
manner*
alluringly, appealingly, attractively, bewitch-
ingly, celestially, charmingly, cutely, delightfully, divinely, elegantly, entrancingly,
excellently, exquisitely, gorgeously, gracefully,
handsomely, ideally, magnificently, prettily, se-
ductively, splendidly, sublimely, superbly, taste-
fully, wonderfully; SEE CONCEPT **544**

beautify [*v*] *make more physically attractive*
adorn, array, bedeck, deck, decorate, dress up,
embellish, enhance, garnish, gild, glamorize,
grace, improve, make up, ornament, prettify, set
off, trim; SEE CONCEPT **162**

beauty [*n1*] *physical attractiveness*
adorableness, allure, allurement, artistry, attraction, bloom, charm, class, comeliness, delicacy,
elegance, exquisiteness, fairness, fascination,
glamor, good looks, grace, handsomeness, loveliness, polish, pulchritude, refinement, shapeliness, style, symmetry, winsomeness; SEE
CONCEPT **718**

beauty [*n2*] *good-looking person*
Adonis*, Apollo*, beaut*, charmer, dream,
dreamboat*, enchanter, eyeful*, good-looker*,
head turner*, looker*, ornament*, stunner*,
Venus*, vision; SEE CONCEPT **424**

beauty [*n3*] *advantage*
asset, attraction, benefit, blessing, boon, excellent, feature, good thing, importance, merit,
value, worth; SEE CONCEPT **668**

because [*conj/prep*] *on account of*
as, as a result of, as long as, as things go, being,
by cause of, by reason of, by virtue of, considering, due to, for, for the reason that, for the sake
of, in as much as, in behalf of, in that, in the in-

terest of, in view of, now that, on the grounds that, over, owing to, seeing, since, thanks to, through, whereas; SEE CONCEPT *676*

beckon [*vl*] *call, signal, or lure*
allure, ask, attract, bid, coax, command, demand, draw, entice, gesticulate, gesture, invite, motion, nod, pull, sign, summon, tempt, wave; SEE CONCEPTS *7,22,53,74*

become [*v1*] *evolve into*
alter to, assume form of, be converted to, be reduced to, be reformed, be remodeled, be transformed into, change into, come, come to be, convert, develop into, emerge as, eventually be, grow into, incline, mature, metamorphose, pass into, ripen into, shift, turn into, turn out, wax; SEE CONCEPT *701*

become [*v2*] *enhance*
accord, adorn, agree, augment, be appropriate, belong to, display, embellish, enrich, fit, flatter, garnish, go together, go with, grace, harmonize, heighten, make handsome, match, ornament, set off, suit; SEE CONCEPT *244*

becoming [*adjl*] *flattering*
acceptable, agreeable, attractive, beautiful, comely, cute, effective, enhancing, excellent, fair, graceful, handsome, neat, nice, presentable, pretty, seemly, tasteful, welcome, well-chosen; SEE CONCEPTS *579,589*

becoming [*adj2*] *suitable; appropriate*
befitting, comme il faut, compatible, conforming, congruous, correct, decent, decorous, fit, fitting, in keeping, nice, proper, right, seemly, worthy; SEE CONCEPT *558*

bed [*nl*] *furniture for sleeping*
bassinet, bedstead, berth, bunk, chaise, cot, couch, cradle, crib, davenport, divan, mattress, pallet, platform, sack, trundle; SEE CONCEPT *443*

bed [*n2*] *patch of ground for planting*
area, border, frame, garden, piece, plot, row, strip; SEE CONCEPTS *509,513*

bed [*n3*] *base, foundation*
basis, bedrock, bottom, ground, groundwork, rest, seat, substratum, understructure; SEE CONCEPT *442*

bed [*v*] *plant*
base, embed, establish, fix, found, implant, insert, settle, set up; SEE CONCEPTS *234,257*

bedazzle [*v*] *captivate*
astound, bewilder, blind, confuse, daze, dazzle, dumbfound, enchant, overwhelm, stagger, stun; SEE CONCEPTS *7,22,42*

bedding [*n*] *covering for sleeping furniture*
bedclothes, bed linen, bedspread, blanket, comforter, cover, coverlet, eiderdown, electric blanket, linen, pillow, pillowcase, quilt, sheet, spread, thermal blanket; SEE CONCEPTS *444,473*

bedlam [*n*] *chaotic situation*
chaos, clamor, commotion, confusion, din, disquiet, disquietude, furor, hubbub, madhouse, maelstrom, noise, pandemonium, racket, shambles, tumult, turmoil, uproar; SEE CONCEPTS *230,674*

bedraggled [*adj*] *unkempt*
decrepit, dilapidated, dirty, disheveled, disordered, dowdy, drenched, dripping, faded, messy, muddied, muddy, run-down, seedy, shabby, sloppy, slovenly, sodden, soiled, stained, sullied, tacky, tattered, threadbare, untidy, wet; SEE CONCEPT *589*

bedridden [*adj*] *sick in bed*
ailing, disabled, flat on one's back*, ill, incapacitated, infirm, invalid, laid up*, prostrate; SEE CONCEPTS *314,485,489*

bedroom [*n*] *place for sleeping*
bedchamber, bunk room, chamber, cubicle, guest room; SEE CONCEPT *448*

bedspread [*n*] *thick, often quilted, covering for bed*
bedcover, blanket, counterpane, cover, coverlet, spread; SEE CONCEPT *444*

bee [*nl*] *honey-making, stinging insect*
bumblebee, drone, honey bee, killer bee, queen bee; SEE CONCEPT *398*

bee [*n2*] *collective task*
communal gathering, harvest, party, social, work party; SEE CONCEPTS *362,386*

beef [*nl*] *strong physical makeup*
arm, brawn, flesh, force, heftiness, meat, might, muscle, physique, power, robustness, sinew, steam, strength, thew, vigor; SEE CONCEPT *757*

beef [*n2*] *complaint*
bickering, criticism, dispute, grievance, gripe, grouse, grumble, objection, protestation, quarrel, rhubarb*, squabble; SEE CONCEPT *52*

beep [*n*] *sound from electronic device*
bell sound, bleep, breedle, computer sound, ding, eep, feep, signal, tone, warning; SEE CONCEPTS *74,284,529,685*

beep [*v*] *call for electronically*
call, page, summon, track down, warn; SEE CONCEPT *74*

beer [*n*] *alcoholic beverage made from malted grain*
ale, amber brew*, barley pop*, brew, brewski*, brown bottle*, chill*, cold coffee*, cold one*, hops, lager, malt, malt liquor, oil*, stout*, suds*; SEE CONCEPT *455*

befall [*v*] *happen to; take place*
action, bechance, betide, break, chance, come down, come off, come to pass, cook*, cook up a storm*, cook with gas*, develop, ensue, fall, fall out, follow, gel, go, go down, hap*, happen, jell*, materialize, occur, shake*, smoke*, supervene, transpire; SEE CONCEPT *4*

befitting [*adj*] *appropriate*
according to Hoyle*, apt, becoming, behooving, beseeming, comme il faut, conforming, correct, decent, decorous, felicitous, fit, fitting, happy, just, kosher*, nice, on the button*, on the nose*, proper, right, right on*, seemly, suitable, what the doctor ordered*; SEE CONCEPTS *533,558*

before [*adv*] *earlier*
afore, aforetime, ahead, ante, antecedently, anteriorly, back, before present, ere, fore, former, formerly, forward, gone, gone by, heretofore, in advance, in days of yore, in front, in old days, in the past, past, precendently, previous, previously, since, sooner, up to now; SEE CONCEPT *820*

before [*prep*] *earlier than*
ahead of, ante, antecedent to, anterior to, ere, in advance of, in front of, preceding, previous to, prior to, since; SEE CONCEPT *820*

beforehand [*adj/adv*] *early*
advanced, ahead, ahead of time, already, ante, antecedently, before, before now, earlier, fore, in advance, in anticipation, precedently, precocious, previous, previously, sooner; SEE CONCEPT *820*

be
be

befriend [*v*] *make social acquaintance; support*
advise, aid, assist, back, benefit, buddy up*, case out*, come on to*, cotton to*, encourage, favor, get chummy with, get in with*, help, hit it off*, patronize, side with, stand by, sustain, take under one's wing*, take up with, uphold, welcome; SEE CONCEPTS **110,384**

befuddle [*v*] *confuse*
addle, baffle, ball up*, bewilder, bother, daze, disorient, distract, dumbfound, fluster, inebriate, intoxicate, make punchy*, mix up, muddle, puzzle, shake, stupefy, throw off*; SEE CONCEPTS **7,19,42**

beg [*v1*] *request*
abjure, advocate, apply to, ask, beseech, besiege, call to, canvass, conjure, crave, desire, entreat, impetrate, implore, importune, invoke, nag, obsecrate, obtest, petition, plead, pray, press, requisition, solicit, sue, supplicate, urge, woo, worry; SEE CONCEPT **48**

beg [*v2*] *seek charity*
ask alms, benefit, bite*, brace, bum*, burn*, buzz*, cadge*, call on, call upon, chisel*, clamor for, dime up*, ding*, freeload*, hit up*, hustle, knock, live hand to mouth*, mendicate, mooch*, nick*, nickel up*, panhandle, pass the hat*, put the bite on*, put the touch on*, score*, scrounge, solicit charity, sponge*, sponge on*, tap, touch, want; SEE CONCEPT **53**

beget [*v*] *create, bear*
afford, breed, bring, bring about, cause, effect, engender, father, generate, get, give rise to, multiply, occasion, procreate, produce, progenerate, propagate, reproduce, result in, sire; SEE CONCEPTS **173,251,374**

beggar [*n1*] *person asking for charity*
asker, borrower, bum, deadbeat, hobo, mendicant, panhandler, rustler, scrounger, supplicant, supplicator, tramp, vagabond; SEE CONCEPTS **412,423**

beggar [*n2*] *person in financial trouble*
alms person, bankrupt, dependent, down-and-out*, guttersnipe*, indigent, mendicant, pauper, poor person, poverty-stricken person, street person*, suppliant, vagrant, ward of state; SEE CONCEPT **423**

begin [*v1*] *start*
activate, actualize, break ground, break the ice*, bring about, bring to pass, cause, commence, create, do, drive, effect, embark on, enter on, enter upon, establish, eventuate, found, generate, get going, give birth to, give impulse to, go ahead, go into, impel, inaugurate, induce, initiate, instigate, institute, introduce, launch, lay foundation for, lead, make, make active, motivate, mount, occasion, open, originate, plunge into, prepare, produce, set about, set in motion, set up, trigger, undertake; SEE CONCEPTS **234,241**

begin [*v2*] *come into being; become functional*
appear, arise, be born, bud, come forth, come into existence, come out, commence, crop up, dawn, derive from, emanate, emerge, enter, germinate, get going, get show on road*, get under way, grow out of, happen, issue forth, result from, rise, sail, send off, set, spring, sprout, start, stem from, take off; SEE CONCEPTS **105,680**

beginner [*n*] *person unskilled in something*
abecedarian, amateur, apprentice, buckwheater*, catechumen, colt, fish*, fledgling, greenhorn, greenie*, initiate, learner, neophyte, newcomer, new kid on the block*, new person, novice, novitiate, probationer, recruit, starter, student, tenderfoot*, trainee, tyro; SEE CONCEPTS **423,424**

beginning [*n1*] *start of an event or action*
alpha, basis, birth, blastoff*, commencement, creation, dawn, dawning, day one*, genesis, inauguration, inception, induction, infancy, initiation, installation, introduction, kickoff, onset, opener, opening, origin, origination, outset, point of departure, preface, prelude, presentation, rise, root, rudiment, source, spring, square one*, starting point, takeoff, threshold, top; SEE CONCEPTS **815,833**

beginning [*n2*] *origin, cause*
antecedent, birth, conception, egg, embryo, font, fount, fountain, fountainhead, generation, genesis, germ, heart, principle, resource, root, seed, stem, well; SEE CONCEPT **229**

begrudge [*v*] *wish that someone did not have*
be jealous, be reluctant, be stingy, covet, eat one's heart out, envy, grudge, pinch, resent, stint; SEE CONCEPTS **17,21**

beguile [*v1*] *fool*
betray, bluff, burn*, cheat, chisel, con, deceive, delude, double-cross, dupe, entice, exploit, finesse, flimflam*, gyp*, have, hoodwink*, impose on, jockey, juggle, lure, manipulate, mislead, play, play for a sucker*, rook*, rope in*, scam, seduce, shave*, snow*, stick*, string along, suck in*, take, take in, trick; SEE CONCEPT **59**

beguile [*v2*] *charm*
amuse, attract, cheer, delight, distract, divert, engross, entertain, entice, knock dead, knock out, lure, occupy, seduce, send, slay, solace, sweep off one's feet, tickle, tickle pink*, tickle to death*, turn on, vamp, wow*; SEE CONCEPTS **7,19,22**

behalf [*n*] *personal interest*
account, advantage, aid, assistance, benefit, cause, concern, countenance, defense, encouragement, favor, furtherance, good, help, part, place, profit, recommendation, representation, sake, service, side, stead, support, welfare; SEE CONCEPTS **410,532**

behave [*v1*] *function*
act, operate, perform, react, run, take, work; SEE CONCEPTS **1,4**

behave [*v2*] *act reasonably, properly*
act correctly, act one's age, act with decorum, be civil, be good, be nice, be on best behavior*, be orderly, comport oneself, conduct oneself properly, control, demean oneself, deport oneself, direct, discipline oneself, keep one's nose clean*, keep the peace, live up to, manage, manage oneself, mind one's manners*, mind one's p's and q's*, observe golden rule*, observe the law, play fair, shape up, toe the mark*, watch one's step*; SEE CONCEPT **633**

behavior [*n*] *manner of conducting oneself*
act, action, address, air, attitude, bag*, bearing, carriage, code, comportment, conduct, convention, course, dealings, decency, decorum, deed, delivery, demeanor, deportment, ethics, etiquette, expression, form, front, guise, habits, management, mien, mode, morals, nature, observance, performance, practice, presence, propriety, ritual, role, routine, savoir-faire, seemliness, social graces, speech, style, tact, talk, taste,

tenue, tone, way, way of life, ways, what's done*; SEE CONCEPTS 633,655

behead [v] *decapitate*
bring to the block, decollate, execute, guillotine, head, kill, neck; SEE CONCEPT 176

behest [n] *order; personal decree*
bidding, charge, command, commandment, demand, dictate, direction, expressed desire, injunction, instruction, mandate, order, precept, prompting, request, solicitation*, wish, word; SEE CONCEPTS 20,53

behind [adv1/prep1] *position farther back; following*
abaft, after, afterwards, at the heels of*, at the rear of, back of, bringing up the rear*, eating the dust*, in the background, in the wake, later than, next, off the pace, subsequently, trailing; SEE CONCEPTS 586,820

behind [adv2] *in debt; late*
backward, behindhand, behind schedule, behind time, belated, delayed, dilatory, have to play catch up*, in arrears, laggard, overdue, slow, sluggish, tardy; SEE CONCEPTS 334,799

behind [n] *buttocks*
backside, bottom, breech, can*, derrière, fanny*, fundament, posterior, rear, rump, seat, tail, tush*; SEE CONCEPT 392

behind [prep2] *being the reason for*
at the bottom of, causing, concerning the circumstances, initiating, instigating, responsible for; SEE CONCEPT 532

behind [prep3] *in support*
backing, for, in agreement, on the side of, supporting; SEE CONCEPT 388

behind one's back [adv] *deceitfully*
covertly, secretly, sneakily, sub rosa, surreptitiously; SEE CONCEPTS 267,548

behind the times [adj] *old-fashioned*
antiquated, dated, obsolete, old hat*, outdated, outmoded, out of date, passe, square; SEE CONCEPTS 578,589,797,799

behold [v] *regard; look at*
catch, consider, contemplate, descry, discern, distinguish, earmark, eye, eyeball*, feast one's eyes*, flash*, lay eyes on*, note, notice, observe, perceive, regard, scan, see, spot, spy, survey, view, watch, witness; SEE CONCEPTS 34,626

beholden [adj] *indebted*
bound, grateful, in hock, into, obligated, obliged, on a string*, on the arm*, on the cuff*, on the tab*, owe one, owing, responsible, under obligation; SEE CONCEPT 403

behoove [v] *be necessary, proper*
be expected, befit, be fitting, be incumbent upon, be needful, be one's obligation, be required, be requisite, be right, beseem, owe it to, suit; SEE CONCEPT 646

beige [n/adj] *light brown color*
biscuit, buff, café au lait, camel, cream, ecru, fawn, khaki, mushroom, neutral, oatmeal, off-white, sand, tan, taupe; SEE CONCEPTS 618,622

being [n1] *existence*
actuality, animation, journey, life, living, presence, reality, subsistence, vitality, world; SEE CONCEPT 407

being [n2] *essential nature*
character, entity, essence, essentia, essentiality, individuality, marrow, personality, quintessence, self, soul, spirit, substance, texture; SEE CONCEPTS 411,673

being [n3] *animate object*
animal, beast, body, conscious thing, creature, entity, human, human being, individual, living thing, mortal, organism, person, personage, soul, thing; SEE CONCEPT 389

belabor [v] *dwell on*
beat a dead horse*, go on about, hammer home, overwork, pound, rehash, repeat; SEE CONCEPT 56

belated [adj] *late, slow*
behindhand, behind time, delayed, long-delayed, overdue, remiss, tardy, unpunctual; SEE CONCEPT 820

belch [v] *burp; spew*
discharge, disgorge, emit, eruct, eructate, erupt, give off, gush, hiccup, irrupt, repeat, ventilate, vomit; SEE CONCEPT 185

beleaguer [v] *harass, besiege*
annoy, badger, bedevil, beset, blockade, bother, gnaw, harry, nag, persecute, pester, plague, put upon, set upon, siege, storm, tease, vex, worry; SEE CONCEPTS 7,19

belfry [n] *tower; part of tower*
bell tower, campanile, carillon, clocher, cupola, dome, head, minaret, spire, steeple, turret; SEE CONCEPT 440

belie [v1] *disprove*
confute, contradict, contravene, controvert, deny, disaffirm, disagree, explode, gainsay, negate, negative, oppose, repudiate; SEE CONCEPTS 54,58

belie [v2] *deceive*
color, conceal, disguise, distort, falsify, garble, give the lie to, gloss over, hide, miscolor, mislead, misrepresent, misstate, pervert, trump up, twist, warp; SEE CONCEPT 63

belief [n1] *putting regard in as true*
acceptance, admission, assent, assumption, assurance, avowal, axiom, certainty, conclusion, confidence, conjecture, conviction, credence, credit, deduction, divination, expectation, faith, fancy, feeling, guess, hope, hypothesis, idea, impression, intuition, judgment, knowledge, mind, mindset, notion, opinion, persuasion, position, postulation, presumption, presupposition, profession, reliance, supposition, surmise, suspicion, theorem, theory, thesis, thinking, trust, understanding, view; SEE CONCEPTS 410,529

belief [n2] *something regarded as true*
assumption, concept, credence, credo, creed, doctrine, dogma, faith, fundamental, gospel, gospel truth*, hypothesis, idea, ideology, law, opinion, postulate, precept, principle, say-so*, tenet, theorem, theory; SEE CONCEPT 689

believable [adj] *trustworthy*
aboveboard, acceptable, authentic, colorable, conceivable, convincing, credential, credible, creditable, fiduciary, honest-to-God*, imaginable, impressive, likely, persuasive, plausible, possible, presumable, presumptive, probable, rational, reasonable, reliable, satisfying, straight, supposable, tenable, tried, trusty, unquestionable, up front*; SEE CONCEPTS 403,582

believe [v1] *trust, rely on*
accept, accredit, admit, affirm, attach weight to, be certain of, be convinced of, be credulous, be of the opinion, buy*, conceive, conclude, consider, count on, credit, deem, fall for*, give credence to, have, have faith in, have no doubt, hold, keep the faith, lap up*, place confidence in, posit, postulate, presume true, presuppose,

reckon on, regard, rest assured, suppose, swallow*, swear by, take as gospel*, take at one's word, take for granted, take it, think, trust, understand; SEE CONCEPT *12*

believe [*v2*] *assume or suppose*
conjecture, consider, credit, deem, expect, feel, gather, guess, hold, imagine, judge, maintain, postulate, presume, reckon, sense, speculate, suppose, suspect, take, think, understand; SEE CONCEPT *28*

believer [*n*] *person who has faith in something*
acceptor, adherent, apostle, canonist, convert, devotee, disciple, doctrinaire, dogmatist, follower, freak, orthodox, prophet, proselyte, religionist, religious person, supporter, upholder, zealot; SEE CONCEPTS *361,423*

belittle [*v*] *detract*
bad-mouth, blister, criticize, cut down to size*, cut to the quick*, decry, deprecate, depreciate, deride, derogate, diminish, discount, discredit, disparage, dispraise, · downgrade, downplay, dump on*, knock*, lower, minimize, pan, pooh pooh*, poor mouth*, put down, rip*, roast*, run down, scoff at, scorch*, scorn, shoot down*, shoot full of holes*, slam*, smear, sneer at, sour grapes*, squash*, squelch, take a swipe at*, take down, take down a peg*, tear down*, underestimate, underrate, undervalue, write off; SEE CONCEPTS *52,54*

bell [*n*] *signaling object or sound*
alarm, buzz, buzzer, carillon, chime, clapper, curfew, ding-dong*, dinger*, gong, peal, ringer, siren, tintinnabulum, tocsin, toll, vesper; SEE CONCEPT *595*

belligerent [*adj*] *nasty, argumentative*
aggressive, antagonistic, ardent, at loggerheads*, battling, bellicose, cantankerous, combative, contentious, fierce, fighting, flip, have a bone to pick*, have chip on shoulder*, have it in for*, hostile, hot, hot-tempered, mean, militant, on the outs*, ornery, pugnacious, quarrelsome, scrappy, truculent, warlike; SEE CONCEPTS *401,404*

bellow [*v*] *holler*
bark, bawl, bay, beller, blare, bluster, bray, call, clamor, cry, howl, low, roar, rout, scream, shout, shriek, wail, whoop, yawp, yell, yelp; SEE CONCEPT *77*

bells and whistles [*n*] *added-value features*
accessories, added features, attractive features, chrome, dressing, extras, gongs, trappings; SEE CONCEPTS *386,829*

belly [*n*] *stomach*
abdomen, bay window*, beer belly*, breadbasket*, corporation*, front porch*, gut, insides, intestines, paunch, pelvis, pot*, pot belly*, solar plexus, spare tire*, tank, tummy, venter; SEE CONCEPT *393*

belong [*v1*] *be part of, be in proper place*
accord, agree, appertain, apply, associate, attach to, be a component, be a constituent, be akin to, be an adjunct of, be a part, bear, bear upon, become, be connected with, befit, be fitting, be linked with, be related, be relevant, chime, concern, correlate, correspond, exist, fit, go, go with, harmonize, have relationship to, have respect to, have to do with, inhere, match, permeate, pertain, refer, regard, reside, set, suit, touch, vest; SEE CONCEPTS *532,543*

belong [*v2*] *be affiliated with*
be allied to, be a member, be a member of, be as-sociated with, be classified among, be contained in, be included in, be one of, be one of the family, be part of, fit in, have a place, in, in with, owe allegiance, owe support, run with*, swing*, swing with*, take one's place with; SEE CONCEPTS *114,388*

belonging [*n*] *sense of security in friendship*
acceptance, affinity, association, attachment, inclusion, kinship, loyalty, rapport, relationship; SEE CONCEPTS *388,410*

belongings [*n*] *personal possessions*
accouterments, appurtenances, assets, chattels, effects, gear, goods, paraphernalia, personal property, property, stuff, things; SEE CONCEPTS *446,710*

belonging to [*adj*] *owned by*
affiliated with, associated with, essential to, held by, inherent in, intrinsic in, native to; SEE CONCEPTS *404,549*

beloved [*adj*] *adored*
admired, cared for, cherished, darling, dear, dearest, doted on, endeared, esteemed, fairhaired, favorite, hallowed, highly regarded, highly valued, idolized, loved, near to one's heart*, pet*, pleasing, popular, precious, prized, respected, revered, sweet, treasured, venerated, well-liked, worshiped; SEE CONCEPTS *568,572*

beloved [*n*] *someone adored*
baby*, beau, boyfriend, darling, dear, dearest, fiancé, flame, girlfriend, heartbeat*, heartthrob, honey, idol, inamorato, love, love of my life*, lover, number one*, numero uno*, object of affection, one and only, pet*, prize, rave*, significant other, steady, sugar*, sweetheart, tootsie*, treasure, true love; SEE CONCEPT *423*

below [*adv/prep*] *lower*
beneath, down, down from, under, underneath; SEE CONCEPTS *581,586,735*

below [*prep2*] *less than; beneath*
inferior, lesser, lower, subject, subordinate, unworthy; SEE CONCEPTS *567,771*

below par [*adj*] *second-rate in quality*
below average, imperfect, inferior, lacking, not oneself, off, off-form, poor, substandard, under the weather*, wanting; SEE CONCEPT *574*

below the belt [*adj/adv*] *nastily and unfairly*
cowardly, dirty, dishonest, foul, unjust, unscrupulous, unsportsmanlike; SEE CONCEPTS *411,674,732*

belt [*n1*] *supporting band*
cincture, cummerbund, girdle, ribbon, ring, sash, strap, string, waistband; SEE CONCEPT *450*

belt [*n2*] *strip of land with characteristic feature*
area, district, layer, region, stretch, territory, tract, zone; SEE CONCEPTS *513,517*

belt [*v*] *hit hard*
bash, bat, biff, blast, blow, bop, clobber, slam, slug, smack, smash, sock, strap, switch, wallop, whip, whop; SEE CONCEPT *189*

bemoan [*v*] *express sorrow*
beat one's breast*, bewail, complain, cry over spilled milk*, deplore, grieve for, lament, moan over, mourn, regret, rue, sing the blues*, weep for; SEE CONCEPTS *49,51*

bemuse [*v*] *confuse*
addle, amaze, bewilder, daydream, daze, gather wool*, moon, muddle, overwhelm, paralyze, perplex, pipe dream*, puzzle, stun, stupefy; SEE CONCEPTS *7,19,22*

bench [*n1*] *furniture for sitting*
bank, chair, form, lawn seat, pew, seat, settee, settle, stall; SEE CONCEPT *443*

bench [*n2*] *large table*
board, counter, desk, easel, ledge, shelf, trestle, workbench, work table; SEE CONCEPT *443*

bench [*n3*] *group of judges*
court, courtroom, judiciary, magistrate, the bar, tribunal, your honors; SEE CONCEPTS *318,355*

benchmark [*n*] *reference point*
criterion, gauge, measure, standard, touchstone, yardstick; SEE CONCEPT *688*

bend [*n*] *curve*
angle, arc, bending, bow, corner, crook, curvation, curvature, deflection, deviation, flection, flexure, hook, lean, loop, round, sag, shift, tack, tilt, turn, twist, yaw, zigzag; SEE CONCEPT *436*

bend [*v1*] *form or cause a curve*
angle away, angle off, arch, bow, buckle, camber, careen, curl, circle, contort, crimp, crinkle, crook, crouch, curl, deflect, deform, detour, double, droop, flex, genuflect, hook, incline, incurvate, lean, loop, pervert, round, spiral, stoop, swerve, tilt, turn, twist, veer, verge, warp, waver, wilt, wind, yaw, zigzag; SEE CONCEPTS *149,184*

bend [*v2*] *persuade; influence*
change mind, compel, direct, mold, shape, subdue, submit, sway, yield; SEE CONCEPT *68*

beneath [*adv*] *in a lower place*
below, underneath; SEE CONCEPT *586*

beneath [*prep*] *inferior*
below, lesser, less than, lower than, subject, subordinate, unbefitting, under, underneath, unworthy of; SEE CONCEPT *567*

benediction [*n*] *closing prayer*
amen, approbation, approval, beatitude, benedictus, benison, blessing, consecration, favor, grace, gratitude, invocation, laying on of hands, okay, orison, praise, sanctification, thanks, thanksgiving; SEE CONCEPT *69*

benefactor [*n*] *donor*
aid, altruist, angel, assistant, backer, contributor, fairy godparent*, fan, good Samaritan, grubstaker, helper, humanitarian, mark*, patron, philanthropist, promoter, protector, Santa Claus*, sponsor, subscriber, subsidizer, supporter, wellwisher; SEE CONCEPTS *416,423*

beneficial [*adj*] *advantageous*
benign, constructive, favorable, favoring, gainful, good, good for what ails you*, healthful, helpful, profitable, propitious, salubrious, salutary, serviceable, toward, useful, valuable, what the doctor ordered*, wholesome, worthy; SEE CONCEPTS *567,572*

beneficiary [*n*] *person who gains, benefits*
almsperson, assignee, devisee, donee, grantee, heir, heiress, inheritor, legatee, payee, possessor, receiver, recipient, stipendiary, successor; SEE CONCEPTS *355,423*

benefit [*n1*] *advantage, profit*
account, aid, asset, assistance, avail, benediction, betterment, blessing, boon, cream*, egg in one's beer*, extras, favor, gain, godsend*, good, gravy*, help, interest, perk*, profit, prosperity, use, welfare, worth; SEE CONCEPTS *337,346,661*

benefit [*n2*] *event to raise money*
ball, bazaar, charitable affair, charity performance, concert, dance, dinner, exhibit, exhibition, fair, pancake breakfast, raffle; SEE CONCEPT *386*

benefit [*v*] *help, enhance*
advance, advantage, aid, ameliorate, assist, avail, be good for, better, build, contribute to, do for one, do the trick, favor, fill the bill*, further, improve, make a killing*, make it*, pay, pay off*, profit, promote, relieve, serve, succor, work for; SEE CONCEPTS *110,244*

benevolence [*n*] *charity*
altruism, amity, comity, compassion, feeling, friendliness, friendship, generosity, gift, goodness, good will, humanity, kindheartedness, kindness, sympathy; SEE CONCEPT *633*

benevolent [*adj*] *charitable, kind*
all heart, altruistic, beneficent, benign, big, big-hearted, bounteous, bountiful, caring, chivalrous, compassionate, considerate, generous, helpful, humane, humanitarian, kindhearted, liberal, magnanimous, philanthropic, tenderhearted, warmhearted, well-disposed; SEE CONCEPT *401*

benign [*adj1*] *kindly*
amiable, beneficent, benevolent, benignant, complaisant, congenial, favorable, friendly, generous, genial, gentle, good, goodhearted, gracious, kind, liberal, merciful, mild, obliging, sympathetic; SEE CONCEPT *542*

benign [*adj2*] *mild, especially describing weather*
auspicious, balmy, bright, favorable, fortunate, gentle, healthful, propitious, refreshing, temperate, warm; SEE CONCEPT *605*

benign [*adj3*] *advantageous*
auspicious, beneficent, benevolent, bright, charitable, dexter, encouraging, favorable, fortunate, good, lucky, merciful, propitious, salutary, smiling; SEE CONCEPTS *537,572*

benign [*adj4*] *not cancerous*
curable, early stage, harmless, limited, remediable, slight, superficial; SEE CONCEPT *314*

bent [*adj1*] *curved*
angled, arced, arched, arciform, bowed, contorted, crooked, curvilinear, doubled over, drooping, droopy, hooked, humped, hunched, inclined, limp, looped, round, rounded, sinuous, slouchy, slumped, stooped, twined, twisted, warped, wilted; SEE CONCEPT *486*

bent [*adj2*] *determined*
bound, decided, decisive, dedicated, disposed, firm, fixed, inclined, insistent, intent, leaning, predisposed, resolute, resolved, set, settled, tending; SEE CONCEPT *403*

bent [*n*] *inclination; talent*
ability, aim, aptitude, bag*, disposition, druthers*, facility, faculty, flair, forte, genius, gift, head-set*, inclining, knack, leaning, mindset*, nose, penchant, predilection, predisposition, preference, proclivity, propensity, set, tack, tendency, thing for*, tilt, turn, weakness for; SEE CONCEPTS *409,630*

bequeath [*v*] *give in a will*
bestow, commit, devise, endow, entrust, grant, hand down, hand on, impart, leave, leave to, legate, pass on, transmit, will; SEE CONCEPTS *108,317*

bequest [*n*] *something given in will*
bequeathal, bequeathment, bestowal, devisal, devise, dower, endowment, estate, gift, heritage, inheritance, legacy, settlement, trust; SEE CONCEPTS *318,337*

berate [*v*] *criticize hatefully*
bawl out*, blister, call down, castigate, censure,

chew*, chew out*, chide, cuss out*, eat out*, give one hell*, give what for*, jaw*, jump all over*, rail at*, rake over the coals*, rate, rebuke, reprimand, reproach, reprove, revile, scold, scorch, tell off, tongue-lash, upbraid, vituperate; SEE CONCEPT 52

bereavement [n] *death; loss*
affliction, deprivation, distress, misfortune, sorrow, tribulation; SEE CONCEPTS 230,674

bereft [adj] *lacking; missing*
beggared, bereaved, cut off, deprived, destitute, devoid, dispossessed, divested, fleeced, impoverished, left without, minus, naked, parted from, robbed, shorn, stripped, wanting, without; SEE CONCEPTS 546,576

berry [n] *small fruit*
bean, drupe, drupelet, grain, haw, hip, kernel, pome, seed; SEE CONCEPT 426

berserk [adj] *crazed*
crazy, demented, deranged, insane, mad, maniacal, manic, violent; SEE CONCEPT 403

berth [n1] *harbor; bunk*
anchorage, bed, bedroom, billet, compartment, cot, dock, hammock, haven, jetty, levee, pier, port, quay, slip, wharf; SEE CONCEPTS 513,516

berth [n2] *position of responsibility*
appointment, billet, capacity, connection, employment, job, living, office, place, post, profession, situation, spot; SEE CONCEPTS 362,668

beseech [v] *beg*
adjure, appeal, ask, call upon, crave, entreat, implore, importune, invoke, petition, plead, pray, solicit, sue, supplicate; SEE CONCEPT 48

beset [v] *plague; hem in*
aggress, assail, attack, badger, bedevil, beleaguer, besiege, bug*, circle*, compass, dog*, drive up the wall*, embarrass, encircle, enclose, encompass, entangle, environ, fall on, fall upon, girdle, give a bad time*, give a hard time*, give one the business*, give the needle*, harass, harry, hassle, infest, invade, jump on one's case*, nag, nudge, overrun, perplex, pester, pick on, put the squeeze on*, ride, ring, start in on, storm, strike, surround; SEE CONCEPTS 7,19

beside [adv/prep] *next to*
abreast of, adjacent to, adjoining, alongside, aside, a step from, at one's elbow, at the edge of, at the side of, bordering on, by, cheek by jowl*, close at hand, close to, close upon, connected with, contiguous to, forment, in juxtaposition, near, nearby, neck and neck*, neighboring, next door to, nigh, opposite, overlooking, round, side by side, verging on, with; SEE CONCEPT 586

beside oneself [adj] *very upset*
berserk, crazed, delirious, demented, distraught, frantic, frenetic, insane, mad, unbalanced, unhinged; SEE CONCEPTS 403,485,570

besides [adv] *in addition; as well*
added to, additionally, along with, also, and all, apart from, aside from, as well as, beyond, conjointly, else, exceeding, exclusive of, extra, further, furthermore, in conjunction with, in distinction to, in excess of, in other respects, likewise, more, moreover, more than, not counting, on the side*, on top of everything, other than, otherwise, over and above, plus, secondly, supplementary to, to boot*, together with, too, what's more*, with the exception of, yet; SEE CONCEPT 772

besides [prep1] *apart from*
aside from, bar, barring, beside, but, except, excepting, excluding, exclusive of, in addition to, other than, outside of, over and above, save, without; SEE CONCEPT 772

besides [prep2] *in addition to*
added to, along with, as well as, beside, beyond, in excess of, more than, on top of, other than, over and above, plus, supplementary, together with; SEE CONCEPT 772

beside the point [adj] *not important*
extraneous, immaterial, inapplicable, incidental, inconsequential, irrelevant, pointless, unimportant, unrelated; SEE CONCEPT 575

besiege [v1] *surround; assault*
assail, attack, beleaguer, beset, blockade, come at from all sides, confine, congregate, encircle, encompass, environ, hem in, invest, lay siege to, shut in, trap, work on, work over; SEE CONCEPTS 86,90

besiege [v2] *bother*
badger, beleaguer, bug*, buttonhole*, harass, harry, hound*, importune, nag, pester, plague, trouble; SEE CONCEPTS 7,19

best [adj1] *most excellent*
10*, A-1*, ace, bad*, beyond compare, boss*, capital, champion, chief, choicest, cool*, culminating, finest, first, first-class, first-rate, foremost, greatest, highest, incomparable, inimitable, leading, matchless, nonpareil, number 1*, optimum, out-of-sight*, outstanding, paramount, peerless, perfect, preeminent, premium, prime, primo*, principal, sans pareil, second to none, super, superlative, supreme, terrific, tops, tough, transcendent, unequaled, unparalleled, unrivaled, unsurpassed; SEE CONCEPTS 568,572

best [adj2] *correct, right*
advantageous, apt, desirable, golden, most suitable, most fitting, preferred, presentable; SEE CONCEPT 558

best [adj3] *most*
biggest, bulkiest, greatest, largest; SEE CONCEPT 771

best [adv] *most excellently*
advantageously, attractively, creditably, extremely, gloriously, greatly, honorably, illustriously, magnanimously, most deeply, most fortunately, most fully, most highly, sincerely; SEE CONCEPTS 568,572

best [n1] *most outstanding thing in class*
choice, cream, cream of the crop*, elite, fat, favorite, finest, first, flower, gem, model, nonpareil, paragon, pick, prime, prize, select, top; SEE CONCEPT 668

best [n2] *highest personal effort*
all one's got, best shot, hardest, highest endeavor, level best*, Sunday best*, utmost; SEE CONCEPT 411

best [v] *defeat; gain advantage*
beat, beat up*, better, blank*, blast*, bulldoze*, clobber*, conquer, cream*, deck*, drub*, exceed, excel, flax*, floor*, get the better of, knock off*, KO*, lambaste, let have it*, lick*, master, outclass, outdo, outshine, outstrip, overcome, prevail, put away, shoot down*, shut down*, surpass, take care of, take down*, tan*, thrash*, top, total, transcend, trash*, triumph, triumph over, trounce, wallop, waste*, wax*, whip*, whomp*, whop*, wipe*, wipe out, wipe the floor with*, zap*; SEE CONCEPT 95

bestow [*v*] *give, allot*
accord, apportion, award, bequeath, come through, commit, confer, devote, donate, entrust, favor, gift, give away, grant, hand out, honor with, impart, kick in, lavish, offer, present, put out, render to; SEE CONCEPTS *98,108*

best-seller [*n*] *top-selling item*
a top ten, chart-buster, favorite, hit*, hot item*, hot seller, mover*, number one, record-breaker, success, winner; SEE CONCEPTS *423,446*

best shot [*n*] *all-out try*
all one's got, best effort, best one can do, maximum effort, one's all, one's damndest, optimum effort; SEE CONCEPTS *87,362,677,724*

bet [*n*] *game of chance; money gambled*
action, ante, betting, chance, down on, hazard, long shot, lot, lottery, odds, odds on, parlay, play, pledge, plunge, pot, raffle, random shot, risk, shot, shot in the dark*, speculation, stake, sweepstakes, uncertainty, venture, wager; SEE CONCEPTS *28,293,329*

bet [*v*] *gamble*
ante, buy in, chance, dice, game, hazard, lay down, lay odds, play against, play for, play the ponies*, pledge, pony up*, put, put money on, risk, set, speculate, tempt fortune*, toss up, trust, venture, wager; SEE CONCEPTS *292,330*

beta [*adj*] *being tested*
dubious, experimental, flaky, mostly working, new, pre-release, suspect, testing, unready; SEE CONCEPTS *529,582*

bête noire [*n*] *trouble*
adversary, anathema, antagonist, bad news*, bane, curse, devil, enemy, pet hate, plague; SEE CONCEPTS *532,674,675,690,728*

betray [*v1*] *be disloyal*
abandon, be unfaithful, bite the hand that feeds you*, blow the whistle*, bluff, break faith, break promise, break trust, break with, commit treason, cross, deceive, deliver up*, delude, desert, double-cross, finger*, forsake, go back on, inform against, inform on, jilt, knife*, let down, mislead, play false*, play Judas*, seduce, sell down the river*, sell out, stab in the back*, take in*, trick, turn in, turn informer, turn state's evidence, walk out on; SEE CONCEPT *384*

betray [*v2*] *divulge, expose information*
blurt out, dime*, disclose, evince, fink on*, give away, inform, lay bare, let slip, make known, manifest, rat on*, reveal, show, sing*, snitch*, spill, squeal*, stool*, tattle, tell, tell on, turn in, uncover, unmask; SEE CONCEPTS *44,60*

betrayal [*n1*] *exhibition of disloyalty*
deception, dishonesty, double-crossing, double-dealing, duplicity, falseness, giveaway, Judas kiss*, let-down, perfidy, sellout, treachery, treason, trickery, unfaithfulness; SEE CONCEPT *633*

betrayal [*n2*] *divulgence of information*
blurting out, diming*, disclosure, giving away, ratting*, revelation, snitching*, spilling*, squealing*, tattling, telling; SEE CONCEPTS *44,60*

betroth [*v*] *marry*
affiance, become engaged, bind, commit, contract, engage, espouse, give one's hand, make compact, plight faith, plight troth, promise, tie oneself to, vow; SEE CONCEPT *297*

betrothal [*n*] *marriage*
affiancing, betrothing, engagement, espousal, plight, promise, troth, vow; SEE CONCEPT *297*

better [*adj1*] *excelling, more excellent*
bigger, choice, exceeding, exceptional, finer, fitter, greater, higher quality, improved, larger, more appropriate, more desirable, more fitting, more select, more suitable, more useful, more valuable, preferable, preferred, prominent, sharpened, sophisticated, souped up*, superior, surpassing, worthier; SEE CONCEPTS *568,572*

better [*adj2*] *improved in health*
convalescent, cured, fitter, fully recovered, healthier, improving, less ill, mending, more healthy, on the comeback trail*, on the mend, on the road to recovery*, out of the woods*, over the hump*, progressing, recovering, stronger, well; SEE CONCEPT *314*

better [*adj3*] *larger*
bigger, greater, longer, more, preponderant, weightier; SEE CONCEPTS *771,773*

better [*adv*] *in a more excellent manner*
finer, greater, in a superior way, more, more advantageously, more attractively, more competently, more completely, more effectively, more thoroughly, preferably, to a greater degree; SEE CONCEPTS *568,572*

better [*v*] *improve performance; outdo*
advance, ameliorate, amend, beat, best, cap, correct, enhance, exceed, excel, forward, further, help, meliorate, mend, outshine, outstrip, promote, raise, rectify, refine, reform, revamp, surpass, top, transcend; SEE CONCEPTS *141,244*

betterment [*n*] *improvement*
advancement, amelioration, mastery, melioration, progress, prosperity, upgrading; SEE CONCEPT *244*

between [*adv/prep*] *middle from two points*
amid, amidst, among, at intervals, betwixt, bounded by, centrally located, enclosed by, halfway, in, inserted, interpolated, intervening, in the middle, in the midst of, in the seam, in the thick of, medially, mid, midway, separating, surrounded by, 'tween, within; SEE CONCEPTS *586,820*

beverage [*n*] *liquid refreshment*
cooler, draft, drink, drinkable, libation, liquor, potable, potation; SEE CONCEPT *454*

bevy [*n*] *swarm*
assembly, band, bunch, cluster, collection, company, covey, crew, crowd, flight, flock, gathering, group, pack, party, troupe; SEE CONCEPT *432*

bewail [*v*] *cry over, lament*
bemoan, deplore, eat heart out*, express sorrow, grieve for, moan, mourn, regret, repent, rue, sing the blues*, take on, wail, weep over; SEE CONCEPT *266*

beware [*v*] *be careful*
attend, avoid, be cautious, be wary, guard against, heed, keep eyes open*, keep one's distance, keep on one's toes*, look out, mind, mind p's and q's*, notice, refrain from, shun, steer clear of*, take care, take heed, walk on eggs*, watch one's step, watch out; SEE CONCEPT *34*

bewilder [*v*] *confuse*
addle, baffle, ball up*, befuddle, bemuse, confound, daze, disconcert, distract, floor*, fluster, mess with one's head*, mix up, muddle, mystify, perplex, puzzle, rattle, snow*, stump, stupefy, throw, upset; SEE CONCEPTS *14,42*

bewildered [*adj*] *confused*
addled, agape, aghast, agog, appalled, astonished, astounded, awed, awe-struck, baffled, be-

fuddled, bowled over*, dazed, dazzled, disconcerted, dizzy, dumbfounded, dumbstruck, flabbergasted, flipped out*, floored*, flustered, giddy, in a dither*, lost, misled, muddled, mystified, perplexed, punchy*, puzzled, rattled, reeling, shocked, shook up, speechless, staggered, startled, stumped, stunned, stupefied, surprised, taken aback, thrown, thunderstruck*, uncertain, unglued*; SEE CONCEPTS *402,403*

bewilderment [*n*] *puzzlement*
bafflement, confusion, daze, discombobulation*, disorientation, perplexity, surprise; SEE CONCEPT *14*

bewitch [*v*] *charm*
allure, attract, bedevil, beguile, captivate, capture, control, dazzle, draw, enchant, enrapture, enthrall, entrance, fascinate, hex, hypnotize, knock dead*, knock out, put horns on*, put the whammy on*, put under magic spell*, send*, slay*, spell*, spellbind, sweep off one's feet*, take, tickle*, tickle pink*, tickle to death*, trick, turn on*, vamp, voodoo, wile, wow*; SEE CONCEPTS *7,22*

bewitched [*adj*] *charmed*
captivated, enamored, enchanted, enraptured, ensorcelled, entranced, fallen for*, fascinated, gaga about*, have a bug in one's ear*, have a thing about*, head over heels*, hooked*, hung up*, mad about*, mesmerized, possessed, spellbound, transformed, turned on*, under a spell; SEE CONCEPTS *32,403*

beyond [*adv/prep*] *further; outside limits*
above, after, ahead, apart from, as well as, at a distance, away from, before, behind, besides, beyond the bounds, clear of, farther, free of, good way off, hyper, in addition to, in advance of, long way off, moreover, more remote, on the far side, on the other side, out of range, out of reach, outside, over, over and above, over there, past, remote, superior to, without, yonder; SEE CONCEPTS *554,772,778*

bias [*n1*] *belief in one way; partiality*
bent, bigotry, chauvinism, disposition, favoritism, flash, head-set*, illiberality, inclination, intolerance, leaning, mind-set*, mind trip*, narrowmindedness, one-sidedness, penchant, preconception, predilection, predisposition, preference, prejudice, prepossession, proclivity, proneness, propensity, spin, standpoint, tendency, tilt, turn, unfairness, viewpoint; SEE CONCEPT *689*

bias [*n2*] *diagonal weave of fabric*
angle, cant, cross, incline, oblique, slant; SEE CONCEPT *606*

bias [*v*] *cause to favor*
distort, incline, influence, make partial, prejudice, prepossess, slant, sway, twist, warp, weight; SEE CONCEPTS *7,19*

bible [*n*] *holy book; authoritative book*
authority, creed, doctrine, guide, guidebook, handbook, manual, sacred writ, sacred writings, scripture, testament, text, the good news; SEE CONCEPTS *280,368*

bicker [*v*] *nastily argue*
altercate, brawl, caterwaul, cause a scene*, cavil, dig, disagree, dispute, fall out, fight, hassle, pick at, quarrel, quibble, row, scrap, scrape, spar, spat, squabble, tiff, trade zingers*, wrangle; SEE CONCEPT *46*

bicycle [*n*] *pedal-driven recreational vehicle*
bike, cycle, tandem, two-wheeler, velocipede, wheels; SEE CONCEPTS *364,505*

bid [*n1*] *offering of money or services*
advance, amount, declaration, feeler, hit, invitation, offer, pass, price, proffer, proposal, proposition, request, submission, suggestion, sum, summons, tender; SEE CONCEPTS *67,330*

bid [*n2*] *endeavor*
attempt, crack, effort, essay, try, venture; SEE CONCEPT *87*

bid [*v1*] *offer money or services*
present, proffer, propose, render, submit, tender, venture; SEE CONCEPTS *67,330*

bid [*v2*] *say*
call, greet, tell, wish; SEE CONCEPT *266*

bid [*v3*] *ask for; command*
call, charge, demand, desire, direct, enjoin, instruct, invite, make a pass at*, make a pitch*, make a play for*, order, proposition, request, require, solicit, summon, tell, warn; SEE CONCEPT *53*

bidding [*n1*] *command*
behest, call, charge, demand, dictate, direction, injunction, instruction, invitation, mandate, order, request, summons, word; SEE CONCEPT *53*

bidding [*n2*] *offering of money, services*
advance, auction, invitation, offer, proffering, proposal, proposition, request, submission, suggestion, tender; SEE CONCEPTS *67,330*

bide [*v*] *wait*
abide, attend, await, continue, dwell, hang around, hang in*, hang out*, hold the phone*, lie in wait*, linger, live, remain, reside, sit tight*, stay, stick around, sweat it*, tarry, watch for; SEE CONCEPT *681*

big [*adj1*] *large, great*
ample, awash, a whale of a*, brimming, bulky, bull*, burly, capacious, chock-full*, colossal, commodious, considerable, copious, crowded, enormous, extensive, fat, full, gigantic, heavy-duty*, heavyweight, hefty, huge, hulking, humongous*, husky, immense, jumbo, mammoth, massive, mondo*, monster*, oversize, packed, ponderous, prodigious, roomy, sizable, spacious, strapping, stuffed, substantial, super colossal*, thundering, tremendous, vast, voluminous, walloping, whopper, whopping; SEE CONCEPTS *771,773*

big [*adj2*] *important*
big league*, big-time*, consequential, considerable, eminent, heavy-duty*, heavyweight, influential, leading, main, major league*, material, meaningful, momentous, paramount, popular, powerful, prime, principal, prominent, serious, significant, substantial, super, super colossal*, valuable, weighty; SEE CONCEPT *568*

big [*adj3*] *grown*
adult, elder, full-grown, grown-up, mature, tall; SEE CONCEPTS *578,797*

big [*adj4*] *generous*
altruistic, benevolent, bighearted, chivalrous, considerate, free, gracious, greathearted, heroic, liberal, lofty, magnanimous, noble, princely, unselfish; SEE CONCEPT *404*

big [*adj5*] *arrogant*
arty, boastful, bragging, conceited, flamboyant, haughty, high-sounding, imperious, imposing, inflated, overblown, pompous, presumptuous, pretentious, proud; SEE CONCEPT *401*

big deal [n] *something or someone important*
big cheese*, big enchilada*, big fish*, biggie*, big gun*, big shot*, big wheel*, bigwig*, boss, boss man*, head honcho*, hotshot*, important person, top dog*, tycoon, very important person, VIP; SEE CONCEPT 347

big-hearted [adj] *very kind*
altruistic, benevolent, compassionate, generous, giving, gracious, noble; SEE CONCEPTS 404,542

big league [adj] *important*
big-time, chief, critical, crucial, exceptional, four-star, front-page*, grave, great, heavy, high-power, major-league, playing hard ball*, professional, serious, strictly business; SEE CONCEPTS 567,568

bigmouth [n] *a loudmouth*
bag of wind*, big talker*, blowhard*, blusterer, boaster, brag, braggart, bragger, bull artist*, bull-thrower*, gasbag*, gossiper, grandstander, know-it-all, show-off, swelled head*, trumpeter*, windbag*; SEE CONCEPTS 412,423

bigot [n] *intolerant, prejudiced person*
chauvinist, diehard, doctrinaire, dogmatist, enthusiast, extremist, fanatic, fiend, maniac, monomaniac, opinionated person, partisan, persecutor, puritan, racist, sectarian, segregationist, sexist, stickler, superpatriot, zealot; SEE CONCEPTS 359,423

bigoted [adj] *intolerant, prejudiced*
biased, chauvinistic, conservative, dogmatic, illiberal, narrow, narrow-minded, obstinate, opinionated, partial, partisan, sectarian, slanted, small-minded, twisted, unfair, warped; SEE CONCEPTS 403,555

bigotry [n] *intolerance, prejudice*
bias, conservatism/conservativism, discrimination, dogmatism, fanaticism, injustice, Jim Crowism*, narrow-mindedness, partiality, provincialism, racialism, racism, sectarianism, sexism, unfairness; SEE CONCEPTS 388,410

big shot [n] *important person*
big cheese*, big gun*, big wheel*, bigwig*, celebrity, dignitary, heavy-hitter*, heavy-weight*, mogul, personage, somebody, VIP; SEE CONCEPT 423

big win [n1] *overwhelming success or victory*
coup, coup d'etat, obliteration; SEE CONCEPT 706

big win [n2] *desirable chance discovery*
accidental discovery, chance discovery, good fortune, luck, serendipity; SEE CONCEPT 693

bilateral [adj] *having two sides*
mutual, reciprocal, respective, two-sided; SEE CONCEPT 562

bilk [v] *cheat*
bamboozle*, beat, circumvent, con, deceive, defraud, disappoint, do*, fleece*, flimflam*, foil, frustrate, gyp*, overreach, rook*, ruin, snow*, swindle, thwart, trick; SEE CONCEPTS 59,139

bill [n1] *account of charges; money owed*
bad news*, check, chit, damage*, debt, invoice, IOU, itemized account, knock*, note, reckoning, request for payment, score, statement, statement of indebtedness, tab; SEE CONCEPTS 329,332

bill [n2] *list; circular*
advertisement, affiche, agenda, bulletin, card, catalogue, flyer, handbill, handout, inventory, leaflet, listing, notice, placard, playbill, poster, program, roster, schedule, syllabus; SEE CONCEPTS 280,283

bill [n3] *piece of legislation*
act, draft, measure, projected law, proposal, proposed act; SEE CONCEPTS 271,318

bill [n4] *piece of paper money*
bank note, buck, certificate, currency, dollar, greenback*, long green*, skin*; SEE CONCEPT 340

bill [n5] *beak of animal*
mandible, neb, nib, pecker, projection; SEE CONCEPT 399

bill [v1] *charge money for goods, services*
bone, chase, debit, draw upon, dun, figure, invoice, put the arm on*, put the bite on*, put the squeeze on*, reckon, record, render, solicit; SEE CONCEPTS 330,342

bill [v2] *advertise*
announce, book, give advance notice, post; SEE CONCEPTS 60,292

billow [n] *surging mass*
beachcomber, breaker, crest, roller, surge, swell, tide, wave; SEE CONCEPTS 437,514

billow [v] *surge*
balloon, belly, bloat, bounce, bulge, ebb and flow, heave, pitch, puff up, ripple, rise and fall, rise up, rock, roll, swell, toss, undulate, wave; SEE CONCEPTS 159,208

billowy [adj] *surging*
bouncing, bouncy, bulgy, distended, ebbing and flowing, heaving, puffy, rippled, rippling, rising, rising and falling, rolling, swelling, swirling, swollen, undulating, waving, wavy; SEE CONCEPTS 486,584

bind [n] *predicament*
between a rock and a hard place*, crunch*, difficulty, dilemma, hot water*, no-win situation*, nuisance, pickle*, predicament, quandary, sticky situation*, tight situation, tight spot*; SEE CONCEPTS 230,674

bind [v1] *fasten, secure*
adhere, attach, bandage, border, chain, cinch, clamp, connect, constrict, cover, dress, edge, encase, enchain, enfetter, fetter, finish, fix, fold, furl, glue, hamper, handcuff, hem, hitch, hitch on, hobble, hook on, hook up, lace, lap, lash, leash, manacle, moor, muzzle, paste, peg down, pin, pin down, pinion, put together, restrain, restrict, rope, shackle, stick, strap, swathe, tack on, tether, tie, tie up, trammel, trim, truss, unite, wrap, yoke; SEE CONCEPTS 85,160

bind [v2] *obligate; restrict*
compel, confine, constrain, detain, engage, enslave, force, hamper, hinder, hogtie*, indenture, lock up, necessitate, oblige, prescribe, put half nelson on*, put lock on*, require, restrain, restrict, yoke; SEE CONCEPTS 14,130

binding [adj1] *necessary*
bounden*, compulsory, conclusive, counted upon, essential, imperative, incumbent on, indissoluble, irrevocable, mandatory, obligatory, required, requisite, unalterable; SEE CONCEPT 546

binding [adj2] *confining*
attached, enslaved, fastened, indentured, limiting, restraining, tied, tying; SEE CONCEPT 554

binding [n] *cover; something which fastens*
adhesive, belt, fastener, jacket, tie, wrapper; SEE CONCEPT 475

binge [n] *spree*
affair, bender, blind*, bout*, carousal, compotation, drunk*, fling, jag*, orgy*, toot*; SEE CONCEPT 386

be
bi

biography [*n*] *account of person's life*
adventures, autobiography, bio, biog, close-up, confessions, diary, experiences, journal, letters, life, life history, life story, memoir, personal account, personal anecdote, personal narrative, personal record, picture, profile, résumé, saga, sketch, vita; SEE CONCEPTS *280,282*

bird [*n*] *flying animal*
feathered creature, fowl, game; SEE CONCEPT *395*

birds of a feather [*n*] *two of a kind*
Bobbsey twins, close friends, compadres, comrades, friends, two minds thinking as one; SEE CONCEPT *423*

birth [*n1*] *becoming alive*
bearing, beginning, birthing, blessed event*, childbearing, childbirth, creation, ct of God, delivery, labor, nascency, natality, nativity, parturition, producing, travail, visit from stork*; SEE CONCEPTS *302,373*

birth [*n2*] *beginning*
commencement, dawn, dawning, emergence, fountainhead, genesis, onset, opening, origin, outset, rise, source, start; SEE CONCEPT *119*

birth [*n3*] *heritage*
ancestry, background, blood, breeding, derivation, descent, extraction, forebears, genealogy, heritance, legacy, line, lineage, parentage, pedigree, position, race, rank, station, status, stock, strain; SEE CONCEPTS *296,648*

birth control [*n*] *method of preventing pregnancy*
abstinence, condom, contraception, contraceptive, diaphragm, IUD, pill, planned parenthood, rhythm method, rubber, safety*, tied tubes, vasectomy; SEE CONCEPTS *121,375*

birth defect [*n*] *congenital defect*
abnormality, congenital malformation, deformity; SEE CONCEPT *580*

birthmark [*n*] *blemish one is born with*
angioma, beauty mark, hemangioma, mole, mother's mark, nevus, port wine stain; SEE CONCEPT *580*

bisect [*v*] *divide in two*
bifurcate, branch off, cleave, cross, cut across, cut in half, cut in two, dichotomize, dimidiate, divaricate, divide in two, fork, furcate, halve, hemisect, intersect, separate, split, split down the middle; SEE CONCEPTS *98,137,176*

bisexual [*adj*] *having relations with either gender*
AC-DC*, androgynous, bi*, epicene, gynandrous, hermaphroditic, intersexual, monoclinous, swings both ways*; SEE CONCEPT *372*

bistro [*n*] *drinkery with food*
bar, lounge, restaurant, tavern; SEE CONCEPTS *439,448,449*

bit [*n1*] *tiny piece*
atom, butt, chicken feed*, chip, chunk, crumb, dab, dash, division, dollop, dose, dot, driblet, droplet, end, excerpt, flake, fraction, fragment, grain, iota, item, jot, lick*, lump, mite, modicum, moiety, molecule, morsel, niggle, parcel, part, particle, peanuts*, pinch, portion, sample, scale, scintilla, scrap, section, segment, shard, share, shaving, shred, slice, sliver, smidgen, snatch, snip, snippet, specimen, speck, splinter, sprinkling, stub, stump, taste, tittle, trace, trickle; SEE CONCEPTS *831,835*

bit [*n2*] *short period of time*
instant, jiffy, little while, minute, moment, second, space, spell, stretch, tick, while; SEE CONCEPT *807*

bit [*n3*] *computer information*
0, 1, binary digit, binary unit, data; SEE CONCEPT *274*

bite [*n1*] *injury from gripping, tearing*
chaw*, chomp*, gob*, itch*, laceration, nip, pain, pinch, prick, smarting, sting, tooth marks*, wound; SEE CONCEPT *309*

bite [*n2*] *mouthful of food*
brunch, drop, light meal, morsel, nibble, nosh*, piece, refreshment, sample, snack, sop*, taste; SEE CONCEPTS *457,459*

bite [*n3*] *pungency; stinging sensation*
burn, edge, guts*, kick, piquancy, punch, spice, sting, zap*, zip*; SEE CONCEPT *614*

bite [*n4*] *allotment*
allowance, cut, lot, part, piece, portion, quota, share, slice; SEE CONCEPT *835*

bite [*v1*] *grip or tear with teeth*
champ, chaw, chaw on, chew, chomp, clamp, crunch, crush, cut, eat, gnaw, hold, lacerate, masticate, munch, nibble, nip, pierce, pinch, rend, ruminate, seize, sever, snap, take a chunk out of*, taste, tooth, wound; SEE CONCEPTS *185,616*

bite [*v2*] *corrode, eat away*
burn, consume, decay, decompose, deteriorate, dissolve, eat into, engrave, erode, etch, oxidize, rot, rust, scour, sear, slash, smart, sting, tingle, wear away; SEE CONCEPTS *215,250*

bite [*v3*] *take a chance*
be victim, get hooked*, nibble, risk, volunteer; SEE CONCEPT *384*

bite the bullet [*v*] *take it*
be forced, bow to fate, face the music*, have no choice, know no alternative, pay the piper*, stand up and take it, swallow the pill*, take one's medicine*, take the rap; SEE CONCEPTS *23,96*

biting [*adj1*] *piercing, sharp*
bitter, bleak, blighting, cold, crisp, cutting, freezing, harsh, nipping, penetrating, raw; SEE CONCEPTS *569,605*

biting [*adj2*] *sarcastic*
acerbic, acrimonious, bitter, caustic, cutting, incisive, mordant, scathing, severe, sharp, stinging, trenchant, withering; SEE CONCEPT *267*

bitter [*adj1*] *pungent, sharp*
absinthal, absinthian, acerb, acerbic, acid, acrid, amaroidal, astringent, harsh, sour, tart, unsweetened, vinegary; SEE CONCEPT *613*

bitter [*adj2*] *hostile, nasty*
acrimonious, alienated, antagonistic, begrudging, biting, caustic, crabby, divided, embittered, estranged, fierce, freezing, hateful, intense, irreconcilable, morose, rancorous, resentful, sardonic, severe, sore, sour, stinging, sullen, virulent, vitriolic, with chip on shoulder*; SEE CONCEPTS *267,404*

bitter [*adj3*] *painful, distressing*
afflictive, annoying, bad, brutal, calamitous, cruel, dire, disagreeable, displeasing, distasteful, disturbing, galling, grievous, hard, harsh, heartbreaking, hurtful, inclement, intemperate, intense, merciless, offensive, poignant, provoking, rigorous, rugged, ruthless, savage, severe, sharp, stinging, unpalatable, unpleasant, vexatious, woeful; SEE CONCEPT *537*

bitterness [*n1*] *sourness*
acerbity, acidity, acridity, astringency, brackish-

ness, brininess, piquancy, pungency, sharpness, tartness, vinegariness; SEE CONCEPT 614

bitterness [n2] *agony*
acrimoniousness, anguish, asperity, distress, grievousness, harshness, hostility, mordancy, pain, painfulness, sarcasm, venom, virulence; SEE CONCEPTS 410,633

bizarre [adj] *strange, wild*
bugged-out*, camp*, comical, curious, eccentric, extraordinary, fantastic, far-out*, freakish, grody*, grotesque, kooky, ludicrous, odd, oddball, offbeat, off the wall*, outlandish, outré, peculiar, queer, ridiculous, singular, unusual, way-out*, weird; SEE CONCEPTS 547,564

blab [v] *gossip*
babble, blather, blurt out, chatter, disclose, divulge, gab, gabble, give away, go on, jabber, let out, let slip, mouth, peach*, prattle, reveal, run off at the mouth*, run on, shoot the breeze*, spill*, spill the beans*, squeal*, talk through one's hat*, tattle, tell, tell on, yak*, yakkety-yak*; SEE CONCEPTS 55,60

blabbermouth [n] *someone who talks too much*
babblemouth, babbler, bag of wind*, bigmouth, blabber, blabberer, blowhard*, chatterbox, chatterer, gabber, gasbag*, gossiper, gossipmonger, jabberer, loudmouth, motor-mouth, squealer*, tattletale, windbag*, yapper; SEE CONCEPTS 412,423

black [adj1] *dark, inky*
atramentous, brunet, charcoal, clouded, coal, dingy, dusky, ebon, ebony, inklike, jet, livid, melanoid, murky, obsidian, onyx, piceous, pitch, pitch-dark, raven, sable, shadowy, slate, sloe, somber, sombre, sooty, starless, stygian, swart, swarthy; SEE CONCEPT 618

black [adj2] *hopeless*
atrocious, bleak, depressing, depressive, dismal, dispiriting, distressing, doleful, dreary, foreboding, funereal, gloomy, horrible, lugubrious, mournful, ominous, oppressive, sad, sinister, sombre, threatening; SEE CONCEPTS 529,570

black [adj3] *dirty*
dingy, filthy, foul, grimy, grubby, impure, nasty, soiled, sooty, spotted, squalid, stained, unclean, uncleanly; SEE CONCEPT 589

black [adj4] *angry*
enraged, fierce, furious, hostile, menacing, resentful, sour, sullen, threatening; SEE CONCEPT 403

black [adj5] *evil*
bad, diabolical, iniquitous, mean, nefarious, villainous, wicked; SEE CONCEPT 545

black [n] *African-American*
African, Afro-American, Negro; SEE CONCEPT 380

blackball [v] *expel from group*
ban, blacklist, debar, exclude, ostracize, oust, reject, repudiate, snub, veto; SEE CONCEPTS 25,384

blacken [v1] *darken*
befoul, begrime, blot, cloud, deepen, ebonize, grow dark, grow dim, ink, make dark, shade, smudge, soil; SEE CONCEPT 250

blacken [v2] *malign; smear*
asperse, attack, bad-mouth*, blot, blotch, calumniate, decry, defame, defile, denigrate, dishonor, do a number on*, give a black eye*, knock*, libel, malign, rip*, rip up and down*, slander, slur, smudge, stain, sully, taint, tarnish, traduce, vilify; SEE CONCEPT 54

black hole [n] *abyss*
great void, supernova, theoretical mass, void; SEE CONCEPTS 509,514

blacklist [v] *ban*
banish, bar, blackball, boycott, debar, exclude, expel, hit list*, ostracize, preclude, proscribe, put on hit list*, reject, repudiate, snub, thumbs down*, vote against; SEE CONCEPT 25

black magic [n] *sorcery*
diabolism, magic, necromancy, voodoo, witchcraft, wizardry; SEE CONCEPTS 370,689

blackmail [n] *intimidation for money; money to quiet informer*
bribe, bribery, exaction, extortion, hush money*, milking*, payoff, protection, ransom, slush fund*, tribute; SEE CONCEPTS 123,192

blackmail [v] *intimidating for money*
badger, bleed, coerce, compel, demand, exact, extort, force, hold to ransom, milk*, put the shake on*, ransom, shake*, shake down*, squeeze*, threaten; SEE CONCEPTS 192,342

black market [n] *illegal sales*
bootleg market, underground, underground market, underworld market; SEE CONCEPT 323

black out [v1] *delete; cover*
batten, conceal, cover up, cross out, cut off, darken, eclipse, eradicate, erase, hold back, make dark, obfuscate, rub out, shade, squash, squelch; SEE CONCEPT 250

black out [v2] *faint*
collapse, crap out*, draw a blank*, go out like a light*, lose consciousness, pass out*, slip into coma, swoon*, zone out*; SEE CONCEPT 303

black sheep [n] *disgraceful person*
ne'er-do-well, outcast, pariah, prodigal, reject, reprobate; SEE CONCEPT 423

blade [n] *cutting tool*
brand, cutlass, edge, épée, knife, shank, sword; SEE CONCEPTS 495,499

blah [adj] *dull, lifeless*
banausic, bland, boring, dim, dreary, humdrum, monotone, monotonous, pedestrian, plodding, yawn producing*; SEE CONCEPT 544

blame [n1] *condemnation*
accusation, animadversion, arraignment, attack, attribution, castigation, censure, charge, chiding, complaint, criticism, denunciation, depreciation, diatribe, disapprobation, disapproval, disfavor, disparagement, expostulation, exprobation, impeachment, implication, imputation, incrimination, inculpation, indictment, invective, objurgation, obloquy, opposition, rebuke, recrimination, remonstrance, reprehension, reprimand, reproach, reprobation, reproof, repudiation, slur, tirade; SEE CONCEPT 54

blame [n2] *responsibility*
accountability, answerability, burden, culpability, fault, guilt, incrimination, liability, onus, rap*; SEE CONCEPTS 639,661

blame [v] *accuse; place responsibility*
admonish, ascribe, attribute, blast, blow the whistle on*, censure, charge, chide, climb all over*, condemn, criticize, denounce, denunciate, disapprove, express disapprobation, find fault with, finger*, frame, hold responsible, impute, indict, jump all over*, jump down one's throat*, knock*, lay a bad trip on*, lay at one's door*, lay to*, let one have it*, lower the boom*, pass the buck*, point the finger*, rap, rebuke, repre-

hend, reproach, reprove, roast*, saddle, skin*, stick it to*, tax, upbraid; SEE CONCEPT 44

blameless [adj] *not responsible*
above suspicion, clean, clean-handed, clear, crimeless, exemplary, faultless, good, guilt-free, guiltless, immaculate, impeccable, inculpable, innocent, in the clear*, irreprehensible, irreproachable, not guilty, perfect, pure, righteous, stainless, unblemished, unimpeachable, unoffending, unspotted, unsullied, untarnished, upright, virtuous; SEE CONCEPT 555

blanch [v] *become afraid*
flinch, pale, recoil, shrink, start, wince; SEE CONCEPT 27

bland [adj1] *tasteless; undistinctive*
banal, blah*, boring, dull, dull as dishwater*, flat, flavorless, ho hum*, humdrum, insipid, milk-and-water*, monotonous, nerdy*, nothing, pabulum*, sapless*, tame, tedious, unexciting, uninspiring, uninteresting, unstimulating, vanilla*, vapid, waterish, watery, weak, wimpy*, wishy-washy*, zero*; SEE CONCEPTS 589,613

bland [adj2] *friendly, gracious*
affable, amiable, civilized, congenial, courteous, gentle, good-natured, ingratiating, oily, pleasant, smooth, suave, unctuous, unemotional, urbane; SEE CONCEPT 401

bland [adj3] *mild, temperate*
balmy, calm, calmative, clear, lenient, mollifying, nonirritant, nonirritating, smooth, soft, soothing; SEE CONCEPTS 485,605

blank [adj1] *clear*
bare, barren, clean, empty, fresh, new, pale, plain, spotless, uncompleted, unfilled, unmarked, untouched, unused, vacant, vacuous, virgin, virginal, void, white; SEE CONCEPTS 485,562

blank [adj2] *expressionless*
deadpan, dull, empty, fruitless, hollow, immobile, impassive, inane, inexpressive, inscrutable, lifeless, masklike, meaningless, noncommittal, poker-faced, stiff, stupid, uncommunicative, unexpressive, vacant, vacuous, vague; SEE CONCEPT 406

blank [adj3] *dumbfounded*
at a loss, awestruck, bewildered, confounded, confused, dazed, disconcerted, muddled, nonplussed, stupefied, uncomprehending, wonderstruck; SEE CONCEPT 402

blank [adj4] *absolute, utter*
complete, downright, out-and-out, outright, perfect, regular, sheer, straight-out, thorough, total, unconditional, unqualified; SEE CONCEPT 531

blank [n] *empty space*
abyss, cavity, chasm, emptiness, gap, gulf, hiatus, hole, hollow, hollowness, interstice, interval, lacuna, nihility, nothingness, nullity, omission, opening, preterition, pretermission, skip, tabula rasa, vacancy, vacuity, vacuum, void, womb; SEE CONCEPT 513

blank check [n] *carte blanche*
free hand, free rein, license, permission, permit, say-so, the run of, total freedom, unconditional authority, unconditional right; SEE CONCEPT 376

blanket [adj] *comprehensive*
absolute, across-the-board, all-inclusive, overall, powerful, sweeping, unconditional, wide-ranging; SEE CONCEPT 772

blanket [n] *cover, covering*
afghan, carpet, cloak, coat, coating, comforter, covering, coverlet, envelope, film, fleece, layer,

mat, puff, quilt, rug, sheath, sheet, throw, wrapper; SEE CONCEPTS 473,475

blanket [v] *cover*
bury, cloak, cloud, coat, conceal, crown, eclipse, envelop, hide, mask, obscure, overcast, overlay, overspread, suppress, surround; SEE CONCEPT 172

blare [v] *make loud noise*
bark, bellow, blast, boom, bray, clamor, clang, honk, hoot, peal, resound, roar, scream, shout, shriek, sound out, toot, trumpet; SEE CONCEPTS 65,77

blarney [n] *flattery*
adulation, a line*, baloney*, blandishment, cajolery, coaxing, compliments, exaggeration, eyewash*, fawning*, honey*, incense, ingratiation, inveiglement, oil*, overpraise, soft soap*, soft words, sweet talk*, wheedling; SEE CONCEPT 69

blasé [adj] *nonchalant*
apathetic, been around twice*, bored, cloyed, cool*, disenchanted, disentranced, done it all*, fed up*, glutted, indifferent, jaded, knowing, laid-back*, lukewarm*, mellow*, mundane, offhand, satiated, sick of, sophisticate, sophisticated, surfeited, unconcerned, unexcited, uninterested, unmoved, weary, worldly, world-weary; SEE CONCEPT 404

blasphemous [adj] *irreverent*
cursing, disrespectful, godless, impious, insulting, irreligious, profanatory, profane, sacrilegious, swearing, ungodly; SEE CONCEPT 545

blasphemy [n] *irreverence*
abuse, cursing, cussing, desecration, execration, heresy, impiety, impiousness, imprecation, indignity, lewdness, profanation, profaneness, profanity, reviling, sacrilege, scoffing, scurrility, swearing, vituperation; SEE CONCEPT 645

blast [n1/v1] *loud sound; make loud sound*
bang, blare, blow, burst, clang, clap, crack, din, honk, peal, roar, scream, slam, smash, toot, trumpet, wail, wham; SEE CONCEPTS 65,521,595

blast [n2] *explosion*
bang, blow-up, burst, crash, detonation, discharge, dynamite, eruption, outbreak, outburst, salvo, volley; SEE CONCEPTS 179,521

blast [n3] *gust of wind*
blow, draft, gale, squall, storm, strong breeze, tempest; SEE CONCEPTS 437,524

blast [n4] *fun time*
amusement, bash*, blow out*, excitement, good time, great time, party, riot*; SEE CONCEPT 386

blast [v2] *explode*
annihilate, blight, blow up, bomb, break up, burst, damage, dash, demolish, destroy, detonate, dynamite, injure, kill, ruin, shatter, shrivel, spoil, stunt, torpedo, wither, wreck; SEE CONCEPTS 86,179

blast [v3] *lambaste; defeat mentally*
attack, beat, castigate, clobber*, criticize, drub*, flay, lash out at, lick*, rail at, shellac*, whip*; SEE CONCEPT 52

blatant [adj] *obvious; brazen*
arrant, bald, barefaced, brassy, clear, conspicuous, crying, flagrant, flashy, flaunting, garish, gaudy, glaring, glitzy, impudent, loud, meretricious, naked, obtrusive, ostentatious, outright, overbold, overt, plain, prominent, pronounced, protrusive, screaming, shameless, sheer, showy, snazzy, unabashed, unblushing, unmitigated; SEE CONCEPTS 540,569

blatant [*adj2*] *deafening*
boisterous, clamorous, crying, ear-splitting, harsh, loud, loudmouthed, noisy, obstreperous, obtrusive, piercing, screaming, scurrilous, strident, vociferant, vociferous, vulgar; SEE CONCEPTS *592,594*

blaze [*n1*] *fire*
bonfire, burning, combustion, conflagration, flame, flames, holocaust, wildfire; SEE CONCEPTS *478,521*

blaze [*n2*] *flash of light*
beam, brilliance, burst, flare, glare, gleam, glitter, glow, radiance; SEE CONCEPT *628*

blaze [*n3*] *torrent*
blast, burst, eruption, flare-up, flash, fury, outbreak, outburst, rush, storm; SEE CONCEPT *673*

blaze [*v*] *burn brightly*
beam, burst out, coruscate, explode, fire, flame, flare, flash, flicker, fulgurate, glare, gleam, glow, illuminate, illumine, incandesce, jet, light, radiate, scintillate, shimmer, shine, sparkle; SEE CONCEPT *249*

bleach [*v*] *whiten*
achromatize, blanch, blench, decolor, decolorize, etiolate, fade, grow pale, lighten, make pale, peroxide, wash out; SEE CONCEPT *250*

bleachers [*n*] *seating for watching event*
benches, boxes, grandstand, Ruthville*, seats, stands; SEE CONCEPTS *440,443*

bleak [*adj1*] *barren*
austere, bare, blank, blighted, bombed, bulldozed, burned, chilly, cleared, cold, deforested, desert, deserted, desolate, dreary, exposed, flat, gaunt, grim, open, raw, scorched, stripped, unpopulated, unsheltered, weather-beaten, wild, windswept; SEE CONCEPT *490*

bleak [*adj2*] *depressing*
black, cheerless, comfortless, dark, discouraging, disheartening, dismal, drear, dreary, funereal, gloomy, grim, hard, harsh, hopeless, joyless, lonely, melancholy, mournful, oppressive, sad, somber, unpromising; SEE CONCEPTS *403,537*

bleed [*v1*] *cause blood to flow*
drain, exude, gush, hemorrhage, leech, ooze, open vein, phlebotomize, run, seep, shed, spurt, trickle, weep; SEE CONCEPT *185*

bleed [*v2*] *extort*
blackmail, confiscate, deplete, drain, exhaust, extract, fleece, impoverish, leech*, milk*, mulct, overcharge, pauperize, put the screws to*, rook*, sap*, skin*, squeeze*, steal, stick*, strong-arm; SEE CONCEPTS *192,342*

bleed [*v3*] *grieve*
agonize, be in pain, che, feel for, pity, suffer, sympathize; SEE CONCEPTS *12,17*

blemish [*n*] *flaw*
beauty spot, birthmark, blackhead, blister, bloom*, blot, blotch, blot on the landscape*, blur, brand, bruise, bug*, catch, chip, cicatrix, defacement, defect, deformity, dent, discoloration, disfigurement, disgrace, dishonor, eyesore, fault, freckle, hickey*, imperfection, impurity, lentigo, lump, macula, maculation, mark, mole, nevus, nodule, patch, pimple, pock, pockmark, scar, second, sight, smudge, snag, speck, speckle, spot, stain, stigma, taint, tarnish, vice, wart, whitehead, zit*; SEE CONCEPT *580*

blemish [*v*] *flaw, disfigure*
blot, blotch, blur, damage, deface, distort, harm, hurt, impair, injure, maim, mangle, mar, mark,
mutilate, pervert, prejudice, scar, smudge, spoil, spot, stain, sully, taint, tarnish, twist, vitiate, wrench; SEE CONCEPTS *54,246*

blend [*n*] *composite, mix*
alloy, amalgam, amalgamation, brew, combination, commixture, composite, compound, concoction, fusion, interfusion, intermixture, mixture, synthesis, union; SEE CONCEPT *432*

blend [*v1*] *mix*
amalgamate, cement, coalesce, combine, commingle, commix, compound, fuse, integrate, interblend, intermix, meld, merge, mingle, synthesize, unite, weld; SEE CONCEPT *109*

blend [*v2*] *harmonize*
arrange, complement, fit, go well, go with, integrate, orchestrate, suit, symphonize, synthesize, unify; SEE CONCEPT *656*

bless [*v1*] *sanctify*
absolve, anoint, baptize, beatify, canonize, commend, confirm, consecrate, cross, dedicate, enshrine, eulogize, exalt, extol, give thanks to, glorify, hallow, honor, invoke benefits, invoke happiness, laud, magnify, make holy, offer, offer benediction, ordain, panegyrize, praise, pray for, pronounce holy, sacrifice, sign, sprinkle, thank; SEE CONCEPTS *69,367*

bless [*v2*] *grant, bestow*
celebrate, endow, favor, give, glorify, grace, laud, magnify, praise, provide; SEE CONCEPTS *50,88*

blessed [*adj1*] *sanctified*
adored, among the angels, beatified, consecrated, divine, enthroned, exalted, glorified, hallowed, holy, inviolable, redeemed, resurrected, revered, rewarded, sacred, sacrosanct, saved, spiritual, unprofane; SEE CONCEPTS *536,568*

blessed [*adj2*] *happy*
blissful, content, contented, endowed, favored, fortunate, glad, granted, joyful, joyous, lucky; SEE CONCEPT *404*

blessing [*n1*] *sanctification*
absolution, benedicite, benediction, benison, commendation, consecration, dedication, divine sanction, grace, invocation, laying on of hands, thanks, thanksgiving; SEE CONCEPT *367*

blessing [*n2*] *good wishes, approval*
approbation, backing, concurrence, consent, favor, Godspeed, leave, okay*, permission, regard, sanction, support, valediction; SEE CONCEPTS *10,50,88*

blessing [*n3*] *advantage*
asset, benediction, benefit, boon, bounty, break, favor, gain, gift, godsend, good, good fortune, good luck, help, kindness, lucky break, manna from heaven*, miracle, profit, service, stroke of luck*, windfall; SEE CONCEPTS *230,679*

blight [*n*] *disease; plague*
affliction, bane, blot on the landscape*, canker, contamination, corruption, curse, decay, dump, evil, eyesore, fungus, infestation, mildew, pest, pestilence, pollution, rot, scourge, sight, withering, woe; SEE CONCEPTS *306,674*

blight [*v*] *ruin, destroy*
annihilate, blast, crush, damage, dash, decay, disappoint, foul up*, frustrate, glitch up*, injure, mar, mess up*, nip in the bud*, nullify, shrivel, spoil, taint, trash*, wither, wreck; SEE CONCEPT *252*

blimp [*n*] *airship*
aircraft, dirigible, zeppelin; SEE CONCEPT *504*

bl
bl

blind [adj 1] *sightless*
amaurotic, blind as a bat*, dark, destitute of vision, eyeless, groping, in darkness, purblind, typhlotic, undiscerning, unseeing, unsighted, visionless; SEE CONCEPT 619

blind [adj 2] *indifferent*
careless, heedless, ignorant, imperceptive, inattentive, inconsiderate, indiscriminate, injudicious, insensitive, myopic, nearsighted, neglectful, oblivious, thoughtless, unaware, unconscious, undiscerning, unmindful, unobservant, unperceiving, unreasoning, unseeing; SEE CONCEPT 402

blind [adj 3] *uncontrolled*
hasty, heedless, impetuous, inconsiderate, irrational, mindless, rash, reckless, senseless, shortsighted, thoughtless, unseeing, unthinking, violent, wild; SEE CONCEPT 544

blind [adj 4] *hidden or covered*
blocked, closed, closed at one end, concealed, dark, dead-end, dim, disguised, impassable, leading nowhere, obscured, obstructed, secluded, unmarked, without egress, without exit; SEE CONCEPTS 490,576

blind [n] *screen, covering*
blinder, blindfold, blinker, camouflage, cloak, cover, curtain, facade, front, mask, trap, veil; SEE CONCEPT 716

blindly [adv 1] *without direction, purpose*
aimlessly, at random, confusedly, frantically, in all directions, indiscriminately, instinctively, madly, pell-mell, purposelessly, wildly; SEE CONCEPT 542

blindly [adv 2] *carelessly*
foolishly, heedlessly, impulsively, inconsiderately, obtusely, passionately, purblindly, recklessly, regardlessly, senselessly, thoughtlessly, tumultuously, unreasonably, unreasoningly, willfully, without rhyme or reason*; SEE CONCEPT 401

blindness [n] *sightlessness*
amaurosis, anopsia, astigmatism, cataracts, darkness, defect, myopia, presbyopia, purblindness, typhlosis; SEE CONCEPT 629

blind-side [v] *attack by surprise*
bushwhack, catch unaware, hit unexpectedly, sucker-punch; SEE CONCEPTS 86,189,200

blink [v 1] *wink of eye; twinkle*
bat, flash, flicker, flutter, glimmer, glitter, nictate, nictitate, scintillate, shimmer, sparkle, squint; SEE CONCEPTS 185,624

blink [v 2] *ignore*
bypass, condone, connive, cushion, discount, disregard, fail, forget, neglect, omit, overlook, overpass, pass by, slight, turn a blind eye*; SEE CONCEPT 30

bliss [n] *ecstasy*
beatitude, blessedness, cool*, euphoria, felicity, gladness, gone*, happiness, heaven*, joy, paradise, rapture; SEE CONCEPTS 32,230

blissful [adj] *happy*
beatific, cool*, crazy, delighted, dreamy, ecstatic, elated, enchanted, enraptured, euphoric, floating*, flying*, gone*, heavenly, in ecstasy, in seventh heaven*, in the twilight zone*, joyful, joyous, mad*, on cloud nine*, rapturous, sent*, spaced-out*, turned-on*; SEE CONCEPT 403

blister [n] *swelling*
abscess, blain, bleb, boil, bubble, bulla, burn, canker, carbuncle, cyst, furuncle, pimple, pus-

tule, sac, sore, ulcer, vesication, vesicle, wale, weal, welt, wheal; SEE CONCEPT 309

blithe [adj] *happy*
animated, buoyant, carefree, cheerful, cheery, chirpy, gay, gladsome, gleeful, jaunty, jocund, jolly, jovial, joyful, lighthearted, merry, mirthful, sprightly, sunny, vivacious; SEE CONCEPT 404

blitz [n] *heavy attack*
assault, blitzkrieg, bombardment, bombing, lightning attack, offensive, onslaught, raid, shelling, strike; SEE CONCEPTS 86,320

blizzard [n] *snow storm*
blast, gale, precipitation, snowfall, squall, tempest, whiteout; SEE CONCEPT 526

bloat [v] *blow up like a balloon*
balloon, belly, bilge, billow, dilate, distend, enlarge, expand, inflate, puff up, swell; SEE CONCEPTS 184,208

block [n 1] *mass of material*
bar, brick, cake, chunk, cube, hunk, ingot, loaf, lump, oblong, piece, section, segment, slab, slice, solid, square; SEE CONCEPTS 470,471

block [n 2] *obstruction*
bar, barrier, blank wall, blockage, chunk, clog, hindrance, impediment, jam, mass, obstacle, obstruction, roadblock, snag, stop, stoppage, wall; SEE CONCEPTS 470,652

block [v] *obstruct*
arrest, bar, barricade, blockade, block out, brake, catch, charge, check, choke, clog, close, close off, close out, congest, cut off, dam, deter, fill, halt, hang up*, hinder, hold up, impede, intercept, interfere with, occlude, plug, prevent, shut off*, shut out, stall, stonewall, stop, stopper, stop up*, stymie, tackle, take out of play*, thwart; SEE CONCEPTS 121,130

blockade [n] *barrier*
bar, barricade, blank wall, clog, closure, embolus, encirclement, hindrance, impediment, infarct, infarction, obstacle, obstruction, restriction, roadblock, siege, snag, stop, stoppage, wall; SEE CONCEPTS 470,652

block out [v 1] *plan course*
arrange, chart, map out, outline, prepare, sketch; SEE CONCEPT 36

block out [v 2] *try to forget*
close, conceal, cover, hide, obscure, obstruct, screen, shroud, shut off, shut out; SEE CONCEPT 40

blond/blonde [adj] *having light-colored hair*
albino, auricomous, bleached, champagne, fair, fair-haired, flaxen, golden-haired, light, pale, pearly, platinum, sallow, sandy-haired, snowy, straw, strawberry, towheaded*, washed-out, yellow-haired; SEE CONCEPT 618

blood [n 1] *red body fluid*
claret, clot, cruor, gore, hemoglobin, juice, plasma, sanguine fluid, vital fluid; SEE CONCEPTS 393,420

blood [n 2] *ancestry*
birth, consanguinity, descendants, descent, extraction, family, kindred, kinship, line, lineage, origin, pedigree, relations, stock; SEE CONCEPT 296

bloodless [adj] *unfeeling*
anesthetic, cold, coldhearted, dull, impassive, indolent, insensible, insensitive, languid, lazy, lifeless, listless, passionless, slow, sluggish, spiritless, torpid, unemotional, unkind; SEE CONCEPT 404

bloodless [*adj2*] *pale*
anemic, ashen, cadaverous, chalky, colorless, ghostly, lifeless, pallid, pasty, sallow, sickly, wan, watery; SEE CONCEPT 618

bloodthirsty [*adj*] *murderous*
barbaric, cruel, homicidal, inhuman, ruthless, sanguinary, savage, slaughterous; SEE CONCEPT 401

bloody [*adj1*] *bleeding*
blood-soaked, blood-spattered, bloodstained, crimson, ensanguined, gaping, gory, grisly, hematic, hemic, imbrued, open, raw, sanguinary, sanguine, unstaunched, unstopped, wounded; SEE CONCEPT 485

bloody [*adj2*] *hard-fought*
bloodthirsty, cruel, cutthroat, decimating, ferocious, fierce, gory, grim, heavy, homicidal, murderous, sanguinary, sanguine, savage, slaughterous; SEE CONCEPTS 540,569

bloom [*n*] *flower*
blossom, blossoming, bud, efflorescence, floret, flourishing, flower, floweret, opening; SEE CONCEPT 425

bloom [*v*] *flower; flourish*
bear fruit, be in flower, blossom, blow, bud, burgeon, burst, develop, effloresce, fare well, fructify, germinate, grow, open, prosper, sprout, succeed, tassel out, thrive, wax; SEE CONCEPTS 427,706

blooper [*n*] *blunder*
boner*, boo-boo*, bungle, error, faux pas, fluff*, gaffe, impropriety, indecorum, lapse, mistake, slip, solecism, trip*; SEE CONCEPTS 384,674

blossom [*n*] *flower*
bloom, bud, efflorescence, floret, floweret, inflorescence, posy, spike; SEE CONCEPT 425

blossom [*v1*] *flower*
bloom, blow, burgeon, burst, effloresce, leaf, open, outbloom, shoot, unfold; SEE CONCEPT 427

blossom [*v2*] *flourish*
batten, bloom, develop, grow, mature, progress, prosper, succeed, thrive; SEE CONCEPT 706

blot [*n*] *mark; flaw*
black eye*, blemish, blotch, blur, brand, defect, discoloration, disgrace, fault, odium, onus, patch, slur, smear, smudge, speck, spot, stain, stigma, taint; SEE CONCEPTS 230,580

blot [*v1*] *disgrace, disfigure*
bespatter, blemish, dirty, discolor, mark, smudge, smut, soil, spoil, spot, stain, sully, tarnish; SEE CONCEPT 240

blot [*v2*] *soak up*
absorb, dry, take up; SEE CONCEPT 211

blotch [*n*] *smudge*
acne, blemish, blot, breakout, eruption, mark, mottling, patch, splash, spot, stain, stigma; SEE CONCEPT 580

blouse [*n*] *shirt for woman*
bodice, bodysuit, middy, pullover, shell, slipover, T-shirt, turtleneck, V-neck; SEE CONCEPT 451

blow [*n1*] *blast, rush of air, wind*
draft, flurry, gale, gust, hurricane, puff, squall, strong breeze, tempest, typhoon; SEE CONCEPT 526

blow [*n2*] *hard hit*
bang, bash, bat, belt, biff, blindside, bop*, buffet, bump, clip, clout, clump, collision, concussion, crack, cut, ding*, impact, jab, jar, jolt, kick, knock, knockout, knuckle sandwich*, KO*, lick,

percussion, poke, pound, punch, rap, shock, slam, slap, slug, smack, smash, sock, strike, stroke, swat, swing, swipe, thrust, thump, thwack*, uppercut, wallop, whack, whomp*, zap*; SEE CONCEPT 189

blow [*n3*] *catastrophe*
affliction, balk, bolt from the blue*, bombshell*, calamity, casualty, chagrin, comedown, debacle, disappointment, disaster, disgruntlement, frustration, jolt, letdown, misadventure, misfortune, mishap, reverse, setback, shock, tragedy, upset; SEE CONCEPT 674

blow [*v1*] *blast, rush of air, wind*
breathe, buffet, drive, exhale, fan, flap, flow, flutter, gasp, heave, huff, inflate, pant, puff, pump, ruffle, rush, stream, swell, swirl, waft, wave, whiff, whirl, whisk, whisper, whistle; SEE CONCEPTS 185,526

blow [*v2*] *make sound, usually with instrument*
blare, blast, honk, mouth, pipe, play, sound, toot, trumpet, vibrate; SEE CONCEPT 65

blow [*v3*] *leave suddenly*
depart, go, hit the road*, split*, take a hike*, take a powder*; SEE CONCEPT 195

blow [*v4*] *ruin chance*
fail, flounder, goof*, miscarry, miss; SEE CONCEPT 699

blow [*v5*] *use up money*
dissipate, lay out, pay out, spend, squander, waste; SEE CONCEPT 341

blowout [*n1*] *explosion; something exploded*
blast, break, burst, detonation, eruption, escape, flat tire, leak, puncture, rupture, tear; SEE CONCEPT 179

blowout [*n2*] *wild party*
bash, binge, feast, riot*, shindig, spree; SEE CONCEPT 383

blow over [*v*] *disappear slowly*
cease, die down, dissipate, end, finish, fizzle out, pass, peter out*, subside, vanish; SEE CONCEPT 699

blow up [*v1*] *inflate*
billow, bloat, distend, enlarge, expand, fill, inflate, puff up, pump up, swell; SEE CONCEPTS 208,236,245

blow up [*v2*] *explode*
blast, bomb, burst, detonate, dynamite, erupt, go off, mushroom, rupture, shatter; SEE CONCEPTS 179,320

blow up [*v3*] *magnify importance*
enlarge, exaggerate, heighten, overstate; SEE CONCEPTS 49,59

blow up [*v4*] *burst with anger*
become angry, become enraged, erupt, go off the deep end*, hit the roof*, lose control, lose temper, rage, rave; SEE CONCEPTS 29,44

blue [*adj1*] *sky, sea color*
azure, beryl, cerulean, cobalt, indigo, navy, royal, sapphire, teal, turquoise, ultramarine; SEE CONCEPT 618

blue [*adj2*] *sad*
dejected, depressed, despondent, disconsolate, dismal, dispirited, downcast, downhearted, down in the dumps*, fed up*, gloomy, glum, low, melancholy, moody, unhappy, woebegone; SEE CONCEPT 403

blue [*adj3*] *vulgar*
bawdy, dirty, indecent, lewd, naughty, obscene, off-color, racy, risqué, salty, shady, smutty, spicy, suggestive, wicked; SEE CONCEPT 545

blueprint [*n*] *plan*
archetype, architectural plan, design, draft, game plan, layout, master plan, model, prototype, rendering, scheme, sketch; SEE CONCEPTS 268,271,625

blues [*n*] *depression*
dejection, despondency, doldrums, dumps*, gloom, gloominess, glumness, heavy heart*, low spirits, melancholy, moodiness, mournfulness, sadness, the dismals*, the mopes*, unhappiness; SEE CONCEPT 410

bluff [*adj*] *abrupt*
barefaced, bearish, blunt, blustering, breviloquent, brief, brusque, candid, crusty, curt, direct, downright, forthright, frank, gruff, hearty, honest, matter-of-fact, no-nonsense, open, outspoken, plain-spoken, rough, rude, short, short-spoken, sincere, snippety, snippy, straightforward, tactless, tart, terse, unceremonious; SEE CONCEPT 267

bluff [*n1*] *boast; deceit*
bluster, braggadocio, bragging, bravado, deception, delusion, facade, fake, false colors, false front, feint, fraud, front, humbug*, jiving*, lie, pretense, pretext, ruse, sham, show, snow*, stall, subterfuge, trick; SEE CONCEPTS 58,59

bluff [*n2*] *precipice*
bank, cliff, crag, escarpment, headland, hill, mountain, peak, promontory, ridge, rock; SEE CONCEPT 509

bluff [*v*] *deceive*
affect, beguile, betray, bunco*, con, counterfeit, defraud, delude, double-cross, fake*, fake out*, feign, fool, humbug*, illude, jive*, juggle, lie, mislead, pretend, psych out*, put on*, sham*, shuck*, simulate, snow*, take in*, trick; SEE CONCEPTS 58,59

blunder [*n*] *mistake*
blooper*, boner*, boo-boo*, bungle, dumb move*, error, fault, faux pas, flub*, flub-up*, fluff*, gaffe, goof*, howler*, impropriety, inaccuracy, indiscretion, lapse, muff*, oversight, slip, slip-up, solecism, trip*; SEE CONCEPTS 101,230

blunder [*v*] *make mistake*
ball up*, blow, bobble, botch, bumble, bungle, confuse, drop the ball*, err, flounder, flub*, foul up, fumble, gum up*, louse up, mess up, misjudge, screw up*, slip up, stumble; SEE CONCEPT 101

blunt [*adj1*] *not sharp*
dull, dulled, edgeless, insensitive, obtuse, pointless, round, rounded, unsharpened; SEE CONCEPTS 485,486

blunt [*adj2*] *straightforward*
abrupt, bluff, brief, brusque, candid, crusty, curt, discourteous, explicit, forthright, frank, gruff, impolite, matter-of-fact, outspoken, plain-spoken, rude, short, snappy, snippy, tactless, trenchant, unceremonious, uncivil, unpolished; SEE CONCEPT 267

blunt [*v*] *make dull*
attenuate, benumb, cripple, dampen, deaden, debilitate, desensitize, disable, enfeeble, numb, obtund, sap, soften, take the edge off, undermine, water down, weaken; SEE CONCEPT 240

blur [*v1*] *cloud, fog*
becloud, bedim, befog, blear, blind, darken, daze, dazzle, dim, glare, make hazy, make indistinct, make vague, mask, muddy, obscure, shade, soften; SEE CONCEPT 627

blur [*v2*] *make dirty*
besmear, blemish, blot, discolor, smear, smudge, spot, stain, taint, tarnish; SEE CONCEPT 254

blush [*n*] *pink coloring*
bloom, blossom, burning, color, flush, flushing, glow, glowing, mantling, pink tinge, reddening, redness, rosiness, rosy tint, ruddiness, scarlet; SEE CONCEPT 622

blush [*v*] *become colored, pinken*
color, crimson, flush, glow, have rosy cheeks, mantle, redden, rouge, turn red, turn scarlet; SEE CONCEPT 250

bluster [*n*] *bullying, intimidation*
bluff, boasting, boisterousness, bombast, braggadocio, bragging, bravado, crowing, rabidity, rampancy, swagger, swaggering; SEE CONCEPT 633

bluster [*v*] *bully, intimidate*
badger, boast, brag, brazen, browbeat, bulldoze*, cow*, crow*, domineer, gloat, hector, rant, rave, ride the high horse*, roar, roister, shoot off one's mouth*, show off, storm, strut, swagger, swell, talk big*, vapor*, vaunt, yap*; SEE CONCEPTS 49,78

board [*n1*] *piece of wood*
lath, panel, plank, slat, strip, timber; SEE CONCEPT 479

board [*n2*] *meal*
daily bread*, eats*, fare, food, keep*, mess, provisions, victuals; SEE CONCEPT 459

board [*n3*] *group of advisers*
advisers, advisory group, brass, cabinet, committee, conclave, council, directorate, directors, execs*, executives, executive suite, front office*, jury, panel, trustees, upstairs*; SEE CONCEPTS 323,333,417

board [*v1*] *embark on vehicle*
catch, climb on, embus, emplane, enter, entrain, get on, hop on, mount; SEE CONCEPTS 159,195

board [*v2*] *provide food and sleeping quarters*
accommodate, bed, canton, care for, feed, harbor, house, let crash*, lodge, put up, quarter, room; SEE CONCEPT 136

boast [*n*] *brag; source of pride*
avowal, bluster, bombast, braggadocio, bravado, exaggeration, gasconade, grandiloquence, heroics, joy, pretension, pride, pride and joy, self-satisfaction, swank, treasure, vaunt; SEE CONCEPTS 410,710

boast [*v1*] *brag*
advertise, aggrandize, attract attention, blow, blow one's own horn*, blow smoke*, bluster, bully, cock-a-doodle-doo*, con, congratulate oneself, crow, exaggerate, exult, fake, flatter oneself, flaunt, flourish, gasconade, give a good account of oneself, gloat, glory, grandstand*, hug oneself*, jive*, lay on thick*, prate, preen, psych*, puff*, shoot*, shovel*, showboat*, show off, shuck*, sling*, sound off, strut, swagger, talk big*, triumph, vapor*; SEE CONCEPT 49

boast [*v2*] *to have advantage*
be proud of, claim, exhibit, have in keeping, own, possess, pride oneself on, show off; SEE CONCEPT 261

boastful [*adj*] *bragging*
arrogant, big, big-headed, bombastic, cocky, conceited, crowing, egotistic, egotistical, exultant, full of hot air*, hifalutin*, hot stuff*, know-

it-all, loudmouth, on ego trip*, pompous, pretentious, puffed-up, self-aggrandizing, self-applauding, smart-alecky*, snooty, strutting, stuck-up, swaggering, swanky, swollen-headed, too big for one's britches*, vainglorious, vaunting, windbag*; SEE CONCEPTS 267,404

boat [*n*] *vehicle for water travel*
ark, barge, bark, bateau, bottom, bucket, canoe, catamaran, craft, dinghy, dory, hulk, ketch, launch, lifeboat, pinnace, raft, sailboat, schooner, scow, ship, skiff, sloop, steamboat, tub, yacht; SEE CONCEPT 506

boating [*n*] *travel, recreation in water*
canoeing, cruising, drifting, paddling, rowing, sailing, sculling, trawling, yachting; SEE CONCEPT 363

bob [*v*] *bounce up and down*
bow, duck, genuflect, hop, jerk, jounce, leap, nod, oscillate, quaver, quiver, ricochet, seesaw, skip, waggle, weave, wobble; SEE CONCEPT 147

bodily [*adj*] *concerning animate structure*
actual, animal, carnal, corporal, corporeal, fleshly, gross, human, material, natural, normal, organic, physical, sensual, somatic, substantial, tangible, unspiritual; SEE CONCEPT 406

bodily [*adv*] *totally*
absolutely, altogether, as a body, as a group, collectively, completely, en masse, entirely, fully, wholly; SEE CONCEPTS 531,772

body [*n1*] *physique*
anatomy, bag of bones*, beefcake*, bod*, boody*, build, carcass, chassis, constitution, embodiment, figure, form, frame, makeup, mortal part, protoplasm, shaft, shape, tenement, torso, trunk; SEE CONCEPT 405

body [*n2*] *corpse*
ashes, bones, cadaver, carcass, carrion, clay, corpus delicti, dead body, deceased, dust, relic, remains, stiff*; SEE CONCEPT 390

body [*n3*] *human being*
being, creature, human, individual, mortal, party, person, personage, soul; SEE CONCEPT 389

body [*n4*] *bulk; central portion*
assembly, basis, bed, box, chassis, core, corpus, crux, essence, frame, fuselage, gist, gravamen, groundwork, hull, main part, majority, mass, material, matter, pith, skeleton, staple, substance, substructure, sum, tenor, total, trunk, whole; SEE CONCEPT 829

body [*n5*] *crowd*
array, batch, bunch, bundle, clump, cluster, group, horde, lot, majority, mass, mob, multitude, parcel, party, set, society, throng; SEE CONCEPTS 417,432

body [*n6*] *main part of written work*
argument, burden, core, discourse, dissertation, evidence, exposition, gist, heart, material, meat, pith, sense, substance, text, thesis, treatise, upshot; SEE CONCEPT 270

bodyguard [*n*] *protector*
bouncer, escort, guardian, minder, muscle*, praetorian, security guard; SEE CONCEPT 348

bog [*n*] *swamp*
fen, lowland, marsh, marshland, mire, morass, moss, peat, quag, quagmire, slough, sump, wetlands; SEE CONCEPT 509

bog down [*v*] *stick; become stuck*
decelerate, delay, detain, halt, hang up, impede, retard, set back, sink, slacken, slow down, slow up, stall; SEE CONCEPT 121

bogus [*adj*] *counterfeit*
artificial, dummy, ersatz, fake, false, fictitious, forged, fraudulent, imitation, not what it is cracked up to be*, phony, pretended, pseudo, sham, simulated, spurious; SEE CONCEPT 582

bohemian [*n*] *nonconformist*
artist, beatnik*, dilettante, flower child*, free spirit, gypsy, hippie*, iconoclast, writer; SEE CONCEPT 423

boil [*n*] *blister*
abscess, blain, blister, carbuncle, excrescence, furuncle, pimple, pustule, sore, tumor, ulcer; SEE CONCEPT 309

boil [*v1*] *heat to bubbling*
agitate, bubble, churn, coddle, cook, decoct, effervesce, evaporate, fizz, foam, froth, parboil, poach, seethe, simmer, smolder, steam, steep, stew; SEE CONCEPTS 170,255

boil [*v2*] *be angry*
be indignant, blow up, bristle, burn, flare, foam at the mouth*, fulminate, fume, rage, rave, sputter, storm; SEE CONCEPT 29

boiling [*adj1*] *very hot*
baking, blistering, broiling, burning, fiery, hot, red-hot, roasting, scalding, scorching, sizzling, torrid, tropical, warm; SEE CONCEPT 605

boiling [*adj2*] *angered*
angry, enraged, fuming, furious, incensed, indignant, infuriated, mad, raging; SEE CONCEPT 403

boisterous [*adj*] *noisy and mischievous*
bouncy, brawling, clamorous, disorderly, effervescent, impetuous, loud, obstreperous, rambunctious, raucous, riotous, rollicking, rowdy, strident, tumultous/tumultuous, unrestrained, unruly, uproarious, vociferant, vociferous, wild; SEE CONCEPT 401

bold [*adj1*] *brave*
adventurous, assuming, audacious, aweless, bantam, courageous, daring, dauntless, enterprising, fearless, forward, gallant, heroic, intrepid, resolute, unafraid, undaunted, valiant, valorous; SEE CONCEPT 401

bold [*adj2*] *brazen, insolent*
assuming, audacious, barefaced, brash, brassy, cheeky, coming on strong*, confident, forward, fresh, gritty, gutsy, immodest, impudent, insolent, nervy, pert, presumptuous, rude, sassy, saucy, shameless, smart, smart-alecky*, spunky; SEE CONCEPTS 401,404

bold [*adj3*] *bright, striking*
clear, colorful, conspicuous, definite, evident, eye-catching, flashy, forceful, lively, loud, manifest, plain, prominent, pronounced, showy, spirited, strong, vivid; SEE CONCEPTS 589,617,618

bolster [*v*] *help*
aid, assist, bear up, boost, brace, buck up, bulwark, buoy, buttress, carry, cushion, help, hold up, maintain, pick up, pillow, prop, reinforce, shore up, stay, strengthen, support, sustain, uphold; SEE CONCEPT 110

bolt [*n1*] *lock; part of lock*
bar, brad, catch, coupling, dowel, fastener, lag, latch, lock, nut, padlock, peg, pin, pipe, rivet, rod, screw, skewer, sliding bar, spike, stake, staple, stud; SEE CONCEPTS 470,471,680

bolt [*n2*] *flash; projectile*
arrow, dart, fulmination, missile, shaft, thunderbolt, thunderstroke; SEE CONCEPTS 624,687

bl
bo

bolt [*n3*] *large roll of material*
coil, curl, cylinder, package, spindle, spiral, twist; SEE CONCEPT *432*

bolt [*v1*] *run quickly away*
abscond, bail out*, bound, cop out*, cut loose*, cut out*, dart, dash, ditch*, drop out*, dump*, escape, flee, flight, fly, hightail*, hotfoot*, hurtle, jump, kiss goodbye*, leap, leave flat*, leave high and dry*, leave holding the bag*, leave in the lurch*, make a break for it*, make off*, make tracks*, opt out*, run like scared rabbit*, run out on, rush, scamper, scoot, skedaddle*, skip, split*, spring, sprint, start, startle, step on it*, take flight, take off*, walk out on; SEE CONCEPTS *150,195*

bolt [*v2*] *fasten securely*
bar, deadbolt, latch, lock, secure; SEE CONCEPT *225*

bolt [*v3*] *eat very fast*
consume, cram, devour, englut, gobble, gorge, gulp, guzzle, ingurgitate, inhale, scarf*, slop, slosh, stuff, swallow whole, wolf*; SEE CONCEPT *169*

bomb [*n*] *exploding weapon*
atom bomb, bombshell, charge, device, explosive, grenade, hydrogen bomb, mine, missile, Molotov cocktail, nuclear bomb, projectile, rocket, shell, ticker*, torpedo; SEE CONCEPT *500*

bomb [*v1*] *detonate weapon*
attack, blast, blitz, blow up, bombard, cannonade, destroy, napalm, prang, raid, rain destruction*, rake, shell, strafe, torpedo, wipe out*, zero in*; SEE CONCEPTS *86,252*

bomb [*v2*] *fail miserably*
blow it*, flop, flummox, go out of business, lose, wash out*, wipe out*; SEE CONCEPT *699*

bombard [*v*] *assault, attack*
assail, barrage, batter, beset, besiege, blast, blitz, bomb, cannonade, catapult, fire upon, harass, hound, launch, open fire, pester, pound, shell, strafe, strike; SEE CONCEPTS *7,19,86*

bombastic [*adj*] *pompous, grandiloquent*
aureate, balderdash, big-talking*, declamatory, euphuistic, flowery, full of hot air*, fustian, grandiose, highfalutin*, high-flown, histrionic, inflated, loudmouthed, magniloquent, orotund, ostentatious, overblown, ranting, rhapsodic, rhetorical, sonorous, stuffed shirt*, swollen, tumid, turgid, verbose, windbag*, windy, wordy; SEE CONCEPT *267*

bona fide [*n*] *genuine*
actual, authentic, honest, kosher, legitimate, real, true, valid; SEE CONCEPT *582*

bonanza [*n*] *windfall*
cash cow*, gold mine, treasure trove; SEE CONCEPTS *332,337,446,710*

bond [*n1*] *binder or fastener*
band, binding, chain, connection, cord, fastening, fetter, gunk, handcuff, hookup, irons, ligature, link, linkage, manacle, network, nexus, rope, shackle, stickum*, tie, tie-in, wire; SEE CONCEPT *497*

bond [*n2*] *association, relation*
affiliation, affinity, attachment, connection, connective, friendship, hookup, interrelationship, liaison, link, marriage, network, obligation, relationship, restraint, tie, tie-in, union; SEE CONCEPT *348*

bond [*n3*] *guarantee; contract*
agreement, bargain, certificate, collateral, compact, convention, covenant, debenture, guaranty, obligation, pact, pledge, promise, security, transaction, warrant, warranty, word; SEE CONCEPTS *318,684*

bond [*v*] *fasten; stick*
bind, connect, fix, fuse, glue, gum, paste, stickum*; SEE CONCEPTS *85,160*

bondage [*n*] *slavery*
chains, enslavement, helotry, peonage, serfage, serfdom, servility, servitude, subjection, subjugation, thrall, thralldom, villenage, yoke; SEE CONCEPTS *136,652*

bone [*n*] *piece of animate skeleton*
bony process, cartilage, ossein, osseous matter; SEE CONCEPTS *393,420*

boner [*n*] *a mistake*
blooper*, blunder, bonehead play, boo-boo*, bungle, error, false move, faux pas*, flub, flummox, foulup, gaffe, goof-up, miscalculation, miscue, misstep, muddle, muff, oversight, screw-up, slipup*, snafu*, whoops; SEE CONCEPTS *101,230,410*

boneyard [*n*] *burial ground*
boot hill*, catacomb, cemetery, charnel, charnel house, churchyard, city of the dead*, crypt, eternal home*, funerary grounds, garden, God's acre*, Golgotha, grave, graveyard, marble town*, memorial park, mortuary, necropolis, ossuary, polyandrium, potter's field, resting place, sepulcher, tomb, vault; SEE CONCEPTS *305,368*

bonfire [*n*] *large prepared fire*
beacon, conflagration, feu de joie, pyre; SEE CONCEPTS *478,521*

bonus [*n*] *unexpected extra*
additional compensation, benefit, bounty, commission, dividend, fringe benefit, frosting*, gift, golden parachute*, goody*, gratuity, gravy*, hand-out*, honorarium, ice*, perk*, plus*, premium, prize, reward, special compensation, tip; SEE CONCEPT *337*

boo boo [*n1*] *small hurt*
black and blue mark, bruise, cut, injury, laceration, scratch, sore; SEE CONCEPTS *309,728*

boo boo [*n2*] *small mistake*
blunder, error, gaffe, goof*, misstep, oversight, screw-up*, slip; SEE CONCEPTS *101,230,410*

book [*n1*] *published document*
album, atlas, bestseller, bible, booklet, brochure, codex, compendium, copy, dictionary, dissertation, edition, encyclopedia, essay, fiction, folio, handbook, hardcover, leaflet, lexicon, magazine, manual, monograph, nonfiction, novel, octavo, offprint, omnibus, opus, opuscule, pamphlet, paperback, periodical, portfolio, preprint, primer, publication, quarto, reader, reprint, roll, scroll, softcover, speller, text, textbook, thesaurus, tome, tract, treatise, vade mecum, volume, work, writing; SEE CONCEPT *280*

book [*n2*] *account; diary*
agenda, album, list, notebook, pad, record, register, roster; SEE CONCEPTS *271,331*

book [*v1*] *register, arrange for*
bespeak, bill, charter, engage, enroll, enter, hire, line up*, make reservation, order, organize, pencil in*, preengage, procure, program, reserve, schedule, set up, sew up*; SEE CONCEPT *36*

book [*v2*] *arrest*
accuse, charge, prefer charges, take into custody; SEE CONCEPT *317*

booking [*n*] *engagement*
gig, performance date, play date, tour date; SEE
CONCEPT *384*

boom [*n1*] *loud sound; crash*
bang, barrage, blare, blast, burst, cannonade,
clap, crack, drumfire, explosion, reverberation,
roar, rumble, slam, smash, thunder, wham; SEE
CONCEPTS *521,595*

boom [*n2*] *prosperity*
advance, boost, development, expansion, gain,
growth, improvement, increase, inflation, jump,
prosperousness, push, rush, spurt, upsurge, upswing, upturn; SEE CONCEPTS *230,335,700*

boom [*v1*] *crash; make loud sound*
bang, blast, burst, clap, crack, drum, explode, resound, reverberate, roar, roll, rumble, slam,
smash, sound, thunder, wham; SEE CONCEPT *65*

boom [*v2*] *prosper*
appreciate, bloom, develop, enhance, expand,
flourish, flower, gain, grow, increase, intensify,
rise in value, spurt, strengthen, succeed, swell,
thrive; SEE CONCEPTS *700,704*

boom box [*n*] *portable music machine*
audio system, CD player, ghetto blaster*, ghetto
box*, radio, stereo, tape player; SEE CONCEPT
463

boomerang [*v*] *backfire*
backlash, bounce back, come back, come home
to roost*, kick back, react, rebound, recoil, return, reverse, ricochet; SEE CONCEPTS *242,695*

boon [*n*] *advantage*
benefaction, benefit, benevolence, blessing,
break, compliment, donation, favor, gift, godsend, good, good fortune, grant, gratuity, help,
largess, present, windfall; SEE CONCEPTS *337,661*

boor [*n*] *clod*
barbarian, bear, boob*, brute, buffoon, cad,
churl, dork*, goon*, lout, oaf, peasant, philistine,
rube*, vulgarian; SEE CONCEPT *423*

boorish [*adj*] *crude, awkward*
bad-mannered, barbaric, bearish, cantankerous,
churlish, cloddish, clodhopping*, clownish,
clumsy, coarse, countrified, gross*, gruff, ill-
bred, ill-mannered, impolite, inurbane, loud,
loutish, lowbred, oafish, ornery, out-of-line, out-
of-order, provincial, rough, rude, rustic, swinish,
tasteless, ugly, uncivilized, uncouth, uncultured,
uneducated, ungracious, unpoised, unpolished,
unrefined, vulgar; SEE CONCEPT *404*

boost [*n1*] *increase*
addition, advance, breakthrough, expansion,
hike, improvement, increment, jump, lift, raise,
rise, step-up, up, upgrade, wax; SEE CONCEPTS
700,780

boost [*n2*] *encouragement*
aid, assistance, backup, buildup, goose*, hand*,
handout, help, helping hand, improvement, leg*,
leg up*, lift, praise, promotion, shot in the arm*,
support; SEE CONCEPT *110*

boost [*n3*] *push, usually up*
advance, goose*, heave, hoist, lift, raise, shove,
thrust; SEE CONCEPTS *196,208*

boost [*v1*] *further, improve*
advance, advertise, assist, encourage, foster, inspire, plug, praise, promote, push, support, sustain; SEE CONCEPT *244*

boost [*v2*] *push, usually up*
advance, elevate, heave, heighten, hoist, lift,
raise, shove, thrust, upraise, uprear; SEE CON-
CEPTS *196,208*

boost [*v3*] *increase*
add to, aggrandize, amplify, augment, beef up*,
develop, enlarge, expand, extend, heighten, hike,
jack up*, jump, magnify, multiply, put up, raise,
up; SEE CONCEPTS *236,245*

boot [*n*] *heavy, often tall, shoe*
brogan, footwear, galoshes, mukluk, oxford,
snow shoes, waders, waters*; SEE CONCEPT *450*

boot [*v1*] *kick; oust*
ax, bounce, can*, chase, chuck*, cut, discharge,
dismiss, drive, dropkick*, eighty-six*, eject,
evict, expel, extrude, fire, heave, kick out, knock,
punt*, sack*, shove, terminate, throw out; SEE
CONCEPTS *180,189*

boot [*v2*] *start operating system*
bootstrap, cold boot, load, reboot, reset, restart,
start, start computer, warm boot; SEE CONCEPT
221

booth [*n*] *small enclosure or building*
berth, box, carrel, compartment, coop, corner,
cote, counter, cubbyhole, cubicle, dispensary,
hut, hutch, nook, pen, pew, repository, shed,
stall, stand; SEE CONCEPTS *439,440,443*

booty [*n*] *loot*
boodle, gain, goods, haul*, pickings*, plunder,
spoils, swag, takings*; SEE CONCEPTS *337,710*

border [*n1*] *outermost edge, margin*
bound, boundary, bounds, brim, brink, circumference, confine, end, extremity, fringe, hem,
limit, line, lip, outskirt, perimeter, periphery,
rim, selvage, skirt, trim, trimming, verge; SEE
CONCEPTS *484,827*

border [*n2*] *boundary; frontier*
beginning, borderline, door, edge, entrance, line,
march, marchland, outpost, pale, perimeter, sideline, threshold; SEE CONCEPTS *484,513*

border [*v*] *bound on; be on the edge*
abut, adjoin, be adjacent to, bind, circumscribe,
communicate, contour, decorate, define, delineate, edge, encircle, enclose, flank, frame, fringe,
hem, join, line, march, margin, mark off, neighbor, outline, rim, set off, side, skirt, surround,
touch, trim, verge; SEE CONCEPT *747*

borderline [*adj*] *inexact*
ambiguous, ambivalent, doubtful, dubitable,
equivocal, indecisive, indefinite, indeterminate,
marginal, open, problematic, uncertain, unclassifiable, unclear, undecided, unsettled; SEE CON-
CEPT *534*

border on [*v*] *come close to; approximate*
abut, adjoin, approach, be like, be similar to,
come near, compare, connect, contact, echo, impinge, join, lie near, lie next to, march, match,
near, neighbor, parallel, resemble, touch, verge
on; SEE CONCEPTS *667,749*

bore [*n*] *nuisance*
bother, bromide, bummer*, creep*, deadhead*,
downer*, drag*, drip*, dull person, flat tire*,
headache, nag, nudge, pain, pain in the neck*,
pest, pill*, soporific, stuffed shirt*, tedious person, tiresome person, wet blanket*, wimp*,
yawn*; SEE CONCEPT *423*

bore [*v1*] *drill hole*
burrow, gouge out, mine, penetrate, perforate,
pierce, pit, prick, punch, puncture, ream, riddle,
sink, tunnel; SEE CONCEPT *178*

bore [*v2*] *cause weariness, disinterest*
afflict, annoy, bend one's ear*, be tedious,
bother, burn out, cloy, discomfort, drag, exhaust,
fatigue, irk, irritate, jade, pall, pester, put to

bo
bo

sleep*, send to sleep*, talk one's ear off*, tire, trouble, turn one off*, vex, wear, wear out, weary, worry; SEE CONCEPTS *7,19*

boredom [*n*] *disinterest; weariness*
apathy, detachment, disgust, distaste, doldrums, dullness, ennui, fatigue, flatness, incuriosity, indifference, irksomeness, jadedness, lack of interest, lassitude, lethargy, listlessness, monotony, pococurantism, sameness, taedium vitae, tediousness, tedium, tiresomeness, unconcern, world-weariness, yawn; SEE CONCEPT *410*

boring [*adj*] *uninteresting*
arid, bomb*, bromidic, bummer*, characterless, cloying, colorless, commonplace, dead*, drab, drag*, drudging, dull, flat*, ho hum*, humdrum, insipid, interminable, irksome, lifeless, monotonous, moth-eaten*, mundane, nothing, nowhere, platitudinous, plebeian, prosaic, repetitious, routine, spiritless, stale, stereotyped, stodgy, stuffy, stupid, tame, tedious, threadbare, tiresome, tiring, trite, unexciting, uninteresting, unvaried, vapid, wearisome, well-worn, zero*; SEE CONCEPT *529*

born [*adj*] *innate*
built-in, congenital, constitutional, deep-seated, essential, inborn, inbred, ingenerate, inherent, intrinsic, natural; SEE CONCEPTS *549,550*

borrow [*v1*] *take for temporary use*
accept loan of, acquire, beg, bite, bum, cadge*, chisel*, give a note for*, hire, hit up*, lift, mooch*, negotiate, obtain, pawn, pledge, raise money, rent, run into debt, scrounge, see one's uncle*, soak, sponge, take on loan, tap, touch, use temporarily; SEE CONCEPT *89*

borrow [*v2*] *adopt from another source; appropriate*
acquire, adopt, assume, copy, filch, imitate, make one's own, obtain, pilfer, pirate, plagiarize, simulate, steal, take, use, usurp; SEE CONCEPT *225*

bosom [*n1*] *breast*
bust, chest, rib cage, teats; SEE CONCEPT *418*

bosom [*n2*] *heart; core*
affections, center, circle, conscience, emotions, feelings, inside, interior, sentiments, soul, spirit, sympathies; SEE CONCEPTS *410,826*

boss [*adj*] *great*
awesome*, bang-up*, capital, champion, excellent, fine, first-rate, fly*, top, whiz-bang*, wonderful; SEE CONCEPT *572*

boss [*n*] *manager over other employees*
administrator, big cheese*, big gun*, big person*, chief, chieftain, controller, director, dominator, employer, exec*, executive, foreperson, head, head honcho*, helmer, honcho*, leader, overseer, owner, person in charge, superintendent, supervisor, taskperson, top dog*, wheel*; SEE CONCEPT *347*

boss [*v*] *control; command*
administer, administrate, chaperon, direct, employ, manage, overlook, oversee, quarterback*, run, superintend, supervise, survey, take charge; SEE CONCEPT *117*

boss around [*v*] *bully*
browbeat, bulldoze, dominate, domineer, dragoon, oppress, order around, push around, tyrannize; SEE CONCEPT *14*

bossy [*adj*] *domineering*
authoritarian, commanding, controlling, despotic, dictatorial, high-handed, imperious, iron-

handed, oppressive, overbearing, overpowering, pushy, strict, tyrannical; SEE CONCEPTS *401,404*

botany [*n*] *study of plants*
anatomy, cytology, dendrology, ecology, floristics, genetics, horticulture, morphology, natural history, paleobotany, pathology, physiology, phytogeography, phytology, pomology, study of flora, study of vegetation, taxonomy; SEE CONCEPT *349*

botch [*v*] *blunder*
blow*, bobble*, boggle*, bollix*, boot, bumble, bungle, butcher*, distort, err, fall down*, flounder, flub*, fumble, goof up*, gum up*, louse up*, mar, mend, mess, mess up*, misapply, miscalculate, miscompute, misconjecture, misconstrue, mishandle, misjudge, mismanage, muck up*, muddle, muff, mutilate, patch, pull a boner*, ruin, screw up*, spoil, stumble, wreck; SEE CONCEPT *101*

both [*det*] *two together*
one and the other, the couple, the pair, the two, twain; SEE CONCEPT *714*

bother [*n*] *trouble, inconvenience*
ado, aggravation, annoyance, anxiety, bellyache*, botheration, bustle, care, concern, difficulty, distress, drag*, exasperation, flurry, fuss, headache*, irritant, irritation, molestation, nudge, nuisance, pain, pain in the neck*, perplexity, pest, plague, pother*, pressure, problem, strain, to-do*, trial, trouble, vexation, worriment, worry; SEE CONCEPT *532*

bother [*v1*] *harass, annoy; give trouble*
afflict, aggravate, agitate, alarm, badger, bedevil, bore, browbeat, carp at, concern, cross, discommode, disconcert, disgust, dismay, displease, disquiet, distress, disturb, eat, embarrass, exacerbate, exasperate, goad, grate on, grieve, harry, hinder, hurt, impede, inconvenience, insult, intrude upon, irk, irritate, molest, nag, needle, nudge, pain, perplex, perturb, pester, pick on, plague, provoke, pursue, put out, ride, scare, spite, tantalize, taunt, tease, torment, trouble, upset, vex, worry; SEE CONCEPTS *7,19*

bother [*v2*] *take the trouble*
be concerned about, concern oneself, exert oneself, fuss over, go out of one's way*, make a fuss about*, make an effort, put oneself out*, take pains, try, worry about; SEE CONCEPT *87*

bothersome [*adj*] *troubling*
aggravating, annoying, distressing, disturbing, exasperating, incommodious, inconvenient, irritating, rebarbative, remote, tiresome, troublesome, vexatious, vexing; SEE CONCEPT *529*

bottle [*n*] *container, usually for liquids*
canteen, carafe, cruet, dead soldier*, decanter, ewer, flagon, flask, glass, jar, jug, phial, soldier, urn, vacuum bottle, vial; SEE CONCEPT *494*

bottleneck [*n*] *obstacle*
barrier, block, blockage, clog, congestion, hindrance, hold-up, impediment, jam, obstruction, snag, traffic jam; SEE CONCEPTS *470,532,666,674*

bottle up [*v*] *keep feeling inside oneself*
box up, check, collar, contain, coop up, corner, cramp, curb, keep back, restrain, restrict, shut in, suppress, trap; SEE CONCEPT *35*

bottom [*adj*] *lowest; fundamental*
basal, base, basement, basic, foundational, ground, last, lowermost, lowest, meat-and-potatoes*, nethermost, primary, radical, rock-bottom,

underlying, undermost; SEE CONCEPTS 585,586,735,799

bottom [n1] *foundation*
base, basement, basis, bed, bedrock, belly, deepest part, depths, floor, foot, footing, ground, groundwork, lowest part, nadir, nether portion, pedestal, pediment, rest, seat, sole, substratum, substructure, support, terra firma, underbelly, underneath, underside; SEE CONCEPT 442

bottom [n2] *base, core*
basis, bottom line, cause, essence, essentiality, ground, heart, mainspring, marrow, origin, pith, principle, quintessence, root, soul, source, stuff, substance, virtuality; SEE CONCEPTS 648,826

bottom [n3] *rear end*
backside, behind, breech, bum*, butt*, buttocks, derriere, eject, fanny*, fundament, posterior, rear, rump, seat, tail, tush*; SEE CONCEPT 418

bottom feeder [n] *lowlife*
base person, bottom fish, hungry puppy, lowest common denominator, riffraff, scum*, slopsucker; SEE CONCEPT 412

bottomless pit [n] *extremely hopeless situation*
abysm, abyss, chasm, crevasse, fire and brimstone*, gulf, Hades, Hell, infernal regions; SEE CONCEPTS 370,435,674

bottom line [n] *conclusion*
determination, final decision, income, last word, loss, main point, net, profit; SEE CONCEPT 230

bough [n] *branch*
arm, fork, limb, offshoot, shoot, sprig, sucker; SEE CONCEPT 428

boulevard [n] *street, often lined with trees*
artery, avenue, drag, highway, passage, path, road, thoroughfare, track, way; SEE CONCEPT 501

bounce [n] *spring*
animation, bound, dynamism, elasticity, energy, give, go, life, liveliness, pep, rebound, recoil, resilience, springiness, vigor, vitality, vivacity, zip; SEE CONCEPTS 150,411

bounce [v1] *spring up; rebound*
backlash, bob, boomerang, bound, buck, bump, carom, fly back, glance off, hop, hurdle, jerk up and down*, jounce, jump, kick back, leap, rebound, recoil, resile, rock, saltate, snap back, spring back, thump, vault; SEE CONCEPTS 150,194

bounce [v2] *evict*
ax*, boot out*, can*, discharge, dismiss, eighty-six*, eject, fire, give one notice, give the heave ho*, heave*, kick out*, oust, sack*, terminate, throw; SEE CONCEPTS 211,351,384

bound [adj] *obligated; destined*
apprenticed, articled, bent, bounden, certain, coerced, compelled, constrained, contracted, doomed, driven, duty-bound, enslaved, fated, firm, forced, having no alternative, impelled, indentured, intent, made, necessitated, obligated, obliged, pledged, pressed, required, restrained, sure, under compulsion, under necessity, urged; SEE CONCEPT 554

bound [v1] *jump, bounce*
bob, caper, frisk, gambol, hop, hurdle, leap, pounce, prance, recoil, ricochet, saltate, skip, spring, vault; SEE CONCEPT 194

bound [v2] *restrict*
circumscribe, confine, define, delimit, delimitate, demarcate, determine, encircle, enclose, hem in, limit, mark, mark out, measure, restrain, restrict, surround, terminate; SEE CONCEPT 130

boundary [n] *outer limit*
abuttals, ambit, barrier, beginning, border, borderland, borderline, bounds, brink, circumference, circumscription, compass, confines, edge, end, environs, extent, extremity, frame, fringe, frontier, hem, horizon, limits, line, line of demarcation, march, margin, mark, mere, mete, outline, outpost, pale, perimeter, periphery, precinct, purlieus, radius, rim, side, skirt, terminal, termination, terminus, verge; SEE CONCEPTS 5,484,745

bound/bounds [n] *farthest limit*
boundary, compass, confine, edge, end, environs, extremity, fringe, limit, limitation, line, march, margin, pale, periphery, precinct, purlieus, rim, term, termination, verge; SEE CONCEPTS 484,788

bounded [adj] *limited, confined*
belted, bordered, boundaried, circumscribed, compassed, contiguous, defined, definite, delimited, determinate, edged, encircled, enclosed, encompassed, enveloped, fenced, finite, flanked, fringed, girdled, hedged, hog-tied*, limitary, restricted, rimmed, ringed, surrounded, walled; SEE CONCEPTS 554,772

boundless [adj] *endless, without limit*
great, illimitable, immeasurable, immense, incalculable, inexhaustible, infinite, limitless, measureless, no catch*, no end of, no end to, no holds barred*, no strings*, no strings attached*, tremendous, unbounded, unconfined, unending, unlimited, untold, vast, wide open; SEE CONCEPTS 554,772

bountiful [adj] *abundant*
ample, aplenty, bounteous, copious, crawling with*, dime a dozen*, exuberant, free, galore*, generous, handsome, lavish, liberal, luxuriant, magnanimous, munificent, no end of*, plenteous, plentiful, plenty, prolific, stink with*, unsparing; SEE CONCEPT 771

bounty [n] *bonus; compensation*
donation, gift, grant, gratuity, largess, pay, premium, present, prize, recompense, reward; SEE CONCEPTS 337,344

bouquet [n1] *flower arrangement*
boutonniere, buttonhole, corsage, festoon, garland, lei, nosegay, posy, pot, spray, vase, wreath; SEE CONCEPTS 425,429

bouquet [n2] *aroma*
aura, balm, fragrance, incense, odor, perfume, redolence, savor, scent, smell, spice; SEE CONCEPT 599

bourgeois [adj] *commonplace*
common, conservative, conventional, hidebound, illiberal, materialistic, middle-class, old-line, Philistine, traditional, Victorian; SEE CONCEPTS 530,589

bout [n1] *period of time in which something occurs*
course, fit*, go*, round, run, session, shift, spell, stint, stretch, tear, term, tour, trick*, turn; SEE CONCEPT 807

bout [n2] *competitive fight*
bat, battle, boxing match, competition, contest, encounter, engagement, go, match, round, set-to, struggle; SEE CONCEPTS 92,106

boutique [n] *shop*
booth, concession, exclusive shop, franchise, gift store, specialty shop, store; SEE CONCEPTS 441,448,449

bow [n1] *bend from waist*
angle, arc, arch, bend, bending, bob, curtsy, cur-

vation, curvature, curve, flection, flexure, genuflection, inclination, kowtow*, nod, obeisance,
round, salaam, turn, turning; SEE CONCEPTS
154,201

bow [n2] *front of boat*
beak, bowsprit, fore, forepart, head, nose, prow,
stem; SEE CONCEPT 502

bow [v1] *bend over*
arch, bob, cower, crook, curtsy, curve, debase,
dip, do obeisance, droop, duck, genuflect, hunch,
incline, nod, round, stoop; SEE CONCEPT 213

bow [v2] *submit, concede*
accept, acquiesce, bend, be servile, capitulate,
cave, comply, defer, give in, knuckle*, knuckle
under*, kowtow*, relent, succumb, surrender,
yield; SEE CONCEPT 23

bowels [n] *insides*
belly, core, deep, depths, entrails, guts, hold, innards, interior, intestines, penetralia, recesses,
viscera, vitals; SEE CONCEPTS 393,830

bowl [n] *hollow, concave container*
basin, boat, casserole, crock, deep dish, dish,
porringer, pot, saucer, tureen, urn, vessel; SEE
CONCEPTS 493,494

bowl [v] *roll a ball down a lane*
fling, hurl, pitch, play duckpins, play tenpins, revolve, rotate, spin, throw, trundle, whirl; SEE
CONCEPT 363

bowl over [v] *amaze*
astonish, astound, dumbfound, flabbergast, floor,
stagger, startle, stun, surprise; SEE CONCEPT 42

box [n] *container, often square or rectangular*
bin, carton, case, casket, chest, coffer, crate,
pack, package, portmanteau, receptacle, trunk;
SEE CONCEPT 494

box [v1] *place in square or rectangular container*
case, confine, crate, encase, pack, package, wrap;
SEE CONCEPT 209

box [v2] *punch competitively*
buffet, clout, cuff, duke*, exchange blows, hit,
mix, scrap, slap, slug, sock, spar, strike, wallop,
whack*; SEE CONCEPTS 106,189

boxing [n] *punching competition*
battle, glove game*, mill*, prelim*, prizefight-
ing, pugilism, slugfest*, sparring, the ring*; SEE
CONCEPTS 92,363

boy [n] *young man*
buck, cadet, chap, child, dude*, fellow, gamin,
guy, half-pint*, junior, lad, little guy*, little
shaver*, master, punk*, puppy*, runt*, schoolboy, shaver*, small fry*, sonny*, sprout*,
squirt*, stripling, tadpole*, whippersnapper*,
youngster, youth; SEE CONCEPTS 419,424

boycott [v] *ban; refrain from using*
avoid, bar, blackball*, blacklist, brush off, cut
off, embargo, exclude, hold aloof from, ice out*,
ostracize, outlaw, pass by*, pass up*, prohibit,
proscribe, refuse, reject, shut out*, snub, spurn,
strike, withhold patronage; SEE CONCEPTS 25,130

boyfriend [n] *male acquaintance or romantic
companion*
admirer, beau, companion, confidant, date, escort, fiancé, flame*, follower, friend, intimate,
partner, soul mate, steady, suitor, swain, sweetheart, young man; SEE CONCEPTS 419,423

brace [n] *support*
arm, band, bar, bearing, block, bolster, boom,
bracer, bracket, buttress, cantilever, clamp,
girder, grip, guy, lever, mainstay, peg, prop,

rafter, reinforcement, rib, shore, skid, splice,
splint, staff, stanchion, stave, stay, stirrup,
strengthener, strut, sustainer, truss, underpinning, vice; SEE CONCEPTS 470,475,499

brace [v] *support*
bandage, bind, bolster, buttress, fasten, fortify,
gird, hold up, prepare, prop, ready, reinforce,
shove, steady, steel, strap, strengthen, support,
tie, tighten, uphold; SEE CONCEPT 191

bracelet [n] *wrist jewelry*
arm band, armlet, bangle, circlet, manacle, ornament, trinket, wristlet; SEE CONCEPT 446

bracing [adj] *brisk; exhilarating*
animating, chilly, cool, crisp, energizing, exhilarative, fortifying, fresh, invigorating, lively,
quickening, refreshing, restorative, reviving,
rousing, stimulating, stimulative, tonic, vigorous;
SEE CONCEPTS 537,605

brag [v] *talk boastingly*
blow one's own horn*, bluster*, boast, crow*,
exult, gasconade, gloat, grandstand*, hotdog*,
jive*, mouth*, pat oneself on the back*, prate,
puff*, rodomontade, showboat*, shuck*, swagger, vaunt; SEE CONCEPTS 49,51

braggart [n] *person who talks boastingly*
bag of wind*, bigmouth, big talker*, big-timer*,
blowhard*, blusterer, boaster, brag, braggadocio,
bragger, egotist, exhibitionist, gasbag*, gascon*,
grandstander*, hotshot*, know-it-all, peacock*,
ranter, raver, show-off, strutter, swaggerer,
swashbuckler*, swelled head*, trumpeter*,
windbag*; SEE CONCEPTS 412,423

braid [n] *interwoven hair style*
pigtail, plait, ponytail, queue; SEE CONCEPTS
418,716

braid [v] *interweave*
complect, cue, entwine, interknit, interlace, intertwine, lace, mesh, pigtail, plait, ravel, twine,
twist, weave; SEE CONCEPTS 184,202

brain [n1] *very smart person*
academician, doctor, egghead*, Einstein*, genius, highbrow, intellect, intellectual, mastermind, prodigy, pundit, sage, scholar; SEE
CONCEPT 350

brain [n2] *mind, intelligence*
cerebellum, cerebrum, encephalon, gray matter*,
head, intellect, medulla oblongata, mentality,
upper story*, wit; SEE CONCEPTS 393,409,420

brain drain [n] *loss of important personnel*
departure, mass exodus, turnover; SEE CONCEPT
195

brainstorm [v] *problem-solve*
analyze, conceive, conceptualize, conjure up,
create, deliberate, dream up, invent, plan, ponder, put heads together*, rack brains*, share
ideas, think; SEE CONCEPTS 35,173,251

brainwash [v] *force to believe or do things*
alter, catechize, condition, convert, convince, educate, indoctrinate, influence, instill, persuade,
proselytize, teach; SEE CONCEPT 14

brainy [adj] *intelligent*
bright, brilliant, clever, intellectual, sapient,
smart; SEE CONCEPT 402

brake [n] *stopping device; check*
anchor, binders, cinchers, constraint, control,
curb, damper, deterrent, discouragement, hamper, hindrance, hurdle, obstacle, rein, restraint,
retarding device; SEE CONCEPTS 130,463

brake [v] *check; stop*
bar, block, dam, decelerate, halt, hinder, impede,

moderate, obstruct, reduce speed, slacken, slow, slow down, stop; SEE CONCEPT *121*

bramble [*n*] *thorny bush*
brier, burr, catch weed, cleaver, furze, goose grass, gorse, hedge, nettle, prick, prickly shrub, shrub, spray, thistle, thistle sage, thorn; SEE CONCEPT *429*

branch [*nl*] *department*
annex, arm, bureau, category, chapter, classification, connection, dependency, derivative, division, extension, local, member, office, outpost, part, portion, section, subdivision, subsection, subsidiary, tributary, wing; SEE CONCEPTS *325,378*

branch [*n2*] *arm, limb*
bough, branchlet, bug, detour, divergence, extension, fork, growth, offshoot, prong, scion, shoot, spray, sprig, wing; SEE CONCEPTS *392,428,471,835*

branch off/branch out [*v*] *extend beyond main part*
add to, develop, diverge, diversify, divide, enlarge, expand, extend, fork, grow, increase, multiply, part, proliferate, ramify, separate, spread out; SEE CONCEPT *756*

brand [*nl*] *type, kind*
cast, character, class, description, grade, make, quality, sort, species, variety; SEE CONCEPT *378*

brand [*n2*] *distinctive label, mark*
brand name, emblem, hallmark, heraldry, imprint, logo, logotype, marker, sign, stamp, symbol, trademark, welt; SEE CONCEPT *284*

brand [*n3*] *stigma*
bar sinister, black eye, blot, blur, disgrace, infamy, mark, mark of Cain, odium, onus, reproach, slur, smirch, spot, stain, stigma, taint; SEE CONCEPT *388*

brand [*v*] *label negatively*
disgrace, mark, stigmatize, taint; SEE CONCEPTS *62,79*

brandish [*v*] *flaunt, swing around*
come on strong*, display, disport, exhibit, expose, flash, gesture, parade, raise, shake, show, show off, sport, swing, threaten, throw weight around*, trot out*, warn, wield; SEE CONCEPT *261*

brash [*adj*] *impulsive, brazen*
audacious, bold, brazenfaced, cheeky*, cocksure, cocky*, effervescent, flip, foolhardy, forward, hasty, headlong, heedless, hotheaded, ill-advised, impertinent, impetuous, impolitic, impudent, incautious, inconsiderate, indiscreet, insolent, madcap, maladroit, nervy, precipitate, presuming, presumptuous, pushing, rash, reckless, rude, self-asserting, self-assertive, tactless, thoughtless, undiplomatic, untactful, uppity, vivacious; SEE CONCEPTS *401,404*

brass [*n*] *impulsiveness; nerve*
assumption, audacity, brashness, cheek*, chutzpah*, confidence, effrontery, gall, impertinence, impudence, insolence, presumption, rudeness; SEE CONCEPT *633*

brassy [*adj*] *vulgar, loud to the senses*
arrant, barefaced, blaring, blatant, bold, brash, brazen, flashy, flirtatious, forward, garish, gaudy, grating, hard, harsh, impudent, insolent, jarring, jazzy, loudmouthed, noisy, obtrusive, overbold, pert, piercing, rude, saucy, shameless, showy, shrill, strident, unabashed, unblushing; SEE CONCEPTS *401,589,592,594*

brat [*n*] *spoiled child*
devil*, enfant terrible*, holy terror*, impudent child, kid, punk*, rascal, unruly child, urchin, whippersnapper*, wild one*, youngster; SEE CONCEPT *424*

bravado [*n*] *boastfulness*
blowing, bluff, bluster, boasting, bombast, braggadocio, bragging, bullying, crowing*, fancy talk*, fuming*, gasconade, grandiosity, guts*, hot air*, pomposity, pretension, raging, railing, rant, selfglorification, storming, swaggering, swelling, talk, tall talk*; SEE CONCEPTS *49,51*

brave [*adj*] *bold*
adventurous, audacious, chin-up*, chivalrous, confident, courageous, daring, dashing, dauntless, defiant, doughty, fearless, firm, foolhardy, forward, gallant, game, gritty, gutsy, hardy, heroic, herolike, imprudent, indomitable, intrepid, lionhearted, militant, nervy, plucky, reckless, resolute, spirited, spunky, stalwart, stout, stouthearted, strong, unabashed, unafraid, unblenching, undauntable, undaunted, undismayed, unfearful, valiant, valorous, venturesome; SEE CONCEPT *401*

brave [*v*] *endure bad situation*
bear, beard, challenge, confront, court, dare, defy, face, face off, fly in the face of*, go through, outdare, risk, stand up to, suffer, support, take on, venture, withstand; SEE CONCEPT *23*

bravery [*n*] *boldness*
courage, daring, dauntlessness, fearlessness, fortitude, gallantry, grit, guts, hardiness, heroism, indomitability, intrepidity, mettle, pluck, pluckiness, spirit, spunk, valor; SEE CONCEPTS *411,633*

brawl [*n*] *nasty fight*
affray, altercation, argument, battle, battle royal*, bickering, broil, clash, disorder, dispute, donnybrook, duke out*, feud, fight, fracas, fray, free-for-all*, fuss, hassle, melee, quarrel, rhubarb*, riot, row, ruckus*, rumble*, rumpus, scrap, scuffle, squabble, tumult, uproar, wrangle; SEE CONCEPTS *46,106*

brawl [*v*] *fight nastily*
altercate, argue, battle, bicker, buck*, caterwaul, dispute, kick up a row*, quarrel, raise Cain*, roughhouse*, row, rumble*, scrap, scuffle, spat, squabble, tussle, wrangle, wrestle; SEE CONCEPTS *46,106*

brawn [*n*] *muscular strength and breadth*
beef, beefiness, clout, energy, flesh, kick, meat, might, moxie*, muscle, muscularity, power, punch, robustness, sinews, sock, steam, thew, vigor; SEE CONCEPTS *723,732*

brawny [*adj*] *muscular, strong*
able-bodied, athletic, beefy, bulky, burly, fleshy, hardy, hefty, husky, powerful, robust, sinewy, stalwart, strapping, sturdy, thewy, tough, vigorous, vital; SEE CONCEPTS *485,489*

brazen [*adj*] *brash, unashamed*
audacious, barefaced, blatant, bold, brassy, cheeky, cocky, contumelious, defiant, flashy, flip, forward, gritty, gutsy, hotshot*, immodest, impertinent, impudent, indecent, insolent, loud, meretricious, nervy, overbold, pert, saucy, shameless, smart-alecky*, smart-ass*, spunky, tawdry, unabashed, unblushing; SEE CONCEPTS *267,401*

breach [*nl*] *gap*
aperture, break, chasm, chip, cleft, crack, discon-

tinuity, fissure, hole, opening, rent, rift, rupture, slit, split; SEE CONCEPT 513

breach [*n2*] *violation of a law*
contravention, delinquency, dereliction, disobedience, disregard, infraction, infringement, neglect, noncompliance, nonobservance, offense, transgression, trespass, violation; SEE CONCEPT 192

breach [*n3*] *change from friendly to unfriendly relationship*
alienation, break, difference, disaffection, disagreement, discord, disharmony, dissension, disunity, division, estrangement, falling-out, fissure, fracture, parting of the ways*, quarrel, rent, rift, rupture, schism, secession, separation, severance, split, strife, variance, withdrawal; SEE CONCEPT 388

bread [*n1*] *daily food*
aliment, bed and board, comestibles, diet, fare, feed, grub*, necessities, nourishment, nurture, nutriment, provender, provisions, shingle*, staff of life*, subsistence, sustenance, viands, victuals; SEE CONCEPT 457

bread [*n2*] *money*
cabbage*, cash, coin, dollars, dough*, finance, funds, greenbacks*, mazuma*, scratch*; SEE CONCEPT 340

breadth [*n1*] *width*
broadness, diameter, distance across, latitude, span, spread, wideness; SEE CONCEPT 760

breadth [*n2*] *extent*
amplitude, area, compass, comprehensiveness, dimension, expanse, extensiveness, fullness, gamut, greatness, inclusiveness, largeness, magnitude, measure, orbit, range, reach, scale, scope, size, space, spread, stretch, sweep, vastness; SEE CONCEPTS 651,756,788

break [*n*] *fissure, opening*
breach, cleft, crack, discontinuity, disjunction, division, fracture, gap, gash, hole, rent, rift, rupture, schism, split, tear; SEE CONCEPTS 230,757

break [*n2*] *interruption of activity*
blow, breather, breathing space, caesura, coffee break, cutoff, downtime*, halt, hiatus, interlude, intermission, interval, lacuna, layoff*, letup*, lull, pause, recess, respite, rest, suspension, ten*, time off, time out; SEE CONCEPT 807

break [*n3*] *change from friendly to unfriendly relationship*
alienation, altercation, breach, clash, difference of opinion, disaffection, dispute, divergence, estrangement, fight, misunderstanding, rift, rupture, schism, separation, split, trouble; SEE CONCEPT 388

break [*n4*] *lucky happening*
accident, advantage, chance, favorable circumstances, fortune, good luck, luck, occasion, opening, opportunity, shot, show, stroke of luck, time; SEE CONCEPT 679

break [*v1*] *destroy; make whole into pieces*
annihilate, batter, burst, bust, bust up, crack, crash, crush, damage, demolish, disintegrate, divide, eradicate, finish off, fracture, fragment, make hash of*, make mincemeat of*, part, pull to pieces, rend, separate, sever, shatter, shiver, smash, snap, splinter, split, tear, torpedo, total, trash*; SEE CONCEPT 252

break [*v2*] *violate law*
breach, contravene, disobey, disregard, infract,

infringe, offend, renege on, transgress, violate; SEE CONCEPT 192

break [*v3*] *weaken, cause instability*
bankrupt, bust, confound, confute, controvert, cow, cripple, declass, degrade, demerit, demoralize, demote, disconfirm, dispirit, disprove, downgrade, enervate, enfeeble, humiliate, impair, impoverish, incapacitate, pauperize, rebut, reduce, refute, ruin, subdue, tame, undermine; SEE CONCEPT 240

break [*v4*] *stop an action*
abandon, cut, discontinue, give up, interrupt, pause, rest, suspend; SEE CONCEPT 121

break [*v5*] *tell news*
announce, come out, communicate, convey, disclose, divulge, impart, inform, let out, make public, pass on, proclaim, reveal, transmit; SEE CONCEPT 60

break [*v6*] *better a performance*
beat, cap, exceed, excel, go beyond, outdo, outstrip, surpass, top; SEE CONCEPT 141

break [*v7*] *emerge, happen*
appear, befall, betide, burst out, chance, come forth, come off, come to pass, develop, erupt, go, occur, transpire; SEE CONCEPT 4

break [*v8*] *run away*
abscond, bust out*, clear out*, cut and run*, dash, decamp, escape, flee, fly, get away, get out; SEE CONCEPTS 102,195

break [*v9*] *cushion something's effect*
diminish, lessen, lighten, moderate, reduce, soften, weaken; SEE CONCEPT 110

breakable [*adj*] *easily hurt or destroyed*
brittle, crisp, crispy, crumbly, delicate, flimsy, fracturable, fragile, frail, frangible, friable, shatterable, shattery, splintery, vitreous, weak; SEE CONCEPTS 489,606

break away [*v*] *depart*
escape, flee, fly, leave, part company*, quit, run away, split*; SEE CONCEPT 195

breakdown [*n1*] *nervous collapse*
basket case*, crackup*, disintegration, disruption, failure, mishap, nervous prostration, neurasthenia, neurosis, psychasthenia; SEE CONCEPT 410

breakdown [*n2*] *account of finances or other business*
analysis, categorization, classification, detailed list, diagnosis, dissection, itemization, resolution; SEE CONCEPT 283

break even [*v*] *be or become equal*
balance books, equalize, experience no loss, recover cost, recover expense; SEE CONCEPTS 126,232

break in [*v1*] *intrude*
barge in, breach, break and enter, burglarize, burgle, burst in*, butt in*, interfere, interject, interrupt, intervene, invade, meddle, raid, rob, steal, trespass; SEE CONCEPTS 139,192

break in [*v2*] *train in new skill*
accustom, condition, educate, gentle, get used to, habituate, initiate, instruct, prepare, tame; SEE CONCEPT 285

break off [*v1*] *snap off something*
detach, disassemble, divide, part, pull off, separate, sever, splinter, take apart; SEE CONCEPT 211

break off [*v2*] *end activity*
cease, desist, discontinue, end, finish, halt, pause, stop, suspend, terminate; SEE CONCEPT 234

break out [v1] *happen, emerge*
appear, arise, begin, burst forth, commence, erupt, explode, occur, set in, spring up, start; SEE CONCEPT 701

break out [v2] *escape*
abscond, bolt, break loose, burst out, bust out*, depart, flee, get free, leave; SEE CONCEPTS 102,195

break the ice [v] *be friendly and talkative*
lead the way, oil the works*, set at ease, socialize, start the ball rolling; SEE CONCEPT 384

breakthrough [n] *advance, progress*
boost, development, discovery, find, finding, gain, hike, improvement, increase, invention, leap, progress, quantum leap*, rise, step forward; SEE CONCEPT 704

breakup [n] *end of relationship*
breakdown, breaking, crackup*, disintegration, dispersal, dissolution, divorce, ending, parting, rift, separation, split, splitsville*, splitting, termination, wind-up; SEE CONCEPT 385

break up [v] *end relationship, activity*
adjourn, disassemble, disband, dismantle, disperse, disrupt, dissolve, divide, divorce, end, halt, part, put an end to, scatter, separate, sever, split, stop, sunder, suspend, take apart, terminate; SEE CONCEPT 234

break with [v] *part ways*
ditch, drop, jilt, reject, renounce, separate; SEE CONCEPTS 21,30,180

breast [n1] *front of upper body*
bosom, bust, chest, front, mammary glands, mammilla, nipple, teat, udder; SEE CONCEPT 418

breast [n2] *feelings, conscience*
being, bosom, character, core, emotions, essential nature, heart, mind, psyche, seat of affections, sentiments, soul, spirit, thoughts; SEE CONCEPTS 410,529

breath [n1] *respiration*
animation, breathing, eupnea, exhalation, expiration, gasp, gulp, inhalation, inspiration, insufflation, pant, wheeze; SEE CONCEPT 163

breath [n2] *wind or something in the air*
aroma, faint breeze, flatus, flutter, gust, odor, puff, sigh, smell, vapor, waft, whiff, zephyr; SEE CONCEPTS 437,599

breath [n3] *respite, break*
blow*, breather, breathing space*, instant, moment, pause, rest, second, ten*; SEE CONCEPT 807

breath [n4] *hint, suggestion*
dash, murmur, shade, soupçon, streak, suspicion, touch, trace, undertone, whiff, whisper; SEE CONCEPTS 278,831

breathe [v1] *take air in and let out*
draw in, exhale, expire, fan, gasp, gulp, inhale, insufflate, open the floodgates*, pant, puff, respire, scent, sigh, sniff, snore, snort, use lungs, wheeze; SEE CONCEPTS 163,601

breathe [v2] *inspire action*
imbue, impart, infuse, inject, instill, transfuse; SEE CONCEPT 242

breathe [v3] *tell information*
articulate, confide, express, murmur, say, sigh, utter, voice, whisper; SEE CONCEPT 60

breathless [adj1] *unable to respire normally*
asthmatic, blown, choking, emphysematous, exhausted, gasping, gulping, out of breath, panting, short of breath, short-winded, spent, stertorous, wheezing, winded; SEE CONCEPT 406

breathless [adj2] *astounded*
agog, anxious, avid, eager, excited, flabbergasted, open-mouthed, thunderstruck, with bated breath; SEE CONCEPT 403

breathtaking [adj] *beautiful, awesome*
amazing, astonishing, awe-inspiring, exciting, hair-raising, heart-stirring, heart-stopping, impressive, magnificent, moving, overwhelming, spine-tingling, stunning, thrilling; SEE CONCEPT 529

breed [n] *kind, class*
brand, character, extraction, family, feather, genus, ilk, likes, line, lineage, lot, nature, number, pedigree, progeny, race, sort, species, stamp, stock, strain, stripe, type, variety; SEE CONCEPT 378

breed [v1] *generate, bring into being*
bear, beget, bring about, bring forth, cause, create, deliver, engender, give birth to, give rise to, hatch, impregnate, induce, make, multiply, originate, procreate, produce, progenerate, propagate, reproduce; SEE CONCEPTS 173,251,302,373

breed [v2] *raise, nurture*
bring up, cultivate, develop, discipline, educate, foster, instruct, nourish, rear; SEE CONCEPTS 285,295

breeding [n] *cultivation of person*
ancestry, civility, conduct, courtesy, culture, development, gentility, grace, lineage, manners, nurture, polish, raising, rearing, refinement, schooling, training, upbringing, urbanity; SEE CONCEPT 388

breeze [n] *light wind*
air, airflow, breath, current, draft, flurry, gust, puff, waft, whiff, zephyr; SEE CONCEPTS 437,524

breeze [v] *work quickly through task*
cruise, flit, glide, hurry, move, pass, sail, sally, skim, slide, slip, sweep, trip, waltz, zip; SEE CONCEPT 704

breezy [adj1] *windy*
airy, blowing, blowy, blusterous, blustery, drafty, fresh, gusty, squally, stormy; SEE CONCEPT 525

breezy [adj2] *easy, lighthearted*
airy, animated, blithe, buoyant, carefree, casual, cheerful, debonair, easy-going, effervescent, free and easy*, gay, informal, jaunty, light, lively, low-pressure, peppy, racy, relaxed, sparkling, spicy, spirited, sprightly, sunny, unconstrained, vivacious; SEE CONCEPT 544

brevity [n] *shortness, briefness*
conciseness, concision, condensation, crispness, curtness, economy, ephemerality, impermanence, pithiness, pointedness, succinctness, terseness, transience, transitoriness; SEE CONCEPTS 730,804

brew [n] *concoction*
beverage, blend, broth, compound, distillation, drink, fermentation, hash, hodgepodge*, infusion, instillation, liquor, melange, miscellany, mishmash*, mixture, potpourri, preparation; SEE CONCEPTS 260,454,457

brew [v1] *prepare by boiling*
boil, concoct, cook, ferment, infuse, mull, seethe, soak, steep, stew; SEE CONCEPT 170

brew [v2] *plan, devise*
breed, compound, concoct, contrive, develop, excite, ferment, form, gather, hatch, impend, loom, mull, plot, project, scheme, start, stir up, weave; SEE CONCEPT 36

br
br

bribe [n] *payoff to influence illegal or wrong activity*

allurement, bait, blackmail, buyoff, compensation, contract, corrupting gift, corrupt money, enticement, envelope*, feedbag*, fringe benefit, gift, goody*, graft, gratuity, gravy*, grease*, hush money*, ice*, incentive, inducement, influence peddling, kickback, lagniappe, lure, payola*, perk*, perquisite, present, price, protection*, remuneration, reward, sop*, sweetener*, sweetening*; take; SEE CONCEPTS 192,329

bribe [v] *request silence, action, or inaction for money*

approach, buy, buy back, buy off, coax, corrupt, do business*, entice, fix*, get at, get to, grease palm*, influence, instigate, lubricate, lure, make a deal, oil palm*, pay off, pervert, reward, seduce, soap*, square, suborn, sugar, sweeten the pot*, take care of, tamper, tempt, tip; SEE CONCEPTS 53,192

bridal [adj] *concerning marriage*

conjugal, connubial, epithalamic, espousal, hymeneal, marital, matrimonial, nubile, nuptial, pre-wedding, prothalamic, spousal; SEE CONCEPT 536

bride [n] *female marriage partner*

helpmate, mate, newly married woman, newly-wed, old woman*, spouse, wife; SEE CONCEPTS 296,415

bridegroom [n] *male marriage partner*

benedict, groom, helpmate, husband, mate, new-lywed, old man*; spouse; SEE CONCEPTS 296,419

bridge [n] *structure or something that makes connection*

arch, bond, branch, catwalk, connection, extension, gangplank, link, overpass, platform, pontoon, scaffold, span, tie, transit, trestle, viaduct, wing; SEE CONCEPTS 501,721

bridge [v] *connect, extend*

arch over, attach, bind, branch, couple, cross, cross over, go over, join, link, reach, span, subtend, traverse, unite; SEE CONCEPTS 113,756

bridle [n] *restraining device*

check, control, curb, deterrent, hackamore, halter, headstall, leash, rein, restraint, trammels; SEE CONCEPT 497

bridle [v] *check, hold back*

constrain, control, curb, govern, inhibit, keep in check, master, moderate, repress, restrain, rule, subdue, suppress, withhold; SEE CONCEPT 121

brief [adj 1] *short, compressed*

abrupt, bluff, blunt, boiled down*, breviloquent, brusque, compendiary, compendious, concise, crisp, curt, hasty, laconic, limited, little, pithy, sharp, short and sweet*, skimpy, small, snippy, succinct, surly, terse, to the point; SEE CONCEPTS 267,773

brief [adj 2] *short in time*

concise, curtailed, ephemeral, fast, fleeting, hasty, little, meteoric, momentary, passing, quick, short-lived, short-term, swift, temporary, transient, transitory; SEE CONCEPT 798

brief [n] *abridgment*

abstract, argument, boildown*, case, condensation, conspectus, contention, data, defense, digest, epitome, outline, précis, sketch, summary, synopsis; SEE CONCEPTS 283,318

brief [v] *inform of facts*

abridge, advise, apprise, edify, enlighten, epito-mize, explain, fill in, give rundown*, give the lowdown*, inform, initiate, instruct, let in on*, orient, prepare, prime, recapitulate, show the lay of the land*, show the ropes*, summarize, tip off*, update; SEE CONCEPT 60

briefcase [n] *carrier for work papers*

attaché, bag, baggage, case, dispatch, folder, portfolio, valise; SEE CONCEPTS 446,494

briefing [n] *preparation by informing of facts*

background meeting, conference, directions, discussion, guidance, information, initiation, instruction, meeting, preamble, priming, rundown, update; SEE CONCEPT 60

brigade [n] *fleet of trained people*

army, band, body, company, contingent, corps, crew, detachment, force, group, organization, outfit, party, posse, squad, team, troop, unit; SEE CONCEPTS 322,381

bright [adj 1] *shining, glowing in appearance*

ablaze, aglow, alight, argent, auroral, beaming, blazing, brilliant, burning, burnished, coruscating, dazzling, effulgent, flashing, fulgent, fulgid, glaring, gleaming, glistening, glittering, glossy, golden, illuminated, illumined, incandescent, intense, irradiated, lambent, light, lighted, limpid, luminous, lustrous, mirrorlike, moonlit, phosphorescent, polished, radiant, relucent, resplendent, scintillating, shimmering, shiny, silvery, sparkling, sunlit, sunny, twinkling, vivid; SEE CONCEPT 617

bright [adj 2] *sunny, clear (weather)*

clement, cloudless, fair, favorable, limpid, lucid, mild, pellucid, pleasant, translucent, transparent, unclouded; SEE CONCEPT 525

bright [adj 3] *intelligent*

acute, advanced, alert, astute, aware, brainy, brilliant, clear-headed, clever, discerning, egg-headed*, Einstein*, having smarts*, ingenious, inventive, keen, knowing, precocious, quick, quick-witted, sharp, smart, whiz kid*, wide-awake; SEE CONCEPT 402

bright [adj 4] *hopeful, promising*

airy, auspicious, benign, breezy, cheering, encouraging, excellent, favorable, golden, good, optimistic, palmy, propitious, prosperous, rosy; SEE CONCEPT 537

bright [adj 5] *cheerful*

alert, animated, gay, genial, glad, happy, jolly, joyful, joyous, keen, lighthearted, lively, merry, optimistic, sanguine, spirited, sprightly, vivacious; SEE CONCEPT 404

bright [adj 6] *famous, outstanding*

distinguished, eminent, glorious, illustrious, magnificent, prominent, remarkable, splendid; SEE CONCEPT 568

bright [adj 7] *vivid in color*

brave, brilliant, clear, colored, colorful, deep, flashy, fresh, gay, glitzy*, hued, intense, psychedelic, razzle-dazzle, rich, ruddy, sharp, showy, tinged, tinted; SEE CONCEPT 618

brighten [v 1] *make shine or glow*

buff up, burnish, clear up, enliven, gleam, grow sunny, illuminate, illumine, intensify, kindle, lighten, light up, polish, punch up*, spiff up*; SEE CONCEPTS 244,250

brighten [v 2] *make happy, feel better*

become cheerful, buck up, buoy up, cheer, cheer up, clear up, encourage, enliven, gladden, hearten, improve, look up, perk up; SEE CONCEPTS 7,22

brilliant [*adj1*] *shining, glowing in appearance*
ablaze, bright, coruscating, dazzling, effulgent, flashy, fulgent, gleaming, glittering, glossy, incandescent, intense, lambent, lucent, luminous, lustrous, radiant, refulgent, resplendent, scintillating, showy, sparkling, vivid; SEE CONCEPT 617

brilliant [*adj2*] *famous, outstanding*
celebrated, distinguished, eminent, excellent, exceptional, glorious, illustrious, magnificent, prominent, splendid, superb; SEE CONCEPT 568

brilliant [*adj3*] *very intelligent*
accomplished, acute, astute, brainy, bright, clever, discerning, eggheaded*, Einstein*, expert, genius, gifted, ingenious, intellectual, inventive, knowing, knowledgeable, masterly, penetrating, profound, quick, quick-witted, sharp, smart, talented, whip, whiz kid*; SEE CONCEPT 402

brim [*n*] *edge of object, usually the top*
border, brink, circumference, fringe, hem, lip, margin, perimeter, periphery, rim, skirt, verge; SEE CONCEPT 836

brim [*v*] *flow over the top*
fill, fill up, hold no more, overflow, run over, spill, swell, teem, well over; SEE CONCEPT 740

brimming/brimful [*adj*] *overflowing; up to the top*
awash, chock-full, crammed, crowded, filled, flush, full, full to the top, jammed, level with, loaded, overfull, packed, running over, stuffed, topfull; SEE CONCEPTS 481,771,774

brine [*n*] *salt solution*
alkali, blue, brackish water, deep, drink, marinade, ocean, pickling solution, preservative, saline, salt water, sea water, sodium chloride solution, vinegar; SEE CONCEPT 514

bring [*v1*] *transport or accompany*
attend, back, bear, buck*, carry, chaperon, companion, conduct, consort, convey, deliver, escort, fetch, gather, guide, gun*, heel*, import, lead, lug, pack, pick up, piggyback*, ride, schlepp*, shoulder, take, take along, tote, transfer, transport, truck, usher; SEE CONCEPT 143

bring [*v2*] *cause; influence*
begin, compel, contribute to, convert, convince, create, dispose, effect, engender, force, induce, inflict, lead, make, move, occasion, persuade, prevail on, prevail upon, produce, prompt, result in sway, wreak; SEE CONCEPT 242

bring [*v3*] *command a price*
afford, bring in, draw, earn, fetch, gross, net, produce, return, sell for, take, yield; SEE CONCEPTS 330,335

bring [*v4*] *file charges in court*
appeal, arraign, cite, declare, indict, initiate legal action, institute, prefer, serve, sue, summon, take to court; SEE CONCEPT 317

bring about [*v*] *cause success*
accomplish, achieve, beget, bring to pass, compass, create, do, draw on, effect, effectuate, engender, generate, give rise to, make happen, manage, occasion, produce, realize, secure, succeed; SEE CONCEPTS 244,706

bring around [*v*] *convince, induce*
argue, convert, draw, get, indoctrinate, persuade, prevail upon, prompt, prove, talk into, win over; SEE CONCEPT 68

bring down [*v*] *reduce or hurt*
abase, cut down, damage, drop, fell, floor, injure, knock down, KO*, lay low, level, lower, mow down, murder*, overthrow, overturn, prostrate, pull down, shoot down, slay*, throw down, tumble, undermine, upset, wound; SEE CONCEPTS 7,19,252

bring in [*v*] *make a profit*
accrue, acquire, bear, be worth, bring, cost, earn, fetch, gain, get, gross, make, pay, produce, realize, return, sell, yield; SEE CONCEPTS 124,330

bring off [*v*] *accomplish*
achieve, bring home the bacon*, bring to pass, carry off, carry out, discharge, effect, effectuate, execute, perform, pull off, realize, succeed; SEE CONCEPTS 704,706

bring on [*v*] *provoke*
accelerate, advance, cause, expedite, generate, give rise to, induce, inspire, lead to, occasion, precipitate, prompt; SEE CONCEPTS 7,19

bring out [*v*] *draw out*
bring to light, emphasize, expose, highlight, introduce, publish, utter; SEE CONCEPTS 49,57

bring up [*v1*] *raise youngster*
breed, cultivate, develop, discipline, educate, feed, form, foster, nourish, nurture, provide for, rear, school, support, teach, train; SEE CONCEPT 295

bring up [*v2*] *initiate, mention in conversation*
advance, advert, allude to, broach, discuss, introduce, moot, move, offer, point out, propose, put forward, raise, raise a subject, refer, submit, tender, touch on, ventilate*; SEE CONCEPT 51

brink [*n*] *edge of an object or area*
border, boundary, brim, fringe, frontier, limit, lip, margin, perimeter, periphery, point, rim, skirt, threshold, verge; SEE CONCEPTS 484,513

brisk [*adj1*] *fast-moving; active*
adroit, agile, alert, animated, bustling, busy, energetic, lively, nimble, quick, speedy, sprightly, spry, vigorous, vivacious, zippy; SEE CONCEPTS 542,584

brisk [*adj2*] *chilly, refreshing (weather)*
biting, bracing, crisp, exhilarating, fresh, invigorating, keen, nippy, sharp, snappy, stimulating; SEE CONCEPT 605

bristle [*n*] *short, prickly hair*
barb, feeler, fiber, point, prickle, quill, spine, stubble, thorn, vibrissa, whisker; SEE CONCEPT 418

bristle [*v*] *become upset, excited*
be angry, be infuriated, be maddened, blow up*, boil, boil over, bridle, flare, flare up, fume, get one's dander up*, rage, rise, ruffle, see red*, seethe, spit*, stand on end*, swell; SEE CONCEPT 410

brittle [*adj1*] *fragile*
breakable, crisp, crumbling, crumbly, delicate, frail, frangible, friable, inelastic, shatterable, shivery, vitreous, weak; SEE CONCEPTS 488,606

brittle [*adj2*] *tense*
curt, edgy, irritable, nervous, prim, short, stiff, stilted; SEE CONCEPT 401

broach [*v1*] *bring up a topic*
advance, approach, bring up, hint at, interject, interpose, introduce, mention, moot, move, offer, open up, propose, raise subject, speak of, submit, suggest, talk of, touch on, ventilate*; SEE CONCEPT 51

broach [*v2*] *open, pierce*
begin, crack, decant, draw off, puncture, start, tap, uncork; SEE CONCEPTS *142,225*

broad [*adj1*] *wide physically*
ample, capacious, deep, expansive, extended, extensive, full, generous, immense, large, latitudinous, outspread, outstretched, roomy, spacious, splay, squat, thick, vast, voluminous, widespread; SEE CONCEPTS *773,796*

broad [*adj2*] *extensive*
all-embracing, all-inclusive, comprehensive, copious, encyclopedic, expansive, extended, far-flung, far-reaching, general, inclusive, nonspecific, scopic, sweeping, ubiquitous, undetailed, universal, unlimited, wide, wide-ranging, widespread; SEE CONCEPT *772*

broad [*adj3*] *full, obvious*
apparent, clear, explicit, open, plain, straightforward, undisguised, unequivocal; SEE CONCEPT *576*

broad [*adj4*] *liberal-minded*
advanced, cultivated, experienced, open, open-minded, permissive, progressive, radical, tolerant, unbiased, wide; SEE CONCEPT *403*

broad [*adj5*] *vulgar*
blue, coarse, dirty, gross, improper, indecent, indelicate, low-minded, off-color, purple, racy, risqué, salty, saucy, smutty, spicy, suggestive, unrefined, unrestrained, wicked; SEE CONCEPT *545*

broad [*n*] *a woman*
babe*, bimbo*, chick*, dame, dish, doll*, doxy, female, floozy, gal, girl, honey*, lady, lassie, miss, moll, skirt*, sweet thing*, tootsie*; SEE CONCEPTS *414,415*

broadcast [*n*] *information on electronic media*
advertisement, air time, announcement, newscast, performance, program, publication, radiocast, show, simulcast, telecast, transmission; SEE CONCEPTS *274,293*

broadcast [*v1*] *put forth on electronic media*
air, announce, beam, be on the air, cable, circulate, colorcast, communicate, get out*, go on the air, go on the airwaves, put on the air, radio, radiograph, relay, send, show, simulcast, telecast, telegraph, telephone, televise, transmit; SEE CONCEPTS *60,292*

broadcast [*v2*] *make public*
advertise, announce, annunciate, blare, blazon, circulate, communicate, declare, disseminate, distribute, proclaim, promulgate, publish, report, sow, spread, strew, troll; SEE CONCEPT *60*

broadcasting [*n*] *informing via electronic media*
airing, air time, announcing, auditioning, newscasting, performing, posting online, putting on program, radio, reporting, telecasting, television, transmission, transmitting; SEE CONCEPTS *263,293*

broaden [*v*] *extend, supplement*
augment, breadthen, develop, enlarge, expand, fatten, grow, increase, open up, ream, spread, stretch, swell, widen; SEE CONCEPT *239*

broad-minded [*adj*] *liberal*
advanced, catholic, cosmopolitan, dispassionate, flexible, free-thinking, indulgent, liberal, open, open-minded, permissive, progressive, radical, receptive, responsive, tolerant, unbiased, unbigoted, undogmatic, unprejudiced, wide; SEE CONCEPT *403*

brochure [*n*] *short, printed document*
advertisement, booklet, circular, flyer, folder, handbill, handout, leaflet, pamphlet; SEE CONCEPT *280*

broil [*v*] *cook under direct heat*
burn, melt, roast, scorch, sear, swelter; SEE CONCEPT *170*

broiling [*adj*] *very hot*
baking, burning, fiery, on fire, red-hot, roasting, scalding, scorching, sizzling, sweltering, torrid; SEE CONCEPT *605*

broke [*adj*] *without money*
bankrupt, beggared, bust*, cleaned out*, destitute, dirt poor*, flat broke*, impoverished, in Chapter 11*, in debt, indebted, indigent, insolvent, needy, penniless, penurious, poor, ruined, stone broke*, strapped*, tapped out; SEE CONCEPT *334*

broken [*adj1*] *destroyed; made into pieces from a whole*
burst, busted, collapsed, cracked, crippled, crumbled, crushed, damaged, defective, demolished, disintegrated, dismembered, fractured, fragmentary, fragmented, hurt, injured, in pieces, mangled, mutilated, pulverized, rent, riven, ruptured, separated, severed, shattered, shivered, shredded, slivered, smashed, split; SEE CONCEPT *485*

broken [*adj2*] *discontinuous*
disconnected, disturbed, erratic, fragmentary, incomplete, intermittent, interrupted, irregular, spasmodic, spastic; SEE CONCEPT *482*

broken [*adj3*] *mentally defeated*
beaten, browbeaten, crippled, crushed, defeated, demoralized, depressed, discouraged, disheartened, heartsick, humbled, oppressed, overpowered, subdued, tamed, vanquished; SEE CONCEPT *403*

broken [*adj4*] *not working*
busted, coming unglued, coming unstuck, defective, disabled, down, exhausted, fallen apart, faulty, feeble, gone, gone to pieces*, gone to pot*, haywire, imperfect, in disrepair, in need of repair, inoperable, in the shop*, kaput*, not functioning, on the blink*, on the fritz*, on the shelf*, out, out of commission*, out of kilter*, out of order, out of whack*, ruined, run-down, screwed up*, shot, spent, unsatisfactory, weak, wracked*, wrecked; SEE CONCEPTS *485,560*

broken [*adj5*] *forgotten, ignored (promise)*
abandoned, dishonored, disobeyed, disregarded, ignored, infringed, isolated, retracted, traduced, transgressed, violated; SEE CONCEPT *544*

broken [*adj6*] *stuttering in speech*
disjointed, halting, hesitant, hesitating, imperfect, incoherent, mumbled, muttered, stammering, unintelligible, weak; SEE CONCEPT *267*

brokenhearted [*adj*] *devastated*
crestfallen, crushed, desolate, despairing, despondent, disappointed, disconsolate, grief-stricken, grieved, heartbroken, heartsick, heartsore, inconsolable, miserable, mournful, prostrated, sorrowful, wretched; SEE CONCEPT *403*

broker [*n*] *financial expert*
agent, business person, dealer, entrepreneur, factor, financier, go-between, interagent, interceder, intercessor, intermediary, intermediate, mediator, merchant, middleperson, negotiator, stockbroker; SEE CONCEPTS *348,353*

bronze [*adj*] *coppery-brown color*
brownish, burnished, chestnut, copper, copper-colored, metallic brown, reddish-brown, reddish-tan, russet, rust, tan; SEE CONCEPT *618*

brooch [*n*] *ornamental pin*
bar pin, breastpin, clip, cluster, jewelry; SEE CONCEPT *446*

brood [*n*] *cluster of children*
begats, breed, chicks, clutch, descendants, family, flock, hatch, infants, issue, litter, offspring, posterity, progeniture, progeny, scions, seed, young; SEE CONCEPT *296*

brood [*v*] *agonize over*
be in brown study*, bleed, chafe inwardly*, consider, daydream, deliberate, despond, dream, dwell upon, eat one's heart out*, fret, gloom, grieve, lament, languish, meditate, mope, mull over, muse, ponder, reflect, repine, ruminate, sigh, speculate, stew over*, sulk, sweat out*, sweat over*, think about, think upon, worry; SEE CONCEPT *17*

brook [*n*] *stream of water*
beck, branch, burn, creek, rill, rindle, river, rivulet, run, runnel, streamlet, watercourse; SEE CONCEPT *514*

brook [*v*] *endure, accept*
abide, allow, bear, be big*, countenance, go, hang in, hang in there*, hear of, live with, put up with, sit tight*, stand, stomach, suffer, support, swallow, take, tolerate, withstand; SEE CONCEPT *23*

broom [*n*] *device for cleaning floors*
besom, carpet sweeper, feather duster, floor brush, mop, swab, sweeper, whisk; SEE CONCEPT *499*

broth [*n*] *soup, usually clear*
borscht, bouillon, bowl, brew, chowder, concoction, consommé, decoction, dishwater*, distillation, elixir, fluid, gumbo, hodge-podge*, olio, porridge, potage, potpourri, pottage, puree, splash, stock, vichyssoise; SEE CONCEPTS *457,467*

brothel [*n*] *house of prostitution*
bagnio, bawdy house*, bordello, call house*, cathouse*, den of iniquity*, house of assignation, house of ill repute, house with red doors*, massage parlor, red-light district, whorehouse; SEE CONCEPT *449*

brother [*n*] *male sibling*
blood brother, kin, kinsperson, relation, relative, twin; SEE CONCEPTS *414,419*

brotherhood [*n*] *association*
affiliation, alliance, clan, clique, community, comradeship, confederacy, coterie, fellowship, fraternity, guild, kinship, league, society, union; SEE CONCEPTS *387,388*

brow [*n*] *forehead*
countenance, eyebrow, face, frons, front, mien, temple, top; SEE CONCEPT *418*

browbeat [*v*] *castigate, nag*
badger, bludgeon, bluster, bulldoze*, bully, coerce, cow, despotize, domineer, dragoon, frighten, harass, hector, intimidate, lean on*, lord it over*, oppress, overawe, overbear, put heat on*, put the chill on*, put through the wringer*, threaten, tyrannize; SEE CONCEPTS *14,52*

brown [*adj*] *dark, burnished color*
amber, auburn, bay, beige, bister, brick, bronze, buff, burnt sienna, chestnut, chocolate, cinnamon, cocoa, coffee, copper, drab, dust, ecru,

fawn, ginger, hazel, henna, khaki, mahogany, nut, ochre, puce, russet, rust, sepia, snuff-colored, sorrel, tan, tawny, terra-cotta, toast, umber; SEE CONCEPT *618*

brownnose [*v*] *suck up to*
apple-polish, back-scratch, bootlick, curry favor, fawn on, flatter, get on the right side of, kiss ass, scratch one's back, suck up to, toady; SEE CONCEPTS *59,69*

brownnoser [*n*] *sycophant, toady*
apple-polisher, ass-kisser, backscratcher*, backslapper*, bootlicker*, brownnose*, doter, fawner, flatterer, flunky*, kiss-ass, kowtower, lackey, minion, teacher's pet, yes-man, yes-person; SEE CONCEPT *423*

browse [*v*] *look around; look through*
check over, dip into*, examine cursorily, feed, flip through, get the cream*, give the once over*, glance at, graze, hit the high spots*, inspect loosely, leaf through, nibble*, once over lightly*, pass an eye over*, peruse, read, read here and there, riffle through, riffle through, run through, scan, skim, skip through, survey, thumb through wander; SEE CONCEPT *623*

browser [*n*] *Internet /Web viewing software*
display program, gateway, Internet service provider, portal, search engine, web directory, web crawler, web spider; SEE CONCEPTS *349,770*

bruise [*n*] *black and blue mark under skin*
black eye, black mark, blemish, boo-boo*, contusion, discoloration, injury, mark, mouse*, swelling, wale, wound; SEE CONCEPT *309*

bruise [*v*] *break blood vessel; discolor*
bang up, batter, beat, black, blacken, blemish, bung up*, contuse, crush, damage, deface, do a number on*, injure, mar, mark, pound, pulverize, wound, zing*; SEE CONCEPTS *137,246,250*

brunette/brunet [*adj*] *dark hair and/or skin*
bistered, brown, dusky, pigmented, swart, swarthy, tanned, tawny; SEE CONCEPTS *406,618*

brunt [*n*] *bad end of a situation*
burden, force, full force, impact, pressure, shock, strain, stress, tension, thrust, violence; SEE CONCEPT *674*

brush [*n1*] *tool with bristles for cleaning*
besom, broom, hairbrush, mop, polisher, sweeper, toothbrush, waxer, whisk; SEE CONCEPT *499*

brush [*n2*] *fight*
clash, conflict, confrontation, encounter, engagement, fracas, rub, run-in, scrap, set-to, skirmish, tap, touch, tussle; SEE CONCEPT *106*

brush [*n3*] *scrappy bushes*
boscage, bracken, brushwood, chaparral, coppice, copse, cover, dingle, fern, gorse, grove, hedge, scrub, sedge, shrubbery, spinney, thicket, undergrowth, underwood; SEE CONCEPT *429*

brush [*v1*] *touch lightly*
caress, contact, flick, glance, graze, kiss, scrape, shave, skim, smooth, stroke, sweep, tickle; SEE CONCEPT *612*

brush [*v2*] *clean, prepare by whisking*
buff, clean, paint, polish, sweep, wash, whisk, wipe; SEE CONCEPTS *165,202*

brush aside/brush off [*v*] *ignore; refuse*
boycott, cold-shoulder*, contradict, cut, deny, disclaim, dismiss, disown, disregard, get rid of, have no time for*, ostracize, override, rebuff, reject, repudiate, scorn, send away, slight, snub, spurn, sweep aside; SEE CONCEPT *30*

brush up [*v*] *improve condition*
clean up, cram, go over, look over, polish up, read up, refresh one's memory, refurbish, relearn, renovate, reread, retouch, revise, revise, study, touch up; SEE CONCEPTS *202,244*

brusque [*adj*] *curt, surly*
abrupt, bluff, blunt, brief, crusty, discourteous, gruff, hasty, impolite, sharp, short, snappy, snippy, tart, terse, unmannerly; SEE CONCEPTS *267,401*

brutal [*adj1*] *cruel, remorseless*
barbarous, bloodthirsty, callous, ferocious, gruff, hard, harsh, heartless, impolite, inhuman, insensitive, merciless, pitiless, remorseless, rough, rude, ruthless, savage, severe, uncivil, uncivilized, unfeeling, unmannerly, unmerciful, vicious; SEE CONCEPT *401*

brutal [*adj2*] *crude, rough*
animal, bearish, beastly, bestial, brute, brutish, carnal, coarse, feral, ferine, inhuman, inhumane, rude, savage, swinish, unfeeling; SEE CONCEPT *544*

brutality [*n*] *cruel treatment*
atrocity, barbarism, barbarity, bloodthirstiness, brutishness, choke hold*, cruelty, ferocity, fierceness, grossness, inhumanity, ruthlessness, sadism, savageness, savagery, third degree*, unfeelingness, viciousness; SEE CONCEPTS *14,86*

brutally [*adv*] *cruelly, without remorse*
atrociously, barbarically, barbarously, brutishly, callously, demoniacally, diabolically, ferally, ferociously, fiercely, hardheartedly, heartlessly, in cold blood, inexorably, inhumanely, inhumanly, meanly, mercilessly, murderously, pitilessly, relentlessly, remorselessly, ruthlessly, savagely, something fierce, something terrible, unkindly, unrelentingly, viciously; SEE CONCEPT *544*

brute [*adj*] *very strong; animal-like*
animal, beastly, bestial, bodily, carnal, feral, ferine, fleshly, instinctive, mindless, physical, senseless, swinish, unthinking; SEE CONCEPTS *489,540*

brute [*n*] *barbarian*
animal, beast, cannibal, creature, critter*, degenerate, devil, fiend, lout, monster, ogre, ruffian, sadist, savage, swine, wild animal; SEE CONCEPTS *394,423*

bubble [*n*] *globule of air*
air ball*, balloon, barm, bead, blister, blob, drop, droplet, effervescence, foam, froth, lather, sac, spume, vesicle; SEE CONCEPT *437*

bubble [*v*] *foam, froth up, especially with sound*
boil, burble, churn, eddy, effervesce, erupt, fester, fizz, gurgle, gush, issue, moil, murmur, percolate, ripple, seep, seethe, simmer, smolder, sparkle, spume, stir, swash, trickle, well; SEE CONCEPTS *179,469*

buck [*n*] *male animal*
bull, stag; SEE CONCEPTS *394,419*

buck [*v*] *resist, kick off*
bound, combat, contest, dislodge, dispute, duel, fight, jerk, jump, leap, oppose, prance, repel, start, throw, traverse, trip, unseat, vault, withstand; SEE CONCEPTS *180,222*

bucket [*n*] *container, often for liquids, with handle*
brazier, can, canister, cask, hod, kettle, pail, pot, scuttle, vat; SEE CONCEPT *494*

buckle [*n*] *fastener with long pin*
catch, clamp, clasp, clip, fastening, fibula, harness, hasp; SEE CONCEPT *450*

buckle [*v*] *contort, warp*
bend, bulge, cave in, collapse, crumple, distort, fold, twist, yield; SEE CONCEPT *702*

buckle down [*v*] *concentrate on*
address, apply oneself, attend to, bend, dedicate oneself to, devote oneself to, exert oneself, give, give oneself over to, keep close to, keep one's mind on, launch into, occupy oneself with, pitch in, set to, throw, turn; SEE CONCEPTS *17,87*

bucolic [*adj*] *rural or rustic*
agrarian, agricultural, Arcadian, countrified, country, pastoral; SEE CONCEPTS *536,583*

bud [*n*] *new sprout on plant*
bloom, blossom, embryo, floret, germ, incipient flower, nucleus, shoot, spark; SEE CONCEPT *428*

bud [*v*] *sprout*
burgeon, burst forth, develop, grow, pullulate, shoot; SEE CONCEPT *427*

budding [*adj*] *developing, flowering*
beginning, blossoming, burgeoning, bursting forth, embryonic, fledgling, fresh, germinal, germinating, growing, incipient, maturing, nascent, opening, potential, promising, pubescent, pullulating, shooting up, sprouting, vegetating, young; SEE CONCEPT *490*

buddy [*n*] *friend*
associate, chum, co-mate, companion, comrade, confidant, co-worker, crony, intimate, mate, pal, peer, sidekick; SEE CONCEPT *423*

budge [*v*] *dislodge from staid position*
bend, change, change position, convince, give way, inch, influence, locomote, move, persuade, propel, push, remove, roll, shift, slide, stir, sway, yield; SEE CONCEPTS *68,147*

budget [*n*] *financial plan*
account, aggregate, allocation, allowance, bulk, cost, estimated expenses, finances, fiscal estimate, funds, means, planned disbursement, quantity, quantum, resources, spending plan, statement, total; SEE CONCEPT *332*

budget [*v*] *plan money or action*
allocate, apportion, calculate, compute, cost, estimate, predict, ration; SEE CONCEPTS *36,330*

buff [*adj*] *sandy color*
bare, blonde, canary, ecru, lemon, light brown, nude, ochre, straw, tan, tawny, yellow-brown, yellowish; SEE CONCEPT *618*

buff [*n*] *enthusiast*
addict, admirer, aficionado, connoisseur, devotee, expert, fan, fiend*, freak*, habitué, hound, lover, votary; SEE CONCEPTS *352,423*

buff [*v*] *polish to a shine*
brush, burnish, furbish, glaze, gloss, pumice, rub, sandpaper, scour, shine, smooth; SEE CONCEPTS *202,215*

buffer [*n*] *safeguard*
bulwark, bumper, cushion, defense, fender, intermediary, screen, shield, shock absorber; SEE CONCEPTS *484,729*

buffet [*n*] *meal set out on table for choosing*
café, cafeteria, cold table, counter, cupboard, lunch wagon, salad bar, shelf, sideboard, smorgasbord, snack bar; SEE CONCEPTS *443,459*

buffet [*v*] *hit repeatedly*
bang, batter, beat, blow, box, bump, clobber, cuff, flail, jolt, knock, pound, pummel, push, rap,

shove, slap, smack, spank, strike, thrash, thump, wallop; SEE CONCEPT *189*

buffoon [*n*] *clownlike person*
antic, bozo*, clown, comedian, comic, droll, fool, harlequin, jester, joker, merry-andrew, wag, zany; SEE CONCEPT *423*

bug [*n1*] *bacterium, microorganism*
bacillus, disease, germ, infection, microbe, virus; SEE CONCEPT *306*

bug [*n2*] *insect*
ant, beetle, cootie, flea, gnat, louse, pest, vermin; SEE CONCEPT *398*

bug [*n3*] *obsession*
craze, enthusiasm, fad, mania, rage, zeal; SEE CONCEPT *532*

bug [*n4*] *computer glitch*
breakdown, computer malfunction, defect, error, failure, fault, flaw, hitch, problem, something wrong, trouble; SEE CONCEPTS *580,674*

bug [*v1*] *bother, disturb*
abrade, annoy, badger, chafe, gall, get on someone*, harass, irk, irritate, needle, nettle, pester, plague, provoke, vex; SEE CONCEPTS *7,19*

bug [*v2*] *listen to without permission*
eavesdrop, listen in, overhear, spy, tap, wiretap; SEE CONCEPTS *192,596*

bugle [*n*] *musical horn*
clarion, cornet, misery pipe*, trumpet; SEE CONCEPT *262*

build [*n*] *physical structure, form*
body, conformation, constitution, figure, frame, habit, habitus, physique, shape; SEE CONCEPT *757*

build [*v1*] *construct structure*
assemble, bring about, carpenter, cast, compile, compose, contrive, engineer, erect, evolve, fabricate, fashion, fit together, forge, form, frame, jerry-build, knock together*, make, manufacture, model, prefabricate, produce, put together, put up, raise, rear, reconstruct, sculpture, set up, superstruct, synthesize, throw together*, throw up*; SEE CONCEPT *168*

build [*v2*] *initiate, found*
base, begin, constitute, establish, formulate, inaugurate, institute, originate, set up, start; SEE CONCEPT *234*

build [*v3*] *increase, accelerate*
aggrandize, amplify, augment, boost, compound, develop, enlarge, escalate, expand, extend, heighten, improve, intensify, magnify, mount, multiply, strengthen, swell, wax; SEE CONCEPTS *236,245*

builder [*n*] *construction worker*
architect, artisan, constructor, contractor, craftsperson, erector, fabricator, framer, inventor, maker, manufacturer, mason, originator, producer; SEE CONCEPT *348*

building [*n*] *constructed dwelling*
architecture, construction, domicile, edifice, erection, fabric, framework, home, house, hut, pile, superstructure; SEE CONCEPTS *439,441*

buildup [*n*] *development; accumulation*
accretion, advertising, enlargement, escalation, expansion, gain, growth, heap, hype, increase, load, mass, plug, promotion, publicity, puff*, stack, stockpile, store; SEE CONCEPTS *230,704,787*

build up [*v*] *amplify, advertise*
add to, boost, develop, expand, extend, fortify, heighten, hype, improve, increase, inten-

sify, plug*, promote, publicize, puff*, reinforce, spotlight, strengthen; SEE CONCEPTS *236,245,266*

built-in [*adj*] *included*
congenital, constitutional, deep-seated, essential, implicit, inborn, inbred, in-built, incorporated, indwelling, ingrained, inherent, innate, inseparable, integral, part and parcel*; SEE CONCEPT *549*

bulb [*n*] *globular object*
ball, bunch, corm, corn, globe, head, knob, nodule, nub, protuberance, swelling, tube, tumor; SEE CONCEPT *436*

bulge [*n*] *swollen object*
appendage, bagginess, blob, bump, bunch, bunching, convexity, dilation, distention, excess, excrescence, gibbosity, growth, hump, intumescence, jut, lump, nodulation, nodule, outgrowth, outthrust, projection, prominence, promontory, protrusion, protuberance, sac, sagging, salience, salient, superfluity, swelling, tuberosity, tumefaction, tumor, wart; SEE CONCEPTS *436,470*

bulge [*v*] *project outward*
bag, balloon, beetle, belly, bilge, billow, bloat, blob, bug out, dilate, distend, enlarge, expand, extrude, jut, overhang, poke, pop out, pouch, protrude, protuberate, puff out, sag, stand out, stick out, swell; SEE CONCEPTS *208,780*

bulk [*n1*] *size, largeness*
aggregate, amount, amplitude, bigness, dimensions, extent, immensity, magnitude, mass, massiveness, quantity, quantum, substance, total, totality, volume, weight; SEE CONCEPT *730*

bulk [*n2*] *main part, most*
best part, better part, biggest share, body, generality, greater number, greater part, gross, lion's share*, majority, major part, mass, nearly all, plurality, predominant part, preponderance, principal part; SEE CONCEPTS *635,829*

bulky [*adj*] *huge*
awkward, beefy, big, colossal, cumbersome, cumbrous, enormous, gross, heavy, hefty, high, hulking, immense, large, long, mammoth, massive, ponderous, substantial, unhandy, unmanageable, unwieldy, voluminous, weighty; SEE CONCEPT *781*

bulldoze [*v1*] *demolish*
drive, elbow, flatten, force, jostle, level, press, propel, push, raze, shove, thrust; SEE CONCEPTS *208,252*

bulldoze [*v2*] *bully, intimidate*
bludgeon, bluster, browbeat, coerce, cow, dragoon, harass, hector; SEE CONCEPT *14*

bullet [*n*] *small missile*
ammo*, ammunition, ball, bolt, cap, cartridge, dose*, lead, love letter*, pellet, projectile, rocket, round, shot, slug, trajectile; SEE CONCEPT *500*

bulletin [*n*] *message, notification*
account, announcement, break, calendar, communication, communiqué, dispatch, flash*, handout, hot wire*, item, list, news, news flash*, notice, program, publication, release, report, scoop*, skinny*, statement, the dope*, what's going down*, what's happening*; SEE CONCEPTS *271,274*

bulletin board [*n*] *electronic messaging system*
bboard, BBS, board, bulletin board system; SEE CONCEPTS *349,770*

bully [*n*] *domineering person*
annoyer, antagonizer, browbeater, bulldozer, coercer, harrier, hector, insolent, intimidator, op-

br
bu

pressor, persecutor, pest, rascal, rowdy, ruffian, tease, tormenter, tough; SEE CONCEPT *423*

bully [v] *intimidate, push around*
bludgeon, bluster, browbeat, buffalo, bulldoze, coerce, cow, despotize, domineer, dragoon, enforce, harass, hector, lean on, menace, oppress, overbear, persecute, ride roughshod*, showboat*, swagger, terrorize, threaten, torment, torture, turn on the heat*, tyrannize, walk heavy*; SEE CONCEPT *14*

bulwark [n] *fortification, support*
barrier, bastion, buffet, buttress, citadel, defense, embankment, fort, fortress, guard, mainstay, outwork, parapet, partition, protection, rampart, redoubt, safeguard, security, stronghold, vallation; SEE CONCEPTS *96,729*

bum [n] *beggar*
bindle*, black sheep*, derelict, drifter, floater, gutterpup*, guttersnipe*, hobo, stiff*, tramp, transient, vagabond, vagrant; SEE CONCEPTS *412,423*

bummer [n] *bad experience*
disappointment, disaster, downer*, drag*, misfortune; SEE CONCEPTS *674,679*

bump [v1] *collide, hit, usually with sound*
bang, bounce, box, buck, bunt, butt, carom, clap, clatter, crack, crash, impinge, jar, jerk, jolt, jostle, jounce, knock, pat, plop, plunk, pound, punch, rap, rattle, shake, slam, slap, smack, smash into, strike, thud, thump, thunder, thwack, whack; SEE CONCEPT *189*

bump [v2] *move over, dislodge*
budge, displace, remove, shift; SEE CONCEPT *213*

bump [v3] *increment*
increase, raise, step up; SEE CONCEPTS *236,245,780*

bump into [v] *happen upon*
chance upon, come across, encounter, hit, light, light upon, luck, meet, meet up with, run across, run into, stumble, tumble; SEE CONCEPT *114*

bumpy [adj] *rough*
choppy, corrugated, jarring, jerky, knobby, lumpy, potholed*, rugged, rutted, uneven; SEE CONCEPTS *485,606*

bum rap [n] *rotten deal*
bad break*, bad deal, bad rap*, bum deal*, bummer*, drag*, frame-up, lousy deal, misfortune, raw deal, stroke of bad luck*, the shaft*; SEE CONCEPTS *674,679*

bun [n] *baked roll*
bread, cruller, Danish, doughnut, eclair, muffin, pastry, scone, sweet roll; SEE CONCEPT *457*

bunch [n] *collection of something*
agglomeration, assemblage, assortment, band, batch, bevy, blob, bouquet, bundle, caboodle*, chunk, clump, cluster, covey, crew, crowd, fascicle, flock, galaxy, gang, gathering, group, heap, host, hunk, knot, lot, mass, mess, mob, multitude, number, oodles*, pack, parcel, party, passel*, pile, quantity, sheaf, shebang*, shock, shooting match*, spray, stack, swarm, team, thicket, troop, tuft; SEE CONCEPT *432*

bunch [v] *gather in group*
assemble, bundle, cluster, collect, congregate, cram, crowd, flock, group, herd, huddle, mass, pack; SEE CONCEPT *109*

bundle [n] *accumulation, package of something*
array, assortment, bag, bale, batch, box, bunch, carton, clump, cluster, collection, crate, group, heap, lot, mass, pack, package, packet, pallet,

parcel, pile, quantity, roll, set, stack, wad; SEE CONCEPTS *432,787*

bundle [v] *accumulate, package*
bale, bind, clothe, fasten, pack, palletize, tie, truss, wrap; SEE CONCEPTS *158,202*

bungle [v] *blunder, mess up*
ball up*, boggle, botch, butcher*, drop the ball*, err, flub, foul up*, fudge*, fumble, goof up*, gum up*, louse up*, make a mess of, mar, mess up, miscalculate, mishandle, mismanage, muff*, ruin, screw up*, spoil; SEE CONCEPT *101*

bungler [n] *person who blunders*
addlebrain*, blockhead*, blunderer, bonehead*, botcher*, bumbler, butcher*, butterfingers*, clod, clumsy oaf*, dolt, donkey*, duffer*, dunce, featherbrain*, fool, foul-up*, fumbler*, goofball*, goof off*, harebrain*, idiot, ignoramus, incompetent, klutz*, mismanager, muddler, muffer*, numskull*, screw up*, spoiler; SEE CONCEPTS *412,423*

bunk [n1] *nonsense*
applesauce*, balderdash, baloney*, bilge*, claptrap, eyewash*, flimflam*, garbage*, hogwash*, hooey*, horsefeathers*, jazz*, piffle*, poppycock, rot*, rubbish, tomfoolery*, tommyrot*, trash*, twaddle*; SEE CONCEPTS *63,278*

bunk [n2] *twin bed, usually stacked; place to sleep*
berth, cot, doss, hay, kip, pallet, sack; SEE CONCEPT *443*

bunt [v] *hit half-heartedly*
butt, lay it down*, meet, sacrifice, throw, toss; SEE CONCEPTS *189,363*

buoy [n] *floating device*
beacon, drift, float, guide, marker, signal; SEE CONCEPT *628*

buoyancy/buoyance [n1] *lightness in weight*
airiness, etheriality, floatability, levity, weightlessness; SEE CONCEPT *734*

buoyancy/buoyance [n2] *lightness in spirit*
animation, bounce, cheerfulness, cheeriness, ebullience, effervescence, exuberance, gaiety, good feeling, good humor, happiness, high spirits, jollity, liveliness, pep, spiritedness, sunniness, vim and vigor, zing*, zip; SEE CONCEPTS *410,411*

buoyant [adj1] *light in weight*
afloat, airy, bouncy, floatable, floating, resilient, supernatant, unsinkable, weightless; SEE CONCEPT *491*

buoyant [adj2] *light in spirit*
animated, blithe, bouncy, breezy, bright, carefree, cheerful, debonair, effervescent, elastic, expansive, full of zip, gay, happy, invigorated, jaunty, jovial, joyful, laid back*, lighthearted, lively, peppy, resilient, sunny, supple, vivacious; SEE CONCEPTS *403,404*

buoy (up) [v] *make light, encourage*
bolster, boost, buck up, cheer, cheer up, encourage, hearten, keep afloat, lift, prop, raise, support, sustain, uphold; SEE CONCEPTS *7,22*

burden [n] *mental weight; stress*
accountability, affliction, albatross*, anxiety, ball and chain*, blame, care, charge, clog, concern, deadweight, difficulty, duty, encumbrance, excess baggage*, grievance, hardship, Herculean task, hindrance, load, millstone, misfortune, mishap, obstruction, onus, punishment, responsibility, sorrow, strain, task, tax, thorn in one's

side*, trial, trouble, weary load, work, worry;
SEE CONCEPTS 532,690

burden [*v*] *encumber, strain*
afflict, bear down on, bother, crush, cumber, depress, dish it out*, dish out*, dump on*, encumber, give it to, hamper, handicap, hinder, impede,
lade, load, make heavy, obligate, oppress, overcharge, overload, overwhelm, pile, press, saddle
with, snow*, snow under*, stick it to, strain, tax,
trouble, try, vex, weigh down, worry; SEE CON-
CEPTS 7,14,19

burdensome [*adj*] *troublesome*
carking, crushing, demanding, difficult, disturbing, exacting, exigent, heavy*, irksome, onerous,
oppressive, superincumbent, taxing, tough, trying, wearing, wearying, weighty; SEE CONCEPT
529

bureau [*n1*] *branch of an organization*
agency, authority, board, commission, committee, department, division, front office*, office,
salt mines*, service, setup, shop, store; SEE CON-
CEPTS 325,441,449

bureau [*n2*] *chest of drawers*
chiffonier, commode, desk, dresser, highboy,
sideboard, writing desk; SEE CONCEPT 443

bureaucracy [*n*] *system which controls organization*
administration, authority, beadledom*, city
hall*, civil service, directorate, government,
management, ministry, officialdom, officials,
powers that be*, red tape*, regulatory commission, the Establishment*, the system*; SEE CON-
CEPTS 325,770

bureaucrat [*n*] *government official*
administrator, civil servant, desk-jockey*, functionary, office-holder, pencil-pusher*, politician,
public servant; SEE CONCEPTS 347,354

burglar [*n*] *person who steals*
cat burglar, crook, filcher*, housebreaker, mid-
nighter*, owl*, picklock*, pilferer*, porch-
climber*, prowler, robber, safecracker,
sneakthief*, thief; SEE CONCEPT 412

burglary [*n*] *stealing from residence, business*
break-in, breaking and entering, caper, crime,
filching, heist, housebreaking, larceny, owl job*,
pilferage, prowl, robbery, safecracking, second-
story work*, sting, theft, thieving; SEE CONCEPT
139

burial [*n*] *laying in of dead body*
burying, deep six*, deposition, entombment, exequies, funeral, inhumation, interment, last rites,
obsequies, sepulture; SEE CONCEPT 367

burlesque [*adj*] *farcical*
caricatural, comic, ironical, ludicrous, mock,
mocking, parodic, satirical, travestying; SEE
CONCEPT 555

burlesque [*n*] *bawdy show; vaudeville*
burly*, caricature, farce, lampoon, lampoonery,
mock, mockery, parody, pastiche, peep show,
revue, satire, send-up, spoof, strip, takeoff, travesty, vaudeville; SEE CONCEPT 263

burly [*adj*] *husky*
able-bodied, athletic, beefcake*, beefy*, big,
brawny, bruising, bulky, gorillalike, hefty, hulking, hulky, hunk, muscular, portly, powerful,
stocky, stout, strapping, strong, sturdy, thickset,
well-built; SEE CONCEPT 773

burn [*v1*] *be on fire; set on fire*
bake, be ablaze, blaze, brand, broil, calcine, cauterize, char, combust, conflagrate, cook, cremate,

enkindle, flame, flare, flash, flicker, glow, heat,
ignite, incinerate, kindle, light, melt, parch, reduce to ashes, rekindle, roast, scald, scorch, sear,
set a match to, singe, smoke, smolder, toast,
torch, wither; SEE CONCEPT 249

burn [*v2*] *feel stinging pain*
bite, hurt, pain, smart, sting, tingle; SEE CONCEPT
590

burn [*v3*] *be excited about; yearn for*
be angry, be aroused, be inflamed, be passionate,
be stirred up, blaze, boil, breathe fire*, bristle,
desire, eat up*, fume, lust, rage, seethe, simmer,
smoulder, tingle, yearn; SEE CONCEPTS 20,29,34

burn [*v4*] *cheat*
beat, bilk, chisel, cozen, deceive, defraud, gyp,
overreach, ream, swindle, take, trick, use; SEE
CONCEPTS 59,142

burning [*adj1*] *blazing, flashing*
afire, aflame, alight, blistering, broiling, conflagrant, enkindled, fiery, flaming, flaring, gleaming, glowing, heated, hot, ignited, illuminated,
incandescent, in flames, kindled, on fire, oxidizing, red-hot*, scorching, searing, sizzling, smoking, smouldering, torrid, white-hot*; SEE
CONCEPTS 485,605

burning [*adj2*] *fervent, excited*
all-consuming, ardent, blazing, eager, earnest,
fervid, feverish, frantic, frenzied, heated, hectic,
impassioned, intense, passionate, red-hot*, vehement, white-hot*, zealous; SEE CONCEPT 403

burning [*adj3*] *stinging, painful*
acrid, biting, caustic, irritating, painful, piercing,
prickling, pungent, reeking, sharp, smarting, tingling; SEE CONCEPTS 314,537

burning [*adj4*] *important*
acute, clamant, clamorous, compelling, critical,
crucial, crying, dire, essential, exigent, imperative, importunate, instant, pressing, significant,
urgent, vital; SEE CONCEPT 568

burnish [*v*] *polish, brighten*
buff, furbish, glance, glaze, gloss, luster, patina,
put on a finish, rub, sheen, shine, smooth, wax;
SEE CONCEPTS 202,215

burrow [*n*] *hole dug by animal*
couch, den, hovel, lair, retreat, shelter, tunnel;
SEE CONCEPT 517

burrow [*v*] *dig a hole*
delve, excavate, hollow out, scoop out, tunnel,
undermine; SEE CONCEPT 178

burst [*n*] *blow-up, blast*
access, bang, barrage, blowout, bombardment,
breach, break, cannonade, crack, discharge,
eruption, explosion, fit, flare, fusillade, gush,
gust, outbreak, outpouring, round, rupture, rush,
sally, salvo, shower, spate, split, spurt, storm,
surge, torrent, volley; SEE CONCEPTS 86,179,208

burst [*v*] *blow up, break out*
barge, blow, break, crack, detonate, discharge,
disintegrate, erupt, explode, fly open, fracture,
fragment, gush forth, perforate, pierce, pop,
prick, puncture, rend asunder, run, rupture, rush,
shatter, shiver, splinter, split, spout, tear apart;
SEE CONCEPTS 179,252

bury [*v1*] *lay to rest after death*
consign to grave, cover up, deposit, embalm, ensepulcher, enshrine, entomb, hold last rites for*,
hold services for, inearth, inhume, inter, inurn,
lay out, mummify, plant*, put away*, put six feet
under*, sepulcher, sepulture, tomb; SEE CONCEPT
367

bury [v2] *conceal, cover*
cache, cover up, ensconce, enshroud, hide, occult, plant, screen, secrete, shroud, stash, stow away; SEE CONCEPTS *172,188*

bury [v3] *plant in ground*
drive in, embed, engulf, implant, sink, submerge; SEE CONCEPTS *172,257*

bury [v4] *engross oneself*
absorb, concentrate, engage, immerse, interest, occupy, rivet, throw oneself into; SEE CONCEPT *24*

bush [n] *shrubs; woodland*
backcountry, backwoods, boscage, bramble, briar, brush, chaparral, creeper, forest, hedge, hinterland, jungle, outback, plant, scrub, scrubland, shrubbery, the wild, thicket, vine, wilderness; SEE CONCEPT *429*

bush-league [adj] *second-rate*
minor league*, small potatoes*; SEE CONCEPTS *334,567,574*

bushy [adj] *shaggy, unkempt*
bristling, bristly, disordered, feathery, fluffy, fringed, full, furry, fuzzy, hairy, heavy, hirsute, leafy, luxuriant, nappy, prickly, rough, rumpled, spreading, stiff, thick, tufted, unruly, wiry, woolly; SEE CONCEPTS *406,606*

busily [adv] *actively; intently*
agilely, animatedly, ardently, arduously, assiduously, briskly, carefully, diligently, eagerly, earnestly, energetically, enthusiastically, expeditiously, fervently, hastily, hurriedly, indefatigably, industriously, laboriously, like all get out*, like the devil*, like the dickens*, nimbly, painstakingly, perseveringly, persistently, purposefully, restlessly, seriously, speedily, spiritedly, strenuously, studiously, unremittingly, unweariedly, vigilantly, vigorously, vivaciously, zealously; SEE CONCEPT *544*

business [n1] *job, profession*
bag*, biz*, calling, career, craft, dodge*, employment, field, function, game, line, livelihood, métier, occupation, pursuit, racket*, specialty, trade, vocation, what one is into*, work; SEE CONCEPT *360*

business [n2] *company, enterprise*
cartel, concern, corporation, establishment, factory, firm, fly-by-night operation*, house, institution, market, megacorp*, mill, Mom and Pop*, monopoly, organization, outfit, partnership, setup, shoestring operation*, shop, store, syndicate, trust, venture; SEE CONCEPTS *325,449*

business [n3] *commerce, trade*
affairs, bargaining, barter, buying and selling, capital and labor, commercialism, contracts, deal, dealings, exchange, free enterprise, game, industrialism, industry, manufacturing, market, merchandising, production and distribution, racket*, sales, selling, trading, traffic, transaction, undertaking; SEE CONCEPTS *325,770*

business [n4] *personal concern*
affair, assignment, beeswax*, carrying on, duty, function, goings-on*, hanky-panky*, happening, interest, issue, lookout, matter, palaver, point, problem, question, responsibility, subject, task, topic; SEE CONCEPT *532*

businesslike [adj] *efficient, professional*
accomplished, careful, concentrated, correct, diligent, direct, disciplined, earnest, effective, enterprising, expeditious, hardworking, industri-

ous, intent, matter-of-fact, methodical, orderly, organized, painstaking, practical, practiced, purposeful, regular, routine, sedulous, serious, skillful, systematic, thorough, well-ordered, workaday; SEE CONCEPTS *326,544*

businessperson [n] *professional working person*
baron, big-time operator*, big wheel*, capitalist, dealer, employer, entrepreneur, executive, financier, franchiser, gray flannel suit*, industrialist, manager, merchandiser, merchant, operator, organization person, small potatoes*, storekeeper, suit*, the bacon*, tradesperson, trafficker, tycoon, wheeler-dealer*; SEE CONCEPTS *347,348*

bust [n1] *chest of human*
bosom, breast, chest, front; SEE CONCEPT *392*

bust [n2] *arrest for illegal action*
apprehension, arrest, capture, cop, detention, nab, pickup, pinch, raid, search, seizure; SEE CONCEPTS *298,317*

bust [v1] *ruin, impoverish*
become insolvent, break, crash, fail, fold up, go bankrupt, go into Chapter 11*, pauperize; SEE CONCEPT *330*

bust [v2] *arrest for illegal action*
apprehend, catch, collar, cop*, detain, nab, pick up, pinch, pull in, raid, run in, search; SEE CONCEPTS *298,317*

bust [v3] *physically break*
burst, fold, fracture, rupture; SEE CONCEPT *252*

bustle [n] *quick and busy activity*
ado, agitation, clamor, commotion, do*, excitement, flurry, furor, fuss, haste, hubbub, hurlyburly*, hurry, pother, rumpus, stir, to-do*, tumult, turmoil, uproar, whirl, whirlpool, whirlwind; SEE CONCEPT *386*

bustle [v] *move around quickly, busily*
bestir, dash, dust, flit, flutter, fuss, hasten, hum, hurry, hustle, run, rush, scamper, scramble, scurry, scuttle, stir, tear, whirl, whisk; SEE CONCEPT *150*

busy [adj1] *engaged, at work*
active, already taken*, assiduous, at it*, buried, diligent, employed, engaged, engrossed, having a full plate*, having enough on one's plate*, having fish to fry*, having many irons in the fire*, hustling, in a meeting, in conference, industrious, in someone else's possession*, in the field, in the laboratory, occupied, on assignment, on duty, on the go, overloaded, persevering, slaving, snowed*, swamped*, tied up, unavailable, up to one's ears*, with a customer, working; SEE CONCEPTS *326,544,555*

busy [adj2] *active, on the go*
bustling, busy as a beaver*, energetic, full, fussy, hectic, humming*, hustling, lively, popping*, restless, strenuous, tireless, tiring; SEE CONCEPT *542*

busy [adj3] *nosy, impertinent*
butting in, curious, forward, inquisitive, interfering, intrusive, meddlesome, meddling, nebby, obtrusive, officious, prying, pushy, snoopy, stirring, troublesome; SEE CONCEPT *404*

busybody [n] *nosy, impertinent person*
backseat driver*, butt-in*, buttinsky*, eavesdropper, fink*, fussbudget, gossip, intermeddler, intruder, meddler, newsmonger*, nosey parker*, rubberneck*, scandalmonger*, sidewalk superintendent*, snoop, snooper, stir, tattletale, troublemaker, yenta*; SEE CONCEPT *423*

butcher [*n*] *meat killer, seller*
boner*, meatmarket person, meat person, processor, skinner*, slaughterer, slayer*; SEE CONCEPT 348

butcher [*v1*] *slay and prepare animal for meat*
beef up, carve, clean, cure, cut, cut down, dress, joint, liquidate, salt, slaughter, smoke, stick; SEE CONCEPTS 170,252

butcher [*v2*] *ruin*
bollix up*, botch, destroy, goof up*, louse up*, make a mess of*, mutilate, screw up*, spoil, wreck; SEE CONCEPT 101

butt [*n1*] *end, shaft*
base, bottom, edge, extremity, fag end, foot, fundament, haft, handle, hilt, shank, stock, stub, stump, tail, tip; SEE CONCEPT 827

butt/buttocks [*n2*] *animate rear end*
back end, backside, behind, bottom, bum*, derrière, fanny*, fundament, gluteus maximus, haunches, hindquarters, posterior, rear, rump, seat, tush*; SEE CONCEPT 392

butt [*n3*] *object of joking*
chump*, clay pigeon*, derision, dupe*, easy mark*, fall guy, fool, goat, jestee*, joke, laughingstock, mark, patsy, pigeon*, sap, setup*, sitting duck*, softie*, subject, sucker, target, turkey, victim; SEE CONCEPT 423

butt [*n4*] *cigarette*
cancer stick*, cig*, coffin nail*, fag*, smoke*, tobacco; SEE CONCEPT 293

butt [*v1*] *bang up against with head*
batter, buck, buffet, bump, bunt, collide, gore, hook, horn, jab, knock, poke, prod, punch, push, ram, run into, shove, smack, strike, thrust, toss; SEE CONCEPT 189

butt [*v2*] *touch, adjoin*
abut, border, bound, communicate, join, jut, meet, neighbor, project, protrude, verge; SEE CONCEPTS 113,747

butterfingers [*n*] *a clumsy person*
bull in a china shop*, bungler, clod, clumsy oaf*, clunker, dolt, duffer*, foozle, fumbler, klutz, lummox, muffer*, schlep; SEE CONCEPTS 412,423

butt in [*v*] *meddle*
barge in, bother, burst in, charge in, chisel in*, cut in, disturb, get into the act*, interject, interrupt, intrude, muscle in, pester, poke one's face in*, pry, put one's two cents in*; SEE CONCEPTS 14,159,208,266,384

button [*n1*] *fastener*
catch, clasp, fastening, frog, knob, stud; SEE CONCEPTS 445,471

button [*n2*] *pushbutton*
adjuster, dial, knob, on/off, power switch, switch, toggle, tuner; SEE CONCEPT 475

buttress [*n*] *brace, support*
abutment, column, mainstay, pier, prop, reinforcement, shore, stanchion, stay, strut, underpinning; SEE CONCEPT 440

buttress [*v*] *support, bolster*
back up, beef up*, brace, build up, bulwark, carry, jack up, jazz up*, prop, reinforce, shore, step up, strengthen, sustain, uphold; SEE CONCEPT 250

buxom [*adj*] *bosomy*
ample, built, busty, chubby, comely, curvaceous, curvy, full-bosomed, full-figured, healthy, hearty, lusty, plump, robust, shapely, stacked*,

voluptuous, well-made, well-proportioned, well-rounded, zaftig*; SEE CONCEPT 406

buy [*n*] *something purchased*
acquisition, bargain, closeout, deal, good deal, investment, purchase, steal, value; SEE CONCEPT 710

buy [*v1*] *purchase*
acquire, bargain for, barter for, contract for, get, get in exchange, go shopping, invest in, market, obtain, pay for, procure, purchase, redeem, score, secure, shop for, sign for, take; SEE CONCEPT 327

buy [*v2*] *bribe*
corrupt, fix, grease palm*, have, land, lubricate, oil palm*, ransom, reach, redeem, sop*, square, suborn, tamper; SEE CONCEPTS 192,341

buyer [*n*] *someone who purchases*
client, consumer, customer, easy make*, emptor, end user, patron, prospect, purchaser, representative, shopper, sucker*, user, vendee; SEE CONCEPT 348

buzz [*n1*] *droning sound*
drone, fizz, fizzle, hiss, hum, murmur, purr, ring, ringing, sibilation, whir, whisper; SEE CONCEPT 595

buzz [*n2*] *gossip*
comment, cry, grapevine*, hearsay, news, report, rumble*, rumor, scandal, scuttlebutt, talk, whisper; SEE CONCEPT 274

buzz [*v1*] *make droning sound*
bombinate, bumble, drone, fizz, fizzle, hum, murmur, reverberate, ring, sibilate, whir, whisper, whiz; SEE CONCEPT 65

buzz [*v2*] *gossip*
call, chatter, inform, natter, rumor, tattle; SEE CONCEPT 60

buzzword [*n*] *popular word or phrase*
argot, cant, doublespeak, fuzzword, jargon, lingo, mediaspeak, phraseology, policyspeak, slang; SEE CONCEPT 275

by [*adv*] *near*
aside, at hand, away, beyond, close, handy, in reach, over, past, through, to one side; SEE CONCEPT 586

by [*prep1*] *next to*
along, alongside, beside, by way of, close to, near, nearby, nigh, over, past, round, via; SEE CONCEPT 586

by [*prep2*] *by means of*
at the hand of, in the name of, on, over, supported by, through, through the agency of, through the medium of, under the aegis of, with, with the assistance of; SEE CONCEPT 544

bygone [*adj*] *in the past*
ancient, antiquated, archaic, belated, dated, dead, defunct, departed, down memory lane*, erstwhile, extinct, forgotten, former, gone, gone by, in oblivion, late, lost, of old, of yore, olden, oldfangled, old-fashioned, old-time, one-time, out-of-date, previous, quondam, sometime, vanished, water over the dam*, water under the bridge*; SEE CONCEPT 820

by hand [*v*] *manually*
arduously, laboriously, strenuously, the hard way, tooth and nail; SEE CONCEPT 544

bypass [*v*] *avoid*
blink at, burke, circumnavigate, circumvent, depart from, detour, deviate from, finesse, get around, go around, go around the barn*, ignore, let go, neglect, omit, outflank, pass around, sidestep, skirt, take back road*, wink at; SEE CONCEPTS 30,102

bu
by

by-product [*n*] *side product*
after-effect, consequence, fall-out, offshoot, outgrowth, repercussion, result, side effect, spinoff; SEE CONCEPTS *230,260*

bystander [*n*] *person who watches*
eyewitness, gaper*, kibitzer*, looker-on, observer, onlooker, passerby, spectator, viewer, watcher, witness; SEE CONCEPT *423*

byte [*n*] *unit of computer memory*
data, eight bits, unit; SEE CONCEPT *274*

byword [*n*] *saying*
adage, aphorism, apophthegm, axiom, catchphrase, catchword, dictum, epithet, gnome, gnomic saying, handle, maxim, motto, nickname, precept, proverb, saw, shibboleth, slogan, standing joke; SEE CONCEPT *275*

C

cab [*n*] *car for hire*
carriage, hack, hackney, jitney, taxi, taxicab, tourist car; SEE CONCEPT *505*

cabaret [*n*] *nightclub with musical performances*
after-hours joint*, bar, café, disco, discothèque, dive, hideaway, hot spot*, nightery, night spot, speakeasy, supper club, tavern, watering hole*; SEE CONCEPTS *447,449*

cabin [*n*] *tiny house; lodging*
berth, box, caboose, camp, chalet, compartment, cot, cottage, crib, deckhouse, home, hovel, hut, lodge, log house, quarters, room, shack, shanty, shed, shelter; SEE CONCEPT *516*

cabinet [*n1*] *cupboard for storage*
case, chiffonier, closet, commode, container, depository, dresser, escritoire, locker, repository, wardrobe; SEE CONCEPTS *443,494*

cabinet [*n2*] *executives serving a leader*
administration, administrators, advisers, assembly, assistants, authority, brain trust*, bureau, bureaucracy, committee, council, counselors, department heads, governing body, government, kitchen cabinet*, ministry, official family; SEE CONCEPT *299*

cabin fever [*n*] *claustrophobia*
climbing the walls*, distress, neurosis, restlessness, SAD, seasonal affective disorder, temporary insanity, winter blues; SEE CONCEPTS *410,657,748*

cache [*n*] *hidden supply*
accumulation, assets, drop, drop joint, drop-off, fund, hideout, hiding place, hoard, kitty*, nest egg*, plant, repository, reserve, shade, stake, stash, stockpile, store, storehouse, supplies, treasure, treasury, wealth; SEE CONCEPTS *446,710*

cache [*v*] *hide a supply of something*
accumulate, bury, conceal, cover, ditch, duck, ensconce, lay away, maintain, park, plant, put away, put in the hole*, save, screen, secrete, squirrel*, squirrel away*, stash, stash away, store; SEE CONCEPT *188*

cackle [*n*] *a loud laugh*
chortle, chuckle, cluck, crow, gibber, giggle, gobble, guffaw, quack, snicker, snigger, titter; SEE CONCEPT *77*

cackle [*v*] *laugh irritatingly*
babble, blather, burble, chortle, chuckle, cluck, crow, gibber, giggle, gobble, jabber, quack, snicker, snigger, titter; SEE CONCEPT *77*

cacophonous [*adj*] *harsh sounding*
clinking, discordant, disharmonic, dissonant, grating, ill-sounding, immusical, inharmonious, jangly, jarring, noisy, raucous, sour, strident, unmusical; SEE CONCEPTS *592,594*

cad [*n*] *sly, dastardly person*
boor, bounder*, clown, creep, cur*, dog*, heel, louse, lout, rake, rascal, rat*, rotter*, rounder*, scoundrel, stinker, worm; SEE CONCEPT *412*

cadaver [*n*] *dead body*
body, cage, carcass, corpse, deceased, mort*, remains, skeleton, stiff*; SEE CONCEPT *390*

cadaverous [*adj*] *pale, corpselike*
ashen, bag of bones, blanched, bloodless, consumptive, dead, deathlike, deathly, emaciated, exsanguinous, gaunt, ghastly, ghostly, haggard, pallid, peaked, peaky, sallow, shadowy, sick, skeletal, skeletonlike, skin and bones*, spectral, thin, wan, wasted; SEE CONCEPTS *406,491,618*

cadence [*n*] *rhythm*
accent, beat, count, inflection, intonation, lilt, measure, meter, modulation, pulse, rhythmus, swing, tempo, throb; SEE CONCEPT *65*

cadre [*n*] *nucleus of effort*
core, force, framework, infrastructure, key group, officers, organization, personnel, staff; SEE CONCEPTS *417,432*

café [*n*] *small, informal restaurant*
bistro, burger joint, cafeteria, cake shop, chophouse, coffee bar, coffee shop, diner, eating house, grease joint*, greasy spoon*, hash house*, luncheonette, lunchroom, noshery*, pit stop*, quick-lunch, snack bar, soup house, tearoom; SEE CONCEPT *449*

cafeteria [*n*] *restaurant*
café, commissary, lunch counter, lunchroom, snack bar, tea room; SEE CONCEPT *449*

cage [*n*] *enclosure with bars*
coop, corral, crate, enclosure, fold, jail, mew, pen, pinfold, pound; SEE CONCEPT *494*

cage [*v*] *hold in enclosure*
close in, confine, coop up, enclose, envelop, fence in, hem, immure, impound, imprison, incarcerate, jail, lock up, mew, pen, restrain, shut in, shut up; SEE CONCEPT *191*

cagey [*adj*] *tricky*
cagey, careful, circumspect, crafty, cunning, leery, secretive, shrewd, sly, wary, wily; SEE CONCEPTS *401,545*

cahoots [*n*] *conspiracy*
alliance, collusion, league, partnership; SEE CONCEPTS *114,660*

cajole [*v*] *attempt to coax; flatter*
apple polish*, argue into, banter, beguile, blandish, bootlick*, brownnose*, build up, butter up*, con, crowd, deceive, decoy, delude, dupe, entice, entrap, get around, get next to*, hand a line*, induce, influence, inveigle, jolly, lay it on thick*, lure, make up to, maneuver, massage, mislead, oil*, play up to, push, rub the right way*, seduce, snow*, soap*, soften, soft-soap*, spread it on*, stroke, suck up to*, sweeten up*, sweet-talk*, tantalize, tempt, urge, wheedle, work on, work over*; SEE CONCEPTS *59,68,75*

cake [*n*] *bar of something*
block, brick, loaf, lump, mass, slab; SEE CONCEPT *470*

calamitous [*adj*] *disastrous; tragic*
adverse, afflictive, blighting, cataclysmic, catastrophic, deadly, deplorable, devastating, dire, fatal, grievous, harmful, heartbreaking, lamentable, messy, pernicious, regrettable, ruinous, unfavorable, unfortunate, woeful; SEE CONCEPT *537*

calamity [*n*] *disaster; tragedy*
adversity, affliction, blue ruin*, cataclysm, catastrophe, collapse, cross, curtains, distress, downfall, hardship, holy mess*, misadventure, mischance, misfortune, mishap, reverse, ruin, scourge, the worst*, trial, tribulation, unholy mess*, visitation, waterloo*, woe, wreck, wretchedness; SEE CONCEPTS *674,675*

calculable [*adj*] *able to be computed or estimated*
accountable, ascertainable, computable, countable, discoverable, estimable, foreseeable, measurable, predictable, reckonable; SEE CONCEPTS *402,762*

calculate [*v1*] *compute or estimate amount*
account, add, adjust, appraise, assay, cast, cipher, consider, count, determine, divide, dope out*, enumerate, figure, forecast, foretell, gauge, guess, judge, keep tabs*, measure, multiply, number, rate, reckon, size up, subtract, sum, take account of, tally, tot, tote up*, value, weigh, work out; SEE CONCEPT *764*

calculate [*v2*] *plan on*
aim, anticipate, assume, bank on, build, count on, depend on, design, intend, judge, plan, reckon, rely on, suppose, think likely, trust; SEE CONCEPTS *26,36*

calculating [*adj*] *scheming to manipulate*
artful, canny, careful, cautious, chary, circumspect, considerate, contriving, crafty, cunning, designing, devious, discreet, gingerly, guarded, guileful, intelligent, Machiavellian, manipulative, politic, premeditating, safe, scheming, sharp, shrewd, sly, wary, wily; SEE CONCEPTS *401,403*

calculation [*n1*] *computing, estimating amount*
adding, arithmetic, ciphering, computation, counting, dividing, estimate, estimation, figuring, forecast, judgment, multiplying, prediction, reckoning, subtracting, summation, totaling; SEE CONCEPTS *28,764*

calculation [*n2*] *computed or estimated amount*
answer, computation, divination, estimate, estimation, figuring, forecast, judgment, prediction, prognosis, prognostication, reckoning, reply; SEE CONCEPT *787*

calculation [*n3*] *forethought*
canniness, caution, circumspection, contrivance, deliberation, discretion, foresight, planning, precaution, prudence, thought; SEE CONCEPT *660*

calculator [*n*] *adding machine*
computer, number cruncher*, PDA, personal digital assistant; SEE CONCEPTS *269,463*

calendar [*n*] *schedule of events*
agenda, almanac, annal, bulletin, card, chronology, daybook, diary, docket, journal, lineup, list, log, logbook, menology, pipeline, program, record, register, sked, system of reckoning, tab, table, time, timetable; SEE CONCEPTS *274,281,809*

calf [*n1*] *leg between knee and ankle*
foreleg, shin; SEE CONCEPT *392*

calf [*n2*] *baby cow*
dogie, freemartin, heifer, maverick, veal, yearling, young bull, young cow; SEE CONCEPT *394*

caliber [*n1*] *capacity; character*
ability, appetency, capability, competence, constitution, dignity, distinction, endowment, essence, faculty, force, gifts, habilitation, merit, nature, parts, power, quality, scope, stature, strength, talent, value, virtue, worth, worthiness; SEE CONCEPT *411*

caliber [*n2*] *size of ammunition*
bore, class, diameter, gauge, grade, length, measure, measurement, quality, striking power, weight; SEE CONCEPT *730*

call [*n1*] *yelled statement*
alarm, calling, command, cry, hail, holler*, scream, shout, signal, whoop, yawp, yell; SEE CONCEPT *278*

call [*n2*] *demand, announcement*
appeal, bidding, command, invitation, notice, order, plea, proposal, request, solicitation, subpoena, summons, supplication, visit; SEE CONCEPT *53*

call [*n3*] *need, cause for action*
claim, excuse, grounds, justification, necessity, obligation, occasion, reason, right, urge; SEE CONCEPT *709*

call [*n4*] *normal sound of animal*
cheep, chirp, cry, note, peep, roar, shriek, song, tweet, twitter, warble; SEE CONCEPT *64*

call [*v1*] *yell declaration*
announce, arouse, awaken, bawl, bellow, cry, cry out, exclaim, hail, holler*, hoot, howl, proclaim, roar, rouse, scream, screech, shout, shriek, vociferate, waken, whoop, yawp*, yoo hoo*, yowl; SEE CONCEPTS *47,266*

call [*v2*] *arrange meeting*
ask, assemble, bid, collect, contact, convene, convoke, gather, invite, muster, phone*, rally, request, ring up, subpoena, summon, telephone; SEE CONCEPT *114*

call [*v3*] *entitle*
address, baptize, christen, denominate, describe as, designate, dub, label, name, style, term, title; SEE CONCEPT *62*

call [*v4*] *demand or announce action*
appeal to, appoint, ask, challenge, charge, claim, command, declare, decree, elect, entreat, exact, ordain, order, postulate, pray to, proclaim, require, requisition, set apart, solicit, summon; SEE CONCEPT *53*

call [*v5*] *estimate, consider*
adumbrate, approximate, augur, forecast, foretell, guess, judge, make rough guess, place, portend, predict, presage, prognosticate, prophesy, put, reckon, regard, think, vaticinate; SEE CONCEPTS *28,70*

call [*v6*] *attempt to communicate by telephone*
beep, blast*, bleep, buzz, contact, get back to*, phone, ring, telephone; SEE CONCEPTS *74,266*

call [*v7*] *visit at residence or business*
come by, come over, crash, drop by, drop in, fall by, fall down, hit, look in on, look up, play, pop in*, run in, see, stop by, stop in, swing by; SEE CONCEPT *227*

call for [*v*] *demand; entail*
ask for, inquire, involve, lack, necessitate, need,

occasion, request, require, suggest, want; SEE CONCEPT *646*

calling [n] *chosen profession*
art, business, career, craft, day gig*, do*, dodge*, employment, gig*, go*, handicraft, hang*, life's work, lifework, line, métier, mission, nine-to-five*, occupation, play, province, pursuit, racket*, rat race*, slot*, swindle*, trade, vocation, walk of life, work; SEE CONCEPT *360*

call off [v] *discontinue*
abandon, abort, break off, cancel, desist, drop, kill*, postpone, scrub*, withdraw; SEE CONCEPTS *18,211,234*

callous [adj] *cruel, insensitive*
apathetic, blind to, careless, case-hardened, cold, cold-blooded, deaf to, hard, hard-bitten, hard-boiled, hardened, hardhearted, heartless, impassive, impenitent, indifferent, indurated, inflexible, insensate, insensible, insensitive, insentient, inured, obdurate, soulless, spiritless, stiff, stony, stubborn, thick-skinned, torpid, tough, toughened, unaffected, unbending, uncaring, uncompassionate, unconcerned, unfeeling, unimpressionable, unresponsive, unsusceptible, unsympathetic; SEE CONCEPT *404*

callow [adj] *immature*
crude, green, guileless, inexperienced, infant, jejune, jellybean*, juvenile, kid, low tech*, naive, not dry behind ears*, puerile, raw, sophomore, tenderfoot, unbaked, unfledged, unripe, unsophisticated, untrained, untried, young; SEE CONCEPTS *578,678,797*

calm [adj1] *peaceful, quiet (inanimate)*
at a standstill, at peace, bland, bucolic, cool, halcyon, harmonious, hushed, inactive, in order, low-key, mild, motionless, pacific, pastoral, placid, quiescent, reposeful, reposing, restful, rural, serene, slow, smooth, soothing, still, stormless, tranquil, undisturbed, unruffled, waveless, windless; SEE CONCEPTS *544,705*

calm [adj2] *composed, cool (animate)*
aloof, amiable, amicable, civil, collected, cool as cucumber*, cool-headed, detached, disinterested, dispassionate, equable, gentle, impassive, imperturbable, inscrutable, kind, laid-back*, level-headed, listless, moderate, neutral, patient, placid, pleased, poised, relaxed, restful, satisfied, sedate, self-possessed, serene, still, temperate, unconcerned, undisturbed, unemotional, unexcitable, unexcited, unflappable, unimpressed, unmoved, unruffled, untroubled; SEE CONCEPTS *401,404*

calm [n] *quietness, composure*
calmness, dispassion, doldrums, hush, impassivity, imperturbation, lull, patience, peace, peacefulness, peace of mind, placidity, quiet, repose, rest, restraint, serenity, silence, stillness, stoicism, tranquility; SEE CONCEPTS *388,411,720*

calm [v] *make composed, quiet*
allay, alleviate, appease, assuage, balm, becalm, compose, cool, cool it*, cool out*, hush, lay back*, lull, mitigate, mollify, pacify, placate, quiet, quieten, relax, relieve, sedate, settle, simmer down, soft-pedal*, soothe, steady, still, stroke, take it easy*, take the edge off*, tranquilize; SEE CONCEPT *231*

camaraderie [n] *friendship*
cheer, companionability, companionship, comradeship, conviviality, esprit de corps, fellowship, gregariousness, intimacy, jollity, sociability, togetherness; SEE CONCEPT *388*

camera [n] *photographic equipment*
camcorder, Kodak*, 35mm, Polaroid*, video camera; SEE CONCEPTS *446,463*

camouflage [n] *disguise*
beard*, blind, cloak, concealment, cover, coverup, deceit, deceptive marking, dissimulation, faking, false appearance, front, guise, mask, masking, masquerade, mimicry, paint, plain brown wrapper*, protective coloring, red herring*, screen, shade, shroud, smokescreen, veil; SEE CONCEPT *260*

camouflage [v] *disguise, cover*
beard*, becloud, befog, cloak, conceal, cover up, deceive, dim, dissemble, dissimulate, dress up, hide, mask, obfuscate, obscure, screen, throw on makeup, veil; SEE CONCEPTS *172,188*

camp [adj] *consciously affecting the unfashionable, weird, or bizarre*
affected, arch, artificial, avant-garde, Daliesque*, far out*, in*, mannered, mod, ostentatious, pop, posturing, wild; SEE CONCEPT *544*

camp [n] *site for outdoor living*
bivouac, campfire, campground, camping ground, caravansary, chalet, cottage, encampment, hut, lean-to, lodge, log cabin, shack, shanty, shed, summer home, tent, tent city, tepee, tilt, wigwam; SEE CONCEPTS *198,516*

campaign [n] *attempt to win; attack*
crusade, drive, expedition, fight, movement, offensive, operation, push, warfare; SEE CONCEPTS *87,320*

campaign [v] *attempt to win political election*
agitate, barnstorm, canvass, contend for, contest, crusade, electioneer, go to grass roots*, hit the trail*, lobby, mend fences*, muckrake, mudsling*, politick, press the flesh*, ring doorbells*, run, run for, shake hands and kiss babies*, solicit votes, stand for, stump*, tour, whistle-stop*; SEE CONCEPT *300*

camper [n] *mobile home*
recreational vehicle, RV, tin can*, Winnebago*; SEE CONCEPT *503*

campus [n] *school grounds*
dorm, grounds, quad, quadrangle, square, yard; SEE CONCEPT *509*

can [n1] *container, usually metallic*
aluminum, bottle, bucket, canister, cannikin, gunboat*, gutbucket*, jar, package, pop top*, receptacle, tin, vessel; SEE CONCEPTS *476,494*

can [n2] *toilet*
head*, john*, johnny*, latrine, lavatory, litter box*, outhouse, pot*, potty*, privy, restroom, sandbox*, throne*, washroom, water closet; SEE CONCEPT *443*

can [n3] *buttocks*
backside, behind, butt*, derrière, fanny*, fundament, gluteus maximus, hind end, posterior, rump, seat, tush*; SEE CONCEPT *418*

can [v1] *preserve fruit, vegetable*
bottle, keep, put up; SEE CONCEPT *170*

can [v2] *be able*
be capable of, be equal to, be up to, be within one's area, be within one's control, can do*, commit, could, cut the mustard*, have it made*, lie in one's power, make it*, make out, make the grade*, manage, may, take care of; SEE CONCEPT *630*

can [v3] *fire from job*
ax*, boot*, bounce*, cashier, discharge, dismiss, expel, give the heave ho*, kick out*, let go, sack*, terminate; SEE CONCEPT *351*

canal [n] *waterway*
aqueduct, bottleneck, channel, choke point, conduit, course, cove, ditch, duct, estuary, firth, trench, water, watercourse; SEE CONCEPT *514*

cancel [v1] *call off; erase*
abolish, abort, abrogate, annul, ax, black out, blot out, break, break off, countermand, cross out, cut, deface, delete, destroy, do away with, do in, efface, eliminate, eradicate, expunge, finish off*, go back on one's word*, kill, obliterate, off*, omit, quash, remove, render invalid, repeal, repudiate, rescind, revoke, rub out, scratch out, scrub*, sink*, smash, squash, stamp across, strike out, torpedo*, total*, trash*, trim*, undo, wash out*, wipe out*, wipe slate clean*, X-out*, zap*; SEE CONCEPTS *18,211,234*

cancel [v2] *equal out*
abort, abrogate, annul, balance out, call off, compensate for, counteract, counterbalance, countercheck, countermand, counterpoise, declare invalid, discard, discharge, frustrate, ignore, invalidate, make up for, negate, neutralize, nullify, offset, overthrow, put an end to, recall, recant, redeem, redress, refute, render inert, render null and void, repeal, repudiate, rescind, retract, revoke, rule out, set aside, suppress, vacate, void; SEE CONCEPTS *232,667*

cancellation [n] *calling off; erasure*
abandoning, abandonment, abolishing, abolition, abrogation, annulment, canceling, deletion, dissolution, dissolving, elimination, invalidating, invalidation, nullification, overruling, quashing, recall, recalling, repeal, repudiation, retirement, retracting, retraction, reversal, reversing, revocation, revoking, undoing, withdrawing; SEE CONCEPT *119*

cancer [n] *malignant growth*
big C*, C*, canker, carcinoma, corruption, disease, long illness, malignancy, sickness, tumor; SEE CONCEPT *306*

candid [adj] *honest*
aboveboard, bluff, blunt, equal, equitable, fair, forthright, frank, free, frontal, genuine, guileless, impartial, ingenuous, just, objective, open, outspoken, plain, right up front*, scrupulous, sincere, straightforward, talking turkey*, telling it like it is*, truthful, unbiased, uncolored, unequivocal, unprejudiced, unpretended, up front*, upright; SEE CONCEPT *267*

candidate [n] *person desiring political office, job*
applicant, aspirant, bidder, claimant, competitor, contender, contestant, dark horse*, entrant, favorite son*, handshaker*, hopeful*, job-hunter, nominee, office-seeker, petitioner, possibility, possible choice, pothunter*, runner, seeker, solicitant, stumper*, successor, suitor, whistle-stopper*, write-in*; SEE CONCEPT *359*

candlestick [n] *holder for candles*
candelabra, candelabrum, menorah, pricket, sconce, taper holder; SEE CONCEPT *444*

candor [n] *complete honesty*
artlessness, directness, fairness, forthrightness, frankness, glasnost, guilelessness, honesty, impartiality, ingenuousness, naïveté, openness, outspokenness, probity, simplicity, sincerity, straightforwardness, truthfulness, unequivocalness, uprightness, veracity; SEE CONCEPT *411*

candy [n] *confection*
bonbon, confectionery, confit, hokum*, jawbreaker*, sweet, sweetmeat; SEE CONCEPT *457*

cane [n] *stick to aid walking of disabled*
pikestaff, pole, rod, staff, vade mecum, walking stick; SEE CONCEPT *479*

canker [n] *blistered infection*
bane, blight, blister, boil, cancer, corrosion, corruption, lesion, rot, scourge, smutch, sore, ulcer; SEE CONCEPT *306*

canker [v] *blight, corrupt*
animalize, bestialize, consume, corrode, debase, debauch, demoralize, deprave, embitter, envenom, inflict, pervert, poison, pollute, rot, ruin, scourge, sore, stain, ulcer, vitiate; SEE CONCEPT *240*

cannibal [n] *beast, beastlike human*
aborigine, anthropophage, anthropophaginian, anthropophagus, brute, bush dweller, cruel person, head-hunter, ogre, ogress, primitive, ruffian, savage; SEE CONCEPT *412*

cannon [n] *large gun*
Big Bertha*, heavy artillery, howitzer, Long Tom*, mortar, ordnance; SEE CONCEPT *500*

canny [adj] *clever, artful*
able, acute, adroit, astute, cagey, careful, cautious, circumspect, cunning, dexterous, discreet, foxy*, frugal, having fancy footwork*, hep*, ingenious, intelligent, judicious, knowing, nimble-witted, perspicacious, prudent, quick, quick-witted, sagacious, shrewd, skillful, slick, slippery*, sly, smart, smooth*, street smart*, streetwise*, subtle, wary, watchful, wise, with it*, worldly-wise; SEE CONCEPT *402*

canoe [n] *light, paddled boat*
coracle, dugout, kayak, outrigger, piragua, pirogue; SEE CONCEPT *506*

can of worms [n] *troublesome problem*
complication, difficulty, entanglement, Gordian knot, hot water*, Pandora's box, predicament, quagmire, quandary, trouble; SEE CONCEPTS *532,674,690*

canon [n1] *rule, edict*
assize, catalogue, command, commandment, criterion, declaration, decree, decretum, dictate, doctrine, dogma, formula, law, list, maxim, order, ordinance, precept, principle, regulation, roll, screed, standard, statute, table, tenet, touchstone, yardstick; SEE CONCEPTS *318,688*

canon [n2] *a body of the most important, influential or superior works in music, literature, or art*
ana, analects, anthology, chrestomathy, classics, collected works, delectus, library, miscellanea, oeuvre, works; SEE CONCEPTS *280,432*

canonical [adj] *accepted, recognized*
approved, authoritative, authorized, lawful, legal, official, orthodox, received, sanctioned, sound, statutory; SEE CONCEPTS *319,535*

canonize [v] *sanctify; idolize*
apotheosize, beatify, besaint, bless, consecrate, dedicate, deify, glorify, idolatrize, love, put on a pedestal*, saint, worship; SEE CONCEPTS *32,367*

canopy [n] *overhanging covering*
awning, baldachin, cover, marquee, shade, sunshade, umbrella; SEE CONCEPTS *440,444*

cant [n1] *hypocritical statement*
affected piety, deceit, dishonesty, humbug, hypocrisy, hypocriticalness, insincerity, lip ser-

vice*, pecksniffery, pharisaicalness, pious platitudes, pomposity, pretense, pretentiousness, sanctimoniousness, sanctimony, sham holiness, show; SEE CONCEPT 63

cant [n2] *jargon*
argot, dialect, diction, idiom, language, lingo, patois, patter, phraseology, slang, vernacular, vocabulary; SEE CONCEPTS 275,278

cant [v] *lean, slant*
angle, bevel, careen, grade, heel, incline, list, recline, rise, slope, tilt, tip; SEE CONCEPTS 154,201

cantankerous [adj] *difficult, crabby*
bad-tempered, bearish, captious, choleric, contrary, cranky, critical, cross, crotchety*, crusty*, disagreeable, dour, grouchy*, grumpy*, huffy*, ill-humored, ill-natured, irascible, irritable, morose, obstinate, ornery*, peevish, perverse, petulant, prickly, quarrelsome, snappish, sour, stuffy*, testy, vinegarish, vinegary; SEE CONCEPT 401

canteen [n1] *portable kitchen*
chuck wagon, mobile kitchen, snack bar, snack shop; SEE CONCEPT 449

canteen [n2] *container for liquids, used in travels*
bota, bottle, flacon, flask, flasket, jug, thermos, water bottle; SEE CONCEPT 494

canvas [n1] *coarse material*
awning cloth, duck, fly, sailcloth, shade, tarp, tarpaulin, tenting; SEE CONCEPT 473

canvas [n2] *painting on coarse material*
art, artwork, oil, picture, piece, portrait, still life, watercolor; SEE CONCEPT 259

canvass [v] *poll; discuss issues*
agitate, analyze, apply, argue, campaign, check, check over, consult, debate, dispute, electioneer, examine, inspect, investigate, review, run, scan, scrutinize, sift, solicit, study, survey, ventilate; SEE CONCEPTS 24,48,56,300

canyon [n] *gulf in mountain area*
coulee, glen, gorge, gulch, gully, ravine, valley; SEE CONCEPTS 509,513

cap [n] *small hat*
beanie*, beret, bonnet, dink*, fez, pillbox, skullcap, tam, tam o'shanter; SEE CONCEPT 450

cap [v] *outdo a performance*
beat, best, better, button down*, button up*, can*, clinch*, cob*, complete, cover, crest, crown, do to a T*, eclipse, exceed, excel, finish, outshine, outstrip, pass, put the lid on*, surmount, surpass, top, top it off*, transcend, trump, wrap up*; SEE CONCEPT 141

capability [n] *ability to perform*
adequacy, aptitude, art, capacity, competence, craft, cunning, effectiveness, efficacy, efficiency, facility, faculty, means, might, potency, potential, potentiality, power, proficiency, qualification, qualifiedness, skill, wherewithal; SEE CONCEPT 630

capable [adj] *able to perform*
able, accomplished, adapted, adept, adequate, apt, au fait, clever, competent, dynamite, efficient, experienced, fireball*, fitted, gifted, good, green thumb*, has what it takes*, having knowhow*, having the goods*, having the right stuff*, intelligent, knowing the ropes*, knowing the score*, like a one-man band*, like a pistol*, masterly, old hand*, old-timer*, on the ball*, proficient, proper, qualified, skillful, suited, talented, there*, up*, up to it*, up to snuff*, up to speed*, veteran; SEE CONCEPT 527

capacious [adj] *ample, extensive*
abundant, broad, comfortable, commodious, comprehensive, dilatable, distensible, expandable, expansive, extended, generous, liberal, plentiful, roomy, sizable, spacious, substantial, vast, voluminous, wide; SEE CONCEPTS 481,772,773,774

capacity [n1] *volume; limit of volume held*
accommodation, amplitude, bulk, burden, compass, contents, dimensions, expanse, extent, full, holding ability, holding power, latitude, magnitude, mass, measure, proportions, quantity, range, reach, retention, room, scope, size, space, spread, standing room only*, sufficiency, sweep; SEE CONCEPTS 481,736,774,794

capacity [n2] *ability; competency*
adequacy, aptitude, aptness, bent, brains, caliber, capability, cleverness, compass, competence, efficiency, facility, faculty, forte, genius, gift, inclination, intelligence, knack, might, power, qualification, readiness, skill, stature, strength, talent, the goods*, up to it*, what it takes*; SEE CONCEPTS 409,630

cape [n1] *promontory into water*
arm, beak, bill, chersonese, finger, foreland, head, headland, jetty, jutty, mole, naze, neck, ness, peninsula, point, tongue; SEE CONCEPTS 509,514

cape [n2] *sleeveless coat*
bertha, capote, cardinal, cloak, cope, dolman, fichu, gabardine, manteau, mantelletta, mantilla, mantle, overdress, paletot, pelerine, pelisse, poncho, shawl, tabard, talma, tippet, Vandyke, victorine, wrap, wrapper; SEE CONCEPT 451

caper [n] *antic, lark*
escapade, gag*, gambol, high jinks*, hop, hot foot*, jest, joke, jump, leap, mischief, monkeyshines*, practical joke, prank, put on*, revel, rib*, rollick, shenanigan*, sport, stunt, tomfoolery*, trick; SEE CONCEPT 386

caper [v] *frolic, cavort*
blow the lid off*, bounce, bound, cut capers*, cut loose*, dance, frisk, gambol, go on a tear*, hop, horse around*, jump, kick up one's heels*, leap, let loose*, play, raise hell*, rollick, romp, skip, spring, whoop it up*; SEE CONCEPT 384

capital [adj1] *main, essential*
basic, cardinal, central, chief, controlling, dominant, first, foremost, fundamental, important, leading, major, number one*, outstanding, overruling, paramount, predominant, preeminent, primary, prime, principal, prominent, underlying, vital; SEE CONCEPTS 546,568,829

capital [adj2] *superior*
best, champion, choice, crack, dandy, delightful, deluxe, excellent, famous, fine, first, first-class*, first-rate*, five-star*, fly, great, prime, splendid, superb, top, top-notch*, world-class*; SEE CONCEPT 574

capital [n1] *financial assets*
business, cash, CD, estate, finances, financing, fortune, funds, gold, interests, investment, IRA, kitty*, means, money, nest egg*, principal, property, resources, savings, stake, stock, substance, treasure, ways and means*, wealth, wherewithal; SEE CONCEPTS 332,710

capital [n2] *city of governmental seat*
control, county seat, metropolis, municipality, political front, principal city, the Hill*; SEE CONCEPTS 507,512

capital [*n3*] *upper case written symbol*
cap, initial, majuscule, small cap, uncial; SEE CONCEPT 284

capitalism [*n*] *economic system of private ownership*
commercialism, competition, democracy, free enterprise, free market, industrialism, laissez faire economics, mercantilism, private enterprise; SEE CONCEPTS 299,689,770

capitalist [*n*] *person engaged in private ownership of business*
backer, banker, bourgeois, businessperson, entrepreneur, financier, investor, landowner, moneybags*, one who signs the checks*, plutocrat, the boss*, the money*; SEE CONCEPT 347

capitalize [*v*] *benefit from situation*
avail oneself of, exploit, gain, make capital of, obtain, profit, realize, subsidize, take advantage of; SEE CONCEPT 120

capitol [*n*] *building or buildings housing chief governmental offices*
Capitol Hill, center, dome, legislative hall, political scene*, seat of government, statehouse; SEE CONCEPTS 299,449

capitulate [*v*] *give in*
bow, buckle under, cave in, cede, come across, come to terms, concede, defer, fold, give away the store*, give out, give up, knuckle under, put out, relent, submit, succumb, surrender, yield; SEE CONCEPTS 35,83

capitulation [*n*] *giving in*
accedence, bowing, buckling, conceding, giving up, knuckling under, relenting, resignation, submission, succumbing, surrender, yielding; SEE CONCEPTS 83,410

caprice [*n*] *sudden change of behavior*
bee*, caper*, changeableness, contrariety, crotchet, fad, fancy, fickleness, fitfulness, fool notion*, freak, gag*, humor, impulse, inconsistency, inconstancy, jerk, kink, mood, notion, peculiarity, perversity, put on*, quirk, rib*, temper, thought, vagary, vein, whim, whimsy; SEE CONCEPTS 13,410

capricious [*adj*] *given to sudden behavior change*
any way the wind blows*, arbitrary, blowing hot and cold*, careless, changeful, contrary, crotchety, effervescent, erratic, every which way*, fanciful, fickle, fitful, flaky*, flighty, freakish, gaga*, helter-skelter*, humorsome, impulsive, inconstant, kinky*, lubricious, mercurial, moody, mutable, notional, odd, picky*, punchy*, queer, quirky, temperamental, ticklish, unpredictable, unreasonable, unstable, up and down*, vagarious, variable, volatile, wayward, whimsical, yo-yo*; SEE CONCEPT 401

capsize [*v*] *overturn*
invert, keel over, roll, tip over, turn over, turn turtle*, upset; SEE CONCEPTS 150,152

capsule [*adj*] *shortened form*
abridged, canned, condensed, epitomized, pocket, potted, tabloid; SEE CONCEPTS 531,773

capsule [*n*] *tablet, usually medicine*
bolus, cap, dose, lozenge, pellet, pill, troche; SEE CONCEPTS 260,307

captain [*n*] *chief of vehicle, effort*
authority, boss, cap, CEO, CFO, chieftain, commander, director, exec*, executive, four-striper*, guide, head, head honcho*, higher up*, leader, master, mistress, number one*, officer, operator,

owner, pilot, royalty, skip*, skipper*, top*, top dog*; SEE CONCEPT 347

caption [*n*] *heading; short description*
explanation, head, inscription, legend, rubric, subtitle, title, underline; SEE CONCEPT 283

captious [*adj*] *very critical*
acrimonious, cantankerous, carping, caviling, cavillous, censorious, contrary, crabby, cross, demanding, deprecating, disparaging, exacting, exceptive, fault-finding, finicky, hypercritical, irritable, nagging, nit-picking, overcritical, peevish, perverse, petulant, sarcastic, severe, testy, touchy; SEE CONCEPTS 267,404

captivate [*v*] *attract, enchant*
allure, beguile, bewitch, charm, dazzle, delight, draw, enamour, enrapture, enslave, ensnare, entertain, enthrall, entrance, fascinate, gratify, grip, hold, hook, hypnotize, infatuate, intrigue, lure, magnetize, make a hit with*, mesmerize, please, rope in*, seduce, spellbind, sweep off one's feet*, take, turn one on, vamp, wile, win; SEE CONCEPTS 7,22

captive [*adj1*] *physically held by force*
bound, caged, confined, enslaved, ensnared, imprisoned, incarcerated, incommunicado, in custody, jailed, locked up, penned, restricted, subjugated, under lock and key*; SEE CONCEPTS 536,554

captive [*adj2*] *mentally enchanted, held*
beguiled, bewitched, charmed, delighted, enraptured, enthralled, fascinated, hypnotized, infatuated; SEE CONCEPT 403

captive [*n*] *person held physically*
bondman, bondservant, bondwoman, con, convict, detainee, hostage, internee, prisoner, prisoner of war, slave; SEE CONCEPTS 412,423

captivity [*n*] *physical detention by force*
bondage, committal, confinement, constraint, custody, durance, duress, enslavement, enthrallment, entombment, impoundment, imprisonment, incarceration, internment, jail, limbo, restraint, serfdom, servitude, slavery, subjection, thralldom, vassalage; SEE CONCEPTS 191,652

capture [*n*] *catching, forceful holding*
abduction, acquirement, acquisition, apprehension, appropriating, appropriation, arrest, bag*, bust*, catch, collar, commandeering, confiscation, drop*, ensnaring, fall, gaining, grab*, grasping, hit the jackpot*, hook*, imprisonment, knock off*, laying hold of*, nab*, nail*, obtaining, occupation, pick up*, pinch*, pull*, run in*, securing, seizing, seizure, snatching*, sweep*, taking, taking captive, taking into custody, trapping, trip, winning; SEE CONCEPT 90

capture [*v*] *catch and forcefully hold*
apprehend, arrest, bag*, bust*, catch, collar, conquer, cop, gain control, get, grab*, hook*, land, nab*, nail*, net, occupy, overwhelm, pick up*, pinch*, prehend, pull in, put the cuffs on*, round up*, run in*, secure, seize, snare, snatch, take, take captive, take into custody, take prisoner, trap, tumble; SEE CONCEPT 90

car [*n*] *vehicle driven on streets*
auto, automobile, bucket*, buggy*, bus, clunker*, compact, convertible, conveyance, coupe, gas guzzler*, hardtop, hatchback, heap*, jalopy*, jeep, junker*, limousine, machine, motor, motorcar, pickup, ride*, roadster, sedan, station wagon, subcompact, touring car, truck, van, wagon, wheels*, wreck*; SEE CONCEPT 505

caravan [n] *group traveling together*
band, camel train, campers, cavalcade, convoy, expedition, procession, safari, train, troop; SEE CONCEPTS *432,503*

carbohydrate [n] *organic compound composed of carbon, hydrogen, and oxygen*
cellulose, dextrin, dextrose, disaccharide, fructose, galactose, glucose, glycogen, lactose, maltose, monosaccharide, polysaccharide, starch, sucrose, sugar; SEE CONCEPT *478*

carcass/carcase [n] *dead body; framework, base structure*
body, cadaver, corpse, framework, hulk, mort*, remains, shell, skeleton, stiff*; SEE CONCEPTS *390,434*

carcinogen [n] *cancer-causing agent*
deadly chemical, health hazard, killer*, mutagen, poison, toxin; SEE CONCEPT *675*

card [n] *piece of paper, often with purposeful writing*
agenda, badge, billet, calendar, cardboard, check, docket, fiberboard, identification, label, pass, poster, program, schedule, sheet, square, tally, ticket, timetable, voucher; SEE CONCEPTS *260,271*

cardiac arrest [n] *heart stoppage*
coronary thrombosis, heart attack, heart failure, myocardial infarction; SEE CONCEPT *308*

cardinal [adj] *important, key*
basal, basic, central, chief, constitutive, essential, first, foremost, fundamental, greatest, highest, indispensable, leading, main, overriding, overruling, paramount, pivotal, preeminent, primary, prime, principal, ruling, vital; SEE CONCEPTS *568,574*

care [n1] *personal interest, concern*
affliction, aggravation, alarm, anguish, annoyance, anxiety, apprehension, bother, burden, chagrin, charge, consternation, discomposure, dismay, disquiet, distress, disturbance, encumbrance, exasperation, fear, foreboding, fretfulness, handicap, hardship, hindrance, impediment, incubus, load, misgiving, nuisance, onus, oppression, perplexity, pressure, responsibility, solicitude, sorrow, stew, strain, stress, sweat, tribulation, trouble, uneasiness, unhappiness, vexation, woe, worry; SEE CONCEPTS *410,532*

care [n2] *carefulness, attention to detail*
alertness, caution, circumspection, concentration, concern, conscientiousness, consideration, diligence, direction, discrimination, effort, enthusiasm, exactness, exertion, fastidiousness, forethought, heed, interest, management, meticulousness, nicety, pains, particularity, precaution, prudence, regard, scrupulousness, solicitude, thought, trouble, vigilance, wariness, watchfulness; SEE CONCEPT *657*

care [n3] *custody of person, usually child*
administration, aegis, auspices, charge, control, direction, guardianship, keeping, management, ministration, protection, safekeeping, superintendence, supervision, trust, tutelage, ward, wardship; SEE CONCEPTS *285,295,388*

care [v1] *tend to*
attend, baby sit, consider, foster, keep an eye on*, keep tabs on*, look after, mind, mind the store*, minister, mother, nurse, nurture, pay attention to, protect, provide for, ride herd on*, sit,

take pains, tend, treasure, wait on, watch, watch over; SEE CONCEPTS *110,295*

care [v2] *regard highly*
be crazy about*, be fond of*, cherish, desire, enjoy, find congenial, hold dear, like, love, prize, respect, take to, want; SEE CONCEPTS *20,32*

careen [v] *tilt; move wildly down path*
bend, lean, lurch, pitch, sway, tilt; SEE CONCEPT *147*

career [n1] *occupation*
bag*, calling, course, dodge*, employment, field, game*, job, lifework, livelihood, number*, pilgrimage, profession, pursuit, racket*, specialty, thing*, vocation, work; SEE CONCEPTS *349,360*

career [n2] *course, path*
course, orbit, passage, pilgrimage, procedure, progress, race, walk; SEE CONCEPTS *501,678,692*

carefree [adj] *lighthearted, untroubled*
airy, at ease, blithe, breezy, buoyant, calm, careless, cheerful, cheery, cool, easy, easy-going, feelgood*, happy, happy-go-lucky, insouciant, jaunty, jovial, laid back*, radiant, secure, sunny, unanxious, unbothered; SEE CONCEPT *404*

careful [adj] *cautious; painstaking*
accurate, alert, apprehensive, assiduous, attentive, chary, choosy, circumspect, concerned, conscientious, conservative, cool, deliberate, discreet, exacting, fastidious, finicky, fussy, going to great lengths*, guarded, heedful, judicious, leery, meticulous, mindful, observant, particular, playing safe*, precise, prim, protective, provident, prudent, punctilious, regardful, religious, rigorous, scrupulous, selfdisciplined, shy, sober, solicitous, solid, thorough, thoughtful, vigilant, wary; SEE CONCEPTS *326,542*

carefully [adv] *cautiously; painstakingly*
anxiously, attentively, circumspectly, concernedly, conscientiously, correctly, deliberately, delicately, dependably, discreetly, exactly, faithfully, fastidiously, fully, gingerly, guardedly, heedfully, honorably, in detail, laboriously, meticulously, particularly, precisely, providently, prudently, punctiliously, regardfully, reliably, rigorously, scrupulously, solicitously, thoroughly, thoughtfully, trustily, uprightly, vigilantly, warily, watchfully, with forethought, with reservations; SEE CONCEPT *542*

caregiver [n] *person caring for child*
au pair, babysitter, caretaker, custodian, father, governess, mother, nanny, nurse, parent; SEE CONCEPT *348*

careless [adj1] *without sufficient attention*
absent-minded, abstracted, casual, cursory, disregardful, forgetful, hasty, heedless, improvident, imprudent, inaccurate, inadvertent, incautious, inconsiderate, indifferent, indiscreet, indolent, injudicious, irresponsible, lackadaisical, lax, loose, mindless, napping, negligent, nonchalant, oblivious, offhand, perfunctory, pococurante, reckless, regardless, remiss, slipshod, sloppy, thoughtless, uncircumspect, unconcerned, unguarded, unheeding, unmindful, unobservant, unreflective, unthinking, wasteful; SEE CONCEPT *542*

careless [adj2] *artless*
casual, modest, naive, natural, nonchalant, simple, unstudied; SEE CONCEPT *557*

caress [n] *loving touch*
cuddle, embrace, endearment, feel, fondling,

hug, kiss, pat, pet, petting, snuggle, squeeze, stroke; SEE CONCEPTS *375*,*590*

caress [*v*] *touch lovingly*
bear hug*, brush, buss, clinch, clutch, coddle, cosset, cuddle, dandle, embrace, feel, fondle, graze, handle, hug, kiss, make love, massage, mug, neck, nestle, nuzzle, pat, pet, play around*, rub, squeeze, stroke, toy; SEE CONCEPTS *375*,*612*

caretaker [*n*] *person who maintains something*
baby sitter, concierge, curator, custodian, house-sitter, janitor, keeper, porter, sitter, super*, su-perintendent, supervisor, warden, watchperson; SEE CONCEPT *348*

cargo [*n*] *baggage; something to be delivered*
burden, consignment, contents, freight, goods, haul, lading, load, merchandise, payload, shipload, shipment, tonnage, ware; SEE CON-CEPTS *338*,*446*

caricature [*n*] *exaggerated description in writ-ing, drawing*
burlesque, cartoon, distortion, farce, imitation, lampoon, libel, mimicry, mockery, parody, pasquinade, pastiche, put-on*, ridicule, satire, send-up*, sham, takeoff*, travesty; SEE CON-CEPTS *271*,*386*,*625*

carillon [*n*] *set of bells*
angelus, chimes, glockenspiel, gong, lyra, peal, tintinnabulation, tocsin; SEE CONCEPT *595*

carnage [*n*] *massacre*
annihilation, blitz, blood, blood and guts*, blood bath*, bloodshed, butchering, butchery, crime, extermination, gore, havoc, hecatomb, holocaust, homicide, killing, liquidation, manslaughter, mass murder, murder, offing*, rapine, search and destroy*, shambles, slaughter, slaying, taking out*, warfare, wasting; SEE CONCEPT *252*

carnal [*adj*] *erotic, sensual*
animal, bodily, corporal, corporeal, earthly, fleshly, genital, impure, lascivious, lecherous, lewd, libidinous, licentious, lustful, physical, prurient, salacious, sensuous, temporal, unchaste, venereal, voluptuous, vulgar, wanton, worldly; SEE CONCEPTS *372*,*403*

carnival [*n*] *outdoor celebration*
amusement park, bacchanal, carny*, carousal, circus, conviviality, exposition, fair, feasting, festival, fete, fiesta, frolic, gala, grind show*, heyday, jamboree, jollification, jubilee, Mardi Gras, masquerade, merrymaking, orgy, ragbag*, revelry, rout, saturnalia, side show, spree, street fair; SEE CONCEPTS *377*,*386*

carnivorous [*adj*] *eating animal flesh*
cannibal, flesh-eating, hungry, omnivorous, predatory, rapacious; SEE CONCEPT *401*

carol [*n*] *joyful hymn*
ballad, canticle, canzonet, chorus, Christmas song, ditty*, lay, madrigal, noel, song, strain; SEE CONCEPTS *263*,*595*

carouse [*v*] *make merry, often with liquor*
booze, drink, frolic, go on a spree*, have fun, imbibe, paint the town*, paint the town red*, play, quaff, raise Cain*, revel, riot, roister, was-sail, whoop it up*; SEE CONCEPT *384*

carp [*v*] *nag*
bother, cavil, censure, complain, criticize, find fault, fuss, grumble, hypercriticize, knock, nit-pick*, objurgate, pan, peck*, pick at, quibble, re-proach; SEE CONCEPT *52*

carpal tunnel syndrome [*n*] *wrist irritation*
repetitive motion disorder, repetitive motion in-jury, sensorimotor disorder; SEE CONCEPT *306*

carpenter [*n*] *person who works with wood*
artisan, builder, cabinetmaker, carps*, chips*, craftsperson, joiner, laborer, mason, wood-worker, worker; SEE CONCEPT *348*

carpet [*n*] *nappy floor covering*
carpeting, matting, rug, runner, tapestry, throw rug, wall-to-wall*; SEE CONCEPT *473*

carriage [*n1*] *delivery of freight*
carrying, conveyance, conveying, delivering, freight, transit, transport, transportation; SEE CONCEPTS *148*,*217*

carriage [*n2*] *posture, physical and mental*
air, aspect, attitude, bearing, behavior, cast, com-portment, conduct, demeanor, deportment, gait, look, manner, mien, pace, positure, presence, stance, step; SEE CONCEPTS *633*,*720*

carry [*v1*] *transport physical object*
backpack*, bear, bring, cart, channel, conduct, convey, convoy, displace, ferry, fetch, freight, funnel, give, haul, heft, hoist, import, lift, lug*, move, pack, pipe, portage, relay, relocate, re-move, schlepp*, shift, shoulder*, sustain, take, tote, traject, transfer, transmit, transplant, truck, waft; SEE CONCEPTS *148*,*217*

carry [*v2*] *win; accomplish*
affect, be victorious, capture, drive, effect, gain, get, impel, impress, influence, inspire, move, prevail, secure, spur, strike, sway, touch, urge; SEE CONCEPTS *68*,*706*

carry [*v3*] *broadcast electronically*
air, bear, communicate, conduct, convey, dis-play, disseminate, give, offer, pass on, publish, relay, release, send, transfer, transport; SEE CON-CEPTS *217*,*266*

carry on [*v1*] *continue activity*
achieve, endure, hang on, keep going, last, main-tain, perpetuate, persevere, persist, proceed; SEE CONCEPT *239*

carry on [*v2*] *manage operations*
administer, conduct, direct, engage in, keep, op-erate, ordain, run; SEE CONCEPT *117*

carry on [*v3*] *lose control emotionally*
act up, be indecorous, blunder, cut up, lose it*, make a fuss*, misbehave, rage, raise Cain*; SEE CONCEPT *633*

carry out [*v*] *complete activity*
accomplish, achieve, carry through, consum-mate, discharge, effect, effectuate, execute, final-ize, fulfill, implement, meet, perform, realize; SEE CONCEPT *706*

cart [*n*] *small attachment for transporting*
barrow, buggy, curricle, dolly, dray, gig, gurney, handcart, palanquin, pushcart, rickshaw, tilbury, truck, tumbrel, two-wheeler, wagon, wheelbar-row; SEE CONCEPTS *499*,*505*

cart [*v*] *carry*
bear, bring, convey, ferry, haul, move, schlepp*, take, tote; SEE CONCEPTS *148*,*217*

carte blanche [*n*] *full power, authority*
blank check, freedom, free hand, free rein, li-cense, permission, power of attorney, preroga-tive, sanction, say, say-so, unconditional right; SEE CONCEPT *376*

cartel [*n*] *group which shares business interest*
bunch*, chain, combine, conglomerate, consor-tium, corporation, crew*, crowd*, gang*, hold-ing company, megacorp*, mob*, monopoly,

multinational*, outfit*, plunderbund*, pool, ring*, syndicate, trust; SEE CONCEPTS *323,325*

carton [*n*] *box for holding items*
bin, case, casket, chest, coffer, container, corrugated box, crate, pack, package, packet; SEE CONCEPT *494*

cartoon [*n*] *funny drawing, often with dialogue or caption*
animation, caricature, comic strip, drawing, lampoon, parody, representation, satire, sketch, takeoff; SEE CONCEPTS *280,625*

cartoonist [*n*] *person who draws cartoons*
artist, caricaturist, comic artist, gag person*, gagster*, illustrator, social critic; SEE CONCEPT *348*

carve [*v*] *cut carefully with sharp instrument*
block out, chip, chisel, cleave, dissect, dissever, divide, engrave, etch, fashion, form, grave, hack, hew, incise, indent, insculpt, model, mold, mould, pattern, rough-hew, sculpt, shape, slash, slice, stipple, sunder, tool, trim, whittle; SEE CONCEPTS *137,176,184*

carved in stone [*adj*] *fixed*
established, etched in stone*, firm, immutable, permanent, set in concrete*, set in stone*, unchangeable; SEE CONCEPTS *488,551,583,649,798*

cascade [*n*] *something falling, especially water*
avalanche, cataract, chute, deluge, downrush, falls, flood, force, fountain, outpouring, precipitation, rapids, shower, spout, torrent, watercourse, waterfall; SEE CONCEPTS *514,787*

cascade [*v*] *fall in a rush*
descend, disgorge, flood, gush, heave, overflow, pitch, plunge, pour, spew, spill, spit up, surge, throw up, tumble, vomit; SEE CONCEPT *179*

case [*n1*] *container; items in container*
bag, baggage, basket, bin, box, cabinet, caddy, caisson, canister, capsule, carton, cartridge, casing, casket, chamber, chassis, chest, coffer, compact, cover, covering, crate, crating, crib, drawer, envelope, folder, grip, holder, integument, jacket, receptacle, safe, scabbard, sheath, shell, suitcase, tray, trunk, wallet, wrapper, wrapping; SEE CONCEPT *494*

case [*n2*] *circumstance, conditions*
context, contingency, crisis, dilemma, event, eventuality, fact, incident, occurrence, plight, position, predicament, problem, quandary, situation, state, status; SEE CONCEPT *696*

case [*n3*] *example*
case history, exemplification, illustration, instance, occasion, occurrence, representative, sample, sampling, specimen; SEE CONCEPT *686*

case [*n4*] *matter brought before a court*
action, argument, cause, claim, dispute, evidence, lawsuit, litigation, petition, proceedings, process, proof, suit, trial; SEE CONCEPT *318*

case [*v*] *check something in detail*
canvass, check out, check over, check up, examine, inspect, scrutinize, study, view; SEE CONCEPT *103*

cash [*n*] *money; assets*
banknote, bread*, buck*, bullion, cabbage*, chicken feed*, coin, coinage, currency, dinero*, dough*, funds, green stuff*, investment, legal tender, lot, mazumah*, note, payment, pledge, principal, ready assets, refund, remuneration, reserve, resources, riches, savings, scratch*, security, skins*, stock, supply, treasure, wampum*, wherewithal; SEE CONCEPTS *340,710*

cash [*v*] *exchange for real money*
acknowledge, break a bill*, change, discharge, draw, honor, liquidate, make change, pay, realize, redeem; SEE CONCEPT *330*

cashier [*n*] *bank worker*
accountant, banker, bursar, clerk, collector, paymaster, purser, receiver, teller, treasurer; SEE CONCEPT *348*

cashier [*v*] *discard, expel*
ax*, boot*, bounce, break, can*, cast off, discharge, dismiss, displace, drum out*, fire, give a pink slip*, give the heave ho*, heave*, remove, sack*, terminate; SEE CONCEPTS *211,324*

casing [*n*] *covering*
hull, jacket, sheath, skin, wrapper; SEE CONCEPTS *484,750*

casino [*n*] *gambling establishment*
bank, betting house, big store*, club, clubhouse, dance hall, dice joint*, dive, gambling den, hall, honky-tonk, house, joint, Monte Carlo, pool hall, roadhouse, rotunda, saloon, track; SEE CONCEPT *447*

cask [*n*] *rounded container for liquids*
barrel, barrelet, butt, firkin, hogshead, keg, pipe, tun, vat; SEE CONCEPT *494*

casket [*n*] *burial box*
bin, carton, case, chest, coffer, crate, funerary box, pine box, pinto, sarcophagus, wood overcoat*; SEE CONCEPTS *368,494*

casserole [*n*] *dish consisting of a combination of cooked food*
covered dish, goulash, hash, meat pie, pot pie, pottage, stew, stroganoff; SEE CONCEPT *457*

cast [*n1*] *a throw to the side*
casting, ejection, expulsion, fling, flinging, heave, heaving, hurl, hurling, launching, lob, lobbing, pitch, pitching, projection, propulsion, shooting, sling, slinging, thrust, thrusting, toss, tossing; SEE CONCEPT *222*

cast [*n2*] *appearance; shade of color*
air, complexion, countenance, demeanor, embodiment, expression, face, hue, look, manner, mien, semblance, stamp, style, tinge, tint, tone, turn, visage; SEE CONCEPTS *622,716*

cast [*n3*] *actors in performance*
actors, actresses, artists, characters, company, dramatis, list, parts, personae, players, roles, troupe; SEE CONCEPT *294*

cast [*n4*] *molded structure*
conformation, copy, duplicate, embodiment, facsimile, figure, form, mold, plaster, replica, sculpture, shape; SEE CONCEPTS *470,475*

cast [*v1*] *throw aside*
boot, bung*, chuck*, drive, drop, fire*, fling, heave, hurl, impel, launch, lob, peg, pitch, project, shed, shy, sling, thrust, toss; SEE CONCEPT *222*

cast [*v2*] *emit, give*
aim, bestow, deposit, diffuse, direct, distribute, point, radiate, scatter, shed, spatter, spray, spread, sprinkle, strew, train; SEE CONCEPTS *108,624*

cast [*v3*] *calculate*
add, compute, count, figure, foot, forecast, number, reckon, sum, summate, tot, total; SEE CONCEPT *764*

cast [*v4*] *select for activity*
allot, appoint, arrange, assign, blueprint, chart, choose, decide upon, delegate, design, designate,

detail, determine, devise, give parts, name, pick, plan, project; SEE CONCEPT *41*

aste [*n*] *social class*
cultural level, degree, estate, grade, lineage, order, position, race, rank, social order, species, sphere, standing, station, status, stratum; SEE CONCEPTS *378,388*

astigate [*v*] *criticize severely*
baste, bawl out*, beat, berate, blister, cane, censure, chasten, chastise, chew, out*, come down on*, correct, criticize, discipline, drag over the coals*, dress down*, drub, excoriate, flay, flog, jump down one's throat*, lambaste, lash, lash out*, lean on*, penalize, pummel, punish, rail, rate, read the riot act*, ream, rebuke, reprimand, scarify, scathe, scold, scorch, scourge, thrash, tongue-lash*, upbraid, whip; SEE CONCEPT *52*

astle [*n*] *magnificent home, often for royalty*
acropolis, alcazar, château, citadel, donjon, estate house, fasthold, fastness, fort, fortification, fortress, hold, keep, manor, mansion, palace, peel, safehold, seat, stronghold, tower, villa; SEE CONCEPT *516*

astrate [*v*] *remove sexual organs*
alter, asexualize, caponize, change, cut, deprive of virility, desexualize, emasculate, eunuchize, fix, geld, mutilate, neuter, spay, sterilize, unsex; SEE CONCEPT *310*

asual [*adj*] *chance, random*
accidental, adventitious, by chance, contingent, erratic, extemporaneous, extempore, fluky, fortuitous, impromptu, improvised, impulsive, incidental, infrequent, irregular, occasional, odd, offhand, serendipitous, spontaneous, uncertain, unexpected, unforeseen, unintentional, unplanned, unpremeditated; SEE CONCEPTS *541,544*

asual [*adj2*] *nonchalant, relaxed in manner*
aloof, apathetic, blasé, breezy, cool*, cursory, detached, down home*, easygoing, folksy*, homey*, incurious, indifferent, informal, insouciant, lackadaisical, laid-back*, loose*, low-pressure, mellow, offhand, perfunctory, pococurante, purposeless, remote, unconcerned, unfussy, uninterested, withdrawn; SEE CONCEPTS *401,542,589*

asualty [*n1*] *accident*
blow, calamity, catastrophe, chance, contingency, debacle, disaster, misadventure, misfortune, mishap; SEE CONCEPT *674*

asualty [*n2*] *victim*
dead, death toll, fatality, injured, killed, loss, missing, prey, sufferer, wounded; SEE CONCEPTS *407,423*

asuistry [*n*] *overgeneral reasoning*
chicanery, deception, deceptiveness, delusion, equivocation, evasion, fallacy, lie, oversubtleness, sophism, sophistry, speciousness, spuriousness, trick; SEE CONCEPTS *54,63*

at [*n*] *feline animal, sometimes a pet*
bobcat, cheetah, cougar, grimalkin, jaguar, kitten, kitty, leopard, lion, lynx, malkin, mouser, ocelot, panther, puma, puss, pussy, tabby, tiger, tom, tomcat; SEE CONCEPTS *394,400*

ataclysm [*n*] *disaster*
calamity, cataract, catastrophe, collapse, convulsion, crunch*, curtains*, debacle, deluge, disturbance, double trouble*, flood, flooding, holy mess*, inundation, misadventure, ruin, torrent, tragedy, unholy mess*, upheaval, waterloo*, woe; SEE CONCEPTS *674,675*

catalog/catalogue [*n*] *written or printed matter featuring a selection of objects*
archive, brief, bulletin, calendar, cartulary, charts, classification, compendium, directory, docket, draft, enumeration, gazette, gazetteer, hit list*, index, inventory, list, prospectus, record, register, roll, roster, schedule, slate, specification, syllabus, synopsis, table; SEE CONCEPTS *271,280*

catalyst [*n*] *something which incites activity*
adjuvant, agitator, enzyme, goad, impetus, impulse, incendiary, incentive, incitation, incitement, motivation, radical stimulus, reactant, reactionary, spark plug*, spur, stimulant, synergist, wave maker*; SEE CONCEPT *712*

catapult [*n*] *implement for shooting weapon*
arbalest, ballista, heaver, hurler, pitcher, propeller, shooter, sling, slingshot, tosser, trebuchet; SEE CONCEPTS *463,500*

catastrophe [*n*] *calamity; unhappy conclusion*
accident, adversity, affliction, alluvion, bad luck, bad news*, blow, calamity, casualty, cataclysm, contretemps, crash, culmination, curtains*, debacle, denouement, desolation, devastation, disaster, emergency, end, failure, fatality, fiasco, finale, grief, hardship, havoc, ill, infliction, meltdown*, misadventure, mischance, misery, misfortune, mishap, reverse, scourge, stroke, termination, the worst*, tragedy, trial, trouble, upshot, waterloo*, wreck; SEE CONCEPT *674*

catatonic [*adj*] *unaware*
comatose, confused, hung, suspended, unconscious, wedged; SEE CONCEPT *402*

catcall [*n*] *heckle*
boo, Bronx cheer*, derision, gibe, hiss, hoot, jeer, raspberry*, shout, whistle; SEE CONCEPTS *44,47*

catch-22 [*n*] *no-win situation*
contradiction, dilemma, lose-lose, paradox, quagmire; SEE CONCEPT *532*

catch [*n1*] *fastener*
bolt, buckle, clamp, clasp, clip, hasp, hook, hook and eye, latch, snap; SEE CONCEPT *497*

catch [*n2*] *trick, hidden disadvantage*
Catch-22, conundrum, deception, decoy, drawback, fly in the ointment*, hitch, joke, puzzle, puzzler, snag, stumbling block, trap; SEE CONCEPTS *674,679*

catch [*v1*] *ensnare, apprehend*
arrest, bag, bust*, capture, clasp, claw, clench, clutch, collar, cop, corral, entangle, entrap, get one's fingers on*, glom, glove, grab, grasp, grip, hook, lasso, lay hold of, nab, nail, net, pick, pluck, pounce on, prehend, secure, seize, snag, snare, snatch, take, take hold of, trap; SEE CONCEPT *90*

catch [*v2*] *find out, discover*
descry, detect, encounter, expose, hit upon, meet with, spot, surprise, take unawares, turn up, unmask; SEE CONCEPT *31*

catch [*v3*] *contract an illness*
become infected ·with, break out with, come down with, develop, fall ill with, fall victim to, get, incur, receive, sicken, succumb to, suffer from, take; SEE CONCEPTS *93,308*

catch [*v4*] *come from behind and grab*
board, climb on, come upon, cotch, get, go after, grab, hop on, jump, make, overhaul, overtake, pass, ram, reach, run down, take; SEE CONCEPT *164*

catch [v5] *hear and understand*
accept, apprehend, comprehend, discern, feel, follow, get, grasp, perceive, recognize, see, sense, take in, understand; SEE CONCEPT 15

catching [adj] *contagious (disease)*
communicable, dangerous, endemic, epidemic, epizootic, infectious, infective, miasmatic, pandemic, pestiferous, pestilential, taking, transferable, transmittable; SEE CONCEPT 314

catchword [n] *motto*
byword, catchphrase, household word, maxim, password, refrain, shibboleth, slogan, watchword; SEE CONCEPTS 275,278

catchy [adj] *captivating, addictive*
fetching, haunting, having a good hook*, memorable, popular; SEE CONCEPT 544

catechize [v] *instruct and question*
ask, cross-examine, drill, educate, examine, grill, inquire, interrogate, query, quiz, teach, train; SEE CONCEPTS 48,285

categorical [adj] *explicit, unconditional*
absolute, all out*, certain, clear-cut, definite, definitive, direct, downright, emphatic, express, flat out*, forthright, no holds barred*, no strings attached*, positive, specific, straight out, sure, ultimate, unambiguous, unequivocal, unmitigated, unqualified, unreserved; SEE CONCEPT 535

categorize [v] *sort by type, classification*
assort, button down*, class, classify, group, identify, peg*, pigeonhole*, put down as, rank, tab, typecast; SEE CONCEPT 39

category [n] *classification, type*
class, department, division, grade, group, grouping, head, heading, kind, league, level, list, order, pigeonhole*, rank, section, sort, tier; SEE CONCEPT 378

cater [v] *provide, help*
baby, coddle, cotton, furnish, gratify, humor, indulge, minister to, outfit, pamper, pander to, procure, provision, purvey, spoil, supply, victual; SEE CONCEPT 136

caterwaul [v] *make screeching, crying noise*
bawl, bicker, howl, quarrel, scream, screech, shriek, squall, wail, yell, yowl; SEE CONCEPT 77

catharsis [n] *purging, purification*
ablution, abreaction, cleansing, expurgation, lustration, purgation, purification, release; SEE CONCEPTS 13,165,230

cathedral [n] *large church*
basilica, bishop's seat, chancel, holy place, house of God, house of prayer, house of worship, minster, place of worship, sanctuary, temple; SEE CONCEPTS 368,439

catholic [adj] *all-embracing, general*
all-inclusive, broad-minded, charitable, comprehensive, cosmic, cosmopolitan, diffuse, eclectic, ecumenical, extensive, generic, global, inclusive, indeterminate, large-scale, liberal, open-minded, planetary, receptive, tolerant, unbigoted, universal, unprejudiced, unsectarian, whole, wide, world-wide; SEE CONCEPTS 557,772

cattle [n] *bovine animals*
beasts, bovid mammals, bulls, calves, cows, dogies*, herd, livestock, longhorn*, moo cows*, oxen, shorthorns, stock, strays; SEE CONCEPT 394

catty [adj] *nasty, malicious*
backbiting, evil, hateful, ill-natured, malevolent, mean, rancorous, spiteful, venomous, vicious, wicked; SEE CONCEPT 404

caucus [n] *group gathered to make decision*
assembly, conclave, convention, council, gathering, get-together, meeting, parley, session; SE CONCEPTS 301,417

cause [n1] *agent, originator*
account, agency, aim, antecedent, author, basi beginning, causation, consideration, creator, de terminant, doer, element, end, explanation, four dation, genesis, ground, grounds, incitemen inducement, instigation, leaven, mainspring maker, matter, motivation, motive, object, occa sion, origin, prime mover, principle, produce purpose, root, source, spring, stimulation; SE CONCEPTS 229,661

cause [n2] *belief; undertaking for belief*
attempt, conviction, creed, enterprise, faith, goa ideal, intention, movement, object, objective plan, principles, purpose; SEE CONCEPT 689

cause [v] *bring into being; bring about*
be at the bottom of*, begin, brainstorm*, brea in*, break the ice*, breed, bring to pass, com out with*, compel, cook up*, create, dream up effect, elicit, engender, evoke, fire up*, generate get things rolling*, give rise to, hatch, incite, ir duce, introduce, kickoff*, kindle, lead to, le make, make up, motivate, muster, occasion open, originate, precipitate, produce, provoke result in, revert, secure, sow the seeds, start th ball rolling*, think up, work up; SEE CONCEPT 228,231,241

cause célèbre [n] *controversial issue*
bone of contention, celebrated case, controvers debate, grist for the gossip mill*, hot potato* moot point, political football*, scandal, war o words; SEE CONCEPTS 46,278,665

caustic [adj1] *burning, corrosive*
abrasive, acerbic, acid, acrid, alkaline, astringen biting, corroding, erosive, keen, mordant, pur gent, tart; SEE CONCEPT 485

caustic [adj2] *sarcastic*
acerb, acerbic, acrimonious, bitter, cutting harsh, incisive, pithy, pungent, rough, salt satiric, scathing, severe, sharp, stinging, tren chant, virulent; SEE CONCEPT 267

caution [n1] *alertness, carefulness*
attention, canniness, care, circumspection, delib eration, discreetness, discretion, Fabian policy foresight, forethought, heed, heedfulness, prov dence, prudence, vigilance, watchfulness; SE CONCEPT 410

caution [n2] *warning*
admonition, advice, bug in one's ear*, cavea commonition, counsel, forewarning, hint, injunc tion, monition, notice, omen, premonition, sig tip*, tip-off*; SEE CONCEPTS 78,274

caution [v] *warn, advise*
admonish, alert, exhort, flag, forewarn, give th high sign*, give the lowdown on*, pull one coat*, put one wise*, tip*, tip off*, urge, wave red flag*, wise one up*; SEE CONCEPT 78

cautionary tale [n] *event illustrating a hazard*
admonition, advisory, caveat, message, omer portent, red flag*, sign of things to come*, wake up call*, warning, word to the wise*; SEE CON CEPTS 78,274

cautious [adj] *careful, guarded*
alert, all ears*, cagey, calculating, chary, circum spect, considerate, discreet, forethoughtful, gin gerly, hedging one's bets*, heedful, judicious keeping on one's toes*, leery, on the lookout*

playing it cool*, playing safe*, politic, provident, prudent, pussyfoot*, safe, shrewd, taking it easy, taking it slow*, tentative, thinking twice*, vigilant, walking on eggs*, wary, watchful, watching one's step*, watching out, with one's eyes peeled*; SEE CONCEPTS 401,403

cavalcade [n] *parade*
array, drill, march-past, procession, promenade, review, spectacle, train; SEE CONCEPT 432

cavalier [adj] *arrogant*
condescending, curt, disdainful, haughty, high-and-mighty*, insolent, lofty, lordly, offhand, overbearing, proud, scornful, snooty*, snotty*, supercilious, superior; SEE CONCEPT 401

cavalry [n] *troops riding horses*
army, bowlegs*, chasseurs, cuirassiers, dragoons, horse, horse soldiers, hussars, lancers, mounted troops, Mounties, rangers, squadron, uhlans; SEE CONCEPT 322

cave [n] *hole in land formation*
cavern, cavity, den, grotto, hollow, pothole, rock shelter, subterrane, subterranean area; SEE CONCEPT 509

caveat [n] *warning*
admonition, alarm, caution, commonition, forewarning, monition, sign; SEE CONCEPTS 78,274

cavern [n] *hollow in land formation*
cave, grotto, hole, pothole, subterrane, subterranean area; SEE CONCEPT 509

cavernous [adj] *hollow and large*
alveolate, broad, chambered, chasmal, commodious, concave, curved inward, deep, deep-set, echoing, gaping, huge, resonant, reverberant, roomy, sepulchral, socketed, spacious, sunken, vast, wide, yawning; SEE CONCEPTS 490,773,796

cavity [n] *sunken or decayed area*
atrium, basin, bursa, caries, chamber, crater, decay, dent, depression, gap, hole, hollow, pit, pocket, sinus, socket, vacuity, void; SEE CONCEPT 513

cavort [v] *frolic, prance*
caper, caracole, carry on*, cut loose*, cut up*, dance, fool around*, frisk, gambol, go places and do things*, horse around*, horseplay, monkey around*, play, revel, rollick, romp, roughhouse*, sport; SEE CONCEPTS 114,384

cease [v] *stop, conclude*
back off, break off, bring to an end, call it a day*, call it quits*, close, close out, come to an end, culminate, cut it out*, desist, die, discontinue, drop, end, fail, finish, give over, halt, intermit, knock off*, leave off, pack in*, quit, quit cold turkey*, refrain, shut down, stay, surcease, terminate, wind up*; SEE CONCEPT 234

cease-fire [n] *stop in fighting*
armistice, suspension of hostilities, truce; SEE CONCEPTS 230,298,684

ceaseless [adj] *never-ending*
amaranthine, constant, continual, continuous, day and night*, endless, eternal, everlasting, incessant, indefatigable, interminable, nonstop, on a treadmill*, perennial, perpetual, round the clock*, unceasing, unending, uninterrupted, unremitting, untiring, world-without-end*; SEE CONCEPT 798

cede [v] *abandon, surrender*
abalienate, abdicate, accord, alien, alienate, allow, capitulate, come across with*, communicate, concede, convey, deed, drop, fold*, fork over*, give in*, give up, grant, hand over*,

leave, make over, part with, relinquish, remise, renounce, resign, sign over, throw in the sponge*, throw in the towel*, transfer, vouchsafe, waive, yield; SEE CONCEPTS 108,127

ceiling [n1] *top of a room*
baldachin, beam, canopy, covert, dome, fan vaulting, groin, highest point, housetop, plafond, planchement, plaster, roof, roofing, timber, topside covering; SEE CONCEPT 440

ceiling [n2] *maximum*
legal price, record, superiority, top; SEE CONCEPT 836

celebrate [v] *commemorate occasion, achievement*
beat the drum*, bless, blow off steam*, carouse, ceremonialize, commend, consecrate, dedicate, drink to, eulogize, exalt, extol, feast, fete, glorify, hallow, have a ball*, honor, jubilate, keep, kick up one's heels*, laud, let loose*, lionize, live it up*, make merry, make whoopee*, mark with a red letter*, memorialize, observe, paint the town red*, party*, perform, praise, proclaim, publicize, raise hell*, rejoice, revel, revere, ritualize, signalize, solemnize; SEE CONCEPT 377

celebrated [adj] *distinguished, famous*
acclaimed, big*, eminent, famed, glorious, great, high-powered, illustrious, immortal, important, large, laureate, lionized, notable, number one*, numero uno*, outstanding, popular, preeminent, prominent, renowned, revered, storied, up there*, well-known, w. k.*; SEE CONCEPT 568

celebration [n] *commemoration of occasion, achievement*
anniversary, bash*, birthday, blast*, blowout*, carousal, ceremony, conviviality, festival, festivity, fete, frolic, gaiety, gala, glorification, hilarity, honoring, hoopla, hullabaloo*, jollification, joviality, jubilation, jubilee, keeping, magnification, memorialization, merriment, merrymaking, observance, party, performance, recognition, remembrance, revelry, saturnalia, solemnization, spree, triumph, wingding*; SEE CONCEPT 377

celebrity [n1] *dignitary*
ace, big cheese*, big deal*, big gun*, big name*, big shot*, big stuff*, bigwig*, celeb*, cynosure, famous person, figure, heavyweight, hero, hotshot*, immortal, lion*, luminary, magnate, mahatma, major leaguer*, name, notable, personage, personality, somebody, someone, star, superstar, the cheese*, VIP, worthy; SEE CONCEPT 423

celebrity [n2] *fame, notoriety*
distinction, éclat, eminence, glory, honor, notability, popularity, preeminence, prestige, prominence, renown, reputation, repute, stardom; SEE CONCEPTS 388,668

celerity [n] *swiftness*
alacrity, briskness, dispatch, expedition, expeditiousness, fleetness, gait, haste, hurry, hustle, legerity, promptness, quickness, rapidity, speed, speediness, swiftness, velocity, vivacity; SEE CONCEPT 755

celestial [adj] *heavenly*
angelic, astral, beatific, blessed, divine, elysian, empyral, empyrean, eternal, ethereal, godlike, hallowed, holy, immortal, Olympian, otherworldly, seraphic, spiritual, sublime, supernal, supernatural, transcendental, transmundane; SEE CONCEPTS 536,673

celibacy [n] *abstinence from sexual activity*
abstention, chastity, continence, frigidity, impotence, maidenhood, purity, singleness, virginity, virtue; SEE CONCEPT 388

celibate [adj] *abstaining from sexual activity*
chaste, continent, pure, virgin, virginal, virtuous; SEE CONCEPT 372

cell [n1] *smallest living organism*
bacterium, cellule, corpuscle, egg, embryo, follicle, germ, haematid, microorganism, spore, unit, utricle, vacuole; SEE CONCEPTS 389,478

cell [n2] *small room, container*
alcove, antechamber, apartment, bastille, booth, burrow, cage, cavity, chamber, cloister, closet, compartment, coop, crib, crypt, cubicle, den, dungeon, hold, hole, keep, lockup, nook, pen, receptacle, recess, retreat, stall, tower, vault; SEE CONCEPTS 448,494,513

cellar [n] *underground story of building*
apartment, basement, subbasement, subterrane, underground room, vault; SEE CONCEPTS 440,448

cement [n] *gluing, binding material*
adhesive, binder, birdlime, bond, concrete, epoxy, glue, grout, gum, gunk*, lime, lute, mortar, mucilage, mud*, paste, plaster, putty, rubber cement, sand, sealant, size, solder, stickum*, tar; SEE CONCEPT 475

cement [v] *attach securely, often with sticky material*
bind, blend, bond, cohere, combine, connect, fasten, fuse, glue, gum, join, merge, mortar, paste, plaster, seal, solder, stick together, unite, weld; SEE CONCEPTS 85,160

cemetery [n] *burial ground*
boot hill*, catacomb, charnel, charnel house, churchyard, city of the dead*, crypt, eternal home*, funerary grounds, garden, God's acre*, Golgotha, grave, graveyard, marble town*, memorial park, mortuary, necropolis, ossuary, polyandrium, potter's field, resting place, sepulcher, tomb, vault; SEE CONCEPTS 305,368

censor [v] *forbid; ban; selectively remove*
abridge, blacklist, black out*, bleach, bleep*, blue-pencil*, bowdlerize, clean up, conceal, control, cork*, criticize, cut, decontaminate, delete, drop the iron curtain*, edit, examine, excise, expurgate, exscind, inspect, launder*, narrow, oversee, prevent publication, purge, purify, put the lid on*, refuse transmission, repress, restrain, restrict, review, revile, sanitize, scissor out*, squelch, sterilize, strike out, supervise communications, suppress, withhold; SEE CONCEPTS 121,266

censorious [adj] *very critical*
accusatory, captious, carping, caviling, cavillous, chiding, complaining, condemnatory, condemning, critical, culpatory, denouncing, disapproving, disparaging, fault-finding, hypercritical, overcritical, reprehending, reproaching, severe; SEE CONCEPT 267

censorship [n] *forbiddance; ban*
blackout*, blue pencil*, bowdlerization, control, forbidding, hush up*, infringing on rights, iron curtain*, restriction, suppression, thought control*; SEE CONCEPTS 376,388

censure [n] *severe criticism*
admonishment, admonition, blame, castigation, condemnation, disapproval, dressing down, objection, obloquy, rebuke, remonstrance, reprehension, reprimand, reproach, reproof, stricture; SEE CONCEPTS 52,410

censure [v] *condemn; criticize severely*
abuse, admonish, animadvert, asperse, attack, backbite, berate, blame, carp at, castigate, cavil, chastise, chide, contemn, cut up*, denigrate, denounce, deprecate, disapprove, discipline, disparage, exprobate, find fault with, get after, impugn, incriminate, judge, knock, lecture, look askance, ostracize, pick apart, pull apart, read out*, rebuff, rebuke, remonstrate, reprehend, reprimand, reproach, reprove, scold, take to task*, tear apart*, tell off, upbraid; SEE CONCEPT 52

census [n] *head count*
demographics, demography, enumeration, poll, population tally, statistics, stats; SEE CONCEPTS 283,786

center [adj] *middle*
at halfway point, centermost, deepest, equidistant, inmost, inner, innermost, inside, interior, intermediary, intermediate, internal, mean, median, mid, middlemost, midpoint, midway; SEE CONCEPTS 583,585,830

center [n1] *middle point*
axis, bull's-eye, centrality, centriole, centrum, core, cynosure, equidistance, essence, focal point, focus, gist, heart, hotbed, hub, inside, interior, intermediacy, kernel, mainstream*, marrow, middle of the road*, midpoint, midst, navel, navel, nucleus, omphalos, pith, pivot, place, polestar, quick, radial point, root, seat; SEE CONCEPT 830

center [n2] *point of attraction for visitors, shoppers, travelers*
capital, city, club, concourse, crossroads, focal point, focus, heart, hub, mall, market, marketplace, mart, meeting place, metropolis, nerve center, plaza, polestar, shopping center, social center, station, town, trading center; SEE CONCEPTS 435,438,507

center [v] *concentrate, draw together*
attract, bring to a focus, bring together, centralize, close on, collect, concenter, consolidate, converge upon, focalize, focus, gather, intensify, join, medialize, meet, unify; SEE CONCEPTS 35,84

central [adj] *main, principal; in the middle*
axial, basic, cardinal, center, centric, centroidal, chief, dominant, equidistant, essential, focal, foremost, fundamental, important, inmost, inner, interior, intermediate, key, leading, master, mean, median, mid, middle, middlemost, midmost, midway, nuclear, outstanding, overriding, paramount, pivotal, predominant, primary, prime, radical, ruling, salient, significant, umbilical; SEE CONCEPTS 567,583,830

centralize [v] *concentrate, draw toward a point*
accumulate, amalgamate, assemble, compact, concenter, condense, consolidate, converge, focus, gather, incorporate, integrate, organize, rationalize, streamline, systematize, unify; SEE CONCEPTS 35,84

centrifugal [adj] *radiating from a central point*
deviating, diffusive, divergent, diverging, eccentric, efferent, outward, radial, spiral, spreading; SEE CONCEPTS 581,584

cereal [n] *edible grain*
bran, breakfast food, corn, grain, oats, rice, rye, wheat; SEE CONCEPTS 428,831

cerebral [*a*] *using one's brain*
analytical, brainy, deep, erudite, intellectual, intelligent, recondite, scholarly, smart; SEE CONCEPT 402

ceremonial [*adj*] *ritual, formal*
august, conventional, imposing, liturgical, lofty, mannered, ritualistic, solemn, stately, studied, stylized; SEE CONCEPT 548

ceremonious [*adj*] *ritual, formal*
civil, courteous, courtly, decorous, deferential, dignified, exact, grandiose, impressive, majestic, moving, precise, proper, punctilious, seemly, solemn, starchy, stately, stiff, striking; SEE CONCEPT 548

ceremony [*n1*] *ritual; celebratory observation*
ceremonial, commemoration, custom, formality, function, liturgy, observance, ordinance, parade, rite, sacrament, service, show, solemnity, tradition; SEE CONCEPT 386

ceremony [*n2*] *etiquette*
ceremonial, conformity, decorum, form, formal courtesy, formalism, formality, nicety, politeness, pomp, preciseness, prescription, propriety, protocol, strictness, usage; SEE CONCEPT 388

certain [*adj1*] *confident*
assertive, assured, believing, calm, cocksure, convinced, positive, questionless, sanguine, satisfied, secure, self-confident, sure, unconcerned, undisturbed, undoubtful, undoubting, unperturbed, untroubled; SEE CONCEPT 403

certain [*adj2*] *undoubtable, valid*
absolute, ascertained, authoritative, clear, conclusive, confirmable, definite, demonstrable, destined, determined, establishable, evident, firm, fixed, genuine, guaranteed, having down pat*, incontrovertible, indubitable, infallible, in the bag*, irrefutable, known, on ice*, plain, positive, predestined, provable, real, reliable, safe, salted away*, set, sound, supreme, sure, sure thing*, true, trustworthy, unambiguous, undeniable, undoubted, unequivocal, unerring, unmistakable, verifiable; SEE CONCEPTS 535,582

certain [*adj3*] *fixed*
assured, bound, certified, concluded, decided, definite, determined, ensured, established, guaranteed, insured, set, settled, stated, stipulated, sure, warranted; SEE CONCEPT 535

certain [*adj4*] *referring to a specifically known amount*
a couple, a few, defined, divers, express, individual, many, marked, numerous, one, particular, precise, regular, several, singular, some, special, specific, specified, sundry, upwards of, various; SEE CONCEPT 557

certainly [*adv*] *without doubt*
absolutely, assuredly, cert*, exactly, for a fact, of course, positively, posolutely*, right on*, surely, unquestionably, without fail; SEE CONCEPT 535

certainty [*n1*] *positive assurance*
all sewn up*, authoritativeness, belief, certitude, cinch, confidence, conviction, credence, definiteness, dogmatism, faith, firmness, indubitableness, inevitability, lock*, lockup*, open and shut case*, positiveness, positivism, rain or shine*, setup, shoo-in*, staunchness, steadiness, stock, store, sure bet*, surefire*, sureness, sure thing*, surety, trust, validity, wrap-up; SEE CONCEPTS 638,725

certainty [*n2*] *fact, resulting truth*
consequence, foregone conclusion, inevitable re-

sult, reality, sure thing*, surety; SEE CONCEPT 230

certificate [*n*] *authorizing document*
affidavit, affirmation, attestation, authentication, authorization, certification, coupon, credential, deed, diploma, docket, documentation, endorsement, guarantee, license, paper, pass, permit, receipt, record, sheepskin*, shingle, testament, testification, testimonial, testimony, ticket, voucher, warrant, warranty; SEE CONCEPTS 271,685

certify [*v*] *declare as true*
accredit, approve, ascertain, assure, attest, authenticate, authorize, aver, avow, commission, confirm, corroborate, endorse, guarantee, license, notify, okay, profess, reassure, rubber-stamp*, sanction, show, state, swear, testify, validate, verify, vouch, witness; SEE CONCEPTS 50,88

cessation [*n*] *ending*
abeyance, arrest, break, break-off*, breather*, cease, ceasing, close, conclusion, cutoff*, desistance, discontinuance, downtime*, end, finish, freeze*, grinding halt, halt, halting, hiatus, intermission, interruption, interval, layoff*, let-up*, pause, recess, remission, respite, rest, screaming halt*, standstill, stay, stop, stoppage, suspension, termination, time off, time-out*; SEE CONCEPT 119

chafe [*v1*] *rub, grind against*
abrade, bark, corrode, damage, erode, excoriate, gall, grate, graze, hurt, impair, inflame, irritate, peel, ruffle, scrape, scratch, skin, wear; SEE CONCEPT 215

chafe [*v2*] *annoy*
abrade, anger, annoy, bother, exasperate, exercise, fret, fume, gall, grate, harass, incense, inflame, irk, irritate, itch, offend, provoke, rage, rasp, rub, ruffle, scrape, scratch, vex, worry; SEE CONCEPTS 7,19

chaff [*n*] *waste*
crust, debris, dregs, husks, pod, refuse, remains, rubbish, shard, shell, trash; SEE CONCEPT 679

chaff [*v*] *joke, ridicule*
banter, deride, fun, jeer, jolly, josh, kid, mock, rag*, rally, razz*, rib*, scoff, taunt, tease; SEE CONCEPT 273

chagrin [*n*] *displeasure*
annoyance, balk, blow, crushing, discomfiture, discomposure, disgruntlement, dismay, disquiet, dissatisfaction, embarrassment, fretfulness, frustration, humiliation, ill-humor, irritation, letdown, mortification, peevishness, shame, spleen, upset, vexation; SEE CONCEPTS 410,674

chagrin [*v*] *cause displeasure*
abash, annoy, confuse, crush, discomfit, discompose, disconcert, disgrace, dismay, displease, disquiet, dissatisfy, embarrass, humiliate, irk, irritate, mortify, peeve, perturb, shame, upset, vex; SEE CONCEPTS 7,19

chain [*n1*] *succession, series*
alternation, catena, concatenation, conglomerate, consecution, continuity, group, order, progression, row, sequence, set, string, syndicate, train, trust; SEE CONCEPTS 432,727,769

chain [*n2*] *connected metal links; jewelry made of such links*
bond, bracelet, cable, clinker*, connection, coupling, fetter, iron, lavaliere, link, locket, manacle, pendant, shackle, trammel; SEE CONCEPTS 446,476,499

ce
ch

chain [*v*] *manacle in metal*
attach, bind, confine, connect, enslave, fetter, handcuff, hold, moor, restrain, shackle, tether, tie up, trammel; SEE CONCEPTS **85,160**

chair [*n1*] *single-seat furniture*
armchair, bench, cathedra, recliner, rocker, sling*; SEE CONCEPT **443**

chair [*n2*] *person in or position of authority*
captain, chairperson, director, fellowship, helm, instructorship, leader, monitor, position of control, principal, professorate, professorship, throne, tutor, tutorship; SEE CONCEPTS **348,376**

chairperson [*n*] *person in charge of proceedings*
administrator, captain, chair, director, introducer, leader, moderator, monitor, president, presider, principal, prolocutor, speaker, spokesperson, symposiarch; SEE CONCEPTS **348,376**

challenge [*n*] *dispute, question*
claiming, confrontation, dare, defiance, demanding, demur, interrogation, objection, protest, provocation, remonstrance, summons to contest, test, threat, trial, ultimatum; SEE CONCEPTS **53,532**

challenge [*v*] *dispute, question*
accost, arouse, ask for, assert, beard, brave, call for, call out, claim, confront, cross, dare, defy, demand, denounce, exact, face down, face off, face the music*, fly in the face of*, hang in*, impeach, impose, impugn, inquire, insist upon, investigate, invite competition, make a point of, make a stand, object to, provoke, query, reclaim, require, search out, stand up to, stick it out, stimulate, summon, tax, test, throw down the gauntlet*, try, vindicate; SEE CONCEPT **53**

chamber [*n1*] *small compartment, room*
alcove, antechamber, apartment, bedchamber, bedroom, box, case, cavity, cell, chest, container, cubicle, enclosure, flat, hall, hollow, lodging, pocket, room, socket; SEE CONCEPTS **448,494**

chamber [*n2*] *legislative body*
assembly, council, legislature, organization, representatives; SEE CONCEPT **299**

champion [*adj*] *best, excellent*
blue-ribbon, boss*, capital, chief, choice, cool, dandy, distinguished, first, greatest, head, illustrious, out of sight*, out of this world*, outstanding, premier, prime, principal, prize-winning, splendid, super, superior, tip top*, top drawer*, topflight*, top-notch*, tops*, unbeaten, undefeated, world class*; SEE CONCEPT **574**

champion [*n*] *defeater in competition; preeminent supporter*
advocate, ally, backer, challenger, champ, conqueror, defender, endorser, exponent, expounder, guardian, hero, heroine, medalist, nonpareil, number one*, numero uno*, paladin, partisan, patron, proponent, protector, supporter, sympathizer, the greatest*, titleholder, top dog*, upholder, vanquisher, victor, vindicator, warrior, winner; SEE CONCEPT **366**

champion [*v*] *advocate, support*
back, battle, contend, defend, espouse, fight for, go to bat for*, patronize, plead for, promote, put in a good word for*, ride shotgun for*, side with, stand behind, stand up for, support, thump for, uphold; SEE CONCEPTS **10,69**

championship [*n*] *contest for ultimate victor*
crown, crowning achievement, elimination, playoffs, showdown, title match, tournament, winner takes all*; SEE CONCEPT **363**

chance [*adj*] *accidental, unforeseeable*
adventitious, at random, casual, contingen, fluky, fortuitous, fortunate, happy, inadverten, incidental, lucky, odd, offhand, unforeseen, un intentional, unlooked for, unplanned; SEE CON CEPT **552**

chance [*nl*] *possibility, probability*
break, contingency, fair shake*, fightin, chance*, indications, liability, likelihood, lon shot*, look-in, occasion, odds, opening, opportu nity, outlook, prospect, scope, shot*, show squeak, time, wager; SEE CONCEPT **650**

chance [*n2*] *fate, luck*
accident, advantage, adventure, bad luck, break cast, casualty, coincidence, contingency, destina tion, destiny, doom, even chance, fluke, fortuit fortune, future, gamble, good luck, hap*, hap hazard, happening, hazard, heads or tails*, hit in the cards*, kismet, lot, lottery, luck out* lucky break, misfortune, occurrence, odds, ou come, peradventure, peril, providence, risl stroke of luck*, throw of the dice*, toss-up* turn of the cards*, way the cookie crumbles* wheel of fortune*; SEE CONCEPT **679**

chance [*n3*] *gamble, risk*
bet, craps game*, fall of the cards*, hazard, jeop ardy, lottery, raffle, speculation, stake, throw the dice*, try, venture, wager; SEE CONCEPT **363**

chance [*vl*] *risk, endanger*
attempt, cast lots, draw lots, gamble, go out on limb, have a fling at, hazard, jeopardize, pla with fire*, plunge, put eggs in one basket*, put on the line*, roll the dice*, run the risk, skate o thin ice*, speculate, stake, stick one's neck out* take shot in the dark*, tempt fate*, tempt fo tune*, toss up*, try, venture, wager, wildcat; SF CONCEPT **87**

chance [*v2*] *happen*
arrive, befall, be one's fate, betide, blunder o break, bump, come, come about, come off, com to pass, fall out, fall to one's lot, go, hap*, h upon, light, light upon, luck, meet, occur, stum ble, stumble on, transpire, tumble, turn up; SE CONCEPT **4**

chancy [*adj*] *dangerous, risky*
capricious, contingent, dicey, erratic, fluctuan fluky, hazardous, iffy*, incalculable, precariou problematic, problematical, rocky, speculative ticklish, touchy, tricky, uncertain, unpredictable unsound, whimsical; SEE CONCEPTS **552,587**

chandelier [*n*] *light hanging from ceiling*
candelabrum, candleholder, corona, crown, elec trolier, gasolier, light fixture, luster; SEE CON CEPT **444**

change [*nl*] *something made different; alteratio*
about-face*, addition, adjustment, advance break, compression, contraction, conversion correction, development, difference, distortion diversification, diversity, innovation, metamo phosis, modification, modulation, mutation, nov elty, permutation, reconstruction, refinemen remodeling, reversal, revision, revolution, shif surrogate, switch, tempering, transformation transition, transmutation, turn, turnover, var ance, variation, variety, vicissitude; SEE CON CEPTS **230,260,701**

change [*n2*] *substitution; replacement*
conversion, exchange, flip-flop*, interchange swap, switch, trade, turnaround; SEE CONCEP **128**

change [*n3*] *smaller currency in exchange for larger*
chicken feed*, coins, copper, dimes, nickels, pennies, pin money*, pocket money, quarters, silver, spending money; SEE CONCEPT **340**

change [*v1*] *make or become different*
accommodate, adapt, adjust, alter, alternate, commute, convert, diminish, diverge, diversify, evolve, fluctuate, make innovations, make over, merge, metamorphose, moderate, modify, modulate, mutate, naturalize, recondition, redo, reduce, reform, regenerate, remake, remodel, renovate, reorganize, replace, resolve, restyle, revolutionize, shape, shift, substitute, tamper with, temper, transfigure, transform, translate, transmute, transpose, turn, vacillate, vary, veer, warp; SEE CONCEPTS **228,232,235,701**

change [*v2*] *substitute, replace*
alternate, barter, convert, displace, exchange, interchange, invert, remove, reverse, shift, supplant, swap, switch around, trade, transmit, transpose; SEE CONCEPT **128**

changeable [*adj*] *erratic*
agitated, capricious, changeful, commutative, convertible, fickle, fitful, flighty, fluctuating, fluid, impulsive, inconstant, indecisive, irregular, irresolute, irresponsible, kaleidoscopic, mercurial, mobile, movable, mutable, permutable, protean, restless, reversible, revocable, shifting, skittish, spasmodic, transformable, transitional, uncertain, unpredictable, unreliable, unsettled, unstable, unsteady, vacillating, vagrant, variable, variant, varying, versatile, volatile, wavering, whimsical; SEE CONCEPT **534**

channel [*n1*] *pathway, usually containing water*
approach, aqueduct, arroyo, artery, avenue, canal, canyon, carrier, chamber, chase, conduit, course, dig, ditch, duct, fluting, furrow, gouge, groove, gully, gutter, main, means, medium, pass, passage, pipe, raceway, route, runway, sewer, slit, sound, strait, tideway, trough, tube, tunnel, vein, watercourse, way; SEE CONCEPTS **501,514**

channel [*n2*] *means*
agency, agent, approach, avenue, course, instrument, instrumentality, instrumentation, medium, ministry, organ, route, vehicle, way; SEE CONCEPTS **6,660,770**

channel [*v*] *direct, guide*
carry, conduct, convey, funnel, pipe, route, send, siphon, traject, transmit, transport; SEE CONCEPTS **187,217**

chant [*n*] *chorus of song*
carol, croon, hymn, incantation, intonation, lilt, melody, psalm, shout, singing, song, trill, tune, warble; SEE CONCEPTS **263,595**

chant [*v*] *sing simple song or song part*
cantillate, carol, chorus, croon, descant, doxologize, drone, intone, recite, shout, tune, vocalize, warble; SEE CONCEPTS **65,77**

chaos [*n*] *utter confusion*
anarchy, ataxia, bedlam, clutter, disarray, discord, disorder, disorganization, entropy, free-for-all*, holy mess*, lawlessness, misrule, mix-up, mobocracy, muddle, pandemonium, rat's nest*, snarl, topsy-turviness*, tumult, turmoil, unruliness; SEE CONCEPTS **230,674**

chaotic [*adj*] *utterly confused*
anarchic, deranged, disordered, disorganized, every which way*, harum-scarum*, helter-skel-

ter*, lawless, purposeless, rampageous, riotous, topsy-turvy*, tumultuous, turbid, turbulent, uncontrolled; SEE CONCEPT **548**

chaperon [*n*] *person who accompanies for supervision*
alarm clock*, babysitter*, bird dog*, companion, escort; SEE CONCEPT **423**

chaperon [*v*] *accompany for supervision*
attend, carry, conduct, consort with, convoy, escort, guide, oversee, protect, safeguard, shepherd, supervise, watch over; SEE CONCEPTS **114,714**

chaplain [*n*] *minister in church*
cleric, member of clergy, pastor, preacher, priest, rabbi, turn-around collar*; SEE CONCEPT **361**

chapter [*n*] *section of book or group of items*
affiliate, branch, clause, division, episode, member, offshoot, part, period, phase, stage, topic, unit, wing; SEE CONCEPTS **270,382,832**

char [*v*] *scorch, sear*
burn, carbonize, cauterize, singe; SEE CONCEPT **249**

character [*n1*] *individuality*
appearance, aspect, attribute, badge, bent, caliber, cast, complex, complexion, constitution, crasis, disposition, emotions, estimation, ethos, frame, frame of mind, genius, grain, habit, humor, kind, makeup, mettle, mood, morale, mystique, nature, personality, quality, record, reputation, repute, sense, set, shape, singularity, sort, specialty, spirit, standing, streak, style, temper, temperament, tone, trait, turn, type, vein; SEE CONCEPT **411**

character [*n2*] *integrity*
courage, fame, honor, intelligence, mind, name, place, position, rank, rectitude, rep, report, reputation, repute, standing, station, status, uprightness; SEE CONCEPT **668**

character [*n3*] *odd person*
card*, case*, clown, crank*, customer*, duck*, eccentric, figure, freak, nut, oddball, oddity, original*, personage, personality, queer, spook*, wack*, weirdo, zombie*; SEE CONCEPTS **412,423**

character [*n4*] *written symbol*
cipher, device, emblem, figure, hieroglyph, letter, logo, mark, monogram, number, numeral, rune, sign, type; SEE CONCEPT **284**

character [*n5*] *portrayal of another*
impersonation, part, personification, role; SEE CONCEPTS **263,352**

characteristic [*adj*] *typical; distinguishing*
appropriate, diagnostic, differentiating, discriminating, discriminative, distinctive, distinguishing, emblematic, especial, essential, exclusive, fixed, idiosyncratic, inborn, inbred, indicative, individual, individualistic, individualizing, ingrained, inherent, innate, local, marked, native, normal, original, particular, peculiar, personal, private, proper, regular, representative, singular, special, specific, symbolic, symptomatic, unique; SEE CONCEPTS **542,547,550**

characteristic [*n*] *typical feature, trait*
affection, aspect, attribute, badge, bag, bearing, bent, caliber, cast, complexion, component, differentia, disposition, distinction, earmark, endowment, essence, essential, faculty, flavor, frame, idiosyncrasy, inclination, individuality, lineament, mannerism, mark, mood, nature, originality, particularity, peculiarity, personality, point, property, quality, singularity, specialty,

streak, stripe, style, symptom, temperament, tendency, thing, thumbprint, tinge, tone, trademark, turn, virtue; SEE CONCEPT 411

characterize [*v*] *typify, distinguish*
belong to, brand, button down*, constitute, define, delineate, describe, designate, differentiate, discriminate, feature, identify, indicate, individualize, individuate, inform, make up, mark, outline, peculiarize, peg, personalize, pigeonhole*, portray, represent, signalize, singularize, stamp, style, symbolize, tab, typecast; SEE CONCEPT 644

charade [*n*] *pretense*
deception, disguise, fake, farce, make-believe, mimicry, pageant, pantomime, parody, pretension, pretentiousness, put-on, travesty, trick; SEE CONCEPT 59

charge [*n1*] *accusation*
allegation, beef*, complaint, gripe, imputation, indictment, plaint, stink*; SEE CONCEPTS 44,317

charge [*n2*] *attack*
assault, blitz, blitzkrieg, invasion, mugging, onset, onslaught, outbreak, push, rush, sortie; SEE CONCEPT 86

charge [*n3*] *burden*
care, commitment, committal, concern, custody, deadweight, duty, millstone, must, need, obligation, office, onus, ought, responsibility, right, safekeeping, task, tax, trust, ward, weight; SEE CONCEPTS 532,709

charge [*n4*] *price asked for something*
amount, bad news*, bite, cost, damage, expenditure, expense, nick, outlay, payment, price, price tag, rate, squeeze, tab, tariff, tick; SEE CONCEPT 329

charge [*n5*] *command*
behest, bidding, dictate, direction, exhortation, injunction, instruction, mandate, order, precept, word; SEE CONCEPTS 53,274

charge [*n6*] *supervisory responsibility*
care, conduct, custody, handling, intendance, management, oversight, running, superintendence, superintendency, supervision, ward; SEE CONCEPT 117

charge [*v1*] *accuse*
arraign, blame, blow the whistle on*, censure, criminate, drag into court*, finger*, hang something on*, impeach, impugn, impute, incriminate, inculpate, indict, involve, peg, point the finger at*, reprehend, reproach, tax, turn on, whistle-blow*; SEE CONCEPTS 44,317

charge [*v2*] *attack*
assail, assault, blindside, bolt, buck, bushwhack*, chase, dash, invade, jump on, lunge, mug, rush, smash, stampede, storm, tear; SEE CONCEPT 86

charge [*v3*] *load, tax*
afflict, burden, choke, clog, commit, cram, crowd, cumber, encumber, entrust, fill, heap, impregnate, instill, lade, pack, penetrate, permeate, pervade, pile, ram, saddle, saturate, suffuse, transfuse, weigh; SEE CONCEPTS 107,156,740

charge [*v4*] *order something done*
adjure, ask, bid, command, direct, enjoin, entrust, exhort, instruct, request, require, solicit, tell, warn; SEE CONCEPTS 53,78

charge [*v5*] *ask a price*
demand, fix price at, impose, levy, price, require, sell for; SEE CONCEPTS 330,345

charge [*v6*] *pay with credit card*
book, buy on credit, chalk up, cuff, debit, encumber, go into hock*, incur debt, nick*, paste*, put on account, put on one's card, put on the cuff, put on the tab, receive credit, run up; SEE CONCEPTS 327,330

charisma [*n*] *great personal charm*
allure, animal magnetism*, appeal, dazzle, drawing power, fascination, flash, glamour, it*, magnetism, pizzazz*, something*, star quality, witchcraft, witchery; SEE CONCEPT 411

charismatic [*adj*] *charming*
alluring, appealing, hypnotic, larger than life*, magnetic, mesmerizing, poised; SEE CONCEPTS 529,537

charitable [*adj1*] *giving, generous*
accommodating, all heart, altruistic, beneficent, benevolent, benign, big*, bighearted*, bountiful, eleemosynary, good, helpful, humane, humanitarian, kind, kindly, lavish, liberal, obliging, philanthropic, sympathetic; SEE CONCEPTS 334,542

charitable [*adj2*] *kind, lenient*
all heart*, benevolent, big*, bighearted*, broadminded, clement, considerate, easy, favorable, forbearing, forgiving, gracious, humane, indulgent, kindly, lenient, magnanimous, merciful, sympathetic, thoughtful, tolerant, understanding; SEE CONCEPT 404

charity [*n1*] *generosity, gift*
alms, alms-giving, assistance, benefaction, beneficence, contribution, dole, donation, endowment, fund, gifting, hand*, hand-out, helping hand*, largesse, oblation, offering, philanthropy, relief, write-off; SEE CONCEPTS 337,657

charity [*n2*] *kindness, compassion*
affection, agape, altruism, amity, attachment, benevolence, benignity, bountifulness, bounty, caritas, clemency, fellow feeling, generosity, goodness, goodwill, grace, humaneness, humanity, indulgence, kindliness, lenity, love, magnanimity, mercy, tenderheartedness; SEE CONCEPTS 32,411

charlatan [*n*] *swindler*
cheat, con, con artist, fake, fraud, imposter, mountebank, phony, pretender, quack, rip-off artist*, sham; SEE CONCEPTS 260,412

charm [*n1*] *enchantment, allure*
agreeableness, allurement, appeal, attraction, attractiveness, beauty, bewitchery, charisma, chemistry, conjuration, delightfulness, desirability, fascination, glamour, grace, it*, lure, magic, magnetism, pizzazz*, something*, sorcery, spell, star quality, witchery; SEE CONCEPTS 411,673

charm [*n2*] *talisman*
amulet, fetish, good-luck piece, juju, lucky piece, madstone, mascot, phylactery, rabbit's foot, trinket, zemi; SEE CONCEPTS 284,446

charm [*v*] *enchant*
allure, attract, beguile, bewitch, cajole, captivate, delight, draw, enamor, enrapture, ensorcell, enthrall, entrance, fascinate, grab, hex, hypnotize, inveigle, kill*, knock dead*, knock out*, magnetize, mesmerize, please, possess, put under a spell*, send*, slay*, spell*, sweep off feet*, take*, tickle, tickle pink*, transport, turn on*, vamp, voodoo, wile, win, win over, wow*; SEE CONCEPTS 7,22

charming [*adj*] *captivating*
absorbing, alluring, amiable, appealing, attractive, bewitching, charismatic, choice, cute, dainty, delectable, delicate, delightful, desirable,

electrifying, elegant, enamoring, engaging, engrossing, enthralling, entrancing, eye-catching, fascinating, fetching, glamorous, graceful, infatuating, inviting, irresistible, likable, lovable, lovely, magnetizing, nice, pleasant, pleasing, provocative, rapturous, ravishing, seducing, seductive, sweet, tantalizing, tempting, titillating, winning, winsome; SEE CONCEPT *404*

hart [*n*] *map, plan*
blueprint, diagram, graph, outline, plat, plot, rough draft, scheme, sketch, table, tabulation; SEE CONCEPTS *625,660*

hart [*v*] *plan, map out*
arrange, block out, blueprint, cast, delineate, design, devise, draft, graph, lay out, outline, plot, project, shape, sketch; SEE CONCEPTS *36,174*

harter [*n*] *treaty, agreement*
allotment, bond, code, concession, constitution, contract, conveyance, deed, document, endowment, franchise, grant, indenture, license, pact, patent, permit, prerogative, privilege, right, settlement; SEE CONCEPTS *684,685*

harter [*v*] *reserve, commission*
allow, authorize, borrow, contract, employ, engage, hire, lease, let, license, permit, rent, sanction; SEE CONCEPTS *48,50,88,89*

hary [*adj*] *careful, cautious*
cagey, calculating, canny, circumspect, considerate, constrained, discreet, economical, fastidious, frugal, guarded, guarded, heedful, hesitant, inhibited, leery, loath, miserly, particular, prudent, reluctant, restrained, safe, scrupulous, sparing, stingy, suspicious, thrifty, uneasy, wary, watchful; SEE CONCEPTS *401,587*

hase [*n*] *pursuit*
hunt, hunting, quest, race, venery; SEE CONCEPT *207*

hase [*v*] *run after, pursue*
bird-dog*, charge, chivy, course, drive, drive away, expel, follow, go after, hound, hunt, run down, rush, seek, shag*, speed, take off after*, tear, track, track down, trail; SEE CONCEPT *207*

hasm [*n*] *gap, abyss*
abysm, alienation, arroyo, blank, breach, cavity, cleavage, cleft, clough, clove, crater, crevasse, fissure, flume, gorge, gulch, gulf, hiatus, hole, hollow, omission, opening, oversight, preterition, ravine, rent, rift, schism, skip, split, void, yawn; SEE CONCEPT *513*

haste [*adj*] *pure, incorrupt*
austere, celibate, clean, continent, controlled, decent, decorous, elegant, immaculate, impotent, inexperienced, innocent, intemerate, modest, monogamous, moral, neat, platonic, proper, prudish, quiet, refined, restrained, simple, spotless, stainless, subdued, unaffected, unblemished, uncontaminated, undefiled, unstained, unsullied, unwed, vestal, virginal, virtuous, wholesome; SEE CONCEPTS *372,404*

hasten [*v*] *correct, humiliate*
abase, admonish, afflict, berate, call down, castigate, chastise, chide, cow, curb, discipline, exprobate, fulminate against, have on the carpet*, humble, objurgate, penalize, punish, rake over the coals*, rebuke, reprehend, repress, reprimand, reproach, reprove, restrain, scold, scourge, soften, subdue, take to task, tame, tongue-lash*, try, upbraid; SEE CONCEPTS *52,122*

hastise [*v*] *scold, discipline*
baste, beat, berate, castigate, censure, chasten,

chew out*, climb all over*, correct, ferule*, flog*, lash*, lay into*, lean on*, pummel, punish, ream, scourge, skelp, slap down*, spank, thrash, upbraid, whip; SEE CONCEPTS *52,122*

chastity [*n*] *celibacy, purity*
abstemiousness, abstinence, chasteness, cleanness, continence, decency, demureness, devotion, honor, immaculacy, innocence, integrity, modesty, monogamy, morality, naïveté, restraint, singleness, sinlessness, spotlessness, temperance, uprightness, virginity, virtue; SEE CONCEPT *633*

chat [*n*] *talk, often short*
babble, bull session, chatter, conversation, converse, gab*, gas*, gossip, heart-to-heart*, hot air*, jabber*, palaver, prattle*, rap*, rap session*, tête-à-tête, visit, yak*; SEE CONCEPT *278*

chat [*v*] *talk, gossip*
babble, blab*, burble, cackle, chatter, chew the fat*, chew the rag*, converse, gab*, go on*, jaw*, prate, prattle*, run on*, shoot the breeze*, yap*; SEE CONCEPT *266*

chat room [*n*] *interaction via computer*
data communication channel, live discussion, net event, room; SEE CONCEPTS *349,770*

chatter [*n*] *constant or rapid talk*
babble, blather, chat, chitchat, gas*, gossip, jabber*, palaver, prattle*, twaddle, yakking*; SEE CONCEPTS *266,278*

chatter [*v*] *speak fast and non-stop*
babble, blab*, blather, cackle, chat, chitchat, clack, gab*, gabble, gas*, gibber, go on and on, gossip, jabber, jaw*, natter, palaver, prate, prattle*, tattle, twaddle, twiddle, yak*; SEE CONCEPT *266*

chatty [*adj*] *talkative*
colloquial, communicative, conversational, familiar, friendly, gabby, garrulous, gossipy, informal, intimate, loose-lipped, loquacious, multieloquent, spontaneous, talky; SEE CONCEPT *267*

chauvinism [*n*] *extreme devotion to a belief or nation*
bellicism, ethnocentricity, fanatical patriotism, fanaticism, jingoism, narrowness, nationalism, zealotry; SEE CONCEPT *689*

cheap [*adj1*] *inexpensive*
at a bargain, bargain, bargain-basement*, bargain-counter, bought for a song*, budget, buy, cheapo*, competitive, cost next to nothing*, cut-price, cut-rate, depreciated, dime a dozen*, easy on the pocketbook*, economical, half-priced, irregular, low-cost, lowered, low-priced, low tariff, marked down, moderate, nominal, on sale, popularly priced, real buy*, reasonable, reduced, sale, slashed, standard, steal, uncostly, undear, utility, worth the money*; SEE CONCEPT *334*

cheap [*adj2*] *inferior, low in quality*
bad, base, bogus, catchpenny, cheesy, common, commonplace, crappy*, cruddy, dud, flashy, garbage, garish, glitzy*, junky*, lousy, mangy, mean, mediocre, meretricious, no bargain*, no good, ordinary, paltry, poor, ratty, raunchy, rinky-dink*, rotten, rubbishy, scroungy, second-rate, shoddy, sleazy, small-time*, tatty, tawdry, terrible, trashy, trumpery, two-bit, valueless, white elephant*, worthless; SEE CONCEPT *589*

cheap [*adj3*] *low, vulgar*
abject, base, beggarly, contemptible, despicable,

dirty, dishonest, mean, pitiable, scurvy, shabby, sordid, sorry, tawdry, vile; SEE CONCEPT 542

cheap [adj4] *concerned with saving money*
mean, mingy, miserly, penny-pinching, stingy, thrifty, tight*, tight-wad*; SEE CONCEPT 332

cheapen [v] *diminish worth*
abase, beat down, belittle, corrupt, damage, debase, decline, decry, degrade, demean, denigrate, depreciate, derogate, devalue, discredit, disparage, downgrade, drop, fall, lose value, lower, mar, mark down, minimize, reduce, render worthless, ruin, spoil, undervalue, write off; SEE CONCEPT 240

cheat [n1] *person who fools others*
bluff, charlatan, chiseler, con artist, confidence operator, conniver, cozener, crook, deceiver, decoy, defrauder, dodger, double-crosser*, double-dealer*, enticer, fake, hypocrite, impostor, inveigler, jockey, masquerader, pretender, quack, rascal, rogue, scammer*, shark, sharper, shyster, swindler, trickster; SEE CONCEPT 412

cheat [n2] *trick*
artifice, baloney, bamboozlement*, bill of goods*, bunco, chicanery, con, con game, cover up, cozening, deceit, deception, dirty pool*, dirty trick*, dodge, double-dealing*, fake, fast one, fast shuffle*, fix, flimflam, frame, fraud, gyp, hanky-panky*, hoax, hoaxing, humbug, hustle, imposture, jazz, jive, plant, put-on, racket, rip-off, run around, scam, sell, shady deal, sham, shell game, snow job*, spoof, sting, stunt, swindle, trickery, whitewash, wrong; SEE CONCEPT 59

cheat [v1] *defraud, fool*
bamboozle*, beat, beguile, bilk, bleed, bunco, burn, caboodle, chisel, con, cozen, crib, cross, deceive, defraud, delude, diddle*, do*, do a number on*, double-cross, double-deal, dupe, fast talk, finagle, fleece, flimflam, fudge*, give bum steer*, gouge, gyp*, hoodwink, hose, jerk around, milk, mislead, pull one's leg*, ream*, rip off*, rook*, rope in*, sandbag, scam, screw, shaft, short, shuck, skin, snow, stiff, sucker, swindle, take, take for a ride*, take in, take out, trick, trim, two-time, victimize; SEE CONCEPTS 59,139,192

cheat [v2] *frustrate, thwart*
baffle, check, defeat, deprive, foil, prevent; SEE CONCEPT 121

check [n1] *inspection, examination*
analysis, audit, checkup, control, inquiry, investigation, poll, rein, research, review, scrutiny, test; SEE CONCEPT 103

check [n2] *restraint, hindrance*
blow, constraint, control, curb, damper, disappointment, frustration, grunt, harness, holdup, impediment, inhibition, limitation, obstruction, rebuff, rejection, restrainer, reversal, reverse, setback, stoppage, trouble; SEE CONCEPTS 121,130,230

check [n3] *symbol for ticking off*
cross, dot, line, mark, score, sign, stroke, tick, X*; SEE CONCEPT 284

check [n4] *pattern of squares*
checkerboard, patchwork, plaid, quilt, tartan; SEE CONCEPT 436

check [v1] *inspect, examine*
analyze, ascertain, audit, balance account, candle, case, compare, confirm, correct, count, enquire about, eyeball*, find out, frisk, go through, investigate, keep account, look at, look over,

look see*, make sure, monitor, note, overlook, probe, prove, quiz, review, scout out, scrutinize, study, take stock, tell, test, try, verify; SEE CONCEPTS 24,103

check [v2] *hinder, restrain*
arrest, baffle, bar, bit, bottleneck*, bridle, checkmate, choke, circumvent, constrain, control, counteract, curb, cut short, delay, discourage, foil, frustrate, halt, harness, hold, hold back, hold down, hold in, impede, inhibit, interrupt, keep back, limit, moderate, neutralize, nip in the bud*, obstruct, obviate, pause, play for time, preclude, prevent, rebuff, reduce, rein in, repress, repulse, retard, slacken pace, slow down, snub, squelch, stay, stop, suppress, tame, terminate, thwart, withhold; SEE CONCEPTS 121,130

checkered [adj] *patterned*
checky, diversified, motley, mutable, patchwork, plaid, quilted, spotted, variegated; SEE CONCEPT 486

cheek [n1] *side of human face*
chop*, choppers*, gill, jowl; SEE CONCEPT 418

cheek [n2] *audacity, boldness*
brashness, brass*, brazenness, chutzpah*, confidence, disrespect, effrontery, gall, impertinence, impudence, insolence, lip*, nerve*, presumption, rudeness, sauce*, temerity; SEE CONCEPT 633

cheeky [adj] *impudent*
audacious, ballsy*, bold, brash, brazen, disrespectful, forward, impertinent, insolent, insulting, nervy, saucy; SEE CONCEPTS 401,404

cheep [v] *vocalize as a bird*
chip, chipper, chirp, chirrup, peek, tweedle, tweet, twitter; SEE CONCEPT 64

cheer [n1] *happiness*
animation, buoyancy, cheerfulness, cheeriness, comfort, delight, encouragement, exuberance, gaiety, geniality, gladness, glee, good cheer, hilarity, hopefulness, jauntiness, jocundity, joy, joyousness, lightheartedness, liveliness, merriment, merry-making, mirth, optimism, solace; SEE CONCEPT 410

cheer [n2] *applause, supportive yell*
acclamation, approbation, approval, cry, encouragement, hurrah, hurray, huzzah, ovation, plaudits, roar, shout; SEE CONCEPTS 69,77

cheer [v1] *make someone feel happier*
animate, brace up, brighten, buck up*, buoy, comfort, console, elate, elevate, embolden, encourage, enliven, exhilarate, give a lift*, gladden, hearten, help, incite, inspirit, let the sun shine in*, perk up, pick up, put on cloud nine*, put on top of the world*, snap out of it*, solace, steel, strengthen, uplift, upraise, warm; SEE CONCEPTS 7,22

cheer [v2] *encourage in activity*
acclaim, applaud, clap, hail, hurrah, plug*, rise to, root, salute, sound off for, support, yell; SEE CONCEPT 69

cheerful [adj] *happy*
airy, animated, blithe, bouncy, bright, bucked, buoyant, cheery, chipper, chirpy, contented, effervescent, enlivening, enthusiastic, full of pep, gay, glad, gladsome, good-humored, good-natured, hearty, high, hilarious, hopeful, in good spirits, in high spirits, jaunty, jocund, jolly, joyful, lighthearted, lively, merry, optimistic, peppy, perky, pleasant, roseate, rosy, sanguine, snappy, sparkling, sprightly, sunny, sunny side up*, up*,

upbeat, vivacious, winsome, zappy, zingy, zippy;
SEE CONCEPTS *403,404*

cheering [*adj*] *encouraging*
auspicious, bright, comforting, heartening, hopeful, promising, propitious; SEE CONCEPT *529*

cheerless [*adj*] *depressing, unhappy*
austere, black, bleak, blue, comfortless, dark, dejected, dejecting, depressed, desolate, despondent, disconsolate, dismal, dispiriting, dolorous, drab, draggy, drearisome, dreary, dull, forlorn, funereal, gloomy, grim, in the dumps*, jarring, joyless, melancholy, miserable, mopey, mournful, oppressive, sad, somber, sorrowful, sullen, tenebrific, uncomfortable, wintry, woebegone, woeful; SEE CONCEPT *403*

chef [*n*] *cook*
chief cook and bottle washer*, cuisinier, culinary artist, gourmet chef, hash slinger*, sous chef; SEE CONCEPT *348*

chemical [*adj*] *concerned with atom and molecule change*
actinic, alchemical, enzymatic, synthesized, synthetic, synthetical; SEE CONCEPT *536*

cherish [*v*] *care about deeply*
admire, adore, appreciate, apprize, care for, clasp, cleave to, cling to, coddle, comfort, cosset, cultivate, defend, dote on, embrace, encourage, enshrine, entertain, fancy, fondle, foster, guard, harbor, hold dear, hold in high esteem, honor, hug, idolize, like, love, nourish, nurse, nurture, pet, preserve, prize, revere, reverence, safeguard, shelter, shield, support, sustain, treasure, value, venerate, worship; SEE CONCEPT *32*

cherry [*adj*] *bright red color*
blooming, blushing, bright red, cerise, claret, crimson, dark red, erubescent, incarnadine, reddish, rosy, rubescent, rubicund, ruddy; SEE CONCEPT *618*

cherry-picker [*n*] *truck with raisable boom*
boom, cable truck, telephone truck, utility truck; SEE CONCEPT *505*

chest [*n1*] *box for storage*
bin, bureau, cabinet, carton, case, casket, chiffonier, coffer, commode, crate, exchequer, pyxis, receptacle, reliquary, strongbox, treasury, trunk; SEE CONCEPT *494*

chest [*n2*] *upper front of body*
bosom, breast, bust, heart, mammary glands, peritoneum, pulmonary cavity, rib cage, ribs, thorax, upper trunk; SEE CONCEPT *392*

chew [*v1*] *grind with teeth*
bite, champ, chaw, chomp, crunch, dispatch, feast upon, gnaw, gulp, gum, manducate, masticate, munch, nibble, rend, ruminate, scrunch; SEE CONCEPTS *169,185*

chew [*v2*] *think about deeply*
consider, deliberate, meditate, mull, mull over, muse on, ponder, reflect upon, ruminate, weigh; SEE CONCEPT *24*

chew out [*v*] *scold*
bawl out, carpet*, criticize, dress down, jaw, revile, tell off, tongue-lash*, vituperate, wig, yell at; SEE CONCEPT *52*

chic [*adj*] *fashionable*
chichi*, clean*, current, dap*, dapper, dashing, elegant, exclusive, faddish, last word*, latest thing*, mod*, modern, modish, natty, sharp, smart, stylish, swank, trendy, voguish, with-it*; SEE CONCEPT *589*

chicanery [*n*] *deception, trickery*
artifice, cheating, chicane, deviousness, dishonesty, dodge, double-crossing, double-dealing*, duplicity, feint, fourberie, fraud, furtiveness, gambit, hanky-panky*, intrigue, machination, maneuver, plot, ploy, ruse, sharp practice, skullduggery, sophistry, stratagem, subterfuge, surreptitiousness, underhandedness, wiles; SEE CONCEPTS *59,660*

chicken [*n1*] *person afraid to try something*
coward, craven, dastard, funk, poltroon, quitter, recreant, scaredy cat*, yellow belly*; SEE CONCEPT *423*

chicken [*n2*] *farm fowl*
banty, barnyard fowl, biddy, capon, chick, cock, cock-a-doodle-do*, cockalorum, cockerel, gump*, heeler, hen, poultry, pullet, rooster; SEE CONCEPTS *394,395*

chicken feed [*n*] *small amount of money*
coins, nickles and dimes*, paltry sum, peanuts*, pin money*, pocket money, small change, small potatoes*, spending money; SEE CONCEPT *340*

chicken out [*v*] *back out*
avoid, back down, back pedal*, beg off*, blow it off*, cancel, chicken out*, cop out*, get cold feet*, give up, go back on, recant, renege, resign, scratch, shy from, surrender, throw in the towel*, turn yellow*, weasel out, welsh, wiggle out, withdraw, worm out*; SEE CONCEPTS *50,88,121,266,697*

chide [*v*] *criticize, lecture*
admonish, berate, blame, call down*, call on the carpet*, castigate, censure, check, condemn, exprobate, find fault, flay, give a hard time*, lesson, monish, rate, rebuke, reprehend, reprimand, reproach, reprove, scold, slap on the wrist*, speak to, take down*, take down a peg*, talk to, tell off, tick off*, upbraid; SEE CONCEPT *52*

chief [*adj*] *most important, essential*
arch, capital, cardinal, central, champion, consequential, controlling, crucial, effective, especial, first, foremost, grand, head, highest, key, leading, main, major, momentous, number one*, outstanding, paramount, potent, predominant, preeminent, premier, primal, primary, prime, principal, ruling, significant, star, stellar, superior, supreme, telling, uppermost, vital, weighty; SEE CONCEPTS *568,574,829*

chief [*n*] *person in charge*
big cheese*, big gun*, big wheel*, bigwig*, boss, captain, chieftain, commander, dictator, director, foreperson, general, governor, head, head honcho*, head person*, honcho*, key player*, leader, manager, monarch, overlord, overseer, president, principal, proprietor, ringleader, ruler, sovereign, superintendent, supervisor, suzerain, top brass*, top cat*; SEE CONCEPTS *347,376*

chiefly [*adv*] *most importantly*
above all, especially, essentially, in general, in the first place, in the main, largely, mainly, mostly, on the whole, overall, predominantly, primarily, principally, usually; SEE CONCEPTS *567,772*

child [*n*] *very young person*
adolescent, anklebiter*, babe, baby, bairn, bambino, brat, cherub, chick, cub, descendant, dickens*, imp, infant, innocent, issue, juvenile, kid, kiddie*, lamb*, little angel*, little darling*, little doll*, little one, minor, mite, moppet, neonate, nestling, newborn, nipper, nursling, offspring,

ch
ch

preteen, progeny, pubescent, shaver, small fry*, sprout, squirt, stripling, suckling, tadpole, teen, teenager, teenybopper*, toddler, tot, tyke, urchin*, whippersnapper*, young one, youngster, youth; SEE CONCEPTS *414,424*

childbirth [n] *giving birth*
accouchement, bearing children, blessed event*, childbed, confinement, delivering, delivery, labor, lying-in, nativity, parturience, parturition, procreation, producing, propagation, reproduction, travail, visit from the stork*; SEE CONCEPTS *302,373*

childhood [n] *period of being young*
adolescence, babyhood, cradle, immaturity, infancy, juniority, juvenility, minority, nonage, nursery, puberty, pupilage, schooldays, teens, tender age, youth; SEE CONCEPTS *816,817*

childish [adj] *immature, silly*
adolescent, baby, babyish, callow, childlike, foolish, frivolous, green, infantile, infantine, innocent, jejune, juvenile, kid stuff*, naive, puerile, unsophisticated, young, youthful; SEE CONCEPTS *401,402,424,578,797*

childlike [adj] *innocent, naive*
artless, childish, credulous, guileless, immature, ingenuous, natural, simple, spontaneous, trustful, trusting, unaffected, unfeigned; SEE CONCEPT *404*

chill [adj1] *cold, raw*
arctic, biting, bleak, brisk, chilly, cool, freezing, frigid, frosty, gelid, glacial, icy, nippy, sharp, wintry; SEE CONCEPT *605*

chill [adj2] *unfriendly, aloof*
cool, depressing, discouraging, dismal, dispiriting, distant, emotionless, formal, frigid, glacial, hateful, hostile, icy, indifferent, reserved, solitary, standoffish, stony, uncompanionable, unemotional, ungenial, unhappy, unresponsive, unwelcoming, wintry, withdrawn; SEE CONCEPTS *401,404*

chill [n] *cold conditions*
bite, coldness, coolness, crispness, frigidity, gelidity, iciness, nip, rawness, rigor, sharpness; SEE CONCEPT *524*

chill [v1] *make cold*
air-condition, congeal, cool, freeze, frost, ice, refrigerate; SEE CONCEPTS *255,521*

chill [v2] *discourage*
cloud, dampen, dash, deject, demoralize, depress, dishearten, dismay, disparage, dispirit; SEE CONCEPTS *7,19*

chilly [adj1] *cold*
arctic, biting, blowy, breezy, brisk, cool, crisp, drafty, freezing, fresh, frosty, glacial, hawkish, icebox, icy, nippy, penetrating, sharp, snappy, wintry; SEE CONCEPT *605*

chilly [adj2] *unfriendly, aloof*
cold, frigid, hostile, unfriendly, unresponsive, unsympathetic, unwelcoming; SEE CONCEPT *404*

chime [v] *ring, peal*
bell, bong, boom, clang, dong, jingle, knell, sound, strike, tinkle, tintinnabulate, toll; SEE CONCEPT *65*

chimera [n] *dream, fantasy*
bogy, bubble, delusion, fabrication, fancy, fata morgana, figment, fool's paradise*, hallucination, ignis fatuus, illusion, mirage, monster, monstrosity, pipe dream*, rainbow*, snare, specter, virtual reality; SEE CONCEPT *529*

chimney [n] *smokestack for building*
chase, chimney pot, chimney stack, fireplace, flue, funnel, furnace, hearth, pipe, smokeshaft, stack, vent, ventilator; SEE CONCEPT *440*

chin [n] *area under mouth*
button, jaw, jawbone, mandible, mentum, point; SEE CONCEPT *399*

china [n] *dishes, often valuable*
ceramics, crockery, porcelain, pottery, service, stoneware, tableware, ware; SEE CONCEPT *493*

chink [n] *opening*
aperture, cleft, crack, crevice, cut, fissure, gap, hole, rift, slit, slot, space; SEE CONCEPT *513*

chintzy [adj] *cheap-looking*
cheap, frowzy, schlocky*, shabby, sleazy, tacky; SEE CONCEPT *485*

chip [n] *shard, flaw*
dent, flake, fragment, gobbet, nick, notch, paring, part, scrap, scratch, shaving, slice, sliver, wafer, wedge; SEE CONCEPTS *580,831*

chip [v] *knock a piece out of*
break, chisel, chop, clip, crack, crack off, crumble, cut away, cut off, damage, flake, fragment, gash, hack, hackle, hew, incise, nick, notch, shape, shear, slash, slice, sliver, snick, snip, splinter, split, whack, whittle; SEE CONCEPTS *137,189,246,250*

chip in [v] *contribute*
ante up*, break in*, chime in*, come through*, conate, go Dutch*, interpose, interrupt, pay, pitch in, subscribe; SEE CONCEPT *110*

chipper [adj] *happy*
alert, animate, animated, bright, brisk, gay, in good spirits, keen, lively, spirited, sprightly, vivacious; SEE CONCEPT *403*

chips [n] *substitute for money; money*
coin, currency, markers, play money, scratch; SEE CONCEPT *340*

chirp [v] *peep, cheep*
call, chip, chipper, chirrup, lilt, pipe, purl, quaver, roll, sing, sound, trill, tweedle, tweet, twitter, warble; SEE CONCEPT *64*

chisel [n] *shaping tool*
adze, blade, edge, gouge, knife; SEE CONCEPTS *495,499*

chisel [v] *cut, wear away*
carve, hew, incise, roughcast, roughhew, sculpt, sculpture, shape; SEE CONCEPTS *137,176,184*

chivalrous [adj] *valiant*
benevolent, big, bold, brave, considerate, courageous, courteous, courtly, gallant, gentlemanlike, great-hearted, heroic, high-minded, honorable, intrepid, lofty, magnanimous, manly, nobleminded, polite, quixotic, spirited, sublime, true, valorous; SEE CONCEPT *401*

chivalry [n] *valor, gallantry*
courage, courtesy, courtliness, fairness, politeness, valiance; SEE CONCEPT *633*

choice [adj] *best, superior*
10*, A-1*, elect, elite, excellent, exceptional, exclusive, exquisite, fine, first-class, hand-picked, 24-karat*, nice, popular, precious, preferential, preferred, prime, prize, rare, select, solid gold*, special, top-drawer*, uncommon, unusual, valuable, winner; SEE CONCEPT *574*

choice [n] *power to select; selection*
alternative, appraisal, choosing, cull, cup of tea*, decision, determination, discretion, discrimination, distinction, druthers*, election, evaluation, extract, favorite, finding, free will, judgment, op-

portunity, option, pick, preference, rating, say, substitute, variety, verdict, volition, vote, weakness; SEE CONCEPTS *41,376*

choke [v] *smother, block*
asphyxiate, bar, check, clog, close, congest, constrict, dam, die, drown, fill, gag, garrote, gasp, gibbet, kill, noose, obstruct, occlude, overpower, retard, squeeze, stifle, stop, stopper, strangle, strangulate, stuff, stunt, suffocate, suppress, throttle, wring; SEE CONCEPTS *121,219*

choose [v] *pick, select*
accept, adopt, appoint, call for, cast, commit oneself, co-opt, crave, cull, decide on, designate, desire, determine, discriminate between, draw lots, elect, embrace, espouse, excerpt, extract, fancy, favor, feel disposed to, finger, fix on, glean, judge, love, make choice, make decision, make up one's mind, name, opt for, predestine, prefer, see fit, separate, set aside, settle upon, sift out, single out, slot, sort, tab, tag, take, take up, tap, want, weigh, will, winnow, wish, wish for; SEE CONCEPT *41*

choosy [adj] *fussy, discriminating*
dainty, eclectic, exacting, fastidious, finical, finicky, nice, overparticular, particular, persnickety*, picky, prissy, select, selective; SEE CONCEPT *404*

chop [v] *cut up with tool*
axe, cleave, clip, cube, dice, divide, fell, fragment, hack, hackle, hash, hew, lop, mangle, mince, sever, shear, slash, truncate, whack; SEE CONCEPT *176*

choppy [adj] *wavy*
inclement, ripply, rough, uneven, violent, wild; SEE CONCEPT *488*

chore [n] *task*
assignment, burden, devoir, duty, effort, errand, grind, housework, job, KP*, routine, scutwork, stint, trial, tribulation, workout; SEE CONCEPT *362*

chortle [v] *laugh gleefully*
cackle, chuckle, crow, giggle, guffaw, hee-haw*, snicker, sniggle, snort, teehee*, titter; SEE CONCEPT *77*

chorus [n1] *group of singers*
carolers, choir, chorale, choristers, ensemble, glee club, singing group, vocalists, voices; SEE CONCEPT *294*

chorus [n2] *refrain*
bob, burden, chorale, main section, melody, motif, music, recurrent verse, response, ritornelle, song, strain, theme, tune, undersong; SEE CONCEPT *264*

chorus [n3] *agreement*
accord, concert, concord, consonance, harmony, tune, unison; SEE CONCEPTS *673,684*

chosen [adj] *preferred*
called, conscript, elect, exclusive, got the nod*, named, pegged, pick, picked, popular, preferential, select, selected, tabbed; SEE CONCEPTS *546,567,574*

christen [v] *named in religious rite*
asperse, baptize, bless, call, dedicate, denominate, designate, dub, entitle, godparent, immerse, sprinkle, style, term, title; SEE CONCEPTS *62,367*

chronic [adj] *incessant, never-ending*
abiding, ceaseless, confirmed, constant, continual, continuing, continuous, deep-rooted, deepseated, enduring, ever-present, fixed, habitual, inborn, inbred, incurable, ineradicable, in-

grained, inveterate, lasting, lifelong, lingering, long-lived, long-standing, obstinate, perennial, persistent, persisting, prolonged, protracted, recurrent, recurring, rooted, routine, settled, stubborn, sustained, tenacious, unabating, unmitigated, unyielding, usual; SEE CONCEPTS *534,551,798*

chronicle [n] *account, narrative*
annals, archives, diary, history, journal, narration, prehistory, recital, record, recountal, register, report, story, version; SEE CONCEPTS *271,282*

chronicle [v] *report, recount*
enter, narrate, record, register, relate, set down, tell; SEE CONCEPTS *60,79*

chronological [adj] *in consecutive time order*
archival, chronographic, chronologic, chronometric, chronometrical, chronoscopic, classified, dated, historical, horological, horometrical, in due course, in due time, in order, in sequence, junctural, ordered, progressive, sequent, sequential, tabulated, temporal; SEE CONCEPTS *548,585*

chubby [adj] *slightly fat*
ample, bearish, big, butterball*, buxom, chunky, fatty, flabby, fleshy, full-figured, hefty, husky, pleasingly plump*, plump, plumpish, podgy, portly, pudgy, rolly-poly*, rotund, round, stout, tubby, zaftig*; SEE CONCEPTS *491,773*

chuck [v] *throw aside, throw away, throw out*
abandon, can, cast, desert, discard, ditch, eightysix*, eject, fire, fling, flip, forsake, give the heave ho*, heave, hurl, jettison, junk, launch, pitch, quit, reject, relinquish, renounce, scrap, shed, shy, sling, slough, toss; SEE CONCEPTS *180,222*

chuckle [v] *giggle*
cackle, chortle, crow, exult, guffaw, hee-haw*, laugh, smile, snicker, snigger, sniggle, teehee*, titter; SEE CONCEPT *77*

chug [v] *drink quickly*
chug-a-lug, down, drink in one draft; SEE CONCEPT *169*

chum [n] *friend*
associate, bro*, buddy, co-mate, companion, comrade, crony, mate, pal, playmate, sis*; SEE CONCEPT *423*

chummy [adj] *friendly*
affectionate, buddy-buddy*, close, confidential, constant, cozy, familiar, intimate, pally*, palsy-walsy*, thick*; SEE CONCEPTS *401,555*

chunk [n] *mass, slab of something*
block, clod, dollop, glob, gob, hunk, lump, nugget, part, piece, portion, wad; SEE CONCEPT *471*

chunky [adj] *fat, plump*
beefy, chubby, dumpy, heavyset, husky, rotund, scrub, squat, stocky, stout, stubby, thick-bodied, thickset; SEE CONCEPTS *491,773*

church [n1] *religious institution, building*
abbey, basilica, bethel, cathedral, chancel, chantry, chapel, fold, house of God, house of prayer, house of worship, Lord's house, minster, mission, mosque, oratory, parish, sacellum, sanctuary, shrine, synagogue, tabernacle, temple; SEE CONCEPTS *368,449*

church [n2] *religious belief, group*
affiliation, body, chapter, communion, congregation, connection, creed, cult, denomination, doctrine, faction, faith, gathering, ism, order, persuasion, religion, schism, sect, society; SEE CONCEPTS *369,689*

churl [n] *rude and ill-bred, a boor; person overly concerned with saving money*
beast, chuff, clodhopper*, miser, mucker*, niggard*, oaf, peasant, provincial, rustic, tightwad, yokel; SEE CONCEPT *423*

churlish [adj] *crude, boorish*
base, blunt, brusque, cantankerous*, cloddish, clodhopping*, crabbed, crude, crusty, curt, cussed*, discourteous, dour, grouchy, gruff, grumpy, harsh, ill-tempered, impolite, loutish, lowbred, mean, miserly, morose, oafish, ornery*, rude, rustic, snippy*, sullen, surly, touchy*, ugly, uncivil, uncivilized, uncultured, unmannerly, unneighborly, unpolished, unsociable, vulgar; SEE CONCEPT *404*

churn [v] *mix up, beat*
agitate, boil, bubble, convulse, ferment, foam, froth, jolt, moil, seethe, simmer, stir up, swirl, toss; SEE CONCEPTS *147,170*

chute [n] *ramp, slope*
channel, course, fall, gutter, incline, rapid, runway, slide, trough; SEE CONCEPTS *440,471*

chutzpah [n] *fearlessness*
arrogance, audacity, backbone*, balls*, boldness, brass, gall, nerve, spine*; SEE CONCEPT *633*

cinch [n] *easy accomplishment*
breeze, cakewalk, child's play*, duck soup*, no sweat*, piece of cake*, snap; SEE CONCEPT *693*

cinder [n] *hot ash*
clinker, ember, hot coal, soot; SEE CONCEPT *260*

cinema [n] *movie industry; movie arena*
big screen*, bijou, cine, drive-in, film, flicks*, motion pictures, movie house, movie theater, moving pictures, nabes*, photoplay, pictures, picture show, playhouse, show, silver screen*; SEE CONCEPTS *293,349*

cipher [n] *zero; nothingness*
blank, diddly squat*, goose egg*, insignificancy, nada*, naught, nil, nobody, nonentity, nothing, nought, nullity, squat, zilch, zip, zippo*, zot*; SEE CONCEPTS *668,787*

cipher [v] *figure out code*
break, calculate, clear up, compute, count, decipher, estimate, figure, reckon, resolve, solve, unravel; SEE CONCEPT *37*

circa [prep] *approximately*
about, around, close on, in the region of, near, nearby, nigh, roughly; SEE CONCEPT *820*

circle [n1] *orb, round figure*
amphitheater, aureole, band, belt, bowl, bracelet, circlet, circuit, circumference, circus, cirque, coil, colure, compass, cordon, corona, crown, cycle, disc, disk, ecliptic, enclosure, equator, full turn, globe, halo, hoop, horizon, lap, meridian, orbit, parallel of latitude, perimeter, periphery, record, revolution, ring, ringlet, round, sphere, stadium, tire, turn, vortex, wheel, wreath, zodiac; SEE CONCEPT *436*

circle [n2] *group of close friends, associates*
assembly, bunch, cabal, camarilla, camp, clan, class, clique, club, companions, company, comrades, coterie, crew, cronies, crowd, crush, fraternity, gang, in-group, insiders, intimates, lot, Mafia, mob, outfit, party, posse, ring, school, set, society, sorority; SEE CONCEPTS *387,417*

circle [v] *go around, circumnavigate*
begird, belt, cincture, circuit, circulate, circumduct, circumscribe, coil, compass, curve, embrace, encircle, enclose, encompass, ensphere, envelop, gird, girdle, gyrate, gyre, hem in, loop,

mill around, pivot, revolve, ring, roll, rotate, round, spiral, surround, tour, wheel, whirl, wind about; SEE CONCEPT *758*

circuit [n] *revolution, track, boundary*
ambit, area, bounds, circle, circling, circulation, circumference, circumnavigation, circumscription, circumvolution, compass, course, cycle, district, gyration, gyre, journey, lap, limit, line, orbit, perambulation, perimeter, periphery, range, region, round, route, tour, tract, turn, turning, twirl, way, wheel, whirl, wind, winding, zone; SEE CONCEPTS *484,501,770*

circuitous [adj] *going around, indirect*
back road*, by way of, circular, collateral, complicated, devious, labyrinthine, long·way*, long way around*, meandering, oblique, rambling, roundabout, tortuous, winding around; SEE CONCEPTS *544,581*

circular [adj] *going around*
annular, circling, dislike, indirect, oblique, orbicular, round, rounded, spheroid; SEE CONCEPT *486*

circular [n] *handbill*
advertisement, booklet, broadside, brochure, flyer, handout, insert, leaflet, literature, notice, pamphlet, poster, publication, throwaway*; SEE CONCEPT *271*

circulate [v1] *make known*
bring out, broadcast, diffuse, disperse, disseminate, distribute, exchange, interview, issue, promulgate, propagate, publicize, publish, radiate, report, spread, strew, troll; SEE CONCEPTS *60,138*

circulate [v2] *flow*
actuate, circle, fly about, get about, get around, go about, gyrate, mill around, mobilize, move around, radiate, revolve, rotate, set off, travel, wander; SEE CONCEPT *147*

circulation [n1] *distribution*
apportionment, currency, dissemination, spread, transmission; SEE CONCEPTS *631,651*

circulation [n2] *moving circularly*
circling, circuit, circumvolution, current, flow, flowing, gyration, gyre, motion, revolution, rotation, round, turn, twirl, wheel, whirl; SEE CONCEPTS *147,738*

circumference [n] *edge, perimeter*
ambit, border, boundary, bounds, circuit, compass, confines, extremity, fringe, girth, limits, lip, margin, outline, periphery, rim, verge; SEE CONCEPT *484*

circumlocution [n] *indirect speech*
beating around the bush*, circumambages, diffuseness, discursiveness, euphemism, gassiness, indirectness, periphrase, periphrasis, pleonasm, prolixity, roundabout, tautology, verbal evasion, verbality, verbiage, wordiness; SEE CONCEPTS *51,266*

circumscribe [v] *mark off, delimit*
bar, bound, confine, define, delineate, demarcate, encircle, enclose, encompass, environ, girdle, hamper, hem in*, limit, nail down*, outline, prelimit, restrain, restrict, surround, trammel; SEE CONCEPTS *18,130*

circumspect [adj] *cautious, discreet*
attentive, cagey, calculating, canny, careful, chary, considerate, deliberate, discriminating, gingerly, guarded, heedful, judicious, meticulous, observant, politic, prudent, punctilious, safe, sagacious, sage, scrupulous, vigilant, wary, watchful; SEE CONCEPTS *403,544*

circumstance [*n*] *situation, condition*
accident, action, adjunct, affair, article, case, cause, coincidence, concern, contingency, crisis, destiny, detail, doom, element, episode, event, exigency, fact, factor, fate, feature, fortuity, go, happening, happenstance, incident, intervention, item, juncture, kismet, lot, matter, Moira, occasion, occurrence, particular, phase, place, point, portion, proviso, respect, scene, status, stipulation, supervention, thing, time, where it's at*; SEE CONCEPT 696

circumstances [*n*] *state of affairs in one's life*
assets, capital, chances, class, command, degree, dowry, financial status, footing, income, lifestyle, lot, means, net worth, outlook, position, precedence, prestige, property, prospects, prosperity, rank, rating, resources, situation, sphere, standing, state, station, status, substance, times, way of life, worldly goods; SEE CONCEPTS 335,388

circumstantial [*adj*] *incidental*
amplified, coincidental, concomitant, concurrent, conjectural, contingent, detailed, environmental, fortuitous, inconclusive, indirect, inferential, presumptive, provisional, uncertain; SEE CONCEPTS 556,582,653

circumvent [*v*] *fool, mislead*
avoid, beat, beguile, bilk, bypass, circumnavigate, cramp, crimp, deceive, detour, disappoint, dodge, dupe, elude, ensnare, entrap, escape, evade, foil, frustrate, get around, hoodwink, outflank, outwit, overreach, prevent, queer, ruin, shun, sidestep, skirt, stave off, steer clear of*, stump, stymie, thwart, trick, ward off; SEE CONCEPTS 59,102,121

circus [*n*] *fair with entertainment*
bazaar, big top, festival, gilly*, hippodrome, kermis, show, spectacle, three-ring*; SEE CONCEPT 293

citadel [*n*] *top, tower*
bastion, blockhouse, burgher, civilian, commoner, fication, fortress, keep, manor, redoubt, stronghold; SEE CONCEPTS 321,836

citation [*n1*] *excerpt*
example, illustration, mention, passage, quotation, quote, quoting, reference, saying, source; SEE CONCEPT 283

citation [*n2*] *award*
bidding, charge, commendation, encomium, mention, panegyric, reward, salutation, summons, tribute; SEE CONCEPTS 69,337

cite [*v1*] *note, quote*
adduce, advance, allege, allude to, appeal to, enumerate, evidence, excerpt, exemplify, extract, get down to brass tacks*, give as example, illustrate with, indicate, instance, lay, mention, name, number, offer, point out, present, recite, recount, reference, refer to, rehearse, remember, reminisce, repeat, specify, spell out, tell; SEE CONCEPT 57

cite [*v2*] *subpoena*
arraign, call, command, name, order, summon; SEE CONCEPT 317

citizen [*n*] *person native of country*
aborigine, burgess, burgher, civilian, commoner, cosmopolite, denizen, dweller, freeman/woman, householder, inhabitant, John/Jane Q. Public*, member of body politic, member of community, national, native, naturalized person, occupant,

resident, settler, subject, taxpayer, townsperson, urbanite, villager, voter; SEE CONCEPT 413

city [*adj*] *metropolitan*
burghal, citified, civic, civil, interurban, intraurban, megalopolitan, municipal, urban; SEE CONCEPT 536

city [*n*] *large town*
apple*, boom town, borough, burg, capital, center, conurbation, downtown, megalopolis, metropolis, metropolitan area, municipality, place, polis, port, urban place, urbs*; SEE CONCEPT 507

civic [*adj*] *community*
borough, civil, communal, local, metropolitan, municipal, national, public, urban; SEE CONCEPTS 536,583

civil [*adj1*] *civic, community*
civilian, domestic, governmental, home, interior, local, municipal, national, political, public; SEE CONCEPTS 536,583

civil [*adj2*] *obliging, kind*
accommodating, affable, civilized, complaisant, cordial, courteous, courtly, cultivated, diplomatic, formal, genteel, gracious, mannerly, polished, polite, politic, refined, suave, urbane, well-bred, wellmannered; SEE CONCEPT 401

civilian [*adj*] *nonmilitary*
noncombatant, noncombative, nonmilitant, not in armed forces, pacificist, private, unhostile; SEE CONCEPT 555

civilian [*n*] *nonmilitary person*
citizen, civ*, civvie*, commoner, noncombatant, private citizen, subject; SEE CONCEPT 423

civilization [*n1*] *culture, sophistication*
acculturation, advancement, breeding, civility, cultivation, development, edification, education, elevation, enlightenment, illumination, polish, progress, refinement, social well-being; SEE CONCEPT 388

civilization [*n2*] *society*
civilized life, community, customs, literate society, modern humanity, mores, nation, people, polity, way of life; SEE CONCEPTS 388,417

civilize [*v*] *make cultured; develop*
acculturate, acquaint, advance, better, cultivate, edify, educate, elevate, enlighten, ennoble, enrich, ethicize, foster, help forward, humanize, idealize, improve, indoctrinate, inform, instruct, polish, promote, reclaim, refine, sophisticate, spiritualize, tame, uplift; SEE CONCEPTS 244,385

civilized [*adj*] *polished*
advanced, civil, cultured, educated, enlightened, humane, refined, sophisticated, urbane; SEE CONCEPT 562

civil rights [*n*] *freedoms of citizens*
civil liberties, constitutional rights, freedom of religion, freedom of speech, freedoms, God-given rights, rights; SEE CONCEPT 376

claim [*n*] *property, right demanded or reserved*
affirmation, allegation, application, assertion, birthright, call, case, counterclaim, declaration, demand, dibs, due, entreaty, interest, lien, part, petition, plea, postulation, prerogative, pretense, pretension, privilege, profession, protestation, reclamation, request, requirement, requisition, suit, title, ultimatum; SEE CONCEPTS 278,318,376,709

claim [*v*] *demand, maintain property or right*
adduce, advance, allege, ask, assert, believe, call for, challenge, collect, declare, defend, exact, have dibs on something*, hit, hit up*, hold, hold

ch
cl

out for*, insist, justify, knock, lay claim to, need, pick up, pop the question*, postulate, pretend, profess, pronounce, require, requisition, solicit, stake out, take, uphold, vindicate; SEE CONCEPTS 53,129

clairvoyance [n] *intuition*
acumen, discernment, ESP*, feeling, foreknowledge, insight, omen, penetration, perception, precognition, premonition, psyche, sixth sense*, telepathy; SEE CONCEPTS 409,410

clairvoyant [adj] *intuitive, psychic*
clear-sighted, discerning, extrasensory, farseeing, far-sighted, fey, judicious, long-sighted, new age*, oracular, penetrating, perceptive, prescient, prophetic, second-sighted, sibylline, spiritualistic, telepathic, vatic, visionary; SEE CONCEPTS 402,403

clairvoyant [n] *person who is psychic*
augur, channeller, diviner, fortune-teller, haruspex, horoscopist, medium, oracle, palm reader, prophet, seer, sibyl, soothsayer, telepath, telepathist, visionary, voodoo doctor*; SEE CONCEPT 423

clam [n] *bivalve living in ocean*
cherrystone, littleneck, mollusk, quahog; SEE CONCEPT 394

clammy [adj] *damp*
close, dank, drizzly, moist, mucid, mucous, muculent, pasty, slimy, soggy, sticky, sweating, sweaty, wet; SEE CONCEPT 603

clamor [n] *loud cry; commotion*
agitation, babel, blare, brouhaha*, bustle, buzz, clinker, complaint, convulsion, din, discord, exclamation, ferment, hassle, hoo-ha*, hubba-hubba*, hubbub, hullabaloo*, hurly-burly*, lament, noise, outcry, pandemonium, protesting, racket, remonstrance, row, ruckus, shout, shouting, to-do, tumult, turmoil, upheaval, uproar, vociferation; SEE CONCEPTS 386,595,674

clamor [v] *cry out, make commotion*
agitate, bark, bawl, bellow, bluster, claim, debate, demand, dispute, holler, put up a howl*, raise Cain*, raise the roof*, roar, rout, shout; SEE CONCEPTS 77,106

clamp [n] *fastener*
bracket, catch, clasp, grip, hold, lock, nipper, press, snap, vice; SEE CONCEPT 499

clamp [v] *fasten*
brace, clench, clinch, fix, impose, make fast, secure; SEE CONCEPTS 85,160

clan [n] *family, clique*
association, band, bunch, club, coterie, crew, crowd, crush, faction, folks, gang, group, house, insiders, kinfolks, mob, moiety, organization, outfit, race, ring, sect, set, society, sodality, stock, tribe; SEE CONCEPTS 296,387

clandestine [adj] *secret, sly*
artful, cloak-and-dagger, closet, concealed, covert, foxy, fraudulent, furtive, hidden, hush-hush*, illegitimate, illicit, in holes and corners*, on the Q. T.*, on the quiet, private, sneaky, stealthy, surreptitious, undercover, underground, underhand, under-the-counter*, under wraps*; SEE CONCEPTS 555,576

clank [n] *metallic noise*
bang, bong, clash, clink, jangle, ring; SEE CONCEPT 595

clank [v] *clang, clatter*
bong, clash, clink, jangle, make noise, resound, reverberate, ring, toll; SEE CONCEPT 65

clannish [adj] *exclusive, select*
akin, alike, associative, cliquish, close, insular, like, narrow, related, reserved, restricting, restrictive, sectarian, unfriendly, unreceptive; SEE CONCEPT 555

clap [n] *loud hitting noise*
applause, bang, blast, boom, burst, crack, crash, handclap, pat, slam, slap, smash, strike, thrust, thunder, thunderclap, thwack, wallop, whack, wham; SEE CONCEPTS 189,595

clap [v] *applaud; slap with approbation*
acclaim, approve, bang, cheer, give a big hand*, give a hand*, hear it for*, pat, praise, slap, strike gently, thwack, whack; SEE CONCEPTS 185,189

clarification [n] *explanation*
description, elucidation, exposition, illumination, interpretation, resolution, simplification, solution, unravelment, vivification; SEE CONCEPTS 57,274

clarify [v1] *explain, make clear*
analyze, break down, clear up, define, delineate, draw a picture, elucidate, formulate, illuminate, illustrate, interpret, make perfectly clear, make plain, resolve, settle, shed light on*, simplify, spell out*, straighten out, throw light on; SEE CONCEPT 57

clarify [v2] *purify*
clean, cleanse, depurate, distill, filter, rarefy, refine; SEE CONCEPT 165

clarion [adj] *clear, stirring sound*
blaring, definite, inspiring, loud, ringing, sharp, shrill, strident; SEE CONCEPTS 562,592,594

clarity [n] *clearness*
accuracy, articulateness, brightness, certainty, cognizability, comprehensibility, conspicuousness, decipherability, definition, directness, distinctness, evidence, exactitude, exactness, explicability, explicitness, intelligibility, legibility, limpidity, limpidness, lucidity, manifestness, obviousness, openness, overtness, palpability, penetrability, perceptibility, perspicuity, plainness, precision, prominence, purity, salience, simplicity, tangibility, transparency, unambiguity, unmistakability; SEE CONCEPTS 409,638

clash [n1] *disagreement or fight, often brief*
affray, argument, battle, brawl, break, broil, brush, bump, collision, concussion, conflict, confrontation, crash, difference of opinion, discord, discordance, disharmony, dispute, donnybrook*, embroilment, encounter, engagement, fracas, fray, have a go at each other*, impact, jam, jar, jolt, jump, melee, misunderstanding, mix up, opposition, rift, riot, row, rumpus, run-in, rupture, scrap, scrimmage, set-to, shock, showdown, skirmish, smash, wallop; SEE CONCEPTS 46,106

clash [v1] *hit with a loud noise*
bang, bump, clang, clank, clatter, collide, crash, grate, grind, jangle, jar, jolt, prang, rattle, scrap, scrimmage, shock, smash, wallop; SEE CONCEPTS 65,189

clash [v2] *fight about, often verbally*
argue, bang heads*, battle, brawl, buck, combat, conflict, contend, cross swords, differ, disagree, encounter, feud, fret, gall, grapple, grate, mix it up*, quarrel, raise Cain*, row, try, war, wrangle; SEE CONCEPTS 46,106

clash [v3] *do not match*
be dissimilar, conflict, contrast, differ, disaccord, discord, disharmonize, mismatch, not go with; SEE CONCEPTS 655,664

clasp [*n*] *fastener; hold on something*
brooch, buckle, catch, clamp, clench, clinch, clip, clutch, embrace, fastening, fibula, grapple, grasp, grip, hasp, hold, hook, hug, pin, safety pin, snap; SEE CONCEPTS *497,641*

clasp [*v*] *grab tightly*
attack, bear hug*, buckle, clamp, clinch, clip, clutch, coll, concatenate, connect, embrace, enfold, fasten, glom onto*, grapple, grasp, grip, hold, hug, pin, press, seize, snatch, squeeze, take; SEE CONCEPTS *85,160,191,219*

class [*adj*] *stylish; with panache*
chic, classy, dashing, fashionable, fine, fly*, foxy*, sharp; SEE CONCEPT *589*

class [*n1*] *kind, sort, category*
branch, brand, breed, cast, caste, character, classification, collection, color, degree, denomination, department, description, designation, distinction, division, domain, estate, family, feather, frame, genre, genus, grade, grain, grouping, hierarchy, humor, ilk, kidney, league, make, mold, name, nature, order, origin, property, province, quality, range, rank, rate, school, sect, section, selection, set, source, species, sphere, standing, status, stripe, style, suit, temperament, value, variety; SEE CONCEPT *378*

class [*n2*] *societal group, background*
ancestry, birth, bourgeoisie, breed, caliber, caste, circle, clan, clique, club, company, condition, connection, coterie, cultural level, degree, derivation, descent, estate, extraction, family, genealogy, grade, hierarchy, influence, intelligentsia, league, lineage, moiety, nobility, origin, pecking order*, pedigree, pigeonhole*, place, position, prestige, quality, sect, social rank, source, sphere, standing, state, station, status, stock, strain, stratum, the right stuff*, tier, title; SEE CONCEPTS *296,387,388,417*

class [*n3*] *group in school*
academy, colloquium, course, course of study, division, form, grade, homeroom, lecture group, line, quiz group, recitation, room, round table, section, seminar, seminary, session, study, study group, subdivision, subject; SEE CONCEPTS *286,287,288,289*

class [*v*] *categorize*
account, allot, appraise, assess, assign, assort, brand, classify, codify, consider, designate, divide, evaluate, gauge, grade, group, hold, identify, judge, mark, part, pigeonhole*, rank, rate, reckon, regard, score, separate; SEE CONCEPTS *39,135*

classic [*adj2*] *characteristic, regular*
prototypal, prototypical, representative, simple, standard, time-honored, typical, usual, vintage; SEE CONCEPTS *533,547*

classic [*n*] *model*
chef d'oeuvre, exemplar, magnum opus, paradigm, prototype, standard, tour de force; SEE CONCEPTS *259,655,686*

classical [*adj*] *concerning ancient culture*
academic, Attic, Augustan, belletristic, bookish, canonic, canonical, classic, classicistic, Doric, Grecian, Greek, Hellenic, Homeric, humanistic, Ionic, Latin, Roman, scholastic, Virgilian; SEE CONCEPTS *536,549*

classical [*adj2*] *simple, chaste*
classic, elegant, harmonious, pure, refined, restrained, symmetrical, understated, well-proportioned; SEE CONCEPT *589*

classic/classical [*adj1*] *best, model*
archetypal, capital, champion, consummate, definitive, distinguished, esthetic, excellent, exemplary, famous, fine, finest, first-rate, flawless, ideal, master, masterly, paradigmatic, paramount, perfect, prime, quintessential, ranking, standard, superior, top, top-notch, vintage, well-known; SEE CONCEPT *574*

classicism [*n*] *simple style; regularity, restraint*
aesthetic principle, Atticism, balance, Ciceronianism, clarity, class, classicalism, conventional formality, dignity, elegance, excellence, finish, formality, formal style, grandeur, grand style, Hellenism, high art, lucidity, majesty, neoclassicism, nobility, objectivity, polish, proportion, propriety, pure taste, purity, rationalism, refinement, rhythm, severity, simplicity, sobriety, sublimity, symmetry; SEE CONCEPT *655*

classification [*n*] *categorization*
allocation, alloting, allotment, analysis, apportionment, arrangement, assignment, assortment, cataloguing, categorizing, codification, collocation, consignment, coordination, denomination, department, designation, disposal, disposition, distributing, distribution, division, echelon, gradation, grade, grading, graduation, group, grouping, kind, order, ordering, ordination, organization, pigeonholing*, regulation, sizing, sorting, systematization, tabulating, taxonomy, typecasting; SEE CONCEPTS *18,39,135,378*

classified [*adj*] *top-secret*
confidential, private, restricted, secret; SEE CONCEPTS *267,576*

classify [*v*] *categorize*
allocate, allot, alphabetize, analyze, arrange, assort, brand, break down, button down*, catalogue, class, codify, collocate, coordinate, correlate, dispose, distinguish, distribute, divide, docket, embody, file, grade, group, incorporate, index, label, match, name, number, order, organize, peg*, pigeonhole*, put away, put down as, put down for, range, rank, rank out, rate, regiment, segregate, size, size up, sort, systematize, tab, tabulate, tag, take one's measure, ticket, type, typecast; SEE CONCEPTS *18,39,135*

classy [*adj*] *stylish, having panache*
chic, dashing, elegant, exclusive, fashionable, high-class, in, in vogue, mod, modish, posh, select, sharp, superior, swank, swanky, tony, uptown; SEE CONCEPT *589*

clatter [*n*] *loud noise*
ballyhoo*, bluster, clack, clangor, hullabaloo*, pandemonium, racket, rattle, rumpus, shattering, smashing; SEE CONCEPTS *181,189,595*

clatter [*v*] *crash; make racket*
bang, bluster, bump, clang, clank, clash, hurtle, noise, rattle, roar, shatter, smash; SEE CONCEPTS *65,181,189*

clause [*n*] *provision in document*
article, catch*, chapter, codicil, condition, fine print*, heading, item, joker*, kicker*, limitation, paragraph, part, passage, point, provision, proviso, requirement, rider, section, small print*, specification, stipulation, string attached to something*, ultimatum; SEE CONCEPTS *270,275*

claw [*n*] *nail of animal; tool shaped like nail of an animal*
barb, cant hook, clapperclaw, crook, fang, fingernail, grapnel, grappler, hook, manus, nail claw,

cl
cl

nipper, paw, pincer, retractile, spur, talon, tentacle, unguis, ungula; SEE CONCEPT *392*

claw [*v*] *using sharp nail*
break, dig, graze, hurt, itch, lacerate, mangle, maul, open, rip, scrabble, scrap, scrape, scratch, tear; SEE CONCEPTS *178,214,220*

clay [*n*] *workable earth material*
adobe, argil, argillaceous earth, bole, brick, china material, clunch, earth, kaolin, loam, loess, marl, mud, porcelain material, pottery, slip, terra cotta, till, wacke; SEE CONCEPT *509*

clean [*adj1*] *not dirty; uncluttered*
apple-pie order*, blank, bright, cleansed, clear, delicate, dirtless, elegant, faultless, flawless, fresh, graceful, hygienic, immaculate, laundered, neat, neat as a button*, neat as a pin*, orderly, pure, sanitary, shining, simple, snowy, sparkling, speckless, spic and span*, spotless, squeaky, stainless, taintless, tidy, trim, unblemished, unpolluted, unsmudged, unsoiled, unspotted, unstained, unsullied, untarnished, vanilla*, washed, well-kept, white; SEE CONCEPT *485*

clean [*adj2*] *sterile*
antiseptic, aseptic, clarified, decontaminated, disinfected, hygienic, pure, purified, sanitary, sterilized, unadulterated, uncontaminated, uninfected, unpolluted, unsullied, wholesome; SEE CONCEPTS *314,485*

clean [*adj3*] *chaste, virtuous*
blameless, crimeless, decent, exemplary, faultless, good, guiltless, honorable, inculpable, innocent, modest, moral, respectable, sinless, undefiled, unguilty, unsullied, upright, wholesome; SEE CONCEPT *404*

clean [*adj4*] *precise, sharp*
clear, clear-cut, correct, definite, distinct, legible, neat, plain, readable, simple, trim, uncluttered; SEE CONCEPT *535*

clean [*adj5*] *complete, thorough*
absolute, conclusive, decisive, entire, final, perfect, total, unimpaired, whole; SEE CONCEPT *531*

clean [*v*] *make undirty, uncluttered*
absterge, bath, bathe, blot, brush, cauterize, clarify, cleanse, clear the decks*, clear up, deodorize, depurate, deterge, disinfect, do up*, dredge, dust, edulcorate, elutriate, erase, expunge, expurgate, flush, hackle, launder, lave, mop, neaten, pick, pick up, polish, purge, purify, rake, rasp, refine, rinse, rout out, sanitize, scald, scour, scrape, scrub, shake out, shampoo, soak, soap, sponge, spruce up*, sterilize, straighten up, swab, sweep, tidy up, vacuum, wash, whisk, winnow, wipe; SEE CONCEPTS *161,165*

clean-cut [*adj*] *neat, clearly outlined*
categorical, chiseled, clear, definite, definitive, etched, explicit, express, sharp, specific, unambiguous, well-defined; SEE CONCEPTS *490,535*

cleanse [*v*] *make undirty; wash*
absolve, clarify, clean, clear, depurate, disinfect, expurgate, launder, lustrate, purge, purify, refine, restore, rinse, sanitize, scour, scrub, sterilize; SEE CONCEPT *165*

cleanser [*n*] *strong disinfectant, solvent*
abrasive, abstergent, antiseptic, cathartic, deodorant, detergent, fumigant, lather, polish, purgative, purifier, scourer, soap, soap powder, suds; SEE CONCEPT *492*

clear [*adj1*] *cloudless, bright*
clarion, crystal, fair, fine, halcyon, light, luminous, pleasant, rainless, shining, shiny, sunny,

sunshiny, unclouded, undarkened, undimmed; SEE CONCEPTS *525,617,627*

clear [*adj2*] *understandable, apparent*
apprehensible, audible, clear-cut, coherent, comprehensible, conspicuous, crystal, definite, distinct, evident, explicit, express, graspable, incontrovertible, intelligible, knowable, legible, loud enough, lucent, lucid, manifest, obvious, open and shut*, palpable, patent, perceptible, perspicuous, plain, precise, pronounced, readable, recognizable, sharp, simple, spelled out*, straightforward, transparent, transpicuous, unambiguous, unblurred, uncomplicated, unequivocal, unmistakable, unquestionable; SEE CONCEPTS *402,562*

clear [*adj3*] *open, unhindered*
bare, empty, free, smooth, stark, unhampered, unimpeded, unlimited, unobstructed, vacant, vacuous, void; SEE CONCEPT *490*

clear [*adj4*] *transparent*
apparent, cloudless, crystal, crystal clear, crystalline, glassy, limpid, pellucid, pure, see-through, thin, tralucent, translucent, translucid; SEE CONCEPTS *618,619*

clear [*adj5*] *not guilty*
absolved, blameless, clean, cleared, discharged, dismissed, exculpated, exonerated, guiltless, immaculate, innocent, pure, sinless, stainless, unblemished, uncensurable, undefiled, untarnished, untroubled; SEE CONCEPTS *319,404*

clear [*adj6*] *certain in one's mind*
absolute, confirmed, convinced, decided, definite, positive, resolved, satisfied, sure; SEE CONCEPT *403*

clear [*v1*] *clean, clear away*
ameliorate, break up, brighten, burn off, clarify, cleanse, disencumber, disengage, disentangle, eliminate, empty, erase, extricate, free, lighten, loosen, lose, meliorate, open, purify, refine, rid, rule out, shake off, sweep, throw off, tidy, unblock, unburden, unclog, unload, unloose, unpack, untie, vacate, void, wipe; SEE CONCEPTS *165,211*

clear [*v2*] *liberate; free from uncertainty*
absolve, acquit, clarify, defog*, discharge, disculpate, emancipate, exculpate, exonerate, explain, find innocent, let go, let off, let off the hook*, release, relieve, set free, vindicate; SEE CONCEPTS *7,22,127*

clear [*v3*] *pass over, often by jumping*
hurdle, leap, miss, negotiate, overleap, surmount, vault; SEE CONCEPT *194*

clear [*v4*] *profit*
accumulate, acquire, clean up*, earn, gain, gather, get, glean, make, net, obtain, pick up, realize, reap, receive, secure, win; SEE CONCEPTS *129,342*

clearance [*n1*] *permission for activity*
approval, authorization, consent, endorsement, go-ahead*, green light*, leave, okay, sanction, say-so*; SEE CONCEPT *376*

clearance [*n2*] *gap above something*
allowance, assart, defoliated area, empty space, expanse, gap, headroom, margin, opening, open space; SEE CONCEPT *513*

clear-cut [*adj*] *definite*
assured, categorical, crystalline, decided, definitive, distinct, evident, explicit, express, indubitable, lucent, lucid, obvious, plain, precise, pronounced, sharp-cut, specific, straightforward,

unambiguous, undisputed, undoubted, unequivocal, unquestioned, well-defined; SEE CONCEPT 535

clearing [n] *gap in area*
allowance, assart, clearance, defoliated area, dell, empty space, expanse, gap, glade, headroom, margin, opening, open space; SEE CONCEPT 513

clearly [adv] *without any doubt*
acutely, apparently, audibly, beyond doubt, certainly, conspicuously, decidedly, definitely, discernibly, distinctly, evidently, incontestably, incontrovertibly, indubitably, lucidly, manifestly, markedly, noticeably, obviously, openly, overtly, patently, penetratingly, perceptibly, plainly, positively, precisely, prominently, purely, recognizably, seemingly, sharply, sonorously, surely, translucently, transparently, undeniably, undoubtedly, unmistakably; SEE CONCEPTS 535,552

clear out [v1] *empty something*
clean out, dispose of, eliminate, exhaust, get rid of, remove, sort, tidy up; SEE CONCEPT 211

clear out [v2] *leave, often quickly*
beat it*, begone, decamp, depart, go, hightail*, kite*, make oneself scarce*, remove oneself, retire, scram, skedaddle*, split*, take a hike*, take off, vamoose*, withdraw; SEE CONCEPT 195

clear up [v1] *explain; resolve*
answer, cipher, clarify, decipher, dissolve, elucidate, figure out, illuminate, illustrate, make plausible, make reasonable, puzzle out, resolve, solve, straighten out, tidy, unfold, unravel; SEE CONCEPTS 37,57

clear up [v2] *become improved*
become fair, become sunny, blow over, brighten, die away, die down, improve, lapse, lift, pick up, run its course*; SEE CONCEPT 700

cleavage [n] *gap*
break, chasm, cleft, discontinuity, divide, division, fracture, hole, rift, schism, separation, severance, split, valley; SEE CONCEPT 513

cleave [v1] *divide, split*
carve, chop, crack, cut, dissect, dissever, disunite, divorce, hack, hew, open, part, pierce, rend, rip, rive, separate, sever, slice, stab, sunder, tear asunder, whack; SEE CONCEPTS 98,137,176

cleave [v2] *stand by, stick together*
abide by, adhere, agree, associate, attach, be devoted to, be tight with*, be true*, cling, cohere, combine, freeze to*, hold, join, link, remain, stay put, unite; SEE CONCEPTS 8,113

cleft [adj] *separated, split*
broken, cloven, cracked, crannied, crenelated, parted, perforated, pierced, rent, riven, ruptured, separated, sundered, torn; SEE CONCEPT 490

cleft [n] *break, gap*
aperture, arroyo, breach, canyon, chasm, chink, cleavage, clough, clove, crack, cranny, crevasse, crevice, fissure, fracture, gorge, gulch, opening, ravine, rent, rift, rima, rimation, rime, schism, slit; SEE CONCEPT 513

clemency [n] *forgiveness*
caritas, charity, compassion, endurance, equitableness, fairness, forbearance, gentleness, grace, humanity, indulgence, justness, kindness, lenience, leniency, lenity, lifesaver, mercifulness, mercy, mildness, moderation, soft-heartedness, sufferance, tenderness, tolerance, toleration; SEE CONCEPTS 410,644

clement [adj1] *calm, mild (weather)*
balmy, clear, fair, fine, moderate, peaceful, temperate, warm; SEE CONCEPT 525

clement [adj2] *forgiving*
benevolent, benign, benignant, charitable, compassionate, easy, forbearing, gentle, humane, humanitarian, indulgent, kind, kind-hearted, kindly, lenient, merciful, mild, soft-hearted, sympathetic, tender, tolerant; SEE CONCEPTS 404,550

clench [v] *grasp*
clamp, clasp, clinch, clutch, constrict, contract, double up, draw together, grapple, grip, hold; SEE CONCEPT 191

clergy [n] *ministry of church*
canonicate, canonry, cardinalate, churchpersons, clerics, conclave, deaconry, diaconate, ecclesiastics, first estate, holy order, pastorate, prelacy, priesthood, rabbinate, the cloth, the desk, the pulpit; SEE CONCEPT 369

clergyperson [n] *minister of church*
abbey, archbishop, bishop, blackcoat*, cardinal, cassock, chaplain, churchperson, cleric, clerk, curate, dean, divine, ecclesiast, ecclesiastic, evangelist, father, missionary, monsignor, padre, parson, pastor, person of God, person of the cloth, pontiff, preacher, predicant, priest, primate, pulpitarian, pulpiteer, rabbi, rector, reverend, sermonizer, shepherd, vicar; SEE CONCEPT 361

clerical [adj1] *secretarial*
accounting, bookkeeping, clerkish, clerkly, office, pink collar*, scribal, stenographic, subordinate, typing, white collar*, written; SEE CONCEPT 536

clerical [adj2] *concerning clergy*
apostolic, canonical, churchly, cleric, ecclesiastic, ecclesiastical, episcopal, holy, ministerial, monastic, monkish, papal, parsonical, parsonish, pastoral, pontifical, prelatic, priestly, rabbinical, sacerdotal, sacred, theocratical; SEE CONCEPT 536

clerk [n] *assistant*
agent, amanuensis, auditor, bookkeeper, cashier, copyist, counter jumper*, counterperson, employee, notary, office helper, operator, paper pusher*, paper shuffler*, pencil pusher*, pen pusher*, receptionist, recorder, registrar, salesperson, secretary, seller, shopperson, stenographer, teller, transcriber, white collar*, worker; SEE CONCEPT 348

clever [adj] *bright, ingenious*
able, adept, adroit, alert, apt, astute, brainy, brilliant, cagey, canny, capable, competent, crackerjack*, cunning, deep, dexterous/dextrous, discerning, egghead*, expert, foxy*, gifted, good, handy, intelligent, inventive, keen, knowing, knowledgeable, many-sided, nimble, nobody's fool*, pretty, pro, qualified, quick, quick on trigger*, quick-witted, rational, resourceful, sagacious, savvy, sensible, sharp, shrewd, skilled, skillful, slick, sly, smart, sprightly, talented, versatile, wise, witty; SEE CONCEPT 402

cleverness [n] *brightness, ingenuity*
ability, adroitness, astuteness, brains, calculation, canniness, dexterity, discernment, flair, gift, gumption, intelligence, quickness, quick wit, resourcefulness, sagacity, sense, sharpness, shrewdness, skill, smartness, talent, wisdom, wit; SEE CONCEPT 409

cl
cl

cliché [*n*] *overused, hackneyed phrase*
adage, banality, boiler plate*, bromide, buzzword, chestnut*, commonplace, corn*, counterword, familiar tune, motto, old story*, platitude, potboiler, prosaism, proverb, rubber stamp*, saying, shibboleth, slogan, stale saying, stereotype, threadbare phrase, triteness, trite remark, triviality, truism, vapid expression; SEE CONCEPTS 275,278

click [*n/v/*] *metallic sound*
bang, beat, clack, snap, tick; SEE CONCEPTS 65,595

click [*v2*] *fall into place*
become clear, be compatible, be on same wavelength*, come off*, feel a rapport*, get on*, go, go off well*, go over, hit it off*, make a hit*, make sense, match, meet with approval, pan out*, prove out, succeed, take to each other*; SEE CONCEPT 704

client [*n*] *customer*
applicant, believer, buyer, chump, consumer, dependent, disciple, follower, front, habitué, head, mark, patient, patron, protégé, protégée, purchaser, shopper, walk-in, ward; SEE CONCEPT 348

clientele [*n*] *customers of business*
audience, business, clientage, clientry, clients, constituency, cortege, dependents, following, market, patronage, patrons, public, regulars, trade; SEE CONCEPT 348

cliff [*n*] *overhang on hill or mountain*
bluff, crag, escarpment, face, precipice, rock face, rocky height, scar, scarp, steep rock, wall; SEE CONCEPT 509

cliffhanger [*n*] *something suspenseful*
close call, close shave*, narrow escape, shocker, spine-chiller, suspenser*, thriller, white knuckle; SEE CONCEPTS 410,679

climactic/climacteric [*adj*] *decisive*
acute, climactical, critical, crucial, desperate, dire, paramount, peak; SEE CONCEPT 567

climate [*n1*] *weather of region*
altitude, aridity, atmospheric conditions, characteristic weather, clime, conditions, humidity, latitude, meteorological character, meteorologic conditions, temperature; SEE CONCEPT 524

climate [*n2*] *mood of situation*
ambience, ambient, atmosphere, disposition, environment, feeling, medium, milieu, mise-en-scène, mood, surroundings, temper, tendency, trend; SEE CONCEPT 673

climax [*n*] *peak, culmination*
acme, apex, apogee, ascendancy, capsheaf, capstone, climacteric, crest, crowning point, extremity, head, height, highlight, high spot, intensification, limit, maximum, meridian, ne plus ultra, orgasm, payoff*, pinnacle, pitch, summit, tiptop, top, turning point, utmost, zenith; SEE CONCEPTS 706,836

climax [*v*] *come to top; culminate*
accomplish, achieve, break the record*, cap, come, come to a head*, conclude, content, crown, end, finish, fulfill, hit high spot, orgasm, peak, please, reach a peak, reach the zenith, rise to crescendo*, satisfy, succeed, terminate, top, tower; SEE CONCEPTS 375,704,706

climb [*v*] *crawl, move up*
ape up*, ascend, clamber, escalade, escalate, go up, mount, rise, scale, soar, top; SEE CONCEPT 166

clinch [*v1*] *secure a goal*
assure, cap, conclude, confirm, decide, determine, seal, seize, set, settle, sew up, verify; SEE CONCEPT 706

clinch [*v2*] *hold securely; grab*
bolt, clamp, clasp, clench, clutch, cuddle, embrace, enfold, fasten, fix, grab hold of, grapple, grasp, grip, hug, lay hands on, make fast, nail, press, rivet, secure, seize, snatch, squeeze; SEE CONCEPTS 191,219

clincher [*n*] *settling event*
capper, closer, coup de grâce, crowning blow*, culmination, deathblow*, deciding moment, finisher, finishing touch; SEE CONCEPTS 230,635,676

cling [*v*] *attach to*
adhere, be true to, cherish, clasp, cleave to, clutch, cohere, continue, embrace, endure, fasten, freeze to, grasp, grip, hang in, hang onto, hold fast, hug, last, linger, squeeze, stay put, stick, stick like glue*; SEE CONCEPTS 85,160,190

clinic [*n*] *medical center*
dispensary, hospital, infirmary, sick bay, surgery center; SEE CONCEPTS 312,439,449

clinical [*adj*] *dispassionate*
analytic, antiseptic, cold, detached, disinterested, emotionless, impersonal, objective, scientific, unemotional; SEE CONCEPT 404

clink [*n/v*] *bang against, ring*
chink, clang, jangle, jingle, sound, tingle, tinkle; SEE CONCEPTS 65,595

clip [*v1*] *cut short*
bob, crop, curtail, cut, cut back, decrease, dock, lower, mow, pare, prune, reduce, shave, shear, shorten, skive, slash, snip, trim, truncate; SEE CONCEPTS 137,176

clip [*v2/n*] *punch*
blow, box, clout, cuff, knock, punch, smack, sock, thump, wallop, whack; SEE CONCEPT 189

clique [*n*] *group of friends*
bunch, cabal, camarilla, camp, circle, clan, club, coterie, crew, crowd, crush, faction, gang, in-group, insiders, lobby, Mafia, mob, organization, outfit, pack, posse, ring, set, society; SEE CONCEPTS 387,417

cloak [*n*] *cover; coat*
beard, blind, camouflage, cape, capote, disguise, facade, face, front, guise, manteau, mantle, mask, pretext, semblance, shawl, shield, show, veneer, wrap; SEE CONCEPTS 451,475,680

cloak [*v*] *disguise*
blanket, camouflage, coat, conceal, cover, curtain, dissemble, dissimulate, dress up, hide, mask, obscure, pretext, screen, shroud, veil; SEE CONCEPT 188

clobber [*v*] *hit, beat*
belt, blast, drub, lambaste*, lick, shellac*, slam, slug, smash, smear, smother, thrash, trim, wallop, whip; SEE CONCEPTS 189,252

clock [*n*] *timekeeping device*
alarm, Big Ben*, chroniker*, chronograph, chronometer, digital watch, hourglass, pendulum, stopwatch, sundial, tattler, ticker*, ticktock*, timekeeper, timemarker, timepiece, timer, turnip*, watch; SEE CONCEPTS 463,819

clockwork [*n*] *being on time; precision*
accuracy, consistency, perfect timing, regularity, smoothness; SEE CONCEPT 818

clod [*n*] *stupid person*
blockhead*, boor, chump, clown, dimwit*, dolt,

dope*, dumbbell, dummy, dunce, fool, imbecile, lame-brain*, lout, oaf, simpleton; SEE CONCEPTS *412,423*

clog [*n*] *blockage*
bar, block, blockade, burden, cumbrance, dead weight, drag, encumbrance, hindrance, impedance, impediment, obstruction, snag; SEE CONCEPTS *121,674*

clog [*v*] *block, hinder*
burden, choke, close, congest, curb, dam up, encumber, entrammel, fetter, fill, glut, hamper, impede, jam, leash, obstruct, occlude, plug, seal, shackle, stopper, stop up, stuff, tie, trammel; SEE CONCEPTS *121,130,190*

cloister [*n*] *secluded religious place*
abbey, cell, chapter house, convent, friary, hermitage, house, lamasery, monastery, nunnery, order, priorate, priory, religious community, retreat, sanctuary; SEE CONCEPTS *368,516*

cloistered [*adj*] *secluded*
cloistral, confined, hermitic, hidden, insulated, recluse, reclusive, restricted, secluse, seclusive, sequestered, sheltered, shielded, shut off, withdrawn; SEE CONCEPTS *554,583*

clone [*n*] *exact duplicate*
act-alike, copy, double, duplicate, look-alike computer, reproduction, twin; SEE CONCEPTS *664,667,716*

clone [*v*] *copy exactly*
copy, duplicate, repeat, replicate, reproduce; SEE CONCEPTS *91,171*

close [*adj1*] *near, nearby*
abutting, across the street, adjacent, adjoining, approaching, around the corner, at hand, contiguous, convenient, give or take a little*, handy, hard by, immediate, imminent, impending, in spitting distance*, in the ball park*, near-at-hand, nearest, nearly, neighboring, next, nigh, proximate, under one's nose*, warm; SEE CONCEPT *586*

close [*adj2*] *dense, cramped*
circumscribed, close-grained, compact, confined, confining, congested, consolidated, cropped, crowded, firm, impenetrable, impermeable, jam-packed, narrow, packed, restricted, short, solid, substantial, thick, tight; SEE CONCEPTS *481,483,774*

close [*adj3*] *accurate, precise*
conscientious, exact, faithful, lifelike, literal, resembling, similar, strict; SEE CONCEPTS *535,563*

close [*adj4*] *intimate*
attached, buddy-buddy*, chummy, confidential, cozy with, dear, devoted, familiar, inseparable, kissing cousins*, loving, making it with*, on top of each other*, palsy-walsy*, private, related, thick*, thick as thieves*, thick with*; SEE CONCEPTS *372,555*

close [*adj5*] *oppressive, humid*
airless, breathless, choky, confined, fusty, heavy, moldy, motionless, muggy, musty, stagnant, stale, stale-smelling, sticky, stifling, stuffy, suffocating, sultry, sweltering, sweltry, thick, tight, uncomfortable, unventilated; SEE CONCEPTS *525,605*

close [*adj6*] *secret, reserved*
buttoning one's lip*, buttoning up*, clamming up*, close-lipped, closemouthed, hidden, hush-hush*, mum's the word*, on the Q. T.*, private, reticent, retired, secluded, secretive, silent, taciturn, tight chops*, tight-lipped*, uncommunica-

tive, unforthcoming, zipping one's lips*; SEE CONCEPTS *267,576*

close [*adj7*] *stingy*
chintzy*, closefisted, illiberal, mean, mingy, miserly, narrow, niggardly, parsimonious, penny-pinching, penurious, skimpy, skinflint*, tight, tight-fisted, ungenerous; SEE CONCEPTS *334,404*

close [*n*] *ending*
adjournment, cease, cessation, completion, conclusion, culmination, denouement, desistance, end, finale, finish, period, stop, termination, windup; SEE CONCEPTS *119,832*

close [*vl*] *obstruct, seal*
bang, bar, block, bolt, button, caulk, choke, clap, clench, clog, confine, congest, cork, dam, exclude, fasten, fill, lock, occlude, plug, prevent passage, put to, retard flow, screen, secure, shut, shut off, shutter, slam, stopper, stop up, stuff, turn off; SEE CONCEPTS *113,121,201*

close [*v2*] *complete, finish, stop*
button down*, button up*, call it a day*, call off, cap, cease, clear, clinch, conclude, consummate, culminate, cut loose, determine, discontinue, do, drop the curtain*, end, fold, fold up, halt, pack it in*, put a lid on*, put to bed*, sew up*, shut down, shutter, terminate, ultimate, wind down*, wind up*, wrap up*; SEE CONCEPT *234*

close [*v3*] *join, unite*
agree, bind, chain, coalesce, come together, connect, couple, encounter, fuse, grapple, inclose, meet, put together, tie, tie up; SEE CONCEPT *113*

close call [*n*] *narrow escape*
cliffhanger, close shave*, heart stopper*, near miss, photofinish, squeaker*, white-knuckler*; SEE CONCEPT *102*

closed [*adj1*] *shut, out of service*
bankrupt, dark, fastened, folded, gone fishing*, locked, not open, out of business*, out of order*, padlocked, sealed, shut down; SEE CONCEPT *576*

closed [*adj2*] *finished, terminated*
concluded, decided, ended, final, over, resolved, settled; SEE CONCEPT *548*

closed [*adj3*] *exclusive, independent*
restricted, self-centered, self-contained, self-sufficient, self-sufficing, self-supported, self-supporting, self-sustained, self-sustaining; SEE CONCEPT *550*

closely [*adv*] *approximately, carefully*
by the skin of one's teeth*, exactly, firmly, hard, heedfully, in conjunction with, intently, intimately, jointly, meticulously, mindfully, minutely, nearly, punctiliously, scrupulously, searchingly, sharply, similarly, strictly, thoughtfully; SEE CONCEPTS *487,557,573*

closemouthed [*adj*] *silent, reserved*
buttoned up*, clammed up*, close, close-lipped, dummied up*, have tight chops*, hush-hush, on the Q. T.*, quiet, reticent, sedate, taciturn, tight-lipped, uncommunicative, zipped one's lips*; SEE CONCEPT *267*

closet [*n*] *storage cupboard, usually tall*
ambry, bin, buffet, cabinet, chest of drawers, clothes room, cold storage, container, depository, locker, receptacle, recess, repository, room, safe, sideboard, vault, walk-in, wardrobe; SEE CONCEPT *440*

closure [*nl*] *conclusion*
cease, cessation, close, closing, desistance, end,

cl
cl

ending, finish, stop, stoppage, termination; SEE CONCEPT *119*

closure [*n2*] *plug, seal*
blockade, bolt, bung, cap, cork, fastener, latch, lid, obstruction, occludent, occlusion, padlock, stop, stopper, stopple, tampon, tap; SEE CONCEPTS *471,680*

clot [*n*] *blockage, mass of coagulation*
array, batch, battery, body, bulk, bunch, bundle, clotting, clump, cluster, coagulum, coalescence, conglutination, consolidation, curd, curdling, embolism, embolus, glob, gob, group, grume, lump, occlusion, precipitate, set, thickness, thrombus; SEE CONCEPTS *432,466,470*

clot [*v*] *coagulate*
clabber, coalesce, congeal, curdle, gel, gelate, gelatinize, glop up*, jell, jellify, jelly, lopper*, lump, set, solidify, thicken; SEE CONCEPT *469*

cloth [*n*] *fabric*
bolt, calico, cotton, dry goods, goods, material, stuff, synthetics, textiles, tissue, twill, weave, yard goods; SEE CONCEPT *473*

clothe [*v*] *cover with apparel*
accouter, apparel, array, attire, bedizen, bedrape, breech, bundle up, caparison, cloak, coat, costume, dandify, deck, disguise, dizen, do up*, drape, dress, dress up, dud*, endow, endue, enwrap, equip, fit, fit out, garb, gown, guise, habilitate, habit, invest, jacket, livery, mantle, outfit, primp, raiment, rig, robe, spruce, suit up, swaddle, swathe, tog, turn out, vest; SEE CONCEPT *167*

clothes/clothing [*n*] *personal attire*
accouterment, apparel, array, caparison, civvies*, costume, covering, drag*, drapery, dress, duds*, ensemble, equipment, finery, frippery, frock, full feather*, garb, garments, gear, get-up*, habiliment, habit, hand-me-downs, livery, mufti, outfit, overclothes, panoply, rags*, raiment, regalia, rigging*, sack*, sportswear, Sunday best*, tailleur, tatters*, things*, threads*, toggery*, togs, tout ensemble, trappings, trousseau, underclothes, vestment, vesture, vines*, wardrobe, wear, weeds*, zoot suit*; SEE CONCEPT *451*

cloud [*n1*] *mass of water particles in air*
billow, brume, darkness, dimness, film, fog, fogginess, frost, gloom, haze, haziness, mare's tail*, mist, murk, nebula, nebulosity, obscurity, ol' buttermilk sky*, overcast, pea soup*, pother, puff, rack, scud, sheep, smog, smoke, smother, steam, thunderhead, vapor, veil, woolpack; SEE CONCEPTS *437,524*

cloud [*n2*] *crowd*
army, dense mass, flock, horde, host, legion, multitude, rout, scores, shower, swarm; throng; SEE CONCEPTS *417,432*

cloud [*v1*] *become foggy or obscured*
adumbrate, becloud, befog, blur, darken, dim, eclipse, envelop, fog, gloom, mist, obfuscate, overcast, overshadow, shade, shadow, veil; SEE CONCEPTS *469,526*

cloud [*v2*] *confuse*
addle, becloud, befuddle, disorient, distort, distract, impair, muddle, muddy, obscure, perplex, puzzle; SEE CONCEPTS *7,19*

cloudy [*adj*] *hazy; darkened*
blurred, confused, dark, dense, dim, dismal, dull, dusky, emulsified, foggy, gloomy, heavy, indefinite, indistinct, leaden, lowering, misty, mucky, muddy, murky, mushy, nebulous, nontranslu-

cent, nontransparent, not clear, nubilous, obscure, opaque, overcast, somber, sullen, sunless, vaporous; SEE CONCEPT *525*

clout [*n*] *power*
authority, influence, prestige, pull*, standing, sway, weight; SEE CONCEPT *686*

clout [*v*] *hit*
blow, box, clip, clobber, cuff, rap, slap, smack, sock, strike, thump, wallop, whack; SEE CONCEPTS *189,200*

clown [*n1*] *joking person*
antic, buffoon, comedian, comic, cut-up*, dolt, droll, farceur, fool, funnyperson, funster, gagman*, gagster*, harlequin, humorist, jester, joker, jokesmith, jokester, life of the party*, madcap, merry-andrew, merrymaker, mime, mountebank, mummer, picador, pierrot, prankster, punch, punchinello*, quipster, ribald, wag, wisecracker, wit*, zany*; SEE CONCEPT *423*

clown [*n2*] *stupid, ignorant person*
blockhead*, boor, bucolic, buffoon, bumpkin*, chuff, churl, clodhopper*, gawk, hayseed*, hick*, hind, jake, lout, mucker*, oaf, peasant, rube, rustic, swain, yahoo*, yokel; SEE CONCEPTS *412,423*

clown [*v*] *joke*
act crazy, act the fool*, bug out*, cut up*, fool around, have fun, jest, kid around; SEE CONCEPT *386*

cloy [*v*] *overfill*
disgust, fill, glut, gorge, jade, nauseate, pall, sate, satiate, satisfy, sicken, stall, stodge, suffice, surfeit, weary; SEE CONCEPT *740*

club [*n1*] *bar, stick*
baton, billy*, blackjack, bludgeon, business*, conk buster*, convincer*, cosh, cudgel, hammer, hickory, mace, mallet, nightstick, persuader*, quarterstaff, rosewood, sap, shill, shillelagh, staff, swatter, truncheon, works*; SEE CONCEPTS *470,499*

club [*n2*] *social organization*
affiliation, alliance, association, bunch, circle, clique, company, crew, faction, gang, guild, hangout*, league, lodge, meeting, mob, order, outfit, ring, set, society, sodality, stamping ground*; union; SEE CONCEPTS *387,439*

club [*n3*] *golfing overclub*
brassie, cleek, driver, iron, mashie, midiron, niblick, putter, spoon, stick, wedge, wood; SEE CONCEPT *364*

club [*v*] *hit hard with object*
bash, baste, batter, beat, blackjack, bludgeon, clobber, clout, cosh, cudgel, fustigate, hammer, pommel, pound, pummel, strike, whack; SEE CONCEPT *189*

clue [*n*] *hint, evidence*
cue, dead giveaway*, hot lead*, indication, inkling, intimation, key, lead, mark, notion, pointer, print, proof, sign, solution, suggestion, suspicion, telltale, tip, tip-off*, trace, track, wind; SEE CONCEPT *274*

clue [*v*] *give information*
acquaint, advise, apprise, fill in, give the low-down*, give the skinny on*, hint, indicate, inform, intimate, lead to, leave evidence, leave trace, leave tracks, notify, point to, post, suggest, tell, warn, wise up; SEE CONCEPT *60*

clump [*n1*] *mass of something*
array, batch, blob, body, bunch, bundle, chunk, cluster, clutter, gob, group, hodgepodge, hunk,

jumble, knot, lot, lump, nugget, parcel, set, shock, wad; SEE CONCEPTS *432,470*

clump [n2] *thumping noise*
clatter, clomp, galumph, scuff, stomp, stumble, thud; SEE CONCEPT *595*

clump [v] *make thumping noise*
barge, bumble, clatter, clomp, galumph, hobble, limp, lumber, plod, scuff, stamp, stomp, stumble, stump, thud, thump, tramp; SEE CONCEPTS *65,595*

clumsy [adj] *not agile; awkward*
all thumbs*, blundering, blunderous, bulky, bumbling, bungling, butterfingered*, clownish, crude, elephantine, gauche, gawkish, gawky, graceless, ham-handed*, heavy, heavy-handed, helpless, hulking, ill-shaped, incompetent, inelegant, inept, inexperienced, inexpert, lubberly, lumbering, lumpish, maladroit, oafish, ponderous, splay, stumbling, unable, unadept, uncoordinated, uncouth, undexterous, uneasy, ungainly, unhandy, unskillful, untactful, untalented, untoward, unwieldy, weedy; SEE CONCEPTS *401,402,584*

cluster [n] *group of something*
array, assemblage, band, batch, bevy, blob, body, bunch, bundle, chunk, clump, clutch, collection, covey, crew, gathering, hunk, knot, lot, pack, party, set; SEE CONCEPT *432*

cluster [v] *assemble, group*
accumulate, aggregate, associate, bunch, bunch up, bundle, collect, crowd around, cumulate, flock, gang around, gather, package, parcel, round up; SEE CONCEPTS *109*

clutch [n] *strong hold*
clamp, clasp, clench, clinch, connection, coupling, grapple, grasp, grip, gripe, link; SEE CONCEPT *190*

clutch [v] *grab, snatch*
catch, cherish, clasp, clench, clinch, cling to, collar, embrace, fasten, glom*, grapple, grasp, grip, harbor, hold, hook, keep, nab, nail*, put the snare on*, seize, snag, snatch, take; SEE CONCEPTS *190,191*

clutches [n] *personal power*
claws, control, custody, grasp, grip, hands, keeping, possession, sway; SEE CONCEPTS *388,641,710*

clutter [n] *disarray, mess*
ataxia, chaos, confusion, derangement, disorder, hodgepodge, huddle, jumble, litter, medley, melange, muddle, rummage, scramble, shuffle, tumble, untidiness; SEE CONCEPTS *432,674*

clutter [v] *cause mess, disarray*
dirty, jumble, litter, muddle, scatter, snarl, strew; SEE CONCEPT *254*

coach [n1] *instructor, usually in recreation*
drill instructor, educator, mentor, physical education instructor, skipper, teacher, trainer, tutor; SEE CONCEPTS *350,366*

coach [n2] *carriage*
bus, car, chaise, charabanc, fourwheeler, gocart, perambulator, stage, tallyho*, train, vehicle, victoria; SEE CONCEPT *505*

coach [v] *instruct, usually in recreation*
break in*, cram, drill, educate, hone, lay it out for*, lick into shape*, prepare, pull one's coat*, put through the grind*, put through the mill*, ready, school, teach, train, tutor; SEE CONCEPTS *285,363*

coagulate [v] *clot*
clabber, coalesce, compact, concentrate, concrete, condense, congeal, consolidate, curdle, dry, gel, gelate, gelatinize, glop up*, harden, inspissate, jell, jellify, jelly, lopper*, set, solidify, thicken; SEE CONCEPT *469*

coagulation [n] *clotting*
agglomeration, caseation, concentration, concretion, condensation, congelation, consolidation, curdling, embolism, gelatination, incrassation, inspissation, jellification, thickening; SEE CONCEPT *469*

coalesce [v] *blend, come together*
adhere, amalgamate, associate, bracket, cleave, cling, cohere, combine, commingle, commix, conjoin, connect, consolidate, fuse, hook up with*, incorporate, integrate, join, join up with, link, merge, mingle, mix, relate, stick, tie in with*, unite, wed; SEE CONCEPTS *112,113*

coalition [n] *allied group, association*
affiliation, alliance, amalgam, amalgamation, anschluss, bloc, coadunation, combination, combine, compact, confederacy, confederation, conjunction, consolidation, conspiracy, faction, federation, fusion, integration, league, melding, mergence, merger, merging, party, ring, unification, union; SEE CONCEPT *381*

coarse [adj1] *not fine, rude*
base, bawdy, blue*, boorish, brutish, cheap, common, crass, crude, dirty, earthy, filthy, foul, foul-mouthed, gross, gruff, immodest, impolite, improper, impure, incult, indelicate, inelegant, loutish, low, lowbred, lowdown and dirty*, mean, nasty, obscene, off-color, offensive, raffish, raunchy, raw, ribald, rough, roughneck*, rude, scatological, smutty*, tacky, uncivil, uncouth, uncultivated, uncultured, unrefined, vulgar, vulgarian; SEE CONCEPTS *401,545*

coarse [adj2] *rough, unrefined*
chapped, coarse-grained, crude, grainy, granular, harsh, homespun, impure, inferior, loose, lumpy, mediocre, particulate, poor quality, rough-hewn, rugged, unfinished, unpolished, unprocessed, unpurified; SEE CONCEPTS *574,606*

coarseness [n] *rudeness, vulgarity*
bawdiness, boorishness, callousness, crassness, crudity, earthiness, harshness, indelicacy, offensiveness, poor taste, rawness, ribaldry, roughness, smut*, smuttiness*, uncouthness, unevenness, unrefinement; SEE CONCEPTS *633,645*

coast [n] *border by water*
bank, beach, coastline, littoral, margin, seaboard, seacoast, seashore, seaside, shore, shoreline, strand; SEE CONCEPTS *509,514*

coast [v] *glide along without much effort*
cruise, drift, float, freewheel, get by*, ride on current, sail, skate, slide, smooth along*, taxi; SEE CONCEPTS *150,704*

coastal [adj] *bordering the water*
along a coast, littoral, marginal, marshy, riverine, seaside, skirting; SEE CONCEPT *583*

coat [n1] *animal hair*
crust, ectoderm, epidermis, felt, fleece, fur, hide, husk, integument, leather, membrane, pelage, pellicle, pelt, peltry, protective covering, rind, scale, scarfskin, shell, skin, wool; SEE CONCEPT *399*

coat [n2] *covering*
bark, coating, crust, finish, glaze, gloss, lacquer,

cl
co

lamination, layer, overlay, painting, plaster, priming, roughcast, set, tinge, varnish, wash, whitewashing; SEE CONCEPTS *259,475*

coat [*n3*] *personal outerwear*
cape, cloak, cutaway, flogger, frock, greatcoat, jacket, mackinaw, mink, overcoat, pea, raincoat, slicker, suit, tails, threads, topcoat, trench, tux, tuxedo, ulster, windbreaker, wrap; SEE CONCEPT *451*

coat [*v*] *cover with layer of material*
apply, cover, crust, enamel, foil, glaze, incrust, laminate, paint, plaster, plate, smear, spread, stain, surface, varnish; SEE CONCEPTS *172,202*

coating [*n*] *covering*
blanket, bloom, coat, crust, dusting, encrustation, film, finish, glaze, lamination, layer, membrane, patina, sheet, skin, varnish, veneer; SEE CONCEPT *475*

coax [*v*] *persuade*
allure, argue into, arm-twist*, barter, beguile, blandish, blarney, butter up*, cajole, come on, con, decoy, entice, flatter, get, hook, importune, induce, influence, inveigle, jawbone*, lure, pester, plague, press, prevail upon, rope in*, soft-soap*, soothe, sweet-talk, talk into, tease, tempt, urge, wangle, wheedle, work on, worm; SEE CONCEPT *68*

cobweb [*n*] *entanglement; filament*
fiber, gossamer, labyrinth, mesh, net, network, snare, tissue, toil, web, webbing; SEE CONCEPTS *517,674*

cocaine [*n*] *illegal drug*
blow*, coke*, controlled substance, crack*, crystal*, freebase*, happy dust*, ice*, joy powder*, mojo*, narcotic, nose candy*, poison*, snort*, snow*, speedball*, stardust*, stuff*, sugar*, white horse*, white lady*, wings*; SEE CONCEPT *307*

cock [*n*] *rooster*
capon, chanticleer, chicken, cock-a-doodle-doo*, cockalorum, cockerel; SEE CONCEPT *394*

cock [*v*] *aim up toward*
erect, hump, perk up, pile, prick, raise, stack, stand erect, stand up, stick up; SEE CONCEPT *201*

cockeyed [*adj*] *crooked, askew*
absurd, askance, askant, asymmetrical, awry, cam, canted, crazy, crooked, cross-eyed, lop-sided, ludicrous, nonsensical, preposterous, squint, strabismic; SEE CONCEPT *586*

cocky/cocksure [*adj*] *self-assured, full of oneself*
arrogant, brash, bumptious, certain, conceited, confident, egotistical, hotdogging*, hotshot*, hubristic, know-it-all*, lordly, nervy, overconfident, overweening, positive, presumptuous, self-confident, smart aleck*, smart guy*, smarty*, smarty pants*, sure, swaggering, swollen-headed, vain, wise guy*; SEE CONCEPTS *401,404*

cocoon [*v*] *protect with covering*
cushion, encase, envelop, insulate, pad, swaddle, swathe, truss, wrap; SEE CONCEPTS *130,134*

coddle [*v1*] *indulge, pamper*
baby, caress, cater to, cosset, cotton, favor, humor, make much of, make over, mollycoddle, nurse, pet, play up to, spoil; SEE CONCEPTS *110,295*

coddle [*v2*] *boil lightly, usually eggs*
brew, cook, poach, simmer, steam; SEE CONCEPT *170*

code [*n1*] *secret language system*
cipher, cryptograph; SEE CONCEPTS *276,284*

code [*n2*] *law, rule*
canon, charter, codex, constitution, convention, custom, digest, discipline, ethics, etiquette, manners, maxim, method, regulation, system; SEE CONCEPTS *318,688*

co-dependent [*adj*] *unhealthy psychological reliance of one person on another*
addicted, attached, hooked, interconnected, interdependent, mutually dependent, slavish trust, unhealthy confidence; SEE CONCEPTS *404,542*

codicil [*n*] *added part to document*
addendum, addition, appendix, postscript, rider, supplement; SEE CONCEPT *270*

codify [*v*] *systematize*
arrange, catalogue, classify, code, collect, condense, digest, order, organize, summarize, tabulate; SEE CONCEPTS *39,84*

coerce [*v*] *compel, press*
beset, browbeat, bulldoze*, bully, concuss, constrain, cow, dragoon, drive, force, high pressure*, hinder, impel, intimidate, lean on, make, make an offer they can't refuse*, menace, oblige, pressurize, push, put the squeeze on*, repress, restrict, shotgun*, strong-arm, suppress, terrorize, threaten, twist one's arm*, urge; SEE CONCEPTS *14,68*

coercion [*n*] *compulsion, pressure*
browbeating, bullying, constraint, duress, force, intimidation, menace, menacing, persuasion, restraint, strong-arm tactic*, threat, threatening, violence; SEE CONCEPTS *14,68*

coexistence [*n*] *happening or being at same time, place*
accord, coetaneousness, coevality, coincidence, concurrence, conformity, conjunction, contemporaneousness, harmony, order, peace, simultaneousness, synchronicity; SEE CONCEPT *407*

coffee [*n*] *hot beverage made from beans of a tree*
battery acid*, brew, café, café au lait, café noir, cappuccino, decaf, decoction, demitasse, espresso, forty weight*, hot stuff*, ink*, jamocha*, java*, joe*, mocha*, mud*, perk*, varnish remover*; SEE CONCEPT *454*

coffer [*n*] *large box*
case, casket, chest, exchequer, repository, strongbox, treasure chest, treasury, war chest*; SEE CONCEPT *494*

coffin [*n*] *box for dead person*
casket, catafalque, crate, funerary box, pall, pine box, pine drape*, sarcophagus; SEE CONCEPTS *368,479,494*

cog [*n*] *main part of device*
cogwheel, differential, fang, gear, pinion, prong, rack, ratchet, tine, tooth, transmission, tusk, wheel; SEE CONCEPT *464*

cogency [*n*] *effectiveness*
bearing, concern, connection, conviction, convincingness, force, forcefulness, pertinence, point, potency, power, punch, relevance, strength, validity, validness; SEE CONCEPTS *376,676*

cogent [*adj*] *effective*
apposite, apt, compelling, conclusive, consequential, convictive, convincing, fitting, forceful, forcible, inducing, influential, irresistible, justified, meaningful, momentous, persuasive, pertinent, potent, powerful, puissant, relevant, satisfactory, satisfying, significant, solid, sound,

strong, suasive, telling, urgent, valid, weighty, well-grounded; SEE CONCEPT 537

cogitate [*v*] *think deeply about*
brainstorm*, cerebrate, chew the cud*, conceive, consider, contemplate, deliberate, envisage, envision, figure, flash on*, imagine, kick around*, meditate, mull over, muse, noodle around*, ponder, reason, reflect, ruminate, speculate, stew over*; SEE CONCEPTS 17,24

cogitation [*n*] *deep thought*
brainwork, cerebration, consideration, contemplation, deliberation, meditation, reflection, rumination, speculation; SEE CONCEPT 410

cognate [*adj*] *alike, associated*
affiliated, agnate, akin, allied, analogous, comparable, connate, connatural, connected, consanguine, general, generic, incident, kindred, like, related, same, similar, universal; SEE CONCEPTS 487,573

cognizance/cognition [*n*] *understanding*
acknowledgment, apprehension, attention, awareness, comprehension, discernment, insight, intelligence, knowledge, mind, need, note, notice, observance, observation, perception, percipience, reasoning, recognition, regard; SEE CONCEPT 409

cognizant [*adj*] *aware*
acquainted, alive, apprehensive, au courant, awake, conscious, conversant, down with, familiar, grounded, hep to*, hip to*, informed, in on, in the know, in the picture*, judicious, knowing, knowledgeable, observant, on the beam*, on to*, perceptive, plugged in, savvy, sensible, sentient, tuned in*, up on*, versed, wise to*, with it*, witting; SEE CONCEPT 402

cohabit [*v*] *live together*
be roommates with, conjugate, couple, have relations, live illegally, live with, mingle, play house*, room together, shack up*, share address, take up housekeeping*; SEE CONCEPTS 226,375,384

cohere [*v1*] *stick to, cling*
adhere, associate, bind, blend, cleave, coalesce, combine, connect, consolidate, fuse, glue, hold, join, merge, unite; SEE CONCEPTS 85,113,160

cohere [*v2*] *agree, conform*
accord, be connected, be consistent, check, check out, comport, conform, correspond, dovetail, fit in, go, hang together, harmonize, hold, hold water, make sense, relate, square; SEE CONCEPTS 8,636,667

coherence [*n*] *agreement*
adherence, attachment, bond, cementation, cling, clinging, comprehensibility, concordance, conformity, congruity, connection, consistency, consonance, construction, continuity, correspondence, inseparability, inseparableness, integrity, intelligibility, rationality, relations, solidarity, stickage, tenacity, union, unity; SEE CONCEPTS 388,684

coherent [*adj*] *understandable*
articulate, comprehensible, consistent, identified, intelligible, logical, lucid, meaningful, orderly, organized, rational, reasoned, sound, systematic; SEE CONCEPT 402

cohort [*adj*] *partner in activity*
accomplice, adherent, aide, ally, assistant, associate, companion, company, comrade, confrere, consociate, contingent, disciple, follower, friend, hand, legion, mate, myrmidon, pal, partisan, reg-iment, satellite, sidekick, stall, supporter; SEE CONCEPT 423

coiffure [*n*] *hairstyle*
afro, beehive, blow dry*, braids, corn rows, crew cut, DA*, dreadlocks, dreads, flip, fuzz cut*, hair, hair-comb, haircut, hairdo, permanent, pigtails, plait, ponytail, razor cut*, tail, tease, trim, wave; SEE CONCEPTS 418,718

coil [*n*] *thread that curls*
bight, braid, circle, convolution, corkscrew, curlicue, gyration, helix, involution, lap, loop, ring, roll, scroll, spiral, tendril, turn, twine, twirl, twist, whorl, wind; SEE CONCEPT 436

coil [*v*] *curl around, entwine*
convolute, convolve, corkscrew, fold, intertwine, intervolve, lap, loop, make serpentine, rotate, scroll, sinuate, snake, spiral, spire, turn, twine, twist, wind, wrap around, wreathe, writhe; SEE CONCEPTS 201,758

coin [*n*] *metallic money*
bread*, cash, change, chicken feed*, chips*, coinage, copper, currency, dough, gold, jack*, legal tender, meter money*, mintage, money, piece, scratch*, silver, small change*, specie; SEE CONCEPT 340

coin [*v*] *create, invent*
brainstorm*, compose, conceive, contrive, counterfeit, dream up, fabricate, forge, formulate, frame, head trip*, make up, make up off the top of one's head*, manufacture, mint, mold, originate, spark, spitball*, stamp, strike, think up, trump up*; SEE CONCEPTS 36,173

coincide [*v*] *go along with; coexist*
accompany, accord, acquiesce, agree, be concurrent, befall, be the same, come about, concert, concur, correspond, equal, eventuate, harmonize, identify, jibe, match, occur simultaneously, quadrate, square, sync, synchronize, tally; SEE CONCEPTS 667,714

coincidence [*n1*] *agreement; coexistence*
accompaniment, accord, accordance, collaboration, concomitance, concurrence, conformity, conjunction, consonance, correlation, correspondence, parallelism, synchronism, union; SEE CONCEPTS 667,684,714

coincidence [*n2*] *accidental happening*
accident, chance, eventuality, fate, fluke, fortuity, happening, happy accident, incident, luck, stroke of luck; SEE CONCEPTS 4,230

coincident [*adj*] *concurring, happening together*
ancillary, attendant, attending, coinciding, collateral, concomitant, consonant, contemporaneous, contemporary, coordinate, correspondent, incident, satellite, simultaneous, synchronous; SEE CONCEPTS 548,820

coincidental [*adj*] *accidental*
casual, chance, circumstantial, fluky, fortuitous, incidental, unintentional, unplanned; SEE CONCEPT 548

cold [*adj1*] *chilly, freezing*
algid, arctic, below freezing, below zero, benumbed, biting, bitter, blasting, bleak, boreal, brisk, brumal, chill, chilled, cool, crisp, cutting, frigid, frore, frosty, frozen, gelid, glacial, have goose bumps*, hawkish, hiemal, hyperborean, icebox, iced, icy, inclement, intense, keen, nipping, nippy, numbed, numbing, one-dog night*, penetrating, piercing, polar, raw, rimy, severe, sharp, shivery, Siberian, sleety, snappy, snowy,

CO
CO

stinging, two-dog night*, wintry; SEE CONCEPT 605

cold [*adj2*] *aloof, unresponsive*
apathetic, cold-blooded, cool, dead, distant, emotionless, frigid, frosty, glacial, icy, impersonal, imperturbable, indifferent, inhibited, inhospitable, joyless, lukewarm, matter-of-fact, passionless, phlegmatic, reserved, reticent, spiritless, standoffish, stony, unconcerned, undemonstrative, unenthusiastic, unfeeling, unimpassioned, unmoved, unresponsive, unsympathetic; SEE CONCEPT 404

cold [*n*] *frigid conditions*
ague, algidity, algor, chill, chilliness, coldness, congelation, draft, freeze, frigidity, frost, frostbite, frostiness, frozenness, gelidity, gelidness, glaciation, goose flesh, iciness, inclemency, rawness, refrigeration, shivering, shivers, snow, wintertime, wintriness; SEE CONCEPTS 524,610

cold-blooded [*adj*] *cruel, heartless*
barbarous, brutal, callous, cold, dispassionate, hard-boiled, hardened, hard-hearted, imperturbable, inhuman, matter-of-fact, merciless, obdurate, pitiless, relentless, ruthless, savage, steely, stony-hearted, uncompassionate, unemotional, unfeeling, unmoved; SEE CONCEPT 542

cold feet [*n*] *fear of carrying out an activity*
anxiety, fear, reservations, second thoughts, timidity; SEE CONCEPT 27

cold fish [*n*] *unemotional person*
aloof person, iceberg*, unfeeling person; SEE CONCEPT 412

cold shoulder [*n*] *snub*
aloofness, brush-off, coldness, dismissal, disregard, iciness; SEE CONCEPTS 30,633

coliseum [*n*] *arena for events*
amphitheater, bowl, hippodrome, open-air theater, stade, stadium, theater; SEE CONCEPT 438

collaborate [*v*] *work together*
be in cahoots*, coact, cofunction, collude, come together, concert, concur, conspire, cooperate, coproduce, do business with, get together, glue oneself to*, go partners*, hook on, hook up*, interface, join forces, join together, join up with, participate, team up, throw in together*, throw in with*, tie in, work with; SEE CONCEPTS 100,351,384

collaborator [*n*] *person who works with another*
assistant, associate, colleague, confederate, co-worker, fellow traveller, helper, partner, quisling, running dog, teammate, team player*; SEE CONCEPTS 348,423

collage [*n*] *mixture of pictures*
abstract composition, found art, photomontage; SEE CONCEPT 259

collapse [*n*] *downfall, breakdown*
bankruptcy, basket case*, cataclysm, catastrophe, cave-in, conk out*, crackup*, crash, debacle, destruction, disintegration, disorganization, disruption, exhaustion, failure, faint, flop, prostration, ruination, ruining, smash, smashup, subsidence, undoing, wreck; SEE CONCEPTS 230,316,410,674

collapse [*v*] *fall apart, break down*
belly up*, bend, break, cave in, conk out*, crack up*, crumple, deflate, disintegrate, droop, drop, exhaust, fail, faint, fall down, flag, flake out, fold, founder, give, give in, give out, give way, go*, go to pieces*, keel over, languish, shatter,

subside, succumb, tire, topple, weaken, weary, wilt, yield; SEE CONCEPTS 252,469,702

collar [*n*] *neck attire*
bertha, choker, dicky, Eton, fichu, fraise, frill, jabot, neckband, ruff, torque, Vandyke; SEE CONCEPTS 450,452

collar [*v*] *apprehend*
abduct, appropriate, arrest, bag, capture, catch, cop*, corner, get, grab, hook, lay hands on, nab, nail*, prehend, secure, seize, take, tree; SEE CONCEPTS 90,317

collate [*v*] *sort collection*
adduce, analogize, assemble, bracket, collect, compare, compose, contrast, examine, gather, group, match, order, relate, verify; SEE CONCEPTS 84,158

collateral [*adj*] *indirect, secondary*
accessory, accompanying, added, adjunctive, adjuvant, ancillary, appurtenant, attendant, auxiliary, circuitous, coincident, complementary, concomitant, concurrent, confirmatory, coordinate, corresponding, corroborative, dependent, incident, lateral, not lineal, parallel, related, roundabout, satellite, side, sub, subordinate, subservient, subsidiary, supporting, tributary, under; SEE CONCEPTS 546,567,831

collateral [*n*] *monetary deposit*
assurance, bond, endorsement, guarantee, pledge, promise, security, surety, warrant, wealth; SEE CONCEPT 344

colleague [*n*] *associate, fellow worker*
aide, ally, assistant, auxiliary, buddy, chum, coadjutor, cohort, collaborator, companion, compatriot, compeer, comrade, confederate, confrere, co-worker, crony, friend, helper, pal, partner, teammate, workmate; SEE CONCEPTS 348,423

collect [*v1*] *accumulate, come together*
aggregate, amass, array, assemble, cluster, compile, congregate, congress, convene, converge, convoke, corral, flock, flock together, gather, get hold of, group, heap, hoard, muster, rally, rendezvous, round up, save, scare up, stockpile; SEE CONCEPTS 109,114

collect [*v2*] *obtain (money)*
acquire, dig up, muster, pass the hat*, raise, requisition, secure, solicit; SEE CONCEPT 342

collected [*adj*] *composed, calm*
confident, cool, easygoing, levelheaded, nonchalant, peaceful, placid, poised, possessed, quiet, sanguine, self-possessed, serene, still, sure, temperate, together, tranquil, unflappable, unperturbable, unperturbed, unruffled; SEE CONCEPT 401

collection [*n*] *group, accumulation*
accumulating, acquiring, acquisition, agglomeration, amassing, amassment, anthology, assemblage, assembling, assembly, assortment, batch, bringing together, caboodle, clump, cluster, collation, combination, company, compilation, congeries, congregation, convocation, crowd, cumulation, digest, gathering, heap, hoard, kit, levy, lot, mass, medley, mess, miscellany, mobilization, muster, number, obtaining, omnibus, pile, quantity, securing, selection, set, stack, stock, stockpile, store; SEE CONCEPTS 109,432

collective [*adj*] *composite*
aggregate, assembled, collated, combined, common, compiled, concentrated, concerted, conjoint, consolidated, cooperative, corporate, cumulative, gathered, grouped, heaped, hoarded,

joint, massed, mutual, piled, shared, unified, united; SEE CONCEPT *585*

college [*n*] *institution of higher education*
alma mater, association, brainery*, halls of ivy*, halls of knowledge*, institute, lyceum, organization, seminary, university; SEE CONCEPTS *287,288,289*

college student [*n*] *person studying at institution of higher education*
first year student, grad student*, graduate student, junior, senior, sophomore, undergrad*, undergraduate student; SEE CONCEPT *350*

collide [*v*] *slam into*
bang, beat, break-up, bump, clash, conflict, crash, crunch*, disagree, fender-bend*, fragment, hit, jolt, meet head-on*, pile up*, plow into*, pulverize*, scrap*, shatter, sideswipe, smash, splinter, strike, wrack up*; SEE CONCEPTS *189,248*

collision [*n*] *accident*
blow, bump, butt, concussion, contact, crash, demolishment, destruction, dilapidation, encounter, fender bender*, head-on*, hit, impact, jar, jolt, knock, percussion, pileup*, rap, ruin, shock, sideswipe, slam, smash, strike, thud, thump, wreck; SEE CONCEPTS *189,230,674*

collocate [*v*] *compile*
accumulate, assemble, collect, collimate, gather, parallel; SEE CONCEPT *84*

colloquial [*adj*] *particular, familiar to an area, informal*
chatty, common, conversational, demotic, dialectal, everyday, idiomatic, jive*, popular, street*, vernacular; SEE CONCEPT *267*

colloquy [*n*] *conversation, debate*
buzz session, chat, chinfest*, chitchat, clambake*, colloquium, confab*, confabulation, conference, converse, dialogue, discourse, discussion, flap*, gab fest*, gam*, groupthink*, huddle*, palaver, parley, powwow*, rap*, rap session*, seminar, talk, talkfest*; SEE CONCEPT *266*

collusion [*n*] *secret understanding, often with intent to defraud*
bait and switch*, bill of goods*, bunco*, cahoots*, complicity, con game*, connivance, conspiracy, craft, deceit, diddling*, dodge, double-cross, fast shuffle*, flam*, flimflam*, fradulent artifice, graft, guilt, guiltiness, gyp, intrigue, plot, racket, scam, scheme, shell game*, skunk*, sting*, trick, whitewash; SEE CONCEPTS *114,660*

cologne [*n*] *fragrance product*
fragrance, perfume, scent, toilet water; SEE CONCEPTS *599,600*

colonial [*adj*] *pioneering, relating to a nonindependent or new territory*
crude, dependent, dominion, early American, emigrant, frontier, immigrant, new, outland, pilgrim, pioneer, prerevolutionary, primitive, provincial, puritan, territorial, transplanted, uncultured, unsettled, unsophisticated, wild; SEE CONCEPTS *549,799*

colonization [*n*] *settlement of area*
clearing, establishment, expanding, expansion, founding, immigration, migration, opening up, peopling, pioneering, populating, settlement, settling, squatting, transplanting; SEE CONCEPTS *198,298*

colony [*n*] *community*
antecedents, clearing, dependency, dominion, mandate, new land, offshoot, outpost, possession, protectorate, province, satellite, settlement, subject state, swarm, territory; SEE CONCEPTS *379,512*

color [*n1*] *pigment, shade*
blush, cast, chroma, chromaticity, chromatism, chromism, colorant, coloration, coloring, complexion, dye, glow, hue, intensity, iridescence, luminosity, paint, pigmentation, polychromasia, saturation, stain, tinct, tincture, tinge, tint, undertone, value, wash; SEE CONCEPT *622*

color [*n2*] *deceptive appearance*
deception, disguise, excuse, facade, face, false show, front, guise, mask, plea, pretense, pretext, put-on, semblance, show; SEE CONCEPTS *59,716*

color [*v1*] *make pigmented; shade*
adorn, blacken, bloom, blush, burn, chalk, crayon, crimson, darken, daub, dye, embellish, emblazon, enamel, enliven, flush, fresco, gild, glaze, gloss, illuminate, imbue, infuse, lacquer, paint, pigment, pinken, redden, rouge, stain, stipple, suffuse, tinge, tint, tone, variegate, wash; SEE CONCEPTS *250,469*

color [*v2*] *distort, exaggerate*
angle*, belie, cook up*, disguise, doctor*, embroider*, fake, falsify, fudge*, garble, gloss over, magnify, misrepresent, misstate, overstate, pad*, pervert, prejudice, slant*, taint, twist*, warp*; SEE CONCEPTS *49,63*

colored [*adj1*] *not white*
dyed, flushed, glowing, hued, shaded, stained, tinged, tinted, washed; SEE CONCEPT *618*

colored [*adj2*] *distorted*
angled, biased, false, falsified, jaundiced, misrepresented, one-sided, partial, partisan, perverted, prejudiced, prepossessed, tampered with, tendentious, warped; SEE CONCEPT *582*

colorful [*adj1*] *brilliant, intensely hued*
bright, chromatic, flashy, florid, gaudy, gay, hued, intense, jazzy, kaleidoscopic, loud, motley, multicolored, picturesque*, prismatic, psychedelic, rich, showy, splashy, variegated, vibrant, vivid; SEE CONCEPTS *617,618*

colorful [*adj2*] *full of life, interesting*
brave, characterful, distinctive, flaky*, gay, glamorous, graphic, jazzy, lively, picturesque, rich, stimulating, unusual, vivid; SEE CONCEPT *404*

colorless [*adj1*] *without hue*
achromatic, achromic, anemic, ashen, ashy, blanched, bleached, cadaverous, doughy, drab, dull, faded, flat, ghastly, livid, lurid, neutral, pale, sickly, uncolored, wan, washed out, waxen, white; SEE CONCEPT *618*

colorless [*adj2*] *unlively, uninteresting*
characterless, dreary, dull, insipid, lackluster, lifeless, prosaic, run-of-the-mill*, tame, unmemorable, unpassioned, vacuous, vapid; SEE CONCEPT *404*

colossal [*adj*] *very large*
barn door*, behemothic, blimp*, cyclopean, elephantine, enormous, gargantuan, giant, gigantic, huge, humongous*, immense, jumbo, mammoth, mondo*, monstrous, mountainous, super, titanic, vast; SEE CONCEPT *781*

colossus [*n*] *giant thing*
behemoth, Cyclops, Gargantua, giant, Godzilla, Goliath, Hercules, leviathan, mammoth, Samson, titan; SEE CONCEPT *424*

CO
CO

colt [*n*] *young horse*
filly, fledgling, foal, rookie, sapling, yearling, youngling, youngster; SEE CONCEPT *394*

column [*n1*] *line, procession*
cavalcade, company, file, list, platoon, queue, rank, row, string, train; SEE CONCEPTS *432,727*

column [*n2*] *pillar*
brace, buttress, caryatid, colonnade, cylinder, mast, minaret, monolith, monument, obelisk, pedestal, peristyle, pier, pilaster, post, prop, pylon, shaft, standard, stay, stele, support, totem, tower, underpinning, upright; SEE CONCEPT *440*

coma [*n*] *deep unconsciousness*
blackout, dullness, faint, hebetude, insensibility, lethargy, oblivion, sleep, slumber, somnolence, stupor, swoon, syncope, torpidity, torpor, trance; SEE CONCEPT *315*

comatose [*adj*] *unconscious*
cold, dead, dead to the world*, dopey, drowsy, drugged, hebetudinous, inconscious, insensible, lethargic, out, out cold*, out to lunch*, senseless, sleepy, sluggish, slumberous, somnolent, soporose, stupefied, stupid, stuporous, torpid, vegged out*; SEE CONCEPT *539*

comb [*v1*] *arrange hair*
adjust, card, cleanse, curry, disentangle, dress, groom, hackle, hatchel, lay smooth, rasp, scrape, separate, smooth, sort, straighten, tease, untangle; SEE CONCEPT *162*

comb [*v2*] *search by ransacking*
beat, beat the bushes*, examine, finecomb*, forage, go through with fine-tooth comb*, grub, hunt, inspect, investigate, leave no stone unturned*, look high and low*, probe, rake, ransack, rummage, scour, screen, scrutinize, search high heaven*, sift, sweep, turn inside-out*, turn upside down*; SEE CONCEPT *216*

combat [*n*] *battle*
action, affray, battle royal*, brush, brush-off, conflict, contest, encounter, engagement, fight, flap, fray, jackpot*, mix-up*, run-in*, service, shoot-out*, skirmish, struggle, war, warfare; SEE CONCEPTS *86,106*

combat [*v*] *fight*
battle, buck, clash, contend, contest, cope, cross swords with*, defy, dispute, do battle with, duel, engage, fight, go up against, oppose, put up a fight*, repel, resist, shoot it out*, strive, traverse, war, withstand; SEE CONCEPTS *86,106*

combatant [*n*] *fighter*
adversary, antagonist, assailant, attacker, battler, belligerent, contender, enemy, foe, serviceman, soldier, warrior; SEE CONCEPT *358*

combative [*adj*] *aggressive*
antagonistic, bellicose, belligerent, cantankerous, contentious, cussed, energetic, fire-eating*, gladiatorial, hawkish, militant, ornery*, pugnacious, quarrelsome, ructious, scrappy, strenuous, trigger-happy*, truculent, warlike, warring; SEE CONCEPTS *401,404*

combination [*n1*] *mixture, blend*
aggregate, amalgam, amalgamation, blending, brew, coalescence, combo, composite, compound, connection, consolidation, everything but kitchen sink*, fusion, junction, medley, merger, miscellany, mishmash*, mix, olio, order, sequence, solution, soup, stew, succession, synthesis, unification, union; SEE CONCEPT *432*

combination [*n2*] *alliance, association*
affiliation, bloc, cabal, cahoots, camarilla, cartel, circle, clique, club, coadunation, coalition, combine, compound, confederacy, confederation, conjunction, connection, consolidation, consortium, conspiracy, coterie, faction, federation, gang, guild, hookup*, mafia, melding, mergence, merger, merging, partnership, party, pool, ring, set, syndicate, tie-up*, trust, unification, union; SEE CONCEPT *381*

combine [*v*] *connect, integrate*
amalgamate, associate, band, bind, blend, bond, bracket, bunch up, coadjute, coalesce, commingle, compound, conjoin, cooperate, couple, dub, fuse, get together, glue oneself to, hitch on*, hook on*, incorporate, interface, join, league, link, marry, merge, mingle, mix, network, plug into, pool, put together, relate, slap on*, stand in with, synthesize, tack on*, tag on*, team up with*, throw in together*, tie up with*, unify, unite, wed; SEE CONCEPT *113*

combustible [*adj*] *able to be exploded*
burnable, comburent, combustive, explosive, fiery, firing, flammable, ignitable, incendiary, inflammable, kindling, volatile; SEE CONCEPTS *485,537*

combustion [*n*] *explosion; on fire*
agitation, candescence, disturbance, flaming, ignition, kindling, oxidization, thermogenesis, tumult, turmoil; SEE CONCEPTS *521,676,724*

come [*v1*] *advance, approach*
appear, arrive, attain, be accessible, be at disposal, become, be convenient, be handy, be obtainable, be ready, blow in*, bob up, breeze in*, burst, buzz*, check in*, clock in*, close in, draw near, drop in, enter, fall by, fall in, flare*, get, get in, happen, hit, hit town*, make it, make the scene*, materialize, move, move toward, near, occur, originate, pop in*, pop up*, punch in*, punch the clock*, reach, ring in*, roll in*, show, show up, sign in, sky in*, spring in, turn out, turn up, wind up at*; SEE CONCEPT *159*

come [*v2*] *happen*
befall, betide, break, chance, come to pass, develop, fall, hap*, occur, take place, transpire, turn out; SEE CONCEPT *4*

come [*v3*] *extend, reach*
add up, aggregate, amount, become, come over, develop, expand, get, go, grow, join, mature, number, run, run into, spread, stretch, sum to, total, turn, wax; SEE CONCEPTS *239,701*

come about [*v*] *happen*
arise, befall, come to pass, occur, result, take place, transpire; SEE CONCEPT *701*

come across [*v*] *encounter, find*
bump into, chance upon, discover, happen upon, hit upon, light upon, meet, notice, stumble upon, uncover, unearth; SEE CONCEPTS *38,183*

come along [*v*] *progress, develop*
do well, get on, improve, mend, perk up, pick up, rally, recover, recuperate, show improvement; SEE CONCEPT *700*

come at [*v1*] *reach, attain*
accomplish, achieve, discover, feel for, find, grasp, succeed, touch, win; SEE CONCEPTS *34,706*

come at [*v2*] *attack*
assail, assault, charge, fall upon, fly at, go for, invade, light into*, rush; SEE CONCEPT *86*

comeback [*n*] *recovery, triumph*
improvement, rally, rebound, resurgence, return, revival, victory, winning; SEE CONCEPT *706*

comeback [*n2*] *snappy retort*
answer back, quip, rejoinder, repartee, reply, response, retaliation, riposte; SEE CONCEPT *278*

come back [*v*] *return*
come again, do better, reappear, recover, recur, re-enter, remigrate, resume, triumph; SEE CONCEPT *239*

come between [*v*] *alienate*
divide, estrange, interfere, interpose, interrupt, intervene, meddle, part, put at odds, separate; SEE CONCEPTS *14,386*

come by [*v1*] *acquire*
get, lay hold of, obtain, procure, secure, take possession of, win; SEE CONCEPTS *124,129*

come by [*v2*] *visit someone*
call, come over, drop by, drop in, look in, look up, meet, pay a call, pop in, run in, see, step in, stop by, visit; SEE CONCEPT *227*

come clean [*v*] *acknowledge information*
admit, confess, explain, make clean breast*, own up, reveal; SEE CONCEPTS *49,57*

comedian [*n*] *funny person, often professional*
actor, banana*, card*, clown, comic, cutup, droll, entertainer, farceur, humorist, jester, joker, jokester, laugh, merry-andrew, million laughs*, quipster, stand-up comic, stooge*, top banana*, wag, wisecracker, wit*, zany*; SEE CONCEPTS *352,423*

comedown [*n*] *letdown, blow*
anticlimax, blow, collapse, comeuppance, crash, cropper*, decline, defeat, deflation, demotion, descent, disappointment, discomfiture, dive, down, downfall, failure, fall, flop*, humiliation, pratfall*, reverse, ruin, setback, undoing, wreck; SEE CONCEPTS *674,699*

come down [*v*] *worsen*
decline, decrease, degenerate, descend, deteriorate, fail, fall, go downhill, reduce, suffer; SEE CONCEPT *698*

come down on [*v*] *criticize strongly*
attack, dress down, jump on, land on, rebuke, reprimand, scold; SEE CONCEPT *52*

come down with [*v*] *contract illness*
be stricken with, catch, contract, fall ill, fall victim to, sicken, take, take sick; SEE CONCEPTS *93,303*

comedy [*n*] *funny entertainment*
ball*, burlesque, camp, chaffing, comicality, comicalness, comic drama, drollery, drollness, facetiousness, farce, field day*, fun, fun and games*, funnies*, funniness, gag show, grins, high camp*, high time, hilarity, hoopla, humor, humorousness, interlude, jesting, joking, laughs, light entertainment, merry-go-round*, picnic, play on, satire, schtick*, send-up, sitcom*, slapstick, takeoff, travesty, vaudeville, wisecracking, witticism, wittiness; SEE CONCEPTS *263,293*

come forward [*v*] *volunteer services*
appear, make proposal, offer services, present oneself, proffer oneself; SEE CONCEPT *67*

come from [*v*] *arise, emanate*
accrue, arise from, ejaculate, emerge, end up, flow, hail from, issue, originate, proceed, result, rise, spring, stem, turn out; SEE CONCEPTS *105,179*

come in [*v*] *enter place*
alight, appear, arrive, cross threshold, disembark, finish, immigrate, intrude, land, pass in, reach, set foot in, show up; SEE CONCEPT *159*

come in for [*v*] *be eligible for something*
acquire, bear brunt, endure, get, receive, suffer; SEE CONCEPTS *23,124*

comely [*adj*] *beautiful*
a ten*, attractive, beauteous, becoming, blooming, buxom, fair, fine, good-looking, gorgeous, graceful, handsome, nice, pleasing, pretty, pulchritudinous, stunning, wholesome, winsome; SEE CONCEPT *579*

come off [*v*] *transpire*
befall, betide, break, chance, click, come about, develop, go, go off, go over, hap*, happen, occur, pan out, prove out, succeed, take place; SEE CONCEPT *4*

come on [*v1*] *advance, progress*
develop, gain, improve, increase, make headway, proceed; SEE CONCEPT *704*

come on [*v2*] *appear, enter*
begin, come across, come into, come upon, encounter, meet, pass in, set foot in*, take place; SEE CONCEPT *119*

come out [*v1*] *make public*
appear, be announced, be brought out, be disclosed, be divulged, be exposed, be issued, be made known, be promulgated, be published, be released, be reported, be revealed, break*, debut, get out, leak*, out, transpire; SEE CONCEPT *60*

come out [*v2*] *conclude*
end, result, terminate, transpire; SEE CONCEPT *119*

come out with [*v*] *disclose information*
acknowledge, bring out, chime in*, come clean, declare, deliver, divulge, lay open, own, own up, say, state, tell, throw out, utter; SEE CONCEPT *60*

come through [*v1*] *accomplish goal*
achieve, be successful, be victorious, carry out, chip in, contribute, kick in, pitch in, prevail, score, succeed, triumph, win; SEE CONCEPT *706*

come through [*v2*] *survive bad situation*
endure, live through, persist, pull through, ride, ride out, survive, weather storm*, withstand; SEE CONCEPT *23*

come unglued [*v*] *go to pieces*
break down, come apart at the seams*, come unstuck, come unwrapped, disintegrate, fall apart, fall to bits*, fall to pieces*, malfunction; SEE CONCEPTS *252,469*

come up [*v*] *happen suddenly*
arise, crop up, occur, rise, spring up, turn up; SEE CONCEPT *119*

come upon [*v*] *happen upon*
bump into*, chance, come across, encounter, meet; SEE CONCEPTS *38,384*

come up to [*v*] *meet expectations*
admit of comparison with, approach, arrive, bear comparison with, come near, compare with, equal, extend, get near, match, measure up to, rank with, reach, resemble, rival, stand comparison with; SEE CONCEPT *667*

come up with [*v*] *suggest, create*
advance, bring forth, compose, detect, discover, find, furnish, invent, offer, originate, present, produce, propose, provide, recommend, stumble upon, submit, uncover; SEE CONCEPTS *75,173*

comfort [*n1*] *good feeling; ease*
abundance, alleviation, amenity, assuagement, bed of roses*, cheer, cheerfulness, complacency, contentment, convenience, coziness, creature comforts*, enjoyment, exhilaration, facility, gratification, happiness, luxury, opulence, peace-

CO
CO

fulness, pleasure, plenty, poise, quiet, relaxation, relief, repose, rest, restfulness, satisfaction, snugness, succor, sufficiency, warmth, well-being; SEE CONCEPTS 230,410,720

comfort [n2] *aid, help*
alleviation, assist, compassion, compensation, consolation, encouragement, hand, lift, pity, relief, secours, solace, succor, support, sympathy; SEE CONCEPTS 337,712

comfort [v] *make to feel better*
abate, aid, allay, alleviate, ameliorate, assist, assuage, bolster, buck up*, calm, cheer, commiserate with, compose, condole, confirm, console, delight, divert, ease, encourage, enliven, free, gladden, grant respite, hearten, help, inspirit, invigorate, lighten burden, make well, mitigate, nourish, put at ease, quiet fears, reanimate, reassure, refresh, relieve, remedy, revitalize, revive, salve, soften, solace, soothe, strengthen, stroke, succor, support, sustain, sympathize, uphold, upraise; SEE CONCEPTS 7,22,572

comfortable [adj] *good feeling*
adequate, agreeable, appropriate, at rest, cared for, cheerful, complacent, contented, convenient, cozy, delightful, easy, enjoyable, enjoying, gratified, hale, happy, healthy, hearty, loose, loose-fitting, made well, pleasant, pleased, protected, relaxed, relaxing, relieved, rested, restful, restored, satisfactory, satisfying, serene, sheltered, snug, snug as a bug in a rug*, soothed, strengthened, untroubled, useful, warm, well-off; SEE CONCEPT 572

comfortable [adj2] *affluent, wealthy*
ample, easy, enough, prosperous, substantial, sufficient, suitable, well-heeled*, well-off, well-to-do; SEE CONCEPT 334

comfortable [adj3] *more than adequate*
ample, commodious, cushy, luxurious, palatial, rich, roomy, spacious; SEE CONCEPT 485

comfort food [n] *satisfying food*
home cooking, meat and potatoes, Mom's food, plain food, prepackaged food; SEE CONCEPTS 457,460,461

comforting [adj] *cheering*
abating, allaying, alleviating, analeptic, assuaging, consolatory, consoling, curing, encouraging, freeing, health-giving, heart-warming, inspiriting, invigorating, lightening, mitigating, reassuring, refreshing, relieving, remedying, restoring, revitalizing, revivifying, softening, solacing, soothing, succoring, sustaining, tranquilizing, upholding, warming; SEE CONCEPT 529

comic [n] *funny person, often professional*
banana*, buffoon*, card*, clown, comedian, droll, humorist, jester, joker, jokester, life of the party*, million laughs*, quipster, stand-up comic, stooge*, top banana*, wag*, wit*; SEE CONCEPTS 352,423

comic/comical [adj] *amusing*
absurd, batty, boffo*, camp*, comical, crazy, dippy, diverting, dizzy, droll, entertaining, facetious, farcical, flaky*, fool, foolheaded, for grins*, freaky, funny, gelastic, goofus*, goofy, gump*, horse's tail*, humorous, ironic, jerky, jocular, joking, joshing, laughable, light, loony, ludicrous, Mickey Mouse*, nutty, off the wall*, priceless, ridiculous, risible, schtick*, screwy, side-splitting, silly, wacky, waggish, whimsical, witty; SEE CONCEPTS 401,529

coming [adj] *approaching, promising*
about to happen, advancing, almost on one, anticipated, aspiring, at hand, certain, close, converging, deserving, docking, drawing near, due, en route, eventual, expected, fated, foreseen, forthcoming, future, gaining upon, getting near, immediate, imminent, impending, in prospect, instant, in store, in the offing, in the wind*, in view, marked, near, nearing, next, nigh, oncoming, ordained, predestined, preparing, progressing, prospective, pursuing, running after, subsequent, to be, up-and-coming; SEE CONCEPTS 537,799

coming [n] *arrival*
accession, advent, approach, landing, reception; SEE CONCEPTS 119,159

command [n1] *directive, instruction*
act, adjuration, ban, behest, bidding, call, canon, caveat, charge, citation, commandment, decree, demand, devoir, dictate, dictation, dictum, direction, duty, edict, enactment, exaction, fiat, imperative, imposition, injunction, interdiction, law, mandate, notification, obligation, order, ordinance, precept, prescript, proclamation, prohibition, proscription, regulation, request, requirement, requisition, responsibility, rule, subpoena, summons, ultimatum, warrant, will, word, writ; SEE CONCEPTS 274,662

command [n2] *rule, power*
ability, absolutism, aplomb, authority, authorization, charge, coercion, compulsion, constraint, control, despotism, domination, dominion, expertise, expertness, government, grasp, grip, hold, jurisdiction, know-how*, leadership, management, might, prerogative, primacy, restraint, right, royalty, skill, sovereignty, strings*, supervision, supremacy, sway, tyranny, upper hand*; SEE CONCEPT 376

command [v1] *demand*
adjure, appoint, authorize, ban, bar, beckon, bid, call, call for, call on, call the signals*, call upon, charge, check, cite, compel, debar, dictate, direct, enact, enjoin, exact, forbid, force upon, give directions, give orders, grant, impose, inflict, inhibit, instruct, interdict, lay down the law, mark out, oblige, ordain, order, ordinate, proclaim, prohibit, put foot down*, require, requisition, restrain, rule out, send for, set, subpoena, summon, take charge, take lead, task, tell, warn; SEE CONCEPT 53

command [v2] *rule, have power*
administer, boss, charge, check, coach, coerce, compel, conduct, conquer, constrain, control, curb, determine, dictate, direct, dominate, domineer, exact, exercise power, force, govern, guide, have authority, head, hinder, hold office, influence, lead, manage, officiate, oppress, overbear, override, predominate, prescribe, preside over, prevail, push, regulate, reign, reign over, repress, restrain, run, stop, subdue, superintend, supervise, sway, take over, tyrannize, wield; SEE CONCEPTS 133,298

commandeer [v] *seize, take over*
accroach, activate, annex, appropriate, arrogate, assume, confiscate, conscript, draft, enslave, expropriate, grab, hijack, liberate, moonlight requisition*, preempt, requisition, sequester, sequestrate, snatch, take, usurp; SEE CONCEPTS 90,142

commander [*n*] *leader of military or other organization*

administrator, big cheese*, boss, captain, chief, CO*, commandant, czar, director, don, exec, guru, head, head honcho*, head person, higher up, high priest/priestess*, kingfish*, kingpin*, lead-off person*, mastermind, officer, point person*, ruler, skipper, top banana*, top brass*, top dog*; SEE CONCEPTS 347,358

commanding [*adj*] *superior, authoritative*

advantageous, arresting, assertive, autocratic, bossy, compelling, controlling, decisive, dictatorial, dominant, dominating, forceful, imperious, imposing, impressive, in charge, lofty, peremptory, striking; SEE CONCEPTS 536,574

commemorate [*v*] *honor, observe occasion*

admire, celebrate, immortalize, keep, memorialize, monument, monumentalize, observe, pay tribute to, perpetuate, remember, salute, solemnize; SEE CONCEPTS 69,377,384

commemoration [*n*] *honoring, observance*

celebration, ceremony, custom, memorial service, monumentalization, recognition, remembrance, tribute; SEE CONCEPT 377

commemorative [*adj*] *in honor of something*

celebratory, commemoratory, dedicatory, in memory of, in remembrance, memorial, observing; SEE CONCEPT 555

commence [*v*] *start action*

arise, begin, come into being, come into existence, embark on, enter upon, get cracking*, get going, get one's feet wet*, get show on road*, hit the ground running*, inaugurate, initiate, jump into, kick off*, launch, lead off, open, originate, start the ball rolling*, take up, tear into; SEE CONCEPTS 119,234

commencement [*n*] *ceremony marking the beginning of stage*

admission, alpha, birth, bow, celebration, convocation, countdown, curtain-raiser*, dawn, dawning, genesis, graduation, initiation, kickoff*, onset, opener, opening, outset, proem, services, start, starting point, tee off*; SEE CONCEPT 377

commend [*v1*] *recommend, praise*

acclaim, accredit, advocate, applaud, approve, boost, build, build up, compliment, countenance, endorse, eulogize, extol, give a posy*, gold star*, hail, hand it to*, hats off to*, hear it for*, kudize, laud, pat on the back*, puff up, sanction, speak highly of, stroke, support; SEE CONCEPTS 69,75

commend [*v2*] *hand over with confidence*

assign, commit, confer, confide, consign, deliver, entrust, proffer, relegate, resign, tender, trust, turn over, yield; SEE CONCEPTS 108,132

commendable [*adj*] *praiseworthy*

admirable, creditable, deserving, estimable, excellent, exemplary, laudable, meritable, meritorious, praisable, thankworthy, worthy; SEE CONCEPTS 527,572

commendation [*n*] *giving of praise; acclaim*

acclamation, approbation, approval, award, bouquet, Brownie points*, credit, encomium, encouragement, good opinion, honor, panegyric, pat on the back*, pat on the head*, pay, plum, points*, posy, PR*, puff, pumping up*, rave, recommendation, shot in the arm*, stroke, stroking, tribute; SEE CONCEPTS 69,337

commensurate [*adj*] *adequate, corresponding*

appropriate, coextensive, comparable, compatible, consistent, due, equal, equivalent, fit, fitting,

in accord, proportionate, sufficient, symmetrical; SEE CONCEPTS 563,566

comment [*n*] *statement of opinion; explanation*

animadversion, annotation, backtalk*, buzz*, comeback*, commentary, crack*, criticism, dictum, discussion, editorial, elucidation, exposition, footnote, gloss, hearsay, illustration, input, judgment, mention, mouthful, note, obiter, observation, opinion, remark, report, review, two cents' worth*, wisecrack*; SEE CONCEPTS 51,278

comment [*v*] *make statement of opinion, explanation*

affirm, animadvert, annotate, assert, bring out, clarify, commentate, conclude, construe, criticize, disclose, elucidate, explain, explicate, expound, express, gloss, illustrate, interject, interpose, interpret, mention, note, notice, observe, opine, pass on, point out, pronounce, reflect, remark, say, state, touch upon; SEE CONCEPTS 51,57

commentary [*n*] *analysis*

annotation, appreciation, comment, consideration, criticism, critique, description, discourse, exegesis, explanation, exposition, gloss, narration, notes, obiter dictum, observation, remark, review, treatise, voice-over; SEE CONCEPTS 51,278

commentator [*n*] *reporter*

analyst, annotator, announcer, correspondent, critic, expositor, interpreter, observer, pundit, reviewer, sportscaster, writer; SEE CONCEPT 356

commerce [*n*] *buying and selling*

business, dealing, dealings, economics, exchange, industry, marketing, merchandising, merchantry, retailing, trade, traffic, truck, wholesaling; SEE CONCEPTS 325,770

commercial [*adj*] *concerning business, marketing*

across the counter*, bartering, commissary, economic, exchange, financial, fiscal, for sale, in demand, in the market, market, marketable, mercantile, merchandising, monetary, pecuniary, popular, profitable, profit-making, retail, retailing, saleable, sales, supplying, trade, trading, wholesale, wholesaling; SEE CONCEPT 536

commercial [*adj2*] *intended for financial gain*

exploited, for profit, investment, materialistic, mercenary, monetary, money-making, pecuniary, profitmaking, venal, Wall Street*; SEE CONCEPT 334

commercialize [*v*] *prepare for saleability*

advertise, cheapen, degrade, depreciate, develop as business, lessen, lower, make bring returns, make marketable, make pay, make profitable, make saleable, market, sell; SEE CONCEPT 324

commingle [*v*] *blend*

amalgamate, combine, commix, compound, inmix, integrate, intermingle, intermix, join, merge, mingle, unite; SEE CONCEPT 109

commiserate [*v*] *listen to woes of another*

ache, compassionate, condole, console, feel, feel for, have mercy, pity, share sorrow, sympathize; SEE CONCEPTS 110,596

commission [*n1*] *task, duty*

agency, appointment, authority, brevet, certificate, charge, consignment, delegation, deputation, diploma, embassy, employment, errand, function, instruction, legation, mandate, mission, obligation, office, permit, power of attorney, proxy, trust, warrant, work; SEE CONCEPT 362

commission [n2] *share of a profit*

allowance, ante, bite*, bonus, brokerage, chunk, compensation, cut, cut-in*, discount, end*, factorage, fee, indemnity, juice, pay, payment, percentage, piece, piece of the action*, rake-off*, remuneration, royalty, salary, slice*, stipend, taste, vigorish; SEE CONCEPTS 329,344

commission [n3] *group working together toward goal*

board, commissioners, committee, delegation, deputation, representative; SEE CONCEPT 381

commission [v] *authorize or delegate task*

accredit, appoint, assign, bespeak, bid, charge, command, commit, confide to, consign, constitute, contract, crown, depute, deputize, dispatch, employ, empower, enable, engage, enlist, enroll, entrust, hire, inaugurate, induct, instruct, invest, license, name, nominate, ordain, order, select, send; SEE CONCEPTS 50,88,324,351

commit [v1] *perform an action*

accomplish, achieve, act, carry out, complete, contravene, do, effectuate, enact, execute, go for broke*, go in for*, go out for*, offend, perpetrate, pull, pull off*, scandalize, sin, transgress, trespass, violate, wreak; SEE CONCEPTS 6,87

commit [v2] *deliver, entrust*

allocate, allot, apportion, authorize, charge, commend, commission, confer trust, confide, consign, convey, delegate, deliver, depend upon, deposit, depute, deputize, destine, dispatch, employ, empower, engage, give, give to do, grant authority, hand over, hold, ice, imprison, institutionalize, intrust, invest, leave to, make responsible for, move, offer, ordain, promise, put away, put in the hands of, relegate, rely upon, remove, send, shift, submit, transfer, turn over to, vest; SEE CONCEPTS 108,143,217

commitment [n] *assurance; obligation*

charge, committal, devoir, duty, engagement, guarantee, liability, must, need, ought, pledge, promise, responsibility, undertaking, vow, word; SEE CONCEPTS 71,271,274

committee [n] *group working on project*

board, bureau, cabinet, chamber, commission, consultants, convocation, council, investigators, jury, panel, representatives, task force, trustees; SEE CONCEPT 381

commodious [adj] *ample, spacious*

big, capacious, comfortable, convenient, expansive, extensive, large, loose, roomy, wide; SEE CONCEPTS 773,781

commodity [n] *merchandise, possession*

article, asset, belonging, chattel, goods, line, material, object, produce, product, property, specialty, stock, thing, vendible, ware; SEE CONCEPTS 338,710

common [adj1] *average, ordinary*

accepted, banal, bourgeois, casual, characteristic, colloquial, comformable, commonplace, conventional, current, customary, daily, everyday, familiar, frequent, general, habitual, hackneyed, homely, humdrum, informal, mediocre, monotonous, natural, obscure, passable, plain, prevailing, prevalent, probable, prosaic, regular, routine, run-of-the-mill*, simple, stale, standard, stereotyped, stock, trite, trivial, typical, undistinguished, universal, unvaried, usual, wearisome, workaday, worn-out; SEE CONCEPT 547

common [adj2] *generally known; held in common*

accepted, coincident, collective, communal, communistic, community, commutual, congruous, conjoint, conjunct, constant, corporate, correspondent, customary, general, generic, in common, intermutual, joint, like, mutual, popular, prevailing, prevalent, public, reciprocal, shared, social, socialistic, united, universal, usual, well-known, widespread; SEE CONCEPT 530

common [adj3] *low, coarse*

baseborn, characterless, cheap, colorless, crass, declassé, hack, hackneyed, impure, inferior, lowgrade, mean, middling, nondescript, passable, pedestrian, Philistine, plebeian, poor, prosy, raffish, second-class, second-rate, shoddy, sleazy, stale, trite, undistinguished, vulgar; SEE CONCEPTS 401,545

commonly [adv] *usually*

as a rule, by ordinary, frequently, generally, more often than not, ordinarily, regularly; SEE CONCEPTS 530,541

commonplace [adj] *usual, everyday*

boiler plate*, characterless, clichéd, colorless, conventional, corny*, customary, dime-a-dozen*, familiar, familiar tune, garden variety*, hackneyed, humdrum, lowly, mainstream, matter-of-course, mediocre, middle-of-the-road*, middling, mundane, natural, normal, obvious, ordinary, pedestrian, plebeian, prevalent, prosaic, run-of-the-mill*, stale, starch, stereotyped, threadbare, trite, typical, uneventful, unexceptional, uninteresting, unnoteworthy, vanilla*, widespread, workaday, worn-out; SEE CONCEPT 530

commonplace [n] *clichéd saying or idea*

banality, bromide*, chestnut*, cliché, corn*, inanity, motto, platitude, prosaicism, prosaism, prose, rubber stamp*, shallowness, shibboleth, stereotype, tag, triteness, truism, triviality; SEE CONCEPTS 278,689

common-sense [adj] *reasonable*

astute, commonsensical, cool, down-to-earth, hard-headed, judicious, levelheaded, matter-of-fact, practical, rational, realistic, sane, sensible, shrewd, sound; SEE CONCEPT 402

common sense [n] *good reasoning*

acumen, cool, good sense, gumption, horse sense*, intelligence, levelheadedness, practicality, prudence, reasonableness, sense, sound judgment, soundness, wisdom, wit; SEE CONCEPT 409

commonwealth [n] *political or geographic area*

body politic, citizenry, citizens, commonality, democracy, federation, nation, people, polity, republic, society; SEE CONCEPTS 301,512

commotion [n] *clamor, uproar*

ado, agitation, annoyance, backwash, ballyhoo*, bedlam, big scene*, big stink*, brouhaha, bustle, clatter, combustion, confusion, convulsion, discomposure, disquiet, dither, excitement, ferment, fermentation, flap, flurry, furor, fuss, hell broke loose*, hubbub, hurly-burly, insurgence, insurrection, lather*, mutiny, outcry, pandemonium, perturbation, pother, racket, rebellion, revolt, riot, rumpus, stew, stir, to-do, tumult, turbulence, upheaval, uprising, upset, upturn, vexation, welter, whirl; SEE CONCEPTS 388,674

communal [adj] *collective; shared*

common, communistic, community, conjoint,

conjunct, cooperative, general, intermutual, joint, mutual, neighborhood, public; SEE CONCEPTS *536,708*

commune [*n*] *group living together*
collective, commonage, commonality, community, cooperative, family, kibbutz, municipality, neighborhood, rank and file, village; SEE CONCEPT *379*

commune [*v*] *communicate, experience with another*
confer, confide in, contemplate, converse, discourse, discuss, mediate, muse, parley, ponder, reflect; SEE CONCEPTS *17,266*

communicable [*adj*] *able to be contracted*
catching, communicative, contagious, expansive, infectious, pandemic, taking, transferable, transmittable; SEE CONCEPT *314*

communicate [*v1*] *give or exchange information, ideas*
acquaint, advertise, advise, announce, be in touch, betray, break, broadcast, carry, connect, contact, convey, correspond, declare, disclose, discover, disseminate, divulge, enlighten, get across, get through, hint, impart, imply, inform, interact, interface, keep in touch, let on, let out, make known, network*, pass on, phone, proclaim, publicize, publish, raise, reach out, relate, report, reveal, ring up, signify, spread, state, suggest, tell, touch base*, transfer, transmit, unfold, write; SEE CONCEPTS *56,266*

communicate [*v2*] *mutually exchange information*
answer, associate with, be close to, be in touch, be near, buzz, cable, chat, commune with, confabulate, confer, converse, correspond, discourse, drop a line*, drop a note*, establish contact, get on the horn*, give a call, give a ring*, have confidence of, hear from, reach, reply, talk, telephone, wire, write; SEE CONCEPTS *56,266*

communication [*n1*] *giving, exchanging information, ideas*
advice, advisement, announcing, articulation, assertion, communion, connection, contact, conversation, converse, correspondence, corresponding, declaration, delivery, disclosing, dissemination, elucidation, expression, intelligence, interchange, intercommunication, intercourse, link, making known, mention, notifying, publication, reading, reception, revelation, talk, talking, telling, transfer, translating, transmission, utterance, writing; SEE CONCEPT *266*

communication [*n2*] *information transmitted*
account, advice, announcement, briefing, bulletin, communiqué, conversation, converse, declaration, directive, disclosure, dispatch, excerpt, goods*, hot story*, ideas, info*, information, inside story*, intelligence, language, lowdown, message, missive, news, note, pipeline, poop*, precis, prophecy, publicity, report, revelation, scoop*, skinny*, speech, statement, summary, tidings, translation, utterance, warning, word, work; SEE CONCEPT *274*

communications [*n*] *systems of information exchange*
information technology, means, media, publicity, public relations, route, telecommunications, transport, travel; SEE CONCEPTS *349,770*

communicative [*adj*] *informative*
candid, chatty, communicable, conversable, conversational, demonstrative, effusive, enlightening, expansive, forthcoming, frank, garrulous, gushing, loquacious, open, outgoing, talkative, unreserved, voluble; SEE CONCEPT *267*

communion [*n1*] *affinity, agreement*
accord, association, closeness, close relationship, communing, concord, contact, converse, fellowship, harmony, intercommunication, intercourse, intimacy, participation, rapport, sympathy, togetherness, unity; SEE CONCEPT *684*

communion [*n2*] *sacrament in church; body of believers sharing a sacrament*
breaking of bread, church, creed, denomination, Eucharist, faith, Lord's Supper, Mass, persuasion, religion, sacrament; SEE CONCEPT *367*

communism [*n*] *socialist government*
Bolshevism, collectivism, Leninism, Marxism, rule of the proletariat, socialism, state ownership, totalitarianism; SEE CONCEPT *301*

community [*n1*] *society, area of people*
association, body politic, center, colony, commonality, commonwealth, company, district, general public, hamlet, locality, nation, neck of the woods*, neighborhood, people, populace, public, residents, society, state, stomping ground*, territory, turf; SEE CONCEPTS *379,512*

community [*n2*] *agreement, similarity*
affinity, identity, kinship, likeness, sameness, semblance; SEE CONCEPTS *664,670*

commute [*v1*] *travel to work*
drive, go back and forth, take the bus/subway/train; SEE CONCEPT *224*

commute [*v2*] *reduce punishment*
alleviate, curtail, decrease, mitigate, modify, remit, shorten, soften; SEE CONCEPTS *236,247, 317*

commute [*v3*] *exchange, trade*
barter, change, convert, interchange, metamorphose, substitute, switch, transfer, transfigure, transform, translate, transmogrify, transmute, transpose; SEE CONCEPTS *104,232*

commuter [*n*] *daily traveler, usually for work*
city worker, driver, straphanger*, suburbanite, traveler; SEE CONCEPT *348*

compact [*adj1*] *condensed*
appressed, bunched, close, compressed, crowded, dense, firm, hard, impenetrable, impermeable, packed, pressed, solid, thick, tight; SEE CONCEPTS *481,483,774*

compact [*adj2*] *short, brief*
boiled down, compendious, concise, epigrammatic, in a nutshell*, laconic, make a long story short*, marrowy, meaty, pithy, pointed, short and sweet*, succinct, terse, to the point; SEE CONCEPTS *773,798*

compact [*n*] *agreement*
alliance, arrangement, bargain, bond, concordat, contract, convention, covenant, deal, engagement, entente, indenture, pact, settlement, stipulation, transaction, treaty, understanding; SEE CONCEPTS *271,684*

compact [*v*] *make condensed*
combine, compress, concentrate, condense, consolidate, contract, cram, integrate, pack, set, solidify, stuff, unify, unite; SEE CONCEPTS *137,208,250*

compact disc [*n*] *recording of music or speech*
album, CD, cut*, cylinder, demo, digital recording, disk, laser disk, record, release, track; SEE CONCEPT *262*

CO
CO.

companion [*n*] *helper, friend*
accompaniment, accomplice, aide, ally, assistant, associate, attendant, buddy, chaperon, colleague, comate, complement, comrade, concomitant, confederate, consort, convoy, counterpart, cousin, co-worker, crony, cuz*, double, escort, guide, match, mate, nurse, pal, pard*, partner, playmate, protector, roomie*, safeguard, side-kick; SEE CONCEPT *423*

companionable [*adj*] *friendly*
affable, amicable, buddy buddy*, clubby*, complacent, congenial, conversable, convivial, cordial, cozy, cozy with, familiar, genial, good-natured, gregarious, intimate, mellow, neighborly, outgoing, pally, palsy*, sociable, social, tight, tight with*; SEE CONCEPT *555*

companionship [*n*] *friendship, accompaniment*
affiliation, alliance, amity, camaraderie, company, comradeship, conviviality, esprit de corps, rapport, society, togetherness, union; SEE CONCEPT *388*

company [*n1*] *crowd of people*
aggregation, assemblage, assembly, association, band, body, circle, clan, clique, club, collection, community, concourse, congregation, convention, corps, cortege, coterie, crew, ensemble, gang*, gathering, group, horde, jungle*, league, mob*, muster, order, outfit, pack, party, retinue, ring, ruck, set, team, throng, troop, troupe, turnout, zoo*; SEE CONCEPT *417*

company [*n2*] *business concern*
association, business, concern, corporation, enterprise, establishment, firm, house, megacorp*, multinational, outfit, partnership, syndicate; SEE CONCEPT *325*

company [*n3*] *social friend, guest*
boarder, caller, companionship, cortege, party, presence, retinue, society, visitor; SEE CONCEPTS *417,423*

comparable [*adj1*] *worthy of comparison*
a match for, as good as, commensurable, commensurate, equal, equipollent, equipotential, equivalent, in a class with, on a par, proportionate, tantamount; SEE CONCEPT *566*

comparable [*adj2*] *corresponding, similar*
agnate, akin, alike, analogous, cognate, consonant, corresponding, like, parallel, related, relative, undifferenced, uniform; SEE CONCEPTS *487,573*

comparative [*adj*] *approximate, close to*
allusive, analogous, approaching, by comparison, comparable, conditional, connected, contingent, contrastive, correlative, corresponding, equivalent, in proportion, like, matching, metaphorical, near, not absolute, not positive, parallel, provisional, qualified, related, relative, restricted, rivaling, similar, vying, with reservation; SEE CONCEPTS *487,566,573*

compare [*v1*] *examine in contrast*
analyze, approach, balance, bracket, collate, confront, consider, contemplate, contrast, correlate, divide, equal, examine, hang, hold a candle to*, inspect, juxtapose, match, match up, measure, observe, oppose, parallel, place in juxtaposition, ponder, rival, scan, scrutinize, segregate, separate, set against, set side by side, size up, stack up against*, study, touch, weigh, weigh against another; SEE CONCEPTS *24,103*

compare [*v2*] *liken, equate*
allegorize, approach, approximate to, assimilate,

balance, bear comparison, be in the same class as*, be on a par with*, bring near, come up to, compete with, connect, correlate, distinguish between, draw parallel, equal, equate, hold a candle to*, identify with, link, make like, match, notice similarities, parallel, put alongside, relate, resemble, show correspondence, stack up with*, standardize, tie up, vie; SEE CONCEPT *39*

comparison [*n*] *contrasting; corresponding*
allegory, analogizing, analogy, analyzing, association, balancing, bringing together, collating, collation, comparability, connection, contrast, correlation, discrimination, distinguishing, dividing, estimation, example, exemplification, identification, illustration, juxtaposition, likeness, likening, measuring, metaphor, observation, opposition, paralleling, ratio, relating, relation, resemblance, segregation, separation, similarity, testing, weighing; SEE CONCEPTS *24,39,529*

compartment [*n*] *section, subdivision*
alcove, area, bay, berth, booth, carrel, carriage, category, cell, chamber, corner, cubbyhole, cubicle, department, division, hole, locker, niche, nook, part, piece, pigeonhole, place, portion, slot, stall; SEE CONCEPT *434*

compass [*n*] *boundary, periphery*
ambit, area, bound, circle, circuit, circumference, circumscription, confines, domain, enclosure, environs, expanse, extent, field, limit, limitation, orbit, perimeter, precinct, purlieus, purview, radius, range, reach, realm, restriction, round, scope, sphere, stretch, sweep, zone; SEE CONCEPTS *484,651,788*

compass [*v1*] *enclose*
beset, besiege, blockade, circle, circumscribe, encircle, encompass, environ, gird, girdle, hem in, ring, round, surround; SEE CONCEPT *758*

compass [*v2*] *achieve, get*
accomplish, annex, attain, bring about, effect, execute, fulfill, gain, have, land, obtain, perform, procure, realize, secure, win; SEE CONCEPTS *142,706*

compassion [*n*] *tender feeling*
benevolence, charity, clemency, commiseration, compunction, condolence, consideration, empathy, fellow feeling, grace, heart, humaneness, humanity, kindness, lenity, mercy, softheartedness, softness, sorrow, sympathy, tenderheartedness, tenderness, yearning; SEE CONCEPTS *410,633*

compassionate [*adj*] *having tender feelings*
all heart, being big*, benevolent, bleeding heart*, charitable, commiserative, forbearing, going easy on*, humane, humanitarian, indulgent, kindhearted, kindly, lenient, living with, merciful, old softie*, piteous, pitying, responsive, softhearted, soft shell*, sparing, sympathetic, tender, tenderhearted, understanding, warm, warmhearted; SEE CONCEPTS *401,403*

compatibility [*n*] *harmony in relationship*
affinity, agreeableness, agreement, amity, congeniality, congruity, consonance, empathy, fit, like-mindedness, rapport, single-mindedness, sympathy, unity; SEE CONCEPT *388*

compatible [*adj*] *agreeable, in harmony*
accordant, adaptable, appropriate, congenial, congruent, congruous, consistent, consonant, cooperative, cotton to*, fit, fitting, getting along with, harmonious, having good vibes*, hitting it off*, in keeping, in sync with*, in the groove*, like-minded, meet, on the same wavelength*,

proper, reconcilable, simpatico, suitable, sympathetic, together; SEE CONCEPT 555

compel [v] *force to act*
bulldoze*, coerce, concuss, constrain, crack down, dragoon, drive, enforce, exact, hustle, impel, make, make necessary, necessitate, oblige, put the arm on*, put the chill on*, restrain, shotgun*, squeeze, throw weight around*, turn on the heat*, urge; SEE CONCEPTS *14,384*

compendious [adj] *abridged*
abbreviated, breviloquent, brief, close, compact, compendiary, comprehensive, concise, condensed, contracted, curt, inclusive, laconic, short, short and sweet*, succinct, summarized, summary, synoptic; SEE CONCEPTS *773,789*

compendium [n] *abridgment*
abstract, aperçu, brief, conspectus, digest, epitome, essence, guide, handbook, manual, overview, pandect, precis, sketch, summary, survey, syllabus, sylloge; SEE CONCEPT *283*

compensate [v1] *make restitution*
atone, come down with*, commit, guerdon, indemnify, make good*, pay, pay up, plank out*, pony up*, recompense, recoup, refund, reimburse, remunerate, repay, requite, reward, satisfy, shell out*, take care of, tickle the palm*; SEE CONCEPTS *108,126,341*

compensate [v2] *offset, make up for*
abrogate, annul, atone for, balance, better, cancel out, counteract, counterbalance, counterpoise, countervail, fix, improve, invalidate, make amends, negate, negative, neutralize, nullify, outweigh, redress, repair, set off; SEE CONCEPTS *126,212*

compensation [n] *repayment; rectification*
advantage, allowance, amends, atonement, benefit, bonus, bread*, consideration, counterclaim, coverage, damages, defrayal, deserts*, earnings, fee*, gain, honorarium, indemnification, indemnity, meet, pay, payment, payoff, premium, profit, quittance, reciprocity, reckoning, recompense, recoupment, redress, reimbursement, remittal, remittance, remuneration, reparation, reprisal, requital, restitution, reward, salary, salt, satisfaction, scale, settlement, shake, stipend, take*, take-home*, wage; SEE CONCEPTS *337,344*

compete [v] *go up against in contest*
attempt, bandy, battle, be in the running*, bid, challenge, clash, collide, contend, contest, cope with, emulate, encounter, essay, face, fence, fight, go after, go for*, go for broke*, go for the gold*, grapple, in the hunt*, jockey for position*, joust, lock horns*, match strength, match wits*, oppose, participate in, pit oneself against*, play, rival, run for, scramble for*, seek prize, spar, strive, struggle, take on, take part, tilt, try, tussle, vie, wrestle; SEE CONCEPT *92*

competence [n] *ability*
adequacy, appropriateness, capability, capacity, competency, cutting it*, cutting the mustard*, expertise, fitness, hacking it*, know-how, makings, making the grade*, might, moxie, proficiency, qualification, qualifiedness, savvy, skill, suitability, the goods*, the right stuff*, what it takes*; SEE CONCEPT *630*

competent [adj] *able*
adapted, adequate, all around, appropriate, au fait, being a pistol*, capable, clever, complete, crisp, decent, dynamite*, efficient, endowed, enough, equal, fireball*, fit, fool, good, know ins

and outs*, know one's business*, know one's stuff*, know the answers*, know the ropes*, know the score*, no slouch*, on the ball*, paid one's dues*, pertinent, polished, proficient, qualified, satisfactory, savvy, skilled, sufficient, suitable, there*, up to it, up to snuff*, up to speed*, wicked*; SEE CONCEPT *527*

competition [n] *contest*
antagonism, athletic event, bout, candidacy, championship, clash, concours, contention, controversy, counteraction, dog eat dog*, do or die*, emulation, encounter, engagement, event, fight, game, go for it, go for the gold*, horse race*, jungle*, match, matchup, meeting, one on one*, one-upping, opposition, pairing off, puzzle, quiz, race, racing, rat race*, rivalry, run, sport, strife, striving, struggle, tilt, tournament, trial, tug-of-war, warfare; SEE CONCEPTS *92,363*

competitive [adj] *willing to oppose*
aggressive, ambitious, antagonistic, at odds, combative, competing, cutthroat, dog-eat-dog*, emulous, killer*, killer instinct*, opposing, rival, streetwise, vying; SEE CONCEPT *542*

competitor [n] *person willing to enter contest*
adversary, antagonist, challenger, competition, contestant, corival, dark horse*, emulator, favorite, opponent, opposition, rival; SEE CONCEPTS *366,423*

compilation [n] *assemblage*
accumulating, accumulation, aggregating, anthology, assembling, assortment, collecting, collection, collocating, combining, compiling, consolidating, garner, garnering, gathering, incorporating, joining, treasury, unifying; SEE CONCEPTS *109,432*

compile [v] *assemble, accumulate*
abridge, amass, anthologize, arrange, assemble, bring together, collate, collect, colligate, collocate, compose, concentrate, congregate, consolidate, cull, draw together, edit, garner, gather, get together, glean, group, heap up, marshal, muster, organize, put together, recapitulate, unite; SEE CONCEPTS *79,84,109*

complacent [adj] *contented*
conceited, confident, easy-going, egoistic, egotistic, gratified, happy, obsequious, pleased, satisfied, self-assured, self-contented, self-pleased, self-possessed, self-righteous, self-satisfied, serene, smug, unconcerned; SEE CONCEPTS *401,403*

complain [v] *grumble about*
accuse, ascribe, attack, beef*, bellyache*, bemoan, bewail, bitch, carp, cavil, charge, contravene, criticize, defy, demur, denounce, deplore, deprecate, differ, disagree, disapprove, dissent, expostulate, find fault, fret, fuss, gainsay, grieve, gripe, groan, grouse, growl, grumble, impute, indict, kick up a fuss*, lament, lay, look askance, make a fuss, moan, nag, object, oppose, protest, refute, remonstrate, repine, reproach, snivel, sound off, take exception to, wail, whimper, whine, yammer; SEE CONCEPT *52*

complaint [n1] *statement of disagreement, discontent*
accusation, annoyance, beef*, cavil, CC*, charge, clamor, criticism, dissatisfaction, expostulation, fault-finding, grievance, gripe, grouse, grumble, guff*, jeremiad, kick, lament, moan, objection, plaint, protest, protestation, rap, remonstrance, remonstration, representation, re-

proach, rumble*, squawk, stink, trouble, wail, whine; SEE CONCEPTS 52,689

complaint [n2] *illness, affliction*
affection, ailment, condition, disease, disorder, ill, indisposition, infirmity, malady, sickness, syndrome, upset; SEE CONCEPTS 306,316

complaisance [n] *agreeableness*
accommodativeness, acquiescence, compliance, courtesy, deference, friendliness, kindness, obligingness, politeness, respect; SEE CONCEPT 633

complaisant [adj] *agreeable*
accommodating, amiable, compliant, conciliatory, deferential, easy, easy-going, friendly, generous, good-humored, good-natured, good-tempered, indulgent, lenient, mild, obliging, polite, solicitous, submissive; SEE CONCEPT 401

complement [n] *companion, counterpart*
accompaniment, addition, aggregate, augmentation, balance, capacity, completion, consummation, correlate, correlative, counterpart, enhancement, enrichment, entirety, filler, finishing touch, makeweight, pendant, quota, remainder, rest, rounding-off*, supplement, total, totality; SEE CONCEPTS 635,824

complement [v] *complete*
accomplish, achieve, cap, clinch, conclude, consummate, crown, finish, fulfill, integrate, perfect, round out, top off; SEE CONCEPTS 91,119,234

complementary [adj] *filling, completing*
commutual, complemental, completing, completory, conclusive, correlative, correspondent, corresponding, crowning, equivalent, fellow, integral, integrative, interconnected, interdependent, interrelated, interrelating, matched, mated, paired, parallel, reciprocal; SEE CONCEPTS 577,824

complete [adj1] *total, not lacking*
all, entire, exhaustive, faultless, full, full-dress, gross, hook line and sinker*, imperforate, intact, integral, integrated, lock stock and barrel*, organic, outright, plenary, replete, the works*, thorough, thoroughgoing, unabbreviated, unabridged, unbroken, uncondensed, uncut, undiminished, undivided, undocked, unexpurgated, unimpaired, unitary, unreduced, whole, whole enchilada*, whole-hog*, whole-length, whole nine yards*; SEE CONCEPT 531

complete [adj2] *finished*
accomplished, achieved, all-embracing, all-inclusive, all over, all over but the shouting*, attained, compassed, concluded, consummate, done, done with, down, effected, ended, entire, executed, fini*, finished off, full, full-fledged, home free*, perfect, plenary, realized, sweeping, terminated, that's it*, through; SEE CONCEPT 528

complete [adj3] *utter, absolute*
blank, blanket, categorical, consummate, downright, dyed-in-the-wool*, flawless, impeccable, out-and-out, outright, perfect, positive, sheer, thorough, thoroughgoing, total, unblemished, unconditional, unmitigated, unqualified, whole; SEE CONCEPTS 531,535

complete [v] *carry out action*
accomplish, achieve, actualize, bring to fruition, bring to maturity, call it a day*, cap, carry off, close, conclude, consummate, crown, determine, develop, discharge, do, do thoroughly, effect, effectuate, elaborate, end, equip, execute, fill, finalize, finish, fulfill, furnish, get through, go the limit*, go through with, go whole hog*, halt, make good*, make up, perfect, perform, put to bed*, realize, refine, round off, round out, settle, sew up*, supplement, terminate, ultimate, wind up*, wrap up*; SEE CONCEPT 91

completely [adv] *entirely*
absolutely, all the way*, altogether, competently, comprehensively, conclusively, effectively, en masse, exclusively, exhaustively, extensively, finally, from A to Z*, from beginning to end*, fully, heart and soul*, hook line and sinker*, in all, in entirety, in full, in toto*, on all counts*, painstakingly, perfectly, quite, solidly, thoroughly, totally, to the end, to the limit, to the max*, to the nth degree*, ultimately, unabridged, unanimously, unconditionally, undividedly, utterly, wholly, without omission; SEE CONCEPT 531

completion [n] *accomplishment, finishing*
achievement, attainment, close, conclusion, consummation, culmination, curtains*, dispatch, end, expiration, finalization, finis, finish, fruition, fulfillment, hips*, integration, perfection, realization, swan song*, windup, wrap-up; SEE CONCEPTS 119,706

complex [adj1] *involved, intricate*
circuitous, complicated, composite, compound, compounded, confused, conglomerate, convoluted, elaborate, entangled, heterogeneous, knotty, labyrinthine, manifold, mingled, miscellaneous, mixed, mixed-up, mosaic, motley, multifarious, multiform, multiple, multiplex, tangled, tortuous, variegated; SEE CONCEPT 562

complex [adj2] *difficult to understand*
abstruse, bewildering, Byzantine, circuitous, complicated, confused, convoluted, crabbed, cryptic, Daedalean, discursive, disordered, disturbing, enigmatic, entangled, excursive, Gordian, hidden, impenetrable, inscrutable, interwoven, intricate, involved, jumbled, knotted, knotty, labyrinthine, mazy, meandering, mingled, mixed, muddled, obscure, paradoxical, perplexing, puzzling, rambling, recondite, roundabout, sinuous, snarled, sophisticated, tangled, tortuous, undecipherable, unfathomable, winding; SEE CONCEPTS 402,529

complex [n1] *composite, aggregate*
association, compound, conglomerate, ecosystem, entanglement, group, network, organization, scheme, structure, syndrome, synthesis, system, totality; SEE CONCEPTS 432,770

complex [n2] *psychological problem*
anxiety, a thing about something*, exaggerated reaction, fear, fixation, fixed idea, hang-up*, idée fixe, insanity, mania, neurosis, obsession, phobia, preoccupation, repression; SEE CONCEPT 410

complexion [n1] *skin coloring, appearance*
cast, color, coloration, coloring, flush, front, glow, hue, looks, mug*, phiz*, pigmentation, skin, skin tone, texture, tinge, tint, tone; SEE CONCEPTS 405,622

complexion [n2] *someone's character*
appearance, aspect, cast, countenance, disposition, guise, humor, ilk, individualism, individuality, kind, light, look, make-up, nature, personality, seeming, semblance, sort, stamp, style, temper, temperament, type; SEE CONCEPT 411

complexity [*n*] *complicatedness*
complication, convolution, elaboration, entanglement, intricacy, involvement, multiplicity, ramification; SEE CONCEPT 663

compliance [*n*] *agreement*
acquiescence, amenability, assent, complaisance, concession, concurrence, conformity, consent, deference, docility, obedience, observance, passivity, resignation, submission, submissiveness, tractability, yielding; SEE CONCEPTS 411,684

complicate [*v*] *confuse, make difficult*
add fuel to fire*, bedevil, clog, combine, confound, convolute, derange, disarrange, disorder, elaborate, embroil, entangle, fold, foul up*, handicap, fancy, gasser*, Gordian, hard, hi-tech*, interweave, involve, jumble, make intricate, make waves*, mix up, muck up*, muddle, multiply, obscure, open can of worms*, perplex, ravel, render unintelligible, screw up*, snafu*, snag, snarl up*, tangle, twist, upset; SEE CONCEPTS 7,19

complicated [*adj*] *difficult, complex*
abstruse, arduous, Byzantine, can of worms*, convoluted, Daedalean, difficult, elaborate, entangled, fancy, gasser*, Gordian, hard, hi-tech*, interlaced, intricate, involved, knotty, labyrinthine, mega factor*, mixed, perplexing, problematic, puzzling, recondite, sophisticated, troublesome, various, wheels within wheels*; SEE CONCEPTS 562,565

complication [*n*] *difficult situation*
aggravation, complexity, confusion, development, difficulty, dilemma, drawback, embarrassment, entanglement, factor, intricacy, obstacle, problem, snag, web; SEE CONCEPTS 230,674

complicity [*n*] *conspiracy*
abetment, agreement, collaboration, collusion, complot, concurrence, confederacy, connivance, engineering, guilt, guiltiness, implication, intrigue, involvement, machination, manipulation, partnership; SEE CONCEPTS 388,660

compliment [*n*] *praise, flattery*
acclaim, acclamation, admiration, adulation, applause, appreciation, approval, blessing, bouquet*, buttering up*, cajolery, commendation, comp, confirmation, congratulations, courtesy, encomium, endorsement, eulogy, favor, felicitation, good word, homage, honor, kudo, laud, laudation, laurels, notice, orchid*, ovation, panegyric, pat on the back*, posy*, regard, respects, sanction, sentiment, tribute, veneration, warm fuzzy*; SEE CONCEPTS 69,278

compliment [*v*] *praise, flatter*
acclaim, adulate, applaud, butter up* cajole, celebrate, charm, cheer, commemorate, commend, congratulate, endorse, eulogize, exalt, extol, fawn upon, felicitate, give bouquet*, glorify, hail, hand it to*, honor, ingratiate oneself with, kudize*, laud, magnify, make much of, panegyrize, pat on the back*, pay respects, pay tribute to, please, puff up*, recommend, roose, salute, sanction, satisfy, sing praises of, soothe, speak highly of, take off hat to*, toast, trade last*, wish joy to, worship; SEE CONCEPT 69

complimentary [*adj* 1] *flattering*
adulatory, appreciative, approbative, approbatory, approving, celebrating, commendatory, congratulatory, courtly, encomiastic, encomiastical, eulogistic, fair-spoken, fawning, highly favorable, honeyed, honoring, laudatory,

panegyrical, plauditory, polite, praiseful, respectful, sycophantic, unctuous, well-wishing, with highest recommendation, with high praise; SEE CONCEPT 267

complimentary [*adj2*] *free*
as a perk*, chargeless, comp, costless, courtesy, donated, free lunch*, free of charge, gratis, gratuitous, honorary, on the house*; SEE CONCEPT 334

comply [*v*] *abide by, follow agreement or instructions*
accede, accord, acquiesce, adhere to, agree to, cave in, come around, conform to, consent to, cry uncle*, defer, discharge, ditto*, don't make waves*, don't rock the boat*, fit in, fold, fulfill, give in, give out, give up, go along with, go with the flow*, keep, knuckle to*, knuckle under*, mind, obey, observe, perform, play ball*, play the game*, put out, quit, respect, roll over and play dead*, satisfy, shape up, stay in line*, straighten up, submit, throw in towel*, toss it in*, yes one*, yield; SEE CONCEPTS 8,35,91

component [*adj*] *constituent*
basic, composing, elemental, fundamental, inherent, integral, intrinsic, part and parcel of*, part of; SEE CONCEPTS 546,567

component [*n*] *part, element*
constituent, factor, fixings, ingredient, item, making, makings, peripheral, piece, plug-in, segment, unit; SEE CONCEPTS 831,834

compose [*v1*] *be part of construction*
be an adjunct, be an element of, belong to, be made of, build, compound, comprise, consist of, constitute, construct, enter in, fashion, form, go into, make, make up, merge in; SEE CONCEPTS 168,642

compose [*v2*] *create writing, artwork, or music*
author, bang out*, cast, clef*, coin a phrase, comp, conceive, contrive, cook up*, design, devise, discover, draw up, dream up, fabricate, forge, form, formulate, frame*, fudge together*, ghost*, ghostwrite, imagine, indite, invent, knock off*, knock out*, make up, note down, orchestrate, originate, pen, poetize, produce, push pencil*, put down, put pen to paper*, score, scribble, script, set type, set up, time, turn out, whip up*, write; SEE CONCEPTS 79,173,174

compose [*v3*] *calm, bring under control*
adjust, allay, appease, arrange, assuage, balm, becalm, check, collect, comfort, console, contain, control, cool, ease, ease up, hold in, lessen, let up, lull, mitigate, moderate, modulate, pacify, placate, quell, quiet, re-collect, reconcile, regulate, rein, relax, relieve, resolve, restrain, settle, simmer down, slacken, smother, soften, solace, soothe, still, suppress, temper, tranquilize, tune down; SEE CONCEPTS 7,22,117

composed [*adj*] *calm, collected*
at ease, calmed, clearheaded, commonsensical, confident, cool, cool as cucumber*, disimpassioned, dispassionate, easy, easygoing, have one's act together*, imperturbable, keeping a stiff upper lip*, keeping one's shirt on*, levelheaded, nonchalant, not turn a hair*, placid, poised, possessed, quieted, relaxed, repressed, sedate, self-assured, self-possessed, sensible, serene, serious, soothed, staid, suppressed, sure of oneself, temperate, together, tranquil, unflappable, unruffled, untroubled; SEE CONCEPT 401

CO
CO

composite [*adj*] *combined, mixed*
blended, complex, compound, conglomerate, melded, synthesized; SEE CONCEPT *490*

composite [*n*] *combination, mixture*
amalgam, amalgamation, blend, combo, commixture, complex, compost, compound, conglomerate, fusion, immixture, intermixture, medley, mix, olio, pastiche, stew*, synthesis, union; SEE CONCEPTS *260,432*

composition [*n1*] *structure, arrangement*
agreement, architecture, balance, beauty, combination, concord, configuration; consonance, constitution, content, design, distribution, form, formation, harmony, layout, make-up, placing, proportion, relation, rhythm, spacing, style, symmetry, weave; SEE CONCEPTS *733,757*

composition [*n2*] *written or musical creation*
arrangement, article, chart, concerto, dissertation, drama, essay, exercise, exposition, fiction, getup*, literary work, manuscript, melody, music, novel, number, opus, paper, piece, play, poetry, rhapsody, romance, score, setup*, short story, song, stanza, study, symphony, theme, thesis, tune, verse, work, writing; SEE CONCEPTS *259,260,263,271*

compost [*n*] *organic material*
admixture, blend, commixture, composition, compound, fertilizer, fusion, humus, manure, mix, mixture, mulch, ordure, pile; SEE CONCEPT *509*

composure [*n*] *calmness, collectedness*
accord, aplomb, assurance, balance, calm, contentment, control, cool*, cool head*, coolheadedness, coolness, dignity, dispassion, ease, equanimity, equilibrium, evenness, even temper, fortitude, harmony, imperturbability, inexcitability, levelheadedness, moderation, nonchalance, peace of mind, placidity, poise, polish, presence of mind, quiet, quietude, repose, sang-froid, sedateness, self-assurance, self-control, self-possession, serenity, sobriety, stability, tranquility; SEE CONCEPT *410*

compound [*n*] *combination, mixture*
admixture, aggregate, alloy, amalgam, amalgamation, blend, combo, commixture, composite, composition, compost, conglomerate, fusion, goulash, medley, mishmash*, soup, stew, synthesis, union; SEE CONCEPTS *260,432*

compound [*v1*] *mix, combine*
admix, amalgamate, associate, blend, bracket, coagment, coalesce, commingle, commix, concoct, connect, couple, fuse, immix, intermingle, join, link, make up, meld, mingle, synthesize, unite; SEE CONCEPTS *109,113*

compound [*v2*] *make difficult; complicate*
add to, aggravate, augment, confound, confuse, exacerbate, extend, heighten, intensify, magnify, make complex, make intricate, multiply, worsen; SEE CONCEPTS *231,240*

comprehend [*v1*] *understand*
appreciate, apprehend, assimilate, capiche*, catch, click, cognize, conceive, dig*, discern, envisage, envision, fathom, get*, get the picture*, gotcha*, grasp, have, know, make out*, perceive, read, savvy*, see, take in, tumble*; SEE CONCEPT *15*

comprehend [*v2*] *include*
comprise, contain, embody, embrace, enclose, encompass, have, involve, subsume, take in; SEE CONCEPT *118*

comprehensible [*adj*] *understandable*
apprehensible, clear, coherent, comprehendible, conceivable, explicit, fathomable, graspable, intelligible, knowable, lucid, luminous, plain; SEE CONCEPTS *402,529*

comprehension [*n*] *understanding*
aha*, apperception, apprehension, awareness, capacity, cognizance, conception, discernment, double take*, grasp, intelligence, judgment, ken, knowledge, perception, prehension, realization, sense, slow take*, take*; SEE CONCEPT *409*

comprehensive [*adj*] *inclusive*
absolute, across the board*, all-embracing, all-inclusive, blanket, broad, catholic, compendious, complete, comprising, containing, discursive, encircling, encyclopedic, exhaustive, expansive, extensive, far-reaching, full, general, global, in depth, infinite, lock stock and barrel*, of great scope, overall, sweeping, synoptic, the big picture*, the whole shebang*, the works*, thorough, umbrella, wall-to-wall*, whole, wide, widespread; SEE CONCEPTS *531,772*

compress [*v*] *compact, condense*
abbreviate, abridge, abstract, bind, boil down, coagulate, concentrate, consolidate, constrict, contract, cram, cramp, crowd, crush, decrease, dehydrate, densen, densify, epitomize, force into space, make brief, narrow, pack, press, press together, ram, reduce, restrict, shorten, shrink, shrivel, squash, squeeze, stuff, summarize, syncopate, telescope, tighten, wedge, wrap; SEE CONCEPTS *208,236,247*

comprise [*v*] *make up, consist of*
add up to, amount to, be composed of, be contained in, compass, compose, comprehend, constitute, contain, cover, embody, embrace, encircle, enclose, encompass, engross, form, hold, include, incorporate, involve, span, subsume, sum up, take in; SEE CONCEPT *643*

compromise [*n*] *agreement, give-and-take*
accommodation, accord, adjustment, arrangement, bargain, compact, composition, concession, contract, copout*, covenant, deal, fifty-fifty*, half and half, half measure, happy medium*, mean, middle course, middle ground, pact, sellout, settlement, trade-off, understanding, win-win situation*; SEE CONCEPTS *230,684*

compromise [*v1*] *give and take*
adjust, agree, arbitrate, compose, compound, concede, conciliate, find happy medium*, find middle ground*, go fifty-fifty*, make a deal, make concession, meet halfway, negotiate, play ball with*, settle, split the difference*, strike balance, trade off; SEE CONCEPT *8*

compromise [*v2*] *put in jeopardy*
blight, cop out*, discredit, dishonor, embarrass, endanger, explode, expose, give in, hazard, imperil, implicate, jeopardize, mar, menace, peril, prejudice, put under suspicion, risk, ruin, sell out, spoil, weaken; SEE CONCEPTS *101,240*

compulsion [*n*] *drive, obligation*
coercion, constraint, demand, drive, driving, duress, duty, engrossment, exigency, force, hang-up, have on the brain*, monkey*, necessity, need, obsession, preoccupation, prepossession, pressure, tiger by the tail*, urge, urgency; SEE CONCEPTS *410,532*

compulsive [*adj*] *driving, obsessive*
besetting, compelling, enthusiastic, irresistible,

overwhelming, passionate, uncontrollable, urgent; SEE CONCEPT 401

compulsory [*adj*] *binding*
compulsatory, de rigueur, forced, imperative, imperious, mandatory, necessary, obligatory, required, requisite; SEE CONCEPT 546

compunction [*n*] *regret, sorrow*
attrition, conscience, contrition, misgiving, penitence, penitency, pity, punctiliousness, qualm, reluctance, remorse, repentance, rue, ruth, second thoughts, shame, stab of conscience, sympathy; SEE CONCEPT 410

computation [*n*] *performing arithmetic*
calculation, ciphering, computing, counting, data processing, estimating, estimation, figuring, gauge, guess, reckoning, summing, totalling; SEE CONCEPT 764

compute [*v*] *calculate, estimate*
add up, cast up, cipher, count, count heads, count noses, cut ice*, dope out*, enumerate, figure, figure out, gauge, keep tabs*, measure, rate, reckon, run down, size up, sum, take account of, take one's measure, tally, tot*, total, tote*, tote up*; SEE CONCEPT 764

computer [*n*] *calculating, data processing machine*
abacus, adding machine, analog, artificial intelligence, brain*, calculator, clone, CPU, data processor, digital, electronic brain*, laptop*, MAC, mainframe, micro*, microcomputer, mini*, minicomputer, number cruncher*, PC, personal computer, thinking machine*; SEE CONCEPTS 269,463

computerese [*n*] *computer technical language*
computer jargon, computer terminology, computer terms, hacker talk, tech talk; SEE CONCEPTS 275,276

computer geek [*n*] *computer expert*
computer specialist, engineer, guru, hacker, programmer, techie; SEE CONCEPT 348

comrade [*n*] *ally*
associate, bosom buddy, buddy, chum, colleague, comate, companion, compatriot, compeer, confederate, confidant, confidante, co-worker, crony, friend, intimate, mate, pal, partner, sidekick; SEE CONCEPT 423

con [*n*] *trick*
bluff, cheat, crime, deception, double-cross, dupe, fraud, gold brick*, graft, mockery, swindle, take in; SEE CONCEPT 59

con [*v*] *deceive, defraud*
bamboozle*, bilk, cajole, cheat, chicane, coax, double-cross, dupe, flimflam*, fool, hoax, hoodwink, hornswoggle*, humbug, inveigle, mislead, rip off*, rook, sweet-talk*, swindle, trick, wheedle; SEE CONCEPT 59

concatenation [*n*] *connection, sequence*
chain, connecting, continuity, integration, interlocking, link, linking, nexus, series, succession, uniting; SEE CONCEPTS 721,727

concave [*adj*] *curved, depressed*
biconcave, cupped, dented, dimpled, dipped, excavated, hollow, hollowed, incurvate, incurvated, incurved, indented, round, rounded, sagging, scooped, sinking, sunken; SEE CONCEPT 486

conceal [*v*] *hide, disguise*
beard, burrow, bury, cache, camouflage, cloak, couch, cover, cover up, dissemble, ditch, duck, ensconce, enshroud, harbor, hole up*, keep dark, keep secret, lie low*, lurk, mask, masquerade,

obscure, plant*, put in a hole*, screen, secrete, shelter, skulk, slink, sneak, stash, stay out of sight, stow, tuck away, veil, wrap; SEE CONCEPT 188

concealed [*adj*] *hidden, secret*
buried, cached, camouflaged, covered, covered up, covert, enshrouded, guarded, holed up, hushed up, hush-hush*, incog*, incognito, inconspicuous, masked, obscure, obscured, on the Q.T.*, perdu, planted, privy, put in the hole*, recondite, screened, secreted, shrouded, stashed, tucked away, ulterior, under wraps*, unseen, veiled; SEE CONCEPT 576,619

concealment [*n*] *hiding, secrecy*
beard, blind, camouflage, cover, covering, cover-up, curtain, disguise, dissimulation, fig leaf*, front, hideaway, hide-out, laundromat, mask, obliteration, obscuration, occultation, privacy, red herring*, secretion, smoke screen*, veil, wraps*; SEE CONCEPTS 188,631

concede [*v*] *acknowledge, give in*
accept, accord, admit, allow, avow, award, bury the hatchet*, capitulate, cave in, cede, confess, cry uncle*, ditto*, fess up*, fold, give up, go along with, go with the flow*, grant, hand over, knuckle under, let on, own, own up, play ball with*, quit, relinquish, say uncle*, surrender, throw in the towel*, waive, yes one*, yield; SEE CONCEPTS 35,57,82,235

conceit [*n*] *egotism*
amour-propre, arrogance, complacence, complacency, consequence, immodesty, narcissism, outrecuidance, pomposity, pride, self-admiration, self-exaltation, self-importance, self-love, self-regard, smugness, snottiness, stuffiness, swagger, swelled head*, vainglory, vainness, vanity; SEE CONCEPT 411

conceited [*adj*] *egotistical*
arrogant, bigheaded*, big talking, cocky, conceity, full of hot air*, gall, ham*, hot stuff*, immodest, know-it-all, loudmouth, narcissistic, overweening, phony, puffed up*, self-important, smart-alecky*, snotty*, stuck up*, swollen-headed*, vain, vainglorious, windbag*; SEE CONCEPT 404

conceivable [*adj*] *reasonable, easy to understand*
believable, convincing, credible, earthly, imaginable, likely, mortal, possible, probable, supposable, thinkable; SEE CONCEPTS 529,552

conceive [*v1*] *understand*
accept, appreciate, apprehend, assume, believe, catch, compass, comprehend, deem, dig, envisage, expect, fancy, feel, follow, gather, get, grasp, imagine, judge, perceive, realize, reckon, suppose, suspect, take, twig; SEE CONCEPT 15

conceive [*v2*] *create*
become pregnant, brainstorm, cogitate, consider, contrive, cook up*, depicture, design, develop, devise, dream up, envisage, envision, fancy, feature, form, formulate, head trip*, image, imagine, make up, meditate, originate, ponder, produce, project, purpose, realize, ruminate, spark, speculate, spitball, think up, trump up*, visualize; SEE CONCEPTS 35,173,251

concentrate [*v1*] *think about closely*
apply, attend, be engrossed in, bring to bear, brood over, center, consider closely, contemplate, crack one's brains*, direct attention, establish, examine, fixate, fix attention, focus, focus attention, get on the beam*, give attention, ham-

mer*, hammer away at*, head trip*, intensify, knuckle down, meditate, muse, need, occupy thoughts, peruse, ponder, pour it on*, put, put mind to, rack one's brains*, rivet, ruminate, scrutinize, set, settle, study, sweat, think hard, weigh; SEE CONCEPT 17

concentrate [v2] *gather, collect*
accumulate, agglomerate, aggregate, amass, assemble, bunch, center, centralize, cluster, coalesce, collect, combine, compact, compress, congest, conglomerate, congregate, consolidate, constrict, contract, converge, cramp, crowd, draw together, eliminate, embody, focalize, focus, forgather, garner, get to the meat*, heap, heap up, hoard, huddle, integrate, intensify, localize, mass, muster, narrow, pile, reduce, salt away, store, strengthen, swarm, unify, zero in*; SEE CONCEPTS 84,109

concentrated [adj1] *condensed, reduced*
boiled down, complete, crashed*, entire, evaporated, fixed, full-bodied, lusty, potent, rich, robust, straight, strong, stuffed*, telescoped*, thick, thickened, total, unadulterated, undiffused, undiluted, undivided, unmingled, unmixed, whole; SEE CONCEPTS 483,554

concentrated [adj2] *intense*
all-out, deep, desperate, exquisite, fierce, furious, hard, intensive, terrible, vehement, vicious; SEE CONCEPTS 326,569

concentration [n1] *consolidation of effort*
absorption, amassing, application, assembly, bringing to bear, centering, centralization, close attention, clustering, coalescing, combination, compacting, compression, concern, congregation, consolidation, convergence, converging, debate, deliberation, fixing, flocking, focusing, heed, huddling, intensification, massing, narrowing, need, single-mindedness, study, unity; SEE CONCEPT 677

concentration [n2] *aggregation*
accumulation, army, array, audience, band, cluster, collection, company, concourse, convergence, flock, group, herd, horde, mass, miscellany, mob, party; SEE CONCEPT 432

concept [n] *idea*
abstraction, apprehension, approach, big idea*, brainchild*, brain wave*, conceit, conception, conceptualization, consideration, fool notion*, hypothesis, image, impression, intellection, notion, perception, slant, supposition, theory, thought, twist, view, wrinkle; SEE CONCEPTS 532,689

conception [n1] *understanding; idea*
apperception, appreciation, apprehension, clue, cogitating, cognition, communing, comprehension, conceit, concentrating, concept, consideration, considering, deliberating, design, dreaming, envisaging, explanation, exposition, fancy, fancying, image, imagining, impression, inkling, intellection, interpretation, meditating, meditation, mental grasp, musing, notion, perception, philosophizing, picture, plan, realization, representation, speculating, speculation, thought, version; SEE CONCEPTS 409,410,689

conception [n2] *beginning, birth*
fertilization, formation, germination, impregnation, inception, initiation, insemination, invention, launching, origin, outset, start; SEE CONCEPTS 119,302,373,375

concern [n1] *business, responsibility*
affair, burden, care, charge, company, corporation, deportment, entanglement, enterprise, establishment, field, firm, house, interest, involvement, job, jungle*, matter, megacorp*, mission, multinational, occupation, organization, outfit, shooting match*, task, thing, transaction, worry, zoo*; SEE CONCEPTS 325,362,532

concern [n2] *interest; anxiety*
apprehension, attention, bearing, care, carefulness, concernment, consideration, disquiet, disquietude, distress, heed, heedfulness, important matter, matter, reference, regard, relation, relevance, solicitude, tender loving care, unease, worry; SEE CONCEPTS 410,690

concern [v1] *affect personally*
apply to, bear on, become involved, be relevant to, bother, disquiet, distress, disturb, interest, involve, make anxious, make uneasy, pertain to, perturb, regard, take pains, touch, trouble, worry; SEE CONCEPTS 7,19,22

concern [v2] *relate to, have reference to*
answer to, appertain to, apply to, be about, be applicable to, bear on, bear upon, be connected with, be dependent upon, be interdependent with, belong to, be pertinent to, be well taken, deal with, depend upon, have a bearing on, have connections with, have implications for, have relation to, have significance for, have to do with, involve, pertain to, refer to, regard; SEE CONCEPT 532

concerned [adj1] *worried*
anxious, biting one's nails*, bothered, butterflies in stomach*, distressed, disturbed, exercised, in a stew*, on pins and needles*, perturbed, tied up in knots*, troubled, uneasy, upset, uptight, worried sick*; SEE CONCEPT 403

concerned [adj2] *involved with*
active, affected, attentive, caring, down with, implicated, in, on, interested, mixed up, privy to, solicitous; SEE CONCEPTS 401,403

concerning [prep] *having to do with*
about, anent, apropos of, as regards, germane to, in regard to, in the matter of, pertaining to, re, regarding, relating to, relevant to, respecting, touching, with reference to, with regard to; SEE CONCEPT 563

concert [n1] *musical performance*
gig, jam session, musical, musicale, recital, rockfest, selections, show; SEE CONCEPT 263

concert [n2] *agreement, harmony*
accord, chorus, collaboration, concord, concordance, consonance, joint, league, togetherness, tune, unanimity, union, unison; SEE CONCEPTS 388,684

concerted [adj] *coordinated*
agreed upon, collaborative, combined, joint, mutual, planned, prearranged, united; SEE CONCEPT 538

concession [n] *yielding, adjustment*
acknowledgment, admission, allowance, assent, authorization, boon, buyback, compromise, concession, copout*, deal, giveback, giving in, grant, indulgence, permission, permit, privilege, rollback, sellout, surrender, trade-off, warrant; SEE CONCEPTS 13,50,67,88

conciliatory [adj] *placid, calm*
appeasing, assuaging, calm, civil, disarming, irenic, mollifying, pacific, peaceable, placating,

placatory, propitiative, quiet, willing; SEE CONCEPT *401*

concise [*adj*] *short, to the point*
abridged, boiled down*, breviloquent, brief, compact, compendiary, compendious, compressed, condensed, curt, epigrammatic, in a nutshell*, laconic, lean, marrowy, meaty, pithy, short and sweet*, succinct, summary, synoptic, terse; SEE CONCEPTS *773,798*

conclave [*n*] *secret meeting*
assembly, buzz session*, cabinet*, confab*, conference, council, encounter, gathering, get-together, huddle, meet, parley, powwow*, private meeting, session; SEE CONCEPTS *324,384*

conclude [*v1*] *finish, come to an end*
achieve, bring down curtain*, call it a day*, cease, cinch, clinch, close, close out, complete, consummate, crown, desist, draw to close, end, halt, knock off, put the lid on*, put to bed*, round off, stop, terminate, top off, ultimate, wind up, wrap up; SEE CONCEPTS *119,234*

conclude [*v2*] *decide, deduce*
add up to, adjudge, analyze, assume, be afraid, boil down to*, collect, derive, draw, figure, gather, have a hunch*, infer, intuit, judge, make, make out, presume, ratiocinate, reason, reckon, sum up, suppose, surmise, the way one sees it*; SEE CONCEPTS *18,37*

conclude [*v3*] *settle, resolve*
accomplish, achieve, bring about, carry out, clinch, confirm, decide, determine, effect, establish, fix, pull off, rule, work out; SEE CONCEPTS *18,91,126*

conclusion [*n1*] *end*
cease, cessation, close, closure, completion, consequence, culmination, denouement, desistance, development, ending, end of the line*, eventuality, finale, finish, issue, outcome, payoff, period, result, stop, termination, upshot, windup, wrap; SEE CONCEPTS *119,832*

conclusion [*n2*] *judgment, decision*
agreement, conviction, corollary, deduction, determination, illation, inference, opinion, ratiocination, resolution, resolve, sequitur, settlement, verdict; SEE CONCEPT *689*

conclusive [*adj*] *definite, final*
absolute, all out*, clear-clinching, cogent, compelling, convincing, deciding, decisive, demonstrative, determinant, determinative, flat out*, incontrovertible, indisputable, irrefragable, irrefrangible, irrefutable, irrevocable, litmus test*, precise, resolving, revealing, settling, straight out, telling, ultimate, unambiguous, unanswerable, unarguable, unconditional, undeniable, unmistakable, unquestionable, what you see is what you get*; SEE CONCEPT *535*

concoct [*v*] *formulate, think up*
ad lib, batch*, brew*, compound, contrive, cook up, create, design, devise, discover, dream up, envisage, envision, fabricate, frame*, hatch, invent, make up, mature, originate, plan, plot, prefab*, prepare, project, scheme, slap together*, throw together*, vamp; SEE CONCEPTS *36,173,251*

concoction [*n*] *creation, blend*
brew, combination, compound, contrivance, intention, medley, mixture, plan, preparation, project, solution; SEE CONCEPTS *260,432,660*

concomitant [*adj*] *contributing, accompanying*
accessory, adjuvant, agreeing, ancillary, associated with, associative, attendant, attending, belonging, coefficient, coetaneous, coeval, coexistent, coincident, coincidental, collateral, complementary, concordant, concurrent, conjoined, conjoined with, connected, contemporaneous, contemporary, coordinate, corollary, coterminous, coupled with, fellow, incident, in tempo, in time, isochronal, isochronous, joint, satellite, synchronal, synchronous, synergetic, synergistic; SEE CONCEPT *577*

concord [*n1*] *unity, harmony*
accord, agreement, amity, calmness, chime, comity, concert, concordance, consensus, consonance, friendship, goodwill, peace, placidity, rapport, serenity, tranquility, tune, unanimity, understanding, unison; SEE CONCEPT *388*

concord [*n2*] *agreement, treaty*
compact, concordat, contract, convention, entente, pact, protocol; SEE CONCEPTS *271,684*

concourse [*n1*] *passageway*
avenue, boulevard, entrance, foyer, hall, highway, lobby, lounge, meeting place, path, rallying point*, road, street; SEE CONCEPTS *440,501*

concourse [*n2*] *crowd, group*
assemblage, assembly, collection, concursion, confluence, convergence, crush, gang, gathering, joining, junction, linkage, meeting, mob, multitude, rout, throng; SEE CONCEPT *432*

concrete [*adj1*] *actual, factual*
accurate, corporeal, definite, detailed, explicit, material, objective, particular, precise, real, sensible, solid, specific, substantial, tangible; SEE CONCEPTS *535,582*

concrete [*adj2*] *hardened*
caked, calcified, cemented, compact, compressed, congealed, conglomerated, consolidated, dried, firm, indurate, monolithic, petrified, poured, precast, set, set in stone*, solid, solidified, steeled, strong, unyielding; SEE CONCEPT *604*

concur [*v*] *agree, approve*
accede, accord, acquiesce, assent, band, be consonant with, be in harmony, coadjute, coincide, collaborate, combine, come together, consent, cooperate, cut a deal*, equal, harmonize, jibe*, join, league*, meet, okay*, pass on*, shake on*, unite; SEE CONCEPTS *8,10,82*

concurrent [*adj1*] *simultaneous*
circumstantial, coeval, coexisting, coincident, concerted, concomitant, contemporaneous, incidental, in sync, parallel, synchronal, synchronous; SEE CONCEPT *799*

concurrent [*adj2*] *agreeing, converging*
allied, at one, centrolineal, coinciding, compatible, concerted, confluent, consentient, consistent, convergent, cooperating, coterminous, harmonious, in agreement, in rapport, joined, likeminded, meeting, mutual, of the same mind, unified, uniting; SEE CONCEPT *563*

concussion [*n*] *collision, shaking*
blast, blow, buffeting, bump, clash, clout, crack, crash, hit, impact, injury, jar, jarring, jolt, jolting, jounce, pounding, punch, shock, trauma; SEE CONCEPTS *189,309,521*

condemn [*v*] *blame, convict*
adjudge, belittle, blow whistle on*, call down*, castigate, censure, chide, come down on*, criticize, damn, decry, denounce, denunciate, deprecate, depreciate, disapprove, disparage, doom, find fault with, find guilty, frame, hang some-

CO
CO

thing on*, judge, knock, lay at one's door*, let have it*, name, pass sentence on*, pin it on*, point finger at*, pronounce, proscribe, punish, put away, put down, reprehend, reproach, reprobate, reprove, send up, send up the river*, sentence, skin, thumbs down on*, upbraid; SEE CONCEPTS *44,52,317*

condemnation [*n*] *blaming, conviction*
accusation, blame, censure, damnation, denouncement, denunciation, disapproval, doom, judgment, proscription, reproach, reprobation, reproof, sentence, stricture; SEE CONCEPTS *44,52,317*

condensation [*n1*] *abridgment*
abstract, boildown*, breviary, brief, compendium, compression, concentration, consolidation, conspectus, contraction, curtailment, digest, epitome, essence, précis, reduction, summary, synopsis; SEE CONCEPTS *283,730*

condensation [*n2*] *water buildup*
condensate, crystallization, deliquescence, dew, distillation, liquefaction, precipitate, precipitation, rainfall; SEE CONCEPT *514*

condense [*v*] *abridge*
abbreviate, blue pencil*, boil down, chop, coagulate, compact, compress, concentrate, constrict, contract, curtail, cut, cut down, decoct, densen, digest, edit, encapsulate, epitomize, inventory, precipitate, précis, press together, put in a nutshell*, reduce, shorten, shrink, snip, solidify, sum, summarize, summate, synopsize, telescope, thicken, trim; SEE CONCEPTS *236,247*

condescend [*v*] *stoop, humble oneself*
accommodate, accord, acquiesce, agree, be courteous, bend, come down off high horse*, comply, concede, degrade oneself, deign, demean oneself, descend, favor, grant, high hat*, lower oneself, oblige, see fit, submit, talk down to, toss a few crumbs*, unbend, vouchsafe, yield; SEE CONCEPT *633*

condescending [*adj*] *snobby, lordly*
arrogant, complaisant, disdainful, egotistic, ladee-da*, lofty, patronizing, snobbish, snooty*, snotty*, supercilious, superior, uppish, uppity; SEE CONCEPT *401*

condescension [*n*] *disdain, superiority*
airs, civility, deference, haughtiness, loftiness, lordliness, patronage, patronizing attitude, superciliousness, toleration; SEE CONCEPT *633*

condiment [*n1*] *flavoring*
catsup, dressing, gravy, horseradish, ketchup, mustard, pepper, relish, salsa, salt, sauce, seasoning, spice, zest; SEE CONCEPTS *457,461*

condition [*n1*] *circumstances*
action, ballgame*, case, estate, happening, how it goes*, how things are*, how things stack up*, lay of the land*, like it is*, mode, order, plight, position, posture, predicament, quality, rank, repair, reputation, riff, scene, shape, situation, size of it*, sphere, spot, standing, state, state of affairs, status, status quo, trim, way things are*, way things shape up*, where it's at*; SEE CONCEPTS *639,696*

condition [*n2*] *requirement, limitation*
arrangement, article, catch, codicil, contingency, demand, essential, exception, exemption, fine print*, kicker*, modification, must, necessity, postulate, precondition, prerequisite, provision, proviso, qualification, requisite, reservation, rule,

sine qua non, small print*, stipulation, strings*, terms; SEE CONCEPTS *270,688*

condition [*n3*] *physical shape, fitness*
appearance, aspect, build, constitution, fettle, form, health, kilter, mint, order, phase, repair, state, status, tone, trim; SEE CONCEPTS *316,757*

condition [*n4*] *illness*
affection, ailment, complaint, disease, ill, infirmity, malady, predicament, problem, syndrome, temper, weakness; SEE CONCEPT *306*

condition [*v*] *adapt, prepare*
accustom, brainwash, build up, educate, equip, habituate, inure, loosen up, make ready, modify, practice, program, ready, shape up, sharpen, tone up, toughen up, train, warm up, whip into shape*, work out, work over; SEE CONCEPTS *35,202*

conditional [*adj*] *dependent*
codicillary, contingent, depending on, fortuitous, granted on certain terms, guarded, iffy*, incidental, inconclusive, limited, modified, not absolute, obscure, provisional, provisory, qualified, relative, reliant, relying on, restricted, restrictive, subject to, tentative, uncertain, with grain of salt*, with reservations, with strings attached*; SEE CONCEPT *554*

condolence [*n*] *sympathy*
comfort, commiseration, compassion, condolement, consolation, fellow feeling, solace; SEE CONCEPT *633*

condom [*n*] *birth control*
contraceptive, French letter*, johnnie*, johnny*, prophylactic, protection, raincoat*, rubber*, safe, sheath; SEE CONCEPTS *307,446*

condominium [*n*] *tenant-owned apartment house*
apartment, condo, co-op, timeshare, townhouse; SEE CONCEPT *516*

condone [*v*] *make allowance for*
buy*, disregard, excuse, forget, forgive, give green light*, go along with, ignore, lap up*, let it come*, let it go by*, let pass*, look the other way*, nod at*, okay, overlook, pardon, pass over, remit, wink at*; SEE CONCEPTS *10,23*

conducive [*adj*] *favorable for*
accessory, calculated to produce, contributive, contributory, helpful, leading, productive of, promotive, tending, useful; SEE CONCEPT *542*

conduct [*n1*] *administration*
care, carrying on*, channels, charge, control, direction, execution, guidance, handling, intendance, leadership, management, manipulation, organization, oversight, plan, policy, posture, red tape*, regimen, regulation, rule, running, strategy, superintendence, supervision, tactics, transaction, treatment, wielding; SEE CONCEPT *117*

conduct [*n2*] *behavior*
address, attitude, bearing, carriage, comportment, demeanor, deportment, manner, manners, mien, posture, stance, tenue, ways; SEE CONCEPT *633*

conduct [*v1*] *administer*
accompany, attend, call the tune*, carry on*, chair, chaperon, control, convey, direct, engineer, escort, govern, guide, handle, head, keep, lead, manage, operate, ordain, order, organize, oversee, pilot, preside over, regulate, ride herd on*, rule, run, run things, shepherd, steer, supervise, trailblaze*, usher, wield baton*; SEE CONCEPT *117*

conduct [v2] *comport oneself*
acquit, act, bear, behave, carry, demean, deport, go on, quit; SEE CONCEPT *384*

conduct [v3] *transport*
accompany, attend, bring, carry, chaperon, companion, convoy, escort, guide, lead, move, pass on, pilot, route, send, shepherd, show, steer, transfer; SEE CONCEPT *187*

conductor [n] *leader*
director, guide, maestro, manager, marshal, master, supervisor; SEE CONCEPTS *347,350,354*

conduit [n] *passage*
aqueduct, cable, canal, channel, conductor, course, culvert, duct, flow, flume, gully, gutter, lead-in, lead-out, main, pipe, pipeline, race, sewer, spout, trough, tube, watercourse; SEE CONCEPTS *499,501*

cone [n] *circular-shaped object with pointed end*
conoid, pyramid, raceme, strobile, strobiloid; SEE CONCEPT *436*

confection [n] *sweet food*
cake, candy, dainty, jam, pastry, sweet; SEE CONCEPT *457*

confederacy [n] *coalition*
alliance, anschluss, bond, compact, confederation, conspiracy, covenant, federation, government, league, organization, union; SEE CONCEPTS *299,301*

confederate [adj] *allied*
amalgamated, associated, combined, corporate, federal, federated, in alliance, incorporated, leagued, organized, syndicated, unionized; SEE CONCEPT *536*

confederate [n] *abettor*
accessory, accomplice, ally, associate, coconspirator, collaborator, colleague, conspirator, fellow, fellow traveler, partner; SEE CONCEPT *412*

confer [v1] *discuss, deliberate*
advise, argue, bargain, blitz*, brainstorm*, breeze*, collogue, confab*, confabulate, consult, converse, deal, debate, discourse, flap*, gab*, get heads together*, give meeting*, groupthink*, huddle, jaw, kick ideas around*, negotiate, parley, pick one's brain*, powwow*, speak, talk, toss ideas around*, treat; SEE CONCEPT *56*

confer [v2] *giving honor, award*
accord, allot, award, bestow, donate, gift with, give, grant, lay on, present, provide, sweeten the kitty*, vouchsafe; SEE CONCEPT *132*

conference [n1] *convention, colloquium*
appointment, argument, chat, colloquy, confabulation, conferring, congress, consultation, conversation, convocation, deliberation, discussion, forum, gabfest*, groupthink*, huddle, interchange, interview, meeting, palaver, parley, powwow*, round robin, round table, seminar, symposium, talk, think-in*, ventilation; SEE CONCEPTS *56,324,386*

conference [n2] *league of athletic teams*
association, athletic union, circuit, league, loop, organization, ring; SEE CONCEPT *365*

confess [v] *admit, confirm*
acknowledge, affirm, allow, assert, attest, aver, avow, blow, blurt out, chirp, clue in, come clean*, come out, concede, confide, declare, disclose, divulge, dump on*, evince, finger*, fink*, grant, humble oneself, leak*, let on*, level with, make clean breast of*, manifest, narrate, open one's heart*, own, own up, post, profess, prove, rat on*, recognize, relate, reveal, sing*, snitch*,

sound off*, spill the beans*, spit out*, squeal*, tip hand*, unload*, vent, weasel*; SEE CONCEPT *60*

confession [n] *admittance of information*
acknowledgment, admission, affirmation, allowance, assenting, assertion, avowal, concession, declaration, disclosing, disclosure, divulgence, enumeration, exposé, exposure, making public, narration, owning up, proclamation, profession, publication, recitation, relation, revealing, revelation, song*, squawk*, squeal*, statement, story, telling, unbosoming, utterance; SEE CONCEPTS *60,274*

confidant [n] *close friend*
acquaintance, adherent, adviser, alter ego, bosom buddy, companion, crony, familiar, intimate, mate, pal; SEE CONCEPT *423*

confide [v1] *divulge information*
admit, bend an ear*, breathe, buzz*, confess, crack to, disclose, hint, impart, insinuate, intimate, lay it on*, lay the guff*, let in on*, reveal, spill to*, suggest, tell, unload on*, whisper; SEE CONCEPT *57*

confide [v2] *entrust*
bestow, charge, commend, commit, consign, delegate, hand over, present, relegate, trust; SEE CONCEPT *108*

confidence [n1] *belief in oneself*
aplomb, assurance, backbone, boldness, brashness, certainty, cool, courage, daring, dash, determination, elan, faith in oneself, fearlessness, firmness, fortitude, grit, hardihood, heart, impudence, intrepidity, mettle, morale, nerve, pluck, poise, presumption, reliance, resoluteness, resolution, self-possession, self-reliance, spirit, spunk, sureness, tenacity; SEE CONCEPT *411*

confidence [n2] *belief in something*
assurance, credence, dependence, faith, hope, reliance, stock, store, sure bet*, trust; SEE CONCEPT *689*

confident [adj1] *certain, assured*
bet on*, bold, brave, cocksure, convinced, counting on, courageous, dauntless, depending on, expectant, expecting, fearless, having faith in, high*, hopeful, intrepid, positive, presuming, presumptuous, puffed up*, pushy, racked, sanguine, satisfied, secure, self-assured, self-reliant, self-sufficient, sure, trusting, unafraid, undaunted, upbeat, uppity*, valiant; SEE CONCEPTS *403,404*

confidential [adj] *secret*
arcane, backdoor, classified, closet, hushed, hush-hush*, inside, intimate, off the record*, private, privy; SEE CONCEPTS *267,576*

confidentially [adv] *in secret*
behind closed doors*, between ourselves, between us, between you and me*, covertly, don't breathe a word*, hushedly, in confidence, in on the ground floor*, off the cuff*, off the record*, personally, privately, sub rosa; SEE CONCEPTS *267,576*

configuration [n] *arrangement*
composition, contour, disposition, figure, form, Gestalt, outline, shape, structure; SEE CONCEPTS *84,727*

confine [v] *enclose, limit*
bar, bind, bound, cage, circumscribe, constrain, cool, cool down, cramp, delimit, detain, enslave, fix, hem in, hinder, hog-tie*, hold back, ice*, immure, imprison, incarcerate, intern, jail, keep,

put a lid on*, put away, put on ice*, repress, restrain, restrict, send up, shorten, shut up; SEE CONCEPTS *121,130*

confined [*adj*] *limited, enclosed*
bedfast, bedridden, bottled up, bound, chilled, circumscribed, compassed, cooped up, cramp, cramped, detained, flattened out, grounded, hampered, held, hog-tied*, iced*, immured, imprisoned, incarcerated, in chains, incommodious, indisposed, in jail, invalided, jailed, laid up, locked up, on ice*, pent, restrained, restricted, sealed up, shut in, sick; SEE CONCEPT *554*

confinement [*n1*] *imprisonment; restriction*
bonds, bounding, bounds, check, circumscription, coercion, constrainment, constraint, control, cramp, curb, custody, delimitation, detention, immuration, incarceration, internment, jail, keeping, limitation, repression, safekeeping, trammels; SEE CONCEPTS *90,191*

confines [*n*] *boundaries*
borders, bounds, circumference, compass, country, dimension, edge, end, environs, extent, limits, orbit, periphery, precinct, proportions, purlieus, purview, radius, range, reach, region, scope, sweep, term, terrain, territory; SEE CONCEPTS *484,745,788*

confirm [*v1*] *ratify, validate, prove*
affirm, approve, attest, authenticate, back, bear out, bless, buy, certify, check, check out, circumstantiate, corroborate, debunk, double-check, endorse, establish, explain, give green light*, give high sign*, give stamp of approval*, give the go-ahead*, give the nod*, justify, lap up, make good*, make sure, okay, rubber-stamp*, sanction, settle, sign, sign off on*, size up, subscribe, substantiate, support, thumbs up*, underpin, uphold, verify, vouch, warrant, witness; SEE CONCEPTS *57,103*

confirm [*v2*] *reinforce*
assure, buttress, clinch, establish, fix, fortify, invigorate, make firm, settle, strengthen; SEE CONCEPTS *244,250*

confirmation [*n*] *ratification, validation, proof*
acceptance, accepting, accord, admission, affirmation, affirming, agreement, approval, assent, attestation, authenticating, authentication, authorization, authorizing, avowal, consent, corroborating, corroboration, endorsement, evidence, go ahead*, green light*, nod, okay, passage, passing, proving, recognition, sanction, sanctioning, stamp of approval*, substantiation, support, supporting, testament, testimonial, testimony, validating, verification, verifying, visa, witness; SEE CONCEPTS *661,685*

confirmed [*adj*] *habitual; rooted*
accepted, accustomed, chronic, deep-rooted, deep-seated, dyed-in-the-wool*, entrenched, firmly established, fixed, habituated, hardened, hard-shell*, ingrained, inured, inveterate, long-established, proved, seasoned, settled, staid, valid, worn; SEE CONCEPTS *542,798*

confiscate [*v*] *steal; seize*
accroach, annex, appropriate, arrogate, assume, commandeer, confisticate, expropriate, glom on to*, grab, hijack, impound, liberate, moonlight requisition*, possess oneself of, preempt, sequester, sequestrate, swipe, take, take over, usurp; SEE CONCEPTS *139,142*

conflagration [*n*] *large fire*
blaze, bonfire, burning, flaming, holocaust, in-

ferno, rapid oxidation, up in smoke*, wildfire; SEE CONCEPTS *249,478*

conflict [*n1*] *fight, warfare*
battle, clash, collision, combat, competition, contention, contest, emulation, encounter, engagement, fracas, fray, rivalry, set-to, strife, striving, struggle, tug-of-war, war; SEE CONCEPTS *106,320*

conflict [*n2*] *disagreement, discord*
affray, animosity, antagonism, bad blood*, brush, competition, coneours, contention, contest, dance, difference, disaccord, dispute, dissension, dissent, dissidence, disunity, divided loyalties, faction, factionalism, flap, fray, friction, fuss, hassle, hostility, interference, meeting, opposition, row, ruckus, run-in, set-to, strife, variance; SEE CONCEPTS *106,388,674*

conflict [*v*] *be at odds*
brawl, bump heads with*, clash, collide, combat, contend, contest, contrast, cross swords with, differ, disaccord, disagree, discord, disharmonize, disturb, fight, interfere, jar, lock horns with*, mismatch, oppose, romp, run against tide*, scrap, slug, square off with, strive, struggle, tangle, vary; SEE CONCEPTS *46,106*

conflicting [*adj*] *contradictory*
adverse, antagonistic, antipathetic, at odds with, clashing, contrarian, contrary, disconsonant, discordant, discrepant, dissonant, incompatible, incongruent, incongruous, inconsistent, inconsonant, opposed, opposing, paradoxical, unfavorable, unmixable; SEE CONCEPTS *542,570*

confluence [*n*] *coming together*
assemblage, assembly, concourse, concurrence, concursion, conflux, convergence, crowd, gathering, host, junction, meeting, mob, multitude, union; SEE CONCEPTS *109,114*

conform [*v1*] *adjust, adapt*
accommodate, attune, be guided by, clean up act*, comply, coordinate, don't make waves*, don't rock the boat*, fall in with, fit, follow, follow beaten path*, follow the crowd, go by the book*, go with the flow*, harmonize, integrate, keep, make room, meet halfway, mind, move over, obey, observe, play the game*, proportion, quadrate, reconcile, reconciliate, roll with punches*, run with the pack*, shape up, square, straighten up, suit, tailor, tailor-make*, toe the line*, tune, yield; SEE CONCEPT *13*

conform [*v2*] *correspond, match*
accord, agree, assimilate, be regular, dovetail, fit in, fit the pattern, go, harmonize, jibe, square, suit, tally; SEE CONCEPT *664*

conformable [*adj*] *appropriate; matching*
adapted, agreeable, alike, amenable, applicable, assorted, comparable, compliant, consistent, docile, fitted, fitting, harmonious, in agreement, like, matched, obedient, orderly, proper, regular, resembling, similar, submissive, suitable, suited, tractable, unified, useable, well-regulated; SEE CONCEPTS *487,558,563,573*

conformation [*n*] *shape*
anatomy, arrangement, build, cast, configuration, figure, form, formation, frame, framework, outline, structure, symmetry, type; SEE CONCEPTS *754,757*

conformist [*n*] *person in agreement*
Babbit, bourgeois, brick in a wall*, conventionalist, emulator, follower, one of the herd*, rubber stamp*, sheep*, traditionalist, yes man*; SEE CONCEPTS *361,423*

conformity [*n1*] *compliance*
acquiescence, allegiance, assent, consent, conventionality, docility, obedience, observance, orthodoxy, resignation, submission, willingness; SEE CONCEPTS *13,689*

conformity [*n2*] *correspondence, harmony*
accord, affinity, agreement, coherence, conformance, congruity, consistency, consonance, likeness, resemblance, similarity; SEE CONCEPT *664*

confound [*v*] *confuse*
abash, amaze, astonish, astound, baffle, befog, bewilder, blend, bug*, commingle, confute, discombobulate*, discomfit, discountenance, dumbfound, embarrass, faze, fiddle, flabbergast, jumble, metagrobolize, misidentify, mix, mix up*, mystify, nonplus, perplex, pose, puzzle, rattle, screw up*, startle, surprise, throw*; SEE CONCEPTS *16,42*

confront [*v*] *challenge*
accost, affront, beard, brave, call one's bluff*, come up against*, dare, defy, encounter, face down*, face up to*, face with*, flout, front, go one-on-one*, make my day*, meet, meet eyeball-to-eyeball*, oppose, repel, resist, scorn, stand up to, tell off, withstand; SEE CONCEPTS *46,52,54*

confrontation [*n*] *conflict*
affray, battle, contest, crisis, dispute, encounter, fight, meeting, set-to, showdown, strife; SEE CONCEPTS *46,106*

confuse [*v1*] *bewilder someone*
abash, addle, amaze, astonish, baffle, becloud, bedevil, befuddle, bemuse, cloud, clutter, complicate, confound, darken, daze, demoralize, discomfit, discompose, disconcert, discountenance, disorient, distract, embarrass, faze, fluster, fog, frustrate, fuddle, involve, lead astray, mess up*, misinform, mislead, mortify, muddle, mystify, nonplus, obscure, perplex, perturb, puzzle, rattle, render uncertain, shame, stir up, stump, throw off, throw off balance*, trouble, unhinge, unsettle, upset, worry; SEE CONCEPT *16*

confuse [*v2*] *mix up; involve*
bedlamize, blend, clutter, confound, disarrange, disarray, discombobulate*, discreate, disorder, disorganize, embroil, encumber, entangle, intermingle, involve, jumble, litter, mess up*, mingle, mistake, muddle, muss up, rumple, snarl up, tangle, tousle, tumble; SEE CONCEPT *112*

confused [*adj*] *disoriented mentally*
abashed, addled, at a loss*, at sea*, at sixes and sevens*, baffled, befuddled, bewildered, come apart*, dazed, discombobulated*, disconcerted, disorganized, distracted, flummoxed, flustered, fouled up*, glassy-eyed*, gone*, misled, mixed up, muddled, nonplussed, not with it*, out to lunch*, perplexed, perturbed, punch-drunk*, punchy*, puzzled, screwy*, shook up*, shot to pieces*, slaphappy, spaced out*, stumped, taken aback, thrown, thrown off balance*, unglued*, unscrewed*, unzipped*; SEE CONCEPT *403*

confused [*adj2*] *mixed up, disordered*
anarchic, blurred, chaotic, disarranged, disorderly, disorganized, haywire, in a muddle, in disarray, involved, jumbled, messy, miscalculated, miscellaneous, mistaken, misunderstood, obscured, out of order, snafu*, snarled, topsy-turvy, unsettled, untidy; SEE CONCEPT *585*

confusion [*n1*] *disorientation*
abashing, abashment, addling, agitation, befuddlement, befuddling, bemusement, bewilderment, blurring, chagrin, cluttering, commotion, confounding, demoralization, disarranging, discomfiting, discomfiture, disorientation, distraction, disturbing, dither, dumbfounding, embarrassing, embarrassment, embroiling, flap, fluster, lather, mixup mystification, obscuring, perplexing, perplexity, perturbation, pother, puzzlement, stew, stirring up, tangling, tumult, turbulence, turmoil, unsettling, upsetting; SEE CONCEPT *14*

confusion [*n2*] *disoriented state*
abashment, ado, anarchy, astonishment, bustle, chaos, clutter, commotion, complexity, complication, consternation, daze, difficulty, disarray, discomposure, dislocation, disorganization, distraction, emotional upset, ferment, fog, fracas, haze, hodge-podge, imbroglio, intricacy, jumble, labyrinth, mess, mistake, muddle, mystification, pandemonium, perturbation, racket, riot, row, shambles, stir, stupefaction, surprise, tangle, trouble, tumult, turmoil, untidiness, upheaval, uproar, wilderness; SEE CONCEPTS *410,727*

confute [*v*] *disprove, refute*
blow sky high*, break, bring to naught, confound, contradict, controvert, defeat, demolish, dismay, disprove, expose, invalidate, knocks props out from under*, negate, oppugn, overcome, overthrow, overturn, overwhelm, parry, prove false, prove wrong, put down, rebut, set aside, shut up, silence, subvert, tap, upset, vanquish; SEE CONCEPTS *46,95*

congeal [*v*] *coagulate*
cake, clabber, clot, concrete, condense, curdle, dry, freeze, gel, gelate, gelatinate, gelatinize, glob up*, harden, indurate, jell, jellify, jelly, refrigerate, set, solidify, stiffen, thicken; SEE CONCEPTS *250,469*

congenial [*adj*] *friendly, compatible*
adapted, affable, agreeable, amical, clubby, companionable, compatible, complaisant, congruous, consistent, consonant, conversable, convivial, cooperative, cordial, delightful, favorable, fit, genial, good-humored, gracious, happy, harmonious, jovial, kindly, kindred, like-minded, mellow, pleasant, pleasing, regular fellow, right neighborly, sociable, social, suitable, sympathetic, well-suited; SEE CONCEPT *555*

congenital [*adj*] *inborn*
complete, connate, connatural, constitutional, inbred, indigenous, indwelling, ingrained, inherent, inherited, innate, intrinsic, inveterate, latent, native, natural, thorough, unacquired, utter; SEE CONCEPTS *314,549*

congested [*adj*] *blocked, clogged*
chock-full, choked, closed, crammed, crowded, filled, glutted, gorged, gridlocked, jam-full, jammed, jam-packed, massed, mobbed, obstructed, occluded, overcrowded, overfilled, overflowing, packed, packed like sardines*, plugged, stopped, stoppered, stuffed, stuffed-up, teeming, up to the rafters*; SEE CONCEPTS *481,483,774*

congestion [*n*] *blockage*
bottleneck*, clogging, crowdedness, crowding, excess, jam, mass, overcrowding, overdevelopment, overpopulation, press, profusion, rubbernecking*, snarl-up*, surfeit, surplus, traffic jam; SEE CONCEPTS *230,432*

CO
CO

conglomerate [*adj*] *composite*
amassed, assorted, blended, clustered, heterogeneous, indiscriminate, massed, melded, miscellaneous, mixed, motley, multifarious, promiscuous, varied, variegated; SEE CONCEPTS 490,589

conglomerate [*n*] *composite organization*
agglomerate, agglomeration, aggregate, aggregation, cartel, chain, combine, conglomeration, group, multinational, pool, syndicate, trust; SEE CONCEPTS 323,325

conglomeration [*n*] *accumulation, potpourri*
agglomeration, aggregate, aggregation, amassment, assortment, collection, combination, combo*, composite, cumulation, everything but the kitchen sink*, hoard, hodge-podge, mass, medley, miscellany, mishmash*, mixed bag*, trove; SEE CONCEPT 432

congratulate [*v*] *compliment on achievement, luck*
applaud, bless, boost, felicitate, give a big cigar*, give bouquet*, give regards, gold star*, hand it to*, hear it for*, laud, pat on back, praise, rejoice with, salute, stroke*, toast, wish happy returns*, wish joy to, wish one well; SEE CONCEPTS 51,69

congratulations [*n*] *complimentation on achievement, luck*
best wishes, compliments, felicitations, give a " hear-hear"*, good going*, good wishes, good work, greetings, hail; SEE CONCEPTS 69,278

congregate [*v*] *assemble, come together*
besiege, bunch up*, collect, concentrate, congress, convene, converge, convoke, corral, flock*, forgather, gang around, gang up, gather, hang out*, make the scene*, mass, meet, meet up, muster, pack, raise, rally, rendezvous, round up, swarm, teem, throng; SEE CONCEPTS 109,114

congregation [*n*] *assembled group, especially concerned with church-going*
aggregation, assemblage, assembly, audience, churchgoers, collection, company, confab*, crowd, disciples, flock, following, gathering, get-together, group, host, laity, meet, meeting, multitude, muster, parish, parishioners, public, sit-in, throng, turnout; SEE CONCEPTS 369,387,417

congress [*n*] *delegation of representatives*
assembly, association, caucus, chamber, club, committee, conclave, conference, convention, convocation, council, delegates, government, guild, league, legislative body, legislature, meeting, order, parliament, senate, society, the Hill, the house, union; SEE CONCEPTS 299,387

congruent [*adj*] *agreeable, harmonious*
coinciding, compatible, concurring, conforming, consistent, corresponding, identical, in agreement; SEE CONCEPT 563

congruous [*adj*] *corresponding, suitable*
accordant, appropriate, apt, becoming, coincidental, compatible, concordant, congruent, consistent, consonant, correspondent, fit, fitting, harmonious, meet, proper, seemly, sympathetic; SEE CONCEPTS 558,563

conical/conic [*adj*] *shaped cylindrically and with a point*
coned, cone-shaped, conoid, conoidal, funnel-shaped, pointed, pyramidal, sharp, strobilate, strobiloid, tapered, tapering; SEE CONCEPT 486

conjectural [*adj*] *speculative*
academic, assumed, doubtful, figured, guessing, guesstimated*, hypothetical, on a hunch*, on a

long shot*, putative, reputed, supposed, suppositional, supposititious, suppositive, surmised, surmising, suspect, tentative, theoretical, uncertain, unresolved; SEE CONCEPT 582

conjecture [*n*] *speculation, assumption*
conclusion, fancy, guess, guesstimate*, guesswork, hunch, hypothesis, inference, notion, opinion, perhaps, presumption, shot in the dark*, sneaking suspicion, stab in the dark*, supposition, surmise, theorizing, theory; SEE CONCEPTS 28,274,689

conjecture [*v*] *speculate*
assume, believe, conceive, conclude, deem, estimate, expect, fancy, feel*, figure, gather, glean, guess, guesstimate*, hazard a guess*, hypothesize, imagine, infer, judge, presume, pretend, suppose, surmise, suspect, take a shot*, take a stab*, take for granted, theorize, think; SEE CONCEPTS 28,51

conjugal [*adj*] *marital*
bridal, connubial, hymeneal, married, matrimonial, nuptial, spousal, wedded; SEE CONCEPT 555

conjunction [*n*] *combination*
affiliation, agreement, alliance, association, cahoots, coincidence, concomitance, concurrence, congruency, conjointment, hookup*, juxtaposition, parallelism, partnership, tie-up*, union; SEE CONCEPTS 388,714

conjure [*v1*] *appeal to, implore*
adjure, ask, beg, beseech, brace, crave, entreat, importune, pray, supplicate, urge; SEE CONCEPT 48

conjure [*v2*] *cast spell*
bewitch, call upon, charm, enchant, ensorcel, entrance, exorcise, fascinate, invoke, levitate, play tricks, raise, rouse, summon, voodoo; SEE CONCEPT 14

conjure up [*v*] *bring to mind*
call, contrive, create, evoke, materialize, produce as by magic, recall, recollect, remember, review, summon, urge; SEE CONCEPT 38

connect [*v*] *combine, link*
affix, ally, associate, attach, bridge, cohere, come aboard, conjoin, consociate, correlate, couple, equate, fasten, get into, hitch on, hook on, hook up, interface, join, join up with, marry, meld with, network with, plug into, relate, slap on, span, tack on, tag, tag on, tie in, tie in with, unite, wed, yoke; SEE CONCEPTS 85,113,160

connected [*adj*] *related, affiliated*
akin, allied, applicable, associated, banded together, bracketed, coherent, combined, consecutive, coupled, in on with*, joined, linked, pertinent, undivided, united; SEE CONCEPTS 482,577

connection [*n1*] *person who aids another in achieving goal*
acquaintance, agent, ally, associate, association, contact, friend, go-between, intermediary, kin, kindred, kinship, mentor, messenger, network, reciprocity, relation, relative, sponsor; SEE CONCEPTS 348,423

connection [*n2*] *something that connects, links*
affiliation, alliance, association, attachment, bond, combination, conjointment, conjunction, coupling, fastening, hookup, joining, joint, junction, juncture, link, linkage, network, partnerhip, seam, tie, tie-in, tie-up, union; SEE CONCEPTS 499,720

connection [n3] *something that communicates, relates*

affinity, application, association, bearing, bond, commerce, communication, correlation, correspondence, intercourse, interrelation, kinship, link, marriage, nexus, partnership, reciprocity, relation, relationship, relevance, tie-in, togetherness; SEE CONCEPTS **388,664**

connive [v] *plot, scheme*

angle, be in cahoots with*, cabal, cogitate, collude, conspire, contrive, cook up, devise, diddle*, finagle, frame, frame up, intrigue, machinate, operate, promote, wangle, wire, work hand in glove*; SEE CONCEPT **36**

connoisseur [n] *authority*

adept, aesthete, aficionado, appreciator, arbiter, bon vivant, buff*, cognoscente, critic, devotee, dilettante, epicure, expert, fan, freak*, gourmet, judge, maven*, nut*, one into*, savant, specialist; SEE CONCEPTS **352,376**

connotation [n] *implication*

association, coloring, essence, hint, meaning, nuance, overtone, significance, suggestion, undertone; SEE CONCEPTS **682,689**

connote [v] *imply*

add up to, betoken, denote, designate, evidence, express, hint at, import, indicate, insinuate, intend, intimate, involve, mean, signify, spell, suggest; SEE CONCEPTS **75,118**

connubial [adj] *marital*

conjugal, hymeneal, married, matrimonial, nuptial, spousal, wedded; SEE CONCEPT **555**

conquer [v1] *defeat, overcome*

beat, bring to knees*, checkmate, circumvent, clobber, control, cream*, crush, discomfit, drub, foil, frustrate, get the better of*, humble, lick, master, outwit, overmaster, overpower, override, overthrow, prevail, quell, reduce, rout, shut down, subdue, subjugate, succeed, surmount, throw, thwart, total*, trample underfoot, trash, triumph, vanquish, whip, wipe off map*, worst, zap*; SEE CONCEPT **95**

conquer [v2] *win; obtain*

achieve, acquire, annex, best, master, occupy, overcome, overrun, prevail, seize, succeed, triumph; SEE CONCEPTS **90,141,706**

conqueror [n] *champion*

conquistador, defeater, hero, subduer, subjugator, vanquisher, victor, winner; SEE CONCEPTS **354,358**

conquest [n1] *defeat, victory*

acquisition, annexation, appropriation, big win*, clean sweep*, conquering, coup, defeating, discomfiture, grand slam*, invasion, killing*, occupation, overthrow, rout, routing, score, splash*, subdual, subjection, subjugation, success, takeover, triumph, vanquishment, win; SEE CONCEPTS **95,706**

conquest [n2] *enchantment; person enchanted*

acquisition, adherent, admirer, captivation, catch, enthrallment, enticement, fan, feather in cap*, follower, prize, seduction, supporter, worshiper; SEE CONCEPTS **410,423**

consanguinity [n] *family relationship*

affiliation, affinity, agnate, blood-relationship, brotherhood, cognate, connection, family tie, filiation, kin, kindred, kindredship, kinship, lineage, race, sisterhood, strain; SEE CONCEPTS **296,388**

conscience [n] *moral sense*

censor, compunction, demur, duty, inner voice, morals, principles, qualms, right and wrong, scruples, shame, small voice*, squeam, still small voice*, superego; SEE CONCEPTS **645,689**

conscientious [adj1] *thorough, careful*

complete, diligent, exact, exacting, faithful, fastidious, fussy, hanging in*, hanging tough*, heart and soul into*, heedful, meticulous, minding p's and q's*, painstaking, particular, playing safe, punctilious, punctual, reliable, tough, walking on eggs*; SEE CONCEPTS **531,538**

conscientious [adj2] *moral, upright*

conscionable, high-minded, high-principled, honest, honorable, incorruptible, just, pious, principled, responsible, right, scrupulous, straightforward, strict, true; SEE CONCEPT **545**

conscious [adj1] *alert, awake*

able to recognize, acquainted, aesthetic, alive to, apperceptive, apprised, assured, attentive, au courant, aware, certain, cognizant, conversant, discerning, felt, hep to*, informed, in on*, in right mind, keen, knowing, known, mindful, noticing, noting, observing, on to*, perceiving, percipient, recognizing, remarking, responsive, seeing, sensible, sensitive to, sentient, supraliminal, sure, understanding, vigilant, watchful, wise to*, with it*, witting; SEE CONCEPTS **402,539**

conscious [adj2] *intentional*

affected, calculated, deliberate, knowing, mannered, premeditated, rational, reasoning, reflective, responsible, self-conscious, studied, willful; SEE CONCEPTS **403,535**

consciousness [n] *knowledge*

alertness, apprehension, awareness, care, carefulness, cognizance, concern, heed, heedfulness, mindfulness, realization, recognition, regard, sensibility; SEE CONCEPT **409**

consecrate [v] *hold in high religious regard*

anoint, beatify, bless, dedicate, devote, exalt, hallow, honor, ordain, sanctify, set apart, venerate; SEE CONCEPTS **69,367**

consecutive [adj] *in sequence*

after, chronological, connected, constant, continuing, continuous, ensuing, following, going on, increasing, in order, in turn, later, logical, numerical, one after another, progressive, running, sequent, sequential, serial, serialized, seriate, seriatim, succedent, succeeding, successional, successive, understandable, uninterrupted; SEE CONCEPTS **585,799**

consensus [n] *general agreement*

accord, concord, concurrence, consent, harmony, unanimity, unison, unity; SEE CONCEPTS **684,689**

consent [n] *agreement; concession*

accord, acquiescence, allowance, approval, assent, authorization, blank check*, blessing, carte blanche*, compliance, concurrence, go-ahead*, green light*, leave, okay*, permission, permit, right on*, sanction, say so*, stamp of approval*, sufferance, understanding, yes; SEE CONCEPTS **684,685**

consent [v] *agree*

accede, accept, acquiesce, allow, approve, assent, bless, comply, concede, concur, fold, give in, give the nod*, give up, knuckle under, let, make a deal, okay*, permit, roll over, sanction, say uncle*, say yes, sign off on*, subscribe, throw in the towel*, yes*, yield; SEE CONCEPTS **8,50,88**

consequence [n1] *result, outcome of action*

aftereffect, aftermath, bottom line*, can of

CO
CO

worms*, chain reaction*, effect, end, event, fall-out, follow through, follow-up, issue, outgrowth, payback, reaction, repercussion, sequel, sequence, spin-off, upshot, waves*; SEE CONCEPT 230

consequence [n2] *importance, significance*
account, concern, exigency, fame, honor, import, interest, magnitude, moment, momentousness, need, note, pith, portent, renown, reputation, repute, signification, value, weight, weightiness; SEE CONCEPT 668

consequence [n3] *person's status*
cachet, dignity, distinction, eminence, notability, position, prestige, rank, repute, standing, state, stature, status; SEE CONCEPT 388

consequent [adj] *resultant*
consistent, ensuing, following, indirect, inferable, intelligent, logical, rational, reasonable, resulting, sensible, sequential, sound, subsequent, successive, understandable; SEE CONCEPTS 537,548

consequential [adj] *significant*
big, considerable, eventful, far-reaching, grave, important, material, meaningful, momentous, serious, substantial, weighty; SEE CONCEPT 568

conservation [n] *preservation*
attention, care, cherishing, conservancy, conserving, control, custody, directing, economy, governing, guardianship, guarding, keeping, maintenance, management, managing, preserval, preserving, protecting, protection, safeguarding, safekeeping, salvation, saving, stewardship, storage, supervising, supervision, sustentation, upkeep; SEE CONCEPTS 134,257

conservationist [n] *environmental activist*
environmentalist, green*, guardian, preservationist, tree hugger*; SEE CONCEPTS 414,423

conservative [adj] *cautious, moderate, tending to preserve the status quo*
bourgeois, constant, controlled, conventional, die-hard, fearful, firm, fogyish*, fuddy-duddy*, guarded, hard hat*, hidebound, holding to, illiberal, in a rut*, inflexible, middle-of-the-road*, not extreme, obstinate, old guard*, old line*, orthodox, quiet, reactionary, redneck*, right, right of center*, right-wing, sober, stable, steady, timid, Tory*, traditional, traditionalistic, unchangeable, unchanging, uncreative, unsabing, unimaginative, unprogressive, white bread*; SEE CONCEPT 542

conservative [n] *person who is cautious, moderate; an opponent of change*
bitter-ender*, classicist, conserver, conventionalist, diehard, hard hat*, middle-of-the-roader*, moderate, moderatist, obstructionist, old guard*, old liner*, preserver, reactionary, redneck*, right, rightist, right-winger, silk-stocking*, standpat, stick-in-the-mud*, Tory*, traditionalist, unprogressive; SEE CONCEPT 359

conservator [n] *caretaker of collection*
curator, custodian, guardian, keeper, protector, restorer; SEE CONCEPT 348

conservatory [n] *greenhouse*
cold frame, glasshouse, hot house, nursery; SEE CONCEPTS 439,449,517

conserve [v] *save, protect*
cut back, cut down on, go easy on*, hoard, keep, maintain, nurse, preserve, safeguard, scrimp, skimp, sock away*, squirrel*, squirrel away*,

stash, steward, store up, support, sustain, take care of, use sparingly; SEE CONCEPT 134

consider [v1] *turn over in one's mind*
acknowledge, allow for, assent to, chew over*, cogitate, concede, consult, contemplate, deal with, deliberate, dream of, envisage, examine, excogitate, favor, flirt with*, grant, inspect, keep in mind, look at, meditate, mull over, muse, perpend, ponder, provide for, reason, reckon with, recognize, reflect, regard, revolve, ruminate, scan, scrutinize, see, see about, speculate, study, subscribe to, take into account, take under advisement, take up, think out, think over, toss around*; SEE CONCEPTS 17,24

consider [v2] *regard a certain way*
analyze, appraise, bear in mind, believe, care for, count, credit, deem, estimate, feel, hold, hold an opinion, judge, keep in view, look upon, make allowance for, reckon with, reflect, remember, respect, sense, set down, suppose, take for, take into account, think, think of, view; SEE CONCEPT 12

considerable [adj1] *abundant, large*
ample, appreciable, astronomical, big, bountiful, comfortable, commodious, extensive, goodly, great, hefty, huge, large-scale, lavish, major, marked, much, noticeable, plentiful, pretty, reasonable, respectable, sizable, substantial, tidy, tolerable; SEE CONCEPT 781

considerable [adj2] *important*
big, consequential, distinguished, doozie*, dynamite, essential, fab*, fat, influential, material, meaningful, momentous, mondo*, noteworthy, renowned, significant, solid gold*, something, something else*, substantial, super, superduper*, to the max*, unreal*, venerable, weighty; SEE CONCEPT 568

considerably [adv] *significantly*
appreciably, far, greatly, markedly, noticeably, quite, rather, remarkably, somewhat, substantially, very much, well; SEE CONCEPT 569

considerate [adj] *respectful of others*
accommodating, amiable, attentive, benevolent, big, charitable, chivalrous, circumspect, compassionate, complaisant, concerned, cool, discreet, forbearing, generous, kind, kindly, like a sport*, magnanimous, mellow, mindful, obliging, patient, polite, solicitous, sympathetic, tactful, tender, thoughtful, unselfish, warmhearted; SEE CONCEPT 401

consideration [n1] *mental analysis*
application, attention, cogitation, concentration, contemplation, debate, deliberation, discussion, examination, forethought, heed, reflection, regard, review, scrutiny, study, thinking, thought; SEE CONCEPT 24

consideration [n2] *concern; something mentally examined*
development, difficulty, emergency, estate, evidence, exigency, extent, factor, fancy, idea, incident, issue, items, judgment, magnitude, minutiae, notion, occasion, occurrence, particulars, perplexity, plan, point, problem, proposal, puzzle, scope, situation, state, thought, trouble; SEE CONCEPT 532

consideration [n3] *high regard*
attentiveness, awareness, concern, considerateness, esteem, estimation, favor, forbearance, friendliness, heed, heedfulness, kindliness, kindness, mercy, mindfulness, respect, solicitude,

tact, thoughtfulness, tolerance; SEE CONCEPTS

consideration [n4] *payment*
baksheesh, commish*, commission, fee*, payback, percentage, perk, perquisite, recompense, remuneration, reward, salary, something to sweeten pot*, tip, wage; SEE CONCEPT 344

considered [adj] *deliberate, thought-out*
advised, aforethought, contemplated, designed, designful, examined, express, given due consideration, gone into, intentional, investigated, mediated, premeditated, prepense, studied, studious, thought-about, thought-through, treated, voluntary, weighed, well advised, well chosen, willful; SEE CONCEPTS 402,529

considering [adj] *taking everything in mind*
all in all, all things considered, as, as long as, because, everything being equal, for, forasmuch as, inasmuch as, in consideration of, in light of, insomuch as, in view of, now, pending, seeing, since, taking into account; SEE CONCEPT 529

consign [v] *entrust, hand over for care*
address, appoint, assign, authorize, commend to, commission, commit, confide, convey, delegate, deliver, deposit with, dispatch, forward, give, issue, put in charge of, relegate, remit, route, send, ship, transfer, transmit, turn over; SEE CONCEPTS 108,143,217

consignment [n1] *entrusting, handing over*
assignment, committal, dispatch, distribution, relegation, sending shipment, transmittal; SEE CONCEPTS 108,143,217

consignment [n2] *something entrusted to another's care*
batch, delivery, goods, shipment; SEE CONCEPT 338

consist [v] *exist, reside*
abide, be, be contained in, be expressed by, be found in, dwell, inhere, lie, repose, rest, subsist; SEE CONCEPT 539

consistency [n1] *thickness*
bendability, bendableness, compactness, density, elasticity, fabric, firmness, flexibility, frangibility, hardness, limberness, moldability, organization, plasticity, pliability, softness, solidity, suppleness, texture, viscidity, viscosity, viscousness; SEE CONCEPTS 611,722

consistency [n2] *constancy, regularity*
accord, agreement, apposition, appropriateness, aptness, coherence, cohesion, compatibility, concord, concurrence, conformability, congruity, consonance, correspondence, evenness, fitness, harmony, homogeneity, invariability, likeness, proportion, similarity, stability, steadfastness, steadiness, suitability, symmetry, uniformity, union, unity; SEE CONCEPTS 637,656,670

consistent [adj1] *constant, regular*
dependable, even, expected, homogeneous, invariable, logical, of a piece, persistent, rational, same, steady, true, true to type, unchanging, undeviating, unfailing, uniform, unvarying; SEE CONCEPT 534

consistent [adj2] *agreeing, compatible*
accordant, according to, agreeable, all of a piece, coherent, conforming with, congenial, congruous, consonant, equable, harmonious, like, logical, matching, sympathetic; SEE CONCEPT 563

consist of [v] *made up of*
amount to, be composed of, comprise, contain,

embody, include, incorporate, involve; SEE CONCEPT 643

consolation [n] *relief, comfort*
alleviation, assuagement, cheer, comfort, compassion, ease, easement, encouragement, fellow feeling, help, lenity, pity, solace, succour, support, sympathy; SEE CONCEPTS 32,410

console [v] *relieve, comfort*
animate, assuage, buck up*, calm, cheer, condole with, encourage, express sympathy, gladden, inspirit, lift, solace, soothe, tranquilize, untrouble, upraise; SEE CONCEPTS 7,22

consolidate [v] *combine; make firm*
add to, amalgamate, amass, band, bind, blend, build up, bunch up, cement, centralize, compact, compound, concatenate, concentrate, condense, conjoin, connect, densen, develop, federate, fortify, fuse, harden, hitch, hitch on, hook up with, incorporate, join, league, mass, meld, mix, plug into, pool, reinforce, render solid, secure, set, slap on, solidify, stabilize, strengthen, tack on, tag on, team up with*, thicken, throw in together*, tie in, tie up with, unify; SEE CONCEPTS 109,250

consolidation [n] *combination, fortification*
alliance, amalgamation, association, coadunation, coalition, compression, concentration, condensation, federation, fusion, incorporation, melding, mergence, merger, merging, reinforcement, solidification, strengthening, unification; SEE CONCEPTS 109,469

consonance [n] *agreement, consistency*
accord, chime, chorus, concert, concord, conformity, congruence, congruity, correspondence, harmony, suitableness, tune; SEE CONCEPT 664

consonant [adj] *agreeing, consistent*
accordant, according, agnate, akin, alike, analogous, blending, coincident, comfortable, comparable, compatible, concordant, congenial, congruous, correspondent, corresponding, harmonious, in agreement, in rapport, like, parallel, similar, suitable, sympathetic, uniform; SEE CONCEPT 563

consort [n] *associate, partner*
accompaniment, companion, concomitant, friend, husband, mate, spouse, wife; SEE CONCEPT 423

consort [v1] *be friendly with; fraternize*
accompany, associate, attend, bear, befriend, bring, carry, chaperon, chum together*, chum with*, clique with, company, conduct, convoy, gang up with*, go around with*, hang around with*, hang out with*, hang with*, join, keep company, mingle, mix, pal, pal around with, pal with, run around with*, run with, take up with, tie up with; SEE CONCEPTS 114,384

consort [v2] *agree*
accord, coincide, comport, concur, conform, correspond, dovetail, harmonize, march, square, tally; SEE CONCEPT 664

conspicuous [adj1] *obvious, easily seen*
apparent, clear, discernible, distinct, evident, manifest, noticeable, open-and-shut*, patent, perceptible, plain, visible; SEE CONCEPT 619

conspicuous [adj2] *important, prominent*
arresting, arrestive, blatant, celebrated, commanding, distinguished, eminent, famed, famous, flagrant, flashy, garish, glaring, glitzy*, illustrious, influential, jazzy, loud, marked, notable, noted, notorious, outstanding, pointed,

CO
CO

rank, remarkable, renowned, salient, screaming, showy, signal, splashy, stick out like sore thumb*, striking, tony*, well-known; SEE CONCEPTS 542,567

conspiracy [n] *collusion in plan*
cabal, complot, confederacy, connivance, countermine, counterplot, covin, disloyalty, fix, frame*, game, hookup*, intrigue, league, little game*, machination, perfidy, plot, practice, put-up job*, scheme, sedition, treacherousness, treachery, treason, trick, trickery; SEE CONCEPT 660

conspirator [n] *schemer*
accomplice, backstabber*, betrayer, caballer, collaborator, colluder, highbinder, plotter, subversive, traitor; SEE CONCEPT 412

conspire [v1] *plot, scheme with someone*
be in cahoots*, cabal, cogitate, collogue, collude, confederate, connive, contrive, cook up*, cooperate, devise, get in bed with*, hatch, intrigue, machinate, maneuver, operate, promote, put out a contract*, wangle, wire, work something out*; SEE CONCEPTS 36,192

conspire [v2] *agree, concur*
cabal, colleague, combine, complot, conduce, consort, contribute, cooperate, join, tend, unite, work together; SEE CONCEPT 8

constancy [n] *fixedness*
abidingness, adherence, allegiance, ardor, attachment, certainty, decision, dependability, determination, devotedness, devotion, doggedness, eagerness, earnestness, endurance, faith, fealty, fidelity, firmness, honesty, honor, integrity, love, loyalty, permanence, perseverance, principle, regularity, resolution, stability, staunchness, steadfastness, steadiness, surety, tenacity, trustiness, trustworthiness, truthfulness, unchangeableness, unfailingness, uniformity, zeal; SEE CONCEPTS 32,410,637

constant [adj1] *fixed*
connected, consistent, continual, equable, even, firm, habitual, homogeneous, immutable, invariable, like the Rock of Gibralter*, monochrome, monophonic, monotonous, nonstop, of a piece, permanent, perpetual, regular, regularized, solid as rock*, stabile, stable, standardized, steadfast, steady, together, unalterable, unbroken, unchanging, unflappable, unfluctuating, uniform, uninterrupted, unvarying; SEE CONCEPT 534

constant [adj2] *neverending*
abiding, ceaseless, chronic, continual, continuous, endless, enduring, eternal, everlasting, incessant, interminable, lasting, nonstop, perpetual, persistent, persisting, relentless, sustained, unending, uninterrupted, unrelenting, unremitting; SEE CONCEPTS 649,798

constant [adj3] *loyal, determined*
allegiant, attached, dependable, devoted, dogged, faithful, fast, persevering, resolute, staunch, tried-and-true, true, trustworthy, trusty, unfailing, unflagging, unshaken, unwavering; SEE CONCEPT 542

consternation [n] *dismay, distress*
alarm, amazement, anxiety, awe, bewilderment, confusion, distraction, dread, fear, fright, horror, muddle, muddlement, panic, perplexity, shock, stupefaction, terror, trepidation, trepidity, wonder; SEE CONCEPT 230

constituency [n] *voting public*
balloters, body of voters, body politic, citizenry,

city, county, district, electorate, electors, faction, nation, people, precinct, state, system, voters, voting area, ward; SEE CONCEPT 379

constituent [adj1] *component, part*
basic, combining, composing, constituting, division, elemental, essential, factor, forming, fraction, fundamental, ingredient, integral, portion; SEE CONCEPTS 826,834,835

constituent [adj2] *voting*
balloter, citizen, electing, electoral, official, overruling; SEE CONCEPT 536

constituent [n] *element*
board, component, division, essential, factor, fixins*, fraction, ingredient, makings, part, part and parcel*, plug-in*, portion, principle, unit; SEE CONCEPTS 826,834

constitute [v1] *comprise, form*
aggregate, complement, complete, compose, compound, construct, cook up*, create, develop, dream up*, embody, enact, establish, fill out, fix, flesh out*, found, frame, fudge together*, incorporate, integrate, make, make up, set up; SEE CONCEPTS 173,184,251

constitute [v2] *authorize*
appoint, commission, decree, delegate, depute, deputize, designate, draft, empower, enact, establish, legislate, make, name, nominate, ordain, order; SEE CONCEPTS 50,88

constitution [n1] *physical make-up and health*
architecture, build, character, composition, construction, content, contents, design, disposition, essence, form, formation, frame, habit, habitus, nature, physique, structure, temper, temperament, type, vitality; SEE CONCEPT 757

constitution [n2] *establishment*
charter, code, composition, custom, formation, lawmaking, legislation, organization, written law; SEE CONCEPTS 271,318

constitutional [adj1] *inherent*
built-in, congenital, deep-seated, essential, inborn, inbred, ingrained, innate, intrinsic, natural, organic, vital; SEE CONCEPT 549

constitutional [adj2] *provided for by law*
approved, chartered, democratic, ensured, lawful, legal, representative, statutory, vested; SEE CONCEPT 319

constitutional [n] *walk*
airing, ambulation, footwork, legwork, perambulation, ramble, saunter, stroll, turn, walk; SEE CONCEPT 149

constrain [v] *force; restrain*
ban, bar, bind, bottle up, bridle, chain, check, coerce, compel, concuss, confine, constrict, cool off*, cork, curb, deny, deprive, disallow, drive, hem in*, hog-tie*, hold back, hold down, hold in, immure, impel, imprison, incarcerate, inhibit, intern, jail, keep lid on*, make, necessitate, oblige, pressure, pressurize, put half nelson on*, shotgun*, stifle, urge, withhold; SEE CONCEPTS 14,121,130

constraint [n1] *force*
a must*, coercion, compulsion, driving, duress, goad, hang-up*, impelling, impulsion, monkey*, motive, necessity, no-no*, pressure, repression, restraint, spring, spur, suppression, violence; SEE CONCEPTS 14,121

constraint [n2] *shyness*
bashfulness, diffidence, embarrassment, hang-up*, humility, inhibition, modesty, repression,

reservation, reserve, restraint, timidity; SEE CON-CEPT *411*

constraint [*n3*] *restriction*

arrest, captivity, check, circumscription, confinement, constrainment, cramp, curb, damper, detention, deterrent, hindrance, limitation, restraint; SEE CONCEPTS *130,652*

constrict [*v*] *inhibit*

astringe, choke, circumscribe, clench, compress, concentrate, condense, confine, constringe, contract, cramp, curb, draw together, limit, narrow, pinch, restrain, restrict, shrink, squeeze, strangle, strangulate, tauten, tense, tighten, tuck; SEE CONCEPTS *130,191,219*

constriction [*n*] *blockage*

binding, choking, compression, constraint, contraction, cramp, impediment, limitation, narrowing, pressure, reduction, restriction, squeezing, stenosis, stricture, tightness; SEE CONCEPTS *130,191,219*

construct [*v*] *assemble, build*

build up, cobble up*, compose, compound, constitute, cook up*, create, design, dream up*, elevate, engineer, envision, erect, establish, fabricate, fashion, forge, form, formulate, found, frame, fudge together*, hammer out*, hoke up*, imagine, invent, make, manufacture, organize, prefab*, produce, put out, put together, put up, raise, rear, set up, shape, throw together, throw up*, trump up*, uprear, whip up*; SEE CONCEPTS *168,173,251*

construction [*n1*] *creation, building*

architecture, arrangement, assembly, build, cast, composition, conception, constitution, contour, cut, development, disposition, edifice, elevation, erecting, erection, fabric, fabricating, fabrication, figuration, figure, form, format, formation, foundation, improvisation, invention, makeup, making, manufacture, mold, origination, outline, plan, planning, prefab, prefabrication, putting up, raising, rearing, roadwork, shape, structure, system, systematization, turn, type; SEE CONCEPTS *168,439,757*

construction [*n2*] *explanation*

apprehension, construal, definition, exegesis, explication, exposé, exposition, inference, interpretation, reading, rendering, rendition, translation, version; SEE CONCEPT *274*

constructive [*adj*] *helpful*

effective, positive, practical, productive, useful, valuable; SEE CONCEPT *401*

construe [*v*] *deduce; explain*

analyze, decipher, define, explicate, expound, figure it to be*, infer, interpret, one's best guess*, parse, read, render, spell out, take, translate, understand; SEE CONCEPTS *37,57*

consul [*n*] *representative*

delegate, emissary, envoy, lawyer, legate; SEE CONCEPTS *354,355*

consulate [*n*] *embassy*

consular office, government office, ministry; SEE CONCEPTS *439,449*

consult [*v*] *ask, confer*

argue, ask advice of, be closeted with, brainstorm*, call in, cogitate, collogue, commune, compare notes, confab, confabulate, consider, debate, deliberate, discuss, examine, flap*, groupthink*, huddle, interrogate, interview, kick ideas around*, negotiate, parlay, pick one's brains*, powwow*, put heads together*, ques-

tion, refer to, regard, respect, review, seek advice, seek opinion of, take account of, take a meeting*, take counsel, talk over, toss ideas around*, treat, turn to; SEE CONCEPTS *17,48,56*

consultant [*n*] *professional advisor*

advisor, authority, counsel, expert, freelancer, guide, master, maven, mentor, pro*, specialist, veteran; SEE CONCEPTS *348,350*

consultation [*n*] *asking, conference*

appointment, argument, buzz session*, clambake*, confab*, conference, council, deliberation, dialogue, discussion, examination, groupthink*, hearing, huddle, interview, meeting, powwow*, second opinion*, session; SEE CONCEPTS *48,114,324*

consume [*v1*] *use up*

absorb, apply, avail oneself of, deplete, devour, dissipate, dominate, drain, drivel, eat up, employ, engross, exhaust, expend, finish, finish up, fritter away, frivol away, go, go through, have recourse to, lavish, lessen, monopolize, obsess, preoccupy, profit by, put away, put to use, run out of, run through, spend, squander, throw away, trifle, utilize, vanish, wash up, waste, wear out; SEE CONCEPT *225*

consume [*v2*] *eat, drink*

absorb, bolt, chow down*, devour, down, eat up, feed, gobble*, gorge, gulp, guzzle, hoover*, ingest, ingurgitate, inhale, meal, mow*, nibble, partake, polish off*, punish, put away*, put down*, scarf*, snack, stuff one's face*, swallow, swill, take, toss down*, wolf*; SEE CONCEPT *169*

consume [*v3*] *destroy*

annihilate, crush, decay, demolish, devastate, eat up, exhaust, expend, extinguish, lay waste, overwhelm, ravage, raze, ruin, suppress, waste, wreck; SEE CONCEPT *252*

consumer [*n*] *person who buys merchandise, services*

buyer, customer, end user, enjoyer, purchaser, shopper, user; SEE CONCEPT *348*

consummate [*adj*] *ultimate, best*

able, absolute, accomplished, complete, conspicuous, downright, faultless, finished, flawless, gifted, ideal, impeccable, inimitable, matchless, out-and-out*, peerless, perfect, perfected, polished, positive, practiced, ripe, skilled, superb, superlative, supreme, talented, thoroughgoing, total, trained, transcendent, unmitigated, unqualified, unsurpassable, utter, virtuosic, whole; SEE CONCEPTS *528,572*

consummate [*v*] *achieve, finish*

accomplish, button down*, call a day*, can*, carry out, clean up, clinch, close, come, come through, compass, complete, conclude, crown, drop curtain*, effectuate, end, fold up, get it together*, go the distance*, halt, knock off, mop up, perfect, perform, polish off*, put away*, put finishing touch on*, put lid on*, put to bed*, sew up, sign, take care of, terminate, top it off, ultimate, wind up, wrap, wrap up; SEE CONCEPTS *234,704,706*

consummation [*n*] *achievement, fulfillment*

cleanup, completion, culmination, doing it to a T*, end, mop-up, payoff, perfection, realization, to a finish, wind-up*, wrap, wrap-up*; SEE CONCEPT *706*

consumption [*n*] *devouring; use*

burning, consuming, damage, decay, decrease, depletion, desolation, destruction, devastation, diminution, dispersion, dissipation, drinking, eating, exhaustion, expenditure, loss, misuse, ruin, swallowing, using up, utilization, waste, wear and tear; SEE CONCEPTS 156,169,225,252

contact [*n1*] *form of communication*
acquaintance, association, channel, commerce, communion, companionship, connection, influence, intercourse, junction, meeting, network, touch, union, unity; SEE CONCEPTS 278,388,687

contact [*n2*] *touching*
approximation, closeness, collision, connection, contiguity, contingence, hit, impingement, junction, juxtaposition, nearness, propinquity, proximity, relation, strike, taction, touch, union; SEE CONCEPT 747

contact [*v*] *communicate with*
approach, be in touch with, buzz*, call, check with, connect, get, get ahold of, get in touch with, interact, interface, network*, phone, reach, reach out, relate, speak to, talk, telephone, touch base*, visit, write to; SEE CONCEPT 266

contagion [*n*] *infection*
bane, contamination, corruption, illness, miasma, pestilence, plague, poison, pollution, taint, transmission, venom, virus; SEE CONCEPT 306

contagious [*adj*] *communicable*
catching, deadly, endemic, epidemic, epizootic, impartible, infectious, inoculable, pestiferous, pestilential, poisonous, spreading, taking, transmissible, transmittable; SEE CONCEPT 314

contain [*v1*] *include, hold*
accommodate, be composed of, comprehend, comprise, consist of, embody, embrace, enclose, encompass, have, have capacity for, hold, incorporate, involve, seat, subsume, take in; SEE CONCEPTS 112,736,742

contain [*v2*] *hold back, control*
bottle up*, check, collect, compose, cool*, cork*, curb, harness, hog-tie*, hold in, keep back, keep lid on*, put half nelson on*, rein, repress, restrain, restrict, simmer down, smother, stifle, stop; SEE CONCEPTS 94,191

container [*n*] *holder for physical object*
alembic, bag, beaker, bin, bottle, bowl, box, bucket, bunker, caisson, can, canister, canteen, capsule, carafe, carton, cask, casket, cauldron, chamber, chest, churn, cistern, cradle, crate, crock, dish, ewer, firkin, flask, hamper, hod, hopper, humidor, hutch, jar, jeroboam, jug, kettle, magnum, package, packet, pail, pit, pod, poke, pot, pottery, pouch, purse, receptacle, reliquary, repository, sac, sack, scuttle, stein, storage, tank, tub, utensil, vase, vat, vessel, vial; SEE CONCEPT 494

contaminate [*v*] *adulterate*
alloy, befoul, corrupt, debase, debauch, defile, deprave, desecrate, dirty, harm, infect, injure, muck up, pervert, poison, pollute, profane, radioactivate, soil, spoil, stain, sully, taint, tarnish, vitiate; SEE CONCEPTS 252,254

contamination [*n*] *adulteration*
contagion, corruption, decay, defilement, dirtying, disease, epidemic, filth, foulness, impurity, infection, pestilence, plague, poisoning, pollution, radioactivation, rottenness, spoliation, taint; SEE CONCEPTS 230,306,674

contemplate [*v1*] *think about seriously; plan*
aim, aspire to, brood over, chew over, consider, cool out*, deliberate, design, envisage, excogitate, expect, foresee, intend, kick around*, mean,

meditate on, mind, mull over, muse over, observe, percolate, perpend, ponder, propose, purpose, reflect upon, ruminate, size up, speculate, study, take in, think of, weigh; SEE CONCEPTS 17,36

contemplate [*v2*] *gaze at*
audit, behold, consider, examine, eye, inspect, notice, observe, peer, penetrate, peruse, pierce, pore over, probe, pry, regard, scan, scrutinize, see, stare at, study, survey, view, witness; SEE CONCEPT 623

contemplation [*n1*] *deep thought; planning*
ambition, cogitation, consideration, deliberation, design, intention, meditation, musing, plan, pondering, purpose, reflection, reverie, rumination, study; SEE CONCEPT 410

contemplation [*n2*] *gazing at*
examination, inspection, looking at, observation, scrutiny, survey, viewing; SEE CONCEPT 623

contemplative [*adj*] *deep in thought*
attentive, cogitative, in brown study*, intent, introspective, lost, meditative, musing, pensive, pondering, rapt, reflecting, reflective, ruminative, speculative, thinking, thoughtful; SEE CONCEPTS 402,403

contemporary [*adj1*] *modern*
abreast, à la mode*, au courant, contempo*, current, existent, extant, hot off press*, in fashion, instant, in vogue, just out*, latest, leading-edge*, mod*, new, newfangled, now, present, present-day, recent, red-hot*, state-of-the-art*, today's, topical, ultramodern, up*, up-to-date, up-to-the-minute, voguish, with it*; SEE CONCEPTS 578,589,797

contemporary [*adj2*] *existing, occurring at same time*
accompanying, associated, attendant, coetaneous, coeval, coexistent, coexisting, coincident, concomitant, concurrent, connected, contemporaneous, current, linked, present, related, simultaneous, synchronal, synchronic, synchronous; SEE CONCEPT 820

contempt [*n1*] *disdain, disrespect*
antipathy, audacity, aversion, condescension, contumely, defiance, derision, despisal, despisement, despite, disesteem, disregard, distaste, hatred, indignity, malice, mockery, neglect, recalcitrance, repugnance, ridicule, scorn, slight, snobbery, stubbornness; SEE CONCEPT 29

contempt [*n2*] *state of disgrace*
discredit, disesteem, disfavor, dishonor, disrepute, humiliation, ignominy, infamy, insignificancy, opprobrium, shame, stigma; SEE CONCEPTS 388,674

contemptible [*adj*] *despicable, shameful*
abhorrent, abject, abominable, bad, base, beggarly, cheap, crass, currish, degenerate, despisable, detestable, dirty, disgusting, hateful, heel, ignoble, ignominious, inferior, low, low-down*, lowest, mean, odious, outcast, paltry, pitiable, pitiful, poor, sad, scummy*, scurvy*, shabby, sordid, sorry*, swinish, unworthy, vile, worthless, wretched; SEE CONCEPT 550

contemptuous [*adj*] *arrogant, insolent*
audacious, bold, cavalier, cheeky, cold-shoulder, condescending, contumelious, cool, derisive, derisory, disdainful, disrespectful, dog it*, hard, hard-nosed, haughty, high and mighty*, high hat*, insulting, on high horse*, opprobrious, sardonic, scornful, sneering, snippy, snobbish,

snooty*, snotty*, supercilious, temperamental, uppity, upstage; SEE CONCEPT *401*

contend [*v1*] *compete, fight*
argue, battle, clash, confront, contest, controvert, cope, dispute, emulate, encounter, face, give all one's got*, give one's all*, go after, go for, go for broke*, go for it*, go for jugular*, grapple, have at*, jockey for position*, jostle, knock oneself out*, litigate, lock horns*, make play for*, meet, mix it up with*, oppose, oppugn, push, push for, resist, rival, scramble for, shoot at, shoot for, skirmish, stand, strive, struggle, tangle with, tug, vie, withstand; SEE CONCEPTS *92,106*

contend [*v2*] *argue*
affirm, allege, assert, aver, avow, blast, charge, claim, come at, cross, debate, defend, dictate, dispute, enjoin, fly in face of*, gang up on, go at, have at*, have bone to pick*, hold, insist, jump on, justify, lace into*, lay into*, let have it*, light into*, lock horns with*, maintain, mix, mix it up*, prescribe, put up argument, report, rip*, say, set to, sock it to one*, stick it to*, take on, tell, urge, vindicate, warrant, zap*; SEE CONCEPT *46*

content [*adj*] *happy, agreeable*
appeased, at ease, can't complain*, comfortable, complacent, contented, fat dumb and happy*, fulfilled, gratified, pleased as punch*, satisfied, smug, tickled pink*, willing; SEE CONCEPT *403*

content [*n1*] *comfort, happiness*
contentment, ease, gratification, peace, peace of mind, pleasure, satisfaction; SEE CONCEPT *410*

content [*n2*] *essence, meaning*
burden, composition, constitution, gist, idea, matter, significance; subject, subject matter, substance, text, thought; SEE CONCEPT *682*

content [*n3*] *capacity, volume*
filling, load, measure, packing, size; SEE CONCEPTS *719,740*

content [*v*] *please*
appease, bewitch, captivate, charm, delight, enrapture, gladden, gratify, humor, indulge, make happy, mollify, placate, reconcile, satisfy, suffice, thrill, tickle; SEE CONCEPTS *7,22*

contented [*adj*] *at ease; happy*
at peace, cheerful, comfortable, complacent, content, glad, gratified, pleased, satisfied, serene, thankful; SEE CONCEPT *403*

contention [*n1*] *competition*
altercation, argument, battle, beef*, belligerency, bone of contention*, bone to pick*, combat, conflict, contest, controversy, difference, disaccord, discord, dispute, dissension, dissent, dissidence, disunity, enmity, feuding, fight, flak*, hassle, hostility, quarrel, rivalry, run-in, scene, scrap, set-to*, squabble, static, strife, struggle, variance, war, wrangle, wrangling; SEE CONCEPTS *92,106*

contention [*n2*] *argument for idea*
advancement, affirmation, allegation, assertion, asseveration, avowal, belief, charge, claim, contestation, declaration, demurrer, deposition, discussion, explanation, ground, hurrah, hypothesis, idea, maintaining, opinion, plea, position, predication, profession, rumpus, stand, thesis, view; SEE CONCEPTS *46,278,689*

contentious [*adj*] *quarrelsome*
antagonistic, argumentative, belligerent, combative, disagreeable, factious, perverse, petulant, querulous, testy; SEE CONCEPTS *401,542*

contentment [*n*] *comfort, happiness*
complacency, content, contentedness, ease, equanimity, fulfillment, gladness, gratification, peace, pleasure, repletion, satisfaction, serenity; SEE CONCEPT *410*

contents [*n*] *elements of larger object*
capacity, cargo, chapters, connotation, constituents, details, divisions, essence, filling, freight, furnishing, gist, guts, implication, ingredients, innards, inside, lading, load, meaning, nub, packing, shipment, significance, size, space, stuffing, subject matter, subjects, substance, sum, text, themes, topics, volume; SEE CONCEPT *835*

contest [*n1*] *competition*
challenge, concours, discussion, game, match, meet, meeting, proving, rencounter, sport, testing, tournament, trial, trying; SEE CONCEPTS *92,363*

contest [*n2*] *fight, struggle*
action, affray, altercation, battle, battle royal*, beef*, brawl, brush, combat, conflict, controversy, debate, discord, dispute, emulation, encounter, engagement, fray, go*, hassle, rivalry, row, rumble*, run-in, scrap, set-to*, shock, skirmish, static, strife, striving, tug-of-war, warfare, wrangle; SEE CONCEPTS *106,320*

contest [*v1*] *argue, challenge*
blast, call in question, debate, dispute, doubt, give it one's all*, go for it*, go for jugular*, jockey for position*, jump on, litigate, mix it up with*, object to, oppose, push, question, scramble for, shoot for*, stand up for, tangle; SEE CONCEPT *46*

contest [*v2*] *fight*
altercate, attack, battle, brawl, break with, buck, compete, conflict, contend, cross, defend, duel, feud, fight over, gang up on, knuckle with, lay a finger on*, lay out, put on gloves*, put up dukes*, quarrel, repel, rival, row, rumpus, scrap, scuffle, set to, sock*, square off, strike, struggle, take on, tilt, traverse, vie, withstand, wrangle; SEE CONCEPT *106*

contestant [*n*] *competitor*
adversary, antagonist, aspirant, battler, candidate, challenger, combatant, contender, contester, dark horse*, disputant, entrant, favorite, hopeful, member, participant, player, rival, scrapper*, team member, warrior; SEE CONCEPT *366*

context [*n*] *framework, circumstances*
ambience, background, conditions, connection, frame of reference, lexicon, relation, situation, substance, text, vocabulary; SEE CONCEPTS *682,696*

contiguous [*adj*] *adjacent, in contact*
abutting, adjoining, approximal, beside, bordering, close, contactual, conterminous, juxtaposed, juxtapositional, meeting, near, near-at-hand, nearby, neighboring, next, next door to, next to, touching; SEE CONCEPTS *586,778*

continence [*n*] *self-restraint*
abstemiousness, abstinence, asceticism, celibacy, chastity, forbearance, moderation, refraining, self-control, sobriety, temperance, virtue; SEE CONCEPT *633*

continent [*adj*] *chaste, pure*
abstemious, abstentious, abstinent, ascetic, austere, bridled, celibate, curbed, inhibited, modest, restrained, self-restrained, sober, temperate; SEE CONCEPT *550*

CO
CO

contingency [*n*] *chance happening; possibility*
accident, break, chance, crisis, crossroads, emergency, event, eventuality, exigency, fortuity, happening, if it's cool*, incident, juncture, likelihood, occasion, odds, opportunity, pass, pinch, predicament, probability, strait, turning point, uncertainty, zero hour*; SEE CONCEPTS *650,679,693*

contingent [*adj*] *conditional; possible*
accidental, casual, chance, controlled by, dependent, fluky, fortuitous, haphazard, incidental, likely, odd, probable, probably, random, subject to, unanticipated, uncertain, unexpected, unforeseeable, unforeseen, unpredictable; SEE CONCEPT *552*

contingent [*n*] *group of followers*
batch, body, bunch, deputation, detachment, disciples, mission, quota, sect, section, set; SEE CONCEPT *417*

continual [*adj*] *constant, incessant*
aeonian, around-the-clock, ceaseless, connected, consecutive, continuous, dateless, endless, enduring, eternal, everlasting, frequent, interminable, oft-repeated, permanent, perpetual, persistent, persisting, recurrent, regular, relentless, repeated, repetitive, running, staying, steady, timeless, unbroken, unceasing, unchanging, unending, unfailing, unflagging, uninterrupted, unremitting, unvarying, unwaning; SEE CONCEPTS *534,798*

continuance [*n*] *duration*
constancy, continuation, endurance, extension, guts*, longevity, period, permanence, perpetuation, protraction, run, survival, term, vitality; SEE CONCEPTS *637,804,807*

continuation [*n*] *addition; maintenance*
assiduity, augmenting, continuance, continuing, continuity, duration, endurance, enduring, extension, furtherance, going on, increase, increasing, line, maintaining, perpetuating, perpetuation, persisting, postscript, preservation, preserving, producing, production, prolongation, prolonging, propagation, protracting, protraction, sequel, succession, supplement, sustaining, sustenance, tenacity; SEE CONCEPTS *640,651,804*

continue [*v1*] *persist, carry on*
abide, advance, carry forward, draw out, endure, extend, forge ahead, get on with it*, go on, hang in*, keep at, keep on, keep on truckin'*, keep the ball rolling*, keep up, last, lengthen, linger, live on, loiter, maintain, make headway, move ahead, never cease, outlast, outlive, perdure, persevere, persist in, press on, progress, project, prolong, promote, pursue, push on, reach, remain, rest, ride, run on, stand, stay, stay on, stick at, stick to, survive, sustain, uphold; SEE CONCEPT *239*

continue [*v2*] *begin again; resume*
begin over, begin where one left off, carry on, carry over, go on with, pick up, proceed, recapitulate, recommence, reestablish, reinstate, reinstitute, renew, reopen, restart, restore, return to, take up; SEE CONCEPT *234*

continuity [*n*] *progression*
chain, cohesion, connection, constancy, continuance, continuousness, continuum, dovetailing, durability, duration, endurance, extension, flow, interrelationship, linking, perpetuity, persistence, prolongation, protraction, sequence, stability, stamina, succession, survival, train, uniting, unity, vitality, whole; SEE CONCEPT *721*

continuous [*adj*] *constant, unending*
connected, consecutive, continued, day and night*, endless, everlasting, extended, for ever and ever, interminable, looped, no end of*, no end to, on a treadmill*, perpetual, prolonged, regular, repeated, stable, steady, timeless, unbroken, unceasing, undivided, unfaltering, uninterrupted; SEE CONCEPTS *482,798*

contort [*v*] *disfigure, distort*
bend, convolute, curve, deform, gnarl, knot, misshape, torture, twist, warp, wind, wrench, writhe; SEE CONCEPTS *147,184*

contortion [*n*] *distortion, mutilation*
anamorphosis, crookedness, deformation, deformity, dislocation, grimace, malformation, misproportion, misshapement, pout, twist, ugliness, unsightliness, wryness; SEE CONCEPTS *436,580*

contour [*n*] *outline, profile*
curve, delineation, figuration, figure, form, lineament, lines, relief, shape, silhouette; SEE CONCEPT *436*

contraband [*adj*] *black-market; unlawful*
banned, bootleg, bootlegged, disapproved, excluded, forbidden, hot*, illegal, illicit, interdicted, prohibited, proscribed, shut out, smuggled, taboo, unauthorized, verboten; SEE CONCEPTS *319,545*

contraband [*n*] *black-market production*
bootlegging, counterfeiting, crime, dealing, goods*, moonshine*, piracy, plunder, poaching, rum-running*, smuggling, stuff, swag, theft, trafficking, violation, wetbacking*; SEE CONCEPTS *192,338*

contraceptive [*n*] *birth control method*
armor, barrier method, coil, condom, diaphragm, foam, hormone, intrauterine device, IUD, jelly, loop, pill, planned parenthood, preventative, preventive medicine, prophylactic, rhythm method, ring, rubber, safety, shield, spermicidal cream, sponge, vaginal suppository; SEE CONCEPTS *307,446*

contract [*n*] *agreement, deal*
arrangement, bargain, bond, commission, commitment, compact, concordat, convention, covenant, deposition, dicker*, engagement, evidence, guarantee, handshake*, indenture, liability, mise, obligation, pact, paper, pledge, promise, proof, record, settlement, stipulation, treaty, understanding; SEE CONCEPTS *271,684*

contract [*v1*] *condense*
abate, abbreviate, abridge, become smaller, clench, compress, confine, constrict, consume, curtail, decline, decrease, deflate, draw in, dwindle, ebb, edit, epitomize, evaporate, fall away, fall off, grow less, lessen, lose, narrow, omit, purse, recede, reduce, shrink, shrivel, subside, syncopate, take in, tighten, wane, waste, weaken, wither, wrinkle; SEE CONCEPTS *169,236,247*

contract [*v2*] *come to terms*
accept offer, adjust, agree, arrange, assent, bargain, become indebted, bound, buy, circumscribe, clinch, close, come around, commit, consent, covenant, dicker*, engage, enter into, firm a deal*, give one's word, go along with*, hammer out deal*, initial*, ink*, it's a deal*, limit, make terms, negotiate, obligate, owe, pact, pledge, promise, put in writing, set, settle, shake hands on it*, sign for, sign papers, sign up, stipulate, swear to, undertake, work out details*; SEE CONCEPTS *8,50,88*

contract [*v3*] *catch disease*
acquire, afflict, be afflicted with, become infected with, be ill with, bring on, cause, come down with, decline, derange, develop, disorder, fall, fall victim to, get, go down with, incur, indispose, induce, obtain, sicken, sink, succumb to, take, take one's death, upset, weaken; SEE CONCEPTS 93,308

contraction [*n*] *drawing in; shortening*
abbreviating, abbreviation, abridging, abridgment, compression, condensation, condensing, confinement, confining, constriction, curtailing, curtailment, cutting down, decrease, decreasing, deflating, deflation, diminishing, diminution, drawing together, dwindling, elision, evaporating, evaporation, lessening, lopping, narrowing, omission, omitting, receding, recession, reducing, reduction, shrinkage, shrinking, shrivelling, tensing, tightening, withdrawal, withdrawing; SEE CONCEPTS 469,776

contradict [*v*] *be at variance with*
belie, buck, call in question*, challenge, confront, contravene, controvert, counter, counteract, cross, dare, deny, differ, disaffirm, disclaim, disprove, dispute, fly in the face of*, gainsay, have bone to pick*, impugn, negate, negative, oppose, refuse to accept, repudiate, take on, thumbs down*, traverse; SEE CONCEPTS 46,54,665

contradiction [*n*] *variance to something*
bucking, conflict, confutation, contravention, defiance, denial, difference, disagreement, discrepancy, dispute, dissension, gainsaying, incongruity, inconsistency, negation, opposite, opposition; SEE CONCEPTS 46,278,665

contradictory [*adj*] *antagonistic*
adverse, against, agin, anti, antipodal, antipodean, antithetic, antithetical, con, conflicting, contrary, converse, counter, counteractive, diametric, discrepant, incompatible, incongruous, inconsistent, irreconcilable, negating, no go*, nullifying, opposing, opposite, ornery*, paradoxical, polar, repugnant, reverse; SEE CONCEPT 542

contraption [*n*] *device*
apparatus, appliance, contrivance, doohickey*, gadget, gizmo*, machine, mechanism, rig, Rube Goldberg device*, thingamajig*, widget; SEE CONCEPTS 463,499

contrary [*adj*] *antagonistic; opposite*
adverse, anti, antipathetic, antipodal, antipodean, antithetical, balky, clashing, conflicting, contradictory, contrariant, contumacious, converse, counter, diametric, discordant, dissentient, dissident, froward, headstrong, hostile, inconsistent, inimical, insubordinate, intractable, negative, nonconforming, nonconformist, obstinate, opposed, ornery*, paradoxical, perverse, rebellious, recalcitrant, recusant, refractory, restive, reverse, stubborn, unruly, wayward, wrongheaded; SEE CONCEPT 401

contrast [*n*] *difference*
adverse, antithesis, comparison, contradiction, contradistinction, contraposition, contrariety, converse, differentiation, disagreement, disparity, dissimilarity, dissimilitude, distinction, divergence, diversity, foil, heterogeneity, incompatibility, incongruousness, inconsistency, inequality, inverse, oppositeness, opposition, reverse, unlikeness, variance, variation; SEE CONCEPTS 561,665

contrast [*v*] *compare, differ*
balance, be a foil to*, be contrary to, be dissimilar, be diverse, be unlike, be variable, bracket, collate, conflict, contradict, depart, deviate, differentiate, disagree, distinguish, diverge, hang, hold a candle to*, match up, mismatch, oppose, separate, set in opposition, set off, stack up against*, stand out, vary, weigh; SEE CONCEPTS 39,561,665

contravene [*v*] *go against, contradict*
abjure, breach, break, combat, conflict with, counteract, cross, defy, disaffirm, disobey, encroach, exclude, fight, gainsay, hinder, impugn, infract, infringe, interfere, interpose, intrude, negate, offend, oppose, overstep, refute, reject, repudiate, resist, spurn, thwart, transgress, traverse, trespass, violate; SEE CONCEPTS 46,106,121,192

contribute [*v1*] *donate, provide*
accord, add, afford, ante up, assign, bequeath, bequest, bestow, chip in, come through, commit, confer, devote, dispense, dole out*, dower, endow, enrich, furnish, give, give away, go Dutch*, grant, hand out, kick in*, pitch in*, pony up*, present, proffer, sacrifice, share, subscribe, subsidize, supply, sweeten the kitty*, tender, will; SEE CONCEPTS 108,140

contribute [*v2*] *be partly responsible for*
add to, advance, aid, assist, augment, be conducive, be instrumental, conduce, do one's bit*, finger in the pie*, fortify, get in the act*, have a hand in*, help, lead, put in two cents*, redound, reinforce, sit in on, strengthen, supplement, support, tend, uphold; SEE CONCEPTS 83,110,244

contribution [*n*] *gift, offering*
addition, a hand, alms, augmentation, benefaction, beneficence, bestowal, charity, donation, do one's part*, gifting, grant, handout, helping hand, improvement, increase, input, present, significant addition, subscription, supplement, write-off*; SEE CONCEPTS 337,340

contrite [*adj*] *regretful*
apologetic, attritional, chastened, compunctious, conscience-stricken, humble, penitent, penitential, remorseful, repentant, sorrowful, sorry; SEE CONCEPT 403

contrition [*n*] *regret*
attrition, compunction, contriteness, humiliation, penance, penitence, penitency, remorse, repentance, rue, ruth, self-reproach, sorrow; SEE CONCEPT 410

contrivance [*n1*] *plan, fabrication*
angle, artifice, brainchild, coinage, design, dodge, expedient, formation, gimmick, intrigue, invention, inventiveness, machination, measure, plot, project, ruse, scheme, slant, stratagem, switch, trick, twist; SEE CONCEPT 660

contrivance [*n2*] *gadget*
apparatus, appliance, brainchild, coinage, contraption, convenience, creation, device, discovery, engine, equipment, gear, gimcrack*, harness, implement, instrument, invention, machine, material, mechanism, tackle, thingamabob*, thingamajig*, tool, utensil, whatsis*, widget*; SEE CONCEPTS 260,463,499

contrive [*v1*] *invent, design*
come up with, concoct, construct, cook up, create, devise, dream up*, engineer, fabricate, fashion, forge, form, formulate, frame*, handle, hatch, improvise, make, make up*, manipulate,

CO
CO

manufacture, move, plan, plot, project, rig*, scheme, throw together*, trump up*, vamp, wangle, whip up*; SEE CONCEPTS *36,173*

contrive [*v2*] *bring about, succeed with difficulty*
achieve, angle, arrange, carry out, cogitate, collude, compass, concoct, connive, develop, devise, effect, elaborate, engineer, execute, finagle*, hatch, hit upon, intrigue, jockey*, machinate, manage, maneuver, manipulate, mastermind, negotiate, pass, plan, play games*, plot, project, scheme, shift, swing, work out, wrangle; SEE CONCEPTS *36,91,94*

contrived [*adj*] *overly planned*
affected, artificial, elaborate, fake, false, forced, labored, manipulated, overdone, phony, recherché, strained, unnatural, unspontaneous; SEE CONCEPTS *564,582*

control [*n*] *command, mastery*
ascendancy, authority, bridle, charge, check, clout, containment, curb, determination, direction, discipline, domination, dominion, driver's seat*, force, government, guidance, inside track, juice, jurisdiction, limitation, management, manipulation, might, oversight, predomination, qualification, regimentation, regulation, restraint, restriction, ropes, rule, strings*, subjection, subordination, superintendence, supervision, supremacy, sway, upper hand*, weight, wire pulling*; SEE CONCEPT *376*

control [*v1*] *have charge of*
administer, administrate, advise, be in saddle*, boss, bully, call, call the signals*, command, conduct, deal with, direct, discipline, dominate, domineer, govern, guide, handle, head, head up*, hold sway over*, hold the reins*, instruct, lead, manage, manipulate, overlook, oversee, pilot, predominate, push buttons*, quarterback*, regiment, regulate, reign over, rule, run*, run the show*, run things*, steer, subject, subjugate, superintend, supervise; SEE CONCEPT *117*

control [*v2*] *curb, hold back*
adjust, awe, bridle, check, collect, compose, constrain, contain, cool, corner, cow, limit, monopolize, quell, regulate, rein in, repress, restrain, simmer down*, smother, subdue; SEE CONCEPT *130*

controversial [*adj*] *at issue*
arguable, argumentative, contended, contentious, contestable, controvertible, debateable, disputable, disputatious, disputed, doubtable, doubtful, dubious, dubitable, in dispute, litigious, moot, open to discussion*, open to question*, polemical, questionable, suspect, uncertain, under discussion; SEE CONCEPTS *535,546*

controversy [*n*] *debate, dispute*
altercation, argument, beef*, bickering, brush, contention, difference, discussion, disputation, dissension, embroilment, falling-out*, flak, fuss, hurrah, miff, polemic, quarrel, row, rumpus, scene, scrap, squabble, strife, tiff*, words, wrangle, wrangling; SEE CONCEPTS *46,278,665*

controvert [*v*] *oppose, argue*
break, challenge, confound, confute, contest, contradict, counter, debate, deny, disconfirm, discuss, disprove, dispute, oppugn, question, rebut, refute, wrangle; SEE CONCEPTS *21,46*

contumacious [*adj*] *headstrong, obstinate*
alienated, contrary, disaffected, estranged, factious, froward, haughty, inflexible, insubordinate, insurgent, intractable, intransigent, irreconcilable, mutinous, obdurate, perverse, pig-headed, rebellious, recalcitrant, refractory, seditious, stubborn, unyielding; SEE CONCEPT *401*

contusion [*n*] *bruise, injury*
bang, bump, cut, discoloration, knock, mouse, swelling, wale, wound; SEE CONCEPT *309*

conundrum [*n*] *puzzle*
brain-teaser, closed book*, enigma, mystery, mystification, poser*, problem, puzzlement, riddle, why*; SEE CONCEPTS *532,666,690*

convalescent [*adj*] *improving, recuperating*
ambulatory, discharged, dismissed, gaining strength, getting better, getting over something*, getting well, healing, mending, on the mend*, past crisis, perked up*, rallying, recovering, rejuvenated, rejuvenating, released, restored, strengthening; SEE CONCEPT *314*

convene [*v*] *bring together; meet*
assemble, call, call in, collect, come together, congregate, convoke, corral, gather, get together, hold meeting, muster, open, rally, round up, scare up*, sit, summon, unite; SEE CONCEPTS *60,114,324*

convenience [*n1*] *availability, usefulness; useful thing*
accessibility, accessory, accommodation, advancement, advantage, agreeableness, aid, amenity, appliance, appropriateness, assistance, avail, benefit, comfort, comforts, contribution, cooperation, decency, ease, enjoyment, facility, fitness, furtherance, handiness, help, life, luxury, means, ministration, ministry, openness, opportuneness, promotion, receptiveness, relief, satisfaction, service, serviceability, succor, suitability, suitableness, support, time saver, use, utility; SEE CONCEPTS *658,712*

convenience [*n2*] *spare time*
chance, freedom, hour, leisure, liberty, occasion, one's own sweet time*, opportunity, place, preference, spare moment*, suitable time, whenever; SEE CONCEPT *807*

convenient [*adj1*] *appropriate, useful*
acceptable, accommodating, adaptable, adapted, advantageous, agreeable, aiding, assisting, available, beneficial, comfortable, commodious, conducive, contributive, decent, favorable, fit, fitted, good, handy, helpful, in public interest, opportune, proper, ready, roomy, seasonable, serviceable, suitable, suited, timely, time-saving, user-friendly*, well-planned; SEE CONCEPT *560*

convenient [*adj2*] *nearby*
accessible, adjacent, adjoining, all around, at elbows*, at fingertips*, at hand, available, central, close, close at hand, close-by, contiguous, easy to reach, handy, immediate, in neighborhood, next, next door, nigh, on deck*, on tap*, under one's nose*, within reach; SEE CONCEPT *586*

convent [*n*] *nunnery*
abbey, cloister, monastery, religious community, retreat, school; SEE CONCEPTS *368,516*

convention [*n1*] *conference*
assemblage, assembly, clambake, confab*, congress, convocation, council, delegates, delegation, get together, meet*, meeting, members, powwow*, rally, representatives, show; SEE CONCEPTS *114,324,417*

convention [*n2*] *practice, tradition*
canon, code, covenance, custom, etiquette, fashion, form, formality, habit, law, percept, precept,

propriety, rule, understanding, usage; SEE CON-
CEPT *688*

convention [*n3*] *agreement*
bargain, bond, compact, concord, concordat,
contract, covenant, pact, protocol, stipulation,
transaction, treaty; SEE CONCEPTS *271,684*

conventional [*adj1*] *common, normal*
accepted, accustomed, button-down, commonplace, correct, current, customary, decorous,
everyday, expected, fashionable, formal, general,
habitual, in established usage, ordinary, orthodox, plain, popular, predominant, prevailing,
prevalent, proper, regular, ritual, routine, square,
standard, stereotyped, straight, traditional,
tralatitious, typical, usual, well-known, wonted;
SEE CONCEPTS *530,547*

conventional [*adj2*] *unoriginal*
bigoted, bourgeois, commonplace, conforming,
conservative, demure, doctrinal, dogmatic,
drippy, hackneyed, hidebound, humdrum, illiberal, inflexible, in rut, insular, isolationist, lame,
literal, moderate, moral, narrow, narrow-minded,
not heretical, obstinate, parochial, pedestrian,
prosaic, puritanical, rigid, routine, rube*, run-of-
the-mill, sober, solemn, square, stereotyped,
straight, straight-laced, strict, stuffy, uptight; SEE
CONCEPT *550*

converge [*v*] *gather*
assemble, coincide, combine, come together,
concenter, concentrate, concur, encounter, enter
in, focalize, focus, join, meet, merge, mingle,
rally, unite; SEE CONCEPTS *113,114*

conversant [*adj*] *experienced, familiar with*
abreast, acquainted, alive, apprehensive, au
courant, au fait, aware, cognizant, comprehending, conscious, cool*, down with*, hep*, hip*,
informed, into, kept posted, knowing, knowledgeable, learned, on the beam*, perceptive, percipient, plugged in*, practiced, proficient,
sensible, sentient, skilled, up*, up-to-date, versant, versed, well-informed, witting; SEE CON-
CEPT *402*

conversation [*n*] *dialogue, discourse*
chat, colloquy, comment, communication, communion, confab*, confabulation, conference,
consultation, converse, debate, discussion, exchange, expression, gab*, gossip, hearing, intercourse, jive*, observation, palaver, parley,
pillow talk*, powwow*, questioning, remark,
repartee, speech, talk, talkfest*, tête-à-tête*, ventilation*, visit, yak*; SEE CONCEPT *266*

converse [*adj*] *opposite*
antipodal, antipodean, antithetical, contradictory,
contrary, counter, counterpole, different, reverse,
reversed, transposed; SEE CONCEPT *564*

converse [*n*] *opposite*
antipode, antipole, antithesis, contra, contrary,
counter, counterpole, inverse, obverse, other
side, reverse; SEE CONCEPT *665*

converse [*v*] *talk*
chat, chew the fat*, chitchat*, commune, confer,
discourse, exchange, gab*, parley, rap*,
schmooze*, speak, use, yak*; SEE CONCEPT *266*

conversion [*n*] *change, adaptation*
about-face*, alteration, born again*, change of
heart*, changeover, exchange, flip-flop*, flux,
growth, innovation, metamorphosis, metanoia,
metasis, modification, novelty, passage, passing,
permutation, progress, proselytization, qualification, reclamation, reconstruction, reformation,

regeneration, remodelling, reorganization, resolution, resolving, reversal, see the light*, switch,
transfiguration, transformation, translation, transmogrification, transmutation, turning, turning
around; SEE CONCEPTS *232,701*

convert [*n*] *new believer*
catechumen, disciple, follower, neophyte,
novice, novitiate, proselyte; SEE CONCEPT *361*

convert [*v1*] *change; adapt*
alter, apply, appropriate, commute, downlink,
download, interchange, make, metamorphose,
modify, remodel, reorganize, restyle, revise,
switch, switch over, transfigure, transform, translate, transmogrify, transmute, transpose, turn;
SEE CONCEPTS *232,701*

convert [*v2*] *change belief, especially regarding
religion*
actuate, alter conviction, assimilate to, baptize,
be born again*, bend, bias, brainwash, bring,
bring around, budge, cause to adopt, change into,
change of heart*, convince, create anew, impel,
incline, lead, lead to believe, make over, move,
persuade, proselyte, proselytize, redeem, reform,
regenerate, save, see the light*, sway, turn; SEE
CONCEPTS *12,14,35*

convex [*adj*] *rounded, curving outward*
arched, bent, biconvex, bulged, bulging, bulgy,
gibbous, outcurved, protuberant, raised; SEE
CONCEPT *486*

convey [*v1*] *transport*
back, bear, bring, carry, channel, conduct, dispatch, ferry, fetch, forward, funnel, grant, guide,
hump, lead, lug, move, pack, pipe, ride,
schlepp*, send, shoulder, siphon, support, tote,
traject, transfer, transmit, truck; SEE CONCEPTS
187,217

convey [*v2*] *express message*
break, carry, communicate, conduct, disclose,
impart, make known, pass on, project, put across,
relate, reveal, send, tell, transmit; SEE CONCEPT
60

conveyance [*n*] *transport*
car, carriage, carrying, communication, machine,
movement, transfer, transference, transmission,
transportation, vehicle; SEE CONCEPTS
143,501,503

convict [*n*] *criminal*
captive, con, culprit, felon, jailbird*, long-ter-
mer*, loser*, malefactor, prisoner, repeater*; SEE
CONCEPT *412*

convict [*v*] *find guilty*
adjudge, attaint, bring to justice, condemn, declare guilty, doom, frame, imprison, pass sentence on, pronounce guilty, put away, put the
screws to*, rap*, send up*, send up the river*,
sentence, throw the book at*; SEE CONCEPTS
18,317

conviction [*n1*] *belief, opinion*
confidence, creed, doctrine, dogma, eye, faith,
feeling, judgment call, mind, persuasion, principle, reliance, say so*, sentiment, slant, tenet,
view; SEE CONCEPT *689*

conviction [*n2*] *guilty sentence; assurance*
assuredness, certainty, certitude, condemnation,
condemning, confidence, determining guilt,
earnestness, fall, fervor, firmness, rap, reliance,
sureness, surety, unfavorable verdict; SEE CON-
CEPTS *317,410*

convince [*v*] *gain the confidence of*
argue into, assure, brainwash, bring around,

CO
CO

bring home to*, bring to reason*, change, demonstrate, draw, effect, establish, get, hook*, induce, make a believer*, overcome, persuade, prevail upon, prompt, prove, put across, refute, satisfy, sell all*, sell one on*, sway, talk into, turn, twist one's arm*, win over; SEE CONCEPT 68

convincing [adj] *persuasive*
acceptable, authentic, believeable, cogent, conclusive, credible, dependable, faithful, hopeful, impressive, incontrovertible, likely, moving, plausible, possible, powerful, presumable, probable, rational, reasonable, reliable, satisfactory, satisfying, solid, sound, swaying, telling, trustworthy, trusty, valid; SEE CONCEPTS *267,537,552*

convivial [adj] *fun-loving*
back-slapping*, cheerful, clubby*, companionable, conversible, entertaining, festal, festive, friendly, gay, genial, glad-handering*, happy, hearty, hilarious, holiday, jocund, jolly, jovial, lively, merry, mirthful, pleasant, sociable, vivacious; SEE CONCEPTS *401,404*

convocation [n] *assembly*
assemblage, conclave, concourse, confab*, conference, congregation, congress, convention, council, diet, get-together, meet, meeting, pow-wow*, synod, turnout; SEE CONCEPT *114*

convolution [n] *loop, spiral*
coil, coiling, complexity, contortion, curlicue, flexing, gyration, helix, intricacy, involution, serpentine, sinuosity, sinuousness, snaking, swirl, tortuousness, twist, undulation, winding; SEE CONCEPT *436*

convoy [n] *guard, escort*
attendance, attendant, companion, protection; SEE CONCEPT *423*

convoy [v] *protect, escort*
accompany, attend, bear, bring, chaperon, companion, company, conduct, consort, defend, guard, pilot, safeguard, shepherd, shield, usher, watch; SEE CONCEPTS *96,110*

convulsion [n1] *muscle spasm*
algospasm, attack, contortion, contraction, cramp, epilepsy, fit, paroxysm, seizure, throe, tremor; SEE CONCEPT *308*

convulsion [n2] *disturbance*
agitation, cataclysm, clamor, commotion, disaster, ferment, furor, outcry, quaking, rocking, seism, shaking, shock, tottering, trembling, tumult, turbulence, upheaval, upturn; SEE CONCEPTS *152,748*

cook [n] *person who prepares food*
baker, chef, hash slinger*, mess sergeant, servant, sous chef; SEE CONCEPT *348*

cook [v] *prepare food, usually using heat*
bake, barbecue, blanch, boil, braise, brew, broil, brown, burn, coddle, curry, decoct, deep fry, devil, doctor*, escallop, fix, French fry, fricassee, fry, griddle, grill, heat, imbue, melt, microwave, mull, nuke*, panfry, parboil, parch, percolate, poach, pressure-cook, reduce, roast, ruin*, sauté, scald, scorch, sear, seethe, simmer, sizzle, spoil*, steam, steep, stew, toast, warm up; SEE CONCEPT *170*

cook up [v] *devise*
arrange, concoct, contrive, dream up, fabricate, falsify, formulate, frame, hatch, improvise, invent, make up, plan, plot, prepare, scheme, vamp; SEE CONCEPTS *17,36*

cool [adj1] *cold, nippy*
air-conditioned, algid, arctic, biting, chill, chilled, chilling, chilly, coldish, frigid, frore, frosty, gelid, hawkish, nipping, refreshing, refrigerated, shivery, snappy, wintry; SEE CONCEPT *605*

cool [adj2] *calm, collected*
assured, composed, coolheaded, deliberate, detached, dispassionate, impassive, imperturbable, levelheaded, nonchalant, philosophical, phlegmatic, placid, quiet, relaxed, self-controlled, self-possessed, serene, stolid, together, tranquil, unagitated, unemotional, unexcited, unflappable, unruffled; SEE CONCEPT *401*

cool [adj3] *aloof, disapproving*
annoyed, apathetic, distant, frigid, impertinent, impudent, incurious, indifferent, insolent, lukewarm, offended, offhand, offish, procacious, reserved, solitary, standoffish, unapproachable, uncommunicative, unenthusiastic, unfriendly, uninterested, unresponsive, unsociable, unwelcoming, withdrawn; SEE CONCEPT *404*

cool [adj4] *excellent*
boss*, dandy, divine, glorious, hunky-dory*, keen, marvelous, neat, nifty, sensational, swell; SEE CONCEPT *572*

cool [v1] *chill*
abate, air-condition, air-cool, ally, calm, freeze, frost, infrigidate, lessen, lose heat, mitigate, moderate, reduce, refrigerate, temper; SEE CONCEPT *255*

cool [v2] *take a break; abate*
allay, assuage, calm, calm down, chill, compose, control, dampen, lessen, mitigate, moderate, quiet, reduce, rein, repress, restrain, simmer down, suppress, temper; SEE CONCEPTS *240,384*

cooperate [v] *aid, assist*
abet, advance, agree, back up, band, befriend, be in cahoots*, chip in, coadjute, coincide, collaborate, combine, comply with, concert, concur, conduce, conspire, contribute, coordinate, espouse, forward, further, go along with, help, join forces, join in, league*, lend a hand*, participate, partner, pitch in*, play ball*, pool resources, pull together, second, share in, show willingness, side with, stick together, succor, take part, unite, uphold, work side by side, work together; SEE CONCEPTS *110,112*

cooperation [n] *mutual effort*
aid, alliance, assistance, cahoots*, coaction, coadjuvancy, coalition, collaboration, combination, combined effort, communion, company, concert, concurrence, confederacy, confederation, confunction, conspiracy, doing business with, esprit de corps, federation, fusion, give-and-take, harmony, help, helpfulness, logrolling*, participation, partisanship, partnership, playing ball*, reciprocity, responsiveness, service, society, symbiosis, synergism, synergy, teaming, teamwork, unanimity, union, unity; SEE CONCEPTS *110,112,388,677*

cooperative [adj1] *joint, unified*
agreeing, coacting, coactive, coadjuvant, coefficient, collaborating, collaborative, collective, collegial, collusive, combined, combining, common, concerted, concurring, coordinated, hand in glove*, harmonious, in league, interdependent, joining, participating, reciprocal, shared, symbiotic, synergetic, synergic, team, united, uniting; SEE CONCEPT *538*

cooperative [adj2] *helpful*
accommodating, companionable, obliging, re-

sponsive, sociable, supportive, useful; SEE CON-CEPTS *538,555*

co-opt [*v*] *to assimilate in order to take over or appropriate*
absorb, accept, admit, adopt, bring in, bring into line, bring into the fold, connaturalize, convert, draw in, elect, embrace, encompass, enfold, homogenize, homologize, include, incorporate, make one's own, take in, take over; SEE CONCEPTS *232,701*

coordinate [*adj*] *equivalent*
alike, coequal, correlative, correspondent, counterpart, equal, equalized, like, parallel, same, tantamount; SEE CONCEPT *566*

coordinate [*v*] *match, relate*
accommodate, adjust, agree, atune, combine, conduce, conform, correlate, get it together*, get one's act together*, harmonize, integrate, mesh, organize, pool, proportion, pull together, quarterback*, reconcile, reconciliate, regulate, shape up, synchronize, systematize, team up; SEE CONCEPTS *36,84,158*

cop [*n*] *policeperson*
deputy, flatfoot*, fuzz*, lawman, officer of the law, patrolman, patrolwoman, peace officer, policeman, police officer, policewoman, sheriff, the man*; SEE CONCEPTS *299,354*

cope [*v*] *manage, contend*
battle with, buffet, carry on, confront, deal, dispatch, encounter, endure, face, get a handle on*, get by, grapple, hack*, hack it*, handle, hold one's own*, live with, make go of it*, make it*, make out*, make the grade*, pit oneself against*, rise to occasion, struggle, struggle through, suffer, survive, tangle, tussle, weather, wrestle; SEE CONCEPTS *23,35*

copious [*adj*] *abundant*
alive with, a mess of*, ample, aplenty, bounteous, bountiful, coming out of ears*, crawling with*, extensive, exuberant, full, galore, generous, heavy, lavish, liberal, lush, luxuriant, no end*, overflowing, plenteous, plentiful, plenty, profuse, prolix, replete, rich, superabundant, thick with, verbose, wordy; SEE CONCEPT *771*

copiousness [*n*] *abundance*
affluence, amplitude, bountifulness, bounty, cornucopia, exuberance, fullness, horn of plenty*, lavishness, luxuriance, plentifulness, plenty, richness, superabundance; SEE CONCEPT *767*

cop out [*v*] *abandon, quit*
back down, back off, back out, backpedal, desert, dodge, excuse, give the slip*, have alibi, rationalize, renege, renounce, revoke, skip, use pretext, welsh, withdraw; SEE CONCEPTS *121,156*

copulate [*v*] *have sexual relations*
be carnal, bed, breed, cohabit, conjugate, couple, do it*, fool around*, fornicate, go all the way*, go to bed*, have coition, have relations, have sex, lay*, lie with, make it*, make love, make out*, mate, sleep together, sleep with, unite; SEE CONCEPT *375*

copy [*n*] *duplicate, imitation*
archetype, carbon, carbon copy*, cast, clone, counterfeit, counterpart, ditto*, ectype, effigy, ersatz, facsimile, forgery, hard copy, image, impersonation, impression, imprint, likeness, microfiche, mimeograph, miniature, mirror, model, offprint, parallel, pattern, photocopy, photograph, photostat, portrait, print, reflection, replica, replication, representation, reprint, re-

production, rubbings, similarity, simulacrum, simulation, study, tracing, transcript, transcription, type, Xerox*; SEE CONCEPTS *269,667,716*

copy [*vl*] *duplicate*
carbon, cartoon, clone, counterfeit, delineate, depict, ditto, draw, dupe, engrave, engross, fake, forge, imitate, knock off*, limn, manifold, mimeo, mirror, mold, paint, paraphrase, photocopy, photostat, picture, plagiarize, portray, reduplicate, reflect, repeat, replicate, represent, reproduce, rewrite, sculpture, simulate, sketch, stat, trace, transcribe, Xerox*; SEE CONCEPT *171*

copy [*v2*] *imitate*
act like, ape, burlesque, do, do a take-off*, do like*, echo, embody, emulate, epitomize, fake, follow, follow example, follow suit, go like*, illustrate, incarnate, knock off*, make like*, mimic, mirror, mock, model, parody, parrot, personify, phony, pirate, play a role, prefigure, repeat, sham, simulate, steal, take leaf out of book*, take off*, travesty, typify; SEE CONCEPTS *59,139,242*

coquet [*v*] *tease*
dally, flirt, fool, gold-dig*, lead on, make eyes at*, operate, philander, string along, titillate, toy, trifle, vamp, wanton, wink at*; SEE CONCEPTS *375,384*

cord [*n*] *rope*
bond, connection, cordage, fiber, line, link, string, tendon, tie, twine; SEE CONCEPTS *470,680*

cordial [*adj*] *friendly, sociable*
affable, affectionate, agreeable, amicable, buddy-buddy*, cheerful, clubby, companionable, congenial, convivial, cozy, earnest, genial, glowing, gracious, happy, heartfelt, heart-to-heart, hearty, invigorating, jovial, mellow, neighborly, palsy-walsy*, polite, red-carpet*, responsive, sincere, social, sympathetic, tender, warm, warmhearted, welcoming, wholehearted; SEE CONCEPT *401*

cordiality [*n*] *friendliness, sociability*
affability, agreeability, agreeableness, amenity, amiability, approbation, approval, earnestness, enjoyableness, favor, geniality, gratefulness, heartiness, mutuality, pleasantness, reciprocity, responsiveness, sincerity, sweetness and light*, sympathy, understanding, warmth, wholeheartedness; SEE CONCEPT *633*

core [*n*] *center, gist*
amount, base, basis, body, bottom line, bulk, burden, consequence, corpus, crux, essence, focus, foundation, heart, import, importance, kernel, main idea, mass, meat*, meat and potatoes*, middle, midpoint, midst, nitty gritty*, nub, nucleus, origin, pith, pivot, purport, quick, root, significance, staple, substance, thrust, upshot; SEE CONCEPTS *442,668,826*

corner [*n1*] *angle*
bend, branch, cloverleaf, crook, crossing, edge, fork, intersection, joint, junction, projection, ridge, rim, shift, V*, veer, Y*; SEE CONCEPTS *436,484,513*

corner [*n2*] *niche*
angle, cavity, compartment, cranny, hideaway, hide-out, hole, indentation, nook, recess, retreat; SEE CONCEPTS *440,471,513*

corner [*n3*] *predicament*
box, difficulty, dilemma, distress, fix, hole, impasse, impediment, jam, knot, pickle, plight, scrape, tight spot; SEE CONCEPTS *674,675*

CO
CO

corner [v] *trap*
bottle, bring to bay, capture, catch, collar*, fool, get on ropes*, have up a tree*, mousetrap*, nab, put out, seize, tree, trick, trouble; SEE CONCEPTS *59,90*

cornerstone [n] *vital element*
anchor, base, essential, foundation, key element, keystone, linchpin, main ingredient, mainspring, mainstay, pillar; SEE CONCEPTS *442,826*

corny [adj] *trite, clichéd*
banal, commonplace, dull, feeble, hackneyed, mawkish, melodramatic, old-fashioned, old hat*, sentimental, shopworn, stale, stereotyped, stupid, tired, warmed-over; SEE CONCEPT *550*

corollary [n] *conclusion, deduction*
aftereffect, analogy, consequence, culmination, effect, end, end product, induction, inference, issue, precipitate, result, sequel, sequence, up-shot; SEE CONCEPTS *230,410,529*

corporal [adj] *bodily, physical*
anatomical, carnal, corporeal, fleshly, fleshy, gross, human, material, objective, phenomenal, sensible, somatic, substantial, tangible; SEE CON-CEPT *542*

corporate [adj] *allied*
amalgamated, associated, collaborative, collective, combined, common, communal, concerted, incorporated, joint, pooled, shared, united; SEE CONCEPTS *563,577*

corporation [n] *business organization, usually large*
association, bunch, business, clan, company, corporate body, crew, crowd, enterprise, gang, hookup*, jungle*, legal entity, megacorp*, mob, multinational, octupus*, outfit, partnership, ring, shell, society, syndicate, zoo*; SEE CONCEPT *325*

corporeal [adj] *bodily, physical*
anatomical, carnal, corporal, fleshly, fleshy, human, material, mortal, objective, phenomenal, sensible, somatic, substantial, tangible; SEE CON-CEPT *542*

corps [n] *group trained for action*
band, body, brigade, company, contingent, crew, detachment, division, outfit, party, posse, regiment, squad, squadron, team, troop, troupe, unit; SEE CONCEPTS *294,322,417*

corpse [n] *dead body*
body, bones*, cadaver, carcass, carrion, deceased, departed, mort*, remains, stiff*; SEE CONCEPTS *390,417*

corpulent [adj] *fat, chubby*
baby elephant*, beefy*, blimp*, bulky, burly, embonpoint, fat, fleshy, gross, having a bay window*, having a spare tire*, heavy, hefty, husky, large, lusty, obese, overblown, overweight, plump, portly, roly-poly*, rotund, stout, tubby, weighty, well-padded*; SEE CONCEPTS *406,491,773*

corpus [n] *body of text*
bulk, collection, compilation, complete works, core, entirety, extant works, mass, oeuvre, opera omnia, staple, substance, whole; SEE CONCEPT *271*

correct [adj 1] *accurate, exact*
according to Hoyle*, actual, amen*, appropriate, cooking with gas*, dead on*, equitable, factual, faithful, faultless, flawless, for sure, free of error, impeccable, just, legitimate, nice, okay, on target*, on the ball*, on the beam*, on the button*, on the money*, on the nose*, on track*, perfect,

precise, proper, regular, right, right as rain*, righteous, right on*, right stuff*, rigorous, stone, strict, true, undistorted, unmistaken, veracious, veridical; SEE CONCEPTS *542,557,574*

correct [adj 2] *proper, appropriate*
acceptable, becoming, careful, comme il faut, conforming, conventional, decent, decorous, diplomatic, done, fitting, meticulous, nice, okay, punctilious, right, right stuff*, scrupulous, seemly, standard, suitable; SEE CONCEPTS *401,558*

correct [v 1] *fix, adjust*
alter, ameliorate, amend, better, change, clean up, clean up act*, cure, debug*, doctor*, do over, edit, emend, fiddle with, fix up, get with it*, go over, help, improve, launder, make over, make right, make up for, mend, pay dues*, pick up, polish, put in order, reclaim, reconstruct, rectify, redress, reform, regulate, remedy, remodel, reorganize, repair, retouch, review, revise, right, scrub*, set right, set straight, shape up, straighten out, touch up, turn around, upgrade; SEE CON-CEPT *126*

correct [v 2] *discipline, chastise*
administer, admonish, castigate, chasten, chide, penalize, punish, reprimand, reprove; SEE CON-CEPTS *52,122*

correction [n 1] *adjustment; fixing*
alteration, amelioration, amending, amendment, changing, editing, emendation, improvement, in-demnification, mending, modification, rectification, redress, reexamination, remodeling, repair, reparation, rereading, revisal, revising, righting; SEE CONCEPTS *126,700*

correction [n 2] *discipline*
admonition, castigation, chastisement, punishment, punition, reformation, reproof, rod; SEE CONCEPT *122*

corrective [adj] *healing, curing*
antidotal, counteracting, curative, disciplinary, palliative, penal, punitive, reformatory, rehabilitative, remedial, restorative, therapeutic; SEE CONCEPT *537*

correctly [adv] *right*
accurately, befittingly, decently, decorously, fitly, fittingly, justly, nicely, perfectly, precisely, properly, rightly, to a T*, well; SEE CONCEPT *558*

correctness [n 1] *accuracy*
definiteness, definitiveness, definitude, exactitude, exactness, faultlessness, fidelity, preciseness, precision, regularity, truth; SEE CONCEPTS *638,654*

correctness [n 2] *propriety*
bon ton, civility, correctitude, decency, decorousness, decorum, fitness, good breeding, order, orderliness, properness, rightness, seemliness; SEE CONCEPTS *633,656*

correlate [v] *equate, compare*
associate, be on same wavelength*, connect, co-ordinate, correspond, have good vibes*, interact, parallel, relate mutually, tie in*, tune in on*; SEE CONCEPT *39*

correlation [n] *equating, equivalence*
alternation, analogue, complement, correspondence, correspondent, counterpart, interaction, interchange, interconnection, interdependence, interrelation, interrelationship, match, parallel, pendant, reciprocity, relationship; SEE CONCEPTS *388,667*

correspond [*v1*] *agree, complement*
accord, amount, approach, assimilate, be consistent, be identical to, be similar to, coincide, compare, conform, correlate, dovetail, equal, fit, harmonize, lip sync, match, partake of, reciprocate, resemble, rival, square, tally, touch; SEE CONCEPT *664*

correspond [*v2*] *communicate in writing*
answer, drop a kite*, drop a line*, drop a note*, epistolize, exchange letters, have pen pal, hear from, keep in touch, pen, put pen to paper*, reply, scribble, send letter, send word, write; SEE CONCEPTS *79,266*

correspondence [*n1*] *agreement*
accord, analogy, coherence, coincidence, comparability, comparison, concurrence, conformity, congruity, consistency, correlation, equivalence, fitness, harmony, likeness, match, regularity, relation, resemblance, similarity, symmetry; SEE CONCEPT *664*

correspondence [*n2*] *communication by writing*
exchange of letters, letters, mail, messages, post, reports, writing; SEE CONCEPTS *79,277,278*

correspondent [*n*] *person communicating in writing*
contributor, epistler, epistolarian, freelancer, gazetteer, journalist, letter writer, pen pal, reporter, stringer*, writer; SEE CONCEPTS *348,423*

corresponding [*adj*] *equivalent, matching*
agnate, akin, alike, analogous, answering, comparable, complementary, consonant, correlative, correspondent, coterminous, identical, interrelated, kin, kindred, like, parallel, reciprocal, similar, synonymous, undifferentiated; SEE CONCEPT *566*

corridor [*n*] *hallway*
aisle, couloir, entrance hall, entranceway, foyer, hall, ingress, lobby, passage, passageway; SEE CONCEPT *440*

corroborate [*v*] *back up information, story*
approve, authenticate, bear out, certify, check on, check out, check up, confirm, declare true, document, double check, endorse, establish, give nod*, justify, okay, prove, ratify, rubber-stamp*, strengthen, substantiate, support, sustain, validate, verify; SEE CONCEPTS *49,57*

corrode [*v*] *wear away; eat away*
bite, canker, consume, corrupt, destroy, deteriorate, erode, gnaw, impair; oxidize, rot, rust, scour, waste; SEE CONCEPTS *156,169,186,250*

corrosion [*n*] *disintegration*
decay, decomposition, degeneration, deterioration, erosion, oxidation, rust, wear; SEE CONCEPTS *309,720*

corrosive [*adj*] *consuming, wearing; bitter*
acerb, acerbic, acrid, biting, caustic, corroding, cutting, destructive, erosive, incisive, sarcastic, strongly acid, trenchant, venomous, virulent, wasting; SEE CONCEPT *537*

corrugated [*adj*] *ridged, grooved*
channelled, creased, crinkled, crumpled, flexed, fluted, folded, furrowed, puckered, roughened, rumpled, wrinkled; SEE CONCEPTS *485,606*

corrupt [*adj1*] *dishonest*
base, bent, bribable, crooked, debauched, double-dealing, exploiting, extortionate, faithless, fast and loose*, fixed, foul, fraudulent, gone to the dogs*, inconstant, iniquitous, knavish, mercenary, nefarious, on the take*, open, padded*,

perfidious, praetorian, profiteering, racket up*, reprobate, rotten, shady, snide, suborned, tainted, treacherous, two-faced, underhanded, unethical, unfaithful, unprincipled, unscrupulous, untrustworthy, venal, wide open*; SEE CONCEPT *545*

corrupt [*adj2*] *debased, vicious*
abandoned, abased, baneful, boorish, degenerate, degraded, deleterious, depraved, dishonored, dissolute, evil, flagitious, infamous, loose, low, miscreant, monstrous, nefarious, perverse, profligate, rotten, villainous; SEE CONCEPTS *401,545*

corrupt [*adj3*] *adulterated, rotten*
altered, contaminated, decayed, defiled, distorted, doctored, falsified, foul, infected, noxious, polluted, putrescent, putrid, tainted; SEE CONCEPTS *485,613*

corrupt [*v*] *pervert; pollute*
abase, abuse, adulterate, animalize, bastardize, blemish, blight, bribe, contaminate, damage, debase, debauch, decay, decompose, deface, defile, deform, degrade, demean, demoralize, deprave, depreciate, despoil, disfigure, disgrace, dishonor, fix, grease palm*, harm, hurt, ill-treat, impair, infect, injure, lower, lure, maltreat, mar, mistreat, misuse, outrage, pull down, putrefy, ravage, reduce, rot, ruin, spoil, square, stain, suborn, subvert, taint, undermine, violate, vitiate, warp, waste; SEE CONCEPTS *14,240*

corruption [*n1*] *dishonesty*
breach of trust, bribery, bribing, crime, crookedness, demoralization, exploitation, extortion, fiddling, fraud, fraudulency, graft, jobbery, malfeasance, misrepresentation, nepotism, on the take*, payoff, payola*, profiteering, racket*, shadiness*, shady deal*, shuffle, skimming, squeeze*, unscrupulousness, venality; SEE CONCEPT *645*

corruption [*n2*] *baseness*
atrocity, decadence, degeneration, degradation, depravity, evil, immorality, impurity, infamy, iniquity, looseness, lubricity, perversion, profligacy, sinfulness, turpitude, vice, viciousness, vulgarity; wickedness; SEE CONCEPTS *633,645*

corruption [*n3*] *adulteration*
debasement, decay, defilement, distortion, doctoring, falsification, foulness, infection, noxiousness, pollution, putrefaction, putrescence, rot, rottenness; SEE CONCEPT *723*

cosmetic [*adj*] *beautifying; relating to appearance*
corrective, gooky*, improving, makeup, nonessential, painted, remedial, restorative, superficial, surface, touching-up; SEE CONCEPT *579*

cosmic [*adj*] *limitless; universal*
catholic, cosmogonal, cosmogonic, cosmopolitan, ecumenical, empyrean, global, grandiose, huge, immense, infinite, measureless, planetary, vast, worldwide; SEE CONCEPT *772*

cosmopolitan [*adj*] *worldly-wise*
catholic, cultivated, cultured, ecumenical, global, gregarious, metropolitan, planetary, polished, public, smooth, sophisticated, universal, urbane, well-travelled, worldly, worldwide; SEE CONCEPT *589*

cosmos [*n1*] *universe*
creation, galaxy, macrocosm, macrocosmos, megacosm, nature, solar system, star system, world; SEE CONCEPTS *511,770*

CO
CO

cosmos [n2] *ordered system*
harmony, order, organization, scheme, structure;
SEE CONCEPTS 727,770

cost [n1] *expense; price paid*
amount, arm and a leg*, bad news*, bite*, bottom dollar*, bottom line*, charge, damage*, disbursement, dues, expenditure, figure, line, nick*, nut*, outlay, payment, price, price tag, rate, score*, setback*, squeeze*, tab, tariff, ticket, toll, top dollar*, value, worth; SEE CONCEPTS 328,336

cost [n2] *penalty, sacrifice*
damage, deprivation, detriment, expense, forfeit, forfeiture, harm, hurt, injury, loss, suffering; SEE CONCEPTS 676,679

cost [v1] *command a price of*
amount to, be asked, be demanded, be given, be marked at, be needed, be paid, be priced at, be received, be valued at, be worth, bring in, come to, mount up, move back, nick*, rap*, require, sell at, sell for, set back, take, to the tune of*, yield; SEE CONCEPTS 328,336

cost [v2] *harm; exact a penalty*
do disservice to, expect, hurt, infuriate, lose, necessitate, obligate, require; SEE CONCEPT 246

cost-effective [adj] *economical*
practical, profitable, worthwhile; SEE CONCEPT 542

costly [adj1] *expensive*
an arm and leg*, cher*, dear, excessive, executive, exorbitant, extortionate, extravagant, fancy, high, highly priced, high-priced, inordinate, precious, premium, pricey, steep, stiff*, top, valuable; SEE CONCEPT 334

costly [adj2] *priceless*
gorgeous, inestimable, invaluable, lavish, luxurious, opulent, precious, rich, splendid, sumptuous, valuable; SEE CONCEPT 567

costly [adj3] *harmful, damaging*
catastrophic, deleterious, disastrous, loss-making, ruinous, sacrificial; SEE CONCEPT 537

costume [n] *set of clothes*
apparel, attire, clothing, dress, duds*, ensemble, fashion, garb, getup*, guise, livery, mode, outfit, rig*, robes*, style, suit, uniform, wardrobe; SEE CONCEPT 451

cot [n] *temporary bed*
army bed, berth, bunk, camp bed, folding bed, gurney, small bed, trundle; SEE CONCEPT 443

cottage [n] *tiny house; lodging*
box, bungalow, cabana, cabin, caboose, camp, carriage house, chalet, cot, home, hut, lean-to, lodge, ranch, shack, shanty, small house; SEE CONCEPT 516

couch [n] *sofa; long, upholstered furniture*
bed, chair, chaise longue, chesterfield, davenport, daybed, divan, lounge, love seat, ottoman, resting place, settee; SEE CONCEPT 443

couch [v] *express in particular way*
formulate, frame, phrase, put, set forth, utter, word; SEE CONCEPT 51

couch potato [n] *inactive person*
bystander, goof-off*, idler, laggard, lazy person, loafer, lotuseater*, lounger, observer, slouch, sluggard, spectator, televiewer*, TV viewer, viewer; SEE CONCEPT 423

cough [n] *expelled air with sound*
ahem, bark, cold, croup, frog in throat*, hack, hem, tickle in throat*, whoop; SEE CONCEPTS 65,316

cough [v] *expelling air with sound*
bark, choke, clear throat, convulse, expectorate, hack, hawk, hem, spit up, vomit, whoop; SEE CONCEPTS 65,308

council [n] *people assembled for purpose*
assembly, board, body, brain trust*, cabinet, chamber, clan, committee, conclave, confab*, conference, congregation, congress, convention, convocation, diet, directorate, gang, gathering, governing body, groupthink*, huddle*, kitchen cabinet*, meet, ministry, mob, official family, outfit, panel, parliament, powwow*, ring, senate, synod; SEE CONCEPTS 299,325,381

counsel [n1] *guidance*
admonition, advice, advisement, caution, consideration, consultation, deliberation, direction, forethought, information, instruction, kibitz*, recommendation, steer, suggestion, tip, tip-off*, two cents' worth*, warning, word to the wise*; SEE CONCEPTS 75,274

counsel [n2] *legal representative*
adviser, advocate, attorney, barrister, bomber*, counselor, legal adviser, legal beagle*, legal eagle*, lip*, mouthpiece*, patch*, shyster*, solicitor; SEE CONCEPT 355

counsel [v] *give advice*
admonish, advise, advocate, caution, charge, confab*, direct, enjoin, exhort, give pointer, give two cents*, guide, huddle*, inform, instruct, keep posted, kibitz*, order, prescribe, prompt, put bug in ear*, put heads together*, put on to, recommend, reprehend, show the ropes*, steer, suggest, teach, tip, tip off*, tout, urge, warn, wise one up*; SEE CONCEPTS 75,317

counselor [n] *legal representative; adviser*
advocate, ambulance chaser*, attorney, counsel, front*, guide, instructor, legal beagle*, legal eagle*, lip*, mentor, mouthpiece*, pleader, solicitor, squeal*, teacher*; SEE CONCEPT 355

count [n] *tally; number*
calculation, computation, enumeration, numbering, outcome, poll, reckoning, result, sum, toll, total, whole; SEE CONCEPT 766

count [v1] *add, check in order*
add up, calculate, cast, cast up, cipher, compute, enumerate, estimate, figure, foot, keep tab, number, numerate, reckon, run down, score, sum, take account of, tally, tell, tick off, total, tot up; SEE CONCEPT 764

count [v2] *consider, deem*
await, esteem, expect, hope, impute, judge, look, look upon, rate, regard, think; SEE CONCEPTS 18,43

count [v3] *have importance*
carry weight, cut ice*, enter into consideration, import, matter, mean, militate, rate, signify, tell, weigh; SEE CONCEPT 668

count [v4] *include*
await, expect, hope, look, number among, take into account, take into consideration; SEE CONCEPTS 26,112

countenance [n1] *appearance, usually of the face*
aspect, biscuit*, cast, demeanor, expression, face, features, gills*, kisser*, look, looks, map*, mask, mien, mug*, phizog*, physiognomy, poker face*, potato*, puss*, visage; SEE CONCEPTS 716,718

countenance [n2] *self-control*
calmness, composure, presence of mind, self-composure; SEE CONCEPT 633

countenance [v] *approve, support*
abet, accept, advocate, aid, applaud, approbate, back, bear with, champion, commend, condone, confirm, cope, encourage, endorse, favor, get behind, give green light*, give stamp of approval*, give the nod*, go along with, go for, grin and bear it*, handle, help, hold with, invite, live with*, nod at, okay*, put John Hancock on*, put up with, sanction, sign off on*, sit still for*, smile on*, stand for, stomach something*, swallow*, thumbs up*, uphold; SEE CONCEPTS 10,50,88

counter [adj] *opposite, opposing*
adverse, against, antagonistic, anti, antipodal, antipodean, antithetical, conflicting, contradictory, contrary, contrasting, converse, diametric, hindering, impeding, obstructive, obverse, opposed, polar, reverse; SEE CONCEPTS 544,581

counter [adv] *contrary, reverse*
against, at variance with, contrarily, contrariwise, conversely, in defiance of, opposite, versus; SEE CONCEPTS 544,581

counter [v] *answer, respond in retaliation*
backtalk, beat, bilk, buck, circumvent, contravene, counteract, counterwork, cross, dash, disappoint, fly in the face of*, foil, frustrate, have bone to pick*, hinder, hit back, match, meet, offset, oppose, parry, pit, play off, resist, respond, retaliate, return, ruin, take on, thumbs down*, vie, ward off; SEE CONCEPTS 45,121

counteract [v] *do opposing action*
annul, buck, cancel, cancel out, check, contravene, correct, counterbalance, countercheck, countervail, counterwork, cross, defeat, fix, foil, frustrate, go against, halt, hinder, invalidate, negate, negative, neutralize, offset, oppose, prevent, rectify, redress, resist, right, thwart; SEE CONCEPTS 87,96,126

counterbalance [v] *offset an action*
amend, atone for, balance, cancel, compensate, correct, counteract, counterpoise, countervail, equalize, make up for, outweigh, rectify, redeem, set off; SEE CONCEPTS 87,96,126

counterfeit [adj] *fake, simulated*
affected, assumed, bent, bogus*, brummagem, copied, crock, deceptive, delusive, delusory, ersatz, faked, false, feigned, fictitious, fishy*, forged, framed, fraudulent, Hollywood*, imitation, misleading, mock, not genuine, not kosher*, phony*, pirate, plant*, pretended, pretentious, pseudo, put-on*, queer, sham, snide, soft shell*, spurious, supposititious, two-faced*, won't fly*, wrong; SEE CONCEPTS 549,582

counterfeit [n] *fake, forgery*
actor, bogus*, bum, copy, deceit, deception, dummy, facsimile, fraud, gyp, hoax, humbug, imitation, imposture, junque*, phony, pseudo, put-on*, reproduction, sell*, sham, simulacrum; SEE CONCEPTS 648,725

counterfeit [v] *make deceitful imitation*
act like, affect, ape, assume, bluff, carbon, cheat, circulate bad money, clone, coin, copy, defraud, delude, ditto, do, do like*, dupe, fabricate, fake, feign, forge, go like*, imitate, impersonate, knock off*, make like*, make money, mimeo, mimic, mint, phony*, phony up*, pretend, put

on*, sham, simulate, stat, Xerox*; SEE CONCEPTS 59,171

countermand [v] *annul, cancel a command*
override, recall, repeal, rescind, retract, retreat, reverse, revoke; SEE CONCEPTS 50,53,88

counterpart [n] *match; identical part or thing*
analogue, carbon copy*, complement, copy, correlate, correlative, correspondent, dead ringer*, ditto*, doppelganger, duplicate, equal, equivalent, fellow, like, look alike, mate, obverse, opposite, opposite number, peas in a pod*, pendant, ringer*, spit and image*, spitting image*, supplement, tally, twin, two of a kind*; SEE CONCEPTS 667,834

countless [adj] *innumerable*
bags of*, endless, gobs*, heap*, immeasurable, incalculable, infinite, innumerous, jillion*, legion, limitless, loads*, lots of, many, measureless, mess*, mint*, mucho*, multitudinous, myriad, numberless, oodles*, passel of*, peck, pile, raft*, scads*, slew*, stack*, tidy sum, umpteen*, uncountable, uncounted, untold, wad*, whole slew*, zillion*; SEE CONCEPTS 762,781

count on/count upon [v] *depend on; rely*
aim for, bank on, bargain for, believe, believe in, bet bottom dollar*, bet on, expect from, heed, lean on, pin faith on, place confidence in, plan on, reckon on, rest on, score, stake on, swear by, tab, take as gospel truth*, take for granted, take on trust, trust; SEE CONCEPTS 12,26

count out [v] *disregard, exclude*
bar, bate, debar, eliminate, except, get rid of, leave out, leave out of account, mark off, pass over, rule out, suspend; SEE CONCEPT 25

country [adj] *rural, pastoral*
agrarian, agrestic, Arcadian, bucolic, campestral, countrified, georgic, homey, out-country, outland, provincial, rustic, uncultured, unpolished, unrefined, unsophisticated; SEE CONCEPTS 401,536,589

country [n1] *political territory; nation*
citizenry, citizens, commonwealth, community, constituents, electors, grass roots, homeland, inhabitants, kingdom, land, native land, patria, people, polity, populace, public, realm, region, society, soil, sovereign state, state, terrain, voters; SEE CONCEPTS 379,508,510

country [n2] *rural area; area away from city*
back country, backwoods, boondocks*, boonies*, bush, countryside, cow country*, farmland, farms, forests, green belt*, hinterland, middle of nowhere*, outback, outdoors, province, sticks*, up country*, wide open space*, wilderness, wilds, woodlands, woods; SEE CONCEPTS 508,513

country mile [n] *long distance*
far piece, good way, great distance; SEE CONCEPTS 651,739,790

county [n] *province or district of area*
canton, constituency, division, shire; SEE CONCEPTS 508,513

coup [n] *achievement, often by maneuver*
accomplishment, action, coup de maître, coup d'état, deed, exploit, feat, overthrow, plot, revolution, stratagem, stroke, stroke of genius*, stunt, successful stroke, tour de force, upset; SEE CONCEPT 706

coup de grâce [n] *finishing blow*
blow, clincher*, comeuppance, deathblow, de-

CO
CO

feat, final blow, final stroke, kill, knockout, mercy stroke, mortal blow, quietus; SEE CONCEPTS 95,252

coup d'état [*n*] *violent seizure*
coup, overthrow, palace revolution, power play*, putsch*, rebellion, revolt, revolution, takeover; SEE CONCEPTS 86,90,320

couple [*n*] *pair of things*
brace, couplet, deuce*, doublet, duo, dyad, husband and wife, item, newlyweds, set, span, team, twain, twosome, yoke; SEE CONCEPTS 432,766

couple [*v*] *join two things*
bracket, bring together, buckle, clasp, coalesce, cohabit, come together, conjoin, conjugate, connect, copulate, harness, hitch, hook up, link, marry, match, pair, unite, wed, yoke; SEE CONCEPTS 113,114,297,375

coupon [*n*] *discount ticket*
advertisement, box top*, card, certificate, credit slip, detachable portion, order blank, premium certificate, ration slip, redeemable part, redemption slip, slip, token, voucher; SEE CONCEPT 331

courage [*n*] *boldness, braveness*
adventuresomeness, adventurousness, audacity, backbone, bravery, bravura, daring, dash, dauntlessness, determination, élan, endurance, enterprise, fearlessness, firmness, fortitude, gallantry, gameness, grit, guts, hardihood, heroism, intrepidity, lion-heartedness, mettle, nerve, pluck, power, prowess, pugnacity, rashness, recklessness, resolution, spirit, spunk, stoutheartedness, temerity, tenacity, valor, venturesomeness; SEE CONCEPTS 411,633

courageous [*adj*] *brave, bold*
adventuresome, adventurous, assured, audacious, cool, daredevil, daring, dauntless, doughty, fearless, fiery, fire-eating*, gallant, game, gritty*, gutsy*, hardy, heroic, high-spirited, impavid, indomitable, intrepid, lionhearted, martial, nervy, plucky*, red-blooded*, resolute, Spartan, stalwart, stand tall*, stouthearted, strong, tenacious, tough, Trojan*, unafraid, undaunted, valiant, valorous, venturesome, venturous; SEE CONCEPTS 401,404

courier [*n*] *messenger*
bearer, carrier, dispatcher, emissary, envoy, express, go-between, gofer*, gopher*, herald, intelligencer, internuncio, runner; SEE CONCEPT 348

course [*n1*] *progress, advance*
advancement, chain, channels, consecution, continuity, development, flow, furtherance, line, manner, march, movement, order, plan, policy, polity, procedure, program, progression, red tape*, row, scheme, sequel, sequence, series, string, succession, system, unfolding, way; SEE CONCEPTS 704,727

course [*n2*] *path, channel*
aisle, aqueduct, boards, byway, canal, circuit, conduit, direction, duct, flow, groove, itinerary, lap, line, movement, orbit, passage, range, road, route, run, rut, scope, stream, tack, track, trail, trajectory, watercourse, way; SEE CONCEPTS 501,514

course [*n3*] *length of action*
duration, elapsing, lapse, passage, passing, progress, sweep, term, time; SEE CONCEPT 804

course [*n4*] *plan of study*
class, conference, curriculum, discussion group, interest, laboratory, lecture, matriculation, meeting, method, period, preparation, procedure, program, regimen, schedule, seminar, session, speciality, subject; SEE CONCEPT 287

course [*v*] *flow; run*
career, chase, dart, dash, follow, gallop, gush, hasten, hunt, hurry, pursue, race, rush, scamper, scoot, scurry, speed, spring, stream, surge, tumble; SEE CONCEPTS 150,152

court [*n1*] *yard, garden of building*
cloister, close, compass, courtyard, curtilage, enclosure, forum, patio, piazza, plaza, quad, quadrangle, square, street; SEE CONCEPTS 509,513

court [*n2*] *ruler's attendants*
castle, cortege, entourage, hall, lords and ladies, palace, retinue, royal household, staff, suite, train; SEE CONCEPTS 296,348

court [*n3*] *judicial system*
bar, bench, court of justice, forum, judge, justice, kangaroo court*, law court, magistrate, seat of judgment, session, tribunal; SEE CONCEPTS 299,318

court [*n4*] *building for legal proceedings*
bar, bench, city hall, county courthouse, courthouse, courtroom, federal building, hall of justice, justice building, law court, municipal building, tribunal; SEE CONCEPTS 318,439

court [*n5*] *wooing*
address, attention, homage, love, respects, suit; SEE CONCEPT 32

court [*v*] *fawn over, pay attention to*
allure, ask in marriage, attract, beseech, bid, bootlick, captivate, charm, chase, cultivate, curry favor, date, entice, entreat, flatter, follow, gallant, go out with, go steady, go together, go with, grovel, importune, invite, keep company with, make love to, make overture, make time with*, pander to, pay addresses to, pay court to, please, pop the question*, praise, propose, pursue, run after*, seek, seek the hand of, serenade, set one's cap*, solicit, spark, spoon*, sue, sweetheart, take out, woo; SEE CONCEPTS 32,384

courteous [*adj*] *gentle, mannerly*
affable, attentive, ceremonious, civil, civilized, complaisant, considerate, courtly, cultivated, debonair, elegant, gallant, genteel, gracious, polished, polite, refined, respectful, soft-spoken, suave, thoughtful, urbane, well-behaved, well-bred, well-mannered, well-spoken; SEE CONCEPTS 267,401

courtesy [*n1*] *good manners*
address, affability, amenities, amiability, attentiveness, ceremony, chivalry, civility, comity, complaisance, consideration, cordiality, courteousness, courtliness, cultivation, culture, deference, elegance, familiarity, favor, friendliness, gallantness, gallantry, generosity, geniality, gentleness, good behavior, good breeding, graciousness, indulgence, kindness, polish, politeness, refinement, respect, reverence, solicitude, suavity, sympathy, tact, thoughtfulness, urbanity; SEE CONCEPTS 633,644

courtesy [*n2*] *favor, indulgence*
accommodation, benevolence, bounty, charity, chivalry, compassion, consent, consideration, dispensation, generosity, kindness, liberality, service, unselfishness; SEE CONCEPTS 337,388, 633

courtly [*adj*] *refined manner*
adulatory, affable, aristocratic, august, ceremonious, chivalrous, civil, civilized, complimentary, conventional, cultured, decorous, dignified, ele-

gant, flattering, formal, gallant, gracious, high-bred, imposing, lofty, obliging, polished, polite, preux, prim, refined, stately, studied, urbane; SEE CONCEPT *401*

courtship [*n*] *dating, romance*
courting, engagement, keeping company*, love, lovemaking, pursuit, suit, wooing; SEE CONCEPT *388*

cove [*n*] *inlet, small niche*
anchorage, arm, bay, bayou, bight, cave, cavern, creek, estuary, firth, frith, gulf, harbor, hole, lagoon, nook, retreat, slough, sound, wash; SEE CONCEPT *509*

covenant [*n*] *pact, promise*
agreement, arrangement, bargain, bond, commitment, compact, concordat, contract, convention, deal, deed, dicker*, handshake*, papers, stipulation, transaction, treaty, trust; SEE CONCEPT *684*

covenant [*v*] *agree*
bargain, concur, contract, engage, pledge, plight, promise, stipulate, swear, undertake, vow; SEE CONCEPTS *8,71,317*

cover [*n1*] *wrapping, cover-up*
awning, bark, binding, camouflage, canopy, canvas, cap, caparison, case, ceiling, cloak, clothing, coating, covering, coverlet, disguise, dome, dress, drop, envelope, facade, false front*, fig leaf, front, guise, hood, integument, jacket, lid, marquee, mask, masquerade, overlay, paint, parasol, polish, pretense, put-on*, roof, screen, seal, semblance, sheath, sheet, shroud, smoke screen*, spread, stopper, tarp, tarpaulin, tegument, tent, top, umbrella, varnish, veil, veneer, window-dressing, wrapper, wraps; SEE CONCEPTS *484,750*

cover [*n2*] *hiding place*
asylum, camouflage, concealment, covert, defense, drop, front, guard, harbor, harborage, haven, port, protection, refuge, retreat, safety, sanctuary, screen, security, shelter; SEE CONCEPT *198*

cover [*v1*] *wrap, hide*
blanket, board up, bury, bush up, cache, camouflage, canopy, cap, carpet, cloak, clothe, coat, conceal, cover up, crown, curtain, daub, disguise, do on the sly*, dress, eclipse, encase, enclose, enfold, ensconce, enshroud, envelop, hood, house, invest, layer, mantle, mask, obscure, overcast, overlay, overspread, protect, put on, screen, secrete, set on, shade, shield, shroud, stash*, superimpose, superpose, surface, veil; SEE CONCEPTS *172,188*

cover [*v2*] *protect, guard*
bulwark, defend, fend, house, reinforce, safeguard, screen, secure, shelter, shield, watch over; SEE CONCEPT *96*

cover [*v3*] *include, contain*
be enough, comprehend, comprise, consider, deal with, embody, embrace, encompass, examine, incorporate, involve, meet, provide for, reach, refer to, suffice, survey, take account of; SEE CONCEPT *643*

cover [*v4*] *describe in published writing*
broadcast, detail, investigate, narrate, recount, relate, report, tell of, write up; SEE CONCEPTS *60,79*

cover [*v5*] *fill in for, compensate*
balance, counterbalance, double for, insure, make good, make up for, offset, relieve, stand in

for*, substitute, take over, take the rap for*; SEE CONCEPTS *110,126*

cover [*v6*] *travel across area*
cross, do, journey over, pass over, pass through, range, track, traverse, trek; SEE CONCEPT *224*

covert [*adj*] *clandestine, underhanded*
buried, camouflaged, cloaked, concealed, disguised, dissembled, furtive, hidden, hush-hush*, incog*, incognito, masked, obscured, private, privy, QT*, secret, shrouded, stealthy, sub rosa, surreptitious, ulterior, undercover, underhand, under-the-table*, under wraps*, unsuspected, veiled; SEE CONCEPTS *544,548*

covertly [*adv*] *clandestine, underhandedly*
by stealth, clandestinely, furtively, hush-hush*, in camera, in holes and corners*, on the QT*, on the quiet, on the sly, privately, secretly, slyly, stealthily, sub rosa, surreptitiously, undercover, under wraps*, wildcat*; SEE CONCEPTS *544,548*

cover-up [*n*] *concealment*
burial*, camouflage, closeting, complicity, conspiracy, disguising, dissimulation, evasion, front, masking, pretense, smoke-screen, whitewash; SEE CONCEPTS *188,631*

covet [*v*] *desire strongly*
aspire to, begrudge, choose, crave, desiderate, envy, fancy, hanker for*, have eye on*, have hots for*, itch for*, long for, lust after, spoil for, thirst for, want, wish for, yearn for, yen for*; SEE CONCEPT *20*

covetous [*adj*] *greedy; very desirous*
acquisitive, avaricious, avid, close-fisted, eager, ensurient, envious, gluttonous, grabby, grasping, green-eyed*, grudging, hogging, itchy*, jealous, keen, mercenary, piggish*, prehensile, rapacious, ravenous, selfish, swinish*, voracious, yearning; SEE CONCEPT *401*

cow [*v*] *browbeat, intimidate*
abash, appall, awe, bludgeon, bluster, buffalo, bulldoze, bully, daunt, discomfit, disconcert, dishearten, dismay, dragoon, embarrass, enforce, faze, frighten, hector, lean on*, overawe, push around*, rattle, scare, showboat*, strong-arm*, subdue, terrorize, turn on the heat*, unnerve, walk heavy*; SEE CONCEPTS *7,19,52*

coward [*n*] *person who is scared, easily intimidated*
alarmist, baby*, caitiff, chicken*, chicken heart*, chicken liver*, craven, cur, dastard, deserter, faintheart, faint-of-heart, fraidy-cat*, funk, gutless*, invertebrate*, jellyfish*, lily liver, malingerer, mouse*, pessimist, poltroon, quitter, rabbit*, recreant, scaredy cat*, shirk, shirker, skulker, sneak, weakling, white liver*, wimp*, yellow*, yellow belly*; SEE CONCEPT *423*

cowardice [*n*] *timidity*
cold feet*, faintheartedness, fear, fearfulness, funk, gutlessness, mousiness, pusillanimity, wimpiness; SEE CONCEPT *27*

cowardly [*adj*] *fearful*
afraid, anxious, apprehensive, backward, base, caitiff, chicken-hearted, cowering, cowhearted, craven, dastardly, diffident, dismayed, fainthearted, frightened, gutless, having the willies*, jittery, lacking courage, lily-livered*, nervous, no guts, panicky, paper tiger*, pigeonhearted*, pusillanimous, recreant, retiring, running scared, scared, shrinking, shy, soft*, spineless*, timid,

timorous, weak, weak-kneed*, worthless, yellow*, yellow-bellied*; SEE CONCEPT *401*

cowboy [*n*] *mounted cattle hand*
bronco, bronco-buster, buckaroo, cattle herder, cattleman, cowhand, cowpoke, cowpuncher, drover, gaucho, herdsman, rancher, stockman, vaquero, wrangler; SEE CONCEPT *258*

cower [*v*] *hide, hover in fear*
apple-polish*, blench, bootlick*, brownnose*, cringe, crouch, draw back, fawn, flinch, grovel, honey*, kowtow*, quail*, recoil, shrink, skulk, sneak, toady*, tremble, truckle, wince; SEE CONCEPTS *188,384*

coy [*adj*] *very modest*
backward, bashful, blushing, coquettish, demure, diffident, evasive, flirtatious, humble, kittenish, overmodest, prudish, rabbity, reserved, retiring, self-effacing, shrinking, shy, skittish, timid, unassertive; SEE CONCEPTS *401,404*

cozy [*adj*] *comforting, soft, warm*
comfortable, comfy, cuddled up, cushy, easeful, in clover, intimate, in velvet*, on bed of roses*, restful, safe, secure, shéltered, snug, snug as bug in rug*, snuggled down, tucked up; SEE CONCEPTS *485,605,606*

crabby/crabbed [*adj*] *in a bad mood*
acid, acrid, acrimonious, awkward, bad-tempered, blunt, brusque, captious, choleric, churlish, cranky*, cross, crotchety, crusty*, cynical, difficult, dour, fretful, gloomy, glum, grouchy*, harsh, huffy, ill-humored, ill-tempered, irascible, irritable, misanthropic, morose, nasty-tempered, peevish, perverse, petulant, prickly, saturnine, snappish, snappy, sour, splenetic, sulky, sullen, surly, tart, testy, tough, trying, unsociable; SEE CONCEPTS *401,403*

crack [*adj*] *super, first-rate*
able, ace, adept, best, capital, choice, crackerjack*, deluxe, elite, excellent, expert, first-class, handpicked, pro*, proficient, skilled, skillful, superior, talented; SEE CONCEPTS *528,542,574*

crack [*n1*] *break, crevice*
breach, chink, chip, cleft, cranny, crevasse, cut, discontinuity, division, fissure, fracture, gap, hole, interstice, interval, rent, rift, rima, rimation, rime, split; SEE CONCEPTS *469,513*

crack [*n2*] *loud sound, usually from hitting*
bang, bash, belt, blast, blow, boom, buffet, burst, clap, clip, clout, crash, cuff, explosion, go, noise, pop, report, shot, slam, slap, smack, smash, snap, splintering, splitting, stab, stroke, thump, thwack, wallop, whack, wham; SEE CONCEPTS *189,595*

crack [*n3*] *attempt to do something*
fling, go, opportunity, pop, shot, stab, try, whack, whirl; SEE CONCEPT *87*

crack [*n4*] *joke*
dig, funny remark, gag, insult, jest, jibe, quip, remark, return, smart remark, wisecrack, witticism; SEE CONCEPT *273*

crack [*v1*] *break, usually into parts*
burst, chip, chop, cleave, crackle, crash, damage, detonate, explode, fracture, hurt, impair, injure, pop, ring, rive, sever, shiver, snap, splinter, split; SEE CONCEPT *248*

crack [*v2*] *lose self-control*
become deranged, become insane, blow one's mind*, blow up, break down, bug out*, collapse, flip*, give way*, go bonkers*, go crazy, go to pieces*, lose it*, succumb, yield; SEE CONCEPT *13*

crack [*v3*] *hit very hard*
bash, buffet, clip, clout, cuff, slap, thump, thun|der, wallop, whack; SEE CONCEPT *189*

crack [*v4*] *discover meaning, answer*
break, cryptanalyze, decipher, decode, decryp|fathom, figure out, get answer, solve, work ou|SEE CONCEPTS *37,38*

crackdown [*n*] *restraint*
clampdown, crush, end, repression, stop, strike|suppression; SEE CONCEPTS *240,832*

cracker [*n*] *hard, often salted, baked wafer*
biscuit, bun, cookie, hardtack, pretzel, rusk|saltine; SEE CONCEPT *457*

crack up [*v*] *break down mentally*
become demented, become psychotic, blow|fuse*, collapse, come apart at seams*, decline|derange, deteriorate, fail, flip out*, freak out*, g|bonkers*, go crazy, go nuts, go off deep end*, g|off rocker*, go out of mind*, go to pieces*, hav|breakdown, schizz out*, sicken; SEE CONCEPT *1.*

cradle [*n1*] *small bed for baby*
baby bed, bassinet, cot, crib, hamper, Moses bas|ket, pannier, trundle bed; SEE CONCEPT *443*

cradle [*n2*] *early childhood; origins*
babyhood, beginning, birthplace, fount, fountain|fountainhead, infancy, nativity, nursery, origin|source, spring, ultimate cause, wellspring; SEE|CONCEPTS *648,817*

cradle [*v*] *hold in arms; nurture*
lull, nestle, nourish, nurse, rock, support, tend|watch over; SEE CONCEPTS *190,295*

craft [*n1*] *expertise, skill*
ability, adeptness, adroitness, aptitude, ar|artistry, cleverness, competence, cunning, dex|terity, expertness, ingenuity, knack, know-how*|proficiency, technique; SEE CONCEPTS *409,706*

craft [*n2*] *deceit, scheme*
art, artfulness, artifice, cageyness, canniness|contrivance, craftiness, cunning, disingenuity|duplicity, foxiness, guile, ruse, shrewdness, sly|ness, stratagem, strategy, subterfuge, subtlety|trickery, wiles, wiliness; SEE CONCEPTS *645,660*

craft [*n3*] *business, discipline*
art, calling, career, employment, handicraft, line|métier, occupation, profession, pursuit, trade, vo|cation, work; SEE CONCEPT *360*

craft [*n4*] *water or air vehicle*
aircraft, airplane, air ship, barge, blimp, boa|bottom, plane, ship, shipping, spacecraft, vesse|watercraft, zeppelin; SEE CONCEPTS *504,506*

craftsperson [*n*] *person skilled in art*
artificer, artisan, journeyperson, machinis|maker, manufacturer, mechanic, skilled worke|smith, specialist, technician, wright; SEE CON|CEPT *348*

crafty [*adj*] *clever, scheming*
adroit, artful, astute, cagey, calculating, canny|crazy like fox*, cunning, deceitful, deep, design|ing, devious, disingenuous, duplicitous, foxy*|fraudulent, guileful, insidious, intelligent, keen|knowing, sharp, shrewd, slick, slippery*, sly|smart, smooth, street smart*, streetwise*, subtle|tricky, vulpine, wily; SEE CONCEPT *401*

craggy [*adj*] *jagged*
asperous, broken, cragged, harsh, precipitous|rock-bound, rocky, rough, rugged, scabrous|scraggy, stony, uneven, unlevel, unsmooth; SE|CONCEPTS *490,606*

cram [*v1*] *fill to overflowing; compress*
charge, choke, compact, crowd, crush, devour, drive, force, gobble, gorge, guzzle, heap, ingurgitate, jam, jam-pack*, load, overcrowd, overeat, overfill, pack, pack 'em in*, pack in, pack it in*, pack like sardines*, press, ram, sardine*, satiate, shove, slop, slosh, squash, squeeze, stive, stuff, tamp*, thrust, wedge, wolf*; SEE CONCEPTS *208,740*

cram [*v2*] *study intensely*
burn midnight oil*, heavy booking*, hit the books*, megabook*, mug up*, read, review, revise; SEE CONCEPT *17*

cramp [*n*] *muscle spasm*
ache, charley horse*, circumscription, confinement, constipation, contraction, convulsion, crick, hindrance, impediment, kink, obstruction, pain, pang, restriction, shooting pain, stiffness, stitch, stricture, twinge; SEE CONCEPTS *308,728*

cramp [*v*] *hinder, restrain*
bottle up*, box up*, check, circumscribe, clamp, clasp, clog, confine, constrain, coop up*, encumber, fasten, grip, hamper, hamstring, handicap, impede, inhibit, limit, object, obstruct, restrict, shackle, stymie, thwart; SEE CONCEPTS *130,191*

cramped [*adj*] *congested, overcrowded*
awkward, circumscribed, close, closed in, confined, crabbed, crowded, hemmed in*, illegible, incommodious, indecipherable, irregular, jammed in, little, minute, narrow, packed, pent, restricted, small, squeezed, tight, tiny, tucked up, two-by-four*, uncomfortable; SEE CONCEPTS *483,773*

cranky [*adj*] *in bad mood*
bad-humored, bearish, cantankerous, choleric, crabby, cross, crotchety, cussed, disagreeable, got up on wrong side of bed*, grouchy, grumpy, hot-tempered, ill-humored, irascible, irritable, like a bear*, mean, ornery*, out of sorts, perverse, quick-tempered, ratty, snappish, tetchy, ugly, vinegary; SEE CONCEPTS *401,403*

cranny [*n*] *nook, opening*
breach, byplace, chink, cleft, crack, crevice, fissure, gap, hole, interstice, niche; SEE CONCEPTS *440,513*

crappy [*adj*] *poor*
cheap, inferior, junky, lousy, shoddy, sub-par, trashy, useless, worthless; SEE CONCEPT *571*

crapshoot [*n*] *big chance*
iffy proposition, risk, risky business, shot in the dark*, spin of the roulette wheel*; SEE CONCEPTS *675,693*

rash [*n1/v1*] *bang; banging sound*
blast, boom, burst, clang, clap, clash, clatter, clattering, crack, din, peal, racket, slam, smash, smashing, sound, thunder, thunderclap, wham; SEE CONCEPTS *65,521,595*

rash [*n2*] *collision, accidental hitting*
accident, bump, collapse, concussion, crack-up*, crunch, debacle, ditch, fender bender*, fender tag*, impact, jar, jolt, percussion, pileup, ram, rear-ender*, shock, sideswipe, smash, smashup*, splashdown*, stack-up*, thud*, thump*, total*, washout*, wreck; SEE CONCEPT *189*

rash [*n3*] *computer system failure*
abend, head crash, program crash, program error, program failure, system crash, system error; SEE CONCEPTS *699,706*

rash [*v2*] *break into pieces*
bang into, crack up, crunch, dash, disintegrate,

fracture, fragment, pile up, shatter, shiver, sideswipe, smash, smash up, splinter, total*, wrack up*; SEE CONCEPT *248*

crash [*v3*] *fall*
bite the dust*, bump, collapse, collide, crash-land, ditch, dive, drive into, drop, fall flat*, fall headlong, fall prostrate, give way, go in*, hurtle, lurch, meet, overbalance, overturn, pancake*, pitch, plough into*, plunge, prang, slip, smash, splash down, sprawl, topple, tumble, upset, washout*; SEE CONCEPT *181*

crass [*adj*] *coarse, insensitive*
asinine, blundering, boorish, bovine, churlish, dense, doltish, gross, indelicate, inelegant, loutish, lowbrow, lumpish, oafish, obtuse, Philistine, raw, rough, rude, stupid, uncouth, unrefined, vulgar, witless; SEE CONCEPT *401*

crate [*n*] *wooden container*
box, cage, carton, case, chest, package; SEE CONCEPT *494*

crave [*v1*] *desire intensely*
ache for, covet, cry out for, die for*, dream, eat one's heart out*, fancy, give eyeteeth for*, hunger for*, itch for*, long for, lust after, need, pine for*, require, sigh for, spoil for, suspire, thirst for*, want, yearn for, yen for*; SEE CONCEPT *20*

crave [*v2*] *beg*
ask, beseech, call for, demand, entreat, implore, necessitate, petition, plead for, pray for, require, seek, solicit, supplicate, take; SEE CONCEPTS *48,53*

craven [*adj*] *weak, timid*
chicken*, cowardly, dastardly, fearful, gutless, lily-livered*, mean-spirited, poltroonish, pusillanimous, scared, timorous, weak-kneed*, wimpish*, wimpy, wussy*, yellow*, yellow-bellied*; SEE CONCEPTS *401,550*

craven [*n*] *timid person*
caitiff, chicken*, coward, dastard, fraidy cat*, nebbish, poltroon, quitter, recreant, scaredy cat*, weakling, wheyface, wimp*, wuss*, yellow belly*; SEE CONCEPT *423*

craving [*n*] *strong desire*
appetite, appetition, hankering, hunger, hurting, itch*, longing, lust, munchies*, need, passion, thirst, urge, yearning, yen*; SEE CONCEPTS *20,709*

crawl [*v1*] *move very slowly*
clamber, creep, drag, drag oneself along, go on all fours, go on belly, grovel, hang back, inch, lag, loiter along, lollygag*, move at snail's pace*, move on hands and knees, plod, poke, pull oneself along, scrabble, slide, slither, squirm, worm, wriggle, writhe; SEE CONCEPT *151*

crawl [*v2*] *humble oneself*
abase oneself, apple-polish*, brownnose*, cringe, fawn, grovel, toady, truckle; SEE CONCEPTS *35,48*

craze [*n*] *fad, strong interest*
chic, cry, enthusiasm, fashion, fever, furor, infatuation, in thing*, kick*, mania, mode, monomania, newest wrinkle*, novelty, passion, preoccupation, rage, the last word*, the latest thing*, trend, vogue, wrinkle; SEE CONCEPTS *532,690*

craze [*v*] *make insane*
bewilder, confuse, dement, derange, distemper, distract, drive mad, enrage, frenzy, infatuate, in-

co
cr

flame, madden, unbalance, unhinge; SEE CONCEPTS 7,19

crazy [adj1] *mentally strange*
ape, barmy, batty, berserk, bonkers*, cracked, crazed, cuckoo, daft, delirious, demented, deranged, dingy*, dippy*, erratic, flaky, flipped*, flipped out*, freaked out*, fruity*, idiotic, insane, kooky, lunatic, mad, maniacal, mental*, moonstruck*, nuts, nutty, nutty as fruitcake*, of unsound mind, out of one's mind, out of one's tree*, out to lunch*, potty*, psycho*, round the bend*, schizo*, screwball*, screw loose*, screwy*, silly, touched*, unbalanced, unglued*, unhinged*, unzipped*, wacky; SEE CONCEPT 403

crazy [adj2] *unrealistic, fantastic*
absurd, balmy, beyond all reason, bizarre, cock-eyed, derisory, eccentric, fatuous, foolhardy, foolish, goofy*, half-baked*, harebrained*, idiotic, ill-conceived, impracticable, imprudent, inane, inappropriate, insane, irresponsible, loony, ludicrous, nonsensical, odd, out of all reason, outrageous, peculiar, preposterous, puerile, quixotic, ridiculous, senseless, short-sighted, silly, strange, unworkable, weird, wild; SEE CONCEPT 529

crazy [adj3] *infatuated, in love*
ardent, beside oneself*, devoted, eager, enamored, fanatical, hysterical, keen, mad, passionate, smitten, wild, zealous; SEE CONCEPT 403

creak [v] *grind, grate with high noise*
chirr, crepitate, groan, rasp, scrape, scratch, screech, sound, squeak, squeal; SEE CONCEPTS 65,186,215

cream [n1] *lotion, oil*
cerate, chrism, cosmetic, demulcent, emulsion, essence, jelly, liniment, moisturizer, ointment, paste, salve, unction, unguent; SEE CONCEPTS 466,467,468

cream [n2] *the best*
choice, crème de la crème*, elite, fat, favorite, finest, flower, pick, pride, prime*, prize, skim*, top; SEE CONCEPT 668

creamy [adj] *smooth, buttery*
creamed, feathery, fluffy, gloppy*, gooey, gooky*, goopy*, greasy, gunky, luscious, lush, milky, oily, rich, soft, velvety; SEE CONCEPT 606

crease [n] *fold, wrinkle*
bend, bulge, cockle, corrugation, furrow, groove, line, overlap, pleat, plica, pucker, ridge, rimple, rivel, ruck, rugosity, tuck; SEE CONCEPTS 452,757

crease [v] *fold, rumple*
bend, cockle, corrugate, crimp, crinkle, crumple, dog-ear*, double up, plait, pleat, pucker, purse, ridge, ruck up, screw up*, wrinkle; SEE CONCEPTS 158,219

create [v] *develop in mind or physically*
actualize, author, beget, bring into being, bring into existence, bring to pass, build, cause to be, coin, compose, conceive, concoct, constitute, construct, contrive, design, devise, discover, dream up, effect, erect, establish, fabricate, fashion, father, forge, form, formulate, found, generate, give birth to, give life to, hatch, imagine, initiate, institute, invent, invest, make, occasion, organize, originate, parent, perform, plan, procreate, produce, rear, set up, shape, sire, spawn, start; SEE CONCEPTS 173,239,251

creation [n1] *development of entity*
conception, constitution, establishment, forma-

tion, formulation, foundation, generation, genesis, imagination, inception, institution, laying down, making, nascency, nativity, origination, procreation, production, setting up, siring; SEE CONCEPT 173

creation [n2] *all living things*
cosmos, life, living world, macrocosm, macrocosm, megacosm, nature, totality, universe, world; SEE CONCEPTS 389,429

creation [n3] *invention, concoction*
achievement, brainchild, chef-d'oeuvre, concept, handiwork, magnum opus, opus, piece, pièce de résistance, production, work, work of genius; SEE CONCEPTS 259,260

creative [adj] *artistic, imaginative*
clever, cool*, demiurgic, deviceful, fertile, formative, gifted, hip*, ingenious, innovational, innovative, innovatory, inspired, inventive, leading-edge*, original, originative, productive, prolific, stimulating, visionary, way out*; SEE CONCEPT 402

creativity [n] *artistry*
cleverness, genius, imagination, imaginativeness, ingenuity, inspiration, inventiveness, originality, resourcefulness, talent, vision; SEE CONCEPTS 409,410

creator [n] *inventor; God*
architect, author, begetter, brain, deity, designer, founder, framer, generator, initiator, maker, originator, prime mover, producer, sire; SEE CONCEPTS 348,352,361

creature [n] *being, beast*
animal, body, brute, creation, critter*, fellow, individual, living being, living thing, lower animal, man, mortal, party, person, personage, quadruped, soul, varmint*, woman; SEE CONCEPT 389

credence [n] *trust, acceptance*
accepting, admission, admitting, assurance, belief, certainty, confidence, credit, dependence, faith, reliance, stock, store; SEE CONCEPT 689

credentials [n] *references, attestation*
accreditation, authorization, card, certificate, character, deed, diploma, docket, document, documentation, endorsement, letter of credence, letter of introduction, license, missive, papers, passport, proof, recommendation, sanction, testament, testimonial, title, token, voucher, warrant; SEE CONCEPTS 271,685

credibility [n] *believeableness*
believability, chance, integrity, likelihood, plausibility, possibility, probability, prospect, reliability, satisfactoriness, solidity, solidness, soundness, tenability, trustworthiness, validity; SEE CONCEPTS 650,725

credible [adj] *believable*
aboveboard, colorable, conceivable, conclusive, creditable, dependable, determinative, honest, honest to God*, imaginable, likely, plausible, possible, probable, probably, rational, reasonable, reliable, satisfactory, satisfying, seeming, sincere, solid, sound, straight, supposable, tenable, thinkable, trustworthy, trusty, up front*, valid; SEE CONCEPTS 552,582

credit [n1] *recognition; trust*
acclaim, acknowledgment, approval, attention, belief, Brownie points*, commendation, confidence, credence, distinction, faith, fame, glory, honor, kudos*, merit, notice, pat on the back*,

points*, praise, reliance, strokes*, thanks, tribute; SEE CONCEPTS 69,410

credit [n2] *reputation, status*
authority, character, clout, esteem, estimation, fame, good name, influence, position, prestige, regard, renown, repute, standing, weight; SEE CONCEPT 388

credit [n3] *deferred payment arrangement; assets*
balance, bond, capital outlay, continuance, debenture, extension, installment buying, installment plan, lien, loan, mortgage, on account, on the arm*, on the cuff*, plastic*, respite, securities, stock, surplus cash, tab, trust, wealth; SEE CONCEPT 335

credit [v1] *believe, depend on*
accept, bank on, buy, consider, deem, fall for*, feel, hand it to one, have faith in, hold, pat on back, rely on, sense, swallow*, take as gospel truth*, take stock in*, think, trust; SEE CONCEPT 12

credit [v2] *accredit, assign to*
ascribe to, attribute to, chalk up to, charge to, defer, impute, lay, refer; SEE CONCEPT 18

creditable [adj] *praiseworthy*
admirable, batting a thousand*, believeable, commendable, decent, deserving, estimable, excellent, exemplary, honest, honorable, laudable, meritorious, nasty*, not too shabby*, organic, palmary, reputable, reputed, respectable, salt of the earth*, satisfactory, suitable, well-thought-of, worthy; SEE CONCEPT 542

credulous [adj] *gullible, naive*
accepting, believing, born yesterday*, dupable, easy mark*, falling for*, green, overtrusting, simple, swallow whole, taken in, trustful, trusting, uncritical, unquestioning, unsophisticated, unsuspecting, unsuspicious, unwary; SEE CONCEPT 404

creed [n] *belief, principles*
articles of faith, canon, catechism, church, confession, conviction, cult, doctrine, dogma, faith, ideology, persuasion, profession, religion, tenet, weltanschauung; SEE CONCEPTS 688,689

creek [n] *stream of water*
brook, brooklet, burn, crick, ditch, race, rill, rindle, river, rivulet, run, runnel, spring, streamlet, tributary, watercourse; SEE CONCEPT 514

creep [v] *crawl along, usually on ground*
approach unnoticed, crawl on all fours, edge, glide, grovel, gumshoe*, inch, insinuate, lurk, pussyfoot, scrabble, scramble, skulk, slink, slither, snake*, sneak, squirm, steal, tiptoe, worm, wriggle, writhe; SEE CONCEPT 151

creepy [adj] *nasty, scary*
awful, direful, disgusting, disturbing, dreadful, eerie, frightening, ghoulish, gruesome, hair-raising, horrible, itching, itchy, macabre, menacing, nightmarish, ominous, shuddersome, sinister, terrifying, threatening, unpleasant, weird; SEE CONCEPT 570

crescendo [n] *increase to climax*
apex, ascension, building, climb, crest, critical mass, culmination, elevation, escalation, intensification, peak, pinnacle, rise, summit, surge, upsurge, zenith; SEE CONCEPT 836

crescent [adj] *sickle-shaped*
bowed, bow-shaped, concave, convex, crescentic, crescentiform, curved, falcate, semicircular; SEE CONCEPT 486

crescent [n] *sickle-shaped object*
bow, concave figure, convex figure, cresentoid, curve, demilune, half-moon, horned moon, lune, meniscus, new moon, old moon, sickle; SEE CONCEPT 436

crest [n1] *highest point*
acme, apex, apogee, climax, crescendo, crown, culmination, fastigium, head, height, noon, peak, pinnacle, ridge, roof, summit, top, vertex; SEE CONCEPT 836

crest [n2] *emblem, symbol*
badge, bearings, charge, device, insignia; SEE CONCEPT 284

crest [n3] *topknot on head of animal*
aigrette, caruncle, chine, cockscomb, comb, crown, feather, hogback, mane, panache, plume, ridge, tassel, tuft; SEE CONCEPT 399

crestfallen [adj] *disappointed*
ass in a sling*, blue, cast down, chapfallen, dejected, depressed, despondent, disconsolate, discouraged, disheartened, dispirited, down, downcast, downhearted, down in the dumps*, in a funk*, inconsolable, low, sad, singing the blues*, taken down*; SEE CONCEPT 403

cretin [n] *obnoxious stupid person*
creep, fool, idiot, imbecile, loser, moron; SEE CONCEPTS 350,423

crevice/crevasse [n] *crack, gap*
abyss, chasm, chink, cleft, crack, cranny, cut, division, fissure, fracture, hole, interstice, opening, precipice, rent, rift, slit, split; SEE CONCEPTS 509,513

crew [n] *group working together*
aggregation, assemblage, band, bevy, bunch, cluster, collection, company, complement, congregation, corps, covey, crowd, faction, gang, hands, herd, horde, lot, mob, organization, pack, party, posse, retinue, sailors, sect, set, squad, swarm, team, troop, troupe, workers, working party; SEE CONCEPTS 381,417

crib [n] *baby bed*
bassinet, bin*, box*, bunk, cot, cradle, manger, Moses basket*, rack*, stall*, trundle bed; SEE CONCEPT 443

crick [n] *muscle spasm*
ache, charley horse*, convulsion, cramp, jarring, kink, pain, stitch, twinge, wrench; SEE CONCEPTS 308,728

crime [n] *offense against the law*
abomination, antisocial behavior, atrocity, breach, break, caper, case, corruption, criminality, delict, delictum, delinquency, depravity, dereliction, enormity, evil, evil behavior, fast one*, fault, felony, hit, illegality, immorality, infraction, infringement, iniquity, job, lawlessness, malefaction, malfeasance, misconduct, misdeed, misdemeanor, mortal sin, outrage, racket, scandal, sneak, tort, transgression, trespass, unlawful act, vice, villainy, violation, wickedness, wrong, wrongdoing; SEE CONCEPT 192

criminal [adj] *lawless, felonious*
bent, caught, corrupt, crooked, culpable, deplorable, dirty, heavy, hung up*, illegal, illegitimate, illicit, immoral, indictable, iniquitous, nefarious, off base*, out of line*, peccant, racket, scandalous, senseless, shady*, smoking gun*, unlawful, unrighteous, vicious, villainous, wicked, wildcat*, wrong; SEE CONCEPT 545

criminal [n] *person who breaks the law*
bad actor*, blackmailer, black marketeer, con,

cr
cr

convict, crook, culprit, delinquent, desperado, deuce, evildoer, ex-con, felon, fugitive, gangster, guerilla, heavy*, hood*, hoodlum, hooligan*, hustler, inside person*, jailbird, lawbreaker, malefactor, mobster, mug, muscle*, offender, outlaw, racketeer, repeater, scofflaw, sinner, slippery eel*, thug*, transgressor, trespasser, wrongdoer, yardbird*; SEE CONCEPT 412

crimp [v] *fold or curl*
coil, crease, crimple, crinkle, crisp, crumple, flow, frizz, pleat, rimple, ruck, screw, scrunch, set, swirl, undulate, wave, wrinkle; SEE CONCEPTS 188,195

cringe [v] *flinch, recoil from danger*
blench, cower, crawl, crouch, dodge, draw back, duck, eat dirt, grovel, kneel, quail, quiver, shrink, shy, start, stoop, tremble, wince; SEE CONCEPTS 188,195

crinkle [v] *crumple, ruffle*
cockle, coil, crackle, crease, crimp, crimple, curl, fold, hiss, pucker, ruck, rumple, rustle, scallop, screw, scrunch, seam, swish, twist, whisper, wind, wreathe, wrinkle; SEE CONCEPTS 65,137,213,250

cripple [v1] *disable; make lame*
attenuate, blunt, debilitate, disarm, dislimb, dismember, enfeeble, hamstring*, hurt, immobilize, incapacitate, injure, lame, maim, mangle, mutilate, palsy, paralyze, prostrate, sap, sideline*, stifle, undermine, unstrengthen, weaken; SEE CONCEPT 246

cripple [v2] *hinder action, progress*
bring to standstill, cramp, damage, destroy, halt, hamstring*, impair, put out of action*, ruin, spoil, stifle, vitiate; SEE CONCEPT 121

crippled [adj] *disabled*
bedridden, broken, damaged, defective, deformed, enfeebled, game, gimp*, halt, hamstrung*, handicapped, harmed, hog-tied*, housebound, impaired, incapacitated, laid up*, lame, maimed, mangled, marred, mutilated, out of commission*, paralyzed, sidelined*; SEE CONCEPTS 314,485

crisis [n] *critical situation*
big trouble*, catastrophe, change, climacteric, climax, confrontation, contingency, corner, crossroad, crunch*, crux, culmination, deadlock, dilemma, dire straits*, disaster, embarrassment, emergency, entanglement, exigency, extremity, height, hot potato*, hour of decision*, imbroglio, impasse, juncture, mess, moment of truth*, necessity, pass, perplexity, pickle*, pinch*, plight, point of no return*, predicament, pressure, puzzle, quandary, situation, stew, strait, trauma, trial, trouble, turning point, urgency; SEE CONCEPT 674

crisp [adj1] *brittle, dry*
crispy, crumbly, crunchy, crusty, firm, fresh, friable, green, plump, ripe, short, unwilted; SEE CONCEPT 606

crisp [adj2] *fresh, chilly*
bracing, brisk, clear, cloudless, invigorating, refreshing, stimulating; SEE CONCEPTS 525,605

crisp [adj3] *short, curt in presentation*
abrupt, biting, brief, brusque, clear, clear-cut, cutting, incisive, penetrating, piquing, pithy, provoking, stimulating, succinct, tart, terse; SEE CONCEPT 267

crisp [adj4] *smart, snappy in appearance*
clean-cut, neat, orderly, spruce, tidy, well-groomed, well-pressed; SEE CONCEPT 579

criterion [n] *test, gauge for judgment*
archetype, basis, benchmark, canon, example, exemplar, fact, foundation, law, measure, model, norm, opinion, original, paradigm, pattern, point of comparison, precedent, principle, proof, prototype, rule, scale, standard, touchstone, yardstick; SEE CONCEPTS 290,688

critic [n1] *analyst, interpreter*
analyzer, annotator, arbiter, authority, caricaturist, cartoonist, commentator, connoisseur, diagnostic, evaluator, expert, expositor, judge, pundit, reviewer, sharpshooter*; SEE CONCEPT 348

critic [n2] *faultfinder, detractor*
aristarch, attacker, backseat driver*, belittler, blamer, carper, caviler, censor, censurer, complainant, complainer, defamer, disapprover, disparager, disputer, doubter, fretter, hypercritic, maligner, muckraker, mud-slinger*, nagger, nit-picker*, panner*, quibbler, reviler, scolder, sidewalk superintendent*, slanderer, vilifier, worrier, zapper*; SEE CONCEPT 412

critical [adj1] *fault-finding, detracting*
analytical, belittling, biting, calumniatory, captious, carping, caviling, cavillous, censorious, censuring, choleric, condemning, critic, cutting, cynical, demanding, demeaning, derogatory, diagnostic, disapproving, discerning, discriminating, disparaging, exacting, exceptive, finicky, fussy, hairsplitting, humbling, hypercritical, lowering, nagging, niggling, nit-picking*, over-critical, particular, penetrating, reproachful, sarcastic, satirical, scolding, severe, sharp, trenchant, withering; SEE CONCEPT 267

critical [adj2] *urgently important*
acute, all-important, climacteric, conclusive, consequential, crucial, dangerous, deciding, decisive, desperate, determinative, dire, exceptive, grave, hairy*, hazardous, high-priority, integral, momentous, perilous, pivotal, precarious, pressing, risky, serious, significant, strategic, urgent, vital, weighty; SEE CONCEPT 568

critical mass [n] *crisis point*
critical point, critical stage, crossroads*, crunch time, do or die time*, high noon*, irreversible momentum, moment of truth, point of no return, sink or swim time*, the Rubicon, turning point; SEE CONCEPT 674

criticism [n1] *interpretation, analysis*
appraisal, appreciation, assessment, comment, commentary, critique, elucidation, essay, estimate, evaluation, examination, exposition, judgment, notice, observation, opinion, pan*, rating, rave*, review, reviewal, scorcher, sideswipe, sleighride*, study, write-up; SEE CONCEPTS 271,277,278

criticism [n2] *verbal disapproval*
animadversion, aspersion, bad press*, blast, brickbats, Bronx cheer*, call down*, carping, cavil, caviling, censure, critical remarks, cut, denunciation, disparagement, faultfinding, flak*, hit*, knock*, nit-picking, objection, opprobrium, pan, panning, put down, quibble, rap on knuckles*, reproof, roast*, slam*, slap*, slap on wrist*, static, stricture, swipe*, vitriol, zapper*; SEE CONCEPT 52

criticize [v1] *disapprove, judge as bad*
animadvert on, bash, blame, blast, blister, carp, castigate, censure, chastise, chide, clobber, come down on, condemn, cut down*, cut to bits*, cut

up*, denounce, denunciate, disparage, do a number on*, dress down*, excoriate, find fault,
fluff*, fulminate against, fustigate, give bad
press*, hit, jump on*, knock*, lambaste*, nag at,
nit-pick, pan, pick at, rap*, reprehend, reprimand, reprobate, reprove, rip*, roast*, scathe,
scorch*, skin*, skin alive*, slam*, slog*, slug*,
take down*, trash*, trim*, zap*; SEE CONCEPT 52

criticize [v2] *analyze, interpret*
appraise, assess, comment upon, evaluate, examine, give opinion, judge, pass judgment on,
probe, review, scrutinize, study; SEE CONCEPTS
37,103

critique [n] *analysis, essay*
appraisal, assessment, comment, commentary,
criticism, editorial, examination, exposition,
flak*, judgment, notice, pan*, putdown*, rap*,
rave*, review, reviewal, slam*, slap*, study,
takedown*, write-up, zapper*; SEE CONCEPTS
51,52,271

croak [v] *make husky, squawking noise*
caw, crow, gasp, grunt, quack, squawk, utter
huskily, utter throatily, wheeze; SEE CONCEPT 77

crony [n] *ally, companion*
accomplice, acquaintance, associate, bosom
buddy*, buddy, chum, colleague, comate, comrade, confidant, friend, good buddy*, intimate,
mate, pal, partner, sidekick*; SEE CONCEPT 423

crook [n] *criminal, thief*
cheat, filcher, knave, pilferer, purloiner, racketeer, robber, rogue, scoundrel, shark*, shyster*,
swindler, villain; SEE CONCEPT 412

crook [v] *bend, angle*
bow, curve, flex, fork, hook, meander, notch,
round, slither, snake, wind, zigzag; SEE CON-
CEPTS 213,738

crooked [adj] *bent, angled*
agee, anfractuous, angular, asymmetric, awry,
bowed, catawampus*, circuitous, cockeyed*,
contorted, crippled, curved, curving, deformed,
deviating, devious, disfigured, distorted, errant,
gnarled, hooked, incurving, indirect, irregular,
kinky, knurly, lopsided, meandering, misshapen,
not straight, oblique, out of shape, rambling,
roundabout, screwy*, serpentine, sinuous,
skewed, slanted, snaky, spiral, tilted, topsy-
turvy*, tortile, tortuous, twisted, twisting, uneven, warped, winding, zigzag; SEE CONCEPTS
486,490,581

crooked [adj2] *evil, corrupt*
crafty, criminal, deceitful, devious, dishonest,
dishonorable, double-dealing, dubious, fraudulent, illegal, indirect, iniquitous, lying, nefarious,
questionable, ruthless, shady, shifty, suborned,
treacherous, underhand, unlawful, unprincipled,
unscrupulous, untruthful; SEE CONCEPT 545

crop [n] *harvest of fruit, vegetable*
annual production, byproduct, crops, fruitage,
fruits, gathering, gleaning, output, produce,
product, reaping, season's growth, vintage, yield;
SEE CONCEPT 429

crop [v] *cut, trim off*
chop, clip, curtail, detach, detruncate, disengage,
hew, lop, mow, pare, pollard, prune, reduce,
shave, shear, shorten, skive, slash, snip, top,
truncate; SEE CONCEPT 176

cross [adj] *very angry; in a bad mood*
annoyed, cantankerous, captious, caviling, choleric, churlish, crabby*, cranky, crotchety*,

crusty, disagreeable, faultfinding, fractious, fretful, grouchy, grumpy, ill-humored, ill-tempered,
impatient, irascible, irritable, jumpy, out of
humor, peeved, peevish, pettish, petulant, put
out*, querulous, quick-tempered, ratty, short,
snappy, splenetic, sullen, surly, testy, tetchy,
touchy, vexed, waspish; SEE CONCEPTS 401,403

cross [v1] *traverse an area*
bridge, cruise, cut across, extend over, ford, go
across, meet, move across, navigate, overpass,
pass over, ply, sail, span, transverse, voyage,
zigzag; SEE CONCEPTS 159,224

cross [v2] *intersect, lie across*
bisect, crisscross, crosscut, decussate, divide, intercross, intertwine, lace, lie athwart of, rest
across; SEE CONCEPTS 738,747

cross [v3] *hybridize, mix*
blend, crossbreed, cross-fertilize, cross-mate,
cross-pollinate, interbreed, intercross, mingle,
mongrelize; SEE CONCEPTS 250,257

cross [v4] *betray, hinder*
backtalk, block, bollix, buck, crab, cramp, crimp,
deny, double-cross, flummox, foul, foul up*,
frustrate, have bone to pick*, impede, interfere,
knock props out*, louse up*, obstruct, oppose,
resist, sell*, sell out*, snafu*, stab in the back*,
stonewall*, stump, stymie, take on, take wind
out of sails*, thwart; SEE CONCEPTS 7,19,59,121

cross-examine [v] *ask pointed questions*
catechize, check, cross-question, debrief, examine, grill, interrogate, investigate, pump, put the
screws to*, question, quiz, sweat, third-degree*;
SEE CONCEPTS 48,53,317

crossing [n] *pathway to traverse larger path*
bridge, cloverleaf, crossroad, crosswalk, crossway, decussation, exchange, grade crossing,
grating, gridiron, interchange, intersection, junction, loop, network, overpass, passage, screen,
traversal, traverse, underpass; SEE CONCEPTS
501,513

crosswise/crossways [adj] *across, at an angle*
angular, aslant, athwart, at right angles, awry,
contrariwise, crisscross, cross, crossing, diagonally, from side to side, horizontally, longways,
on the bias, over, perpendicular, sideways,
thwart, transversal, transverse, transversely, traverse, vertically; SEE CONCEPT 581

crotchety [adj] *irritable, often due to old age*
awkward, bad-tempered, bearish, cantankerous,
contrary, crabby*, cranky, cross, cross-grained,
crusty, curmudgeonly, difficult, disagreeable, eccentric, fractious, grouchy, grumpy, irritable, obstinate, obstreperous, odd, ornery*, peevish,
queer, surly, testy, unusual, vinegary*, waspish,
waspy; SEE CONCEPTS 401,403

crouch [v] *stoop low; cringe*
bend, bend down, bow, cower, dip, duck, grovel,
huddle, hunch, hunker down, kneel, quail, quat,
scrooch down, squat, stoop, wince; SEE CONCEPT
213

crow [v] *brag, exult*
babble, blow, bluster, boast, cackle, caw, cock-a-
doodle-doo*, cry, flourish, gas*, gloat, glory in,
gurgle, jubilate, mouth, prate, puff, rodomontade, squawk, strut, swagger, triumph, vaunt,
whoop; SEE CONCEPT 49

crowd [n1] *large assembly*
army, array, blowout, bunch, cattle, circle,
clique, cloud, cluster, company, concourse, con-

cr
cr

fluence, conflux, congeries, congregation, coterie, crew, crush, deluge, drove, faction, flock,
flood, gaggle, great unwashed*, group, herd,
horde, host, jam, legion, lot, mass, masses, meet,
mob, multitude, muster, organization, pack,
party, people, posse, press, rabble, rank and file*,
scores, sellout, set, stream, surge, swarm, throng,
troupe, tumult; SEE CONCEPTS *381,417*

crowd [n2] *special group of friends*
bunch, circle, clique, coterie, faction, group, in-
crowd, lot, posse, push, set; SEE CONCEPTS
387,417

crowd [v] *cram, press into area*
bear, bunch, bundle, chock, cluster, congest,
congregate, crush, deluge, elbow, flock, gather,
huddle, jam, jam-pack*, justle, mass, muster,
overcrowd, pack, pack 'em in*, pack like sardines*, pile, push, ram, sardine*, shove, squash,
squeeze, squish*, stream, surge, swamp, swarm,
throng, top off, troop; SEE CONCEPTS *208,740*

crowded [adj] *busy, congested*
awash, brimful, brimming, chock-full, clean,
close, compact, crammed, cramped, crushed,
dense, elbow-to-elbow*, filled to the rafters*, fit
to bust*, full, full house*, full up*, huddled,
jammed, jam-packed*, loaded, lousy with*,
massed, mobbed, mob scene*, overflowing,
packed, populous, sardined*, sold out, SRO*,
standing room only*, stiff with*, stuffed, swarming, teeming, thick, thickset, thronged, tight,
topped off, up to here*, up to the hilt*, wall-to-
wall*; SEE CONCEPTS *481,483,774*

crown [n1] *top; best*
acme, apex, climax, crest, culmination,
fastigium, head, meridian, peak, perfection, pinnacle, roof, summit, tip, top, ultimate, vertex,
zenith; SEE CONCEPTS *706,836*

crown [n2] *tiara for royalty*
chaplet, circlet, coronal, coronet, diadem, garland, headband, headdress, wreath; SEE CONCEPT
452

crown [n3] *royalty*
crowned head, monarch, monarchy, potentate,
ruler, sovereign, sovereignty, supreme ruler, the
throne; SEE CONCEPT *422*

crown [v1] *reward, dignify*
adorn, arm, authorize, commission, coronate,
delegate, determine, dower, enable, endow,
endue, ennoble, enthrone, erect, establish, exalt,
festoon, fix, heighten, honor, inaugurate, induct,
install, invest, raise, sanction, settle, set up, stabilize, strengthen; SEE CONCEPTS *50,69,88*

crown [v2] *be the culmination of*
cap, climax, complete, consummate, crest, finish,
fulfill, perfect, put finishing touch on, round off,
surmount, terminate, top, top off; SEE CONCEPTS
234,706

crown [v3] *hit, usually on head*
biff, box, cuff, knock, punch, smite, strike; SEE
CONCEPT *189*

crowning [adj] *climactic*
consummate, culminating, excellent, final, paramount, principal, sovereign, supreme, ultimate;
SEE CONCEPTS *531,548*

crucial [adj] *critical, important*
acute, central, clamorous, climacteric, climatic,
compelling, deciding, decisive, desperate, dire,
essential, hanging by thread*, high-priority, imperative, insistent, momentous, necessary, on
thin ice*, pivotal, pressing, searching, show-

down*, touch and go*, touchy, urgent, vital; SEE
CONCEPT *568*

crucify [v1] *execute; torture near to death*
excruciate, hang, harrow, kill, martyr, martyrize,
nail to cross, persecute, rack, torment, torture;
SEE CONCEPT *252*

crucify [v2] *browbeat, destroy with words*
afflict, agonize, bedevil, bother, harrow, ill-treat,
lampoon, pan, ridicule, smite, tear to pieces*,
torment, torture, try, wipe the floor with*; SEE
CONCEPTS *7,19,52*

crude [adj1] *vulgar, unpolished in manner*
awkward, backward, barnyard*, boorish, cheap,
cloddish, clumsy, coarse, crass, dirty, earthy,
filthy, foul, grody*, gross*, ignorant, ill-bred, indecent, indelicate, inelegant, insensible, lewd,
loud, loud-mouthed, loutish, lowbred, oafish, obscene, raunchy*, raw, rough, rude, savage,
smutty*, tacky*, tactless, uncouth, unenlightened, ungainly, unskillful; SEE CONCEPTS
267,401

crude [adj2] *unrefined, natural*
amateurish, callow, coarse, green, harsh, homemade, homespun, immature, impure, inexpert, in
the rough*, makeshift, outline, prentice, primitive, raw, rough, rough-hewn, rude, rudimentary,
rustic, simple, sketchy, thick, undeveloped, unfinished, unformed, ungraded, unmatured, un-
milled, unpolished, unprepared, unprocessed,
unproficient, unsorted, untaught, untrained, un-
worked, unwrought; SEE CONCEPTS
562,578,589,797

cruel [adj] *vicious, pitiless; causing pain*
atrocious, barbarous, bestial, bitter, bloodthirsty,
brutal, brutish, callous, cold-blooded, degenerate, demoniac, depraved, evil, excruciating, ferocious, fierce, flinty, hard, hard-hearted, harsh,
hateful, heartless, hellish, implacable, inexorable, inhuman, inhumane, malevolent, merciless, monstrous, painful, pernicious, poignant,
rancorous, relentless, revengeful, ruthless, sadistic, sinful, spiteful, tyrannical, unfeeling, unkind,
unnatural, unrelenting, vengeful, vicious, virulent, wicked; SEE CONCEPTS *401,570*

cruelty [n] *brutality, harshness*
animality, barbarism, barbarity, bestiality, bloodthirstiness, brutishness, callousness, coarseness, coldness, depravity, despotism, ferocity,
fiendishness, fierceness, hard-heartedness,
heartlessness, inhumanity, insensibility, insensi-
tiveness, malice, malignity, masochism,
mercilessness, murderousness, persecution, rancor, ruthlessness, sadism, savageness, savagery,
severity, spite, spitefulness, torture, truculence,
unfeelingness, unkindness, venom, viciousness,
wickedness; SEE CONCEPT *633*

cruise [n] *sailing expedition*
boat trip, crossing, jaunt, journey, sail, sailing,
sea trip, voyage; SEE CONCEPTS *224,292,363*

cruise [v] *sail*
boat, coast, drift, fare, gad, gallivant, go, hie,
jaunt, journey, keep steady pace, meander, navigate, pass, proceed, push on, repair, travel, voyage, wander about, wend; SEE CONCEPTS
147,151,159,224

crumb [n] *tiny bit, morsel*
atom, dab, dash, dram, drop, grain, iota, jot,
mite, ounce, particle, pinch, scrap, seed, shred,
sliver, smidgen, snippet, soupçon, speck; SEE
CONCEPT *831*

crumble [v] *break or fall into pieces*
break up, collapse, crumb, crush, decay, decompose, degenerate, deteriorate, disintegrate, dissolve, fragment, go to pieces, granulate, grind, molder, perish, powder, pulverize, putrefy, triturate, tumble; SEE CONCEPTS *181,248,469*

crumbly [adj] *brittle*
breakable, corroded, crisp, crunchy, decayed, degenerated, deteriorated, disintegrated, disintegrated, eroded, fragile, frail, frangible, friable, oxidized, perishing, powdery, pulverizable, rotted, rotten, rusted, shivery, short, soft, worn; SEE CONCEPTS *571*

crummy [adj] *lousy*
cheap, contemptible, crappy*, grotty, inferior, miserable, pathetic, poor, rotten, second-rate, shabby, sub-par, third-rate, useless, worthless; SEE CONCEPT *571*

crumple [v] *make or become wrinkled*
break down, buckle, cave in, collapse, crease, crimp, crimple, crinkle, crush, fall, fold, give way, go to pieces, pucker, rimple, ruck, rumple, screw, scrunch, shrivel, wad, wrinkle; SEE CONCEPTS *184,208,252*

crunch [n] *crucial point*
crisis, critical point, crux, difficulty, emergency, hour of decision*, moment of truth*, problem, test, trouble, trying time*; SEE CONCEPTS *388,674,675*

crunch [v] *grind, chew*
beat, bite, champ, chaw, chomp, crush, gnaw, masticate, munch, ruminate, scrunch; SEE CONCEPTS *169,186*

crunchy [adj] *brittle*
chewy, crackling, crisp, crispy, crumbly, crusty; SEE CONCEPT *606*

crusade [n] *campaign for cause*
cause, demonstration, drive, evangelism, expedition, holy war, jihad, march, movement, push; SEE CONCEPT *300*

crush [n1] *crowd of animate beings*
drove, gathering, horde, huddle, jam, multitude, party, press, push, throng, tumult; SEE CONCEPTS *417,432*

crush [n2] *infatuation*
beguin, desire, flame, love affair, passion, puppy love*, torch; SEE CONCEPT *20*

crush [v1] *compress, smash*
beat, bray, break, bruise, buck, comminute, contriturate, contuse, crease, crowd, crumble, crunch, embrace, enfold, express, hug, jam, kablooey*, mash, pound, powder, press, pulverize, push, romp, rumple, squash, squeeze, squish, total*, trample, tread, triturate, wrinkle; SEE CONCEPTS *208,219,246,252*

crush [v2] *defeating soundly*
annihilate, bear down, beat, blot out*, blow away*, conquer, defeat, demolish, extinguish, force down, ice*, kill, obliterate, overcome, overpower, overwhelm, quelch, quell, reduce, ruin, squelch, stamp out*, strangle, subdue, subjugate, suppress, vanquish, wreck; SEE CONCEPTS *95,252*

crush [v3] *humiliate*
abash, browbeat, chagrin, dispose of, dump, hurt, mortify, overwhelm, put away*, put down*, quash, quell, shame, suppress; SEE CONCEPTS *7,19*

crust [n] *stiff outer layer; coating*
band, bloom, border, caking, coat, concretion, covering, edge, encrustation, film, hull, incrustation, integument, layer, outside, rind, scab, shell, skin, surface, verge; SEE CONCEPT *34*

crusty [adj1] *irritable, often due to old age*
abrupt, bluff, blunt, brief, brusque, cantankerous, captious, choleric, crabbed, crabby*, cranky, cross, curt, dour, gruff, harsh, ill-humored, irascible, peevish, prickly, sarcastic, saturnine, scornful, short, short-tempered, snappish, snarling, snippety, snippy, splenetic, surly, testy, touchy, vinegary*; SEE CONCEPT *401*

crusty [adj2] *brittle on outside*
crisp, crispy, crunchy, friable, hard, short, well-baked, well-done; SEE CONCEPTS *462,606*

crux [n] *most important part*
body, bottom line*, core, decisive point, essence, gist, heart, kernel, matter, meat*, meat and potatoes*, nitty-gritty, nub, pith, purport, substance, thrust; SEE CONCEPTS *668,826*

cry [n1] *weeping and making sad sounds*
bawl, bawling, bewailing, blubber, blubbering, howl, howling, keening, lament, lamentation, mourning, shedding tears, snivel, snivelling, sob, sobbing, sorrowing, tears, the blues*, wailing, weep, whimpering, yowl; SEE CONCEPTS *77,469*

cry [n2] *calling out; yelling*
acclamation, bark, bawl, bay, bellow, cackle, call, caw, chatter, cheer, clack, clamor, cluck, coo, crow, ejaculation, exclamation, expletive, fuss, gobble, groan, grunt, hiss, holler, hoot, howl, hullabaloo, hurrah, meow, mewling, moo, motto, nicker, note, outcry, pipe, quack, report, roar, ruckus, scream, screech, shout, shriek, song, squall, squawk, squeak, trill, uproar, vociferation, wail, whine, whinny, whistle, whoop, yammer, yawp*, yell, yelp, yoo-hoo; SEE CONCEPTS *47,77,278*

cry [v1] *weep and make sad sounds*
bawl, bemoan, bewail, blub, blubber, boohoo*, break down, burst into tears*, caterwaul, choke up, complain, crack up*, deplore, dissolve in tears*, fret, grieve, groan, howl, keen, lament, let go, let it all out*, mewl, moan, mourn, put on the weeps*, regret, ring the blues*, shed bitter tears*, shed tears, sigh, sniff, snivel, sob, sorrow, squall, turn on waterworks*, wail, weep, whimper, whine, yammer, yowl; SEE CONCEPTS *77,469*

cry [v2] *call out, yell*
bark, bawl, bay, bellow, bleat, cackle, call, caw, chatter, cheer, clack, clamor, cluck, coo, croak, crow, ejaculate, exclaim, gabble, growl, grunt, hail, hiss, holler, holler out, hoot, howl, low, meow, moo, nicker, pipe, quack, roar, scream, screech, shout, shriek, sing out, snarl, squawk, trill, tweet, twitter, vociferate, whinny, whistle, whoop, yawp*, yelp; SEE CONCEPTS *47,77*

cry [v3] *advertise*
announce, bark*, broadcast, build up, hawk, hype*, press-agent*, proclaim, promulgate, publicize, publish, puff*, trumpet*; SEE CONCEPT *324*

crybaby [n] *malcontent*
bellyacher, cissy, complainer, critic, faultfinder, griper, grumbler, moaner, softy*, whiner, wimp*, wuss*; SEE CONCEPT *412*

crypt [n] *burial place*
catacomb, cave, cavern, cell, chamber, compartment, grave, grotto, mausoleum, room, sepulcher, tomb, undercroft, vault; SEE CONCEPT *305*

cr
cr

cryptic [*adj*] *secret; obscure in meaning*
abstruse, ambiguous, apocryphal, arcane, cabbalistic, dark, Delphian, Delphic, enigmatic, equivocal, esoteric, evasive, hidden, incomprehensible, inexplicable, murky, mysterious, mystic, mystical, mystifying, occult, opaque, oracular, perplexing, puzzling, recondite, secretive, strange, tenebrous, unclear, unfathomable, uninformative, vague, veiled; SEE CONCEPTS 267,576,682

crystal [*adj*] *clear, transparent*
clear-cut, limpid, lucent, lucid, luminous, pellucid, translucent, transpicuous, unblurred; SEE CONCEPTS 617,618

cubicle [*n*] *office compartment*
booth, cell, chamber, cubbyhole, desk, nook, office, pigeonhole, room, stall, work area; SEE CONCEPT 434

cuddle [*v*] *hold fondly, closely*
bundle, burrow, caress, clasp, cosset, curl up, dandle, embrace, enfold, feel up*, fondle, huddle, hug, kiss, love, nestle, nuzzle, pet, snug, snuggle, touch; SEE CONCEPTS 190,375

cuddly [*adj*] *huggable, embraceable*
caressible, cuddlesome, kissable, lovable, plump, snuggly, soft, warm; SEE CONCEPT 485

cudgel [*n*] *baton for hitting*
bastinado, bat, billy*, billyclub, birch, blackjack, bludgeon, cane, club, cosh*, ferule, mace, nightstick, paddle, rod, sap, shill, shillelagh, spontoon, stick, switch, truncheon; SEE CONCEPT 500

cue [*n*] *signal to act*
catchword, clue, hint, hot lead*, idea, indication, inkling, innuendo, in the wind*, intimation, job, key, lead, mnemonic, nod, notion, prod, prompt, prompting, reminder, sign, suggestion, telltale*, tip-off, warning; SEE CONCEPTS 278,284,628

cuff [*n*] *beating with hands*
belt, biff, box, buffet, chop, clip, clout, hit, knock, poke, punch, rap, slap, smack, sock, thump, wallop, whack; SEE CONCEPT 189

cuff [*v*] *beat with hands*
bat, belt, biff, box, buffet, clap, clobber*, clout, hit, knock, pummel, punch, slap, smack, spank, thump, whack; SEE CONCEPT 189

cuisine [*n*] *food*
cooking, dishes, eats*, fare, grub*, meal, menu; SEE CONCEPT 459

cull [*v1*] *pick out for reason*
choose, discriminate, elect, extract, glean, mark, optate, opt for, pluck, prefer, select, sift, single out, take, thin, thin out, winnow; SEE CONCEPTS 41,142

cull [*v2*] *gather*
accumulate, amass, collect, extract, garner, glean, pick up, round up; SEE CONCEPT 109

culminate [*v*] *come to a climax*
cap, climax, close, come to a head*, conclude, crown, end, end up, finish, go over the mountain*, go the route*, rise to crescendo, round off, shoot one's wad*, terminate, top off*, wind up*; SEE CONCEPT 119

culmination [*n*] *conclusion; climactic stage*
acme, all the way*, apex, apogee, blow off*, capper*, climax, completion, consummation, critical mass, crown, crowning touch, finale, finish, height, limit, maximum, meridian, ne plus ultra, noon, payoff, peak, perfection, pinnacle, punch line*, summit, top, zenith; SEE CONCEPTS 230,635,676

culpable [*adj*] *responsible for action*
amiss, answerable, at fault, blamable, blameful, blameworthy, caught, caught in the act*, caught red-handed*, censurable, demeritorious, dirty, found wanting, guilty, hung up, impeachable, indictable, in the wrong, liable, off base, out of line*, punishable, reprehensible, responsible, sinful, smoking gun*, to blame, unholy, wrong; SEE CONCEPTS 404,545

culprit [*n*] *person responsible for wrongdoing*
con, convict, criminal, delinquent, evildoer, ex-con, felon, fugitive, guilty party, jailbird*, malefactor, miscreant, offender, rascal, sinner, transgressor, wrongdoer, yardbird*; SEE CONCEPT 412

cult [*n1*] *group sharing belief*
band, body, church, clan, clique, creed, denomination, faction, faith, following, party, persuasion, religion, school, sect; SEE CONCEPTS 369,387

cult [*n2*] *worship; form of ceremony*
admiration, ceremony, craze, creed, cultus, devotion, faddism, faith, idolization, liturgy, persuasion, religion, reverence, rite, ritual, veneration; SEE CONCEPTS 410,689

cultivate [*v1*] *develop land for growing*
breed, crop, dress, farm, fertilize, garden, harvest, labor, manage, mature, plant, plow, prepare, propagate, raise, ripen, seed, tend, till, work; SEE CONCEPTS 253,257

cultivate [*v2*] *enrich situation; give special attention*
advance, ameliorate, better, bolster, bring on, brownnose*, butter up*, cherish, civilize, court, develop, discipline, elevate, encourage, enrich, foster, further, get in with*, get next to*, get on good side of*, improve, nourish, nurse, nurture, play up to*, polish, promote, refine, run after, seek friendship, shine up to*, suck up to*, take pains with, train; SEE CONCEPTS 244,384

cultivate [*v3*] *nurture, take care of*
aid, ameliorate, better, cherish, devote oneself to, educate, encourage, forward, foster, further, help, improve, instruct, nurse, patronize, promote, pursue, raise, rear, refine, support, teach, train; SEE CONCEPTS 110,295

cultivation [*n1*] *development of land for growing*
agrology, agronomics, agronomy, farming, gardening, horticulture, planting, plowing, tillage, tilling, working; SEE CONCEPT 257

cultivation [*n2*] *culture, sophistication, education*
advancement, aestheticism, breeding, civility, civilization, delicacy, discernment, discrimination, enlightenment, gentility, good taste, grounding, improvement, learning, letters, manners, polish, progress, refined taste, refinement, schooling, taste; SEE CONCEPTS 411,655,673

cultivation [*n3*] *nurture, help*
advancement, advocacy, development, encouragement, enhancement, fostering, furtherance, patronage, promotion, support; SEE CONCEPTS 110,657

cultural [*adj*] *educational, enlightening*
adorning, advancing, artistic, beautifying, beneficial, broadening, civilizing, constructive, corrective, developmental, dignifying, disciplining, edifying, educative, elevating, ennobling, enriching, expanding, glorifying, helpful, humane, humanizing, influential, inspirational, instructive,

learned, liberal, liberalizing, nurturing, ornamenting, polishing, promoting, raising, refined, refining, regenerative, socializing, stimulating, uplifting, widening; SEE CONCEPTS 537,555,589

culture [n1] *breeding, education, sophistication*
ability, accomplishment, address, aestheticism, art, capacity, civilization, class, courtesy, cultivation, delicacy, dignity, discrimination, dress, elegance, elevation, enlightenment, erudition, experience, fashion, finish, gentility, good taste, grace, improvement, kindness, learning, manners, nobility, perception, polish, politeness, practice, proficiency, refinement, savoir-faire, science, skill, tact, training, urbanity; SEE CONCEPTS 388,633,678

culture [n2] *ideas, values of a people*
arts and sciences, civilization, convention, customs, development, ethnology, folklore, folkways, grounding, habit, humanism, knowledge, lifestyle, mores, society, the arts, way of life; SEE CONCEPTS 388,689

culture [n3] *development of land*
agriculture, agrology, agronomics, agronomy, cultivation, farming, gardening, raising, tending; SEE CONCEPT 257

cultured [adj] *well-bred, experienced*
able, accomplished, advanced, aesthetic, appreciative, au courant, blue-stocking*, chivalrous, civilized, courteous, cultivated, distingue, educated, elegant, enlightened, erudite, gallant, genteel, highbrow*, high-class, informed, intellectual, intelligent, knowledgeable, lettered, liberal, literary, literate, mannerly, polished, polite, refined, savant, scholarly, sensitive, sophisticated, tasteful, tolerant, traveled, understanding, up-to-date, urbane, versed, well-informed; SEE CONCEPT 550

culvert [n] *ditch for flow of water*
canal, channel, conduit, drain, duct, gutter, pipe, watercourse; SEE CONCEPT 509

cumbersome [adj] *clumsy, awkward*
bulky, burdensome, clunker, clunking, clunky, cumbrous, embarrassing, galumphing, heavy, hefty, incommodious, inconvenient, leaden, massive, oppressive, ponderous, tiresome, unhandy, unmanageable, unwieldy, wearisome, weighty; SEE CONCEPTS 544,773

cumulative [adj] *accruing; growing in size or effect*
accumulative, additive, additory, advancing, aggregate, amassed, augmenting, chain, collective, heaped, heightening, increasing, increscent, intensifying, magnifying, multiplying, snowballing*, summative; SEE CONCEPTS 540,548,786

cunning [adj1] *devious*
acute, artful, astute, cagey, canny, crafty, crazy like fox*, deep, fancy footwork*, foxy, guileful, insidious, keen, knowing, Machiavellian, sharp, shifty, shrewd, slick, slippery, sly, sly boots*, smart, smarts, smooth, street-smart*, streetwise*, subtle, tricky, wary, wily; SEE CONCEPTS 401,545

cunning [adj2] *imaginative*
able, adroit, canny, clever, crackerjack*, deft, dexterous, ingenious, intelligent, masterful, skillful, slighty, sly, smart, smooth, subtle, well-laid, well-planned; SEE CONCEPT 402

cup [n] *container for drinking*
beaker, bowl, cannikin, chalice, cupful, demitasse, draught, drink, goblet, grail, mug, potion, stein, taster, teacup, tumbler, vessel; SEE CONCEPT 494

cupboard [n] *storage cabinet*
buffet, closet, depository, facility, locker, press, repository, sideboard, storeroom, wardrobe; SEE CONCEPT 443

cupidity [n] *greed, strong desire*
acquisitiveness, avarice, avariciousness, avidity, covetousness, craving, eagerness, graspingness, greediness, hunger, infatuation, itching*, longing, lust, passion, possessiveness, rapaciousness, rapacity, voracity, yearning; SEE CONCEPTS 20,709

cur [n1] *rotten, lowly animate being*
blackguard, black sheep*, bum, cad, coward, dog*, good-for-nothing*, heel*, hound*, ne'er-do-well*, rat*, riffraff*, scoundrel, scum*, skunk*, snake*, stinker*, toad*, villain, worm*, wretch, yellow dog*; SEE CONCEPTS 389,412

cur [n2] *animal of mixed breed*
crossbreed, hybrid, mongrel, mutt; SEE CONCEPT 394

curable [adj] *able to be improved, fixed*
amenable, capable, correctable, corrigible, healable, improvable, mendable, not hopeless, not too bad, reparative, restorable, subject to cure; SEE CONCEPTS 314,485

curative [adj] *healing, health-giving*
alleviative, beneficial, corrective, curing, healthful, helpful, invigorating, medicable, medicative, medicinal, pick-me-up*, remedial, remedying, restorative, salutary, sanative, shot in the arm*, therapeutic, tonic, vulnerary, what the doctor ordered*, wholesome; SEE CONCEPTS 314,537

curator [n] *caretaker of collection*
administrator, conservator, custodian, director, guardian, keeper, manager, steward; SEE CONCEPT 348

curb [n] *restraining device; check*
barrier, border, brake, bridle, chain, control, deterrent, edge, harness, hindrance, ledge, limitation, lip, rein, restrainer, restraint, restriction, rim; SEE CONCEPTS 376,497,652,745

curb [v] *repress, restrict*
abstain, bit, bottle up*, box in bridle, bring to screeching halt*, check, clog, constrain, contain, control, cook*, cool down, cool off, deny, entrammel, fetter, hamper, hinder, hobble, hogtie*, hold back, hold down, hold in, ice*, impede, inhibit, keep lid on*, keep tight rein on*, leash, manacle, moderate, muzzle, refrain, rein in, restrain, retard, scrub*, send up, shackle, subdue, suppress, tame, tie, tie up, withhold; SEE CONCEPTS 121,130

curdle [n] *sour; change into coagulated substance*
acerbate, acidify, acidulate, clabber, clot, coagulate, condense, congeal, curd, ferment, go off, spoil, thicken, turn, turn sour; SEE CONCEPT 456

cure [n] *solution to problem, often health*
aid, alleviation, antidote, assistance, catholicon, corrective, counteractant, counteragent, countermeasure, drug, elixir, elixir vitae, fix, healing, healing agent, help, medicament, medicant, medication, medicine, nostrum, panacea, pharmacon, physic, placebo, proprietary, quick fix*, recovery, redress, remedy, reparation, restorative, therapeutic, treatment; SEE CONCEPTS 110,307,311

cure [*v1*] *heal, ease bad situation*
alleviate, ameliorate, attend, better, cold turkey*, correct, doctor, dose, dress, dry out*, help, improve, kick, kick the habit*, make better, make healthy, make whole, medicate, mend, minister to, nurse, palliate, quit cold*, rectify, redress, rehabilitate, relieve, remedy, repair, restore, restore to health, right, shake, sweat it out*, treat; SEE CONCEPTS 126,244,310

cure [*v2*] *cook, age food*
dry, fire, harden, keep, kipper, pickle, preserve, salt, smoke, steel, temper; SEE CONCEPT 170

curio [*n*] *knickknack*
antique, bauble, bibelot, bygone, collectible, collector's item, objet d'art, toy, trifle, trinket, whatnot; SEE CONCEPT 446

curiosity [*n1*] *intense desire to know, understand*
concern, eagerness, inquiring mind, inquiringness, inquisitiveness, interest, interestingness, intrusiveness, investigation, meddlesomeness, meddling, mental acquisitiveness, nosiness, officiousness, prying, questioning, regard, searching, snoopiness, snooping, thirst for knowledge; SEE CONCEPTS 20,410

curiosity [*n2*] *odd item*
anomaly, bibelot, bygone, conversation piece, curio, exoticism, freak, knickknack, marvel, monstrosity, nonesuch, objet d'art, oddity, peculiar object, prodigy, rarity, singular object, trinket, unusual object, wonder; SEE CONCEPT 260

curious [*adj1*] *desiring knowledge, understanding*
analytical, disquisitive, examining, impertinent, inquiring, inquisitive, inspecting, interested, interfering, intrusive, investigative, meddlesome, meddling, nosy, peeping, peering, prurient, prying, puzzled, questioning, scrutinizing, searching, snoopy*, tampering; SEE CONCEPTS 403,542

curious [*adj2*] *very odd*
bizarre, exotic, extraordinary, marvelous, mysterious, novel, oddball, peculiar, puzzling, quaint, queer, rare, remarkable, singular, strange, unconventional, unexpected, unique, unorthodox, unusual, weird, wonderful; SEE CONCEPTS 547,564

curl [*n*] *loop, ringlet, curve*
coil, crimp, crispation, curlicue, flourish, frizz, kink, quirk, spiral, swirl, twist, wave, whorl; SEE CONCEPTS 418,436

curl [*v*] *bend, loop*
buckle, coil, contort, convolute, corkscrew, crimp, crinkle, crisp, crook, curve, entwine, fold, form into ringlets, frizz, indent, kink, lap, meander, ringlet, ripple, roll, scallop, snake, spiral, swirl, turn, twine, twirl, twist, undulate, wave, wind, wreathe, writhe, zigzag; SEE CONCEPTS 147,184,213

curly [*adj*] *looping, forming ringlets*
coiled, convoluted, corkscrew, crimped, crimpy, crinkling, crinkly, crisp, curled, curling, frizzed, frizzy, fuzzy, kinky, looped, permed, spiralled, waved, waving, wavy, winding, wound; SEE CONCEPTS 406,486

currency [*n*] *paper and coin money of a country*
almighty dollar*, bills, bread*, cabbage*, cash, chicken feed*, coinage, coins, cold cash*, dinero*, dough*, folding money, green stuff*, legal tender, medium of exchange, moolah*, notes, piece of change*, roll*, specie, wad*; SEE CONCEPT 340

current [*adj*] *contemporary; common*
accepted, accustomed, afoot, circulating, common knowledge, customary, cutting-edge*, doing, existent, extant, fad, fashionable, general, going around, hot*, in, in circulation, in progress, instant, in the mainstream, in the news, in use, in vogue, leading-edge*, mod*, modern, now*, on front burner*, ongoing, popular, present, present-day, prevailing, prevalent, rampant, regnant, rife, ruling, state-of-the-art, swinging, topical, trendy, up-to-date, widespread; SEE CONCEPTS 530,820

current [*n*] *flow of something, usually water*
course, draught, drift, ebb and flow, flood, flux, jet, juice, progression, river, run, rush, spate, stream, tidal motion, tide; SEE CONCEPTS 514,519,738

curse [*n1*] *hateful, swearing remark*
anathema, ban, bane, blaspheming, blasphemy, commination, cursing, cussing*, cuss word*, damning, denunciation, dirty name*, dirty word*, double whammy*, execration, expletive, four-letter word*, fulmination, imprecation, malediction, malison, naughty words*, no-no*, oath, objuration, obloquy, obscenity, profanation, profanity, sacrilege, swearing, swear word, vilification, whammy*; SEE CONCEPTS 54,278

curse [*n2*] *misfortune wished upon someone*
affliction, bane, burden, calamity, cancer, cross, disaster, evil, evil eye*, hydra, jinx, ordeal, pestilence, plague, scourge, torment, tribulation, trouble, vexation, voodoo; SEE CONCEPTS 674,675

cursed [*adj1*] *damned, doomed for bad ending*
accursed, bedeviled, blankety-blank*, blasted, blessed, blighted, cast out, confounded, doggone*, excommunicate, execrable, fey, foredoomed, hell fire*, ill-fated, infernal, snakebit*, star-crossed, unholy, unsanctified, villainous, voodooed*; SEE CONCEPTS 548,571

cursed [*adj2*] *detestable, hateful*
abominable, accursed, atrocious, damnable, devilish, disgusting, execrable, fiendish, flatitous, heinous, infamous, infernal, loathsome, odious, pernicious, pestilential, vile; SEE CONCEPTS 404,571

cursory [*adj*] *casual, hasty*
brief, careless, depthless, desultory, fast, half-assed*, half-baked*, haphazard, hit or miss*, hurried, offhand, passing, perfunctory, quick, random, rapid, shallow, short, sketchy, slapdash, slight, sloppy, speedy, summary, superficial, swift, uncritical; SEE CONCEPTS 562,588,589

curt [*adj*] *abrupt, rude*
blunt, breviloquent, brief, brusque, churlish, compendiary, compendious, concise, crusty, gruff, imperious, laconic, offhand, peremptory, pithy, sharp, short, short and sweet, snappish, snippety, snippy, succinct, summary, tart, terse, unceremonious, uncivil, ungracious; SEE CONCEPT 267

curtail [*v*] *cut short; abridge*
abbreviate, boil down, chop, clip, contract, cramp, cut, cut back, decrease, diminish, dock, downsize, get to meat*, halt, lessen, lop, minify, pare down, put in nutshell*, reduce, retrench, roll back, shorten, slash, trim, truncate; SEE CONCEPTS 130,236,247

curtain [*n*] *window covering*
blind, decoration, drape, drapery, film, hanging,

jalousie, oleo, portiere, rag, roller, screen, shade, shield, shroud, shutter, valance, veil, Venetian blind; SEE CONCEPT 444

curtains [n] *the end*
bitter end, death, end of life, end of the line*, exit, extinction, lights out*, taps*; SEE CONCEPTS 195,304

curvaceous [adj] *voluptuous, full-figured*
bosomy, buxom, curvesome, curvilinear, curvy, rounded, shapely, statuesque, well-developed, well-proportioned, well-rounded, zaftig*; SEE CONCEPTS 406,490

curvature [n] *rounded part of thing, usually body part*
arc, arch, arching, bend, bow, curve, curving, curvity, deflection, flexure, incurvation, round, shape; SEE CONCEPTS 754,757

curve [n] *arched, rounded line or object*
ambit, arc, arch, bend, bight, bow, camber, catenary, chord, circle, circuit, circumference, compass, concavity, contour, crook, curlicue, curvation, curvature, ellipse, festoon, flexure, hairpin, half-moon, helix, horseshoe, hyperbola, incurvation, incurvature, loop, meniscus, ogee, parabola, quirk, rondure, round, sinuosity, sweep, swerve, trajectory, turn, vault, whorl; SEE CONCEPT 436

curve [v] *bending in a shape or course*
arc, arch, bend, bow, buckle, bulge, coil, concave, convex, crook, crumple, curl, deviate, divert, gyrate, hook, incurve, inflect, loop, round, skew, snake, spiral, stoop, swerve, turn, twist, veer, wind, wreathe; SEE CONCEPTS 147,184,213,738

curved [adj] *bowed, bent*
arced, arched, arciform, arrondi, biflected, circular, compass, crooked, curly, curvaceous, curvilinear, declinate, elliptical, enbowed, humped, incurvate, incurved, looped, loopy, round, rounded, serpentine, sigmoid, sinuous, skewed, snaky, S-shaped, sweeping, swirly, turned, twisted, twisting, twisty; SEE CONCEPTS 486,490

cushion [n] *pillow, pad*
beanbag, bolster, buffer, bumper, fender, hassock, headrest, mat, rest, seat, sham, squab, woolsack; SEE CONCEPTS 444,464,484

cushion [v] *pad, protect from blow*
bolster, buttress, cradle, dampen, deaden, insulate, muffle, pillow, seclude, soften, stifle, support, suppress; SEE CONCEPT 680

cushy [adj] *lush, comfortable*
agreeable, comfy*, easy, pleasant, plum, soft*, undemanding; SEE CONCEPT 334

custodian [n] *caretaker, maintenance person*
baby sitter, bodyguard, cerebus, claviger, cleaner, cleaning person, concierge, curator, escort, guardian, housesitter, keeper, maintenance person, manager, overseer, protector, sitter, steward, super*, superintendent, supervisor, swamper*, warden, watchdog, watchperson; SEE CONCEPT 348

custody [n1] *supervision, charge of something*
aegis, auspices, care, conservation, custodianship, guardianship, keeping, management, observation, preservation, protection, safekeeping, salvation, superintendence, trusteeship, tutelage, ward, wardship, watch; SEE CONCEPTS 117,376,710

custody [n2] *confinement, jailing*
arrest, detention, duress, imprisonment, incarceration, jail, keeping; SEE CONCEPTS 90,691

custom [n1] *habitual action*
addiction, beaten path*, characteristic, consuetude, daily grind*, fashion, form, grind*, groove, habit, habitude, hang-up*, into*, manner, matter of course, mode, observance, practice, praxis, precedent, procedure, proprieties, routine, rule, second nature*, shot, swim, thing, trick, usage, use, way, wont; SEE CONCEPT 633

custom [n2] *ritual, traditional action*
attitude, canon, ceremony, character, convention, conventionalism, design, dictates, established way, etiquette, fashion, folkways, form, formality, inheritance, manner, matter of course, method, mode, mold, mores, observance, observation, pattern, performance, policy, practice, praxis, precedent, precept, rite, routine, rule, second nature*, style, system, taste, type, unwritten law, unwritten rule, usage, use, vogue, way; SEE CONCEPTS 644,688

customarily [adv] *ordinarily; as a rule*
as a matter of course, as usual, commonly, consistently, conventionally, frequently, generally, habitually, naturally, normally, regularly, routinely, traditionally, usually, wontedly; SEE CONCEPTS 530,547

customary [adj] *usual, established*
accepted, according to Hoyle*, accustomed, acknowledged, by the numbers*, chronic, common, confirmed, conventional, established, everyday, familiar, fashionable, frequent, general, habitual, household, in a rut*, in the groove*, normal, ordinary, orthodox, playing it safe*, popular, prescriptive, recognized, regular, regulation, routine, same old*, SOP*, standard, standard operating procedure*, stipulated, traditional, understood, universal, wonted; SEE CONCEPTS 530,547

customer [n] *buyer of goods, services*
client, clientele, consumer, habitué, patron, prospect, purchaser, regular shopper; SEE CONCEPT 348

cut [n1] *incision*
carving, chip, chop, cleavage, cleft, dissection, fissure, furrow, gash, graze, groove, intersection, kerf, laceration, mark, nick, nip, notch, opening, passage, penetration, pierce, prick, rabbet, rent, rip, scarification, sculpture, section, shave, slash, slit, slot, snip, stab, stroke, trench, trim, wound; SEE CONCEPT 309

cut [n2] *reduction, diminution*
cutback, decrease, decrement, downsize, economy, fall, lessening, lowering, reduction, saving; SEE CONCEPTS 698,776

cut [n3] *portion of profit*
allotment, allowance, bite, chop*, division, kickback*, lot, member, moiety, part, partage, percentage, piece, quota, section, segment, share, slice; SEE CONCEPT 344

cut [n4] *style, shape of clothing*
configuration, construction, fashion, figure, form, look, mode; SEE CONCEPTS 655,754

cut [n5] *insult*
abuse, hateful remark, indignity, offense; SEE CONCEPT 52

cut [n6] *type, kind*
cast, description, feather, ilk, lot, mold, sort, stamp; SEE CONCEPT 378

CU
CU

cut [*vI*] *sever, chop with sharp instrument; incise*
amputate, behead, bisect, bite, carve, chine, chip, chisel, cleave, clip, crop, curtail, decussate, dice, dispatch, dissect, dissever, divide, facet, fell, flitch, gash, guillotine, hack, hash, hew, hew, intersect, lacerate, lay open, level, lop, lop, massacre, mince, mow, mow, mow, mow down, nick, notch, part, penetrate, perforate, pierce, prune, puncture, quarter, rabbet, raze, reap, rend, rip, rive, saber, saw, scarify, scissor, score, scythe, separate, shave, shear, sickle, skive, slash, slaughter, slay, slice, slit, sliver, snip; SEE CONCEPT 252

cut a deal [*v*] *make a deal*
bargain, barter, bicker, dicker*, do business, hammer out a deal*, negotiate, trade, work out a deal*; SEE CONCEPT 324

cutback [*n*] *decrease*
abatement, belt-tightening, curtailment, decline, decrement, economy, lessening, lowering, reduction, reversal; SEE CONCEPT 698

cute [*adj*] *perky, attractive*
adorable, beautiful, charming, dainty, delightful, pleasant, pretty; SEE CONCEPTS 404,579

cut in [*v*] *interrupt*
break in, butt in*, chisel in*, horn in*, interfere, interpose, intervene, intrude, move in, obtrude; SEE CONCEPT 234

cut off [*vI*] *prevent; interrupt*
block, break in, bring to end, catch, close off, disconnect, discontinue, halt, insulate, intercept, intersect, intervene, intrude, isolate, obstruct, renounce, segregate, separate, sequester, suspend; SEE CONCEPT 234

cut off [*v2*] *disinherit in will*
cut out of will, disown, renounce; SEE CONCEPT 317

cut out [*v*] *excise, remove*
carve, cease, delete, displace, eliminate, exclude, exsect, extirpate, extract, give up, oust, pull out, refrain from, sever, stop, supersede, supplant, usurp; SEE CONCEPT 211

cut out for [*adj*] *adapted*
adequate, competent, designed, equipped, fit, fitted, good for, qualified, suitable, suited; SEE CONCEPT 558

cut short [*v*] *bring to an end; leave unfinished*
abbreviate, abort, abridge, break off, check, diminish, end, finish, halt, hinder, intercept, interrupt, postpone, quit, shorten, stop, terminate; SEE CONCEPTS 121,234

cutthroat [*adj*] *ruthless*
barbarous, bloodthirsty, cruel, dog-eat-dog*, ferocious, hard as nails*, merciless, pitiless, relentless, savage, unprincipled, vicious; SEE CONCEPTS 401,404

cutting [*adj*] *nasty, hateful*
acerbic, acid, acrimonious, barbed, biting, bitter, caustic, clear-cut, crisp, hurtful, incisive, ingoing, malicious, penetrating, piercing, pointed, probing, raw, sarcastic, sardonic, scathing, severe, sharp, stinging, trenchant, wounding; SEE CONCEPT 267

cutting edge [*n*] *newest technology*
advancement, avant-garde, fore, forefront, front line, innovation, invention, leading edge, new wave, point, vanguard; SEE CONCEPT 668

cut up [*vI*] *make fun of; criticize*
censure, condemn, crucify, denounce, give a rough time*, knock, pan*, rap, reprehend, reprobate, ridicule, skin, vilify; SEE CONCEPT 52

cut up [*v2*] *be rowdy*
act up, caper, carry on*, cavort, clown, fool around, joke, misbehave, play, play jokes, romp, roughhouse, show off, whoop it up*; SEE CONCEPT 384

cut up [*v3*] *chop, mince*
carve, dice, divide, slice; SEE CONCEPT 176

cybernetics [*n*] *science studying brain function to design analagous mechanical systems*
artificial intelligence, automatic technology, automation, autonetics, electronic communication, radiodynamics, robotization, telemechanics; SEE CONCEPTS 274,349

cyberpunk [*n*] *computer hacker*
computer nerd, engineer, geek, hacker, programmer; SEE CONCEPT 348

cyberspace [*n*] *computer world*
communications, computer network, data bank, data network, electronic highway, electronic mail, email, global village, infobahn*, information space, information superhighway*, inforrnation technology, Internet, online community, virtual community, virtual library, virtual reality, Web, World Wide Web, WWW; SEE CONCEPTS 349,770

cycle [*n*] *era, phase*
aeon, age, alternation, chain, circle, circuit, course, eon, isochronism, loop, orbit, period, periodicity, revolution, rhythm, ring, rotation, round, run, sequel, sequence, series, succession, wheel; SEE CONCEPTS 816,817

cynic [*n*] *nonbeliever*
carper, caviler, detractor, disbeliever, doubter, doubting Thomas*, egoist, egotist, flouter, misanthrope, misanthropist, misogamist, misogynist, mocker, pessimist, questioner, satirist, scoffer, skeptic, sneerer, unbeliever; SEE CONCEPTS 361,423

cynical [*adj*] *nonbelieving; doubtful*
contemptuous, derisive, ironic, misanthropic, misanthropical, mocking, pessimistic, sarcastic, sardonic, scoffing, scornful, skeptical, sneering, suspicious, unbelieving, wry; SEE CONCEPTS 267,403

cyst [*n*] *unusual growth*
bag, bleb, blister, injury, pouch, sac, sore, vesicle, wen; SEE CONCEPTS 306

D

dab [*n*] *small quantity*
bit, blob, dollop, drop, fleck, flick, pat, peck, smidgen, smudge, speck, spot, stroke, tap, touch; SEE CONCEPT 835

dab [*v*] *blot up; touch lightly*
bedaub, besmear, daub, pat, peck, plaster, smear, smudge, stipple, swab, tap, wipe; SEE CONCEPT 612

dabble [*v*] *play at; tinker*
amuse oneself with, be amateur, dally, dilly-dally*, fiddle with*, flirt with*, horse around*, idle, kid around*, mess around*, monkey*, monkey around*, muck around*, not be serious*,

play, play around*, play games with, toy with, trifle, trifle with, work superficially; SEE CONCEPT 87

dabbler [n] *amateur*
abecedarian, beginner, dilettante, loafer, nonprofessional, novice, potterer, pretender, smatterer, tinkerer, trifler, tyro, uninitiate; SEE CONCEPTS 348,366

dad [n] *father*
daddy*, old man*, pa*, papa*, pappy*, parent, pop; SEE CONCEPTS 394,400,414,419,423

daffy [adj] *silly, crazy*
clownish, crackers*, daft, demented, deranged, dotty, foolish, goofy* loony*, nuts, nutty*; SEE CONCEPT 403

daft [adj] *stupid; crazy*
absurd, asinine, bedlamite, bonkers, cracked*, crackers*, daffy*, demented, deranged, dopey*, flaky*, foolish, fried*, giddy, half-baked*, idiotic, inane, insane, in the ozone*, lunatic, mad, mental*, nuts, nutty*, off the wall*, out of one's gourd*, ridiculous, screwy*, silly, simple, touched, unbalanced, unhinged*, unsound, wacky, whacko*, witless; SEE CONCEPT 403

dagger [n] *knife*
anlace, bayonet, blade, bodkin, cutlass, dirk, poniard, sidearm, skean, stiletto, stylet, switchblade, sword; SEE CONCEPTS 495,499

daily [adj] *occurring every day; during the day*
circadian, common, commonplace, constantly, cyclic, day after day, day by day, day-to-day, diurnal, everyday, from day to day, often, once a day, once daily, ordinary, per diem, periodic, quotidian, regular, regularly, routine; SEE CONCEPTS 541,801

dainty [adj1] *delicate, fragile, fine*
airy, attractive, beautiful, bonny, charming, choice, comely, cute, darling, delectable, delicious, delightful, diaphanous, elegant, ethereal, exquisite, fair, feeble, frail, graceful, lacy, light, lovely, neat, nice, palatable, petite, pleasing, precious, pretty, rare, recherché, refined, savory, select, soft, subtle, superior, sweet, tasteful, tasty, tender, thin, toothsome, trim, well-made; SEE CONCEPTS 490,491,606

dainty [adj2] *finicky, particular*
acute, choosy, delicate, fastidious, finical, finicking, fussy, mincing, nice, perceptive, persnickety*, refined, scrupulous, tasteful; SEE CONCEPT 404

dairy [n] *producer of milk products*
buttery, cow barn, creamery, dairy farm, factory, farm, pasteurizing plant; SEE CONCEPTS 449,517

dalliance [n1] *dawdling*
dabbling, delay, delaying, dilly-dallying*, frittering, frivoling, idling, loafing, loitering, playing, poking*, procrastinating, procrastination, puttering, toying, trifling; SEE CONCEPTS 151,210,681

dalliance [n2] *love affair*
affair, a little on the side*, amorous play, carrying on*, fling, fooling around*, frolicking, hanky-panky*, messing around*, relationship, seduction, toying*, working late at office*; SEE CONCEPTS 114,375,388

dally [v1] *dawdle, delay*
boondoggle*, drag, fool around, fool with, fritter away, hang about*, horse around*, idle, jerk off*, lag, linger, loiter, lollygag*, play around*, play games with*, procrastinate, put off, putter,

tarry, trail, trifle with, waste time, while away; SEE CONCEPTS 151,210,681

dally/dally with [v2] *have love affair*
be insincere with, carry on, cosset, fool around*, frivol, frolic, gambol, have a fling, lead on, play around*, rollick, romp, tamper, wanton; SEE CONCEPTS 114,375

dam [n] *embankment, wall*
bank, barrage, barrier, dike, ditch, gate, grade, hindrance, levee, milldam, millpond, obstruction, weir; SEE CONCEPT 470

dam [v] *hold back; block*
bar, barricade, brake, check, choke, clog, close, confine, hinder, hold in, impede, obstruct, repress, restrain, restrict, retard, slow, stop up, suppress; SEE CONCEPTS 130,191

damage [n1] *injury, loss*
accident, adulteration, adversity, affliction, bane, blemish, blow, breakage, bruise, casualty, catastrophe, cave-in, contamination, corruption, debasement, depreciation, deprivation, destruction, deterioration, detriment, devastation, disservice, disturbance, evil, hardship, harm, hurt, illness, impairment, infliction, knockout, marring, mischief, mishap, mutilation, outrage, pollution, ravage, reverse, ruin, ruining, spoilage, stroke, suffering, waste, wound, wreckage, wrecking, wrong; SEE CONCEPTS 309,674

damage [v] *cause injury, loss*
abuse, bang up*, batter, bleach, blight, break, burn, contaminate, corrode, corrupt, crack, cripple, deface, defile, dirty, discolor, disfigure, disintegrate, dismantle, fade, gnaw, harm, hurt, impair, incapacitate, infect, injure, lacerate, maim, maltreat, mangle, mar, mutilate, pollute, ravage, rot, ruin, rust, scathe, scorch, scratch, smash, split, spoil, stab, stain, tamper with, tarnish, tear, undermine, vitiate, weaken, wear away, wound, wreak havoc on*, wreck, wrong; SEE CONCEPTS 246,252

damaged [adj] *broken, not working*
beat-up, bent, blemished, busted, dinged, down, flawed, flubbed*, fouled up, glitched*, gone, hurt, impaired, imperfect, injured, in need of repair, in poor condition, in smithereens*, kaput*, loused up*, marred, messed up*, mucked up*, no go*, on the blink*, on the fritz*, out of action*, out of kilter*, out of whack*, run-down, screwed up*, shot, snafued*, spoiled, sunk*, totaled*, unsound; SEE CONCEPTS 485,560

damage(s) [n2] *cost for problem*
amends, bill, charge, compensation, expense, fine, forfeit, indemnity, reimbursement, reparation, satisfaction, total; SEE CONCEPTS 123,329

damaging [adj] *hurtful to reputation*
bad, deleterious, detrimental, disadvantageous, evil, harmful, injurious, mischievous, nocent, nocuous, prejudicial, ruinous; SEE CONCEPT 537

damn [v] *condemn, denounce*
abuse, anathematize, attack, ban, banish, blaspheme, blast, castigate, cast out, censure, complain of, confound, convict, criticize, cry down, curse, cuss*, darn, denunciate, doom, drat, excommunicate, excoriate, execrate, expel, flame, fulminate against, imprecate, inveigle against, jinx, object to, objurgate, pan*, penalize, proscribe, punish, revile, sentence, slam, swear, thunder against*; SEE CONCEPTS 52,54

damnable [adj] *atrocious, horrible*
abhorrent, abominable, accursed, blamed,

cu da

blessed, culpable, cursed, dang*, darn, depraved, despicable, detestable, dratted, execrable, hateful, odious, offensive, outrageous, wicked; SEE CONCEPTS 545,570

damnation [n] *everlasting punishment*
condemnation, doom, hell, perdition, suffering, torment; SEE CONCEPT 679

damned [adj] *hateful, unwelcome*
accursed, all-fired*, anathematized, bad, blankety-blank*, blasted, blessed*, bloody*, blooming*, condemned, confounded, cursed, cussed*, damnable, dang*, darn*, darned*, despicable, detestable, doggone*, done for*, doomed, dratted*, execrable, gone to blazes*, infamous, infernal*, loathsome, lost, lousy, reprobate, revolting, unhappy, voodooed*; SEE CONCEPTS 545,570

damp [adj] *wet, humid*
clammy, cloudy, dank, dewy, drenched, dripping, drippy, drizzly, irriguous, misty, moist, muggy, oozy, saturated, soaked, soaking, sodden, soggy, sopping, steam bath*, steamy, sticky, vaporous, waterlogged, wettish; SEE CONCEPT 603

dampen [v1] *make wet*
bedew, besprinkle, dabble, humidify, moisten, rinse, spray, sprinkle, water, wet; SEE CONCEPT 256

dampen [v2] *spoil spirits*
allay, check, chill, cloud, cool, curb, dash, deaden, deject, depress, diminish, discourage, dismay, dispirit, dull, humble, inhibit, moderate, muffle, mute, restrain, stifle; SEE CONCEPTS 7,19

damsel [n] *maiden*
colleen, lady, lass, lassie, miss, virgin, woman, young girl, young woman; SEE CONCEPTS 414,415

dance [n1/v] *moving feet and body to music*
bob*, boogie, boogie down*, bunny hop, caper, careen, cavort, Charleston, conga, cut a rug*, disco, flit*, foot it*, foxtrot, frolic, gambol, get down*, hoof it*, hop, hustle, jig, jitter*, jitterbug, jive*, jump, leap, one-step, prance, promenade, rhumba, rock, rock 'n' roll, samba, shimmy, skip, spin, step, strut, sway, swing, tango, tap, tread, trip, trip the light fantastic*, twist, two-step, waltz, whirl; SEE CONCEPTS 292,363

dance [n2] *party for moving to music*
ball, brawl, disco, formal, hoedown, hop, jump, masquerade, mingle, prom, promenade, shindig, social, sock hop; SEE CONCEPT 383

dancer [n] *ballerina*
ballet dancer, belly-dancer, chorus girl, coryphee, danseur, danseuse, go-go dancer, hoofer*, line-dancer, prima ballerina, show girl, tap-dancer; SEE CONCEPT 352

dandle [v] *caress, cuddle*
amuse, cosset, coddle, dance, fondle, love, nuzzle, pet, play, ride on knee, rock, sport, toss, toy*, toy with*; SEE CONCEPTS 147,190

dandruff [n] *scurf*
flakes, seborrhea; SEE CONCEPT 831

dandy [adj] *fine, excellent*
capital, cool*, exemplary, famous, first-class, first-rate, five-star*, fly*, glorious, grand, great, groovy*, hunky-dory*, keen, marvelous, model, neat, nifty, paragon, peachy*, prime, splendid, superior, swell, terrific; SEE CONCEPT 574

danger [n] *hazard, troublesome situation*
clouds, crisis, double trouble*, dynamite, emergency, endangerment, exigency, exposure, hot potato*, insecurity, instability, jeopardy, menace, peril, pitfall, possibility, precariousness, precipice, probability, risk, risky business*, slipperiness, storm, thin ice*, threat, uncertainty, venture, vulnerability; SEE CONCEPT 675

dangerous [adj] *hazardous, troubling*
alarming, bad, breakneck*, chancy, critical, dangersome, deadly, delicate, dynamite, exposed, fatal, formidable, hairy*, heavy*, hot*, impending, impregnable, insecure, jeopardous, loaded, malignant, menacing, mortal, nasty, on collision course*, parlous, perilous, portentous, precarious, pressing, queasy, risky, serious, serpentine, shaky, speculative, terrible, thorny*, threatening, ticklish*, touch-and-go*, touchy, treacherous, ugly*, unhealthy, unsafe, unstable, urgent, viperous, vulnerable, wicked; SEE CONCEPT 548

dangerously [adv] *precariously*
alarmingly, carelessly, critically, daringly, desperately, gravely, harmfully, hazardously, perilously, precariously, recklessly, riskily, seriously, severely, unsafely, unsecurely; SEE CONCEPT 548

dangle [v] *suspend*
brandish, depend, droop, entice, flap, flaunt, flourish, hang, hang down, lure, sling, sway, swing, tantalize, tempt, trail, wave; SEE CONCEPTS 153,190

dank [adj] *clammy*
chilly, close, damp, dewy, dripping, humid, moist, muggy, slimy, soggy, steamy, sticky, wet, wettish; SEE CONCEPT 603

dapper [adj] *well-groomed, neat*
bandbox, brisk, chic, chichi, classy, clean, dainty, dashing, doggy*, dressed to kill*, dressed to nines*, jaunty, natty, nice, nifty, nimble, nobby, posh, prim, rakish, ritzy, sassy, sharp, showy, smart, snazzy*, snug, spiff, spiffy, spruce, spry, stylish, swank, swanky, swell, trim, turned out, well turned out; SEE CONCEPT 579

dappled [adj] *mottled, freckled*
brindle, brindled, checkered, discolored, flecked, motley, multicolor, multicolored, multihued, parti-colored, piebald, pied, speckled, spotted, stippled, varicolored, variegated, versicolor, versicolored; SEE CONCEPT 618

dare [n] *challenge, defiance*
cartel, defy, provocation, stump, taunt; SEE CONCEPTS 53,87

dare [v1] *challenge, defy someone*
beard, brave, bully, call one's bluff, confront, cope, denounce, disregard, face, face off, front, goad, insult, knock chip off shoulder*, laugh at, make my day*, meet, mock, muster courage, oppose, outdare, provoke, resist, run the gauntlet, scorn, spurn, square off, step over the line, take one on, taunt, threaten, throw down gauntlet; SEE CONCEPTS 14,53

dare [v2] *take a risk; be courageous*
adventure, attempt, be bold, brave, endanger, endeavor, gamble, go ahead, hazard, make bold, pluck up, presume, risk, run the risk, speculate, stake, take a chance, take heart, try, try one's hand*, undertake, venture; SEE CONCEPTS 35,87

daredevil [n] *thrill-seeker*
adventurer, hotdog*, madcap, risk-taker, showoff, stuntman, stuntperson, stuntwoman; SEE CONCEPT 423

daring [*adj*] *adventurous*

adventuresome, audacious, bold, brassy*, brave, cheeky, cocky, courageous, crusty, fearless, fire eating*, foolhardy, forward, game, go for broke*, gritty, gutsy*, gutty*, hot shot*, impudent, impulsive, intrepid, nervy, obtrusive, out on a limb*, plucky, rash, reckless, salty*, smart, smart-alecky*, spunky*, temerarious, valiant, venturesome; SEE CONCEPT 401

dark [*adj1*] *lack of light*

aphotic, atramentous, black, blackish, caliginous, Cimmerian, clouded, cloudy, crepuscular, darkened, dim, dingy, drab, dull, dun, dusk, dusky, faint, foggy, gloomy, grimy, ill-lighted, indistinct, inky, lightless, lurid, misty, murky, nebulous, obfuscous, obscure, opaque, overcast, pitch-black, pitch-dark, pitchy, rayless, shaded, shadowy, shady, somber, sooty, stygian, sunless, tenebrous, unlighted, unlit, vague; SEE CONCEPT 617

dark [*adj2*] *shaded complexion, hair*

adumbral, bistered, black, brunet, brunette, dark-complexioned, dark-skinned, dusky, ebon, ebony, sable, swart, swarthy, tan; SEE CONCEPTS 406,618

dark [*adj3*] *hidden, secret*

abstruse, anagogic, arcane, cabalistic, complicated, concealed, cryptic, deep, Delphian, enigmatic, esoteric, intricate, knotty, mysterious, mystic, mystical, mystifying, not known, obscure, occult, puzzling, recondite; SEE CONCEPTS 402,576,582

dark [*adj4*] *grim, hopeless*

bleak, cheerless, dismal, doleful, drab, foreboding, gloomy, joyless, morbid, morose, mournful, ominous, sinister, somber, unpropitious; SEE CONCEPT 548

dark [*adj5*] *evil, satanic*

atrocious, bad, corrupt, damnable, foul, hellish, horrible, immoral, infamous, infernal, nefarious, sinful, sinister, vile, wicked; SEE CONCEPT 545

dark [*adj6*] *ignorant*

benighted, uncultivated, unenlightened, unlettered, unread; SEE CONCEPT 402

dark [*adj7*] *angry, upset*

dour, forbidding, frowning, glowering, glum, ominous, scowling, sulky, sullen, threatening; SEE CONCEPT 401

dark [*n1*] *place, time without light*

caliginosity, darkness, dead of night, dimness, dusk, duskiness, evening, gloom, midnight, murk, murkiness, night, nightfall, nighttime, obscurity, opacity, semidarkness, shade, shadows, twilight, witching hour; SEE CONCEPTS 620,810

dark [*n2*] *ignorance; mystery*

concealment, denseness, inscrutability, seclusion, secrecy, thickness; SEE CONCEPTS 409,410

darken [*v*] *become shaded, unlit*

becloud, bedim, blacken, cloud over, cloud up, deepen, dim, eclipse, fog, gray, haze, make dim, murk, obfuscate, obscure, overcast, overshadow, shade, shadow, tone down*; SEE CONCEPTS 250,469

dark horse [*n*] *long shot*

hundred-to-one shot, improbability, outside chance, sleeper, small chance, underdog, unexpected winner*, unknown, unlikelihood, unlikely winner; SEE CONCEPTS 366,423

darkness [*n1*] *place, time that is unlit*

black, blackness, blackout, brownout, calignos-

ity, Cimmerian shade, cloudiness, crepuscule, dark, dimness, dusk, duskiness, eclipse, gloom, lightlessness, murk, murkiness, nightfall, obscurity, pitch darkness, shade, shadiness, shadows, smokiness, tenebrosity, twilight; SEE CONCEPT 620

darkness [*n2*] *ignorance; mystery*

blindness, concealment, denseness, inscrutability, isolation, privacy, seclusion, secrecy, unawareness; SEE CONCEPTS 409,410

darling [*n*] *sweetheart, favorite person*

angel*, apple of one's eye*, baby*, beloved, boyfriend, dear, dearest, dearie*, dear one, fair-haired boy*, flame, friend, girlfriend, heart's desire*, honeybunch, lamb*, light of my life*, love, lover, one and only*, pet*, precious, sugar*, sweetie, treasure*, truelove; SEE CONCEPT 423

darn [*interj*] *damn*

confound it, cripes, damn it, dang*, darnation, doggone, drat*, gosh-darn; SEE CONCEPTS 52,54

dart [*v*] *race away; propel*

bound, career, cast, course, dash, flash, fling, flit, float, fly, gallop, hasten, heave, hurry, hurtle, launch, move quickly, pitch, plunge, run, rush, sail, scamper, scoot, scud, scurry, shoot, skim, speed, spring, sprint, spurt, start, tear, throw, thrust, whiz; SEE CONCEPTS 150,195,222

dash [*n1*] *fast race for short distance*

birr, bolt, dart, haste, onset, run, rush, sortie, sprint, spurt, zip; SEE CONCEPT 150

dash [*n2*] *flair, style*

animation, birr, brio, éclat, élan, energy, esprit, flourish, force, impressiveness, intensity, life, might, oomph*, panache, power, spirit, strength, vehemence, verve, vigor, vim, vivacity, zing, zip; SEE CONCEPTS 411,655,673

dash [*n3*] *small amount; suggestion*

bit, drop, few drops, flavor, grain, hint, lick, little, part, pinch, scattering, seasoning, smack, smidgen, soupçon, sprinkle, sprinkling, squirt, streak, suspicion, taste, tincture, tinge, touch, trace, trifle, zest; SEE CONCEPT 831

dash [*v1*] *run very fast for short distance*

boil, bolt, bound, career, charge, chase, course, dart, fly, gallop, get on it*, haste, hasten, hurry, lash, make a run for it*, make it snappy*, race, rush, rush at, scamper, scoot, scurry, shoot, speed, spring, sprint, tear; SEE CONCEPT 150

dash [*v2*] *break by hitting or throwing violently*

beat, bludgeon, cast, charge, crash, cudgel, destroy, fling, hit, hurl, hurtle, lunge, plunge, shatter, shiver, slam, sling, smash, splash, splatter, splinter, throw; SEE CONCEPTS 189,222,248

dash [*v3*] *discourage, frustrate*

abash, baffle, balk, beat, bilk, blast, blight, chagrin, chill, circumvent, cloud, confound, dampen, disappoint, discomfort, dismay, dispirit, foil, nip, ruin, spoil, thwart; SEE CONCEPTS 7,19,121

dashboard [*n*] *instrument panel*

control panel, indicator panel, instrument board; SEE CONCEPTS 463,499

dashing [*adj*] *bold, flamboyant*

adventurous, alert, animated, chic, dapper, daring, dazzling, debonair, elegant, exclusive, exuberant, fashionable, fearless, gallant, gay, jaunty, keen, lively, modish, plucky, rousing, showy, smart, spirited, sporty, stylish, swank, swash-

da
da

buckling, swish, vivacious; SEE CONCEPTS *404,589*

dastardly [*adj*] *rotten*
base, contemptible, cowardly, craven, despicable, low, mean, pusillanimous, underhanded, vile; SEE CONCEPTS *404,545,570,571,574*

data [*n*] *information in visible form*
abstracts, brass tacks*, chapter and verse*, circumstances, compilations, conclusions, details, documents, dope, dossier, evidence, experiments, facts, figures, goods, info, input, knowledge, materials, measurements, memorandums, notes, picture, proof, reports, results, scoop, score, statistics, testimony, whole story*; SEE CONCEPT *274*

data bank [*n*] *database*
computerized information, data processing, storage; SEE CONCEPT *274*

data processor [*n*] *computer*
calculator, CPU, laptop, MAC, Macintosh, mainframe, microcomputer, number cruncher, PC, personal computer, word processor; SEE CONCEPTS *269,463*

date [*n1*] *point in time; particular day or time*
age, century, course, day, duration, epoch, era, generation, hour, juncture, moment, period, quarter, reign, span, spell, stage, term, time, while, year; SEE CONCEPTS *800,801,802,815*

date [*n2*] *social engagement*
appointment, assignation, call, interview, meeting, rendezvous, tryst, visit; SEE CONCEPTS *114,386*

date [*n3*] *person accompanying another socially*
blind date, boyfriend, companion, escort, friend, girlfriend, lover, partner, steady, sweetheart; SEE CONCEPT *423*

date [*v1*] *assign a time*
affix a date to, belong to, carbon-date, chronicle, come from, determine, exist from, fix, fix the date of, isolate, mark, measure, originate in, put in its place, record, register; SEE CONCEPTS *18,37*

date [*v2*] *see person socially*
associate with, attend, consort with, court, deuce it*, escort, fix up, go around together*, go around with*, go out with, go steady, go together, keep company, make a date, see, step around, take out, woo; SEE CONCEPT *114*

date [*v3*] *become obsolete*
antiquate, archaize, obsolesce, obsolete, outdate, show one's age; SEE CONCEPT *105*

dated [*adj*] *out-of-date*
antiquated, archaic, behind the times, obsolescent, obsolete, old-fashioned, old hat, outdated, outmoded, out of style, passé, unfashionable; SEE CONCEPTS *530,578,797*

daub [*v*] *coat; make dirty*
begrime, besmear, bespray, blur, cover, dab, deface, dirty, fleck, grime, paint, plaster, slap on, smear, smirch, smudge, spatter, speckle, splatter, spot, spread, stain, sully, variegate, varnish; SEE CONCEPTS *172,250*

daughter [*n*] *female child*
female offspring, girl, offspring, woman; SEE CONCEPTS *415,424*

daunt [*v*] *frighten, alarm*
appall, baffle, browbeat, bully, consternate, cow, deter, discourage, dishearten, dismay, dispirit, foil, horrify, intimidate, overawe, put off*, scare, shake, subdue, terrify, thwart; SEE CONCEPTS *7,19*

dauntless [*adj*] *bold, courageous*
aweless, brave, daring, doughty, fearless, gallant, game, heroic, indomitable, intrepid, invincible, lionhearted, resolute, stouthearted, unafraid, unconquerable, undaunted, unfearing, unflinching, valiant, valorous; SEE CONCEPT *401*

davenport [*n*] *sofa; small desk*
chesterfield, convertible sofa, couch, daybed, futon, secretary, sofa bed, writing desk; SEE CONCEPT *443*

dawdle [*v*] *delay; waste time*
amble, bum around*, dally, diddle-daddle*, dilly-dally*, drag, fool around*, fritter away*, get no place fast*, goof off*, hang around*, hang out*, idle, lag, laze, lazy, loaf, loiter, loll, lounge, mosey*, poke*, procrastinate, put off, saunter, scrounge around, shlep along*, sit around*, sit on one's butt*, stay, stroll, tarry, toddle, trifle, wait, warm a chair*; SEE CONCEPTS *210,681*

dawn [*n1*] *beginning of day*
aurora, break of day, bright, cockcrow, crack of dawn, dawning, daybreak, daylight, day peep, early bright, first blush, first light, light, morn, morning, sunrise, sunup, wee hours*; SEE CONCEPTS *810,815*

dawn [*n2*] *a beginning*
advent, alpha, birth, commencement, dawning, emergence, foundation, genesis, head, inception, onset, opening, origin, outset, outstart, rise, source, start, unfolding; SEE CONCEPT *832*

dawn [*v*] *start*
appear, begin, develop, emerge, glimmer, initiate, lighten, loom, open, originate, rise, show itself, unfold; SEE CONCEPT *119*

day [*n1*] *light part of every 24 hours*
astronomical day, bright, dawn-to-dark, daylight, daytime, diurnal course, early bright, light, light of day, mean solar day, nautical day, sidereal day, sunlight, sunrise-to-sunset, sunshine, working day; SEE CONCEPTS *801,803,810,821*

day [*n2*] *era*
age, ascendancy, cycle, epoch, generation, height, heyday, period, prime, term, time, years, zenith; SEE CONCEPTS *802,816*

daybook [*n*] *journal*
album, datebook, diary, Filofax®, ledger, log, logbook, memo pad, notebook, record, scrapbook; SEE CONCEPTS *280,283*

daybreak [*n*] *beginning of light hours*
aurora, break of day, bright, cockcrow, crack of dawn, dawn, dawning, daylight, day peep, dayspring, early bright, first light, morn, morning, sunrise, sunup; SEE CONCEPTS *810,815*

daycare [*n*] *child care center*
babysitter, kindergarten, nursery school, playgroup, pre-K, pre-school; SEE CONCEPT *295*

daydream [*n*] *fantasy thought of when awake*
castle in the air*, conceiving, dream, fancy, fancying, figment of imagination, fond hope, fool's paradise*, head trip*, imagination, imagining, in a zone*, mind trip*, musing, phantasm, phantasy, pie in the sky*, pipe dream*, reverie, stargazing, trip*, vision, wish, woolgathering; SEE CONCEPT *529*

daydream [*v*] *make up fantasy*
build castles in air*, conceive, dream, envision, fancy, fantasize, hallucinate, imagine, moon, muse, pipe dream*, stargaze, trip out*, woolgather; SEE CONCEPTS *17,36*

daylight [*n*] *light part of 24 hours*
aurora, dawn, day, daybreak, daytime, during the day, light, light of day, sunlight, sunrise, sunshine; SEE CONCEPT 810

daze [*n*] *confusion*
befuddlement, bewilderment, distraction, gauze, glaze, haze, lala-land*, maze, muddledness, nadaville*, narcosis, shock, stupefaction, stupor, trance; SEE CONCEPT 410

daze [*v*] *confuse, shock*
addle, amaze, astonish, astound, befog, befuddle, benumb, bewilder, blind, blur, confound, dazzle, disorder, distract, dizzy, dumbfound, flabbergast, fuddle, mix up, muddle, mystify, numb, overpower, overwhelm, paralyze, perplex, petrify, puzzle, rock, stagger, startle, stun, stupefy, surprise; SEE CONCEPTS 16,42

dazzle [*v*] *confuse, amaze*
astonish, awe, bedazzle, blind, blur, bowl over*, daze, excite, fascinate, glitz*, hypnotize, impress, overawe, overpower, overwhelm, razzle-dazzle, strike dumb*, stupefy, surprise; SEE CONCEPTS 16,42

dazzling [*adj*] *radiant*
beaming, bright, brilliant, flashy, glaring, glittering, ravishing, resplendent, sensational, shining, sparkling, splendid, stunning; SEE CONCEPT 617

deacon [*n*] *clergyperson*
church officer, cleric, elder, priest; SEE CONCEPT 361

deactivate [*v*] *decommission*
demilitarize, disband, make inactive, shut down, shut off; SEE CONCEPTS 25,121,188

dead [*adj1*] *no longer alive*
asleep, bereft of life, bloodless, bought the farm*, breathless, buried, cadaverous, checked out*, cold, cut off, deceased, defunct, departed, done for*, erased, expired, extinct, gone, gone to meet maker*, gone to reward*, inanimate, inert, late, lifeless, liquidated, mortified, no more, not existing, offed*, out of one's misery*, passed away, perished, pushing up daisies*, reposing, resting in peace, spiritless, stiff, unanimated, wasted; SEE CONCEPT 539

dead [*adj2*] *indifferent, cold*
anesthetized, apathetic, asleep, boring, callous, deadened, dull, flat, frigid, glazed, inert, insensitive, insipid, lukewarm, numb, numbed, paralyzed, senseless, spiritless, stagnant, stale, still, tasteless, torpid, unfeeling, uninteresting, unresponsive, vapid, wooden; SEE CONCEPT 550

dead [*adj3*] *not working*
barren, bygone, defunct, departed, exhausted, extinct, gone, inactive, inoperable, inoperative, lost, obsolete, spent, stagnant, sterile, still, tired, unemployed, unprofitable, useless, vanished, wearied, worn, worn out; SEE CONCEPT 560

dead [*adj4*] *complete, total*
absolute, bloody, downright, entire, final, out-and-out*, outright, perfect, sure, thorough, unconditional, unmitigated, unqualified, utter, whole; SEE CONCEPT 531

dead [*adv*] *completely, totally*
absolutely, direct, directly, due, entirely, exactly, right, straight, straightly, undeviatingly, wholly; SEE CONCEPTS 531,772

deadbeat [*n*] *freeloader*
bum, debtor, leech, loafer, moocher, parasite, sponge; SEE CONCEPTS 412,423

deaden [*v*] *diminish, muffle, quiet*
abate, alleviate, anesthetize, benumb, blunt, check, chloroform, consume, cushion, damp, dampen, depress, deprive, desensitize, destroy, devitalize, dim, dope, drown, dull, etherize, exhaust, freeze, frustrate, gas, hush, impair, incapacitate, injure, knock out, KO*, lay out, lessen, mute, numb, paralyze, put out of order*, put to sleep, quieten, reduce, repress, retard, slow, smother, soften, stifle, stun, stupefy, suppress, tire, tone down, unnerve, weaken; SEE CONCEPTS 130,240

dead end [*n*] *cul-de-sac; deadlock*
blank wall, blind alley, Catch-22, corner, draw, impasse, nowhere to turn, obstacle, road block, stalemate, standoff, stumbling block; SEE CONCEPT 674

deadline [*n*] *due date*
bound, cutoff, limit, period, target date, time frame, time limit, zero hour; SEE CONCEPTS 513,745,815,832

deadlock [*n*] *stalemate, impasse*
box*, Catch-22*, cessation, checkmate, corner, dead end, dead heat, dilemma, draw, full stop, gridlock, halt, hole, pause, pickle, plight, posture, predicament, quandary, standoff, standstill, tie, wall*; SEE CONCEPT 674

deadly [*adj1*] *causing end of life*
baleful, baneful, bloodthirsty, bloody, cannibalistic, carcinogenic, cruel, dangerous, death-dealing, deathly, deleterious, destroying, destructive, fatal, grim, harmful, homicidal, injurious, internecine, killing, lethal, malignant, mortal, mortiferous, murderous, noxious, pernicious, pestiferous, pestilent, pestilential, poisonous, ruthless, savage, slaying, suicidal, toxic, unrelenting, venomous, violent, virulent; SEE CONCEPT 537

deadly [*adj2*] *ghostly*
ashen, corpselike, dead, deadened, deathful, deathlike, deathly, ghastly, pallid, wan, white; SEE CONCEPT 539

dead-on [*adj*] *accurate*
by the book, dead-center, definite, direct, exact, on the button*, on the mark*, on the money*, on the nose*, precise, to the point; SEE CONCEPT 535

deadpan [*adj*] *expressionless*
blank, impassive, nobody home*, poker-faced, serious, stony, straight-faced, unreadable, vacant, wooden; SEE CONCEPT 406

deaf [*adj1*] *without hearing*
deafened, earless, hard of hearing, stone deaf*, unable to hear; SEE CONCEPT 591

deaf [*adj2*] *unwilling*
bullheaded*, headstrong, indifferent, intractable, mulish*, oblivious, obstinate, pertinacious, perverse, pigheaded*, self-willed, strong-willed, stubborn, to listen blind, unaware, unconcerned, unhearing, unmoved; SEE CONCEPT 401

deafening [*adj*] *very loud*
at full volume, blaring, booming, ear-piercing*, ear-popping*, ear-splitting*, noisy, ringing, roaring, rowdy, screaming, thunderous, turned up, vociferous; SEE CONCEPTS 592,594

deal [*n1*] *agreement, bargain*
accord, arrangement, buy, compromise, conception, contract, pact, pledge, prearrangement, transaction, understanding; SEE CONCEPT 684

deal [*n2*] *amount, share*
abundance, degree, distribution, extent, plenty,

da
de

plethora, portion, quantity, shake, superabundance, transaction; SEE CONCEPTS 344,787,835

deal [*n3*] *distribution of playing cards*
appointment, chance, cut and shuffle*, fresh start, game, hand, opportunity, round; SEE CONCEPT 363

deal [*v2*] *do business*
bargain, barter, bicker, buy and sell, dicker*, hammer out deal*, handle, horse trade*, knock down price*, negotiate, sell, stock, swap, trade, traffic, treat, work out deal; SEE CONCEPT 324

deal [*v3*] *distribute*
administer, allot, apportion, assign, bestow, come across with*, deliver, disburse, dish out*, dispense, disperse, disseminate, divide, divvy*, dole out*, drop, fork out*, fork over*, give, hand out, impart, inflict, measure, mete out, partake, participate, partition, render, reward, share, strike; SEE CONCEPTS 108,140

deal/deal with [*vt*] *handle, manage*
act, approach, attend to, behave, behave toward, clear, concern, conduct oneself, consider, control, cope with, direct, discuss, get a handle on something*, hack it*, handle, have to do with, live with*, make a go of it*, make it*, oversee, play, review, rid, see to, serve, take, take care of, treat, unburden, use; SEE CONCEPTS 94,117

dealer [*n*] *business owner*
banker, bursar, businessperson, chandler, changer, dispenser, marketer, merchandiser, merchant, retailer, trader, tradesperson, trafficker, vendor, wholesaler; SEE CONCEPT 347

dealings [*n*] *business relations*
affairs, balls in air*, business, commerce, concerns, doings, intercourse, irons in fire*, matters, proceedings, ropes*, sale, strings*, things, trade, traffic, transactions, truck, wire pulling*, wires*; SEE CONCEPT 324

dean [*n*] *leader of institution*
administrator, authority, dignitary, doyen, ecclesiastic, guide, lead, legislator, pilot, president, principal, professor, senior, tack; SEE CONCEPT 350

dear [*adj1*] *beloved, favorite*
cherished, close, darling, doll face, endeared, esteemed, familiar, intimate, loved, pet, precious, prized, respected, treasured; SEE CONCEPTS 555,567

dear [*adj2*] *very expensive*
an arm and a leg*, at a premium, cher*, costly, fancy, high, high-priced, out of sight*, over-priced, pretty penny*, pricey*, prized, steep, stiff*, valuable; SEE CONCEPT 334

dear [*n*] *beloved person*
darling, favorite, heartthrob, honey, love, loved one, lover, pet, precious, sweetheart, treasure; SEE CONCEPT 423

dearly [*adv1*] *extremely*
greatly, profoundly, to a great extent, very, very much; SEE CONCEPT 772

dearly [*adv2*] *lovingly*
affectionately, devotedly, fondly, tenderly, yearningly; SEE CONCEPT 403

dearth [*n*] *insufficiency, scarcity*
absence, default, defect, deficiency, exiguousness, famine, inadequacy, infrequency, lack, meagerness, miss, need, paucity, poverty, privation, rareness, scantiness, scantness, shortage, slim pickings*, sparsity, uncommonness, want; SEE CONCEPTS 646,674,709

death [*n*] *end of life*
afterlife, annihilation, bereavement, casualty, cessation, curtains*, darkness, decease, demise, departure, destruction, dissolution, downfall, dying, end, ending, eradication, eternal rest, euthanasia, exit, expiration, extermination, extinction, fatality, finis*, finish, grave, grim reaper*, heaven, loss, mortality, necrosis, obliteration, oblivion, paradise, parting, passing, passing over, quietus, release, repose, ruin, ruination, silence, sleep, termination, tomb; SEE CONCEPT 304

deathly [*adj1*] *suggesting end of life*
appalling, cadaverous, corpselike, deathlike, defunctive, dreadful, gaunt, ghastly, grim, gruesome, haggard, horrible, macabre, pale, pallid, wan, wasted; SEE CONCEPTS 579,618

deathly [*adj2*] *fatal*
deadly, extreme, intense, lethal, mortal, mortiferous, noxious, pestilent, pestilential, terrible; SEE CONCEPT 537

debacle [*n*] *catastrophe*
beating, blue ruin*, breakdown, collapse, crackup*, crash, defeasance, defeat, devastation, disaster, dissolution, downfall, drubbing, failure, fiasco, havoc, licking, overthrow, reversal, rout, ruin, ruination, shellacking*, smash, smashup, trouncing, vanquishment, washout, wreck; SEE CONCEPT 674

debase [*v1*] *degrade, shame*
abase, bemean, cast down, cheapen, corrupt, cripple, debauch, debilitate, demean, demoralize, deprave, devaluate, devalue, disable, disgrace, dishonor, drag down*, dump on*, enfeeble, fluff off*, humble, humiliate, lower, put away, put down, reduce, sap, shoot down, sink, take down*, take down a peg*, undermine, weaken; SEE CONCEPTS 7,19,52,54

debase [*v2*] *adulterate*
abase, animalize, bastardize, bestialize, contaminate, corrupt, damage, defile, depreciate, doctor, dope up*, impair, load, pervert, pollute, sophisticate, spoil, taint, vitiate, weight, worsen; SEE CONCEPTS 240,250

debatable [*adj*] *controversial*
arguable, between rock and hard place*, between sixes and sevens*, betwixt and between*, bone of contention*, borderline, chancy*, contestable, disputable, doubtful, dubious, iffy*, in dispute, moot, mootable*, open to question, problematic, problematical, questionable, the jury's out*, touch and go*, uncertain, undecided, unsettled, up for discussion; SEE CONCEPTS 267,535

debate [*n*] *discussion of issues; consideration*
agitation, altercation, argument, argumentation, blah-blah*, cogitation, contention, contest, controversy, controverting, deliberation, dialectic, disputation, dispute, forensic, hassle, match, meditation, mooting, polemic, rebutting, reflection, refuting, tiff, words, wrangle; SEE CONCEPTS 56,532

debate [*v*] *argue, discuss*
agitate, altercate, answer, bandy, bicker, bump heads*, canvass, chew the fat*, cogitate, confab*, confute, consider, contend, contest, controvert, cross swords*, deliberate, demonstrate, differ, discept, disprove, dispute, hammer away at*, hash over*, hassle, have at it*, kick around*, knock around*, lock horns*, moot, oppose, pettifog, pick a bone*, prove, put up argument, ques-

tion, reason, rebut, refute, rehash, set to, talk back*, talk game*, thrash out*, toss around*, wrangle; SEE CONCEPTS 24,56

debauch [v] *deprave, corrupt*
abuse, bastardize, bestialize, betray, brutalize, debase, defile, deflower, demoralize, fornicate, fraternize, go bad*, go to hell*, intrigue, inveigle, lead astray*, live in the gutter*, lure, pervert, pollute, ravish, ruin, seduce, subvert, tempt, violate, vitiate, warp; SEE CONCEPTS 14,240,375

debauched [adj] *violated, corrupted*
abandoned, corrupt, debased, defiled, degenerate, degraded, depraved, deteriorated, dissipated, dissolute, fast, gone bad*, gone to the dogs*, immoral, in the gutter*, licentious, perverted, profligate, reprobate, vitiate, vitiated, wanton, wicked; SEE CONCEPT 545

debauchery [n] *immoral self-indulgence*
bender, binge, blowout*, burning candle at both ends*, bust, carousal, depravity, dissipation, dissoluteness, drunk*, excess, fast living*, fornication, gluttony, incontinence, indulgence, intemperance, intimacy, la dolce vita*, lasciviousness, lechery, lewdness, license, licentiousness, life in fast lane*, lust, orgy, overindulgence, revel, revelry, seduction, sensuality, sybaritism, tear*; SEE CONCEPTS 633,645

debenture [n] *certificate of debt*
bond, I.O.U., promise to pay, voucher; SEE CONCEPTS 318,684

debilitate [v] *incapacitate*
attenuate, blunt, cripple, devitalize, disable, enervate, enfeeble, eviscerate, exhaust, extenuate, harm, hurt, injure, mar, prostrate, relax, sap, spoil, unbrace, undermine, unstrengthen, weaken, wear out; SEE CONCEPTS 240,246

debility [n] *incapacity, weakness*
decrepitude, disease, enervation, enfeeblement, exhaustion, faintness, feebleness, frailty, infirmity, languor, malaise, sickliness, unhealthiness; SEE CONCEPT 316

debonair [adj] *charming, elegant*
affable, buoyant, casual, cheerful, courteous, dashing, detached, happy, jaunty, lighthearted, nonchalant, pleasant, refined, smooth, sprightly, suave, urbane, well-bred; SEE CONCEPT 401

debrief [v1] *question*
ask questions, cross-examine, examine, gather intelligence, give the third degree*, grill, interrogate, interview, investigate, probe, put through the wringer*, quiz, work over*; SEE CONCEPTS 48,53

debrief [v2] *silence*
censor, dummy up*, gag, hold one's tongue*, hush up, mute, muzzle, put the lid on, quash, say nothing, shut up, sit on*, soft-pedal*, squelch, stifle, suppress; SEE CONCEPT 266

debris [n] *litter, waste*
bits, crap*, detritus, dregs, dross, fragments, garbage, junk, offal, pieces, refuse, remains, riffraff, rubbish, rubble, ruins, trash, wreck, wreckage; SEE CONCEPT 260

debt [n] *money owed to others*
albatross*, arrearage, arrears, bad news*, baggage*, below the line*, bill, bite*, capital, check, chit*, claim, commitment, credit, cuff*, damage*, dead horse*, debenture, debit, deficit, due, dues, duty, encumbrance, indebtedness, in hock*, in the hole*, in the red*, invoice, IOU, liability, manifest, mortgage, note, obligation, out-

standings*, price tag*, promissory note, receipt, reckoning, red ink*, responsibility, score, tab, tally, voucher; SEE CONCEPTS 329,344

debug [v] *troubleshoot*
adjust, correct, fix, iron out, remedy, remove errors, repair, sort out, straighten out, unravel, unscramble, untangle, work the bugs out of*; SEE CONCEPTS 49,60

debunk [v] *disprove, ridicule*
cut down to size*, deflate, demystify, discover, disparage, expose, lampoon, mock, puncture, show up*, uncloak, unmask, unshroud; SEE CONCEPTS 49,60

debut [n] *first public appearance*
admission, appearance, beginning, bow, coming out*, coming out party*, entrance, entree, first step*, graduating, graduation, inauguration, incoming, initiation, introduction, launching, opener, presentation; SEE CONCEPT 386

debutante [n] *young woman*
deb, teenage girl, young girl, young lady; SEE CONCEPTS 415,424

decadence [n] *perversion; deterioration of morality*
corruption, debasement, decay, declension, decline, degeneracy, degeneration, degradation, devolution, dissipation, dissolution, downfall, downgrade, evil, excess, fall, gluttony, incontinence, intemperance, lasciviousness, lechery, lewdness, licentiousness, regression, sensuality, sybaritism; SEE CONCEPT 645

decadent [adj] *corrupt, self-indulgent*
debased, debauched, decaying, declining, degenerate, degraded, depraved, dissolute, effete, evil, gone bad, gone to the dogs*, immoral, lost, moribund, overripe, perverted, wanton, wicked; SEE CONCEPT 545

decal [n] *sticker*
advertisement, decalcomania, decorative picture, emblem, symbol, token; SEE CONCEPTS 259,284, 625

decamp [v] *depart suddenly*
beat it, bolt, break camp, clear out, depart, disappear, escape, evacuate, flee, head for the hills*, hightail*, hit the road*, make a break for it, make oneself scarce*, make tracks*, run away, scram, skedaddle*, slip away, vamoose; SEE CONCEPTS 102,150,195

decanter [n] *vessel*
bottle, canteen, carafe, container, cruet, flask, jug, magnum, pitcher, wine bottle; SEE CONCEPT 494

decapitate [v] *behead*
ax, bring to the block*, chop off one's head, decollate, execute, guillotine; SEE CONCEPT 176

decay [n] *breaking down, collapse*
adulteration, atrophy, blight, caries, cariosity, consumption, corrosion, crumbling, decadence, decline, decomposition, decrease, decrepitude, degeneracy, degeneration, depreciation, deterioration, dilapidation, disintegration, disrepair, dissolution, downfall, dying, extinction, fading, failing, gangrene, impairment, mortification, perishing, putrefaction, putrescence, putridity, putridness, rot, rotting, ruin, ruination, rust, senescence, spoilage, spoilation, wasting, wasting away, withering; SEE CONCEPTS 230,674,716

decay [v] *deteriorate, crumble*
atrophy, become contaminated, be impaired, blight, break up, collapse, corrode, curdle, de-

de
de

cline, decompose, defile, degenerate, depreciate, discolor, disintegrate, dissolve, dry-rot, dwindle, fade, fail, get worse, go bad, go to seed*, go to the dogs*, hit rock bottom*, hit the skids*, lessen, mildew, mold, molder, mortify, pejorate, perish, pollute, putrefy, putresce, reach depths, rot, sap, shrivel, sicken, sink, slump, spoil, suppurate, turn, wane, waste away, weaken, wear away, wither; SEE CONCEPTS 240,246,469

decayed [adj] *rotten, falling apart*
addled, bad, carious, carrion, corroded, decomposed, effete, gangrenous, moldered, overripe, perished, putrefied, putrescent, putrid, rank, riddled, rotted, ruined, spoiled, wasted, withered; SEE CONCEPT 485

decease [n] *death*
buying the farm*, curtains*, defunction, demise, departure, dissolution, dying, grim reaper*, passing, passing away, passing over, quietus, release, silence, sleep, taps*, the end; SEE CONCEPT 304

decease [v] *pass away; expire*
buy a one-way ticket*, call off all bets*, cease, check out*, cool off*, croak*, deep six*, depart, die, drop, go, pass, pass away, pass on, pass over, perish, succumb; SEE CONCEPT 304

deceased [adj] *dead*
asleep, bit the dust*, cold*, defunct, departed, exanimate, expired, extinct, finished, former, gave up the ghost*, gone, inanimate, kicked the bucket*, late, lifeless, lost, passed on, pushing up daisies*; SEE CONCEPT 539

deceit [n1] *practice of misleading*
ambidexterity, ambidextrousness, artifice, cheating, chicane, chicanery, cozening, craft, craftiness, cunning, deceitfulness, deception, defrauding, dirty dealing*, dirty pool*, dishonesty, dissemblance, dissimulation, double-dealing, duplicity, entrapping, fraud, fraudulence, guile, hypocrisy, imposition, overreaching, pretense, slyness, smoke and mirrors*, trapping, treachery, trickery, two-facedness*, two-timing*, underhandedness; SEE CONCEPTS 59,633

deceit [n2] *particular type of trick, misleading*
artifice, blind, cheat, chicanery, crocodile tears*, deception, dirty trick*, dirty work*, duplicity, fake, feint, flimflam*, fraud, fraudulence, hoax, humbug, imposture, misrepresentation, pretense, ruse, sell, sellout, sham, shift, smoke and mirrors*, snow job*, soft soap*, spoof, stratagem, subterfuge, sweet talk*, swindle, trick, whitewash*, wile; SEE CONCEPTS 59,660

deceitful [adj] *dishonest, insincere*
artful, astucious, astute, beguiling, clandestine, counterfeit, crafty, cunning, deceiving, deceptive, delusive, delusory, designing, disingenuous, double-dealing, duplicitous, fallacious, false, feline, foxy, fraudulent, furtive, guileful, hypocritical, illusory, impostrous, indirect, insidious, knavish, lying, mendacious, misleading, rascal, roguish, shifty, slick, sly, sneaky, stealthy, subtle, treacherous, tricky, two-faced*, underhand, underhanded, untrustworthy, untruthful, wily; SEE CONCEPT 401

deceive [v] *mislead; be dishonest*
bamboozle*, beat, beat out of, beguile, betray, bilk, buffalo*, burn, cheat, circumvent, clip, con, cozen, cross up, defraud, delude, disappoint, double-cross, dupe, ensnare, entrap, fake, falsify, fleece, fool, gouge, gull, hoax, hoodwink, hook*, humbug, impose upon, lead on, outwit, play joke

on, pull fast one*, put on, rob, scam, screw, sell, skin, suck in*, swindle, take advantage of, take for, take for ride*, take in, take to cleaners*, trick, victimize; SEE CONCEPTS 7,19,59

decency [n] *respectable behavior*
appropriateness, ceremoniousness, civility, conventionality, correctness, courtesy, decorum, dignity, etiquette, fitness, fittingness, formality, good form, good manners, honesty, modesty, propriety, respectability, righteousness, seemliness, virtue; SEE CONCEPT 633

decent [adj1] *respectable, appropriate*
approved, becoming, befitting, chaste, clean, comely, comme il faut, conforming, continent, correct, decorous, delicate, ethical, fit, fitting, good, honest, honorable, immaculate, mannerly, modest, moral, nice, noble, on the up and up*, polite, presentable, proper, prudent, pure, reserved, right, seemly, spotless, stainless, standard, straight, straight arrow*, straight shooting*, suitable, trustworthy, unblemished, undefiled, untarnished, upright, virtuous, worthy; SEE CONCEPTS 401,558

decent [adj2] *kind, generous*
accommodating, courteous, friendly, gracious, helpful, obliging, thoughtful, virtuous; SEE CONCEPTS 404,542

decent [adj3] *sufficient, tolerable*
acceptable, adequate, all right, ample, average, comfortable, common, competent, enough, fair, fair to middling*, good, mediocre, middling, moderately good, passable, presentable, reasonable, respectable, right, satisfactory, sufficing, unexceptional, unimpeachable, unobjectionable; SEE CONCEPTS 533,558,572

deception [n1] *misleading; being dishonest*
beguilement, betrayal, blarney*, boondoggle*, cheat, circumvention, cozenage, craftiness, cunning, deceit, deceitfulness, deceptiveness, defraudation, dirt, disinformation, dissimulation, double-dealing, dupery, duplicity, equivocation, falsehood, fast one*, flimflam*, fraud, fraudulence, guile, hokum*, hypocrisy, imposition, insincerity, juggling, legerdemain, lying, mendacity, pretense, prevarication, snow job*, sophism, treachery, treason, trickery, trickiness, trumpery, untruth; SEE CONCEPTS 7,19,59

deception [n2] *trick*
artifice, bilk, bluff, catch, cheat, chicane, con, confidence game, con game*, cover-up, crock, decoy, device, dodge, fallacy, fast one*, fast shuffle*, feint, fib, fraud, gimmick, hoax, hogwash*, hustle, illusion, imposture, jive*, lie, malarkey*, mare's-nest*, pretext, ride*, ruse, scam, sham, shift, shuck, snare, snow job*, stall, sting, story, stratagem, subterfuge, swindle, trap, trick, whitewash*, wile, wrinkle*; SEE CONCEPTS 59,230

deceptive [adj] *dishonest*
ambiguous, astucious, beguiling, bum*, catchy, crafty, cunning, deceitful, deceiving, deluding, delusive, delusory, designing, disingenuous, fake, fallacious, false, fishy, foxy, fraudulent, illusory, impostorous, indirect, insidious, lying, misleading, mock, oblique, off*, phony, plausible, rascal, roguish, scheming, seeming, serpentine, shifty, slick, slippery, sly, sneaky, snide, specious, spurious, subtle, treacherous, tricky, two-faced*, underhand, underhanded, unreliable, wily; SEE CONCEPTS 401,582

decide [*v*] *make a determination; settle an issue*
adjudge, adjudicate, agree, arrive at conclusion, award, call shots*, cast the die*, choose, cinch, clinch, come to agreement, come to conclusion, come to decision, commit oneself, conclude, conjecture, decree, determine, draw a conclusion, elect, end, establish, figure, fix upon, form opinion, gather, go down line*, guess, have final word*, judge, make a decision, make up mind, mediate, opt, pick, poll, purpose, reach decision, resolve, rule, select, set, surmise, take a stand, tap, vote, will; SEE CONCEPT *18*

decided [*adj*] *certain, definite*
absolute, assured, categorical, cinched, clear, clear-cut, clinched, destined, determined, distinct, emphatic, explicit, express, fated, for sure*, indisputable, in the bag*, nailed*, on ice*, positive, prearranged, predetermined, pronounced, resolved, runaway*, settled, sure, unalterable, unambiguous, undeniable, undisputed, unequivocal, unmistakable, unquestionable; SEE CONCEPT *535*

decided [*adj2*] *determined, strong-willed*
assertive, bent, certain, cocksure, decisive, deliberate, earnest, emphatic, established, firm, fixed, inflexible, intent, iron-jawed*, mulish, positive, purposeful, resolute, resolved, serious, set, settled, strong-minded, sure, unbending, unfaltering, unhesitating, unwavering, unyielding; SEE CONCEPTS *401,403*

decidedly [*adv*] *certainly*
absolutely, bloody*, by all means, clearly, decisively, determinedly, distinctly, downright, emphatically, flat out*, for a fact*, in spades*, no catch*, no holds barred*, no ifs ands or buts*, no mistake*, no strings attached*, of course, positively, powerful, real, really, right, straight out, strongly, sure, surely, terribly, terrifically, unequivocally, unmistakably; SEE CONCEPT *535*

deciding [*adj*] *determining*
chief, conclusive, critical, crucial, decisive, important, influential, key, necessary, prime, principal, significant; SEE CONCEPTS *546,568*

decimate [*v*] *destroy*
annihilate, butcher*, commit genocide, execute, exterminate, kill off, massacre, obliterate, slaughter, stamp out, wipe out; SEE CONCEPT *252*

decipher [*v*] *figure out, understand*
analyze, break, break down, bring out, cipher, construe, crack, decode, deduce, disentangle, dope out, elucidate, encipher, explain, expound, find the key, interpret, make clear, make out, puzzle out, read, render, reveal, solve, spell, translate, unfold, unravel, unriddle; SEE CONCEPTS *15,31,37*

decision [*n1*] *conclusion; resolution reached*
accommodation, accord, adjudication, adjudicature, adjustment, agreement, arbitration, arrangement, choice, compromise, declaration, determination, end, finding, judgment, opinion, outcome, prearrangement, preference, reconciliation, resolution, result, ruling, selection, sentence, settlement, showdown, the call, the nod, understanding, verdict; SEE CONCEPTS *278,689*

decision [*n2*] *strength of mind or will*
backbone, decidedness, decisiveness, determination, doggedness, earnestness, firmness, fortitude, grit, iron will, obstinacy, obstinance, perseverance, persistence, pluck*, purpose, purposefulness, purposiveness, resoluteness, resolu-

tion, resolve, seriousness, spine, stubbornness, volition, will, will power; SEE CONCEPTS *410,411*

decisive [*adj*] *definite*
absolute, all out*, assured, bent, certain, conclusive, crisp, critical, crucial, decided, definitive, determined, fateful, final, firm, flat out*, forceful, imperative, imperious, incisive, influential, intent, litmus test*, momentous, peremptory, positive, resolute, resolved, set, settled, significant, straight out*, strong-minded, trenchant; SEE CONCEPT *535*

deck [*v*] *put on clothing, usually nice*
accouter, adorn, appoint, array, attire, beautify, bedeck, clothe, decorate, dress, dress up, embellish, festoon, garland, garnish, grace, gussy up*, ornament, prettify, primp, slick, trim; SEE CONCEPT *167*

declaim [*v*] *proclaim; get on a soapbox*
attack, bloviate, blow hot air*, declare, decry, denounce, harangue, hold forth, inveigh, lecture, mouth, orate, perorate, pile it on*, proclaim, rail, rant, recite, soapbox*, speak, spiel*, spout*, talk big*; SEE CONCEPTS *49,51*

declaration [*n1*] *assertion of belief or knowledge*
acknowledgment, admission, advertisement, affirmation, allegation, announcement, answer, attestation, averment, avowal, bomb*, broadcast, communication, deposition, disclosure, enunciation, explanation, exposition, expression, hot air*, information, notice, notification, oath, pitch, presentation, profession, promulgation, protestation, publication, remark, report, revelation, saying, say so*, spiel*, statement, story, testimony, two cents' worth*, utterance; SEE CONCEPTS *49,274,278*

declaration [*n2*] *official proclamation*
acclamation, affidavit, allegation, announcement, article, attestation, bulletin, canon, charge, confirmation, constitution, credo, creed, denunciation, deposition, document, edict, gospel, indictment, manifesto, notice, notification, plea, proclamation, profession, promulgation, pronouncement, pronunciamento, resolution, testament, testimony, ultimatum; SEE CONCEPTS *271,274,278*

declare [*v1*] *make known clearly or officially*
acknowledge, advance, advocate, affirm, allegate, allege, announce, argue, assert, asservate, attest, aver, avow, be positive, blaze, bring forward, certify, cite, claim, confess, confirm, contend, convey, demonstrate, disclose, enunciate, give out, inform, insist, maintain, manifest, notify, pass, proclaim, profess, promulgate, pronounce, propound, publish, put forward, reaffirm, reassert, render, repeat, reveal, set forth, show, sound, state, stress, swear, tell, testify, validate, vouch; SEE CONCEPTS *49,60*

declare [*v2*] *claim as possession*
acknowledge, admit, avouch, avow, confess, convey, disclose, divulge, impart, indicate, manifest, notify, own, profess, represent, reveal, state, swear; SEE CONCEPTS *57,60*

declassify [*v*] *open to the public*
display, exhibit, make available, make public, publicize, show; SEE CONCEPT *261*

decline [*n1*] *lessening*
abatement, backsliding, comedown, cropper*, decay, decrepitude, degeneracy, degeneration, descent, deterioration, devolution, diminution, dissolution, dive, downfall, downgrade, down-

de
de

turn, drop, dwindling, ebb, ebbing, enfeeblement, failing, failure, fall, falling off, flop, lapse, on the skids*, pratfall, recession, relapse, senility, skids*, slump, wane, waning, weakening, worsening; SEE CONCEPTS 674,698,699

decline [n2] *downward change in value, position*
declivity, decrease, depression, descent, dip, downslide, downswing, downtrend, downturn, drop, drop-off, fall-off, hill, incline, lapse, loss, lowering, pitch, sag, slide, slip, slope, slump; SEE CONCEPTS 336,346,738

decline [v1] *say no*
abjure, abstain, avoid, balk, beg to be excused, bypass, demur, deny, desist, disapprove, dismiss, don't buy*, forbear, forgo, gainsay, nix*, not accept, not hear of, not think of, pass on*, refrain, refuse, reject, renounce, reprobate, repudiate, send regrets, shy, spurn, turn down, turn thumbs down*; SEE CONCEPTS 45,51

decline [v2] *lessen, become less*
abate, backslide, cheapen, decay, decrease, degenerate, depreciate, deteriorate, diminish, disimprove, disintegrate, droop, drop, dwindle, ebb, fade, fail, fall, fall off, flag, go downhill*, go to pot*, go to the dogs*, hit the skids*, languish, lapse, lose value, lower, pine, recede, relapse, retrograde, return, revert, rot, sag, settle, shrink, sink, slide, subside, wane, weaken, worsen; SEE CONCEPTS 240,698

decline [v3] *descend*
dip, droop, drop, fall, go down, lower, sag, set, settle, sink, slant, slope; SEE CONCEPTS 151,181

decode [v] *decipher*
break, clear up, crack, crack the code, decrypt, figure out, find the solution, interpret, make clear, read, solve, translate, unravel, unriddle, unscramble, untangle, work out; SEE CONCEPTS 15,31,37

decommission [v] *withdraw from active service*
deactivate, demilitarize, make inactive, retire, shut down, shut off; SEE CONCEPTS 25,121,188

decompose [v1] *rot, break up*
break down, crumble, decay, disintegrate, dissolve, fall apart, fester, molder, putrefy, putresce, spoil, taint, turn; SEE CONCEPT 469

decompose [v2] *analyze by taking apart*
anatomize, atomize, break down, break up, decompound, disintegrate, dissect, dissolve, distill, resolve, separate; SEE CONCEPTS 24,103

decomposition [n] *rot, breakdown*
atomization, corruption, decay, disintegration, dissipation, dissolution, division, putrefaction, putrescence, putridity; SEE CONCEPTS 230,674

deconstructionist [n/adj] *exposing a text's multiple meanings*
critical, debunking, demystifying, demythifying, hermeneutical, reinterpretive, revisionist; SEE CONCEPT 268

decontaminate [v] *clean*
antiseptize, cleanse, disinfect, fumigate, make sterile, purify, sanitize, sterilize, wash; SEE CONCEPTS 161,165

decor [n] *colors, furnishings of a place*
adornment, color scheme, decoration, interior design, ornamentation; SEE CONCEPTS 622,723

decorate [v1] *beautify, embellish*
add finishing touches, adorn, bedeck, bedizen, brighten, burnish, color, deck, do up*, dress out*, dress up*, enhance, enrich, festoon, finish, fix up, frill, furbish, garnish, gild, grace, gussy

up*, idealize, illuminate, jazz up*, ornament, paint, perfect, prank, renovate, spruce up*, trim; SEE CONCEPTS 162,177

decorate [v2] *honor and give medal*
cite, laureate, pin medal on, plume; SEE CONCEPT 132

decoration [n1] *beautification, embellishment*
adornment, beautifying, bedecking, bedizenment, designing, elaboration, enhancement, enrichment, festooning, flounce, flourish, frill, furbelow, garnish, garnishing, illumination, improvement, ornament, ornamentation, redecorating, spangle, trimming; SEE CONCEPTS 162,177

decoration [n2] *particular type of embellishment*
appliqué, arabesque, bauble, bays, braid, color, curlicue, désign, dingbat*, doodad*, extravagance, fandangle*, festoon, filigree, finery, flounce, flourish, fretwork, frill, frippery, furbelow, fuss, garbage*, garnish, garniture, gewgaws, gilt, gimcracks*, gingerbread, inlay, jazz*, lace, ornament, parquetry, plaque, ribbon, scroll, sequin, spangle, thing*, tinsel, tooling, trimming, trinket, wreath; SEE CONCEPTS 259,260

decoration [n3] *medal of honor*
accolade, award, badge, bays, citation, colors, cross, distinction, emblem, garter, kudos, laurels, medal, mention, order, Purple Heart, ribbon, star; SEE CONCEPT 337

decorative [adj] *beautifying*
adorning, cosmetic, embellishing, enhancing, fancy, florid, nonfunctional, ornamental, prettifying, pretty; SEE CONCEPT 579

decorous [adj] *appropriate, suitable*
au fait, becoming, befitting, ceremonial, ceremonious, civilized, comely, comme il faut, conforming, conventional, correct, decent, demure, de rigueur, dignified, done, elegant, fit, fitting, formal, good, mannerly, meet, moral, nice, polite, prim, proper, punctilious, refined, respectable, right, seasonable, sedate, seemly, staid, well-behaved; SEE CONCEPTS 401,558

decorum [n] *appropriate behavior, good manners*
breeding, civility, conduct, convenance, convention, correctitude, correctness, courtliness, decency, demeanor, deportment, dignity, etiquette, form, formality, gentility, good grace, gravity, habits, order, orderliness, politeness, politesse, properness, propriety, protocol, punctilio, respectability, seemliness, tact, usage; SEE CONCEPT 633

decoy [n] *bait, trap*
allurement, attraction, beard*, blind, blow off*, booster, camouflage, catch, chicane, chicanery, come-on, deception, drawing card, ensnarement, enticement, facade, fake, front, imitation, inducement, inveiglement, lure, nark*, plant, pretense, seducement, shill, sitting duck*, snare, stick, stoolie*, stool pigeon*, temptation, trick, trickery; SEE CONCEPTS 59,230,680

decoy [v] *bait, entrap*
allure, come on, con, deceive, delude, egg one on*, ensnare, ensorcell, entice, fascinate, inveigle, lead on*, lead up garden path*, lure, mislead, mousetrap*, rope in*, seduce, shill, steer, suck in*, tempt, toll, tout, trap, wile; SEE CONCEPTS 16,59

decrease [n] *diminishing, lessening*
abatement, compression, condensation, constriction, contraction, cutback, decline, declining, de-

crescence, depression, diminution, discount, downturn, dwindling, ebb, falling off, loss, reduction, shrinkage, striction, subsidence, waning; SEE CONCEPT 698

decrease [v] *grow less or make less*
abate, calm down, check, contract, crumble, curb, curtail, cut down, decay, decline, degenerate, depreciate, deteriorate, devaluate, die down, diminish, droop, drop, drop off, dry up, dwindle, ease, ebb, evaporate, fade, fall off, lessen, let up, lighten, lose edge, lower, modify, narrow down, peter out, quell, quiet, reduce, restrain, run low, settle, shrink, shrivel, sink, slacken, slack off, slash, slow down, slump, soften, subside, tail off, wane, waste, weaken, wear away, wear down, wither; SEE CONCEPTS *240,698*

decree [n] *mandate, legal order*
act, announcement, behest, bidding, charge, charging, command, commandment, declaration, decretum, dictum, direction, directive, edict, enactment, injunction, instruction, judgment, law, order, ordinance, precept, prescript, proclamation, promulgation, pronouncement, rap*, regulation, rule, ruling, say, statute, the riot act*, the word*, ukase; SEE CONCEPTS *318,685*

decree [v] *order rule or action*
announce, command, compel, constrain, decide, declare, demand, determine, dictate, enact, force, impose, lay down the law*, oblige, ordain, prescribe, proclaim, pronounce, put one's foot down*, read the riot act*, require, rule, set; SEE CONCEPTS *50,53,81,88,317*

decrepit [adj] *deteriorated, debilitated, especially as a result of age*
aged, anile, antiquated, battered, bedraggled, broken-down, creaky, crippled, dilapidated, doddering, effete, feeble, flimsy, fragile, frail, haggard, incapacitated, infirm, insubstantial, old, quavering, ramshackle, rickety, run-down, seedy, senile, shabby, shaking, superannuated, tacky, threadbare, tired, tottering, tumble-down, unsound, used, wasted, weak, weakly, weather-beaten, worn, worn-out; SEE CONCEPTS *406,485*

decriminalize [v] *legalize*
allow, declare lawful, legitimize, make legal, permit, regulate, sanction; SEE CONCEPTS *298,317*

decry [v] *criticize, blame*
abuse, asperse, bad-mouth*, belittle, calumniate, censure, condemn, cry down, defame, denounce, depreciate, derogate, detract, devalue, diminish, discount, discredit, disgrace, disparage, do a number on*, downgrade, dump on*, hit*, knock*, lower, malign, mark down, minimize, opprobriate, pan*, poor-mouth*, put down, rail against, rap, reprehend, reprobate, run down, slam*, take away, take swipe at*, throw stones at*, traduce, underestimate, underrate, undervalue, vilify, write off; SEE CONCEPTS *44,52*

dedicate [v1] *donate, set aside for special use*
address, allot, apply, apportion, appropriate, assign, commit, consign, devote, give, give over to, inscribe, offer, pledge, restrict, surrender; SEE CONCEPTS *18,50,88,135*

dedicate [v2] *sanctify*
anoint, bless, consecrate, hallow, set apart; SEE CONCEPTS *69,367*

dedicated [adj] *loyal, hard-working*
committed, devoted, enthusiastic, faithful, given over to, old faithful*, purposeful, single-hearted,

single-minded, sworn, true blue*, true to the end*, wholehearted, zealous; SEE CONCEPTS *404,542*

dedication [n1] *faithfulness, loyalty*
adherence, allegiance, commitment, devotedness, devotion, single-mindedness, wholeheartedness; SEE CONCEPTS *411,657*

dedication [n2] *speech of praise; sanctification*
address, celebration, consecration, devotion, envoy, glorification, hallowing, inscription, message; SEE CONCEPTS *69,367*

deduce [v] *figure out, understand*
add up, analyze, assume, be afraid, boil down, cogitate, collect, conceive, conclude, consider, deduct, deem, derive, draw, fancy, figure, gather, glean, have a hunch*, imagine, infer, judge, make, make out, presume, presuppose, ratiocinate, read into, reason, regard, surmise, take to mean; SEE CONCEPTS *15,24*

deducible [adj] *understandable*
a priori, consequent, deductive, derivable, dogmatic, following, inferable, inferential, provable, reasoned, traceable; SEE CONCEPTS *402,529*

deduct [v] *take away or out; reduce*
abstract, allow, bate, cut back, decrease by, diminish, discount, dock, draw back, knock off, lessen, rebate, reduce, remove, roll back, subtract, take, take from, take off, withdraw, write off; SEE CONCEPTS *236,247,330*

deduction [n1] *conclusion, understanding*
answer, assumption, cogitation, concluding, consequence, consideration, contemplation, corollary, deliberation, derivation, finding, illation, inference, inferring, judgment, meditation, mulling, musing, opinion, pondering, ratiocination, reasoning, reflection, result, rumination, sequitur, speculation, thinking, thought; SEE CONCEPTS *15,24,689*

deduction [n2] *something subtracted*
abatement, abstraction, allowance, credit, cut, decrease, decrement, depreciation, diminution, discount, dockage, excision, rebate, reduction, removal, subtraction, withdrawal, write-off; SEE CONCEPTS *763,776*

deed [n1] *achievement*
accomplishment, act, action, adventure, ball-game, big idea*, bit, byplay, cause, commission, crusade, do, enterprise, exploit, fact, feat, follow through, game, happenin'*, performance, plan, quest, reality, securing, stunt, thing*, tour de force, truth, winning; SEE CONCEPTS *4,706*

deed [n2] *legal paper assigning property; contract*
agreement, bargain, certificate, charter, compact, conveyance, covenant, document, indenture, instrument, lease, papers, proof, record, release, security, title, transaction, voucher, warranty; SEE CONCEPTS *271,318*

deem [v] *regard, consider*
account, allow, appraise, assume, be afraid, believe, calculate, conceive, conjecture, credit, daresay, divine, esteem, estimate, expect, feel, guess, hold, imagine, judge, know, presume, reckon, sense, set store by, suppose, surmise, suspect, think, understand, view; SEE CONCEPTS *12,28*

deep [adj1] *extending very far, usually down*
abysmal, abyssal, below, beneath, bottomless, broad, buried, deep-seated, distant, downreaching, far, fathomless, immersed, inmost, low, pro-

found, rooted, subaqueous, submarine, submerged, subterranean, sunk, underground, unfathomable, wide, yawning; SEE CONCEPTS
737,777

deep [*adj2*] *abstract, complicated in meaning*
abstruse, acute, arcane, complex, concealed, Delphic, difficult, discerning, esoteric, hard to understand, heavy*, hermetic, hidden, incisive,
intricate, learned, mysterious, obscure, occult,
Orphic, penetrating, profound, recondite, sagacious, secret, serious, Sibylline, wise; SEE CON-
CEPTS 402,529

deep [*adj3*] *scheming, devious*
acute, artful, astute, canny, contriving, crafty,
cunning, designing, foxy, guileful, insidious, intriguing, keen, knowing, plotting, sharp, shrewd,
sly, tricky, wily; SEE CONCEPT 404

deep [*adj4*] *absorbed, engrossed in activity*
abstracted, centered, concentrated, enfolded, engaged, fixed, focused, immersed, intent, into,
lost, musing, preoccupied, rapt, set, wrapped,
wrapped up; SEE CONCEPT 542

deep [*adj5*] *intense in effect on senses*
bass, booming, dark, extreme, full-toned, grave,
great, hard, low, low-pitched, low-toned, profound, resonant, rich, sonorous,˙ strong, vivid;
SEE CONCEPTS 537,594,618

deep [*n*] *the sea*
blue*, brine, briny*, Davy Jones's locker*,
drink*, main, middle, ocean, Poseidon's realm*,
the high seas; SEE CONCEPT 514

deepen [*v1*] *make depth greater*
dig, dig out, dredge, excavate, expand, extend,
hollow, scoop out, scrape out; SEE CONCEPT 250

deepen [*v2*] *make more intense*
aggravate, develop, enhance, expand, extend,
grow, heighten, increase, intensate, intensify,
magnify, mount, redouble, reinforce, rise, rouse,
strengthen; SEE CONCEPTS 236,245,697

deeply [*adv*] *completely, intensely*
acutely, affectingly, distressingly, feelingly, genuinely, gravely, intensely, mournfully, movingly,
passionately, profoundly, sadly, seriously, severely, surely, thoroughly, to the quick; SEE CON-
CEPTS 531,772

deep-seated [*adj*] *ingrained*
built-in, chronic, confirmed, deep down, deeply
felt, deep-rooted, dyed-in-the-wool, established,
fixed, habitual, inborn, inbred, inherent, lodged
in one's brain*, longstanding, longtime, subconscious; SEE CONCEPTS 535,549

deep space [*n*] *region beyond Earth's solar system*
intergalactic space, interplanetary space, inter-
stellar space, outer space; SEE CONCEPTS 370,511

deface [*v*] *mar, mutilate*
blemish, contort, damage, deform, demolish, destroy, dilapidate, disfigure, distort, harm, impair,
injure, mangle, misshape, obliterate, ruin,
scratch, spoil, sully, tarnish, trash*, vandalize,
wreck; SEE CONCEPTS 246,252

de facto [*adv*] *in reality*
actual, actually, existing, genuinely, in effect, in
fact, real, really, tangible, truly, veritably; SEE
CONCEPT 582

defamation [*n*] *libel, slander*
aspersion, backbiting, backstabbing, belittlement, black eye*, calumny, character assassination, cheap shot*, denigration, depreciation,
detraction, dirt, dirty laundry*, disparagement,

dump*, dynamite, hit, knock, lie, low-down
dirty*, mud, obloquy, opprobrium, scorcher,
slam*, slap in face*, slime, slur, smear, traducement, vilification; SEE CONCEPT 54

defamatory [*adj*] *libelous, slanderous*
abusive, calumnious, contumelious, denigrating,
derogatory, detracting, detractive, disparaging,
injurious, insulting, maligning, opprobrious, traducing, vilifying, vituperative; SEE CONCEPTS
267,537

defame [*v*] *inflict libel or slander*
asperse, bad-mouth*, belie, besmirch, blacken,
blister, calumniate, cast aspersions on, cast slur
on, denigrate, detract, discredit, disgrace, dishonor, disparage, do a number on*, knock, malign, pan*, put zingers on*, roast, scandalize,
scorch, slam, smear, speak evil of*, stigmatize,
throw mud at*, traduce, vilify, villainize, vituperate; SEE CONCEPTS 7,19,54

default [*n*] *failure; want*
absence, blemish, blunder, dearth, defect, deficiency, delinquency, dereliction, disregard, error,
fault, imperfection, inadequacy, insufficiency,
lack, lapse, miss, neglect, nonpayment, offense,
omission, overlooking, oversight, privation,
shortcoming, slight, transgression, vice, weakness, wrongdoing; SEE CONCEPTS 335,699,709

default [*v*] *dodge payment*
bilk, defraud, dishonor, evade, fail, leave town*,
meet under arch*, neglect, put on the cuff*, rat*,
repudiate, run out on*, see in the alley, shirk,
skate*, skip, skip out on*, stiff*, swindle, welch,
welsh; SEE CONCEPTS 59,63,330

defeat [*n1*] *overthrow, beating*
ambush, annihilation, beating, blow, break,
breakdown, check, collapse, conquest, count, debacle, defeasance, destruction, discomfiture,
downthrow, drubbing*, embarrassment, extermination, failure, fall, insuccess, killing*, KO*,
lacing, licking, loss, massacre, mastery, nonsuccess, paddling, rebuff, repulse, reverse, rout,
ruin, scalping, setback, shellacking*, slaughter,
subjugation, thrashing, trap, trashing, trimming,
triumph, trouncing, vanquishment, waxing,
whaling, whipping, whitewashing*; SEE CON-
CEPT 95

defeat [*n2*] *frustration*
disappointment, discomfiture, downfall, failure,
foil, loss, rebuff, repulse, reversal, reverse, setback, thwarting; SEE CONCEPT 410

defeat [*v1*] *conquer in military manner*
ambush, annihilate, bar, bear down, beat, best,
block, butcher, crush, decimate, demolish, discomfit, drown, entrap, finish off, halt, hinder, impede, lick, mow down, obliterate, obstruct,
outflank, outmaneuver, overpower, overrun,
overthrow, overwhelm, parry, prevail over,
quell, reduce, repel, repress, repulse, roll back,
rout, route, sack, scatter, shipwreck, sink,
slaughter, smash, subdue, subjugate, suppress,
surmount, swamp, torpedo*, trample, trash,
upset, vanquish, whip, wipe out; SEE CONCEPTS
95,320

defeat [*v2*] *conquer in athletic contest*
beat, bust*, clobber*, cream*, deck*, drop*,
drub*, edge, flax*, flog*, floor*, knock out*,
KO*, lambaste*, lick, outhit, outjump, outplay,
outrun, overpower, plow under*, pommel*,
pound*, powder*, pulverize*, run roughshod
over*, skin*, steamroll*, take, take it all*, take to

cleaners*, tan*, thrash, total, trounce, wallop*, whack*, whomp*, win, work over*, zap*; SEE CONCEPTS 95,363

defeat [v3] *frustrate*
baffle, balk, beat down*, beat the system*, blank, block, bury, cast down, cause setback, checkmate, circumvent, confound, contravene, cook*, counterplot, cross, disappoint, discomfit, disconcert, disprove, edge out*, foil, invalidate, neutralize, nonplus, nose out*, nullify, outwit, overturn, put end to*, puzzle, quell, reduce, refute, ruin, scuttle, shave*, shellac*, skunk*, spoil, squash, stump, subdue, subjugate, surmount, take wind out of sails*, throw for loop*, thwart, undo, victimize; SEE CONCEPTS 14,121

defect [n] *blemish, imperfection*
birthmark, blot, blotch, break, bug, catch, check, crack, deficiency, deformity, discoloration, drawback, error, failing, fault, flaw, foible, frailty, gap, glitch, gremlin, hole, infirmity, injury, irregularity, kink, knot, lack, mark, marring, mistake, patch, rift, rough spot, scar, scarcity, scratch, seam, second, shortage, shortcoming, sin, speck, spot, stain, taint, unsoundness, vice, want, weakness, weak point; SEE CONCEPTS 309,580,646

defect [v] *break from belief, faith*
abandon, abscond, apostatize, back out, break faith*, change sides, depart, desert, fall away from, forsake, go, go back on, go over, go over the fence*, lapse, leave, pull out, quit, rat*, rebel, reject, renege, renounce, revolt, run out, schism, sell out*, spurn, take a walk*, tergiversate, tergiverse, turn, turn coat*, walk out on, withdraw; SEE CONCEPTS 198,367

defection [n] *abandonment*
alienation, apostasy, backsliding, deficiency, dereliction, desertion, disaffection, disloyalty, disownment, divorce, estrangement, failing, failure, faithlessness, forsaking, lack, parting, rebellion, recreancy, rejection, repudiation, retreat, revolt, separation, severance, sundering, tergiversation, withdrawal; SEE CONCEPTS 195,198, 367

defective [adj] *broken, not working*
abnormal, amiss, blemished, damaged, deficient, faulty, flawed, impaired, imperfect, inadequate, incomplete, injured, insufficient, lacking, on the bum*, out of order, poor, seconds, sick, subnormal, unfinished, unhealthy, unsound, wanting; SEE CONCEPTS 560,565

defend [v1] *protect*
avert, battle, beat off, bulwark, care for, cherish, conserve, contend, cover, entrench, espouse, fend off, fight, fight for, fortify, foster, garrison, guard, guard against, hedge, hold, hold at bay, house, insure, keep safe, look after, maintain, mine, nourish, oppose, panoply, preserve, prevent, provide sanctuary, repel danger, resist, retain, safeguard, save, screen, secure, shelter, shield, stave off, sustain, take in, uphold, war, ward off, watch, watch over, withstand; SEE CONCEPTS 96,110

defend [v2] *show support for*
advocate, aid, apologize for, argue, assert, back, back up, bear one out*, befriend, champion, come to defense of, cover for, endorse, espouse, exculpate, exonerate, explain, go to bat for*, guarantee, justify, maintain, plead, prove a case, put in a good word*, rationalize, recommend,

ride shotgun for*, say in defense, second, speak up for, stand by, stand up for, stick up for, stonewall*, support, sustain, thump for, uphold, vindicate, warrant; SEE CONCEPTS 10,49

defendant [n] *accused*
appellant, litigant, offender, prisoner, suspect; SEE CONCEPT 412

defense [n1] *armament; protection system*
aegis, armor, arms, barricade, bastille, bastion, bulwark, buttress, citadel, cover, deterrence, dike, embankment, fastness, fence, fort, fortification, fortress, garrison, guard, immunity, munitions, palisade, parapet, position, protection, rampart, redoubt, resistance, safeguard, security, shelter, shield, stockade, stronghold, trench, wall, ward, warfare, weaponry, weapons; SEE CONCEPTS 321,322,500

defense [n2] *explanation, justification*
answer, apologetics, apologia, apologizing, apology, argument, cleanup, copout*, exculpation, excuse, excusing, exoneration, explaining, extenuation, fish story*, jive, off-time*, plea, rationalization, rejoinder, reply, response, retort, return, song and dance*, story, vindication, whitewash*; SEE CONCEPTS 57,278

defenseless [adj] *powerless, vulnerable*
caught, endangered, exposed, hands tied*, helpless, indefensible, in line of fire*, like a clay pigeon*, like a sitting duck*, naked*, on the line*, on the spot*, open, out on limb*, pigeon*, poor, unarmed, unguarded, unprotected, up the creek*, weak, wide open*; SEE CONCEPTS 555,576

defensible [adj] *justifiable*
condonable, defendable, excusable, fit, logical, pardonable, permissible, plausible, proper, tenable, valid, vindicable, warrantable; SEE CONCEPT 528

defensive [adj] *protective, watchful*
arresting, averting, balking, checking, conservative, coping with, defending, foiling, forestalling, frustrating, guarding, in opposition, interrupting, opposing, preservative, preventive, protecting, resistive, safeguarding, thwarting, uptight*, warding off, withstanding; SEE CONCEPTS 401,550

defer [v1] *hold off, put off*
adjourn, block, delay, detain, extend, give rain check*, hang fire*, hinder, hold up, impede, intermit, lay over, lengthen, obstruct, postpone, procrastinate, prolong, prorogue, protract, put on back burner*, put on hold*, put on ice*, remit, retard, set aside, shelve, slow, stall, stay, suspend, table, waive; SEE CONCEPTS 121,130

defer [v2] *yield*
accede, accommodate, acquiesce, adapt, adjust, admit, agree, assent, bow, buckle, capitulate, cave, comply, concede, cringe, fawn, give in to, knuckle*, knuckle under*, kowtow*, obey, submit, succumb, truckle; SEE CONCEPT 83

deference [n1] *obedience, compliance*
acquiescence, capitulation, complaisance, condescension, docility, obeisance, submission, yielding; SEE CONCEPT 633

deference [n2] *attention, homage*
acclaim, civility, consideration, courtesy, esteem, honor, obeisance, politeness, regard, respect, reverence, thoughtfulness, veneration; SEE CONCEPTS 10,410

deferential [adj] *respectful, considerate*
civil, complaisant, courteous, disarming, du-

de
de

teous, dutiful, ingratiating, ingratiatory, insinuating, insinuative, obedient, obeisant, obsequious, polite, regardful, reverential, saccharine, silken, silky, submissive; SEE CONCEPT 401

deferment/deferral [n] *postponement*
adjournment, delay, holdover*, moratorium, pause, putting off*, stay, suspension; SEE CONCEPTS 121,130

deferred [adj] *put off till a later time*
adjourned, assessed, charged, delayed, funded, held up, indebted, in waiting, negotiated, on hold*, on the shelf*, pigeonholed*, postponed, prolonged, protracted, remanded, renegotiated, retarded, scrubbed*, stalled, staved off, temporized; SEE CONCEPT 820

defiance [n] *disobedience, disregard*
affront, audacity, back talk*, big talk*, boldness, bravado, brazenness, call, cartel, challenge, command, confrontation, contempt, contrariness, contumacy, dare, defy, effrontery, enjoinder, factiousness, gas*, guts*, hot air*, impudence, impugnment, insolence, insubordination, insurgence, insurgency, intractableness, lip*, muster*, opposition, order, perversity, provocation, rebellion, rebelliousness, recalcitrance, revolt, sass*, spite, stump, summons, temerity, throwing of the gauntlet*, unruliness; SEE CONCEPTS 633,657

defiant [adj] *disobedient, disregardful*
aggressive, audacious, bold, challenging, contumacious, daring, gutsy*, insolent, insubmissive, insubordinate, mutinous, obstinate, provocative, rebellious, recalcitrant, reckless, refractory, resistant, resistive, sassy*, truculent; SEE CONCEPT 401

deficiency [n] *imperfection, inadequacy*
absence, bug*, dearth, defalcation, default, defect, deficit, demerit, dereliction, failing, failure, fault, flaw, frailty, glitch*, inability to hack it*, insufficience, insufficiency, lack, loss, need, neglect, paucity, privation, scantiness, scarcity, shortage, shortcoming, sin, want, weakness; SEE CONCEPTS 635,666,674

deficient [adj] *imperfect, inadequate*
amiss, bad, damaged, defective, exiguous, faulty, flawed, found wanting, impaired, incomplete, inferior, infrequent, injured, insufficient, lacking, marred, meager, not cut out for*, not enough, not make it*, not up to scratch*, outta gas*, rare, scant, scanty*, scarce, second fiddle*, second string, short, shy, sketchy, skimpy, third string*, unassembled, unequal, unfinished, unsatisfactory, wanting, weak; SEE CONCEPTS 531,565

deficit [n] *shortage of something needed, required*
arrears, dead horse*, defalcation, default, deficiency, due bill, dues, inadequacy, in hock*, insufficience, insufficiency, in the hole*, in the red, lack, loss, paucity, red ink*, scantiness, shortcoming, shortfall, underage; SEE CONCEPTS 335,646

deficit spending [n] *paying out in excess of income*
debt, debt explosion, deficit financing, in the red, megadebt, negative cash flow, no assets, overspending; SEE CONCEPTS 324,330,344

defile [v] *corrupt, violate*
abuse, adulterate, befoul, besmirch, contaminate, debase, deflower, degrade, desecrate, dirty, discolor, disgrace, dishonor, hurt, maculate, make

foul, mess up*, molest, muck up*, pollute, profane, rape, ravish, scuzz up*, seduce, shame, smear, soil, stain, sully, taint, tar, tarnish, trash, vitiate; SEE CONCEPTS 54,156,246

defiled [adj] *corrupted, violated*
besmirched, common, cooked, desecrated, dirty, dishonored, exposed, impure, mucked up*, polluted, profaned, ravished, spoilt, tainted, trashed*, unclean, vitiated; SEE CONCEPT 570

define [v1] *give description*
ascertain, assign, call a spade a spade*, characterize, construe, decide, delineate, denominate, denote, describe, designate, detail, determine, dub, elucidate, entitle, etch, exemplify, explain, expound, formalize, illustrate, interpret, label, lay it out*, nail it down*, name, prescribe, represent, specify, spell out, tag, translate; SEE CONCEPTS 55,57,62

define [v2] *delimit, outline*
belt, border, bound, circumscribe, compass, confine, curb, delineate, demarcate, distinguish, edge, encircle, enclose, encompass, envelop, establish, fence in, fix, flank, gird, girdle, limit, mark, mark out, rim, set, set bounds to, settle, stake out, surround, verge, wall in; SEE CONCEPTS 18,60,758

definite [adj1] *exact, clear*
audible, bold, categorical, clean-cut, clear-cut, clearly defined, complete, crisp, definitive, determined, distinct, distinguishable, downright, explicit, express, fixed, forthright, full, graphic, incisive, marked, minute, not vague, obvious, palpable, particular, plain, positive, precise, pronounced, ringing, severe, sharp, silhouetted, specific, straightforward, tangible, unambiguous, undubitable, unequivocal, unmistakable, visible, vivid, well-defined, well-grounded, well-marked; SEE CONCEPT 557

definite [adj2] *fixed, certain, positive*
assigned, assured, beyond doubt, circumscribed, convinced, decided, defined, determinate, determined, established, guaranteed, limited, narrow, precise, prescribed, restricted, set, settled, sure; SEE CONCEPT 535

definitely [adv] *certainly*
absolutely, beyond any doubt, categorically, clearly, decidedly, doubtless, doubtlessly, easily, explicitly, expressly, far and away*, finally, indubitably, no ifs ands or buts about it*, obviously, plainly, positively, specifically, surely, undeniably, unequivocally, unmistakably, unquestionably, without doubt, without fail, without question; SEE CONCEPTS 535,552

definition [n] *description*
analogue, annotation, answer, characterization, clarification, clue, comment, commentary, cue, delimitation, delineation, demarcation, denotation, determination, diagnosis, drift, elucidation, exemplification, explanation, explication, exposition, expounding, fixing, formalization, gloss, individuation, interpretation, key, outlining, rationale, rendering, rendition, representation, settling, signification, solution, statement of meaning, terminology, translation; SEE CONCEPTS 274,278,689

definitive [adj] *authoritative*
absolute, actual, categorical, clear-cut, closing, complete, completing, concluding, conclusive, decisive, definite, determining, downright*, ending, exhaustive, express, final, finishing, flat

out*, last, limiting, nailed down, perfect, plain, precise, real, reliable, settling, specific, straight out, terminal, terminating, ultimate, unambiguous; SEE CONCEPTS 531,535,574

deflate [*v1*] *reduce or cause to contract*
collapse, decrease, depreciate, depress, devalue, diminish, empty, exhaust, flatten, puncture, shrink, squash, void; SEE CONCEPTS 236,247,776

deflate [*v2*] *humiliate*
chasten, cut down to size*, dash, debunk, disconcert, dispirit, humble, kick in the teeth*, knock down*, let down easy*, let wind out of sails*, mortify, puncture balloon*, put down*, shoot down*, take down*; SEE CONCEPTS 7,19

deflect [*v*] *bounce off; turn aside*
avert, bend, cover up, curve, deviate, disperse, diverge, divert, fend, glance off, hold off, hook, keep off, parry, pivot, ricochet, sheer, shy, sidetrack, slew, slip, swerve, twist, veer, volte-face, wheel, whip, whirl, wind; SEE CONCEPTS 147,189,194

deflower [*v*] *ravish; take away beauty*
assault, defile, deflorate, depredate, desecrate, despoil, devour, force, harm, have, mar, molest, outrage, possess, ravage, ravish, ruin, seduce, spoil, violate; SEE CONCEPT 375

deforestation [*n*] *clear-cutting*
denuding, desertification, erosion, logging; SEE CONCEPTS 252,257,698

deform [*v*] *distort, disfigure*
batter, blemish, buckle, contort, cripple, damage, deface, flaw, gnarl, grimace, impair, injure, knot, maim, malform, mangle, mar, misshape, mutilate, ruin, skew, spoil, twist, warp, wince; SEE CONCEPTS 246,250

deformed [*adj*] *disfigured, distorted*
askew, awry, bent, blemished, bowed, buckled, contorted, cramped, crippled, crooked, curved, damaged, disjointed, gnarled, grotesque, humpbacked, hunchbacked, ill-made, irregular, knotted, maimed, malformed, mangled, marred, misproportioned, misshapen, out of shape, scarred, twisted, ugly, warped; SEE CONCEPTS 485,486

deformity [*n*] *disfigurement, distortion*
aberration, abnormality, asymmetry, buckle, contortion, corruption, crookedness, damage, defacement, defect, depravity, evil, grossness, hideousness, impairment, injury, irregularity, knot, malconformation, malformation, misproportion, misshape, misshapenness, repulsiveness, ugliness, unattractiveness, unnaturalness, unsightliness, warp; SEE CONCEPT 580

defraud [*v*] *cheat, bilk*
bamboozle, beguile, burn, chouse, circumvent, clip, con, cozen, deceive, delude, do, do number on*, do out of*, dupe, embezzle, fleece, flimflam, foil, hoax, jive*, milk*, outwit, pilfer, pull fast one*, rip off*, rob, shaft*, shuck*, stick*, sucker into*, swindle, take*, take in*, take to the cleaner's*, trick, victimize; SEE CONCEPT 59

defray [*v*] *pay*
bear the cost*, chip in*, cover cost, finance, foot the bill*, fund, pay for, pick up the bill*, pick up the check*, pick up the tab*, settle; SEE CONCEPTS 108,115,327,341,351

deft [*adj*] *agile, clever*
able, adept, adroit, apt, crack, crackerjack*, cute, dexterous, expert, fleet, handy, having good hands, having know-how, ingenious, neat, nimble, proficient, prompt, quick, ready, skilled, skillful; SEE CONCEPT 527

defunct [*adj*] *extinct, not functioning*
asleep, bygone, cold, dead, deceased, departed, done for*, down the drain*, exanimate, expired, gone, had it*, inanimate, inoperative, invalid, kaput*, late, lifeless, lost, nonexistent, obsolete, out of commission*, vanished; SEE CONCEPTS 539,560

defuse [*v*] *disarm; smooth over*
alleviate, cripple, deactivate, demilitarize, diminish, disable, lessen, moderate, mollify, pacify, pad, restrain, soften, soothe, subdue, weaken; SEE CONCEPTS 7,22,142,211,320

defy [*v*] *challenge, frustrate*
baffle, beard, brave, confront, contemn, dare, defeat, deride, despise, disregard, elude, face, flout, fly in face of*, foil, front, gibe*, hang tough*, hurl defiance at, ignore, insult, make my day*, mock, oppose, outdare, provoke, repel, repulse, resist, ridicule, scorn, slight, spurn, stick*, stick fast*, take one on*, thwart, venture, violate, withstand; SEE CONCEPTS 78,87

degeneracy [*n1*] *corruption*
abasement, decadence, degradation, depravity, dissoluteness, downfall, immorality, inferiority, meanness, poorness; SEE CONCEPT 645

degeneracy [*n2*] *decay, deterioration*
atrophy, debasement, declination, decline, decrease, depravation, devolution, downfall, downgrade; SEE CONCEPTS 230,469

degenerate [*adj*] *corrupt, deteriorated*
base, debased, debauched, decadent, decayed, degenerated, degraded, demeaned, depraved, dissolute, effete, failing, fallen, flatitious, immoral, infamous, low, mean, miscreant, nefarious, overripe, perverted, retrograde, retrogressive, rotten, sinking, unhealthy, vicious, villainous, vitiated, wicked, worsen; SEE CONCEPTS 545,570

degenerate [*v*] *decay, deteriorate*
backslide, come apart at seams*, corrode, corrupt, decline, decrease, deprave, descend, die on vine*, disimprove, disintegrate, fall off, go downhill*, go to pieces*, go to the dogs*, lapse, lessen, regress, retrogress, return, revert, rot, sink, slip, vitiate, worsen; SEE CONCEPTS 469,698,702

degradation [*n*] *depravity, shame*
abasement, debasement, decadence, decline, degeneracy, degeneration, demotion, derogation, deterioration, discredit, disgrace, dishonor, downgrading, evil, humiliation, ignominy, mortification, perversion, reduction; SEE CONCEPTS 230,410

degrade [*v*] *shame, humiliate*
abase, belittle, bemean, bench, break, bump, bust, canker, cast down, cheapen, corrupt, cut down to size*, debase, debauch, declass, decry, degenerate, demean, demote, depose, deprave, derogate, deteriorate, detract, diminish, disbar, discredit, disgrace, dishonor, disparage, downgrade, humble, impair, injure, lessen, lower, mudsling*, pan*, pervert, put down, reduce, rule out, run down*, shoot down*, sink, slam, take down*, take down a peg*, tear down*, vitiate, weaken; SEE CONCEPTS 7,19,240

degrading [*adj*] *debasing*
cheapening, demeaning, derogatory, disgraceful, downgrading, humiliating, lowering; SEE CONCEPTS 267,555,570

de
de

degree [*n1*] *unit of measurement*
amount, amplitude, caliber, dimension, division, expanse, extent, gauge, gradation, grade, height, intensity, interval, length, limit, line, link, mark, notch, period, plane, point, proportion, quality, quantity, range, rate, ratio, reach, rung, scale, scope, severity, shade, size, space, stage, stair, standard, step, stint, strength, tenor, term, tier; SEE CONCEPTS 651,783,792

degree [*n2*] *recognition of achievement; rank or grade of position*
approbation, approval, baccalaureate, caliber, class, compass, credentials, credit, dignification, dignity, distinction, eminence, grade, height, honor, level, magnitude, order, pitch, point, position, potency, qualification, quality, quantity, range, rank, reach, scope, sheepskin, shingle, sort, stage, standard, standing, station, status, strength, testimonial, testimony; SEE CONCEPTS 388,706

dehydrate [*v*] *take moisture out of*
cotton-mouth, desiccate, drain, dry, dry out, dry up, evaporate, exsiccate, parch, sear; SEE CONCEPTS 250,469

deify [*v*] *elevate, glorify*
adore, apostheosize, consecrate, ennoble, enthrone, exalt, extol, idealize, idolize, immortalize, venerate, worship; SEE CONCEPTS 69,367

deign [*v*] *lower oneself*
condescend, consent, deem worthy, patronize, see fit*, stoop, think fit*, vouchsafe; SEE CONCEPT 35

deity [*n*] *god, worshiped being*
celestial, celestial being, creator, divine being, divinity, goddess, godhead, idol, immortal, supreme being; SEE CONCEPTS 368,370

déjà vu [*n*] *already seen or experienced*
familiarity, past-life experience, recall, recognition, remembrance; SEE CONCEPTS 40,529

dejected [*adj*] *depressed, blue*
abject, all torn up*, atrabilious, black, bleak, broody, bummed out*, cast down, cheerless, clouded, crestfallen, dampened, dashed, despondent, disconsolate, discouraged, disheartened, dismal, dispirited, doleful, down, downcast, downhearted, down in the dumps*, down in the mouth*, dragged, drooping, droopy, gloomy, glum, heavyhearted, hurting*, in the pits*, low, low-spirited, melancholy, miserable, moody, mopey*, mopish*, morose, sad, sagging, shot down*, spiritless, woebegone, wretched; SEE CONCEPT 403

delay [*n*] *deferment, interruption*
adjournment, bind, check, cooling-off period*, cunctation, dawdling, demurral, detention, discontinuation, downtime*, filibuster, hangup*, hindrance, holding, holding pattern*, hold-up*, impediment, interval, jam, lag, lingering, logjam*, loitering, moratorium, obstruction, postponement, problem, procrastination, prorogation, putting off*, remission, reprieve, retardation, retardment, setback, showstopper*, stall, stay, stop, stoppage, surcease, suspension, tarrying, tie-up, wait; SEE CONCEPTS 121,130,666

delay [*v*] *cause stop in action*
adjourn, arrest, bar, bide time, block, check, choke, clog, confine, curb, dawdle, defer, detain, deter, dilly-dally*, discourage, drag, encumber, filibuster, gain time, hamper, hold, hold over, impede, inhibit, interfere, intermit, keep, keep back, lag, lay over, linger, loiter, obstruct, postpone, prevent, procrastinate, prolong, prorogue, protract, put off, remand, repress, restrict, retard, shelve, slacken, stall, stave off, stay, suspend, table, tarry, temporize, withhold; SEE CONCEPTS 121,130,237

delectable [*adj*] *delicious, enjoyable*
adorable, agreeable, ambrosial, appetizing, charming, choice, dainty, darling, delicate, delightful, delish, divine, enticing, exquisite, gratifying, heavenly, inviting, luscious, lush, palatable, pleasant, pleasurable, rare, sapid, satisfying, savory, scrumptious, tasty, toothsome, yummy; SEE CONCEPTS 574,579,613

delegate [*n*] *representative, often governmental*
agent, alternate, ambassador, appointee, catchpole*, commissioner, consul, deputy, emissary, envoy, factor, front*, legate, member, member of congress, minister, mouthpiece, nominee, people's choice, pinch hitter*, plenipotentiary, proxy, regent, rep*, replacement, senator, spokesperson, stand-in, substitute, surrogate, vicar, viceroy; SEE CONCEPT 354

delegate [*v1*] *give authority; empower*
accredit, appoint, assign, authorize, cast, charge, choose, commission, constitute, depute, deputize, designate, elect, give nod, invest, license, mandate, name, nominate, ordain, place trust in, select, swear in, warrant; SEE CONCEPTS 50,88

delegate [*v2*] *assign responsibility*
authorize, consign, devolve, entrust, give, hand over, hold responsible for, parcel out*, pass on*, relegate, send on errand, send on mission, shunt, transfer; SEE CONCEPTS 50,88,143

delegation [*n1*] *assignment of responsibility*
appointment, apportioning, authorization, charge, commissioning, committal, consigning, consignment, conveyance, conveying, deputation, deputization, deputizing, devolution, entrustment, giving over, installation, investiture, mandate, nomination, ordination, reference, referring, relegation, sending away, submittal, submitting, transferal, transference, transferring, trust; SEE CONCEPTS 50,88,143,685

delegation [*n2*] *group of representatives*
commission, contingent, deputation, embassy, envoys, gathering, legation, mission, organization; SEE CONCEPTS 299,301

delete [*v*] *erase, remove*
annul, black out, bleep, blot out, blue-pencil*, cancel, clean, clean up, cross out, cut, cut out, decontaminate, destroy, drop, edit, efface, eliminate, exclude, expunge, obliterate, omit, pass up, rub, rub out, rule out, sanitize, snip, squash, squelch, sterilize, strike out, trim, wipe out, X-out*; SEE CONCEPT 211

deleterious [*adj*] *harmful, damaging*
bad, destroying, destructive, detrimental, hurtful, injurious, mischievous, nocent, nocuous, pernicious, prejudicial, prejudicious, ruining, ruinous; SEE CONCEPTS 537,570

deliberate [*adj*] *intentional*
advised, aforethought, calculated, careful, cautious, cold-blooded, conscious, considered, cut-and-dried*, designed, designful, done on purpose, express, fixed, intended, judged, meticulous, planned, pondered, prearranged, predesigned, predeterminate, predetermined, premeditated, prepense, projected, provident, prudent, purposed, purposeful, purposive, rea-

soned, resolved, schemed, scrupulous, studied, studious, thoughtful, thought out, voluntary, wary, weighed, willful, with forethought, witting; SEE CONCEPTS *401,542*

deliberate [*v*] *think about seriously; discuss*
argue, bat it around*, cerebrate, chew over*, cogitate, consider, consult, contemplate, debate, excogitate, hammer away at*, judge, kick around, knock around, meditate, mull over, muse, ponder, pour it on*, put on thinking cap*, rack brains*, reason, reflect, revolve, roll, ruminate, run up a flagpole*, speculate, stew over*, study, sweat over*, talk over, turn over, weigh; SEE CONCEPTS *17,24,56*

deliberately [*adv*] *intentionally*
advisedly, after consideration, apurpose, by design, calculatingly, consciously, designed, determinedly, emphatically, freely, in cold blood, independently, knowingly, meaningfully, on purpose, pointedly, premeditatively, prepensely, purposely, purposively, resolutely, studiously, to that end, voluntarily, willfully, with a view to, with eyes wide open*, with malice aforethought*, without qualms, wittingly; SEE CONCEPTS *401,542*

deliberation [*n*] *serious thought, discussion*
application, attention, brainwork, calculation, care, carefulness, caution, cerebration, circumspection, cogitation, confabulation, conference, consideration, consultation, debate, forethought, heed, meditation, prudence, purpose, rap, ratiocination, reflection, speculation, study, ventilation, wariness; SEE CONCEPTS *17,24,56*

delicacy [*n1*] *daintiness, fineness of structure*
airiness, banquet, bonne bouche, dainty, delight, dessert, feast, goody, indulgence, luxury, gossameriness, infirmity, lightness, slenderness, smoothness, softness, subtlety, tenderness, tenuity, translucency, transparency, weakness; SEE CONCEPTS *611,733*

delicacy [*n2*] *delicious, gourmet food*
ambrosia, banquet, bonne bouche, dainty, delight, dessert, feast, goody, indulgence, luxury, morsel, nectar, pleasure, rarity, regale, relish, savory, special, sweet, tidbit, treat; SEE CONCEPT *457*

delicate [*adj1*] *dainty, weak*
aerial, balmy, breakable, choice, delectable, delicious, delightful, elegant, ethereal, exquisite, faint, filmy, fine, fine-grained, finespun, flimsy, fracturable, fragile, frail, frangible, gauzy, gentle, gossamery, graceful, hairline, mild, muted, nice, pale, pastel, rare, recherché, select, shatterable, shattery, slight, soft, subdued, subtle, superior, tender; SEE CONCEPTS *490,574,606*

delicate [*adj2*] *sickly*
ailing, debilitated, decrepit, feeble, flimsy, fragile, frail, infirm, shatterable, shattery, slender, slight, susceptible, tender, unhealthy, weak; SEE CONCEPT *314*

delicate [*adj3*] *fussy, discriminating*
alert, careful, critical, dainty, fastidious, finical, finicking, finicky, gentle, nice, particular, persnickety, prudish, pure, refined, scrupulous, sensitive, squeamish, thin-skinned; SEE CONCEPT *404*

delicate [*adj4*] *difficult, sticky (situation)*
critical, hair-trigger*, precarious, sensitive, ticklish, touchy, tricky, uncertain, unpredictable, volatile; SEE CONCEPT *565*

delicate [*adj5*] *careful, tactful*
accurate, adept, cautious, considerate, deft, detailed, diplomatic, discreet, expert, foresighted, heedful, masterly, minute, politic, precise, proficient, prudent, sensitive, skilled, tactical, wary; SEE CONCEPTS *401,542*

delicately [*adv*] *carefully*
beautifully, cautiously, daintily, deftly, elegantly, exquisitely, fastidiously, finely, gracefully, lightly, precisely, sensitively, skillfully, softly, subtly, tactfully; SEE CONCEPTS *542,544*

delicatessen [*n*] *eatery*
café, cafeteria, charcuterie, deli, restaurant, sandwich shop, subway shop; SEE CONCEPT *449*

delicious [*adj*] *pleasing, especially to the taste*
adorable, ambrosial, appetizing, choice, dainty, darling, delectable, delightful, delish*, distinctive, divine, enjoyable, enticing, exquisite, fit for king*, good, gratifying, heavenly, luscious, lush, mellow, mouthwatering, nectarous, nice, palatable, piquant, pleasant, rare, rich, sapid, savory, scrumptious, spicy, sweet, tasteful, tasty, tempting, titillating, toothsome, well-prepared, well-seasoned, yummy*; SEE CONCEPTS *572,613*

delight [*n*] *enjoyment, happiness*
contentment, delectation, ecstasy, enchantment, felicity, fruition, gladness, glee, gratification, hilarity, jollity, joy, joyance, mirth, pleasure, rapture, relish, satisfaction, transport; SEE CONCEPT *410*

delight [*v*] *make happy; experience happiness*
allure, amuse, arride, attract, be the ticket*, charm, cheer, content, delectate, divert, enchant, enrapture, entertain, exult, fascinate, freak out, gladden, glory, go over big*, gratify, groove*, hit the spot*, jubilate, knock dead*, knock out*, please, pleasure, ravish, rejoice, satisfy, score, send, slay, thrill, tickle pink*, tickle to death*, turn on, wow; SEE CONCEPTS *7,22*

delighted [*adj*] *very happy*
captivated, charmed, ecstatic, elated, enchanted, entranced, excited, fulfilled, gladdened, gratified, joyous, jubilant, overjoyed, pleasantly surprised, pleased, thrilled; SEE CONCEPT *403*

delightful [*adj*] *pleasant, charming*
adorable, agreeable, alluring, ambrosial, amusing, attractive, beautiful, captivating, cheery, clever, congenial, darling, delectable, delicious, enchanting, engaging, enjoyable, entertaining, fair, fascinating, gratifying, heavenly, ineffable, lovely, luscious, lush, pleasing, pleasurable, rapturous, ravishing, refreshing, satisfying, scrumptious, thrilling, yummy*; SEE CONCEPTS *401,404*

delight in [*v*] *take pleasure from*
admire, adore, amuse oneself, appreciate, be content, be pleased, cherish, dig*, eat up*, enjoy, feast on, get a kick out of*, get high on*, get off on*, glory in, groove on*, indulge in, like, live a little*, live it up*, love, luxuriate in, relish, revel in, savor; SEE CONCEPTS *32,410*

delineate [*v*] *describe; outline*
characterize, chart, define, depict, detail, draft, draw, figure, lay out, limn, mark, plot, portray, represent, sketch out, trace; SEE CONCEPTS *36,55,174*

delinquency [*n*] *misconduct*
crime, default, dereliction, failure, fault, lapse, misbehavior, misdeed, misdemeanor, neglect, nonobservance, offense, oversight, weakness, wrongdoing; SEE CONCEPTS *192,645*

de
de

delinquent [*adj*] *irresponsible, defaulting*
behind, blamable, blameworthy, careless, censurable, criminal, culpable, defaultant, derelict, disregardful, faulty, guilty, lax, neglectful, negligent, offending, overdue, procrastinating, redhanded*, remiss, reprehensible, shabby, slack, tardy, unpaid; SEE CONCEPTS *401,570*

delinquent [*n*] *criminal, often young*
behind, blackguard, black sheep*, culprit, dawdler, deadbeat*, deadhead*, debtor, defaulter, derelict, desperado, evader, fallen angel*, felon, hoodlum*, jailbird*, JD*, juvenile delinquent, juvie*, lawbreaker, loafer, lounger, malefactor, miscreant, neglecter, no show*, offender, outlaw, punk*, recreant, reprobate, sinner, wrongdoer, young offender; SEE CONCEPT *412*

delirious [*adj1*] *mentally imbalanced*
aberrant, bewildered, confused, crazed, crazy, demented, deranged, deviant, deviate, disarranged, disordered, distracted, disturbed, flipped*, flipped out*, hallucinatory, incoherent, insane, irrational, lightheaded, lunatic, mad, maniac, maniacal, manic, off one's head*, out of one's head*, out of one's skull*, rambling, raving, unhinged, unreasonable, unsettled, wandering; SEE CONCEPTS *402,403*

delirious [*adj2*] *excited; very happy*
beside oneself*, carried away*, corybantic, crazy, delighted, drunk*, ecstatic, enthused, frantic, frenetic, frenzied, furious, hysterical, intoxicated, mad, overwrought, rabid*, rapturous, thrilled, transported, wild; SEE CONCEPTS *401,403*

delirium [*n*] *madness*
aberration, ardor, dementia, derangement, ecstasy, enthusiasm, fervor, fever, frenzy, furor, fury, hallucination, hysteria, insanity, lunacy, mania, passion, rage, raving, transport, zeal; SEE CONCEPT *410*

deliver [*v1*] *transfer, carry*
bear, bring, cart, come across with*, convey, dish out*, distribute, drop, fork over*, gimme*, give, hand, hand-carry, hand over, pass, put on, put out, remit, transport, truck; SEE CONCEPTS *108,217*

deliver [*v2*] *relinquish possession*
abandon, cede, commit, give up, grant, hand over, let go, resign, surrender, transfer, turn over, yield; SEE CONCEPTS *116,131*

deliver [*v3*] *free, liberate*
acquit, discharge, emancipate, loose, ransom, redeem, release, rescue, save, unshackle; SEE CONCEPT *127*

deliver [*v4*] *announce, proclaim*
address, bring out, broach, chime in, come out with, communicate, declare, express, give, give forth, impart, present, pronounce, publish, read, say, state, tell, throw out, utter, vent, voice; SEE CONCEPTS *51,60*

deliver [*v5*] *administer; throw*
aim, deal, direct, dispatch, fling, give, hurl, inflict, launch, pitch, send, strike, transmit; SEE CONCEPTS *217,222*

deliver [*v6*] *discharge, give forth*
accouch, bear, birth, born, dispense, feed, find, hand, hand over, produce, provide, release, supply, turn over; SEE CONCEPTS *179,374*

deliverance [*n*] *liberation*
acquittal, delivery, emancipation, extrication,

freeing, redemption, release, rescue, salvation, saving; SEE CONCEPT *134*

delivery [*n1*] *transfer, transmittal*
carting, commitment, consignment, conveyance, dispatch, distribution, drop, freighting, giving over, handing over, impartment, intrusting, mailing, parcel post, portage, post, rendition, shipment, surrender, transmission; SEE CONCEPTS *108,217*

delivery [*n2*] *articulation of message*
accent, diction, elocution, emphasis, enunciation, inflection, intonation, modulation, pronunciation, speech, utterance; SEE CONCEPTS *47,595*

delivery [*n3*] *childbirth*
accouchement, bearing, birth, birthing, bringing forth, Caesarian section, childbearing, confinement, geniture, labor, lying-in, parturition, travail; SEE CONCEPTS *302,373,374*

delivery [*n4*] *giving of freedom*
deliverance, emancipation, escape, freeing, liberation, pardon, release, rescue, salvage, salvation; SEE CONCEPT *127*

delivery room [*n*] *birthing room*
birthing center, hospital room; SEE CONCEPTS *312,439,449*

delude [*v*] *deceive, fool*
beguile, betray, bluff, caboodle*, cheat, con, cozen, disinform, do a number on*, doublecross, dupe*, gull*, hoax*, hoodwink*, illude, impose on, jive*, juggle*, lead up garden path*, misguide, mislead, mousetrap*, outfox, play trick on, snow*, string along, sucker*, take in, trick; SEE CONCEPT *59*

deluge [*n*] *downpour, flood of something*
avalanche, barrage, cataclysm, cataract, drencher, flux, inundation, niagara, overflowing, overrunning, pour, rush, spate, torrent; SEE CONCEPTS *432,524,787*

deluge [*v1*] *inundate with water*
douse, drench, drown, engulf, flood, flush, gush, overflow, overrun, overwhelm, pour, sluice, soak, sop, souse, stream, submerge, swamp, wet, whelm; SEE CONCEPT *256*

deluge [*v2*] *overwhelm*
abound, crowd, engulf, flood, glut, inundate, overcome, overcrowd, overload, overrun, oversupply, snow*, snow under*, swamp, teem; SEE CONCEPTS *42,140*

delusion [*n*] *misconception, misbelief*
apparition, blunder, casuistry, chicanery, daydream, deception, deceptiveness, dream, eidolon, error, fallacy, false impression, fancy, fantasy, figment*, fool's paradise*, ghost, hallucination, head trip*, ignis fatuus, illusion, lapse, mirage, misapprehension, mistake, optical illusion, oversight, phantasm, phantom, pipe dream*, self-deception, shade, speciousness, spuriousness, trickery, trip, vision; SEE CONCEPTS *409,410,689*

delusive [*adj*] *deceptive*
apparent, beguiling, chimerical, deceiving, deluding, fallacious, false, fanciful, fantastic, illusive, illusory, imaginary, misleading, ostensible, quixotic, seeming, specious, spurious, visionary; SEE CONCEPT *582*

deluxe [*adj*] *superior, plush*
choice, costly, dainty, delicate, elegant, exclusive, expensive, exquisite, first-class, grand, luscious, lush, luxuriant, luxurious, opulent, palatial, posh, rare, recherché, rich, ritzy, select,

special, splendid, sumptuous, super, swank, swanky; SEE CONCEPT *574*

delve [*v*] *dig into task, action*
burrow, dig, dredge, examine, excavate, explore, ferret out*, go into, gouge out, inquire, investigate, jump into, leave no stone unturned*, look into, probe, prospect, ransack, really get into*, research, rummage, scoop out, search, seek, shovel, sift, spade, trowel, turn inside out*, unearth; SEE CONCEPTS *87,103,216*

demagogue [*n*] *agitating person*
agitator, fanatic, firebrand*, fomenter, haranger, hothead*, incendiary, inciter, inflamer, instigator, politician, rabble-rouser*, radical, rebel, revolutionary, soapbox orator*, troublemaker; SEE CONCEPTS *359,412*

demand [*n*] *question, request*
appeal, application, arrogation, bid, bidding, call, call for, charge, claim, clamor, command, counterclaim, entreatment, entreaty, exaction, impetration, imploration, importunity, imposition, inquiry, insistence, interest, interrogation, lien, necessity, need, occasion, order, petition, plea, prayer, pursuit, requirement, requisition, rush, sale, search, solicitation, stipulation, suit, supplication, trade, ultimatum, use, vogue, want; SEE CONCEPT *662*

demand [*v*] *ask strongly for something*
abuse, appeal, apply, arrogate, badger, beg, beseech, besiege, bid, challenge, charge, cite, claim, clamor for, coerce, command, compel, constrain, counterclaim, direct, dun, enjoin, entreat, exact, expect, force, hit, hit up, impetrate, implore, importune, inquire, insist on, interrogate, knock, nag, necessitate, oblige, order, pester, petition, postulate, pray, press, question, request, require, requisition, solicit, stipulate, sue for, summon, supplicate, tax, urge, whistle for; SEE CONCEPT *53*

demand [*v2*] *require*
ask, call for, command, crave, cry out for, fail, involve, lack, necessitate, need, oblige, take, want; SEE CONCEPTS *26,646*

demanding [*adj*] *challenging, urgent*
ambitious, backbreaker*, bothersome, clamorous, critical, dictatorial, difficult, exacting, exhausting, exigent, fussy, grievous, hard, imperious, importunate, insistent, nagging, onerous, oppressive, pressing, querulous, strict, stringent, taxing, tough, troublesome, trying, wearing, weighty; SEE CONCEPTS *542,565*

demarcation [*n*] *boundary, division*
bound, confine, delimitation, differentiation, distinction, enclosure, limit, margin, separation, split, terminus; SEE CONCEPT *745*

demean [*v*] *humble, humiliate*
abase, bad-mouth*, belittle, bemean, cast down, contemn, cut down to size*, cut rate, debase, decry, degrade, derogate, descend, despise, detract, dis*, disparage, dump on*, knock down*, lower, pan*, poor-mouth*, scorn, sink, stoop*; SEE CONCEPTS *7,19,54*

demeanor [*n*] *behavior, manner*
address, air, attitude, bearing, carriage, comportment, conduct, deportment, disposition, mien, poise, port, presence, set; SEE CONCEPTS *411,633*

demented [*adj*] *crazy, insane*
bananas*, bemused, crackbrained*, daft, deliri-
ous, deranged, distracted, distraught, flipped out*, foolish, frenzied, fruity*, hysterical, idiotic, in the ozone*, lunatic, mad, maniac, maniacal, manic, non compos mentis, nutty as a fruitcake*, out of one's gourd*, out of one's tree*, psycho, psychopathic, psychotic, schitzy*, schizoid*, unbalanced, unglued*, unhinged*, unsound, whacko*; SEE CONCEPT *403*

dementia [*n*] *senility*
Alzheimer's disease, derangement, insanity, madness, mental decay, mental deterioration, mental disorder, personality change, softening of the brain*, unbalance; SEE CONCEPTS *316,410*

demise [*n*] *fate, usually death*
annihilation, collapse, curtains, decease, departure, dissolution, downfall, dying, end, ending, expiration, extinction, failure, fall, final thrill*, last out*, last roundup*, lights out*, number's up*, passing, quietus, ruin, silence, sleep, termination; SEE CONCEPTS *105,304,679*

democracy [*n*] *government in which people participate*
commonwealth, egalitarianism, emancipation, equalitarianism, equality, freedom, justice, liberal government, representative government, republic, suffrage; SEE CONCEPTS *299,688,689*

democratic [*adj*] *representative, self-governing*
autonomous, common, communal, constitutional, egalitarian, equal, free, friendly, individualistic, informal, just, libertarian, orderly, popular, populist, self-ruling, socialist; SEE CONCEPTS *319,536*

demography [*n*] *study of human population*
anthropology, census-taking, population analysis, population density, population growth, population size, population studies, population vital statistics; SEE CONCEPT *349*

demolish [*v*] *destroy; consume*
annihilate, break, bulldoze, burst, crack, crush, decimate, defeat, devastate, devour, dilapidate, dismantle, eat, flatten, gobble up, knock down, level, obliterate, overthrow, overturn, pulverize, put away, put in toilet*, raze, ruin, sink, smash, take apart, take out, tear down, torpedo*, total*, trash*, undo, wax*, wipe off map*, wrack, wreck; SEE CONCEPTS *169,252*

demolition [*n*] *destruction*
annihilation, bulldozing, explosion, extermination, knocking down, leveling, razing, wrecking; SEE CONCEPT *252*

demon [*n*] *evil, devilish being or influence*
archfiend, beast, brute, fiend, goblin, hellion, imp, incubus, little devil*, malignant spirit, monster, rascal, rogue, Satan, succubus, vampire, villain; SEE CONCEPTS *370,412*

demonic [*adj*] *evil*
aroused, bad, crazed, demoniac, demoniacal, devilish, diabolic, diabolical, fiendish, fired, frantic, frenetic, frenzied, hellish, impious, infernal, insane, inspired, mad, maniacal, manic, possessed, satanic, serpentine, unhallowed, violent, wicked; SEE CONCEPTS *404,545*

demonstrable [*adj*] *provable, evident*
ascertainable, attestable, axiomatic, certain, conclusive, deducible, evincible, incontrovertible, indubitable, inferable, irrefutable, obvious, palpable, positive, self-evident, undeniable, unmistakable, verifiable; SEE CONCEPTS *529,535*

de
de

demonstrate [*v1*] *display, show*
authenticate, determine, establish, evidence, evince, exhibit, expose, flaunt, indicate, make evident, make out, manifest, prove, roll out*, show and tell*, test, testify to, trot out*, try, validate; SEE CONCEPT 97

demonstrate [*v2*] *explain, illustrate*
confirm, debunk, describe, express, give for instance, make clear, ostend, proclaim, set forth, show how, teach, testify to, walk one through*; SEE CONCEPT 57

demonstrate [*v3*] *display or take public action for a cause*
exhibit, fast, lie in, manifest, march, march on, parade, picket, protest, rally, sit in, stage walkout, strike, walkout; SEE CONCEPTS 261,300

demonstration [*n1*] *display of proof*
affirmation, confirmation, description, evidence, exhibition, explanation, exposition, expression, illustration, induction, manifestation, presentation, proof, show, spectacle, substantiation, test, testimony, trial, validation; SEE CONCEPT 97

demonstration [*n2*] *display of belief in cause by taking public action*
fast, lie-in*, love-in*, march, mass lobby, parade, peace march, picket, picket line, protest, rally, sit-in*, strike, teach-in*, walkout; SEE CONCEPTS 261,300

demonstrative [*adj1*] *expressive, communicative*
affectionate, candid, effusive, emotional, evincive, expansive, explanatory, expository, frank, gushing, histrionic, illustrative, indicative, loving, open, outgoing, outpouring, outspoken, plain, profuse, symptomatic, tender, unconstrained, unreserved, unrestrained, warmhearted; SEE CONCEPTS 267,401

demonstrative [*adj2*] *conclusive*
authenticating, certain, convincing, decisive, definite, final, proving, showing, specific, validating; SEE CONCEPTS 531,537

demonstrator [*n*] *protester*
agitator, boycotter, disrupter, dissenter, marcher, objector, picketer, radical, revolter, revolutionary, rioter, striker, troublemaker; SEE CONCEPT 412

demoralize [*v1*] *depress, unnerve*
abash, blow out, blow up, chill, cripple, damp, dampen, daunt, debilitate, deject, disarrange, disconcert, discountenance, discourage, dishearten, disorder, disorganize, disparage, dispirit, disturb, embarrass, enfeeble, get to*, jumble, muddle, nonplus, psych out*, rattle, sap, send up*, shake, snarl, take apart*, take steam out*, undermine, unglue*, unman, unsettle, unzip*, upset, weaken; SEE CONCEPTS 7,19

demoralize [*v2*] *corrupt, pervert*
bastardize, bestialize, brutalize, debase, debauch, deprave, lower, vitiate, warp; SEE CONCEPT 14

demote [*v*] *downgrade, lower in rank*
bench*, break, bump, bust, declass, degrade, demean, demerit, dismiss, disrate, hold back, kick downstairs*, lower, reduce, relegate, set back; SEE CONCEPTS 233,351

demur [*v*] *disagree*
balk, cavil, challenge, combat, complain, deprecate, disapprove, dispute, doubt, fight, hem and haw*, hesitate, object, oppose, pause, protest, pussyfoot*, refuse, remonstrate, resist, scruple, shy, stick, stickle, strain, take exception*, vacillate, wait and see*, waver; SEE CONCEPTS 46,54

demure [*adj*] *reserved, affected*
backward, bashful, blushing, close, coy, decorous, diffident, earnest, humble, modest, nice, prim, prissy, proper, prudish, reticent, retiring, sedate, serious, shy, silent, skittish, sober, solemn, staid, strait-laced, timid, unassertive, unassuming, unassured; SEE CONCEPTS 401,404

den [*n1*] *cavern, hideaway*
atelier, burrow, cave, cloister, couch, cubbyhole, haunt, hideout, hole, hotbed, lair, lodge, nest, retreat, sanctuary, sanctum, shelter, snuggery, study; SEE CONCEPTS 448,513

den [*n2*] *room for relaxation or informal entertaining*
family room, library, media room, playroom, recreation room, rec room*, rumpus room, studio, TV room; SEE CONCEPTS 440,448

denial [*n*] *dismissal, refusal of belief in statement*
abnegation, abstaining, adjuration, brush-off, cold shoulder*, contradiction, controversion, declination, disallowance, disapproval, disavowal, disclaimer, dismissing, disproof, dissent, forswearing, gainsaying, nay, negation, negative, nix*, nonacceptance, noncommittal, no way*, prohibition, protestation, rebuff, rebuttal, refraining, refusing, refutal, refutation, rejecting, rejection, renegement, renouncement, renunciation, repudiating, repudiation, repulse, retraction, turndown, veto; SEE CONCEPTS 45,54

denigrate [*v*] *belittle, malign*
asperse, bad mouth*, besmirch, blacken, blister, calumniate, decry, defame, dis*, disparage, give black eye*, impugn, knock*, libel, mudsling*, put down*, revile, rip up*, roast*, run down*, scandalize, slander, tear down*, traduce, vilify; SEE CONCEPTS 52,54

denizen [*n*] *resident*
citizen, dweller, habitant, indweller, inhabitant, inhabiter, liver, national, native, occupant, resider, subject; SEE CONCEPT 413

denomination [*n1*] *religious belief*
church, communion, connection, creed, cult, faith, group, persuasion, religion, school, sect; SEE CONCEPTS 368,689

denomination [*n2*] *classification*
body, category, class, grade, group, size, type, unit, value; SEE CONCEPT 378

denomination [*n3*] *name*
appellation, appellative, brand, cognomen, compellation, designation, flag, handle, identification, label, moniker, nomen, slot, style, surname, tab, tag, term, title; SEE CONCEPT 683

denotation [*n*] *meaning, description*
designation, explanation, implication, indication, signification, specification; SEE CONCEPTS 268,682

denote [*v*] *designate, mean*
add up, announce, argue, bespeak, betoken, connote, evidence, express, finger, flash, hang sign on*, imply, import, indicate, insinuate, intend, make, mark, peg, prove, put down for, put finger on*, show, signify, spell, stand for, symbol, symbolize, tab, tag, typify; SEE CONCEPTS 55,682

denouement [*n*] *the end result*
climax, close, completion, conclusion, culmination, end, final curtain*, finale, last act*, resolution, windup*; SEE CONCEPT 832

denounce [*v*] *condemn, attack*
accuse, adjudicate, arraign, blacklist, blame, boycott, brand, castigate, censure, charge, charge

with, criticize, damn, decláim, decry, denunciate, derogate, dress down, excoriate, expose, finger*, hang something on*, impeach, implicate, impugn, incriminate, indict, inveigh against, knock, ostracize, proscribe, prosecute, rap, rat*, rebuke, reprehend, reprimand, reproach, reprobate, reprove, revile, scold, show up, skin*, smear, stigmatize, take to task, threaten, upbraid, vilify, vituperate; SEE CONCEPTS 44,52

dense [*adj*] *compressed, thick*
close, close-knit, compact, condensed, crammed, crowded, heaped, heavy, impenetrable, jammed, jam-packed*, massed, opaque, packed, packed like sardines*, piled, solid, substantial, thickset; SEE CONCEPT 483

dense [*adj2*] *slow, stupid*
blockheaded*, boorish, doltish, dull, dumb, fat-headed*, ignorant, imbecile, impassive, lethargic, numskulled*, oafish, obtuse, phlegmatic, simple, slow-witted, sluggish, stolid, thick, torpid; SEE CONCEPT 402

density [*n*] *bulk, mass*
body, closeness, compactness, concretion, consistency, crowdedness, denseness, frequency, heaviness, impenetrability, massiveness, quantity, solidity, substantiality, thickness, tightness; SEE CONCEPT 722

dent [*n*] *depression, scrape, chip*
cavity, concavity, crater, crenel, cut, dimple, dint, dip, embrasure, furrow, hollow, impression, incision, indentation, nick, notch, pit, scallop, score, scratch, sink, trough; SEE CONCEPT 580

dent [*v*] *chip, scrape, depress*
dig, dimple, dint, furrow, gouge, hollow, imprint, indent, make concave, mark, nick, notch, perforate, pit, press in, push in, ridge, scratch; SEE CONCEPTS 176,189,208,246

dentures [*n*] *false teeth*
artificial teeth, bridge, choppers*, dental plate, implants, partial, set of teeth; SEE CONCEPT 393

denude [*v*] *strip*
bare, disrobe, expose, fleece, lay bare*, peel, uncover, undress; SEE CONCEPT 211

denunciation [*n*] *condemnation, criticism*
accusation, arraignment, blame, castigation, censure, charge, cursing, damning, denouncement, derogation, dressing down*, fulmination, incrimination, indictment, invective, knock*, obloquy, rap*, reprehension, reprimand, reprobation, smearing, stigmatization, upbraidment, vilification; SEE CONCEPT 52

deny [*v*] *disagree, renounce, decline*
abjure, abnegate, ban, begrudge, call on, contradict, contravene, controvert, curb, disacknowledge, disallow, disavow, disbelieve, discard, disclaim, discredit, disown, disprove, doubt, enjoin from, eschew, exclude, forbid, forgo, forsake, gainsay, hold back, keep back, negate, negative, not buy, nullify, oppose, rebuff, rebut, recant, refuse, refute, reject, repudiate, restrain, revoke, sacrifice, say no to, spurn, taboo, take exception to, turn down, turn thumbs down*, veto, withhold; SEE CONCEPTS 46,49,52

deodorant [*n*] *something that freshens*
air freshener, antiperspirant, cleanser, cosmetic, deodorizer, disinfectant, fumigant, fumigator, smoke screen*; SEE CONCEPT 492

depart [*v1*] *leave, retreat*
abandon, abdicate, absent, beat it*, blast off*, cut and run*, cut out*, decamp, desert, disappear,

emigrate, escape, evacuate, exit, get away, git*, go, go away, go forth, hit the bricks*, hit the road*, hit the trail*, make a break*, march out, migrate, move on, move out, part, perish, pull out, quit, remove, retire, sally forth*, say goodbye*, scram*, secede, set forth, shove off*, slip away*, split*, start, start out, take leave, tergiversate, troop*, vacate, vanish, withdraw; SEE CONCEPT 195

depart [*v2*] *diverge from normal, expected*
abandon, cast, desert, deviate, differ, digress, disagree, discard, dissent, excurse, forsake, ramble, reject, repudiate, stray, swerve, turn aside, vary, veer, wander; SEE CONCEPTS 665,697

departed [*adj*] *dead*
bought the farm*, buried, deceased, expired, gone, in the grave*, laid to rest*, late, passed away, pushing up daisies*, six feet under*, stiff; SEE CONCEPT 539

department [*n1*] *section of organization, area*
administration, agency, area, arena, beat, board, branch, bureau, canton, circuit, commission, commune, constituency, division, force, office, parish, precinct, quarter, range, staff, station, subdivision, territory, tract, unit, ward; SEE CONCEPTS 381,440,508

department [*n2*] *area of interest, expertise*
activity, administration, assignment, avocation, bailiwick, berth, bureau, business, capacity, class, classification, domain, dominion, duty, field, function, incumbency, jurisdiction, line, niche, occupation, office, province, realm, responsibility, slot, specialty, sphere, spot, station, vocation, walk of life, wing; SEE CONCEPT 349

department store [*n*] *retail store*
anchor store, chain store, dime store, discount store, five-and-dime store, outlet store, shop, store; SEE CONCEPTS 325,439,448,449

departure [*n1*] *leaving*
abandonment, adieu, bow out*, congé, decampment, desertion, egress, egression, embarkation, emigration, escape, evacuation, exit, exodus, expatriation, farewell, flight, getaway*, going, going away, goodbye*, hegira, migration, parting, passage, powder*, quitting, recession, removal, retirement, retreat, sailing, separation, setting forth, setting out, stampede, start, takeoff, taking leave, taking off, vacation, vanishing act*, walkout, withdrawal, withdrawing; SEE CONCEPT 195

departure [*n2*] *deviation from normal, expected*
aberration, branching off, branching out, change, declination, deflection, difference, digression, divergence, diversion, innovation, in thing*, last word*, latest thing*, new wrinkle*, novelty, rambling, shift, straying, turning, variance, variation, veering, wandering; SEE CONCEPTS 665,697

depend [*v1*] *count on, rely upon*
bank on*, bet bottom dollar on*, bet on*, build upon, calculate on, confide in, gamble on*, lay money on*, lean on*, reckon on, trust in, turn to; SEE CONCEPT 26

depend [*v2*] *be contingent on*
be at mercy of, be based on, be conditioned, be connected with, be determined by, be in control of, be in the power of, be subject to, be subordinate to, bottom, found, ground, hang, hang in suspense, hang on, hinge on, pend, rest, rest on, rest with, revolve around, revolve on, stand on, stay, trust to, turn on; SEE CONCEPT 711

de
de

dependable [*adj*] *reliable, responsible*
always there, carrying the load*, certain, constant, faithful, good as one's word*, loyal, rocklike*, secure, stable, staunch, steadfast, steady, sturdy, sure,,to be counted on, tried, tried-and-true, true, trustworthy, trusty, unfailing; SEE CONCEPTS 542,560

dependence/dependency [*n1*] *confidence, reliance*
assurance, belief, credence, expectation, faith, hope, interdependence, responsibility, responsibleness, stability, steadiness, stock, trust, trustiness, trustworthiness; SEE CONCEPTS 410,689

dependence/dependency [*n2*] *addiction, need*
attachment, contingency, habit, helplessness, hook, inability, security blanket, servility, subjection, subordination, subservience, vulnerability, weakness, yoke; SEE CONCEPTS 20,709

dependent [*adj*] *weak, helpless*
abased, clinging, counting on, debased, defenseless, humbled, immature, indigent, inferior, lesser, minor, poor, reliant, relying on, secondary, subordinate, tied to apron strings*, under, under thumb*, unsustaining, vulnerable; SEE CONCEPTS 404,574

dependent [*adj2*] *contingent, determined by*
accessory to, ancillary, appurtenant, conditional, controlled by, counting, depending, incidental to, liable to, provisory, reckoning, regulated by, relative, reliant, relying, subject to, subordinate, subservient, susceptible, sustained by, trusting, under control of; SEE CONCEPT 546

depict [*v*] *describe, render in drawing or writing*
characterize, delineate, design, detail, illustrate, image, interpret, limn, narrate, outline, paint, picture, portray, relate, report, represent, reproduce, sculpt, sketch, state; SEE CONCEPTS 79,174

depiction [*n*] *description, rendering*
delineation, drawing, illustration, image, likeness, outline, picture, portraiture, portrayal, presentment, representation, sketch; SEE CONCEPTS 259,268

deplete [*v*] *consume, exhaust supply*
bankrupt, bleed*, decrease, dig into, diminish, drain, draw, dry up, empty, evacuate, expend, finish, impoverish, lessen, milk*, reduce, sap, spend, squander, suck dry*, undermine, use up, wash up, waste, weaken; SEE CONCEPTS 142,169,225

depleted [*adj*] *consumed, exhausted*
all in*, bare, bleary*, collapsed, decreased, depreciated, destitute, devoid of, drained, effete, emptied, far-gone*, in want, kaput*, lessened, out of, pooped out*, reduced, sapped, short of, sold, sold out, spent, sucked out*, used, used up, vacant, washed out, wasted, weakened, without resources, worn, worn out; SEE CONCEPTS 576,771

deplorable [*adj*] *unfortunate, shameful*
afflictive, awful, blameworthy, bummer*, calamitous, dire, dirty, disastrous, disgraceful, dishonorable, disreputable, distressing, dolorous, downer*, dreadful, execrable, faulty, godawful*, grievous, grim, heartbreaking, heartrending, horrifying, intolerable, lamentable, lousy, melancholy, miserable, mournful, opprobrious, overwhelming, pitiable, poor, regrettable, reprehensible, rotten, sad, scandalous, sickening, stinking, terrible, tragic, unbearable, unsatisfactory, woeful, wretched; SEE CONCEPTS 529,570, 574

deplore [*v*] *regret; condemn*
abhor, be against, bemoan, bewail, carry on, censure, complain, cry, denounce, deprecate, disapprove of, eat one's heart out*, grieve for, hate, hurt, lament, moan, mourn, object to, repent, rue, sing the blues*, sorrow over, take on, weep; SEE CONCEPTS 21,29

deploy [*v*] *redistribute, station troops or weapons*
arrange, display, dispose, expand, extend, fan out, form front, open, position, put out patrol, set out, set up, spread out, take battle stations, unfold, use, utilize; SEE CONCEPTS 158,213,320

deport [*v*] *banish*
cast out, dismiss, displace, exile, expatriate, expel, expulse, extradite, oust, relegate, ship out, transport; SEE CONCEPTS 198,211,217

deportation [*n*] *banishment*
displacement, eviction, exile, expatriation, expulsion, extradition, ostracism, relegation, removal, transportation; SEE CONCEPTS 198,211, 217

deportment [*n*] *carriage, manner of person*
actions, address, air, appearance, aspect, bearing, behavior, cast, comportment, conduct, demeanor, mien, port, posture, set, stance; SEE CONCEPT 633

depose [*v*] *oust from position*
boot out, bounce, break, can*, cashier, chuck, degrade, demote, dethrone, discrown, dismiss, displace, downgrade, drum out, eject, freeze out*, give heave-ho*, impeach, kick out*, overthrow, remove from office, ride out on rail*, run out of town*, send packing*, subvert, throw out, throw out on ear*, uncrown, unfrock, unmake, unseat, upset; SEE CONCEPTS 133,298,320

deposit [*n1*] *down payment; money saved*
drop, installment, money in the bank, partial payment, pledge, retainer, security, stake, warranty; SEE CONCEPTS 340,344

deposit [*n2*] *accumulation of solid*
alluvium, delta, deposition, dregs, drift, grounds, lees, precipitate, precipitation, sediment, settlings, silt; SEE CONCEPTS 432,470,471

deposit [*v*] *locate, put in place for safekeeping*
accumulate, amass, bank, collect, commit, deliver, ditch, drop, entrust, garner, give in trust, hoard, install, invest, keep, lay, lay away, park, place, plant*, plop*, plunk*, plunk down*, precipitate, put aside, put by, repose, rest, salt away*, save, settle, sit down, sock away*, squirrel away*, stash, stock up, store, stow, transfer, treasure; SEE CONCEPTS 134,201,330

deposition [*n1*] *dethroning, ousting*
degradation, discharge, dismissal, displacement, ejection, impeachment, overthrow, removal, unfrocking; SEE CONCEPTS 133,298,320

deposition [*n2*] *attestation of truth, especially in legal matters*
affidavit, affirmation, allegation, announcement, declaration, evidence, sworn statement, testimony; SEE CONCEPTS 271,318

depository [*n*] *storage place*
archive, arsenal, bank, bunker, cache, collection, depot, gallery, magazine, museum, repertory, repository, safe, safe-deposit box, store, storehouse, tomb, vault, warehouse; SEE CONCEPT 435

depot [*n*] *storage place; station*
annex, armory, base, depository, destination,

garage, halting-place, haven, junction, loft, lot, magazine, office, repository, stopping-place, store, storehouse, storeroom, terminal, terminus, waiting room, warehouse, yard; SEE CONCEPTS 435,449

deprave [*v*] *corrupt, lead astray*
bastardize, bestialize, brutalize, debase, debauch, degrade, demoralize, pervert, seduce, subvert, vitiate, warp; SEE CONCEPT 14

depraved [*adj*] *corrupt, immoral*
abandoned, bad, base, debased, debauched, degenerate, degraded, dirty*, dirty-minded, dissolute, evil, fast*, filthy*, flagitous, gone to the dogs*, kinky*, lascivious, lewd, licentious, low, mean, miscreant, nefarious, perverted, profligate, putrid, rotten, shameless, sinful, twisted, unhealthy, unnatural, vicious, vile, villainous, vitiate, vitiated, wanton, warped, wicked; SEE CONCEPT 545

depravity [*n*] *corruption, immorality*
abandonment, baseness, contamination, criminality, debasement, debauchery, degeneracy, degradation, depravation, evil, iniquity, lewdness, licentiousness, perversion, profligacy, sensuality, sinfulness, vice, viciousness, vitiation, wickedness; SEE CONCEPT 645

deprecate [*v*] *belittle, condemn*
cut down to size*, depreciate, derogate, detract, disapprove of, discommend, discountenance, disesteem, disfavor, disparage, expostulate, frown, mudsling*, not go for*, object, poohpooh*, poor mouth*, protest against, put down*, rip*, run down*, take dim view of, take down, take exception to; SEE CONCEPTS 7,19,52

depreciate [*v1*] *devalue, lose value*
abate, cheapen, decay, decrease, decry, deflate, depress, deteriorate, devalorize, diminish, downgrade, drop, dwindle, erode, fall, lessen, lower, mark down, reduce, soften, underrate, undervalue, worsen, write down, write off; SEE CONCEPTS 698,776

depreciate [*v2*] *belittle, ridicule*
abuse, asperse, attack, calumniate, censure, clamor against, condemn, contemn, decry, defame, denigrate, denounce, deprecate, deride, derogate, detract, discount, discountenance, discredit, disgrace, disparage, dispraise, fault, find fault with, humble, knock, look down on*, lower, malign, minimize, put down, rap, revile, roast*, run down*, scoff at, scorn, slam, slander, slight, slur, smear, sneer at, spurn, take down a peg*, traduce, underestimate, underrate, undervalue, vilify; SEE CONCEPTS 7,19,52

depreciation [*n*] *devaluation*
accounting allowance, deflation, fall, loss of value, reduction, slump; SEE CONCEPTS 137,236, 240,247,698

depredation [*n*] *devastation, destruction*
burglary, crime, desecration, desolation, despoiling, laying waste, marauding, pillage, plunder, ransacking, rapine, ravaging, robbery, sacking, spoliation, stealing, theft, wasting; SEE CONCEPTS 192,252

depress [*v1*] *deject, make despondent; exhaust*
abase, afflict, ail, bear down, beat, beat down, bother, bug*, bum out*, cast down, chill*, cow*, damp, dampen, darken, daunt, debase, debilitate, degrade, desolate, devitalize, discourage, dishearten, dismay, dispirit, distress, disturb, drag*, drain, dull, enervate, faze, keep under, lower,

mock, mortify, oppress, perturb, press, put down*, reduce, reduce to tears*, run down*, sadden, sap*, scorn, slow, throw cold water on*, torment, trouble, try, turn one off*, upset, weaken, weary, weigh down*; SEE CONCEPTS 7,19,240

depress [*v2*] *devalue*
cheapen, debase, depreciate, diminish, downgrade, impair, lessen, lower, reduce; SEE CONCEPTS 240,330

depress [*v3*] *push down*
couch, demit, dip, droop, flatten, let down, level, lower, press down, settle, sink, smoosh, squash; SEE CONCEPT 208

depressant [*n*] *sedative*
calmant, downer, intoxicant, relaxant, tranquilizer; SEE CONCEPTS 7,22,310

depressed [*adj*] *discouraged*
bad, bleeding*, blue*, bummed out*, cast-down, crestfallen, crummy*, dejected, despondent, destroyed, disconsolate, dispirited, down, down and out*, downcast, downhearted, down in the dumps*, down in the mouth*, dragged*, fed up*, glum, grim, hurting, in a blue funk*, in pain*, in the dumps*, in the pits*, in the toilet*, let down, low, low-down, low-spirited, lugubrious, melancholy, moody, morose, on a downer*, pessimistic, ripped, sad, sob story*, spiritless, taken down*, torn up*, unhappy, weeping, woebegone; SEE CONCEPT 403

depressed [*adj2*] *concave, pushed down*
hollow, indented, recessed, set back, sunken; SEE CONCEPT 490

depressed [*adj3*] *disadvantaged*
cheapened, depreciated, deprived, destitute, devalued, distressed, ghetto, ghost, impaired, needy, poor, poverty-stricken, run-down, shanty, skid row*, underprivileged, weakened; SEE CONCEPTS 334,555

depressing [*adj*] *discouraging, upsetting*
black, bleak, daunting, dejecting, disheartening, dismal, dispiriting, distressing, dreary, funereal, gloomy, heartbreaking, hopeless, joyless, melancholic, melancholy, mournful, oppressive, sad, saddening, somber; SEE CONCEPT 529

depression [*n1*] *low spirits; despair*
abasement, abjection, abjectness, blahs*, bleakness, blue funk*, bummer, cheerlessness, dejection, desolation, desperation, despondency, disconsolation, discouragement, dispiritedness, distress, dole, dolefulness, dolor, downheartedness, dreariness, dullness, dumps, ennui, gloom, gloominess, heaviness of heart, heavyheartedness, hopelessness, lowness, lugubriosity, melancholia, melancholy, misery, mortification, qualm, sadness, sorrow, the blues*, trouble, unhappiness, vapors*, woefulness, worry; SEE CONCEPT 410

depression [*n2*] *economic decline*
bad times*, bankruptcy, bear market*, big trouble*, bottom out*, bust, crash, crisis, deflation, dislocation, downturn, drop, failure, hard times*, inactivity, inflation, overproduction, panic, paralysis, rainy days*, recession, retrenchment, sag, slide, slowness, slump, stagflation, stagnation, unemployment; SEE CONCEPTS 324,330,335

depression [*n3*] *concavity, cavity*
basin, bowl, crater, dent, dimple, dip, excavation, hole, hollow, impression, indentation, pit,

pocket, sag, scoop, sink, sinkage, sinkhole, vacuity, vacuum, valley, void; SEE CONCEPT 513

deprivation [n] *taking, keeping away; need*
denial, deprival, destitution, detriment, disadvantage, dispossession, distress, divestiture, divestment, expropriation, hardship, loss, privation, removal, seizure, want, withdrawal, withholding; SEE CONCEPTS 121,142,709

deprive [v] *keep or take away something wanted, needed*
bankrupt, bare, bereave, denude, despoil, disinherit, dismantle, dispossess, disrobe, divest, dock, expropriate, hold back, lose, oust, rob, seize, skim, stiff, strip, wrest; SEE CONCEPTS 121,142

depth [n1] *distance down or across*
base, bottom, declination, deepness, draft, drop, expanse, extent, fathomage, intensity, lower register, lowness, measure, measurement, pit, pitch, profoundness, profundity, remoteness, sounding; SEE CONCEPTS 737,790

depth [n2] *insight, wisdom*
acuity, acumen, astuteness, brain, discernment, intellect, intelligence, keenness, penetration, profoundness, profundity, sagacity, sense, sharpness, weightiness; SEE CONCEPT 409

deputy [n] *assistant, agent*
aide, ambassador, appointee, assembly member, backup, commissioner, councilor, delegate, dogcatcher*, factor, legate, lieutenant, minister, proxy, regent, replacement, representant, representative, second-in-command, sub, subordinate, substitute, surrogate; SEE CONCEPTS 348,354

derange [v] *make crazy; confuse*
confound, craze*, dement, disarrange, disarray, discommode, discompose, disconcert, disorder, disorganize, displace, distract, disturb, drive mad, frenzy, madden, make insane, mess up*, misplace, muss*, perplex, ruffle, rummage, unbalance, unhinge*, unsettle, upset; SEE CONCEPTS 16,84

deranged [adj] *crazy, insane*
ape*, baked*, bananas*, berserk, cracked*, crazed, delirious, demented, disarranged, disconcerted, disordered, displaced, distracted, dotty*, flipped*, flipped out*, frantic, frenzied, fried*, irrational, loco*, lunatic, mad, maddened, maniac, maniacal, nuts*, perplexed, schizzo*, unbalanced, unglued*, unhinged*, unscrewed*, unsettled, unsound, unzipped*, whacko*; SEE CONCEPT 403

deregulate [v] *remove imposed controls on a system*
decontrol, denationalize, leave be, let alone, not interfere, not meddle, not tamper; SEE CONCEPTS 94,117

deregulation [n] *the removal of imposed controls on a system*
disinvolvement, free competition, free enterprise; free trade, isolationism, laissez-faire, liberalism, noninterference, nonintervention, self-regulating market; SEE CONCEPT 299

derelict [adj1] *careless, negligent*
behindhand, delinquent, disregardful, irresponsible, lax, regardless, remiss, slack, undependable, unreliable, untrustworthy; SEE CONCEPT 542

derelict [adj2] *deserted, forsaken*
abandoned, castoff, desolate, dilapidated, dingy, discarded, faded, lorn, neglected, ownerless, relinquished, ruined, run-down, seedy, shabby, solitary, threadbare, uncouth; SEE CONCEPT 560

derelict [n] *destitute or down-and-out person*
beggar, bum, castaway, dawdler, drifter, floater, grifter, hobo, ne'er-do-well*, outcast, renegade, skidrow bum, stiff, stumblebum*, tramp, vagabond, vagrant; SEE CONCEPTS 412,423

deride [v] *make fun of; insult*
banter, chaff, contemn, detract, dis*, disdain, disparage, do a number on*, dump on*, flout, gibe, jeer, jolly, kid, knock, laugh at, lout, mock, pan, pooh-pooh*, put down*, quiz, rag*, rally, razz*, rib*, ridicule, roast*, scoff, scorn, slam, sneer, taunt, twit; SEE CONCEPTS 52,54

de rigueur [adj] *proper, right*
au fait, becoming, comme il faut, conventional, correct, decent, decorous, done, fitting, necessary, required; SEE CONCEPT 558

derision [n] *insult, disrespect*
backhanded compliment*, brickbat*, Bronx cheer*, butt*, comeback, contempt, contumely, crack, dig*, disdain, disparagement, dump*, jab, jest, joke, laughingstock, laughter, mockery, object of ridicule, parting shot, pilgarlic, put-down, raillery, ridicule, satire, scoffing, scorn, slam*, slap, sneering; SEE CONCEPTS 52,278,689

derisive [adj] *ridiculing*
cheeky*, cocky, contemptuous, crusty, disdainful, flip*, fresh, gally, insulting, jeering, mocking, nervy, out-of-line, rude, sarcastic, sassy, scoffing, scornful, smart*, smart-alecky*, taunting; SEE CONCEPT 267

derivable [adj] *deducible*
a priori, attributable, available, determinable, dogmatic, extractable, inferable, likely, obtainable, reasoned, resultant, traceable; SEE CONCEPT 529

derivation [n] *root, source*
ancestry, basis, beginning, descent, etymology, foundation, genealogy, inception, origin, provenance, provenience, spin-off, well, wellspring, whence it came; SEE CONCEPT 648

derivative [adj] *borrowed, transmitted from source*
acquired, ancestral, caused, cognate, coming from, connate, copied, evolved, hereditary, imitative, inferential, inferred, not original, obtained, plagiaristic, plagiarized, procured, rehashed, secondary, secondhand, subordinate, uninventive, unoriginal; SEE CONCEPT 549

derivative [n] *product, descendant*
by-product, offshoot, outgrowth, spin-off, wave; SEE CONCEPT 260

derive [v] *deduce a conclusion*
acquire, arrive, assume, collect, determine, develop, draw, educe, elaborate, elicit, evolve, excogitate, extract, follow, formulate, gain, gather, get, glean, infer, judge, make, make out, obtain, procure, put together, reach, receive, trace, work out; SEE CONCEPTS 15,18

derive from [v] *come from; arise*
descend, emanate, flow, head, issue, originate, proceed, rise, spring from, stem from; SEE CONCEPT 648

dernier cri [n] *the latest thing*
fad, look, the last word*, the newest fashion, vogue; SEE CONCEPT 655

derogatory [adj] *offensive, uncomplimentary*
aspersing, belittling, calumnious, censorious, contumelious, critical, damaging, decrying,

defamatory, degrading, demeaning, deprecatory, depreciative, despiteful, detracting, disdainful, dishonoring, disparaging, fault-finding, humiliating, injurious, malevolent, malicious, maligning, minimizing, opprobrious, reproachful, sarcastic, scornful, slanderous, slighting, spiteful, unfavorable, unflattering, vilifying; SEE CONCEPTS **267,570**

derriere [*n*] *backside*
ass, bottom, buns, buttocks, can, cheeks, fanny, heinie, keister, posterior, rear, rear end, seat; SEE CONCEPT **392**

descend [*v1*] *move down, lower a*
cascade, cataract, cave in*, coast, collapse, crash, crouch, decline, deplane, detrain, dip, disembark, dismount, dive, dribble*, drop, fall, fall prostrate, get down, get off, go down, gravitate, ground, incline, light, light, lose balance, penetrate, pitch, plop, plummet, plunge, prolapse, set, settle, sink, slant, slide, slip, slope, slough off, slump, stoop, stumble, submerge, subside, swoop, toboggan, topple, trickle, trip, tumble, weep; SEE CONCEPTS **147,181,213**

descend [*v2*] *condescend*
abase oneself, concede, degenerate, deteriorate, humble oneself, lower oneself, patronize, stoop; SEE CONCEPTS **23,35**

descend [*v3*] *trace ancestry from; be passed or handed down*
arise, derive, issue, originate, proceed, spring; SEE CONCEPT **108**

descendant [*n*] *person in line of ancestry*
brood, child, children, chip off old block*, get*, heir, issue, kin, offshoot, offspring, posterity, product, progeniture, progeny, scion, seed, spin-off*; SEE CONCEPTS **296,414**

descent [*n1*] *moving down; lowering*
cave-in, coast, coming down, crash, declension, declination, decline, declivity, dip, downgrade, droop, drop, drop-off, fall, falling, grade, gradient, header, hill, inclination, incline, landslide, plummeting, plunge, plunging, precipitation, prolapse, sag, settlement, sinkage, sinking, slant, slide, slip, slope, swoop, tailspin, topple, tumble; SEE CONCEPTS **147,181,213,738**

descent [*n2*] *line of ancestry*
blood, extraction, family, family tree, genealogy, heredity, lineage, origin, parentage, pedigree, relationship; SEE CONCEPT **296**

descent [*n3*] *deterioration*
abasement, anticlimax, cadence, comedown, debasement, decadence, decline, degradation, discomfiture, down, downcome, downfall, lapse, pathos, slump; SEE CONCEPTS **230,674**

descent [*n4*] *assault, attack*
advance, foray, incursion, invasion, pounce, raid, swoop; SEE CONCEPTS **86,320**

describe [*v*] *explain in speech, writing*
call, characterize, chronicle, communicate, construe, convey image, define, delineate, depict, detail, distinguish, draw, elucidate, epitomize, exemplify, explicate, expound, express, illuminate, illustrate, image, impart, interpret, label, limn, make apparent, make clear, make sense of, make vivid, mark out, name, narrate, outline, paint, particularize, picture, portray, recite, recount, rehearse, relate, report, represent, sketch, specify, state, tell, term, trace, transmit, write up; SEE CONCEPT **55**

description [*n1*] *account in speech, writing*
ABCs*, blow by blow, brief, characterization, chronicle, confession, declaration, definition, delineation, depiction, detail, explanation, explication, fingerprint, information, make, monograph, narration, narrative, picture, portraiture, portrayal, presentment, recital, recitation, record, recountal, rehearsal, report, representation, rundown, sketch, specification, statement, story, summarization, summary, tale, version, vignette, writeup, yarn; SEE CONCEPT **268**

description [*n2*] *class, kind*
brand, breed, category, character, classification, feather, genre, genus, ilk, kidney, nature, order, sort, species, stripe, type, variety; SEE CONCEPT **378**

descriptive [*adj*] *explanatory*
anecdotic, characteristic, characterizing, circumstantial, classificatory, clear, definitive, delineative, depictive, describing, designating, detailed, eloquent, explicative, expository, expressive, extended, graphic, identifying, illuminating, illuminative, illustrative, indicative, interpretive, lifelike, narrative, particularized, pictorial, picturesque, revealing, specific, true to life, vivid; SEE CONCEPTS **267,557**

desecrate [*v*] *abuse, violate*
befoul, blaspheme, commit sacrilege, contaminate, defile, depredate, desolate, despoil, devastate, devour, dishonor, make lose face*, mess up*, pervert, pillage, pollute, profane, prostitute, ravage, sack*, spoil, spoliate, waste; SEE CONCEPTS **246,252**

desecration [*n*] *violation, abuse*
blasphemy, debasement, defilement, impiety, irreverence, profanation, sacrilege; SEE CONCEPTS **246,252**

desegregate [*v*] *eliminate segregation*
abolish segregation, commingle, give equal access, integrate, open, unify; SEE CONCEPTS **113,114**

desensitize [*v*] *dull*
anesthetize, benumb, deaden, make inactive, make less sensitive, numb, render insensible; SEE CONCEPTS **130,240**

desert [*adj*] *barren, uncultivated*
arid, bare, desolate, infertile, lonely, solitary, sterile, uninhabited, unproductive, untilled, waste, wild; SEE CONCEPT **560**

desert [*n*] *wasteland; dry area*
arid region, badland, barren, barren land, flats, lava bed, Sahara, sand dunes, solitude, wild, wilderness, wilds; SEE CONCEPTS **508,517**

desert [*v*] *abandon, defect*
abscond, apostatize, bail out*, beach, betray, bolt, check out*, chuck, cop out*, crawl out, decamp, depart, duck*, escape, flee, fly, forsake, give up, go, go AWOL*, go back on, go over the hill*, go west*, jilt, leave, leave high and dry*, leave in the lurch*, leave stranded, light, maroon, opt out, play truant, pull out, quit, relinquish, renounce, resign, run out on*, sneak off*, split*, strand, take a hike*, take off, tergiversate, throw over, vacate, violate oath, walk; SEE CONCEPTS **195,297**

deserted [*adj*] *abandoned, unoccupied*
bare, barren, bereft, cast off, derelict, desolate, empty, forlorn, forsaken, godforsaken*, isolated, left, left in the lurch*, left stranded, lonely, lorn,

neglected, relinquished, solitary, uncouth, uninhabited, vacant; SEE CONCEPTS 485,577

deserter [n] *fugitive from responsibility*
absconder, apostate, AWOL*, backslider, betrayer, criminal, defector, delinquent, derelict, escapee, escaper, hookey player*, lawbreaker, maroon, no-show*, recreant, refugee, renegade, runaway, shirker, slacker, traitor, truant; SEE CONCEPTS 358,412,423

desertion [n] *abandonment*
abrogation, absconding, apostasy, avoidance, backsliding, betrayal, castoff, defecting, departing, departure, derelict, dereliction, disaffection, disavowal, disavowing, divorce, elusion, escape, evasion, falling away, falseness, flight, forsaking, going back on*, leaving, marooning, perfidy, recreancy, rejection, relinquishment, renunciation, repudiation, resignation, retirement, retreat, running out on*, secession, tergiversation, treachery, truancy, withdrawal; SEE CONCEPTS 195,297

deserts [n] *what is due one*
chastening, chastisement, comeuppance, compensation, deserving, discipline, disciplining, due, get hers*, get his*, guerdon, lumps*, meed, merit, payment, penalty, punishment, recompense, requital, retribution, return, revenge, reward, right, talion, what is coming to one*, what one is asking for*; SEE CONCEPTS 129,710

deserve [v] *be entitled to*
be given one's due*, be in line for*, be worthy of, demand, earn, gain, get, get comeuppance*, get what is coming to one*, have it coming*, have the right to, justify, lay claim to, merit, procure, rate, warrant, win; SEE CONCEPT 129

deserving [adj] *worthy, meritorious*
admirable, commendable, due, estimable, fitting, laudable, needy, praisable, praiseworthy, righteous, rightful, thankworthy; SEE CONCEPT 404

desiccate [v] *take moisture out of*
anhydrate, dehydrate, deplete, devitalize, divest, drain, dry, dry up, evaporate, exsiccate, parch, sear, shrivel, wither, wizen; SEE CONCEPTS 137,250

design [n1] *sketch, draft*
architecture, arrangement, blueprint, chart, comp, composition, conception, constitution, construction, delineation, depiction, diagram, doodle, drawing, dummy, form, formation, idea, layout, makeup, map, method, model, outline, paste-up, pattern, perspective, picture, plan, scheme, study, tracery, tracing, treatment; SEE CONCEPTS 268,625,660

design [n2] *artful conception*
arrangement, configuration, construction, depiction, device, doodle, drawing, figure, form, illustration, motif, motive, organization, painting, pattern, picture, portrait, shape, sketch, style; SEE CONCEPT 259

design [n3] *intention*
action, aim, angle, animus, big picture*, brainchild*, child*, conation, conspiracy, deliberation, end, enterprise, game plan*, gimmick, goal, intendment, intrigue, lay of the land*, machination, meaning, notion, object, objective, picture, pitch, plan, play, plot, point, project, proposition, purport, purpose, recipe, reflection, scenario, scene, schema, scheme, setup, story, target, thinking, thought, trick, undertaking, view, volition, what's cooking*, will; SEE CONCEPTS 410,660

design [v1] *plan, outline*
accomplish, achieve, arrange, block out, blueprint, cast, chart, construct, contrive, create, delineate, describe, devise, diagram, dope out, draft, draw, effect, execute, fashion, form, frame, fulfill, invent, lay out, perform, produce, project, set out, sketch, sketch out, trace, work out; SEE CONCEPT 36

design [v2] *create, conceive*
compose, contrive, cook up*, devise, dream up*, fabricate, fashion, form, frame, invent, make up, originate, produce, think up; SEE CONCEPTS 43,173

design [v3] *intend, mean to do*
aim, contemplate, contrive, destine, devise, make, mind, plan, prepare, project, propose, purpose, scheme, tailor; SEE CONCEPTS 35,36

designate [v1] *name, entitle*
baptize, call, christen, cognominate, denominate, dub, label, nickname, nominate, style, term, title; SEE CONCEPT 62

designate [v2] *specify as selection*
allocate, allot, appoint, apportion, appropriate, assign, authorize, button down*, characterize, charge, choose, commission, connote, constitute, define, delegate, denote, depute, deputize, describe, dictate, earmark*, elect, evidence, favor, finger*, indicate, individualize, make, mark, mete, name, nominate, opt, peg*, pick, pin down, pinpoint, prefer, put down for*, reserve, set apart, set aside, show, single, slot, stipulate, tab*, tag*, tap*; SEE CONCEPTS 41,129

designation [n1] *name, label, mark*
appellation, appellative, class, classification, cognomen, compellation, denomination, description, epithet, identification, key word, moniker, nickname, nomen, style, title; SEE CONCEPT 683

designation [n2] *delegation, selection*
appointment, classification, identification, indication, pigeonhole*, recognition, specification; SEE CONCEPT 41

designedly [adv] *intentionally*
apurpose, by design, calculatedly, deliberately, knowingly, on purpose, prepensely, purposedly, purposely, purposively, studiously, willfully, wittingly; SEE CONCEPTS 402,535

designing [adj] *plotting, crafty*
artful, astute, conniving, conspiring, crooked, cunning, deceitful, devious, heedful, intriguing, Machiavellian, observant, scheming, sharp, shrewd, sly, treacherous, tricky, unscrupulous, wily; SEE CONCEPT 542

desirable [adj1] *attractive, seductive*
adorable, alluring, beautiful*, charming, covetable, enticing, fascinating, fetching, sexy; SEE CONCEPTS 372,579

desirable [adj2] *advantageous, good*
acceptable, advisable, agreeable, beneficial, covetable, eligible, enviable, expedient, grateful, gratifying, helpful, pleasing, preferable, profitable, useful, welcome, worthwhile; SEE CONCEPTS 560,572

desire [n1] *want, longing*
admiration, ambition, appetite, ardor, aspiration, attraction, avidity, concupiscence, covetousness, craving, craze, cupidity, devotion, doting, eagerness, fancy, fascination, fervor, fondness, frenzy, greed, hankering*, hunger, inclination, infatua-

tion, itch*, lasciviousness, lechery, libido, liking, love, lust, mania, motive, need, passion, predilection, proclivity, propensity, rapaciousness, rapture, ravenousness, relish, salacity, solicitude, thirst, urge, voracity, will, wish, yearning; SEE CONCEPTS 20,709

desire [n2] *request*
appeal, entreaty, hope, importunity, petition, solicitation, supplication, want, wish; SEE CONCEPT 662

desire [v1] *want, long for*
aim, aspire to, be smitten, be turned on by*, choose, covet, crave, desiderate, die over*, enjoy, fall for*, fancy, give eyeteeth for*, go for*, hanker after*, have eyes for*, have the hots for*, hunger for, like, lust after, make advances to, partial to, pine, set heart on*, spoil for, sweet on*, take a liking to*, take a shine to*, take to*, thirst, wish for, yearn for; SEE CONCEPT 20

desire [v2] *ask, request*
beg, bespeak, entreat, importune, petition, seek, solicit; SEE CONCEPT 48

desirous [adj] *aspiring, hopeful*
acquisitive, ambitious, amorous, anxious, avid, covetous, craving, desiring, eager, enthusiastic, grasping, greedy, hot*, itchy*, keen, longing, lustful, passionate, prehensile, ready, stimulated, turned on*, willing, wishful, wishing, yearning; SEE CONCEPT 529

desist [v] *stop, refrain from*
abandon, abstain, avoid, break off, cease, discontinue, end, forbear, give over, give up, halt, have done with*, knock off*, leave off, not do, pause, quit, relinquish, resign, surcease, suspend, yield; SEE CONCEPTS 119,234

desk [n] *table*
counter, davenport, escritoire, lectern, reading stand, rolltop, school desk, secretary, workspace, writing desk; SEE CONCEPT 443

desk jockey [n] *an office worker*
clerical worker, desk worker, pencil driver, pencil pusher, pen pusher, white-collar worker; SEE CONCEPT 348

desktop publishing [n] *producing publications with computer software*
desktop*, electronic publishing, formatting, outputting, typesetting; SEE CONCEPT 277

desolate [adj1] *unused, barren*
abandoned, bare, bleak, derelict, desert, destroyed, dreary, empty, forsaken, godforsaken*, isolated, lonely, lonesome, lorn, ruined, solitary, unfrequented, uninhabited, unoccupied, vacant, waste, wild; SEE CONCEPTS 485,560

desolate [adj2] *depressed, despondent*
abandoned, acheronian, bereft, black, bleak, blue, cheerless, comfortless, companionless, dejected, disconsolate, dismal, dolorous, down, downcast, forlorn, forsaken, funereal, gloomy, hurting, in a blue funk*, inconsolable, joyless, lonely, lonesome, lorn, melancholy, miserable, somber, tragic, wretched; SEE CONCEPT 403

desolate [v] *ravage, destroy*
depopulate, depredate, desecrate, despoil, devastate, devour, lay low, lay waste, pillage, plunder, ruin, sack, spoliate, waste; SEE CONCEPT 252

desolation [n1] *uninhabited area; barrenness*
bareness, bleakness, desert, devastation, dissolution, extinction, forlornness, isolation, loneliness, ruin, solitariness, solitude, waste, wildness, wreck; SEE CONCEPTS 517,710

desolation [n2] *distress, unhappiness*
anguish, dejection, despair, gloom, gloominess, loneliness, melancholy, misery, mourning, sadness, sorrow, woe, wretchedness; SEE CONCEPT 410

despair [n] *depression, hopelessness*
anguish, dashed hopes, dejection, desperation, despondency, discouragement, disheartenment, forlornness, gloom, melancholy, misery, ordeal, pain, sorrow, trial, tribulation, wretchedness; SEE CONCEPT 410

despair [v] *give up hope*
abandon, be hopeless, despond, destroy, drop, flatten, give way, have heavy heart*, let air out*, lose faith, lose heart, relinquish, renounce, resign, surrender, take down, yield; SEE CONCEPT 21

despairing [adj] *upset, despondent*
anxious, at end of one's rope*, blue, brokenhearted, can't win*, cynical, dejected, depressed, desperate, disconsolate, downcast, forlorn, frantic, grief-stricken, hopeless, inconsolable, in pain*, in the dumps*, in the pits*, in the soup*, melancholic, melancholy, miserable, not a prayer*, no-win*, oppressed, pessimistic, sad, shot down*, strabilious, suicidal, sunk*, weighed down*, wretched; SEE CONCEPT 403

desperado [n] *criminal*
bandit, convict, cutthroat, gangster, hoodlum, lawbreaker, mugger, outlaw, ruffian, thug; SEE CONCEPT 412

desperate [adj1] *reckless, outrageous*
atrocious, audacious, bold, careless, dangerous, daring, death-defying, determined, devil-may-care, foolhardy, frantic, frenzied, furious, hasty, hazardous, headlong, headstrong, heinous, impetuous, incautious, madcap, monstrous, precipitate, rash, risky, scandalous, shocking, venturesome, violent, wild; SEE CONCEPT 401

desperate [adj2] *extreme, intense*
acute, climacteric, concentrated, critical, crucial, dire, drastic, exquisite, fierce, furious, great, terrible, urgent, vehement, very grave, vicious, violent; SEE CONCEPTS 537,540,569

desperate [adj3] *hopeless*
at end of one's rope*, back to the wall*, can't win*, dead duck*, despairing, despondent, desponding, downcast, forlorn, futile, gone*, goner*, hard up*, inconsolable, in the soup*, in the toilet*, irrecoverable, irremediable, irretrievable, no-chance*, no-way*, no-win*, running out of time*, sad, sunk*, up against it*, up the creek*, useless, vain, wretched; SEE CONCEPT 548

desperately [adv1] *severely*
badly, carelessly, dangerously, dramatically, fiercely, gravely, greatly, harmfully, hysterically, like crazy*, like mad*, perilously, seriously; SEE CONCEPT 569

desperately [adv2] *frightfully*
appallingly, fearfully, hopelessly, shockingly; SEE CONCEPT 403

desperation [n1] *hopelessness*
agony, anguish, anxiety, concern, dejection, depression, desolation, despair, despondency, discomfort, disconsolateness, distraction, distress, fear, gloom, grief, heartache, melancholy, mis-

de
de

ery, pain, pang, sorrow, torture, trouble, unhappiness, worry; SEE CONCEPT *410*

desperation [*n2*] *rashness*
carelessness, defiance, foolhardiness, frenzy, heedlessness, impetuosity, madness, recklessness; SEE CONCEPT *633*

despicable [*adj*] *hateful; beyond contempt*
abject, awful, base, beastly, cheap, contemptible, degrading, detestable, dirty, disgraceful, disreputable, down, ignominious, infamous, insignificant, loathsome, low, low-life*, mean, no-good*, pitiful, reprehensible, shameful, slimy*, sordid, vile, worthless, wretched; SEE CONCEPTS *404,570*

despise [*v*] *look down on*
abhor, abominate, allergic to*, contemn, deride, detest, disdain, disregard, eschew, execrate, feel contempt for, flout, hate, have no use for*, loathe, look down nose at*, misprize, neglect, put down*, reject, renounce, repudiate, revile, scorn, shun, slight, snub, spurn, undervalue, wipe out*; SEE CONCEPT *29*

despite [*prep*] *in spite of, regardless of*
against, although, even though, even with, in contempt of, in defiance of, in the face of, notwithstanding, undeterred by; SEE CONCEPT *544*

despoil [*v*] *ravage, destroy*
denude, depopulate, depredate, deprive, desecrate, desolate, devastate, devour, dispossess, divest, loot, maraud, pillage, plunder, raid, rifle, rob, sack, spoil, spoliate, strip, vandalize, waste, wreak havoc, wreck; SEE CONCEPT *252*

despondent [*adj*] *depressed*
all torn up*, blue*, bummed-out*, cast-down, dejected, despairing, disconsolate, discouraged, disheartened, dispirited, doleful, down, downcast, downhearted, forlorn, gloomy, glum, grief-stricken, grieving, hopeless, in a blue funk*, in despair, in the pits*, low, low-spirited, melancholy, miserable, morose, mourning, sad, shot down*, sorrowful, woebegone, wretched; SEE CONCEPT *403*

desposition [*n*] *absolute power*
authoritarianism, autocracy, dictatorship, tyranny; SEE CONCEPTS *133,299,641*

despot [*n*] *dictator*
autocrat, Hitler*, monocrat, oppressor, slave-driver, tyrant; SEE CONCEPTS *354,412*

destination [*n*] *goal; place one wants to go*
aim, ambition, design, end, harbor, haven, intention, journey's end, landing-place, object, objective, purpose, resting-place, station, stop, target, terminal, terminus; SEE CONCEPTS *198,659*

destine [*v*] *predetermine, ordain*
allot, appoint, assign, consecrate, decide, decree, dedicate, design, determine, devote, doom, doom to, earmark*, fate, foreordain, intend, mark out, predestine, preform, preordain, purpose, reserve; SEE CONCEPT *18*

destined [*adj*] *bound for, fated in near future*
at hand, brewing*, certain, closed, coming, compelled, compulsory, condemned, designed, directed, doomed, foreordained, forthcoming, hanging over*, impending, ineluctable, inescapable, inevitable, inexorable, in prospect, instant, in store, intended, in the cards*, in the wind*, looming, meant, menacing, near, ordained, overhanging, predesigned, predestined, predetermined, que sera sera*, sealed, settled, stated, that is to be, that will be, threatening, to come, unavoidable, way the ball bounces*; SEE CONCEPTS *537,820*

destined [*adj2*] *en route, on the road to*
appointed, appropriated, assigned, bent upon, booked, bound for, chosen, consigned, delegated, designated, determined, directed, entrained, heading, ordered to, prepared, routed, scheduled, specified; SEE CONCEPT *584*

destiny [*n*] *fate*
afterlife, break*, breaks*, certainty, circumstance, conclusion, condition, constellation, course of events, cup, design, divine decree, doom, expectation, finality, foreordination, fortune, future, happenstance, hereafter, horoscope, inevitability, intent, intention, karma, kismet*, lot, luck, Moirai, objective, ordinance, portion, predestination, predetermination, prospect, serendipity, the stars*, way the ball bounces*, way the cookie crumbles*, what is written*, wheel of fortune*, world to come*; SEE CONCEPT *679*

destitute [*adj*] *down and out; wanting*
bankrupt, beggared, bereft, busted, dead broke*, deficient, depleted, deprived of, devoid of, dirt poor*, divested, drained, empty, exhausted, flat*, flat broke*, impecunious, impoverished, indigent, in need of, insolvent, lacking, moneyless, necessitous, needy, on the breadline*, on the rocks*, penniless, penurious, pinched, played out*, poor, poverty-stricken, stony, strapped, stripped, totaled, wiped out*, without; SEE CONCEPT *334*

destroy [*v*] *demolish, devastate*
abort, annihilate, annul, axe*, blot out, break down, butcher*, consume, cream*, crush, damage, deface, desolate, despoil, dismantle, dispatch, end, eradicate, erase, exterminate, extinguish, extirpate, gut*, impair, kill, lay waste, level, liquidate, maim, mar, maraud, mutilate, nuke*, nullify, overturn, quash, quell, ravage, ravish, raze, ruin, sabotage, shatter, slay, smash, snuff out*, spoliate, stamp out, suppress, swallow up*, tear down, torpedo*, total, trash*, vaporize, waste, wax*, wipe out, wreck, zap*; SEE CONCEPT *252*

destruction [*n*] *demolition, devastation*
abolishing, abolition, annihilation, assassinating, bane, carnage, crashing, crushing, disintegrating, disrupting, dissolving, downfall, elimination, end, eradication, extermination, extinction, extinguishing, extirpation, havoc, invalidating, invalidation, liquidation, loss, massacre, murder, overthrow, ravaging, ruin, ruination, sacking, shattering, slaughter, slaying, subjugation, subversion, subverting, undoing, wreckage, wrecking; SEE CONCEPTS *230,252*

destructive [*adj1*] *injurious, devastating*
annihilative, baleful, baneful, calamitous, cancerous, cataclysmic, catastrophic, consumptive, cutthroat, damaging, deadly, deleterious, detrimental, dire, disastrous, eradicative, evil, extirpative, fatal, fell, harmful, hurtful, internecine, lethal, lethiferous, mortal, noisome, noxious, pernicious, pestiferous, pestilential, ruinous, slaughterous, suicidal, toxic, venomous, wrackful, wreckful; SEE CONCEPT *537*

destructive [*adj2*] *hurtful, disparaging*
abrasive, adverse, antagonistic, cankerous, caustic, contrary, corrosive, deleterious, derogatory, detrimental, discouraging, discrediting, erosive,

hostile, injurious, invalidating, negative, offensive, opposed, troublesome, undermining, vicious; SEE CONCEPTS 267,537

desultory [adj] *random*
aimless, chance, chaotic, deviating, erratic, haphazard, orderless, rambling, unmethodical, unstable, unsystematic, without purpose; SEE CONCEPTS 535,548,557

detach [v] *disconnect, cut off*
abstract, disaffiliate, disassemble, disassociate, disengage, disentangle, disjoin, dismount, dissociate, disunite, divide, divorce, free, isolate, loose, loosen, part, remove, segregate, separate, sever, sunder, take apart, tear off, uncouple, unfasten, unfix, unhitch, withdraw; SEE CONCEPT 135

detached [adj1] *disconnected*
alone, apart, discrete, disjoined, divided, emancipated, free, isolate, isolated, loose, loosened, removed, separate, severed, unaccompanied, unconnected; SEE CONCEPT 490

detached [adj2] *aloof, disinterested; neutral*
abstract, apathetic, casual, cool*, dispassionate, distant, impartial, impersonal, incurious, indifferent, laid-back*, objective, out of it*, poker-faced*, remote, removed, reserved, spaced-out, spacey*, staid, stolid, unbiased, uncommitted, unconcerned, uncurious, uninvolved, unpassioned, unprejudiced, withdrawn; SEE CONCEPTS 401,404

detachment [n1] *disconnection*
disengagement, disjoining, dissolution, disunion, division, divorce, divorcement, partition, rupture, separation, severing, split-up; SEE CONCEPTS 388,747

detachment [n2] *aloofness*
brown study*, coldness, coolness, disinterestedness, dreaminess, impartiality, incuriosity, indifference, neutrality, nonpartisanship, objectivity, preoccupation, remoteness, reverie, unconcern, woolgathering*; SEE CONCEPT 633

detachment [n3] *military troop*
army, body, detail, division, force, organization, party, patrol, special force, squad, task force, troupe, unit; SEE CONCEPT 322

detail [n1] *feature, specific aspect*
ABCs*, accessory, article, brass tacks*, chapter and verse*, circumstantiality, component, count, cue, design, dope*, element, fact, factor, fine point, fraction, item, meat and potatoes*, minor point, minutia, nicety, nitty-gritty*, nuts and bolts*, part, particular, peculiarity, plan, point, portion, respect, schedule, singularity, specialty, specification, structure, technicality, thing, trait, trivia, triviality; SEE CONCEPT 831

detail [n2] *military troop*
army, assignment, body, detachment, duty, fatigue, force, kitchen police, KP*, organization, party, special force, squad, unit; SEE CONCEPT 322

detail [v1] *specify, make clear*
analyze, catalog, circumstantiate, communicate, delineate, depict, describe, designate, elaborate, embellish, enumerate, epitomize, exhibit, fly speck*, get down to brass tacks*, individualize, itemize, lay out, narrate, particularize, portray, produce, quote chapter and verse*, recapitulate, recite, recount, rehearse, relate, report, reveal, set forth, show, specialize, spell out, spread, stipu-

late, summarize, sweat details*, tell, uncover; SEE CONCEPTS 55,57,60

detail [v2] *assign specific task*
allocate, appoint, charge, commission, delegate, detach, send; SEE CONCEPTS 50,88

detailed [adj] *itemized, particularized*
abundant, accurate, all-inclusive, amplified, at length, blow-by-blow*, circumstantial, circumstantiated, clocklike, complete, complicated, comprehensive, copious, definite, described, developed, disclosed, elaborate, elaborated, enumerated, exact, exhausting, exhaustive, finicky*, full, fussy*, individual, individualized, intricate, meticulous, minute, narrow, nice, point-by-point, precise, seriatim, specific, specified, thorough, unfolded; SEE CONCEPT 557

detain [v] *hold, keep back; arrest*
apprehend, bog down*, bust*, buttonhole*, check, confine, constrain, decelerate, delay, hang up*, hinder, hold up*, ice*, impede, inhibit, intern, jail, mire, nab*, pick up, pinch*, pull in*, put away*, reserve, restrain, retard, run in, send up, set back, slow down, slow up, withhold; SEE CONCEPTS 191,317

detect [v] *discover*
ascertain, catch, descry, dig up*, disclose, distinguish, encounter, espy, expose, find, hit on*, hit upon*, identify, meet, meet with, nose out*, note, notice, observe, recognize, reveal, scent, see, smell out*, smoke out*, spot, stumble on, track down, tumble into, turn up, uncover, unmask, wise up to*; SEE CONCEPTS 38,183

detection [n] *discovery*
apprehension, disclosure, espial, exposé, exposure, ferreting out, find, revelation, strike, tracking down, uncovering, unearthing, unmasking; SEE CONCEPTS 38,183

detective [n] *investigator of crime*
agent, analyst, bird dog*, bloodhound*, bull*, constable, cop, dick*, eavesdropper, eye*, fed*, fink*, flatfoot*, gumshoe*, informer, nark*, peeper*, P. I.*, plainclothes officer, police officer, private eye, private investigator, prosecutor, reporter, roper, scout, sergeant, shadow*, shamus*, Sherlock Holmes*, shoofly*, sleuth, slewfoot*, snoop*, spy, tail*; SEE CONCEPT 348

détente [n] *peace*
amity, cooling off, equal power, harmony, relaxation, relief, tranquility, truce; SEE CONCEPTS 388,691

detention [n] *confinement, imprisonment*
apprehension, arrest, arrestation, bust*, custody, delay, detainment, hindrance, holding back, holding pen*, immurement, impediment, incarceration, internment, keeping in, nab, pen*, pickup, pinch*, quarantine, restraint, retention, time up the river*, withholding; SEE CONCEPTS 191,317

deter [v] *check, inhibit from action*
act like a wet blanket*, avert, block, caution, chill, cool, damp, dampen, daunt, debar, disadvise, discourage, dissuade, divert, forestall, forfend, frighten, hinder, impede, intimidate, obstruct, obviate, preclude, prevent, prohibit, put a damper on, put off, restrain, rule out, scare, shut out, stave off, stop, talk out of, throw cold water on*, turn off, warn; SEE CONCEPT 121

detergent [n] *soap*
cleaner, solvent; SEE CONCEPT 492

de
de

deteriorate [*v*] *decay, degenerate*
adulterate, alloy, become worse, be worse for wear*, break, corrode, corrupt, crumble, debase, debilitate, decline, decompose, degrade, deprave, depreciate, descend, disimprove, disintegrate, ebb, fade, fail, fall apart, flag, go downhill*, go to pieces*, go to pot*, go to the dogs*, hit the skids*, impair, injure, languish, lapse, lessen, lose it, lose quality, lower, mar, pervert, regress, retrograde, retrogress, rot, sink, skid, slide, spoil, undermine, vitiate, weaken, wear away, worsen; SEE CONCEPT *698*

deterioration [*n*] *decay, degeneration*
abasement, adulteration, atrophy, corrosion, crumbling, debasement, decadence, decaying, declension, declination, decline, decomposition, degradation, degringolade, depreciation, descent, devaluation, dilapidation, disintegration, dislocation, disrepair, downfall, downgrade, downturn, drop, fall, lapse, lessening, perversion, retrogression, rotting, ruin, slump, spoiling, vitiation, worsening; SEE CONCEPTS *230,698*

determination [*n1*] *perseverance*
assurance, backbone*, boldness, bravery, certainty, certitude, constancy, conviction, courage, dauntlessness, decision, dedication, doggedness, dogmatism, drive, energy, fearlessness, firmness, fortitude, grit, guts*, hardihood, heart*, independence, indomitability, intrepidity, nerve*, obstinacy, persistence, pluck*, purpose, purposefulness, resoluteness, resolution, resolve, self-confidence, single-mindedness, spine*, spunk*, steadfastness, stiff upper lip*, stubbornness, tenacity, valor, willpower; SEE CONCEPTS *411, 657*

determination [*n2*] *conclusion*
decision, judgment, measurement, opinion, perception, purpose, resolution, resolve, result, settlement, solution, verdict, visualization; SEE CONCEPTS *685,689*

determine [*v1*] *conclude, decide*
actuate, arbitrate, call the shots*, cinch, clinch, complete, dispose, drive, end, figure, finish, fix upon, halt, impel, incline, induce, move, nail down*, opt, ordain, persuade, pin down*, predispose, regulate, resolve, rule, settle, take a decision, tap, terminate, ultimate, wind up*, wrap up*; SEE CONCEPTS *18,35,234*

determine [*v2*] *discover, find out*
add up to*, ascertain, boil down to*, catch on, certify, check, demonstrate, detect, divine, establish,˙figure, figure out, have a hunch*, hear, learn, make out, see, size up, tell, tumble, unearth, verify, work out; SEE CONCEPTS *15,31*

determine [*v3*] *choose, decide*
destine, doom, elect, establish, fate, finger*, fix, foreordain, make up mind, predestine, predetermine, preform, preordain, purpose, resolve, settle; SEE CONCEPT *18*

determine [*v4*] *dictate, govern, regulate*
affect, bound, circumscribe, command, condition, control, decide, delimit, devise, direct, impel, impose, incline, induce, influence, invent, lead, limit, manage, mark off, measure, modify, plot, rule, shape; SEE CONCEPT *94*

determined [*adj*] *driven, persistent*
bent, bent on, buckled down*, constant, decided, decisive, dogged, earnest, firm, fixed, hard-as-nails*, hardboiled*, intent, mean business*, obstinate, on ice*, pat, persevering, purposeful,

resolute, resolved, serious, set, set on, settled, single-minded, solid, steadfast, strong-minded, strong-willed, stubborn, tenacious, unfaltering, unflinching, unhesitating, unwavering; SEE CONCEPTS *404,542*

deterrent [*n*] *impediment, restraint*
bridle, check, curb, defense, determent, discouragement, disincentive, hindrance, leash, obstacle, preventative, preventive, rein, shackle; SEE CONCEPT *680*

detest [*v*] *hate; feel disgust toward*
abhor, abominate, be allergic to, despise, dislike intensely, down on, execrate, feel aversion toward, feel hostility toward, feel repugnance toward, have no use for*, loathe, recoil from, reject, repudiate; SEE CONCEPT *29*

detestable [*adj*] *loathsome, abominable*
abhorred, abhorrent, accursed, atrocious, awful, despicable, disgusting, execrable, godawful*, grody*, gross*, hateable, hateful, heinous, horrid, lousy, low-down, maggot, monstrous, obnoxious, odious, offensive, outrageous, repugnant, repulsive, revolting, rotten, shocking, sorry, vile; SEE CONCEPTS *529,542*

dethrone [*v*] *oust*
degrade, depose, discrown, dismiss, displace, uncrown, unmake; SEE CONCEPTS *298,320*

detonate [*v*] *set off bomb*
bang, blast, blow up, burst, discharge, explode, fulminate, kablooey*, let go, mushroom*, push the button*, shoot off, touch off, va-voom*; SEE CONCEPT *179*

detonation [*n*] *explosion*
bang, blast, blowout, blow-up, boom, discharge, ignition; SEE CONCEPTS *179,320,521*

detour [*n*] *indirect course*
alternate route, back road, branch, bypass, bypath, byway, circuit, circuitous route, circumbendibus*, circumnavigation, circumvention, crotch, deviation, divergence, diversion, fork, roundabout way, runaround, secondary highway, service road, substitute, temporary route; SEE CONCEPT *501*

detract [*v*] *take away a part; lessen*
backbite*, belittle, blister, cheapen, cut rate, decrease, decry, depreciate, derogate, devaluate, diminish, discount, discredit, disesteem, draw away, knock*, laugh at, lower, minimize, misprize, reduce, subtract from, underrate, undervalue, vilipend, withdraw, write off; SEE CONCEPTS *52,54,236,247*

detraction [*n*] *misrepresentation; slander*
abuse, aspersion, backbiting*, backstabbing*, belittlement, calumny, damage, defamation, denigration, deprecation, derogation, disesteem, disparagement, harm, hit, hurt, injury, injustice, innuendo, insinuation, knock*, libel, libeling, lie, maligning, minimization, muckraking*, obloquy, pejorative, revilement, ridicule, running down*, scandal, scandalmongering, scurrility, slam, smear campaign*, tale, traducement, traducing, vilification, vituperation, wrong; SEE CONCEPTS *52,54,63*

detriment [*n*] *disadvantage*
damage, disability, disservice, drawback, handicap, harm, hurt, impairment, injury, liability, loss, marring, mischief, prejudice, spoiling; SEE CONCEPTS *309,674*

detrimental [*adj*] *damaging, disadvantageous*
adverse, bad, baleful, deleterious, destructive,

disturbing, evil, harmful, hurtful, ill, inimical, injurious, mischievous, negative, nocuous, pernicious, prejudicial, unfavorable; SEE CONCEPTS 537,570

detritus [*n*] *debris*
deposit, fragments, grains, leavings, rubble, scree, sediment, shavings; SEE CONCEPT 260

devalue [*v*] *depreciate*
cheapen, cut rate, debase, decrease, decry, devalorize, devaluate, knock off, lower, mark down, nose dive, revalue, take down, underrate, undervalue, write down, write off; SEE CONCEPTS 330,335

devastate [*v*] *demolish, destroy*
depredate, desecrate, desolate, despoil, devour, do one in*, lay waste, level, pillage, plunder, raid, ravage, raze, ruin, sack, smash, spoil, spoliate, stamp out*, take apart, total*, trash*, waste, wipe off map*, wreck; SEE CONCEPTS 246,252

devastation [*n*] *destruction*
confusion, defoliation, demolition, depredation, desolation, havoc, loss, pillage, plunder, ravages, ruin, ruination, spoliation, waste; SEE CONCEPT 674

develop [*v1*] *cultivate, prosper*
advance, age, enroot, establish, evolve, expand, flourish, foster, grow, grow up, maturate, mature, mellow, progress, promote, ripen, thrive; SEE CONCEPTS 253,427,704

develop [*v2*] *expand, work out*
actualize, advance, amplify, augment, beautify, broaden, build up, cultivate, deepen, dilate, elaborate, enlarge, enrich, evolve, exploit, extend, finish, heighten, improve, intensify, lengthen, magnify, materialize, perfect, polish, promote, realize, refine, spread, strengthen, stretch, unfold, widen; SEE CONCEPTS 700,775

develop [*v3*] *begin; occur*
acquire, arise, befall, betide, break, break out, breed, chance, come about, come off, commence, contract, ensue, establish, follow, form, generate, go, happen, invest, originate, pick up, result, start, transpire; SEE CONCEPT 119

develop [*v4*] *unfold; be made known*
account for, acquire, actualize, disclose, disentangle, elaborate, evolve, exhibit, explain, explicate, foretell, form, materialize, produce, reach, realize, recount, state, uncoil, uncover, unfurl, unravel, unroll, untwist, unwind; SEE CONCEPTS 60,261

developer [*n*] *real estate developer*
builder, planner, real estate investor; SEE CONCEPT 348

development [*n1*] *growth*
adding to, addition, adulthood, advance, advancement, advancing, augmentation, augmenting, boost, buildup, developing, elaborating, enlargement, evolution, evolvement, evolving, expansion, flowering, hike, improvement, increase, increasing, making progress, maturation, maturing, maturity, ongoing, perfecting, progress, progression, reinforcement, reinforcing, ripening, spread, spreading, unfolding, unraveling, upgrowth, upping; SEE CONCEPTS 700,704,775

development [*n2*] *happening, incident*
change, circumstance, conclusion, denouement, event, eventuality, eventuation, issue, materialization, occurrence, outcome, phenomenon, result, situation, transpiration, turn of events, upshot; SEE CONCEPT 3

deviant [*adj*] *abnormal, different*
aberrant, anomalous, atypical, bent, devious, divergent, freaky, heretical, heteroclite, irregular, kinky, off-key, perverse, perverted, preternatural, queer, twisted, unorthodox, unrepresentative, untypical, variant, varying, wandering, wayward, weird; SEE CONCEPT 564

deviate [*v*] *stray from normal path*
aberrate, angle off, avert, bear off, bend, bend the rules*, break pattern, circumlocate, contrast, deflect, depart, depart from, differ, digress, divagate, diverge, drift, edge off*, err, get around, go amiss, go haywire*, go off on tangent*, go out of control*, go out of way, leave beaten path*, not conform, part, shy, swerve, swim against stream*, take a turn, turn, turn aside, vary, veer, wander; SEE CONCEPTS 195,665,697

deviation [*n*] *change, departure*
aberration, alteration, anomaly, breach, crotch, deflection, detour, difference, digression, discrepancy, disparity, divergence, diversion, fluctuation, fork, heresy, heterodoxy, inconsistency, irregularity, modification, shift, transgression, turning, variance, variation; SEE CONCEPTS 665,697,738

device [*n1*] *instrument, tool*
accessory, agent, apparatus, appliance, arrangement, article, construction, contraption, contrivance, creation, doohickey*, equipment, expedient, gadget, gear, gimmick, implement, invention, machine, makeshift, material, means, mechanism, medium, outfit, resort, resource, rigging*, Rube Goldberg invention*, shift, tackle, thingamabob*, utensil, whatchamacallit*, whatnot*, whatsit*; SEE CONCEPTS 463,499

device [*n2*] *ploy, scheme, maneuver*
artifice, cabal, chicanery, clever move, craft, craftiness, cunningness, design, dodge, evasion, expedient, fake, feint, finesse, gambit, game, gimmick, improvisation, loophole*, machination, method, pattern, plan, plot, project, proposition, purpose, racket, ruse, shift, stratagem, strategy, stunt, subterfuge, trap, trick, wile; SEE CONCEPT 660

device [*n3*] *symbol, emblem*
badge, colophon, crest, design, ensign, figure, insignia, logo, motif, motto, pattern, scroll, sign, slogan, token; SEE CONCEPT 284

devil [*n*] *demon*
adversary, archfiend, beast, Beelzebub, bête noire, brute, common enemy, dastard, diablo, djinn, dybbuk, enfant terrible*, evil one, fiend, genie, hellion, imp, knave, Lucifer, Mephistopheles, monster, ogre, Prince of Darkness, rogue, Satan, scamp, scoundrel, the dickens*, the Erinyes, the Furies, villain; SEE CONCEPTS 370,412

devilish [*adj*] *wicked*
accursed, atrocious, bad, brutish, cloven-footed, cursed, damnable, demoniac, demonic, detestable, diabolic, diabolical, evil, execrable, fiendish, hellborn, hellish, infernal, inhuman, iniquitous, Mephistophelian, nefarious, satanic, serpentine, unhallowed, villainous; SEE CONCEPT 545

devil's advocate [*n*] *mediator*
apologist, pleader, polemicist, sophist; SEE CONCEPTS 348,423

de
de

devious [*adj*] *dishonest, crafty*
artful, calculating, crooked, deceitful, double-dealing, duplicitous, errant, erring, evasive, faking one out*, fishy*, foxy*, fraudulent, guileful, indirect, insidious, insincere, not straightforward, oblique, obliquitous, playing games, playing politics*, put on, roundabout, scheming, shady, shifty, shrewd, sly, sneaking, sneaky, surreptitious, treacherous, tricky, underhanded, wily; SEE CONCEPTS *401,404*

devious [*adj*] *crooked; indirect*
ambiguous, bending, circuitous, confounding, confusing, curving, detouring, deviating, digressing, digressory, diverting, errant, erratic, excursive, flexuous, misleading, obscure, out-of-the-way, rambling, remote, removed, roundabout, serpentine, straying, tortuous, twisting, wandering; SEE CONCEPT *581*

devise [*v*] *conceive, dream up*
ad-lib, arrange, blueprint*, brainstorm*, cast, chart, cogitate, come up with, concoct, construct, contrive, cook up*, craft, create, design, discover, dope out*, fake it, forge, form, formulate, frame*, get off*, hatch, head trip*, imagine, improvise, intrigue, invent, machinate, make up, mastermind*, plan, play it by ear*, plot, prepare, project, scheme, shape, spark, think up, throw together, trump up*, vamp, whip up*, work out; SEE CONCEPTS *36,43*

devoid [*adj*] *empty, wanting*
bare, barren, bereft, deficient, denuded, destitute, free from, innocent, lacking, needed, sans*, unprovided with, vacant, void, without; SEE CONCEPTS *483,485*

devote [*v*] *commit one's energies, thoughts*
allot, apply, apportion, appropriate, assign, bestow, bless, concern oneself, confide, consecrate, consign, dedicate, donate, enshrine, entrust, give, give away, hallow, hand out, occupy oneself, pledge, present, reserve, sanctify, set apart, vow; SEE CONCEPTS *17,108,112*

devoted [*adj*] *committed, loyal*
adherent, affectionate, ardent, behind one, caring, concerned, consecrated, constant, crazy about*, dear, dedicated, devout, doting, dutiful, faithful, fervid, fond, gone on*, lovesome, loving, staunch, steadfast, stuck on*, thoughtful, true, true-blue*, wild about*, zealous; SEE CONCEPT *542*

devotee [*n*] *ardent supporter; fan*
addict, adherent, admirer, aficionado, amateur, believer, booster, buff, disciple, enthusiast, fanatic, fancier, fiend, follower, groupie, habitué, junkie, lover, rooter, supporter, votarient, votary; SEE CONCEPT *423*

devotion [*n*] *commitment; loyalty*
adherence, adoration, affection, allegiance, ardor, attachment, consecration, constancy, dedication, deference, devotedness, devotement, devoutness, earnestness, enthusiasm, faithfulness, fealty, fervor, fidelity, fondness, intensity, love, observance, passion, piety, reverence, sanctity, service, sincerity, spirituality, worship, zeal; SEE CONCEPTS *32,657*

devour [*v*] *swallow, consume*
absorb, annihilate, appreciate, be engrossed by, be preoccupied, bolt, bolt down*, chow down*, cram*, delight in, destroy, dispatch, do compulsively, do voraciously, drink in, eat, enjoy, exhaust, feast on, feed on, gloat over, gobble,

gorge*, go through, gulp, guzzle, hoover*, imbibe, ingest, inhale, partake of, pig out*, polish off*, ravage, rejoice in, relish, revel in, scarf down*, spend, stuff, take, take in, use up, waste, wipe out, wolf*, wolf down*; SEE CONCEPTS *169,225*

devout [*adj*] *sincerely believing; devoted*
adherent, adoring, ardent, deep, earnest, faithful, fervent, fervid, genuine, godly, goody-goody*, goody two-shoes*, heart-and-soul, heartfelt, holy, intense, orthodox, passionate, pietistic, pious, prayerful, profound, religious, reverent, revering, serious, sincere, venerating, worshiping, zealous; SEE CONCEPT *542*

dew [*n*] *moisture*
condensation, water droplets; SEE CONCEPTS *467,524*

dewy-eyed [*adj*] *innocent*
dovelike, green, inexperienced, naïve, pure, sinless, uncorrupted, undefiled, unworldly, wide-eyed; SEE CONCEPTS *404,542*

dexterity [*n*] *aptitude, ability*
address, adroitness, aptness, art, artistry, cleverness, craft, cunning, deftness, effortlessness, expertise, expertness, facility, finesse, handiness, ingenuity, knack, know-how, mastery, neatness, nimbleness, proficiency, readiness, skill, skillfulness, smoothness, tact, touch; SEE CONCEPTS *409,630*

dexterous [*adj*] *ingenious, proficient*
able, active, acute, adept, adroit, agile, apt, artful, canny, clever, crack*, crackerjack*, deft, effortless, expert, facile, handy, having the know-how*, masterly, neat, nimble, nimble-fingered, prompt, quick, savvy, skilled, skillful, slick, sly, smooth; SEE CONCEPTS *402,527*

diabolic [*adj*] *evil, fiendish*
atrocious, cruel, damnable, demoniac, demonic, devilish, hellish, impious, infernal, Mephistophelian, monstrous, nasty, nefarious, satanic, serpentine, shocking, unhallowed, unpleasant, vicious, vile, villainous, wicked; SEE CONCEPT *545*

diagnose [*v*] *identify problem, disease*
analyze, determinate, determine, diagnosticate, distinguish, interpret, investigate, pinpoint, place, pronounce, recognize, spot; SEE CONCEPTS *38,310*

diagnosis [*n*] *identification of problem, disease*
analysis, conclusion, examination, interpretation, investigation, opinion, pronouncement, scrutiny, summary; SEE CONCEPTS *283,689*

diagonal [*adj*] *angled*
askew, bevel, beveled, bias, biased, cater-cornered, catty-cornered, cornerways, cross, crossways, crosswise, inclining, kitty-cornered*, oblique, skewing, slanted, slanting, transversal, transverse; SEE CONCEPT *581*

diagonally [*adv*] *at an angle*
askew, aslant, cater-corner, catty-corner, cornerwise, crosswise, kitty-corner*, obliquely, on a slant, on the bias, slantingways, slantways, slantwise, slaunchways; SEE CONCEPT *581*

diagram [*n*] *drawing, sketch of form or plan*
big picture*, blueprint, chart, description, design, draft, figure, floor plan, game, game plan, ground plan, layout, outline, perspective, representation, rough draft; SEE CONCEPTS *625,660*

dial [*v*] *tune to desired position*
punch, ring, rotate, turn, twist, wheel, zero in on*; SEE CONCEPT *201*

dialect [*n*] *local speech*
accent, argot, can, idiom, jargon, language, lingo, localism, patois, patter, pronunciation, provincialism, regionalism, slang, terminology, tongue, vernacular, vocabulary; SEE CONCEPT 276

dialectic [*adj*] *logical, rational*
analytic, argumentative, controversial, dialectical, persuasive, polemical, rationalistic; SEE CONCEPT 529

dialectic [*n*] *logic, reasoning*
argumentation, contention, debate, deduction, discussion, disputation, forensic, logical argument, mooting, persuasion, polemics, question-and-answer method, ratiocination; SEE CONCEPT 37

dialogue/dialog [*n*] *talk, exchange of ideas*
chat, colloquy, communication, confab*, confabulation, conference, conversation, converse, discourse, discussion, duologue, interlocution, lines*, parlance, parley, powwow, remarks, repartee, script, sides, small talk*; SEE CONCEPTS 56,278

diameter [*n*] *measurement across object*
bore, breadth, broadness, caliber, module, width; SEE CONCEPT 760

diametric/diametrical [*adj*] *opposed, conflicting*
adverse, antipodal, antipodean, antithetical, contradictory, contrary, contrasting, converse, counter, facing, opposite, polar, reverse; SEE CONCEPT 564

diaphanous [*adj*] *fine, see-through*
chiffon, clear, cobweblike, delicate, filmy, flimsy, gauzy, gossamer, light, pellucid, pure, sheer, thin, translucent, transparent; SEE CONCEPTS 490,606

diarrhea [*n*] *loose bowels*
dysentery, flux, Montezuma's revenge*, the runs*, the trots*; SEE CONCEPT 306

diary [*n*] *recounting of activities in writing*
account, agenda, appointment book, chronicle, daily record, daybook, engagement book, journal, log, minutes, notebook, record; SEE CONCEPT 283

diaspora [*n*] *the spreading out of a group of people*
disbandment, dispersal, dispersion, dissolution, escape, exodus, mass exodus, refugee flow; SEE CONCEPT 195

diatribe [*n*] *harangue, criticism*
abuse, castigation, denunciation, disputation, invective, jeremiad, objection, onslaught, philippic, reviling, screed, stricture, tirade, vituperation; SEE CONCEPT 52

dibs [*n*] *claim*
dueness, entitlement, preemptive declaration, privilege, request, rights; SEE CONCEPTS 278,318, 376,709

dicey [*adj*] *risky*
capricious, chancy, dangerous, difficult, erratic, fluctuant, iffy*, incalculable, ticklish, tricky, uncertain, unpredictable, whimsical; SEE CONCEPTS 535,552

dichotomy [*n*] *division*
difference, difference of opinion, disagreement, disunion, separation, split; SEE CONCEPTS 98,135

dicker [*v*] *bargain; argue about*
barter, buy and sell, chaffer, cut a deal*, haggle*, hammer out a deal*, huckster*, negotiate, palter, trade, work out a deal*; SEE CONCEPTS 46,330

dictate [*n*] *command; rule*
behest, bidding, code, decree, dictum, direction, edict, fiat, injunction, law, mandate, order, ordinance, precept, principle, requirement, statute, ultimatum, word; SEE CONCEPTS 274,318,688

dictate [*v1*] *command; give instructions*
bid, bulldoze*, call-the play*, call the shots*, call the tune*, charge, control, decree, direct, enjoin, govern, guide, impose, instruct, lay down, lay down the law, lead, manage, ordain, order, prescribe, pronounce, put foot down*, read the riot act*, regiment, rule, set, take the reins*, walk heavy*; SEE CONCEPTS 53,60

dictate [*v2*] *read out for the record*
compose, deliver, draft correspondence, emit, formulate, give account, give forth, interview, orate, prepare draft, say, speak, talk, transmit, utter, verbalize; SEE CONCEPTS 60,324

dictator [*n*] *absolute ruler*
absolutist, adviser, authoritarian, autocrat, boss, chief, commander, despot, disciplinarian, fascist, Hitler*, leader, magnate, mogul, oligarch, oppressor, ringleader, slavedriver, totalitarian, tycoon, tyrant, usurper; SEE CONCEPT 354

dictatorial [*adj*] *tyrannical, authoritarian*
absolute, arbitrary, arrogant, autocratic, bossy, clamorous, crack-the-whip*, despotic, dictative, doctrinaire, dogmatic, domineering, egotistic, firm, haughty, imperative, imperious, iron-handed, oppressive, overbearing, peremptory, pompous, proud, stern, throwing weight around, totalitarian, unlimited, unrestricted; SEE CONCEPT 542

dictatorship [*n*] *absolute rule*
authoritarianism, autocracy, coercion, despotism, fascism, garrison state, Nazism, reign of terror*, totalitarianism, tyranny, unlimited rule; SEE CONCEPTS 133,299,641

diction [*n*] *style of speech; articulation*
command of language, delivery, elocution, eloquence, enunciation, expression, fluency, gift of gab*, inflection, intonation, language, line, lingo, locution, oratory, parlance, phrase, phraseology, phrasing, pronunciation, rhetoric, usage, verbalism, verbiage, vocabulary, wordage, wording; SEE CONCEPTS 47,276

dictionary [*n*] *book of word meanings*
concordance, cyclopedia, encyclopedia, glossary, language, lexicon, palaver, promptory, reference, terminology, vocabulary; SEE CONCEPT 280

dictum [*n1*] *saying; proverb*
adage, aphorism, apothegm, axiom, brocard, gnome, maxim, moral, motto, precept, rule, saw, truism; SEE CONCEPTS 278,689

dictum [*n2*] *decree, pronouncement*
affirmation, assertion, command, declaration, dictate, edict, fiat, order; SEE CONCEPT 278

didactic [*adj*] *educational*
academic, advisory, donnish, edifying, enlightening, exhortative, expository, homiletic, hortative, instructive, moral, moralizing, pedagogic, pedantic, preachy, preceptive, schoolmasterist, sermonic, sermonizing, teacherish, teacherly, teachy; SEE CONCEPT 548

die [*v1*] *pass away; stop living*
be no more*, be taken, breathe one's last*, cease to exist, conk*, croak*, decease, demise, depart, drop, drop off, drown, expire, finish, give up the ghost*, go way of all flesh*, kick the bucket*,

de
di

perish, relinquish life, rest in peace, succumb, suffocate; SEE CONCEPT *304*

die [*v2*] *wither, dwindle*
abate, bate, break down, crumble, decay, decline, degenerate, deteriorate, dilapidate, diminish, disappear, droop, ease off, ebb, end, expire, fade, fade away, fade out, fail, fall, fizzle out*, go bad*, go downhill*, halt, lapse, let up, lose power, melt away, moderate, molder, pass, peter out*, rankle, recede, retrograde, rot, run down, run low, run out, sink, slacken, stop, subside, vanish, wane, weaken, wear away, wilt; SEE CONCEPTS *469,698*

die-hard [*adj*] *uncompromising*
conservative, convinced, dyed-in-the-wool*, extremist, firm, fogyish, immovable, inflexible, intransigent, old-line*, orthodox, Philistine, reactionary, right, standpat, Tory*, traditionalistic, ultraconservative, unreconstructed; SEE CONCEPTS *404,542*

diehard [*n*] *overenthusiastic person*
bitter ender*, Bourbon*, dyed-in-the-wool*, extremist, fanatic, fogy, fundamentalist, intransigent, mossback*, old liner*, praetorian, pullback*, reactionary, right, rightist, rightwinger, standpat, standpatter, stick-in-the-mud*, Tory*, true blue*, ultraconservative, zealot; SEE CONCEPTS *359,423*

diet [*n1*] *abstinence from food*
dietary, fast, nutritional therapy, regime, regimen, restriction, starvation, weight-reduction plan; SEE CONCEPT *660*

diet [*n2*] *daily intake of food*
aliment, bite, comestibles, commons, daily bread, edibles, fare, goodies, grubbery, menu, nourishment, nutriment, nutrition, provisions, rations, snack, subsistence, sustenance, viands, victuals; SEE CONCEPTS *457,459*

diet [*v*] *abstain from food*
count calories*, eat sparingly, fall off, fast, go without, lose weight, reduce, skinny down*, slim, slim down, starve, tighten belt*, watch weight*; SEE CONCEPT *169*

differ [*v1*] *be dissimilar, distinct*
alter, bear no resemblance, be distinguished from, be off the beaten path*, be unlike, clash with, conflict with, contradict, contrast, depart from, deviate from, digress, disagree, divaricate from, diverge, diversify, jar with, lack resemblance, modify, not conform, not look like, qualify, reverse, run counter to, show contrast, sing a different tune*, stand apart, take exception, turn, vary; SEE CONCEPT *665*

differ [*v2*] *clash; hold opposing views*
bicker*, bump heads*, contend, debate, demur, disaccord, disagree, discept, discord, dispute, dissent, divide, fight, go after each other, go at it*, hit a clinker*, hit a sour note*, jar*, lock horns*, object, oppose, protest against, quarrel, squabble, take issue, vary, war; SEE CONCEPT *46*

difference [*n1*] *dissimilarity, distinctness*
aberration, alteration, anomaly, antithesis, asymmetry, change, characteristic, contrariety, contrariness, contrast, departure, deviation, digression, discongruity, discrepancy, disparity, dissemblance, distinction, divergence, diversity, exception, heterogeneity, idiosyncrasy, inequality, irregularity, nonconformity, opposition, particularity, peculiarity, separateness, separation, singularity, unconformity, unlikeness, unortho-

doxness, variance, variation, variety; SEE CONCEPT *665*

difference [*n2*] *opposing views*
argument, beef*, blowup*, bone to pick*, brannigan, brawl, brush*, brush-off*, catamaran, clash, conflict, contention, contrariety, contretemps, controversy, debate, disaccord, disagreement, discord, discordance, dispute, dissension, dissent, dissidence, disunity, dustup*, estrangement, hassle, quarrel, row*, run-in*, scrap*, setto*, spat*, strife, tiff*, variance, words*, wrangle; SEE CONCEPTS *46,388*

different [*adj1*] *dissimilar, unlike*
a far cry from*, altered, antithetic, at odds, at variance, changed, clashing, colorful, contradistinct, contradistinctive, contrary, contrasting, contrastive, deviating, differential, discrepant, disparate, distant, distinct, distinctive, divergent, divers, diverse, incommensurable, incomparable, inconsistent, individual, like night and day*, mismatched, mismated, offbeat, opposed, other, otherwise, particular, peculiar, poles apart*, single, unalike, unequal, unrelated, unsimilar, variant, various; SEE CONCEPTS *487,564,573*

different [*adj2*] *separate, distinct*
another, another story, atypical, bizarre, discrete, diverse, especial, express, extraordinary, individual, novel, original, other, out of the ordinary, particular, peculiar, rare, several, singular, something else, special, specialized, specific, startling, strange, uncommon, unconventional, unique, unusual, various; SEE CONCEPT *564*

different [*adj3*] *miscellaneous, various*
anthologized, assorted, asymmetrical, collected, disparate, dissonant, divergent, divers, diverse, diversified, diversiform, heterogeneous, incongruous, inconsistent, indiscriminate, jarring, manifold, many, multifarious, multiform, numerous, omnifarious, omniform, several, some, sundry, varicolored, varied, variegated, varietal, variform; SEE CONCEPT *772*

differentiate [*v1*] *make a distinction*
antithesize, characterize, comprehend, contrast, demarcate, discern, discrepate, discriminate, extricate, individualize, individuate, know, know what's what*, mark, mark off, redline*, separate, set apart, set off, sever, severalize, split hairs*, tell apart, understand; SEE CONCEPTS *15,38*

differentiate [*v2*] *change; make different*
adapt, alter, assort, convert, diversify, mismatch, mismate, modify, transform, variegate, vary; SEE CONCEPT *232*

differently [*adv*] *in another way; otherwise*
abnormally, adversely, antagonistically, antithetically, asymmetrically, conflictingly, contradictorily, contrarily, contrastingly, contrastively, discordantly, disparately, dissimilarly, distinctively, divergently, diversely, hostilely, in a different manner, incompatibly, incongruously, individually, negatively, nonconformably, on the contrary, on the other hand, oppositely, poles apart, separately, uniquely, unorthodoxly, unusually, variously, vice versa; SEE CONCEPT *564*

difficult [*adj1*] *hard on someone; hard to do*
ambitious, arduous, backbreaker*, bothersome, burdensome, challenging, crucial, demanding, difficile, easier said than done*, effortful, exacting, formidable, galling, Gargantuan*, hard-won, heavy, Herculean*, immense, intricate, irritating, labored, laborious, no picnic*, not easy, onerous,

operose, painful, problem, problematic, prohibitive, rigid, severe, stiff, strenuous, titanic, toilsome, tough, troublesome, trying, unyielding, uphill, upstream, wearisome; SEE CONCEPT 538

difficult [*adj1*] *complicated; hard to comprehend*
abstract, abstruse, baffling, bewildering, complex, confounding, confusing, dark, deep, delicate, enigmatic, enigmatical, entangled, esoteric, formidable, hard to explain, hard to solve, hidden, inexplicable, intricate, involved, knotty, labyrinthine, loose, meandering, mysterious, mystical, mystifying, nice, obscure, obstinate, paradoxical, perplexing, problematical, profound, puzzling, rambling, subtle, tangled, thorny, ticklish, troublesome, unclear, unfathomable, unintelligible, vexing; SEE CONCEPT 529

difficult [*adj3*] *unmanageable socially*
argumentative, bearish, boorish, dark, demanding, fastidious, finicky, fractious, fussy, grim, hard to please, impolite, intractable, irritable, oafish, obstreperous, perverse, picky, refractory, rigid, rude, tiresome, tough, troublesome, trying, unaccommodating, unamenable; SEE CONCEPTS 404,542,555

difficulty [*n1*] *problem; situation requiring great effort*
adversity, arduousness, awkwardness, barricade, check, complication, crisis, crux, dead end, deadlock, deep water*, dilemma, distress, emergency, exigency, fix*, frustration, hardship, hazard, hindrance, hitch*, hot water*, impasse, knot*, labor, laboriousness, mess, misfortune, muddle, obstacle, obstruction, pain, painfulness, paradox, perplexity, pickle*, predicament, quagmire, quandary, scrape*, snag*, stew*, strain, strait, strenuousness, struggle, stumbling block*, tribulation, trouble; SEE CONCEPTS 674,677

difficulty [*n2*] *mental burden*
ado, aggravation, annoyance, anxiety, bafflement, bother, care, charge, complication, crisis, depression, discouragement, distress, embarrassment, emergency, exigency, frustration, grievance, hangup, harassment, imbroglio, inconvenience, irritation, jam, maze, mess, millstone*, misery, oppression, perplexity, pickle*, pinch, predicament, pressure, puzzle, quandary, ramification, responsibility, scrape*, setback, strain, strait, stress, strife, struggle, to-do*, trouble, vicissitude, weight, worry; SEE CONCEPTS 410,532,690

difficulty [*n3*] *argument*
altercation, beef*, bickering, controversy, dispute, falling-out*, fight, hassle, misunderstanding, quarrel, squabble, strife, trouble; SEE CONCEPT 46

diffidence [*n*] *hesitancy; lack of confidence*
backwardness, bashfulness, constraint, doubt, fear, hesitation, humility, insecurity, meekness, modesty, mousiness, reluctance, reserve, self-consciousness, sheepishness, shyness, timidity, timidness, timorousness, unassertiveness; SEE CONCEPT 633

diffident [*adj*] *hesitant; unconfident*
backward, bashful, blenching, chary, constrained, coy, demure, distrustful, doubtful, dubious, flinching, humble, insecure, meek, modest, mousy, rabbity, reluctant, reserved, retiring, self-conscious, self-effacing, sheepish, shrinking, shy, suspicious, timid, timorous, unassertive,

unassuming, unassured, unobtrusive, unpoised, unsure, withdrawn; SEE CONCEPT 401

diffuse [*adj1*] *spread out*
broadcast, catholic, circulated, diluted, dispersed, disseminated, distributed, expanded, extended, general, prevalent, propagated, radiated, scattered, separated, strewn, thin, unconcentrated, universal, widespread; SEE CONCEPTS 530,583, 772

diffuse [*adj2*] *wordy*
circumlocutory, copious, diffusive, digressive, discursive, dull, exuberant, lavish, lengthy, long, long-winded, loose, meandering, palaverous, profuse, prolix, rambling, random, redundant, vague, verbose, waffling, windy; SEE CONCEPT 267

diffusion [*n*] *spread; wide distribution*
circulation, dispersal, dispersion, dissemination, dissipation, expansion, propaganda, propagation, scattering; SEE CONCEPTS 634,651

dig [*n*] *insult*
crack, cut, cutting remark, gibe, innuendo, jeer, quip, slur, sneer, taunt, wisecrack; SEE CONCEPT 54

dig [*v1*] *delve into; hollow out*
bore, break up, bulldoze, burrow, cat, channel, clean, concave, deepen, depress, dig down, discover, dredge, drill, drive, enter, excavate, exhume, fork out, go into, gouge, grub, harvest, hoe, investigate, mine, penetrate, pierce, pit, probe, produce, quarry, root, root out, rout, sap, scoop, scoop out, search, shovel, sift, spade, till, tunnel, turn over, uncover, undermine, unearth; SEE CONCEPT 178

dig [*v2*] *thrust object into*
drive, gouge, jab, jog, nudge, plunge, poke, prod, punch, ram, sink, stab, stick; SEE CONCEPT 208

dig [*v3*] *investigate; discover*
bring to light*, come across, come up with, delve, dig down, expose, extricate, find, go into, inquire, look into, probe, prospect, research, retrieve, root, search, search high and low*, shake down*, sift*, turn inside out*, turn upside down*, uncover, unearth; SEE CONCEPTS 31,103,216

dig [*v4*] *enjoy, like*
appreciate, follow, go for*, groove*, love, mind, relish, understand; SEE CONCEPT 32

dig [*v5*] *understand*
accept, apprehend, catch, comprehend, follow, grasp, recognize, see, take, take in; SEE CONCEPT 15

digest [*n*] *abridgement of something written*
abstract, aperçu, brief, compendium, condensation, epitome, pandect, précis, résumé, short form, sketch, summary, survey, syllabus, sylloge, synopsis; SEE CONCEPT 271

digest [*v1*] *assimilate food*
absorb, chymify, consume, dissolve, eat, incorporate, macerate, swallow, take; SEE CONCEPT 169

digest [*v2*] *make shorter; abridge*
abbreviate, abstract, boil down, classify, codify, compress, condense, cut, cut down, cut to bone*, decrease, epitomize, get to the meat*, inventory, methodize, nutshell*, put in a nutshell*, reduce, shorten, sum, summarize, summate, sum up, survey, synopsize, systematize, tabulate, trim; SEE CONCEPTS 236,247

di
di

digest [v3] *come to understand*
absorb, analyze, assimilate, consider, contemplate, deliberate, grasp, master, meditate, ponder, study, take in, think about, think over; SEE CONCEPT 15

digest [v4] *tolerate, endure*
abide, bear, brook, go, stand, stomach, swallow, take; SEE CONCEPT 23

dig in [v] *begin with enthusiasm*
bite, burrow, chew, commence, consume, delve, eat, rise, set about, spring, start eating; SEE CONCEPTS 100,169

digit [n1] *number*
arabic, chiffer, cipher, figure, integer, notation, numeral, symbol, whole number; SEE CONCEPTS 765,784

digit [n2] *small appendage of animate being*
claw, extremity, fang, feeler, finger, fork, hook, index finger, phalange, pinkie, pointer, ring finger, thumb, toe; SEE CONCEPT 392

digital library [n] *multimedia library*
digital object library, electronic library, information superhighway, national information infrastructure, virtual library; SEE CONCEPT 274

dignified [adj] *honorable*
aristocratic, august, courtly, decorous, distingué, distinguished, eminent, formal, grand, grave, great, highbrow*, highfalutin'*, imperial, imperious, lofty, magisterial, magnificent, nifty*, noble, proud, refined, regal, reserved, respected, solemn, somber, stately, superior, upright; SEE CONCEPTS 404,555,574

dignify [v] *make honorable; glorify*
adorn, advance, aggrandize, distinguish, elevate, ennoble, erect, exalt, grace, honor, magnify, prefer, promote, raise, sublime, uprear; SEE CONCEPTS 244,700

dignitary [n] *high ranking person*
big gun*, big kahuna*, bigshot*, bigwig*, celebrity, luminary, official, person of influence, star, top cat*, VIP*; SEE CONCEPTS 388,668

dignity [n] *excellence, nobility*
address, cachet, character, consequence, courtliness, culture, decency, decorum, distinction, elevation, eminence, ethics, etiquette, glory, grace, grandeur, gravity, greatness, hauteur, honor, importance, loftiness, majesty, merit, morality, nobleness, perfection, poise, prestige, propriety, quality, rank, regard, renown, respectability, seemliness, self-respect, significance, solemnity, splendor, standing, state, stateliness, station, stature, status, sublimity, virtue, worth, worthiness; SEE CONCEPTS 388,411,668

digress [v] *stray, deviate*
aberrate, beat about the bush*, be diffuse, circumlocute, depart, divagate, drift, excurse, get off the point, get off the subject, get sidetracked, go by way of*, go off on a tangent*, long way*, meander, ramble, roam, swerve, turn aside, veer, wander, wander away; SEE CONCEPTS 195,266, 697

digression [n] *deviation; straying*
apostrophe, aside, deflection, departure, detour, difference, discursion, divagation, divergence, diversion, drifting, episode, excursion, excursus, footnote, incident, note, obiter dictum, parenthesis, rambling, variation, wandering; SEE CONCEPTS 278,665,697

dilapidated [adj] *falling apart; in ruins*
battered, beat-up, broken-down, crumbling, crumbly, crummy*, damaged, decayed, decaying, decrepit, derelict, dingy, dog-eared*, faded, fallen-in, impaired, in a bad way*, injured, marred, neglected, old, ramshackle, ratty*, raunchy, rickety, rinky-dink*, run-down, seedy, shabby, shaky, slummy, tacky, threadbare, tumble-down, uncared for, unimproved, unkempt, used-up, worn-out; SEE CONCEPTS 485,560

dilate [v] *stretch, widen*
amplify, augment, be profuse, be prolix, broaden, develop, distend, enlarge, expand, expatiate, expound, extend, increase, inflate, lengthen, prolong, protract, puff out, spin off, swell; SEE CONCEPTS 57,236,245

dilatory [adj] *procrastinating*
backward, behindhand, dallying, delaying, deliberate, laggard, late, lax, lazy, leisurely, lingering, loitering, moratory, neglectful, negligent, putting off, remiss, slack, slow, sluggish, snail-like*, tardy, tarrying, time-wasting, unhasty, unhurried; SEE CONCEPTS 542,799

dilemma [n] *crisis*
bind*, box*, Catch-22*, corner, difficulty, double bind*, embarrassment, fix, hole, hooker*, impasse, jam, mess, mire, perplexity, pickle*, plight, predicament, problem, puzzle, quandary, scrape, spot, strait, tight corner*; SEE CONCEPTS 674,675

dilettante [adj] *amateurish*
artsy fartsy*, dabbling, green*, half-baked*, half-cocked*, rookie, tenderfoot*, unaccomplished, ungifted, unskilled; SEE CONCEPT 527

dilettante [n] *amateur*
abecedarian, aesthete, connoisseur, dabbler, dallier, greenhorn*, nonprofessional, rookie, smatterer, tenderfoot*, trifler, tyro, uninitiate; SEE CONCEPT 423

diligence [n] *perseverance in carrying out action*
activity, alertness, application, assiduity, assiduousness, attention, attentiveness, briskness, care, carefulness, constancy, earnestness, exertion, heed, heedfulness, industry, intensity, intent, intentness, keenness, laboriousness, pertinacity, quickness, sedulousness, vigor; SEE CONCEPTS 657,677

diligent [adj] *persevering, hard-working*
active, assiduous, attentive, busy, careful, conscientious, constant, eager, eager beaver*, earnest, grind*, indefatigable, industrious, laborious, occupied, operose, painstaking, persistent, persisting, pertinacious, plugging*, sedulous, steadfast, studious, tireless, unflagging, unrelenting, untiring; SEE CONCEPTS 326,538,542

dilly-dally [v] *waste time*
dawdle, delay, hem and haw*, hesitate, linger, loiter, meander, mosey, move slowly, procrastinate, vacillate; SEE CONCEPTS 151,210,681

dilute [v] *make thinner; weaken*
adulterate, alter, attenuate, cook, cut, decrease, deliquesce, diffuse, diminish, doctor*, doctor up*, irrigate, lace, lessen, liquefy, mitigate, mix, moderate, modify, needle*, phony up*, plant, qualify, reduce, shave*, spike, temper, water, water down; SEE CONCEPT 250

diluted/dilute [adj] *thinned, weakened*
adulterated, attenuated, cut, impaired, impoverished, laced, light, moderated, reduced, shaved*, spiked, tempered, washy, watered down, waterish, watery, wishy-washy*; SEE CONCEPTS 485,606

dim [*adj1*] *darkish*
blah, bleary, blurred, caliginous, cloudy, dark, dingy, dreary, dull, dusk, dusky, faded, faint, flat, fuzzy, gloomy, gray, ill-defined, indistinct, lackluster, lightless, mat, monotone, monotonous, murky, muted, obscured, opaque, overcast, pale, poorly lit, shadowy, sullied, tarnished, tenebrous, unclear, unilluminated, vague, weak; SEE CONCEPT 617

dim [*adj2*] *unfavorable with regard to opinion*
depressing, disapproving, discouraging, gloomy, skeptical, somber, suspicious, unpromising; SEE CONCEPT 542

dim [*adj3*] *not very intelligent*
boorish, dense, dim-witted, doltish, dull, dumb, oafish, obtuse, slow, slow on uptake*, stupid, thick*, weak-minded; SEE CONCEPT 402

dim [*v*] *darken; obscure*
becloud, bedim, befog, blear, blur, cloud, dull, eclipse, fade, fog, haze, lower, muddy, obfuscate, pale, tarnish, turn down; SEE CONCEPTS 250,627

dimensions/dimension [*n*] *proportions; range*
admeasurement, ambit, amplitude, bigness, bulk, capacity, compass, depth, dimensionality, extension, extensivity, extent, greatness, height, importance, largeness, length, magnitude, measure, measurement, reach, scale, scope, size, volume, width; SEE CONCEPTS 698,776

diminish [*v1*] *become or cause to be less*
abate, abbreviate, attenuate, become smaller, close, contract, curtail, cut, decline, decrease, depreciate, die out, drain, dwindle, ebb, extenuate, fade away, lessen, lower, minify, moderate, peter out, recede, reduce, retrench, shrink, shrivel, slacken, subside, taper, temper, wane, weaken; SEE CONCEPTS 698,776

diminish [*v2*] *belittle*
abuse, bad-mouth*, cheapen, cut down to size*, decry, demean, depreciate, derogate, detract from, devalue, disparage, dump on*, give comeuppance*, knock off high horse*, minimize, pan*, poormouth*, put away*, put down*, run down*, tear down*; SEE CONCEPT 54

diminution [*n*] *lessening, reduction*
abatement, alleviation, contraction, curtailment, cut, cutback, decay, decline, decrease, deduction, retrenchment, weakening; SEE CONCEPTS 698, 776

diminutive [*adj*] *tiny, petite*
bantam, bitsy*, bitty*, button*, Lilliputian, little, midget, mini, miniature, minute, peewee*, pint-sized, pocket, pocket-sized, small, teensy*, teensy-weensy*, teeny*, teeny-weeny*, undersize, wee*, weeny*; SEE CONCEPT 789

dimwit [*n*] *a stupid person*
blockhead, bonehead, dolt, dullard, dunce, fool, idiot, ignoramus, imbecile, moron, numbskull, simpleton, twit; SEE CONCEPT 412

din [*n*] *loud, continuous noise*
babel, bedlam, boisterousness, brouhaha, buzz, clamor, clangor, clash, clatter, commotion, confusion, crash, disquiet, hoo-ha*, hubbub, hullabaloo*, hurly-burly*, jangle, music, outcry, pandemonium, percussion, racket, row, shout, sound, stridency, tintamarre*, tintinnabulation, tumult; SEE CONCEPT 595

dine [*v*] *eat, often formally*
banquet, breakfast, consume, do lunch*, eat

out*, fall to*, feast, feed on, lunch, sup, supper; SEE CONCEPT 169

diner [*n*] *casual restaurant with varied menu*
Automat*, bistro, booth, café, canteen, chuck wagon*, coffee shop, concession, dump*, eatery, eating house, facility, fast-food outlet, greasy spoon*, grill, hash house*, ice-cream parlor, lunch counter, lunchroom, lunch wagon, mess hall, quick-lunch, saloon, sandwich shop, snack bar, tearoom; SEE CONCEPT 449

dingy [*adj*] *soiled, tacky*
bedimmed, broken-down, colorless, dark, darkish, dilapidated, dim, dirty, discolored, drab, dreary, dull, dusky, faded, gloomy, grimy, muddy, murky, obscure, run-down, seedy, shabby, smirched, somber, sullied, tarnished, threadbare, tired; SEE CONCEPTS 485,617

dinky [*adj*] *tiny, small*
bush-league*, dainty, insignificant, lesser, Lilliputian, mini, miniature, minor, minor-league*, neat, petite, secondary, second rate*, small-fry*, small-time*, trim; SEE CONCEPT 789

dinner [*n*] *evening meal*
banquet, blowout*, chow*, collation, din-din*, eats*, feast, feedbag*, fete, main meal, major munch*, potluck, principal meal, refection, regale, repast, ribs*, spread*, supper, table d'hôte; SEE CONCEPT 459

dip [*n1*] *submersion in liquid*
bath, dive, douche, drenching, ducking, immersion, plunge, soak, soaking, swim; SEE CONCEPT 256

dip [*n2*] *something for dunking*
concoction, dilution, infusion, mixture, preparation, solution, suffusion, suspension; SEE CONCEPTS 260,466

dip [*n3*] *depression; decline*
basin, concavity, declivity, descent, downslide, downswing, downtrend, drop, fall, fall-off, hole, hollow, inclination, incline, lowering, pitch, sag, sink, sinkage, sinkhole, slip, slope, slump; SEE CONCEPTS 513,697,738

dip [*v1*] *put into liquid*
baptize, bathe, douse, drench, duck, dunk, immerse, irrigate, lave, lower, moisten, pitch, plunge, rinse, slop, slosh, soak, souse, splash, steep, submerge, submerse, wash, water, wet; SEE CONCEPTS 201,256

dip [*v2*] *lower, descend*
bend, decline, disappear, droop, drop down, fade, fall, go down, incline, nose-dive, plummet, plunge, reach, recede, sag, set, settle, sheer, sink, skew, skid, slant, slip, slope, slue, slump, spiral, subside, swoop, tilt, tumble, veer, verge; SEE CONCEPT 181

dip [*v3*] *scoop, ladle*
bail, bale, bucket, decant, dish, draft off, draw, draw out, dredge, handle, lade, lift, offer, reach into, shovel, spoon, strain; SEE CONCEPTS 196,225

dip into [*v*] *try, sample*
appropriate, browse, dabble, flip through, get, glance at, glance over, leaf through, peruse, play at, rifle through*, run over, run through, scan, seize, skim, take, taste, thumb through*; SEE CONCEPTS 87,623

diploma [*n*] *certificate for achievement*
authority, award, charter, commission, confirmation, credentials, degree, honor, recognition,

di
di

sheepskin, shingle, voucher, warrant; SEE CONCEPTS 271,337

diplomacy [*n*] *tact*
address, artfulness, craft, delicacy, delicatesse, discretion, expedience, finesse, negotiation, poise, politics, savoir-faire, skill, statecraft, subtlety; SEE CONCEPTS 388,633

diplomat [*n*] *politician, consul*
agent, ambassador, attaché, cabinet member, chargé d'affaires, conciliator, emissary, envoy, expert, go-between, legate, mediator, minister, moderator, negotiator, plenipotentiary, public relations person, representative, tactician; SEE CONCEPTS 354,359

diplomatic [*adj*] *politic, tactful*
adept, arch, artful, astute, bland, brainy, cagey, calculating, capable, clever, conciliatory, conniving, contriving, courteous, crafty, cunning, deft, delicate, dexterous, discreet, gracious, guileful, intriguing, opportunistic, polite, prudent, savvy, scheming, sensitive, sharp, shrewd, sly, smooth, strategic, suave, subtle, wily; SEE CONCEPTS 401,542

dire [*adj1*] *urgent; crucial*
acute, burning, clamant, clamorous, climacteric, critical, crying, desperate, drastic, exigent, extreme, immoderate, imperative, importunate, instant, pressing; SEE CONCEPTS 546,568,799

dire [*adj2*] *terrible, ominous*
afflictive, alarming, appalling, awful, black, calamitous, cataclysmic, catastrophic, cruel, deplorable, depressing, disastrous, dismal, distressing, dreadful, fearful, fierce, frightful, gloomy, grievous, grim, heartbreaking, horrible, horrid, lamentable, oppressing, portentous, redoubtable, regrettable, ruinous, scowling, shocking, terrific, ugly, unfortunate, woeful; SEE CONCEPTS 537,548,570

direct [*adj1*] *honest*
absolute, bald, blunt, candid, categorical, downright, explicit, express, forthright, frank, matter-of-fact, open, outspoken, person-to-person, plain, plainspoken, point-blank, sincere, straight, straightforward, straight from the shoulder*, talk turkey*, unambiguous, unconcealed, undisguised, unequivocal, unreserved; SEE CONCEPT 267

direct [*adj2*] *undeviating; uninterrupted*
beeline*, continuous, even, horizontal, in bee line*, in straight line, linear, nonstop, not crooked, point-blank, right, shortest, straight, straight ahead, straightaway, through, true, unbroken, unswerving; SEE CONCEPTS 482,581

direct [*adj3*] *face-to-face; next to*
contiguous, firsthand, head-on, immediate, lineal, next, personal, primary, prompt, proximate, resultant, succeeding; SEE CONCEPTS 585,586

direct [*v1*] *manage, oversee*
administer, advise, be in the driver's seat*, boss, call the shots*, carry on, conduct, control, control the affairs of, dispose, dominate, govern, guide, handle, have the say, head up*, influence, keep, lead, operate, ordain, preside over, quarterback*, regulate, rule, run, run the show*, run things*, shepherd, superintend, supervise, take the reins*; SEE CONCEPTS 94,117

direct [*v2*] *give instructions; teach*
address, advise, bid, charge, command, deliver, dictate, enjoin, give directions, give orders, inform, instruct, lecture, order, read, tell, warn; SEE CONCEPTS 53,61

direct [*v3*] *point in a direction; guide*
address, aim, beam, cast, conduct, escort, fix, focus, head, incline, indicate, intend, lay, lead, level, mean, move in, pilot, point, point the way, present, route, see, set, shepherd, show, sight, sight on, slant, steer, target, train, turn, zero in; SEE CONCEPTS 187,201

direct [*v4*] *send, usually by mail system*
address, designate, inscribe, label, mail, mark, route, superscribe; SEE CONCEPT 217

direct [*v5*] *put all of efforts toward*
address, aim, apply, bend, buckle down, devote, endeavor, fix, give, set, settle, strive, throw, try, turn; SEE CONCEPTS 87,677

direction [*n1*] *management*
administration, charge, command, control, government, guidance, leadership, order, oversight, superintendence, supervision; SEE CONCEPTS 299,325

direction [*n2*] *course, route*
aim, angle, area, aspect, bearing, beeline*, bent, bias, current, drift, end, inclination, line, objective, orientation, outlook, path, point of compass, proclivity, range, region, road, set, side, slant, spot, standpoint, stream, tack, tendency, that-a-way*, tide, track, trajectory, trend, viewpoint, way; SEE CONCEPTS 657,738

direction(s) [*n3*] *instructions, guidance*
advice, advisement, assignment, briefing, directive, guidelines, indication, lowdown*, notification, plan, prescription, recommendation, regulation, sealed order, specification, specs*, steer*, summons, tip, word*; SEE CONCEPTS 271,274

directive [*n*] *command, instruction*
charge, communication, decree, dictate, edict, injunction, mandate, memo, memorandum, message, notice, order, ordinance, regulation, ruling, ukase, word; SEE CONCEPTS 271,274,662

directly [*adv1*] *the shortest route*
as a crow flies*, beeline*, dead, direct, due, exactly, plump, precisely, right, slam bang*, slap, smack, smack dab*, straight, straightly, undeviatingly, unswervingly, without deviation; SEE CONCEPTS 581,778

directly [*adv2*] *as soon as possible*
anon, at once, contiguously, dead*, due, first off, forthwith, immediately, in a second, instantaneously, instanter, instantly, presently, promptly, pronto*, quickly, right away, shortly, speedily, straightaway, straight off; SEE CONCEPT 820

directly [*adv3*] *straightforwardly*
candidly, face-to-face, honestly, in person, literally, openly, personally, plainly, point-black, truthfully, unequivocally, verbatim, without prevarication, word for word; SEE CONCEPT 267

director [*n*] *manager*
administrator, big person*, boss, chair, chief, controller, exec, executive, executive officer, governor, head, head honcho*, helmer, key player*, kingpin*, leader, organizer, overseer, person upstairs*, player, principal, producer, skipper*, supervisor, top dog*, top person*; SEE CONCEPTS 347,352

directory [*n*] *reference book; guide*
agenda, almanac, atlas, blue book, book, catalogue, charts, gazeteer, hit list*, index, laundry list*, lineup, list, little black book*, record, regis-

ter, roster, scorecard, short list*, social register, syllabus, white pages*, who's who*, yellow pages*; SEE CONCEPTS *280,283*

direful [*adj*] *fearful; horrible*
apocalyptic, appalling, awful, baleful, baneful, calamitous, dreadful, fateful, ghastly, gloomy, horrid, ill-boding, inauspicious, ominous, shocking, terrible, terrific, unlucky, unpropitious; SEE CONCEPTS *537,570*

dirge [*n*] *sad song*
chant, coronach, cry, death march, death song, elegy, funeral song, hymn, jeremiad, keen, lament, march, monody, requiem, threnody; SEE CONCEPT *595*

dirigible [*n*] *airship*
blimp, hot-air balloon, zeppelin; SEE CONCEPT *504*

dirt [*n1*] *grime, impurity*
crud*, dreck, dregs, excrement, feculence, filth, filthiness, gook*, ground, gunk*, mire, muck, mud, rottenness, scuz*, sleaze, slime, smudge, smut, soil, stain, tarnish; SEE CONCEPT *509*

dirt [*n2*] *obscenity; immorality*
chicanery, double-dealing, filth, fourberie, fraud, indecency, lubricity, pornography, smut; SEE CONCEPT *645*

dirt [*n3*] *soil*
clay, dust, earth, loam, real estate, terra firma; SEE CONCEPT *509*

dirt [*n4*] *gossip*
buzz, intimate intelligence, juicy morsel, news, rumor, talk, the lowdown*; SEE CONCEPTS *274,278*

dirty [*adj*] *soiled, unclean*
bedraggled, begrimed, black, contaminated, cruddy*, crummy, defiled, disarrayed, dishabille, disheveled, dreggy, dungy, dusty, filthy, foul, fouled, greasy, grimy, grubby, grungy*, icky*, lousy, messy, mucky*, muddy, mung*, murky, nasty, pigpen*, polluted, raunchy, scummy*, scuzzy*, slatternly, slimy, sloppy, slovenly, smudged, smutty, sooty, spattered, spotted, squalid, stained, straggly, sullied, undusted, unhygienic, unkempt, unlaundered, unsanitary, unsightly, unswept, untidy, unwashed, yucky*; SEE CONCEPT *485*

dirty [*adj2*] *obscene, pornographic*
base, blue, coarse, contemptible, despicable, filthy, immoral, impure, indecent, lewd, low, mean, nasty, off-color, ribald, risqué, salacious, scatological, scurvy, smutty, sordid, squalid, unchaste, unclean, uncleanly, vile, vulgar; SEE CONCEPTS *542,545*

dirty [*adj3*] *dishonest*
below the belt*, cheating, corrupt, crooked, deceitful, double-dealing, foul, shabby, shady, shifty, sleazy, sneaky, sordid, underhanded, unethical, unscrupulous, untruthful; SEE CONCEPT *267*

dirty [*v*] *cause to be soiled*
begrime, besoil, blacken, blotch, blur, botch, coat, contaminate, corrupt, debase, decay, defile, discolor, draggle, encrust, foul, grime, make dusty, make impure, mess up, mold, muddy, pollute, rot, smear, smirch, smoke, smudge, smutch, spatter, spoil, spot, stain, sully, sweat, taint, tar, tarnish; SEE CONCEPT *254*

dirty old man [*n*] *pervert*
degenerate, lecher, sex maniac, sleazebag; SEE CONCEPT *412*

dirty tricks [*n*] *dishonest practices*
dirty pool*, funny business*, malicious tactics, monkey business*, shady business, skullduggery, unethical behavior; SEE CONCEPTS *59,633, 657*

disability [*n*] *disadvantage, restriction*
affliction, ailment, defect, detriment, disqualification, drawback, impairment, inability, incapacity, incompetency, inexperience, infirmity, injury, invalidity, lack, unfitness, weakness; SEE CONCEPTS *309,316,410,720*

disable [*v*] *render inoperative; cripple*
attenuate, batter, blunt, damage, debilitate, disarm, disenable, disqualify, enervate, enfeeble, exhaust, hamstring*, handicap, harm, hock*, hogtie*, hurt, immobilize, impair, incapacitate, invalidate, kibosh*, knock out*, maim, mangle, mar, mutilate, muzzle, paralyze, pinion, prostrate, put out of action*, render incapable, ruin, sabotage, sap, shatter, shoot down*, spoil, take out*, throw monkey wrench in*, total*, unbrace, undermine, unfit, unstrengthen, weaken, wreck; SEE CONCEPTS *130,246*

disabled [*adj*] *incapacitated*
broken-down, confined, decrepit, disarmed, hamstrung*, handicapped, helpless, hurt, incapable, infirm, laid-up, lame, maimed, out-of-action*, out-of-commission*, paralyzed, powerless, rundown, sidelined, stalled, weakened, worn-out, wounded, wrecked; SEE CONCEPTS *314,527*

disadvantage [*n2*] *hurt, loss*
damage, deprivation, detriment, disservice, harm, injury, prejudice; SEE CONCEPTS *230,309, 679*

disadvantaged [*adj*] *underprivileged*
deprived, discriminated against, handicapped, hindered, impaired, impoverished, poor; SEE CONCEPT *334*

disadvantageous [*adj*] *detrimental, inconvenient*
adverse, contrary, damaging, debit-side, deleterious, depreciative, depreciatory, derogatory, detracting, disparaging, downside, dyslogistic, harmful, hurtful, ill-timed, inexpedient, injurious, inopportune, objectionable, on the debit side, pejorative, prejudicial, slighting, uncomplimentary, unfavorable, unprofitable; SEE CONCEPTS *334,537,555*

disadvantage(s) [*n1*] *difficulty, trouble*
adverse circumstance, bar, blocking, burden, defect, deficiency, deprivation, detriment, disability, discommodity, drawback, failing, fault, flaw, fly in the ointment*, hamper, handicap, hardship, hindrance, impediment, imperfection, imposition, inadequacy, inconvenience, inutility, lack, liability, limitation, minus, nuisance, objection, obstacle, privation, problem, restraint, snag, stumbling block*, weakness, weak point; SEE CONCEPTS *666,674*

disaffect [*v*] *lose affection for, estrange*
agitate, alienate, antagonize, discompose, disquiet, disturb, disunify, disunite, divide, repel, upset, wean; SEE CONCEPTS *7,19,135,384*

disaffected [*adj*] *alienated, estranged*
antagonistic, discontented, disloyal, dissatisfied, hostile, indifferent, mutinous, rebellious, seditious, uncompliant, unfriendly, unsubmissive; SEE CONCEPTS *403,555*

disaffection [*n*] *alienation, estrangement*
animosity, antagonism, antipathy, aversion, breach, disagreement, discontent, dislike, disloy-

di
di

alty, dissatisfaction, hatred, hostility, ill will, repugnance, resentment, unfriendliness; SEE CON-
CEPTS *388,410*

disagree [*v1*] *be different*
be discordant, be dissimilar, clash, conflict, contradict, counter, depart, deviate, differ, discord,
disharmonize, dissent, diverge, run counter to,
vary, war; SEE CONCEPT *665*

disagree [*v2*] *argue; hold differing opinion*
altercate, battle, bicker, brawl, break with, bring
action, clash, contend, contest, controversialize,
controvert, debate, differ, disaccord, discept, discord, dispute, dissent, divide, fall out*, feud,
fight, go for the jugular*, haggle, have words*,
jump on*, lay into*, let have it, logomachize, object, oppose, palter, quarrel, quibble, rip, row,
scrap, set to, skirmish, spar, spat, sue, take issue,
take on, war, wrangle, zap*; SEE CONCEPTS *12,46*

disagree [*v3*] *be injurious*
be distasteful, be disturbing, be sickening, be unsuitable, bother, discomfort, distress, go against
the grain*, hurt, injure, make ill, nauseate,
sicken, trouble, upset; SEE CONCEPT *246*

disagreeable [*adj1*] *bad-tempered, irritable*
bellicose, brusque, cantankerous, churlish, contentious, contrary, cross, difficult, disobliging,
disputatious, eristic, grouchy, ill-natured, nasty,
obnoxious, offensive, out of sorts, peevish, pettish, petulant, querulous, rude, snappy, surly,
ugly, unfriendly, ungracious, unlikable, unpleasant, uptight, waspish, whiny; SEE CONCEPT *401*

disagreeable [*adj2*] *disgusting, offensive*
annoying, awful, bad, bothersome, displeasing,
distasteful, distressing, drag, nasty, objectionable, obnoxious, pain, repellent, repugnant, repulsive, rotten, sour, unhappy, uninviting,
unpalatable, unpleasant, unsavory, upsetting,
woeful; SEE CONCEPTS *537,548*

disagreement [*n1*] *dispute, quarrel*
altercation, animosity, antagonism, argument, at-
mospherics, bickering, breach, break, clash,
clashing, conflict, contention, contest, controversy, cross-purposes, debate, difference, discord, dissent, dissidence, disunion, disunity,
division, divisiveness, falling out, feud, fight,
friction, hassle, hostility, ill feeling, ill will, jarring, misunderstanding, opposition, rupture, spat,
split, squabble, strife, tension, variance, vendetta,
words, wrangle; SEE CONCEPTS *46,388*

disagreement [*n2*] *difference, unlikeness*
clash, disaccord, discordance, discrepancy,
disharmonism, disharmony, disparity, dissimilarity, dissimilitude, divergence, divergency,
diversity, incompatibility, incongruity, incongruousness, inconsistency, variance; SEE CONCEPT
665

disallow [*v*] *reject, prohibit*
abjure, cancel, censor, debar, deny, disacknowledge, disavow, disclaim, dismiss, disown, embargo, exclude, forbid, keep back, kill, nix*, pass
on, proscribe, put down, rebuff, refuse, repudiate, shut out, taboo*, veto, withhold, zing*; SEE
CONCEPTS *21,25,30*

disappear [*v*] *vanish; cease*
abandon, abscond, be done for, be gone, be lost,
be no more*, be swallowed up, cease to exist,
clear, come to naught, decamp, dematerialize,
depart, die, die out, disperse, dissipate, dissolve,
drop out of sight*, ebb, end, end gradually, escape, evanesce, evanish, evaporate, exit, expire,

fade, fade away, flee, fly, go, go south*, leave,
leave no trace, melt, melt away, pass, pass away,
perish, recede, retire, retreat, sink, take flight, vacate, vamoose*, wane, withdraw; SEE CONCEPTS
102,105,195

disappearance [*n*] *vanishing*
ceasing to exist, decline and fall, dematerialization, departure, desertion, disappearing act, disintegration, dispersal, dissipation, dissolution,
ebbing, eclipse, escape, evanescence, evaporation, exit, exodus, fading, flight, going, loss,
melting, passing, receding, recession, removal,
retirement, wane, wearing away, withdrawal; SEE
CONCEPTS *102,105,195*

disappoint [*v*] *sadden, dismay; frustrate*
abort, baffle, balk, bring to naught, bungle, cast
down, chagrin, circumvent, come to nothing,
dash, dash hopes*, deceive, delude, disconcert,
disenchant, disgruntle, dishearten, disillusion,
dissatisfy, dumbfound, embitter, fail, fall down
on, fall flat, fall short of, foil, founder, hamper,
hinder, leave in the lurch*, let down, miscarry,
mislead, not show, put out, ruin prospects, stand
up, tease, thwart, torment, vex; SEE CONCEPTS
7,19,699

disappointed [*adj*] *let down, saddened*
aghast, balked, beaten, chapfallen, complaining,
crestfallen, defeated, depressed, despondent, disconcerted, discontented, discouraged, disenchanted, disgruntled, disillusioned, dissatisfied,
distressed, down, downcast, downhearted, down
in the dumps*, foiled, frustrated, hopeless, objecting, shot down, taken down, thwarted, unhappy, unsatisfied, upset, vanquished, worsted;
SEE CONCEPT *403*

disappointment [*n1*] *saddening situation; letdown*
bitter pill*, blind alley*, blow, blunder, bring-
down, bummer, bust*, calamity, defeat, disaster,
discouragement, downer*, downfall, drag, dud,
error, failure, false alarm*, faux pas*, fiasco, fizzle, flash in the pan*, impasse, inefficacy,
lemon*, miscalculation, mischance, misfortune,
mishap, mistake, obstacle, old one-two*, setback, slip, washout; SEE CONCEPTS *230,674*

disappointment [*n2*] *mental upset; displeasure*
adverse fate, adversity, bafflement, blow, chagrin, defeat, despondency, discontent, discouragement, disenchantment, disgruntlement,
disillusion, disillusionment, dissatisfaction, distress, failure, frustration, lack of success, letdown, mortification, nonsuccess, regret, setback,
the knocks*, unfulfillment; SEE CONCEPT *410*

disapproval [*n*] *condemnation*
blackball*, black list*, blame, boo*, boycott,
brickbat, call down, castigation, catcall*, censure, criticism, denunciation, deprecation,
disapprobation, discontent, disfavor, dislike, disparagement, displeasure, dissatisfaction, hiss*,
nix*, objection, opprobrium, ostracism, reproach, reproof, slap on wrist*, stricture, thumbs
down*, vitriol, zing*; SEE CONCEPTS *278,689*

disapprove [*v*] *condemn*
blame, censure, chastise, criticize, damn, decry,
denounce, deplore, deprecate, detract, disallow,
discommend, discountenance, disesteem, disfavor, dislike, dismiss, dispraise, expostulate, find
fault with, find unacceptable, frown on, look
askance at, look down on, nix*, object to, op-

pose, pan*, pass on, refuse, reject, remonstrate, reprehend, reprobate, reprove, set aside, slam, spurn, take dim view of, take exception to, turn down, veto, zing*; SEE CONCEPTS *18,21,52*

disarm [v1] *render defenseless*
conciliate, cripple, deactivate, debilitate, deescalate, demilitarize, demobilize, disable, disband, disqualify, incapacitate, invalidate, neutralize, occupy, pacify, paralyze, prostrate, skin, strip, subdue, subjugate, unarm, weaken; SEE CONCEPTS *142,211,320*

disarm [v2] *persuade*
allure, attract, bewitch, captivate, charm, coax, convince, enchant, fascinate, seduce, set at ease, unarm, urge, win over; SEE CONCEPTS *7,19,22,68*

disarmament [n] *reduction of weapons*
arms limitation, arms reduction, conquest, crippling, de-escalation, demilitarization, demobilization, disablement, disqualification, freeze, neutralizing, occupation, pacification, paralyzing, rendering powerless, subjugation; SEE CONCEPTS *142,211,320*

disarming [adj] *charming*
bewitching, convincing, deferential, ingratiating, ingratiatory, insinuating, insinuative, inveigling, irresistible, likable, persuasive, saccharine, seductive, silken, silky, winning; SEE CONCEPT *401*

disarrange [v] *disorder*
derange, discompose, disturb, get out of order, jumble, mess, mix up, ruffle, scramble, shuffle, unsettle, untidy; SEE CONCEPTS *240,250*

disarray [n] *disorder, confusion, mess*
anarchy, ataxia, chaos, clutter, disarrangement, discomposure, disharmony, dishevelment, disorganization, holy mess*, indiscipline, jumble, muddle, shambles*, snarl, tangle, topsy-turviness*, unholy mess*, unruliness, untidiness, upset; SEE CONCEPTS *230,727*

disaster [n] *accident, trouble*
act of God*, adversity, affliction, bad luck, bad news*, bale, bane, blight, blow, bust, calamity, casualty, cataclysm, catastrophe, collapse, collision, crash, debacle, defeat, depression, emergency, exigency, failure, fall, fell stroke*, fiasco, flood, flop, grief, hard luck, harm, hazard, holocaust, hot water*, ill luck, misadventure, mischance, misfortune, mishap, reverse, rock, rough, ruin, ruination, setback, slip, stroke, the worst*, tragedy, undoing, upset, washout*, woe; SEE CONCEPTS *674,675*

disaster area [n] *scene of destruction*
area of devastation, chaos, confusion, crisis zone, earthquake zone, emergency area, flood zone, havoc, hot spot, war zone; SEE CONCEPTS *230,674*

disastrous [adj] *detrimental, devastating*
adverse, calamitous, cataclysmal, cataclysmic, catastrophic, destructive, dire, dreadful, fatal, fateful, hapless, harmful, ill-fated, ill-starred, luckless, ruinous, terrible, tragic, unfavorable, unfortunate, unlucky, unpropitious, untoward; SEE CONCEPTS *537,548*

disavow [v] *reject*
abjure, contradict, deny, disacknowledge, disallow, disclaim, disown, drop out, forswear, gainsay, go back on word*, impugn, negate, negative, refuse, renege, renig, repudiate, wash hands of*, weasel out of*, welsh, worm out of*; SEE CONCEPTS *18,25*

disband [v] *break up*
demobilize, destroy, disperse, dissolve, fold, scatter, separate, thin out; SEE CONCEPT *234*

disbelief [n] *doubt, skepticism*
atheism, distrust, dubiety, incredulity, mistrust, nihilism, rejection, repudiation, spurning, unbelief, unbelievingness, unfaith; SEE CONCEPTS *21,689*

disbelieve [v] *doubt*
discount, discredit, distrust, eschew, give no credence to, mistrust, not accept, not buy, not credit, not swallow*, question, reject, repudiate, scoff at, scorn, scout, suspect, unbelieve; SEE CONCEPT *21*

disbelieving [adj] *suspicious, doubting*
aporetic, cagey, cynical, incredulous, leery, mistrustful, questioning, quizzical, show-me*, skeptical, unbelieving; SEE CONCEPT *403*

disburse [v] *spend money*
acquit, ante up*, come across, come through, come up with, contribute, cough up*, deal, defray, dispense, disperse, distribute, divide, divvy*, dole out*, expend, foot the bill*, give, lay out*, measure out, outlay, partition, pay out, pony up*, put out, shell out*, use; SEE CONCEPTS *108,341*

disbursement [n] *payment*
cost, disposal, expenditure, expense, outgoing, outlay, spending; SEE CONCEPT *344*

discard [v] *get rid of*
abandon, abdicate, abjure, adios*, banish, can*, cancel, cashier, cast aside, chuck, deep-six*, desert, dispatch, dispense with, dispose of, dispossess, ditch, divorce, do away with, drop, dump, eject, eliminate, expel, forsake, free of, give up, have done with, jettison, junk*, oust, part with, protest, put by, reject, relinquish, remove, renounce, repeal, repudiate, scrap, shake off, shed, sweep away, throw away, throw out, throw overboard*, toss aside, write off; SEE CONCEPT *180*

discern [v] *catch sight of; recognize and understand*
anticipate, apprehend, ascertain, behold, descry, detect, determine, difference, differentiate, discover, discrepate, discriminate, distinguish, divine, espy, extricate, figure out, find out, focus, foresee, get a load of*, get the picture*, get wise to, judge, know, make distinction, make out, note, notice, observe, perceive, pick out, read, remark, rubberneck*, secern, see the light*, see through, separate, severalize, spot, take in, view; SEE CONCEPTS *15,38*

discernible [adj] *recognizable; distinct*
apparent, appreciable, audible, clear, detectable, discoverable, distinguishable, noticeable, observable, obvious, palpable, perceivable, perceptible, plain, sensible, tangible, visible; SEE CONCEPTS *535,576,619*

discerning [adj] *discriminating*
acute, astute, bright, brilliant, clear-sighted, clever, critical, gnostic, ingenious, insighted, insightful, intelligent, judicious, knowing, knowledgeable, penetrating, perceptive, percipient, perspicacious, piercing, sagacious, sage, sensitive, sharp, shrewd, subtle, wise; SEE CONCEPT *402*

discharge [n1] *setting free*
acquittal, clearance, disimprisonment, exonera-

tion, liberation, pardon, parole, probation, release, remittance; SEE CONCEPT *127*

discharge [*n2*] *dismissal from responsibility*
ax, bounce, bum's rush*, congé, demobilization, ejection, gate, old heave ho*, pink slip*, the boot*, the door*, walking papers*; SEE CONCEPTS *324,351*

discharge [*n3*] *detonation*
barrage, blast, burst, explosion, firing, fusillade, report, salvo, shot, shower, volley; SEE CONCEPT *521*

discharge [*n4*] *pouring forth*
elimination, emission, emptying, excretion, exudation, flow, ooze, pus, secretion, seepage, shower, suppuration, vent, voiding; SEE CONCEPTS *179,748*

discharge [*n5*] *unloading*
disburdening, emptying, unburdening, unlading; SEE CONCEPT *211*

discharge [*n6*] *carrying out of responsibility*
accomplishment, achievement, execution, fulfillment, observance, performance; SEE CONCEPT *706*

discharge [*n7*] *payment of debt*
acquittal, disbursement, liquidation, satisfaction, settlement; SEE CONCEPTS *341,344*

discharge [*v1*] *set free*
absolve, acquit, allow to go*, clear, disimprison, dismiss, emancipate, exonerate, expel, liberate, loose, loosen, manumit, oust, pardon, release, unbind, unchain, unshackle; SEE CONCEPT *127*

discharge [*v2*] *dismiss from responsibility*
absolve, ax, boot out*, bounce, bump, bust, can*, cashier, disburden, discard, disencumber, dispense, displace, eject, excuse, exempt, expel, fire, freeze out*, give one notice, kick out, lay off, let go, let off, let one go, let out, lock out*, nix*, oust, privilege from, relieve, remove, replace, ride out on rail*, run out of town*, show the door*, spare, supersede, supplant, terminate, unload; SEE CONCEPTS *324,351*

discharge [*v3*] *detonate weapon*
blast, explode, fire, let off, set off, shoot, shoot off; SEE CONCEPT *179*

discharge [*v4*] *pour forth*
break out, disembogue, dispense, ejaculate, emit, empty, erupt, excrete, exude, give off, gush, leak, ooze, release, send forth, spew, void, vomit; SEE CONCEPTS *152,179*

discharge [*v5*] *unload*
carry away, disburden, empty, off-load, remove, remove cargo, send, take away, take off, unburden, unlade, unpack, unship, unstow; SEE CONCEPT *211*

discharge [*v6*] *carry out responsibility*
accomplish, achieve, do, execute, fulfill, meet, observe, perform; SEE CONCEPT *91*

discharge [*v7*] *pay, settle debt*
clear, honor, liquidate, meet, pay up, quit, relieve, satisfy, square up; SEE CONCEPT *341*

discharge [*v8*] *invalidate agreement*
abrogate, annul, cancel, dissolve, quash, render void, vacate, void; SEE CONCEPT *121*

disciple [*n*] *believer, follower*
adherent, apostle, attendant, booster, buff, bug*, catechumen, cohort, convert, devotee, enthusiast, fan, fanatic, fiend, freak, groupie, hound*, junkie*, learner, nut*, partisan, proselyte, pupil, rooter*, satellite, sectary, sectator, student, supporter, votary, witness, zealot; SEE CONCEPTS *361,423*

disciplinarian [*n*] *person who makes others work hard*
authoritarian, bully, despot, drill sergeant, enforcer, formalist, master, sergeant, stickler, strict teacher, sundowner, teacher, trainer, tyrant; SEE CONCEPTS *350,354,423*

discipline [*n1*] *regimen, training*
conduct, control, cultivation, curb, development, domestication, drill, drilling, education, exercise, inculcation, indoctrination, limitation, method, orderliness, practice, preparation, regulation, restraint, self-command, self-control, self-government, self-mastery, self-restraint, strictness, subordination, will, willpower; SEE CONCEPTS *94,326,410*

discipline [*n2*] *punishment*
castigation, chastisement, comeuppance, correction, getting yours*, hell to pay*, punition, rod; SEE CONCEPTS *122,123*

discipline [*n3*] *field of study; subject of interest*
area, branch of knowledge, course, curriculum, specialty; SEE CONCEPT *349*

disc jockey [*n*] *radio personality*
announcer, broadcaster, deejay*, dj*, pancake turner*, radio performer, shock jock*, video jockey, vj*; SEE CONCEPT *348*

disclaim [*v*] *deny*
abandon, abjure, abnegate, belittle, contradict, contravene, criticize, decline, deprecate, disacknowledge, disaffirm, disallow, disavow, discard, disown, disparage, divorce oneself from, forswear, gainsay, minimize, negate, recant, refuse, reject, renounce, repudiate, retract, revoke, spurn, traverse, turn back on, wash hands of*; SEE CONCEPT *54*

disclaimer [*n*] *repudiation*
abjuration, abnegation, clause, denial, disavowal, dissociation, renunciation, retraction, waiver; SEE CONCEPTS *45,54*

disclose [*v*] *reveal, make public*
acknowledge, admit, avow, bare, betray, blab, bring to light*, broadcast, come out of the closet*, communicate, confess, discover, display, divulge, exhibit, expose, give away, impart, lay bare, leak, let slip, make known, mouth*, open, own, publish, relate, reveal, show, snitch*, spill, spill the beans*, squeal*, tell, uncover, unfurl, unveil, utter; SEE CONCEPT *60*

disclosure [*n*] *announcement, revelation*
acknowledgment, admission, advertisement, betrayal, blow-by-blow*, broadcast, confession, declaration, discovery, divulgation, divulgence, enlightenment, exposal, exposé, exposure, handout, impartance, impartation, leak, make, picture, publication, revealing, revealment, rundown, snitch*, squeal*, tip*, tip-off*, uncovering, unveilment, ventilation; SEE CONCEPT *274*

disco [*n*] *discotheque*
club, dance hall, nightclub, nightspot; SEE CONCEPTS *293,439,449*

discolor [*v*] *fading, dirtying of hue*
besmear, besmirch, blot, defile, mar, mark, rust, smear, soil, stain, streak, sully, tar, tarnish, tinge; SEE CONCEPTS *250,469*

discomfit [*v*] *defeat, frustrate; confuse*
abash, annoy, baffle, balk, beat, bother, checkmate, confound, demoralize, discompose, disconcert, discountenance, disturb, embarrass,

faze, fluster, foil, irk, outwit, overcome, perplex, perturb, prevent, rattle, ruffle, take aback, thwart, trump, unsettle, upset, vex, worry, worst; SEE CONCEPTS 7,19,95

discomfiture [n] *embarrassment, frustration*
abashment, agitation, beating, chagrin, comedown, confusion, conquest, defeasance, defeat, demoralization, descent, disappointment,* discomposure, disconcertion, disconcertment, disquiet, failure, humiliation, overthrow, perturbation, rout, ruin, shame, undoing, unease, uneasiness, upset, vanquishment, vexation; SEE CONCEPTS 410,674

discomfort [n] *irritation, pain*
ache, annoyance, discomfiture, discomposure, displeasure, disquiet, distress, embarrassment, hardship, hurt, inquietude, malaise, nuisance, soreness, trouble, uneasiness, unpleasantness, upset, vexation; SEE CONCEPTS 410,728

discomfort [v] *irritate; cause pain*
discomfit, discompose, disquiet, distress, disturb, embarrass, make uncomfortable, nettle, perturb, upset, vex; SEE CONCEPTS 7,19,246,313

discommode [v] *annoy*
bother, burden, disoblige, disquiet, disturb, fluster, harass, incommode, inconvenience, irk, molest, perturb, put out, trouble, upset, vex; SEE CONCEPTS 7,19

discompose [v] *provoke, agitate*
annoy, bewilder, bother, confuse, discombobulate, discomfit, disconcert, dismay, disorganize, displease, disquiet, disturb, embarrass, faze, flurry, fluster, harass, harry, irk, irritate, nettle, perplex, perturb, pester, plague, rattle, ruffle, unhinge, unsettle, upset, vex, worry; SEE CONCEPTS 7,19

disconcert [v] *shake up; confuse*
abash, agitate, baffle, balk, bewilder, bug, confound, demoralize, disarrange, discombobulate, discomfit, discompose, discountenance, disturb, embarrass, faze, fluster, foul up, frustrate, get to, hinder, nonplus, perplex, perturb, psych out*, put off, puzzle, rattle, ruffle, take aback, throw off balance, trouble, unbalance, undo, unsettle, upset, upset apple cart*, worry; SEE CONCEPTS 7,16,19

disconcerted [adj] *confused; shaken*
annoyed, bewildered, caught off balance, come apart, distracted, disturbed, embarrassed, fazed, flustered, in botheration, messed-up, mixed-up, nonplussed, out of countenance, perturbed, psyched-out*, rattled, ruffled, shook-up*, spaced-out*, taken aback, thrown, troubled, unglued, unsettled, unzipped*; upset; SEE CONCEPT 403

disconnect [v] *take apart; uncouple*
abstract, break it off, break it up, cut off, detach, disassociate, disengage, disjoin, dissever, dissociate, disunite, divide, drop it, part, separate, sever, sideline, unfix; SEE CONCEPTS 98,135

disconnected [adj] *confused; discontinuous*
broken, detached, disjointed, disordered, garbled, illogical, inchoate, incoherent, incohesive, interrupted, irrational, irregular, jumbled, loose, mixed-up, muddled, rambling, separated, uncontinuous, uncoordinated, unintelligible, wandering; SEE CONCEPTS 267,482

disconsolate [adj] *depressed, unhappy*
bad, black, blue, cheerless, cold, comfortless, crestfallen, crushed, dark, dejected, desolate, despairing, destroyed, dispirited, distressed, doleful, down, downcast, downhearted, dreary, forlorn, gloomy, grief-stricken, heartbroken, hopeless, hurting, inconsolable, in pain*, in the pits*, low, melancholy, miserable, ripped*, sad, somber, sorrowful, torn-up*, woebegone, woeful, wretched; SEE CONCEPT 403

discontent [n] *dissatisfaction*
depression, discontentment, displeasure, envy, fretfulness, regret, restlessness, uneasiness, unhappiness, vexation; SEE CONCEPT 410

discontented/discontent [adj] *unhappy, dissatisfied*
blue, complaining, crabby, disaffected, disgruntled, displeased, disquieted, disturbed, exasperated, fed up, fretful, griping, kvetching*, malcontent, malcontented, miserable, perturbed, picky, restless, ungratified, upset, vexed; SEE CONCEPT 403

discontinuance [n] *stop, suspension of activity*
adjournment, alternation, cease, cessation, close, closing, desistance, desuetude, discontinuation, disjunction, disruption, ending, finish, intermission, interruption, separation, stopping, termination; SEE CONCEPT 119

discontinue [v] *prevent activity from going on*
abandon, bag it*, blow off*, break off*, call it quits, cease, close, desist, disconnect, disjoin, dissever, disunite, drop, end, finish, give over, give up, halt, interpose, interrupt, intervene, kill, knock off*, leave off, part, pause, put an end to, quit, refrain from, scrub, separate, stop, surcease, suspend, terminate; SEE CONCEPTS 121,234

discontinuous [adj] *broken; intermittent*
alternate, desultory, disconnected, disjointed, disordered, fitful, gaping, inchoate, incoherent, incohesive, interrupted, irregular, muddled, spasmodic, unconnected, unorganized; SEE CONCEPT 482

discord [n1] *conflict, disagreement*
animosity, antagonism, antipathy, clash, clashing, collision, contention, difference, disaccord, discordance, discrepancy, disharmony, dispute, dissension, dissent, dissidence, dissonance, disunion, disunity, division, enmity, friction, fuss, hassle, hostility, incompatibility, incongruity, inharmony, lack of concord, mischief, opposition, polarization, rancor, row, ruckus, rupture, scene, spat, split, static, strife, variance, wrangling; SEE CONCEPT 388

discord [n2] *noise*
cacophony, clamor, clinker, din, disharmony, dissonance, harshness, jangle, jarring, racket, sour note, tumult; SEE CONCEPT 595

discordant [adj] *not in harmony; conflicting*
antagonistic, antipathetic, at odds, cacophonous, clashing, contradictory, contrarient, contrary, different, disagreeing, discrepant, dissonant, divergent, grating, harsh, incompatible, incongruous, inconsistent, inconsonant, inharmonious, jangling, jarring, on a sour note*, opposite, quarreling, strident, uncongenial, unharmonious, unmelodious, unmixable*; SEE CONCEPTS 558,564, 592,594

discount [n] *reduction in cost*
abatement, allowance, commission, concession, cut, cut rate, decrease, deduction, depreciation, diminution, drawback, exemption, knock-off*, markdown, modification, percentage, premium, qualification, rebate, remission, rollback, sal-

di
di

vage, something off, subtraction, tare; SEE CONCEPTS *335,763*

discount [*vl*] *lower, reduce cost*
abate, allow, deduct, depreciate, diminish, hold a sale, knock off*, make allowance for, mark down, modify, rebate, redeem, remove, sell at discount, strike off, subtract, take away, take off, undersell; SEE CONCEPTS *236,247,330*

discount [*v2*] *ignore; treat as insignificant*
belittle, blink at*, brush off*, depreciate, derogate, detract from, disbelieve, discredit, dispraise, disregard, doubt, fail, forget, minimize, mistrust, neglect, omit, overlook, overpass, pass over, question, reject, scoff at, scout, slight; SEE CONCEPTS *21,30*

discountenance [*vl*] *reject, oppose*
condemn, count me out*, deprecate, disapprove, discommend, discourage, disesteem, disfavor, dispute, frown on*, hold no brief for*, not go for*, not stand for*, object to, put down, resist, take a dim view of*, take exception to*; SEE CONCEPT *21*

discountenance [*v2*] *embarrass, disconcert*
abash, chagrin, confuse, discomfit, discompose, faze, humiliate, rattle, shame; SEE CONCEPTS *7,19,54*

discourage [*vl*] *dishearten, dispirit*
abash, afflict, alarm, appall, awe, beat down, bother, break one's heart*, bully, cast down, chill, confuse, cow, dampen, dash, daunt, deject, demoralize, deprecate, depress, dismay, disparage, distress, droop, frighten, intimidate, irk, overawe, prostrate, repress, scare, throw cold water on*, trouble, try, unnerve, vex, weigh; SEE CONCEPT *14*

discourage [*v2*] *deter, dissuade; restrain*
check, chill, control, curb, deprecate, disadvise, discountenance, disfavor, disincline, divert, frighten, hinder, hold back, hold off, impede, indispose, inhibit, interfere, keep back, obstruct, prevent, put off, quiet, repress, scare, shake, talk out of, throw cold water on*, turn aside, turn off, warn, withhold; SEE CONCEPTS *68,121*

discouraged [*adj*] *disheartened*
beat, beat-down, blue, caved-in, come-apart, crestfallen, dashed, daunted, depressed, deterred, dismayed, dispirited, down, downbeat, downcast, down-in-mouth*, glum*, gone to pieces*, in a funk*, in blue funk*, in the dumps*, lost momentum, pessimistic, sad; SEE CONCEPT *403*

discouragement [*nl*] *despondency*
cold feet*, dejection, depression, despair, disappointment, discomfiture, dismay, downheartedness, hopelessness, loss of confidence, low spirits, melancholy, pessimism, sadness, the blues*; SEE CONCEPT *410*

discouragement [*n2*] *restraint*
bar, constraint, curb, damper, deterrent, disincentive, hindrance, impediment, obstacle, opposition, rebuff, setback; SEE CONCEPT *674*

discouraging [*adj*] *upsetting*
black, bleak, dampening, daunting, depressing, depressive, deterring, disadvantageous, disappointing, disheartening, dismal, dismaying, dispiriting, dissuading, dreary, gloomy, hindering, inopportune, off-putting, oppressive, repressing, unfavorable, unpropitious; SEE CONCEPTS *403,529*

discourse [*n*] *dialogue; dissertation*
address, article, chat, communication, conversation, converse, descant, discussion, disquisition, essay, gabfest*, homily, huddle, lecture, memoir, monograph, monologue, oration, paper, rhetoric, sermon, speaking, speech, talk, thesis, tractate, treatise, utterance, verbalization; SEE CONCEPT *266*

discourse [*v*] *discuss, speak about*
argue, chew*, comment, commentate, confab*, confer, converse, debate, declaim, descant, develop, dilate upon, dispute, dissert, dissertate, elaborate, enlarge, expand, expatiate, explain, expound, give a meeting, harangue, hold forth, lecture, modulate, orate, perorate, remark, sermonize, talk, treat, voice; SEE CONCEPTS *51,56*

discourteous [*adj*] *rude, impolite*
abrupt, bad-mannered, boorish, brusque, cavalier, cheeky*, churlish, contumelious, crude, crusty*, curt, disrespectful, flip, fresh, ill-bred, ill-mannered, impertinent, inaffable, indelicate, insolent, inurbane, oafish, offhand, rustic, sassy, smart-alecky*, uncivil, uncouth, ungenteel, ungracious, unmannerly, unrefined; SEE CONCEPT *401*

discover [*v*] *find, uncover*
ascertain, bring to light, catch, come across, come upon, conceive, contrive, debunk, design, detect, determine, devise, dig up, discern, disclose, distinguish, elicit, espy, explore, ferret out*, get wind of*, get wise to*, glimpse, hear, identify, invent, learn, light upon, locate, look up, nose out*, notice, observe, originate, perceive, pick up on*, pioneer, realize, recognize, reveal, see, sense, smoke out*, spot, think of, turn up, unearth; SEE CONCEPTS *31,183*

discovery [*nl*] *finding, uncovering*
analysis, ascertainment, authentication, calculation, certification, detection, determination, diagnosis, discernment, disclosure, distinguishing, empiricism, encounter, espial, experimentation, exploration, exposition, exposure, feeling, hearing, identification, introduction, invention, learning, locating, location, origination, perception, revelation, sensing, sighting, strike, unearthing, verification; SEE CONCEPTS *31,183*

discovery [*n2*] *treasure; invention*
algorithm, bonanza*, breakthrough, conclusion, contrivance, coup, data, design, device, find, finding, formula, godsend*, innovation, law, luck, luck out*, machine, method, principle, process, result, secret, theorem, way; SEE CONCEPTS *260,532*

discredit [*vl*] *blame, detract from*
blow up*, bring into disrepute, bring to naught, censure, defame, degrade, destroy, disconsider, disesteem, disfavor, disgrace, dishonor, disparage, disprove, explode, expose, frown upon*, knock bottom out of*, mudsling*, poke full of holes*, pooh-pooh*, puncture, put down, reflect on, reproach, ruin, run down, shoot, show up, slander, slur, smear, take rug out from under*, tear down*, vilify; SEE CONCEPTS *44,54*

discredit [*v2*] *doubt, question*
challenge, deny, disbelieve, discount, dispute, distrust, mistrust, put under suspicion, reject, scoff at; SEE CONCEPT *21*

discreet [*adj*] *cautious, sensible*
alert, attentive, awake, cagey, calculating, careful, chary, circumspect, civil, conservative, considerate, controlled, diplomatic, discerning, discriminating, gingerly, guarded, having fore-

sight, heedful, intelligent, judicious, like a clam*, moderate, noncommittal, not rash, observant, on lookout*, politic, precautious, prudent, reasonable, reserved, restrained, safe, sagacious, strategic, tactful, temperate, thoughtful, vigilant, wary, watchful, wise, worldly-wise; SEE CONCEPT 401

discrepancy [n] *conflict, disagreement*
alterity, contrariety, difference, discordance, disparity, dissemblance, dissimilarity, dissimilitude, dissonance, distinction, divergence, divergency, error, far´cry*, incongruity, inconsistency, miscalculation, otherness, split, unlikeness, variance, variation; SEE CONCEPT 665

discrepant [adj] *disagreeing*
at variance, conflicting, contradictory, contrary, different, differing, disconsonant, discordant, disparate, dissonant, divergent, diverse, incompatible, incongruent, incongruous, inconsistent, inconsonant, unmixable, varying; SEE CONCEPT 564

discrete [adj] *individual*
detached, different, disconnected, discontinuous, distinct, diverse, separate, several, unattached, various; SEE CONCEPT 564

discretion [n] *caution, judgment*
acumen, attention, calculation, canniness, care, carefulness, chariness, circumspection, concern, considerateness, consideration, deliberation, diplomacy, discernment, discrimination, foresight, forethought, good sense, gumption, heed, heedfulness, judiciousness, maturity, observation, perspicacity, precaution, presence of mind, providence, prudence, responsibility, sagacity, sense, shrewdness, solicitude,. tact, thoughtfulness, vigilance, wariness, warning, watchfulness, wisdom; SEE CONCEPT 657

discretionary [adj] *open to choice*
at the call*, elective, facultative, judge and jury, leftover, nonmandatory, nonobligatory, open, optional, unrestricted; SEE CONCEPT 546

discriminate [v1] *show prejudice*
be bigot, be partial, contradistinguish, disfavor, favor, hate, incline, judge, segregate, separate, set apart, show bias, single out, treat as inferior, treat differently, victimize; SEE CONCEPTS 32,384

discriminate [v2] *differentiate, distinguish*
assess, collate, compare, contradistinguish, contrast, difference, discern, discrepate, evaluate, extricate, judge, know, know what's what*, make out*, note, perceive, remark, segregate, separate, sever, severalize, sift, specify, split hairs*, tell apart, tell the difference; SEE CONCEPTS 15,38

discriminating [adj] *critical*
acute, astute, careful, choicy, choosy, cultivated, discerning, distinctive, eclectic, fastidious, finical, finicky, fussy, individualizing, judicious, keen, opinionated, particular, persnickety*, picky, prudent, refined, select, selective, sensitive, tasteful, wise; SEE CONCEPTS 404,542

discrimination [n1] *bias*
bigotry, favoritism, hatred, inequity, injustice, intolerance, partiality, prejudice, unfairness, wrong; SEE CONCEPTS 29,689

discrimination [n2] *particularity in taste*
acumen, acuteness, astucity, astuteness, bias, clearness, decision, difference, differentiation, discernment, distinction, judgment, keenness, penetration, perception, percipience, perspicac-

ity, preference, refinement, sagacity, sense, separation, shrewdness, subtlety, taste, understanding; SEE CONCEPTS 32,410,655

discursive [adj] *rambling*
deviating, digressive, erratic, excursive, long-winded, meandering, prolix, roaming, roving, spreading, wandering; SEE CONCEPT 267

discuss [v] *talk over with another*
altercate, argue, bounce off*, canvass, compare notes, confabulate, confer, consider, consult with, contend, contest, converse, debate, deliberate, descant, discept, discourse about, dispute, dissert, dissertate, examine, exchange views on*, explain, figure, get together, go into, group-think*, hash over*, hold forth, jaw*, kick about*, knock around*, moot, put heads together*, reason about, review, sift, take up, thrash out*, toss around*, ventilate, weigh; SEE CONCEPT 56

discussion [n] *talk with another*
altercation, analysis, argument, argumentation, canvass, colloquy, confabulation, conference, consideration, consultation, contention, controversy, conversation, debate, deliberation, dialogue, discourse, disputation, dispute, dissertation, examination, exchange, excursus, group-think*, huddle, interview, meet, meeting, powwow*, quarrel, review, scrutiny, symposium, ventilation, wrangling; SEE CONCEPT 56

disdain [n] *hate; indifference*
antipathy, arrogance, aversion, contempt, contumely, derision, despisal, despisement, despite, dislike, disparagement, hatred, haughtiness, hauteur, insolence, loftiness, pride, ridicule, scorn, sneering, snobbishness, superbity, superciliousness; SEE CONCEPT 29

disdain [v] *scorn*
abhor, be allergic to*, belittle, chill, contemn, deride, despise, disregard, hate, ignore, look down nose at*, look down on, misprize, pooh-pooh*, put down*, refuse, reject, scout, slight, sneer at, spurn, undervalue; SEE CONCEPTS 29,30

disdainful [adj] *scornful*
aloof, antipathetic, arrogant, averse, cavalier, contemning, contemptuous, cool, derisive, despising, egotistic, haughty, high-and-mighty*, hoity-toity*, indifferent, insolent, lordly, overbearing, proud, rejecting, repudiating, scouting, sneering, snooty*, supercilious, superior, toplofty, unsympathetic, uppity*; SEE CONCEPT 401

disease [n] *ailment, affliction*
ache, affection, attack, blight, breakdown, bug*, cancer, canker, collapse, complaint, condition, contagion, contamination, convulsions, debility, decrepitude, defect, disorder, distemper, endemic, epidemic, feebleness, fever, fit, flu, hemorrhage, ill health, illness, indisposition, infection, infirmity, inflammation, malady, misery, pathosis, plague, seizure, sickliness, sickness, spell, stroke, syndrome, temperature, unhealthiness, unsoundness, upset, virus, visitation; SEE CONCEPT 306

diseased [adj] *unhealthy*
afflicted, ailing, indisposed, infected, infectious, infirm, rotten, sick, sickly, tainted, unsound, unwell, unwholesome; SEE CONCEPT 314

disembark [v] *get off transportation*
alight, anchor, arrive, come ashore, debark, deplane, detrain, dismount, go ashore, land, put in, step out of; SEE CONCEPT 159

di
di

disembowel [v] *gut*
clean, disbowel, draw, empty, eviscerate, exenterate, extract; SEE CONCEPTS 206,211

disenchanted [adj] *let down*
blasé, cynical, disappointed, disenthralled, disentranced, disillusioned, embittered, indifferent, jaundiced, knowing, mondaine, out of love, sick of, sophisticate, sophisticated, soured, undeceived, worldly, worldly-wise; SEE CONCEPT 403

disengage [v] *free from connection*
abstract, back off, back out, cut loose, cut out, detach, disassociate, disconnect, disentangle, disjoin, dissociate, disunite, divide, drop out, ease, extricate, liberate, loose, loosen, opt out, pull the plug, release, separate, set free, unbind, uncouple, undo, unfasten, unfix, unloose, untie, weasel out*, withdraw; SEE CONCEPT 135

disentangle [v] *unwind, disconnect; solve*
bail one out*, clear up, detach, discumber, disembroil, disencumber, disengage, disinvolve, emancipate, expand, extricate, free, let go, let off, loose, open, part, resolve, separate, sever, simplify, sort out, sunder, unbraid, undo, unfold, unravel, unscramble, unsnarl, untangle, untie, untwine, untwist, work out; SEE CONCEPTS 127,135

disfavor [n] *dislike; disgrace*
aversion, disapprobation, disapproval, discredit, disesteem, dishonor, disinclination, displeasure, disregard, disrepute, disrespect, dissatisfaction, distaste, distrust, doghouse*, indisposition, mistrust, shame, thumbs down*, unpopularity; SEE CONCEPTS 29,388

disfigure [v] *make ugly*
blemish, damage, deface, defile, deform, disfashion, disfeature, distort, hurt, injure, maim, mangle, mar, mutilate, scar; SEE CONCEPTS 137,246,250

disgorge [v] *vomit*
be sick*, discharge, lose one's lunch*, regurgitate, retch, spew, throw up, upchuck*; SEE CONCEPTS 179,185,308

disgrace [n] *state of shame; bad reputation*
abasement, abuse, baseness, black eye*, blemish, blur, brand, comedown, contempt, contumely, corruption, culpability, debasement, debasing, defamation, degradation, derision, disbarment, discredit, disesteem, disfavor, dishonor, disrepute, disrespect, humbling, humiliation, ignominy, ill repute, infamy, ingloriousness, meanness, obloquy, odium, opprobrium, pollution, prostitution, put-down, reproach, scandal, scorn, slander, slight, slur, spot, stain, stigma, taint, tarnish, turpitude, venality; SEE CONCEPT 388

disgrace [v] *bring shame upon*
abase, attaint, besmirch, blot, debase, defame, defile, degrade, depress, deride, derogate, desecrate, discredit, disfavor, dishonor, disparage, disregard, disrespect, expel, give a black eye*, humble, humiliate, libel, 'lose face*, lower, mock, put down, reduce, reproach, ridicule, slander, slur, snub, stain, stigmatize, sully, taint, take down a peg*, tar and feather*, tarnish; SEE CONCEPTS 14,54,384

disgraceful [adj] *shameful, low*
blameworthy, contemptible, degrading, detestable, discreditable, dishonorable, disreputable, ignoble, ignominious, infamous, inglorious, mean, offensive, opprobrious, scandalous, shabby, shady, shocking, shoddy, unrespectable, unworthy; SEE CONCEPT 555

disgruntled [adj] *unhappy; critical*
annoyed, bad tempered, bellyaching*, crabbing*, crabby, cranky, disappointed, discontent, discontented, displeased, dissatisfied, griping, grouchy, grousing, grumpy, irritable, irritated, kicking, kvetching*, malcontent, malcontented, peeved, peevish, petulant, put out, sulky, sullen, testy, uncontent, ungratified, vexed; SEE CONCEPTS 401,403

disguise [n] *covering, makeup for deception*
beard, blind, camouflage, charade, cloak, color, coloring, concealment, costume, counterfeit, cover-up, dissimulation, dress, facade, face, faking, false front*, fig leaf*, front*, get-up, guise, illusion, make-believe, mask, masquerade, pageant, pen name, pretense, pretension, pretentiousness, pseudonym, put-on, red herring*, screen, semblance, smoke screen*, trickery, veil, veneer; SEE CONCEPTS 446,451,680

disguise [v] *mask; misrepresent*
affect, age, alter, antique, assume, beard, belie, camouflage, change, cloak, color, conceal, counterfeit, cover, cover up, deceive, dissemble, dissimulate, doctor up*, dress up, fake, falsify, feign, front, fudge*, garble, gloss over, hide, make like, make up, masquerade, muffle, obfuscate, obscure, pretend, put on a false front*, put on a front*, put on an act*, put up a front*, redo*, screen, secrete, sham, shroud, simulate, touch up, varnish, veil, wear cheaters*, whitewash*; SEE CONCEPTS 59,137,172,188,202

disguised [adj] *unrecognizable*
camouflaged, changed, cloaked, covered, covert, fake, false, feigned, hidden, incog, masked, pretend, undercover; SEE CONCEPTS 547,619

disgust [n] *aversion; repulsion*
abhorrence, abomination, antipathy, detestation, dislike, distaste, hatefulness, hatred, loathing, nausea, nauseation, nauseousness, objection, repugnance, revolt, revulsion, satiation, satiety, sickness, surfeit; SEE CONCEPTS 410,720

disgust [v] *cause aversion; repel*
abominate, be repulsive, bother, cloy on, disenchant, displease, disturb, fill with loathing, gross out*, insult, irk, make one sick*, nauseate, offend, offend morals of, outrage, pall, pique, put off, reluct, repulse, revolt, scandalize, shock, sicken, surfeit, turn off, turn one's stomach*, upset; SEE CONCEPTS 7,19

disgusted [adj] *sickened; offended*
abhorred, appalled, displeased, fastidious, fed up*, full up*, grossed out*, had bellyful*, had enough*, had it*, nauseated, nauseous, outraged, overwrought, queasy, repelled, repulsed, revolted, satiated, scandalized, sick, sick and tired of*, sick of*, squeamish, teed off*, tired, turned off*, unhappy, up to here*, weary; SEE CONCEPT 403

disgusting [adj] *sickening; repulsive*
abominable, awful, beastly, cloying, creepy, detestable, distasteful, foul, frightful, ghastly, grody*, gross*, gruesome, hateful, hideous, horrid, horrific, icky*, loathsome, lousy, macabre, monstrous, nasty, nauseating, nerdy*, noisome, objectionable, obnoxious, odious, offensive, outrageous, repellent, repugnant, revolting, rotten, satiating, scandalous, scuzzy*, shameless, shocking, sleazeball*, sleazy*, stinking, surfeiting,

vile, vulgar, yecchy*, yucky*; SEE CONCEPTS 485,548

dish [*n1*] *eating receptacle*
bowl, casserole, ceramic, china, container, cup, mug, pitcher, plate, platter, porringer, pot, pottery, salver, saucer, tray, vessel; SEE CONCEPT 494

dish [*n2*] *main part of meal*
course, eats*, entrée, fare, food, helping, recipe, serving; SEE CONCEPTS 457,460,461

dish [*n3*] *attractive woman*
angel, babe*, bathing beauty, beauty queen, broad*, bunny*, centerfold, chick*, cover girl, cupcake*, cutie, cutie-pie*, doll*, dollface, dreamboat*, dream girl, fox*, glamor girl, good-looking woman, honey*, hot dish*, hot number*, peach*, pin-up, raving beauty, sex bunny*, sex kitten*, sex pot*, tomato*; SEE CONCEPTS 415,424

disharmony [*n*] *conflict, discord*
clash, contention, difference, disaccord, dissension, dissonance, dissonancy, friction, inharmoniousness, strife, variance; SEE CONCEPTS 388,665

dishearten [*v*] *depress, ruin one's hopes*
cast down, chill*, crush, damp, dampen, dash, daunt, deject, demoralize, deter, discourage, disincline, dismay, disparage, dispirit, get down*, humble, humiliate, indispose, put a damper on*, put down, shake, throw a pall over*; SEE CONCEPTS 7,19

disheveled [*adj*] *wrinkled, unkempt in appearance*
bagged out*, beat up*, bedraggled, blowzy*, dirty, disarranged, disarrayed, disordered, frowzy*, grubby*, messed up*, messy, mussed up*, mussy, ruffled, rumpled, scuzzy, slipshod, sloppy, slovenly, tousled, unbuttoned, uncombed, unfastidious, untidy, unzipped*; SEE CONCEPTS 485,579

dishonest [*adj*] *lying, untruthful*
backbiting, bent, bluffing, cheating, corrupt, crafty, crooked, cunning, deceitful, deceiving, deceptive, designing, disreputable, double-crossing, double-dealing, elusive, false, fraudulent, guileful, hoodwinking*, mendacious, misleading, perfidious, recreant, shady, shifty, sinister, slippery*, sneaking, sneaky, swindling, traitorous, treacherous, tricky, two-faced*, two-timing*, unctuous, underhanded, unfair, unprincipled, unscrupulous, untrustworthy, villainous, wily; SEE CONCEPT 267

dishonesty [*n*] *lying; unwillingness to tell the truth*
artifice, bunk, cheating, chicane, chicanery, corruption, craft, criminality, crookedness, cunning, deceit, double-dealing, duplicity, faithlessness, falsehood, falsity, flimflam*, fourberie, fraud, fraudulence, graft, guile, hanky-panky*, hocus-pocus*, improbity, infamy, infidelity, insidiousness, mendacity, perfidiousness, perfidy, racket, rascality, sharp practice*, slyness, stealing, swindle, treachery, trickery, trickiness, unscrupulousness, wiliness; SEE CONCEPTS 59,633,657

dishonor [*n*] *state of shame*
abasement, abuse, affront, blame, degradation, discourtesy, discredit, disesteem, disfavor, disgrace, disrepute, ignominy, indignity, infamy, insult, obloquy, odium, offense, opprobrium,

outrage, reproach, scandal, slight; SEE CONCEPT 388

dishonor [*v*] *shame, degrade*
abase, attaint, blot, corrupt, debase, debauch, defame, defile, disconsider, discredit, disgrace, disoblige, give a black eye*, libel, make lose face*, reflect on, slander, sully; SEE CONCEPT 54

dishonorable [*adj*] *shameful, corrupt*
base, blackguardly, contemptible, crooked, deceitful, despicable, devious, discreditable, disgraceful, disreputable, fraudulent, ignoble, ignominious, infamous, inglorious, low, miscreant, offensive, opprobrious, putrid, scandalous, shabby, shady, treacherous, unprincipled, unrespectable, unscrupulous, untrustworthy; SEE CONCEPT 555

dish out [*v*] *distribute*
allocate, deliver, dispense, dole out*, fork over*, furnish, give out, hand, hand out, hand over, inflict, ladle, mete out, present, produce, scoop, serve, serve up, spoon, supply, transfer, turn over; SEE CONCEPT 140

disillusioned [*adj*] *disappointed*
blasé, broken, brought down to earth*, debunked, disabused, disenchanted, disenthralled, disentranced, embittered, enlightened, freed, indifferent, knowing, let-down, mondaine, out of love*, punctured, sadder and wiser*, shattered, sophisticated, undeceived, worldly, worldly-wise*; SEE CONCEPT 403

disinclination [*n*] *unwillingness to do or believe something*
alienation, antipathy, aversion, demur, disfavor, dislike, disliking, displeasure, disrelish, dissatisfaction, distaste, hatred, hesitance, indisposition, lack of desire, lack of enthusiasm, loathness, objection, opposition, reluctance, repugnance, resistance; SEE CONCEPTS 29,410,657

disinclined [*adj*] *unwilling*
afraid, antipathetic, averse, backward, balking, doubtful, dubious, hesitating, indisposed, loath, not in the mood*, objecting, opposed, protesting, reluctant, resistant, shy, shying, slow, sticking, uneager, unsympathetic; SEE CONCEPTS 403,542

disinfect [*v*] *make clean, pure*
antisepticize, cleanse, decontaminate, deodorize, fumigate, purify, sanitize, sterilize; SEE CONCEPT 165

disingenuous [*adj*] *insincere*
artful, crooked, cunning, deceitful, designing, dishonest, duplicitous, false, feigned, foxy, guileful, indirect, insidious, mendacious, oblique, shifty*, sly, tricky, two-faced*, uncandid, underhanded, unfair, unfrank, wily; SEE CONCEPTS 401,542

disinherit [*v*] *cut off in will of bequeathal*
bereave, cut off without a cent*, deprive, disaffiliate, disown, dispossess, divest, evict, exclude, exheridate, neglect, oust, repudiate, rob; SEE CONCEPTS 25,317

disintegrate [*v*] *fall apart; reduce to pieces*
atomize, break apart, break down, break up, come apart, crumble, decay, decline, decompose, degenerate, deliquesce, descend, detach, dilapidate, disband, disconnect, disimprove, dismantle, disorganize, disperse, disunite, divide, fade away, fall to pieces*, molder, pulverize, putrefy, rot, separate, sever, shatter, sink, splinter, spoil, taint, take apart, turn, turn to dust*, wash away, wash out, wither, worsen; SEE CONCEPTS 252,469

di
di

disinterested [adj] *detached, uninvolved*
aloof, candid, casual, dispassionate, equitable, even-handed, impartial, impersonal, incurious, indifferent, just watching the clock*, lackadaisical, negative, neutral, nonpartisan, not giving a damn*, outside, perfunctory, remote, unbiased, unconcerned, uncurious, unprejudiced, unselfish, withdrawn; SEE CONCEPTS 401,403

disjointed [adj] *loose, disconnected*
aimless, confused, cool, discontinuous, disordered, displaced, disunited, divided, far-out, fitful, fuzzy, inchoate, incoherent, incohesive, irrational, jumbled, muddled, out-of-it*, out-to-lunch*, rambling, separated, spaced-out*, spacey*, spasmodic, split, unattached, unconnected, unorganized; SEE CONCEPTS 267,482,585

disk [n] *round object*
circle, disc, discoid, discoidal, discus, dish, flan, plate, platter, quoit, sabot, saucer, shell; SEE CONCEPT 436

dislike [n] *antagonism, hatred toward something*
animosity, animus, antipathy, aversion, deprecation, detestation, disapprobation, disapproval, disesteem, disfavor, disgust, disinclination, displeasure, dissatisfaction, distaste, enmity, hostility, indisposition, loathing, objection, offense, opposition, prejudice, repugnance; SEE CONCEPT 29

dislike [v] *be antagonistic toward something; hate*
abhor, abominate, antipathize, avoid, be allergic to*, bear malice toward, be averse to, be turned off to*, condemn, contemn, deplore, despise, detest, disapprove, disesteem, disfavor, disrelish, eschew, execrate, grossed out on*, have hard feelings*, have no stomach for*, have no taste for, loathe, look down on, lose interest in, make faces at*, mind, not appreciate, not care for, not endure, not feel like, not take kindly to, object to, regret, resent, scorn, shudder at, shun; SEE CONCEPT 29

dislocate [v] *displace*
break, disarticulate, disconnect, disengage, disjoint, disorder, disrupt, disturb, disunite, divide, jumble, misplace, mix up, move, put out of joint, remove, rummage, separate, shift, transfer, unhinge, upset; SEE CONCEPTS 135,147,213

dislocation [n] *displacement*
break, confusion, disarray, disarticulation, disconnection, discontinuity, disengagement, disorder, disorganization, disruption, disturbance, division, luxation, misplacement, unhinging; SEE CONCEPTS 316,720,727

dislodge [v] *knock loose*
dig out, disentangle, dislocate, displace, disturb, eject, evict, extricate, force out, oust, remove, uproot; SEE CONCEPTS 147,213

disloyal [adj] *unfaithful*
alienated, apostate, cheating, disaffected, double-crossing, estranged, faithless, false, perfidious, recreant, seditious, snaky*, subversive, traitorous, treacherous, treasonable, two-faced*, two-timing*, unloyal, unpatriotic, untrue, untrustworthy, wormlike*; SEE CONCEPT 401

disloyalty [n] *unfaithfulness*
apostasy, bad faith, betrayal of trust, breach of trust, breaking of faith, deceitfulness, disaffection, double-dealing, faithlessness, falseness, falsity, inconstancy, infidelity, perfidiousness,

perfidy, recreancy, sedition, seditiousness, subversive activity, treachery, treason, untrueness, violation; SEE CONCEPT 633

dismal [adj] *bleak, dreary, gloomy*
afflictive, black, boring, cheerless, cloudy, dark, depressed, depressing, desolate, despondent, dim, dingy, disagreeable, discouraging, disheartening, dispiriting, doleful, dolorous, dull, forlorn, frowning, funereal, ghastly, gruesome, hopeless, horrible, horrid, inauspicious, in the pits*, joyless, lonesome, lowering, lugubrious, melancholy, miserable, monotonous, morbid, murky, oppressive, overcast, sad, shadowy, somber, sorrowful, tedious, tenebrous, troublesome, unfortunate, unhappy; SEE CONCEPTS 525,536,548

dismantle [v] *take apart*
annihilate, bankrupt, bare, break down, break up, decimate, demolish, denudate, denude, deprive, destroy, disassemble, dismember, dismount, disrobe, divest, fell, knock down, level, part out, pull down, raze, ruin, strike, strip, subvert, take down, take to pieces, tear down, undo, unrig, wrack, wreck; SEE CONCEPTS 135,168,252

dismay [n] *disappointed feeling; distress*
agitation, alarm, anxiety, apprehension, blue funk*, blues*, bummer*, chagrin, cold feet*, consternation, discouragement, disheartenment, disillusionment, downer*, dread, dumps*, fear, fright, funk*, hassle, horror, letdown, panic, terror, the blahs*, trepidation, upset; SEE CONCEPTS 27,410,690

dismay [v] *disappoint, fill with consternation*
abash, affright, agitate, alarm, appall, bewilder, bother, chill, confound, daunt, discomfit, discompose, disconcert, discourage, dishearten, disillusion, dispirit, disquiet, distress, disturb, dumbfound, embarrass, faze, flummox*, fluster, foul up*, frighten, get to, horrify, louse up*, mess up*, muck up*, mystify, nonplus, paralyze, perplex, put off, puzzle, rattle, scare, screw up*, shake, snafu*, take aback, terrify, terrorize, throw, throw into a tizzy*, unhinge*, unnerve, upset; SEE CONCEPTS 7,19

dismember [v] *cut into pieces*
amputate, anatomize, cripple, disassemble, disjoint, dislimb, dislocate, dismantle, dismount, dissect, divide, maim, mutilate, part, rend, sever, sunder, take down; SEE CONCEPTS 98,135,176

dismiss [v1] *send away, remove; free*
abolish, banish, boot*, brush off*, bundle, cast off*, cast out*, chase, chuck, clear, decline, deport, detach, disband, discard, dispatch, dispense with, disperse, dispose of, dissolve, divorce, do without, drive out, eject, expel, force out, have done with*, kick out*, let go, let out, lock out*, outlaw, push aside, push back, reject, release, relegate, relinquish, repel, repudiate, rid, send off, send packing*, shed, show out*, slough off, supersede, sweep away*, turn out; SEE CONCEPTS 127,217

dismiss [v2] *remove from job, responsibility*
ax*, boot*, boot out*, bounce*, bump*, can*, cashier*, defrock, depone, depose, deselect, discharge, disemploy, disfrock, displace, disqualify, drop, fire, furlough, give notice to, give the ax*, give the gate*, give the heave-ho*, give walking papers*, give warning, impeach, kick out*, lay off, let go*, let out*, oust, pension, pink-slip*, put away*, recall, retire, sack*, send packing*,

shelve*, shut out*, suspend, terminate, turn away, unfrock, unseat, wash out*; SEE CONCEPTS 324,351

dismiss [v3] *put out of one's mind*
banish, contemn, deride, despise, discard, disdain, dispel, disregard, drop, flout, gibe, gird, jeer, kiss off*, laugh away*, lay aside, mock, pooh-pooh*, rally, reject, relegate, repudiate, repulse, ridicule, scoff, scorn, scout, set aside, shelve*, spurn, taunt, twit; SEE CONCEPT 35

dismissal [n] *release*
adjournment, banishment, bounce, brush-off, cold shoulder*, congé, deportation, deposal, deposition, discharge, dislodgment, displacement, dispossession, dissolution, door*, end, eviction, exile, exorcism, expatriation, expulsion, freedom, freeing, housecleaning*, kiss-off*, layoff, liberation, marching orders*, notice, old heave-ho*, ostracism, ouster, permission, pink slip*, relegation, removal, suspension; SEE CONCEPTS 127,217,351

dismount [v] *get off something higher*
alight, debark, deplane, descend, detrain, disembark, get down, light; SEE CONCEPT 195

disobedience [n] *misbehavior; noncompliance with rules*
defiance, dereliction, disregard, indiscipline, infraction, infringement, insubmission, insubordination, insurgence, intractableness, mutiny, neglect, nonobservance, perversity, rebellion, recalcitrance, refractoriness, revolt, revolution, riot, sabotage, sedition, strike, stubbornness, transgression, unruliness, violation, waywardness; SEE CONCEPT 633

disobedient [adj] *defiant, mischievous*
contrary, contumacious, disorderly, fractious, froward, headstrong, insubordinate, intractable, naughty, noncompliant, nonobservant, obstreperous, perverse, recalcitrant, refractory, resistive, uncompliant, undisciplined, unruly, wayward, willful; SEE CONCEPT 401

disobey [v] *disregard rules; refuse to conform*
balk, be remiss, break rules, contravene, counteract, dare, decline, defy, desert, differ, disagree, evade, flout, fly in face of*, go counter to, ignore, infringe, insurrect, misbehave, mutiny, neglect, not heed, not listen, not mind, object, overstep, pay no attention to, rebel, recalcitrate, resist, revolt, revolution, revolutionize, riot, rise in arms*, run riot*, set aside, shirk, strike, take law into own hands*, transgress, violate, withstand; SEE CONCEPTS 30,192,384

disoblige [v] *displease, annoy*
affront, bother, discommode, disturb, incommode, inconvenience, insult, offend, put about, put out, slight, trouble, upset, vex; SEE CONCEPTS 7,19

disobliging [adj] *rude, annoying*
awkward, disagreeable, discourteous, ill-disposed, ill-natured, unaccommodating, unamiable, uncivil, uncongenial, uncooperative, unhelpful, unpleasant; SEE CONCEPT 401

disorder [n1] *chaos, clutter*
anarchy, ataxia, confusion, derangement, disarrangement, disarray, discombobulation, disorderliness, disorganization, huddle, irregularity, jumble, mess, muddle, rat's nest*, shambles, snarl, topsyturviness*, untidiness; SEE CONCEPT 230

disorder [n2] *social commotion; mental confusion*
agitation, anarchism, anarchy, brawl, bustle, chaos, clamor, complication, convulsion, discombobulation*, discord, disorganization, distemper, disturbance, dither, entanglement, fight, flap, fracas, fuss, hubbub, hullabaloo*, imbroglio, insurrection, lawlessness, mayhem, misrule, mob rule*, quarrel, rebellion, reign of terror*, revolution, riot, rioting, ruckus, rumpus, static, strike, terrorism, tizzy*, trouble, tumult, turbulence, turmoil, unrest, unruliness, uproar; SEE CONCEPTS 388,410

disorder [n3] *illness*
affliction, ailment, cachexia, complaint, disease, diseasedness, indisposition, infirmity, malady, sickness, unhealth, upset; SEE CONCEPT 306

disorder [v] *mix up, disarrange*
clutter, confound, confuse, derange, discompose, discreate, dishevel, disjoint, dislocate, disorganize, disrupt, distemper, disturb, embroil, jumble, mess up, muddle, muss up*, rummage, rumple, scatter, shuffle, tumble, unsettle, upset; SEE CONCEPTS 240,250

disordered [adj] *in a mess*
all over the place*, confused, deranged, disarranged, discombobulated, disconnected, discontinuous, disjointed, dislocated, disorganized, displaced, incoherent, in confusion, jumbled, mislaid, misplaced, molested, moved, muddled, out-of-place, removed, roiled, ruffled, rumpled, shifted, shuffled, stirred up*, tampered-with, tangled, tossed, tousled, tumbled, unsettled, untidy; SEE CONCEPTS 485,535

disorderly [adj] *messy, untidy*
all over the place*, chaotic, cluttered, confused, dislocated, disorganized, heterogeneous, indiscriminate, irregular, jumbled, mixed up, out-of-control*, out-of-line*, out-of-step*, out-of-whack*, scattered, scrambled, slovenly, topsy-turvy*, tumult, uncombed, undisciplined, unkempt, unmethodical, unrestrained, unsystematic, untrained; SEE CONCEPTS 485,535

disorderly [adj2] *causing trouble; unlawful*
boisterous, disobedient, disruptive, drunk, fractious, indisciplined, intemperate, noisy, obstreperous, off-base*, on-a-tear*, out-of-line*, out-of-order*, raucous, rebellious, refractory, riotous, rowdy, stormy, termagant, tumultuous/tumultous, turbulent, uncompliant, uncontrollable, ungovernable, unmanageable, unruly, wayward; SEE CONCEPTS 401,545

disorganization [n] *unordered situation or thing*
anarchy, chaos, confusion, derangement, disarray, disjointedness, disorder, disruption, dissolution, disunion, foul-up*, incoherence, mix-up, rat's nest*, screw-up*, unconnectedness, unholy mess*; SEE CONCEPTS 674,727

disorganize [v] *disrupt arrangement; make shambles of*
break down, break up, clutter, complicate, confound, confuse, demobilize, derange, destroy, disarrange, disarray, disband, discompose, discreate, dishevel, dislocate, disorder, disperse, disturb, embroil, jumble, litter, mess up, mislay, misplace, muddle, perturb, put out of order, scatter, scramble, shuffle, toss, turn topsy-turvy, unsettle, upset; SEE CONCEPTS 250,252,384

disorganized [adj] *unmethodical; messed up*
chaotic, confused, disordered, disorderly, hap-

hazard, jumbled, mixed up, muddled, screwed up*, shuffled, unsystematic; SEE CONCEPTS *485,585*

disoriented [*adj*] *confused, unstable*
adrift, all at sea*, astray, bewildered, discombobulated, lost, mixed-up, not adjusted, off-beam*, off-course, out-of-joint*, perplexed, unbalanced, unhinged, unsettled; SEE CONCEPT *403*

disown [*v*] *refuse to acknowledge*
abandon, abjure, abnegate, cast off, deny, disacknowledge, disallow, disavow, discard, disclaim, divorce oneself from, refuse to recognize, reject, renounce, repudiate, retract; SEE CONCEPTS *50,54,88*

disparage [*v*] *criticize; detract from*
abuse, belittle, chill*, cry down, decry, defame, degrade, deject, demoralize, denigrate, deprecate, depreciate, deride, derogate, dis*, discourage, discredit, disdain, dishearten, dismiss, dispirit, dispraise, downcry, dump on*, lower, malign, minimize, pan*, put down, put hooks in*, rap*, ridicule, roast*, run down*, scorch, scorn, slam*, slander, smear*, sour grapes*, tear down, traduce, underestimate, underrate, undervalue, vilify, write off; SEE CONCEPTS *7,19,52,54*

disparagement [*n*] *strong criticism; detraction*
aspersion, backbiting*, backstabbing*, belittlement, blame, calumny, censure, condemnation, contempt, contumely, debasement, degradation, denunciation, depreciation, derision, derogation, discredit, disdain, impairment, lessening, lie, prejudice, reproach, ridicule, scandal, scorn, slander, tale, underestimation; SEE CONCEPTS *52,54*

disparate [*adj*] *at odds, different*
at . variance, contrary, contrasting, discordant, discrepant, dissimilar, distant, distinct, divergent, diverse, far cry, incommensurate, incompatible, inconsistent, inconsonant, like night and day*, poles apart, separate, unalike, unequal, unequivalent, uneven, unlike, unsimilar, various; SEE CONCEPT *564*

disparity [*n*] *difference*
alterity, discrepancy, disproportion, dissemblance, dissimilarity, dissimilitude, distinction, divergence, divergency, diverseness, gap, imbalance, imparity, incongruity, inequality, otherness, unevenness, unlikeness, variation; SEE CONCEPT *665*

dispassionate [*adj*] *unfeeling, impartial*
abstract, aloof, calm, candid, cold-blooded, coldfish*, collected, composed, cool, cool cat*, couldn't care less*, detached, disinterested, fair, iceberg*, impersonal, imperturbable, indifferent, judicial, just, laid back, moderate, neutral, nondiscriminatory, nonpartisan, objective, poker-faced*, quiet, serene, sober, temperate, tough, unbiased, unemotional, unexcitable, unexcited, unflappable, uninvolved, unmoved, unprejudiced, unruffled; SEE CONCEPTS *401,404*

dispatch [*n1*] *speed in carrying out action*
alacrity, celerity, expedition, expeditiousness, haste, hurry, hustle, precipitateness, promptitude, promptness, quickness, rapidity, rustle, speediness, swiftness; SEE CONCEPTS *755,818*

dispatch [*n2*] *communication*
account, bulletin, communiqué, document, instruction, item, letter, message, missive, news, piece, report, story; SEE CONCEPTS *271,277,278*

dispatch [*v1*] *hurry, send fast*
accelerate, address, consign, dismiss, express, forward, hand-carry, hasten, issue, quicken, railroad*, remit, route, run with, run with ball*, ship, speed, transmit, walk through; SEE CONCEPTS *152,217*

dispatch [*v2*] *finish; consume*
conclude, devour, discharge, dispose of, eat up, expedite, lay low, perform, polish off*, scarf down*, settle; SEE CONCEPTS *169,234*

dispatch [*v3*] *kill*
assassinate, bump off*, butcher*, destroy, eliminate, execute, finish, finish off*, murder, put away*, put end to, slaughter, slay, take out*; SEE CONCEPTS *238,252*

dispel [*v*] *drive away thought, belief*
allay, banish, beat off*, break it up*, break up*, bust up*, cancel, chase away, crumble, deploy, disband, disintegrate, dismiss, disperse, dissipate, distribute, eject, eliminate, expel, oust, repel, resolve, rout, scatter, scramble, split up*; SEE CONCEPTS *14,35*

dispensable [*adj*] *not necessary; able to be thrown away*
disposable, excessive, expendable, minor, needless, nonessential, removable, superfluous, trivial, unimportant, unnecessary, unrequired, useless; SEE CONCEPT *546*

dispensation [*n1*] *allocation of supply*
allotment, appointment, apportionment, award, bestowal, conferment, consignment, courtesy, dealing out, disbursement, distribution, dole, endowment, favor, indulgence, kindness, part, portion, quota, service, share; SEE CONCEPTS *140,337*

dispensation [*n2*] *management*
administration, direction, economy, plan, regulation, scheme, stewardship, system; SEE CONCEPTS *325,660,770*

dispensation [*n3*] *permission*
exception, exemption, immunity, indulgence, license, privilege, relaxation, relief, remission, reprieve; SEE CONCEPT *685*

dispense [*v1*] *dole out supply*
allocate, allot, apportion, assign, come across with, deal, deal out, disburse, dish out*, distribute, divide, divvy*, fork out*, furnish, give, give away, give with, hand out, hand over, lot, measure, mete out, partition, portion, prepare, prorate, share, shell out*; SEE CONCEPT *140*

dispense [*v2*] *operate, administer*
apply, carry out, command, direct, discharge, enforce, execute, handle, implement, manage, maneuver, manipulate, swing, undertake, wield; SEE CONCEPT *117*

dispense [*v3*] *exempt from responsibility*
absolve, discharge, except, excuse, exonerate, let off, privilege from, release, relieve, reprieve, spare; SEE CONCEPT *110*

dispense with [*v*] *omit; do away with*
abolish, abstain from, brush aside, cancel, dispose of, disregard, do without, forgo, get rid of, give up, ignore, pass over, relinquish, render needless, shake off, waive; SEE CONCEPT *30*

disperse [*v*] *distribute; scatter*
banish, besprinkle, break up, broadcast, cast forth, circulate, deal, diffuse, disappear, disband, disburse, discharge, dislodge, dismiss, dispel, disseminate, dissipate, dissolve, divvy*, drive out, eject, intersperse, measure out, partition,

propagate, radiate, rout, scatter, scramble, send off, separate, shed, sow, split up, spray, spread, strew, take off in all directions*, vanish; SEE CONCEPTS *135,217*

dispirited [*adj*] *dejected, sad*
blue*, bummed-out*, crestfallen, depressed, despondent, disconsolate, discouraged, disheartened, down*, downbeat, downcast, downhearted, dragged*, funky*, gloomy, glum, in the doldrums, low, melancholy, morose, shot-down*, spiritless, woebegone; SEE CONCEPT *403*

displace [*v1*] *move, remove from normal place*
change, crowd out, derange, disarrange, disestablish, dislocate, dislodge, displant, dispossess, disturb, eject, evict, expel, expulse, force out, lose, mislay, misplace, relegate, shift, transpose, unsettle, uproot; SEE CONCEPTS *147,213*

displace [*v2*] *remove from position of responsibility*
banish, can*, cashier*, cut out*, deport, depose, dethrone, discard, discharge, discrown, disenthrone, dismiss, disthrone, exile, expatriate, fire, oust, relegate, remove, replace, sack*, step into shoes of*, succeed, supersede, supplant, take over, take the place of, transport, uncrown, unseat, usurp; SEE CONCEPTS *133,298,300*

display [*n*] *public showing; spectacle*
act, affectation, arrangement, array, arrayal, blaze, bravura, dash, demonstration, example, exhibit, exhibition, expo*, exposition, exposure, fanfare, flourish, for show, frame-up*, frippery, front, grandstand play*, layout, manifestation, ostentation, ostentatiousness, pageant, panorama, parade, pedantry, pomp, presentation, pretension, pretentiousness, revelation, sample, scheme, shine, showboat*, splash, splendor, splurge, spread, unfolding, vanity; SEE CONCEPTS *261,386*

display [*v*] *show for public viewing, effect*
advertise, arrange, bare, betray, boast, brandish, bring to view, demonstrate, disclose, emblazon, evidence, evince, exhibit, expand, expose, express, feature, flash, flaunt, flourish, glaze, grandstand*, illustrate, impart, lay bare*, lay out, make clear, make known, manifest, model, open, open out, parade, perform, present, promote, promulgate, publish, represent, reveal, set out, showcase, show off, sport, spread out, stretch out, trot out*, uncover, unfold, unfurl, unmask, unroll, unveil, vamp; SEE CONCEPT *261*

displease [*v*] *make unhappy*
aggravate, anger, annoy, antagonize, bother, cap, chagrin, cool, curdle*, cut to the quick*, disappoint, discontent, disgruntle, disgust, disoblige, dissatisfy, enrage, exasperate, fret, frustrate, gall, hurt, incense, irk, irritate, nettle, offend, perplex, pique, play dirty, provoke, put out, repel, revolt, rile, roil, sound, turn off*, upset, vex, -wing*, worry, zing*; SEE CONCEPTS *7,19*

displeasure [*n*] *unhappiness, anger*
annoyance, aversion, disapprobation, disapproval, discontentment, disfavor, disgruntlement, disinclination, dislike, disliking, disrelish, dissatisfaction, distaste, incensement, indignation, indisposition, irritation, offense, pique, resentment, umbrage, vexation, wrath; SEE CONCEPT *410*

disposal [*n1*] *parting with or throwing something away*
auctioning, bartering, chucking, clearance, conveyance, demolishing, demolition, destroying, destruction, discarding, dispatching, dispensa-

tion, disposition, dumping, ejection, jettison, jettisoning, junking, relegation, relinquishment, removal, riddance, sacrifice, sale, scrapping, selling, trading, transfer, transference, vending; SEE CONCEPT *180*

disposal [*n2*] *conclusion, settlement of situation*
action, allocation, arrangement, array, assignment, assortment, bequest, bestowal, consignment, control, conveyance, determination, dispensation, disposition, distribution, division, effectuation, end, gift, grouping, order, ordering, placing, position, provision, sequence, transfer, winding up; SEE CONCEPTS *119,230*

dispose [*v*] *place, order; deal with*
actuate, adapt, adjust, arrange, array, bend, bias, call the tune*, condition, determine, distribute, fix, govern, group, incline, induce, influence, lay down the law*, lead, locate, make willing, marshal, methodize, motivate, move, organize, predispose, prepare, promote, prompt, put, put one's foot down*, put to rights, range, rank, read the riot act*, regulate, ride herd on*, set, set in order, settle, shepherd, stand, sway, systematize, tailor, tempt; SEE CONCEPTS *84,117,158,180*

disposed [*adj*] *inclined to a type of behavior*
apt, at drop of hat*, biased, fain, game*, game for, given, liable, likely, minded, of a mind to*, partial, predisposed, prone, ready, subject, tending toward, willing; SEE CONCEPTS *542,552*

dispose of [*v1*] *throw away*
adios*, bestow, chuck*, deep six*, destroy, discard, dump, eighty-six*, eliminate, file in circular file*, get rid of, give, jettison, junk*, kiss*, kiss off*, make over, part with, relinquish, scrap, sell, transfer, unload; SEE CONCEPT *180*

dispose of [*v2*] *settle a matter*
chop, cut, cut off, deal with, decide, determine, do the trick*, end, finish, knock off*, polish off*, put away, take care of; SEE CONCEPTS *18,234*

disposition [*n1*] *personal temperament*
bag*, being, bent, bias, cast, character, complexion, constitution, cup of tea*, druthers*, emotions, flash, frame of mind, groove*, habit, humor, identity, inclination, individualism, individuality, leaning, make-up, mind-set*, mood, nature, penchant, personality, predilection, predisposition, proclivity, proneness, propensity, readiness, spirit, stamp, temper, tendency, tenor, thing*, tone, type, vein; SEE CONCEPT *411*

disposition [*n2*] *arrangement, management of a situation*
adjustment, classification, control, decision, direction, disposal, distribution, grouping, method, order, ordering, organization, placement, plan, regulation, sequence; SEE CONCEPTS *6,660*

dispossess [*v*] *deprive*
appropriate, eject, evict, expel, expropriate, oust, put out, throw into the street*; SEE CONCEPTS *121,142*

disproportion [*n*] *imbalance*
asymmetry, difference, discrepancy, disparity, imparity, inadequacy, inequality, insufficiency, irregularity, lopsidedness, unevenness, unsuitableness; SEE CONCEPTS *665,667*

disproportionate [*adj*] *out of balance*
asymmetric, excessive, incommensurate, inordinate, irregular, lopsided, nonsymmetrical, out of proportion, overbalanced, superfluous, too much, unequal, uneven, unreasonable, unsymmetrical; SEE CONCEPTS *564,566,771*

disprove [v] *prove false*
belie, blow sky high*, blow up*, break, confound, confute, contradict, contravene, controvert, deny, disconfirm, discredit, explode, expose, find unfounded, impugn, invalidate, knock bottom out of*, knock props out*, negate, negative, overthrow, overturn, poke holes in*, puncture, rebut, refute, set aside, shoot, shoot holes in*, tear down*, throw out, traverse, weaken; SEE CONCEPT 58

disputable [adj] *debatable; open to discussion*
arguable, controversial, doubtful, dubious, moot, mootable, problematic, questionable, uncertain; SEE CONCEPTS 529,535

disputation [n] *controversy*
argumentation, debate, dialectic, dispute, dissension, forensic, mooting, polemics; SEE CONCEPTS 278,532

disputatious [adj] *argumentative*
cantankerous, captious, caviling, contentious, controversial, dissentious, litigious, polemical, pugnacious, quarrelsome; SEE CONCEPTS 401,542

dispute [n] *argument*
altercation, beef*, bickering, bone of contention*, brawl, brouhaha, commotion, conflict, contention, controversy, debate, difference of opinion, disagreement, discord, discussion, dissension, disturbance, embroilment, falling-out, feud, fireworks*, flare-up, fracas, friction, fuss, hubbub, miff*, misunderstanding, polemic, quarrel, row, rumpus*, squabble, squall, strife, tiff, uproar, variance, words, wrangle; SEE CONCEPTS 46,106,278

dispute [v] *argue*
agitate, altercate, bicker, brawl, bump heads*, canvass, challenge, clash, confute, contend, contest, contradict, controvert, debate, deny, disaffirm, discept, discuss, disprove, doubt, gainsay, hassle, have at*, impugn, jump on one's case*, kick around*, lock horns*, moot, negate, pick a bone*, quarrel, question, quibble, rebut, refute, squabble, take on, thrash out, toss around*, wrangle; SEE CONCEPT 46

disqualification [n] *disability; rejection for participation*
awkwardness, clumsiness, debarment, disenablement, disentitlement, elimination, exclusion, incapacitation, incapacity, incompetence, incompetency, ineligibility, ineptitude, lack, unfitness, unproficiency; SEE CONCEPT 630

disqualify [v] *be unfit for; be ineligible*
bar, bate, debar, disable, disenable, disentitle, disfranchise, eighty-six*, except, exclude, impair, incapacitate, invalidate, nix*, not make the cut*, paralyze, preclude, prohibit, rule out, suspend, unfit, weaken; SEE CONCEPTS 121,699

disquiet [n] *worry; mental upset*
ailment, alarm, angst, anxiety, care, concern, concernment, disquietude, distress, disturbance, fear, ferment, foreboding, fretfulness, inquietude, nervousness, restiveness, restlessness, solicitude, storm, trouble, turmoil, uneasiness, unrest; SEE CONCEPTS 410,532,690

disquiet [v] *worry; make uneasy*
agitate, annoy, bother, concern, discompose, distress, disturb, fluster, fret, harass, incommode, perplex, perturb, pester, plague, trouble, unhinge, unsettle, upset, vex; SEE CONCEPTS 7,19

disquieting [adj] *upsetting*
annoying, bothersome, disconcerting, distress-

ing, disturbing, irritating, perplexing, perturbing, troublesome, troubling, unnerving, unsettling, vexing, worrying; SEE CONCEPT 529

disregard [n] *ignoring*
apathy, brush-off*, contempt, disdain, disesteem, disfavor, disinterest, disrespect, forgetting, heedlessness, inadvertence, inattention, indifference, insouciance, lassitude, lethargy, listlessness, neglect, neglecting, negligence, oblivion, omission, omitting, overlooking, oversight, scorn, slight, slighting, the cold shoulder*, unconcern, unmindfulness; SEE CONCEPTS 30,633

disregard [v] *ignore; make light of*
blink at*, brush aside, brush away, brush off*, cold-shoulder*, contemn, despise, discount, disdain, disobey, disparage, fail, forget, have no use for*, laugh off*, leave out of account, let go, let off easy*, let pass*, live with*, look the other way*, miss, neglect, omit, overlook, overpass, pass over, pay no attention to, pay no heed to, pay no mind*, pooh-pooh*, scorn, shut eyes to*, slight, snub, take no notice of, tune out*, turn a blind eye*, turn a deaf ear*, vilipend, wink at*; SEE CONCEPT 30

disrepair [adj] *broken; deteriorated*
busted*, damaged, dead, decayed, decrepit, down, kaput*, not functioning, on the blink*, on the fritz*, out of commission*, out of order, worn out, wracked*; SEE CONCEPT 485

disrepair [n] *state of deterioration*
collapse, decay, decrepitude, dilapidation, ruination; SEE CONCEPTS 230,674

disreputable [adj] *dishonorable, lowly*
abject, bad, base, beggarly, cheap, contemptible, derogatory, despicable, discreditable, disgraceful, disorderly, dissolute, ignominious, in bad, infamous, inglorious, in low esteem, in the doghouse*, lewd, libidinous, licentious, mean, no good*, notorious, opprobrious, pitiable, scandalous, scurvy, shabby, shady, shameful, shocking, shoddy, sordid, sorry, unprincipled, vicious, vile; SEE CONCEPT 404

disrepute [n] *dishonor, shame*
blemish, blot, brand, cloud, discredit, disesteem, disfavor, disgrace, ignominy, ill fame, ill favor, ill repute, infamy, ingloriousness, notoriety, obloquy, odium, opprobrium, reproach, scandal, scar, slur, smear, spot, stain, stigma, taint, unpopularity; SEE CONCEPT 411

disrespect [n] *disregard, rudeness toward someone*
boldness, coarseness, contempt, discourtesy, dishonor, flippancy, hardihood, impertinence, impiety, impoliteness, impudence, incivility, insolence, insolency, insolentness, irreverence, lack of respect, sacrilege, unmannerliness; SEE CONCEPTS 29,633

disrespectful [adj] *insulting, rude*
aweless, bad-mannered, blasphemous, bold, cheeky*, contemptuous, discourteous, disgracious, flip*, flippant, fresh, ill-bred, ill-mannered, impertinent, impious, impolite, impudent, insolent, irreverent, misbehaved, nervy*, out-of-line*, profanatory, profane, sacrilegious, sassy*, saucy*, smart-alecky*, snippy*, uncivil, unfilial, ungracious; SEE CONCEPTS 267,401

disrobe [v] *take off one's clothes*
bare, denudate, denude, deprive, dismantle, divest, doff, husk*, peel*, remove, shed, shuck*,

...ip out of, strip, take it off, unbutton*, unclothe, ncover, undress; SEE CONCEPT 167

srupt [v1] *upset, disorganize*
gitate, bollix, confuse, disarray, discombobu-ate, discompose, disorder, disturb, mess up, mix p, muck up*, muddle, muddy the waters*, sych out*, put off, rattle, rattle one's cage*, ummage, screw up*, shake, spoil, throw, un-ettle, upset the apple cart*; SEE CONCEPTS *6,84,234*

srupt [v2] *break, interrupt*
reach, break into, break up, fracture, hole, inter-ere with, intrude, obstruct, open, rupture, unset-le, upset; SEE CONCEPTS *98,135*

sruptive [adj] *causing trouble, confusion*
lisorderly, distracting, disturbing, obstreperous, ff-base*, out-of-line*, out-of-order*, rowdy, roublemaking, troublesome, unruly, unsettling, psetting; SEE CONCEPTS *401,537*

ssatisfaction [n] *discontent, unhappiness*
nnoyance, anxiety, aversion, boredom, chagrin, omplaint, desolation, disapproval, discomfort, liscouragement, disfavor, disgruntlement, disin-lination, dislike, disliking, dismay, displeasure, lisquiet, disrelish, distaste, distress, ennui, envy, xasperation, fretfulness, frustration, heartburn, opelessness, indisposition, irritation, jealousy, amentation, malcontent, malcontentedness, op-ression, querulousness, regret, resentment, trou-le, uneasiness, weariness, worry; SEE CONCEPTS *9,410*

ssatisfactory [adj] *unsatisfactory*
ad, damaged, deficient, disappointing, displeas-ng, distressing, inadequate, insufficient, junky*, ame, mediocre, no good, not satisfying, not up o par*, offensive, poor, rotten, unacceptable, un-atisfying, unsuitable, unworthy, useless; SEE ONCEPTS *529,558,570*

ssatisfied [adj] *discontented, unhappy*
nnoyed, begrudging, bothered, complaining, crabby*, critical, disaffected, disappointed, dis-gruntled, displeased, ennuied, envious, faultfind-ng, fed-up*, fretful, frustrated, griping, grudging, grumbling, grumpy*, insatiable, irked, aundiced, jealous, kvetching*, malcontent, mal-contented, not satisfied, offended, picky, plain-ive, put-out*, querulous, sniveling, sulky, sullen, unappeased, unassuaged, unfulfilled, un-gratified, unsated, unsatisfied, vexed; SEE CON-:EPT *403*

ssect [v1] *cut up; take apart*
anatomize, break up, cut, dichotomize, disjoin, disjoint, dislimb, dismember, dissever, divide, exscind, exsect, lay open, operate, part, prosect, quarter, section, sever, slice, sunder; SEE CON-CEPTS *98,176*

ssect [v2] *analyze*
anatomize, break down, decompose, decom-pound, examine, explore, inquire about, inspect, nvestigate, resolve, scrutinize, study; SEE CON-:EPT *24*

ssection [n1] *cutting up, particularly of a dead body*
anatomization, anatomy, autopsy, dismember-ment, examination, necropsy, operation, post-mortem, vivisection; SEE CONCEPTS *176,310*

ssection [n2] *thorough analysis*
breakdown, breakup, criticism, critique, exami-nation, inquest, inspection, investigation, resolu-

tion, review, scrutiny, study; SEE CONCEPTS *24,290*

dissemble [v] *disguise, pretend*
affect, camouflage, cloak, conceal, counterfeit, cover, cover up, dissimulate, doublespeak*, dou-ble-talk*, dress up, fake, falsify, feign, four-flush*, hide, let on*, make like*, mask, pass, play possum*, pussyfoot*, put on a false front*, put on a front*, put on an act*, put up a front*, put up a smoke screen*, sham*, shroud, shuck and jive*, signify, simulate, sinuate, stonewall*, white-wash*; SEE CONCEPTS *59,188,716*

disseminate [v] *distribute, scatter*
advertise, announce, annunciate, blaze, blazon, broadcast, circulate, declare, diffuse, disject, dis-perse, dissipate, proclaim, promulgate, propa-gate, publicize, publish, radiate, sow, spread, strew; SEE CONCEPTS *108,140,201,222*

dissemination [n] *distribution*
airing, broadcasting, circulation, diffusion, dissi-pation, promulgation, propagation, publication, publishing, spread; SEE CONCEPTS *651,746*

dissension [n] *conflict of opinion*
altercation, argument, bad vibes*, bickering, clinker*, contention, controversy, difference, disaccord, disagreement, discord, discordance, dispute, dissent, dissidence, disunity, faction, factionalism, flak*, friction, fuss, quarrel, scene, sour note*, static, strife, trouble, variance, wran-gle; SEE CONCEPTS *46,278,665*

dissent [n] *disagreement, disapproval*
bone*, bone of contention*, bone to pick*, clinker*, conflict, contention, denial, difference, disaccord, discord, dissension, dissidence, dis-unity, far cry*, flak*, hassle, heresy, heterodoxy, misbelief, nonagreement, nonconcurrence, non-cortformism, nonconformity, nope*, objection, opposition, poles apart*, protest, refusal, resis-tance, schism, sour note*, spat, split, strife, un-orthodoxy, variance; SEE CONCEPTS *29,665,689*

dissent [v] *disagree*
argue, balk, break with, buck, contradict, de-cline, demur, differ, disaccord, discord, divide, fly in the face of*, object, oppose, pettifog, protest, put up a fight*, put up an argument, refuse, say not a chance*, say nothing doing*, say no way*, shy, stickle, vary, wrangle; SEE CONCEPTS *21,46*

dissertation [n] *scholarly thesis*
argumentation, commentary, critique, discourse, disputation, disquisition, essay, exposition, memoir, monograph, tractate, treatise; SEE CON-CEPTS *271,287*

disservice [n] *unkindness*
bad turn, detriment, disfavor, harm, hurt, injury, injustice, insult, outrage, prejudice, wrong; SEE CONCEPTS *309,645,674*

dissidence [n] *difference of opinion*
bad vibes*, contention, disaccord, disagreement, discordance, disharmony, dispeace, dispute, dis-sension, dissent, feud, heresy, heterodoxy, mis-belief, nonconformism, nonconformity, rupture, schism, sour note*, strife, unorthodoxy; SEE CONCEPTS *278,633,689*

dissident [adj] *disagreeing, differing*
discordant, dissentient, dissenting, heretical, het-erodox, nonconformist, schismatic, sectarian, un-orthodox; SEE CONCEPT *403*

dissident [n] *person who holds different belief*
agitator, dissenter, heretic, misbeliever, noncon-

formist, protester, rebel, recusant, schismatic, schismatist, sectary, separatist; SEE CONCEPTS *359,423*

dissimilar [*adj*] *not alike; not capable of comparison*
antithetical, antonymous, contradictory, contrary, different, disparate, distant, divergent, diverse, far cry*, heterogeneous, individual, like night and day*, march to a different drummer*, mismatched, mismated, not similar, offbeat, opposite, poles apart*, unequal, unique, unlike, unrelated, unsimilar, various, weird*; SEE CONCEPT *564*

dissimilarity [*n*] *unlikeness*
alterity, contrast, difference, discord, discordance, discrepancy, disparity, dissemblance, dissimilitude, distance, distinction, divarication, divergence, divergency, diversity, heterogeneity, incomparability, incongruity, inconsistency, inconsonance, nonuniformity, offset, otherness, separation, severance, unrelatedness, variance, variation; SEE CONCEPT *665*

dissimulate [*v*] *conceal, disguise*
beard*, camouflage, cloak, deceive, dissemble, dress up, fake, feign, hide, make-believe, mask, present a false face*, present a false front*, pretend; SEE CONCEPTS *59,172,188*

dissipate [*v1*] *expend, spend*
be wasteful with, blow*, burn up*, consume, deplete, dump*, fritter away, indulge oneself, kiss goodbye*, lavish, misspend, misuse, run through, squander, throw away, trifle away, use up, waste; SEE CONCEPTS *156,169*

dissipate [*v2*] *disappear*
dispel, disperse, dissolve, drive away, evanesce, evaporate, melt away, run dry, scatter, spread, vanish; SEE CONCEPTS *105,469*

dissipated [*adj1*] *used up*
blown, burnt out*, consumed, destroyed, exhausted, kaput*, played out*, scattered, spent, squandered, wasted; SEE CONCEPTS *560,576*

dissipated [*adj2*] *self-indulgent*
abandoned, corrupt, debauched, dissolute, gone bad*, gone to seed*, gone to the dogs*, hellbent*, intemperate, profligate, rakish, wicked; SEE CONCEPTS *401,545*

dissipation [*n1*] *amusement, entertainment, occasionally to excess*
bender*, binge, blow-out, bust*, celebration, circus, distraction, diversion, divertissement, gratification, party, recreation, self-indulgence, tear*, toot*, wingding*; SEE CONCEPTS *363,386*

dissipation [*n2*] *wantonness*
abandonment, debauchery, dissoluteness, dissolution, drunkenness, evil, excess, extravagance, free-living, high-living*, indulgence, intemperance, lavishness, life in the fast lane*, prodigality, profligacy, self-gratification, squandering, to hell in handbasket*, waste; SEE CONCEPT *633*

dissipation [*n3*] *disappearance*
diffusion, disintegration, dispersal, dispersion, dissemination, dissolution, distribution, emission, extravagance, improvidence, radiation, scattering, spread, vanishing, wastage, waste; SEE CONCEPTS *230,651,720*

dissociate [*v*] *part company with; separate*
abstract, alienate, break off, detach, disassociate, disband, disconnect, disengage, disjoin, disperse, disrupt, distance, disunite, divide, divorce, es-

trange, isolate, quit, scatter, segregate, set apar[t] uncouple, unfix; SEE CONCEPTS *135,384*

dissociation [*n*] *detachment, separation*
break, disconnection, disengagement, disjunc[tion], distancing, disunion, division, divorce, iso[lation], segregation, severance; SEE CONCEPT *388*

dissolute [*adj*] *lacking restraint, indulgent*
abandoned, corrupt, debauched, degenerate, de[praved], dissipated, evil, fast*, fast and loose*[,] gone bad*, high living*, intemperate, in the fas[t] lane*, lascivious, lax, lecherous, lewd, libertine licentious, light, loose*, nighthawk*, night owl[*] on the take*, open, player*, profligate, raffish rakish, reprobate, slack, swift, sybaritic, uncon[strained], unprincipled, unrestrained, viciou[s] wanton, wayward, wicked, wild; SEE CONCEPT *401,545*

dissolution [*n1*] *separation, rupture*
breaking up, detachment, disintegration, dis[union], division, divorce, divorcement, parting partition, resolution, split-up; SEE CONCEPT *230,388*

dissolution [*n2*] *death; destruction*
adjournment, conclusion, curtains, decay, de[cease], decomposition, defunction, demise disappearance, disbandment, discontinuatio[n] dismissal, dispersal, end, ending, evaporatio[n] extinction, finish, liquefaction, melting, ove[r]throw, passing, quietus, release, resolution, rui[n] silence, sleep, solution, suspension, terminatio[n] SEE CONCEPTS *105,304,469,703*

dissolve [*v1*] *melt from solid to liquid; mix in*
defront, deliquesce, diffuse, fluidify, flux, fus[e] liquefy, liquesce, render, run, soften, thaw, was[h] away; SEE CONCEPTS *469,702*

dissolve [*v2*] *disappear, disintegrate*
break down, break into pieces, break up, crum[ble], decline, decompose, diffuse, dilapidate, dis[band], disperse, dissipate, dwindle, evanesc[e] evaporate, fade, melt away, perish, separate, un[make], vanish, waste away; SEE CONCEPT *105,469*

dissolve [*v3*] *annul, discontinue*
abrogate, adjourn, annihilate, break up, cance[l] collapse, decimate, demolish, destroy, destruc[t] discharge, dismiss, disorganize, disunite, di[vorce], do away with, end, eradicate, invalidate loose, overthrow, postpone, put an end to, quash render void, repeal, resolve into, ruin, separate sever, shatter, shoot, suspend, terminate, un[make], vacate, void, wind up, wrack, wreck; SE[E] CONCEPTS *121,234,252*

dissonance [*n1*] *disagreement*
antagonism, conflict, contention, controversy difference, disaccord, discord, discrepancy disharmony, disparity, dissension, dissidence, in[con]gruity, inconsistency, strife, variance; SE[E] CONCEPTS *278,665,689*

dissonance [*n2*] *noise, discord*
cacophony, harshness, jangle, jarring, unmelodi[ousness]; SEE CONCEPT *595*

dissonant [*adj1*] *different, conflicting*
anomalous, at variance, differing, disagreeing disconsonant, discordant, discrepant, dissentien[t] incompatible, incongruent, incongruous, incon[sistent], inconsonant, irreconcilable, irregula[r] sour note*, unmixable; SEE CONCEPT *564*

dissonant [*adj2*] *unharmonious*
cacophonic, cacophonous, discordant, dishar[monic], disharmonious, grating, harsh, inhar[monious]

-monic, inharmonious, jangling, jarring, out of tune, raucous, strident, tuneless, unmelodious, unmusical; SEE CONCEPTS *592,594*

issuade [*v*] *talk out of*
advise against, caution against, chicken out*, counsel, cry out against, deprecate, derail, deter, disadvise, discourage, disincline, divert, exhort, expostulate, faze, hinder, lean on*, persuade not to, prevent, prick, put off, remonstrate, throw a wet blanket on*, throw cold water on*, throw off, thwart, turn off*, urge not to, warn; SEE CONCEPTS *68,78*

istance [*n1*] *interval, range*
absence, ambit, amplitude, area, bit, breadth, compass, country mile*, expanse, extension, extent, farness, far piece*, gap, good ways*, heavens, hinterland, horizon, lapse, length, objective, orbit, outpost, outskirts, provinces, purlieu, purview, radius, reach, remoteness, remove, scope, separation, size, sky, space, span, spread, stretch, sweep, way, width; SEE CONCEPTS *651,739,790*

istance [*n2*] *aloofness*
coldness, coolness, frigidity, reserve, restraint, stiffness; SEE CONCEPT *633*

istance [*v*] *dissociate oneself; leave behind*
break away from the pack, outdo, outpace, outrun, outstrip, pass, put in proportion, separate oneself; SEE CONCEPT *195*

istant [*adj1*] *faraway*
abroad, abstracted, apart, a piece, arm's length*, asunder, away, backwoods, beyond range, far, far back, far-flung, far-off, farther, further, inaccessible, indirect, in the background, in the boonies*, in the distance, in the sticks*, isolated, middle of nowhere*, not home*, obscure, outlying, out of earshot*, out of range, out of reach, out-of-the-way, remote, removed, retired, secluded, secret, separate, sequestered, telescopic, unapproachable, ways*, wide of*, yonder*; SEE CONCEPTS *576,778*

istant [*adj2*] *aloof*
arrogant, ceremonious, cold, cool, formal, haughty, insociable, laid back, modest, offish, on ice*, proud, put on airs*, remote, reserved, restrained, reticent, retiring, shy, solitary, standoff, standoffish, stiff, stuck-up*, unapproachable, uncompanionable, unconcerned, unfriendly, unsociable, uppity*, withdrawn; SEE CONCEPTS *401,404*

istaste [*n*] *dislike, hate*
abhorrence, antipathy, aversion, detestation, disfavor, disgust, disinclination, displeasure, disrelish, dissatisfaction, hatred, horror, hostility, indisposition, loathing, repugnance, repulsion, revolt, revulsion; SEE CONCEPT *29*

istasteful [*adj*] *repulsive, unpleasant*
abhorrent, abominable, afflictive, bitter, detestable, disagreeable, dislikable, displeasing, flat, flavorless, galling, grievous, grody*, gross*, hateful, icky*, insipid, loathsome, nauseous, objectionable, obnoxious, odious, offensive, painful, repellent, repugnant, savorless, tasteless, unappetizing, undesirable, uninviting, unlikable, unpalatable, unsavory, yicky*, yucky*; SEE CONCEPTS *529,589,613*

istend [*v*] *bulge, swell*
amplify, augment, balloon, bloat, dilate, distort, enlarge, expand, increase, inflate, lengthen, puff, stretch, widen; SEE CONCEPTS *157,469,780*

distended [*adj*] *swollen*
bloated, bulging, enlarged, expanded, inflated, puffed out, puffy, stretched, tumescent, tumid, turgid; SEE CONCEPT *485*

distill [*v*] *make pure; draw out something*
boil down, brew, clarify, concentrate, condense, cook, cut, cut down, cut to the bone*, dribble, drip, drop, evaporate, express, extract, ferment, get to the meat*, infuse, precipitate, press, press out, purify, rarefy, rectify, refine, squeeze out, steam, sublimate, trickle, trim, vaporize, volatilize; SEE CONCEPTS *165,170,211,219*

distillation [*n*] *distillate*
cleansing, purification, refining; SEE CONCEPTS *165,367*

distinct [*adj1*] *apparent, obvious*
audible, categorical, clean-cut, clear, clear-cut, decided, definite, enunciated, evident, explicit, express, incisive, lucid, manifest, marked, noticeable, palatable, patent, perspicuous, plain, prescribed, recognizable, sharp, sharp-cut, specific, transparent, trenchant, unambiguous, unequivocal, unmistakable, well-defined; SEE CONCEPTS *535,591,619*

distinct [*adj2*] *different; unconnected*
detached, discrete, disparate, dissimilar, distinctive, disunited, divergent, diverse, especial, individual, offbeat, particular, peculiar, poles apart*, separate, separated, several, single, sole, special, specific, unassociated, unattached, unique, various; SEE CONCEPT *564*

distinction [*n1*] *differentiation; feature*
acumen, acuteness, alterity, analysis, characteristic, clearness, contrast, diagnosis, difference, differential, discernment, discrepancy, discreteness, discretion, discrimination, dissemblance, dissimilarity, dissimilitude, divergence, divergency, division, earmark, estimation, individuality, judgment, mark, marking, nicety, otherness, particularity, peculiarity, penetration, perception, qualification, quality, refinement, sensitivity, separation, sharpness, tact, unlikeness; SEE CONCEPTS *411,665*

distinction [*n2*] *prominence; achievement*
accolade, account, award, badge, bays, celebrity, consequence, credit, decoration, eminence, excellence, fame, flair, greatness, illustriousness, importance, kudos, laurels, manner, merit, name, note, perfection, preeminence, prestige, quality, rank, renown, reputation, repute, style, superiority, worth; SEE CONCEPTS *388,671,706*

distinctive [*adj*] *different, unique*
characteristic, cool, diacritic, diagnostic, discrete, distinguishing, excellent, extraordinary, far cry, gnarly*, idiosyncratic, individual, like night and day*, offbeat, original, outstanding, peculiar, perfect, poles apart*, proper, separate, single, singular, special, superior, typical, uncommon, unreal, weird, wicked; SEE CONCEPTS *564,574*

distinguish [*v1*] *tell the difference*
analyze, ascertain, categorize, characterize, classify, collate, decide, demarcate, determinate, determine, diagnose, diagnosticate, differentiate, discriminate, divide, estimate, extricate, figure out, finger*, identify, individualize, individuate, judge, know, label, make out, mark, mark off, name, part, pinpoint, place, qualify, recognize, select, separate, set apart, set off, sift, signalize, single out, singularize, sort out, specify, spot,

di
di

tag, tell apart, tell between, tell from; SEE CON-
CEPTS 15,18,38

distinguish [v2] *discern, identify*

beam*, catch, descry, detect, dig, discover, discriminate, eye, eyeball*, flash*, focus, get a load
of*, get an eyeful*, know, make out, mark, note,
notice, observe, perceive, pick out, pick up on*,
read, recognize, remark, see, spot, spy, take in,
tell, view; SEE CONCEPTS 38,626

distinguish [v3] *make famous*

acknowledge, admire, celebrate, dignify, honor,
immortalize, pay tribute to, praise, signalize; SEE
CONCEPT 69

distinguished [adj] *famous, outstanding*

acclaimed, aristocratic, arresting, big name*,
brilliant, celebrated, conspicuous, dignified, distingué, eminent, especial, esteemed, extraordinary, famed, foremost, glorious, great, highly
regarded, honored, illustrious, imposing,
marked, memorable, name, noble, nonpareil, notable, noted, noteworthy, peerless, prominent, remarkable, renowned, reputable, royal, salient,
shining, signal, singular, special, stately, striking,
superior, talked of, unforgettable, venerable,
well-known; SEE CONCEPT 574

distort [v] *deform; falsify*

alter, angle, belie, bend, bias, buckle, change,
collapse, color, con, contort, crush, curve, deceive, decline, deteriorate, deviate, disfigure,
doctor*, fake, fudge*, garble, gnarl, knot, lie,
make out like, mangle, melt, misconstrue, misinterpret, misrepresent, misshape, pervert, phony
up*, put one on, sag, scam*, slant, slump,
snow*, torture, trump up*, twist, warp, whitewash*, wind, wrench, writhe; SEE CONCEPTS
63,137,232,250

distortion [n] *deformity; falsification*

baloney*, bend, bias, BS*, buckle, coloring, contortion, crock, crookedness, exaggeration, intor-
sion, jazz*, jive*, lie, line, malconformation,
malformation, misinterpretation, misrepresentation, misshape, misstatement, misuse, mutilation,
perversion, slant, smoke*, story*, tall story*, torture, twist, twistedness, warp; SEE CONCEPTS
63,580

distract [v] *divert attention; confuse*

abstract, addle, agitate, amuse, befuddle, beguile,
bewilder, call away, catch flies*, confound, derange, detract, discompose, disconcert, disturb,
divert, draw away, engross, entertain, fluster,
frenzy, harass, lead astray*, lead away, madden,
mislead, mix up, occupy, perplex, puzzle, sidetrack, stall, throw off*, torment, trouble, turn
aside, unbalance, unhinge*; SEE CONCEPTS 14,16

distraction [n] *having one's attention drawn
away*

aberration, abstraction, agitation, amusement,
beguilement, bewilderment, commotion, complication, confusion, disorder, dissipation, disturbance, diversion, divertissement, engrossment,
entertainment, frenzy, game, interference, interruption, pastime, perplexity, preoccupation,
recreation; SEE CONCEPTS 293,410,532,690

distraught [adj] *very upset, worked-up*

addled, agitated, anxious, beside oneself, bothered, concerned, confused, crazed*, crazy, discomposed, distracted, distrait, distressed,
flustered, frantic, harassed, hysterical, in a panic,
like a chicken with its head cut off*, mad, muddled, nonplussed, nuts*, out of one's mind*,

overwrought, perturbed, rattled, raving, shook
up, thrown*, tormented, troubled, unglued*, unscrewed*, unzipped*, wild, worried; SEE CON-
CEPTS 401,403,690

distress [n1] *pain, agony*

ache, affliction, anguish, anxiety, bad news*,
blues*, care, concern, cross, dejection, desolation, disappointment, discomfort, disquietude,
dolor, embarrassment, grief, headache, heartache, heartbreak, irritation, malaise, misery,
mortification, ordeal, pang, perplexity, sadness,
shame, sorrow, stew, suffering, throe, torment,
torture, trial, tribulation, trouble, twinge, uncon-
solability, unhappiness, vexation, visitation,
woe, worriment, worry, wretchedness; SEE CON-
CEPTS 410,532,690,720,728

distress [n2] *hardship, adversity*

bad luck, bummer*, calamity, can of worms*,
catastrophe, crunch*, destitution, difficulty, disaster, downer*, drag*, exigency, hard knocks*,
hard time*, holy mess*, hot water*, indigence,
jam*, misfortune, need, pickle*, pinch*, poverty,
privation, rigor, rotten luck*, scrape*, straits,
throe, ticklish spot*, tough break*, tough luck*,
trial, trouble, unholy mess*, vicissitude, want;
SEE CONCEPT 674

distress [v] *worry, upset*

afflict, aggrieve, agonize, ail, be on one's case*,
bother, break, bug, burn up, depress, desolate,
discombobulate*, disquiet, disturb, do a numbe▯
on*, dog*, eat*, get*, get to*, give a hard time*,
grieve, harass, harry, hound, hurt, injure, irk, irritate, make it tough for*, miff, nag, needle, nit-
pick, oppress, pain, peeve, perplex, pester, pick
on, plague, push, push buttons*, rack, sadden,
strain, strap, stress, tick off*, torment, torture,
trouble, try, vex, weigh, wound; SEE CONCEPTS
7,19,313

distressed [adj] *upset*

afflicted, agitated, all torn up*, antsy, anxious,
basket case*, bothered, bugged, bummed out*,
bundle of nerves*, concerned, cut up*, discom▯
bobulated*, disconsolate, distracted, distrait, dis▯
traught, dragged, exercised, fidgety, harassed,
hyper*, in a stew*, in a tizzy*, inconsolable, jit▯
tery, jumpy, miffed, peeved, perturbed, ripped*,
saddened, shaky, shook*, shook up*, sho▯
down*, spooked*, strung out*, tormented, trou▯
bled, unconsolable, unglued*, up the wall*, up▯
tight*, wired, worried, wrecked*, wretched; SE▯
CONCEPT 403

distress signal [n] *alarm*

burglar alarm, call for help*, danger signal, fir▯
alarm, mayday, SOS, warning signal; SEE CON▯
CEPTS 269,463

distribute [v1] *allocate, deliver, spread*

administer, allot, apportion, appropriate, assig▯
bestow, circulate, consign, convey, cut up, dea▯
deal out, diffuse, disburse, dish out*, dispens▯
disperse, dispose, disseminate, divide, divv▯
up*, dole out*, donate, endow, fork out*, giv▯
give away, hand out, issue, lot out, measure ou▯
mete, parcel, partition, pass out, pay out, presen▯
prorate, radiate, ration, scatter, share, shell out▯
slice up, sow, strew; SEE CONCEPTS 98,140,217

distribute [v2] *classify*

arrange, assort, categorize, class, file, grou▯
order; SEE CONCEPT 84

distribution [n1] *allocation, dispersion*

administration, alloting, allotment, apportionin▯

apportionment, assessment, assigning, circulating, circulation, dealing, delivery, diffusion, dispensation, dispersal, disposal, disposing, dissemination, dissipating, division, dole, handing out, handling, mailing, marketing, partition, partitioning, propagation, prorating, rationing, scattering, sharing, spreading, trading, transport, transportation; SEE CONCEPTS 98,140,217

distribution [n2] *classification*
arrangement, assortment, disposal, disposition, grouping, location, order, ordering, organization, placement, sequence; SEE CONCEPTS 109,727

distributor [n] *wholesaler*
dealer, jobber, merchandiser, middleperson, salesperson, trader; SEE CONCEPT 347

district [n] *geographical area*
commune, community, department, locale, locality, neck of the woods*, neighborhood, parcel, parish, precinct, quarter, region, section, sector, stomping ground*, territory, turf*, vicinage, vicinity, ward; SEE CONCEPT 508

distrust [n] *lack of faith in something*
disbelief, doubt, misdoubt, misgiving, mistrust, qualm, question, skepticism, suspicion, wariness; SEE CONCEPTS 21,689

distrust [v] *be suspicious, skeptical of*
be wary of, disbelieve, discredit, doubt, misbelieve, mistrust, question, smell a rat*, suspect, wonder about; SEE CONCEPT 21

distrustful [adj] *disbelieving*
been hit before*, cagey, cautious, chary, cynical, doubtful, doubting, dubious, fearful, jealous, leery, mistrustful, skeptical, suspicious, uneasy, uptight, wary; SEE CONCEPTS 403,542

disturb [v1] *bother, upset*
afflict, agitate, ail, alarm, amaze, annoy, arouse, astound, badger, burn up*, complicate, confound, confuse, depress, discompose, dishearten, disrupt, distract, distress, excite, fluster, frighten, gall, grieve, harass, interfere, interrupt, intrude, irk, irritate, make uneasy, molest, muddle, outrage, pain, perplex, perturb, pester, pique, plague, provoke, puzzle, rattle, rouse, ruffle, shake, shake up*, startle, tire, trouble, unhinge*, unnerve, unsettle, vex, worry; SEE CONCEPTS 7,19

disturb [v2] *disorder; dislocate*
confuse, derange, disarrange, disarray, discompose, disorganize, displace, distort, foul up*, interfere, jumble, louse up*, mess up, mix up, move, muddle, remove, replace, shift, tamper, unsettle, upset; SEE CONCEPTS 84,137,250

disturbance [n] *commotion; upset*
agitation, annoyance, big scene*, big stink*, bother, brawl, brouhaha, clamor, confusion, convulsion, derangement, disarrangement, disorder, disruption, distraction, eruption, explosion, ferment, fisticuffs, flap, fracas, fray, fuss, hindrance, hubbub, hullabaloo*, insurrection, interruption, intrusion, molestation, perturbation, quake, quarrel, racket, rampage, restlessness, riot, ruckus, rumble, shock, spasm, stink*, stir*, storm, to-do*, tremor, tumult, turmoil, upheaval, uprising, uproar, violence; SEE CONCEPTS 388,410,674,720

ditch [n] *gulley*
canal, channel, chase, cut, dike, drain, excavation, furrow, gutter, mine, moat, trench, watercourse; SEE CONCEPTS 509,513

ditch [v] *get rid of*
abandon, desert, discard, dispose of, drop, dump*, eighty-six*, forsake, jettison, junk*, leave, reject, scrap*, throw away, throw out, throw overboard*; SEE CONCEPT 180

ditsy [adj] *silly*
airbrained, airheaded, daffy*, dippy*, dipsy*, dizzy*, dopey, eccentric, empty, giddy, goofy*, inane, kooky*, rattlebrained, scatterbrained; SEE CONCEPTS 314,401

ditto [n] *the same; duplicate*
clone, copy, double, duplication, facsimile, likewise, reproduction, the above, the very words*; SEE CONCEPTS 664,667,716

ditty [n] *song*
ballad, composition, jingle, tune; SEE CONCEPT 595

ditz [n] *scatterbrain*
airbrain, airhead, birdbrain*, dingbat*, fluffhead*, ninny, rattlebrain, silly person, space case; SEE CONCEPTS 412,423

diva [n] *prima donna*
famous singer, lead singer, opera singer; SEE CONCEPT 352

dive [n1] *descent, usually underwater*
belly flop*, dash, dip, duck, ducking, fall, header* headlong* jump, leap, lunge, nosedive, pitch, plunge, spring, submergence, submersion, swoop; SEE CONCEPTS 147,181,194

dive [n2] *dirty, sleazy establishment*
bar, barroom, beer garden* cabaret, dump, flea trap*, flophouse*, hangout, hole, honky-tonk*, joint, lounge, night club, pool hall, pub, saloon, taproom, tavern; SEE CONCEPT 449

dive [v] *descend, usually going underwater*
belly flop*, dip, disappear, drop, duck, fall, go headfirst, gutter, header*, jump, leap, lunge, nose-dive, pitch, plumb, plummet, plunge, spring, submerge, swoop, vanish, vault; SEE CONCEPTS 147,181,194

diverge [v1] *go in different directions*
bend, bifurcate, branch, branch off, depart, deviate, digress, divagate, divaricate, divide, excurse, fork, part, radiate, ramble, separate, split, spread, stray, swerve, veer, wander; SEE CONCEPTS 195,738

diverge [v2] *be different from; be at odds*
argue, conflict, contrast, depart, deviate, differ, digress, disagree, disapprove, dissent, oppose, stray, swerve, turn aside, vary, wander; SEE CONCEPTS 46,665

divergence [n] *branching out; difference*
aberration, alteration, alterity, crotch, deflection, departure, detour, deviation, digression, disagreeing, discrepancy, disparity, dissemblance, dissimilarity, dissimilitude, distinction, divagation, divergency, diversity, division, fork, mutation, otherness, parting, radiation, ramification, separation, turning, unlikeness, variety, varying; SEE CONCEPTS 665,738

divergent [adj] *differing*
aberrant, abnormal, anomalous, antithetical, atypical, conflicting, contradictory, contrary, deviating, different, disagreeing, disparate, dissimilar, dissonant, distant, diverging, diverse, factional, factious, irregular, off-key, opposite, poles apart*, separate, unalike, unequal, unlike, unnatural, unsimilar, untypical, variant, various; SEE CONCEPT 564

di
di

diverse [*adj*] *different; various*
assorted, contradictory, contrary, contrasted, contrasting, contrastive, differing, discrete, disparate, dissimilar, distant, distinct, divergent, diversified, diversiform, incommensurable, like night and day*, manifold, miscellaneous, mixed bag*, multifarious, opposite, separate, several, sundry, unalike, unequal, unlike, varied, varying; SEE CONCEPTS 564,772

diversify [*v*] *spread out; branch out*
alter, assort, change, expand, mix, modify, transform, variegate, vary; SEE CONCEPTS 232,697

diversion [*n1*] *change in a course, path*
aberration, alteration, deflection, departure, detour, deviation, digression, divergence, fake out*, red herring*, turning, variation; SEE CONCEPTS 501,738

diversion [*n2*] *entertainment, recreation*
amusement, ball, beguilement, delectation, delight, disport, dissipation, distraction, divertissement, enjoyment, field day*, frivolity, fun, fun and games*, game, gratification, grins*, high time*, hoopla*, laughs*, levity, merry-go-round*, pastime, picnic*, play, pleasure, relaxation, relish, sport, whoopee*; SEE CONCEPTS 292,363,386

diversity [*n*] *variety, difference*
assortment, dissimilarity, distinction, distinctiveness, divergence, diverseness, diversification, heterogeneity, medley, mixed bag*, multeity, multifariousness, multiformity, multiplicity, range, unlikeness, variance, variegation, variousness; SEE CONCEPTS 651,665

divert [*v1*] *turn a different direction*
alter, avert, change, deflect, modify, pivot, redirect, sheer, swerve, switch, turn aside, veer, volte-face, wheel, whip, whirl; SEE CONCEPTS 187,213

divert [*v2*] *amuse, entertain*
beguile, break one up*, delight, fracture one*, get one's jollies*, gladden, gratify, knock 'em dead*, make happy, panic, please, put 'em away*, recreate, regale, relax, slay, tickle, wow; SEE CONCEPT 9

divert [*v3*] *take attention away*
abstract, attract attention, bend the rules*, catch flies*, circumlocute, detach, deter, detract, disadvise, discourage, disengage, dissuade, distract, disturb, draw away, get around, lead astray, lead away, send on a wild-goose chase*, sidetrack, stall; SEE CONCEPTS 7,19,22

divest [*v*] *dispossess; take off*
bankrupt, bare, bereave, bleed, denudate, denude, deprive, despoil, disinherit, dismantle, disrobe, ditch*, doff, dump, eighty-six*, lose, milk*, oust, plunder, remove, rob, seize, spoil, strip, take from, unclothe, uncover, undress, unload; SEE CONCEPTS 139,142,211

divide [*v1*] *separate, disconnect*
abscind, bisect, branch, break, break down, carve, chop, cleave, cross, cut, cut up, demarcate, detach, dichotomize, disengage, disentangle, disjoin, dislocate, dismember, dissect, dissever, dissociate, dissolve, disunite, divorce, halve, intersect, isolate, loose, part, partition, pull away, quarter, rend, rupture, section, segment, segregate, sever, shear, split, subdivide, sunder, tear, unbind, undo; SEE CONCEPTS 98,135,137

divide [*v2*] *distribute*
allocate, allot, apportion, articulate, cut, cut in*,

cut one in*, cut up, deal, deal out, disburse, dish out*, dispense, disperse, divvy up*, dole out*, factor, fork out*, go fifty-fifty*, hand out, hand over, lot out, measure out, parcel, partition, piece up, portion, prorate, quota, ration, share, shell out*, shift, slice, slice up, split up; SEE CONCEPTS 98,140

divide [*v3*] *put in order; classify*
arrange, categorize, grade, group, separate, sort; SEE CONCEPT 84

divide [*v4*] *disagree, alienate*
break up, cause to disagree, come between, differ, disaccord, dissent, disunite, estrange, part, pit against, separate, set against, set at odds*, sow dissension*, split, vary; SEE CONCEPTS 46,266

dividend [*n*] *one's share, profit*
allotment, allowance, appropriation, bonus, carrot*, check, coupon, cut*, dispensation, divvy*, extra, gain, gravy*, guerdon, interest, lagniappe*, meed, pay, portion, premium, prize, proceeds, remittance, returns, reward, surplus, taste*; SEE CONCEPTS 337,344

divination [*n*] *fortune-telling*
augury, clairvoyancy, horoscopy, occultism, palmistry, prediction, premonition, prognostication, prophecy, soothsaying; SEE CONCEPTS 70,278,689

divine [*adj*] *godlike, perfect*
all-powerful, almighty, ambrosial, angelic, anointed, beatific, beautiful, blissful, celestial, consecrated, deific, deistic, eternal, exalted, excellent, glorious, godly, hallowed, heavenly, holy, immaculate, magnificent, marvelous, mystical, omnipotent, omnipresent, omniscient, rapturous, religious, sacramental, sacred, sacrosanct, sanctified, spiritual, splendid, superhuman, superlative, supernatural, supreme, theistic, transcendent, transcendental, transmundane, unearthly, wonderful; SEE CONCEPTS 568,574

divine [*v*] *prophesy*
anticipate, apprehend, conjecture, deduce, discern, forebode, foretell, foreknow, foresee, foretell, go out on a limb*, guess, infer, intuit, perceive, predict, previse, prognosticate, see, see in the cards*, suppose, surmise, suspect, take a shot*, take a stab*, understand, visualize; SEE CONCEPT 28

divinity [*n*] *absolute being; divine nature*
celestial, deity, genius, god, goddess, godhead, godhood, godliness, godship, guardian spirit, higher power, holiness, lord, prime mover, sanctity, spirit; SEE CONCEPTS 368,370,689

division [*n1*] *separation, disconnection*
analysis, apportionment, autopsy, bisection, breaking, breaking down, breaking up, carving, contrasting, cutting up, demarcation, departmentalizing, detaching, detachment, diagnosis, disjunction, dismemberment, disparting, disseverance, dissolution, distinguishing, distribution, disunion, disuniting, dividing, divorce, parceling, parting, partition, reduction, rending, rupture, segmentation, selection, separating, severance, splitting up, subdivision, vivisection; SEE CONCEPTS 98,135

division [*n2*] *something produced from separating*
affiliate, associate, border, boundary, branch, category, chunk, class, compartment, cut, degree,

demarcation, department, divide, dividend, divider, dividing line, divvy*, end, fraction, fragment, grouping, head, kind, lobe, lump, member, moiety, offset, offshoot, parcel, partition, piece, piece of action*, portion, rake-off*, ramification, section, sector, segment, share, slice, sort, split, subdivision, wedge; SEE CONCEPTS 378,382,710,835

division [n3] *breach, estrangement*
conflict, difference of opinion, difficulty, disaccord, disagreement, discord, disharmony, dispute, dissension, dissent, dissidence, dissonance, disunion, feud, rupture, split, trouble, variance, words; SEE CONCEPT 388

divisive [ad] *dissenting*
alienating, at odds, discordant, disruptive; SEE CONCEPTS 401,537

divorce [n] *split-up of marriage*
annulment, breach, break, breakup, decree nisi, dedomiciling, detachment, disparateness, dissociation, dissolution, disunion, division, divorcement, on the rocks*, parting of the ways*, partition, rupture, separate maintenance, separation, severance, split, splitsville*; SEE CONCEPT 297

divorce [v] *split up a marriage*
annul, break up, cancel, disconnect, disjoin, dissever, dissociate, dissolve, disunite, divide, nullify, part, put away, separate, sever, split, sunder, unmarry; SEE CONCEPT 297

divulge [v] *make known; confess*
admit, betray, blab, blow the whistle*, broadcast, communicate, cough up*, declare, disclose, discover, exhibit, expose, fess up*, give away, go public*, gossip, impart, leak, let hair down*, let slip*, mouth, open up*, own up*, proclaim, promulgate, publish, reveal, spill, spill the beans*, spring, tattle, tell, tip off*, uncover; SEE CONCEPT 60

divvy up [v] *divide*
allocate, apportion, cut, cut up the pie*, dole out, go halves*, measure out, mete out, share, split; SEE CONCEPTS 98,140

dizzy [adj1] *light-headed, confused*
addled, befuddled, bemused, bewildered, blind, blinded, dazed, dazzled, distracted, disturbed, dumb, dumbfounded, faint, gaga*, giddy, groggy*, hazy, light, muddled, off balance*, out of control*, punch-drunk*, punchy*, puzzled, reeling, shaky, slap-happy*, staggered, staggering, swimming*, tipsy, unsteady, upset, vertiginous, weak in the knees*, weak-kneed*, whirling, wobbly, woozy; SEE CONCEPTS 314,480

dizzy [adj2] *flighty, scatterbrained*
capricious, changeable, crazy, empty-headed, fatuous, feather-brained, fickle, foolish, frivolous, giddy, harebrained, heady, inane, light-headed, silly, skittish, unstable; SEE CONCEPT 402

DNA [n] *deoxyribonucleic acid*
chromosome, gene, genetic code, heredity, nucleic acid, RNA; SEE CONCEPT 648

do [v1] *carry out*
accomplish, achieve, act, arrange, be responsible for, bring about, cause, close, complete, conclude, cook*, create, determine, discharge, do one's thing*, effect, end, engage in, execute, finish, fix, fulfill, get ready, get with it*, go for it*, look after, make, make ready, move, operate, organize, perform, prepare, produce, pull off*, see to, succeed, take care of business*, take on,

transact, undertake, wind up*, work, wrap up*; SEE CONCEPT 91

do [v2] *be sufficient*
answer, avail, be adequate, be enough, be good enough for, be of use, be useful, give satisfaction*, pass muster*, satisfy, serve, suffice, suit; SEE CONCEPTS 646,656

do [v3] *figure out, solve*
adapt, decipher, decode, interpret, puzzle out, render, resolve, translate, transliterate, transpose, work out; SEE CONCEPTS 15,37

do [v4] *act, behave*
acquit oneself, appear, bear, carry, come on like*, comport, conduct, demean, deport, discourse, enact, fare, get along, get by, give, go on, impersonate, make out*, manage, muddle through*, operate, perform, personate, play, playact, portray, present, produce, put on*, quit, render the role, seem, stagger along*; SEE CONCEPT 633

do [v5] *travel, visit*
cover, explore, journey, look at, pass through, stop in, tour, track, traverse; SEE CONCEPT 224

do [v6] *cheat*
beat, bilk, chouse, con, cozen, deceive, defraud, dupe, fleece*, flimflam*, gyp*, hoax, overreach, swindle, take for a ride*, trick; SEE CONCEPT 59

do away with [v] *get rid of; destroy*
abolish, bump off*, cancel, discard, discontinue, do in*, eliminate, exterminate, finish, kill, liquidate, murder, put an end to, put to death, remove, slaughter, slay, take away, wipe out*; SEE CONCEPTS 180,252

docile [adj] *compliant, submissive*
accommodating, acquiescent, adaptable, agreeable, amenable, biddable, childlike, complacent, cool, docious, ductile, easily influenced, easy, easygoing, gentle, governable, humble, laid-back, manageable, meek, mellow, mild, obedient, obliging, orderly, pliable, pliant, quiet, resigned, soft, tame, teachable, tractable, usable, weak-kneed*, well-behaved, willing, yielding; SEE CONCEPTS 401,404

dock [n] *waterfront*
berth, embarkment, harbor, jetty, landing, landing pier, levee, lock, marina, pier, quay, slip, wharf; SEE CONCEPT 439

dock [v] *land on the waterfront*
anchor, berth, drop anchor, hook up, join, link up, moor, put in, rendezvous, tie up, unite; SEE CONCEPT 159

docket [n] *program, agenda*
calendar, card, schedule, tab, tally, ticket, timetable; SEE CONCEPT 271

doctor [n] *medical practitioner*
bones*, doc*, expert, general practitioner, healer, intern, MD, medic, medical person, medico, physician, professor*, quack*, scientist, specialist, surgeon; SEE CONCEPT 357

doctor [v1] *fix up, treat*
administer, apply medication, attend, do up, fix, give treatment, medicate, mend, overhaul, patch up*, rebuild, recondition, reconstruct, repair, revamp, supply; SEE CONCEPTS 110,310

doctor [v2] *adulterate, pervert*
add to, alter, change, cut, deacon, debase, dilute, disguise, dope up*, falsify, fudge*, gloss, load, misrepresent, mix with, sophisticate, spike*, tamper with, water down, weight; SEE CONCEPT 240

di
do

doctrinaire [*adj*] *dogmatic, opinionated*
authoritarian, authoritative, biased, bigoted, bull-headed*, dictative, dictatorial, dogged, fanatical, impractical, inflexible, insistent, magisterial, mulish, obstinate, one-sided, pertinacious, pig-headed*, rigid, speculative, stiff-necked*, stubborn, unrealistic; SEE CONCEPTS *267,401*

doctrine [*n*] *opinion; principle*
article, article of faith, attitude, axiom, basic, belief, canon, concept, convention, conviction, credenda, creed, declaration, dogma, fundamental, gospel, implantation, inculcation, indoctrination, instruction, position, precept, pronouncement, propaganda, proposition, regulation, rule, statement, teaching, tenet, tradition, universal law, unwritten rule; SEE CONCEPTS *688,689*

document [*n*] *written communication*
archive, certificate, credentials, deed, diary, evidence, form, instrument, language, pages, paper, record, report, script, testimony, token; SEE CONCEPT *271*

documentary [*adj*] *investigative report*
account, broadcast, docudrama, feature, film, information, narrative; SEE CONCEPTS *271,282*

dodder [*v*] *shake*
quiver, shiver, shudder, stagger, sway, teeter, totter, tremble, wobble; SEE CONCEPTS *150,152*

doddering [*adj*] *aged, feeble*
anile, decrepit, dotard, faltering, floundering, infirm, senile, shaky, tottering, trembling, unsteady, weak; SEE CONCEPTS *314,488,578,797*

dodge [*n*] *trick, feint*
contrivance, device, machination, method, plan, plot, ploy, ruse, scheme, stratagem, strategy, subterfuge, wile; SEE CONCEPT *660*

dodge [*v*] *avoid*
circumlocute, dark, deceive, ditch, duck, elude, equivocate, escape, evade, fence, fend off, fudge*, get around, get out of, give the slip*, hedge, juke, lurch, malinger, move to the side*, parry, pussyfoot*, put the move on*, shake, shake off*, shift, shirk, short-circuit, shuffle, sidestep, skip out on*, skirt, slide, slip, swerve, tergiversate, tergiverse, trick, turn aside, weasel*; SEE CONCEPTS *59,102*

doer [*n*] *go-getter*
achiever, busy person, dynamo*, energetic person, man of action, motivator, mover and shaker*, risk-taker, woman of action; SEE CONCEPT *706*

doff [*v*] *remove*
cast off, discard, disrobe, peel, put aside, shed, shuck, slip off, strip, take off, undress; SEE CONCEPTS *211,453*

do for [*v1*] *destroy*
defeat, deprive, finish, kill, ruin, shatter, slaughter, slay; SEE CONCEPTS *238,252*

do for [*v2*] *help*
abet, aid, assist, benefact, care for, help out, lend a hand*, look after, provide for, steady, support; SEE CONCEPT *110*

dog [*n*] *canine mammal*
bitch, bowwow*, cur, doggy, fido*, flea bag*, hound, man's best friend*, mongrel, mutt, pooch*, pup, puppy, stray, tail-wagger*, tyke; SEE CONCEPT *400*

dog [*v*] *chase after; bother*
bedog, haunt, hound, plague, pursue, shadow, tag, tail, track, trail, trouble; SEE CONCEPT *207*

dog-eat-dog [*adj*] *competitive*
aggressive, brutal, cutthroat, every person for themselves*, fierce, ruthless, vicious; SEE CONCEPT *542*

dogged [*adj*] *determined, persistent*
adamant, bullheaded*, firm, hanging tough*, hardheaded*, hard-nosed*, indefatigable, inexorable, inflexible, insistent, mulish, obdurate, obstinate, perseverant, perseverative, persevering, pertinacious, pigheaded*, relentless, resolute, rigid, single-minded, staunch, steadfast, steady, stubborn, tenacious, tough nut*, unbending, unflagging, unshakable, unyielding; SEE CONCEPTS *401,542*

dogleg [*n*] *bend*
curve, hairpin curve, sharp turn; SEE CONCEPT *436*

dogma [*n*] *belief, principle*
article, article of faith, canon, conviction, credenda, credo, creed, doctrine, gospel, opinion, persuasion, precept, rule, teachings, tenet, view; SEE CONCEPTS *688,689*

dogmatic [*adj1*] *dictatorial, opinionated*
arbitrary, arrogant, assertive, bigoted, bullheaded*, categorical, cocksure*, confident, definite, despotic, determined, dictative, doctrinaire, domineering, downright, egotistical, emphatic, fanatical, fascistic, formal, high and mighty*, imperious, intolerant, magisterial, narrow-minded, obdurate, obstinate, one-sided, overbearing, peremptory, pigheaded*, prejudiced, stiff-necked*, stubborn, tenacious, tyrannical, unequivocal, wrong-headed; SEE CONCEPTS *267, 542*

dogmatic [*adj2*] *based on absolute truth*
a priori, as a matter of course, assertive, authoritarian, authoritative, axiomatic, by fiat, by natural law, by nature, canonical, categorical, deducible, deductive, derivable, doctrinaire, doctrinal, eternal, excathedra, formal, imperative, inevitable, on faith, oracular, orthodox, peremptory, positive, pragmatic, prophetic, reasoned, systematic, theoretical, unchangeable, unerring, unqualified; SEE CONCEPTS *530,567,582*

do-gooder [*n*] *idealist*
altruist, bleeding heart, good Samaritan, humanitarian, philanthropist, volunteer; SEE CONCEPTS *416,423*

do in [*v*] *destroy; exhaust*
assassinate, bankrupt, bump off*, butcher*, cool*, dilapidate, dispatch, do away with*, eliminate, execute, fatigue, finish, frazzle*, kill, knock out*, liquidate, murder, put away*, ruin, shatter, slaughter, slay, tire, wear out, weary, wreck; SEE CONCEPTS *137,250,252*

doing [*n*] *achievement*
accomplishing, accomplishment, achieving, act, action, carrying out, deed, execution, exploit, handiwork, implementation, performance, performing, thing; SEE CONCEPT *706*

doings [*n*] *actions*
acts, affairs, deal, deed, events, goings-on, happenings, matters, proceeding; SEE CONCEPT *1*

doldrums [*n*] *depression*
apathy, black mood*, blahs*, blue funk*, blues*, boredom, bummer*, dejection, disinterest, dismals, downer, dullness, dumps*, ennui, funk*, gloom, inactivity, indifference, inertia, lassitude, letdown, listlessness, malaise, mopes*, slump,

stagnation, stupor, tedium, torpor, yawn*; SEE CONCEPT 410

dole [*n*] *allowance, allocation*
allotment, alms, apportionment, benefit, charity, dispensation, distribution, division, donation, gift, grant, gratuity, handout, living wage, mite, modicum, parcel, pittance, portion, quota, relief, share, subsistence, trifle; SEE CONCEPTS 337,344

doleful [*adj*] *depressing*
afflicted, cast down, cheerless, crestfallen, dejected, depressed, dirgeful, dismal, dispirited, distressing, dolent, dolorous, down, downcast, downhearted, down in the mouth*, dreary, forlorn, funereal, gloomy, grieving, lamentable, lugubrious, melancholy, mournful, painful, piteous, pitiful, plaintive, rueful, sad, somber, sorrowful, woebegone, woeful, wretched; SEE CONCEPTS 403,529

dole out [*v*] *allocate, distribute*
administer, allot, apportion, assign, deal, deal out, dispense, disperse, divide, divvy*, give, hand out, lot, measure, mete, mete out, parcel, partition, share, share out; SEE CONCEPTS 108,140

doll [*n1*] *toy person*
baby, dolly, effigy, figure, figurine, manikin, marionette, model, moppet*, puppet; SEE CONCEPT 446

doll [*n2*] *generous person*
darling, decent person, helpful person, honey*, prince*, sweetheart, sweetie; SEE CONCEPTS 296,423

doll [*n3*] *attractive woman*
angel, babe*, bathing beauty, beauty queen, broad*, bunny*, centerfold, chick*, cover girl, cupcake*, cutie, cutie-pie*, dish*, dollface, dreamboat*, dream girl, fox*, glamour girl, good-looking woman, honey*, hot dish*, hot number*, peach*, pin-up, raving beauty, sex bunny*, sex kitten*, sexpot*, tomato*; SEE CONCEPTS 415,424

dollar [*n*] *paper money*
ace*, bank note, bill, buck*, certificate, clam*, cucumber*, currency, folding money, greenback*, legal tender, note, one-spot*, single; SEE CONCEPT 340

dollop [*n*] *lump*
bit, blob, glob, gob, mass, piece, portion; SEE CONCEPTS 432,786,835

doll up [*v*] *beautify oneself; dress up*
deck out*, fix up, gussy up*, preen, primp, put on best clothes, smarten up*, spiff*, spruce up*; SEE CONCEPTS 162,167,202

dolly [*n*] *handtruck*
carrier, cart, pushcart; SEE CONCEPTS 499,505

dolor [*n*] *misery, anguish*
agony, distress, grief, heartache, heartbreak, passion, ruth, sadness, sorrow, suffering; SEE CONCEPT 410

dolorous [*adj*] *miserable, anguished*
afflicted, afflictive, calamitous, deplorable, dire, distressing, doleful, dolent, dolesome, grievous, harrowing, heart-rending, lamentable, lugubrious, melancholy, mournful, painful, plaintive, regrettable, rueful, ruthful, sad, sorrowful, woebegone, woeful, wretched; SEE CONCEPTS 401,403

dolt [*n*] *stupid person*
airhead*, blockhead*, boob*, chump*, dimwit*, dodo*, dope, dork*, dumbbell*, dumdum*, dunce, fool, goon*, idiot, ignoramus, lamebrain*, lunkhead*, meathead*, nitwit*, sap*, simpleton, stupid, yo-yo*; SEE CONCEPTS 412,423

domain [*n*] *area of expertise, rule*
authority, bailiwick, concern, demesne, department, discipline, district, dominion, empire, estate, field, home park*, jurisdiction, land, neck of the woods*, occupation, orbit*, power, province, quarter, realm, region, scope, slot, specialty, sphere, stomping grounds*, terrain, territory, turf, walk, wing; SEE CONCEPTS 349,518,710

dome [*n*] *arched part of ceiling*
arcade, arch, bubble, bulge, covering, cupola, mosque, roof, span, top, vault; SEE CONCEPT 440

domestic [*adj1*] *household*
calm, devoted, domiciliary, family, home, homelike, home-loving, homely, indoor, pet, private, sedentary, settled, stay-at-home, subdued, submissive, tame, trained, tranquil; SEE CONCEPT 542

domestic [*adj2*] *not foreign*
handcrafted, home-grown, homemade, indigenous, inland, internal, intestine, intramural, municipal, national, native; SEE CONCEPTS 536,549

domesticate [*v*] *tame; habituate*
acclimatize, accustom, break, break in, breed, bring up, bust, corral, domiciliate, familiarize, gentle, herd, hitch, housetrain, naturalize, raise, reclaim, round up, subdue, teach, train, yoke; SEE CONCEPTS 202,285

domesticity [*n*] *home life*
domestication, family life, staying at home; SEE CONCEPT 516

domestic partner [*n*] *live-in significant other*
beneficiary, cohabitant, companion, housemate, longtime companion, lover, partner, spouse; SEE CONCEPT 414

domicile [*n*] *human habitat*
abode, accommodation, apartment, castle, commorancy, condo*, condominium, co-op, crash pad*, dump, dwelling, habitation, home, house, joint, legal residence, mansion, pad*, rack*, residence, residency, roof over head*, roost*, settlement; SEE CONCEPTS 439,516

dominance [*n*] *supremacy*
ascendancy, authority, command, control, domination, dominion, government, influence, paramountcy, power, preeminence, preponderance, prepotence, prepotency, rule, sovereignty, sway, upper hand, whip hand; SEE CONCEPTS 376,668

dominant [*adj1*] *superior, controlling*
ascendant, assertive, authoritative, bossy, chief, commanding, demonstrative, despotic, domineering, effective, first, foremost, governing, imperative, imperious, leading, main, obtaining, outweighing, overbalancing, overbearing, overweighing, paramount, powerful, predominant, predominate, preeminent, preponderant, presiding, prevailing, prevalent, principal, regnant, reigning, ruling, sovereign, supreme, surpassing, transcendent; SEE CONCEPT 574

dominant [*adj2*] *main, primary*
capital, chief, influential, major, number one*, outstanding, paramount, predominant, preeminent, prevailing, prevalent, principal, prominent, stellar; SEE CONCEPT 568

dominate [*v1*] *govern, rule*
boss, call the shots*, command, control, detract from, dictate, direct, domineer, eclipse, handle,

do
do

have one's way*, have upper hand*, head, hold sway over*, influence, keep under thumb*, lay down the law*, lead, lead by the nose*, manage, monopolize, outshine, overbear, overrule, overshadow, play first fiddle*, predominate, preponderate, prevail, prevail over, reign, rule the roost*, run, run the show*, sit on top of*, subject, subjugate, superabound, sway, tyrannize; SEE CONCEPTS 94,117,298

dominate [v2] *tower above*
bestride, look down upon, loom over, overlie, overlook, overtop, stand over, survey; SEE CONCEPTS 741,752

domination [n] *control; subjection*
ascendancy, authority, command, despotism, dictatorship, dominance, dominion, influence, jurisdiction, might, oppression, power, preponderancy, prepotence, prepotency, repression, rule, sovereignty, strings*, subordination, superiority, suppression, supremacy, sway, tyranny; SEE CONCEPT 376

domineer [v] *oppress; assume authority*
be in the saddle*, bend, bluster, boss around*, browbeat, bulldoze*, bully*, call the shots*, dominate, hector, henpeck*, in the driver's seat*, intimidate, keep under thumb*, kick around*, lead by the nose*, menace, overbear, predominate, preponderate, prevail, push the buttons*, reign, rule, rule the roost*, run the show*, run things*, swagger, threaten, throw weight around*, tyrannize; SEE CONCEPTS 14,94

domineering [adj] *oppressive, authoritarian*
arrogant, autocratic, bossy, coercive, crack the whip*, despotic, dictatorial, egotistical, high-handed, imperative, imperial, imperious, in driver's seat*, insolent, iron-handed*, on high horse*, overbearing, peremptory, tyrannical; SEE CONCEPT 401

dominion [n] *area of rule; authority*
ascendancy, authorization, bailiwick, command, commission, control, country, demesne, district, domain, dominance, domination, empire, enclave, field, government, jurisdiction, management, power, preeminence, prepotence, prepotency, prerogative, privilege, property, province, realm, regency, regiment, regimentation, region, reign, rule, seniority, sovereignty, sphere, state, stomping grounds*, supremacy, sway, terrain, territory, turf, walk; SEE CONCEPTS 198,376,1707

donate [v] *make a gift of*
accord, ante up*, award, bequeath, bestow, chip in*, confer, contribute, devote, dole out*, do one's part*, feed the kitty*, get in the act*, get it up*, give, give away, grant, hand out, lay on, pass the hat*, present, provide, subscribe, sweeten the pot*; SEE CONCEPT 108

donation [n] *gift*
a hand*, aid, allowance, alms, appropriation, assistance, benefaction, beneficence, bequest, boon, charity, contribution, dole, do one's part*, endowment, gifting, grant, gratuity, handout, help, helping hand* largess, lump, offering, philanthropy, pittance, present, presentation, ration, relief, subscription, subsidy, subvention, write-off*; SEE CONCEPTS 337,340

done [adj1] *accomplished, finished*
all in*, all over*, a wrap*, brought about, brought to pass, buttoned up*, compassed, complete, completed, concluded, consummated, depleted, down, drained, effected, effete, ended, executed, exhausted, fixed, fulfilled, over, perfected, performed, realized, rendered, set, spent, succeeded, terminated, through, used up, wired, wrought; SEE CONCEPTS 528,531

done [adj2] *thoroughly cooked*
baked, boiled, brewed, broiled, browned, crisped, fried, ready, stewed; SEE CONCEPTS 462,613

done [adj3] *approved, agreed upon*
compacted, determined, okay, settled, you're on*; SEE CONCEPT 558

done for [adj] *beaten, defeated*
broken, conquered, dashed, destroyed, doomed, finished, foiled, lost, ruined, through, undone, vanquished, washed-up*, wrecked; SEE CONCEPTS 537,570

done in [adj] *exhausted*
all in*, bushed*, dead, depleted, done, effete, fagged, far-gone*, on last leg*, ready to drop*, spent, tired, used up, washed-out*, weary, worn-out; SEE CONCEPTS 314,485

Don Juan [n] *ladies' man*
Casanova*, charmer, lady-killer*, libertine, lover, philanderer, playboy, Romeo*, seducer, skirt chaser, smooth operator, stud, woman chaser; SEE CONCEPT 423

donkey [n] *small domestic horselike mammal*
ass, burro, horse, jackass, jennet, jenny, maud, moke, mule, neddy, pony, Rocky Mountain canary*; SEE CONCEPT 400

donnybrook [n] *brawl*
battle royal, fight, fracas, fray, free-for-all, hoedown*, melee, rhubarb*, riot, row, rumble, shindig, slugfest*, turmoil, uproar; SEE CONCEPTS 46,106

donor [n] *giver of gift*
almsgiver, altruist, angel*, backer, benefactor, benefactress, bestower, conferrer, contributor, donator, grantor, heavy hitter*, patron, philanthropist, presenter, Santa Claus*, savior, subscriber; SEE CONCEPTS 359,423

do-nothing [n] *bum*
couch potato*, goof-off*, idler, lazybones, lazy person, loafer, moocher, slacker; SEE CONCEPTS 412,423

doodad [n] *gadget*
contraption, contrivance, doohickey*, gismo, object, thing, thingamabob*, thingamajig*, whatchamacallit*, widget; SEE CONCEPTS 463, 499

doohickey [n] *gadget*
contraption, contrivance, doodad*, gismo, object, thing, thingamabob*, thingamajig*, whatchamacallit*, widget; SEE CONCEPTS 463,499

doom [n] *fate or decision, usually unpleasant*
annihilation, calamity, cataclysm, catastrophe, circumstance, conclusion, condemnation, death, decree, destination, destiny, destruction, disaster, downfall, end, fixed future, foreordination, fortune, handwriting on wall*, judgment, Judgment Day, karma, kismet, lap of the gods*, lot, Moira, opinion, portion, predestination, predetermination, ruin, sentence, tragedy, verdict, way the ball bounces*, way the cookie crumbles*; SEE CONCEPT 679

doomed [adj] *condemned, hopeless*
bedeviled, bewitched, convicted, cursed, cut down, damned, dead duck*, destroyed, done,

done for*, fated, foreordained, ill-fated, ill-omened, in the cards*, kiss of death*, lost, luckless, menaced, overthrown, overwhelmed, predestined, que sera sera*, reprobate, ruined, sentenced, star-crossed, sunk, suppressed, threatened, thrown down, undone, unfortunate, unredeemed, wrecked; SEE CONCEPT 537

doomsayer [n] *alarmist*
Chicken Little, doom merchant, pessimist, scaremonger; SEE CONCEPTS 412,423

door [n] *entrance to room, building*
aperture, egress, entry, entryway, exit, gate, gateway, hatch, hatchway, ingress, opening, portal, postern, slammer; SEE CONCEPT 440

doorbell [n] *chime*
buzzer, door knocker, ringer; SEE CONCEPTS 74,284,529,685

do-out of [v] *cheat*
balk, beat out of*, bilk, con, deceive, deprive, steal, swindle, trick; SEE CONCEPTS 59,139

doozy [n] *winner*
beauty, humdinger*, killer*, lulu*, smash hit, something; SEE CONCEPTS 366,416

dope [n1] *stupid person*
ass, blockhead*, dimwit*, dolt, donkey*, dunce, fool, idiot, lame-brain*, simpleton; SEE CONCEPTS 412,423

dope [n2] *drug*
narcotic, opiate, stimulant; SEE CONCEPT 307

dope [n3] *inside news*
account, details, developments, facts, info*, information, knowledge, lowdown*, tip*; SEE CONCEPT 274

dope [v] *drug someone*
adulterate, anesthetize, deaden, debase, inject, knock out*, load, narcotize, put to sleep, sedate, soak, sophisticate, stupefy; SEE CONCEPTS 156,310

dopey [adj] *stupid*
comatose, dense, dumb, foolish, heavy, hebetudinous, idiotic, lethargic, senseless, silly, simple, slow, sluggish, slumberish, thick, torpid; SEE CONCEPT 402

dormant [adj] *inactive; sleeping*
abeyant, asleep, closed down, comatose, down, fallow, hibernating, inert, inoperative, latent, lethargic, lurking, on the shelf*, out of action*, passive, potential, prepatent, quiescent, sidelined, slack, sluggish, slumbering, smoldering, suspended, torpid; SEE CONCEPT 539

dormitory [n] *living quarters*
bedroom, dorm, dorm room, sleeping quarters; SEE CONCEPT 448

dose [n] *portion of drug or other consumable*
application, dosage, dram, draught, fill, fix*, hit*, lot, measure, measurement, nip*, potion, prescription, quantity, share, shot*, slug*, spoonful; SEE CONCEPTS 307,835

dossier [n] *file*
archives, information, personal account, portfolio, profile, record, recorded information, report, summary; SEE CONCEPTS 271,281

dot [n] *tiny mark, drop*
atom, circle, dab, droplet, fleck, flyspeck, grain, iota, jot, mite, mote, particle, period, pinpoint, point, speck, spot, tittle; SEE CONCEPTS 284,831

dot [v] *make spot(s)*
bespeckle, dab, dabble, fleck, freckle, pepper, pimple, sprinkle, stipple, stud; SEE CONCEPTS 79,174

dotage [n] *feebleness, old age*
advanced age, decrepitude, elderliness, fatuity, imbecility, infirmity, second childhood*, senectitude, senility, weakness; SEE CONCEPTS 405,715

dote on/dote upon [v] *lavish affection on*
admire, adore, be fond of, be infatuated with, be sweet on*, cherish, enjoy, fancy, hold dear, idolize, like, love, pet, prize, treasure, worship; SEE CONCEPT 32

doting [adj] *indulgent; serving*
adoring, affectionate, devoted, fascinated, fatuous, fond, foolish, lovesick, lovesome, loving, silly, simple, struck; SEE CONCEPT 401

dotty [adj] *crazy*
absurd, daft, demented, disturbed, eccentric, foolish, goofy*, loony*, mentally unbalanced, nuts*, nutty, odd, peculiar, queer, ridiculous, strange, twisted, unconventional, weird; SEE CONCEPT 403

double [adj] *in a pair*
as much again, bifold, binary, binate, coupled, dual, dualistic, duple, duplex, duplicate, duplicated, geminate, paired, repeated, second, twice, twin, twofold, two times; SEE CONCEPT 771

double [n] *something which exactly resembles another*
angel, clone, companion, coordinate, copy, counterpart, dead ringer*, duplicate, image, impersonator, lookalike*, match, mate, picture, portrait, reciprocal, replica, ringer*, simulacrum, spitting image*, stand-in*, twin; SEE CONCEPTS 664,716

double [v] *make two of; make twice as large*
amplify, augment, dualize, dupe, duplicate, duplify, enlarge, fold, grow, increase, infold, loop, magnify, multiply, plait, pleat, plicate, redouble, repeat, replicate, supplement; SEE CONCEPTS 236,245

double back [v] *reverse path*
backtrack, circle, dodge, loop, retrace one's steps, return, turn; SEE CONCEPTS 224,232

double-cross [v] *betray*
beguile, bluff, cheat, con, cross, deceive, defraud, four-flush*, hoodwink*, humbug*, illude, juggle, mislead, sell, sell out*, split, swindle, take in, trick, two-time*; SEE CONCEPTS 7,19,59

double-dealing [adj] *cheating, deceitful*
ambidextrous, crooked, dishonest, double, duplicitous, fraudulent, hypocritical, insincere, left-handed*, lying, perfidious, sneaky, swindling, treacherous, tricky, two-faced*, two-timing*, underhanded, untrustworthy, wily; SEE CONCEPT 401

double-dealing [n] *betrayal, cheating*
bad faith, chicane, chicanery, deceit, deception, dishonesty, duplicity, foul play*, fourberie, fraud, hanky-panky*, hypocrisy, mendacity, perfidy, sharp practice*, treachery, trickery, two-timing*; SEE CONCEPT 59

double entendre [n] *play on words*
ambiguity, amphibiology, double meaning, equivocality, equivocation, equivoque, innuendo, joke, pun, tergiversation; SEE CONCEPTS 278,682

double standard [n] *contrasting principles*
contradictory standard, two sets of rules; SEE CONCEPTS 46,278,665

double-talk [n] *nonsense communicated*
amphibiology, balderdash, baloney*, bull*, dri-

do
do

vel, equivocation, flimflam*, gibberish, jazz*, mumbo jumbo*, rigmarole; SEE CONCEPT 278

doubt [n] *lack of faith, conviction; questioning*
agnosticism, ambiguity, apprehension, confusion, demurral, difficulty, diffidence, dilemma, disbelief, discredit, disquiet, distrust, dubiety, dubiousness, faithlessness, faltering, fear, hesitancy, hesitation, incertitude, incredulity, indecision, irresolution, lack of confidence, misgiving, mistrust, perplexity, problem, qualm, quandary, rejection, reluctance, scruple, skepticism, suspense, suspicion, uncertainty, vacillation, wavering; SEE CONCEPTS 21,410,689,690

doubt [v] *lack confidence in; question*
be apprehensive of, be curious, be dubious, be in a quandary, be puzzled, be uncertain, be undetermined, call in question, challenge, demur, disbelieve, discredit, dispute, distrust, fear, fluctuate, give no credence, harbor suspicion, have qualms, hesitate, imagine, impugn, insinuate, misdoubt, misgive, mistrust, not buy*, query, read differently, scruple, shilly-shally*, skepticize, smell a rat*, surmise, suspect, take dim view of, vacillate, waver, wonder at; SEE CONCEPT 21

doubter [n] *person who does not believe*
agnostic, cynic, disbeliever, headshaker*, questioner, skeptic, unbeliever, zetetic; SEE CONCEPTS 361,423

doubtful [adj] *questionable, unclear*
ambiguous, borderline, chancy, clouded, contingent, debatable, dicey, disreputable, doubtable, dubious, dubitable, equivocal, far-fetched, fat chance, fishy*, hazardous, hazy, iffy*, impugnable, inconclusive, indecisive, indefinite, indeterminate, indistinct, insecure, long shot*, obscure, on thin ice*, open, pending, precarious, problematic, shady, sneaky*, speculative, suspect, suspicious, touch-and-go*, touchy, uncertain, unconfirmed, undecided, uneasy, unsettled, unstable, unsure, up for grabs*; SEE CONCEPTS 529,535

doubtful [adj2] *not believing*
agnostic, baffled, confused, discomposed, disconcerted, distracted, distrustful, disturbed, doubting, dubious, equivocal, faithless, faltering, flustered, hesitant, hesitating, in a quandary, in clouds*, indecisive, in dilemma, irresolute, like doubting Thomas*, lost, not following, of two minds*, perplexed, puzzled, questioning, skeptical, suspicious, tentative, theoretical, troubled, uncertain, unconvinced, undecided, unresolved, unsettled, unsure, vacillating, wavering, without belief; SEE CONCEPTS 403,542

doubting Thomas [n] *skeptic*
disbeliever, doubter, questioner, unbeliever; SEE CONCEPTS 361,423

doubtless [adv] *certainly; most likely*
absolutely, apparently, assuredly, clearly, easily, for sure, indisputably, no ifs ands or buts*, of course, ostensibly, positively, precisely, presumably, probably, seemingly, supposedly, surely, truly, undoubtedly, unequivocally, unquestionably, without doubt; SEE CONCEPTS 535,552

dough [n] *money*
beans*, boodle*, bread*, bucks*, cabbage*, cash, change, chips, clams*, coin, coinage, cold cash, currency, dinero, funds, greenback*, hard cash*, legal tender, lettuce*, loot, moola, pesos*, wealth; SEE CONCEPT 340

doughnut [n] *sweet ring-shaped fried cake*
bun, cruller, danish, dunker*, pastry, sinker*, sweet roll; SEE CONCEPTS 457,461

do up [v] *physically prepare; fix*
clean, doctor, enclose, finish, gift-wrap, launder, mend, overhaul, package, patch, rebuild, recondition, reconstruct, repair, revamp, wash, wrap; SEE CONCEPTS 126,165,182,202

dour [adj] *gloomy, grim*
bleak, crabbed, dismal, dreary, forbidding, glum, hard, harsh, morose, saturnine, severe, sour, stringent, sulky, sullen, surly, ugly, unfriendly; SEE CONCEPTS 401,542

douse [v] *drench, extinguish with liquid*
blow out, deluge, drown, duck, dunk, immerse, plunge, put out, quench, saturate, slop, slosh, smother, snuff, snuff out, soak, sop, souse, spatter, splash, splatter, squench, steep, submerge, submerse, wet; SEE CONCEPTS 250,256

dovetail [v] *link, fit together*
accord, agree, check out, coincide, conform, correspond, go, harmonize, interlock, jibe, join, match, mortise, square, sync*, sync up*, tally, tenon, unite; SEE CONCEPTS 113,664

dowdy [adj] *poorly dressed; old-fashioned*
antiquated, archaic, baggy, bedraggled, blowsy*, bygone, dated, dingy, drab, dull, frowzy*, frumpy*, homely, moldy, old hat*, outdated, outmoded, out-of-date, passé, plain, run-down, scrubby*, shabby, slatternly, sloppy, slovenly, stodgy, tacky, tasteless, unfashionable, unkempt, unseemly, unstylish, untidy, vintage, wrinkled; SEE CONCEPT 589

do without [v] *get along without*
abstain from, dispense, endure, forgo, give up; SEE CONCEPTS 23,646

down [adj1/adv] *below; physically lower*
bottomward, cascading, declining, depressed, descending, downgrade, downhill, downward, dropping, earthward, falling, gravitating, groundward, inferior, nether, precipitating, sagging, sinking, sliding, slipping, slumping, subjacent, to the bottom, under, underneath; SEE CONCEPTS 583,586,735

down [adj2] *unhappy*
bad, blue*, cast down, chapfallen, crestfallen, dejected, depressed, disheartened, dispirited, downcast, downhearted, low, miserable, off, sad, slack, sluggish; SEE CONCEPT 403

down-and-out [adj] *poverty-stricken*
beaten, beggared, defeated, derelict, destitute, finished, impoverished, needy, outcast, penniless, ruined, vagabond, vagrant; SEE CONCEPT 334

downbeat [adj] *pessimistic*
cheerless, defeatist, dejected, dispirited, gloomy, hopeless, negative, unhappy, unhopeful; SEE CONCEPTS 403,548

downcast [adj] *depressed, unhappy*
bad, blue, brooding, bummed out*, cast down, chapfallen, cheerless, crestfallen, daunted, dejected, despondent, disappointed, disconsolate, discouraged, disheartened, dismayed, dispirited, distressed, doleful, down, downhearted, down in the dumps*, down-in-the-mouth*, dragged*, droopy, dull, forlorn, gloomy, glum, heartsick, in pain, listless, low, low-spirited, miserable, moody, mopey*, morose, oppressed, sad, shot down*, singing the blues*, sunk*, troubled, weighed down*, woebegone; SEE CONCEPT 403

downer [n] *depressing experience*
bad deal*, bad scene*, bad trip*, bummer*, drag*, misfortune, raw deal, rotten hand; SEE CONCEPTS *674,679*

downfall [n] *disgrace, ruin*
atrophy, bane, breakdown, cloudburst, collapse, comedown, comeuppance, debacle, decadence, declension, degeneracy, degeneration, deluge, descent, destruction, deterioration, devolution, discomfiture, down, drop, failure, fall, flood, on the rocks*, overthrow, rack and ruin*, road to ruin*, ruination, storm, the skids*, undoing; SEE CONCEPTS *674,679,699*

downgrade [n] *slope*
decline, declivity, descent, dip, hill, inclination, pitch; SEE CONCEPTS *509,738*

downgrade [v] *lower in opinion or rank*
abase, bench*, break*, bump*, bust*, declass, decrease, decry, degrade, demerit, demote, denigrate, depreciate, detract from, devalorize, devalue, disparage, disrate, humble, mark down, minimize, reduce, run down, set back, take down a peg*, undervalue, write off*; SEE CONCEPTS *7,19,54,240*

downhearted [adj] *depressed, unhappy*
blue*, chapfallen, crestfallen, dejected, despondent, disconsolate, discouraged, disheartened, dismayed, dispirited, down, downcast, low, low-spirited, sad, sorrowful, spiritless, woebegone; SEE CONCEPT *403*

downhill [adj] *descending*
declining, dipping, dropping, falling, sloping downward; SEE CONCEPTS *583,586,735*

downlink [n] *transmission path for data*
circuit, communications pathway, network, pathway, signal route; SEE CONCEPT *269*

download [v] *transfer data from one computer system to another*
boot up, compute, computerize, crunch numbers*, digitize, initialize, input, keyboard, key in, load, log in, log out, program, run; SEE CONCEPTS *211,217,223*

downplay [v] *minimize*
attach little importance to, deemphasize, devalue, give little weight to, lessen, make light of, play down, soften, think nothing of, whitewash; SEE CONCEPTS *54,240,247*

downpour [n] *tremendous pouring of rain*
cloudburst, deluge, drencher, flood, inundation, monsoon, rainstorm, storm, torrential rain; SEE CONCEPT *526*

downright [adj] *thorough, absolute*
blatant, blunt, categorical, certain, clear, complete, damned, explicit, flat, gross, honest, indubitable, open, out-and-out, outright, plain, positive, simple, sincere, straight, straightforward, sure, thoroughgoing, total, undisguised, unequivocal, unmitigated, unqualified, unquestionable, utter, whole; SEE CONCEPT *531*

downside [n] *a negative aspect of a situation*
defect, disadvantage, drawback, fault, flaw, inconvenience, minus, problem, trouble; SEE CONCEPTS *666,674*

downsize [v] *to decrease in size, especially of a workforce*
curtail, cut, cut back, cut down, decrease, deduct, diminish, phase down, phase out, reduce, retrench, roll back, roll down, scale back, scale down, shrink, step down, trim, trim away, tune down; SEE CONCEPTS *236,240,247*

downtime [n] *time during which an activity is stopped*
break, breathing spell, freedom, free time, halt, interim, interlude, intermission, letup, lull, pause, recess, repose, respite, rest, spare time, spell, stay, suspension, time on one's hands, time out, time to burn, time to kill; SEE CONCEPT *807*

down-to-earth [adj] *reasonable, practical*
common, commonsense, easy, hard, hardboiled, hardheaded, matter-of-fact, mundane, no-nonsense, plainspoken, pragmatic, rational, realistic, sane, sensible, sober, unfantastic, unidealistic, unsentimental; SEE CONCEPTS *402,558*

downtrodden [adj] *afflicted, abused*
abject, a slave to*, at one's beck and call*, at one's feet*, at one's mercy*, destitute, distressed, exploited, have-not, helpless, in one's clutches*, in one's pocket*, in one's power*, led by the nose*, maltreated, mistreated, needy, oppressed, overcome, persecuted, subjugated, subservient, suppressed, tyrannized, underdog*, underfoot*, under one's thumb*; SEE CONCEPT *542*

downturn [n] *drop*
decline, descent, deterioration, dip, downtick, fall, plunge, retreat, sinking, slide, slump; SEE CONCEPTS *336,346,738*

downy [adj] *fluffy*
featherlike, feathery, fleecy, fuzzy, light, plumate, plumose, pubescent, silky, soft, velutinous, velvety, woolly; SEE CONCEPTS *604,606*

doze [n] *light sleep*
catnap, drowse, forty winks*, nap, shut-eye*, siesta, slumber, snooze*; SEE CONCEPTS *315,681*

doze [v] *take a nap*
catch a wink*, catnap, cop some z's*, drift off*, drop off*, drowse, nod off*, sleep, sleep lightly, slumber, snooze; SEE CONCEPTS *315,681*

drab [adj] *dull, colorless*
arid, blah*, bleak, boring, brown, characterless, cheerless, desolate, dingy, dismal, dreary, dry, dull as dishwater*, faded, flat, gloomy, gray, grungy, lackluster, lusterless, muddy, murky, run-down, same, shabby, somber, subfuse, unchanging, uninspired, vapid, zero*; SEE CONCEPTS *536,617,618*

draconian [adj] *harsh*
brutal, cruel, drastic, exorbitant, extreme, heavy-handed, oppressive, rough, severe, strict, very severe; SEE CONCEPT *401*

draft [n1] *something formulated; plan*
abstract, blueprint, delineation, outline, preliminary form, rough sketch, version; SEE CONCEPTS *271,660*

draft [n2] *check for paying money*
bank draft, bill, bond, cheque, coupon, debenture, IOU, letter of credit, money order, order, promissory note, receipt, warrant; SEE CONCEPTS *332,344*

draft [n3] *gust of air*
breeze, current, eddy, puff, wind; SEE CONCEPT *437*

draft [n4] *military conscription*
allotment, assignment, call of duty, call-up*, greetings*, impressment, induction, letter from Uncle Sam*, levy, lottery, recruiting, registration, roll call*, selection, selective service; SEE CONCEPT *321*

do
dr

draft [n5] *drink of beverage*
drag*, drain, drench, glass, peg*, quaff, swallow, swig*, swill*; SEE CONCEPTS *169,454*

draft [v1] *formulate*
adumbrate, block out, characterize, compose, concoct, contrive, delineate, design, devise, draw, draw up, fabricate, fashion, forge, form, frame, invent, make, manufacture, outline, plan, prepare, project, rough, shape, skeleton, sketch; SEE CONCEPTS *36,79,173*

draft [v2] *select for military force*
call up, choose, conscribe, conscript, dragoon, enlist, enroll, impress, indite, induct, muster, press, recruit, sign on, sign up; SEE CONCEPTS *8,320*

drag [n1] *bad situation*
annoyance, bore, bother, burden, encumbrance, hang-up, hindrance, impediment, nuisance, pain, pest, pill, sway, trouble; SEE CONCEPT *674*

drag [n2] *a puff while smoking*
breathing, draw, inhalation, pull, smoke; SEE CONCEPT *185*

drag [v1] *haul something to a new place*
draw, hale, lug, magnetize, move, pull, schlepp*, tow, trail, transport, truck, tug, yank; SEE CONCEPTS *206,213*

drag [v2] *move very slowly*
be delayed, be quiescent, crawl, creep, dally*, dawdle*, delay, encounter difficulty*, hang*, inch*, lag, lag behind, limp along, linger, loiter, mark time*, poke*, procrastinate, put off*, sag, shamble, shuffle, slow down, stagnate, straggle, tarry, trail behind*, traipse; SEE CONCEPTS *151,681*

dragging [adj] *tiresome, monotonous*
boring, drawn-out, dull, going slowly, humdrum, lengthy, long, overlong, prolonged, protracted, tedious, wearisome; SEE CONCEPTS *482,798*

dragnet [n] *manhunt*
all points bulletin, chase, pursuit, search; SEE CONCEPT *207*

drag on/drag out [v] *extend time of action*
continue, draw out, endure, extend, go on slowly, keep going, lengthen, persist, prolong, protract, spin out, stretch out; SEE CONCEPT *239*

drag queen [n] *cross-dresser*
female impersonator, transvestite; SEE CONCEPT *412*

drain [n] *channel through which liquid runs off*
cesspool, cloaca, conduit, culvert, ditch, duct, outlet, pipe, sewer, sink, trench, watercourse; SEE CONCEPT *501*

drain [v1] *remove liquid; remove supply*
abate, bankrupt, bleed, bleed dry*, catheterize, consume, debilitate, decrease, deplete, devitalize, diminish, dissipate, divert, draft, draw off, drink up, dry, empty, evacuate, exhaust, expend, fatigue, filter off, finish, free from, get last drop*, get rid of, gulp down, impoverish, lessen, milk*, pump, pump out, quaff, reduce, sap, siphon, spend, strain, suck, suck dry*, swallow, tap, tax, tire out, use up, waste, wear, wear down, weary, withdraw; SEE CONCEPTS *142,211,225*

drain [v2] *seep, discharge liquid*
abate, decline, decrease, diminish, dwindle, effuse, exude, filter off, flow, flow out, leak, leave dry, ooze, osmose, percolate, reduce, run off, taper off, trickle, well; SEE CONCEPTS *179,698*

drained [adj] *used up; exhausted*
all in*, beat*, bleary, burned out*, dead, dead

tired*, depleted, dragging, effete, far-gone, hacked*, pooped*, spent, washed-out, weary, wiped-out*, worn-out; SEE CONCEPTS *485,560*

drama [n1] *theatrical piece; acting*
boards*, Broadway*, climax, comedy, dramatic art, dramatization, dramaturgy, farce, footlights, histrionic art, melodrama, play, production, scene, show, show business, showmanship, stagecraft, stage show, tear-jerker*, theater, theatricals, thespian art, tragedy, vehicle*; SEE CONCEPTS *263,271,293*

drama [n2] *turmoil in real life*
climax, comedy, crisis, dramatics, emotion, excitement, farce, histrionics, melodrama, scene, spectacle, tension, theatrics, tragedy; SEE CONCEPT *674*

dramatic [adj] *exciting, moving*
affecting, breathtaking, climactic, comic, effective, electrifying, emotional, expressive, farcical, histrionic, impressive, melodramatic, powerful, sensational, startling, striking, sudden, suspenseful, tense, theatrical, thespian, thrilling, tragic, vivid; SEE CONCEPTS *537,548*

dramatization [n] *drama*
dramatics, entertainment, melodrama; SEE CONCEPTS *263,271,293*

dramatize [v] *make a performance of*
act, amplify, burlesque, enact, exaggerate, execute, farcialize, give color to, ham it up*, lay it on*, make a production of, melodramatize, overdo, overstate, perform, playact, play on heartstrings*, play to gallery, play up, present, produce, show, splash, stage, tragedize; SEE CONCEPTS *49,59,292*

drape [v] *hang over, adorn*
array, cloak, clothe, cover, dangle, display, don, dress, droop, drop, enclose, enswathe, envelop, enwrap, fold, hang, lean over, let fall, line, model, roll, sprawl, spread, spread-eagle, suspend, swathe, wrap; SEE CONCEPT *172*

drastic [adj] *severe, extreme*
desperate, dire, exorbitant, extravagant, forceful, harsh, immoderate, radical, strong; SEE CONCEPTS *537,569*

draw [n] *tie in competition*
dead end*, dead heat*, deadlock, even steven*, photo finish*, stalemate, standoff, tie; SEE CONCEPT *706*

draw [v1] *move something by pulling*
attract, bring, carry, convey, cull, draft, drag, drain, educe, elicit, evoke, extract, fetch, gather, haul, hook, jerk, lug, magnetize, pick, pluck, pump, rake, siphon, tap, tow, trail, trawl, tug, wind in, wrench, yank; SEE CONCEPT *206*

draw [v2] *create a likeness in a picture*
caricature, chart, compose, crayon, delineate, depict, describe, design, draft, engrave, etch, express, form, formulate, frame, graph, limn, map out, mark, model, outline, paint, pencil, portray, prepare, profile, sketch, trace, write; SEE CONCEPTS *79,174*

draw [v3] *deduce*
collect, conclude, derive, gather, get, infer, judge, make, make out, take; SEE CONCEPT *15*

draw [v4] *allure, influence*
argue into, attract, bewitch, bring around, bring forth, call forth, captivate, charm, convince, elicit, enchant, engage, entice, evoke, fascinate, get, induce, invite, lure, magnetize, persuade,

prompt, take, wile, win over; SEE CONCEPTS 7,19,22,68

draw [v5] *take out, extend*
attenuate, choose, drain, elongate, extort, extract, lengthen, pick, pull out, respire, select, single out, stretch, suck, take; SEE CONCEPTS *142,163,* *239*

drawback [n] *disadvantage*
check, defect, deficiency, detriment, difficulty, disability, evil, failing, fault, flaw, fly in the ointment*, handicap, hindrance, hitch, ill, impediment, imperfection, inconvenience, lack, nuisance, obstacle, shortcoming, snag, stumbling block*, trouble, weakness; SEE CONCEPTS *666,674*

draw back [v] *retract from position*
deduct, discount, pull back, recede, recoil, reel in, retreat, sheathe, shrink, start back, subtract, take away, withdraw; SEE CONCEPTS *195,213*

drawing [n] *illustration*
cartoon, commercial art, comp, delineation, depiction, design, doodle, etching, graphics, layout, likeness, outline, painting, picture, portrayal, representation, sketch, storyboard, study, tracing, work of art; SEE CONCEPT *625*

drawl [v] *lengthen, draw out*
chant, drag out, drone, extend, intone, nasalize, prolong, pronounce slowly, protract, utter; SEE CONCEPTS *77,239*

drawn [adj] *tense, fatigued*
fraught, haggard, harassed, harrowed, peaked, pinched, sapped, starved, strained, stressed, taut, thin, tired, worn; SEE CONCEPT *485*

draw on [v] *use to advantage*
effect, employ, exploit, extract, fall back on, have recourse to, make use of, rely on, require, take from; SEE CONCEPT *225*

draw out [v] *prolong*
attract, continue, drag, drag out, elongate, extend, lead on, lengthen, make longer, prolongate, protract, pull, spin, spin out*, stretch, string out*, tug; SEE CONCEPTS *236,239,245*

draw up [v] *draft document*
compose, formulate, frame, indite, make, prepare, write, write out; SEE CONCEPT *79*

dread [adj] *horrible, terrifying*
alarming, awe-inspiring, awful, creepy*, dire, frightening, frightful, shuddersome, terrible; SEE CONCEPT *537*

dread [n] *fear*
affright, alarm, apprehension, aversion, awe, cold feet*, consternation, creeps*, dismay, fright, funk*, goose bumps*, horror, jitters, panic, phobia, stage fright, terror, trepidation, trepidity, worriment; SEE CONCEPT *27*

dread [v] *anticipate with horror*
apprehend, be afraid, cringe, fear, have cold feet*, misdoubt, quake, shrink from, shudder, tremble; SEE CONCEPT *27*

dreadful [adj] *horrible, frightening*
abominable, alarming, appalling, atrocious, awful, bad, beastly, creepy*, dire, distressing, fearful, formidable, frightful, frozen, ghastly, godawful*, grievous, grim, grody*, gross*, hideous, horrendous, horrific, icky*, lousy, mean, monstrous, rotten, shameful, shocking, shuddersome, spooky, terrible, terrific, tragic, tremendous, wicked; SEE CONCEPTS *537,550*

dream [n1] *illusion, vision*
bubble*, castle in the air*, chimera, daydream, delusion, fancy, fantasy, hallucination, head trip*, idea, image, imagination, impression, incubus, mental picture, nightmare, pie in the sky*, pipe dream*, rainbow, reverie, specter, speculation, thought, trance, vagary, wraith; SEE CONCEPT *529*

dream [n2] *goal*
ambition, aspiration, design, desire, flight of fancy*, hope, notion, pipe dream*, wish; SEE CONCEPT *659*

dream [v] *conjure up scenario*
be delirious, be moonstruck, be up in clouds*, brainstorm, build castles in air*, conceive, concoct, cook up*, crave, create, daydream, devise, envisage, fancy, fantasize, formulate, hallucinate, hanker*, hatch*, have a flash*, have a nightmare*, have a notion*, have a vision, hunger, idealize, imagine, invent, long, lust, make up, picture, pine, search for pot of gold*, sigh, stargaze*, sublimate, think, think up, thirst, visualize; SEE CONCEPTS *17,529*

dreamer [n] *visionary*
daydreamer, escapist, fantasizer, idealist, romantic, star-gazer, theorizer, Walter Mitty*; SEE CONCEPTS *361,416*

dream up [v] *concoct plan*
contrive, cook up*, create, devise, frame, hatch*, imagine, invent, make up, spin*, think up; SEE CONCEPTS *17,36*

dreamy [adj] *illusory, romantic*
abstracted, astral, calming, chimerical, daydreaming, excellent, fanciful, fantastic, gentle, idealistic, imaginary, immaterial, impractical, intangible, introspective, introvertive, lulling, marvelous, misty, musing, mythical, nightmarish, otherworldly, out of this world*, pensive, phantasmagoric, phantasmagorical, preoccupied, quixotic, relaxing, shadowy, soothing, speculative, unreal, unsubstantial, utopian, vague, visionary, whimsical; SEE CONCEPT *582*

dreary [adj] *gloomy, lifeless*
black, blah, bleak, boring, cheerless, colorless, comfortless, damp, depressing, depressive, dingy, dismal, dispiriting, doleful, downcast, drab, dull, forlorn, funereal, glum, humdrum, joyless, lonely, lonesome, melancholy, monotonous, mournful, oppressive, pedestrian, raw, routine, sad, somber, sorrowful, tedious, uneventful, uninteresting, wearisome, windy, wintry, wretched; SEE CONCEPTS *525,544*

dredge [v] *deepen*
bring up, clean, dig up, raise, unearth, widen; SEE CONCEPT *178*

dregs [n1] *sediment*
deposits, dirt, draff, lees, residue, settlings, slag, waste; SEE CONCEPT *260*

dregs [n2] *bad person*
loser, outcast, rabble, riffraff, scum, trash; SEE CONCEPT *412*

drench [v] *wet thoroughly*
deluge, dip, douse, drown, duck, dunk, flood, imbrue, immerse, impregnate, inundate, pour, saturate, seethe, soak, sodden, sop, souse, steep, submerge, teem; SEE CONCEPT *256*

dress [n] *clothing; woman's garment*
accouterment, apparel, attire, attirement, civvies*, costume, covering, drape, dry goods, duds*, ensemble, evening clothes, frock, garb, gear, gown, guise, habiliment, habit, muumuu, outfit, raiment, robe, shift, skirt, smock, suit,

dr
dr

Sunday best*, things*, threads*, tog, toga, toggery, trappings, uniform, vestment, wardrobe; SEE CONCEPT *451*

dress [*v1*] *put on clothing*
adorn, apparel, array, attire, bedeck, bundle up, change, clad, clothe, costume, cover, deck, decorate, don, drape, embellish, fit out, furbish, garb, ornament, outfit, primp, put on, raiment, rig, robe, slip into, slip on, spruce up, suit up, trim, turn out, wear; SEE CONCEPT *167*

dress [*v2*] *physically prepare; groom*
adjust, align, arrange, comb, decorate, dispose, do up, fit, make ready, ornament, set, straighten, trim; SEE CONCEPT *202*

dress [*v3*] *cover a wound*
attend, bandage, bind, cauterize, cleanse, give first aid, heal, plaster, sew up, sterilize, treat; SEE CONCEPTS *172,310*

dress down [*v*] *scold*
bawl out, berate, carpet, castigate, censure, chew out*, lash, rail, rake over coals*, ream, rebuke, reprimand, reprove, tear into*, tell off*, tonguelash*, upbraid; SEE CONCEPT *52*

dresser [*n*] *chest of drawers*
bureau, cabinet, chiffonier, closet, highboy, wardrobe; SEE CONCEPT *443*

dressing-down [*n*] *severe scolding*
bawling-out, castigation, chiding, lambasting, reprimand, reproach, tongue-lashing, upbraiding; SEE CONCEPTS *123,278*

dress up [*v*] *put on one's best clothes*
array, attire, beautify, clothe, deck out*, embellish, fit out*, fix up, gussy up*, improve, overdress, preen, prettify, primp, prink, slick, smarten, spiff up*, spruce up*, titivate; SEE CONCEPT *167*

dressy [*adj*] *formal, fashionable*
chic, classy, dressed to kill*, dressed to the nines*, dressed up*, elaborate, elegant, fancy, in high feather*, looking sharp, ornate, ritzy, smart, stylish; SEE CONCEPTS *579,589*

dribble [*v*] *trickle*
distill, drip, drivel, drizzle, drool, drop, fall in drops, leak, ooze, run, salivate, seep, slaver, slobber, spout, squirt, trill, weep; SEE CONCEPTS *179,185*

drift [*n1*] *accumulation*
alluvion, bank, batch, bunch, bundle, clump, cluster, deposit, heap, hill, lot, mass, mound, mountain, parcel, pile, set, shock, stack; SEE CONCEPTS *432,524*

drift [*n2*] *meaning, significance of communication*
aim, design, direction, end, gist, implication, import, intention, object, progress, progression, purport, scope, significance, tendency, tenor; SEE CONCEPT *682*

drift [*v*] *move aimlessly*
accumulate, aim, amass, amble, be carried along, coast, dance, draw near, flicker, flit, flitter, float, flow, flutter, gad*, gallivant*, gather, go-that-a-way*, go with the tide*, gravitate, hover, kick around*, linger, malinger, meander, mosey*, muck*, ride, sail, saunter, scud, skim, slide, stray, stroll, tend, waft, wander, wash*; SEE CONCEPT *147*

drifter [*n*] *wanderer*
derelict, hobo, itinerant, nomad, rolling stone, tramp, transient, vagabond, vagrant; SEE CONCEPTS *412,423*

drill [*n1*] *practice, exercise*
assignment, call, conditioning, constitutional, daily dozen*, discipline, dress, drilling, dry run*, gym, homework, instruction, learning by doing, maneuvers, marching, preparation, repetition, run-through*, shakedown*, training, tryout, warm-up, workout; SEE CONCEPTS *87,290*

drill [*n2*] *tool for boring*
auger, awl, bit, borer, corkscrew, countersink, dibble, gimlet, implement, jackhammer, punch, riveter, rotary tool, trepan, trephine, wimble; SEE CONCEPT *499*

drill [*v1*] *train, discipline*
accustom, break, break in, exercise, get into shape, habituate, hone, instruct, lick into shape, practice, rehearse, teach, tune up, walk through, work out; SEE CONCEPTS *117,285*

drill [*v2*] *bore hole*
dig, penetrate, perforate, pierce, prick, punch, puncture, sink in; SEE CONCEPT *220*

drink [*n*] *beverage; alcoholic beverage*
alcohol, booze*, brew, cup, draft, glass, gulp, libation, liquid, liquor, potable, potation, potion, refreshment, shot, sip, slug*, spirits, spot*, swallow, swig, taste, thirst quencher*, toast; SEE CONCEPT *454*

drink [*v*] *take in liquid*
absorb, belt*, booze*, consume, dissipate, down, drain, gargle, gulp, guzzle*, hit the bottle*, imbibe, indulge, inhale, irrigate, lap*, liquor up*, nip*, partake of, put away, quaff, sip, slosh, slurp, soak up, sop, sponge, suck, sup, swallow, swig, swill, tank up*, thirst, tipple*, toast, toss off*, wash down*, wet whistle*; SEE CONCEPT *169*

drip [*v*] *drop, trickle*
dribble, drizzle, exude, filter, plop, rain, splash, sprinkle, trill, weep; SEE CONCEPT *181*

drive [*n1*] *journey by vehicle*
airing, commute, excursion, expedition, hitch, jaunt, joyride, lift, outing, pickup, ramble, ride, run, spin, Sunday drive*, tour, trip, turn, whirl; SEE CONCEPT *224*

drive [*n2*] *campaign for cause*
action, advance, appeal, crusade, effort, enterprise, get-up-and-go*, initiative, push, surge; SEE CONCEPTS *87,300*

drive [*n3*] *person's will to achieve*
ambition, clout, effort, energy, enterprise, fire in belly*, get-up-and-go, goods*, gumption*, guts*, impellent, impetus, impulse, initiative, momentum, motivation, motive, moxie*, pep, pressure, punch*, push*, right stuff*, spunk*, steam*, stuff*, vigor, vitality, what it takes*, zip*; SEE CONCEPTS *411,706*

drive [*v1*] *move or urge on*
actuate, act upon, animate, arouse, bulldoze*, chase, coerce, compel, constrain, dog*, egg on*, encourage, force, goad, goose*, harass, hasten, herd, hound*, hurl, hurry, hustle, impel, induce, inspire, instigate, kick, lean on*, make, motivate, nag, oblige, overburden, overwork, pound, press, pressure, prod, prompt, propel, provoke, push, put up to*, railroad*, ride herd on*, rouse, rush, send, shepherd, shove, spirit up, spur, steamroll*, stimulate, work on, worry; SEE CONCEPTS *68,147,208*

drive [*v2*] *moving, controlling a vehicle*
actuate, advance, bear down, bicycle, bike, burn rubber*, burn up the road*, coast, cruise, cycle,

dash, direct, drag, fire up*, floor it*, fly, guide, handle, impel, lean on it*, make sparks fly*, manage, mobilize, motor, operate, pour it on*, propel, push, ride, roll, run, send, speed, spin, start, steer, step on it*, step on the gas*, tailgate, tool*, transport, travel, turn, vehiculate*, wheel; SEE CONCEPTS 148,187

drive [v3] *hit with heavy blow*
batter, beat, butt, dash, dig, hammer, jackhammer, knock, maul, plunge, pop, punch, ram, run, shoot, sink, smite, sock, stab, stick, strike, throw, thrust, thump, twack*, whack*, wham*; SEE CONCEPT 189

drive at [v] *mean, suggest as meaning*
aim, allude to, contemplate, design, get at, have in mind, hint at, imply, indicate, intend, intimate, propose, refer to, signify; SEE CONCEPTS 73,682

drivel [n] *foolish talk*
babble, balderdash*, blather, bunk*, double-talk, gibberish, gobbledygook*, Greek*, hogwash*, hooey*, jabber*, nonsense, poppycock*, prating, rot*, rubbish*, tripe*, twaddle*; SEE CONCEPT 278

drivel [v1] *talk foolishly*
babble, blabber, blather*, blethe, gab, gabble, prate, prattle, ramble, twaddle*, waffle*; SEE CONCEPT 266

drivel [v2] *drool*
dribble, salivate, slaver, slobber; SEE CONCEPTS 185,256

driver [n] *person who engineers vehicle*
autoist, automobilist, cabbie, chauffeur, coach person, hack*, handler, jockey, leadfoot*, motorist, operator, road hog*, trainer, whip*; SEE CONCEPT 423

driving [adj] *forceful*
active, compelling, dynamic, energetic, enterprising, galvanic, impellent, lively, propulsive, sweeping, urging, vigorous, violent; SEE CONCEPT 540

drizzle [v] *fine rain*
dribble, drip, drop, mist, mizzle, shower, spit, spray, sprinkle; SEE CONCEPT 526

droid [n] *robot*
android, clone, cyborg, drone; SEE CONCEPT 463

droll [adj] *amusing, farcical*
absurd, camp, campy, clownish, comic, comical, crack-up, diverting, eccentric, entertaining, for grins*, funny, gagged up*, gelastic, humorous, jocular, joshing, laffer, laughable, ludicrous, odd, preposterous, quaint, queer, quizzical, ridiculous, riot, risible, waggish, whimsical; SEE CONCEPTS 267,548

drone [n1] *person who is lazy*
idler, leech, loafer, lounger, parasite, slug, sluggard, sponger*; SEE CONCEPT 412

drone [n2] *continuous noise*
buzz, hum, murmur, purr, sound, vibration, whirr; SEE CONCEPT 595

drone [v] *making noise continuously*
bombinate, buzz, chant, drawl, hum, intone, nasalize, purr, sound, strum, thrum, vibrate, whirr; SEE CONCEPTS 65,77

drool [n] *saliva*
drivel, expectoration, salivation, slaver, slobber, spit, spittle; SEE CONCEPT 467

drool [v1] *drivel*
dribble, lick one's chops*, salivate, slaver, slobber, water at the mouth; SEE CONCEPT 467

drool [v1] *salivate*
dribble, drivel, froth, ooze, run, slabber, slaver, slobber, spit, water, water at the mouth; SEE CONCEPTS 185,256

drool [v2] *desire, lust after*
dote on, enthuse, fondle, gush, lick chops*, make much of, pet, rave, rhapsodize, rhapsody, slobber over*, spoil, want; SEE CONCEPT 20

droop [v] *hang down; languish*
bend, dangle, decline, depress, diminish, drop, fade, fail, faint, fall down, flag, lean, let down, loll, lop, sag, settle, sink, sling, slouch, slump, subside, suspend, weaken, wilt, wither; SEE CONCEPTS 181,699

droopy [adj] *limp*
bent, drooping, flabby, floppy, languid, languorous, lassitudinous, pendulous, sagging, saggy, slouchy, stooped, wilting; SEE CONCEPT 485

drop [n1] *globule*
bead, bit, bubble, crumb, dab, dash, dewdrop, driblet, drip, droplet, iota, molecule, morsel, nip, ounce, particle, pearl, pinch, sip, smidgen, speck, splash, spot, taste, tear, teardrop, trace, trickle; SEE CONCEPTS 467,468,831,835

drop [n2] *steep decline; hole*
abyss, chasm, declivity, deepness, depth, descent, dip, fall, plunge, precipice, slope, tumble; SEE CONCEPTS 181,509

drop [n3] *decrease*
cut, decline, descent, deterioration, dip, downfall, downslide, downswing, downtrend, downturn, fall, fall-off, landslide, lapse, lowering, precipitation, reduction, sag, slide, slip, slump, tumble, upset; SEE CONCEPTS 698,776

drop [v1] *fall in globules*
bead, bleed, descend, distill, drain, dribble, drip, emanate, hail, leak, ooze, percolate, precipitate, seep, snow, splash, trickle, trill; SEE CONCEPT 179

drop [v2] *let go of; fall*
abandon, bring down, cave in, collapse, decline, depress, descend, dive, duck, dump, fell, floor, flop, give up, go down, ground, keel over*, knock, loosen, lower, nose-dive*, pitch, plummet, plump, plunge, release, relinquish, shed, shoot, sink, slide, slip, slump, topple, tumble, unload; SEE CONCEPTS 181,200

drop [v3] *abandon; ignore*
abort, adios*, be alienated from, break with, call off, cancel, cast off, cease, desert, discontinue, dismiss, disown, ditch*, divorce, dust off*, eighty-six*, end, forfeit, forget about, forsake, give up, have done with*, interrupt, jilt, kick*, leave, lose, part from, part with, quit, reject, relinquish, remit, renounce, repudiate, resign, sacrifice, scratch*, scrub*, separate, shake, stop, terminate, throw over, wash out*, waste one*, wipe out*, write off*; SEE CONCEPTS 30,121,195

drop in [v] *visit*
blow in*, call, call upon, come by, come over, go and see*, look in on, look up, pop in*, run in*, stop, stop by, stop in, turn up; SEE CONCEPT 227

drop in the bucket [n] *small amount*
bit, drop in the ocean*, not enough, pittance, small change*, small potatoes*, small quantity, speck, trivial amount; SEE CONCEPT 831

drop off [v1] *decrease*
decline, diminish, dwindle, fall away, fall off,

dr
dr

lessen, sag, slacken, slide, slip, slump; SEE CONCEPTS 698,776

drop off [*v2*] *deliver*
deposit, give, hand over, leave, let off, present, set down, unload; SEE CONCEPT 108

drop off [*v3*] *fall asleep*
catnap, doze, doze off*, drowse, have forty winks*, nod, nod off*, snooze; SEE CONCEPTS 210,315

drop out [*v*] *stop doing an activity*
abandon, back out, cease, forsake, give notice, give up, leave, quit, renege, retreat, withdraw; SEE CONCEPT 121

droppings [*n*] *excrement*
cow pies*, cowplop*, crap, dung, feces, fertilizer, guano, manure, meadow muffin*, night soil*, ordure, poop*; SEE CONCEPT 260

drought [*n*] *dryness; shortage of supply*
aridity, dearth, deficiency, dehydration, desiccation, dry spell, insufficiency, lack, need, parchedness, rainlessness, scarcity, want; SEE CONCEPTS 607,646

drove [*n*] *large gathering*
collection, company, crowd, crush, drive, flock, herd, horde, mob, multitude, pack, press, rout, run, swarm, throng; SEE CONCEPTS 397,432

drown [*v*] *submerge in liquid; submerge and die*
asphyxiate, deluge, dip, douse, drench, engulf, flood, go down, go under, immerse, inundate, knock over, obliterate, overcome, overflow, overpower, overwhelm, plunge, prostrate, sink, soak, sop, souse, stifle, suffocate, swamp, whelm, wipe out; SEE CONCEPTS 252,256

drowsy [*adj*] *sleepy*
comatose, dazed, dopy, dozing, dozy, dreamy, drugged, half asleep, heavy, indolent, lackadaisical, languid, lazy, lethargic, lulling, napping, nodding, out of it*, restful, sluggish, slumberous, snoozy, somnolent, soothing, soporific, tired, torpid; SEE CONCEPTS 406,539

drub [*v*] *thrash*
beat, cane, clobber, defeat, flog, hit, lash, pound, spank, strike, tan, trounce, wallop, whip; SEE CONCEPT 95

drudge [*n*] *slave, very hard worker*
factotum, grind*, laborer, menial, nose to grindstone*, peon*, plodder*, servant, toiler, workaholic, worker, workhorse; SEE CONCEPT 348

drudge [*v*] *work very hard*
back to the salt mines*, dig, grind*, hammer*, keep nose to grindstone*, labor, muck*, perform, plod, plow, plug away*, pound*, schlepp*, slave, slog, sweat, toil, travail; SEE CONCEPTS 87,100,324

drudgery [*n*] *hard, tedious work*
backbreaker*, chore, daily grind*, elbow grease*, grind*, gruntwork*, labor, menial labor, rat race, slavery, struggle, sweat, toil, travail, workout; SEE CONCEPT 362

drug [*n*] *medication*
biologic, cure, depressant, dope, essence, medicament, medicinal, medicine, narcotic, opiate, pharmaceutic, pharmaceutical, physic, pill, poison, potion, prescription, remedy, sedative, stimulant, tonic; SEE CONCEPT 307

drug [*v*] *put under influence of medication*
analgize, anesthetize, benumb, blunt, deaden, desensitize, dope*, dope up, dose, dose up*, fix, hit, knock out*, medicate, narcotize, numb, poison, relax, sedate, stupefy, treat; SEE CONCEPT 310

drugged [*adj*] *under the influence of medication*
benumbed, blown away*, coked*, comatose, dazed, doped, dopey*, floating*, flying*, high*, junked-up*, loaded*, narcotized, on a trip*, out of it*, ripped*, smashed*, spaced-out*, stoned*, strung out*, stupefied, unconscious; SEE CONCEPT 314

druggist [*n*] *pharmacist*
apothecary, pharmacologist, posologist; SEE CONCEPT 357

drum [*v*] *beat, tap a beat*
boom*, pulsate, rap, reverberate, roar, strum, tattoo, throb, thrum, thunder*; SEE CONCEPTS 65,189

drum into [*v*] *make a point strongly*
din into, drive home*, hammer away*, harp on*, instill, reiterate; SEE CONCEPTS 49,75

drum up [*v*] *gather support for something*
attract, bid for, canvass, discover, obtain, petition, round up, solicit, succeed in finding; SEE CONCEPTS 68,300

drunk [*adj*] *intoxicated by alcohol*
bashed, befuddled, boozed up*, buzzed*, crocked*, feeling no pain*, flushed*, flying*, fuddled, glazed*, groggy, high*, inebriated, juiced*, laced*, liquored up*, lit*, lush, muddled, plastered*, potted*, seeing double*, sloshed*, stewed*, stoned*, tanked*, three sheets to the wind*, tight*, tipsy, totaled*, under the influence, under the table*, wasted*; SEE CONCEPTS 314,545

drunk/drunkard [*n*] *person who is inebriated*
alcoholic, boozer*, carouser*, dipsomaniac, drinker, guzzler*, inebriate, lush*, sot*, sponge*, wino*; SEE CONCEPT 423

dry [*adj1*] *moistureless*
anhydrous, arid, athirst, baked, bald, bare, barren, dehydrated, depleted, desert, desiccant, desiccated, drained, dried-up, droughty, dusty, evaporated, exhausted, hard, impoverished, juiceless, not irrigated, parched, rainless, sapless, sapped, sear, shriveled, stale, thirsty, torrid, unmoistened, waterless; SEE CONCEPT 603

dry [*adj2*] *dull, uninteresting*
apathetic, blah, boring, bromidic, draggy, dreary, dull as dishwater*, dusty, ho hum*, impassive, inelaborate, insipid, matter-of-fact, modest, monotonous, naked, phlegmatic, plain, simple, tedious, tiresome, trite, weariful, wearisome; SEE CONCEPT 529

dry [*adj3*] *sarcastic, sharp-tongued*
acerbic, arcane, biting, caustic, cutting, cynical, deadpan, droll, harsh, humorous, ironical, keen, low-key, restrained, salty, sardonic, satirical, sharp, sly, sour, subtle, tart; SEE CONCEPT 267

dry [*v*] *take moisture out of*
anhydrate, bake, blot, concentrate, condense, dehumidify, dehydrate, deplete, desiccate, drain, empty, evaporate, exhaust, exsiccate, freeze-dry, harden, kiln, mummify, parch, scorch, sear, shrivel, soak up, sponge, stale, swab, torrefy, towel, wilt, wipe, wither, wizen; SEE CONCEPTS 250,469

dual [*adj*] *two-fold*
bifold, binal, binary, coupled, double, double-header, duple, duplex, duplicate, matched, paired, twin; SEE CONCEPTS 762,771

dub [v] *name, label something*
baptize, bestow, call, christen, confer, denominate, designate, entitle, knight, nickname, style, tag, term, title; SEE CONCEPT 62

dubious [adj1] *doubtful*
arguable, chancy, debatable, diffident, disputable, dubitable, equivocal, far-fetched, fishy*, fly-by-night*, hesitant, iffy*, improbable, indecisive, moot, mootable, open, perplexed, problematic, questionable, reluctant, shady, skeptical, suspect, suspicious, touch and go*, trustless, unassured, uncertain, unclear, unconvinced, undecided, undependable, unlikely, unreliable, unsure, untrustworthy, untrusty, wavering; SEE CONCEPT 552

dubious [adj2] *vague, unclear*
ambiguous, debatable, disinclined, doubtful, equivocal, indefinite, indeterminate, mistrustful, obscure, open, problematic, problematical, undecided, unsettled; SEE CONCEPTS 535,576

duck [v] *drop down; avoid*
bend, bob, bow, crouch, dip, dive, dodge, double, elude, escape, evade, fence, lower, lurch, move to side, parry, plunge, shirk, shun, shy, sidestep, stoop, submerge; SEE CONCEPTS 102,154,181

duck soup [n] *easily accomplished task*
a breeze, a snap, cakewalk, child's play, easy thing, easy to do, piece of cake; SEE CONCEPT 693

duct [n] *channel, pipe*
aqueduct, canal, conduit, course, funnel, passage, tube, vessel, watercourse; SEE CONCEPT 501

ductile [adj] *pliant, flexible*
adaptable, amenable, biddable, docile, extensile, malleable, manageable, moldable, plastic, pliable, responsive, submitting, supple, tractable, yielding; SEE CONCEPTS 488,490

dud [n] *failure*
bomb, bummer, bust, debacle, flop, lemon, loser, washout; SEE CONCEPT 674

dude [n1] *friend*
buddy, chap, fellow, guy; SEE CONCEPT 423

dude [n2] *dapper man*
Beau Brummel*, coxcomb, dandy, fancy Dan*, fashion plate, fine gentleman, fop, slicker*, stud; SEE CONCEPT 423

duds [n] *clothes*
accouterment, apparel, array, civvies*, costume, covering, dress, finery, frippery, frock, garb, garments, habiliment, outfit, rags*, raiment, sportswear, Sunday best*, tatters*, threads*, wardrobe; SEE CONCEPT 451

due [adj1] *unpaid; owing money*
chargeable, collectible, expected, in arrears, IOU, mature, not met, outstanding, overdue, owed, payable, receivable, scheduled, to be paid, unliquidated, unsatisfied, unsettled; SEE CONCEPT 334

due [adj2] *appropriate, proper*
becoming, coming, condign, deserved, earned, equitable, fair, fit, fitting, good, just, justified, merited, obligatory, requisite, rhadamanthine, right, rightful, suitable; SEE CONCEPT 558

due [adv] *directly*
dead, direct, exactly, right, straight, straightly, undeviatingly; SEE CONCEPTS 581,799

due [n] *expected reward*
be in line for*, claim, comeuppance, compensation, deserts*, entitlement, guerdon, interest,

merits, need, payment, perquisite, prerogative, privilege, rate, recompense, repayment, reprisal, retaliation, retribution, revenge, right, rights, satisfaction, title, vengeance, what is coming to one*; SEE CONCEPTS 337,710

duel [n] *fight*
affair of honor, bout, challenge, engagement, fencing, joust, shootout, single combat, sword fight; SEE CONCEPTS 53,532

dues [n] *payment for membership*
ante, arrearage, assessment, charge, charges, collection, contribution, custom, debit, debt, duty, fee, kickback, levy, liability, obligation, pay, protection, rates, tax, toll; SEE CONCEPTS 344,679

duff [n] *rear end*
ass, backside, behind, buns*, butt*, buttocks, cheeks*, derriere, fanny*, gluteus maximus, heinie*, keister, posterior, seat*; SEE CONCEPT 392

dulcet [adj] *melodious*
agreeable, musical, pleasing to the ear, pleasurable, sweet, sweet-sounding; SEE CONCEPT 594

dull [adj1] *unintelligent*
addled, backward, besotted, boring, brainless, daffy, daft, dense, dim, dim-witted, doltish, dumb, feeble-minded, half-baked, ignorant, imbecilic, indolent, insensate, low, moronic, not bright, numskulled, obtuse, scatterbrained, shallow, simple, simple-minded, slow, sluggish, stolid, stupid, tedious, thick, unintellectual, vacuous, wearisome, witless; SEE CONCEPT 402

dull [adj2] *insensitive*
accustomed, apathetic, blank, boring, callous, colorless, dead, depressed, empty, even, flat, heavy, impassible, inactive, indifferent, inert, insensible, jejune, languid, lifeless, listless, lumpy, monotonous, passionless, placid, prosaic, quiet, regular, routine, slack, slow, sluggish, spiritless, stagnant, still, stolid, torpid, unexciting, unresponsive, unsympathetic, usual, vacuous; SEE CONCEPT 542

dull [adj3] *boring, uninteresting*
abused, archaic, arid, big yawn*, blah, colorless, common, commonplace, dead, dismal, dreary, driveling, dry, familiar, flat, hackneyed, heavy, hoary, ho hum*, humdrum*, insipid, jejune, longwinded, monotonous, oft-repeated*, ordinary, out-of-date, plain, pointless, prolix, prosaic, prosy, repetitious, repetitive, routine, run-of-the-mill*, soporific, stale, stock, stupid, tame, tedious, tired, tiresome, trite, unimaginative, uninspiring, usual, usual thing, vapid, worn-out; SEE CONCEPTS 529,530

dull [adj4] *not sharp*
blunt, blunted, edentate, edgeless, flat, not keen, obtuse, pointless, round, square, toothless, turned, unpointed, unsharpened; SEE CONCEPT 486

dull [adj5] *uneventful*
accustomed, apathetic, blah, boring, dead, depressed, draggy*, even, falling off, flat, inactive, inert, languid, lifeless, listless, monotonous, placid, quiet, regular, routine, sitting tight*, slack, slothful, slow, sluggish, stagnant, still, stolid, tight, torpid, unexciting, unresponsive, usual, without incident, yawn; SEE CONCEPT 548

dull [adj6] *drab, lackluster in effect on senses*
ashen, black, blind, cloudy, cold, colorless, dark, dead, dim, dingy, dismal, dun, dusky, faded, feeble, flat, grimy, hazy, indistinct, leaden, lifeless,

dr
du

low, matte, mousy, muddy, muffled, murky, muted, obscure, opaque, overcast, plain, shadowy, sober, soft, softened, somber, sooty, subdued, subfusc, toned-down, unlit; SEE CONCEPTS *594,617*

dullard [*n*] *dolt*
airhead*, blockhead*, boob*, dimwit, dope*, dork*, dumbbell*, dunce, fool, idiot, imbecile, lamebrain*, lunkhead*, meathead*, nitwit, simpleton, stupid person; SEE CONCEPTS *412,423*

dullsville [*adj*] *boring*
blah*, dead*, deadsville, dragsville, hicksville, tedious; SEE CONCEPTS *529,548*

duly [*adv*] *accordingly, properly*
appropriately, at the proper time, befittingly, correctly, decorously, deservedly, on time, punctually, rightfully, suitably; SEE CONCEPTS *558,799*

dumb [*adj1*] *unable to speak*
at a loss for words*, inarticulate, incoherent, mousy*, mum, mute, quiet, silent, soundless, speechless, tongue-tied, uncommunicative, voiceless, wordless; SEE CONCEPT *593*

dumb [*adj2*] *stupid, unintelligent*
dense, dim-witted, doltish, dull, feebleminded, foolish, moronic, simple-minded, thick*; SEE CONCEPT *402*

dumbbell [*n*] *stupid person*
dodo*, dolt, dullard, dumbo*, dumdum*, dummy, dunce, idiot, ignoramus, moron, simpleton; SEE CONCEPTS *412,423*

dumbfound [*v*] *astound, confuse*
amaze, astonish, bewilder, blow away*, blow one's mind*, boggle, bowl over*, confound, flabbergast, knock over with feather*, nonplus, overwhelm, puzzle, stagger, startle, stun, surprise, take aback, throw, throw into a tizzy*; SEE CONCEPTS *16,42*

dumbfounded [*adj*] *astounded, confused*
agape, aghast, amazed, astonished, bamboozled*, beat, bewildered, blown away*, bowled over*, breathless, buffaloed*, confounded, dismayed, dumb, flabbergasted, floored, knocked, licked, nonplused, overcome, overwhelmed, puzzled, shocked, speechless, staggered, startled, stuck, stumped, stunned, surprised, taken aback, thrown, thunderstruck*; SEE CONCEPT *403*

dumbstruck [*adj*] *shocked*
amazed, astonished, astounded, blown away, dumbfounded, flabbergasted, jolted, rendered speechless, startled, stunned, stupefied; SEE CONCEPT *42*

dummy [*n1*] *mannequin*
copy, counterfeit, duplicate, figure, form, imitation, manikin, model, ringer*, sham*, stand-in, sub, substitute; SEE CONCEPTS *436,716*

dummy [*n2*] *stupid person*
blockhead*, dimwit*, dolt*, dullard*, dunce, fool, idiot, ignoramus, moron, numbskull, oaf, simpleton; SEE CONCEPTS *412,423*

dump [*n1*] *junkyard*
ash heap*, cesspool, depot, dumping ground, garbage lot, junk pile*, magazine, refuse heap, rubbish pile, swamp; SEE CONCEPTS *438,449,680*

dump [*n2*] *slummy establishment*
hole, hovel, joint*, mess*, pigpen*, pigsty*, shack, shanty, slum, sty; SEE CONCEPTS *449,673*

dump [*v*] *drop, throw away*
cast, chuck, clear out, deep-six*, deposit, discard, discharge, dispose of, ditch, drain, eject, empty, evacuate, expel, exude, fling, fling down,

get rid of, jettison, junk, leave, let fall, scrap, throw down, throw out, throw overboard*, tip, unload, unpack; SEE CONCEPTS *180,181*

dumps [*n*] *depression*
blahs*, blues*, bummer, cheerlessness, doldrums, dreariness, gloom, gloominess, low spirits, melancholy, sulks, the blues*, trouble, unhappiness, woefulness; SEE CONCEPT *410*

dumpy [*adj*] *short and stout*
chubby, chunky, fat, homely, plump, podgy, pudgy, roly-poly, squat, stocky, stumpy, tubby; SEE CONCEPT *491*

dunce [*n*] *stupid person*
ass, birdbrain*, blockhead*, bonehead*, buffoon, dimwit*, dolt, donkey*, dope*, dork*, drip*, dullard, dunderhead*, fool, goof, goof ball*, half-wit, idiot, ignoramus, imbecile, jerk, knucklehead*, lame-brain*, lightweight*, moron, nerd*, nincompoop*, ninny*, nitwit, numskull, oaf, pinhead*, scatterbrain*, schnook*, simpleton, twit*; SEE CONCEPTS *412,423*

dune [*n*] *hill*
hillock, hummock, knoll, ridge, sand drift, sand dune, sand pile; SEE CONCEPT *509*

dung [*n*] *excrement*
cow pies*, cowplop*, crap, droppings, feces, fertilizer, guano, manure, meadow muffin*, night soil*, ordure, poop*; SEE CONCEPT *260*

dungarees [*n*] *blue jeans*
denims, jeans, pants, trousers; SEE CONCEPT *451*

dungeon [*n*] *prison*
cell, oubliette, torture chamber, vault; SEE CONCEPTS *439,449,516*

dunk [*v*] *dip in liquid*
douse, duck, immerse, saturate, soak, sop, souse, submerge, submerse; SEE CONCEPT *256*

duo [*n*] *twosome*
brace, couple, doublet, dyad, pair; SEE CONCEPT *787*

dupe [*n*] *person who is fooled*
butt*, chump*, easy mark*, fish*, fool, mark*, patsy*, pigeon*, pushover*, sap*, sitting duck*, sucker, victim; SEE CONCEPT *423*

dupe [*v*] *fool someone*
baffle, bamboozle*, beguile, betray, catch, cheat, chicane, circumvent, con, cozen, deceive, defraud, delude, double-cross, dust*, flimflam*, gull, hoax, hoodwink*, hornswoggle, jerk around*, kid, mislead, outwit, overreach, pull one's leg*, pull something*, rip off*, rook*, rope in*, shaft, spoof, swindle, trick, victimize; SEE CONCEPT *59*

duplex [*adj*] *twofold*
double, paired, twin; SEE CONCEPT *771*

duplicate [*adj*] *matching*
alike, corresponding, dualistic, duple, duplex, equal, equivalent, identic, identical, indistinguishable, same, self-same, tantamount, twin, twofold, very same; SEE CONCEPTS *563,566*

duplicate [*n*] *copy, reproduction*
analogue, carbon, carbon copy*, chip off the old block*, clone, companion, coordinate, copycat*, correlate, counterfeit, counterpart, counterscript, dead ringer*, ditto*, double, dupe*, duplication, facsimile, fake, fellow, germination, imitation, knockoff*, likeness, lookalike, match, mate, obverse, parallel, phony, photocopy, photostat, pirate, reciprocal, recurrence, repetition, replica, replication, repro*, ringer*, second, similarity,

spitting image*, stat, twin, Xerox*; SEE CONCEPTS 664,667,716

duplicate [v] *make a copy; repeat*
act like, clone, copy, counterfeit, ditto*, do again, do a takeoff*, do like*, double, dualize, dupe, echo, fake, go like*, imitate, knock off*, make like*, make replica, make twofold, manifold, mimeo, mirror, multiply, phony, photocopy, photostat, pirate*, redo, redouble, reduplicate, remake, replicate, repro, reproduce, rework, stat, take off as*, trace, Xerox*; SEE CONCEPTS 91,171

duplicitous [adj] *deceptive*
cheating, deceitful, dishonest, double-dealing, shady, two-faced, two-timing; SEE CONCEPTS 401,582

duplicity [n] *deception*
artifice, chicanery, cunning, deceit, dirty dealing*, dirty pool*, dirty trick, dirty work*, dishonesty, dissemblance, dissimulation, double-dealing, dualism, duality, faithlessness, falsehood, fraud, guile, hypocrisy, Judas kiss*, one-upmanship, perfidiousness, perfidy, skullduggery, stab in back*, treacherousness, treachery, two-facedness*, twoness; SEE CONCEPTS 59,63

durability [n] *sturdiness over time*
backbone, constancy, durableness, endurance, grit, guts*, gutsiness, hard as nails*, heart*, imperishability, intestinal fortitude, lastingness, moxie*, permanence, persistence, stamina, starch*, staying power*, stick-to-itiveness*; SEE CONCEPTS 721,731,732

durable [adj] *sturdy, long-lasting*
abiding, constant, dependable, diuturnal, enduring, fast, firm, fixed, impervious, lasting, long-continued, perdurable, perduring, permanent, persistent, reliable, resistant, sound, stable, stout, strong, substantial, tenacious, tough; SEE CONCEPTS 482,488,489

duration [n] *length of action, event*
continuance, continuation, continuity, endurance, extent, period, perpetuation, persistence, prolongation, run, span, spell, stretch, term, tide, time; SEE CONCEPT 804

duress [n] *threat, hardship*
bondage, captivity, coercion, compulsion, confinement, constraint, control, detention, discipline, force, imprisonment, incarceration, pressure, restraint, violence; SEE CONCEPTS 14,674

during [prep] *concurrently with an activity, event*
all along, all the while, amid, as, at the same timeas, at the time, for the time being, in the course of, in the interim, in the meanwhile, in the middle of, in the time of, meanwhile, mid, midst, over, pending, the time between, the whole time, throughout, until, when, while; SEE CONCEPT 820

dusk [n] *early evening*
dark, dimday, dimmet, eventide, gloaming, gloom, night, nightfall, sundown, sunset, twilight; SEE CONCEPT 810

dusky [adj] *dark-hued; murky*
adusk, bistered, bleak, brunette, caliginous, cheerless, cloudy, crepuscular, dark, dark-complexioned, darkish, desolate, dim, dismal, dull, funereal, gloomy, joyless, lightless, obscure, overcast, sable, shadowy, shady, swart, swarthy, tenebrous, twilight, twilit, unilluminated, veiled; SEE CONCEPTS 617,618

dust [n] *tiny particles in the air*
ashes, cinders, dirt, dust bunnies*, earth, filth, flakes, fragments, gilings, granules, grime, grit, ground, lint, loess, powder, refuse, sand, smut, soil, soot; SEE CONCEPT 437

dust [v] *sprinkle tiny particles*
besprinkle, cover, dredge, powder, scatter, sift, spray, spread; SEE CONCEPTS 172,222

dusty [adj] *filled with or covered with powdery particles*
arenaceous, arenose, chalky, crumbly, dirty, friable, granular, grubby, sandy, sooty, unclean, undusted, unswept, untouched; SEE CONCEPT 485

dutiful [adj] *obedient*
binding, compliant, conscientious, deferential, devoted, docile, duteous, faithful, incumbent on, obligatory, punctilious, regardful, respectful, reverential, submissive; SEE CONCEPT 542

duty [n1] *responsibility, assignment*
burden, business, calling, charge, chore, commission, commitment, committal, contract, devoir, dues, engagement, function, hook*, job, load, millstone*, minding the store*, mission, must, need, obligation, occupation, office, onus, ought*, pains, part, province, role, service, station, string*, taking care of business*, task, trouble, trust, undertaking, weight, work; SEE CONCEPTS 362,376,679

duty [n2] *tax on foreign goods*
assessment, custom, customs, due, excise, impost, levy, rate, revenue, tariff, toll; SEE CONCEPT 329

duty [n3] *moral obligation*
accountability, accountableness, allegiance, amenability, answerability, burden, call of duty, charge, conscience, deference, devoir, faithfulness, good faith, honesty, integrity, liability, loyalty, obedience, pledge, respect, reverence; SEE CONCEPT 388

dwarf [adj] *miniature, tiny*
baby, diminutive, low, petite, pocket, small, undersized; SEE CONCEPT 773

dwarf [n] *very small person*
bantam, dwarfling, homunculus, Lilliputian*, midget, Tom Thumb*; SEE CONCEPT 424

dwarf [v] *minimize*
belittle, check, detract from, dim, diminish, dominate, hinder, look down upon, lower, make small, micrify, minify, overshadow, predominate, retard, rise above, stunt, suppress, tower above, tower over; SEE CONCEPTS 7,19,698,741

dwell [v] *live in*
abide, bide, bunk*, continue, crash*, establish oneself, exist, flop*, hang one's hat*, hang out*, hole up*, inhabit, keep house, locate, lodge, make one's home, nest, occupy, park*, perch*, pitch tent*, quarter, remain, rent, reside, rest, room, roost*, settle, sojourn, squat*, stay, stop, tarry, tenant, tent; SEE CONCEPT 226

dwelling [n] *home*
abode, castle, commorancy, den, digs*, domicile, dump*, establishment, habitat, habitation, haunt, hole in the wall*, house, lodging, pad, quarters, residence, residency; SEE CONCEPT 516

dwell on/dwell upon [v] *linger over; be engrossed in*
consider, continue, elaborate, emphasize, expatiate, harp on*, involve oneself, tarry over; SEE CONCEPTS 17,239

du
dw

dwindle [v] *waste away; taper off*
abate, bate, become smaller, close, contract, decay, decline, decrease, die away, die down, die out, diminish, drain, drop, ebb, fade, fall, grow less, lessen, peter out*, pine, shrink, shrivel, sink, slack off*, subside, taper, wane, weaken, wither; SEE CONCEPTS **698,776**

dye [n] *coloring agent*
color, colorant, dyestuff, pigment, stain, tincture, tinge, tint; SEE CONCEPT **259**

dye [v] *change color with mixture*
impregnate, pigment, stain, tincture, tinge, tint; SEE CONCEPT **250**

dyed-in-the-wool [adj] *through and through*
absolute, complete, deep-down, deeply ingrained, deep-rooted, die-hard, entrenched, fixed, genuine, hardened, long-standing, to the core*, unchangeable, uncompromising; SEE CONCEPT **554**

dying [adj] *failing, expiring*
at death's door*, at end of rope*, decaying, declining, disintegrating, done for*, doomed, ebbing, fading, fated, final, giving up the ghost*, going, in extremis, moribund, mortal, one foot in grave*, on last leg*, passing, perishing, sinking, vanishing, withering; SEE CONCEPT **539**

dynamic [adj] *active, vital*
activating, aggressive, changing, charismatic, coming on strong*, compelling, driving, effective, electric, energetic, energizing, enterprising, forceful, forcible, go-ahead*, go-getter*, go-getting*, highpowered, hyped-up, influential, intense, lively, lusty, magnetic, peppy*, play for keeps*, play hard ball*, potent, powerful, productive, progressive, red-blooded*, strenuous, vehement, vigorous, vitalizing, zippy*; SEE CONCEPTS **404,540,542**

dynamite [n] *explosive*
gelignite, nitroglycerin, TNT, trinitrotoluene; SEE CONCEPT **500**

dynamo [n] *go-getter*
achiever, ball of fire*, bundle of energy*, busy person, doer, eager beaver*, energetic person, fireball*, generator, hard worker, hot shot, live wire*, mover and shaker*, pistol*, risk-taker, spark plug*, whiz kid*; SEE CONCEPT **706**

dynasty [n] *area of rule*
absolutism, ascendancy, dominion, empire, government, house, regime, sovereignty, sway; SEE CONCEPTS **435,508,710**

dysfunctional [adj] *socially impaired*
broken, debilitated, decayed, defective, deteriorated, flawed, inhibited, maladjusted, malfunctional, sick, undermined, unfit, wounded; SEE CONCEPT **314**

E

each [adj] *every*
all, any, exclusive, individual, one by one*, particular, personal, piece by piece*, respective, separate, several, single, specific, various, without exception; SEE CONCEPT **577**

each [adv] *apiece; for one*
all, a pop*, a shot*, aside, a throw*, by the, every, individually, per, per capita, per head, per person, per unit, proportionately, respectively, separately, singly, without exception; SEE CONCEPT **577**

each [prep] *each one*
each and every one*, each other, every last one, every one, one, one and all*, one another; SEE CONCEPT **577**

eager [adj] *anxious, enthusiastic*
acquisitive, agog, ambitious, antsy, appetent, ardent, athirst, avid, breathless, champing at the bit*, covetous, craving, desiring, desirous, dying to, earnest, fervent, fervid, greedy, gung ho*, hankering, heated, hot*, hot to trot*, hungry*, impatient, intent, keen, longing, pining, rarin' to go*, ready and willing*, restive, restless, self-starting, solicitous, thirsty, vehement, voracious, warmblooded*, wild, wishful, yearning, zealous; SEE CONCEPTS **326,401,542**

eager beaver [n] *active person*
ambitious person, ball of fire*, busy bee*, busy person, doer, dynamo, fireball*, go-getter, hot shot, live wire*, pistol*, self-starter, spark plug*, workhorse; SEE CONCEPT **706**

eagerness [n] *enthusiasm, anxiousness*
alacrity, ambition, anticipation, ardor, avidity, earnestness, excitement, fervor, greediness, gusto, heartiness, hunger, impatience, impetuosity, intentness, keenness, longing, promptness, quickness, solicitude, thirst, vehemence, voracity, yearning, zeal, zest, zing*; SEE CONCEPTS **20,633,657**

eagle-eyed [adj] *keen-eyed*
clear-sighted, hawk-eyed, observant, perceptive, perspicacious, sharp-eyed, X-ray eye; SEE CONCEPTS **402,542**

ear [n] *attention*
appreciation, consideration, discrimination, hearing, heed, mark, mind, note, notice, observance, observation, perception, regard, remark, sensitivity, taste; SEE CONCEPT **532**

early [adj1] *in the beginning*
a bit previous, aboriginal, ancient, antecedent, antediluvian, antiquated, brand-new, budding, early bird*, fresh, initial, new, original, preceding, premier, prevenient, previous, primal, prime, primeval, primitive, primordial, prior, pristine, proleptical, raw, recent, undeveloped, young; SEE CONCEPTS **799,828**

early [adj2] *sooner than expected*
advanced, ahead of time, anticipative, anticipatory, before appointed time, beforehand, direct, immature, immediate, matinal, on short notice*, on the dot*, overearly, oversoon, preceding, precipitant, precocious, preexistent, premature, previous, prompt, pronto, punctual, quick, seasonable, soon, speedy, unanticipated, unexpected, untimely; SEE CONCEPT **820**

early [adv1] *sooner than expected*
a bit previous, ahead of time, anon, beforehand, before long, betimes, briefly, bright and early*, directly, early bird*, ere long, far ahead, immediately, in advance, in good time*, in the bud*, in time, on short notice*, on the dot*, oversoon, prematurely, presently, previous, promptly, pronto, proximately, quick, shortly, soon, too soon, unexpectedly, with time to spare*; SEE CONCEPT **820**

early [adv2] *immediately*
at once, betimes, directly, first, freshly, in a

jiffy*, in an instant*, in no time*, instantaneously, instantly, newly, presto, primitively, promptly, recently, right away, seasonably, soon, straightaway, summarily, thereon, thereupon, timely, without delay; SEE CONCEPTS *799,828*

earmark [*n*] *signature characteristic*
attribute, differential, distinction, feature, hallmark, label, marking, peculiarity, quality, stamp, tag, token, trademark, trait; SEE CONCEPT *644*

earmark [*v*] *reserve*
allocate, designate, keep back, label, maintain, mark out, name, set aside, slot, tab, tag; SEE CONCEPT *129*

earn [*v1*] *make money*
acquire, attain, be gainfully employed, be in line for*, bring home*, bring home the bacon*, bring home the groceries*, bring in, clean up*, clear*, collect, consummate, cop*, derive, draw, effect, gain, gather, get, gross, hustle, make, make fast buck*, make it big*, net, obtain, pay one's dues*, perform, pick up, procure, profit, pull*, pull down*, rate, realize, reap, receive, scare up*, score*, scrape together*, secure, snag*, sock*, turn, win, wrangle; SEE CONCEPTS *330,351*

earn [*v2*] *deserve a reward*
acquire, attain, bag, be entitled to, be worthy of, come by, gain, harvest, merit, net, rate, reap, score, warrant, win; SEE CONCEPTS *120,129*

earnest [*adj1*] *very enthusiastic*
ardent, busy, devoted, diligent, eager, fervent, fervid, heartfelt, impassioned, industrious, keen, passionate, perseverant, purposeful, sedulous, sincere, urgent, vehement, warm, wholehearted, zealous; SEE CONCEPTS *326,401,542*

earnest [*adj2*] *serious; very important*
close, constant, determined, firm, fixed, for real, grave, intent, mean business, meaningful, nofooling, no-nonsense, playing hard ball*, resolute, resolved, sedate, sincere, sober, solemn, somber, stable, staid, steady, thoughtful, weighty; SEE CONCEPT *568*

earnestness [*n*] *determination; seriousness*
absorption, ardor, attentiveness, concentration, decision, deliberation, devotion, doggedness, eagerness, engrossment, enthusiasm, fervor, firmness, gravity, intensity, intentness, keenness, passion, perseverance, persistence, purposefulness, resolution, resolve, serious-mindedness, sincerity, sobriety, solemnity, stress, tenacity, urgency, vehemence, warmth, zeal; SEE CONCEPTS *633,657*

earnings [*n*] *money for work performed*
balance, bottom line*, emolument, gain, gate, groceries*, income, in the black*, lucre, net, pay, payoff, piece of the pie*, proceeds, profit, receipts, remuneration, return, revenue, reward, salary, salt*, stipend, take-home*, takings, wages; SEE CONCEPT *344*

earsplitting [*adj*] *loud*
blaring, deafening, noisy, penetrating, piercing, ringing, shrill, strident, thunderous; SEE CONCEPTS *592,594*

Earth [*n1*] *the world*
apple*, big blue marble*, cosmos, creation, dust*, globe, macrocosm, orb, planet, sphere, star, sublunary world, terra, terra firma, terrene, terrestrial sphere, universe, vale; SEE CONCEPT *511*

earth [*n2*] *ground, soil*
alluvium, clay, clod, coast, compost, deposit, dirt, dry land, dust, fill, glebe, gravel, humus, land, loam, marl, mold, muck, mud, peat moss, sand, shore, sod, subsoil, surface, terra firma, terrain, terrane, topsoil, turf; SEE CONCEPT *509*

earthling [*n*] *human being*
earth dweller, humankind, man, person, tellurian, woman; SEE CONCEPT *417*

earthly [*adj1*] *physically concerning land or its inhabitants*
alluvial, carnal, corporeal, geotic, global, human, in all creation, material, mortal, mundane, nonspiritual, physical, profane, secular, substratal, sublunary, tellurian, telluric, temporal, terraqueous, terrene, terrestrial, uncelestial, under the sun*, unspiritual, worldly; SEE CONCEPT *536*

earthly [*adj2*] *conceivable*
feasible, imaginable, likely, mortal, possible, potential, practical, probable; SEE CONCEPT *552*

earthmover [*n*] *bulldozer*
backhoe, excavator, grader, heavy machinery, tracked vehicle; SEE CONCEPT *505*

earthquake [*n*] *tremor from inside the earth*
convulsion, fault, macroseism, microseism, movement, quake, quaker*, seimicity, seism, seismism, shake, shock, slip, temblor, trembler*, undulation, upheaval; SEE CONCEPTS *144,526*

earthy [*adj*] *unsophisticated*
bawdy, coarse, crude, down, down home*, down-to-earth*, dull, easygoing, folksy, funky*, hard-boiled*, home folk*, homely, homey, indelicate, lowbred, lusty, mundane, natural, pragmatic, ribald, robust, rough, simple, unidealistic, uninhibited, unrefined; SEE CONCEPT *542*

ease [*n1*] *peace, quiet; lack of difficulty*
affluence, ataraxia, bed of roses*, calm, calmness, comfort, content, contentment, easiness, enjoyment, gratification, happiness, idleness, inactivity, inertia, inertness, leisure, luxury, passivity, peace of mind*, prosperity, quietness, quietude, relaxation, repose, requiescence, rest, restfulness, satisfaction, security, serenity, supinity, tranquility; SEE CONCEPTS *388,410,673*

ease [*n2*] *facility, freedom*
adroitness, affability, aplomb, breeze, child's play*, cinch, cleverness, composure, dexterity, dispatch, duck soup*, easygoingness, efficiency, effortlessness, expertise, expertness, familiarity, flexibility, fluency, informality, insouciance, knack, liberty, naturalness, nonchalance, poise, pushover, quickness, readiness, relaxedness, setup, simplicity, skillfulness, smoothness, smooth sailing*, snap, unaffectedness, unconstraint, unreservedness; SEE CONCEPTS *376,388, 630*

ease [*v1*] *alleviate, help*
abate, aid, allay, ameliorate, anesthetize, appease, assist, assuage, attend to, calm, cheer, clear the way*, comfort, cure, disburden, disengage, doctor, expedite, facilitate, forward, free, further, improve, lessen, let up on, lift, lighten, make easier, meliorate, mitigate, moderate, mollify, nurse, open the door*, pacify, palliate, promote, quiet, relax, relent, relieve, run interference for*, simplify, slacken, smooth, soften, soothe, speed, speed up, still, tranquilize, untighten; SEE CONCEPTS *110,310*

ease [*v2*] *guide, move carefully*
disentangle, edge, extricate, facilitate, handle,

dw ea

inch, induce, insert, join, loose, loosen, maneuver, relax, remove, right, set right, slack, slacken, slide, slip, squeeze, steer, untighten; SEE CONCEPT *187*

easel [*n*] *stand*
frame, mount, tripod; SEE CONCEPTS *442,733,757*

easement [*n*] *right of way*
access, legal right, means of access, passage; SEE CONCEPTS *318,685*

easily [*adv1*] *without difficulty*
calmly, comfortably, competently, conveniently, coolly, dexterously, efficiently, effortlessly, evenly, facilely, fluently, freely, handily, hand over fist*, hands down*, just like that*, lightly, like nothing*, no sweat*, nothing to it*, piece of cake*, plainly, quickly, readily, regularly, simply, smoothly, steadily, surely, swimmingly, uncomplicatedly, well, with ease, with no effort, without a hitch*, without trouble; SEE CONCEPT *565*

easily [*adv2*] *without a doubt*
absolutely, actually, almost certainly, assuredly, beyond question, by far, certainly, clearly, decidedly, definitely, doubtless, doubtlessly, far and away, indeed, indisputably, indubitably, no doubt, plainly, positively, probably, really, surely, truly, undeniably, undoubtedly, unequivocally, unquestionably; SEE CONCEPTS *535,552*

easy [*adj1*] *not difficult*
accessible, apparent, basic, child's play*, cinch, clear, easily done, effortless, elementary, evident, facile, inconsiderable, light, little, manageable, manifest, mere, no bother*, no problem*, no sweat*, not burdensome, nothing to it*, no trouble*, obvious, painless, paltry, picnic*, piece of cake*, plain, plain sailing*, pushover*, royal, simple, simple as ABC*, slight, smooth, snap, straightforward, uncomplicated, undemanding, uninvolved, untroublesome, wieldy, yielding; SEE CONCEPT *565*

easy [*adj2*] *leisurely, relaxed*
at ease, calm, carefree, comfortable, comfy, commodious, composed, content, contented, cozy, cursive, cushy, easeful, effortless, flowing, fluent, forthright, gentle, in clover*, languid, light, mild, moderate, peaceful, pleasant, prosperous, quiet, running, satisfied, secure, serene, slow, smooth, snug, soft, spontaneous, substantial, successful, temperate, thriving, tranquil, undemanding, undisturbed, unexacting, unhurried, untroubled, unworried, well-to-do; SEE CONCEPTS *542,544*

easy [*adj3*] *tolerant, permissive*
accommodating, amenable, benign, biddable, charitable, clement, compassionate, compliant, condoning, deceivable, deludable, dupable, easygoing, excusing, exploitable, fleeceable, flexible, forbearing, forgiving, gentle, gullible, humoring, indulgent, kindly, lax, lenient, liberal, light, merciful, mild, moderate, mollycoddling*, naive, pampering, pardoning, soft, spoiling, submissive, susceptible, sympathetic, temperate, tractable, trusting, unburdensome, unoppressive, unsuspicious; SEE CONCEPT *401*

easy [*adj4*] *good-humored*
affable, amiable, at ease, carefree, casual, complaisant, diplomatic, familiar, friendly, gentle, good-natured, good-tempered, graceful, gracious, gregarious, informal, mild, natural, obliging, open, pleasant, polite, relaxed, secure,

smooth, sociable, suave, tolerant, unaffected, unanxious, undemanding, unforced, unpretentious, urbane; SEE CONCEPT *404*

easy as pie [*adj*] *very easy*
duck soup, easily done, easily managed, easy as can be, like falling off a log*, like shooting fish in a barrel*, like stealing candy from a baby*, no sweat, simple, simple as ABC; SEE CONCEPTS *527,565*

easygoing [*adj*] *complacent, permissive*
amenable, breezy, calm, carefree, casual, collected, complaisant, composed, devil-may-care*, even-tempered*, flexible, free and easy*, hang-loose*, happy-go-lucky*, indolent, indulgent, informal, insouciant, laid-back*, lazy, lenient, liberal, low-pressure, mild, moderate, nonchalant, offhand, outgiving, patient, placid, poised, relaxed, self-possessed, serene, tolerant, tranquil, unconcerned, uncritical, undemanding, unhurried, uninhibited; SEE CONCEPT *404*

eat [*v1*] *consume food*
absorb, attack, banquet, bite, bolt*, break bread*, breakfast, chew, chow down*, cram*, devour, digest, dine, dispatch, dispose of, fall to, feast upon, feed, gobble up*, gorge, gormandize, graze*, have a bite*, have a meal, have for, ingest, inhale*, lunch, make pig of oneself*, masticate, munch, nibble, nosh*, partake of, peck at*, pick, pig out*, polish off*, pork out*, put away*, ruminate, scarf*, scoff, snack, sup, swallow, take food, take in, take nourishment, wolf; SEE CONCEPT *169*

eat [*v2*] *erode, wear away; use up*
bite, condense, corrode, crumble, decay, decompose, disappear, disintegrate, dissipate, dissolve, drain, exhaust, gnaw, liquefy, melt, nibble, rot, run through, rust, spill, squander, vanish, waste away; SEE CONCEPTS *225,469*

eatable [*adj*] *able to be consumed*
appetizing, comestible, culinary, delicious, delish*, dietary, digestible, edible, esculent, fit, good, harmless, kosher*, nutritious, nutritive, palatable, piquant, safe, satisfying, savory, scrumptious, succulent, tasty, tempting, wholesome, yummy*; SEE CONCEPTS *462,613*

eat high on the hog [*v*] *live well*
be in fat city*, be in hog heaven*, be sitting pretty, have it good, have it made, sit pretty; SEE CONCEPTS *5539,544,589*

eating disorder [*n*] *unhealthy disturbance in eating behavior*
anorexia nervosa, bingeing, bulimarexia, bulimia, compulsive eating, hyperagia, pica, psychological disorder, purging; SEE CONCEPT *316*

eat up [*v*] *to accept*
buy, stand still for, swallow; SEE CONCEPT *12*

eavesdrop [*v*] *listen without permission*
be all ears*, bend an ear*, bug, ears into*, listen in, monitor, overhear, pry, snoop, spy, tap, tune in on*, wire, wiretap; SEE CONCEPTS *188,596*

ebb [*n*] *regression; decline*
abatement, backflow, decay, decrease, degeneration, depreciation, deterioration, diminution, drop, dwindling, fading away, flagging, going out, lessening, low tide, low water, outward flow, petering out*, recession, refluence, reflux, retreat, retrocession, retroflux, shrinkage, sinking, slackening, subsidence, sweep, wane, waning, weakening, withdrawal; SEE CONCEPTS *195,698*

ebb [v] *subside; decline*
abate, decay, decrease, degenerate, deteriorate, die down, die out, diminish, drop, dwindle, ease off, fade away, fall, fall away, fall back, flag, flow back, go out, languish, lessen, let up, melt, moderate, peter out, recede, relent, retire, retreat, retrocede, shrink, sink, slacken, wane, weaken, withdraw; SEE CONCEPTS *195,698*

ebullience [n] *enthusiasm*
agitation, animation, buoyancy, effervescence, effusiveness, elation, excitement, exhilaration, exuberance, exuberancy, ferment, gaiety, high-spiritedness, high spirits, liveliness, vitality, vivaciousness, vivacity, zest; SEE CONCEPT *633*

ebullient [adj] *enthusiastic*
agitated, bouncy, brash, buoyant, chipper*, chirpy*, effervescent, effusive, elated, excited, exhilarated, exuberant, frothy*, gushing, high-spirited, in high spirits*, irrepressible, vivacious, zestful, zippy*; SEE CONCEPT *401*

eccentric [adj] *bizarre, unusual*
aberrant, abnormal, anomalous, beat*, bent*, bizarre, capricious, characteristic, cockeyed, crazy, curious, droll, erratic, far out*, flaky, freak, freakish, funky*, funny, idiosyncratic, irregular, kooky, nutty, odd, oddball, offbeat, off-center, off the wall*, out in left field*, outlandish, peculiar, quaint, queer, quirky, quizzical, singular, strange, uncommon, unconventional, unnatural, way out*, weird, whimsical, wild; SEE CONCEPTS *547,564*

eccentric [n] *person who is bizarre, unusual*
beatnik, character, freak, hippie, kook, loner, maverick, nonconformist, nut*, oddball, oddity, odd person, original, queer duck*, rare bird*, three-dollar bill*, weirdo; SEE CONCEPT *423*

eccentricity [n] *bizarreness, unusualness*
aberration, abnormality, anomaly, caprice, capriciousness, foible, freakishness, hereticism, idiocrasy, idiosyncrasy, irregularity, kink, nonconformity, oddity, oddness, outlandishness, peculiarity, queerness, quirk, singularity, strangeness, unconventionality, unorthodoxness, waywardness, weirdness, whimsicality, whimsicalness; SEE CONCEPTS *647,665*

ecclesiastical [adj] *churchly*
clerical, diaconal, episcopal, holy, ministerial, orthodox, parochial, pastoral, religious, sectarian, spiritual; SEE CONCEPTS *536,582*

echelon [n] *class, level*
degree, file, grade, line, office, place, position, queue, rank, row, string, tier; SEE CONCEPTS *378,388*

echo [n] *repeat, copy*
answer, imitation, mirror, mirror image, onomatopoeia, parallel, parroting, rebound, reflection, reiteration, repercussion, repetition, reply, reproduction, reverberation, ringing, rubber stamp*; SEE CONCEPTS *595,695,716*

echo [v] *repeat, copy*
ape, ditto*, do like*, go like*, imitate, impersonate, make like*, mimic, mirror, parallel, parrot, react, recall, redouble, reflect, reiterate, reproduce, resemble, resound, respond, reverberate, ring, rubber-stamp*, second, vibrate; SEE CONCEPTS *91,171*

eclectic [adj] *comprehensive, general*
all-embracing, assorted, broad, catholic, dilettantish, diverse, diversified, heterogeneous, inclusive, liberal, many-sided, mingled, mixed, multifarious, multiform, selective, universal, varied, wide-ranging; SEE CONCEPTS *537,772*

eclipse [n] *shadowing of the sun*
concealment, darkening, decline, diminution, dimming, extinction, extinguishment, obliteration, obscuration, occultation, penumbra, shading, shroud, veil; SEE CONCEPTS *522,624*

eclipse [v1] *obscure, veil*
adumbrate, becloud, bedim, blot out, cloud, darken, dim, extinguish, murk, overshadow, shadow, shroud; SEE CONCEPT *250*

eclipse [v2] *surpass achievement*
exceed, excel, outdo, outshine, overrun, surmount, tower above, transcend; SEE CONCEPT *141*

ecology [n] *environmental science*
bionomics, conservation, preservation; SEE CONCEPTS *134,257*

economic [adj] *business-related; financial*
bread-and-butter*, budgetary, commercial, fiscal, industrial, material, mercantile, monetary, money-making, pecuniary, productive, profitable, profit-making, remunerative, solvent, viable; SEE CONCEPTS *334,536*

economical [adj1] *conservative with resources; careful*
avaricious, canny, chary, circumspect, close, closefisted, cost-effective, curmudgeonly, efficient, frugal, meager, mean, methodical, miserly, money-saving, niggardly*, on the rims*, parsimonious, penny-pinching*, penny-wise*, penurious, practical, provident, prudent, prudential, saving, scrimping, skimping, spare, sparing, stingy, thrifty, tight, time-saving, unwasteful, watchful, work-saving; SEE CONCEPT *542*

economical [adj2] *inexpensive*
bought for a song*, cheap, cost next to nothing*, cost nothing, cut rate, dime a dozen*, dirt cheap*, dog cheap*, fair, low, low-priced, low tariff, marked down, moderate, modest, on sale, quite a buy*, reasonable, reduced, sound, steal*; SEE CONCEPT *334*

economize [v] *save money*
be frugal, be prudent, be sparing, conserve, cut back, cut corners*, cut down, keep within means, make ends meet*, manage, meet a budget, pay one's way*, pinch pennies*, retrench, run tight ship*, scrimp, shepherd, skimp, stint, stretch a dollar*, tighten one's belt*; SEE CONCEPT *330*

economy [n] *saving, frugality*
abridgement, austerity, care, carefulness, caution, curtailment, cutback, decrease, deduction, direction, discretion, husbandry, layoff, meanness, miserliness, moratorium, niggardliness, parcity, parsimony, providence, prudence, recession, reduction, regulation, restraint, retrenchment, rollback, scrimping, shrinkage, skimping, sparingness, stinginess, supervision, thrift, thriftiness; SEE CONCEPTS *117,330,335*

eco-rich [adj] *possessing an abundance of natural resources*
bountiful, clean, flowing, full, green, natural, plentiful, pure, rich; SEE CONCEPT *518*

ecosystem [n] *environment*
ecological community, environs; SEE CONCEPTS *515,673,696*

ecstasy [n] *bliss*
beatitude, blessedness, cool*, delectation, delight, delirium, ebullience, elation, enchantment, enthusiasm, euphoria, exaltation, felicity, fervor,

ea
ec

frenzy, gladness, happiness, heaven, inspiration, intoxication, joy, joyfulness, paradise, rapture, ravishment, rhapsody, seventh heaven*, trance, transport, twilight zone*; SEE CONCEPT 410

ecstatic [adj] very happy, blissful

athrill, beatific, crazy, delirious, dreamy, elated, enraptured, enthusiastic, entranced, euphoric, fervent, floating, flying high*, frenzied, gone*, high*, in exaltation, in seventh heaven*, joyful, joyous, mad, on cloud nine*, out, overjoyed, pleased as punch*, rapturous, ravished, rhapsodic, sent*, sunny, thrilled, tickled pink*, tickled to death*, transported*, turned on*, upbeat, wild; SEE CONCEPT 403

ecumenical [adj] general

all-comprehensive, all-inclusive, all-pervading, catholic, comprehensive, cosmic, cosmopolitan, global, inclusive, planetary, unifying, universal, worldwide; SEE CONCEPTS 537,772

eddy [n] current

swirl, tide, vortex, whirlpool; SEE CONCEPT 514

Eden [n] Paradise

Arcadia, garden, Garden of Eden, heaven, heaven on earth, promised land, Shangri-La, Utopia; SEE CONCEPTS 370,410,515

edge [n1] border, outline

bend, berm, bound, boundary, brim, brink, butt, circumference, contour, corner, crook, crust, curb, end, extremity, frame, fringe, frontier, hem, hook, ledge, limb, limit, line, lip, margin, molding, mouth, outskirt, peak, perimeter, periphery, point, portal, rim, ring, shore, side, skirt, split, strand, term, threshold, tip, trimming, turn, verge; SEE CONCEPTS 484,513

edge [n2] advantage

allowance, ascendancy, bulge, dominance, draw, handicap, head start, lead, odds, start, superiority, upper hand*, vantage; SEE CONCEPT 712

edge [v1] border, trim

bind, bound, decorate, fringe, hem, margin, outline, rim, shape, skirt, surround, verge; SEE CONCEPTS 751,758

edge [v2] defeat narrowly

creep, ease, inch, infiltrate, nose out*, sidle, slip by, slip past, squeeze by*, squeeze past*, steal, worm*; SEE CONCEPT 95

edge [v3] sharpen

file, grind, hone, polish, sharpen, strop, whet; SEE CONCEPTS 137,250

edgy [adj] nervous

anxious, critical, excitable, excited, high-strung, ill at ease, impatient, irascible, irritable, keyed up*, overstrung, restive, restless, skittish, tense, touchy, uneasy, uptight; SEE CONCEPT 401

edible [adj] able to be eaten

comestible, digestible, eatable, esculent, fit, good, harmless, nourishing, nutritious, nutritive, palatable, savory, succulent, tasty, toothsome, wholesome; SEE CONCEPTS 462,613

edict [n] pronouncement, order

act, canon, command, commandment, decree, decretum, dictate, dictum, directive, enactment, fiat, injunction, instrument, judgment, law, mandate, manifesto, ordinance, precept, prescript, proclamation, pronunciamento, regulation, rule, ruling, statute, ukase, writ; SEE CONCEPTS 278,662,688

edification [n] improvement, education

betterment, elevation, elucidation, enhancement, enlightenment, guidance, illumination, information, instruction, irradiation, knowledge, learning, nurture, schooling, teaching, tuition, uplifting; SEE CONCEPTS 31,287,700

edifice [n] structure

building, construction, erection, habitation, house, monument, pile, rockpile*, skyscraper, towers; SEE CONCEPT 439

edit [v] rewrite, refine

adapt, alter, amplify, analyze, annotate, arrange, assemble, assign, blue-pencil*, boil down*, butcher, censor, check, choose, compile, compose, condense, correct, cut, delete, discard, doctor, draft, emend, excise, feature, fine-tune, finish, fly speck*, go over, make up, massage*, polish, prepare, prescribe, proofread, publish, put together, rearrange, recalibrate, rectify, redact, regulate, rehash, rephrase, report, revise, scrub*, select, set up, strike out, style, tighten, trim, write over; SEE CONCEPTS 79,126,203

edition [n] issue of publication

copy, impression, imprint, number, printing, program, publication, reissue, release, reprint, reprinting, version, volume; SEE CONCEPT 280

editorial [n] commentary

article, critique, opinion, report, review; SEE CONCEPTS 51,278

educate [v] teach information, experience

brainwash*, brief, civilize, coach, cultivate, develop, discipline, drill, drum into, edify, enlighten, exercise, explain, foster, improve, indoctrinate, inform, instruct, let in on, mature, nurture, put hip*, put through the grind*, rear, school, show the ropes*, train, tutor; SEE CONCEPTS 61,285

educated [adj] learned, experienced

accomplished, acquainted with, brainy, civilized, coached, corrected, cultivated, cultured, developed, enlightened, enriched, erudite, expert, finished, fitted, formed, informed, initiated, instructed, intelligent, knowledgeable, lettered, literary, literate, nurtured, polished, prepared, professional, refined, scholarly, schooled, scientific, shaped, skilled, tasteful, taught, trained, tutored, versed in, well-informed, well-read, well-taught, well-versed; SEE CONCEPT 402

education [n] instruction, development of knowledge

apprenticeship, background, book learning*, brainwashing*, breeding, catechism, civilization, coaching, cultivation, culture, direction, discipline, drilling, edification, enlightenment, erudition, finish, guidance, improvement, inculcation, indoctrination, information, learnedness, learning, literacy, nurture, pedagogy, preparation, propagandism, proselytism, reading, rearing, refinement, scholarship, schooling, science, study, teaching, training, tuition, tutelage, tutoring; SEE CONCEPTS 285,287,409

educational [adj] instructional

academic, cultural, didactic, informational, informative, instructive, scholarly, scholastic, tutorial; SEE CONCEPT 536

educator [n] teacher

coach, dean, department head, educationist, instructor, lecturer, mentor, monitor, professor, schoolteacher, trainer, tutor; SEE CONCEPT 350

educe [v] bring out, elicit

come out, conclude, deduce, derive, develop, distill, drag, draw, draw out, evince, evoke, evolve, excogitate, extort, extract, gain, get, infer, milk*, obtain, procure, pull, reason, secure, think out, wrest, wring; SEE CONCEPTS *37,142*

eerie [*adj*] *spooky*
awesome, bizarre, crawly, creepy, fantastic, fearful, frightening, ghostly, mysterious, scary, spectral, strange, supernatural, superstitious, uncanny, unearthly, weird; SEE CONCEPT *537*

efface [*v*] *erase*
blot out, blue-pencil, cancel, cross out, delete, destroy, edit, eliminate, expunge, fade, obliterate, rub out, scratch out, white out, wipe out; SEE CONCEPTS *211,215*

effect [*n1*] *result*
aftereffect, aftermath, backlash, backwash, can of worms*, causatum, chain reaction*, conclusion, consequence, corollary, denouement, development, end, end product, event, eventuality, fallout, flak*, follow through, follow-up, fruit, issue, outcome, outgrowth, precipitate, pursuance, ramification, reaction, reflex, repercussion, response, sequel, sequence, side effect, spin-off, upshot*, waves*; SEE CONCEPT *230*

effect [*n2*] *impact, impression*
action, clout, drift, effectiveness, efficacy, efficiency, enforcement, essence, execution, fact, force, implementation, import, imprint, influence, mark, meaning, power, purport, purpose, reality, sense, significance, strength, tenor, use, validity, vigor, weight; SEE CONCEPT *687*

effect [*v*] *carry out, accomplish*
achieve, actualize, actuate, begin, bring about, bring off, bring on, buy, carry through, cause, complete, conceive, conclude, consummate, create, do a number*, do one's thing*, do the job*, do the trick*, do a T*, draw on, effectuate, enact, enforce, execute, fulfill, generate, get across, get to, give rise to, implement, induce, initiate, invoke, make, make it*, make waves*, perform, procure, produce, pull it off*, put across, realize, render, secure, sell, turn out, turn the trick*, unzip*, yield; SEE CONCEPTS *91,706*

effective [*adj*] *productive, persuasive*
able, active, adequate, capable, cogent, compelling, competent, convincing, direct, effectual, efficacious, efficient, emphatic, energetic, forceful, forcible, having lead in pencil*, impressive, live, moving, on the ball*, operative, playing hardball*, potent, powerful, powerhouse*, practical, producing, resultant, serviceable, serving, sound, striking, sufficient, telling, trenchant, useful, valid, virtuous, wicked*, yielding; SEE CONCEPTS *537,540*

effective [*adj2*] *in use at the time*
active, actual, current, direct, dynamic, in effect, in execution, in force, in operation, operative, real; SEE CONCEPTS *560,582,799*

effectiveness [*n*] *influence*
capability, clout, cogency, effect, efficacy, efficiency, force, forcefulness, performance, point, potency, power, punch, strength, success, use, validity, validness, verve, vigor, weight; SEE CONCEPTS *676,687*

effects [*n*] *belongings*
accouterments, chattels, goods, holdings, paraphernalia, possessions, property, stuff, things, trappings; SEE CONCEPTS *446,710*

effectual [*adj*] *influential; authoritative*
accomplishing, achieving, adequate, binding, capable, conclusive, decisive, determinative, effecting, effective, efficacious, efficient, forcible,

fulfilling, in force, lawful, legal, licit, potent, powerful, practicable, productive, qualified, serviceable, sound, strong, successful, telling, useful, valid, virtuous, workable; SEE CONCEPTS *319,528,537*

effeminate [*adj*] *having female qualities*
epicene, feminine, womanish, womanlike, womanly; SEE CONCEPTS *401,404*

effervescence [*n1*] *fizz, foam*
bubbles, bubbling, ebullition, ferment, fermentation, froth, frothing, sparkle; SEE CONCEPTS *437,522*

effervescence [*n2*] *enthusiasm, vivacity*
animation, buoyancy, ebullience, excitedness, excitement, exhilaration, exuberance, exuberancy, gaiety, happiness, high spirits, joy, liveliness, vim, vitality, volatility, zing*; SEE CONCEPTS *633,657*

effervescent [*adj*] *fizzing, foaming*
airy, boiling, bouncy, bubbling, bubbly, carbonated, elastic, expansive, fermenting, frothing, frothy, resilient, sparkling, volatile; SEE CONCEPTS *462,485*

effervescent [*adj2*] *enthusiastic, vivacious*
animated, bouncy, brash, bubbly, buoyant, ebullient, excited, exhilarated, exuberant, gleeful, happy, high-spirited, hilarious, in high spirits*, irrepressible, jolly, joyous, lively, merry, mirthful, sprightly, vital, zingy; SEE CONCEPTS *401,542*

effete [*adj1*] *spoiled, exhausted*
burnt out*, corrupt, debased, decadent, decayed, declining, decrepit, degenerate, dissipated, dissolute, drained, enervated, enfeebled, far-gone*, feeble, immoral, obsolete, overrefined, overripe, played out*, soft, spent, vitiated, washed-out*, wasted, weak, worn out; SEE CONCEPT *560*

effete [*adj2*] *unproductive*
barren, fruitless, impotent, infecund, infertile, sterile, unfruitful, unprolific; SEE CONCEPT *527*

efficacious [*adj*] *efficient, productive*
active, adequate, capable, competent, effective, effectual, energetic, influential, operative, potent, powerful, puissant, serviceable, strong, successful, useful, virtuous; SEE CONCEPTS *528,537*

efficacy [*n*] *efficiency; productiveness*
ability, adequacy, capability, capableness, capacity, competence, effect, effectiveness, efficaciousness, energy, force, influence, performance, potency, power, strength, success, sufficiency, use, vigor, virtue, weight; SEE CONCEPTS *641,676,706*

efficiency [*n*] *adeptness, effectiveness*
ability, abundance, adaptability, address, adequacy, capability, capableness, competence, competency, completeness, economy, effectualness, efficacy, energy, expertise, facility, faculty, know-how, performance, potency, power, powerfulness, productiveness, productivity, proficiency, prowess, quantity, readiness, resourcefulness, response, skill, skillfulness, suitability, suitableness, talent, thoroughness; SEE CONCEPTS *409,630,658*

efficient [*adj*] *adept, effective*
able, accomplished, active, adapted, adequate, apt, businesslike, capable, clever, competent, conducive, decisive, deft, dynamic, economic, economical, effectual, efficacious, energetic, equal to, experienced, expert, familiar with, fitted, good at, good for, handy, masterly, orga-

ec
ef

nized, potent, powerful, practiced, productive, proficient, profitable, qualified, ready, saving, shrewd, skilled, skillful, systematic, talented, tough, useful, valuable, virtuous, well-organized; SEE CONCEPTS *402,527,560*

effigy [*n*] *dummy*
figure, icon, idol, image, likeness, model, picture, portrait, puppet, representation, statue; SEE CONCEPT *436*

effort [*n*] *work, exertion*
accomplishment, achievement, act, aim, application, aspiration, attempt, battle, crack*, creation, deed, discipline, drill, elbow grease*, endeavor, energy, enterprise, essay, exercise, feat, fling*, force, go*, industry, intention, job, labor, old college try*, pains, power, product, production, pull, purpose, push, resolution, shot*, spurt, stab*, strain, stress, stretch, strife, striving, struggle, sweat, tension, toil, training, travail, trial, trouble, try, tug*, undertaking, venture, whack*; SEE CONCEPTS *87,362,677,724*

effortless [*adj*] *easy*
child's play*, cursive, duck soup*, facile, flowing, fluent, light, no problem*, no sweat*, offhand, painless, picnic*, piece of cake*, royal, running, simple, smooth, snap*, uncomplicated, undemanding, untroublesome; SEE CONCEPT *565*

effrontery [*n*] *nerve, boldness*
arrogance, assurance, audacity, backtalk, brashness, brass*, brazenness, cheek*, cheekiness, chutzpah*, crust*, disrespect, face, gall, guff, hardihood, impertinence, impudence, incivility, insolence, lip*, presumption, rudeness, sass, sauce*, self-assurance, self-confidence, shamelessness, smart talk, temerity; SEE CONCEPTS *411,633*

effulgent [*adj*] *glowing, luminous*
beaming, blazing, bright, brilliant, dazzling, flaming, fluorescent, incandescent, lambent, lucent, lustrous, radiant, resplendent, shining, splendid, vivid; SEE CONCEPT *617*

effusion [*n*] *outpouring*
address, diffusion, discharge, effluence, effluvium, efflux, emanation, emission, exudate, gush, gushing, ooze, outflow, pouring, shedding, stream, verbosity, wordiness; SEE CONCEPTS *179,266*

effusive [*adj*] *gushing, profuse*
all jaw*, big mouthed*, demonstrative, ebullient, enthusiastic, expansive, extravagant, exuberant, free-flowing, fulsome, gabby*, gushy*, lavish, outpouring, overflowing, prolix, talkative, unconstrained, unreserved, unrestrained, verbose, windbag*, windy*, wordy; SEE CONCEPTS *267,542*

egalitarian [*adj*] *equal*
democratic, equitable, even-handed, impartial, just, unbiased; SEE CONCEPTS *319,536*

egg [*n*] *seed, cell; embryo of an animal*
bud, cackle*, cackleberry*, germ, nucleus, oospore,᾽ ovum, roe, rudiment, spawn, yellow eye*; SEE CONCEPTS *389,392*

egghead [*n*] *intellectual*
bluestocking, bookworm*, brain*, geek*, genius, highbrow, know-it-all*, longhair*, rocket scientist*, scholar, thinker*; SEE CONCEPTS *350,416*

egg on [*v*] *push to do something*
agitate, arouse, drive, encourage, excite, exhort, goad, incite, instigate, pique, prick, prod,

prompt, propel, rally, sic, spur, stimulate, stir up, urge, whip up; SEE CONCEPT *68*

ego [*n*] *personality*
character, psyche, self, self-admiration, selfdom, self-pride; SEE CONCEPT *411*

egocentric [*adj*] *thinking very highly of oneself*
conceited, egoistic, egoistical, egomaniacal, egotistic, egotistical, individualist, individualistic, megalomaniac, narcissistic, pompous, self-absorbed, self-centered, self-concerned, self-indulgent, selfinterested, selfish, self-loving, self-serving, stuck-up, vainglorious, wrapped up in oneself; SEE CONCEPT *404*

egoism/egotism [*n*] *self-centeredness*
arrogance, assurance, boastfulness, boasting, bragging, conceit, conceitedness, egocentricity, egomania, gasconade, haughtiness, insolence, megalomania, narcissism, ostentation, overconfidence, preoccupation with self, presumption, pride, self-absorption, self-admiration, self-confidence, self-importance, self-interest, selfishness, self-love, self-possession, self-regard, self-worship, superiority, swellheadedness, vainglory, vanity, vaunting; SEE CONCEPT *411*

egotistic/egoistic [*adj*] *thinking very highly of oneself*
affected, aloof, autocratic, boastful, boasting, bragging, conceited, egocentric, egomaniacal, haughty, individualistic, inflated, inner-directed, intimate, intrinsic, introverted, isolated, narcissistic, obsessive, opinionated, personal, pompous, prideful, proud, puffed up*, self-absorbed, self-admiring, self-centered, self-important, snobbish, stuck on oneself*, stuck-up*, subjective, superior, swollen, vain, vainglorious; SEE CONCEPT *404*

egregious [*adj*] *outstandingly bad; outrageous*
arrant, atrocious, capital, deplorable, extreme, flagrant, glaring, grievous, gross*, heinous, infamous, insufferable, intolerable, monstrous, nefarious, notorious, outright, preposterous, rank, scandalous, shocking, stark; SEE CONCEPTS *545,548,570*

egress [*n*] *passage out*
departure, doorway, emanation, emergence, escape, exit, exiting, exodus, issue, opening, outlet, setting-out, vent, way out, withdrawal; SEE CONCEPTS *195,440*

ejaculate [*v*] *eject semen*
climax, come*, discharge, have an orgasm, spurt; SEE CONCEPTS *152,179*

eject [*v*] *throw or be thrown out*
banish, bounce*, bump, cast out, debar, disbar, discharge, disgorge, dislodge, dismiss, displace, dispossess, ditch, do away with*, drive off, dump*, eighty-six*, ejaculate, eliminate, emit, eradicate, eruct, erupt, evict, exclude, expel, expulse, extrude, fire, force out, get rid of, give the boot*, heave out*, irrupt, kick out*, kiss goodbye*, oust, reject, rout, sack, send packing*, show the gate to*, spew, spit out, spout, squeeze out, throw overboard*, turn out, unloose, vomit; SEE CONCEPTS *179,222*

ejection [*n*] *expulsion*
banishment, disbarment, discharge, dismissal, elimination, eviction, exile, ouster, removal, the boot*, the heave-ho*, the sack*, throwing out; SEE CONCEPTS *179,748*

eke out [*v*] *make something last*
barely exist, be economical with, be frugal with,

be sparing with, economize on, get by*, stretch out; SEE CONCEPT 239

elaborate [*adj*] *intricate; involved*
busy, careful, complex, complicated, decorated, detailed, elegant, embellished, exact, extensive, extravagant, fancy, fussy, garnished, highly wrought, high tech*, imposing, knotty, labored, labyrinthine, luxurious, many-faceted, minute, ornamented, ornate, ostentatious, overdone, overworked, painstaking, perfected, plush, posh, precise, prodigious, refined, showy, skillful, sophisticated, studied, thorough, with all the extras*, with all the options*, with bells and whistles*; SEE CONCEPT 562

elaborate [*v*] *make detailed; expand*
amplify, bedeck, clarify, comment, complicate, deck, decorate, develop, devise, discuss, embellish, enhance, enlarge, evolve, expatiate, explain, expound, flesh out, garnish, improve, interpret, ornament, particularize, polish, produce, refine, specify, unfold, work out; SEE CONCEPT 57

élan [*n*] *vivacity*
animation, ardor, brio, dash, esprit, flair, impetuosity, impetus, life, oomph*, panache, spirit, style, verve, vigor, vim, zest, zing*; SEE CONCEPT 411

elapse [*v*] *go by; slip away*
expire, flow, glide by, lapse, pass, pass away, pass by, roll by, roll on, run out, transpire, vanish; SEE CONCEPTS 6,144,818

elastic [*adj1*] *pliant, rubbery*
adaptable, bouncy, buoyant, ductile, extendible, extensible, flexible, irrepressible, limber, lithe, malleable, moldable, plastic, pliable, resilient, rubberlike, springy, stretchable, stretchy, supple, tempered, yielding; SEE CONCEPTS 490,606

elastic [*adj2*] *adaptable, tolerant*
accommodating, adjustable, airy, animated, bouncy, buoyant, complaisant, compliant, ebullient, effervescent, expansive, flexible, gay, high-spirited, lively, recuperative, resilient, soaring, spirited, sprightly, supple, variable, vivacious, volatile, yielding; SEE CONCEPT 404

elated [*adj*] *very happy*
animated, aroused, blissful, cheered, delighted, ecstatic, elevated, enchanted, enraptured, euphoric, exalted, excited, exhilarated, exultant, fired up*, flying*, flying high*, gleeful, high, hopped up*, in heaven*, in high spirits*, in seventh heaven*, intoxicated, joyful, joyous, jubilant, looking good*, on cloud nine*, overjoyed, proud, puffed up*, roused, set up, transported, turned-on*; SEE CONCEPTS 22,403

elation [*n*] *extreme happiness*
bliss, buoyancy, buzz, charge, cloud nine*, delight, ecstasy, enthusiasm, euphoria, exaltation, excitement, exhilaration, exultation, glee, high, high spirits, intoxication, jollies*, joy, joyfulness, joyousness, jubilation, kick*, kicks*, rapture, stars in one's eyes*, transport, triumph, up*, upper*; SEE CONCEPT 410

elbow [*n*] *angular part of arm; angularly shaped item*
ancon, angle, bend, bow, corner, crazy bone*, crook, crutch, curve, fork, funny bone*, half turn, hinge, joint, turn; SEE CONCEPTS 418,436

elbow [*v*] *push aside*
bend, bulldoze, bump, crowd, hook, hustle, jostle, knock, nudge, press, rough and tumble*, shoulder, shove; SEE CONCEPT 208

elbow grease [*n*] *physical effort*
effort, exertion, labor, muscle, oomph*, strain, strength, sweat, toil; SEE CONCEPTS 87,100,351, 360,362

elder [*adj*] *born earlier*
ancient, earlier, first-born, more mature, older, senior; SEE CONCEPTS 578,797

elder [*n*] *older person*
ancestor, ancient, forebearer, golden ager*, matriarch, oldest, old fogey*, oldster*, patriarch, senior, senior citizen, superior, veteran; SEE CONCEPT 424

elderly [*adj*] *in old age*
aged, aging, ancient, been around*, declining, gray*, hoary, long in tooth*, lot of mileage*, no spring chicken*, old, olden, on last leg*, over the hill*, retired, tired, venerable; SEE CONCEPTS 578,797

elect [*v*] *select as representative; choose*
accept, admit, appoint, ballot, conclude, cull, decide upon, designate, determine, go down the line, judge, mark, name, nominate, optate, opt for, pick, pick out, prefer, receive, resolve, settle, settle on, single out, take, tap, vote, vote for; SEE CONCEPTS 41,300

election [*n*] *choosing; voting*
alternative, appointment, ballot, balloting, choice, decision, determination, franchise, judgment, option, poll, polls, preference, primary, referendum, selection, ticket, vote-casting; SEE CONCEPTS 41,300

electioneering [*n*] *campaigning*
barnstorming*, canvassing, polling, voting; SEE CONCEPTS 87,320

elective [*adj*] *able to be chosen*
constituent, discretionary, electoral, facultative, nonobligatory, not compulsory, optional, selective, voluntary, voting; SEE CONCEPT 535

electric/electrical [*adj*] *charged; energetic*
AC, DC, dynamic, electrifying, excite, juiced*, magnetic, motor-driven, power-driven, rousing, stimulating, stirring, tense, thrilling, voltaic; SEE CONCEPT 540

electricity [*n*] *energized matter, power*
AC, current, DC, electromagneticism, electron, galvanism, heat, hot stuff*, ignition, juice*, light, magnetism, service, spark, tension, utilities, voltage; SEE CONCEPT 520

electrify [*v*] *thrill, stimulate*
amaze, animate, astonish, astound, charge, commove, disturb, dynamize, energize, enthuse, excite, fire, frenzy, galvanize, invigorate, jar, jolt, magnetize, power, provoke, rouse, send, shock, stagger, startle, stir, strike, stun, take one's breath away*, wire*; SEE CONCEPTS 7,22,42

electronics [*n*] *electronic devices*
camcorders, CD players, computer chips, computers, electronic components, integrated circuitry, radios, stereos, televisions, transistors, VCRs, video cameras; SEE CONCEPTS 463,499

elegance [*n*] *cultivated beauty, taste*
breeding, charm, class, courtliness, cultivation, culture, delicacy, dignity, discernment, distinction, exquisiteness, felicity, gentility, good taste, grace, gracefulness, grandeur, hauteur, lushness, luxury, magnificence, nicety, nobility, noblesse, ornateness, polish, politeness, poshness, propriety, purity, refinement, restraint, rhythm, sophistication, splendor, style, sumptuousness,

ef
el

symmetry, tastefulness; SEE CONCEPTS
655,671,718

elegant [*adj*] *beautiful, tasteful*
affected, appropriate, apt, aristocratic, artistic,
august, chic, choice, classic, clever, comely,
courtly, cultivated, cultured, dainty, delicate,
dignified, effective, exquisite, fancy, fashionable,
fine, genteel, graceful, grand, handsome, ingenious, luxurious, majestic, modish, neat, nice,
noble, opulent, ornamented, ornate, ostentatious,
overdone, polished, rare, recherché, refined, rich,
select, simple, stately, stuffy, stylish, stylized,
sumptuous, superior, turgid, well-bred; SEE CON-
CEPTS 574,579,589

elegiac [*adj*] *lamenting*
doleful, funereal, melancholy, mournful, sad,
sorrowful, threnodial; SEE CONCEPT 403

elegy [*n*] *dirge*
death song, funeral song, knell, lament, plaint,
requiem, threnody; SEE CONCEPTS 262,293,595

element [*n1*] *essential feature*
aspect, basic, basis, bit, component, constituent,
detail, drop, facet, factor, fundamental, hint, ingredient, item, material, matter, member, part,
particle, particular, piece, portion, principle, root,
section, stem, subdivision, trace, unit, view; SEE
CONCEPTS 668,826,829

element [*n2*] *place where one feels comfortable*
domain, environment, field, habitation, medium,
milieu, sphere; SEE CONCEPTS 198,516

elementary [*adj*] *simple, basic*
ABCs, abecedarian, basal, beginning, child's
play*, clear, duck soup*, easy, elemental, essential, facile, foundational, fundamental, initial, introductory, meat and potatoes*, original, plain,
prefatory, preliminary, primary, primitive,
primo*, rudimentary, simplest, simplex, simpli-
fied, straightforward, substratal, uncomplex, uncomplicated, underlying; SEE CONCEPTS 546,562

elephantine [*adj*] *huge*
behemothic, big, colossal, enormous, extensive,
gargantuan, giant, gigantic, grand, great, humongous, immense, jumbo*, large, mammoth, massive, monstrous, monumental, mountainous,
titanic, towering; SEE CONCEPTS 771,773

elevate [*v1*] *lift up*
erect, fetch up*, heighten, hike up*, hoist, jack
up*, levitate, poise, pump, put up, pyramid*,
raise, ramp, rear, shoot up*, stilt, take up, tilt, uphold, uplift, upraise; SEE CONCEPT 196

elevate [*v2*] *promote; augment*
advance, aggrandize, appoint, boost, build up,
dignify, enhance, ennoble, exalt, further, glorify,
heighten, honor, increase, intensify, magnify,
prefer, put up, skip, swell, upgrade; SEE CON-
CEPTS 69,351,700

elevate [*v3*] *raise spirits*
animate, boost, brighten, bring up, buoy up*,
cheer, elate, excite, exhilarate, glorify, hearten,
inspire, lift up*, perk up*, refine, rouse, sublimate, uplift; SEE CONCEPTS 7,22

elevated [*adj1*] *highly moral or dignified*
animated, big-time*, bright, elated, eloquent,
eminent, ethical, exalted, exhilarated, formal,
grand, grandiloquent, heavy, high, high-flown*,
high-minded, honorable, inflated, lofty, noble,
righteous, stately, sublime, superb, upright, upstanding, virtuous; SEE CONCEPTS 402,545,567

elevated [*adj2*] *raised up*
aerial, high, high-rise, lifted, raised, stately, tall,

towering, upheaved, uplifted, upraised, uprisen;
SEE CONCEPT 779

elevation [*n1*] *height; high ground*
acclivity, altitude, ascent, boost, eminence,
heave, hill, hillock, hoist, levitation, mountain,
platform, ridge, rise, roof, top, uplift, upthrow;
SEE CONCEPTS 509,741

elevation [*n2*] *advancement, promotion*
aggrandizement, apotheosis, boost, deification,
eminence, ennoblement, exaltation, exaltedness,
glorification, grandeur, immortalization, lionization, loftiness, magnification, nobility, nobleness, preference, preferment, prelation, raise,
sublimity, upgrading; SEE CONCEPTS 69,351,668

elevator [*n*] *lift*
conveyor, dumbwaiter, escalator, hoist; SEE CON-
CEPT 196

elf [*n*] *small, fairytale character*
brownie, elfin, fairy, fay, leprechaun, nisse,
pixie; SEE CONCEPT 370

elfin [*adj*] *mischievous; small*
delicate, devilish, disobedient, elfish, frolicsome,
impish, little, minute, misbehaving, naughty, petite, playful, prankish, puckish, puny, rascally,
slight, sprightly, tiny; SEE CONCEPTS 401,545

elicit [*v*] *draw out*
arm-twist*, badger, bite*, bring, bring forth,
bring out, bring to light*, call forth, cause, derive, educe, evince, evoke, evolve, exact, extort,
extract, fetch, give rise to, milk*, obtain, put
muscle on*, put the arm on*, rattle, shake, shake
down*, squeeze, wrest, wring; SEE CONCEPTS
68,142

eligible [*adj*] *fit, worthy*
acceptable, appropriate, becoming, capable of,
desirable, discretionary, elective, employable,
equal to, fitted, in line for*, in the running*, licensed, likely, preferable, privileged, proper,
qualified, satisfactory, seemly, suitable, suited,
trained, up to*, usable; SEE CONCEPTS 527,558

eliminate [*v*] *remove, throw out*
annihilate, blot out*, bump off*, cancel, cast out,
count out, cut out, defeat, discard, discharge, dismiss, dispense with, dispose of, disqualify, disregard, do away with, drive out, drop, eject,
eradicate, erase, evict, exclude, expel, exterminate, get rid of, ignore, invalidate, kill, knock
out*, leave out, liquidate, murder, omit, oust,
phase out, put out, reject, rub out*, rule out, set
aside, shut the door on*, slay, stamp out*, take
out, terminate, waive, waste, wipe out*; SEE
CONCEPTS 30,211

elimination [*n*] *removal*
cut, destruction, discard, displacement, dropping,
ejection, eradication, exclusion, expulsion, extermination, omission, rejection, riddance, taking
away, weeding out, withdrawal; SEE CONCEPT
180

elite [*adj*] *best, first-class*
aristocratic, choice, cool*, crack*, elect, exclusive, gilt-edged, greatest, noble, out of sight*,
out of this world*, pick, selected, super, tip-top*,
top, top drawer*, topflight, top-notch, upper-
class, world-class; SEE CONCEPTS 555,574

elite [*n*] *high-class persons*
aristocracy, beautiful people*, best, blue blood*,
carriage trade*, celebrity, choice, country club
set*, cream, crème de la crème*, crowd, elect,
establishment, fast lane*, fat*, flower, gentility,
gentry, glitterati, high society*, in-crowd*, jet-

set*, main line*, nobility, old money*, optimacy, pride, prime, prize, quality, select, society, top, upper class, upper crust*; SEE CONCEPTS 387,388,417

elitist [*n*] *snob*
highbrow, name-dropper, pompous ass, pompous person, social climber, stiff, stuffed shirt; SEE CONCEPT 423

elixir [*n*] *remedy*
cure-all, elixir of life, extract, medicine, mixture, panacea, philosopher's stone, potion, principle, solution; SEE CONCEPTS 307,311,693,712

elliptical [*adj*] *oval-shaped*
egg-shaped, ellipsoidal, oblong, ovoid; SEE CONCEPT 486

elocution [*n*] *articulation*
declamation, delivery, diction, dramatic, eloquence, enunciation, expression, locution, oratory, pronunciation, public speaking, reading, rhetoric, speech, speechcraft, speechmaking, utterance, voice culture, voice production; SEE CONCEPT 47

elongate [*v*] *make longer*
drag one's feet*, drag out, draw, draw out, extend, fill, lengthen, let out, pad*, prolong, prolongate, protract, put rubber in*, spin out, stretch; SEE CONCEPTS 137,239,250

elongated [*adj*] *lengthened*
dragged out, drawn out, expanded, extended, increased, made longer, outstretched, prolonged, protracted, stretched, strung out; SEE CONCEPTS 482,779,798

elope [*v*] *run away to be married*
abscond, bolt, decamp, disappear, escape, flee, fly, go secretly, go to Gretna Green*, leave, run off, skip*, slip away, slip out, steal away; SEE CONCEPT 297

eloquence [*n*] *skillful way with words*
ability, appeal, articulation, command of language, delivery, diction, dramatic, expression, expressiveness, expressivity, facility, fervor, flow, fluency, force, forcefulness, gift of gab*, grandiloquence, loquacity, meaningfulness, mellifluousness, oration, oratory, passion, persuasiveness, poise, power, rhetoric, spirit, style, vigor, vivacity, volubility, wit, wittiness; SEE CONCEPTS 68,278,630

eloquent [*adj*] *having a skillful way with words*
affecting, ardent, articulate, expressive, facund, fervent, fervid, fluent, forceful, glib, grandiloquent, graphic, impassioned, impressive, indicative, magniloquent, meaningful, moving, outspoken, passionate, persuasive, poignant, potent, powerful, revealing, rhetorical, sententious, significant, silver-tongued*, smooth-spoken*, stirring, suggestive, telling, touching, vivid, vocal, voluble, well-expressed; SEE CONCEPT 267

elsewhere [*adv*] *in another place*
abroad, absent, away, formerly, gone, hence, not here, not present, not under consideration, otherwhere, outside, remote, removed, somewhere, somewhere else, subsequently; SEE CONCEPT 586

elucidate [*v*] *explain in detail*
annotate, clarify, clear, clear up, decode, demonstrate, draw a picture*, enlighten, exemplify, explicate, expound, get across*, gloss, illuminate, illustrate, interpret, make perfectly clear, make plain, make see daylight*, prove, shed light on*, spell out*, throw light on*, unfold; SEE CONCEPT 57

elude [*v*] *avoid; escape*
baffle, beat around the bush*, be beyond someone*, bilk, circumvent, confound, cop out*, ditch, dodge, double, duck, eschew, evade, flee, fly, foil, frustrate, get around, get away from, give the runaround*, give the slip*, give wide berth to*, hem and haw*, not touch, outrun, outwit, pass the buck*, pass up, puzzle, run around, shirk, shuck, shun, shy, stall, stay shy of*, steer clear of*, stonewall*, stump, thwart; SEE CONCEPTS 30,38,59,102

elusive [*adj*] *evasive, mysterious*
ambiguous, baffling, cagey, deceitful, deceptive, difficult to catch, elusory, equivocal, evanescent, fallacious, fleeting, fraudulent, fugacious, fugitive, greasy, illusory, imponderable, incomprehensible, indefinable, insubstantial, intangible, misleading, occult, phantom, puzzling, shifty, shy, slippery, stonewalling*, subtle, transient, transitory, tricky, unspecific, volatile; SEE CONCEPTS 529,542

emaciated [*adj*] *undernourished; thin*
anorexic, atrophied, attenuate, attenuated, bony, cadaverous, consumptive, famished, gaunt, haggard, lank, lean, like a bag of bones*, meager, peaked, pinched, scrawny, skeletal, skeletonlike, skin-andbones*, skinny, starved, thin as rail*, underfed, wasted, wizened; SEE CONCEPTS 490,491

el
em

E-mail [*n*] *electronic mail*
chat message, online correspondence, online mail, voice mail; SEE CONCEPT 266

emanate [*v*] *come forth; give off*
arise, birth, derive, discharge, egress, emerge, emit, exhale, exit, exude, flow, initiate, issue, originate, proceed, radiate, rise, send forth, spring, stem; SEE CONCEPTS 179,221,648

emanation [*n*] *emergence, discharge*
arising, beginning, derivation, drainage, effluence, effluent, efflux, effusion, ejaculation, emerging, emission, escape, exhalation, exudation, flow, flowing, gush, issuance, issuing, leakage, oozing, origin, origination, outflow, outpour, proceeding, radiation, springing, welling; SEE CONCEPTS 179,221,648

emancipate [*v*] *set free*
affranchise, deliver, discharge, disencumber, disenthral, enfranchise, liberate, loose, loosen, manumit, release, unbind, unchain, unfetter, unshackle; SEE CONCEPT 127

emancipation [*n*] *freedom*
deliverance, delivery, enfranchisement, independence, liberation, liberty, release, setting free; SEE CONCEPT 691

emasculate [*v*] *weaken, deprive of force*
alter, debilitate, devitalize, enervate, fix*, impoverish, vitiate; SEE CONCEPTS 240,250

embalm [*v*] *preserve, immortalize*
anoint, cherish, consecrate, conserve, enshrine, freeze, lay out, mummify, prepare, process, store, treasure, wrap; SEE CONCEPT 202

embargo [*n*] *prohibition, restriction*
ban, bar, barrier, blockage, check, hindrance, impediment, interdict, interdiction, proscription, restraint, stoppage; SEE CONCEPTS 119,130

embark [*v*] *get on transportation object*
board, commence, emplane, enter, entrain, go aboard ship, launch, leave port, plunge into, put on board, set about, set out, set sail, take on board, take ship; SEE CONCEPTS 159,195,224

embark on [v] *begin undertaking, journey*
broach, commence, engage, enter, get off, initiate, jump off, launch, open, plunge into, set about, set out, set to, start, take up, tee off*; SEE CONCEPTS 100,221

embarrass [v] *cause mental discomfort*
abash, agitate, annoy, bewilder, bother, bug, catch one short*, chagrin, confuse, discombobulate*, discomfit, discompose, disconcert, discountenance, distract, distress, disturb, dumbfound, faze, fluster, give a bad time*, give a hard time*, hang up*, irk, let down*, make a monkey of*, mortify, nonplus, perplex, perturb, plague, put in a hole*, put in a spot*, put on the spot*, put out of countenance*, puzzle, rattle, shame, show up*, stun, tease, throw, throw into a tizzy*, upset; SEE CONCEPTS 7,19,54

embarrassing [adj] *humiliating, shaming*
awkward, bewildering, compromising, confusing, delicate, difficult, disagreeable, discomfiting, discommoding, discommodious, disconcerting, distracting, distressing, disturbing, equivocal, exasperating, impossible, incommodious, inconvenient, inopportune, mortifying, perplexing, puzzling, rattling, sensitive, shameful, sticky, ticklish, touchy, tricky, troublesome, troubling, uncomfortable, uneasy, unpropitious, unseemly, upsetting, worrisome; SEE CONCEPTS 537,548

embarrassment [n] *humiliation, shame*
awkwardness, awkward situation, bashfulness, bind, boo boo*, chagrin, clumsiness, complexity, confusion, destitution, difficulty, dilemma, discomfiture, discomposure, disconcertion, distress, egg on face*, faux pas, fix, hitch, hot seat*, hot water*, impecuniosity, indebtedness, indiscretion, inhibition, mess, mistake, mortification, pickle*, pinch, plight, poverty, predicament, puzzle, quandary, scrape, self-consciousness, shyness, snag, stew, strait, tangle, timidity, unease, uneasiness; SEE CONCEPTS 410,674

embassy [n] *residence, offices of overseas representatives*
commission, committee, consular office, consulate, delegation, diplomatic office, legation, ministry, mission; SEE CONCEPTS 439,449,516

embattle [v] *prepare for battle*
arm, array, equip, fortify, furnish, make ready, militarize, mobilize, prepare for combat, strengthen, supply; SEE CONCEPT 202

embed [v] *sink, implant*
bury, deposit, dig in, drive in, enclose, fasten, fix, hammer in, impact, infix, ingrain, inlay, insert, install, lodge, pierce, plant, plunge, press, put into, ram in, root, set, stick in, stuff in, thrust in, tuck in; SEE CONCEPTS 178,188

embellish [v] *make beautiful; decorate*
add bells and whistles*, adorn, amplify, array, beautify, bedeck, color, deck, dress up*, elaborate, emblaze, embroider, enhance, enrich, exaggerate, festoon, fix up*, fudge*, garnish, gild, give details, grace, gussy up*, magnify, ornament, overstate, spiff up*, spruce up*, trim; SEE CONCEPTS 49,162,177,700

embellishment [n] *beautification; decorating*
adornment, coloring, decoration, doodad*, elaboration, embroidering, embroidery, enhancement, enrichment, exaggeration, fandangle*, floridity, flowery speech, frill, froufrou*, fuss*, garnish, gilding, gingerbread*, hyperbole, icing

on the cake*, jazz*, ornament, ornamentation, ostentation, overstatement; SEE CONCEPTS 177, 278,700,718

embers [n] *hot ashes from fire*
ash, brand, cinders, clinkers, coals, firebrand, live coals, slag, smoking remnants, smoldering remains; SEE CONCEPTS 260,478

embezzle [v] *steal money, often from employer*
abstract, appropriate, defalcate, filch, forge, loot, misapply, misappropriate, misuse, peculate, pilfer, purloin, put hand in cookie jar*, put hand in till*, skim, thieve; SEE CONCEPT 139

embezzlement [n] *stealing money, often from employer*
abstraction, appropriation, defalcation, filching, fraud, larceny, misapplication, misappropriation, misuse, peculation, pilferage, pilfering, purloining, skimming, theft, thieving; SEE CONCEPT 139

embitter [v] *upset, alienate*
acerbate, acidulate, aggravate, anger, annoy, bitter, bother, disaffect, disillusion, envenom, exacerbate, exasperate, irritate, make bitter, make resentful, poison, sour, venom, worsen; SEE CONCEPTS 7,14,19

embittered [adj] *resentful*
bitter, disaffected, full of hate, irritated, rancorous, sore, spiteful; SEE CONCEPTS 267,404

emblazon [v] *adorn*
add finishing touches, beautify, brighten, color, deck, decorate, do up*, embellish, fix up, gussy up*, jazz up*, ornament, paint, spruce up*; SEE CONCEPTS 162,177

emblem [n] *crest*
adumbration, arms, attribute, badge, banner, brand, character, coat of arms, colophon, colors, design, device, figure, flag, hallmark, identification, image, impress, insignia, logo, mark, marker, medal, memento, miniature, monogram, motto, pennant, regalia, reminder, representation, scepter, seal, sign, standard, symbol, token, trademark, type; SEE CONCEPTS 259,284,625

embodiment [n] *representation, manifestation*
apotheosis, archetype, cast, collection, comprehension, conformation, embracement, encompassment, epitome, example, exemplar, exemplification, expression, form, formation, incarnation, inclusion, incorporation, integration, matter, organization, personification, prosopopoeia, quintessence, realization, reification, structure, symbol, systematization, type; SEE CONCEPTS 118,686

embody [v1] *represent; materialize*
actualize, complete, concretize, demonstrate, emblematize, epitomize, evince, exemplify, exhibit, express, exteriorize, externalize, hypostatize, illustrate, incarnate, incorporate, manifest, mirror, objectify, personalize, personify, realize, reify, show, stand for, substantiate, symbolize, typify; SEE CONCEPT 118

embody [v2] *include, integrate*
absorb, amalgamate, assimilate, blend, bring together, codify, collect, combine, comprehend, comprise, concentrate, consolidate, contain, embrace, encompass, establish, fuse, have, incorporate, involve, merge, organize, subsume, systematize, take in, unify; SEE CONCEPTS 112,113

embolden [v] *encourage*
boost, buoy, cheer, energize, enhearten, exhilarate, give courage, give pep talk*, goad, inspire,

inspirit, invigorate, psyche up, push, rally, reassure, refresh, revitalize, spur, stir, sway; SEE CONCEPTS 7,22

emboss [v] *imprint*
adorn, carve, decorate, etch, impress, punch, sculpt, stamp; SEE CONCEPT 79

embrace [v1] *hold tightly in one's arms*
bear hug*, clasp, clinch, cling, clutch, cradle, cuddle, encircle, enfold, entwine, envelop, fold, fondle, grab, grasp, grip, hug, lock, nuzzle, press, seize, snuggle, squeeze, take in arms*, wrap; SEE CONCEPTS 190,191

embrace [v2] *include in one's beliefs; take into account*
accept, accommodate, admit, adopt, avail oneself of, comprehend, comprise, contain, cover, deal with*, embody, enclose, encompass, espouse, get into*, go in for*, grab, have, incorporate, involve, make use of, provide for, receive, seize, subsume, take advantage of, take in, take on, take up, welcome; SEE CONCEPTS 12,15,112

embroider [v1] *add fancy stitching, adornment*
beautify, bedeck, braid, color, cross-stitch, deck, decorate, embellish, fix up, garnish, gild, gussy up*, knit, ornament, pattern, quilt, spruce up*, stitch, weave pattern, work; SEE CONCEPTS 177,218

embroider [v2] *exaggerate information*
aggrandize, amplify, blow-up*, build up, color, distend, dramatize, elaborate, embellish, enhance, enlarge, expand, falsify, fudge*, heighten, hyperbolize, lie, magnify, make federal case*, make mountain out of molehill*, overdo, overelaborate, overembellish, overemphasize, overestimate, overstate, pad*, play up*, puff*, romanticize, spread on thick*, stretch, stretch the truth*, yeast*; SEE CONCEPTS 58,63

embroidery [n] *fancy stitching*
adornment, appliqué, arabesque, bargello, brocade, crewel, crochet, cross-stitch, decoration, lace, lacery, needlepoint, needlework, quilting, sampler, tapestry, tatting, tracery; SEE CONCEPTS 218,259

embroil [v] *involve in dispute; complicate*
cause trouble, compromise, confound, confuse, derange, disorder, disturb, disunite, encumber, enmesh, ensnare, entangle, implicate, incriminate, involve, mire, mix up, muddle, perplex, snarl, tangle, trouble; SEE CONCEPTS 7,19,86

embryonic [adj] *rudimentary*
beginning, developing, early, elementary, evolving, germinal, immature, incipient, undeveloped; SEE CONCEPTS 485,578,797

emend [v] *correct*
alter, amend, better, edit, emendate, improve, polish, rectify, redact, retouch, revise, right, touch up; SEE CONCEPT 126

emerge [v] *come out, arise*
appear, arrive, become apparent, become known, become visible, come forth, come into view, come on the scene, come to light, come up, crop up, dawn, derive, develop, egress, emanate, flow, gush, issue, loom, make appearance, materialize, originate, proceed, rise, show, spring, spring up, spurt, steam, stem, surface, transpire, turn up; SEE CONCEPTS 105,118

emergency [n] *crisis, danger*
accident, climax, clutch*, compulsion, crossroad, crunch*, depression, difficulty, distress, exigency, extremity, fix, hole, impasse, juncture,

meltdown*, misadventure, necessity, pass, pinch*, plight, predicament, pressure, push, quandary, scrape, squeeze, strait, tension, turning point, urgency, vicissitude, zero hour*; SEE CONCEPTS 674,675

emergency room [n] *trauma center*
critical care facility, emergency clinic, ER, ICU, intensive care unit, triage room; SEE CONCEPTS 312,439,449

emergent [adj] *resulting*
appearing, budding, coming, developing, efflorescent, emanant, emanating, issuing forth, outgoing, rising; SEE CONCEPT 537

emigrant [n] *person who leaves his or her native country*
alien, colonist, departer, displaced person, émigré, evacuee, exile, expatriate, fugitive, migrant, migrator, outcast, pilgrim, refugee, traveler, wanderer, wayfarer; SEE CONCEPTS 413,423

emigrate [v] *move to new country*
depart, migrate, move abroad, quit, remove, transmigrate; SEE CONCEPT 198

émigré [n] *emigrant*
displaced person, DP, exile, expatriate, foreigner, migrant, refugee; SEE CONCEPT 413

eminence [n1] *importance, fame*
authority, celebrity, credit, dignity, distinction, esteem, famousness, glory, greatness, honor, illustriousness, influence, kudos, loftiness, notability, note, power, preeminence, prepotency, prestige, prominence, prominency, rank, renown, reputation, repute, significance, standing, superiority, weight; SEE CONCEPTS 388,668,671

eminence [n2] *high ground*
altitude, elevation, height, highland, highness, hill, hillock, knoll, loftiness, peak, project, prominence, promontory, raise, ridge, rise, summit, upland; SEE CONCEPTS 509,741

eminent [adj] *very important; famous*
august, big-gun*, big-league*, big-name*, big-time*, celeb*, celebrated, celebrious, conspicuous, distinguished, dominant, elevated, esteemed, exalted, famed, grand, great, high, high-ranking, illustrious, lionlike, lofty, name, noble, notable, noted, noteworthy, of note, outstanding, page-oner*, paramount, preeminent, prestigious, prominent, redoubted, renowned, star, superior, superstar, VIP*, well-known; SEE CONCEPTS 555,568

eminently [adv] *exceptionally; well*
conspicuously, exceedingly, extremely, greatly, highly, notably, outstandingly, prominently, remarkably, strikingly, suitably, surpassingly, very; SEE CONCEPT 574

emir [n] *prince*
amir, chieftain, governor, leader, shah, sheik; SEE CONCEPTS 347,354

emissary [n] *deputy*
agent, ambassador, bearer, carrier, consul, courier, delegate, envoy, front, go-between, herald, hired gun*, intermediary, internuncio, legate, messenger, rep*, representative, scout, spy; SEE CONCEPTS 348,423

emission [n] *issuance, diffusion*
discharge, ejaculation, ejection, emanation, exhalation, exudation, issue, radiation, shedding, transmission, utterance, venting; SEE CONCEPT 179

emit [v] *diffuse, discharge*
afford, beam, belch, breathe, cast out, disem-

em
em

bogue, drip, eject, emanate, erupt, evacuate, excrete, exhale, expectorate, expel, expend, expire,
extrude, exude, give off, give out, give vent to,
gush, issue, jet, let off, loose, ooze, pass, perspire, pour, pronounce, purge, radiate, reek, secrete, send forth, send out, shed, shoot, speak,
spew, spill, spit, squirt, throw out, transmit, utter,
vent, voice, void, vomit, yield; SEE CONCEPTS
108,179,266

emollient [adj] soothing
balsamic, demulcent, healing, lenitive, palliative,
relieving, remedial, softening; SEE CONCEPTS
7,22,110,384

emollient [n] lotion
balm, cream, lenitive, liniment, moisturizer, oil,
ointment, salve, soothing agent, unguent; SEE
CONCEPTS 311,446,466

emote [v] express emotion
act, dramatize, exaggerate, ham it up*, overact,
overdramatize, overplay; SEE CONCEPT 292

emoticon [n] keyboard symbol code, :-)
emotag, smiley, winkey; SEE CONCEPT 284

emotion [n] mental state
affect, affection, affectivity, agitation, anger,
ardor, commotion, concern, desire, despair, despondency, disturbance, drive, ecstasy, elation,
empathy, excitability, excitement, feeling, fervor, grief, gut reaction, happiness, inspiration,
joy, love, melancholy, passion, perturbation,
pride, rage, remorse, responsiveness, sadness,
satisfaction, sensation, sensibility, sensitiveness,
sentiment, shame, sorrow, sympathy, thrill,
tremor, vehemence, vibes, warmth, zeal; SEE
CONCEPT 410

emotional [adj] demonstrative about feelings
affecting, ardent, disturbed, ecstatic, emotive,
enthusiastic, excitable, exciting, falling apart*,
fanatical, feeling, fervent, fervid, fickle, fiery,
heartwarming, heated, histrionic, hot-blooded*,
hysterical, impassioned, impetuous, impulsive,
irrational, moving, nervous, overwrought, passionate, pathetic, poignant, responsive, roused,
sensitive, sentient, sentimental, spontaneous,
stirred, stirring, susceptible, tear-jerking*, temperamental, tender, thrilling, touching, warm,
zealous; SEE CONCEPTS 403,542

emotionless [adj] unfeeling, undemonstrative
blank, chill, cold, cold-blooded*, cold fish*,
cool, cool cat*, deadpan, detached, dispassionate, distant, flat, frigid, glacial*, heartless, icy,
immovable, impassive, impersonal, in cold
blood*, indifferent, laid back*, matter-of-fact,
nonemotional, nowhere*, poker face*, remote,
reserved, stony-eyed*, thick-skinned*, toneless,
unemotional, unimpassioned, with straight face;
SEE CONCEPTS 401,403,542

empathize [v] identify with
comprehend, feel for, imagine, put oneself in another's place, relate to, share, stand in one's
shoes, suffer with, sympathize, understand; SEE
CONCEPTS 34,110

empathy [n] understanding
affinity, appreciation, being on same wavelength*, being there for someone*, communion,
community of interests, compassion, comprehension, concord, cottoning to*, good vibrations*,
hitting it off*, insight, picking up on*, pity, rapport, recognition, responsiveness, soul, sympathy, warmth; SEE CONCEPTS 32,409,411

emperor [n] ruler
czar, dictator, empress, king, monarch, prince,
sovereign, sultan; SEE CONCEPTS 347,354

emphasis [n] importance, prominence
accent, accentuation, attention, decidedness,
force, headline, highlight, impressiveness, insistence, intensity, moment, positiveness, power,
preeminence, priority, significance, strength,
stress, underlining, underscoring, weight; SEE
CONCEPTS 668,682

emphasize [v] stress, give priority to
accent, accentuate, affirm, articulate, assert, bear
down, charge, dramatize, dwell on, enlarge,
enunciate, headline, highlight, hit*, impress, indicate, insist on, italicize, labor the point*, limelight*, maintain, make a point, make clear, make
emphatic, make much of*, mark, pinpoint, play
up*, point out*, point up*, press, pronounce,
punctuate, put accent on*, reiterate, repeat, rub
in*, spotlight*, underline, underscore, weight;
SEE CONCEPTS 49,57

emphatic [adj] insistent, unequivocal
absolute, accented, assertive, assured, categorical, certain, cogent, confident, decided, definite,
definitive, determined, direct, distinct, dogmatic,
dynamic, earnest, energetic, explicit, express,
flat, for a face*, forceful, forcible, important, impressive, marked, momentous, no mistake*,
pointed, positive, potent, powerful, pronounced,
resounding, significant, sober, solemn, stressed,
striking, strong, sure, telling, trenchant, unmistakable, vigorous; SEE CONCEPTS 267,535

empire [n] place ruled by sovereign; rule
authority, command, commonwealth, control,
domain, dominion, federation, government, people, power, realm, sovereignty, supremacy,
sway, union; SEE CONCEPTS 198,299,376

empirical/empiric [adj] practical; based on experience
experient, experiential, experimental, factual, ob-
servational, observed, pragmatic, provisional,
speculative; SEE CONCEPTS 548,582

employ [v1] make use of
apply, bestow, bring to bear*, engage, exercise,
exert, exploit, fill, handle, keep busy*, manipulate, occupy, operate, put to use*, spend, take
up*, use, use up*, utilize; SEE CONCEPT 225

employ [v2] give money in exchange for work
performed
bring on board*, come on board*, commission,
contract, contract for, engage, enlist, hire, ink*,
obtain, place, procure, put on*, retain, secure,
sign on*, sign up*, take on, truck with*; SEE
CONCEPT 351

employed [adj] working
active, at it*, at work, busy, engaged, hired, in a
job, in collar*, in harness*, inked*, in place, laboring, occupied, on board*, on duty*, on the
job*, on the payroll*, operating, plugging
away*, selected, signed*; SEE CONCEPTS 538,560

employee [n] person being paid for working for
another or a corporation
agent, apprentice, assistant, attendant, blue collar*, breadwinner*, clerk, cog*, company person, craftsperson, desk jockey*, domestic, hand,
help, hired gun*, hired hand*, hireling, job-
holder, laborer, member, operator, pink collar*,
plug*, representative, sales help, salesperson,
servant, slave, staff member, wage-earner, white

collar*, worker, working stiff*; SEE CONCEPT *348*

employer [*n*] *person, business who hires workers*
big cheese*, big shot*, boss, businessperson, capitalist, CEO*, chief, CO*, company, corporation, director, entrepreneur, establishment, executive, firm, front office, head, head honcho*, juice*, kingpin*, management, manager, manufacturer, meal ticket*, organization, outfit, overseer, owner, patron, president, proprietor, slavedriver*, superintendent, supervisor; SEE CONCEPT *347*

employment [*n1*] *working for a living; engagement in activity*
application, assignment, avocation, awarding, business, calling, carrying, commissioning, contracting, craft, employ, engaging, enlistment, enrollment, exercise, exercising, exertion, field, function, game*, hire, hiring, job, line, métier, mission, number, occupation, occupying, office, position, post, profession, pursuit, racket*, recruitment, retaining, service, servicing, setup, signing on*, situation, taking on, thing*, trade, using, vocation, what one is into*, work; SEE CONCEPTS *349,351,360*

employment [*n2*] *using something*
adoption, appliance, application, disposition, exercise, exercising, exertion, exploitation, handling, operation, play, purpose, usage, usance, use, utilization; SEE CONCEPTS *225,658,694*

emporium [*n*] *market*
bazaar, boutique, chain, co-op, cut-rate store*, discount store, five-and-dime*, flea market, galleria, mall, mart, outlet, outlet store, shop, shopping center, shopping plaza, stand, store, supermarket, thrift shop; SEE CONCEPT *449*

empower [*v*] *authorize, enable*
accredit, allow, capacitate, charge, commission, delegate, entitle, entrust, grant, invest, legitimize, license, okay, permit, privilege, qualify, sanction, vest, warrant; SEE CONCEPTS *50,88*

empress [*n*] *female ruler*
princess, queen, sovereign; SEE CONCEPTS *347,354*

emptiness [*n*] *void, bareness*
blank, blankness, chasm, depletedness, desertedness, desolation, destitution, exhaustion, gap, hollowness, inanition, vacancy, vacuity, vacuum, waste; SEE CONCEPTS *720,733*

empty [*adj1*] *containing nothing*
abandoned, bare, barren, blank, clear, dead, deflated, depleted, desert, deserted, desolate, despoiled, destitute, devoid, dry, evacuated, exhausted, forsaken, godforsaken*, hollow, lacking, stark, unfilled, unfurnished, uninhabited, unoccupied, vacant, vacated, vacuous, void, wanting, waste; SEE CONCEPTS *481,774,786*

empty [*adj2*] *fruitless, ineffective*
aimless, banal, barren, cheap, dead, deadpan, devoid, dishonest, dumb, expressionless, fatuous, flat, frivolous, futile, hollow, idle, ignorant, inane, ineffectual, inexpressive, insincere, insipid, jejune, meaningless, nugatory, otiose, paltry, petty, purposeless, senseless, silly, trivial, unintelligent, unreal, unsatisfactory, unsubstantial, vacuous, vain, valueless, vapid, worthless; SEE CONCEPTS *402,570,575*

empty [*adj3*] *hungry*
famished, ravenous, starving, unfed, unfilled; SEE CONCEPT *406*

empty [*v*] *remove contents*
clear, consume, decant, deplete, discharge, disgorge, drain, drink, dump, ebb, eject, escape, evacuate, exhaust, expel, flow out, gut, leak, leave, make void, pour out, purge, release, run out, rush out, tap, unburden, unload, use up, vacate, void; SEE CONCEPT *211*

empty-headed [*adj*] *flighty, scatterbrained*
brainless, dizzy, featherbrained, frivolous, giddy, harebrained, ignorant, illiterate, inane, knownothing, silly, skittish, stupid, uneducated, unschooled, untaught, vacant, vacuous; SEE CONCEPT *402*

emulate [*v*] *copy the actions of*
challenge, compete, compete with, contend, contend with, ditto*, do*, do like*, follow, follow in footsteps*, follow suit*, follow the example of*, go like*, imitate, make like*, mimic, mirror, outvie, pattern after*, rival, rivalize, take after*, vie with; SEE CONCEPTS *87,171*

enable [*v*] *allow, authorize*
accredit, approve, capacitate, commission, condition, empower, endow, facilitate, fit, give power, implement, invest, let, license, make possible, permit, prepare, provide the means*, qualify, ready, sanction, set up, warrant; SEE CONCEPTS *50,83,88,99*

enact [*v1*] *act out; accomplish*
achieve, appear as, depict, discourse, do, execute, go on*, perform, personate, play, playact, play the part of, portray, represent; SEE CONCEPTS *91,292*

enact [*v2*] *authorize, legislate*
accomplish, appoint, bring about, carry through, command, constitute, decree, determine, dictate, effect, effectuate, establish, execute, fix, formulate, get the floor*, institute, jam through*, make, make into law, make laws, ordain, order, pass, proclaim, put in force, put through, railroad*, railroad through*, ratify, sanction, set, steamroll*, transact, vote favorably*, vote in*; SEE CONCEPTS *50,88,298,317*

enactment [*n1*] *playacting*
achievement, acting, depiction, execution, impersonation, performance, personation, personification, playing, portrayal, representation; SEE CONCEPTS *263,292*

enactment [*n2*] *law; authorization*
command, commandment, decree, dictate, edict, execution, legislation, order, ordinance, proclamation, ratification, regulation, statute; SEE CONCEPTS *318,685*

enamel [*n*] *paint, often shiny*
cloisonné, coating, finish, glaze, gloss, japan, lacquer, polish, stain, topcoat, varnish, veneer; SEE CONCEPTS *259,260,467*

enamor [*v*] *fascinate, captivate*
attract, bewitch, charm, enchant, endear, enrapture, enthrall, entice, entrance, fall in love with*, grab, infatuate, make hit with*, please, slay*, sweep off feet*, turn on*; SEE CONCEPTS *7,22,375*

enamored [*adj*] *in love*
amorous, attracted, besotted, bewitched, captivated, charmed, crazy about*, devoted, dotty, enchanted, enraptured, entranced, fascinated, fond, gone*, has a thing about*, hooked*, infatuated, loving, nuts about*, silly about*, smitten, stuck on*, swept off one's feet*, taken*, wild about*; SEE CONCEPTS *32,403*

em
en

encampment [n] *camp*
bivouac, campground, campsite, rest area, site; SEE CONCEPTS *198,516*

encapsulate [v] *encase*
box, cover, enclose, envelop, sheathe, wrap; SEE CONCEPTS *112,209,758*

encapsulate [v2] *epitomize*
abbreviate, abridge, capsulize, condense, cut, digest, precis, shorten, summarize, sum up, synopsize; SEE CONCEPTS *236,247*

enchant [v] *delight, mesmerize*
allure, beguile, bewitch, captivate, carry away*, cast a spell on*, charm, delectate, draw, enamor, enrapture, ensorcell, enthrall, entice, entrance, fascinate, grab, gratify, hex, hypnotize, kill*, knock dead*, magnetize, make a hit with*, make happy*, please, send*, slay*, spell, spellbind, sweep off feet*, take, thrill, turn on*, voodoo*, wile, wow*; SEE CONCEPTS *7,22*

enchanting [adj] *fascinating, delightful*
alluring, appealing, attractive, beguiling, bewitching, captivating, charming, delectable, endearing, enthralling, entrancing, exciting, glamorous, intriguing, lovely, pleasant, pleasing, ravishing, seductive, siren, sirenic, winsome; SEE CONCEPTS *404,529*

enchantress [n] *sorceress*
charmer, diviner, femme fatale, seductress, siren, vamp, witch; SEE CONCEPTS *361,412,415*

encircle [v] *circumscribe*
band, begird, cincture, circle, circuit, compass, cover, enclose, encompass, enfold, envelop, environ, gird in, girdle, halo, hem in*, inclose, invest, ring, surround, wreathe; SEE CONCEPT *758*

enclose [v] *put inside, surround*
blockade, block off, bound, box up, cage, circle, circumscribe, close in, confine, coop, corral, cover, encase, encircle, encompass, enfold, enshroud, environ, fence, fence off*, hedge, hem in*, imbue, immure, implant, impound, imprison, include, induct, insert, intern, jail, limit, lock in*, lock up*, mew, mure, pen, restrict, set apart, shut in, veil, wall in, wrap; SEE CONCEPTS *112,209,758*

enclosure [n1] *area bounded by something*
asylum, aviary, bowl, building, cage, camp, cell, close, coliseum, coop, corral, court, courtyard, den, dungeon, garden, ghetto, hutch, jail, pale, park, patch, pen, place, plot, pound, precinct, prison, quad, quadrangle, region, room, stadium, stockade, sty, vault, walk, yard, zone; SEE CONCEPTS *439,448,513*

enclosure [n2] *something included with a letter*
check, circular, copy, document, form, information, money, printed matter, questionnaire; SEE CONCEPT *271*

encode [v] *encrypt*
cipher, conceal, cryptograph, make secret, put into code; SEE CONCEPT *188*

encompass [v1] *surround, circumscribe*
beset, circle, compass, encircle, enclose, envelop, environ, gird, girdle, hem in, ring; SEE CONCEPT *758*

encompass [v2] *include, contain*
admit, comprehend, comprise, cover, embody, embrace, have, hold, incorporate, involve, subsume, take in; SEE CONCEPT *112*

encore [n] *another round of applause; repeat*
acclamation, cheers, number, plaudits, praise,

reappearance, repeat performance, repetition, response, return; SEE CONCEPT *264*

encounter [n1] *chance meeting*
appointment, brush, concurrence, confrontation, interview, rendezvous; SEE CONCEPT *384*

encounter [n2] *fight, argument*
action, battle, bout, brush, clash, collision, combat, conflict, contention, contest, dispute, engagement, flap*, fray, hassle, quarrel, rumpus*, run-in*, scrap, set-to*, skirmish, velitation, violence; SEE CONCEPTS *46,86,106*

encounter [v1] *happen upon*
alight upon, bear, bump into, chance upon, close, come across, come upon, confront, cross the path*, descry, detect, espy, experience, face, fall in with*, find, front, hit upon, meet, meet up with, rub eyeballs*, run across, run into, run smack into*, suffer, sustain, turn up, undergo; SEE CONCEPTS *38,384*

encounter [v2] *fight, attack*
affront, battle, clash with, collide, combat, conflict, confront, contend, cross swords*, do battle*, engage, face, grapple, meet, strive, struggle; SEE CONCEPTS *86,106*

encourage [v1] *stimulate spiritually*
animate, applaud, boost, brighten, buck up*, buoy, cheer, cheer up, comfort, console, embolden, energize, enhearten, enliven, excite, exhilarate, fortify, galvanize, give shot in arm*, gladden, goad, hearten, incite, inspire, inspirit, instigate, praise, prick, prop up*, psych up*, push, rally, reassure, refresh, restore, revitalize, revivify, rouse, spur, steel, stir, strengthen, sway; SEE CONCEPTS *7,22*

encourage [v2] *give support; help*
abet, advance, advocate, aid, approve, assist, back, back up, befriend, bolster, boost, brace, comfort, console, countenance, develop, ease, egg on*, endorse, favor, fortify, forward, foster, further, get behind, give a leg up*, go for*, improve, instigate, invite, pat on the back, prevail, promote, pull for*, push, reassure, reinforce, relieve, root for*, sanction, second, serve, side with*, smile upon*, solace, spur, strengthen, subscribe to, subsidize, succor, support, sustain, uphold; SEE CONCEPTS *8,110*

encouragement [n] *help, support*
advance, advocacy, aid, animation, assistance, backing, boost, cheer, comfort, confidence, consolation, consoling, easement, enlivening, faith, favor, firmness, fortitude, helpfulness, hope, incentive, incitement, inspiration, inspiritment, invigoration, optimism, promotion, reassurance, reassuring, refreshment, relief, relieving, reward, shot in the arm*, softening, solacing, stimulation, stimulus, succor, supporting, trust, urging; SEE CONCEPTS *7,22,110,410*

encroach [v] *invade another's property, business*
appropriate, arrogate, barge in*, butt in*, crash, elbow in*, entrench, horn in*, impinge, infringe, interfere, interpose, intervene, intrude, make inroads*, meddle, muscle in*, overstep, put two cents in*, squeeze in*, stick nose into*, trench, trespass, usurp, work in, worm in*; SEE CONCEPTS *7,19,86,159*

encumber [v] *bother, burden*
block, charge, clog, cramp, discommode, embarrass, hamper, handicap, hang up, hinder, hog-tie*, hold up, impede, incommode, inconvenience, lade, load, make difficult, obstruct, op-

press, overburden, overload, retard, saddle, saddle with*, slow down, tax, trammel, weigh down, weight; SEE CONCEPTS *121,130*

encumbrance [*n*] *burden*
albatross, ball and chain*, cross, debt, duty, guilt, handicap, hindrance, impediment, load, millstone, monkey on one's back*, obstruction, responsibility, saddle, thorn in one's side*, weight, worry; SEE CONCEPTS *532,690*

encyclopedic [*adj*] *comprehensive*
all-embracing, all-encompassing, all-inclusive, broad, catholic, complete, discursive, exhaustive, extensive, general, thorough, thorough-going, universal, vast, wide-ranging, widespread; SEE CONCEPTS *267,772*

end [*n1*] *extreme, limit*
borderline, bound, boundary, butt end, confine, cusp, deadline, edge, extent, extremity, foot, head, heel, limitation, neb, nib, point, prong, spire, stub, stump, tail, tail end, term, terminal, termination, terminus, tip, top, ultimate; SEE CONCEPTS *745,827,833*

end [*n2*] *completion, stop*
accomplishment, achievement, adjournment, attainment, bottom line*, cease, cessation, close, closing, closure, conclusion, consequence, consummation, culmination, curtain, denouement, desistance, desuetude, determination, discontinuance, execution, expiration, expiry, finale, finis, finish, fulfillment, issue, last word*, omega, outcome, payoff, perfection, realization, resolution, result, retirement, sign-off*, target, termination, terminus, upshot*, windup, wrap-up*; SEE CONCEPTS *119,230,832*

end [*n3*] *intention, aim*
aspiration, design, drift, goal, intent, mark, object, objective, point, purpose, reason, where one's heading*; SEE CONCEPT *659*

end [*n4*] *leftover part*
bit, butt end, dregs, fragment, leaving, lees, particle, piece, portion, remainder, remnant, residue, scrap, share, side, stub, tag end; SEE CONCEPT *835*

end [*n5*] *death, destruction*
annihilation, demise, dissolution, doom, expiration, extermination, extinction, finish, passing, ruin, ruination; SEE CONCEPT *304*

end [*v1*] *bring to an end*
abolish, abort, accomplish, achieve, break off, break up, call it a day*, call off*, cease, close, close out, complete, conclude, consummate, crown, culminate, cut short, delay, determine, discontinue, dispose of, dissolve, drop, expire, finish, get done, give up, halt, interrupt, pack it in*, perorate, postpone, pull the plug*, put the lid on*, quit, relinquish, resolve, settle, sew up*, shut down*, stop, switch off*, terminate, top off*, ultimate, wind up*, wrap, wrap up*; SEE CONCEPT *234*

end [*v2*] *die or kill*
abolish, annihilate, cease, depart, desist, destroy, die, expire, exterminate, extinguish, lapse, put to death, ruin, run out, wane; SEE CONCEPTS *252,304*

endanger [*v*] *put in jeopardy*
be careless, chance, chance it*, expose, hazard, imperil, lay on the line*, lay open*, leave defenseless, leave in the middle*, make liable, menace, peril, play into one's hands*, put at risk, put in danger, put on the spot*, risk, stick one's

neck out*, subject to loss, threaten, venture; SEE CONCEPTS *246,252,384*

endangered [*adj*] *imperiled*
at risk, facing extinction, in danger, threatened; SEE CONCEPTS *231,407*

endear [*v*] *attract attention*
attach, bind, captivate, charm, cherish, engage, prize, treasure, value, win; SEE CONCEPTS *7,22,32*

endearing [*adj*] *lovable*
adorable, captivating, charming, dear, irresistible, sweet, winning; SEE CONCEPT *404*

endeavor [*n*] *attempt to achieve something*
aim, all*, best shot*, crash project*, dry run*, effort, enterprise, essay, exertion, fling, full blast*, full court press*, full steam*, go, header*, labor, lick*, old college try*, one's all*, one's level best*, push, shot*, stab*, striving, struggle, toil, travail, trial, try, try-on*, undertaking, venture, whack*, whirl*, work; SEE CONCEPT *87*

endeavor [*v*] *attempt to achieve something*
address, aim, apply, aspire, assay, bid for, buck, determine, dig, do one's best*, drive at, essay, go for*, go for broke*, grind, hammer away*, hassle, have a crack*, have a shot at*, have a swing at*, hump*, hustle, intend, labor, make an effort, make a run at*, offer, peg away*, plug, pour it on*, purpose, push, risk, scratch, seek, strain, strive, struggle, sweat, take on, take pains*, try, undertake, venture; SEE CONCEPT *87*

endemic [*adj*] *native*
local, regional; SEE CONCEPT *536*

ending [*n*] *conclusion*
catastrophe, cessation, close, closing, closure, completion, consummation, coup de grace, culmination, denouement, desistance, dissolution, epilogue, expiration, finale, finish, lapse, omega, outcome, period, resolution, stop, summation, swan song*, termination, terminus, upshot, wane, windup; SEE CONCEPTS *119,230,832*

endless [*adj*] *not stopping, not finishing*
amaranthine, boundless, ceaseless, constant, continual, continuous, countless, deathless, enduring, eternal, everlasting, illimitable, immeasurable, immortal, incalculable, incessant, indeterminate, infinite, interminable, limitless, measureless, monotonous, multitudinous, never-ending, no end of, no end to, numberless, overlong, perpetual, self-perpetuating, unbounded, unbroken, undivided, undying, unending, unfathomable, uninterrupted, unlimited, unsurpassable, untold, without end; SEE CONCEPTS *482,551,798*

endorse [*v1*] *support, authorize*
accredit, advocate, affirm, approve, attest, authenticate, back, back up*, bless, boost, certify, champion, commend, confirm, countenance, defend, favor, give a boost to, give green light*, give one's word*, give the go-ahead*, give the nod*, go along with*, go to bat for*, go with, guarantee, lend one's name to, okay, praise, push, ratify, recommend, rubber-stamp*, sanction, second, stand behind, stand up for*, stump for*, subscribe to, sustain, underwrite, uphold, vouch for, warrant, witness; SEE CONCEPTS *10,50,69,88,300*

endorse [*v2*] *countersign a check*
add one's name to, authenticate, autograph, cosign, notarize, put John Hancock on*, put signature on, rubber-stamp*, say amen to*, sign, sign off on, sign on dotted line*, subscribe, su-

en
en

perscribe, undersign, underwrite; SEE CONCEPTS 50,79,88,330

endorsement [n] *support, authorization*

advocacy, affirmation, approbation, approval, backing, championing, commercial, confirmation, countersignature, favor, fiat, go-ahead*, green light*, hubba-hubba*, okay, pat on back*, permission, qualification, ratification, recommendation, sanction, seal of approval, signature, stroke, subscription to, superscription, the nod*, warrant; SEE CONCEPT 685

endow [v] *give large gift*

accord, award, back, bequeath, bestow, come through with, confer, contribute, donate, empower, enable, endue, enhance, enrich, establish, favor, finance, found, fund, furnish, grant, heighten, invest, lay on*, leave, make over*, organize, promote, provide, settle on, sponsor, subscribe, subsidize, supply, support, vest in, will; SEE CONCEPTS 108,341

endowment [n1] *large gift*

award, benefaction, benefit, bequest, bestowal, boon, bounty, dispensation, donation, fund, funding, gifting, grant, gratuity, income, inheritance, largess, legacy, nest egg, pension, presentation, property, provision, revenue, stake, stipend, subsidy, trust; SEE CONCEPTS 337,340

endowment [n2] *personal talent, ability*

aptitude, attribute, capability, capacity, faculty, flair, genius, gift, habilitation, power, qualification, quality, turn; SEE CONCEPTS 411,630

end up [v] *become eventually; come to a close*

arrive finally, cease, come to a halt, finish, finish as, finish up, stop, turn out to be, wind up; SEE CONCEPT 119

endurable [adj] *tolerable*

bearable, livable, sufferable, supportable, sustainable; SEE CONCEPT 548

endurance [n1] *bearing hardship; staying power*

ability, allowance, backbone, bearing, capacity, continuing, cool, coolness, courage, enduring, forebearance, fortitude, grit, guts, gutsiness, heart*, holding up*, intestinal fortitude, mettle, moxie*, patience, perseverance, persistence, pertinacity, pluck, resignation, resistance, resolution, restraint, spunk, stamina, standing, starch*, strength, submission, sufferance, suffering, tenacity, tolerance, toleration, undergoing, vitality, will, withstanding; SEE CONCEPTS 411,633

endurance [n2] *continuity, lastingness*

continuance, continuation, durability, duration, immutability, longevity, permanence, persistence, stability; SEE CONCEPT 804

endure [v1] *bear hardship*

abide, accustom, allow, bear the brunt*, be patient with, brave, brook, cope with, countenance, eat, encounter, experience, face, feel, go through, grin and bear it*, hang in*, keep up, know, live out, live through, meet with, never say die*, permit, put up with, repress feelings, resign oneself, ride out*, sit through, stand, stick, stick it out*, stomach*, subject to, submit to, suffer, support, sustain, swallow*, take, take it*, take patiently, tolerate, undergo, weather, withstand; SEE CONCEPT 23

endure [v2] *continue; be durable*

abide, be, be left, be long lived, be timeless, bide, carry on, carry through, cling, exist, go on, hang on*, have no end, hold, hold on, hold out, keep on, last, linger, live, live on, never say die*, outlast, outlive, perdure, persist, prevail, remain, ride out*, run on, stand, stay, stay on, stick to*, superannuate, survive, sustain, wear, wear on, wear well*; SEE CONCEPTS 239,407,804

enemy [n] *someone hated or competed against*

adversary, agent, antagonist, archenemy, asperser, assailant, assassin, attacker, backbiter, bad person*, bandit, betrayer, calumniator, competitor, contender, criminal, defamer, defiler, detractor, disputant, emulator, falsifier, fifth column*, foe, guerrilla, informer, inquisitor, invader, murderer, opponent, opposition, other side*, prosecutor, rebel, revolutionary, rival, saboteur, seditionist, slanderer, spy, terrorist, traducer, traitor, vilifier, villain; SEE CONCEPTS 322,412

energetic [adj] *full of life; forceful*

active, aggressive, animated, ball of fire*, breezy, brisk, demonic, driving, dynamic, enterprising, forcible, fresh, hardy, high-powered, indefatigable, industrious, kinetic, lively, lusty, peppy, potent, powerful, red-blooded*, rugged, snappy, spirited, sprightly, spry, stalwart, strenuous, strong, sturdy, tireless, tough, unflagging, untiring, vigorous, vital, vivacious, zippy*; SEE CONCEPTS 404,542

energize [v] *activate; give more life*

actify, activize, animate, arm, build up, electrify, empower, enable, enliven, excite, fortify, goose*, innervate, inspirit, invigorate, jazz up*, juice up*, liven up, motivate, pep up, prime, pump up*, put zip into*, quicken, reinforce, start up, stimulate, strengthen, sustain, switch on, trigger, turn on, vitalize, work up, zap*; SEE CONCEPTS 7,22,231,700

energy [n1] *person's spirit and vigor*

activity, animation, application, ardor, birr, dash, drive, effectiveness, efficacy, efficiency, élan, endurance, enterprise, exertion, fire, force, forcefulness, fortitude, get-up-and-go*, go, hardihood, initiative, intensity, juice, life, liveliness, might, moxie*, muscle, operativeness, pep, pizzazz, pluck, potency, power, puissance, punch, spirit, spontaneity, stamina, steam, strength, toughness, tuck, vehemence, verve, vim, virility, vitality, vivacity, zeal, zest, zing, zip*; SEE CONCEPT 411

energy [n2] *generated power*

application, burn, conductivity, current, dynamism, electricity, force, friction, gravity, heat, horsepower, juice, kilowatts, magnetism, potential, pressure, radioactivity, rays, reaction, response, service, steam, strength, voltage, wattage; SEE CONCEPT 520

enervate [v] *tire, wear out*

debilitate, devitalize, disable, enfeeble, exhaust, fatigue, incapacitate, jade, paralyze, sap, unnerve, vitiate, weaken, weary; SEE CONCEPTS 156,225,250

enervated [adj] *exhausted, worn out*

debilitated, deteriorated, devitalized, done in, enfeebled, fatigued, feeble, gone to seed*, incapacitated, lackadaisical, languid, languishing, languorous, limp, listless, on the ropes*, out of condition*, out of gas*, out of shape*, paralyzed, prostrate, prostrated, run-down, rusty, sapped, soft, spent, spiritless, tired, undermined, unnerved, vitiated, washed out, weak, weakened; SEE CONCEPTS 485,560

enfeeble [v] *make very weak*
attenuate, blunt, cripple, debilitate, devitalize, diminish, disable, exhaust, fatigue, incapacitate, sap, undermine, unhinge, unnerve,
weaken, wear out; SEE CONCEPTS 240,252

enfold [v] *embrace, hug*
bear hug, cinch, clasp, clinch, clutch, cover,
drape, encase, enclose, encompass, enshroud, envelop, envelope, enwrap, fold, girdle, grab, hold,
invest, press, shroud, squeeze, surround, swathe,
veil, wrap, wrap up; SEE CONCEPTS 191,219

enforce [v] *put a rule, plan in force*
accomplish, administer, administrate, apply,
carry out, coerce, commandeer, compel, constrain, crack down, demand, dictate, discharge,
dragoon, drive, effect, egg on*, emphasize,
exact, execute, exert, expect, extort, force upon,
fortify, fulfill, goad, hound, impel, implement,
impose, incite, insist on, invoke, lash, lean on,
make, necessitate, oblige, perform, press, prosecute, put into effect, put screws to*, reinforce, require, sanction, spur, strain, stress, strong-arm,
support, urge, whip, wrest; SEE CONCEPTS
50,88,133,298,317

enforcement [n] *requirement to obey; implementation of rule(s)*
administration, application, carrying out, coercion, compulsion, compulsory law, constraint,
duress, enforcing, exaction, execution, fulfilling,
imposition, impulsion, insistence, lash, martial
law, necessitation, obligation, prescription, pressure, prosecution, reinforcement, spur, whip; SEE
CONCEPTS 298,317,685

engage [v1] *hire for job, use*
appoint, bespeak, book, bring on board*, charter,
come on board*, commission, contract, employ,
enlist, enroll, ink*, lease, place, prearrange, put
on, rent, reserve, retain, secure, sign on, sign up,
take on, truck with*; SEE CONCEPTS 129,351

engage [v2] *occupy oneself; engross*
absorb, allure, arrest, bewitch, busy, captivate,
catch, charm, draw, embark on, employ, enamor,
enchant, enter into, enthrall, fascinate, give a
try*, give a whirl*, go for broke*, go in for*, go
out for*, grip*, have a fling at*, have a go at*,
have a shot at*, imbue, immerse, interest, involve, join, keep busy, monopolize, partake, participate, pitch in, practice, preengage, preoccupy,
set about, soak, tackle*, take part, tie up, try on
for size*, undertake; SEE CONCEPTS 87,363

engage [v3] *promise to marry*
affiance, agree, betroth, bind, catch, commit,
contract, covenant, give one's word*, guarantee,
hook, obligate, oblige, pass, pledge, tie, troth,
turn on*, undertake, vouch, vow; SEE CONCEPT
297

engage [v4] *start a fight; attack*
assail, assault, combat, do battle with, encounter,
face, fall on, give battle to, join battle with,
launch, meet, strike, take on; SEE CONCEPTS
86,106,320

engage [v5] *interconnect; bring into operation*
activate, apply, attach, dovetail, energize, fasten,
get going, interact, interlace, interlock, inter-
mesh, interplay, join, lock, mesh, switch on; SEE
CONCEPTS 85,113,160,221

engaged [adj] *promised to be married*
affianced, asked for, betrothed, bound, committed, contracted, future, given one's word*, going
steady*, hooked*, intended, matched, pinned,

pledged, plighted, ringed, spoken for, steady; SEE
CONCEPT 555

engaged [adj2] *operating; busy*
absorbed, at work, committed, connected with,
dealing in, deep, doing, employed, engrossed,
immersed, in place, intent, interested, in use, involved, occupied, performing, practicing, preoccupied, pursuing, rapt, signed, tied up,
unavailable, working, wrapped up*; SEE CON-
CEPTS 542,555,576

engagement [n1] *pledge to marry*
assurance, betrothal, betrothing, betrothment,
bond, commitment, compact, contract, espousal,
match, oath, obligation, pact, plight, promise,
troth, undertaking, vow, word; SEE CONCEPT 297

engagement [n2] *meeting; date*
appointment, arrangement, assignation, blind
date*, commission, commitment, date, errand,
get-together, gig, going out*, interview, invitation, meet, seeing one*, stint, tryst, visit; SEE
CONCEPT 384

engagement [n3] *battle*
action, combat, conflict, confrontation, contest,
encounter, fight, fray, skirmish; SEE CONCEPTS
106,320

engaging [adj] *charming*
agreeable, alluring, appealing, attractive, bewitching, captivating, enchanting, enticing, entrancing, fascinating, fetching, glamorous,
interesting, intriguing, inviting, likable, lovable,
magnetic, mesmeric, pleasant, pleasing, prepossessing, siren, sweet, winning, winsome; SEE
CONCEPT 404

engender [v] *cause to happen; cause an action*
arouse, beget, breed, bring about, bring forth,
create, develop, excite, foment, generate, give
birth to, give rise to, hatch, incite, induce, instigate, lead to, make, muster, occasion, precipitate,
procreate, produce, propagate, provoke, quicken,
rouse, spawn, stimulate, stir, work up; SEE CON-
CEPTS 221,242

engine [n] *device that drives a machine*
agent, apparatus, appliance, barrel, contrivance,
cylinder, diesel, dynamo, fan, generator, horses*,
implement, instrument, means, mechanism,
motor, piston, pot*, powerhouse, power plant,
power train, putt-putt*, rubber band*, tool, transformer, turbine, weapon, what's under the
hood*; SEE CONCEPTS 463,464

engineer [n] *person who puts together things*
architect, builder, contriver, designer, deviser,
director, inventor, manager, manipulator, originator, planner, schemer, sights*, surveyor,
techie*, technie*; SEE CONCEPT 348

engineer [v] *devise; bring about*
angle, arrange, cause, come up with, con, conceive, concoct, contrive, control, cook*, create,
direct, doctor, effect, encompass, finagle*,
jockey*, machinate, manage, maneuver, manipulate, negotiate, operate, organize, originate, plan,
plant, play games*, plot, pull strings*, pull
wires*, put one on*, put one over*, put over*,
put through, rig*, scam, scheme, set up, superintend, supervise, swing, upstage, wangle, work;
SEE CONCEPTS 36,173,251

engrave [v] *carve letters or designs into*
bite, burn, chase, chisel, crosshatch, cut, diaper,
embed, enchase, etch, fix, grave, hatch, impress,
imprint, infix, ingrain, initial, inscribe, instill, in-

en
en

taglio, lithograph, lodge, mezzotint, ornament, print, scratch, stipple; SEE CONCEPTS 79,174,176

engraving [n] *carving of letters or design into something*
blocking, chasing, chiselling, cutting, dry point, enchasing, etching, illustration, impression, inscribing, inscription, intaglio, lithograph, mezzotint, photoengraving, photogravure, print, rotogravure, scratch, woodcut; SEE CONCEPTS 79,174,176,625

engross [v] *hold one's attention*
absorb, apply, arrest, assimilate, attract, become lost, be hung*, bewitch, busy, captivate, consume, corner, engage, engulf, enrapture, enthrall, fascinate, fill, grip, hog*, immerse, involve, monopolize, occupy, preoccupy, sew up*, soak, take up, up on*; SEE CONCEPTS 14,17

engrossed [adj] *preoccupied; attentive to*
absorbed, all wound up*, assiduous, bugged*, busy, captivated, caught up, caught up in, consumed, deep, diligent, engaged, enthralled, fascinated, fiend for*, gone*, gripped, head over heels*, heavily into*, hooked, hung up, immersed, industrious, intent, into*, intrigued, lost, monopolized, occupied, rapt, really into*, riveted, sedulous, submerged, taken up with, tied up, turned on*, up to here in*, wrapped up*; SEE CONCEPTS 403,542

engrossing [adj] *very interesting*
absorbing, all-consuming, captivating, compelling, consuming, controlling, enthralling, exciting, fascinating, gripping, intriguing, monopolizing, obsessing, preoccupying, provoking, riveting, stimulating; SEE CONCEPT 529

engulf [v] *absorb, overwhelm*
bury, consume, deluge, drown, encompass, engross, envelop, flood, imbibe, immerse, inundate, overflow, overrun, overwhelm, plunge, submerge, swallow up, swamp, whelm; SEE CONCEPTS 169,172,256

enhance [v] *improve, embellish*
add to, adorn, aggrandize, amplify, appreciate, augment, beautify, boom, boost, build up, complement, elevate, embroider, enlarge, exaggerate, exalt, flesh out*, heighten, increase, intensify, lift, magnify, pad*, pyramid*, raise, reinforce, strengthen, swell, upgrade; SEE CONCEPTS 162,177,244

enigma [n] *mystery*
bewilderment, cliffhanger, conundrum, crux, cryptogram, Gordian knot*, grabber*, knot*, mind-boggler*, mind-twister*, mystification, parable, perplexity, problem, puzzle, puzzlement, puzzler, question, question mark, riddle, secret, sixty-four dollar question*, sphinx*, sticker, stickler, stumper, teaser, tough nut to crack*, twister, why*; SEE CONCEPT 532

enigmatic/enigmatical [adj] *mysterious*
ambiguous, cryptic, dark, Delphian*, doubtful, equivocal, incomprehensible, indecipherable, inexplicable, inscrutable, obscure, occult, oracular, perplexing, puzzling, recondite, secret, Sibylline*, sphinxlike, stickling, stumping, teasing, uncertain, unfathomable, unintelligible; SEE CONCEPTS 529,576,582

enjoin [v1] *order, command*
adjure, admonish, advise, appoint, bid, call upon, caution, charge, counsel, decree, demand, dictate, direct, forewarn, impose, instruct, ordain, prescribe, require, rule, tell, urge, warn; SEE CONCEPTS 53,78

enjoin [v2] *forbid*
ban, bar, deny, disallow, inhibit, interdict, outlaw, place injunction on, preclude, prohibit, proscribe, restrain, taboo; SEE CONCEPTS 50,53,88, 130

enjoy [v1] *take pleasure in, from something*
adore, appreciate, be entertained, be fond of, be pleased, cotton to*, delight in, dig*, dote on*, drink in*, eat up*, fancy, flip over*, freak out on*, get a charge out of*, get a kick out of*, get high on*, go, have a ball*, have a good time, have fun, like, live a little*, live it up*, love, luxuriate in, mind, paint the town*, rejoice in, relish, revel in, savor, take joy in, thrill to; SEE CONCEPTS 32,384

enjoy [v2] *have the benefit or use of*
be blessed, be favored, boast, command, experience, have, hold, maintain, occupy, own, possess, process, reap the benefits*, retain, use; SEE CONCEPT 710

enjoyable [adj] *pleasing; to one's liking*
agreeable, amusing, clear sailing*, delectable, delicious, delightful, entertaining, fun, genial, gratifying, groovy*, just for grins*, just for kicks*, just for laughs*, just for the heck of it*, likable, lots of laughs*, pleasant, pleasurable, preferable, relishable, satisfying, welcome; SEE CONCEPTS 529,548

enjoyment [n1] *delight in something*
amusement, delectation, diversion, enjoying, entertainment, fruition, fun, gladness, gratification, gusto, happiness, hedonism, indulgence, joy, loving, luxury, pleasure, recreation, rejoicing, relaxation, relish, satisfaction, savor, self-indulgence, sensuality, thrill, triumph, zest; SEE CONCEPTS 32,410

enjoyment [n2] *possession; use of*
advantage, benefit, exercise, having, indulgence, ownership, spending, using; SEE CONCEPT 710

enlarge [v] *make or grow bigger; increase*
add to, aggrandize, amplify, augment, beef up*, blow up*, boost, broaden, build, bulk, develop, diffuse, dilate, distend, elaborate, elongate, embroider, exaggerate, expand, expatiate, extend, give details, grow, grow larger, heighten, inflate, jack up*, jazz up*, lengthen, magnify, make larger, mount, multiply, pad*, pyramid*, rise, slap on*, snowball*, spread, stretch, swell, upsurge, wax, widen; SEE CONCEPTS 137,236,245, 780

enlargement [n] *increase, expansion*
aggrandizement, amplification, augmentation, blow up, elongation, extension, growth, spread; SEE CONCEPT 780

enlighten [v] *explain thoroughly; make aware*
acquaint, advise, apprise, brief, catechize, cause to understand, civilize, convert, counsel, direct, disclose, divulge, edify, educate, elucidate, give faith*, give the lowdown*, give the word*, guide, illume, illuminate, illumine, imitate, improve, inculcate, indoctrinate, inform, inspirit, instruct, let in on, open up, persuade, preach, put on to*, reveal, save, school, teach, tell, train, update, uplift; SEE CONCEPTS 57,60,75

enlightened [adj] *informed, educated*
aware, broad-minded, civilized, cultivated, hip to*, instructed, in the picture*, knowing what's what*, knowledgeable, learned, liberal, literate,

open-minded, plugged in*, reasonable, refined, savvy, sharp, sophisticated, tuned in*, wised up*; SEE CONCEPT 402

enlightenment [n] *awareness, understanding*
broad-mindedness, civilization, comprehension, cultivation, culture, edification, education, information, insight, instruction, knowledge, learning, literacy, open-mindedness, refinement, sophistication, teaching, wisdom; SEE CONCEPT 409

enlist [v] *sign up for responsibility*
admit, appoint, assign, attract, call to arms, call up, conscribe, conscript, draft, embody, employ, engage, enroll, enter, enter into, gather, get, hire, hitch, incorporate, induct, initiate, inscribe, interest, join, join up, levy, list, mobilize, muster, oblige, obtain, place, press into service, procure, record, recruit, register, reserve, secure, serve, sign on, take on, volunteer; SEE CONCEPTS 8,320

enliven [v] *inspire, vitalize*
animate, brace up, brighten, buck up, buoy, cheer, cheer up, divert, entertain, excite, exhilarate, fire, fire up, galvanize, give a lift, give life to, gladden, hearten, inspirit, invigorate, jazz up*, juice up*, let sunshine in*, pep up*, perk up*, pick up, put pep into, quicken, recreate, refresh, rejuvenate, renew, restore, rouse, snap out of it*, spark, spice, spice up*, stimulate, vivificate, vivify, wake up, work up*, zap*; SEE CONCEPTS 7,22

en masse [adj] *all at once*
all in all, all together, altogether, as a body, as a group, as a whole, as one, bodily, by and large*, ensemble, generally, in a body, in a group, in a mass, jointly, on the whole, together; SEE CONCEPT 577

enmesh [v] *involve in a situation*
box in, catch, drag into*, draw in, embroil, ensnare, entangle, entrap, hook, implicate, incriminate, lay a trap for*, lay for*, make party to*, net, snare, snarl, tangle, trammel, trap; SEE CONCEPTS 59,112

enmity [n] *hatred, animosity*
acrimony, alienation, animus, antagonism, antipathy, aversion, bad blood*, bitterness, daggers*, detestation, dislike, hate, hostility, ill will, loathing, malevolence, malice, malignancy, malignity, rancor, spite, spleen, uncordiality, unfriendliness, venom; SEE CONCEPT 29

ennui [n] *boredom*
apathy, blahs, blues, dejection, depression, dissatisfaction, doldrums, dumps*, fatigue, ho hums*, lack of interest, languidness, languor, lassitude, listlessness, melancholy, sadness, satiety, spiritlessness, surfeit, tedium, weariness, yawn*; SEE CONCEPT 410

enormity [n1] *horribleness*
abomination, atrociousness, atrocity, crime, depravity, disgrace, evil, evilness, flagrancy, grossness, heinousness, horror, monstrosity, monstrousness, nefariousness, outrage, outrageousness, rankness, turpitude, vice, viciousness, vileness, villainy, wickedness; SEE CONCEPTS 645,666

enormity [n2] *extreme largeness*
bigness, bulk, enormousness, greatness, hugeness, immensity, magnitude, massiveness, size, tremendousness, vastness; SEE CONCEPT 730

enormous [adj] *very large*
astronomic, barn door*, blimp*, colossal, excessive, gargantuan, gigantic, huge, huge, humongous, immense, jumbo*, mammoth, massive, monstrous, mountainous, prodigious, stupendous, super-colossal*, titanic*, tremendous, vast, whopping; SEE CONCEPT 773

enough [adj] *plenty*
abundant, acceptable, adequate, all right already*, ample, bellyful*, bounteous, bountiful, comfortable, competent, complete, copious, decent, enough already*, fed up*, full, had it*, last straw*, lavish, plenteous, plentiful, replete, satisfactory, satisfying, sick and tired of*, sufficient, sufficing, suitable, unlimited, up to here*; SEE CONCEPTS 546,771

enough [adv] *adequately*
abundantly, acceptably, admissibly, amply, averagely, barely, commensurately, decently, fairly, moderately, passably, proportionately, rather, reasonably, satisfactorily, so-so*, sufficiently, tolerably; SEE CONCEPTS 546,558,771

enough [n] *plenty*
abundance, adequacy, ampleness, ample supply, competence, plenitude, right amount, sufficiency, sufficient; SEE CONCEPTS 646,767

enquire [v] *ask about*
analyze, check, examine, explore, go over, inquire, inspect, investigate, look into, probe, pry, query, question, scrutinize, search, seek, seek an answer, want to know; SEE CONCEPTS 24,48

enquiry [n] *inquest*
analysis, examination, exploration, inquiry, inquisition, inspection, interrogation, investigation, probe, query, questioning, research, study; SEE CONCEPTS 24,48,290

enrage [v] *make very upset*
aggravate, anger, ask for it*, exasperate, get under skin*, hack*, incense, incite, inflame, infuriate, ire, irritate, madden, make blood boil*, make see red*, needle, provoke, rile, steam up*, T-off*, umbrage, whip up*; SEE CONCEPTS 7,14,19

enraged [adj] *furious*
aggravated, angered, angry, boiling*, exasperated, fuming, incensed, inflamed, infuriated, irate, livid, mad, pushed too far*, riled, upset; SEE CONCEPT 403

enrapture [v] *captivate*
allure, attract, beguile, bewitch, charm, delight, elate, enamor, enchant, enthrall, entrance, fascinate, gladden, gratify, please, ravish, rejoice, score, send, spellbind, transport; SEE CONCEPTS 7,22

enrich [v] *improve, embellish*
adorn, aggrandize, ameliorate, augment, beef up*, better, build, build up, cultivate, decorate, develop, endow, enhance, figure in, flesh out*, grace, hike up*, hop up*, jack up*, jazz up*, make rich, ornament, pad, parlay, pour it on*, pyramid*, refine, run up*, soup up*, spike*, step up, supplement, sweeten*, up*, upgrade; SEE CONCEPTS 177,244

enroll [v1] *sign up for membership*
accept, admit, become student, call up, employ, engage, enlist, enter, join, join up, matriculate, muster, obtain, recruit, register, serve, sign on, subscribe, take course, take on; SEE CONCEPTS 114,129

enroll [v2] *list, record*
affix, bill, book, catalog, chronicle, engross, enlist, enter, file, fill out, index, inscribe, insert, in-

ventorize, mark, matriculate, note, poll, register, schedule, slate; SEE CONCEPTS *79,125*

enrollment [*n*] *registration for membership*
acceptance, accession, admission, conscription, engagement, enlistment, entrance, entry, induction, influx, listing, matriculation, rally, reception, record, recruitment, response, student body, students, subscription; SEE CONCEPTS *288,388, 417*

en route [*adj*] *on the way to destination*
advancing, along the way, bound, driving, entrained, en voyage*, flying, heading toward, in passage, in transit, making headway*, midway, on the road*, pressing on, progressing, traveling; SEE CONCEPTS *577,586*

ensconce [*v*] *hide; tuck away*
bury, cache, conceal, cover, curl up, ditch, establish, fix, install, locate, nestle, place, plant, protect, screen, seat, secrete, set, settle, shelter, shield, situate, snuggle up, stash, station; SEE CONCEPTS *188,201*

ensemble [*adv*] *at the same time*
all at once, altogether, as a body, as a group, as a whole, as one, at once, en masse, in concert; SEE CONCEPT *577*

ensemble [*n1*] *collection*
aggregate, assemblage, band, cast, choir, chorus, company, composite, entirety, gathering, glee club, group, octet, orchestra, organization, outfit, quartet, quintet, set, sextet, sum, total, totality, trio, troupe, whole; SEE CONCEPTS *294,432*

ensemble [*n2*] *clothing outfit*
coordinates, costume, garb*, get-up*, suit, togs*; SEE CONCEPT *451*

enshrine [*v*] *hold as sacred*
apotheosize, bless, cherish, consecrate, dedicate, embalm, exalt, hallow, idolize, preserve, revere, sanctify, treasure; SEE CONCEPTS *69,367*

enshroud [*v*] *cover*
cloak, conceal, hide, mask, pall, shroud; SEE CONCEPTS *172,188*

ensign [*n*] *flag*
banderole, banner, colors, emblem, gonfalon, insignia, pennant, standard, streamer, symbol; SEE CONCEPTS *284,473*

enslave [*v*] *make someone a servant*
bind, capture, chain, check, circumscribe, coerce, compel, confine, deprive, disenfranchise, disfranchise, dominate, enchain, enclose, enthrall, fetter, get hooks into*, hobble, hold, immure, imprison, incarcerate, indenture, jail, keep under thumb*, oppress, put in irons*, reduce, restrain, restrict, secure, shackle, shut in, subdue, subject, subjugate, suppress, tether, tie, yoke; SEE CONCEPTS *14,90,130,191*

ensnare [*v*] *trap*
bag*, bat eyes at*, capture, catch, cheat, come on, deceive, decoy, embroil, enmesh, entangle, entice, entrap, hook, inveigle, lure, mislead, net, rope in, snag, snare, snarl, suck in*, tangle, trick; SEE CONCEPTS *59,90*

ensue [*v*] *start to happen; come to pass*
appear, arise, attend, be consequent on, befall, be subsequent to, come after, come next, come up, derive, develop, emanate, eventualize, eventuate, flow, follow, issue, occur, proceed, result, stem, succeed, supervene, turn out, turn up; SEE CONCEPTS *119,242*

ensuing [*adj*] *resultant*
after, coming, coming up, consequent, conse-

quential, following, later, next, next off, posterior, postliminary, subsequent, subsequential; SEE CONCEPTS *548,820*

ensure [*v*] *guarantee; make secure*
arrange, assure, certify, cinch, clinch, confirm, effect, establish, guard, insure, lock on*, lock up*, make certain, make safe, make sure, nail down*, okay, protect, provide, put on ice*, safeguard, secure, set out, warrant; SEE CONCEPTS *71,96*

entail [*v*] *require; result in*
bring about, call for, cause, demand, encompass, entangle, evoke, give rise to, impose, involve, lead to, necessitate, occasion, require, tangle; SEE CONCEPTS *242,646*

entangle [*v*] *involve, mix up*
bewilder, burden, catch, clog, come on, complicate, compromise, confuse, corner, dishevel, duke in, embarrass, embrangle, embroil, enchain, enmesh, ensnare, entrap, fetter, hamper, hook, impede, implicate, intertangle, intertwine, interweave, jumble, knot, lead on, mat, muddle, perplex, puzzle, ravel, rope in, set up, snag, snare, snarl, swindle, tangle, trammel, trap, twist, unsettle; SEE CONCEPTS *59,90,112*

entanglement [*n*] *complication, predicament*
affair, association, cobweb, complexity, confusion, difficulty, embarrassment, embroilment, enmeshment, ensnarement, entrapment, imbroglio, intricacy, intrigue, involvement, jumble, knot, liaison, mesh, mess, mix-up, muddle, snare, tangle, tie-up, toil, trap, web; SEE CONCEPTS *666,674*

entente [*n*] *agreement*
accord, arrangement, deal, pact, settlement, treaty, understanding; SEE CONCEPTS *271,331*

enter [*v1*] *come, put into a place*
access, arrive, barge in*, blow in*, break in, breeze in*, burst in, bust in*, butt in*, come in, crack, crawl, creep, crowd in*, drive in, drop in, fall into, gain entree, get in, go in, horn in*, immigrate, infiltrate, ingress, insert, insinuate, introduce, intrude, invade, jump in, make an entrance, make way, move in, pass into, penetrate, pierce, pile in, pop in*, probe, rush in, set foot in, slip, sneak, work in, worm in*, wriggle; SEE CONCEPT *159*

enter [*v2*] *embark on; take part in*
become member, begin, commence, commit oneself, enlist, enroll, get oneself into*, inaugurate, join, join up, lead off, muster*, open, participate in, set about, set out on, set to, sign on, sign up, start, subscribe, take up, tee off*; SEE CONCEPTS *114,234*

enter [*v3*] *record, list*
admit, docket, inject, inscribe, insert, intercalate, interpolate, introduce, log, note, post, put in, register, set down, take down; SEE CONCEPT *125*

enterprise [*n1*] *adventure, undertaking*
action, activity, affair, attempt, baby*, bag*, ballgame*, biggie*, big idea*, bit*, business, campaign, cause, company, concern, crusade, deal, deed, do*, effort, endeavor, engagement, essay, establishment, firm, flier*, follow through*, game*, happening, hazard, house, move, operation, outfit, performance, pet project*, plan, plunge*, program, project, proposition, purpose, pursuit, risk, scheme, speculation, stake, striving, stunt, task, thing*, trade, try, venture, work; SEE CONCEPTS *87,324,325,362*

enterprise [*n2*] *resourcefulness, energy*
activity, adventurousness, alertness, ambition, audacity, boldness, courage, daring, dash, drive, eagerness, enthusiasm, force, foresight, get-up-and-go*, gumption, hustle, industry, initiative, inventiveness, pluck, push, readiness, resource, self-reliance, spirit, venturesomeness, vigor, zeal; SEE CONCEPTS *411,657*

enterprising [*adj*] *resourceful, energetic*
active, advancing, adventurous, aggressive, alert, ambitious, aspiring, audacious, bold, busy, coming on strong*, craving, daring, dashing, diligent, driving, eager, enthusiastic, go-ahead*, go-go*, gumptious, hard ball*, hardworking, hungry, hustling, industrious, intrepid, itching, keen, lively, lusting, peppy, progressive, pushing, ready, self-starting, snappy, spanking, spark plug*, spirited, stirring, take-over, up-and-coming*, venturesome, vigorous, yearning, zealous, zippy*; SEE CONCEPTS *326,404,542*

entertain [*v1*] *amuse*
absorb, beguile, captivate, charm, cheer, comfort, crack up*, delight, distract, divert, ecstasize, elate, engross, enliven, enthrall, gladden, grab, gratify, humor, indulge, inspire, inspirit, interest, knock dead*, make merry, occupy, pique, please, recreate, regale, relax, satisfy, slay, solace, stimulate, tickle; SEE CONCEPTS *9,292*

entertain [*v2*] *accommodate visitors*
admit, be host, board, chaperone, dine, do the honors*, feed, foster, give a party, harbor, have a do*, have a get-together*, have company, have guests, have visitors, house, invite, lodge, nourish, pick up the check*, pop for*, put up*, quarter, receive, recreate, regale, room, show hospitality, spring for*, throw a party*, treat, welcome, wine and dine*; SEE CONCEPTS *377,384*

entertain [*v3*] *think about seriously*
cherish, cogitate on, conceive, consider, contemplate, deliberate, foster, harbor, heed, hold, imagine, keep in mind, maintain, muse over, ponder, recognize, support, think over; SEE CONCEPT *17*

entertaining [*adj*] *amusing, pleasing*
absorbing, affecting, be a ball*, captivating, charming, cheerful, cheering, clever, compelling, delightful, diverting, droll, enchanting, engaging, engrossing, enjoyable, enthralling, enticing, entrancing, exciting, fascinating, fun, funny, gas*, gay, humorous, impressive, inspiring, interesting, lively, moving, piquant, pleasant, pleasurable, poignant, priceless, provocative, recreative, relaxing, restorative, riot, rousing, scream, side-splitting, stimulating, stirring, striking, thrilling, witty; SEE CONCEPTS *529,537*

entertainment [*n*] *amusement, pleasure*
ball*, bash*, big time*, blast*, blow out*, celebration, cheer, clambake*, delight, dissipation, distraction, diversion, divertissement, enjoyment, feast, frolic, fun, fun and games*, gaiety, game, good time*, grins*, high time*, laughs*, leisure activity, lots of laughs*, merriment, merrymaking, party, pastime, picnic, play, recreation, regalement, relaxation, relief, revelry, satisfaction, shindig*, sport, spree, surprise, treat, winging*; SEE CONCEPTS *383,384,386,388*

enthrall [*v*] *captivate*
absorb, beguile, bewitch, charm, enchant, engage, enrapture, enslave, entrance, fascinate,

grab, grip, hold spellbound, hook, hypnotize, intrigue, mesmerize, preoccupy, rivet, spellbind, subdue, subject, subjugate; SEE CONCEPTS *7,19,22*

enthusiasm [*n*] *keen interest, excitement*
activity, ardency, ardor, avidity, conviction, craze; dash, devotion, eagerness, earnestness, ecstasy, elan, emotion, energy, exhilaration, fad, fanaticism, feeling, fervor, fever, fieriness, fire, flame, flare, frenzy, fury, gaiety, glow, go*, heat, hilarity, hobby, impetuosity, intensity, interest, joy, joyfulness, keenness, life, mania, mirth, nerve, oomph*, orgasm, passion, pep, rapture, red heat*, relish, snap, spirit, transport, vehemence, verve, vim, vivacity, warmth, zeal, zealousness, zest; SEE CONCEPTS *633,657*

enthusiast [*n*] *person active in interest*
addict, admirer, aficionado, believer, buff, bug*, bum*, devotee, eccentric, fan, fanatic, follower, freak, habitué, lover, maniac, monomaniac, nut*, optimist, participant, partisan, rooter, supporter, votary, worshiper, zealot; SEE CONCEPT *423*

enthusiastic [*adj*] *interested, excited*
agog, animated, anxious, ardent, athirst, attracted, avid, bugged*, concerned, crazy about*, devoted, dying to*, eager, earnest, ebullient, exhilarated, exuberant, fanatical, fascinated, fervent, fervid, forceful, gaga*, gone on*, gung ho*, hearty, intent, keen, keyed up*, lively, nutty*, obsessed, passionate, pleased, rabid, red-hot*, rhapsodic, spirited, tantalized, thrilled, titillated, unqualified, vehement, vigorous, wacky*, warm, wholehearted, willing, zealous; SEE CONCEPTS *401,542*

entice [*v*] *allure; persuade*
attract, bait, bat eyes at*, beguile, cajole, coax, decoy, draw, entrap, inveigle, lead on, lure, prevail on, seduce, tempt, toll, turn on*, wheedle; SEE CONCEPTS *7,19,22,68*

enticement [*n*] *allurement; persuasion*
attraction, bait, blandishment, cajolery, coaxing, come hither*, come-on*, decoy, fascination, inducement, inveiglement, lure, mousetrap*, promise, seduction, snare, sweetener*, sweetening, temptation, trap; SEE CONCEPTS *7,19,22,68*

entire [*adj*] *complete, whole*
absolute, all, choate, consolidated, continuous, full, gross, intact, integral, integrated, outright, perfect, plenary, sound, thorough, total, unbroken, undamaged, undiminished, undivided, unified, unimpaired, uninjured, unmarked, unmarred, unmitigated, unreserved, unrestricted, untouched; SEE CONCEPTS *482,531*

entirely [*adv*] *completely*
absolutely, alone, altogether, exclusively, fully, in every respect, only, perfectly, plumb, quite, reservedly, solely, thoroughly, totally, undividedly, uniquely, utterly, well, wholly, without exception, without reservation; SEE CONCEPTS *531,535*

entirety [*n*] *wholeness, whole*
absoluteness, aggregate, all, allness, collectiveness, collectivity, completeness, complex, comprehensiveness, ensemble, entireness, everything, fullness, gross, intactness, integrality, integrity, omneity, omnitude, oneness, perfection, plenitude, sum, sum total, the works*, total, totality, undividedness, unity, universality, whole ball of wax*, whole bit*, whole enchilada*, whole nine yards*; SEE CONCEPTS *635,837*

en
en

entitle [v1] *name, label*

baptize, call, characterize, christen, denominate, designate, dub, nickname, style, subtitle, term, title; SEE CONCEPT 62

entitle [v2] *hold right to*

accredit, allow, authorize, be in line for*, confer a right, empower, enable, enfranchise, fit for, have coming*, let, license, make eligible, permit, qualify for, rate, warrant; SEE CONCEPTS 50,83,88,129

entity [n1] *object that exists*

article, being, body, creature, existence, individual, item, material, matter, organism, presence, quantity, single, singleton, stuff, substance, subsistence, substance, thing; SEE CONCEPT 433

entity [n2] *nature of a being*

actuality, essence, existence, integral, integrate, quiddity, quintessence, reality, subsistence, substance, sum, system, totality; SEE CONCEPTS 411,644

entomb [v] *bury*

embalm, ensepulcher, enshrine, hold last rites for*, hold services for*, inhume, inter, inurn, lay to rest*, put six feet under*, sepulcher, sepulture, tomb; SEE CONCEPT 367

entourage [n] *followers*

associates, attendants, companions, company, cortege, court, courtiers, escort, following, groupies*, hangers-on*, retainers, retinue, staff, suite, sycophants, toadies*, train; SEE CONCEPTS 387,417

entrails [n] *internal organs*

bowels, guts, innards, insides, internal parts, viscera, vitals; SEE CONCEPT 393

entrance [n1] *a way into a place*

access, approach, archway, avenue, corridor, door, doorway, entry, entryway, gate, gateway, hall, hallway, ingress, inlet, lobby, opening, passage, passageway, path, porch, port, portal, portico, staircase, threshold, vestibule, way; SEE CONCEPT 440

entrance [n2] *coming into a place; introduction*

access, accession, adit, admission, admittance, appearance, approach, arrival, baptism, beginning, commencement, debut, enlistment, enrollment, entree, entry, immigration, import, importation, inception, incoming, ingoing, ingress, ingression, initiation, invasion, outset, passage, penetration, progress, start, trespass; SEE CONCEPTS 119,159

entrance [v] *captivate, hypnotize*

anesthetize, attract, bewitch, charm, delight, enchant, enrapture, enthrall, fascinate, gladden, mesmerize, please, put in a trance, ravish, rejoice, spellbind, transport; SEE CONCEPTS 7,14,22

entrant [n] *person entering competition, starting new activity*

aspirant, beginner, candidate, competitor, contestant, convert, entry, incomer, initiate, neophyte, newcomer, new member, novice, participant, petitioner, player, probationer, rival, solicitor, tenderfoot*; SEE CONCEPTS 366,423

entrap [v] *capture, involve*

allure, bag*, beguile, benet, box in*, catch, decoy, embroil, enmesh, ensnare, entangle, entice, hook, implicate, inveigle, lay for*, lead on, lure, net, reel in*, rope in*, seduce, set up, snare, suck in*, tempt, trap, trick; SEE CONCEPTS 59,90,112

entreat [v] *plead with*

appeal to, ask, beg, beseech, blandish, coax, conjure, crave, enjoin, exhort, implore, importune, invoke, pester, petition, plague, pray, press, request, supplicate, urge, wheedle; SEE CONCEPTS 48,53

entreaty [n] *plea*

appeal, application, imploration, imprecation, petition, prayer, request, suit, supplication; SEE CONCEPTS 318,662

entrée [n] *admittance*

access, adit, admission, connection, contact, debut, door, entrance, entry, importation, in, incoming, induction, ingress, introduction, open arms*, open door*, way; SEE CONCEPTS 388,685

entrench [v1] *establish, make inroads*

anchor, confirm, define, dig in, embed, ensconce, fence, fix, fortify, found, ground, hole up, implant, infix, ingrain, install, lodge, plant, protect, root, seat, set, settle, strengthen; SEE CONCEPTS 518,710

entrench [v2] *trespass*

break in on, encroach, impinge, infringe, interfere, interlope, intervene, intrude, invade, make inroads*, stick nose into*; SEE CONCEPT 192

entrepreneur [n] *person who starts a business alone*

administrator, backer, businessperson, contractor, executive, founder, impressario, industrialist, manager, organizer, producer, promoter, undertaker; SEE CONCEPT 347

entropy [n] *deterioration*

breakup, collapse, decay, decline, degeneration, destruction, falling apart, worsening; SEE CONCEPTS 230,698

entrust [v] *give custody, authority to*

allocate, allot, assign, authorize, bank, bend an ear*, charge, commend, commit, confer, confide, consign, count, delegate, deliver, depend, deposit with, hand over, impose, invest, leave with, reckon, relegate, rely, trust, turn over; SEE CONCEPTS 50,88,108

entry [n1] *way in to a place*

access, adit, approach, avenue, door, doorway, entrance, foyer, gate, hall, ingress, ingression, inlet, lobby, opening, passage, passageway, portal, threshold, vestibule; SEE CONCEPT 440

entry [n2] *introduction; permission to enter*

access, adit, admission, admittance, appearance, coming in, entering, entrance, entree, free passage*, ingress, initiation, introgression, way; SEE CONCEPTS 388,685

entry [n3] *person participating in competition; effort*

attempt, candidate, competitor, contestant, entrant, participant, player, submission; SEE CONCEPT 366

entry [n4] *listing in a record*

account, item, jotting, memo, memorandum, minute, note, registration; SEE CONCEPT 270

entwine [v] *twist around*

braid, coil, corkscrew, curl, embrace, encircle, enmesh, entangle, interlace, interplait, intertwine, interweave, knit, lace, plait, spiral, surround, twine, weave, wind, wreathe; SEE CONCEPTS 147,201,754

enumerate [v] *list, count*

add up, calculate, cite, compute, count noses*, detail, figure, identify, inventory, itemize, keep tabs*, mention, name, number, particularize, quote, recapitulate, recite, reckon, recount, rehearse, relate, run down, run off*, specialize, specify, spell out, sum, take account of, tally, tell, tick off*, total; SEE CONCEPTS 57,125,764

enunciate [v] *speak clearly*
affirm, announce, articulate, declare, deliver, develop, enounce, express, intone, lay down, modulate, outline, phonate, postulate, proclaim, promulgate, pronounce, propound, publish, say, show, sound, state, submit, utter, vocalize, voice; SEE CONCEPTS 47,51

envelop [v] *encase, hide*
blanket, cage, cloak, conceal, contain, coop, corral, cover, drape, embrace, encircle, enclose, encompass, enfold, engulf, enshroud, enwrap, fence, gird, girdle, guard, hem, immure, invest, obscure, overlay, overspread, pen, protect, roll, sheathe, shield, shroud, shut in, superimpose, surround, swaddle, swathe, veil, wrap, wrap up; SEE CONCEPTS 172,188

envelope [n] *wrapper*
bag, box, case, casing, cloak, coat, coating, container, cover, covering, enclosure, hide, jacket, pocket, pouch, receptacle, sheath, shell, skin, vesicle, wrapping; SEE CONCEPT 494

enviable [adj] *desired, blessed*
advantageous, covetable, desirable, excellent, favored, fortunate, good, lucky, privileged, superior, welcome; SEE CONCEPT 574

envious [adj] *jealous, resentful*
appetent, aspiring, begrudging, coveting, covetous, craving, desiring, desirous, distrustful, fain, grasping, greedy, green-eyed*, green with envy*, grudging, hankering, invidious, jaundiced, longing for, malicious, spiteful, suspicious, umbrageous, watchful, wishful, yearning; SEE CONCEPTS 401,403

environment [n] *surroundings, atmosphere*
ambiance, aura, backdrop, background, circumstances, climate, conditions, context, domain, element, encompassment, entourage, habitat, hood*, jungle*, locale, medium, milieu, neck of the woods*, neighborhood, purlieus, scene, scenery, setting, situation, status, stomping ground*, surroundings, terrain, territory, turf, zoo*; SEE CONCEPTS 515,673,696

environment [n2] *Earth's system of natural resources*
atmosphere, biosphere, ecosphere, ecosystem, environs, Gaia; SEE CONCEPTS 511,515

environmentalist [n] *conservationist*
eagle freak*, ecologist, greenie*, naturalist, preservationist, tree-hugger*; SEE CONCEPTS 515,673,696

environs [n] *neighborhood*
bound, boundary, compass, confine, district, fringes*, limits, locality, outskirts, precinct, purlieus, suburb, surroundings, territory, turf, vicinity; SEE CONCEPT 516

envisage/envision [v] *picture in one's mind*
anticipate, behold, conceive, conceptualize, contemplate, externalize, fancy, feature, foresee, form mental picture of*, grasp, have a picture of*, image, imagine, look upon, materialize, objectify, predict, realize, regard, see, survey, think up, view, view in mind's eye*, vision, visualize; SEE CONCEPTS 17,43

envoy [n] *deputy*
agent, ambassador, attaché, bearer, carrier, chargé d'affaires, consul, courier, delegate,

diplomat, emissary, intermediary, internuncio, legate, medium, messenger, minister, nuncio, plenipotentiary, representative, vicar; SEE CONCEPTS 348,354

envy [n] *jealousy*
backbiting, coveting, covetousness, enviousness, evil eye*, green-eyed monster*, grudge, grudging, grudgingness, hatred, heartburn, ill will, invidiousness, jaundiced eye*, lusting,. malevolence, malice, maliciousness, malignity, opposition, prejudice, resentfulness, resentment, rivalry, spite; SEE CONCEPT 410

envy [v] *be jealous of another*
be envious, begrudge, covet, crave, desire, die over*, eat one's heart out*, grudge, hanker, have hard feelings*, hunger, long, lust, object to, resent, thirst, turn green*, want, yearn; SEE CONCEPTS 10,20

eon [n] *an age*
aeon, ages, time period, years; SEE CONCEPT 807

ephemeral [adj] *momentary, passing*
brief, episodic, evanescent, fleeting, flitting, fugacious, fugitive, impermanent, short, shortlived, temporary, transient, transitory, unenduring, volatile; SEE CONCEPTS 798,801

epic [n] *long story*
heroic poem, legend, narrative, saga, tale; SEE CONCEPT 282

epicure [n] *gourmet*
bon vivant, connoisseur, Epicurean, gastronome, gastronomer, gastronomist, gourmand; SEE CONCEPTS 348,423

epicurean [adj] *loving food and finer things*
gluttonous, gourmandizing, gourmet, hedonistic, libertine, lush, luxurious, pleasure-seeking, self-indulgent, sensual, sensuous, sybaritic, voluptuous; SEE CONCEPT 401

epicurean [n] *gourmet*
bon vivant, connoisseur, critic, epicure, gastronome, gastronomer, glutton, gourmand, hedonist, pleasure seeker, sensualist, specialist, sybarite; SEE CONCEPT 423

epidemic [adj] *widespread*
catching, communicable, contagious, endemic, general, infectious, pandemic, prevailing, prevalent, rampant, rife, sweeping, wide-ranging; SEE CONCEPTS 314,537

epidemic [n] *widespread disease*
contagion, endemic, growth, outbreak, pest, pestilence, plague, rash, scourge, spread, upsurge, wave, what's going around*; SEE CONCEPTS 306,316

epigram [n] *witticism*
aphorism, bon mot, joke, motto, pithy saying, quip, quirk; SEE CONCEPT 278

epilogue [n] *afterword*
coda, concluding speech, conclusion, ending, finale, follow-up, peroration, postlude, postscript, sequel, summation, swan song*; SEE CONCEPTS 264,270,278

episode [n] *adventure; scene*
affair, business, chapter, circumstance, doings, event, experience, goings-on*, happening, incident, installment, interlude, matter, occasion, occurrence, part, passage, section, thing*, what's going down*; SEE CONCEPTS 3,4

episodic [adj] *intermittent; composed of several tales*
anecdotal, digressive, disconnected, discursive, disjointed, incidental, irregular, occasional, pi-

en
ep

caresque, rambling, roundabout, segmented, soap opera*, sporadic, wandering; SEE CONCEPT *482*

epistle [*n*] *letter*
billet doux*, cannonball*, card, communication, dispatch, FYI*, get-well, invite, kite*, line*, love letter, memo, message, missive, note, poison pen*, postcard, scratch*, tab*, thank-you; SEE CONCEPT *271*

epitaph [*n*] *inscription on a gravestone*
commemoration, elegy, epigraph, eulogy, hic jacet, legend, memorial, monument, remembrance, requiscat in pacem, sentiment; SEE CONCEPT *278*

epithet [*n*] *nickname*
appellation, description, designation, name, sobriquet, tag, title; SEE CONCEPT *683*

epitome [*n1*] *perfect example*
apotheosis, archetype, embodiment, essence, exemplar, exemplification, illustration, last word*, personification, quintessence, representation, type, typification, ultimate; SEE CONCEPT *686*

epitome [*n2*] *abbreviation*
abridgment, abstract, brief, compendium, condensation, conspectus, contraction, digest, precis, recapitulation, résumé, summary, summation, syllabus, synopsis; SEE CONCEPT *283*

epitomize [*v1*] *typify*
characterize, embody, exemplify, illustrate, mean, model, personify, represent, stand for, symbolize; SEE CONCEPT *644*

epitomize [*v2*] *encapsulate*
abbreviate, abridge, capsulize, compress, condense, contract, cut, digest, reduce, shorten, summarize, sum up, synopsize; SEE CONCEPTS *236,247*

epoch [*n*] *period*
age, date, era, span, time; SEE CONCEPTS *807,822*

equable [*adj*] *steady, calm*
agreeable, composed, consistent, constant, easygoing, even, even-tempered, imperturbable, level-headed, methodical, orderly, placid, regular, serene, smooth, stabile, stable, systematic, temperate, tranquil, unchanging, unexcitable, unflappable, unfluctuating, uniform, unruffled, unvarying; SEE CONCEPTS *401,542,544*

equal [*adj1*] *alike*
according, balanced, break even, commensurate, comparable, coordinate, correspondent, corresponding, double, duplicate, egalitarian, equivalent, evenly matched, fifty-fifty*, homologous, identic, identical, indistinguishable, invariable, level, look-alike, matched, matching, one and the same, parallel, proportionate, same, same difference*, spit and image*, stack up with*, tantamount, to the same degree, two peas in pod*, uniform, unvarying; SEE CONCEPTS *487,566,573*

equal [*adj2*] *fair, unbiased*
dispassionate, egalitarian, equable, even-handed, impartial, just, nondiscriminatory, nonpartisan, objective, uncolored, unprejudiced, without distinction; SEE CONCEPTS *401,542*

equal [*n*] *peer*
alter ego, coequal, companion, compeer, competitor, complement, copy, counterpart, double, duplicate, equivalent, like, likeness, match, mate, parallel, rival, twin; SEE CONCEPT *423*

equal [*v*] *make even, be even with*
agree, amount to, approach, balance, be commensurate, be identical, be level, be tantamount, break even, come up to, compare, comprise, consist of, coordinate, correspond, emulate, equalize, equate, equipoise, equiponderate, keep pace with*, level, live up to*, match, measure up, meet, parallel, partake of, rank with, reach, rise to, rival, run abreast, square with, tally, tie, touch; SEE CONCEPT *667*

equality [*n*] *similarity, balance; egalitarianism*
adequation, civil rights, commensurateness, coordination, correspondence, equal opportunity, equatability, equilibrium, equipoise, equivalence, evenness, fairness, fair play*, fair practice, fair shake*, homology, identity, impartiality, isonomy, likeness, par, parallelism, parity, sameness, tolerance, uniformity; SEE CONCEPTS *388,645,667*

equalize [*v*] *make the same; balance*
adjust, commeasure, communize, compare, coordinate, democratize, emulate, equal, equate, establish, even, even up, handicap, level, match, parallel, regularize, rival, smooth, socialize, square, standardize, trim; SEE CONCEPTS *126,232*

equanimity [*n*] *levelheadedness*
aplomb, assurance, ataraxia, ataraxy, calm, calmness, composure, confidence, cool, coolness, detachment, equability, imperturbability, patience, peace, phlegm, placidity, poise, presence of mind*, sangfroid, self-possession, serenity, steadiness, tranquillity; SEE CONCEPTS *410,633*

equate [*v*] *balance; think of together*
agree, assimilate, associate, average, be commensurate, compare, consider, correspond to, correspond with, equalize, even, hold, level, liken, make equal, match, offset, pair, paragon, parallel, regard, relate, represent, similize, square, tally, treat; SEE CONCEPTS *37,39,667*

equilibrium [*n*] *balance; evenness*
calm, calmness, composure, cool, coolness, counterbalance, counterpoise, equanimity, equipoise, poise, polish, rest, serenity, stability, stasis, steadiness, steadying, symmetry; SEE CONCEPTS *633,731*

equip [*v*] *make ready with supplies*
accouter, adorn, appoint, arm, array, attire, deck, deck out*, decorate, dress, endow, feather nest*, fit out, fix up, furnish, gear, gear up*, heel*, implement, line nest*, man, outfit, prep*, prepare, provide, qualify, ready, rig, set up, stake, stock, supply, turn out; SEE CONCEPTS *140,182*

equipment [*n*] *supplies, gear for activity*
accessories, accompaniments, accouterments, apparatus, appliances, appurtenances, articles, attachments, baggage, belongings, contraptions, contrivances, devices, equipage, facilities, fittings, fixtures, furnishings, furniture, gadgets, habiliments, impedimenta, kit and kaboodle*, machinery, material, materiel, miscellaneous, outfit, paraphernalia, provisioning, provisions, rig*, setup, shebang*, stock, store, stuff, tackle, things, tools, trappings, traps, utensils; SEE CONCEPTS *364,446,496*

equitable [*adj*] *impartial*
candid, cricket, decent, disinterested, dispassionate, due, ethical, even-handed, even-steven*, fair, fair and square*, fair shake*, fair-to-middling*, honest, impersonal, just, level, moral, nondiscriminatory, nonpartisan, objective, proper, proportionate, reasonable, right, rightful, square, square deal*, stable, unbiased, uncolored, unprejudiced; SEE CONCEPTS *542,545*

equity [*n1*] *impartiality*
disinterestedness, equitableness, even-handedness, fairness, fair play, honesty, integrity, justice, justness, nonpartisanship, piece, reasonableness, rectitude, righteousness, square deal*, uprightness; SEE CONCEPTS 645, 657

equity [*n2*] *money invested in possession*
capital, investment, outlay; SEE CONCEPTS 332, 344

equivalence [*n*] *sameness, similarity*
adequation, agreement, alikeness, compatibility, conformity, correlation, correspondence, equality, evenness, exchangeability, identity, interchangeableness, interchangeableness, likeness, match, par, parallel, parity, synonym, synonymy; SEE CONCEPTS 667,670

equivalent [*adj*] *same, similar*
agnate, akin, alike, analogous, carbon*, commensurate, comparable, convertible, copy, correlative, correspondent, corresponding, ditto*, duplicate, equal, even, homologous, identical, indistinguishable, interchangeable, like, of a kind, parallel, proportionate, reciprocal, same difference*, substitute, synonymous, tantamount; SEE CONCEPTS 487,566,573

equivalent [*n*] *equal, counterpart*
carbon copy*, correspondent, dead ringer*, ditto, like, match, obverse, opposite, parallel, peer, reciprocal, same difference*, spitting image*, substitute, twin; SEE CONCEPTS 667,670

equivocal [*adj*] *doubtful, uncertain*
ambiguous, ambivalent, amphibological, borderline, clear as mud*, clouded*, disreputable, dubious, evasive, fishy*, fuzzy*, hazy*, indefinite, indeterminate, indistinct, misleading, muddled, muzzy*, oblique, obscure, open, problematic, puzzling, questionable, suspect, suspicious, tenebrous, unclear, undecided, unexplicit, unintelligible, vague, with mixed feelings*; SEE CONCEPTS 529,535

equivocate [*v*] *avoid an issue*
beat around the bush*, beg the question*, blow hot and cold*, cavil, cloud the issue*, con, cop a plea*, cop out*, cover up*, dodge, double-talk, elude, escape, eschew, evade, falsify, fence, fib, flip-flop*, fudge*, give run around*, hedge, hem and haw*, jive*, lie, mince words, palter, parry, pass the buck*, prevaricate, pussyfoot, quibble, run around, shuck, shuffle, sidestep, sit on the fence*, stonewall*, tell white lie*, tergiversate, tergiverse, waffle*, weasel*; SEE CONCEPTS 63,102

equivocation [*n*] *avoidance of an issue*
ambiguity, amphibology, casuistry, coloring, con, cop out, cover, cover-up, deceit, deception, deceptiveness, delusion, dissimulation, distortion, double entendre, double meaning, double talk, doubtfulness, duplicity, equivocality, evasion, fallacy, fib, fibbing, hedging, lie, line*, lying, misrepresentation, prevarication, quibbling, routine, run-around, shuffling, song*, song and dance*, sophistry, speciousness, spuriousness, stall, stonewall*, tergiversation, waffle*; SEE CONCEPTS 63,278

era [*n*] *time period in history*
aeon, age, cycle, date, day, days, eon, epoch, generation, stage, term, time; SEE CONCEPTS 807,816

eradicate [*v*] *destroy; remove*
abate, abolish, annihilate, blot out*, demolish, deracinate, do away with, efface, eliminate, erase, expunge, exterminate, extinguish, extirpate, liquidate, mow down*, obliterate, off*, purge, raze, root out*, rub out*, scratch*, scrub, shoot down, squash, stamp out*, take out*, torpedo*, total, trash, unroot, uproot, wash out, waste, weed out*, wipe out*; SEE CONCEPTS 211,252

erase [*v*] *remove; rub out*
abolish, annul, black out, blank, blot, blue pencil*, cancel, cross out, cut, cut out, delete, disannul, dispatch, efface, eliminate, excise, expunge, extirpate, gut, kill, launder*, negate, nullify, obliterate, scratch out*, stamp out*, strike, strike out, take out, trim, wipe out*, withdraw, X-out*; SEE CONCEPTS 211,215

erect [*adj*] *straight up*
arrect, cocked, elevated, erectile, firm, perpendicular, raised, rigid, standing, stiff, upright, upstanding, vertical; SEE CONCEPTS 485,581,604

erect [*v*] *build; establish*
assemble, bring about, cobble up*, cock, compose, construct, create, effect, elevate, fabricate, fashion, fit together, forge, form, found, frame, fudge together*, heighten, hoist, initiate, institute, join, knock together*, lift, make, make up, manufacture, mount, organize, pitch, plant, prefabricate*, produce, put together, put up, raise, rear, run up, set up, shape, stand, stand up, throw together*, throw up, upraise, uprear; SEE CONCEPTS 168,221

ergo [*adv*] *for that reason*
accordingly, consequently, hence, in consequence, so, then, therefore, thereupon, thus, thusly; SEE CONCEPT 544

ergonomics [*n*] *human engineering*
comfort design, functional design, human factors, user-friendly systems, workplace efficiency; SEE CONCEPT 349

erode [*v*] *deteriorate; wear away*
abrade, bite, consume, corrode, crumble, destroy, disintegrate, eat, gnaw, grind down, scour, spoil, waste, wear down; SEE CONCEPTS 252,469

erosion [*n*] *deterioration; wearing away*
abrasion, attrition, consumption, corrosion, decrease, desedimentation, despoliation, destruction, disintegration, eating away, grinding down, spoiling, washing away, wear, wearing down; SEE CONCEPTS 252,257,698

erotic [*adj*] *sexy*
amative, amatory, amorous, aphrodisiac, bawdy, blue*, carnal, concupiscent, earthy, erogenous, fervid, filthy, fleshly, hot*, impassioned, kinky*, lascivious, lecherous, lewd, obscene, off-color*, prurient, purple*, raunchy, raw, romantic, rousing, salacious, seductive, sensual, sexual, spicy, steamy, stimulating, suggestive, titillating, venereal, voluptuous; SEE CONCEPTS 372,545

erotica [*n*] *pornography*
adult literature, adult materials, dirt*, obscene art, obscene literature, porn, sexually explicit art, sexually explicit literature, smut, soft porn, X-rated materials; SEE CONCEPT 280

eroticism [*n*] *sexual excitement*
arousal, libido, lust, stimulation, titillation; SEE CONCEPTS 20,709

err [*v*] *make a mistake; do wrong*
be inaccurate, be incorrect, be in error, be mis-

ep
er

taken, blow*, blunder, bollix*, boo-boo*, deviate, drop the ball*, fall, flub*, foul up*, go astray, goof*, go wrong, lapse, louse up*, make a mess of*, mess up*, misapprehend, misbehave, miscalculate, misjudge, muff*, offend, screw up*, sin, slip up*, snafu*, snarl up, stray, stumble, transgress, trespass, wander; SEE CONCEPT 101

errand [n] *task*
assignment, charge, commission, duty, job, message, mission; SEE CONCEPT 362

errant [adj] *wrong; deviant*
aberrant, deviating, devious, drifting, errable, erratic, erring, fallible, heretic, meandering, misbehaving, mischievous, miscreant, naughty, offending, off straight and narrow*, rambling, ranging, roaming, roving, shifting, sinning, stray, straying, unorthodox, unreliable, wandering, wayward; SEE CONCEPTS 542,545,581

erratic [adj] *unpredictable; wandering*
aberrant, abnormal, anomalous, arbitrary, bizarre, capricious, changeable, desultory, devious, dicey, directionless, dubious, eccentric, fitful, flaky*, fluctuant, idiosyncratic, iffy*, incalculable, inconsistent, inconstant, irregular, meandering, mercurial, nomadic, oddball*, peculiar, planetary, rambling, roving, shifting, spasmodic, strange, stray, uncertain, undirected, unnatural, unreliable, unstable, unusual, vagarious, variable, volatile, wayward, weird, whimsical; SEE CONCEPTS 535,542,581

erroneous [adj] *wrong, incorrect*
all off*, all wet*, amiss, askew, awry, defective, fallacious, false, faulty, flawed, inaccurate, inexact, invalid, misguided, mistaken, off, specious, spurious, unfounded, unsound, untrue, way off, wrong number*; SEE CONCEPTS 267,570,582

error [n] *mistake; wrong*
absurdity, bad job*, blunder, boner*, boo-boo*, delinquency, delusion, deviation, erratum, failure, fall, fallacy, falsehood, falsity, fault, faux pas, flaw, glitch, goof*, howler*, inaccuracy, lapse, misapprehension, misbelief, miscalculation, misconception, miscue, misdeed, misjudgment, mismanagement, miss, misstep, misunderstanding, offense, omission, oversight, screamer*, screw-up*, sin, slight, slip, slipup, solecism, stumble, transgression, trespass, untruth, wrongdoing, X*; SEE CONCEPTS 101,230, 674,699

ersatz [adj] *artificial*
bogus, copied, counterfeit, fake, false, imitation, manufactured, phony, pretended, sham, simulated, spurious, substitute, synthetic; SEE CONCEPT 582

erstwhile [adj] *former*
bygone, ex, late, old, once, one-time, past, preceding, previous, quondam, sometime; SEE CONCEPT 820

erudite [adj] *well-educated, cultured*
brainy, cultivated, educated, highbrow, in the know, into*, knowledgeable, learned, lettered, literate, savvy, scholarly, scholastic, studious, well-read, wise up*; SEE CONCEPT 402

erudition [n] *higher education*
bookishness, brains, cultivation, culture, enlightenment, intellectuality, knowledge, learnedness, learning, letters, literacy, lore, pedantry, refinement, savvy, scholarliness, scholarship, science, studiousness; SEE CONCEPTS 287,409

erupt [v] *give forth, eject with force*
appear, belch, blow up, boil, break out, burst, cast out, detonate, discharge, emit, eruct, explode, extravasate, flare up*, go off*, gush, hurl, jet, pour forth, rupture, spew, spit, spout, spurt, throw off*, touch off*, vent, vomit; SEE CONCEPTS 179,222

eruption [n] *ejection*
access, blast, blow-up, breakout, burst, discharge, explosion, flare-up, flow, gust, outbreak, outburst, sally, venting, vomiting; SEE CONCEPTS 179,467

escalate [v] *increase, be increased*
amplify, ascend, broaden, climb, enlarge, expand, extend, grow, heighten, intensify, magnify, make worse, mount, raise, rise, scale, step up, widen; SEE CONCEPTS 236,245

escapade [n] *adventure, usually lighthearted*
antic, caper, fling, folly, frolic, gag, high jinks, lark, mischief, monkeyshines*, prank, rib*, roguery, rollick, romp, scrape, shenanigans*, spree, stunt, trick, vagary; SEE CONCEPTS 384,386

escape [n] *breaking away; getaway*
abdication, avoidance, AWOL*, beat, bolt, break, breakout, bypassing, circumvention, decampment, deliverance, departure, desertion, disappearance, dodging, ducking, elopement, elusion, elusiveness, eschewal, evasion, evasiveness, extrication, fadeout, flight, freedom, hegira, lam, leave, liberation, out, outbreak, powder, release, rescue, retreat, runaround, shunning, sidestepping, slip, spring, withdrawal; SEE CONCEPT 102

escape [v] *break away from*
abscond, avoid, bail out*, bolt, burst out, circumvent, cut and run*, cut loose*, decamp, depart, desert, disappear, dodge, double, duck, duck out*, elope, elude, emerge, evade, flee, fly, fly the coop*, gafiate, get away with*, get off*, go scot-free*, leave, make getaway*, make off*, make oneself scarce*, pass, play hooky*, run, run away, run off*, run out on*, shun, skip, slip, slip away, steal away, take a powder*, take flight, take on the lam*, vanish, work out of, wriggle out*; SEE CONCEPT 102

escapee [n] *fugitive*
defector, deserter, dodger, escaped prisoner, hunted person, jail-breaker, refugee, runaway; SEE CONCEPT 412

eschew [v] *have nothing to do with*
abandon, abjure, abstain, avoid, double, duck, elude, evade, forgo, forswear, give up, have no truck with*, let well enough alone*, not touch, refrain, renounce, sacrifice, shun, shy, shy away from, steer clear of*, swear off*; SEE CONCEPTS 30,102

escort [n] *protection; accompaniment*
alarm clock*, attendant, beau, bird dog*, bodyguard, cavalier, chaperon, companion, company, consort, convoy, convoyer, cortege, date, entourage, fellow, friend, gallant, guard, guide, partner, protector, retinue, safeguard, squire, train, warden*; SEE CONCEPTS 419,423

escort [v] *act as a companion, guard*
accompany, attend, bear, bring, carry, chaperon, company, conduct, consort with, convoy, date, direct, drag, go with, guide, lead, partner, pilot, protect, route, see, shepherd, show, squire, steer, take out, usher; SEE CONCEPTS 114,384,714

escrow [n] *collateral*

bond, deed, guarantee, insurance, pledge, security; SEE CONCEPTS *71,271,685*

esoteric [adj] *mysterious, obscure*

abstruse, acroamatic, arcane, cabbalistic, cryptic, deep, Delphic, heavy, hermetic, hidden, inner, inscrutable, mystic, mystical, occult, Orphic, private, profound, recondite, secret, Sibylline; SEE CONCEPTS *529,576,582*

especial [adj] *exceptional, particular*

chief, distinguished, dominant, exclusive, express, extraordinary, individual, marked, notable, noteworthy, outstanding, paramount, peculiar, personal, predominant, preeminent, preponderant, principal, private, set, signal, singular, special, specific, supreme, surpassing, uncommon, unique, unusual; SEE CONCEPTS *535,564,574*

especially [adv] *exceptionally, particularly*

abnormally, above all, before all else, chiefly, conspicuously, curiously, eminently, exclusively, expressly, extraordinarily, in particular, in specie, mainly, markedly, notably, oddly, outstandingly, peculiarly, preeminently, primarily, principally, remarkably, signally, singularly, specially, specifically, strangely, strikingly, supremely, unaccountably, uncommonly, uncustomarily, uniquely, unusually, wonderfully; SEE CONCEPTS *535,564,574*

espionage [n] *spying*

intelligence, reconnaissance, secret service, shadowing, tailing, undercover operations, undercover work, underground activities; SEE CONCEPTS *348,412*

esplanade [n] *promenade*

avenue, boardwalk, path, walk, walkway; SEE CONCEPTS *6,501*

espouse [v1] *stand up for; support*

accept, adopt, advocate, approve, back, champion, defend, embrace, get into*, go in for*, maintain, stand behind*, take on, take up, uphold; SEE CONCEPT *10*

espouse [v2] *marry*

betroth, catch, take as spouse, unite, wed; SEE CONCEPT *297*

esprit de corps [n] *group spirit*

camaraderie, common bond, cooperation, group loyalty, morale, solidarity, team spirit; SEE CONCEPTS *410,411*

essay [n1] *written discourse*

article, composition, discussion, disquisition, dissertation, explication, exposition, manuscript, paper, piece, study, theme, thesis, tract, treatise; SEE CONCEPT *271*

essay [n2] *try, attempt*

aim, bid, dry run*, effort, endeavor, exertion, experiment, hassle, labor, one's all*, one's level best*, shot*, striving, struggle, test, toil, travail, trial, try on*, tryout, undertaking, venture, whack*, work; SEE CONCEPT *87*

essay [v] *try, attempt*

aim, assay, endeavor, have a crack*, have a go*, have a shot*, have at it*, labor, make a run at*, offer, put to the test*, seek, strive, struggle, take a stab at*, take a whack at*, take on, test, toil, travail, try out, undertake, venture, work; SEE CONCEPT *87*

essence [n1] *heart, significance*

aspect, attribute, backbone, base, basis, be-all and end-all*, being, bottom, bottom line*, burden, caliber, character, chief constituent, constitution, core, crux, element, entity, essentia, essentiality, fiber, form, fundamentals, germ, grain, kernel, life, lifeblood, main idea, marrow, meaning, meat*, name of game*, nature, nitty-gritty*, nub, nucleus, pith, point, principle, property, quality, quiddity, quintessence, reality, root, soul, spirit, structure, stuff, substance, timber, vein, virtuality; SEE CONCEPTS *411,661,668,688*

essence [n2] *distillate, concentrate*

balm, cologne, drug, effusion, elixir, extract, fragrance, juice, liquor, perfume, potion, scent, spirits, tincture; SEE CONCEPTS *260,467*

essential [adj1] *important, vital*

capital, cardinal, chief, constitutive, crucial, foremost, fundamental, imperative, indispensable, leading, main, necessary, necessitous, needed, needful, prerequisite, principal, required, requisite, right-hand, wanted; SEE CONCEPT *567*

essential [adj2] *basic, fundamental*

absolute, basal, cardinal, cold, complete, congenital, connate, constitutional, deep-seated, elemental, elementary, ideal, inborn, inbred, inherent, innate, intrinsic, key, main, material, meat and potatoes*, name of the game*, nitty-gritty*, nub, perfect, primary, prime, primitive, principal, quintessential, substratal, underlying; SEE CONCEPTS *546,549*

essential [n] *necessity, basic*

ABCs*, bottom line*, brass tacks*, condition, element, essence, fire and ice*, fundamental, groceries*, guts*, heart, meat and potatoes*, must, name of the game*, nitty-gritty*, nuts and bolts*, part and parcel*, precondition, prerequisite, principle, quintessence, requirement, requisite, rudiment, sine qua non, stuff, substance, vital part, where one's at*; SEE CONCEPTS *646,661,826*

establish [v1] *set up, organize*

authorize, base, build, constitute, create, decree, domiciliate, enact, endow, ensconce, entrench, erect, fix, form, found, ground, implant, inaugurate, inculcate, install, institute, land, lay foundation, live, lodge, moor, originate, place, plant, practice, provide, put, ring in, rivet, root, secure, set down, settle, stabilize, start, start ball rolling*, station, stick; SEE CONCEPTS *168,173, 221,251*

establish [v2] *authenticate; demonstrate*

ascertain, authorize, base, certify, circumstantiate, confirm, constitute, corroborate, decree, determine, discover, enact, find out, formulate, learn, legislate, make, make out, predicate, prescribe, prove, ratify, rest, show, stay, substantiate, validate, verify; SEE CONCEPTS *49,50,88,97*

establishment [n1] *organization; creation*

enactment, endowment, formation, formulation, foundation, founding, inauguration, installation, institution, setting up; SEE CONCEPTS *173,221*

establishment [n2] *business, institution*

abode, building, company, concern, corporation, enterprise, factory, firm, foundation, house, institute, office, organization, outfit, plant, quarters, residence, setup, structure, system, workplace; SEE CONCEPTS *323,325,449*

establishment [n3] *ruling class; bureaucracy*

authority, city hall*, conservatives, diehards*, established order, Old Guard*, powers that be*, them, the system*; SEE CONCEPTS *347,354*

estate [n1] *extensive manor and its property*

acreage, area, country home, country place, demesne, domain, dominion, farm, finca, free-

er
es

hold, grounds, holdings, lands, parcel, plantation, quinta, ranch, residence, rural seat, territory, villa; SEE CONCEPT 516

estate [n2] *person's possessions, property, wealth*
assets, belongings, bequest, capital, chattels, devise, earthly possessions, effects, endowment, fortune, goods, heritage, inheritance, legacy, patrimony, substance; SEE CONCEPTS 340,710

estate [n3] *class, rank*
bracket, caste, category, classification, condition, echelon, footing, form, grade, level, lot, order, period, place, position, quality, repair, shape, situation, sphere, standing, state, station, status, stratum; SEE CONCEPTS 378,388

esteem [v1] *think highly of*
admire, appreciate, apprise, be fond of, cherish, consider, hold dear, honor, idolize, like, look up to*, love, prize, regard, regard highly, respect, revere, reverence, think the world of*, treasure, value, venerate, worship; SEE CONCEPT 32

esteem [v2] *consider, believe*
account, calculate, deem, estimate, hold, judge, rate, reckon, regard, think, view; SEE CONCEPT 12

estimable [adj] *honorable, worthy*
admirable, admired, appreciable, august, big name*, big time*, commendable, decent, deserving, esteemed, excellent, good, high-powered, honored, in limelight*, laudable, major league*, meretorious, meritable, name, noble, palmary, praisable, praiseworthy, reputable, reputed, respectable, respected, sterling, valuable, valued, venerable, well-thought-of*; SEE CONCEPTS 567,572

estimate [n] *approximate calculation; educated guess*
appraisal, appraisement, assay, assessment, ballpark figure*, belief, conclusion, conjecture, estimation, evaluation, gauging, guess, guesstimate*, impression, judgment, measure, measurement, mensuration, opinion, point of view, projection, rating, reckoning, sizing up*, stock, surmise, survey, thought, valuation; SEE CONCEPTS 28,37,689,784

estimate [v] *guess, try to value*
account, appraise, assay, assess, believe, budget, calculate roughly, cast, cipher, class, classify, compute, conjecture, consider, count, decide, deduce, determine, enumerate, evaluate, examine, expect, figure, form opinion, gauge, guess, guesstimate*, judge, look into, look upon, number, outline, plan, predict, prophesy, rank, rate, reason, reckon, regard, run over*, scheme, set a figure*, size up*, sum, suppose, surmise, suspect, tax, think, think through*; SEE CONCEPTS 28,37,764

estimation [n] *belief, guess*
admiration, appraisal, appreciation, arithmetic, assessment, calculating, ciphering, computation, consideration, considered opinion, credit, esteem, estimate, estimating, evaluation, favor, figuring, impression, judgment, opinion, predicting, reckoning, regard, respect, stock, valuation, veneration, view; SEE CONCEPTS 28,689

estrange [v] *destroy the affections of*
alien, alienate, antagonize, break up, disaffect, disunify, disunite, divert, divide, divorce, drive apart, leave, make hostile, part, put on the outs*, separate, set at odds*, sever, split, sunder, turn

off*, wean, withdraw, withhold; SEE CONCEPTS 7,19,297,384

estrangement [n] *destruction of affections*
alienation, antagonization, breach, break-up, disaffection, disassociation, disunity, division, divorce, hostility, leave, leaving, parting, removal, schism, separation, split, withdrawal, withholding; SEE CONCEPTS 297,388

estuary [n] *mouth*
arm, creek, firth, fjord, inlet, tidewater, waterway; SEE CONCEPTS 509,514

et cetera [adj] *and so forth*
along with others, and all, and on and on, and others, and so on, and the like, and the rest, blah blah blah*, et al., whatever, whatnot; SEE CONCEPTS 267,577

etch [v] *carve*
compose, corrode, cut, define, delineate, depict, describe, eat into, engrave, erode, execute, furrow, grave, impress, imprint, incise, ingrain, inscribe, outline, picture, portray, reduce, represent, set forth, stamp; SEE CONCEPTS 174,176

etching [n] *art created by carving*
engraving, impression, imprint, inscription, mezzotint, photoengraving, photogravure, print, reproduction, rotogravure, transferring; SEE CONCEPT 259

eternal [adj] *without pause; endless*
abiding, ageless, always, amaranthine, boundless, ceaseless, constant, continual, continued, continuous, dateless, deathless, enduring, everlasting, forever, illimitable, immemorial, immortal, immutable, imperishable, incessant, indefinite, indestructible, infinite, interminable, lasting, never-ending, perdurable, perennial, permanent, perpetual, persistent, relentless, termless, timeless, unbroken, unceasing, undying, unending, unfading, uninterrupted, unremitting, without end; SEE CONCEPTS 482,798

eternally [adv] *endlessly*
always, continually, ever, evermore, forever, forevermore, for ever so long*, for keeps, in perpetuum, perpetually, regularly, till cows come home*; SEE CONCEPT 798

eternity [n] *forever*
aeon, afterlife, age, ages, blue moon*, dog's age*, endlessness, endless time, everlastingness, forever and a day*, future, immortality, imperishability, infiniteness, infinitude, infinity, kingdom come*, other world*, perpetuity, timelessness, time without end, wild blue yonder*, world without end*; SEE CONCEPTS 370,804,818

ethereal [adj] *delicate, heavenly*
aerial, airy, celestial, dainty, divine, empyreal, empyrean, exquisite, fairy, filmy, fine, gaseous, ghostly, gossamer, impalpable, insubstantial, intangible, light, rarefied, refined, spiritual, sublime, subtle, supernal, tenuous, unearthly, unsubstantial, unworldly, vaporous, vapory; SEE CONCEPTS 491,549,582,606

ethical [adj] *moral, righteous*
Christian, clean, conscientious, correct, decent, elevated, equitable, fair, fitting, good, high-principled, honest, honorable, humane, just, kosher*, moralistic, noble, principled, proper, respectable, right, right-minded, square, straight, true blue*, upright, upstanding, virtuous; SEE CONCEPT 545

ethics/ethic [*n*] *moral philosophy, values*
belief, conduct, conscience, convention, conventionalities, criteria, descency, ethos, goodness, honesty, honor, ideal, imperative, integrity, moral code, morality, mores, natural law, nature, practice, principles, right and wrong, "rules of conduct, standard, standards, the Golden Rule*; SEE CONCEPTS *645,688,689*

ethnic [*adj*] *racial, cultural*
indigenous, national, native, traditional, tribal; SEE CONCEPT *549*

etiquette [*n*] *manners, politeness*
amenities, civility, code, convention, courtesy, customs, decency, decorum, deportment, dignity, form, formalities, good behavior*, mores, politesse, proper behavior, propriety, protocol, p's and q's*, rules, seemlessness, social graces, suavities, usage; SEE CONCEPT *633*

eulogize [*v*] *praise, glorify*
acclaim, applaud, bless, celebrate, commend, compliment, cry up, exalt, extol, flatter, give a bouquet*, give a posy*, hymn, idolize, laud, magnify, panegyrize, pay tribute to, sing praises; SEE CONCEPT *69*

eulogy [*n*] *praise, acclamation*
acclaim, accolade, adulation, applause, citation, commendation, compliment, encomium, exaltation, glorification, laudation, paean, panegyric, plaudit, salutation, tribute; SEE CONCEPTS *69,278*

euphemism [*n*] *nice way of saying something*
circumlocution, delicacy, floridness, grandiloquence, inflation, pomposity, pretense, purism; SEE CONCEPTS *275,278*

euphonious [*adj*] *pleasing to the ear*
agreeable, clear, dulcet, harmonious, mellifluous, melodious, musical, rhythmic, smooth, sweet-sounding, tuneful, well-pitched; SEE CONCEPT *563*

euphoria [*n*] *extreme happiness*
bliss, dreamland, ecstasy, elation, exaltation, exhilaration, exultation, frenzy, glee, health, high spirits, intoxication, joy, joyousness, jubilation, madness, rapture, relaxation, transport; SEE CONCEPT *410*

euthanasia [*n*] *mercy killing*
assisted suicide, putting out of misery*; SEE CONCEPT *252*

evacuate [*v*] *clear an area; empty*
abandon, bail out*, cut out, decamp, depart, desert, discharge, displace, eject, expel, forsake, hightail, leave, move out, pack up, pull out, quit, relinquish, remove, run for the hills*, skidaddle*, vacate, withdraw; SEE CONCEPTS *179,195*

evade [*v*] *get away from*
avoid, baffle, balk, beat around bush*, beg the question*, bypass, cavil, circumvent, conceal, confuse, cop out, deceive, decline, dodge, double, duck, elude, equivocate, escape, eschew, fence, fend off*, flee, fly, fudge*, get around, give the runaround*, hedge, hide, keep distance*, lay low*, lead on a merry chase*, lie, parry, pass up, pretend, prevaricate, pussyfoot, put off, shift, shirk, shuck, shuffle, shun, shy, sidestep, slip out, sneak away*, steer clear of*, tergiversate, trick, waffle*, weasel*; SEE CONCEPTS *30,102*

evaluate [*v*] *judge*
appraise, assay, assess, calculate, check, check out, class, classify, criticize, decide, estimate, figure out, fixture, gauge, grade, guesstimate*,

look over, peg*, price out, rank, rate, read, reckon, set at, size, size up*, survey, take account of, take measure, valuate, value, weigh; SEE CONCEPTS *18,24,103*

evaluation [*n*] *judgment*
appraisal, appraisement, assessment, calculation, decision, estimate, estimation, guesstimation*, interpretation, opinion, rating, stock, take, valuation; SEE CONCEPTS *24,103,689*

evanescent [*adj*] *transient*
brief, disappearing, fading, fleeting, momentary, passing, short-lived, temporary, tenuous, vanishing; SEE CONCEPTS *551,798*

evangelism [*n*] *preaching*
ministration, sermonizing, spreading the word, teaching; SEE CONCEPT *361*

evangelist [*n*] *preacher*
circuit rider, minister, missionary, pastor, religious teacher, revivalist, televangelist, television evangelist, television preacher, TV evangelist; SEE CONCEPT *361*

evaporate [*v*] *dry up, dissolve*
clear, concentrate, dehumidify, dehydrate, dematerialize, desiccate, disappear, dispel, disperse, dissipate, evanesce, evanish, fade, fade away, melt, parch, pass, vanish, vaporize, weaken; SEE CONCEPTS *469,698*

evaporation [*n*] *drying up; dissolution*
dehydration, dematerialization, desiccation, disappearance, dispelling, dispersal, dissipation, escape, evanescence, fading, melting, vanishing, vaporescence, vaporization; SEE CONCEPTS *469,607,698*

evasion [*n*] *escape, avoidance*
artifice, circumvention, cop-out*, cunning, ditch*, dodge*, dodging, elusion, equivocating, equivocation, eschewal, evading, evasiveness, excuse, fancy footwork*, fudging*, jive, lie, obliqueness, pretext, prevarication, quibble, routine, run-around, ruse, shift, shirking, shuffling, shunning, slip*, sophism, sophistry, stall, stonewall*, subterfuge, trick, trickery; SEE CONCEPTS *59,63,102*

evasive [*adj*] *deceitful, tricky*
ambiguous, cagey, casuistic, casuistical, cunning, deceptive, devious, dissembling, elusive, elusory, equivocating, false, fugitive, greasy, indirect, intangible, lying, misleading, oblique, prevaricating, shifty, shuffling, slippery, sly, sophistical, stonewalling*, unclear, vague; SEE CONCEPTS *267,401,542*

even [*adj1*] *flat, uniform*
alike, balanced, consistent, constant, continual, continuous, direct, equal, flush, homogenous, horizontal, level, matching, metrical, parallel, planate, plane, plumb, proportional, regular, right, same, smooth, square, stabile, stable, steady, straight, surfaced, true, unbroken, unchanging, undeviating, unfluctuating, uninterrupted, unvaried, unvarying, unwavering, unwrinkled; SEE CONCEPTS *480,490*

even [*adj2*] *calm, undisturbed*
composed, cool, equable, equanimous, even-tempered, imperturbable, peaceful, placid, serene, stable, steady, tranquil, unexcitable, unruffled, well-balanced; SEE CONCEPT *401*

even [*adj3*] *commensurate; having no advantage*
balanced, coequal, comparable, coterminous, drawn, equal, equalized, equivalent, even-steven*, exact, fifty-fifty*, horse to horse*, iden-

tical, level, matching, neck and neck*, on a par*, parallel, proportional, proportionate, same, similar, smack in the middle*, square, tied, uniform; SEE CONCEPT 566

even [adj4] *fair, impartial*
balanced, disinterested, dispassionate, equal, equitable, fair and square*, honest, just, matching, nonpartisan, square, straightforward, unbiased, unprejudiced; SEE CONCEPTS 267,542

even [adv] *still, yet*
all the more, despite, disregarding, indeed, in spite of, much, notwithstanding, so much as; SEE CONCEPT 544

even [v] *balance, make smooth*
align, equal, equalize, flatten, flush, grade, lay, level, match, pancake*, plane, regularize, roll, square, stabilize, steady, symmetrize, uniform; SEE CONCEPTS 231,757

even-handed [adj] *fair*
aboveboard, balanced, disinterested, equitable, honest, honorable, impartial, just, neutral, nonpartisan, objective, on the level*, on the up-and-up*, reasonable, square, straight, unbiased, unprejudiced, upright, virtuous; SEE CONCEPT 542

evening [n] *latter part of a day*
black, close, dark, decline, dim, dusk, duskiness, early black*, eve, even, eventide, late afternoon, nightfall, sundown, sunset, twilight; SEE CONCEPTS 801,806,810

event [n1] *occurrence, happening*
accident, act, action, advent, adventure, affair, appearance, business, calamity, case, catastrophe, celebration, ceremony, chance, circumstance, coincidence, conjuncture, crisis, deed, development, emergency, episode, experience, exploit, fact, function, holiday, incident, juncture, marvel, matter, milestone, miracle, misfortune, mishap, mistake, occasion, occurrence, pass, phase, phenomenon, predicament, proceeding, shift, situation, story, thing*, tide, transaction, triumph, turn, wonder; SEE CONCEPT 2

event [n2] *effect, result*
aftereffect, aftermath, case, causatum, chance, conclusion, consequence, end, end result, eventuality, fortuity, hap, happenstance, issue, offshoot, outcome, outgrowth, product, resultant, sequel, sequent, termination, upshot; SEE CONCEPT 230

event [n3] *performance, competition*
bout, contest, game, match, meet, tournament; SEE CONCEPTS 263,363

even-tempered [adj] *easygoing*
calm, collected, complacent, composed, cool, level-headed, patient, relaxed, stable, steady, unexcitable, unruffled; SEE CONCEPTS 401,404

eventful [adj] *significant, busy*
active, consequential, critical, crucial, decisive, exciting, fateful, full, historic, important, lively, memorable, momentous, notable, noteworthy, outstanding, remarkable, signal; SEE CONCEPT 548

eventual [adj] *future, concluding*
closing, conditional, consequent, contingent, dependent, down the pike*, down the road*, ending, endmost, ensuing, final, hindmost, indirect, inevitable, in the cards*, last, later, latter, overall, possible, prospective, resulting, secondary, succeeding, terminal, ulterior, ultimate, vicarious; SEE CONCEPTS 552,820

eventuality [n] *something that probably will happen*
aftereffect, aftermath, any case, case, chance, consequence, contingency, effect, event, godown*, goings-on*, happening, issue, likelihood, outcome, possibility, probability, result, sequel, toss-up, upshot*; SEE CONCEPTS 230,650

eventually [adv] *in the course of time*
after all, at last, at the end of the day*, finally, hereafter, in future, in the end, in the long run*, one day, someday, sometime, sooner or later*, ultimately, when all is said and done*; yet; SEE CONCEPTS 552,820

eventuate [v] *be a consequence*
be consequent, befall, come about, come to pass, end, ensue, eventualize, follow, happen, issue, occur, result, stop, take place, terminate; SEE CONCEPTS 2,242

ever [adv] *always, at any time*
anytime, at all, at all times, at any point, by any chance*, consistently, constantly, continually, endlessly, eternally, everlastingly, evermore, forever, for keeps, in any case*, incessantly, in perpetuum, invariably, on any occasion*, perpetually, regularly, relentlessly, till cows come home*, to the end of time*, unceasingly, unendingly, usually; SEE CONCEPTS 798,799

everlasting [adj] *infinite, never-ending*
abiding, amaranthine, boundless, ceaseless, constant, continual, continuous, deathless, endless, eternal, immortal, imperishable, incessant, indestructible, interminable, lasting, limitless, perdurable, permanent, perpetual, termless, timeless, unceasing, undying, unending, uninterrupted, unremitting; SEE CONCEPT 798

every [adj] *each, all*
each one, whole, without exception; SEE CONCEPT 531

everybody/everyone [n] *all involved, all human beings; the whole world*
all, all and sundry*, anybody, each one, each person, every person, generality, masses, people, populace, the public, the whole, young and old*; SEE CONCEPT 417

everyday [adj] *common*
accustomed, average, commonplace, conventional, customary, daily, dime a dozen*, dull, familiar, frequent, garden variety*, habitual, informal, lowly, mainstream, middle-of-the-road*, mundane, normal, ordinary, per diem, plain, prosaic, quotidian, routine, run-of-the-mill*, stock, unexceptional, unimaginative, unremarkable, usual, vanilla*, whitebread*, wonted, workaday; SEE CONCEPTS 530,547

everything [n] *entirety*
aggregate, all, all in all, all that, all things, business, complex, each thing, every little thing*, fixins'*, lock stock and barrel*, lot, many things, sum, the works*, total, universe, whole, whole ball of wax*, whole caboodle*, whole enchilada*, whole lot*, whole shebang*; SEE CONCEPTS 432,837

everywhere [adv] *in all places*
all around, all over, all over creation*, all over the map*, far and wide*, here and there*, here till Sunday*, high and low*, in all quarters, in each place, in every direction, in every place, inside and out, near and far*, omnipresent, overall, pole to pole*, the world over*, throughout, ubiq-

uitous, ubiquitously, universally, wherever; SEE CONCEPT *583*

evict [*v*] *throw out from residence*
boot out*, bounce*, chase, dislodge, dismiss, dispossess, eject, expel, extrude, force out, heave-ho*, kick out*, oust, out, put out, remove, send packing*, show out, show the door*, shut out, toss out on ear*, turn out; SEE CONCEPTS *122,198,211*

eviction [*n*] *throwing out of a residence*
boot*, bounce*, bum's rush*, clearance, dislodgement, dispossession, ejection, expulsion, kicking out*, ouster, removal, rush, the gate*, walking papers*; SEE CONCEPTS *123,198,211*

evidence [*n*] *proof*
affirmation, attestation, averment, cincher*, clincher*, clue, confirmation, corroboration, cue, data, declaration, demonstration, deposition, documentation, dope*, goods*, gospel, grabber*, grounds, index, indication, indicia, info*, information, manifestation, mark, sign, significant, smoking gun*, substantiation, symptom, testament, testimonial, testimony, token, witness; SEE CONCEPTS *274,318*

evidence [*v*] *prove*
attest, bespeak, betoken, confirm, connote, demonstrate, denote, designate, display, evince, exhibit, expose, illustrate, indicate, manifest, mark, ostend, proclaim, reveal, show, signify, testify to, witness; SEE CONCEPTS *57,97,317*

evident [*adj*] *apparent, clear*
axiomatic, barefaced*, clear-cut, conspicuous, crystal clear*, distinct, fact, incontestable, incontrovertible, indisputable, logical, manifest, noticeable, obvious, open-and-shut*, palpable, patent, perceptible, plain, plain as day*, reasonable, straightforward, tangible, unambiguous, unmistakable, visible; SEE CONCEPTS *529,535*

evidently [*adv*] *apparently, clearly*
doubtless, doubtlessly, incontestably, incontrovertibly, indisputably, it seems, it would seem, manifestly, obviously, officially, ostensibly, outwardly, patently, plainly, professedly, seemingly, to all appearances*, undoubtedly, unmistakably, without question; SEE CONCEPT *535*

evil [*adj*] *sinful, immoral*
angry, atrocious, bad, baneful, base, beastly, calamitous, corrupt, damnable, depraved, destructive, disastrous, execrable, flagitious, foul, harmful, hateful, heinous, hideous, iniquitous, injurious, loathsome, low, maleficent, malevolent, malicious, malignant, nefarious, no good, obscene, offensive, pernicious, poison, rancorous, reprobate, repugnant, repulsive, revolting, spiteful, stinking, ugly, unpleasant, unpropitious, vicious, vile, villainous, wicked, wrathful, wrong; SEE CONCEPTS *545,570*

evil [*n*] *badness, immorality; disaster*
affliction, baseness, blow, calamity, catastrophe, corruption, crime, criminality, curse, debauchery, depravity, devilry, diabolism, harm, hatred, heinousness, hurt, ill, impiety, indecency, infamy, iniquity, injury, knavery, lewdness, licentiousness, looseness, malevolence, malignity, meanness, mischief, misery, misfortune, obscenity, outrage, pain, perversity, ruin, sin, sinfulness, sorrow, suffering, turpitude, vice, viciousness, vileness, villainy, wickedness, woe, wrong, wrongdoing; SEE CONCEPT *645*

evildoer [*n*] *wrongdoer*
bad person, criminal, devil, evil person, felon, gangster, lawbreaker, murderer, psychopath, sinner, sociopath, troublemaker, villain; SEE CONCEPT *412*

evince [*v*] *manifest*
attest, declare, demonstrate, disclose, display, furnish, indicate, prove, reveal, show; SEE CONCEPTS *118,261*

evoke [*v*] *induce, stimulate*
arouse, awaken, call, call forth, conjure, educe, elicit, evince, evolve, excite, extort, extract, give rise to, invoke, milk*, provoke, raise, rally, recall, rouse, stir up, summon, waken; SEE CONCEPTS *228,242*

evolution [*n*] *development, progress*
change, enlargement, evolvement, expansion, flowering, growth, increase, maturation, natural process, progression, transformation, unfolding, working out; SEE CONCEPT *704*

evolve [*v*] *develop, progress*
advance, derive, disclose, educe, elaborate, emerge, enlarge, excogitate, expand, get, grow, increase, mature, obtain, open, result, ripen, unfold, work out; SEE CONCEPTS *236,245,704*

exacerbate [*v*] *infuriate; make worse*
add insult to injury*, aggravate, annoy, egg on*, embitter, enrage, envenom, exasperate, excite, fan the flames*, feed the fire*, go from bad to worse*, heat up*, heighten, hit on*, increase, inflame, intensify, irritate, madden, provoke, push one's button*, rattle one's cage*, rub salt in a wound*, vex, worsen; SEE CONCEPTS *7,19*

exact [*adj*] *accurate, precise*
bull's-eye*, careful, clear, clear-cut, correct, dead on*, definite, distinct, downright, explicit, express, faithful, faultless, identical, literal, methodical, nailed down*, nice, on target*, on the button*, on the money*, on the numbers*, orderly, particular, perfect, right, right on*, rigorous, sharp, specific, true, unequivocal, unerring, veracious, verbal, verbatim; SEE CONCEPTS *535,557*

exact [*adj2*] *careful, painstaking*
conscientious, conscionable, demanding, exacting, finicky, fussy, heedful, meticulous, punctilious, punctual, rigorous, scrupulous, severe, strict; SEE CONCEPT *542*

exact [*v*] *demand, call for*
assess, bleed, call, challenge, claim, coerce, command, compel, constrain, extort, extract, force, gouge, impose, insist upon, lean on, levy, oblige, pinch, postulate, put on, require, requisition, shake down*, solicit, squeeze, wrench, wrest, wring; SEE CONCEPTS *53,142*

exacting [*adj*] *demanding*
burdensome, by the book*, careful, critical, difficult, exigent, finicky, fussy, grievous, hard, harsh, hypercritical, imperious, nit-picking, onerous, oppressive, painstaking, particular, persnickety, picky, precise, rigid, rigorous, severe, stern, strict, stringent, taxing, tough, trying, unsparing, weighty; SEE CONCEPTS *401,404*

exactly [*adv*] *accurately, particularly*
absolutely, altogether, bang*, carefully, completely, correctly, definitely, explicitly, expressly, faithfully, faultlessly, for a fact, for certain, for sure*, indeed, in every respect, just, literally, methodically, no mistake, on the dot*, on the money*, on the nail*, on the nose*, posi-

ev
ex

tively, precisely, quite, right, rigorously, scrupulously, severely, sharp, specifically, square, strictly, the ticket*, totally, truly, truthfully, unequivocally, unerringly, utterly, veraciously, wholly; SEE CONCEPTS 535,557

exactness [n] *accuracy, precision*
carefulness, correctness, definiteness, definitiveness, definitude, exactitude, faithfulness, faultlessness, nicety, orderliness, painstakingness, preciseness, promptitude, regularity, rigor, rigorousness, scrupulousness, strictness, truth, unequivocalness, veracity; SEE CONCEPTS 638,654

exaggerate [v] *overstate, embellish*
amplify, blow out of proportion*, boast, boost, brag, build up, caricature, color, cook up*, corrupt, distort, embroider, emphasize, enlarge, exalt, expand, fabricate, falsify, fudge*, go to extremes*, heighten, hike, hyperbolize, inflate, intensify, lay it on thick*, lie, loud talk*, magnify, make too much of*, misquote, misreport, misrepresent, overdo, overdraw, overemphasize, overestimate, pad*, pretty up*, puff, put on, pyramid*, romance, romanticize, scam, stretch, up*; SEE CONCEPT 63

exaggerated [adj] *overstated, embellished*
a bit thick*, abstract, amplified, artificial, bouncing, caricatural, distorted, embroidered, exalted, excessive, extravagant, fabricated, fabulous, false, fantastic, farfetched, hammy, highly colored, histrionic, hyperbolic, impossible, inflated, magnified, melodramatic, out of proportion, overblown, overdone, overestimated, overkill, overwrought, preposterous, pretentious, schmaltzy, sensational, spectacular, steep, strained, stylized, tall, too much*, too-too*, unrealistic; SEE CONCEPTS 267,542,562

exaggeration [n] *overstatement, embellishment*
aggrandizement, amplification, baloney*, boasting, caricature, coloring, crock*, elaboration, embroidery, emphasis, enlargement, exaltation, excess, extravagance, fabrication, falsehood, fancy, fantasy, figure of speech, fish story*, flight of fancy*, hogwash*, hyperbole, inflation, jazz*, line*, magnification, misjudgment, misrepresentation, overemphasis, overestimation, pretension, pretentiousness, rant, romance, stretch, tall story*, untruth, whopper*, yarn*; SEE CONCEPTS 63,278,663

exalt [v] *promote, praise*
acclaim, advance, aggrandize, apotheosize, applaud, bless, boost, build up*, commend, dignify, distinguish, ennoble, erect, eulogize, extol, glorify, halo, honor, idolize, intensify, laud, magnify, pay homage to, pay tribute to, raise, revere, set on pedestal*, sublime, transfigure, upgrade, uprear, worship; SEE CONCEPTS 10,69

exaltation [n] *promotion, praise*
acclaim, acclamation, advancement, aggrandizement, apotheosis, applause, blessing, dignity, elevation, eminence, ennoblement, extolment, glorification, glory, grandeur, high rank, homage, honor, idolzation, laudation, lionization, loftiness, magnification, panegyric, plaudits, prestige, reverence, rise, tribute, upgrading, uplifting, worship; SEE CONCEPTS 69,278

exaltation [n2] *great joy*
animation, bliss, blessing, delight, ecstasy, elation, elevation, euphoria, excitement, exhilaration, exultation, inspiration, intoxication, joyousness, jubilation, rapture, stimulation, transport, uplift; SEE CONCEPTS 32,410

exalted [adj] *praised; held in high esteem*
astral, august, dignified, elevated, eminent, exaggerated, excessive, first, grand, high, highest, highest-ranking, high-minded, high-ranking, honorable, honored, ideal, illustrious, immodest, imposing, inflated, intellectual, leading, lofty, magnificent, noble, number one, outstanding, overblown, pompous, prestigious, pretentious, proud, self-important, sublime, superb, superior, top-drawer*, top-ranking, uplifting; SEE CONCEPTS 404,529

examination [n1] *test, analysis*
assay, audit, battery, blue book*, breakdown, canvass, catechism, checking, checkup, cross-examination, diagnosis, dissection, exam, experiment, exploration, final, grilling, inquest, inquiry, inquisition, inspection, interrogation, investigation, legwork*, make-up, observation, once-over*, oral, perlustration, perusal, probe, quest, questioning, questionnaire, quiz, raid, reconnaissance, research, review, scan, scrutiny, search, study, survey, the eye*, third degree*, trial, tryout, view, written; SEE CONCEPT 290

examination [n2] *medical checkup*
autopsy, biopsy, exam, inquiry, observation, physical, postoperative, probe, test; SEE CONCEPTS 103,310

examine [v1] *analyze, test*
appraise, assay, audit, canvass, case, check, check out, chew over*, consider, criticize, delve into, dig into, explore, eye*, finger*, frisk, go into, go over, go through, gun*, inquire, inspect, investigate, look over, look see*, parse, pat down, peruse, pick at, ponder, pore over, probe, prospect, prove, read, reconnoiter, research, review, scan, scope, screen, scrutinate, scrutinize, search into, sift, size up*, study, survey, sweep, take stock of*, try, turn over*, vet, view, weigh, winnow*; SEE CONCEPTS 24,103

examine [v2] *ask questions pointedly*
catechize, check, cross-examine, experiment, give the third*, give the third degree*, grill, inquire, interrogate, judge, measure, pump, put through the wringer*, query, quiz, try, try out, weigh; SEE CONCEPT 48

example [n] *instance, model*
archetype, case, case history, case in point, citation, copy, excuse, exemplar, exemplification, for instance, ideal, illustration, kind of thing, lesson, object, original, paradigm, paragon, part, pattern, precedent, prototype, quotation, representation, sample, sampling, specimen, standard, stereotype, symbol; SEE CONCEPT 686

exasperate [v] *upset, provoke*
aggravate, agitate, anger, annoy, bug*, disturb, drive up the wall*, embitter, enrage, exacerbate, excite, gall, get*, get under one's skin*, incense, inflame, infuriate, irk, irritate, madden, make waves*, needle*, nettle, peeve, pique, rankle, rile, roil, rouse, T-off*, try the patience of, vex, work up; SEE CONCEPTS 7,19

exasperation [n] *upset, provocation*
aggravation, anger, annoyance, besetment, bother, botheration, displeasure, exacerbation, fury, ire, irritant, irritation, nuisance, passion, pest, pique, plague, rage, resentment, vexation, wrath; SEE CONCEPTS 29,410

excavate [v] *dig up*
burrow, cut, delve, empty, gouge, grub, hollow, mine, quarry, scoop, scrape, shovel, spade, trench, tunnel, uncover, unearth; SEE CONCEPT 178

excavation [n] *site of digging; digging*
blasting, burrow, cavity, cut, cutting, dig, disinterring, ditch, dugout, exhuming, hole, hollow, mine, mining, pit, quarry, removal, scooping, shaft, shoveling, trench, trough, unearthing; SEE CONCEPTS 178,509,513

excavator [n] *earthmover*
backhoe, bulldozer, digger, heavy machinery; SEE CONCEPT 505

exceed [v] *be superior to; surpass*
beat, best, better, break record*, cap, distance, eclipse, excel, get upper hand*, go beyond, go by, have advantage, have a jump on*, have it all over*, out-distance, outdo, outpace, outreach, outrun, outshine, outstrip, overstep, overtake, overtax, pass, rise above*, run circles around*, surmount, top, transcend; SEE CONCEPT 141

exceedingly [adv] *very; exceptionally*
awfully, enormously, especially, excessively, extraordinarily, extremely, greatly, highly, hugely, immoderately, in a marked degree, inordinately, powerful, really, remarkably, strikingly, superlatively, surpassingly, terribly, too much, unusually, vastly, vitally; SEE CONCEPT 569

excel [v] *be superior; surpass*
beat, be good, be master of, be proficient, be skillful, best, be talented, better, cap, come through, eclipse, exceed, go beyond, go to town*, improve upon, make it, outdo, outrival, outshine, outstrip, pass, predominate, shine, show talent, surmount, take precedence, top, transcend, wax*; SEE CONCEPTS 141,671,706

excellence [n] *superiority*
arete, class, distinction, éclat, eminence, excellency, fineness, goodness, greatness, high quality, merit, perfection, preeminence, purity, quality, superbness, supremacy, transcendence, virtue, worth; SEE CONCEPT 671

excellent [adj] *superior, wonderful*
A-1*, accomplished, admirable, attractive, capital, certified, champion, choice, choicest, desirable, distinctive, distinguished, estimable, exceptional, exemplary, exquisite, fine, finest, first, first-class, first-rate, good, great, high, incomparable, invaluable, magnificent, meritorious, notable, noted, outstanding, peerless, piked*, premium, priceless, prime, select, skillful, sterling, striking, superb, superlative, supreme, tiptop*, top-notch, transcendent, world-class; SEE CONCEPT 574

except [prep] *other than*
apart from, aside from, bar, barring, besides, but, excepting, excluding, exclusive of, exempting, if not, lacking, leaving out, minus, not for, omitting, outside of, rejecting, save, saving, short of, without, with the exception of; SEE CONCEPT 577

except [v] *leave out*
ban, bar, bate, count out, debar, disallow, eliminate, exclude, exempt, expostulate, inveigh, object, omit, pass over, protest, reject, remonstrate, rule out, suspend, taboo; SEE CONCEPTS 25,30, 211

exception [n1] *leaving out*
barring, debarment, disallowment, excepting, exclusion, excusing, expulsion, noninclusion,

omission, passing over, rejection, repudiation, reservation; SEE CONCEPTS 25,30,211

exception [n2] *special case; irregularity*
allowance, anomalism, anomaly, departure, deviation, difference, dispensation, eccentricity, exemption, freak, inconsistency, nonconformity, oddity, peculiarity, perquisitor, privilege, privileged person, quirk; SEE CONCEPTS 423,665

exceptional [adj1] *irregular*
aberrant, abnormal, anomalous, atypical, deviant, distinct, extraordinary, inconsistent, infrequent, notable, noteworthy, odd, peculiar, phenomenal, rare, remarkable, scarce, singular, special, strange, uncommon, uncustomary, unheard-of, unimaginable, unique, unordinary, unprecedented, unthinkable, unusual; SEE CONCEPT 564

exceptional [adj2] *excellent, wonderful*
brainy, extraordinary, fine, first-class, first-rate, good, high, marvelous, outstanding, phenomenal, premium, prodigious, remarkable, singular, special, superior, world-class; SEE CONCEPTS 572,574

excerpt [n] *citation; something taken from a whole*
extract, fragment, notation, note, part, passage, pericope, piece, portion, quotation, quote, saying, section, selection; SEE CONCEPTS 270,274, 835

excerpt [v] *take a part from a whole*
choose, cite, cull, extract, glean, note, pick, pick out, quote, select, single out; SEE CONCEPTS 41,142,211

excess [n1] *overabundance of something*
balance, by-product, enough, exorbitance, exuberance, fat, fulsomeness, glut, inundation, lavishness, leavings, leftover, luxuriance, nimiety, overdose, overflow, overkill, overload, overmuch, overrun, oversupply, overweight, plenty, plethora, profusion, recrement, redundance, redundancy, refuse, remainder, residue, rest, spare, superabundance, supererogation, superfluity, surfeit, surplus, the limit, too much*, too much of a good thing*, waste, wastefulness; SEE CONCEPTS 787,824,835

excess [n2] *overindulgence in personal desires*
debauchery, dissipation, dissoluteness, exorbitance, extravagance, extreme, extremity, immoderacy, immoderation, indulgence, inordinateness, intemperance, overdoing, prodigality, saturnalia, selfindulgence, unrestraint; SEE CONCEPTS 633, 645

excessive [adj] *too much; overdone*
boundless, disproportionate, dissipated, dizzying, enormous, exaggerated, exorbitant, extra, extravagant, extreme, immoderate, indulgent, inordinate, intemperate, limitless, more, needless, over, overboard, overkill, overmuch, plethoric, prodigal, profligate, recrementitious, redundant, self-indulgent, sky-high*, steep, stiff, stratospheric*, super, superabundant, superfluous, supernatural, too many, towering, unbounded, unconscionable, undue, unmeasurable, unreasonable, way out*; SEE CONCEPTS 560,771,781

exchange [n1] *trade; deal*
barter, buying and selling, castling, change, commerce, commutation, conversion, correspondence, dealing, interchange, interdependence, interrelation, network, quid pro quo, rearrangement, reciprocation, reciprocity, replacement, revision, shift, shuffle, shuffling, substitution,

ex
ex

supplanting, supplantment, swap, switch, tit for tat*, traffic, transaction, transfer, transposing, transposition, truck*; SEE CONCEPTS *104,324*

exchange [n2] *place where stocks are bought, sold*
curb, market, net, network, over the counter, stock exchange, store, the Big Board*, the Street*, Wall Street*; SEE CONCEPTS *325,449*

exchange [v] *trade*
alternate, bandy, bargain, barter, buy and sell, cash in, castle, change, change hands*, commute, contact with, convert into, correspond, deal in, displace, flip-flop*, give and take*, go over to*, hook up, horse trade, interchange, invert, link up, market, network, pass to, pay back, rearrange, reciprocate, replace, return the compliment*, reverse, revise, seesaw, shift, shuffle, shuttle, substitute, swap, swap horses*, switch, traffic, transact, transfer, transpose, truck*, turn the tables*; SEE CONCEPT *104*

excise [n] *tax on goods*
customs, duty, import tax, levy, surcharge, tariff, toll; SEE CONCEPT *329*

excise [v] *remove, delete*
amputate, black out, blot out*, blue pencil*, cross out, cut, cut off, cut out, cut up, destroy, edit, elide, eradicate, erase, expunge, exscind, exsect, exterminate, extirpate, extract, gut, knock off*, launder*, lop off*, resect, scissor out, scratch out, slash, stamp out*, strike, trim, wipe out, X out*; SEE CONCEPT *211*

excitable [adj] *easily upset or inspired*
agitable, alarmable, demonstrative, edgy, emotional, enthusiastic, fidgety, fierce, fiery, galvanic, hasty, high-strung, hot-headed, hot-tempered, hysterical, impatient, impetuous, impulsive, inflammable, intolerant, irascible, mercurial, moody, nervous, neurotic, overzealous, passionate, peevish, quick, quick-tempered, rash, reckless, restless, sensitive, short fused, skittish, susceptible, temperamental, testy, touchy, uncontrolled, uneasy, vehement, violent, volatile, volcanic; SEE CONCEPTS *401,404*

excite [v] *inspire; upset*
accelerate, agitate, amaze, anger, animate, annoy, arouse, astound, awaken, bother, chafe, delight, discompose, disturb, electrify, elicit, energize, evoke, feed the fire*, fire, fluster, foment, galvanize, goad, incite, induce, inflame, infuriate, instigate, intensify, irritate, jar, jolt, kindle, madden, mock, move, offend, precipitate, provoke, quicken, rouse, start, stimulate, stir up, taunt, tease, thrill, titillate, touch off, vex, waken, wake up, warm, whet, work up, worry; SEE CONCEPTS *7,14,19,22*

excited [adj] *inspired; upset*
aflame, agitated, animated, annoyed, aroused, awakened, beside oneself*, charged, delighted, discomposed, disconcerted, disturbed, eager, enthusiastic, feverish, fired up*, frantic, high*, hot*, hot and bothered*, hyperactive, hysterical, in a tizzy*, inflamed, juiced up*, jumpy*, keyed up*, moved, nervous, on edge*, on fire*, overwrought, passionate, piqued, provoked, roused, ruffled, steamed up*, stimulated, stirred, thrilled, tumultous/tumultuous, wild, wired*, worked up, zipped up*; SEE CONCEPTS *401,403*

excitement [n] *enthusiasm; incitement*
action, activity, ado, adventure, agitation, animation, bother, buzz*, commotion, confusion, dis-

composure, disturbance, dither*, drama, elation, emotion, excitation, feeling, ferment, fever, flurry, frenzy, furor, fuss, heat*, hubbub*, hullabaloo*, hurry, hysteria, impulse, instigation, intoxication, kicks*, melodrama, motivation, motive, movement, passion, perturbation, provocation, rage, stimulation, stimulus, stir, thrill, titillation, to-do*, trepidation, tumult, turmoil, urge, warmth, wildness; SEE CONCEPTS *388,410, 633*

exciting [adj] *inspiring, exhilarating*
agitative, animating, appealing, arousing, arresting, astonishing, bracing, breathtaking, commoving, dangerous, dramatic, electrifying, exhilarant, eye-popping*, far-out*, fine, flashy, groovy*, hair-raising*, heady*, hectic, impelling, impressive, interesting, intoxicating, intriguing, lively, melodramatic, mind-blowing, moving, neat, overpowering, overwhelming, provocative, racy; rip-roaring*, rousing, sensational, showy, spine-tingling*, stimulating, stirring, thrilling, titillating, wild, zestful; SEE CONCEPTS *529,542,548*

exclaim [v] *shout out*
assert, bellow, blurt, burst out, call, call aloud, call out, cry, cry out, declare, ejaculate, emit, figure, holler, proclaim, rend the air*, roar, say loudly, shout, state, utter, vociferate, yawp*; yell; SEE CONCEPTS *529,542,548*

exclamation [n] *shout; assertion*
bellow, call, clamor, cry, ejaculation, expletive, holler, interjection, outcry, roar, utterance, vociferation, yawp*, yell; SEE CONCEPTS *49,77*

exclude [v] *expel, forbid*
ban, bar, bate, blackball*, blacklist, block, bounce, boycott, close out, count out, debar, disallow, drive out, eject, eliminate, embargo, estop, evict, except, force out, get rid of, ignore, interdict, keep out, leave out, lock out, obviate, occlude, omit, ostracize, oust, pass over, preclude, prevent, prohibit, proscribe, put out, refuse, refuse admittance, reject, remove, repudiate, rule out, set aside, shut out, shut the door on*, sideline, suspend, throw out, veto, ward off; SEE CONCEPTS *25,30,121*

exclusion [n] *expulsion; forbiddance*
ban, bar, blackball*, blockade, boycott, coventry, cut, debarment, debarring, discharge, dismissal, ejection, elimination, embargo, eviction, exception, excommunication, interdict, interdicting, interdiction, keeping out, lockout, nonadmission, occlusion, omission, ostracism, ousting, preclusion, prevention, prohibition, proscription, refusal, rejection, relegation, removal, repudiation, segregation, separation, suspension, veto; SEE CONCEPTS *25,30,121*

exclusive [adj] *unshared, restricted*
absolute, aloof, aristocratic, chic, choice, chosen, circumscribed, clannish, classy, cliquish, closed, complete, confined, country club, discriminative, elegant, entire, exclusionary, exclusory, fashionable, full, independent, licensed, limited, narrow, only, particular, peculiar, posh, preferential, private, privileged, prohibitive, restrictive, ritzy, segregated, select, selfish, single, snobbish, socially correct, sole, swank, total, undivided, unique, upper crust*, whole; SEE CONCEPTS *554,567*

exclusively [adv] *particularly*
alone, but, completely, entirely, one and only,

onliest, only, singularly, solely, wholly; SEE
CONCEPT 554

exclusive of [*prep*] *except for*
aside from, bar, barring, bating, besides, but, debarring, excepting, excluding, leaving aside, not
counting, omitting, outside of, restricting, ruling
out, save; SEE CONCEPT 554

excogitate [*v*] *think about seriously*
conceive, consider, contemplate, contrive, deliberate, derive, develop, devise, educe, evolve,
frame, invent, mind, mull over, perpend, ponder,
ruminate, study, think out, think up, weigh, work
out; SEE CONCEPTS 17,24

excommunicate [*v*] *banish*
anathematize, ban, cast out, curse, denounce, dismiss, eject, exclude, expel, oust, proscribe, remove, repudiate, unchurch; SEE CONCEPTS
317,367

excoriate [*v1*] *scrape layers off*
abrade, chafe, flay, fret, gall, peel, rub, scarify,
scratch, skin, strip; SEE CONCEPTS 211,215

excoriate [*v2*] *denounce, criticize*
attack, berate, blister, castigate, censure, chastise, condemn, flay, lambaste, lash, rebuke, reproach, reprove, revile, scathe, scold, scorch,
slash, tear into, upbraid, vilify; SEE CONCEPT 52

excrement [*n*] *feces*
crap, droppings, dung, guano, manure, poop,
sewage, stool, waste, waste matter; SEE CONCEPT
260

excrete [*v*] *discharge, usually liquified substance*
defecate, egest, ejaculate, eject, eliminate, emanate, evacuate, exhale, expel, exudate, exude,
give off, leak, pass, perspire, produce, remove,
secrete, sweat, throw off, urinate, void; SEE CON-
CEPTS 179,185

excruciating [*adj*] *torturous, painful*
acute, agonizing, burning, chastening, consuming, exquisite, extreme, grueling, harrowing, insufferable, intense, piercing, punishing, racking,
rending, searing, severe, sharp, shooting, stabbing, tearing, tormenting, torturesome, torturing,
unbearable, unendurable, violent; SEE CONCEPTS
314,548,609

exculpate [*v*] *forgive*
absolve, acquit, amnesty, clear, condone, discharge, disculpate, dismiss, excuse, exonerate,
explain, free, justify, let off*, pardon, rationalize,
release, remit, vindicate, wipe slate clean*; SEE
CONCEPTS 10,127,317

excursion [*n*] *journey*
circuit, cruise, day trip, digression, expedition,
jaunt, junket, outing, picnic, pleasure trip, ramble, round trip, safari, tour, trek, trip, walk, wandering; SEE CONCEPTS 224,384

excusable [*adj*] *allowable*
all right, condonable, defensible, exculpatory,
explainable, fair, forgivable, justifiable, minor,
moderate, not too bad*, okay, pardonable, passable, permissible, plausible, reasonable, remit-
table, reprievable, slight, specious, temperate,
tenable, trivial, understandable, venial, vindicable, vindicatory, warrantable, within limits; SEE
CONCEPT 558

excuse [*n*] *reason, explanation*
alibi, apology, cleanup*, cop-out*, cover*, cover
story*, coverup, defense, disguise, evasion, expedient, extenuation, fish story*, grounds, jive*,
justification, makeshift, mitigation, plea, pretext,
rationalization, regrets, routine, semblance, shift,

song*, song and dance*, stall, stopgap*, story,
substitute, subterfuge, trick*, vindication, whitewash*, why and wherefore*; SEE CONCEPTS
59,661

excuse [*v*] *forgive, absolve; justify*
acquit, alibi, apologize for, appease, bear with,
clear, condone, cover, defend, discharge, dispense from, exculpate, exempt, exempt from, exonerate, explain, extenuate, forgive, free, give
absolution, grant amnesty, indulge, let go*, let
off*, liberate, make allowances for, mitigate,
overlook, pardon, pass over*, plead ignorance,
pretext, purge, rationalize, release, relieve, remit,
reprieve, shrive, shrug off*, spare, take rap for*,
tolerate, vindicate, whitewash*, wink at*; SEE
CONCEPTS 10,57,83

execrable [*adj*] *horrible, sickening*
abhorrent, abominable, accursed, atrocious, confounded, cursed, damnable, defective, deplorable, despicable, detestable, disgusting, foul,
hateful, heinous, horrific, loathsome, low, monstrous, nauseous, obnoxious, odious, offensive,
repulsive, revolting, vile, wretched; SEE CONCEPT
542

execrate [*v*] *hate*
abhor, abominate, accurse, anathematize, censure, condemn, curse, damn, denounce, deplore,
despise, detest, excoriate, imprecate, loathe, objurgate, reprehend, reprobate, reprove, revile,
vilify; SEE CONCEPT 29

execration [*n*] *hating*
abhorrence, abomination, anathema, blasphemy,
condemnation, contempt, curse, cursing, cussing,
damnation, denunciation, detestation, detesting,
excoriation, hatred, imprecation, loathing, malediction, odium, profanity, swearing, vilification;
SEE CONCEPT 29

execute [*v1*] *kill*
assassinate, behead, bump off*, do in*, electrocute, eliminate, finish, gas, guillotine, hang,
knock off*, liquidate, murder, purge, put away*,
put to death, shoot; SEE CONCEPT 252

execute [*v2*] *carry out a task*
accomplish, achieve, act, administer, administrate, bring off, bring to fruition, cause, come
through, complete, consummate, deal with, discharge, do, do the job*, do the trick*, do to a T*,
earn wings*, effect, enact, enforce, finish, fulfill,
get there*, govern, hack it*, hit*, implement,
make it*, meet, percolate*, perform, play, polish
off*, prosecute, pull off*, put into effect, put
over*, put through, realize, render, sail through*,
score*, take care of, take care of business*,
transact; SEE CONCEPTS 91,706

execution [*n1*] *killing*
beheading, capital punishment, contract killing*,
crucifixion, decapitation, electrocution, gassing,
guillotining, hanging, hit, impalement, lethal injection, necktie party*, punishment, rub out*,
shooting, strangling, strangulation; SEE CONCEPT
252

execution [*n2*] *carrying out of a task*
accomplishment, achievement, administration,
completion, consummation, delivery, discharge,
doing, effect, enactment, enforcement, fulfilling,
implementation, nuts and bolts*, operation, performance, prosecution, realization, rendering,
style; SEE CONCEPTS 91,706

executive [*adj*] *administrative*
controlling, decision-making, directing, govern-

ex
ex

ing, managerial, managing, ruling; SEE CONCEPT 527

executive [n] *person who manages an organization*
administration, administrator, big wheel*, boss, brass, businessperson, CEO*, chief, CO*, commander, director, directorate, entrepreneur, exec*, government, governor, head, head honcho*, head person*, heavyweight*, hierarchy, higher-up*, industrialist, key player*, leader, leadership, management, manager, officer, official, skipper*, supervisor, top brass*, tycoon, VIP*; SEE CONCEPTS 347,354

exemplar [n] *ideal*
archetype, copy, criterion, epitome, example, exemplification, illustration, instance, mirror, model, paradigm, paragon, pattern, prototype, specimen, standard, type; SEE CONCEPT 686

exemplary [adj] *ideal*
admirable, batting a thousand*, blameless, bueno*, characteristic, classic, classical, commendable, correct, estimable, excellent, good, guiltless, honorable, illustrative, inculpable, innocent, irreprehensible, laudable, meritorious, model, neato*, not bad*, not too shabby*, paradigmatic, praiseworthy, prototypical, punctilious, pure, quintessential, representative, righteous, sterling, typical, virtuous, worthy; SEE CONCEPTS 404,572,574

exemplify [v] *serve as an example*
body, cite, clarify, clear up, demonstrate, depict, display, elucidate, emblematize, embody, enlighten, epitomize, evidence, exhibit, illuminate, illustrate, instance, manifest, mirror, personify, quote, represent, show, spell out, symbolize, typify; SEE CONCEPTS 97,118

exempt [adj] *freed from responsibility*
absolved, beat the rap*, clear, cleared, discharged, excepted, excluded, excused, favored, free, immune, let go*, let off*, liberated, not liable, not responsible, not subject, off the hook*, outside, privileged, released, set apart, spared, special, unbound, unchecked, unrestrained, unrestricted, unshackled, void of, walked*; SEE CONCEPTS 319,554

exempt [v] *relieve, absolve*
clear, discharge, dispense, except, excuse, exonerate, free, go easy on*, grant immunity, let off*, let off the hook*, liberate, pass by, privilege from, release, spare, wipe the slate*, write off; SEE CONCEPTS 50,83,88,127

exemption [n] *freedom from a responsibility*
absolution, discharge, dispensation, exception, exoneration, immunity, impunity, privilege, release; SEE CONCEPTS 652,685,691

exercise [n1] *work, effort*
act, action, activity, calisthenics, constitutional*, daily dozen*, discharge, discipline, drill, drilling, examination, exercising, exertion, gym, labor, lesson, movement, occupation, operation, performance, problem, pursuit, recitation, schoolwork, study, task, test, theme, toil, training, warm-up, workout; SEE CONCEPTS 87,362,363

exercise [n2] *accomplishment, use*
application, discharge, employment, enjoyment, exertion, fulfillment, implementation, operation, performance, practice, pursuit, utilization; SEE CONCEPTS 225,706

exercise [v1] *put to use*
apply, bestow, bring to bear, devote, drill, era-

ploy, enjoy, execute, exert, exploit, handle, operate, practice, put into practice, rehearse, sharpen, use, utilize, wield; SEE CONCEPT 225

exercise [v2] *do repeatedly, especially to improve*
break, break in, condition, cultivate, develop, discipline, drill, dry run*, exert, fix, foster, groom, habituate, hone, improve, inure, labor, lick into shape*, limber up, loosen up, maneuver, ply, practice, prepare, pump iron*, put out, put through grind*, put through mill*, rehearse, run through, set, strain, teach, train, tune up, walk through, warm up, work, work out; SEE CONCEPTS 87,363

exercise [v3] *upset, worry*
abrade, afflict, agitate, annoy, bother, burden, chafe, distress, disturb, gall, irk, occupy, pain, perturb, preoccupy, provoke, trouble, try, vex; SEE CONCEPTS 7,19

exert [v] *make use of*
apply, apply oneself, bring into play*, bring to bear*, dig*, employ, endeavor, exercise, expend, give all one's got*, give best shot*, labor, make effort, peg away*, plug*, ply, pour it on*, push, put forth, put out, strain, strive, struggle, sweat it*, throw, toil, try hard, use, utilize, wield, work; SEE CONCEPTS 87,225

exertion [n] *hard work*
action, activity, application, attempt, effort, elbow grease*, employment, endeavor, exercise, hard pull*, industry, labor, long pull*, operation, pains, strain, stretch, striving, struggle, toil, travail, trial, trouble, use, utilization; SEE CONCEPTS 87,362,677

exfoliate [v] *peel*
desquamate, doff, flake off, scale off, shed; SEE CONCEPTS 142,176,211

exhale [v] *breathe out*
breathe, discharge, eject, emanate, emit, evaporate, expel, give off, issue, let out, respire, steam, vaporize; SEE CONCEPT 163

exhaust [v1] *tire or wear out*
bankrupt, burn out*, conk out*, cripple, debilitate, disable, do in*, drain, draw, enervate, enfeeble, fag, fatigue, frazzle, impoverish, overdo, overexert, overextend, overfatigue, overtire, overwork, peter out*, poop*, poop out*, prostrate, run ragged*, sap*, suck dry*, tucker*, use up, weaken, wear down, weary; SEE CONCEPTS 250,469

exhaust [v2] *consume, use up*
bankrupt, bleed dry*, deplete, devour, dispel, disperse, dissipate, drain, draw, dry, eat, eat up*, empty, expend, finish, impoverish, run out, run through, spend, squander, strain, suck dry*, take last of, void, wash up, waste; SEE CONCEPTS 169,225

exhausted [adj1] *extremely tired*
all in*, beat*, bleary, bone-weary, bushed, crippled, dead*, dead tired*, debilitated, disabled, dog-tired*, done for*, done in*, drained, effete, enervated, frazzled, had it*, kaput*, limp, out on one's feet*, outta gas*, prostrated, ready to drop*, run-down, sapped*, shot*, spent, tired out, wasted*, weak, weakened, wearied, worn, worn out; SEE CONCEPTS 406,485

exhausted [adj2] *used up*
all gone, at an end, bare, consumed, depleted, dissipated, done, drained, dry, empty, expended,

finished, gone, spent, squandered, void, washed-out, wasted; SEE CONCEPTS 560,771

exhaustion [*n*] *tiredness*
burnout*, collapse, consumption, debilitation, debility, enervation, expenditure, fatigue, feebleness, lassitude, prostration, weariness; SEE CONCEPTS 410,720

exhaustive [*adj*] *all-inclusive, complete*
all-embracing, all-encompassing, all-out, catholic, comprehensive, embracive, encyclopedic, extensive, far-reaching, from A to Z*, full, full-blown, full-dress*, full-scale, in-depth, intensive, no stone unturned*, out-and-out*, profound, radical, sweeping, the word, thorough, thoroughgoing, total, whole-hog*; SEE CONCEPTS 531,772

exhibit [*n*] *viewing; presentation*
display, exhibition, exposition, fair, illustration, model, performance, show; SEE CONCEPTS 259,261

exhibit [*v*] *put on view; present*
advertise, air, brandish, demonstrate, disclose, display, disport, evidence, evince, expose, express, feature, flash, flaunt, illustrate, indicate, let it all hang out*, make clear, make plain, manifest, mark, offer, ostend, parade, parade wares*, proclaim, reveal, roll out, show, show and tell*, showcase, show off, strut stuff*, trot out*, wave around*; SEE CONCEPT 261

exhibition [*n*] *showing, demonstration*
advertisement, airing, an act*, a scene*, carnival, display, exhibit, expo, exposition, fair, fireworks, flash*, front*, manifestation, offering, pageant, performance, presentation, representation, show, sight, spectacle; SEE CONCEPTS 261,386

exhibitionism [*n*] *attention-seeking behavior*
exposing oneself, flashing*, immodesty, indecent exposure, self-display, showing off; SEE CONCEPTS 261,386

exhilarate [*v*] *make very happy*
animate, boost, buoy, cheer, commove, delight, elate, enliven, exalt, excite, gladden, inspire, inspirit, invigorate, juice*, lift, pep up*, perk up*, pick up, put zip into*, quicken, rejoice, send, snap up*, stimulate, thrill, turn on*, uplift, vitalize; SEE CONCEPTS 7,22

exhilarating [*adj*] *stimulating, cheering*
animating, animative, bracing, breathtaking, electric, elevating, enlivening, exalting, exciting, exhilarant, exhilarative, exhilaratory, eye-popping*, gladdening, inspiring, inspiriting, intoxicating, invigorating, quickening, rousing, stimulative, stirring, thrilling, tonic, uplifting, vitalizing; SEE CONCEPTS 529,568

exhilaration [*n*] *great happiness, excitement*
animation, a rush*, cheerfulness, delight, elation, electrification, elevation, enlivenment, euphoria, exaltation, excitation, firing, gaiety, galvanization, gladness, gleefulness, head rush*, high spirits*, hilarity, inspiration, invigoration, joy, joyfulness, liveliness, mirth, quickening, sprightliness, stimulation, uplift, vitalization, vivacity, vivification; SEE CONCEPT 410

exhort [*v*] *urge, warn*
admonish, advise, beseech, bid, call upon, caution, counsel, egg on*, encourage, enjoin, entreat, goad, incite, insist, persuade, plead, preach, press, pressure, prick, prod, prompt, propel, spur, stimulate; SEE CONCEPTS 75,78

exhortation [*n*] *warning, urging*
admonition, advice, beseeching, bidding, caution, counsel, encouragement, enjoinder, entreaty, goading, incitement, instigation, lecture, persuasion, preaching, sermon; SEE CONCEPTS 75,78,274

exhume [*v*] *dig up, especially the dead*
disclose, disembalm, disentomb, disinhume, disinter, resurrect, reveal, unbury, uncharnel, unearth; SEE CONCEPT 178

exigency/exigence [*n*] *difficulty; demand*
acuteness, constraint, contingency, crisis, criticalness, crossroad, demandingness, dilemma, distress, duress, emergency, extremity, fix, hardship, imperativeness, jam, juncture, necessity, need, needfulness, pass, pickle*, pinch, plight, predicament, pressingness, pressure, quandary, requirement, scrape*, stress, turning point*, urgency, vicissitude, want, wont, zero hour*; SEE CONCEPTS 646,674,709

exigent [*adj1*] *urgent, pressing*
acute, burning, clamant, clamorous, constraining, critical, crucial, crying, imperative, importunate, insistent, instant, menacing, necessary, needful, threatening; SEE CONCEPTS 548,568

exigent [*adj2*] *difficult, taxing*
arduous, burdensome, demanding, exacting, grievous, hard, harsh, onerous, oppressive, rigorous, severe, stiff, strict, stringent, superincumbent, tough, weighty; SEE CONCEPTS 537,542

exiguous [*adj*] *scanty*
bare, confined, diminutive, inadequate, limited, little, meager, narrow, negligible, paltry, petty, poor, restricted, skimpy, slender, slight, small, spare, sparse, tenuous, thin, tiny; SEE CONCEPTS 771,789

exile [*n1*] *deportation from a place*
banishment, diaspora, dispersion, displacement, exclusion, expatriation, expulsion, extradition, migration, ostracism, proscription, relegation, scattering, separation; SEE CONCEPT 298

exile [*n2*] *person deported from a place*
deportee, displaced person, DP*, émigré, expatriate, expellee, fugitive, nonperson*, outcast, outlaw, person without country*, refugee; SEE CONCEPTS 354,412,423

exile [*v*] *deport from place*
banish, cast out, displace, dispossess, drive out, eject, evacuate, expatriate, expel, expulse, extradite, ostracize, oust, outlaw, proscribe, relegate, transport, turn out; SEE CONCEPTS 122,198,298

exist [*v1*] *be living*
abide, be, be extant, be latent, be present, breathe, continue, endure, happen, last, lie, live, move, obtain, occur, prevail, remain, stand, stay, subsist, survive; SEE CONCEPT 407

exist [*v2*] *get along in life*
consist, dwell, eke out a living*, endure, get by*, go on, inhere, kick*, lie, live, make it*, reside, stay alive*, subsist, survive; SEE CONCEPTS 100,226

existence [*n*] *life*
actuality, animation, being, breath, continuance, continuation, duration, endurance, entity, essence, hand one is dealt*, individuality, journey, lifing, permanence, perseverance, presence, rat race*, reality, real world*, something, subsistence, survival, the big game*, world; SEE CONCEPTS 407,639

ex
ex

exit [*n1*] *way out of a place*
avenue, door, egress, fire escape, gate, hole, opening, outlet, passage out, vent; SEE CONCEPT **440**

exit [*n2*] *leaving*
adieu, death, demise, departure, egress, egression, evacuation, exodus, expiration, expiry, farewell, going, goodbye, leave-taking, offgoing, retirement, retreat, stampede, withdrawal; SEE CONCEPT **195**

exit [*v*] *leave a place*
bid farewell, blow*, depart, do vanishing act*, flake off*, get*, get away, get off, git*, go, go away, go out, issue, move, move out, quit, retire, retreat, say goodbye, split*, take a hike*, take one's leave*, withdraw; SEE CONCEPT **195**

exodus [*n*] *leaving*
departure, egress, egression, emigration, evacuation, exit, exiting, flight, going out, journey, migration, offgoing, retirement, retreat, withdrawal; SEE CONCEPT **195**

exonerate [*v*] *excuse, clear of responsibility or blame*
absolve, acquit, disburden, discharge, dismiss, except, exculpate, exempt, free, justify, let off*, let off hook*, liberate, pardon, release, relieve, sanitize, vindicate, whitewash*, wipe slate clean*; SEE CONCEPTS **10,127,317**

exorbitant [*adj*] *extravagant, excessive*
absonant, dear, enormous, exacting, expensive, extortionate, extreme, high, highway robbery*, immoderate, inordinate, out of sight*, outrageous, overboard, overmuch, over one's head*, preposterous, pricey, steep*, stiff*, towering, unconscionable, undue, unreasonable, unwarranted, up to here*, wasteful; SEE CONCEPTS **334,547, 558**

exorcise [*v*] *free from evil spirits*
cast out, dismiss, drive out, expel, purge, purify, remove; SEE CONCEPT **179**

exorcism [*n*] *expelling evil spirits*
casting out, ceremony, ejection, expulsion, purification, ritual; SEE CONCEPTS **165,367**

exotic [*adj*] *not native or usual; mysterious*
alien, alluring, avant garde, bizarre, colorful, curious, different, enticing, external, extraneous, extraordinary, extrinsic, far out*, fascinating, foreign, glamorous, imported, introduced, kinky*, outlandish, outside, peculiar, peregrine, romantic, strange, striking, unfamiliar, unusual, way out*, weird*; SEE CONCEPTS **542,549**

expand [*v1*] *extend, augment*
aggrandize, amplify, beef up*, bloat, blow up*, bolster, broaden, bulk up*, burgeon, detail, develop, diffuse, dilate, distend, elaborate, embellish, enlarge, explicate, fan out*, fatten, fill out, grow, heighten, hike, increase, inflate, lengthen, magnify, mount, multiply, mushroom, open, open out, outspread, pad, piggyback*, prolong, protract, puff up*, pyramid*, slap on*, soup up*, spread, spread out, stretch, stretch out, swell, tack on*, thicken, unfold, unfurl, unravel, unroll, upsurge, wax*, widen; SEE CONCEPTS **236,245**

expand [*v2*] *go into detail*
amplify, beef up*, build up, develop, dilate, discourse, drag out*, elaborate, embellish, enlarge, expatiate, expound, extend, flesh out*, spell out, sweeten; SEE CONCEPT **57**

expanse [*n*] *large space, usually open*
amplitude, area, belt, breadth, compass, distance, domain, extension, extent, field, immensity, latitude, length, margin, orbit, plain, radius, range, reach, region, remoteness, room, scope, span, sphere, spread, stretch, sweep, territory, tract, uninterrupted space, width, wilderness; SEE CONCEPTS **509,513,651,788**

expansion [*n*] *growth*
amplification, augmentation, breadth, development, diffusion, dilation, distance, distension, enlargement, evolution, expanse, extension, increase, inflation, magnification, maturation, multiplication, opening out, space, spread, stretch, swelling, unfolding, unfurling; SEE CONCEPTS **700,704,780**

expansionism [*n*] *growth*
development, economic expansion, imperialism, progress; SEE CONCEPTS **427,469,703,704,775**

expansive [*adj1*] *broad, comprehensive*
all-embracing, ample, big, dilatant, elastic, expanding, expansile, extensive, far-reaching, great, inclusive, large, scopic, scopious, stretching, thorough, unrepressed, unsuppressed, voluminous, wide, wide-ranging, widespread; SEE CONCEPT **772**

expansive [*adj2*] *talkative*
affable, communicative, demonstrative, easy, effervescent, effusive, extroverted, free, friendly, garrulous, generous, genial, gregarious, gushy, lavish, liberal, loquacious, open, outgoing, sociable, unconstrained, uninhibited, unreserved, unrestrained, warm; SEE CONCEPT **267**

expatriate [*n*] *person thrown out of a country*
departer, deportee, displaced person, emigrant, émigré, evacuee, exile, expellee, migrant, outcast, refugee; SEE CONCEPTS **354,412,423**

expatriate [*v*] *throw out of a country*
banish, deport, displace, exile, expel, expulse, ostracize, oust, proscribe, relegate, transport; SEE CONCEPTS **130,198,211**

expect [*v1*] *believe strongly; anticipate*
apprehend, assume, await, bargain for, bargain on, be afraid, calculate, conjecture, contemplate, count on, divine, envisage, feel, figure, forecast, foreknow, foresee, gather, hope, hope for, imagine, in the cards*, look, look ahead to, look for, look forward to*, predict, presume, presuppose, reckon, see coming*, sense, suppose, surmise, suspect, take, think, trust, understand, wait for, watch for; SEE CONCEPTS **12,26**

expect [*v2*] *want, wish*
call for, count on, demand, exact, insist on, look for, rely upon, require; SEE CONCEPT **20**

expectancy [*n*] *anticipation*
assumption, assurance, belief, calculation, confidence, conjecture, expectation, hope, likelihood, looking forward, outlook, prediction, presentation, presentiment, presumption, probability, prospect, reliance, supposition, surmise, suspense, trust, view, waiting; SEE CONCEPTS **410,689**

expectant [*adj1*] *anticipating*
alert, anticipative, anxious, apprehensive, awaiting, breathless, eager, expecting, hopeful, hoping, in suspense, looking for, on edge*, on tenterhooks*, prepared, raring*, ready, vigilant, waiting, waiting on, watchful, with bated breath*; SEE CONCEPTS **403,406**

expectant [*adj2*] *preparing to give birth*
enceinte, expecting, gravid, parturient, pregnant, with child*; SEE CONCEPT **485**

expectation [*n*] *belief, anticipation*
apprehension, assumption, assurance, calculation, chance, confidence, conjecture, design, expectancy, fear, forecast, hope, intention, likelihood, looking forward, motive, notion, outlook, possibility, prediction, presumption, probability, promise, prospect, reliance, supposition, surmise, suspense, trust, view; SEE CONCEPTS *410,689*

expecting [*adj*] *pregnant*
carrying, expectant, in a family way*, with child*; SEE CONCEPTS *406,485*

expediency/expedience [*n1*] *appropriateness; worth*
advantage, advantageousness, advisability, appositeness, aptness, benefit, convenience, desirability, effectiveness, efficiency, fitness, helpfulness, judiciousness, meetness, opportunism, opportunity, order, policy, practicality, pragmatism, profitability, profitableness, properness, propitiousness, propriety, prudence, rightness, suitability, usefulness, utilitarianism, utility; SEE CONCEPTS *656,658*

expediency/expedience [*n2*] *resource*
band-aid*, contrivance, design, device, dodge, easy way out*, gimmick*, makeshift*, maneuver, means, measure, method, recourse, resort, scheme, shift, step, stopgap*, stratagem, strategy, substitute, surrogate, tactic, trick; SEE CONCEPTS *660,712*

expedient [*adj*] *worthwhile, appropriate*
ad hoc, advantageous, advisable, beneficial, convenient, desirable, discreet, effective, feasible, fit, fitting, helpful, judicious, meet, opportune, politic, possible, practicable, practical, pragmatic, profitable, proper, prudent, seasonable, suitable, tactical, timely, useful, utilitarian, wise; SEE CONCEPTS *558,560*

expedient [*n*] *resource*
contrivance, device, gency, instrument, instrumentality, makeshift, maneuver, means, measure, medium, method, recourse, refuge, resort, scheme, shift, stopgap, stratagem, substitute; SEE CONCEPTS *660,712*

expedite [*v*] *make happen faster*
accelerate, advance, assist, cut the red tape*, dispatch, facilitate, fast track*, forward, grease wheels*, hand-carry, handle personally, handwalk*, hasten, hurry, precipitate, press, promote, quicken, railroad*, run interference*, run with the ball*, rush, shoot through*, speed, speed up, urge, walk it through*; SEE CONCEPT *242*

expedition [*n1*] *journey; people on a journey*
campaign, caravan, cavalcade, company, crew, crowd, cruise, crusade, enterprise, entrada, excursion, exploration, explorers, fleet, jaunt, junket, mission, outing, party, patrol, peregrination, picnic, posse, quest, safari, squadron, swing, team, tour, travel, travellers, trek, trip, undertaking, voyage, voyagers, wayfarers; SEE CONCEPTS *224,417*

expedition [*n2*] *speed; speeding up*
alacrity, celerity, dispatch, expeditiousness, goodwill, haste, hurry, hustle, promptitude, promptness, punctuality, quickness, rapidity, readiness, swiftness; SEE CONCEPTS *242,755*

expeditious [*adj*] *immediate, speedy*
active, alert, breakneck, brisk, diligent, effective, effectual, efficient, fast, fleet, hasty, instant, nimble, prompt, punctual, quick, rapid, ready, swift; SEE CONCEPTS *542,588*

expel [*v1*] *discharge*
belch, blow out, cast out, disgorge, dislodge, drive out, ejaculate, eruct, erupt, evacuate, exhaust, exudate, exude, get rid of, irrupt, pass, remove, spew, throw out, vomit; SEE CONCEPT *179*

expel [*v2*] *throw out, banish*
ban, bar, blackball*, bust, cast-out, chase, deport, discharge, dismiss, displace, dispossess, drum out, eject, eliminate, evict, exclude, exile, expatriate, expulse, fire, give the boot*, give the hook*, give walking papers*, kick out, oust, proscribe, send packing*, show the door*, suspend, throw out on ear*, turn out; SEE CONCEPTS *122,130,198*

expend [*v*] *exhaust; spend*
ante up*, blow*, consume, disburse, dish out*, dispense, dissipate, distribute, employ, finish, foot the bill*, fork out*, give, go through*, lay out, outlay, pay, pay out, put out*, shell out*, splurge*, spring for*, throw money at*, use up, wash up*; SEE CONCEPTS *225,341*

expendable [*adj*] *not important*
dispensable, disposable, excess, inessential, nonessential, replaceable, superfluous, unimportant; SEE CONCEPTS *546,575*

expenditure [*n*] *payment*
amount, application, bottom line*, cash on barrelhead*, charge, come to*, consumption, cost, disbursement, dissipation, expense, figure, investment, kickback*, outgo, outlay, output, payoff, price, rate, setback*, spending, splurge, squander, throw*, tune*, use, valuation, value, waste; SEE CONCEPT *344*

expense [*n*] *cost, payment*
amount, assessment, bite*, bottom line*, budget, charge, consumption, debit, debt, decrement, deprivation, disbursement, duty, expenditure, forfeit, forfeiture, insurance, investment, liability, loan, loss, mortgage, obligation, outdo*, outlay, out of pocket*, output, overhead, payroll, price, price tag, rate, responsibility, risk, sacrifice, spending, sum, surcharge, tariff, toll, upkeep, use, value, worth; SEE CONCEPTS *328,329,336, 344*

expensive [*adj*] *high-priced*
an arm and a leg*, at a premium, big-ticket*, costly, dear, excessive, exorbitant, extravagant, fancy, high, highway robbery*, holdup*, immoderate, inordinate, invaluable, lavish, out of sight*, overpriced, plush, posh, pretty penny*, pricey*, rich, ritzy*, sky-high*, steep*, stiff*, swank*, too high, uneconomical, unreasonable, upscale*, valuable; SEE CONCEPT *334*

experience [*n1*] *knowledge*
acquaintance, action, actuality, background, caution, combat, contact, doing, empiricism, evidence, existence, exposure, familiarity, forebearance, intimacy, involvement, inwardness, judgment, know-how*, maturity, observation, participation, patience, perspicacity, practicality, practice, proof, reality, savoir-faire, seasoning, sense, skill, sophistication, strife, struggle, training, trial, understanding, wisdom, worldliness; SEE CONCEPT *409*

experience [*n2*] *happening, occurrence*
adventure, affair, encounter, episode, event, incident, ordeal, test, trial, trip; SEE CONCEPTS *2,696*

experienced [*adj*] *knowledgeable, knowing*
accomplished, accustomed, adept, been around*, been there*, broken in*, capable, competent, cultivated, dynamite, expert, familiar, having something on the ball*, instructed, in the know*, knowing one's stuff*, knowing the score*, mature, matured, old, old hand*, practical, practiced, pro, professional, qualified, rounded, seasoned, skillful, sophisticated, sport, tested, the right stuff*, trained, tried, versed, vet, veteran, well-versed, wise, worldly, worldly-wise*; SEE CONCEPTS 402,527

experiment [*n*] *investigation, test*
agreement, analysis, assay, attempt, check, dissection, dry run*, enterprise, essay, examination, exercise, experimentation, fling*, measure, observation, operation, practice, probe, procedure, proof, quiz, R and D*, rehearsal, research, research and development, scrutiny, search, speculation, study, trial, trial and error*, trial run*, try, try-on, tryout, undertaking, venture, verification; SEE CONCEPTS 103,290

experiment [*v*] *investigate, test*
analyze, assay, diagnose, examine, explore, fool with*, futz around*, mess around*, play around with*, practice with, probe, prove, put to the test*, research, sample, scrutinize, search, shake down*, speculate, study, try, try on, try on for size*, try out, venture, verify, weigh; SEE CONCEPTS 24,87,103

experimental [*adj*] *exploratory*
beginning, developmental, empirical, experiential, first stage, laboratory, momentary, on approval, pilot, preliminary, preparatory, primary, probationary, provisional, speculative, temporary, tentative, test, trial, trial-and-error, unconcluded, under probation, unproved; SEE CONCEPT 535

expert [*adj*] *knowledgeable, proficient*
able, adept, adroit, apt, big league*, clever, crack, crackerjack*, deft, dexterous, experienced, facile, handy, practiced, professional, qualified, savvy, schooled, sharp, skilled, skillful, slick, trained, virtuoso; SEE CONCEPTS 402,527

expert [*n*] *master, specialist*
ace*, adept, artist, artiste, authority, buff, connoisseur, doyen, graduate, guru*, hot shot*, old hand*, old pro*, phenomenon, pro, professional, proficient, shark*, virtuoso, whiz*, wizard; SEE CONCEPTS 348,350,416

expertise/expertness [*n*] *knowledge, proficiency*
ability, ableness, adroitness, aptness, art, cleverness, command, competence, craft, cunning, deftness, dexterity, dodge*, facility, finesse, goods*, ingeniousness, judgment, knack*, know-how*, line*, makings*, oil*, one's thing*, prowess, readiness, savvy, sharpness, skill, skillfulness, stuff*; SEE CONCEPTS 409,630

expiate [*v*] *make amends for*
absolve, amend, appease, atone, atone for, compensate, correct, do penance, excuse, forgive, pay one's dues*, rectify, redeem, redress, remedy, square things*; SEE CONCEPTS 67,126

expiration [*n*] *finish, demise*
cessation, close, closing, conclusion, death, decease, departure, dying, elapsing, end, expiry, going, passing, termination, terminus; SEE CONCEPTS 119,304

expire [*v1*] *come to an end*
bite the dust*, buy it*, cash in chips*, cease, close, conclude, croak*, decease, depart, die, elapse, end, finish, go, kick the bucket*, lapse, pass, pass away, pass on, pass over, perish, quit, run out, stop, strike out*, terminate, up and die*; SEE CONCEPTS 119,304

expire [*v2*] *breathe out*
emit, exhale, expel; SEE CONCEPTS 163,185

explain [*v*] *make clear; give a reason for*
account for, analyze, annotate, break down, bring out, clarify, clear up, construe, decipher, define, demonstrate, describe, diagram, disclose, elucidate, excuse, explicate, expound, get across*, go into detail, illustrate, interpret, justify, make plain*, manifest, paraphrase, point out, put across, put in plain English*, rationalize, read, refine, render, resolve, reveal, set right, solve, spell out*, teach, tell, throw light upon*, translate, unfold, unravel, untangle; SEE CONCEPT 57

explanation [*n*] *clarification; reason*
account, annotation, answer, breakdown, brief, cause, comment, commentary, confession, definition, demonstration, description, details, display, elucidation, evidence, example, excuse, explication, exposition, expression, gloss, history, illustration, information, interpretation, justification, meaning, mitigation, motive, narration, note, recital, rendition, report, resolution, sense, showing, significance, specification, statement, story, summary, tale, talking, telling, vindication, writing; SEE CONCEPTS 271,274,661

explanatory [*adj*] *descriptive*
allegorical, analytical, annotative, critical, declarative, demonstrative, diagrammatic, discursive, elucidatory, enlightening, exegetic, exegetical, explicative, expositional, expository, graphic, guiding, hermeneutic, illuminative, illustrative, informative, informing, instructive, interpretive, justifying, summary, supplementary; SEE CONCEPT 267

expletive [*n*] *swear word; exclamation*
curse, cuss, cuss word, interjection, oath; SEE CONCEPT 275

explicate [*v*] *clarify, expand*
amplify, clear up, construe, demonstrate, develop, dilate, elucidate, enlarge upon, enucleate, expatiate, explain, expound, give the big picture*, illustrate, interpret, make clear, make explicit, make plain*, run down, spell out*, tell why, unfold, untangle, work out; SEE CONCEPT 57

explicit [*adj*] *specific, unambiguous*
absolute, accurate, categorical, certain, clean-cut, clear, clear-cut, correct, definite, definitive, direct, distinct, exact, express, frank, lucid, obvious, on the nose*, open, outspoken, patent, perspicuous, plain, positive, precise, stated, straightforward, sure, understandable, unequivocal, unqualified, unreserved; SEE CONCEPTS 267,529,535

explode [*v1*] *blow up*
backfire, blast, blaze, blow, blow to kingdom come*, break out, burst, collapse, convulse, detonate, discharge, erupt, flame up, flare up, fracture, jet, kablooey*, let go*, mushroom*, rupture, set off, shatter, shiver, split, thunder; SEE CONCEPTS 179,320

explode [v2] *discredit*
belie, confute, debunk, deflate, discard, disprove, invalidate, puncture, refute, repudiate, shoot down*, shoot full of holes*; SEE CONCEPT 54

xploit [n] *achievement*
accomplishment, adventure, attainment, coup, deed, do, effort, enterprise, escapade, feat, job, maneuver, performance, stroke, stunt, tour de force, venture; SEE CONCEPT 706

xploit [v] *take advantage of; misuse*
abuse, apply, avail oneself of, bleed*, capitalize on, cash in on*, employ, exercise, finesse, fleece*, get mileage out of*, handle, impose upon, jockey*, make capital of, make use of, maneuver, manipulate, milk*, mine*, play*, play on, profit by, profit from, put to use, skin*, soak*, stick*, use, utilize, work; SEE CONCEPTS 156,225

exploitation [n] *taking advantage*
bleeding*, profiteering, using; SEE CONCEPTS 156,225

exploration [n] *investigation; survey*
analysis, examination, expedition, inquiry, inspection, probe, reconnaissance, research, scrutiny, search, study, tour, travel, trip; SEE CONCEPTS 216,224

explore [v] *investigate; survey*
analyze, burrow, delve into, dig into, examine, go into*, have a look*, hunt, inquire into, inspect, leave no stone unturned*, look into, probe, prospect, question, reconnoitre, research, scout, scrutinize, search, seek, sift, test, tour, travel, traverse, try, turn inside out*; SEE CONCEPTS 103,216,224

explorer [n] *trailblazer*
adventurer, experimenter, inquisitive person, pathfinder, pilgrim, pioneer, searcher, seeker, traveler; SEE CONCEPTS 348,413

explosion [n] *eruption, discharge*
access, backfire, bang, blast, blowout, blowup, burst, clap, combustion, concussion, crack, detonation, firing, fit, flare-up, fulmination, gust, ignition, outbreak, outburst, paroxysm, percussion, pop, report, roar, salvo; SEE CONCEPTS 179,320, 521

explosive [adj] *volatile, dangerous*
at the boiling point*, bursting, charged, consequential, convulsive, detonating, detonative, ebullient, eruptive, fiery, forceful, frenzied, fulminant, fulminating, hazardous, impetuous, meteoric, overwrought, perilous, raging, rampant, stormy, tense, touchy, ugly, uncontrollable, unstable, vehement, violent, wild; SEE CONCEPT 542

explosive [n] *something that blows up*
ammunition, bomb, booby trap*, charge, detonator, dynamite, fireworks, grease*, grenade, gunpowder, mine, missile, mulligan, munition, nitroglycerin, pineapple*, powder, propellant, shell, shot, soup*, TNT*; SEE CONCEPT 500

exponent [n1] *person who supports, advocates*
backer, booster, champion, defender, demonstrator, expositor, expounder, interpreter, partisan, promoter, propagandist, proponent, protagonist, second, seconder, spokesperson, supporter, upholder; SEE CONCEPT 423

xponent [n2] *example*
denotation, exemplar, illustration, index, indication, model, representative, sample, sign, specimen, token, type; SEE CONCEPTS 284,686

export [v] *sell or trade abroad*
consign, convey, dump, find market, find outlet, freight, send out, ship, smuggle, transport, transship; SEE CONCEPTS 217,324

exposé [n] *disclosure*
betrayal, confession, construction, divulgence, exegesis, explanation, explication, exposal, exposition, exposure, interpretation, revelation, truth, uncovering; SEE CONCEPT 274

expose [v1] *reveal*
advertise, air, bare, betray, brandish, bring to light*, broadcast, crack, debunk, denude, dig up*, disclose, display, disport, divulge, exhibit, feature, flash, flaunt, give away, lay bare*, lay open*, leak, let cat out of bag*, let out*, make known, manifest, open, open to view, parade, present, prove, publish, put on view, report, show, show off, smoke out*, spill, streak, tip off*, trot out*, unclothe, uncover, unearth, unfold, unmask, unshroud, unveil; SEE CONCEPTS 60,261

expose [v2] *subject to danger*
endanger, hazard, imperil, jeopardize, lay open*, leave open*, make liable, make vulnerable, peril, put in harm's way*, risk; SEE CONCEPT 246

exposed [adj1] *made public*
apparent, bare, bared, brought to light*, caught, clear, debunked, defined, denuded, disclosed, discovered, divulged, dug up*, evident, exhibited, for show, found out, laid bare*, made manifest, manifest, naked, on display, on the spot*, on view, open, peeled, resolved, revealed, shown, solved, stripped, unconcealed, uncovered, unhidden, unmasked, unprotected, unsealed, unsheltered, unveiled, visible; SEE CONCEPT 576

exposed [adj2] *in danger*
accessible, in peril, laid bare*, laid open*, left open*, liable, menaced, open, prone, sensitive, subject, susceptible, threatened, unguarded, unprotected, vulnerable; SEE CONCEPTS 485,548

exposition [n1] *written description*
account, analysis, annotation, article, comment, commentary, composition, construal, construction, critique, delineation, details, discourse, discussion, disquisition, dissertation, editorial, elucidation, enucleation, enunciation, essay, exegesis, explanation, explication, exposé, expounding, history, illustration, interpretation, monograph, paper, piece, position paper, presentation, report, review, statement, story, study, tale, text, theme, thesis, tract, tractate, treatise; SEE CONCEPTS 268,271

exposition [n2] *fair*
bazaar, circus, county fair, demonstration, display, exhibition, expo, marketplace, mart, pageant, presentation, production, show, showing; SEE CONCEPT 386

expository [adj] *descriptive*
critical, disquisitional, elucidative, exegetic, explanatory, explicative, explicatory, hermeneutic, illustrative, informative, interpretive; SEE CONCEPT 267

expostulate [v] *reason with*
argue, dissuade, oppose, protest, remonstrate; SEE CONCEPT 46

exposure [n] *uncovering; putting in view or danger*
acknowledgment, airing, baring, betrayal, confession, defenselessness, denudation, denuncia-

tion, disclosure, display, divulgence, divulging, exhibition, exposé, giveaway, hazard, introduction, jeopardy, laying open, liability, manifestation, nakedness, openness, peril, presentation, publicity, revelation, risk, showing, susceptibility, susceptiveness, susceptivity, unfolding, unmasking, unveiling, vulnerability, vulnerableness; SEE CONCEPTS 60,261

expound [v] *talk about in great detail*
clarify, comment, construe, delineate, describe, discourse, elucidate, enucleate, exemplify, explain, explicate, express, illustrate, interpret, present, set forth, spell out, state, unfold; SEE CONCEPT 57

express [adj1] *certain, precise*
accurate, categorical, clean-cut*, clear, clear-cut, considered, definite, definitive, deliberate, designful, direct, distinct, especial, exact, explicit, expressed, individual, intended, intentional, out-and-out*, outright, particular, plain, pointed, premeditated, set, singular, special, specific, unambiguous, unconditional, unmistakable, unqualified, uttered, voiced, voluntary, willing, witting; SEE CONCEPTS 535,556,653

express [adj2] *direct, speedy*
accelerated, fast, high-speed, nonstop, quick, rapid, swift, velocious; SEE CONCEPTS 548,588

express [v1] *articulate; signify, mean*
add up to*, air, assert, asseverate, bespeak, broach, circulate, communicate, connote, convey, couch, declare, denote, depict, designate, disclose, divulge, embody, enunciate, evince, exhibit, formulate, frame*, give, hint, import, indicate, insinuate, intend, intimate, make known, manifest, phrase, pop off*, proclaim, pronounce, put, put across, put into words*, represent, reveal, say, show, speak, spell, stand for, state, suggest, symbolize, tell, testify, utter, vent, ventilate, verbalize, voice, word; SEE CONCEPTS 51,682

express [v2] *discharge by squeezing or force*
crush, dispatch, distill, expel, extract, force out, forward, press out, ship, squeeze out; SEE CONCEPT 179

expression [n1] *verbalization*
announcement, argument, articulation, assertion, asseveration, choice of words, commentary, communication, declaration, definition, delivery, diction, elucidation, emphasis, enunciation, execution, explanation, exposition, formulation, idiom, interpretation, intonation, issue, language, locution, mention, narration, phrase, phraseology, phrasing, pronouncement, remark, rendition, set phrase, speaking, speech, statement, style, term, turn of phrase, utterance, vent, voice, voicing, word, writ; SEE CONCEPTS 47,268,276

expression [n2] *facial appearance*
air, aspect, cast, character, contortion, countenance, face, grimace, grin, look, mien, mug*, pout*, simper, smile, smirk, sneer, visage; SEE CONCEPT 716

expressionless [adj] *having a blank look on face*
dead*, deadpan, dull, empty, fish-eyed*, impassive, inexpressive, inscrutable, lackluster, lusterless, nobody home*, poker-faced*, stolid, straight-faced, stupid, unexpressive, vacant, vacuous, wooden; SEE CONCEPT 406

expressive [adj] *telling, revealing*
alive, allusive, articulate, artistic, brilliant, colorful, demonstrative, dramatic, eloquent, emphatic,

energetic, forcible, graphic, indicative, ingenious, lively, masterly, meaningful, mobile, moving, passionate, pathetic, pictorial, picturesque, poignant, pointed, pregnant, representative, responsive, revelatory, showy, significant, silver-tongued*, spirited, stimulating, stirring, striking, strong, suggestive, sympathetic, tender, thoughtful, touching, understanding, vivid, warm; SEE CONCEPTS 267,537

expressly [adv1] *purposely*
especially, exactly, in specie, intentionally, on purpose, particularly, precisely, specially, specifically; SEE CONCEPT 556

expressly [adv2] *definitely, unambiguously*
absolutely, categorically, clearly, decidedly, directly, distinctly, explicitly, in no uncertain terms*, manifestly, outright, plainly, pointedly, positively, specifically, unequivocally, unmistakably; SEE CONCEPT 535

expressway [n] *large, well-travelled road*
freeway, interstate, parkway, superhighway, thruway, turnpike; SEE CONCEPT 501

expropriate [v] *seize*
accroach, annex, appropriate, arrogate, assume, commandeer, confiscate, deprive of property, dispossess, impound, preempt, requisition, sequester, take, take over; SEE CONCEPTS 90,142

expulsion [n] *banishing*
banishment, boot*, bounce, debarment, deportment, discharge, dislodgment, dismissal, displacement, dispossession, driving out, ejection, eviction, exclusion, exile, expatriation, extrusion, forcing out, ostracism, ouster, ousting, proscription, purge, relegation, removal, rush, suspension; SEE CONCEPTS 130,211,298

expunge [v] *destroy, obliterate*
abolish, annihilate, annul, black, black out*, blot out, blue pencil*, call all bets off*, call off, cancel, cut, delete, discard, drop, efface, eradicate, erase, exclude, exterminate, extinguish, extirpate, gut, kayo*, kill, knock off*, KO*, launder*, omit, raze, remove, scrub*, strike out, take out, trim, wipe out, X out*, zap*; SEE CONCEPTS 211,252

expurgate [v] *censor, cut*
bleep*, bleep out*, blip*, blue pencil*, bowdlerize, cleanse, clean up, decontaminate, lustrate, purge, purify, sanitize, screen, scrub*, squash, sterilize; SEE CONCEPTS 165,232

exquisite [adj1] *beautiful, excellent, finely detailed*
admirable, attractive, charming, choice, comely, consummate, cultivated, dainty, delicate, delicious, discerning, discriminating, elegant, errorless, ethereal, fastidious, fine, flawless, impeccable, incomparable, irreproachable, lovely, matchless, meticulous, outstanding, peerless, perfect, pleasing, polished, precious, precise, rare, recherché, refined, select, selective, splendid, striking, subtle, superb, superior, superlative; SEE CONCEPTS 574,579,589

exquisite [adj2] *intense*
acute, concentrated, consummate, desperate, excruciating, extreme, fierce, furious, keen, piercing, poignant, sharp, terrible, transcending, vehement, vicious, violent; SEE CONCEPT 569

extant [adj] *in existence*
actual, alive, around, being, contemporary, current, existent, existing, immediate, in current use, instant, living, not lost, present, present-day,

al, remaining, subsisting, surviving, unde-
oyed; SEE CONCEPTS 539,582

emporaneous/extemporary [adj] unre-
arsed, improvised

hoc, ad lib, at first glance, automatic, by ear*,
sual, expedient, extempore, free, immediate,
promptu, improv*, improvisatory, improviso,
ormal, jamming*, made-up, makeshift, off-
nd, off the cuff*, off the top of head*, on
pulse, on-the-spot*, snap, spontaneous, spur-
-the-moment*, taking for ride*, thought out
ad*, tossed off*, tossed out*, unplanned, un-
emeditated, unprepared, unstudied, winging
*; SEE CONCEPTS 267,799

emporize [v] improvise
-lib, dash out, devise, do offhand*, impro-
sate, invent, knock off*, make up, play by
r*, toss off*; SEE CONCEPT 51

end [vl] make larger, longer
ld to, aggrandize, amplify, augment, beef up*,
oost, broaden, carry on, continue, crane, de-
lop, dilate, drag one's feet*, drag out, draw,
aw out, elongate, enhance, enlarge, expand,
n out, go on, heighten, increase, last, lengthen,
t out, magnify, mantle, multiply, open, pad,
olong, prolongate, protract, run on, spin out,
read, spread out, stall, stretch, string out, sup-
ment, unfold, unfurl, unroll, widen; SEE
ONCEPTS 236,239,245

end [v2] offer
cord, advance, allocate, allot, award, bestow,
ing forward, confer, donate, give, grant, hold
t, impart, place at disposal, pose, present, prof-
r, put forth, put forward, reach out, stretch out,
bmit, tender, yield; SEE CONCEPTS 66,67

ended [adjl] lengthened
ontinued, drawn-out, elongate, elongated, en-
rged, lengthy, long, prolonged, protracted,
read, spread out, stretched out, unfolded, un-
rled, very long; SEE CONCEPTS 782,798

ended [adj2] widespread, comprehensive
oad, enlarged, expanded, expansive, extensive,
r-flung, far-reaching, large-scale, outspread,
opic, scopious, spread, sweeping, thorough,
ide; SEE CONCEPT 772

ension [n] enlargement, continuation
ddendum, addition, adjunct, amplification,
nnex, appendage, appendix, arm, augmentation,
anch, broadening, compass, continuing, delay,
evelopment, dilatation, distension, drawing out,
ongation, expansion, extent, increase, length-
ning, orbit, postponement, production, prolon-
ation, protraction, purview, radius, reach,
ope, span, spread, spreading out, stretch,
etching, supplement, sweep, widening, wing;
EE CONCEPT 772

tensive [adj] far-reaching, thorough
cross the board*, all-encompassing, all-inclu-
ve, big, blanket*, boundless, broad, capacious,
ommodious, comprehensive, comprising, con-
erable, expanded, extended, far-flung*, gen-
al, great, hefty, huge, inclusive, indiscriminate,
rge, large-scale, lengthy, long, major, perva-
ve, prevalent, protracted, roomy, scopic, scopi-
us, sizable, spacious, sweeping, unexclusive,
niversal, unrestricted, vast, voluminous, wall to
rall*, wholesale, wide, wide-ranging, wide-
pread; SEE CONCEPTS 772,773

tent [n] range, magnitude
dmeasurement, ambit, amount, amplitude, area,

bounds, breadth, bulk, capaciousness, compass,
degree, dimensions, duration, elbowroom*, expanse, expansion, extension, intensity, leeway,
length, limit, mass, matter, measure, neighborhood, orbit, order, period of time, play, proliferation, proportions, purview, quantity, radius,
reach, scope, size, space, spaciousness, span,
sphere, stretch, sweep, term, territory, time, tract,
tune, vicinity, volume, wideness, width; SEE
CONCEPTS 651,730,743,745,783,788,804

extenuate [v] lessen, mitigate
decrease, diminish, downplay, excuse, justify,
make allowances, minimize, moderate, palliate,
qualify, reduce, soften; SEE CONCEPTS
247,698,776

extenuating [adj] serving as an excuse
condoning, diminishing, justifying, lessening,
mitigating, moderating, palliating, qualifying, reducing, sanitizing, softening, varnishing, whitewashing*; SEE CONCEPT 537

exterior [adj] outside
exoteric, external, extraneous, extraterrestrial,
extraterritorial, extrinsic, foreign, marginal, outdoor, outer, outermost, outlying, outmost, outward, over, peripheral, superficial, surface; SEE
CONCEPT 583

exterior [n] visible part
appearance, aspect, coating, cover, covering, exteriority, external, facade, face, finish, outside,
polish, rind, shell, skin, superficies, superstra-
tum, surface; SEE CONCEPT 484

exterminate [v] kill
abolish, annihilate, blot out*, decimate, destroy,
do away with*, eliminate, eradicate, erase, execute, extinguish, extirpate, finish off, massacre,
obliterate, put an end to*, rub out*, send to kingdom come*, slaughter, stamp out*, wipe out*;
SEE CONCEPT 252

external [adj] outside, extrinsic
alien, apparent, exterior, extraneous, foreign, independent, out, outer, outermost, outmost, outward, over, peripheral, superficial, surface,
visible; SEE CONCEPT 583

extinct [adj] dead, obsolete
abolished, archaic, asleep, bygone, cold*, dead
and gone*, deceased, defunct, departed, disappeared, done for*, doused, ended, exanimate, exterminated, extinguished, fallen, gone, inactive,
late, lifeless, lost, no longer known, out, outmoded, passé, passed on, snuffed out*, superseded, terminated, unknown, vanished,
vanquished, void; SEE CONCEPT 539

extinction [n] dying out
annihilation, death, destruction, elimination, end
of life, no life, obsolescence, thing of the past*;
SEE CONCEPT 252

extinguish [v1] put out a fire
blot out, blow out, choke, douse, drown, out,
quench, smother, snuff out, stamp out, stifle, suffocate, trample; SEE CONCEPT 256

extinguish [v2] kill; quash
abate, abolish, annihilate, blot out*, check,
crush, destroy, eliminate, end, eradicate, erase,
expunge, exterminate, extirpate, obliterate, obscure, put down, put the lid on*, quell, remove,
squash, stamp out, suppress, wipe out*; SEE CON-
CEPTS 95,252

extirpate [v] destroy; uproot
abate, abolish, annihilate, blot out*, cut out, demolish, deracinate, efface, eliminate, eradicate,

ex
ex

erase, excise, expunge, exsect, exterminate, extinguish, kill, raze, remove, root out, wipe out*; SEE CONCEPTS *211,252*

extol [v] *sing the praises of*
acclaim, applaud, bless, boost, brag about, celebrate, commend, cry up*, eulogize, exalt, give a boost to, give a bouquet*, glorify, hand it to*, hats off to*, hear it for*, hymn, laud, magnify, make much of, panegyrize, pay tribute to, praise, puff up*, push, rave, root, stroke*; SEE CONCEPT *69*

extort [v] *cheat; blackmail*
bleed*, bully, clip, coerce, demand, educe, elicit, evince, exact, extract, fleece, force, get, gouge, hold up*, ice*, make pay through nose*, milk*, obtain, pinch, pull one's leg*, put screws to*, put the arm on*, secure, shake down*, skin*, soak, squeeze, stick, sting, wrench, wrest, wring; SEE CONCEPTS *53,59,139,342*

extortion [n] *blackmail; cheating*
arm, badger, bite, coercion, compulsion, demand, exaction, force, fraud, oppression, payoff, payola*, pressure, protection, racket, rapacity, shake, shakedown*, squeeze, stealing, swindle, theft; SEE CONCEPTS *53,139,192,342*

extra [adj] *accessory; excess*
added, additional, ancillary, another, auxiliary, beyond, button*, extraneous, extraordinary, fresh, further, fuss*, gingerbread*, gravy*, ice*, in addition, inessential, in reserve, in store, lagniappe*, leftover, more, needless, new, one more, optional, other, over and above*, perk*, plus, redundant, reserve, spare, special, superfluous, supernumerary, supplemental, supplementary, surplus, tip, unnecessary, unneeded, unused; SEE CONCEPTS *546,771*

extra [adv] *particularly*
considerably, especially, exceptionally, extraordinarily, extremely, markedly, noticeably, rarely, remarkably, uncommon, uncommonly, unusually; SEE CONCEPTS *557,569*

extra [n] *accessory*
addendum, addition, adjunct, affix, appendage, appurtenance, attachment, bonus, complement, extension, supernumerary, supplement; SEE CONCEPT *824*

extract [n] *something condensed from whole*
abstract, citation, clipping, concentrate, cutting, decoction, distillate, distillation, elicitation, essence, excerpt, infusion, juice*, passage, quotation, selection; SEE CONCEPTS *270,835*

extract [v1] *physically remove, draw out*
avulse, bring out, catheterize, cull, derive, distill, eke out, elicit, eradicate, evoke, evulse, exact, express, extirpate, extort, extricate, garner, gather, get, glean, obtain, pick up, pluck, press out, pry, pull, reap, secure, select, separate, siphon, squeeze, take, tear, uproot, weed out*, withdraw, wrest, wring, yank; SEE CONCEPTS *206,211*

extract [v2] *select a quotation*
abridge, abstract, bring forth, choose, cite, condense, copy, cull, cut out, deduce, derive, educe, elicit, evolve, excerpt, glean, quote, shorten; SEE CONCEPTS *79,142,211*

extraction [n1] *removal from whole; distillation*
abstraction, derivation, drawing, elicitation, eradication, evocation, evulsion, expression, extirpation, extrication, pulling, separation, taking

out, uprooting, withdrawal, wrenching, wresting; SEE CONCEPT *211*

extraction [n2] *ancestry, origin*
birth, blood, derivation, descent, family, lineage, parentage, pedigree, race, stock; SEE CONCEPTS *296,648*

extradite [v] *send to another place by force*
abandon, apprehend, arrest, bring to justice, bring to trial, deliver, give up, release, surrender; SEE CONCEPTS *217,317*

extraneous [adj1] *unneeded; irrelevant*
accidental, additional, adventitious, beside the point, extra, foreign, immaterial, impertinent, inadmissible, inapplicable, inapposite, inappropriate, incidental, inessential, needless, nonessential, off the subject, peripheral, pointless, redundant, superfluous, supplementary, unconnected, unessential, unnecessary, unrelated; SEE CONCEPT *546*

extraneous [adj2] *foreign*
adventitious, alien, exotic, external, extrinsic, out of place, strange; SEE CONCEPT *549*

extraordinary [adj] *strange and wonderful*
amazing, bizarre, boss*, curious, exceptional, fab*, fantastic, flash*, gnarly*, heavy*, inconceivable, incredible, marvelous, odd, off beaten path*, out of the ordinary, outstanding, particular, peculiar, phenomenal, rare, remarkable, singular, special, strange, stupendous, surprising, terrific, uncommon, unfamiliar, unheard-of unimaginable, unique, unprecedented, unthinkable, unusual, unwonted, weird, wicked*; SEE CONCEPTS *564,572*

extrapolate [v] *infer*
anticipate, assume, conclude, deduce, envision, figure, foresee, foretell, guess, hypothesize, make an educated guess*, predict, project, see ahead, theorize; SEE CONCEPTS *12,15,37*

extrasensory perception [n] *psychic powers*
clairvoyance, ESP, intuition, keen intuition, second sight, sixth sense, telepathy, vision; SEE CONCEPTS *409,410*

extraterrestrial [n] *alien*
E.T.*, little green man*, Martian, men from outer space*, space being, space inhabitant; SEE CONCEPT *423*

extravagance [n] *indulgence; waste*
absurdity, amenity, dissipation, exaggeration, excess, exorbitance, expenditure, folly, frill, icing on the cake*, immoderation, improvidence, lavishness, luxury, outrageousness, overdoing overindulgence, overspending, preposterousness, prodigality, profligacy, profusion, recklessness, squander, squandering, superfluity, unreasonableness, unrestraint, unthrift, wastefulness, wildness; SEE CONCEPTS *335,337,787*

extravagant [adj] *indulgent; wasteful*
absurd, bizarre, costly, crazy, exaggerated, excessive, exorbitant, expensive, extortionate, extreme, fanciful, fancy, fantastic, flamboyant flashy, foolish, garish, gaudy, grandiose, immoderate, implausible, improvident, imprudent, inordinate, lavish, ludicrous, nonsensical, ornate ostentatious, outrageous, overpriced, preposterous, pretentious, prodigal, profligate, reckless ridiculous, showy, silly, spendthrift, steep, unbalanced, unconscionable, unreasonable, unrestrained; SEE CONCEPTS *334,560,771*

extravaganza [n] *spectacle*
caricature, display, divertissement, flight o

fancy*, pageant, parody, show, spectacular; SEE CONCEPTS *263,293*

xtreme [*adj1*] *very great*
acute, consummate, high, highest, intense, maximal, maximum, severe, sovereign, supreme, top, ultimate, utmost, uttermost; SEE CONCEPTS *569,771,781*

xtreme [*adj2*] *beyond reason and convention*
absolute, desperate, dire, downright, drastic, egregious, exaggerated, exceptional, excessive, extraordinary, extravagant, fabulous, fanatical, flagrant, gross, harsh, immoderate, improper, imprudent, inordinate, intemperate, irrational, nonsensical, out-and-out*, out of proportion, outrageous, overkill, preposterous, rabid, radical, remarkable, rigid, severe, sheer, stern, strict, thorough, unbending, uncommon, uncompromising, unconventional, unreasonable, unseemly, unusual, utter, zealous; SEE CONCEPTS *547,558, 569*

xtreme [*adj3*] *faraway*
far-off, farthest, final, furthermost, last, most distant, outermost, outmost, remotest, terminal, ultimate, utmost, uttermost; SEE CONCEPT *778*

xtreme [*n*] *ultimate; limit*
acme, apex, apogee, bitter end, boundary, ceiling, climax, consummation, crest, crown, culmination, depth, edge, end, excess, extremity, height, inordinancy, maximum, nadir, nth degree*, peak, pinnacle, pole, termination, top, utmost, uttermost, zenith; SEE CONCEPTS *484,706, 745,836*

xtremely [*adv*] *greatly, intensely*
acutely, almighty, awfully, drastically, exceedingly, exceptionally, excessively, exorbitantly, extraordinarily, highly, hugely, immensely, immoderately, inordinately, intensely, markedly, mortally, notably, over, overly, overmuch, parlous, plenty, powerful, prohibitively, quite, radically, rarely, remarkably, severely, strikingly, surpassingly, terribly, terrifically, to nth degree*, too, too much*, totally, ultra*, uncommonly, unduly, unusually, utterly, very*, violently, vitally; SEE CONCEPTS *569,771,781*

xtremist [*n*] *person zealous about a belief*
agitator, die-hard, fanatic, radical, revolutionary, revolutionist, ultra, ultraist, zealot; SEE CONCEPTS *359,423*

xtremity [*n1*] *ultimate; limit*
acme, acuteness, adversity, apex, apogee, border, bound, boundary, brim, brink, butt, climax, consummation, crisis, depth, dire straits, disaster, edge, end, excess, extreme, extremes, frontier, height, last, margin, maximum, nadir, outside, pinnacle, plight, pole, remote, rim, setback, terminal, termination, terminus, tip, top, trouble, verge, vertex, zenith; SEE CONCEPTS *484,706,745,836*

xtremity [*n2*] *animate being's appendage*
backside, finger, flipper, foot, hand, leg, limb, paw, posterior, toe; SEE CONCEPT *392*

xtricate [*v*] *get out of a situation; relieve of responsibility*
bail out*, clear, deliver, detach, difference, differentiate, disburden, discumber, disembarrass, disencumber, disengage, disentangle, disinvolve, extract, free, get off the hook*, get out from under*, let go, let off*, liberate, loose, loosen, pull out, release, remove, rescue, resolve, save one's neck*, separate, sever, untie, withdraw, wriggle out of*; SEE CONCEPTS *102,127*

extrinsic [*adj*] *foreign*
acquired, alien, exotic, exterior, external, extraneous, gained, imported, outer, outside, outward, superficial; SEE CONCEPT *549*

extrovert [*n*] *sociable person*
character*, exhibitionist, gregarious person, life of the party*, showboat*, show-off*; SEE CONCEPT *423*

extroverted [*adj*] *outgoing*
congenial, cordial, demonstrative, friendly, gregarious, personable, sociable, social, unreserved; SEE CONCEPT *404*

extrude [*v*] *force out*
boot*, chase, dismiss, eject, evict, expel, kick out, press, project, squeeze*, throw out, thrust; SEE CONCEPTS *208,222*

exuberance [*n1*] *energy, enthusiasm*
abandon, animation, ardor, bounce, buoyancy, cheerfulness, eagerness, ebullience, effervescence, excitement, exhilaration, fervor, friskiness, gayness, get up and go*, high spirits, juice*, life, liveliness, pep, pepper*, spirit, sprightliness, vigor, vitality, zap*, zest*, zip*; SEE CONCEPT *633*

exuberance [*n2*] *profusion*
abundance, affluence, copiousness, effusiveness, exaggeration, excessiveness, fulsomeness, lavishness, lushness, luxuriance, plenitude, plenty, prodigality, richness, superabundance, superfluity, teemingness; SEE CONCEPTS *710,767*

exuberant [*adj1*] *energetic, enthusiastic*
animated, ardent, bouncy, brash, buoyant, cheerful, chipper, eager, ebullient, effervescent, elated, excited, exhilarated, feeling one's oats*, frolicsome, gay, high-spirited, lively, passionate, sparkling, spirited, sprightly, vigorous, vivacious, zappy*, zestful, zingy*, zippy*; SEE CONCEPT *401*

exuberant [*adj2*] *profuse*
abundant, affluent, copious, diffuse, effusive, exaggerated, excessive, fecund, fertile, fruitful, fulsome, lavish, lush, luxuriant, opulent, overdone, overflowing, plenteous, plentiful, prodigal, prolific, rampant, rich, riotous, superabundant, superfluous, teeming; SEE CONCEPT *781*

exude [*v*] *display, emit*
bleed, discharge, emanate, evacuate, excrete, exhibit, expel, flow out, give forth, give off, issue, leak, manifest, ooze, pass, percolate, radiate, secrete, seep, show, sweat, throw off, trickle, weep; SEE CONCEPTS *118,179*

exult [*v1*] *be joyful*
be delighted, be elated, be happy, be in high spirits*, be jubilant, be overjoyed, celebrate, cheer, jubilate, jump for joy*, make merry*, rejoice; SEE CONCEPTS *32,266*

exult [*v2*] *boast*
bluster, brag, bully, crow, gloat, glory, revel, show off, take delight in*, triumph, vaunt; SEE CONCEPT *49*

exultant [*adj*] *very happy*
blown away*, delighted, ecstatic, elated, exulting, flipping, flushed, flying, gleeful, high, joyful, joyous, jubilant, overjoyed, rejoicing, revelling, transported, triumphant, turned on*, wowed*; SEE CONCEPT *403*

exultation [*n*] *celebration, reveling*
crowing, delight, elation, glee, gloating, glory,

ex
ex

happiness, high spirits, joy, joyousness, jubilance, jubilation, merriment, rejoicing, satisfaction, triumph; SEE CONCEPTS 32,410

eye [n1] *judgment, opinion*
appreciation, belief, conviction, discernment, discrimination, eagle eye*, feeling, mind, perception, persuasion, point of view, recognition, scrutiny, sentiment, surveillance, tab, taste, view, viewpoint, watch; SEE CONCEPTS 411,689

eye [n2] *optical organ of an animate being*
baby blue*, blinder*, eyeball, headlight*, lamp*, ocular, oculus, optic, peeper*, pie*; SEE CONCEPT 392

eye [v] *gaze at, scrutinize*
check out, consider, contemplate, eyeball*, gape, give the eye*, glance at, have a look, inspect, keep eagle eye on*, leer, look at, ogle, peruse, regard, rubberneck*, scan, size up*, stare at, study, survey, take a look, take in, view, watch; SEE CONCEPTS 17,623,626

eye-catching [adj] *noticeable*
attractive, beautiful, can't miss it*, conspicuous, gorgeous, manifest, obvious, showy, spectacular, striking, stunning; SEE CONCEPTS 529,579

eyeful [n] *spectacular-looking person*
beauty, dazzler*, knockout*, looker, lovely, show, spectacle, stunner*, vision; SEE CONCEPT 424

eyeglasses [n] *glasses*
bifocals, cheaters*, contact lenses, contacts, goggles, lorgnette, monocle, pair of glasses, pince-nez, reading glasses, shades, specs*, spectacles, sunglasses, trifocals; SEE CONCEPT 446

eyesight [n] *vision*
optics, perceiving, perception, range of view, seeing, sight, view; SEE CONCEPT 629

eyesore [n] *mess, ugliness*
atrocity, blemish, blight, blot, blot on landscape*, deformity, disfigurement, disgrace, distortion, dump, horror, monstrosity, sight, ugly thing; SEE CONCEPTS 674,716

eyewitness [n] *person who sees an event occur*
beholder, bystander, looker-on, observer, onlooker, passer-by, spectator, viewer, watcher, witness; SEE CONCEPT 423

F

fable [n] *fantasy, story*
allegory, apologue, bestiary, bunk*, crock*, fabrication, fairy story, fairy tale, falsehood, fantasy, fib, fiction, figment, fish story*, hogwash*, invention, legend, lie, myth, old chestnut*, old saw*, one for the birds*, parable, romance, tale, tall story, untruth, white lie*, whopper*, yarn; SEE CONCEPT 282

fabled [adj] *legendary*
fabulous, famed, famous, fanciful, fictional, mythical, mythological, storied, unreal; SEE CONCEPT 568

fabric [n1] *cloth, material*
bolt, fiber, goods, stuff, textile, texture, web; SEE CONCEPT 473

fabric [n2] *structure*
building, consistency, constitution, construction,

foundation, frame, framework, infrastructure, make-up, mold, organization, stamp, substance, texture; SEE CONCEPTS 733,757

fabricate [v1] *manufacture*
assemble, brainstorm, build, cobble up*, compose, concoct, construct, contrive, cook up*, create, devise, dream up, erect, fashion, fit together, form, formulate, frame, head trip*, invent, join, knock together*, make, make up, mix, organize, piece together, prefab*, produce, put together, shape, structure, think up, throw together*, throw up*, turn out, whip up*, whomp up*; SEE CONCEPTS 36,173,205,251

fabricate [v2] *falsify, make up a story*
coin, concoct, contrive, counterfeit, devise, fake, feign, fib, forge, form, fudge*, invent, jive*, lie, make like*, misrepresent, pretend, prevaricate, trump up*; SEE CONCEPTS 58,63

fabrication [n1] *lie*
artifact, concoction, deceit, fable, fairy story*, fake*, falsehood, fib, fiction, figment, forgery, hogwash*, invention, jazz*, jive*, line*, myth, opus, smoke*, song and dance*, untruth, work, yarn; SEE CONCEPTS 63,278

fabrication [n2] *something manufactured*
assemblage, assembly, building, construction, creation, erection, product, production; SEE CONCEPTS 205,260,338

fabulous [adj] *amazing, wonderful*
10*, A-1*, aces*, A-OK*, astonishing, astounding, awesome, best, breathtaking, cool*, doozie*, extravagant, fab*, fantastic, fictitious, first-class, greatest, groovy*, immense, inconceivable, incredible, legendary, marvelous, mind-blowing*, out-of-sight*, out-of-this-world*, outrageous, peachy*, phenomenal, primo*, prodigious, rad*, remarkable, spectacular, striking, stupendous, super, superb, terrific, top drawer*, tops*, turn on*, unbelievable, unreal, wicked*; SEE CONCEPTS 529,572

facade [n] *appearance, often deceptive*
beard*, bluff, color, disguise, exterior, face, fake, false colors*, false front*, front, frontage, guise, look, mask, phony, pretense, put-on*, semblance, show, veneer, window dressing*; SEE CONCEPT 716

face [n1] *front of something; expression, exterior*
air, appearance, aspect, cast, clock, countenance, dial*, disguise, display, facet, features, finish, frontage*, frontal, frontispiece, frown, glower, grimace, guise, kisser*, light*, lineaments, look, makeup, map*, mask, mug*, obverse, paint*, physiognomy, pout, presentation, profile, scowl, seeming, semblance, show, showing, silhouette, simulacrum, smirk, surface, top, visage; SEE CONCEPTS 484,716,836

face [n2] *pretense, nerve*
air, audacity, boldness, brass*, cheek*, chutzpah*, cloak, confidence, cover, disguise, effrontery, facade, false front*, front, gall, impertinence, impudence, mask, presumption, semblance, show, veil; SEE CONCEPTS 633,657

face [n3] *authority, status*
dignity, honor, image, prestige, reputation, self respect, social position, standing; SEE CONCEPT 388

face [v1] *come up against a situation*
abide, accost, affront, allow, bear, beard, be confronted by, bit the bullet*, brace, brave, brook, challenge, confront, contend, cope with, counter,

nance, court, cross, dare, deal with, defy, encounter, endure, experience, eyeball*, fight, fly in face of*, go up against*, grapple with, make a stand*, meet, oppose, resist, risk, run into, square off*, stand, stomach*, submit, suffer, sustain, swallow*, take, take it, take on, take the bull by the horns*, tell off*, tolerate, venture, withstand; SEE CONCEPTS 23,35,117

ace [v2] *be opposite; look at*
be turned toward, border, confront, front, front onto, gaze, glare, meet, overlook, stare, watch; SEE CONCEPTS 623,747

ace [v3] *put paint or finish on*
clad, coat, cover, decorate, dress, finish, front, level, line, overlay, plaster, polish, redecorate, refinish, remodel, sheathe, shingle, side, skin, smooth, surface, veneer; SEE CONCEPTS 172,202

ace-lift [n] *beautification; cosmetic surgery*
new look, nose job, plastic surgery, renovation, repair, restoration, revival, rhytidectomy; SEE CONCEPT 162

acet [n] *surface; aspect*
angle, appearance, character, face, feature, front, hand, level, obverse, part, phase, plane, side, slant, switch, twist; SEE CONCEPT 835

e the music [v] *face up to*
be punished, bite the bullet*, grin and bear it*, pay the piper*, swallow the pill*, take one's lumps*, take one's medicine*; SEE CONCEPT 23

acetious [adj] *tongue-in-cheek, kidding*
amusing, blithe, capering, clever, comic, comical, droll, dry, facetial, farcical, flip*, flippant, frivolous, funny, gay, humorous, indecorous, ironic, irreverent, jesting, jocose, jocular, joking, joshing, laughable, ludicrous, merry, not serious, playful, pleasant, pulling one's leg*, punning, putting one on*, ridiculous, salty, sarcastic, satirical, smart, sportive, sprightly, waggish, whimsical, wisecracking, witty, wry; SEE CONCEPT 267

acile [adj] *easy; easily mastered*
accomplished, adept, adroit, apparent, articulate, breeze, child's play*, cursory, deft, dexterous, easy as pie*, effortless, fast talk*, flip*, fluent, glib, hasty, light, obvious, picnic*, practiced, proficient, pushover*, quick, ready, shallow, simple, skillful, slick*, smooth, superficial, uncomplicated, untroublesome, voluble; SEE CONCEPTS 527,565

acilitate [v] *assist the progress of*
aid, ease, expedite, forward, further, grease the wheels*, hand-carry*, help, make easy, open doors*, promote, run interference for*, simplify, smooth, speed, speed up, walk through*; SEE CONCEPTS 110,242

acility [n1] *ease; ability*
address, adroitness, aptitude, bent, child's play*, competence, dexterity, efficiency, effortlessness, expertness, fluency, knack, leaning, lightness, poise, proficiency, propensity, quickness, readiness, skill, skillfulness, smoothness, smooth sailing*, spontaneity, tact, turn, wit; SEE CONCEPTS 630,666

acility [n2] *convenience*
accommodation, advantage, aid, amenity, appliance, comfort, equipment, fitting, material, means, opportunity, resource, tool; SEE CONCEPTS 693,712

simile [n1] *reproduction*
carbon, carbon copy*, chip off old block*, clone, copy, copycat*, dead ringer*, ditto*, double,

dupe*, duplicate, knock-off*, likeness, look-alike, mimeo, miniature, mirror, photocopy, photostat, print, reduplication, replica, replication, repro*, ringer*, spitting image*, stat, transcript, twin, Xerox*; SEE CONCEPTS 271,625,716

fact [n1] *verifiable truth; reality*
actuality, appearance, authenticity, basis, bottom line*, brass tacks*, case, certainty, certitude, concrete happening, dope*, evidence, experience, genuineness, gospel, gospel truth*, how it is*, intelligence, law, like it is*, matter*, naked truth*, palpability, permanence, scene, scripture, solidity, stability, substantiality, verity, what's what*; SEE CONCEPTS 688,725

fact [n2] *event; detail of action*
accomplishment, act, action, actuality, adventure, affair, being, case, circumstance, conception, consideration, construction, creation, data, datum, deed, entity, episode, evidence, experience, factor, fait accompli, feature, happening, incident, information, item, manifestation, occurrence, organism, particular, performance, phenomenon, point, proceeding, specific, statistic, transaction, truism; SEE CONCEPTS 2,274,433

faction [n1] *group sharing a belief or cause*
band, bloc, bunch, cabal, camp, caucus, cell, circle, clan, clique, club, coalition, combination, combine, combo, concern, conclave, confederacy, conspiracy, contingent, coterie, crew, crowd, design, division, entente, gang, guild, insiders, intrigue, junta, knot, lobby, machine, minority, mob, network, offshoot, outfit, partnership, party, pressure group, ring, schism, sect, section, sector, set, side, splinter group, team, unit, wing; SEE CONCEPTS 301,387

faction [n2] *conflict, strife*
disagreement, discord, disharmony, dissension, disunity, division, divisiveness, friction, infighting, quarrelsomeness, rebellion, sedition, tumult, turbulence; SEE CONCEPTS 106,684

factious [adj] *conflicting, warring*
alienated, belligerent, contending, contentious, contumacious, disaffected, disputatious, dissident, divisive, estranged, fighting, hostile, insubordinate, insurgent, insurrectionary, litigious, malcontent, mutinous, partisan, quarrelsome, rebellious, refractory, rival, sectarian, seditious, troublemaking, tumultous/tumultuous, turbulent; SEE CONCEPT 542

factor [n] *determinant*
agency, agent, aid, antecedent, aspect, board, cause, circumstance, component, consideration, constituent, element, fixin's*, influence, ingredient, instrument, instrumentality, item, makin's*, means, part, part and parcel*, point, portion, thing; SEE CONCEPTS 831,835

factory [n] *manufacturing plant*
branch, cooperative, firm, forge, foundry, industry, laboratory, machine shop, manufactory, mill, mint, salt mines*, shop, sweatshop*, warehouse, workroom, works, workshop; SEE CONCEPTS 439,441,449

facts [n] *inside information*
bottom line*, brass tacks*, certainty, clue, cue, data, details, dope*, gospel, info*, inside dope*, like it is*, lowdown*, numbers, poop*, reality, scoop*, score*, story, whole story*; SEE CONCEPT 274

factual [adj] *real, correct*
absolute, accurate, actual, authentic, card-carry-

ey
fa

ing*, certain, circumstantial, close, credible, descriptive, exact, faithful, genuine, hard, kosher*, legit*, legitimate, literal, objective, on the level*, positive, precise, righteous, specific, straight from horse's mouth*, sure, sure-enough*, true, true-to-life*, unadorned, unbiased, undoubted, unquestionable, valid, veritable; SEE CONCEPTS 535,582

faculty [n1] *ability, skill*
adroitness, aptitude, aptness, bent, capability, capacity, cleverness, dexterity, facility, flair, forte, genius, gift, instinct, intelligence, knack, knowing way around*, leaning, nose*, peculiarity, penchant, pistol*, power, predilection, proclivity, propensity, property, quality, readiness, reason, right stuff*, sense, strength, talent, turn, what it takes*, wits; SEE CONCEPT 630

faculty [n2] *teachers in educational institution*
academics, advisers, body, clinic, college, corps, department, employees, institute, instructors, lecturers, literati, mentors, organization, pedagogues, personnel, professorate, professors, profs*, researchers, scholars, society, staff, tutors, university, workers; SEE CONCEPTS 288,350

fad [n] *craze*
affectation, amusement, caprice, chic, conceit, cry, custom, dernier cri, eccentricity, fancy, fantasy, fashion, fool notion*, frivolity, furor, hobby, humor, in, innovation, in thing*, kick, kink, latest word*, mania, mode, newest wrinkle*, new look*, passing fancy*, passion, quirk, rage, sport, style, thing, trend, vagary, vogue, whim, whimsy, wrinkle; SEE CONCEPT 655

fade [v1] *lose color*
achromatize, become colorless, blanch, bleach, blench, clear, decolorize, dim, disappear, discolor, dissolve, dull, etiolate, evanish, evaporate, grow dim, lose brightness, lose luster, muddy, neutralize, pale, tarnish, tone down, vanish, wash out; SEE CONCEPTS 250,469,622

fade [v2] *dwindle, die out*
abate, attenuate, clear, decline, deliquesce, deteriorate, die away, die on vine*, dim, diminish, disappear, disperse, dissolve, droop, ebb, etiolate, evanesce, evanish, evaporate, fag out*, fail, fall, flag, fold, hush, languish, lessen, melt, melt away, moderate, perish, peter out*, poop out*, quiet, rarefy, shrivel, sink, slack off*, taper, thin, tire, tucker out*, vanish, wane, waste away, weaken, wilt, wither; SEE CONCEPTS 105,698

faded [adj] *bleached; used*
achromatic, ashen, bedraggled, dim, dingy, discolored, dull, etiolated, indistinct, lackluster, lusterless, murky, not shiny, pale, pallid, run-down, seedy, shabby, shopworn, tacky, tattered, threadbare, tired, wan, washed out, wasted, worn; SEE CONCEPTS 560,617,618

fail [v1] *be unsuccessful*
abort, backslide, back wrong horse*, be defeated, be demoted, be found lacking*, be in vain*, be ruined, blunder, break down, come to naught, come to nothing, decline, deteriorate, fall, fall flat*, fall short*, fall through*, fizzle, flop, flounder, fold, founder, go astray*, go down*, go downhill*, go down swinging*, go up in smoke*, go wrong, hit bottom*, hit the skids*, lose control, lose out, lose status, meet with disaster, miscarry, miss, miss the boat*, play into, run aground*, slip, turn out badly; SEE CONCEPT 699

fail [v2] *abandon, forsake*
abort, back out, blink, break one's word, desert, disappoint, discount, disregard, fault, forget, funk, go astray, ignore, let down, miscarry, neglect, omit, overlook, overpass, slight, slip; SEE CONCEPTS 7,19

fail [v3] *lose money*
be cleaned out*, become insolvent, be in arrears, be ruined, be taken to the cleaners*, break, close, close down*, close one's doors*, crash, defalcate, default, dishonor, drop, drop a bundle*, end, finish, fold, go bankrupt, go belly up*, go broke*, go bust*, go into chapter 11*, go out of business*, go to the wall*, go under*, go up*, lose big*, lose one's shirt*, overdraw, repudiate, terminate; SEE CONCEPTS 330,335

failing [adj] *not well, weak*
declining, defeated, deficient, faint, feeble, inadequate, insufficient, scant, scanty, scarce, short, shy, unavailing, unprosperous, unsuccessful, unsufficient, unthriving, vain, wanting; SEE CONCEPTS 485,489

failing [n] *lapse, shortcoming*
blind spot*, defect, deficiency, drawback, error, failure, fault, flaw, foible, frailty, imperfection, infirmity, miscarriage, misfortune, vice, weakness, weak point*; SEE CONCEPTS 411,674

fail-safe [adj] *guaranteed not to fail*
confident, covered, foolproof, protected, reliable, reliant, safeguarded, secure, sound, sure; SEE CONCEPTS 535,542,544

failure [n1] *lack of success*
abortion, bankruptcy, bomb, botch*, breakdown, bungle*, bust, checkmate, collapse, decay, decline, defeat, deficiency, deficit, deterioration, downfall, failing, false step*, faux pas, fiasco, flash in the pan*, flop*, frustration, implosion, inadequacy, lead balloon*, lemon*, loser, loss, mess, misadventure, miscarriage, misstep, nonperformance, nonsuccess, overthrow, rout, rupture, sinking ship*, stalemate, stoppage, total loss, turkey*, washout*, wreck; SEE CONCEPTS 699,706

failure [n2] *person who does not succeed*
also-ran*, bankrupt, beat*, born loser*, bum, castaway, deadbeat, defaulter, derelict, disappointment, dud*, flop, good-for-nothing*, hasbeen, incompetent, insolvent, loafer, loser, lumpy*, might-have-been*, moocher*, nobody, no-good, nonperformer, prodigal, turkey*, underachiever, washout*; SEE CONCEPTS 412,423

faint [adj1] *having little effect on senses*
aside, bated, bland, bleached, blurred, breathless, deadened, deep, delicate, dim, distant, dull, dusty, faded, faltering, far-off, feeble, gentle, hazy, hoarse, hushed, ill-defined, imperceptible, inaudible, indistinct, lenient, light, low, low-pitched, mild, moderate, muffled, murmuring, muted, muttering, obscure, out of earshot*, padded, pale, piano, quiet, remote, shadowy, slight, smooth, soft, softened, soothing, stifled, subdued, tenuous, thin, unclear, vague, wan, weak, whispered; SEE CONCEPTS 537,594,617

faint [adj2] *weak*
delicate, dizzy, drooping, enervated, exhausted, faltering, fatigued, feeble, fragile, languid, lethargic, lightheaded, slight, tender, unenthusiastic, woozy; SEE CONCEPTS 314,485

faint [n] *unconsciousness*
blackout, collapse, dizziness, grayout, insensibil-

ity, knockout, stupor, swoon, syncope, vertigo; SEE CONCEPTS 308,316

faint [*v*] *lose consciousness*
become unconscious, be overcome, black out, collapse, drop, fade, fail, fall, flicker, go out like light*, keel over, languish, pass out, succumb, swoon, weaken; SEE CONCEPTS 303,308

fainthearted [*adj*] *timid*
afraid, cowardly, cowed, cowering, fearful, frightened, gutless, having cold feet*, intimidated, lily-livered*, meek, mousy, spineless, unassertive, weak, wimpy*, yellow*; SEE CONCEPT 401

fair [*adj1*] *impartial, unprejudiced*
aboveboard, benevolent, blameless, candid, civil, clean, courteous, decent, disinterested, dispassionate, equal, equitable, even-handed, frank, generous, good, honest, honorable, impartial, just, lawful, legitimate, moderate, nonpartisan, objective, on the level*, on up-and-up*, open, pious, praiseworthy, principled, proper, reasonable, respectable, righteous, scrupulous, sincere, square, straight, straightforward, temperate, trustworthy, unbiased, uncolored, uncorrupted, upright, virtuous; SEE CONCEPT 542

fair [*adj2*] *light-complexioned, light-haired*
argent, blanched, bleached, blond, blonde, chalky, colorless, creamy, faded, fair-haired, fair-skinned, flaxen-haired, light, milky, neutral, pale, pale-faced, pallid, pearly, sallow, silvery, snowy, tow-haired, tow-headed, white, whitish; SEE CONCEPTS 406,618

fair [*adj3*] *mediocre, satisfactory*
adequate, all right, average, common, commonplace, decent, fairish, indifferent, intermediate, mean, medium, middling, moderate, not bad*, okay, ordinary, passable, pretty good*, reasonable, respectable, satisfactory, so-so*, tolerable, up to standard*, usual; SEE CONCEPT 530

fair [*adj4*] *beautiful*
attractive, beauteous, bonny, charming, chaste, comely, dainty, delicate, enchanting, exquisite, good-looking, handsome, lovely, pretty, pulchritudinous, pure; SEE CONCEPT 579

fair [*adj5*] *bright, cloudless (weather)*
balmy, calm, clarion, clear, clement, dry, favorable, fine, mild, placid, pleasant, pretty, rainless, smiling, sunny, sunshiny, tranquil, unclouded, undarkened, unthreatening; SEE CONCEPT 525

fair [*n*] *exposition, carnival*
bazaar, celebration, centennial, display, exhibit, exhibition, expo*, festival, fete, gala, market, observance, occasion, pageant, show, spectacle; SEE CONCEPTS 377,386

fairly [*adv1*] *somewhat*
adequately, averagely, enough, kind of, moderately, more or less, passably, pretty well, quite, rather, ratherish, reasonably, some, something, sort of, so-so*, tolerably; SEE CONCEPT 786

fairly [*adv2*] *justly*
deservedly, equitably, honestly, honorably, impartially, objectively, properly, reasonably, without favor, without fear; SEE CONCEPT 542

fairness [*n*] *justice*
candor, charitableness, charity, civility, consideration, courtesy, decency, decorum, disinterestedness, due, duty, equitableness, equity, exactitude, fair-mindedness, fair shake*, give and take*, good faith, goodness, honesty, honor, humanity, impartiality, integrity, justness, legitimacy, mod-

eration, open-mindedness, propriety, rationality, reasonableness, right, righteousness, rightfulness, rightness, seemliness, square deal*, suitability, tolerance, truth, uprightness, veracity; SEE CONCEPTS 645,657

fairy [*n*] *supernatural being*
bogie, brownie, elf, enchanter, fay, genie, gnome, goblin, gremlin, hob, imp, leprechaun, mermaid, nisse, nymph, pixie, puck, siren, spirit, sprite, sylph; SEE CONCEPT 370

fait accompli [*n*] *done deed*
accomplished fact, certainty, fact of life, hard facts, irreversible accomplishment, irreversible act, irreversible truth, matter of fact, reality, undeniable fact; SEE CONCEPTS 689,725

faith [*n1*] *trust in something*
acceptance, allegiance, assent, assurance, belief, certainty, certitude, confidence, constancy, conviction, credence, credit, credulity, dependence, faithfulness, fealty, fidelity, hope, loyalty, reliance, stock, store, sureness, surety, troth, truth, truthfulness; SEE CONCEPT 689

faith [*n2*] *belief in a higher being; community of believers*
canon, church, communion, confession, connection, conviction, credo, creed, cult, denomination, doctrine, dogma, doxy, gospel, orthodoxy, persuasion, piety, piousness, principle, profession, religion, revelation, sect, teaching, tenet, theism, theology, worship; SEE CONCEPTS 368,689

faithful [*adj1*] *loyal, reliable*
affectionate, allegiant, ardent, attached, behind one, circumspect, confiding, conscientious, constant, dependable, devoted, dutiful, dyed-in-the-wool*, enduring, fast, firm, genuine, hard-core*, honest, honorable, incorruptible, loving, obedient, on the level*, patriotic, resolute, scrupulous, sincere, staunch, steadfast, steady, straight, string along with*, sure, tried, tried and true*, true, true-blue*, trustworthy, trusty, truthful, unchanging, unswerving, unwavering, upright, veracious; SEE CONCEPTS 401,545

faithful [*adj2*] *authentic, accurate*
close, credible, exact, just, lifelike, precise, right, similar, strict, true, trusty, undistorted, veracious, veridical; SEE CONCEPTS 487,573

faithfulness [*n*] *devotion*
adherence, adhesion, allegiance, ardor, attachment, care, constancy, dependability, duty, fealty, fidelity, loyalty, piety, trustworthiness, truth; SEE CONCEPTS 633,645,689

faithless [*adj*] *disloyal*
capricious, changeable, changeful, cheating, deceitful, dishonest, double-crossing*, double-dealing*, doubting, dubious, false, fickle, fluctuating, inconstant, perfidious, recreant, skeptical, traitorous, treacherous, two-faced*, two-timing*, unbelieving, unconverted, unfaithful, unloyal, unreliable, unstable, untrue, untrustworthy, untruthful, wavering; SEE CONCEPTS 401,545

faithlessness [*n*] *disloyalty*
betrayal, disbelief, dishonesty, doubt, falseness, fickleness, fraud, inconstancy, infidelity, perfidiousness, perfidy, skepticism, treacherousness, treachery, treason, unfaithfulness; SEE CONCEPTS 633,645

fake [*adj*] *false, imitation*
affected, artificial, assumed, bogus, concocted,

fa
fa

counterfeit, fabricated, fictitious, forged, fraudulent, invented, make-believe, mock, phony, pretended, pseudo*, reproduction, sham, simulated, spurious; SEE CONCEPTS *401,582*

fake [*n*] *imposter, copy*
actor, bluffer, charlatan, cheat, counterfeit, deception, fabrication, faker, flimflam*, forgery, four-flusher*, fraud, gold brick*, hoax, imitation, imposition, imposture, junque, make-believe, mountebank, phony, plant*, pretender, pretense, pseudo*, put-on, reproduction, scam, sham*, sleight, spoof, swindle, trick; SEE CONCEPTS *260,412*

fake [*v*] *pretend*
act, affect, assume, bluff, copy, counterfeit, disguise, dissimulate, fabricate, feign, forge, put on, put on an act*, sham, simulate, spoof; SEE CONCEPT *59*

falderal [*n*] *folderol, foolishness*
absurdity, baloney, bunk*, craziness, garbage, gibberish, gobbledygook*, horse feathers*, lunacy, nonsense, stupidity, twaddle; SEE CONCEPT *633*

fall [*n1*] *descent; lowering*
abatement, belly flop*, cut, decline, declivity, decrease, diminution, dip, dive, downgrade, downward slope, drop, dwindling, ebb, falling off, header*, incline, lapse, lessening, nose dive*, plummet, plunge, pratfall*, recession, reduction, slant, slip, slope, slump, spill, tumble; SEE CONCEPTS *152,181,776*

fall [*n2*] *defeat, overthrow*
abasement, breakdown, capitulation, collapse, death, degradation, destruction, diminution, disaster, dive, downfall, drop, failure, humiliation, loss, resignation, ruin, surrender, tumble; SEE CONCEPTS *116,230,674,699*

fall [*v1*] *descend; become lower*
abate, backslide, be precipitated, break down, buckle, cascade, cave in, collapse, crash, decline, decrease, depreciate, diminish, dip, dive, drag, droop, drop down, dwindle, ease, ebb, flag, flop, fold up, go down, gravitate, hit the dirt*, keel over, land, lapse, lessen, nose-dive, pitch, plummet, plunge, recede, regress, relapse, settle, sink, slip, slope, slump, spin, stumble, subside, take a header*, tip over, topple, totter, trail, trip, tumble, wane; SEE CONCEPTS *152,181,776*

fall [*v2*] *be overthrown by an enemy; surrender*
back down, be casualty, be destroyed, be killed, be lost, bend, be taken, capitulate, defer to, die, drop, eat dirt*, fall to pieces*, give in, give up, give way, go down, go under, lie down, obey, pass into enemy hands*, perish, resign, slump, submit, succumb, yield; SEE CONCEPTS *116,699*

fall [*v3*] *happen*
arrive, become, befall, chance, come about, come to pass, occur, take place; SEE CONCEPT *119*

fallacious [*adj*] *false, wrong*
beguiling, deceiving, deceptive, deluding, delusive, delusory, erroneous, fictitious, fishy*, fraudulent, illogical, illusory, incorrect, invalid, irrational, mad, misleading, mistaken, off*, phony, reasonless, sophistic, sophistical, spurious, unfounded, ungrounded, unreal, unreasonable, unreasoned, unsound, untrue, way off*; SEE CONCEPTS *267,570,582*

fallacy [*n*] *illusion, misconception*
aberration, ambiguity, artifice, bias, casuistry,

cavil, deceit, deception, deceptiveness, delusion, deviation, elusion, equivocation, erratum, erroneousness, error, evasion, falsehood, faultiness, flaw, heresy, illogicality, inconsistency, inexactness, invalidity, misapprehension, miscalculation, misconstrual, misinterpretation, mistake, non sequitur, notion, paradox, perversion, preconception, prejudice, quibbling, quirk, solecism, sophism, sophistry, speciousness, subterfuge, untruth; SEE CONCEPTS *410,689,725*

fall back [*v*] *retreat*
back, draw back, give back, recede, recoil, retire, retrocede, retrograde, surrender, withdraw, yield; SEE CONCEPT *195*

fallen [*adj1*] *disgraced, ruined*
collapsed, decayed, dishonored, immoral, loose, ruinous, shaken, shamed, sinful, unchaste; SEE CONCEPTS *539,555*

fallen [*adj2*] *dead*
casualty, killed, lost, perished, slain, slaughtered; SEE CONCEPT *539*

fall for [*v*] *become infatuated with*
desire, fall in love with, flip over, go head over heels*, lose one's head over*, succumb; SEE CONCEPT *32*

fall guy [*n*] *scapegoat*
chopping block, dupe, patsy, pigeon, sacrifice, sap, schmuck, stooge, sucker, victim, whipping boy; SEE CONCEPT *412*

fallible [*adj*] *able or prone to err*
careless, deceptive, errable, errant, erring, faulty, frail, heedless, human, ignorant, imperfect, in question, liable, mortal, questionable, uncertain, unreliable, untrustworthy, weak; SEE CONCEPT *542*

falling-out [*n*] *disagreement*
altercation, argument, clash, dispute, exchange, feud, fight, friction, misunderstanding, quarrel; SEE CONCEPTS *46,388*

fall out [*v1*] *argue*
altercate, bicker, clash, differ, disagree, fight, quarrel, spar, squabble; SEE CONCEPT *46*

fall out [*v2*] *come to pass*
befall, chance, happen, occur, result, take place, turn out; SEE CONCEPT *4*

fallow [*adj*] *inactive*
dormant, idle, inert, neglected, quiescent, resting, slack, uncultivated, undeveloped, unplanted, unplowed, unproductive, unseeded, untilled, unused, vacant, virgin; SEE CONCEPTS *485,560*

fall to [*v*] *set about doing*
apply oneself to, begin, be up to, buckle down*, commence, jump in, pitch in*, start, undertake, wade into*; SEE CONCEPTS *100,221*

false [*adj1*] *wrong, made up*
apocryphal, beguiling, bogus, casuistic, concocted, contrary to fact, cooked-up*, counterfactual, deceitful, deceiving, delusive, dishonest, distorted, erroneous, ersatz*, fake, fallacious, fanciful, faulty, fictitious, fishy, fraudulent, illusive, imaginary, improper, inaccurate, incorrect, inexact, invalid, lying, mendacious, misleading, misrepresentative, mistaken, off the mark*, phony, sham, sophistical, specious, spurious, trumped up*, unfounded, unreal, unsound, untruthful; SEE CONCEPTS *267,570,582*

false [*adj2*] *dishonest, hypocritical*
apostate, base, beguiling, canting, corrupt, crooked, deceitful, deceiving, deceptive, deluding, delusive, devious, dishonorable, disloyal,

double-dealing*, duplicitous, faithless, false-hearted, forsworn, foul, lying, malevolent, malicious, mean, misleading, mythomaniac, perfidious, perjured, rascally, recreant, renegade, scoundrelly, traitorous, treacherous, treasonable, two-faced*, underhanded, unfaithful, unscrupulous, untrustworthy, venal, villainous, wicked; SEE CONCEPTS 267,401

false [adj3] *fake, counterfeit*
adulterated, alloyed, artificial, assumed, bent, bogus*, brummagem, bum*, colored, contrived, copied, crock*, deceptive, disguised, ersatz*, fabricated, factitious, feigned, fishy*, forged, framed*, hollow, imitation, made-up, make-believe, manufactured, meretricious, mock, ostensible, phony, pretended, pseudo*, seeming, shady, sham*, simulated, snide, so-called*, spurious, substitute, synthetic, unreal, wrong; SEE CONCEPT 582

falsehood [n] *lie*
canard, cover-up, deceit, deception, dishonesty, dissimulation, distortion, equivocation, erroneousness, error, fable, fabrication, fakery, fallaciousness, fallacy, falseness, falsity, feigning, fib, fibbery, fiction, figment, fraud, half truth, hogwash*, line, mendacity, misstatement, perjury, pretense, prevarication, sham*, story, tale, tall tale*, untruism, untruth, untruthfulness, whopper*, yarn; SEE CONCEPTS 63,278

falsely [adv] *deceitfully*
basely, behind one's back*, crookedly, dishonestly, dishonorably, disloyally, faithlessly, falseheartedly, malevolently, maliciously, perfidiously, roguishly, traitorously, treacherously, underhandedly, unfaithfully, unscrupulously; SEE CONCEPTS 267,401

false teeth [n] *dentures*
artificial teeth, bridge, choppers*, dental plate, implants, partial, set of teeth; SEE CONCEPT 393

falsies [n] *padded bra*
props, Wonderbra™; SEE CONCEPT 451

falsify [v] *alter, misrepresent*
adulterate, belie, change, color, con, contort, contradict, contravene, cook, counterfeit, deacon, deceive, deny, distort, doctor, dress up*, embroider, equivocate, exaggerate, fake, fake it, fib, forge, four-flush*, frame up*, garble, gloss, lie, misquote, misstate, palter, pervert, phony up*, prevaricate, promote, put on an act*, salt*, tamper with, traverse, trump up*, twist, warp; SEE CONCEPT 63

falsity [n] *dishonesty, deception*
canard, cheating, deceit, deceptiveness, disingenuousness, double-dealing, duplicity, erroneousness, error, faithlessness, fake, fallacy, falsehood, fib, fraud, fraudulence, hypocrisy, inaccuracy, infidelity, insincerity, lie, mendacity, misrepresentation, perfidiousness, perfidy, prevarication, sham, story, tale, treachery, uncandidness, unfaithfulness, unreality, untruth; SEE CONCEPTS 278,645,725

falter [v] *stumble, stutter*
be undecided, bobble, break, drop the ball*, flounder, fluctuate, fluff, halt, hem and haw*, hesitate, lurch, quaver, reel, rock, roll, scruple, shake, speak haltingly, stagger, stammer, stub toe*, teeter, topple, totter, tremble, trip up, vacillate, waver, whiffle, wobble; SEE CONCEPTS 18,147,266

fame [n] *celebrity*
acclaim, acclamation, account, acknowledgment, character, credit, dignity, distinction, éclat, elevation, eminence, esteem, estimation, exaltation, favor, glory, greatness, heyday, honor, illustriousness, immortality, kudos, laurels, luster, majesty, name, nobility, note, notoriety, place, popularity, position, preeminence, prominence, public esteem, rank, recognition, regard, renown, rep*, report, reputation, repute, splendor, standing, stardom, station, superiority; SEE CONCEPT 388

familiar [adj1] *common, well-known*
accustomed, commonplace, conventional, customary, domestic, everyday, frequent, garden variety*, habitual, homespun, household, humble, informal, intimate, known, matter-of-fact, mundane, native, natural, old hat*, ordinary, plain, prosaic, proverbial, recognizable, repeated, routine, simple, stock, unceremonious, unsophisticated, usual, wonted, workaday; SEE CONCEPTS 530,547

familiar [adj2] *knowledgeable*
abreast, acquainted, apprised, at home with*, au courant, au fait, aware, cognizant, conscious, conversant, grounded*, informed, in on*, in the know*, introduced, kept posted*, mindful, no stranger to*, plugged in*, savvy, tuned in*, up*, up on*, versant, versed in, well up in*, with it*; SEE CONCEPT 402

familiar [adj3] *friendly, bold*
affable, amicable, buddy-buddy*, chummy*, close, comfortable, confidential, cordial, cozy, dear, easy, forward, free, free-and-easy*, fresh, genial, gracious, impudent, informal, intimate, intrusive, near, neighborly, nervy, obtrusive, officious, open, palsy, palsy-walsy*, presuming, presumptuous, relaxed, sassy*, smart, snug, sociable, thick, tight, unceremonious, unconstrained, unreserved, wise; SEE CONCEPT 555

familiarity [n1] *friendliness*
acquaintance, acquaintanceship, boldness, closeness, ease, fellowship, freedom, freshness, friendship, informality, intimacy, liberty, naturalness, openness, presumption, sociability, unceremoniousness; SEE CONCEPT 388

familiarity [n2] *knowledgeableness*
acquaintance, awareness, cognition, comprehension, experience, feel, grasp, knowledge, sense, understanding; SEE CONCEPT 409

familiarize [v] *make or become acquainted with, knowledgeable about*
accustom, adapt, adjust, awaken to, become adept in, become aware of, break the ice*, bring into use, case*, check out, coach, come to know, condition, enlighten, gain friendship, get in, get lay of land*, get lowdown on*, get together, get to know, get with it*, habituate, inform, instruct, inure, let down hair*, let know, let next to, make conversant, make used to, mix, naturalize, popularize, post, prime, put on to*, school, season, tip off*, train, use, wont; SEE CONCEPTS 15,38

family [n] *kin, offspring; classification*
ancestors, ancestry, birth, blood, brood, children, clan, class, descendants, descent, dynasty, extraction, folk, forebears, genealogy, generations, genre, group, heirs and assigns, house, household, inheritance, in-laws, issue, kind, kindred, kith and kin, line, lineage, ménage, network, parentage, pedigree, people, progenitors, prog-

eny, race, relations, relationship, relatives, siblings, strain, subdivision, system, tribe; SEE CONCEPTS 296,378,397

family tree [*n*] *family history*
ancestral tree, ancestry, bloodline, descent, genealogical chart, genealogy, heredity, lineage, pedigree; SEE CONCEPT 296

famine [*n*] *hunger*
dearth, destitution, drought, misery, paucity, poverty, scarcity, starvation, want; SEE CONCEPTS 674,709

famished [*adj*] *starving*
could eat a horse*, dog-hungry*, empty, flying light*, having the munchies*, hollow, hungering, hungry, ravening, ravenous, starved, starved to death*, voracious; SEE CONCEPTS 20,406,546

famous [*adj*] *legendary, notable to many*
acclaimed, applauded, august, brilliant, celebrated, conspicuous, distinguished, elevated, eminent, exalted, excellent, extraordinary, foremost, glorious, grand, great, honored, illustrious, important, imposing, influential, in limelight*, in spotlight*, leading, lionized, memorable, mighty, much-publicized, noble, noted, noteworthy, notorious, of note, outstanding, peerless, powerful, preeminent, prominent, recognized, remarkable, renowned, reputable, signal, splendid, talked about*, well-known; SEE CONCEPT 568

fan [*n*] *blower of air*
air conditioner, blade, draft, flabellum, leaf, palm leaf, propeller, thermantidote, vane, ventilator, windmill; SEE CONCEPT 463

fan [*n2*] *person enthusiastic about an interest*
addict, adherent, admirer, aficionado, amateur, buff, devotee, follower, freak*, groupie*, habitué, hound, lover, rooter, supporter, votary, zealot; SEE CONCEPTS 352,366,423

fan [*v1*] *blow on*
aerate, air-condition, air-cool, cool, refresh, ruffle, spread, ventilate, wind, winnow; SEE CONCEPTS 199,208

fan [*v2*] *provoke*
add fuel, agitate, arouse, enkindle, excite, expand, extend, impassion, increase, rouse, stimulate, stir up, whip up, work up; SEE CONCEPT 14

fanatic [*n*] *person overenthusiastic about an interest*
activist, addict, bigot, bug*, crank*, crazy, demon, devotee, enthusiast, extremist, fiend*, fool, freak, maniac, militant, monomaniac, nut*, radical, ultraist, visionary, zealot; SEE CONCEPTS 352,359,366

fanatical [*adj*] *overenthusiastic*
biased, bigoted, bugged*, burning*, contumacious, credulous, devoted, dogmatic, domineering, enthusiastic, erratic, extreme, fervent, feverish, fiery, frenzied, headstrong, high on*, immoderate, impassioned, impulsive, incorrigible, infatuated, mad, monomaniacal, narrowminded, nuts for*, obsessed, obsessive, obstinate, opinionated, partial, partisan, passionate, possessed, prejudiced, rabid, radical, raving, single-minded, stubborn, turned on*, unruly, violent, visionary, wild, willful, zealous; SEE CONCEPT 401

fanaticism [*n*] *overenthusiasm*
abandonment, arbitrariness, bias, bigotry, contumacy, dedication, devotion, dogma, enthusiasm, extremism, faction, frenzy, hatred, illiberality, immoderation, incorrigibility, infatuation, injustice, intolerance, madness, monomania, obsessiveness, obstinacy, partiality, partisanship, passion, prejudice, rage, single-mindedness, stubbornness, superstition, tenacity, transport, unfairness, unreasonableness, unruliness, violence, willfulness, zeal, zealotry; SEE CONCEPTS 633,689

fanciful [*adj*] *imaginary, romantic*
absurd, aerial, bizarre, blue sky*, capricious, castles in the air*, chimerical, curious, dreamlike, extravagant, fabulous, fairy-tale, fancied, fantastic, fantastical, fictional, fictitious, fictive, flaky*, floating, ideal, illusory, imaginative, imagined, incredible, kinky*, legendary, mythical, notional, offbeat, on cloud nine*, pie in the sky*, pipe dream*, poetic, preposterous, shadowy, suppositious, unreal, visionary, whimsical, wild; SEE CONCEPTS 529,572

fancy [*adj*] *extravagant, ornamental*
adorned, baroque, beautifying, chichi*, complicated, cushy, custom, decorated, decorative, deluxe, elaborate, elegant, embellished, fanciful, florid, frilly, froufrou*, garnished, gaudy, gingerbread*, intricate, lavish, ornate, ostentatious, resplendent, rich, rococo, showy, special, spiffy*, sumptuous, unusual; SEE CONCEPTS 562,579

fancy [*n1*] *impulse, urge*
caprice, conceit, conception, contrariness, creation, cup of tea*, desire, druthers*, flash, fool's paradise*, groove*, humor, idea, image, imagination, impression, inclination, irrationality, liking, mind, notion, perverseness, pleasure, thing*, thought, vagary, velleity, visualization, weakness for, whim, will; SEE CONCEPTS 20,532

fancy [*n2*] *liking, dream*
big eyes*, chimera, conception, daydream, delusion, envisagement, envisioning, eyes for*, fabrication, fantasy, figment, fondness, hallucination, hankering, idea, illusion, imagination, imaginativeness, inclination, invention, itch*, mirage, nightmare, notion, partiality, penchant, phantasm, picture, pie in the sky*, pipe dream*, predilection, preference, relish, reverie, romancing, sweet tooth*, vision, yearning; SEE CONCEPTS 20,32,409

fancy [*v1*] *imagine, create*
be inclined to think, believe, conceive, conjecture, dream up, envisage, envision, fantasize, feature*, guess, head trip*, image, infer, make up, make up off top of one's head*, phantom, picture, realize, reckon, spark, spitball*, suppose, surmise, think, think likely, think up, trump up*, vision, visualize; SEE CONCEPT 43

fancy [*v2*] *love, desire*
approve, be attracted to, be captivated by, be enamored of, be in love with, care for, crave, crazy about*, desire, dream of, endorse, fall for, favor, like, long for, lust after, mad for*, prefer, relish, sanction, set one's heart on*, take a liking to*, take to, wild for*, wish for, yearn for; SEE CONCEPTS 17,20,32

fanfare [*n*] *cheering*
alarum, array, ballyhoo*, demonstration, display, flourish, hullabaloo*, panoply, parade, pomp, shine, show, trump, trumpet call*; SEE CONCEPT 377

fanny [*n*] *buttocks*
ass, backside, behind*, bottom*, buns*, butt*, cheeks*, derriere, gluteus maximus, heinie*,

hindquarters, posterior, rear end, rump*, seat*, tail; SEE CONCEPT 17

fantasize [v] *dream about desires*
build castles in air*, daydream, envision, hallucinate, head trip*, imagine, invent, live in a dream world*, moon, romance, trip out*, woolgather*; SEE CONCEPT 17

fantastic [adj1] *strange, different; imaginary*
absurd, artificial, capricious, chimerical, comical, crazy, eccentric, erratic, exotic, extravagant, extreme, fanciful, far-fetched, fictional, foolish, foreign, freakish, grotesque, hallucinatory, illusive, imaginative, implausible, incredible, insane, irrational, ludicrous, mad, misleading, nonsensical, odd, outlandish, out of sight*, peculiar, phantasmagorical, preposterous, quaint, queer, ridiculous, singular, suppositious, unbelievable, unlikely, unreal, wacky*, weird, whimsical; SEE CONCEPTS 564,582

fantastic [adj2] *enormous*
cracking, extreme, great, huge, humongous, massive, monstrous, monumental, overwhelming, prodigious, severe, stupendous, towering, tremendous; SEE CONCEPT 781

fantastic [adj3] *wonderful, excellent*
A-1*, awesome, best, best ever, cat's meow*, delicious, far out*, first-class, first-rate, great, like wow*, marvelous, out of sight*, out of this world*, primo*, sensational, superb, unreal*; SEE CONCEPTS 572,574

fantasy [n] *imagination, dream*
air castle, apparition, appearance, Atlantis*, bubble*, chimera, conceiving, creativity, daydream, delusion, envisioning, externalizing, fabrication, fairyland*, fancy, fancying, fantasia, figment*, flight, flight of imagination, fool's paradise*, hallucination, head trip*, illusion, imaginativeness, imagining, invention, mind trip*, mirage, nightmare, objectifying, originality, rainbow*, reverie, trip, Utopia, vagary, vision; SEE CONCEPTS 20,529,689

FAQ [n] *frequently asked questions*
common answers, common questions, listed questions and answers; SEE CONCEPTS 48,53

far [adj/adv1] *at a great distance*
afar, a good way, a long way, bit, deep, distant, end of rainbow*, faraway, far-flung*, far-off, far piece*, far-removed, good ways*, long, middle of nowhere*, miles, outlying, out-of-the-way*, piece, remote, removed, stone's throw*, ways*; SEE CONCEPTS 586,778

far [adv2] *considerably*
decidedly, extremely, greatly, incomparably, much, notably, quite, significantly, somewhat, very, very much, well; SEE CONCEPTS 772,781

faraway [adj] *remote, distant*
absent, abstracted, beyond the horizon, distant, dreamy, far, far-flung*, far-off, far-removed, lost, outlying, preoccupied, quite a ways*, removed, well away; SEE CONCEPTS 586,778

farce [n] *nonsense, satire*
absurdity, broad comedy, buffoonery, burlesque, camp, caricature, comedy, high camp*, horseplay*, interlude, joke, low camp*, mock, mockery, parody, play, pratfall comedy, ridiculousness, sham*, skit, slapstick, travesty; SEE CONCEPTS 263,293

farcical [adj] *absurd*
amusing, camp, campy*, comic, comical, derisory, diverting, droll, for grins*, funny, gelas-

tic, joshing, laughable, ludicrous, nonsensical, outrageous, preposterous, ridiculous, risible, slapstick, stupid; SEE CONCEPTS 267,542

fare [n1] *amount charged for transportation*
book, charge, check, expense, passage, price, slug, tariff, ticket, token, toll; SEE CONCEPT 329

fare [n2] *food served at meals*
commons, diet, eatables, eats*, edibles, meals, menu, provision, rations, slop*, sustenance, swill*, table, victuals; SEE CONCEPTS 457,459

fare [v] *get along; turn out*
advance, do, get by, get on, go, handle, happen, hie, journey, make headway, make out, manage, muddle through, pass, proceed, progress, prosper, prove, shift, stagger; SEE CONCEPTS 100,117,704

farewell [n] *departing saying; departure*
adieu, adieus, adieux, adios, bye-bye, cheerio, ciao, goodbye, hasta la vista, have a nice day, leave-taking, parting, salutation, sendoff, so long, ta-ta, valediction; SEE CONCEPTS 195,278

far-fetched [adj] *hard to believe*
bizarre, doubtful, dubious, eccentric, fantastic, fishy*, forced, hard to swallow*, illogical, implausible, improbable, labored, incoherent, inconsequential, incredible, preposterous, queer, recondite, strained, strange, suspicious, unbelievable, unconvincing, unlikely, unnatural, unrealistic; SEE CONCEPTS 529,552,582

far-flung [adj] *wide-ranging*
comprehensive, distant, extensive, far-reaching, global, remote, spacious, widely distributed, widespread; SEE CONCEPTS 576,778

farm [n] *land for agriculture or animal breeding*
acreage, acres, arboretum, claim, demense, enclosure, estate, farmstead, field, freehold, garden, grange, grassland, holding, homestead, lawn, meadow, nursery, orchard, pasture, patch, plantation, ranch, soil, vineyard; SEE CONCEPTS 258,449,509,517

farm [v] *produce crops, raise animals*
bring under cultivation, crop, cultivate, direct, dress, garden, graze, grow, harrow, harvest, homestead, husband, landscape, look after, operate, pasture, plant, plow, ranch, reap, run, seed, sow, subdue, superintend, tend, till, till the soil, work; SEE CONCEPTS 117,253,324

farmer [n] *person who produces crops, raises animals*
agriculturalist, agriculturist, agronomist, breeder, clodhopper*, cob*, country person, cropper, cultivator, feeder, gardener, gleaner, grazer, grower, harvester, hired hand, homesteader, horticulturist, laborer, peasant, planter, plower, producer, rancher, reaper, sharecropper, sower, tender, tiller, villein; SEE CONCEPTS 347,348

farming [n] *producing crops, raising animals*
agriculture, agronomics, agronomy, breeding, crop-raising, cultivation, culture, feeding, fertilizing, gardening, geoponics, gleaning, grazing, growing, harvesting, homesteading, hydroponics, landscaping, operating, production, ranching, reaping, seeding, share-cropping, soil culture, threshing, tilling; SEE CONCEPTS 117,253,324

far-out [adj] *very unconventional*
boss*, cool*, deep*, excellent, fabulous, fantastic, groovy*, hip*, neat, nifty, rad*, sensational, strange, super, swell, trendy, unorthodox, way-out, weird, wild, wonderful; SEE CONCEPT 572

fa
fa

far-reaching [adj] *broad, widespread*
extensive, far-ranging, important, momentous, pervasive, significant, sweeping, wide; SEE CONCEPT 772

far-sighted [adj] *looking ahead wisely*
acute, canny, cautious, clairvoyant, commonsensical, cool-headed*, discerning, judicious, level-headed, perceptive, politic, prescient, provident, prudent, sagacious, sage, shrewd, well-balanced, wise; SEE CONCEPT 402

fart [n] *flatulence*
gas, vapors, wind; SEE CONCEPT 465

fart [v] *expel gas*
break wind, cut one*, cut the cheese*, pass gas, rip one*, toot; SEE CONCEPT 465

farther [adv] *at a greater distance*
beyond, further, longer, more distant, more remote, remoter, yon, yonder; SEE CONCEPTS 586,778

farthest [adv] *most distant*
extreme, farthermost, furthermost, furthest, last, lattermost, outermost, outmost, remotest, ultimate, utmost, uttermost; SEE CONCEPTS 586,778

fascinate [v] *captivate, hold spellbound*
absorb, allure, animate, arouse, attach, attract, beguile, bewitch, charm, compel, delight, draw, enamor, enchant, engage, engross, enrapture, enslave, ensnare, enthrall, entice, entrance, excite, fire, gladden, hypnotize, infatuate, interest, intoxicate, intrigue, invite, kindle, lure, mesmerize, overpower, overwhelm, pique, please, provoke, ravish, rivet, seduce, spellbind, stimulate, stir, subdue, tantalize, tempt, thrill, titillate, transfix, transport, win; SEE CONCEPTS 7,11,22

fascinated [adj] *captivated, spellbound*
absorbed, aroused, attracted, beguiled, bewitched, charmed, dazzled, delighted, enamored, enchanted, engrossed, enraptured, enthralled, enticed, entranced, excited, fond of, hypnotized, infatuated, in love with, intoxicated, mesmerized, overpowered, seduced, sent, smitten, sold on*, stuck on*, tantalized, thrilled, titillated, transfixed, transported, under a spell*; SEE CONCEPTS 32,403

fascinating [adj] *interesting, spellbinding*
alluring, appealing, attractive, bewitching, captivating, charming, compelling, delectable, delightful, enchanting, engaging, engrossing, enticing, glamorous, gripping, intriguing, irresistible, ravishing, riveting, seducing, seductive, siren; SEE CONCEPT 529

fascination [n] *strong interest*
allure, appeal, attraction, bug*, charisma, charm, enchantment, enthrallment, glamour, grabber*, hang-up*, lure, magic, magnetism, obsession, piquancy, power, pull*, sorcery, spell, thing*, thing for*, trance, witchcraft, witchery; SEE CONCEPTS 20,32,532,690

fascism [n] *political system of dictatorship*
absolutism, authoritarianism, autocracy, bureaucracy, despotism, Nazism, one-party system, party government, racism, regimentation, totalitarianism; SEE CONCEPTS 299,301,689

fascist [n] *dictator*
authoritarian, autocrat, Nazi, totalitarian, tyrant; SEE CONCEPT 354

fashion [n1] *latest style, prevailing taste*
appearance, bandwagon*, chic, configuration, convention, craze, cry, cultism, cultus, custom, cut, dernier cri, fad, faddism, figure, form, furor,
in thing*, last word*, latest*, latest thing*, line*, look, make, mode, model, mold, newest wrinkle*, pattern, rage, shape, thing*, tone, trend, usage, vogue; SEE CONCEPT 655

fashion [n2] *attitude, manner*
convention, custom, demeanor, device, etiquette, form, formality, formula, guise, method, mode, modus operandi, mores, observance, order, practice, precedent, prescription, prevalence, procedure, sort, style, system, technique, tendency, tone, trend, usage, vein, vogue, way; SEE CONCEPTS 644,657

fashion [v] *adjust, design, create*
accommodate, adapt, build, carve, construct, contrive, cook up*, cut, devise, dream up*, erect, fabricate, fit, forge, form, frame*, knock together*, make, manufacture, model, mold, plan, plot, produce, sculpture, shape, suit, tailor, throw together*, turn out*, work; SEE CONCEPTS 168,173,232

fashionable [adj] *stylish, up-to-date*
a go-go*, à la mode*, all the rage*, chic, chichi*, contemporary, current, customary, dashing, faddy*, favored, fly*, genteel, hot*, in style, in-thing*, in vogue, last word*, latest*, latest thing*, mod*, modern, modish*, natty*, new, newfangled, now, popular, prevailing, rakish, smart, swank, trendsetting, trendy, upscale*, up-to-the-minute*, usual, well-liked, with it*; SEE CONCEPTS 579,589

fast [adj1] *speedy*
accelerated, active, agile, blue streak*, breakneck*, brisk, chop-chop*, dashing, double-time*, electric, expeditious, expediting, flashing, fleet, fleeting, flying, hairtrigger*, hasty, hot, hurried, hypersonic, in a jiffy*, in nothing flat*, lickety split*, like a bat out of hell*, like all get out*, like crazy*, like mad*, nimble, on the double*, PDQ*, posthaste, presto, pronto, quick, racing, rapid, ready, screamin'*, snap*, snappy*, speedball*, supersonic, swift, velocious, winged; SEE CONCEPTS 588,799

fast [adj2] *fixed, immovable*
adherent, ardent, attached, close, constant, constrained, durable, faithful, fastened, firm, fortified, glued, held, impregnable, indelible, inextricable, lasting, loyal, permanent, resistant, resolute, secure, set, sound, stable, staunch, steadfast, stuck, sure, tenacious, tight, true, true blue*, unwavering, wedged; SEE CONCEPTS 488,542

fast [adj3] *immoral, promiscuous*
bawdy, careless, debauched, depraved, devil-may-care*, dissipated, dissolute, easy, extravagant, flirtatious, frivolous, gadabout*, giddy, incontinent, indecent, intemperate, lascivious, lecherous, lewd, libertine, libidinous, licentious, light, loose, lustful, profligate, rakish, reckless, salacious, self-gratifying, self-indulgent, sportive, sporty, unchaste, wanton, wild; SEE CONCEPT 545

fast [adv1] *speedily*
apace, chop-chop*, expeditiously, flat-out*, fleetly, full tilt*, hastily, hurriedly, in a flash*, in haste, in nothing flat*, in short order*, like a flash*, like a shot*, like greased lightning*, like wildfire*, posthaste, presto, promptly, pronto, quick, quickly, rapidly, soon, swift, swiftly; SEE CONCEPTS 588,799

fast [*adv2*] *fixedly*
deeply, firm, firmly, hard, securely, solidly, soundly, steadfastly, tight, tightly; SEE CONCEPT *488*

fast [*n*] *abstention from eating*
abstinence, diet, fasting, xerophagy; SEE CONCEPT *169*

fast [*v*] *go without food*
abstain, deny oneself, diet, famish, forbear, go hungry, not eat, refrain, starve; SEE CONCEPT *169*

fasten [*v*] *make secure; join together*
adhere, affix, anchor, attach, band, bar, batten, belt, bind, bolt, bond, brace, button, catch, cement, chain, cleave, close, cohere, connect, couple, embed, establish, fix, freeze to*, girth, glue, grip, hitch, hitch on, hold, hook, hook up, implant, infix, jam, knot, lace, leash, link, lock, lodge, make firm, moor, mortise, nail, rivet, rope, screw, seal, set, settle, solder, stay put, stick, strengthen, string, tack on, tag, tie, tighten, truss, unite, wedge, weld; SEE CONCEPTS *85,113,160*

fastener [*n*] *holder*
bolt, buckle, button, catch, clasp, fastening, latch, lock, rivet, screw, snap; SEE CONCEPT *499*

fastidious [*adj*] *very careful, meticulous*
captious, choosy, critical, dainty, demanding, difficult, discriminating, easily disgusted, exacting, finical, finicky, fussbudgety*, fussy, hard to please*, hypercritical, nice, nit-picky, overdelicate, overnice, particular, persnickety*, picky, punctilious, queasy, squeamish, stickling; SEE CONCEPTS *542,550*

fat [*adj1*] *overweight*
beefy*, big, blimp, bovine, brawny, broad, bulging, bulky, bull, burly, butterball*, chunky*, corpulent, distended, dumpy, elephantine, fleshy, gargantuan, gross, heavy, heavyset*, hefty, husky, inflated, jelly-belly*, lard, large, meaty*, obese, oversize, paunchy, plump, plumpish, ponderous, porcine, portly, potbellied, pudgy*, roly-poly*, rotund, solid, stout, swollen, thickset*, weighty, whalelike*; SEE CONCEPT *491*

fat [*adj2*] *containing an oily substance*
adipose, fatlike, fatty, greasy, oleaginous, suety, unctuous; SEE CONCEPT *485*

fat [*adj3*] *productive, rich*
affluent, cushy, fertile, flourishing, fruitful, good, lucrative, lush, profitable, prosperous, remunerative, thriving; SEE CONCEPT *334*

fat [*n*] *overweight; adipose tissue*
blubber, bulk, cellulite, corpulence, excess, fatness, flab, flesh, grease, lard, obesity, overabundance, overflow, paunch, plethora, suet, superfluity, surfeit, surplus, tallow; SEE CONCEPTS *723,734*

fatal [*adj1*] *deadly, lethal*
baleful, baneful, calamitous, cataclysmic, catastrophic, deathly, destructive, disastrous, fateful, final, ill-fated, ill-starred, incurable, inevitable, killing, malefic, malignant, mortal, mortiferous, noxious, pernicious, pestilent, pestilential, poisonous, ruinous, terminal, virulent; SEE CONCEPTS *537,539*

fatal [*adj2*] *critical, very important*
crucial, decisive, destined, determining, doomed, fateful, final, foreordained, inevitable, predestined, unlucky; SEE CONCEPTS *531,568*

fatalism [*n*] *resignation to a fate*
acceptance, destinism, determinism, necessitari-anism, passivity, predestinarianism, predestination, stoicism; SEE CONCEPT *689*

fatality [*n*] *death, loss; ability to cause such*
accident, casualty, deadliness, destructiveness, disaster, dying, inevitability, lethality, lethalness, mortality, necrosis, noxiousness, poisonousness, virulence; SEE CONCEPTS *304,675*

fat chance [*n*] *no chance*
impossible, not a prayer, no way, snowball's chance in hell*, unthinkable, very little chance, when hell freezes over*; SEE CONCEPT *552*

fat city [*n*] *paradise*
cloud nine*, hog heaven*, pig heaven*; SEE CONCEPTS *370,410,515*

fate [*n*] *predetermined course*
break, chance, circumstance, consequence, cup*, destination, destiny, divine will*, doom, effect, end, ending, fortune, future, handwriting on the wall*, horoscope, inescapableness, issue, karma, kismet, lot, luck, Moirai, nemesis, outcome, portion, predestination, providence, stars*, termination, upshot, wheel of fortune*; SEE CONCEPT *679*

fated [*adj*] *governed by fate*
decided by fate, destined, doomed, foreordained, imminent, impending, inescapable, inevitable, in the stars*, predestined, predetermined, prejudged, preordained, unavoidable; SEE CONCEPTS *548,820*

fateful [*adj1*] *significant*
acute, apocalyptic, conclusive, critical, crucial, decisive, determinative, direful, doomful, eventful, important, inauspicious, momentous, ominous, portentous, resultful; SEE CONCEPT *568*

fateful [*adj2*] *deadly*
calamitous, cataclysmic, catastrophic, destructive, disastrous, fatal, lethal, mortal, ominous, ruinous; SEE CONCEPT *537*

father [*n1*] *male person who begets children*
ancestor, begetter, dad, daddy*, forebearer, origin, pa, padre, papa, parent, pop*, predecessor, procreator, progenitor, sire, source; SEE CONCEPTS *394,400,414,419,423*

father [*n2*] *priest*
abbé, clergyman, confessor, curé, ecclesiastic, minister, padre, parson, pastor, preacher, reverend; SEE CONCEPT *361*

father/mother [*n3*] *founder, inventor*
administrator, architect, author, builder, creator, dean, elder, encourager, generator, initiator, introducer, leader, maker, matriarch, motor*, mover, organizer, originator, patriarch, patron, prime mover*, promoter, promulgator, publisher, sire, sponsor, supporter; SEE CONCEPTS *347,423*

father [*v*] *sire*
beget, conceive, create, dream up, engender, establish, found, generate, invent, originate, procreate, produce, sow the seeds of*, spawn, trigger; SEE CONCEPTS *173,239,251*

fatherland [*n*] *homeland*
home, motherland, native land, the old country; SEE CONCEPTS *510,515,648*

fathom [*v*] *discern, understand*
appreciate, apprehend, catch, cognize, comprehend, dig, divine, estimate, figure out, follow, gauge, get, get to the bottom*, grasp, have, interpret, know, measure, penetrate, perceive, pierce, pinpoint, plumb, probe, recognize, savvy, sound, unravel; SEE CONCEPTS *15,38*

fa
fa

fatigue [*n*] *tiredness*
brain fag*, burnout*, debility, dullness, enervation, ennui, exhaustion, faintness, fatigation, feebleness, heaviness, languor, lassitude, lethargy, listlessness, overtiredness, weakness, weariness; SEE CONCEPTS 316,405

fatigue [*v*] *tire, wear out*
bedraggle, burn out*, bush*, conk out*, debilitate, deplete, disable, drain, droop, drop, enervate, exhaust, fag, fizzle, flag, jade*, knock out*, languish, overtire, peter out*, poop*, poop out*, prostrate, sag, sink, succumb, take, tucker, weaken, wear down, weary; SEE CONCEPTS 137,225,240,250

fatigued [*adj*] *tired*
all in*, beat*, bedraggled, blasé, burned out*, bushed*, dead*, dead-beat*, dead-tired*, dog-tired*, dog-weary*, done in*, droopy, dropping, enervated, exhausted, fagged out*, jaded*, languid, languorous, lassitudinous, listless, out of gas*, overtired, played out*, pooped*, prostrate, ready to drop*, spent*, tuckered*, washed out*, wasted*, weary, worn, worn-out, zonked*; SEE CONCEPT 485

fatness [*n*] *overweight*
adiposity, breadth, bulkiness, corpulence, distension, flab*, flesh, fleshiness, girth, grossness, heaviness, heftiness, inflation, largeness, obesity, plumpness, portliness, protuberance, pudginess, rotundity, size, stoutness, tumidity, weight; SEE CONCEPT 734

fatten [*v*] *grow or make bigger; nourish*
augment, bloat, broaden, build up, coarsen, cram, distend, expand, feed, fill, gain weight, increase, overfeed, plump, put flesh on*, put on weight, round out, spread, stuff, swell, thicken, thrive, wax; SEE CONCEPTS 236,245,250

fatty [*adj*] *full of adipose tissue*
blubbery, fatlike, greasy, lardaceous, lardy, oily, oleaginous, rich, suety, unctuous; SEE CONCEPT 485

fatuous [*adj*] *stupid*
absurd, asinine, birdbrained*, boneheaded*, brainless*, dense, dull, foolish, idiotic, imbecile, inane, insensate, jerky*, lamebrained*, ludicrous, lunatic, mad, mindless, moronic, puerile, sappy, silly, simple, vacuous, witless; SEE CONCEPT 402

faucet [*n*] *spigot*
bibb, bibcock, hydrant, nozzle, spout, stopcock, tap, valve; SEE CONCEPTS 445,464,499

fault [*n1*] *blame, sin; mistake*
accountability, answerability, blunder, crime, culpability, defect, delinquency, dereliction, error, evil doing, failing, flaw, foible, frailty, guilt, impropriety, inaccuracy, indiscretion, infirmity, lapse, liability, loss of innocence, malfeasance, malpractice, misconduct, miscue, misdeed, misdemeanor, negligence, offense, omission, onus, oversight, peccancy, responsibility, slip, slip-up*, solecism, transgression, trespass, vice, weakness, wrong, wrongdoing; SEE CONCEPTS 101,192,699

fault [*n2*] *physical defect*
blemish, debility, deficiency, demerit, imperfection, infirmity, lack, pimple, shortcoming, weakness, weak point, zit*; SEE CONCEPT 580

fault-finding [*adj*] *critical*
captious, carping, fussy, hairsplitting*, hard to please, hypercritical, nagging, niggling, nit-picking, overcritical, pettifogging, quibbling; SEE CONCEPT 267

faultless [*adj*] *having nothing wrong with it*
above reproach, accurate, blameless, classic, clean, correct, crimeless, errorless, exemplary, exquisite, faithful, flawless, foolproof, guiltless, ideal, immaculate, impeccable, inculpable, innocent, intact, irreproachable, model, on target*, perfect, pure, right on*, sinless, spotless, stainless, supreme, textbook*, unblemished, unguilty, unspotted, unsullied, whole; SEE CONCEPTS 545,572

faulty [*adj*] *not working; incorrect*
adulterated, amiss, awry, below par, blamable, blemished, botched, broken, cracked, damaged, debased, defective, deficient, distorted, erroneous, fallacious, fallible, false, flawed, frail, impaired, imperfect, imprecise, inaccurate, inadequate, incomplete, inexact, injured, insufficient, invalid, lame, leaky, lemon, maimed, malformed, malfunctioning, marred, out of order, rank, sick, tainted, unfit, unreliable, unretentive, unsound, warped, weak, wrong; SEE CONCEPTS 560,570

faux pas [*n*] *blunder in etiquette*
blooper*, boo-boo*, breach, break, bungle, error, flop, flub*, gaffe*, goof*, impropriety, indecorum, indiscretion, mess-up, misconduct, misjudgment, misstep, mistake, oversight, solecism; SEE CONCEPTS 101,384

favor [*n*] *approval, good opinion; help*
accommodation, account, admiration, aid, approbation, assistance, backing, benediction, benefit, benevolence, benignity, bias, blessing, boon, championship, compliment, consideration, cooperation, courtesy, dispensation, encouragement, esteem, estimation, friendliness, gift, good turn*, good will*, grace, indulgence, kindness, largess, obligation, okay, partiality, patronage, present, regard, respect, service, support, token; SEE CONCEPTS 10,110,689

favor [*v1*] *pamper, reward; help*
abet, accommodate, advance, aid, assist, befriend, be partial to, do a kindness, do right by*, esteem, facilitate, further, gratify, humor, indulge, make exception, oblige, play favorites*, promote, pull strings*, show consideration, side with, smile upon*, spare, spoil, treat well, value; SEE CONCEPT 110

favor [*v2*] *prefer, like*
accept, advocate, appreciate, approbate, approve, back, be in favor of, be on one's side*, buck for*, champion, choose, commend, cotton to*, countenance, encourage, endorse, esteem, eulogize, fancy, flash on*, for, go for*, hold with, honor, incline, lean toward, look up to, opt for, patronize, pick, praise, prize, regard highly, root for, sanction, single out*, support, take a liking to*, take a shine to*, take to*, think well of, tilt toward*, value; SEE CONCEPT 32

favor [*v3*] *look like*
be the image of*, be the picture of*, feature, resemble, simulate, take after*; SEE CONCEPT 716

favorable [*adj*] *approving, friendly*
acclamatory, affirmative, agreeable, amicable, approbative, approbatory, assenting, benevolent, benign, benignant, commending, complimentary, encouraging, enthusiastic, inclined, in favor of, kind, kindly, laudatory, okay, positive, praiseful, predisposed, reassuring, recommendatory, supportive, sympathetic, understanding, welcoming,

well-disposed, well-intentioned; SEE CONCEPT *401*

favorable [*adj2*] *good, timely, advantageous*
appropriate, auspicious, benefic, beneficial, benign, bright, cheering, convenient, encouraging, fair, fit, fortunate, full of promise, gratifying, happy, healthful, helpful, hopeful, kindly, lucky, nice, opportune, pleasant, pleasing, pleasurable, pleasureful, promising, propitious, prosperous, providential, reassuring, seasonable, suitable, toward, useful, welcome, well-timed, wholesome, worthy; SEE CONCEPTS *537,558,572*

favorably [*advl*] *genially, in a kindly manner*
agreeably, amiably, approvingly, cordially, courteously, enthusiastically, fairly, generously, graciously, heartily, helpfully, positively, receptively, usefully, willingly, with approbation, with approval, without prejudice; SEE CONCEPT *401*

favorably [*adv2*] *opportunely, advantageously*
auspiciously, conveniently, fortunately, happily, profitably, prosperously, satisfyingly, successfully, swimmingly, to one's advantage, well; SEE CONCEPTS *537,558,572*

favored [*adj*] *popular*
advantaged, best-liked, blessed, chosen, elite, fair-haired*, lucky, pet*, preferred, privileged, recommended, selected, singled out, sweetheart, well-liked; SEE CONCEPTS *529,568*

favorite [*adj*] *preferred*
admired, adored, beloved, best-loved, cherished, choice, darling, dear, dearest, desired, especial, esteemed, favored, intimate, liked, main, number one*, personal, pet*, pleasant, popular, precious*, prized, revered, sweetheart*, treasured, wished-for; SEE CONCEPTS *529,568*

favorite [*n*] *something or someone cherished, prized*
apple of eye*, beloved, chalk*, choice, darling, dear, fave*, front-runner*, ideal, idol, love, main, minion, number one*, paramour, pet*, pick, preference, shoo-in*, teacher's pet*; SEE CONCEPTS *423,446*

favoritism [*n*] *bias, partiality*
discrimination, inclination, inequity, nepotism, one-sidedness, partisanship, preference, preferential treatment, unfairness; SEE CONCEPTS *41,388,645*

fawn [*n*] *baby deer*
baby buck, baby doe, yearling; SEE CONCEPTS *394,400*

fawn [*v*] *ingratiate oneself to; serve*
abase, apple-polish*, be at beck and call*, be obsequious, be servile, blandish, bow, brownnose*, buddy up*, butter up*, cajole, cater to, cave in to*, cotton*, court, cower, crawl, creep, cringe, crouch, curry favor*, debase, defer, fall all over, fall on one's knees*, flatter, grovel, honey up*, invite, jolly, kneel, kowtow*, lay it on*, lick boots*, make up to, massage*, oil*, pander, pay court*, play up to*, scrape, slaver, snow*, stoop, stroke*, submit, toady*, truckle*, woo*, yield; SEE CONCEPTS *110,384*

fawning [*adj*] *deferential, groveling*
abject, adulatory, bootlicking*, bowing, brownnosing*, compliant, cowering, crawling, cringing, flattering, humble, ingratiating, kowtowing*, mealy-mouthed*, obsequious, parasitic, prostrate, scraping, servile, slavish, sniveling, spineless, submissive, subservient, sycophant, sycophantic; SEE CONCEPT *401*

fax [*n*] *facsimile*
copy, duplicate, electronic message, reproduction, transmission; SEE CONCEPTS *269,667,716*

fax [*v*] *copy*
deliver, relay, send, transmit; SEE CONCEPTS *269,667,716*

faze [*v*] *embarrass*
abash, annoy, appall, bother, confound, confuse, daunt, discomfit, disconcert, discountenance, dismay, dumbfound, horrify, irritate, muddle, mystify, nonplus, perplex, puzzle, rattle, vex; SEE CONCEPTS *7,19*

fear [*n*] *alarm, apprehension*
abhorrence, agitation, angst, anxiety, aversion, awe, bête noire, chickenheartedness*, cold feet*, cold sweat*, concern, consternation, cowardice, creeps, despair, discomposure, dismay, disquietude, distress, doubt, dread, faintheartedness, foreboding, fright, funk*, horror, jitters, misgiving, nightmare, panic, phobia, presentiment, qualm, recreancy, reverence, revulsion, scare, suspicion, terror, timidity, trembling, tremor, trepidation, unease, uneasiness, worry; SEE CONCEPT *27*

fear [*v*] *feel alarm; be scared of*
anticipate, apprehend, avoid, be afraid, be anxious, be apprehensive, be disquieted, be frightened, be in awe, blanch, break out in a sweat*, cower, crouch, dare not, dread, expect, falter, feel concern, flinch, foresee, fret, have butterflies*, have qualms, lose courage*, quail, quaver, shrink, shudder, shun, shy, start, suspect, tremble, wilt, worry; SEE CONCEPT *27*

fearful [*adjl*] *alarmed, apprehensive*
aflutter, afraid, aghast, agitated, anxious, chicken, chickenhearted*, diffident, discomposed, disquieted, disturbed, fainthearted, frightened, goose-bumpy*, have cold feet*, hesitant, in a dither*, intimidated, jittery, jumpy, lily-livered*, mousy, nerveless, nervous, nervy, panicky, perturbed, phobic, pusillanimous, quivery, rabbity*, running scared*, scared, shaky, sheepish*, shrinking, shy, skittish, solicitous, spineless, tense, timid, timorous, tremulous, uneasy, unmanly, weak-kneed*, worried, yellow*; SEE CONCEPT *401*

fearful [*adj2*] *horrifying*
appalling, astounding, atrocious, awful, baleful, bloodcurdling, creepy, dire, distressing, dreadful, eerie, formidable, frightful, ghastly, ghoulish, grievous, grim, grisly, gruesome, hair-raising*, hideous, horrendous, horrible, horrific, lurid, macabre, monstrous, morbid, overwhelming, redoubtable, shocking, shuddersome, sinister, strange, sublime, terrible, tremendous, unearthly, unspeakable; SEE CONCEPTS *529,537,570*

fearless [*adj*] *brave, unafraid*
assured, aweless, bodacious, bold, brassy, cheeky, chesty*, cocky, confident, cool hand*, courageous, crack*, daring, dashing, dauntless, doughty, flip*, fresh*, gallant, game, gritty, gutsy, heroic, icy*, indomitable, intrepid, lionhearted, nervy, plucky, salty*, sanguine, sassy*, smart, spunky, sure, temerarious, unabashed, undaunted, unflinching, valiant, valorous, wise; SEE CONCEPT *401*

feasible [*adj*] *possible, doable*
achievable, advantageous, appropriate, attain-

able, beneficial, breeze, cinch, duck soup*, easy as pie*, expedient, fit, fitting, likely, no sweat*, performable, pie*, piece of cake*, practicable, practical, probable, profitable, pushover, realizable, reasonable, simple as ABC's*, snap, suitable, viable, workable, worthwhile; SEE CONCEPTS 528,552,558

feast [n] *banquet and celebration*
barbecue, big feed*, blow*, blowout*, carnival, carousal, clambake, dinner, entertainment, fest, festival, festivity, fete, fiesta, gala, jollification, merrymaking, picnic, refreshment, regale, repast, spread, treat, wassail; SEE CONCEPTS 377,459

feast [v] *eat a great amount or very well*
banquet, dine, eat sumptuously, entertain, gorge, gormandize, indulge, overindulge, regale, stuff, stuff one's face*, treat, wine and dine*; SEE CONCEPT 169

feat [n] *achievement*
accomplishment, act, action, adventure, attainment, conquest, consummation, coup, deed, effort, enterprise, execution, exploit, performance, stunt, tour de force, triumph, venture, victory; SEE CONCEPTS 1,706

feather [n] *tuft of bird; plumage*
calamus, crest, down, fin, fluff, fringe, penna, pinion, pinna, plume, plumule, pompon, quill, shaft, spike, wing; SEE CONCEPT 399

feature [n1] *characteristic*
affection, angle, article, aspect, attribute, character, component, constituent, detail, differential, earmark*, element, facet, factor, gag*, gimmick, hallmark, idiosyncrasy, individuality, ingredient, integrant, item, mark, notability, particularity, peculiarity, point, property, quality, savor, slant*, speciality, specialty, trait, twist*, unit, virtue; SEE CONCEPTS 831,834,835

feature [n2] *highlight, special attraction*
big show*, crowd puller*, draw, drawing card*, headliner*, innovation, main item, peculiarity, prominent part, speciality, specialty; SEE CONCEPTS 386,829

feature [n3] *special article in publication*
column, comment, item, piece, report, story; SEE CONCEPT 270

feature [v] *give prominence to*
accentuate, advertise, blaze*, call attention to, emphasize, headline*, italicize, make conspicuous, mark, play up*, point up*, present, promote, set off*, spotlight*, star, stress, underline, underscore; SEE CONCEPT 60

featureless [adj] *nondescript*
bland, characterless, faceless, forgettable, nameless, plain, stark, unadorned; SEE CONCEPTS 485,589

features [n] *facial characteristics*
appearance, countenance, face, lineaments, looks, mien, mug*, physiognomy, puss*, visage; SEE CONCEPT 418

featuring [adj] *giving prominence to*
calling attention to, displaying, drawing attention to, giving center stage to*, headlining*, highlighting, making much of*, pointing up*, presenting, promoting, pushing, recommending, showing, showing off*, starring, turning, turning the spotlight on*; SEE CONCEPT 292

febrile [adj] *feverish*
delirious, fevered, fiery, flushed, hallucinatory, hot, inflamed, pyretic; SEE CONCEPTS 314,605

feckless [adj] *without purpose*
aimless, carefree, careless, feeble, fustian, futile, good-for-nothing*, hopeless, incautious, incompetent, ineffective, ineffectual, irresponsible, meaningless, reckless, shiftless, uncareful, useless, weak, wild, worthless; SEE CONCEPTS 404, 542

fecund [adj] *productive*
breeding, fertile, fructiferous, fruitful, generating, pregnant, proliferant, prolific, propagating, reproducing, rich, spawning, teeming; SEE CONCEPT 537

federation [n] *partnership, organization*
alliance, amalgamation, association, bunch, coalition, combination, confederacy, crew, crowd, entente, family, federacy, gang, league, mob, outfit, pool, ring, syndicate, syndication, tribe, union; SEE CONCEPTS 323,381,417

fed up [adj] *disgusted with*
annoyed, blasé, blue*, bored, depressed, discontented, dismal, dissatisfied, down, gloomy, glum, jaded, sated, satiated, sick and tired*, surfeited, tired, up to here*, weary; SEE CONCEPT 403

fee [n] *charge for service or privilege*
account, ante*, bill, bite*, chunk*, commission, compensation, consideration, cost, cut*, emolument, end*, expense, gravy*, handle, hire, honorarium, house*, juice*, pay, payment, percentage, piece*, piece of the action*, price, rakeoff*, recompense, remuneration, reward, salary, share, slice*, stipend, take*, take-in*, toll, wage; SEE CONCEPTS 329,344

feeble [adj] *not strong; ineffective*
aged, ailing, chicken*, debilitated, decrepit, delicate, doddering, dopey*, effete, emasculated, enervated, enfeebled, etiolated, exhausted, failing, faint, flabby*, flat, fragile, frail, gentle, helpless, impotent, inadequate, incompetent, indecisive, ineffectual, inefficient, infirm, insubstantial, insufficient, lame, languid, low, out of gas*, paltry, poor, powerless, puny, sapless, sickly, slight, strengthless, tame, thin, unconvincing, vitiated, weak, weakened, weakly, wimpy*, woozy*, zero*; SEE CONCEPTS 267,489,527

feebleminded [adj] *mentally handicapped*
dim-witted, dull-witted, dumb, half-witted, imbecilic, moronic, retarded, simple, slow, soft in the head, stupid, unintelligent, weak-minded; SEE CONCEPTS 402,548

feebleness [n] *lack of strength; ineffectiveness*
debility, decrepitude, delicacy, disease, effeteness, enervation, etiolation, exhaustion, flimsiness, frailness, frailty, inability, inadequacy, incapacity, incompetence, ineffectualness, infirmity, infirmness, insignificance, insufficiency, lameness, languor, lassitude, malaise, senility, sickliness, unhealthiness, weakness; SEE CONCEPTS 630,676,732

feed [n] *food*
animal food, barley, corn, fodder, forage, grain, grass, grub, hay, meal, pasturage, provender, provisions, silage, straw, vittles; SEE CONCEPTS 457,460,461

feed [v] *give nourishment; augment*
banquet, bolster, cater, cram, deliver, dine, dish out*, dispense, encourage, fatten, feast, fill, find, foster, fuel, furnish, give, gorge, hand, hand over, maintain, minister, nourish, nurse, nurture, provide, provision, regale, satisfy, stock,

strengthen, stuff, supply, support, sustain, victual, wine and dine*; SEE CONCEPTS 107,140

feedback [n] *response*
answer, assessment, comeback, comment, criticism, evaluation, observation, reaction, rebuttal, reply, retaliation, sentiment; SEE CONCEPT 278

feed on [v] *consume*
devour, eat, exist on, fare, feast, graze, have a bite*, ingest, live on*, meal, munch, nibble, nurture, partake, pasture*, peck*, pig out*, prey on, scarf*, snack, sponge, subsist, take, take nourishment; SEE CONCEPT 169

feel [n] *texture; air*
ambience, atmosphere, aura, feeling, finish, impression, mood, palpation, quality, semblance, sensation, sense, surface, tactility, taction, touch, vibes; SEE CONCEPTS 611,673

feel [v1] *touch, stroke*
apperceive, caress, clasp, clutch, explore, finger, fondle, frisk, fumble, grapple, grasp, grip, grope, handle, manipulate, maul, palm, palpate, paw, perceive, pinch, ply, poke, press, run hands over*, sense, squeeze, test, thumb, tickle, try, twiddle, wield; SEE CONCEPT 612

feel [v2] *experience*
accept, acknowledge, appear, appreciate, be affected, be aware of, be excited, be impressed, be sensible of, be sensitive, be turned on to*, comprehend, discern, encounter, endure, enjoy, exhibit, get*, get in touch*, get vibes*, go through*, have, have a hunch*, have funny feeling*, have vibes*, know, meet, note, notice, observe, perceive, receive, remark, resemble, savor, see, seem, sense, suffer, suggest, take to heart*, taste, undergo, understand, welcome; SEE CONCEPTS 15,34,38

feel [v3] *believe*
assume, be convinced, be of the opinion, conclude, conjecture, consider, credit, deduce, deem, esteem, gather, guess, have a hunch*, have the impression*, hold, infer, intuit, judge, know, presume, repute, sense, suppose, surmise, suspect, think; SEE CONCEPT 12

feeling [n1] *sensation, especially of touch*
activity, awareness, consciousness, enjoyment, excitability, excitation, excitement, feel, innervation, motility, motor response, pain, perceiving, perception, pleasure, reaction, receptivity, reflex, responsiveness, sense, sensibility, sensitivity, sensuality, tactility, tangibility, titillation; SEE CONCEPT 608

feeling [n2] *idea, impression*
apprehension, belief, consciousness, conviction, eye*, hunch*, inclination, inkling, instinct, mind, notion, opinion, outlook, persuasion, point of view, presentiment, reaction, sense, sentiment, suspicion, thought, view; SEE CONCEPTS 532,689, 690

feeling [n3] *a state of mind, often strong*
action, affection, appreciation, ardor, behavior, capacity, compassion, concern, cultivation, culture, delicacy, discernment, discrimination, emotion, empathy, faculty, fervor, fondness, heat, imagination, impression, intelligence, intensity, intuition, judgment, keenness, palpability, passion, pathos, pity, reaction, refinement, sensibility, sensitivity, sentiment, sentimentality, sharpness, spirit, sympathy, tangibility, taste, tenderness, understanding, warmth; SEE CONCEPTS 409,410

feeling [n4] *ambience*
air, atmosphere, aura, impression, imprint, mood, quality, semblance; SEE CONCEPT 673

feign [v] *pretend*
act, affect, assume, bluff*, counterfeit, devise, dissemble, dissimulate, do a bit*, fabricate, fake, forge, four-flush*, give appearance of, imagine, imitate, invent, make show of*, phony up*, play, play possum*, put on, put on act*, put up a front*, sham*, simulate, stonewall*; SEE CONCEPTS 59,63,292

feigned [adj] *pretended*
affected, artificial, assumed, counterfeit, fabricated, fake, faked, false, fictitious, imaginary, imagined, imitation, insincere, phony, pretended, pseudo*, put-on*, sham*, simulated, spurious; SEE CONCEPTS 401,582

feint [n] *pretense*
artifice, bait, blind, bluff, cheat, deceit, distraction, dodge, duck, expedient, fake, gambit, hoax, hoodwinking*, imposture, make-believe, maneuver, mock attack, play, ploy, pretension, pretext, ruse, sham*, shift, snare, stall, stratagem, subterfuge, trick, wile; SEE CONCEPTS 633,660,725

feisty [adj] *spirited; touchy*
active, alive, bubbly, courageous, difficult, enthusiastic, excitable, fiery, frisky, full of pep, game, gritty, gutsy, gutty, high-strung, hot-blooded, lively, mettlesome, ornery, peppy, quarrelsome, scrappy, sensitive, spunky, thin-skinned, tough, truculent, zestful; SEE CONCEPTS 404,542

felicitate [v] *congratulate*
commend, compliment, praise, recommend, rejoice with, salute, wish joy to; SEE CONCEPT 69

felicitous [adj] *appropriate, suitable*
applicable, apposite, apropos, apt, convincing, fit, fitting, germane, happy, inspired, just, meet, neat, opportune, pat, pertinent, proper, propitious, relevant, seasonable, telling, timely, well-chosen, well-timed; SEE CONCEPTS 558,799

felicity [n1] *happiness*
bliss, cheerfulness, contentment, delight, ecstasy, elation, enjoyment, euphoria, exhilaration, exuberance, glee, good spirits, joviality, joy, jubilation, merriment, mirth, pleasure, rapture, well-being; SEE CONCEPT 410

felicity [n2] *appropriateness*
applicability, aptness, becomingness, suitability; SEE CONCEPT 558

fell [v] *chop down*
blow down, bowl over*, bring down, cause to fall, cleave, cut, cut down, dash, demolish, down, drop, flatten, floor*, gash, ground, hack, hew, knock down, knock over, lay low*, level, mangle, mow down*, prostrate, pull down, raze, rive, sever, shoot, shoot down*, slash, split, strike down, sunder, throw down, tumble; SEE CONCEPTS 176,181

fellow [n2] *male or female colleague, friend*
assistant, associate, cohort, companion, compeer, comrade, concomitant, confrere, consort, coordinate, counterpart*, coworker, double, duplicate, equal, instructor, lecturer, match, mate, member, partner, peer, professor, reciprocal, twin; SEE CONCEPTS 348,423

fellowship [n] *sociability, association*
acquaintance, affability, alliance, amity, camaraderie, club, communion, companionability, companionship, company, comradeship, convivi-

fe
fe

ality, familiarity, friendliness, guild, intimacy, kindliness, league, order, society, sodality, togetherness; SEE CONCEPTS 387,388

felon [n] criminal
con, convict, delinquent, ex-con*, jailbird*, lawbreaker, lifer*, loser*, malefactor, offender, outlaw, yardbird*; SEE CONCEPT 412

felonious [adj] criminal
base, corrupt, evil, illegal, illicit, lawbreaking, villainous, wrongful; SEE CONCEPT 545

felony [n] crime
arson, assault, burglary, criminal offense, foul play, murder, offense, rape, robbery, violation, wrongdoing; SEE CONCEPT 192

female [adj] having the qualities or characteristics of a woman
effeminate, fecund, feminine, fertile, maternal, muliebrous, womanish, womanly; SEE CONCEPTS 371,408

female [n] woman
daughter, femme, gal, gentlewoman, girl, grandmother, lady, madam, matron, Miss/Mrs./Ms., mother, she, sister; SEE CONCEPT 415

femininity/feminine [n/adj] womanly
effeminate, effete, fertile, gender, gynic, womanhood, womanish, womanliness; SEE CONCEPTS 371,372,408,648

femme fatale [n] seductress
attractive woman, dangerous woman, enchantress, enticing woman, siren, temptress, vamp; SEE CONCEPTS 361,412,415

fence [n] barrier used to enclose a piece of land
backstop, balustrade, bar, barbed wire, barricade, block, boards, chains, Cyclone, defense, dike, guard, hedge, net, paling, palisade, pickets, posts, rail, railing, rampart, roadblock, shield, stakes, stockade, stop, wall; SEE CONCEPTS 260,476,479

fence [v1] enclose or separate an area
bound, cage, circumscribe, confine, coop, corral, defend, encircle, fortify, girdle, guard, hedge, hem, immure, mew, pen, protect, rail, restrict, secure, surround, wall; SEE CONCEPT 758

fence [v2] dodge; beat around the bush
avoid, baffle, cavil, duck, equivocate, evade, feint, foil, hedge, maneuver, outwit, parry, prevaricate, quibble, shift, shirk, sidestep, stonewall*, tergiversate; SEE CONCEPTS 30,59

fend [v] defend
bulwark, cover, dodge, guard, oppose, parry, protect, repel, resist, safeguard, screen, secure, shield; SEE CONCEPT 96

fender [n] piece protecting part of a vehicle
apron, buffer, bumper, cover, curb, cushion, frame, guard, mask, mudguard*, protector, screen, shield, splashboard, ward; SEE CONCEPT 502

fend for [v] take care of
eke out existence*, look after, make do, make provision for, provide for, stay alive*, subsist, support, survive, sustain; SEE CONCEPTS 100,117

fend off [v] keep at bay
avert, avoid, beat off*, deflect, drive back*, hold at bay*, keep at a distance, keep at arm's length*, keep off, parry, rebuff, rebuke, rebut, refuse, reject, repel, repulse, resist, snub, spurn, stave off, turn aside, ward off; SEE CONCEPT 96

feral [adj] untamed
animal, brutal, ferocious, fierce, raging, savage, tameless, uncultivated, undomesticated, wild; SEE CONCEPTS 401,542

ferment [n1] substance causing chemicals to split into simpler substances
bacteria, bacterium, barm, ebullition, enzyme, fermentation agent, leaven, leavening, mold, seethe, simmer, yeast; SEE CONCEPT 478

ferment [n2] agitation, uprising
ailment, brouhaha, clamor, commotion, convulsion, disquiet, disquietude, disruption, disturbance, excitement, fever, flap, frenzy, furor, fuss, heat, hell broke loose*, hubbub, imbroglio, outcry, restiveness, restlessness, row, rumble, scene, state of unrest, stew*, stink*, stir, storm, to-do*, tumult, turbulence, turmoil, unrest, upheaval, uproar, upturn; SEE CONCEPTS 106,674

ferment [v] split into simpler substances; be agitated
acidify, be violent, boil, brew, bubble, churn, concoct, dissolve, effervesce, evaporate, excite, fester, fizz, foam, foment, froth, heat, incite, inflame, leaven, moil, overflow, provoke, ripen, rise, rouse, seethe, simmer, sour, sparkle, stir up, work; SEE CONCEPTS 7,19,22,250

ferocious [adj] violent, barbaric
barbarous, bloodthirsty, brutal, brutish, cruel, fell, feral, fierce, frightful, grim, implacable, inhuman, inhumane, lupine, merciless, murderous, pitiless, predatory, rapacious, ravening, ravenous, relentless, ruthless, sanguinary, savage, tigerish, truculent, unmerciful, unrestrained, untamed, vehement, vicious, voracious, wild, wolfish; SEE CONCEPTS 401,542

ferocity [adj] fierceness
barbarity, bloodthirstiness, brutality, cruelty, ferociousness, murderousness, savagery, viciousness, violence, wildness; SEE CONCEPTS 401,542

ferret out [v] trace, search out
ascertain, be on to, bring to light*, chase, determine, dig up*, disclose, discover, drive out, elicit, extract, follow, get at*, hunt, learn, nose out*, penetrate, pick up on, pierce, probe, pry, pursue, quest, root out*, seek, smell out*, smoke out*, track down, trail, unearth; SEE CONCEPTS 183,216

ferry [n] transportation boat
barge, ferryboat, packet, packet boat, passage boat; SEE CONCEPT 506

ferry [v] carry across
bear, buck, carry, chauffeur, convey, lug*, move across, pack, run, schlepp*, send, ship, shuttle, tote*, transport; SEE CONCEPTS 187,217

fertile [adj] ready to bear, produce
abundant, arable, bearing, black, bountiful, breeding, breedy, bringing forth, childing, fecund, feracious, flowering, flowing with milk and honey*, fruitful, generative, gravid, hebetic, loamy, lush, luxuriant, plenteous, plentiful, pregnant, procreant, producing, productive, proliferant, prolific, puberal, pubescent, rank, rich, spawning, teeming, uberous, vegetative, virile, with child*, yielding; SEE CONCEPTS 372,485

fertility [n] readiness to bear, produce
abundance, copiousness, fecundity, feracity, fruitfulness, generative capacity, gravidity, luxuriance, plentifulness, potency, pregnancy, productiveness, productivity, prolificacy, prolificity, puberty, pubescence, richness, uberty, virility; SEE CONCEPTS 372,723

fertilize [*v*] *make ready to bear, produce*

beget, breed, compost, cover, dress, enrich, fecundate, feed, fructify, generate, germinate, impregnate, inseminate, lime, make fruitful, make pregnant, manure, mulch, pollinate, procreate, propagate, top-dress, treat; SEE CONCEPTS *257,374,375*

fertilizer [*n*] *dressing to aid production of crops*

buffalo chips*, compost, cow chips*, dung, guano, humus, manure, maul*, mulch, peat moss, plant food, potash, top dressing*; SEE CONCEPTS *260,399,429*

fervent/fervid [*adj*] *enthusiastic, excited*

animated, ardent, blazing, burning, devout, dying to*, eager, earnest, ecstatic, emotional, enthused, falling all over oneself*, fiery, glowing, go great guns*, heartfelt, hearty, hot*, hot-blooded*, impassioned, intense, passionate, perfervid, pious, religious, responsive, serious, sincere, unfeigned, vehement, warm, warmhearted, wholehearted, zealous; SEE CONCEPTS *401,542*

fervor [*n*] *excitement, enthusiasm*

animation, ardency, ardor, devoutness, eagerness, earnestness, fervency, fire*, heartiness, heat*, hurrah, intensity, jazz*, love, oomph*, passion, pep talk*, piety, piousness, religiousness, seriousness, sincerity, solemnity, vehemence, warmth, weakness, wholeheartedness, zeal, zealousness; SEE CONCEPTS *633,657*

fester [*v*] *intensify; become inflamed*

aggravate, blister, canker, chafe, decay, gall, gather, irk, maturate, putrefy, rankle, rot, smolder, suppurate, ulcer, ulcerate; SEE CONCEPTS *469,698*

festival [*n*] *celebration*

anniversary, carnival, commemoration, competition, entertainment, fair, feast, festivities, fete, field day, fiesta, gala, holiday, jubilee, merrymaking, treat; SEE CONCEPT *377*

festive [*adj*] *decorated, celebratory*

blithe, bouncy, carnival, cheery, chipper*, chirpy, convivial, festal, gala, gay, gleeful, gogo*, grooving, happy, hearty, holiday, jocund, jolly, jovial, joyful, joyous, jubilant, juiced up*, jumping, lighthearted, merry, mirthful, peppy*, perky, rocking*, snappy*, swinging, upbeat, zippy*; SEE CONCEPTS *403,548*

festivity [*n*] *celebration, revelry*

amusement, bash*, blowout*, carousal*, clambake*, conviviality, do*, entertainment, festival, fun, fun and games*, gaiety, happiness, hilarity, hoopla, jamboree, jollity, joviality, joyfulness, levity, merriment, merrymaking, mirth, party, pleasure, revel, reveling, revelment, shindig*, sport, whoopee*, wingding*; SEE CONCEPTS *377,383*

festoon [*v*] *decorate*

adorn, deck, drape, garnish, hang, trim, wreath; SEE CONCEPTS *162,177*

fetch [*v*] *go get, bring in*

back, bear, be sold for, bring, bring back, bring to, buck, call for, carry, conduct, convey, deliver, draw forth, earn, elicit, escort, get, give rise to, go for, gun, heel, lead, lug*, make, obtain, pack, piggyback*, produce, realize, retrieve, ride, sell, sell for, shlep*, shoulder*, tote, transport, truck*, yield; SEE CONCEPTS *90,124,131*

fetching [*adj*] *alluring, attractive*

beautiful, captivating, charming, cute, enchanting, enticing, fascinating, intriguing, luring, pleasing, sweet, taking, tempting, winsome; SEE CONCEPTS *537,579*

fete [*n*] *celebration, party*

ball, banquet, bazaar, do*, fair, festival, fiesta, gala; SEE CONCEPT *377*

fete [*v*] *throw a party for someone*

celebrate, entertain, feast, festival, hold reception for, holiday, honor, lionize, make much of*, roll out the red carpet*, treat, wine and dine*; SEE CONCEPT *384*

fetid [*adj*] *foul, rancid*

corrupt, fusty, grody*, gross*, icky*, loathsome, lousy, malodorous, mephitic, noisome, noxious, offensive, putrid, rank, reeking, repugnant, repulsive, revolting, rotten, smelly, stenchy, stinking, stinky, strong, yecchy*, yucky*; SEE CONCEPT *598*

fetish [*n1*] *obsession*

bias, craze*, desire, fixation, golden calf*, idée fixe, leaning, luck, mania, partiality, penchant, periapt, predilection, prejudice, preoccupation, prepossession, proclivity, propensity, stimulant, thing*; SEE CONCEPTS *529,689*

fetish [*n2*] *object believed to have supernatural powers*

amulet, charm, cult object, idol, image, juju*, mascot, phylactery, superstition, talisman, voodoo doll*, zemi; SEE CONCEPTS *446,687*

fetter [*v*] *tie up, hold*

bind, chain, check, clog, confine, cuff, curb, drag feet, encumber, hamper, hamstring*, handcuff, hang up, hinder, hobble, hog-tie*, hold captive, leash, manacle, put straitjacket on*, repress, restrain, restrict, shackle, throw monkey wrench in*, trammel; SEE CONCEPTS *130,191*

fetters [*n*] *bindings; bondage*

bilboes, bonds, captivity, chains, check, cuffs, curb, handcuffs, hindrance, irons, manacles, obstruction, restraint, shackles, trammels; SEE CONCEPTS *130,191,500*

fettle [*n*] *spirits*

condition, emotional state, mental state, order, shape, sound condition, state of mind; SEE CONCEPTS *407,411*

fetus [*n*] *unborn young*

blastosphere, blastula, developing infant, embryo, fertilized egg; SEE CONCEPTS *414,424*

feud [*n*] *major argument; estrangement*

altercation, bad blood*, bickering, broil*, combat, conflict, contention, contest, controversy, disagreement, discord, dispute, dissension, enmity, faction, falling out*, fight, fracas, grudge, hostility, quarrel, rivalry, row, run-in*, squabble, strife, vendetta; SEE CONCEPTS *46,106,388*

feud [*v*] *fight bitterly; fall out*

be at daggers with*, be at odds*, bicker, brawl, clash, contend, dispute, duel, quarrel, row, squabble, war; SEE CONCEPTS *46,106*

fever [*n*] *state of high temperature or agitation*

burning up*, delirium, ecstasy, excitement, febrile disease, ferment, fervor, fire, flush, frenzy, heat, intensity, passion, pyrexia, restlessness, running a temperature*, the shakes*, turmoil, unrest; SEE CONCEPTS *410,610*

feverish [*adj1*] *having a high temperature*

above normal*, aguey, burning, burning up*, febrile, fevered, fiery, flushed, having the shakes*, hectic, hot, inflamed, on fire, pyretic, running a temperature*; SEE CONCEPT *605*

fe
fe

feverish [adj2] *excited, agitated*
burning, distracted, fervid, fevered, frantic, frenetic, frenzied, furious, heated, hectic, high-strung*, impatient, keyed up*, nervous, obsessive, overwrought, passionate, restless; SEE CONCEPT 401

few [adj] *hardly any*
exiguous, few and far between*, imperceptible, inconsequential, inconsiderable, infrequent, insufficient, lean, less, meager, middling, minor, minority, minute, negligible, not many, not too many*, occasional, paltry, petty, piddling, rare, scant, scanty, scarce, scarcely any, scattered, scattering, seldom, semioccasional, short, skimpy, slender, slight, slim, some, sparse, sporadic, stingy, straggling, thin, trifling, uncommon, infrequent, widely spaced; SEE CONCEPTS 771,789

few [prep] *scarcely any*
not many, not too many*, scattering, several, slim pickings*, small number, smatter, smattering, some, spattering, sprinkling; SEE CONCEPT 787

fiancé/fiancée [n] *person engaged to marry*
affianced person, betrothed, engaged person, future*, husband-to-be, prospective spouse, steady*, wife-to-be; SEE CONCEPTS 414,423

fiasco [n] *catastrophe*
abortion, blunder, botched situation, breakdown, debacle, disaster, dumb thing to do*, dumb trick*, embarrassment, error, failure, farce, flap, flop, mess, miscarriage, route, ruin, screwup*, stunt, washout*; SEE CONCEPT 674

fiat [n] *order, proclamation*
authorization, command, decree, dictate, dictum, edict, endorsement, mandate, ordinance, permission, precept, sanction, ukase, warrant; SEE CONCEPT 685

fib [n] *undetailed lie*
canard, crock*, equivocation, evasiveness, fabrication, fairy tale*, falsehood, falsity, fiction, invention, jazz*, line*, mendacity, misrepresentation, prevarication, spinach*, story, tale, untruth, untruthfulness, white lie*, whopper*, yarn*; SEE CONCEPTS 278,282

fib [v] *tell an undetailed lie*
concoct, create fiction, equivocate, fabricate, falsify, invent, jive*, make up, palter, plant, prevaricate, promote, shovel*, speak with forked tongue*, stretch the truth*, tell a little white lie*, trump up*; SEE CONCEPT 63

fiber [n1] *strand of material*
cilia, cord, fibril, filament, footlet, grain, grit, hair, shred, staple, string, strip, tendril, thread, tissue, tooth, vein, warp, web, woof; SEE CONCEPTS 392,428,611,831

fiber [n2] *texture*
essence, fabric, feel, hand, nap, nature, pile, spirit, substance; SEE CONCEPTS 411,682

fibrous [adj] *stringy*
coarse, fibroid, hairy, muscular, pulpy, ropy, sinewy, stalky, threadlike, tissued, veined, wiry, woody; SEE CONCEPT 606

fickle [adj] *vacillating, blowing hot and cold*
arbitrary, capricious, changeable, cheating, coquettish, double-crossing, faithless, fitful, flighty, frivolous, inconstant, irresolute, lubricious, mercurial, mutable, quicksilver, sneaking, temperamental, ticklish, two-timing, unfaithful, unpredictable, unstable, unsteady, untrue, variable, volatile, whimsical, yo-yo*; SEE CONCEPTS 401,534,545

fiction [n] *made-up story*
anecdote, best seller, book, cliff-hanger*, clothesline*, concoction, crock*, drama, fable, fabrication, falsehood, fancy, fantasy, fib, figment of imagination*, fish story*, hooey*, imagination, improvisation, invention, legend, lie, misrepresentation, myth, narrative, novel, potboiler*, prevarication, romance, smoke*, storytelling, tale, tall story*, terminological inexactitude, untruth, whopper*, work of imagination, yarn*; SEE CONCEPTS 63,271,280,282

fictitious [adj] *untrue, made-up*
apocryphal, artificial, assumed, bogus*, chimerical, concocted, cooked-up*, counterfeit, created, deceptive, delusive, delusory, dishonest, ersatz*, fabricated, factitious, fake, faked, false, fanciful, fantastic, fashioned, feigned, fictional, fictive, figmental, hyped up*, illusory, imaginary, imagined, improvised, invented, made, make-believe, misleading, mock, mythical, phony, queer, romantic, sham*, simulated, spurious, supposititious, suppositious, synthetic, trumped-up*, unreal; SEE CONCEPTS 267,582

fiddle [v] *mess with, tinker*
dabble, doodle, feel, fidget, finger, fool, handle, interfere, mess, mess around*, monkey*, play, potter, puddle, putter, tamper, touch, toy, trifle, twiddle; SEE CONCEPTS 87,291

fidelity [n1] *faithfulness in a relationship*
allegiance, ardor, attachment, constancy, dependability, devotedness, devotion, faith, fealty, integrity, loyalty, piety, reliability, staunchness, steadfastness, true-heartedness, trustworthiness; SEE CONCEPTS 32,388

fidelity [n2] *conformity to a standard*
accuracy, adherence, adhesion, attachment, closeness, constancy, correspondence, exactitude, exactness, faithfulness, loyalty, naturalism, preciseness, precision, realism, scrupulousness, verism; SEE CONCEPT 636

fidget [v] *move restlessly*
be antsy*, be hyper*, be nervous, be on pins and needles*, be spooked*, be wired*, bustle, chafe, fiddle, fret, fuss, hitch, jiggle, jitter, joggle, jump, play, squirm, stir, toss, trifle, twiddle, twitch, wiggle, worry; SEE CONCEPT 147

fidgety [adj] *restlessly moving*
antsy*, apprehensive, high-strung*, hyper*, impatient, jerky, jittery, jumpy, nervous, nervous wreck*, nervy, on edge*, on pins and needles*, restive, restless, spooked*, spooky*, twitchy, uneasy, unrestful, up the walls*, wired*; SEE CONCEPT 401

field [n1] *open land that can be cultivated*
acreage, cropland, enclosure, farmland, garden, glebe, grassland, green, ground, lea, mead, meadow, moorland, pasture, patch, plot, ranchland, range, terrain, territory, tillage, tract, vineyard; SEE CONCEPTS 509,517

field [n2] *persons taking part in competition*
applicants, candidates, competition, competitors, contestants, entrants, entries, nominees, participants, possibilities, runners; SEE CONCEPTS 325,365,417

field [n3] *sphere of influence, activity, interest, study*
area, avocation, bailiwick, bounds, calling,

champaign, circle, compass, confines, cup of tea*, demesne, department, discipline, domain, dominion, environment, job, jurisdiction, limits, line, long suit*, margin, métier, occupation, orbit, precinct, province, purview, racket, range, reach, region, scope, speciality, specialty, sweep, terrain, territory, thing, vocation, walk, weakness, work; SEE CONCEPT 349

field [n4] *arena with special use, as athletics*
amphitheater, battlefield, circuit, course, court, diamond, fairground, golf course, green, gridiron, grounds, landing strip, lot, park, playground, playing area, racecourse, race track, range, rink, stadium, terrain, theater, track, turf; SEE CONCEPTS 364,438,449

field [v] *catch a hit or thrown object*
cover, deal with, deflect, handle, hold, occupy, patrol, pick up, play, retrieve, return, stop, turn aside; SEE CONCEPT 164

field trip [n] *outing*
day trip, excursion, expedition, school outing, school trip; SEE CONCEPTS 224,386

fiend [n1] *dastardly person*
barbarian, beast, brute, degenerate, demon, devil, diablo*, evil spirit, hellion, imp, little devil*, Mephistopheles, monster, ogre, Satan, savage, serpent, troll; SEE CONCEPT 412

fiend [n2] *person overenthusiastic about interest*
addict, aficionado, bigot, devotee, enthusiast, fan, fanatic, freak, maniac, monomaniac, nut*, votarist, votary, zealot; SEE CONCEPT 423

fiendish [adj] *diabolical*
atrocious, beastly, brutish, cruel, demonic, demonical, devilish, diabolic, evil, hellish, inhuman, malicious, nefarious, sadistic, satanic, savage, vicious, wicked; SEE CONCEPT 545

fierce [adj] *violent, menacing*
angry, animal, ape, awful, barbarous, bloodthirsty, blustery, boisterous, bold, brutal, brutish, cruel, cutthroat*, dangerous, enraged, fell, feral, ferocious, fiery, flipped*, frightening, furious, horrible, howling, impetuous, infuriated, intense, malevolent, malign, murderous, passionate, powerful, primitive, raging, raving, relentless, savage, stormy, strong, tempestuous, terrible, threatening, tigerish, truculent, tumultuous/tumultuous, uncontrollable, untamed, vehement, venomous, vicious, wild; SEE CONCEPTS 525,537,540

fiercely [adv] *violently, menacingly*
angrily, awfully, boldly, brutally, ferociously, forcefully, forcibly, frantically, frenziedly, frighteningly, furiously, hard, horribly, impetuously, in a frenzy, irresistibly, like cats and dogs*, madly, maleficiently, malevolently, malignly, mightily, monstrous, no holds barred*, passionately, riotously, roughly, savagely, severely, stormily, tempestuously, terribly, threateningly, tigerishly, tooth and nail*, turbulently, uncontrollably, vehemently, venomously, viciously, wildly, with bared teeth*; SEE CONCEPTS 525,537,540

fiery [adj] *passionate; on fire*
ablaze, afire, aflame, agitable, alight, blazing, burning, choleric, combustible, conflagrant, enthusiastic, excitable, febrile, fervid, fevered, feverish, fierce, flaming, flaring, flickering, flushed, glowing, heated, hot, hot-blooded, hotheaded*, hot-tempered*, igneous, ignited, impassioned, impetuous, impulsive, inflamed, in flames, intense, irascible, irritable, madcap, pep-

---

pery, perfervid, precipitate, red-hot*, spirited, unrestrained, vehement, violent; SEE CONCEPTS 401,542,605

fiesta [n] *day of rest; religious celebration*
carnival, feast, festival, holiday, holy day, saint's day, vacation; SEE CONCEPTS 377,386

fight [n1] *physical encounter*
action, affray, altercation, argument, battle, battle royal*, bout, brawl, broil, brush, clash, combat, conflict, confrontation, contention, contest, controversy, difficulty, disagreement, dispute, dissension, dogfight, duel, engagement, exchange, feud, fisticuffs*, fracas, fray, free-for-all*, fuss, hostility, joust, match, melee, quarrel, riot, rivalry, round, row, ruckus, rumble, scrap*, scrimmage, scuffle, set-to*, skirmish, sparring match, strife, struggle, tiff, to-do*, tussle, war, wrangling; SEE CONCEPT 106

fight [n2] *courage, will to resist*
aggression, aggressiveness, attack, backbone, belligerence, boldness, combativeness, gameness, hardihood, mettle, militancy, pluck, pugnacity, resistance, spirit; SEE CONCEPT 411

fight [v1] *engage in physical encounter*
altercate, assault, attack, bandy with*, battle, bear arms, bicker, box, brawl, brush with*, buck, carry on war, challenge, clash, contend, cross swords, dispute, do battle, duel, exchange blows, feud, flare up, go to war, grapple, joust, meet, mix it up*, oppugn, ply weapons, protect, quarrel, repel, resist, rowdy, scrap, scuffle, skirmish, spar, strive, struggle, take all comers*, take the field*, take up the gauntlet*, tiff*, tilt*, traverse, tug, tussle, wage war, war, withstand, wrangle, wrestle; SEE CONCEPT 106

fight [v2] *oppose action, belief*
argue, bicker, buck*, buckle down*, carry on, combat, conduct, contest, continue, defy, dispute, effect, endure, engage in, exert oneself, fall out, force, further, hammer away*, hassle, lay into*, light into*, maintain, make a stand against*, oppose, persevere, persist, prosecute, push forward, put up an argument*, repel, resist, row, spare no effort*, squabble, stand up to*, strive, struggle, support, take on, take pains*, tangle with, toil on, travail, traverse, uphold, wage, withstand, wrangle; SEE CONCEPTS 46,100,384

fight back/fight off [v] *defend oneself*
beat off*, bottle up*, check, contain, control, curb, fend off, hold at bay*, hold back, keep at bay*, oppose, put up fight, repel, reply, repress, repulse, resist, restrain, retaliate, stave off, ward off; SEE CONCEPTS 96,106

fighter [n] *person engaged in hostile encounter*
aggressor, antagonist, assailant, battler, belligerent, boxer, brawler, bruiser*, bully, champion, combatant, competitor, contender, contestant, disputant, duelist, GI, gladiator, heavy*, jouster, mercenary, militant, opponent, person-at-arms, pugilist, punching bag*, rival, scrapper, serviceperson, slugger, soldier, tanker*, warrior, wildcat*; SEE CONCEPTS 358,366,412

fighting [adj] *aggressive, warlike*
angry, argumentative, battling, bellicose, belligerent, boxing, brawling, combative, contending, contentious, determined, disputatious, disputative, fencing, ferocious, hawkish, hostile, jingoistic, jousting, martial, militant, militaristic, pugnacious, quarrelsome, ready to fight, resolute,

fe
fi

scrappy, skirmishing, sparring, tilting, truculent, unbeatable, under arms*, up in arms*, warmongering, wrestling; SEE CONCEPT 401

fighting [n] *battle, encounter*
argument, battle royal*, beef*, bloodshed, blowup, bout, brannigan, brawling, brush, combat, conflict, contention, dispute, donnybrook*, exchange, flap*, fracas, free-for-all*, go, hassle, hell broke loose*, hostility, joust, match, melee, mix, punch out*, riot, roughhouse*, row, rowdy, rumble, rumpus, run-in*, scramble, scrap*, scrimmage, scuffle, set-to*, spat, strife, struggle, tiff, war, warfare, words, wrangle; SEE CONCEPT 106

figment [n] *creation in one's mind*
bubble*, castle in the air*, chimera, daydream, dream, fable, fabrication, falsehood, fancy, fantasy, fiction, illusion, invention, lie, nightmare, production; SEE CONCEPT 529

figurative [adj] *not literal, but symbolic*
allegorical, denotative, descriptive, emblematic, emblematical, fanciful, florid, flowery, illustrative, metaphoric, metaphorical, ornate, pictorial, poetical, representative, signifying, typical; SEE CONCEPTS 267,582

figure [n1] *numeral; numeric value*
amount, character, chiffer, cipher, cost, digit, integer, number, price, quotation, rate, sum, symbol, terms, total, worth; SEE CONCEPTS 784,787

figure [n2] *form, shape; physical structure*
anatomy, appearance, attitude, bod*, body, build, carriage, cast, chassis*, configuration, conformation, constitution, delineation, development, frame, mass, measurements, outline, physique, pose, posture, proportions, shadow, silhouette, substance, torso; SEE CONCEPTS 733,754,757

figure [n3] *object with design; depiction*
cast, composition, decoration, device, diagram, drawing, effigy, embellishment, emblem, illustration, image, model, mold, motif, motive, ornamentation, pattern, piece, portrait, representation, sketch, statue; SEE CONCEPTS 259,625

figure [n4] *famous person*
celebrity, character, dignitary, force, leader, notability, notable, personage, personality, presence, somebody, worthy; SEE CONCEPTS 354,423

figure [v1] *calculate, compute*
add, cast, cipher, count, count heads*, count noses*, cut ice*, dope out*, enumerate, estimate, fix a price, foot*, guess, keep tabs*, number, reckon, run down, sum, summate, take account of, tally, tot*, total, totalize, tote*, tot up*, work out; SEE CONCEPTS 197,764

figure [v2] *understand; decide, infer*
catch on to, cipher, clear up, comprehend, conclude, crack, decipher, decode, determine, discover, disentangle, dope out*, fathom, follow, get*, make heads or tails of*, make out*, master, opine, puzzle out, reason, resolve, rule, see, settle, solve, suppose, think, think out, unfold, unravel, unriddle, unscramble, untangle; SEE CONCEPTS 15,18,37

figurehead [n] *person who is leader in name only*
cipher, front*, mouthpiece*, nominal head, nonentity, nothing, puppet*, straw boss*, straw person, titular head, token; SEE CONCEPTS 354,423

figure in [v] *contribute to*
act, appear, be conspicuous, be featured, be in-

cluded, be mentioned, have a place in, play a part*; SEE CONCEPT 112

figure of speech [n] *communication that is not meant literally; stylistic device*
adumbration, allegory, alliteration, allusion, analogue, anaphora, anticlimax, antistrophe, antithesis, aposiopesis, apostrophe, asyndeton, bathos, comparison, conceit, echoism, ellipsis, euphemism, euphuism, exaggeration, hyperbole, image, imagery, irony, litotes, metaphor, metonymy, onomatopoeia, oxymoron, parable, paradox, parallel, personification, proteron, rhetoric, satire, simile, synecdoche, trope, tropology, turn of phrase, understatement; SEE CONCEPTS 275,278

filch [v] *steal*
cop*, crib*, embezzle, hustle*, lift*, misappropriate, pilfer*, pinch*, purloin, rip off*, rob, scrounge, sneak, snipe, snitch*, swipe, take, thieve, walk off with*; SEE CONCEPTS 139,142

file [n1] *system of order, placement for ease of use*
book, cabinet, case, census, charts, circular file*, data, directory, docket, documents, dossier, folder, index, information, list, notebook, pigeonhole*, portfolio, record, register, repository; SEE CONCEPTS 271,770

file [n2] *line, queue*
column, echelon, list, parade, rank, row, string, tier, troop; SEE CONCEPT 727

file [v1] *put in place, order*
alphabetize, arrange, catalog, catalogue, categorize, classify, deposit, docket, document, enter, index, list, pigeonhole*, record, register, slot, tabulate; SEE CONCEPTS 84,158

file [v2] *rub down, grind*
abrade, burnish, erode, finish, furbish, grate, level, polish, rasp, raze, refine, scrape, shape, sharpen, smooth; SEE CONCEPTS 137,186,215,250

filibuster [n] *obstruction of progress, especially in verbal argument*
delay, hindrance, holding the floor*, interference, opposition, postponement, procrastination, stonewalling*, talkathon*; SEE CONCEPT 298

filigree [n] *ornamental art*
fretwork, interlace, lacework, lattice, ornamentation, tracery; SEE CONCEPT 473

fill [n] *capacity*
all one wants, ample, enough, filler, padding, plenty, satiety, stuffing, sufficiency, sufficient; SEE CONCEPTS 719,736,794

fill [v1] *to put in and occupy the whole of*
block, blow up, brim over, bulge out, charge, choke, clog, close, congest, cram, crowd, distend, fulfill, furnish, glut, gorge, heap, impregnate, inflate, jam-pack, lade, load, meet, overflow, overspread, pack, pack like sardines*, permeate, pervade, plug, puff up*, pump up, ram, ram in*, replenish, sate, satiate, satisfy, saturate, shoal, stock, stopper*, store, stretch, stuff, supply, swell, take up, top, top off*; SEE CONCEPTS 107,209

fill [v2] *execute, fulfill*
answer, assign, carry out, discharge, dispatch, distribute, elect, engage, fix, hold, meet, name, occupy, officiate, perform, satisfy, take up; SEE CONCEPT 91

fill in [v1] *answer in writing*
advise, apprise, clue, complete, fill out, inform,

insert, notify, post, sign, tell, warn, write in; SEE CONCEPTS 45,79

fill in [v2] *act as substitute*
deputize, insinuate, interject, interpose, replace, represent, stand in, substract, take the place of, understudy; SEE CONCEPT 128

filling/filler [n] *something that takes up capacity*
batting, bushing, cartridge, center, content, contents, cylinder, dressing, fill, guts*, impletion, inlay, innards, inside, layer, liner, mixture, pack, packing, pad, padding, refill, replenishment, shim, stuffing, wad, wadding; SEE CONCEPTS 826,830

film [n1] *coating, tissue; mist*
blur, brume, cloud, coat, covering, dusting, fabric, foil, fold, gauze, haze, haziness, integument, layer, leaf, membrane, mistiness, nebula, obscuration, opacity, partition, pellicle, scum*, sheet, skin, transparency, veil, web; SEE CONCEPTS 478,524

film [n2] *movie*
cinema, dailies*, flick*, footage, motion picture, moving picture, photoplay, picture, picture show, rushes, show, silent*, talkie*; SEE CONCEPT 293

film [v] *take photographs*
photograph, put in the can*, record, roll, shoot, take, turn; SEE CONCEPTS 173,205

filmy [adj1] *finespun, fragile*
chiffon, cobwebby*, dainty, delicate, diaphanous, fine, fine-grained, flimsy, floaty, gauzy, gossamer, insubstantial, see-through*, sheer, tiffany, transparent, wispy; SEE CONCEPT 606

filmy [adj2] *covered with mist; blurry*
bleary, blurred, cloudy, dim, hazy, membranous, milky, misty, opalescent, opaque, pearly; SEE CONCEPTS 525,603

filter [v] *separate to refine; seep through*
clarify, clean, distill, drain, dribble, escape, exude, filtrate, leak, metastasize, ooze, osmose, penetrate, percolate, permeate, purify, refine, screen, sieve, sift, soak through, strain, trickle, winnow; SEE CONCEPTS 135,165

filth [n] *dirt, pollution*
carrion, contamination, corruption, crud*, defilement, dregs, dung, excrement, feces, feculence, filthiness, foul matter, foulness, garbage, grime, impurity, manure, mire, muck, mud, nastiness, ordure, putrefaction, putrescence, putridity, refuse, rottenness, sediment, sewage, silt, sleaze, slime, slop, sludge, slush, smut, trash, uncleanness; SEE CONCEPTS 260,674

filthy [adj1] *dirty, polluted*
begrimed, black, blackened, cruddy*, crummy*, disheveled, fecal, feculent, foul, grimy*, gross*, grubby*, grungy*, impure, loathsome, miry, mucky*, muddy, nasty, obscene, offensive, putrid, repulsive, revolting, scummy, sleazy, slimy, slipshod, sloppy, slovenly, smoky, soiled, sooty, squalid, unclean, uncleanly, unkempt, unwashed, verminous, vile, yecchy*; SEE CONCEPTS 485,570

filthy [adj2] *vulgar, obscene*
base, bawdy, blue*, coarse, contemptible, corrupt, depraved, despicable, dirty-minded*, foul, foul-mouthed, impure, indecent, lewd, licentious, low, mean, nasty, offensive, pornographic, raunchy, scatological, scurvy, smutty, suggestive, vicious, vile; SEE CONCEPTS 267,545

finagle [v] *maneuver*
cheat, contrive, deceive, manipulate, plot, scheme, swindle, trick, wheel and deal*; SEE CONCEPTS 36,59

final [adj1] *ending, last*
closing, concluding, crowning, end, eventual, finishing, hindmost, lag, last-minute, latest, latter, supreme, terminal, terminating, ultimate; SEE CONCEPTS 531,820

final [adj2] *conclusive, definitive*
absolute, decided, decisive, definite, determinate, determinative, finished, incontrovertible, irrefutable, irrevocable, settled, unanswerable, unappealable; SEE CONCEPT 535

finale [n] *ending of an event*
afterpiece, blow-off*, button*, cessation, chaser*, climax, close, closer*, conclusion, consummation, crowning glory*, culmination, denouement, end, end piece, epilogue, finis, finish, last act, payoff*, peroration, summation, swan song*, termination, windup*; SEE CONCEPT 832

finality [n] *definiteness, conclusiveness*
certitude, completeness, decidedness, decisiveness, entirety, finish, inevitableness, intactness, integrity, irrevocability, perfection, resolution, terminality, totality, unavoidability, wholeness; SEE CONCEPTS 635,638,832

finalize [v] *finish, complete action*
agree, clinch*, conclude, consummate, decide, settle, sew up*, tie up*, work out, wrap up; SEE CONCEPT 91

finally [adv1] *beyond any doubt*
assuredly, beyond recall*, beyond shadow of doubt*, certainly, completely, conclusively, convincingly, decisively, definitely, determinately, done with, enduringly, for all time*, for ever, for good*, in conclusion, inescapably, inexorably, irrevocably, lastly, once and for all*, past regret*, permanently, settled, with conviction; SEE CONCEPT 535

finally [adv2] *in the end; after period of time*
after all, after a while, already, as a sequel, at last, at length, at long last*, at the end, at the last moment, belatedly, despite delay*, eventually, in conclusion, in spite of all*, in the eleventh hour*, in the long run*, lastly, someday, sometime, sooner or later*, subsequently, tardily, ultimately, yet; SEE CONCEPT 799

finance [n] *economic affairs*
accounts, banking, business, commerce, economics, financial affairs, investment, money, money management; SEE CONCEPTS 360,770

finance [v] *offer loan money; set up in business*
back, bank, bankroll, capitalize, endow, float*, fund, go for*, grubstake*, guarantee, juice*, lay on one*, loan shark*, patronize, pay for, pick up the check*, pick up the tab*, prime the pump*, promote, provide funds, provide security, put up money, raise dough*, sponsor, stake, subsidize, support, underwrite; SEE CONCEPTS 108,115,341

finances [n] *person or corporation's money, property*
affairs, assets, balance sheet, budget, capital, cash, condition, funds, net, net worth, resources, revenue, wealth, wherewithal, worth; SEE CONCEPTS 340,710

financial [adj] *having to do with money*
banking, budgeting, business, commercial, economic, fiscal, monetary, numbers*, numeric, pecuniary, pocket; SEE CONCEPT 334

fi
fi

financier [n] *person who lends money, advises*
backer, banker, bankroller, broker, businessperson, capitalist, entrepreneur, fat cat*, grubstaker*, manipulator*, merchant, money, moneybags*, money lender, operator*, person who writes the checks*, rich person, Santa Claus*, speculator, sponsor, staker, stockbroker, tycoon, usurer; SEE CONCEPTS 347,348,353

financing [n] *money for operating expenses*
costs, expenditure, funding, loan, matching funds, outgo, outlay, payment; SEE CONCEPTS 340,344

find [n] *discovery*
acquisition, asset, bargain, boast, bonanza, catch, gem, good buy, jewel, one in a million*, pride, treasure, treasure trove; SEE CONCEPTS 337,712

find [v1] *catch sight of, lay hands on*
arrive at, bring to light*, chance upon, collar*, come across, come upon, come up with*, corral, descry, detect, dig up*, discern, discover, distinguish, encounter, espy, expose, fall in with*, ferret out, happen upon*, hit upon*, identify, lay fingers on, light upon*, locate, make out, meet, notice, observe, perceive, pinpoint, recognize, recover, run across, run into, scare up*, sight, smoke out*, spot, strike, stumble upon, track down, trip on*, turn up*, uncover, unearth; SEE CONCEPT 183

find [v2] *achieve, win*
acquire, attain, be one's lot*, earn, fall to the lot*, gain, get, meet, meet with, obtain, procure; SEE CONCEPTS 124,706

finding [n] *judgment, verdict*
award, conclusion, data, decision, decree, discovery, pronouncement, recommendation, sentence; SEE CONCEPT 685

find out [v] *discover, learn*
ascertain, catch, catch on, detect, determine, disclose, divine, expose, hear, identify, note, observe, perceive, realize, reveal, see, uncover, unearth, unmask; SEE CONCEPTS 31,183

fine [adj1] *excellent, masterly*
accomplished, aces*, admirable, attractive, beautiful, capital, choice, cool*, crack*, dandy*, elegant, enjoyable, exceptional, expensive, exquisite, fashionable, first-class, first-rate, first-string, five-star*, gilt-edged*, gnarly*, good-looking, great, handsome, lovely, magnificent, mean, neat*, not too shabby*, ornate, outstanding, pleasant, rare, refined, select, showy, skillful, smart, solid, splendid, striking, subtle, superior, supreme, top, top-notch, unreal*, well-made, wicked*; SEE CONCEPTS 528,574,579

fine [adj2] *cloudless, sunny*
balmy, bright, clarion, clear, clement, dry, fair, pleasant, rainless, undarkened; SEE CONCEPT 525

fine [adj3] *dainty, delicate; sheer*
diaphanous, ethereal, exquisite, filmy, fine-drawn, fine-grained, fine-spun, flimsy, fragile, gauzy, gossamer, gossamery, granular, impalpable, light, lightweight, little, loose, minute, porous, powdered, powdery, pulverized, quality, slender, small, thin, threadlike, transparent; SEE CONCEPTS 491,606

fine [adj4] *discriminating, exact*
abstruse, acute, clear, critical, cryptic, delicate, distinct, enigmatic, esoteric, fastidious, fine-spun, hairline, hairsplitting, intelligent, keen, minute, nice, obscure, petty, precise, pure, quick, recondite, refined, sensitive, sharp, sterling,

strict, subtle, tasteful, tenuous, trifling, unadulterated, unpolluted; SEE CONCEPT 557

fine [n] *penalty in money*
amends, amercement, assessment, damages, forfeit, mulct, punishment, reparation, rip; SEE CONCEPT 123

fine [v] *penalize in monetary way*
alienate, amerce, confiscate, dock*, exact, extort, hit with*, levy, make pay, mulct, pay through the nose*, punish, sconce, seize, sequestrate, slap with*, tax, throw book at*; SEE CONCEPTS 122,342

finery [n] *best clothing*
apparel, bib and tucker*, caparison, decoration, fancy dress, formals, frippery*, full dress, gear, regalia, splendor, suit, Sunday best* trappings, trimmings, trinkets; SEE CONCEPT 451

finesse [n] *know-how, maneuver*
acumen, adeptness, adroitness, artfulness, artifice, big stick*, bluff, cleverness, competence, con, craft, craftiness, cunning, delicacy, diplomacy, discernment, discretion, feint, gimmick, grift, guile, polish, quickness, racket*, runaround*, ruse, savoir-faire, savvy, skill, sophistication, stratagem, subtlety, tact, trick, wile; SEE CONCEPTS 409,657

finesse [v] *maneuver, manipulate*
angle, beguile, bluff, exploit, finagle*, jockey*, operate, play, play games*, pull strings*, pull wires*, rig*, wangle; SEE CONCEPTS 36,59

fine-tune [v] *make small adjustments*
adjust, calibrate, make improvements, set, tune up, tweak; SEE CONCEPTS 202,212

finger [n] *appendage of hand*
antenna*, claw, digit, extremity, feeler*, hook*, pinky*, pointer*, ring finger, tactile member, tentacle*, thumb; SEE CONCEPT 392

finger [v1] *touch lightly*
feel, fiddle, grope, handle, manipulate, maul, meddle, palpate, paw, play with, thumb, toy with; SEE CONCEPT 612

finger [v2] *choose, designate*
appoint, determine, identify, indicate, locate, make, name, nominate, pin down*, point out, specify, tap; SEE CONCEPT 41

finicky [adj] *overparticular*
choosy, critical, dainty, difficult, fastidious, finical, finicking, fussbudget*, fussy, hard to please, nice, nit-picking, overnice, persnickety*, picky, scrupulous, squeamish, stickling; SEE CONCEPTS 401,404,556

finish [n1] *conclusion; completion*
accomplishment, achievement, acquirement, acquisition, annihilation, attainment, cease, cessation, close, closing, culmination, curtain*, curtains*, death, defeat, denouement, desistance, end, ending, end of the line*, end of the road*, finale, finis, last, last stage, ruin, stop, termination, terminus, winding-up*, wind-up, wrap, wrap-up*; SEE CONCEPTS 119,832

finish [n2] *coating; perfecting*
appearance, beauty, burnish, cultivation, culture, elaboration, glaze, grace, grain, lacquer, luster, patina, perfection, polish, refinement, shine, smoothness, surface, texture, veneer; SEE CONCEPTS 611,655

finish [v1] *bring to a conclusion; get done*
accomplish, achieve, bag it*, break up, bring to a close, carry through, cease, clinch, close, complete, conclude, crown*, culminate, deal with,

determine, discharge, do, effect, end, execute, finalize, fold, fulfill, get out of the way*, halt, hang it up*, have done with*, make, make short work of*, mop up*, perfect, put finishing touches on*, round off*, round up*, scratch, scrub, settle, sew up*, shut down, shutter*, stop, terminate, top off*, ultimate, wind up*, wrap, wrap up*; SEE CONCEPTS 91,234,706

finish [*v2*] *consume, use up*
deplete, devour, dispatch, dispose of, drain, drink, eat, empty, exhaust, expend, go, run through*, spend, use, wash up*; SEE CONCEPTS 169,225

finish [*v3*] *defeat; kill*
annihilate, assassinate, best*, bring down*, carry off*, destroy, dispatch, dispose of, do in*, down, execute, exterminate, get rid of*, liquidate, overcome, overpower, put an end to, put away*, rout, rub out*, ruin, slaughter, slay, take off*, take out*, vaporize, worst*; SEE CONCEPTS 95,252

finish [*v4*] *put a coating on; perfect*
coat, develop, elaborate, face, gild, lacquer, polish, refine, smooth, stain, texture, veneer, wax; SEE CONCEPTS 172,202

finished [*adj1*] *cultivated, refined*
accomplished, all-around, classic, consummate, cultured, elegant, expert, exquisite, flawless, impeccable, many-sided, masterly, perfected, polished, professional, proficient, skilled, smooth, suave, urbane, versatile; SEE CONCEPTS 404,528

finished [*adj2*] *complete, done*
accomplished, achieved, brought about, ceased, closed, come to an end, compassed, concluded, consummated, decided, discharged, dispatched, disposed of, done for, done with, effected, effectuated, elaborated, ended, entire, executed, final, finalized, fulfilled, full, in the past, lapsed, made, over, over and done*, perfected, performed, put into effect*, realized, resolved, satisfied, settled, sewn up*, shut, stopped, terminated, through, tied up*, worked out*, wound up*, wrapped up*; SEE CONCEPTS 528,531

finished [*adj3*] *consumed, used up*
bankrupt, devastated, done, done for*, done in*, drained, empty, exhausted, gone, liquidated, lost, played out*, ruined, spent, through, undone, washed up*, wiped out*, wrecked*; SEE CONCEPTS 334,560

finite [*adj*] *subject to limitations*
bound, bounded, circumscribed, conditioned, confined, definable, definite, delimited, demarcated, determinate, exact, fixed, limited, precise, restricted, specific, terminable; SEE CONCEPTS 535,554

fink [*n*] *informer*
canary*, narc, nark, rat*, scab, snake*, snitch, squealer, stoolie, stool pigeon, tattletale, tipster, weasel, whistle-blower; SEE CONCEPTS 412,423

fire [*n1*] *burning*
blaze, bonfire, campfire, charring, coals, combustion, conflagration, devouring, element, embers, flame and smoke, flames, flare, glow, hearth, heat, holocaust, hot spot*, incandescence, inferno, luminosity, oxidation, phlogiston, pyre, rapid oxidation, scintillation, scorching, sea of flames*, searing, sparks, tinder, up in smoke*, warmth; SEE CONCEPTS 478,521

fire [*n2*] *barrage of projectiles*
attack, bombarding, bombardment, bombing, cannonade, cannonading, crossfire, explosion,

fusillade, hail, round, salvo, shelling, sniping, volley; SEE CONCEPTS 86,320

fire [*n3*] *animation, vigor*
ardor, brio, calenture, dash, drive, eagerness, élan, energy, enthusiasm, excitement, exhilaration, fervency, fervor, force, ginger*, gusto, heartiness, heat, impetuosity, intensity, life, light, liveliness, luster, passion, pep*, punch*, radiance, red heat*, scintillation, snap*, sparkle, spirit, splendor, starch, verve, vim, virtuosity, vivacity, white heat*, zeal, zing, zip; SEE CONCEPT 411

fire [*v1*] *cause to burn*
enkindle, ignite, kindle, light, put a match to*, set ablaze, set aflame, set alight, set fire to, set on fire, start a fire, touch off*; SEE CONCEPT 249

fire [*v2*] *detonate or throw a weapon*
cast, discharge, eject, explode, fling, heave, hurl, launch, let off*, loose, pitch, pull trigger, set off*, shell, shoot, toss, touch off*; SEE CONCEPTS 179,222

fire [*v3*] *excite, arouse*
animate, electrify, enliven, exalt, galvanize, heighten, impassion, incite, inflame, inform, inspire, intensify, intoxicate, irritate, provoke, quicken, rouse, stir, thrill; SEE CONCEPT 14

fire [*v4*] *dismiss from responsibility*
ax*, boot*, can*, discharge, drop, eject, expel, give bum's rush*, give marching orders*, give one notice*, give pink slip*, give the sack*, hand walking papers*, kick out*, lay off, let one go*, oust, pink slip*, sack*, terminate; SEE CONCEPTS 50,88,351

fire alarm [*n*] *smoke detector*
danger signal, emergency alarm, fire bell, heat sensor, siren, smoke alarm; SEE CONCEPTS 269,463

firearm [*n*] *gun*
handgun, heat*, musket, pistol, revolver, rifle, shotgun, weapon; SEE CONCEPT 500

firebrand [*n*] *agitator*
demonstrator, guerrilla, instigator, malcontent, protester, rabble-rouser, rebel, revolutionist, troublemaker; SEE CONCEPTS 359,412,423

firecracker [*n*] *fireworks*
bottle rockets, bursts, cherry bomb, fire flowers, illuminations, pyrotechnics, rockets, Roman candles, sparklers; SEE CONCEPT 293

fireplace [*n*] *hearth for burning wood*
bed of coals, blaze, chimney, fireside, furnace, grate, hearthside, hob, ingle, inglenook, ingleside, settle, stove; SEE CONCEPTS 440,443

fireproof [*adj*] *resistant to burning*
asbestos, concrete, fire-resistant, incombustible, noncandescent, noncombustible, nonflammable, noninflammable; SEE CONCEPT 485

fireworks [*n*] *pyrotechnic display at celebrations*
bottle rockets, bursts, firecrackers, fire flowers, illuminations, rockets, Roman candles, sparklers; SEE CONCEPT 293

firm [*adj1*] *inflexible*
close, close-grained, compact, compressed, concentrated, concrete, condensed, congealed, dense, fine-grained, hard, hardened, heavy, impenetrable, impermeable, impervious, inelastic, jelled, nonporous, refractory, rigid, set, solid, solidified, stiff, sturdy, substantial, thick, tough, unyielding; SEE CONCEPTS 604,606

fi
fi

firm [*adj2*] *stable, unmoving*
anchored, bolted, braced, cemented, closed, durable, embedded, fast, fastened, fixed, immobile, immovable, motionless, mounted, nailed, petrified, riveted, robust, rooted, screwed, secure, secured, set, settled, soldered, solid, sound, spiked, stationary, steady, strong, sturdy, substantial, taut, tenacious, tight, tightened, unfluctuating, unshakable, welded; SEE CONCEPT *488*

firm [*adj3*] *unalterable, definite*
abiding, adamant, bent, bound, consistent, constant, dead set on*, determined, enduring, established, exact, explicit, fixed, flat, going, hang tough*, inflexible, intent, never-failing, obdurate, persevering, persistent, prevailing, resolute, resolved, set, settled, specific, stable, stand pat*, stated, staunch, steadfast, steady, stipulated, strict, strong, sure, tenacious, true, unbending, unchangeable, undeviating, unflinching, unqualified, unshakable, unshaken, unwavering, unyielding; SEE CONCEPTS *267,403,542*

firm [*n*] *business*
association, bunch, company, concern, conglomerate, corporation, crew, crowd, enterprise, gang, house, megacorp, mob, multinational, organization, outfit, partnership, ring; SEE CONCEPTS *323,325*

firmament [*n*] *heaven*
empyrean, lid*, sky, the blue*, the skies, vault, welkin, wild blue yonder*; SEE CONCEPT *437*

firmly [*adv1*] *immovably*
durably, enduringly, fast, fixedly, hard, inflexibly, like a rock*, motionlessly, rigidly, securely, solid, solidly, soundly, stably, steadily, stiffly, strongly, substantially, thoroughly, tight, tightly, unflinchingly, unshakeably; SEE CONCEPTS *488,489,604*

firmly [*adv2*] *with determination*
adamantly, constantly, decisively, doggedly, indefatigably, intently, obdurately, obstinately, perseveringly, persistently, pertinaciously, purposefully, resolutely, staunchly, steadfastly, stolidly, strictly, stubbornly, tenaciously, through thick and thin*, unchangeably, unwaveringly, with heavy hand*; SEE CONCEPTS *534,542*

firmness [*n1*] *stiffness*
compactness, density, durability, fixedness, hardness, impenetrability, impermeability, imperviousness, impliability, inelasticity, inflexibility, resistance, rigidity, solidity, temper, tensile strength, toughness; SEE CONCEPTS *722,726*

firmness [*n2*] *immovability*
durability, solidity, soundness, stability, steadiness, strength, substantiality, tautness, tension, tightness; SEE CONCEPTS *731,732*

firmness [*n3*] *resolution, resolve*
constancy, decidedness, decision, determination, fixedness, fixity, inflexibility, obduracy, obstinacy, purposefulness, purposiveness, staunchness, steadfastness, strength, strictness; SEE CONCEPTS *410,633*

first [*adj1*] *earliest in order*
aboriginal, ahead, antecedent, anterior, basic, beginning, cardinal, early, elementary, first off*, front, fundamental, head, headmost, inaugural, inceptive, incipient, initial, in the beginning, introductory, key, leading, lead off*, least, number one*, numero uno*, opening, original, pioneer, premier, primary, prime, primeval, primitive, primogenial, primordial, pristine, right up front*,

rudimentary, slightest, smallest; SEE CONCEPTS *585,632,820*

first [*adj2*] *highest in importance*
advanced, A-number-1*, arch, champion, chief, dominant, eminent, first-class, first-string*, foremost, greatest, head, head of the line*, leading, main, number one*, outstanding, paramount, predominant, preeminent, premier, primary, prime, primo*, principal, ranking, ruling, sovereign, supreme, top-flight*, top of the list; SEE CONCEPT *568*

first [*adv*] *at the beginning*
at the outset, before all else, beforehand, initially, in the first place, originally, to begin with, to start with; SEE CONCEPTS *585,820*

first-class/first-rate [*adj*] *superior, excellent*
capital, choice, dandy, fine, first-string*, five-star*, in class by itself*, prime*, shipshape, sound, supreme, tiptop*, top, top-notch*, very good; SEE CONCEPT *574*

firsthand [*adj*] *direct*
eyewitness, immediate, primary, straight, straight from the horse's mouth*; SEE CONCEPT *267*

fiscal [*adj*] *monetary*
budgetary, commercial, economic, financial, money, pecuniary, pocket; SEE CONCEPT *334*

fish [*v*] *throwing bait to catch seafood*
angle, bait, bait the hook*, bob, cast, cast one's hook*, cast one's net*, chum, extract, extricate, find, go fishing, haul out*, net, produce, pull out, seine, trawl, troll; SEE CONCEPT *363*

fisherman [*n*] *angler*
clam digger, fisher, lobsterman, piscator, rodman, trawler, troller; SEE CONCEPT *423*

fish for [*v*] *look for; hint*
angle, angle for, elicit, hope for, hunt for, invite, search for, seek, solicit, try to evoke; SEE CONCEPTS *20,75*

fishing [*n*] *angling*
fly-fishing, freshwater fishing, piscary, trawling, trolling; SEE CONCEPT *363*

fishy [*adj*] *doubtful, suspicious*
ambiguous, doubtable, dubious, dubitable, equivocal, far-fetched, funny, implausible, improbable, odd, problematic, queer, questionable, shady, suspect, uncertain, unlikely; SEE CONCEPT *552*

fission [*n*] *splitting*
atomic reaction, atom smashing, dividing, division, nuclear fission, parting, severance, splitting the atom, thermonuclear reaction; SEE CONCEPT *500*

fit [*adj1*] *suitable, appropriate*
able, adapted, adequate, advantageous, apposite, apt, becoming, befitting, beneficial, capable, comely, comme il faut, competent, conformable, convenient, correct, correspondent, deserving, desirable, due, equipped, equitable, expedient, favorable, feasible, felicitous, fitted, fitting, good enough, happy, just, likely, meet, opportune, practicable, preferable, prepared, proper, qualified, ready, right, rightful, seasonable, seemly, tasteful, timely, trained, well-suited, wise, worthy; SEE CONCEPT *558*

fit [*adj2*] *healthy, in good physical shape*
able-bodied, competent, fit as a fiddle*, hale, in good condition, muscled, robust, slim, sound, strapping*, toned, trim, up to snuff*, well,

wholesome, wrapped tight*; SEE CONCEPTS 314,485

fit [*n*] *seizure; sudden emotion*
access, attack, blow, bout, burst, caprice, conniption*, convulsion, epileptic attack, frenzy, humor, jumps*, mood, outbreak, outburst, paroxysm, rage, rush, spasm, spate, spell, stroke, tantrum, throe, torrent, turn, twitch, whim, whimsy; SEE CONCEPTS 13,303

fit [*v1*] *belong, correspond*
accord, agree, answer, apply, be apposite, be apt, become, be comfortable, be consonant, befit, be in keeping, click*, concur, conform, consist, dovetail*, go, go together, go with, harmonize, have its place, interlock, join, match, meet, parallel, relate, respond, set, suit, tally; SEE CONCEPT 664

fit [*v2*] *equip*
accommodate, accoutre, arm, fix, furnish, get, implement, kit out*, make, make up, outfit, prepare, provide, ready, rig*; SEE CONCEPT 182

fit [*v3*] *adapt, change*
adjust, alter, arrange, conform, dispose, fashion, modify, place, position, quadrate, reconcile, shape, square, suit, tailor, tailor-make*; SEE CONCEPT 232

fitful [*adj*] *irregular, sporadic*
bits and pieces*, broken, capricious, catchy*, changeable, desultory, disturbed, erratic, flickering, fluctuating, haphazard, herky-jerky*, hit-or-miss*, impulsive, inconstant, intermittent, interrupted, on-again-off-again, periodic, random, recurrent, restive, restless, shifting, spasmodic, spastic*, spotty, unstable, variable; SEE CONCEPTS 482,534

fitness [*n1*] *good condition*
fettle*, good health, health, kilter*, repair, robustness, shape, strength, trim, vigor; SEE CONCEPTS 316,723

fitness [*n2*] *appropriateness*
accommodation, accordance, adaptation, adequacy, admissibility, agreeableness, applicability, appositeness, aptitude, aptness, assimilation, auspiciousness, compatibility, competence, concurrency, congeniality, congruousness, consistency, consonance, convenience, correspondence, decency, decorum, eligibility, expediency, harmony, keeping, order, patness, pertinence, preparedness, propriety, qualification, readiness, relevancy, rightness, seasonableness, seemliness, suitability, timeliness; SEE CONCEPT 656

fitted [*adj1*] *appropriate, right*
adapted, conformable, cut out for, equipped, matched, proper, qualified, suitable, suited, tailor-made*; SEE CONCEPT 558

fitted [*adj2*] *equipped*
accoutered, appointed, armed, furnished, implemented, outfitted, provided, rigged out*, set up, supplied; SEE CONCEPTS 560,589

fitting [*adj*] *appropriate, suitable*
applicable, apt, becoming, comme il faut, correct, decent, decorous, desirable, due, felicitous, happy, just, just what was ordered*, meet, on the button*, on the nose*, proper, right, right on*, seemly, that's the ticket*; SEE CONCEPT 558

fitting [*n*] *accessory*
accouterment, appointment, attachment, component, connection, convenience, equipment, extra,

furnishing, furniture, instrument, paraphernalia, part, piece, trimming, unit; SEE CONCEPT 824

fix [*n*] *difficult or ticklish situation*
box*, corner*, dilemma, embarrassment, hole*, hot water*, jam*, mess*, pickle*, plight, predicament, quandary, scrape, spot*; SEE CONCEPT 674

fix [*v1*] *establish, make firm*
affix, anchor, attach, bind, catch, cement, congeal, connect, consolidate, couple, embed, entrench, fasten, freeze to*, glue, graft, harden, implant, inculcate, infix, ingrain, install, instill, link, locate, lodge, moor, nail down*, pin, place, plant, position, rigidify, rivet, root, secure, set, settle, solidify, stabilize, stay put, steady, stick, stiffen, thicken, tie; SEE CONCEPTS 85,113,160, 201

fix [*v2*] *determine, decide*
agree on, appoint, arrange, arrive at, conclude, define, establish, limit, name, resolve, set, settle, solve, specify, work, work out; SEE CONCEPT 18

fix [*v3*] *mend, repair*
adjust, amend, correct, debug, doctor, do up*, emend, face-lift*, fiddle with, overhaul, patch, put to rights*, rebuild, recondition, reconstruct, regulate, restore, retread, revamp, revise, see to*, sort, tune up; SEE CONCEPTS 126,212

fix [*v4*] *prepare, plan ahead*
arrange, dispose, frame, prearrange, precontrive, predesign, preorder, preplan, put up, rig*, set up, stack the deck*; SEE CONCEPT 36

fix [*v5*] *focus on*
concenter, concentrate, direct, fasten, fixate, level at, put, rivet; SEE CONCEPT 623

fix [*v6*] *cook a meal*
fit, get, get ready, heat, make, make up, microwave, prepare, ready, warm, whip up*; SEE CONCEPT 170

fix [*v7*] *manipulate, influence an event*
bribe, buy, buy off, corrupt, fiddle*, have, lubricate, maneuver, pull strings*, reach, square, suborn, tamper with; SEE CONCEPTS 192,232

fix [*v8*] *wreak vengeance on*
cook someone's goose*, get*, get even, get revenge, hurt, pay back, punish, take retribution; SEE CONCEPT 86

fixate [*v*] *focus*
become attached, center on, direct, haunt, infatuate, obsess, rivet one's eyes*, zero in on; SEE CONCEPTS 17,623

fixation [*n*] *obsession*
addiction, case, complex, craze, crush, fascination, fetish, hang-up*, idée fixe, infatuation, mania, preoccupation, thing; SEE CONCEPTS 532,690

fixed [*adj1*] *permanent, steady*
anchored, attached, established, fast, firm, hitched, hooked, immobile, immotile, immovable, located, locked, made fast, nailed*, quiet, rigid, rooted, secure, set, settled, situated, solid, stable, steadfast, stiff, still, tenacious, tight; SEE CONCEPTS 488,551,583,649

fixed [*adj2*] *intent, resolute; established*
abiding, agreed, arranged, certain, changeless, circumscribed, confirmed, decided, defined, definite, definitive, determinate, enduring, firm, inalterable, inflexible, in the bag*, inveterate, level, limited, narrow, never-failing, planned, prearranged, precise, resolved, restricted, rigged, rooted, set, settled, set-up, stated, steadfast,

fi
fi

steady, still, stipulated, sure, unbending, unblinking, unchangeable, undeviating, unfaltering, unflinching, unmodifiable, unmovable, unqualified, unwavering; SEE CONCEPTS 535,554

fixed [*adj3*] *repaired*
back together, going, in order, in working order, mended, put right, rebuilt, refitted, sorted, whole; SEE CONCEPT 560

fixture [*n*] *fitting, appliance*
accessory, appendage, appurtenance, attachment, component, device, equipment; SEE CONCEPT 463

fix up [*v*] *prepare, beautify*
deck*, dress up, furnish, gussy up*, primp, provide, rehabilitate, repair, smarten, spiff*, spruce up*; SEE CONCEPTS 162,202

fizz [*v*] *bubble*
buzz, effervesce, fizzle, froth, hiss, seethe, sibilate, simmer, sparkle, sputter, whisper, whoosh; SEE CONCEPT 469

fizzle [*v*] *collapse, fall through*
abort, be a fiasco*, come to nothing*, die, end, end in defeat*, end in disappointment*, fail, fold, miscarry, misfire, miss the mark*, peter out*, wane; SEE CONCEPT 699

flabbergast [*v*] *surprise*
abash, amaze, astonish, astound, blow away*, bowl over*, confound, daze, disconcert, dumbfound, make speechless, nonplus, overcome, overwhelm, put away*, shock, stagger, stun, throw, throw for a loop*; SEE CONCEPT 42

flabby [*adj*] *baggy, fat*
drooping, enervated, flaccid, flexuous, floppy*, gone to seed*, hanging, irresilient, lax, limp, loose, out of condition*, out of shape*, pendulous, rusty, sagging, shapeless, slack, sloppy, soft, tender, toneless, unfit, yielding; SEE CONCEPTS 486,490

flaccid [*adj*] *drooping*
debilitated, emasculated, enervated, enfeebled, flabby, flimsy, inelastic, irresilient, lax, limp, loose, nerveless, quaggy, sapped, slack, soft, weak, weakened; SEE CONCEPTS 485,604

flag [*n*] *pennant, symbol*
banderole, banner, bannerol, burgee, colors, emblem, ensign, gonfalon, jack, pennon, standard, streamer; SEE CONCEPTS 284,473

flag [*v1*] *decline, fall off*
abate, deteriorate, die, droop, ebb, fade, fail, faint, languish, peter out*, pine, sag, sink, slump, succumb, taper off*, wane, weaken, weary, wilt; SEE CONCEPTS 698,699

flag [*v2*] *signal*
gesture, give a sign to, hail, indicate, motion, salute, warn, wave; SEE CONCEPT 74

flagrant [*adj*] *flaunting, blatant; without shame*
arrant, atrocious, awful, bare-faced*, bold, brazen, capital, conspicuous, crying, disgraceful, dreadful, egregious, enormous, flagitous, flaming, flashy*, glaring, grody*, gross*, hanging out*, heinous, immodest, infamous, noticeable, notorious, obvious, open, ostentatious, out-and-out*, outrageous, rank, scandalous, shameful, shameless, shocking, stick out like sore thumb*, striking, undisguised, wicked; SEE CONCEPTS 401,545,576

flagship [*n*] *leader*
bellwether, chief, crown jewel, flotilla leader, forerunner, front runner, head, lead ship, mother ship; SEE CONCEPTS 347,354

flail [*v*] *beat, strike*
bash, batter, club, flog, hit, knock, lash, maltreat, pummel, slug, smack, smash, sock, thrash, thwack, whale; SEE CONCEPTS 189,246

flair [*n*] *talent, style*
ability, accomplishment, aptitude, aptness, bent, chic, dash, elegance, faculty, feel, genius, gift, glamour, head, knack, mastery, panache, pizzazz*, presence, shine*, splash*, taste, turn, zip*; SEE CONCEPTS 630,706

flak [*n*] *complaint, criticism*
abuse, bad press*, brickbat*, censure, condemnation, disapprobation, disapproval, disparagement, fault-finding, hostility, knock*, opposition, pan*, rap*, swipe*; SEE CONCEPTS 52,278

flake [*n*] *scale, peel*
cell, disk, drop, foil, lamella, lamina, layer, leaf, membrane, pellicle, plate, scab, section, shaving, sheet, skin, slice, sliver, wafer; SEE CONCEPT 831

flake [*v*] *peel off*
blister, chip, delaminate, desquamate, drop, exfoliate, pare, scab, scale, shed, slice, sliver, trim, wear away; SEE CONCEPTS 157,469

flaky [*adj*] *eccentric*
birdy*, crazy, goofy*, half-cracked, haywire, nutty, odd, peculiar, queer, screwy, unconventional, wacky; SEE CONCEPTS 547,564

flamboyant [*adj*] *extravagant, theatrical*
baroque, bombastic, brilliant, camp, chichi*, colorful, dashing, dazzling, elaborate, exciting, flaky*, flaming, flashy, florid, gassy*, gaudy, glamorous, jazzy*, luscious, luxuriant, ornate, ostentatious, peacockish, pretentious, resplendent, rich, rococo, showy, splashy, sporty, swank*, swashbuckling*; SEE CONCEPTS 401,589

flame [*n1*] *fire*
blaze, brightness, conflagration, flare, flash, holocaust, light, rapid oxidation, wildfire; SEE CONCEPTS 478,521

flame [*n2*] *lover; passion*
affection, ardor, baby, beau, beloved, boyfriend, darling, dear, desire, enthusiasm, fervor, fire, girlfriend, heartthrob, honey, inamorata, inamorato, keenness, love, paramour, spark, steady, swain, sweetheart, sweetie, truelove; SEE CONCEPTS 32,423

flame [*n3*] *insulting e-mail message*
abusive e-mail message, abusive newsgroup message, abusive newsgroup posting, flamemail, flame war, insulting newsgroup message, insulting newsgroup posting; SEE CONCEPTS 52,54,278

flame [*v*] *burn*
blaze, coruscate, fire, flare, flare up, flash, glare, glint, glow, ignite, kindle, light, oxidize, shine; SEE CONCEPT 249

flaming [*adj1*] *burning*
ablaze, afire, aflame, alight, blazing, brilliant, conflagrant, fiery, flaring, glowing, ignited, in flames, raging, red, red-hot*; SEE CONCEPT 485

flaming [*adj2*] *very angry, vehement*
ardent, aroused, blazing, bright, burning, fervent, frenzied, hot, hot-blooded*, impassioned, intense, passionate, raging, red-hot*, scintillating, vivid, white-hot*; SEE CONCEPTS 267,403

flammable [*adj*] *easily set afire*
burnable, combustible, ignitable, incendiary, inflammable; SEE CONCEPT 485

flank [*n*] *haunch of an animate being*
ham, hand, hip, loin, pleuron, quarter, side, thigh, wing; SEE CONCEPT *392*

flap [*n1*] *winged or extended part of an object*
accessory, adjunct, appendage, apron, cover, drop, fly, fold, hanging, lapel, lobe, lug, overlap, pendant, pendulosity, ply, queue, skirt, strip, tab, tag, tail, tippet; SEE CONCEPTS *471,824*

flap [*n2*] *commotion*
agitation, banging, brouhaha, confusion, dither, fluster, flutter, fuss, lather*, panic, pother*, state*, stew*, sweat*, tizzy, to-do, tumult, turbulence, turmoil, twitter*; SEE CONCEPTS *230,674*

flap [*v*] *flutter*
agitate, beat, dangle, flail, flash, flop, hang, lop, shake, swing, swish, thrash, thresh, vibrate, wag, wave; SEE CONCEPT *149*

flare [*n*] *erupt, blow*
blaze, boil over, break out, burn, burn up, burst, dart, dazzle, explode, fire up, flash, flicker, flutter, fume, glare, glow, go off, lose control, rant, seethe, shimmer, shoot, waver; SEE CONCEPTS *13,179,249*

flare [*v2*] *spread*
broaden, grow, splay, widen; SEE CONCEPT *469*

flare-up [*n*] *sudden outbreak*
blowup, epidemic, eruption, explosion, gush, outburst, rise; SEE CONCEPT *633*

flash [*n1*] *shimmer, flicker*
beam, bedazzlement, blaze, burst, coruscation, dazzle, flame, flare, glance, glare, gleam, glimmer, glint, glisten, glitter, glow, illumination, imprint, impulse, incandescence, luster, phosphorescence, quiver, radiation, ray, reflection, scintillation, shine, spark, sparkle, streak, stream, twinkle, twinkling, vision; SEE CONCEPTS *521,624*

flash [*n2*] *instant, split second*
breathing, burst, jiffy, minute, moment, outburst, shake, show, trice, twinkling; SEE CONCEPTS *808,821*

flash [*n3*] *demonstration*
burst, display, manifestation, outburst, show, sign, splash, swank; SEE CONCEPT *261*

flash [*v1*] *shimmer, flicker*
beam, bedazzle, blaze, blink, coruscate, dazzle, flame, flare, glance, glare, gleam, glimmer, glint, glisten, glitter, glow, incandesce, light, phosphoresce, radiate, reflect, scintillate, shine, shoot out, spangle, spark, sparkle, twinkle; SEE CONCEPT *624*

flash [*v2*] *move fast and display*
bolt, brandish, dart, dash, disport, exhibit, expose, flaunt, flit, flourish, fly, parade, race, shoot, show, show off, speed, spring, streak, sweep, trot out, whistle, zoom; SEE CONCEPTS *150,261*

flashback [*n*] *remembrance*
flash from the past*, hallucination, memory, nostalgia, recall, recollection, reliving, reminiscence, thoughts of the past*, voice from the past*; SEE CONCEPTS *40,529*

flash point [*n*] *crucial moment*
breaking point, crisis, critical moment, hour of decision, moment of truth, turning point, zero hour; SEE CONCEPT *674*

flashy [*adj*] *flamboyant, in poor taste*
blatant, brazen, catchpenny*, cheap, chintzy, flaunting, florid, garish, gaudy, glaring, glittering, glittery, glitzy, jazzy*, loud, meretricious, ornate, ostentatious, showy, snazzy, sparkling,

tacky*, tasteless, tawdry, tinsel, vulgar; SEE CONCEPT *589*

flask [*n*] *small container for liquid*
alembic, ampulla, bag, beaker, bottle, canteen, carafe, caster, chalice, crock, cruel, crystal, decanter, demijohn, ewer, fiasco, flacon, flagon, flasket, glass, goblet, gourd, horn, jar, jug, noggin, phial, retort, tumbler, urn, vial; SEE CONCEPT *494*

flat [*adj1*] *level, smooth*
collapsed, complanate, decumbent, deflated, depressed, empty, even, extended, fallen, flush, horizontal, laid low, low, oblate, outstretched, pancake*, planar, planate, plane, procumbent, prone, prostrate, punctured, reclining, recumbent, splay, spread out, supine, tabular, unbroken; SEE CONCEPTS *486,490*

flat [*adj2*] *dull, lackluster to the senses*
banal, blah, bland, blind, boring, colorless, dead, dim, drab, draggy, flavorless, ho hum*, inane, innocuous, insipid, jejune, lead balloon*, lifeless, matte, monotonous, muted, pointless, prosaic, prosy, sapless, spiritless, stale, tasteless, tedious, uninteresting, unpalatable, unsavory, unseasoned, vanilla*, vapid, watery, weak, whitebread*; SEE CONCEPTS *529,537*

flat [*adj3*] *absolute, positive*
categorical, direct, downright, explicit, final, fixed, indubitable, out-and-out*, peremptory, plain, straight, unconditional, unequivocal, unmistakable, unqualified, unquestionable; SEE CONCEPT *535*

flat [*n*] *apartment*
chambers, condo, co-op*, crash pad*, floorthrough, go-down, joint*, lodging, pad*, railroad apartment, rental, room, rooms, suite, tenement, walk-up; SEE CONCEPT *516*

flat-out [*adv*] *at top speed*
all-out, all the way, at a good clip*, for all one's worth*, full blast, head over heels*, in full gallop*, lickety-split, the whole nine yards*, to the max, unrestrainedly, wide open, without reservation; SEE CONCEPTS *574,762,781*

flatten [*v*] *level out*
abrade, beat down, compress, crush, debase, deflate, depress, even out, fell, floor, flush, grade, ground, iron out, knock down, lay, lay low, mow down, plane, plaster*, prostrate, raze, roll, smash, smooth, spread out, squash, straighten, subdue, trample; SEE CONCEPTS *137,250,469,702*

flatter [*v1*] *compliment excessively*
adulate, beslaver, blandish, bootlick*, brownnose*, build up*, butter up*, cajole, cater to, charm, con, court, fawn*, get next to*, glorify, grovel, humor, inveigle, jolly, lay it on thick*, massage, oil*, overpraise, play up to*, praise, rub the right way*, salve, sell, snow*, soften*, soft-soap*, spread it on*, stroke, suck up to*, sweeten up*, sweet-talk*, toady*, wheedle, work on*, work over*; SEE CONCEPTS *59,69*

flatter [*v2*] *complement, enhance*
adorn, beautify, become, decorate, do something for*, embellish, enrich, finish, go with*, grace, ornament, perfect, put in best light*, set off, show to advantage, suit; SEE CONCEPTS *162,664*

flatterer [*n*] *complimenter*
apple polisher*, backscratcher, booster, bootlicker*, brownnose*, cajoler, charmer, fawner, flunkey, lackey, puffer*, sweet talker*, syco-

phant, teacher's pet, toady, yes-person*; SEE CONCEPTS *59,69*

flattery [*n*] *false praise, compliments*
adulation, applause, approbation, blandishment, blarney*, bootlicking*, cajolery, commendation, encomium, eulogy, eyewash*, fawning*, flattering, flummery, fulsomeness, gallantry, gratification, hokum*, honeyed words, incense, ingratiation, jive*, laud, mush*, obsequiousness, palaver, plaudits, pretty speech, puffery*, servility, smoke*, snow*, snow job*, soft-soap*, soft words, stroke*, sweet talk*, sycophancy, toadyism, tribute, truckling, unctuousness; SEE CONCEPTS *59,69*

flatulent [*adj*] *pretentious, long-winded*
bombastic, inflated, oratorical, overblown, pompous, prolix, shallow, superficial, swollen, tedious, tumescent, tumid, turgid, windy, wordy; SEE CONCEPTS *267,404*

flaunt [*v*] *make an exhibition, show off*
advertise, air, boast, brandish, break out, broadcast, declare, disclose, display, disport, divulge, expose, fan it*, flash, flash about, flourish, gasconade, grandstand*, hotdog*, let it all hang out*, make a scene*, parade, proclaim, put on an act*, reveal, roll out, show and tell, showcase, smack with*, sport, spring on*, streak, throw weight around*, trot out*, vaunt, wave around, whip out*; SEE CONCEPT *261*

flavor [*n1*] *odor and taste*
acidity, aroma, astringency, bitterness, essence, extract, gusto, hotness, piquancy, pungency, relish, saltiness, sapidity, sapor, savor, seasoning, smack, sourness, spiciness, sweetness, tang, tartness, twang, vim, wallop, zest, zing; SEE CONCEPT *614*

flavor [*n2*] *aura, essence*
aspect, character, feel, feeling, property, quality, soupçon, stamp, style, suggestion, tinge, tone, touch; SEE CONCEPT *673*

flavor [*v*] *add seasoning*
add zing, add zip, ginger, hot it up*, imbue, impart, infuse, lace, leaven, pepper, pep up*, salt, season, spice; SEE CONCEPT *170*

flavoring [*n*] *spice, extract added to food*
additive, condiment, distillation, essence, herb, quintessence, relish, sauce, seasoning, spirit, tincture, zest; SEE CONCEPT *428*

flaw [*n*] *imperfection*
blemish, bug, catch*, Catch-22*, defect, disfigurement, failing, fault, foible, glitch*, gremlin*, pitfall, slipup, speck, spot, stain, typo*, vice, wart*, weakness, weak spot; SEE CONCEPTS *580,674*

flawless [*adj*] *spotless, intact*
absolute, entire, faultless, immaculate, impeccable, irreproachable, perfect, sound, unblemished, unbroken, undamaged, unimpaired, unmarred, unsullied, whole; SEE CONCEPTS *574,579*

fleck [*n*] *spot, pinpoint mark*
bit, dot, mite, mote, patch, pinpoint, speck, speckle, stipple, streak, stripe; SEE CONCEPTS *284,831*

fleck [*v*] *mark with spots*
bespeckle, besprinkle, dapple, dot, dust, maculate, mottle, speckle, stipple, streak, variegate; SEE CONCEPT *79*

fledgling [*n*] *beginner in activity*
apprentice, chick, colt, greenhorn*, learner, neophyte, nestling, newcomer, novice, rookie, tenderfoot*, trainee, tyro*; SEE CONCEPTS *352,366,424*

flee [*v*] *run away to escape*
abscond, avoid, beat a hasty retreat*, blow*, bolt*, break, cut and run*, cut out*, decamp, depart, desert, elude, evade, fly, fly the coop*, get*, get away, get the hell out*, hotfoot*, jump, leave, make a getaway*, make off*, make oneself scarce*, make one's escape*, make quick exit*, make tracks*, retreat, scamper, scoot, scram*, skedaddle*, skip*, split*, step on it*, step on the gas*, take a hike*, take flight, take off, vamoose*, vanish; SEE CONCEPTS *102,150, 195*

fleece [*v*] *plunder, steal*
bleed*, burn*, cheat*, clip*, con, cozen, defraud, despoil, flimflam*, gouge, hustle, jerk around*, milk*, mulct, overcharge, pluck, rifle, rip off*, rob, rook*, rope in*, run a game on*, sell a bill of goods*, shaft*, strip, swindle, take for a ride*, take to the cleaners*; SEE CONCEPTS *59,139,342*

fleecy [*adj*] *downy, woolly; like a lamb's coat*
floccose, flocculent, fluffy, hairy, hirsute, lanose, pileous, pilose, shaggy, soft, whiskered; SEE CONCEPT *606*

fleet [*adj*] *quick in movement*
agile, barreling, breakneck*, brisk, expeditious, expeditive, fast, flying, hasty, in nothing flat*, like greased lightning*, lively, mercurial, meteoric, nimble, nimble-footed, on the double*, rapid, screaming, speedball*, speedy, swift, winged; SEE CONCEPTS *584,588*

fleet [*n*] *group of ships*
argosy, armada, flotilla, formation, line, naval force, navy, sea power, squadron, tonnage, vessels, warships; SEE CONCEPTS *322,432,506*

fleeting [*adj*] *brief, transient*
cursory, ephemeral, evanescent, fading, flash in the pan*, flitting, flying, fugacious, fugitive, impermanent, meteoric, momentary, passing, short, short-lived, sudden, temporary, transitory, vanishing, volatile; SEE CONCEPTS *551,798*

flesh [*n1*] *body tissue, skin*
beef, brawn, cells, corpuscles, fat, fatness, flesh and blood, food, meat, muscle, plasm, plasma, protoplasm, sinews, thews, weight; SEE CONCEPT *392*

flesh [*n2*] *humankind*
animality, carnality, homo sapiens, humanity, human nature, human race, living creatures, mortality, people, physicality, physical nature, race, sensuality, stock, world; SEE CONCEPTS *407,417*

fleshly [*adv1*] *lecherous, desiring sex*
animal, animalistic, bodily, carnal, erotic, gross, lascivious, lewd, lustful, profane, sensual, venereal, voluptuous; SEE CONCEPTS *372,529,545*

fleshly [*adv2*] *bodily*
corporal, corporeal, earthly, human, material, mundane, of this world, physical, secular, somatic, terrestrial, worldly; SEE CONCEPT *536*

fleshy [*adj*] *overweight*
adipose, ample, beefy*, brawny, chubby*, chunky*, corpulent, fat, gross, heavy, hefty, husky, meaty*, obese, plump, porcine, portly, pudgy*, pulpy, sarcous, stout, tubby*, weighty, well-padded*, zaftig*; SEE CONCEPTS *406,491, 773*

flex [*v*] *bend*
angle, contract, crook, curve, lean, mold, ply,

spring, stretch, tighten, tilt, yield; SEE CONCEPTS 147,149

flexibility [*n*] *elasticity, adaptability*
adjustability, affability, compliance, compliance, docility, extensibility, flaccidity, flexibleness, give, limberness, litheness, plasticity, pliability, pliancy, resilience, springiness, suppleness, tensility, tractability; SEE CONCEPTS 652,731

flexible [*adj1*] *pliable, bendable*
adjustable, bending, ductile, elastic, extensible, extensile, flexile, formable, formative, impressionable, like putty*, limber, lithe, malleable, moldable, plastic, pliant, soft, spongy, springy, stretch, stretchable, stretchy, supple, tensile, tractable, tractile, whippy*, willowy, yielding; SEE CONCEPTS 485,488

flexible [*adj2*] *adaptable, responsive*
acquiescent, adjustable, amenable, biddable, complaisant, compliant, discretionary, docile, gentle, going every which way*, hanging loose*, like putty in hands*, manageable, open, rolling with punches*, tractable, variable; SEE CONCEPTS 401,542

flick [*v*] *light touch*
dab, flicker, flip, hit, pat, snap, tap, tip, touch lightly; SEE CONCEPT 612

flicker [*n*] *spark, glimmer*
beam, flare, flash, gleam, oscillation, quivering, ray, scintillation, twinkle, vibration; SEE CONCEPTS 145,624,831

flicker [*v*] *sparkle, flutter*
blare, blaze, blink, burn, dance, flare, flash, flit, flitter, fluctuate, glance, gleam, glimmer, glint, glitter, glow, hover, oscillate, quaver, quiver, scintillate, shimmer, swing, tremble, twinkle, vibrate, waver; SEE CONCEPTS 152,624

flier [*n*] *flyer, pilot*
ace*, aeronaut, air person, aviator, aviatrix, jet*, navigator; SEE CONCEPT 348

flight [*n1*] *flying; journey*
aerial navigation, aeronautics, arrival, aviation, avigation, departure, gliding, hop, jump, mounting, navigation, shuttle, soaring, take-off, transport, trip, volitation, voyage, winging; SEE CONCEPT 224

flight [*n2*] *fleeing; departure*
beat*, break*, breakout, escape, escapement, escaping, exfiltration, exit, exodus, fugue, getaway, getaway car*, lam, out*, powder*, retreat, retreating, running away, slip*, spring*; SEE CONCEPTS 102,195

flightiness [*n*] *irresponsibility*
airheadedness*, capriciousness, changeability, dizziness, fickleness, flippancy, frivolity, giddiness, inconstancy, instability, levity, lightness, mercurialness, variability, volatility, whimsicality, whimsicalness; SEE CONCEPT 633

flighty [*adj*] *fickle, irresponsible*
airheaded*, birdbrained*, bubbleheaded*, capricious, changeable, dingbat*, dingdong*, dizzy*, effervescent, empty-headed, featherbrained*, frivolous, gaga*, giddy, harebrained*, impetuous, impulsive, inconstant, lightheaded, lively, mercurial, scatterbrained, silly, thoughtless, twit, unbalanced, unstable, unsteady, volatile, whimsical, wild; SEE CONCEPT 401

flimflam [*v*] *deceive, swindle*
bilk, burn*, cheat, chisel, con, defraud, diddle*, dupe*, fleece, fool, gip*, gull, gyp*, hose*, pull

a fast one*, rip off*, rook*, sandbag, scam, shaft, steal, take for a ride*, trick; SEE CONCEPTS 59,139,192

flimsy [*adj1*] *not strong; light, thin*
chiffon, cut-rate*, decrepit, defective, delicate, diaphanous, feeble, fragile, frail, gauzy, gossamer, house of cards*, inadequate, infirm, insubstantial, meager, papery, rickety, rinkydink*, shaky, shallow, sheer, slapdash*, sleazy, slight, superficial, tacky, transparent, unsound, unsubstantial, weak, wobbly; SEE CONCEPTS 489,606

flimsy [*adj2*] *unconvincing, implausible*
assailable, baseless, contemptible, controvertible, fallacious, false, feeble, frivolous, groundless, illogical, improbable, inadequate, inane, inconceivable, incredible, inept, lame, poor, puerile, superficial, thin, transparent, trifling, trivial, unbelievable, ungrounded, unpersuasive, unreasonable, unsatisfactory, unsubstantial, weak, weakly, wishful; SEE CONCEPT 267

flinch [*v*] *shy away, wince*
avoid, balk, blanch, blench, blink, cower, cringe, crouch, draw back, duck, elude, escape, eschew, evade, flee, quail, recede, recoil, retire, retreat, shirk, shrink, shun, start, swerve, withdraw; SEE CONCEPTS 102,150

fling [*n1*] *casual throw*
cast, chuck, firing, heave, hurl, launching, lob, peg, pitch, shot, slinging, toss; SEE CONCEPT 222

fling [*n2*] *unrestrained behavior*
affair, attempt, binge, celebration, crack*, essay, fun, gamble, go*, good time, indulgence, orgy, party, rampage, shot*, splurge, spree, stab*, trial, try, venture, whirl; SEE CONCEPT 386

fling [*v*] *throw with abandon*
cast, catapult, chuck*, dump, fire, heave, hurl, jerk, launch, let fly*, lob, peg*, pitch, precipitate, propel, send, shy*, sling, toss; SEE CONCEPT 222

flinty [*adj*] *stern*
cruel, firm, hard, inflexible, rigid, steely, stony, unsympathetic, unyielding; SEE CONCEPT 604

flip [*n/v*] *throw, jump with abandon*
cast, chuck, flick, jerk, pitch, snap, spin, toss, twist; SEE CONCEPTS 194,222

flip-flop [*n*] *reversal*
about-face, change, change of heart, turn-around, U-turn; SEE CONCEPTS 674,679

flip out [*v*] *lose one's cool*
blow a gasket*, blow one's mind*, blow one's stack*, blow one's top*, crack up*, fly off the handle*, freak out*, go ape*, go ballistic*, go berserk*, go crazy*, go haywire*, go nuts*, go off the deep end*, hit the ceiling*, lose control of oneself, lose it*, lose one's composure, lose one's mind, lose one's temper, wig out*; SEE CONCEPT 13

flippancy [*n*] *irreverence*
archness, cheek, cheekiness, cockiness, disrespectfulness, flightiness, freshness, frivolity, impertinence, impishness, impudence, levity, lightness, mischievousness, pertness, playfulness, roguishness, rudeness, sauciness, volatility, waggishness; SEE CONCEPT 633

flippant [*adj*] *irreverent*
brassy, breezy, cheeky*, cocky, disrespectful, flighty, flip*, fresh, frivolous, glib, impertinent, impudent, insolent, lippy*, nervy*, offhand, pert, playful, rude, sassy*, smart*, smart-alecky*, superficial; SEE CONCEPT 401

flip side [*n*] *reverse side*
back, B-side*, contraposition, opposite side, other side, other side of the fence*; SEE CONCEPT **665**

flirt [*n*] *person who makes advances*
coquette, cruiser*, heartbreaker, operator*, philanderer, player, seducer, siren, swinger, tease, trifler, vamp, vixen, wanton, wolf*; SEE CONCEPT **423**

flirt [*v*] *make advances toward someone*
banter, bat eyes at*, come hither*, come on*, coquet, dally, disport, eyeball*, fool, gam*, hit on*, lead on, linger with, make a move*, make a pass*, ogle, philander, pick up*, pitch*, proposition, tease, wink at*; SEE CONCEPTS **375,384**

flirtation [*n*] *amorous advance*
amour, coquetry, courting, cruising, dalliance, flirting, intrigue, pickup*, romance, romancing, tease, teasing, toying*, trifling*; SEE CONCEPTS **32,375,384**

flirtatious [*adj*] *provocative, teasing*
amorous, arch, come-hither*, come-on*, coquettish, coy, dallying, enticing, flirty, libidinous, spoony*, sportive; SEE CONCEPTS **401,404**

flit [*v*] *flutter, move rapidly*
dance, dart, flash, fleet, flicker, float, fly, hover, hurry, pass, run, rush, sail, scud*, skim, speed, sweep, whisk, whiz, wing, zip; SEE CONCEPT **150**

float [*v*] *lie on the surface*
be buoyant, bob, drift, glide, hang, hover, move gently, poise, rest on water, ride, sail, skim, slide, slip along, smooth along, stay afloat, swim, waft, wash; SEE CONCEPT **153**

flock [*n*] *congregation*
army, assembly, bevy, brood, cloud, collection, colony, company, convoy, crowd, crush, drift, drove, flight, gaggle, gathering, group, herd, host, legion, litter, mass, multitude, pack, progeny, rout, scores, skein, throng; SEE CONCEPTS **391,432**

flock [*v*] *congregate*
collect, converge, crowd, gather, group, herd, huddle, mass, throng, troop; SEE CONCEPTS **109,384**

flog [*v*] *whip, lash*
beat, belt, cane, castigate, chastise, ferule, flagellate, flax, flay, give the cat o'nine tails*, hide, hit, larrup, lather, leather*, paddle, scourge, spank, strike, stripe, tan one's hide*, thrash, trounce, wax*, whack, whale*, whomp, whop*; SEE CONCEPT **189**

flood [*n*] *overwhelming flow, quantity*
abundance, alluvion, bore, bounty, cataclysm, cataract, current, deluge, downpour, drencher, drift, eager, excess, flow, flux, freshet, glut, inundation, multitude, niagara, outgushing, outpouring, overflow, plenty, pour, profusion, rush, spate, stream, superabundance, superfluity, surge, surplus, tide, torrent, tsunami, wave; SEE CONCEPTS **179,524,787**

flood [*v*] *inundate or submerge*
brim over, choke, deluge, drown, engulf, fill, flow, glut, gush, immerse, overflow, oversupply, overwhelm, pour over, rush, saturate, surge, swamp, swarm, sweep, whelm; SEE CONCEPTS **179,209,740**

floor [*n*] *bottom of a room; level of a multistory building*
basement, boards, canvas, carpet, cellar, deck, downstairs, flat, flooring, ground, landing, lowest point, mat, mezzanine, nadir, rug, stage, story, tier, upstairs; SEE CONCEPT **440**

floor [*v*] *perplex, confound*
baffle, beat, bewilder, bowl over*, bring down*, bring up short*, conquer, defeat, discomfit, disconcert, down, drop, dumbfound, fell, flatten, ground, knock down, lay low*, level, nonplus, overthrow, prostrate, puzzle, stump, throw; SEE CONCEPTS **16,95**

floor it [*v*] *drive at full speed*
accelerate, barrel, gather momentum, go flat-out, nail it*, open the throttle, put the pedal to the metal*, sprint, step on it*, step on the gas; SEE CONCEPTS **234,242**

floozy [*n*] *sexually promiscuous woman*
bimbo, broad, doxy, easy make, hooker, moll, nympho, piece of tail*, prostitute, tramp, whore; SEE CONCEPTS **348,412,415,419**

flop [*n*] *miserable failure*
bomb, bust, debacle, disaster, dud*, fiasco, lemon*, loser, miscarriage, nonstarter, washout*; SEE CONCEPTS **674,699**

flop [*v1*] *fall limply, collapse*
dangle, droop, drop, flag, flap, flounder, flutter, hang, jerk, lop, quiver, sag, slump, stagger, teeter, topple, toss, totter, tumble, wave, wiggle; SEE CONCEPTS **144,181**

flop [*v2*] *fail miserably*
bomb*, close, come apart*, come to nothing*, fall flat*, fall short*, flummox, fold, founder, miscarry, misfire, wash out*; SEE CONCEPT **699**

flophouse [*n*] *cheap hotel*
fleabag, fleabox, fleahouse, fleatrap, flop joint, run-down boarding house, run-down hotel; SEE CONCEPTS **439,449,516**

floral [*adj*] *decorated with flowers*
blooming, blossoming, blossomy, botanic, decorative, dendritic, efflorescent, flower-patterned, flowery, herbaceous, sylvan, verdant; SEE CONCEPT **589**

florid [*adj1*] *very elaborate*
aureate, baroque, busy, decorative, embellished, euphuistic, figurative, flamboyant, flowery, fussy, garnished, grandiloquent, high-flown, luscious, magniloquent, ornamental, ornamented, ornate, overblown, pretentious, rhetorical, rich, sonorous; SEE CONCEPTS **267,589**

florid [*adj2*] *flushed, ruddy*
blowzy, flush, glowing, high-colored, pink, reddened, rubicund, sanguine; SEE CONCEPTS **406,618**

flotilla [*n*] *small fleet*
argosy, armada, group, navy, squadron, unit, vessels; SEE CONCEPTS **322,432,506**

flotsam [*n*] *floating debris*
cargo, castoffs, jetsam, junk, odds and ends, sea-drift, wreckage; SEE CONCEPTS **260,674**

flounce [*v*] *bounce; intermittently move*
fling, jerk, mince, nancy, prance, sashay, spring, stamp, storm, strut, swish, throw, toss; SEE CONCEPT **149**

flounder [*v*] *struggle; be in the dark*
blunder, bobble, cast about, come apart at the seams*, drop the ball*, fall down, flop, flummox, foul up*, fumble, go at backwards*, go to pieces*, grope, labor, lurch, make a mess of, miss one's cue*, muddle, plunge, pratfall*, screw up*, slip up*, snafu*, strive, stub one's toe*, stumble, thrash, toil, toss, travail, trip up*, tumble, wallow, work at; SEE CONCEPTS **101,699**

flourish [*n*] *curlicue, decoration*
curl, embellishment, furbelow, garnish, ornamentation, plume, quirk, spiral, sweep, twist; SEE CONCEPTS 259,284

flourish [*v*] *grow, prosper*
amplify, arrive, augment, batten, bear fruit, be on top of heap*, blossom, boom, burgeon, come along, develop, do well, expand, flower, get ahead, get on*, go, go great guns*, hit it big*, increase, live high on hog*, make out*, multiply, score, succeed, thrive, wax; SEE CONCEPTS 141,704,706

flourish [*v2*] *wave about*
brandish, display, flaunt, flutter, shake, sweep, swing, swish, twirl, vaunt, wag, wield; SEE CONCEPTS 147,152

flourishing [*adj*] *prospering, going well*
blooming, burgeoning, doing well, expanding, exuberant, going strong, growing, in full swing*, in the pink*, in top form*, lush, luxuriant, mushrooming, profuse, prosperous, rampant, rank, rich, roaring, robust, successful, thriving, vigorous; SEE CONCEPT 528

flout [*v*] *show contempt for*
affront, defy, deride, disregard, gibe, gird, insult, jeer, laugh at, mock, outrage, quip, repudiate, ridicule, scoff, scorn, slight, sneer, spurn, taunt, thumb nose at*; SEE CONCEPT 54

flow [*n*] *issue, abundance*
breeze, continuance, continuation, continuity, course, current, deluge, discharge, draft, draw, dribble, drift, ebb, effusion, electricity, emanation, flood, flux, gush, juice, leak, movement, oozing, outflow, outpouring, plenty, plethora, progress, progression, river, run, sequence, series, spate, spout, spurt, stream, succession, tide, train, wind; SEE CONCEPTS 146,179,467,787

flow [*v*] *issue, surge, run out*
abound, arise, brim, cascade, circulate, continue, course, deluge, discharge, disembogue, dribble, ebb, emanate, emerge, emit, exudate, exude, flood, glide, gurgle, gush, inundate, jet, leak, move, ooze, overflow, pass, percolate, pour, proceed, progress, pullulate, regurgitate, result, ripple, roll, rush, slide, sluice, smooth along, spew, spill, splash, spring, spurt, sputter, squirt, stream, sweep, swell, swirl, teem, trickle, tumble, void, well forth; SEE CONCEPTS 146,179

flowchart [*n*] *sequential diagram*
flow diagram, flow sheet; SEE CONCEPTS 625,660

flower [*n1*] *bloom of a plant*
annual, blossom, bud, cluster, efflorescence, floret, floweret, head, herb, inflorescence, perennial, pompon, posy, shoot, spike, spray, vine; SEE CONCEPTS 425,428

flower [*n2*] *best, choicest part*
cream, elite, finest point, freshness, greatest point, height, pick, pride, prime, prize, top; SEE CONCEPTS 668,829

flower [*v*] *bloom, flourish*
batten, blossom, blow, burgeon, effloresce, mature, open, outbloom, prosper, thrive, unfold; SEE CONCEPTS 253,704

flowery [*adj*] *ornate, especially referring to speech or writing*
aureate, baroque, bombastic, declamatory, diffuse, embellished, euphemistic, euphuistic, fancy, figurative, florid, grandiloquent, highflown, magniloquent, ornamented, overwrought, prolix, purple, redundant, rhetorical, rococo,

sonorous, swollen, verbose, windy, wordy; SEE CONCEPTS 267,589

flowing [*adj*] *gushing, abounding*
brimming, continuous, cursive, easy, falling, flooded, fluent, fluid, fluidic, full, issuing, liquefied, liquid, overrun, pouring out, prolific, rich, rippling, rolling, running, rushing, sinuous, smooth, spouting, streaming, sweeping, teeming, tidal, unbroken, uninterrupted; SEE CONCEPTS 482,584

fluctuate [*v*] *vacillate, change*
alter, alternate, be undecided, blow hot and cold*, ebb and flow, flutter, go up and down*, hem and haw*, hesitate, oscillate, rise and fall*, seesaw*, shift, swing, undulate, vary, veer, vibrate, wave, waver, yo-yo*; SEE CONCEPTS 13,469,697

flue [*n*] *pipe*
channel, chimney, duct, exhaust pipe, passage, smoke duct, tube, vent; SEE CONCEPT 440

fluent [*adj*] *articulate*
chatty, cogent, copious, cursive, declamatory, disputatious, easy, effortless, effusive, eloquent, facile, flowing, garrulous, glib, liquid, loquacious, mellifluent, mellifluous, natural, persuasive, prompt, quick, ready, running, silver-tongued*, smooth, smooth-spoken, talkative, verbose, vocal, voluble, well-versed, wordy; SEE CONCEPTS 267,584

fluff [*n1*] *down*
eiderdown, feathers, fleece, floss, fuzz, lint, wool; SEE CONCEPT 606

fluff [*n2*] *mistake*
blooper*, bungling, error, false step, flub*, fumble, miscalculation, miscue, miss, muddle, muff, oversight, slip, slipup*, stumble; SEE CONCEPTS 101,230,410

fluffy [*adj*] *soft, furry*
creamy, downy, featherlike, feathery, fleecy, flocculent, flossy, gossamer, linty, pile, silky, velutinous; SEE CONCEPT 606

fluid [*adj1*] *liquid*
aqueous, flowing, fluent, in solution, juicy, liquefied, lymphatic, melted, molten, running, runny, serous, uncongealed, watery; SEE CONCEPTS 603,757

fluid [*adj2*] *adaptable, changeable*
adjustable, changeful, flexible, floating, fluctuating, indefinite, malleable, mercurial, mobile, mutable, protean, shifting, unsettled, unstable, unsteady, variable; SEE CONCEPTS 534,542

fluid [*n*] *liquid*
agua, broth, chaser, cooler, goo*, goop*, juice, liquor, solution, vapor; SEE CONCEPT 467

fluke [*n*] *chance occurrence*
accident, blessing, break, contingency, fortuity, fortunate, fortune, good fortune*, good luck, incident, lucky break*, odd chance, quirk, stroke of luck*, windfall; SEE CONCEPTS 4,679,693

fluky [*adj*] *chance*
accidental, casual, chancy, coincidental, contingent, fortuitous, incalculable, incidental, lucky, odd, uncertain, variable; SEE CONCEPT 552

flume [*n*] *chute*
channel, conduit, run, sluice, spillway; SEE CONCEPTS 501,514

flurry [*n*] *commotion, burst*
ado, agitation, brouhaha, bustle, confusion, disturbance, excitement, ferment, flap*, flaw, fluster, flutter, furor, fuss, gust, haste, hurry,

fl
fl

flurry [*v*] *agitate, confuse*
bewilder, bother, bustle, discombobulate*, discompose, disconcert, disquiet, distract, disturb, excite, fluster, flutter, frustrate, fuss, galvanize, hassle, hurry, hustle, perplex, perturb, provoke, quicken, rattle, ruffle, stimulate, unhinge, unsettle, upset; SEE CONCEPTS *7,19*

flush [*adj*] *flat*
even, horizontal, level, planate, plane, smooth, square, true; SEE CONCEPTS *486,490*

flush [*adj2*] *overflowing, abundant*
affluent, close, full, generous, lavish, liberal, opulent, prodigal, rich, wealthy, well-off; SEE CONCEPTS *334,771*

flush [*n*] *blush*
bloom, color, freshness, glow, pinkness, redness, rosiness, ruddiness; SEE CONCEPT *622*

flush [*v1*] *become or make pink or red*
blush, burn, color, color up, crimson, flame, glow, go red, mantle, pink, pinken, redden, rose, rouge, suffuse; SEE CONCEPTS *250,469*

flush [*v2*] *inundate with liquid*
cleanse, douche, drench, eject, expel, flood, hose, rinse, swab, wash; SEE CONCEPTS *165,179*

flushed [*adj*] *pink, glowing*
ablaze, animated, aroused, blushing, burning, crimson, elated, embarrassed, enthused, exhilarated, feverish, florid, full-blooded, high, hot, inspired, intoxicated, red, rosy, rubicund, ruddy, sanguine, thrilled; SEE CONCEPTS *401,403,618*

fluster [*n*] *perturbation, upset*
agitation, brouhaha, commotion, disturbance, dither, flap*, flurry, flutter, furor, ruffle, state*, to-do*, turmoil; SEE CONCEPT *410*

fluster [*v*] *upset, perturb*
addle, agitate, bewilder, bother, confound, confuse, craze*, discombobulate*, discompose, disquiet, distract, disturb, excite, flip*, flurry, frustrate, fuddle*, get to*, hassle, heat*, hurry, make nervous, make waves*, muddle, mystify, nonplus, perplex, psych*, puzzle, rattle, ruffle, spook*, stir up*, throw off balance*, unhinge*, work up*; SEE CONCEPTS *7,16,19*

flutter [*v*] *wave rapidly, flap*
agitate, bat, beat, dance, drift, flicker, flit, flitter, flop, fluctuate, hover, lop, oscillate, palpitate, pulsate, quaver, quiver, ripple, ruffle, shake, shiver, swing, throb, tremble, vibrate, wiggle, wobble; SEE CONCEPTS *150,152*

flux [*n*] *state of constant change*
alteration, change, flow, fluctuation, fluidity, instability, modification, motion, mutability, mutation, transition, unrest; SEE CONCEPT *697*

fly [*v1*] *take to the air, usually employing wings*
aviate, barnstorm*, bend the throttle*, buzz*, circle, circumnavigate, climb, control, cross, dart, dash, dive, drift, flat-hat*, fleet, flit, float, flutter, glide, hop, hover, hurry, jet, jet out, jet over, maneuver, mount, operate, pilot, reach, remain aloft, rush, sail, scud*, seagull*, shoot, skim, skirt, sky out*, soar, speed, swoop, take a hop*, take flight, take off, take wing, travel, whisk*, whiz*, whoosh*, wing*, wing in*, zip*, zoom*; SEE CONCEPTS *148,150,224*

fly [*v2*] *run or pass swiftly*
barrel, bolt, breeze, career, dart, dash, elapse, flee, flit, glide, go like the wind*, hasten, hurry, hustle, make off*, pass, race, roll, run its course*, rush, scamper, scoot, shoot, slip away*, speed, sprint, tear, whiz*, zoom*; SEE CONCEPTS *150,818*

fly [*v3*] *escape, flee*
abscond, avoid, bolt, break, clear, clear out*, cut and run*, decamp, disappear, get away, hasten away, hide, hightail*, light out*, make a getaway*, make a quick exit*, make off, run*, run for it, run from, skedaddle*, skip, steal away, take flight, take off, withdraw; SEE CONCEPTS *102,195*

fly-by-night [*adj*] *undependable*
brief, cowboy*, dubious, here-today-gone-tomorrow*, impermanent, questionable, shady, shifty, short-lived, slimy*, slippery*, treacherous, trustless, unreliable, unsure, untrustworthy; SEE CONCEPTS *542,551*

flyer [*n*] *person who navigates an aircraft*
ace*, air person, aviator, flier, jet*, navigator, pilot; SEE CONCEPT *348*

flying [*adj*] *in the air, winged*
aerial, aeronautical, airborne, avian, drifting, express, flapping, fleet, floating, fluttering, gliding, hovering, mercurial, mobile, on the wing, plumed, soaring, speedy, streaming, swooping, volant, volar, volitant, waving, winging, zooming; SEE CONCEPT *584*

flying saucer [*n*] *spaceship*
extraterrestrial vessel, spacecraft, UFO, unidentified flying object; SEE CONCEPTS *504,506*

foam [*n*] *bubbles formed from a liquid*
cream, fluff, froth, head, lather, scum, spray, spume, suds, surf, yeast; SEE CONCEPT *260*

foam [*v*] *become bubbly*
aerate, boil, burble, effervesce, ferment, fizz, froth, gurgle, hiss, lather, seethe, simmer, sparkle; SEE CONCEPTS *170,469*

foamy [*adj*] *bubbly*
barmy, boiling, burbling, carbonated, creamy, ebullient, effervescent, fermented, fizzy, frothy, lathery, scummy*, seething, simmering, spumescent, spumous, spumy, sudsy, yeasty; SEE CONCEPT *485*

focus [*n*] *center of attraction*
bull's eye*, center, core, cynosure, focal point, headquarters*, heart, hub, limelight*, locus, meeting place, nerve center*, point of convergence, polestar, seat, spotlight, target; SEE CONCEPTS *532,826,829*

focus [*v*] *aim attention at*
adjust, attract, bring out, center, centralize, concenter, concentrate, convene, converge, direct, fasten, fix, fixate, get detail, home in*, home in on*, hone in*, join, key on*, knuckle down*, meet, move in, pinpoint, pour it on*, put, rivet, sharpen, spotlight*, sweat*, zero in*, zoom in*; SEE CONCEPTS *17,623*

fodder [*n*] *animal feed*
animal food, barley, corn, food, forage, grain, grass, grub, hay, meal, pasturage, provender, provisions, silage, straw, vittles; SEE CONCEPTS *457,460,461*

foe [*n*] *person who is an opponent*
adversary, antagonist, anti*, enemy, hostile party, rival; SEE CONCEPT *412*

fog [*n1*] *heavy mist that reduces visibility*
brume, cloud, effluvium, film, gloom, grease, ground clouds, haze, London fog, miasma, murk, murkiness, nebula, obscurity, pea soup*, smaze,

outbreak, pother, spell, spurt, squall, stir*, to-do, tumult, turbulence, turmoil, whirl, whirlwind; SEE CONCEPTS *230,524*

smog, smoke, smother, soup*, steam, vapor, visibility zero-zero*, wisp; SEE CONCEPTS 524,627

fog [*n2*] *mental unclarity*
befuddlement, blindness, confusion, daze, haze, maze, mist, muddledness, muddlement, obscurity, perplexity, stupor, trance, vagueness; SEE CONCEPT 410

fog [*v*] *muddle, obscure*
addle, becloud, bedim, befuddle, bewilder, blind, blur, cloud, confuse, darken, daze, dim, eclipse, mist, muddy, mystify, obfuscate, perplex, puzzle, steam up, stupefy; SEE CONCEPTS 250,526

foggy [*adj*] *hazy, obscure*
blurred, ceiling zero*, closed in, clouded, cloudy, dark, dim, filmy, fogged in, fuzzy, gray, indistinct, misty, murky, mushy, nebulous, pea-soupy*, smazy, smoggy, socked in*, soupy*, unclear, vague, vaporous, vapory, zero-zero*; SEE CONCEPTS 403,525

foghorn [*n*] *warning signal*
alarm, danger signal, signal, siren; SEE CONCEPTS 269,463

foible [*n*] *personal imperfection*
characteristic, defect, eccentricity, failing, fault, frailty, idiosyncrasy, infirmity, kink, mannerism, oddity, peculiarity, quirk, shortcoming, singularity, vice, weakness, weak point; SEE CONCEPTS 411,644

foil [*n*] *contrast*
antithesis, background, complement, counterblow, defense, guard, setting; SEE CONCEPT 665

foil [*v*] *circumvent, nip in the bud*
baffle, balk, beat, bilk, bollix*, buffalo*, check, checkmate, counter, crab, cramp, crimp, curb, dash, defeat, disappoint, disconcert, ditch, dodge, duck, elude, faze, foul up*, frustrate, get around*, give the run-around*, give the slip*, hang up*, hinder, juke, nullify, outwit, prevent, rattle, restrain, run circles around*, run rings around*, shake, shake off, shuffle off, skip, stop, stymie, throw monkey wrench in*, thwart, upset the apple cart*; SEE CONCEPTS 121,130

foist [*v*] *force upon*
compel to accept, fob off, impose, insert fraudulently, palm off, pass off, pull a fast one*, ram down one's throat*, sneak in; SEE CONCEPT 14

fold [*n*] *double thickness*
bend, circumvolution, cockle, convolution, corrugation, crease, crimp, crinkle, dog's ear*, flection, flexure, furrow, gather, gathering, groove, knife-edge*, lap, lapel, layer, loop, overlap, plait, pleat, plica, plication, plicature, ply, pucker, ridge, rimple, rivel, ruche, ruck, ruffle, rumple, shirring, smocking, tuck, turn, wrinkle; SEE CONCEPT 754

fold [*v1*] *lay in creases*
bend, cockle, corrugate, crimp, crisp, crumple, curl, dog-ear*, double, double over, furrow, gather, groove, hem, intertwine, knit, lap, overlap, overlay, plait, pleat, plicate, pucker, purse, replicate, ridge, ruche, ruck, ruffle, telescope, tuck, turn under, wrinkle; SEE CONCEPT 184

fold [*v2*] *encase, enclose*
do up, enfold, entwine, envelop, involve, wrap, wrap up; SEE CONCEPT 209

fold [*v3*] *fail, close*
become insolvent, be ruined, break, bust, collapse, crash, crumple, give, go bankrupt, go bust, go into Chapter 11*, go under*, impoverish, pauper, pauperize, shut down, yield; SEE CONCEPTS 324,699

folder [*n*] *paper envelope for holding items*
binder, case, file, pocket, portfolio, sheath, wrapper, wrapping; SEE CONCEPT 260

foliage [*n*] *leaves*
frondescence, greenness, growth, herbage, leafage, umbrage, vegetation, verdure; SEE CONCEPT 428

folk [*n*] *person's relations, acquaintances*
body politic, clan, community, confederation, culture group, ethnic group, family, general public, group, house, household, inhabitants, kin, kindred, lineage, masses, ménage, nation, nationality, people, population, proletariat, public, race, settlement, society, state, stock, tribe; SEE CONCEPTS 296,379

folklore [*n*] *tales from the past*
ballad, custom, fable, folk story, legend, myth, mythology, mythos, oral literature, superstition, tradition, wisdom; SEE CONCEPT 282

folks [*n*] *family*
brood, clan, horde, household, kin, parents, people, relatives, tribe; SEE CONCEPTS 296,378,397

folksy [*adj*] *informal, simple*
cozy, down-to-earth*, homely, homey, low-key, modest, natural, plain, rustic, unassuming, unpretentious; SEE CONCEPTS 562,589

follow [*v1*] *take the place of*
be subsequent to, chase, come after, come from, come next, displace, ensue, go after, go next, postdate, proceed from, pursue, replace, result, spring from, succeed, supersede, supervene, supplant; SEE CONCEPTS 128,242,813

follow [*v2*] *trail, pursue physically*
accompany, attend, bring up the rear*, catenate, chase, come with, concatenate, convoy, dog*, dog the footsteps of*, draggle, escort, freeze, give chase, go after, go with, hound*, hunt, onto*, persecute, put a tail on*, run after, run down, schlepp along*, search, seek, shadow, shag*, spook*, stalk, stick to, string along, tag, tag after*, tag along*, tail, tailgate*, take out after, track; SEE CONCEPT 207

follow [*v3*] *act in accordance with*
abide by, accord, adhere to, adopt, attend, be consistent with, be devoted to, be guided by, be in keeping, be interested in, comply, conform, copy, cultivate, do like, emulate, follow suit, give allegiance to, harmonize, heed, hold fast, imitate, keep, keep abreast of, keep an eye on, live up to, match, mimic, mind, mirror, model on, note, obey, observe, pattern oneself upon, reflect, regard, serve, string along*, support, take after, take as an example, watch; SEE CONCEPTS 8,91,171

follow [*v4*] *understand*
accept, appreciate, apprehend, catch*, catch on*, comprehend, dig*, fathom, get*, get the picture*, grasp, realize, see, take in*; SEE CONCEPT 15

follower [*n*] *person who believes or has great interest*
addict, adherent, admirer, advocate, apostle, attendant, backer, believer, bootlicker*, buff, client, cohort, companion, convert, copycat, devotee, disciple, fan, fancier, freak*, habitué, hanger-on*, helper, imitator, lackey*, member, minion, parasite, participant, partisan, patron, promoter, proselyte, protégé, pupil, representative, satellite, sectary, servant, sidekick, stooge*,

fl
fo

supporter, sycophant, toady*, vassal, votary, worshiper, zealot; SEE CONCEPTS 352,366,423

following [*adj*] *happening, being next or after*
after a while, afterward, attendant, a while later, back, by and by, coming, coming after, coming next, consecutive, consequent, consequential, directly after, ensuing, henceforth, hinder, in pursuit, in search of, in the wake of, later, later on, latter, next, next off*, on the scent*, posterior, presently, proximate, pursuing, rear, resulting, sequent, sequential, serial, seriate, specified, subsequent, succeeding, successive, supervenient, then, trailing, when; SEE CONCEPTS 585,811,818, 820

following [*n*] *persons of an interest or belief*
adherents, audience, circle, clientage, clientele, cortege, coterie, dependents, entourage, fans, group, groupies*, hangers-on*, patronage, patrons, public, retinue, rout, suite, support, supporters, train; SEE CONCEPTS 294,387,417

follow through [*v*] *bring to a conclusion*
complete, conclude, consummate, pursue, see through; SEE CONCEPT 91

follow up [*v*] *make inquiries*
check out, find out about, investigate, look into, make sure, pursue; SEE CONCEPT 103

folly [*n*] *nonsense, ridiculous idea*
absurdity, craziness, daftness, dottiness, dumb thing to do*, dumb trick*, fatuity, foolishness, idiocy, imbecility, impracticality, imprudence, inadvisability, inanity, indiscretion, irrationality, lunacy, madness, obliquity, preposterousness, rashness, recklessness, senselessness, silliness, stupidity, triviality, unsoundness, vice, witlessness; SEE CONCEPTS 410,633

foment [*v*] *instigate, provoke*
abet, agitate, arouse, brew, cultivate, encourage, excite, fan the flames*, foster, goad, incite, nurse, nurture, promote, quicken, raise, set, set on, sow the seeds*, spur, start, stimulate, stir up, whip up*; SEE CONCEPTS 14,221

fond [*adj*] *have a liking or taste for*
addicted, adoring, affectionate, amorous, attached, caring, devoted, doting, enamored, indulgent, keen on, lovesome, lovey-dovey*, loving, mushy*, partial, predisposed, responsive, romantic, sentimental, silly over, sympathetic, tender, warm; SEE CONCEPTS 32,542

fondle [*v*] *touch lovingly*
bear hug*, caress, clutch, cosset, cuddle, dandle, embrace, feel, fool around*, grab, grope, hug, love, make love to, neck, nestle, nuzzle, pat, paw, pet, play footsie*, snuggle, squeeze, stroke; SEE CONCEPTS 190,375

fondness [*n*] *liking or taste for*
affection, attachment, devotion, fancy, kindness, love, partiality, penchant, predilection, preference, soft spot, susceptibility, tenderness, weakness; SEE CONCEPT 32

font [*n1*] *source*
fount, fountain, genesis, origin, root, seed, wellspring; SEE CONCEPT 648

font [*n2*] *print type*
face, typeface; SEE CONCEPTS 79,284

food [*n*] *edible material*
aliment, bite*, board, bread, cheer, chow*, comestible, cookery, cooking, cuisine, diet, drink, eatable, eats*, entrée, fare, fast food, feed, fodder*, foodstuff, goodies*, grit*, groceries*, grub*, handout*, home cooking, keep, larder, meal, meat, menu, mess*, moveable feast, nourishment, nutriment, nutrition, pabulum, provision, ration, refreshment, slop*, snack, store, subsistence, support, sustenance, table, take out, tuck, viand, victual, vittles*; SEE CONCEPTS 457,460,461

food court [*n*] *public area where variety of food is sold*
cafe, counter, fast food, food festival, restaurant, smorgasbord; SEE CONCEPTS 439,448,449

food poisoning [*n*] *poisoning caused by eating food*
botulism, ptomaine poisoning, salmonella; SEE CONCEPT 537

fool [*n*] *stupid or ridiculous person*
ass, birdbrain*, blockhead*, bonehead*, boob*, bore, buffoon, clod*, clown, cretin*, dimwit*, dolt*, dope*, dumb ox*, dunce, dunderhead*, easy mark*, fair game*, fathead*, goose*, halfwit, idiot, ignoramus, illiterate, imbecile, innocent, jerk*, lamebrain*, lightweight*, loon*, moron, nerd*, nincompoop*, ninny*, nitwit, numskull*, oaf, sap*, schlemiel*, silly, simpleton, stooge*, sucker*, turkey*, twerp*, twit*, victim; SEE CONCEPTS 412,423

fool [*v*] *trick, mislead*
bamboozle*, bluff, cheat, chicane, con, deceive, delude, diddle, dupe, fake out*, flimflam*, fox*, gull, hoax, hoodwink*, jive*, juke*, kid, lead on, make believe, outfox, play-act*, play a trick on, pretend, put on, put one over on*, scam*, snow*, spoof*, suck in*, take in*, trifle; SEE CONCEPT 59

fool around [*v*] *waste time*
dawdle, hang around*, idle, kill time*, lark, mess around*, play around*; SEE CONCEPT 681

fooled [*adj*] *tricked*
bamboozled*, conned, deceived, deluded, duped, flimflammed*, hornswoggled*, misled, outfoxed*, snowed*, sucked in*; SEE CONCEPT 537

foolhardy [*adj*] *impetuous, rash*
adventuresome, adventurous, audacious, bold, breakneck*, daredevil, daring, devil-may-care*, harebrained*, headstrong, imprudent, incautious, irresponsible, madcap, off deep end*, out on limb*, precipitate, reckless, temerarious, venturesome, venturous, wide open; SEE CONCEPT 401

fooling [*n*] *joking, tricks*
bluffing, buffoonery, clownishness, farce, frolicking, high jinks*, horseplay, jesting, joshing, kidding, making light*, mockery, nonsense, pretense, roughhouse*, roughhousing*, rowdiness, sham*, skylarking*, spoofing, teasing, trifling; SEE CONCEPT 59

foolish [*adj*] *nonsensical, idiotic*
absurd, asinine, brainless, cockamamy*, crazy, daffy*, daft, dippy*, doltish*, dotty*, fantastic, fatuous, feebleminded*, half-baked*, half-witted*, harebrained*, ill-advised, ill-considered, imbecilic, imprudent, incautious, indiscreet, injudicious, insane, irrational, jerky*, kooky*, loony*, ludicrous, lunatic, mad, moronic, nerdy*, nutty*, preposterous, ridiculous, senseless, short-sighted, silly, simple, stupid, unintelligent, unreasonable, unwise, wacky*, weak, witless, zany*; SEE CONCEPTS 401,542,544

foolishly [*adv*] *idiotic, without due consideration*
absurdly, ill-advisedly, imprudently, incautiously, indiscreetly, injudiciously, mistakenly,

short-sightedly, stupidly, unwisely; SEE CON-
CEPTS 401,542,544

foolishness [*n*] *idiocy, nonsense*
absurdity, absurdness, bunk*, carrying-on*,
claptrap*, craziness, dumb trick*, folly, foolery,
fool trick, horse feathers*, impracticality, imprudence, inanity, indiscretion, insanity, insensibility, irrationality, irresponsibility, ludicrousness,
lunacy, mistake, poppycock*, preposterousness,
rubbish*, senselessness, silliness, stupidity, tommyrot*, twaddle, unreasonableness, unwiseness,
weakness, witlessness; SEE CONCEPT 633

foolproof [*adj*] *infallible*
certain, dependable, fail-safe, faultless, flawless,
goofproof, guaranteed, idiot-proof*, never-failing, perfect, reliable, safe, sure, sure-fire, tested,
tried, unassailable, unerring, unfailing; SEE CON-
CEPTS 535,582

foot [*n1*] *extremity of an animate being*
hoof, pad, paw; SEE CONCEPT 392

foot [*n2*] *base of an object*
bottom, foundation, lowest point, nadir, pier; SEE
CONCEPT 442

foot [*n3*] *twelve inches/30.48 centimeters measured*
cubic; square; SEE CONCEPTS 790,791

footing [*n1*] *foundation, basis*
basement, bedrock, bottom, establishment, foot,
foothold, ground, groundwork, infrastructure, installation, resting place, seat, seating, settlement,
substratum, substructure, underpinning, understructure, warrant, base; SEE CONCEPTS 442,661

footing [*n2*] *social status*
capacity, character, condition, grade, place, position, rank, relations, relationship, situation,
standing, state, station, terms; SEE CONCEPT 388

footloose [*adj*] *free*
easygoing, free and easy, go-as-you-please,
loose, unattached, uncommitted, unengaged; SEE
CONCEPTS 401,542

footprint [*n*] *footmark*
footstep, hoofprint, impression, imprint, spoor,
track, trail, tread; SEE CONCEPTS 513,628

fop [*n*] *dandy*
beau, Beau Brummel, clotheshorse, coxcomb,
dude, fashion plate, macaroni, peacock, popin-
jay; SEE CONCEPT 423

for [*conj*] *in consequence of the fact that*
as, as long as, because, being, considering, inasmuch as, now, since, whereas; SEE CONCEPT 544

for [*prep*] *in consideration of*
after, as, beneficial to, concerning, conducive to,
during, for the sake of, in contemplation of, in
exchange for, in favor of, in furtherance of, in
order to, in order to get, in place of, in pursuance
of, in spite of, in the direction of, in the interest
of, in the name of, notwithstanding, on the part
of, on the side of, pro, supposing to, to counterbalance, to go to, to the amount of, to the extent
of, toward, under the authority of, with a view to,
with regard to, with respect; SEE CONCEPT 544

forage [*v*] *search madly for*
beat, cast about, comb, explore, fine-tooth-
comb*, grub, hunt, pilfer, plunder, raid, rake,
ransack, ravage, rummage, scour, scrounge,
seek; SEE CONCEPT 216

foray [*n*] *incursion, attempt*
attack, depredation, descent, inroad, invasion, irruption, raid, reconnaissance, sally, sortie; SEE
CONCEPTS 86,90,159

forbear [*v*] *resist the temptation to*
abstain, avoid, bridle, cease, curb, decline, desist,
escape, eschew, evade, forgo, go easy*, hold
back*, inhibit, keep, keep from, omit, pause, refrain, restrain, sacrifice, shun, stop, withhold; SEE
CONCEPTS 35,121,130,681

forbearance [*n*] *resisting, avoidance*
abstinence, endurance, fortitude, going easy on*,
living with*, longanimity, moderation, patience,
patientness, refraining, resignation, restraint,
self-control, temperance, tolerance; SEE CON-
CEPTS 410,633

forbearing [*adj*] *tolerant*
being big*, charitable, clement, considerate,
easy, forgiving, gentle, going easy on*, going
easy with*, humane, humanitarian, indulgent, lenient, living with*, longanimous, long-suffering,
merciful, mild, moderate, patient, soft-shell*,
thoughtful; SEE CONCEPTS 404,542

forbid [*v*] *outlaw, prohibit an action*
ban, block, cancel, censor, debar, declare
illegal, deny, deprive, disallow, embargo, enjoin,
exclude, forestall, forfend, freeze*, halt, hinder,
hold up, impede, inhibit, interdict, lock up, nix*,
obstruct, obviate, oppose, preclude, prevent, proscribe, put the chill on*, restrain, restrict, rule
out, say no*, shut down*, shut out*, spike*, stop,
stymie*, taboo*, veto, withhold; SEE CONCEPT
121

forbidden [*adj*] *outlawed, prohibited*
banned, closed, closed-down*, closed-up*, contraband, no-no*, off limits, out of bounds, proscribed, refused, taboo*, verboten, vetoed; SEE
CONCEPT 548

forbidden fruit [*n*] *taboo*
desired object, golden apple, illicit love, no-no*,
prohibition; SEE CONCEPTS 532,687

forbidding [*adj*] *ominous, daunting*
abhorrent, disagreeable, dour, foreboding, frightening, glowering, grim, hostile, menacing, odious, offensive, off-putting, repellent, repulsive,
sinister, threatening, tough, ugly, unapproachable, unfriendly, unpleasant; SEE CONCEPTS
537,550

force [*n1*] *physical energy, power*
arm, brunt, clout, coercion, compulsion, conscription, constraint, draft, duress, dynamism, effort, enforcement, exaction, extortion, full head
of steam*, fury, horsepower, impact, impetus,
impulse, might, momentum, muscle, pains*, potency, potential, pow*, pressure, punch, push,
sinew, sock*, speed, steam, stimulus, strain,
strength, stress, strong arm*, stuff*, subjection,
tension, trouble, velocity, vigor, violence, what it
takes*; SEE CONCEPTS 641,724

force [*n2*] *mental power, energy*
ability, authority, bite*, capability, coercion, cogency, competence, determination, dominance,
drive, duress, effect, effectiveness, efficacy, emphasis, fierceness, forcefulness, gumption, guts*,
impressiveness, influence, intensity, intestinal
fortitude, obligation, persistence, persuasiveness,
point, pressure, puissance, punch, push, requirement, sapience, stress, validity, validness, vehemence, vigor, willpower; SEE CONCEPTS 410,677

force [*n3*] *military organization*
armed forces, army, battalion, body, cell, corps,
crew, detachment, division, guard, horses, host,
legion, patrol, regiment, reserves, shop, soldiers,

fo
fo

squad, squadron, troop, unit; SEE CONCEPTS 322,417

force [v1] *obligate to do something*
apply, bear down, bear hard on, bind, blackmail, bring pressure to bear upon*, burden, cause, charge, choke, coerce, command, compel, concuss, conscript, constrain, contract, demand, draft, drag, dragoon*, drive, enforce, enjoin, exact, extort, fix, impel, impose, impress, inflict, insist, limit, make, move, necessitate, oblige, obtrude, occasion, order, overcome, pin down, press, pressure, pressurize, put screws to*, put squeeze on*, require, restrict, sandbag*, shotgun*, strong-arm*, urge, wrest, wring; SEE CONCEPT 14

force [v2] *use violence upon*
assault, blast, break in, break open, burst, bust open, crack open, defile, extort, jimmy*, propel, pry, push, rape, ravish, spoil, squeeze, thrust, twist, undo, violate, wrench, wrest, wring; SEE CONCEPTS 156,208

forced [adj] *compulsory, strained*
affected, artificial, begrudging, binding, bound, coerced, coercive, compelled, conscripted, constrained, contrived, enforced, factitious, false, grudging, inflexible, insincere, involuntary, labored, mandatory, obligatory, peremptory, rigid, slave, stiff, stringent, unnatural, unwilling, wooden*; SEE CONCEPTS 542,548

forceful [adj] *effective, powerful*
ball of fire*, bullish*, cogent, coming on strong, commanding, compelling, constraining, convincing, dominant, dynamic, electric, elemental, energetic, forcible, gutsy*, mighty, persuasive, pithy, potent, powerhouse, puissant, punch, punchy*, steamroller*, stringent, strong, takecharge, take-over, telling, titanic, vehement, vigorous, violent, virile, weighty; SEE CONCEPTS 267,401,550

forcible [adj] *powerful, aggressive*
active, armed, assertive, coercive, cogent, compelling, compulsory, drastic, effective, efficient, energetic, forceful, impressive, intense, mighty, militant, persuasive, potent, puissant, strong, telling, valid, vehement, vigorous, violent, weighty; SEE CONCEPTS 267,537

forcibly [adv] *against one's will*
by force, coercively, compulsorily, effectively, energetically, hard, mightily, powerfully, strongly, under protest, vigorously; SEE CONCEPTS 544,548

fore [adv] *in the front*
ahead, ante*, antecedently, before, beforehand, forward, in advance, near, nearest, precedently, previous; SEE CONCEPTS 585,820

forebearer [n] *family predecessor*
ancestor, antecedent, ascendant, author, begetter, forerunner, founder, materfamilias, matriarch, originator, parent, paterfamilias, patriarch, precursor, primogenitor, procreator, progenitor, relative, sire; SEE CONCEPT 414

forebode [v] *predict, warn*
augur, betoken, bode, divine, forecast, foresee, foreshadow, foretell, foretoken, forewarn, indicate, omen, portend, premonish, presage, prognosticate, promise; SEE CONCEPTS 70,78

foreboding [n] *misgiving, bad omen*
anxiety, apprehension, apprehensiveness, augury, bad vibes*, chill, dread, fear, foreshadowing, foretoken, forewarning, funny feeling*,

handwriting on the wall*, portent, prediction, premonition, prenotion, presage, presentiment, prognostic, prophecy, sinking feeling*, vibes*, warning, wind change*; SEE CONCEPTS 78,689, 690

forecast [n] *prediction, often of weather or business*
anticipation, augury, budget, calculation, cast, conjecture, divination, estimate, foreknowledge, foreseeing, foresight, foretelling, forethought, foretoken, guess, outlook, planning, precognition, prescience, prevision, prognosis, prognostication, projection, prophecy; SEE CONCEPTS 28,37,70,78

forecast [v] *predict, guess*
adumbrate, anticipate, augur, calculate, call the turn*, conclude, conjecture, demonstrate, determine, divine, dope out*, estimate, figure, figure out*, foresee, foretell, gather, gauge, infer, in the cards*, plan, portend, predetermine, presage, prognosticate, prophesy, reason, see it coming*, soothsay, surmise, telegraph; SEE CONCEPTS 28,37,70,78

forefather [n] *ancestor*
antecedent, ascendant, forebearer, patriarch, precursor, predecessor, primogenitor, procreator, progenitor; SEE CONCEPT 414

forefront/foreground [n] *prominence*
beginning, center, cutting-edge*, focus, fore, forepart, front, lead, leading-edge*, limelight*, on the line*, spearhead*, state-of-the-art, vanguard; SEE CONCEPT 668

foregoing [adj] *come before; previous*
above, aforementioned, aforesaid, aforestated, antecedent, anterior, former, past, precedent, preceding, prior; SEE CONCEPTS 585,820

foreign [adj1] *from another country, experience*
adopted, alien, alienated, antipodal, barbarian, barbaric, borrowed, derived, different, distant, estranged, exiled, exotic, expatriate, external, extralocal, extraneous, extrinsic, far, faraway, far-fetched, far-off, from abroad, immigrant, imported, inaccessible, nonnative, nonresident, not domestic, not native, offshore, outlandish, outside, overseas, remote, strange, transoceanic, unaccustomed, unexplored, unfamiliar, unknown; SEE CONCEPTS 536,549

foreign [adj2] *irrelevant*
accidental, adventitious, extraneous, extrinsic, heterogeneous, immaterial, impertinent, inapposite, incompatible, incongruous, inconsistent, inconsonant, irrelative, repugnant, unassimilable, uncharacteristic, unrelated; SEE CONCEPTS 267,537

foreigner [n] *person from another country*
alien, fresh off the boat*, greenhorn*, immigrant, incomer, newcomer, outlander, outsider, stranger; SEE CONCEPT 413

foremost [adj] *first in rank, order*
A-1*, A-number-1*, arch, at the cutting edge*, at the leading edge*, champion, chief, front, head, headmost, heavy, heavy stuff*, heavyweight*, highest, hotdog*, hotshot*, hot stuff*, inaugural, initial, leading, most important, number one*, original, paramount, preeminent, premier, primary, prime, primo*, principal, supreme; SEE CONCEPTS 568,585,799

forensic [adj] *judicial, legal*
argumentative, debatable, dialectic, dialectical,

foreordain [v] *doom, fate*
destine, destine, foredoom, foreshadow, foretell, prearrange, predestine, predetermine, preform, preordain, reserve; SEE CONCEPT 70

foreplay [n] *fondling*
action*, caress, cuddling, heavy petting, kissing, lovemaking, making out, necking, oral sex, petting, sex, sexual activity; SEE CONCEPTS 375,388

forerunner [n1] *messenger, herald*
advertiser, advocate, ancestor, announcer, author, envoy, forebearer, foregoer, harbinger, initiator, originator, pioneer, precursor, progenitor, prognostic, prototype; SEE CONCEPTS 414,423

forerunner [n2] *example, sign*
advertisement, announcement, antecedent, antecessor, augury, exemplar, foregoer, foreshadow, foretoken, forewarning, indication, mark, model, omen, pattern, portent, precursor, predecessor, premonition, presage, prognostic, prototype, sign, token, warning; SEE CONCEPT 529

foresee [v] *anticipate, predict*
apprehend, call the turn*, crystal ball it*, discern, divine, dope out*, envisage, espy, expect, forebode, forecast, foreknow, foretell, have a hunch*, perceive, preknow, presage, previse, prevision, prognosticate, prophesy, psych out*, see, see it coming*, understand, visualize; SEE CONCEPTS 26,70

foreshadow [v] *indicate*
adumbrate, augur, be in the wind*, betoken, bode, forebode, foretell, hint, imply, omen, portend, predict, prefigure, presage, promise, prophesy, shadow, signal, suggest, telegraph; SEE CONCEPTS 70,75,261

foresight [n] *mental preparedness*
anticipation, canniness, care, carefulness, caution, circumspection, clairvoyance, discernment, discreetness, discretion, economy, far-sightedness, foreknowledge, forethought, insight, long-sightedness, perception, precaution, precognition, preconception, premeditation, premonition, prenotion, prescience, prospect, providence, provision, prudence, sagacity; SEE CONCEPTS 409,410

forest [n] *area with a large number of trees*
backwoods, brake, chase, clump, coppice, copse, cover, covert, grove, growth, jungle, park, shelter, stand, thicket, timber, timberland, weald, wildwood, wood, woodland, woodlot, woods; SEE CONCEPTS 509,517

foretell [v] *predict, warn*
adumbrate, announce, anticipate, apprehend, augur, auspicate, betoken, bode, call, call it*, call the shot*, crystal ball it*, declare, disclose, divine, divulge, dope*, dope out*, figure, figure out*, forebode, forecast, foreknow, foreshadow, forewarn, make book*, portend, prefigure, presage, proclaim, prognosticate, prophesy, psych, read, reveal, see something coming*, signify, soothsay, tell; SEE CONCEPTS 70,78

forethought [n] *mental preparedness*
anticipation, canniness, caution, deliberation, discreetness, discretion, far-sightedness, foresight, gumption, judgment, planning, precaution, premeditation, providence, provision, prudence, sense; SEE CONCEPT 410

forever [adj1] *for all time; everlasting*
always, durably, endlessly, enduringly, eternally,

evermore, everything considered*, for always, forevermore, for good*, for keeps*, for life*, immortally, infinitely, in perpetuity, in perpetuum, interminably, lastingly, now and forever*, on and on*, permanently, perpetually, till blue in the face*, till death do us part*, till Doomsday*, till the cows come home*, till the end of time*, unchangingly, world without end*; SEE CONCEPTS 551,649,798,799

forever [adj2] *not ceasing, continually*
all the time, constantly, endlessly, eternally, everlastingly, incessantly, interminably, perpetually, regularly, unendingly, unremittingly; SEE CONCEPTS 534,798

forewarn [v] *caution that something may happen*
admonish, advise, alarm, alert, apprise, dissuade, flag, forbode, give fair warning*, give the high sign*, portend, premonish, pull one's coat*, put a bug in one's ear*, put one wise*, put on guard*, telegraph, tip, tip off, wave a red flag*; SEE CONCEPT 78

foreword [n] *introduction to a document*
exordium, overture, preamble, preface, preliminary, prelude, prelusion, proem, prolegomenon, prologue; SEE CONCEPT 270

forfeit [n] *something given as sacrifice*
cost, damages, fine, loss, mulct, penalty, relinquishment; SEE CONCEPT 123

forfeit [v] *give up something in sacrifice*
abandon, be deprived of, be stripped of, drop, give over, lose, relinquish, renounce, sacrifice, surrender; SEE CONCEPT 116

forge [v1] *counterfeit*
coin, copy, design, duplicate, fabricate, fake, falsify, fashion, feign, frame, imitate, invent, make, phony up*, pirate*, produce, reproduce, scratch, trace, transcribe, trump up*; SEE CONCEPTS 59,171

forge [v2] *make something from scratch*
beat, build, construct, contrive, create, devise, fabricate, fashion, form, frame, hammer out*, invent, manufacture, mold, pound, put together, shape, turn out, work; SEE CONCEPTS 168,173, 175,205,251

forgery [n] *counterfeiting; counterfeit item*
bogus*, carbon*, carbon copy, cheat, coining, copy, fabrication, fake, faking, falsification, fraudulence, imitating, imitation, imposition, imposture, lookalike, phony, pseudo, sham*, twin, workalike*; SEE CONCEPTS 59,171,716

forget [v1] *not be able to remember*
blow, clean forget*, consign to oblivion*, dismiss from mind, disremember, draw a blank*, escape one's memory*, fail to remember, let slip from memory*, lose consciousness of, lose sight of*, misrecollect, obliterate, think no more of*; SEE CONCEPT 40

forget [v2] *leave behind*
blink, discount, disregard, drop, fail, ignore, lose sight of*, neglect, omit, overlook, overpass, pass over, skip, slight, transgress, trespass; SEE CONCEPTS 30,116

forgetful [adj] *tending to not remember*
absent, absent-minded, abstracted, airheaded*, amnemonic, amnesic, asleep on the job*, bemused, careless, distracted, dreamy, heedless, inattentive, lax, like an absent-minded professor*, looking out window*, mooning, moony*, neglectful, negligent, nirvanic, not on the job*, oblivious, out of it*, out to lunch*, pipe dream-

ing*, preoccupied, remiss, slack, sloppy, unmindful, unwitting, woolgathering*; SEE CON-
CEPTS 403,550

forgetfulness [*n*] *consistent inability to remember*
absentmindedness, abstraction, amnesia, blackout, blank, blockout, carelessness, dreaminess,
fugue, heedlessness, hypomnesia, inattention,
lapse of memory, laxness, lethe, limbo, loss of
memory, negligence, nirvana, oblivion, obliviousness, paramnesia, repression, short memory,
suppression; SEE CONCEPTS 410,644

forgive [*v*] *stop blame and grant pardon*
absolve, accept apology, acquit, allow for,
amnesty, bear no malice*, bear with, bury the
hatchet*, clear, commute, condone, dismiss from
mind, efface, exculpate, excuse, exempt, exonerate, extenuate, forget, kiss and make up*, laugh
off*, let bygones be bygones*, let it go*, let off*,
let off easy*, let pass*, let up on*, make allowance, overlook, palliate, pocket, purge, release, relent, remit, reprieve, respite, spring,
think no more of*, turn other cheek*, wink at*,
wipe slate clean*; SEE CONCEPTS 12,50,88

forgiveness [*n*] *pardon; end of blame*
absolution, acquittal, amnesty, charity, clemency, compassion, condonation, dispensation,
exculpation, exoneration, extenuation, grace, immunity, impunity, indemnity, justification, lenience, lenity, mercy, overlooking, palliation,
purgation, quarter, quittance, remission, remittal,
reprieve, respite, vindication; SEE CONCEPTS
685,689

forgo [*v*] *give up, do without*
abandon, abdicate, abjure, abstain, cede, desist,
eschew, forbear, forsake, give in, go on the
wagon*, leave alone, leave out, pack in*, pass,
pass on, pass up, quit, refrain, relinquish, renounce, resign, resist, sacrifice, sit out*, surrender, swear off*, take the cure*, take the oath*,
waive, yield; SEE CONCEPTS 121,130,681

forgotten [*adj*] *out of one's mind*
abandoned, blanked out*, blotted out*, blown
over*, buried, bygone, clean forgot*, consigned
to oblivion*, disremembered*, drew a blank*,
erased, fell between the cracks*, gone, lapsed,
left behind, left out, lost, obliterated, omitted,
past, past recollection, repressed, slipped one's
mind*, suppressed, unrecalled, unremembered;
SEE CONCEPTS 402,403,529

fork [*v*] *go separate ways*
angle, bifurcate, branch off, branch out, divaricate, diverge, divide, part, split; SEE CONCEPTS
98,738

forked [*adj*] *going separate ways*
angled, bifid, bifurcate, bifurcated, branched,
branching, dichotomous, dichotonic, divaricate,
divided, furcate, furcated, pronged, split, tined,
tridented, zigzag; SEE CONCEPTS 485,581

for keeps [*adv*] *forever*
for good, permanently, till hell freezes over*;
SEE CONCEPTS 551,649,798,799

for kicks [*adv*] *for fun*
for mere pleasure, for no useful reason, for the
hell of it; SEE CONCEPTS 537,572

forlorn [*adj*] *hopeless, inconsolable*
abandoned, alone, bereft, blue*, cheerless,
comfortless, cynical, defenseless, depressed,
deserted, desolate, despairing, desperate, despondent, destitute, destroyed, disconsolate, down

and out*, dragging*, forgotten, forsaken, friendless, fruitless, futile, godforsaken*, helpless,
homeless, in the dumps*, lonely, lonesome, lost,
miserable, oppressed, pathetic, pessimistic,
pitiable, pitiful, solitary, tragic, unhappy, vain,
weighed down, woebegone, wretched; SEE CON-
CEPT 403

form [*n1*] *shape; arrangement*
anatomy, appearance, articulation, cast, configuration, conformation, construction, contour, cut,
design, die, embodiment, fashion, figure, formation, framework, mode, model, mold, outline,
pattern, plan, profile, scheme, silhouette, skeleton, structure, style, system; SEE CONCEPTS
184,660,754,757

form [*n2*] *animate body and its condition*
anatomy, being, build, condition, fettle*, figure,
fitness, frame, health, object, outline, person,
phenomenon, physique, shape, silhouette, thing,
torso, trim*; SEE CONCEPTS 316,389,720

form [*n3*] *accepted procedure; ceremony*
behavior, by the book*, by the numbers*, canon,
ceremonial, channels*, conduct, convenance,
convention, custom, decorum, done thing*, etiquette, fashion, formality, habit, law, layout,
manner, manners, method, mode, practice, precept, proceeding, process, propriety, protocol,
regulation, rite, ritual, ropes*, rule, setup, style,
usage, way; SEE CONCEPT 688

form [*n4*] *document that requires answers or information*
application, blank, chart, data sheet, letter, paper,
questionnaire, sheet; SEE CONCEPT 271

form [*n5*] *type, kind*
arrangement, character, class, description, design, grade, guise, make, manifestation, manner,
method, mode, order, practice, rank, semblance,
sort, species, stamp, style, system, variety, way;
SEE CONCEPTS 6,378

form [*n6*] *organization, arrangement*
format, framework, harmony, order, orderliness,
placement, plan, proportion, scheme, structure,
symmetry; SEE CONCEPT 727

form [*v1*] *bring into existence; make, produce*
arrange, assemble, block out, bring about, build,
cast, complete, compose, conceive, concoct, constitute, construct, consummate, contrive, cook
up*, create, cultivate, cut, design, develop, devise, dream up, erect, establish, fabricate, fashion, finish, fix, forge, found, frame, hammer
out*, invent, knock off*, make up, manufacture,
model, mold, organize, outline, pattern, perfect,
plan, plot, project, put together, scheme, set, set
up, shape, structure, throw together, trace, turn
out*, work; SEE CONCEPTS 168,173,205,251

form [*v2*] *come into being; arise*
accumulate, acquire, appear, become a reality,
become visible, condense, crystallize, develop,
eventuate, fall into place*, grow, harden, materialize, mature, rise, set, settle, shape up, show up,
take on character, take shape*; SEE CONCEPTS
105,704

form [*v3*] *educate, discipline*
breed, bring up, give character, instruct, rear,
school, teach, train; SEE CONCEPTS 285,295

form [*v4*] *comprise, be a part of*
act as, compose, constitute, figure in, make,
make up, serve as; SEE CONCEPT 643

formal [*adj1*] *established, orderly*
academic, approved, ceremonial, ceremonialis-

tic, ceremonious, confirmed, conventional, decorous, directed, explicit, express, fixed, formalistic, lawful, legal, methodical, official, precise, prescribed, pro forma, proper, punctilious, regular, rigid, ritual, ritualistic, set, solemn, stately, stereotyped, stereotypical, strict, systematic; SEE CONCEPTS 533,547

formal [*adj2*] *stiff, affected, correct*
aloof, by the numbers*, ceremonious, conventional, decorous, distant, exact, nominal, playing the game*, polite, precise, prim, punctilious, reserved, seemly, sententious, starched*, stilted*, straight arrow*, stuffy*, unbending; SEE CONCEPT 401

formality [*n1*] *convention, custom*
academism, ceremony, convenance, conventionality, form, gesture, liturgy, matter of form*, officialism, procedure, red tape*, rite, ritual, rituality, rubric, rule, service, solemnity, solemnness, stereotype, tradition; SEE CONCEPT 688

formality [*n2*] *etiquette, protocol*
ceremoniousness, conventionalism, correctness, decorum, formalism, honors, mummery, politesse, propriety, p's and q's*, punctiliousness; SEE CONCEPT 633

format [*n*] *layout, plan*
arrangement, composition, configuration, dimensions, figure, form, formation, formula, look, makeup, pattern, scheme, setup, shape, size; SEE CONCEPTS 625,660

formation [*n*] *composition, establishment*
accumulation, architecture, arrangement, compilation, configuration, constitution, construction, creation, crystallization, deposit, design, development, dispersal, disposition, embodiment, evolution, fabrication, figure, forming, generation, genesis, grouping, induction, makeup, manufacture, order, organization, pattern, production, rank, structure, synthesis; SEE CONCEPTS 173,260

formative [*adj*] *influential, impressionable*
determinative, developmental, immature, impressible, malleable, moldable, pliant, sensitive, shaping, susceptible; SEE CONCEPTS 534,537

former [*adj*] *previous in time or order*
above, aforementioned, aforesaid, ancient, antecedent, anterior, bygone, departed, earlier, erstwhile, ex-*, first, foregoing, late, long ago*, long gone, of yore, old, once, one-time, past, preceding, prior, quondam, sometime, whilom; SEE CONCEPTS 585,820

formerly [*adv*] *previously in time or order*
aforetime, already, anciently, at one time, away back, a while back, back, back when*, before, before now, before this, down memory lane*, earlier, eons ago*, erewhile, erstwhile, heretofore, in former times, in the olden days*, in the past, lately, long ago, of old, of yore, olden days*, once, once upon a time*, radically, some time ago, time was*, used to be*, water under the bridge*; SEE CONCEPTS 585,820

formidable [*adj1*] *horrible, terrifying*
appalling, awful, dangerous, daunting, dire, dismaying, dreadful, fearful, fierce, frightful, horrific, imposing, impregnable, intimidating, menacing, redoubtable, shocking, terrible, terrific, threatening; SEE CONCEPT 537

formidable [*adj2*] *difficult, overwhelming*
all-powerful, arduous, awesome, ballbuster, challenging, colossal, dismaying, effortful, great, hard, impressive, indomitable, intimidating, la-

bored, laborious, mammoth, mighty, murder*, onerous, overpowering, powerful, puissant, rough*, rough go*, staggering, strenuous, tall order*, toilsome, tough*, tough proposition*, tremendous, uphill*; SEE CONCEPT 565

formless [*adj*] *disorganized, vague*
amorphous, baggy*, blobby*, chaotic, crude, inchoate, incoherent, indefinite, indeterminate, indistinct, nebulous, obscure, orderless, raw, rough, rude, shapeless, unclear, undefined, unformed, unorganized; SEE CONCEPTS 485,535, 589

formula [*n*] *set preparation; rule, recipe*
blueprint, canon, code, credo, creed, custom, description, direction, equation, form, formulary, maxim, method, modus operandi, precept, prescription, principle, procedure, rite, ritual, rote, rubric, specifications, theorem, way; SEE CONCEPTS 268,688

formulate [*v*] *plan, specify systematically*
codify, coin, compose, concoct, contrive, cook up, couch, define, detail, develop, devise, draft, draw up*, dream up*, evolve, express, forge, frame, give form to, hatch, indite, invent, make, make up*, map, originate, particularize, phrase, prepare, put, set down*, systematize, vamp, work, work out; SEE CONCEPTS 36,173,202

fornicate [*v*] *have sexual intercourse*
be promiscuous, commit adultery, philander, sleep around; SEE CONCEPTS 375,384

fornication [*n*] *sexual intercourse*
coition, coitus, copulation, intimacy, lovemaking, relations, screwing around, sex, sleeping around; SEE CONCEPTS 375,384

for openers [*adv*] *as a beginning*
first off, for starters, to begin with; SEE CONCEPTS 815,833

forsake [*v*] *abandon, turn one's back on*
abdicate, cast off, change one's tune*, desert, disclaim, disown, drift away*, forgo, forswear, give up, have done with, jettison, jilt, kiss goodbye*, leave, leave flat*, leave high and dry*, quit, relinquish, renounce, repudiate, resign, run out on*, set aside, show the door*, spurn, surrender, take the oath*, throw over*, walk out on*, wash one's hands of*, yield; SEE CONCEPTS 30,195,384

forsaken [*adj*] *abandoned*
cast off, derelict, deserted, desolate, destitute, disowned, forlorn, friendless, godforsaken*, ignored, isolated, jilted, left at the altar*, left behind, left in the lurch*, lonely, lorn, marooned, outcast, solitary, thrown over*; SEE CONCEPT 555

for sure [*adv*] *definitely*
certainly, dead sure, for a fact, for certain, for real, no doubt, no question, no two ways about it, really, sure thing, unquestionably; SEE CONCEPTS 535,552

forswear [*v*] *abandon, disavow*
abjure, deny, disclaim, disown, drop, forgo, forsake, give up, recall, recant, reject, renege, renounce, repudiate, retract, swear off, take back, withdraw; SEE CONCEPTS 44,54

forte [*n*] *person's strong point*
ability, ableness, aptitude, competence, effectiveness, efficiency, eminency, faculty, gift*, long suit*, medium, métier, oyster*, speciality, strength, strong suit*, talent, thing*; SEE CONCEPTS 409,411

fo
fo

fort/fortress [n] *stronghold*
acropolis, blockhouse, camp, castle, citadel, fastness, fortification, garrison, redoubt, station; SEE CONCEPTS *321,439*

forth [adv] *outward*
ahead, alee, along, away, first, forward, into, into the open*, on, onward, out; SEE CONCEPT *581*

forthcoming [adj] *expected, imminent*
accessible, anticipated, approaching, at hand, available, awaited, coming, destined, fated, future, impending, inescapable, in evidence, inevitable, in preparation, in prospect, in store*, in the cards*, in the wind*, nearing, obtainable, oncoming, on tap*, open, pending, predestined, prospective, ready, resulting, upcoming; SEE CONCEPTS *548,799*

forthright [adj] *straightforward, honest*
aboveboard, bald, blunt, call a spade a spade*, candid, categorical, direct, directly, forward, frank, from the hip*, like it is*, no lie*, open, outspoken, plain, plainspoken, real, simple, sincere, straight, undisguised, up front*; SEE CONCEPT *267*

forthwith [adv] *immediately*
abruptly, at once, away, directly, instantly, now, quickly, right away*, right now*, straightaway, suddenly, tout de suite, without delay; SEE CONCEPTS *544,820*

fortification [n] *reinforced position*
barricade, barrier, bastion, battlement, block, blockhouse, breastwork, buffer, bulwark, castle, citadel, consolidation, defense, earthwork, embattlement, entrenchment, fastness, fort, fortress, garrison, keep, outpost, parapet, preparation, presidio, protection, reinforcement, stockade, strengthening, stronghold, support, wall; SEE CONCEPTS *439,729*

fortify [v1] *make strong and secure; add to*
brace, build up, bulwark, buttress, charge up, consolidate, embattle, entrench, garrison, gird, prepare, prop, protect, punch up*, ready, reinforce, secure, shore up*, soup up*, steel*, step up, strengthen, support; SEE CONCEPT *202*

fortify [v2] *encourage, reassure*
arouse, brace, buck up*, build up, cheer, confirm, embolden, energize, enliven, hearten, invigorate, pour it on*, punch up*, rally, refresh, reinforce, renew, restore, rouse, stiffen, stir, strengthen, sustain; SEE CONCEPTS *7,22*

fortitude [n] *strength of mind; guts*
backbone*, boldness, braveness, bravery, constancy, courage, courageousness, dauntlessness, determination, endurance, fearlessness, firmness, grit*, gutsiness, hardihood, heart, intrepidity, mettle, moxie, nerve, patience, perseverance, pith, pluck, resoluteness, resolution, spine*, spirit, spunk, stamina, starch, staying power, stick-to-itiveness*, stomach, stoutheartedness, tenacity, true grit*, valiancy, valor, valorousness, what it takes*; SEE CONCEPTS *410,411*

fortuitous [adj] *lucky, accidental*
arbitrary, casual, chance, contingent, fluke*, fluky*, fortunate, haphazard, happy, incidental, luck in*, luck out*, lucky-dog*, odd, providential, random, serendipitous, unforeseen, unplanned; SEE CONCEPTS *548,552*

fortunate [adj] *having good luck*
advantageous, affluent, auspicious, blessed, born with a silver spoon*, bright, charmed, convenient, encouraging, favorable, favored, felicitous, flourishing, fortuitous, gaining, get a break*, golden, happy, healthy, helpful, hopeful, in luck*, in the gravy*, lucky, on a roll*, opportune, overcoming, profitable, promising, propitious, prosperous, providential, rosy, sitting pretty, successful, sunny side*, thriving, timely, triumphant, victorious, wealthy, well-off, well-to-do; SEE CONCEPTS *404,542,572*

fortunately [adv] *luckily*
auspiciously, by good luck, by happy chance*, favorably, happily, in good time*, in the nick of time*, opportunely, prosperously, providentially, satisfyingly, seasonably, successfully, swimmingly, well; SEE CONCEPTS *537,544,572*

fortune [n1] *wealth, possessions*
affluence, capital, estate, gold mine*, inheritance, opulence, portion, property, prosperity, resources, riches, substance, treasure, worth; SEE CONCEPTS *335,710*

fortune [n2] *fate, lot in life*
accident, break*, certainty, chance, circumstances, contingency, destiny, doom, expectation, experience, fifty-fifty*, fighting chance*, fluke*, fortuity, fortunateness, good break, hazard, history, karma*, kismet*, life, luck, lucked into*, lucked out*, luckiness, lucky break*, lucky hit*, Moirai, portion, providence, roll of the dice*, run of luck*, star, streak of luck, success, way the ball bounces*, way the cookie crumbles*, wheel of fortune*; SEE CONCEPT *679*

fortune-teller [n] *person attempting to tell the future*
augur, clairvoyant, crystal ball gazer, diviner, medium, mind reader, oracle, palmist, palm reader, predicter, prophet, psychic, seer, soothsayer, spiritualist, tarot reader, tea-leaf reader; SEE CONCEPTS *348,423*

forward [adj1] *advancing, early*
ahead, forth, forward-looking, in advance, leading, onward, precocious, premature, progressing, progressive, propulsive, well-developed; SEE CONCEPT *528*

forward [adj2] *in front, first*
advance, anterior, facial, fore, foremost, front, head, leading, ventral; SEE CONCEPTS *581,583, 585*

forward [adj3] *brash, impertinent*
aggressive, assuming, audacious, bantam, barefaced, bold, brazen, cheeky*, coming on strong*, confident, familiar, fresh, impudent, nervy*, overassertive, overweening, pert, presuming, presumptuous, pushing, pushy*, rude, sassy*, saucy*, self-assertive, smart, smart-alecky*, uppity*, wise; SEE CONCEPTS *401,404*

forward [adv] *toward the front in order, time*
ahead, alee, along, ante, antecedently, before, forehand, fore, forth, in advance, into prominence, into view, on, onward, out, precedently, previous, to the fore*, vanward; SEE CONCEPTS *581,585,799*

forward [v1] *aid, expedite*
advance, assist, back, champion, cultivate, encourage, favor, foster, further, hasten, help, hurry, promote, serve, speed, support, uphold; SEE CONCEPTS *68,110*

forward [v2] *send, ship*
address, consign, deliver, dispatch, express, freight, post, remit, route, transmit, transport; SEE CONCEPT *217*

fossil [*n*] *organic remains of a previous time*
deposit, eolith, impression, neolith, paleolith, petrifaction, reconstruction, relic, skeleton, specimen, trace; SEE CONCEPTS 429,470,509

foster [*v1*] *promote, support*
advance, back, champion, cherish, cultivate, encourage, feed, foment, forward, further, harbor, nurse, nurture, serve, stimulate, uphold; SEE CONCEPT 110

foster [*v2*] *give care or accommodation to*
assist, bring up, care for, cherish, entertain, favor, harbor, help, house, lodge, minister to, nourish, nurse, oblige, raise, rear, serve, shelter, sustain, take care of; SEE CONCEPTS 110,140,295

foul [*adj1*] *disgusting, dirty*
abhorrent, abominable, base, contaminated, despicable, detestable, disgraceful, dishonorable, egregious, fetid, filthy, gross*, hateful, heinous, horrid, icky*, impure, infamous, iniquitous, loathsome, malodorous, mucky*, nasty, nauseating, nefarious, noisome, notorious, offensive, pigpen*, polluted, putrid, rank*, raunchy*, repellent, repulsive, revolting, rotten, scandalous, shameful, squalid, stinking*, sullied, tainted, unclean, vicious, vile, wicked, yecchy*, yucky*; SEE CONCEPTS 485,529

foul [*adj2*] *vulgar, offensive*
abusive, blasphemous, blue*, coarse, dirty, filthy, foul-mouthed, gross*, indecent, lewd, low, nasty, obscene, profane, raunchy, scatological, scurrilous, smutty*; SEE CONCEPTS 267

foul [*adj3*] *corrupt, dishonest*
caitiff, crooked, dirty, fraudulent, inequitable, monstrous, shady, underhand, underhanded, unfair, unjust, unscrupulous, vicious; SEE CONCEPTS 537,548

foul [*n*] *infraction*
breach, encroachment, error, faux pas, infringement, offense, slip*, violation; SEE CONCEPTS 192,691

foul [*v*] *make or become dirty*
befoul, begrime, besmear, besmirch, block, catch, choke, clog, contaminate, defile, desecrate, discolor, ensnare, entangle, fill, jam, pollute, profane, smear, smudge, snarl, soil, spot, stain, sully, taint, tarnish, twist; SEE CONCEPTS 250,469

foul play [*n*] *treacherous action*
bad deed, corruption, crime, cruel act, dirty trick, dirty work, felony, fraud, funny business, lawbreaking, murder, violence, wrong; SEE CONCEPT 645

foul up [*v*] *make a mess of*
botch, bungle, confuse, jumble, mismanage, mix up*, muck up*, muddle, screw up*, snafu*, snarl, tumble; SEE CONCEPTS 16,234

found [*v1*] *bring into being*
begin, commence, constitute, construct, create, endow, erect, establish, fashion, fix, form, get going, inaugurate, initiate, institute, launch, organize, originate, plant, raise, ring in*, settle, settle up, start, start the ball rolling*, start up; SEE CONCEPT 221

found [*v2*] *put on a base*
bottom, build, erect, establish, ground, predicate, raise, rear, rest, root, stay, support, sustain; SEE CONCEPTS 168,221

foundation [*n1*] *basis for something physical or mental*
ABCs*, authority, base, basics, bed, bedrock, bottom, bottom line*, brass tacks*, foot, footing, ground, groundwork, guts*, heart*, infrastructure, justification, nitty-gritty*, nub*, nuts and bolts*, prop, reason, root, stay, substratum, substructure, support, underpinning, understructure; SEE CONCEPTS 442,826

foundation [*n2*] *established institution*
association, charity, company, corporation, endowment, establishment, guild, inauguration, institute, organization, plantation, settlement, set-up, society, trusteeship; SEE CONCEPT 381

founder [*n*] *person who establishes an institution*
architect, author, beginner, benefactor, builder, constructor, creator, designer, establisher, forebearer, framer, generator, initiator, institutor, inventor, maker, organizer, originator, patron, planner, prime mover*; SEE CONCEPTS 347,423

founder [*v*] *go under, fail*
abort, be lost, break down, collapse, come to nothing, fall, fall through, go down, go lame, go to bottom, lurch, miscarry, misfire, sink, sprawl, stagger, stumble, submerge, submerse, trip; SEE CONCEPTS 181,699

fountain [*n*] *source, often of liquid*
bubbler, cause, font, fount, geyser, gush, inception, inspiration, jet, lode, mainspring, mine, origin, play, provenance, provenience, pump, reservoir, root, spout, spray, spring, stream, well, wellhead, wellspring; SEE CONCEPTS 514,648

fountainhead [*n*] *principal source; person who originates*
administrator, architect, author, builder, creator, father, fount, fountain, generator, initiator, leader, maker, mother, originator, spring, wellspring; SEE CONCEPTS 348,350

foxy [*adj*] *shrewd*
artful, astute, canny, crafty, cunning, deceitful, deep, devious, dishonest, experienced, guileful, insidious, intelligent, knowing, retiary, sharp, slick, sly, subtle, tricky, vulpine, wily; SEE CONCEPTS 401,404

foyer [*n*] *receiving area*
antechamber, anteroom, entrance hall, lobby, reception, vestibule; SEE CONCEPTS 440,441,448

fracas [*n*] *disturbance, fight*
affray, altercation, battle, battle royal*, bickering, brawl, broil*, brouhaha, dispute, donnybrook*, feud, flap*, fray, free-for-all*, hassle, knock-down-drag-out*, melee, mix up*, quarrel, riot, row, ruction, ruffle, rumpus, run-in*, scrimmage, scuffle, set-to*, squabble, stew*, trouble, tumult, uproar, words*; SEE CONCEPTS 46,106

fraction [*n1*] *part*
bite, chunk, cut, division, end, fragment, half, piece, portion, section, share, slice; SEE CONCEPT 835

fraction [*n2*] *incomplete number*
bit, division, fragment, part, partial, piece, portion, quotient, ratio, section, segment, slice, subdivision; SEE CONCEPT 765

fractional [*adj*] *partial*
apportioned, compartmental, compartmentalized, constituent, dismembered, dispersed, divided, fragmentary, frationary, incomplete, parceled, part, piecemeal, sectional, segmented; SEE CONCEPT 785

fractious [*adj*] *grouchy, cross*
awkward, captious, crabby*, disorderly, fretful, froward, huffy*, indocile, indomitable, intractable, irritable, mean, ornery*, peevish, per-

fo
fr

verse, pettish, petulant, querulous, recalcitrant, refractory, restive, scrappy, snappish, testy, thin-skinned, touchy, uncompliant, undisciplined, unmanageable, unruly, wayward, wild; SEE CONCEPTS 267,401

fracture [n] *break, rupture*
breach, cleavage, cleft, crack, discontinuity, disjunction, displacement, fissure, fragmentation, gap, mutilation, opening, rent, rift, schism, severance, splinter, split, wound; SEE CONCEPTS 309,513

fragile [adj] *breakable, dainty*
brittle, crisp, crumbly, decrepit, delicate, feeble, fine, flimsy, fracturable, frail, frangible, friable, infirm, insubstantial, shatterable, shivery, slight, unsound, weak, weakly; SEE CONCEPTS 485,489

fragment [n] *part, chip*
ace, atom, bit, bite, chunk, crumb, cut, end, fraction, gob*, grain, hunk, iota, job*, lump*, minim, morsel, particle, piece, portion, remnant, scrap, share, shiver, shred, slice, sliver, smithereen*; SEE CONCEPT 835

fragment [v] *break into pieces*
burst, come apart, crumble, disintegrate, disunite, divide, rend, rive, shatter, shiver, smash, splinter, split, split up; SEE CONCEPTS 98,135, 137,246,469

fragmentary [adj] *broken, incomplete*
bitty, disconnected, discrete, disjointed, fractional, incoherent, part, partial, piecemeal, scattered, scrappy, sketchy, unsystematic; SEE CONCEPT 785

fragrance [n] *pleasant odor*
aroma, aura, balm, bouquet, incense, perfume, redolence, scent, smell, spice; SEE CONCEPT 600

fragrant [adj] *smelling pleasant*
ambrosial, aromal, aromatic, balmy, delectable, delicious, delightful, odoriferous, odorous, perfumed, perfumy, redolent, savory, spicy, sweet, sweet-scented, sweet-smelling; SEE CONCEPT 598

frail [adj] *breakable, weak*
brittle, dainty, decrepit, delicate, feeble, fishy, flimsy, fracturable, fragile, frangible, infirm, insubstantial, puny, sad, shatterable, shattery, sickly, slender, slight, slim, tender, tenuous, thin, unsound, unsubstantial, vulnerable, wimpy*, wishy-washy*, wispy; SEE CONCEPTS 485,489

frailty [n] *weakness, flaw*
Achilles heel*, blemish, daintiness, debility, decrepitude, defect, deficiency, delicacy, error, failing, fallibility, fault, feebleness, flimsiness, foible, foil, imperfection, infirmity, peccability, peccadillo, shortcoming, solecism, suscept, weak point*; SEE CONCEPTS 101,230,411,580

frame [n] *skeleton, casing*
anatomy, architecture, body, build, cage, carcass, construction, enclosure, fabric, flounce, form, framework, fringe, groundwork, hem, mount, mounting, outline, physique, scaffold, scaffolding, scheme, setting, shell, stage, structure, support, system, trim, trimming, truss, valance; SEE CONCEPTS 442,733,757

frame [v] *build*
assemble, back, border, constitute, construct, encase, enclose, erect, fabricate, fashion, forge, form, institute, invent, lath, make, manufacture, mat, model, mold, mount, panel, produce, put together, raise, set up, shingle; SEE CONCEPTS 168,758

frame [v2] *compose, plan*
block out, conceive, concoct, contrive, cook up, design, devise, draft, draw up, dream up*, form, formulate, hatch, indite, invent, make, make up, map out, outline, prepare, shape, sketch, vamp, write; SEE CONCEPTS 36,173

frame of mind [n] *state of mind*
attitude, constitution, disposition, emotions, inner nature, makeup, mentality, mood, nature, spirit, state, temperament; SEE CONCEPTS 410,689

framework [n] *foundation, core*
bare bones*, cage, fabric, frame, frame of reference*, groundwork, plan, schema, scheme, shell, skeleton, structure; SEE CONCEPTS 439,479,733

franchise [n] *authority, right*
authorization, ballot, charter, exemption, freedom, immunity, patent, prerogative, privilege, suffrage, vote; SEE CONCEPT 376

frank [adj] *completely honest*
aboveboard, apparent, artless, bare-faced*, blunt, bold, brazen, call a spade a spade*, candid, direct, downright, easy, familiar, flat-out*, forthright, free, from the hip*, guileless, heart-to-heart*, ingenuous, lay it on the line*, like it is*, matter-of-fact, naive, natural, open, outright, outspoken, plain, plain-spoken, real, saying what one thinks*, scrupulous, sincere, straight, straightforward, transparent, truthful, unconcealed, undisguised, uninhibited, unreserved, unrestricted, up front*, upright; SEE CONCEPTS 267,582

frankfurter [n] *cylindrical meat sausage*
bowwow*, Coney Island*, dog*, footlong*, frank, hot dog, link, weenie*, wiener, wienerwurst; SEE CONCEPTS 457,460

frankly [adv] *very honestly*
bluntly, candidly, dead level*, dead on*, directly, forthrightly, freely, from the hip*, in truth, laid on the line*, level, on the level*, on the line*, openly, plainly, straight, straightforwardly, without reserve; SEE CONCEPT 267

frantic [adj] *distressed, distracted*
agitated, angry, at wits' end*, berserk, beside oneself*, corybantic, crazy, delirious, deranged, distraught, excited, flipped out*, fraught, freaked out*, frenetic, frenzied, furious, hectic, hot and bothered*, hot under the collar*, hyper*, in a stew*, in a tizzy*, insane, keyed up*, mad, out of control, overwrought, rabid, raging, raving, shook up*, spazzed out*, unglued*, unscrewed*, unzipped*, violent, weird, weirded out*, wigged out*, wild, wired*, worked up*, zonkers*; SEE CONCEPTS 403,542

fraternity [n] *brotherhood*
affiliation, camaraderie, club, fellowship, frat*, guild, house, kinship, order, sisterhood, society, sorority; SEE CONCEPTS 381,387

fraternize [v] *associate with*
be friendly, be sociable with, club together, consort with, fall in with, go around with, hang out with, hobnob*, keep company with, make friends, mingle with, mix with, rub elbows with, rub shoulders with, run with, socialize with; SEE CONCEPTS 114,384

fraud [n1] *trickery, deception*
artifice, bamboozlement*, blackmail, cheat, chicane, chicanery, con, craft*, deceit, double-dealing*, dupery, duping, duplicity, extortion, fake, fast one*, fast shuffle*, flimflam*, fourberie,

fraudulence, graft, guile, hanky-panky*, hoax, hocus-pocus*, hoodwinking*, hustle*, imposture, line, misrepresentation, racket, scam, sell, shakedown*, sham*, sharp practice*, skunk*, smoke*, song*, song and dance*, spuriousness, sting, string, swindle, swindling, treachery; SEE CONCEPTS 59,192,645

fraud [n2] *person who is false, deceitful*
bastard, bluffer, charlatan, cheat, counterfeit, crook, deceiver, double-dealer*, fake, forger, four-flusher*, hoaxer, horse trader*, impostor, mechanic*, mountebank, phony, play actor*, pretender, quack*, racketeer, sham*, shark*, swindler; SEE CONCEPT 412

fraudulent [adj] *deceptive, false*
bamboozling*, counterfeit, crafty, criminal, crooked, deceitful, devious, dishonest, dishonorable, double-dealing*, duplicitous, fake, forged, mock, phony, pseudo, sham*, spurious, swindling, treacherous, tricky; SEE CONCEPTS 545,582

fraught [adj] *full of*
abounding, attended, bristling, charged, filled, heavy, laden, replete, stuffed; SEE CONCEPTS 483,771

fray [n] *fight, battle*
affray, battle royal*, brawl, broil*, brouhaha*, clash, combat, conflict, contest, disturbance, donnybrook*, engagement, fracas, melee, quarrel, riot, row, ruckus, rumble, rumpus, scuffle, set-to*; SEE CONCEPTS 86,106

fray [v] *shred, come apart*
become ragged, become threadbare, chafe, erode, frazzle, fret, ravel, rip, rub, tatter, tear, unravel, wear, wear away, wear thin; SEE CONCEPT 214

frazzle [n] *exhaustion; something very worn*
collapse, enervation, lassitude, prostration, rag, remnant, shred; SEE CONCEPTS 410,720

frazzle [v] *wear out*
exhaust, fray, knock out, poop*, prostrate, rip, shred, tear, tire, tucker*, wear; SEE CONCEPTS 156,186

freak [n1] *something, someone very abnormal*
aberration, abortion, anomaly, chimera, curiosity, geek*, grotesque, malformation, miscreation, misshape, monster, monstrosity, mutant, mutation, oddity, queer, rarity, sport, weirdo*; SEE CONCEPTS 424,580

freak [n2] *irregularity, whim*
caprice, conceit, crochet, fad, fancy, folly, humor, megrim, quirk, turn, twist, vagary, whimsy; SEE CONCEPT 679

freak [n3] *person enthused about something*
addict, aficionado, buff, bug*, devotee, enthusiast, fan, fanatic, fiend*, maniac, nut*, zealot; SEE CONCEPTS 352,366,423

freak [v] *become extraordinarily upset*
flip out*, go beserk, go insane, go mad, lose control, rave, unhinge*, wig out*; SEE CONCEPTS 7,19,80

freakish [adj] *abnormal, unusual*
aberrant, arbitrary, bizarre, capricious, crazy, erratic, fantastic, far-out, freaky, grotesque, malformed, monstrous, odd, outlandish, outré, preternatural, queer, strange, unconventional, vagarious, wayward, weird, whimsical, wild; SEE CONCEPT 564

freak out [v] *lose one's cool*
blow a gasket*, blow one's mind*, blow one's stack*, blow one's top*, break down, come unglued, crack up*, flip out*, fly off the handle*, freak out*, go ape*, go ballistic*, go berserk*, go crazy*, go haywire*, go nuts*, go off the deep end*, hit the ceiling*, lose control of oneself, lose it*, lose one's composure, lose one's mind, lose one's temper, wig out*; SEE CONCEPTS 7,19,80

freckle [n] *small discoloration on skin*
blemish, blotch, daisy, dot, lentigo, macula, mole, patch, pepper, pigmentation, pit, pock, pockmark, speck, speckle, sprinkle, stipple; SEE CONCEPT 392

free [adj1] *without charge*
chargeless, comp*, complimentary, costless, for love*, for nothing*, freebie*, free of cost, free ride*, gratis, gratuitous, handout, on the cuff*, on the house*, paper*, unpaid, unrecompensed*; SEE CONCEPT 334

free [adj2] *unrestrained personally*
able, allowed, at large, at liberty, casual, clear, disengaged, easy, escaped, familiar, fancy-free*, footloose, forward, frank, free-spirited, freewheeling, independent, informal, lax, liberal, liberated, loose, off the hook*, on one's own*, on the loose*, open, permitted, relaxed, unattached, uncommitted, unconfined, unconstrained, unengaged, unfettered, unhampered, unimpeded, unobstructed, unregulated, unrestricted, untrammeled; SEE CONCEPTS 401,542

free [adj3] *unrestrained politically*
at liberty, autarchic, autonomic, autonomous, democratic, emancipated, enfranchised, freed, independent, individualistic, liberated, self-directing, self-governing, self-ruling, separate, sovereign, sui juris, unconstrained, unenslaved, unregimented; SEE CONCEPTS 319,536

free [adj4] *not busy; unoccupied*
at leisure, available, clear, empty, extra, idle, loose, not tied down*, spare, unemployed, unengaged, unhampered, unimpeded, uninhabited, unobstructed, unused, vacant; SEE CONCEPT 485

free [adj5] *generous, unsparing*
big, big-hearted*, bounteous, bountiful, charitable, eager, handsome, hospitable, lavish, liberal, munificent, open-handed*, prodigal, unstinging, willing; SEE CONCEPT 404

free [v1] *liberate, let go*
absolve, acquit, bail, bail out*, clear, cut loose*, deliver, demobilize, discharge, disengage, disenthrall, disimprison, dismiss, emancipate, enfranchise, extricate, let loose*, let off*, let off the hook*, let out, loose, loosen, manumit, pardon, parole, put on the street*, ransom, redeem, release, relieve, reprieve, rescue, save, set free, spring*, turn loose, turn out, unbind, uncage, unchain, undo, unfetter, unfix, unleash, untie; SEE CONCEPT 127

free [v2] *take burden from*
cast off, clear, cut loose, decontaminate, deliver, discharge, disembarrass, disencumber, disengage, disentangle, empty, excuse, exempt, extricate, put off, ransom, redeem, relieve, rescue, rid, unburden, undo, unlade, unload, unpack, unshackle; SEE CONCEPTS 110,211

freebie [n] *something for nothing*
complimentary ticket, free lunch, free pass, gift, giveaway, handout; SEE CONCEPT 337

freedom [n1] *independence, license to do as one wants*
abandon, abandonment, ability, bent, carte

fr
fr

blanche, compass, discretion, elbowroom*, exemption, facility, flexibility, free rein*, full play*, full swing*, immunity, indulgence, laissez faire, latitude, laxity, leeway, liberty, margin, opportunity, own accord*, play, plenty of rope*, power, prerogative, privilege, profligacy, rampancy, range, rein, right, rope*, scope, sweep, swing, unrestraint; SEE CONCEPT 693

freedom [n2] *political independence*
abolition, abolitionism, autarchy, autonomy, citizenship, deliverance, delivery, democracy, discharge, disengagement, disimprisonment, emancipation, enfranchisement, exemption, extriction, franchise, home rule*, immunity, impunity, liberation, liberty, manumission, parole, prerogative, privilege, probation, redemption, release, relief, representative government, rescue, salvage, salvation, selfdetermination, self-government, sovereignty; SEE CONCEPT 691

freedom [n3] *easy attitude*
abandon, boldness, brazenness, candor, directness, disrespect, ease, facility, familiarity, forthrightness, forwardness, frankness, impertinence, informality, ingenuousness, lack of reserve, lack of restraint, laxity, license, openness, overfamiliarity, presumption, readiness, spontaneity, unconstraint; SEE CONCEPT 633

free-for-all [n] *fight*
affray, battle, brawl, broil*, brouhaha*, fracas, fray, knock-down-drag-out*, melee, riot, row, ruction; SEE CONCEPT 106

freelance [adj] *independent*
free agent, non-staff, self-employed, unaffiliated; SEE CONCEPT 554

freely [adj1] *without restriction*
advisedly, as you please*, at one's discretion, at one's pleasure, at will, candidly, deliberately, designedly, fancy-free*, frankly, intentionally, of one's own accord*, of one's own free will*, openly, plainly, purposely, spontaneously, unchallenged, unreservedly, voluntarily, willingly, without hindrance, without prompting, without reserve, without restraint, without urging; SEE CONCEPT 401

freely [adv2] *easily, smoothly done*
abundantly, amply, as one pleases*, bountifully, cleanly, copiously, effortlessly, extravagantly, facilely, lavishly, liberally, lightly, like water*, loosely, open-handedly, readily, unhindered, unobstructedly, unstintingly, well, with a free hand*, without encumbrance*, without hindrance*, without restraint*, without stint*; SEE CONCEPT 544

free spirit [n] *maverick*
bohemian, dissenter, eccentric, nonconformist, radical; SEE CONCEPT 359

freeware [n] *free software*
public-domain software, shareware; SEE CONCEPTS 274,660

freeway [n] *expressway*
artery, beltway, highway, interstate, parkway, road, superhighway, thoroughfare, thruway; SEE CONCEPT 501

free will [n] *person's full intent and purpose*
assent, choice, consent, desire, determination, discretion, free choice, freedom, inclination, intention, mind, option, own say so*, own sweet way*, pleasure, power, say so*, velleity, volition, voluntary decision, willingness, wish; SEE CONCEPTS 20,410

freeze [v1] *make cold enough to become solid*
benumb, bite, chill, chill to the bone*, congeal, frost, glaciate, harden, ice over, ice up, nip, pierce, refrigerate, solidify, stiffen; SEE CONCEPTS 255,521

freeze [v2] *stop*
dampen, depress, discourage, dishearten, fix, hold up, inhibit, peg, suspend; SEE CONCEPTS 14,121

freezer [n] *icebox*
cold storage, cooler, refrigerator; SEE CONCEPTS 202,255

freezing [adj] *very cold*
arctic, biting, bitter, chill, chilled, chilly, cutting, frigid, frost-bound, frosty, gelid, glacial, hawkish, icy, nippy, numbing, one-dog night*, penetrating, polar, raw, shivery, Siberian*, snappy*, two-dog night*, wintry; SEE CONCEPT 605

freight [n] *goods being shipped*
bales, ballast, bulk, burden, carriage, consignment, contents, conveyance, encumbrance, fardel, haul, lading, load, merchandise, pack, packages, payload, shipment, shipping, tonnage, transportation, wares, weight; SEE CONCEPT 338

frenetic [adj] *maniacal*
corybantic, delirious, demented, distraught, excited, fanatical, frantic, frenzied, furibund, furious, hyper*, in a lather*, insane, lost it*, mad, obsessive, overwrought, phrenetic, rabid, unbalanced, unscrewed*, weirded out*, wigged out*, wild, wired*; SEE CONCEPT 403

frenzied [adj] *uncontrolled*
agitated, berserk, convulsive, corybantic, delirious, distracted, distraught, excited, feverish, frantic, frenetic, furious, hysterical, mad, maniacal, nuts*, rabid, wild; SEE CONCEPTS 542,544

frenzy [n] *uncontrolled state or situation*
aberration, agitation, blow, blow a fuse*, blow one's cork*, blow one's stack*, blow one's top*, bout, burst, conniption*, convulsion, craze, delirium, derangement, distemper, distraction, dithers*, excitement, ferment, fever, fit, flap*, flip one's lid*, free-for-all*, furor, fury, fuss, hell broke loose*, hysteria, insanity, lather, lunacy, madness, mania, outburst, paroxysm, passion, rage, row, ruckus, ruction, rumble, rumpus, seizure, spasm, stew, stir, to-do*, transport, turmoil, wingding*; SEE CONCEPTS 230,410,674

frequency [n] *commonness, repetitiveness*
abundance, beat, constancy, density, frequentness, iteration, number, oscillation, periodicity, persistence, prevalence, pulsation, recurrence, regularity, reiteration, repetition, rhythm; SEE CONCEPT 634

frequent [adj] *common, repeated*
a good many*, commonplace, constant, continual, customary, everyday, expected, familiar, general, habitual, incessant, intermittent, iterated, manifold, many, monotonous, numberless, numerous, periodic, perpetual, persistent, pleonastic, profuse, recurrent, recurring, redundant, reiterated, reiterative, successive, thick, ubiquitous, usual, various; SEE CONCEPT 530

frequent [v] *be a regular customer of*
affect, attend, attend regularly, be at home in*, be found at, be often in, drop in, go to, hang about*, hang around*, hang out at*, haunt*, hit*, infest, overrun, patronize, play*, resort, revisit, visit often; SEE CONCEPTS 227,384

frequently [*adv*] *commonly, repeatedly*
again and again*, as a rule*, at regular intervals, at short intervals, at times, by ordinary, customarily, every now and then*, generally, habitually, in many instances*, in quick succession, intermittently, many a time*, many times, much, not infrequently, not seldom, oft, often, oftentimes, ofttimes, ordinarily, over and over, periodically, recurrently, regularly, spasmodically, successively, thick and fast*, time and again*, usually, very often; SEE CONCEPTS 530,544,799

fresh [*adj1*] *new, just produced*
beginning, brand-new*, comer, contemporary, crisp, crude, current, different, gleaming, glistening, green*, hot*, hot off the press*, immature, just out*, late, latest, mint*, modern, modernistic, natural, neoteric, newborn, newfangled*, novel, now, original, radical, raw, recent, sparkling, state-of-the-art, the latest*, this season's*, unconventional, unprocessed, unseasoned, untouched, unusual, up-to-date, virginal, what's happening*, young, youthful; SEE CONCEPTS 578,797

fresh [*adj2*] *additional*
added, another, auxiliary, else, extra, farther, further, increased, more, new, other, renewed, supplementary; SEE CONCEPTS 546,824

fresh [*adj3*] *refreshing to the senses*
bracing, bright, brisk, clean, clear, colorful, cool, crisp, definite, fair, invigorating, not stale, pure, quick, sharp, spanking, sparkling, stiff, stimulating, sweet, uncontaminated, unpolluted, vivid; SEE CONCEPT 537

fresh [*adj4*] *energetic, healthy*
active, alert, blooming, bouncing, bright, bright-eyed, bushy-tailed*, chipper*, clear, dewy, fair, florid, glowing, good, hardy, invigorated, keen, like new, lively, refreshed, rehabilitated, relaxed, relieved, rested, restored, revived, rosy, ruddy, sprightly, spry, stimulated, undimmed, unfaded, unused, unwearied, unwithered, verdant, vigorous, vital, wholesome, young; SEE CONCEPTS 485,542

fresh [*adj5*] *inexperienced*
artless, callow, green*, natural, new, raw, tender-footed*, uncultivated, unpracticed, unskilled, untrained, untried, unversed, young, youthful; SEE CONCEPT 404

fresh [*adj6*] *sassy, brazen*
bold, cheeky*, disrespectful, familiar, flip*, flippant, forward, impertinent, impudent, insolent, nervy*, pert, presumptuous, rude, saucy*, smart*, smart-alecky*, snippy*, wise; SEE CONCEPTS 267,401

freshen [*v*] *make like new; revitalize*
activate, air, cleanse, enliven, invigorate, purify, refresh, restore, revive, rouse, spruce up, sweeten, titivate, ventilate; SEE CONCEPT 244

freshman [*n*] *first-year student*
beginner, frosh*, greenhorn, novice, rookie, underclassman, undergrad*, undergraduate; SEE CONCEPTS 348,350,423

freshness [*n*] *newness*
bloom, brightness, callowness, cleanness, clearness, dew, dewiness, glow, greenness, inexperience, innovativeness, inventiveness, novelty, originality, rawness, shine, sparkle, vigor, viridity, youth; SEE CONCEPT 715

fret [*v1*] *worry, be annoyed*
affront, agonize, anguish, bleed, bother, brood,

carp, carry a heavy load*, chafe, chagrin, distress oneself, eat one's heart out*, fume, fuss, get into a dither*, grieve, lose sleep over*, mope*, pother*, stew, sweat it out*, take on, torment, upset oneself; SEE CONCEPT 410

fret [*v2*] *upset someone*
abrade, agitate, bother, displease, distress, disturb, gall, get on nerves*, goad, harass, irk, irritate, nag, nettle, peeve, pique, provoke, rile, ruffle, torment, trouble, vex; SEE CONCEPTS 7,19

fret [*v3*] *rub hard*
abrade, chafe, corrode, erode, excoriate, fray, gall, riffle, ripple, wear away, wear threadbare; SEE CONCEPT 215

fretful [*adj*] *irritable*
captious, carping*, caviling, complaining, contrary, crabby*, cranky*, critical, cross, crotchety*, edgy, faultfinding, fractious, huffy*, mean, ornery*, out of sorts*, peevish, perverse, petulant, querulous, short-tempered, snappish*, splenetic, testy, touchy, uneasy, worried, wreck*; SEE CONCEPTS 401,403

friction [*n1*] *rubbing*
abrasion, agitation, attrition, chafing, erosion, filing, fretting, grating, grinding, irritation, massage, rasping, resistance, scraping, soreness, traction, trituration, wearing away; SEE CONCEPT 215

friction [*n2*] *disagreement*
animosity, antagonism, bad blood*, bad feeling*, bickering, bone to pick*, conflict, counteraction, discontent, discord, disharmony, dispute, dissension, faction, factionalism, flak*, hassle, hatred, hostility, impedance, incompatibility, interference, opposition, quarrel, resentment, resistance, rivalry, row*, ruckus*, rumpus*, set-to*, sour note*, strife, trouble, wrangling*; SEE CONCEPTS 46,106,674

friend [*n1*] *confidant, companion*
acquaintance, ally, alter ego, associate, bosom buddy*, buddy, chum*, classmate, cohort, colleague, companion*, compatriot, comrade, consort, cousin, crony, familiar, intimate, mate, pal, partner, playmate, roommate, schoolmate, sidekick, soul mate*, spare*, well-wisher; SEE CONCEPT 423

friend [*n2*] *benefactor*
accomplice, adherent, advocate, ally, associate, backer, partisan, patron, supporter, well-wisher; SEE CONCEPT 348

friendless [*adj*] *without companionship or confidant*
abandoned, adrift, alienated, all alone*, all by one's self*, alone, cut off*, deserted, estranged, forlorn, forsaken, isolated, lonely, lonesome, marooned*, ostracized, shunned, solitary, unattached, without ties; SEE CONCEPT 555

friendliness [*n*] *companionability*
affability, amiability, amity, benevolence, camaraderie, comity, comradery, congeniality, conviviality, cordiality, friendship, geniality, goodwill, kindliness, kindness, neighborliness, open arms*, sociability, warmth; SEE CONCEPT 388

friendly [*adj*] *intimate, companionable*
affable, affectionate, amiable, amicable, attached, attentive, auspicious, beneficial, benevolent, benign, buddy-buddy*, chummy*, civil, close, clubby, comradely, conciliatory, confiding, convivial, cordial, faithful, familiar, favor-

fr
fr

able, fond, genial, good, helpful, kind, kindly, loving, loyal, neighborly, on good terms*, outgoing, peaceable, peaceful, propitious, receptive, sociable, solicitous, sympathetic, tender, thick, welcoming, well-disposed*; SEE CONCEPT 555

friendship [n] *companionship*
accord, acquaintanceship, affection, affinity, agreement, alliance, amiability, amicability, amity, association, attachment, attraction, benevolence, closeness, coalition, comity, company, concord, consideration, consonance, devotion, empathy, esteem, familiarity, favor, favoritism, fondness, friendliness, fusion, good will, harmony, intimacy, league, love, pact, partiality, rapport, regard, sociability, society, sodality, solidarity, understanding; SEE CONCEPTS 388,714

fright [n1] *extreme apprehension*
alarm, cold sweat*, consternation, dismay, dread, fear, horror, panic, quaking, scare, shiver, shock, terror, trepidation, trepidity; SEE CONCEPT 410

fright [n2] *horrifying or unpleasant sight*
bother, eyesore*, frump*, mess, monstrosity, nuisance, scarecrow, ugliness; SEE CONCEPT 718

frighten [v] *shock, scare*
affright, agitate, alarm, appall, astound, awe, browbeat*, bulldoze*, chill, chill to the bone*, cow, curdle the blood*, daunt, demoralize, deter, disburb, discomfort, disconcert, discourage, dishearten, dismay, disquiet, faze, horrify, intimidate, make blood run cold*, make teeth chatter*, panic, perturb, petrify, repel, scare away, scare off, scare to death*, spook, startle, stiff, strike terror into*, terrify, terrorize, unhinge*, unnerve*; SEE CONCEPTS 14,42

frightened [adj] *very scared*
abashed, affrighted, afraid, aghast, alarmed, anxious, butterflies*, chicken*, chicken-hearted*, cowed*, dismayed, fearful, frozen, have cold feet*, having kittens*, hung up*, in a cold sweat*, in a panic*, in a sweat*, jellyfish*, jittery, jumpy, lily-livered*, mousy*, numb, panicky, petrified, pushing the panic button*, rabbity*, running scared*, scared stiff*, shaky, shivery, sissy*, spooked, startled, terrified, terrorized, terror-stricken, unnerved, uptight, yellow*; SEE CONCEPTS 403,690

frightful [adj2] *offensive*
annoying, awful, bad, calamitous, disagreeable, dreadful, extreme, ghastly, great, hideous, horrible, insufferable, lewd, shocking, terrible, terrific, unpleasant, vile, wicked, wrong; SEE CONCEPTS 529,545

frightful/frightening [adj1] *scary, shocking*
alarming, appalling, atrocious, awesome, awful, chilling, daunting, dire, direful, dismaying, disquieting, dread, dreadful, fearful, fearsome, formidable, ghastly, grabber, grim, grisly, gruesome, hair-raising, hairy, harrowing, hideous, horrendous, horrible, horrid, horrifying, inconceivable, intimidating, lurid, macabre, menacing, morbid, ominous, petrifying, portentous, repellent, spooky, terrible, terrifying, traumatic, unnerving, unspeakable; SEE CONCEPTS 529,537

frigid [adj1] *extremely cold*
antarctic, arctic, chill, chilly, cool, freezing, frost-bound, frosty, frozen, gelid, glacial, hyperboreal, icebox*, ice-cold, icy, refrigerated, Siber-

ian*, snappy, three-dog night*, wintry; SEE CONCEPT 605

frigid [adj2] *unresponsive*
aloof, austere, chilly, cold, cold-hearted*, coldshoulder*, cool, forbidding, formal, frosty, icy, impotent, indifferent, lifeless, passionless, passive, repellent, rigid, stiff, unapproachable, unbending, unfeeling, unloving; SEE CONCEPT 404

frill [n] *luxury, nice touch*
amenity, decoration, doodad*, extravagance, fandangle, flounce, foppery*, frippery*, fuss, garbage*, garnish, gathering, gimcrack*, gingerbread*, jazz*, lace, ruffle, superfluity, thing*, tuck; SEE CONCEPTS 646,655,824

fringe [n] *border, trimming*
binding, borderline, brim, brink, edge, edging, flounce, hem, limit, mane, march, margin, outside, outskirts, perimeter, periphery, rickrack, ruffle, skirt, tassel, verge; SEE CONCEPTS 484,825

frippery [n] *waste, nonsense*
adornment, bauble, decoration, fanciness, fandangle*, flashiness, frill, fussiness, gaudiness, knickknack, meretriciousness, ornament, ostentation, pretentiousness, showiness, tawdriness, toy, trinket; SEE CONCEPTS 655,824

frisk [v1] *cavort*
bounce, caper, dance, frolic, gambol, hop, jump, lark, leap, play, prance, rollick, romp, skip, sport, trip; SEE CONCEPT 384

frisk [v2] *search*
check, fan, inspect, run over, shake down; SEE CONCEPT 216

frisky [adj] *full of spirit*
active, antic, bouncy, coltish*, dashing, feeling one's oats*, frolicsome, full of beans*, gamesome, high-spirited, in high spirits*, jumpy, kittenish*, larkish, lively, peppy, playful, prankish, rollicking, romping, spirited, sportive, wicked, zesty, zippy; SEE CONCEPTS 401,542,555

fritter [v] *waste away*
be wasteful with, blow*, cast away, consume, dally, diddle away, dissipate, frivol, go through*, idle, lavish, misspend, run through*, spend like water*, squander, throw away, trifle; SEE CONCEPTS 156,341

frivolity [n] *silliness, childishness*
coquetting, dallying, flightiness, flippancy, flirting, flummery, folly, fribble, frippery, frivolousness, fun, gaiety, game, giddiness, jest, levity, lightheartedness, lightness, nonsense, play, puerility, shallowness, sport, superficiality, toying, trifling, triviality, volatility, whimsicality, whimsy; SEE CONCEPTS 388,633

frivolous [adj] *trivial, silly*
barmy*, childish, dizzy*, empty-headed*, facetious, featherbrained*, flighty, flip, flippant, foolish, gay, giddy*, harebrained*, idiotic, idle, ill-considered, impractical, juvenile, light, lightminded, minor, niggling*, nonserious, not serious, paltry, peripheral, petty, playful, pointless, puerile, scatterbrained*, senseless, shallow, sportive, superficial, tongue-in-cheek*, unimportant, unprofound, volatile, whimsical; SEE CONCEPTS 401,402,575

frock [n] *women's garment*
apron, clothing, dress, gown, habit, muumuu, robe; SEE CONCEPT 451

frog [n] *jumping amphibian*
bullfrog, croaker*, polliwog, toad; SEE CONCEPT 394

frolic [*n*] *amusement, revel*
antic, drollery, escapade, fun, fun and games*, gaiety, gambol, game, high jinks*, joke, joviality, lark, merriment, monkeyshines*, play, prank, romp, shenanigan*, skylarking*, sport, spree, tomfoolery*, trick; SEE CONCEPTS *59,386*

frolic [*v*] *have fun, make merry*
caper, carouse, cavort, cut capers, cut loose*, fool around*, frisk, gambol, go on a tear*, kick up one's heels*, lark, let go*, let loose*, play, prance, raise hell*, revel, riot, rollick, romp, sport, spree, whoop it up*; SEE CONCEPTS *384,386*

frolicsome [*adj*] *playful*
antic, coltish, frisky, fun, gamesome, gay, gleeful, happy, impish, jocular, jovial, kittenish, lively, merry, mischievous, roguish, rollicking, sportive, sprightly; SEE CONCEPT *542*

from [*prep1*] *outside of, separating*
against, in distinction to, out of possession of, taken away; SEE CONCEPT *583*

from [*prep2*] *arising out of*
beginning at, coming out of, deriving out of, originating at, starting with; SEE CONCEPT *549*

from scratch [*adv*] *from the very beginning*
from square one, from the ground up, from the top, initially; SEE CONCEPTS *585,799,828*

front [*adj*] *lead, beginning*
advanced, ahead, anterior, facial, first, fore, foremost, forward, frontal, head, headmost, in the foreground, leading, obverse, topmost, vanward, ventral; SEE CONCEPTS *567,583,585,632*

front [*n1*] *forward, beginning part of something*
anterior, bow, breast, brow, exterior, facade, face, facing, fore, foreground, forehead, forepart, frontage, frontal, frontispiece, front line, head, lead, obverse, proscenium, top, van, vanguard; SEE CONCEPTS *833,835,836*

front [*n2*] *appearance put on for show*
air, aspect, bearing, blind, carriage, coloring, countenance, cover, cover-up*, demeanor, disguise, display, expression, exterior, facade, face, fake, figure, manner, mask, mien, phony, port, presence, pretext, put-on*, show, veil, window dressing*; SEE CONCEPT *716*

front [*v*] *look out on to*
border, confront, cover, encounter, face, look over, meet, overlay, overlook; SEE CONCEPT *746*

frontier [*n1*] *boundary*
borderland, borderline, bound, confines, edge, limit, march, perimeter, verge; SEE CONCEPTS *513,745*

frontier [*n2*] *unexplored, unoccupied area of land*
backcountry, backwater, backwoods, boondocks*, boonies*, bush, hinterland, outback, outskirts, sticks*, unknown*; SEE CONCEPT *509*

front runner [*n*] *leader*
best bet*, favorite, first choice, forerunner, top seed; SEE CONCEPTS *347,354*

frost [*n*] *extreme cold*
blight, dip, drop, freeze, hoarfrost, ice, Jack Frost*, rime; SEE CONCEPTS *524,610*

frosting [*n*] *icing*
covering, glaze, spread, sugar coating, topping; SEE CONCEPTS *457,460,461*

frosty [*adj*] *very cold*
antarctic, arctic, chill, chilly, cool, frigid, frozen, gelid, glacial, hoar, ice-capped, icicled, icy, nippy*, rimy, shivery, wintry; SEE CONCEPT *605*

froth [*n*] *lather, bubbles*
barm, ebullition, effervescence, fizz, foam, head, scud, scum, spindrift, spray, spume, suds, yeast; SEE CONCEPTS *260,467,468*

frothy [*adj*] *bubbly*
barmy, bubbling, fermenting, fizzing, fizzy, foaming, foamy, soapy, spumescent, spumous, spumy, sudsy, with a head on*, yeasty; SEE CONCEPT *485*

frown [*v1*] *scowl*
cloud up*, do a slow burn*, give a dirty look*, give the evil eye*, glare, gloom, glower, grimace, knit brows*, look black*, look daggers*, look stern*, lower, pout, sulk; SEE CONCEPT *185*

frown [*v2*] *disapprove*
deprecate, discommend, discountenance, discourage, disesteem, disfavor, dislike, look askance at*, not take kindly to*, object, show displeasure, take a dim view of*; SEE CONCEPTS *21,29*

frozen [*adj1*] *very cold*
antarctic, arctic, chilled, frigid, frosted, icebound, ice-cold, ice-covered, iced, icy, numb, Siberian*; SEE CONCEPT *605*

frozen [*adj2*] *stopped*
fixed, pegged, petrified, rooted, stock-still, suspended, turned to stone; SEE CONCEPTS *534,584*

frugal [*adj*] *economical*
abstemious, canny, careful, chary, conserving, discreet, meager, meticulous, mingy*, niggardly*, parsimonious, penny-pinching*, pennywise*, preserving, provident, prudent, saving, scrimping, sparing, Spartan*, stingy, thrifty, tight, tightwad*, unwasteful, wary; SEE CONCEPT *334*

frugality [*n*] *economizing*
avarice, avariciousness, carefulness, conservation, economy, forehandedness, good management, miserliness, moderation, niggardliness, parsimoniousness, parsimony, penuriousness, providence, prudence, saving, scrimping, stinginess, thrift, thriftiness; SEE CONCEPTS *330,335*

fruit [*n1*] *edible part of vegetative growth developed after flowering*
berry, crop, drupe, grain, harvest, nut, pome, produce, product, yield; SEE CONCEPTS *426,428*

fruit [*n2*] *result of labor*
advantage, benefit, consequence, effect, outcome, pay, profit, result, return, reward; SEE CONCEPTS *230,337*

fruitful [*adj*] *productive*
abounding, abundant, advantageous, beneficial, blooming, blossoming, breeding, childing, conducive, copious, effective, fecund, fertile, flourishing, flush, fructiferous, gainful, plenteous, plentiful, profitable, profuse, proliferant, prolific, propagating, reproducing, rewarding, rich, spawning, successful, useful, well-spent, worthwhile; SEE CONCEPTS *528,537,560*

fruition [*n*] *achievement, maturation*
accomplishment, actualization, attainment, completion, consummation, enjoyment, fulfillment, gratification, materialization, maturity, perfection, pleasure, realization, ripeness, satisfaction, success; SEE CONCEPTS *704,706*

fruitless [*adj*] *bringing no advantage, product*
abortive, barren, empty, futile, gainless, idle, ineffective, ineffectual, infertile, in vain, pointless, profitless, spinning one's wheels*, sterile, to no avail*, to no effect*, unavailable, unavailing, un-

fr
fr

fruitful, unproductive, unprofitable, unprolific, unsuccessful, useless, vain, wild goose chase*; SEE CONCEPTS 528,537,560

frumpy [*adj*] *dowdy*
badly dressed, baggy, blowsy*, dingy, drab, dull, frumpish, homely, old-fashioned, outdated, plain, poorly dressed, shabby, sloppy, stodgy, unfashionable, unkempt, unstylish; SEE CONCEPT 589

frustrate [*v*] *thwart, disappoint*
annul, arrest, baffle, balk, bar, beat, block, cancel, check, circumvent, confront, conquer, counter, counteract, cramp, cramp one's style*, crimp, dash, dash one's hope*, defeat, depress, discourage, dishearten, foil, forbid, forestall, foul up*, give the run around*, halt, hang up*, hinder, hold up, impede, inhibit, lick, negate, neutralize, nullify, obstruct, obviate, outwit, overcome, preclude, prevent, prohibit, render null and void*, ruin, stump*, stymie*, upset the applecart*; SEE CONCEPTS 7,19,121

frustrated [*adj*] *disappointed, thwarted*
balked*, crabbed*, cramped, crimped, defeated, discontented, discouraged, disheartened, embittered, foiled, fouled up*, hung up on*, irked, resentful, stonewalled*, stymied*, through the mill*, ungratified, unsated, unslaked, up the wall*; SEE CONCEPT 403

frustration [*n*] *disappointment, thwarting*
annoyance, bitter pill*, blocking, blow, bummer, chagrin, circumvention, contravention, curbing, defeat, disgruntlement, dissatisfaction, downer*, drag*, failure, fizzle, foiling, grievance, hindrance, impediment, irritation, letdown, nonfulfillment, nonsuccess, obstruction, old one-two*, resentment, setback, unfulfillment, vexation; SEE CONCEPTS 410,674

fry [*v*] *cook in hot oil*
brown, french fry, fricassee, frizzle, pan fry, sauté, sear, singe, sizzle; SEE CONCEPT 170

frying pan [*n*] *skillet*
fry pan, gridiron, spider, wok; SEE CONCEPTS 493,494

fuddy-duddy [*n*] *fussy person*
fussbudget, fusspot*, old fogy*, old geezer*, old poop*, square*, stick-in-the-mud*, stuffed shirt*; SEE CONCEPT 423

fudge [*v*] *fake, misrepresent*
avoid, color, cook up*, dodge, embellish, embroider, equivocate, evade, exaggerate, falsify, hedge, magnify, overstate, pad, patch, shuffle, slant, stall; SEE CONCEPTS 59,63

fuel [*n*] *something providing energy*
ammunition, combustible, electricity, encouragement, food, gas, incitement, juice, material, means, nourishment, propellant, provocation; SEE CONCEPTS 467,520,523,661

fuel [*v*] *give energy to*
charge, fan, feed, fill 'er up*, fill up, fire, gas, gas up*, incite, inflame, nourish, service, stoke up*, supply, sustain, tank up*; SEE CONCEPTS 107,140

fugitive [*adj*] *fleeing, transient*
avoiding, brief, criminal, elusive, ephemeral, errant, erratic, escaping, evading, evanescent, fleeting, flitting, flying*, fugacious, hot*, impermanent, lamster, momentary, moving, on the lam*, passing, planetary, running away*, short*, short-lived, temporary, transitory, unstable, volatile, wandering, wanted; SEE CONCEPTS 551,584,798

fugitive [*n*] *person escaping from law or other pursuer*
bolter, derelict, deserter, displaced person, dodger, émigré, escapee, escaper, evacuee, exile, fly-by-night*, hermit, hunted person, outcast, outlaw, recluse, refugee, runagate, runaway, stray, transient, truant, vagabond, waif, walkout; SEE CONCEPT 412

fulfill [*v*] *bring to completion*
accomplish, achieve, answer, be just the ticket*, carry out, comply with, conclude, conform, discharge, do, effect, effectuate, execute, fill, fill the bill*, finish, hit the bull's-eye*, implement, keep, make it*, make the grade*, meet, obey, observe, perfect, perform, please, realize, render, satisfy, score*, suffice, suit; SEE CONCEPTS 7,22,91,706

fulfilled [*adj*] *completed*
accomplished, achieved, actualized, attained, brought about, brought to a close, carried out, compassed, concluded, consummated, crowned, delighted, dispatched, effected, effectuated, executed, finished, gratified, made good*, matured, obtained, perfected, performed, pleased, put into effect, reached, realized, satisfied; SEE CONCEPTS 403,531

fulfillment [*n*] *accomplishment, completion*
achievement, attainment, carrying out, carrying through, consummation, contentedness, contentment, crowning, discharge, discharging, effecting, end, gratification, implementation, just the ticket*, kick*, kicks* observance, perfection, realization, you got it*; SEE CONCEPTS 230,706

full [*adj1*] *brimming, filled*
abounding, abundant, adequate, awash, big, bounteous, brimful, burdened, bursting, chockablock, chock-full, competent, complete, crammed, crowded, entire, extravagant, glutted, gorged, imbued, impregnated, intact, jammed, jammed full*, jam-packed*, laden, lavish, loaded, overflowing, packed, packed like sardines, padded, plenteous, plentiful, plethoric, profuse, replete, running over, sated, satiated, satisfied, saturated, stocked, stuffed, sufficient, suffused, surfeited, teeming, voluminous, weighted; SEE CONCEPTS 481,483,773,774,786

full [*adj2*] *thorough*
absolute, abundant, adequate, all-inclusive, ample, blow-by-blow*, broad, choate, circumstantial, clocklike, complete, comprehensive, copious, detailed, entire, exhaustive, extensive, generous, integral, itemized, maximum, minute, particular, particularized, perfect, plenary, plenteous, plentiful, unabridged, unlimited, whole; SEE CONCEPT 531

full [*adj3*] *deep in sound*
clear, distinct, loud, resonant, rich, rounded, throaty; SEE CONCEPT 594

full [*adj4*] *satiated in hunger*
glutted, gorged, jaded, lousy with*, sated, satiate, stuffed, surfeited, up to here*; SEE CONCEPTS 406,481,774

full-blooded [*adj*] *purebred; strong*
hardy, hearty, powerful, robust, sound, thoroughbred, unmixed, vigorous, virile, vital; SEE CONCEPTS 314,489,613

full-bodied [*adj*] *robust*
concentrated, fruity, full-flavored, heady*, heavy, lusty, mellow, potent, redolent, rich, strong, well-matured; SEE CONCEPTS 489,613

full-grown/full-fledged [*adj*] *developed, ripe, ready*
adult, full-blown*, grown, grown-up, in one's prime*, marriageable, mature, nubile, of age, perfected, prime, ripened; SEE CONCEPTS *558, 578,797*

fullness [*n*] *abundance, breadth*
adequateness, ampleness, amplitude, broadness, completeness, completion, comprehensiveness, congestion, copiousness, curvaceousness, dilation, distension, enlargement, entirety, extensiveness, fill, glut, plenitude, plenty, plenum, profusion, repletion, roundness, satiation, satiety, saturation, scope, sufficiency, surfeit, swelling, totality, tumescence, vastness, voluptuousness, wealth, wholeness, wideness; SEE CONCEPTS *635,730*

full-scale [*adj*] *total, all-out*
all-encompassing, comprehensive, exhaustive, extensive, full-blown*, full-dress*, full-out*, in-depth, major, proper, sweeping, thorough, thoroughgoing, total, unlimited, wide-ranging; SEE CONCEPTS *531,772*

fully [*adv1*] *completely, in all respects*
absolutely, all out*, all the way*, altogether*, entirely, every inch*, from A to Z*, from soup to nuts*, heart and soul*, intimately, outright, perfectly, positively, quite, royal*, thoroughly, through and through*, totally, utterly, wholly, without exaggeration; SEE CONCEPTS *531,772*

fully [*adv2*] *sufficiently, adequately*
abundantly, amply, comprehensively, enough, plentifully, satisfactorily, well; SEE CONCEPT *558*

fulminate [*v*] *criticize harshly*
animadvert, berate, blow up, bluster, castigate, censure, condemn, curse, declaim, denounce, denunciate, execrate, explode, fume, intimidate, inveigh against, menace, protest, rage, rail, reprobate, swear at, thunder, upbraid, vilify, vituperate; SEE CONCEPTS *52,54*

fulmination [*n*] *tirade; condemnation*
blast, curse, denunciation, diatribe, discharge, explosion, intimidation, invective, obloquy, outburst, philippic, reprobation, warning; SEE CONCEPTS *52,54,278*

fulsome [*adj*] *sickening or excessive behavior*
adulatory, bombastic, buttery*, canting, cloying, coarse, extravagant, fawning, flattering, glib, grandiloquent, hypocritical, immoderate, ingratiating, inordinate, insincere, magniloquent, mealy-mouthed*, nauseating, offensive, oily*, oleaginous, overdone, saccharine, sanctimonious, slick*, slimy*, smarmy*, smooth, suave, sycophantic, unctuous, wheedling*; SEE CONCEPTS *267,401*

fumble [*v*] *bumble, mess up*
bollix*, botch*, bungle*, err, feel, flounder, flub*, fluff*, goof*, grapple, grope, lose the handle*, louse up*, misfield, mishandle, mismanage, scrabble*, screw up*, spoil, stumble; SEE CONCEPTS *101,181*

fume [*v*] *get very upset about*
anger, blow up*, boil, bristle, burn, chafe, chomp at the bit*, get hot*, get steamed up*, rage, rant, rave, seethe, smoke*, storm*; SEE CONCEPTS *21,29,410*

fumes [*n*] *pollution, gas in air*
effluvium, exhalation, exhaust, haze, miasma, reek, smog, smoke, stench, vapor; SEE CONCEPTS *437,600*

fumigate [*v*] *disinfect, ventilate*
air out, antisepticize, circulate, decontaminate, deodorize, fan, freshen, purify, sanitize, sterilize, vaporize; SEE CONCEPTS *51,60*

fun [*adj*] *good, happy*
amusing, boisterous, convivial, diverting, enjoyable, entertaining, lively, merry, pleasant, witty; SEE CONCEPTS *537,572*

fun [*n*] *amusement, play*
absurdity, ball*, big time*, blast*, buffoonery, celebration, cheer, clowning, distraction, diversion, enjoyment, entertainment, escapade, festivity, foolery, frolic, gaiety, gambol, game*, good time*, grins*, high jinks*, holiday, horseplay*, jesting, jocularity, joke, joking, jollity, joy, junketing, laughter, living it up*, merriment, merrymaking, mirth, nonsense, pastime, picnic*, playfulness, pleasure, recreation, rejoicing, relaxation, riot, romp, romping, solace, sport, tomfoolery*, treat, whoopee*; SEE CONCEPTS *386, 388*

function [*n1*] *capacity, job*
action, activity, affair, behavior, business, charge, concern, duty, employment, exercise, faculty, goal, mark, mission, object, objective, occupation, office, operation, part, post, power, province, purpose, raison d'être*, responsibility, role, service, situation, target, task, use, utility, work; SEE CONCEPTS *362,659*

function [*n2*] *social occasion*
affair, celebration, do*, gathering, get-together*, meeting, party, reception; SEE CONCEPT *386*

function [*v*] *perform, work*
act, act the part*, behave, be in action, be in commission, be in operation, be running, cook, do, do duty*, do one's thing*, get with it*, go, go to town*, move, officialize, officiate, operate, percolate*, react, run, serve, take, take care of business*; SEE CONCEPTS *87,362*

functional [*adj*] *working*
handy, occupational, operative, practicable, practical, serviceable, useful, utile, utilitarian, utility; SEE CONCEPT *560*

fund [*n*] *repository, reserve*
armamentarium, capital, endowment, foundation, hoard, inventory, kitty*, mine, pool*, reservoir, source, stock, store, storehouse, supply, treasury, trust, vein; SEE CONCEPTS *332,340,710*

fund [*v*] *provide money for*
back, bankroll, capitalize, endow, finance, float, grubstake*, juice*, patronize, pay for, pick up the check*, pick up the tab*, promote, stake, subsidize, support; SEE CONCEPTS *115,341*

fundamental [*adj*] *basic, important*
axiological, axiomatic, basal, bottom, bottom-line*, cardinal, central, constitutional, constitutive, crucial, elemental, elementary, essential, first, foundational, grass-roots*, indispensable, integral, intrinsic, key, major, meat-and-potatoes*, necessary, organic, original, paramount, primary, prime, primitive, primordial, principal, radical, requisite, rudimentary, significant, structural, substratal, substantive, supporting, sustaining, theoretical, underived, underlying, vital; SEE CONCEPTS *546,567*

fundamental [*n*] *basic, essential part*
ABCs*, axiom, basis, bottom line*, brass tacks*, coal and ice*, component, constituent, cornerstone, element, factor, foundation, guts*, heart, law, nitty-gritty*, principium, principle, rock

fr
fu

bottom*, rudiment, rule, sine qua non*, theorem; SEE CONCEPTS *668,688,826,829*

fundraiser [*n*] *pledge drive*
appeal for funds, bazaar, charity event, charity sale, philanthropic enterprise, radiothon, telethon; SEE CONCEPTS *337,657*

funds [*n*] *cash reserve*
accounts receivable, affluence, assets, backing, bankroll, belongings, bread*, budget, capital, collateral, currency, dough*, earnings, finance, fluid assets, hard cash*, kitty*, lucre, means, money, money in the bank*, money on hand*, nest egg*, nut*, petty cash, pork barrel*, possessions, proceeds, profits, property, ready money*, resources, revenue, savings, scratch*, securities, specie, stakes*, store*, stuff*, substance, treasure, wealth, wherewithal*, winnings*; SEE CONCEPTS *340,710*

funeral [*n*] *ceremony for the dead*
burial, cremation, entombment, exequies, funeration, inhumation, interment, last rites, obit, obsequies, planting, requiem, sepulture, services, solemnities; SEE CONCEPTS *172,386*

funereal [*adj*] *depressing*
black, bleak, dark, deathlike, dirgelike, disheartening, dismal, doleful, dreary, elegiac, gloomy, grave, grim, lamenting, lugubrious, melancholy, mournful, oppressive, sad, sepulchral, serious, solemn, somber, woeful; SEE CONCEPTS *403,537, 542*

funk [*n*] *fear, depression*
alarm, cold sweat*, despondency, fright, gloom, misery, panic, trembling; SEE CONCEPTS *27,410*

funnel [*v*] *direct down a path*
carry, channel, conduct, convey, filter, move, pass, pipe, pour, siphon, traject, transmit; SEE CONCEPTS *187,217*

funny [*adj1*] *comical, humorous*
absurd, amusing, antic, blithe, capricious, clever, diverting, droll, entertaining, facetious, farcical, for grins*, gas*, gay, gelastic, good-humored, hilarious, humdinger, hysterical, jocose, jocular, joking, jolly, killing*, knee-slapper*, laughable, ludicrous, merry, mirthful, playful, priceless, rich, ridiculous, riot, riotous, risible, screaming, side-splitting*, silly, slapstick, sportive, waggish, whimsical, witty; SEE CONCEPTS *267,529, 537*

funny [*adj2*] *odd, peculiar*
bizarre, curious, dubious, fantastic, mysterious, perplexing, puzzling, queer, remarkable, strange, suspicious, unusual, weird; SEE CONCEPTS *552,564*

funny money [*n*] *counterfeit money*
bad currency, bad money, counterfeit currency, fake currency, fake money, false currency, false money, play money; SEE CONCEPTS *648,725*

fur [*n*] *hair on animals*
brush, coat, down, fluff, fuzz, hide, jacket, lint, pelage, pelt, pile, skin, wool; SEE CONCEPT *399*

furbish [*v*] *polish, renovate*
brighten, buff, burnish, clean, deck out*, fix up, glaze, gloss, gussy up*, improve, recondition, refurbish, rehabilitate, renew, restore, rub, shine, smarten up*, spruce up*; SEE CONCEPTS *162,165,700*

furious [*adj1*] *extremely angry, very mad*
bent*, bent out of shape*, beside oneself*, boiling*, browned off*, bummed out*, corybantic, crazed, demented, desperate, enraged, fierce, fit

to be tied*, frantic, frenetic, frenzied, fuming, hacked, hopping mad*, incensed, infuriated, insane, irrational, livid, maddened, maniac, on the warpath*, rabid, raging, smoking*, steamed, unreasonable, up in arms*, vehement, vicious, violent, wrathful; SEE CONCEPT *403*

furious [*adj2*] *stormy, turbulent*
agitated, blustering, blustery, boisterous, concentrated, excessive, exquisite, extreme, fierce, flaming, impetuous, intense, intensified, raging, rampageous, rough, savage, tempestuous, terrible, tumultuous/tumultuous, ungovernable, unrestrained, vehement, vicious, violent, wild; SEE CONCEPTS *525,537,548*

furlough [*n*] *leave of absence*
layoff, leave, liberty, rest and recreation, rest and recuperation, rest and relaxation, R&R, sabbatical, shore leave, shutdown, vacation; SEE CONCEPTS *802,807*

furnace [*n*] *heating mechanism*
boiler, calefactor, cinerator, cremator, forge, Franklin stove, heater, heating system, incinerator, kiln, oil burner, smithy, stove; SEE CONCEPT *463*

furnish [*v1*] *decorate, supply*
accoutre, apparel, appoint, arm, array, clothe, endow, equip, feather a nest*, fit, fit out*, fix up*, gear, line a nest*, make habitable, outfit, provide, provision, purvey, rig, stock, store, turn out; SEE CONCEPTS *140,177,182*

furnish [*v2*] *give, reveal information*
afford, bestow, deliver, dispense, endow, feed, grant, hand, hand over, offer, present, provide, supply, transfer, turn over; SEE CONCEPTS *60,67,108*

furnishings [*n*] *appliances, furniture*
accessories, accoutrements, appointments, décor, equipment, fittings, fixtures, gear, provisions, trappings; SEE CONCEPT *443*

furniture [*n*] *household property*
appliance, appointment, bed, bookcase, buffet, bureau, cabinet, chair, chattel, chest, commode, couch, counter, cupboard, davenport, desk, dresser, effect, equipment, fittings, furnishing, goods, highboy, hutch, movables, possession, sideboard, sofa, stool, table, thing, wardrobe; SEE CONCEPT *443*

furor [*n*] *disturbance, excitement*
ado*, agitation, big scene*, big stink*, bustle, commotion, craze, enthusiasm, fad, ferment, flap*, free-for-all*, frenzy, fury, fuss, hell broke loose*, hullabaloo*, hysteria, lunacy, madness*, mania, outburst, outcry, rage, row, ruckus, stir*, to-do*, tumult, uproar, whirl; SEE CONCEPTS *230,388,410*

furrow [*n*] *ditch*
channel, corrugation, crease, crinkle, crow's-foot*, dike, fluting, fold, groove, gutter, hollow, line, plica, rabbet, ridge, rimple, rivel, ruck, rut, seam, trench, wrinkle; SEE CONCEPT *513*

further [*adj*] *additional*
added, another, else, extra, farther, fresh, in addition, more, new, other, supplementary; SEE CONCEPT *771*

further [*adv*] *additionally*
again, also, as well as, besides, beyond, distant, farther, in addition, moreover, on top of*, over and above*, then, to boot, what's more*, yet, yonder; SEE CONCEPT *771*

further [*v*] *advance, lend support*

aid, assist, back up, bail out*, ballyhoo*, champion, contribute, encourage, engender, expedite, facilitate, forward, foster, generate, give a boost to*, go with, hasten, help, lend a hand*, open doors*, patronize, plug, promote, propagate, push, serve, speed, succor, take care of, work for; SEE CONCEPTS *69,87,110*

furtherance [*n*] *advancement*

advocacy, backing, boosting, carrying-out, championship, progress, progression, promotion, prosecution, pursuit; SEE CONCEPTS *110,704*

furthermore [*adv*] *in addition*

additionally, along, as well, besides, likewise, moreover, not to mention, to boot, too, what's more*, withal, yet; SEE CONCEPTS *577,824*

furthest [*adj*] *most distant*

extreme, farthest, most remote, outermost, outmost, remotest, ultimate, uttermost; SEE CONCEPTS *586,778*

furtive [*adj*] *sneaky, secretive*

artful, calculating, cautious, circumspect, clandestine, cloaked, conspiratorial, covert, crafty*, creepy*, cunning, disguised, elusive, evasive, foxy, guileful, hidden, hush-hush*, insidious, masked, scheming, shifty*, skulking, slinking*, sly, stealthy, sub-rosa*, surreptitious, tricky*, undercover, underhand, underhanded, under-the-table*, under wraps*, wily; SEE CONCEPTS *548,576*

fury [*n*] *anger, wrath*

acerbity, acrimony, asperity, boiling point*, conniption, energy, ferocity, fierceness, fire, flare-up, force, frenzy, furor, impetuosity, indignation, intensity, ire, madness, might, passion, power, rabidity, rage, rampancy, rise, savagery, severity, slow burn*, sore, stew*, storm*, tempestuousness, turbulence, vehemence, violence; SEE CONCEPTS *29,410*

fuse [*v*] *meld, intermix*

agglutinate, amalgamate, bind, blend, cement, coalesce, combine, commingle, compound, dissolve, federate, flux, integrate, interblend, interfuse, intermingle, join, liquefy, liquesce, melt, merge, mingle, run, run together, smelt, solder, thaw, unite, weld; SEE CONCEPT *113*

fusillade [*n*] *rapid outburst*

barrage, broadside, burst of fire, hail, salvo, volley; SEE CONCEPT *633*

fusion [*n*] *melding; mixture*

admixture, alloy, amalgam, amalgamation, blend, blending, coadunation, coalescence, coalition, commingling, commixture, compound, federation, heating, immixture, integration, intermixture, junction, liquefaction, liquification, melting, merger, merging, smelting, soldering, synthesis, unification, union, uniting, welding; SEE CONCEPTS *113,260,432*

fuss [*n*] *disturbance, trouble*

ado, agitation, altercation, argument, bickering, bother, broil*, bustle, commotion, complaint, confusion, controversy, difficulty, display, dispute, excitement, falling-out*, fight, flap, flurry, flutter, fret, furor, hassle, kick-up*, objection, palaver, perturbation, quarrel, row, ruckus, scene, squabble, stew*, stink*, stir, storm, to-do*, turmoil, unrest, upset, winging*, worry; SEE CONCEPTS *46,106,388,633*

fussy [*adj*] *meticulous, particular*

careful, choosy, conscientious, conscionable, dainty, difficult, discriminating, exact, exacting, fastidious, finical, finicky, fretful, fuddy-duddy*, hard to please*, heedful, nit-picking*, overfastidious, painstaking, persnickety, picky, picky-picky*, punctilious, punctual, querulous, scrupulous, squeamish, stickling; SEE CONCEPTS *401,404*

fustian [*adj*] *pompous*

arrogant, boastful, bombastic, conceited, flaunting, high and mighty*, highfalutin, lofty, ostentatious, pontifical, portentous, pretentious, puffed up*, ranting, self-centered, self-important, vain, vainglorious; SEE CONCEPTS *267,401,542*

futile [*adj*] *hopeless, pointless*

abortive, barren, bootless, delusive, empty, exhausted, forlorn, fruitless, hollow, idle, impracticable, impractical, ineffective, ineffectual, insufficient, in vain, no dice*, nugatory, on a treadmill*, otiose, out the window*, profitless, resultless, save one's breath*, sterile, to no avail*, to no effect*, to no purpose*, trifling, trivial, unavailing, unimportant, unneeded, unproductive, unprofitable, unreal, unsatisfactory, unsubstantial, unsuccessful, useless, vain, valueless, worthless; SEE CONCEPTS *528,548,560*

futility [*n*] *uselessness*

emptiness, frivolousness, fruitlessness, hollowness, idleness, ineffectiveness, ineffectuality, meaninglessness, pointlessness, senselessness, unprofitableness, worthlessness; SEE CONCEPT *560*

futon [*n*] *sofa bed*

convertible sofa, couch, davenport, daybed, sofa; SEE CONCEPT *443*

future [*adj*] *to come; expected*

approaching, booked, budgeted, close at hand*, coming, coming up, destined, down the line*, down the pike, down the road*, eventual, fated, final, forthcoming, from here in, from here on, from here to eternity*, from now on in*, imminent, impending, inevitable, in the cards*, in the course of time, in the offing*, just around the corner*, later, likely, looked toward, near, next, planned, prospective, scheduled, subsequent, to be*, ulterior, ultimate, unborn, unfolding, up; SEE CONCEPT *820*

future [*n*] *time to come*

aftertime, afterward, by and by*, destiny, eternity, expectation, fate, futurity, hereafter, infinity, life to come, millennium, morrow, offing, outlook, posterity, prospect, subsequent time, to be*, tomorrow, world to come*; SEE CONCEPTS *679,807,811,818*

futuristic [*adj*] *ahead of one's time*

advanced, cutting edge, innovative, modern, pioneering, revolutionary, visionary; SEE CONCEPTS *578,589,797*

fuzz [*n*] *fluff*

down, dust ball*, dust bunnies*, fiber, floss, fur, hair, lanugo, lint, nap, pile; SEE CONCEPT *260*

fuzzy [*adj1*] *fluffy*

down-covered, downy, flossy, frizzy, furry, hairy, linty, napped, pilate, velutinous, woolly; SEE CONCEPT *606*

fuzzy [*adj2*] *out of focus*

bleary, blurred, dim, distorted, faint, foggy, hazy, ill-defined, indefinite, indistinct, misty, muffled, murky, obscure, shadowy, unclear, unfocused, vague; SEE CONCEPT *619*

fu
fu

G

gab [*n*] *conversation*
blab*, blather*, chat, chitchat*, gossip, idle talk*, loquacity*, palaver*, prattle, small talk*, talk, tête-à-tête, tongue-wagging*, yak*, yakkety-yak*; SEE CONCEPT 278

gab [*v*] *talk a lot*
blabber*, blather*, buzz*, chatter, gossip, jabber*, jaw*, prate, prattle, yak*, yakkety-yak*; SEE CONCEPT 266

gabby [*adj*] *talkative*
chattering, chatty, effusive, garrulous, glib, gossiping, gushing, jabbering, long-winded*, loose-lipped*, loquacious, mouthy*, prattling, prolix, talky, verbose, voluble, windy*, wordy; SEE CONCEPT 267

gad [*v*] *roam about*
cruise, gallivant, hit the road*, hit the trail*, jaunt, knock about*, knock around*, maunder, mooch*, ramble, range, rove, run around*, stray, traipse, wander; SEE CONCEPTS 149,224

gadfly [*n*] *goad; nuisance*
annoyance, energizer, excitant, irritant, motivator, mover, pest, prod, spur, stimulator; SEE CONCEPTS 412,674

gadget [*n*] *device, novelty*
apparatus, appliance, business, concern, contraption, contrivance, doodad*, doohickey*, gimmick, gizmo*, invention, object, thing*, thingamajig, tool, utensil, whatchamacallit*, widget*; SEE CONCEPTS 463,499

gadgetry [*n*] *mechanism*
appliances, bells and whistles, contraptions, ingenious device, instrumentation, machinery, works; SEE CONCEPTS 463,499

gaffe [*n*] *mistake, goof*
blooper*, blunder, boner*, boo-boo*, faux pas*, howler*, impropriety, indecorum, indiscretion, putting foot in mouth*, slip*, solecism; SEE CONCEPTS 101,230

gag [*n*] *practical joke*
crack, drollery, hoax, jest, quip, ruse, trick, wile, wisecrack, witticism; SEE CONCEPT 59

gag [*v*] *silence, stop up*
balk, bottle up*, choke, constrain, cork*, cork up*, curb, deaden, demur, garrote, keep the lid on*, muffle, muzzle, obstruct, put the lid on*, quiet, repress, restrain, shut down, shy, squash*, squelch, stifle, still, stumble, suppress, tape up*, throttle*, tongue-tie*; SEE CONCEPTS 121,130

gag [*v*] *vomit, choke*
be nauseated, disgorge, gasp, heave, nauseate, pant, puke*, retch, sicken, spew, strain, struggle, throw up; SEE CONCEPTS 179,308

gaiety [*n*] *happiness, celebration*
animation, blitheness, brightness, brilliance, cheer, color, colorfulness, conviviality, effervescence, elation, entertainment, exhilaration, festivity, frolic, fun, geniality, gladness, glee, glitter, good humor*, grins*, high spirits*, hilarity, joie de vivre, jollity, joviality, joyousness, lightheartedness, liveliness, merriment, merrymaking, mirth, pleasantness, radiance, revel, reveling, revelry, shindig*, showiness, sparkle, sport, sprightliness, vivacity, whoopee*, wingding*; SEE CONCEPTS 377,388

gaily [*adv*] *happily, brightly*
blithely, brilliantly, cheerfully, colorfully, flamboyantly, flashily, gleefully, glowingly, joyfully, laughingly, lightheartedly, merrily, showily, sparklingly, spiritedly, splendidly, vivaciously, with élan*, with spirit*; SEE CONCEPTS 542,589

gain [*n*] *acquisition, winnings*
accretion, accrual, accumulation, achievement, addition, advance, advancement, advantage, attainment, benefit, boost, buildup, cut, dividend, earnings, emolument, gravy*, growth, headway*, hike*, improvement, income, increase, increment, lucre, payoff, proceeds, produce, profit, progress, receipts, return, rise, share, take, up*, upping*, velvet*, yield; SEE CONCEPTS 337,344, 706,710

gain [*v*] *acquire, win*
accomplish, achieve, advance, ameliorate, annex, attain, augment, benefit, boost, bring in, build up, capture, clear, collect, complete, consummate, earn, enlarge, enlist, expand, fulfill, gather, get, glean, grow, harvest, have, improve, increase, land, make, make a killing*, move forward, net, obtain, overtake, parlay, perfect, pick up, procure, produce, profit, progress, promote, rack up*, reach, realize, reap, score*, secure, succeed, win over; SEE CONCEPTS 120,124,129

gainful [*adj*] *very productive, profitable*
advantageous, beneficial, fat, fruitful, generous, going, going concern*, good, in the black*, lucrative, lush, moneymaking, paid off, paying, remunerative, rewarding, rich, satisfying, substantial, sweet*, useful, well-paying, worthwhile; SEE CONCEPT 334

gainsay [*v*] *contradict*
combat, contravene, controvert, cross, deny, disaffirm, disagree, disclaim, disprove, dispute, fight, impugn, negate, negative, oppose, refute, repudiate, resist, traverse, withstand; SEE CONCEPTS 52,54

gait [*n*] *way an animal or person moves, walks*
amble, bearing, canter, carriage, clip, gallop, get along, lick, march, motion, movement, pace, run, speed, step, stride, tread, trot, walk; SEE CONCEPT 149

gala [*adj*] *celebratory*
bright, colorful, convivial, festal, festive, gay, happy, jovial, joyful, merry; SEE CONCEPT 548

gala [*n*] *festival*
affair, ball, bash, blast*, blowout*, carnival, celebration, clambake, dance, do, festivity, fete, fiesta, function, get-together*, hop, jamboree, moveable feast, pageant, party, prom, roast, shindig*, stag, to-do*, wingding*; SEE CONCEPTS 377,383

galaxy [*n*] *nebula*
elliptical galaxy, irregular galaxy, island universe, Milky Way, spiral galaxy, star cluster, star system; SEE CONCEPTS 370,511

gale [*n*] *violent storm*
blast, blow, burst, chinook, cyclone, hurricane, mistral, monsoon, outbreak, outburst, squall, tempest, tornado, typhoon, wind, windstorm; SEE CONCEPTS 524,526

gall [*n*] *nerve, brashness*
acrimony, animosity, arrogance, bitterness, brass, brazenness, cheek*, chutzpah*, conceit, confidence, crust, cynicism, effrontery, guts*, haughtiness, hostility, impertinence, impudence, insolence, malevolence, malice; overbearance,

pomposity, presumption, rancor, sauciness, self-importance, spite, venom; SEE CONCEPTS *411, 633*

gall [v1] *upset, irritate*
aggravate, annoy, bedevil, bother, burn, chafe, chide, disturb, exasperate, fret, grate, harass, harry, inflame, irk, nag, peeve, pester, plague, provoke, rile, roil, rub, ruffle, scrape, torment, trouble, vex, worry; SEE CONCEPTS *7,19*

gall [v2] *rub raw*
abrade, bark, burn, chafe, corrode, erode, excoriate, file, fray, frazzle, fret, grate, graze, irritate, scrape, scratch, scuff, skin, wear; SEE CONCEPT *215*

gallant [adj] *brave, splendid*
attentive, bold, considerate, courageous, courteous, courtly, daring, dashing, dauntless, dignified, doughty, fearless, fire-eating*, game*, glorious, gracious, grand, gritty*, hairy*, heroic, honorable, intrepid, lionhearted*, lofty, magnanimous, noble, plucky*, polite, quixotic, stately, stouthearted, suave, thoughtful, urbane, valiant, valorous; SEE CONCEPTS *404,542*

gallantry [n] *bravery, civility*
address, attentiveness, audacity, boldness, courage, courageousness, courteousness, courtesy, daring, dauntlessness, deference, derring-do*, duty, elegance, fearlessness, graciousness, honor, intrepidity, mettle, nerve, nobility, pluck*, poise, politeness, prowess, resolution, reverence, savoir-faire, spirit, tact, urbanity, valiance, valor; SEE CONCEPTS *411,657*

gallery [n1] *balcony*
arcade, loggia, mezzanine, patio, porch, upstairs, veranda; SEE CONCEPT *440*

gallery [n2] *showplace for wares*
exhibit, exhibition room, hall, museum, salon, showroom, studio, wing; SEE CONCEPTS *448,449*

gallery [n3] *audience, usually seated high*
attendance, onlookers, peanut gallery*, public, spectators; SEE CONCEPTS *294,417*

galling [adj] *very upsetting*
acid, afflictive, aggravating, annoying, bitter, bothersome, distasteful, exasperating, grievous, harassing, humiliating, irksome, irritating, nettlesome, painful, plaguing, provoking, rankling, unpalatable, vexatious, vexing; SEE CONCEPTS *7,19*

gallivant [v] *run around, gad about*
cruise, jaunt, meander, mooch, ramble, range, roam, rove, stray, traipse, wander; SEE CONCEPTS *149,224*

gallop [v] *bolt, race with slight jumping motion*
amble, canter, career, course, dart, dash, fly, hasten, hurdle, hurry, jump, leap, lope, pace, rack, run, rush, shoot, speed, spring, sprint, stride, tear along, trot, zoom; SEE CONCEPTS *150,194*

galvanize [v] *inspire, stimulate*
animate, arouse, astonish, awaken, commove, electrify, energize, excite, fire*, frighten, innervate, invigorate, jolt, motivate, move, pique, prime, provoke, quicken, shock, spur, startle, stir, stun, thrill, vitalize, wake, zap*; SEE CONCEPTS *7,14,22*

gambit [n] *plan, plot*
artifice, design, device, gimmick, jig, maneuver, play, ploy, ruse, trick; SEE CONCEPT *660*

gamble [n] *chance, speculation*
action, bet, fling, leap*, long shot*, lottery, outside chance*, raffle, risk, shot in the dark*, spec*, stab*, throw of the dice*, toss up*, uncertainty, venture, wager; SEE CONCEPTS *28,363*

gamble [v] *take a chance on winning*
back, bet, brave, buck the odds*, cast lots*, challenge, cut the cards, dare, defy, endanger, face, flip the coin*, game, go for broke*, hazard, imperil, jeopardize, lay money on*, lot, make a bet, play, plunge, put, put faith in, put trust in, risk, set, shoot the moon*, shoot the works*, speculate, stake, stick one's neck out*, take a flyer*, tempt fortune*, trust to luck, try one's luck, venture, wager; SEE CONCEPTS *28,363*

gambol [v] *tumble playfully*
bound, caper, carry on, cavort, cut, cut a caper*, cut loose*, fool around*, frisk, frolic, hop, horse around*, jump, kibitz around*, kick up one's heels*, lark, leap, play, prance, revel, roister, rollick, romp, skip, sport, spring, whoop it up*; SEE CONCEPTS *149,194,363*

game [adj1] *brave, willing*
bold, courageous, dauntless, desirous, disposed, dogged, eager, fearless, gallant, hardy, heroic, inclined, interested, intrepid, nervy*, persevering, persistent, plucky*, prepared, ready, resolute, spirited, spunky, unafraid, unflinching, up for*, valiant, valorous; SEE CONCEPT *404*

game [adj2] *debilitated*
ailing, bad, crippled, deformed, disabled, incapacitated, injured, lame, maimed, weak; SEE CONCEPTS *314,485*

game [n1] *entertainment*
adventure, amusement, athletics, business, distraction, diversion, enterprise, festivity, frolic, fun, jest, joke, lark, line, merriment, merrymaking, occupation, pastime, plan, play, proceeding, pursuit, recreation, romp, scheme, sport, sports, undertaking; SEE CONCEPTS *292,363*

game [n2] *individual sporting event*
competition, contest, match, meeting, round, tournament; SEE CONCEPT *364*

game [n3] *undomesticated animals chased for food*
chase, fish, fowl, kill, meat, prey, quarry, ravin, victim, wild animals; SEE CONCEPTS *394,457,460*

game [n4] *plot, trick*
butt, derision, design, device, hoax, joke, object of ridicule, plan, ploy, practical joke, prank, scheme, stratagem, strategy, tactic; SEE CONCEPTS *59,660*

gamely [adv] *bravely*
boldly, courageously, dauntlessly, eagerly, enthusiastically, fearlessly, stoutly, with one's head held high*; SEE CONCEPT *401*

gamut [n] *range*
area, catalogue, compass, diapason, extent, field, panorama, scale, scope, series, spectrum, sweep; SEE CONCEPTS *651,788*

gamy [adj] *ill-smelling; corrupt*
fetid, foul, malodorous, pungent, rancid, rank, reeking, seamy, sordid, strong-flavored, strong-smelling, strong-tasting, tainted; SEE CONCEPT *598*

gang [n] *group, mob of people*
assemblage, band, bunch, circle, clan, clique, club, cluster, combo*, company, coterie, crew, crowd, herd, horde, knot, lot, organization, outfit, pack, party, posse, ring, set, shift, squad, syndicate, team, tribe, troop, troupe, workers, zoo*; SEE CONCEPT *387*

ga
ga

gangling [*adj*] *rangy*
awkward, bony, gawky, lanky, leggy, long-legged, long-limbed, lumbering, skinny, spindly, tall, thin; SEE CONCEPTS *490,491*

gangster [*n*] *person involved in illegal activities*
bandit, bruiser*, criminal, crook, dealer, desperado, goon*, hit person, hood, hoodlum, hooligan*, Mafioso*, member of the family, mobster, pusher, racketeer, robber, ruffian, soldier*, thug, tough; SEE CONCEPT *412*

gap [*n*] *break, breach*
aperture, arroyo, blank, caesura, canyon, chasm, cleft, clove, crack, cranny, crevice, cut, defile, difference, disagreement, discontinuity, disparity, divergence, divide, division, fracture, gorge, gulch, gully, hiatus, hole, hollow, inconsistency, interlude, intermission, interruption, interspace, interstice, interval, lacuna, lull, notch, opening, orifice, pause, ravine, recess, rent, respite, rest, rift, rupture, separation, slit, slot, space, vacuity, void; SEE CONCEPTS *513,665*

gape [*v1*] *gawk*
beam, bore, eye, eyeball*, focus, get a load of*, get an eyeful*, give the eye*, glare, gloat, goggle*, look, ogle, peer, rubberneck*, size up*, stare, take in*, wonder, yawp*; SEE CONCEPT *623*

gape [*v2*] *be wide open*
cleave, crack, dehisce, divide, frondesce, gap, part, split, yaw, yawn; SEE CONCEPT *135*

gaping [*adj*] *wide open*
broad, cavernous, chasmal, great, vast, yawning; SEE CONCEPTS *485,490*

garage [*n*] *storage building for vehicles, workplace*
barn, carport*, car stall*, parking lot, parking space, repair shop, shop, storage; SEE CONCEPTS *439,449*

garb [*n*] *clothing*
apparel, appearance, array, attire, clothes, costume, dress, duds*, feathers*, form, garment, gear, guise, habiliment, habit, outfit, raiment, robes*, semblance, things*, threads*, uniform, vestments, wear; SEE CONCEPT *451*

garb [*v*] *fit with clothes*
apparel, array, attire, clad, clothe, cover, deck, deck out*, drape, dress, dud*, fit out*, garment, raiment, rig out*, rig up*, robe, suit up*, tog*, turn out*; SEE CONCEPT *167*

garbage [*n*] *refuse, litter*
bits and pieces*, debris, detritus, dreck, dregs, dross, filth, junk, muck, odds and ends*, offal, rubbish, rubble, scrap, scrapings, sewage, slop*, sweepings, swill, trash, waste; SEE CONCEPT *260*

garble [*v*] *mix up, misrepresent*
belie, color, confuse, corrupt, distort, doctor, falsify, jumble, misinterpret, mislead, misquote, misstate, mutilate, obscure, pervert, slant, tamper with, twist, warp; SEE CONCEPTS *59,63*

garden [*n*] *cultivated plants, flowers*
back yard, bed, cold frame, conservatory, enclosure, field, greenhouse, hothouse, nursery, oasis, patch, patio, plot, terrace; SEE CONCEPTS *509,517*

gargantuan [*adj*] *very large*
big, colossal, elephantine, enormous, giant, gigantic, heavyweight, huge, humongous, immense, jumbo, leviathan, mammoth, massive, monstrous, monumental, mountainous, prodigious, super-colossal*, super-duper*, titanic, towering, tremendous, vast, whopping*; SEE CONCEPTS *491,773*

gargle [*v*] *rinse the mouth with liquid*
irrigate, swish, trill, use mouthwash; SEE CONCEPTS *169,308,616*

garish [*adj*] *flashy, tasteless*
blatant, brassy, brazen, cheap, chintzy, flaunting, gaudy, glaring, glittering, kitschy*, loud, meretricious, ornate, ostentatious, overdone, overwrought, raffish, screaming*, showy, tawdry, tinsel, vulgar; SEE CONCEPT *589*

garland [*n*] *strand of material, usually hung*
bays, chaplet, coronal, crown, festoon, honors, laurel, palm, wreath; SEE CONCEPTS *260,429*

garment [*n*] *article of clothing*
apparel, array, attire, costume, covering, drapes*, dress, duds*, feathers*, garb, gear, get-up*, habiliment, habit, outfit, raiment, robe, things*, threads*, togs*, uniform, vestments, wear, weeds*; SEE CONCEPT *451*

garner [*v*] *collect, accumulate*
amass, assemble, cull, cumulate, deposit, extract, gather, glean, harvest, hive, hoard, lay in*, lay up*, pick up, put by*, reap, reserve, roll up*, save, stockpile, store, stow away, treasure; SEE CONCEPTS *109,135*

garnish [*n*] *embellishment, improvement*
adornment, decoration, enhancement, furbelow, gingerbread*, ornament, ornamentation, tinsel, trim, trimming; SEE CONCEPT *824*

garnish [*v*] *embellish, improve*
adorn, beautify, bedeck, deck, decorate, dress up, enhance, fix up, grace, gussy up*, ornament, set off*, spiff up*, spruce up*, trim; SEE CONCEPT *244*

garrison [*n*] *military post, fort*
barracks, base, camp, citadel, command post, encampment, fortification, fortress, stronghold; SEE CONCEPTS *321,439*

garrulous [*adj*] *talkative*
babbling, blabbermouth*, chattering, chatty, effusive, flap jaw*, gabby, glib, gossiping, gushing, long-winded*, loose-lipped*, loose-tongued*, loquacious, motormouth*, mouthy, prating, prattling, prolix, prosy, running on at the mouth*, verbose, voluble, wind-bag*, windy*, wordy, yakkity*, yakky*; SEE CONCEPTS *267,404*

gas [*n*] *something not liquid or solid*
effluvium, fumes, miasma, smoke, stream, vapor, volatile substance; SEE CONCEPT *465*

gash [*n*] *cut made by slicing*
cleft, furrow, gouge, incision, laceration, mark, nip, notch, rent, slash, slit, split, tear, wound; SEE CONCEPT *309*

gash [*v*] *cut by slicing*
carve, cleave, furrow, gouge, incise, injure, lacerate, lance, mark, nip, notch, pierce, rend, slash, slit, split, tear, wound; SEE CONCEPTS *137,176*

gasket [*n*] *seal*
cap, covering, packing, stopper; SEE CONCEPTS *85,160*

gasoline [*n*] *fuel*
diesel fuel, gasohol, juice*, oil, petrol, propellant; SEE CONCEPTS *467,520,523,661*

gasp [*n*] *sharply drawn breath*
blow, ejaculation, exclamation, gulp, heave, pant, puff, wheeze, whoop; SEE CONCEPTS *163,595*

gasp [*v*] *draw breath in sharply*
blow, catch one's breath, choke, convulse, fight for breath, gulp, heave, inhale, inspire, pant,

puff, respire, sniffle, snort, wheeze, whoop; SEE CONCEPT 163

gate [n] *movable barrier at entrance*
access, bar, conduit, door, doorway, egress, exit, gateway, issue, lock, opening, passage, port, portal, revolving door, slammer*, turnstile, way, weir; SEE CONCEPTS 440,445

gatekeeper [n] *watchperson*
doorkeeper, guard, lookout, monitor, protector, security officer, sentinel, sentry; SEE CONCEPT 348

gather [v1] *come or bring together*
accumulate, aggregate, amass, assemble, associate, bunch up, capture, choose, close with, cluster, collect, concentrate, congregate, convene, converge, corral, crowd, cull, draw, draw in, flock, forgather, gang up, garner, get together, group, hang around*, hang out*, heap, herd, hoard, huddle, make the scene*, marshal, mass, meet, muster, pick, pile up, pluck, poke*, pour in, punch*, rally, reunite, round up*, scare up*, scrape together*, show up, stack up, stockpile, swarm, throng, unite; SEE CONCEPTS 109,114

gather [v2] *be led to believe; infer*
assume, conclude, deduce, draw, expect, find, hear, imagine, judge, learn, make, presume, reckon, suppose, surmise, suspect, take, think, understand; SEE CONCEPT 15

gather [v3] *harvest, pick out*
crop, cull, draw, extract, garner, glean, heap, ingather, mass, pick up, pile, pluck, reap, select, stack, take in; SEE CONCEPT 257

gather [v4] *gain, increase*
build, deepen, enlarge, expand, grow, heighten, intensify, rise, swell, thicken, wax; SEE CONCEPT 780

gathering [n] *assemblage, accumulation*
acquisition, affair, aggregate, aggregation, association, band, body, bunch, caucus, clambake*, collection, company, concentration, conclave, concourse, conference, congregation, congress, convention, convocation, crowd, crush, drove, flock, function, gain, get-together*, group, herd, horde, huddle, junction, knot, levy, mass, meet, meeting, muster, parley, party, pile, pow-wow*, rally, roundup, social function, society, stock, stockpile, swarm, throng, turnout, union; SEE CONCEPTS 324,386,417

gauche [adj] *tactless, unsophisticated*
awkward, bumbling, clumsy, crude, graceless, green, halting, ham-handed*, heavy-handed*, ignorant, ill-bred, ill-mannered, inelegant, inept, insensitive, lacking, maladroit, oafish, uncouth, uncultured, unhappy, unpolished, wooden*; SEE CONCEPT 404

gaudy [adj] *bright and vulgar*
blatant, brazen, brilliant, catchpenny*, chichi*, chintzy, coarse, crude, flashy, flaunting, florid, frou-frou*, garish, gay, glaring, gross, gussied up*, jazzy, kitschy*, loud, meretricious, obtrusive, ostentatious, pizzazz*, pretentious, putting on the ritz*, raffish, ritzy, screaming*, showy, snazzy, splashy, splendiferous, tasteless, tawdry, tinsel; SEE CONCEPTS 589,618

gauge [n] *measure, standard*
barometer, basis, benchmark, bore, capacity, check, criterion, degree, depth, example, exemplar, extent, guide, guideline, height, indicator, magnitude, mark, meter, model, norm, pattern, rule, sample, scale, scope, size, span, test, thickness, touchstone*, type, width, yardstick; SEE CONCEPTS 647,680,688,792

gauge [v] *measure, judge*
adjudge, appraise, ascertain, assess, calculate, calibrate, check, check out, compute, count, determine, estimate, evaluate, eye*, figure, figure in, guess, guesstimate, have one's number*, look over, meter, peg*, quantify, quantitate, rate, reckon, scale, size, size up*, take account of, tally, value, weigh; SEE CONCEPTS 37,764

gaunt [adj] *skinny*
angular, anorexic, attenuated, bare, bleak, bony, cadaverous, desolate, dismal, dreary, emaciated, forbidding, forlorn, grim, haggard, harsh, lank, lean, like a bag of bones*, meager, peaked, peaky, pinched, rawboned, scraggy, scrawny, skeletal, skeleton, skin and bones*, spare, thin, wasted; SEE CONCEPTS 406,490,491

gauzy [adj] *see-through, gossamer in texture*
delicate, diaphanous, filmy, flimsy, insubstantial, light, lucid, pellucid, sheer, thin, tiffany, translucent, transparent; SEE CONCEPT 606

gawk [v] *stare at in amazement*
bore*, eyeball*, gape, gaze, glare, gloat, goggle*, look, ogle, peer, rubberneck*, yawp*; SEE CONCEPT 623

gawky [adj] *clumsy*
awkward, bumbling, clownish, gauche, loutish*, lumbering, lumpish*, lumpy, maladroit, oafish, rude, rustic, splay, uncouth, ungainly; SEE CONCEPTS 550,584

gay [adj1] *happy*
alert, animate, animated, blithe, blithesome, bouncy, brash, carefree, cheerful, cheery, chipper*, chirpy, confident, convivial, devil-may-care*, festive, forward, frivolous, frolicsome, fun-loving, gamesome, glad, gleeful, hilarious, insouciant, jocund, jolly, jovial, joyful, joyous, keen, lighthearted, lively, merry, mirthful, playful, pleasure-seeking, presuming, pushy, rollicking, self-assertive, sparkling, spirited, sportive, sprightly, sunny, vivacious, wild, zippy*; SEE CONCEPTS 403,542

gay [adj2] *colorful, vivid*
brave, bright, brilliant, flamboyant, flashy, fresh, garish, gaudy, intense, rich, showy; SEE CONCEPTS 589,618

gay [adj3] *homosexual*
homoerotic, homophile, lesbian, Sapphic; SEE CONCEPT 372

gaze [n] *long, fixed stare*
fish eye*, glaring, gun*, look, looking, ogling, peek, peep, rubbernecking*, scrutiny, seeing, survey, watching; SEE CONCEPT 623

gaze [v] *stare at*
admire, beam*, bore*, contemplate, eye, eyeball*, gape, gawk, get a load of*, get an eyeful*, glare, gloat, inspect, lamp*, look, look fixedly, moon*, observe, ogle, peek, peep, peer, pin*, pipe*, regard, rubber*, rubberneck*, scrutinize, see, size up*, survey, take in*, view, watch, wonder; SEE CONCEPTS 623,626

gazebo [n] *pavilion*
arbor, bandstand, belvedere, bower, kiosk, platform, rotunda, summerhouse; SEE CONCEPTS 440,443

gear [n1] *equipment*
accessory, accoutrement, adjunct, apparatus, appendage, appurtenance, baggage, belongings, contraption, effects, encumbrances, fittings, ha-

ga
ge

biliment, harness, impedimenta, instrument, kit, kit and kaboodle*, luggage, machinery, material, materiel, means, outfit, paraphernalia, possessions, rigging, setup, stuff, supply, tackle, things, tools, trappings; SEE CONCEPT *496*

gear [*n2*] *toothed part of wheel*
cog, cogwheel, gearwheel, pinion, ragwheel, sprocket, spurwheel; SEE CONCEPT *464*

gear [*n3*] *clothing*
apparel, array, attire, clothes, costume, drapes*, dress, duds*, feathers*, garb, garments, habit, outfit, rags*, threads*, toggery*, togs*, wear; SEE CONCEPT *451*

gear [*v*] *prepare, equip*
accouter, adapt, adjust, appoint, arm, blend, fit, fit out*, furnish, harness, match, organize, outfit, ready, regulate, rig*, suit, tailor, turn out; SEE CONCEPTS *182,202*

geek [*n2*] *odd person; computer expert*
buffoon, computer specialist, curiosity, dolt, dork, freak, goon, guru, nerd, techie, weirdo; SEE CONCEPTS *352,366,423*

gelatinous [*adj*] *coagulated*
gluey, glutinous, gummy, jelled, jellied, jelly-like, mucilaginous, pudding*, sticky, thick, viscid, viscous; SEE CONCEPT *606*

geld [*v*] *castrate*
alter*, emasculate, eunuchize, fix*, neuter, spay, sterilize, unman; SEE CONCEPTS *240,250*

gem [*n*] *precious stone; treasure*
bauble*, glass*, hardware*, jewel, jewelry, masterpiece, nonpareil, ornament, paragon, pearl, pick, prize, rock*, sparkler*, stone, trump*; SEE CONCEPTS *337,446,474*

gender [*n*] *grammatical rules applying to nouns that connote sex or animateness*
common, feminine, gender-specific, masculine, neuter; SEE CONCEPT *408*

genealogy [*n*] *person's family tree*
ancestry, blood line, derivation, descent, extraction, generation, genetics, heredity, history, line, lineage, parentage, pedigree, progeniture, stemma, stirps, stock, strain; SEE CONCEPT *296*

general [*adj1*] *common, accepted*
accustomed, broad, commonplace, conventional, customary, everyday, extensive, familiar, generic, habitual, humdrum, inclusive, matter-of-course*, natural, normal, ordinary, popular, prevailing, prevalent, public, regular, routine, run-of-the-mill*, typical, uneventful, universal, usual, wide, widespread, wonted; SEE CONCEPTS *530,547*

general [*adj2*] *inexact, approximate*
ill-defined, imprecise, inaccurate, indefinite, loose, not partial, not particular, not specific, uncertain, undetailed, unspecific, vague; SEE CONCEPT *557*

general [*adj3*] *comprehensive*
across-the-board*, all-around*, all-embracing*, all-inclusive*, ample, blanket, broad, catholic, collective, comprehending, diffuse, ecumenical, encyclopedic, endless, extensive, far-reaching, generic, global, inclusive, indiscriminate, infinite, limitless, miscellaneous, overall, panoramic, sweeping, taken as a whole, total, ubiquitous, unconfined, universal, unlimited, wide, worldwide; SEE CONCEPTS *537,772*

generality [*n*] *vague notion*
abstraction, abstract principle, generalization, half-truth, law, loose statement, observation,

principle, sweeping statement, universality; SEE CONCEPTS *688,689*

generalize [*v*] *make a sweeping assumption, statement*
be metaphysical, conclude, derive, discern, discover, establish, hypothesize, induce, observe, philosophize, postulate, speculate, stay in the clouds*, theorize, vapor; SEE CONCEPTS *37,49*

generally [*adv*] *mainly, in most cases*
about, all in all, almost always, altogether, approximately, as a rule, broadly, by and large, chiefly, commonly, conventionally, customarily, en masse, extensively, for the most part, habitually, largely, mostly, normally, on average, on the whole, ordinarily, overall, popularly, practically, predominantly, primarily, principally, publicly, regularly, roughly, roundly, thereabouts, typically, universally, usually, widely; SEE CONCEPTS *530,547,772*

generate [*v*] *produce, create*
accomplish, achieve, bear, beget, breed, bring about, bring to pass, cause, develop, effect, engender, form, found, get up, give birth to, give rise to, hatch, inaugurate, induce, initiate, institute, introduce, make, multiply, muster, occasion, originate, parent, perform, procreate, propagate, provoke, reproduce, set up, spawn, whip up*, work up; SEE CONCEPTS *173,205,251, 374*

generation [*n1*] *creation, production*
bearing, begetting, breeding, bringing forth, engenderment, formation, fructifying, genesis, multiplying, origination, procreation, propagation, reproduction, spawning; SEE CONCEPTS *173,205,374*

generation [*n2*] *era; age group*
aeon, breed, contemporaries, crop, day, days, eon, epoch, peers, period, rank, span, step, time, times; SEE CONCEPTS *807,816*

generic [*adj*] *common, general*
all-encompassing, blanket, collective, comprehensive, inclusive, nonexclusive, sweeping, universal, wide; SEE CONCEPT *530*

generosity [*n*] *spirit of giving*
all heart*, alms-giving, altruism, beneficence, benevolence, bounteousness, bounty, charitableness, charity, free giving, goodness, heart, high-mindedness, hospitality, kindness, largesse, liberality, magnanimity, munificence, nobleness, openhandedness, philanthropy, profusion, readiness, unselfishness; SEE CONCEPTS *411,657*

generous [*adj1*] *giving, big-hearted*
acceptable, altruistic, beneficent, benevolent, big, bounteous, bountiful, charitable, considerate, easy, equitable, excellent, fair, free, good, great-hearted, helpful, high-minded, honest, honorable, hospitable, just, kind, kindhearted, kindly, lavish, liberal, lofty, loose, magnanimous, moderate, munificent, noble, open-handed, philanthropic, prodigal, profuse, reasonable, soft-touch*, thoughtful, tolerant, ungrudging, unselfish, unsparing, unstinting, willing; SEE CONCEPTS *404,542*

generous [*adj2*] *plentiful*
abundant, affluent, ample, aplenty, bounteous, bountiful, copious, dime a dozen*, full, galore, handsome, large, lavish, liberal, luxuriant, no end*, no end in sight*, overflowing, plenteous, rich, stinking with*, unstinting, wealthy; SEE CONCEPTS *334,589,781*

genesis [*n*] *beginning, creation*
alpha, birth, commencement, dawn, dawning, engendering, formation, generation, inception, opening, origin, outset, propagation, provenance, provenience, root, source, start; SEE CONCEPTS *119,832*

genetic [*adj*] *coming from heredity*
abiogenetic, ancestral, digenetic, eugenic, genesiological, genital, hereditary, historical, matriclinous, patrimonial, phytogenetic, sprogenous, xenogenetic; SEE CONCEPTS *314,549*

genial [*adj*] *extremely nice and happy*
affable, agreeable, amiable, amicable, blithe, cheerful, cheering, cheery, chipper*, chirpy*, congenial, convivial, cordial, easygoing, enlivening, favorable, friendly, gentle, glad, good-natured, gracious, hearty, high, jocund, jolly, jovial, joyous, kind, kindly, merry, neighborly, perky, pleasant, sociable, sunny*, sunny side up*, up*, upbeat, upper*, warm, warm-hearted; SEE CONCEPTS *401,404*

geniality [*n*] *extreme niceness*
affability, agreeability, agreeableness, amenity, amiability, cheerfulness, cheeriness, congenialness, conviviality, cordiality, enjoyableness, friendliness, gladness, good cheer, good nature, gratefulness, happiness, heartiness, jollity, joviality, joy, joyousness, kindliness, kindness, mirth, pleasance, pleasantness, sunniness*, sweetness and light*, warmheartedness, warmth; SEE CONCEPTS *411,633*

genie [*n*] *mythical being*
demon, djinni, jinnee, jinni, spirit, wizard; SEE CONCEPT *361*

genius [*n*] *gift of high intellect*
ability, accomplishment, acumen, acuteness, adept, aptitude, aptness, astuteness, bent, brain, brilliance, capability, capacity, creativity, discernment, Einstein*, endowment, expert, faculty, flair, grasp, head, imagination, inclination, ingenuity, inspiration, intelligence, inventiveness, knack, mature, originality, percipience, perspicacity, power, precocity, prodigy, propensity, prowess, reach, sagacity, superability, talent, turn, understanding, virtuoso, wisdom; SEE CONCEPTS *350,409,416*

genocide [*n*] *mass extermination*
annihilation, carnage, decimation, ethnic cleansing, holocaust, massacre, mass execution, mass murder, race extermination, slaughter; SEE CONCEPT *252*

genre/genus [*n*] *type, class*
brand, category, character, classification, fashion, group, kind, school, sort, species, style; SEE CONCEPTS *378,388,655*

genteel [*adj*] *sophisticated, cultured*
affected, aristocratic, artificial, chivalrous, civil, confined, courteous, courtly, cultivated, distingué, elegant, fashionable, formal, graceful, hollow, intolerant, la-di-da*, mannerly, noble, ostentatious, polished, polite, pompous, precious, pretentious, priggish, prim, prissy, prudish, refined, respectable, straitlaced, stuffy*, stylish, urbane, well-behaved, well-bred, well-mannered; SEE CONCEPTS *401,404*

gentility [*n*] *sophistication, cultivation*
aristocracy, blue blood*, civility, courtesy, courtliness, culture, decorum, elegance, elite, etiquette, flower*, formality, gentle birth*, gentlefolk, gentry, good breeding*, good fam-

ily*, good manners*, high birth*, mannerliness, nobility, optimacy, polish, politeness, propriety, quality, rank, refinement, respectability, ruling class*, society, upper class, upper crust*, urbanity; SEE CONCEPT *388,411*

gentle [*adj*] *having a mild or kind nature*
affable, agreeable, amiable, benign, biddable, bland, compassionate, considerate, cool*, cultivated, disciplined, docile, domesticated, dove-like*, easy, genial, humane, kindly, laid back*, lenient, manageable, meek, mellow, merciful, moderate, pacific, peaceful, placid, pleasant, pleasing, pliable, quiet, soft, softhearted, sweet-tempered, sympathetic, tame, taught, temperate, tender, tractable, trained, warmhearted; SEE CONCEPTS *404,542*

gentle [*adj2*] *mild, temperate in effect on senses*
balmy, bland, calm, clement, delicate, easy, faint, feeble, gradual, halcyon, hushed, imperceptible, lenient, light, low, low-pitched, low-toned, mellow, mild, moderate, muted, peaceful, placid, quiet, sensitive, serene, slight, slow, smooth, soft, soothing, subdued, tender, tranquil, untroubled; SEE CONCEPTS *525,537,594*

gentle [*adj3*] *of noble birth*
aristocratic, blue-blooded*, Brahmin*, courteous, cultured, elegant, genteel, high-born, high-bred, noble, polished, polite, refined, upper-class, well-born, well-bred; SEE CONCEPT *555*

gentleperson [*n*] *polite, well-mannered person*
aristocrat, brick*, good egg*, good person, nice person, noble, scholar; SEE CONCEPT *423*

genuine [*adj1*] *authentic, real*
absolute, accurate, actual, authenticated, bona fide, -carat*, 24-carat*, certain, certified, demonstrable, exact, existent, factual, for real*, good, hard, honest, honest-to-goodness*, indubitable, in the flesh*, kosher*, legit, legitimate, literal, natural, official, original, palpable, plain, positive, precise, proved, pure, real stuff*, sound, sterling, sure-enough*, tested, true, unadulterated, unalloyed, undoubted, unimpeachable, unquestionable, unvarnished, valid, veritable, very, whole; SEE CONCEPT *582*

genuine [*adj2*] *unaffected; honest*
actual, artless, candid, earnest, frank, heartfelt, known, natural, open, positive, real, reliable, righteous, sincere, true, trustworthy, undesigning, unfeigned, unimpeachable, unpretended, unquestionable, up front*, valid, well-established; SEE CONCEPTS *267,542*

geography [*n*] *the earth's features; study of land*
cartography, chorography, earth science, geology, geopolitical study, geopolitics, physiographics, physiography, topography, topology; SEE CONCEPTS *349,509*

germ [*n1*] *microscopic organism, often causing illness*
antibody, bacterium, bug*, disease, microbe, microorganism, parasite, pathogen, plague, virus, what's going around*; SEE CONCEPTS *306,392*

germ [*n2*] *beginning*
bud, cause, egg, embryo, inception, nucleus, origin, ovule, ovum, root, rudiment, seed, source, spark, spore, sprig, sprout; SEE CONCEPTS *392,648,826,832*

germane [*adj*] *appropriate*
ad rem, akin, allied, applicable, applicative, applicatory, apposite, apropos, apt, cognate, connected, fitting, kindred, kosher*, legit*, material,

on target*, on the button*, on the nose*, pertinent, proper, related, relating, relevant, right on*,
suitable, that's the ticket*, to the point, to the
purpose; SEE CONCEPT *558*

germinate [*v*] *grow*
bud, develop, generate, live, originate, pullulate,
shoot, sprout, swell, vegetate; SEE CONCEPT *427*

gestation [*n*] *process of early development*
evolution, fecundation, gravidity, growth, incubation, maturation, pregnancy, reproduction,
ripening; SEE CONCEPTS *316,704,809*

gesture [*n*] *motion as communication*
action, body language, bow, curtsy, expression,
genuflection, gesticulation, high sign, indication,
intimation, kinesics, mime, nod, pantomime, reminder, salute, shrug, sign, signal, sign language,
token, wave, wink; SEE CONCEPTS *74,185*

gesture/gesticulate [*v*] *make signs, motions to
communicate*
act out, flag, indicate, mime, pantomime, signal,
signalize, use one's hands, use sign language,
wave; SEE CONCEPT *74*

get [*v1*] *come into possession of; achieve*
access, accomplish, acquire, annex, attain, bag*,
bring, bring in, build up, buy into, buy off, buy
out, capture, cash in on*, chalk up*, clean up*,
clear, come by, compass, cop*, draw, earn,
educe, effect, elicit, evoke, extort, extract, fetch,
gain, get hands on*, glean, grab, have, hustle*,
inherit, land, lock up, make, make a buy, make a
killing*, net, obtain, parlay, pick up, procure,
pull, rack up*, realize, reap, receive, score, secure, snag*, snap up*, snowball*, succeed to,
take, wangle*, win; SEE CONCEPTS *120,706,710*

get [*v2*] *fall victim to*
accept, be afflicted with, become infected with,
be given, be smitten by, catch, come down
with*, contract, get sick, receive, sicken, succumb, take; SEE CONCEPT *93*

get [*v3*] *seize*
apprehend, arrest, bag*, beat, capture, catch, collar*, defeat, grab, lay hold of*, lay one's hands
on*, nab*, nail*, occupy, overcome, overpower,
secure, take, trap; SEE CONCEPT *90*

get [*v4*] *come to be*
achieve, attain, become, come over, develop
into, effect, go, grow, realize, run, turn, wax*;
SEE CONCEPTS *697,706*

get [*v5*] *understand*
acquire, catch, catch on to, comprehend, fathom,
figure out, follow, gain, get into one's head*,
hear, know, learn, look at, memorize, notice, perceive, pick up*, receive, see, take in, work out;
SEE CONCEPTS *15,31*

get [*v6*] *arrive*
advance, blow in*, come, come to, converge,
draw near, land, make it, reach, show, show up,
turn up; SEE CONCEPT *159*

get [*v7*] *contact for communication*
get in touch, reach; SEE CONCEPT *266*

get [*v8*] *arrange, manage desired goal*
adjust, contrive, dispose, dress, fit, fix, make,
make up, order, prepare, ready, straighten, succeed, wangle*; SEE CONCEPT *202*

get [*v9*] *convince, induce*
argue into, beg, bring around, coax, compel,
draw, influence, persuade, press, pressure, prevail upon, prompt, provoke, sway, talk into,
urge, wheedle, win over; SEE CONCEPT *68*

get [*v10*] *have an effect on*
affect, amuse, arouse, bend, bias, carry, dispose,
entertain, excite, gratify, impress, influence, inspire, move, predispose, prompt, satisfy, stimulate, stir, stir up, strike, sway, touch; SEE
CONCEPTS *7,22*

get [*v11*] *produce offspring*
beget, breed, generate, procreate, produce, propagate, sire; SEE CONCEPT *374*

get [*v12*] *irritate, upset*
aggravate, annoy, bother, bug*, burn, exasperate,
gall, get someone's goat*, irk, nettle, peeve,
pique, provoke, put out*, rile, rub the wrong
way*, try, vex; SEE CONCEPTS *7,19*

get [*v13*] *confuse*
baffle, beat, bewilder, buffalo*, confound, discomfit, disconcert, distress, disturb, embarrass,
mystify, nonplus, perplex, perturb, puzzle,
stick*, stump, upset; SEE CONCEPT *16*

get across [*v*] *communicate an idea*
bring home*, convey, get through to, impart,
make clear, make understood, pass on, put over,
transmit; SEE CONCEPT *60*

get ahead [*v*] *excel, succeed*
advance, be successful, climb, do well, flourish,
get on, leave behind, make good, outdo, outmaneuver, overtake, progress, prosper, surpass,
thrive; SEE CONCEPTS *141,706*

get a kick out of [*v*] *delight in*
be pleased, dig*, enjoy, get a bang out of*, get a
charge out of*, get pleasure from, gloat over,
take pleasure in; SEE CONCEPTS *32,384*

get along [*v1*] *make progress*
cope, develop, do, fare, flourish, get by*, get
on*, make out, manage, muddle through*, prosper, shift, succeed, thrive; SEE CONCEPTS *117,704*

get along [*v2*] *depart*
advance, be off, go, go away, leave, march,
move, move off, move on, proceed, progress,
push ahead, take a hike*; SEE CONCEPT *195*

get along [*v3*] *be compatible*
agree, be friendly, get on*, harmonize, hit it off*;
SEE CONCEPT *388*

get at [*v1*] *attain*
access, achieve, acquire, arrive, ascertain, gain
access, get hold of, reach; SEE CONCEPT *120*

get at [*v2*] *mean, intend*
aim, hint, imply, lead up to, purpose, suggest;
SEE CONCEPT *75*

getaway [*n*] *escape*
break, breakout, decampment, flight, lam, slip;
SEE CONCEPT *102*

get back [*v1*] *regain*
reclaim, recoup, recover, repossess, retrieve, salvage; SEE CONCEPT *120*

get back [*v2*] *return*
arrive home, come back, come home, reappear,
revert, revisit, turn back; SEE CONCEPT *159*

get back at [*v*] *settle a score*
be avenged, get even, pay back, retaliate, revenge, take vengeance; SEE CONCEPTS *14,246*

get by [*v*] *manage, survive*
contrive, cope, do, do well enough, exist, fare,
flourish, get along, get on, make ends meet*,
make out, muddle through*, prosper, shift, subsist, succeed, thrive; SEE CONCEPT *117*

get down [*v*] *dismount*
alight, bring down, climb down, come down, descend, disembark, get off, lower, step down; SEE
CONCEPT *154*

get even [v] *to get revenge*
even the score, get back at, get square, settle the score; SEE CONCEPTS *126,384*

get in [v] *infiltrate; find a way in*
alight, appear, arrive, blow in*, come, embark, enter, gain ingress, get inside, include, insert, interpose, land, mount, penetrate, reach, show, show up, turn up; SEE CONCEPT *159*

get off [v] *depart*
alight, blow*, descend, disembark, dismount, escape, exit, go, go away, leave, light, pull out, quit, retire, withdraw; SEE CONCEPTS *154,195*

get off someone's back [v] *leave alone*
back off, get off someone's case, let someone breathe, stop annoying, stop nagging; SEE CONCEPTS *30,83*

get on [v1] *mount*
ascend, board, climb, embark, enplane, entrain, go up, scale; SEE CONCEPTS *159,166*

get on [v2] *cope, progress*
advance, do, do well enough, fare, get along, get by, make out, manage, muddle through*, prosper, shift, succeed; SEE CONCEPTS *117,704*

get on [v3] *be compatible*
agree, be friendly, concur, get along, harmonize, hit it off; SEE CONCEPT *388*

get on [v4] *put clothing on*
assume, attire, don, draw on, dress, slip into, throw on, wear; SEE CONCEPT *167*

get out [v] *escape*
alight, avoid, beat it*, begone, be off, break out, bug off*, buzz off*, clear out, decamp, depart, dodge, duck, egress, evacuate, evade, exit, extricate oneself, flee, fly, free oneself, go, hightail*, kite*, leave, make tracks*, run away, scram*, shirk, shun, skedaddle*, split, take a hike*, take off, vacate, vamoose*, withdraw; SEE CONCEPTS *102,195*

get over [v] *recover*
come round, get better, mend, overcome, pull through, recuperate, shake off, survive; SEE CONCEPT *35*

get the lead out [v] *hurry*
get a move on, get cracking*, get going, get it on, hop to it, hustle, look alive, make it snappy, shake a leg*, snap to it, step on it; SEE CONCEPTS *91,150*

get together [v] *gather, accumulate*
assemble, collect, congregate, convene, converge, join, meet, muster, rally, unite; SEE CONCEPTS *109,113*

get up [v] *mount; get out of bed*
arise, ascend, awake, awaken, climb, increase, move up, pile out*, rise, rise and shine*, roll out, scale, spring out, stand, turn out, uprise, upspring; SEE CONCEPT *154*

geyser [n] *fountain*
gusher, hot spring, jet, spout, thermal spring; SEE CONCEPTS *514,648*

ghastly [adj] *horrifying, dreadful; pale*
abhorrent, anemic, appalling, ashen, awful, bloodless, cadaverous, corpselike, deathlike, dim, disgusting, faint, frightening, frightful, funereal, ghostly, ghoulish, grim, grisly, gruesome, haggard, hideous, horrendous, horrible, horrid, livid, loathsome, lurid, macabre, mortuary, nauseating, offensive, pallid, repellent, repulsive, sepulchral, shocking, sickening, spectral, supernatural, terrible, terrifying, uncanny, unearthly,

unnatural, unpleasant, wan, weak, wraithlike; SEE CONCEPTS *485,529,537*

ghetto [n] *slum*
public squalor, rundown section of a city; SEE CONCEPTS *334,485,570*

ghetto box [n] *large portable stereo*
boom box, ghetto blaster, radio; SEE CONCEPT *279*

ghost [n] *spirit of the dead*
apparition, appearance, banshee, daemon, demon, devil, eidolon, ethereal being, haunt, incorporeal being, kelpie, manes, phantasm, phantom, poltergeist, revenant, shade, shadow, soul, specter, spook, vampire, vision, visitor, wraith, zombie; SEE CONCEPT *370*

ghostly [adj] *spooky*
apparitional, cadaverous, corpselike, deathlike, divine, eerie, eidolic, ghastly, haunted, holy, illusory, insubstantial, pale, phantasmal, phantom, scary, shadowy, spectral, spiritual, supernatural, uncanny, unearthly, vampiric, wan, weird, wraithlike, wraithy; SEE CONCEPTS *485,537*

ghoul [n] *evil demon*
bogeyman, devil, evil spirit, fiend, grave robber, monster; SEE CONCEPTS *370,412*

ghoulish [adj] *hideous, scary*
cruel, demonic, devilish, diabolical, eerie, fiendish, frightening, ghastly, grim, grisly, gruesome, horrible, macabre, monstrous, morbid, revolting, spine-chilling, spooky, terrifying; SEE CONCEPTS *529,548*

GI [n] *government issue; soldier*
army personnel, doughboy, enlisted person, GI Joe, serviceperson; SEE CONCEPT *358*

giant [adj] *very large*
big, blimp*, brobdingnagian*, colossal, cyclopean, elephantine*, enormous, gargantuan, gigantic, gross*, Herculean*, huge, hulking, humongous*, immense, jumbo*, mammoth, monstrous*, mountainous, prodigious, superduper*, titanic, vast, whale of a*, whaling*; SEE CONCEPTS *491,773,779,781*

giant [n] *extremely large person*
behemoth, bulk, colossus, cyclops, elephant*, goliath, Hercules*, hulk, jumbo*, leviathan, mammoth, monster*, mountain*, ogre, polypheme, titan, whale*, whopper*; SEE CONCEPT *424*

gibberish [n] *nonsense talk*
babble, balderdash*, blah-blah*, blather, chatter, claptrap*, double talk*, drivel, gobbledygook*, hocus-pocus*, jabber*, jargon, mumbo jumbo*, palaver*, prattle, scat*, twaddle*, yammer*; SEE CONCEPT *278*

gibe [n] *ridicule*
comeback, cutting remark, derision, dig*, dump*, jab, jeer, joke, mockery, parting shot*, put-down*, rank-out*, sarcasm, scoffing, slam*, sneer, swipe, taunt; SEE CONCEPT *278*

gibe [v] *ridicule*
deride, dis*, disrespect, flout, jeer, make fun of*, mock, poke fun at*, scoff, scorn, sneer, taunt; SEE CONCEPTS *52,54*

giddy [adj] *silly, impulsive*
bemused, brainless, bubbleheaded*, capricious, careless, changeable, changeful, ditzy*, dizzy, empty-headed*, erratic, fickle, flighty*, flustered, frivolous, gaga*, heedless, inconstant, irresolute, irresponsible, lightheaded*, punchy*, reckless, reeling, scatterbrained*, skittish*, slaphappy*,

swimming*, thoughtless, unbalanced, unsettled, unstable, unsteady, vacillating, volatile, whimsical, whirling, wild, woozy*; SEE CONCEPTS *314,401*

gift [*n1*] *something given freely, for no recompense*

allowance, alms, award, benefaction, benefit, bequest, bestowal, bonus, boon, bounty, charity, contribution, courtesy, dispensation, donation, endowment, fairing, favor, giveaway, goodie, grant, gratuity, hand, hand-me-down*, handout, honorarium, lagniappe, largesse, legacy, libation, oblation, offering, offertory, philanthropy, pittance, premium, present, presentation, provision, ration, relief, remembrance, remittance, reward, souvenir, subscription, subsidy, tip, token, tribute, write-off*; SEE CONCEPT *337*

gift [*n2*] *talent, aptitude*

ability, accomplishment, acquirement, aptness, attainment, attribute, bent, capability, capacity, endowment, faculty, flair, forte, genius, head*, instinct, knack, leaning, nose*, numen, power, propensity, set, specialty, turn; SEE CONCEPTS *409,630,706*

gifted [*adj*] *talented, intelligent*

able, accomplished, adroit, brilliant, capable, class act, clever, expert, got it*, have on the ball*, have smarts*, have the goods*, hot*, hotshot, ingenious, mad, masterly, phenomenal, shining at*, skilled, smart; SEE CONCEPTS *402,527,528*

gig [*n*] *show*

appearance, concert, employment, engagement, job, performance, recital; SEE CONCEPT *706*

gigantic [*adj*] *very large*

blimp, brobdingnagian*, colossal, cyclopean*, elephantine, enormous, gargantuan, giant, gross*, Herculean*, huge, immense, jumbo*, mammoth, massive, Moby*, monster, monstrous, prodigious, stupendous, super-colossal*, titan, tremendous, vast, whopping*; SEE CONCEPTS *491,773,779,781*

giggle [*n/v*] *snickering laugh*

cackle, chortle, chuckle, guffaw*, hee-haw*, snicker, snigger, teehee*, titter, twitter; SEE CONCEPT *77*

gigolo [*n*] *male escort*

Casanova, Don Juan, inamorato, ladies' man, lady-killer, Lothario, lover, male prostitute, seducer; SEE CONCEPT *423*

gild [*v*] *embellish, decorate*

adorn, aureate, aurify, beautify, bedeck, begild, brighten, coat, deck, dress up, embroider, engild, enhance, overlay, paint, plate, tinsel, varnish, wash, whitewash*; SEE CONCEPTS *172,177,202*

gimcrack [*n*] *gewgaw*

bagatelle, bauble, curio, doodad*, knickknack, novelty, souvenir, trinket; SEE CONCEPT *446*

gimmick [*n*] *contrived object; scheme*

aid, apparatus, artifice, catch, concern, counterfeit, deceit, device, dodge*, fake, feint, fixture, fun, gadget, gambit, game, gizmo*, imposture, instrument, jest, maneuver, means, method, ploy, ruse, secret, shift, sport, stratagem, stunt, trick, widget*; wile; SEE CONCEPTS *59,260,660*

gingerly [*adj*] *careful*

calculating, cautious, chary, circumspect, considerate, dainty, delicate, discreet, fastidious, guarded, hesitant, reluctant, safe, squeamish, suspicious, timid, wary; SEE CONCEPTS *542,550*

gingerly [*adv*] *carefully*

cautiously, charily, circumspectly, daintily, delicately, discreetly, fastidiously, guardedly, hesitantly, reluctantly, safely, squeamishly, suspiciously, timidly, warily; SEE CONCEPTS *542,550*

gin mill [*n*] *barroom*

alehouse, beer garden, cocktail lounge, drinkery, pub, public house, saloon, taproom, tavern, watering hole; SEE CONCEPTS *439,448,449*

gird [*v1*] *encircle; strengthen*

band, belt, bind, block, blockade, bolster, brace, buttress, cincture, circle, enclose, encompass, enfold, environ, fasten, fortify, girdle, hem in*, make ready, pen, prepare, ready, reinforce, ring, round, secure, steel, support, surround; SEE CONCEPTS *250,758*

gird [*v2*] *make fun of*

deride, flout, fun at, gibe, jeer, jest, mock, poke, quip, ridicule, scoff, scorn, sneer, taunt; SEE CONCEPTS *52,54*

girder [*n*] *main support beam*

I-beam, joist, rafter, tiebeam, truss; SEE CONCEPTS *471,479*

girdle [*n*] *corset*

band, belt, sash, undergarment, underwear, waistband; SEE CONCEPT *451*

girl [*n*] *young female person*

adolescent, damsel, daughter, lady, lassie, mademoiselle, Ms, schoolgirl, she, teenager, young lady, young woman; SEE CONCEPTS *415,424*

girlfriend [*n*] *female acquaintance or romantic companion*

companion, confidante, date, financee, flame*, friend, intimate, partner, soul mate, steady, sweetheart; SEE CONCEPTS *415,423*

gist [*n*] *meaning, essence*

basis, bearing, bottom line*, burden, core, drift, force, heart, idea, import, kernel*, keynote, marrow, matter, meat*, name of the game*, nature of the beast*, nitty gritty*, nuts and bolts*, pith*, point, punch line, quintessence, score, sense, short, significance, soul, spirit, stuff*, subject, substance, summary, tenor, theme, thrust, topic, upshot*; SEE CONCEPT *682*

give [*v1*] *contribute, supply, transfer*

accord, administer, allow, ante up, award, bequeath, bestow, cede, come across, commit, confer, consign, convey, deed, deliver, dish out*, dispense, dispose of, dole out, donate, endow, entrust, fork over*, furnish, gift, grant, hand down, hand out, hand over, heap upon, lavish upon, lay upon, lease, let have, make over*, parcel out, part with, pass down, pass out, permit, pony up*, present, provide, relinquish, remit, sell, shell out*, subsidize, throw in, tip, transmit, turn over, vouchsafe, will; SEE CONCEPTS *108,223,243*

give [*v2*] *communicate*

air, announce, be a source of, broadcast, carry, deliver, emit, express, furnish, impart, issue, notify, present, pronounce, publish, put, read, render, state, supply, transfer, transmit, utter, vent, ventilate; SEE CONCEPTS *60,266*

give [*v3*] *demonstrate, proffer*

administer, bestow, confer, dispense, display, evidence, extend, furnish, hold out, indicate, issue, manifest, minister, offer, pose, present, produce, provide, put on, render, return, set forth, show, tender, yield; SEE CONCEPTS 97,118

give [v4] *yield, collapse*
allow, bend, bow to, break, cave, cede, concede, contract, crumble, crumple, devote, fail, fall, flex, fold, fold up, give way, go, grant, hand over, lend, open, recede, relax, relent, relinquish, retire, retreat, sag, shrink, sink, slacken, surrender, weaken; SEE CONCEPTS 13,469

give [v5] *perform action*
address, apply, bend, buckle down, cause, devote, direct, do, engender, lead, make, occasion, produce, throw, turn; SEE CONCEPT 100

give-and-take [n] *compromise*
adaptability, cooperation, exchange, reciprocity, swap, trade-off; SEE CONCEPTS 230,684

give away [v1] *reveal*
betray, blab*, disclose, discover, divulge, expose, inform, leak, let out, let slip, mouth*, spill, tell, uncover; SEE CONCEPT 60

give away [v2] *unselfishly transfer*
award, bestow, devote, donate, hand out, present; SEE CONCEPT 108

give in/give up [v] *admit defeat*
abandon, back down*, bail out*, bow out*, buckle under*, capitulate, cave in*, cease, cede, chicken out*, collapse, comply, concede, cry uncle*, cut out, desist, despair, drop, drop like a hot potato*, fold, forswear, hand over, leave off, pull out, quit, relinquish, resign, stop, submit, surrender, take the oath*, throw in the towel*, waive, walk out on, wash one's hands of*, yield; SEE CONCEPTS 8,45,119,385

given to [adj] *likely to*
accustomed, addicted, apt, disposed, habituated, inclined, in the habit of, inured, liable, obsessed, prone; SEE CONCEPT 542

give off/give out [v] *discharge*
beam, belch, diffuse, emanate, emit, exhale, exude, flow, give forth, issue, pour, produce, radiate, release, send out, smell of, throw out, vent, void; SEE CONCEPT 179

give the cold shoulder [v] *snub*
act cool*, brush off*, disregard, eject, ignore, make unwelcome, neglect, ostracize, shun, turn up one's nose*, upstage; SEE CONCEPT 30

gizmo [n] *gadget*
appliance, contraption, contrivance, device, doohickey, instrument, machine, mechanical device, thingamabob, thingamajig, tool, whatchamacallit, widget; SEE CONCEPTS 463,499

glacial [adj1] *extremely cold*
antarctic, arctic, biting, bitter, chill, chilly, cool, freezing, frigid, frosty, frozen, gelid, icy, nippy, piercing, polar, raw, wintry; SEE CONCEPT 605

glacial [adj2] *unfriendly*
aloof, antagonistic, chill, cold, cool, distant, emotionless, frigid, hostile, icy, inaccessible, indifferent, inimical, remote, reserved, seclusive, standoffish, unapproachable, unemotional, withdrawn; SEE CONCEPTS 401,404

glacier [n] *mountain of ice, snow*
berg, floe, glacial mass, iceberg, icecap, ice field, ice floe, snow slide; SEE CONCEPT 509

glad [adj] *happy, delightful*
animated, beaming, beautiful, blithesome, bright, can't complain*, cheerful, cheering, cheery, contented, exhilarated, felicitous, floating on air*, gay, genial, gleeful, gratified, gratifying, hilarious, jocund, jovial, joyful, joyous, lighthearted, merry, mirthful, overjoyed, pleasant, pleased, pleased as punch*, pleasing, radiant, rejoicing, sparkling, tickled, tickled pink*, tickled to death*, up, willing; SEE CONCEPTS 403,529

gladden [v] *please*
brighten, cheer, delight, elate, hearten, make happy, warm; SEE CONCEPTS 7,22

gladiator [n] *combatant*
boxer, contender, fighter; SEE CONCEPTS 358,366,412

gladly [adv] *happily*
acquiescently, ardently, beatifically, blissfully, blithely, cheerfully, cheerily, contentedly, cordially, delightedly, delightfully, ecstatically, enchantedly, enthusiastically, felicitously, freely, gaily, genially, gleefully, gratefully, heartily, jocundly, jovially, joyfully, joyously, lovingly, merrily, paradisiacally, passionately, pleasantly, pleasingly, pleasurably, rapturously, readily, sweetly, warmly, willingly, with good grace, with pleasure, with relish, zealously, zestfully; SEE CONCEPTS 403,538,542

gladness [n] *happiness*
animation, blitheness, cheer, cheerfulness, delight, felicity, gaiety, glee, high spirits*, hilarity, jollity, joy, joyousness, mirth, pleasure; SEE CONCEPT 410

glamorous [adj] *sophisticated in style*
alluring, attractive, bewitching, captivating, charismatic, charming, classy, dazzling, drop-dead gorgeous*, elegant, enchanting, entrancing, exciting, fascinating, flashy, foxy*, glittering, glossy, looking like a million*, lovely, magnetic, nifty, prestigious, righteous, seductive, siren, smart; SEE CONCEPTS 579,589

glamour [n] *sophisticated style*
allure, allurement, animal magnetism, appeal, attraction, beauty, bewitchment, charisma, charm, color, enchantment, fascination, interest, magnetism, prestige, ravishment, razzle-dazzle*, romance, star quality; SEE CONCEPTS 655,718

glance [n1] *brief look*
eye*, eyeball*, flash*, fleeting look, gander, glimpse, lamp*, look, look-see*, peek, peep, quick look, sight, slant*, squint, swivel*, view; SEE CONCEPT 623

glance [n2] *reflection of light*
coruscation, flash, gleam, glimmer, glint, glisten, shimmer, sparkle, twinkle; SEE CONCEPTS 624,628

glance [v1] *look at briefly*
browse, check out, dip into*, flash*, flip through, gaze, get a load of*, glimpse, leaf through, peek, peep, peer, riffle through*, run over, run through, scan, see, skim through*, take a gander*, take in, thumb through*, view; SEE CONCEPT 623

glance [v2] *reflect light*
coruscate, flash, gleam, glimmer, glint, glisten, glitter, shimmer, shine, sparkle, twinkle; SEE CONCEPT 624

glance [v3] *ricochet, hit off of something*
bounce, brush, careen, carom, contact, dart, graze, kiss*, rebound, scrape, shave*, sideswipe, skim, skip, slant, slide, strike, touch; SEE CONCEPT 189

glare [n1] *very bright light, shine*
blaze, blinding light, brilliance, dazzle, flame, flare, glow; SEE CONCEPT 628

glare [n2] *dirty look*
angry stare, bad eye*, black look*, evil eye*,

gi
gl

frown, glower, lower, scowl; SEE CONCEPTS
623,716
glare [v1] *give a dirty look*
bore, do a slow burn*, fix, frown, gape, gawk,
gaze, glower, look daggers*, lower, menace,
peer, pierce, scowl, stare, stare angrily*, stare
icily*, wither; SEE CONCEPT 623
glare [v2] *shine very brightly*
beam, blare, blaze, blind, blur, daze, dazzle,
flame, flare, glaze, glow, radiate; SEE CONCEPT
624
glaring [adj1] *obvious, unconcealed*
audacious, blatant, brazen, capital, conspicuous,
crying, egregious, evident, excessive, extreme,
flagrant, gross, inordinate, manifest, noticeable,
obtrusive, open, outrageous, outstanding, overt,
patent, protrusive, rank, visible; SEE CONCEPTS
576,619
glaring [adj2] *bright, dazzling; flashy*
blatant, blazing, blinding, brazen, chintzy, florid,
garish, gaudy, glowing, loud, meretricious, shining, tawdry; SEE CONCEPTS 589,617
glass [n1] *object that reflects an image*
looking glass, mirror, reflector, seeing glass; SEE
CONCEPTS 260,470
glass [n2] *object used for drinking liquids*
beaker, bottle, chalice, cup, decanter, goblet,
highball, jar, jigger, jug, mug, pilsener, pony,
snifter, tumbler; SEE CONCEPT 494
glasses [n] *object worn to correct vision*
bifocals, blinkers*, cheaters*, contact lenses,
eyeglasses, four eyes*, frames, goggles,
lorgnette, pince-nez, rims*, shades*, specs*,
spectacles, trifocals; SEE CONCEPT 446
glassy [adj1] *polished, smooth*
burnished, clear, glazed, glazy, glossy, hyaline,
hyaloid, icy, lustrous, shiny, sleek, slick, slippery, transparent, vitreous, vitric; SEE CONCEPT
606
glassy [adj2] *expressionless, especially referring
to eyes*
blank, cold, dazed, dull, empty, fixed, glazed,
lifeless, stupid, vacant; SEE CONCEPTS 406,619
glaze [n] *varnish, lacquer*
coat, enamel, finish, glint, gloss, luster, patina,
polish, sheen, shine; SEE CONCEPTS 259,475
glaze [v] *varnish, lacquer*
buff, burnish, coat, cover, enamel, furbish,
glance, glass, gloss, incrust, make lustrous, make
vitreous, overlay, polish, rub, shine, vitrify; SEE
CONCEPTS 172,202,215
gleam [n] *brightness, sparkle*
beam, brilliance, coruscation, flash, flicker,
glance, glim, glimmer, glint, glitz, gloss, glow,
luster, ray, scintillation, sheen, shimmer, splendor, twinkle; SEE CONCEPTS 620,624
gleam [v] *sparkle*
beam, burn, coruscate, flare, flash, glance, glimmer, glint, glisten, glister, glitter, glow, radiate,
scintillate, shimmer, shine, twinkle; SEE CON-
CEPTS 620,624
glean [v] *pick out, collect*
accumulate, amass, ascertain, conclude, cull, deduce, extract, garner, gather, harvest, learn, pick,
reap, select, sift, winnow; SEE CONCEPTS 31,135
glee [n] *extreme happiness*
blitheness, cheerfulness, delectation, delight, elation, enjoyment, exhilaration, exuberance, exultation, fun, gaiety, gladness, hilarity, jocularity,
jollity, joviality, joy, joyfulness, joyousness,

liveliness, merriment, mirth, pleasure, sprightliness, triumph, verve; SEE CONCEPT 410
gleeful [adj] *very happy*
blithe, blithesome, boon, cheerful, delighted,
elated, exalted, exuberant, exultant, frolicsome,
gay, gratified, hilarious, jocund, jolly, jovial,
joyful, joyous, jubilant, lighthearted, merry,
mirthful, overjoyed, pleased, triumphant; SEE
CONCEPT 403
glen [n] *valley*
canyon, combe, dale, dell, glade, gorge, vale; SEE
CONCEPT 509
glib [adj] *slick, smooth-talking*
artful, articulate, easy, eloquent, facile, fast-talk-
ing*, flip, fluent, garrulous, hot-air*, insincere,
loquacious, plausible, quick, ready, silver-
tongued*, slippery, smooth operator*, smooth-
spoken*, smooth-tongued*, suave, talkative,
urbane, vocal, vocative, voluble; SEE CONCEPTS
267,404
glide [v] *move smoothly and quickly on a surface*
coast, decline, descend, drift, flit, float, flow, fly,
glissade, roll, run, sail, scud, shoot, skate, skim,
skip, skirr, slide, slink, slip, slither, smooth
along, soar, spiral, stream, trip, waft, wing; SEE
CONCEPT 150
glimmer [n] *flash, sparkle*
blink, coruscation, flicker, glance, gleam, glint,
glow, grain, hint, inkling, ray, scintillation, shimmer, suggestion, trace, twinkle; SEE CONCEPTS
624,831
glimmer [v] *sparkle*
blink, coruscate, fade, flash, flicker, glance,
gleam, glint, glisten, glister, glitter, glow, scintillate, shimmer, shine, twinkle; SEE CONCEPT 624
glimpse [n] *brief look*
eye, eyeball*, flash*, gander*, glance, glom*,
gun*, impression, lamp*, look-see*, peek, peep,
quick look, sight, sighting, slant, squint, swivel*;
SEE CONCEPT 623
glimpse [v] *look briefly*
catch sight of, check out, descry, espy, eye, flash,
get a load of*, get an eyeful*, peek, sight, spot,
spy, take a gander*, take in*, view; SEE CONCEPT
623
glint [n] *sparkle*
flash, glance, gleam, glimmer, glitter, look,
shine, trace, twinkle; SEE CONCEPTS 411,624,628
glisten [v] *shimmer*
coruscate, flash, flicker, glance, glare, gleam,
glimmer, glint, glister, glitter, glow, scintillate,
shine, sparkle, twinkle; SEE CONCEPT 624
glitch [n] *error*
bug*, defect, flaw, hitch, malfunction, misfire,
mishap, problem, setback, snafu, snag, something wrong; SEE CONCEPTS 101,230,674,699
glitter [n] *brilliance, sparkle*
beam, brightness, coruscation, display, flash,
gaudiness, glamour, glare, gleam, glint, glisten,
glister, glitz, luster, pageantry, radiance, scintillation, sheen, shimmer, shine, show, showiness,
splendor, tinsel, twinkle, zap*; SEE CONCEPTS
620,655
glitter [v] *sparkle*
coruscate, flash, glance, glare, gleam, glimmer,
glint, glisten, glister, glow, scintillate, shimmer,
shine, spangle, twinkle; SEE CONCEPT 624
glitz [n] *showiness*
appeal, flashiness, gaudiness, glamour, ostentation, speciousness; SEE CONCEPT 261

oat [v] *exclaim triumph*
elebrate, crow*, exult, glory, rejoice, relish, rub in*, triumph, vaunt, whoop*; SEE CONCEPT 49

ob [n] *thick lump*
atch, blob, chunk, clump, gob, hunk, mass, rad; SEE CONCEPTS 432,470,471

obal [adj] *worldwide, all-encompassing*
ll-around, all-inclusive, all-out, blanket, atholic, comprehensive, cosmic, cosmopolitan, arthly, ecumenical, encyclopedic, exhaustive, eneral, grand, international, mundane, overall, andemic, planetary, spherical, sweeping, thorugh, total, unbounded, universal, unlimited, vorld; SEE CONCEPTS 536,772

obe [n] *Earth, sphere*
pple*, ball, balloon*, big blue marble*, map, rb, planet, rondure, round, spheroid, terrene, vorld; SEE CONCEPTS 436,511

oom [n1] *melancholy, depression*
nguish, bitterness, blue devils*, blue funk*, lues*, catatonia, chagrin, cheerlessness, dejecon, desolation, despair, despondency, disconsoateness, discouragement, dismals, distress, oldrums, dolor, downheartedness, dullness, umps*, foreboding, grief, heaviness, heavyeartedness, horror, low spirits*, malaise, misry, misgiving, mopes, morbidity, mourning, ppression, pensiveness, pessimism, sadness, aturninity, sorrow, unhappiness, vexation, veariness, woe; SEE CONCEPT 410

oom [n2] *darkness, blackness*
leakness, cloud, cloudiness, dimness, dullness, usk, duskiness, gloominess, murk, murkiness, bscurity, shade, shadow, twilight; SEE CONEPTS 620,622,810

oomy [adj1] *dark, black*
leak, caliginous, cheerless, clouded, cloudy, repuscular, desolate, dim, dismal, dreary, dull, usky, forlorn, funereal, lightless, murky, obcure, overcast, overclouded, sepulchral, shadwy, somber, tenebrous, unilluminated, unlit, vintry; SEE CONCEPTS 525,617,618

oomy [adj2] *feeling down, blue*
lue funk*, broody, chapfallen, cheerless, rabbed*, crestfallen, dejected, depressed, desoate, despondent, disconsolate, dismal, dispirited, our, downcast, downhearted, down in the umps*, down in the mouth*, dragged, forlorn, lum, in low spirits*, in the dumps*, joyless, ow, melancholy, mirthless, miserable, moody, noping, mopish, morose, mournful, oppressed, essimistic, sad, saturnine, solemn, sulky, sullen, urly, ugly, unhappy, weary, woebegone, woeul; SEE CONCEPT 403

oomy [adj3] *sad, depressing*
cheronian, acherontic, bad, black, bleak, cheerss, cold, comfortless, depressive, desolate, disonsolate, discouraging, disheartening, dismal, ispiriting, drab, dreary, dull, dusky, funereal, oyless, lugubrious, morose, oppressive, saddenng, somber, tenebrific; SEE CONCEPTS 537,548

orify [v1] *praise*
cclaim, bless, boost, build up, celebrate, commend, cry up, eulogize, exalt, extol, hike, honor, ymn, laud, lionize, magnify, panegyrize, put on pedestal*, put up, sing the praises of*; SEE ONCEPT 69

orify [v2] *adore, idolize*
dorn, aggrandize, apotheosize, augment, beatfy, bless, canonize, deify, dignify, distinguish,

elevate, enhance, ennoble, enshrine, erect, exalt, halo*, honor, illuminate, immortalize, lift up, magnify, pay homage to, raise, revere, sanctify, transfigure, uprear, venerate, worship; SEE CONCEPT 12

glorious [adj] *adored, idolized; divine*
august, beautiful, bright, brilliant, celebrated, dazzling, delightful, distinguished, effulgent, elevated, eminent, enjoyable, esteemed, exalted, excellent, famed, famous, fine, gorgeous, grand, gratifying, great, heavenly, heroic, honored, illustrious, immortal, magnificent, majestic, marvelous, memorable, noble, notable, noted, pleasurable, preeminent, radiant, remarkable, renowned, resplendent, shining, splendid, sublime, superb, time-honored, triumphant, venerable, well-known, wonderful; SEE CONCEPTS 568,574,579

glory [n1] *fame, importance*
celebrity, dignity, distinction, eminence, exaltation, grandeur, greatness, honor, illustriousness, immortality, kudos, magnificence, majesty, nobility, praise, prestige, renown, reputation, splendor, sublimity, triumph; SEE CONCEPTS 388,668

glory [n2] *great beauty*
brightness, brilliance, effulgence, fineness, gorgeousness, grandeur, luster, magnificence, majesty, pageantry, pomp, preciousness, radiance, resplendence, richness, splendor, sublimity, sumptuousness; SEE CONCEPTS 673,718

glory [v] *boast, exult*
crow, gloat, jubilate, pride oneself, relish, revel, take delight, triumph; SEE CONCEPTS 12,49

gloss [n1] *shine, sheen*
appearance, brightness, brilliance, burnish, facade, finish, front, glaze, gleam, glint, glossiness, luster, polish, shimmer, silkiness, sleekness, slickness, surface, varnish, veneer; SEE CONCEPTS 611,620

gloss [n2] *definition*
annotation, comment, commentary, elucidation, explanation, footnote, interpretation, note, translation; SEE CONCEPT 268

gloss [v1] *make shiny*
buff, burnish, finish, furbish, glance, glaze, lacquer, polish, rub, shine, varnish, veneer; SEE CONCEPTS 202,215

gloss [v2] *conceal truth*
belie, camouflage, cover up, deacon, disguise, doctor, explain, extenuate, falsify, hide, justify, mask, misrepresent, palliate, rationalize, smooth over, soft-pedal, sugarcoat*, varnish, veil, veneer, white, whiten, whitewash*; SEE CONCEPTS 49,63

gloss [v3] *define*
annotate, comment, construe, elucidate, explain, interpret, justify, translate; SEE CONCEPT 57

glossary [n] *word list*
dictionary, lexicon, vocabulary, word index; SEE CONCEPT 280

glossy [adj] *shiny*
bright, brilliant, burnished, glassy, glazed, gleaming, glistening, lustrous, polished, reflecting, silken, silky, sleek, slick, smooth; SEE CONCEPTS 606,617

glove [n] *hand covering for warmth, protection*
gage, gauntlet, mitt, mitten, muff; SEE CONCEPT 451

glow [n] *burning, brightness*
afterglow, bloom, blossom, blush, brilliance, ef-

gl
gl

fulgence, flush, glare, gleam, glimmer, glitter, gusto, heat, incandescence, intensity, lambency, light, luminosity, passion, phosphorescence, radiance, ray, splendor, vividness, warmth; SEE CONCEPTS 610,620,622,673

glow [v] *burn, radiate*
be suffused, blare, blaze, blush, brighten, color, crimson, fill, flame, flare, flush, gleam, glimmer, glisten, glitter, ignite, kindle, light, mantle, pink, pinken, redden, rose, rouge, shine, smolder, thrill, tingle, twinkle; SEE CONCEPTS 249,469,624

glower [v] *frown*
glare, gloom, look, look daggers*, lower, scowl, stare, sulk, watch; SEE CONCEPT 623

glowing [adj1] *burning, bright*
aglow, beaming, flaming, florid, flush, flushed, gleaming, lambent, luminous, lustrous, phosphorescent, red, rich, rubicund, ruddy, sanguine, suffused, vibrant, vivid, warm; SEE CONCEPTS 617,618

glowing [adj2] *very happy, enthusiastic*
adulatory, ardent, avid, blazing, burning, complimentary, desirous, eager, ecstatic, eulogistic, fervent, fervid, fierce, fiery, flaming, heated, hot-blooded, impassioned, keen, laudatory, panegyrical, passionate, rave, rhapsodic, zealous; SEE CONCEPTS 267,401

glue [n] *adhesive*
cement, gum, gunk*, mucilage, paste, plaster, spit*, stickum*; SEE CONCEPT 475

glum [adj] *sullen*
blue, bummed out, dejected, depressed, dismal, dispirited, down, gloomy, low, melancholy, morose, sad, sulky; SEE CONCEPT 403

glut [n] *overabundance*
excess, nimiety, oversupply, plenitude, saturation, superfluity, surfeit, surplus, too much*; SEE CONCEPTS 740,787

glut [v] *choke; oversupply*
burden, clog, cloy, congest, cram, deluge, devour, feast, fill, flood, gorge, hog*, inundate, jade, load, make a pig of*, overfeed, overload, overstock, overwhelm, pack*, pall, raven, sate, satiate, saturate, stuff, surfeit, wolf*; SEE CONCEPTS 140,169,209,740

glutton [n] *person who overeats*
epicure, gorger*, gormandizer, gourmand, hefty eater, hog*, pig*, sensualist, stuffer*; SEE CONCEPT 412

gluttonous [adj] *voracious*
covetous, devouring, edacious, gorging, gourmandizing, greedy, gross, hoggish*, insatiable, never full, omnivorous, piggish*, piggy*, prodigious, rapacious, ravening, ravenous, sating, starved, starving, unquenchable, wolfish*; SEE CONCEPTS 20,401

gnarled [adj] *knotted*
bent, contorted, crooked, deformed, distorted, gnarly, knurled, leathery, out of shape, rough, rugged, tortured, twisted, weather-beaten, wrinkled; SEE CONCEPTS 485,486

gnarly [adj] *cool, excellent*
boss*, finest, great, hairy*, keen, magnificent, marvelous, neat, nifty, sensational, superb, swell, wonderful; SEE CONCEPT 574

gnash [v] *grind*
clamp, crush, grate, grit, rub; SEE CONCEPTS 186,204

gnaw [v1] *bite, chew*
champ, chaw, chomp, consume, corrode, crunch,

devour, eat, eat away, erode, gum, masticate, munch, nibble, wear; SEE CONCEPTS 169,185

gnaw [v2] *be bothered, worried about*
annoy, bedevil, beleague, distress, eat at*, fret, harass, harry, haunt, irritate, nag, pester, plague, prey on one's mind*, rankle, tease, trouble, wear down; SEE CONCEPTS 17,34

gnome [n] *troll*
elf, fairy; SEE CONCEPT 424

go [n1] *spirit, vitality*
activity, animation, bang, birr*, drive, energy, force, get-up-and-go*, hardihood, life, moxie*, oomph*, pep, potency, push, snap*, starch*, tuck*, verve, vigor, vivacity, zest; SEE CONCEPT 411

go [n2] *try, attempt*
bid, crack, effort, essay, fling, pop, shot, slap, stab, turn, whack, whirl; SEE CONCEPTS 87,677

go [v1] *advance, proceed physically*
abscond, approach, beat it*, bug out*, cruise, decamp, depart, escape, exit, fare, flee, fly, get away, get going*, get lost, get off*, hie, hightail*, hit the road*, journey, lam, leave, light out*, make a break for it*, make for*, make one's way*, mosey, move, move out, near, pass, progress, pull out, push off, push on, quit, repair, retire, run along, run away, set off, shove off*, skip out*, split*, take a hike*, take a powder*, take flight, take leave*, take off*, travel, vamoose*, wend, withdraw; SEE CONCEPTS 159,195

go [v2] *operate, function*
act, carry on, click*, continue, flourish, maintain, make out, move, pan out*, perform, persist, prosper, run, score, succeed, thrive, work; SEE CONCEPTS 4,239

go [v3] *span, stretch*
connect, cover, extend, fit, give access, lead, make, range, reach, run, spread, vary; SEE CONCEPTS 651,756

go [v4] *contribute, work towards an end*
avail, befall, chance, come, concur, conduce, develop, eventuate, fall out, fare, happen, incline, lead to, occur, persevere, persist, proceed, result, serve, tend, transpire, turn, turn out, wax*, work out; SEE CONCEPTS 87,704

go [v5] *agree, harmonize*
accord, be adapted for, be designed for, belong, blend, chime, complement, conform, correspond, dovetail*, enjoy, fit, jibe*, like, match, mesh, relish, set, square, suit; SEE CONCEPTS 8,664,714

go [v6] *die, collapse*
bend, break, cave, conclude, consume, crumble, decease, decline, demise, depart, deplete, devour, dissipate, drop, exhaust, expend, expire, fail, finish, fold up, fritter, give, pass away*, pass on*, perish, run through*, spend, squander, succumb, terminate, use up, waste, weaken, worsen, yield; SEE CONCEPTS 105,698,699

go [v7] *elapse*
be spent, expire, flow, lapse, pass, pass away, slip away, transpire, waste away; SEE CONCEPT 804

go [v8] *endure*
abide, allow, bear, brook, consent to, let, permit, put up with*, stand, stomach*, suffer, swallow*, take, tolerate; SEE CONCEPT 23

go about [v] *undertake*
approach, be employed, begin, devote oneself to

goad [n] *stimulus*
catalyst, compulsion, desire, drive, impetus, impulse, impulsion, incentive, incitation, incitement, irritation, lash, lust, motivation, passion, pressure, prod, spur, urge, whip, zeal; SEE CONCEPTS 20,661

goad [v] *egg on, incite*
animate, annoy, arouse, bully, coerce, drive, encourage, excite, exhort, fire up*, force, goose*, harass, hound, impel, inspirit, instigate, irritate, key up*, lash, move, needle*, press, prick*, prod, prompt, propel, provoke, push, put up to*, rowel, sic*, sound, spark*, spur, stimulate, sting*, tease, thrust, trigger, turn on*, urge, whip*, work up, worry; SEE CONCEPTS 14,68

go-ahead [adj] *progressive*
ambitious, enterprising, entrepreneurial, go-getting*, gumptious*, pioneering, up-and-coming*; SEE CONCEPTS 538,542

go-ahead [n] *authorization*
assent, consent, green light*, leave, okay, permission; SEE CONCEPT 685

go ahead [v] *proceed*
advance, begin, continue, dash ahead, edge forward, go forward, go on, move on, progress, shoot ahead; SEE CONCEPTS 149,159,704

goal [n] *aim, purpose of an action*
ambition, design, destination, duty, end, ground zero*, intent, intention, limit, mark, mission, object, objective, target, use, zero*; SEE CONCEPT 659

go along/go along with [v] *agree, cooperate*
accompany, acquiesce, act jointly, assent, collaborate, concur, conspire, follow, share in, work together; SEE CONCEPTS 8,18

goat [n] *hollow-horned mammal*
billy, buck, kid; SEE CONCEPTS 394,400

go back/go back on [v] *break promise; change one's mind*
abandon, betray, be unfaithful, desert, forsake, leave in the lurch*, renege, repudiate, retract, return, revert, run out on; SEE CONCEPTS 13,71

go back to square one [v] *start all over*
begin again, go back to the drawing board, make a fresh start, make a new beginning, start from scratch, wipe the slate clean*; SEE CONCEPTS 221,241

gobble [v] *eat hurriedly*
cram*, devour, gorge, gulp*, guzzle, ingurgitate, scarf*, stuff*, suck up*, swallow, wolf*; SEE CONCEPT 169

gobbledygook [n] *jargon*
balderdash*, baloney*, bosh, bull*, bunk*, cant, drivel, gibberish, hooey*, rigmarole, rubbish*; SEE CONCEPTS 275,276

go-between [n] *person acting as an agent*
arbitrator, attorney, broker, dealer, delegate, deputy, emissary, entrepreneur, envoy, factor, interagent, interceder, intercessor, intermediary, intermediate, intermediator, liaison, matchmaker, mediator, medium, messenger, negotiator, proxy, referee, representative; SEE CONCEPTS 348,423

goblin [n] *elf*
bogeyman, brownie, demon, fiend, gnome, gremlin, imp, kobold, nixie, pixie, spirit, sprite; SEE CONCEPT 370

go by [v1] *elapse*
exceed, flow on, make one's way, move onward, pass, proceed; SEE CONCEPT 141

go by [v2] *adopt, conform*
abide by, adjust to, agree, be guided by, comply, cooperate, fall in with, follow, heed, judge from, observe, take as guide; SEE CONCEPTS 8,18

go crazy [v] *become insane*
blow a gasket*, blow one's mind*, blow one's stack*, blow one's top*, crack up*, flip one's lid*, flip out, fly off the handle*, freak out*, go ballistic*, go bananas*, go batty*, go berserk*, go bonkers*, go buggy*, go cuckoo*, go daffy*, go haywire*, go kooky*, go loco*, go loony*, go mental, go nuts*, go nutty*, go off, go off one's rocker*, go off the deep end*, go off the wall*, go psycho*, go wacko*, go wacky*, lose control of oneself, lose it*, lose one's cool, lose one's mind, wig out*; SEE CONCEPT 13

god [n] *supernatural being worshipped by people*
Absolute Being, Allah, All Knowing, All Powerful, Almighty, Creator, daemon, deity, demigod, demon, Divine Being, divinity, Father, God, holiness, Holy Spirit, idol, Infinite Spirit, Jah, Jehovah, King of Kings, Lord, Maker, master, numen, omnipotent, power, prime mover, providence, soul, spirit, totem, tutelary, universal life force, world spirit, Yahweh; SEE CONCEPT 370

God-fearing [adj] *religious*
churchgoing, dedicated, devoted, devout, ecclesiastical, faithful, godly, goody-goody*, holy, orthodox, pious, prayerful, reverent, righteous, sacred, spiritual, theological; SEE CONCEPTS 536,545

godforsaken [adj] *desolate*
abandoned, backward, deserted, dismal, distant, empty, forgotten, forlorn, gloomy, isolated, lonely, miserable, neglected, out-of-the-way, remote, secluded, wicked; SEE CONCEPTS 485,560

godless [adj] *without a god or divine faith*
adiamorphic, agnostic, atheistic, freethinking, iconoclastic, irreligious, nonbelieving, skeptical, undogmatic; SEE CONCEPT 542

godly [adj] *religious*
angelic, born-again, celestial, charismatic, deific, devout, divine, god-fearing, good, holy, pietistic, pious, prayerful, righteous, saintlike, saintly, virtuous; SEE CONCEPT 542

go down [v] *lose, fall*
be beaten, be defeated, cave in, collapse, crumple, decline, decrease, descend, droop, drop, fold, founder, go under, keel, lessen, make less, pitch, plunge, reduce, sag, set, sink, slump, submerge, submerse, submit, succumb, suffer defeat, topple, tumble; SEE CONCEPTS 181,698,699

godsend [n] *gift, benefit*
advantage, benediction, blessing, boon, good, manna*, stroke of luck*, windfall; SEE CONCEPTS 337,679

go far [v] *be successful*
achieve, advance, do well, get ahead, get on, make a name*, move up in the world*, progress, rise, succeed; SEE CONCEPTS 704,706

gofer [n] *errand boy or girl*
bottom person on the totem pole*, gal Friday, go getter*, grunt, guy Friday, hired help, low person on the totem pole*, office boy, office girl, peon, scrub; SEE CONCEPT 348

gl
go

go for [*v1*] *reach*
clutch at, fetch, obtain, outreach, seek, stretch for; SEE CONCEPT *149*

go for [*v2*] *like, choose*
accept, admire, approbate, approve, be attracted to, be fond of, care for, countenance, fancy, favor, hold with, prefer; SEE CONCEPTS *10,32*

go for [*v3*] *attack*
assail, assault, launch at, run at, rush, rush upon, set upon, spring at; SEE CONCEPT *86*

go for it [*v*] *take a risk*
bet the farm, bet the ranch, exert oneself, go all out, go for broke, pull out all the stops, put one's heart and soul into it, shoot the works, use every muscle; SEE CONCEPTS *87,100*

go into [*v1*] *take an interest in; participate*
be absorbed in, begin, develop, engage in, enter, get involved with, take on*, take up*, take upon oneself*, undertake; SEE CONCEPT *100*

go into [*v2*] *investigate*
analyze, consider, delve into, dig*, dig into*, discuss, examine, explore, inquire, look into, probe, prospect, pursue, review, scrutinize, sift, study; SEE CONCEPTS *24,103*

golden [*adj2*] *beautiful, advantageous*
auspicious, best, blissful, bright, brilliant, delightful, excellent, favorable, flourishing, glorious, happy, joyful, joyous, opportune, precious, promising, propitious, prosperous, resplendent, rich, rosy, shining, successful, valuable; SEE CONCEPTS *529,574*

gold/golden [*adj1*] *dark yellow*
aureate, auric, auriferous, aurous, aurulent, blond, blonde, caramel, dusty, flaxen, honeyed, mellow yellow, ochroid, straw, tan, tawny, wheat; SEE CONCEPT *618*

gold mine [*n*] *very profitable venture*
bonanza, cash cow*, golden goose*, goose that laid the golden egg*, gravy train*, license to print money*, mother lode, source of supply, vein; SEE CONCEPTS *334,537,572*

gone [*adj*] *not present, no longer in existence*
absent, astray, away, AWOL*, burned up*, consumed, dead, decamped, deceased, defunct, departed, disappeared, disintegrated, displaced, dissipated, dissolved, done, down the drain*, dried up, elapsed, ended, extinct, finished, flown, lacking, left, lost, missing, moved, no more, nonextant, not a sign of*, not here, out the window*, over, passed, past, quit, removed, retired, run-off, shifted, spent, split, taken a powder*, taken leave*, transferred, traveling, turned to dust*, vanished, withdrawn; SEE CONCEPTS *407,586*

gonzo [*adj*] *bizarre*
crazy, far-fetched, insane, odd, strange, unconventional, weird, wild; SEE CONCEPTS *547,564*

good [*adj1*] *pleasant, fine*
acceptable, ace*, admirable, agreeable, bad, boss*, bully, capital, choice, commendable, congenial, crack*, deluxe, excellent, exceptional, favorable, first-class, first-rate, gnarly*, gratifying, great, honorable, marvelous, neat*, nice, pleasing, positive, precious, prime, rad*, recherché*, reputable, satisfactory, satisfying, select, shipshape*, sound, spanking*, splendid, sterling, stupendous, super, superb, super-eminent, superexcellent, superior, tip-top*, up to snuff*, valuable, welcome, wonderful, worthy; SEE CONCEPTS *529,572*

good [*adj2*] *moral, virtuous*
admirable, blameless, charitable, dutiful, estimable, ethical, exemplary, guiltless, honest, honorable, incorrupt, inculpable, innocent, irreprehensible, irreproachable, lily-white*, obedient, praiseworthy, pure, reputable, respectable, right, righteous, sound, tractable, uncorrupted, untainted, upright, well-behaved, worthy; SEE CONCEPT *545*

good [*adj3*] *competent, skilled*
able, accomplished, adept, adroit, au fait, capable, clever, dexterous, efficient, expert, first-rate, proficient, proper, qualified, reliable, satisfactory, serviceable, skillful, suitable, suited, talented, thorough, trustworthy, useful; SEE CONCEPT *527*

good [*adj4*] *useful, adequate*
acceptable, advantageous, all right, ample, appropriate, approving, apt, auspicious, becoming, benefic, beneficial, benignant, brave, commendatory, commending, common, conformable, congruous, convenient, decent, desirable, favorable, favoring, fit, fitting, fruitful, healthful, healthy, helpful, hygienic, meet, needed, opportune, profitable, proper, propitious, respectable, right, salubrious, salutary, satisfying, seemly, serviceable, suitable, tolerable, toward, unobjectionable, wholesome; SEE CONCEPTS *537,558,560*

good [*adj5*] *reliable; untainted*
dependable, eatable, fit to eat, flawless, fresh, intact, loyal, normal, perfect, safe, solid, sound, stable, trustworthy, unblemished, uncontaminated, uncorrupted, undamaged, undecayed, unhurt, unimpaired, unspoiled, vigorous, whole; SEE CONCEPT *485*

good [*adj6*] *kind, giving*
altruistic, approving, beneficent, benevolent, charitable, considerate, friendly, gracious, humane, humanitarian, kindhearted, merciful, obliging, philanthropic, tolerant, well-disposed; SEE CONCEPTS *404,542*

good [*adj7*] *authentic, real*
bona fide, conforming, dependable, genuine, honest, justified, kosher*, legitimate, loyal, orthodox, proper, regular, reliable, sound, strict, true, trustworthy, valid, well-founded; SEE CONCEPT *582*

good [*adj8*] *well-behaved*
considerate, decorous, dutiful, kindly, mannerly, obedient, orderly, polite, proper, respectful, seemly, thoughtful, tolerant, tractable, well-mannered; SEE CONCEPT *401*

good [*adj9*] *considerable*
adequate, advantageous, ample, big, complete, entire, extensive, full, great, immeasurable, large, long, lucrative, much, paying, profitable, respectable, sizable, solid, substantial, sufficient, whole, worthwhile; SEE CONCEPTS *334,771,781*

good [*n1*] *advantage, benefit*
asset, avail, behalf, benediction, blessing, boon*, commonwealth, favor, gain, godsend, good fortune, interest, nugget*, plum*, prize, profit, prosperity, service, treasure, use, usefulness, welfare, well-being, windfall; SEE CONCEPTS *337,658,679*

good [*n2*] *morality*
class, dignity, excellence, ideal, merit, prerogative, probity, quality, rectitude, right, righteousness, straight, uprightness, value, virtue, worth; SEE CONCEPT *645*

goodbye [n] *farewell statement*
adieu, adios, bye-bye, cheerio, ciao, godspeed*, leave-taking, parting, so long*, swan song*, toodle-oo*; SEE CONCEPTS 195,278

good-for-nothing [n] *person who is idle, worthless*
bad lot*, black sheep*, bum, loafer, ne'er-do-well*, no-good*, profligate, rapscallion, scalawag, scamp, tramp, vagabond, waster*, wastrel; SEE CONCEPT 412

good-humored [adj] *funny, happy*
affable, amiable, buoyant, cheerful, cheery, complaisant, congenial, easy, genial, good-natured, good-tempered, lenient, merry, mild, obliging, pleasant, smiling; SEE CONCEPT 404

good-looking [adj] *handsome*
attractive, beauteous, beautiful, clean-cut, comely, fair, impressive, lovely, pretty, pulchritudinous, righteous; SEE CONCEPT 579

good-natured [adj] *easygoing, easily pleased*
acquiescent, agreeable, altruistic, amiable, benevolent, bighearted, breezy, charitable, complaisant, compliant, cordial, easy, even-tempered, friendly, good-hearted, good-humored, gracious, helpful, kind, kindly, lenient, marshmallow*, mild, moderate, nice, obliging, softie*, tolerant, warmhearted, well-disposed, willing to please; SEE CONCEPT 404

goodness [n] *decency, excellence*
advantage, beneficence, benefit, benevolence, ethicality, friendliness, generosity, good will, grace, graciousness, honesty, honor, humaneness, integrity, kindheartedness, kindliness, kindness, mercy, merit, morality, nourishment, obligingness, probity, quality, rectitude, righteousness, rightness, superiority, uprightness, value, virtue, wholesomeness, worth; SEE CONCEPTS 411,645

goods [n1] *personal possessions*
appurtenances, belongings, chattels, effects, encumbrances, equipment, furnishings, furniture, gear, impedimenta, movables, paraphernalia, property, stuff, things, trappings; SEE CONCEPT 446

goods [n2] *merchandise*
bolt, cargo, commodities, fabric, freight, line, load, materials, seconds, stock, stuff, textile, vendibles, wares; SEE CONCEPT 338

good will/goodwill [n] *kindliness*
altruism, amity, benevolence, brownie points*, charity, comity, cordiality, favor, friendliness, friendship, generosity, good deed, good side of*, helpfulness, rapport, right side of*, sympathy, tolerance; SEE CONCEPTS 411,645

goody-goody [adj] *straight-laced*
God-fearing, goody two-shoes*, holier-than-thou*, moral, nice, PC, pious, politically correct, priggish, prissy, prudish, Puritan, self-righteous, unctuous, Victorian, virtuous; SEE CONCEPT 401

gooey [adj] *sticky, gummy*
adhesive, gluey, glutinous, mucilaginous, soft, tacky, viscous; SEE CONCEPT 606

goof [v] *mistake*
blow it, blunder, botch*, bungle, err, flub*, foul up, get wrong, louse up, make a boner*, mess up, miscalculate, mix up, screw up*, slip, snarl; SEE CONCEPTS 101,230,410

go off [v1] *explode*
befall, blow, blow up, burst, detonate, discharge,

fire, happen, mushroom, occur, pass, take place; SEE CONCEPT 179

go off [v2] *leave*
decamp, depart, exit, go away, move out, part, quit; SEE CONCEPT 195

goof off [v] *avoid work*
bum around, coast, diddle, dog it*, doodle, drag one's feet*, featherbed, fiddle around, fluff off, fool around, hang around, hang out, horse around, lollygag, mess around, monkey around, putz around, screw off, shirk, slack, take it easy; SEE CONCEPTS 30,59,681

goofy [adj] *silly*
crazy, daffy*, dippy*, ditzy*, dopey, dotty, empty-headed*, flaky*, foolish, idiotic, kooky*, nutty*, screwy, stupid, wacky*, weird; SEE CONCEPTS 401,403,542

goon [n] *ruffian*
bozo*, bruiser*, dope, gorilla*, hood*, hooligan*, jerk, lummox, moron, nincompoop, ninny, sap, strong-arm, thug, tough guy*; SEE CONCEPTS 412,423

go on [v] *continue*
act, advance, bear, behave, carry on, come about, comport, conduct, deport, endure, execute, go ahead, hang on, happen, hold on, keep on, last, occur, persevere, persist, proceed, ramble, stay, take place; SEE CONCEPTS 100,239

go out [v1] *become extinguished*
become dark, burn out, cease, darken, die, die out, dim, expire, fade out, flicker, stop shining; SEE CONCEPTS 105,469

go out [v2] *leave*
decamp, depart, exit, go on strike, walk out; SEE CONCEPT 195

go over [v1] *review*
analyze, examine, inspect, investigate, look at, peruse, practice, read, rehearse, reiterate, repeat, revise, riffle through*, scan, skim, study, thumb through*; SEE CONCEPTS 24,103

go over [v2] *succeed*
be impressive, be successful, click*, come off*, go, pan out*, prove; SEE CONCEPT 706

gore [n] *bloodshed*
blood, carnage, slaughter; SEE CONCEPT 252

gore [v] *pierce*
gouge, impale, lance, perforate, puncture, spear, stab, stick, wound; SEE CONCEPT 220

gorge [n] *valley*
abyss, arroyo, canyon, chasm, cleft, clough, clove, crevasse, fissure, flume, gap, glen, gulch, pass, ravine; SEE CONCEPT 509

gorge [v] *eat voraciously*
blimp out*, bolt*, cloy, congest, cram, devour, eat like a horse*, feed, fill, glut, gobble, gormandize, gulp, guzzle, hoover*, jade, jam, make a pig of*, overeat, overindulge, pack, sate, satiate, stuff*, surfeit, swallow, wolf*; SEE CONCEPT 169

gorgeous [adj] *beautiful, magnificent*
attractive, beaut*, bright, brilliant, centerfold*, colorful, dazzling, delightful, dream, drop-dead*, easy on the eyes*, elegant, enjoyable, exquisite, fine, flamboyant, foxy*, gaudy, glittering, glorious, good-looking, grand, handsome, imposing, impressive, knockout*, lavish, lovely, lulu*, luxuriant, luxurious, opulent, ostentatious, pleasing, plush, pulchritudinous, ravishing, resplendent, showy, splendid, splendiferous, stunning, sublime, sumptuous, superb; SEE CONCEPTS 579,589

go
go

gormandize [v] *gorge*
binge, devour, eat like a horse*, eat to excess, glut, gluttonize, gobble, gulp, guzzle, hoover*, overeat, overindulge, pig out*, stuff, wolf*; SEE CONCEPTS **169,225**

gory [adj] *bloody, horrible*
bleeding, blood-soaked, bloodstained, imbrued, murderous, offensive, sanguinary, sanguine; SEE CONCEPTS **314,537**

gospel [n] *fact, doctrine*
actuality, authority, belief, certainty, credo, creed, dogma, faith, last word, scripture, testament, truism, truth, veracity, verity; SEE CONCEPT **689**

gossamer [adj] *gauzy, thin*
airy, cobweb, delicate, diaphanous, fibrous, fine, flimsy, light, sheer, silky, tiffany, translucent, transparent; SEE CONCEPT **606**

gossip [n1] *talk about others; rumor*
account, babble, back-fence talk*, blather, blether, buzz*, calumny, chatter, chitchat*, chronicle, clothesline*, conversation, cry, defamation, dirty laundry*, dirty linen*, dirty wash*, earful*, grapevine*, hearsay, idle talk, injury, malicious talk, meddling, news, prate, prattle, report, scandal, scuttlebutt*, slander, small talk*, story, tale, talk, whispering campaign*, wire*; SEE CONCEPTS **274,278**

gossip [n2] *person who talks a lot, spreads rumors*
babbler*, blabbermouth*, busybody, chatterbox, chatterer, circulator, flibbertigibbet*, gossipmonger, informer, meddler, newsmonger, parrot*, prattler, rumormonger*, scandalizer*, scandalmonger*, snoop*, talebearer, tattler, telltale; SEE CONCEPT **412**

gossip [v] *talk about others; spread rumors*
babble, bad-mouth*, bend one's ear*, blab, blather, blether, chat, chatter, cut to pieces*, cut up*, dish, hint, imply, insinuate, intimate, jaw*, prate, prattle, rattle on*, repeat, report, rumor, schmoose*, spill the beans*, spread*, suggest, talk, talk idly, tattle, tell secrets*, tell tales*, wiggle-waggle*; SEE CONCEPTS **56,60**

go straight [v] *reform*
be honorable, go legit, mend one's ways*, turn over a new leaf*, walk the straight and narrow*; SEE CONCEPTS **35,110,126,202**

go through [v1] *endure*
bear, brave, experience, suffer, support, survive, swallow, tolerate, undergo, withstand; SEE CONCEPT **23**

go through [v2] *use up*
consume, deplete, exhaust, pay out, spend, squander; SEE CONCEPT **169**

go through [v3] *search*
audit, check, examine, explore, hunt, inspect, investigate, look, pass through; SEE CONCEPT **103**

go to bat for [v] *show support for*
back up, cover for, defend, endorse, go to the wall for*, recommend, stand behind, stand by, stand up for, stick up for, support; SEE CONCEPTS **10,49,110**

go together/go with [v1] *agree, match*
accompany, accord, become, befit, be suitable, blend, complement, concur, correspond, fit, go, harmonize, make a pair*, not clash, suit; SEE CONCEPT **664**

go together/go with [v2] *accompany socially*
attend, be with, court, date, escort, go out with*,

go steady with*, keep company with*; SEE CONCEPT **384**

gouge [n] *groove, hole*
channel, cut, excavation, furrow, gash, hollow, notch, scoop, score, scratch, trench; SEE CONCEPT **220**

gouge [v] *cut, scoop*
burrow, claw, dig, dredge, excavate, gash, groove, scrape, scratch, shovel, tunnel; SEE CONCEPT **220**

go under [v] *fail, submerge*
bankrupt, default, die, drown, fall, fold, founder, go down, sink, submerse, submit, succumb, suffocate, surrender; SEE CONCEPTS **181,699**

gourmet [n] *person who likes, knows about food*
bon vivant, connoisseur, critic, epicure, epicurean, gastronome, gastronomer, gastronomist, gourmand; SEE CONCEPTS **348,423**

govern [v1] *take control; rule*
administer, assume command, be in power, be in the driver's seat*, call the shots*, call the signals*, captain*, carry out, command, conduct, control, dictate, direct, execute, exercise authority, guide, head, head up, hold dominion, hold office, hold sway, lay down the law*, lead, manage, occupy throne, order, overrule, oversee, pilot, pull the strings*, regulate, reign, render, run, serve the people*, steer, superintend, supervise, sway, tyrannize, wear the crown*; SEE CONCEPT **133**

govern [v2] *influence; hold in check*
boss, bridle, check, contain, control, curb, decide, determine, direct, directionalize, discipline, dispose, dominate, get the better of*, guide, handle, incline, inhibit, manage, predispose, regulate, restrain, rule, shepherd, steer, subdue, sway, tame, underlie; SEE CONCEPTS **7,19,22,130**

government [n] *management, administration*
authority, bureaucracy, command, control, direction, domination, dominion, empire, execution, executive, governance, guidance, influence, jurisdiction, law, ministry, patronage, political practice, politics, polity, power, powers-that-be*, predominance, presidency, regency, regime, regimentation, regulation, restraint, rule, sovereignty, state, statecraft, superintendence, superiority, supervision, supremacy, sway, the feds*, Uncle Sam*, union, Washington*; SEE CONCEPT **299**

governor [n] *person administering government*
administrator, boss, chief, chief of state, commander, comptroller, controller, director, executive, gubernatorial leader, guv*, head, head honcho*, leader, manager, overseer, presiding officer, ruler, superintendent, supervisor; SEE CONCEPT **354**

go without [adj] *deny or be denied*
abstain, be deprived of, do without, fall short*, go short*, lack, need, want; SEE CONCEPT **646**

gown [n] *robe, dress*
clothes, costume, frock, garb, garment, habit; SEE CONCEPT **451**

grab [v] *latch on to*
capture, catch, catch hold of, clutch, collar*, corral*, get one's fingers on*, get one's hands on*, glom*, grapple, grasp, grip, hook, land, lay one's hands on*, nab, nail, pluck, seize, snag, snap up, snatch, take, take hold of; SEE CONCEPTS **90,190**

grace [n1] *charm, loveliness*
address, adroitness, agility, allure, attractiveness,

balance, beauty, breeding, comeliness, consideration, cultivation, decency, decorum, dexterity, dignity, ease, elegance, etiquette, finesse, finish, form, gracefulness, lissomeness, lithesomeness, mannerliness, manners, nimbleness, pleasantness, pliancy, poise, polish, propriety, refinement, shapeliness, smoothness, style, suppleness, symmetry, tact, tastefulness; SEE CONCEPTS *633,655,718*

grace [*n2*] *mercy, forgiveness*
benefaction, beneficence, benevolence, caritas, charity, clemency, compassion, compassionateness, favor, forbearance, generosity, goodness, good will, indulgence, kindliness, kindness, leniency, lenity, love, pardon, quarter, reprieve, responsiveness, tenderness; SEE CONCEPTS *278,657,685*

grace [*n3*] *prayer*
benediction, blessing, invocation, petition, thanks, thanksgiving; SEE CONCEPTS *278,368*

grace [*v*] *beautify, embellish*
adorn, bedeck, crown, deck, decorate, dignify, distinguish, elevate, enhance, enrich, favor, garnish, glorify, honor, laureate, ornament, set off; SEE CONCEPTS *202,700*

graceful [*adj*] *agile, charming, lovely*
adroit, aesthetic, artistic, balletic, beautiful, becoming, comely, controlled, curvaceous, dainty, decorative, delicate, dexterous, easy, elastic, elegant, exquisite, fair, fine, flowing, handsome, harmonious, limber, lissome, lithe, natural, neat, nimble, pleasing, pliant, poised, practiced, pretty, refined, rhythmic, seemly, shapely, skilled, slender, smooth, springy, statuesque, supple, symmetrical, tasteful, trim, willowy; SEE CONCEPTS *579,584,589*

graceless [*adj*] *clumsy, unsophisticated*
awkward, barbarian, barbaric, barbarous, boorish, clunky*, coarse, corrupt, crude*, forced, gauche, gawky*, ill-mannered, improper, indecorous, inelegant, inept, infelicitous, klutzy*, loutish, oafish, outlandish, rough, rude, shameless, tasteless, two left feet*, uncouth, uncultured, unfortunate, ungainly, unhappy, unmannered; SEE CONCEPTS *401,584*

gracious [*adj*] *kind, giving*
accommodating, affable, amiable, amicable, approachable, beneficent, benevolent, benign, benignant, big-hearted, bland, bonhomous, charitable, chivalrous, civil, compassionate, complaisant, congenial, considerate, cordial, courteous, courtly, easy, forthcoming, friendly, gallant, genial, good-hearted, good-natured, hospitable, indulgent, lenient, loving, merciful, mild, obliging, pleasing, polite, sociable, stately, suave, tender, unctuous, urbane, well-mannered; SEE CONCEPTS *401,542*

gradation [*n*] *classification, step*
arrangement, calibration, change, degree, difference, distinction, divergence, grade, grouping, level, mark, measurement, modification, notch, nuance, ordering, place, point, position, progression, rank, scale, sequence, series, shade, sorting, stage, succession, variation; SEE CONCEPTS *378,665,727,744*

grade [*n1*] *rank, step*
brand, caliber, category, class, classification, condition, degree, division, echelon, estate, form, gradation, group, grouping, league, level, mark, notch, order, pigeonhole*, place, position, quality, rung*, size, stage, standard, station, tier; SEE CONCEPTS *286,378,665,727,744*

grade [*n2*] *incline, slope*
acclivity, ascent, bank, cant, climb, declivity, descent, downgrade, elevation, embankment, gradient, height, hill, inclination, inclined plane, lean, leaning, level, obliquity, pitch, plane, ramp, rise, slant, tangent, tilt, upgrade; SEE CONCEPTS *738,757*

grade [*v*] *evaluate, rank*
arrange, assort, brand, class, classify, group, order, range, rate, sort, value; SEE CONCEPTS *103,291*

gradient [*n*] *slope*
acclivity, angle, bank, cant, declivity, grade, hill, inclination, incline, lean, leaning, pitch, ramp, rise, slant, tilt; SEE CONCEPTS *738,757*

gradual [*adj*] *happening slowly, evenly*
bit-by-bit*, by degrees, continuous, creeping, even, gentle, graduate, moderate, piecemeal, progressive, regular, slow, steady, step-by-step*, successive, unhurried; SEE CONCEPTS *544,588, 799*

gradually [*adv*] *happening slowly, evenly*
bit by bit*, by degrees, by installments, constantly, continuously, deliberately, gently, imperceptibly, inch by inch*, increasingly, in small doses*, little by little*, moderately, perceptibly, piece by piece*, piecemeal, progressively, regularly, sequentially, serially, steadily, step by step*, successively, unhurriedly; SEE CONCEPTS *544,588,799*

graduate [*n*] *person who completes education, pursuit*
alum*, alumnus, baccalaureate, bachelor, collegian, diplomate, doctor, former student, grad, holder, licentiate, master, Ph.D., product, recipient; SEE CONCEPT *350*

graduate [*v1*] *complete education, pursuit*
be commissioned, certify, confer degree, earn, finish, get a degree, get out*, give sheepskin*, grant diploma, take a degree, win; SEE CONCEPT *234*

graduate [*v2*] *classify, grade*
arrange, calibrate, class, group, mark off, measure, measure out, order, proportion, range, rank, regulate, sort; SEE CONCEPTS *84,103*

graduation [*n*] *commencement*
commencement exercises, convocation; SEE CONCEPTS *119,706*

graffiti [*n*] *wall writing*
cave painting, defacement, doodles, scribbling; SEE CONCEPTS *79,284*

graft [*n1*] *transplant*
bud*, hybridization, implant, jointure, scion, shoot, slip, splice, sprout, union; SEE CONCEPTS *113,257*

graft [*n2*] *payoff for fraud*
bribe, corruption, gain, hat*, hush money*, juice*, money, money under the table*, pay, payola*, peculation, shake*, share, skimming*, squeeze*, thievery; SEE CONCEPTS *192,344*

graft [*v*] *transplant, splice*
affix, implant, ingraft, insert, join, plant, propagate, unite; SEE CONCEPTS *113,257*

grain [*n1*] *seed, piece*
atom, bit, cereal, corn, crumb, drop, fragment, granule, grist, iota, jot, kernel, mite, modicum, molecule, morsel, mote, ounce, particle, pellet,

go
gr

scintilla, scrap, scruple, smidgen, spark, speck, tittle, trace, whit; SEE CONCEPTS *428,831*

grain [*n2*] *texture of fabric*
character, current, direction, fiber, make-up, nap, pattern, staple, striation, surface, tendency, tissue, tooth, warp and woof, weave, weft; SEE CONCEPT *611*

grammar [*n*] *language rules*
ABCs*, accidence, alphabet, elements, fundaments, linguistics, morphology, principles, rudiments, sentence structure, stratification, structure, syntax, tagmemics; SEE CONCEPTS *275,276,770*

grand [*adj1*] *impressive, great*
admirable, ambitious, august, awe-inspiring, dignified, dynamite, elevated, eminent, exalted, excellent, fab*, fine, first-class, first-rate, glorious, grandiose, haughty, illustrious, imposing, large, lofty, luxurious, magnificent, majestic, marvelous, monumental, noble, opulent, ostentatious, outstanding, palatial, pompous, pretentious, regal, rich, smashing, something else*, splendid, stately, striking, sublime, sumptuous, super, superb, terrific, unreal, very good; SEE CONCEPTS *574,589,773*

grand [*adj2*] *most important*
chief, dignified, elevated, exalted, grave, head, highest, leading, lofty, main, majestic, mighty, noble, preeminent, principal, regal, supreme, transcendent; SEE CONCEPT *568*

grandeur [*n*] *great importance*
amplitude, augustness, beauty, breadth, brilliance, celebrity, circumstance, dignity, distinction, elevation, eminence, expansiveness, fame, fineness, glory, grandiosity, gravity, greatness, handsomeness, immensity, impressiveness, inclusiveness, loftiness, luxuriousness, magnificence, majesty, might, nobility, opulence, pomp, preeminence, richness, splendor, state, stateliness, sublimity, sumptuousness, superbity, sway, transcendency, vastness; SEE CONCEPT *668*

grandiloquent [*adj*] *pretentious, flowery (communication)*
aureate, big-talking*, bombastic, declamatory, euphuistic, fustian, high-flown, histrionic, inflated, magniloquent, oratorical, orotund, overblown, pompous, purple*, rhetorical, sonorous, swollen, tall-talking*, verbose, windbag*, windy*; SEE CONCEPT *267*

grandiose [*adj*] *theatrical, extravagant*
affected, ambitious, august, bombastic, cosmic, egotistic, flamboyant, fustian, grand, high-falutin'*, high-flown, imposing, impressive, lofty, lordly, magnificent, majestic, monumental, noble, ostentatious, overwhelming, pompous, pretentious, purple*, royal, showy, splashy, stately, unfathomable, vast; SEE CONCEPTS *401,542,589*

grandstand [*v*] *show off*
be ostentatious, be vain, flaunt it*, hot dog*, parade, play to the crowd, prance, put on airs*, showboat*, strut, swagger; SEE CONCEPT *261*

grange [*n*] *farm*
acreage, farmstead, hacienda, manor, plantation, ranch; SEE CONCEPTS *258,516,517*

grant [*n*] *allowance, gift*
admission, allocation, allotment, alms, appropriation, assistance, award, benefaction, bequest, boon, bounty, charity, concession, contribution, dole, donation, endowment, fellowship, gratuity,

handout, lump, present, privilege, reward, scholarship, stipend, subsidy; SEE CONCEPTS *337,344*

grant [*v*] *authorize, allow*
accede, accept, accord, acknowledge, acquiesce, admit, agree to, allocate, allot, assign, assume, avow, award, bestow, bless, cede, come across, come around, come through, concede, confer, consent to, convey, donate, drop, gift with*, give, give in, give out, give the nod*, give thumbs-up*, go along with*, impart, invest, own, own up*, permit, present, profess, relinquish, shake on*, sign off on*, sign on*, stake, suppose, surrender, transfer, transmit, vouchsafe, yield; SEE CONCEPTS *8,50,82,83,88*

granted [*adv*] *allowed, accepted*
acknowledged, admitted, assumed, indeed, just so, yes; SEE CONCEPT *558*

granulate [*v*] *crush into tiny pieces*
atomize, comminute, crumble, crystallize, disintegrate, grate, grind, make coarse, make grainy, pound, powder, pulverize, triturate; SEE CONCEPT *186*

graphic [*adj1*] *clear, explicit*
colorful, compelling, comprehensible, concrete, convincing, definite, descriptive, detailed, distinct, eloquent, expressive, figurative, forcible, illustrative, incisive, intelligible, lively, lucid, moving, perspicuous, picturesque, precise, realistic, stirring, striking, strong, telling, unequivocal, vivid; SEE CONCEPTS *267,535,562*

graphic [*adj2*] *pictorial, visible*
blocked-out, delineated, depicted, descriptive, diagrammatic, drawn, engraved, etched, iconographic, illustrated, illustrational, illustrative, marked-out, outlined, painted, photographic, pictoric, pictured, portrayed, representational, seen, sketched, traced, visual; SEE CONCEPTS *576,589,619*

graphics [*n*] *drawings*
artwork, computer graphics, illustrations, pictures, visuals; SEE CONCEPT *625*

grapple [*v*] *grab, wrestle*
attack, battle, catch, clash, clasp, close, clutch, combat, confront, contend, cope, deal with, do battle*, encounter, engage, face, fasten, fight, grasp, grip, hold, hook, hug, nab, nail, scuffle, seize, snatch, struggle, tackle, take, take on*, tussle; SEE CONCEPTS *106,191*

grasp [*n1*] *hold, grip*
butt, cinch, clamp, clasp, clench, clinch, clutches, embrace, grapple, lug, possession, purchase, tenure; SEE CONCEPTS *191,710*

grasp [*n2*] *understanding*
awareness, comprehension, ken, knowledge, mastery, perception, realization; SEE CONCEPT *409*

grasp [*v1*] *grab*
bag*, catch, clasp, clinch, clutch, collar*, corral, enclose, glom*, grapple, grip, hold, hook, land, seize, snatch, take, take hold of; SEE CONCEPTS *90,191*

grasp [*v2*] *understand*
accept, appreciate, apprehend, catch, catch on*, cognize, compass, comprehend, dig*, envisage, fathom, follow, get, get the drift*, get the picture*, have, know, latch on*, make, perceive, pick up*, realize, see, take, take in*; SEE CONCEPT *15*

grasping [*adj*] *greedy*
acquisitive, avaricious, avid, close-fisted, cov-

etous, desirous, extorting, extortionate, grabby*, itchy*, mean, miserly, niggardly*, penny-pinching*, penurious, prehensile, rapacious, selfish, stingy*, tightfisted*, usurious, venal; SEE CONCEPTS 326,334,542

grass [n] *lawn*
barley, grama, hay, meadow, pasture, sod, turf, verdure; SEE CONCEPT 429

grassland [n] *meadow*
campo, field, llano, pampas, pasture, plain, prairie, range, savanna, steep, sward, swarth, veldt; SEE CONCEPT 509

grate [v1] *shred, grind down*
abrade, bark, bray, file, fray, gall, mince, pound, pulverize, rasp, raze, rub, scrape, scratch, scuff, skin, triturate; SEE CONCEPTS 186,215

grate [v2] *irritate*
aggravate, annoy, burn, chafe, exasperate, fret, gall, get on one's nerves*, irk, nettle, peeve, pique, provoke, rankle, rile, rub the wrong way*, vex; SEE CONCEPTS 7,14,19

grateful [adj1] *appreciative*
beholden, gratified, indebted, obliged, pleased, thankful; SEE CONCEPT 403

grateful [adj2] *pleasing, nice*
acceptable, agreeable, comforting, congenial, consoling, delectable, delicious, delightful, desirable, favorable, good, gratifying, pleasant, pleasurable, pleasureful, refreshing, rejuvenating, renewing, restful, restorative, restoring, satisfactory, satisfying, solacing, welcome; SEE CONCEPTS 537,548,572

gratification [n] *satisfaction*
delight, enjoyment, fruition, fulfillment, glee, hit, indulgence, joy, kicks*, luxury, pleasure, recompense, regalement, relish, reward, sure shock*, thrill; SEE CONCEPT 410

gratify [v] *give pleasure; satisfy*
appease, arride, baby*, cater to, coddle, content, delectate, delight, do one proud*, do the trick*, enchant, favor, fill the bill*, fulfill*, get one's kicks*, gladden, hit the spot*, humor, indulge, make a hit*, make happy, oblige, pamper, please, recompense, requite, thrill; SEE CONCEPTS 7,22

grating [adj] *irritating; scraping*
annoying, disagreeable, discordant, displeasing, dissonant, dry, grinding, harsh, harsh-sounding, hoarse, irksome, jarring, offensive, rasping, raucous, rough, shrill, squeaky, strident, stridulent, stridulous, unpleasant, vexatious; SEE CONCEPTS 529,592,594

gratis [adj] *free*
as a gift, chargeless, complimentary, costless, for love*, for nothing, freebie*, freely given, free of charge, free ride*, gratuitous, on someone*, on the house*, unpaid for, without charge, without recompense; SEE CONCEPT 334

gratitude [n] *appreciation*
acknowledgment, appreciativeness, grace, gratefulness, honor, indebtedness, obligation, praise, recognition, requital, response, responsiveness, sense of obligation, thankfulness, thanks, thanksgiving; SEE CONCEPTS 32,76,278,410

gratuitous [adj1] *free*
chargeless, complimentary, costless, for nothing, gratis, spontaneous, unasked-for, unpaid, voluntary, willing; SEE CONCEPTS 334,542

gratuitous [adj2] *not necessary*
assumed, baseless, bottomless, causeless, groundless, indefensible, inessential, needless,

reasonless, supererogatory, superfluous, uncalled-for, unessential, unfounded, unjustified, unmerited, unprovoked, unsupportable, unwarranted, wanton; SEE CONCEPT 546

gratuity [n] *gift, tip*
alms, benefaction, bonus, boon, bounty, contribution, donation, fringe benefit, grease palm*, largesse, little something*, offering, perk*, perquisite, present, recompense, reward, salve*, sweetener*, token; SEE CONCEPTS 337,344

grave [adj1] *serious; gloomy*
cold sober*, deadpan*, dignified, dour, dull, earnest, grim, grim-faced, heavy, leaden, longfaced, meaningful, muted, no-nonsense*, ponderous, quiet, sad, sage, saturnine, sedate, sober, solemn, somber, staid, strictly business*, subdued, thoughtful, unsmiling; SEE CONCEPT 401

grave [adj2] *crucial, dangerous*
acute, afflictive, consequential, critical, deadly, destructive, dire, exigent, fatal, fell, grievous, hazardous, heavy*, important, killing*, life-and-death*, major, momentous, of great consequence, ominous, perilous, pressing, serious, severe, significant, threatening, ugly, urgent, vital, weighty; SEE CONCEPTS 537,548,567

grave [n] *burial place*
catacomb, crypt, final resting place*, last home*, mausoleum, mound, permanent address*, place of interment, resting place, sepulcher, shrine, six feet under*, tomb, vault; SEE CONCEPT 305

graveyard [n] *burial area*
boneyard*, burial ground, cemetery, charnel house, God's acre*, memorial park, necropolis; SEE CONCEPT 305

gravitate [v] *be drawn toward; fall to*
approach, be attracted, be influenced, be pulled, descend, drift, drop, incline, lean, move, precipitate, settle, sink, tend; SEE CONCEPTS 34,159

gravity [n1] *force of attraction*
force, heaviness, pressure, weight; SEE CONCEPT 641

gravity [n2] *seriousness, importance*
acuteness, concern, consequence, exigency, hazardousness, momentousness, perilousness, severity, significance, solemnity, urgency, weightiness; SEE CONCEPT 668

gray/grey [adj] *muted silver in color*
ash, ashen, battleship*, cinereal, clouded, dingy, dove, drab, dusky, dusty, granite, heather, iron, lead, leaden, livid, mousy, neutral, oyster, pearly, peppery, powder, sere, shaded, silvered, silvery, slate, smoky, somber, stone; SEE CONCEPT 618

graze [v1] *touch*
abrade, brush, carom, chafe, glance off, kiss*, ricochet, rub, scrape, scratch, shave*, skim, skip; SEE CONCEPT 612

graze [v2] *feed on*
bite, browse, champ, crop, crunch, eat, forage, gnaw, masticate, munch, nibble, pasture, ruminate, uproot; SEE CONCEPT 169

grease [n] *fat*
animal oil, drippings, lard, lubricant, oil, tallow, vegetable oil; SEE CONCEPTS 723,734

grease [v1] *lubricate*
anoint, butter, oil, slick; SEE CONCEPT 202

grease [v2] *bribe*
buy off, corrupt, do business*, entice, fix*, influence, oil someone's palm*, pay off, take care of, tamper; SEE CONCEPTS 53,192

gr
gr

greasy [adj] *slippery, oily*
anointed, creamy, daubed, fatty, lubricated, lubricious, oleaginous, pomaded, salved, slick, slimy*, slithery, smeared, swabbed, unctuous; SEE CONCEPT 606

greasy spoon [n] *inexpensive restaurant*
beanery, bean wagon, cheap restaurant, dump*, eatery, grease pit*, hashery, hashhouse; SEE CONCEPTS 439,448,449

great [adj 1] *very large*
abundant, ample, big, big league*, bulky, bull, colossal, considerable, decided, enormous, excessive, extended, extensive, extravagant, extreme, fat, gigantic, grievous, high, huge, humongous, husky, immense, inordinate, jumbo*, lengthy, long, major league*, mammoth, mondo*, numerous, oversize, prodigious, prolonged, pronounced, protracted, strong, stupendous, terrible, titanic*, towering, tremendous, vast, voluminous; SEE CONCEPTS 773,781

great [adj 2] *important, celebrated*
august, capital, chief, commanding, dignified, distinguished, eminent, exalted, excellent, famed, famous, fine, glorious, grand, heroic, highly regarded, high-minded, honorable, idealistic, illustrious, impressive, leading, lofty, magnanimous, main, major, noble, notable, noted, noteworthy, outstanding, paramount, primary, principal, prominent, puissant, regal, remarkable, renowned, royal, stately, sublime, superior, superlative, talented; SEE CONCEPT 568

great [adj 3] *excellent, skillful*
able, absolute, aces*, adept, admirable, adroit, awesome, bad*, best, brutal, cold*, complete, consummate, crack*, downright, dynamite, egregious, exceptional, expert, fab*, fantastic, fine, first-class*, first-rate*, good, heavy*, hellacious*, marvelous, masterly, number one*, out-and-out*, out of sight*, out of this world*, perfect, positive, proficient, super-duper*, surpassing, terrific, total, tough, transcendent, tremendous, unmitigated, unqualified, utter, wonderful; SEE CONCEPTS 527,528,574

greatly [adv] *considerably*
abundantly, by much, conspicuously, eminently, emphatically, enormously, exceedingly, exceptionally, extremely, famously, glaringly, highly, hugely, immeasurably, immensely, incalculably, incomparably, incredibly, indeed, infinitely, in great measure, inimitably, intensely, largely, markedly, mightily, most, much, notably, on a large scale, powerfully, remarkably, strikingly, superlatively, supremely, surpassingly, tremendously, vastly, very much; SEE CONCEPTS 537,569,772

greatness [n 1] *large size*
abundance, amplitude, bigness, bulk, enormity, force, high degree, hugeness, immensity, infinity, intensity, length, magnitude, mass, might, potency, power, prodigiousness, sizableness, strength, vastness; SEE CONCEPTS 730,767

greatness [n 2] *nobleness of character; eminence*
celebrity, chivalry, dignity, distinction, fame, generosity, glory, grandeur, heroism, high-mindedness, idealism, illustriousness, importance, loftiness, magnanimity, majesty, merit, morality, nobility, note, prominence, renown, stateliness, sublimity, worthiness; SEE CONCEPTS 411,645, 668

greed [n] *overwhelming desire for more*
acquisitiveness, avarice, avidity, covetousness, craving, cupidity, eagerness, edacity, esurience, excess, gluttony, gormandizing, graspingness, hunger, indulgence, insatiableness, intemperance, longing, piggishness*, rapacity, ravenousness, selfishness, swinishness*, the gimmies*, voracity; SEE CONCEPT 20

greedy [adj] *desiring excessively*
acquisitive, avaricious, avid, carnivorous, close, close-fisted*, covetous, craving, desirous, devouring, eager, edacious, esurient, gluttonous, gobbling, gormandizing, grabby, grasping, grudging, gulping, guzzling, hoggish*, hungry, impatient, insatiable, insatiate, intemperate, itchy*, miserly, niggardly, omnivorous, parsimonious, pennypinching*, penurious, piggish*, prehensile, rapacious, ravening, ravenous, selfish, stingy, swinish, tight*, tight-fisted*, voracious; SEE CONCEPTS 326,403,542

green [adj 1] *young, new, blooming*
bosky, budding, burgeoning, callow, developing, flourishing, foliate, fresh, grassy, growing, half-formed, immature, infant, juvenile, leafy, lush, maturing, pliable, puerile, pullulating, raw, recent, sprouting, supple, tender, undecayed, undried, unfledged, ungrown, unripe, unseasoned, verdant, verduous, visculent, youthful; SEE CONCEPTS 485,578,797

green [adj 2] *inexperienced*
callow, credulous, fresh, gullible, ignorant, immature, inexpert, ingenuous, innocent, naive, new, raw, tenderfoot*, unconversant, unpolished, unpracticed, unseasoned, unskillful, unsophisticated, untrained, unversed, wet behind the ears*, young, youthful; SEE CONCEPT 404

green [adj 3] *emerald in color*
apple, aquamarine, beryl, chartreuse, fir, forest, grass, jade, kelly, lime, malachite, moss, olive, pea, peacock, pine, sage, sap, sea, spinach, verdigris, vert, viridian, willow; SEE CONCEPT 618

green [adj 4] *referring to practices or policies that do not negatively affect the environment*
biodegradable, ecological, environmental, environmentally-safe, environment-friendly; SEE CONCEPT 485

green [n] *square or park in center of town*
common, field, grass, grassplot, green, plaza, sward, terrace, turf; SEE CONCEPTS 509,513

green around the gills [adj] *sick*
blah, crummy, miserable, nauseated, pale, queasy, shaky, sick as a dog*, sick to one's stomach, throwing up, under the weather, vomiting; SEE CONCEPT 314

green card [n] *working card*
pass, passport, permit, visa; SEE CONCEPTS 271,376,685

greenhorn [n] *inexperienced person*
amateur, apprentice, babe*, beginner, colt*, hayseed*, ingénue, learner, naif, neophyte, newcomer, new hand, novice, recruit, rube*, simpleton, tenderfoot*, tyro*, virgin; SEE CONCEPT 423

greet [v] *welcome*
accost, acknowledge, address, approach, attend, bow, call to, compliment, curtsy, embrace, exchange greetings, extend one's hand, flag, hail, herald, highball*, high-five*, meet, move to, nod, pay respects, receive, recognize, roll out the red carpet*, salaam*, salute, say hello, say hi*,

shake hands, shoulder, speak to, stop, tip one's hat*, usher in*, whistle for; SEE CONCEPT 51

greeting [n] *welcome; message of kindness*
accosting, acknowledgment, address, aloha*, attention, best wishes*, blow*, card*, ciao*, compellation, compliments, good wishes*, hail, hello, heralding, hi, highball*, high five*, how-do-you-do*, howdy*, letter*, nod, note, notice, ovation, reception, regards, respects, rumble, salaam*, salutation, salute, speaking to, testimonial, ushering in, what's happening*; SEE CONCEPT 51

gregarious [adj] *friendly*
affable, clubby*, companionable, convivial, cordial, fun, outgoing, sociable, social; SEE CONCEPT 404

gridlock [n] *traffic jam*
barrier, blockage, bottleneck, clog, congestion, impasse, logjam, obstacle, stoppage; SEE CONCEPTS 230,432

grief [n] *mental suffering*
affliction, agony, anguish, bemoaning, bereavement, bewailing, care, dejection, deploring, depression, desolation, despair, despondency, discomfort, disquiet, distress, dole, dolor, gloom, grievance, harassment, heartache, heartbreak, infelicity, lamentation, lamenting, malaise, melancholy, misery, mortification, mournfulness, mourning, pain, purgatory, regret, remorse, repining, rue, sadness, sorrow, torture, trial, tribulation, trouble, unhappiness, vexation, woe, worry, wretchedness; SEE CONCEPTS 410,728

grief-stricken [adj] *sad, sorrowful*
anguished, cheerless, dejected, depressed, despairing, devastated, distressed, down, heartbroken, heartsick, heavyhearted, hurting, inconsolable, melancholy, miserable, morose, overcome, troubled, unhappy, woebegone; SEE CONCEPT 403

grievance [n] *complaint, gripe*
affliction, ax to grind*, beef*, bellyache*, big stink*, blast, case, cross*, damage, distress, flack*, grief, grouse*, hardship, holler*, hooha*, howl*, injury, injustice, jeremiad*, kick, knock*, objection, outrage, pain, pain in the neck*, rap*, resentment, rigor, roar, rumble, sorrow, squawk*, stink*, trial, tribulation, trouble, unhappiness, violence, wrong, yell; SEE CONCEPTS 52,278,689

grieve [v1] *mourn, feel deep distress*
ache, bear, bemoan, bewail, carry on, complain, cry, cry a river*, deplore, eat one's heart out*, endure, hang crepe*, keen, lament, regret, rue, sing the blues*, sorrow, suffer, take it hard*, wail, weep; SEE CONCEPTS 17,410

grieve [v2] *upset, distress someone*
afflict, aggrieve, agonize, break the heart of*, constrain, crush, hurt, injure, pain, sadden, wound; SEE CONCEPTS 7,19

grievous [adj] *severe, painful; serious*
afflicting, agonizing, appalling, atrocious, calamitous, damaging, deplorable, dire, dismal, disquieting, distressing, disturbing, dreadful, egregious, flagrant, glaring, grave, harmful, heart-rending, heavy*, heinous, hurtful, injurious, intolerable, lamentable, monstrous, mournful, offensive, onerous, oppressive, outrageous, pathetic, pitiful, sad, shameful, sharp, shocking, sorrowful, taxing, tough, tragic, troublesome,

unbearable, upsetting, villainous, weighty*, wounding; SEE CONCEPTS 537,544,548

grift [n] *swindle*
cheating, confidence game, con game*, deceit, dirty pool*, double-dealing*, extortion, fix, fraud, racket*, rip-off*, scam, shady deal*, shell game*, stealing, sting, trickery; SEE CONCEPTS 59,139,192

grill [v1] *broil food*
barbecue, burn, charcoal-broil, cook, cook over an open pit, roast, rotisserie, sear; SEE CONCEPT 170

grill [v2] *ask questions aggressively*
catechize, cross-examine, give the third degree*, go over*, inquisition, interrogate, interview, put the pressure on*, put the screws to*, question, roast*, third degree*; SEE CONCEPTS 48,53

grim [adj] *hopeless, horrible in manner, appearance*
austere, barbarous, bleak, cantankerous, churlish, crabbed*, cruel, crusty, dogged, ferocious, fierce, forbidding, foreboding, formidable, frightful, funereal, ghastly, gloomy, glowering, glum, grisly, grouchy, gruesome, grumpy*, harsh, hideous, horrid, implacable, inexorable, intractable, merciless, morose, ominous, relentless, resolute, ruthless, scowling, severe, shocking, sinister, somber, sour, splenetic, stern, stubborn, sulky, sullen, surly, terrible, truculent, unrelenting, unyielding; SEE CONCEPTS 534,544,570

grimace [n] *scowling facial expression*
face, frown, moue, mouth, mouthing, mug*, scowl, smile, smirk, sneer, wry face; SEE CONCEPT 716

grimace [v] *make a pained expression*
contort, deform, distort, frown, make a face, make a wry face, misshape, mouth, mug*, scowl, screw up one's face*, smirk, sneer; SEE CONCEPT 185

grime [n] *dirt*
crud*, dust, film, filth, gook*, gunk*, muck*, smudge, smut*, soil, soot, tarnish; SEE CONCEPT 260

grimy [adj] *dirty*
begrimed, besmirched, cruddy*, dingy*, filthy, foul, grubby*, grungy*, messy, mucky*, nasty, scuzzy*, sleazy*, smeared, smutty*, soiled, sooty, sordid, squalid, unclean; SEE CONCEPTS 485,621

grin [n/v] *smile widely*
beam, crack, simper, smirk; SEE CONCEPTS 185,716

grind [n] *tedious job*
chore, drudgery, groove*, grubwork*, hard work, labor, moil, pace, rote, routine, rut*, sweat*, task, toil, travail, treadmill*; SEE CONCEPT 362

grind [v1] *crush, pulverize*
abrade, atomize, attenuate, beat, bray, chop up, comminute, crumble, crumple, disintegrate, file, granulate, grate, kibble*, levigate, mill, pestle, pound, powder, pulverize*, rasp, reduce, roll out*, scrape, shiver, triturate; SEE CONCEPTS 186,204

grind [v2] *sharpen*
abrade, file, give an edge to, gnash, grate, grit, polish, rub, sand, scrape, smooth, whet; SEE CONCEPTS 186,215

grind [v3] *oppress*
afflict, annoy, harass, hold down, hound, perse-

gr
gr

cute, plague, trouble, tyrannize, vex; SEE CONCEPTS *14,130*

grip [*n1*] *clasp, embrace*
anchor, brace, catch, cinch, cincture, clamp, clamping, clench, clinch, clutch, coercion, constraint, crushing, duress, enclosing, enclosure, fastening, fixing, grapnel, grapple, grasp, gripe, handclasp, handgrip, handhold, handshake, hold, hook, ligature, lug, purchase, restraint, snatch, squeeze, strength, tenure, vise, wrench; SEE CONCEPT *191*

grip [*n2*] *perception, understanding*
clutches*, comprehension, control, domination, grasp, hold, influence, keeping, ken, possession, power, tenure; SEE CONCEPT *409*

grip [*v1*] *hold tightly*
clap a hand on, clasp, clench, clinch, clutch, get one's hands on*, grasp, latch on to*, lay hands on, nab, seize, snag, snatch, take, take hold of; SEE CONCEPT *191*

grip [*v2*] *entrance, enchant*
catch up, compel, engross, enthrall, fascinate, hold, hypnotize, involve, mesmerize, rivet, spellbind; SEE CONCEPTS *7,11,22*

gripe [*n1*] *complaint*
ache, aching, affliction, disorder, distress, grievance, groan, grouse, grumble, illness, indisposition, infirmity, moan, objection, pain, pang; SEE CONCEPTS *52,278,313*

gripe [*n2*] *strong hold*
clamp, clasp, clench, clinch, clutch, crunch, grab, grapple, grasp, grip, tenure; SEE CONCEPT *191*

gripe [*v1*] *complain*
bellyache*, blow off*, carp, crab*, fuss, groan, grouch, grouse, grumble, kvetch*, moan, murmur, mutter, nag, squawk, take on*, whine, yammer*, yawp*; SEE CONCEPTS *44,52*

gripe [*v2*] *pain, annoy*
ache, bother, compress, cramp, disturb, hurt, irritate, pinch, press, squeeze, vex; SEE CONCEPTS *7,19,219,246*

grisly [*adj*] *horrifying*
abominable, appalling, awful, blood-stained, bloody, disgusting, dreadful, eerie, frightful, ghastly, grim, grody*, gross*, gruesome, hideous, horrible, horrid, lurid, macabre, sanguine, shocking, sick, sickening, terrible, terrifying, yucky*; SEE CONCEPTS *537,544,570*

grit [*n1*] *particles of dirt*
dust, foreign matter, gravel, lumps, pebbles, powder, sand; SEE CONCEPTS *260,831*

grit [*n2*] *courage, determination*
backbone, daring, doggedness, fortitude, gameness, guts*, hardihood, intestinal fortitude*, mettle, moxie*, nerve, perseverance, pluck, resolution, spine*, spirit, spunk, steadfastness, tenacity, toughness; SEE CONCEPTS *411,633*

gritty [*adj1*] *granular*
abrasive, branlike, calculous, crumbly, dusty, friable, grainy, gravelly, in particles, loose, lumpy, permeable, porous, powdery, pulverant, rasping, rough, sabulous, sandy, scratchy; SEE CONCEPT *606*

gritty [*adj2*] *brave*
courageous, determined, dogged, game*, hardy, mettlesome, plucky*, resolute, spirited, steadfast, tenacious, tough; SEE CONCEPTS *401,404*

groan [*n*] *moan, complaint*
cry, gripe, grouse, grumble, grunt, objection, sigh, sob, whine; SEE CONCEPTS *278,595*

groan [*v*] *moan, complain*
bemoan, cry, gripe, grouse, grumble, keen, lament, mumble, murmur, object, sigh, whine; SEE CONCEPTS *44,52,77*

grocery store [*n*] *supermarket*
bodega, convenience store, corner store*, food mart, food store, market, mom-and-pop store, retail food store; SEE CONCEPTS *323,333,449*

groggy [*adj*] *dizzy, stunned*
befuddled, confused, dazed, dopey*, drunken, faint, hazy, out of it*, punch-drunk*, punchy*, reeling, shaky, slaphappy*, staggering, stupefied, swaying, tired, unsteady, weak, whirling, wobbly, woozy*; SEE CONCEPT *314*

groom [*n1*] *man being married*
benedict, bridegroom, fiancé, husband, spouse, suitor; SEE CONCEPT *419*

groom [*n2*] *stable attendant; servant*
equerry, hostler, stable person; SEE CONCEPTS *348,419*

groom [*v*] *make ready, prepare physically*
brush, clean, coach, comb, curry, dress, drill, educate, lick into shape*, make attractive, make presentable, nurture, preen, prep*, pretty up*, prim, prime, primp, put through grind*, put through mill*, ready, refine, refresh, rub down, shape up, sleek, slick up*, smarten up*, spiff up*, spruce up*, tend, tidy, train, turn out; SEE CONCEPTS *162,202,285*

groove [*n1*] *channel, indentation*
canal, corrugation, crease, crimp, cut, cutting, depression, ditch, flute, fluting, furrow, gouge, gutter, hollow, incision, notch, pucker, rabbet, rut, scallop, score, scratch, slit, trench, valley; SEE CONCEPT *513*

groove [*n2*] *daily routine*
daily grind*, grind, pace, rote, rut*, same old stuff*, schtick*, slot*; SEE CONCEPTS *362,677*

groovy [*adj*] *cool, wonderful*
boss*, chic, deep*, excellent, fabulous, fantastic, far-out*, great, hip, neat*, nifty*, rad*, sensational, splendid, super, swell*, trendy, unorthodox, way-out*, wild, with it; SEE CONCEPT *572*

grope [*v*] *feel about for*
cast about, examine, explore, feel blindly, finger*, fish*, flounder, fumble, grabble, handle, manipulate, poke, pry, root, scrabble, search, touch; SEE CONCEPTS *34,216,612*

gross [*adj1*] *large, fat*
adipose, big, bulky, chubby*, corpulent, dense, fleshy, great, heavy, hulking, husky, lumpish, massive, obese, overweight, porcine, portly, stout, thick, unwieldy, weighty; SEE CONCEPTS *773,781*

gross [*adj2*] *whole*
aggregate, all, before deductions, before tax, complete, entire, in sum, outright, total, whole ball of wax*, whole enchilada*, whole nine yards*, whole schmear*, whole shebang*; SEE CONCEPT *785*

gross [*adj3*] *crude, vulgar*
barnyard*, boorish, breezy, callous, carnal, cheap, coarse, corporeal, crass, dull, fleshly, foul, ignorant, improper, impure, indecent, indelicate, inelegant, insensitive, in the gutter*, lewd, loud-mouthed, low, low-minded, lustful, obscene, offensive, rank, raunchy, raw, ribald, rough, rude, scatological, sensual, sexual, sleazy*, smutty*, swinish*, tasteless, ugly, uncouth, uncultured, undiscriminating, unfeeling, unrefined, un-

seemly, unsophisticated, voluptuous; SEE CON-
CEPTS 267,542,545

gross [adj4] obvious, apparent
absolute, arrant, blatant, capital, complete,
downright, egregious, excessive, exorbitant, extreme, flagrant, glaring, grievous, heinous, immoderate, inordinate, manifest, out-and-out*,
outrageous, outright*, perfect, plain, rank, serious, shameful, sheer, shocking, unmitigated, unqualified, utter; SEE CONCEPTS 535,537

gross [n] total, whole
aggregate, all, entirety, sum, sum total, totality;
SEE CONCEPTS 344,837

gross [v] bring in as total
earn, make, take in; SEE CONCEPTS 330,351

grotesque [adj] ugly, misshapen
aberrant, abnormal, absurd, antic, bizarre, deformed, distorted, eerie, extravagant, extreme,
fanciful, fantastic, flamboyant, freakish, grody*,
gross*, incongruous, ludicrous, malformed,
monstrous, odd, outlandish, perverted, preposterous, queer, ridiculous, strange, surrealistic,
uncanny, unnatural, weird, whimsical; SEE CON-
CEPTS 486,537,579

grotto [n] cave
antre, cavern, cavity, chamber, den, hollow, rock
shelter, subterrane, underground chamber; SEE
CONCEPT 509

grouch [n] person who complains a lot
bear*, bellyacher*, bug*, crab*, crank, crosspatch*, curmudgeon, faultfinder, griper, grouser,
growler, grumbler, grump*, kicker*, malcontent,
moaner, sorehead*, sourpuss*, whiner; SEE CON-
CEPTS 412,423

grouch [v] complain a lot
bellyache*, carp, find fault, gripe, grouse, grumble, moan, murmur, mutter, scold, whine; SEE
CONCEPT 52

grouchy [adj] complaining, irritable
cantankerous*, cross, crusty*, discontented,
grumbling, grumpy*, ill-tempered, irascible,
peevish, petulant, querulous, snappy, sulky,
surly, testy; SEE CONCEPTS 267,401

ground [n] earth, land
arena, dirt, dust, field, landscape, loam, old sod,
park, real estate, sand, sod, soil, terra firma, terrain, turf; SEE CONCEPT 509

ground [v1] base, set; educate
acquaint, bottom, coach, discipline, establish, familiarize, fit, fix, found, indoctrinate, inform, initiate, instruct, introduce, predicate, prepare,
prime, qualify, rest, settle, stay, teach, train,
tutor; SEE CONCEPTS 18,285

ground [v2] restrict; drop in place
bar, beach, bring down, dock, down, fell, floor,
knock down, land, level, mow down*, prevent,
strand; SEE CONCEPTS 130,181

groundbreaking [adj] pioneering
avant-garde, cutting-edge, innovating, innovative, leading-edge, radical, revolutionary, spear-
heading, trailblazing, trendsetting; SEE CONCEPTS
529,578,589,797

groundless [adj] without reason, justification
baseless, bottomless, causeless, chimerical,
empty, false, flimsy, foundationless, gratuitous,
idle, illogical, illusory, imaginary, unauthorized,
uncalled-for, unfounded, unjustified, unprovoked, unsupported, unwarranted; SEE CONCEPTS
267,552,582

grounds [n1] estate, domain
acreage, area, campus, country, district, environs, fields, gardens, habitat, holding, land, lot,
premises, property, real estate, realm, sphere,
spot, terrace, terrain, territory, tract, zone; SEE
CONCEPTS 508,516

grounds [n2] basis, premise
account, antecedent, argument, base, bedrock*,
call, cause, chapter and verse*, demonstration,
determinant, dope*, evidence, excuse, factor,
footing, foundation, goods*, groundwork, inducement, info*, information*, infrastructure,
justification, motive, numbers, occasion, pretext,
proof, rationale, reason, root*, seat, straight
stuff*, substratum, test, testimony, trial, underpinning, wherefore, why, whyfor; SEE CONCEPTS
274,661

grounds [n3] sediment
deposit, dregs, grouts, leavings, lees, precipitate,
precipitation, residue, settlings; SEE CONCEPT
260

groundwork [n] basis, fundamentals
ABCs*, background, base, bedrock*, cornerstone*, footing, foundation, ground, infrastructure, origin, preliminaries, preparation, root,
substratum, underpinning, understructure; SEE
CONCEPTS 274,442,660,661

group [n] number of individuals collectively
accumulation, aggregation, assemblage, assembly, association, assortment, band, batch, battery,
bevy, body, bunch, bundle, cartel, category,
chain, circle, class, clique, clot, club, clump,
cluster, clutch, collection, combination, combine, company, conglomerate, congregation, coterie, covey, crew, crowd, faction, formation,
gang, gathering, grade, league, lot, mess, organization, pack, parcel, party, passel, platoon, pool,
posse, set, shooting match, society, sort, suite,
syndicate, troop, trust; SEE CONCEPTS 391,432

group [v1] bring together
arrange, assemble, associate, band together,
bracket, bunch, bunch up*, cluster, collect, congregate, consort, corral, crowd, gang around*,
gang up*, gather, get together, hang out*, harmonize, huddle, link, make the scene*, meet, organize, poke, punch*, round up*, scare up*,
systematize; SEE CONCEPTS 109,114

group [v2] classify, sort
arrange, assemble, associate, assort, bracket, categorize, class, dispose, file, gather, marshal,
order, organize, pigeonhole*, put together,
range, rank; SEE CONCEPTS 18,84,158

groupie [n] devoted fan
admirer, buff, devotee, follower, hanger-on, supporter; SEE CONCEPTS 352,366,423

grove [n] cluster of trees
brake, coppice, copse, covert, forest, orchard,
plantation, spinney, stand, thicket, wood, woodland; SEE CONCEPTS 429,517

grovel [v] abase, demean oneself
apple-polish*, beg, beg for mercy, beseech, blandish, bootlick*, bow and scrape*, brown-nose*,
butter up*, cater to, court, cower, crawl, creep,
cringe, crouch, eat crow*, eat dirt*, eat humble
pie*, fall all over*, fawn*, flatter, humble oneself, humor, implore, kiss one's feet*, kneel,
kowtow*, make much of*, make up to*, pamper,
play up to*, prostrate*, revere, snivel, soft-
soap*, stoop, suck up to*, truckle*, wheedle,
yes*; SEE CONCEPTS 384,633

grow [v] *become larger, evolve*

abound, advance, age, amplify, arise, augment, become, branch out, breed, build, burgeon, burst forth, come, come to be, cultivate, develop, dilate, enlarge, expand, extend, fill out, flourish, gain, germinate, get bigger, get taller, heighten, increase, issue, luxuriate, maturate, mature, mount, multiply, originate, pop up*, produce, propagate, pullulate, raise, ripen, rise, shoot*, spread, spring up, sprout, stem, stretch, swell, thicken, thrive, turn, vegetate, wax*, widen; SEE CONCEPTS 427,469,704,775

growl [n/v] *animal-like sound*

bark, bellow, gnarl, gnarr, grumble, grunt, howl, moan, roar, roll, rumble, snarl, thunder; SEE CONCEPTS 77,595

grown-up [n] *adult*

gentleman, grown person, lady, mam, man, Miss, mister, Mr., Mrs., Ms., woman; SEE CONCEPT 424

growth [n1] *development, progress*

advance, advancement, aggrandizement, augmentation, beefing up*, boost, buildup, crop, cultivation, enlargement, evolution, evolvement, expansion, extension, fleshing out*, flowering, gain, germination, heightening, hike, improvement, increase, maturation, maturing, multiplication, produce, production, proliferation, prosperity, rise, sprouting, stretching, success, surge, swell, thickening, unfolding, up, upping, vegetation, waxing*, widening; SEE CONCEPTS 427,469,703,704,775

growth [n2] *tumor*

cancer, cancroid, excrescence, fibrousness, fibrous tissue, fungus, lump, mole, outgrowth, parasite, polyp, swelling, thickening, wen; SEE CONCEPT 306

grub [n1] *larva*

caterpillar, entozoon, maggot, worm; SEE CONCEPT 398

grub [n2] *food*

chow*, comestibles, eats*, edibles, feed, nosh*, nurture, provisions, rations, sustenance, viands, victuals, vittles*; SEE CONCEPTS 457,460

grub [v1] *dig, uncover*

beat, break, burrow, clean, clear, comb, delve, excavate, ferret, fine-tooth-comb*, forage, hunt, poke, prepare, probe, pull up, rake, ransack, root, rummage, scour, search, shovel, spade, unearth, uproot; SEE CONCEPTS 178,216

grub [v2] *work very hard*

drudge, grind, labor, moil, plod, slave, slog, sweat, toil; SEE CONCEPT 100

grubby [adj] *dirty, disheveled*

besmeared, black, filthy, foul, frowzy*, grimy, grungy*, impure, messy, mucky*, nasty, scruffy, scuzzy*, seedy*, shabby, sloppy, slovenly, smutty*, soiled, sordid, squalid, unclean, uncleanly, unkempt, untidy, unwashed; SEE CONCEPTS 485,621

grudge [n] *hard feelings*

animosity, animus, antipathy, aversion, bad blood*, bitterness, bone to pick*, dislike, enmity, grievance, hate, hatred, ill will, injury, injustice, malevolence, malice, maliciousness, malignancy, peeve, pet peeve*, pique, rancor, resentment, spite, spitefulness, spleen, venom; SEE CONCEPT 29

grudge [v] *feel resentful; give unwillingly*

begrudge, be reluctant, be stingy*, complain,

covet, deny, envy, hold back, mind, pinch, refuse, resent, stint; SEE CONCEPT 21

grueling [adj] *difficult, taxing*

arduous, backbreaking, brutal, chastening, crushing, demanding, excruciating, exhausting, fatiguing, fierce, grinding, hairy*, hard, harsh, heavy*, laborious, punishing, racking, severe, stiff, strenuous, tiring, torturous, trying; SEE CONCEPT 565

gruesome [adj] *horrible, awful*

abominable, appalling, daunting, fearful, frightful, ghastly, grim, grisly, grody*, gross*, hideous, horrendous, horrid, horrific, horrifying, loathsome, lurid, macabre, monstrous, morbid, offensive, repugnant, repulsive, shocking, sick*, spine-tingling*, terrible, terrifying, ugly, weird*; SEE CONCEPTS 485,548

gruff [adj1] *bad-tempered, rude*

abrupt, bearish, blunt, boisterous, boorish, brusque, churlish, crabbed*, crabby*, crude, crusty*, curt, discourteous, dour, fierce, grouchy*, grumpy*, ill-natured, impolite, morose, nasty, offhand, rough, saturnine, short, snappy*, snippy*, sour, sullen, surly, truculent, uncivil, ungracious, unmannerly; SEE CONCEPTS 267,401

gruff [adj2] *rasping in sound*

cracked, croaking, croaky, grating, guttural, harsh, hoarse, husky, low, rough, throaty; SEE CONCEPT 594

grumble [v] *complain*

bellyache*, carp, find fault, fuss, gripe, groan, grouch*, grouse, kick, kvetch*, moan, protest, pule, repine, scold, snivel*, squawk*, whine; SEE CONCEPTS 44,52

grumble [v2] *murmur, rumble*

bark, croak, gnarl, gnarr, growl, grunt, gurgle, mumble, mutter, roar, roll, snap, snarl, snuffle, splutter, whine; SEE CONCEPTS 65,77

grump [n] *cranky person*

bear*, complainer, crab*, curmudgeon, grouch, malcontent, sorehead*, sourpuss*, whiner; SEE CONCEPTS 412,423

grumpy [adj] *in a bad mood*

bad-tempered, cantankerous*, crabby*, cross, crotchety, disgruntled, dissatisfied, griping, grouchy*, grumbling, irritable, peevish, pettish, petulant, querulous, sulky, sullen, surly, testy, truculent; SEE CONCEPTS 401,403

grungy [adj] *dirty and unkempt*

cruddy*, dilapidated, disgusting, disheveled, filthy, flimsy, foul, greasy, grimy, grubby, messy, nasty, offensive, repellent, revolting, rundown, scummy*, scuzzy*, shoddy, slimy, sloppy, trashy, unclean, unwashed, vile, wretched; SEE CONCEPTS 485,579

guarantee [n] *pledge, promise*

agreement, assurance, attestation, bail, bargain, bond, certainty, certificate, certification, charter, collateral, contract, covenant, deposit, earnest, gage, guaranty, insurance, lock, oath, pawn, pipe, recognizance, security, sure thing*, surety, testament, token, undertaking, vow, warrant, warranty, word, word of honor; SEE CONCEPTS 71,271,685

guarantee [v] *pledge, promise*

affirm, angel, answer for, assure, attest, aver, back, bankroll, be surety for, bind oneself, certify, confirm, cosign, endorse, ensure, evidence, evince, get behind*, give bond, grubstake, guaranty, insure, juice*, maintain, make bail*, make certain, make sure, mortgage, pick up the check*, pick up the tab*, protect, prove, reassure, secure, sign for, stake, stand behind*, stand up for*, support, swear, testify, vouch for, wager, warrant, witness; SEE CONCEPTS 71,110

guaranteed [*adj*] *made certain*
affirmed, approved, ascertained, assured, attested, bonded, certified, confirmed, endorsed, for a fact, for sure, have a lock on*, insured, on ice*, pledged, plighted, protected, sealed, secured, sure, sure enough*, sure-fire*, warranted; SEE CONCEPT 535

guard [*n1*] *protector*
bouncer*, chaperon, chaperone, chaser*, convoyer, custodian, defender, escort, guardian, lookout, picket, sentinel, sentry, shepherd, shield, ward, warden, watch, watchperson; SEE CONCEPT 348

guard [*n2*] *defense*
aegis, armament, armor, buffer, bulwark, pad, protection, rampart, safeguard, screen, security, shield, ward; SEE CONCEPT 712

guard [*v*] *protect, watch*
attend, baby-sit, bulwark, chaperon, chaperone, conduct, convoy, cover, cover up, defend, escort, fend, keep, keep an eye on*, keep in view, keep under surveillance, look after, lookout, mind, observe, oversee, patrol, police*, preserve, ride shotgun for*, safeguard, save, screen, secure, tend after, shelter, shepherd, shield, shotgun, stonewall*, superintend, supervise, tend; SEE CONCEPTS 96,134

guarded [*adj*] *suspicious*
attentive, cagey, calculating, canny, careful, cautious, chary, circumspect, discreet, gingerly, leery, noncommittal, on the lookout*, overcautious, prudent, reserved, restrained, reticent, safe, vigilant, wary, watchful, with eyes peeled*; SEE CONCEPT 542

guardian [*n*] *keeper, protector*
angel*, attendant, baby-sitter, bird dog*, cerberus, champion, chaperon, chaperone, conservator, cop*, curator, custodian, defender, escort, guard, keeper, nurse, overseer, paladin, patrol, preserver, safeguard, sentinel, shepherd, sitter, sponsor, superintendent, supervisor, trustee, vigilante, warden, watchdog*; SEE CONCEPTS 414, 423

guerrilla [*n*] *bushfighter*
commando, freedom fighter, irregular, mercenary, professional soldier, resistance fighter, soldier of fortune, terrorist, underground fighter; SEE CONCEPT 358

guess [*n*] *belief, speculation*
assumption, ballpark figure*, conclusion, conjecture, deduction, divination, estimate, fancy, feeling, guesstimate*, guesswork, hunch*, hypothesis, induction, inference, judgment, notion, opinion, postulate, postulation, prediction, presumption, presupposition, reckoning, shot*, shot in the dark*, sneaking suspicion*, stab*, supposal, supposition, surmisal, surmise, suspicion, theory, thesis, view; SEE CONCEPT 689

guess [*v*] *try to figure out; imagine*
believe, calculate, chance, conjecture, dare say, deduce, deem, divine, estimate, fancy*, fathom, go out on a limb*, guesstimate*, happen upon*, hazard*, hypothesize, infer, judge, jump to a conclusion*, lump it*, opine, penetrate, pick, postulate, predicate, predict, presume, pretend,

reason, reckon, select, size up*, solve, speculate, suggest, suppose, surmise, survey, suspect, take a shot at*, take a stab at*, theorize, think, think likely, venture, work out*; SEE CONCEPT 28

guest [*n*] *person accommodated, given hospitality*
bedfellow, boarder, caller, client, companion, company, customer, frequenter*, habitué, inmate, lodger, mate, out-of-towner*, partaker, patron, recipient, renter, roomer, sharer, sojourner, tenant, transient, vacationer, visitant, visitor; SEE CONCEPT 423

guffaw [*n*] *burst of laughter*
belly laugh, deep laugh, howl, howling, laughter, loud laugh, roar, shout, shriek, snort; SEE CONCEPTS 77,185

guidance [*n*] *counseling*
advice, auspices, conduct, conduction, control, conveyance, direction, government, help, instruction, intelligence, leadership, management, navigation, supervision, teaching; SEE CONCEPTS 75,274,278

guide [*n1*] *something that or someone who leads*
adviser, attendant, captain, chaperon, cicerone, conductor, controller, convoy, counselor, criterion, design, director, docent, escort, example, exemplar, exhibitor, genie, genius, guiding spirit, guru, ideal, inspiration, lead, leader, lodestar, mentor, model, monitor, paradigm, pathfinder, pattern, pilot, pioneer, rudder, scout, standard, superintendent, teacher, usher, vanguard; SEE CONCEPTS 348,423,686

guide [*n2*] *information, instructions*
ABCs*, beacon*, bellwether*, bible, catalog, chapter and verse*, clue, compendium, directory, enchiridion, guidebook, guiding light*, handbook, hot lead*, key, landmark, lodestar, manual, mark, marker, no-no's*, pointer, print, sign, signal, signpost, telltale, the book*, the numbers*, tip-off*, vade mecum; SEE CONCEPT 274

guide [*v*] *direct, lead*
accompany, advise, attend, beacon*, chaperon, command, conduct, contrive, control, convoy, counsel, coxswain, educate, engineer, escort, govern, handle, have a handle on*, influence, instruct, manage, maneuver, marshal, navigate, oversee, pilot, quarterback*, regulate, route, rule, see, shepherd, show, show the way, spearhead*, steer, superintend, supervise, sway, teach, trailblaze*, train, usher; SEE CONCEPTS 75,110,117, 187

guidebook [*n*] *handbook*
enchiridion, field guide, how-to book, instruction book, manual, map, reference book, road map, travel book, vade mecum; SEE CONCEPT 280

guideline [*n*] *direction*
clue, code, ground rule, guidance, guide, instruction, key, mark, marker, precept, protocol, rule, signal, standard procedure; SEE CONCEPTS 271,274

guild [*n*] *association, fellowship*
club, company, corporation, federation, group, interest group, league, lodge, order, organization, profession, society, sodality, trade, union; SEE CONCEPTS 381,387

guile [*n*] *slyness, cleverness*
artfulness, artifice, chicanery, craft, craftiness, cunning, deceit, deception, dirty dealing*, dirty pool*, dirty trick*, dirty work*, dishonesty, dissemblance, dissimulation, double-cross*, duplic-

gr
gu

ity, foul play*, jive*, run-around*, ruse, sellout*, sharp practice*, stab in the back*, treachery, trickery, trickiness, wiliness; SEE CONCEPTS 645,657

guileless [*adj*] *honest*
aboveboard, artless, candid, frank, genuine, ingenuous, innocent, naive, natural, open, simple, simple-minded, sincere, straightforward, truthful, unaffected, undesigning, unsophisticated, unstudied; SEE CONCEPTS 267,542,545

guilt [*n*] *blame; bad conscience over responsibility*
answerability, blameworthiness, contrition, crime, criminality, culpability, delinquency, dereliction, disgrace, dishonor, error, failing, fault, indiscretion, infamy, iniquity, lapse, liability, malefaction, malfeasance, malpractice, misbehavior, misconduct, misstep, offense, onus, peccability, penitence, regret, remorse, responsibility, self-condemnation, self-reproach, shame, sin, sinfulness, slip, solecism, stigma, transgression, wickedness, wrong; SEE CONCEPTS 101,532, 645,690

guiltless [*adj*] *blameless, not responsible*
clean, clear, crimeless, exemplary, faultless, free, good, immaculate, impeccable, inculpable, innocent, irreproachable, pure, righteous, sinless, spotless, unimpeachable, unsullied, untainted, untarnished, virtuous; SEE CONCEPT 545

guilty [*adj*] *blameworthy; found at fault*
accusable, caught, censurable, censured, chargeable, condemned, conscience-stricken, contrite, convictable, convicted, criminal, culpable, damned, delinquent, depraved, doomed, erring, evil, felonious, hangdog*, impeached, incriminated, in error, iniquitous, in the wrong, judged, liable, licentious, offending, on one's head*, out of line*, proscribed, regretful, remorseful, reprehensible, responsible, rueful, sentenced, sheepish, sinful, sorry, wicked, wrong; SEE CONCEPT 545

guinea pig [*n*] *test subject*
examinee, experimental subject, lab animal, laboratory animal, test animal, testee, victim; SEE CONCEPTS 5,290

guise [*n*] *appearance, pretense*
air, aspect, behavior, cloak, color, cover, demeanor, disguise, disguisement, dress, facade, face, false front*, false show*, fashion, form, front, mask, mien, mode, pose, posture, role, seeming, semblance, shape, show, showing, simulacrum; SEE CONCEPTS 645,716

gulch [*n*] *small ravine*
arroyo, channel, cut, ditch, gap, gorge, gulley, trench, valley; SEE CONCEPTS 509,513

gulf [*n1*] *sea inlet*
basin, bay, bayou, bight, cove, firth, harbor, slough, sound, whirlpool; SEE CONCEPTS 509,514

gulf [*n2*] *deep, gaping hole*
abyss, breach, cave, cavity, chasm, cleft, crevasse, depth, depths, distance, expanse, gap, gulch, hiatus, hollow, opening, pit, ravine, rent, rift, separation, shaft, split, void, well, whirlpool; SEE CONCEPTS 509,513

gullible [*adj*] *naive, trusting*
being a sucker*, believing, biting, credulous, easily taken in*, easy mark*, falling hook line and sinker*, foolish, green*, innocent, kidding oneself*, mark*, silly, simple, sucker, susceptible, swallowing whole*, taken in*, taking the

bait*, trustful, tumbling for*, unskeptical, unsophisticated, unsuspecting, wide-eyed*; SEE CONCEPTS 402,542

gully [*n*] *ravine, ditch*
channel, chase, chasm, crevasse, culvert, gutter, notch, trench, watercourse; SEE CONCEPTS 509,513

gulp [*n*] *swallow*
choke, draught, gasp, mouthful, swig, swill; SEE CONCEPT 185

gulp [*v*] *eat, drink fast*
belt*, choke down*, chugalug*, consume, devour, dispatch, dispose, drop*, englut, gobble*, guzzle*, imbibe, ingurgitate, inhale*, pour, quaff, scarf down*, slop*, slosh*, stuff, swallow, swig, swill, take in, toss off*, wolf*, wolf down*; SEE CONCEPTS 169,185

gum [*n*] *sticky substance*
adhesive, amber, cement, cohesive substance, exudate, glue, mucilage, paste, pitch, plaster, resin, rosin, tar, wax; SEE CONCEPT 466

gumption [*n*] *nerve, initiative*
ability, acumen, astuteness, cleverness, commonsense, discernment, enterprise, get-up-and-go*, good sense, horse sense*, industry, judgment, perspicaciousness, perspicacity, resourcefulness, sagaciousness, sagacity, savvy, sense, shrewdness, spirit, wisdom, wit; SEE CONCEPT 411

gun [*n*] *weapon that shoots*
blaster*, cannon, difference*, equalizer*, flintlock, forty-five*, handgun, hardware*, howitzer, magnum, 9 mm.*, mortar, musket, ordnance, peashooter*, persuader*, piece*, pistol, revolver, rifle, rod*, Saturday-night special*, shotgun, thirty-eight*, Uzi*; SEE CONCEPT 500

gung ho [*adj*] *extremely enthusiastic*
anxious, ardent, dedicated, eager, enthused, excited, fanatical, fired up*, keyed up*, lively, passionate, spirited, zealous; SEE CONCEPTS 401,542

gurgle [*n/v*] *burble, murmur*
babble, bubble, crow, lap, plash, purl, ripple, slosh, splash, wash; SEE CONCEPTS 65,595

guru [*n*] *mentor, guide*
authority, guiding light*, leader, master, sage, teacher, tutor; SEE CONCEPT 350

guru [*n2*] *technical expert*
computer expert, computer geek, computer specialist, geek, techie; SEE CONCEPTS 348,350,416

gush [*n*] *outpouring*
burst, cascade, flood, flow, flush, issue, jet, run, rush, spate, spout, spring, spurt, stream, surge; SEE CONCEPTS 467,687

gush [*v1*] *pour out*
burst, cascade, emanate, emerge, flood, flow, flush, issue, jet, pour, roll, run, rush, sluice, spew, spout, spring, spurt, stream, surge, well; SEE CONCEPT 179

gush [*v2*] *speak with overwhelming enthusiasm*
babble*, blather, carry on about*, chatter, effervesce, effuse, enthuse, fall all over*, go on about*, jabber, make a to-do over*, overstate, prate, prattle, rave; SEE CONCEPT 49

gust [*n*] *rush, eruption*
access, blast, blow, breeze, burst, explosion, fit, flare-up, flurry, gale, outburst, paroxysm, passion, puff, sally, squall, storm, surge; SEE CONCEPTS 524,787

gusto [*n*] *great enthusiasm*
appetite, appreciation, ardor, brio, delectation,

delight, enjoyment, exhilaration, fervor, heart, liking, palate, passion, pleasure, relish, savor, taste, verve, zeal, zest; SEE CONCEPTS *411,657*

gusty [*adj*] *windy*
airy, blowy, blustering, blustery, breezy, hearty, robust, squally, stormy, tempestuous; SEE CONCEPT *525*

gut [*adj*] *intuitive*
basic, deep-seated, emotional, heartfelt, innate, inner, instinctive, interior, internal, intimate, involuntary, natural, spontaneous, unthinking, visceral, viscerous; SEE CONCEPT *403*

gut [*n*] *stomach and abdomen*
belly, bowels, duodenum, entrails, innards, intestines, paunch, tripes, tummy*, venter, viscera; SEE CONCEPT *393*

gut [*v*] *clean out, strip*
bowel, decimate, despoil, dilapidate, disembowel, draw, dress, empty, eviscerate, exenterate, loot, pillage, plunder, ransack, ravage, rifle, sack; SEE CONCEPTS *165,211*

gutless [*adj*] *timid*
abject, chicken*, chicken-hearted*, coward, cowardly, craven, faint-hearted*, feeble, irresolute, lily-livered*, pusillanimous, spineless*, submissive, weak, wimpy*, yellow*, yellow-bellied*; SEE CONCEPTS *404,542*

guts [*n*] *nerve, boldness*
audacity, backbone*, courage, daring, dauntlessness, effrontery, forcefulness, fortitude, grit*, hardihood, heart*, intestinal fortitude*, mettle, moxie*, pluck, resolution, sand*, spine*, spirit, spunk*, willpower; SEE CONCEPTS *411,657*

gutsy [*adj*] *bold, brave*
courageous, determined, gallant, game*, indomitable, intrepid, mettlesome, plucky, resolute, spirited, spunky*, staunch, unfearful, valiant; SEE CONCEPTS *404,542*

gutter [*n*] *ditch*
channel, conduit, culvert, dike, drain, duct, eaves, fosse, funnel, gully, moat, pipe, runnel, sewer, sluice, spout, sulcation, trench, trough, tube, watercourse; SEE CONCEPTS *440,513*

guttural [*adj*] *deep in sound*
glottal, grating, gravely, growling, gruff, harsh, hoarse, husky, inarticulate, low, rasping, rough, sepulchral, thick, throaty; SEE CONCEPT *594*

guy [*n*] *man*
bird*, bloke*, boy, brother, bud, buddy, cat*, chap, chum, dude*, feller*, fellow, gentleman, individual, male, person; SEE CONCEPTS *414,419*

guzzle [*v*] *drink down fast*
bolt*, booze*, carouse*, cram, devour, englut, gobble*, gorge, gormandize, imbibe, ingurgitate, knock back*, quaff, slop*, slosh*, soak, swig, swill, tipple; SEE CONCEPT *169*

gymnasium [*n*] *arena for sports, recreation*
alley, amphitheater, athletic club, center, circus, coliseum, course, exercise room, field house, floor, gym, health club, hippodrome, pit, recreation center, ring, rink, spa, stadium, sweatshop*, theater; SEE CONCEPTS *364,438,439*

gymnastics [*n*] *acrobatic exercise*
aerobics, balance beam, bars, body-building, calisthenics, floor exercise, free exercise, gym, horse, rings, trampoline, trapeze, tumbling, vaulting, workout; SEE CONCEPT *363*

gyp [*v*] *rip-off*
bamboozle, bilk, cheat, deceive, defraud, dupe, fleece, flimflam*, gip, gull, hoodwink, hustle*, pull something*, rook, scam, stick*, swindle, take for a ride*, trick; SEE CONCEPT *59*

gyrate [*v*] *revolve*
circle, circulate, circumduct, gyre, pirouette, purl, roll, rotate, spin, spiral, turn, twirl, whirl, whirligig; SEE CONCEPTS *147,149*

H

habit [*n1*] *tendency, practice*
addiction, bent, bias, constitution, consuetude, convention, custom, dependence, disposition, fashion, fixation, fixed attitude, frame of mind*, gravitation, groove, habitude, hangup, impulsion, inclination, make-up*, manner, mannerism, mode, nature, obsession, pattern, penchant, persuasion, praxis, predisposition, proclivity, proneness, propensity, quirk, routine, rule, rut, second nature*, set, style, susceptibility, thing*, turn, usage, use, way, weakness, wont; SEE CONCEPT *644*

habit [*n2*] *dress, clothing, often for a particular purpose*
apparel, costume, garb, garment, habiliment, riding clothes, robe, vestment; SEE CONCEPT *451*

habitat/habitation [*n*] *place where someone resides*
abode, accommodations, address, apartment, berth, biosphere, cave, commoracy, condo, condominium, co-op, den, digs*, domicile, dwelling, element, environment, fireside, flat, haunt*, haven, hearth, hole*, home, home plate*, homestead, house, housing, locale, locality, lodging, neck of the woods*, nest, nook, occupancy, occupation, pad*, place, quarters, range, residence, residency, roof*, roost*, seat*, settlement, site, stamping ground*, stomping ground*, surroundings, terrain, territory, turf; SEE CONCEPT *515*

habitual [*adj*] *usual, established*
accepted, accustomed, addicted, addicting, automatic, chronic, common, confirmed, constant, continual, conventional, customary, cyclic, disciplined, familiar, fixed, frequent, hardened, ingrained, inveterate, iterated, iterative, mechanical, methodical, natural, normal, ordinary, perfunctory, permanent, perpetual, persistent, practiced, recurrent, regular, reiterative, repeated, repetitious, rooted, routine, seasoned, set, standard, steady, systematic, traditional, wonted; SEE CONCEPTS *530,547*

habituate [*v*] *prepare, accustom*
acclimate, acclimatize, addict, adjust, break in, condition, confirm, devote, discipline, endure, familiarize, harden, inure, make used to, school, season, take to, tolerate, train; SEE CONCEPTS *35,202*

hacienda [*n*] *large estate*
cattle ranch, farmhouse, large house, mansion, plantation, ranch; SEE CONCEPTS *439,516*

hack [*n1*] *person who does easy work for money*
drudge*, greasy grind*, grind*, hireling, lackey*, old pro*, plodder*, pro*, servant, slave, workhorse*; SEE CONCEPT *348*

gu
ha

hack [n2] *taxicab*

cab, carriage, coach, hackney, taxi, vehicle; SEE CONCEPT 505

hack [n3/v] *cut without care*

chop, clip, fell, gash, hackle, hew, lacerate, mangle, mutilate, notch, slash, whack; SEE CONCEPTS 137,176

hacker [n] *someone proficient at computers, especially a hobbyist*

application programmer, computer architect, computer designer, computer jock, key puncher, operator, programmer, systems analyst, systems engineer, systems software specialist, systems programmer, technician; SEE CONCEPTS 360,366

hack it [v] *to succeed*

accomplish, avail, be successful, bring home the bacon*, carry off*, come out on top*, come through, cut it, cut the mustard*, deliver the goods*, get to the top*, hit the mark*, make a go of it*, make it*, make the cut*, make the grade*, prevail, pull it off, score, win; SEE CONCEPTS 141,706

hackneyed [adj] *clichéd, tired*

antiquated, banal, common, commonplace, conventional, corny*, everyday, familiar tune*, hokey*, moth-eaten*, obsolete, old, old-chestnut*, old-hat*, old-saw*, outdated, outmoded, out-of-date, overworked, pedestrian*, played-out*, quotidian, run-of-the-mill*, stale, stereotyped, stock, threadbare*, timeworn, tripe, trite, unoriginal, well-worn, worn-out*; SEE CONCEPTS 267,530

haggard [adj] *worn, weakened*

ashen, careworn, drawn, emaciated, exhausted, faded, fagged, fatigued, fretted, gaunt, ghastly, lank, lean, pale, pallid, pinched, scraggy, scrawny, shrunken, skinny, spare, starved, thin, tired, wan, wasted, weak, wearied, worn-down, wrinkled; SEE CONCEPTS 314,406,491

haggle [v] *bicker, quarrel*

argue, bargain, barter, beat down*, cavil, chaffer, deal, dicker*, dispute, hammer out a deal*, horse-trade*, make a deal*, palter, quibble, squabble, wrangle; SEE CONCEPT 46

hail [n] *torrent*

barrage, bombardment, broadside, cannonade, hailstorm, pelting, rain, salvo, shower, storm, volley; SEE CONCEPTS 189,524

hail [v1] *call to, yell for*

accost, address, flag, flag down*, greet, hello, holler*, salute, shoulder, shout, signal, sing out*, speak to, wave down, welcome, whistle down*, whistle for*, yawp*, yoo-hoo*; SEE CONCEPTS 47,74,77

hail [v3] *come from; originate*

be a native of, be born in, begin, claim as birthplace; SEE CONCEPT 648

hail [v4] *rain down on*

barrage, batter, beat down upon, bombard, pelt, shower, storm, volley; SEE CONCEPT 526

hair [n] *threadlike growth on animate being*

beard, bristle, cilium, coiffure, cowlick, cut, down, eyebrow, eyelash, feeler, fiber, filament, fluff, fringe, frizzies*, fur, grass, haircut, hairstyle, lock, mane, mop*, moustache, quill, ruff, shock, sideburn, split ends, strand, thatch, tress, tuft, vibrissa, villus, whiskers, wig, wool; SEE CONCEPT 392

hairdresser [n] *hair stylist*

barber, beautician, coiffeur, coiffeuse, friseur; SEE CONCEPT 348

hairless [adj] *without growth on body part*

bald, baldheaded, beardless, clean-shaven, cue ball*, depilated, egghead*, glabrate, glabrescent, glabrous, shaved, shaven, shorn, skinhead*, smooth, smooth-faced, tonsured, whiskerless; SEE CONCEPT 406

hair-raising [adj] *causing excitement*

bloodcurdling, breathtaking, chilling, cliff-hanging, electrifying, exciting, frightening, shocking, spine-chilling, spine-tingling, suspenseful, terrifying; SEE CONCEPTS 529,542,548

hairsplitting [n] *nitpicking*

bickering, carping, caviling, faultfinding, perfectionism, pettiness, quibbling, sophistry; SEE CONCEPTS 671,706

hairstyle [n] *cut, style of a head of hair*

afro*, beehive*, blow dry*, bob*, bouffant, braid, brushcut, bubble*, bun, coiffure, crewcut, cut, do*, dreadlocks, ducktail, fade, feather cut, flattop*, flip, haircut, hairdo, headdress, horse tail, mohawk, natural, pageboy, pigtails, pixie, ponytail, razor cut; SEE CONCEPT 718

hairy [adj1] *having much hair*

bearded, bewhiskered, bristly, bushy, downy, fleecy, flocculent, fluffy, furry, fuzzy, hirsute, lanate, pileous, piliferous, pilose, pubescent,* rough, shaggy, stubbly, tufted, unshaven, unshorn, villous, whiskered, woolly; SEE CONCEPT 406

hairy [adj2] *dangerous*

chancy, difficult, hazardous, jeopardous, perilous, risky, scary, treacherous, uncertain, unhealthy, unsound, wicked; SEE CONCEPT 548

halcyon [adj] *calm, peaceful*

at peace, balmy, bucolic, gentle, golden, happy, harmonious, palmy, pastoral, quiet, serene, soothing, still, sunny, tranquil, untroubled; SEE CONCEPTS 401,404,525,542,594

hale [adj] *strong and healthy*

able-bodied, alive and kicking*, blooming, fit, fit as a fiddle*, flourishing, healthy, hearty, husky, in fine fettle*, in the pink*, right, robust, sane, sound, stout, strapping, strong, trim, vigorous, well, well-conditioned, wholesome; SEE CONCEPTS 314,489

half [adj] *partial*

bisected, divided, even-steven*, fifty-fifty*, fractional, halved, incomplete, limited, moderate, partly; SEE CONCEPT 785

half [n] *one of two equal parts of a whole*

bisection, division, fifty percent, fraction, hemisphere, moiety; SEE CONCEPT 835

half-baked [adj] *stupid; not thought through*

backward, batty*, birdbrained*, blockheaded*, boneheaded*, brainless, crazy, dumb, feeble-minded, foolish, harebrained*, idiotic, ignorant, ill-conceived, imbecilic, impractical, indiscreet, moronic, poorly planned, retarded, senseless, short-sighted, silly, slow, sophomoric, underdeveloped, unformed, witless; SEE CONCEPTS 403,529,548

half-breed [n] *mixed creation*

amalgam, blend, combination, conglomeration, cross, cross-breed, hodgepodge*, hybrid, medley, melange, miscegnation, mishmash*, mule, mutt*; SEE CONCEPTS 260,394

halfhearted [*adj*] *without enthusiasm*
apathetic, cool, impassive, indifferent, irresolute, lackluster, listless, lukewarm, neutral, passive, perfunctory, spiritless, tame, tepid, unenthusiastic, uninterested; SEE CONCEPTS 401,542

halfway [*adj*] *not complete; in the middle*
betwixt and between*, center, centermost, central, equidistant, imperfect, intermediate, medial, median, mid*, middlemost, midway, moderate, part, partial, part-way*, smack dab*, smack in the middle*; SEE CONCEPTS 531,586

halfway [*adv*] *not complete; in the middle*
comparatively, compromising, conciliatory, half the distance, imperfectly, incompletely, in part, insufficiently, medially, middling, midway, moderately, nearly, partially, partly, pretty*, rather, restrictedly, to a degree, to some extent, to the middle, unsatisfactorily; SEE CONCEPTS 531,586

half-wit [*n*] *stupid person*
blockhead*, cretin, dimwit, dingbat*, dolt, dope*, dork*, dullard, dumbbell*, dummy*, dunce, dunderhead, fool, idiot, ignoramus, imbecile, lamebrain*, moron, nitwit, pea brain*, simpleton; SEE CONCEPTS 350,423

hall [*n1*] *corridor*
anteroom, entrance, entranceway, entry, foyer, gallery, hallway, lobby, pass, passage, passageway, room, rotunda, vestibule; SEE CONCEPT 440

hall [*n2*] *room for large affairs*
amphitheater, arena, armory, assembly room, auditorium, ballroom, casino, chamber, church, gallery, gym, gymnasium, lounge, lyceum, mart, meeting place, refectory, salon, stateroom, theater; SEE CONCEPTS 438,439,441,448

hallmark [*n*] *symbol, authentication*
badge, certification, device, emblem, endorsement, indication, mark, ratification, seal, sign, signet, stamp, sure sign, telltale sign, trademark; SEE CONCEPTS 284,628

hallowed [*adj*] *holy, revered*
anointed, beatified, blessed, consecrated, dedicated, divine, enshrined, holy, honored, inviolable, sacred, sacrosanct, sanctified, unprofane; SEE CONCEPT 568

hallucinate [*v*] *imagine vividly*
blow one's mind*, daydream, envision, fantasize, freak out*, have visions, head trip*, hear voices*, trip*, visualize; SEE CONCEPT 34

hallucination [*n*] *dream, delusion*
aberration, apparition, fantasy, figment of the imagination*, head trip*, illusion, mirage, phantasm, phantasmagoria, phantom, trip*, vision, wraith; SEE CONCEPTS 529,532,690

halo [*n*] *ring of light*
aura, aureola, aureole, aurora, corona, crown of light, glory, halation, nimbus, radiance; SEE CONCEPTS 624,628

halt [*n*] *end, stoppage*
arrest, break, break-off*, close, cutoff, freeze*, grinding halt, impasse, interruption, layoff, letup, pause, screaming halt*, screeching halt*, stand, standstill, stop, termination; SEE CONCEPT 119

halt [*v1*] *stop, cause to stop*
adjourn, arrest, balk, bar, block, blow the whistle on*, break off*, bring to an end, bring to standstill, call it a day*, cease, cease fire, check, close down, come to an end, cool it*, curb*, cut short, desist, deter, draw up, drop anchor*, end, frus-

trate, hamper, hold at bay*, hold back, impede, intermit, interrupt, obstruct, pause, pull up*, punctuate, put a cork in*, rest, stall, stand still, stay, stem, stop, suspend, terminate, wait; SEE CONCEPTS 121,234

halt [*v2*] *hesitate, stutter*
be defective, dither, falter, hobble, limp, pause, shilly-shally*, stagger, stammer, stumble, vacillate, waver, whiffle*, wiggle-waggle*; SEE CONCEPTS 234,721,804

halting [*adj*] *hesitant*
awkward, bumbling, clumsy, doubtful, faltering, gauche, imperfect, indecisive, inept, irresolute, labored, limping, lumbering, maladroit, slow, stammering, stumbling, stuttering, tentative, uncertain, unhandy, vacillating, vacillatory, wavering, wooden*; SEE CONCEPTS 534,550

halve [*v*] *cut in half*
bisect, divide equally, reduce by fifty percent, share equally, split in two; SEE CONCEPT 98

hamburger [*n*] *ground beef sandwich*
beefburger, burger, cheeseburger, chopped beefsteak, ground chuck, ground round, ground sirloin, Salisbury steak; SEE CONCEPTS 457,460

hamlet [*n*] *small village*
community, crossroads, district, small town, suburb; SEE CONCEPT 507

hammer [*v*] *beat, hit*
bang, batter, bear down, clobber, defeat, drive, drub, fashion, forge, form, knock, make, pound, pummel, shape, strike, tap, thrash, trounce, wallop, whack, whomp; SEE CONCEPT 189

hammer away/hammer into [*v*] *work hard at*
continue, drive home*, drub into*, drudge, drum into*, endeavor, grind*, grind into*, impress upon, instruct, keep on, peg away*, persevere, persist, plug away*, pound away*, repeat, stick to*, try hard, try repeatedly, work; SEE CONCEPTS 68,87,239

hammer out [*v*] *bring to a conclusion*
accomplish, bring about, build, complete, construct, erect, establish, excogitate, fight through, finish, form, make, negotiate, produce, settle, set up, sort out, thrash out*, work out; SEE CONCEPTS 91,706

hamper [*n*] *basket for storage*
bassinet, carton, crate, creel, laundry basket, pannier; SEE CONCEPT 494

hamper [*v*] *impede, restrict*
baffle, balk, bar, bind, block, check, clog, cramp, cramp one's style*, cumber, curb, drag one's feet*, embarrass, encumber, entangle, fetter, foil, frustrate, get in the way*, hamstring*, handicap, hang up*, hinder, hobble, hog-tie*, hold up*, inconvenience, inhibit, interfere with, leash, obstruct, prevent, restrain, retard, shackle, slow down, stymie, thwart, tie, tie one's hands*, tie up, trammel; SEE CONCEPT 130

hamstring [*v*] *disable*
cripple, debilitate, handicap, hinder, hobble, immobilize, impair, lame, maim, mangle, paralyze, weaken; SEE CONCEPTS 130,246

hand [*n1*] *appendage at end of human arm, including fingers*
duke*, extremity, fin*, fist, grasp, grip, ham*, hold, hook, metacarpus, mitt*, palm, paw*, phalanges, shaker*; SEE CONCEPT 392

hand [*n2*] *person who does labor*
aide, artificer, artisan, craftsperson, employee,

ha
ha

help, helper, hired person, laborer, operative, roustabout, worker; SEE CONCEPT 348

hand [n3] help, aid

ability, agency, assistance, control, direction, guidance, influence, instruction, knack, lift, part, participation, relief, share, skill, succor, support; SEE CONCEPTS 110,630

hand [n4] handwriting

calligraphy, chirography, longhand, script; SEE CONCEPT 79

hand [n5] round of applause

clap, handclapping, ovation, thunderous reception; SEE CONCEPT 189

handbag [n] person's carryall

backpack, bag, clutch, evening bag, grip, hide, knapsack, leather, pocketbook, portmanteau, purse, reticule; SEE CONCEPT 446

handbook [n] document giving instruction, information

bible, compendium, directory, enchiridion, encyclopedia, fundamentals, guide, guidebook, instruction book, manual, text, textbook, vade mecum; SEE CONCEPT 280

handful [adj] a small quantity

few, scattering, small number, smattering, some, spattering, sprinkling; SEE CONCEPT 789

handicap [n1] disadvantage

affliction, baggage*, barrier, block, burden, detriment, disability, drawback, encumbrance, hangup*, hindrance, impairment, impediment, injury, limitation, load, millstone, obstacle, psychological baggage*, restriction, shortcoming, stumbling block*; SEE CONCEPTS 666,674

handicap [n2] advantage

bulge, edge*, favor, head start*, odds, penalty, points*, start, upper hand*, vantage; SEE CONCEPT 693

handicap [v] give disadvantage

burden, cripple, encumber, hamper, hamstring*, hinder, hog-tie*, hold back, impede, limit, put out of commission*, restrict, sideline*, take out*; SEE CONCEPTS 130,246

handicraft [n] artwork, skill

achievement, art, artifact, artisanship, calling, craft, craftship, creation, design, handiwork, invention, métier, product, production, profession, result, trade, vocation; SEE CONCEPTS 259,630

handle [n1] something to grip

arm, bail, crank, ear, grasp, haft, handgrip, helve, hilt, hold, holder, knob, shaft, stem, stock, tiller; SEE CONCEPTS 445,502,831

handle [n2] nickname

appellation, byname, byword, cognomen, denomination, designation, moniker, name, nomen, sobriquet, style, title; SEE CONCEPT 683

handle [v1] touch

check, examine, feel, finger*, fondle, grasp, hold, manipulate, maul, palpate, paw*, pick up, poke, test, thumb*; try; SEE CONCEPT 612

handle [v2] manage, take care of

administer, advise, apply, behave toward, bestow, call the signals*, command, conduct, control, cope with, cut the mustard*, deal with, direct, discuss, dispense, dominate, employ, exercise, exploit, get a handle on*, govern, guide, hack it*, make out*, make the grade*, maneuver, manipulate, operate, play, ply, run things, serve, steer, supervise, swing, take, treat, use, utilize, wield, work; SEE CONCEPTS 91,117

handle [v3] carry as merchandise

deal in, market, offer, retail, sell, stock, trade, traffic in; SEE CONCEPT 345

handling [n] management

administration, approach, care, charge, conduct, direction, manipulation, running, styling, superintendence, supervision, treatment; SEE CONCEPT 117

hand-me-down [adj] secondhand

not new, passed down, previously owned, used; SEE CONCEPTS 575,585

hand out [v] give to others

bestow, deal out, deliver, devote, disburse, dish out, dispense, disseminate, distribute, donate, give away, give out, hand over, mete, present, provide; SEE CONCEPTS 108,140

hand over [v] give back; release

abandon, cede, commend, commit, consign, deliver, dispense, donate, entrust, feed, find, fork out*, fork up*, give up, hand, leave, present, provide, relegate, relinquish, supply, surrender, transfer, turn over, waive, yield; SEE CONCEPTS 108,131

handsome [adj1] attractive

admirable, aristocratic, athletic, august, beautiful, becoming, clean-cut, comely, dapper, elegant, fair, fashionable, fine, good-looking, graceful, impressive, lovely, majestic, noble, personable, pulchritudinous, robust, sharp, smart, smooth, spruce, stately, strong, stylish, suave, virile, well-dressed, well-proportioned*; SEE CONCEPT 579

handsome [adj2] abundant

ample, bounteous, bountiful, considerable, extensive, full, generous, gracious, large, lavish, liberal, magnanimous, munificent, openhanded, plentiful, princely, sizable, unsparing; SEE CONCEPT 781

handsomely [adv] abundantly

amply, bountifully, generously, lavishly, liberally, magnanimously, munificently, nobly, plentifully, richly; SEE CONCEPT 781

handwriting [n] the way a person writes

autography, calligraphy, chicken scratch*, chirography, ductus, griffonage, hand, hieroglyphics, longhand, manuscript, manuscription, mark, pencraft, penscript, scratching*, scrawl, scribble, script, scription, scrivenery, scrivening, style, writing; SEE CONCEPTS 284,625,628

handy [adj1] nearby

accessible, adjacent, at hand, available, close, close-at-hand, close by, convenient, near, near-at-hand, on hand, ready, within reach; SEE CONCEPT 586

handy [adj2] easy to use

adaptable, advantageous, available, beneficial, central, convenient, functional, gainful, helpful, manageable, neat, practicable, practical, profitable, ready, serviceable, useful, utile, wieldy; SEE CONCEPT 560

handy [adj3] adept physically

able, adroit, clever, deft, dexterous, expert, fit, ingenious, nimble, proficient, ready, skilled, skillful; SEE CONCEPT 527

hang [v1] suspend or be suspended

adhere, attach, beetle, be fastened, be in mid-air, be loose, bend, be pendent, be poised, bow, cling, cover, dangle, deck, decorate, depend, drape, drift, droop, drop, fasten, fix, flap, float, flop, furnish, hold, hover, impend, incline, lean, loll, lop, lower, nail, overhang, pin, project, remain, rest, sag, stay up, stick, swing, tack, trail, wave; SEE CONCEPTS 144,201,746

hang [*v2*] *kill by suspension from a rope*
execute, gibbet, hoist, lynch, noose, scrag, send to the gallows, stretch*, string up*, swing*; SEE CONCEPT 252

hang [*v3*] *depend on future action*
await, be conditional upon, be contingent on, be dependent on, be determined by, be in limbo, be in suspense, cling, hinge, pend, rest, turn on; SEE CONCEPT 681

hang about/hang around/hang out [*v*] *associate with; be residing in*
abide, affect, dally, frequent, get along with, haunt, have relations with, linger, live, loiter, reside, resort, roam, spend time, stand around, swell, tarry, waste time; SEE CONCEPTS 114,226

hangdog [*adj*] *shamefaced*
ashamed, browbeaten, conscience-stricken, cowering, defeated, downcast, guilty, intimidated, sheepish, wretched; SEE CONCEPT 403

hanger-on [*n*] *person who attends the powerful for status or benefit*
dependent, flunky*, follower, freeloader*, lackey*, leech*, nuisance, parasite, sponger*, sycophant, truckler*; SEE CONCEPT 423

hang on [*v*] *continue; endure*
be tough, carry on, cling, clutch, go on, grasp, grip, hold fast, hold on, hold out, persevere, persist, remain; SEE CONCEPTS 23,239

hangout [*n*] *place for socializing*
bar, den*, dive*, haunt*, home, honky-tonk*, joint*, purlieu, resort, stomping ground*, watering hole*; SEE CONCEPTS 439,447,449

hangover [*n*] *result of heavy drinking*
aftereffect, big head*, delirium tremens, drunkenness, DTs*, headache, morning after*, shakes*, under the weather*, willies*, withdrawal; SEE CONCEPT 316

hang tough [*v*] *endure*
bear, bear the brunt*, be patient with, brave, cope with, face up, go through, grin and bear it*, gut it out*, hang in*, hang in there, keep up, live out, live through, meet with, never say die*, put up with, ride out*, sit through, stand, stick in there, stick it out*, stomach*, suffer, swallow*, take, take it*, tough it out*, weather, withstand; SEE CONCEPT 23

hang-up [*n*] *preoccupation*
block, difficulty, dilemma, disturbance, impasse, inhibition, obsession, predicament, problem, reserve, restraint, thing; SEE CONCEPTS 532,674,690

hanker after/hanker for [*v*] *desire strongly*
ache, covet, crave, hunger, itch, long, lust, partial to, pine, sigh, thirst, want, wish, yearn, yen; SEE CONCEPT 20

hankering [*n*] *strong desire*
ache, craving, druthers*, fire in belly*, hunger, itch*, longing, munchies*, pining, thirst, urge, want, weakness, wish, yearning, yen; SEE CONCEPTS 20,709

hanky-panky [*n*] *mischief*
chicane, chicanery, deception, devilry, double-dealing, fourberie, fraud, funny business*, knavery, machinations, monkey business*, sharp practice*, shenanigans*, skullduggery*, subterfuge, trickery; SEE CONCEPTS 59,384

haphazard [*adj*] *without plan or organization*
accidental, aimless, all over the map*, any old way*, any which way*, arbitrary, careless, casual, chance, designless, desultory, devil-may-care*, disorderly, disorganized, erratic, fluke, helter-skelter*, hit-or-miss*, incidental, indiscriminate, irregular, loose, offhand, purposeless, random, reckless, slapdash, slipshod, spontaneous, sudden, unconcerned, unconscious, unconsidered, uncoordinated, unexpected, unmethodical, unorganized, unpremeditated, unsystematic, unthinking, willy-nilly*; SEE CONCEPTS 535,581

hapless [*adj*] *unfortunate*
behind the eightball*, cursed, hexed, ill-fated, ill-starred, infelicitous, jinxed, jonah*, loser, luckless, miserable, poor fish*, sad sack*, snakebit*, star-crossed*, unhappy, unlucky, untoward, voodooed*, woeful, wretched; SEE CONCEPT 548

happen [*v*] *come to pass; occur*
appear, arise, arrive, become a fact, become known, become of, befall, be found, betide, bump, chance, come about, come after, come into being, come into existence, come off, crop up*, develop, down, ensue, eventuate, fall, follow, go on, hit, issue, light, luck, materialize, meet, pass, present itself, proceed, recur, result, shake, smoke*, spring, stumble, stumble upon, supervene, take effect, take place, transpire, turn out, turn up, what goes*; SEE CONCEPT 4

happening [*n*] *occurrence*
accident, adventure, affair, case, chance, circumstance, episode, event, experience, go*, incident, milestone, occasion, phenomenon, proceeding, scene, thing*; SEE CONCEPT 4

happily [*adv1*] *with joy, pleasure*
agreeably, blissfully, blithely, brightly, buoyantly, cheerfully, contentedly, delightedly, delightfully, devotedly, elatedly, enthusiastically, exhilaratingly, exultantly, freely, gaily, gladly, gleefully, graciously, heartily, hilariously, jovially, joyfully, joyously, laughingly, lightheartedly, lightly, lovingly, merrily, optimistically, peacefully, playfully, sincerely, smilingly, sportively, vivaciously, willingly, with relish, with zeal, zestfully; SEE CONCEPTS 403,542

happily [*adv2*] *successfully*
appropriately, aptly, auspiciously, favorably, felicitously, fortunately, gracefully, propitiously, prosperously, providentially, satisfyingly, seasonably, swimmingly, well; SEE CONCEPT 548

happiness [*n*] *high spirits, satisfaction*
beatitude, blessedness, bliss, cheer, cheerfulness, cheeriness, content, contentment, delectation, delight, delirium, ecstasy, elation, enchantment, enjoyment, euphoria, exhilaration, exuberance, felicity, gaiety, geniality, gladness, glee, good cheer, good humor, good spirits, hilarity, hopefulness, joviality, joy, jubilation, laughter, lightheartedness, merriment, mirth, optimism, paradise, peace of mind, playfulness, pleasure, prosperity, rejoicing, sanctity, seventh heaven*, vivacity, well-being; SEE CONCEPT 410

happy [*adj1*] *in high spirits; satisfied*
blessed, blest, blissful, blithe, can't complain*, captivated, cheerful, chipper, chirpy, content, contented, convivial, delighted, ecstatic, elated, exultant, flying high*, gay, glad, gleeful, gratified, intoxicated, jolly, joyful, joyous, jubilant,

ha
ha

laughing, light, lively, looking good*, merry, mirthful, on cloud nine*, overjoyed, peaceful, peppy, perky, playful, pleasant, pleased, sparkling, sunny, thrilled, tickled, tickled pink*, up, upbeat, walking on air*; SEE CONCEPT *403*

happy [*adj2*] *lucky*
accidental, advantageous, appropriate, apt, auspicious, befitting, casual, convenient, correct, effective, efficacious, enviable, favorable, felicitous, fitting, fortunate, incidental, just, meet, nice, opportune, promising, proper, propitious, providential, right, satisfactory, seasonable, successful, suitable, timely, well-timed; SEE CONCEPT *558*

happy-go-lucky [*adj*] *carefree and untroubled*
blithe, casual, cheerful, cool, devil-may-care*, easy, easygoing, feckless, free-minded, heedless, improvident, insouciant, irresponsible, lackadaisical*, lighthearted, nonchalant, reckless, unconcerned; SEE CONCEPTS *404,542*

hara-kiri [*n*] *ritual suicide*
belly cutting, ceremonious suicide, disembowelment, self-immolation, seppuku; SEE CONCEPTS *192,252*

harangue [*n*] *long lecture*
address, chewing out*, declamation, diatribe, discourse, exhortation, hassle, jeremiad, oration, philippic, reading out*, screed, sermon, speech, spiel*, spouting, tirade; SEE CONCEPTS *51,278*

harangue [*v*] *give a long lecture*
accost, address, apostrophize, buttonhole*, chew out*, declaim, exhort, get on a soapbox*, go on about*, hold forth, orate, perorate, rant, rave, soapbox*, spiel*, spout, stump, talk to, yell at; SEE CONCEPT *51*

harass [*v*] *badger*
annoy, attack, bait, bedevil, beleaguer, bother, bug*, burn*, despoil, devil*, distress, disturb, eat*, exasperate, exhaust, fatigue, foray, get to*, give a bad time*, give a hard time*, gnaw*, harry, hassle, heckle, hound*, intimidate, irk, irritate, jerk around*, macerate, maraud, noodge*, pain*, perplex, persecute, pester, plague, raid, rattle one's cage*, ride, strain, stress, tease, tire, torment, trouble, try, vex, weary, work on*, worry; SEE CONCEPTS *7,14,19*

harassment [*n*] *badgering*
aggravation, annoyance, bedevilment, bother, bothering, disturbance, exasperation, hassle, irking, irritation, molestation, nuisance, persecution, perturbation, pestering, provocation, provoking, torment, trouble, vexation, vexing; SEE CONCEPTS *14,313*

harbinger [*n*] *indication*
augury, forerunner, foretoken, herald, messenger, omen, portent, precursor, sign, signal; SEE CONCEPTS *74,284,529*

harbor [*n1*] *place for storing boats in the water*
anchorage, arm, bay, bight, breakwater, chuck, cove, dock, embankment, firth, gulf, haven, inlet, jetty, landing, mooring, pier, port, road, roadstead, wharf; SEE CONCEPTS *439,509,514*

harbor [*n2*] *place for seclusion*
asylum, cover, covert, harborage, haven, port, refuge, retreat, sanctuary, sanctum, security, shelter; SEE CONCEPT *515*

harbor [*v1*] *hide, protect*
accommodate, board, bunk, conceal, defend, domicile, entertain, guard, hold back, house, lodge, nurse, nurture, provide refuge, put up,

quarter, relieve, safeguard, screen, secrete, secure, shelter, shield, suppress, withhold; SEE CONCEPTS *134,188*

harbor [*v2*] *hold in imagination*
believe, brood over, cherish, cling to, consider, entertain, foster, hold, imagine, maintain, nurse, nurture, regard, retain; SEE CONCEPT *17*

hard [*adj1*] *rocklike*
adamantine, callous, compact, compacted, compressed, concentrated, consolidated, dense, firm, hardened, impenetrable, indurate, indurated, inflexible, iron*, packed, rigid, rocky, set, solid, stiff, stony, strong, thick, tough, unyielding; SEE CONCEPT *604*

hard [*adj2*] *difficult, exhausting*
arduous, backbreaking, bothersome, burdensome, complicated, demanding, difficile, distressing, effortful, exacting, fatiguing, formidable, grinding, hairy*, heavy*, Herculean*, intricate, involved, irksome, knotty*, labored, laborious, mean, merciless, murder, onerous, operose, rigorous, rough, rugged, scabrous, serious, severe, slavish, sticky, strenuous, terrible, tiring, toilful, toilsome, tough, troublesome, unsparing, uphill*, uphill battle*, wearing, wearisome, wearying; SEE CONCEPTS *529,538,565*

hard [*adj3*] *cruel, ruthless*
acrimonious, angry, antagonistic, austere, bitter, bleak, brutal, callous, cold, cold-blooded*, cold fish*, dark, disagreeable, distressing, dour, exacting, grievous, grim, hard as nails*, hardboiled*, harsh, hostile, inclement, intemperate, intolerable, obdurate, painful, perverse, pitiless, rancorous, resentful, rigorous, rugged, severe, stern, strict, stringent, stubborn, thick-skinned*, tough, unfeeling, unjust, unkind, unpleasant, unrelenting, unsparing, unsympathetic, vengeful; SEE CONCEPTS *401,542*

hard [*adj4*] *true, indisputable*
absolute, actual, bare, cold, definite, down-to-earth, genuine, plain, positive, practical, pragmatic, realistic, sure, undeniable, unvarnished, verified; SEE CONCEPTS *535,582*

hard [*adv1*] *with great force*
actively, angrily, animatedly, boisterously, briskly, brutally, cruelly, earnestly, energetically, ferociously, fiercely, forcibly, frantically, furiously, heavily, intensely, keenly, like fury, madly, meanly, painfully, powerfully, relentlessly, rigorously, roughly, rowdily, savagely, seriously, severely, sharply, spiritedly, sprightly, stormily, strongly, tumultuously/tumultuously, turbulently, uproariously, urgently, viciously, vigorously, violently, vivaciously, wildly, with all one's might; SEE CONCEPT *540*

hard [*adv2*] *with determination*
assiduously, closely, diligently, doggedly, earnestly, exhaustively, industriously, intensely, intensively, intently, painstakingly, persistently, searchingly, sharply, steadily, strenuously, thoroughly, unremittingly, untiringly; SEE CONCEPT *538*

hard [*adv3*] *with difficulty*
agonizingly, arduously, awkwardly, badly, burdensomely, carefully, cumbersomely, cumbrously, distressingly, exhaustingly, gruelingly, hardly, harshly, inconveniently, laboriously, painfully, ponderously, roughly, severely, stren-

uously, tiredly, toilsomely, unwieldily, vigorously, with great effort; SEE CONCEPT 565

hard [*adv4*] *with resentment*
bitterly, hardly, keenly, rancorously, reluctantly, slowly, sorely; SEE CONCEPT 403

hard [*adv5*] *in a fixed manner*
close, fast, firm, firmly, solidly, steadfastly, tight, tightly; SEE CONCEPTS 488,586

hard-boiled [*adj*] *tough*
callous, firm, hard as nails*, hard-line*, hard-nosed*, hard-shelled*, headstrong, inflexible, obdurate, obstinate, rough, stern, strict, unbending, unfeeling; SEE CONCEPTS 403,542

hard-core [*adj*] *dedicated*
determined, devoted, die-hard*, dyed-in-the-wool*, explicit, extreme, faithful, intransigent, obstinate, resolute, rigid, staunch, steadfast, stubborn, uncompromising, unwaivering, unyielding; SEE CONCEPTS 535,542

harden [*v1*] *make or become solid*
amalgamate, anneal, bake, brace, buttress, cake, calcify, callous, cement, close, clot, coagulate, compact, congeal, consolidate, contract, crystallize, curdle, densify, dry, firm, fix, fortify, fossilize, freeze, gird, indurate, jell, nerve, ossify, petrify, precipitate, press, reinforce, set, settle, solidify, starch, steel, stiffen, strengthen, temper, thicken, toughen, vitrify; SEE CONCEPTS 250,469

harden [*v2*] *accustom*
acclimate, acclimatize, adapt, adjust, blunt, brutalize, callous, callus, case-harden, climatize, coarsen, conform, deaden, develop, discipline, dull, embitter, habituate, indurate, inure, make callous, numb, paralyze, render insensitive, roughen, season, steel, stiffen, strengthen, stun, stupefy, teach, train; SEE CONCEPTS 35,235

hardened [*adj*] *unfeeling*
accustomed, benumbed, callous, case-hardened, coldhearted*, contemptuous, cruel, disdainful, habituated, hard-as-nails*, hard-bitten*, hard-boiled*, hardhearted*, heartless, impenetrable, impious, inaccessible, indurated, inured, irreverent, obdurate, obtuse, prepared, resistant, seasoned, steeled, toughened, unashamed, unbending, uncaring, uncompassionate, unemotional, unrepenting, unsubmissive; SEE CONCEPTS 404,542

hardhearted [*adj*] *cold, cruel*
brutish, callous, cold-blooded*, coldhearted*, hard, hard-boiled*, heartless, indifferent, inhuman, insensitive, intolerant, merciless, obdurate, pitiless, stony, uncaring, uncompassionate, unemotional, unfeeling, unkind, unsympathetic; SEE CONCEPTS 401,404

hard-line [*adj*] *firm*
adamant, hard-boiled*, hard-core, hard-nosed*, inflexible, militant, stand pat*, staunch, steadfast, stern, stiff, strict, unbending, uncompromising, ungiving, unyielding; SEE CONCEPTS 267,403,542

hardly [*adv*] *scarcely; with difficulty*
almost inconceivably, almost not, barely, by a hair, by no means, comparatively, detectably, faintly, gradually, imperceptibly, infrequently, just, little, no more than, not a bit, not at all, not by much, not likely, not markedly, not measurably, not much, not notably, not noticeably, not often, not quite, no way, once in a blue moon*, only, only just, perceptibly, practically, pretty near, rarely, scantly, seldom, simply, slightly,

somewhat, sparsely, sporadically, with trouble; SEE CONCEPTS 541,552,771

hard-nosed/hardheaded [*adj*] *stubborn*
astute, bullheaded*, hard*, hard-boiled*, headstrong, intractable, levelheaded, locked in*, mulish, obstinate, pertinacious, perverse, pigheaded*, practical, pragmatic, rational, realistic, resolute, sensible, shrewd, sober, stand pat, tough, tough-nut*, unsentimental, unyielding, willful; SEE CONCEPTS 404,542

hardship [*n*] *personal burden*
accident, adversity, affliction, asperity, austerity, calamity, case, catastrophe, curse, danger, destitution, difficulty, disaster, discomfort, distress, drudgery, fatigue, grief, grievance, hard knocks*, hazard, Herculean task*, injury, labor, mischance, misery, misfortune, need, oppression, peril, persecution, privation, rainy day*, rigor, rotten luck*, sorrow, suffering, toil, torment, tough break*, tough luck*, travail, trial, tribulation, trouble, uphill battle*, vicissitude, want, worry; SEE CONCEPTS 674,675

hardware [*n*] *tools; fittings, especially made of metal*
accouterments, appliances, fasteners, fixtures, household furnishings, housewares, implements, ironware, kitchenware, metalware, plumbing, utensils; SEE CONCEPTS 338,499

hardy [*adj*] *strong, tough*
able, able-bodied, acclimatized, brawny, burly, capable, enduring, firm, fit, fresh, hale, hardened, healthy, hearty, hefty, indefatigable, in fine fettle*, in good condition, in good shape, inured, lusty, mighty, muscular, physically fit, powerful, resistant, robust, rugged, seasoned, solid, sound, stalwart, staunch, stout, sturdy, substantial, tenacious, unflagging, vigorous, well; SEE CONCEPTS 314,485,489

harebrained [*adj*] *stupid, unthinking*
absurd, asinine, barmy, bizarre, careless, changeable, crazy, dizzy*, empty-headed*, featherbrained*, flighty, foolish, frivolous, giddy, half-baked*, heedless, inane*, irresponsible, loony*, mindless, preposterous, rash, rattlebrained, reckless, scatterbrained*, unstable, unsteady, wacky*, wild; SEE CONCEPTS 402,529

harlot [*n*] *prostitute*
call girl, concubine, courtesan, fallen woman*, floozy*, hooker, hussy, lady of the evening, loose woman, nymphomaniac*, painted woman, slut, streetwalker, strumpet, tramp, whore; SEE CONCEPTS 348,412,415,419

harm [*n*] *injury, evil*
abuse, banefulness, damage, deleteriousness, detriment, disservice, foul play*, hurt, ill, immorality, impairment, infliction, iniquity, loss, marring, mischance, mischief, misfortune, misuse, noxiousness, outrage, perniciousness, prejudice, ravage, ruin, ruination, sabotage, sin, sinfulness, vandalism, vice, violence, wear and tear*, wickedness, wrong; SEE CONCEPTS 309,674,728

harm [*v*] *injure; cause evil*
abuse, blemish, bruise, cripple, crush, damage, dilapidate, discommode, disserve, do violence to, dump on*, get, hurt, ill-treat, impair, incommode, inconvenience, louse up*, maim, maltreat, mangle, mar, mess up*, misuse, molest, muck up*, mutilate, nick, outrage, prejudice, put down, ruin, sabotage, sap*, scathe, shatter, shock, spoil,

stab, tarnish, total, trample, traumatize, tweak*, undermine, vandalize, vitiate, wing*, wound, wreck, wrench, wrong, zing*; SEE CONCEPTS 7,19,246,313

harmful [*adj*] *injurious, hurtful*
adverse, bad, baleful, baneful, calamitous, cataclysmic, catastrophic, consumptive, corroding, corrupting, crippling, damaging, deleterious, destructive, detrimental, dire, disadvantageous, disastrous, evil, harassing, incendiary, inimical, internecine, malefic, malicious, malignant, menacing, mischievous, murderous, nocuous, noxious, painful, pernicious, pestiferous, pestilential, risky, ruinous, sinful, sinister, subversive, toxic, undermining, unhealthy, unsafe, unwholesome, virulent; SEE CONCEPT 537

harmless [*adj*] *not injurious or dangerous*
controllable, disarmed, gentle, guiltless, hurtless, innocent, innocuous, innoxious, inoffensive, inoperative, kind, manageable, naive, nonirritating, nontoxic, painless, paper-tiger*, powerless, pussycat*, reliable, safe, sanitary, simple, soft*, softie*, sound, sure, trustworthy, unobjectionable, unoffensive; SEE CONCEPT 537

harmonious [*adj*] *agreeable, corresponding; friendly*
accordant, adapted, amicable, balanced, compatible, concordant, congenial, congruous, consonant, coordinated, cordial, dulcet, euphonious, harmonic, harmonizing, in accord, in chorus, in concert, in harmony, in step, in tune, in unison, like, matching, mellifluous, melodic, melodious, mix, musical, of one mind*, on same wavelength*, peaceful, rhythmical, silvery, similar, simpatico, sonorous, suitable, sweet-sounding, symmetrical, sympathetic, symphonic, symphonious, tuneful; SEE CONCEPT 563

harmonize [*v*] *correspond, match*
accord, adapt, adjust, agree, arrange, attune, be in unison, be of one mind*, blend, carol, chime with, cohere, combine, compose, cooperate, coordinate, correlate, fit in with*, integrate, orchestrate, proportion, reconcile, reconciliate, relate, set, sing, suit, symphonize, synthesize, tune, unify, unite; SEE CONCEPTS 77,664

harmony [*n1*] *social agreement*
accord, affinity, amicability, amity, compatibility, concord, conformity, consensus, consistency, cooperation, correspondence, empathy, friendship, good will, kinship, like-mindedness, meeting of minds*, peace, rapport, sympathy, tranquility, unanimity, understanding, unity; SEE CONCEPT 388

harmony [*n2*] *correspondence, balance*
accord, agreement, articulation, chime, concord, concordance, conformance, conformity, congruity, consistency, consonance, fitness, form, integration, integrity, oneness, order, parallelism, proportion, regularity, suitability, symmetry, togetherness, tune, unity; SEE CONCEPT 664

harmony [*n3*] *musical accordance*
arrangement, attunement, blend, blending, chime, chord, chorus, composition, concentus, concert, concinnity, concurrence, consonance, diapason, euphony, harmonics, mellifluousness, melodiousness, melody, organum, overtone, piece, polyphony, richness, symphony, triad, tune, tunefulness, unison, unity; SEE CONCEPTS 65,262,595

harness [*n*] *gear for controlling an animal*
belt, equipment, strap, tack, tackle, trappings; SEE CONCEPT 496

harness [*v*] *rein in; control*
accouter, apply, bind, bridle, channel, check, cinch, collar, constrain, couple, curb, domesticate, employ, equip, exploit, fasten, fetter, fit, furnish, gear, govern, hitch, hold, leash, limit, make productive, mobilize, muzzle, outfit, put in harness, render useful, rig, saddle, secure, strap, tackle, tame, tie, utilize, yoke; SEE CONCEPTS 94,130,191

harried [*adj*] *pressured*
agitated, anxious, at wit's end*, beset, bothered, distressed, harassed, hard-pressed, stressed, troubled, worried; SEE CONCEPTS 403,690

harrowing [*adj*] *dangerous, frightening*
agonizing, alarming, chilling, distressing, disturbing, excruciating, heartbreaking, heart-rending, nerve-racking, painful, racking, soaring, tearing, terrifying, tormenting, torturing, torturous, traumatic; SEE CONCEPTS 529,548

harry [*v*] *pester, annoy*
attack, badger, bedevil, beleaguer, chivy, depredate, devastate, disturb, fret, gnaw, harass, hassle, irk, irritate, lay waste, molest, persecute, perturb, pillage, plague, plunder, ravage, sack, tease, torment, trouble, upset, vex, worry; SEE CONCEPTS 7,19

harsh [*adj1*] *rough, crude (to the senses)*
acrid, asperous, astringent, bitter, bleak, cacophonous, caterwauling, clashing, coarse, cracked, craggy, creaking, croaking, disagreeing, discordant, dissonant, disturbing, earsplitting, flat, glaring, grating, grim, guttural, hard, hoarse, incompatible, jagged, jangling, jarring, noisy, not smooth, off-key*, out-of-key*, out-of-tune*, rasping, raucous, rigid, rugged, rusty, screeching, severe, sharp, sour, strident, stridulous, tuneless, uneven, unlevel, unmelodious, unmusical, unrelenting; SEE CONCEPTS 537,569

harsh [*adj2*] *nasty, abusive*
austere, bitter, brutal, comfortless, cruel, cussed, discourteous, dour, grim, gruff, hairy*, hard, hard-boiled, hard-nosed*, hard-shell*, mean, pitiless, punitive, relentless, rude, ruthless, severe, sharp, stern, stringent, tough, uncivil, unfeeling, ungracious, unkind, unpleasant, unrelenting, wicked; SEE CONCEPTS 267,542

harum-scarum [*adj*] *reckless*
carefree, careless, daring, disorderly, erratic, flighty, foolhardy, giddy, haphazard, hasty, imprudent, irresponsible, light-minded, negligent, rash, regardless, romping, scatty, thoughtless, wild; SEE CONCEPTS 401,542

harvest [*n*] *crops; taking in of crops*
autumn, by-product, consequence, cropping, effect, fall, fruitage, fruition, garnering, gathering, harvesting, harvest-time, ingathering, intake, output, produce, reaping, repercussion, result, return, season, storing, summer, yield, yielding; SEE CONCEPTS 257,338,429

harvest [*v*] *gathering of produce*
accumulate, acquire, amass, bin, cache, collect, crop, cull, cut, garner, gather, get, glean, harrow, hoard, mow, pick, pile up, plow, pluck, reap, squirrel*, stash, store, stow, strip, take in; SEE CONCEPTS 142,257

hash [*n*] *mess, mix-up*
assortment, clutter, confusion, hodgepodge*,

hotchpotch*, jumble, litter, medley, melange, miscellany, mishmash*, muddle*, salmagundi*, shambles*, stew*; SEE CONCEPTS *260,432*

hashish [*n*] *cannabis resin*
black hash*, black oil*, cannabis, dope, drug, ganja*, grass*, hash, hemp, marijuana, narcotic, pot*; SEE CONCEPT *307*

hassle [*n*] *problem, fight*
altercation, argument, bickering, bother, clamor, commotion, difficulty, disagreement, dispute, inconvenience, quarrel, row, run-in*, squabble, struggle, trial, trouble, try, tumult, turmoil, tussle, uproar, upset, whirl, wrangle; SEE CONCEPTS *46,106,674*

hassle [*v*] *bother, harass*
annoy, argue, argufy, badger, bedevil, beleaguer, bicker, dispute, dun, harry, hound, pester, plague, quibble, squabble, worry, wrangle; SEE CONCEPTS *14,16,46*

haste [*n*] *extreme speed, hurry*
alacrity, briskness, bustle, carelessness, celerity, dash, dispatch, drive, expedition, expeditiousness, fleetness, flurry, foolhardiness, hastiness, heedlessness, hurly-burly*, hurriedness, hustle, hustling, impatience, impetuosity, incautiousness, nimbleness, pace, precipitancy, precipitateness, prematureness, press, promptitude, promptness, quickness, rapidity, rapidness, rashness, recklessness, rush, scamper, scramble, scurry, scuttle, swiftness, urgency, velocity; SEE CONCEPTS *755,818*

hasten [*v*] *speed something; hurry*
accelerate, advance, bolt, bound, burn, bustle, clip*, cover ground*, dash, dispatch, expedite, express, flee, fly, gallop, get cracking*, get the lead out*, goad, haste, hie, hustle, leap, make haste, make tracks*, move quickly, not lose a minute*, pace, plunge, precipitate, press, push, quicken, race, run, rush, scamper, scoot, scurry, scuttle, shake a leg*, skip, sprint, spurt, step on it*, step up*, take wing*, tear, trot, urge, waste no time*, whip around; SEE CONCEPTS *150,152*

hastily [*adv*] *with great speed*
agilely, apace, carelessly, double-quick, expeditiously, fast, flat-out*, heedlessly, hurriedly, impetuously, impulsively, lickety-split*, nimbly, on spur of the moment*, posthaste, precipitately, prematurely, promptly, quickly, rapidly, rashly, recklessly, speedily, straightaway, subito, suddenly, swiftly, thoughtlessly, too quickly, unpremeditatedly; SEE CONCEPTS *544,588*

hasty [*adj*] *speedy; without much thought*
abrupt, agile, brash, breakneck*, brief, brisk, careless, chop-chop*, cursory, eager, expeditious, fast, fiery, fleet, fleeting, foolhardy, harefooted*, headlong, heedless, hurried, ill-advised, impatient, impetuous, impulsive, incautious, inconsiderate, madcap*, on the double*, passing, PDQ*, perfunctory, precipitate, prompt, pronto*, quick, quickened, quickie, rapid, rash, reckless, rushed, short, slambang*, slapdash*, snappy*, sudden, superficial, swift, thoughtless, urgent; SEE CONCEPTS *542,588,799*

hat [*n*] *covering for the head*
boater, bonnet, bowler, bucket, chapeau, fedora, headgear, headpiece, helmet, lid*, millinery, Panama, sailor*, skimmer, sombrero, Stetson, stove pipe*, straw*, tam, tam o'shanter*, tengallon*, topper*; SEE CONCEPT *451*

hatch [*v*] *create, plan*
bear, brainstorm*, breed, bring forth, brood, cause, come up with, conceive, concoct, contrive, cook up*, design, devise, dream up*, engender, formulate, generate, get up, give birth, incubate, induce, invent, lay eggs, make, make up, occasion, originate, parent, plot, prepare, procreate, produce, project, provoke, scheme, set, sire, spawn, spitball*, think up*, throw together*, trump up*, whip up*, work up*; SEE CONCEPTS *36,173,251*

hate [*n*] *extreme dislike*
abhorrence, abomination, anathema, animosity, animus, antagonism, antipathy, aversion, bête noire*, black beast*, bother, bugbear*, detestation, disgust, enmity, execration, frost*, grievance, gripe, hatred, horror, hostility, ill will, irritant, loathing, malevolence, malignity, mislike, nasty look, no love lost*, nuisance, objection, odium, pain, rancor, rankling, repugnance, repulsion, resentment, revenge, revulsion, scorn, spite, trouble, venom; SEE CONCEPT *29*

hate [*v*] *dislike very strongly*
abhor, abominate, allergic to*, anathematize, bear a grudge against, be disgusted with, be hostile to, be loath, be reluctant, be repelled by, be sick of, be sorry, can't stand*, contemn, curse, deprecate, deride, despise, detest, disapprove, disdain, disfavor, disparage, down on*, execrate, feel malice to, have an aversion to*, have enough of*, have no use for*, loathe, look down on, nauseate*, not care for*, object to, recoil from, scorn, shudder at, shun, spit upon*, spurn; SEE CONCEPT *29*

hateful [*adj*] *nasty, obnoxious*
abhorrent, abominable, accursed, awful, bitter, blasted, catty*, confounded, cursed, cussed, damnable, damned, despicable, despiteful, detestable, disgusting, evil, execrable, forbidding, foul, gross, heinous, horrid, infamous, invidious, loathsome, malevolent, malign, mean, odious, offensive, ornery*, pesky, pestiferous, repellent, repugnant, repulsive, resentful, revolting, shuddersome, spiteful, uncool*, undesirable, vicious, vile; SEE CONCEPTS *267,404*

hatred [*n*] *severe dislike*
abhorrence, abomination, acrimony, alienation, allergy to*, animosity, animus, antagonism, antipathy, aversion, bitterness, coldness, contempt, detestation, disapproval, disfavor, disgust, displeasure, distaste, enmity, envy, execration, grudge, hard feelings*, hate, horror, hostility, ignominy, ill will, invidiousness, loathing, malevolence, malice, malignance, military, no use for*, odium, pique, prejudice, rancor, repugnance, repulsion, revenge, revulsion, scorn, spite, spleen, venom; SEE CONCEPT *29*

haughtiness [*n*] *air of supremacy*
aloofness, arrogance, conceit, contempt, contemptuousness, disdain, disdainfulness, hauteur, insolence, loftiness, pomposity, pride, snobbishness, superbity, superciliousness; SEE CONCEPT *633*

haughty [*adj*] *arrogant*
assuming, cavalier*, conceited, contemptuous, detached, disdainful, distant, egotistic, egotistical, high, high and mighty*, hoity-toity*, imperious, indifferent, lofty, on high horse*, overbearing, overweening, proud, reserved, scornful, sniffy*, snobbish, snooty*, snotty*,

ha
ha

stuck-up*, supercilious, superior, uppity*; SEE CONCEPT *401*

haul [*n*] *something obtained or moved*
booty, burden, cargo, catch, find, freight, gain, harvest, lading, load, loot*, payload*, spoils, takings*, yield; SEE CONCEPTS *337,338*

haul [*v*] *move, pull to another spot*
back, boost, bring, buck, carry, cart, convey, drag, draw, elevate, gun, heave, heel, hoist, hump, jag, lift, lug, pack, piggy back*, raise, rake, remove, ride, shift, shlep*, shoulder, tote, tow, trail, transport, trawl, truck, tug; SEE CONCEPTS *147,148*

haunt [*n*] *place for socializing*
abode, bar, clubhouse, cubbyhole*, den, dwelling, gathering place, habitat, hangout*, headquarters, home, lair, living quarters, locality, meeting place, niche, place, purlieu, range, rendezvous, resort, retreat, site, stomping ground*, trysting place, watering hole*; SEE CONCEPTS *435,516*

haunt [*v1*] *visit as a spirit*
agitate, agonize, annoy, appall, appear, bedevil, be ever present, beset, besiege, come back, disquiet, dwell, float, frighten, harass, harrow, hound*, hover, infest, inhabit, intrude, madden, manifest, materialize, molest, nettle, obsess, overrun, permeate, pervade, pester, plague, possess, prey on, rack*, reappear, recur, return, rise, spook*, stay with, tease, terrify, terrorize, torment, trouble, vex, voodoo*, walk, weigh on, worry; SEE CONCEPT *14*

haunt [*v2*] *spend a lot of time at*
affect, frequent, habituate, hang about*, hang around*, hang out*, infest, repair, resort, tarry at, visit; SEE CONCEPT *384*

haunting [*adj*] *unforgettable*
eerie, memorable, nagging, nostalgic, obsessive, ongoing, persistent, recurrent, repeated, spooky; SEE CONCEPTS *529,537*

hauteur [*n*] *arrogance*
airs, audacity, conceit, conceitedness, condescension, contempt, disdain, disdainfulness, egotism, gall, haughtiness, high-handedness, nerve, pomposity, pompousness, presumption, pride, self-importance, snobbishness, vanity; SEE CONCEPTS *411,633*

have [*v1*] *be in possession*
accept, acquire, admit, annex, bear, carry, chalk up, compass, corner, enjoy, gain, get, get hands on*, get hold of*, have in hand, hog*, hold, include, keep, land, latch on to*, lock up*, obtain, occupy, own, pick up, possess, procure, receive, retain, secure, sit on*, take, take in, teem with; SEE CONCEPTS *124,142,710*

have [*v2*] *endure, bear*
allow, become, be compelled to, be forced to, be one's duty to, be up to, consider, enjoy, entertain*, experience, fall on, feel, know, leave, let, meet with, must, need, ought, permit, put up with*, rest with, see, should, suffer, sustain, think about, tolerate, undergo; SEE CONCEPTS *23,83,646*

have [*v3*] *contain*
comprehend, comprise, embody, embrace, encompass, include, involve, subsume, take in; SEE CONCEPTS *642,742*

have [*v4*] *cheat, trick*
buy off*, deceive, dupe*, fix*, fool, outfox, outmaneuver, outsmart, outwit, overreach, swindle,

take in*, tamper with, undo*; SEE CONCEPTS *59,192*

have [*v5*] *bring into the world*
bear, beget, bring forth, deliver, give birth; SEE CONCEPT *374*

have a ball [*v*] *have fun*
beat the drum*, cut loose, enjoy, feast, get down*, get it on*, go to town*, jubilate, kick up one's heels*, let loose*, let off steam*, live it up*, make merry, paint the town red*, party, raise hell*, raise the roof*, rejoice, revel, revere; SEE CONCEPT *377*

haven [*n*] *refuge, port*
anchorage, asylum, cover, covert, harbor, harborage, retreat, roadstead, sanctuary, sanctum, shelter; SEE CONCEPTS *435,515*

have someone's number [*v*] *know someone's motives*
be onto someone, be wise to someone*, have someone pegged*, have someone sized · up*, know what makes someone tick*, read someone; SEE CONCEPTS *15,18,37*

havoc [*n*] *chaotic situation*
calamity, cataclysm, catastrophe, chaos, confusion, damage, desolation, despoiling, destruction, devastation, dilapidation, disorder, disruption, loss, mayhem, plunder, rack and ruin*, ravages, ruination, shambles*, vandalism, waste, wreck, wreckage; SEE CONCEPT *674*

hawker [*n*] *peddler*
colporteur, costermonger, huckster, pitchperson, salesperson, seller, street seller, street vendor; SEE CONCEPTS *347,348*

hayseed [*n*] *bumpkin, yokel*
backwoodsman/woman, boor*, clodhopper*, country boy/girl, country bumpkin, country cousin*, hick*, hillbilly, rustic; SEE CONCEPT *413*

haywire [*adj*] *broken; crazy*
amiss, amok, batty, berserk, bonkers*, chaotic, confused, cracked, crazed, defective, disordered, disorganized, erratic, flipped, in a mess*, in pieces, insane, mad, messy, nuts, orderless, out of order, out of whack*, out to lunch*, psycho*, schizo*, screwball*, screwy*, touched*, unbalanced, unglued*, unhinged, wacky; SEE CONCEPTS *403,485*

hazard [*n1*] *danger*
double trouble*, dynamite, endangerment, hot potato*, imperilment, jeopardy, peril, risk, risky business*, thin ice*, threat; SEE CONCEPT *675*

hazard [*n2*] *luck, chance*
accident, adventure, coincidence, dynamite, fling*, fluke*, go*, hundred-to-one*, long shot, lucky break*, lucky hit*, misfortune, mishap, possibility, risk, risky business*, stroke of luck*, toss-up, venture, wager, way the ball bounces*, way the cookie crumbles*; SEE CONCEPT *693*

hazard [*v*] *take a chance; risk*
adventure, conjecture, dare, endanger, gamble, go for broke*, go out on limb*, guess, imperil, jeopardize, presume, proffer, skate on thin ice*, speculate, stake, submit, suppose, take a plunge*, throw out, try, venture, volunteer, wager; SEE CONCEPTS *28,87*

hazardous [*adj*] *dangerous, unpredictable*
chancy, dicey*, difficult, hairy*, haphazard, hot*, insecure, parlous, perilous, precarious, risky, touchy, uncertain, unhealthy, unsafe, unsound, venturesome, wicked; SEE CONCEPT *548*

haze [n] *cloudy air*
brume, cloud, dimness, film, fog, fumes, ground clouds, haziness, indistinctness, miasma, mist, murk, obscurity, smog, smokiness, smother, soup*, steam, vapor; SEE CONCEPT 524

hazy [adj1] *cloudy*
bleared, bleary, blurred, blurry, clouded, crepuscular, dim, dull, dusky, faint, foggy, frosty, fuliginous, fumy, fuzzy, gauzy, indefinite, indistinct, misty, murky, mushy*, nebulous, obfuscated, obfuscous, obscure, opaque, overcast, rimy, screened, shadowy, smoggy, smoky, soupy*, steaming, thick, unclear, vague, vaporous, veiled; SEE CONCEPT 525

hazy [adj2] *confused*
dazed, dizzy, dreamy, groggy, ill-defined, indefinite, indistinct, muddled, murky, nebulous, obscure, stuporous, tranced, uncertain, unclear, unintelligible, unsound, vague, whirling; SEE CONCEPTS 402,529

head [adj] *most important; chief*
arch, champion, first, foremost, front, highest, leading, main, pioneer, preeminent, premier, prime, principal, stellar, supreme, topmost; SEE CONCEPTS 568,574

head [n1] *top part of an animate body*
attic*, belfry*, brain, coconut*, cranium, crown, dome*, gray matter, noggin*, noodle*, pate, scalp, skull, thinker*, think tank*, top story*, upper story*, upstairs*; SEE CONCEPT 392

head [n2] *leader*
boss, captain, chief, chieftain, commander, commanding officer, director, dominator, executive, honcho*, lead-off person*, manager, officer, president, principal, superintendent, supervisor, top dog*; SEE CONCEPT 347

head [n3] *top part*
apex, banner, beak, bill, cap, cork, crest, crown, heading, headline, height, peak, pitch, point, promontory, streamer, summit, tip, vertex; SEE CONCEPT 836

head [n4] *front, beginning*
commencement, first place, fore, forefront, fountainhead, origin, rise, source, start, van, vanguard; SEE CONCEPTS 648,727

head [n5] *ability, intelligence*
aptitude, aptness, bent, brains, capacity, faculty, flair, genius, gift, intellect, knack, mentality, mind, talent, thought, turn, understanding; SEE CONCEPTS 409,630

head [n6] *turning point*
acme, climax, conclusion, crisis, culmination, end; SEE CONCEPT 832

head [v] *manage, oversee*
address, be first, be in charge, command, control, direct, dominate, go first, govern, guide, hold sway over*, lead, lead the way*, pioneer, precede, rule, run, supervise; SEE CONCEPT 117

headache [n1] *difficulty, problem*
annoyance, bane, bother, dilemma, frustration, hassle, hindrance, inconvenience, nuisance, pain in the neck*, pest, predicament, quagmire, trouble, vexation, worry; SEE CONCEPTS 674,677

headache [n2] *migraine*
cephalalgia, megrim, pounding head, splitting headache, throbbing head; SEE CONCEPTS 316,728

headhunting [n] *recruiting*
executive recruiting, executive recruitment, recruitment, talent search; SEE CONCEPT 351

heading [n1] *title*
caption, description, descriptor, headline, label, legend, lemma, rubric; SEE CONCEPT 283

heading [n2] *course*
aim, angle, bearing, compass reading, direction, line, point, point of compass, route, track, trajectory, way; SEE CONCEPTS 501,514

headlong [adj] *dangerous, reckless*
abrupt, brash, breakneck, daredevil, daring, foolhardy, hasty, hurried, impetuous, impulsive, inconsiderate, precipitant, precipitate, rash, rough, rushing, sudden, tempestuous, thoughtless; SEE CONCEPTS 542,588

headquarters [n] *center of operations*
base, base of operations, central station, command post, company headquarters, high command, HQ, main office, nerve center; SEE CONCEPTS 312,439,441,448,449

headstrong [adj] *stubborn*
bullheaded*, contrary, determined, foolhardy, froward, hard-core*, hard-nosed, hard-shell*, heedless, imprudent, impulsive, intractable, locked-in*, mule, mulish, murder, obstinate, perverse, pig-headed*, rash, reckless, refractory, self-willed, strong-minded, uncontrollable, ungovernable, unruly, unyielding, willful; SEE CONCEPTS 401,403

headway [n] *progress*
advance, advancement, anabasis, ground, improvement, increase, march, proficiency, progression, promotion, way; SEE CONCEPTS 230,704

heady [adj] *thrilling, intoxicating*
exciting, exhilarating, inebriating, overwhelming, potent, powerful, provocative, spirituous, stimulating, strong; SEE CONCEPT 529

heal [v] *cure, recover*
alleviate, ameliorate, attend, bring around, compose, conciliate, convalesce, doctor, dress, fix, free, get well, harmonize, improve, knit, make healthy, make sound, make well, make whole, medicate, meliorate, mend, minister to, patch up, physic, put on feet again*, reanimate, rebuild, reconcile, regenerate, rehabilitate, rejuvenate, remedy, renovate, repair, restore, resuscitate, revive, revivify, salve, set, settle, soothe, treat; SEE CONCEPTS 308,310

healer [n] *faith healer*
curer, doctor, medicine man, mender, physician, shaman, therapist; SEE CONCEPT 357

health [n] *physical, mental wellness*
bloom*, clean bill*, complexion, constitution, energy, eupepsia, euphoria, fettle, fine feather*, fitness, form, good condition, haleness, hardihood, hardiness, healthfulness, healthiness, lustiness, pink*, prime*, robustness, salubriousness, salubrity, shape, soundness, stamina, state, strength, tone, tonicity, top form, verdure, vigor, well-being, wholeness; SEE CONCEPTS 316,410,720

healthful/healthy [adj1] *good for one's wellness*
advantageous, aiding, aseptic, beneficial, benign, body-building, bracing, cathartic, clean, compensatory, conducive, corrective, desirable, disease-free, energy-giving, fresh, harmless, healing, health-giving, helpful, hygienic, innocuous, invigorating, mitigative, nourishing, nutritious, nutritive, profitable, pure, restorative, salubrious, salutary, sanatory, sanitary, stimulating, sustain-

ing, tonic, unadulterated, unpolluted, untainted, useful, wholesome; SEE CONCEPT 537

healthy [adj2] in good condition
able-bodied, active, all right, athletic, blooming, bright-eyed*, bushy-tailed*, chipper*, firm, fit, flourishing, fresh, full of life*, hale, hardy, healthful, hearty, husky, in fine feather*, in fine fettle*, in good shape, in the pink*, lively, lusty, muscular, normal, physically fit, potent, restored, robust, rosy-cheeked*, safe and sound*, sound, stout, strong, sturdy, tough, trim, unimpaired, vigorous, virile, well, whole; SEE CONCEPTS 314,403

heap [n] pile, accumulation
abundance, agglomeration, aggregation, a lot*, amassment, assemblage, bank, batch, bulk, bunch, bundle, cargo, clump, cluster, collection, concentration, congeries, deposit, fullness, gathering, gobs*, great deal, harvest, haul, hill, hoard, jumble, load, lot, lots, lump, mass, million, mint, mound, mountain, much, ocean, oodles*, plenty, pot, profusion, quantity, scad*, stack, stock, stockpile, store, sum, thousand, ton, total, trillion, volume, whole; SEE CONCEPTS 432,787

heap [v] amass, collect in pile
accumulate, add, arrange, augment, bank, bunch, concentrate, deposit, dump, fill, fill up, gather, group, hoard, increase, load, lump, mass, mound, pack, stack, stockpile, store, swell; SEE CONCEPT 109

hear [v1] detect by perceiving sound
apprehend, attend, auscultate, be all ears*, become aware, catch, descry, devour, eavesdrop, get*, get an earful*, get wind of*, give an audience to*, give attention, give ears*, hark, hearken, heed, listen, make out*, overhear, pick up*, read, strain, take in*; SEE CONCEPTS 590,596

hear [v2] become aware of information
apperceive, ascertain, be advised, be informed, be led to believe, be told of, catch, catch on, descry, determine, discover, find out, gather, get the picture*, get wind of*, get wise to*, glean, have on good authority*, learn, pick up*, receive, see, tumble*, understand, unearth; SEE CONCEPTS 15,31

hearing [n1] ability to perceive sound
audition, auditory, auditory range, detecting, distinguishing, ear, earshot, effect, extent, faculty, hearing distance, listening, perception, range, reach, recording, sense; SEE CONCEPT 597

hearing [n2] opportunity to present views, knowledge, or skill
admittance, attendance, attention, audience, audit, audition, chance, conference, congress, consultation, council, discussion, inquiry, interview, investigation, meeting, negotiation, notice, parley, performance, presentation, reception, review, test, trial, tryout; SEE CONCEPTS 48,103,357,693

hearsay [n] unsubstantiated information
clothesline*, comment, cry, gossip, grapevine*, leak*, mere talk*, noise*, report, rumble*, rumor, scandal, scuttlebutt*, talk, talk of the town*, word of mouth*; SEE CONCEPTS 51,278

heart [n1] person's emotions
affection, benevolence, character, compassion, concern, disposition, feeling, gusto, humanity, inclination, love, nature, palate, pity, relish, response, sensitivity, sentiment, soul, sympathy,

temperament, tenderness, understanding, zest; SEE CONCEPT 410

heart [n2] courage
boldness, bravery, dauntlessness, fortitude, gallantry, guts*, mettle, mind, moxie*, nerve, pluck, purpose, resolution, soul, spirit, spunk*, will; SEE CONCEPT 411

heart [n3] essence, central part
basic, bosom, bottom line*, center, coal and ice*, core, crux, focal point, focus, gist, hub, kernel, marrow, middle, nitty-gritty*, nub, nucleus, pith, polestar*, quick*, quintessence, root, seat, soul; SEE CONCEPT 826

heart [n4] blood-pumping organ in an animate being
cardiac organ, clock*, ticker*, vascular organ; SEE CONCEPTS 393,420

heartache [n] anguish, sorrow
affliction, agony, bitterness, broken heart, dejection, depression, despair, despondency, distress, dolor, grief, heartbreak, heavy heart, hurting, misery, pang, remorse, sadness, suffering, torment, torture; SEE CONCEPT 410

heart attack [n] acute myocardial infarction
angina pectoris, cardiac arrest, cardiovascular disease, coronary, coronary thrombosis; SEE CONCEPT 308

heartbreak [n] mental or emotional misery
affliction, agony, anguish, bale, bitterness, broken heart, care, desolation, despair, distress, grief, heartache, heartsickness, heavy heart*, pain, regret, remorse, rue, sorrow, suffering, torment, torture, woe; SEE CONCEPTS 410,728

heartbreaking [adj] disappointing
affecting, afflictive, agonizing, bitter, calamitous, cheerless, deplorable, dire, distressing, grievous, heart-rending, joyless, lamentable, moving, pitiful, poignant, regrettable, sad, touching, tragic, unfortunate; SEE CONCEPTS 529,537

hearten [v] raise someone's spirits
animate, arouse, assure, buck up, buoy, cheer, comfort, console, embolden, encourage, energize, enliven, incite, inspire, inspirit, rally, reassure, revivify, rouse, steel, stimulate, stir, strengthen; SEE CONCEPTS 7,22

heartfelt [adj] genuine
ardent, bona fide, cordial, deep, devout, earnest, fervent, heart-to-heart, hearty, honest, profound, sincere, true, unfeigned, warm, wholehearted; SEE CONCEPTS 267,582

heartless [adj] without feeling; cold
brutal, callous, cold-blooded*, cold fish*, cold-hearted*, cruel, hard, hard as nails*, hardboiled*, hard-hearted*, harsh, inhuman, insensitive, merciless, obdurate, pitiless, ruthless, savage, thick-skinned*, uncaring, uncompassionate, unemotional, unfeeling, unkind, unsympathetic; SEE CONCEPTS 401,542

heartrending [adj] arousing deep sympathy
agonizing, distressing, doleful, excruciating, harrowing, heartbreaking, heartsickening, moving, piteous, pitiful, sad, tear-jerking, touching, tragic; SEE CONCEPTS 529,537

heartsick [adj] despondent
all torn up*, blue, bummed-out*, dejected, depressed, despairing, disappointed, disconsolate, disheartened, down, forlorn, grieving, heavy-hearted, inconsolable, low, melancholy, mournful, sad, unhappy, woebegone; SEE CONCEPT 403

heartwarming [*adj*] *pleasant*
cheering, encouraging, exhilarating, gladdening, heartening, heartfelt, inspiring, joyous, loving, stirring, sweet; SEE CONCEPTS *542,548,572*

hearty [*adj1*] *energetic, enthusiastic*
affable, animated, ardent, avid, back-slapping*, cheerful, cheery, cordial, deep, deepest, deep-felt, devout, eager, earnest, ebullient, effusive, exuberant, frank, friendly, gay, generous, genial, genuine, glad, gushing, heartfelt, honest, impassioned, intense, jolly, jovial, neighborly, passionate, profuse, real, responsive, sincere, true, unfeigned, unreserved, unrestrained, vivacious, warm, warmhearted, wholehearted, zealous; SEE CONCEPTS *401,542*

hearty [*adj2*] *healthy, full*
active, ample, energetic, filling, glowing, good, hale, hardy, nourishing, robust, sizable, solid, sound, square, strong, substantial, vigorous, well; SEE CONCEPTS *314,773*

heat [*n1*] *high temperature*
calefaction, calidity, dog days*, fever, fieriness, heatwave, hotness, hot spell, hot weather, incalescence, incandescence, sultriness, swelter, torridity, torridness, warmness, warmth; SEE CONCEPT *610*

heat [*n2*] *anger, passion*
agitation, ardor, desire, earnestness, excitement, ferocity, fervor, fever, fury, impetuosity, intensity, rage, vehemence, violence, warmth, zeal; SEE CONCEPTS *410,657*

heat [*v*] *make or become hot*
bake, bask, blaze, boil, broil, calorify, chafe, char, enflame, enkindle, fire, flame, flush, frizzle, fry, glow, grill, grow hot, grow warm, ignite, incandesce, incinerate, inflame, kindle, melt, oxidate, oxidize, perspire, raise the temperature, reheat, roast, scald, scorch, sear, seethe, set on fire, singe, smelt, steam, sun, swelter, tepefy, thaw, toast, warm, warm up; SEE CONCEPTS *255,469*

heated [*adj1*] *angry*
acrimonious, ardent, avid, bitter, excited, fervent, fervid, feverish, fierce, fiery, frenzied, furious, hectic, impassioned, indignant, intense, irate, ireful, mad, passionate, raging, stormy, tempestuous, vehement, violent, wrathful; SEE CONCEPT *267*

heated [*adj2*] *warmed*
baked, baking, boiling, broiled, broiling, burned, burning, burnt, cooked, fiery, fired, fried, hot, parched, scalding, scorched, scorching, sizzling, toasted; SEE CONCEPT *605*

heathen [*adj*] *not believing in Christian god*
agnostic, atheistic, barbarian, godless, idolatrous, infidel, irreligious, nonbeliever, pagan, profane, skeptic; SEE CONCEPT *545*

heave [*v1*] *lift, throw with effort*
boost, cast, chuck, drag, elevate, fling, haul, heft, hoist, hurl, launch, pitch, pull, raise, send, sling, toss, tug; SEE CONCEPTS *196,222*

heave [*v2*] *discharge with force; expel from digestive system by mouth*
billow, breathe, cast, dilate, disgorge, exhale, expand, gag, groan, huff, palpitate, pant, puff, puke*, retch, rise, sign, sob, spew, spit up, surge, suspire, swell, throb, throw up, upchuck*, vomit; SEE CONCEPTS *163,179*

heaven [*n*] *place where God lives; wonderful feeling*
afterworld, Arcadia, atmosphere, azure*, beyond, bliss, Canaan, dreamland, ecstasy, Elysium, empyrean, enchantment, eternal home, eternal rest, eternity, fairyland*, felicity, firmament, glory, great unknown*, happiness, happy hunting ground*, harmony, heights, hereafter, immortality, kingdom, kingdom come, life everlasting, life to come, next world, nirvana, paradise, pearly gates*, promised land*, rapture, Shangri-la*, sky*, the blue*, transport, upstairs*, Utopia, wonderland*, Zion; SEE CONCEPTS *370,410,435*

heavenly [*adj*] *very pleasant*
adorable, alluring, ambrosial, angelic, beatific, beautiful, blessed, blissful, celestial, cherubic, darling, delectable, delicious, delightful, divine, empyrean, enjoyable, entrancing, excellent, exquisite, extraterrestrial, glorious, godlike, holy, immortal, lovely, luscious, lush, paradisaical, rapturous, ravishing, scrumptious, seraphic, sublime, superhuman, supernal, supernatural, sweet, wonderful, yummy; SEE CONCEPTS *537,572*

heavy [*adj1*] *having great weight*
abundant, ample, awkward, beefy*, big, built, bulky, burdensome, chunky*, considerable, copious, corpulent, cumbersome, cumbrous, elephantine, enceinte, excessive, expectant, fat, fleshy, gravid, gross*, hefty, huge, laden, large, lead-footed*, loaded, lumbering, massive, obese, oppressed, overweight, parturient, ponderous, porcine, portly, pregnant, stout, substantial, top-heavy, two-ton*, unmanageable, unwieldy, weighted, weighty, zaftig*; SEE CONCEPT *491*

heavy [*adj2*] *difficult, severe*
abstruse, acroamatic, arduous, boisterous, burdensome, complex, complicated, confused, effortful, esoteric, formidable, grave, grievous, hard, harsh, intolerable, knotty*, labored, laborious, onerous, oppressive, profound, recondite, rough, serious, solemn, stormy, strenuous, tedious, tempestuous, toilsome, tough, troublesome, turbulent, vexatious, violent, wearisome, weighty, wild; SEE CONCEPTS *538,565,569*

heavy [*adj3*] *depressed, gloomy*
close, cloudy, crestfallen, damp, dark, dejected, despondent, disconsolate, dismal, downcast, dull, grieving, leaden, lowering, melancholy, oppressive, overcast, sad, sodden, soggy, sorrowful, stifling, wet; SEE CONCEPTS *403,525,548*

heavy [*adj4*] *listless, slow*
apathetic, comatose, dull, hebetudinous, indifferent, lethargic, sluggish, slumberous, torpid; SEE CONCEPT *584*

heckle [*v*] *jeer*
badger, bait, bother, bully, chivy, dis*, discomfit, disconcert, disrupt, disturb, embarrass, faze, gibe, hound*, interrupt, pester, plague, rattle, ride*, ridicule, shout at, taunt, tease, torment, worry; SEE CONCEPTS *44,47*

hectic [*adj*] *frantic, turbulent*
animated, boisterous, burning, chaotic, confused, disordered, excited, exciting, fervid, fevered, feverish, flurrying, flustering, frenetic, frenzied, furious, hassle, heated, hell broke loose*, jungle*, madhouse*, nutsy*, restless, riotous, riproaring, tumultuous, unsettled, wild, woolly*, zoolike*; SEE CONCEPT *548*

hedge [*n*] *boundary, obstacle, especially one made of plants*
barrier, bush, enclosure, fence, guard, hedgerow, hurdle, protection, quickset, screen, shrubbery, thicket, windbreak; SEE CONCEPTS 429,470

hedge [*vl*] *avoid, dodge*
beat around the bush*, be noncommittal, blow hot and cold*, cop a plea*, cop out*, duck, equivocate, evade, flip-flop*, fudge*, give the run around*, hem and haw*, jive*, pass the buck*, prevaricate, pussyfoot*, quibble, run around, shilly-shally*, shuck*, shuffle, sidestep, sit on the fence*, stall, stonewall*, temporize, tergiversate, tergiverse, waffle*; SEE CONCEPTS 18,30

hedge [*v2*] *enclose*
block, border, cage, confine, coop, corral, edge, fence, girdle, hem in, hinder, immure, obstruct, pen, restrict, ring, siege, surround; SEE CONCEPT 758

hedonist [*n*] *person who seeks pleasure above other values*
bon vivant, debauchee, epicure, epicurean, glutton, gourmand, lecher, libertine, pleasuremonger, pleasureseeker, profligate, sensualist, sybarite, thrill-seeker, voluptuary; SEE CONCEPT 423

heed [*n*] *care, thought*
application, attention, carefulness, caution, cognizance, concentration, concern, consideration, debate, deliberation, ear*, heedfulness, interest, listen up*, mark, mind*, note, notice, observance, observation, regard, remark, respect, spotlight*, study, tender loving care*, TLC*, watchfulness; SEE CONCEPTS 17,532

heed [*v*] *give care, thought to*
attend, baby-sit, bear in mind, be aware, be guided by, catch, consider, dig*, do one's bidding*, follow, follow orders, get a load of*, give ear*, hark, hear, hearken, keep eye peeled*, keep tabs*, listen, mark, mind, mind the store*, note, obey, observe, pay attention, pick up, regard, ride herd on*, see, sit, spot, stay in line*, take notice of, take to heart*, toe the line*, watch, watch one's step*, watch out, watch over, watch the store*; SEE CONCEPTS 17,623

heedless [*adj*] *careless*
asleep at the switch*, daydreaming, disregardful, fast and loose*, feckless, foolhardy, goofing off*, impetuous, imprudent, inadvertent, inattentive, incautious, inconsiderate, irreflective, neglectful, negligent, oblivious, out to lunch*, precipitate, rash, reckless, slapdash*, sloppy, thoughtless, uncaring, unmindful, unobservant, unthinking, unwary; SEE CONCEPT 401

hefty [*adj*] *big, bulky*
ample, awkward, beefy*, brawny, burly, colossal, cumbersome, extensive, fat, forceful, heavy, hulking, husky, large, large-scale, major, massive, muscular, ponderous, powerful, robust, sizable, strapping*, strong, sturdy, substantial, thumping*, tremendous, unwieldy, vigorous, weighty; SEE CONCEPTS 491,773

height [*n1*] *altitude, top part*
acme, apex, apogee, brow, ceiling, crest, crown, cusp, elevation, extent, highness, hill, loftiness, mountain, peak, pinnacle, pitch, prominence, rise, solstice, stature, summit, tallness, tip, tiptop, vertex, zenith; SEE CONCEPTS 741,743,791,836

height [*n2*] *climax; importance*
acme, crest, crisis, crowning point, culmination,

dignity, eminence, end, exaltation, extremity, grandeur, heyday*, high point, limit, loftiness, maximum, ne plus ultra*, prominence, sublimity, top, ultimate, utmost degree, uttermost; SEE CONCEPTS 388,668,832

heighten [*v*] *intensify*
add to, amplify, augment, boost, build up, elevate, enhance, enlarge, exalt, extend, improve, increase, lift, magnify, make higher, raise, send up, strengthen; SEE CONCEPTS 233,250

heinous [*adj*] *horrifying, monstrous*
abhorrent, abominable, accursed, atrocious, awful, bad, beastly, crying, cursed, evil, execrable, flagitious, flagrant, frightful, godawful*, grave, gross*, hateful, hideous, horrendous, infamous, iniquitous, nefarious, odious, offensive, outrageous, raunchy, revolting, scandalous, shocking, stinking*, unspeakable, vicious, villainous; SEE CONCEPTS 529,548,570

heir [*n*] *person who inherits possessions*
beneficiary, crown prince/princess, devisee, grantee, heritor, inheritor, next in line, scion, successor; SEE CONCEPTS 355,414

heirloom [*n*] *something inherited, often antique*
antique, bequest, birthright, gift, heritage, inheritance, legacy, patrimony, reversion; SEE CONCEPT 337

heist [*n*] *burglary, robbery*
break-in, breaking and entering, caper, crime, five-finger discount, holdup, larceny, pilferage, rip-off, stickup, sting, theft; SEE CONCEPT 139

helicopter [*n*] *aircraft*
autogiro, chopper, copter, eggbeater*, whirlybird; SEE CONCEPT 504

hell [*n*] *place of the condemned; bad situation*
Abaddon*, abyss, affliction, agony, anguish, blazes*, bottomless pit*, difficulty, everlasting fire*, fire and brimstone*, Gehenna*, grave, Hades, hell-fire, infernal regions, inferno, limbo, lower world, misery, nether world, nightmare, ordeal, pandemonium, perdition, pit, place of torment, purgatory, suffering, torment, trial, underworld, wretchedness; SEE CONCEPTS 370,435,674

hell-bent [*adj*] *determined*
bent on, bound and determined, constant, decided, driven, firm, fixed, intent, obsessed, persevering, persistent, resolute, resolved, serious, set on, steadfast, strong-minded, strong-willed, stubborn, tenacious, unhesitating, unwavering; SEE CONCEPTS 404,542

hellion [*n*] *troublemaker*
agent provocateur, agitator, demon, evildoer, firebrand*, heel*, incendiary, inciter, inflamer, instigator, loose cannon*, mischief-maker, punk*, rabblerouser*, rascal, recreant, rogue, rowdy*, smart aleck*, wise guy*; SEE CONCEPT 412

hellish [*adj*] *fiendish; unpleasant*
abominable, accursed, atrocious, barbarous, cruel, damnable, damned, demonic, devilish, diabolical, horrible, infernal, monstrous, nefarious, satanic, terrible, vicious, wicked; SEE CONCEPTS 529,570

helm [*n*] *wheel*
command, control, controls, driver's seat, leadership, reins, rudder, steering wheel, tiller; SEE CONCEPTS 436,464,502

helmet [*n*] *headgear*
armor, busby, crash helmet, hard hat, hat, head

protector, kepi, safety helmet, shako; SEE CONCEPT 451

help [n1] *assistance, relief*
advice, aid, assist, avail, balm*, benefit, comfort, cooperation, corrective, cure, guidance, hand, helping hand*, lift*, maintenance, nourishment, remedy, service, succor, support, sustenance, use, utility; SEE CONCEPTS 658,694

help [n2] *employee*
abettor, adjutant, aide, ally, ancilla, assistant, attendant, auxiliary, collaborator, colleague, deputy, domestic, hand, helper, helpmate, mate, partner, representative, right-hand person*, servant, subsidiary, supporter, worker; SEE CONCEPT 348

help [vl] *aid, assist*
abet, accommodate, advocate, back, ballyhoo*, befriend, benefit, be of use, bolster, boost, buck up*, cheer, cooperate, do a favor, do a service, do one's part*, encourage, endorse, further, go to bat for*, go with, hype*, intercede, lend a hand*, maintain, open doors*, patronize, plug*, promote, prop, puff*, push, relieve, root for*, sanction, save, second, see through, serve, stand by, stick up for*, stimulate, stump for*, succor, support, sustain, take under one's wing*, uphold, work for; SEE CONCEPT 110

help [v2] *improve*
alleviate, ameliorate, amend, attend, better, cure, doctor, ease, facilitate, heal, meliorate, mitigate, nourish, palliate, relieve, remedy, restore, revive, treat; SEE CONCEPT 244

helper [n] *assistant*
abettor, accessory, accomplice, adherent, adjunct, aide, ally, appointee, apprentice, attendant, backer, backup*, coadjutant, coadjutor, collaborator, colleague, companion, deputy, fellow worker, follower, friend, gal Friday*, girl Friday*, gofer*, help, helpmate, henchman, man Friday*, paraprofessional, partner, right-hand man/woman, right-hand person, secretary, servant, subordinate, supporter, temp*, temporary worker; SEE CONCEPTS 348,423

helpful [adj] *beneficial, beneficent*
accessible, accommodating, advantageous, applicable, benevolent, bettering, caring, conducive, considerate, constructive, contributive, convenient, cooperative, crucial, effectual, efficacious, essential, favorable, fortunate, friendly, good for, important, improving, instrumental, invaluable, kind, neighborly, operative, practical, pragmatic, productive, profitable, serendipitous, serviceable, significant, suitable, supportive, symbiotic, sympathetic, timely, usable, useful, utilitarian, valuable; SEE CONCEPTS 537,560

helping [n] *portion of food*
allowance, course, dollop, meal, order, piece, plateful, ration, serving, share; SEE CONCEPT 457

helpless [adj] *incapable, incompetent; vulnerable*
abandoned, basket-case*, debilitated, defenseless, dependent, destitute, disabled, exposed, feeble, forlorn, forsaken, friendless, handcuffed, impotent, inefficient, inexpert, infirm, invalid, over a barrel*, paralyzed, pinned*, powerless, prostrate, shiftless, tapped, tapped out*, unable, unfit, unprotected, up creek without paddle*, weak, with hands tied*; SEE CONCEPTS 401,542

helter-skelter [adv] *carelessly, confused*
about, anyhow, any which way*, anywise, around, at random, cluttered, disorderly, haphaz-

ard, hastily, headlong, higgledy-piggledy*, hit-or-miss*, hotfoot*, hurriedly, impetuously, incautiously, in confusion, incontinently, irregular, jumbled, muddled, pell-mell*, random, randomly, rashly, recklessly, topsy-turvy*, tumultous/tumultuous, unmindfully, wildly; SEE CONCEPT 544

hem [n] *border, edge*
brim, brink, define, edging, fringe, margin, perimeter, periphery, piping, rim, selvage, skirt, skirting, trimming, verge; SEE CONCEPTS 484,513

he-man [adj] *masculine*
macho*, male, manful, manly, mannish, muscular, potent, virile; SEE CONCEPTS 371,408,648

he-man [n] *masculine man*
caveman*, hunk*, macho man*, man's man, strong man, virile man; SEE CONCEPTS 414,419

hem/hem in [v] *enclose, restrict*
begird, beset, border, bound, cage, circle, circumscribe, close in, confine, corral, define, edge, encircle, encompass, envelop, environ, fence, fringe, girdle, hedge in, immure, margin, pen, rim, ring, round, shut, shut in, skirt, surround, verge; SEE CONCEPTS 130,758

hemorrhage [v] *bleed*
drain, extravasate, gush, lose blood, ooze, open vein, outflow, phlebotomize, seep, spill blood; SEE CONCEPT 185

hence [adv] *for that reason; therefore*
accordingly, as a deduction, away, consequently, ergo, forward, from here, from now on, henceforth, henceforward, hereinafter, in the future, it follows that, on that account, onward, out, so, then, thence, thereupon, thus, wherefore; SEE CONCEPT 799

henchman [n] *follower*
abettor, accessory, accomplice, adherent, adjunct, aide, ally, appointee, apprentice, assistant, attendant, backer, backup*, bodyguard, coadjutant, coadjutor, cohort, collaborator, colleague, companion, deputy, fellow worker, flunky, friend, gal Friday*, girl Friday*, gofer*, hanger-on, hatchet man/woman, help, helper, helpmate, lackey, man Friday*, partner, right-hand man/woman, right-hand person, secretary, servant, sidekick*, stooge*, subordinate, supporter, yes-person*; SEE CONCEPTS 348,423

henpeck [v] *nag*
badger, berate, bother, bug*, bully, carp, fuss, give a hard time*, harass, hector, hound, intimidate, irritate, needle, pester, pick on*, ride, scold, torment; SEE CONCEPTS 7,19,52

herald [n] *omen, messenger*
adviser, bearer, courier, crier, forerunner, harbinger, indication, outrider, precursor, prophet, reporter, runner, sign, signal, token; SEE CONCEPTS 274,284,423

herald [v] *bring message*
advertise, announce, ballyhoo*, broadcast, declare, forerun, fozetoken, harbinger, indicate, pave the way*, portend, precede, preindicate, presage, proclaim, publicize, publish, pzomise, show, tout, trumpet*, usher in*; SEE CONCEPT 60

herbicide [n] *poison*
DDT, defoliant, fungicide, insecticide, paraquat, pesticide, weedkiller; SEE CONCEPTS 307,475, 674,675

Herculean [adj] *powerful, strong*
almighty, backbreaking, colossal, courageous, forceful, gargantuan, gigantic, hard, heroic,

he
he

herd [n] *large group*

assemblage, bevy, brood, clan, collection, covey, crowd, crush, drif , drove, flight, flock, gaggle, gathering, hoi polloi*, horde, lot, mass, mob, multitude, nest, (pack, people, populace, press, rabble, school, swarm, throng; SEE CONCEPTS 397,432

herd [v] *gather; shepherd*

assemble, associate, collect, congregate, corral, drive, flock, force, goad, guide, huddle, lead, muster, poke, punch, rally, round up*, run, scare up*, spur; SEE CONCEPT 109

here [adv] *in this place*

attendant, attending, available, hereabouts, hither, hitherto, in this direction, on board, on deck, on hand, on-the-spot, on this spot, present, within reach; SEE CONCEPT 583

hereafter [adv] *from now on*

after this, eventually, hence, henceforth, henceforward, hereupon, in the course of time, in the future, ultimately; SEE CONCEPT 799

hereafter [n] *life after death*

afterlife, aftertime, afterward, afterworld, by-and-by*, future, future existence, future life, heaven, hell, next world, offing, otherworld, the beyond*, to-be*, underworld, world to come*; SEE CONCEPT 370

hereditary [adj] *inherited; transmitted at birth*

ancestral, bequeathed, $family, genealogical, genetic, handed down, heritable, inborn, inbred, inheritable, inherited, lineal, maternal, paternal, patrimonial, traditional, transmissible, transmitted, willed; SEE CONCEPT 549

heredity [n] *transmission of traits from parents to offspring*

ancestry, congenital traits, constitution, eugenics, genesiology, genetic make-up, genetics, inborn character, inheritance; SEE CONCEPT 648

heresy [n] *unorthodox opinion, especially in religious matters*

agnosticism, apostasy, atheism, blasphemy, defection, disbelief, dissent, dissidence, divergence, error, fallacy, heterodoxy, iconoclasm, impiety, infidelity, misbelief, nonconformism, nonconformity, paganism, revisionism, schism, sectarianism, secularism, sin; SEE CONCEPT 689

heretical [adj] *unorthodox*

agnostic, apostate, atheistic, differing, disagreeing, dissenting, dissentive, dissident, freethinking, heterodox, iconoclastic, idolatrous, impious, infidel, misbelieving, miscreant, nonconformist, revisionist, schismatic, sectarian, skeptical, unbelieving; SEE CONCEPTS 529,545

heritage [n] *person's background, tradition*

ancestry, bequest, birthright, convention, culture, custom, dowry, endowment, estate, fashion, heirship, heritance, inheritance, legacy, lot, patrimony, portion, right, share, tradition; SEE CONCEPTS 296,648,678

hermeneutical [adj] *interpretive*

critical, demonstrative, explanatory, explicative, expository, illustrative, investigative, revealing; SEE CONCEPT 268

hermeneutics [n] *the science of searching for hidden meaning in texts*

exegetics, exploration, interpretation, investigation, literary criticism, psychoanalytic criticism, revealing, unmasking; SEE CONCEPT 349

hermit [n] *person who chose to live alone outside of human society*

anchoret, anchorite, ascetic, eremite, misanthrope, pillarist, recluse, skeptic, solitaire, solitarian, solitary, stylite; SEE CONCEPTS 361,423

hero [n] *submarine sandwich*

grinder, hoagie, sub*, submarine*, torpedo; SEE CONCEPTS 457,460,461

hero/heroine [n] *brave person; champion*

ace, adventurer, celebrity, combatant, conqueror, daredevil, demigod, diva, exemplar, gallant, god, goddess, great person, heavy, ideal, idol, lead, leading person*, lion, martyr, model, paladin, person of the hour*, popular figure, prima donna*, principal, protagonist, saint, star, superstar, tin god*, victor, worthy; SEE CONCEPTS 352,416

heroic [adj] *brave, champion*

bigger than life*, bold, classic, courageous, daring, dauntless, doughty, elevated, epic, exaggerated, fearless, fire-eating*, gallant, grand, grandiose, gritty, gutsy*, gutty*, high-flown, impavid, inflated, intrepid, lion-hearted, mythological, noble, stand tall*, stouthearted, unafraid, undaunted, valiant, valorous; SEE CONCEPTS 401,404

heroin [n] *smack*

big H*, candy*, crap*, diacetylmorphine, doojee*, dope, drug, flea powder*, H*, hard stuff*, horse*, junk*, mojo*, narcotic, opium, scag*, white stuff*; SEE CONCEPT 307

heroism [n] *bravery*

boldness, courage, courageousness, daring, doughtiness, fearlessness, fortitude, gallantry, intrepidity, nobility, prowess, spirit, strength, valiance, valiancy, valor, valorousness; SEE CONCEPTS 411,633

hesitant [adj] *uncertain, waiting*

afraid, averse, backward, dawdling, delaying, diffident, disinclined, doubtful, doubting, faltering, half-hearted, halting, hanging back, hesitating, indecisive, irresolute, lacking confidence, lazy, loath, reluctant, shy, skeptical, slow, tentative, timid, uneager, unpredictable, unsure, unwilling, vacillating, wavering; SEE CONCEPTS 534,535,542

hesitate [v] *wait; be uncertain*

alternate, balance, balk, be irresolute, be reluctant, be unwilling, blow hot and cold*, dally, debate, defer, delay, demur, dillydally*, dither, doubt, equivocate, falter, flounder, fluctuate, fumble, hang*, hang back, hedge, hem and haw*, hold back, hold off, hover, linger, oscillate, pause, ponder, pull back, pussyfoot*, scruple, seesaw*, shift, shrink, shy away, sit on fence*, stammer, stop, straddle, stumble, stutter, swerve, tergiversate, think about, think twice*, vacillate, waffle*, waver, weigh; SEE CONCEPTS 21,121,681

hesitation [n] *waiting; uncertainty*

averseness, dawdling, delay, delaying, demurral, doubt, dubiety, equivocation, faltering, fluctuation, fumbling, hemming and hawing*, hesitancy, indecision, indecisiveness, indisposition, irresolution, misgiving, mistrust, oscillation, pause, procrastination, qualm, reluctance, scruple, skepticism, stammering, stumbling, stuttering, unwillingness, vacillation, wavering; SEE CONCEPTS 21,121,410,681

heterogeneous [*adj*] *assorted, miscellaneous*
amalgamate, composite, confused, conglomerate, contrary, contrasted, different, discordant, discrepant, disparate, dissimilar, divergent, diverse, diversified, incongruous, independent, inharmonious, jumbled, mingled, mixed, mongrel, mosaic, motley, multifarious, multiplex, odd, opposed, unallied, unlike, unrelated, variant, varied, variegated; SEE CONCEPT *564*

hex [*n*] *curse, spell*
abracadabra*, allure, bewitching, bewitchment, charm, conjuration, double whammy*, enchantment, evil eye, hexing, hocus-pocus*, jinx, magic, magic spell, mumbo-jumbo*, sorcery, voodoo*, whammy*; SEE CONCEPTS *370,673,689*

hiatus [*n*] *pause, interruption*
aperture, blank, breach, break, chasm, discontinuity, gap, interim, interval, lacuna, lapse, opening, rift, space; SEE CONCEPT *807*

hibernate [*v*] *lie dormant; sleep through cold weather*
hide, hole up, immure, lie torpid, sleep, vegetate, winter; SEE CONCEPT *315*

hick [*n*] *rustic*
backwoodsman/woman, boor, bumpkin, clodhopper, cornfed*, country boy/girl, country cousin*, countryman/woman, farmer, hayseed*, hillbilly, local yokel*, redneck*, rube, rural, yokel*; SEE CONCEPT *413*

hidden [*adj*] *unseen, secret*
abstruse, buried, clandestine, cloaked, close, clouded, concealed, covered, covert, cryptic, dark, disguised, eclipsed, esoteric, hermetic, hermetical, imperceivable, indiscernible, in the dark, invisible, latent, masked, mysterious, mystic, mystical, obscure, occult, out of view, private, QT*, recondite, screened, secluded, sequestered, shadowy, shrouded, surreptitious, ulterior, undercover, underground, undetected, undisclosed, unexposed, unknown, unrevealed, veiled, withheld; SEE CONCEPT *576*

hide [*v*] *conceal; remain unseen*
adumbrate, blot out, bury, cache, camouflage, cloak, cover, curtain*, disguise, dissemble, ditch, duck, eclipse, ensconce, go into hiding, go underground, harbor, hold back, hole up*, hush up, keep from, keep secret, lie low*, lock up, mask, not give away, not tell, obscure, plant, protect, put out of the way, reserve, salt away*, screen, secrete, shadow, shelter, shield, shroud, smuggle, squirrel*, stash, stifle, stow away, suppress, take cover, tuck away, veil, withhold; SEE CONCEPTS *17,188*

hideous [*adj*] *grotesque, horrible*
abominable, animal, appalling, awful, beast, bestial, detestable, disgusting, dreadful, frightful, ghastly, grim, grisly, gross*, gruesome, hateful, horrendous, horrid, loathsome, macabre, monstrous, morbid, nasty, odious, offensive, repellent, repugnant, repulsive, revolting, shocking, sick, sickening, terrible, terrifying, ugly, uncomely, unsightly, weird; SEE CONCEPTS *537,579*

hideout [*n*] *hiding place*
cover, den, hideaway, refuge, safe house, safe place, sanctuary, shelter; SEE CONCEPTS *198,515*

hierarchy [*n*] *order*
chain of command*, due order, echelons, grouping, pecking order, placing, position, pyramid, ranking, scale; SEE CONCEPT *727*

high [*adj 1*] *tall; at a great distance aloft*
aerial, alpine, altitudinous, big, colossal, elevated, eminent, flying, formidable, giant, gigantic, grand, great, high-reaching, high rise, hovering, huge, immense, large, lofty, long, sky-high, sky-scraping, soaring, steep, towering, tremendous, uplifted, upraised; SEE CONCEPTS *779,782*

high [*adj2*] *extreme*
costly, dear, excessive, exorbitant, expensive, extraordinary, extravagant, grand, great, high-priced, intensified, lavish, luxurious, precious, rich, sharp, special, steep, stiff, strong, unusual; SEE CONCEPTS *334,569*

high [*adj3*] *important*
arch, capital, chief, consequential, crucial, distinguished, eminent, essential, exalted, extreme, grave, influential, leading, necessary, noble, powerful, prominent, ruling, serious, significant, superior; SEE CONCEPT *567*

high [*adj4*] *very happy*
boisterous, bouncy, cheerful, elated, excited, exhilarated, exuberant, joyful, lighthearted, merry, psyched*, pumped*; SEE CONCEPT *403*

high [*adj5*] *intoxicated, drugged*
delirious, doped, drunk, euphoric, flying*, freaked out*, inebriated, on a trip*, potted*, spaced out*, stoned*, tanked*, tipsy; SEE CONCEPT *314*

high [*adj6*] *shrill, strong (on the senses)*
acute, high-pitched, loud, malodorous, penetrating, piercing, piping, putrid, rancid, rank, reeking, sharp, shrill, soprano, strident, treble; SEE CONCEPTS *406,594,598*

high and mighty [*adj*] *haughty, overbearing*
arrogant, cavalier, cocky*, conceited, contemptuous, disdainful, egotistic, egotistical, highfalutin*, high-handed*, hoity-toity*, imperious, lofty, lordly, on high horse*, presumptuous, sniffy*, snobbish, snooty*, snotty, stuck-up*, stuffy, superior, uppity*; SEE CONCEPTS *401,404*

highbrow [*adj*] *intellectual*
bookish, brainy*, cerebral, cultivated, cultured, erudite, intellective, intelligent, learned, scholarly, studious, wise; SEE CONCEPT *402*

highbrow [*n*] *intellectual, very smart person*
academic, academician, bluestocking, brain*, egghead*, Einstein*, genius, illuminati, intelligentsia, literato, longhair, philosopher, sage, savant, scholar, thinker, whiz*; SEE CONCEPT *402*

high-class [*adj*] *first-class*
best, choice, classy, deluxe, elite, superior, supreme, upper-class, upper-crust*; SEE CONCEPTS *568,572*

highfalutin [*adj*] *pompous*
arrogant, boastful, conceited, flaunting, grandiose, high and mighty*, important, lofty, ostentatious, overbearing, presumptuous, pretentious, puffed up*, puffy, self-centered, stuck-up*, swanky, uppity*, vain; SEE CONCEPTS *267,401,542*

high-flown [*adj*] *exalted, lofty*
bombastic, elaborate, exaggerated, extravagant, grandiloquent, grandiose, inflated, showy, turgid; SEE CONCEPT *562*

high-handed [*adj*] *domineering*
authoritarian, autocratic, bossy, dictatorial, imperious, ironhanded, oppressive, overbearing, tyrannical; SEE CONCEPTS *319,401*

he
hi

highlight [*n*] *memorable part*

best part, climax, feature, focal point, focus, high point, high spot, main feature, peak; SEE CONCEPT 832

highly [*adv*] *very, well*

awful, awfully, bloody*, but good*, decidedly, deeply, eminently, exceedingly, exceptionally, extraordinarily, extremely, greatly, hugely, immensely, jolly, mighty, mucho*, notably, parlous, plenty, powerful, profoundly, real, really, remarkably, right, so, so much*, strikingly, supremely, surpassingly, terribly, terrifically, too much*, tremendously, vastly, very much; SEE CONCEPTS 537,569

high-minded [*adj*] *principled*

chivalrous, conscientious, ethical, honest, moral, noble, righteous, upright, virtuous; SEE CONCEPT 545

high-powered [*adj*] *powerful*

authoritarian, authoritative, commanding, controlling, dominant, dynamic, effective, effectual, forceful, forcible, in control, influential, in the saddle*, mighty, potent, robust, ruling, strong, supreme, weighty; SEE CONCEPTS 489,527,540, 574

high society [*n*] *cultured class*

aristocracy, beau monde, beautiful people*, best people, cream of society, elite, fashionable society, high life, jet set*, polite society, privileged class, smart set, upper class; SEE CONCEPTS 387,388,417

high-strung [*adj*] *nervous*

all shook up*, choked*, easily upset, edgy, excitable, fidgety, hyper*, impatient, irascible, irritable, jittery, jumpy, nervy, neurotic, on pins and needles*, on ragged edge, restless, sensitive, spooked*, stressed, taut, temperamental, tense, tight*, unrestful, uptight*, wired*, zonkers*; SEE CONCEPTS 401,404

highway [*n*] *heavily traveled, capacious road*

artery, avenue, boulevard, drag*, four-lane*, freeway, interstate, parking lot*, parkway, path, pike*, roadway, skyway, street, superhighway, super slab*, thoroughfare, toll road, track, turnpike; SEE CONCEPT 501

hijack [*v*] *seize control*

carjack, commandeer, kidnap, shanghai, skyjack, steal, take hostage; SEE CONCEPTS 90,139

hijacker [*n*] *abductor*

carjacker, kidnapper, robber, skyjacker, terrorist, thief; SEE CONCEPTS 90,139

hike [*n*] *journey by foot*

backpack, constitutional, excursion, exploration, march, ramble, tour, traipse, tramp, trek, trip, walk, walkabout; SEE CONCEPTS 149,224,363

hike [*v1*] *walk for recreation*

backpack, explore, hit the road*, hoof*, leg it*, ramble, rove, stroll, stump, tour, tramp, travel, tromp; SEE CONCEPTS 149,224,363

hike [*v2*] *raise, increase*

advance, boost, jack, jump, lift, pull up, put up, up*, upgrade; SEE CONCEPTS 236,245

hilarious [*adj*] *very funny*

amusing, comical, convivial, entertaining, exhilarated, frolicsome, gay, gleeful, gut-busting*, happy, humorous, jocular, jolly, jovial, joyful, joyous, laughable, lively, merry, mirthful, noisy, priceless, riot, rollicking, scream, side-splitting*, uproarious, witty; SEE CONCEPT 529

hill [*n*] *uprising of earth's surface; pile*

acclivity, ascent, bluff, butte, cliff, climb, down, drift, dune, elevation, eminence, esker, fell, gradient, headland, heap, height, highland, hillock, hilltop, hummock, inclination, incline, knoll, mesa, mound, mount, precipice, prominence, promontory, protuberance, range, ridge, rise, rising ground, shock, slope, stack, summit, talus, tor, upland; SEE CONCEPT 509

hillbilly [*n*] *hayseed*

backwoodsman/woman, boor*, bumpkin, clodhopper*, country boy/girl, country bumpkin, country cousin*, hick*, rube, rustic, yokel; SEE CONCEPT 413

hillock [*n*] *small hill*

acclivity, ascent, bluff, butte, cliff, drift, dune, elevation, esker, headland, heap, highland, hilltop, hummock, inclination, incline, knoll, mesa, mound, mount, precipice, prominence, promontory, ridge, rise, slope, summit; SEE CONCEPT 509

hinder [*v*] *prevent, slow down*

arrest, balk, bar, block, bottleneck, box in, burden, check, choke, clog, contravene, counteract, crab, cramp, crimp, cripple, curb, debar, delay, deter, encumber, fetter, frustrate, get in the way*, hamper, hamstring*, handicap, hog-tie*, hold back, hold up, impede, inhibit, interfere, interrupt, louse up*, muzzle, neutralize, obstruct, offset, oppose, preclude, prohibit, resist, retard, shut out, snafu*, stay, stop, stymie*, terminate, thwart, trammel; SEE CONCEPTS 121,130

hindrance [*n*] *obstruction, difficulty*

albatross*, baggage*, ball and chain*, bar, barrier, catch, Catch-22*, check, clog, crimp, cumbrance, deterrent, drag, drawback, encumbrance, excess baggage*, foot dragging*, glitch*, gridlock, handicap, hang-up*, hitch, impedance, impediment, interference, interruption, intervention, jam-up*, joker, limitation, lock, millstone*, monkey wrench*, obstacle, restraint, restriction, snag, stoppage, stumbling block*, trammel; SEE CONCEPTS 666,674

hindsight [*n*] *retrospect*

experience, knowledge, looking back, Monday morning quarterbacking, recollection, remembering, 20/20 vision*, wisdom; SEE CONCEPTS 17,40,410

hinge [*n*] *pivot, turning point*

articulation, axis, ball-and-socket, butt, elbow, hook, joint, juncture, knee, link, pin, spring, swivel; SEE CONCEPTS 471,498

hinge [*v*] *be contingent on*

be subject to, be undecided, depend, hang, pend, pivot, rest, revolve around, stand on, turn, turn on; SEE CONCEPT 711

hint [*n*] *indication; suggestion*

adumbration, advice, allusion, announcement, clue, communication, connotation, denotation, evidence, flea in ear*, glimmering, help, idea, implication, impression, inference, information, inkling, innuendo, insinuation, intimation, iota, lead, mention, notice, notion, observation, omen, pointer, print, reference, reminder, scent, sign, signification, smattering, suspicion, symptom, taste, telltale, tinge, tip, tip-off*, token, trace, warning, whiff*, whisper, wink*, word to wise*, wrinkle*; SEE CONCEPT 274

hint [*v*] *suggest; indicate*

acquaint, adumbrate, advise, allude to, angle, apprise, bring up, broach, coax, connote, cue, drop, expose, fish*, foreshadow, give an inkling*, impart, imply, infer, inform, insinuate, intimate, jog memory, leak*, let it be known, let out of bag*, make*, mention, point, prefigure, press, prompt, put flea in ear*, recall, refer to, remind, say in passing, shadow, signify, solicit, spring, tip off*, tip one's hand*, touch on*, whisper, wink*; SEE CONCEPTS 60,74,75

hinterland [n] *backcountry*
boondocks*, boonies*, borderland, brush, bush country, frontier, outback, sticks*, wasteland, wilderness, woods; SEE CONCEPTS 513,745

hip [adj] *fashionable, stylish*
all the rage*, chic, chichi*, contemporary, cool*, current, faddy*, hot*, in style, in-thing*, in vogue, latest*, latest thing*, mod*, modern, modish*, natty*, new, now, popular, smart, sophisticated, trendsetting, trendy, with it*; SEE CONCEPTS 579,580

hippie [n] *nonconformist*
beatnik, Bohemian, drop-out, flower child, freak, free spirit, freethinker, yippie; SEE CONCEPT 423

hire [v] *commission for responsibility, use*
add to payroll, appoint, authorize, book, bring in, bring on board, carry, charter, contract for, delegate, draft, employ, empower, engage, enlist, exploit, fill a position, find help, give a break*, give job to, give work, ink*, lease, let, make use of, obtain, occupy, pick, place, pledge, procure, promise, put on*, put to work, rent, retain, secure, select, sign on, sign up*, sublease, sublet, take on, truck with*, utilize; SEE CONCEPT 351

hiss [n] *buzzing sound; jeer*
boo, Bronx cheer*, buzz, catcall, contempt, derision, hoot, sibilance, sibilation; SEE CONCEPTS 278,595

hiss [v] *make buzzing sound; ridicule*
blow, boo, catcall, condemn, damn, decry, deride, disapprove, hoot, jeer, mock, rasp, revile, seethe, shout down, shrill, sibilate, siss, spit, wheeze, whirr, whisper, whistle, whiz; SEE CONCEPTS 52,77

historic [adj] *momentous, remarkable*
celebrated, consequential, extraordinary, famous, important, memorable, notable, outstanding, red-letter*, significant, well-known; SEE CONCEPTS 548,568

historical [adj] *recorded as actually having happened*
actual, ancient, archival, attested, authentic, chronicled, classical, commemorated, documented, factual, important, in truth, old, past, real, verifiable; SEE CONCEPTS 548,582,820

history [n1] *past events, experiences*
ancient times, antiquity, bygone times, days of old*, days of yore*, good old days*, old days*, olden days*, past, yesterday, yesteryear; SEE CONCEPTS 678,807

history [n2] *chronicle of events*
account, annals, autobiography, biography, diary, epic, journal, memoirs, narration, narrative, prehistory, recapitulation, recital, record, relation, report, saga, story, tale, version; SEE CONCEPTS 268,271

histrionic [adj] *overly dramatic*
melodramatic, overacting, overplayed, theatrical, thespian; SEE CONCEPTS 537,548

histrionics [n] *theatrics*
dramatics, dramatization, performance, performing; SEE CONCEPT 674

hit [n1] *strike, bump*
bang, bat, bell-ringer*, belt, blow, bonk, box*, buffet, butt, chop, clash, clip, clout, collision, cuff*, fisticuff, glance, impact, knock, lick*, one-two punch*, paste*, pat, plunk, punch, rap, roundhouse*, shock, shot, slap, slog, smack, smash, sock, spank, stroke, swat, swing, swipe, tap, uppercut, wallop, whammy*, whop, zap*, zinger*; SEE CONCEPTS 189,200

hit [n2] *entertainment success*
achievement, bang, click, favorite, knockout, masterstroke, sellout, sensation, smash, SRO*, triumph, winner, wow; SEE CONCEPT 706

hit [v1] *strike*
bang, bash, bat, batter, beat, belt, blast, blitz, box*, brain*, buffet, bump, clap, clip, clobber, clout, club, crack, cudgel, cuff*, dab, ding*, flail, flax, flog, give a black eye*, hammer*, hook, jab, kick, knock, knock around, knock out, KO*, lace, lambaste, larrup, lather, let fly*, let have it*, lob, nail*, pellet, pelt, percuss, pop, pound, punch, rap, ride roughshod*, slap, smack, sock, stone, swat, tap, thrash, thump, thwack, trash, uppercut, wallop, whack*, whang*; SEE CONCEPTS 189,200

hit [v2] *collide, bump into*
bang into, buffet, butt, carom, clash, crash, glance, jostle, knock, light, meet, meet head-on*, pat, rap, run into, scrape, sideswipe, smash, stumble, tap, thud, thump; SEE CONCEPTS 189,208

hit [v3] *accomplish*
achieve, affect, arrive at, attain, gain, influence, leave a mark, occur, overwhelm, reach, secure, strike, touch; SEE CONCEPTS 199,706

hitch [n] *problem, difficulty*
block, bug*, catch, check, delay, discontinuance, drawback, glitch*, hang-up, hindrance, hold-up, impediment, interruption, joker, mishap, snafu*, snag, stoppage, stumbling block, tangle, trouble; SEE CONCEPTS 666,674

hitch [v] *join, fasten*
attach, chain, connect, couple, harness, hook, lash, make fast, moor, strap, tether, tie, unite, yoke; SEE CONCEPTS 85,113,160

hit it off [v] *get along well*
be of one mind*, be on the same wavelength*, click, make friends, see eye to eye, take to; SEE CONCEPT 388

hit man [n] *professional killer*
assassin, contract killer, executioner, gunman, hatchet man, hired gun*, hired killer, murderer, triggerman; SEE CONCEPT 412

hit-or-miss [adj] *random*
accidental, aimless, arbitrary, casual, chance, contingent, fluky, fortuitous, haphazard, incidental, irregular, slipshod, trial-and error, unplanned, unpremeditated; SEE CONCEPTS 535,548,557

hoard [n] *stockpile*
abundance, accumulation, agglomeration, aggregation, amassment, backlog, cache, collection, conglomeration, cumulation, fund, garner, heap, inventory, mass, nest egg*, pile, reserve, reservoir, riches, stock, store, supply, treasure, treasure-trove*, trove, wealth; SEE CONCEPT 712

hoard [v] *put away, accumulate*
acquire, amass, buy up, cache, collect, deposit, garner, gather, hide, keep, lay away, lay up, pile up, put aside for rainy day*, put by, save, scrimp,

hi
ho

sock away*, squirrel*, stash, stockpile, store, stow away, treasure; SEE CONCEPTS *135,710*

hoarse [*adj*] *raspy in voice*
blatant, breathy, cracked, croaking, croaky, croupy, discordant, dry, grating, gravelly, growling, gruff, guttural, harsh, husky, indistinct, jarring, piercing, ragged, raucous, rough, scratching, squawking, stertorous, strident, stridulous, thick, throaty, uneven, whispering; SEE CONCEPT *594*

hoary [*adj1*] *ancient*
aged, age-old, antiquated, antique, elderly, lot of mileage*, old, older, old-fashioned, oldie*, out-of-date, relic, rusty, timeworn, venerable, very old; SEE CONCEPTS *578,797*

hoary [*adj2*] *gray or white*
frosty, gray-haired, graying, salt and pepper, silvery, snowy-haired, white-haired, whitish; SEE CONCEPT *618*

hoax [*n*] *trick*
cheat, cock-and-bull story*, con*, con game*, crock*, deceit, deception, dodge, fabrication, fake, falsification, fast one*, fast shuffle*, fib, flimflam*, fraud, gimmick, gyp*, hooey*, humbug*, hustle, imposture, joke, lie, practical joke, prank, put-on, racket, ruse, scam, sell, shift, snow job*, spoof, sting, swindle, whopper*; SEE CONCEPTS *59,63*

hoax [*v*] *trick*
bamboozle*, bluff, chicane, con, deceive, delude, dupe, fake out, fleece, flimflam*, fool, frame, gammon, gull, hoodwink*, Murphy*, play games with*, pull one's leg*, rook*, run a game on*, set up*, sting*, swindle, take for a ride*, take in*; SEE CONCEPT *59*

hobble [*v1*] *limp*
clump, dodder, falter, halt, hitch, scuff, shuffle, stagger, stumble, totter; SEE CONCEPT *151*

hobble [*v2*] *cripple, restrict*
clog, cramp, cramp one's style, crimp, curb, entrammel, fasten, fetter, gimp, hamper, hamstring*, hang up*, hinder, hog-tie*, leash, put a crimp in*, shackle, tie, trammel; SEE CONCEPT *130*

hobby [*n*] *pleasurable pastime*
amusement, art, avocation, bag*, craft, craze, distraction, diversion, divertissement, fad*, fancy, favorite occupation, fun, game, interest, kick*, labor of love*, leisure activity, leisure pursuit, obsession, occupation, pet topic, play, quest, relaxation, schtick*, shot, sideline, specialty, sport, thing*, vagary, weakness, whim, whimsy; SEE CONCEPTS *363,364*

hobgoblin [*n*] *mischievous goblin*
bogeyman, brownie, elf, fairy, fay, imp, leprechaun, pixie, puck, sprite; SEE CONCEPT *370*

hobo [*n*] *homeless person*
beggar, bum, derelict, drifter, migrant worker, street person, tramp, transient, vagabond, vagrant, wanderer, wino; SEE CONCEPTS *412,423*

hock [*v*] *pawn*
borrow, give security, pledge; SEE CONCEPTS *115,330*

hocus-pocus [*n*] *deception, magic*
abracadabra*, artifice, cant, chant, charm, cheating, chicanery, conjuring, deceit, delusion, flimflam*, fraud, gibberish, gobbledegook*, hoax, humbug, imposture, incantation, jargon, juggling, legerdemain, mumbo-jumbo*, mummery, nonsense, open-sesame*, rigmarole*, sleight of

hand*, spell, swindle, trick, trickery; SEE CONCEPTS *59,278*

hodgepodge [*n*] *mixture, mess*
collection, combination, goulash*, hash, jumble, medley, mélange, miscellany, mishmash*, mixed bag, olio, patchwork, potpourri, salmagundi*; SEE CONCEPTS *260,432*

hog [*n1*] *pig*
boar, cob roller*, oinker*, piggy, piglet, porker*, razorback, shoat, sow, swine, warthog; SEE CONCEPTS *394,400*

hog [*n2*] *glutton*
cormorant, epicure, gorger*, gormandizer, gourmand, greedy eater, hefty eater, pig*, swine*; SEE CONCEPT *412*

hog [*v*] *be selfish*
be greedy, gobble up, grab all of, have all to oneself*, monopolize; SEE CONCEPTS *90,190*

hogwash [*n*] *nonsense*
absurdity, balderdash*, baloney, BS*, bull*, bunk*, debris, drivel*, foolishness, hokum, hooey*, horsefeathers*, poppycock*, refuse, ridiculousness, rot, rubbish, trash, twaddle*; SEE CONCEPT *278*

hoi polloi [*n*] *the masses*
commonality, commoners, common people, rank and file, the herd, the multitude, the proletariat, the working class; SEE CONCEPTS *379,417*

hoist [*v*] *lift*
elevate, erect, heave, pick up, raise, rear, take up, uphold, uplift, upraise, uprear; SEE CONCEPT *196*

hokey [*adj*] *corny*
banal, commonplace, dull*, feeble, hackneyed, mawkish, old-fashioned, old hat*, sentimental, shopworn, stale, trite; SEE CONCEPT *550*

hold [*n*] *grasp, possession*
authority, clasp, clench, clinch, clout, clutch, control, dominance, dominion, grip, influence, occupancy, occupation, ownership, pull, purchase, retention, sway, tenacity, tenure; SEE CONCEPTS *190,343,710*

hold [*v1*] *have in one's hands, possession; grasp*
adhere, arrest, bind, bottle up, carry, catch, check, cherish, clasp, cleave, clench, clinch, cling, clutch, confine, contain, cork up*, cradle, detain, embrace, enclose, enjoy, fondle, freeze to*, grip, handle, hang on, have, hug, imprison, keep, keep close, keep out, lock up, maintain, not let go, nourish, occupy, own, palm, possess, press, put a lock on, restrain, retain, secure, seize, squeeze, stay put, stick, take, trammel, vise, wield, withhold, wring; SEE CONCEPTS *190,191,200,710*

hold [*v2*] *believe*
assume, aver, bet bottom dollar*, buy*, consider, credit, cross one's heart*, deem, entertain, esteem, feel, have hunch*, have sneaking suspicion*, judge, lap up, lay money on, maintain, okay, presume, reckon, regard, sense, set store by*, swear by, swear up and down*, take as gospel truth*, take stock in*, think, view; SEE CONCEPT *12*

hold [*v3*] *continue, endure*
apply, be in effect, be in force, be the case, be valid, exist, have bearing, hold good, hold true, last, operate, persevere, persist, remain, remain true, resist, stand up, stay, stay staunch, wear; SEE CONCEPT *239*

hold [*v4*] *support*
bear, bolster, brace, buttress, carry, lock, prop,

shore up, shoulder, stay, sustain, take, underpin, uphold; SEE CONCEPTS *110,190*

hold [*v5*] *have a capacity for*
accommodate, be equipped for, carry, comprise, contain, include, seat, take; SEE CONCEPTS *719,742*

hold [*v6*] *conduct meeting, function*
assemble, call, carry on, celebrate, convene, have, officiate, preside, run, solemnize; SEE CONCEPTS *324,384*

hold back/hold off [*v*] *repress*
bit, bridle, check, control, curb, defer, delay, deny, forbear, hold down, hold in, inhibit, keep, keep back, keep out, postpone, prevent, put off, refrain, refuse, restrain, stop, suppress, withhold; SEE CONCEPTS *121,130*

holdup [*n1*] *problem*
bottleneck*, delay, difficulty, gridlock*, hitch, obstruction, setback, snag, stoppage, traffic jam*, trouble, wait; SEE CONCEPTS *192,674*

holdup [*n2*] *take goods illegally by force*
burglary, crime, mugging, robbery, stickup, theft; SEE CONCEPT *192*

hold up [*v1*] *postpone*
delay, detain, hinder, hold off, impede, interfere, interrupt, pause, prorogue, retard, set back, slow down, stay, stop, suspend, waive; SEE CONCEPTS *121,130*

hold up [*v2*] *rob*
burglarize, mug, steal from, stick up, waylay; SEE CONCEPTS *139,192*

hole [*n1*] *opening in a solid object*
aperture, breach, break, burrow, cave, cavern, cavity, chamber, chasm, chink, cistern, cleft, covert, crack, cranny, crater, cut, den, dent, depression, dimple, dip, excavation, eyelet, fissure, foramen, fracture, gap, gash, gorge, hollow, hovel, keyhole, lacuna, lair, leak, mouth, nest, niche, nick, notch, orifice, outlet, passage, peephole, perforation, pit, pocket, pockmark, puncture, rent, retreat, scoop, shaft, shelter, space, split, tear, tunnel, vacuity, vent, void, window; SEE CONCEPT *513*

hole [*n2*] *predicament*
box*, corner*, difficulty, dilemma, emergency, fix, imbroglio, impasse, jam, mess, pickle*, plight, quandary, scrape, spot, tangle; SEE CONCEPT *674*

holiday [*n*] *celebratory day; time off*
anniversary, break, celebration, day of rest, feast, festival, festivity, fete, few days off*, fiesta, gala, gone fishing*, holy day, jubilee, layoff, leave, liberty, long weekend*, recess, red-letter day*, saint's day, vacation; SEE CONCEPTS *364,802*

holier-than-thou [*adj*] *self-righteously pious*
goody-goody, high-hat, judgmental, pietistic, sanctimonious, smug, snobbish, unctuous; SEE CONCEPT *401*

holiness [*n*] *religiousness*
asceticism, beatitude, blessedness, consecration, devotion, devoutness, divineness, divinity, faith, godliness, grace, humanity, inviolability, piety, purity, religiosity, reverence, righteousness, sacredness, saintliness, sanctity, spirituality, unction, venerableness, virtuousness, worship; SEE CONCEPTS *368,645*

holistic [*adj*] *complete, whole*
aggregate, comprehensive, entire, full, integrated, total, universal; SEE CONCEPT *531*

holler [*v*] *shout, yell*
bawl, bellow, call, cheer, complain, cry, hoot, howl, roar, scream, screech, shriek, shrill, squawk, squeal, ululate, vociferate, wail, whoop, yap, yelp; SEE CONCEPTS *47,595*

hollow [*adj1*] *empty, hollowed out*
alveolate, arched, carved out, cavernous, cleft, concave, cupped, cup-shaped, curved, deep-set, depressed, dimpled, excavated, incurved, indented, infundibular, notched, not solid, pitted, striated, sunken, troughlike, unfilled, vacant, vaulted, void; SEE CONCEPTS *483,490*

hollow [*adj2*] *deep, resonant in sound*
cavernous, clangorous, dull, echoing, flat, ghostly, low, muffled, mute, muted, resounding, reverberant, ringing, roaring, rumbling, sepulchral, sounding, thunderous, toneless, vibrant, vibrating; SEE CONCEPT *594*

hollow [*adj3*] *meaningless*
empty, fruitless, futile, idle, nugatory, otiose, pointless, specious, unavailing, useless, vain, worthless; SEE CONCEPT *560*

hollow [*adj4*] *false, artificial*
cynical, deceitful, faithless, flimsy, hypocritical, insincere, treacherous, unsound, weak; SEE CONCEPT *267*

hollow [*n*] *empty or dented area*
basin, bottom, bowl, cave, cavern, cavity, chamber, channel, cleft, concavity, crater, cup, dale, den, depression, dimple, dip, dish, excavation, groove, gulf, hole, indentation, notch, pit, pocket, sag, scoop, sinkage, sinkhole, socket, trough, vacuity, valley, void; SEE CONCEPTS *740,754*

hollow [*v*] *empty out; make concave*
channel, chase, corrugate, dent, dig, dish, ditch, excavate, furrow, gorge, groove, indent, notch, pit, rabbet, remove, rut, scoop, shovel, trench; SEE CONCEPTS *178,211*

holocaust [*n*] *widespread destruction*
annihilation, carnage, catastrophe, devastation, extermination, extinction, genocide, immolation, inferno, massacre, mass murder, slaughter; SEE CONCEPT *252*

holy [*adj*] *religious, sacred*
angelic, believing, blessed, chaste, clean, consecrated, dedicated, devoted, devotional, devout, divine, faithful, faultless, glorified, god-fearing, godlike, godly, good, hallowed, humble, immaculate, innocent, just, moral, perfect, pietistic, pious, prayerful, pure, revered, reverent, righteous, sacrosanct, sainted, saintlike, saintly, sanctified, seraphic, spiritual, spotless, sublime, uncorrupt, undefiled, untainted, unworldly, upright, venerable, venerated, virtuous; SEE CONCEPTS *545,567,574*

homage [*n*] *devotion, admiration*
adoration, adulation, allegiance, awe, deference, duty, esteem, faithfulness, fealty, fidelity, genuflection, honor, kneeling, loyalty, obeisance, praise, respect, reverence, service, tribute, worship; SEE CONCEPTS *32,69*

home [*adj*] *domestic*
at ease, at rest, central, down home*, familiar, family, homely, homey, household, inland, in one's element*, internal, in the bosom*, local, national, native; SEE CONCEPT *536*

home [*n1*] *place where a human lives*
abode, address, apartment, asylum, boarding house, bungalow, cabin, castle, cave*, com-

ho
ho

morancy, condo, condominium, co-op, cottage, crash pad*, diggings*, digs*, domicile, dormitory, dump*, dwelling, farm, fireside*, flat, habitation, hangout*, haunt, hearth, hideout, hole in the wall*, home plate*, homestead, hospital, house, hut, joint*, living quarters, manor, mansion, nest*, orphanage, pad*, palace, parking place*, place, residence, resort, roof*, rooming house, roost*, shanty, shelter, trailer, turf, villa, where the hat is*; SEE CONCEPT 516

home [n2] *birthplace, environment*
abode, camping ground*, country, element, family, farm, fireside*, habitat, habitation, haunt, haven, hearth, hills, home ground, homeland, homestead, hometown, household, land, locality, neck of the woods*, neighborhood, range, roof, site, soil, stamping ground*, stomping ground*, territory; SEE CONCEPTS 510,515,648

homeboy [n] *friend*
bro*, brother*, buddy, fellow gang member, homie, neighbor; SEE CONCEPT 423

homegrown [adj] *grown at home*
domestic, homemade, native; SEE CONCEPT 536

homeless [adj] *displaced*
abandoned, banished, deported, derelict, desolate, destitute, disinherited, displaced, dispossessed, down-and-out*, estranged, exiled, forlorn, forsaken, friendless, houseless, itinerant, outcast, refugee, uncared-for, unhoused, unsettled, unwelcome, vagabond, vagrant, wandering, without a roof*; SEE CONCEPT 555

homely [adj1] *ordinary, comfortable*
comfy, cozy, domestic, everyday, familiar, friendly, homelike, homespun, homey, inelaborate, informal, modest, natural, plain, simple, snug, unaffected, unassuming, unostentatious, unpretentious, welcoming; SEE CONCEPTS 579,589

homely [adj2] *unattractive*
animal, disgusting, plain, ugly, unaesthetic, unalluring; SEE CONCEPT 579

homemade [adj] *made in the home*
do-it-yourself, handcrafted, handmade, homegrown, homespun, natural; SEE CONCEPT 536

homesick [adj] *nostalgic*
hankering, heartsick, lonely, longing for home, missing, wistful, yearning; SEE CONCEPTS 403,529

homespun [adj] *spun from home*
crude, handcrafted, handmade, homemade, ordinary, plain, rough, rustic, simple, unrefined, unsophisticated; SEE CONCEPT 536

homey [adj] *comfortable*
adequate, cared for, cheerful, comfy*, complacent, contented, cozy, delightful, easy, familiar, folksy, friendly, intimate, plain, pleasant, relaxed, rested, restful, simple, snug, snug as a bug in a rug*, soft, soothed, warm; SEE CONCEPT 572

homicidal [adj] *murderous*
bloodthirsty, deadly, lethal, maniacal, slaughterous, violent; SEE CONCEPTS 538,548,565

homicide [n] *killing*
assassination, big chill*, bloodshed, bump-off*, butchery, carnage, crime, death, erase*, foul play, hit, manslaughter, murder, offing, ride, rubout*, slaying; SEE CONCEPT 252

homogenous [adj] *similar, comparable*
akin, alike, analogous, cognate, consistent, homologous, identical, kindred, like, uniform, unvarying; SEE CONCEPTS 487,573

homosexual [adj] *sexually attracted to the same sex*
gay, homoerotic, homophile, lesbian; SEE CONCEPT 372

hone [v] *sharpen*
acuminate, edge, file, grind, make sharp, put an edge on, put a point on, whet; SEE CONCEPTS 137,250

honest [adj] *truthful, candid*
above-board, authentic, bona fide*, conscientious, decent, direct, equitable, ethical, fair, fair and square*, forthright, frank, genuine, high-minded*, honorable, impartial, ingenuous, just, law-abiding*, lay it on the line*, like it is*, no lie*, on the level*, on the up and up*, open, outright, plain, proper, real, reliable, reputable, scrupulous, sincere, straight, straightforward, true, true blue*, trustworthy, trusty, undisguised, unfeigned, upfront*, upright, veracious, virtuous, what you see is what you get*; SEE CONCEPTS 267,545

honest-to-God [adj] *genuine*
absolute, accurate, actual, authentic, authenticated, bona fide*, certain, certified, factual, for real*, for-sure, honest, honest-to-goodness*, kosher*, legit, legitimate, no buts about it*, official, on the level*, on the up-and-up, positive, real, really-truly*, real stuff*, straight, sure-enough, sure-thing, true, unquestionable, valid; SEE CONCEPT 582

honesty [n] *truthfulness, candidness*
bluntness, candor, confidence, conscientiousness, equity, evenhandedness, fairness, faithfulness, fidelity, frankness, genuineness, goodness, honor, impeccability, incorruptibility, integrity, justness, loyalty, morality, openness, outspokenness, plainness, principle, probity, rectitude, reputability, responsibility, right, scrupulousness, self-respect, sincerity, soundness, straightforwardness, straightness, trustiness, trustworthiness, uprightness, veracity, virtue; SEE CONCEPTS 633,645

honeyed [adj] *sweetened*
cajoling, candied, dulcet, flattering, ingratiating, sugarcoated, sugary; SEE CONCEPT 170

honk [v] *toot*
beep, blare, blast, blow, blow the horn, sound, sound one's horn, tootle; SEE CONCEPT 65

honor [n1] *respect*
account, adoration, adulation, aggrandizement, apotheosis, approbation, attention, canonization, celebration, confidence, consideration, credit, deference, deification, dignity, distinction, elevation, esteem, exaltation, faith, fame, fealty, glorification, glory, greatness, high standing, homage, immortalization, laud, laurel, lionization, notice, obeisance, popularity, praise, prestige, rank, recognition, renown, reputation, repute, reverence, tribute, trust, veneration, worship, wreath; SEE CONCEPTS 668,689

honor [n2] *integrity*
character, chastity, courage, decency, fairness, goodness, honestness, honesty, incorruption, incorruptness, innocence, modesty, morality, morals, principles, probity, purity, rectitude, righteousness, trustworthiness, truthfulness, uprightness, virtue; SEE CONCEPTS 411,645

honor [n3] *praise, award*
acclaim, accolade, adoration, badge, bays, com-

mendation, compliment, credit, decoration, deference, distinction, favor, homage, kudos, laurels, pleasure, privilege, recognition, regard, respect, reverence, source of pride, tribute, veneration; SEE CONCEPTS 278,337,689

honor [v] *recognize, treat with respect*
acclaim, admire, adore, aggrandize, appreciate, be faithful, be true, celebrate, commemorate, commend, compliment, decorate, dignify, distinguish, ennoble, erect, esteem, exalt, give glad hand*, give key to city*, glorify, hallow, keep, laud, lionize, live up to, look up to, magnify, observe, praise, prize, revere, roll out red carpet*, sanctify, sublime, uprear, value, venerate, worship; SEE CONCEPTS 10,633

honorable [adj] *reputable*
acclaimed, celebrated, chivalrous, conscientious, dependable, distinguished, eminent, esteemed, ethical, faithful, forthright, high-principled, honest, honored, illustrious, just, knightly, law-abiding, noble, notable, of good repute, on the up-and-up*, principled, reliable, respectable, righteous, sincere, sterling, straightforward, trustworthy, truthful, unstained, upright, virtuous; SEE CONCEPTS 545,567,574

honorary [adj] *honorific*
celebratory, congratulatory, titular; SEE CONCEPTS 668,689

hood/hoodlum [n] *gangster*
criminal, delinquent, gangster, goon*, hooligan, mobster, punk, rioter, rowdy, ruffian, thug, troublemaker; SEE CONCEPT 545

hoodwink [v] *deceive*
bamboozle*, beat out of, bilk, bluff, buffalo*, burn, cheat, con, defraud, double-cross, dupe, fake, fleece, fool, gull, gyp*, hoax, hornswoggle, kid, mislead, pull a fast one*, pull the wool over one's eyes*, scam, screw, suck in*, swindle, take advantage of, take for a ride*, take to the cleaners*, trick, victimize; SEE CONCEPTS 7,19,59

hook [n] *curved fastener*
angle, catch, clasp, crook, curve, grapnel, grapple, hasp, holder, link, lock, peg; SEE CONCEPTS 260,498

hook [v] *grab, catch*
angle, bag, clasp, crook, curve, enmesh, ensnare, entrap, fasten, fix, hasp, lasso, net, pin, secure, snare, trap; SEE CONCEPT 190

hooked [adj] *addicted*
absorbed, captivated, dependent, devoted, enamored, obsessed, prone, strung out*, under the influence; SEE CONCEPT 542

hooker [n] *prostitute*
bawd, call girl, concubine, courtesan, fallen woman*, floozy*, harlot, hustler, lady of the evening, moll, nymphomaniac*, painted*, pro*, streetwalker, strumpet, whore, woman of the streets, working girl*; SEE CONCEPTS 348,412, 415,419

hooligan [n] *hoodlum*
criminal, delinquent, gangster, goon*, hood, mobster, punk, rioter, rowdy, ruffian, thug, troublemaker; SEE CONCEPT 545

hoopla [n] *excitement*
action, activity, brouhaha, bustle, buzz*, commotion, drama, elation, emotion, excitation, feeling, fever, fireworks*, flurry, frenzy, furor, fuss, heat*, hubbub*, hullabaloo*, hysteria, passion,

racket, rage, ruckus, rumpus, stir, thrill; SEE CONCEPTS 388,410,633

hoot [v] *cry*
boo, catcall, heckle, hiss, howl, jeer, razz*, scoff at, scorn, scream, shout down, whistle; SEE CONCEPTS 44,47

hop [n/v] *jump on one leg*
bounce, bound, caper, dance, hurdle, leap, lop, lope, skip, skitter, spring, step, trip, vault; SEE CONCEPT 194

hope [n] *longing; dream*
achievement, ambition, anticipation, aspiration, assumption, belief, bright side*, buoyancy, castles in air*, concern, confidence, daydream, dependence, desire, endurance, expectancy, expectation, faith, fancy, fool's paradise*, fortune, gain, goal, greedy glutton*, hopefulness, light at end of tunnel*, optimism, pipe dream*, promise, promised land*, prospect, reliance, reverie, reward, rosiness, sanguineness, security, stock, thing with feathers*, Utopia, wish; SEE CONCEPTS 20,410,709

hope [v] *long for, dream about*
anticipate, aspire, assume, await, believe, be sure of, cherish, contemplate, count on, deem likely, depend on, desire, expect, feel confident, foresee, hang in*, have faith, hold, keep fingers crossed*, knock on wood*, look at sunny side*, look forward to, pray, presume, promise oneself, rely, suppose, surmise, suspect, sweat*, sweat it*, sweat it out*, take heart*, think to, trust, watch for, wish; SEE CONCEPT 20

hopeful [adj1] *optimistic, expectant*
anticipating, anticipative, assured, at ease, blithe, buoyant, calm, cheerful, comfortable, confident, content, eager, elated, emboldened, enthusiastic, expecting, faithful, forward-looking*, high, hoping, inspirited, keeping the faith*, lighthearted, looking forward to, reassured, rose-colored*, rosy*, sanguine, satisfied, serene, trustful, trusting, unflagging, upbeat; SEE CONCEPT 403

hopeful [adj2] *promising, auspicious*
advantageous, arousing, beneficial, bright, cheerful, cheering, conducive, convenient, elating, encouraging, enlivening, exciting, expeditious, fair, favorable, fine, fit, flattering, fortifying, fortunate, golden, good, gracious, halcyon, heartening, helpful, inspiring, inspiriting, likely, lucky, opportune, pleasant, pleasing, probable, promiseful, propitious, providential, reasonable, reassuring, roseate, rosy*, rousing, stirring, suitable, sunny, timely, uplifting, well-timed; SEE CONCEPT 548

hopeless [adj] *futile, pessimistic*
bad, beyond recall, cynical, dejected, demoralized, despairing, desperate, despondent, disconsolate, discouraging, downhearted, fatal, forlorn, gone*, goner*, helpless, ill-fated, impossible, impracticable, incurable, in despair, irredeemable, irreparable, irreversible, irrevocable, lost, menacing, no-win, past hope, pointless, sad, shot down*, sinister, sunk, threatening, tragic, unachievable, unavailing, unfortunate, unmitigable, up the creek*, useless, vain, woebegone, worsening; SEE CONCEPTS 529,548

horde [n] *uncontrolled throng, pack*
band, crew, crowd, crush, drove, everybody, gang, gathering, host, jam, mob, multitude,

ho
ho

press, push, squash, swarm, troop, turnout, wall-to-wall*; SEE CONCEPTS 397,417

horizon [n] *skyline, extent*
border, boundary, compass, field of vision, ken, limit, perspective, prospect, purview, range, reach, realm, scope, sphere, stretch, vista; SEE CONCEPTS 484,509,529

horizontal [adj] *lying flat*
accumbent, aligned, even, flush, level, parallel, plane, recumbent, regular, smooth, straight, uniform; SEE CONCEPTS 581,583

horny [adj] *sexually aroused*
concupiscent, desiring, hard up, hot*, hot to trot*, lascivious, libidinous, lustful, oversexed, passionate, randy, turned on; SEE CONCEPT 372

horoscope [n] *astrological forecast*
astrology, crystal gazing, prediction; SEE CONCEPT 70

horrible/horrendous/horrid [adj] *repulsive, very unpleasant*
abhorrent, abominable, appalling, awful, beastly, cruel, detestable, disagreeable, disgusting, dreadful, eerie, execrable, fearful, frightful, ghastly, grim, grisly, gross*, gruesome, heinous, hideous, loathsome, lousy, lurid, mean, nasty, obnoxious, offensive, repellent, revolting, scandalous, scary, shameful, shocking, terrible, terrifying, ungodly, unholy, unkind; SEE CONCEPTS 529,537

horrify [v] *scare*
affright, alarm, appall, chill off*, consternate, daunt, disgust, dismay, frighten, intimidate, outrage, petrify, scare to death*, shake, shock, sicken, terrify, terrorize; SEE CONCEPTS 7,14,19

horror [n] *fear, revulsion*
abhorrence, abomination, alarm, antipathy, apprehension, aversion, awe, chiller, consternation, detestation, disgust, dislike, dismay, dread, fright, hate, hatred, loathing, monstrosity, panic, repugnance, terror, trepidation; SEE CONCEPTS 27,29,532,690

hors d'oeuvre [n] *appetizer*
antipasto, aperitif, canape, cocktail, dip, finger food, finger sandwich, munchies, sample, starter; SEE CONCEPTS 457,828

horse [n] *equine species*
bronco, colt, filly, foal, gelding, mare, mustang, nag, plug*, pony, stallion, steed; SEE CONCEPT 394

horse around [v] *fool around*
carry on, cavort, cut up, lark, monkey around*, play around; SEE CONCEPTS 114,384

horseplay [n] *rough play*
antics, buffoonery, capers, clowning, fooling around, fun and games, hijinks, misbehavior, pranks, rough-housing, rowdiness, shenanigans, tomfoolery; SEE CONCEPT 386

horticulture [n] *gardening*
agriculture, arboriculture, cultivation, farming, floriculture, groundskeeping, viniculture, viticulture; SEE CONCEPTS 205,257

hospitable [adj] *sociable, accommodating*
accessible, amenable, amicable, bountiful, charitable, companionable, convivial, cooperative, cordial, courteous, friendly, generous, genial, gracious, gregarious, kind, liberal, magnanimous, neighborly, obliging, open, open-minded, philanthropic, receptive, red-carpet treatment*, responsive, tolerant, welcoming; SEE CONCEPTS 542,555

hospital [n] *place where ill, injured are treated*
clinic, emergency room, health service, hospice, infirmary, institution, nursing home, rest home, sanatorium, sanitarium, sick bay*, surgery, ward; SEE CONCEPTS 312,439,449

hospitality [n] *neighborliness*
accommodation, affability, amiability, cheer, companionship, comradeship, consideration, conviviality, cordiality, entertainment, friendliness, generosity, geniality, good cheer, heartiness, hospitableness, obligingness, reception, sociability, warmth, welcome; SEE CONCEPTS 388,657

host [n1] *person who entertains, performs*
anchor, anchor person, emcee, entertainer, innkeeper, keeper, manager, moderator, owner, person of the house, presenter, proprietor; SEE CONCEPT 352

host [n2] *large group*
army, array, cloud, crowd, crush, drove, flock, gathering, horde, legion, multitude, myriad, rout, score, swarm, throng; SEE CONCEPTS 417,432

host [v] *entertain, accommodate*
do the honors*, introduce, pick up the check*, present, receive, spread oneself*, throw a party, treat, wine and dine*; SEE CONCEPTS 292,384

hostage [n] *person held captive until captor's demand is met*
captive, earnest, guaranty, pawn, pledge, prisoner, sacrificial lamb*, scapegoat*, security, surety, token, victim; SEE CONCEPTS 359,423

hostile [adj] *antagonistic, mean*
adverse, alien, allergic, anti*, argumentative, bellicose, belligerent, bitter, catty*, chill*, cold*, competitive, contentious, contrary, disapproving, dour, hateful, ill-disposed, inhospitable, inimical, malevolent, malicious, malignant, militant, nasty, opposed, opposite, oppugnant, ornery*, pugnacious, rancorous, scrappy*, sour*, spiteful, surly, unfavorable, unfriendly, unkind, unpropitious, unsociable, unsympathetic, unwelcoming, viperous, virulent, vitriolic, warlike; SEE CONCEPTS 401,542

hostility [n] *antagonism, meanness*
abhorrence, aggression, animosity, animus, antipathy, aversion, bad blood*, bellicosity, belligerence, bitterness, detestation, disaffection, enmity, estrangement, grudge, hatred, ill will, imicality, malevolence, malice, opposition, rancor, resentment, spite, spleen, unfriendliness, venom, virulence, war, warpath; SEE CONCEPTS 633,657

hot [adj1] *very high in temperature*
baking, blazing, blistering, boiling, broiling, burning, calescent, close, decalescent, febrile, fevered, feverish, feverous, fiery, flaming, heated, humid, igneous, incandescent, like an oven*, on fire, ovenlike, parching, piping, recalescent, red*, roasting, scalding, scorching, searing, sizzling, smoking, steaming, stuffy, sultry, summery, sweltering, sweltry, thermogenic, torrid, tropic, tropical, very warm, warm, white*; SEE CONCEPT 605

hot [adj2] *spicy to taste*
acrid, biting, peppery, piquant, pungent, racy, sharp, spicy, zestful; SEE CONCEPT 613

hot [adj3] *passionate, vehement*
angry, animated, ardent, aroused, distracted, eager, enthusiastic, excited, fervent, fervid,

fierce, fiery, furious, ill-tempered, impassioned, impetuous, indignant, inflamed, intense, irascible, lustful, raging, stormy, temperamental, touchy, violent; SEE CONCEPTS *401,403*

hot [*adj4*] *new, in vogue*
approved, cool*, dandy, favored, fresh, glorious, groovy*, in demand, just out*, keen, latest*, marvelous, neat*, nifty*, peachy*, popular, recent, sought-after, super, trendy, up-to-the-minute*; SEE CONCEPT *589*

hot [*adj5*] *sexually excited*
aroused, carnal, concupiscent, erotic, lascivious, lewd, libidinous, lustful, passionate, prurient, salacious, sensual; SEE CONCEPTS *372,555*

hot dog [*n1*] *frankfurter*
foot long*, frank, pigs in a blanket, red-hot, weenie*, wiener; SEE CONCEPTS *399,457,460*

hot dog [*n2*] *showoff*
boaster, braggart, crowd-pleaser, granstander, showboat; SEE CONCEPT *412*

hotel [*n*] *place where one pays for accommodation*
auberge, boarding house, caravansary, dump*, fleabag*, flophouse*, hospice, hostel, hostelry, house, inn, lodging, motel, motor inn, public house, resort, roadhouse, rooming house, spa, tavern; SEE CONCEPTS *439,449,516*

hotheaded [*adj*] *quick-tempered*
easily provoked, excitable, explosive, hot-tempered, impetuous, passionate, rash, short-fused, touchy, volatile; SEE CONCEPTS *401,542,548*

hound [*n*] *dog*
afghan, airedale, akita, basset, beagle, bow-wow*, canine, dachshund, man's best friend*, mongrel, mutt, pointer, pooch, poodle, retriever; SEE CONCEPTS *394,400*

hound [*v*] *chase, badger*
annoy, bait, be at, beat the bushes*, be on one's back*, be on one's case*, be on one's tail*, bird-dog*, bother, bug, chivy, curdle, dog*, drive, give chase, goad, harass, harry, hassle, heckle, hector, hunt, hunt down, impel, leave no stone unturned*, persecute, pester, prod, provoke, pursue, rag*, rag on*, ride, scout, scratch, scratch around, search high heaven*, tail, take out after*, track down, turn inside out, turn upside down, yap at*; SEE CONCEPTS *7,19,207*

house [*n1*] *human habitat*
abode, apartment, box*, building, bullpen, castle, cave*, commoracy, condo, condominium, co-op, coop, crash pad*, crib*, cubbyhole*, den, diggings*, digs*, domicile, dump*, dwelling, edifice, flat, flophouse*, habitation, hole in the wall*, home, home plate*, homestead, joint, kennel, layout, lean-to*, mansion, pad, pied-à-terre, pigpen*, pigsty*, rack*, residence, residency, roof, roost*, setup, shack, shanty, turf*; SEE CONCEPTS *439,516*

house [*n2*] *family, ancestry*
clan, dynasty, family tree, folk, folks, household, kin, kindred, line, lineage, ménage, race, stock, tradition, tribe; SEE CONCEPT *296*

house [*n3*] *business establishment*
company, concern, corporation, firm, organization, outfit, partnership; SEE CONCEPT *325*

house [*n4*] *government body, sometimes elected, responsible for laws*
commons, congress, council, legislative body, legislature, parliament; SEE CONCEPT *299*

household [*adj*] *domestic*
domiciliary, everyday, family, home, homely, homey, ordinary, plain; SEE CONCEPT *536*

household [*n*] *domestic establishment*
family, family unit, folks, home, house, ménage; SEE CONCEPTS *296,516*

housekeeper [*n*] *domestic*
caretaker, chambermaid, house cleaner, housemaid, housewife, maid, servant; SEE CONCEPTS *348,415*

housework [*n*] *cleaning, maintaining a home*
administration, bed-making, cooking, domestic art, domestic science, dusting, home economics, homemaking, housecraft, housekeeping, ironing, laundering, management, mopping, sewing, stewardship, sweeping, washing; SEE CONCEPTS *165,170,202*

housing [*n*] *place of accommodation*
construction, digs*, dwelling, habitation, home, house, lodgment, quarter, quarterage, residence, roof, shelter, sheltering, stopping place; SEE CONCEPTS *388,516*

hovel [*n*] *tiny unkempt house*
burrow, cabin, cottage, den, dump*, hole*, hut, hutch, lean-to, pigpen*, pigsty*, rathole*, rat-trap*, shack, shanty, shed, stall, sty*; SEE CONCEPT *516*

hover [*v*] *hang, float over*
be suspended, brood over, dance, drift, flicker, flit, flitter, flutter, fly, hang about, linger, poise, wait nearby, waver; SEE CONCEPT *154*

how [*adv*] *in what way or manner*
according to what, after what precedent, by means of, by virtue of what, by what means, by what method, by whose help, from what source, through what agency, through what medium, to what degree, whence, whereby, wherewith; SEE CONCEPT *544*

however [*adv*] *still, nevertheless*
after all, all the same, anyhow, be that as it may, but, despite, for all that, howbeit, in spite of, nonetheless, notwithstanding, on the other hand, per contra, though, withal, without regard to, yet; SEE CONCEPT *544*

howl [*n/v*] *long, painful cry*
bark, bawl, bay, bellow, blubber, clamor, groan, growl, hoot, keen, lament, moan, outcry, quest, roar, scream, shout, shriek, ululate, wail, weep, whimper, whine, yell, yelp, yip, yowl; SEE CONCEPTS *64,77,595*

hub [*n*] *center, focal point*
core, focus, heart, middle, nerve center*, pivot, polestar, seat; SEE CONCEPT *826*

hubbub [*n*] *commotion, disorder*
babel, bedlam, brouhaha*, clamor, confusion, din, disturbance, fuss, hassle, hell broke loose*, hue and cry*, hullabaloo*, hurly-burly*, jangle, noise, pandemonium, racket, riot, rowdydow*, ruckus, ruction, rumpus, to-do*, tumult, turmoil, uproar, whirl; SEE CONCEPTS *230,384,388*

hubris [*n*] *arrogance*
airs, audacity, brass*, cheek*, chutzpah*, cockiness, conceitedness, contemptuousness, disdain, insolence, loftiness, nerve, ostentation, overbearance, pomposity, pompousness, presumption, pretension, pretentiousness, self-importance, vanity; SEE CONCEPTS *411,633*

huckster [*n*] *peddler*
colporteur, costermonger, hawker, pitchperson,

ho
hu

salesperson, seller, street seller, street vendor;
SEE CONCEPTS *347,348*

huddle [*n*] *assemblage, crowd, often disorganized*
bunch, chaos, cluster, clutter, confab*, conference, confusion, disarray, discussion, disorder, gathering, group, heap, jumble, mass, meeting, mess*, muddle; SEE CONCEPTS *230,260,417,432*

huddle [*v*] *meet, discuss*
bunch, cluster, confer, consult, converge, crouch, crowd, cuddle, curl up, draw together, flock, gather, herd, hug, hunch up*, mass, nestle, parley, powwow*, press, press close, snuggle, throng; SEE CONCEPTS *56,114,154*

hue [*n*] *color, shade*
aspect, cast, chroma, complexion, dye, tincture, tinge, tint, tone, value; SEE CONCEPT *622*

hue and cry [*n*] *public clamor*
brouhaha, bugle call, hullabaloo, outcry, protest, rallying cry, uproar; SEE CONCEPTS *46,65,106,674*

huff [*n*] *bad mood*
anger, annoyance, dudgeon, miff, offense, passion, perturbation, pet*, pique, rage, snit*, stew*, temper, tiff, umbrage; SEE CONCEPT *410*

huff [*v*] *sigh, breathe out forcefully*
blow, expire, gasp, heave, pant, puff; SEE CONCEPT *163*

huffy [*adj*] *angry, in a bad mood*
angered, annoyed, crabbed, crabby, cross, crotchety, crusty, curt, disgruntled, exasperated, fractious, grumpy, huffish, hurt, insulted, irked, irritable, miffed, moody, moping, nettled, offended, peeved, peevish, pettish, petulant, piqued, provoked, put out*, querulous, resentful, riled, short, snappish, snappy, stewed, sulky, sullen, surly, testy, touchy, vexed, waspish; SEE CONCEPTS *401,403*

hug [*n*] *embrace*
affection, bear hug*, bunny hug*, caress, clasp, clinch, lock, squeeze, tight grip; SEE CONCEPTS *190,375*

hug [*v*] *hold close, cling to*
bear hug, be near to, cherish, clasp, clinch, cradle, cuddle, embrace, enbosom, enfold, envelop, fold in arms, follow closely, grasp, hold onto, keep close, lie close, lock, love, nestle, nurse, press, receive, retain, seize, squeeze, stay near, take in one's arms, welcome; SEE CONCEPTS *190,375*

huge [*adj*] *extremely large*
behemothic, bulky, colossal, cyclopean, elephantine, enormous, extensive, gargantuan, giant, gigantic, great, gross*, humongous, immeasurable, immense, jumbo, leviathan, lusty, magnificent, mammoth, massive, mighty, mondo*, monster*, monstrous*, monumental, mountainous, outsize, oversize, planetary, prodigious, stupendous, titanic*, towering, tremendous, vast, walloping, whopping*; SEE CONCEPTS *771,773*

hulk [*n*] *large piece, lump; remains*
blob, body, bulk, chunk, clod, clump, frame, hull, hunk, mass, ruins, shambles, shell, shipwreck, skeleton, wreck; SEE CONCEPT *829*

hulking [*adj*] *massive*
big, bulky, clumsy, colossal, cumbersome, elephantine, enormous, extensive, gargantuan, gigantic, grand, great, heavy, hefty, huge, immense, imposing, large, lumbering, mammoth, monumental, solid, titanic, towering,

tremendous, unwieldy, weighty; SEE CONCEPTS *773,781*

hull [*n*] *skeleton, body*
bark, case, casing, cast, covering, frame, framework, husk, mold, peel, peeling, pod, rind, shell, shuck, skin, structure; SEE CONCEPTS *484,829*

hullabaloo [*n*] *uproar*
bedlam, big scene*, brouhaha, chaos, clamor, commotion, confusion, free-for-all*, furor, fuss, hassle, hubbub, hue and cry, mayhem, melee, noise, pandemonium, racket*, riot, row, ruckus, to-do*; SEE CONCEPTS *46,65,106,230,384,388,674*

hum [*v*] *buzz, vibrate*
bombilate, bombinate, bum, bumble, croon, drone, moan, mumble, murmur, purr, rustle, sing, sing low, sound, strum, throb, thrum, trill, warble, whir, whisper, zoom; SEE CONCEPTS *65,77*

human [*adj*] *characteristic of people*
animal, anthropoid, anthropological, anthropomorphic, biped, bipedal, civilized, creatural, ethnologic, ethological, fallible, fleshly, forgivable, hominal, homonid, homonine, humanistic, individual, mortal, personal, vulnerable; SEE CONCEPTS *406,549*

human [*n*] *person, homosapien*
being, biped, body, character, child, creature, homo sapien, individual, life, mortal, personage, soul, wight; SEE CONCEPT *417*

humane [*adj*] *kind, compassionate*
accommodating, altruistic, amiable, approachable, benevolent, benign, benignant, broadminded, charitable, clement, considerate, cordial, democratic, forbearing, forgiving, friendly, generous, genial, gentle, good, good-natured, gracious, helpful, human, humanitarian, indulgent, kindhearted, kindly, lenient, liberal, magnanimous, merciful, mild, natural, obliging, openminded, philanthropic, pitying, righteous, sympathetic, tender, tenderhearted, tolerant, understanding, unselfish, warmhearted; SEE CONCEPTS *401,542*

humanitarian [*adj*] *giving, compassionate*
altruistic, beneficent, benevolent, charitable, eleemosynary, generous, good, humane, idealistic, kindly, philanthropic, public-spirited; SEE CONCEPT *542*

humanitarian [*n*] *person who gives generously*
altruist, benefactor, bleeding heart*, do-gooder*, Good Samaritan*, good scout*, helper, patron, philanthropist; SEE CONCEPTS *416,423*

humanity [*n1*] *human race*
Homo sapiens, human beings, humankind, humanness, mankind, people, society; SEE CONCEPT *417*

humanity [*n2*] *benevolence*
altruism, amity, brotherly love, charity, compassion, empathy, feeling, friendship, generosity, goodness, goodwill, heart, kindheartedness, kindness, mercy, sympathy; SEE CONCEPT *410,633*

humankind [*n*] *the human race*
community, flesh, Homo sapiens, human beings, humanity, human species, mortality, mortals, people, populace, society; SEE CONCEPT *417*

humble [*adj1*] *meek, unassuming*
apprehensive, backward, bashful, biddable, blushing, content, courteous, deferential, demure, diffident, docile, fearful, gentle, hesitant,

lowly, manageable, mild, modest, obliging, obsequious, ordinary, polite, quiet, reserved, respectful, retiring, reverential, sedate, self-conscious, self-effacing, servile, sheepish, shy, simple, soft-spoken, standoffish, submissive, subservient, supplicatory, tentative, timid, timorous, tractable, unambitious, unobtrusive, unostentatious, unpretentious, withdrawn; SEE CONCEPTS *401,404*

humble [*adj2*] *poor, inferior*
base, beggarly, common, commonplace, contemptible, humdrum, ignoble, inglorious, insignificant, little, low, low-born, lowly, low-ranking, meager, mean, measly, menial, miserable, modest, obscure, ordinary, paltry, petty, pitiful, plebeian, proletarian, puny, rough, scrubby, seemly, servile, severe, shabby, simple, small, sordid, trivial, unassuming, uncouth, underprivileged, undistinguished, unfit, unimportant, unpretentious, unrefined, vulgar, wretched; SEE CONCEPTS *334,549,589*

humble [*v*] *shame, put down*
abase, abash, bemean, break, bring down*, cast down, chagrin, chasten, confound, confuse, crush*, cut to the quick*, debase, deflate, degrade, demean, demote, deny, discomfit, discredit, disgrace, embarrass, hide, humiliate, lower*, make eat dirt*, make one feel small*, mortify, overcome, pop one's balloon*, pull down*, put away*, put one away*, put to shame, reduce, silence, sink, snub, squash*, squelch, strike dumb, subdue, take down*, take down a peg*, upset; SEE CONCEPTS *14,16,44,52*

humbug [*n1*] *nonsense*
babble, balderdash*, baloney*, BS*, bull*, bunk*, drivel, empty talk, gibberish, hogwash*, hooey*, hot air*, poppycock*, pretense, rubbish, silliness, trash*; SEE CONCEPTS *230,388,633*

humbug [*n2*] *hoax*
con*, con game*, deceit, fast one*, flimflam*, fraud, gyp*, hustle, prank, put-on, scam, snow job*, spoof, sting, swindle; SEE CONCEPTS *59,63*

humdinger [*n*] *something extraordinary*
ace, beauty, champ, champion, crackerjack*, doozy, hit, hot stuff*, knockout, lulu, pip*, pistol*, smash hit, something, something else, whopper, winner; SEE CONCEPT *668*

humdrum [*adj*] *boring, uneventful*
arid, banausic, blah, bromidic, common, commonplace, dim, dime a dozen*, drab, dreary, dull, everyday, garden-variety*, insipid, lifeless, monotone, monotonous, mundane, ordinary, pedestrian, plodding, prosy, repetitious, routine, tedious, tiresome, toneless, treadmill, uninteresting, unvaried, vanilla*, wearisome, whitebread*; SEE CONCEPT *548*

humid [*adj*] *very damp, referring to weather*
boiling, clammy, close, dank, irriguous, moist, mucky, muggy, oppressive, sodden, soggy, steamy, sticky, stifling, sultry, sultry, sweaty, sweltering, watery, wet; SEE CONCEPTS *525,603*

humidity [*n*] *very damp weather*
clamminess, dampness, dankness, dew, dewiness, evaporation, fogginess, heaviness, humectation, humidness, moistness, moisture, mugginess, oppressiveness, sogginess, steam, steaminess, stickiness, sultriness, sweatiness, swelter, thickness, vaporization, wet, wetness; SEE CONCEPTS *524,607*

humiliate [*v*] *embarrass, put down*
abase, abash, base, bemean, blister, break, bring down*, bring low*, cast down, chagrin, chasten, confound, confuse, conquer, crush*, cut down to size*, debase, degrade, demean, denigrate, deny, depress, discomfit, discountenance, disgrace, dishonor, downplay, humble, lower, make a fool of*, make ashamed, mortify, pan, play down, put out of countenance*, put to shame, rip*, run down*, shame, shoot down*, slam*, smear, snub, squash*, subdue, take down*, take down a peg*, tear down*, vanquish, wither; SEE CONCEPTS *14,44,52*

humiliation [*n*] *embarrassment*
abasement, affront, chagrin, comedown*, comeuppance, condescension, confusion, degradation, discomfiture, disgrace, dishonor, humbling, ignominy, indignity, loss of face*, mental pain, mortification, put-down, resignation, self-abasement, shame, submission, submissiveness, touché*; SEE CONCEPTS *388,410*

humility [*n*] *humbleness, modesty*
abasement, bashfulness, demureness, diffidence, docility, fawning, inferiority complex, lack of pride, lowliness, meekness, mortification, nonresistance, obedience, obsequiousness, passiveness, reserve, resignation, self-abasement, self-abnegation, servility, sheepishness, shyness, subjection, submissiveness, subservience, timidity, timorousness, unobtrusiveness, unpretentiousness; SEE CONCEPTS *633,657*

humor [*n1*] *comedy, funniness*
amusement, badinage, banter, buffoonery, clowning, comicality, comicalness, drollery, facetiousness, farce, flippancy, fun, gag, gaiety, happiness, high spirits, jest, jesting, jocoseness, jocularity, joke, joking, joyfulness, kidding, levity, lightness, playfulness, pleasantry, raillery, tomfoolery, whimsy, wisecrack, wit, witticism, wittiness; SEE CONCEPT *293*

humor [*n2*] *mood, temperament*
bee, bent, bias, caprice, character, complexion, conceit, disposition, fancy, frame of mind, individualism, individuality, makeup, mind, nature, notion, personality, propensity, quirk, spirits, strain, temper, tone, vagary, vein, whim; SEE CONCEPTS *9,410,411*

humorist [*n*] *comedian*
card*, clown, comedienne, comic, cutup, entertainer, jester, joker, jokesmith, jokester, satirist, stand-up comic, wisecracker, wit; SEE CONCEPTS *352,423*

humorous [*adj*] *funny, comical*
amusing, camp*, campy*, comic, droll, entertaining, facetious, farcical, hilarious, jocose, jocular, jokey, joshing, laughable, ludicrous, merry, playful, pleasant, priceless, ribald, screaming*, side-splitting*, too funny for words*, waggish, whimsical, witty; SEE CONCEPTS *267,529*

hump [*n*] *swelling, projection*
bulge, bump, convexedness, convexity, dune, elevation, eminence, excrescence, gibbosity, hill, hummock, hunch, knap, knob, knurl, kyphosis, mound, prominence, protrusion, protuberance, ridge, swell, tumescence; SEE CONCEPTS *471,513*

hunch [*n*] *feeling, idea*
anticipation, apprehension, auguration, augury, boding, clue, expectation, feeling in one's bones*, foreboding, forecast, foreknowledge, forewarning, forewisdom, funny feeling*, glim-

hu
hu

hunch [v] *cower, crouch*
arch, bend, bow, curve, draw in, draw together, huddle, hump, lean, scrooch down, squat, stoop, tense; SEE CONCEPT 154

hunger [n] *appetite for food, other desire*
ache, appetence, appetency, appetition, a stomach for*, big eyes*, bottomless pit*, craving, desire, emptiness, esurience, eyes for*, famine, famishment, gluttony, greed, greediness, hungriness, longing, lust, mania, munchies*, ravenousness, starvation, sweet tooth*, vacancy, void, voracity, want, yearning, yen; SEE CONCEPTS 20,709

hungry [adj] *starving; desirous*
athirst, avid, carnivorous, could eat a horse*, covetous, craving, eager, edacious, empty, esurient, famished, famishing, flying light*, got the munchies*, greedy, hankering, hoggish, hollow, hungered, insatiate, keen, omnivorous, on empty stomach*, piggish*, rapacious, ravenous, starved, unfilled, unsatisfied, voracious, yearning; SEE CONCEPTS 20,406

hunk [n] *chunk of solid material*
a lot*, batch, bit, block, bulk, bunch, clod, glob, gob*, large piece, loads*, loaf, lump, mass, morsel, nugget, piece, pile, portion, quantity, slab, slice, wad, wedge; SEE CONCEPTS 470,471

hunt [n] *search, chase*
coursing, exploration, field sport, following, frisking, game, hounding, hunting, inquest, inquiry, inquisition, interrogation, investigation, look-see*, meddling, probe, prosecution, prying, pursuance, pursuing, pursuit, quest, race, raid, reconnaissance, research, rummage, scrutiny, seeking, sifting, snooping, sporting, steeplechase, study, tracing, trailing; SEE CONCEPTS 207,216

hunt [v] *chase for killing*
beat the bushes*, bird-dog*, capture, course, dog, drag, drive, fish, follow, give chase, grouse, gun*, gun for*, hawk, heel, hound, kill, look for, poach, press, pursue, ride, run, scent, scratch, scratch around, seek, shadow, shoot, snare, stalk, start, track, trail; SEE CONCEPTS 207,216,252,363

hunt [v2] *look, search for*
be on the lookout*, cast about, delve, drag, examine, ferret out, fish for, forage, go after, grope, inquire, interrogate, investigate, look all over hell*, look high and low*, nose around*, probe, prowl, quest, question, ransack, rummage, run down, scour, scratch around*, search high heaven*, seek, sift, trace, trail, try to find, winnow; SEE CONCEPT 216

hurdle [n] *barrier, obstacle*
bar, barricade, blockade, complication, difficulty, fence, hamper, handicap, hedge, hindrance, impediment, interference, mountain, obstruction, rub, snag, stumbling block, traverse, wall; SEE CONCEPTS 470,674

hurdle [v] *jump over an obstacle*
bounce, bound, clear, conquer, down, hop, jump across, leap over, lick, lop, master, negotiate, over, overcome, saltate, scale, spring, surmount, vault; SEE CONCEPT 194

hurl [v] *throw forcefully*
bung, cast, chuck, chunk, fire, fling, gun, heave, launch, let fly, lob, peg, pitch, project, propel, send, sling, toss; SEE CONCEPT 222

hurricane [n] *violent windstorm*
blow, cyclone, gale, line storm, monsoon, storm, tempest, tornado, tropical cyclone, tropical storm, twister, typhoon, whirlwind; SEE CONCEPTS 524,526

hurried [adj] *quick, rushed*
abrupt, breakneck, brief, cursory, fast, hasty, headlong, hectic, impetuous, perfunctory, precipitant, precipitate, precipitous, rushing, short, slapdash, speedy, subitaneous, sudden, superficial, swift; SEE CONCEPTS 548,588,799

hurry [n] *speed in action, motion*
bustle, celerity, commotion, dash, dispatch, drive, expedition, expeditiousness, flurry, haste, precipitance, precipitateness, precipitation, promptitude, push, quickness, rush, rustle, scurry, speediness, swiftness, urgency; SEE CONCEPTS 657,748,755

hurry [v] *act, move speedily*
accelerate, barrel, beeline*, be quick, bestir, breeze, bullet, burst, bustle, dash, dig in, drive, expedite, fleet, flit, fly, get a move on*, goad, go like lightning*, haste, hasten, hurry up, hustle, jog, lose no time, make haste, make short work of*, make time*, make tracks*, nip, push, quicken, race, rip, rocket, roll, run, rush, sally, scoot, scurry, shake a leg*, smoke, speed, speed up, spur, step on gas*, step on it*, turn on steam*, urge, whirl, whish, whisk, whiz, zip; SEE CONCEPTS 150,234

hurt [adj] *physically or mentally injured*
aching, aggrieved, agonized, all torn up*, battered, bleeding, bruised, buffeted, burned, busted up*, contused, crushed, cut, damaged, disfigured, distressed, disturbed, grazed, harmed, hit, impaired, indignant, in pain, lacerated, marred, mauled, miffed, mutilated, nicked, offended, pained, piqued, put away, resentful, rueful, sad, scarred, scraped, scratched, shook, shot, sore, stricken, struck, suffering, tender, tortured, umbrageous, unhappy, warped, wounded; SEE CONCEPTS 314,403

hurt [n] *injury; damage*
ache, black and blue*, blow, boo-boo*, bruise, chop, detriment, disadvantage, disaster, discomfort, disservice, distress, down, gash, harm, ill, ill-treatment, loss, mark, mischief, misfortune, nick, ouch, outrage, pain, pang, persecution, prejudice, ruin, scratch, sore, soreness, suffering, wound, wrong; SEE CONCEPTS 316,728

hurt [v1] *cause physical pain; experience pain*
abuse, ache, afflict, ail, belt, be sore, be tender, bite, blemish, bruise, burn, cramp, cut, cut up, damage, disable, do violence, flail, flog, harm, impair, injure, kick, lacerate, lash, maltreat, mar, maul, mess up, nip, pierce, pinch, pommel, prick, pummel, punch, puncture, punish, rough up, shake up, slap, slug, smart, spank, spoil, squeeze, stab, sting, tear, throb, torment, torture, total, trouble, wax, whack, whip, wing, wound, wrack up, wring; SEE CONCEPTS 246,313

hurt [v2] *cause mental pain*
abuse, afflict, aggrieve, annoy, burn, chafe, constrain, cut to the quick*, discomfit, discommode, displease, distress, excruciate, faze, give no quarter*, go for jugular*, grieve, hit where one

lives*, injure, lambaste, lay a bad trip on*, lean on*, martyr, martyrize, prejudice, punish, put down, put out, sadden, sting*, thumb nose at*, torment, torture, try, upset, vex, vitiate, work over*, wound, zing*; SEE CONCEPTS 7,14,19

hurtful [*adj*] *injurious, cruel*
aching, afflictive, bad, cutting, damaging, dangerous, deadly, deleterious, destructive, detrimental, disadvantageous, distressing, evil, harmful, hurting, malicious, mean, mischievous, nasty, nocuous, noxious, ominous, pernicious, poisonous, prejudicial, spiteful, unkind, upsetting, wounding; SEE CONCEPTS 537,542

hurtle [*v*] *plunge, charge*
bump, collide, fly, lunge, push, race, rush, rush headlong, scoot, scramble, shoot, speed, spurt, tear; SEE CONCEPT 150

husband [*n*] *married man*
bridegroom, companion, consort, groom, helpmate, hubby, mate, monogamist, monogynist, other half, partner, spouse; SEE CONCEPTS 414,419

hush [*n*] *quiet*
calm, lull, peace, peacefulness, quietude, silence, still, stillness, tranquility; SEE CONCEPT 65

hush [*v*] *attempt to make quiet*
burke, choke, gag, muffle, mute, muzzle, quiet, quieten, shush*, shut up, silence, stifle, still, stop, suppress; SEE CONCEPTS 65,87

hush-hush [*adj*] *secret*
clandestine, classified, closet, confidential, covert, dark, private, restricted, sub-rosa*, surreptitious, undercover, under-the-table*; SEE CONCEPT 576

hush up [*v*] *keep secret*
burke, conceal, cover, cover up, keep dark, sit on, smother, squash, stifle, suppress; SEE CONCEPT 266

husk [*n*] *covering, case*
aril, bark, case, chaff, glume, hull, outside, pod, rind, shell, shuck, skin; SEE CONCEPTS 428,484

husky [*adj1*] *deep, scratchy in sound*
croaking, croaky, growling, gruff, guttural, harsh, hoarse, loud, rasping, raucous, rough, throaty; SEE CONCEPT 594

husky [*adj2*] *big, burly*
brawny, gigantic, hefty, Herculean*, mighty, muscular, powerful, rugged, sinewy, stalwart, stocky, stout, strapping, strong, sturdy, thickset, well-built; SEE CONCEPT 773

hussy [*n*] *loose woman*
broad, floozy, jade, Jezebel, minx, slut, strumpet, tart*, tramp, trollop, vamp, wench, whore; SEE CONCEPTS 348,412,415,419

hustle [*v*] *hurry; work hurriedly*
apply oneself, be conscientious, bulldoze*, bustle, elbow, fly, force, haste, hasten, hotfoot*, impel, jog, press, push, race, rush, shove, speed, thrust, use elbow grease*; SEE CONCEPTS 91,150

hustler [*n*] *con artist; prostitute*
call girl, cheater, fast talker, floozy, grifter, hooker, rip-off artist*, scam artist, streetwalker, swindler, whore; SEE CONCEPTS 348,412,415,419

hut [*n*] *tiny, often roughly built, house*
box*, bungalow, cabana, cabin, camp, chalet, cot, cottage, crib*, den, dugout, dump*, hovel*, hutch, lean-to, lodge, log house, pigeonhole*, rathole*, refuge, shack, shanty, shed, shelter, summer house, tepee, wigwam; SEE CONCEPT 516

hybrid [*n*] *composite, mixture*
amalgam, bastard, combination, compound, cross, crossbreed, half-blood, half-breed, half-caste, incross, miscegenation, mongrel, mule, outcross; SEE CONCEPTS 260,394,414,429

hygiene [*n*] *cleanliness*
healthful living, hygienics, preventive medicine, public health, regimen, salutariness, sanitation, wholesomeness; SEE CONCEPTS 316,405

hygienic [*adj*] *clean*
aseptic, disinfected, germ-free, good, healthful, healthy, pure, salubrious, salutary, salutiferous, sanitary, sterile, uncontaminated, uninfected, wholesome; SEE CONCEPT 621

hymn [*n*] *religious song*
aria, canticle, carol, chant, choral, chorale, descant, ditty, evensong, hosanna, laud, lay, lied, litany, ode, oratorio, paean, psalm, shout, song of praise, worship song; SEE CONCEPTS 262,595

hype [*n*] *extensive publicity*
advertising, buildup*, plugging*, promotion; SEE CONCEPTS 292,324

hyperactive [*adj*] *excessively active*
excitable, high-strung, hyper*, overactive, overzealous, uncontrollable, wild; SEE CONCEPTS 401,404

hyperbole [*n*] *exaggeration*
amplification, big talk*, coloring*, distortion, embellishment, embroidering, enlargement, hype*, laying it on thick*, magnification, metaphor, mountain out of molehill*, overstatement, PR*, tall talk*; SEE CONCEPT 268

hypercritical [*adj*] *captious*
carping, caviling, censorious, critical, demanding, faultfinding, finicky, fussy, hair-splitting, hard to please, niggling, nit-picking, overcritical, persnickety; SEE CONCEPTS 267,404

hyperinflation [*n*] *extremely high, rising economic inflation*
devaluation, overextension, run-away inflation, wheelbarrow economics; SEE CONCEPT 335

hypermedia [*n*] *system giving access to multimedia information on a single subject*
data base, information bank, information retrieval; SEE CONCEPT 274

hypnotic [*adj*] *spellbinding, sleep-inducing*
anesthetic, anodyne, calmative, lenitive, mesmeric, mesmerizing, narcotic, opiate, sleepy, somniferous, somnolent, soothing, soporific, soporose, trance-inducing; SEE CONCEPTS 529,537

hypnotize [*v*] *put in trance; spellbind*
anesthetize, bring under control, captivate, charm, drug, dull the will, entrance, fascinate, hold under a spell, induce, lull to sleep, magnetize, make drowsy, make sleepy, mesmerize, narcotize, put to sleep, soothe, stupefy, subject to suggestion; SEE CONCEPT 250

hypocrisy [*n*] *deceitfulness, pretense*
affectation, bad faith*, bigotry, cant, casuistry, deceit, deception, dishonesty, display, dissembling, dissimulation, double-dealing, duplicity, false profession, falsity, fraud, glibness, imposture, insincerity, irreverence, lie, lip service*, mockery, pharisaicalness, pharisaism, phoniness, pietism, quackery, sanctimoniousness, sanctimony, speciousness, unctuousness; SEE CONCEPTS 63,633,657

hypocrite [*n*] *person who pretends, is deceitful*
actor, attitudinizer, backslider*, bigot, bluffer, casuist, charlatan, cheat, con artist, crook,

deceiver, decoy, dissembler, dissimulator, fake, faker, four-flusher*, fraud, hook*, humbug, impostor, informer, lip server*, malingerer, masquerader, mountebank, Pharisee, phony, playactor*, poser, pretender, quack*, smoothie*, sophist, swindler, trickster, two-face*, two-timer*, wolf in sheep's clothing*; SEE CONCEPT 412

hypocritical [*adj*] *deceitful, pretending*
affected, artificial, assuming, bland, canting, captious, caviling, deceptive, deluding, dissembling, double, double-dealing, duplicitous, faithless, false, feigning, fishy*, fraudulent, glib, hollow, insincere, jivey, left-handed, lying, moralistic, oily, pharisaical, phony, pietistic, pious, sanctimonious, self-righteous, smooth, smooth-spoken, smooth-tongued*, snide, specious, spurious, two-faced*, unctuous, unnatural, unreliable; SEE CONCEPTS 267,401,542

hypothesis [*n*] *theory*
antecedent, apriority, assignment, assumption, attribution, axiom, basis, belief, conclusion, condition, conjecture, data, deduction, demonstration, derivation, explanation, foundation, ground, guess, inference, interpretation, layout, lemma, philosophy, plan, position, postulate, premise, presupposition, principle, proposal, proposition, rationale, reason, scheme, shot in the dark*, speculation, starting point, suggestion, supposition, surmise, system, tentative law, term, theorem, thesis; SEE CONCEPTS 661,689

hypothetical [*adj*] *guessed, assumed*
academical, assumptive, casual, concocted, conditional, conjectural, conjectural, contestable, contingent, debatable, disputable, doubtful, equivocal, imaginary, imagined, indefinite, indeterminate, postulated, presumptive, presupposed, pretending, problematic, provisory, putative, questionable, refutable, speculative, stochastic, supposed, suppositional, suppositious, suspect, theoretic, theoretical, uncertain, unconfirmed, vague; SEE CONCEPTS 529,552,582

hysteria [*n*] *state of extreme upset*
agitation, delirium, excitement, feverishness, frenzy, hysterics, madness, mirth, nervousness, panic, unreason; SEE CONCEPT 410

hysterical [*adj*] *very upset, excited*
agitated, berserk, beside oneself, blazing, carried away*, convulsive, crazed, crazy, delirious, distracted, distraught, emotional, fiery, frantic, frenzied, fuming, furious, impassioned, impetuous, in a fit, incensed, irrepressible, mad, maddened, nervous, neurotic, overwrought, panic-stricken, passionate, possessed, rabid, raging, rampant, raving, seething, spasmodic, tempestuous, turbulent, uncontrollable, uncontrolled, unnerved, unrestrained, uproarious, vehement, violent, wild, worked up*; SEE CONCEPTS 403,542

I

ice [*n*] *frozen water*
chunk, crystal, cube ice, diamonds*, dry ice, floe, glacier, glaze, hail, hailstone, iceberg, ice cube, icicle, permafrost, sleet; SEE CONCEPTS 470,514

icky [*adj*] *not pleasant*
disgusting, horrible, loathsome, nasty, noisome, offensive, repellent, revolting, sickening, vile; SEE CONCEPT 570

icon [*n*] *image*
figure, graphical user interface, graphic image, idol, ikon, likeness, painted image, picture, portrait, portrayal, representation, symbol; SEE CONCEPTS 259,667,716

iconoclast [*n*] *detractor*
critic, cynic, denouncer, dissenter, dissident, heretic, image-breaker, nonbeliever, non-conformist, questioner, radical, rebel, revolutionist, ruiner, sceptic, unbeliever; SEE CONCEPTS 359,423

icy [*adj*] *frozen; slippery when frozen*
antarctic, arctic, biting, bitter, chill, chilled to the bone*, chilling, chilly, cold, freezing, frigid, frost-bound, frosty, frozen over, gelid, glacial, glaring, iced, polar, raw, refrigerated, rimy, shivering, shivery, sleeted, smooth as glass*; SEE CONCEPTS 605,606

icy [*adj2*] *aloof*
chill, cold, distant, emotionless, forbidding, frigid, frosty, glacial, hostile, indifferent, steely, stony, unemotional, unfriendly, unwelcoming; SEE CONCEPTS 401,404

idea [*n*] *something understood, planned, or believed*
abstraction, aim, approximation, belief, brainstorm*, clue, concept, conception, conclusion, conviction, design, doctrine, end, essence, estimate, fancy, feeling, flash*, form, guess, hint, hypothesis, import, impression, inkling, intention, interpretation, intimation, judgment, meaning, notion, object, objective, opinion, pattern, perception, plan, purpose, reason, scheme, sense, significance, solution, suggestion, suspicion, teaching, theory, thought, understanding, view, viewpoint; SEE CONCEPTS 529,660,661,689

ideal [*adj1*] *model, perfect*
absolute, archetypal, classic, classical, complete, consummate, excellent, exemplary, fitting, flawless, have-it-all*, indefectible, optimal, paradigmatic, pie-in-the-sky*, prototypical, quintessential, representative, Shangri-la*, supreme; SEE CONCEPTS 533,574

ideal [*adj2*] *conceptual; impractical*
abstract, chimerical, dreamlike, extravagant, fanciful, fictitious, high-flown, hypothetical, imaginary, intellectual, in the clouds*, ivory-tower*, mental, mercurial, notional, out-of-reach*, quixotic, theoretical, transcendent, transcendental, unattainable, unearthly, unreal, Utopian*, visionary; SEE CONCEPTS 529,552

ideal [*n*] *model*
archetype, criterion, epitome, example, exemplar, goal, idol, jewel, last word*, mirror, nonesuch, nonpareil, paradigm, paragon, pattern, perfection, prototype, standard; SEE CONCEPTS 671,686

idealist [*n*] *person who holds fancies in mind, who believes in perfection*
dreamer, enthusiast, escapist, optimist, Platonist, radical, romancer, romantic, romanticist, seer, stargazer, theorizer, transcendentalist, utopian, visionary; SEE CONCEPTS 359,416,423

idealistic [*adj*] *visionary*
abstracted, chimerical, dreaming, idealized, impractical, optimistic, quixotic, radical, romantic,

starry-eyed, unrealistic, utopian; SEE CONCEPTS *529,560,582*

ideals [*n*] *moral beliefs*
ethics, goals, principles, standards, values; SEE CONCEPTS *645,689*

identical [*adj*] *alike, equal*
carbon copy*, corresponding, dead ringer*, ditto*, double, duplicate, equivalent, exact, identic, indistinguishable, interchangeable, like, like two peas in a pod*, look-alike, matching, same, same difference*, selfsame, spitting image*, tantamount, twin, very, very same, Xerox*; SEE CONCEPTS *487,566,573*

identification [*n*] *labeling; means of labeling*
apperception, assimilation, badge, bracelet, cataloging, classifying, credentials, description, dog tag, establishment, ID*, identity bracelet, letter of introduction, letter of recommendation, naming, papers, passport, recognition, tag, testimony; SEE CONCEPTS *268,271*

identify [*v*] *recognize; label*
analyze, button down*, card, catalog, classify, describe, determinate, determine, diagnose, diagnosticate, distinguish, establish, find, make out, name, peg*, pick out, pinpoint, place, put one's finger on*, select, separate, single out*, spot, tab*, tag*; SEE CONCEPTS *38,62*

identify with [*v*] *put oneself in the place of another*
ally, associate, empathize, feel for*, put in same category*, put oneself in another's shoes*, relate to, respond to, see through someone's eyes*, sympathize, think of in connection*, understand; SEE CONCEPTS *15,39*

identity [*n1*] *person's individuality*
character, circumstances, coherence, distinctiveness, existence, identification, integrity, ipseity, name, oneness, particularity, personality, self, selfdom, selfhood, selfness, singleness, singularity, status, uniqueness; SEE CONCEPT *411*

identity [*n2*] *similarity, correspondence*
accord, agreement, congruence, congruity, empathy, equality, equivalence, identicalness, likeness, oneness, rapport, resemblance, sameness, selfsameness, semblance, similitude, unanimity, uniformity, unity; SEE CONCEPTS *664,670*

ideology [*n*] *beliefs*
articles of faith*, credo, creed, culture, dogma, ideas, outlook, philosophy, principles, system, tenets, theory, view, Weltanschauung*; SEE CONCEPTS *688,689*

idiocy [*n*] *utter stupidity*
asininity, cretinism, derangement, fatuity, fatuousness, foolishness, imbecility, inanity, insanity, insipidity, lunacy, madness, senselessness, tomfoolery; SEE CONCEPTS *409,410*

idiom [*n*] *manner of speaking, turn of phrase*
argot, colloquialism, dialect, expression, idiosyncrasy, jargon, language, lingo*, localism, locution, parlance, patois, phrase, provincialism, set phrase, street talk*, style, talk, tongue, usage, vernacular, vernacularism, word; SEE CONCEPT *275*

idiosyncrasy [*n*] *oddity, quirk*
affectation, bit, characteristic, distinction, eccentricity, feature, habit, mannerism, peculiarity, singularity, trait, trick; SEE CONCEPTS *411,644*

idiot [*n*] *very stupid person*
blockhead, bonehead*, cretin, dimwit, dork, dumbbell, dunce, fool, ignoramus, imbecile, jerk,

kook*, moron, nincompoop, ninny*, nitwit, out to lunch*, pinhead*, simpleton, stupid, tomfool, twit*; SEE CONCEPT *412*

idiotic [*adj*] *very stupid*
asinine, batty*, birdbrained*, crazy, daffy*, daft, dull, dumb, fatuous, foolhardy, foolish, harebrained*, imbecile, imbecilic, inane, insane, lunatic, moronic, senseless, silly, squirrelly*, thick-witted*, unintelligent; SEE CONCEPT *402*

idle [*adj1*] *not used; out of action*
abandoned, asleep, barren, closed down, dead, deserted, down, dusty, empty, gathering dust*, inactive, inert, jobless, laid-off, leisured, mothballed, motionless, on the bench*, on the shelf*, out of operation, out of work*, passive, quiet, redundant, resting, rusty, sleepy, stationary, still, uncultivated, unemployed, unoccupied, untouched, unused, vacant, void, waste, workless; SEE CONCEPTS *542,560*

idle [*adj2*] *lazy*
at rest, indolent, lackadaisical, resting, shiftless, slothful, sluggish, taking it easy*; SEE CONCEPTS *401,538*

idle [*adj3*] *worthless, ineffective*
abortive, bootless, empty, frivolous, fruitless, futile, groundless, hollow, insignificant, irrelevant, not serious, nugatory, of no avail*, otiose, pointless, rambling, superficial, trivial, unavailing, unhelpful, unnecessary, unproductive, unsuccessful, useless, vain; SEE CONCEPTS *267,560*

idleness [*n*] *laziness, inaction*
dawdling, dilly-dallying*, dormancy, droning, goof-off time*, hibernation, inactivity, indolence, inertia, joblessness, laze, lazing, leisure, lethargy, loafing, loitering, otiosity, own sweet time*, pottering, shiftlessness, sloth, slothfulness, slouch, slowness, sluggishness, stupor, time on one's hands*, time to burn*, time to kill*, time-wasting, torpidity, torpor, trifling, truancy, unemployment, vegetating; SEE CONCEPTS *657,677,681*

idol [*n*] *person greatly admired*
beloved, darling, dear, deity, desire, eidolon, false god, favorite, fetish, god, goddess, golden calf*, graven image, hero, icon, image, inamorata, pagan symbol, simulacrum, superstar; SEE CONCEPTS *352,423*

idolize [*v*] *think of very highly; worship*
admire, adore, apotheosize, bow down, canonize, deify, dote on, exalt, glorify, look up to*, love, put on a pedestal*, revere, reverence, venerate; SEE CONCEPTS *10,32*

idyllic [*adj*] *perfect; extremely pleasant*
arcadian, bucolic, charming, comfortable, halcyon, heavenly, ideal, idealized, out-of-this-world*, pastoral, peaceful, picturesque, pleasing, rustic, unspoiled; SEE CONCEPTS *529,572*

iffy [*adj*] *uncertain*
capricious, chancy, conditional, dicey, doubtful, erratic, fluctuant, incalculable, in lap of gods*, problematic, undecided, unpredictable, unsettled, up in the air*, whimsical; SEE CONCEPT *552*

ignite [*v*] *set on fire*
burn, burst into flames, catch fire, enkindle, fire, flare up, inflame, kindle, light, put match to*, set alight, set fire to, start up, take fire, touch off; SEE CONCEPT *249*

ignoble [*adj*] *lowly, unworthy*
abject, base, baseborn, coarse, common, con-

hy ig

temptible, corrupt, craven, dastardly, degenerate, degraded, despicable, disgraceful, dishonorable, heinous, humble, infamous, inferior, lewd, low, mean, menial, modest, ordinary, peasant, petty, plain, plebeian, poor, rotten, scurvy, servile, shabby, shameful, simple, sordid, unwashed, vile, vulgar, wicked, wretched, wrong; SEE CONCEPTS 542,545,549

ignorance [n] *unintelligence, inexperience*
benightedness, bewilderment, blindness, callowness, crudeness, darkness, denseness, disregard, dumbness, empty-headedness*, fog*, halfknowledge, illiteracy, incapacity, incomprehension, innocence, inscience, insensitivity, lack of education, mental incapacity, naiveté, nescience, oblivion, obtuseness, philistinism, rawness, sciolism, shallowness, simplicity, unawareness, unconsciousness, uncouthness, unenlightenment, unfamiliarity, unscholarliness, vagueness; SEE CONCEPTS 409,678

ignorant [adj] *unaware, unknowing*
apprenticed, benighted, birdbrained*, blind to*, cretinous, dense, green*, illiterate, imbecile, inexperienced, innocent, insensible, in the dark*, mindless, misinformed, moronic, naive, nescient, oblivious, obtuse, shallow, thick, unconscious, unconversant, uncultivated, uncultured, uneducated, unenlightened, uninformed, uninitiated, unintellectual, unknowledgeable, unlearned, unlettered, unmindful, unread, unschooled, unsuspecting, untaught, untrained, unwitting, witless; SEE CONCEPTS 402,542

ignore [v] *disregard on purpose*
avoid, be oblivious to, blink, brush off*, bury one's head in sand*, cold-shoulder*, discount, disdain, evade, fail, forget, let it go*, neglect, omit, overlook, overpass, pass over, pay no attention to, pay no mind*, pooh-pooh*, reject, scorn, shut eyes to*, slight, take no notice, tune out*, turn back on*, turn blind eye*, turn deaf ear; SEE CONCEPT 30

ilk [n] *kind, type*
brand, class, classification, denomination, gender, kin, lot, order, persuasion, race, set, sort, species, variety; SEE CONCEPTS 378,411,673

ill [adj1] *sick*
afflicted, ailing, a wreck*, below par*, bummed*, diseased, down, down with, feeling awful, feeling rotten, feeling terrible, got the bug*, indisposed, infirm, laid low*, off one's feet*, on sick list*, out of sorts*, peaked, poorly, queasy, rotten, run-down, running temperature, sick as a dog*, under the weather*, unhealthy, unwell, woozy*; SEE CONCEPT 314

ill [adj2] *bad, evil*
acrimonious, adverse, antagonistic, cantankerous, cross, damaging, deleterious, detrimental, disrespectful, disturbing, foreboding, foul, harmful, harsh, hateful, hostile, hurtful, ill-mannered, impertinent, inauspicious, inimical, iniquitous, injurious, malevolent, malicious, nocent, nocuous, noxious, ominous, ruinous, sinister, sullen, surly, threatening, unfavorable, unfortunate, unfriendly, ungracious, unhealthy, unkind, unlucky, unpromising, unpropitious, unwholesome, vile, wicked, wrong; SEE CONCEPTS 537,545,570

ill [n] *misfortune*
abuse, affection, affliction, ailment, badness, complaint, condition, cruelty, damage, depravity, destruction, disease, disorder, evil, harm, hurt, illness, indisposition, infirmity, injury, insult, malady, malaise, malice, mischief, misery, pain, sickness, suffering, syndrome, trial, tribulation, trouble, unpleasantness, wickedness, woe, wrong; SEE CONCEPTS 316,674,675

ill-advised [adj] *unwise, not thought out*
brash, confused, foolhardy, foolish, half-baked*, hotheaded*, ill-considered, ill-judged, impolitic, imprudent, inappropriate, incautious, inconsiderate, indiscreet, inexpedient, injudicious, madcap*, misguided, off the top of one's head*, overhasty, rash, reckless, short-sighted*, thoughtless, unseemly, wrong; SEE CONCEPTS 544,548

ill at ease [adj] *uncomfortable, nervous*
anxious, awkward, discomfited, disquieted, disturbed, doubtful, edgy, faltering, fidgety, hesitant, insecure, on edge*, on pins and needles*, on tenterhooks*, out of place*, restless, self-conscious, shy, suspicious, tense, uneasy, unrelaxed, unsettled, unsure; SEE CONCEPTS 401,403

illegal [adj] *against the law*
actionable, banned, black-market*, bootleg*, contraband, criminal, crooked, extralegal, felonious, forbidden, heavy*, hot*, illegitimate, illicit, interdicted, irregular, lawless, not approved, not legal, outlawed, outside the law, prohibited, proscribed, prosecutable, racket, shady, smuggled, sub rosa, taboo, unauthorized, unconstitutional, under the table*, unlawful, unlicensed, unofficial, unwarrantable, unwarranted, verboten, violating, wildcat*, wrongful; SEE CONCEPTS 319,545

illegible [adj] *unreadable*
cacographic, crabbed, cramped, difficult to read, faint, hard to make out*, hieroglyphic, indecipherable, indistinct, obscure, scrawled, unclear, undecipherable, unintelligible; SEE CONCEPTS 535,576

illegitimate [adj] *not legal*
contraband, illegal, illicit, improper, invalid, misbegotten, spurious, supposititious, unauthorized, unconstitutional, unlawful, unsanctioned, wicked, wrong; SEE CONCEPTS 319,549

ill-fated/ill-starred [adj] *doomed*
blighted, catastrophic, destroyed, disastrous, hapless, ill-omened, inauspicious, luckless, misfortunate, ruined, star-crossed*, unfortunate, unhappy, unlucky, untoward; SEE CONCEPTS 537,548

illicit [adj] *not legal; forbidden*
adulterous, black-market*, bootleg*, clandestine, contraband, contrary to law, criminal, crooked, dirty*, felonious, furtive, guilty, heavy*, illegal, illegitimate, immoral, improper, in violation of law, lawless, out of line*, prohibited, racket, unauthorized, unlawful, unlicensed, wrong, wrongful; SEE CONCEPTS 319,545

illiterate [adj] *unable to read well; lacking education*
benighted, catachrestic, ignorant, inerudite, solecistic, uneducated, unenlightened, ungrammatical, uninstructed, unlearned, unlettered, unread, unschooled, untaught, untutored; SEE CONCEPT 402

ill-mannered [adj] *badly behaved*
bad-mannered, boorish, cheap, churlish, coarse, discourteous, disrespectful, ill-behaved, ill-bred, impertinent, impolite, insolent, loud, loudmouthed, loutish, raunchy*, raw, rough, rough-

neck*, rude, tacky*, uncivil, uncouth, ungracious, unmannerly, unrefined, vulgar; SEE CONCEPT 401

ill-natured [adj] *bad-tempered*
catty, churlish, crabbed, crabby, cross, crotchety, cussed*, dirty*, disagreeable, disobliging, dyspeptic, hot-tempered, ill-humored, irritable, malevolent, malicious, mean, nasty, ornery*, perverse, petulant, spiteful, sulky, sullen, surly, temperamental, tempersome, touchy, unfriendly, unkind, unpleasant; SEE CONCEPTS 401,404

illness [n] *disease; bad health*
affliction, ailing, ailment, attack, breakdown, bug*, collapse, complaint, confinement, convalescence, disability, diseasedness, disorder, disturbance, dose, failing health, fit, flu, ill health, indisposition, infirmity, malady, malaise, poor health, prostration, relapse, seizure, sickness, syndrome, unhealth, virus, what's going around*; SEE CONCEPT 306

illogical [adj] *not making sense*
absurd, casuistic, cockeyed*, fallacious, false, fatuous, faulty, groundless, hollow, implausible, inconclusive, incongruous, inconsequent, inconsistent, incorrect, invalid, irrational, irrelevant, mad, meaningless, not following, nutty*, off the wall*, preposterous, screwy*, self-contradictory, senseless, sophistic, sophistical, specious, spurious, unconnected, unproved, unreasonable, unscientific, unsound, unsubstantial, untenable, wacky, without basis, without foundation; SEE CONCEPTS 267,529

ill-suited [adj] *inappropriate*
bad form, ill-fitted, ill-matched, ill-timed, improper, inapt, incompatible, incorrect, irrelevant, malapropos, mismatched, out of character, out of its element, out of place, unbecoming, unfit, unfitting, unseemly, unsuitable, wrong; SEE CONCEPT 558

ill-tempered [adj] *irritable*
annoyed, bad-tempered, bearish, cantankerous, choleric, crabby, cross, crotchety, grouchy, grumpy, irascible, moody, nasty, quick-tempered, sharp, snappy, sour, spiteful, surly, testy, touchy, vicious; SEE CONCEPTS 401,403

ill-timed [adj] *not occurring at a suitable time*
awkward, badly timed, improper, inappropriate, inconvenient, inept, inopportune, malapropos, mistimed, unbecoming, unbefitting, unfavorable, unseasonable, unseemly, unsuitable, untimely, unwelcome; SEE CONCEPT 548

illuminate [v1] *make light*
brighten, fire, flash, floodlight, highlight, hit with a light*, ignite, illume, illumine, irradiate, kindle, light, lighten, light up, limelight*, spot, spotlight; SEE CONCEPT 624

illuminate [v2] *make clear; educate*
better, clarify, clear up, construe, define, dramatize, edify, elucidate, enlighten, explain, expound, express, finish, give insight, gloss, illustrate, improve, instruct, interpret, perfect, polish, shed light on*, uplight; SEE CONCEPTS 57,285

illumination [n1] *light; making light*
beam, brightening, brightness, brilliance, flame, flash, gleam, lighting, lights, radiance, ray; SEE CONCEPTS 620,624

illumination [n2] *clear understanding*
awareness, clarification, edification, education, enlightenment, information, insight, inspiration, instruction, perception, revelation, teaching; SEE CONCEPTS 274,409

illusion [n] *false appearance; false belief*
apparition, bubble*, chimera, confusion, daydream, deception, déjà vu*, delusion, error, fallacy, false impression, fancy, fantasy, figment of imagination*, fool's paradise*, ghost, hallucination, head trip*, hocus-pocus*, idolism, ignus fatuus, image, invention, make-believe, mirage, misapprehension, misbelief, misconception, misimpression, mockery, myth, optical illusion, paramnesia, phantasm, pipe dream*, rainbow*, seeming, semblance, trip*, virtual reality; SEE CONCEPTS 689,716

illusory/illusive [adj] *deceptive, false*
apparent, blue-sky*, chimerical, deceitful, delusive, delusory, fake, fallacious, fanciful, fantastic, fictional, fictitious, fictive, hallucinatory, ideal, imaginary, misleading, mistaken, ostensible, pseudo*, seeming, semblant, sham*, supposititious, unreal, untrue, visionary, whimsical; SEE CONCEPTS 529,552,582

illustrate [v1] *demonstrate, exemplify*
allegorize, bring home*, clarify, clear up, delineate, depict, disclose, draw a picture*, elucidate, emblematize, embody, emphasize, epitomize, evidence, evince, exhibit, explain, expose, expound, get across*, get over*, highlight, illuminate, imitate, instance, interpret, lay out*, limelight*, make clear, make plain, manifest, mark, mirror, ostend, personify, picture, point up*, portray, proclaim, represent, reveal, show, show and tell*, spotlight*, symbolize, typify, vivify; SEE CONCEPT 57,97

illustrate [v2] *explain by drawing, decorating*
adorn, delineate, depict, embellish, illuminate, limn, ornament, paint, picture, portray, represent, sketch; SEE CONCEPTS 57,174

illustration [n1] *demonstration, exemplification*
analogy, case, case history, case in point, clarification, elucidation, example, explanation, for instance, instance, interpretation, model, representative, sample, sampling, specimen; SEE CONCEPTS 268,686

illustration [n2] *drawing, artwork that assists explanation*
adornment, cartoon, decoration, depiction, design, engraving, etching, figure, frontispiece, halftone, image, line drawing, painting, photo, photograph, picture, plate, sketch, snapshot, tailpiece, vignette; SEE CONCEPT 259

illustrative [adj] *explanatory*
allegorical, clarifying, comparative, corroborative, delineative, descriptive, diagrammatic, emblematic, exemplifying, explicatory, expository, figurative, graphic, iconographic, illuminative, illustrational, illustratory, imagistic, indicative, interpretive, metaphoric, pictorial, pictoric, representative, revealing, sample, specifying, symbolic, typical; SEE CONCEPT 267

illustrious [adj] *famous, prominent*
big league*, brilliant, celeb*, celebrated, distinguished, eminent, esteemed, exalted, famed, glorious, great, heavy, lofty, monster*, name*, noble, notable, noted, outstanding, remarkable, renowned, resplendent, signal, splendid, star, sublime, superstar, well-known; SEE CONCEPT 568

ill will [n] *hatred; hard feelings*
acrimony, animosity, animus, antagonism, an-

ig
il

tipathy, aversion, bad blood*, bad will, blame, despite, dislike, enmity, envy, feud, grudge, hate, hostility, malevolence, malice, maliciousness, no love lost*, objection, rancor, resentment, spite, spitefulness, spleen, unfriendliness, venom; SEE CONCEPT 29

image [n1] *representation; counterpart*
angel*, appearance, carbon*, carbon copy, carved figure, chip off old block*, copy, dead ringer*, double, drawing, effigy, equal, equivalent, facsimile, figure, form, icon, idol, illustration, likeness, match, model, photocopy, photograph, picture, portrait, reflection, replica, reproduction, similitude, simulacre, simulacrum, spitting image*, statue; SEE CONCEPTS *259,667,716*

image [n2] *concept*
apprehension, conceit, conception, construct, figure, idea, impression, intellection, mental picture, notion, perception, phantasm, thought, trope, vision; SEE CONCEPTS *529,689*

imaginable [adj] *believable, possible*
apprehensible, calculable, comprehensible, conceivable, conjecturable, convincing, credible, likely, plausible, sensible, supposable, thinkable, under the sun*; SEE CONCEPTS *529,552*

imaginary [adj] *fictitious, invented*
abstract, apocryphal, apparitional, assumed, chimerical, deceptive, delusive, dreamed-up*, dreamlike, dreamy, fabulous, fancied, fanciful, fantastic, fictional, figmental, fool's paradise*, hallucinatory, hypothetical, ideal, illusive, illusory, imaginative, imagined, legendary, made-up, mythological, nonexistent, notional, phantasmal, phantasmic, quixotic, shadowy, spectral, supposed, supposititious, theoretical, trumped up*, unreal, unsubstantial, visionary, whimsical; SEE CONCEPTS *529,582*

imagination [n] *power to create in one's mind*
acuteness, artistry, awareness, chimera, cognition, conception, creation, creative thought, creativity, enterprise, fabrication, fancy, fantasy, flight of fancy*, idea, ideality, illusion, image, imagery, ingenuity, insight, inspiration, intelligence, invention, inventiveness, mental agility, notion, originality, perceptibility, realization, resourcefulness, sally, supposition, thought, thoughtfulness, unreality, verve, vision, visualization, wit, wittiness; SEE CONCEPTS *409,410*

imaginative [adj] *creative, inventive*
artistic, avant-garde, blue-sky*, brain wave, breaking ground, clever, dreamy, enterprising, extravagant, fanciful, fantastic, fertile, festive, high-flown*, ingenious, inspired, offbeat, original, originative, pie-in-the-sky*, poetic, poetical, productive, quixotic, romantic, utopian, visionary, vivid, way out*, whimsical; SEE CONCEPTS *529,542*

imagine [v1] *dream up, conceive*
brainstorm, build castles in air*, conceptualize, conjure up, cook up*, create, depict, devise, envisage, envision, fabricate, fancy, fantasize, fantasy, feature, figure, form, frame, harbor, image, invent, make up, nurture, perceive, picture, plan, project, realize, scheme, see in one's mind*, spark, think of, think up, vision, visualize; SEE CONCEPT *43*

imagine [v2] *assume, deduce*
apprehend, believe, conjecture, deem, expect, fancy, gather, guess, infer, presume, realize,

reckon, suppose, surmise, suspect, take for granted, take it, think, understand; SEE CONCEPTS *12,26*

imbecile [adj] *stupid, foolish*
asinine, backward, deranged, dim-witted, dull, fatuous, feeble-minded, idiotic, imbecilic, inane, ludicrous, moronic, simple, simple-minded, slow, thick, witless; SEE CONCEPT *402*

imbecile [n] *very stupid person*
birdbrain, dimwit, dolt, dummy, dunce, fool, idiot, jerk, lamebrain*, moron, pinhead*, simpleton; SEE CONCEPT *412*

imbibe [v] *drink, often heavily*
absorb, assimilate, belt*, consume, down, gorge, guzzle*, ingest, ingurgitate, irrigate, partake, put away*, quaff, raise a few's, sip, swallow, swig*, swill*, toss*; SEE CONCEPT *169*

imbroglio [n] *misunderstanding; fight*
altercation, argument, bickering, brawl, broil*, brouhaha*, complexity, complication, dispute, embarrassment, embroilment, entanglement, falling-out*, flack*, involvement, knock-down-drag-out*, miff*, quandary, quarrel, row, runin*, soap opera*, spat, squabble; SEE CONCEPTS *46,106*

imbue [v] *infuse, saturate*
bathe, diffuse, impregnate, inculcate, infix, ingrain, inoculate, instill, invest, leaven, permeate, pervade, steep, suffuse; SEE CONCEPTS *209,236,245*

imitate [v] *pretend to be; do an impression of*
act like, affect, ape, assume, be like, borrow, burlesque, carbon*, caricature, clone, copy, counterfeit, ditto*, do like*, do likewise, duplicate, echo, emulate, falsify, feign, follow, follow in footsteps*, follow suit*, forge, impersonate, look like, match, mime, mimic, mirror, mock, model after, parallel, parody, pattern after, personate, play a part, pretend, put on*, reduplicate, reflect, repeat, replicate, reproduce, resemble, send up*, sham, simulate, spoof, take off*, travesty, Xerox*; SEE CONCEPTS *87,111,171*

imitation [n] *simulation, substitution*
apery, aping, carbon copy, clone, copy, counterfeit, counterfeiting, counterpart, ditto*, dupe*, duplicate, duplication, echoing, ersatz*, fake, forgery, image, impersonation, impression, likeness, match, matching, mime, mimicry, mirroring, mockery, parallel, paralleling, paraphrasing, parody, parroting, patterning, phony, picture, reflection, replica, representing, reproduction, resemblance, ringer, semblance, sham*, simulacrum, takeoff*, transcription, travesty, Xerox*; SEE CONCEPTS *171,260,716*

imitative [adj] *simulated, unoriginal*
artful, copied, copycat, copying, counterfeit, deceptive, derivative, echoic, emulative, emulous, following, forged, mimetic, mimic, mimicking, mock, onomatopoeic, parrot*, plagiarized, pseudo*, put-on*, reflecting, reflective, secondhand, sham*, simulant; SEE CONCEPT *582*

immaculate [adj] *very clean; unspoiled*
bright, clean, errorless, exquisite, faultless, flawless, impeccable, irreproachable, neat, pure, snowy*, spick-and-span*, spotless, spruce, stainless, taintless, trim, unexceptionable, unsoiled, unsullied; SEE CONCEPT *621*

immaculate [adj2] *innocent, uncorrupted*
above reproach, chaste, clean, decent, faultless, flawless, guiltless, incorrupt, modest, perfect,

pure, sinless, spotless, stainless, unblemished, uncontaminated, undefiled, unpolluted, unsullied, untarnished, virtuous; SEE CONCEPTS 404,545

immaterial [*adj1*] *irrelevant*
extraneous, foreign, impertinent, inapplicable, inapposite, inappropriate, inconsequential, inconsiderable, inconsiderate, inessential, insignificant, irrelative, matter of indifference, meaningless, no big deal*, no never mind*, of no account*, of no consequence*, of no importance*, trifling, trivial, unimportant, unnecessary; SEE CONCEPT 575

immaterial [*adj2*] *not existing in physical form*
aerial, airy, apparitional, asomatous, bodiless, celestial, disbodied, discarnate, disembodied, dreamlike, dreamy, ethereal, ghostly, heavenly, impalpable, imponderable, incorporate, incorporeal, insensible, intangible, metaphysical, nonmaterial, nonphysical, psychic, shadowy, spectral, spiritlike, spiritual, subjective, supernatural, unearthly, unembodied, unfleshly, unsubstantial, unworldly, wraithlike; SEE CONCEPT 539

immature [*adj*] *young, inexperienced*
adolescent, baby, babyish, callow, childish, crude, green*, half-grown, imperfect, infantile, infantine, jejune, juvenile, kid, kidstuff*, premature, puerile, raw, sophomoric, tender*, tenderfoot*, underdeveloped, undergrown, undeveloped, unfinished, unfledged, unformed, unripe, unseasonable, unseasoned, unsophisticated, untimely, wet behind ears*, youthful; SEE CONCEPTS 485,578,797

immeasurable [*adj*] *infinite, incalculable*
alive with, bottomless, boundless, countless, crawling with, endless, extensive, illimitable, immense, indefinite, inestimable, inexhaustible, jillion*, large, limitless, measureless, no end of*, no end to*, umpteen*, unbounded, uncountable, unfathomable, unlimited, unmeasurable, unreckonable, vast, zillion*; SEE CONCEPTS 762,773,781

immediate [*adj1*] *instantaneous; without delay*
actual, at once, at present time, at this moment, critical, current, existing, extant, first, hair-trigger*, instant, live, next, now, on hand*, paramount, present, pressing, prompt, up-to-date*, urgent; SEE CONCEPTS 567,585,812,820

immediate [*adj2*] *near, next*
adjacent, close, contiguous, direct, firsthand, near-at-hand, nearby, nearest, nigh, primary, proximal, proximate, recent; SEE CONCEPTS 586,778

immediately [*adv*] *at once, right away*
anon, at short notice, away, directly, double-time*, forthwith, hereupon, in a flash*, in a jiffy*, in a New York minute*, in nothing flat*, instantaneously, instanter, instantly, like now*, now, now or never*, on the dot*, on the double*, on the spot*, PDQ*, promptly, pronto*, rapidly, right now, shortly, soon, soon afterward, straight away*, straight off*, summarily, thereupon, this instant, this minute, tout de suite*, unhesitatingly, urgently, without delay, without hesitation; SEE CONCEPTS 544,820

immemorial [*adj*] *ancient, old*
age-old, archaic, fixed, forever, long-standing, of yore, olden, prehistoric, primeval, rooted, time-honored, traditional; SEE CONCEPTS 578,797,799

immense [*adj*] *extremely large*
barn door*, boundless, Brobdingnagian*, colossal, elephantine, endless, enormous, eternal, extensive, giant, gigantic, great, gross, huge, humongous, illimitable, immeasurable, infinite, interminable, jumbo*, limitless, mammoth, massive, measureless, mighty, monstrous, monumental, prodigious, stupendous, super, titanic*, tremendous, unbounded, vast; SEE CONCEPT 773

immerse [*v1*] *submerge in liquid*
asperse, baptize, bathe, bury, christen, dip, douse, drench, drown, duck, dunk, merge, plunge, saturate, sink, slop, soak, souse, sprinkle, steep, submerse; SEE CONCEPT 256

immerse [*v2*] *become deeply involved*
absorb, busy, engage, engross, interest, involve, occupy, soak, take up; SEE CONCEPTS 17,100

immersed [*adj*] *deeply involved with*
absorbed, bound-up*, buried*, busy, consumed, deep, eat sleep and breathe*, engaged, engrossed, intent, into*, mesmerized, occupied, preoccupied, rapt, spellbound, taken up*, tied up*, turned on*, wrapped up*; SEE CONCEPT 542

immigrant [*n*] *person from a foreign land*
adoptive citizen, alien, colonist, documented alien, foreigner, incomer, migrant, naturalized citizen, newcomer, outsider, pioneer, settler, undocumented alien; SEE CONCEPT 413

immigrate [*v*] *enter a foreign area intending to live there*
arrive, colonize, come in, go in, migrate, settle; SEE CONCEPT 159

imminent [*adj*] *at hand, on the way*
about to happen, approaching, brewing*, close, coming, expectant, fast-approaching, following, forthcoming, gathering, handwriting-on-the-wall*, immediate, impending, ineluctable, inescapable, inevasible, inevitable, in store*, in the air*, in the cards*, in the offing*, in the wind*, in view*, likely, looming, menacing, near, nearing, next, nigh, on its way, on the horizon, on the verge, overhanging, possible, probable, see it coming*, threatening, to come, unavoidable, unescapable; SEE CONCEPTS 548,820

immobile [*adj*] *motionless, fixed*
anchored, at a standstill, at rest, frozen, immobilized, immotile, immovable, nailed, nailed down, pat, quiescent, rigid, riveted, rooted, stable, stagnant, static, stationary, steadfast, stiff, still, stock-still, stolid, unmovable, unmoving; SEE CONCEPTS 488,584

immoderate [*adj*] *excessive, extreme*
dizzying, egregious, enormous, exaggerated, exorbitant, extravagant, inordinate, intemperate, overindulgent, profligate, steep, too much*, too-too*, towering, unbalanced, unbridled, uncalled-for*, unconscionable, uncontrolled, undue, unjustified, unmeasurable, unreasonable, unrestrained, unwarranted, wanton; SEE CONCEPTS 544,569

immodest [*adj*] *shameless*
bawdy, bold, brazen, coarse, depraved, forward, indecent, lewd, obscene, revealing, risque, unashamed, unchaste, unseemly; SEE CONCEPTS 401,545

immoral [*adj*] *evil, degenerate*
abandoned, bad, corrupt, debauched, depraved, dishonest, dissipated, dissolute, fast*, graceless, impure, indecent, iniquitous, lewd, licentious, loose*, nefarious, obscene, of easy virtue*, pornographic, profligate, rakish, reprobate, saturnalian, shameless, sinful, speedy, unchaste, un-

clean*, unethical, unprincipled, unscrupulous, vicious, vile, villainous, wicked, wrong, X-rated*; SEE CONCEPT 545

immortal [adj1] *death-defying, imperishable*
abiding, amaranthine, ceaseless, constant, deathless, endless, enduring, eternal, evergreen, everlasting, incorruptible, indestructible, indissoluble, interminable, lasting, never-ceasing, never-ending, perdurable, perennial, permanent, perpetual, phoenixlike, sempiternal, timeless, undying, unfading; SEE CONCEPTS 539,798

immortal [adj2] *famous*
celebrated, eminent, epic, genius, glorious, heroic, illustrious, laureate, paragon, storied; SEE CONCEPT 568

immortality [n1] *endless life*
athanasia, deathlessness, endurance, eternal life, eternity, everlasting life, perpetuity, timelessness; SEE CONCEPTS 539,798

immortality [n2] *enduring fame*
celebrity, fame, famousness, glorification, glory, greatness, lasting fame, renown; SEE CONCEPTS 388,668

immovable [adj] *fixed, stubborn*
adamant, constant, dead set on*, dug in, fast, firm, hard-nosed, immobile, immotile, immutable, impassive, inflexible, intransigent, locked in*, motionless, obdurate, quiescent, resolute, rooted, secure, set, set in concrete*, set in stone*, solid, stable, stand pat*, stationary, steadfast, stick to guns*, stuck, tough nut*, unalterable, unchangeable, uncompromising, unmodifiable, unshakable, unwavering, unyielding; SEE CONCEPTS 404,488,534

immune [adj] *invulnerable*
allowed, clear, exempt, favored, free, hardened to, insusceptible, irresponsible, licensed, not affected, not liable, not subject, privileged, protected, resistant, safe, unaffected, unanswerable, unliable, unsusceptible; SEE CONCEPTS 314,552

immunity [n] *privilege, exemption*
amnesty, charter, exoneration, franchise, freedom, impunity, indemnity, invulnerability, liberty, license, prerogative, protection, release, resistance, right; SEE CONCEPTS 316,376,388

immutable [adj] *unchangeable*
abiding, ageless, changeless, constant, enduring, fixed, immovable, inflexible, invariable, permanent, perpetual, sacrosanct, stable, steadfast, unalterable, unmodifiable; SEE CONCEPT 534

imp [n] *mischievous child, small person*
brat, demon, devil, deviling, devilkin, elf, fiend, gamin, gnome, gremlin, hellion, minx, pixie, puck, rascal, rogue, scamp, sprite, troll, tyke, urchin, villain; SEE CONCEPT 412

impact [n1] *collision, force*
appulse, bang, blow, bounce, brunt, buffet, bump, clash, concussion, contact, crash, crunch, crush, encounter, hit, impingement, jar, jolt, jounce, kick, knock, meeting, percussion, pound, punch, quake, quiver, ram, rap, rock, shake, shock, slap, smash, smashup, strike, stroke, thump, tremble, tremor, wallop; SEE CONCEPTS 189,641

impact [n2] *effect*
brunt, burden, consequences, full force, impression, imprint, influence, mark, meaning, power, repercussion, significance, thrust, weight; SEE CONCEPT 230

impact [v] *hit with force*
bang into, clash, collide, crack up, crash, crush, jolt, kick, register, smash, smash up, strike, wrack up*; SEE CONCEPT 189

impair [v] *harm, hinder*
blemish, blunt, cheapen, damage, debase, debilitate, decrease, destroy, deteriorate, devaluate, devalue, diminish, ding*, disqualify, enervate, enfeeble, hurt, injure, invalidate, lessen, lose strength, make useless, mar, prejudice, queer, reduce, rough up*, spoil, tarnish, total, tweak, undermine, unfit, vitiate, weaken, worsen; SEE CONCEPTS 130,240,246

impaired [adj] *injured, faulty*
broken, busted, damaged, debilitated, defective, down*, flawed, harmed, hurt, imperfect, kaput*, marred, on the blink*, on the fritz*, spoiled, unsound; SEE CONCEPTS 485,560

impale [v] *stab*
lance, perforate, pierce, prick, punch, puncture, run through, skewer, skiver, spear, spike, stick, transfix; SEE CONCEPT 220

impalpable [adj] *intangible, unsubstantial*
airy, delicate, disembodied, fine, imperceptible, imponderable, imprecise, inappreciable, incorporeal, indiscernible, indistinct, insensible, insubstantial, nebulous, shadowy, tenuous, thin, unapparent, unobservable, unperceivable, vague; SEE CONCEPTS 485,529,619

impart [v1] *make known*
admit, announce, break, communicate, convey, disclose, discover, divulge, expose, inform, pass on, publish, relate, reveal, tell, transmit; SEE CONCEPT 60

impart [v2] *give*
accord, afford, allow, bestow, cede, confer, contribute, grant, lead, offer, part with, present, relinquish, render, yield; SEE CONCEPT 108

impartial [adj] *fair, unprejudiced*
candid, detached, disinterested, dispassionate, equal, equitable, evenhanded, fair-minded, impersonal, just, middle-of-the-road*, neutral, nondiscriminating, nondiscriminatory, nonpartisan, objective, on-the-fence, open-minded, unbiased, unbigoted, uncolored, unslanted, without favor; SEE CONCEPTS 403,542

impasse [n] *stalemate*
box*, Catch-22*, cessation, corner*, cul-de-sac*, dead end, deadlock, dilemma, fix, gridlock, jam, mire*, morass*, pause, pickle*, plight, predicament, quandary, rest, scrape*, standoff, standstill; SEE CONCEPT 674

impassioned [adj] *excited, vehement*
animated, ardent, blazing, burning, deep, fervent, fervid, fierce, fiery, fired up*, flaming, furious, glowing, heated*, hot-blooded*, inflamed, inspired, intense, melodramatic, moving, mushy, overemotional, passionate, perfervid, powerful, profound, red-hot*, romantic, rousing, sentimental, starry-eyed*, steamed up*, stirring, torrid, violent, vivid, warm, white-hot*, wild about, worked up*, zealous; SEE CONCEPT 403

impassive [adj] *aloof, cool*
apathetic, callous, cold, cold-blooded*, collected, composed, dispassionate, dry, emotionless, hardened, heartless, imperturbable, indifferent, indurated, inexcitable, inexpressive, inscrutable, insensible, insusceptible, matter-of-fact, nonchalant, passionless, phlegmatic, placid, poker-faced*, reserved, reticent, sedate, self-con-

tained, serene, spiritless, stoic, stoical, stolid, taciturn, unconcerned, unemotional, unexcitable, unfeeling, unflappable, unimpressible, unmoved, unruffled, wooden; SEE CONCEPTS *404,542*

impatience [*n*] *inability, unwillingness to wait*
agitation, anger, annoyance, ants in pants*, anxiety, avidity, disquietude, eagerness, edginess, excitement, expectancy, fretfulness, haste, hastiness, heat*, impetuosity, intolerance, irritability, irritableness, nervousness, quick temper, rashness, restiveness, restlessness, shortness, snappiness, suspense, uneasiness, vehemence, violence; SEE CONCEPTS *633,657*

impatient [*adj*] *unable, unwilling to wait*
abrupt, agog, antsy, anxious, appetent, ardent, athirst, avid, breathless, brusque, chafing, choleric, curt, demanding, dying to*, eager, edgy, feverish, fretful, hasty, having short fuse*, headlong, hot-tempered, hot under collar*, impetuous, indignant, intolerant, irascible, irritable, itchy, keen, on pins and needles*, quick-tempered, racing one's motor*, restless, ripe*, snappy, straining, sudden, testy, thirsty, unforbearing, unindulgent, vehement, violent; SEE CONCEPTS *401,542*

impeach [*v*] *denounce, censure*
accuse, arraign, blame, bring charges against, call into question, call to account, cast aspersions on, cast doubt on, challenge, charge, criminate, criticize, discredit, disparage, hold at fault, impugn, incriminate, inculpate, indict, query, question, reprehend, reprimand, reprobate, tax, try; SEE CONCEPTS *44,52,317*

impeccable [*adj*] *above suspicion; flawless*
accurate, aces, A-okay*, apple-pie*, clean, correct, errorless, exact, exquisite, faultless, fleckless, immaculate, innocent, infallible, innocent, irreproachable, nice, note-perfect, on target*, perfect, precise, pure, right, sinless, stainless, ten*, unblemished, unerring, unflawed, unimpeachable; SEE CONCEPTS *535,574,621*

impecunious [*adj*] *poverty-stricken*
beggared, broke*, cleaned out*, destitute, dirt poor*, homeless, impoverished, indigent, insolvent, necessitous, needy, penniless, penurious, poor, strapped*, unprosperous; SEE CONCEPT *334*

impede [*v*] *obstruct, hinder*
bar, block, blow whistle on*, brake, check, clog, close off, cramp one's style*, curb, cut off, dam, delay, deter, discomfit, disconcert, disrupt, embarrass, faze, flag one*, freeze, hamper, hang up, hold up, interfere, oppose, rattle, restrain, retard, saddle with*, shut down, shut off, slow, slow down, stonewall*, stop, stymie, thwart; SEE CONCEPTS *121,130*

impediment [*n*] *obstruction, hindrance*
bar, barricade, barrier, block, blockage, bottleneck*, burden, catch*, Catch-22*, chain, check, clog, cramp, curb, dead weight*, defect, delay, deterrent, detriment, difficulty, disadvantage, drag*, drawback, encumbrance, fault, flaw, handicap, hazard, hitch, holdup, hurdle, inhibition, load, manacle, millstone*, obstacle, prohibition, red tape*, restraint, restriction, retardation, retardment, road block*, rub*, setback, shackle, snag, stoppage, stricture, stumbling block*, tie, trammel, wall; SEE CONCEPT *666*

impel [*v*] *prompt, incite*
actuate, boost, compel, constrain, drive, excite,

foment, force, goad, induce, influence, inspire, instigate, jog, lash, mobilize, motivate, move, oblige, poke, power, press, prod, propel, push, require, set in motion, shove, spur, start, stimulate, thrust, urge; SEE CONCEPTS *14,68,221,242*

impending [*adj*] *forthcoming*
approaching, at hand, brewing, coming, gathering, handwriting-on-the-wall*, hovering, imminent, in the cards*, in the offing*, in the wind*, looking to*, looming, menacing, near, nearing, ominous, on the horizon*, overhanging, portending, proximate, see it coming*, threatening, waiting to; SEE CONCEPTS *548,820*

impenetrable [*adj1*] *dense*
bulletproof, close, compact, firm, hard, hermetic, impassable, impermeable, impervious, inviolable, solid, substantial, thick, unpierceable; SEE CONCEPTS *483,604*

impenetrable [*adj2*] *incomprehensible*
arcane, baffling, cabalistic, dark, Delphic, enigmatic, enigmatical, hidden, incognizable, indiscernible, inexplicable, inscrutable, mysterious, mystic, obscure, sibylline, unaccountable, unfathomable, ungraspable, unintelligible, unknowable; SEE CONCEPTS *529,576*

imperative [*adj1*] *necessary*
acute, burning, clamant, clamorous, compulsory, critical, crucial, crying, essential, exigent, immediate, important, importunate, indispensable, inescapable, insistent, instant, no turning back*, obligatory, pressing, urgent, vital; SEE CONCEPT *546*

imperative [*adj2*] *authoritative*
aggressive, autocratic, bidding, bossy, commanding, dictatorial, dominant, domineering, harsh, high-handed, imperial, imperious, ordering, overbearing, peremptory, powerful, stern; SEE CONCEPTS *267,574*

imperceptible [*adj*] *hard to sense; faint*
ephemeral, evanescent, fine, gradual, impalpable, imponderable, inappreciable, inaudible, inconsiderable, inconspicuous, indiscernible, indistinct, indistinguishable, infinitesimal, insensible, insignificant, invisible, microscopic, minute, momentary, shadowy, slight, small, subtle, tiny, trivial, undetectable, unnoticeable, vague; SEE CONCEPTS *406,537*

imperfect [*adj*] *flawed*
amiss, below par, bottom-of-barrel*, broken, damaged, defective, deficient, disfigured, dud*, faulty, few bugs*, garbage*, immature, impaired, incomplete, inexact, injured, junk*, lemon*, limited, low, marred, minus, partial, patchy, rudimentary, schlocky*, sick, sketchy, two-bit*, undeveloped, unfinished, unsound, vicious, warped; SEE CONCEPTS *570,574,579*

imperfection [*n*] *flaw*
blemish, bug*, catch, defect, deficiency, deformity, demerit, disfigurement, failing, fallibility, fault, foible, frailty, glitch*, gremlin*, inadequacy, incompleteness, infirmity, insufficiency, peccadillo, problem, shortcoming, sin, stain, taint, weakness, weak point; SEE CONCEPTS *230,671,718*

imperil [*v*] *cause to be in danger*
chance it, compromise, endanger, expose, hazard, jeopard, jeopardize, jeopardy, menace, peril, risk; SEE CONCEPT *240*

imperious [*adj*] *bossy, overbearing*
arrogant, authoritative, autocratic, commanding,

im
im

compulsatory, compulsory, despotic, dictatorial, domineering, exacting, haughty, high-handed, imperative, imperial, mandatory, obligatory, oppressive, overweening, peremptory, required, tyrannical, tyrannous; SEE CONCEPTS *267,574*

impermeable [*adj*] *impenetrable*
airtight, dense, hermetic, impassable, impervious, leak-proof, nonporous, sealed, waterproof, water-resistant, watertight; SEE CONCEPTS *483, 604*

impersonal [*adj*] *cold, unfriendly*
abstract, bureaucratic, businesslike, candid, cold-blooded*, cold turkey*, colorless, cool, detached, disinterested, dispassionate, emotionless, equal, equitable, fair, formal, impartial, indifferent, inhuman, neutral, nondiscriminatory, objective, poker-faced*, remote, straight, strictly business*, unbiased, uncolored, unpassioned; SEE CONCEPTS *401,542,544*

impersonate [*v*] *pretend to be another*
act, act a part, act like, act out, ape, assume character, ditto*, do, do an impression of, double as, dress as, enact, fake, imitate, make like*, masquerade as, mimic, mirror, pass oneself off as*, perform, personate, play, playact, play a role, portray, pose as, put on an act*, represent, take the part of; SEE CONCEPTS *59,292*

impertinence [*n*] *boldness*
assurance, audacity, backchat, back talk*, brazenness, cheek*, chutzpah*, come-back*, crust*, disrespect, disrespectfulness, effrontery, forwardness, freshness, gall, guff, hardihood, impropriety, impudence, incivility, insolence, insolency, lip*, nerve, pertness, presumption, rudeness, sass*, smart mouth*, wisecrack*, wise guy*; SEE CONCEPT *633*

impertinent [*adj*] *bold, disrespectful*
arrogant, brash, brassy*, brazen, contumelious, discourteous, disgracious, flip*, forward, fresh, ill-mannered, impolite, impudent, inappropriate, incongruous, inquisitive, insolent, interfering, intrusive, lippy*, meddlesome, meddling, nosy*, off base*, offensive, out of line*, pert, presumptuous, procacious, prying, rude, sassy*, smart, smart alecky*, uncalled-for*, uncivil, ungracious, unmannerly, unsuitable; SEE CONCEPT *401*

imperturbable [*adj*] *calm, collected*
assured, complacent, composed, cool, cool as cucumber*, disimpassioned, equanimous, hard as nails*, immovable, nerveless, nonchalant, roll with punches*, sedate, self-possessed, self-satisfied, smug, stiff upper lip*, stoical, thick-skinned, tranquil, unaffected, undisturbed, unexcitable, unflappable, unmoved, unruffled, untouched; SEE CONCEPT *404*

impervious [*adj*] *unable to be penetrated*
closed to, hermetic, immune, impassable, impassive, impenetrable, impermeable, imperviable, inaccessible, invulnerable, resistant, sealed, tight, unaffected, unapproachable, unmoved, unpierceable, unreceptive, watertight; SEE CONCEPTS *485,534,604*

impetuous [*adj*] *acting without thinking*
abrupt, ardent, eager, fervid, fierce, furious, going off deep end*, hasty, headlong, hurried, impassioned, impulsive, passionate, precipitant, precipitate, precipitous, rash, restive, rushing, spontaneous, spur-of-the-moment, subitaneous, sudden, swift, unbridled, unexpected, unplanned, unpremeditated, unreflecting, unrestrained, un-

thinking, vehement, violent; SEE CONCEPTS *404,542*

impetus [*n*] *stimulus, force*
catalyst, energy, goad, impulse, impulsion, incentive, incitation, incitement, momentum, motivation, power, pressure, push, spur, stimulant, urge; SEE CONCEPTS *641,661*

impinge [*v*] *trespass*
affect, bear upon, disturb, encroach, influence, infringe, intrude, invade, make inroads, meddle, obtrude, pry, touch, violate; SEE CONCEPTS *14,156*

impious [*adj*] *not religious*
agnostic, apostate, atheistic, blasphemous, canting, contrary, deceitful, defiling, desecrating, desecrative, diabolic, disobedient, disrespectful, godless, hardened, hypocritical, iconoclastic, immoral, iniquitous, irreligious, irreverent, perverted, pietistical, profane, recusant, reprobate, sacrilegious, sanctimonious, satanic, scandalous, sinful, unctuous, undutiful, unethical, unfaithful, ungodly, unhallowed, unholy, unregenerate, unrighteous, unsanctified, wayward, wicked; SEE CONCEPT *545*

impish [*adj*] *mischievous*
casual, devilish, devil-may-care*, elfin, elvish, fiendish, flippant, free and easy*, fresh, frolicsome, giddy, jaunty, naughty, offhand, pert, pixieish, playful, prankish, puckish, rascally, saucy*, sportive, waggish; SEE CONCEPT *401*

implacable [*adj*] *merciless, cruel*
grim, inexorable, inflexible, intractable, iron-fisted, mortal, pitiless, rancorous, relentless, remorseless, ruthless, unappeasable, unbending, uncompromising, unflinching, unforgiving, unrelenting, unyielding, vindictive; SEE CONCEPT *542*

implausible [*adj*] *not likely*
doubtful, dubious, farfetched, far out*, fishy*, flimsy, for the birds*, full of holes*, impossible, improbable, inconceivable, incredible, obscure, problematic, puzzling, reachy, suspect, thin*, too much*, unbelievable, unconvincing, unreasonable, unsubstantial, weak, won't hold water*, won't wash*; SEE CONCEPT *552*

implement [*n*] *agent, tool*
apparatus, appliance, contraption, contrivance, device, equipment, gadget, instrument, machine, utensil; SEE CONCEPT *499*

implement [*v*] *start, put into action*
achieve, actualize, bring about, carry out, complete, effect, enable, enforce, execute, fulfill, invoke, make good*, make possible, materialize, perform, provide the means, put into effect, realize, resolve; SEE CONCEPTS *91,99,221*

implicate [*v*] *imply, involve*
accuse, affect, associate, blame, charge, cite, compromise, concern, connect, embroil, entangle, frame, hint, impute, include, incriminate, inculpate, insinuate, lay at one's door*, link, mean, mire, name, pin on*, point finger at*, relate, stigmatize, suggest, tangle*; SEE CONCEPTS *44,112*

implication [*n*] *association, suggestion*
assumption, conclusion, connection, connotation, entanglement, guess, hint, hypothesis, incrimination, indication, inference, innuendo, intimation, involvement, link, meaning, overtone, presumption, ramification, reference, significance, signification, undertone, union; SEE CONCEPTS *28,39,278*

implicit [adj] *included without question, inherent, absolute*

accurate, certain, complete, constant, constructive, contained, definite, entire, firm, fixed, full, implicative, implied, inarticulate, inevitable, inferential, inferred, latent, practical, steadfast, tacit, taken for granted, total, undeclared, understood, unexpressed, unhesitating, unqualified, unquestioned, unreserved, unsaid, unshakable, unspoken, unuttered, virtual, wholehearted; SEE CONCEPTS *267,535,549*

implied [adj] *hinted at*

adumbrated, alluded to, allusive, connoted, constructive, figured, foreshadowed, hidden, implicit, indicated, indicative, indirect, inferential, inferred, inherent, insinuated, intended, involved, latent, lurking, meant, occult, parallel, perceptible, potential, significative, signified, suggested, symbolized, tacit, tacitly assumed, undeclared, understood, unexpressed, unsaid, unspoken, unuttered, wordless; SEE CONCEPTS *267,535*

implode [v] *collapse inward*

cave in, fall down, fall in, fold, fold up; SEE CONCEPTS *230,316,410,674*

implore [v] *beg*

appeal, beseech, conjure, crave, entreat, go on bended knee*, importune, plead, pray, solicit, supplicate, urge; SEE CONCEPT *48*

imply [v] *indicate, mean*

betoken, connote, denote, designate, entail, evidence, give a hint, hint, import, include, insinuate, intend, intimate, involve, mention, point to, presuppose, refer, signify, suggest; SEE CONCEPTS *75,97,682*

impolite [adj] *having bad manners*

bad-mannered, boorish, churlish, crude, discourteous, disgracious, disrespectful, ill-bred, ill-mannered, indecorous, indelicate, insolent, irritable, loutish, moody, oafish, rough, rude, sullen, uncivil, ungracious, unmannered, unmannerly, unrefined; SEE CONCEPT *401*

impolitic [adj] *unwise, careless*

brash, ill-advised, ill-judged, imprudent, inadvisable, inconsiderate, indiscreet, inexpedient, injudicious, maladroit, misguided, rash, stupid, tactless, undiplomatic, untimely; SEE CONCEPTS *401,544*

import [n1] *meaning*

acceptation, bearing, bottom line*, construction, drift*, gist*, heart*, implication, intendment, intention, interpretation, meat*, message, name of the game*, nature of beast*, nuts and bolts*, point, punch line*, purport, score*, sense, significance, signification, stuff*, thrust, understanding; SEE CONCEPT *682*

import [n2] *significance, weight*

consequence, design, emphasis, importance, intent, magnitude, moment, momentousness, object, objective, pith, purpose, signification, stress, substance, value, weightiness, worth; SEE CONCEPTS *346,668*

importance [n1] *significance, weight*

accent, attention, bearing, caliber, concern, concernment, consequence, denotation, distinction, drift*, effect, emphasis, force, gist*, gravity, import, influence, interest, materiality, moment, momentousness, notability, paramountcy, point, precedence, preponderance, preponderancy, priority, purport, relevance, sense, seriousness, signification, standing, stress, substance, tenor,

usefulness, value, weightiness; SEE CONCEPTS *346,668,682*

importance [n2] *prominence, standing*

consequence, conspicuousness, distinction, eminence, esteem, fame, greatness, influence, lionization, mark, notability, note, noteworthiness, rank, reputation, salience, status, usefulness, worth; SEE CONCEPTS *388,671*

important [adj1] *valuable, substantial*

big, big-league*, chief, considerable, conspicuous, critical, crucial, decisive, determining, earnest, essential, esteemed, exceptional, exigent, extensive, far-reaching, foremost, front-page*, grave, great, heavy, imperative, importunate, influential, large, marked, material, mattering much, meaningful, momentous, necessary, of moment, of note, of substance, paramount, ponderous, pressing, primary, principal, relevant, salient, serious, signal, significant, something, standout, urgent, vital, weighty; SEE CONCEPT *567*

important [adj2] *eminent, influential, outstanding*

aristocratic, big-time*, distinctive, distinguished, effective, esteemed, extraordinary, famous, first-class*, foremost, four-star*, front-page*, grand, heavy*, high-level, high profile, high-ranking, high-up, honored, illustrious, imposing, incomparable, leading, majestic, major-league*, noble, notable, noted, noteworthy, of note, page-one*, potent, powerful, preeminent, prominent, remarkable, seminal, signal, solid, superior, talented, top-drawer*, top-notch*, upper-class, VIP*, well-known; SEE CONCEPTS *555,574*

imported [adj] *brought in from another place*

alien, carried, choice, exotic, ferried, foreign, introduced, rare, sent, shipped, transported, trucked; SEE CONCEPT *549*

importunate [adj] *demanding, insistent*

burning, clamant, clamorous, crying, disturbing, dogged, earnest, exigent, harassing, imperative, instant, overly solicitous, persevering, persistent, pertinacious, pressing, solicitous, troublesome, urgent; SEE CONCEPTS *267,401*

importune [v] *demand, insist*

appeal, ask, badger, beg, beseech, beset, besiege, con*, crave, dun, egg on*, entreat, goose*, harass, hound*, implore, invoke, nag, persuade, pester, plague, plead, pray, press, sell, solicit, supplicate, urge, work on*; SEE CONCEPT *53*

impose [v] *set, dictate*

appoint, burden, charge, command, compel, constrain, decree, demand, encroach, enforce, enjoin, establish, exact, fix, foist, force, force upon, horn in, inflict, infringe, institute, introduce, intrude, lade, lay, lay down, lay down the law, levy, move in on, oblige, obtrude, ordain, order, place, prescribe, presume, promulgate, put, put foot down*, read riot act*, require, saddle*, take advantage, trespass, visit, wish, wreak, wreck; SEE CONCEPTS *18,53,133*

imposing [adj] *impressive*

august, big, commanding, dignified, effective, exciting, grand, grandiose, imperial, magnificent, majestic, massive, mega*, mind-blowing*, monumental, moving, noble, ominous, one for the book*, overblown, overwhelming, pretentious, regal, royal, something else*, something to write home about*, stately, stirring, striking, towering; SEE CONCEPTS *537,574,773*

im
im

imposition [*n1*] *deception*
artifice, cheating, con, craftiness, dissimulation, fraud, hoax, hocus-pocus*, hypocrisy, illusion, imposture, stratagem, trick, trickery; SEE CONCEPTS *59,645*

imposition [*n2*] *burden*
charge, command, constraint, demand, drag, duty, encroachment, encumbrance, intrusion, levy, pain, pain in the neck*, pressure, presumption, restraint, tax; SEE CONCEPTS *14,130*

impossible [*adj1*] *beyond the bounds of possibility*
absurd, beyond, contrary to reason, cureless, futile, hardly possible, hopeless, hundred-to-one*, impassable, impervious, impracticable, impractical, inaccessible, inconceivable, inexecutable, infeasible, insurmountable, irrealizable, irreparable, no-go*, not a prayer*, no-way*, no-win*, out of the question*, preposterous, too much, unachievable, unattainable, uncorrectable, unfeasible, unimaginable, unobtainable, unreasonable, unrecoverable, unthinkable, unworkable, useless, visionary, way out; SEE CONCEPT *552*

impossible [*adj2*] *intolerable, ungovernable*
absurd, egregious, hopeless, improper, incongruous, ludicrous, objectionable, offensive, outrageous, preposterous, unacceptable, unanswerable, undesirable, unreasonable, unsuitable; SEE CONCEPT *401*

impostor [*n*] *person pretending to be something else*
actor, beguiler, bluffer, charlatan, cheat, con artist, deceiver, empiric, fake, faker, four-flusher*, fraud, hypocrite, imitator, impersonator, masquerader, mimic, mocker, mountebank, pettifogger, phony, pretender, pseudo, quack, scorner, sham, sharper, shyster, trickster; SEE CONCEPT *412*

imposture [*n*] *fraud, trick*
artifice, cheat, con, copy, counterfeit, deceit, deception, fabrication, fake, feint, fiddle, flimflam*, forgery, gambit, hoax, hocus-pocus*, illusion, imitation, impersonation, imposition, make-believe, maneuver, masquerade, phony, ploy, pretense, pretension, put-on*, quackery, ruse, sell*, sham, sleight, spoof, stratagem, swindle, wile; SEE CONCEPTS *59,192,645,674*

impotent [*adj*] *disabled; unable to perform action*
barren, crippled, dud, effete, enervated, enfeebled, feeble, forceless, frail, gutless, helpless, inadequate, incapable, incapacitated, incompetent, ineffective, ineffectual, inept, infecund, infirm, nerveless, paper tiger*, paralyzed, powerless, prostrate, sterile, unfruitful, unproductive, weak; SEE CONCEPT *485*

impound [*v*] *confine*
cage, coop up, enclose, fence in, hold, imprison, keep, pen, seize, shut in, take; SEE CONCEPTS *121,130*

impoverished [*adj*] *poor, exhausted*
bankrupt, barren, beggared, broke, clean, depleted, destitute, distressed, drained, empty, flat*, flat broke*, have-not*, hurting, impecunious, indigent, insolvent, necessitous, needy, penurious, played out*, poverty-stricken, reduced, ruined, spent, sterile, strapped; SEE CONCEPTS *334,560*

impractical/impracticable [*adj*] *unrealistic*
abstract, absurd, chimerical, idealistic, illogical, impossible, impracticable, improbable, inapplicable, inefficacious, infeasible, inoperable, irrealizable, ivory-tower*, no-go*, nonfunctional, nonviable, not a prayer*, otherworldly, out of the question*, quixotic, romantic, speculative, starry-eyed*, theoretical, unattainable, unbusinesslike, unfeasible, unreal, unserviceable, unusable, unwise, unworkable, useless, visionary, wild, won't fly*; SEE CONCEPT *552*

impregnable [*adj*] *unyielding*
firm, fortified, impenetrable, indestructible, invincible, invulnerable, secure, solid, strong, unassailable; SEE CONCEPTS *489,540,551*

impregnate [*v*] *infuse, fill; make pregnant*
charge, conceive, drench, fecundate, fertilize, imbrue, implant, inoculate, inseminate, leaven, overflow, percolate, permeate, pervade, procreate, produce, reproduce, saturate, seethe, soak, sodden, souse, steep, suffuse, transfuse; SEE CONCEPTS *179,375*

impresario [*n*] *manager, producer*
director, showperson, sponsor, stage manager; SEE CONCEPT *347*

impress [*v1*] *influence*
affect, arouse, awe, be conspicuous, blow away*, buffalo*, bulldoze*, carry, electrify, enforce, enthuse, excite, faze, galvanize, get*, grab, grandstand*, inspire, kill*, knock out*, make a hit*, make an impression, make splash*, move, overawe, pique, provoke, push around*, register, score, show off, slay*, stimulate, stir, strike, sway, thrill, touch*; SEE CONCEPTS *7,19,22,261*

impress [*v2*] *press down to make design*
carve, dent, emboss, engrave, etch, imprint, indent, inscribe, mark, print, stamp; SEE CONCEPT *174*

impress [*v3*] *emphasize*
bring home*, drive home*, establish, fix, get into head*, inculcate, instill, press, set, stress; SEE CONCEPT *49*

impression [*n1*] *influence*
consequence, effect, feeling, impact, reaction, response, result, sway; SEE CONCEPT *230*

impression [*n2*] *feeling, idea*
apprehension, belief, conceit, concept, conception, conjecture, conviction, fancy, feel, hunch, image, inkling, intellection, memory, notion, opinion, perception, recollection, sensation, sense, supposition, suspicion, theory, thought, view; SEE CONCEPTS *529,689*

impression [*n3*] *design made by pressing*
brand, cast, dent, depression, dint, fingerprint, footprint, form, hollow, impress, imprint, indentation, mark, matrix, mold, outline, pattern, print, sign, spoor, stamp, stamping, trace, track, vestige; SEE CONCEPTS *284,625*

impression [*n4*] *pretending to be somebody*
imitation, impersonation, masquerade, parody, sendup, takeoff; SEE CONCEPT *263*

impressionable [*adj*] *easily taught; gullible*
affectable, affected, feeling, impressible, influenceable, ingenuous, open, perceptive, plastic*, receptive, responsive, sensible, sensile, sensitive, sentient, suggestible, susceptible, susceptive, vulnerable, wax-like; SEE CONCEPTS *402,403*

impressive [*adj*] *powerful, influential*
absorbing, affecting, arresting, august, awe-inspiring, consequential, cool*, deep*, dramatic,

effective, eloquent, excited, exciting, extraordinary, forcible, grand, impassioned, important, imposing, inspiring, intense, lavish, luxurious, majestic, massive, momentous, monumental, moving, noble, notable, penetrating, prime*, profound, remarkable, rousing, splendid, stately, stirring, striking, sumptuous, superb, thrilling, touching, towering, vital, well-done; SEE CONCEPTS *574,773*

imprint [n] *impression; symbol*
banner, dent, design, effect, emblem, heading, impress, indentation, influence, mark, name, print, sign, signature, stamp, trace, trademark; SEE CONCEPTS *284,625*

imprint [v] *stamp*
designate, engrave, establish, etch, fix, impress, inscribe, mark, offset, print; SEE CONCEPT *174*

imprison [v] *confine; put in jail*
apprehend, bastille, bottle up*, cage, check, circumscribe, closet, commit, constrain, curb, detain, fence in, hold, hold captive, hold hostage, hold in custody, ice*, immure, impound, incarcerate, intern, jail, keep, keep captive, keep in custody, limit, lock in, lock up, nab*, occlude, pen, put away, put behind bars, rail in, remand, restrain, send to prison, send up*, shut in, stockade, take prisoner, trammel; SEE CONCEPTS *90,191,317*

improbable [adj] *not likely*
doubtful, dubious, fanciful, far-fetched, flimsy*, hundred-to-one*, iffy*, implausible, inconceivable, not expected, outside chance*, questionable, rare, slim, slim and none*, unbelievable, uncertain, unconvincing, unheard of, unimaginable, unlikely, unsubstantial, weak; SEE CONCEPT *552*

impromptu [adj/adv] *unrehearsed, improvised*
ad-lib*, dashed off, extemporaneous, extempore, extemporized, fake, faked, improv*, improviso, offhand, off the cuff*, played by ear*, shot from the hip*, spontaneous, spur-of-the-moment, thrown off*, tossed off*, unpremeditated, unprepared, unscripted, unstudied, vamped, whipped up*, winged*; SEE CONCEPT *267*

improper [adj1] *not suitable*
abnormal, at odds, awkward, bad form, discordant, discrepant, erroneous, false, ill-advised, ill-timed, imprudent, inaccurate, inadmissible, inadvisable, inapplicable, inapposite, inappropriate, inapt, incongruous, incorrect, inexpedient, infelicitous, inharmonious, inopportune, irregular, ludicrous, malapropos, odd, off-base*, out-of-place*, out-of-season*, preposterous, unapt, unbefitting, uncalled-for*, uncomely, undue, unfit, unfitting, unseasonable, unsuitable, unsuited, untimely, unwarranted, wrong; SEE CONCEPT *558*

improper [adj2] *vulgar, immoral*
blue*, dirty, impolite, indecent, indecorous, indelicate, lewd, malodorous, naughty, risqué, rough, salacious, suggestive, unbecoming, unconventional, unequitable, unethical, ungodly, unjust, unrighteous, unrightful, unseemly, untoward, wrong, wrongful; SEE CONCEPTS *542,545*

impropriety [n] *bad taste, mistake*
barbarism, blunder, faux pas, gaffe, gaucherie, goof*, immodesty, impudence, incongruity, incorrectness, indecency, indecorum, inelegance, rudeness, slip*, solecism, unseemliness, unsuit-

ability, vulgarism, vulgarity; SEE CONCEPTS *101,278,674*

improve [v] *make or become better*
advance, ameliorate, amend, augment; better, boost, civilize, come around*, convalesce, correct, cultivate, develop, doctor up*, edit, elevate, emend, enhance, gain ground*, help, increase, lift, look up*, make strides, meliorate, mend, perk up*, pick up*, polish, progress, promote, purify, raise, rally, recover, rectify, recuperate, refine, reform, revamp, revise, rise, set right*, shape up*, sharpen, skyrocket*, straighten out*, take off*, touch up*, turn the corner*, update, upgrade; SEE CONCEPTS *244,700*

improvement [n] *bettering; something bettered*
advance, advancement, amelioration, amendment, augmentation, betterment, change, civilization, correction, cultivation, development, elevation, enhancement, enrichment, furtherance, gain, growth, increase, preferment, progress, progression, promotion, rally, reclamation, recovery, rectification, reformation, regeneration, renovation, revision, rise, upbeat, upgrade, upswing; SEE CONCEPTS *230,700*

improvident [adj] *careless, spendthrift*
extravagant, heedless, imprudent, inconsiderate, lavish, negligent, prodigal, profligate, profuse, reckless, shiftless, shortsighted, thoughtless, thriftless, uneconomical, unthrifty, wasteful; SEE CONCEPTS *334,542*

improvise [v] *make up*
ad-lib, brainstorm, coin, concoct, contrive, dash off*, devise, do offhand, do off top of head*, dream up, extemporize, fake, fake it, improv*, improvisate, invent, jam*, knock off*, make do*, slapdash*, spark, speak off the cuff*, throw together*, wing it*; SEE CONCEPTS *173,266*

improvised [adj] *made-up*
ad-lib, autoschediastic, Band-Aid*, extemporaneous, extempore, extemporized, fly-by-night*, hit-or-miss*, impromptu, improviso, makeshift, offhand, spontaneous, spur-of-the-moment*, unprepared, unrehearsed, unstudied; SEE CONCEPTS *267,589*

imprudent [adj] *without much thought*
brash, careless, foolhardy, foolish, heedless, ill-advised, ill-considered, ill-judged, impolitic, improvident, incautious, inconsiderate, indiscreet, inexpedient, injudicious, irresponsible, leaving self wide open*, off the deep end*, overhasty, playing with fire*, rash, reckless, temerarious, thoughtless, unadvisable, unthinking, unwise; SEE CONCEPTS *267,542*

impudent [adj] *bold, shameless*
arrant, audacious, barefaced, blatant, boldfaced, brassy, brazen, bumptious, cheeky*, cocky*, contumelious, cool*, flip*, forward, fresh, immodest, impertinent, insolent, nervy*, off-base*, overbold, pert, presumptuous, procacious, rude, sassy*, saucy*, smart*, smart-alecky*, unabashed, unblushing, wise*; SEE CONCEPT *401*

impugn [v] *criticize, challenge*
assail, attack, blast, break, call into question, cast aspersions upon, cast doubt upon, come down on*, contradict, contravene, cross, cut to shreds*, deny, disaffirm, dispute, gainsay, knock*, negate, negative, oppose, pin something on*, put down*, question, resist, run down, skin alive*, slam*, smear*, stick it to*, swipe at*, tar*, throw doubt on, throw the book at*, thumb nose at*,

traduce, trash, traverse, zap*, zing*; SEE CONCEPTS *52,58*

impulse [*n1*] *drive, resolve*
actuation, appeal, bent, caprice, catalyst, desire, disposition, excitant, extemporization, fancy, feeling, flash*, goad, hunch, impellent, impulsion, incitation, incitement, inclination, influence, inspiration, instinct, itch*, lash, lust, mind, motivation, motive, notion, passion, spontaneity, spur, thought, urge, vagary, whim, whimsy, wish, yen; SEE CONCEPTS *20,410*

impulse [*n2*] *throb, stimulus*
augmentation, beat, bump, catalyst, drive, force, impetus, impulsion, lash, momentum, movement, pressure, propulsion, pulsation, pulse, push, rush, shock, shove, stroke, surge, thrust, vibration; SEE CONCEPT *641*

impulsive [*adj*] *tending to act without thought*
abrupt, ad-lib*, automatic, careless, devil-may-care*, emotional, extemporaneous, flaky*, gone off deep end*, hasty, headlong, hot-and-cold*, impetuous, instinctive, intuitive, involuntary, jumping the gun*, mad, offhand, passionate, precipitate, quick, rash, spontaneous, sudden, swift, unconsidered, unexpected, unmeditated, unpredictable, unpremeditated, unprompted, up-and-down*, violent, winging it*; SEE CONCEPTS *401,542*

impunity [*n*] *freedom*
dispensation, exception, exemption, immunity, liberty, license, nonliability, permission, privilege, security; SEE CONCEPT *376*

impure [*adj*] *not clean mentally, physically; mixed*
admixed, adulterated, alloyed, carnal, coarse, common, contaminated, corrupt, debased, defiled, desecrated, diluted, dirty, doctored*, filthy, foul, gross*, grubby*, immodest, immoral, indecent, infected, lewd, nasty, not pure, obscene, polluted, profaned, smutty*, squalid, sullied, tainted, unchaste, unclean, unrefined, unwholesome, vile, vitiated, weighted, wicked; SEE CONCEPTS *545,621*

impurity [*n*] *contaminant*
adulteration, contamination, corruption, defilement, dirt, filth, foreign matter, grime, pestilence, poisoning, pollutant, pollution, scum, stain, taint, uncleanness; SEE CONCEPTS *230,306,674*

impute [*v*] *attribute*
accredit, accuse, adduce, ascribe, assign, blame, brand, censure, charge, credit, hang something on*, hint, indict, insinuate, intimate, lay, pin on*, refer, reference, stigmatize; SEE CONCEPTS *44,49*

inability [*n*] *disabling lack of talent, skill*
disqualification, failure, frailty, impotence, inadequacy, inaptitude, incapability, incapacitation, incapacity, incompetence, ineffectiveness, ineffectualness, inefficacy, inefficiency, ineptitude, ineptness, insufficiency, inutility, lack, necessity, powerlessness, shortcoming, unfitness, weakness; SEE CONCEPT *630*

inaccessible [*adj*] *out of reach*
aloof, away, beyond, distant, elusive, far, faraway, far-off, impassable, impervious, impracticable, insurmountable, not at hand*, out-of-the-way*, remote, unachievable, unapproachable, unattainable, unavailable, unfeasible, ungettable, unobtainable, unreachable, unrealizable, unworkable; SEE CONCEPT *576*

inaccuracy [*n*] *error, erroneousness*
blunder, corrigendum, deception, defect, erratum, exaggeration, fault, howler*, imprecision, incorrectness, inexactness, miscalculation, mistake, slip*, solecism, typo*, unfaithfulness, unreliability, wrong; SEE CONCEPTS *101,230*

inaccurate [*adj*] *erroneous*
all wet*, careless, counterfactual, defective, discrepant, doesn't wash*, fallacious, false, faulty, imprecise, incorrect, in error, inexact, mistaken, off, off base*, out*, specious, unfaithful, unreliable, unsound, untrue, way-off*, wide*, wild*, wrong; SEE CONCEPTS *565,582*

inactive [*adj*] *not engaged in action; inert, lazy*
abeyant, asleep, blah*, disengaged, do-nothing*, dormant, down, draggy, dull, idle, immobile, indolent, in holding pattern*, inoperative, jobless, latent, lax, lethargic, limp, low-key, moth-balled*, motionless, on hold, ossified, out of action, out of commission*, out of service, out of work*, passive, quiescent, quiet, sedentary, slack, sleepy, slothful, slow, sluggish, somnolent, stable, static, still, torpid, unemployed, unoccupied, unused; SEE CONCEPTS *401,560,584*

inadequacy [*n*] *shortage, defect, inability*
blemish, dearth, defalcation, defectiveness, deficiency, deficit, drawback, failing, faultiness, flaw, imperfection, inadequateness, inaptness, incapacity, incompetence, incompetency, incompleteness, ineffectiveness, ineffectualness, inefficacy, inefficiency, ineptitude, insufficiency, lack, meagerness, paucity, poverty, scantiness, shortcoming, skimpiness, underage, unfitness, unsuitableness, weakness; SEE CONCEPTS *335,674,709*

inadequate [*adj*] *defective, insufficient, incompetent*
bare, barren, bush-league*, deficient, depleted, dry, failing, faulty, feeble, found wanting, glitch*, imperfect, impotent, inappreciable, inapt, incapable, incommensurate, incompetent, incomplete, inconsiderable, insubstantial, junk*, lacking, lame*, lemon*, lousy, low, meager, minus, miserly, niggardly, not enough, parsimonious, poor, scanty, scarce, short, shy*, sketchy*, skimpy*, small, spare, sparse, sterile, stinted, stunted*, thin*, too little, unequal, unproductive, unqualified, weak; SEE CONCEPTS *546,570,771*

inadmissible [*adj*] *not appropriate*
exceptionable, ill-favored, ill-timed, immaterial, improper, inappropriate, inapt, incompetent, inept, irrelevant, malapropos, objectionable, unacceptable, unallowable, unbecoming, undesirable, unfit, unqualified, unreasonable, unsatisfactory, unseemly, unsuited, unwanted, unwelcome; SEE CONCEPTS *319,558*

inadvertent [*adj*] *accidental*
careless, chance, feckless, heedless, irreflective, negligent, not on purpose, reckless, thoughtless, uncaring, unconcerned, undesigned, undevised, unheeding, unintended, unintentional, unmindful, unplanned, unpremeditated, unthinking, unthought, unwitting; SEE CONCEPTS *542,544*

inadvisable [*adj*] *not recommended*
careless, foolhardy, foolish, harebrained*, ill-advised, impolitic, improper, imprudent, inappropriate, incautious, inconvenient, indiscreet, inexpedient, injudicious, pointless, rash, undesirable, unsensible, unsuitable, unwise, wrong; SEE CONCEPTS *529,558*

inalienable [*adj*] *absolute, inherent*
basic, entailed, inbred, inviolable, natural, non-negotiable, nontransferable, sacrosanct, unassailable, untransferable; SEE CONCEPT 535

inane [*adj*] *stupid*
absurd, asinine, daft, empty, fatuous, flat, foolish, frivolous, futile, harebrained*, idiotic, illogical, imbecilic, innocuous, insipid, jejune, laughable, meaningless, mindless, pointless, puerile, ridiculous, sappy*, senseless, silly, trifling, unintelligent, vacant, vacuous, vain, vapid, weak, wishy-washy*, worthless; SEE CONCEPTS 542,548

inanimate [*adj*] *not alive, not organic*
azoic, cold, dead, defunct, dull, exanimate, extinct, idle, inactive, inert, inoperative, insensate, insentient, lifeless, mineral, motionless, nonanimal, nonvegetable, quiescent, soulless, spiritless; SEE CONCEPT 539

inapplicable [*adj*] *not relevant*
extraneous, foreign, garbage*, immaterial, impertinent, inapposite, inappropriate, inappurtenant, inapropos, inapt, inconsistent, irrelative, irrelevant, remote, unsuitable, unsuited; SEE CONCEPTS 546,558

inappropriate [*adj*] *not proper, suitable*
bad form, disproportionate, foot-in-mouth*, garbage*, ill-fitted, ill-suited, ill-timed, improper, inapplicable, inapropos, incongruous, inconsonant, incorrect, indecorous, inept, irrelevant, left-field*, malapropos, off*, out of line, out of place, tasteless, unbecoming, unbefitting, undue, unfit, unfitting, unmeet, unseasonable, unseemly, unsuitable, untimely, way off*, wrong, wrong-number*; SEE CONCEPT 558

inapt [*adj*] *incompetent; not suitable*
awkward, banal, clumsy, dull, flat, gauche, ill-adapted, ill-fitted, ill-suited, improper, inadept, inapposite, inappropriate, incongruous, inept, inexperienced, inexpert, infelicitous, insipid, jejune, maladroit, malapropos, slow, stupid, unable, undexterous, unfacile, unfit, unhandy, unmeet, unproficient, unskilled, unsuitable, unsuited, untimely; SEE CONCEPTS 527,558

inarticulate [*adj*] *unable to speak well*
blurred, dumb, faltering, halting, hesitant, hesitating, inaudible, incoherent, incomprehensible, indistinct, maundering, muffled, mumbled, mumbling, mute, obscure, reticent, silent, speechless, stammering, tongue-tied, unclear, unintelligible, unspoken, unuttered, unvocal, unvoiced, vague, voiceless, wordless; SEE CONCEPT 267

inattentive [*adj*] *negligent, not paying attention*
absent, absentminded, apathetic, blind, bored, careless, distracted, distrait, distraught, diverted, dreamy, faraway, heedless, inadvertent, indifferent, inobservant, listless, lost*, musing, neglectful, oblivious, off-guard*, out to lunch*, preoccupied, rapt, regardless, remiss, removed, scatterbrained*, thoughtless, unconscious, undiscerning, unheeding, unmindful, unnoticing, unobservant, unobserving, unperceiving, unthinking, unwatchful, vague; SEE CONCEPTS 403,542

inaudible [*adj*] *silent*
closemouthed, faint, hushed, imperceptible, low, muffled, mum, mumbled, mute, muted, noiseless, nonvocal, not talkative, quiet, soundless, still, unclear, uncommunicative, unhearable, voiceless, wordless; SEE CONCEPT 594

inaugurate [*v*] *begin; install*
bow, break in, break the ice*, commence, commission, dedicate, get things rolling*, get under way*, induct, initiate, instate, institute, introduce, invest, jump, kick off*, launch, make up, open, ordain, originate, set in motion*, set up, start, usher in; SEE CONCEPT 221

inauguration [*n*] *installation of newcomers*
commencement, inaugural, induction, initiation, institution, investiture, launch, launching, opening, setting up; SEE CONCEPT 386

inauspicious [*adj*] *ominous, unpromising*
bad, baleful, baneful, black, dire, discouraging, evil, fateful, foreboding, ill-boding, ill-omened, impending, inopportune, sinister, threatening, unfavorable, unfortunate, unlucky, unpromising, unpropitious, untimely, untoward; SEE CONCEPTS 548,570

inborn/inbred [*adj*] *coming from birth; natural*
congenital, connate, connatural, constitutional, deep-seated, essential, hereditary, inbred, indigenous, indwelling, ingenerate, ingrained, inherent, inherited, innate, instinctive, intrinsic, intuitive, native, unacquired; SEE CONCEPTS 406,549

incalculable [*adj*] *countless, limitless*
boundless, capricious, chancy, enormous, erratic, fluctuant, iffy*, immense, incomputable, inestimable, infinite, innumerable, jillion*, measureless, no end of*, no end to*, numberless, uncertain, uncountable, unfixed, unforeseen, unpredictable, unreckonable, untold, vast, whimsical, without number, zillion*; SEE CONCEPTS 535,773,781

incandescent [*adj*] *glowing*
beaming, brilliant, effulgent, fulgent, intense, lambent, lucent, luminous, phosphorescent, radiant, red-hot*, refulgent, shining, white-hot*; SEE CONCEPT 617

incantation [*n*] *spell, magic*
abracadabra*, ala kazam*, bewitchment, black magic, chant, charm, conjuration, conjuring, enchantment, formula, hex, hocus-pocus*, hoodoo*, hymn, invocation, mumbo-jumbo*, necromancy, open sesame*, rune, sorcery, voodoo*, witchcraft, wizardry; SEE CONCEPTS 370,689

incapable [*adj*] *not adequate; helpless*
butterfingers*, disqualified, feeble, impotent, inadequate, incompetent, ineffective, ineligible, inept, inexperienced, inexpert, inproficient, insufficient, losing, naive, not equal to, not up to*, poor, powerless, unable, uncool*, unequipped, unfit, unqualified, unskilled, unskillful, unsuited, weak; SEE CONCEPT 527

incapacitate [*v*] *put out of action*
clip wings*, cripple, damage, disable, disarm, disenable, disqualify, hamstring*, hinder, hogtie*, hurt, immobilize, lame, lay up*, maim, paralyze, prostrate, put out of commission*, take out, undermine, weaken; SEE CONCEPTS 121,246

incapacitated [*adj*] *disabled*
bedridden, broken-down, confined, crippled, debilitated, handicapped, helpless, hurt, immobilized, impaired, impotent, incapable, infirm, laid-up, lame, maimed, out-of-action*, out of commission*, paralyzed, powerless, sidelined, weak, weakened, wornout; SEE CONCEPTS 314,527

im
in

incarcerate [v] *put in jail, confinement*
bastille, book*, cage*, commit, confine, constrain, coop up*, detain, hold, immure, impound, imprison, intern, jail, lock up, put away, put on ice*, put under lock and key*, railroad*, restrain, restrict, send up the river*, settle, slough, take away, throw book at*; SEE CONCEPTS 90,191,317

incarnate [adj] *in bodily form*
embodied, exteriorized, externalized, human, in human form, in the flesh*, made flesh, manifested, materialized, personified, physical, real, substantiated, tangible, typified; SEE CONCEPTS 490,539

incautious [adj] *not careful*
any old way*, bold, brash, careless, caught napping*, devil-may-care*, fast-and-loose*, foot-in-mouth*, hasty, heedless, hotheaded*, ill-advised, ill-judged, impetuous, improvident, imprudent, impulsive, inconsiderate, indiscreet, injudicious, madcap*, neglectful, negligent, off guard*, pay no mind*, playing with fire*, precipitate, rash, reckless, regardless, sticking one's neck out*, thoughtless, unalert, unguarded, unmindful, unthinking, unvigilant, unwatchful, wary, wide open*; SEE CONCEPTS 542,544

incendiary [adj] *causing trouble, damage*
dangerous, demagogic, dissentious, inflammatory, malevolent, provocative, rabble-rousing*, seditious, subversive, treacherous, wicked; SEE CONCEPTS 537,570

incendiary [n] *person who causes fire, trouble*
agitator, arsonist, criminal, demagogue, demonstrator, firebrand*, insurgent, pyromaniac, rabble-rouser*, rebel, revolutionary, rioter; SEE CONCEPT 412

incense [n] *strongly fragrant smoke*
aroma, balm, bouquet, burnt offering, essence, flame, frankincense, fuel, myrrh, odor, perfume, punk, redolence, scent, spice; SEE CONCEPTS 599,600

incense [v] *make very angry*
anger, ask for it*, bother, disgust, egg on*, enrage, exasperate, excite, fire up*, get a rise out of*, get under one's skin*, inflame, infuriate, ire, irritate, mad, madden, make blood boil*, make see red*, provoke, rile, umbrage; SEE CONCEPT 14

incensed [adj] *very angry*
at end of one's rope*, buffaloed*, bugged*, bummed out*, burned up*, dogged, enraged, exasperated, fuming, furious, hacked, hot and bothered*, huffy*, indignant, infuriated, irate, ireful, mad, maddened, miffed, on the warpath*, peeved, riled, rousted, rubbed the wrong way*, steamed up*, up in arms*, uptight*, wrathful; SEE CONCEPT 403

incentive [n] *lure, inducement*
allurement, bait, carrot*, catalyst, come-on*, consideration, determinant, drive, encouragement, enticement, excuse, exhortation, goad, ground, impetus, impulse, incitement, influence, insistence, inspiration, instigation, motivation, motive, persuasion, provocation, purpose, rationale, reason, reason why, spring, spur, stimulant, stimulation, stimulus, temptation, urge, whip; SEE CONCEPT 661

inception [n] *beginning*
birth, commencement, dawn, derivation, fountain, inauguration, initiation, kickoff, origin, outset, provenance, provenience, rise, root, source, start, well, wellspring; SEE CONCEPTS 648,832

incessant [adj] *never-ending, persistent*
ceaseless, constant, continual, continuous, day-and-night*, endless, eternal, everlasting, interminable, interminate, monotonous, nonstop, perpetual, relentless, round-the-clock*, timeless, unbroken, unceasing, unending, unrelenting, unremitting; SEE CONCEPTS 798

inch [n] *one-twelfth of a foot/2.54 centimeters measured*
fingerbreadth, one thirty-sixth of a yard, square; SEE CONCEPTS 790,791

inchoate [adj] *undeveloped, beginning*
amorphous, elementary, embryonic, formless, immature, imperfect, inceptive, incipient, just begun, nascent, preliminary, rudimentary, shapeless, unfinished, unformed, unshaped; SEE CONCEPTS 485,578,797

incident [n] *occurrence*
adventure, circumstance, episode, event, fact, happening, matter, milestone, occasion, scene, trip; SEE CONCEPT 2

incidental [adj] *related; minor*
accidental, accompanying, adventitious, ancillary, attendant, by-the-way*, casual, chance, circumstantial, coincidental, concomitant, concurrent, contingent, contributing, contributory, fluke*, fortuitous, irregular, nonessential, occasional, odd, random, secondary, subordinate, subsidiary; SEE CONCEPTS 547,548,577

incidentally [adv] *by chance*
accidentally, as a by-product, as side effect, by the bye*, by the way, casually, fortuitously, in passing, in related manner, not by design, obiter, parenthetically, remotely, subordinately, unexpectedly; SEE CONCEPT 544

incinerate [v] *reduce to ashes*
blaze, burn, combust, consume, cremate, flame, ignite, light, parch, scald, scorch, set a match to, torch; SEE CONCEPT 249

incinerator [n] *furnace*
boiler, burner, cinerator, crematory, heater, heating system, oil burner; SEE CONCEPT 463

incipient [adj] *developing*
basic, beginning, commencing, elementary, embryonic, fundamental, inceptive, inchoate, initial, initiative, initiatory, introductory, nascent, originating, start; SEE CONCEPT 585

incision [n] *cut, slit*
carving, cleavage, cleft, dissection, gash, groove, laceration, mark, nick, nip, notch, opening, pierce, slash, stab, wound; SEE CONCEPT 309

incisive [adj] *intelligent*
acute, bright, clever, concise, keen, penetrating, perspicacious, piercing, profound, sharp, trenchant; SEE CONCEPT 402

incisive [adj2] *sarcastic*
acerb, acerbic, acid, biting, caustic, clear-cut, concise, crisp, cutting, drilling, laconic, mordant, penetrating, sardonic, satirical, scathing, severe, sharp, slashing, succinct, tart, terse, trenchant; SEE CONCEPT 267

incite [v] *encourage, provoke*
abet, activate, actuate, agitate, animate, arouse, coax, craze, drive, egg on*, encourage, excite, exhort, fan the fire*, foment, force, forward, further, get to*, goad, impel, induce, inflame, influence, inspire, instigate, instigate, juice*, key up*, motivate, persuade, prick, promote, prompt, pro-

voke, psych*, push, put up to*, raise, rouse, set, set off*, solicit, spur, stimulate, stir up*, talk into, taunt, trigger, urge, whip up*, work up*; SEE CONCEPTS *14,221,242*

incivility [n] *discourtesy*
bad manners, coarseness, discourteousness, disrespect, impoliteness, rudeness, unmannerliness; SEE CONCEPTS *29,633*

inclement [adj1] *bitter, nasty (weather)*
brutal, cold, foul, hard, harsh, intemperate, raw, rigorous, rough, rugged, severe, stormy, tempestuous, violent, wintry; SEE CONCEPT *525*

inclement [adj2] *cruel, merciless*
callous, draconian, harsh, intemperate, pitiless, rigorous, ruthless, savage, severe, tyrannical, unfeeling, unkind, unmerciful; SEE CONCEPT *401*

inclination [n1] *tendency, bent*
affection, appetite, aptitude, aptness, attachment, attraction, bias, capability, capacity, cup of tea*, desire, disposition, drift, druthers*, fancy, fondness, groove*, idiosyncrasy, impulse, leaning, liking, mind, movement, partiality, penchant, persuasion, pleasure, predilection, predisposition, preference, prejudice, proclivity, proneness, propensity, slant*, soft spot*, stomach*, susceptibility, taste, temperament, thing*, trend, turn*, type, urge, velleity, weakness, whim, will, wish; SEE CONCEPTS *20,411,630*

inclination [n2] *slant, angle*
acclivity, bank, bend, bending, bevel, bow, bowing, cant, declivity, deviation, direction, downgrade, grade, gradient, hill, incline, lean, leaning, list, pitch, ramp, slope, tilt; SEE CONCEPT *738*

incline [n] *slope*
acclivity, approach, ascent, cant, declivity, descent, dip, grade, gradient, inclination, lean, leaning, plane, ramp, rise, slant, tilt; SEE CONCEPT *738*

incline [v1] *tend toward*
affect, be disposed, bend, be partial, be predisposed, be willing, bias, drive, favor, govern, gravitate toward, impel, induce, influence, lean to, look, make willing, move, not mind, persuade, predispose, prefer, prejudice, prompt, sway, turn, verge; SEE CONCEPT *657*

incline [v2] *bend, lean*
aim, bevel, bow, cant, cock, deviate, diverge, heel, lay, level, list, lower, nod, point, recline, skew, slant, slope, stoop, tend, tilt, tip, train, turn, veer, yaw; SEE CONCEPT *738*

inclined [adj] *having a preference*
apt, bent on, disposed, given, in the mood, likely, predisposed, prone, tending, willing; SEE CONCEPTS *542,552*

include [v] *contain, involve*
accommodate, add, admit, allow for, append, bear, be composed of, be made up of, build, build in, carry, combine, comprehend, comprise, consist of, constitute, count, cover, cut in on, embody, embrace, encircle, enclose, encompass, entail, enter, have, hold, implicate, incorporate, inject, insert, interject, interpolate, introduce, make allowance for, make room for, number, number among, receive, subsume, take in, take into account, teem with, work in; SEE CONCEPTS *112,532,643*

including [adj] *containing*
along with, among other things, as well as, containing, counting, in addition to, inclusive of, in

conjunction with, made up of, not to mention, plus, together with, with; SEE CONCEPT *577*

inclusion [n] *addition*
admittance, composition, comprisal, embodiment, embracement, encompassment, formation, incorporation, insertion, involvement, subsumption; SEE CONCEPT *642*

inclusive [adj] *all-encompassing, all-embracing*
across-the-board*, all-around, all the options*, all together, ball-of-wax*, blanket*, broad, catchall*, comprehensive, encyclopedic, full, general, global, in toto*, overall, sweeping, umbrella*, wall-to-wall*, whole, without exception; SEE CONCEPT *772*

incognito [adj] *in disguise*
anonymous, bearded, camouflaged, concealed, disguised, hidden, incog*, isolated, masked, masquerading, obscure, under assumed name, unknown, unrecognized; SEE CONCEPTS *576,589*

incoherent [adj] *unintelligible*
breathless, confused, disconnected, discontinuous, discordant, disjointed, disordered, dumb, faltering, inarticulate, incohesive, incomprehensible, incongruous, inconsistent, indistinct, indistinguishable, irrational, jumbled, maundering, muddled, muffled, mumbling, mute, muttered, puzzling, rambling, stammering, stuttering, tongue-tied*, uncommunicative, unconnected, uncoordinated, uneven, unvocal, wandering, wild; SEE CONCEPT *267*

income [n] *money earned by work or investments*
assets, avails, benefits, bottom line*, cash, cash flow, commission, compensation, dividends, drawings, earnings, gains, gravy*, gross, harvest, honorarium, interest, in the black*, livelihood, means, net, pay, payoff, proceeds, profit, receipts, returns, revenue, royalty, salary, take home, wage; SEE CONCEPTS *340,344*

incomparable [adj] *superlative*
beyond compare, excellent, exceptional, ideal, inimitable, matchless, paramount, peerless, perfect, preeminent, second to none, sovereign, superior, supreme, surpassing, towering, transcendent, ultimate, unequalled, unmatchable, unmatched, unparalleled, unrivalled, unsurpassable; SEE CONCEPT *574*

incompatible [adj] *antagonistic, contradictory*
adverse, antipathetic, antipodal, antithetical, clashing, conflicting, contrary, counter, disagreeing, discordant, discrepant, disparate, factious, inadmissible, inappropriate, incoherent, inconformable, incongruous, inconsistent, inconsonant, inconstant, irreconcilable, jarring, marching to a different drummer*, mismatched, night and day*, offbeat*, opposed, opposite, poles apart*, unadapted, uncongenial, unsuitable, unsuited, warring, whale of difference*; SEE CONCEPT *564*

incompetent [adj] *unskillful, unable*
amateur, amateurish, awkward, bungling, bush-league*, clumsy, disqualified, floundering, helpless, inadequate, incapable, ineffectual, inefficient, ineligible, inept, inexperienced, inexpert, insufficient, maladroit, not cut out for*, not equal to, not have it*, out to lunch*, raw, unadapted, unequipped, unfit, unfitted, unhandy, uninitiated, unproficient, unqualified, unskilled, untrained, useless; SEE CONCEPT *527*

incomplete [adj] *unfinished, wanting*
abridged, broken, crude, defective, deficient, ex-

purgated, fractional, fragmentary, garbled, half-done, immature, imperfect, inadequate, incoherent, insufficient, lacking, meager, part, partial, rough, rude, rudimentary, short, sketchy, unaccomplished, unconsummated, under construction, undeveloped, undone, unexecuted, unpolished; SEE CONCEPT 531

incomprehensible [*adj*] *not understandable*
baffling, beats me*, beyond comprehension, beyond one's grasp*, clear as mud*, cryptic, Delphic*, enigmatic, fathomless, Greek*, impenetrable, incognizable, inconceivable, inscrutable, mysterious, mystifying, obscure, opaque, over one's head*, perplexing, puzzling, sibylline, unclear, unfathomable, ungraspable, unimaginable, unintelligible, unknowable; SEE CONCEPTS 402,529

inconceivable [*adj*] *beyond reason, belief*
extraordinary, fantastic, imcomprehensible, implausible, impossible, improbable, incogitable, incredible, insupposable, mind-boggling*, phony, rare, reachy, staggering, strange, thin*, unbelievable, unconvincing, unheard-of, unimaginable, unknowable, unlikely, unsubstantial, unthinkable, weak*, won't fly*, won't wash*; SEE CONCEPTS 529,532

inconclusive [*adj*] *up in the air*
ambiguous, deficient, incomplete, indecisive, indeterminate, lacking, open, uncertain, unconvincing, undecided, uneventful, unfateful, unfinished, unsatisfactory, unsettled, vague; SEE CONCEPTS 537,548

incongruous [*adj*] *out of place, absurd*
alien, bizarre, conflicting, contradictory, disconsonant, discordant, disparate, distorted, divergent, extraneous, fantastic, fitful, illogical, improper, inappropriate, inapropos, inapt, incoherent, incompatible, incongruent, inconsistent, irreconcilable, irregular, jumbled, lopsided, mismatched, out of keeping*, rambling, shifting, twisted, unavailing, unbalanced, unbecoming, unconnected, uncoordinated, uneven, unintelligible, unpredictable, unrelated, unsuitable, unsuited; SEE CONCEPTS 547,558

inconsequential/inconsiderable [*adj*] *of no significance*
casual, dinky*, entry-level*, exiguous, immaterial, inadequate, inappreciable, inconsequent, insignificant, insufficient, light, little, measly, minor, negligible, paltry, petty, picayune, puny, runt, scanty, shoestring*, skimpy, small, small potatoes*, small-time*, trifling, trivial, two-bit*, unconsidered, unimportant, wimpy*, worthless; SEE CONCEPT 575

inconsiderate [*adj*] *insensitive to others*
boorish, brash, careless, discourteous, hasty, impolite, incautious, indelicate, intolerant, reckless, rude, self-centered, selfish, sharp, short, tactless, thoughtless, unceremonious, uncharitable, ungracious, unkind, unthinking; SEE CONCEPT 401

inconsistent [*adj*] *contradictory, irregular*
at odds, at variance, capricious, changeable, conflicting, contrary, discordant, discrepant, dissonant, erratic, fickle, illogical, incoherent, incompatible, in conflict, incongruent, incongruous, inconstant, irreconcilable, lubricious, mercurial, out of step*, temperamental, uncertain, unpredictable, unstable, variable, warring; SEE CONCEPTS 534,564

inconsolable [*adj*] *brokenhearted*
comfortless, dejected, desolate, despairing, disconsolate, discouraged, distressed, forlorn, heartbroken, heartsick, sad, unconsolable; SEE CONCEPT 403

inconspicuous [*adj*] *hidden, unnoticeable*
camouflaged, concealed, dim, faint, hidden, indistinct, insignificant, low-key*, low-profile*, modest, muted, ordinary, plain, quiet, retiring, secretive, shy, soft-pedalled*, subtle, tenuous, unassuming, unemphatic, unobtrusive, unostentatious; SEE CONCEPTS 485,576

inconstant [*adj*] *changeable*
capricious, changeful, erratic, fickle, flickering, fluctuating, impulsive, inconsistent, intermittent, irregular, irresolute, mercurial, shifting, uncertain, undependable, unreliable, unsettled, unstable, vacillating, variable, varying, volatile, waffling, wavering; SEE CONCEPT 534

incontrovertible [*adj*] *beyond dispute*
accurate, authentic, certain, established, incontestable, indisputable, indubitable, irrefutable, nailed down*, no mistake*, no two ways about it*, positive, sure, surefire*, sure thing*, uncontestable, undeniable, unequivocable, unquestionable, unshakable; SEE CONCEPT 535

inconvenience [*n*] *bother, trouble*
aggravation, annoyance, awkwardness, bothersomeness, cumbersomeness, difficulty, disadvantage, disruption, disturbance, drawback, exasperation, fuss, hindrance, nuisance, pain*, stew*, trial, troublesomeness, uneasiness, unfitness, unhandiness, unsuitableness, untimeliness, unwieldiness, upset, vexation; SEE CONCEPT 674

inconvenience [*v*] *bother, trouble*
aggravate, discombobulate, discommode, discompose, disoblige, disrupt, disturb, exasperate, give a hard time*, give trouble*, hang up*, interfere, irk, make it tough*, meddle, put in a spot*, put on the spot*, put to trouble*, try, upset; SEE CONCEPTS 14,242

inconvenient [*adj*] *bothersome, troublesome*
annoying, awkward, cumbersome, detrimental, difficult, disadvantageous, discommoding, discommodious, disturbing, embarrassing, incommodious, inexpedient, inopportune, pestiferous, prejudicial, remote, tiresome, troublesome, unhandy, unmanageable, unseasonable, unsuitable, untimely, unwieldy, vexatious; SEE CONCEPTS 537,548

incorporate [*v*] *include, combine*
absorb, add to, amalgamate, assimilate, associate, blend, charter, coalesce, consolidate, cover, dub, embody, form, fuse, gang up*, hook in*, imbibe, integrate, join, link, merge, mix, organize, pool, put together, start, subsume, tie in*, unite; SEE CONCEPTS 112,113,324

incorrect [*adj*] *wrong*
counterfactual, erroneous, false, faulty, flawed, imprecise, improper, inaccurate, inappropriate, inexact, mistaken, not trustworthy, out*, specious, unfitting, unreliable, unseemly, unsound, unsuitable, untrue, way off*, wide of the mark*, wrong number*; SEE CONCEPTS 558,570

incorrigible [*adj*] *bad, hopeless*
abandoned, beastly, hardened, incurable, intractable, inveterate, irredeemable, irreparable, loser, recidivous, uncorrectable, unreformed, useless, wicked; SEE CONCEPT 570

incorruptible [*adj*] *honest, honorable*
above suspicion, imperishable, indestructible, inextinguishable, just, loyal, moral, perpetual, persistent, pure, reliable, straight, trustworthy, unbribable, undestroyable, untouchable, upright; SEE CONCEPTS 485,545

increase [*n*] *addition, growth*
access, accession, accretion, accrual, accumulation, aggrandizement, augmentation, boost, breakthrough, burgeoning, cumulation, development, elaboration, enlargement, escalation, exaggeration, expansion, extension, gain, hike, incorporation, increment, inflation, intensification, maximization, merger, multiplication, optimization, raise, rise, spread, step-up, surge, swell, swelling, upgrade, upsurge, upturn, waxing; SEE CONCEPTS 763,780

increase [*v*] *add or grow*
advance, aggrandize, aggravate, amplify, annex, augment, boost, broaden, build, build up, deepen, develop, dilate, distend, double, enhance, enlarge, escalate, exaggerate, expand, extend, further, heighten, inflate, intensify, lengthen, magnify, mark up, mount, multiply, pad*, progress, proliferate, prolong, protract, pullulate, raise, redouble, reinforce, rise, sharpen, slap on*, snowball*, spread, step up, strengthen, supplement, swarm, swell, tack on*, teem, thicken, triple, wax, widen; SEE CONCEPTS 236,245,780

increasingly [*adv*] *to a greater extent*
more, more and more, progressively, with acceleration; SEE CONCEPT 772

incredible [*adj*] *beyond belief*
absurd, far-fetched, fishy*, flimsy*, implausible, impossible, improbable, incogitable, inconceivable, insupposable, outlandish, out of the question*, phony, preposterous, questionable, ridiculous, rings phony*, suspect, thin*, unbelievable, unconvincing, unimaginable, unsubstantial, untenable, unthinkable; SEE CONCEPT 552

incredible [*adj2*] *marvellous*
ace*, amazing, astonishing, astounding, awe-inspiring, awesome, extraordinary, fabulous, glorious, great, prodigious, superhuman*, unreal*, wonderful; SEE CONCEPTS 529,572

incredulous [*adj*] *unbelieving*
disbelieving, distrustful, doubtful, doubting, dubious, hesitant, mistrustful, questioning, quizzical, show-me*, skeptical, suspect, suspicious, uncertain, unconvinced, unsatisfied, wary; SEE CONCEPTS 403,529

increment [*n*] *small step toward gain*
accession, accretion, accrual, accrument, addition, advancement, augmentation, enlargement, increase, profit, raise, rise, supplement; SEE CONCEPTS 763,780

incriminate [*v*] *accuse*
allege, attack, attribute, blame, brand, bring charges, charge, cite, finger*, frame, hold accountable, implicate, inculpate, indict, involve, name, pin on*, point the finger at*, prosecute, serve summons; SEE CONCEPT 44

incubus [*n*] *evil spirit*
demon, devil, fiend, goblin, hobgoblin, nightmare, succuba, succubus; SEE CONCEPTS 370,412

inculcate [*v*] *implant, infuse information*
brainwash*, break down, communicate, drill, drum into*, educate, hammer into*, impart, impress, indoctrinate, inseminate, instill, instruct, plant, program, shape up, teach, work over*; SEE CONCEPTS 14,285

incur [*v*] *bring upon oneself*
acquire, arouse, be subjected to, bring down on*, catch, contract, draw, earn, expose oneself to, gain, get, induce, meet with, obtain, provoke; SEE CONCEPT 93

incurable [*adj*] *unfixable, unchangeable*
cureless, deadly, fatal, hopeless, immedicable, impossible, inoperable, irrecoverable, irremediable, irreparable, nowhere to go*, out of time*, remediless, serious, terminal, uncorrectable, unrecoverable; SEE CONCEPTS 485,548

incursion [*n*] *invasion*
aggression, attack, foray, infiltration, inroad, intrusion, irruption, penetration, raid; SEE CONCEPTS 86,320

indebted [*adj*] *under an obligation*
accountable, answerable for, appreciative, beholden, bound, bounden, chargeable, dutybound, grateful, honor-bound, hooked*, in debt, in hock*, liable, obligated, obliged, owed, owing, responsible, thankful; SEE CONCEPTS 334,546

indecency [*n*] *obscenity, vulgarity*
bawdiness, coarseness, crudity, drunkenness, evil, foulness, grossness, immodesty, impropriety, impurity, incivility, indecorum, indelicacy, lewdness, licentiousness, offense, outrageousness, pornography, ribaldry, smuttiness, unseemliness, vileness; SEE CONCEPTS 633,645

indecent [*adj*] *obscene, vulgar; offensive*
blue*, coarse, crude, dirty*, filthy, foul, foulmouthed, gross*, ill-bred, immodest, immoral, improper, impure, in bad taste, indecorous, indelicate, lewd, licentious, malodorous, off-color*, outrageous, pornographic, raunchy*, raw, ridiculous, rough, salacious, scatological, shameless, shocking, smutty*, tasteless, unbecoming, undecorous, unseemly, untoward, vile, wicked, X-rated*; SEE CONCEPT 545

indecisive [*adj*] *uncertain, indefinite*
astraddle, changeable, doubtful, faltering, halting, hemming and hawing*, hesitant, hesitating, hot and cold*, inconclusive, indeterminate, irresolute, of two minds*, on the fence*, tentative, unclear, undecided, undetermined, uneventful, unsettled, unstable, vacillating, waffling, wavering, weak-kneed*, wishy-washy*; SEE CONCEPTS 534,535

indeed [*adv*] *actually*
absolutely, amen*, certainly, doubtlessly, easily, even, for real, in point of fact, in truth, much, naturally, of course, positively, really, strictly, surely, sure thing*, to be sure, truly, undeniably, undoubtedly, verily, veritably, very, very much, well; SEE CONCEPT 535

indefatigable [*adj*] *untiring*
active, assiduous, bound and determined*, dead set on*, determined, diligent, dogged, energetic, hell-bent*, industrious, inexhaustible, ironclad, nose to grindstone*, painstaking, patient, persevering, persistent, pertinacious, relentless, sedulous, steadfast, stop at nothing*, strenuous, tireless, unfaltering, unflagging, unflinching, unremitting, unwavering, unwearied, unwearying, vigorous; SEE CONCEPT 542

indefensible [*adj*] *inexcusable*
bad, faulty, inexpiable, insupportable, unforgiv-

in
in

able, unjustifiable, unpardonable, untenable, unwarrantable, wrong; SEE CONCEPTS *545,548*

indefinite [*adj*] *ambiguous, vague*

broad, confused, doubtful, dubious, equivocal, evasive, general, ill-defined, imprecise, indeterminable, indeterminate, indistinct, inexact, inexhaustible, infinite, innumerable, intangible, loose, obscure, shadowy, uncertain, unclear, undefined, undependable, undetermined, unfixed, unknown, unlimited, unsettled, unspecific, unsure, wide; SEE CONCEPT *535*

indefinitely [*adv*] *continually*

considerably, endlessly, forever, frequently, regularly, sine die, without end; SEE CONCEPT *798*

indelible [*adj*] *not able to be erased, indestructible*

enduring, ineffaceable, ineradicable, inerasable, inexpungible, inextirpable, ingrained, lasting, memorable, permanent, rememberable, stirring, unforgettable; SEE CONCEPTS *482,529*

indelicate [*adj*] *obscene, vulgar*

base, brash, brutish, callow, coarse, crude, earthy, embarrassing, immodest, improper, indecent, indecorous, lewd, low, lowbred, off-color*, offensive, outrageous, risqué, rude, suggestive, tasteless, unbecoming, unblushing, uncouth, unseemly, untactful, untoward; SEE CONCEPTS *544,545*

indent [*v*] *make a space; push in slightly*

bash, cave in, cut, dent, depress, dint, hollow, jag, mark, nick, notch, pink, pit, rabbet, rut, scallop, score, serrate; SEE CONCEPTS *158,201,208*

independence [*n*] *liberty, freedom*

ability, aptitude, autarchy, autonomy, home rule*, license, qualification, self-determination, self-government, self-reliance, self-rule, self-sufficiency, separation, sovereignty; SEE CONCEPTS *376,691*

independent [*adj*] *liberated, free*

absolute, autarchic, autarchical, autonomous, freewheeling, individualistic, nonaligned, nonpartisan, on one's own, self-contained, self-determining, self-governing, self-reliant, self-ruling, self-sufficient, self-supporting, separate, separated, sovereign, unaided, unallied, unconnected, unconstrained, uncontrolled, unregimented; SEE CONCEPT *554*

independently [*adv*] *alone*

all by one's self, apart, autonomously, by oneself, exclusive of, freely, individually, of one's own volition, one at a time, one by one, on one's own, separately, severally, singly, solo, unaided, unrestrictedly, unsupervised, without regard to, without support; SEE CONCEPT *554*

indescribable [*adj*] *beyond words*

impossible, incommunicable, indefinable, ineffable, inexpressible, nondescript, sublime, subtle, unspeakable, untellable, unutterable; SEE CONCEPT *267*

indestructible [*adj*] *lasting, unable to be destroyed*

abiding, deathless, durable, enduring, everlasting, immortal, immutable, imperishable, incorruptible, indelible, indissoluble, inexterminable, inextinguishable, inextirpable, irrefragable, irrefrangible, nonperishable, permanent, perpetual, unalterable, unbreakable, unchangeable, undestroyable, undying, unfading; SEE CONCEPTS *489,534*

indeterminate [*adj*] *uncertain, vague*

borderless, general, imprecise, inconclusive, indefinite, indistinct, inexact, undefined, undetermined, unfixed, unspecified, unstipulated; SEE CONCEPT *535*

index [*n*] *indication*

basis, clue, evidence, formula, guide, hand, indicant, indication, indicator, indicia, mark, model needle, pointer, ratio, rule, sign, significant, symbol, symptom, token; SEE CONCEPTS *284,290*

index [*v*] *arrange, order*

alphabetize, catalogue, docket, file, list, record tabulate; SEE CONCEPT *84*

indicate [*v*] *signify, display*

add up to, announce, argue, attest, augur, bespeak, be symptomatic, betoken, button down* card, connote, demonstrate, denote, designate evidence, evince, express, finger, hint, illustrate imply, import, intimate, make, manifest, mark mean, name, peg*, pin down*, pinpoint*, poin out, point to, prove, read, record, register, reveal show, sign, signal, slot, specify, suggest, symbolize, tab, tag, testify, witness; SEE CONCEPTS *74,118,266*

indication [*n*] *evidence, clue*

adumbration, attestation, augury, auspice, cue earnest, explanation, expression, forewarning gesture, hint, implication, index, indicia, inkling intimation, manifestation, mark, nod, note, notion, omen, pledge, portent, preamble, prefiguration, prognostic, prolegomenon, proof, reminder show, sign, signal, significant, signifier, suggestion, symptom, telltale, token, trace, vestige warning, wind*, wink*; SEE CONCEPTS *74,278,284*

indicative [*adj*] *exhibitive*

apocalyptic, augural, auspicious, characteristic connotative, demonstrative, denotative, denotive designative, diagnostic, emblematic, evidential evincive, expressive, inauspicious, indicatory indicial, ominous, pointing to, prognostic, signif icant, significatory, suggestive, symbolic, symp tomatic, testatory, testimonial; SEE CONCEPT *267*

indicator [*n*] *sign*

barometer, beacon, clue, dial, gauge, guide, hint index, mark, meter, omen, pointer, signal, sym bol, warning; SEE CONCEPTS *274,529,673,689*

indict [*v*] *accuse*

arraign, censure, charge, criminate, face with charges, finger*, frame*, impeach, incriminate inculpate, prosecute, summon, tax; SEE CONCEPTS *44,317*

indictment [*n*] *accusation*

allegation, arraignment, bill, blame, censure charge, citation, detention, findings, impeach ment, incrimination, presentment, prosecution statement, summons, warrant, writ; SEE CONCEPTS *44,317,318*

indifference [*n*] *absence of feeling, interest*

alienation, aloofness, apathy, callousness, care lessness, cold-bloodedness, coldness, cold shoul der*, coolness, detachment, disdain, disinterest disinterestedness, dispassion, disregard, equity heedlessness, immunity, impartiality, impassive ness, impassivity, inattention, inertia, insensitiv ity, insouciance, isolationism, lack, lethargy listlessness, negligence, neutrality, nonchalance noninterference, objectivity, stoicism, torpor, un concern, unmindfulness; SEE CONCEPTS *410,657*

indifferent [*adj*] *unfeeling, uninterested*
aloof, apathetic, blasé, callous, cold, cool, detached, diffident, disinterested, dispassionate, distant, equitable, haughty, heartless, heedless, highbrow, impartial, impervious, inattentive, listless, neutral, nonchalant, nonpartisan, objective, passionless, phlegmatic, regardless, scornful, silent, stoical, supercilious, superior, unaroused, unbiased, uncaring, uncommunicative, unconcerned, unemotional, unimpassioned, uninvolved, unmoved, unprejudiced, unresponsive, unsocial, unsympathetic; SEE CONCEPTS 403,542

indigenous [*adj*] *native, inborn*
aboriginal, autochthonous, chthonic, congenital, connate, domestic, endemic, homegrown, inbred, inherent, inherited, innate, natural, original, primitive, unacquired; SEE CONCEPT 549

indigent [*adj*] *poor*
beggared, busted, destitute, down and out*, flat broke*, hard up*, homeless, impecunious, impoverished, in want, necessitous, needy, penniless, penurious, poverty-stricken; SEE CONCEPT 334

indigestion [*n*] *upset stomach*
acid indigestion, acidosis, digestive upset, dyspepsia, dyspepsy, flatulence, flu, gas, gaseous stomach, heartburn, nausea, pain; SEE CONCEPT 306

indignant [*adj*] *angry*
acrimonious, annoyed, bent out of shape*, boiling*, bugged*, burned up*, disgruntled, displeased, exasperated, fuming, furious, heated, huffy*, in a huff*, incensed, irate, livid, mad, miffed, peeved, piqued, p.o.'d*, provoked, resentful, riled, scornful, seeing red*, up in arms*, upset, wrathful; SEE CONCEPTS 403,542

indignation [*n*] *anger*
animus, boiling point*, danger, displeasure, exasperation, fury, huff*, ire, mad, miff*, pique, rage, resentment, rise, scorn, slow burn*, umbrage, wrath; SEE CONCEPTS 29,657

indignity [*n*] *embarrassment, humiliation*
abuse, affront, backhanded compliment*, contumely, discourtesy, dishonor, disrespect, grievance, injury, injustice, insult, obloquy, opprobrium, outrage, put-down*, reproach, slap*, slight, slur, snub, take-down*, taunt; SEE CONCEPTS 278,410

indirect [*adj*] *roundabout; unintended*
ambiguous, ancillary, circuitous, circular, circumlocutory, collateral, complicated, contingent, crooked, devious, discursive, duplicitous, erratic, eventual, implied, incidental, long, long-drawn-out*, long way home*, long-winded*, meandering, oblique, obscure, out-of-the-way, periphrastic, rambling, secondary, serpentine*, sidelong, sinister, sinuous, snaking*, sneaking, sneaky, subsidiary, tortuous, twisting, underhand, vagrant, wandering, winding, zigzag; SEE CONCEPTS 544,581

indiscreet [*adj*] *injudicious*
careless, foolish, hasty, heedless, imprudent, inconsiderate, insensitive, rash, reckless, unthinking; SEE CONCEPT 542

indiscretion [*n*] *mistake*
bumble, crudeness, dropping the ball*, dumb move*, error, excitability, faux pas, folly, foolishness, fool mistake*, foul-up, gaffe, gaucherie, goof*, hastiness, imprudence, indiscreetness, ingenuousness, lapse, miscue, misjudgment, miss-

peak, naïveté, rashness, recklessness, screw-up*, simple-mindedness, slip*, slip of the tongue*, slip-up*, stumble, stupidity, tactlessness, thoughtlessness, unseemliness; SEE CONCEPTS 101,633,674

indiscriminate [*adj*] *random, chaotic*
aimless, assorted, broad, careless, confused, designless, desultory, extensive, general, haphazard, heterogeneous, hit-or-miss*, imperceptive, jumbled, mingled, miscellaneous, mixed, mongrel, motley*, multifarious, promiscuous, purposeless, shallow, spot, superficial, sweeping, unconsidered, uncritical, undiscriminating, unmethodical, unplanned, unselective, unsystematic, varied, variegated, wholesale*, wide; SEE CONCEPTS 403,542,585,772

indispensable [*adj*] *necessary*
basal, basic, cardinal, crucial, essential, fundamental, imperative, key, necessitous, needed, needful, prerequisite, primary, required, requisite, vital; SEE CONCEPT 546

indisposed [*adj1*] *not well*
ailing, below par, confined, down, down with*, feeling rotten*, got a bug*, ill, infirm, laid up*, on sick list*, out of action*, poorly, sick, sickly, under the weather*, unwell; SEE CONCEPT 314

indisposed [*adj2*] *unwilling*
afraid, antagonistic, antipathetic, averse, backward, disinclined, hesitant, hostile, inimical, loath, reluctant, uncaring, uneager, uninclined; SEE CONCEPT 542

indisputable [*adj*] *beyond doubt*
absolute, accurate, actual, certain, double-checked, evident, incontestable, incontrovertible, indubitable, irrefutable, no ifs ands or buts about it*, no mistake*, open and shut*, positive, real, sure, that's a fact*, true, unassailable, undeniable, undoubted, unfabled, unquestionable, veridical; SEE CONCEPTS 535,582

indistinct [*adj*] *obscure, ambiguous*
bleared, bleary, blurred, confused, dark, dim, doubtful, faint, fuzzy, hazy, ill-defined, inaudible, inconspicuous, indefinite, indeterminate, indiscernible, indistinguishable, inexact, misty, muffled, murky, out of focus, shadowy, unclear, undefined, undetermined, unheard, unintelligible, vague, weak; SEE CONCEPTS 485,535

indistinguishable [*adj*] *alike*
duplicate, equivalent, identic, identical, like, same, tantamount, twin; SEE CONCEPT 566

individual [*adj*] *distinctive, exclusive*
alone, characteristic, definite, diacritic, diagnostic, different, discrete, distinct, especial, express, idiosyncratic, indivisible, lone, odd, only, original, own, particular, peculiar, personal, personalized, proper, reserved, respective, secluded, select, separate, several, single, singular, sole, solitary, special, specific, uncommon, unique, unitary, unusual; SEE CONCEPTS 404,564

individual [*n*] *singular person, thing*
being, body, character, child, creature, dude*, entity, existence, human being, man, material, matter, mortal, number, party, person, personage, self, singleton, somebody, something, soul, stuff, substance, type, unit, woman; SEE CONCEPTS 389,433

individuality [*n*] *personality*
air, character, complexion, difference, discreteness, disposition, dissimilarity, distinction, distinctiveness, eccentricity, habit, humor, identity,

in
in

idiosyncrasy, independence, individualism, ipseity, makeup, manner, nature, oddity, oneness, originality, particularity, peculiarity, rarity, seity, selfdom, selfhood, selfness, separateness, singleness, singularity, singularness, temper, temperament, uniqueness, unity, unlikeness, way; SEE CONCEPT *411*

individually [*adv*] *separately*
alone, apart, by oneself, distinctively, exclusively, independently, one at a time, one by one, personally, restrictedly, severally, singly, without help; SEE CONCEPT *544*

individual retirement account [*n*] *IRA*
Keogh plan, retirement plan, Roth IRA, self-funded retirement plan, tax-free savings account; SEE CONCEPTS *335,340,446,710*

indoctrinate [*v*] *brainwash*
break down, convince, drill, ground, imbue, implant, inculcate, influence, initiate, instill, instruct, plant, program, school, teach, train, work over; SEE CONCEPTS *14,285*

indolent [*adj*] *lazy*
drony, easygoing, fainéant, idle, inactive, inert, lackadaisical, languid, lax, lazy, lethargic, listless, resting, shiftless, slothful, slow, slow-going, sluggish, torpid; SEE CONCEPTS *538,542,584*

indomitable [*adj*] *steadfast, unyielding*
dogged, impassable, impregnable, insuperable, insurmountable, invincible, invulnerable, obstinate, pertinacious, resolute, ruthless, staunch, stubborn, unassailable, unbeatable, unconquerable, undefeatable, unflinching, willful; SEE CONCEPTS *404,489,534*

indubitably [*adv*] *unquestionably*
certainly, definitely, for sure, indeed, no question, of course, positively, surely, undoubtedly, without doubt; SEE CONCEPT *535*

induce [*v*] *cause to happen; encourage*
abet, activate, actuate, argue into, breed, bring about, bring around, bulldoze*, cajole, cause, coax, convince, draw, draw in, effect, engender, generate, get*, get up, give rise to, goose*, impel, incite, influence, instigate, lead to, make, motivate, move, occasion, persuade, press, prevail upon, procure, produce, promote, prompt, sell one on*, set in motion, soft-soap*, squeeze, steamroll*, suck in*, sway, sweet-talk*, talk into*, twist one's arm*, urge, wheedle, win over*; SEE CONCEPTS *14,68,242*

inducement [*n*] *incentive, motive*
attraction, bait, brainwash*, carrot*, cause, come-on*, con*, consideration, desire, encouragement, hard sell*, hook*, impulse, incitement, influence, leader, lure, reward, snow job*, soft soap*, spur, stimulus, sweet talk*, temptation, twist, urge; SEE CONCEPTS *68,661*

induct [*v*] *take into an organization*
conscript, draft, enlist, inaugurate, initiate, install, instate, introduce, invest, recruit, sign on, sign up, swear in; SEE CONCEPTS *50,88,320,384*

induction [*n1*] *taking in, initiation*
consecration, draft, entrance, greetings, inaugural, inauguration, installation, instatement, institution, introduction, investiture, ordination, selection; SEE CONCEPTS *320,384,685*

induction [*n2*] *inference*
conclusion, conjecture, deducement, generalization, judgment, logical reasoning, ratiocination, rationalization, reason; SEE CONCEPTS *37,689*

indulge [*v1*] *treat oneself or another to*
allow, baby, cater, coddle, cosset, delight, entertain, favor, foster, give in, give rein to*, go along, go easy on*, gratify, humor, mollycoddle*, nourish, oblige, pamper, pander, pet, please, regale, satiate, satisfy, spoil, spoil rotten*, take care of*, tickle, yield; SEE CONCEPT *110*

indulge [*v2*] *luxuriate in*
bask in, ego trip*, enjoy, go in for*, live it up*, look out for number one*, revel in, rollick*, take part, wallow in; SEE CONCEPT *20*

indulgence [*n*] *luxury; gratification*
allowance, appeasement, attention, babying*, coddling*, courtesy, endurance, excess, extravagance, favor, favoring, fondling, fondness, forbearance, fulfillment, goodwill, gratifying, hedonism, immoderation, intemperance, intemperateness, kindness, kowtowing*, lenience, leniency, pampering, partiality, patience, permissiveness, petting, placating, pleasing, privilege, profligacy, profligateness, satiation, satisfaction, service, spoiling, toadying*, tolerance, toleration, treating, understanding; SEE CONCEPTS *337,657,712*

indulgent [*adj*] *lenient, giving*
able to live with*, big*, charitable, clement, compassionate, complaisant, compliant, considerate, easy, easygoing, favorable, fond, forbearing, gentle, going along with*, going easy on*, gratifying, kind, kindly, liberal, merciful, mild, overpermissive, permissive, soft-shelled*, tender, tolerant, understanding; SEE CONCEPTS *404,542*

industrial [*adj*] *related to manufacturing*
automated, business, factory-made, industrialized, in industry, machine-made, manufactured, manufacturing, mechanical, mechanized, modern, smokestack, streamlined, technical; SEE CONCEPT *536*

industrious [*adj*] *hardworking*
active, assiduous, ball of fire*, burning, busy, conscientious, diligent, dynamic, eager, energetic, grind*, in full swing*, intent, involved, jumping, laborious, on the go*, operose, perky*, persevering, persistent, plugging, productive, psyched up*, purposeful, sedulous, spirited, steady, tireless, zealous; SEE CONCEPT *538*

industry [*n1*] *manufacturing*
big business*, business, commerce, commercial enterprise, corporation, management, manufactory, megacorp*, mob, monopoly, multinational, outfit*, production, trade, traffic; SEE CONCEPTS *323,325*

industry [*n2*] *hard work*
activity, application, assiduity, attention, care, determination, diligence, dynamism, effort, energy, enterprise, intentness, inventiveness, labor, pains, patience, perseverance, persistence, tirelessness, toil, vigor, zeal; SEE CONCEPT *677*

inebriated [*adj*] *drunk*
blind drunk*, bombed, boozy, high*, inebriate, intoxicated, loaded*, plastered*, smashed*, tight*, tipsy, under the influence, wasted*; SEE CONCEPT *314*

ineffable [*adj*] *too great for words*
beyond words, celestial, divine, empyreal, empyrean, ethereal, heavenly, holy, ideal, impossible, incommunicable, incredible, indefinable, indescribable, inexpressible, nameless, sacred

spiritual, too sacred for words*, transcendent, transcendental, unspeakable, untellable, unutterable; SEE CONCEPTS 267,574

ineffective/ineffectual [adj] *weak, useless*
abortive, anticlimactic, barren, bootless, defeasible, feckless, feeble, forceless, fruitless, futile, idle, impotent, inadequate, incompetent, indecisive, inefficacious, inefficient, inept, inferior, innocuous, inoperative, invertebrate, lame, limited, neutralized, nugatory, null, null and void*, paltry, powerless, spineless, unable, unavailing, unfruitful, unproductive, unprofitable, unsuccessful, vain, void, withered, worthless; SEE CONCEPTS 537,560

inefficient [adj] *not working well; wasteful*
can't hack it*, careless, disorganized, extravagant, faulty, feeble, half-baked*, improficient, improvident, incapable, incompetent, ineffective, ineffectual, inefficacious, inept, inexpert, not cut out for*, prodigal, shooting blanks*, slack, slipshod, sloppy, slovenly, unfit, unprepared, unqualified, unskilled, unskillful, untrained, weak; SEE CONCEPTS 402,527,560

inelegant [adj] *clumsy, crude*
awkward, coarse, crass, gauche, graceless, gross, indelicate, labored, oafish, raw, rough, rude, stiff*, uncouth, uncultivated, uncultured, ungainly, ungraceful, unpolished, unrefined, vulgar, wooden*; SEE CONCEPTS 267,542,555

ineligible [adj] *not qualified*
disqualified, inappropriate, incompetent, objectionable, ruled out, unacceptable, unavailable, undesirable, unequipped, unfit, unqualified, unsuitable; SEE CONCEPTS 402,558

inept [adj1] *clumsy, unskilled; incompetent*
all thumbs*, artless, awkward, bumbling, bungling, butterfingers*, gauche, halting, inadept, incapable, incompetent, inefficient, inexpert, loser, maladroit, unapt, undexterous, unfacile, ungraceful, unhandy, unproficient, unskillful, wooden*; SEE CONCEPTS 402,527

inept [adj2] *not suitable; improper*
absurd, ill-timed, inappropriate, inapt, infelicitous, malapropos, meaningless, not adapted, out of place*, pointless, ridiculous, undue, unfit, unseasonable, unseemly, unsuitable; SEE CONCEPT 558

inequality [n] *prejudice; lack of balance*
asperity, bias, contrast, difference, discrimination, disparity, disproportion, dissimilarity, dissimilitude, diversity, imparity, incommensurateness, injustice, irregularity, one-sidedness, partisanship, preferentiality, roughness, unequivalence, unevenness, unfairness, unjustness, variation; SEE CONCEPT 665

inequitable [adj] *unfair*
arbitrary, biased, discriminatory, one-sided, partial, partisan, prejudiced, unbalanced, unequal, unethical, uneven, unjust; SEE CONCEPTS 480,544,545,548

inert [adj] *not moving; lifeless*
apathetic, asleep, dead, dormant, down, dull, idle, immobile, impassive, impotent, inactive, inanimate, indolent, languid, languorous, lazy, leaden, listless, motionless, numb, paralyzed, passive, phlegmatic, powerless, quiescent, quiet, slack, sleepy, slothful, sluggard, sluggish, slumberous, static, still, stolid, torpid, unmoving, unreactive, unresponsive; SEE CONCEPTS 542,584

inertia [n] *disinclination to move; lifelessness*
apathy, deadness, drowsiness, dullness, idleness, immobility, immobilization, inactivity, indolence, languor, lassitude, laziness, lethargy, listlessness, oscitancy, paralysis, passivity, sloth, sluggishness, stillness, stupor, torpidity, torpor, unresponsiveness; SEE CONCEPTS 657,681

inevitable [adj] *certain; cannot be avoided*
all locked up*, assured, binding, compulsory, decided, decreed, destined, determined, doomed, fated, fateful, for certain, foreordained, imminent, impending, ineluctable, ineludible, inescapable, inexorable, inflexible, in the bag*, irresistible, irrevocable, necessary, no ifs ands or buts*, obligatory, ordained, pat*, prescribed, settled, sure, unalterable, unavoidable, undeniable, unpreventable, without recourse; SEE CONCEPTS 535,552

inexcusable [adj] *not forgivable*
blamable, blameworthy, censurable, criticizable, impermissible, indefensible, inexpiable, intolerable, outrageous, reprehensible, unallowable, unforgivable, unjustifiable, unpardonable, unpermissible, untenable, unwarrantable, wrong; SEE CONCEPTS 545,570

inexhaustible [adj1] *unlimited*
bountiful, endless, infinite, limitless, never-ending, no end to*, numberless; SEE CONCEPT 772

inexhaustible [adj2] *tireless*
enduring, indefatigable, unflagging, untiring, unwearying, vigorous; SEE CONCEPTS 538,542

inexorable [adj] *cruel, pitiless*
adamant, adamantine, bound, bound and determined*, compulsory, dead set on*, dogged, hard, harsh, hell bent on*, immobile, immovable, implacable, ineluctable, inescapable, inflexible, ironclad, like death and taxes*, locked in*, mean business*, merciless, necessary, no going back*, obdurate, obstinate, relentless, remorseless, resolute, rigid, set in stone*, severe, single-minded, stubborn, unappeasable, unbending, uncompromising, unmovable, unrelenting, unyielding; SEE CONCEPTS 401,534

inexpensive [adj] *not high priced*
bargain, budget, buy, cheap, cost next to nothing*, cut-rate, dime a dozen*, dirt-cheap*, economical, for a song*, half-price, low-cost, low-priced, marked down, modest, nominal, popular, popularly priced, real buy*, real steal*, reasonable, reduced, steal, thrifty; SEE CONCEPT 334

inexperienced [adj] *unskilled, unfamiliar*
amateur, callow, fresh, green*, ignorant, immature, inept, inexpert, innocent, kid*, naive, new, prentice, raw*, rookie, rude, sophomoric, spring chicken*, tenderfoot*, unaccustomed, unacquainted, unconversant, undisciplined, unfamiliar with, unfledged, unpracticed, unschooled, unseasoned, unsophisticated, untrained, untried, unused, unversed, unworldly, verdant, wet behind ears*, young; SEE CONCEPTS 402,404,527

inexplicable [adj] *beyond comprehension, explanation*
baffling, enigmatic, incomprehensible, indecipherable, indescribable, inexplainable, inscrutable, insoluble, mysterious, mystifying, obscure, odd, peculiar, puzzling, strange, unaccountable, undefinable, unexplainable, unfathomable, unintelligible, unsolvable; SEE CONCEPTS 267,529

in
in

infallible [*adj*] *unerring, dependable*
acceptable, accurate, agreeable, apodictic, authoritative, certain, correct, effective, effectual, efficacious, efficient, exact, faultless, flawless, foolproof, handy, helpful, impeccable, incontrovertible, inerrable, inerrant, omniscient, perfect, positive, reliable, satisfactory, satisfying, sure, surefire, true, trustworthy, unbeatable, undeceivable, unfailing, unimpeachable, unquestionable, useful; SEE CONCEPTS 535,560,574

infamous [*adj*] *shameful, bad in reputation*
abominable, atrocious, base, caitiff, contemptible, corrupt, degenerate, despicable, detestable, disgraceful, dishonorable, disreputable, egregious, evil, flagitious, foul, hateful, heinous, ignominious, ill-famed, iniquitous, loathsome, miscreant, monstrous, nefarious, notorious, odious, offensive, opprobrious, outrageous, perverse, questionable, rotten, scandalous, scurvy, shady, shocking, sorry, unhealthy, vicious, vile, villainous, wicked; SEE CONCEPTS 404,545,570

infamy [*n*] *shameful, bad reputation*
abomination, atrocity, disapprobation, discredit, disesteem, disgrace, dishonor, disrepute, enormity, evil, ignominy, immorality, impropriety, notoriety, notoriousness, obloquy, odium, opprobrium, outrageousness, scandal, shame, stigma, villainy, wickedness; SEE CONCEPTS 411,645

infant [*n*] *baby*
babe, bairn, bambino, bantling, bundle, child, kid, little one, neonate, newborn, small child, suckling, toddler, tot; SEE CONCEPTS 414,424

infant/infantile [*adj*] *very young*
baby, babyish, callow, childish, childlike, dawning, developing, early, emergent, green*, growing, immature, infantine, initial, juvenile, kid, naive, nascent, newborn, puerile, tender, unfledged, unripe, weak, youthful; SEE CONCEPTS 542,578,797,820

infatuated [*adj*] *in love with; obsessed*
beguiled, besotted, bewitched, captivated, carried away*, charmed, crazy about*, enamored, enraptured, far gone on*, fascinated, foolish, inflamed, intoxicated, possessed, seduced, silly*, smitten, spellbound, under a spell*; SEE CONCEPTS 32,403

infect [*v*] *pollute, contaminate*
affect, blight, corrupt, defile, disease, influence, poison, spoil, spread among, spread to, taint, touch, vitiate; SEE CONCEPTS 143,246

infection [*n*] *contamination*
bug*, communicability, contagion, contagiousness, corruption, defilement, disease, epidemic, flu, germs, impurity, insanitation, poison, pollution, septicity, virus, what's going around*; SEE CONCEPTS 230,306

infectious [*adj*] *catching, spreading*
communicable, contagious, contaminating, corrupting, defiling, diseased, epidemic, infective, mephitic, miasmic, noxious, pestilent, pestilential, poisoning, polluting, toxic, transferable, transmittable, virulent, vitiating; SEE CONCEPTS 314,559

infer [*v*] *conclude*
arrive at, ascertain, assume, believe, collect, conjecture, construe, deduce, derive, draw, draw inference, figure, figure out, gather, glean, guess, induce, interpret, intuit, judge, presume, presuppose, reach conclusion, read between lines*, read

into*, reason, reckon, speculate, suppose, surmise, think, understand; SEE CONCEPTS 12,15,37

inference [*n*] *conclusion, deduction*
assumption, conjecture, corollary, guess, hint, interpretation, presumption, reading, reasoning, supposition; SEE CONCEPT 689

inferior [*adj1*] *less in rank, importance*
back seat*, bottom, bottom-rung*, entry-level, junior, less, lesser, lower, menial, minor, minus, nether, peon, second, secondary, second-banana*, second-fiddle*, second-string*, smaller, subjacent, subordinate, subsidiary, under, underneath; SEE CONCEPT 567

inferior [*adj2*] *poor, second-rate*
average, bad, base, common, déclassé, fair, good-for-nothing*, hack*, imperfect, indifferent, junk*, lemon*, lousy, low-grade, low-rent*, mean, mediocre, middling, ordinary, paltry, poorer, sad, second-class, sorry*, substandard, tawdry, two-bit*, worse, wretched; SEE CONCEPT 574

inferior [*n*] *person of lesser rank, importance*
adherent, attendant, auxiliary, deputy, disciple, follower, hanger-on, hireling, junior, menial, minion, minor, peon, satellite, second banana*, subaltern, subject, subordinate, sycophant, underling; SEE CONCEPTS 348,423

infernal [*adj*] *damned; underworld*
accursed, blamed, blasted, chthonian, confounded, cursed, cussed, damnable, demonic, devilish, diabolical, execrable, fiendish, hellish, lower, malevolent, malicious, monstrous, nether, satanic, subterranean, sulphurous, wicked; SEE CONCEPTS 536,545

inferno [*n*] *hell*
blazes*, bottomless pit*, everlasting fire*, fire and brimstone*, Hades, hellfire, netherworld, purgatory, underworld; SEE CONCEPTS 370,435, 674

infertile [*adj*] *not bearing fruit, young*
barren, depleted, drained, effete, exhausted, impotent, impoverished, infecund, nonproductive, sterile, unbearing, unfertile, unfruitful, unproductive; SEE CONCEPTS 406,560

infest [*adj*] *flood, overrun*
abound, annoy, assail, beset, crawl, crowd, defile, fill, flock, harass, harry, infect, invade, overspread, overwhelm, pack, penetrate, pester, plague, pollute, press, ravage, swarm, teem, throng, worry; SEE CONCEPTS 14,86,179

infidel [*n*] *nonbeliever*
agnostic, atheist, gentile, heathen, heretic, nonworshiper, pagan, unbeliever; SEE CONCEPT 689

infidelity [*n*] *disloyalty to an obligation*
adultery, affair, bad faith, betrayal, cheating, duplicity, extramarital relations, faithlessness, falseness, falsity, inconstancy, lewdness, perfidiousness, perfidy, treacherousness, treachery, treason, two-timing*, unfaithfulness; SEE CONCEPTS 388,645

infiltrate [*v*] *creep in*
access, crack*, edge in, filter through, foist, impregnate, insinuate, penetrate, percolate*, permeate, pervade, saturate, sneak in, tinge, work in, worm into*; SEE CONCEPTS 159,179

infinite [*adj*] *limitless, without end*
absolute, all-embracing, bottomless, boundless, enduring, enormous, eternal, everlasting, illimitable, immeasurable, immense, incalculable, incessant, inestimable, inexhaustible, interminable,

measureless, million, never-ending, no end of, no end to, numberless, perdurable, perpetual, sempiternal, stupendous, supertemporal, supreme, total, unbounded, uncounted, unending, untold, vast, wide, without limit, without number; SEE CONCEPTS *762,781,798*

infinitesimal [*adj*] *small*
atomic, imperceptible, inappreciable, inconsiderable, insignificant, little, microscopic, miniature, minuscule, minute, negligible, teeny*, tiny, unnoticeable; SEE CONCEPTS *773,789*

infinity [*n*] *endlessness*
beyond, boundlessness, continuity, continuum, endless time, eternity, expanse, extent, immeasurability, immensity, infinitude, limitlessness, myriad, perpetuity, sempiternity, space, ubiquity, unlimited space, vastitude, vastness; SEE CONCEPTS *730,807*

infirm [*adj*] *sick, weak*
ailing, anemic, anile, debilitated, decrepit, delicate, enfeebled, failing, faint, faltering, feeble, flimsy, fragile, frail, halting, ill, insecure, irresolute, laid low*, lame, sensile, shaky, unsound, unstable, unsubstantial, vacillating, wavering, wobbly; SEE CONCEPTS *314,485,489*

infirmity [*n*] *weakness, sickness*
affliction, ailing, ailment, confinement, debilitation, debility, decay, decrepitude, defect, deficiency, disease, diseasedness, disorder, failing, fault, feebleness, flu, frailty, ill health, imperfection, indisposition, malady, malaise, shortcoming, sickliness, unhealth, unhealthiness, unwellness, vulnerability; SEE CONCEPTS *306, 674,732*

inflame [*v*] *anger, aggravate*
agitate, annoy, arouse, burn, disturb, embitter, enrage, exacerbate, exasperate, excite, fan, fire, fire up, foment, gall, get*, grate, heat, heat up, ignite, impassion, incense, increase, infuriate, intensify, intoxicate, irritate, kindle, light, madden, provoke, put out*, rile, roil, rouse, steam up, stimulate, vex, worsen; SEE CONCEPTS *7,14,19, 22,249*

inflammable [*adj*] *ready to burn*
burnable, combustible, dangerous, flammable, hazardous, ignitable, incendiary, risky, unsafe; SEE CONCEPT *485*

inflammation [*n*] *redness, swelling*
burning, infection, irritation, pain, rash, sore, tenderness; SEE CONCEPTS *306,309*

inflammatory [*adj*] *instigative, angering*
anarchic, demagogic, exciting, explosive, fiery, incendiary, incitive, inflaming, insurgent, intemperate, provocative, rabble-rousing*, rabid, rebellious, revolutionary, riotous, seditionary, seditious; SEE CONCEPTS *537,542*

inflate [*v*] *blow up, increase*
aerate, aggrandize, amplify, augment, balloon*, beef up*, bloat, boost, build up, cram*, dilate, distend, enlarge, escalate, exaggerate, exalt, expand, flesh out*, magnify, maximize, overestimate, pad*, puff up*, pump up*, pyramid, raise, spread, stretch, surcharge, swell up*, widen; SEE CONCEPTS *236,245,780*

inflated [*adj*] *exaggerated*
aggrandized, amplified, augmented, aureate, bloated, bombastic, diffuse, dilated, distended, dropsical, enlarged, euphuistic, extended, filled, flatulent, flowery, fustian, grandiloquent, grown, magnified, magniloquent, ostentatious, overblown, overestimated, pompous, pretentious, prolix, puffed, pumped up, ranting, rhapsodical, rhetorical, showy, spread, stretched, surcharged, swollen, tumescent, tumid, turgid, verbose, windy, wordy; SEE CONCEPTS *267,773*

inflation [*n*] *increase, swelling*
aggrandizement, blowing up, boom, boost, buildup, distension, enhancement, enlargement, escalation, expansion, extension, hike, intensification, prosperity, puffiness, rise, spread, tumefaction; SEE CONCEPTS *335,763,780*

inflection [*n*] *accent, intonation*
articulation, change, emphasis, enunciation, modulation, pitch, pronunciation, sound, timbre, tonality, tone, tone of voice, variation; SEE CONCEPTS *65,595*

inflexible [*adj*] *stubborn*
adamant, adamantine, determined, dogged, dyed-in-the-wool*, firm, fixed, hard, hard-and-fast*, immovable, immutable, implacable, indomitable, inexorable, intractable, iron, obdurate, obstinate, relentless, resolute, rigid, rigorous, set, set in one's ways*, single-minded, stand one's ground*, staunch, steadfast, steely, stiff, strict, stringent, unadaptable, unbending, unchangeable, uncompliant, uncompromising, unrelenting, unswayable, unyielding; SEE CONCEPT *404*

inflexible [*adj2*] *hardened, stiff*
hard, immalleable, impliable, inelastic, nonflexible, rigid, set, starched, taut, unbending; SEE CONCEPT *604*

inflict [*v*] *impose something*
administer, apply, bring upon, command, deal out, deliver, dispense, exact, expose, extort, force, force upon, give, give it to*, lay down the law*, levy, mete out, require, stick it to*, strike, subject, visit, wreak; SEE CONCEPTS *50,53,88,242*

influence [*n*] *power, authority*
access, agency, ascendancy, character, clout, command, connections, consequence, control, credit, direction, domination, dominion, drag, effect, esteem, fame, fix, force, grease*, guidance, hold, impact, importance, imprint, in*, juice*, leadership, leverage, magnetism, mark, moment, money, monopoly, network, notoriety, predominance, prerogative, pressure, prestige, prominence, pull, repercussion, reputation, ropes*, rule, significance, spell, supremacy, sway, weight*; SEE CONCEPT *687*

influence [*v*] *lead to believe, do*
act upon, affect, alter, argue into, arouse, be recognized, bias, brainwash*, bribe, bring to bear, carry weight, change, channel, compel, control, count, determine, direct, dispose, form, get at*, guide, have a part in, impact on, impel, impress, incite, incline, induce, instigate, manipulate, modify, mold, move, persuade, predispose, prejudice, prevail, prompt, pull strings*, regulate, rouse, rule, seduce, sell, shape, snow*, sway, talk into, train, turn, urge, work upon; SEE CONCEPTS *18,68,242*

influential [*adj*] *effective, powerful*
affecting, authoritative, big-gun*, big-wheel*, controlling, dominant, efficacious, famous, forcible, governing, guiding, hot-dog*, important, impressive, inspiring, instrumental, leading, major-league*, meaningful, momentous, moving, name, persuasive, potent, prominent, significant, strong, substantial, telling, touching, weighty; SEE CONCEPTS *537,568*

in
in

influx [*n*] *flow, rush*
arrival, coming in, convergence, entrance, incursion, inflow, inpouring, inrush, introduction, inundation, invasion, penetration; SEE CONCEPTS 159,179,786

infomercial [*n*] *full-length television program existing solely to market a product*
advertorial, commercial, demonstration, documentainment, infotainment, paid announcement; SEE CONCEPT 277

inform [*v*] *communicate knowledge, information*
acquaint, advise, apprise, betray, blab*, brief, caution, clue, edify, educate, endow, endue, enlighten, familiarize, fill in, forewarn, give a pointer, give a tip, give away, give two cents'*, illuminate, inspire, instruct, invest, leak, let in on*, let know, level, make conversant with, notify, post, relate, send word, show the ropes*, snitch, squeal, tattle, teach, tell, tell on, tip, tout, update, warn, wise; SEE CONCEPT 60

informal [*adj*] *casual, simple*
breezy, colloquial, congenial, cool*, democratic, down home*, easy, easygoing, everyday, extempore, familiar, folksy, frank, free, free-and-easy*, homey, improv*, inconspicuous, intimate, laid back*, loose, low-pressure, mellow, mixed, motley, natural, off-the-cuff*, open, ordinary, relaxed, spontaneous, sporty, straightforward, throwaway*, unceremonious, unconstrained, unconventional, unfussy, unofficial, unrestrained, urbane, without ceremony; SEE CONCEPTS 548,589

informant/informer [*n*] *person who delivers news*
accuser, adviser, announcer, betrayer, blabbermouth*, canary*, crier, deep throat*, double-crosser, herald, interviewer, journalist, messenger, newscaster/newsperson, notifier, preacher, propagandist, rat*, reporter, sneak, source, stool pigeon*, tattler, tattletale; SEE CONCEPTS 348,354,423

information [*n*] *facts, news*
advice, ammo*, break*, chapter and verse*, clue, confidence, counsel, cue, data, dirt*, dope*, dossier, earful*, enlightenment, erudition, illumination, info*, inside story*, instruction, intelligence, knowledge, leak, learning, lore, lowdown*, material, message, network, notice, notification, orientation, propaganda, report, science, scoop, score, tidings, tip, what's what*, whole story*, wisdom, word*; SEE CONCEPT 274

informative [*adj*] *educational*
advisory, chatty, communicative, descriptive, edifying, educative, elucidative, enlightening, explanatory, forthcoming, gossipy, illuminating, informational, instructional, instructive, newsy, revealing, revelatory, significant; SEE CONCEPT 267

informed [*adj*] *cognizant, conversant*
abreast, acquainted, apprized, au courant*, au fait*, briefed, enlightened, erudite, expert, familiar, in the know*, into*, knowledgeable, know the score*, know what's what*, learned, on top of*, posted*, primed*, reliable, savvy*, tuned in*, up*, up on*, up-to-date, versant, versed, well-read, wise to*; SEE CONCEPT 402

infraction [*n*] *violation*
breach, breaking, contravention, crime, error, faux pas, infringement, lapse, offense, sin, slip*, transgression, trespass; SEE CONCEPTS 192,645

infrastructure [*n*] *foundation*
base, footing, framework, groundwork, root, support, underpinning; SEE CONCEPTS 442,826

infrequent [*adj*] *not happening regularly*
exceptional, few, few and far between*, isolated, limited, meager, occasional, odd, rare, scant, scanty, scarce, scattered, seldom, semioccasional, sparse, spasmodic, sporadic, stray, uncommon, unusual; SEE CONCEPT 530

infringe [*v*] *violate*
borrow, breach, break, contravene, crash, disobey, encroach, entrench, impose, infract, intrude, invade, lift, meddle, obtrude, offend, pirate, presume, steal, transgress, trespass; SEE CONCEPTS 192,384

infuriate [*v*] *make angry*
aggravate, anger, enrage, exasperate, incense, ire, irritate, madden, make blood boil*, provoke, rile, T-off*, umbrage; SEE CONCEPT 14

infuse [*v*] *introduce; soak*
animate, breathe into, imbue, impart, implant, impregnate, inculcate, indoctrinate, ingrain, inoculate, inspire, instill, intersperse, invest, leaven, permeate, pervade, plant, saturate, steep, suffuse; SEE CONCEPTS 140,179,187

ingenious [*adj*] *clever; brilliant*
able, adroit, artistic, bright, canny, crafty, creative, cunning, deviceful, dexterous, gifted, imaginative, innovational, innovative, innovatory, intelligent, inventive, original, ready, resourceful, shrewd, skillful, sly, subtle; SEE CONCEPT 402

ingenuity [*n*] *cleverness*
ability, adroitness, astuteness, brains, brightness, brilliance, creativity, cunning, dexterity, flair, genius, gumption, intelligence, inventiveness, resourcefulness, shrewdness, skill, smartness, talent, wisdom, wit; SEE CONCEPT 409

ingenuous [*adj*] *honest, trustful*
artless, candid, childlike, frank, green*, guileless, innocent, like a babe in the woods*, naive, natural, open, outspoken, plain, simple, sincere, square, straightforward, trusting, unaffected, unartful, unartificial, undisguised, unreserved, unschooled, unsophisticated, unstudied, up front*; SEE CONCEPTS 267,542,589

ingest [*v*] *swallow*
absorb, consume, devour, digest, down, drink, eat, inhale; SEE CONCEPT 169

inglorious [*adj*] *disgraceful*
blameworthy, contemptible, degrading, detestable, dishonorable, disreputable, ignoble, ignominious, offensive, reprehensible, shameful, unrespectable, unworthy; SEE CONCEPT 555

ingrained [*adj*] *deep-rooted*
built-in, chronic, confirmed, congenital, constitutional, deep-seated, fixed, fundamental, hereditary, implanted, inborn, inbred, inbuilt, indelible, indwelling, ineradicable, inherent, innate, in the blood*, intrinsic, inveterate, rooted; SEE CONCEPTS 535,549

ingratiate [*v*] *get on the good side of someone*
attract, blandish, brownnose*, captivate, charm, crawl, flatter, get in with*, grovel, hand a line*, insinuate oneself, kowtow*, play up to*, seek favor, truckle; SEE CONCEPTS 7,22,68

ingratiating [*adj*] *fawning, servile*
charming, crawling, deferential, disarming, flattering, humble, insinuating, obsequious, saccha-

rine, serving, silken, smarmy, soft, sycophantic, toadying*, unctuous; SEE CONCEPT 401

ingredient [n] *component of concoction*
additive, constituent, element, factor, fixing, fundamental, innards, integral, integrant, making, part, part and parcel*, piece; SEE CONCEPT 835

inhabit [v] *take up residence in*
abide, crash, dwell, indwell, live, locate, lodge, make one's home, occupy, park, people, perch, populate, possess, reside, roost, settle, squat, stay, tenant; SEE CONCEPT 226

inhabitant [n] *person who is resident of habitation*
aborigine, addressee, autochthon, boarder, citizen, colonist, denizen, dweller, householder, incumbent, indweller, inmate, lessee, lodger, native, neighbor, occupant, occupier, renter, resider, roomer, settler, squatter, suburbanite, tenant, urbanite; SEE CONCEPTS 354,413

inhale [v] *breathe in*
drag, draw in, gasp, inspire, insufflate, puff, pull, respire, smell, sniff, snort, suck in; SEE CONCEPTS 163,601

inherent [adj] *basic, hereditary*
built-in, characteristic, congenital, connate, constitutional, deep-rooted, deep-seated, distinctive, elementary, essential, fixed, fundamental, genetic, immanent, implicit, inborn, inbred, inbuilt, indigenous, indispensable, individual, indwelling, ingrained, inherited, innate, inner, instinctive, integral, integrated, internal, in the grain, intimate, intrinsic, inward, latent, native, natural, original, part and parcel*, resident, running in the family*, subjective, unalienable; SEE CONCEPTS 404,549

inherit [v] *gain as possession from someone's death*
accede, acquire, be bequeathed, be granted, be left, come in for, come into, derive, fall heir, get, obtain, receive, succeed, take over; SEE CONCEPTS 124,317

inheritance [n] *possession gained through someone's death*
bequest, birthright, devise, estate, gift, heirloom, heritage, heritance, legacy, primogeniture; SEE CONCEPT 337

inherited [adj] *hereditary*
congenital, connate, genetic, handed down, inborn, inbred, innate, in the blood, in the genes, passed down, rooted; SEE CONCEPT 549

inhibit [v] *restrict, prevent*
arrest, avert, bar, bit, bridle, check, constrain, cramp, curb, discourage, enjoin, faze, forbid, frustrate, hang up*, hinder, hog-tie*, hold back, hold down, hold in, impede, interdict, keep in, obstruct, outlaw, prohibit, put on brakes*, repress, restrain, sandbag*, stop, stymie, suppress, taboo*, ward, withhold; SEE CONCEPTS 121,130

inhibited [adj] *shy*
bottled up*, cold, constrained, frustrated, guarded, hung up*, passionless, repressed, reserved, reticent, self-conscious, subdued, undemonstrative, unresponsive, uptight, withdrawn; SEE CONCEPTS 404,542

inhibition [n] *restriction, hindrance*
bar, barrier, blockage, check, embargo, hangup, interdict, interference, obstacle, prevention, prohibition, reserve, restraint, reticence, self-consciousness, shyness, sublimation, suppression; SEE CONCEPTS 411,657

inhospitable [adj] *unfriendly*
brusque, cold, cool, hostile, rude, short, uncongenial, unfavorable, ungenerous, unkind, unreceptive, unsociable, unwelcoming; SEE CONCEPT 401

inhuman/inhumane [adj] *animal, savage*
barbaric, barbarous, bestial, brutal, cannibalistic, cold-blooded, cruel, devilish, diabolical, fell, ferocious, fiendish, fierce, grim, hateful, heartless, implacable, malicious, malign, malignant, mean, merciless, pitiless, relentless, remorseless, ruthless, truculent, uncompassionate, unfeeling, unkind, unrelenting, unsympathetic, vicious; SEE CONCEPTS 401,545

inhumanity [n] *lack of compassion*
atrocity, barbarism, bloodthirstiness, brutality, brutishness, callousness, cold-bloodedness, cruelty, ferocity, heartlessness, maliciousness, ruthlessness, savagery, viciousness, violence; SEE CONCEPTS 29,645

inimical [adj] *antagonistic, contrary*
adverse, antipathetic, destructive, disaffected, harmful, hostile, hurtful, ill, ill-disposed, inimicable, injurious, noxious, opposed, oppugnant, pernicious, repugnant, unfavorable, unfriendly, unwelcoming; SEE CONCEPTS 401,537

inimitable [adj] *incomparable*
consummate, matchless, nonpareil, peerless, perfect, supreme, unequalled, unexampled, unique, unmatched, unparalleled, unrivalled, unsurpassable; SEE CONCEPT 574

iniquity [n] *sin, evil*
abomination, baseness, crime, evildoing, heinousness, immorality, infamy, injustice, miscreancy, misdeed, offense, sinfulness, unfairness, unrighteousness, wickedness, wrong, wrongdoing; SEE CONCEPT 645

initial [adj] *beginning, primary*
antecedent, basic, commencing, earliest, early, elementary, embryonic, first, foremost, fundamental, germinal, headmost, inaugural, inceptive, inchoate, incipient, infant, initiative, initiatory, introductory, leading, nascent, opening, original, pioneer, virgin; SEE CONCEPTS 585,799,828

initiate [v1] *start, introduce*
admit, begin, break the ice*, come out with, come up with, commence, dream up, enter, get ball rolling*, get feet wet*, get under way, inaugurate, induct, install, instate, institute, intro*, invest, kick off*, launch, make up, open, originate, pioneer, set in motion, set up, take in, take up, trigger, usher in; SEE CONCEPT 221

initiate [v2] *teach*
brief, coach, edify, enlighten, familiarize, indoctrinate, induct, inform, instate, instruct, introduce, invest, train; SEE CONCEPT 285

initiation [n] *start, introduction*
admission, baptism, beginning, commencement, debut, enrollment, entrance, inaugural, inauguration, inception, indoctrination, induction, installation, instatement, investiture, preliminaries; SEE CONCEPTS 221,386

initiative [n] *eagerness to do something*
action, ambition, drive, dynamism, energy, enterprise, enthusiasm, get-up-and-go*, gumption*, inventiveness, leadership, moxie*, originality, punch, push, resource, resourcefulness, spunk*, steam*, vigor; SEE CONCEPTS 411,657

in
in

inject [*v1*] *put in, introduce*
add, drag in, force into, imbue, implant, impregnate, include, infuse, insert, instill, interjaculate, interject, place into, squeeze in, stick in, throw in; SEE CONCEPTS *187,208,209*

inject [*v2*] *introduce into bloodstream by use of a needle*
give a shot, inoculate, jab, mainline*, shoot, vaccinate; SEE CONCEPTS *179,310*

injection [*n*] *introduction into bloodstream*
booster, dose, dram, enema, inoculation, needle, vaccine; SEE CONCEPT *311*

injunction [*n*] *decree*
admonition, ban, bar, behest, bidding, charge, command, demand, dictate, embargo, enjoinder, exhortation, instruction, mandate, order, precept, prohibition, ruling, word, writ; SEE CONCEPTS *271,318*

injure [*v*] *hurt, harm*
abuse, aggrieve, batter, blemish, blight, break, contort, cripple, cut up, damage, deface, deform, disable, disfigure, distort, distress, do in*, draw blood*, foul, foul up, grieve, hack up, impair, maim, maltreat, mangle, mar, mutilate, pain, pique, prejudice, ruin, shake up, spoil, sting, tarnish, torment, torture, total, undermine, vitiate, wax, weaken, wound, wrong; SEE CONCEPT *246*

injurious [*adj*] *hurtful*
abusive, adverse, bad, baneful, corrupting, damaging, dangerous, deadly, deleterious, destructive, detrimental, disadvantageous, evil, harmful, iniquitous, insulting, libeling, mischievous, nocent, nocuous, noxious, opprobrious, pernicious, poisonous, prejudicial, ruinous, slanderous, unconducive, unhealthy, unjust, wrongful; SEE CONCEPTS *537,570*

injury [*n*] *hurt, harm*
abrasion, abuse, affliction, affront, agony, bad, bite, blemish, boo-boo*, bruise, burn, chop, cramp, cut, damage, deformation, detriment, discomfiture, disservice, distress, evil, fracture, gash, grievance, hemorrhage, ill, impairment, indignity, injustice, insult, laceration, lesion, libel, loss, mischief, misery, mutilation, nick, ouch*, outrage, pang, ruin, scar, scratch, shock, slander, sore, sprain, stab, sting, suffering, swelling, trauma, twinge, wound, wrong; SEE CONCEPTS *309,728*

injustice [*n*] *unfair treatment; bias*
abuse, breach, crime, crying shame*, damage, dirty deal*, discrimination, encroachment, favoritism, grievance, inequality, inequity, infraction, infringement, iniquity, malfeasance, malpractice, maltreatment, miscarriage, mischief, negligence, offense, onesidedness, oppression, outrage, partiality, partisanship, prejudice, railroad*, ruin, sellout*, transgression, trespass, unfairness, unjustness, unlawfulness, villainy, violation, wrong, wrongdoing; SEE CONCEPTS *192,645,674*

inkling [*n*] *idea, clue*
conception, cue, faintest idea*, foggiest idea*, glimmering, hint, hot lead*, hunch*, impression, indication, innuendo, intimation, lead, notion, sneaking suspicion*, suggestion, suspicion, tip, tipoff, whisper; SEE CONCEPT *689*

inlet [*n*] *arm of the sea*
basin, bay, bayou, bight, canal, channel, cove, creek, delta, entrance, estuary, firth, fjord, gulf, harbor, ingress, loch, narrows, passage, slew, slough, sound, strait; SEE CONCEPTS *509,514*

inn [*n*] *accommodation for travellers*
auberge, hospice, hostel, hostelry, hotel, lodge, motel, public house, resort, roadhouse, saloon, tavern; SEE CONCEPTS *439,449,516*

innate [*adj*] *inherited, native*
congenital, connate, connatural, constitutional, deep-seated, elemental, essential, hereditary, in-born, inbred, indigenous, ingrained, inherent, instinctive, intrinsic, intuitive, natural, normal, regular, standard, typical, unacquired; SEE CONCEPTS *406,549*

inner [*adj1*] *central, middle physically*
close, constitutional, essential, familiar, focal, inherent, innermore, inside, interior, internal, intestinal, intimate, intrinsic, inward, nuclear; SEE CONCEPTS *826,830*

inner [*adj2*] *mental, private*
central, concealed, deep-rooted, deep-seated, emotional, esoteric, essential, focal, gut*, hidden, individual, inherent, innate, inside, interior, internal, intimate, intrinsic, intuitive, inward, personal, psychological, repressed, secret, spiritual, subconscious, unrevealed, visceral, viscerous; SEE CONCEPTS *529,576*

innocence [*n1*] *blamelessness*
chastity, clean hands*, clear conscience*, guiltlessness, immaculateness, impeccability, incorruptibility, incorruption, inculpability, probity, purity, righteousness, sinlessness, stainlessness, uprightness, virtue; SEE CONCEPT *645*

innocence [*n2*] *harmlessness, naïveté*
artlessness, candidness, credulousness, forthrightness, frankness, freshness, guilelessness, gullibility, ignorance, inexperience, ingenuousness, innocuousness, innoxiousness, inoffensiveness, lack, nescience, plainness, purity, simplicity, sincerity, unaffectedness, unawareness, unfamiliarity, unknowingness, unsophistication, unworldliness, virtue; SEE CONCEPTS *409,411*

innocent [*adj1*] *blameless*
above suspicion, angelic, chaste, clean, cleanhanded, clear, crimeless, exemplary, faultless, free of, good, guilt-free, guiltless, honest, immaculate, impeccable, impeccant, inculpable, in the clear*, irreproachable, lawful, legal, legitimate, licit, not guilty, pristine, pure, righteous, safe, sinless, spotless, stainless, unblemished, uncensurable, uncorrupt, unimpeachable, uninvolved, unoffending, unsullied, untainted, upright, virginal, virtuous; SEE CONCEPT *545*

innocent [*adj2*] *harmless, naive*
artless, childlike, credulous, frank, fresh, guileless, gullible, hurtless, ignorant, inexperienced, ingenuous, innocuous, innoxious, inobnoxious, inoffensive, offenseless, open, raw, safe, simple, soft, square, unacquainted, unartificial, uncool, unfamiliar, unhurtful, uninjurious, unmalicious, unobjectionable, unoffensive, unschooled, unsophisticated, unstudied, unsuspicious, unworldly, well-intentioned, wellmeant, wide-eyed, youthful; SEE CONCEPTS *404,542*

innocuous [*adj*] *harmless*
banal, bland, flat, innocent, innoxious, inobnoxious, inoffensive, insipid, jejune, kind, painless, safe, sapless, unobjectionable, unoffending, weak; SEE CONCEPTS *401,572*

innovation [*n*] *change, novelty*
addition, alteration, contraption, cutting edge*, departure, deviation, introduction, last word*, latest thing*, leading edge*, modernism, modernization, modification, mutation, newness, notion, permutation, shift, variation, vicissitude, wrinkle*; SEE CONCEPTS 260,529,660,665

innovative [*adj*] *creative*
avant-garde, breaking new ground*, contemporary, cutting-edge*, deviceful, ingenious, innovational, innovatory, inventive, just out*, leading-edge*, new, newfangled*, original, originative, state-of-the-art*; SEE CONCEPTS 529,578, 589,797

innovator [*n*] *inventor*
avant-garde, creator, discoverer, groundbreaker, pioneer, trailblazer, trendsetter, vanguard; SEE CONCEPTS 348,413

innuendo [*n*] *suggestion*
allusion, aside, aspersion, hint, implication, imputation, insinuation, intimation, overtone, reference, whisper; SEE CONCEPTS 75,278

innumerable [*adj*] *many, infinite*
alive with*, beyond number, countless, frequent, incalculable, multitudinous, myriad, numberless, numerous, uncountable, unnumbered, untold; SEE CONCEPT 762

inoculation [*n*] *immunization*
injection, prevention, shot, vaccination; SEE CONCEPT 310

inoffensive [*adj*] *not obnoxious; harmless*
calm, clean, friendly, humble, innocent, innocuous, innoxious, mild, neutral, nonprovocative, peaceable, pleasant, quiet, retiring, safe, unobjectionable, unobtrusive, unoffending; SEE CONCEPTS 267,542

inopportune [*adj*] *not appropriate or suitable*
contrary, disadvantageous, disturbing, ill-chosen, ill-timed, inappropriate, inauspicious, inconvenient, malapropos, mistimed, troublesome, unfavorable, unfortunate, unpropitious, unseasonable, unsuitable, untimely; SEE CONCEPT 558

inordinate [*adj*] *excessive, extravagant*
disproportionate, dizzying, exorbitant, extortionate, extreme, gratuitous, immoderate, intemperate, irrational, outrageous, overindulgent, overmuch, preposterous, supererogatory, superfluous, surplus, too much, towering, uncalled-for, unconscionable, uncurbed, undue, unmeasurable, unreasonable, unrestrained, untempered, unwarranted, wanton, wasteful; SEE CONCEPTS 570,781

inquest [*n*] *investigation*
delving, examination, hearing, inquiry, inquisition, probe, probing, quest, research, trial; SEE CONCEPTS 48,290,318

inquire [*v*] *ask; look into*
analyze, catechize, examine, explore, feel out, go over, grill, hit, hit up, inspect, interrogate, investigate, knock, probe, prospect, pry, query, question, request information, roast, scrutinize, search, seek, seek information, sift, study, test the waters*; SEE CONCEPTS 24,48

inquiring [*adj*] *wondering, curious*
analytical, catechistic, doubtful, examining, fact-finding, heuristic, inquisitive, interested, interrogative, investigative, investigatory, nosy, outward-looking, probing, prying, questioning, quizzical, searching, Socratic, speculative, studious; SEE CONCEPTS 402,542

inquiry [*n*] *asking; looking into*
analysis, audit, catechizing, check, cross-examination, delving, disquisition, examination, exploration, fishing expedition*, grilling, hearing, inquest, inquisition, inspection, interrogation, interrogatory, investigation, legwork*, poll, probe, probing, pursuit, Q and A*, query, quest, question, questioning, quizzing, request, research, scrutiny, search, study, survey, third degree*, trial balloon*; SEE CONCEPTS 24,48,290

inquisitive [*adj*] *curious*
big-eyed*, challenging, forward, impertinent, inquiring, inquisitorial, interested, intrusive, investigative, meddlesome, meddling, naytical, nosy, peering, personal, poking, presumptuous, probing, prying, questioning, scrutinizing, searching, sifting, snooping, speculative; SEE CONCEPT 402

inroad [*n*] *advance, foray*
encroachment, impingement, incursion, intrusion, invasion, irruption, onslaught, raid, trespass; SEE CONCEPTS 86,704

insane [*adj*] *mentally ill; foolish*
batty*, bizarre, cracked*, crazed, crazy, cuckoo*, daft, demented, derailed, deranged, fatuous, frenzied, idiotic, impractical, irrational, irresponsible, loony*, lunatic, mad, maniacal, mental, moonstruck*, nuts*, nutty*, off one's rocker*, of unsound mind, out of one's mind*, paranoid, preposterous, psychopathic, psychotic, rabid, raging, raving, schizophrenic, screwy, senseless, touched, unhinged, unsettled, wild; SEE CONCEPTS 314,403,548

insanely [*adv*] *extremely*
crazily, ferociously, fiercely, furiously, idiotically, irrationally, stupidly, violently, wildly; SEE CONCEPT 569

insanity [*n*] *mental illness; foolishness*
aberration, absurdity, alienation, craziness, delirium, delusion, dementia, derangement, distraction, dotage, folly, frenzy, hallucination, hysteria, illusion, inanity, irrationality, irresponsibility, lunacy, madness, mania, mental disorder, neurosis, phobia, preposterousness, psychopathy, psychosis, senselessness, unbalance, unreasonableness, witlessness; SEE CONCEPTS 316,410

insatiable [*adj*] *voracious, wanting*
clamorous, crying, demanding, desiring, exigent, gluttonous, greedy, importunate, insatiate, insistent, intemperate, pressing, quenchless, rapacious, ravenous, unappeasable, unquenchable, unsatisfiable, unsatisfied, urgent, yearning; SEE CONCEPTS 20,403,546

inscribe [*v*] *imprint, write*
book, carve, cut, engrave, engross, etch, impress, indite, list, record, register, scribe; SEE CONCEPT 79

inscription [*n*] *message*
autograph, caption, dedication, engraving, epitaph, heading, imprint, label, legend, lettering, saying, signature, wording; SEE CONCEPT 283

inscrutable [*adj*] *hidden, mysterious; blank*
ambiguous, arcane, cabalistic, deadpan*, difficult, enigmatic, impenetrable, incomprehensible, inexplicable, mysterial, mystic, poker-faced*, secret, sphinxlike, unaccountable, undiscoverable, unexplainable, unfathomable, unintelligible, unknowable, unreadable; SEE CONCEPTS 529,576

in
in

insect [n] *bug*

ant, aphid, bedbug, bee, beetle, bumblebee, butterfly, cockroach, cootie, daddy longlegs, dragonfly, flea, fly, fruit fly, gnat, grasshopper, hornet, ladybug, louse, mite, mosquito, moth, pest, praying mantis, termite, tick, vermin, yellowjacket; SEE CONCEPT 398

insecure [adj] *uncertain, worried*

afraid, anxious, apprehensive, choked, Delphic, diffident, hanging by thread*, hesitant, jumpy, on thin ice*, questioning, shaky, touch and go*, touchy*, troubled, unassured, unconfident, unpoised, unsure, up in the air*, uptight*, vague; SEE CONCEPTS 403,542

insecure [adj2] *dangerous, precarious*

defenseless, exposed, fluctuant, frail, hazardous, immature, insubstantial, loose, open to attack*, perilous, rickety, rocky, rootless, shaky, unguarded, unprotected, unreliable, unsafe, unshielded, unsound, unstable, unsteady, vacillating, vulnerable, wavering, weak, wobbly; SEE CONCEPTS 488,570

insensitive [adj1] *indifferent, callous*

aloof, bloodless*, coldhearted*, crass, feelingless, hard, hard as nails*, hard-boiled*, hardened, hardhearted*, heartless, imperceptive, incurious, obtuse, stony, tactless, thick-skinned*, tough, uncaring, unconcerned, unfeeling, unkind, unresponsive, unsusceptible; SEE CONCEPT 401

insensitive [adj2] *numb*

anesthetized, asleep, benumbed, dead, deadened, immune to, impervious to, insensible, nonreactive, senseless, unfeeling; SEE CONCEPT 406

inseparable [adj] *unable to be divided*

as one, attached, conjoined, connected, entwined, inalienable, indissoluble, indivisible, inseverable, integral, integrated, intertwined, interwoven, molded, secure, tied up, unified, united, whole; SEE CONCEPT 531

insert [v] *put, tuck in*

admit, drag in, embed, enter, fill in, imbed, implant, include, infix, infuse, inject, inlay, insinuate, instill, intercalate, interject, interlope, interpolate, interpose, introduce, intrude, lug in, obtrude, place, pop in*, root, set, shoehorn*, shove in, squeeze in, stick, work in; SEE CONCEPTS 201,209

inside [adj1] *in the middle; interior*

central, indoors, inner, innermost, internal, intramural, inward, surrounded, under a roof; SEE CONCEPTS 583,830

inside [adj2] *secret*

classified, closet, confidential, esoteric, exclusive, hushed, internal, limited, private, restricted; SEE CONCEPTS 529,576

inside [adv] *within*

indoors, under a roof, under cover, within doors, within walls; SEE CONCEPT 583

inside [n] *middle, lining*

belly, bowels, breast, center, contents, gut, heart, innards, inner portion, interior, recess, soul, stuffing, womb; SEE CONCEPT 830

insidious [adj] *sneaky, tricky*

artful, astute, corrupt, crafty, crooked, cunning, dangerous, deceitful, deceptive, deep, designing, dishonest, disingenuous, duplicitous, ensnaring, false, foxy, guileful, intriguing, like a snake in the grass*, Machiavellian, perfidious, perilous, secret, slick, sly, smooth, snaky*, sneaking,

stealthy, subtle, surreptitious, treacherous, wily, wormlike*; SEE CONCEPTS 401,542,545

insight [n] *intuitiveness, awareness*

acumen, click*, comprehension, discernment, divination, drift*, intuition, judgment, observation, penetration, perception, perceptivity, perspicacity, sagaciousness, sagacity, sageness, sapience, shrewdness, understanding, vision, wavelength*, wisdom; SEE CONCEPTS 409,410

insightful [adj] *perceptive*

alert, astute, awake, aware, brainy, conscious, cute, discerning, ear to the ground*, intelligent, intuitive, keen, knowing, knowledgeable, knows what's what*, observant, penetrating, penetrative, quick, responsive, savvy, sensitive, sharp, shrewd, smart, tuned in*, understanding, wise; SEE CONCEPTS 402,542

insignia [n] *emblem*

badge, coat of arms, crest, decoration, earmark, ensign, mark, paraphernalia, regalia, symbol; SEE CONCEPTS 259,284

insignificant [adj] *not important; of no consequence*

casual, immaterial, inappreciable, inconsequential, inconsiderable, infinitesimal, irrelevant, lesser, light, lightweight*, little, meager, meaningless, minim, minimal, minor, minuscule, minute, negligible, nondescript, nonessential, not worth mentioning*, nugatory, paltry, petty, pointless, purportless, scanty, secondary, senseless, small, trifling, trivial, unimportant, unsubstantial; SEE CONCEPT 575

insincere [adj] *dishonest, pretended*

ambidextrous, backhanded, deceitful, deceptive, devious, disingenuous, dissembling, dissimulating, double, double-dealing, duplicitous, evasive, faithless, fake, false, hollow, hypocritical, lying, mendacious, perfidious, phony, pretentious, put-on*, shifty, slick, sly, snide, two-faced*, unfaithful, untrue, untruthful; SEE CONCEPTS 267,542,545

insinuate [v] *hint, suggest*

allude, ascribe, connote, imply, impute, indicate, intimate, mention, propose, purport, refer, signify; SEE CONCEPTS 49,75

insinuate [v2] *force one's way into*

curry favor*, edge in, fill in, foist, get in with*, horn in*, infiltrate, infuse, ingratiate, inject, insert, instill, intercalate, interject, interpose, introduce, muscle in*, slip in, wedge in, work in, worm in*; SEE CONCEPTS 159,208,384

insipid [adj1] *dull, uninteresting*

anemic, arid, banal, beige, blah*, bland, characterless, colorless, commonplace, dead*, drab, driveling, dry, feeble, flat, ho-hum*, inane, innocuous, jejune, lifeless, limp, mild, mundane, nebbish, nothing, ordinary, plain, pointless, prosaic, prosy, slight, soft*, spiritless, stale, stupid, subdued, tame, tedious, tenuous, thin, tired, trite, unimaginative, vapid, watery, weak, weariful, wearisome, wishy-washy*; SEE CONCEPTS 402,404,537

insipid [adj2] *tasteless*

bland, distasteful, flat, flavorless, jejune, mild, savorless, stale, unappetizing, unpalatable, unsavory, vapid, watered-down, watery; SEE CONCEPT 613

insist [v] *order and expect; claim*

assert, asseverate, aver, be firm, contend, demand, hold, importune, lay down the law*, maintain, persist, press, reiterate, repeat, request, require, stand firm, swear, take a stand*, urge, vow; SEE CONCEPTS *49,53*

insistent [*adj*] *demanding*
assertive, burning, clamant, clamorous, continuous, crying, dire, dogged, emphatic, exigent, forceful, imperative, imperious, importunate, incessant, obstinate, peremptory, perseverant, persevering, persistent, pressing, reiterative, resolute, resounding, unrelenting, urgent; SEE CONCEPTS *267,534,540*

insolence [*n*] *boldness, disrespect*
abuse, arrogance, audacity, back talk, brass*, brazenness, cheek*, chutzpah*, contempt, contemptuousness, contumely, effrontery, gall, guff*, hardihood, impertinence, impudence, incivility, insubordination, lip*, offensiveness, pertness, presumption, rudeness, sass*, sauce*, uncivility; SEE CONCEPTS *633*

insolent [*adj*] *bold, disrespectful*
abusive, arrogant, barefaced, brassy*, brazen, breezy, contemptuous, contumelious, dictatorial, discourteous, disdainful, flip*, fresh, imperative, impertinent, impolite, impudent, insubordinate, insulting, magisterial, nervy, off-base*, offensive, out-of-line*, overbearing, peremptory, pert, procacious, put down, rude, sassy*, saucy*, smart, smart-alecky*, uncivil, ungracious; SEE CONCEPTS *267,401*

insoluble [*adj*] *mysterious, unable to be solved or answered*
baffling, difficult, impenetrable, indecipherable, inexplicable, inextricable, irresolvable, mystifying, obscure, unaccountable, unconcluded, unfathomable, unresolved, unsolvable, unsolved; SEE CONCEPTS *529,576*

insolvent [*adj*] *financially ruined*
bankrupt, broke*, broken, busted*, failed, foreclosed, in Chapter 11*, in Chapter 13*, indebted, in receivership, in the red*, lost, on the rocks*, out of money, strapped*, taken to the cleaners*, unbalanced, undone, wiped out*; SEE CONCEPT *334*

insomnia [*n*] *inability to sleep soundly*
indisposition, insomnolence, restlessness, sleeplessness, stress, tension, vigil, vigilance, wakefulness; SEE CONCEPT *315*

insouciant [*adj*] *easygoing, casual*
airy, breezy, buoyant, carefree, careless, free and easy*, gay, happy-go-lucky*, heedless, jaunty, lighthearted, nonchalant, sunny*, thoughtless, unconcerned, untroubled, unworried; SEE CONCEPTS *404,542*

inspect [*v*] *examine, check*
audit, canvass, case, catechize, check out, clock*, eye*, give the once-over*, go over, go through, inquire, interrogate, investigate, kick the tires*, look over, notice, observe, oversee, probe, question, review, scan, scope, scout, scrutinize, search, study, superintend, supervise, survey, vet, view, watch; SEE CONCEPTS *103,623*

inspection [*n*] *examination, check*
analysis, checkup, frisk, inquest, inquiry, inquisition, inventory, investigation, look-over, maneuvers, once-over*, pageant, parade, perlustration, probe, read, research, review, scan, scrutiny, search, superintendence, supervision, surveillance, survey, view; SEE CONCEPTS *103,290*

inspector [*n*] *examiner*
assessor, auditor, checker, controller, detective,

investigator, monitor, overseer, police officer, private eye, reviewer, scrutinizer, sleuth, tester; SEE CONCEPT *348*

inspiration [*n*] *idea, stimulus*
afflatus, animus, approach, arousal, awakening, brainchild*, brainstorm*, creativity, deep think*, elevation, encouragement, enthusiasm, exaltation, fancy, flash*, genius, hunch*, illumination, impulse, incentive, inflatus, influence, insight, motivation, motive, muse, notion, revelation, rumble, spark, spur, stimulation, thought, vision, whim; SEE CONCEPTS *529,661*

inspire [*v*] *encourage, stimulate*
affect, animate, arouse, be responsible for, carry, cause, commove, elate, embolden, endue, enkindle, enliven, exalt, excite, exhilarate, fire up*, galvanize, get*, give impetus, give one an idea*, give rise to, hearten, imbue, impress, infect, inflame, influence, inform, infuse, inspirit, instill, invigorate, motivate, occasion, produce, provoke, quicken, reassure, set up, spark, spur, start off, stir, strike, sway, touch, trigger, urge, work up; SEE CONCEPTS *7,22,221,242*

instability [*n*] *imbalance, inconstancy*
alternation, anxiety, capriciousness, changeability, changeableness, disequilibrium, disquiet, fickleness, fitfulness, flightiness, fluctuation, fluidity, frailty, hesitation, immaturity, impermanence, inconsistency, inquietude, insecurity, irregularity, irresolution, mutability, oscillation, pliancy, precariousness, restlessness, shakiness, transience, uncertainty, unfixedness, unpredictability, unreliability, unsteadiness, vacillation, variability, volatility, vulnerability, wavering, weakness; SEE CONCEPTS *410,637,731*

install [*v*] *set up, establish*
build in, ensconce, fix, fix up, furnish, inaugurate, induct, instate, institute, introduce, invest, lay, line, lodge, place, plant, position, put in, settle, station; SEE CONCEPTS *201,221*

installation [*n1*] *establishment, inauguration*
accession, coronation, fitting, furnishing, inaugural, induction, installment, instatement, investiture, investment, launching, ordination, placing, positioning, setting up; SEE CONCEPTS *201,221,832*

installation [*n2*] *equipment*
base, establishment, fort, fortification, furnishings, lighting, machinery, plant, post, power, station, system, wiring; SEE CONCEPTS *439,463,496*

installment [*n*] *part, section*
chapter, division, earnest, episode, partial payment, payment, portion, repayment, token; SEE CONCEPTS *344,835*

instance [*n*] *case, situation*
case history, case in point, detail, example, exemplification, exponent, ground, illustration, item, occasion, occurrence, particular, precedent, proof, reason, representative, sample, sampling, specimen, time; SEE CONCEPTS *686,696,815*

instance [*v*] *name*
adduce, cite, exemplify, illustrate, mention, quote, refer, show, specify; SEE CONCEPT *73*

instant [*adj*] *immediate, urgent*
burning, clamant, contemporary, crying*, current, dire, direct, exigent, existent, extant, fast, imperative, importunate, insistent, instantaneous, on-the-spot*, present, present-day, pressing, prompt, quick, split-second*; SEE CONCEPTS *544,588,799*

in
in

instant [*n*] *moment*
bat of the eye*, breath, crack, flash, jiffy*, juncture, minute, nothing flat*, occasion, point, sec*, second, shake*, short while, split second*, tick, time, trice, twinkling*, while, wink*; SEE CONCEPTS 802,808

instantaneous [*adj*] *immediate*
direct, fast, hair-trigger*, in a flash*, instant, momentary, quick, rapid, spontaneous, transitory; SEE CONCEPT 820

instantly [*adv*] *right now*
at once, away, directly, double-time*, first off*, forthwith, immediately, in a flash*, instantaneously, instanter, now, on a dime*, PDQ*, pronto*, right, right away, spontaneously, straight away*, there and then*, this minute, tout de suite*, without delay; SEE CONCEPTS 544,588,799

instead [*adv*] *alternatively*
alternately, alternative, as a substitute, in lieu, in place of, in preference, on behalf of, on second thought, preferably, rather, rather than; SEE CONCEPT 560

instigate [*v*] *influence, provoke*
abet, actuate, add fuel, bring about, egg on*, encourage, fire up*, foment, goad, hint, impel, incite, inflame, initiate, insinuate, kindle, make waves*, move, needle*, persuade, plan, plot, prompt, put up to, rabble-rouse*, raise, rouse, scheme, set on, spur, start, steam up, stimulate, stir up, suggest, turn on, urge, whip up*, work up; SEE CONCEPTS 7,19,22,221,242

instigator [*n*] *troublemaker*
agent provocateur, agitator, firebrand, hellion, incendiary, inciter, inflamer, knave, meddler, mischief-maker, nuisance, provocateur*, punk*, rabble-rouser*, ringleader, sparkplug*, wise guy*; SEE CONCEPT 412

instill [*v*] *implant, introduce*
brainwash*, catechize, diffuse, disseminate, engender, engraft, force in, imbue, impart, impregnate, impress, inculcate, indoctrinate, infiltrate, infix, infuse, inject, inoculate, inseminate, insert, insinuate, inspire, interject, intermix, program, propagandize, put in head*, suffuse, transfuse; SEE CONCEPTS 14,221,285

instinct [*n*] *gut feeling, idea*
aptitude, faculty, feeling, funny feeling*, gift, gut reaction*, hunch, impulse, inclination, intuition, knack, know-how*, nose*, predisposition, proclivity, savvy*, sense, sentiment, sixth sense*, talent, tendency, urge; SEE CONCEPTS 529,689

instinctive [*adj*] *reflex, automatic*
accustomed, by seat of one's pants*, congenital, habitual, impulsive, inborn, ingrained, inherent, innate, instinctual, intrinsic, intuitional, intuitive, involuntary, knee-jerk*, mechanical, native, natural, normal, regular, rooted, second-nature*, spontaneous, typical, unlearned, unmeditated, unpremeditated, unprompted, unthinking, visceral; SEE CONCEPT 544

institute [*n2*] *law; custom*
convention, decree, decretum, doctrine, dogma, edict, establishment, fixture, habit, maxim, ordinance, practice, precedent, precept, prescript, principle, regulation, rite, ritual, rule, statute, tenet, tradition; SEE CONCEPTS 318,688

institute [*v*] *begin; put into operation*
appoint, bow, break in, bring into being, come

out with, come up with, commence, constitute, create, enact, establish, fix, found, inaugurate, induct, initiate, install, introduce, invest, launch, make up, open, open up, ordain, organize, originate, pioneer, rev*, set in motion, settle, set up, start, usher in*; SEE CONCEPTS 173,221,242

institute/institution [*n1*] *organization, usually educational*
academy, association, asylum, business, clinic, college, company, conservatory, establishment, fixture, foundation, guild, hospital, orphanage, school, seminar, seminary, society, system, think tank, university; SEE CONCEPTS 288,381,439

instruct [*v1*] *inform, teach*
acquaint, advise, apprise, brainwash*, break in, break it to, brief, clue in, coach, counsel, discipline, disclose, drill, drum into*, educate, engineer, enlighten, give lessons, ground, guide, keep posted*, lead, lecture, level, notify, pilot, reveal, school, steer, tell, train, tutor, update, wise up*; SEE CONCEPTS 60,285

instruct [*v2*] *order, command*
assign, bid, charge, define, direct, enjoin, prescribe, tell, warn; SEE CONCEPTS 53,61

instruction [*n1*] *education*
apprenticeship, chalk talk*, coaching, direction, discipline, drilling, edification, enlightenment, grounding, guidance, information, lesson, preparation, schooling, teaching, training, tuition, tutelage; SEE CONCEPTS 274,285

instruction [*n2*] *demand, command*
advice, briefing, direction, directive, information, injunction, mandate, order, plan, ruling; SEE CONCEPTS 274,278

instructive [*adj*] *informative*
educational, educative, enlightening, explanatory, helpful, illuminating, informational, instructional, useful; SEE CONCEPT 267

instructor [*n*] *person who educates*
adviser, coach, demonstrator, exponent, guide, lecturer, mentor, pedagogue, preceptor, professor, teacher, trainer, tutor; SEE CONCEPT 350

instrument [*n1*] *tool, implement*
apparatus, appliance, contraption, contrivance, device, doodad*, equipment, gadget, gear, gizmo*, machine, machinery, mechanism, paraphernalia, tackle, utensil; SEE CONCEPTS 463,499

instrument [*n2*] *means, agent*
agency, channel, factor, force, instrumentality, material, mechanism, medium, ministry, organ, vehicle, wherewithal; SEE CONCEPTS 6,687

instrumental [*adj*] *influential, assisting*
active, auxiliary, conducive, contributory, helpful, helping, involved, of help, of service, partly responsible, serviceable, subsidiary, useful; SEE CONCEPT 560

insubordinate [*adj*] *rebellious*
contrary, contumacious, defiant, disaffected, disobedient, disorderly, dissentious, factious, fractious, insurgent, intractable, mutinous, naughty, perverse, recalcitrant, refractory, riotous, seditious, treacherous, turbulent, uncompliant, uncomplying, undisciplined, ungovernable, unruly; SEE CONCEPT 401

insubordination [*n*] *disobedience*
defiance, dereliction, disregard, dissension, indiscipline, infringement, insurrection, mutiny, noncompliance, noncooperation, nonobservance, rebellion, revolt, revolution, riot, sabotage; SEE CONCEPT 633

insubstantial [adj] weak, imaginary
aerial, airy, chimerical, decrepit, ephemeral, false, fanciful, feeble, flimsy, fly-by-night*, fragile, frail, idle, illusory, immaterial, imponderable, incorporeal, infirm, intangible, metaphysical, petty, poor, puny, slender, slight, tenuous, thin, too little too late*, unreal, unsound, unsubstantial; SEE CONCEPT 485

insufferable [adj] horrible, intolerable
detestable, distressing, dreadful, impossible, insupportable, outrageous, painful, unacceptable, unbearable, unendurable, unspeakable; SEE CONCEPTS 529,537

insufficient [adj] not enough; lacking
bereft, defective, deficient, destitute, devoid, drained, dry, failing, faulty, imperfect, inadequate, incapable, incommensurate, incompetent, incomplete, infrequent, meager, minus, out of, poor, rare, scant, scarce, short, short of, shy, thin*, too little too late*, unample, unfinished, unfitted, unqualified, unsatisfactory, wanting; SEE CONCEPTS 546,771

insular [adj] narrow-minded
bigoted, circumscribed, closed, confined, contracted, cut off, detached, illiberal, inward-looking, isolated, limited, narrow, parochial, petty, prejudiced, provincial, restricted, secluded, separate, separated, sequestered; SEE CONCEPTS 403,583

insulate [v] protect; close off
coat, cocoon, cushion, cut off, inlay, island, isolate, keep apart, line, seclude, separate, sequester, set apart, shield, tape, treat, wrap; SEE CONCEPT 172

insult [n] hateful communication
abuse, affront, aspersion, black eye*, blasphemy, cheap shot*, contempt, contumely, derision, despite, discourtesy, disdainfulness, disgrace, disrespect, ignominy, impertinence, impudence, incivility, indignity, insolence, invective, libel, mockery, obloquy, offense, opprobrium, outrage, put-down, rudeness, scorn, scurrility, shame, slam, slander, slap, slap in the face*, slight, snub, superciliousness, taunt, unpleasantry, vilification, vituperation; SEE CONCEPTS 52,54,278

insult [v] abuse, offend
abase, affront, aggravate, annoy, blister, curse, cut to the quick*, debase, degrade, deride, dishonor, disoblige, dump on*, flout, gird, humiliate, injure, irritate, jeer, libel, mock, outrage, pan*, provoke, put down*, revile, ridicule, roast*, scoff, slam*, slander, slight, sneer, snub, step on one's toes*, taunt, tease, underestimate, vex; SEE CONCEPTS 52,54

insulting [adj] abusive
biting, degrading, derogatory, discourteous, disparaging, disrespectful, hurtful, insolent, offensive, repulsive, ridiculing, rude, slighting, uncivil; SEE CONCEPTS 267,529,537

insurance [n] protection, security
allowance, assurance, backing, cover, coverage, guarantee, indemnification, indemnity, provision, safeguard, support, warrant, warranty; SEE CONCEPTS 318,332

insure [v] protect, secure
assure, cinch, cover, guarantee, guard, hedge, indemnify, register, safeguard, shield, underwrite, warrant; SEE CONCEPTS 317,330

insurgent [adj] rebellious
anarchical, contumacious, disobedient, factious, insubordinate, insurrectionary, mutinous, revolting, revolutionary, riotous, seditious; SEE CONCEPT 401

insurgent [n] rebel
agitator, anarch, anarchist, demonstrator, frondeur, insurrectionist, malcontent, mutineer, radical, resister, revolter, revolutionary, revolutionist, rioter; SEE CONCEPTS 359,412

insurmountable [adj] impossible
forget it, hopeless, impassable, impregnable, inaccessible, indomitable, ineluctable, insuperable, invincible, not a prayer*, no way*, no-win*, overwhelming, unbeatable, unconquerable, unmasterable; SEE CONCEPTS 552,565

insurrection [n] rebellion
coup, disorder, insurgence, insurgency, mutiny, revolt, revolution, riot, rising, sedition, uprising; SEE CONCEPTS 86,320

intact [adj] undamaged; all in one piece
complete, entire, flawless, imperforate, indiscrete, perfect, scatheless, sound, together, unblemished, unbroken, uncut, undefiled, unharmed, unhurt, unimpaired, uninjured, unmarred, unscathed, untouched, unviolated, whole; SEE CONCEPTS 485,531

intangible [adj] indefinite, obscured
abstract, abstruse, airy, dim, eluding, elusive, ethereal, evading, evanescent, evasive, hypothetical, impalpable, imperceptible, imponderable, inappreciable, incorporeal, indeterminate, insensible, invisible, rare, shadowy, slender, slight, unapparent, uncertain, unobservable, unreal, unsubstantial, unsure, vague; SEE CONCEPTS 535,582

integral [adj1] necessary, basic
component, constituent, elemental, essential, fundamental, indispensable, intrinsic, requisite; SEE CONCEPT 546

integral [adj2] complete
aggregate, choate, elemental, entire, full, indivisible, intact, part-and-parcel*, perfect, unbroken, undivided, whole; SEE CONCEPT 531

integrate [v] mix, merge
accommodate, amalgamate, arrange, articulate, assimilate, associate, attune, blend, coalesce, combine, come together, compact, concatenate, concentrate, conform, conjoin, consolidate, coordinate, desegregate, embody, fuse, get together, harmonize, incorporate, interface, intermix, join, knit, link, meld with, mesh, orchestrate, organize, proportion, reconcile, reconciliate, symphonize, synthesize, systematize, throw in together, tune, unify, unite, wed; SEE CONCEPTS 113,114

integrity [n1] honor, uprightness
candor, forthrightness, goodness, honestness, honesty, honorableness, incorruptibility, incorruption, principle, probity, purity, rectitude, righteousness, sincerity, straightforwardness, virtue; SEE CONCEPT 411

integrity [n2] completeness
absoluteness, coherence, cohesion, entireness, perfection, purity, simplicity, soundness, stability, totality, unity, wholeness; SEE CONCEPT 635

intellect [n] capability of the mind; someone with capable mind
ability, acumen, brains*, cerebration, comprehension, egghead*, genius, intellectual, intellectuality, intelligence, intuition, judgment, mentality, mind, psyche, pundit, reason, savvy,

in
in

sense, smarts, thinker, understanding, what it takes*, wits; SEE CONCEPTS *409,416*

intellectual [*adj*] *very smart*
bookish, brainy*, cerebral, creative, highbrow*, highbrowed*, intellective, intelligent, inventive, learned, mental, phrenic, psychological, rational, scholarly, studious, subjective, thoughtful; SEE CONCEPT *402*

intellectual [*n*] *very smart person*
academic, academician, avant-garde, brain*, braintruster*, doctor, egghead*, Einstein*, genius, highbrow*, intelligentsia, philosopher, pundit, sage, scholar, thinker, whiz*, wizard; SEE CONCEPTS *350,416*

intelligence [*n1*] *ability to perceive, understand*
acuity, acumen, agility, alertness, aptitude, brainpower, brains*, brightness, brilliance, capacity, cleverness, comprehension, coruscation, discernment, gray matter*, intellect, IQ*, judgment, luminosity, mentality, mind, penetration, perception, perspicacity, precocity, quickness, quotient, reason, sagacity, savvy, sense, skill, smarts, subtlety, the right stuff*, trenchancy, understanding, what it takes*, wit; SEE CONCEPT *409*

intelligence [*n2*] *secret information*
advice, clue, data, dirt, disclosure, facts, findings, hot tip*, info*, inside story*, knowledge, leak, lowdown*, news, notice, notification, picture, report, rumor, tidings, tip-off*, word*; SEE CONCEPT *274*

intelligent [*adj*] *very smart*
able, acute, alert, alive, all there*, apt, astute, brainy*, bright, brilliant, calculating, capable, clever, comprehending, creative, deep*, discerning, enlightened, exceptional, highbrow*, imaginative, ingenious, instructed, inventive, keen, knowing, knowledgeable, original, penetrating, perceptive, perspicacious, profound, quick, quick-witted, rational, ready, reasonable, resourceful, responsible, sage, sharp, smart, thinking, together*, understanding, well-informed, whiz*, wise, witty; SEE CONCEPT *402*

intelligible [*adj*] *understandable*
apprehensible, clear, comprehensible, distinct, fathomable, graspable, knowable, lucid, luminous, obvious, open, plain, unambiguous, unequivocal, unmistakable; SEE CONCEPT *529*

intend [*v*] *have in mind; determine*
add up, aim, appoint, aspire to, attempt, be determined, be resolved, connote, contemplate, decree, dedicate, denote, design, designate, destine, devote, endeavor, essay, expect, express, figure on, have in mind, hope to, import, indicate, look forward, mean, meditate, ordain, plan, plot, propose, purpose, reserve, resolve, scheme, set apart, set aside, signify, spell, strive, think, try; SEE CONCEPTS *18,36,73,129*

intended [*adj*] *engaged; destined*
accidentally on purpose*, advised, affianced, aforethought, asked for, betrothed, calculated, contemplated, contracted, designed, expected, future, intentional, meant, pinned, planned, plighted, prearranged, predestined, predetermined, promised, proposed, set, steady; SEE CONCEPT *552*

intense [*adj*] *forceful, severe; passionate*
acute, agonizing, all-consuming, ardent, biting, bitter, burning, close, concentrated, consuming, cutting, deep, diligent, eager, earnest, energetic,

exaggerated, exceptional, excessive, exquisite, extraordinary, extreme, fanatical, fervent, fervid, fierce, forcible, full, great, hard, harsh, heightened, impassioned, intensified, intensive, keen, marked, piercing, powerful, profound, protracted, pungent, sharp, shrill, stinging, strained, strong, supreme, undue, vehement, violent, vivid, zealous; SEE CONCEPT *569*

intensify [*v*] *make more forceful, severe*
accent, accentuate, add fuel*, add to, aggrandize, aggravate, augment, beef up*, boost, brighten, build up, concentrate, darken, deepen, emphasize, enhance, escalate, exacerbate, exalt, heat up*, heighten, increase, intensate, lighten, magnify, point, pour it on*, quicken, raise, redouble, reinforce, rise, rouse, set off, sharpen, spike*, step up, strengthen, stress, tone up, whet; SEE CONCEPTS *233,250*

intensity [*n*] *passion, force*
acuteness, anxiety, ardor, concentration, deepness, depth, earnestness, emotion, emphasis, energy, excess, excitement, extreme, extremity, fanaticism, ferment, ferociousness, ferocity, fervency, fervor, fierceness, fire, force, forcefulness, fury, high pitch*, intenseness, keenness, magnitude, might, nervousness, potency, power, severity, sharpness, strain, strength, tenseness, tension, vehemence, vigor, violence, voltage, weightiness, wildness; SEE CONCEPTS *641,669*

intensive [*adj*] *exhaustive*
accelerated, all-out*, complete, comprehensive, concentrated, deep, demanding, fast, hard, in-depth, out-and-out*, profound, radical, severe, speeded-up*, thorough, thoroughgoing; SEE CONCEPT *531*

intent [*adj*] *determined, resolute*
absorbed, alert, attending, attentive, bent, bound, committed, concentrated, concentrating, decided, decisive, deep, eager, earnest, engaged, engrossed, enthusiastic, firm, fixed, hell-bent*, immersed, industrious, minding, occupied, piercing, preoccupied, rapt, resolved, riveted*, set, settled, steadfast, steady, watchful, watching, wrapped up*; SEE CONCEPTS *403,542*

intent/intention [*n*] *aim, purpose*
acceptation, animus, bottom line*, conation, design, desire, drift, end, goal, heart, hope, idea, import, intendment, meaning, meat*, name of the game*, nature, notion, nub, nuts and bolts*, object, objective, plan, point, project, purport, scheme, score, sense, significance, significancy, signification, target, understanding, volition, will, wish; SEE CONCEPT *659*

intentional [*adj*] *deliberate*
advised, aforethought, calculated, considered, designed, designful, done on purpose, intended, meant, meditated, planned, prearranged, premeditated, proposed, purposed, studied, unforced, voluntary, willful, willing, witting; SEE CONCEPT *544*

intently [*adv*] *with concentration*
attentively, closely, fixedly, hard, keenly, searchingly, sharply, steadily, watchfully; SEE CONCEPTS *403,544*

inter [*v*] *bury*
cover up, entomb, inhume, inurn, lay to rest, plant, put away, sepulcher, sepulture, tomb; SEE CONCEPTS *172,178,367*

interact [*v*] *communicate*
collaborate, combine, connect, contact, cooper-

ate, get across*, get the message*, interface, interplay, interreact, join, keep in touch, merge, mesh, network, reach out, relate, touch, touch base*, unite; SEE CONCEPT 266

intercede [v] *mediate*
advocate, arbitrate, barge in, butt in*, intermediate, interpose, intervene, intrude, mix in, monkey with*, negotiate, plead, reconcile, speak, step in; SEE CONCEPT 56,110

intercept [v] *head off; interrupt*
ambush, appropriate, arrest, block, catch, check, curb, cut in, cut off, deflect, head off at pass*, hijack, hinder, interlope, interpose, make off with, obstruct, prevent, seize, shortstop*, stop, take, take away; SEE CONCEPTS 121,164

interchange [n] *switch, exchange*
altering, alternation, barter, change, crossfire, give-and-take*, intersection, junction, mesh, networking, reciprocation, shift, trade, transposition, variation, varying; SEE CONCEPTS 104,697

interchange [v] *switch, exchange*
alternate, bandy, barter, commute, connect, contact, convert, interact, interface, mesh, network, reciprocate, relate, reverse, substitute, swap, trade, transpose; SEE CONCEPTS 56,104

interchangeable [adj] *identical, transposable*
changeable, commutable, compatible, converse, convertible, correspondent, equivalent, exchangeable, fungible, interconvertible, mutual, reciprocal, reciprocative, same, substitutable, synonymous, workalike; SEE CONCEPTS 487,573

intercourse [n1] *sexual act*
carnal knowledge, coition, coitus, copulation, fornication, intimacy, love-making, relations, sex, sexual relations; SEE CONCEPT 375

intercourse [n2] *communication; business exchange*
association, commerce, communion, connection, contact, converse, correspondence, dealings, give-and-take, interchange, intercommunication, mesh, networking, team play, teamwork, trade, traffic, transactions; SEE CONCEPTS 266,324

interest [n1] *attraction, curiosity*
absorption, activity, affection, attentiveness, care, case, concern, concernment, consequence, diversion, engrossment, enthusiasm, excitement, game, hobby, importance, interestedness, into, leisure activity, matter, moment, note, notice, passion, pastime, preoccupation, pursuit, racket, recreation, regard, relaxation, relevance, significance, sport, suspicion, sympathy, thing; SEE CONCEPTS 20,532,690

interest [n2] *advantage*
benefit, gain, good, profit, prosperity, welfare, well-being; SEE CONCEPT 693

interest [n3] *share, investment*
accrual, authority, bonus, claim, commitment, credit, discount, due, earnings, gain, influence, involvement, participation, percentage, piece, points, portion, premium, right, stake, title; SEE CONCEPTS 332,344,835

interest [v] *hold the attention of*
affect, amuse, appeal, appeal to, arouse, attract, be interesting to, concern, divert, engage, engross, entertain, enthrall, excite, fascinate, grab, hook, intrigue, involve, lure, move, perk up, pique, please, pull, sit up, snare, tantalize, tempt, titillate, touch, turn on; SEE CONCEPTS 7,11,22

interested [adj] *concerned, curious*
absorbed, affected, attentive, attracted, awakened,

biased, caught, drawn, eat sleep and breathe*, engrossed, enticed, excited, fascinated, fired*, gone*, hooked*, implicated, impressed, inspired, inspirited, intent, into*, involved, keen, lured, moved, obsessed, occupied, on the case*, open, partial, partisan, predisposed, prejudiced, responsive, roused, sold, stimulated, stirred, struck, sympathetic, taken, touched; SEE CONCEPT 403

interesting [adj] *appealing, entertaining*
absorbing, affecting, alluring, amusing, arresting, attractive, beautiful, captivating, charismatic, compelling, curious, delightful, elegant, enchanting, engaging, engrossing, enthralling, entrancing, exceptional, exotic, fascinating, fine, gracious, gripping, impressive, intriguing, inviting, lovely, magnetic, pleasing, pleasurable, prepossessing, provocative, readable, refreshing, riveting, stimulating, stirring, striking, suspicious, thought-provoking, unusual, winning; SEE CONCEPTS 529,572

interfere [v] *meddle, intervene*
baffle, balk, barge in, busybody*, butt in*, conflict, discommode, foil, fool with, frustrate, get in the way*, get involved, hamper, handicap, hang up*, hinder, hold up, horn in*, impede, incommode, inconvenience, inhibit, intercede, interlope, intermeddle, intermediate, intermit, interpose, intrude, jam, make*, mix in, obstruct, obtrude, oppose, poke nose in*, prevent, remit, step in, stop, suspend, tamper, thwart, trammel, trouble; SEE CONCEPTS 121,384

interference [n] *meddling, impedance*
arrest, background, backseat driving*, barging in*, barring, blocking, checking, choking, clashing, clogging, conflict, hampering, hindrance, intermeddling, interposition, intervention, intrusion, meddlesomeness, obstruction, opposition, prying, resistance, retardation, tackling, tampering, trespassing; SEE CONCEPTS 121,384

interim [adj] *temporary*
acting, ad interim, caretaker*, improvised, intervening, makeshift, pro tem, pro tempore, provisional, stopgap, thrown-together*; SEE CONCEPT 560

interim [n] *interval*
breach, break, breather, breathing spell, coffee break, cutoff, downtime*, gap, hiatus, interlude, interregnum, interruption, lacuna, layoff, letup*, meantime, meanwhile, pause, take*, ten*, time*, time-out; SEE CONCEPTS 807,822

interior [adj] *inside, central*
autogenous, domestic, endogenous, gut, home, in-house, inland, inner, innermost, internal, intimate, inward, private, remote, secret, visceral, visceral, within; SEE CONCEPTS 583,826,830

interior [n] *center, core*
belly, bosom, contents, heart, heartland, innards, inner parts, inside, internals, intrinsicality, lining, marrow, midst, pith, pulp, soul, substance, viscera, within; SEE CONCEPTS 742,826,830

interject [v] *throw in; interrupt*
add, fill in, force in, implant, import, include, infiltrate, infuse, ingrain, inject, insert, insinuate, intercalate, interpolate, interpose, intersperse, introduce, intrude, parenthesize, put in, splice, squeeze in; SEE CONCEPTS 14,51

interloper [n] *person who intrudes, meddles*
alien, busybody, intermeddler, intruder, meddler, obtruder, trespasser, uninvited guest, unwanted visitor; SEE CONCEPTS 412,423

in
in

interlude [*n*] *pause, break*

breathing space*, delay, episode, halt, hiatus, idyll, interim, intermission, interregnum, interruption, interval, lull, meantime, meanwhile, parenthesis, recess, respite, rest, spell, stop, stoppage, wait; SEE CONCEPT *807*

intermediary [*n*] *person who negotiates*

agent, broker, channel, connection, cutout, delegate, emissary, entrepreneur, fixer, go-between*, influence, instrument, interagent, interceder, intercessor, intermediate, mediator, medium, middle person, negotiator, organ, vehicle; SEE CONCEPTS *348,354*

intermediate [*adj*] *middle, in-between*

average, between, center, central, common, compromising, fair, halfway, indifferent, intermediary, interposed, intervening, mean, medial, median, mediocre, medium, mid, middling, midway, moderate, neutral, so-so*, standard, transitional; SEE CONCEPTS *585,830*

interment [*n*] *burial*

burying, entombment, funeral, inhumation, inurning, obsequy, sepulture; SEE CONCEPT *367*

interminable [*adj*] *infinite*

boring, boundless, ceaseless, constant, continuous, day-and-night*, dragged out*, dull, endless, eternal, everlasting, immeasurable, incessant, interminate, limitless, long, long-drawn-out*, long-winded, looped, never-ending, no end of*, no end to*, on a treadmill*, permanent, perpetual, protracted, spun out*, strung out*, timeless, unbound, unceasing, uninterrupted, unlimited, wearisome; SEE CONCEPT *798*

intermingle [*v*] *blend, mix*

amalgamate, associate, combine, come together, commingle, commix, fuse, immingle, interblend, interfuse, interlace, intermix, interweave, join, merge, mesh, network, pool, throw in with, throw together, wed; SEE CONCEPTS *113,114*

intermission [*n*] *break, recess*

abeyance, abeyancy, break-off, breather, breathing spell, cessation, doldrums, dormancy, downtime*, interim, interlude, interregnum, interruption, interval, latency, layoff, let-up*, lull, parenthesis, pause, quiescence, quiescency, respite, rest, spell, stop, stoppage, suspense, suspension, time, time-out, wait; SEE CONCEPT *807*

intermittent [*adj*] *irregular, sporadic*

alternate, arrested, broken, by bits and pieces*, checked, cyclic, cyclical, discontinuing, discontinuous, epochal, every other, fitful, here and there*, hit-or-miss*, infrequent, interrupted, isochronal, isochronous, iterant, iterative, metrical, now and then*, occasional, on and off*, periodic, periodical, punctuated, recurrent, recurring, rhythmic, rhythmical, seasonal, serial, shifting, spasmodic, stop-and-go*; SEE CONCEPTS *482,534,799*

internal [*adj*] *within*

centralized, circumscribed, civic, constitutional, domestic, enclosed, gut, home, indigenous, inherent, in-house, inmate, inner, innermore, inside, interior, intestine, intimate, intramural, intrinsic, inward, municipal, national, native, private, subjective, visceral, viscerous; SEE CONCEPTS *536,585,826,830*

international [*adj*] *worldwide*

all-embracing, cosmopolitan, ecumenical, foreign, global, intercontinental, universal, world; SEE CONCEPTS *536,772*

Internet [*n*] *computer network*

ARPANET, computer network, cyberspace, hyperspace, infobahn, information highway, information superhighway, national information infrastructure, online network, the Net*, the Web*, W3, World Wide Web, WWW; SEE CONCEPTS *381,388,770*

interplay [*n*] *interaction*

coaction, exchange, give-and-take*, mesh, meshing, networking, reciprocation, reciprocity, team play*, teamwork, tit for tat*, transaction; SEE CONCEPT *266*

interpolate [*v*] *add*

admit, annex, append, enter, fill in, include, inject, insert, insinuate, intercalate, interjaculate, interject, interlope, interpose, introduce, intrude, throw in; SEE CONCEPTS *112,201,209*

interpret [*v*] *make sense of; define*

adapt, annotate, clarify, comment, commentate, construe, decipher, decode, delineate, depict, describe, elucidate, enact, exemplify, explain, explicate, expound, gather, gloss, illustrate, image, improvise, limn, make of, mimic, paraphrase, perform, picture, play, portray, read, reenact, render, represent, solve, spell out, take*, throw light on*, translate, understand, view; SEE CONCEPTS *57,292*

interpretation [*n*] *understanding*

analysis, apprehension, assimilation, awareness, clarification, comprehension, discernment, explanation, grasp, grip, insight, judgment, knowing, meaning, perception, reading, slant, translation; SEE CONCEPT *409*

interrogate [*v*] *ask pointed questions*

catechize, cross-examine, cross-question, examine, give the third degree*, go over*, grill, inquire, investigate, pump, put the screws to*, put through the wringer*, query, question, quiz, roast*, sweat out*, work over*; SEE CONCEPTS *48,53*

interrupt [*v*] *bother, interfere*

arrest, barge in, break, break in, break off, break train of thought*, bust in*, butt in*, check, chime in*, come between, crash, crowd in, cut, cut in on*, cut off*, cut short*, defer, delay, disconnect, discontinue, disjoin, disturb, disunite, divide, edge in, get in the way, halt, heckle, hinder, hold up, horn in, impede, in, infringe, inject, insinuate, intrude, lay aside, obstruct, prevent, punctuate, put in, separate, sever, shortstop*, stay, stop, suspend, work in; SEE CONCEPTS *51,121,384*

interruption [*n*] *break; interference*

abeyance, abeyancy, arrest, blackout, breach, break-off, cessation, check, cutoff, delay, disconnection, discontinuance, disruption, dissolution, disturbance, disuniting, division, doldrums, dormancy, gap, halt, hiatus, hindrance, hitch, impediment, interim, intermission, interval, intrusion, lacuna, latency, layoff, letup*, obstacle, obstruction, parenthesis, pause, quiescence, rift, rupture, separation, severance, split, stop, stoppage, suspension; SEE CONCEPTS *807,832*

intersect [*v*] *cut across; cross at a point*

bisect, break in two, come together, converge, crisscross, cross, crosscut, cut, decussate, divide, intercross, join, meet, separate, touch, traverse; SEE CONCEPTS *113,738,749*

intersection [n] *crossroads*
circle, cloverleaf, crossing, crosswalk, crossway, interchange, junction, stop; SEE CONCEPT 501

intersperse [v] *scatter*
bestrew, diffuse, distribute, infuse, interfuse, interlard, intermix, intersow, intersprinkle, pepper, sprinkle; SEE CONCEPTS 201,222

interstice [n] *opening, crack*
aperture, chink, cleft, cranny, crevice, fissure, gap, hole, interval, slit, space; SEE CONCEPT 513

intertwine/interweave [v] *twist around*
associate, braid, connect, convolute, crisscross, cross, entwine, interknit, interlace, intertwist, intervolve, interwind, interwreathe, link, mesh, network, relate, reticulate, tangle, tat, weave; SEE CONCEPTS 113,114

interval [n] *break, pause*
breach, breathing space*, comma, delay, distance, downtime, five*, gap, hiatus, interim, interlude, intermission, interregnum, interruption, lacuna, layoff, letup, lull, meantime, opening, parenthesis, pausation, period, playtime, rest, season, space, spell, ten*, term, time, time-out, wait, while; SEE CONCEPTS 807,822

intervene [v1] *mediate*
arbitrate, barge in, butt in*, come between, divide, horn in*, intercede, interfere, intermediate, interpose, interrupt, intrude, involve, meddle, mix in, muscle in*, negotiate, obtrude, part, put in two cents*, reconcile, separate, settle, sever, step in, take a hand*; SEE CONCEPTS 110,234,266

intervene [v2] *happen*
bedevil, befall, come to pass, ensue, occur, succeed, supervene, take place; SEE CONCEPTS 4,242

interview [n] *questioning and evaluation*
account, audience, call, call back, cattle call*, communication, conference, consultation, conversation, dialogue, examination, hearing, meeting, oral, parley, press conference, record, statement, talk; SEE CONCEPTS 48,351

interview [v] *ask questions and evaluate*
consult, converse, examine, get for the record, get opinion, give oral examination, hold inquiry, interrogate, question, quiz, sound out, talk, talk to; SEE CONCEPTS 48,351

interviewer [n] *questioner*
inquirer, inquistor, interrogator, reporter, talk-show host; SEE CONCEPTS 348,356

intestinal/intestine [adj] *pertaining to digestive organs*
abdominal, alimentary, bowel, celiac, duodenal, gut, inner, inside, interior, internal, inward, rectal, stomachic, ventral, visceral; SEE CONCEPT 406

in the bag [adj] *certain*
assured, bound, certified, cinched, concluded, decided, definite, ensured, fixed, guaranteed, insured, set, settled, sure; SEE CONCEPT 535

intimacy [n] *closeness between people*
acquaintance, affection, affinity, close relationship, communion, confidence, confidentiality, experience, familiarity, friendship, inwardness, understanding; SEE CONCEPT 388

intimate [adj] *friendly, devoted*
affectionate, bosom, buddy-buddy*, cherished, chummy*, close, clubby*, comfy, confidential, cozy, dear, dearest, faithful, fast, fond, loving, mellow, mix, near, nearest, next, nice, regular, roommate, snug, warm; SEE CONCEPT 555

intimate [adj2] *private, personal*
confidential, deep, deep-seated, detailed, elemental, essential, exhaustive, experienced, firsthand, guarded, gut*, immediate, inborn, inbred, in-depth, indwelling, ingrained, inherent, inmost, innate, innermost, interior, internal, intrinsic, penetrating, privy, profound, secret, special, thorough, trusted, uptight, visceral, viscerous; SEE CONCEPTS 529,549

intimate [n] *a close friend; familiar person*
associate, bosom buddy*, chum, companion, comrade, confidant, confidante, crony, familiar, family, lover, mate, pal; SEE CONCEPTS 416,423

intimate [v] *suggest; tip off*
affirm, air, allude, announce, assert, aver, avouch, communicate, connote, declare, drop a hint*, expose, express, hint, impart, imply, indicate, infer, insinuate, leak, let cat out of bag*, let it be known, make known, make noise*, profess, remind, spill the beans*, spring, state, utter, vent, voice, warn; SEE CONCEPTS 49,60,75

intimation [n] *clue, hint*
allusion, announcement, breath, communication, cue, declaration, implication, indication, inkling, innuendo, insinuation, notice, notion, reminder, shade, shadow, strain, streak, suggestion, suspicion, telltale, tinge, tip, trace, warning, wind; SEE CONCEPTS 274,689

intimidate [v] *frighten, threaten*
alarm, appall, awe, badger, bait, bludgeon, bluster, bowl over*, browbeat*, buffalo*, bulldoze*, bully, chill, coerce, compel, constrain, cow*, daunt, dishearten, dismay, dispirit, disquiet, dragoon, enforce, force, hound*, lean on*, oblige, overawe, push around*, ride*, ruffle, scare, showboat, spook, strong-arm, subdue, terrify, terrorize, twist someone's arm*; SEE CONCEPTS 7,14,19

intimidating [adj] *threatening*
aggressive, bullying, frightening, pressuring, terrifying, terrorizing; SEE CONCEPTS 525,548,570

intolerable [adj] *unacceptable; beyond bearing*
a bit much, enough already*, excruciating, extreme, impossible, insufferable, insupportable, last straw*, offensive, painful, unbearable, undesirable, unendurable; SEE CONCEPT 529

intolerant [adj] *impatient, prejudiced*
antipathetic, averse, biased, bigoted, chauvinistic, communist, conservative, contemptuous, dictatorial, disdainful, dogmatic, fanatical, fractious, hateful, illiberal, indignant, individualistic, inflexible, irate, irritable, jaundiced, narrow, narrow-minded, obdurate, one-sided, outraged, racialist, racist, short-fuse*, small-minded*, snappy, stuffy, tilted, uncharitable, unfair, unforbearing, unindulgent, unsympathetic, unwilling, upset, waspish, worked-up*, xenophobic; SEE CONCEPTS 403,404,542

intonation [n] *inflection*
accent, articulation, emphasis, enunciation, modulation, pitch, pronunciation, sound, tonality, tone, tone of voice; SEE CONCEPTS 65,595

intoxicated [adj] *drunk*
blind*, bombed*, boozed, buzzed*, drunken, high*, inebriated, loaded*, looped*, muddled, potted*, sloppy, smashed*, tanked*, three sheets to the wind*, tied one on*, tight*, tipsy, under the influence, unsober; SEE CONCEPT 406

intoxicated [adj2] *extremely happy*
absorbed, affected, beside oneself, captivated,

concerned, delirious, dizzy, drunk, ecstatic, elated, enraptured, euphoric, excited, exhilarated, galvanized, high*, infatuated, interested, moved, piqued, quickened, sent*, stimulated, turned-on*; SEE CONCEPT 403

intoxicating [adj] causing great happiness
exciting, exhilarant, exhilarating, exhilarative, eye-popping, heady, inspiring, provocative, rousing, stimulating, stirring, thrilling; SEE CONCEPT 537

intractable /intransigent [adj] difficult, stubborn
awkward, bullheaded*, cantankerous, contrary, hang tough*, hard-line*, headstrong, immovable, incompliant, incurable, indocile, indomitable, insoluble, locked in*, mulish, obdurate, obstinate, pat, pertinacious, perverse, pigheaded*, recalcitrant, refractory, resolute, self-willed, set in stone, tenacious, tough, tough-nut*, unbending, uncompromising, uncooperative, undisciplined, ungovernable, unmanageable, unpliable, unruly, unyielding, wayward, wild, willful; SEE CONCEPTS 401,534,542

intrepid [adj] brave, nervy
audacious, bodacious*, bold, courageous, daring, dauntless, doughty, fearless, gallant, game, gritty, gutsy*, heroic, impavid, lionhearted, nerveless, plucky, resolute, spunky*, stalwart, unafraid, undaunted, unflinching, valiant, valorous; SEE CONCEPT 401

intricate [adj] complicated, elaborate
abstruse, baroque, Byzantine*, can of worms*, complex, convoluted, Daedal*, difficult, entangled, fancy, hard, high-tech*, involved, labyrinthine, obscure, perplexing, rococo, sophisticated, tangled, tortuous, tricky; SEE CONCEPT 562

intrigue [n1] scheme
artifice, cabal, chicanery, collusion, complication, conspiracy, contrivance, deal, design, dodge, double-dealing*, fix, frame-up*, fraud, game, graft, hookup, little game*, machination, maneuver, manipulation, plan, plot, ruse, stratagem, trickery, wile; SEE CONCEPTS 192,660

intrigue [n2] love affair
affair, amour, attachment, case, flirtation, infatuation, interlude, intimacy, liaison, romance; SEE CONCEPT 388

intrigue [v1] arouse curiosity
appeal, attract, bait, captivate, charm, con, delight, draw, enchant, entertain, excite, fascinate, grab, hook, interest, lead on*, mousetrap*, pique, please, pull, rivet, tickle, titillate, tout; SEE CONCEPTS 7,11,22

intrigue [v2] plot
angle, be in cahoots*, cogitate, collude, connive, conspire, contrive, cook up*, devise, finagle, frame up*, machinate, maneuver, operate, plan, promote, scheme, set up*, work hand in glove*; SEE CONCEPT 36

intriguing [adj] interesting
absorbing, alluring, appealing, arousing, attractive, beguiling, captivating, compelling, curious, enchanting, enthralling, exciting, fascinating, gripping, provocative, puzzling, riveting, stimulating, stirring, thought-provoking; SEE CONCEPTS 529,572

intrinsic [adj] basic, inborn
built-in, central, congenital, connate, constitutional, constitutive, deep-seated, elemental, essential, fundamental, genuine, hereditary, inbred, indwelling, inherent, inmost, innate, intimate, material, native, natural, particular, peculiar, real, true, underlying; SEE CONCEPTS 404,406,546

introduce [v1] make known; present
acquaint, advance, air, announce, bring out, bring up, broach, come out with, do the honors*, familiarize, fix up, get things rolling*, get together, give introduction, harbinger*, herald, kick off, knock down, lead into, lead off, moot, offer, open, open up, originate, pave the way*, precede, preface, propose, put forward, recommend, set forth, spring with, start ball rolling*, submit, suggest, usher, ventilate; SEE CONCEPTS 60,384

introduce [v2] begin, institute
admit, bring forward, bring in, commence, enter, establish, found, inaugurate, induct, initiate, innovate, install, invent, kick off*, launch, organize, pioneer, plan, preface, present, set up, start, unveil, usher in; SEE CONCEPT 221

introduce [v3] add, insert
carry, enter, fill in, freight, import, include, infix, inject, inlay, inlet, inset, insinuate, instill, intercalate, interject, interpolate, interpose, put in, send, ship, throw in, transport, work in; SEE CONCEPTS 112,113,209

introduction [n] something new; something that begins
addition, admittance, awakening, baptism, basic principles, basic text, beginning, commencement, debut, essentials, establishment, exordium, first acquaintance, first taste, foreword, inauguration, inception, induction, influx, ingress, initiation, insertion, installation, institution, interpolation, intro*, launch, lead, lead-in, opening, opening remarks, overture, pioneering, preamble, preface, preliminaries, prelude, presentation, primer, proem, prolegomenon, prologue, survey; SEE CONCEPTS 270,727,828

introductory [adj] preliminary, first
anterior, basic, beginning, early, elementary, inaugural, incipient, inductive, initial, initiatory, opening, original, precursory, prefatory, prelusive, preparative, preparatory, primary, prior, proemial, provisional, rudimentary, starting; SEE CONCEPTS 546,585

introspection [n] self-analysis
brooding, contemplation, deep thought, egoism, heart-searching, introversion, meditation, reflection, rumination, scrutiny, self-absorption, self-examination, self-observation, self-questioning, soul-searching; SEE CONCEPTS 24,410

introvert [n] person who retreats mentally
autist, brooder, egoist, egotist, loner*, narcissist, self-observer, solitary, wallflower*; SEE CONCEPT 423

introverted [adj] reserved
bashful, cautious, close-mouthed, cold*, collected, cool, demure, introspective, modest, offish, quiet, reclusive, restrained, secretive, shy, soft-spoken, solitary, standoffish, uncommunicative, withdrawn; SEE CONCEPTS 401,404

intrude [v] trespass, interrupt
barge in, bother, butt in*, chisel in*, cut in, disturb, encroach, entrench, go beyond, hold up, horn in*, infringe, insinuate, intercalate, interfere, interject, interlope, intermeddle, interpolate, interpose, introduce, invade, meddle, obtrude,

overstep, pester, push in, thrust, violate; SEE CONCEPTS *14,159,208,266*

intruder [*n*] *person who trespasses*
burglar, criminal, gate-crasher*, infiltrator, interferer, interloper, interrupter, invader, meddler, nuisance, obtruder, prowler, raider, snooper, squatter, thief, trespasser; SEE CONCEPTS *412,423*

intrusive [*adj*] *obtrusive*
forward, interfering, invasive, meddlesome, meddling, nosy*, presumptuous, protruding, prying; SEE CONCEPTS *401,542*

intuition [*n*] *insight*
clairvoyance, discernment, divination, ESP*, feeling*, foreknowledge, gut reaction*, hunch*, innate knowledge, inspiration, instinct, intuitiveness, nose*, penetration, perception, perceptivity, premonition, presentiment, second sight*, sixth sense*; SEE CONCEPTS *409,689*

intuitive [*adj*] *instinctive*
automatic, direct, emotional, habitual, immediate, inherent, innate, instinctual, involuntary, natural, perceptive, spontaneous, understood, unreflecting, untaught, visceral; SEE CONCEPT *402*

inundate [*v*] *drown, overwhelm*
deluge, dunk, engulf, flood, glut, immerse, overflow, overrun, pour down on, snow*, submerge, swamp, whelm; SEE CONCEPTS *172,179*

inure [*v*] *accustom*
acclimate, familiarize, habituate, harden, make ready, season, toughen, train; SEE CONCEPTS *15,38*

invade [*v*] *attack and encroach*
access, assail, assault, breach, burglarize, burst in, crash, descend upon, entrench, fall on, foray, go in, infect, infest, infringe, inroad, interfere, loot, make inroads*, maraud, meddle, muscle in*, occupy, overrun, overspread, overswarm, penetrate, permeate, pervade, pillage, plunder, raid, ravage, storm, swarm over, trespass, violate; SEE CONCEPTS *86,159,320*

invalid [*adj*] *worthless; unfounded*
bad, baseless, fallacious, false, ill-founded, illogical, inoperative, irrational, mad, not binding, not working, nugatory, null, null and void*, reasonless, sophistic, unreasonable, unreasoned, unscientific, unsound, untrue, void, wrong; SEE CONCEPTS *552,560*

invalid [*adj2*] *sickly*
ailing, bedridden, below par, debilitated, disabled, down, feeble, frail, ill, infirm, laid low*, on the sick list*, out of action*, peaked, poorly, run-down, sick, weak; SEE CONCEPT *314*

invalid [*n*] *sick person*
consumptive, convalescent, incurable, patient, shut-in, sufferer; SEE CONCEPT *424*

invalidate [*v*] *render null and void*
abate, abolish, abrogate, annihilate, annul, blow sky-high*, cancel, circumduct, counteract, counterbalance, disannul, discredit, disqualify, impair, negate, negative, neutralize, nix, nullify, offset, overrule, overthrow, quash, refute, revoke, shoot full of holes*, undermine, undo, unfit, weaken, X-out*; SEE CONCEPTS *121,234*

invaluable [*adj*] *priceless*
beyond price, costly, dear, expensive, helpful, inestimable, precious, serviceable, valuable; SEE CONCEPTS *334,568*

invariable [*adj*] *not changing*
changeless, consistent, constant, fixed, immovable, immutable, inalterable, inflexible, monotonous, perpetual, regular, rigid, same, set, static, unalterable, unchangeable, unchanging, undiversified, unfailing, uniform, unmodifiable, unrelieved, unvarying, unwavering; SEE CONCEPT *534*

invasion [*n*] *attack, encroachment*
aggression, assault, breach, entrenchment, foray, forced entrance, incursion, infiltration, infraction, infringement, inroad, intrusion, irruption, maraud, offense, offensive, onslaught, overstepping, raid, transgression, trespass, usurpation, violation; SEE CONCEPTS *86,159,320*

invective [*n*] *verbal abuse*
accusation, berating, billingsgate, blame, blasphemy, castigation, censure, condemnation, contumely, denunciation, diatribe, epithet, jeremiad, obloquy, philippic, reproach, revilement, sarcasm, scurrility, tirade, tongue-lashing*, vilification, vituperation; SEE CONCEPTS *44,52,54,278*

inveigh [*v*] *blame, denounce*
admonish, berate, blast, castigate, censure, condemn, crack down on*, except, expostulate, go after*, have at*, jump down one's throat*, kick, lambaste, lay into, lay out, let have it, object, protest, rail, read out*, recriminate, remonstrate, reproach, rip into, roast, scold, scorch, sound off, tongue-lash, trash*, upbraid, vituperate, work over*; SEE CONCEPTS *44,52,54*

inveigle [*v*] *entice, manipulate*
allure, bait, bamboozle, beguile, blandish, butter*, cajole, charm, coax, con*, decoy, egg on*, ensnare, entrap, get around*, honey*, hook, influence, jolly, lay it on thick*, lead on*, lure, maneuver, massage, oil*, overdo it, persuade, play up to, rope in*, seduce, snow*, soap*, soften up*, string along*, stroke*, sweet talk*, tempt, toll, urge, wheedle, work over*; SEE CONCEPTS *11,14,59*

invent [*v1*] *create, think up*
ad-lib, author, bear, bring into being, coin, come upon, come up with, compose, conceive, contrive, cook up*, design, devise, discover, dream up, envision, execute, fake, fashion, find, forge, form, formulate, frame, hatch, imagine, improve, improvise, inaugurate, initiate, jam*, knock off*, make, make up, mint, off-the-cuff*, originate, plan, produce, project, toss off*, turn out, wing*; SEE CONCEPTS *36,173,221*

invent [*v2*] *fabricate*
concoct, conjure up, create out of thin air*, equivocate, fake, falsify, feign, fib, forge, lie, make believe, make up, misrepresent, misstate, pretend, prevaricate, simulate, tell a white lie*, tell untruth, think up, trump up*, vamp; SEE CONCEPTS *59,63*

invention [*n1*] *creation, creativeness*
apparatus, black box*, brainchild*, coinage, concoction, contraption, contrivance, creativity, design, development, device, discovery, doodad*, gadget, genius, gimmick, gizmo*, imagination, ingenuity, innovation, inspiration, inventiveness, novelty, opus, original, originality, resourcefulness; SEE CONCEPTS *260,409,660*

invention [*n2*] *fabrication, lie*
deceit, fake, falsehood, fancy, fantasy, fib, fiction, figment, forgery, prevarication, sham*, story, tall story*, untruth, yarn*; SEE CONCEPTS *63,278*

inventive [*adj*] *creative*
adroit, artistic, avant-garde, breaking new

in
in

ground, causative, constructive, demiurgic, deviceful, fertile, forgetive, formative, fruitful, gifted, imaginative, ingenious, innovational, innovative, innovatory, inspired, original, originative, poetical, productive, resourceful, teeming; SEE CONCEPTS 402,542

inventor [n] *discoverer*
architect, author, builder, coiner, creator, designer, experimenter, father, founder, innovator, maker, originator, pioneer; SEE CONCEPTS 348,352,361

inventory [n] *list of stock; stock*
account, backlog, catalogue, file, fund, hoard, index, itemization, record, register, reserve, reservoir, roll, roster, schedule, stock book, stockpile, store, summary, supply, table, tabulation; SEE CONCEPTS 283,338

inverse [adj] *opposite*
changed, contrary, converse, flipped, inverted, reverse, reversed, reverted, transposed, turned, turned over; SEE CONCEPT 564

invert [v] *reverse; turn upside down*
alter, backtrack, capsize, change, convert, double back, evert, flip, flip-flop*, introvert, inverse, modify, overturn, revenge, revert, tip, transplace, transpose, turn, turn down, turn inside out, turn over, turn the tables*, upend, upset, upturn; SEE CONCEPTS 213,232

invest [v1] *contribute money to make money*
advance, back, bankroll, buy into, buy stock, devote, endow, endue, get into, go in for, imbue, infuse, intrust, lay out, lend, loan, pick up the tab*, plow back into*, plunge, provide, put in, put up dough*, salt away*, sink, spend, stake, supply; SEE CONCEPTS 115,330,341

invest [v2] *give power or authority*
adopt, authorize, bequeath, charge, consecrate, empower, endow, endue, enthrone, establish, honor, inaugurate, induct, initiate, install, instate, license, ordain, sanction, vest; SEE CONCEPTS 50,88

investigate [v] *check into thoroughly*
be all ears*, bug, case*, check out, check over, check up, consider, delve, dig, examine, explore, eyeball*, feel out, frisk, give the once over*, go into, inquire, inquisite, inspect, interrogate, listen in, look into, look over, look-see, make inquiry, muckrake, nose around*, poke, probe, prospect, pry, put to the test*, question, read, reconnoiter, research, review, run down, scout, scrutinize, search, sift, spy, stake out, study, tap, wiretap; SEE CONCEPTS 48,103,216

investigation [n] *thorough check*
analysis, case, delving, examination, exploration, fact-finding, gander, hearing, hustle, inquest, inquiry, inquisition, inspection, legwork, observation, observing, pike, probe, probing, quest, quiz, research, review, scrutiny, search, sounding, study, survey, surveying; SEE CONCEPTS 48,103,216,290

investigator [n] *person who checks thoroughly*
agent, analyst, attorney, auditor, detective, examiner, gumshoe*, hound*, inquirer, inspector, plainclothes officer, police, private detective, private eye, prosecutor, researcher, reviewer, Sherlock Holmes*, sleuth, snooper, spy, tester, undercover cop; SEE CONCEPTS 348,355

investment [n] *something given, lent for a return*
advance, ante, asset, backing, bail, contribution, endowment, expenditure, expense, finance, financing, flutter, grant, hunch, inside, interests, investing, loan, money, piece, plunge, property, purchase, smart money*, spec*, speculation, stab*, stake, transaction, venture, vested interests; SEE CONCEPTS 330,332,340

investor [n] *financier*
backer, banker, capitalist, lender, shareholder, stockholder, venture capitalist; SEE CONCEPTS 347,348,353

inveterate [adj] *long-standing, established*
abiding, accustomed, addicted, chronic, confirmed, continuing, customary, deep-rooted, deep-seated, dyed-in-the-wool*, enduring, entrenched, fixed, habitual, habituated, hard-core*, hardened, inbred, incorrigible, incurable, indurated, ineradicable, ingrained, innate, lifelong, long-lasting, long-lived, obstinate, old, perennial, permanent, persistent, persisting, set, settled, stubborn, sworn, usual; SEE CONCEPTS 404,534,798

invidious [adj] *hateful*
abominable, calumnious, defamatory, detestable, detracting, detractive, detractory, discriminatory, envious, envying, green-eyed*, jealous, libelous, maligning, obnoxious, odious, offensive, repugnant, scandalous, slanderous, slighting, undesirable, vilifying; SEE CONCEPTS 401,403

invigorate [v] *stimulate*
activate, animate, brace, buck up, energize, enliven, excite, exhilarate, fortify, freshen, galvanize, harden, inspirit, liven up, nerve, pep up, perk up, pick up, quicken, rally, refresh, reinforce, rejuvenate, renew, restore, revitalize, rouse, snap up*, stir, strengthen, trigger, turn on*, vitalize, vivify, zap; SEE CONCEPTS 7,14,22,110

invigorating [adj] *stimulating*
aesthetic, bracing, brisk, charged, energizing, exhilarating, exhilarative, fascinating, fresh, healthful, high*, hyper*, interesting, lively, quickening, refreshing, rejuvenating, rejuvenative, restorative, salubrious, tonic, uplifting, vitalizing; SEE CONCEPT 537

invincible [adj] *indestructible*
bulletproof, impassable, impregnable, indomitable, insuperable, inviolable, invulnerable, irresistible, powerful, strong, unassailable, unattackable, unbeatable, unconquerable, undefeatable, unsurmountable, untouchable, unyielding; SEE CONCEPTS 489,540,551

invisible [adj] *unable to be seen; hidden*
concealed, covert, deceptive, disguised, ethereal, gaseous, ghostly, ideal, impalpable, imperceptible, imponderable, inappreciable, inconspicuous, indiscernible, infinitesimal, insensible, intangible, masked, microscopic, not in sight, obliterated, obscured, occult, out of sight, perdu, screened, supernatural, ulterior, unapparent, undisclosed, ungraspable, unnoticeable, unobservable, unperceivable, unreal, unseeable, unseen, unviewable, vaporous, veiled, wraithlike; SEE CONCEPTS 485,582,619

invitation [n] *proposal; asking*
allurement, appeal, attraction, begging, bid, bidding, call, challenge, compliments, coquetry, date, encouragement, enticement, feeler*, ground, hit, incitement, inducement, invite, lure, motive, offer, open door*, overture, paper, pass, petition, pressure, proffer, prompting, proposition, provocation, rain check*, reason, request,

solicitation, suggestion, summons, supplication, temptation, urge; SEE CONCEPTS *48,384*

invite [*v*] *ask to do something socially*
allure, appeal to, attract, beg, bid, bring on, call, command, countenance, court, draw, encourage, entice, entreat, give invitation, have in, have over, include as guest, insist, inveigle, invitation, issue, lead, lure, persuade, petition, ply, pray, press, prevail on, propose, provoke, request, send invitation, solicit, suggest, summon, supplicate, tempt, toll, urge, vamp, welcome, woo; SEE CONCEPTS *48,68,384*

inviting [*adj*] *alluring, captivating*
agreeable, appealing, attractive, beguiling, bewitching, charming, cordial, delightful, encouraging, engaging, enticing, fascinating, intriguing, magnetic, mouthwatering, open, persuasive, pleasing, provocative, seductive, tempting, warm, welcoming, winning, winsome; SEE CONCEPTS *404,529,537*

in vitro [*adj*] *artificial*
artificial insemination, outside the womb, test-tube; SEE CONCEPTS *372,723*

invocation [*n*] *prayer*
abracadabra*, appeal, beseeching, calling, command, conjuration, entreaty, hocus-pocus*, hoodoo*, mumbo-jumbo*, petition, rune, summons, supplication, voodoo*; SEE CONCEPTS *48,278,368*

invoice [*n*] *itemized bill*
account, bill of sale, check, IOU, note, statement; SEE CONCEPTS *329,332*

invoke [*v1*] *call upon*
adjure, appeal to, beg, beseech, call forth, conjure, crave, entreat, implore, importune, petition, plead, pray, request, send for, solicit, summon, supplicate; SEE CONCEPT *48*

invoke [*v2*] *put into effect*
apply, call in, effect, enforce, have recourse to, implement, initiate, resort to, use; SEE CONCEPTS *50,88*

involuntary [*adj*] *automatic; not done willingly*
automatic, begrudging, blind, compulsory, conditioned, forced, grudging, habitual, impulsive, instinctive, instinctual, knee-jerk*, obligatory, reflex, reflexive, reluctant, spontaneous, uncalculated, unconscious, uncontrolled, unintended, unintentional, unmeditated, unpremeditated, unprompted, unthinking, unwilling, unwitting, will-less; SEE CONCEPT *544*

involve [*v*] *draw in; include*
absorb, affect, argue, associate, bind, catch, commit, complicate, comprehend, comprise, compromise, concern, connect, contain, cover, denote, embrace, embroil, engage, engross, enmesh, entail, entangle, grip, hold, hook, implicate, imply, incorporate, incriminate, inculpate, link, mean, mire, mix up*, necessitate, number, point to, preoccupy, presuppose, prove, relate, require, rivet, rope in, snarl up, suggest, take in, tangle, touch, wrap up in*; SEE CONCEPT *112*

involved [*adj1*] *complicated*
Byzantine*, complex, confusing, convoluted, difficult, elaborate, Ghordian*, high-tech*, intricate, knotty*, labyrinthine, mazy, muddled, ramified, sophisticated, tangled, tortuous, winding; SEE CONCEPT *562*

involved [*adj2*] *implicated in action*
affected, caught, concerned, eat sleep and breathe*, embarrassed, embroiled, enmeshed,

entangled, hooked, immersed in, incriminated, interested, into, knee-deep in*, mixed up in*, mixed up with*, occupied, participating, taking part in, tangled, up to here in*, up to one's neck in*; SEE CONCEPTS *542,545*

invulnerable [*adj*] *invincible*
bulletproof, impassable, impenetrable, impregnable, indestructible, powerful, secure, strong, unbeatable, untouchable; SEE CONCEPTS *489,540,551*

inward [*adj1*] *ingoing*
entering, inbound, incoming, infiltrating, inflowing, inpouring, penetrating; through; SEE CONCEPT *581*

inward [*adj2*] *private*
confidential, hidden, inmost, inner, innermost, inside, intellectual, interior, internal, intimate, personal, privy, psychological, religious, secret, spiritual; SEE CONCEPT *529*

iota [*n*] *small bit*
atom, crumb, grain, hint, infinitesimal, jot, mite, molecule, nucleus, ounce, particle, ray, scintilla, scrap, smidgen, speck, trace, whit; SEE CONCEPT *831*

IRA [*n*] *individual retirement account*
Keogh plan, retirement plan, Roth IRA, self-funded retirement plan, tax-free savings account; SEE CONCEPTS *335,340,446,710*

irascible [*adj*] *crabby*
angry, bearish, bristly, cantankerous, choleric, crabbed, cranky, cross, feisty, fractious, grouchy, hasty, hot-tempered, huffy, ireful, irritable, ogre, passionate, peevish, petulant, querulous, quick-tempered, short-tempered, snappish, surly, testy, thin-skinned*, touchy, uptight; SEE CONCEPT *401*

irate [*adj*] *angry*
angered, annoyed, blown a gasket*, enraged, exasperated, fuming, furious, incensed, indignant, infuriated, irritated, livid, mad, piqued, provoked, riled, steamed*, ticked off*, up in arms*, worked up*, wrathful, wroth; SEE CONCEPTS *403,542*

ire [*n*] *anger*
annoyance, boiling point*, conniption, conniption fit*, displeasure, exasperation, fury, indignation, more heat than light*, passion, rage, slow burn*, wrath; SEE CONCEPT *410*

iridescent [*adj*] *rainbow-colored*
irised, lustrous, many-colored, nacreous, opalescent, opaline, pearly, polychromatic, prismatic, rainbowlike, shimmering; SEE CONCEPT *618*

irk [*v*] *aggravate; rub the wrong way*
abrade, annoy, bother, bug*, discommode, disturb, eat*, fret, gall, get on nerves*, get to*, give a hard time*, harass, incommode, inconvenience, irritate, make waves*, miff, nettle, peeve, provoke, put out*, rasp, rile, ruffle, trouble, vex; SEE CONCEPTS *7,19*

irksome [*adj*] *annoying*
aggravating, boring, bothersome, burdensome, irritating, tedious, tiresome, troublesome, troubling, vexing; SEE CONCEPT *529*

iron [*adj*] *hard, tough; inflexible*
adamant, adamantine, cruel, dense, ferric, ferrous, firm, heavy, immovable, implacable, indomitable, inexorable, insensible, obdurate, relentless, rigid, robust, steel, steely, strong, stubborn, thick, unbending, unyielding; SEE CONCEPTS *534,604*

in
ir

iron [n1] *hard, ferrous metal*
cast, coke, pig; SEE CONCEPT 476
iron [n2] *restraint made of metal*
bond, chain, cuffs, fetter, handcuffs, leg irons, manacles, shackles; SEE CONCEPT 476
ironclad [adj] *fixed, rigid*
abiding, agreed, arranged, certain, changeless, confirmed, definite, determinate, enduring, firm, inflexible, in the bag*, planned, prearranged, settled, stated, stubborn, sure, unalterable, uncompromising, unwavering; SEE CONCEPTS 535,554
ironic/ironical [adj] *sarcastic*
acrid, alert, arrogant, backbiting, biting, bitter, burlesque, caustic, chaffing, clever, contemptuous, contradictory, critical, cutting, cynical, defiant, derisive, disparaging, double-edged, exaggerated, implausible, incisive, incongruous, jibing, keen, mocking, mordant, paradoxical, pungent, quick-witted, ridiculous, sardonic, satiric, satirical, scathing, scoffing, sharp, sneering, spicy, trenchant, twisted, uncomplimentary, witty, wry; SEE CONCEPTS 267,548
iron out [v] *reconcile a situation*
agree, arbitrate, clear up*, compromise, eliminate, eradicate, erase, expedite, get rid of*, harmonize, negotiate, put right*, reach agreement, resolve, settle, settle differences, simplify, smooth over*, sort out*, straighten out*, unravel; SEE CONCEPT 126
irony [n] *sarcasm*
banter, burlesque, contempt, contrariness, criticism, derision, humor, incongruity, jibe, mockery, mordancy, paradox, quip, raillery, repartee, reproach, ridicule, sardonicism, satire, taunt, twist, wit; SEE CONCEPTS 230,278
irrational [adj] *illogical, senseless*
aberrant, absurd, brainless, cockamamie*, crazy, delirious, demented, disconnected, disjointed, distraught, fallacious, flaky*, foolish, freaky, incoherent, injudicious, insane, invalid, kooky*, loony*, mad, mindless, nonsensical, nutty*, off-the-wall*, preposterous, raving, reasonless, ridiculous, silly, sophistic, specious, stupid, unreasonable, unreasoning, unsound, unstable, unthinking, unwise, wacky*, wild, wrong; SEE CONCEPTS 402,403,529
irreconcilable [adj] *hostile, conflicting*
clashing, diametrically opposed, discordant, discrepant, dissonant, hard-line, implacable, incompatible, incongruous, inconsistent, inexorable, inflexible, inharmonious, intransigent, opposed, reluctant, unappeasable, uncompromising, unfriendly; SEE CONCEPTS 401,564
irrefutable [adj] *beyond question*
accurate, apodictic, can bet on it*, certain, double-checked, evident, final, inarguable, incontestable, incontrovertible, indisputable, indubitable, invincible, ironclad, irrebuttable, irrefragable, irresistible, nof ifs ands or buts*, obvious, odds-on*, positive, proven, set, sure, unanswerable, unassailable, undeniable, unimpeachable, unquestionable; SEE CONCEPTS 529,535,582
irregular [adj1] *random, variable*
aberrant, aimless, capricious, casual, changeable, designless, desultory, disconnected, discontinuous, eccentric, erratic, faltering, fitful, fluctuating, fragmentary, haphazard, hit-or-miss*, inconstant, indiscriminate, infrequent, intermittent, jerky, nonuniform, occasional, out of order, patchy, purposeless, recurrent, shaky, shifting, spasmodic, sporadic, uncertain, unconsidered, uneven, unmethodical, unpunctual, unreliable, unsettled, unsteady, unsystematic, up and down*, weaving; SEE CONCEPTS 534,799
irregular [adj2] *abnormal, peculiar*
aberrant, anomalous, atypical, capricious, deviant, different, disorderly, divergent, eccentric, exceptional, extraordinary, immoderate, improper, inappropriate, inordinate, odd, off-key*, queer, quirky, singular, strange, unconventional, unique, unnatural, unofficial, unorthodox, unsuitable, unusual; SEE CONCEPT 547
irregular [adj3] *bumpy, uneven*
aberrant, amorphous, asymmetrical, bent, broken, cockeyed*, craggy, crooked, devious, disproportionate, eccentric, elliptic, elliptical, hilly, jagged, lopsided, lumpy, meandering, notched, not uniform, off-balance, off-center, out of proportion, pitted, protuberant, rough, scarred, serrate, serrated, unaligned, unbalanced, unequal, unsymmetrical, variable, wobbly, zigzagged; SEE CONCEPTS 490,606
irregularly [adv] *intermittently*
anyhow, any which way*, at intervals, by fits and starts*, by turns, disconnectedly, eccentrically, erratically, fitfully, haphazardly, helter-skelter*, infrequently, in snatches*, jerkily, now and again, occasionally, off and on*, out of sequence, periodically, slapdash, spasmodically, sporadically, uncertainly, uncommonly, unevenly, unmethodically, unpunctually, willy-nilly*; SEE CONCEPTS 544,548,799
irrelevant [adj] *beside the point*
extraneous, foreign, garbage, immaterial, impertinent, inapplicable, inapposite, inappropriate, inappurtenant, inapropos, inapt, inconsequent, inconsequential, insignificant, not connected with, not germane, not pertaining to, off the point, off the topic, out of order, out of place, outside, pointless, remote, trivial, unapt, unconnected, unimportant, unnecessary, unrelated, without reference; SEE CONCEPTS 560,575
irreligious [adj] *ungodly*
agnostic, atheistic, blasphemous, faithless, free-thinking, godless, heathen, iconoclastic, impious, irreverent, pagan, sacrilegious, sinful, unbelieving, undevout, unholy; SEE CONCEPT 545
irreparable [adj] *unable to be fixed*
beyond repair, broken, cureless, destroyed, hopeless, impossible, incorrigible, incurable, irrecoverable, irredeemable, irremediable, irremedial, irreplaceable, irretrievable, irreversible, ruined, uncorrectable, unrecoverable; SEE CONCEPTS 314,485
irrepressible [adj] *effervescent, vivacious*
boisterous, bubbling, buoyant, ebullient, enthusiastic, insuppressible, rebellious, rhapsodical, tumultous/tumultuous, unconstrained, uncontainable, uncontrollable, unmanageable, unquenchable, unrestrainable, unrestrained, unruly, unstoppable; SEE CONCEPT 401
irreproachable [adj] *innocent*
beyond reproach, blameless, exemplary, faultless, good, guiltless, impeccable, inculpable, innocent, irreprehensible, irreprovable, perfect, pure, reproachless, righteous, unblamable, unblemished, unimpeachable, virtuous; SEE CONCEPTS 545,574

irresistible [adj] compelling; inescapable

alluring, beckoning, charming, enchanting, fascinating, glamorous, imperative, indomitable, ineluctable, inevitable, inexorable, invincible, lovable, overpowering, overwhelming, potent, powerful, ravishing, scrumptious, seductive, stunning, tempting, unavoidable, unconquerable, urgent; SEE CONCEPTS *529,574,579*

irresolute [adj] indecisive

changing, doubtful, doubting, faltering, fearful, fickle, fluctuating, halfhearted*, halting, hesitant, hesitating, hot-and-cold*, infirm, on-the-fence*, shaky, tentative, timid, uncertain, undecided, undetermined, unsettled, unstable, unsteady, vacillating, waffling*, wavering, weak, weak-kneed*, wimpy*, wishy-washy*, wobbly; SEE CONCEPTS *403,535*

irresponsible [adj] careless, reckless

capricious, carefree, devil-may-care*, feckless, fickle, flighty, fly-by-night*, giddy, harebrained, ill-considered, immature, immoral, incautious, lax, loose*, no-account*, rash, scatterbrained*, shiftless, thoughtless, unaccountable, unanswerable, uncareful, undependable, unpredictable, unreliable, unstable, untrustworthy, wild; SEE CONCEPTS *404,544*

irreverence [n] disrespect

blasphemy, cheek, derision, discourtesy, flippancy, heresy, impertinence, impiety, impudence, insult, mockery, profanity, ridicule, rudeness, sauciness, sin, sinfulness; SEE CONCEPT *633*

irreverent [adj] disrespectful

aweless, cheeky*, cocky*, contemptuous, crusty*, derisive, flip*, flippant, fresh, iconoclastic, impertinent, impious, impudent, insolent, irreverential, mocking, out-of-line*, profane, rude, sacrilegious, sassy*, saucy*, tongue-in-cheek*, ungodly, unhallowed, unholy; SEE CONCEPT *401*

irrevocable [adj] fixed, unchangeable

certain, changeless, constant, doomed, established, fated, final, immutable, indelible, inevitable, invariable, irremediable, irretrievable, irreversible, lost, permanent, predestined, predetermined, settled, unalterable, unrepealable, unreversible; SEE CONCEPTS *534,551*

irritable [adj] bad-tempered, crabby

annoyed, bearish, brooding, cantankerous, carping, choleric, complaining, contentious, crabbed, cross, crotchety, disputatious, dissatisfied, dyspeptic, easily offended, exasperated, fiery, fractious, fretful, fretting, gloomy, grouchy, grumbling, hasty, hot, huffy, hypercritical, ill-humored, irascible, moody, morose, out of humor, oversensitive, peevish, petulant, plaintive, prickly, querulous, quick-tempered, resentful, sensitive, snappy, snarling, surly, tense, testy, touchy; SEE CONCEPTS *401,403*

irritate [v1] upset, anger

abrade, affront, aggravate, annoy, bother, bug*, burn*, chafe, confuse, distemper, disturb, drive up the wall*, enrage, exasperate, fret, gall, get, get on nerves*, get under skin*, grate, harass, incense, inflame, infuriate, irk, madden, needle*, nettle, offend, pain, peeve, pester, pique, provoke, put out, rankle, rasp, rattle, rile, roil, rub the wrong way*, ruffle, sour, try, vex; SEE CONCEPTS *7,19*

irritate [v2] hurt, chafe

aggravate, burn, erupt, fret, inflame, intensify, itch, pain, redden, rub, sensitize, sharpen, sting, swell; SEE CONCEPT *246*

island [n] land surrounded by body of water

archipelago, atoll, bar, cay, enclave, haven, isle, islet, key, peninsula, reef, refuge, retreat, sanctuary, shelter; SEE CONCEPT *509*

isolate [v] cut off, set apart

abstract, block off, close off, confine, detach, disconnect, disengage, divide, divorce, insulate, island, keep apart, part, quarantine, remove, seclude, segregate, separate, sequester, sever, sunder; SEE CONCEPTS *188,201*

isolated [adj] unique; private

abandoned, abnormal, alone, anomalous, apart, backwoods*, confined, deserted, detached, exceptional, far-out, forsaken, hidden, incommunicado*, lonely, lonesome, off beaten track*, outlying, out-ofthe-way*, random, remote, retired, screened, secluded, segregated, sequestered, single, solitary, special, stranded, unaccompanied, unfrequented, unrelated, untypical, unusual, withdrawn; SEE CONCEPTS *577,583*

isolation [n] seclusion

aloneness, aloofness, beleaguerment, concealment, confinement, desolation, detachment, exile, hiding, monkhood, privacy, privateness, quarantine, reclusion, reclusiveness, remoteness, retreat, seclusiveness, segregation, sequestration, solitude, withdrawal; SEE CONCEPTS *135,188, 388,631*

issue [n1] point in question

affair, argument, concern, contention, controversy, matter, matter of contention, point, point of departure, problem, puzzle, question, subject, topic; SEE CONCEPTS *278,532*

issue [n2] result

causatum, conclusion, consequence, culmination, effect, end, end product, eventuality, finale, fruit, outcome, payoff, sequel, termination, upshot; SEE CONCEPT *230*

issue [n3] edition of publication

copy, impression, installment, number, printing; SEE CONCEPT *280*

issue [n4] distribution

circulation, delivery, dispersion, dissemination, granting, issuance, issuing, publication, sending out, supply, supplying; SEE CONCEPT *140*

issue [n5] children

brood, descendants, get, heirs, offspring, posterity, progeniture, progeny, scions, seed; SEE CONCEPTS *296,414*

issue [v1] distribute

air, allot, announce, assign, bring out, broadcast, circulate, consign, declare, deliver, dispatch, dispense, emit, get out, give out, promulgate, publish, put in circulation, put out, release, send, send out, transmit; SEE CONCEPTS *60,140,292*

issue [v2] emit, emerge; come from

appear, arise, be a consequence, birth, come forth, derive from, emanate, exude, flow, give off, give out, ooze, originate, proceed, release, rise, send forth, spring, spurt, stem, throw off, vent, well; SEE CONCEPTS *179,648*

itch [n1] scratching; tingling

crawling, creeping, irritation, itchiness, prickling, psoriasis, rawness, tickle; SEE CONCEPTS *608,728*

itch [n2] strong desire

aphrodisia, appetite, appetition, concupiscence, craving, eroticism, hankering, hunger, impulse,

ir
it

longing, lust, lustfulness, motive, passion, prurience, restlessness, urge, yearning, yen; SEE CON-
CEPTS 20,529

itch [*v1*] *scratch; tingle*
crawl, creep, irritate, prick, prickle, sting, tickle,
titillate; SEE CONCEPTS 185,313,612

itch [*v2*] *desire strongly*
ache, be impatient, burn, chafe, crave, hanker,
have a yen for, hunger, long, lust, pant, pine,
sigh, thirst, want, yearn; SEE CONCEPT 20

item [*n*] *part, article*
account, aspect, bit, blurb*, bulletin, column,
component, consideration, conversation piece,
detail, dispatch, element, entry, feature, incidental, information, matter, minor point, minutia,
news, note, notice, novelty, paragraph, particular, piece, point, report, scoop*, scrap, specific,
story, thing, write-up; SEE CONCEPTS 270,831,
835

itemize [*v*] *keep detailed record*
catalog, circumstantiate, cite, count, detail, document, enumerate, individualize, instance, inventory, lay out, list, mention, number, particularize,
quote, recite, record, recount, rehearse, relate, set
out, specify, spell out, tally; SEE CONCEPTS
57,125

itinerant [*adj*] *roaming*
afoot, ambulant, ambulatory, floating, gypsy,
journeying, migratory, moving, nomadic, on
foot, peripatetic, ranging, riding the rails*, roving, shifting, travelling, unsettled, vagabond, vagrant, wandering, wayfaring; SEE CONCEPTS
536,584

itinerary [*n*] *plan of travel*
beat, circuit, course, guide, guidebook, journey,
line, outline, path, program, route, run, schedule,
tour, way; SEE CONCEPTS 281,660

J

jab [*n/v*] *poke*
blow, buck, bump, bunt, dig, hit, jog, lunge,
nudge, prod, punch, push, stab, tap, thrust; SEE
CONCEPT 189

jabber [*v*] *talk incessantly and trivially*
babble, blather*, chatter, drivel, gab, go on and
on*, jaw, mumble, murmur, mutter, prate, ramble, run off at mouth*, shoot the breeze*, talk,
tattle, utter, yak, yap; SEE CONCEPTS 51,56

jacket [*n*] *covering*
case, casing, coat, envelope, folder, fur, hide,
parka, pelt, sheath, skin, threads, tunic, wrapper,
wrapping; SEE CONCEPTS 451,484

jaded [*adj*] *exhausted, indifferent*
been around, blah*, blasé, bored, cool*, done it
all*, dulled, fagged, fatigued, fed up*, had it*,
mellow, sated, satiated, sick of*, spent, surfeited,
tired, tired-out*, up to here*, wearied, weary,
worn, worn-down, worn-out; SEE CONCEPTS
401,406

jagged [*adj*] *ragged, notched*
asperous, barbed, broken, cleft, craggy, denticulate, harsh, indented, irregular, pointed, ridged,
rough, rugged, scabrous, serrated, snaggy,

spiked, toothed, uneven, unlevel, unsmooth; SEE
CONCEPTS 490,606

jail [*n*] *place for incarceration*
bastille, black hole*, brig, bullpen*, can*, cell,
clink*, cooler*, detention camp, dungeon, house
of correction, inside*, jailhouse, joint*, lockup,
pen, penal institution, penitentiary, pound,
prison, rack*, reformatory, slammer*, solitary*,
stir*, stockade, up the river*; SEE CONCEPTS
439,449,516

jail [*v*] *incarcerate*
bastille, book, cage, can*, confine, constrain, detain, hold, immure, impound, imprison, lock up,
prison, put away*, put behind bars*, put on ice*,
railroad*, send up*, sentence, take away*, throw
away the keys*, throw in dungeon, throw the
book at*; SEE CONCEPT 317

jailer [*n*] *prison warden*
correctional officer, corrections officer, guard,
prison guard, turnkey; SEE CONCEPT 348

jalopy [*n*] *old, dilapidated automobile*
bucket of bolts*, clunker, heap*, junker*, rattletrap*, tin lizzie*, wreck; SEE CONCEPTS 260,674

jam [*n*] *troublesome situation*
bind, box, corner, difficulty, dilemma, fix, hole,
hot water*, pickle*, plight, predicament, problem, quandary, scrape, spot, strait, trouble; SEE
CONCEPT 674

jam [*v*] *squeeze in; compress*
bear, bind, block, cease, clog, congest, cram,
crowd, crush, elbow, force, halt, jam-pack, jostle, obstruct, pack, press, push, ram, squash,
squish, stall, stick, stuff, tamp, throng, wad,
wedge; SEE CONCEPTS 121,208

jamboree [*n*] *noisy celebration*
bash*, blowout*, ceremony, convention, festival,
gathering, hoopla, jubilee, party, rally, revelry,
shindig, wingding*; SEE CONCEPT 377

jangle [*n*] *cacophony of noises*
babel, clang, clangor, clash, din, dissonance,
hubbub*, hullabaloo*, jar, pandemonium, racket,
rattle, reverberation, roar, tumult, uproar; SEE
CONCEPT 595

jangle [*v*] *make clinking noises*
chime, clank, clash, clatter, conflict, disaccord,
discord, disharmonize, hit a sour note*, jar, jingle, mismatch, rattle, vibrate; SEE CONCEPT 65

janitor [*n*] *person who cleans and maintains*
attendant, caretaker, cleaning person, concierge,
custodian, doorkeeper, doorperson, gatekeeper,
house sitter, porter, sitter, super, superintendent,
sweeper, watchperson; SEE CONCEPT 348

jar [*n1*] *container*
basin, beaker, bottle, burette, can, chalice, crock,
cruet, decanter, ewer, flagon, flask, jug, pitcher,
pot, tun, urn, vase, vat, vessel; SEE CONCEPT 494

jar [*n2*] *shocking hit*
bump, clash, collision, concussion, crash, impact, jolt, jounce, rock, smash, succussion, thud,
thump; SEE CONCEPT 189

jar [*v1*] *shock, jolt*
agitate, bang, bounce, bump, clash, convulse,
crash, disturb, grate, grind, hit, irritate, jerk, jiggle, jounce, jump, offend, quake, rasp, rattle,
rock, shake, slam, thump, tremor, vibrate, wiggle, wobble; SEE CONCEPTS 65,189

jar [*v2*] *clash, disharmonize*
annoy, bicker, contend, disaccord, disagree, discompose, discord, grate, grind, interfere, irk, irri-

tate, jangle, mismatch, nettle, oppose, outrage, quarrel, shock, wrangle; SEE CONCEPTS 7,19

jargon [n] *specialized language; dialect*
abracadabra*, argot, balderdash*, banality, bombast, bunk*, buzzwords*, cant, cliché, colloquialism, commonplace term, doublespeak, drivel, fustian, gibberish, hackneyed term, idiom, insipidity, lexicon, lingo*, mumbo jumbo*, neologism, newspeak, nonsense, overused term, palaver, parlance, patois, patter, rigmarole, shoptalk, slang, slanguage*, speech, stale language, street talk*, tongue, trite language, twaddle*, usage, vernacular, vocabulary; SEE CONCEPTS 275,276

jaundiced [adj] *tainted, prejudiced*
biased, bigoted, bitter, colored, cynical, disapproving, distorted, envious, grudging, hostile, intolerant, jealous, one-sided, opprobrious, partial, partisan, preconceived, prepossessed, resentful, skeptical, spiteful, suspicious, tendentious, unfair, unfriendly, unindifferent, warped, yellow; SEE CONCEPTS 401,403,542

jaunt [n] *expedition*
adventure, airing, amble, beat, canter, circuit, constitutional, course, cruise, drive, excursion, frolic, gallop, hike, jog, journey, junket, march, outing, patrol, peregrination, picnic, promenade, prowl, ramble, ride, round, roundabout, run, sally, saunter, stroll, tour, tramp, travel, trek, trip, turn, voyage, walk; SEE CONCEPTS 159,195,224

jaunty [adj] *lively*
airy, animated, bold, brash, breezy, buoyant, carefree, careless, cocky, dapper, dashing, debonair, devilish, devil-may-care*, easy, exhilarated, flip*, flippant, forward, free, fresh, frisky, frolicsome, gamesome, gay, high-spirited, hilarious, impetuous, impish, impudent, jocose, joking, jolly, jovial, light, natty, nervy, perky, playful, prankish, provocative, reckless, rollicking, self-confident, showy, smart, sportive, sporty, sprightly, spruce, swaggering, trim, venturesome, vivacious; SEE CONCEPTS 401,404

jaw [n] *bones of chin*
bone, chops*, jowl, mandible, maxilla, mouth, muzzle*, orifice; SEE CONCEPT 392

jaw [v1] *talk a lot*
babble, chat, chatter, gab*, gossip, jabber, lecture, orate, prate, prattle, yak; SEE CONCEPTS 51,56

jaw [v2] *criticize*
abuse, baste, berate, blame, call on the carpet*, censure, rail, rate, revile, scold, tongue-lash*, upbraid, vituperate; SEE CONCEPT 52

jazz [n] *style of music*
bebop*, blues, boogie*, boogie-woogie*, Dixieland, fusion jazz, hot jazz, improvisational music, jive*, ragtime, swing; SEE CONCEPT 595

jazzed-up [adj] *souped up*
gassed-up, high geared, high performance, high speed, hopped-up*, pepped-up*, pumped-up*, revved-up*, speedy, supercharged; SEE CONCEPTS 401,404

jazzy [adj] *fancy*
animated, exciting, flashy, gaudy, lively, salacious, sexy, smart, snazzy*, spirited, vivacious, wild, zestful, zippy*; SEE CONCEPTS 537,589

jealous [adj] *desirous; wary*
anxious, apprehensive, attentive, begrudging, covetous, demanding, doubting, emulous, envi-

ous, envying, grabby, grasping, green-eyed, grudging, guarded, intolerant, invidious, jaundiced, mistrustful, monopolizing, possessive, possessory, protective, questioning, resentful, rival, skeptical, solicitous, suspicious, vigilant, watchful, zealous; SEE CONCEPTS 403,542

jealousy [n] *envy*
backbiting, begrudging, covetousness, enviousness, evil eye*, green-eyed monster*, grudge, grudgingness, jaundiced eye*, resentfulness, resentment, spite; SEE CONCEPT 410

jeans [n] *dungarees*
blue jeans, chaps, denims, Lees℗, Levi's℗, pants, trousers, Wranglers℗; SEE CONCEPT 451

jeer [v] *heckle*
banter, comeback, contemn, deride, dig*, fleer, flout, gibe, hector, hoot, jab, jest, laugh at, make a crack*, mock, poke fun, put down, put on, quip, ridicule, scoff, sneer, snipe, taunt; SEE CONCEPT 54

jell [v] *coagulate*
clot, cohere, come together, condense, congeal, crystallize, finalize, form, freeze, gel, gelate, gelatinize, harden, jellify, jelly, materialize, set, solidify, stick, stiffen, take shape, thicken; SEE CONCEPTS 250,469

jeopardize [v] *endanger*
be careless, chance, chance it*, gamble, hazard, imperil, lay on the line*, peril, put at risk, put in danger, put in jeopardy, risk, stake, subject to, tempt fate, threaten; SEE CONCEPTS 246,252,384

jeopardy [n] *danger, trouble*
accident, chance, double-trouble*, endangerment, exposure, hazard, insecurity, liability, on the line*, on the spot*, out on a limb*, peril, precariousness, risk, venture, vulnerability; SEE CONCEPT 675

jerk [n1] *a lurching move*
bounce, bump, flick, flop, jolt, pull, quake, quiver, shiver, snag, thrust, tug, tweak, twitch, wiggle, wrench, wriggle, yank; SEE CONCEPTS 80,149,150

jerk [n2] *stupid, bumbling person*
brute, fool, idiot, nincompoop, ninny, oaf, rascal; SEE CONCEPT 423

jerk [v] *move with lurch*
bounce, bump, dance, flick, fling, flip, flop, grab, hook, hurtle, jolt, lug, pluck, pull, quake, quiver, seize, shiver, shrug, sling, snag, snatch, throw, thrust, tug, tweak, twitch, vellicate, whisk, wiggle, wrench, wrest, wriggle, wring, yank; SEE CONCEPTS 150,152

jerry-built [adj] *flimsy*
cheap, defective, insubstantial, jerry-rigged, junky, makeshift, ramshackle, rickety, shoddy, slipshod, unsound, unsubstantial; SEE CONCEPT 267

jest [n] *joke*
banter, bon mot, crack, fun, funny, gag, game, hoax, jive, jolly, laugh, one-liner*, play, pleasantry, prank, quip, rib, rib-tickler*, ridicule, sally, spoof, sport, wisecrack, witticism; SEE CONCEPT 273

jest [v] *joke*
banter, chaff, deride, flout, fool, fun*, gibe*, gird*, jeer, jive*, jolly*, josh*, kid, mock, needle*, put on, quip, rag*, razz*, rib*, roast*, scoff, sneer, spoof, tease; SEE CONCEPT 273

jester [n] *person who jokes, plays jokes*
actor, antic, banterer, buffoon, card*, clown, co-

it
je

median, comic, cutup*, droll, fool, harlequin, humorist, japer, joker, jokester, larker, life of the party*, madcap*, pantaloon, practical joker, prankster, quipster, standup comic, trickster, wag*, wisecracker*, wit; SEE CONCEPT 423

jet [adj] black
atramentous, coal-black, dark, ebon, ebony, inky, midnight, obsidian, pitch-black, pitch-dark, raven, sable; SEE CONCEPT 618

jet [n1] rush, gush of substance
flow, fountain, spout, spray, spring, spritz, spurt, squirt, stream; SEE CONCEPTS 465,467

jet [n2] vehicle propelled by ejection of pressurized gas or liquid
airbus, airplane, plane, supersonic, supersonic transport, turbo; SEE CONCEPTS 463,503

jet [v] spurt, gush
flow, fly, issue, pour, roll, rush, shoot, soar, spew, spout, spritz, squirt, surge, travel, zoom; SEE CONCEPT 179

jet set [n] high society
beau monde, beautiful people, cream of society, elite, fashionable society, in-crowd, leisured class, moneyed class, polite society, smart set, the well-to-do, upper crust; SEE CONCEPTS 387,388,417

jettison [v] eject; throw overboard
abandon, abdicate, cast, cast off, deep-six*, discard, dump, expel, heave, hurl, junk*, maroon, reject, scrap*, shed, slough, throw away, unload*; SEE CONCEPTS 180,222

jetty [n] pier
barrier, breakwater, dock, groin, landing, quay, seawall, slip, wharf; SEE CONCEPTS 439,443,479

jewel [n1] precious stone
baguette, bauble, bead, bijou, birthstone, brilliant, gem, gemstone, glass, gullion, hardware*, ornament, rock*, sparkler*, stone, trinket; SEE CONCEPTS 446,474,478

jewel [n2] something, someone precious
charm, find, gem, genius, ideal, masterpiece, nonesuch, nonpareil, paragon, pearl*, phenomenon, phoenix*, prize, prodigy, rarity, specialty, treasure, wonder; SEE CONCEPT 671

jewelry [n] precious stones, metals worn as decoration
adornment, anklet, band, bangle, bauble, beads, bijou, bracelet, brass, brooch, cameo, chain, charm, choker, costume, cross, crown, diamonds, earring, finery, frippery, gem, glass*, gold, ice*, jewel, junk*, knickknack, lavaliere, locket, necklace, ornament, pendant, pin, regalia, ring, rock, rosary, silver, solitaire, sparkler, stickpin, stone, tiara, tie pin, treasure, trinket; SEE CONCEPT 446

Jewish [adj] Israelite
Hasidic, Hebrew, Judaistic, Semitic; SEE CONCEPT 369

Jezebel [n] prostitute
broad, fallen woman*, femme fatale, floozy*, harlot, hooker, hussy, jade, loose woman, scarlet, slut, strumpet, tart, trollop, vamp, whore; SEE CONCEPTS 348,412,415,419

jibe [v] agree
accord, conform, correspond, dovetail, fit, fit in, go, harmonize, match, resemble, square, tally; SEE CONCEPT 664

jiffy [n] instant
breath, crack, flash, jiff*, minute, moment, second, shake*, split second*, trice, twinkling*; SEE CONCEPT 808

jiggle [v] bounce up and down
agitate, bob, fidget, jerk, jig, jigger, jog, joggl[e], shake, shimmer, shimmy, twitch, vellicate, wig[gle]; SEE CONCEPTS 150,152

jilt [v] abandon, betray
break off*, coquette, deceive, desert, disappoin[t], discard, ditch*, drop*, dump*, forsake, get r[id] of, leave, leave at the altar*, leave flat*, reje[ct], throw over*; SEE CONCEPTS 195,297,384

jingle [v] make metallic clinking noise
chime, chink, chinkle, clamor, clang, clatte[r], clink, ding, jangle, rattle, reverberate, rin[g], sound, tingle, tinkle, tintannabulate; SEE CON[-]
CEPT 65

jinx [n] curse
black magic, charm, enchantment, evil eye[*], hex, hoodoo*, kiss of death*, nemesis, plagu[e], spell, voodoo*; SEE CONCEPTS 230,679

jinx [v] curse
bedevil, bewitch, cast a spell on, charm, co[n]demn, damn*, enchant, give the evil eye*, he[x]; SEE CONCEPTS 14,192

jitters [n] nervousness
anxiety, dither, fidgets, heebie-jeebies*, jump[y], nerves, shakes, shivers, tenseness, willies*; SE[E] CONCEPTS 230,410,690

jittery [adj] nervous
antsy*, anxious, apprehensive, edgy, excitable[*], fidgety, high-strung*, jumpy, on edge*, on pin[s] and needles*, panicky, quivering, restless, shak[y], skittish, spooked, tense, trembling, uneasy, up[-]tight; SEE CONCEPTS 401,690

job [n1] employment
activity, appointment, assignment, berth, bille[t], business, calling, capacity, career, chore, co[n]nection, craft, daily grind*, engagement, facult[y], function, gig*, grind*, handicraft, line, livel[i]hood, means, métier, niche, nine-to-five*, occu[-]pation, office, opening, operation, place[,] position, post, posting, profession, pursui[t], racket*, rat race*, situation, spot, stint, swindle[*], task, trade, vocation, work; SEE CONCEP[TS] 351,360

job [n2] task
act, action, affair, assignment, burden, busines[s], care, charge, chore, commission, concern, contri[-]bution, deed, devoir, duty, effort, enterprise, er[-]rand, function, matter, mission, obligation[,] office, operation, project, province, pursuit, re[-]sponsibility, role, stint, task, taskwork, thing[*,] tour of duty, undertaking, venture, work; SE[E] CONCEPT 362

jobless [adj] unemployed
between jobs*, collecting unemployment bene[-]fits, laid off, on the dole*, out of a job, out o[f] work, without employment, without gainful em[-]ployment, workless; SEE CONCEPT 538

jock [n] athlete
competitor, letterman/woman, letterperson[,] player, sportsman/woman, sportsperson; SE[E] CONCEPT 366

jockey [v] maneuver
direct, guide, handle, move, navigate, negotiate[,] pilot, position, ride, steer, turn, twist; SEE CON[-]CEPTS 187,225

jocular/jocose/jocund [adj] funny, playful
amusing, blithe, camp, cheerful, comic, comica[l*,] crazy, daffy, droll, facetious, flaky*, frolicsome[,] gay, gleeful, happy, humorous, jesting, jokey[,] joking, jolly, joshing, jovial, joyous, laughable[,]

lighthearted, lively, ludicrous, merry, mischievous, pleasant, roguish, sportive, teasing, wacky, waggish, whimsical, witty; SEE CONCEPTS 267,529

jog [*v1*] *activate, push*
agitate, arouse, bounce, dig, hit, jab, jar, jiggle, joggle, jolt, jostle, jounce, nudge, press, prod, prompt, punch, remind, rock, shake, shove, stimulate, stir, suggest, whack; SEE CONCEPTS 14,208

jog [*v2*] *run for recreation*
amble, canter, dash, dogtrot, lope, pace, sprint, trot; SEE CONCEPT 151

John Hancock [*n*] *signature*
autograph, endorsement, inscription, mark, seal, undersignature; SEE CONCEPT 284

join [*v1*] *unite*
accompany, add, adhere, affix, agglutinate, annex, append, assemble, associate, attach, blend, bracket, cement, clamp, clasp, clip, coadunate, coalesce, combine, compound, concrete, conjoin, conjugate, connect, copulate, couple, entwine, fasten, fuse, grapple, hitch on, incorporate, interlace, intermix, juxtapose, knit, leash, link, lock, lump together, marry, mate, melt, mix, pair, put together, slap on, span, splice, stick together, tack on, tag on, tie, tie up, touch, weave, wed, weld, yoke; SEE CONCEPT 113

join [*v2*] *affiliate with organization*
align, associate with, be in, come aboard*, consort, cooperate, enlist, enroll, enter, fall in with*, follow, go to, mingle with, pair with, plug into*, side with, sign on, sign up, take part in, take up with, team up with, throw in with*, tie up with; SEE CONCEPT 114

join [*v3*] *touch; border on*
abut, adjoin, be at hand, be close to, be contiguous to, bound, butt, communicate, conjoin, extend, fringe, hem, lie beside, lie near, lie next to, line, march, meet, neighbor, open into, parallel, reach, rim, skirt, trench on, verge on; SEE CONCEPT 747

joint [*adj*] *shared, combined*
collective, common, communal, concerted, conjoint, conjunct, consolidated, cooperative, hand in hand, intermutual, joined, mutual, public, united; SEE CONCEPTS 577,708

joint [*n1*] *intersection, juncture*
abutment, articulation, bend, bond, bracket, bridge, concourse, confluence, conjuncture, connection, copula, coupling, crux, elbow, hinge, hyphen, impingement, interconnection, junction, knot, link, meeting, nexus, node, point, seam, splice, suture, swivel, tangency, tie, union, vinculum; SEE CONCEPTS 393,830,831

joint [*n2*] *cheap hangout*
bar, club, dive*, hole in the wall*, honky-tonk*, juke joint*, roadhouse, tavern; SEE CONCEPTS 439,449

jointly [*adv*] *as one*
accordingly, agreeably, alike, arm in arm*, coincidentally, collectively, combined, companionably, concomitantly, concurrently, conjointly, connectedly, cooperatively, en masse, hand in glove*, hand in hand*, harmoniously, in a group, in common, in company with, in concert, in conjunction, inextricably, in league, in partnership, inseparably, intimately, in unison, mutually, reciprocally, side by side*, similarly, simultane-

ously, synchronically, together, unitedly, with one another; SEE CONCEPT 577

joke [*n1*] *fun, quip*
antic, bon mot, buffoonery, burlesque, caper, caprice, chestnut*, clowning, drollery, epigram, escapade, farce, frolic, gag, gambol, game, haha*, hoodwinking*, horseplay*, humor, jape, jest, lark, laugh, mischief, monkeyshine*, mummery, one-liner*, parody, payoff, play, pleasantry, prank, pun, put-on, quirk, raillery, repartee, revel, rib, sally, saw, shaggy-dog story*, shenanigan*, snow job*, sport, spree, stunt, tomfoolery, trick, vagary, whimsy, wisecrack, witticism, yarn; SEE CONCEPT 273

joke [*n2*] *person that is made fun of*
buffoon, butt, clown, derision, fool, goat, jackass, jestee, laughingstock, mockery, simpleton, sport, target; SEE CONCEPTS 412,423

joke [*v*] *kid, tease*
banter, chaff, deceive, deride, fool, frolic, fun, gambol, horse around*, jape, jest, jive*, jolly, josh, kid around, laugh, make merry, mock, needle, play, play the clown, play tricks, poke fun*, pull one's leg*, pun, put on, quip, rag, revel, rib, ridicule, roast*, spoof, sport, taunt, trick, wisecrack*; SEE CONCEPT 273

joker [*n*] *person who kids, teases*
actor, banana*, buffoon, card*, clown, comedian, comic, cutup*, farceur, fool, funster*, gagster*, humorist, jester, jokesmith, jokester, josher*, kidder, life of the party*, prankster*, punster*, quipster*, second banana*, stand-up comic, stooge, straight person, top banana*, trickster*, wag, wisecracker*, wit; SEE CONCEPTS 352,423

jolly [*adj*] *laughing, joyful*
blithe, blithesome, bouncy, carefree, cheerful, chipper, chirpy, convivial, daffy, delightful, enjoyable, entertaining, festive, frolicsome, funny, gay, gladsome, gleeful, happy, hilarious, jocund, jokey, joshing, jovial, joyous, jubilant, larking, lighthearted, lots of laughs, merry, mirthful, playful, pleasant, sportive, sprightly, zippy*; SEE CONCEPTS 267,542,548

jolt [*n*] *surprise; sudden push*
blow, bombshell*, bounce, bump, clash, collision, concussion, double whammy*, impact, jar, jerk, jog, jounce, jump, kick, lurch, percussion, punch, quiver, reversal, setback, shake, shock, shot, start, surprise, thunderbolt; SEE CONCEPTS 42,208

jolt [*v*] *surprise; push suddenly*
astonish, bowl over*, bump, churn, convulse, discompose, disturb, floor, jar, jerk, jog, jostle, knock, knock over*, lay out*, perturb, rock, shake, shake up*, shock, shove, spring something on*, stagger, start, startle, stun, throw a curve*, upset; SEE CONCEPTS 42,208

jostle [*v*] *bump, shake*
bang into, bulldoze*, bump heads*, butt*, crash, crowd, elbow, hustle, jab, jog, joggle, jolt, nudge, press, push, push around, push aside, rough and tumble*, scramble, shoulder, shove, squeeze, thrust; SEE CONCEPTS 152,189,208

journal [*n*] *chronicle*
account, almanac, annals, annual, calendar, chronology, comic book, daily, daybook, diary, gazette, ledger, log, magazine, memento, memoir, minutes, monthly, newspaper, note, observation, organ, paper, periodical, publication, rag,

je
jo

record, register, reminder, reminiscence, review, scandal sheet*, statement, tabloid, weekly; SEE CONCEPTS 271,280,801

journalism [n] *reporting*
broadcast writing, news, newspaper writing, the fourth estate, the press, writing; SEE CONCEPTS 280,349,356

journalist [n] *person who writes about factual events for a living*
announcer, broadcaster, columnist, commentator, contributor, correspondent, cub, editor, hack, media person, newspaper person, newsperson, pencil pusher*, press, publicist, reporter, scribe, scrivener, stringer*, television commentator, writer; SEE CONCEPTS 348,356

journey [n] *excursion*
adventure, airing, beat, campaign, caravan, circuit, constitutional, course, crossing, drive, expedition, exploration, hike, itinerary, jaunt, junket, march, migration, odyssey, outing, passage, patrol, peregrination, pilgrimage, progress, promenade, quest, ramble, range, roaming, round, route, run, safari, sally, saunter, sojourn, stroll, survey, tour, tramp, transit, transmigration, travel, traveling, traverse, trek, trip, vagabondage, vagrancy, venture, visit, voyage, wandering, wayfaring; SEE CONCEPT 224

journey [v] *travel*
circuit, cruise, fare, fly, globe trot*, go, go places, hie, hop, jaunt, jet, junket, knock about*, pass, peregrinate, proceed, process, push on, ramble, range, repair, roam, rove, safari, take a trip, tour, traverse, trek, voyage, wander, wend; SEE CONCEPT 224

jovial [adj] *happy*
affable, airy, amiable, animated, bantering, blithe, blithesome, bouncy, buoyant, chaffing, cheery, chipper, chirpy, companionable, conversable, convivial, cordial, daffy*, delightful, dizzy*, enjoyable, facetious, festal, festive, gay, glad, gleeful, good-natured, hilarious, humorous, jocose, jocund, jokey, jolly, jollying, joshing, jubilant, larking, lighthearted, loony, lots of laughs*, merry, mirthful, nutty*, off-the-wall*, pleasant, sociable; SEE CONCEPTS 401,403

joy [n] *great happiness, pleasure*
alleviation, amusement, animation, bliss, charm, cheer, comfort, delectation, delight, diversion, ecstasy, elation, exultation, exulting, felicity, festivity, frolic, fruition, gaiety, gem, gladness, glee, good humor, gratification, hilarity, humor, indulgence, jewel, jubilance, liveliness, luxury, merriment, mirth, pride, pride and joy, prize, rapture, ravishment, refreshment, regalement, rejoicing, revelry, satisfaction, solace, sport, transport, treasure, treat, wonder; SEE CONCEPTS 410,529

joyful/joyous [adj] *happy*
blithesome, cheerful, cheery, delighted, ecstatic, effervescent, elated, enjoyable, enraptured, expansive, festive, flying*, gay, glad, gladsome, gratified, heartening, high*, high as a kite*, jubilant, lighthearted, merry, overjoyed, pleased, pleasurable, popping*, rapturous, satisfied, sunny*, sunny-side up*, transported, upbeat; SEE CONCEPTS 403,542,548

joyless [adj] *unhappy*
black, bleak, blue, cheerless, dejected, depressant, depressed, depressing, dismal, dispirited,

dispiriting, doleful, downcast, down in the mouth*, dragged, dreary, droopy, gloomy, having the blahs*, heavy*, low, melancholic, melancholy, miserable, mopey, mournful, sad, saddening, somber; SEE CONCEPTS 403,542,548

jubilant [adj] *happy*
celebrating, doing handsprings*, elated, enraptured, euphoric, excited, exuberant, exultant, exulting, flipping, flying*, glad, gleeful, joyous, overjoyed, pleased, rejoicing, rhapsodic, thrilled, tickled*, triumphal, triumphant; SEE CONCEPTS 401,403

Judas [n] *traitor*
backstabber, Benedict Arnold, betrayer, conspirator, deceiver, rat, turncoat, two-timer*, weasel; SEE CONCEPT 412

judge [n] *person who arbitrates*
adjudicator, appraiser, arbiter, assessor, authority, bench, chancellor, conciliator, court, critic, evaluator, expert, honor, inspector, intercessor, intermediary, interpreter, judiciary, justice, justice of peace, legal official, magister, magistrate, marshal, moderator, negotiator, peacemaker, reconciler, referee, umpire, warden; SEE CONCEPT 355

judge [v] *make decision from evidence; deduce*
act on, adjudge, adjudicate, appraise, appreciate, approximate, arbitrate, arrive, ascertain, assess, check, collect, conclude, condemn, consider, criticize, decide, decree, deduct, derive, determine, discern, distinguish, doom, draw, esteem, estimate, evaluate, examine, find, gather, give a hearing, make, make out, mediate, pass sentence, place, pronounce sentence, put, rate, reckon, referee, resolve, review, rule, sentence, settle, size up, suppose, test, try, umpire, value; SEE CONCEPTS 18,317

judgment [n1] *common sense*
acumen, acuteness, apprehension, astuteness, awareness, brains, capacity, comprehension, discernment, discrimination, experience, genius, grasp, incisiveness, ingenuity, intelligence, intuition, keenness, knowledge, mentality, penetration, perception, percipience, perspicacity, prudence, quickness, range, rationality, reach, readiness, reason, reasoning, sagacity, sanity, sapience, savvy, sense, sharpness, shrewdness, sophistication, soundness, taste, understanding, wisdom, wit; SEE CONCEPTS 37,409

judgment [n2] *decision about blame*
analysis, appraisal, appreciation, arbitration, assaying, assessment, award, belief, close study, conclusion, contemplation, conviction, decree, deduction, determination, estimate, estimation, evaluation, examination, exploration, finding, idea, inference, inquest, inquiry, inquisition, inspection, observation, opinion, order, probing, pursuit, quest, reconnaissance, regard, report, research, resolution, result, review, ruling, scrutiny, search, sentence, sifting, summary, verdict, view, weigh-in; SEE CONCEPTS 103,689

judgment [n3] *doom, fate*
affliction, castigation, chastisement, correction, damnation, infliction, manifestation, misfortune, mortification, punishment, retribution, visitation; SEE CONCEPT 679

judicial [adj] *legal*
administrative, authoritative, constitutional, discriminating, distinguished, equitable, forensic, impartial, judgelike, judiciary, juridical, jurisdic-

tional, juristic, lawful, legalistic, magisterial, official, pontifical, principled, regular, statutory; SEE CONCEPT 319

judicious [adj] *wise, thoughtful*
accurate, acute, astute, calculating, careful, cautious, circumspect, clear-sighted, considerate, considered, diplomatic, discerning, discreet, discriminating, efficacious, enlightened, expedient, far-sighted, informed, judicial, keen, perceptive, perspicacious, politic, profound, prudent, quick-witted, rational, reasonable, sagacious, sage, sane, sapient, seasonable, seemly, sensible, sharp, shrewd, skillful, sober, sophisticated, sound, thorough, wary, well-advised, well-judged, worldly-wise; SEE CONCEPTS 402,403, 542

jug [n] *container for liquid*
amphora, beaker, bottle, bucket, canteen, carafe, crock, cruet, decanter, ewer, flagon, flask, growler, hooker, jar, pitcher, pot, tub, urn, vase, vessel; SEE CONCEPT 494

juggle [v] *mislead, falsify; handle several things at once*
alter, beguile, betray, bluff, change, conjure, delude, disguise, doctor*, double-cross, fix, humbug*, illude, maneuver, manipulate, misrepresent, modify, perform magic, prestidigitate, shuffle, take in, tamper with, trim; SEE CONCEPTS 59,63

juice [n] *liquid squeezed from fruit, plant*
abstract, alcohol, aqua vitae, distillation, drink, essence, extract, fluid, liquor, milk, nectar, oil, sap, sauce, secretion, serum, spirit, syrup, water; SEE CONCEPTS 428,467

juicy [adj1] *moist*
dank, dewy, dripping, humid, liquid, luscious, lush, mellow, oily, oozy, pulpy, sappy, saturated, sauced, slippery, slushy, soaked, sodden, succulent, syrupy, viscid, watery, wet; SEE CONCEPT 603

juicy [adj2] *exciting, interesting*
colorful, fascinating, intriguing, piquant, provocative, racy, risqué, sensational, spicy, suggestive, tantalizing, vivid; SEE CONCEPTS 537,548

jumble [n] *hodgepodge*
assortment, chaos, clutter, confusion, derangement, disarrangement, disarray, disorder, farrago, gallimaufry, garbage, goulash, hash*, litter, medley, mélange, mess, miscellany, mishmash, mixture, muddle, olio, pastiche, patchwork, potpourri, salmagundi, scramble, shuffle, snarl, tangle, tumble; SEE CONCEPT 432

jumble [v] *mix up, confuse*
clutter, confound, derange, disarrange, disarray, dishevel, disorder, disorganize, disturb, entangle, foul up, mess up, mistake, muddle, rummage, shuffle, snarl, tangle, tumble; SEE CONCEPTS 16,84

jumbled [adj] *confused, mixed-up*
blurred, chaotic, cluttered, disarranged, disordered, disorderly, disorganized, in disarray, messy, misunderstood, out of order, scrambled, tangled, unsettled, unsorted, untidy; SEE CONCEPT 585

jumbo [adj] *gigantic*
colossal, cyclopean, elephantine, giant, huge, immense, large, mammoth, mighty, oversized, prodigious; SEE CONCEPT 781

jump [n1] *leap*
bob, bounce, bound, buck, canter, caper, capriole, dance, dive, drop, fall, gambade, gambol, hop, hopping, hurdle, jar, jerk, jolt, leapfrog, leapfrogging, leaping, lurch, nosedive, plummet, plunge, pounce, rise, saltation, shock, skip, skipping, spring, start, swerve, twitch, upspring, upsurge, vault, wrench; SEE CONCEPT 194

jump [n2] *increase, advantage*
advance, ascent, augmentation, boost, handicap, head start, increment, inflation, rise, spurt, start, upper hand, upsurge, upturn; SEE CONCEPTS 704,763

jump [n3] *obstacle*
bar, barricade, barrier, fence, hurdle, impediment, rail, stretch; SEE CONCEPTS 470,674

jump [v1] *leap, spring*
bail out, barge, bob, bounce, bound, buck, canter, caper, clear, curvet, dive, drop, fall, gambol, hop, hurdle, hurtle, jerk, jiggle, jounce, lollop, lop, lunge, lurch, parachute, plummet, pop, quiver, rattle, ricochet, saltate, shake, skip, sky, somersault, surge, take, top, trip, vault, waver, wobble; SEE CONCEPT 194

jump [v2] *recoil*
bob, bolt, bounce, carom, flinch, jerk, jounce, rebound, ricochet, spring, start, startle, wince; SEE CONCEPT 213

jump [v3] *omit, avoid*
abandon, cancel, clear out, cover, cross out, digress, evade, leave, miss, nullify, overshoot, pass over, skip, switch; SEE CONCEPT 25

jump [v4] *increase*
advance, ascend, boost, escalate, gain, hike, jack up, mount, put up, raise, rise, surge, up; SEE CONCEPTS 236,245,763

jumpy [adj] *nervous*
agitated, antsy*, anxious, apprehensive, creepy*, excitable, excited, fidgety, frisky, high-strung*, jittery, on edge*, on pins and needles*, restless, sensitive, shaky, skittish, spooked, tense, timorous, unrestful; SEE CONCEPTS 401,690

junction/juncture [n1] *link, connection*
alliance, annexation, articulation, assemblage, attachment, bond, coalition, coherence, collocation, combination, combine, concatenation, concourse, concursion, confluence, conjugation, consolidation, convergence, coupling, crossing, crossroads, dovetail, elbow, gathering, gore, hinge, hookup, interface, intersection, joining, joint, knee, linking, meeting, miter, mortise, node, pivot, plug-in, reunion, seam, splice, terminal, tie-in, tie-up, union, weld; SEE CONCEPTS 746,830

juncture [n2] *turning point*
choice, circumstance, condition, contingency, crisis, crossroad, crux, emergency, exigency, instant, meeting point, moment, occasion, pass, pinch, plight, point, position, posture, predicament, quandary, state, status, strait, time, zero hour*; SEE CONCEPTS 388,693,815

jungle [n] *wilderness full of plant and animal life*
boscage, bush, chaparral, forest, labyrinth, maze, morass, primeval forest, tangle, undergrowth, wasteland, web, wood, zoo; SEE CONCEPT 517

junior [adj] *subordinate, younger*
inferior, lesser, lower, minor, second, secondary, second-string*; SEE CONCEPTS 574,578,797

junk [n] *odds and ends; garbage*
clutter, collateral, debris, filth, hogwash*, litter,

jo
ju

miscellany, offal, refuse, rubbish, rubble, rummage, salvage, scrap, trash, waste; SEE CONCEPTS *260,432*

jurisdiction [n] *area of authority*
administration, arbitration, area, authority, bailiwick, bounds, circuit, command, commission, compass, confines, control, discretion, district, domination, dominion, empire, extent, field, hegemony, influence, inquisition, judicature, limits, magistracy, might, orbit, power, prerogative, province, purview, range, reach, reign, right, rule, say, scope, slot, sovereignty, sphere, stomping grounds*, supervision, sway, territory, turf*, zone; SEE CONCEPTS *198,376,651*

jurist [n] *jurisprudent*
attorney, barrister, counsel, counsellor, counselor, defender, judge, justice, lawyer, legal adviser, legal expert, legal scholar, magistrate; SEE CONCEPT *355*

jury [n] *panel that hears legal matter*
board, judges, peers, tribunal; SEE CONCEPTS *299,318*

just [adj 1] *fair, impartial*
aloof, blameless, condign, conscientious, decent, dependable, dispassionate, due, equal, equitable, ethical, evenhanded, fair-minded, good, honest, honorable, lawful, nondiscriminatory, nonpartisan, objective, pure, reliable, right, righteous, rightful, rigid, scrupulous, strict, tried, true, trustworthy, unbiased, uncolored, upright, virtuous; SEE CONCEPTS *319,545*

just [adj2] *accurate, precise*
cogent, correct, exact, faithful, good, justified, normal, proper, regular, right, sound, strict, true, undistorted, veracious, veridical, well-formed, well-grounded; SEE CONCEPTS *535,582*

just [adj3] *suitable, appropriate*
apt, befitting, condign, deserved, due, felicitous, fit, fitting, happy, justified, legitimate, meet, merited, proper, reasonable, requisite, right, rightful, well-deserved; SEE CONCEPT *558*

just [adv1] *definitely*
absolutely, accurately, completely, directly, entirely, exactly, expressly, perfectly, precisely, right, sharp, smack-dab*, square, squarely, unmistakably; SEE CONCEPT *535*

just [adv2] *only now*
almost, a moment ago, approximately, at this moment, barely, by very little, hardly, just a while ago, just now, lately, nearly, now, presently, recently, right now, scarce, scarcely; SEE CONCEPTS *544,820*

just [adv3] *merely*
at most, but, no more than, nothing but, only, plainly, simply, solely; SEE CONCEPT *557*

just about [adv] *almost*
about, all but, approximately, around, as good as, close to, nearly, nigh, not quite, practically, well-nigh; SEE CONCEPTS *762,771,799*

justice [n1] *lawfulness, fairness*
amends, appeal, authority, authorization, charter, code, compensation, consideration, constitutionality, correction, credo, creed, decree, due process, equity, evenness, fair play, fair treatment, hearing, honesty, impartiality, integrity, judicatory, judicature, justness, law, legality, legalization, legal process, legitimacy, litigation, penalty, reasonableness, recompense, rectitude, redress, reparation, review, right, rule, sanction,

sentence, square deal*, truth; SEE CONCEPTS *376,645,691*

justice [n2] *person who oversees court of law*
chancellor, court, judge, magistrate, umpire*; SEE CONCEPT *354*

justifiable [adj] *reasonable, well-founded*
acceptable, admissible, allowable, condonable, defensible, excusable, fair, fit, forgivable, lawful, legit*, legitimate, licit, logical, pardonable, probable, proper, reasonable, remissible, right, rightful, sound, suitable, tenable, understandable, valid, vindicable, warrantable; SEE CONCEPTS *545,558*

justification [n] *reason, excuse*
absolution, account, acquittal, advocacy, answer, apologia, apology, approval, argument, basis, confirmation, defense, exculpation, exoneration, explanation, extenuation, grounds, idea, mitigation, palliation, palliative, plea, pretext, raison d'être, rationale, rationalization, rebuttal, redemption, reply, response, salvation, sanctification, song and dance*, story, support, validation, vindication, warrant, whatfor*, wherefore*, whitewashing*, whole idea*, why and wherefore*; SEE CONCEPT *661*

justify [v] *legitimize, substantiate*
absolve, acquit, advocate, alibi*, answer for, apologize for, approve, argue for, assert, be answerable for, bear out, brief, claim, clear, condone, confirm, contend, cop a plea*, countenance, crawl, defend, do justice to, establish, exculpate, excuse, exonerate, explain, favor, legalize, maintain, make allowances, make good*, palliate, pardon, plead, rationalize, rebut, show cause, speak in favor, square, stand up for, support, sustain, uphold, validate, verify, vindicate, warrant; SEE CONCEPTS *49,57*

justly [adv] *fairly*
accurately, befittingly, beneficently, benevolently, benignly, candidly, charitably, correctly, decently, decorously, duly, duteously, dutifully, equally, equitably, evenhandedly, fitly, fittingly, frankly, helpfully, honestly, honorably, impartially, lawfully, legally, legitimately, moderately, nicely, piously, properly, reasonably, respectably, righteously, rightfully, rightly, straightforwardly, temperately, tolerantly, unreservedly, uprightly, virtuously, well; SEE CONCEPTS *544,545*

jut [v] *extend*
beetle, bulge, elongate, impend, lengthen, overhang, poke, pop, pouch, project, protrude, protuberate, stand out, stick out; SEE CONCEPT *201*

juvenile [adj] *childish*
adolescent, babyish, beardless, blooming, boyish, budding, callow, childlike, developing, formative, fresh, girlish, green, growing, immature, inexperienced, infant, infantile, jejune, junior, kid stuff*, milk-fed*, naive, pubescent, puerile, teenage, tender, undeveloped, unfledged, unripe, unsophisticated, unweaned, vernal, young, younger, youthful; SEE CONCEPTS *401,578,797*

juvenile [n] *young person*
adolescent, boy, child, girl, infant, kid*, minor, youngster, youth; SEE CONCEPT *424*

juvenile delinquent [n] *hooligan, punk*
criminal, first offender, gangster, goon*, hood, hoodlum, punk, rowdy, ruffian, thug, troublemaker; SEE CONCEPT *412*

juxtapose [*v*] *place side by side*
appose, bring near, bring together, connect, pair, place in proximity, set side by side; SEE CONCEPTS *85,113,160*

K

kaput [*adj*] *ruined, wrecked*
all washed up*, belly-up*, burned out, cooked*, dead*, destroyed, done for, down and out, down for the count*, down the drain*, down the tubes*, finished, floored, had it, nonfunctioning, on the skids*, out of business, out of circulation, sunk, totaled, washed up, wiped out; SEE CONCEPT *252*

keel over [*v*] *fall, faint*
black out, capsize, collapse, drop, founder, go down, overturn, pass out, pitch, plunge, slump, swoon, topple, tumble, upset; SEE CONCEPTS *152,181*

keen [*adj1*] *enthusiastic*
agog, alert, animate, animated, anxious, appetent, ardent, athirst, avid, breathless, devoted, dying to*, eager, earnest, ebullient, fervent, fervid, fierce, fond of, gung ho*, impassioned, impatient, intense, intent, interested, lively, perfervid, spirited, sprightly, thirsty, vehement, vivacious, warm, zealous; SEE CONCEPTS *401,403*

keen [*adj2*] *sharp, piercing*
acid, acute, caustic, cutting, edged, extreme, fine, honed, incisive, intense, observant, penetrating, perceptive, pointed, quick-witted, razor-sharp*, sardonic, satirical, strong, tart, trenchant, unblunted; SEE CONCEPT *267*

keen [*adj3*] *intelligent*
astute, bright, brilliant, canny, clever, discerning, discriminating, Einstein*, nobody's fool*, perceptive, perspicacious, quick, sagacious, sapient, sensitive, sharp, sharp as a tack*, shrewd, whiz, wise; SEE CONCEPT *402*

keep [*v1*] *hold, maintain*
accumulate, amass, cache, care for, carry, conduct, conserve, control, deal in, deposit, detain, direct, enjoy, garner, grasp, grip, have, heap, hold back, manage, own, pile, place, possess, preserve, put, put up, reserve, retain, save, season, stack, stock, store, trade in, withhold; SEE CONCEPT *710*

keep [*v2*] *tend; provide for*
administer, attend, board, care for, carry on, command, conduct, continue, defend, direct, endure, feed, foster, guard, look after, maintain, manage, mind, minister to, nourish, nurture, operate, ordain, protect, provision, run, safeguard, shelter, shield, subsidize, support, sustain, victual, watch over; SEE CONCEPTS *110,140*

keep [*v3*] *prevent*
arrest, avert, block, check, constrain, control, curb, delay, detain, deter, hamper, hamstring, hinder, hold back, impede, inhibit, limit, obstruct, restrain, retard, shackle, stall, stop, withhold; SEE CONCEPT *121*

keep [*v4*] *commemorate; pay attention to*
adhere to, bless, celebrate, comply with, consecrate, fulfill, hold, honor, laud, obey, observe, perform, praise, regard, respect, ritualize, sanctify, solemnize; SEE CONCEPT *377*

keep at [*v*] *continue, endure*
be steadfast, carry on, complete, drudge, finish, grind, labor, last, maintain, persevere, persist, remain, slave, stay, stick, toil; SEE CONCEPTS *23,87*

keeper [*n*] *guardian*
archivist, attendant, caretaker, conservator, curator, custodian, defender, guard, jailer, lookout, overseer, protector, sentinel, sentry, steward, superintendent, supervisor, warden; SEE CONCEPTS *414,423*

keep one's cool [*v*] *remain calm*
control one's temper, go with the flow*, keep calm, keep cool*, keep one's shirt on*, restrain oneself; SEE CONCEPTS *121,130,191*

keepsake [*n*] *something precious*
emblem, favor, memento, memorial, relic, remembrance, reminder, souvenir, symbol, token, trophy; SEE CONCEPT *446*

keep up [*v*] *maintain, sustain*
balance, compete, contend, continue, emulate, go on, hold on, keep pace, keep step, match, pace, persevere, preserve, rival, run with, vie; SEE CONCEPTS *23,87,363*

keg [*n*] *barrel*
butt, cask, container, drum, firkin, hogshead, pipe, tub, tun, vat; SEE CONCEPT *494*

ken [*n*] *perception*
acumen, apprehending, apprehension, attention, attitude, awareness, cognizance, comprehension, concept, consciousness, grasp, idea, impression, insight, judgment, knowledge, light, notion, picture, realizing, recognition, sense, sight, understanding, vision; SEE CONCEPTS *409,410,689*

kernel [*n*] *seed, essence*
atom, bit, center, core, crux, fruit, germ, gist, grain, heart, hub, keynote, marrow, matter, meat, morsel, nub, nubbin, nut, part, piece, pith, root, substance, upshot; SEE CONCEPTS *668,826*

kettle [*n*] *metal pot*
boiler, cauldron, pot, steamer, teakettle, vat, vessel; SEE CONCEPT *494*

key [*adj*] *essential, important*
basic, chief, crucial, decisive, fundamental, indispensable, leading, main, major, material, pivotal, primary, principal, vital; SEE CONCEPT *568*

key [*n1*] *item that unlocks*
latchkey, opener, passkey, screw*, skeleton; SEE CONCEPT *499*

key [*n2*] *answer, solution*
blueprint, brand, cipher, clue, code, core, crux, cue, earmark, explanation, fulcrum, guide, hinge, index, indicator, interpretation, lead, lever, marker, means, nexus, nucleus, passport, password, pivot, pointer, root, sign, symptom, ticket, translation; SEE CONCEPTS *274,668*

keynote/keystone [*n*] *essence, theme*
basic idea, basis, center, core, cornerstone, criterion, crux, gist, heart, idea, kernel, linchpin, mainspring, marrow, measure, motive, nub, pith, principle, root, source, spring, standard, substance; SEE CONCEPTS *532,661,688*

kick [*n1*] *thrill, enjoyment*
bang*, buzz*, excitement, fun, gratification, hoot*, joy, pleasure, refreshment, sensation, stimulation, wallop*; SEE CONCEPTS *388,410*

kick [*n2*] *power, strength*
backlash, blow, boot*, force, intensity, jar, jolt,

ju
ki

pep, punch, pungency, snap, sparkle, tang, verve, vitality, zest, zing*; SEE CONCEPTS 641,732

kick [*v1*] *hit with foot*
boot, calcitrate, dropkick, give the foot, jolt, punt; SEE CONCEPT 189

kick [*v2*] *complain*
anathematize, carp, combat, condemn, criticize, curse, damn, except, execrate, expostulate, fight, fuss, gripe, grumble, inveigh, mumble, object, oppose, protest, rebel, remonstrate, repine, resist, spurn, wail, whine, withstand; SEE CONCEPT 52

kick [*v3*] *quit a habit*
abandon, desist, give up, go cold turkey*, leave off, stop; SEE CONCEPT 234

kickback [*n*] *bribe*
cut, gift, graft, money under the table*, oil*, payment, payoff, payola, percentage, recompense, reward, share; SEE CONCEPTS 192,344

kick back [*v*] *relax*
breathe easy*, calm down*, catch one's breath, chill out*, collect oneself, compose oneself, cool off*, feel at home, hang loose*, lie down, loosen up, make oneself at home*, mellow out*, put one's feet up*, recline, rest, settle back, sit around, sit back, take a break*, take a breather*, take a load off*, take it easy*, take ten*, unwind, wind down; SEE CONCEPT 210

kick in [*v*] *contribute*
ante up, chip in, commit, dish out*, dole out*, donate, fork over*, furnish, give, hand out, hand over, pitch in*, pony up*, provide; SEE CONCEPTS 108,140

kick out [*v*] *get rid of*
ax, boot*, bounce*, can*, cashier*, chase, chuck, discharge, dismiss, drop, eject, evict, expel, extrude, fire, oust, out, reject, remove, sack*, throw out, toss out; SEE CONCEPTS 180,351,384

kid [*n*] *young person*
baby, bairn, boy, child, daughter, girl, infant, juvenile, lad, lass, little one*, son, teenager, tot, youngster, youth; SEE CONCEPTS 414,424

kid [*v*] *fool, ridicule*
bamboozle*, banter, beguile, bother, cozen, delude, dupe, flimflam*, fun*, gull, hoax, hoodwink, jape, jest, joke, jolly, josh, make fun of, make sport of, mock, pretend, rag*, razz, rib, roast, spoof, tease, trick; SEE CONCEPTS 59,273

kid around [*v*] *tease*
annoy, badger, bait, banter, bother, chaff, disturb, dog*, fool around, give a hard time*, goad, harass, josh, lead on*, mock, needle*, nudge, pester, pick on*, rag*, razz*, rib*, ride, ridicule, roast*, taunt; SEE CONCEPTS 7,11,19,22

kidnap [*v*] *abduct; hold for ransom*
bodysnatch*, bundle off, capture, carry away, carry off, coax, decoy, entice, grab, hijack, impress, inveigh, lay hands on, lure, make off with*, pirate, remove, run away with, seduce, seize, shanghai*, skyjack, snatch, spirit away*, steal, waylay; SEE CONCEPTS 90,139

kill [*v1*] *deprive of existence; destroy*
annihilate, asphyxiate, assassinate, crucify, dispatch, do away with*, do in*, drown, dump, electrocute, eradicate, erase*, execute, exterminate, extirpate, finish, garrote, get*, guillotine, hang, hit*, immolate, liquidate, lynch, massacre, murder, neutralize, obliterate, off*, poison, polish off*, put away*, put to death, rub out*, sacrifice, slaughter, slay, smother, snuff, strangle, suffocate, waste*, wipe out*, X-out*, zap*; SEE CONCEPT 252

kill [*v2*] *turn off; cancel*
annul, cease, counteract, deaden, defeat, extinguish, forbid, halt, negative, neutralize, nix*, nullify, prohibit, quash, quell, recant, refuse, revoke, ruin, scotch*, shut off, smother, stifle, still, stop, suppress, turn out, veto; SEE CONCEPTS 121,239

killer [*n*] *murderer*
assassin, butcher, cut-throat, executioner, exterminator, gunman/woman, gunperson, hitman/woman, hit person, hunter, slayer, soldier; SEE CONCEPT 412

killing [*n*] *murder*
assassination, bloodshed, bumping off*, capital punishment, carnage, execution, extermination, homicide, manslaughter, massacre, slaughter, slaying; SEE CONCEPTS 192,252

killjoy [*n*] *spoilsport*
complainer, dampener, doomsdayer, grinch*, grouch*, moaner, partypooper, pessimist, prophet of doom*, stick in the mud*, wet blanket*, whiner; SEE CONCEPTS 412,423

kin [*n*] *blood relative*
affinity, blood, clan, connection, consanguinity, cousin, extraction, family, folk, house, kindred, kinsfolk, kinship, kinsperson, kith, lineage, member, people, race, relation, relationship, sibling, stock, tribe; SEE CONCEPTS 296,414,421

kind [*adj*] *generous, good*
affectionate, all heart*, altruistic, amiable, amicable, beneficent, benevolent, benign, big, bleeding-heart*, bounteous, charitable, clement, compassionate, congenial, considerate, cordial, courteous, eleemosynary, friendly, gentle, good-hearted, gracious, heart in right place*, humane, humanitarian, indulgent, kindhearted, kindly, lenient, loving, mild, neighborly, obliging, philanthropic, propitious, softhearted, soft touch, sympathetic, tenderhearted, thoughtful, tolerant, understanding; SEE CONCEPTS 401,404,542

kind [*n1*] *class, species*
brand, breed, classification, family, genus, ilk, kin, order, race, set, sort, type, variety; SEE CONCEPT 378

kind [*n2*] *type, character*
breed, complexion, connection, denomination, description, designation, essence, fiber, gender, habit, ilk, likes, lot, manner, mold, nature, number, persuasion, set, sort, stamp, stripe, style, temperament, tendency, tribe, variety, way; SEE CONCEPTS 411,673

kindhearted [*adj*] *compassionate, helpful*
altruistic, amiable, amicable, considerate, generous, good, good-natured, gracious, humane, kind, merciful, responsive, softhearted, sympathetic, tender, tenderhearted, warm, warmhearted; SEE CONCEPTS 404,542

kindle [*v1*] *start a fire*
blaze, burn, fire, flame, flare, glow, ignite, inflame, light, set alight, set fire; SEE CONCEPT 249

kindle [*v2*] *excite, incite*
agitate, animate, arouse, awaken, bestir, burn up*, challenge, egg on*, enkindle, exasperate, fire up*, foment, get smoking*, induce, inflame, inspire, key up*, provoke, rally, rouse, sharpen, stimulate, stir, thrill, turn on*, wake, waken, whet, work up*; SEE CONCEPTS 7,14,22,221

kindly [*adj*] *compassionate, helpful*
attentive, beneficial, benevolent, benign, benignant, cool, cordial, favorable, friendly, generous, genial, gentle, good, good-hearted, good-natured, gracious, hearty, humane, kind, kindhearted, mellow, merciful, mild, neighborly, pleasant, polite, sociable, sympathetic, thoughtful, warm; SEE CONCEPTS 404,542

kindly [*adv*] *with compassion*
affectionately, agreeably, benevolently, benignly, carefully, charitably, compassionately, considerately, cordially, courteously, delicately, generously, genially, good-naturedly, graciously, heedfully, helpfully, humanely, politely, solicitously, sympathetically, tenderly, thoughtfully, tolerantly, understandingly, well; SEE CONCEPTS 542,544

kindness [*n1*] *compassion, generosity*
affection, altruism, amiability, beneficence, benevolence, charity, clemency, consideration, cordiality, courtesy, decency, delicacy, fellow feeling, forbearance, gentleness, good intention, goodness, good will, grace, graciousness, heart, helpfulness, hospitality, humanity, indulgence, kindliness, magnanimity, mildness, patience, philanthropy, serviceability, solicitousness, solicitude, sweetness, sympathy, tact, tenderness, thoughtfulness, tolerance, understanding, unselfishness; SEE CONCEPTS 633,657

kindness [*n2*] *helping act; service*
accommodation, aid, alms, assistance, benediction, benefaction, benevolence, benison, blessing, boon, boost, bounty, charity, dispensation, favor, generosity, good deed, good turn, help, indulgence, lift, mercy, philanthropy, relief, succor; SEE CONCEPTS 110,657

kindred [*adj*] *corresponding, matching*
affiliated, agnate, akin, alike, allied, analogous, cognate, congeneric, congenial, connate, connatural, consanguine, germane, homogeneous, incident, kin, likable, parallel, related, similar; SEE CONCEPT 563

kindred [*n*] *blood relative*
affinity, blood, clan, connection, consanguinity, cousin, family, flesh, folk, homefolk, house, kin, kinsfolk, kinsperson, lineage, race, relation, relationship, stock, tribe; SEE CONCEPTS 296,414,421

kingdom [*n*] *historically, an area ruled by a monarch*
commonwealth, country, county, crown, division, domain, dominion, dynasty, empire, field, lands, monarchy, nation, possessions, principality, province, realm, reign, rule, scepter, sovereignty, sphere, state, suzerainty, sway, territory, throne, tract; SEE CONCEPTS 508,510

kink [*n1*] *bend, twist*
coil, corkscrew, crimp, crinkle, curl, curve, entanglement, frizz, knot, loop, tangle, wrinkle; SEE CONCEPT 436

kink [*n2*] *spasm of muscular tissue*
charley horse*, cramp, crick, knot, muscle spasm, pain, pang, pinch, stab, stitch, tweak, twinge; SEE CONCEPTS 185,728

kink [*n3*] *complication*
defect, difficulty, flaw, hitch, impediment, imperfection, knot, tangle; SEE CONCEPT 674

kink [*n4*] *person's idiosyncrasy*
eccentricity, fetish, foible, notion, peculiarity, quirk, singularity, vagary, whim; SEE CONCEPT 411

kinky [*adj1*] *twisted*
coiled, crimped, curled, curly, frizzled, frizzy, knotted, matted, matty, rolled, tangled; SEE CONCEPT 486

kinky [*adj2*] *bizarre, perverted*
degenerated, depraved, deviant, eccentric, far-out, licentious, odd, outlandish, outre, peculiar, queer, quirky, sick, strange, unconventional, unnatural, unusual, warped, weird; SEE CONCEPTS 372,542,589

kinship [*n*] *family relationship*
affinity, blood, clan, family, flesh, folk, kin, kindred, lineage, relations, tribe; SEE CONCEPTS 296,414,421

kiosk [*n*] *gazebo*
bandstand, booth, rotunda, stall, stand; SEE CONCEPTS 442,443

kismet [*n*] *fate, fortune*
chance, destination, destiny, divine will*, doom, handwriting on the wall*, horoscope, karma, Lady Luck*, lot, luck, portion, predestination, providence; SEE CONCEPT 679

kiss [*n*] *touching lips to another*
butterfly*, caress, embrace, endearment, osculation, peck, salutation, salute, smack*, smooch*; SEE CONCEPTS 185,375

kiss [*v*] *touch one's lips to another's*
blow, brush, butterfly*, French*, glance, graze, greet, lip*, make out*, mush*, neck*, osculate, peck, pucker up*, salute, smack*, smooch*; SEE CONCEPTS 185,375

kit [*n*] *provisions, equipment*
accoutrements, apparatus, assortment, bag, collection, container, effects, gear, impedimenta, implements, material, outfit, pack, paraphernalia, rig, satchel, selection, set, stock, stuff, suitcase, supplies, tackle, things, tools, trappings, utensils; SEE CONCEPTS 494,496

kitchen [*n*] *room for cooking food*
canteen, cookery, cookhouse, cook's room, cuisine, eat-in, gallery, galley, kitchenette, mess, scullery; SEE CONCEPT 448

kittenish [*adj*] *frisky, playful*
childish, coquettish, coy, elvish, flirtatious, frolicsome, fun-loving, impish, jaunty, mischievous, sportive; SEE CONCEPT 401

klutz [*n*] *clumsy person*
bungler, butterfingers*, dolt, dullard, lummox, oaf; SEE CONCEPT 412

knack [*n*] *ability, talent*
adroitness, aptitude, aptness, bent, capacity, command, dexterity, expertise, expertism, expertness, facility, faculty, flair, forte, genius, gift, handiness, hang of it*, head*, ingenuity, know-how, mastership, nose*, propensity, quickness, readiness, savvy*, set, skill, skillfulness, trick, turn; SEE CONCEPTS 409,630

knead [*v*] *mix by pressing*
aerate, alter, blend, form, manipulate, massage, mold, ply, press, push, rub, shape, squeeze, stroke, twist, work; SEE CONCEPTS 170,208

kneel [*v*] *get down on one's knees*
bow, bow down, curtsey, do obeisance, genuflect, kowtow, prostrate oneself, stoop; SEE CONCEPT 154

knickknack [*n*] *trinket; decorative piece*
bagatelle, bauble, bibelot, bric-a-brac, conversation piece, curio, curiosity, device, embellishment, flummery, frill, furbelow, gadget*, miniature, notion, novelty, objet d'art, ornament,

ki
kn

plaything*, showpiece, souvenir, thingamajig*, toy, trapping, trifle, whatnot*, whimsy; SEE CONCEPTS 259,260,446

knife [*n*] *cutting tool*
bayonet, blade, bolo, cutlass, cutter, cutting edge, dagger, edge, lance, lancet, machete, point, ripper, sabre, scalpel, scimitar, scythe, shank, shiv, sickle, skewer, skiver, steel, stiletto, switchblade, sword, tickler; SEE CONCEPTS 495,499

knife [*v*] *stab with pointed tool*
brand, carve, chop down, clip, cut, hurt, impale, jag, kill, lacerate, lance, open up, pierce, shank, shiv, slash, slice, spit, stick, thrust, wound; SEE CONCEPTS 176,220,246

knit [*v*] *intertwine*
affiliate, affix, ally, bind, cable, connect, contract, crochet, fasten, heal, interlace, intermingle, join, link, loop, mend, net, purl, repair, secure, sew, spin, tie, unite, weave, web; SEE CONCEPTS 113,202,218

knob [*n*] *lump, handle*
bulge, bulk, bump, bunch, doorknob, hump, knot, knurl, latch, lever, nub, opener, projection, protrusion, protuberance, snag, stud, swell, swelling, trigger, tumor; SEE CONCEPTS 445,471

knock [*n1*] *pushing, striking*
beating, blow, box, clip, conk, cuff, hammering, hit, injury, lick, rap, slap, smack, swat, swipe, thump, whack; SEE CONCEPT 189

knock [*n2*] *strong criticism*
blame, censure, condemnation, defeat, failure, flak, pan, rap, rebuff, rejection, reversal, setback, stricture, swipe; SEE CONCEPTS 52,278

knock [*v1*] *push over; strike*
abuse, bash, batter, beat, beat up, bob, bruise, buffet, clap, clout, cuff, damage, deck, drub*, fell, flatten, floor, hit, hurt, KO*, level, maltreat, manhandle, maul, mistreat, pound, punch, rap, roughhouse, slap, smack, tap, thrash, thump, thwack*, total, wallop, whack*, wound; SEE CONCEPT 189

knock [*v2*] *criticize harshly*
abuse, alive*, belittle, blame, carp, cavil, censure, condemn, denounce, denunciate, deprecate, disparage, find fault, lambaste, reprehend, reprobate, run down*, skin*, slam; SEE CONCEPT 52

knock about/knock around [*v*] *roam, wander*
drift, ramble, range, rove, traipse, travel, walk; SEE CONCEPTS 151,224

knock off [*v1*] *kill*
assassinate, do away with*, do in*, dust*, eliminate, execute, finish, liquidate, murder, rub out*, shoot, slay, stab, waste; SEE CONCEPT 252

knock off [*v2*] *steal*
filch, knock over, loot, pilfer, pinch, plunder, purloin, ransack, relieve, rifle, rip off*, rob, thieve; SEE CONCEPTS 139,192

knock off [*v3*] *stop action; accomplish*
achieve, cease, complete, conclude, desist, discontinue, eliminate, finish, give over, halt, leave off, quit, stop work, succeed, surcease, terminate; SEE CONCEPTS 119,234

knoll [*n*] *small hill*
acclivity, ascent, bluff, butte, cliff, drift, dune, elevation, esker, headland, heap, highland, hillock, hilltop, hummock, inclination, incline, knoll, mesa, mound, mount, precipice, prominence, promontory, ridge, rise, slope, summit; SEE CONCEPT 509

knot [*n1*] *bow, loop*
bond, braid, bunch, coil, connection, contortion entanglement, gnarl, helix, hitch, joint, kink, ligament, ligature, link, mat, nexus, perplexity rosette, screw, snag, snarl, spiral, splice, tangle tie, twirl, twist, vinculum, warp, whirl, whorl yoke; SEE CONCEPTS 436,471

knot [*n2*] *lump; crowd*
aggregation, assemblage, assortment, band bunch, circle, clique, clump, cluster, collection company, crew, gang, gathering, group, heap mass, mob, pack, pile, set, squad, swarm, tuft SEE CONCEPT 432

knot [*v*] *weave, complicate*
bind, cord, entangle, knit, loop, secure, tat tether, tie; SEE CONCEPTS 85,113,160

knotty [*adj*] *troublesome*
baffling, complex, complicated, difficult, effort ful, elaborate, formidable, Gordian*, hard, intricate, involved, labyrinthine, mazy, mystifying perplexing, problematical, puzzling, ramified, re ticular, rough, rugged, sophisticated, sticky*, terrible, thorny*, tough, tricky, uphill*; SEE CONCEPTS 529,565

know [*v1*] *understand information*
apperceive, appreciate, apprehend, be acquainted, be cognizant, be conversant in, be informed, be learned, be master of, be read, be schooled, be versed, cognize, comprehend, differentiate, discern, discriminate, distinguish, experience, fathom, feel certain, get the idea*, grasp, have, have down pat*, have information have knowledge of, keep up on, ken, learn, notice, on top of*, perceive, prize, realize, recognize, see, undergo; SEE CONCEPTS 15,38

know [*v2*] *be familiar with*
associate, be acquainted with, be friends with, experience, feel, fraternize, get acquainted, have dealings with, identify, savor, see, sustain, taste, undergo; SEE CONCEPT 384

know-how [*n*] *skill, talent*
ability, adroitness, aptitude, art, background, capability, command, craft, cunning, dexterity, experience, expertise, expertness, faculty, flair, ingenuity, knack, knowledge, proficiency, savoir-faire, wisdom; SEE CONCEPTS 409,630

knowing [*adj*] *experienced, aware*
alive, apprehensive, astute, awake, brainy, bright, brilliant, canny, clever, cognizant, competent, conscious, conversant, cool*, crack*, deliberate, discerning, expert, insightful, intelligent, intended, intentional, judicious, knowledgeable, observant, perceiving, percipient, qualified, quick, quick-witted, sagacious, sage, sensible, sentient, sharp, skillful, slick*, smart, sophic, sophisticated, tuned-in, vigilant, watchful, well-informed, wise, with-it, witting, worldly, worldly-wise; SEE CONCEPT 402

know-it-all [*n*] *intellectual, smart aleck*
braggart, brain*, smarty-pants*, walking encyclopedia, windbag, wiseacre, wise guy*; SEE CONCEPTS 412,423

knowledge [*n*] *person's understanding; information*
ability, accomplishments, acquaintance, apprehension, attainments, awareness, cognition, comprehension, consciousness, dirt*, discernment, doctrine, dogma, dope*, education, enlightenment, erudition, expertise, facts, familiarity, goods*, grasp, inside story*, insight, instruction,

intelligence, judgment, know-how*, learning, light*, lore, observation, philosophy, picture, power*, principles, proficiency, recognition, scholarship, schooling, science, scoop*, substance, theory, tuition, wisdom; SEE CONCEPTS 274,409,529

knowledgeable [*adj*] *aware, educated*
abreast, acquainted, alert, appreciative, apprised, au courant, au fait, brainy*, bright, brilliant, clever, cognizant, conscious, conversant, discerning, erudite, experienced, familiar, informed, insightful, intelligent, in the know, knowing, learned, lettered, omniscient, perceptive, plugged in*, posted, prescient, privy, quick-witted, sagacious, sage, savvy, scholarly, sensible, sharp, smart, sophic, sophisticated, tuned-in*, understanding, versed, well-informed, well-rounded, wise, with-it; SEE CONCEPT 402

known [*adj*] *famous, popular*
accepted, acknowledged, admitted, avowed, celebrated, certified, common, confessed, conscious, down pat*, established, familiar, hackneyed, manifest, noted, notorious, obvious, patent, plain, proverbial, published, received, recognized, well-known; SEE CONCEPTS 529,567,576

knurled [*adj*] *knotted*
bumpy, coarse, gnarled, knobby, knotty, rough; SEE CONCEPTS 485,606

kook [*n*] *eccentric person*
crackpot, crank, crazy*, dingbat*, flake*, fruitcake*, lamebrain, lunatic, nut, screwball*, wacko*, weirdo; SEE CONCEPTS 412,423

kosher [*adj1*] *ritually proper*
apropos, clean, decent, ritually pure, undefiled; SEE CONCEPTS 401,404

kosher [*adj2*] *legitimate*
acceptable, according to law, authentic, genuine, legal, permissible, permitted, proper; SEE CONCEPTS 319,558,582

kowtow [*v*] *grovel*
bow, brownnose*, cave in*, court, cower, cringe, fawn, flatter, fold, genuflect, give in, go along with, kneel, knuckle under, lie down and roll over*, pander, prostrate, say uncle*, stoop, toe the mark*; SEE CONCEPT 384

kudos [*n*] *praise, acclaim*
applause, credit, distinction, eminence, esteem, fame, flattery, glory, honor, illustriousness, laudation, notability, pat on the back*, plaudits, plum*, PR*, preeminence, prestige, prominence, puff*, pumping up*, raves*, regard, renown, repute, strokes*; SEE CONCEPTS 69,268

L

label [*n*] *marker, description; brand*
characterization, classification, company, design, epithet, hallmark, identification, insignia, logo, mark, number, price mark, stamp, sticker, tag, tally, ticket, trademark; SEE CONCEPTS 268,270,284

label [*v*] *mark, describe; brand*
call, characterize, class, classify, define, designate, identify, name, specify, stamp, sticker, tag, tally; SEE CONCEPTS 62,79

labor [*n1*] *work, undertaking*
activity, chore, daily grind, diligence, drudgery, effort, employment, endeavor, energy, exercise, exertion, grind*, gruntwork*, industry, job, moonlight*, operation, pains*, pull, push, strain, stress, struggle, sweat, toil, travail; SEE CONCEPTS 87,100,351,360,362

labor [*n2*] *person(s) performing service*
apprentice, blue collar, breadwinner, employee, hack*, hand*, hard hat*, help, helper, hireling, instrument, laborer, learner, operative, prentice, proletariat, rank and file*, toiler, worker, work force, working people; SEE CONCEPTS 325,348

labor [*n3*] *childbirth process*
birth, birth pangs, childbearing, contractions, delivery, giving birth, pains, parturition, throes, travail; SEE CONCEPT 374

labor [*v*] *work very hard*
bear down, cultivate, drive, drudge, endeavor, exert oneself, grind, plod, plug away*, pour it on*, slave, strain, strive, struggle, sweat, tend, toil, travail, work oneself to the bone*; SEE CONCEPTS 87,100

laboratory [*n*] *testing room*
chemistry laboratory, lab, research laboratory, workshop; SEE CONCEPTS 312,439,441,448,449

labored [*adj*] *difficult to understand, unclear*
affected, arduous, awkward, clumsy, contrived, effortful, forced, hard, heavy, inept, maladroit, operose, overdone, overwrought, ponderous, stiff, strained, strenuous, studied, toilsome, unnatural, uphill*, weighty; SEE CONCEPT 538

laborer [*n*] *worker*
blue-collar worker, drudge, farmhand, grunt, hand, hireling, manual worker, migrant worker, peon, unskilled worker, working man/woman, working stiff*; SEE CONCEPT 348

laborious [*adj1*] *hard, difficult*
arduous, backbreaking, burdensome, effortful, fatiguing, forced, heavy, herculean*, labored, onerous, operose, ponderous, rough go*, stiff, strained, strenuous, tiresome, toilsome, tough, tough job*, wearing, wearisome, wicked*; SEE CONCEPTS 538,565

laborious [*adj2*] *hardworking*
active, assiduous, diligent, indefatigable, industrious, operose, painstaking, persevering, sedulous, tireless, unflagging; SEE CONCEPTS 538,550

labyrinth [*n*] *maze, complexity*
coil, complication, convolution, entanglement, intricacy, jungle, knot, mesh, morass, perplexity, problem, puzzle, riddle, skein, snarl, tangle, web; SEE CONCEPTS 436,663,666

lace [*n1*] *netted material*
appliqué, banding, border, crochet, edging, filigree, mesh, net, netting, openwork, ornament, tatting, threadwork, tissue, trim, trimming; SEE CONCEPT 473

lace [*n2*] *string used to connect*
band, cord, rope, shoelace, thong, thread, tie; SEE CONCEPT 475

lace [*v*] *fasten, intertwine*
add, attach, bind, close, do up, fortify, interlace, interweave, mix, plat, spike, strap, thread, tie, twine; SEE CONCEPT 113

lacerate [*v*] *tear, cut; wound*
claw, gash, harm, hurt, injure, jag, lance, maim, mangle, mutilate, puncture, rend, rip, score, serrate, slash, stab, torment, torture; SEE CONCEPTS 137,176,214,220,246

kn
la

laceration [n] *cut, wound*
gash, injury, lesion, pierce, rip, slash, slice, slit, stab, tear; SEE CONCEPT *309*

lack [n] *deficiency, need*
abridgement, absence, curtailment, dearth, decrease, default, defect, deficit, depletion, deprivation, destitution, distress, exigency, exiguity, inadequacy, inferiority, insufficience, insufficiency, loss, meagerness, miss, necessity, paucity, poverty, privation, reduction, retrenchment, scantiness, scarcity, shortage, shortcoming, shortfall, shortness, shrinkage, shrinking, slightness, stint, want; SEE CONCEPTS *707,709*

lack [v] *do not have*
be deficient in, be short of, be without, have need of, hurting for*, minus, miss, need, not got* out, require, too little too late*, want; SEE CONCEPTS *20,646*

lackadaisical [adj] *careless, indifferent*
abstracted, apathetic, daydreaming, disinterested, dreamy, dull, energyless, enervated, faineant, halfhearted, idle, inattentive, incurious, indolent, inert, laid-back, languid, languishing, languorous, lazy, lethargic, limp, listless, moony*, passive, romantic, sentimental, slothful, spiritless, spring fever*, unconcerned; SEE CONCEPTS *403,542,544*

lacking [adj] *wanting, deficient*
can't cut it*, coming up short*, defective, deprived of, flawed, impaired, inadequate, incomplete, minus, missing, needed, needing, not hacking it*, not making it*, sans, short, without; SEE CONCEPTS *546,771*

lackluster [adj] *dull, lifeless*
blah*, blind, boring, colorless, dark, dead, dim, drab, draggy*, dry, flat*, ho-hum*, laid-back*, leaden, lusterless, matte, muted, nothing*, obscure, pabulum*, prosaic, sombre, unimaginative, uninspired, vanilla*, vapid, zero*; SEE CONCEPTS *542,548,617*

laconic [adj] *short, to the point*
breviloquent, brief, brusque, compact, compendiary, compendious, concise, crisp, curt, pithy, sententious, short and sweet*, succinct, terse; SEE CONCEPTS *267,773,798*

lacquer [n] *coating*
covering, finish, glaze, lamination, layer, varnish, veneer; SEE CONCEPT *475*

lacy [adj] *delicate, netlike*
elegant, fancy, filigree, fine, frilly, gauzy, gossamer, lacelike, meshy, open, ornate, patterned, sheer, thin, transparent; SEE CONCEPT *606*

lad [n] *young man*
boy, buddy, child, fellow, guy, half-pint*, juvenile, kid*, runt*, schoolboy, son, stripling, youngster, youth; SEE CONCEPTS *419,424*

laden [adj] *loaded down*
burdened, charged, encumbered, fraught, full, hampered, oppressed, taxed, weighed down, weighted; SEE CONCEPTS *485,538*

lag [v] *move slowly; delay*
be behind, dally, dawdle, decrease, dillydally*, diminish, drag, drag one's feet*, ebb, fail, fall off, falter, flag, get no place fast*, hang back, hobble, idle, inch, inch along*, jelly, limp, linger, loiter, lose strength, lounge, plod, poke, procrastinate, put off, retard, saunter, shuffle, slacken, slouch, slow, slow up, stagger, stay, straggle, tail, tarry, tool, trail, trudge, wane; SEE CONCEPTS *151,153*

laggard [n] *straggler*
dawdler, idler, lingerer, loafer, lounger, slowpoke, slow starter; SEE CONCEPT *151*

lagoon [n] *shallow body of water*
bayou, gulf, marsh, pond, pool, shallows, shoal, tidal pond; SEE CONCEPT *514*

laid-back [adj] *relaxed*
easygoing, lax, low-pressure, mellow, undemanding, unhurried; SEE CONCEPT *404*

lair [n] *hideout, habitat*
burrow, cave, den, earth, form, hideaway, hole, nest, pen, refuge, resting place, retreat, sanctuary; SEE CONCEPT *515*

laissez-faire [n] *free enterprise, for the most part unrestrained by law*
free trade, indifference, individualism, live and let live*, neutrality, nonintervention; SEE CONCEPTS *388,691*

lake [n] *inland body of water*
basin, creek, inland sea, lagoon, lakelet, loch, mere, millpond, mouth, pond, pool, reservoir, sluice, spring, tarn; SEE CONCEPT *514*

lambaste [v] *punish, beat*
assail, attack, berate, blister, bludgeon, castigate, censure, criticize, cudgel, denounce, excoriate, flay, flog, hammer, hit, lash into*, pan, pelt, pound, pummel, rake over the coals*, read the riot act*, rebuke, reprimand, rip into, roast, scathe, scold, scorch, scourge, shellac, slam, slap, slash, smear, smother, strike, thrash, trim, upbraid, wallop, whip; SEE CONCEPTS *52,54,86*

lame [adj] *unable to walk properly*
bruised, deformed, disabled, game, gimp, gimpy, halt, handicapped, hobbling, limping, pained, raw, sidelined, sore, stiff; SEE CONCEPTS *314,489*

lame [adj2] *feeble, weak*
faltering, faulty, flabby, flimsy, inadequate, ineffective, inefficient, insufficient, poor, thin, unconvincing, unpersuasive, unpleasing, unsatisfactory, unsuitable; SEE CONCEPTS *558,570*

lament [v] *to mourn or grieve deeply*
bawl, beat one's breast*, bemoan, bewail, bleed, cry, deplore, eat one's heart out*, howl, hurt, kick self*, moan, rain, regret, repine, rue, sing, sob, sorrow, take it hard*, wail, weep; SEE CONCEPTS *52,54*

lamentable [adj] *upsetting, miserable*
afflictive, awful, bad, calamitous, deplorable, dire, dirty, distressing, doleful, dolorous, godawful, grievous, grim, heartbreaking, hurting, lousy, low, lugubrious, meager, mean, melancholy, mournful, pitiful, plaintive, poor, regretful, rotten, rueful, sad, sorrowful, stinking, tragic, unfavorable, unfortunate, unsatisfactory, woeful, wretched; SEE CONCEPTS *529,537*

lament/lamentation [n] *grief, complaint*
complaining, dirge, elegy, grieving, jeremiad, keen, keening, lament, moan, moaning, mourning, plaint, requiem, sob, sobbing, sorrow, tears, threnody, ululation, wail, wailing, weeping; SEE CONCEPTS *29,278,410*

laminate [v] *cover with veneer*
coat, exfoliate, face, flake, foil, foliate, layer, overlayer, plate, separate, split, stratify, veneer; SEE CONCEPT *172*

lamp [n] *lantern*
beacon, flashlight, gas lamp, gaslight, hurricane lamp, kerosene lamp, light, searchlight, torch; SEE CONCEPTS *620,624,628,810*

ampoon [n] *parody, satire*
burlesque, caricature, invective, pasquil, pasquinade, pastiche, ridicule, roast*, send-up*, skit, squib, takedown, takeoff*; SEE CONCEPTS 263,273

ampoon [v] *ridicule, make fun of*
burlesque, caricature, jape, mock, parody, pasquinade, put on*, rail, roast*, satirize, send up*, squib, take off*, travesty; SEE CONCEPT 273

ance [v] *pierce*
bore, cut, cut into, gash, gore, incise, penetrate, prick, puncture, slash, slice, slit, stab, stick into; SEE CONCEPTS 137,159,176,220

and [n] *earth's surface; ownable property*
acreage, acres, area, beach, continent, country, countryside, dirt, district, earth, estate, expanse, extent, farming, farmland, field, ground, grounds, holding, home, homeland, loam, mainland, manor, nation, old sod, parcel, plot, province, purlieu, quarry, quinta, ranch, real estate, realty, region, shore, sod, soil, stretch, sweep, terra firma, terrain, territory, tillage, tract; SEE CONCEPTS 508,509,510,515

and [v] *arrive, come to rest on*
alight, berth, bring in, check in, come ashore, come down, come in, come to berth, debark, descend upon, disembark, ditch, dock, drop anchor, flatten out, get down, ground, level off, light on, make land, pilot, put down, put in, set down, set on deck, settle, sit down, splash down, steer, take down, thump, touch down; SEE CONCEPTS 159,181

and [v2] *achieve, acquire*
annex, bring in, gain, get, have, obtain, pick up, procure, secure, win; SEE CONCEPTS 120,706

andfill [n] *dump*
ash heap*, depot, disposal area, dumping ground, garbage lot, hazardous waste dump, junk pile*, junkyard, recycling station, refuse heap, rubbish pile, toxic waste site, transfer station; SEE CONCEPTS 438,449,680

andlord [n] *owner of property leased*
freeholder, hotelier, hotelkeeper, innkeeper, lessor, property owner, proprietor, saw, squire; SEE CONCEPT 347

andmark [nl] *historical or notable sight*
battleground, benchmark, bend, blaze, feature, fragment, guide, hill, mark, marker, memorial, milepost, milestone, monument, mountain, museum, promontory, remnant, ruins, souvenir, specimen, stone, survival, trace, tree, vantage point, vestige, waypost; SEE CONCEPTS 198,284,447

andmark [n2] *turning point*
crisis, event, milepost, milestone, stage, watershed, waypost; SEE CONCEPTS 696,817

andscape [n] *countryside; picture of countryside*
mural, outlook, painting, panorama, photograph, prospect, scene, scenery, sketch, view, vista; SEE CONCEPTS 259,509

andslide [nl] *landslip*
avalanche, earthfall, mudslide, rockslide, snowslide; SEE CONCEPTS 509,524,786

andslide [n2] *great victory*
advantage, clean sweep*, conquest, defeat, grand slam*, killing*, overthrow, superiority, sweep, triumph, win; SEE CONCEPTS 95,671,706,832

ane [n] *road*
alley, artery, avenue, back street, boulevard, byway, drive, expressway, highway, parkway,

passage, pathway, roadway, route, street, thoroughfare, throughway, thruway, turnpike; SEE CONCEPT 501

language [n] *system of words for communication*
accent, argot, articulation, brogue, cant, communication, conversation, dialect, diction, dictionary, discourse, doublespeak*, expression, gibberish, idiom, interchange, jargon, lexicon, lingua franca, palaver, parlance, patois, phraseology, prose, signal, slang, sound, speech, style, talk, terminology, tongue, utterance, verbalization, vernacular, vocalization, voice, word, wording; SEE CONCEPT 276

languid [adj] *drooping, dull, listless*
apathetic, blah*, blahs*, comatose, dopey, easy, energyless, enervated, faint, feeble, heavy, impassive, inactive, indifferent, inert, infirm, lackadaisical, laid-back, languishing, languorous, lazy, leaden, leisurely, lethargic, limp, moony*, nebbish, phlegmatic, pining, sickly, sleepyhead*, slow, sluggish, snoozy*, spiritless, supine, torpid, unconcerned, unenthusiastic, unhurried, uninterested, weak, weary, wimpy*; SEE CONCEPTS 403,542,584

languish [v] *droop; become dull, listless*
be disregarded, be neglected, brood, conk out*, decline, desire, despond, deteriorate, die on vine*, dwindle, ebb, fade, fag, fag out, fail, faint, fizzle out, flag, go soft*, go to pieces*, grieve, hanker, hunger, knock out, long, pine, repine, rot, sicken, sigh, snivel, sorrow, suffer, tucker, waste, waste away, weaken, wilt, yearn; SEE CONCEPTS 20,105,469

languor [n] *lethargy*
apathy, dullness, fatigue, idleness, inaction, inactivity, laziness, listlessness, sluggishness, tiredness, torpor, weakness; SEE CONCEPTS 315,410,633,748

lanky [adj] *tall and thin*
angular, attenuated, beanpole*, beanstalk*, bony, broomstick*, extenuated, gangling, gangly, gaunt, lean, meager, rangy, rawboned, scraggy, scrawny, slender, spare, spindling, spindly, stilt, stringy, twiggy*, weedy; SEE CONCEPTS 491,779

lantern [n] *lamp*
beacon, flashlight, gas lamp, gaslight, hurricane lamp, kerosene lamp, light, searchlight, torch; SEE CONCEPTS 620,624,628,810

lap [n] *orbit, circuit*
circle, course, distance, loop, round, tour; SEE CONCEPTS 364,436

lap [vl] *slosh, wash against*
bathe, bubble, burble, drink, gurgle, lave, lick, lip, plash, purl, ripple, sip, slap, splash, sup, swish; SEE CONCEPT 144

lap [v2] *overlap*
cover, enfold, envelop, fold, imbricate, overlie, override, ride, shingle, swaddle, swathe, turn, twist, wrap; SEE CONCEPTS 172,201

lapse [nl] *mistake*
blunder, breach, bungle, crime, error, failing, failure, fault, flub, foible, frailty, gaff, goof, goof-up*, indiscretion, miscue, negligence, offense, omission, oversight, screw-up*, sin, slip, slip-up, transgression, trespass, trip*, vice, violation; SEE CONCEPTS 101,674

lapse [n2] *break in action*
gap, intermission, interruption, interval, lacuna, lull, passage, pause; SEE CONCEPT 807

la
la

lapse [n3] *backsliding*
decadence, declension, decline, degeneration, descent, deterioration, devolution, drop, fall, recession, regression, relapse, retrogradation, retrogression; SEE CONCEPTS 230,316,388

lapse [v] *become void; fall back into previous pattern*
apostatize, backslide, become obsolete, cease, decline, degenerate, descend, deteriorate, die, elapse, end, expire, go by, pass, recede, recidivate, relapse, retrograde, return, revert, run out, slide, slip, subside, terminate, weaken; SEE CONCEPTS 119,698

larceny [n] *theft*
burglary, crime, lift, misappropriation, pilfering, pinch, purloining, robbery, steal, stealing, thievery, thieving, touch*; SEE CONCEPTS 139,192

larder [n] *provisions*
food supply, groceries, pantry, provender, stock, storage, supplies; SEE CONCEPTS 140,712

large [adj] *big, abundant*
ample, barn door*, blimp*, booming, broad, bulky, capacious, colossal, comprehensive, considerable, copious, enormous, excessive, exorbitant, extensive, extravagant, full, generous, giant, gigantic, goodly, grand, grandiose, great, gross, hefty, huge, humongous*, immeasurable, immense, jumbo*, liberal, massive, monumental, mountainous, plentiful, populous, roomy, sizable, spacious, stupendous, substantial, super, sweeping, thumping, tidy, vast, voluminous, whopping*, wide; SEE CONCEPTS 773,781

largely [adv] *to a great extent*
abundantly, as a rule, broadly, by and large, chiefly, commodiously, comprehensively, considerably, copiously, expansively, extensively, extravagantly, generally, generously, grandly, immoderately, imposingly, in a big way, in a grand manner, lavishly, liberally, magnificently, mainly, mostly, on a large scale, overall, predominantly, primarily, principally, prodigally, prodigiously, voluminously, widely; SEE CONCEPTS 544,772

larger than life [adj] *legendary*
awesome, celebrated, extraordinary, famed, famous, immortal, imposing, impressive, mythical, renowned, towering; SEE CONCEPT 568

largess [adj] *generosity*
aid, alms, altruistic, benefaction, benevolent, charitable, charity, donation, endowment, generous, gift, giving, philanthropy, thoughtful; SEE CONCEPTS 404,542

lascivious [adj] *sexually aroused; displaying excessive interest in sex*
bawdy, blue, bodily, carnal, coarse, crude, evil-minded, fast*, fleshly, gross*, hard-core*, hot*, immoral, incontinent, indecent, lecherous, lewd, libertine, libidinous, licentious, low-down*, lubricious, lustful, nasty, obscene, off-color*, offensive, orgiastic, pornographic, prurient, randy, raunchy*, raw, ribald, rough, salacious, scurrilous, sensual, smutty*, soft-core*, steamy, suggestive, unchaste, voluptuous, vulgar, wanton, X-rated*; SEE CONCEPTS 372,403

lash [v1] *beat, whip*
baste, batter, buffet, chastise, dash, drum, flagellate, flay, flog, hammer, hide, hit, horsewhip, knock, lam, lather, pound, pummel, scourge, smack, strap, strike, thrash, wear out, whale*; SEE CONCEPT 189

lash [v2] *criticize harshly*
abuse, attack, baste, bawl out*, belabor, berate, blister, castigate, censure, chew out*, exprobate, flay, fulminate, jaw, lambaste, lampoon, ridicule, satirize, scold, tear into*, tell off*, tongue-lash*, upbraid; SEE CONCEPT 52

lass [n] *young woman*
colleen, damsel, female, girl, lassie, maid, maiden, miss, missy; SEE CONCEPTS 548,585

lassitude [n] *lethargy*
apathy, dullness, exhaustion, fatigue, idleness, inaction, inactivity, languor, laziness, listlessness, sleepiness, sluggishness, tiredness, torpor, weakness, weariness; SEE CONCEPTS 315,410, 633,748

lasso [n] *lariat*
bola, halter, rope, snare; SEE CONCEPT 475

last [adj] *final; newest*
aftermost, antipodal, at the end, bitter end, climactic, closing, concluding, conclusive, crowning, curtains*, definitive, determinate, determinative, end, ending, eventual, extreme, far, far-off, farthest, finishing, furthest, hindmost, lag, latest, least, lowest, meanest, most recent, once and for all*, outermost, rearmost, remotest, supreme, swan song*, terminal, ulterior, ultimate, utmost, uttermost; SEE CONCEPTS 585,778,799

last [n] *end*
close, completion, conclusion, ending, finale, finis, finish, omega, termination; SEE CONCEPT 832

lasting [adj] *enduring, unending*
abiding, constant, continual, continuing, deep-rooted, durable, endless, eternal, everlasting, forever, incessant, indelible, indissoluble, inexhaustible, inexpungible, in for the long haul*, lifelong, longstanding, long-term, old, perdurable, perennial, permanent, perpetual, persisting, stable, till the cows come home*, unceasing, undying, unremitting; SEE CONCEPTS 551,798

lastly/last [adv] *in the end*
after, after all, all in all, at last, at the end, behind, bringing up rear*, finally, in conclusion, in the rear, to conclude, to sum up, ultimately; SEE CONCEPTS 585,799

latch [n] *lock*
bar, bolt, catch, clamp, fastening, hasp, hook, padlock; SEE CONCEPTS 445,499

latch [v] *fasten with lock*
bar, bolt, cinch, close, close up, lock, make fast, secure; SEE CONCEPTS 85,160

late [adj1] *not on time*
backward, behind, behindhand, behind time, belated, blown*, delayed, dilatory, eleventh-hour*, gone, held up, hung up*, in a bind*, in the lurch*, jammed*, lagging, last-minute, missed the boat*, out of luck*, overdue, postponed, put off, remiss, slow, strapped*, tardy, too late, unpunctual; SEE CONCEPTS 548,799

late [adj2] *new*
advanced, fresh, just out, modern, recent; SEE CONCEPTS 578,797

late [adj3] *dead*
asleep, bygone, cold, deceased, defunct, departed, erstwhile, ex-*, exanimate, extinct, former, inanimate, lifeless, old, once, onetime, past, preceding, previous, quondam, sometime; SEE CONCEPT 539

late [adv] *at the last minute*
backward, behind, behindhand, behind time, belatedly, dilatorily, slowly, tardily, unpunctual; SEE CONCEPT 799

lately [adv] *new, recently*
afresh, anew, a short time ago, in recent times, just now, latterly, newly, not long ago, of late; SEE CONCEPT 820

latent [adj] *dormant, hidden*
abeyant, between the lines, concealed, contained, covert, idle, immature, implied, in abeyance, inactive, inert, inferential, inferred, inherent, inoperative, intrinsic, invisible, involved, lurking, passive, possible, potential, quiescent, rudimentary, secret, sleeping, smoldering, suppressed, suspended, tacit, torpid, underdeveloped, underlying, undeveloped, unexposed, unexpressed, unrealized, unripe, unseen, veiled, vestigial; SEE CONCEPTS 404,576

later [adj] *coming after*
downstream, ensuing, following, more recent, next, posterior, postliminary, proximate, subsequent, subsequential, succeeding, ulterior; SEE CONCEPT 799

later [adv] *happening after*
after, afterward, again, at another time, behind, by and by*, come Sunday*, down the line*, down the road*, in a while, infra, in time, later on, latterly, more recent, next, subsequently, succeeding, thereafter; SEE CONCEPT 799

lateral [adj] *sideways*
crabwise, edgeways, flanking, oblique, side, side-by-side, sidelong, sideward, sidewise, skirting; SEE CONCEPTS 581,583

lather [n1] *bubbles*
cream, foam, froth, head, soap, soapsuds, spume, suds, yeast; SEE CONCEPTS 260,437

lather [n2] *commotion, fuss*
agitation, bustle, clamor, confusion, dither, fever, flap*, fluster, hassle, hoopla*, hubbub*, hullabaloo*, state, stew*, storm*, sweat*, tizzy*, tumult, turbulence, turmoil, twitter*; SEE CONCEPTS 230,388

lather [v] *cause to bubble*
beat, foam, froth, scrub, soap, wash, whip; SEE CONCEPT 165

latitude [n] *freedom, room to move; scope*
breadth, compass, elbow room, extent, independence, indulgence, laxity, leeway, liberty, license, margin, play, range, reach, room, run, run of, space, span, spread, sweep, swing, unrestrictedness, width; SEE CONCEPTS 651,739,756,788

latter [adj] *latest, concluding*
closing, eventual, final, following, hindmost, lag, last, last-mentioned, later, modern, rearmost, recent, second, terminal; SEE CONCEPTS 585,799

lattice [n] *mesh, trellis*
filigree, frame, fretwork, grating, grid, grill, latticework, net, network, openwork, reticulation, screen, structure, tracery, web; SEE CONCEPT 259

laud [v] *acclaim, praise*
admire, adore, approve, bless, boost, build up, celebrate, commend, compliment, cry up, eulogize, extol, flatter, glorify, hand it to*, honor, hymn, magnify, panegyrize, pat on the back*, reverence, sing the praises of*, stroke, venerate, worship; SEE CONCEPT 69

laudable [adj] *admirable*
commendable, creditable, deserving, estimable, excellent, mean, meritable, meritorious, of note,

praisable, praiseworthy, stellar, terrific, thankworthy, worthy; SEE CONCEPT 574

laudatory [adj] *complimentary*
acclamatory, adulatory, approbative, approbatory, approving, commendatory, encomiastic, eulogistic, flattering, laudative, panegyrical, praiseful; SEE CONCEPT 267

laugh [v] *expressing amusement, happiness with sound be*
be in stitches*, break up*, burst*, cachinnate, chortle, chuckle, convulsed*, crack up*, crow, die laughing*, fracture*, giggle, grin, guffaw, howl, roar, roll in the aisles*, scream, shriek, snicker, snort, split one's sides*, titter, whoop*; SEE CONCEPTS 77,185

laughable [adj] *easily made fun of*
absurd, amusing, asinine, bizarre, camp, campy, comic, comical, derisive, derisory, diverting, droll, eccentric, entertaining, facetious, fantastic, farcical, funny, gelastic, har-har*, hilarious, humorous, inane, jocose, jocular, jokey, joshing, ludicrous, mirthful, mocking, nonsensical, preposterous, rich, ridiculous, riot, risible, scream, unusual, witty; SEE CONCEPTS 267,550

laugh at [v] *ridicule*
belittle, deride, hoot, jeer, lampoon, make fun of, mock, scoff, taunt; SEE CONCEPT 54

laugh/laughter [n] *audible expression of amusement*
amusement, cachinnation, cackle, chortle, chuckle, chuckling, crack-up*, crow, fit, gesture, giggle, giggling, glee, guffaw, hilarity, howling, merriment, mirth, peal, rejoicing, roar, shout, shriek, snicker, snigger, snort, sound, titter, yuck*; SEE CONCEPTS 77,185

launch [v1] *send off*
barrage, bombard, bung, cast, catapult, discharge, dispatch, drive, eject, fire, fling, heave, hurl, lance, pitch, project, propel, send forth, set afloat, set in motion, shoot, sling, throw, toss; SEE CONCEPTS 179,222

launch [v2] *begin, initiate*
bow, break the ice*, break the seal*, commence, embark upon, get show on road*, inaugurate, instigate, institute, introduce, jump, kick off*, open, originate, set going, start, start ball rolling*, usher in*; SEE CONCEPT 221

launder [v] *wash*
clean, cleanse, do the laundry*, do the washing*, rinse; SEE CONCEPT 165

laurels [n] *credit, praise*
acclaim, accolade, award, badge, bays, blue ribbon, commendation, crown, decoration, distinction, fame, feather in cap*, glory, gold, gold star*, kudos, prestige, recognition, renown, reward; SEE CONCEPTS 69,278,337

lavatory [n] *bathroom*
latrine, powder room, restroom, shower, toilet, washroom, water closet, WC; SEE CONCEPT 448

lavish [adj] *profuse; splendid*
abundant, bountiful, copious, effusive, exaggerated, excessive, extravagant, exuberant, first-class, free, generous, gorgeous, grand, immoderate, impressive, improvident, inordinate, intemperate, liberal, lush, luxuriant, luxurious, munificent, openhanded, opulent, plentiful, plush, posh, prodigal, profligate, profusive, prolific, riotous, ritzy, sumptuous, swanky, thriftless, unreasonable, unrestrained, unsparing,

unstinging, wasteful, wild; SEE CONCEPTS
334,589,781

lavish [v] *pamper, shower*
be generous, be wasteful, deluge, dissipate, expend, fritter, give, go through, heap, pour, run through*, scatter, spend, spend money like water*, squander, thrust upon, waste; SEE CONCEPTS 110,327,341

law [n1] *rules of a government, society*
act, assize, behest, bidding, bylaw, canon, case, caveat, charge, charter, code, command, commandment, constitution, covenant, decision, decree, decretum, demand, dictate, divestiture, due process, edict, enactment, equity, garnishment, injunction, institute, instruction, jurisprudence, legislation, mandate, measure, notice, order, ordinance, precedent, precept, prescript, prescription, reg, regulation, requirement, ruling, statute, subpoena, summons, warrant, writ; SEE CONCEPT 318

law [n2] *standard, principle of behavior*
assumption, axiom, base, canon, cause, criterion, exigency, formula, foundation, fundamental, generalization, ground, guide, maxim, origin, postulate, precept, principium, proposal, proposition, reason, regulation, rule, source, theorem, ,truth, usage; SEE CONCEPT 688

lawbreaker [n] *criminal*
blackmailer, black marketeer, con, convict, crook, culprit, delinquent, felon, fugitive, gangster, hood*, hoodlum, hooligan, jailbird, malefactor, mobster, offender, outlaw, racketeer, scofflaw; SEE CONCEPT 412

lawful [adj] *allowable, legitimate*
authorized, bona fide, canonical, card-carrying*, commanded, condign, constitutional, decreed, due, enacted, enforced, enjoined, established, innocent, judged, judicial, jural, juridical, jurisprudent, just, justifiable, kosher*, legal, legalized, legislated, legit*, legitimatized, licit, mandated, official, of right, on the level*, on the up and up*, ordained, ordered, passed, permissible, proper, protected, rightful, ruled, statutory, valid, vested, warrantable, warranted; SEE CONCEPTS 319,545

lawless [adj] *reckless, ungoverned*
anarchic, anarchical, anarchistic, bad, barbarous, chaotic, contumacious, criminal, despotic, disobedient, disordered, disorderly, evil, fierce, heterodox, infringing, insubordinate, insurgent, mutinous, nihilistic, noncompliant, nonconformist, piratical, rebellious, recusant, revolutionary, riotous, savage, seditious, tempestuous, terrorizing, traitorous, turbulent, tyrannous, uncivilized, uncultivated, unorthodox, unpeaceful, unrestrained, unruly, untamed, violent, warlike, wild; SEE CONCEPTS 319,545

lawn [n] *cultivated area of green grass*
backyard, garden, grass, grassplot, green, park, plot, terrace, yard; SEE CONCEPTS 509,513,517

lawsuit [n] *case brought to court*
accusation, action, argument, arraignment, assumpsit, bill, cause, claim, contest, dispute, impeachment, indictment, litigation, presentment, proceedings, prosecution, replevin, suit, trial; SEE CONCEPT 318

lawyer [n] *person who is trained to counsel or argue in cases of law*
advocate, attorney, attorney-at-law, barrister, counsel, counsellor, counselor, defender, jurisprudent, jurist, legal adviser, legal eagle*, legist, member of the bar, mouthpiece*, pleader, practitioner, proctor, procurator, solicitor; SEE CONCEPT 355

lax [adj] *slack, remiss*
any way*, asleep on job*, behindhand, broad, careless, casual, delinquent, derelict, devil-may-care*, disregardful, easygoing, flaccid, forgetful, general, imprecise, inaccurate, indefinite, indifferent, inexact, lenient, neglectful, negligent, nonspecific, oblivious, overindulgent, paying no mind*, regardless, shapeless, slipshod, sloppy, soft, unmindful, vague, yielding; SEE CONCEPTS 401,542,557

laxative [n] *aperient*
cathartic, purgative; SEE CONCEPT 307

lay [adj] *amateur, not trained in a religious or other profession*
inexpert, nonclerical, nonprofessional, nonspecialist, ordinary, secular, temporal, unsacred; SEE CONCEPT 530

lay [v1] *put, place*
arrange, deposit, dispose, establish, fix, leave, locate, order, organize, plant, posit, position, repose, rest, set, set down, set out, settle, spread, stick, systematize; SEE CONCEPTS 158,201

lay [v2] *produce, advance*
adduce, allege, bear, bring forth, bring forward, cite, deposit, generate, lodge, offer, present, put forward, submit, yield; SEE CONCEPTS 66,205

lay [v3] *credit, allocate*
accredit, address, aim, allot, apply, ascribe, assess, assign, attribute, burden, cast, charge, direct, encumber, impose, impute, incline, level, point, refer, saddle, tax, train, turn, zero in*; SEE CONCEPTS 49,50,88,187

lay [v4] *design, plan*
concoct, contrive, devise, hatch, plot, prepare, work out; SEE CONCEPT 36

lay [v5] *make smooth*
allay, alleviate, appease, assuage, calm, even, flatten, flush, iron, level, plane, press, quiet, relieve, steam, still, suppress; SEE CONCEPTS 235,250

lay [v6] *bet, wager*
gamble, game, give odds, hazard, play, risk, stake; SEE CONCEPT 363

layer [n] *coating, tier*
band, bed, blanket, coat, coping, couch, course, cover, covering, film, flag, flap, floor, fold, girdle, lamina, lamination, lap, mantle, overlap, overlay, panel, ply, row, seam, sheet, slab, story, stratum, stripe, substratum, thickness, zone; SEE CONCEPTS 744,835

lay into [v] *criticize, attack*
assail, battle, belabor, fire at*, invade, lambaste, let fly at*, set about; SEE CONCEPTS 52,86

layoff [n] *dismissal from job or responsibility*
cutback, discharge, early retirement, respite, unemployment; SEE CONCEPT 351

lay off [v1] *stop doing*
cease, desist, end, give a rest, give up, halt, leave alone, leave off, let up, lie by, quit, rest, spell; SEE CONCEPTS 119,234

lay off [v2] *relieve of responsibility*
discharge, dismiss, drop, fire, let go, oust, pay off, retire early; SEE CONCEPT 351

layout [n] *physical arrangement*
blueprint, chart, design, diagram, draft, forma-

tion, geography, map, organization, outline, plan, purpose; SEE CONCEPTS *625,660*

lay out [*v1*] *spend money*
disburse, expend, give, invest, lend, outlay, pay, put out, put up, shell out*; SEE CONCEPTS *327,341*

lay out [*v2*] *design, plan*
arrange, chart, diagram, display, exhibit, map, outline, set out, spread out; SEE CONCEPTS *36,158,174*

layperson [*n*] *amateur person, not trained in religious or other profession*
believer, dilettante, follower, laic, member, neophyte, nonprofessional, novice, outsider, parishioner, proselyte, recruit, secular; SEE CONCEPTS *361,423*

lay up [*v*] *hurt, incapacitate*
beat up, confine, disable, harm, hospitalize, injure; SEE CONCEPT *246*

lay up/lay by [*v1*] *set aside, store*
accumulate, amass, build up, bury, conserve, cumulate, garner, hide, hoard, keep, lay in, preserve, put away, roll up, salt away, save, spare, store up, treasure; SEE CONCEPTS *120,134*

laziness [*n*] *unwillingness to work, be active*
apathy, dilatoriness, do-nothingness, dormancy, dreaminess, drowsiness, dullness, faineance, faineancy, heaviness, idleness, inactivity, indolence, inertia, inertness, lackadaisicalness, languidness, languorousness, laxness, leadenness, leisureliness, lethargy, listlessness, neglectfulness, negligence, otioseness, otiosity, passivity, remissness, slackness, sleepiness, sloth, slothfulness, slowness, sluggishness, stolidity, supineness, tardiness, torpescence, torpidness, weariness; SEE CONCEPTS *411,633*

lazy [*adj*] *inactive, sluggish*
apathetic, asleep on the job*, careless, comatose, dallying, dilatory, drowsy, dull, flagging, idle, inattentive, indifferent, indolent, inert, lackadaisical, laggard, lagging, languid, languorous, lethargic, lifeless, loafing, neglectful, out of it*, passive, procrastinating, remiss, shiftless, slack, sleepy, slothful, slow, slow-moving, snoozy*, somnolent, supine, tardy, tired, torpid, trifling, unconcerned, unenergetic, unindustrious, unpersevering, unready, weary; SEE CONCEPTS *401,404*

leach [*v*] *drain, empty*
extract, filter, filtrate, lixiviate, percolate, seep, strain, wash away; SEE CONCEPTS *142,211,225*

lead [*n1*] *first place, supremacy*
advance, advantage, ahead, bulge, cutting edge*, direction, edge, example, facade, front rank, guidance, head, heavy, leadership, margin, model, over, pilot, point, precedence, primacy, principal, priority, protagonist, spark, star, start, title role, top, top spot, vanguard; SEE CONCEPTS *668,693,828*

lead [*n2*] *clue*
evidence, guide, hint, indication, proof, sign, suggestion, tip, trace; SEE CONCEPTS *274,284*

lead [*v1*] *guide physically*
accompany, attend, be responsible for, chaperone, coerce, compel, conduct, convey, convoy, direct, drive, escort, find a way, force, get, go along with, guard, impel, induce, manage, pass along, persuade, pilot, point out, point the way, precede, prevail, protect, quarterback*, route, safeguard, see, shepherd, show, show around,

show in, show the way, span, squire, steer, traverse, usher, watch over; SEE CONCEPT *187*

lead [*v2*] *guide mentally; influence*
affect, bring, bring on, call the shots*, cause, command, conduce, contribute, convert, direct, dispose, draw, get the jump on*, go out in front*, govern, head, helm, incline, induce, introduce, manage, motivate, move, persuade, preside over, prevail, produce, prompt, quarterback*, result in, run things*, serve, shepherd, spearhead*, spur, supervise, tend, trail-blaze*; SEE CONCEPTS *68,117,221*

lead [*v3*] *surpass*
be ahead, blaze a trail*, come first*, exceed, excel, outdo, outstrip, precede, preface, transcend, usher; SEE CONCEPT *141*

lead (a life) [*v4*] *experience*
have, live, pass, spend, undergo; SEE CONCEPT *678*

leader [*n*] *person who guides*
boss, captain, chief, chieftain, commander, conductor, controller, counsellor, dean, dignitary, director, doyen, eminence, exec, forerunner, general, governor, guide, harbinger, head, herald, lead, lion*, luminary, manager, mistress, notability, notable, officer, pacesetter, pilot, pioneer, precursor, president, principal, rector, ringleader, ruler, shepherd, skipper, superintendent, superior; SEE CONCEPTS *347,354*

leadership [*n*] *guidance*
administration, authority, capacity, command, conduction, control, conveyance, direction, directorship, domination, foresight, hegemony, influence, initiative, management, pilotage, power, preeminence, primacy, skill, superintendency, superiority, supremacy, sway; SEE CONCEPTS *376,687*

leading [*adj*] *chief, superior*
arch, best, champion, dominant, dominating, famous, first, foremost, governing, greatest, headmost, highest, inaugural, initial, main, noted, notorious, number one*, outstanding, popular, preeminent, premier, primary, principal, prominent, ruling, stellar, top, well-known; SEE CONCEPTS *574,585*

leaf [*n1*] *green foliage of plant*
blade, bract, flag, foliole, frond, leaflet, needle, pad, petal, petiole, scale, stalk, stipule; SEE CONCEPT *428*

leaf [*n2*] *page of document*
folio, paper, sheet; SEE CONCEPT *270*

leaf [*v*] *flip through*
browse, dip into, glance, riff, riffle, run through, scan, skim, thumb; SEE CONCEPTS *72,623*

leafy [*adj*] *abundant in foliage*
abounding, abundant, covered, green, hidden, leafed, leaved, shaded, shady, umbrageous, verdant, wooded; SEE CONCEPTS *485,583*

league [*n1*] *association, federation*
alliance, band, bunch, circle, circuit, club, coalition, combination, combine, compact, company, confederacy, confederation, conference, consortium, crew, gang, group, guild, loop, mob, order, organization, outfit, partnership, pool, ring, society, sodality, union, unit; SEE CONCEPTS *365,381,387*

league [*n2*] *group of a certain ability*
category, circle, class, grade, grouping, level, pigeonhole*, rank, status, tier; SEE CONCEPTS *388,630*

la
le

league [*v*] *associate*

ally, amalgamate, band, coadjute, collaborate, combine, concur, confederate, conjoin, consolidate, cooperate, federate, join forces, unite; SEE CONCEPTS *8,10,114*

leak [*n*] *opening; seepage through opening*

aperture, chink, crack, crevice, decrease, destruction, detriment, drip, drop, escape, expenditure, exposure, fissure, flow, hole, leakage, leaking, loss, outgoing, percolation, pit, puncture, short circuit, slip; SEE CONCEPTS *116,513*

leak [*v*] *seep; make known*

break, come out, discharge, disclose, divulge, drip, drool, escape, exude, get out, give away, let slip*, make public, ooze, out, pass, pass on, percolate, reveal, slip, spill, spill the beans, tell, transpire, trickle; SEE CONCEPTS *60,116,179*

lean [*adj*] *bare, thin*

angular, anorexic, barren, beanpole*, bony, emaciated, gangling, gangly, gaunt, haggard, inadequate, infertile, lank, lanky, meager, no fat, pitiful, poor, rangy, rawboned, scanty, scraggy, scrawny, shadow*, sinewy, skinny, slender, slim, spare, sparse, stick, stilt, stringy, svelte, sylphlike, twiggy*, unfruitful, unproductive, wasted, wiry, wizened, worn; SEE CONCEPTS *485,491*

lean [*vI*] *bend, angle toward*

bear on, beetle, be off, be slanted, bow, cant, careen, cock, curve, decline, deflect, dip, divert, drift, droop, fasten on, hang on, heel, incline, jut, list, nod, overhang, pitch, place, prop, put weight on, recline, repose, rest, rest on, roll, sag, sheer, sink, slant, slope, tilt, tip, turn, twist, veer; SEE CONCEPTS *147,201,738*

lean [*v2*] *be disposed*

be prone, be willing, favor, gravitate toward, have propensity, incline, look, not mind, prefer, tend; SEE CONCEPT *20*

lean [*v3*] *count, depend on*

bank on*, believe in, bet bottom dollar*, bet on*, confide, gamble on*, have faith, hinge on*, lay money on*, put faith in, rely, trust; SEE CONCEPTS *12,26*

leaning [*n*] *tendency, bias*

aptitude, bent*, cup of tea*, disposition, drift, favor, favoritism, inclination, inclining, liking, mindset, partiality, penchant, predilection, predisposition, proclivity, proneness, propensity, sentiment, taste, thing, weakness; SEE CONCEPTS *20,32,689*

leap [*n*] *jump; increase*

bound, caper, escalation, frisk, hop, rise, skip, spring, surge, upsurge, upswing, vault; SEE CONCEPTS *194,780*

leap [*v*] *jump, jump over; increase*

advance, arise, ascend, bounce, bound, caper, cavort, clear, escalate, frisk, hop, hurdle, lop, mount, rise, rocket, saltate, skip, soar, spring, surge, vault; SEE CONCEPTS *194,780*

learn [*vI*] *acquire information*

apprentice, attain, become able, become versed, be taught, be trained, brush up on*, burn midnight oil*, commit to memory, con, crack the books*, cram*, determine, drink in*, enroll, gain, get, get down pat*, get the hang of*, get the knack of*, grasp, grind, imbibe, improve mind, lucubrate, major in, master, matriculate, memorize, minor in, peruse, pick up*, pore over, prepare, read, receive, review, soak up*, specialize

in, study, take course*, take in, train in, wade through*; SEE CONCEPTS *31,33*

learn [*v2*] *discover, find out*

ascertain, catch on, detect, determine, dig up*, discern, gain, gather, hear, see, smoke out*, stumble upon*, trip over, tumble, uncover, understand, unearth; SEE CONCEPTS *34,183*

learned [*adj*] *well-informed*

abstruse, academic, accomplished, bookish, brainy*, conversant, cultivated, cultured, deep*, educated, erudite, esoteric, experienced, expert, grave, grounded, highbrow*, intellectual, in the know*, judicious, lettered, literary, literate, omniscient, pansophic, pedantic, philosophic, philosophical, polymath, posted, professorial, recondite, sage, sapient, scholarly, scientific, sharp, skilled, solemn, solid, sound, studied, studious, versed, well-educated, well-grounded, well-read, well-rounded; SEE CONCEPT *402*

learner [*n*] *person who receives education*

abecedarian, apprentice, beginner, bookworm, catechumen, disciple, initiate, neophyte, novice, probationer, pupil, scholar, student, trainee; SEE CONCEPT *350*

learning [*n*] *education, knowledge*

acquirements, attainments, culture, erudition, information, letters, literature, lore, research, scholarship, schooling, science, study, training, tuition, wisdom; SEE CONCEPTS *274,409*

lease [*v*] *rent object, residence*

charter, hire, let, loan, rent out, sublease, sublet; SEE CONCEPTS *89,115*

leash [*n*] *rein*

bridle, chain, check, control, cord, curb, deterrent, hold, lead, restraint, rope, strap, tether; SEE CONCEPT *475*

leash [*v*] *rein, hold*

bridle, check, clog, control, curb, entrammel, fasten, fetter, hamper, hobble, hog-tie*, hold back, restrain, secure, shackle, suppress, tether, tie, tie up, trammel; SEE CONCEPT *191*

least [*adj*] *slightest, smallest*

atomic, bottom, entry-level, feeblest, fewest, finical, first, gutter, infinitesimal, last, lowest, meanest, microcosmic, microscopic, minimal, minimum, minute, minutest, molecular, most trivial, nadir, next to nothing*, niggling*, piddling*, poorest, second, short-end*, third*, tiniest, trivial, unimportant; SEE CONCEPTS *585,789*

leathery [*adj*] *hard, durable*

coriaceous, hardened, leatherlike, rough, rugged, strong, tough, wrinkled; SEE CONCEPTS *489,606*

leave [*nI*] *permission*

allowance, assent, authorization, concession, consent, dispensation, freedom, go-ahead*, green light*, liberty, okay, permit, sanction, sufferance, tolerance; SEE CONCEPTS *376,685*

leave [*n2*] *holiday, time off*

adieu, departure, farewell, furlough, goodbye, leave of absence, leave-taking, liberty, parting, retirement, sabbatical, vacation, withdrawal; SEE CONCEPTS *802,807*

leave [*vI*] *depart, abandon physically*

abscond, beat it*, break away, clear out*, come away, cut out, decamp, defect, desert, disappear, ditch*, elope, embark, emigrate, escape, exit, flee, flit, fly, forsake, give the slip*, go, go away, go forth, head out*, issue, migrate, move, move out, part, pull out*, push off*, quit, relinquish, remove oneself, retire, retire off*, run along*, sally, say goodbye*, scram, set out, slip out, split*, start, step down, take a hike*, take leave, take off, vacate, vamoose*, vanish, walk out, withdraw; SEE CONCEPT 195

leave [*v2*] *abandon, renounce*
back out*, cease, cede, desert, desist, drop, drop out*, evacuate, forbear, forsake, give notice, give up*, hand over, knock off, maroon, quit, refrain, relinquish, resign, stop, surrender, terminate, waive, yield; SEE CONCEPT 234

leave [*v3*] *forget, neglect*
allow, drop, have, lay down, leave behind, let, let be, let continue, let go, let stay, mislay, omit, permit, suffer; SEE CONCEPTS 108,317

leave [*v4*] *give, especially after death*
allot, apportion, assign, bequeath, bequest, cede, commit, confide, consign, demise, devise, entrust, give over, hand down, leave behind, legate, refer, transmit, will; SEE CONCEPTS 108,317

leave off [*v*] *stop*
abstain, break off, cease, desist, discontinue, end, give over, give up, halt, knock off*, quit, refrain, surcease; SEE CONCEPT 234

lecherous [*adj*] *lustful, lewd*
carnal, concupiscent, corrupt, fast*, hot and heavy*, incontinent, lascivious, libertine, libidinous, licentious, low-down*, lubricous, prurient, raunchy*, salacious, satyric, sensual, unchaste, wanton; SEE CONCEPTS 372,401

lechery [*n*] *lewdness*
carnality, debauchery, lasciviousness, libertinism, licentiousness, lust, lustfulness, raunchiness, salaciousness, wantonness; SEE CONCEPTS 20,709

lectern [*n*] *reading desk*
ambo, platform, pulpit, reading stand, rostrum, stand, support; SEE CONCEPTS 440,443

lecture [*n1*] *lesson, speech*
address, allocution, chalk talk*, discourse, disquisition, harangue, instruction, oration, pep talk*, pitch*, soapbox*, spiel*, talk; SEE CONCEPTS 60,278

lecture [*n2*] *speech of criticism*
castigation, censure, chiding, dressing-down*, going-over*, harangue, moralism, preaching, preachment, rebuke, reprimand, reproof, scolding, sermon, talking-to*, telling off*; SEE CONCEPTS 52,54

lecture [*v1*] *give a lesson, speech*
address, declaim, deliver, discourse, expound, get on a soapbox*, give a talk, harangue, hold forth, orate, prelect, recite, speak, spiel*, spout, talk, teach; SEE CONCEPTS 60,266

lecture [*v2*] *criticize lengthily*
admonish, berate, chide, exprobate, flay, give going-over*, give piece of mind*, moralize, preach, rank on, rate, reprimand, reprove, scold, sermonize, tell off; SEE CONCEPT 52

ledge [*n*] *shelf*
bar, bench, berm, bracket, console, edge, jut, mantle, offset, path, projection, reef, ridge, rim, route, sill, step, strip, tier, track, trail, walk, way; SEE CONCEPTS 445,513

ledger [*n*] *account book*
books, daybook, journal, record book, register; SEE CONCEPTS 271,280,801

leech [*n*] *parasite*
barnacle, bloodsucker*, bum*, freeloader, scrounger, sponge*, sycophant; SEE CONCEPTS 394,412

leer [*n/v*] *look at longingly*
eye, eyeball*, gloat, goggle*, ogle, smirk, sneer, squint, stare, wink; SEE CONCEPT 623

leery [*adj*] *suspicious*
careful, cautious, chary, distrustful, doubting, dubious, on one's guard*, shy, skeptical, uncertain, unsure, wary; SEE CONCEPT 529

leeway [*n*] *room to move, grow*
elbow room*, extent, headway, latitude, margin, play, scope, space; SEE CONCEPT 739

left [*adj1*] *on west side when facing north*
hard to left, larboard, near, nigh side, port, portside, sinister, sinistral, south; SEE CONCEPTS 581,583

left [*adj2*] *politically radical*
leftist, left-wing, liberal, progressive, revolutionary, socialist; SEE CONCEPT 529

left [*adj3*] *abandoned*
continuing, departed, extra, forsaken, gone out, leftover, marooned, over, remaining, residual, split, staying; SEE CONCEPT 577

leftover [*adj*] *remaining, excess*
extra, residual, surplus, unconsumed, uneaten, untouched, unused, unwanted; SEE CONCEPTS 560,771

leftover [*n*] *remainder, remains*
debris, leavings, legacy, oddments, odds and ends*, orts, remnants, residue, scraps, surplus, survivor, trash; SEE CONCEPTS 260,457

left-wing [*adj*] *liberal*
communist, leftist, radical, socialist; SEE CONCEPTS 529,542

leg [*n*] *appendage used for support*
brace, column, lap, limb, member, part, pile, pole, portion, post, prop, section, segment, shank, stage, stake, stilt, stretch, stump, support, upright; SEE CONCEPTS 392,471,832

legacy [*n*] *inheritance, heritage*
bequest, birthright, devise, endowment, estate, gift, heirloom, throwback, tradition; SEE CONCEPTS 337,710

legal [*adj*] *allowable, permissible*
acknowledged, allowed, authorized, card-carrying*, chartered, clean*, condign, constitutional, contractual, decreed, due, enforced, enforcible, enjoined, fair, forensic, granted, innocent, judged, judicial, juridical, just, justifiable, justified, lawful, legalized, legit*, legitimate, licit, on the level*, on the up and up*, ordained, passed, precedented, prescribed, proper, protected, right, rightful, sanctioned, sound, statutory, straight, sure enough, valid, warranted, within the law; SEE CONCEPT 319

legalize [*v*] *allow, validate*
approve, authorize, clean up, codify, constitute, decree, decriminalize, enact, formulate, launder, legislate, legitimate, legitimatize, license, ordain, permit, regulate, sanction; SEE CONCEPTS 298,317

legend [*n1*] *story of the past, often fictitious*
fable, fiction, folklore, folk story, folk tale, lore, myth, mythology, mythos, narrative, saga, tale, tradition; SEE CONCEPT 282

legend [*n2*] *brief description in document*
cipher, code, device, epigraph, epitaph, head, heading, inscription, key, motto, rubric, table, underline; SEE CONCEPTS 268,270

legendary [*adj*] *fictitious but well known*
allegorical, apocryphal, created, customary, doubtful, dubious, fabled, fabricated, fabulous,

le
le

fanciful, figmental, handed-down, imaginary, imaginative, improbable, invented, mythical, mythological, related, romantic, storied, told, traditional, unhistoric, unhistorical, unreal, unverifiable; SEE CONCEPTS 267,552

legendary [adj2] famous
celebrated, famed, illustrious, immortal, renowned, well-known; SEE CONCEPT 568

legerdemain [n] sleight of hand
artfulness, chicanery, conjuring, craftiness, cunning, deceit, deception, hocus-pocus, manipulation, trickery; SEE CONCEPTS 59,278

legible [adj] easy to read
clear, coherent, decipherable, distinct, easily read, intelligible, lucid, neat, plain, readable, sharp, understandable; SEE CONCEPTS 267,535, 576

legion [adj] numerous
countless, many, multifarious, multitudinal, multitudinous, myriad, numberless, populous, several, sundry, various, very many, voluminous; SEE CONCEPTS 762,781

legion [n] mass, force of people
army, body, brigade, cloud, company, division, drove, flock, group, horde, host, multitude, myriad, number, phalanx, rout, scores, throng, troop; SEE CONCEPTS 322,387,417

legislation [n] law of a government
act, bill, charter, codification, constitution, enactment, lawmaking, measure, prescription, regulation, ruling, statute; SEE CONCEPT 318

legislative [adj] lawmaking
congressional, decreeing, enacting, jurisdictive, lawgiving, legislational, legislatorial, ordaining, parliamentarian, parliamentary, senatorial, statute-making, synodical; SEE CONCEPT 319

legislator [n] person in government who makes laws
administrator, aldermember, assemblymember, council member, deputy, lawgiver, lawmaker, leader, member, member of Congress, parliamentarian, representative, senator; SEE CONCEPT 354

legislature [n] governmental body, most often elected, that makes laws
assembly, body, chamber, congress, council, diet, house, house of representatives, lawmakers, parliament, plenum, senate, voice of the people; SEE CONCEPT 299

legitimate [adj] authentic, valid, legal
accepted, accredited, acknowledged, admissible, appropriate, authorized, canonical, certain, cogent, consistent, correct, customary, fair, genuine, innocent, just, justifiable, lawful, licit, logical, natural, normal, official, on the level, on the up and up, orthodox, probable, proper, real, reasonable, received, recognized, regular, reliable, rightful, sanctioned, sensible, sound, statutory, sure, true, typical, usual, verifiable, warranted, well-founded; SEE CONCEPTS 319,558,582

leisure [n] free time and its activities
chance, convenience, ease, freedom, holiday, idle hours, intermission, leave of absence, liberty, one's own sweet time*, opportunity, pause, quiet, range, recess, recreation, relaxation, repose, requiescence, respite, rest, retirement, sabbatical, scope, spare moments*, spare time, time, time off*, unemployment, vacant hour*, vacation; SEE CONCEPTS 363,681,807

leisurely [adj] casual, unhurried
comfortable, delayed, deliberate, dilatory, easy, free, gentle, laggard, laid-back*, languid, lax, lazy, relaxed, restful, slack, slackened, slow, slow-moving, unhasty; SEE CONCEPTS 550,584, 799

leisurely [adv] casually, unhurriedly
at one's convenience*, at one's leisure, calmly, comfortably, composedly, deliberately, dilatorily, easily, gradually, inactively, indolently, laggardly, langorously, languidly, lazily, lethargically, lingeringly, listlessly, slowly, sluggishly, taking one's time*, tardily, torpidly, with delay, without haste; SEE CONCEPTS 544,584,799

lemon [n] dud
failure, flop, junk, piece of junk, reject; SEE CONCEPTS 412,423

lend [v] loan, accommodate
add, advance, afford, allow, bestow, confer, contribute, entrust, extend, furnish, give, grant, impart, lay on one, lend-lease, let, loan shark*, oblige, permit, present, provide, shark, stake, supply, trust; SEE CONCEPTS 115,140

length [n] extent of object, distance, time
breadth, compass, continuance, diameter, dimension, duration, elongation, endlessness, expanse, expansion, extensiveness, height, interval, lastingness, lengthiness, limit, linearity, loftiness, longitude, longness, magnitude, measure, mileage, orbit, panorama, period, piece, portion, protractedness, purview, quantity, radius, range, ranginess, reach, realm, remoteness, season, section, segment, space, spaciousness, span, stretch, stride, tallness, term, unit, width, year; SEE CONCEPTS 651,721,743,788,804

lengthen [v] extend
amplify, augment, continue, dilate, distend, drag out, draw, draw out*, elongate, expand, increase, let out, make longer, pad, proceed, prolong, prolongate, protract, reach, spin out*, stretch, string out*; SEE CONCEPTS 236,239,245

lengthy [adj] extended
diffuse, dragging, drawn-out, elongate, elongated, interminable, lengthened, long, longish, long-winded, overlong, padded, prolix, prolonged, protracted, tedious, tiresome, verbose, very long, wearisome, windy, wordy; SEE CONCEPTS 267,482,782

lenient [adj] permissive
allowing, amiable, assuaging, assuasive, being big*, benign, benignant, charitable, clement, compassionate, complaisant, compliant, condoning, easy, easygoing, emollient, excusing, favoring, forbearing, forgiving, gentle, going easy on*, good-natured, humoring, indulgent, kind, kindly, letting, live with*, loving, merciful, mild, mollycoddling*, obliging, pampering, pardoning, permitting, soft, softhearted, soft-shell*, sparing, spoiling, sympathetic, tender, tolerant, yielding; SEE CONCEPTS 401,542

leprechaun [n] elf
brownie, elfin, fairy, fay, gnome, nisse, pixie, sprite; SEE CONCEPT 370

lesion [n] injury, wound
abrasion, bruise, contusion, cut, gash, laceration, scrape, scratch, sore; SEE CONCEPT 309

less [adj] smaller, inferior
beneath, declined, deficient, depressed, diminished, excepting, fewer, lacking, lesser, limited, lower, minor, minus, negative, not as great, re-

duced, secondary, shortened, shorter, slighter, subordinate, subtracting, unsubstantial, without; SEE CONCEPTS *574,762,789*

ess [*adv*] *little*
barely, in a lower degree, meagerly, to a smaller extent; SEE CONCEPTS *530,544*

essen [*v*] *lower, reduce*
abate, abridge, amputate, attenuate, become smaller, clip, close, contract, crop, curtail, cut, cut back, decline, decrease, de-escalate, degrade, die down, dilute, diminish, downsize, drain, dwindle, ease, erode, grow less, impair, lighten, minify, minimize, mitigate, moderate, narrow, roll back, shrink, slacken, slack up, slow down, soft-pedal*, take the bite out*, take the edge off*, take the sting out*, taper, taper off, thin, truncate, weaken, wind down; SEE CONCEPTS *247,698,776*

esser [*adj*] *inferior, secondary*
a notch under*, bottom, bush, bush-league*, dinky*, insignificant, less important, low, lower, minor, minor-league*, nether, second-fiddle*, second-string*, slighter, small, small-fry*, small-time*, subjacent, subordinate, third-string*, undersized; SEE CONCEPTS *575,793*

esson [*n1*] *information taught*
assignment, chalk talk*, class, coaching, drill, education, exercise, homework, instruction, lecture, period, practice, quiz, reading, recitation, schooling, study, task, teaching, test, tutoring; SEE CONCEPTS *274,285,287*

esson [*n2*] *helpful example, communication*
admonition, censure, chiding, deterrent, exemplar, helpful word, message, model, moral, noble action, notice, precept, punishment, rebuke, reprimand, reproof, scolding, warning; SEE CONCEPTS *123,661,686*

et [*v1*] *allow*
accredit, approve, authorize, be big*, cause, certify, commission, concede, enable, endorse, free up, give, give leave, give okay, give permission, grant, have, hear of, leave, license, live with, make, permit, sanction, sit still for*, suffer, tolerate, warrant; SEE CONCEPTS *50,83,88*

et [*v2*] *rent out object, property*
charter, hire, lease, sublease, sublet; SEE CONCEPTS *89,115*

etdown [*n*] *disappointment*
anticlimax, balk, bitter pill*, blow, chagrin, comedown, disgruntlement, disillusionment, frustration, setback, washout*; SEE CONCEPTS *410,728*

et down [*v*] *disappoint*
abandon, depress, disenchant, disillusion, dissatisfy, fail, fall short, leave in lurch*, leave stranded*, lower, pull down, take down; SEE CONCEPTS *7,19*

ethal [*adj*] *deadly*
baleful, dangerous, deathly, destructive, devastating, fatal, harmful, hurtful, malignant, mortal, mortiferous, mortuary, murderous, necrotic, noxious, pernicious, pestilent, pestilential, poisonous, virulent; SEE CONCEPT *537*

ethargic [*adj*] *lazy, sluggish*
apathetic, blah*, comatose, debilitated, dilatory, dopey, dormant, draggy*, drowsy, dull, enervated, having spring fever*, heavy, idle, impassive, inactive, indifferent, inert, lackadaisical, laggard, laid-back*, languid, languorous, listless, moony*, nebbish, out of it*, passive, phlegmatic,

sleepy, sleepyhead*, slothful, slow, slumberous, snoozy, somnolent, spiritless, stolid, stretchy, stupefied, supine, torpid, wimpy*; SEE CONCEPTS *401,403,584*

lethargy [*n*] *laziness, sluggishness*
apathy, coma, disinterest, disregard, drowsiness, dullness, hebetude, heedlessness, idleness, impassivity, inaction, inactivity, inanition, indifference, indolence, inertia, inertness, insouciance, languor, lassitude, listlessness, passiveness, phlegm, sleep, sleepiness, sloth, slowness, slumber, stupor, supineness, torpidity, torpidness, torpor, unconcern, unmindfulness; SEE CONCEPTS *315,410,633,748*

let off [*v*] *make not subject to punishment or action*
abandon, absolve, discharge, dispense, drop, excuse, exempt, exonerate, forgive, let go, pardon, privilege from, release, relieve, remove, spare; SEE CONCEPTS *50,83,88,317*

let on [*v*] *acknowledge, admit*
allow, avow, betray, concede, confess, disclose, divulge, give away, grant, hint, imply, indicate, let out, make known, mouth*, own, own up*, reveal, say, spill*, suggest, tell, uncover, unveil; SEE CONCEPTS *57,60*

letter [*n1*] *symbol of an alphabet*
ABCs*, alphabet, cap, capital, character, majuscule, minuscule, rune, sign, small letter, type, uncial; SEE CONCEPT *284*

letter [*n2*] *written communication*
acknowledgment, answer, billet, dispatch, epistle, junk mail*, kite, line, memo, memorandum, message, missive, note, postcard, reply, report, thank you; SEE CONCEPTS *271,278*

letup [*n*] *pause*
abatement, break, cessation, interval, lapse, lessening, lull, recess, remission, respite, slackening; SEE CONCEPT *807*

let up [*v*] *pause*
abate, cease, decrease, die down, die out, diminish, ease, ease off, ease up, ebb, fall, moderate, release, relent, slacken, slow down, stop, subside, wane; SEE CONCEPTS *240,698*

levee [*n*] *embankment*
bank, breakwater, dam, earthwork, mound; SEE CONCEPT *509*

level [*adj*] *smooth, balanced*
akin, aligned, alike, calm, commensurate, common, comparable, consistent, constant, continuous, equable, equivalent, even, exact, flat, flush, horizontal, identical, in line, leveled, like, lined up, matched, matching, of same height, on a line, on a par, on one plane, parallel, plain, planate, plane, planed, polished, precise, proportionate, regular, rolled, same, stable, steady, straight, trim, trimmed, unbroken, unfluctuating, uniform, uninterrupted; SEE CONCEPTS *401,490,566*

level [*n1*] *horizontal position or thing*
altitude, elevation, floor, height, layer, plain, plane, story, stratum, surface, zone; SEE CONCEPTS *738,744*

level [*n2*] *rank, position*
achievement, degree, grade, stage, standard, standing, status; SEE CONCEPTS *286,388*

level [*v1*] *make even*
equalize, equate, even, even off, even out, flatten, flush, grade, lay, make equal, make flat, mow, plane, press, roll, smooth, smoothen, straighten, surface; SEE CONCEPT *250*

le
le

level [*v2*] *destroy, demolish*
bring down, bulldoze*, devastate, down*, drop, equalize, fell, flatten, floor, ground, knock down, knock over, lay low, mow*, pull down, raze, ruin, smooth, tear down, waste*, wreck; SEE CONCEPTS *208,252*

level [*v3*] *be honest*
be above-board, be frank, be on the up and up*, be open, be straight, be straightforward, be up-front*, come clean*, come to terms*, keep nothing back*, talk straight*, tell the truth; SEE CONCEPT *49*

level [*v4*] *aim, direct*
address, beam, cast, focus, incline, lay, point, slant, train, turn, zero in on; SEE CONCEPT *187*

levelheaded [*adj*] *reasonable, calm*
all there*, balanced, collected, commonsensical, composed, cool, cool as cucumber*, coolheaded*, dependable, discreet, even-tempered, far-sighted, in one's right mind*, judicious, practical, prudent, rational, sane, self-possessed, sensible, steady, together, unflappable, wise, with all marbles*; SEE CONCEPTS *403,542*

leverage [*n*] *influence*
advantage, ascendancy, authority, bargaining chip*, break, clout, drag, edge, grease*, jump on*, power, pull, rank, ropes*, suction, weight; SEE CONCEPTS *687,693*

levity [*n*] *funniness, silliness*
absurdity, amusement, buoyancy, facetiousness, festivity, fickleness, flightiness, flippancy, folly, foolishness, frivolity, giddiness, happiness, high spirits, hilarity, jocularity, laughs, lightheartedness, mirth, picnic*, pleasantry, repartee, trifling, triviality, volatility, wit; SEE CONCEPTS *273,410*

levy [*n*] *assessment, tax*
burden, collection, custom, duty, exaction, excise, fee, gathering, imposition, impost, muster, tariff, toll; SEE CONCEPT *329*

levy [*v*] *assess, impose*
call up, call up, charge, collect, demand, exact, extort, gather, lay on, place, put on, raise, set, summon, tax, wrest, wring; SEE CONCEPT *330*

lewd [*adj*] *vulgar, indecent*
bawdy, blue, coarse, erotic, fast*, filthy*, foul-mouthed, gross*, hard-core*, immodest, immoral, improper, impure, in bad taste, incontinent, indelicate, lascivious, lecherous, libertine, libidinous, licentious, loose*, lustful, naughty, obscene, off-color*, pornographic, profligate, questionable, racy*, rakish, ribald, risqué, salacious, scandalous, scurrilous, shameless, smutty*, suggestive, taboo, unchaste, unclean, unconventional, unvirtuous, vile, wanton, wicked, X-rated*; SEE CONCEPTS *372,542,545*

lexicon [*n*] *collection of word meanings, usage*
dictionary, glossary, terminology, thesaurus, vocabulary, wordbook, wordlist, word stock; SEE CONCEPTS *276,280*

liability [*n1*] *answerability, responsibility*
accountability, accountableness, amenability, amenableness, arrearage, blame, burden, compulsion, culpability, debt, duty, indebtedness, obligation, onus, owing, subjection, susceptibility; SEE CONCEPT *645*

liability [*n2*] *burden, debt*
account, arrear, arrearage, bad news*, baggage*, balance, bite*, chance, chit*, contingency, contract, damage, debit, disadvantage, drag*, drawback, due*, encumbrance, handicap, hindrance, impediment, inconvenience, indebtedness, debtment, involvement, IOU*, lease, loan, m[...] stone*, minus, misfortune, mortgage, nuisan[...] obligation, onus, pledge, possibility, remaind[...] responsibility, tab; SEE CONCEPTS *332,674*

liability [*n3*] *chance, probability*
exposure, likelihood, openness, proneness, s[...] ceptibility, tendency, vulnerability, vulnerab[...] ness; SEE CONCEPTS *650,657*

liable [*adj1*] *answerable, responsible*
accountable, amenable, bound, chargeable, [...] ligated, subject, tied; SEE CONCEPT *545*

liable [*adj2*] *open, likely*
apt, assailable, attackable, beatable, conquerab[...] disposed, exposed, given, inclined, in dang[...] penetrable, prone, sensitive, subject, susceptib[...] tending, verisimilar, vincible, vulnerable; s[...] CONCEPTS *542,552*

liaison [*n1*] *person who acts as go-between*
communication, connection, contact, fix[...] hookup, in, interchange, interface, intermedia[...] link; SEE CONCEPTS *348,354,423*

liaison [*n2*] *love affair*
amour, encounter, entanglement, fling, illicit [...] mance, interlude, intrigue, romance; SEE CO[...] CEPTS *32,388*

liar [*n*] *person who tells falsehood*
cheat, con artist, deceiver, deluder, dissimula[...] equivocator, fabler, fabricator, fabulist, false w[...] ness, falsifier, fibber, maligner, misleader, p[...] jurer, phony, prevaricator, promoter, storytel[...] trickster*; SEE CONCEPT *412*

libel [*n*] *purposeful lie about someone, often m[...] licious*
aspersion, calumny, defamation, denigrati[...] lying, malicious, obloquy, smear, vituperati[...] SEE CONCEPTS *63,318*

libel [*v*] *purposefully lie about someone*
asperse, bad-mouth*, blister, burlesque, calum[...] ate, caricature, crack, defame, denigrate, de[...] gate, drag name through mud*, give a bla[...] eye*, knock, malign, mark*, mark wrong, revi[...] roast, scandalize, scorch, sizzle, slur, smear, te[...] down, traduce, travesty, vilify; SEE CONCE[...] *63,192*

libelous [*adj*] *derogatory*
aspersive, backbiting, calumniatory, calumnio[...] contumelious, debasing, defamatory, deprec[...] tive, detracting, detractory, disparaging, false, [...] jurious, invidious, malevolent, malicio[...] maligning, opprobrious, pejorative, sarcas[...] scurrilous, traducing, untrue, vilifying, vitupe[...] tive; SEE CONCEPT *267*

liberal [*adj1*] *progressive*
advanced, avant-garde, broad, broad-minde[...] catholic, enlightened, flexible, free, gene[...] high-minded, humanistic, humanitarian, ind[...] gent, intelligent, interested, latitudinarian, l[...] lenient, libertarian, loose, magnanimous, perm[...] sive, radical, rational, reasonable, receiving, [...] ceptive, reformist, tolerant, unbiased, unbigote[...] unconventional, understanding, unorthodox, u[...] prejudiced; SEE CONCEPTS *529,542*

liberal [*adj2*] *giving, generous*
altruistic, beneficent, benevolent, bighearte[...] bounteous, bountiful, casual, charitab[...] eleemosynary, exuberant, free, free-and-ea[...] handsome, kind, lavish, loose, munificent, ope[...] handed, openhearted, philanthropic, prince[...]

prodigal, profuse, soft-touch, unselfish, unsparing, unstinging; SEE CONCEPTS *334,401,404*

liberal [*adj3*] *abundant, profuse*
ample, aplenty, bounteous, bountiful, copious, dime a dozen*, galore, generous, handsome, lavish, munificent, no end, plentiful, plenty, rich; SEE CONCEPT *771*

liberate [*v*] *give freedom*
bail one out*, deliver, detach, discharge, disembarrass, emancipate, free, free up*, get out from under*, let loose*, let out*, loose, loosen, manumit, redeem, release, rescue, save, save one's neck*, set free, unbind, unchain, unhook, unshackle; SEE CONCEPTS *83,110*

liberation [*n*] *freedom*
abolition, deliverance, democracy, emancipation, freeing, liberty, release, salvation, setting free, sovereignty, unchaining, unshackling; SEE CONCEPT *691*

liberty [*n*] *freedom*
autarchy, authorization, autonomy, birthright, carte blanche, choice, convenience, decision, deliverance, delivery, dispensation, emancipation, enfranchisement, enlightenment, exemption, franchise, free speech, immunity, independence, leave, leisure, liberation, license, opportunity, permission, power of choice, prerogative, privilege, relaxation, release, rest, right, sanction, self-determination, selfgovernment, sovereignty, suffrage, unconstraint; SEE CONCEPTS *388,691*

libidinous [*adj*] *lustful*
carnal, coarse, concupiscent, debauched, fast, hot*, impure, incontinent, lascivious, lecherous, libertine, loose*, obscene, passionate, prurient, salacious, satyric, sensual, unchaste, wanton, wicked; SEE CONCEPTS *372,545*

libido [*n*] *sex instinct*
eroticism, lust, passion, sex drive, sexual desire, sexuality, sexual urge, the hots*; SEE CONCEPTS *20,709*

library [*n*] *book repository*
athenaeum, atheneum, bibliotheca, book collection, book room, information center, media center, reference center, study; SEE CONCEPT *435*

license [*n1*] *authority, permission*
authorization, carte blanche*, certificate, charter, consent, dispensation, entitlement, exemption, freedom, go-ahead*, grant, green light*, immunity, independence, latitude, leave, liberty, okay*, permit, privilege, right, self-determination, ticket, unconstraint, warrant; SEE CONCEPT *685*

license [*n2*] *abandon, indulgence*
anarchy, animalism, arrogance, audacity, boldness, complacency, debauchery, disorder, effrontery, excess, forwardness, gluttony, immoderation, impropriety, irresponsibility, lawlessness, laxity, looseness, presumptuousness, prodigality, profligacy, refractoriness, relaxation, relaxedness, sauciness*, self-indulgence, sensuality, slackness, temerity, unrestraint, unruliness, wantonness, wildness; SEE CONCEPTS *633,645*

license [*v*] *authorize*
accredit, allow, certify, commission, empower, enable, let, permit, privilege, sanction, suffer, warrant; SEE CONCEPTS *50,83,88*

licentious [*adj*] *immoral, uncontrolled*
abandoned, amoral, animal, carnal, corrupt, debauched, depraved, desirous, disorderly, dissolute, fast, fast and loose*, fleshly, impure,

incontinent, in the fast lane*, lascivious, lax, lecherous, lewd, libertine, libidinous, lickerish, loose*, lubricious, lustful, oversexed, profligate, promiscuous, relaxed, reprobate, salacious, satyric, scabrous, sensual, swinging, unconstrained, uncontrollable, uncurbed, unmoral, unprincipled, unruly, wanton; SEE CONCEPTS *372,401,545*

lick [*n*] *light touch; little amount*
bit, brush, cast, dab, dash, hint, sample, smack, speck, stroke, suggestion, taste, tinge, trace, whiff; SEE CONCEPTS *612,831*

lick [*v1*] *touch with tongue*
brush, calm, caress, fondle, glance, gloss, graze, lap, lap against, move over, osculate, pass over, play, quiet, ripple, rub, soothe, stroke, sweep, taste, tongue, touch, wash; SEE CONCEPTS *185,612*

lick [*v2*] *play over with fire*
blaze, burn, dart, flick, flicker, fluctuate, flutter, ignite, kindle, leap, palpitate, quiver, ripple, run over, shoot, touch, tremble, vacillate, vibrate, waver; SEE CONCEPTS *249,612*

lick [*v3*] *defeat, sometimes by hitting*
beat, best, clobber, conquer, down, excel, flog, hit, hurdle, lambaste, master, outdo, outstrip, overcome, overwhelm, rout, slap, smear, smother, spank, strike, surmount, surpass, thrash, throw, top, trim, trounce, vanquish, wallop, whip; SEE CONCEPTS *95,141,189*

lid [*n*] *top covering*
cap, cover, hood, roof, top; SEE CONCEPT *836*

lie [*n*] *untruth*
aspersion, backbiting, calumniation, calumny, deceit, deception, defamation, detraction, dishonesty, disinformation, distortion, evasion, fable, fabrication, falsehood, falseness, falsification, falsity, fib, fiction, forgery, fraudulence, guile, hyperbole, inaccuracy, invention, libel, mendacity, misrepresentation, misstatement, myth, obloquy, perjury, prevarication, revilement, reviling, slander, subterfuge, tale, tall story*, vilification, white lie*, whopper; SEE CONCEPTS *63,278*

lie [*v1*] *tell an untruth*
bear false witness, beguile, be untruthful, break promise, BS*, bull*, con, concoct, deceive, delude, dissemble, dissimulate, distort, dupe*, equivocate, exaggerate, fabricate, fake, falsify, fib, forswear, frame, fudge, go back on*, invent, make believe, malign, misguide, misinform, misinstruct, mislead, misrepresent, misspeak, misstate, overdraw, palter, perjure, pervert, phony, plant*, prevaricate, promote, put on*, put up a front*, snow*, soft-soap*, string along*, victimize; SEE CONCEPT *63*

lie [*v2*] *be prostrate, flat*
be prone, be recumbent, be supine, couch, go to bed*, laze, lie down, loll, lounge, nap, recline, repose, rest, retire, siesta, sleep, sprawl, stretch out, turn in; SEE CONCEPTS *154,201*

lie [*v3*] *be situated*
be, be beside, be buried, be established, be even, be fixed, be found, be interred, be level, be located, belong, be on, be placed, be seated, beset, be smooth, exist, extend, have its seat in, occupy, prevail, reach, remain, spread, stretch; SEE CONCEPT *746*

life [*n1*] *animation, spirit*
activity, being, breath, brio, dash, élan*, élan

vital*, energy, enthusiasm, entity, esprit, essence, excitement, get-up-and-go*, go*, growth, heart, high spirits, impulse, lifeblood, liveliness, oomph*, sentience, soul, sparkle, verve, viability, vigor, vitality, vivacity, zest*, zing*; SEE CONCEPT 411

life [n2] *existence, duration*
being, career, continuance, course, cycle, days, endurance, epoch, era, expectancy, extent, generation, history, length, life span, lifetime, longevity, orbit, period, pilgrimage, record, season, span, survival, time; SEE CONCEPTS 816,817

life [n3] *being*
animal, animateness, animation, body, breath, consciousness, continuance, creature, endurance, entity, essence, existence, flesh, flesh and blood*, growth, human, human being, individual, living, living being, living thing, man, metabolism, mortal, mortal being, organism, person, personage, presence, soul, subsistence, substantiality, survival, symbiosis, viability, vitality, vital spark*, wildlife, woman; SEE CONCEPT 389

life [n4] *history, biography*
autobiography, bio, career, confession, curriculum vitae, journal, life story, memoir, memorial, story; SEE CONCEPT 271

life [n5] *person's experiences*
attainment, behavior, circumstances, conduct, development, enjoyment, enlightenment, growth, hand one is dealt*, happiness, human condition, journey, knowledge, lifestyle, participation, personality, realization, suffering, trials and tribulations*, vicissitudes, way of life*, world; SEE CONCEPT 678

life-and-death [adj] *vitally important*
critical, crucial, determining, earth-shaking, essential, imperative, meaningful, paramount, pivotal, serious, significant, urgent, vital; SEE CONCEPT 567

lifeless [adj1] *not living, not containing living things*
asleep, bare, barren, brute, cold, comatose, dead, deceased, defunct, departed, desert, empty, exanimate, extinct, faint, inanimate, inert, inorganic, insensate, insensible, late, out cold*, sterile, unconscious, uninhabited, waste; SEE CONCEPTS 485,539

lifeless [adj2] *dull, spiritless*
blah*, cold, colorless, drab, draggy*, flat, hollow, insipid, lackluster, lethargic, listless, lusterless, nothing*, pabulum*, passive, prosaic, prosy, slothful, slow*, sluggish, spent, static, stiff*, torpid, wooden*, zero*; SEE CONCEPTS 401,542,584

lifelike [adj] *realistic*
authentic, faithful, graphic, natural, original, real, representational, representative, true, true to life; SEE CONCEPT 582

lifelong [adj] *lasting*
constant, continuing, deep-rooted, enduring, for life, inveterate, lifetime, livelong, long-lasting, long-lived, long-standing, old, perennial, permanent, persistent; SEE CONCEPT 798

lifestyle [n] *way of life*
behavior, conduct, habits, style of living, way of acting; SEE CONCEPT 633

lifetime [n] *span of animate being's existence*
all one's born days*, career, continuance, course, cradle to grave*, days, endurance, existence, life,

life span, natural life, period, time; SEE CONCEPT 817

lifework [n] *person's calling*
business, career, interest, mission, occupatio profession, purpose, pursuit, vocation, work; s CONCEPTS 349,360

lift [n1] *transportation*
car ride, drive, journey, passage, ride, run, trar port; SEE CONCEPT 155

lift [n2] *help, aid*
assist, assistance, boost, comfort, encourag ment, hand, leg up*, pick-me-up*, reassuran relief, secours, shot in the arm*, succor, suppo SEE CONCEPTS 110,700

lift [v1] *move upwards; ascend*
arise, aspire, bear aloft, boost, bring up, build buoy up, climb, come up, disappear, disper dissipate, draw up, elevate, erect, goose*, he hike, hike up, hoist, jack up, jump up, mou move up, pick up, put up, raise, raise high, re rise, soar, take up, up, upheave, uphold, upl upraise, uprear, vanish; SEE CONCEF 196,200,236,245

lift [v2] *repeal, revoke*
annul, cancel, countermand, dismantle, end, call, relax, remove, rescind, reverse, stop, terr nate; SEE CONCEPTS 234,317

lift [v3] *steal*
abstract, appropriate, cop, copy, crib, filch, ho nip, pilfer, pinch, pirate, plagiarize, pocket, p loin, snitch, swipe, take, thieve; SEE CONCE 139,200

lift [v4] *promote, improve*
advance, ameliorate, boost, build up, dignify, evate, enhance, exalt, hike, jack up, raise, s port, upgrade; SEE CONCEPTS 110,244

liftoff [n] *rocket launch*
blast-off, rocket firing, rocket ignition, sh take-off; SEE CONCEPTS 179,222

ligature [n] *link*
band, bandage, binding, bond, connection, kn ligament, nexus, rope, tie, yoke; SEE CONCE 471,831

light [adj1] *illuminated*
ablaze, aglow, bright, brilliant, burnished, cle cloudless, flashing, fluorescent, glossy, glowi lambent, lucent, luminous, lustrous, phosphor cent, polished, radiant, refulgent, resplende rich, scintillant, shining, shiny, sunny, clouded, unobscured, vivid, well-lighted, w lit; SEE CONCEPTS 617,618

light [adj2] *blond, fair*
bleached, faded, fair-skinned, light-hued, lig skinned, light-toned, pale, pastel, tow-head SEE CONCEPTS 406,618

light [adj3] *not heavy*
agile, airy, atmospheric, buoyant, crumb dainty, delicate, downy, easy, effervescent, et real, featherweight, feathery, filmy, flimsy, flc able, floating, fluffy, friable, frothy, gossame graceful, imponderous, inconsequential, ins stantial, light-footed, lightweight, lithe, liv loose, meager, nimble, petty, porous, portal sandy, sheer, slender, slight, small, spon sprightly, sylphlike, thin, tissuelike, trifling, tr ial, unheavy, unsubstantial, weightless; SEE C CEPT 491

light [adj4] *small in amount, content*
casual, digestible, faint, fractional, fragment frivolous, frugal, gentle, hardly any, har

enough, inadequate, inconsequential, inconsiderable, indistinct, insignificant, insufficient, mild, minor, minuscule, minute, moderate, modest, not many, not much, not rich, puny, restricted, scanty, shoestring*, slight, soft, sparse, superficial, thin, tiny, trifling, trivial, unimportant, unsubstantial, weak, wee; SEE CONCEPTS 762,789

light [adj5] *simple, easy*
effortless, facile, manageable, moderate, smooth, undemanding, unexacting, untaxing, untroublesome; SEE CONCEPT 538

light [adj6] *funny, cheery*
airy, amusing, animated, blithe, carefree, cheerful, chipper*, chirpy, diverting, dizzy, entertaining, fickle, flighty, frivolous, gay, giddy, high, humorous, lighthearted, lively, merry, perky, pleasing, sunny, sunny-side up*, superficial, trifling, trivial, up, upbeat, witty; SEE CONCEPTS 401,542

light [n1] *luminescence from sun or other source*
aurora, beacon, blaze, brightness, brilliance, brilliancy, bulb, candle, coruscation, dawn, daybreak, daylight, daytime, effulgence, emanation, flare, flash, fulgor, glare, gleam, glimmer, glint, glitter, glow, illumination, incandescence, irradiation, lambency, lamp, lantern, lighthouse, luminosity, luster, morn, morning, phosphorescence, radiance, radiation, ray, refulgence, scintillation, sheen, shine, sparkle, splendor, star, sun, sunbeam, sunrise, sunshine, taper, torch, window; SEE CONCEPTS 620,624,628,810

light [n2] *context, point of view; understanding*
angle, approach, aspect, attitude, awareness, comprehension, condition, education, elucidation, enlightenment, example, exemplar, explanation, illustration, information, insight, interpretation, knowledge, model, paragon, slant, standing, vantage point, viewpoint; SEE CONCEPTS 274,409,682,686

light [v1] *illuminate*
animate, brighten, cast, fire, flood, floodlight, furnish with light, highlight, ignite, illume, illumine, inflame, irradiate, kindle, lighten, light up, limelight, make bright, make visible, put on, shine, spot, spotlight, switch on, turn on; SEE CONCEPTS 250,624

light [v2] *start on fire*
burn, enkindle, fire, flame, ignite, inflame, kindle, set fire to, set on fire, spark, strike a match; SEE CONCEPT 249

light [v3] *step down; land*
alight, arrive, come down, deplane, detrain, disembark, drop, fly down, get down, perch, rest, roost, set down, settle, settle down, sit, sit down, stop, touch down; SEE CONCEPTS 159,181

lighten [v1] *illuminate*
become light, brighten, flash, gleam, illume, irradiate, light, light up, make bright, shine; SEE CONCEPT 624

lighten [v2] *reduce weight, load*
allay, alleviate, ameliorate, assuage, attenuate, buoy, change, comfort, cut down, decrease, dilute, disburden, disencumber, ease, empty, eradicate, extenuate, facilitate, free, jettison, lessen, levitate, make less, make lighter, mitigate, mollify, pour out, put off, reduce, relieve, remove, shift, take, take a load off*, thin, throw out, unburden, unload, uplight, upraise; SEE CONCEPTS 110,244,250

lighten [v3] *cheer up; inspire*
brighten, buoy up, cheer, elate, encourage, gladden, hearten, lift, perk up, revive, take a load off; SEE CONCEPTS 7,22

light-headed [adj] *silly; feeling faint*
changeable, delirious, dizzy, empty, featherbrained*, fickle, flighty, flippant, foolish, frivolous, gaga*, giddy, harebrained*, hazy, punchy*, reeling, rocky, scatterbrained*, shallow, superficial, swimming, swimmy, tired, trifling, vertiginous, whirling, woozy*; SEE CONCEPTS 314,401

lighthearted [adj] *carefree, untroubled*
blithe, blithesome, bright, buoyant, cheerful, effervescent, expansive, feelgood*, frolicsome, gay, glad, gleeful, happy, happy-go-lucky*, high-spirited, insouciant, jocund, jolly, jovial, joyful, joyous, laid-back, lightsome, lively, merry, playful, resilient, spirited, sprightly, sunny, upbeat, vivacious, volatile; SEE CONCEPTS 404,542

lightly [adv] *gently, effortlessly*
agilely, airily, breezily, carelessly, casually, daintily, delicately, easily, ethereally, faintly, flippantly, freely, frivolously, gingerly, heedlessly, indifferently, leniently, mildly, moderately, nimbly, peacefully, quietly, readily, simply, slightingly, slightly, smoothly, softly, sparingly, sparsely, subtly, tenderly, tenuously, thinly, thoughtlessly, timidly, unsubstantially, well; SEE CONCEPTS 538,544,584

light out [v] *run away*
abscond, depart, escape, head, leave, make, make off, quit, set out, strike out, take a hike, take off; SEE CONCEPT 195

lightweight [adj] *inconsequential*
failing, featherweight, foolish, imponderous, incompetent, insignificant, of no account, paltry, petty, slight, trifling, trivial, unimportant, weightless, worthless; SEE CONCEPTS 491,575

likable [adj] *nice, pleasant*
agreeable, amiable, appealing, attractive, charismatic, charming, engaging, enjoyable, friendly, genial, good, good-natured, pleasing, preferable, relishable, sweet, sweet-natured, sympathetic, winning, winsome; SEE CONCEPT 404

like [adj] *similar*
according to, agnate, akin, alike, allied, allying, analogous, approximating, approximative, close, coextensive, cognate, commensurate, comparable, compatible, conforming, congeneric, congenerous, consistent, consonant, corresponding, double, equal, equaling, equivalent, homologous, identical, in the manner of, jibing, matching, much the same, near, not far from, not unlike, on the order of, parallel, related, relating, resembling, same, selfsame, such, twin, undifferentiated, uniform; SEE CONCEPTS 487,573

like [v1] *enjoy, be fond of*
admire, adore, appreciate, approve, be gratified by, be keen on, be partial to, be pleased by, be sweet on, care for, care to, cherish, delight in, derive pleasure from, dig*, dote on, esteem, exclaim, fancy, feast on, find appealing, get a kick out of*, go for*, hanker for, hold dear, indulge in, love, luxuriate in, prize, rejoice in, relish, revel in, savor, stuck on*, take an interest in, take delight in, take satisfaction in, take to; SEE CONCEPT 32

like [v2] *choose, feel inclined*
care to, desire, elect, fancy, feel disposed, feel

like, have a preference for, incline toward, please, prefer, select, want, will, wish; SEE CONCEPTS 20,41

likelihood [n] *chance of something happening*
coin flip*, direction, even break, fair shake, fifty-fifty*, fighting chance*, good chance*, liability, likeliness, long shot*, outside chance*, plausibility, possibility, presumption, probability, prospect, reasonableness, shot at*, strong possibility, tendency, toss-up*, trend; SEE CONCEPT 650

likely [adj] *probable, apt, hopeful*
acceptable, achievable, anticipated, assuring, attainable, believable, conceivable, conjecturable, credible, destined, disposed, expected, fair, favorite, feasible, given to, imaginable, inclined, in favor of, inferable, in the cards*, in the habit of*, liable, odds-on*, on the verge of, ostensible, plausible, possible, practicable, predisposed, presumable, promising, prone, rational, reasonable, seeming, subject to, supposable, tending, thinkable, true, up-and-coming*, verisimilar, workable; SEE CONCEPT 552

likely [adv] *probably*
assumably, doubtless, doubtlessly, in all likelihood, in all probability, like as not, most likely, no doubt, presumably, presumptively, prima facie, seemingly, to all appearances; SEE CONCEPT 552

like-minded [adj] *similar*
agreeing, compatible, harmonious, in accord, in agreement, in harmony, of one mind, unanimous; SEE CONCEPTS 487,573

liken [v] *compare*
allegorize, approach, approximate to, assimilate, balance, bear comparison, be in the same class as*, be on a par with*, come up to, correlate, distinguish between, draw parallel, equal, equate, identify with, link, make like, match, notice similarities, parallel, put alongside, relate, resemble, show correspondence; SEE CONCEPT 39

likeness [n] *correspondence in appearance; something that corresponds*
affinity, agreement; alikeness, analogousness, analogy, appearance, carbon, clone, comparableness, comparison, conformity, copy, counterpart, dead ringer*, delineation, depiction, ditto*, double, effigy, equality, equivalence, facsimile, form, guise, identicalness, identity, image, knock-off*, lookalike*, model, parallelism, photocopy, photograph, picture, portrait, replica, representation, reproduction, resemblance, sameness, semblance, similarity, simile, similitude, study, uniformity, Xerox*; SEE CONCEPTS 664,670,716

likewise [adj] *also, similarly*
additionally, along, as well, besides, correspondingly, further, furthermore, in addition, in like manner, in the same way, more, moreover, so, too, withal; SEE CONCEPT 563

liking [n] *fondness, taste*
affection, affinity, appetite, appreciation, attachment, attraction, bent, bias, desire, devotion, fancy, favoritism, inclination, love, mind, palate, partiality, passion, penchant, pleasure, predilection, preference, proneness, propensity, relish, soft spot*, stomach, sympathy, tendency, tooth, velleity, weakness, will; SEE CONCEPTS 20,32,529

limb [n] *appendage*
arm, bough, branch, extension, extremity, fi gam*, leg, lobe, member, offshoot, part, pin, pin ion, process, projection, spray, sprig, spur, ster switch, unit, wheel, wing; SEE CONCEPTS 392,42

limber [adj] *flexible*
agile, deft, elastic, graceful, lissome, lithe, lithe some, loose, nimble, plastic, pliable, pliant, re silient, springy, spry, supple; SEE CONCEPT 406,488

limbo [n] *state of uncertainty*
demilitarized zone, left field*, nothingnes nowhere, oblivion, out there*, Siberia*; si CONCEPTS 679,705

limit [nl] *greatest extent*
absolute, bitter end*, border, bottom line bound, bourne, breaking point*, brim, brink, ca ceiling, check, circumscription, conclusion, con finement, confines, curb, cutoff point*, deadlin destination, edge, end, end point, extremity, f out, farthest point, farthest reach, fence, finalit goal, limitation, margin, maximum, obstructio restraint, restriction, rim, termination, the max the most*, tops*, ultimate, utmost, verge; si CONCEPTS 529,548,832

limit [n2] *physical boundary*
border, borderland, compass, confines, edg end, extent, extreme, extremity, frontier, perime ter, periphery, precinct, purlieu; SEE CONCEPT 513,745

limit [v] *confine, restrict*
appoint, assign, bar, bottle up, bound, cap, check circumscribe, constrict, contract, cork, cramp curb, define, delimit, delimitate, demarcate, dra the line, fix, hem in, hinder, inhibit, keep the li on*, lessen, narrow, prescribe, ration, reduce, re strain, set, specify; SEE CONCEPTS 5,130

limitation [n] *restraint, disadvantage*
bar, block, check, circumspection, conditio constraint, control, cramp, curb, definition, draw back, impediment, inhibition, injunction, modif cation, obstruction, qualification, reservation restriction, snag, stint, stricture, taboo; SEE CON CEPTS 666,674

limited [adj1] *restricted, definite*
bound, bounded, checked, circumscribed, con fined, constrained, controlled, curbed, defined delimited, determinate, finite, fixed, hampered hemmed in, local, modified, narrow, particula precise, qualified, reserved, restrained, sectiona topical; SEE CONCEPTS 554,557

limited [adj2] *inadequate, short*
cramped, diminished, faulty, ineffectual, insuffi cient, little, mean, minimal, narrow, paltry, poo reduced, restricted, set, small, unsatisfactory; SE CONCEPT 771

limitless [adj] *never-ending, infinite*
bottomless, boundless, countless, endless, illim itable, immeasurable, immense, incomprehensi ble, indefinite, inexhaustible, innumerable measureless, no end of*, no end to*, no hold barred*, no strings*, numberless, unbounded uncalculable, undefined, unending, unfath omable, unlimited, untold, vast, wide-open; SE CONCEPTS 762,771,798

limp [adj] *not stiff; weak*
bending, debilitated, drooping, droopy, ductile enervated, exhausted, feeble, flabby, flaccid flexible, flexuous, flimsy, floppy, impressible, w firm, languid, languishing, lax, lethargic, limber

listless, loose, plastic, pliable, pliant, relaxed, slack, soft, spent, spiritless, supple, tired, unsubstantial, weakened, wearied, worn out, yielding; SEE CONCEPTS *490,604*

limp [*n*] *faltering walk*
bad wheel, falter, flat wheel, floppy, gimp, halt, hitch, hobble, lameness; SEE CONCEPT *151*

limp [*v*] *walk with faltering step*
clump, dodder, falter, flag, gimp, halt, hitch, hobble, hop, lag, scuff, shamble, shuffle, stagger, stumble, teeter, totter, waddle, walk lamely; SEE CONCEPT *151*

limpid [*adj*] *clear, comprehensible*
bright, comprehensible, crystal-clear, crystalline, definite, distinct, filmy, intelligible, lucid, luculent, obvious, pellucid, perspicuous, pure, see-through, thin, translucent, transparent, transpicuous, unambiguous; SEE CONCEPT *535*

line [*n1*] *mark, stroke; border*
band, bar, borderline, boundary, channel, configuration, contour, crease, dash, delineation, demarcation, edge, figuration, figure, frontier, furrow, groove, limit, lineament, lineation, outline, profile, rule, score, scratch, silhouette, streak, stripe, tracing, underline, wrinkle; SEE CONCEPTS *284,436*

line [*n2*] *row, succession; course*
arrangement, array, axis, band, block, border, catalogue, channel, column, concatenation, crack, direction, division, drain, echelon, file, fissure, formation, furrow, groove, group, lane, length, list, magazine, mark, order, path, progression, queue, rank, ridge, road, route, row, scar, seam, sequence, series, street, string, thread, tier, track, train, trajectory, trench, way; SEE CONCEPTS *501,727,738,744*

line [*n3*] *cord, rope*
cable, filament, strand, string, thread, wire; SEE CONCEPT *475*

line [*n4*] *belief, policy*
approach, avenue, course, course of action, ideology, method, polity, position, practice, principle, procedure, program, route, scheme, system; SEE CONCEPTS *688,689*

line [*n5*] *person's calling, interest*
activity, area, business, department, employment, field, forte, job, occupation, profession, province, pursuit, racket*, specialization, trade, vocation, work; SEE CONCEPTS *349,360*

line [*n6*] *ancestry*
breed, descent, family, heredity, lineage, pedigree, race, stock, strain, succession; SEE CONCEPT *296*

line [*n7*] *written communication*
card, letter, message, note, postcard, report, word; SEE CONCEPT *271*

line [*n8*] *hint; influential communication*
clue, indication, information, lead, patter, persuasion, pitch, prepared speech, song and dance*, spiel*; SEE CONCEPT *278*

line [*n9*] *merchandise carried by store*
commodity, goods, involvement, materials, produce, trade, vendibles, wares; SEE CONCEPT *338*

line [*v1*] *border, mark*
abut, adjoin, align, allineate, array, bound, butt against, communicate, crease, cut, delineate, draw, edge, fix, follow, fringe, furrow, group, inscribe, join, line up, march, marshal, neighbor, order, ordinate, outline, place, queue, range,

rank, rim, rule, score, skirt, touch, trace, underline, verge; SEE CONCEPTS *79,84,753*

line [*v2*] *put covering inside object*
bush, ceil, cover, encrust, face, fill, incrust, interline, overlay, panel, quilt, reinforce, sheath, stuff, wad, wainscot; SEE CONCEPTS *172,218*

lineage [*n*] *ancestry*
birth, blood, breed, clan, descendants, descent, extraction, family, folk, forbears, genealogy, heredity, house, kin, kindred, line, offspring, origin, pedigree, progenitors, progeny, race, stirps, stock, succession, tribe; SEE CONCEPT *296*

linger [*v1*] *loiter, delay*
amble, be dilatory, be long, be tardy, crawl, dally, dawdle, dillydally*, drift, falter, fool around*, fritter away*, goof off*, hang around*, hang out*, hesitate, hobble, idle, lag, loll, lumber, mope, mosey, plod, poke, procrastinate, put off, putter, remain, saunter, shuffle, sit around, slouch*, stagger, stay, stick around, stop, stroll, take one's time*, tarry, tool, totter, trail, traipse, trifle, trudge, vacillate, wait, wait around; SEE CONCEPTS *151,681*

linger [*v2*] *continue, endure*
abide, bide, cling, hang on, last, persist, remain, stand, stay, stick around, survive, wait; SEE CONCEPTS *23,239*

lingo [*n*] *dialect spoken by a group*
argot, cant, idiom, jargon, language, patois, patter, slang, speech, talk, tongue, vernacular, vocabulary; SEE CONCEPT *276*

liniment [*n*] *ointment*
balm, cream, dressing, embrocation, emollient, lenitive, lotion, medicine, salve, unguent; SEE CONCEPTS *311,466*

link [*n*] *component, connection*
articulation, association, attachment, bond, channel, connective, constituent, contact, copula, coupler, coupling, division, element, fastening, hitch, hookup, in, interconnection, interface, intersection, joining, joint, junction, knot, ligament, ligation, ligature, loop, member, network, nexus, part, piece, relationship, ring, seam, section, splice, tie, tie-up, vinculum, weld, yoke; SEE CONCEPTS *471,835*

link [*v*] *connect*
associate, attach, bind, bracket, combine, conjoin, conjugate, couple, fasten, group, hitch on, hook up, identify, incorporate, interface, join, meld with, network, plug into, relate, slap on, tack on, tag along, tag on, team up with, throw in with*, tie, tie in with, unite, yoke; SEE CONCEPTS *113,114,193*

lionize [*v*] *celebrate*
acclaim, adulate, aggrandize, eulogize, exalt, glorify, hero-worship, honor, idolize, immortalize, praise, roll out the red carpet*, show respect, worship; SEE CONCEPT *69*

lip [*n1*] *edge, brink*
border, brim, chops, flange, flare, labium, labrum, margin, nozzle, overlap, portal, projection, rim, spout; SEE CONCEPTS *392,484,513*

lip [*n2*] *insolence*
back talk, cheek*, effrontery, guff*, impertinence, jaw*, mouth*, rudeness, sass*, sauce*, sauciness*; SEE CONCEPTS *54,278*

lip service [*n*] *empty talk*
duplicity, hollow words, insincerity, token agreement, tongue in cheek, unctuousness; SEE CONCEPTS *267,542,545*

liquefy [v] *melt*
deliquesce, dissolve, thaw; SEE CONCEPTS 250, 255

liqueur [n] *liquor*
alcohol, alcoholic beverage, aperitif, booze*, brandy, cognac, cordial, flavored drink, intoxicant, port, spirits; SEE CONCEPT 455

liquid [adj1] *fluid, flowing, melting*
aqueous, damp, deliquescent, dissolvable, dissolved, dulcet, fluent, fluidic, fusible, ichorous, juicy, liquefied, liquescent, liquiform, luscious, mellifluent, mellifluous, mellow, meltable, melted, moist, molten, moving, pulpy, running, runny, sappy, serous, smooth, soft, solvent, splashing, succulent, thawed, thin, uncongealed, viscous, watery, wet; SEE CONCEPTS 485,584,603

liquid [adj2] *readily available*
convertible, fluid, free, marketable, negotiable, quick, ready, realizable, usable; SEE CONCEPT 334

liquid [n] *fluid*
aqua, aqueous material, broth, elixir, extract, flow, flux, goo*, goop*, juice, liquor, melted material, nectar, sap, secretion, slop*, solution, swill*; SEE CONCEPT 467

liquidate [v1] *pay; change into cash*
cash, cash in, cash out, clear, convert, discharge, exchange, honor, pay off, quit, realize, reimburse, repay, satisfy, sell off, sell up, settle, square; SEE CONCEPT 330

liquidate [v2] *destroy, dissolve*
abolish, annihilate, annul, cancel, dispatch, do away with*, do in*, eliminate, exterminate, finish off*, get rid of*, kill, murder, purge, remove, rub out*, silence, terminate, vaporize, wipe out*; SEE CONCEPT 252

liquor [n] *drink; alcoholic beverage*
alcohol, aqua vitae, booze*, broth, decoction, drinkable, elixir, extract, firewater*, fluid, hard stuff*, inebriant, infusion, intoxicant, liquid, moonshine*, poison*, potable, sauce*, solvent, spirits, stock, the bottle*, whiskey; SEE CONCEPT 455

lissom [adj] *supple*
adaptable, agile, bendable, bending, elastic, flexible, graceful, limber, lithe, lithesome, loose, malleable, moldable, pliable, pliant, resilient, rubber, springy, stretchy, wiry; SEE CONCEPTS 488,604

list [n] *record, tabulation*
account, agenda, archive, arrangement, ballot, bill, brief, bulletin, calendar, canon, catalog, catalogue, census, checklist, contents, dictionary, directory, docket, draft, enumeration, file, gazette, index, inventory, invoice, lexicon, lineup, listing, loop, manifest, memorandum, menu, outline, panel, poll, program, prospectus, register, roll, roll call, row, schedule, screed, scroll, series, slate, statistics, syllabus, table, tally, thesaurus, ticket, timetable, vocabulary; SEE CONCEPT 281

list [v] *keep a record; tabulate*
arrange, bill, book, button down, calender, catalogue, census, chart, chronicle, classify, detail, docket, enroll, enter, enumerate, file, index, inscribe, insert, inventory, invoice, itemize, keep count, manifest, note, numerate, particularize, peg, place, poll, post, put down as, put down for, record, register, run down, schedule, set down,

specialize, specify, spell out, tab, tally, tick off, write down; SEE CONCEPTS 79,125

list [v2] *lean, slant*
cant, careen, heel, incline, pitch, recline, slope, tilt, tip; SEE CONCEPTS 154,201,738

listen [v] *hear and pay attention*
accept, admit, adopt, attend, audit, auscult, auscultate, be all ears*, be attentive, catch, concentrate, eavesdrop, entertain, get, get a load of*, give an audience to, give attention, give heed to, hang on words*, hark, harken, hearken, hear out, hear tell, lend an ear*, mind, monitor, obey, observe, overhear, pick up on*, prick up ears*, receive, take advice*, take into consideration*, take notice, take under advisement*, tune in, tune in on*, welcome; SEE CONCEPT 596

listless [adj] *spiritless, without energy*
absent, abstracted, apathetic, blah*, bored, careless, dormant, dreamy, drowsy, dull, easygoing, energyless, enervated, faint, heavy, heedless, impassive, inanimate, inattentive, indifferent, indolent, inert, insouciant, lackadaisical, lagging, laid-back*, languid, languishing, languorous, leaden, lethargic, lifeless, limp, lukewarm, lymphatic, mopish, neutral, out of it*, passive, phlegmatic, slack, sleepy, slow, sluggish, stupid, supine, thoughtless, torpid, uninterested, vacant; SEE CONCEPTS 401,584

litany [n] *recital of items, often part of religious services*
account, catalogue, enumeration, invocation, list, petition, prayer, recitation, refrain, repetition, supplication, tale; SEE CONCEPTS 278,368

literacy [n] *ability to read*
articulacy, articulateness, background, cultivation, education, knowledge, learning, proficiency, refinement, scholarship; SEE CONCEPTS 409,630

literal [adj] *word for word; exact, real*
accurate, actual, apparent, authentic, bona fide, close, critical, faithful, genuine, gospel, methodical, natural, not figurative, ordinary, plain, scrupulous, simple, strict, to the letter*, true, undeviating, unerring, unexaggerated, unvarnished, usual, veracious, verbal, verbatim, veritable, written; SEE CONCEPTS 267,557

literally [adv] *word for word; exactly*
actually, completely, correctly, direct, directly, faithfully, indisputably, letter by letter*, literatim, not figuratively, plainly, precisely, really, rightly, rigorously, sic*, simply, straight, strictly, to the letter*, truly, undeviatingly, undisputably, unerringly, unmistakably, verbatim, veritably; SEE CONCEPTS 267,557

literary [adj] *concerning books*
belletristic, bookish, classical, erudite, formal, learned, lettered, literate, scholarly, well-read; SEE CONCEPTS 267,536

literate [adj] *able to read and write*
cultivated, cultured, educated, instructed, knowledgeable, learned, lettered, scholarly, schooled; SEE CONCEPT 402

literature [n] *written matter, both fictional and nonfictional*
abstract, article, belles-lettres, biography, books, brochure, classics, comment, composition, critique, discourse, discussion, disquisition, dissertation, drama, essay, exposition, findings, history, humanities, information, leaflet, letters, lit*, literary works, lore, novel, observation,

pamphlet, paper, poetry, precis, prose, report, research, story, summary, theme, thesis, tract, treatise, treatment, writings, written work; SEE CONCEPT 280

lithe [*adj*] *flexible, graceful and slender*
agile, lean, lightsome, limber, lissome, loose, nimble, pliable, pliant, slight, slim, spare, supple, thin; SEE CONCEPTS 488,491,584

litigate [*v*] *bring matter before court of law*
appeal, contest, dispute, drag into court*, file suit, go to court, go to law, institute legal proceedings, press charges, prosecute, see one in court*, sue, take the law on*; SEE CONCEPT 317

litigation [*n*] *matter coming before court of law*
action, case, cause, contention, dispute, lawsuit, process, prosecution, suit, trial; SEE CONCEPT 318

litigious [*adj*] *quarrelsome*
argumentative, belligerent, combative, contentious, disputable; SEE CONCEPTS 401,542

litter [*n1*] *mess, debris*
clutter, collateral, confusion, detritus, disarray, disorder, garbage, hash, hodgepodge, jumble, jungle, junk, mishmash, muck, muddle, offal, rash, refuse, rubbish, rummage, scattering, scramble, shuffle, trash, untidiness, waste; SEE CONCEPTS 260,432

litter [*n2*] *animal offspring*
brood, cubs, family, kittens, piglets, progeny, puppies, school, young; SEE CONCEPTS 394,397

litter [*v*] *make a mess*
clutter, confuse, derange, dirty, disarrange, disarray, disorder, jumble, mess up, scatter, strew; SEE CONCEPT 254

little [*adj1*] *small in size, amount*
babyish, bantam, brief, cramped, diminutive, dinky, elfin, embryonic, fleeting, hardly any, hasty, immature, imperceptible, inappreciable, inconsiderable, infant, infinitesimal, insufficient, junior, light, Lilliputian*, limited, meager, microscopic, mini, miniature, minute, not big, not large, peanut*, petite, scant, short, short-lived, shrimpy*, shriveled, skimpy, slight, snub, sparse, stubby, stunted, teeny, tiny, toy, truncated, undersized, undeveloped, wee, wizened, young; SEE CONCEPTS 773,789

little [*adj2*] *not important*
casual, inconsiderable, insignificant, light, minor, minute, negligible, paltry, petty, shoestring*, small, trifling, trivial, unimportant; SEE CONCEPT 575

little [*adj3*] *narrow-minded*
base, bigoted, cheap, contemptible, hidebound, illiberal, ineffectual, limited, mean, narrow, paltry, petty, provincial, self-centered, selfish, set, small, small-minded, vulgar, wicked; SEE CONCEPT 404

little [*adv*] *infrequently, not much*
a little, barely, hardly, hardly ever, not many, not often, not quite, only just, rarely, scarcely, seldom, somewhat; SEE CONCEPTS 530,544

little [*n*] *small amount of something*
bit, dab, dash, fragment, hint, modicum, particle, pinch, soupçon, speck, spot, taste, touch, trace, trifle, whit; SEE CONCEPT 835

liturgy [*n*] *worship, ceremony*
celebration, ceremonial, form, formality, formula, observance, rite, ritual, sacrament, service, services; SEE CONCEPT 368

livable [*adj*] *adequate, acceptable*
bearable, comfortable, cozy, endurable, fit, habitable, homey, inhabitable, lodgeable, passable, satisfactory, snug, sufferable, supportable, sustainable, tenantable, tolerable, worthwhile; SEE CONCEPTS 485,558

live [*adj1*] *existent*
alive, animate, aware, breathing, conscious, living, vital; SEE CONCEPT 539

live [*adj2*] *energetic, vigorous*
active, alert, brisk, burning, controversial, current, dynamic, earnest, effective, effectual, efficacious, efficient, functioning, hot*, lively, operative, pertinent, pressing, prevalent, running, topical, unsettled, vital, vivid, working; SEE CONCEPTS 542,560

live [*v1*] *exist*
abide, be, be alive, breathe, continue, draw breath, endure, get along, get by, have life, last, lead, maintain, make it, move, pass, persist, prevail, remain, remain alive, subsist, survive; SEE CONCEPT 407

live [*v2*] *inhabit a dwelling*
abide, bide, bunk*, crash*, dwell, hang one's hat*, hang out*, locate, lodge, nest, occupy, perch, reside, roost, settle; SEE CONCEPT 226

live [*v3*] *enjoy being alive*
be happy, delight, experience, flourish, love, luxuriate, make the most of, prosper, relish, savor, take pleasure, thrive; SEE CONCEPT 678

live [*v4*] *make money to support living*
acquire a livelihood, earn a living, earn money, fare, feed, get along*, get by*, maintain, make ends meet*, make it, profit, subsist, support; SEE CONCEPT 351

livelihood [*n*] *occupation*
alimentation, art, bread and butter*, business, circumstances, craft, employment, game*, grind*, income, job, keep*, living, maintenance, means, nine-to-five*, profession, racket*, rat race*, resources, slot, source of income, subsistence, support, sustenance, thing*, trade, vocation, what one is into*, work; SEE CONCEPTS 349,351,360

lively [*adj*] *energetic, active, busy*
agile, alert, animate, animated, astir, blithe, blithesome, bouncy, bright, brisk, buoyant, bustling, buzzing, cheerful, chipper*, chirpy*, complex, dashing, driving, effervescent, enjoyable, enterprising, entertaining, festive, frisky, frolicsome, full of pep*, gay, go-go*, happy, hyper*, industrious, involved, jocund, jumping, keen, merry, nimble, peppy*, perky, pert, provocative, quick, refreshing, rousing, snappy, sparkling, spirited, sprightly, spry, stimulating, stirring, vigorous, vivacious, zippy*; SEE CONCEPTS 401,542,548

livid [*adj1*] *pale, ashen*
ashy, blanched, bloodless, colorless, discolored, dusky, gloomy, greyish, grisly, leaden, lurid, murky, pallid, pasty, wan, waxen; SEE CONCEPT 618

livid [*adj2*] *bruised*
black-and-blue, contused, purple; SEE CONCEPT 618

livid [*adj3*] *extremely angry*
beside oneself, black*, boiling, enraged, exasperated, flaming, fuming, furious, hot*, incensed, indignant, infuriated, mad, offended, outraged*; SEE CONCEPTS 403,542

living [*adj*] *existing, active*
alert, alive, animated, around, awake, breathing,

li
li

brisk, contemporary, continuing, current, developing, dynamic, existent, extant, in use, live, lively, ongoing, operative, persisting, strong, subsisting, ticking, vigorous, vital, warm; SEE CONCEPTS 539,560

living [n] *lifestyle; source of income*
alimentation, bread and butter*, existence, income, job, keep*, livelihood, maintenance, means, mode, occupation, salt*, subsistence, support, sustainment, sustenance, sustentation, way, work; SEE CONCEPTS 335,351

load [n1] *cargo, freight*
amount, bale, bundle, capacity, charge, consignment, contents, encumbrance, goods, haul, heft, hindrance, lading, mass, pack, parcel, part, payload, shipment, shot, weight; SEE CONCEPTS 338,432

load [n2] *burden, pressure*
affliction, albatross, care, charge, cumber, deadweight*, drag, drain, duty, encumbrance, excess baggage*, incubus, liability, millstone*, obligation, onus, oppression, responsibility, task, tax, trouble, trust, weight, worry; SEE CONCEPT 674

load [v1] *burden, saddle*
arrange, ballast, bear, carry, charge, chock, choke, containerize, cram, fill, flood, freight, glut, gorge, heap, heap up, jam*, lade, lumber, mass, oversupply, pack, pile, pile it on, pile up, place, pour in, put aboard, ram in, stack, store, stow, stuff, surfeit, swamp, top, top off, weigh, weigh down, weight; SEE CONCEPT 209

load [v2] *overburden, pressure*
burden, charge, encumber, hamper, lade, oppress, saddle, task, tax, trouble, weigh down, weight, worry; SEE CONCEPT 14

loaf [n] *block of something*
bun, cake, cube, dough, lump, mass, pastry, roll, slab, twist; SEE CONCEPTS 436,457,460,461

loaf [v] *be idle, lazy*
be inactive, be indolent, be slothful, be unoccupied, bum*, bum around*, dally, dillydally*, dream, drift, evade, fool around*, fritter away*, goldbrick, hang out*, idle, kill time*, knock around*, laze, let down, lie, loiter, loll, lounge, lounge around, malinger, not lift a finger*, pass time, piddle, relax, saunter, shirk, sit around, slack, slow down, stall, stand around, stroll, take it easy, trifle, twiddle thumbs*, vegetate, waste time, while away hours*; SEE CONCEPTS 210,681

loafer [n] *person who is idle, lazy*
beachcomber, deadbeat, do-nothing, good-for-nothing*, goof-off*, idler, lazybones*, lounger, malingerer, ne'er-do-well*, shirker, slacker, slouch, sluggard, sponger, wanderer, waster, wastrel; SEE CONCEPT 412

loan [n] *money given temporarily*
accommodation, advance, allowance, credit, extension, floater, investment, mortgage, time payment, trust; SEE CONCEPT 332

loan [v] *give money, possession temporarily*
accommodate, advance, allow, credit, lay on one, lend, let out, provide, score, scratch, stake, touch; SEE CONCEPT 115

loath [adj] *against, averse*
afraid, counter, disinclined, hesitant, indisposed, opposed, reluctant, remiss, resisting, uneager, unwilling; SEE CONCEPTS 29,542

loathe [v] *dislike strongly*
abhor, abominate, be allergic to*, be down on, decline, despise, detest, execrate, feel repugnance, find disgusting, hate, have aversion to, have no use for*, refuse, reject, repudiate, revolt, spurn; SEE CONCEPT 29

loathing [n] *abhorrence*
contempt, detestation, disgust, dislike, enmity, hatred, repugnance, revulsion; SEE CONCEPT 29

loathsome [adj] *hateful*
abhorrent, abominable, beastly, bitchy*, creepy, deplorable, detestable, disgusting, execrable, gross, hideous, horrible, invidious, lousy, nasty, nauseating, obnoxious, odious, offensive, pesky, pestiferous, repellent, repugnant, repulsive, revolting, sleazy*, slimy*, uncool*, vile; SEE CONCEPTS 485,529,570

lob [v] *toss*
chuck, flip, hurl, launch, loft, pitch, project, propel; SEE CONCEPT 222

lobby [n] *entrance hall*
antechamber, corridor, doorway, foyer, gateway, hall, hallway, passage, passageway, porch, vestibule, waiting room; SEE CONCEPTS 441,448

lobby [v] *press for political action*
advance, affect, alter, bill, billboard*, boost, bring pressure to bear*, build up, campaign for, change, drum, exert influence, further, hard sell*, high pressure, hype*, induce, influence, make a pitch for*, modify, persuade, pitch, plug, politick, press, pressure, procure, promote, pull strings*, push, put pressure on, request, sell, sell on*, soft-sell*, soft-soap*, solicit, solicit votes, splash, spot, sway, sweet-talk*, thump, urge; SEE CONCEPTS 68,300

lobbyist [n] *special interest representative*
activist, influence peddler, mover and shaker, person of influence, powerbroker, pressure group; SEE CONCEPTS 348,354

local [adj] *of a community, restricted to immediate area*
bounded, civic, confined, district, divisional, geographical, insular, legendary, limited, narrow, neighborhood, parish, parochial, provincial, regional, sectarian, sectional, small-town, territorial, town, vernacular; SEE CONCEPT 536

local [n] *person deeply rooted in community*
character, inhabitant, native, resident; SEE CONCEPTS 413,423

locale/locality [n] *physical setting*
area, bailiwick, belt, district, domain, haunt, hole, home, location, locus, neck of the woods*, neighborhood, place, position, region, scene, sector, site, sphere, spot, stage, stomping ground*, territory, theater, tract, turf, venue, vicinity, zone; SEE CONCEPT 198

localize [v] *confine*
center, contain, limit, narrow, pinpoint, restrain, restrict, stop from spreading; SEE CONCEPTS 121,130

locate [v1] *find*
come across, come upon, detect, determine, discover, establish, ferret out*, get at, happen upon, hit upon, hook*, lay one's hands on*, light upon*, meet with, pick up on, pin down, pinpoint, place, position, read, search out, smell out, smoke out*, spot, station, strike, stumble on, track down, trip over*, uncover, unearth, zero in on*; SEE CONCEPT 183

locate [v2] *settle*
dig in, dispose, dwell, establish, fix, hang one's hat*, inhabit, park, place, put, reside, seat, set, situate, squat, stand; SEE CONCEPT 226

located [adj] *situated*
based, occupying, placed, positioned, posted, stationed; SEE CONCEPTS *158,201*

location [n] *place of residence or activity*
area, bearings, district, fix*, hole, locale, locality, locus, neck of the woods*, neighborhood, part, point, position, post, region, scene, section, site, situation, spot, station, tract, turf, venue, whereabouts; SEE CONCEPT *198*

lock [n] *device that fastens and bars free passage*
bar, bolt, bond, catch, clamp, clasp, clinch, connection, fastening, fixture, grapple, grip, hasp, hook, junction, latch, link, padlock; SEE CONCEPT *499*

lock [v] *fasten, clasp*
bar, bolt, button, button up, clench, close, clutch, embrace, encircle, enclose, engage, entwine, grapple, grasp, hug, join, latch, link, mesh, press, seal, secure, shut, turn the key, unite; SEE CONCEPTS *85,160*

locker [n] *compartment*
cabinet, chest, closet, trunk; SEE CONCEPT *440*

locomotion [n] *movement*
action, mobileness, mobility, motion, moving, progression, travel, travelling; SEE CONCEPTS *2,145,697*

locution [n] *phrasing*
accent, articulation, dialect, diction, expression, inflection, language, phraseology; SEE CONCEPT *77*

lodge [n] *cabin; vacation residence*
abode, auberge, burrow, camp, chalet, cottage, couch, country house, den, dormitory, dwelling, gatehouse, haunt, home, hospice, hostel, hostelry, hotel, house, hut, inn, motel, public house, retreat, roadhouse, shack, shanty, shelter, stopover, tavern, villa; SEE CONCEPT *516*

lodge [v1] *become fixed or wedged*
abide, catch, come to rest, embed, entrench, fix, imbed, implant, infix, ingrain, install, plant, remain, root, stay, stick; SEE CONCEPT *201*

lodge [v2] *stay at temporary residence*
abide, accommodate, bestow, board, bunk, canton, crash, domicile, dwell, entertain, harbor, hole up*, hostel, house, locate, nest, park*, perch*, put up, quarter, rent, reside, room, roost*, shelter, sojourn, squat, station, stay, stay over, stop; SEE CONCEPT *226*

lodging [n] *accommodation for rent*
abode, address, apartment, bed and breakfast, boarding house, camp, castle, chambers, cover, domicile, dorm, dwelling, habitation, harbor, home, hostel, hotel, inn, lodge, lodgment, motel, palace, pied-à-terre, place, port, protection, quarters, residence, resort, roof, room, room and board, rooming house, shelter; SEE CONCEPT *516*

loft [n] *room on upper floor*
apartment, attic, dormer, garret, storage, studio; SEE CONCEPT *448*

lofty [adj1] *high, elevated*
aerial, airy, high-rise, lifted, raised, sky-high, skyscraping, skyward, soaring, spiring, tall, towering; SEE CONCEPT *779*

lofty [adj2] *grand, stately*
arresting, benevolent, big, chivalrous, commanding, considerate, dignified, distinguished, elevated, exalted, generous, great, illustrious, imposing, magnanimous, majestic, noble, renowned, striking, sublime, superb, superior, utopian, visionary; SEE CONCEPT *574*

lofty [adj3] *arrogant, high and mighty*
ambitious, cavalier, condescending, disdainful, grandiose, haughty, high-minded, immodest, insolent, overbearing, patronizing, pretentious, proud, snooty, supercilious; SEE CONCEPT *401*

log [n1] *stump of tree*
block, bole, chunk, length, piece, stick, timber, trunk, wood; SEE CONCEPTS *428,479*

log [n2] *record*
account, book, chart, daybook, diary, journal, listing, logbook, register, tally; SEE CONCEPT *271*

logic [n] *science of reasoning*
antithesis and synthesis, argumentation, coherence, connection, course of thought, deduction, dialectic, good sense, induction, inference, linkage, philosophy, ratiocination, rationale, relationship, sanity, sense, sound judgment, syllogism, syllogistics, thesis, train of thought; SEE CONCEPTS *37,349,689*

logical [adj1] *probable, reasonable*
analytic, analytical, clear, cogent, coherent, commonsensical, compelling, congruent, consequent, consistent, convincing, deducible, discerning, discriminating, extensional, fair, germane, holding together, holding water*, inferential, intelligent, judicious, juridicious, justifiable, kosher*, legit*, legitimate, lucid, most likely, necessary, obvious, perceptive, perspicuous, pertinent, plausible, rational, relevant, sensible, sound, subtle, telling, valid, well-organized, wise; SEE CONCEPTS *402,529,552*

logistics [n] *management*
coordination, engineering, masterminding, organization, planning, plans, strategy, systematization; SEE CONCEPT *660*

logo [n] *trademark*
brand, brand name, emblem, identification, imprint, label, logotype, symbol, tag; SEE CONCEPTS *259,284*

loiter [v] *hang around; stroll*
amble, dabble, dally*, dawdle, delay, diddle, drag, flag, fritter away, get no place fast*, halt, hover, idle, lag, linger, loaf, loll, lounge, pass time, pause, poke, procrastinate, put off, ramble, saunter, shamble, shuffle, slacken, slough, tarry, trail, traipse, wait, waste time; SEE CONCEPTS *151,210,681*

loll [v] *lay sprawled*
bum, dangle, dawdle, droop, drop, flap, flop, goof off, hang, hang loose, idle, laze, lean, loaf, loiter, lounge, recline, relax, rest, sag, slouch, slump, sprawl; SEE CONCEPTS *154,210*

lone [adj] *by oneself; only*
abandoned, alone, deserted, forsaken, isolated, lonely, lonesome, one, onliest, particular, secluded, separate, separated, single, singular, sole, solitary, solo, stag, unaccompanied, unique; SEE CONCEPT *577*

loneliness [n] *isolation*
alienation, aloneness, desolation, forlornness, friendlessness, heartache, lonesomeness, remoteness, seclusion, solitariness, solitude, withdrawal; SEE CONCEPTS *135,188,388,631*

lonely [adj1] *feeling friendless, forlorn*
abandoned, alone, apart, by oneself, comfortless, companionless, deserted, desolate, destitute, disconsolate, down, empty, estranged, forsaken, godforsaken, homeless, isolated, left, lone, lonesome, outcast, reclusive, rejected, renounced, secluded, single, solitary, troglodytic, unattended,

li
lo

unbefriended, uncherished, unsocial, withdrawn; SEE CONCEPTS *403,555*

lonely [*adj2*] *out-of-the-way*
alone, deserted, desolate, godforsaken, isolated, obscure, off the beaten track*, private, quiet, remote, removed, retired, secluded, secret, sequestered, solitary, unfrequented, uninhabited; SEE CONCEPT *583*

loner [*n*] *recluse*
anomic, hermit, introvert, lone wolf*, outsider, solitary; SEE CONCEPTS *361,423*

lonesome [*adj*] *forlorn, friendless*
alone, cheerless, companionless, deserted, desolate, dreary, gloomy, homesick, isolated, lone, lonely, solitary; SEE CONCEPTS *403,555*

long [*adj1*] *extended in space or time*
continued, deep, distant, drawn out, elongate, elongated, enduring, enlarged, expanded, extensive, faraway, far-off, far-reaching, gangling, great, high, lanky, lasting, lengthened, lengthy, lingering, lofty, longish, outstretched, prolonged, protracted, rangy, remote, running, spread out, spun out, stretch, stretched, stretching, stringy, sustained, tall, towering; SEE CONCEPTS *482,779,798*

long [*adj2*] *interminable, excessive in length*
boundless, delayed, diffuse, diffusive, dilatory, dragging, drawn-out, for ages*, forever and a day*, late, lengthy, limitless, lingering, long-drawn-out*, long-winded*, overlong, prolix, prolonged, protracted, slow, sustained, tardy, unending, verbose, without end, wordy; SEE CONCEPTS *544,798*

long [*v*] *desire, crave*
ache, aim, aspire, covet, dream of, hanker, have a yen for, hunger, itch, lust, miss, pine, sigh, spoil for, suspire, thirst, want, wish, yearn; SEE CONCEPT *20*

longevity [*n*] *long life*
durability, endurance, lastingness, old age; SEE CONCEPTS *411,633*

longing [*adj*] *desirous*
anxious, ardent, avid, craving, eager, hungry, languishing, pining, ravenous, wishful, wistful, yearning; SEE CONCEPT *403*

longing [*n*] *strong desire*
ambition, aspiration, coveting, craving, fire in the belly*, hankering, hunger, hungering, itch, pining, thirst, urge, wish, yearning, yen; SEE CONCEPTS *20,709*

long shot [*n*] *outside chance*
fluke, hundred-to-one shot, little chance, lucky shot, no chance, off-chance, one in a million*, slim chance, small chance; SEE CONCEPT *679*

long-standing [*adj*] *existing for some time*
abiding, durable, enduring, established, fixed, lasting, long-established, long-lasting, long-lived, traditional; SEE CONCEPTS *551,798*

long-winded [*adj*] *wordy*
bombastic, chatty*, gabby*, garrulous, loquacious, palaverous, prolix, rambling, talkative, verbose, voluble; SEE CONCEPT *267*

look [*n1*] *visual examination*
attention, beholding, case, contemplation, evil eye*, eye*, flash, gander, gaze, glance, glimpse, gun, inspection, introspection, keeping watch, leer, look-see*, marking, noticing, observation, once-over, peek, reconnaissance, regard, regarding, review, scrutiny, sight, slant, specula-

tion, squint, stare, surveillance, survey, swivel, view, viewing; SEE CONCEPT *623*

look [*n2*] *characteristic, stylish appearance*
air, aspect, bearing, cast, complexion, countenance, demeanor, effect, expression, face, fashion, guise, manner, mien, mug*, physiognomy, presence, seeming, semblance, visage; SEE CONCEPTS *655,673,716*

look [*v1*] *examine visually*
admire, attend, behold, beware, consider, contemplate, eye, feast one's eyes*, flash, focus, gape, gawk, gaze, get a load of, glance, glower, goggle, heed, inspect, mark, mind, note, notice, observe, ogle, peep, peer, pore over, read, regard, rubberneck*, scan, scout, scrutinize, see, spot, spy, stare, study, survey, take a gander*, take in the sights*, tend, view, watch; SEE CONCEPT *623*

look [*v2*] *appear, seem to be*
display, evidence, exhibit, express, indicate, look like, make clear, manifest, present, resemble, show, sound, strike as; SEE CONCEPTS *261,716*

look [*v3*] *expect, anticipate*
await, count on, divine, forecast, foretell, hope, hunt, reckon on, search, seek; SEE CONCEPT *26*

look [*v4*] *face*
front, front on, give onto, overlook; SEE CONCEPT *746*

look-alike [*n*] *double*
carbon copy, clone, copy, dead ringer*, duplicate, impersonator, match, replica, ringer*, spitting image*, stand-in*, twin; SEE CONCEPTS *664,716*

look down on [*v*] *hold in contempt*
abhor, contemn, despise, disdain, scorn, scout, sneer, spurn, turn nose up at*; SEE CONCEPT *29*

look into [*v*] *check, research*
audit, check out, delve into, dig, examine, explore, follow up, go into, inquire, inspect, investigate, look over, make inquiry, probe, prospect, scrutinize, sift, study; SEE CONCEPT *103*

lookout [*n*] *guard; place from which to guard*
anchor, beacon, belvedere, case, catbird seat*, citadel, crow's nest*, cupola, eagle eye*, hawk, observance, observation, observatory, outlook, overlook, panorama, patrol, post, scene, scout, sentinel, sentry, spotter, station, surveillance, tip, tower, view, vigil, vigilance, ward, watch, watcher, watch person watchtower*, weather eye*; SEE CONCEPTS *198,358,623*

look out [*v*] *be wary*
be alert, be careful, be on guard, beware, check out, have a care, heads up*, hearken, keep an eye out*, keep tabs*, listen, mind, notice, pay attention, peg*, pick up on*, scope, shotgun*, size up, spot, spy, watch out; SEE CONCEPTS *35,623*

look up [*v1*] *research*
come upon, confirm, discover, find, hunt for, peruse, scan, search for, seek, seek out, track down; SEE CONCEPTS *72,216*

look up [*v2*] *improve*
advance, ameliorate, come along, convalesce, gain, get better, mend, perk up, pick up, progress, recuperate, shape up, show improvement; SEE CONCEPTS *303,700*

loom [*v*] *appear, often imposingly*
approach, await, be at hand*, become visible, be coming, be imminent, be in the cards*, be in the wind*, be near, break through, brew, bulk, come forth, come into view, come on, come on the scene*, dawn, dominate, em-

anate, emerge, figure, gather, hang over, hover, impend, impress, issue, lower, make up, menace, mount, near, overhang, overshadow, overtop, portend, rear, rise, seem huge, seem large, show, soar, stand out, take shape, threaten, top, tower; SEE CONCEPTS *118,159,261*

loony [*adj*] *crazy*
ape, barmy, batty, berserk, bonkers*, cracked, crazed, cuckoo, daffy*, daft, delirious, demented, deranged, flaky, flipped out*, insane, kooky, lunatic, mad, maniacal, mental*, nuts, nutty, out of one's mind*, out to lunch*, psycho*, screwball*, screwy*, silly, touched*, unbalanced, wacky; SEE CONCEPT *403*

loony bin [*n*] *mental health facility*
bughouse*, funny farm*, insane asylum, madhouse*, mental hospital, mental institution, nut house*, psychiatric hospital, psychiatric ward, sanatorium; SEE CONCEPTS *312,439,516*

loop [*n*] *circle, spiral*
bend, circuit, circumference, coil, convolution, curl, curve, eyelet, hoop, kink, knot, loophole, noose, ring, twirl, twist, whorl, wreath; SEE CONCEPT *436*

loop [*v*] *circle, spiral*
arc, arch, begird, bend, bow, braid, coil, compass, connect, crook, curl, curve, curve around, encircle, encompass, fold, gird, girdle, join, knot, ring, roll, surround, tie together, turn, twist, wind around; SEE CONCEPTS *147,201,754*

loophole [*n*] *escape*
alternative, escape clause, means of escape, outlet, technicality, way out; SEE CONCEPT *102*

loose [*adj*] *not tight; unconstrained*
apart, asunder, at large, baggy, clear, detached, disconnected, easy, escaped, flabby, flaccid, floating, free, hanging, insecure, lax, liberated, limp, loosened, movable, not fitting, relaxed, released, separate, slack, slackened, sloppy, unattached, unbolted, unbound, unbuttoned, uncaged, unclasped, unconfined, unconnected, undone, unfastened, unfettered, unhinged, unhooked, unlatched, unlocked, unpinned, unrestrained, unrestricted, unsecured, unshackled, untied, wobbly; SEE CONCEPT *485*

loose [*adj*] *indefinite, vague*
detached, diffuse, disconnected, disordered, ill-defined, imprecise, inaccurate, indistinct, negligent, obscure, rambling, random, remiss; SEE CONCEPTS *267,529*

loose [*adj*] *promiscuous*
abandoned, capricious, careless, corrupt, debauched, disreputable, dissipated, dissolute, easy, fast, heedless, high living*, immoral, imprudent, inconstant, lax, lewd, libertine, licentious, light, negligent, out of control*, playing, profligate, rash, reckless, speeding, swinging, thoughtless, unchaste, unmindful, unrestrained, wanton; SEE CONCEPTS *372,401,545*

loose/loosen [*v*] *set free; unbind*
alleviate, become unfastened, break up, deliver, detach, discharge, disconnect, disengage, disenthrall, disjoin, ease, ease off, emancipate, extricate, free, let go, let out, liberate, manumit, mitigate, relax, release, separate, slacken, unbar, unbolt, unbuckle, unbutton, unchain, unclasp, undo, unfasten, unfix, unhitch, unhook, unlace, unlash, unlatch, unleash, unlock, unloose, unpin, unscrew, unsnap, unstick, unstrap, untie,

untighten, work free, work loose; SEE CONCEPTS *127,250*

loot [*n*] *stolen goods*
booty, dough*, graft, haul, hot goods*, lift*, make*, money, pickings*, pillage, plunder, plunderage, prize, seizure, spoils, squeeze, take*; SEE CONCEPTS *337,340*

loot [*v*] *steal goods*
appropriate, boost, burglarize, despoil, grab, gut, liberate, lift, loft, make, moonlight requisition*, pillage, plunder, raid, ransack, ravage, relieve, requisition, rifle, rip off*, rob, sack, salvage, smash and grab*, snatch, snitch*, stick up, swipe, take, thieve, tip over; SEE CONCEPTS *139,192*

looter [*n*] *thief*
criminal, marauder, pilferer, pillager, plunderer, raider, ransacker, ravager, spoiler; SEE CONCEPT *412*

lop [*v*] *trim*
chop, clip, crop, cut, cut back, cut down, mow, pare, pare down, prune, shear, snip, truncate; SEE CONCEPTS *176,236,247*

lope [*v*] *stride*
bound, canter, gallop, run, trot; SEE CONCEPT *149*

lopsided [*adj*] *leaning, falling to one side; larger on one side*
askew, asymmetrical, awry, cockeyed, crooked, disproportional, disproportionate, inclinatory, irregular, nonsymmetrical, off-balance, one-sided, out of shape, overbalanced, squint, tilting, top-heavy, unbalanced, unequal, uneven, unsteady, warped; SEE CONCEPT *480*

loquacious [*adj*] *talkative*
babbling, chattering, chatty, fluent, gabby*, garrulous, gossipy, jabbering, long-winded*, loose-lipped*, motormouth*, multiloquent, prolix, verbose, voluble, wordy, yacking*; SEE CONCEPTS *267,401*

lore [*n*] *myths, traditional wisdom*
adage, belief, custom, doctrine, enlightenment, erudition, experience, fable, folklore, information, knowledge, learning, legend, letters, mythology, mythos, saga, saw, saying, scholarship, science, superstition, tale, teaching, tradition; SEE CONCEPTS *274,282,287*

lose [*v1*] *be deprived of; mislay*
be careless, become poorer, be impoverished, bereave, be reduced, capitulate, consume, default, deplete, disinherit, displace, dispossess, dissipate, divest, drain, drop, exhaust, expend, fail, fail to keep, fall short, forfeit, forget, give up, lavish, misplace, miss, misspend, oust, pass up, relinquish, rob, sacrifice, squander, suffer, suffer loss, surrender, use up, waste, yield; SEE CONCEPTS *116,156*

lose [*v2*] *be defeated*
be humbled, be outdistanced, be sunk, be taken to cleaners*, be the loser, be worsted*, come up short, decline, drop, drop a bundle*, fall, kiss goodbye*, lose out, miss, succumb, suffer defeat, take a beating*, take the count*, take the heat*, yield; SEE CONCEPTS *384,674*

lose [*v3*] *escape, avoid*
clear, dodge, duck, elude, evade, give the slip*, leave behind, outrun, rid, shake, shake off*, slip away, stray, throw off*, unburden, wander from; SEE CONCEPTS *30,102*

loser [*n*] *person, thing that fails*
also-ran*, deadbeat*, defeated, disadvantaged,

down-and-outer*, dud*, failure, flop*, flunkee*, has-been, underdog, underprivileged; SEE CONCEPTS 412,423,433

loss [*n*] *misfortune, deficit; something misplaced or lost*
accident, bad luck, bereavement, calamity, casualty, cataclysm, catastrophe, cost, damage, death, debit, debt, defeat, deficiency, depletion, deprivation, destitution, destruction, detriment, disadvantage, disappearance, disaster, dispossession, failure, fall, fatality, forfeiture, harm, hurt, impairment, injury, losing, misadventure, mishap, mislaying, misplacing, need, perdition, privation, retardation, ruin, sacrifice, shrinkage, squandering, trial, trouble, undoing, want, waste, wreckage; SEE CONCEPTS 407,674,707

lost [*adj1*] *missing, off-track*
absent, adrift, astray, at sea, cast away, disappeared, disoriented, down the drain*, fallen between cracks*, forfeit, forfeited, gone, gone astray, hidden, invisible, irrecoverable, irretrievable, irrevocable, kiss goodbye*, lacking, minus, mislaid, misplaced, missed, nowhere to be found*, obscured, off-course, out the window*, strayed, unredeemed, vanished, wandering, wayward, without; SEE CONCEPT 576

lost [*adj2*] *extinct, destroyed*
abolished, annihilated, bygone, consumed, dead, demolished, devastated, dissipated, eradicated, exterminated, forgotten, frittered, gone, lapsed, misspent, misused, obliterated, obsolete, out-of-date, past, perished, ruined, squandered, unremembered, wasted, wiped out*, wrecked; SEE CONCEPTS 539,560

lost [*adj3*] *distracted, dreaming*
absent, absentminded, absorbed, abstracted, bemused, bewildered, distrait, dreamy, engrossed, entranced, faraway, feeble, going in circles*, ignorant, inconscient, musing, perplexed, preoccupied, rapt, spellbound, taken in*, taken up*, unconscious, wasted; SEE CONCEPT 403

lot [*n1*] *piece of property*
acreage, allotment, apportionment, area, block, clearing, division, field, frontage, parcel, part, patch, percentage, piece, plat, plot, plottage, portion, property, real estate, tract; SEE CONCEPTS 509,510

lot [*n2*] *quantity, often large*
abundance, aggregate, aggregation, amplitude, assortment, barrel, batch, body, bunch, bundle, circle, clump, cluster, clutch, collection, conglomerate, conglomeration, consignment, crowd, great deal, group, heap, load, mass, mess*, much, multiplicity, number, ocean, oodles, order, pack, pile, plenitude, plenty, push, reams, requisition, scores, set, stack, stacks; SEE CONCEPTS 432,787

lot [*n3*] *portion, share*
allotment, allowance, bite, cut, parcel, part, percentage, piece, quota, ration, slice, take; SEE CONCEPTS 710,835

lot [*n4*] *fate, destiny*
accident, break, breaks, chance, circumstance, decree, doom, foreordination, fortune, hand one is dealt*, hazard, karma, kismet, Moirai, plight, portion, predestination, run of luck*, way cookie crumbles*, wheel of fortune*; SEE CONCEPT 679

lothario [*n*] *womanizer*
Casanova, Don Juan, gigolo, ladies' man, ladykiller, lecher, libertine, lover, philanderer, rake,

Romeo, seducer, skirt chaser, stud*, wolf*; SEE CONCEPTS 372,401

lotion [*n*] *creamy solution*
balm, cosmetic, cream, demulcent, embrocation, lenitive, liniment, medicine, ointment, palliative, preparation, salve, unguent, wash; SEE CONCEPTS 311,446,466

lottery [*n*] *drawing*
chance, door prize, gambling, game of chance, Lotto, luck of the draw, numbers game, raffle, sweepstake; SEE CONCEPTS 28,363

loud [*adj1*] *blaring, noisy*
big, blatant, blustering, boisterous, booming, cacophonous, clamorous, crashing, deafening, deep, ear-piercing, ear-splitting, emphatic, forte, full, full-mouthed, fulminating, heavy, highsounding, intense, loud-voiced, lusty, obstreperous, pealing, piercing, powerful, rambunctious, raucous, resonant, resounding, ringing, roaring, rowdy, sonorous, stentorian, strident, strong, thundering, tumultuous, turbulent, turned up, uproarious, vehement, vociferous, wakes the dead*; SEE CONCEPTS 592,594

loud [*adj2*] *offensive, gaudy*
brash, brassy, brazen, chintzy, coarse, crass, crude, flamboyant, flashy, garish, glaring, gross, lurid, meretricious, obnoxious, obtrusive, ostentatious, raucous, rude, showy, tasteless, tawdry, vulgar; SEE CONCEPTS 401,542,589

loudmouthed [*adj*] *loud-voiced*
bellowing, bigmouthed, big-voiced, blustering, boisterous, full-throated, obnoxious, vociferous; SEE CONCEPT 401

lounge [*n*] *club, socializing place*
bar, barroom, club room, cocktail lounge, dive*, drinkery, hideaway, lobby, mezzanine, parlor, pub, reception, saloon, spot, tap, taproom, watering hole*; SEE CONCEPTS 293,449

lounge [*v*] *lie about, waste time*
bum*, dawdle, fritter away, goldbrick*, goof off*, idle, kill time*, laze, loaf, loiter, loll*, pass time, recline, relax, repose, saunter, sprawl, take it easy*; SEE CONCEPTS 154,210,681

lousy [*adj*] *very bad*
awful, base, contemptible, despicable, dirty, disliked, execrable, faulty, harmful, hateful, horrible, inferior, low, mean, miserable, no good*, outrageous, poor, rotten, second-rate*, shoddy, slovenly, terrible, unpopular, unwelcome, vicious, vile; SEE CONCEPT 571

lout [*n*] *boor*
barbarian, bear, boob*, brute, buffoon, bumpkin, cad, churl, clod, clodhopper, dolt, dork*, goon*, lummox, oaf, philistine, rube, slob*, vulgarian; SEE CONCEPT 423

loutish [*adj*] *boorish*
bad-mannered, barbaric, bearish, bungling, cantankerous, churlish, cloddish, clodhopping*, clownish, clumsy, coarse, dense, doltish, gross*, gruff, ill-bred, ill-mannered, impolite, loud, oafish, ornery, rough, rude, rustic, swinish, uncivilized, uncouth, uncultured, uneducated, unmannerly, unpolished, unrefined, vulgar; SEE CONCEPT 404

lovable [*adj*] *very likable; endearing*
adorable, agreeable, alluring, amiable, angelic, appealing, attractive, bewitching, captivating, charming, cuddly, delightful, desirable, enchanting, engaging, enthralling, entrancing, fascinating, fetching, friendly, genial, lovely, lovesome,

pleasing, ravishing, seductive, sweet, winning, winsome; SEE CONCEPT 404

love [*n1*] *adoration; very strong liking*
adulation, affection, allegiance, amity, amorousness, amour, appreciation, ardency, ardor, attachment, case*, cherishing, crush, delight, devotedness, devotion, emotion, enchantment, enjoyment, fervor, fidelity, flame, fondness, friendship, hankering, idolatry, inclination, infatuation, involvement, like, lust, mad for, partiality, passion, piety, rapture, regard, relish, respect, sentiment, soft spot*, taste, tenderness, weakness, worship, yearning, zeal; SEE CONCEPT 32

love [*n2*] *person who is loved by another*
admirer, angel, beau, beloved, boyfriend, courter, darling, dear, dearest, dear one, flame, girlfriend, honey, inamorata, inamorato, Juliet*, loved one, lover, paramour, passion, Romeo*, spark, suitor, swain, sweet, sweetheart, trueLove, valentine; SEE CONCEPT 423

love [*v1*] *adore, like very much*
admire, adulate, be attached to, be captivated by, be crazy about, be enamored of, be enchanted by, be fascinated with, be fond of, be in love with, canonize, care for, cherish, choose, deify, delight in, dote on, esteem, exalt, fall for, fancy, glorify, go for*, gone on*, have affection for, have it bad*, hold dear, hold high, idolize, long for, lose one's heart to*, prefer, prize, put on pedestal*, think the world of*, thrive with, treasure, venerate, wild for*, worship; SEE CONCEPT 32

love [*v2*] *have sexual relations*
caress, clasp, cling, cosset, court, cuddle, draw close, embrace, feel, fondle, hold, hug, kiss, lick, look tenderly, make love, neck*, pet*, press, shine, soothe, stroke, take into one's arms, tryst, woo; SEE CONCEPTS 375,384

love affair [*n*] *sexual relationship outside of marriage*
adultery, affair, amour, devotion, extracurricular activity*, flirtation, intrigue, liaison, love, menage à trois, passion, romance, thing, triangle; SEE CONCEPTS 375,388

love handles [*n*] *bulging waistline*
fat, flab, hate handles*, keg*, middle age spread*, spare tire*; SEE CONCEPTS 723,734

lovelorn [*n*] *unloved*
bereft, crossed in love, dejected, forsaken, jilted, loveless, lovesick, rejected, spurned; SEE CONCEPTS 21,30,384

lovely [*adj*] *beautiful, charming; agreeable*
admirable, adorable, alluring, amiable, attractive, beauteous, bewitching, captivating, comely, dainty, delectable, delicate, delicious, delightful, enchanting, engaging, enjoyable, exquisite, fair, good-looking, gorgeous, graceful, gratifying, handsome, knockout, lovesome, nice, picture, pleasant, pleasing, pretty, pulchritudinous, rare, scrumptious, splendid, stunning, sweet, winning; SEE CONCEPTS 537,579,589

lovemaking [*n*] *sexual activity*
carnal knowledge, coition, coitus, copulation, coquetting, courting, courtship, cuddling, dalliance, fondling, fooling around, foreplay, hugging, intercourse, intimacy, kissing, mating, screwing, sexual intercourse, sexual relations, smooching*, snuggling, sucking face*; SEE CONCEPT 375

lover [*n*] *person having sexual relationship*
admirer, beau, beloved, boyfriend, companion,

courter, darling, dear, dearest, escort, fiancé, fiancée, flame, girlfriend, idolizer, inamorata, inamorato, infatuate, Juliet*, paramour, petitioner, Romeo*, significant other, solicitor, steady, suitor, suppliant, swain, sweetheart, trueLove, valentine, wooer; SEE CONCEPT 423

lovesick [*adj*] *longing*
desiring, infatuated, languishing, lovelorn, pining, yearning; SEE CONCEPTS 21,30,384

loving [*adj*] *expressing adoration*
admiring, affectionate, amatory, amiable, amorous, anxious, appreciative, ardent, attached, attentive, benevolent, bound up, caring, concerned, considerate, cordial, dear, demonstrative, devoted, doting, earnest, enamored, erotic, expressive, faithful, fervent, fond, friendly, generous, idolatrous, impassioned, infatuated, kind, liking, loyal, passionate, respecting, reverent, reverential, romantic, sentimental, solicitous, tender, thoughtful, valuing, warm, warm-hearted, worshipful, zealous; SEE CONCEPTS 372,401,542

low [*adj1*] *close to the ground; short*
below, beneath, bottom, bottommost, crouched, decumbent, deep, depressed, flat, ground-level, inferior, junior, lesser, level, little, lowering, low-hanging, low-lying, low-set, minor, nether, not high, profound, prostrate, rock-bottom, shallow, small, squat, squatty, stunted, subjacent, subsided, sunken, under, unelevated; SEE CONCEPTS 583,779,782,793

low [*adj2*] *reduced; mediocre*
cheap, cut, cut-rate*, deficient, depleted, economical, inadequate, inexpensive, inferior, insignificant, little, low-grade, marked down, meager, moderate, modest, nominal, paltry, poor, puny, reasonable, scant, second-rate*, shoddy, slashed, small, sparse, substandard, trifling, uncostly, worthless; SEE CONCEPTS 334,574,789

low [*adj3*] *crude, vulgar*
abject, base, blue, coarse, common, contemptible, crass, crumby, dastardly, degraded, depraved, despicable, disgraceful, dishonorable, disreputable, gross*, ignoble, ill-bred, inelegant, mean, menial, miserable, nasty, obscene, off-color*, offensive, raw, rough, rude, scrubby, scruffy*, scurvy, servile, sordid, unbecoming, uncouth, undignified, unrefined, unworthy, vile, woebegone, woeful, wretched; SEE CONCEPTS 404,542

low [*adj4*] *living in, coming from poor circumstances*
base, baseborn, humble, ignoble, lowborn, lowly, mean, meek, obscure, plain, plebeian, poor, rude, simple, unpretentious, unwashed; SEE CONCEPT 549

low [*adj5*] *depressed*
bad, blue*, crestfallen, dejected, despondent, disheartened, down, down and out*, downcast, downhearted, down in the dumps*, down in the mouth*, dragged, fed up, forlorn, gloomy, glum, in the pits*, low-down*, miserable, moody, morose, sad, singing the blues*, spiritless, unhappy; SEE CONCEPT 403

low [*adj6*] *not feeling well*
ailing, debilitated, dizzy, dying, exhausted, faint, feeble, frail, ill, indisposed, poorly, prostrate, reduced, sick, sickly, sinking, stricken, unwell, weak; SEE CONCEPT 314

lo
lo

low [*adj7*] *not loud*
faint, gentle, hushed, muffled, muted, quiet, soft, subdued, whispered; SEE CONCEPT *594*

lowbrowed [*adj*] *uncultivated, vulgar*
ignorant, illiterate, uneducated, unlearned, unlettered, unread, unrefined, unschooled, unsophisticated, untaught, untutored; SEE CONCEPT *402*

lower [*adj*] *under, inferior*
bush-league*, curtailed, decreased, diminished, junior, lessened, lesser, low, lower rung, minor, nether, pared down, reduced, secondary, second-class, second-fiddle*, second-string*, smaller, subjacent, subordinate, under; SEE CONCEPTS *586,772*

lower [*v1*] *let down; fall*
bring low, cast down, couch, demit, depress, descend, detrude, droop, drop, ground, let down, make lower, push down, reduce, set down, sink, submerge, take down; SEE CONCEPT *181*

lower [*v2*] *reduce, minimize*
abate, clip, curtail, cut, cut back, cut down, decrease, decry, de-escalate, deflate, demote, depreciate, devaluate, devalue, diminish, downgrade, downsize, lessen, mark down, moderate, pare, prune, roll back, scale down, shave, slash, soften, tone down, undervalue, write off; SEE CONCEPTS *236,240,247*

lower [*v3*] *belittle, disgrace*
abase, bemean, cast down, condescend, debase, degrade, deign, demean, depress, devalue, downgrade, humble, humiliate, stoop; SEE CONCEPTS *7,19*

low-key [*adj*] *subdued*
easygoing, laid-back*, loose, low-pitched, muffled, muted, played down, quiet, relaxed, restrained, sober, softened, soft-sell*, subtle, toned down, understated; SEE CONCEPTS *542,544,548*

lowly [*adj*] *inferior, plain*
average, base, baseborn, cast down, common, commonplace, docile, dutiful, everyday, gentle, humble, ignoble, low, lowborn, mean, meek, menial, mild, modest, mundane, obscure, obsequious, ordinary, plebeian, poor, proletarian, prosaic, retiring, reverential, servile, simple, submissive, subordinate, unassuming, unpretentious, withdrawing; SEE CONCEPTS *404,547,549*

loyal [*adj*] *faithful, dependable*
allegiant, ardent, attached, behind one, believing, coming through, constant, devoted, dutiful, dyed-in-the-wool*, firm, on one's side*, patriotic, resolute, staunch, steadfast, steady, tried-and-true*, true, true-blue*, trustworthy, trusty, unfailing, unswerving, unwavering; SEE CONCEPTS *404,545*

loyalty [*n*] *faithfulness, dependability*
adherence, allegiance, ardor, attachment, bond, conscientiousness, constancy, devotedness, devotion, duty, earnestness, faith, fealty, fidelity, homage, honesty, honor, incorruptibility, integrity, inviolability, obedience, patriotism, probity, reliability, resolution, scrupulousness, sincerity, single-mindedness, singleness, staunchness, steadfastness, subjection, submission, support, tie, troth, trueheartedness, trueness, trustiness, trustworthiness, truth, truthfulness, uprightness, zeal; SEE CONCEPTS *411,645*

LSD [*n*] *lysergic acid diethylamide*
acid, blotter acid*, blue heaven*, California sunshine*, cubes*, dots*, drug, electric Kool-aid*, hallucinogen, instant Zen*, Lucy in the sky with diamonds*, mellow yellows*, microdots*, Owsley, Owsley's acid, purple haze, strawberry fields*, sunshine, tabs*, yellow sunshine*; SEE CONCEPT *307*

lubricant [*n*] *lubricator*
coating, grease, oil, silicone, wax, WD40℠; SEE CONCEPT *606*

lubricate [*v*] *make slippery*
anoint, cream, grease, lard, lube, make, oil, oil the wheels*, slick, smear, smooth, tallow, wax; SEE CONCEPT *202*

lucid [*adj1*] *evident, obvious*
apprehensible, clear, clear-cut, comprehendible, comprehensible, crystal clear, distinct, explicit, fathomable, graspable, intelligible, knowable, limpid, luminous, pellucid, plain, translucent, transparent, transpicuous, unambiguous, unblurred, understandable; SEE CONCEPT *529*

lucid [*adj2*] *brilliant, shining*
beaming, bright, effulgent, gleaming, incandescent, lambent, luminous, lustrous, radiant, refulgent, resplendent; SEE CONCEPT *617*

lucid [*adj3*] *clear, transparent*
clear, crystalline, diaphanous, gauzy, glassy, limpid, obvious, pellucid, pure, sheer, translucent, transpicuous, unblurred; SEE CONCEPTS *606,619*

lucid [*adj4*] *clearheaded, sensible*
all there, compos mentis, cool, got head together*, in right mind, normal, rational, reasonable, right, sane, sober, sound, together; SEE CONCEPTS *402,403*

Lucifer [*n*] *Satan*
archangel, beast, Beelzebub, devil, diablo, evil one, fallen angel, Mephistopheles, Prince of Darkness; SEE CONCEPTS *370,412*

luck [*n1*] *good fortune*
advantage, big break*, blessing, break*, fluke*, fortunateness, godsend*, good luck, happiness, health, in the cards*, karma*, kismet*, luckiness, lucky break*, occasion, opportunity, profit, prosperity, run of luck*, serendipity, smile*, streak of luck, stroke, success, triumph, victory, weal, wealth, win, windfall; SEE CONCEPT *693*

luck [*n2*] *chance*
accident, break, destiny, fate, fifty-fifty*, fortuity, fortune, hap*, happenstance, hazard, occasion, occurrence, toss-up*, unforeseen event; SEE CONCEPT *679*

luckily [*adv*] *happily*
by chance, favorably, fortuitously, fortunately, opportunely, propitiously, providentially; SEE CONCEPTS *544,572*

lucky [*adj*] *fortunate, opportune*
advantageous, adventitious, all systems go*, auspicious, beneficial, benign, blessed, charmed, coming up roses*, everything going*, favored, felicitous, fortuitous, getting a break*, golden, happy, hit it big*, holding aces*, hopeful, hot*, in the groove*, into something, on a roll*, on a streak, promising, propitious, prosperous, providential, serendipitous, striking it rich*, successful, timely, well; SEE CONCEPTS *537,572*

lucrative [*adj*] *productive, well-paid*
advantageous, cost effective, fatness, fruitful, gainful, good, high-income*, in the black*, money-making, paying, profitable, remunerative, sweet, worthwhile; SEE CONCEPT *334*

lucre [n] *money, profits*
capital, cash, earnings, funds, gain, gate*, gravy*, income, proceeds, receipts, resources, revenue, riches, take*, wealth; SEE CONCEPTS *332,340,344,693*

ludicrous [adj] *absurd, ridiculous*
antic, bizarre, burlesque, comic, comical, crazy, droll, fantastic, farcical, foolish, funny, gelastic, grotesque, incongruous, laughable, nonsensical, odd, outlandish, preposterous, risible, silly, zany; SEE CONCEPT *548*

lug [v] *drag something around*
bear, buck, carry, convey, draw, ferry, haul, heave, hump, jerk, lift, lurch, pack, pull, rake, schlepp*, snap, tote, tow, transport, trawl, tug, vellicate, yank; SEE CONCEPT *206*

luggage [n] *bag, suitcase*
baggage, carry-on, case, fortnighter, gear, impedimenta, paraphernalia, suit bag, things*, tote bag, trunk, valise; SEE CONCEPTS *446,494*

lukewarm [adj1] *slightly heated*
blood-warm, milk-warm, tepid, warm, warmish; SEE CONCEPT *605*

lukewarm [adj2] *indifferent, unenthusiastic*
apathetic, chilly, cold, cool, halfhearted, hesitant, indecisive, irresolute, phlegmatic, tepid, uncertain, uncommitted, unconcerned, undecided, uninterested, unresolved, unresponsive, wishy-washy*; SEE CONCEPTS *403,542*

lull [n] *pause, calm*
abeyance, break, breather, breathing spell, calmness, coffee break, comma*, downtime*, hiatus, hush, layoff, letup, pausation, quiescence, quiet, respite, silence, stillness, stop, time-out*, tranquility; SEE CONCEPT *807*

lull [v] *calm, ease off*
abate, allay, balm, becalm, cease, chill out*, compose, cool*, cool off*, decrease, die down, diminish, dwindle, ebb, fall, hush, lay back, let up, lullaby, moderate, pacify, put a lid on*, qualify, quell, quiet, quiet down, settle, slacken, softpedal*, soothe, still, stroke, subdue, subside, take it easy*, take the edge*, take the sting out*, temper, tranquilize, wane; SEE CONCEPTS *7,22,210,698*

lumber [v1] *walk heavily, clumsily*
barge, clump, galumph, lump, plod, shamble, shuffle, slog, stump, trudge, trundle, waddle; SEE CONCEPT *151*

lumber [v2] *burden*
charge, cumber, encumber, impose upon, lade, land, load, saddle, tax, weigh; SEE CONCEPT *14*

lumbering [adj] *clumsy, awkward*
blundering, bovine, bumbling, clodhopping*, clunking, elephantine, gauche, gawky, halting, heavy, heavy-footed, hulking, inept, klutzy*, lead-footed*, lumpish, maladroit, overgrown, ponderous, splay, two left feet*, ungainly, unhandy, unwieldy, wooden; SEE CONCEPTS *406,584*

luminary [n] *very important person*
big name*, celeb*, celebrity, dignitary, eminence, leader, lion*, name, notability, notable, personage, personality, somebody*, star, superstar, VIP*, worthy; SEE CONCEPTS *352,423*

luminescent [adj] *glowing, shining*
bright, effulgent, fluorescent, luminous, phosphorescent, radiant; SEE CONCEPT *617*

luminous [adj1] *bright, glowing*
beaming, brilliant, clear, crystal, effulgent, ful-

gent, illuminated, incandescent, lambent, lighted, lit, lucent, lucid, luminescent, lustrous, radiant, refulgent, resplendent, shining, translucent, transparent, vivid; SEE CONCEPT *617*

luminous [adj2] *obvious, understandable*
apprehensible, bright, brilliant, clear, comprehendible, comprehensible, evident, fathomable, graspable, intelligible, knowable, lucid, perspicacious, perspicuous; SEE CONCEPT *529*

lummox [n] *oaf*
beast, blunderer, boor, bruiser, brute, bumpkin, chump*, clod, clodhopper, clown, dolt, dumb ox*, dunce, fool, goon*, half-wit*, hayseed, idiot, imbecile, klutz*, loser, lout*, lunkhead, moron, nincompoop*, ox*, sap*, simpleton*, yokel; SEE CONCEPT *412*

lump [n] *clump, mass*
agglomeration, ball, bit, block, bulge, bulk, bump, bunch, cake, chip, chunk, cluster, crumb, dab, gob, group, growth, handful, hunk, knot, knurl, lot, morsel, mountain, much, nugget, part, peck, piece, pile, portion, protrusion, protuberance, scrap, section, solid, spot, swelling, tumescence, tumor, wad, wedge; SEE CONCEPTS *432,470,471*

lump [v] *tolerate, withstand*
abide, bear, brook, digest, endure, put up with, stand, stomach, suffer, swallow, take; SEE CONCEPT *23*

lunacy [n] *craziness, madness*
aberration, absurdity, alienation, asininity, dementia, derangement, distraction, fatuity, folly, foolhardiness, foolishness, idiocy, imbalance, imbecility, inanity, ineptitude, insanity, mania, psychopathy, psychosis, senselessness, silliness, stupidity; SEE CONCEPTS *410,633*

lunatic [adj] *crazy, mad*
absurd, baked*, balmy*, bananas*, bonkers*, cracked, crazed, daft, demented, deranged, dippy*, flaky*, flipped out*, foolish, freaked out*, fried*, idiotic, insane, irrational, kooky*, loco, maniac, maniacal, nonsensical, nutty*, preposterous, psyched out*, psychotic, schizoid*, screwy*, stupid, unsound, whacko*, zany; SEE CONCEPTS *401,403*

lunatic [n] *person who is crazy, mad*
crackpot*, crank, cuckoo*, demoniac, flake*, fruitcake*, kook*, lamebrain*, loon*, maniac, neurotic, nut*, paranoid, psycho*, psychopath, psychotic, scatterbrain, schizophrenic, sociopathic; SEE CONCEPTS *412,809*

lunge [n] *pounce*
charge, cut, jab, jump, pass, spring, stab, swing, swipe, thrust; SEE CONCEPTS *159,194*

lunge [v] *pounce, dive for*
bound, burst, charge, cut, dash, drive, fall upon, hit, jab, jump, leap, lurch, pitch, plunge, poke, push, set upon, stab, strike, surge, thrust; SEE CONCEPTS *159,194*

lurch [v] *move toward with jerk*
blunder, bumble, careen, dodge, duck, falter, flounder, heave, jerk, lean, list, move to the side, pitch, reel, rock, roll, seesaw, slide, slip, stagger, stumble, sway, swing, teeter, tilt, toss, totter, wallow, weave, wobble, yaw; SEE CONCEPTS *80,150,152,194*

lure [n] *bait*
allurement, ambush, appeal, attraction, bribe, call, camouflage, carrot*, come-on*, con game*, decoy, delusion, draw, enticement, fake, gim-

lo
lu

mick, hook, illusion, incentive, inducement, inveiglement, invitation, magnet*, mousetrap*, pull, seducement, seduction, siren song*, sitting duck*, snare, sweetener*, temptation, tout, trap, trick; SEE CONCEPTS *32,529*

lure [v] *attract, seduce*
allure, bag, bait, beckon, beguile, bewitch, cajole, captivate, capture, catch, charm, come on*, decoy, drag, draw, enchant, ensnare, entice, fascinate, grab, haul, hit on*, hook, inveigle, invite, lead on, pull, rope, steer, suck in*, sweep off one's feet*, tempt, train, turn on; SEE CONCEPT *11*

lurid [adj] *shocking, gruesome*
ashen, bloody, deep, disgusting, distinct, exaggerated, extreme, fiery, ghastly, gory*, graphic, grim, grisly, hideous, horrible, horrid, horrifying, livid, low-down, macabre, melodramatic, obscene, off-color*, offensive, purple*, racy, raunchy, revolting, rough, salty, sanguine*, savage, sensational, sinister, startling, terrible, terrifying, violent, vivid, yellow*; SEE CONCEPTS *267,537*

lurk [v] *hide; move stealthily*
conceal oneself, creep, crouch, go furtively, gumshoe, lie in wait, prowl, skulk, slide, slink, slip, snake, sneak, snoop, stay hidden, steal, wait; SEE CONCEPTS *151,188*

luscious [adj] *delicious, delectable*
adorable, ambrosial, appetizing, choice, darling, delish, deluxe, distinctive, divine, exquisite, flamboyant, flavorsome, heavenly, honeyed, juicy, lush, luxurious, mellow, mouth-watering, nectarious, opulent, ornate, palatable, palatial, piquant, rare, rich, savory, scrumptious, succulent, sumptuous, sweet, toothsome, voluptuous, yummy*; SEE CONCEPTS *574,613*

lush [adj] *profuse and delightful*
abundant, ambrosial, delectable, delicious, deluxe, dense, elaborate, extensive, extravagant, exuberant, flourishing, fresh, grand, green, heavenly, juicy, lavish, luscious, luxuriant, luxurious, opulent, ornate, overgrown, palatial, plush, prodigal, prolific, rank, rich, riotous, ripe, ritzy, scrumptious, sensuous, succulent, sumptuous, teeming, tender, verdant, voluptuous; SEE CONCEPTS *574,589,771*

lust [n] *appetite, passion*
animalism, aphrodisia, appetence, appetition, avidity, carnality, concupiscence, covetousness, craving, cupidity, desire, eroticism, excitement, fervor, greed, hunger, itch, lasciviousness, lechery, lewdness, libido, licentiousness, longing, prurience, pruriency, salaciousness, salacity, sensualism, sensuality, thirst, urge, wantonness, weakness, yen; SEE CONCEPTS *20,709*

lust [v] *desire strongly*
ache, be consumed with desire, be hot for*, covet, crave, hanker, hunger for, itch, long, need, pine, thirst, want, wish, yearn, yen; SEE CONCEPT *20*

luster [n] *gloss, shine*
afterglow, brightness, brilliance, brilliancy, burnish, candescence, dazzle, effulgence, glaze, gleam, glint, glitter, glow, incandescence, iridescence, lambency, luminousness, opalescence, polish, radiance, refulgence, resplendence, sheen, shimmer, sparkle; SEE CONCEPT *620*

lustrous [adj] *glossy, shining*
bright, burnished, dazzling, effulgent, fulgent,

glacé, gleaming, glinting, glistening, glorious, glowing, incandescent, lambent, lucent, luminous, polished, radiant, refulgent, shimmering, shiny, sparkling, splendid, waxy; SEE CONCEPT *617*

lusty [adj] *energetic, healthy*
brawny, dynamic, hale, hearty, potent, powerful, red-blooded, robust, rugged, stalwart, stout, strapping, strenuous, strong, sturdy, tough, vigorous, vital; SEE CONCEPTS *314,485,489*

luxuriant [adj] *profuse, plush*
abundant, ample, copious, deluxe, dense, elaborate, excessive, extravagant, exuberant, fancy, fecund, fertile, flamboyant, flourishing, fruitful, lavish, luscious, lush, opulent, overflowing, palatial, plenteous, plentiful, prodigal, productive, profusive, prolific, rampant, rank, rich, riotous, sumptuous, superabundant, teeming, thriving; SEE CONCEPTS *574,771*

luxuriate [adj] *indulge, prosper*
abound, bask, be in clover*, bloom, burgeon, delight, eat up*, enjoy, feast, flourish, grow, increase, live extravagantly, live high on hog*, live in luxury*, live it up*, love, overdo, relish, revel, riot, roll, rollick, take it easy*, thrive, wallow, wanton; SEE CONCEPTS *539,544,589*

luxurious [adj] *affluent, indulgent*
comfortable, costly, deluxe, easy, elaborate, epicurean, expensive, extravagant, fancy, fit for a king/queen*, gorgeous, grand, grandiose, gratifying, hedonistic, immoderate, imposing, impressive, in the lap of luxury, lavish, luscious, lush, magnificent, majestic, opulent, ostentatious, palatial, pampered, pleasurable, pleasure-loving, plush, plushy, posh, pretentious, rich, ritzy*, self-indulgent, sensual, sensuous, splendid, stately, sumptuous, sybaritic, upscale, voluptuous, well-appointed; SEE CONCEPTS *544,574,589*

luxury [n] *great pleasure, indulgence*
affluence, bliss, comfort, delight, enjoyment, exorbitance, extravagance, frill, gratification, hedonism, high living, immoderation, intemperance, leisure, luxuriousness, opulence, rarity, richness, satisfaction, splendor, sumptuousness, treat, well-being; SEE CONCEPTS *337,388,712*

lying [adj] *dishonest*
committing perjury, deceitful, deceptive, delusive, delusory, dissembling, dissimulating, double-crossing*, double-dealing*, equivocating, false, falsifying, fibbing, guileful, inventing, mendacious, misleading, misrepresenting, misstating, perfidious, prevaricating, shifty, treacherous, tricky, two-faced*, two-timing*, unreliable, untruthful, wrong; SEE CONCEPT *267*

lynching [n] *hanging*
capital punishment, execution, mob justice*, stringing up*, the gallows*, vigilante justice; SEE CONCEPT *252*

lyric [adj] *musical*
choral, coloratura, mellifluous, melodic, melodious, poetic, songful, songlike, tuneful; SEE CONCEPT *594*

lyrical [adj] *musical*
agreeable, blending, chiming, choral, dulcet, emotional, euphonious, expressive, harmonious, lilting, melodic, melodious, operatic, orchestral, passionate, pleasing, poetic, rhapsodic, rhythmic, songful, songlike, soulful, sweet-sounding, symphonic, symphonious, tuneful; SEE CONCEPT *594*

lyricist [*n*] *songwriter*
composer, lyrist, musician, music writer, poet, songsmith, songwriter; SEE CONCEPT *352*

M

macabre [*adj*] *eerie; deathlike*
cadaverous, deathly, dreadful, frightening, frightful, ghastly, ghostly, ghoulish, grim, grisly, gruesome, hideous, horrible, horrid, lurid, morbid, offensive, scary, spookish, spooky, terrible, unearthly, weird; SEE CONCEPTS *537,547*

macaroni [*n*] *pasta*
noodles, penne, shells, spaghetti, tortellini; SEE CONCEPTS *457,460,461*

Machiavellian [*adj*] *scheming*
artful, astute, calculating, conniving, contriving, crafty, cunning, deceitful, devious, expedient, opportunist, plotting, shrewd, sly, underhanded, unscrupulous, wily; SEE CONCEPTS *401,545*

machinate [*v*] *maneuver, plot*
cogitate, collude, come up with, connive, conspire, contrive, design, devise, engineer, finagle, hatch, intrigue, invent, plan, play games*, promote, pull strings*, scheme, trump up*, wangle; SEE CONCEPT *36*

machination [*n*] *maneuver, plot*
artifice, cabal, conspiracy, design, device, dirty work*, dodge*, intrigue, monkey business*, on the make*, ploy, practice, ruse, scheme, sellout, skullduggery*, song and dance*, stratagem, trick; SEE CONCEPT *660*

machine [*n1*] *device that performs a task*
apparatus, appliance, automaton, automobile, computer, contraption, contrivance, engine, gadget, implement, instrument, mechanism, motor, robot, thingamabob*, tool, vehicle, widget*; SEE CONCEPT *463*

machine [*n2*] *well-run political organization*
agency, lineup, machinery, movement, party, ring, setup, structure, system; SEE CONCEPT *301*

machine [*n3*] *person who acts automatically*
agent, automaton, clone, drudge, grind, laborer, mechanical, puppet, robot, zombie*; SEE CONCEPTS *348,423*

machinery [*n*] *devices performing work*
accouterment, agency, agent, apparatus, appliance, channel, contraption, contrivance, engine, equipment, gadget, gear, habiliments, implement, instrument, materiel, means, mechanism, medium, method, motor, organ, outfit, paraphernalia, shifts, structure, system, tackle, tool, utensil, vehicle, works; SEE CONCEPTS *463,770*

machismo [*n*] *masculinity*
macho*, male, manful, manliness, mannish, masculine, muscular, virile; SEE CONCEPTS *371,408,648*

macho [*adj*] *masculine*
aggressive, cocky, courageous, manful, manly, potent, ultramasculine, virile; SEE CONCEPTS *371,408,648*

mad [*adj1*] *crazy, insane*
aberrant, absurd, bananas*, batty, crazed, cuckoo*, daft, delirious, demented, deranged, distracted, fantastic, foolhardy, foolish, frantic, frenetic, frenzied, illogical, imprudent, invalid, irrational, kooky*, loony*, ludicrous, lunatic, mental, non compos mentis, nonsensical, nutty*, off one's rocker*, of unsound mind, out of one's mind*, preposterous, psychotic, rabid, raving, senseless, unbalanced, unhinged, unreasonable, unsafe, unsound, unstable, wacky*; SEE CONCEPTS *403,529*

mad [*adj2*] *angry*
abandoned, agitated, berserk, distracted, distraught, enraged, exasperated, excited, frantic, frenetic, fuming, furious, incensed, infuriated, irritated, livid, provoked, raging, resentful, seeing red*, uncontrolled, very upset, wild, wrathful; SEE CONCEPT *403*

mad [*adj3*] *enthusiastic; in love*
ardent, avid, crazy, daft, devoted, enamoured, enthused, fanatical, fond, hooked*, impassioned, infatuated, keen, nuts*, wild, zealous; SEE CONCEPTS *32,403*

madcap [*adj*] *crazy, impulsive*
brash, foolhardy, foolish, frivolous, harebrained*, heedless, hotheaded, ill-advised, imprudent, incautious, inconsiderate, lively, rash, reckless, stupid, thoughtless, wild; SEE CONCEPT *548*

madden [*v*] *make angry*
anger, annoy, bother, craze, derange, distract, drive crazy, drive insane, drive out of mind*, drive to distraction*, enrage, exasperate, frenzy, incense, inflame, infuriate, ire, irritate, make see red*, pester, possess, provoke, shatter, steam up*, umbrage, unbalance, unhinge*, upset, vex; SEE CONCEPTS *7,19*

maddening [*adj*] *irritating*
aggravating, annoying, exasperating, frustrating, infuriating, provoking, riling, troubling, trying, vexatious; SEE CONCEPTS *529,565*

made-up [*adj*] *invented mentally*
fabricated, false, fictional, imaginary, make-believe, mythical, prepared, specious, trumped-up, unreal, untrue; SEE CONCEPT *582*

madhouse [*n*] *place where mentally ill live; place full of commotion*
asylum, bedlam, chaos, insane asylum, loony bin*, mental hospital, mental institution, pandemonium, psychiatric hospital, sanitarium, turmoil, uproar; SEE CONCEPTS *312,449,516,674*

madly [*adj*] *wildly, fiercely*
absurdly, crazily, deliriously, dementedly, desperately, devotedly, distractedly, energetically, exceedingly, excessively, excitedly, extremely, foolishly, frantically, frenziedly, furiously, hard, hastily, hurriedly, hysterically, insanely, intensely, irrationally, like mad, ludicrously, nonsensically, passionately, psychotically, quickly, rabidly, rapidly, rashly, recklessly, senselessly, something fierce, speedily, stormily, to distraction, tumultously/tumultuously, turbulently, unreasonably, violently; SEE CONCEPTS *537,540,544*

madness [*n*] *insanity*
aberration, absurdity, craziness, delirium, delusion, dementia, derangement, fanaticism, foolishness, hysteria, irrationality, lunacy, madness, mania, mental disorder, mental illness, neurosis, phobia, psychopathy, psychosis, stupidity, unbalance; SEE CONCEPTS *316,410*

lu
ma

mad person [n] *person who is considered mentally ill*

bedlamite, crazy person, demented, deranged, idiot, imbecile, loon, lunatic, maniac, mental case*, patient, psycho*, psychopath, psychotic, raver*, schizophrenic, sociopath; SEE CONCEPTS 412,423

maelstrom [n1] *agitation*

bedlam, chaos, confusion, disorder, flap*, fuss, pandemonium, turbulence, turmoil, uproar; SEE CONCEPTS 230,674

maelstrom [n2] *whirlpool*

eddy, stir, swirl, undercurrent, undertow, vortex, whirl; SEE CONCEPT 514

magazine [n1] *periodic publication*

annual, bimonthly, biweekly, booklet, broadside, brochure, circular, daily, digest, gazette, glossy, joint, journal, manual, monthly, newsletter, newspaper, organ, pamphlet, paper, periodical, pulp*, quarterly, rag*, review, semiweekly, sheet*, slick, throwaway*, weekly; SEE CONCEPT 280

magazine [n2] *arsenal of weapons*

ammunition dump, armory, cache, depository, depot, munitions dump, repertory, repository, store, storehouse, warehouse; SEE CONCEPTS 321,500

magic [n] *supernatural power; appearance of impossible feats by tricks*

abracadabra*, alchemy, allurement, astrology, augury, bewitchment, black art, conjuring, conjury, devilry, diabolism, divination, enchantment, exorcism, fascination, foreboding, fortune-telling, hocuspocus*, horoscopy, illusion, incantation, legerdemain, magnetism, necromancy, occultism, power, prediction, presage, prestidigitation, prophecy, rune, sleight of hand, soothsaying, sorcery, sortilege, spell, superstition, taboo, thaumaturgy, trickery, voodoo, voodooism, witchcraft, wizardry; SEE CONCEPTS 370,689

magician [n] *person who performs supernatural feats or tricks*

archimage, charmer, conjurer, diabolist, diviner, enchanter, enchantress, exorciser, exorcist, fortune-teller, genie, genius, illusionist, marvel, medicine person, medium, miracle worker, necromancer, prophet, satanist, seer, shaman, siren, soothsayer, sorcerer, spellbinder, thaumaturge, theurgist, trickster, virtuoso, voodoo, warlock, witch, witch doctor, wizard; SEE CONCEPTS 352,361

magic/magical [adj] *bewitching, charming*

bewitched, charismatic, clairvoyant, conjuring, demoniac, diabolic, eerie, enchanted, enchanting, ensorcelled, entranced, entrancing, extraordinary, fascinating, fiendish, ghostly, haunted, imaginary, magnetic, marvelous, miraculous, mysterious, mystic, mythical, necromantic, occult, otherworldly, parapsychological, runic, sorcerous, spectral, spellbinding, spellbound, spiritualistic, spooky, telekinetic, thaumaturgic, tranced, uncanny, unusual, weird, witching, witchlike, wizardly, wonderful; SEE CONCEPTS 537,548,582

magistrate [n] *civil officer*

bailiff, JP, judge, justice, justice of the peace; SEE CONCEPT 354

magnanimous [adj] *giving and kind*

all heart, altruistic, beneficent, benevolent, big, bighearted, bountiful, charitable, considerate, forgiving, free, generous, great, greathearted, handsome, has heart in right place*, highminded, kindly, knightly, liberal, lofty, loose, munificent, noble, openhanded, Santa Claus*, selfless, soft*, soft-touch*, ungrudging, unselfish, unstinting; SEE CONCEPTS 404,542

magnate [n] *important person, usually in business*

aristocrat, bigwig*, businessperson, capitalist, captain of industry, chief, figure, financier, industrialist, leader, lion*, merchant, mogul, name, noble, notable, peer, personage, plutocrat, tycoon, VIP*; SEE CONCEPT 347

magnetic [adj] *drawing, attractive*

alluring, appealing, arresting, bewitching, captivating, charismatic, charming, enchanting, entrancing, fascinating, hypnotic, inviting, irresistible, mesmerizing, pulling, seductive; SEE CONCEPTS 404,537

magnetism [n] *charm, attractiveness*

allure, appeal, attraction, captivatingness, charisma, draw, drawing power, enchantment, fascination, glamour, hypnotism, influence, lure, magic, mesmerism, power, pull, seductiveness, spell, witchcraft, witchery; SEE CONCEPTS 411,676

magnificent [adj] *glorious, wonderful*

arresting, august, brilliant, chivalric, commanding, elegant, elevated, exalted, excellent, fine, glittering, gorgeous, grand, grandiose, highminded, imperial, imposing, impressive, lavish, lofty, luxurious, magnanimous, magnific, majestic, noble, opulent, outstanding, palatial, plush, pompous, posh, proud, radiant, regal, resplendent, rich, royal, smashing, splendid, standout, stately, striking, sublime, sumptuous, superb, superior, superlative, swanky, towering, transcendent; SEE CONCEPTS 485,572

magnify [v1] *enlarge, intensify*

aggrandize, aggravate, amplify, augment, bless, blow up, boost, build up, deepen, dignify, dilate, distend, enhance, ennoble, eulogize, exalt, expand, extend, glorify, heighten, hike, hike up, increase, inflate, intensate, jack up, jump up, mount, multiply, pad, pyramid, redouble, rise, rouse, run up, step up, sweeten, swell; SEE CONCEPTS 236,244,245

magnify [v2] *exaggerate, blow out of proportion*

aggravate, blow up*, boost, color, dramatize, embellish, embroider, enhance, fudge*, inflate, make mountain of molehill*, overcharge, overdo, overdraw, overemphasize, overestimate, overplay, overrate, overstate, overstress, pad*, puff up*, pyramid; SEE CONCEPTS 49,69,266

magnitude [n1] *importance*

consequence, degree, eminence, grandeur, greatness, import, mark, moment, momentousness, note, pith, significance, signification, weight, weightiness; SEE CONCEPT 668

magnitude [n2] *size*

admeasurement, amount, amplitude, bigness, breadth, bulk, capacity, compass, dimension, dimensions, enormity, enormousness, expanse, extent, greatness, hugeness, immensity, intensity, largeness, mass, measure, measurement, proportion, proportions, quantity, range, reach, sizableness, space, strength, tremendousness, vastness, volume; SEE CONCEPT 730

maharishi [n] *spiritual leader*
guru, master, mentor, mystic, spiritual guide, swami, teacher; SEE CONCEPT *350*

maiden [adj] *earliest*
beginning, first, fresh, inaugural, initial, initiatory, intact, introductory, new, original, pioneer, primary, prime, unbroached, untapped, untried, unused; SEE CONCEPTS *548,585*

mail [n] *written correspondence; system for sending correspondence*
air mail, communication, junk mail, letter, package, parcel, post, postal service, postcard, post office; SEE CONCEPTS *271,770*

mail [v] *send through the postal system*
dispatch, drop, express, forward, post, send by mail, transmit; SEE CONCEPT *217*

maim [v] *cripple, put out of action*
batter, blemish, break, castrate, crush, damage, deface, disable, disfigure, dismember, disqualify, gimp*, hack, hamstring*, harm, hog-tie*, hurt, impair, incapacitate, injure, lame, mangle, mar, massacre, maul, mayhem, mutilate, spoil, truncate, warp, wound; SEE CONCEPT *246*

main [adj1] *principal, predominant*
capital, cardinal, central, chief, controlling, critical, crucial, essential, foremost, fundamental, head, leading, major, necessary, outstanding, paramount, particular, preeminent, premier, prevailing, primary, prime, special, star, stellar, supreme, vital; SEE CONCEPTS *546,567,829*

main [adj2] *absolute, utter*
brute, direct, downright, entire, mere, only, pure, sheer, simple, undisguised, utmost; SEE CONCEPT *535*

main [n] *pipe for system*
cable, channel, conduit, duct, line, trough, trunk; SEE CONCEPT *494*

mainly [adv] *for the most part*
above all, chiefly, essentially, first and foremost, generally, in general, in the main, largely, mostly, most of all, on the whole, overall, predominantly, primarily, principally, substantially, to the greatest extent, usually; SEE CONCEPTS *530,544,772*

mainstay [n] *chief support*
anchor, backbone, brace, bulwark, buttress, crutch*, good right arm*, linchpin*, maintainer, pillar, prop, right-hand person*, sinew, staff, standby, stay, strength, supporter, sustainer, upholder; SEE CONCEPTS *646,712*

mainstream [adj] *prevailing*
accepted, average, common, conventional, current, dominant, established, general, normal, popular, predominant, primary, regular, standard, typical, widespread; SEE CONCEPT *530*

maintain [v1] *care for, keep up*
advance, carry on, conserve, continue, control, cultivate, finance, go on with, guard, keep, keep going, look after, manage, nurture, perpetuate, persevere, preserve, prolong, protect, provide, renew, repair, retain, save, supply, support, sustain, take care of, uphold; SEE CONCEPTS *134,140*

maintain [v2] *assert, claim; argue for*
advocate, affirm, allege, asseverate, attest, aver, avow, back, champion, contend, correct, declare, defend, emphasize, fight for, hold, insist, justify, persist, plead for, profess, protest, rectify, report, right, say, stand by, state, stress, uphold, vindicate; SEE CONCEPTS *46,49,68*

maintenance [n] *perpetuation, support; sustenance*
aliment, alimentation, alimony, allowance, bacon*, bread, bread and butter*, care, carrying, conservation, continuance, continuation, food, keep, keeping, livelihood, living, nurture, preservation, prolongation, provision, repairs, resources, retainment, salt*, subsistence, supply, sustaining, sustainment, sustention, upkeep, wherewithal; SEE CONCEPTS *134,340,457,712*

majestic [adj] *impressive, splendid*
august, awesome, ceremonious, cool, courtly, dignified, elevated, exalted, fab*, grand, grandiose, imperial, imposing, lofty, magnific, magnificent, marvelous, mind-blowing*, monumental, noble, out of this world*, pompous, regal, royal, smashing, sovereign, stately, stunning, sublime, sumptuous, superb; SEE CONCEPTS *567,572,574*

major [adj1] *bigger*
above, better, big, chief, considerable, dominant, elder, exceeding, extensive, extreme, greater, hefty, higher, large, larger, large-scale, leading, main, most, oversized, primary, senior, sizable, superior, supreme, ultra, upper, uppermost; SEE CONCEPTS *574,773*

major [adj2] *important*
big, chief, critical, crucial, dangerous, grave, great, grievous, heavyweight, influential, life and death*, main, major-league, meaningful, notable, outstanding, overshadowing, preeminent, principal, radical, serious, significant, star, stellar, top, vital, weighty; SEE CONCEPT *568*

majority [n1] *plurality, most*
best part*, bulk, greater number, greater part, larger part, lion's share*, mass, max*, more, more than half*, preponderance, superiority; SEE CONCEPTS *766,829,835*

majority [n2] *adulthood*
age of consent, drinking age, estate, full age, legal maturity, manhood, maturity, prime, prime of life*, ripe age*, seniority, voting age, womanhood; SEE CONCEPTS *715,817*

make [v1] *create, build*
accomplish, adjust, arrange, assemble, beget, brew, bring about, cause, compose, conceive, constitute, construct, cook, cook up*, dash off*, draw on, dream up, effect, engender, fabricate, fashion, forge, form, frame, generate, get ready, give rise to, hatch, initiate, invent, knock off*, lead to, manufacture, mold, occasion, originate, parent, prepare, procreate, produce, put together, secure, shape, spawn, synthesize, tear off, throw together*, whip, whip out*; SEE CONCEPTS *168,173,205,221*

make [v2] *induce, compel*
bring about, cause, coerce, concuss, constrain, dragoon, drive, effect, force, horn in*, impel, impress, initiate, interfere, meddle, oblige, press, pressurize, prevail upon, require, secure, shotgun, start, tamper; SEE CONCEPTS *14,221*

make [v3] *designate, appoint*
advance, assign, constitute, create, delegate, elect, finger, install, invest, name, nominate, ordain, proffer, select, tap, tender; SEE CONCEPTS *50,88*

make [v4] *enact, execute*
act, carry on, carry out, carry through, conduct, declare, decree, do, draft, draw up, effect, engage in, establish, fix, form, formulate, frame, legis-

late, pass, perform, practice, prepare, prosecute, wage; SEE CONCEPTS 91,100,242

make [*v5*] *add up to; constitute*
amount to, come to, compose, compound, comprise, construct, embody, equal, fabricate, form, make up, mix, organize, put together, represent, structure, synthesize, texture; SEE CONCEPTS 664,667

make [*v6*] *estimate, infer*
calculate, collect, conclude, deduce, deduct, derive, dope out, draw, figure, gather, gauge, judge, reckon, suppose, think; SEE CONCEPTS 15,37

make [*v7*] *earn, acquire*
bring home bacon*, bring in, clean up*, clear, gain, get, harvest, hustle, net, obtain, pull, pull down*, rate, realize, reap, receive, secure, sock*, take in; SEE CONCEPTS 120,124,351

make [*v8*] *arrive, aim at*
advance, arrive at, arrive in time, attain, bear, break for, catch, get to, go, head, light out, meet, move, proceed, progress, reach, set out, strike out, take off; SEE CONCEPTS 159,224

make-believe [*adj*] *imagined, unreal*
acted, dream, false, fantasized, fantasy, fictional, fraudulent, imaginary, made-up, mock, pretend, pretended, sham, simulated; SEE CONCEPTS 529,582

make-believe [*n*] *unreality*
charade, disguise, dissimulation, dream, fairy tale, fakery, fantasy, imagination, pageant, playacting, pretense, pretension, pretentiousness, sham; SEE CONCEPTS 689,725

make-believe [*v*] *pretend, dream*
act as if, act as though, counterfeit, enact, fantasize, feign, fool, imagine, play, playact*, simulate; SEE CONCEPTS 12,59

make off [*v*] *flee, run away*
abscond, bolt*, clear, cut and run, decamp, depart, escape, fly*, go, leave, make away, quit, retire, run, run for it, run off, scamper, scoot, skedaddle*, skip*, withdraw; SEE CONCEPTS 102,150,195

make out [*v1*] *see, recognize*
detect, discern, discover, distinguish, espy, notice, observe, perceive, remark; SEE CONCEPT 626

make out [*v2*] *understand*
accept, catch, collect, compass, comprehend, conclude, decipher, deduce, deduct, derive, dig, fathom, follow, gather, grasp, infer, judge, perceive, realize, recognize, see, take in, work out; SEE CONCEPTS 15,18

make out [*v3*] *get by, succeed*
accomplish, achieve, do, do well enough, do with, endure, fare, flourish, get along, get on, manage, muddle through, prosper, score, thrive; SEE CONCEPTS 23,91,140

makeshift [*adj*] *temporary*
alternative, Band-Aid*, expedient, hit-or-miss*, make-do*, provisional, quick-and-dirty*, slapdash*, stopgap, substitute, temp, throwaway*; SEE CONCEPTS 551,560

makeshift [*n*] *temporary help*
expediency, expedient, last resort, pis aller, recourse, refuge, replacement, resort, resource, shift, stopgap, substitute; SEE CONCEPTS 658,712

makeup [*n1*] *cosmetics*
blush, face*, foundation, greasepaint, lipstick, maquillage, paint, pancake, powder*; SEE CONCEPT 446

makeup [*n2*] *structure, composition*
architecture, arrangement, assembly, configuration, constitution, construction, content, contents, design, form, format, formation, layout, order, ordering, organization, plan, scheme, setup, shape, spread, style; SEE CONCEPT 757

makeup [*n3*] *person's character*
build, cast, complexion, constitution, disposition, fiber, figure, frame of mind, grain, humor, individualism, individuality, make, mold, nature, personality, stamp, stripe, temper, temperament, vein; SEE CONCEPT 411

make up [*v1*] *create*
ad-lib*, blend, coin, combine, compose, compound, concoct, construct, contrive, cook up*, devise, dream up, fabricate, fake it, fashion, fix, formulate, frame, fuse, hatch, improv*, improvise, invent, join, knock off, make, meld, merge, mingle, mix, originate, play by ear*, prepare, pretend, put together, ready, trump up, whip up*, wing it*, write; SEE CONCEPTS 173,202

make up [*v2*] *comprise, constitute*
complete, compose, consist, fill, form, furnish, include, make, meet, provide, supply; SEE CONCEPT 643

make up [*v3*] *compensate, reconcile*
accommodate, atone, balance, bury the hatchet*, come to terms, compose, conciliate, counterbalance, counterpoise, countervail, forgive and forget, make amends, make peace, mend, offset, outweigh, pacify, recompense, redeem, redress, requite, set off, settle, shake hands; SEE CONCEPTS 126,384

maladjusted [*adj*] *maladapted*
abnormal, disturbed*, messed up*, muddled, neurotic, unfit, unstable; SEE CONCEPT 547

maladroit [*adj1*] *awkward, clumsy*
all thumbs*, blundering, bumbling, bungling, clunky, floundering, gauche, halting, heavy-handed, inept, inexpert, klutzy*, lumbering, stumbling, two left feet*, ungraceful, unhandy, unskillful; SEE CONCEPTS 401,584

maladroit [*adj2*] *tactless*
brash, gauche, impolitic, inconsiderate, inelegant, insensitive, thoughtless, undiplomatic, untactful, untoward; SEE CONCEPT 401

malady [*n*] *disease*
ache, affection, affliction, ailment, attack, blight, bug*, cancer, complaint, condition, contagion, debility, disability, disorder, distemper, epidemic, fever, flu, ill health, illness, infection, infirmity, inflammation, plague, sickness, syndrome, virus; SEE CONCEPT 306

malaise [*n*] *depression, sickness*
angst, anxiety, debility, decrepitude, despair, discomfort, disquiet, distress, doldrums, enervation, feebleness, illness, infirmity, infirmness, lassitude, melancholy, pain, sickliness, unease, uneasiness, unhealthiness, weakness; SEE CONCEPTS 316,410

malarky [*n*] *nonsense*
absurdity, babble, balderdash*, baloney*, bombast, bull*, bunk*, drivel, foolishness, gibberish, giddiness, hogwash*, hot air*, jive*, poppycock*, prattle, rubbish, silliness, trash*; SEE CONCEPTS 230,388,633

malcontent [*adj*] *dissatisfied*
belly-aching, complaining, discontented, disgruntled, unhappy, unsatisfied; SEE CONCEPT 403

male [*adj*] *masculine*
macho*, manful, manlike, manly, paternal, potent, virile; SEE CONCEPTS 371,408

male [*n*] *man*
boy, brother, father, fellow, gent*, gentleman, grandfather, guy, he, husband, Mr., sir, son; SEE CONCEPT 419

malediction [*n*] *curse*
anathema, commination, curse word, cuss, cuss word, damn, damnation, damning, darn, denunciation, dirty name*, dirty word*, execration, expletive, four-letter word*, imprecation, jinx, no-no*, oath, swear word, whammy*; SEE CONCEPT 278

malevolent [*adj*] *hateful*
bad-natured, baleful, catty*, despiteful, dirty, evil, evil-minded, hellish, hostile, lousy, malicious, malign, malignant, murder, murderous, pernicious, poison, rancorous, rough, sinister, spiteful, tough, vengeful, vicious, vindictive, waspish, wicked; SEE CONCEPTS 401,542

malformation [*n*] *deformity*
abberation, abnormality, defect, disfigurement, impairment, injury, malconformation, misshape, monstrosity, mutation; SEE CONCEPT 580

malformed [*adj*] *distorted*
abnormal, contorted, crooked, deformed, grotesque, irregular, misshapen, twisted, warped; SEE CONCEPT 486

malfunction [*n*] *breakdown, failure*
bug*, defect, fault, flaw, glitch*, gremlin*, impairment, slip; SEE CONCEPTS 658,674

malice [*n*] *hate, vengefulness*
acerbity, animosity, animus, antipathy, bad blood, bane, bile, bitterness, despite, despitefulness, dirt, dislike, down, enmity, evil, grudge, hatefulness, hatred, hostility, ill will, implacability, malevolence, maliciousness, malignance, malignity, meanness, mordacity, poison, rancor, repugnance, resentment, spite, spitefulness, spleen, umbrage, venom, viciousness, vindictiveness; SEE CONCEPT 29

malicious [*adj*] *hateful*
awful, bad-natured, baleful, beastly, bitter, catty*, cussed, deleterious, despiteful, detrimental, envious, evil, evil-minded, green*, greeneyed*, gross*, ill-disposed, injurious, jealous, low, malevolent, malign, malignant, mean, mischievous, nasty, noxious, ornery, pernicious, petty, poisonous, rancorous, resentful, spiteful, uncool*, vengeful, venomous, vicious, virulent, wicked; SEE CONCEPTS 267,401,542

malign [*adj*] *hurtful, injurious*
antagonistic, antipathetic, bad, baleful, baneful, deleterious, despiteful, destructive, detrimental, evil, harmful, hateful, hostile, inimical, malefic, maleficent, malevolent, malignant, noxious, pernicious, rancorous, sinister, spiteful, vicious, wicked; SEE CONCEPTS 267,537,542

malign [*v*] *slander, defame*
abuse, accuse, asperse, backbite*, bad-mouth*, befoul, besmirch, bespatter, blacken, calumniate, cast aspersion, curse, decry, defile, denigrate, depreciate, derogate, detract, dirty*, disparage, harm, injure, insult, misrepresent, mudsling, opprobriate, pollute, rap, revile, roast*, run down*, scandalize, slur, smear, soil, spatter*, speak ill of, stain, sully, taint, take a swipe at*, tarnish, tear down, traduce, vilify, villainize, vituperate; SEE CONCEPTS 44,52,54,63

malignant [*adj*] *diseased*
cancerous, deadly, destructive, fatal, internecine, lethal, mortal, pestilential, poisonous; SEE CONCEPT 314

malingerer [*n*] *slacker*
dodger, goof-off, idler, loafer, shirker; SEE CONCEPT 412

mall [*n*] *commercial complex with many individual retail stores*
commercial center, market, mart, mini-mart, plaza, shopping center, shopping mall; SEE CONCEPTS 325,439,449

mall [*n1*] *shopping center*
marketplace, shopping complex, shopping mall, shopping plaza; SEE CONCEPTS 323,333,449

mall [*n2*] *promenade*
alameda, boardwalk, boulevard, esplanade, parade, public walk, walk; SEE CONCEPT 501•

malleable [*adj*] *pliable*
adaptable, compliant, ductile, flexible, governable, go-with-the-flow*, impressionable, manageable, moldable, plastic, pliant, putty in hands*, rolls with punches*, soft, submissive, supple, tractable, tractile, transformable, workable, yielding; SEE CONCEPTS 403,485

malnutrition [*n*] *poor nutrition*
anorexia nervosa, bulimia, dietary deficiency, hunger, malnourishment, starvation, undernourishment; SEE CONCEPT 20,709

malodorous [*adj*] *foul-smelling*
bad, decayed, decomposed, fetid, foul, frowzy, funky*, fusty, gamy*, high*, infested, lousy, mephitic, musty, nasty, nauseating, noisome, noxious, off*, offensive, pestilential, poisonous, polluted, putrid, rancid, rank, reeking, rotten, smelly, stale, stenchful, stinking, strong, tainted, vile; SEE CONCEPT 598

malpractice [*n*] *abuse, misconduct*
carelessness, dereliction, malefaction, misbehavior, misdeed, mismanagement, negligence, offense, transgression, violation; SEE CONCEPTS 101,156,310,324

mammoth [*adj*] *huge*
behemothic, colossal, elephantine, enormous, gargantuan, giant, gigantic, high, immense, jumbo, large, leviathan, long, massive, mighty, monstrous, monumental, mountainous, prodigious, stupendous, titanic, vast; SEE CONCEPT 773

man [*n2*] *male human*
beau, boyfriend, brother, father, fellow, gentleman, grandfather, guy, he, husband, Mr., nephew, papa, sir, son, spouse, swain*, uncle; SEE CONCEPT 419

manacle [*n*] *handcuff*
bond, bracelet, chain, fetter, iron, pinion, shackle; SEE CONCEPT 497

manage [*vI*] *be in charge, control*
administer, advocate, boss, call the shots*, call upon, captain, care for, carry on, command, concert, conduct, counsel, designate, direct, disburse, dominate, engage in, engineer, execute, govern, guide, handle, head, hold down*, influence, instruct, maintain, manipulate, minister, officiate, operate, oversee, pilot, ply, preside, regulate, request, rule, run, run the show, steer, superintend, supervise, take care of, take over, take the helm*, train, use, watch, watch over, wield; SEE CONCEPTS 94,117

ma
ma

manage [v2] *accomplish*
achieve, arrange, bring about, bring off, carry out, con*, contrive, cook*, cope with, deal with, doctor*, effect, engineer, execute, finagle, fix, jockey*, plant*, play games*, pull strings*, push around, put one over*, rig*, scam*, succeed, swing, upstage, wangle*, work; SEE CONCEPTS *91,706*

manage [v3] *survive, get by*
bear up, carry on, cope, endure, fare, get along*, get on*, make do*, make out*, muddle, scrape by*, shift, stagger; SEE CONCEPTS *23,407*

manageable [adj] *controllable*
amendable, convenient, docile, easy, feasible, governable, obedient, submissive, tamable, tractable, trained, workable; SEE CONCEPTS *401,404*

management [n1] *persons running an organization*
administration, authority, board, bosses, brass, directorate, directors, employers, execs*, executive, executives, executive suite, front office*, head, mainframe*, management, micro management*, person upstairs*, top brass*, upstairs*; SEE CONCEPT *325*

management [n2] *running an organization*
administration, care, charge, command, conduct, control, direction, governance, government, guidance, handling, intendance, manipulation, operation, oversight, rule, superintendence, superintendency, supervision; SEE CONCEPTS *117,324*

manager [n] *person who runs organization*
administrator, boss, comptroller, conductor, controller, director, exec*, executive, governor, handler, head, head person, officer, official, organizer, overseer, producer, proprietor, slavedriver*, straw boss*, superintendent, supervisor, zookeeper*; SEE CONCEPT *347*

mandate [n] *authority, order*
authorization, behest, bidding, blank check*, carte blanche*, charge, command, commission, decree, dictate, directive, edict, fiat, go-ahead*, green light*, imperative, injunction, instruction, okay*, precept, sanction, warrant, word*; SEE CONCEPTS *318,685*

mandatory [adj] *required, necessary*
binding, commanding, compelling, compulsatory, compulsory, de rigueur, essential, forced, imperative, imperious, indispensable, involuntary, irremissible, needful, obligatory, requisite; SEE CONCEPT *546*

maneuver [n1] *move, tactic*
action, angle, artifice, contrivance, curveball, demarche, device, dodge, fancy footwork*, feint, finesse, gambit, game, gimmick, intrigue, jig*, machination, manipulation, measure, movement, plan, play, plot, ploy, procedure, proceeding, ruse, scheme, shenanigans*, shuffle*, step, stratagem, stunt, subterfuge, trick; SEE CONCEPTS *6,660*

maneuver [n2] *military practice, operation*
battle, deployment, drill, evolution, exercise, measure, movement, parade, plan, procedure, proceeding, stratagem, tactics, war games; SEE CONCEPT *320*

maneuver [v1] *plan, scheme*
angle, beguile, cheat, come up with, con*, conspire, contrive, cook, design, devise, doctor, engineer, exploit, fence, finagle, finesse, go around,

intrigue, jockey, leave holding the bag*, machinate, manage, manipulate, move, navigate, operate, play, play games*, plot, proceed, pull strings*, push around, put one over*, rig, scam, sham, shift, trick, upstage, wangle, work; SEE CONCEPTS *36,59*

maneuver [v2] *direct physically*
deploy, dispense, drive, exercise, guide, handle, manipulate, move, navigate, negotiate, pilot, ply, steer, swing, wield; SEE CONCEPTS *187,225*

mangle [v] *mutilate, deform*
batter, break, bruise, butcher, carve, contort, crush, cut, damage, deface, destroy, disfigure, distort, flay, hack, hash, impair, injure, lacerate, maim, mar, maul, rend, ruin, separate, slash, slay, slice, slit, spoil, tear, wound, wreck; SEE CONCEPTS *176,246,252*

mangy [adj] *scruffy*
decrepit, dirty, impoverished, indigent, mean, moth-eaten*, poor, ragtag*, shabby, shoddy, sick, sleazy*, squalid, tattered; SEE CONCEPTS *485,621*

manhood/womanhood [n] *physical maturity and strength of adult male or female*
adulthood, coming of age*, fecundity, femininity, fertility, manfulness, manliness, masculinity, mettle, potency, virility, womanliness, womanness; SEE CONCEPTS *633,715*

mania [n] *fixation, madness*
aberration, ax to grind*, bee*, bee in bonnet*, bug*, bug in ear*, compulsion, craving, craze, craziness, delirium, dementia, derangement, desire, disorder, enthusiasm, fad, fancy, fascination, fetish, fixed idea, frenzy, furor, grabber*, hang-up*, idée fixe, infatuation, insanity, lunacy, monomania, obsession, on the brain*, partiality, passion, preoccupation, rage, thing, tiger*, tiger by the tail*; SEE CONCEPTS *20,32,410,529*

maniac [n] *person who is crazy, overenthusiastic*
bedlamite, bigot, crackpot*, enthusiast, fan, fanatic, fiend, flake*, freak, fruitcake*, kook*, loon, loony*, lunatic, madperson, nut*, nutcase*, psycho*, psychopath, schizoid*, screwball*, Section 8*, zealot; SEE CONCEPT *412*

manic/maniacal [adj] *overexcited, crazy*
berserk, crazed, demented, deranged, excited, flipped*, flipped out*, freaked out*, freaky*, frenzied, high*, insane, lunatic, mad, nutty*, psychotic, rabid, raving, turned-out, unbalanced, up*, wild; SEE CONCEPTS *403*

manifest [adj] *clear, obvious*
apparent, big as life*, bold, clear-cut*, conspicuous, crystal clear*, disclosed, distinct, divulged, evidenced, evident, evinced, glaring, noticeable, open, palpable, patent, plain, prominent, revealed, shown, straightforward, told, unambiguous, unmistakable, visible; SEE CONCEPTS *529,576*

manifest [v] *exhibit, make plain*
confirm, declare, demonstrate, display, embody, establish, evidence, evince, expose, express, exteriorize, externalize, flash, illustrate, incarnate, let it all hang out*, mark, materialize, objectify, ostend, parade, personalize, personify, personize, proclaim, prove, reveal, set forth, show, show and tell*, showcase, signify, sport, strut, substantiate, suggest, utter, vent, voice, wave around*; SEE CONCEPTS *118,261*

manifestation [n] *exhibition, proof*
appearance, demonstration, disclosure, display,

explanation, exposure, expression, indication, instance, mark, materialization, meaning, phenomenon, revelation, show, sign, symptom, token; SEE CONCEPTS 642,672

manifesto [n] *public declaration*
announcement, notice, platform, policy, proclamation, promulgation, public notice, statement of belief; SEE CONCEPTS 271,274,278

manifold [adj] *abundant, many*
assorted, complex, copious, different, diverse, diversified, diversiform, multifarious, multifold, multiform, multiple, multiplied, multitudinous, multivarious, numerous, sundry, varied, various; SEE CONCEPTS 564,762,781

manipulate [v1] *maneuver, handle physically*
employ, feel, finger*, form, manage, mold, operate, ply, shape, swing, thumb*, use, wield, work; SEE CONCEPTS 225,612

manipulate [v2] *change to suit one's desire*
beguile, conduct, control, direct, engineer, exploit, finagle, finesse, guide, handle, influence, jockey, machinate, maneuver, massage, mold, negotiate, play, play games*, pull strings*, pull wires*, push around, shape, steer, upstage, use; SEE CONCEPTS 14,234

manner [n1] *person's behavior, conduct*
address, affectation, affectedness, air, appearance, aspect, bearing, comportment, demeanor, deportment, idiosyncrasy, look, mannerism, mien, peculiarity, presence, style, tone, turn, way; SEE CONCEPTS 411,633,644

manner [n2] *method, approach*
consuetude, custom, fashion, form, genre, habit, habitude, line, means, mode, modus, practice, procedure, process, routine, style, system, tack, technique, tenor, tone, trick, usage, use, vein, way, wise, wont; SEE CONCEPTS 6,660

manner [n3] *class, category*
brand, breed, form, kind, nature, sort, type, variety; SEE CONCEPT 378

mannered [adj] *affected, put-on*
airish*, apish*, artificial, artsy, campy*, chichi*, conscious, gone Hollywood*, highfaluting*, posed, pretentious, self-conscious, stilted, stuck up*, unnatural; SEE CONCEPT 401

mannerism [n] *peculiarity of how someone behaves, acts*
affectation, air, characteristic, eccentricity, foible, habit, idiosyncrasy, oddness, pose, pretension, queerness, quirk, singularity, trait, trick; SEE CONCEPT 644

mannerly [adj] *polite, well-behaved*
charming, civil, civilized, considerate, courteous, decorous, genteel, gracious, polished, refined, respectful, well-bred, well-mannered; SEE CONCEPT 401

manners [n] *polite, refined social behavior*
amenities, bearing, behavior, breeding, carriage, ceremony, civilities, comportment, conduct, courtesy, culture, decorum, demeanor, deportment, dignity, elegance, etiquette, formalities, good breeding, good form, mien, mores, polish, politeness, politesse, propriety, protocol, p's and q's*, refinement, social graces, sophistication, taste, urbanity; SEE CONCEPT 633

mansion [n] *very large house*
abode, building, castle, chateau, dwelling, estate, habitation, hall, home, manor, palace, residence, seat, villa; SEE CONCEPTS 439,516

manslaughter [n] *killing without malicious forethought*
crime, foul play*, hit*, homicide, killing, murder; SEE CONCEPT 252

manual [adj] *done by hand*
chiral, hand-operated, human, not automatic, physical, standard; SEE CONCEPT 544

manual [n] *book giving instruction*
bible, compendium, cookbook, enchiridion, guide, guidebook, handbook, primer, reference book, schoolbook, text, textbook, workbook; SEE CONCEPT 280

manufacture [v1] *build, produce*
accomplish, assemble, carve, cast, cobble*, complete, compose, construct, create, execute, fabricate, fashion, forge, form, frame, fudge together*, machine, make, make up, mass-produce, mill, mold, prefab, process, put together, shape, synthesize, throw together, tool, turn out; SEE CONCEPT 205

manufacture [v2] *concoct, invent*
contrive, cook up*, create, devise, fabricate, hatch, make up, produce, think up, trump up*; SEE CONCEPTS 35,36

manufacture/manufacturing [n] *production of processed goods*
accomplishment, assembling, assembly, casting, completion, composing, composition, construction, creation, doing, erection, fabrication, finishing, forging, formation, making, mass-production, preparing, produce, tooling; SEE CONCEPT 324

manure [n] *fertilizer*
buffalo chips*, compost, cow chips*, cowplop*, droppings, dung, excrement, guano, maul*, meadow muffins*, mulch; SEE CONCEPTS 260,399,429

manuscript [n] *book, script*
article, composition, document, hard copy, palimpsest, text; SEE CONCEPTS 263,271

many [adj] *profuse, abundant*
abounding, alive with, bounteous, bountiful, copious, countless, crowded, divers, frequent, innumerable, legion, lousy with*, manifold, multifarious, multifold, multiplied, multitudinous, myriad, no end of*, numberless, numerous, plentiful, populous, prevalent, rife, several, sundry, teeming, umpteen, uncounted, varied, various; SEE CONCEPTS 762,771

many [n] *abundance; a lot*
gobs*, heaps*, horde, jillion*, large numbers, mass, multitude, oodles*, piles*, plenty, scads*, scores, thousands, throng, tons, umpteen*, whole slew*; SEE CONCEPTS 432,787

map [n] *chart of geographic area*
atlas, delineation, design, diagram, draft, drawing, elevation, globe, graph, ground plan, outline, picture, plan, plat, portrayal, print, projection, sketch, topographical depiction, tracing; SEE CONCEPT 625

mapmaker [n] *cartographer*
mapper, surveyor, topographer; SEE CONCEPTS 37,103,291

mar [v] *hurt, damage*
bend, blemish, blight, blot, break, bruise, deface, deform, detract, ding*, disfigure, foul up, harm, impair, injure, louse up, maim, mangle, mess up*, mutilate, queer*, rough up, ruin, scar, scratch, shake up, spoil, stain, sully, taint, tar-

ma
ma

nish, tweak, vitiate, warp, wreck; SEE CONCEPT *246*

marathon [*n*] *long-distance race*
cross-country race, endurance run, test of endurance; SEE CONCEPT *363*

maraud [*v*] *pillage and plunder*
despoil, forage, foray, harass, harry, loot, raid, ransack, ravage, sack; SEE CONCEPTS *86,139*

marauder [*n*] *pillager, raider*
bandit, buccaneer, corsair, freebooter, looter, outlaw, pirate, plunderer, ravager, robber, thief; SEE CONCEPT *412*

march [*v*] *walk with deliberation*
advance, boot, debouch, drill, file, forge ahead, go on, hoof it*, journey, mount, move, move out, pace, parade, patrol, pound, pound the pavement*, proceed, progress, promenade, range, space, stalk, step, step out, stomp, stride, strut, traipse, tramp, tread; SEE CONCEPT *150*

margin [*n*] *border; room around something*
allowance, bound, boundary, brim, brink, compass, confine, edge, elbowroom*, extra, field, frame, hem, latitude, leeway, limit, lip, perimeter, periphery, play, rim, scope, selvage, shore, side, skirt, space, surplus, trimming, verge; SEE CONCEPTS *270,484,513*

marginal [*adj*] *borderline; slight*
bordering, insignificant, low, minimal, minor, negligible, on the edge, peripheral, rimming, small, verging; SEE CONCEPTS *513,789*

marijuana [*n*] *grass, pot*
Acapulco gold*, bhang*, cannabis, Columbian*, doobie*, dope*, ganja*, hash, hashish, hemp, herb*, Jamaican*, joint, loco weed*, maryjane*, Maui wowie*, Mexican*, Panama red*, reefer, roach, sinsemilla, tea*, weed*; SEE CONCEPT *307*

marina [*n*] *dock*
berth, boat basin, boatyard, harbor, landing, moorings, pier, port, quay, slip, wharf; SEE CONCEPT *439*

marinate [*v*] *soak*
bathe, brine, immerse, marinade, pickle, season, souse, steep; SEE CONCEPT *256*

marine/maritime [*adj*] *concerning the sea*
abyssal, aquatic, coastal, deep-sea, hydrographic, littoral, maritime, natatorial, nautical, naval, navigational, Neptunian, oceangoing, oceanic, oceanographic, of the sea, pelagic, saltwater, sea, seafaring, seagoing, seashore, seaside, shore; SEE CONCEPT *536*

mariner [*n*] *person who makes living on the sea*
bluejacket*, captain, crew, mate, navigator, sailor, salt*, sea dog*, seafarer, shipmate, swab*, yachtie*; SEE CONCEPTS *348,366*

marionette [*n*] *puppet*
doll, dummy, fantoccini, figurine, manikin, moppet; SEE CONCEPTS *423,446*

marital [*adj*] *concerning marriage*
conjugal, connubial, married, matrimonial, nuptial, spousal, wedded; SEE CONCEPT *555*

maritime [*adj*] *nautical*
aquatic, deep-sea, marine, naval, oceangoing, oceanic, pelagic, seafaring, seagoing; SEE CONCEPT *536*

mark [*n1*] *blemish; character*
autograph, blaze, blot, blotch, brand, brand name, bruise, check, cross, dent, dot, impression, imprint, ink, John Hancock*, John Henry*, label, line, logo, nick, pock, point, record, register, representation, scar, score, scratch, sign, signature, smudge, splotch, spot, stain, stamp, streak, stroke, symbol, tag, ticket, trace, trademark, underlining, X*; SEE CONCEPTS *79,284*

mark [*n2*] *characteristic, symptom*
affection, attribute, badge, blaze, brand, character, device, distinction, earmark, emblem, evidence, feature, hallmark, idiosyncrasy, image, impression, incision, index, indication, indicia, label, marking, note, particularity, peculiarity, print, proof, property, quality, seal, sign, significant, stamp, symbol, token, trait, type, virtue; SEE CONCEPTS *411,644,716*

mark [*n3*] *criterion, standard*
gauge, level, measure, norm, yardstick; SEE CONCEPTS *561,783*

mark [*n4*] *goal, target*
aim, ambition, bull's eye*, duty, end, function, object, objective, prey, purpose, use; SEE CONCEPT *659*

mark [*n5*] *importance*
consequence, dignity, distinction, effect, eminence, fame, influence, manifestation, notability, note, notice, prestige, quality, regard, result, standing, value; SEE CONCEPTS *346,668*

mark [*v1*] *blemish, stain*
autograph, blaze, blot, blotch, brand, bruise, chalk, check, dent, dot, impress, imprint, initial, ink, inscribe, label, letter, nick, pinpoint, point, print, scar, score, scratch, seal, sign, smudge, splotch, stamp, streak, stroke, trace, underline, write, X*; SEE CONCEPTS *79,250*

mark [*v2*] *characterize*
bespeak, betoken, brand, check off, demonstrate, denote, designate, distinguish, earmark, evidence, evince, exemplify, exhibit, feature, identify, illustrate, indicate, individualize, individuate, label, manifest, mark off, ostend, point out, point up*, proclaim, qualify, remark, set apart, show, show up, signalize, signify, singularize, stake out*, stamp; SEE CONCEPT *261*

mark [*v3*] *see, notice*
attend, behold, chronicle, discern, distinguish, eye, hearken, mind, note, observe, pay attention, pay heed, perceive, regard, register, remark, take notice of, view, watch, write down; SEE CONCEPTS *38,626*

marked [*adj*] *apparent, obvious*
arresting, clear, considerable, conspicuous, decided, distinct, evident, manifest, notable, noted, noticeable, outstanding, patent, pointed, prominent, pronounced, remarkable, salient, signal, striking; SEE CONCEPTS *485,535,589*

markedly [*adv*] *distinctly*
clearly, considerably, conspicuously, decidedly, especially, evidently, greatly, manifestly, notably, noticeably, obviously, outstandingly, particularly, patently, remarkably, signally, strikingly, to a great extent; SEE CONCEPTS *535,544*

market [*v*] *package and sell goods*
advertise, barter, display, exchange, merchandise, offer for sale, retail, vend, wholesale; SEE CONCEPTS *324,345*

marketable [*adj*] *easily sold; in demand*
bankable, commercial, fit, for sale, good, hot*, merchandisable, merchantable, profitable, salable, sellable, selling, sought after, sound, trafficable, vendible, wanted; SEE CONCEPTS *334,546*

market/mart [*n*] *place, venue for selling goods*
bazaar, bodega, booth, business, chain store, co-

op, corner store, deli, delicatessen, department store, dimestore, drugstore, emporium, exchange, fair, general store, grocery store, mall, mart, outlet, shop, shopping mall, showroom, souk, square, stall, stock exchange, store, supermarket, trading post, truck, variety store, warehouse; SEE CONCEPTS *323,333,449*

maroon [*v*] *abandon*
beach, cast ashore, cast away, desert, forsake, isolate, leave, leave high and dry*, strand; SEE CONCEPTS *195,384*

marriage [*n*] *legal joining of two people; a union*
alliance, amalgamation, association, confederation, conjugality, connubiality, consortium, coupling, espousal, holy matrimony, link, match, mating, matrimony, merger, monogamy, nuptials, pledging, sacrament, spousal, tie, tie that binds*, wedded bliss*, wedded state, wedding, wedding bells*, wedding ceremony, wedlock; SEE CONCEPTS *297,388*

marrow [*n*] *heart, essence*
bottom, core, cream, essentiality, gist, kernel, meat, pith, quick, quintessence, quintessential, soul, spirit, stuff, substance, virtuality; SEE CONCEPT *826*

marry [*v*] *become husband and wife in legal ceremony*
ally, associate, become one, bond, catch*, combine, conjoin, conjugate, contract, couple, drop anchor*, espouse, get hitched*, get married, join, knit, land*, lead to altar, link, match, mate, merge, one, pledge, plight one's troth, promise, relate, settle down*, take vows, tie, tie the knot*, unify, unite, walk down aisle*, wed, yoke; SEE CONCEPT *297*

marsh [*n*] *swamp*
bog, estuary, everglade, fen, mire, morass, moss, quag, quagmire, slough, swampland, wetland; SEE CONCEPT *509*

marshal [*v*] *organize, guide*
align, arrange, array, assemble, collect, conduct, deploy, direct, dispose, distribute, draw up, escort, gather, group, lead, line up, methodize, mobilize, muster, order, rally, rank, shepherd, space, systematize, usher; SEE CONCEPTS *84,117,187*

marshy [*adj*] *swampy*
boggy, fenny, miry, moory, mucky, paludal, quaggy, soggy; SEE CONCEPT *509*

martial [*adj*] *having to do with armed hostilities*
aggressive, bellicose, belligerent, combative, hostile, military, pugnacious, soldierly, warlike; SEE CONCEPT *401*

martinet [*n*] *disciplinarian*
authoritarian, bully, despot, drillmaster, drill sergeant, enforcer, hard master, slavedriver, stickler, taskmaster, tyrant; SEE CONCEPTS *350,354,423*

martyrdom [*n*] *suffering endured for sake of a cause*
affliction, agonizing, agony, anguish, crucifixion, devotion, distress, mortification, ordeal, pain, persecution, sacrifice, self-immolation, self-sacrifice, torment, torture, unselfishness; SEE CONCEPTS *410,411*

marvel [*n*] *wonder*
curiosity, genius, miracle, one for the books*, phenomenon, portent, prodigy, sensation, something else*, stunner, whiz; SEE CONCEPTS *529,671*

marvel [*v*] *be amazed*
be awed, be surprised, feel surprise, gape, gaze, goggle, stand in awe, stare, wonder; SEE CONCEPT *17*

marvelous [*adj*] *hard to believe; amazing*
astonishing, astounding, awe-inspiring, awesome, awful, bewildering, breathtaking, confounding, difficult to believe, extraordinary, fabulous, fantastic, implausible, improbable, incomprehensible, inconceivable, incredible, miraculous, phenomenal, prodigious, remarkable, singular, spectacular, staggering, strange, striking, stunning, stupendous, supernatural, surprising, unbelievable, unimaginable, unlikely, unusual, wonderful, wondrous; SEE CONCEPTS *529,552*

marvelous [*adj2*] *superb, great*
agreeable, astonishing, bad*, boss*, colossal, cool*, divine, dreamy*, enjoyable, excellent, fab*, fabulous, fantastic, glorious, greatest, groovy*, hot*, keen, magnificent, neat*, out of this world*, outrageous, peachy, pleasant, pleasurable, prime*, rewarding, satisfying, sensational, smashing, solid*, solid gold*, spectacular, splendid, stupendous, super, supreme, swell, terrific, wonderful; SEE CONCEPT *574*

masculinity/masculine [*n/adj*] *manly*
andric, gender, macho*, male, manful, mannish, potent, virile; SEE CONCEPTS *371,372,408,648*

mash [*v*] *smash, squash*
brew, bruise, chew, crush, decoct, grind, hash, infuse, macerate, masticate, mush up, pound, press, pulp, pulverize, push, reduce, scrunch, squeeze, squish, steep, triturate; SEE CONCEPTS *170,186,208*

mask [*n*] *false face, cover*
affectation, air*, appearance, aspect, beard*, blind, camouflage, cloak*, concealment, cover-up, disguise, disguisement, dissembling, dissimulation, domino*, facade, fig leaf*, front, guise, hood, masquerade, pose, posture, pretense, pretext, put-on*, screen, semblance, show*, simulation, veil*, veneer, visage, visor, window dressing*; SEE CONCEPTS *450,716*

mask [*v*] *disguise*
beard, camouflage, cloak, conceal, cover, cover up, defend, dissemble, dissimulate, dress up, front, guard, hide, obscure, protect, safeguard, screen, secrete, shield, veil; SEE CONCEPTS *172,188,384*

masquerade [*n*] *disguise; social occasion for disguises*
carnival, circus, cloak, color, costume, costume ball, cover, cover-up, deception, dissimulation, domino*, facade, festivity, front, guise, impersonation, imposture, Mardi Gras*, mask, masked ball, masking, mummery, personation, pose, pretense, put-on, revel, screen, show, subterfuge, veil; SEE CONCEPTS *172,188,383,451*

masquerade [*v*] *disguise*
attitudinize, dissemble, dissimulate, frolic, impersonate, mask, pass as, pass for, pass off, pose, posture, pretend, revel; SEE CONCEPT *59*

mass [*n*] *body of matter; considerable portion*
accumulation, aggregate, assemblage, band, batch, block, bulk, bunch, chunk, clot, coagulation, collection, combination, concretion, conglomeration, core, corpus, crowd, entirety, gob, great deal, greater part, group, heap, horde, host, hunk, knot, lion's share*, load, lot, lump, major-

ity, mob, mound, mountain, much, number, object, peck, piece, pile, plurality, preponderance, pyramid, quantity, shock, stack, staple, stockpile, sum, sum total, throng, totality, troop, volume, wad, whole; SEE CONCEPTS 432,787,835

mass [n2] *bulk, measurement*
dimension, extent, greatness, magnitude, size, span, volume; SEE CONCEPT 792

massacre [n] *killing of many*
annihilation, assassination, bloodbath, bloodshed, butchery, carnage, decimation, extermination, genocide, internecion, murder, slaughter, slaying; SEE CONCEPT 252

massacre [v] *kill, often in great numbers*
annihilate, butcher, decimate, depopulate, exterminate, mass murder, murder, slaughter, slay; SEE CONCEPT 252

massage [n] *kneading of body parts*
back rub, beating, chirapsia, manipulation, rolfing*, rubbing, rubbing-down, stroking; SEE CONCEPTS 308,310

massage [v] *knead body parts*
caress, manipulate, pat, press, push, rolf*, rub, rub down, stimulate, stroke; SEE CONCEPTS 208,308,310

masses [n] *public, crowd*
commonalty, common people, great unwashed*, hoi polloi*, lower class, mob, multitude, proletariat, rabble, rank and file*, riffraff*; SEE CONCEPT 417

massive [adj] *large*
big, bulky, colossal, cracking, cumbersome, cumbrous, elephantine, enormous, extensive, gargantuan, gigantic, grand, great, gross, heavy, hefty, huge, hulking, immense, imposing, impressive, mammoth, mighty, monster, monumental, mountainous, ponderous, prodigious, solid, stately, substantial, titanic, towering, tremendous, unwieldy, vast, walloping, weighty, whopping*; SEE CONCEPTS 773,781

master [adj1] *expert*
ace*, adept, crack*, crackerjack*, experienced, masterly, proficient, skilled, skillful; SEE CONCEPT 527

master [adj2] *main*
ascendant, chief, controlling, foremost, grand, great, leading, major, original, overbearing, paramount, predominant, predominate, preponderant, prevalant, prime, principal, regnant, sovereign, supreme; SEE CONCEPT 568

master [n1] *person in charge, female or male*
administrator, boss, captain, chief, chieftain, commandant, commander, commanding officer, conqueror, controller, director, employer, general, governor, guide, guru, head, head person, instructor, judge, lord, manager, matriarch, overlord, overseer, owner, patriarch, pedagogue, preceptor, principal, pro, ruler, schoolmaster/mistress, skipper, slave driver*, spiritual leader, superintendent, supervisor, swami*, taskmaster, teacher, top dog*, tutor, wheel*; SEE CONCEPTS 347,350,354

master [n2] *expert, skilled person, female or male*
ace*, adept, artist, artiste, authority, buff*, champion, connoisseur, conqueror, doctor, doyen, doyenne, genius, guru, maestro, maven, old hand*, old pro*, past master, prima donna*, pro, professional, proficient, pundit, real pro*, sage,

savant, scientist, shark*, victor, virtuoso, whiz*, whiz-bang*, winner, wizard; SEE CONCEPTS 350,366,423

master [v1] *learn; become proficient*
acquire, beat the game*, beat the system*, bone up*, bury yourself in*, comprehend, cram, excel in, gain mastery, get down cold*, get down pat*, get hold of*, get the hang of*, get the knack of*, grasp, grind, hit the books*, learn the ropes*, megastudy*, pick up, study, swamp*, understand; SEE CONCEPTS 31,630

masterful [adj] *expert, skilled*
adept, adroit, clever, consummate, crack, crackerjack*, deft, dexterous, excellent, exquisite, fine, finished, first-rate, master, masterly, preeminent, proficient, skillful, superior, superlative, supreme, transcendent; SEE CONCEPT 527

masterpiece [n] *respected work of art*
chef d'oeuvre, classic, cream*, cream of the crop*, flower, gem*, jewel*, magnum opus, masterstroke, master work, model, monument, perfection, pièce de résistance*, prize, showpiece, standard, tour de force*, treasure; SEE CONCEPT 259

mastery [n1] *command, expertise*
ability, acquirement, adeptness, adroitness, attainment, capacity, cleverness, comprehension, cunning, deftness, dexterity, expertism, expertness, familiarity, finesse, genius, grasp, grip, ken, knack, know-how, knowledge, mastership, power, proficiency, prowess, skill, understanding, virtuosity, wizardry; SEE CONCEPT 630

match [n1] *competition*
bout, contest, engagement, event, game, meet, race, rivalry, sport, test, trial; SEE CONCEPT 363

match [n2] *counterpart, equal*
adversary, analogue, antagonist, approximation, companion, competitor, complement, copy, correlate, counterpart, dead ringer*, double, duplicate, equivalent, like, lookalike, mate, opponent, parallel, peer, replica, ringer*, rival, spitting image*, twin; SEE CONCEPTS 664,667,716

match [n3] *couple*
affiliation, alliance, combination, duet, espousal, marriage, mating, pair, pairing, partnership, union; SEE CONCEPTS 297,388

matching [adj] *corresponding, equal*
analogous, comparable, coordinating, double, duplicate, equivalent, identical, like, paired, parallel, same, twin; SEE CONCEPT 566

matchless [adj] *unequalled, unique*
alone, consummate, excellent, exquisite, incomparable, inimitable, nonpareil, only, peerless, perfect, superior, superlative, supreme, unapproached, unmatched, unparalleled, unrivaled; SEE CONCEPT 574

mate [n] *one of a pair; partner*
acquaintance, alter ego, analog, assistant, associate, bedmate, bride, buddy*, chum*, classmate, cohort, colleague, companion, compeer, complement, comrade, concomitant, consort, coordinate, counterpart, coworker, crony, double, duplicate, familiar, friend, groom, helper, helpmate, intimate, match, pal*, peer, playmate, reciprocal, roommate, schoolmate, sidekick*, spouse, twin; SEE CONCEPTS 296,423,664

mate [v] *marry and breed*
cohabit, copulate, couple, crossbreed, generate, join, land*, match, merge, pair, procreate, serve,

tie, tie the knot*, wed, yoke; SEE CONCEPTS 297,375

material [adj1] *bodily, tangible*
actual, animal, appreciable, carnal, concrete, corporeal, earthly, fleshly, incarnate, nonspiritual, objective, palpable, perceptible, phenomenal, physical, real, sensible, sensual, substantial, true, worldly; SEE CONCEPT 485

material [adj2] *important, relevant*
ad rem, applicable, applicative, apposite, apropos, big, cardinal, consequential, considerable, essential, fundamental, germane, grave, indispensable, intrinsic, key, meaningful, momentous, pertinent, pointful, primary, serious, significant, substantial, vital, weighty; SEE CONCEPT 567

material [n1] *matter, fabric*
being, body, bolt, cloth, component, constituent, crop, element, entity, equipment, gear, goods, habiliments, individual, ingredient, machinery, materiel, object, outfit, paraphernalia, staple, stock, stuff, substance, supply, tackle, textile, thing; SEE CONCEPTS 475,523

material [n2] *written matter*
data, evidence, facts, information, notes, reading, text, work; SEE CONCEPTS 271,274

materialistic [adj] *thinking mainly about physical things*
acquisitive, banausic, carnal, earthly-minded, earthy, greedy, material, mundane, object-oriented, possessive, profane, secular, sensual, temporal, terrestrial, unspiritual; SEE CONCEPT 542

materialize [v] *come into being*
actualize, appear, become concrete, become real, become visual, be incarnate, be realized, coalesce, come about, come to pass, corporealize, develop, embody, emerge, entify, evolve, exteriorize, externalize, happen, hypostatize, make real, manifest, metamorphose, objectify, occur, personalize, personify, personize, pragmatize, realize, reify, substantialize, substantiate, symbolize, take form, take place, take shape, turn up, typify, unfold, visualize; SEE CONCEPTS 105,173,184,231,251

maternity [n] *period of being pregnant with child*
gestation, maternology, motherhood, parenthood; SEE CONCEPTS 316,817

mathematical [adj] *concerning manipulation of numbers*
algebraic, algorithmic, analytical, arithmetical, computative, geometrical, math, measurable, numerical, scientific, trigonometric; SEE CONCEPT 762

mathematics [n] *arithmetic*
addition, algebra, calculation, calculus, division, figures, geometry, math, multiplication, numbers, subtraction, trigonometry; SEE CONCEPTS 349,764

matriculate [v] *begin, enroll*
enter, join, register, sign up for; SEE CONCEPTS 114,119

matrimonial [adj] *married*
betrothed, conjugal, connubial, engaged, epithalamic, espoused, marital, nuptial, spousal, wedded, wedding; SEE CONCEPT 555

matrimony [n] *being joined in marriage*
alliance, bells*, conjugality, connubiality, marital rites, marriage, match, nuptials, shotgun wedding*, union, wedding, wedding bells*, wedding ceremony, wedlock; SEE CONCEPT 297

matrix [n] *something from which another originates*
cast, forge, form, grid, model, mold, origin, pattern, source, womb; SEE CONCEPT 648

matronly [adj] *womanly*
dignified, female, honorable, ladylike, mature, motherly, respected, stately; SEE CONCEPTS 404,555,574

matted [adj] *tangled*
disordered, kinky, knotted, rumpled, snarled, tousled, twisted, uncombed; SEE CONCEPT 606

matter [n1] *substance*
amount, being, body, constituents, corporeality, corporeity, element, entity, individual, material, materialness, object, phenomenon, physical world, protoplasm, quantity, stuff, substantiality, sum, thing; SEE CONCEPTS 407,433,470

matter [n2] *concern, tissue*
affair, bag, business, circumstance, episode, event, goings-on*, incident, job, lookout, nub, occurrence, proceeding, question, shooting match*, situation, subject, thing, topic, transaction, undertaking; SEE CONCEPTS 532,696

matter [n3] *subject, thesis*
argument, context, focus, head, interest, motif, motive, point, purport, resolution, sense, subject matter, substance, text, theme, topic; SEE CONCEPTS 349,529

matter [n4] *significance, meaning*
amount, body, burden, consequence, content, core, extent, gist*, import, importance, magnitude, meat, moment, neighborhood, note, order, pith, range, sense, substance, text, tune, upshot, vicinity, weight; SEE CONCEPTS 651,668

matter [n5] *difficulty, problem*
circumstance, complication, distress, grievance, perplexity, predicament, to-do*, trouble, upset, worry; SEE CONCEPTS 666,674

matter [n6] *secretion of a sore*
discharge, infection, maturation, purulence, pus, suppuration, ulceration; SEE CONCEPTS 311,467

matter [v] *be of consequence, importance*
affect, be important, be of value, be substantive, carry weight, count, cut ice*, express, have influence, imply, import, involve, make a difference, mean, mean something, signify, value, weigh; SEE CONCEPTS 7,19,22,130,682

matter-of-fact [adj] *realistic, unembellished*
apathetic, calm, cold, cold-blooded*, deadpan, down-to-earth*, dry, dull, earthy, emotionless, factual, feasible, flat, hard-boiled*, impassive, impersonal, lifeless, mundane, naked*, objective, phlegmatic, plain, practical, pragmatic, prosaic, prosy, serious, sober, stoic, stolid, unaffected, unidealistic, unimaginative, unimpassioned, unsentimental, unvarnished; SEE CONCEPTS 267,582

mature [adj] *adult, grown-up*
complete, cultivated, cultured, developed, fit, full-blown, full-fledged, full-grown, fully grown, grown, in full bloom, in one's prime, matured, mellow, mellowed, of age, perfected, prepared, prime, ready, ripe, ripened, seasoned, settled, sophisticated; SEE CONCEPTS 485,578,797

mature [v] *become adult, fully grown*
advance, age, arrive, attain majority, become experienced, become wise, bloom, blossom, come of age, culminate, develop, evolve, fill out, flower*, grow, grow up, maturate, mellow*, mushroom*, perfect, prime, progress, reach

adulthood, reach majority, ripen, round, season, settle down*, shoot up*; SEE CONCEPT 704

maturity [n] *adulthood, full growth*

ability, advancement, capability, civilization, completion, cultivation, development, experience, fitness, full bloom, fullness, majority, manhood, maturation, matureness, maturescence, mellowness, mentality, perfection, postpubescence, prime, prime of life, readiness, ripeness, sophistication, wisdom, womanhood; SEE CONCEPTS *678,715,720*

maudlin [adj] *teary, overemotional*

bathetic, befuddled, confused, cornball*, drippy*, gushing, insipid, lachrymose, mawkish, mushy*, romantic, schmaltzy*, sentimental, slush*, soap*, soapy*, soppy*, syrupy*, tearful, tear-jerking*, weak, weepy; SEE CONCEPTS *529,542*

maul [v] *mangle, abuse*

bang, bash, batter, beat, beat up, bludgeon, break face, buffet, claw, clean, drub, flagellate, flail, handle roughly, hit, hurt, ill-treat, knock about*, knock around*, lacerate, lash, lean on*, let have it*, maltreat, molest, mug, muscle, paste*, paw, pelt, pound, pummel, put in the hospital*, rough up, skin, take care of*, thrash, trample, wax, whip, work over*; SEE CONCEPTS *189,246*

mausoleum [n] *tomb*

burial, burial chamber, burial place, catacomb, cemetery, charnel house, coffin, crypt, grave, monument, sepulcher, vault; SEE CONCEPT 305

mauve [adj] *purplish color*

lavender, lilac, plum, violaceous, violet; SEE CONCEPT 618

maverick [n] *person who takes chances, departs from accepted course*

bohemian, dissenter, extremist, malcontent, nonconformist, radical; SEE CONCEPTS *348,423*

mawkish [adj] *sentimental, emotional*

bathetic, cloying, feeble, gooey*, gushing, gushy*, lovey-dovey*, maudlin, mushy*, nauseating, romantic, sappy*, schmaltzy*, sickening, sloppy, tear-jerking*, teary; SEE CONCEPTS *401,542*

maxim [n] *saying*

adage, aphorism, apophthegm, axiom, belief, brocard, byword, canon, commonplace, device, dictum, epithet, formula, law, moral, motto, platitude, precept, prescript, proverb, rule, saw, tenet, theorem, truism; SEE CONCEPTS *278,689*

maximum [adj] *highest, utmost*

best, biggest, greatest, largest, maximal, most, mostest, outside, paramount, superlative, supreme, top, topmost, ultimate; SEE CONCEPTS *574,762,781*

maximum [n] *upper limit, greatest amount*

apex, apogee, ceiling, climax, crest, culmination, extremity, height, max*, maxi*, most, nonpareil, peak, pinnacle, preeminence, record, summit, supremacy, the end*, top, utmost, uttermost, zenith; SEE CONCEPTS *706,766,836*

maybe [adv] *possibly*

as it may be, can be, conceivable, conceivably, could be, credible, feasible, imaginably, it could be, might be, obtainable, perchance, perhaps, weather permitting; SEE CONCEPT 552

mayhem [n] *chaos, confusion*

anarchy, commotion, destruction, disorder, fracas, havoc, pandemonium, trouble, violence; SEE CONCEPTS *106,675*

maze [n] *labyrinth; confusion*

bewilderment, convolution, entanglement, hodgepodge, imbroglio, intricacy, jungle, knot, meander, meandering, mesh, miscellany, morass, muddle, network, perplexity, puzzle, quandary, skein, snarl, tangle, torsion, twist, uncertainty, web, winding; SEE CONCEPTS *436,529,674*

meadow [n] *grassy field*

bottoms*, carpet*, grassland, heath, lea, mead, pasturage, pasture, plain, prairie, rug*, steppe, veldt; SEE CONCEPT 509

meager [adj1] *small, inadequate; poor*

bare, barren, deficient, exiguous, flimsy, inappreciable, inconsiderable, infertile, insubstantial, insufficient, little, mere, minimum, miserable, paltry, puny, scant, scanty, scrimp, scrimpy, shabby, short, skimp, skimpy, slender, slight, spare, sparse, subtle, tenuous, too little too late*, unfinished, unfruitful, unproductive, wanting, weak; SEE CONCEPTS *546,789*

meager [adj2] *very thin*

angular, bare, beanpole*, beanstalk*, bony, broomstick*, emaciated, gangling, gangly, gaunt, hungry, lacking, lank, lanky, lean, lithe, little, narrow, rattleboned, rawboned, scraggy, scrawny, skin and bones*, skinny, slender, slim, spare, starved, stinted, stunted, tenuous, underfed, wanting, willowy, withered; SEE CONCEPT 491

meal [n] *food, often taken by several individuals together*

banquet, blue plate*, board, breakfast, brunch, carryout, chow*, chow time*, collation, cookout, dessert, din-din*, dinner, eats*, fare, feast, feed, grub*, lunch, luncheon, mess, munchies*, picnic, potluck, refection, refreshment, regalement, repast, snack, special*, spread, square meal*, supper, table, tea; SEE CONCEPT 459

mean [adj1] *ungenerous*

close, greedy, mercenary, mingy, miserly, niggard, parsimonious, penny-pinching*, penurious, rapacious, scrimpy, selfish, stingy, tight, tightfisted*; SEE CONCEPT 334

mean [adj2] *hostile, rude*

bad-tempered, callous, cantankerous, churlish, contemptible, dangerous, despicable, difficult, dirty*, disagreeable, dishonorable, down*, evil, formidable, hard, hard-nosed*, ignoble, ill-tempered, infamous, knavish, liverish, lousy*, lowdown and dirty*, malicious, malign, nasty, perfidious, pesky, rotten, rough, rugged, scurrilous, shameless, sinking, snide, sour, the lowest*, touch, treacherous, troublesome, ugly, unfriendly, unpleasant, unscrupulous, vexatious, vicious, vile; SEE CONCEPTS *267,401,542*

mean [adj3] *poor; of or in inferior circumstances*

base, beggarly, common, contemptible, déclassé, down-at-heel*, hack, humble, ignoble, ineffectual, inferior, insignificant, limited, low, lowborn, lowly, mediocre, menial, miserable, modest, narrow, obscure, ordinary, paltry, petty, pitiful, plebeian, proletarian, run-down*, scruffy*, second-class*, second-rate, seedy*, servile, shabby*, sordid, squalid, tawdry, undistinguished, unwashed, vulgar, wretched; SEE CONCEPTS *334,485,589*

mean [adj4] *average*

common, conventional, halfway, intermediate, medial, median, mediocre, medium, middle, middling, normal, popular, standard, traditional; SEE CONCEPTS 547,585

mean [n] *average*

balance, center, compromise, happy medium, median, middle, middle course, midpoint, norm, par; SEE CONCEPTS 727,830

mean [v1] *signify, convey*

add up, adumbrate, allude, allude to, argue, attest, augur, betoken, connote, denote, designate, determine, drive at*, express, foreshadow, foretell, herald, hint at, imply, import, indicate, intimate, involve, name, point to, portend, presage, promise, purport, represent, say, speak of, spell, stand for, suggest, symbolize, tell the meaning of, touch on; SEE CONCEPTS 55,73,682

mean [v2] *have in mind; intend*

aim, anticipate, aspire, contemplate, design, desire, destine, direct, expect, fate, fit, make, match, plan, predestine, preordain, propose, purpose, resolve, set out, suit, want, wish; SEE CONCEPTS 26,36

meander [v] *wander, zigzag*

be all over the map*, change, drift, extravagate, gallivant, get sidetracked, peregrinate, ramble, range, recoil, roam, rove, snake, stray, stroll, traipse, turn, twine, twist, vagabond, wind; SEE CONCEPTS 151,738

meaning [n1] *message, signification*

acceptation, allusion, bearing, bottom line*, connotation, content, context, definition, denotation, drift, effect, essence, explanation, force, gist, heart*, hint, implication, import, interpretation, intimation, meat, name of the game*, nature of beast*, nitty-gritty*, nuance, nuts and bolts*, pith, point, purport, sense, significance, spirit, stuff, subject, subject matter, substance, suggestion, symbolization, tenor, thrust, understanding, upshot, use, value, worth; SEE CONCEPTS 278,661,682

meaning [n2] *intention, aim*

animus, design, end, goal, idea, intent, interest, object, plan, point, purpose, trend; SEE CONCEPT 659

meaningful [adj] *significant*

allusive, big, clear, concise, consequential, considerable, deep, eloquent, essential, exact, explicit, expressive, heavy, important, indicative, intelligible, material, momentous, pointed, pregnant, purposeful, relevant, sententious, serious, substantial, succinct, suggestive, useful, valid, weighty, worthwhile; SEE CONCEPTS 267,567

meaningless [adj] *without use, value, worth*

absurd, aimless, blank, doesn't cut it*, doubles-peak*, double-talk*, empty, feckless, fustian, futile, good-for-nothing, hollow, hot air*, inane, inconsequential, insignificant, insubstantial, nonsensical, nothing, nugatory, pointless, purportless, purposeless, senseless, suggestive, trifling, trivial, unimportant, unmeaning, unpurposed, useless, vacant, vague, vain, valueless, vapid, worthless; SEE CONCEPT 575

means [n1] *way, method*

agency, agent, aid, apparatus, auspices, avenue, channel, course, dodge*, equipment, expedient, factor, fashion, gimmick*, instrument, instrumentality, instrumentation, intermediary, machinery, manner, measure, mechanism, mode, ministry, mode, modus operandi, organ, organization, paraphernalia, path, power, process, road, route, step, stepping-stone, system, tactic, tech-

nique, trick, vehicle, ways and means*; SEE CONCEPT 6

means [n2] *wealth, resources*

ace in the hole*, affluence, assets, backing, bankroll, budget, bundle, capital, dough*, estate, finances, fortune, funds, holdings, income, intangibles, kitty*, money, nest egg*, nut*, pocket, possessions, property, purse, rainy day*, reserves, revenue, riches, savings, securities, sock*, stake, stuff, substance, ways and means*, wherewithal; SEE CONCEPTS 332,340

meantime [n/adv] *in the intervening time*

at the same time, concurrently, for now, for the duration, for the moment, for then, interim, interregnum, interruption, interval, in the interim, in the interval, in the meanwhile, meanwhile, recess, simultaneously, while; SEE CONCEPTS 799,807

meanwhile [adv] *at the same time*

ad interim, concurrently, during the interval, for now, for the duration, for the moment, for then, for the time being, in the interim, in the interval, in the intervening time, in the meantime, meantime, simultaneously, till, until, up to, when; SEE CONCEPT 799

measly [adj] *skimpy*

beggarly, contemptible, insignificant, meager, mean, miserable, miserly, niggling*, paltry, pathetic, petty, picayune, piddling*, pitiful, poor, puny, scanty, stingy, trifling, trivial, ungenerous, unimportant, valueless, worthless; SEE CONCEPT 789

measurable [adj] *determinable*

assessable, calculable, commensurate, computable, fathomable, gaugeable, material, mensurable, perceptible, quantifiable, quantitative, significant, surveyable, weighable; SEE CONCEPT 529

measure [n1] *portion, scope*

admeasurement, admensuration, allotment, allowance, amount, amplification, amplitude, area, bang, breadth, bulk, capacity, degree, depth, dimension, distance, duration, extent, fix, frequency, height, hit, magnitude, mass, meed, mensuration, nip, part, pitch, proportion, quantity, quantum, quota, range, ratio, ration, reach, share, shot, size, slug, span, strength, sum, volume, weight; SEE CONCEPTS 787,792,835

measure [n2] *standard, rule*

benchmark*, canon, criterion, example, gauge, meter, method, model, norm, pattern, scale, system, test, touchstone*, trial, type, yardstick; SEE CONCEPTS 686,688

measure [n3] *preventive or institutive action*

act, action, agency, bounds, control, course, deed, device, effort, expedient, limit, limitation, makeshift, maneuver, means, moderation, move, procedure, proceeding, project, proposal, proposition, resort, resource, restraint, shift, step, stopgap*, strategem; SEE CONCEPT 5

measure [n4] *bill, law*

act, enactment, project, proposal, proposition, resolution, statute; SEE CONCEPT 318

measure [n5] *beat, rhythm*

accent, cadence, cadency, division, melody, meter, rhyme, step, stress, stroke, swing, tempo, throb, time, tune, verse, vibration; SEE CONCEPTS 65,262

measure [v] *calculate, judge*

adapt, adjust, align, appraise, assess, average,

beat, blend, bound, calibrate, caliper, check, check out, choose, compute, delimit, demarcate, determine, dope out*, estimate, evaluate, even, eye*, figure, fit, gauge, gradate, grade, graduate, level, limit, line, look over, mark, mark out, mete, pace off, peg*, plumb, portion, quantify, rank, rate, read, reckon, regulate, rhyme, rule, scale, shade, size, size up, sound, square, stroke, survey, tailor, take account, time, value, weigh; SEE CONCEPTS 103,197,764

measurement [n] *calculation*
altitude, amount, amplitude, analysis, appraisal, area, assessment, calibration, capacity, computation, degree, density, depth, determination, dimension, distance, estimation, evaluation, extent, frequency, height, judgment, length, magnitude, mass, measure, mensuration, metage, pitch, quantification, quantity, range, reach, scope, size, survey, thickness, time, valuation, volume, weight, width; SEE CONCEPTS 730,792

meat [n1] *flesh of animal consumed as food*
aliment, brawn, chow, comestible, eats*, edible, fare, food, foodstuff, grub*, muscle, nourishment, nutriment, provision, ration, subsistence, sustenance, victual; SEE CONCEPTS 399,457,460

meat [n2] *core, gist*
burden, essence, heart, kernel, marrow, matter, nub, nucleus, pith, point, sense, short, substance, thrust, upshot; SEE CONCEPTS 682,826

meat-eating [adj] *carnivorous*
cannibalistic, flesh-eating, omophagous, predacious; SEE CONCEPT 401

meaty [adj] *significant*
compact, epigrammatic, factual, full of content, interesting, meaningful, pithy, pointed, profound, rich, substantial, weighty; SEE CONCEPT 267

mecca [n] *center, goal*
aim, capital, destination, focal point, focus, heart, hub, nerve center, objective, purpose; SEE CONCEPTS 435,438,507,659

mechanical [adj] *done by machine; machinelike*
automated, automatic, cold, cursory, emotionless, fixed, habitual, impersonal, instinctive, involuntary, laborsaving, lifeless, machine-driven, matter-of-fact, monotonous, perfunctory, programmed, routine, spiritless, standardized, stereotyped, unchanging, unconscious, unfeeling, unthinking, useful; SEE CONCEPT 544

mechanism [n1] *machine, device*
apparatus, appliance, black box*, components, contrivance, doohickey*, gadget, gears, gimmick, innards, instrument, machinery, motor, structure, system, tool, workings, works; SEE CONCEPT 463

mechanism [n2] *means, method*
agency, execution, functioning, medium, operation, performance, procedure, process, system, technique, workings; SEE CONCEPT 6

mechanize [v] *automate*
equip, industrialize, motorize, rig; SEE CONCEPTS 538,549

medal [n] *decoration of honor*
badge, commemoration, gold, hardware*, laurel, medallion, reward, ribbon, wreath; SEE CONCEPTS 337,476

meddle [v] *intervene, interfere*
abuse rights, advance, barge in, break in on, busybody*, butt in*, chime in, come uninvited, crash the gates*, dabble in, encroach, encumber,

fool with, hinder, horn in*, impede, impose, infringe, inquire, interlope, intermeddle, interpose, intrude, invade, kibitz*, mess around*, mix in, molest, obtrude, pry, push in, put two cents in*, sidewalk-superintend*, snoop*, stick nose in*, tamper, trespass, worm in*; SEE CONCEPTS 14,384

meddlesome [adj] *interfereing*
busy, busybody*, chiseling*, curious, encumbering, hindering, impeding, impertinent, intermeddling, interposing, interrupting, intruding, intrusive, kibitzing*, meddling, mischievous, nosy, obstructive, officious, prying, pushy, snooping*, snoopy*, tampering, troublesome; SEE CONCEPT 555

media [n] *communication by publication or broadcast*
announcement, announcing, cable, communications, correspondence, disclosure, expression, intelligence, news, publishing, radio, television; SEE CONCEPT 279

median [n/adj] *middle*
average, center, centermost, central, equidistant, halfway, intermediary, intermediate, mean, medial, mid, middlemost, midmost, midpoint, midway, par; SEE CONCEPTS 585,727,746,830

mediate [v] *try to bring to an agreement*
act as middle*, arbitrate, bring to terms, conciliate, deal, go fifty-fifty*, intercede, interfere, intermediate, interpose, intervene, make a deal, make peace, meet halfway*, moderate, negotiate, propitiate, reconcile, referee, resolve, restore harmony, settle, step in, strike happy medium*, trade off, umpire; SEE CONCEPTS 126,324,384

mediation [n] *attempt to bring to agreement*
arbitration, conciliation, intercession, interposition, intervention, negotiation, reconciliation; SEE CONCEPTS 126,324,384

mediator [n] *person who negotiates agreement*
advocate, arbiter, arbitrator, broker, conciliator, fixer, go-between*, interagent, interceder, intermediary, intermediator, judge, medium, middle person, moderator, negotiator, peacemaker, ref*, referee, rent-a-judge*, troubleshooter*, umpire; SEE CONCEPTS 348,423

medicine/medication [n] *substance that helps cure, alleviate, or prevent illness*
anesthetic, antibiotic, antidote, antiseptic, antitoxin, balm, biologic, capsule, cure, dose, drug, elixir, injection, inoculation, liniment, lotion, medicament, ointment, pharmaceutical, pharmacon, physic, pill, potion, prescription, remedy, salve, sedative, serum, tablet, tincture, tonic, vaccination, vaccine; SEE CONCEPT 307

medieval [adj] *having to do with the Middle Ages; old*
antediluvian, antiquated, antique, archaic, feudal, Gothic, old, old-fashioned, primitive, unenlightened; SEE CONCEPTS 549,578,797

mediocre [adj] *average, commonplace*
characterless, colorless, common, conventional, decent, dull, fair, fairish, fair to middling*, humdrum*, indifferent, inferior, insignificant, intermediate, mainstream, mean, medium, middling, moderate, no great shakes*, of poor quality, ordinary, passable, pedestrian, run-of-the-mill*, second-rate, so-so*, standard, tolerable, undistinguished, unexceptional, uninspired, vanilla*; SEE CONCEPTS 533,547

meditate [*v*] *think deeply about*
brood over, cogitate, consider, contemplate, deliberate, design, devise, dream, entertain idea*, figure, have in mind*, intend, moon*, mull over, muse, plan, ponder, purpose, put on thinking cap*, puzzle over, reflect, revolve, roll, ruminate, say to oneself, scheme, speculate, study, think, think over, track, view, weigh; SEE CONCEPT *17*

meditation [*n*] *deep thought*
concentration, contemplation, introspection, pondering, quiet time, reflection, rumination, self-examination; SEE CONCEPTS *17,24*

medium [*adj*] *midway, average*
common, commonplace, fair, fairish, intermediate, mean, medial, median, mediocre, middle, middling, moderate, neutral, normal, ordinary, par, passable, popular, run-of-the-mill*, so-so*, standard, tolerable; SEE CONCEPTS *533,547*

medium [*n1*] *means, mode*
agency, agent, avenue, channel, clairvoyant, factor, form, instrument, instrumentality, intermediate, measure, mechanism, ministry, organ, psychic, seer, tool, vehicle, way; SEE CONCEPTS *658,712*

medium [*n2*] *atmosphere, setting*
ambience, ambient, climate, conditions, element, habitat, influences, milieu, surroundings; SEE CONCEPTS *673,696*

medium [*n3*] *area of artistic expression*
art, drama, interpretation, manifestation, mark, music, painting, revelation, sculpture, speech, writing; SEE CONCEPTS *259,263,293*

medley [*n*] *miscellany*
assortment, brew, collection, combo, composition, confusion, conglomeration, farrago, hodgepodge, jumble, mélange, melee, mingling, mishmash, mixed bag, mixture, pasticcio, pastiche, patchwork, potpourri, salmagundi, variety; SEE CONCEPTS *262,432*

meek [*adj*] *shy; compliant*
acquiescent, deferential, docile, forbearing, gentle, humble, lenient, longanimous, long-suffering, lowly, manageable, mild, milquetoast*, modest, nothing, orderly, pabulum*, passive, patient, peaceful, plain, resigned, serene, soft, spineless, spiritless, subdued, submissive, tame, timid, tolerant, unassuming, unpretentious, unresisting, weak, weak-kneed*, wishy-washy*, yielding, zero*; SEE CONCEPT *401*

meet [*adj*] *fitting*
accommodated, applicable, appropriate, apt, conformed, equitable, expedient, fair, felicitous, fit, good, happy, just, proper, reconciled, right, suitable, timely; SEE CONCEPT *558*

meet [*n*] *sporting event involving several participants*
athletic event, competition, conflict, contest, event, match, meeting, tournament, tourney; SEE CONCEPT *363*

meet [*v1*] *happen on*
accost, affront, brush against, bump into, chance on, clash, collide, come across, come up against, confront, contact, cross, dig up*, encounter, engage, experience, face, fall in with*, find, front, get together, grapple, greet, hit, light, luck*, make a meet, meet face to face, rendezvous with, rub eyeballs*, run across, run into, run up against, salute, see, strike, stumble, touch shoulders*, tumble, tussle, wrestle; SEE CONCEPTS *183,384,626*

meet [*v2*] *connect, join*
abut, adhere, adjoin, border, coincide, connect, converge, cross, intersect, link, link up, reach, touch, unite; SEE CONCEPTS *612,759*

meet [*v3*] *perform, carry out*
answer, approach, come up to, comply, cope with, discharge, equal, execute, fit, fulfill, gratify, handle, match, measure up, rival, satisfy, suffice, tie, touch; SEE CONCEPT *91*

meet [*v4*] *come together, convene*
appear, assemble, be introduced, be present, be presented, collect, congregate, converge, enter in, flock, foregather, gather, get together, get to know, join, make acquaintance, muster, open, rally, rendezvous, show, sit; SEE CONCEPTS *114,324*

meeting [*n1*] *gathering, conference*
affair, assemblage, assembly, assignation, audience, bunch, call, cattle call*, company, competition, conclave, concourse, concursion, confab*, conflict, confrontation, congregation, congress, contest, convention, convocation, date, encounter, engagement, gang, get-together, huddle, introduction, meet, one on one*, parley, powwow*, rally, rendezvous, reunion, session, showdown, talk, tryst, turnout*; SEE CONCEPTS *324,363,384*

meeting [*n2*] *convergence, intersection*
abutment, agreement, apposition, concourse, confluence, conjunction, connection, contact, crossing, joining, junction, juxtaposition, unification, union; SEE CONCEPTS *113,684*

melancholy [*adj*] *depressed, sad*
blue*, dejected, despondent, destroyed, disconsolate, dismal, dispirited, doleful, dolorous, down*, down and out*, downbeat, downcast, downhearted, down in the dumps*, down in the mouth*, dragged, droopy, funereal, gloomy, glum, grim, heavyhearted, in blue funk*, joyless, lachrymose, low, low-spirited, lugubrious, mirthless, miserable, moody, moony*, mournful, pensive, saddened, saddening, somber, sorrowful, sorry*, torn up, trite, unhappy, wet blanket*, wistful, woebegone, woeful; SEE CONCEPT *403*

melancholy [*n*] *depression, sadness*
blahs*, blue devils*, blue funk*, blues*, boredom, bummer*, dejection, despair, desperation, despondency, dismals, dolefuls, dolor, downer*, down trip*, dumps, ennui, funk, gloom, gloominess, grief, letdown, low spirits, miserableness, misery, mopes*, mournfulness, pensiveness, sorrow, tedium, unhappiness, wistfulness, woe, wretchedness; SEE CONCEPT *410*

mélange [*n*] *mixture*
assortment, combo, confusion, farrago, gallimaufry, hodgepodge, jumble, medley, miscellany, mishmash, mix, mixed bag, pasticcio, pastiche, patchwork, potpourri, salmagundi, soup, stew; SEE CONCEPT *432*

meld [*v*] *blend, bring together*
amalgamate, associate, compound, dissolve, feather in, fuse, interblend, interface, interfuse, intermingle, marry, merge, mingle, mix, unite; SEE CONCEPTS *113,193*

melee [*n*] *battle, fight*
affray, battle royal*, brawl, broil, brouhaha*, brush, clash, donnybrook*, fracas, fray, free-for-all*, knock-down-drag-out*, row, ruckus, ruction, rumpus, scrimmage, scuffle, set-to*,

mellifluous [*adj*] *smooth and sweet sounding*
agreeable, dulcet, euphonic, fluid, harmonic, honeyed, mellow, pleasing, resonant, songful, soothing, symphonious, tuned, tuneful; SEE CONCEPT 594

mellow [*adj*] *ripe, mature; softened*
aged, cultured, cured, delicate, developed, dulcet, flavorful, full, full-flavored, fully developed, juicy, matured, mellifluent, mellifluous, melodious, perfect, perfected, rich, ripened, rounded, sapid, savory, seasoned, smooth, soft, soothing, sweet, tuneful; SEE CONCEPTS 462,578,594,797

mellow [*v*] *ripen, mature*
age, arrive, develop, grow, grow up, improve, maturate, milden, mollify, perfect, ripe, season, settle down, soften, sweeten; SEE CONCEPTS 678,704

melodious/melodic [*adj*] *harmonious, musical*
accordant, agreeable, assonant, canorous, clear, concordant, dulcet, euphonic, euphonious, harmonic, in tune, mellifluous, mellow, pleasing, resonant, silvery, soft, songful, sweet, sweet-sounding, symphonic, symphonious, tuned, tuneful, well-tuned; SEE CONCEPT 594

melodramatic [*adj*] *extravagant in speech, behavior*
artificial, blood-and-thunder*, cliff-hanging*, cloak-and-dagger*, exaggerated, ham*, hammy*, histrionic, hokey*, overdramatic, overemotional, sensational, spectacular, stagy, theatrical; SEE CONCEPT 542

melody [*n*] *harmony, tune*
air, aria, assonance, carillon, chant, chime, concord, consonance, descant, diapason, euphony, inflection, lay, lyric, measure, melodiousness, music, musicality, refrain, resonance, run, song, strain, theme, tunefulness, unison; SEE CONCEPTS 262,595

melt [*v1*] *liquefy; dissolve*
cook, deliquesce, diffuse, disappear, disintegrate, disperse, evanesce, evaporate, fade, flow, flux, fuse, go, heat, merge, pass away, render, run, smelt, soften, thaw, vanish, warm, waste away; SEE CONCEPTS 250,255

melt [*v2*] *give in, yield*
become lenient, disarm, forgive, mollify, relax, relent, show mercy, soften, touch; SEE CONCEPT 35

member [*n1*] *part of a group*
affiliate, associate, branch, chapter, component, comrade, constituent, cut, division, joiner, offshoot, parcel, piece, portion, post, representative, section, segment, unit; SEE CONCEPTS 417,834,835

member [*n2*] *appendage*
arm, component, constituent, element, extremity, feature, fragment, leg, limb, organ, part, portion, segment; SEE CONCEPT 392

membership [*n*] *belonging to organization; those belonging to a group*
associates, association, body, club, company, enrollment, fellows, group, members, participation, society; SEE CONCEPTS 381,417

membrane [*n*] *covering layer*
film, lamina, leaf, mucosa, sheath, sheet; SEE CONCEPT 484

memento [*n*] *souvenir*
keepsake, memorial, relic, remembrance, re-
membrancer, reminder, token, trace, trophy, vestige; SEE CONCEPTS 337,446

memoir [*n*] *record of experiences*
account, anecdote, annal, autobiography, bio*, biography, chronicle, confessions, diary, discourse, dissertation, essay, journal, life, life story, memory, monograph, narrative, note, recollection, register, reminiscence, thesis, tractate, transactions, treatise, vita; SEE CONCEPTS 271,280,282

memorabilia [*n*] *mementos*
annals, archives, collectibles, keepsakes, relics, remembrances, reminders, souvenirs, tokens, trophies; SEE CONCEPT 337

memorable [*adj*] *noteworthy, significant*
A-1*, big-league*, bodacious, catchy, celebrated, critical, crucial, decisive, distinguished, doozie*, enduring, eventful, extraordinary, famous, great, heavy*, heavyweight*, historic, hot*, illustrious, important, impressive, indelible, interesting, lasting, major-league, meaningful, mind-blowing*, momentous, monumental, notable, observable, red-letter*, remarkable, rememberable, rubric, serious, signal, something, standout, striking, super, surpassing, terrible, terrific, top-drawer, unforgettable; SEE CONCEPTS 529,548

memorandum/memo [*n*] *written note*
announcement, chit, diary, directive, dispatch, epistle, jotting, letter, message, minute, missive, notation, notice, record, reminder, tickler; SEE CONCEPTS 271,277,278

memorial [*adj*] *commemorative*
canonizing, celebrative, commemoratory, consecrating, consecrative, dedicatory, deifying, enshrining, in tribute, memorializing, monumental, remembering; SEE CONCEPT 537

memorial [*n*] *monument, testimonial in honor, praise*
cairn, ceremony, column, headstone, inscription, keepsake, mausoleum, memento, monolith, obelisk, pillar, plaque, record, relic, remembrance, reminder, shaft, slab, souvenir, statue, stele, tablet, token, tombstone, trophy; SEE CONCEPTS 337,386

memorize [*v*] *remember*
commit to memory, cram, fix in the mind, keep forever, know, know by heart, learn, learn by heart, master, nail down, recall, recollect, remind, retain, store; SEE CONCEPT 40

memory [*n1*] *ability to hold in the mind*
anamnesis, awareness, camera-eye*, cognizance, consciousness, dead-eye*, flashback, memorization, mind, mindfulness, mind's eye*, recall, recapture, recognition, recollection, reflection, remembrance, reminiscence, retention, retentiveness, retrospection, subconsciousness, thought; SEE CONCEPT 409

memory [*n2*] *specific thing remembered*
concept, cue, fantasy, hint, image, jog, memo, memoir, mnemonic, picture, prod, prompt, reminder, representation, suggestion, thought, vision; SEE CONCEPTS 529,678

menace [*n*] *danger; pest*
annoyance, caution, commination, hazard, intimidation, jeopardy, nuisance, peril, plague, risk, scare, threat, thunder, trouble, troublemaker, warning; SEE CONCEPTS 412,675

menace [*v*] *bother, frighten*
alarm, bad-eye*, browbeat, bully, chill, compro-

mise, endanger, hazard, impend, imperil, intimidate, jeopardize, lean on, loom, lower, overhang,
peril, portend, push around, put heat on*, risk,
scare, scare hell out of*, spook, terrorize,
threaten, torment, whip around*; SEE CONCEPTS
7,19

menacing [*adj*] *intimidating, ominous*
alarming, approaching, dangerous, frightening,
imminent, impending, intimidatory, looming,
louring, lowering, minacious, minatory, overhanging, threatening; SEE CONCEPTS *401,537,548*

menagerie [*adj*] *zoo*
aquarium, collection, exhibition, safari park,
wildlife park, zoological garden; SEE CONCEPTS
509,513

mend [*v*] *correct, improve, fix*
aid, ameliorate, amend, better, condition, convu-
lesce, cure, darn, doctor, emend, fiddle with,
gain, get better, get well, heal, knit, look up,
overhaul, patch, perk up, ready, rebuild, recondition, reconstruct, recover, rectify, recuperate, redress, refit, reform, refurbish, rejuvenate,
remedy, renew, renovate, repair, restore, retouch,
revamp, revise, right, service, sew; SEE CON-
CEPTS *126,244,303,700*

mendacious [*adj*] *dishonest*
deceitful, deceptive, duplicitous, equivocating,
erroneous, fallacious, false, fibbing, fraudulent,
insincere, lying, paltering, perfidious, perjured,
prevaricating, shifty, spurious, untrue, untruthful, wrong; SEE CONCEPT *267*

menial [*adj*] *lowly, low-status*
abject, base, baseborn, boring, common, degrading, demeaning, dull, fawning, grovelling, humble, humdrum, ignoble, ignominious, low, mean,
obeisant, obsequious, routine, servile, slavish,
sorry, subservient, sycophantic, unskilled, vile;
SEE CONCEPTS *574,575*

men's movement [*n*] *men's attempt to redefine
gender roles*
gender revisionism, male reform, men's liberation, men's studies; SEE CONCEPT *388*

mental [*adj*] *concerning the mind*
brainy*, cerebral, clairvoyant, deep, heavy, ideological, imaginative, immaterial, inner, intellective, intellectual, mysterious, phrenic, psychic,
psychical, psychological, rational, reasoning,
spiritual, subconscious, subjective, subliminal,
telepathic, thinking, thoughtful, unreal; SEE CON-
CEPTS *402,403*

mental [*adj2*] *insane*
deranged, disturbed, fruity, loco*, lunatic, mad,
maniac, mentally ill, mindless, non compos mentis, nuts*, nutsy*, psychiatric, psychotic, unbalanced, unstable; SEE CONCEPTS *314,403*

mental hospital [*n*] *psychiatric hospital*
bughouse*, funny farm*, insane asylum, loony
bin*, madhouse*, mental health facility, mental
institution, nuthouse*, psychiatric ward, sanatorium; SEE CONCEPTS *312,439,516*

mental illness [*n*] *mental disorder*
depression, emotional disorder, emotional instability, insanity, maladjustment, mania, mental
sickness, nervous breakdown, neurosis, neurotic
disorder, personality disorder, phobia, psychosis,
schizophrenia; SEE CONCEPTS *316,410*

mentality [*n*] *state of mind; intelligence*
attitude, brainpower, brains, cast, character,
comprehension, disposition, frame of mind*,
headset*, intellect, intelligence quotient, IQ,

makeup, mental age, mind, mindset*, outlook,
personality, psychology, rationality, reasoning,
routine, sense, turn of mind*, understanding,
way of thinking*, wit; SEE CONCEPTS *409,411*

mention [*n*] *referral, observation*
acknowledgment, allusion, citation, comment,
footnote, indication, naming, note, notice, notification, recognition, reference, remark, specifying, tribute, utterance; SEE CONCEPTS *73,278*

mention [*v*] *refer to*
acknowledge, acquaint, adduce, advert, allude to,
bring up, broach, call attention to, cite, communicate, declare, designate, detail, disclose, discuss, divulge, enumerate, hint at, impart, infer,
instance, intimate, introduce, make known,
name, notice, notify, observe, point out, point to,
quote, recount, remark, report, reveal, speak
about, speak of, specify, state, suggest, tell,
throw out, touch on; SEE CONCEPT *73*

mentor [*n*] *person who advises*
adviser, coach, counsellor, guide, instructor,
teacher, trainer, tutor; SEE CONCEPT *350*

menu [*n*] *list from which to choose, often to
choose food*
bill of fare, card, carte, carte du jour, cuisine,
food, spread, table; SEE CONCEPT *283*

mercenary [*adj*] *greedy for money*
acquisitive, avaricious, bribable, corrupt, covetous, grabby, grasping, miserly, money-grub-
bing, selfish, sordid, stingy, unethical,
unprincipled, unscrupulous, venal; SEE CONCEPT
401

mercenary [*n*] *person who fights, kills for money*
hireling, legionnaire, merc, professional soldier,
slave, soldier of fortune, warrior; SEE CONCEPTS
358,412

merchandise [*n*] *goods for sale*
commodity, effects, job lot, line, material, number, produce, product, seconds, staple, stock,
stuff, truck, vendible, wares; SEE CONCEPT *338*

merchandise [*v*] *sell goods*
advertise, buy and sell, deal in, distribute, do
business in, market, promote, publicize, retail,
trade, traffic in, vend, wholesale; SEE CONCEPT
345

merchant [*n*] *person who sells goods*
broker, businessperson, consigner, dealer, ex-
porter, handler, jobber, marketer, operator, retailer, salesperson, seller, sender, shipper,
shopkeeper, storekeeper, trader, tradesperson,
trafficker, tycoon, vendor, wholesaler; SEE CON-
CEPT *347*

merciful [*adj*] *kind, sparing*
all heart*, beneficent, benign, benignant, bleeding heart*, charitable, clement, compassionate,
condoning, easygoing, feeling, forbearing, forgiving, generous, gentle, gracious, heart in right
place*, humane, humanitarian, indulgent, kindly,
lenient, liberal, mild, pardoning, pitiful, pitying,
soft*, softhearted*, sympathetic, tender, tenderhearted, tolerant; SEE CONCEPTS *401,542*

merciless [*adj*] *mean, heartless*
barbarous, callous, compassionless, cruel, cutthroat, dog-eat-dog*, fierce, gratuitous, grim,
hard, hardhearted, harsh, hatchet job*, having a
killer instinct*, implacable, inexorable, inhumane, iron-fisted, mean machine*, mortal, pitiless, relentless, ruthless, severe, unappeasable,
uncalled-for, unfeeling, unflinching, unforgiving,
unmerciful, unpitying, unrelenting, unsparing,

unsympathetic, unyielding, wanton; SEE CON-
CEPTS *401,542*

mercurial [*adj*] *flighty, temperamental*
blowing hot and cold*, bubbleheaded*, buoyant,
capricious, changeable, effervescent, elastic, erratic, expansive, fickle, flaky, flip*, fluctuating,
gaga*, gay, impulsive, inconstant, irregular, irrepressible, lighthearted, lively, lubricious, mad,
mobile, movable, quicksilver, resilient, short-
fuse*, spirited, sprightly, ticklish, unpredictable,
unstable, up-and-down*, variable, volatile, yo-
yo*; SEE CONCEPTS *401,404*

mercy [*n*] *kindness, compassion*
benevolence, benignancy, blessing, boon, charity, clemency, commiseration, favor, forbearance, forgiveness, generosity, gentleness,
godsend, goodwill, grace, humanity, kindliness,
lenience, leniency, lenity, lifesaver, luck, mildness, pity, quarter, relief, ruth, softheartedness,
sympathy, tenderness, tolerance; SEE CONCEPTS
32,633

mere [*adj*] *nothing more; absolute*
bald, bare, blunt, common, complete, entire, insignificant, little, minor, plain, poor, pure, pure
and simple, sheer, simple, small, stark, unadorned, unadulterated, unmitigated, unmixed,
utter, very; SEE CONCEPTS *535,589*

meretricious [*adj*] *gaudy, flashy*
blatant, bogus, brazen, chintzy, counterfeit, garish, glaring, insincere, loud, misleading, ornate,
phony, plastic*, put-on*, sham, showy, spurious,
superficial, tawdry, tinsel, trashy; SEE CONCEPTS
542,589

merge [*v*] *bring or come together*
absorb, amalgamate, assimilate, become lost in,
become partners, be swallowed up*, blend, cement, centralize, coalesce, combine, come
aboard*, compound, conglomerate, consolidate,
converge, deal one in, fuse, hitch on*, hook up*,
immerge, incorporate, interface, intermingle, intermix, join, join up, line up, marry, meet, meld,
melt into, mingle, mix, network, plug into, pool,
slap on, submerge, synthesize, tack on*, tag,
team up*, throw in together*, tie in, unite; SEE
CONCEPTS *113,193,324*

merger [*n*] *consolidation*
alliance, amalgamation, cahoots*, coadunation,
coalition, combination, fusion, hookup, incorporation, lineup, melding, mergence, merging, organization, pool, takeover, tie-in, tie-up,
unification, union; SEE CONCEPTS *323,324,703*

meridian [*n*] *summit, climax*
acme, apex, apogee, crest, culmination, extremity, high noon, high-water mark, peak, pinnacle,
zenith; SEE CONCEPTS *832,836*

merit [*n*] *advantage*
arete, asset, benefit, caliber, credit, desert, dignity, excellence, excellency, good, goodness,
honor, integrity, perfection, quality, stature,
strong point, talent, value, virtue, worth, worthiness; SEE CONCEPT *693*

merit [*v*] *be entitled to*
be in line for, be worthy, deserve, earn, get one's
comeuppance*, get one's due*, get one's just
desserts*, get what is coming*, have a claim,
have a right, have coming, incur, justify, rate,
warrant; SEE CONCEPT *129*

meritorious [*adj*] *honorable, commendable*
admirable, boss*, choice, creditable, deserving,
estimable, excellent, exemplary, golden, good,

laudable, meritable, noble, praisable, praiseworthy, right, righteous, thankworthy, top drawer*,
virtuous, winner, world-beating*, worthy; SEE
CONCEPTS *404,548,572*

merriment/merrymaking [*n*] *enjoyment, amusement*
brawl, buffoonery, cheerfulness, conviviality,
festivity, frolic, fun, fun and games*, gaiety,
glee, happiness, hilarity, hoopla*, indulgence,
jocularity, jocundity, jollity, joviality, joy,
laughs, laughter, levity, liveliness, mirth, picnic,
recreation, revel, revelry, self-indulgence,
shindig, sport, whoopee*, wingding*; SEE CON-
CEPTS *386,410*

merry [*adj*] *very happy; festive*
amusing, blithe, blithesome, boisterous, boon,
carefree, cheerful, comic, comical, convivial, enjoyable, entertaining, facetious, frolicsome, fun-
loving, funny, gay, glad, gleeful, grooving*,
hilarious, humorous, jocund, jolly, joyful, joyous, jumping, larking, lighthearted, lively, mad,
mirthful, perky, pleasant, riotous, rip-roaring*,
rocking, rollicking, saturnalian, sportive, sunny,
unconstrained, uproarious, vivacious, wild, winsome, zappy*, zingy*, zippy*; SEE CONCEPTS
403,548,572

mesa [*n*] *plateau*
butte, elevation, highland, plain, tableland, upland; SEE CONCEPTS *509,744*

mesh [*n*] *netting, entanglement*
cobweb, jungle, knot, labyrinth, maze, morass,
net, network, plexus, reticulation, screen, skein,
snare, snarl, tangle, toils, tracery, trap, web; SEE
CONCEPTS *473,770,733*

mesh [*v*] *entangle, connect*
agree, catch, coincide, combine, come together,
coordinate, dovetail, engage, enmesh, ensnare,
fit, fit together, harmonize, interlock, knit, net,
snare, tangle, trap; SEE CONCEPTS *113,193*

mesmerize [*v*] *captivate*
catch up, control, deaden, drug, ensorcell, enthrall, entrance, fascinate, grip, hold spellbound,
hypnotize, magnetize, numb, render unconscious, spellbind, stupefy; SEE CONCEPTS *11,14*

mess [*n1*] *disorder, litter*
botch, chaos, clutter, combination, compound,
confusion, debris, dirtiness, disarray, discombob-
ulation*, disorganization, every which way*,
eyesore, fright, hash, hodgepodge, jumble, mayhem, mishmash, monstrosity, salmagundi, shambles, sight, turmoil, untidiness, wreck, wreckage;
SEE CONCEPTS *230,260*

mess [*n2*] *difficulty, predicament*
dilemma, fix, imbroglio, jam, mix-up, muddle,
perplexity, pickle*, plight, stew; SEE CONCEPT
674

message [*n1*] *communication, often written*
bulletin, cannonball, communiqué, directive, dispatch, dope, earful, epistle, information, intelligence, intimation, letter, memo, memorandum,
missive, news, note, notice, paper, report, tidings, wire, word; SEE CONCEPTS *271,274*

message [*n2*] *meaning, idea*
acceptation, import, intendment, moral, point,
purport, sense, significance, significancy, signification, theme, understanding; SEE CONCEPTS
661,682

mess around [*v*] *fiddle; goof off*
amuse oneself, dabble, dawdle, doodle, fool
around, loiter, muck around*, play, play around,

play the fool*, potter, puddle, putter, tinker, tri-fle; SEE CONCEPTS 87,363

messenger [n] *person carrying information to another*
agent, ambassador, bearer, carrier, commission-aire, courier, crier, delegate, delivery person, de-tachment, detail, dispatcher, emissary, envoy, errand person*, flag-bearer, forerunner, go-be-tween*, gofer*, harbinger, herald, intermediary, mediator, minister, post, precursor, prophet, run-ner, schlepper*; SEE CONCEPT 348

mess up [v] *disorder, dirty*
befoul, besmirch, bobble, bollix*, botch, bungle, clutter, confuse, damage, derange, destroy, dis-arrange, discompose, dishevel, disorganize, dis-turb, foul, goof up*, gum up*, jumble, litter, louse up, muddle, pollute, ruin, rummage, scram-ble, screw up*, smear, soil, spoil, unsettle, upset; SEE CONCEPTS 158,252,254

messy [adj] *cluttered, dirty*
blotchy*, careless, chaotic, confused, disheveled, disordered, disorganized, grimy, grubby*, lit-tered, muddled, raunchy*, rumpled, slapdash*, slipshod*, sloppy, slovenly, unfastidious, un-kempt, untidy; SEE CONCEPTS 485,621

metal [n] *lustrous chemical element*
alloy, casting, deposit, foil, hardware, ingot, leaf, load, mail, mineral, native rock, ore, plate, sol-der, vein; SEE CONCEPT 476

metamorphose [v] *convert, transform*
age, alter, be reborn, change, commute, develop, diverge, mature, mutate, remake, remodel, re-shape, ripen, transfigure, translate, transmogrify, transmute, transubstantiate, vary; SEE CONCEPTS 469,697,701

metamorphosis [n] *conversion, transformation*
alteration, change, changeover, evolution, muta-tion, rebirth, transfiguration, transfigurement, translation, transmogrification, transmutation, transubstantiation; SEE CONCEPTS 469,697,701

metaphor [n] *figure of speech, implied compari-son*
allegory, analogy, emblem, hope, image, metonymy, personification, similitude, symbol, trope; SEE CONCEPT 275

metaphorical [adj] *figurative*
allegorical, denotative, descriptive, emblematic, illustrative, metaphoric, representative, sym-bolic, tropological; SEE CONCEPTS 267,582

metaphysical [adj] *not physical; without physi-cal presence*
abstract, abstruse, bodiless, deep, difficult, dis-carnate, esoteric, eternal, fundamental, high-flown, ideal, immaterial, impalpable, incorporeal, insubstantial, intangible, intellec-tual, jesuitic, mystical, nonmaterial, nonphysical, numinous, oversubtle, philosophical, preternat-ural, profound, recondite, spiritual, superhuman, superior, supermundane, supernatural, suprahu-man, supramundane, supranatural, theoretical, transcendental, unearthly, unfleshly, universal, unphysical, unreal, unsubstantial; SEE CONCEPTS 529,582

mete [v] *administer, distribute*
admeasure, allocate, allot, allow, apportion, as-sign, deal, dispense, divide, dole, give, lot, mea-sure, parcel, portion, ration, share; SEE CONCEPTS 98,108

meteoric [adj] *brief, sudden*
dazzling, ephemeral, flashing, fleeting, momen-tary, overnight, rapid, spectacular, speedy, swift, transient; SEE CONCEPTS 548,798,799

meteorology [n] *weather science*
aerology, climatology, weather forecasting; SEE CONCEPTS 522,524

meter [n] *rhythm, beat*
cadence, cadency, feet, lilt, measure, mora, music, pattern, poetry, rhyme, structure, swing; SEE CONCEPTS 65,262

method [n1] *means, procedure*
adjustment, approach, arrangement, channels, course, custom, design, disposal, disposition, fashion, form, formula, habit, line, manner, mechanism, method, mode, modus, modus operandi, nuts and bolts*, plan, practice, pro-ceeding, process, program, receipt, recipe, red tape*, ritual, rote, routine, rubric, rule, rut, schema, scheme, shortcut, style, system, tack, tactics, technic, technique, tenor, the book*, usage, way, ways and means*, wise, wrinkle*; SEE CONCEPTS 6,660

method [n2] *order, pattern*
arrangement, classification, design, form, order-liness, organization, plan, planning, purpose, regularity, structure, system; SEE CONCEPTS 727,770

methodical/methodic [adj] *organized, precise*
all together, analytical, businesslike, by the book*, by the numbers, careful, cut-and-dried*, deliberate, disciplined, efficient, exact, fixed, framed, in a groove*, logical, methodized, meticulous, neat, ordered, orderly, painstaking, planned, regular, scrupulous, set-up*, structured, systematic, tidy, together, well-regulated; SEE CONCEPTS 326,542,544,585

methodology [n] *methods*
approach, channels, design, manner, mode, plan, practice, procedure, process, program, style, technique, way; SEE CONCEPTS 6,644

meticulous [adj] *detailed, perfectionist*
accurate, cautious, conscientious, conscionable, crossing the t's*, dotting the i's*, exact, fastidi-ous, fussy, heedful, microscopic, nitpicking*, painstaking, particular, persnickety*, picky, pre-cise, punctilious, punctual, scrupulous, stickling, strict, thorough; SEE CONCEPTS 542,544,557

metier [n] *occupation*
calling, chosen work, craft, day gig*, employ-ment, field, forte, job, line of work, one's spe-cialty, profession, pursuit, racket*, thing*, trade, vocation, walk of life*, work; SEE CONCEPTS 349,351,360

metropolis [n] *major city*
capital, downtown, megalopolis, metropolitan area, municipality; SEE CONCEPT 507

metropolitan [adj] *concerning a city*
city, cosmopolitan, modern, municipal, urban, urbane; SEE CONCEPT 536

mettle [n] *boldness, strength of character*
animation, ardor, backbone, bravery, caliber, courage, daring, dauntlessness, disposition, en-ergy, fire, force, fortitude, gallantry, gameness, grit*, guts*, hardihood, heart*, indomitability, kidney*, life*, makeup, moxie, nature, nerve, pluck, quality, resolution, resolve, spirit, spunk, stamina, stamp*, starch, temper, temperament, valor, vigor, vitality; SEE CONCEPT 411

miasma [n] *effluvium*
fetor, foul air, fumes, gas, mephitis, odor, pollu-

tion, reek, smell, smog, stench, stink, vapor; SEE CONCEPT 465

microbe [n] *bacteria*
bacillus, bacterium, bug*, crud, germ, microorganism, pathogen, plague, virus; SEE CONCEPT 306

microorganism [n] *germ*
bacterium, bug*, disease, disease-causing agent, microbe, parasite, pathogen, plague, virus; SEE CONCEPTS 306,392

microscopic [adj] *tiny, almost undetectable*
atomic, diminutive, imperceptible, infinitesimal, invisible, little, minuscule, minute, negligible, teeny*, wee*; SEE CONCEPTS 773,789

microwave [v] *cook*
bake, heat, melt, nuke*, warm up, zap*; SEE CONCEPT 170

middle [adj] *central*
average, between, betwixt and between*, center, centermost, equidistant, halfway, inner, inside, intermediate, intervening, mainstream, mean, medial, median, medium, mezzo*, middlemost, middle of the road*, midmost, smack in the middle, straddling the fence*; SEE CONCEPTS 547,583,830

middle [n] *center*
core, deep, focus, halfway, halfway point, heart, inside, marrow, mean, media, midpoint, midriff, midsection, midst, thick, waist; SEE CONCEPTS 746,761,830,833

middle-of-the-road [adj] *moderate*
balanced, cautious, compromising, conservative, controlled, disciplined, even, impartial, indifferent, inexpensive, midway, mild, modest, neutral, noncommittal, nonpartisan, not excessive, on the fence*, reasonable, straight; SEE CONCEPTS 533,575

middle person [n] *person who acts as intermediary*
agent, broker, connection, distributor, entrepreneur, fixer, go-between*, influence, interagent, interceder, intercessor, intermediate, intermediator, jobber*, mediator, representative, salesperson, wholesaler; SEE CONCEPT 348

middling [adj] *adequate, okay*
all right, average, common, conventional, decent, fair, fairish, good, indifferent, intermediate, mean, mediocre, medium, moderate, modest, okay, ordinary, passable, run-of-the-mill*, so-so*, tolerable, traditional, unexceptional, unremarkable; SEE CONCEPT 547

midget [adj] *short, small*
baby, diminutive, knee-high*, Lilliputian, miniature, minikin, pocket, teensy*, teeny*, tiny; SEE CONCEPTS 773,779

midget [n] *small person*
bantam, gnome, homunculus, homunculus, Lilliputian*, little person, manikin, midge, runt*; SEE CONCEPT 424

midnight [n] *middle of the night*
bewitching hour*, dead of night*, 12 o'clock at night, small hours*, twelve o'clock at night, witching hour*; SEE CONCEPTS 801,802,806

midst [n] *middle, core*
betwixt and between*, bosom, center, deep, depths, halfway, heart, hub, interior, mean, medium, midpoint, nucleus, thick; SEE CONCEPT 830

mien [n] *person's presence, manner*
act, address, air, appearance, aspect, aura, bearing, carriage, countenance, demeanor, deportment, expression, front, image, look, mannerism, port, set, style; SEE CONCEPTS 411,644

miff [v] *annoy*
aggrieve, bother, displease, hurt, irk, irritate, nettle, offend, pester, pique, provoke, put out, resent, upset, vex; SEE CONCEPTS 7,19

might [n] *ability, power*
adequacy, arm, authority, capability, capacity, clout, command, competence, control, domination, efficacy, efficiency, energy, force, forcefulness, forcibleness, get-up-and-go*, jurisdiction, lustiness, mastery, moxie*, muscle*, potency, powerfulness, prowess, puissance, punch, qualification, qualifiedness, sinew*, steam, strength, strenuousness, strong arm*, sway, valor, vigor, vigorousness; SEE CONCEPTS 411,641,732

mightily [adv1] *very much, extremely*
decidedly, exceedingly, greatly, highly, hugely, intensely, mighty, notably, surpassingly, very; SEE CONCEPT 569

mightily [adv2] *forcefully*
arduously, energetically, forcibly, hard, hardly, laboriously, lustily, might and main*, powerfully, strenuously, strongly, vigorously, with all one's strength; SEE CONCEPTS 540,544

mighty [adj1] *forceful, powerful*
boss*, doughty, hardy, indomitable, lusty, muscular, omnipotent, potent, powerhouse, puissant, robust, stalwart, steamroller*, stout, strapping, strengthy, strong, strong as ox*, sturdy, vigorous, wieldy; SEE CONCEPTS 489,540

mighty [adj2] *gigantic, monumental*
august, bulky, colossal, considerable, dynamic, eminent, enormous, extensive, extraordinary, grand, great, heroic, high, huge, illustrious, immense, imposing, impressive, intense, irresistible, large, magnificent, majestic, massive, moving, notable, prodigious, renowned, stupendous, titanic, towering, tremendous, vast; SEE CONCEPTS 537,773,781

migrant [n] *person who moves to a foreign place*
departer, drifter, emigrant, evacuee, expatriate, gypsy, immigrant, itinerant, migrator, mover, nomad, rover, tinker, transient, traveler, vagrant, wanderer; SEE CONCEPT 413

migrant/migratory [adj] *moving, traveling*
casual, changing, drifting, emigrating, errant, gypsy, immigrant, immigrating, impermanent, itinerant, migrative, migratorial, mobile, nomad, nomadic, on the move, passing over, passing through, peripatetic, ranging, roving, seasonal, shifting, temporary, tramp, transient, transmigratory, unsettled, vagabond, vagrant, wandering; SEE CONCEPT 584

migrate [v] *move, travel to another place*
drift, emigrate, immigrate, journey, leave, nomadize, range, roam, rove, shift, transmigrate, trek, voyage, wander; SEE CONCEPTS 198,224

mild [adj1] *gentle, temperate, nonirritating*
balmy, benign, benignant, blah*, bland, breezy, calm, choice, clear, clement, cool, dainty, delicate, demulcent, easy, emollient, exquisite, faint, fine, flat, genial, ho-hum*, lenient, lenitive, light, lukewarm, medium, mellow, moderate, mollifying, nothing, nothing much*, pabulum, pacific, peaceful, placid, smooth, soft, soothing, sunny, tempered, tepid, untroubled, vanilla*, warm, weak, wimpy*; SEE CONCEPTS 485,525,537

mild [*adj2*] *easygoing, pleasant in personality*
amiable, balmy, bland, calm, clement, compassionate, complaisant, deferential, docile, dull, easy, equable, feeble, flat, forbearant, forbearing, forgiving, gentle, good-humored, good-natured, good-tempered, humane, indulgent, insipid, jejune, kind, lenient, meek, mellow, merciful, mild-mannered, moderate, obeisant, obliging, pacific, patient, peaceable, placid, serene, smooth, soft, spiritless, subdued, submissive, subservient, tame, temperate, tender, tranquil, unassuming, vapid, warm; SEE CONCEPTS 401,404

mile [*n*] *5, 280 feet/1.609 kilometers measured*
nautical, square, statute; SEE CONCEPTS 790,791

milestone [*n*] *achievement*
anniversary, breakthrough, discovery, event, landmark, milepost, occasion, turning point, waypost; SEE CONCEPTS 2,706

milieu [*n*] *environment, atmosphere*
ambience, ambient, background, bag, climate, element, locale, location, medium, mise-en-scène, nabe, neighborhood, place, scene, setting, space, sphere, surroundings, turf; SEE CONCEPT 673

militant [*adj*] *aggressive, combative*
active, assertive, assertory, bellicose, belligerent, combating, contending, contentious, embattled, fighting, gladiatorial, in arms, martial, militaristic, military, offensive, pugnacious, pushy, quarrelsome, scrappy, self-assertive, truculent, up in arms, vigorous, warlike, warring; SEE CONCEPT 401

militant [*n*] *person who fights, is aggressive*
activist, belligerent, combatant, demonstrator, fighter, objector, partisan, protester, rioter, warrior; SEE CONCEPTS 358,359

military [*adj*] *soldierlike; concerning the armed forces*
aggressive, armed, army, combatant, combative, fighting, martial, militant, militaristic, noncivil, soldierly, warlike, warmongering; SEE CONCEPT 536

military [*n*] *armed force*
air force, army, force, marines, navy, service, servicepeople, soldiery, troop; SEE CONCEPT 322

milk [*n*] *liquid produced by mammals*
buttermilk, chalk*, condensed, cream, evaporated, formula, goat, half-and-half, homogenized, laiche, low fat, moo juice*, pasteurized, powdered, raw, skim, two-percent, whole; SEE CONCEPT 467

milk [*v*] *tap; exploit*
bleed, drain, draw off, elicit, empty, evince, evoke, exhaust, express, extort, extract, fleece, impose on, let out, press, pump, siphon, suck, take advantage, take out, use, wring; SEE CONCEPTS 139,142,156,225

milksop [*n*] *coward*
baby*, caitiff, chicken*, chicken heart*, chicken liver*, cry-baby, deserter, fraidy-cat*, jellyfish*, lily liver, momma's boy*, namby-pamby, pansy, pantywaist, quitter, scaredy cat*, sissy*, weakling, wimp, wuss*, wussy*, yellow, yellow belly*; SEE CONCEPT 423

milky [*adj*] *white, cloudy*
alabaster, clouded, frosted, lacteal, lacteous, lactescent, milk-white, opalescent, opaline, opaque, pearly, whitish; SEE CONCEPT 618

mill [*n*] *factory*
foundry, manufactory, plant, shop, sweatshop, works; SEE CONCEPTS 439,449

mill [*v*] *grind*
comminute, crush, granulate, grate, pound, powder, press, pulverize; SEE CONCEPT 186

millenium [*n*] *one thousand years*
one-thousandth anniversary, turn of the century; SEE CONCEPTS 807,816

millstone [*n*] *burden*
accountability, affliction, albatross*, anxiety, ball and chain*, blame, charge, concern, cross, deadweight, difficulty, encumbrance, grievance, hardship, hindrance, load, mental weight, misfortune, onus, punishment, responsibility, strain, stress, task, thorn in one's side*, trial, trouble, worry; SEE CONCEPTS 532,690

mimic [*n*] *person who imitates*
actor, caricaturist, comedian, copycat, imitator, impersonator, impressionist, mime, mummer, parodist, parrot, performer, playactor, player, thespian, trouper; SEE CONCEPT 352

mimic [*v*] *imitate, mock*
act, ape, burlesque, caricature, copy, copycat, ditto*, do, do like*, echo, enact, fake, go like*, impersonate, look like*, make believe, make fun of, make like*, mime, mirror, pantomime, parody, parrot, perform, personate, play, resemble, ridicule, sham, simulate, take off*, travesty; SEE CONCEPTS 54,59,111,171

mince [*v1*] *chop up*
chip, crumble, cut, dice, divide, grind, hack, hash, whack; SEE CONCEPT 176

mince [*v2*] *pose, put on airs*
attitudinize, flounce, posture, prance, sashay, strut; SEE CONCEPT 59

mince [*v3*] *euphemize, hold back in communication*
alleviate, decrease, diminish, extenuate, lessen, minimize, moderate, palliate, soften, spare, tone down, weaken; SEE CONCEPT 266

mincing [*adj*] *affected, pretentious*
artificial, dainty, delicate, effeminate, fastidious, finical, finicky, fussy, genteel, insincere, la-di-da*, nice, particular, persnickety, precious, sissy, squeamish, stilted, too-too*, unnatural; SEE CONCEPTS 401,404

mind [*n1*] *intelligence*
apperception, attention, brain*, brainpower, brains*, capacity, cognizance, conception, consciousness, creativity, faculty, function, genius, head, imagination, ingenuity, instinct, intellect, intellectual, intellectuality, intuition, judgment, lucidity, marbles*, mentality, observation, perception, percipience, power, psyche, ratiocination, reason, reasoning, regard, sanity, sense, soul, soundness, spirit, talent, thinker, thought, understanding, wisdom, wits; SEE CONCEPTS 393,409

mind [*n2*] *memory*
attention, cognizance, concentration, head, mark, note, notice, observance, observation, recollection, regard, remark, remembrance, subconscious, thinking, thoughts; SEE CONCEPTS 409,630

mind [*n3*] *inclination, tendency; belief*
attitude, bent, conviction, desire, determination, disposition, eye, fancy, feeling, humor, impulse, intention, judgment, leaning, liking, mood, notion, opinion, outlook, persuasion, pleasure,

mi
mi

point of view, purpose, sentiment, strain, temper, temperament, thoughts, tone, urge, vein, view, way of thinking, will, wish; SEE CONCEPTS *20,657,689*

mind [*v1*] *be bothered; care*
be affronted, be opposed, complain, deplore, disapprove, dislike, look askance at, object, resent, take offense; SEE CONCEPTS *21,29*

mind [*v2*] *comply, obey*
adhere to, attend, behave, do as told, follow, follow orders, heed, keep, listen, mark, note, notice, observe, pay attention, pay heed, regard, respect, take heed, watch; SEE CONCEPTS *23,91*

mind [*v3*] *attend, tend*
baby-sit, be attentive, behold, care for, discern, discipline, ensure, give heed to, govern, guard, have charge of, keep an eye on*, listen up, look, make certain, mark, mind the store*, note, notice, observe, oversee, perceive, regard, ride herd on*, see, sit, superintend, supervise, watch; SEE CONCEPTS *110,295,596,623*

mind [*v4*] *be careful*
be cautious, be concerned, be on guard, be solicitous, be wary, have a care, mind one's p's and q's*, take care, tend, toe the line*, trouble, watch, watch one's step*, watch out*; SEE CONCEPT *34*

mind [*v5*] *remember*
bethink, bring to mind, cite, recall, recollect, remind, reminisce, retain; SEE CONCEPT *40*

mind-blowing [*adj*] *amazing, intense*
astonishing, eye-opening, hallucinatory, mind-altering, mind-boggling, overwhelming, psychedelic, staggering, stunning, wonderful; SEE CONCEPTS *547,572*

mind-boggling [*adj*] *overwhelming*
amazing, astonishing, breathtaking, eye-opening, mind-blowing, spectacular, staggering, startling, stunning, stupendous, surprising, wonderful; SEE CONCEPTS *547,572*

mindful [*adj*] *attentive, aware*
alert, alive to, apprehensive, au courant, be up on*, cagey, careful, cautious, chary, cognizant, conscientious, conscious, conversant, heedful, in the know, know all the answers*, knowing, know ins and outs*, knowledgeable, observant, observative, observing, on one's toes*, on the ball*, on the job*, on to*, plugged in*, regardful, respectful, sensible, solicitous, thoughtful, tuned in*, vigilant, wary, watchful, with eyes peeled*; SEE CONCEPTS *402,403,542*

mindless [*adj*] *oblivious, stupid; automatic*
asinine, brutish, careless, daydreaming, foolish, forgetful, gratuitous, heedless, idiotic, imbecilic, inattentive, mooning, moony, moronic, neglectful, negligent, nitwitted, obtuse, out, out of it*, rash, senseless, silly, simple, spaced-out*, thoughtless, unaware, unintelligent, unmindful, unthinking, witless; SEE CONCEPTS *403,538*

mind reader [*n*] *psychic*
augur, channeller, clairvoyant, diviner, fortune-teller, haruspex, horoscopist, medium, mentalist, oracle, palm reader, prophet, seer, soothsayer, telepathis; SEE CONCEPT *423*

mind-set [*n*] *mental attitude*
air, approach, belief, character, demeanor, disposition, frame of mind, headset, inclination, mental outlook, mental state, mood, opinion, perspective, philosophy, point of view, position, sentiment, stance, stand, standing, standpoint, temperament, view, way of thinking; SEE CONCEPTS *410,689*

mine [*n*] *deposit, supply*
abundance, bed, bonanza, ditch, excavation, field, fount, fountain, fund, gold mine, hoard, lode, pit, quarry, reserve, shaft, source, spring, stock, store, treasure trove, treasury, trench, vein, wealth, well, wellspring; SEE CONCEPTS *449,509,712*

mine [*v*] *dig up*
burrow, delve, dig for, drill, excavate, extract, hew, pan, quarry, sap, scoop, shovel, unearth, work; SEE CONCEPT *178*

mingle [*v1*] *physically join*
admix, alloy, blend, coalesce, commingle, compound, intermingle, intermix, interweave, make up, marry, meld, merge, mix, unite, wed; SEE CONCEPT *193*

mingle [*v2*] *socialize*
associate, circulate, consort, fraternize, gang up*, hang out*, hobnob, mix, network, pool, rub shoulders*, tie in, work the room*; SEE CONCEPT *384*

miniature [*adj*] *tiny*
baby, diminutive, itsy-bitsy*, itty-bitty*, Lilliputian*, little, midget, mini, minikin, minuscule, minute, mite, model, petite, pint-sized*, pocket, reduced, scaled-down, small, small-scale, teensy*, teeny*, toy, wee; SEE CONCEPTS *773,789*

miniature [*n*] *tiny thing*
baby, insignificancy, midget, model, pocket edition, toy; SEE CONCEPT *730*

minimal [*adj*] *littlest, slightest*
basal, basic, essential, fundamental, least, least possible, lowest, minimum, nominal, smallest, token; SEE CONCEPTS *762,773,789*

minimize [*v*] *make smaller; underrate*
abbreviate, attenuate, belittle, cheapen, curtail, cut down to size, cut rate, decrease, decry, deprecate, depreciate, derogate, detract, diminish, discount, disparage, downplay*, dwarf*, knock*, knock down*, lessen, make light of*, make little of, miniaturize, pan, play down, pooh-pooh*, poor-mouth*, prune, put down, reduce, run down, shrink, underestimate, underplay; SEE CONCEPTS *54,240,247*

minimum [*adj*] *least, lowest*
least possible, littlest, merest, minimal, slightest, smallest, tiniest; SEE CONCEPTS *762,789*

minimum [*n*] *lowest amount*
atom, bottom, dab, depth, dot, gleam, grain, hair, iota, jot, least, lowest, margin, modicum, molecule, nadir, narrowest, particle, pittance, point, scintilla, scruple, shadow, slightest, smallest, smidgen, soupçon, spark, speck, trifle, whit; SEE CONCEPTS *787,831*

minion [*n*] *sycophant*
backscratcher*, backslapper*, bootlicker*, brownnoser*, dependent, doormat, fan, fawner, flatterer, flunky*, follower, groupie, hanger-on*, lackey, parasite, puppet, slave, stooge*, subordinate, toady, yes-man/woman, yes-person; SEE CONCEPTS *352,366,423*

miniscule/minuscule [*adj*] *tiny, very small*
diminutive, dwarf, infinitesimal, itsy-bitsy, Lilliputian, little, meager, microscopic, mini*, miniature, minute, pint-sized*, puny*, short, slight, small-scale, stunted, teensy*, teeny, trivial, undersized, wee*; SEE CONCEPTS *773,789*

minister [n1] *person in charge of church*
abbot, archdeacon, archdeacon, bishop, chaplain, clergy, clergyperson, cleric, clerical, clerk, confessor, curate, deacon, dean, diocesan, divine, ecclesiastic, lecturer, missionary, monk, parson, pastor, preacher, prelate, priest, pulpiteer, rector, reverend, shepherd, vicar; SEE CONCEPT *361*

minister [n2] *person high in government*
administrator, agent, aide, ambassador, assistant, cabinet member, consul, delegate, diplomat, envoy, executive, legate, liaison, lieutenant, officeholder, official, plenipotentiary, premier, prime minister, secretary; SEE CONCEPT *354*

minister [v] *help, serve*
accommodate, administer, aid, answer, attend, be solicitous of, cater to, cure, doctor, do for, foster, heal, nurse, pander, pander to, remedy, succor, take care of, tend, treat, wait on, watch over; SEE CONCEPT *110*

minor [adj] *insignificant, small*
accessory, below the mark, bush-league*, casual, dependent, dinky*, inconsequential, inconsiderable, inferior, junior, lesser, light, low, minus, negligible, paltry, petty, piddling, secondary, second-string*, slight, smaller, small-fry*, small-time, subordinate, subsidiary, tacky, trifling, trivial, two-bit*, unimportant, younger; SEE CONCEPTS *575,773,789*

minor [n] *person under legal age of maturity*
adolescent, baby, boy, child, girl, infant, junior, juvenile, lad, little one, schoolboy, schoolgirl, teenager, underage, youngster, youth; SEE CONCEPT *424*

mint [adj] *brand-new*
excellent, first-class, fresh, intact, original, perfect, spanking-new*, spick-and-span*, unblemished, undamaged, unmarred, untarnished, virgin; SEE CONCEPTS *574,578,797*

mint [n] *a lot of money*
boodle, bundle, fortune, heap, million, packet, pile, pot, roll, wad; SEE CONCEPTS *340,787*

mint [v] *create, coin*
cast, construct, devise, fabricate, fashion, forge, invent, issue, make, make up, mold, monetize, produce, provide, punch, stamp, strike, think up; SEE CONCEPTS *43,173,205,251*

minute [adj1] *very small*
atomic, diminutive, exact, exiguous, fine, inconsiderable, infinitesimal, insignificant, invisible, little, microbic, microscopic, miniature, minim, minimal, minuscule, molecular, peewee*, piddling, precise, puny, slender, teeny-weeny*, tiny, wee; SEE CONCEPTS *773,789*

minute [adj2] *unimportant*
immaterial, inconsiderable, insignificant, light, little, minor, negligible, nonessential, paltry, petty, picayune, piddling, puny, slight, small, trifling, trivial; SEE CONCEPT *575*

minute [adj3] *exact, precise*
blow-by-blow*, careful, circumstantial, clocklike, close, critical, detailed, elaborate, exhaustive, full, itemized, meticulous, painstaking, particular, particularized, punctilious, scrupulous, specialized, thorough; SEE CONCEPT *557*

minute [n] *brief time period*
bat of an eye*, breath, breathing, crack, flash, instant, jiffy*, min*, mo*, moment, nothing flat*, sec*, second, shake, short time*, sixtieth of hour, sixty seconds, split second, twinkling*; SEE CONCEPTS *803,807,821*

minutiae [n] *trivial detail*
incidental, minor detail, small detail, trifle, trivia, triviality, trivial matter, unimportant detail, useless information; SEE CONCEPTS *274,543*

miracle [n] *wonderful, surprising event or thing*
marvel, phenomenon, portent, prodigy, rarity, revelation, surprise, stunner, supernatural occurrence, surprise, thaumaturgy, unusualness, wonder; SEE CONCEPTS *671,689,693*

miraculous [adj] *surprisingly wonderful*
amazing, anomalous, astonishing, astounding, awesome, extraordinary, fabulous, freakish, heavy, incredible, inexplicable, magical, marvelous, monstrous, numinous, phenomenal, preternatural, prodigious, spectacular, staggering, strange, stupefying, stupendous, superhuman, superior, supermundane, supernatural, supranatural, thaumaturgic, the utmost, unaccountable, unbelievable, unearthly, unimaginable, unreal, wonderworking, wondrous; SEE CONCEPTS *529,548,572*

mirage [n] *imaginary vision*
delusion, fantasy, hallucination, ignis fatuus, illusion, optical illusion, phantasm; SEE CONCEPTS *529,628*

mire [n] *muck, morass*
bog, dirt, fen, glop*, goo*, gunk*, marsh, moss, mud, ooze*, quagmire, quicksand, slime*, swamp; SEE CONCEPTS *509,674*

mire [v] *delay, catch up in*
bog down, cling, decelerate, detain, dirty, embroil, enmesh, ensnare, entangle, entrap, flounder, hang up, implicate, involve, retard, set back, sink, slow down, slow up, snare, soil, stick, tangle, trap; SEE CONCEPTS *112,121*

mirror [n] *glass that reflects image*
cheval glass, gaper, hand glass, imager, looking glass, pier glass, polished metal, reflector, seeing glass, speculum; SEE CONCEPTS *443,470*

mirror [v] *copy, reflect*
act like, depict, double, echo, embody, emulate, epitomize, exemplify, follow, glass, illustrate, image, imitate, make like*, mimic, personify, represent, show, simulate, symbolize, take off*, typify; SEE CONCEPTS *111,118,171*

mirth [n] *great joy*
amusement, cheer, cheerfulness, convulsions, entertainment, festivity, frivolity, frolic, fun, gaiety, gladness, glee, happiness, hilarity, hysteria, hysterics, jocularity, jocundity, jollity, joviality, joyousness, kicks*, laughs, laughter, levity, lightheartedness, merriment, merrymaking, pleasure, rejoicing, revelry, sport, whoopee*; SEE CONCEPTS *388,410*

mirthful [adj] *merry*
amusing, blithe, blithesome, carefree, cheerful, cheery, convivial, enjoyable, entertaining, festive, frolicsome, fun-loving, funny, gay, glad, gleeful, happy, jocund, jolly, joyful, joyous, larking, lighthearted, lively, perky, playful, sunny, vivacious; SEE CONCEPTS *403,548,572*

misadventure [n] *bad luck, mishap*
accident, adversity, bad break*, blunder, calamity, casualty, cataclysm, catastrophe, debacle, disaster, error, failure, faux pas, ill fortune, lapse, mischance, misfortune, reverse, setback, slip, tragedy, woe; SEE CONCEPT *674*

misanthrope [n] *person who hates others*
cynic, doubter, egoist, egotist, hater, isolate,

loner, misanthropist, recluse, skeptic; SEE CON-
CEPT 412

misanthropic [adj] *unsociable, cynical*
antisocial, egoistic, egotistical, eremitic, hating,
inhumane, malevolent, misanthropical, reclusive,
reserved, sarcastic, selfish, solitary, standoffish,
unfriendly; SEE CONCEPT 404

misapprehend [v] *get the wrong idea, impression*
blunder, confuse, err, misconceive, misconstrue,
misinterpret, misread, miss, mistake, misunderstand; SEE CONCEPT 15

misappropriate [v] *use wrongly; steal*
abuse, appropriate, defalcate, embezzle, misapply, misspend, misuse, peculate, plunder, pocket,
rob, swindle; SEE CONCEPTS 139,156,341

misbegotten [adj] *illegitimate, illicit*
baseborn, bastard, dishonest, disreputable, illegal, natural, poor, shady, spurious, stolen, suppositious, unlawful, unrespectable; SEE CONCEPTS
319,549

misbehave [v] *act in inappropriate manner*
act up, be at fault, be bad, be dissolute, be guilty,
be immoral, be indecorous, be insubordinate, be
mischievous, bend the law*, be out of line*, be
out of order*, be reprehensible, carry on, cut up,
deviate, do evil, do wrong, fail, fool around*, get
into mischief, go astray, go wrong, make trouble,
misconduct, offend, roughhouse*, sin, sow wild
oats*, take a wrong turn*, transgress, trespass;
SEE CONCEPTS 633,645

misbehavior [n] *naughty act, conduct*
acting up*, fault, immorality, impropriety, incivility, indiscipline, insubordination, mischief,
misconduct, misdeed, misdemeanor, misdoing,
monkey business*, naughtiness, rudeness,
shenanigans*, transgression, wrongdoing; SEE
CONCEPTS 633,645

miscalculate [v] *make a mistake*
blow*, blunder, discount, disregard, drop the
ball*, err, get signals crossed*, get wrong, go
wrong, mess up*, misconstrue, miscount, misinterpret, misjudge, misread, misreckon, miss by a
mile*, misunderstand, mix up, overestimate,
overlook, overrate, overvalue, slip up, stumble,
underestimate, underrate, undervalue; SEE CON-
CEPT 101

miscarriage [n] *failure*
abortion, botch, breakdown, defeat, error, interruption, malfunction, misadventure, mischance,
misfire, mishap, miss, mistake, nonsuccess, perversion, undoing; SEE CONCEPTS 230,699

miscellaneous [adj] *diversified, various*
assorted, confused, conglomerate, different, disordered, disparate, divergent, divers, diverse,
heterogeneous, indiscriminate, jumbled, many,
mingled, mixed, motley, muddled, multifarious,
multiform, odd, promiscuous, scattered, scrambled, sundry, unmatched, unsorted, varied, variegated; SEE CONCEPT 564

miscellany [n] *varied collection*
accumulation, aggregation, anthology, assortment, brew, collectanea, combination, combo,
compilation, conglomeration, cumulation, diversity, farrago, gallimaufry, garbage*, hash,
hodgepodge, jumble, medley, mélange, melee,
mess, mishmash, mix, mixed bag, mixture, muddle, odds and ends*, olio, pasticcio, pastiche,
patchwork, potpourri, salad, salmagundi, smorgasbord, stew, variety; SEE CONCEPTS 432,665

mischief [n] *trouble, damage*
atrocity, catastrophe, devilment, devilry, dirty
trick*, evil, fault, friskiness, frolicsomeness,
funny business*, gag, harm, high jinks*, hurt, ill,
impishness, injury, misbehavior, mischievousness, misconduct, misdoing, misfortune, monkey
business*, naughtiness, outrage, playfulness,
prank, rascality, roguery, roguishness, sabotage,
shenanigans, sportiveness, transgression, vandalism, waggery, waggishness, waywardness,
wrong, wrongdoing; SEE CONCEPTS 192,633,645

mischievous [adj] *devilish, wicked*
arch, artful, bad, bothersome, damaging, dangerous, deleterious, destructive, detrimental, dickens*, evil, exasperating, foxy*, frolicsome,
harmful, hazardous, holy terror*, hurtful, ill, ill-
behaved, impish, injurious, insidious, irksome,
malicious, malignant, misbehaving, naughty,
nocuous, perilous, pernicious, playful, precarious, puckish, rascal, rascally, risky, rude, sinful,
sly, spiteful, sportive, teasing, tricky, troublesome, vexatious, vexing, vicious, wayward; SEE
CONCEPTS 401,545

misconception [n] *wrong idea, impression*
delusion, error, fallacy, fault, misapprehension,
misconstruction, misinterpretation, mistake, mistaken belief, misunderstanding; SEE CONCEPTS
409,689

misconduct [n] *bad or unethical behavior*
delinquency, dereliction, evil, immorality, impropriety, malfeasance, malpractice, malversa-
tion, misbehavior, mischief, misdemeanor,
misdoing, mismanagement, naughtiness, offense,
rudeness, transgression, wrongdoing; SEE CON-
CEPTS 192,633,645

misconstrue [v] *get a wrong or false impression*
distort, exaggerate, misapprehend, misconceive,
misinterpret, misjudge, misread, mistake, mis-
translate, misunderstand, pervert, take the wrong
way; SEE CONCEPT 15

miscreant [adj] *evil, immoral*
corrupt, criminal, degenerate, depraved, flagitious, infamous, iniquitous, nefarious, perverse,
rascally, reprehensible, reprobate, unhealthy, unprincipled, vicious, villainous, wicked; SEE CON-
CEPTS 401,545

miscreant [n] *person who is very bad, immoral*
blackguard, black sheep*, bootlegger, bully, cad,
caitiff, convict, criminal, culprit, delinquent,
drunkard, evildoer, felon, fink*, heel*, hoodlum,
jailbird, loafer, louse*, lowlife*, malefactor, outcast, outlaw, pickpocket, racketeer, rapscallion,
rascal, rat*, reprobate, rowdy, ruffian, scalawag,
scamp, scoundrel, scum*, sinner, sneak,
vagabond, villain, wretch, wrongdoer; SEE CON-
CEPT 412

misdeed/misdemeanor [n] *sin, crime*
breach of law, criminality, dirt*, dirty deed*,
dirty pool*, fault, infringement, malefaction,
misbehavior, misconduct, miscue, offense, peccadillo, slipup, transgression, trespass, villainy,
violation, wrong, wrongdoing; SEE CONCEPTS
192,633,645

miser [n] *person who hoards money, possessions*
cheapskate*, churl, harpy*, hoarder, moneygrubber*, penny-pincher*, pinchfist*, pinchpenny*,
Scrooge*, stiff*, tightwad*; SEE CONCEPTS
348,412,423

miserable [adj] *unhappy, depressed*
afflicted, agonized, ailing, anguished, broken-

hearted, crestfallen, dejected, desolate, despairing, despondent, destroyed, disconsolate, discontented, distressed, doleful, dolorous, down, downcast, down in the mouth*, forlorn, gloomy, heartbroken, hopeless, hurt, hurting, ill, injured, in pain, melancholy, mournful, on a downer*, pained, pathetic, pitiable, racked, rueful, ruthful, sad, sick, sickly, sorrowful, strained, suffering, tormented, tortured, tragic, troubled, woebegone, wounded, wretched; SEE CONCEPT *403*

miserable [*adj2*] *destitute, shabby*
abject, bad, contemptible, deplorable, despicable, detestable, disgraceful, godforsaken, impoverished, indigent, inferior, lamentable, low, meager, mean, needy, paltry, pathetic, penniless, piteous, pitiable, poor, poverty-stricken, sad, scanty, scurvy, shameful, sordid, sorry, squalid, tragic, vile, worthless, wretched; SEE CONCEPTS *485,570*

miserly [*adj*] *greedy, stingy*
abject, avaricious, beggarly, cheapskate*, churlish, close, close-fisted, covetous, grasping, ignoble, illiberal, mean, parsimonious, penny-pinching*, penurious, skinflint*, sordid, tightfisted*, ungenerous; SEE CONCEPTS *326,334,401,404*

misery [*n1*] *pain, mental or physical*
ache, agony, anguish, anvil chorus, bad news*, blues*, depression, desolation, despair, despondency, discomfort, distress, dolor, gloom, grief, hardship, headache, heartache, hurting, melancholy, pang, passion, sadness, sorrow, squalor, stitch, suffering, throe, torment, torture, twinge, unhappiness, woe, worriment, worry, wretchedness; SEE CONCEPT *728*

misery [*n2*] *trouble, torment*
adversity, affliction, anxiety, bitter pill*, burden, calamity, catastrophe, curse, destitution, difficulty, grief, indigence, load, misfortune, need, ordeal, penury, poverty, privation, problem, sordidness, sorrow, squalor, trial, tribulation, want, woe; SEE CONCEPTS *335,666,674*

misfire [*v*] *fail*
abort, backfire, blunder, break down, come to nothing, explode, fall flat*, fall short*, fizzle, fizzle out, fizz out, flop, flounder, go up in smoke*, go wrong, miscarry, miss, peter out, poop out, slip; SEE CONCEPT *699*

misfit [*n*] *nonconformist*
beatnik*, bohemian*, different breed*, dissenter, dissident, dropout, eccentric, fish out of water*, freak*, individualist, lone wolf, loser, oddball, odd man out, offbeat, outsider, weirdo*; SEE CONCEPTS *359,423*

misfortune/mishap [*n*] *bad luck; disaster*
accident, adversity, affliction, annoyance, anxiety, bad break*, bad news*, blow*, burden, calamity, casualty, cataclysm, catastrophe, contretemps, cross, crunch, debacle, disadvantage, disappointment, discomfort, dole, failure, hard luck*, hardship, harm, inconvenience, infelicity, loss, misadventure, mischance, misery, nuisance, reverse, rotten luck, setback, stroke of bad luck*, tough luck*, tragedy, trial, tribulation, trouble, unpleasantness, visitation, worry; SEE CONCEPTS *674,679*

misgiving [*n*] *uncertainty*
anxiety, apprehension, apprehensiveness, distrust, doubt, fear, foreboding, hesitation, mistrust, premonition, prenotion, presage, presentiment, qualm, reservation, scruple, suspicion, unbelief, unease, worry; SEE CONCEPTS *21,689,690*

misguided [*adj*] *ill-advised, deluded*
bearded, bum-steer*, confused, deceived, disinformed, erroneous, faked-out*, foolish, imprudent, indiscreet, inexpedient, injudicious, led up the garden path*, misled, misplaced, mistaken, stonewalled*, uncalled for, unreasonable, unwarranted, unwise, wrong; SEE CONCEPTS *544,548,570*

mishandle/mismanage [*v*] *mess up*
abuse, be incompetent, be inefficient, blow, blunder, botch*, bungle, confound, err, flub*, foul up, fumble, goof*, goof up*, gum up*, harm, make a hash of*, make a mess of*, maladminister, misapply, misconduct, misdirect, misemploy, misgovern, mistreat, misuse, muff*, overlook, pervert, prostitute, put foot in*, screw up*, shoot oneself in foot*; SEE CONCEPTS *101,156,384*

mishap [*n*] *accident*
blow, blunder, calamity, collision, crack-up*, disaster, fender-bender*, fluke*, hazard, ill-fortune, misadventure, misfortune, mistake, pileup*, rear-ender*, setback, smash*, smashup*, stack-up*, total*, wrack-up*; SEE CONCEPT *674*

mishmash [*n*] *hodgepodge*
collection, combination, goulash*, hash, jumble, medley, melange, mess, miscellany, mixed bag, mixture, olio, patchwork, potpourri, salmagundi*; SEE CONCEPTS *260,432*

misinform [*v*] *give wrong information intentionally*
bait and switch*, cover up, deceive, disinform, doublespeak*, double-talk*, lead astray, lie, misdirect, misguide, mislead, misstate, mousetrap*, pervert, prevaricate, put on*, put on an act*, put on false front*, put up smoke screen*, signify, string along*; SEE CONCEPT *63*

misjudge [*v*] *get the wrong idea*
bark up wrong tree*, be misled, be overcritical, be partial, be unfair, be wrong, come to hasty conclusion, dogmatize, drop the ball*, err, misapprehend, miscalculate, miscomprehend, misconceive, misconjecture, misconstrue, misdeem, misreckon, miss by a mile*, mistake, misthink, misunderstand, overestimate, overrate, prejudge, presume, presuppose, put foot in*, stumble, suppose, underestimate, underrate; SEE CONCEPTS *12,18,101*

mislead [*v*] *give someone the wrong idea, information*
bait, beguile, betray, bilk, bluff, bunk, cheat, cozen, deceive, defraud, delude, double-cross*, dupe, enmesh, ensnare, entangle, entice, fool, fudge*, gull, hoax, hoodwink*, hose*, illude, inveigle, juggle, lead astray, lead on*, lie, lure, misdirect, misguide, misinform, misrepresent, outwit, overreach, pervert, pull wool over eyes*, put on*, rip off*, rook, rope in*, scam, seduce, shaft, snow*, take in, tempt, trick, victimize; SEE CONCEPTS *59,63*

misleading [*adj*] *deceptive, confusing*
ambiguous, beguiling, bewildering, casuistical, catchy, confounding, deceitful, deceiving, deluding, delusive, delusory, demagogic, disingenuous, distracting, evasive, fallacious, false,

inaccurate, perplexing, puzzling, sophistical, specious, spurious, tricky, wrong; SEE CONCEPTS 267,548

mismatch [*n*] *disparity*
discrepancy, disproportion, dissemblance, dissimilarity, divergence, divergency, diverseness, imbalance, imparity, incongruity, inequality, unevenness; SEE CONCEPT 665

misogynist [*n*] *woman-hater*
anti-feminist, male chauvinist, misanthrope, sexist; SEE CONCEPT 689

misplace [*v*] *lose; be unable to find*
be unable to lay hands on*, confuse, disarrange, dishevel, disorder, disorganize, displace, disturb, forget whereabouts of, lose track of, misfile, mislay, miss, mix, muss, place unwisely, place wrongly, put in wrong place, remove, scatter, unsettle; SEE CONCEPTS 116,201

misrepresentation [*n*] *falsehood*
adulteration, coloring, distortion, exaggeration, fabrication, false light, falsification, lie, misstatement, mutilation, not a true picture*, slant, story*, stretch, tall story*, twist, untruth; SEE CONCEPTS 63,580

misrepresent/misquote [*v*] *lie, distort*
adulterate, angle, beard*, belie, build up, cloak, color, con, confuse, cover up, disguise, distort, dress, embellish, embroider, equivocate, exaggerate, falsify, garble, give snow job*, mangle, mask, miscolor, misinterpret, misreport, misstate, overdraw, overstate, palter, pervert, phony up*, pirate*, prevaricate, promote, puff*, skew, slant, snow*, spread it on*, stretch, take out of context*, throw a curve*, trump up*, twist, warp; SEE CONCEPT 63

miss [*n*] *failure*
absence, blunder, default, defect, error, fault, loss, mishap, mistake, omission, oversight, slip, want; SEE CONCEPTS 101,699

miss [*v*] *fail, make a mistake*
be late for, blow, blunder, botch, disregard, drop, drop the ball*, fall, fall flat on face*, fall short, flub*, forget, fumble, ignore, juggle, let go, let slip, lose, miscarry, misfire, mislay, misplace, muff*, neglect, omit, overlook, overshoot, pass over, pass up, skip, slight, slip, trip, trip up, undershoot; SEE CONCEPTS 101,699

miss [*v2*] *want; feel a loss*
crave, desire, long, need, pine, wish, yearn; SEE CONCEPT 20

misshapen [*adj*] *deformed*
askew, awry, bent, blemished, bowed, buckled, contorted, crooked, curved, damaged, disfigured, disjointed, distorted, grotesque, ill-made, irregular, malformed, mangled, marred, out of shape, twisted, ugly, unshapely, warped; SEE CONCEPTS 485,486

missile [*n*] *projectile weapon*
ammunition, arrow, bat, bird*, bolt, bomb, bullet, cartridge, dart, MX*, pellet, projectile, rocket, shot, stealth, trajectile; SEE CONCEPT 500

missing [*adj*] *gone, absent*
astray, away, AWOL*, disappeared, lacking, left behind, left out, lost, mislaid, misplaced, not present, nowhere to be found*, omitted, removed, short, unaccounted for, wanting; SEE CONCEPTS 539,576

mission [*n*] *person's task, responsibility*
aim, assignment, business, calling, charge, commission, duty, end, errand, goal, job, lifework,
object, objective, office, operation, profession, purpose, pursuit, quest, sortie, trade, trust, undertaking, vocation, work; SEE CONCEPTS 360,362,659

missionary [*n*] *person who aids, does religious work*
apostle, clergy, clergyperson, converter, evangelist, herald, messenger, minister, missioner, pastor, preacher, promoter, propagandist, proselytizer, revivalist, teacher; SEE CONCEPTS 361,416

missive [*n*] *written communication*
dispatch, epistle, letter, line, memo, memorandum, message, note, report, word; SEE CONCEPTS 271,278

misspent [*adj*] *wasted*
blown*, dissipated, down the drain*, idle, imprudent, misapplied, prodigal, profitless, squandered, thrown away; SEE CONCEPTS 544,560,570

misstatement [*n*] *misrepresentation*
adulteration, coloring, distortion, exaggeration, fabrication, falsehood, false light, falsification, inaccuracy, lie, misstatement, mutilation, not a true picture*, slant, story*, stretch, tall story*, twist, untruth; SEE CONCEPTS 63,580

misstep [*n*] *mistake, wrong move*
bad move*, blunder, bungle, error, failure, false step, faux pas, fluff*, gaffe, indiscretion, lapse, miscue, miss, slip, slipup*, stumble, trip; SEE CONCEPTS 101,674,699

mist [*n*] *film, vapor*
brume, cloud, condensation, dew, drizzle, fog, ground clouds, haze, moisture, rain, smog, soup*, spray, steam, visibility zero*; SEE CONCEPT 524

mist [*v*] *cloud, steam up*
becloud, befog, blur, dim, drizzle, film, fog, haze, mizzle, murk, obscure, overcast, overcloud, rain, shower, sprinkle, steam; SEE CONCEPT 526

mistake [*n*] *error, misunderstanding*
aberration, blooper*, blunder, boo-boo*, bungle, confusion, delusion, erratum, false move, false step, fault, faux pas, flub*, fluff*, gaffe, illusion, inaccuracy, inadvertence, lapse, misapplication, misapprehension, miscalculation, misconception, misinterpretation, misjudgment, misprint, misstatement, misstep, muddle, neglect, omission, overestimation, oversight, slight, slip, slip of tongue*, slipup*, snafu*, solecism, trip*, typographical error, underestimation; SEE CONCEPTS 101,230,410

mistake [*v*] *mix up, misunderstand*
addle, be off the mark*, be wrong, blunder, botch*, bungle, confound, confuse, deceive oneself, err, fail, get wrong, goof*, have wrong impression, jumble, lapse, make a mess*, misapprehend, miscalculate, misconceive, misconstrue, miscount, misdeem, misinterpret, misjudge, misknow, misread, miss, miss the boat*, not know, omit, overestimate, overlook, put foot in*, slip*, slip up*, snarl, take for*, tangle, underestimate; SEE CONCEPTS 15,101

mistaken [*adj*] *wrong, incorrect*
all wet*, at fault, barking up wrong tree*, confounded, confused, confused with, deceived, deluded, duped, erroneous, fallacious, false, faulty, fooled, ill-advised, illogical, inaccurate, inappropriate, misconstrued, misguided, misinformed, misinterpreting, misjudging, misled, misunder-

standing, off base*, off track*, tricked, unadvised, under wrong impression, unfounded, unreal, unsound, untrue, warranted, way off*, wide of mark*, wrongly identified, wrong number*; SEE CONCEPTS *402,529*

mistreat [v] *treat badly or wrongly*
abuse, backbite, bash, brutalize, bung up*, chop, do wrong, dump on*, give black eye*, handle roughly, harm, injure, kick around, knock around, maltreat, maul, mess up, misuse, molest, outrage, push around, rip, roughhouse*, rough up, shake up, total*, trash*, wax*, wound, wrong; SEE CONCEPTS *14,156,246*

mistrust [n] *doubtfulness*
apprehension, chariness, concern, distrust, doubt, dubiety, dubiosity, fear, foreboding, incertitude, misgiving, presentiment, scruple, skepticism, suspicion, uncertainty, wariness, wonder; SEE CONCEPTS *21,27,690*

mistrust [v] *doubt*
apprehend, beware, be wary, challenge, disbelieve, dispute, distrust, fear, have doubts, question, scruple, suspect, suspicion; SEE CONCEPT *21*

misty [adj] *filmy, obscure*
bleary, blurred, closed in, clouded, cloudy, dark, dewy, dim, enveloped, foggy, fuzzy, hazy, indistinct, murky, mushy, nebulous, opaque, overcast, shrouded, socked in, soupy*, unclear, vague, vaporous; SEE CONCEPTS *525,603,617*

misunderstand [v] *get the wrong idea*
be at cross purposes*, be bewildered, be confused, be perplexed, confound, confuse, fail, get signals crossed*, get signals mixed*, get wrong, get wrong impression*, misapply, misapprehend, miscalculate, miscomprehend, misconceive, misconstrue, misinterpret, misjudge, misknow, misread, misreckon, miss*, miss the point*, mistake, not register*, take amiss, take wrongly; SEE CONCEPT *15*

misunderstanding [n1] *instance of having the wrong idea*
confounding, confusion, delusion, error, false impression, misapprehension, misconception, misconstruction, misinterpretation, misjudgment, misreckoning, mistake, mix-up; SEE CONCEPT *409*

misunderstanding [n2] *argument, fight*
bad vibes*, blowup*, breach, break, clash, conflict, crossed wires*, debate, difference, difficulty, disagreement, discord, dissension, falling-out*, feud, fuss, quarrel, rift, row, run-in*, rupture, set-to, sour note*, spat, squabble, tiff*, variance, words*; SEE CONCEPTS *46,106*

misuse [n] *abuse; wrong application*
abusage, barbarism, catachresis, corruption, cruel treatment, desecration, dissipation, exploitation, harm, ill-treatment, injury, malapropism, maltreatment, misapplication, misemployment, mistreatment, misusage, perversion, profanation, prostitution, rough handling, solecism, squandering, waste; SEE CONCEPT *156*

misuse [v] *abuse; apply wrongly*
blow*, brutalize, corrupt, cut up, desecrate, dissipate, exploit, go through, handle roughly, illtreat, maltreat, maul, mess up*, misapply, misemploy, mistreat, molest, outrage, pervert, profane, prostitute, run through*, shake up, squander, waste, wrong; SEE CONCEPT *156*

mitigate [v] *check, diminish, lighten*
abate, allay, alleviate, appease, assuage, blunt, calm, come together, cool*, dull, ease, extenuate, lessen, meet halfway*, moderate, modify, mollify, pacify, palliate, placate, quiet, reduce, relieve, remit, soften, soothe, subdue, take the edge off*, temper, tone down, tranquilize, weaken; SEE CONCEPTS *233,240*

mix [v1] *combine, join*
admix, adulterate, alloy, amalgamate, associate, blend, braid, coalesce, commingle, commix, compound, conjoin, cross, embody, fuse, hybridize, incorporate, infiltrate, infuse, instill, interbreed, intermingle, interweave, jumble, knead, link, lump, make up, merge, mingle, mix up, put together, saturate, stir, suffuse, synthesize, tangle, transfuse, unite, weave, work in; SEE CONCEPTS *113,193*

mix [v2] *socialize*
associate, come together, consort, get along, hang out, hobnob, join, mingle; SEE CONCEPT *114*

mixed [adj] *assorted, combined*
alloyed, amalgamated, assimilated, assorted, blended, brewed, composite, compound, conglomerate, crossbred, crossed, different, disordered, diverse, diversified, embodied, fused, heterogeneous, hybrid, hybridized, incorporated, infused, interbred, interdenominational, joint, kneaded, married, merged, mingled, miscellaneous, mongrel, motley, multifarious, tied, transfused, united, varied, woven; SEE CONCEPTS *485,564,772*

mixed bag [n] *assortment*
all shapes and sizes, array, choice, collection, combination, combo*, diversity, hodgepodge, jumble, medley, melange, miscellany, mishmash, mixture, potpourri; SEE CONCEPTS *432,665*

mixed-up [adj] *confused*
baffled, befuddled, bewildered, come apart*, confounded, dazed, discombobulated*, disconcerted, disorganized, disoriented, flummoxed, flustered, lost, muddled, out to lunch*, perplexed, puzzled, stumped, thrown off balance*; SEE CONCEPT *403*

mix/mixture [n] *assortment, combination*
admixture, adulteration, alloy, amalgam, amalgamation, assimilation, association, batter, blend, brew, combine, combo, commixture, composite, compound, concoction, confection, conglomeration, cross, crossing, dough, fusion, goulash, grab bag*, hodgepodge, hybrid, hybridization, incorporation, infiltration, interfusion, jumble, mash, medley, melange, merger, mingling, miscellany, mishmash, mixed bag, mosaic, package, patchwork, potpourri, salmagundi, saturation, soup*, stew*, transfusion, union, variety; SEE CONCEPTS *260,432*

mix-up [n] *confusion, misunderstanding*
botch*, chaos, commotion, disorder, jumble, mess, mistake, muddle, shambles*, tangle, turmoil; SEE CONCEPTS *230,674*

mix up [v] *confuse*
addle, befuddle, bewilder, confound, derange, disorder, disorganize, disrupt, distract, disturb, dizzy, fluster, foul up*, jumble, mess up*, mistake, muddle, perplex, puzzle, snafu*, upset; SEE CONCEPTS *16,158*

moan [n] *groan, complaint*
beef, cry, gripe, grouse, grumble, lament, lamen-

tation, plaint, sigh, sob, wail, whine; SEE CON-
CEPTS 52,77

moan [v] *groan, complain*
bemoan, bewail, carp, deplore, grieve, gripe,
grouse, grumble, keen, lament, mourn, sigh, sob,
wail, whine; SEE CONCEPTS 52,77

moat [n] *ditch*
canal, channel, fosse, gully, trench; SEE CON-
CEPTS 509,513

mob [n] *large group of people*
assemblage, body, cabal, camp, canaille, cattle,
circle, clan, class, clique, collection, commonality, company, coterie, crew, crowd, crush, drove,
flock, gang, gathering, herd, horde, host, jam, lot,
mass, masses, multitude, pack, populace, posse,
press, proletariat, rabble, riffraff*, ring, riot,
scum, set, swarm, throng, troop; SEE CONCEPTS
378,417,432

mob [v] *come upon by pushing; surround*
attack, cram, crowd, fill, hustle, jam, jostle, overrun, pack, riot, set upon, swarm, throng; SEE
CONCEPTS 208,758

mobile [adj] *movable, travelling*
adaptable, ambulatory, changeable, fluid, free,
itinerant, liquid, locomotive, loose, migrant, migratory, motile, motorized, moving, mutable, nomadic, peripatetic, portable, roaming, roving,
unsettled, unstable, unstationary, unsteadfast, unsteady, versatile, wandering; SEE CONCEPTS
576,584

mobilize [v] *ready for action, movement*
activate, actuate, animate, assemble, call to arms,
call up, catalyze, circulate, drive, gather, get
ready, impel, make ready, marshal, muster, organize, prepare, propel, put in motion, rally, ready,
set in motion, set off; SEE CONCEPTS
148,187,221,320

mobster [n] *gangster*
criminal, crook, godfather, goon, gunman/
woman, hit man/woman, hood, hoodlum, hooligan*, Mafioso*, member of the family*, outlaw,
racketeer, soldier*, thug, wiseguy*; SEE CON-
CEPT 412

mock [adj] *artificial, fake*
apish*, bogus*, counterfeit, dummy, ersatz*,
faked, false, feigned, forged, fraudulent, hokey*,
imitation, imitative, make-believe, mimic,
phony, pretended, pseudo*, put-on*, quasi*,
sham*, simulated, so-called*, spurious, substitute, unreal; SEE CONCEPTS 566,582

mock [v1] *ridicule*
buffoon, burlesque, caricature, chaff, deride,
flout, hoot, insult, jape, jeer, kid, laugh at, make
fun of, needle, parody, poke fun at*, rally, rib*,
scoff, scorn, show contempt, sneer, taunt, tease,
thumb nose at*, travesty; SEE CONCEPTS 7,19,49

mock [v2] *mimic*
affect, ape, assume, burlesque, caricature, counterfeit, ditto*, do, fake, feign, hoke, imitate, lampoon, mime, mirror, parody, satirize, send up*,
simulate, take off*, travesty; SEE CONCEPT 111

mock [v3] *deceive*
beguile, belie, betray, challenge, cheat, defeat,
defy, delude, disappoint, double-cross*, dupe,
elude, foil, fool, frustrate, juggle, let down*, mislead, sell out*, thwart; SEE CONCEPTS 59,63

mockery [n1] *joke, parody*
burlesque, butt*, caricature, deception, farce, imitation, jest, lampoon, laughingstock, mimicry,

mock, pretense, send-up*, sham*, spoof, sport*,
take-off*, travesty; SEE CONCEPTS 111,278

mockery [n2] *insult, disrespect*
contempt, contumely, derision, disdain, disparagement, gibe, jeer, ridicule, scoffing, scorn,
sport; SEE CONCEPTS 49,278

mode [n1] *manner, way*
approach, book, channels, condition, course, custom, fashion, form, mechanism, method, modus,
nuts and bolts*, plan, posture, practice, procedure, process, quality, rule, situation, state, status, style, system, technique, tone, vein, wise;
SEE CONCEPTS 6,644

mode [n2] *trend, fad*
chic, convention, craze, cry, dernier cri*, fashion, furor, last word*, latest thing*, latest wrinkle*, look, mainstream, now*, rage*, style,
thing*, vogue; SEE CONCEPTS 529,655

model [adj] *typical, ideal*
archetypal, classic, classical, commendable,
copy, dummy, exemplary, facsimile, flawless, illustrative, imitation, miniature, paradigmatic,
perfect, prototypical, quintessential, representative, standard, typical, very; SEE CONCEPTS
566,574

model [n1] *imitation, replica*
cartoon, clone, copy, copycat, dead ringer*,
ditto*, dummy, duplicate, effigy, engraving, facsimile, figure, figurine, game plan, illustration,
image, knock-off, layout, look-alike, miniature,
mock-up, painting, paste-up, photograph, picture, pocket, portrait, print, relief, representation,
ringer*, setup, sketch, spitting image*, statue,
statuette, tracing, visual; SEE CONCEPTS
259,625,628,667

model [n2] *example, standard*
apotheosis, archetype, beau ideal, criterion, design, emblem, embodiment, epitome, exemplar,
gauge, hero, ideal, lodestar, mirror, mold, nonesuch, nonpareil, original, paradigm, paragon,
pattern, prototype, quintessence, role model,
saint, symbol, touchstone, type; SEE CONCEPTS
686,688

model [n3] *person, thing that poses*
dummy, manikin, mannequin, nude, sitter, subject; SEE CONCEPT 348

model [n4] *type, version*
configuration, design, form, kind, mark, mode,
style, variety; SEE CONCEPTS 378,463,505,654

model [v1] *form, shape*
base, carve, cast, create, design, fashion, mold,
pattern, plan, sculpt; SEE CONCEPT 184

model [v2] *display, pose*
parade, represent, set example, show off, sit,
sport, wear; SEE CONCEPT 138

moderate [adj1] *calm, temperate*
abstinent, balanced, bearable, careful, cautious,
compromising, conservative, considerate, considered, controlled, cool, deliberate, disciplined,
dispassionate, equable, even, gentle, impartial,
inconsiderable, inexpensive, judicious, limited,
low-key, measured, middle-of-the-road*, midway, mild, modest, monotonous, neutral, nonpartisan, not excessive, pacific, peaceable, pleasant,
reasonable, reserved, restrained, sober, soft,
steady, straight, tame, tolerable, tolerant, tranquil, untroubled; SEE CONCEPTS 533,563

moderate [adj2] *fair, average, so-so*
bland, fairish*, fair to middling*, inconsequential, inconsiderable, indifferent, intermediate,

mean, mediocre, medium, middling*, ordinary, paltry, passable, piddling*, trifling, trivial, unexceptional; SEE CONCEPTS 547,575

moderate [*v1*] *restrain, control*
abate, allay, alleviate, appease, assuage, calm, chasten, check, constrain, cool*, cool out*, curb, decline, decrease, die down, diminish, ease off, fall, lessen, let up, meet halfway, mitigate, modify, modulate, mollify, pacify, play down, qualify, quiet, reduce, regulate, relent, relieve, repress, slacken, slow, soften, soft-pedal, subdue, subside, tame, temper, tone down, wane; SEE CONCEPTS 94,130,240

moderate [*v2*] *mediate, arbitrate*
chair, judge, make peace*, negotiate, preside, referee, take the chair*, umpire; SEE CONCEPTS 18,317

moderately [*adv*] *to a degree, to some extent*
a little, averagely, enough, fairly, gently, in moderation, in reason, kind of, more or less*, more than not*, not exactly, passably, pretty, quite, quite a bit, rather, reasonably, slightly, some, something, somewhat, sort of, so-so*, temperately, tolerable, tolerably, tolerantly, within limits*, within reason*; SEE CONCEPTS 544,772

moderation [*n*] *temperance*
balance, calmness, composure, constraint, coolness, dispassionateness, equanimity, fairness, forbearance, golden mean, judiciousness, justice, justness, lenity, measure, moderateness, restraint, sedateness, sedation, sobriety, steadiness, toleration; SEE CONCEPTS 633,657

moderator [*n*] *mitigator*
alleviator, mediator, pacifier, peacemaker, referee, soother, stabilizer; SEE CONCEPTS 348,366

modern [*adj*] *new, up-to-date*
avant-garde, coincident, concomitant, concurrent, contempo, contemporary, current, cutting-edge*, fresh, last word*, late, latest, latter-day*, leading-edge*, modernistic, modernized, modish, neoteric, newfangled*, new-fashioned, novel, now, present, present-day, prevailing, prevalent, recent, state-of-the-art*, stylish, today, twenty-first century*, up-to-the-minute, with-it*; SEE CONCEPTS 578,589,797

modernize [*v*] *bring up to date; remodel*
improve, refresh, regenerate, rejuvenate, remake, renew, renovate, restore, revamp*, revive, update; SEE CONCEPTS 168,177,202

modest [*adj1*] *shy*
bashful, blushing, chaste, coy, demure, diffident, discreet, humble, lowly, meek, moderate, nice, proper, prudent, quiet, reserved, resigned, reticent, retiring, seemly, self-conscious, self-effacing, sheepish, silent, simple, temperate, timid, unassertive, unassuming, unassured, unboastful, unobtrusive, unpresuming, unpretending, unpretentious, withdrawing; SEE CONCEPTS 401,404

modest [*adj2*] *limited, ordinary*
average, cheap, discreet, dry, economical, fair, humble, inelaborate, inexpensive, middling, moderate, natural, plain, reasonable, simple, small, unadorned, unaffected, unembellished, unembroidered, unexceptional, unexcessive, unextravagant, unextreme, unobtrusive, unornamented, unostentatious, unpretentious, unradical, unstudied; SEE CONCEPTS 334,547,562

modesty [*n*] *shyness*
bashfulness, celibacy, chastity, constraint, coyness, decency, delicacy, demureness, diffidence, discreetness, humbleness, humility, inhibition, innocence, lack of pretension, meekness, propriety, prudery, purity, quietness, reserve, reticence, self-effacement, simplicity, timidity, unobtrusiveness, unostentatiousness, unpretentiousness, virtue; SEE CONCEPT 633

modicum [*n*] *bit, small amount*
atom, crumb, dash, drop, fraction, fragment, grain, inch, iota, jot, little, minim, mite, molecule, ounce, particle, pinch, scrap, shred, smidge, speck, tinge, touch, trifle, whit; SEE CONCEPT 831

modify [*v1*] *alter, change*
adapt, adjust, become, convert, correct, customize, doctor, mutate, recast, redo, refashion, reform, remodel, reorganize, repair, reshape, revise, rework, shift gears*, switch over, transfigure, transform, transmogrify, transmute, turn, turn one around*, turn over new leaf*, turn the corner*, turn the tables*, tweak*, vary; SEE CONCEPT 232

modify [*v2*] *lessen, reduce*
abate, curb, decrease, limit, lower, mitigate, moderate, modulate, qualify, relax, remit, restrain, restrict, slacken, soften, temper, tone down; SEE CONCEPTS 236,240,247

modish [*adj*] *fashionable*
a la mode*, all the rage*, chic, contemporary, current, dashing, exclusive, faddy, fresh, happening, hip*, in*, in-thing*, last-word, latest, mod*, now*, smart, stylish, swank, swish*, trendy, up-to-date, up-to-the-minute, vogue, voguish, with-it*; SEE CONCEPTS 578,589,797

modulate [*v*] *adjust, harmonize*
attune, balance, fine-tune, inflect, regulate, restrain, revamp, switch, temper, tone, transmogrify, tune, tweak, vary; SEE CONCEPT 202

modus operandi [*n*] *mode of operation*
manner, method, method of operation, M.O., procedure, process, rule of thumb, technique, way, way of doing things, workings; SEE CONCEPTS 6,630

mogul [*n*] *person who has great power, many possessions*
executive, key player*, king, magnate, notable, personage, potentate, prince, princess queen, royalty, top brass*, tycoon, VIP*; SEE CONCEPTS 347,354

moist [*adj*] *wet, wettish*
clammy, damp, dampish, dank, dewy, dripping, drippy, drizzly, humid, irriguous, muggy, not dry, oozy*, rainy, soggy, teary, watery; SEE CONCEPT 603

moisten [*v*] *make wet, damp*
bathe, bedew, dampen, dip, drench, humidify, lick, mist, moisturize, rain on, rinse, saturate, shower, soak, sog, sop, splash, splatter, spray, sprinkle, squirt, steam, steep, wash, water, water down, waterlog, wet; SEE CONCEPT 256

moisture [*n*] *dampness; liquid*
damp, dankness, dew, drizzle, fog, humidity, mist, perspiration, precipitation, rain, sweat, water, wateriness, wet, wetness; SEE CONCEPTS 467,524

moisturizer [*n*] *lotion*
balm, cream, demulcent, emollient, liniment, oil, ointment, salve, unction, unguent; SEE CONCEPTS 311,446,466,467,468

mold [*n*] *form, pattern*
cast, cavity, character, class, depression, descrip-

tion, design, die, frame, image, impression, kind, lot, matrix, model, nature, shape, sort, stamp, type, womb; SEE CONCEPTS *378,411,436*

mold [*v*] *form, give shape*
build, construct, devise, erect, fashion, forge, form, frame, make, pat, plan, plant, plot, put together, round, scheme, sculpt, whittle; SEE CONCEPTS *173,175,184,251*

moldy [*adj*] *musty*
airless, dirty, funky, mildewed, mildewy, putrid, rotten, rotting, smelly, stale, stuffy; SEE CONCEPTS *578,598,603,797*

mole [*n1*] *blemish*
beauty mark, beauty spot, birthmark, blot, freckle, nevus, strawberry mark; SEE CONCEPT *580*

mole [*n2*] *spy*
agent, double agent, infiltrator, informer, inside man/woman, secret agent; SEE CONCEPTS *348,412*

molecule [*n*] *smallest part*
bit, fragment, iota, jot, minim, mite, modicum, mote, ounce, particle, ray, speck, unit; SEE CONCEPTS *393,831*

molest [*v1*] *physically abuse*
accost, assail, attack, disorganize, displace, disturb, encroach, fondle, harm, hinder, hurt, illtreat, injure, interfere, intrude, maltreat, meddle, misuse, rape; SEE CONCEPTS *246,375*

molest [*v2*] *bother, annoy*
abuse, afflict, badger, bait, bedevil, beset, break in, bug*, confuse, discommode, discompose, disquiet, disturb, encroach, frighten, harass, harry, heckle, hector, interrupt, intrude, irk, irritate, obtrude, persecute, perturb, pester, plague, pother, pursue, scare, tease, terrify, torment, trouble, upset, vex, worry; SEE CONCEPTS *7,14,19*

mollify [*v*] *pacify, soothe*
abate, allay, alleviate, ameliorate, appease, assuage, blunt, calm, compose, conciliate, cool, cushion, decrease, diminish, dulcify, ease, fix up, lessen, lighten, lull, mellow, mitigate, moderate, modify, pacify, patch things up*, placate, propitiate, quell, quiet, reduce, relieve, soften, sweeten, take sting out*, temper, tranquilize; SEE CONCEPTS *7,22,244,698*

mollycoddle [*v*] *pamper*
baby, caress, cater to, coddle, cosset, dandle*, fondle, indulge, overindulge, overprotect, pet, spoil, wait on; SEE CONCEPTS *136,295*

molt [*v*] *shed*
cast off, decorticate, doff, exuviate, peel, pull off, slough, take off; SEE CONCEPTS *142,176,179,180,181,211*

molten [*adj*] *melted*
fused, glowing, igneous, liquefied, smelted; SEE CONCEPTS *250,255*

mom [*n*] *mother*
child-bearer, grandmother, ma*, mama*, matriarch, matron, mommy*, mum*, mumsy*, parent; SEE CONCEPTS *394,400,414*

moment [*n1*] *brief time period*
bit, breathing, crack, date, flash, hour, instant, jiff*, jiffy*, juncture, minute, nothing flat*, no time*, occasion, point, point in time, sec*, second, shake, split second*, stage, three winks*, tick*, time, trice*, twinkle*, twinkling*, while, wink*; SEE CONCEPTS *807,808*

moment [*n2*] *importance*
advantage, avail, concern, consequence, gravity, import, magnitude, momentousness, note, pith, profit, seriousness, significance, signification, substance, use, value, weight, weightiness, worth; SEE CONCEPT *668*

momentarily [*adv*] *for a short time*
briefly, for a little while, for a minute, for a moment, for an instant, for a second, for a short time, for a short while, immediately, instantly, now, right now, temporarily; SEE CONCEPT *820*

momentary [*adj*] *brief, fleeting*
cursory, dreamlike, ephemeral, evanescent, flashing, flitting*, flying, fugacious, fugitive, gone in flash*, hasty, impermanent, impulsive, instantaneous, in wink of an eye*, like lightning, passing, quick, shifting, short, short-lived, spasmodic, summary, temporary, transient, transitory, vanishing, volatile; SEE CONCEPT *798*

momentous [*adj*] *important; serious*
big, chips are down*, consequential, considerable, critical, crucial, decisive, earth-shaking, earth-shattering, epochal, eventful, far-reaching, fateful, grave, heavy, heavy number, historic, material, meaningful, memorable, notable, of moment, outstanding, pivotal, significant, substantial, vital, weighty; SEE CONCEPT *568*

momentum [*n*] *impetus, push*
drive, energy, force, impulse, power, propulsion, strength, thrust; SEE CONCEPTS *641,712*

monarch [*n*] *ruler*
autocrat, crowned head, despot, emperor, empress, king, majesty, potentate, prince, princess, queen, sovereign; SEE CONCEPTS *354,422*

monastery [*n*] *place where monks live*
abbey, cloister, friary, house, lamasery, priory, religious community; SEE CONCEPTS *368,439,516*

monetary [*adj*] *concerning money, finances*
budgetary, capital, cash, commercial, financial, fiscal, pecuniary, pocket; SEE CONCEPT *334*

money [*n*] *currency accepted as exchange for goods, services*
almighty dollar*, banknote, bankroll, bill, bread*, bucks*, capital, cash, check, chips, coin, coinage, dough*, finances, fund, funds, gold, gravy*, greenback*, hard cash*, legal tender, loot*, medium of exchange, pay, payment, pesos*, property, resources, riches, roll, salary, silver, specie, treasure, wad*, wage, wealth, wherewithal*; SEE CONCEPT *340*

moneyed [*adj*] *rich*
affluent, fat-cat*, flush*, leisure-class*, loaded*, opulent, prosperous, upper-class, upscale, uptown, wealthy, well-heeled*, well-off*, well-to-do*; SEE CONCEPT *334*

moneymaking [*adj*] *producing profit*
advantageous, gainful, going, good, lucrative, paying, profitable, remunerative, successful, thriving, well-paying; SEE CONCEPT *334*

mongrel [*n*] *animal of mixed background*
bastard, cross, crossbreed, cur, half-blood, half-breed, hybrid, mixed breed, mixture, mule, mutt; SEE CONCEPT *394*

moniker [*n*] *nickname*
appellation, byname, denomination, handle*, label, pet name*, sobriquet, tag*; SEE CONCEPTS *268,683*

monitor [*n*] *person who watches, oversees*
adviser, auditor, counselor, director, eavesdropper, guide, informant, invigilator, listener, overseer, supervisor, watchdog; SEE CONCEPTS *348,350*

monitor [v] *listen, watch carefully*
advise, audit, check, control, counsel, follow, keep an eye on*, keep track of*, observe, oversee, record, scan, supervise, survey, track; SEE CONCEPTS 117,596,623

monk [n] *man who devotes life to contemplation of god*
abbot, anchorite, ascetic, brother, cenobite, eremite, friar, hermit, monastic, priest, recluse, religious, solitary; SEE CONCEPT 361

monkey [n] *primate*
anthropoid, ape, baboon, chimpanzee, gorilla, imp, lemur, monk, orangutan, rascal, scamp, simian; SEE CONCEPT 394

monkey [v] *fiddle, tamper with*
busybody, butt in*, fool, fool around*, fool with*, horn in*, interfere, interlope, intermeddle, make*, meddle, mess, play, pry, tinker, trifle; SEE CONCEPTS 87,612

monkey business [n] *foolishness*
absurdity, absurdness, antics, carrying-on*, craziness, disobedience, foolery, high jinks, horse feathers*, horseplay, inanity, insanity, irresponsibility, ludicrousness, lunacy, misbehavior, mischief-making, nonsense, poppycock*, silliness, stupidity, tommyrot*; SEE CONCEPT 633

monolithic [adj] *massive*
big, bulky, colossal, consistent, elephantine, enormous, gargantuan, giant, gigantic, grand, great, huge, hulking, immense, immovable, imposing, mammoth, permanent, solid, titanic, towering, uniform, vast, whopping*; SEE CONCEPTS 773,781

monologue [n] *speech by one person*
address, descant, discourse, disquisition, harangue, lecture, sermon, soliloquy, speech, stand-up bit*, talk; SEE CONCEPTS 266,278

monopolize [v] *dominate, control*
absorb, acquire, bogart, consume, copyright, corner, corner the market*, devour, employ, engross, exclude, exercise control, have, hog*, hold, keep to oneself, lock up*, manage, own, own exclusively, patent, possess, restrain, sew up*, sit on*, syndicate, take over, take up, use, utilize; SEE CONCEPTS 94,324,710

monopoly [n] *something held, owned exclusively*
cartel, consortium, copyright, corner, holding, oligopoly, ownership, patent, pool, possessorship, proprietorship, syndicate, trust; SEE CONCEPT 710

monotonous [adj] *all the same, remaining the same*
banausic, blah*, boring, colorless, dreary, droning, dull, dull as dishwater*, flat, flat as pancake*, ho-hum*, humdrum*, monotone, nothing, pedestrian, plodding, prosaic, puts one to sleep*, recurrent, reiterated, repetitious, repetitive, samely, sing-song*, soporific, tedious, tiresome, toneless, treadmill, unchanged, unchanging, uniform, uninflected, uninteresting, unrelieved, unvaried, unvarying, wearisome, wearying; SEE CONCEPTS 529,534,544

monotony [n] *boredom; sameness*
colorlessness, continuance, continuity, dreariness, dryness, dullness, ennui, equability, evenness, flatness, humdrum*, identicalness, invariability, levelness, likeness, monotone, monotonousness, oneness, repetitiousness, repetitiveness, routine, same old thing*, similarity, tediousness, tedium, tiresomeness, unchange-

ableness, uniformity, wearisomeness; SEE CONCEPTS 410,637,673

monster [n] *giant animal; supernatural being*
abnormality, barbarian, beast, behemoth, brute, centaur, colossus, demon, devil, dragon, fiend, Frankenstein, freak, giant, hellion, horror, leviathan, lusus naturae, mammoth, miscreation, monstrosity, mutant, ogre, phoenix, savage, titan, villain, werewolf, whale; SEE CONCEPTS 370,394,412

monstrosity [n] *freak*
abnormality, atrocity, deformity, dreadfulness, enormity, eyesore, freakishness, frightfulness, grotesqueness, heinousness, hideousness, horror, monster, mutant, mutation; SEE CONCEPTS 411,657

monstrous [adj1] *unnatural, shocking*
aberrant, abnormal, atrocious, cruel, desperate, devilish, diabolical, disgraceful, dreadful, egregious, evil, fiendish, flagitious, foul, freakish, frightful, grotesque, gruesome, heinous, hellish, hideous, horrendous, horrible, horrifying, infamous, inhuman, intolerable, loathsome, macabre, miscreated, morbid, obscene, odious, ominous, outrageous, preposterous, rank, satanic, scandalous, teratoid, terrible, uncanny, unusual, vicious, villainous; SEE CONCEPTS 537,564,582

monstrous [adj2] *very large*
colossal, cracking, elephantine, enormous, fantastic, gargantuan, giant, gigantic, grandiose, great, huge, immense, impressive, magnificent, mammoth, massive, monumental, prodigious, stupendous, titanic, towering, tremendous, vast, whopping; SEE CONCEPTS 773,781

monument [n] *memorial, remembrance*
cairn, cenotaph, column, commemoration, erection, footstone, gravestone, headstone, ledger, magnum opus, marker, masterpiece, mausoleum, memento, monolith, obelisk, pile, pillar, record, reminder, shrine, slab, statue, stele, stone, tablet, testament, token, tomb, tombstone, tower, tribute, witness; SEE CONCEPTS 259,271,305,470

monumental [adj] *impressive, overwhelming*
awe-inspiring, awesome, classic, enduring, enormous, fantastic, gigantic, grand, great, historic, huge, immense, immortal, important, lasting, lofty, majestic, mammoth, massive, memorable, mighty, mortal, mountainous, outstanding, prodigious, significant, stupendous, towering, tremendous, unforgettable, vast; SEE CONCEPTS 568,773

mooch [v] *cadge*
beg, borrow, bum*, bum off*, freeload, leach off*, scrounge, sponge; SEE CONCEPT 89

mood [n] *state of mind*
affection, air, atmosphere, attitude, aura, bent*, blues*, caprice, character, color*, condition, crotchet, cue, depression, desire, disposition, doldrums, dumps*, emotion, fancy, feel*, feeling, frame of mind*, high spirits, humor, inclination, individuality, low spirits, melancholy, mind, personality, pleasure, propensity, response, scene, semblance, soul, spirit, strain, temper, temperament, tendency, tenor, timbre, vagary, vein, whim, wish; SEE CONCEPTS 410,411,673

moody [adj] *crabby, temperamental*
angry, cantankerous, capricious, changeable, crabbed*, crestfallen, cross, dismal, doleful, dour, downcast, down in the dumps*, down in the mouth*, erratic, fickle, fitful, flighty, frown-

mo
mo

ing, gloomy, glum, huffy, ill-humored, ill-tempered, impulsive, in a huff*, in the doldrums, introspective, irascible, irritable, lugubrious, melancholy, mercurial, miserable, moping, morose, offended, out of sorts*, pensive, petulant, piqued, sad, saturnine, short-tempered, splenetic, sulky, sullen, testy, touchy; SEE CONCEPT *403*

moon [*n*] *Earth's satellite*
celestial body, crescent, full moon, half-moon, heavenly body, new moon, old moon, orb of night*, planetoid, pumpkin*, quarter-moon, satellite; SEE CONCEPTS *511,809*

moon [*v*] *dream about; desire*
daydream, idle, languish, mope, pine, waste time, yearn; SEE CONCEPT *20*

moonshine [*n*] *illegally distilled alcohol*
bathtub gin*, bootleg, firewater*, home brew, hooch*, mountain dew*, rotgut*, white lightning; SEE CONCEPTS *454,467*

moor [*v*] *anchor, fasten securely*
berth, catch, chain, dock, fix, lash, make fast, picket, secure, tether, tie, tie up; SEE CONCEPTS *85,160*

mooring [*n*] *landing*
anchorage, berth, dock, harbor, marina, pier, port, station, wharf; SEE CONCEPTS *439*

moot [*adj*] *doubtful, arguable*
at issue, contestable, controversial, debatable, disputable, dubious, open, open to debate, problematic, questionable, suspect, uncertain, undecided, unresolved, unsettled; SEE CONCEPT *535*

mop [*n*] *tangle of material, often used to absorb liquid*
duster, sponge, squeegee, swab, sweeper, towel; SEE CONCEPTS *392,499*

mop [*n2*] *thick mass of hair*
mane, shock, tangle, thatch, tresses; SEE CONCEPT *399*

mop [*v*] *clean by using water and cloth*
dab, dust, pat, polish, rub, soak up, sponge, squeegee, swab, towel off, wash, wipe; SEE CONCEPT *165*

mope [*v*] *pout, be dejected*
ache, be apathetic, be down in the mouth*, be gloomy, be in a funk*, bleed*, brood, chafe, despair, despond, droop, eat one's heart out, fret, grieve, grumble, grump, idle, lament, languish, lose heart, moon, pine, pine away*, regret, repine, sink, stew over*, sulk, sweat over*, waste time*, wear a long face*, yearn; SEE CONCEPTS *20,410*

moral [*adj*] *ethical, honest*
aboveboard, blameless, chaste, conscientious, correct, courteous, decent, decorous, dutiful, elevated, exemplary, good, high-minded, honorable, immaculate, incorruptible, innocent, just, kindly, kosher*, laudable, meet, meritorious, modest, moralistic, noble, praiseworthy, principled, proper, pure, respectable, right, righteous, saintly, salt of the earth*, scrupulous, seemly, square, straight, true-blue*, trustworthy, truthful, upright, upstanding, virtuous, worthy; SEE CONCEPT *545*

moral [*n*] *lesson, proverb*
adage, aphorism, apophthegm, axiom, dictum, epigram, gnome, maxim, meaning, message, moralism, motto, point, precept, rule, saw, saying, sermon, significance, truism; SEE CONCEPTS *278,283*

morale [*n*] *confidence, self-esteem*
assurance, attitude, disposition, drive, esprit, esprit de corps, heart, humor, mettle, mood, outlook, resolve, self-confidence, self-possession, spirit, temper, temperament, turn, vigor; SEE CONCEPTS *410,411*

morality [*n*] *ethics, honesty*
chastity, conduct, decency, ethicality, ethicalness, gentleness, godliness, good habits, goodness, honor, ideals, incorruptibility, incorruption, integrity, justice, manners, moral code, morals, mores, philosophy, principle, principles, probity, purity, rectitude, righteousness, rightness, saintliness, standards, uprightness, virtue, worthiness; SEE CONCEPT *645*

moralize [*v*] *preach*
admonish, edify, lecture, pass judgment, pontificate, pontify, preachify, sermonize, teach; SEE CONCEPTS *51,75*

morals [*n*] *personal principles, standards*
behavior, beliefs, conduct, customs, dogmas, ethic, ethics, habits, ideals, integrity, manners, morality, mores, policies, scruples; SEE CONCEPTS *411,645,688*

morass [*n*] *bog; mess*
chaos, confusion, fen, jam, jungle, knot, labyrinth, marsh, maze, mesh, mix-up, muddle, quagmire, skein, snarl, swamp, tangle, web; SEE CONCEPTS *230,509*

moratorium [*n*] *suspension*
abeyance, abeyancy, adjournment, ban, break, breather*, breathing spell*, deferment, delay, downtime*, five*, freeze, grace period, halt, pause, postponement, reprieve, respite, stay, truce; SEE CONCEPTS *119,807,832*

morbid [*adj*] *gloomy, nasty, sickly*
aberrant, abnormal, ailing, brooding, dark, deadly, depressed, despondent, diseased, dreadful, frightful, ghastly, ghoulish, grim, grisly, gruesome, hideous, horrid, infected, irascible, macabre, malignant, melancholy, monstrous, moody, pessimistic, saturnine, sick, somber, sullen, unhealthy, unnatural, unsound, unusual, unwholesome; SEE CONCEPTS *314,403,537*

mordant [*adj*] *sarcastic*
acerb, acerbic, acid, biting, bitter, caustic, cutting, cynical, disparaging, disrespectful, mean, poignant, pointed, sardonic, scathing, sharp; SEE CONCEPT *267*

more [*adj*] *additional, greater*
added, aggrandized, also, amassed, and, another, augmented, besides, bounteous, deeper, else, enhanced, exceeding, expanded, extended, extra, farther, fresh, further, heavier, higher, in addition, increased, innumerable, larger, likewise, major, massed, more than that, new, numerous, other, over and above, spare, supplementary, too many, wider; SEE CONCEPTS *762,771*

more [*adv*] *to a greater extent*
additionally, along with, also, as well, besides, better, beyond, further, furthermore, in addition, likewise, longer, moreover, over, too, withal; SEE CONCEPTS *544,772*

more or less [*adv*] *approximately*
about, almost, around, ballpark figure*, bordering on, circa, close to, in the ballpark*, in the neighborhood of, in the vicinity of, just about, not far from, not quite, on average, relatively, roughly, thereabouts, very close; SEE CONCEPT *566*

moreover [*adv*] *additionally*
also, as well, besides, by the same token*, further, furthermore, in addition, likewise, more, to boot*, too, what is more*, withal, yet; SEE CONCEPTS 544,772

mores [*n*] *traditional customs*
attitude, codes, established ways, etiquette, formalities, manners, morals, policies, practices, principles, protocol, rites, rituals, routines, rules, social conduct, standards, way of life; SEE CONCEPTS 644,687

morgue [*n*] *mortuary*
charnel house, crematory, funeral home, funeral parlor; SEE CONCEPTS 172,386

moribund [*adj*] *dying*
at death's door*, at the end of the rope*, declining, done for*, doomed, expiring, fading, fated, going, mortal, mortally ill, one foot in the grave*, on one's deathbed, on one's last leg*, passing, perishing; SEE CONCEPT 539

morning [*n*] *first part of the day*
after midnight, AM, ante meridiem, aurora, before lunch, before noon, breakfast time*, break of day, cockcrow*, crack of dawn*, dawn, daybreak, daylight, dayspring, early bright*, first blush*, foreday, forenoon, morn*, morningtide, morrow, prime*, sunrise, sunup, wee hours*; SEE CONCEPTS 801,802,806,810

moron [*n*] *stupid person*
addlepate, blockhead*, boob*, dimwit, dingbat*, dolt, dope*, dork*, dumbbell*, dummy*, dunce, fool, halfwit, idiot, ignoramus, imbecile, lamebrain*, loony*, loser*, mental defective*, nerd*, simpleton; SEE CONCEPT 423

moronic [*adj*] *stupid*
asinine, brainless, dense, dimwitted, doltish, dopey*, dumb, foolish, half-baked*, idiotic, illadvised, imbecilic, inane, irresponsible, ludicrous, mindless, nonsensical, pointless, senseless, unintelligent, unthinking; SEE CONCEPTS 402,548

morose [*adj*] *depressed, pessimistic*
acrimonious, blue*, brusque, cantankerous, choleric, churlish, crabbed*, crabby*, cranky*, cross, dolorous, dour, down, down in the dumps*, down in the mouth*, frowning, gloomy, glum, grouchy, gruff, harsh, having blue devils*, having the blahs*, ill-humored, ill-tempered, in a bad mood*, in a blue funk*, irritable, low, melancholy, moody, moping, mournful, perverse, perversive, sad, saturnine, singing the blues*, snappish, sour, splenetic, sulky, sullen, surly, taciturn, testy, troubled, ugly; SEE CONCEPT 403

morsel [*n*] *tiny piece*
bait, bit, bite, chunk, crumb, cut, delicacy, drop, fraction, fragment, grain, hunk, lump, mouthful, nibble, nosh, part, sample, scrap, segment, slice, snack, soupcon, taste, tidbit, treat; SEE CONCEPTS 457,458,831,835

mortal [*adj1*] *deadly*
bitter, death-dealing, deathly, destructive, dire, ending, extreme, fatal, grave, great, grievous, grim, intense, killing, last, lethal, malignant, merciless, monstrous, mortiferous, murderous, noxious, pestilent, pestilential, poisonous, relentless, remorseless, ruthless, severe, terminal, terrible, unrelenting; SEE CONCEPT 537

mortal [*adj2*] *human*
animate, bipedal, corporeal, creatural, earthly,

ecce homo, ephemeral, evanescent, fading, finite, frail, fugacious, impermanent, momentary, passing, perishable, precarious, sublunary, temporal, transient, weak, worldly; SEE CONCEPT 549

mortal [*n*] *human being*
animal, being, body, character, creature, earthling, human, individual, living soul, man, naked ape, party, person, personage, soul, woman; SEE CONCEPT 417

mortality [*n1*] *death*
bloodshed, carnage, deadliness, destruction, dying, extinction, fatality, killing, lethality, loss of life; SEE CONCEPT 407

mortality [*n2*] *humanness*
being, ephemerality, flesh, Homo sapiens, humanity, humankind, human race, impermanence, temporality, transience; SEE CONCEPTS 417,648

mortally [*adv*] *fatally*
badly, critically, gravely, painfully, seriously; SEE CONCEPTS 544,565,568

mortgage [*n*] *loan agreement*
contract, debt, deed, homeowner's loan, pledge, title; SEE CONCEPT 332

mortician [*n*] *undertaker*
embalmer, funeral director; SEE CONCEPT 304

mortification [*n*] *humiliation*
abasement, affront, bring down, chagrin, condescension, degradation, disgrace, dishonor, embarrassment, humbling, ignominy, loss of face*, put-down, resignation, shame; SEE CONCEPTS 388,410

mortify [*v*] *embarrass*
abase, abash, affront, annoy, belittle, chagrin, chasten, confound, control, crush, deflate, deny, disappoint, discipline, discomfit, disgrace, displease, get one's comeuppance*, harass, humble, humiliate, put to shame, ridicule, shame, subdue, take down a peg*, take the wind out*, vex, worry; SEE CONCEPTS 7,19,52,54

mortuary [*n*] *funeral home*
charnel house, crematory, funeral parlor, morgue; SEE CONCEPT 304

mosaic [*n*] *collage*
checker, montage, motley, patchwork, plaid, tessellation, variegation; SEE CONCEPTS 259,625

mosey [*v*] *saunter*
amble, dally, dilly-dally, drift, linger, loiter, meander, mope*, move slowly, ramble, stroll along, take a stroll, take it easy, traipse, walk slowly; SEE CONCEPT 151

mosque [*n*] *temple*
cathedral, chapel, church, holy place, house of God, house of worship, masjid, place of worship, sanctuary, shrine, synagogue, tabernacle; SEE CONCEPTS 368,439

mossback [*n*] *old-fashioned person*
conservative, fuddy-duddy*, geezer*, old fogy*, old geezer*, square*; SEE CONCEPT 424

most [*adj*] *best, greatest*
better, biggest, greater, highest, largest, lion's share*, max*, maximum, ultimate, utmost, uttermost; SEE CONCEPTS 771,772

most [*adv*] *nearly all; extremely*
about, all but, almost, approximately, close, eminently, exceedingly, in the majority, mightily, much, nearly, nigh, practically, remarkably, super, surpassingly, too, very, well-nigh; SEE CONCEPTS 544,569,771

mostly [*adv*] *generally, mainly*
above all, almost entirely, as a rule*, chiefly,

customarily, essentially, for the most part*, frequently, in many instances*, largely, many times, most often, often, on the whole*, overall, particularly, predominantly, primarily, principally, regularly, usually; SEE CONCEPTS 544,548,772

mote [n] *speck*

atom, bit, crumb, dot, fleck, fragment, grain, iota, particle, small thing, smidgen, speckle, tiny bit, trace; SEE CONCEPT 831

motel [n] *temporary, short-term residence, often for travelers*

cabin, court, hotel, inn, lodge, motor court, resort, roadhouse; SEE CONCEPTS 439,449,516

moth-eaten [adj] *shabby; stale*

ancient, antiquated, archaic, dated, decayed, decrepit, dilapidated, moribund, old-fashioned, outdated, ragged, tattered, threadbare, worn-out; SEE CONCEPT 485

mother [n] *female person who has borne children*

ancestor, child-bearer, creator, forebearer, mom*, mommy*, origin, parent, predecessor, procreator, progenitor, source; SEE CONCEPTS 394,400,414,415,423

motif [n] *central theme*

concept, design, idea, logo, notion, pattern, structure, subject; SEE CONCEPTS 278,682,689

motion [n1] *movement, action*

act, advance, agitation, ambulation, body English*, change, changing, direction, drift, dynamics, flow, fluctuation, flux, full swing*, gesticulation, gesture, high sign*, inclination, kinetics, locomotion, mobility, motility, move, oscillation, passage, passing, progress, sign, signal, stir, stirring, stream, sway, sweep, swing, tendency, travel, wave, wavering; SEE CONCEPT 145

motion [n2] *formal suggestion in a meeting*

plan, proposal, proposition, recommendation, submission; SEE CONCEPTS 75,278

motion [v] *gesture, direct*

beckon, flag, gesticulate, guide, invite, move, nod, sign, signal, signalize, wave; SEE CONCEPT 149

motionless [adj] *calm, not moving*

apoplectic, at a standstill*, at rest, becalmed, dead, deadlocked, deathly, firm, fixed, frozen, halted, immobile, immotile, inanimate, inert, lifeless, numb, palsied, paralyzed, petrified, quiescent, quiet, spellbound, stable, stagnant, stalled, standing, static, stationary, steadfast, still, stock-still, torpid, transfixed, unmovable, unmoved, unmoving; SEE CONCEPTS 488,584

motion picture [n] *movie*

cine, cinema, cinematics, cinematograph, feature film, film, flick*, moving picture, picture show, silver screen*, talkie*, talking picture, videotape; SEE CONCEPTS 263,293

motivate [v] *stimulate, instigate*

actuate, arouse, bring, cause, dispose, draw, drive, egg on*, excite, fire, galvanize, give incentive, goad, goose*, impel, incite, incline, induce, innervate, innerve, inspire, inspirit, lead, move, persuade, pique, predetermine, predispose, prevail upon, prompt, propel, provoke, quicken, rouse, set afoot, set astir, sound, spark, spur, suggest, sway, touch off, trigger, whet; SEE CONCEPTS 14,68,242

motivation [n] *ambition, inspiration*

action, actuation, angle, catalyst, desire, disposi-

tion, drive, encouragement, fire, get up and go*, gimmick, goose*, hunger, impetus, impulse, impulsion, incentive, incitation, incitement, inclination, inducement, instigation, interest, kick*, motive, persuasion, predetermination, predisposition, provocation, push, reason, right stuff*, spur, stimulus, suggestion, wish; SEE CONCEPTS 20,411,689

motive [n] *reason, purpose*

aim, antecedent, basis, cause, consideration, design, determinant, drive, emotion, end, feeling, grounds, idea, impulse, incentive, incitement, inducement, influence, inspiration, intent, intention, mainspring, motivation, object, occasion, passion, rationale, root, spring, spur, stimulus, thinking; SEE CONCEPTS 20,661,689

motley [adj] *mixed, varied*

assorted, conglomerate, dappled, discrepant, disparate, dissimilar, diversified, heterogeneous, indiscriminate, kaleidoscopic, mingled, miscellaneous, mixed, mottled, multicolor, multicolored, multiform, multihued, polychromatic, prismatic, rainbow, unlike, varicolored, variegated, various, versicolor; SEE CONCEPTS 564,618,772

motor [n] *engine*

cylinder, diesel, generator, mechanism, piston, power train, transformer, turbine, what's under the hood*; SEE CONCEPTS 463,464

motorcade [n] *procession of motor vehicles*

caravan, convoy, parade; SEE CONCEPTS 432,503

motorcycle [n] *motorbike*

chopper*, dirt bike, enduro, hog*, minibike, moped, scooter; SEE CONCEPTS 364,505

motor home [n] *recreational vehicle*

camper, mobile home, RV; SEE CONCEPT 505

motorized [adj] *power-driven*

mechanical, mechanized, powered; SEE CONCEPT 544

mottled [adj] *speckled*

blotchy, checkered, dappled, flecked, freckled, maculate, marbled, motley, piebald, pied, skewbald, spotted, streaked, tabby, variegated; SEE CONCEPTS 606,618

motto [n] *saying, slogan*

adage, aphorism, apothegm, battle cry, byword, catchphrase, cry, epigram, formula, maxim, precept, proverb, rallying cry, rule, saw, sentiment, shibboleth, war cry, watchword, word; SEE CONCEPT 278

mound [n] *heap, hill*

anthill, bank, drift, dune, embankment, hillock, knoll, mass, molehill, mountain, pile, rise, shock, stack, tumulus; SEE CONCEPTS 432,509

mount [v1] *climb*

arise, ascend, back, bestride, clamber up, climb onto, climb up on, escalade, escalate, get astride, get up on, go up, jump on, lift, rise, scale, soar, tower, up, vault; SEE CONCEPTS 149,154,166

mount [v2] *increase, grow*

accumulate, aggravate, augment, build, deepen, enhance, enlarge, escalate, expand, heighten, intensate, intensify, multiply, pile up, redouble, rise, rouse, swell, upsurge, wax; SEE CONCEPTS 704,780

mount [v3] *affix, frame*

emplace, exhibit, fit, install, place, position, prepare, produce, put in place, put on, set up, show, stage; SEE CONCEPTS 174,261

mountain [*n*] *very large hill*
abundance, alp, bank, bluff, butte, cliff, crag, dome, drift, elevation, eminence, glob, heap, height, hump, mass, mesa, mound, mount, palisade, peak, pike, pile, precipice, pyramid, range, ridge, shock, sierra, stack, ton, tor, volcano; SEE CONCEPTS *432,509*

mountaineer [*n*] *mountain climber*
alpinist, backpacker, climber, cragsman, cragswoman, hiker, rock climber; SEE CONCEPTS *149,224,363*

mountaineering [*n*] *mountain climbing*
alpinism, backpacking, hiking, hill-climbing, rock-climbing; SEE CONCEPTS *149,224,363*

mountainous [*adj*] *hilly; large*
alpine, big, colossal, gigantic, highland, huge, mammoth, tall, towering; SEE CONCEPT *509*

mountebank [*n*] *charlatan*
cheat, con man/woman*, grifter, imposter, rip-off artist*, swindler; SEE CONCEPT *412*

mourn [*v*] *be sad over loss*
ache, agonize, anguish, be brokenhearted*, bemoan, be sad, bewail, bleed, blubber, carry on, complain, cry, deplore, fret, grieve, hurt, keen, lament, languish, long for, miss, moan, pine, regret, repine, rue, sigh, sob, sorrow, suffer, take it hard*, wail, wear black*, weep, wring hands*, yearn; SEE CONCEPTS *23,410*

mournful [*adj*] *sorrowful*
anguished, bereft, cheerless, depressed, disconsolate, distressing, doleful, dolent, forlorn, full of sorrow, grief-stricken, grieving, grievous, heartbroken, in mourning, in pain, in sorrow, lamentable, pitiful, sad, sombre, woeful; SEE CONCEPT *403*

mourning [*n*] *sadness, time of sadness*
aching, bereavement, blackness, crying, darkness, grief, grieving, keening, lamentation, lamenting, languishing, moaning, pining, repining, sorrowing, wailing, weeping, woe; SEE CONCEPTS *388,410*

mousy [*adj*] *drab; quiet*
bashful, colorless, diffident, dull, indeterminate, ineffectual, pale, plain, self-effacing, shy, timid, timorous, unassertive, unassuming; SEE CONCEPTS *401,618*

mouth [*n*] *opening*
aperture, beak, box, cavity, chops*, clam, crevice, delta, door, embouchure, entrance, estuary, firth, fly trap, funnel, gate, gills, gob, harbor, inlet, jaws, kisser*, lips, mush*, orifice, portal, rim, trap*, yap*; SEE CONCEPTS *392,513*

mouth [*n*] *backtalk*
boasting, braggadocio, bragging, cheek, empty talk*, freshness, gas*, guff*, hot air*, idle talk, impudence, insolence, lip*, rudeness, sass*, sauce*; SEE CONCEPTS *54,278*

mouth off [*v*] *talk back*
answer back, come back at, sass, sass back, wise off; SEE CONCEPTS *44,52*

mouthpiece [*n*] *spokesperson*
agent, delegate, PR person, representative, speaker, spokesman, spokeswoman; SEE CONCEPTS *348,354,359*

mouth-watering [*adj*] *appetizing*
aperitive, appealing, delectable, delicious, divine*, flavorsome, full of flavor, heavenly*, luscious, palatable, piquant, saporous, savory, scrumptious, succulent, tasty, tempting, yummy*; SEE CONCEPT *613*

mouthy [*adj*] *talkative*
big-mouthed*, chattering, chatty*, full of hot air*, gabby, garrulous, gossipy, long-winded*, loose-lipped*, loudmouthed*, ranting, talky, vociferous, windy*; SEE CONCEPT *267*

movable [*adj*] *transportable*
adaptable, adjustable, ambulatory, conveyable, deployable, detachable, in parts, liftable, loose, mobile, motile, moving, not fastened, not fixed, on wheels, portable, portative, removable, separable, shiftable, transferable, turnable, unattached, unfastened, unstationary, unsteady; SEE CONCEPTS *488,584*

move [*n*] *progress, deed*
act, action, alteration, change, maneuver, measure, modification, motion, movement, ploy, procedure, proceeding, shift, step, stir, stirring, stratagem, stroke, turn, variation; SEE CONCEPTS *2,660*

move [*v1*] *be in motion, put in motion*
actuate, advance, blow, budge, bustle, carry, change, climb, crawl, cross, depart, dislocate, disturb, drift, drive, exit, flow, fly, get away, get going, get off, glide, go, go away, head for, hurry, impel, jump, leap, leave, locomote, march, migrate, off-load, position, proceed, progress, propel, pull out, push, quit, relocate, remove, roll, run, scram, shift, ship, shove, skip out, split, stir, switch, take off, transfer, transport, transpose, travel, traverse, walk, withdraw; SEE CONCEPTS *147,149,198*

move [*v2*] *motivate, influence*
activate, actuate, advocate, affect, agitate, bring, bring up, budge, carry, cause, convert, draw up, drive, excite, get going, give rise to, impel, impress, incite, induce, inspire, inspirit, instigate, introduce, lead, operate, persuade, play on, prevail upon, prompt, propel, propose, push, put forward, quicken, recommend, rouse, shift, show, start, stimulate, stir, strike, submit, suggest, sway, touch, tug at, turn, urge, work on; SEE CONCEPTS *7,19,22,75,242*

movement [*n1*] *motion, activity*
act, action, advance, agitation, alteration, change, changing, deed, development, displacement, dynamism, evolution, evolving, exercise, flight, flow, flux, gesture, journey, journeying, locomotion, maneuver, migration, mobility, motility, movableness, move, moving, operation, operativeness, passage, progress, progression, regression, roaming, shift, shifting, steps, stir, stirring, transferal, transit, translating, transplanting, undertaking, velocity, voyaging, wandering; SEE CONCEPTS *2,145,697*

movement [*n2*] *drive, campaign*
change, crusade, current, demonstration, displacement, drift, evolution, faction, flight, flow, front, group, grouping, march, mobilization, organization, party, patrol, shift, sweep, swing, tendency, transfer, transition, trend, unrest, withdrawal; SEE CONCEPTS *381,697*

mover and shaker [*n*] *doer*
achiever, catalyst, enterprising person, entrepreneur, generator, go-getter*, mover, player*, producer, spark plug*, upstart, wheeler and dealer*; SEE CONCEPT *347*

movie [*n*] *presentation of action on continuous film*
cine, cinema, cinematics, cinematograph, feature, film, flick*, motion picture, moving picture,

photoplay, picture, screenplay, show, silent*, silver screen*, talkie*, talking picture, videotape; SEE CONCEPTS 263,293

moving [adj1] *affecting, exciting*
affective, arousing, awakening, breathless, dynamic, eloquent, emotional, emotive, expressive, facund, far-out*, felt in gut*, grabbed by*, gripping, hairy*, heartbreaking, heartrending, impelling, impressive, inspirational, inspiring, meaningful, mind-bending*, mind-blowing*, motivating, persuasive, poignant, propelling, provoking, quickening, rallying, rousing, sententious, significant, something*, stimulating, stimulative, stirring, stunning, touching, turned on by*; SEE CONCEPTS 529,537

moving [adj2] *mobile*
advancing, changing, climbing, evolving, flying, going, jumping, motile, movable, nomadic, portable, progressing, roaming, roving, running, shifting, traversing, unfixed, unstable, unsteadfast, unsteady, walking; SEE CONCEPTS 488,584

mow [v] *cut*
clip, crop, scythe, shear, sickle, trim; SEE CONCEPTS 137,176,236,247

moxie [n] *courage*
adventuresomeness, adventurousness, audacity, backbone, boldness, braveness, bravery, daring, dash, dauntlessness, determination, fearlessness, fortitude, gameness, grit, guts, hardihood, mettle, nerve, pluck, prowess, spirit, spunk, stamina, tenacity, toughness, valor; SEE CONCEPTS 411,633

much [adj] *plenty*
abundant, adequate, a lot of*, ample, complete, considerable, copious, countless, endless, enough, everywhere, extravagant, full, galore, generous, great, heaps*, immeasurable, jam-packed*, lavish, loads*, lotsa*, many, mega*, mucho*, no end*, plenteous, plentiful, profuse, satisfying, scads*, sizable, substantial, sufficient, very many, voluminous; SEE CONCEPTS 772,781

much [adv] *greatly, a lot*
again and again, a great deal*, considerably, decidedly, eminently, exceedingly, exceptionally, extremely, frequently, highly, hugely, indeed, notably, oft, often, over and over*, regularly, repeatedly, surpassingly, time and time again*, very; SEE CONCEPTS 530,544,548

much [n] *a great deal*
abundance, all kinds of*, a lot*, amplitude, appreciable amount, barrel, breadth, completeness, copiousness, excess, exuberance, fullness, gobs*, great quantity, heaps*, loads*, lots*, lump, mass, mess*, mountain, multiplicity, oodles*, overage, oversupply, pack, peck, pile, plentifulness, plenty, plethora, profuseness, riches, scads*, sufficiency, superabundance, superfluity, thousands, tons*, very much, volume, wealth; SEE CONCEPT 771

mud [n] *wet dirt*
clay, mire, muck, ooze, silt, slab, sludge, slush; SEE CONCEPT 509

muddle [n] *confused state*
ataxia, awkwardness, botch, chaos, clutter, complexity, complication, confusion, daze, difficulty, dilemma, disarrangement, disarray, disorder, disorganization, emergency, encumbrance, fog, foul-up*, hash, haze, intricacy, involvement, jumble, mess, mess and a half*, mix-up*, muss*, perplexity, plight, predicament, quandary, rat's

nest*, screw-up*, shambles*, snarl, struggle, tangle, trouble; SEE CONCEPTS 230,410,666

muddle [v] *confuse, disorganize*
addle, befuddle, bewilder, blunder, botch, bungle, clutter, complicate, confound, daze, derange, disarrange, discombobulate*, disorder, disorient, disturb, entangle, fluster, foul, foul up*, jumble, louse up, make a mess of*, mess, misarrange, mix, mix up*, muck, mumble, murmur, nonplus, perplex, perturb, psych out*, rattle, ravel, ruffle, scramble, shuffle, snafu*, snarl, spoil, stir up, stumble, stupefy, tangle, throw, throw off, tumble; SEE CONCEPTS 16,84,242

muddled [adj] *confused*
addled, befuddled, bewildered, blurred, chaotic, convoluted, dazed, disarranged, disarrayed, disordered, disorderly, disorganized, in disarray, jumbled, messy, mixed up, scrambled, topsy-turvy, untidy; SEE CONCEPT 585

muddy [adj] *dark and cloudy*
addled, bemired, bespattered, black, blurred, boggy*, caked, confused, dingy, dirty, dull, filthy, flat, foul, fuzzy, gloomy, greasy, grimy, grubby*, gummy*, gunky*, hazy, impure, indistinct, marshy, miry, mucky*, obscure, opaque, roily, sloppy, slushy, smoky, sodden, soggy, soiled, subfuse, swampy, turbid, unclean, unclear; SEE CONCEPTS 485,606,618

mudslinging [n] *smear campaign*
character assassination, defamation, dirty politics, dragging one's name through the mud, negative campaign, slander; SEE CONCEPT 54

muff [v] *bungle*
blunder, boggle, botch, choke*, drop the ball*, err, flub, foul up, fumble, goof up*, make a mess of, mess up, miscalculate, mishandle, mismanage, screw up*, slip; SEE CONCEPT 101

muffle [v] *suppress, make quiet*
conceal, cover, cushion, dampen, deaden, decrease, drown, dull, envelop, gag, hide, hush, mellow, mute, muzzle, put the lid on*, quieten, shut down, silence, sit down on*, smother, soften, soft-pedal*, squelch, stifle, subdue, tone down*, wrap*; SEE CONCEPTS 65,121,240

muffled [adj] *quietened*
deadened, dim, dull, faint, flat, indistinct, mute, muted, obscure, silenced, stifled, strangled, subdued, suppressed; SEE CONCEPT 594

mug [n1] *drinking cup*
coffee cup, demitasse, flagon, jug, stoup, tankard, toby; SEE CONCEPT 494

mug [n2] *face*
countenance, frown, grimace, kisser*, mask, profile, puss*; SEE CONCEPTS 484,716,836

mug [v] *hold up*
assault, hold up*, purse-snatch, rob, steal, stick up*; SEE CONCEPTS 52,86

muggy [adj] *humid*
clammy*, close, damp, dampish, dank, moist, mucky*, oppressive, soggy, sticky, stuffy, sultry; SEE CONCEPTS 525,603

mulish [adj] *obstinate*
adamant, bullheaded, dead set on*, dogged, firm, hardheaded, headstrong, immovable, inflexible, intractable, obdurate, opinionated, persistent, pigheaded*, recalcitrant, relentless, single-minded, steadfast, strong-minded, stubborn, tenacious; SEE CONCEPTS 401,404,542

mull [v] *think about seriously*
brood over, chaw, consider, contemplate, delay,

deliberate, examine, figure, hammer away at*, linger, meditate, moon*, muse on, ponder, pore over, procrastinate, rack one's brains*, reflect, review, revolve, ruminate, stew over*, study, sweat over*, think over, turn over, weigh, woolgather*; SEE CONCEPT 17

multicolored [*adj*] *having various hues*
checkered, dappled, flecked, kaleidoscopic, marbled, motley, mottled, multicolor, particolored, piebald, pied, polychrome, prismatic, speckled, spotted, streaked, varicolored, veined, versicolor; SEE CONCEPT 618

multiculturalism [*n*] *doctrine acknowledging contributions and interests of many cultures*
cross-culturalism, cultural diversity, diversity, ethnic inclusiveness, ethnic mosaic, multiracialism, pluralism; SEE CONCEPTS 665,689

multimedia [*n*] *combined use of several media*
interactive media, intermedia, mixed media; SEE CONCEPT 274

multinational [*adj*] *international*
continental, global, intercontinental, multicultural, universal, worldwide; SEE CONCEPTS 536,772

multiple/multifarious [*adj*] *diversified, miscellaneous*
assorted, collective, conglomerate, different, diverse, diversiform, heterogeneous, indiscriminate, legion, manifold, many, mixed, motley, multiform, multiplex, multitudinal, multitudinous, numerous, populous, several, sundry, varied, variegated, various, voluminous; SEE CONCEPTS 564,762,772

multiply [*v*] *increase; reproduce*
accumulate, add, aggrandize, aggregate, augment, boost, breed, build up, compound, cube, double, enlarge, expand, extend, generate, heighten, magnify, manifold, mount, populate, procreate, produce, proliferate, propagate, raise, repeat, rise, spread, square; SEE CONCEPTS 171,374

multitude [*n*] *large group*
aggregation, army, assemblage, assembly, collection, commonalty, concourse, congregation, crowd, crush, drove, great number, heap, herd, horde, host, infinitude, infinity, jam*, legion, loads, lot, lots*, majority, mass, mob, much, myriad, number, numbers, ocean*, oodles*, people, plenitude, plurality, populace, proletariat, public, push*, quantity, scores*, sea, slew*, swarm, throng, turnout; SEE CONCEPTS 417,432

multitudinous [*adj*] *many, considerable*
abounding, abundant, copious, countless, great, heaps*, infinite, innumerable, innumerous, legion, manifold, multifarious, myriad, numberless, numerous, populous, profuse, several, sundry, teeming, uncountable, uncounted, unnumbered, untold, various, voluminous; SEE CONCEPTS 762,781

mum [*adj*] *silent*
bashful, buttoned up*, clammed up*, closemouthed, hushed, mute, muted, nonvocal, not forthcoming, not talkative, quiet, reserved, secretive, shy, soundless, speechless, still, tightlipped, tongue-tied, uncommunicative, unsociable, unspeaking, voiceless, wordless, zipped*; SEE CONCEPT 594

mumble [*v*] *say low and inarticulately*
grumble, maunder, murmur, mutter, ramble, rumble, say to oneself, speak, stammer, stutter,

swallow, talk, utter, verbalize, vocalize, voice, whimper, whine, whisper; SEE CONCEPTS 47,77

munch [*v*] *chew, eat*
bite, break up, champ, chomp, crunch, crush, grind, mash, masticate, press, reduce, ruminate, scrunch, smash, soften; SEE CONCEPTS 169,185

mundane [*adj*] *ordinary*
banal, commonplace, day-to-day, earthly, everyday, humdrum*, lowly, normal, prosaic, routine, workaday*, workday, worldly; SEE CONCEPT 547

municipal [*adj*] *concerning cities*
borough, burghal, city, civic, civil, community, corporate, domestic, home, incorporated, internal, local, metropolitan, native, public, town, urban; SEE CONCEPT 536

municipality [*n*] *city*
borough, community, district, metropolis, precinct, town, township, village; SEE CONCEPT 507

munificent [*adj*] *giving, generous*
beneficent, benevolent, big, big-hearted, bounteous, bountiful, charitable, free, handsome, kind, lavish, liberal, loose, magnanimous, openhanded, philanthropic, rich, unsparing, unstinting; SEE CONCEPTS 334,401

munitions [*n*] *ammunition*
ammo*, armament, arsenal, bombs, bullets, explosives, grenades, gunpowder, missiles, shells, torpedos, weapons; SEE CONCEPTS 498,500

murder [*n*] *killing*
annihilation, assassination, blood, bloodshed, butchery, carnage, crime, death, destruction, dispatching, felony, foul play*, hit*, homicide, knifing, liquidation, lynching, manslaughter, massacre, off*, offing*, one-way ticket*, rub out*, shooting, slaying, taking out*, terrorism, the business*, the works*; SEE CONCEPTS 192,252

murder [*v*] *kill*
abolish, asphyxiate, assassinate, behead, blot out*, bump off*, butcher, chill*, cool*, decapitate, defeat, destroy, dispatch, do in*, drub*, dust off*, electrocute, eliminate, eradicate, execute, exterminate, extinguish, finish, garotte, guillotine, hang, hit*, knife, knock off*, liquidate, lynch, mangle, mar, massacre, misuse, off*, put away*, rub out*, ruin, shoot, slaughter, slay, smother, snuff, spoil, strangle, take a life, take for a ride*, take out*, thrash*, waste*; SEE CONCEPTS 192,252

murderer [*n*] *person who kills*
assassin, butcher, criminal, cutthroat, enforcer, executioner, hit-and-run*, hit person*, homicide, killer, manslaughterer, perpetrator, slaughterer, slayer, soldier, trigger person*; SEE CONCEPT 412

murderous [*adj*] *difficult*
arduous, brutal, criminal, cruel, dangerous, deadly, destroying, destructive, devastating, exhausting, fell, ferocious, harrowing, hellish, killing, lethal, ruinous, sapping, savage, strenuous, unpleasant; SEE CONCEPTS 538,548,565

murk [*n*] *darkness*
dimness, dusk, gloom, murkiness; SEE CONCEPT 620

murky [*adj*] *gloomy, obscure*
black, caliginous, cheerless, cloudy, dark, darkened, dim, dingy, dirty, dismal, drab, dreary, dull, dun*, dusk, dusky, filthy, foggy, foul, fuzzy, glowering, gray, grubby*, impenetrable, lowering, misty, mucky, muddy, nasty, nebulous,

mo
mu

nubilous, overcast, roily, sad, smoky, somber, squalid, stormy, tenebrous, turbid, unclean; SEE CONCEPTS *617,618*

murmur [*n*] *low, continuous sound*
babble, buzz, buzzing, drone, grumble, hum, humming, mumble, murmuration, mutter, muttering, purr, rumble, rumor, undertone, whisper, whispering; SEE CONCEPTS *65,595*

murmur [*v*] *make low, continuous sound*
babble, burble, buzz, drip, drone, flow, growl, gurgle, hum, meander, moan, mumble, mutter, purl, purr, ripple, rumble, stage-whisper, stammer, stutter, susurrate, tinkle, trickle, utter, verbalize, vocalize, voice, whisper; SEE CONCEPTS *65,77*

muscle [*n1*] *large fibers of animal body*
beef, brawn, flesh, meat, might, sinew, tendon, thew, tissue; SEE CONCEPTS *393,420*

muscle [*n2*] *power, influence*
brawn, clout, energy, force, forcefulness, might, potency, sinew, stamina, strength, strong arm*, sturdiness, weight; SEE CONCEPTS *641,687*

muscular [*adj*] *powerfully built*
able-bodied, athletic, brawny, bruising, burly, fibrous, hefty, Herculean*, hulky, husky, lusty, mighty, muscled, powerful, powerhouse*, pumped up*, ripped*, robust, ropy, sinewy, stalwart, stout, strapping, stringy, strong, sturdy, tiger*, tough, vigorous, well-built, wiry; SEE CONCEPTS *485,489*

muse [*v*] *think about, dream*
be lost in thought*, brood, build castles in air*, chew over*, cogitate, consider, contemplate, deliberate, feel, meditate, moon*, mull over, percolate, ponder, puzzle over, reflect, revolve, roll, ruminate, speculate, think, think over, turn over, weigh; SEE CONCEPT *17*

museum [*n*] *place for viewing artifacts or exhibits*
archive, building, depository, exhibition, foundation, gallery, hall, institution, library, menagerie, repository, salon, storehouse, treasury, vault; SEE CONCEPTS *439,449*

mushroom [*v*] *sprout; grow quickly*
augment, blow up, boom, burgeon, burst, detonate, expand, explode, flourish, go off, grow, grow rapidly, increase, luxuriate, proliferate, shoot up, spread, spring up; SEE CONCEPTS *179,704*

mushy [*adj1*] *doughy, soft*
gelatinous, jelled, mashy*, muddy, pap*, pastelike, pulpous, pulpy, quaggy, semiliquid, semisolid, slushy, spongy, squashy*, squishy*; SEE CONCEPTS *604,606*

mushy [*adj2*] *romantic, corny*
bathetic, effusive, emotional, lovey-dovey*, maudlin, mawkish, saccharine, schmaltzy*, sentimental, sloppy*, slushy*, soppy*, sugary, syrupy, tear-jerking, weepy, wet; SEE CONCEPTS *267,542*

music [*n*] *sounds that are pleasant, harmonized*
a cappella, acoustic, air, bebop, bop, chamber, classical, folk, fusion, hard rock, harmony, heavy metal, hymn, instrumental, jazz, measure, melody, modern, opera, piece, plainsong, popular, ragtime, rap, refrain, rock, rock and roll, singing, song, soul, strain, swing, tune; SEE CONCEPTS *263,595*

musical [*adj*] *harmonic, lyrical*
agreeable, blending, chiming, choral, consonant, dulcet, euphonious, harmonious, lilting, mellow, melodic, melodious, operatic, orchestral, pleasing, rhythmic, silvery, songful, sweet, sweet-sounding, symphonic, symphonious, tuned, tuneful, vocal; SEE CONCEPT *594*

music hall [*n*] *concert hall*
amphitheater, auditorium, opera house, theater; SEE CONCEPTS *263,293,439,448*

musician [*n*] *person who performs music*
artist, artiste, composer, conductor, diva, entertainer, instrumentalist, performer, player, session player, soloist, virtuoso, vocalist; SEE CONCEPT *352*

muss [*n*] *disorder*
chaos, confusion, disarrangement, hash, mess, mess-up, mix-up*, muddle, shambles, turmoil; SEE CONCEPTS *230,674*

muss [*v*] *dishevel, disorder*
clutter, crumple, disarrange, disarray, disorganize, disrupt, disturb, jumble, mess up, mix up*, muddle, ruffle, rummage, rumple, tangle, tousle, upset, wrinkle; SEE CONCEPT *158*

must [*n*] *necessity, essential*
charge, commitment, committal, condition, devoir, duty, fundamental, imperative, necessary, need, obligation, ought, precondition, prerequisite, requirement, requisite, right, sine qua non; SEE CONCEPTS *646,709*

must [*v*] *ought, should*
be compelled, be destined, be directed, be doomed*, be driven*, be made, be necessitated, be obliged, be one's fate, be ordered, be required, got to, have, have got to*, have no choice, have to, must needs*, need, pushed to the wall*; SEE CONCEPT *650*

muster [*n*] *gathering*
aggregation, assemblage, assembly, call-up*, collection, company, congeries, convocation, crowd, draft, group, head count*, meeting, mobilization, nose count*, rally, roll, roll call*, roster, roundup*; SEE CONCEPTS *417,432*

muster [*v*] *gather, come together*
assemble, call together, call up, collect, congregate, congress, convene, convoke, enroll, enter, group, join up, marshal, meet, mobilize, organize, raise, rally, rendezvous, round up, sign on, sign up, summon; SEE CONCEPT *109*

musty [*adj1*] *stuffy, aged*
airless, ancient, antediluvian, antique, crumbling, dank, decayed, decrepit, dirty, dried-out*, dry, fetid, filthy, frowzy*, malodorous, mildewed, mildewy, moldy, moth-eaten*, noisome, old, putrid, rotten, smelly, spoiled, squalid, stale, stuffy; SEE CONCEPTS *578,598,603,797*

musty [*adj2*] *worn-out, clichéd*
ancient, antiquated, banal, common, commonplace, dull, hackneyed, hoary, obsolete, old-fashioned, old hat*, shopworn*, stale, stereotypical, threadbare, timeworn*, tired, trite, warmed-over*, worn; SEE CONCEPTS *267,530,578,797*

mutant [*n*] *mutation*
abnormality, deformity, deviation, freak, freak of nature, monster; SEE CONCEPTS *424,580*

mutation [*n*] *metamorphosis*
alteration, anomaly, change, deviant, deviation, evolution, innovation, modification, mutant, novelty, permutation, transfiguration, transformation, variation, vicissitude; SEE CONCEPTS *665,697*

mute [*adj*] *unable to speak*
aphasiac, aphasic, aphonic, muffled, mum, quiet, silenced, silent, speechless, tongueless, tongue-tied, unexpressed, unpronounced, unsounded, unspeaking, unspoken, voiceless, wordless; SEE CONCEPT *593*

mute [*v*] *muffle, tone down sound*
benumb, bottle up*, cork up*, dampen, deaden, decrease the volume, drown, gag, hush, keep it down*, lower, moderate, muzzle, pipe down*, put damper on*, put the lid on*, reduce, silence, soften, soft-pedal*, subdue, turn down; SEE CONCEPTS *65,240*

mutilate [*v*] *maim, damage*
adulterate, amputate, batter, bowdlerize, butcher, cripple, crush, cut to pieces, cut up, deface, disable, disfigure, dismember, distort, expurgate, hack*, hash up*, hurt, injure, lacerate, lame, mangle, mar, mess up*, ravage, scratch, spoil, weaken; SEE CONCEPTS *176,246*

mutilated [*adj*] *dismembered*
amputated, disfigured, maimed, mangled, marred; SEE CONCEPTS *137,246,250*

mutinous [*adj*] *rebellious*
anarchistic, contumacious, defiant, disloyal, disobedient, disorderly, dissident, factious, iconoclastic, insubordinate, insurgent, insurrectionary, radical, rebel, revolutionary, rioting, riotous, subversive, traitorous, treasonable, ungovernable, unmanageable; SEE CONCEPTS *401,529,542*

mutiny [*n*] *defiance, resistance*
disobedience, insubordination, insurrection, refusal to obey, revolt, revolution, riot, rising, strike, uprising; SEE CONCEPTS *300,388,633*

mutiny [*v*] *defy, revolt*
be insubordinate, disobey, insurrect, kick over, rebel, refuse to obey, resist, rise against, rise up, strike; SEE CONCEPTS *300,384*

mutter [*v*] *grumble, mumble*
complain, creak, groan, grouch*, grouse, growl, grunt, moan, muddle, murmur, rumble, snarl, sputter, swallow, whisper; SEE CONCEPTS *52,77*

mutual [*adj*] *shared, common*
associated, bilateral, collective, communal, conjoint, conjunct, connected, convertible, correlative, dependent, give-and-take*, given and taken*, interactive, interchangeable, interchanged, interdependent, intermutual, joint, partaken, participated, public, reciprocal, reciprocated, related, requited, respective, returned, two-sided*, united; SEE CONCEPTS *563,708*

mutual fund [*n*] *stock fund*
bond fund, hedge fund, individual retirement account, investment fund, IRA, 401(k) fund, money market funds, retirement plan; SEE CONCEPTS *330,332,340*

mutually [*adv*] *together*
all at once, as a group, by agreement, by contract, commonly, conjointly, cooperatively, en masse, in collaboration, in combination, in conjunction, jointly, reciprocally, respectively; SEE CONCEPTS *544,577*

muzzle [*n*] *covering for control*
cage, cover, envelope, gag, guard, sheath, wrap; SEE CONCEPT *172*

muzzle [*v*] *gag, quiet*
bottle up*, censor, check, choke, clamp down on*, cork, crack down on*, curb, dry up*, dummy up*, hush, ice*, muffle, prevent, quieten,

repress, restrain, restrict, shush, shut down, silence, squash, squelch, stifle, still, stop, suppress, tongue-tie*, trammel; SEE CONCEPTS *121,250*

myopic [*adj*] *able only to see things near at hand*
astigmatic, biased, blind, halfsighted, nearsighted, presbyopic, shortsighted; SEE CONCEPT *619*

myriad [*adj*] *innumerable*
countless, endless, gobs*, heaping, immeasurable, incalculable, infinite, multiple, multitudinous, no end of*, numberless, thousand-and-one*, uncounted, untold, variable; SEE CONCEPTS *762,781*

myriad [*n*] *a lot*
army, flood, heap, horde, host, loads*, mint, mountain*, multitude, oodles*, scores, slew, stacks*, swarm, thousands*; SEE CONCEPT *787*

mysterious [*adj*] *secret, concealed*
abstruse, alchemistic, arcane, astrological, baffling, cabalistic, covert, cryptic, curious, dark, difficult, enigmatic, enigmatical, equivocal, esoteric, furtive, hidden, impenetrable, incomprehensible, inexplicable, inscrutable, insoluble, magical, mystical, mystifying, necromantic, obscure, occult, oracular, perplexing, puzzling, recondite, secretive, sphinxlike, spiritual, strange, subjective, symbolic, transcendental, uncanny, unfathomable, unknowable, unknown, unnatural, veiled, weird; SEE CONCEPTS *529,576*

mystery [*n*] *puzzle, secret*
abstruseness, brainteaser*, braintwister*, charade, chiller, cliffhanger*, closed book*, conundrum, crux, cryptogram, difficulty, enigma, grabber, inscrutability, inscrutableness, mindboggler*, mystification, occult, oracle, perplexity, poser, problem, puzzlement, question, rebus, riddle, rune, secrecy, sixty-four-thousand-dollar question*, sphinx, stickler, stumper, subtlety, teaser, thriller, tough nut to crack*, twister, whodunit*, why*; SEE CONCEPTS *282,532,696*

mystic/mystical [*adj*] *secret, esoteric*
abstruse, anagogic, arcane, cabalistic, cryptic, enigmatical, hidden, imaginary, impenetrable, inscrutable, magic, magical, metaphysical, mysterial, mysterious, necromantic, nonrational, numinous, occult, otherworldly, paranormal, preternatural, quixotic, sorcerous, spiritual, supernatural, telestic, thaumaturgic, transcendental, unaccountable, unknowable, visionary, wizardly; SEE CONCEPTS *529,549,582*

mystify [*v*] *bewilder, confuse*
baffle, bamboozle*, beat*, befog*, buffalo*, confound, deceive, elude, escape, floor*, fog in*, hoodwink*, lick*, lie, perplex, puzzle, stump*, throw*, trick; SEE CONCEPT *16*

mystique [*n*] *person's strong impression*
attitude, awe, character, charisma, charm, complex, fascination, glamour, magic, nature, spell, temperament; SEE CONCEPT *411*

myth [*n*] *fictitious story, often ancient*
allegory, apologue, creation, delusion, fable, fabrication, fairy story, fancy, fantasy, fiction, figment, folk ballad, folk tale, illusion, imagination, invention, legend, lore, mythos, parable, saga, superstition, tale, tall story*, tradition; SEE CONCEPT *282*

mythical/mythological [*adj*] *make-believe, fairy-tale*
allegorical, chimerical, created, fabled, fabricated, fabulous, false, fanciful, fantasy, fictitious,

fictive, folkloric, imaginary, invented, legendary, made-up, mythic, nonexistent, pretended, storied, supposititious, traditional, unreal, untrue, visionary, whimsical; SEE CONCEPTS 267,582

mythology [*n*] *folklore*
belief, conviction, folk tales, legend, lore, mythicism, mythos, myths, stories, tradition; SEE CONCEPT 282

N

nab [*v*] *seize*
apprehend, arrest, capture, catch, clutch, cop*, detain, grab, nail*, pick up*, run in*, snatch*, take*, take into custody; SEE CONCEPTS 90,317

nadir [*n*] *lowest point*
all-time low, base, bottom, floor, low point, record low, rock bottom, zero level; SEE CONCEPT 442

nag [*v*] *harass, bother*
annoy, badger, bait, berate, bug*, carp at, dog*, eat*, egg*, find fault, fuss, give a hard time*, goad, harry, heckle, hector, hound, importune, irk, irritate, needle, nudge*, pester, pick at, plague, prod, provoke, ride, scold, take it out on*, tease, torment, upbraid, urge, vex, work on*, worry; SEE CONCEPTS 7,19,52

nail [*v1*] *fasten, fix with pointed object*
attach, beat, bind, drive, hammer, hit, hold, join, pin, pound, secure, sock*, spike, strike, tack, whack*; SEE CONCEPTS 85,160,189

nail [*v2*] *capture, arrest*
apprehend, bag, catch, collar*, detain, get*, hook*, nab, pinch*, prehend, secure, seize, take*; SEE CONCEPTS 90,317

naive [*adj*] *childlike, trusting*
aboveboard, artless, callow, candid, confiding, countrified, credulous, forthright, frank, fresh, green*, guileless, gullible, harmless, ignorant, impulsive, ingenuous, innocent, innocuous, instinctive, jejune, lamb*, like a babe in the woods*, natural, open, original, patsy*, plain, simple, simple-minded, sincere, spontaneous, square, sucker*, unaffected, unjaded, unpretentious, unschooled, unsophisticated, unsuspecting, unsuspicious, untaught, unworldly, virgin, wide-eyed*; SEE CONCEPTS 401,542,678

naïveté [*n*] *innocence, gullibility*
artlessness, callowness, candor, childishness, credulity, frankness, guilelessness, inexperience, ingenuousness, naturalness, openness, simplicity; SEE CONCEPTS 657,678

naked [*adj1*] *without covering*
au naturel, bald, bare, bared, bare-skinned, barren, defenseless, denuded, disrobed, divested, exposed, helpless, in birthday suit*, in dishabille*, in the altogether*, in the buff*, in the raw*, leafless, natural, nude, open, peeled*, raw, stark-naked*, stripped, threadbare, unclad, unclothed, unconcealed, uncovered, undraped, undressed, unprotected, unveiled, vulnerable, without a stitch*; SEE CONCEPTS 485,589

naked [*adj2*] *manifest, evident*
artless, blatant, disclosed, discovered, dry, matter-of-fact, obvious, open, overt, palpable,

patent, plain, pure, revealed, sheer, simple, stark, unadorned, undisguised, unexaggerated, unmistakable, unqualified, unvarnished; SEE CONCEPTS 267,529

namby-pamby [*n*] *pansy*
baby*, caitiff, chicken*, chicken heart*, chicken liver*, coward, cry-baby, fraidy-cat*, jellyfish*, lily liver, milksop, momma's boy*, pantywaist, quitter, scaredy cat*, sissy*, weakling, wimp, wuss*, wussy*, yellow, yellow belly*; SEE CONCEPT 423

name [*n1*] *title given to something, someone*
agname, agnomen, alias, appellation, autograph, autonym, brand, cognomen, compellation, denomination, designation, epithet, eponym, flag*, handle*, head, heading, label, matronymic, moniker, monogram, nickname, nom de guerre, nom de plume, nomen, patronymic, pen name, pet name, place name, prenomen, proper name, pseudonym, rubric, sign, signature, sobriquet, stage name, style, surname, tag, term, trade name; SEE CONCEPTS 268,683

name [*n2*] *fame, distinction*
character, credit, eminence, esteem, honor, note, praise, renown, rep*, report, reputation, repute; SEE CONCEPTS 388,668

name [*n3*] *celebrity*
big name*, celeb*, entertainer, headliner, hero, lion*, luminary, notability, notable, personality, somebody*, star, superstar; SEE CONCEPTS 352,366

name [*v1*] *give a title*
baptize, call, characterize, christen, classify, cognominate, define, denominate, designate, dub, entitle, give a handle*, identify, label, nickname, nomenclature, put tag on, style, tag, term, ticket, title; SEE CONCEPT 62

name [*v2*] *choose, designate*
announce, appoint, cite, classify, commission, connote, declare, delegate, denote, elect, identify, index, instance, list, make, mark, mention, nominate, peg*, pin down*, point to, put down for, put finger on*, recognize, refer to, remark, select, signify, single out, slot, specify, suggest, tab, tag, tap; SEE CONCEPTS 41,50,88

name-dropper [*n*] *snob*
social climber, status seeker; SEE CONCEPT 423

nameless [*adj*] *unknown, anonymous*
incognito, inconspicuous, innominate, obscure, pseudonymous, unacknowledged, uncelebrated, undesignated, undistinguished, unfamed, unheard-of, unnamed, unnoted, unsung, untitled, whatchamacallit*, X*; SEE CONCEPTS 267,576

namely [*adv*] *that is to say*
by way of explanation, especially, expressly, id est*, i.e., in other words, in plain English*, particularly, scilicet, specially, specifically, strictly speaking, that is, to wit, videlicet, viz.; SEE CONCEPT 557

nanny [*n*] *children's nurse*
au pair, baby-sitter, governess, nursemaid, wet nurse; SEE CONCEPT 295

nap [*n1*] *short, light sleep*
break, catnap, doze, few z's*, forty winks*, interlude, intermission, microsleep*, nod, pause, respite, rest, shuteye*, siesta, snooze*, spot; SEE CONCEPT 315

nap [*n2*] *grain of material*
down, feel, fiber, grit, outside, pile, roughness,

shag, smoothness, surface, tooth, wale, warp, weave, weft, woof; SEE CONCEPTS *473,611*

nap [*v*] *take a short, light sleep*
catch forty winks*, catnap, doze, drop off*, drowse, get some shut-eye*, grab some z's*, nod, nod off, rack*, relax, rest, sleep, snooze, take a siesta*, take a snooze*; SEE CONCEPTS *210,315*

napkin [*n*] *linen*
cloth, doily, moist towelette, serviette, towel, wipe; SEE CONCEPT *473*

nappy [*adj*] *fuzzy*
downy, frizzy, furry, hairy, kinky, napped, velutinous, woolly; SEE CONCEPT *606*

narcissistic [*adj*] *concerned only with oneself*
conceited, egotistic, egotistical, self-centered, self-involved, self-loving, stuck-up*, vain, vainglorious; SEE CONCEPTS *401,404*

narcotic [*adj*] *dulling, painkilling*
analgesic, anesthetic, calming, deadening, hypnotic, numbing, opiate, sedative, somnifacient, somnific, somnolent, somnorific, soporiferous, soporific, stupefacient, stupefactive, stupefying; SEE CONCEPT *537*

narcotic [*n*] *powerful drug inducing anesthesia or sleep*
analgesic, anesthetic, anodyne, dope*, downer*, fix*, hard drug, hard stuff*, heroin, hypnotic, junk*, laudanum, lenitive, merchandise*, nepenthe, opiate, opium, painkiller, sedative, somnifacient, soporific, stuff*, stupefacient, tranquilizer; SEE CONCEPT *307*

narrate [*v*] *describe, detail*
characterize, chronicle, delineate, depict, descant, disclose, discourse, enumerate, expatiate, give an account of, hold forth, make known, paint, picture, portray, proclaim, recite, recount, rehearse, relate, repeat, report, reveal, set forth, spin, state, tell, tell a story, unfold; SEE CONCEPTS *55,72*

narration [*n*] *description, reading*
account, anecdote, explanation, narrative, recital, recountal, recounting, rehearsal, relation, report, story, storytelling, tale, telling, voice-over*, yarn*; SEE CONCEPTS *55,72,282*

narrative [*adj*] *storylike, chronological*
anecdotal, fictional, fictive, historical, narrated, recounted, reported, retold, sequential; SEE CONCEPT *267*

narrative [*n*] *story, tale*
account, anecdote, book, chronicle, chronology, description, detail, fiction, history, line, long and short of it*, narration, plot, potboiler*, recount, report, statement, version, yarn*; SEE CONCEPTS *271,282*

narrator [*n*] *storyteller*
author, chronicler, describer, novelist, raconteur, reporter, teller of tales, writer, yarn spinner; SEE CONCEPTS *348,356*

narrow [*adj1*] *confined, restricted*
attenuated, circumscribed, close, compressed, confining, constricted, contracted, cramped, definite, determinate, exclusive, exiguous, fine, fixed, incapacious, limited, linear, meager, near, paltry, pent, pinched, precarious, precise, scant, scanty, select, set, shrunken, slender, slim, small, spare, strait, taper, tapered, tapering, thin, threadlike, tight; SEE CONCEPTS *554,773*

narrow [*adj2*] *intolerant, small-minded*
biased, bigoted, conservative, conventional, dog-matic, hidebound, illiberal, inexorable, inflexible, narrow-minded, obdurate, parochial, partial, prejudiced, reactionary; SEE CONCEPTS *403,542*

narrow [*adj3*] *cheap, stingy*
avaricious, close, mean, mercenary, scrimpy*, tight*, ungenerous; SEE CONCEPT *334*

narrow [*v*] *reduce, simplify*
circumscribe, constrict, contract, diminish, limit, taper, tighten; SEE CONCEPTS *130,236,247*

narrowly [*adv*] *just, closely*
almost, barely, by a hair*, by a whisker*, by narrow margin, carefully, close, nearly, only just, painstakingly, scarcely, scrutinizingly; SEE CONCEPTS *544,799*

narrow-minded [*adj*] *biased, intolerant*
bigoted, conservative, conventional, hidebound, illiberal, insular, narrow, opinionated, parochial, petty, prejudiced, provincial, reactionary, short-sighted, small-minded, strait-laced, unenlarged; SEE CONCEPTS *403,542*

nasty [*adj1*] *disgusting, offensive*
awful, beastly, bum*, dirty, disagreeable, fierce, filthy, foul, gross, grubby, hellish, horrible, horrid, icky*, impure, loathsome, lousy, malodorous, mephitic, murderous*, nauseating, noisome, noxious, objectionable, obnoxious, obscene, odious, ornery, outrageous, poison, polluted, raunchy*, repellent, repugnant, repulsive, revolting, rough, sickening, soiled, squalid, stinking, tough, unappetizing, unclean, uncleanly, ungodly, unholy, unpleasant, vile, vulgar, yucky*; SEE CONCEPTS *485,548,571*

nasty [*adj2*] *indecent, smutty*
blue*, coarse, dirty, filthy, foul, gross, immodest, immoral, improper, impure, indecorous, indelicate, lascivious, lewd, licentious, obscene, pornographic, raunchy*, ribald, scatological, shameful, unseemly, vulgar, wicked, X-rated*; SEE CONCEPTS *372,545*

nasty [*adj3*] *bad-tempered, mean*
abusive, annoying, beastly, critical, cruel, despicable, disagreeable, distasteful, evil, fierce, hateful, malevolent, malicious, malign, malignant, ornery, ruthless, sarcastic, sordid, spiteful, squalid, unkind, unpleasant, vicious, vile, wicked; SEE CONCEPT *401*

nasty [*adj4*] *injurious, dangerous*
bad, critical, damaging, harmful, noxious, painful, poisonous, serious, severe, ugly; SEE CONCEPT *537*

nation [*n*] *country with its own government*
body politic, commonwealth, community, democracy, domain, dominion, empire, land, monarchy, people, populace, population, principality, public, race, realm, republic, society, sovereignty, state, tribe, union; SEE CONCEPT *510*

national [*adj*] *concerning a country with a government*
civic, civil, communal, countrywide, domestic, ethnic, federal, general, governmental, home, imperial, inland, internal, interstate, nationwide, native, politic, political, public, royal, social, societal, sovereign, state, sweeping, vernacular, widespread; SEE CONCEPT *536*

nationality [*n*] *place of birth*
allegiance, body politic, citizenship, community, country, ethnic group, nation, native land, origin, political home, race, society; SEE CONCEPTS *380,510*

my
na

native [*adj1*] *innate, inherent*
built-in, congenital, connate, connatural, constitutional, endemic, essential, fundamental, genuine, hereditary, implanted, inborn, inbred, indigenous, ingrained, inherited, instinctive, intrinsic, inveterate, inwrought, natal, natural, original, real, unacquired, wild; SEE CONCEPTS *404,549*

native [*adj2*] *domestic, home*
aboriginal, autochthonous, belonging, endemic, from, homegrown, homemade, indigenous, inland, internal, local, municipal, national, original, primary, primeval, primitive, regional, related, vernacular; SEE CONCEPT *536*

native [*n*] *person born in the country in which he/she dwells*
aboriginal, aborigine, ancient, autochthon, citizen, dweller, home towner, indigene, inhabitant, local, national; SEE CONCEPT *413*

native land [*n*] *homeland*
fatherland, God's country, home, mother country, motherland, native soil, the old country*; SEE CONCEPTS *510,515,648*

natty [*adj*] *dapper*
chic, chichi, classy, clean, dainty, dashing, dressed to kill*, dressed to the nines*, elegant, fashionable, neat, prim, sharp, slick, smart, snazzy*, spiffy*, spruce, spruced up, stylish, swanky, trim, well-groomed; SEE CONCEPT *579*

natural [*adj1*] *normal, everyday*
accustomed, anticipated, characteristic, common, commonplace, congenital, connatural, consistent, constant, counted on, customary, essential, familiar, general, habitual, inborn, indigenous, ingenerate, inherent, innate, instinctive, intuitive, involuntary, legitimate, logical, looked for, matter-of-course, natal, native, ordinary, prevailing, prevalent, probable, reasonable, regular, relied on, spontaneous, typic, typical, unacquired, uncontrolled, uniform, universal, usual; SEE CONCEPTS *530,547*

natural [*adj2*] *open, unaffected*
artless, being oneself, candid, childlike, credulous, direct, easy, folksy, forthright, frank, genuine, homey*, ignorant, impulsive, inartificial, ingenuous, innocent, instinctive, laid-back*, naive, plain, primitive, provincial, real, rustic, simple, simplehearted, sincere, spontaneous, straightforward, trusting, unassumed, uncontrived, undesigning, unembarrassed, unfeigned, unforced, unlabored, unpolished, unpretentious, unschooled, unsophisticated, unstudied, unworldly, up-front*; SEE CONCEPTS *267,401,404*

natural [*adj3*] *organic, unrefined*
agrarian, agrestal, crude, native, plain, pure, raw, unbleached, uncultivated, undomesticated, unmixed, unpolished, unprocessed, whole, wild; SEE CONCEPTS *462,485*

naturally [*adv*] *as anticipated*
artlessly, but of course*, by birth, by nature, candidly, casually, characteristically, commonly, consistently, customarily, easily, freely, generally, genuinely, habitually, impulsively, informally, innocently, instinctively, normally, openly, ordinarily, readily, simply, spontaneously, typically, unaffectedly, uniformly, unpretentiously, usually; SEE CONCEPT *544*

natural selection [*n*] *Darwinism*
Darwinian theory, evolution, evolutionism, social Darwinism, survival of the fittest; SEE CONCEPT *704*

nature [*n1*] *character, disposition*
attributes, being, bottom line*, complexion, constitution, description, drift, essence, essentiality, features, heart*, humor, individualism, individuality, like, makeup, meat*, mood, name of game*, name of tune*, nature of beast*, outlook, personality, point, quality, score, stuff, temper, temperament, texture, traits, type; SEE CONCEPTS *411,682*

nature [*n2*] *type, kind*
anatomy, brand, cast, category, character, color, conformation, description, figure, framework, ilk, shape, sort, species, stripe*, structure, style, variety, way; SEE CONCEPT *378*

nature [*n3*] *earth, creation*
cosmos, country, countryside, environment, forest, generation, landscape, macrocosm, megacosm, natural history, outdoors, scenery, seascape, setting, universe, view, world; SEE CONCEPTS *407,429,509,511*

naughty [*adj1*] *bad, misbehaved*
annoying, badly behaved*, contrary, disobedient, disorderly, evil, exasperating, fiendish, fractious, froward, headstrong, impish, indecorous, insubordinate, intractable, mischievous, obstreperous, perverse, playful, rascally, raunchy, recalcitrant, refractory, rough, rowdy, sinful, teasing, tough, ungovernable, unmanageable, unruly, wanton, wayward, wicked, willful, worthless, wrong; SEE CONCEPT *401*

naughty [*adj2*] *obscene, vulgar*
adult, bawdy, blue*, dirty*, hot*, improper, lascivious, lewd, loose*, off-color*, pornographic, purple*, ribald, risqué, steamy*; SEE CONCEPTS *372,545*

nausea [*n*] *sickness in stomach; revulsion*
abhorrence, aversion, biliousness, disgust, hatred, loathing, offense, qualm, qualms, queasiness, regurgitation, rejection, repugnance, retching, squeamishness, vomiting; SEE CONCEPTS *316,410*

nauseate [*v*] *make sick; disgust*
bother, disturb, horrify, offend, reluct, repel, repulse, revolt, sicken; SEE CONCEPTS *14,308*

nauseating [*adj*] *nauseous*
abhorrent, detestable, disgusting, distasteful, fulsome, loathsome, offensive, repugnant, repulsive, revolting, sickening; SEE CONCEPTS *314,529*

nauseous [*adj*] *disgusting*
abhorrent, brackish, detestable, distasteful, ill, loathsome, nauseated, nauseating, offensive, queasy, repugnant, repulsive, revolting, rocky*, seasick, sick, sick as dog*, sickening, squeamish; SEE CONCEPTS *314,529*

nautical/naval [*adj*] *concerning ships, sea*
abyssal, aquatic, boating, cruising, deep-sea, marine, maritime, navigating, navigational, oceangoing, oceanic, oceanographic, pelagic, rowing, sailing, sailorly, salty, seafaring, seagoing, sealoving, thalassic, yachting; SEE CONCEPT *536*

navigate [*v*] *guide along route, often over water*
captain*, cross, cruise, direct, drive, handle, head out for*, helm, journey, lay the course*, maneuver, operate, pilot, plan, pilot, ride out, sail, skipper*, steer, voyage; SEE CONCEPTS *148,187,224*

navigation [*n*] *traveling, guiding along route, often over water*
aeronautics, boating, cruising, exploration, fly-

na
ne

ing, helmsmanship, nautics, navigating, ocean travel, pilotage, piloting, plotting a course, sailing, seafaring, seamanship, shipping, steerage, steering, voyage, voyaging, yachting; SEE CONCEPTS 155,187,224

navigator [*n*] *course plotter*
helmsman, pilot, steersman, wheelman; SEE CONCEPT 348

navy [*n*] *fleet*
argosy, armada, flotilla, marine defense, merchant marine, naval force, sea force, sea power, vessels, warships; SEE CONCEPTS 322,432,506

naysayer [*n*] *pessimist*
complainer, cynic, defeatist, downer, gloomy, killjoy*, misanthrope, party pooper*, prophet of doom*, sourpuss*, wet blanket*; SEE CONCEPTS 412,423

near [*adj*] *close by physically*
abreast, abutting, adjacent, adjoining, alongside, along toward, approximal, around, at close quarters, available, beside, bordering, burning, close, close-at-hand, close-by, close shave*, contiminous, contiguous, convenient, hair's breadth*, handy, immediate, in close proximity*, near-at-hand*, nearby, neighboring, next door*, nigh*, not remote, practically, proximal, proximate, ready, side-by-side, touching, vincinal, warm*, within stone's throw*; SEE CONCEPTS 586,778

near [*adj2*] *close in time; forthcoming*
approaching, approximate, at hand, coming, comparative, expected, imminent, impending, in the offing*, looming, near-at-hand*, next, relative; SEE CONCEPTS 812,820

near [*adj3*] *familiar*
affecting, akin*, allied, attached, close, connected, dear, friendly, intimate, related, touching; SEE CONCEPT 555

nearby [*adj*] *adjoining*
adjacent, close, close-at-hand, close-by, contiguous, convenient, handy, immediate, neighboring, proximate, ready; SEE CONCEPTS 586,778

nearby [*adv*] *within reach*
about, at close quarters, close, close at hand, hard, near, near-at-hand*, nigh*, not far away; SEE CONCEPTS 586,778

nearing [*adj*] *approaching*
advancing, approximating, oncoming, forthcoming, imminent, impending, oncoming, threatening, upcoming; SEE CONCEPTS 548,820

nearly [*adv*] *almost*
about, all but*, approaching, approximately, as good as*, circa*, close but no cigar*, closely, give or take a little*, in effect, in essence, in substance, in the ballpark*, in the neighborhood*, just about, more or less, most, much, nearabout, not quite, practically, pretty near, roughly, round, roundly, some, somewhere, upwards of*, virtually, well-nigh*, within a little*; SEE CONCEPT 566

near miss [*n*] *close call*
close shave, narrow escape, near hit; SEE CONCEPT 747

nearsighted [*adj*] *myopic*
blind as a bat*, purblind, shortsighted; SEE CONCEPT 619

neat [*adj*] *arranged well, uncluttered*
accurate, apple-pie order*, chic*, correct, dainty, dapper, elegant, exact, fastidious, finical, finicky, immaculate, in good order, in good shape, methodical, natty, neat as a pin*, nice, orderly, pre-

cise, prim, proper, regular, shipshape*, sleek, slick, smart, spick-and-span*, spotless, spruce, systematic, tidy, trim, well-groomed, well-kept; SEE CONCEPTS 485,589,621

neat [*adj2*] *clever, practiced*
able, adept, adroit, agile, apt, artful, deft, dexterous, efficient, effortless, elegant, expert, finished, graceful, handy, nimble, precise, proficient, quick, ready, skillful, speedy, stylish, well-judged; SEE CONCEPTS 527,542

neaten [*v*] *tidy*
arrange, clean, clear the decks*, fix up, groom, order, put in good shape, put in order, shape up, spruce up*, straighten up, whip into shape*; SEE CONCEPT 250

neatly [*adv*] *tidily*
accurately, adeptly, adroitly, aptly, cleanly, efficiently, expertly, fastidiously, handily, methodically, nicely, orderly, precisely, skillfully, sprucely; SEE CONCEPTS 326,485,585,589

nebulous [*adj*] *confused, obscure*
ambiguous, amorphous, cloudy, dark, dim, hazy, imprecise, indefinite, indeterminate, indistinct, misty, murky, shadowy, shapeless, uncertain, unclear, unformed, vague; SEE CONCEPTS 535,617

necessarily [*adv*] *inevitably, certainly*
accordingly, as a matter of course*, automatically, axiomatically, beyond one's control*, by definition, by its own nature*, cardinally, come what may*, compulsorily, consequently, exigently, from within*, fundamentally, incontrovertibly, indubitably, ineluctably, inescapably, inexorably, irresistibly, naturally, no doubt, of course, of necessity, perforce, positively, pressingly, significantly, undoubtedly, unpreventably, unquestionably, vitally, willy-nilly*, without fail*; SEE CONCEPTS 535,544

necessary [*adj*] *essential*
all-important, basic, binding, bottom-line*, cardinal, chief, compelling, compulsory, crucial, decisive, de rigueur*, elementary, exigent, expedient, fundamental, imperative, incumbent on, indispensable, mandatory, momentous, name of game*, needed, needful, obligatory, paramount, prerequisite, pressing, prime, principal, quintessential, required, requisite, significant, specified, unavoidable, urgent, vital, wanted; SEE CONCEPTS 546,568

necessary [*adj2*] *inevitable*
assured, certain, fated, imminent, ineluctable, ineludible, inerrant, inescapable, inevasible, inexorable, infallible, returnless, unavoidable, undeniable, unescapable; SEE CONCEPTS 535,548

necessitate [*v*] *call for, make necessary*
ask, behoove, cause, coerce, command, compel, constrain, crave, demand, drive, entail, force, impel, make, oblige, postulate, require, take; SEE CONCEPTS 53,242,646

necessity [*n*] *need, essentiality*
call, cause, claim, compulsion, demand, desideratum, duress, essence, essential, exaction, exigency, fundamental, godsend*, imperative, indispensability, inevitability, inexorableness, life or death*, must, necessary, needfulness, no alternative, no choice, obligation, pinch, precondition, prerequisite, privation, requirement, requisite, sine qua non, stress, undeniability, urgency, vital part, vitals, want; SEE CONCEPTS 646,709

necking [*n*] *kissing*
canoodling, caressing, cuddling, embracing, fondling, lovemaking, making love*, making out*, parking*, petting, smooching, sucking face*; SEE CONCEPTS *185,375*

necklace [*n*] *chain*
beads, carcanet, choker, jewelry, lavalliere, locket, pearls, pendant, riviere, strand, string; SEE CONCEPT *446*

necromancy [*n*] *sorcery*
abracadabra*, alchemy, bewitchment, black art, black magic, charm, conjuring, devilry, divination, enchantment, evil eye, hocus-pocus*, incantation, jinx, magic, mumbo-jumbo*, mysticism, occultism, spell, thaumaturgy, voodoo, witchcraft, witchery, witching, wizardry; SEE CONCEPTS *370,689*

necropolis [*n*] *cemetery*
boot hill*, catacomb, charnel, charnel house, churchyard, city of the dead*, crypt, funerary grounds, God's acre*, graveyard, potter's field, sepulcher, tomb, vault; SEE CONCEPTS *305,368*

need [*n1*] *want, requirement*
charge, commitment, committal, compulsion, demand, desideratum, devoir, duty, essential, exigency, extremity, longing, must, obligation, occasion, ought, requisite, right, the urge, urgency, use, weakness, wish; SEE CONCEPTS *20,709*

need [*n2*] *poverty*
deprivation, destitution, distress, extremity, impecuniousness, impoverishment, inadequacy, indigence, insufficiency, lack, neediness, paucity, pennilessness, penury, privation, shortage, want; SEE CONCEPTS *335,709*

need [*n3*] *emergency; pressing lack*
deficiency, exigency, inadequacy, insufficiency, necessity, obligation, shortage, urgency, want; SEE CONCEPTS *646,709*

need [*v*] *want something*
be deficient, be deprived, be down and out*, be hard up*, be inadequate, be in need of, be in want, be needy, be poor, be short, be without, call for, claim, covet, crave, demand, desire, die for*, do without, drive for*, exact, feel a dearth of*, feel the necessity for, feel the pinch*, go hungry*, hanker, have occasion for, have occasion to, have use for*, hunger, hurt for, lack, long, lust, miss, necessitate, pine, require, suffer privation, thirst, wish, yearn, yen for; SEE CONCEPTS *20,646*

needle [*v*] *tease, annoy*
aggravate, badger, bait, bedevil, bother, examine, gnaw, goad, harass, hector, irk, irritate, nag, nettle, pester, plague, prick, prod, provoke, question, quiz, ride*, rile, ruffle, spur, sting, taunt, tweak*, worry; SEE CONCEPTS *7,19,54*

needless [*adj*] *unnecessary, groundless*
causeless, dispensable, excessive, expendable, gratuitous, inessential, nonessential, pointless, redundant, superfluous, uncalled-for, undesired, unrequired, unwanted, useless; SEE CONCEPTS *546,575*

needlework [*n*] *needlepoint*
crocheting, darning, embroidery, knitting, lace, quilting, sewing, stitchery, stitching, tatting; SEE CONCEPT *128*

needy [*adj*] *deprived, impoverished*
beggared, dead broke*, destitute, dirt poor*, disadvantaged, down-and-out*, down at heel*,

down to last cent*, flat*, impecunious, indigent, necessitous, penniless, penurious, poor, poverty-stricken, underprivileged, unprosperous; SEE CONCEPT *334*

ne'er-do-well [*n*] *irresponsible person*
bum*, good-for-nothing, idler, lazybones*, loafer, sloucher, wastrel; SEE CONCEPT *412*

nefarious [*adj*] *bad, sinful*
abominable, atrocious, base, corrupt, criminal, degenerate, depraved, detestable, dreadful, evil, execrable, flagitious, flagrant, foul, glaring, gross, heinous, horrible, infamous, infernal, iniquitous, miscreant, monstrous, odious, opprobrious, outrageous, perverse, putrid, rank, rotten, shameful, treacherous, vicious, vile, villainous, wicked; SEE CONCEPTS *401,545,548*

negate [*v*] *contradict, countermand*
abate, abolish, abrogate, annihilate, annul, belie, blackball*, break with*, cancel, cancel out, controvert, countercheck, cross*, deny, ding*, disaffirm, disallow, disprove, dump*, fly in the face of*, frustrate, gainsay, impugn, invalidate, kill, negative, neutralize, nullify, oppose, put down, quash*, rebut, redress, refute, repeal, rescind, retract, reverse, revoke, stonewall*, traverse, turn down, turn thumbs down*, undo, vitiate, void; SEE CONCEPTS *46,50,88,121*

negation [*n*] *contradiction, denial*
antithesis, antonym, blank, cancellation, contrary, converse, counterpart, disavowal, disclaimer, forget it*, gainsaying, inverse, negatory, neutralization, no, nonexistence, nothingness, nullification, nullity, opposite, opposition, proscription, refusal, rejection, renunciation, repudiation, reverse, vacuity, veto, void; SEE CONCEPTS *121,278,685*

negative [*adj*] *bad, contradictory*
abrogating, adverse, against, annulling, antagonistic, anti, balky, colorless, con, contrary, contravening, counteractive, cynical, denying, detrimental, disallowing, disavowing, dissentient, dissenting, gainsaying, gloomy, impugning, invalidating, jaundiced, naysaying, neutralizing, nugatory, nullifying, opposing, pessimistic, privative, recusant, refusing, rejecting, removed, repugnant, resisting, resistive, unaffirmative, unenthusiastic, unfavorable, uninterested, unwilling, weak; SEE CONCEPTS *267,403,570*

negative [*n*] *contradiction*
denial, disavowal, nay, refusal, refutation; SEE CONCEPT *278*

negative attitude [*n*] *pessimism*
chip on one's shoulder*, cynicism, dim view*, expectation of the worst, gloomy outlook, hopelessness, lack of confidence, low spirits, negativism; SEE CONCEPTS *410,689*

neglect [*n1*] *disregard*
carelessness, coolness, delinquency, disdain, disregardance, disrespect, heedlessness, inadvertence, inattention, inconsideration, indifference, laxity, laxness, oversight, scorn, slight, thoughtlessness, unconcern; SEE CONCEPTS *410,657*

neglect [*n2*] *failure, default*
carelessness, chaos, delay, delinquency, dereliction, dilapidation, forgetfulness, lapse, laxity, laxness, limbo, neglectfulness, negligence, omission, oversight, pretermission, remissness, slackness, slovenliness; SEE CONCEPTS *674,699*

neglect [v1] *be indifferent, leave alone*
affront, brush aside, brush off, condemn, depreciate, despise, detest, discount, disdain, dismiss, disregard, have nothing to do with*, ignore, keep at arm's length*, keep one's distance*, laugh off*, let go*, live with*, make light of*, not care for*, overlook, pass by, pass over, pass up, pay no attention to, pay no mind*, pretermit, rebuff, reject, scant, scorn, shrug off*, slight, slur, spurn, tune out*, underestimate; SEE CONCEPTS 30,681

neglect [v2] *fail to do; forget*
be careless, be derelict, be irresponsible, be negligent, be remiss, bypass, defer, discard, dismiss, disregard, elide, evade, gloss over*, let pass*, let slide*, look the other way*, lose sight of*, miss, not trouble oneself*, omit, overleap, overlook, overpass, pass over, postpone, procrastinate, shirk, skimp, skip, suspend, think little of*, trifle; SEE CONCEPTS 101,699

neglectful [adj] *careless, failing*
behindhand, delinquent, derelict, disregardful, heedless, inattentive, indifferent, lax, lazy, negligent, regardless, remiss, slack, thoughtless, uncaring, unmindful; SEE CONCEPTS 401,542

negligee [n] *nightgown*
camisole, dishabille, nightdress, nightie, peignoir, robe, teddy, wrap, wrapper; SEE CONCEPT 451

negligence [n] *carelessness*
disregard, failure, forgetfulness, heedlessness, inattention, inattentiveness, laxity, laxness, neglect, neglectfulness, oversight, thoughtlessness, unpreparedness; SEE CONCEPTS 30,633

negligent [adj] *careless, indifferent*
asleep at switch*, behindhand, cursory, delinquent, derelict, discinct, disregardful, forgetful, heedless, inadvertent, inattentive, inconsiderate, incurious, lax, neglectful, nonchalant, offhand, regardless, remiss, slack, slapdash*, slipshod*, sloppy*, slovenly, thoughtless, unconcerned, unheedful, unmindful, unthinking; SEE CONCEPTS 401,542

negligible [adj] *insignificant*
imperceptible, inconsequential, minor, minute, off*, outside, petty, remote, slender, slight, slim, small, trifling, trivial, unimportant; SEE CONCEPTS 552,575,789

negotiate [v1] *bargain, discuss*
accommodate, adjudicate, adjust, agree, arbitrate, arrange, bring to terms*, bury the hatchet*, come across with*, compose, concert, conciliate, confer, connect, consult, contract, covenant, cut a deal*, deal, debate, dicker*, haggle, hammer out a deal*, handle, horse trade*, intercede, make a deal, make peace*, make terms*, manage, mediate, moderate, network, parley*, referee, settle, step in*, stipulate, swap, transact, treat, umpire*, work out*, work out a deal; SEE CONCEPTS 8,56,68

negotiate [v2] *traverse, cross*
clear, get around, get over, get past, hurdle, leap over, overleap, pass, pass through, surmount, vault; SEE CONCEPTS 149,224

negotiation [n] *bargaining*
agreement, arbitration, colloquy, compromise, conference, consultation, debate, diplomacy, discussion, intervention, mediation, meeting, transaction; SEE CONCEPTS 56,68,684

negotiator [n] *person who bargains, controls discussion*
adjudicator, ambassador, arbitrator, broker, delegate, diplomat, fixer*, go-between*, interagent, intermediary, intermedium, judge, mediator, middleperson, moderator; SEE CONCEPTS 348,354,423

neighbor [n] *person who lives close by*
acquaintance, bystander, friend, homebody*, nearby resident, next-door neighbor; SEE CONCEPT 423

neighbor [v] *be next to*
abut, adjoin, be adjacent, be contiguous, be near, be nearby, border, butt against, communicate, connect, join, line, march, surround, touch, verge; SEE CONCEPT 759

neighborhood [n] *community, surroundings*
adjacency, area, block, closeness, confines, contiguity, district, environs, ghetto, hood, jungle*, locale, locality, nearness, neck of the woods*, parish, part, precinct, propinquity, proximity, purlieus, quarter, region, section, slum, stomping ground*, street, suburb, territory, tract, turf, vicinage, vicinity, ward, zone, zoo*; SEE CONCEPTS 198,379,516

neighborly [adj] *friendly*
amiable, civil, companionable, considerate, cooperative, cordial, genial, gracious, gregarious, harmonious, helpful, hospitable, kind, obliging, sociable, social, well-disposed; SEE CONCEPT 401

neither here nor there [adj] *irrelevant*
beside the point, extraneous, immaterial, impertinent, inconsequential, not connected with, not germane, not pertaining to, off the point, off the topic, pointless, trivial, unconnected, unimportant; SEE CONCEPTS 560,575

nemesis [n] *bane*
adversary, affliction, bête noire, curse, infliction, opponent, plague, rival, ruination, scourge, torment; SEE CONCEPTS 529,674

neologism [n] *new word*
buzz word*, coinage, neology, new phrase, slang, synthetic word*, vogue word*; SEE CONCEPT 275

neophyte [n] *beginner*
abecedarian, amateur, apprentice, colt*, fledgling, freshman, greenhorn, new boy/girl, newcomer, new kid on the block*, novice, recruit, rookie*, tenderfoot*, trainee, tyro*; SEE CONCEPTS 423,424

nepotism [n] *favoritism*
bias, discrimination, inequity, one-sidedness, partiality, partisanship, preference, preferential treatment; SEE CONCEPTS 41,388,645

nerd [n] *geek*
dolt, dork*, dweeb*, fool, goober*, goofball*, jerk*, oaf, techie*, trekkie*, weirdo*; SEE CONCEPTS 564,570

nerve [n] *daring, boldness*
assumption, assurance, audacity, backbone, brass*, bravery, brazenness, cheek*, chutzpah*, confidence, coolness, courage, crust*, determination, effrontery, endurance, energy, face*, fearlessness, firmness, force, fortitude, gall*, gameness, grit*, guts*, hardihood, hardiness, heart*, impertinence, impudence, insolence, intestinal fortitude, intrepidity, mettle, might, moxie*, pluck*, presumption, resolution, sauce*, spirit, spunk*, starch*, steadfastness, stomach*, temerity, vigor, will; SEE CONCEPT 411

nerve [v] *strengthen, hearten*
animate, brace, cheer, embolden, encourage, enhearten, fortify, inspirit, invigorate, steel; SEE CONCEPTS 7,14,22

nerve center [n] *control center*
command post, core, focal point, focus, headquarters, heart, HQ, hub; SEE CONCEPTS 532,826,829

nerveless [adj1] *calm, cool*
collected, composed, controlled, impassive, imperturbable, intrepid, patient, self-possessed, tranquil, unemotional; SEE CONCEPT 542

nerveless [adj2] *scared to death*
afraid, cowardly, debilitated, enervated, fearful, feeble, nervous, petrified, spineless*, timid, weak, yellow-bellied*; SEE CONCEPTS 401,403

nerve-racking [adj] *distressing*
aggravating, annoying, disquieting, disturbing, exasperating, irksome, irritating, maddening, stressful, taxing, tense, trying, upsetting; SEE CONCEPTS 548,565

nerves [n] *extreme anxiety*
fretfulness, hysteria, imbalance, irritation, nervousness, neurasthenia, sleeplessness, strain, stress, tenseness, tension; SEE CONCEPT 410

nervous [adj] *anxious, fearful*
afraid, agitated, annoyed, apprehensive, basket case*, bothered, concerned, distressed, disturbed, edgy, excitable, fidgety, fitful, flustered, fussy*, hesitant, high-strung*, hysterical, irritable, jittery*, jumpy*, nervy*, neurotic, on edge*, overwrought, querulous, restive, ruffled, sensitive, shaky*, shrinking, shy, skittish, snappish, solicitous, spooked*, taut, tense, timid, timorous, troubled, twitchy*, uneasy, unrestful, unstrung*, upset, uptight, volatile, weak, wired*, worried; SEE CONCEPTS 403,542

nervous breakdown [n] *mental collapse*
burnout*, crackup*, depression, emotional collapse, nervous exhaustion, nervous prostration, shattered nerves; SEE CONCEPT 410

nervousness [n] *anxious state*
agitation, all-overs*, anger, animation, butterflies*, cold sweat*, creeps*, delirium, discomfiture, disquiet, disquietude, dithers*, excitability, feverishness, fidgets*, flap*, fluster*, fuss*, impatience, jitters*, jumps*, moodiness, neurasthenia, neuroticism, perturbation, quivers, sensitivity, shakes, stage fright, stimulation, stress, tension, timidity, tizzy*, to-do*, touchiness, trembles*, tremulousness, turbulence, uneasiness, willies*, worry; SEE CONCEPTS 410,657

nervy [adj] *bold, pushy*
cheeky*, crass, crude, forward, fresh*, impudent, inconsiderate, pert, plucky*, rude, sassy*, smart, smart-alecky*, wise; SEE CONCEPT 401

nest [n] *home*
aerie, breeding ground, burrow, den, haunt, hideaway, lair, refuge, roost; SEE CONCEPTS 198,515

nest egg [n] *savings*
backup, cache, funds, investment, life savings, mad money*, means, money in the bank, piggy bank, provisions, rainy day fund*, reserves, resources, savings account, stash*, stockpile; SEE CONCEPTS 335,340,446,710

nestle [v] *curl up*
bundle, burrow, cuddle, huddle, lie against, lie close, make snug*, move close, nuzzle, settle down, snug*, snuggle, take shelter; SEE CONCEPTS 154,612

net [adj] *profiting*
after deductions, after taxes, clear, excluding, exclusive, final, irreducible, pure, remaining, take-home, undeductible; SEE CONCEPT 334

net [n] *mesh, web*
cloth, fabric, lace, lacework, lattice, netting, network, openwork, reticulum, screen, tracery; SEE CONCEPTS 473,770

net [v1] *capture*
bag*, catch, enmesh, ensnare, entangle, hook*, lasso*, nab*, trap; SEE CONCEPT 90

net [v2] *gain after expenses*
accumulate, bring in, clean up, clear, earn, make, profit, realize, reap; SEE CONCEPT 330

nettle [v] *provoke, upset*
annoy, chafe, disgust, disturb, exasperate, fret, get*, goad, harass, huff, incense, insult, irritate, miff, peeve*, pester, pet, pique, put out*, rile, roil, ruffle, snit*, stew*, sting*, tease, tiff*, vex; SEE CONCEPTS 7,14,19

nettlesome [adj] *irritating*
aggravating, annoying, bothersome, burdensome, distressing, disturbing, exasperating, irksome, nagging, troublesome, trying, vexatious, vexing; SEE CONCEPTS 529,537

network [n] *system of connections*
arrangement, artery, chain, checkerboard*, circuitry, complex, convolution, crisscross*, fabric, fiber, grid, grill*, grillwork, hookup, interconnections, jungle, labyrinth, maze, mesh, net, netting, nexus, organization, patchwork*, plexus, reticulation, reticule, screening, structure, system, tessellation, tracks, wattle, weave, web, wiring; SEE CONCEPTS 381,388,770

network [v] *to socialize for professional or personal gain*
associate, circulate, hobnob, make contacts, meet, meet and greet*, mingle, rub elbows*, schmooze*; SEE CONCEPT 384

neurosis [n] *mental disturbance, disorder*
aberration, abnormality, affliction, breakdown, compulsion, crack-up*, derangement, deviation, hysteria, inhibition, insanity, instability, madness, maladjustment, mental illness, neurasthenia, obsession, personality disorder, phobia, psychological disorder, psychopathy; SEE CONCEPTS 316,410

neurotic [adj] *mentally maladjusted*
aberrant, abnormal, anxious, basket case*, bundle of nerves*, choked*, clutched*, compulsive, deviant, disordered, disoriented, distraught, disturbed, erratic, hung up*, hysteric, inhibited, manic, nervous, nervous wreck*, obsessive, overwrought, psychoneurotic, unhealthy, unstable, upset, uptight, wired*; SEE CONCEPTS 314,403

neuter [v] *remove sex organs*
alter, castrate, change, desexualize, doctor, dress, fix, geld, make barren, make impotent, make infertile, make sexless, mutilate, spay, sterilize, unsex; SEE CONCEPTS 157,250

neutral [adj1] *impartial, noncommittal*
aloof, bystanding, calm, clinical, collected, cool, detached, disengaged, disinterested, dispassionate, easy, evenhanded, fair-minded, impersonal, inactive, indifferent, inert, middle-of-road*, nonaligned, nonbelligerent, nonchalant, noncombatant, nonparticipating, nonpartisan, on sidelines*, on the fence*, pacifistic, poker-faced*, relaxed, unaligned, unbiased, uncommitted, unconcerned,

undecided, uninvolved, unprejudiced; SEE CONCEPTS 403,542

neutral [*adj2*] *flat, dull to senses*
abstract, achromatic, colorless, drab, expressionless, indeterminate, indistinct, indistinguishable, intermediate, toneless, undefined, vague, vanilla; SEE CONCEPTS 485,537,618

neutralize [*v*] *counteract*
abrogate, annul, balance, cancel, compensate for, conquer, counterbalance, countercheck, counterpoise, countervail, defeat, frustrate, invalidate, negate, negative, nullify, offset, overcome, override, overrule, redress, subdue, undo; SEE CONCEPTS 121,232

never [*adv*] *not at any time*
at no time, don't hold your breath*, forget it, nevermore, not at all, not ever, not in any way, not in the least, not on your life*, not under any condition, no way*; SEE CONCEPT 799

never-ending [*adj*] *continual, unceasing*
amaranthine, boundless, ceaseless, constant, continuous, endless, eternal, everlasting, immortal, incessant, interminable, nonstop, perpetual, persistent, relentless, timeless, unbroken, unchanging, uninterrupted, unremitting; SEE CONCEPTS 482,798

nevertheless [*adv*] *however*
after all, although, but, even so, even though, howbeit, nonetheless, not the less, notwithstanding, regardless, still, still and all, though, withal, yet; SEE CONCEPT 544

new [*adj1*] *recent, fresh*
advanced, au courant, brand-new, contemporary, current, cutting-edge*, dewy, different, dissimilar, distinct, fashionable, inexperienced, just out*, late, latest, modern, modernistic, modish*, neoteric, newfangled, novel, now*, original, recent, spick-and-span*, state-of-the-art, strange, topical, ultramodern, unaccustomed, uncontaminated, unfamiliar, unique, unknown, unlike, unseasoned, unskilled, unspoiled, untouched, untrained, untried, untrodden, unused, unusual, up-to-date, virgin, youthful; SEE CONCEPTS 564,578,797

new [*adj2*] *additional*
added, another, else, extra, farther, fresh, further, increased, more, other, supplementary; SEE CONCEPTS 771,824

new [*adj3*] *modernized, restored*
altered, changed, improved, redesigned, refreshed, regenerated, renewed, revived; SEE CONCEPT 589

new [*adv*] *recently*
afresh, anew, freshly, lately, newly, of late; SEE CONCEPT 820

new age [*adj*] *of a broad-ranging consciousness-raising movement*
Age of Aquarius*, alternative, astrological, balanced, crystal healing, holistic, mystic, occult, planetary, spiritual, supernaturalist; SEE CONCEPTS 403,529

newborn [*n*] *infant*
babe, baby, bairn, bambino, bantling, bundle, child, kid, little one, neonate, nursling, small child, suckling, tot; SEE CONCEPTS 414,424

newcomer [*n*] *person who has just arrived in area*
alien, arrival, beginner, blow-in*, colt*, foreigner, greenhorn*, immigrant, incomer, Johnny-come-lately*, late arrival, latecomer, maverick,

neophyte, new kid on the block*, novice, novitiate, outsider, rookie, settler, stranger, tenderfoot*; SEE CONCEPTS 413,423

newfangled [*adj*] *quite recent*
contemporary, fashionable, fresh, gimmicky*, in vogue, modern, modernistic, neoteric, new, new-fashioned, novel, popular, unique; SEE CONCEPTS 578,589,797

newly [*adv*] *recently*
anew, freshly, just, lately, latterly, of late; SEE CONCEPT 820

news [*n*] *information, revelation*
account, advice, announcement, broadcast, bulletin, cable, cognizance, communication, communiqué, copy, data, description, disclosure, discovery, dispatch, enlightenment, exposé, eye-opener*, front-page news*, headlines, hearsay, intelligence, itemization, knowledge, leak, lowdown, message, narration, news flash, particularization, recital, recognition, release, report, rumor, scandal, scoop*, specification, statement, story, telecast, telegram, telling, the goods*, tidings*, word*; SEE CONCEPTS 268,274,293

newscaster [*n*] *broadcaster*
anchor, anchor man/woman, anchor person, announcer, commentator, news anchor, news commentator, reporter; SEE CONCEPTS 60,292

newsletter [*n*] *special interest publication*
bulletin, journal, magazine, pamphlet, report; SEE CONCEPTS 279,280

newsman/newswoman [*n*] *reporter*
anchor, anchor man/woman, anchor person, announcer, columnist, copy editor, correspondent, cub*, editor, foreign correspondent, ink slinger*, interviewer, investigative reporter, journalist, legman/woman*, newscaster, newshound, newspaperman/woman, newswriter, pressman/woman, stringer, war correspondent, writer; SEE CONCEPTS 348,356

newspaper [*n*] *regular, continuous publication containing information*
biweekly, bulldog*, community, daily, extra, gazette, journal, magazine, metropolitan, organ, paper, periodical, press, rag*, record, review, scandal sheet*, sheet, tabloid, trade, weekly; SEE CONCEPTS 279,280

newsworthy [*adj*] *important*
consequential, critical, crucial, essential, far-reaching, front-page*, great, influential, material, meaningful, momentous, of note, of substance, paramount, relevant, serious, significant, urgent, vital; SEE CONCEPT 567

next [*adj*] *coming immediately after in space, time, order*
abutting, adjacent, adjoining, after, alongside, attached, back-to-back, beside, close, closest, coming, consequent, co-terminous, ensuing, following, hard by*, later, meeting, nearest, neighboring, on the side, proximate, side-by-side, subsequent, succeeding, touching; SEE CONCEPTS 585,586,799

next [*adv*] *immediately after in time, space, order*
after, afterward, afterwhile, behind, by and by, closely, coming up, following, later, latterly, next off, subsequently, thereafter; SEE CONCEPTS 585,586,799

nibble [*n*] *morsel, bite*
crumb, peck, snack, soupçon, taste, tidbit; SEE CONCEPTS 458,831

ne
ni

nibble [v] *bite, pick at*
crop, eat, eat like a bird*, gnaw, munch, nip*, nosh on*, peck*, snack; SEE CONCEPT *169*

nice [adj] *likable, agreeable*
admirable, amiable, approved, attractive, becoming, charming, commendable, considerate, copacetic, cordial, courteous, decorous, delightful, ducky, fair, favorable, fine and dandy*, friendly, genial, gentle, good, gracious, helpful, ingratiating, inviting, kind, kindly, lovely, nifty*, obliging, okay*, peachy*, pleasant, pleasurable, polite, prepossessing, seemly, simpatico, superior, swell, unpresumptuous, welcome, well-mannered, winning, winsome; SEE CONCEPTS *404,548,572*

nice [adj2] *precise, neat, refined*
accurate, becoming, befitting, careful, choosy, conforming, correct, critical, cultured, dainty, decent, delicate, discerning, discriminating, distinguishing, exact, exacting, fastidious, fine, fine-spun, finical, finicking, finicky*, fussy*, genteel, hairsplitting*, meticulous, minute, particular, persnickety*, picky*, proper, respectable, right, rigorous, scrupulous, seemly, squeamish, strict, subtle, tidy, trim, trivial*, virtuous, well-bred; SEE CONCEPTS *542,557,558*

niche [n] *place all one's own*
alcove, byplace, calling, compartment, corner, cranny*, cubbyhole*, hole, hollow, indentation, nook, opening, pigeonhole*, position, recess, slot, vocation; SEE CONCEPTS *440,513,630*

nick [n/v] *chip, scratch*
cut, damage, dent, dint, indent, jag, knock, mark, mill, notch, scar, score, slit; SEE CONCEPTS *137,176,208*

nickname [n] *informal title*
appellation, byname, byword, denomination, diminutive, epithet, familiar name, handle*, label, moniker, pet name*, sobriquet, style, tag*; SEE CONCEPTS *268,683*

nifty [adj] *marvelous*
chic, clever, cool*, dandy, enjoyable, excellent, groovy*, keen, neat, peachy*, pleasing, quick, sharp, smart, spruce, stylish, super, swell, terrific; SEE CONCEPT *572*

night [n] *part of day after sundown and before sunrise*
after dark, after hours*, bedtime, before dawn, black*, blackness, dark, dark hours, darkness, dead of night*, dim, duskiness, dusk to dawn, evening, eventide, gloom, midnight, nightfall, nighttide, nighttime, obscurity*, pitch dark, twilight, witching hour*; SEE CONCEPTS *620,801,806,810*

nightclub [n] *place for evening entertainment*
bar, bistro, cabaret, café, casino, disco*, discotheque, dive*, hideaway*, honky-tonk*, joint*, nightery, night spot, nitery, restaurant, roadhouse, saloon, speakeasy*, spot, supper club, tavern, theatre, watering hole*; SEE CONCEPTS *293,439,449*

nightfall [n] *beginning of darkness*
black*, crepuscule, dim, dusk, eve, eventide, sundown, sunset, twilight, vespers; SEE CONCEPT *810*

nightgown [n] *dress in which to sleep*
bedgown, lingerie, negligee, nightdress, nightie*, nightrobe, nightshirt, pajamas, PJs*, sleeper*; SEE CONCEPT *451*

nightly [adj/adv] *each evening; after dark*
at night, by night, every night, in the night, night after night, nights, nighttime, nocturnal, nocturnally; SEE CONCEPTS *541,799,801*

nightmare [n] *bad dream or experience*
dream, fancy, fantasy, hallucination, horror, illusion, incubus, ordeal, phantasm, succubus, torment, trial, tribulation, vision; SEE CONCEPTS *315,674*

nightmarish [adj] *frightening*
alarming, awful, chilling, creepy, dire, direful, disquieting, dreadful, eerie, fearful, fearsome, ghastly, ghoulish, grim, grisly, hair-raising, hellish, horrible, horrid, horrifying, macabre, morbid, ominous, petrifying, scary, spooky, terrible, terrifying, traumatic, unnerving; SEE CONCEPTS *529,537*

night stick [n] *billy club*
billy*, blackjack, cudgel, police officer's club, shillelagh; SEE CONCEPTS *470,499*

nihilism [n] *refusal to believe*
abnegation, agnosticism, anarchy, atheism, denial, disbelief, disorder, lawlessness, mob rule*, nonbelief, rejection, renunciation, repudiation, skepticism, terrorism; SEE CONCEPT *689*

nil [adj] *nonexistent*
naught, nihil, nix*, none, nothing, nought, zero; SEE CONCEPTS *539,762,771*

nimble [adj] *dexterous, smart*
active, adept, adroit, agile, alert, bright, brisk, clever, deft, handy, light, lissome, lithe, lively, proficient, prompt, quick, quick-witted, ready, skillful, sprightly, spry, swift, vigilant, wide-awake; SEE CONCEPTS *402,527,584*

nip [n] *swallow, taste*
bite, catch, dram, drop, finger, jolt, morsel, mouthful, nibble, pinch, portion, shot*, sip, slug*, snifter, soupçon, toothful; SEE CONCEPTS *458,831*

nip [v1] *bite; take small part*
catch, clip, compress, grip, munch, nab at*, nibble, pinch, sink teeth into*, snag, snap*, snip*, squeeze*, take a chunk out of*, tweak, twinge, twitch; SEE CONCEPTS *142,169,190*

nip [v2] *stop, thwart*
arrest, balk, blight, check, dash, end, frustrate; SEE CONCEPTS *121,234*

nirvana [n] *enlightenment*
awakening, bliss, cloud nine*, ecstasy, happiness, heaven, joy, paradise, peace, serenity, tranquility; SEE CONCEPT *409*

nitty-gritty [n] *heart of the matter*
basics, bottom line*, chief part, chief thing, core, essential part, focus, fundamentals, gist, important matter, nuts and bolts*, root, the facts*; SEE CONCEPTS *442,668,826*

nitwit [n] *idiot*
blockhead, bonehead*, cretin, dimwit, dork, dumbbell, dummy, dunce, fool, halfwit, ignoramus, imbecile, jerk, moron, nincompoop, ninny*, numbskull, pinhead*, simpleton, stupid person; SEE CONCEPT *412*

nobility [n] *aristocracy; eminence*
dignity, elevation, elite, ennoblement, exaltation, excellence, generosity, gentry, glorification, grandeur, greatness, high society, honor, illustriousness, incorruptibility, integrity, loftiness, magnanimity, magnificence, majesty, nobleness, patricians, peerage, royalty, ruling class, society, stateliness, sublimity, superiority, upper class,

noble [*adj 1*] *aristocratic*
gentle, highborn, imperial, kingly, nobiliary, patrician, queenly, titled, wellborn; SEE CONCEPTS **549,555**

noble [*adj 2*] *dignified, excellent*
august, beneficent, benevolent, benign, big, bounteous, brilliant, charitable, courtly, cultivated, dignified, distinguished, elevated, eminent, extraordinary, first-rate, generous, gracious, grand, great, great-hearted, high-minded, honorable, humane, imposing, impressive, liberal, lofty, magnanimous, magnificent, meritorious, preeminent, refined, remarkable, reputable, splendid, stately, sublime, supreme, sympathetic, tolerant, upright, virtuous, worthy; SEE CONCEPTS **401,404,572**

noble [*n*] *member of royal or important family*
archduchess, archduke, aristocrat, blue blood*, count, countess, duchess, duke, emperor, empress, gentleman, gentlewoman, lady, lord, patrician, peer, prince, princess, royalty, silk stocking*; SEE CONCEPTS **422,423**

nobody/nonentity [*n*] *person of little importance*
cipher, insignificancy, lightweight*, menial, nix*, nothing, parvenu*, small potato*, squirt*, upstart, wimp*, zero*, zip; SEE CONCEPT **423**

nocturnal [*adj*] *happening at night*
after dark, late, night, night-loving, nightly, nighttime; SEE CONCEPTS **799,801**

nod [*n*] *gesture of the head*
acceptance, acknowledgment, affirmative, beckon, bow, dip, greeting, inclination, indication, permission, salute, sign, signal, yes; SEE CONCEPTS **74,185,685**

nod [*v1*] *gesture with head*
acknowledge, acquiesce, agree, approve, assent, beckon, bend, bow, concur, consent, curtsy, dip, duck, greet, indicate, recognize, respond, salute, say yes, sign, signal; SEE CONCEPTS **10,50,74,88,185**

nod [*v2*] *fall asleep*
become inattentive, be sleepy, doze, drift, drift off, droop, drowse, nap, sleep, slump; SEE CONCEPTS **210,315,681**

node/nodule [*n*] *knot, growth*
bud, bulge, bump, burl, clot, knob, lump, protuberance, swelling, tumor; SEE CONCEPTS **471,831**

noise [*n*] *sound that is loud or not harmonious*
babble, babel, bang, bedlam, bellow, bewailing, blare, blast, boisterousness, boom, buzz, cacophony, caterwauling, clamor, clang, clatter, commotion, crash, cry, detonation, din, discord, disquiet, disquietude, drumming, eruption, explosion, fanfare, fireworks, fracas*, fuss*, hooha*, hubbub*, hullabaloo*, jangle, lamentation, outcry, pandemonium, peal, racket, ring, roar, row, shot, shouting, sonance, squawk, stridency, talk, thud, tumult, turbulence, uproar, uproariousness, yelling, yelp; SEE CONCEPTS **521,595**

noiseless [*adj*] *quiet*
hushed, hushful, inaudible, mute, muted, silent, soundless, speechless, still, voiceless, wordless; SEE CONCEPT **594**

noiseproof [*adj*] *soundproof*
insulated, nonresonant, silent; SEE CONCEPT **594**

noisome [*adj*] *immoral, bad, offensive*
baneful, dangerous, deadly, deleterious, disgusting, fetid, foul, harmful, horrid, hurtful, injuri-

ous, insalubrious, insalutary, loathsome, malodorous, mephitic, mischievous, nauseating, noxious, pernicious, pestiferous, pestilential, poisonous, putrid, rank, reeking, repulsive, sickening, sickly, smelly, stinking, unhealthful, unhealthy, unwholesome, vile, yucky*; SEE CONCEPTS **537,571,598**

noisy [*adj*] *very loud and unharmonious in sound*
blatant, blusterous, boisterous, booming, cacophonous, chattering, clamorous, clangorous, clattery, deafening, disorderly, ear-popping*, ear-splitting*, jumping, loudmouth, obstreperous, piercing, rackety, raising Cain*, raising the roof*, rambunctious, raspy, riotous, rowdy, screaming, strepitous, strident, tumultuous/tumultuous, turbulent, turned up, uproarious, vociferous; SEE CONCEPTS **592,594**

nomad [*n*] *person who wanders from place to place*
hobo, itinerant, migrant, pilgrim, rambler, roamer, rover, vagabond, wanderer, wayfarer; SEE CONCEPT **413**

nomadic [*adj*] *itinerant*
drifting, gypsy, itinerate, migrant, migratory, pastoral, perambulant, perambulatory, peripatetic, roaming, roving, traveling, vagabond, vagrant, wandering, wayfaring; SEE CONCEPTS **401,536,584**

nom de plume [*n*] *pen name*
AKA*, alias, anonym, assumed name, nickname, nom de guerre, professional name, pseudonym; SEE CONCEPTS **268,683**

nomenclature [*n*] *vocabulary*
classification, codification, glossary, locution, phraseology, taxonomy, terminology; SEE CONCEPTS **275,276,683**

nominal [*adj 1*] *supposed, theoretical*
alleged, apparent, as advertised, formal, given, honorary, in effect only, in name only, mentioned, named, ostensible, pretended, professed, puppet, purported, seeming, self-styled, simple, so-called, stated, suggested, titular; SEE CONCEPT **582**

nominal [*adj 2*] *insignificant*
cheap, inconsiderable, inexpensive, low, low-priced, meaningless, minimal, small, symbolic, token, trifling, trivial, unnecessary; SEE CONCEPTS **334,575,789**

nominate [*v*] *designate, select*
appoint, assign, call, choose, cognominate, commission, decide, denominate, draft, elect, elevate, empower, intend, make, mean, name, offer, present, proffer, propose, purpose, put down for, put up, recommend, slate, slot, specify, submit, suggest, tab, tap, tender, term; SEE CONCEPTS **41,50,75,88,300**

nomination [*n*] *appointment for responsibility*
choice, designation, election, naming, proposal, recommendation, selection, suggestion; SEE CONCEPTS **41,50,75,88,300**

nominee [*n*] *candidate*
applicant, appointee, aspirant, contender, contestant, entrant, hopeful*, office-seeker, runner, seeker; SEE CONCEPT **359**

nonaggression [*n*] *pacifism*
nonviolence, passivity, peaceableness; SEE CONCEPTS **7,22,250**

nonchalant [*adj*] *easygoing, laid back*
airy, aloof, apathetic, blasé, calm, careless, casual, cold, collected, composed, cool, detached,

ni
no

disimpassioned, disinterested, dispassionate, easy, effortless, happy, impassive, imperturbable, incurious, indifferent, insouciant, lackadaisical, light, listless, loose, lukewarm, mellow, neglectful, negligent, neutral, offhand, placid, serene, smooth, trifling, uncaring, unconcerned, unemotional, unexcited, unfeeling, unflappable, unimpressible, unperturbed, unruffled, untroubled; SEE CONCEPTS 401,404,542

noncommittal [*adj*] *unwilling to decide*
ambiguous, buttoned up*, careful, cautious, circumspect, clammed up*, constrained, discreet, equivocal, evasive, even-steven*, guarded, hush-hush*, incommunicable, indefinite, judicious, middle-ground*, middle-of-the-road*, neutral, on-the-fence*, politic, reserved, restrained, tactful, temporizing, tentative, unrevealing, vague, wary, zipped*; SEE CONCEPTS 267,403,542

noncompliant [*adj*] *unwilling to go along with something*
belligerent, contumacious, declinatory, declining, divergent, impatient, irregular, negative, objecting, rebellious, recalcitrant, refractory, refusing, restive, truculent; SEE CONCEPTS 401,542

nonconforming [*adj*] *nonobservant*
independent, individualistic, marching to the beat of a different drummer*, nonadhering, noncompliant, one's own sweet way*, radical, unorthodox; SEE CONCEPT 554

nonconformist [*adj*] *unwilling to behave, believe as most do*
beatnik*, bohemian*, dissident, freak*, heretical, heterodox, hippie*, iconoclastic, maverick, oddball, offbeat, original, rebel, schismatic*, sectarian, swinger, unorthodox, weird*; SEE CONCEPTS 401,542

nonconformist [*n*] *person who goes against normal behavior, beliefs*
beatnik*, bohemian*, demonstrator, different breed*, dissenter, dissentient, dissident, dropout, eccentric, fish out of water*, freak*, heretic, iconoclast, individualist, liberal, malcontent, maverick, misbeliever, night person, oddball, offbeat, original, protester, radical, rebel, sectary, separatist, swinger, weirdo*; SEE CONCEPTS 359,423

nonconformity [*n*] *belief, behavior different from most*
bohemianism, breach, contumaciousness, denial, disaffection, disagreement, disapprobation, disapproval, discordance, disobedience, dissent, eccentricity, exception, heresy, heterodoxy, iconoclasm, insubordination, lawlessness, mutinousness, negation, nonacceptance, nonagreement, noncompliance, nonconsent, objection, opposition, originality, recalcitrance, recusance, recusancy, rejection, strangeness, transgressiveness, unconventionality, uniqueness, unorthodoxy, unruliness, veto, violation; SEE CONCEPTS 633,657,689

nondescript [*adj*] *undistinguished, commonplace*
characterless, colorless, common, dull, empty, featureless, garden*, indescribable, indeterminate, mousy*, ordinary, unclassifiable, unclassified, unexceptional, uninspiring, uninteresting, unmemorable, unremarkable, vague; SEE CONCEPTS 529,537,547

none [*prep*] *not one thing*
nil, nobody, no one, no one at all, no part, not a

bit, not any, not anyone, not anything, not a soul, not a thing, nothing, not one, zero, zilch*; SEE CONCEPT 407

nonessential [*adj*] *not needed or important*
deadwood*, dispensable, excess baggage*, excessive, expendable, extraneous, inessential, insignificant, peripheral, petty, superfluous, trivial, unimportant, unnecessary; SEE CONCEPTS 546,575

nonexistent [*adj*] *fictional, not real*
absent, airy, baseless, blank, chimerical, dead, defunct, departed, dreamlike, dreamy, empty, ethereal, extinct, extinguished, fancied, flimsy, gone, gossamery, groundless, hallucinatory, hypothetical, illusory, imaginary, imagined, immaterial, imponderable, insubstantial, legendary, lost, missing, mythical, negative, null and null and void*, passed away, passed on, perished, shadowy, tenuous, ungrounded, unreal, unsubstantial, vacant, vague, vaporous, void, without foundation; SEE CONCEPTS 539,582

nonpartisan [*adj*] *impartial; not political*
detached, equitable, fair, free-wheeling*, independent, indifferent, just, middle-of-the-road*, neutral, nonaligned, nondiscriminatory, objective, on one's own*, on-the-fence*, playing it cool*, unaffected, unaffiliated, unbiased, unbigoted, uncolored, unimplicated, uninfluenced, uninvolved, unprejudiced; SEE CONCEPT 542

nonplus [*v*] *confuse, perplex*
astonish, astound, baffle, balk, beat, bewilder, boggle, buffalo*, confound, daze, discomfit, disconcert, discountenance, dismay, dumbfound, embarrass, faze, floor*, flurry, fluster, frustrate, get*, mess with one's head*, muddle, mystify, overcome, paralyze, puzzle, rattle, rattle one's cage*, stagger, stick, stump, stun, stymie*, take aback, throw*, throw into tizzy*, thwart; SEE CONCEPTS 14,16

nonsense [*n*] *craziness, ridiculousness*
absurdity, babble, balderdash*, baloney*, bananas*, bombast, bull*, bunk*, claptrap*, drivel, fatuity, flightiness, folly, foolishness, fun, gibberish, giddiness, hogwash*, hooey*, hot air*, imprudence, inanity, irrationality, jazz, jest, jive*, joke, ludicrousness, madness, mumbo jumbo*, palaver, poppycock*, prattle, pretense, ranting, rashness, rot, rubbish, scrawl, scribble, senselessness, silliness, soft soap*, stupidity, thoughtlessness, trash*, tripe*; SEE CONCEPTS 230,388,633

nonstop [*adj*] *continuous, direct*
ceaseless, constant, endless, incessant, interminable, relentless, round-the-clock*, steady, unbroken, unending, unfaltering, uninterrupted, unremitting; SEE CONCEPTS 482,584,798

nonviolence [*n*] *abstention from violence*
nonagression, pacification, pacifism, passiveness, passivity, peaceableness; SEE CONCEPTS 388,691

nonviolent [*adj*] *peaceful*
irenic, nonbelligerent, pacifist, passive, peaceable, quiet, resistant, without violence; SEE CONCEPT 401

nook [*n*] *corner, cubbyhole*
alcove, byplace, cavity, compartment, cranny, crevice, den, hideout, hole, inglenook, niche, opening, quoin, recess, retreat; SEE CONCEPTS 440,513

noon [n] *the middle of a day*
apex, high noon, meridian, midday, noonday, noontide, noontime, twelve noon, twelve o'clock; SEE CONCEPTS 801,802,806

norm [n] *average, standard*
barometer, benchmark*, criterion, gauge, mean, measure, median, medium, model, par, pattern, rule, scale, touchstone*, type, yardstick; SEE CONCEPTS 647,686,688

normal [adj1] *common, usual*
accustomed, acknowledged, average, commonplace, conventional, customary, general, habitual, mean, median, methodical, natural, orderly, ordinary, popular, prevalent, regular, routine, run-of-the-mill*, standard, traditional, typic, typical, unexceptional; SEE CONCEPT 547

normal [adj2] *sane, rational*
all there*, compos mentis*, cool*, healthy, in good health, in one's right mind*, lucid, reasonable, right, right-minded, sound, together, well-adjusted, whole, wholesome; SEE CONCEPTS 314,403

normally [adv] *usually*
as a rule, commonly, habitually, in accordance with, ordinarily, regularly, typically; SEE CONCEPT 547

north [adj/adv] *toward the top pole of the earth*
arctic, boreal, cold, frozen, hyperborean, northbound, northerly, northern, northmost, northward, polar, septentrional, toward North Pole, tundra; SEE CONCEPTS 581,583

nose [n] *smelling organ of animate being*
adenoids, beak*, bill*, horn*, muzzle*, nares, nostrils, olfactory nerves, proboscis, schnoz*, smeller*, sneezer*, sniffer*, snoot*, snout*, snuffer*, whiffer*; SEE CONCEPTS 392,601

nose [v] *detect, search*
busybody*, examine, inspect, meddle, mouse*, pry, scent, smell, sniff, snoop*; SEE CONCEPTS 103,216

nosh [n] *snack*
bite, bite to eat*, break, goodies*, grub, light meal, midnight snack, pickings, refreshment, tidbit, tiny meal; SEE CONCEPTS 457,459

nosh [v] *snack*
eat between meals, munch, nibble, pick at, taste; SEE CONCEPT 169

nostalgia [n] *pleasant remembrances*
fond memories*, hearts and flowers*, homesickness, longing, pining, reminiscence, remorse, schmaltz*, sentimentality, tear-jerker*, wistfulness, yearning; SEE CONCEPTS 20,410

nostalgic [adj] *longingly remembering*
cornball*, down memory lane*, drippy*, homesick, like yesterday*, lonesome, longing, mushy*, regretful, sappy*, sentimental, sloppy, syrupy*, wistful, yearning; SEE CONCEPTS 403,529

nostrum [n] *cure-all, often ineffective*
catholicon, cure, drug, elixir, fix, formula, home remedy, medicine, panacea, patent medicine, potion, quack medicine*, quick fix*, remedy, treatment; SEE CONCEPTS 307,311

nosy [adj] *curious; prying*
eavesdropping, inquisitive, inquisitorial, inquisitory, interested, interfering, intermeddling, intrusive, meddlesome, personal, searching, snooping, snoopy; SEE CONCEPT 401

notable [adj] *important; famous*
big-league*, bodacious*, celebrated, celebrious,

conspicuous, distingué, distinguished, eminent, eventful, evident, extraordinary, famed, great, heavy*, high-profile*, illustrious, major-league*, manifest, marked, memorable, momentous, nameable, noteworthy, noticeable, notorious, observable, outstanding, preeminent, prominent, pronounced, rare, red-letter*, remarkable, renowned, rubric, serious, something else*, striking, top-drawer*, uncommon, unusual, well-known; SEE CONCEPT 568

notable [n] *person who is famous, important*
big name*, big shot*, big-time operator*, big wheel*, celebrity, chief, dignitary, eminence, executive, figure*, heavyweight*, high-up, hot-dog*, leader, lion*, luminary, magnate, mogul, name, notability, personage, pooh-bah*, power, somebody*, star, superstar, VIP*, worthy; SEE CONCEPTS 347,352,423

notably [adv] *especially*
conspicuously, distinctly, exceedingly, exceptionally, extremely, greatly, highly, hugely, markedly, noticeably, outstandingly, particularly, prominently, remarkably, reputably, signally, strikingly, uncommonly, very; SEE CONCEPT 569

notarize [v] *certify*
attest, authenticate, document, endorse, register, sign and seal, swear, validate, verify, witness; SEE CONCEPTS 50,88

notary [n] *notary public*
certifier, commissioner for oaths, court clerk, endorser, public official, recorder, registrar, scrivener, signatory, witness; SEE CONCEPTS 355,423

notation [n] *written remarks*
characters, chit, code, documentation, figures, jotting, memo, memorandum, note, noting, record, representation, script, signs, symbols, system; SEE CONCEPTS 268,284

not born yesterday [adj] *experienced*
battle-scarred, been around, canny, cunning, on the ball*, savvy, seasoned, trained, unbelieving, wise, worldly; SEE CONCEPTS 402,527

notch [n1] *indentation*
cleft, cut, gap, gash, groove, incision, indent, indenture, mark, mill, nick, nock, rabbet, rut, score, scratch; SEE CONCEPT 513

notch [n2] *level within classification*
cut, degree, grade, rung, stage, step; SEE CONCEPTS 388,744

notch [v] *indent*
chisel, cleave, crenelate, crimp, cut, dent, gash, incise, jag, mark, mill, nick, scallop, score, scratch; SEE CONCEPTS 137,176,208

note [n2] *symbol, often used in reference to music*
character, degree, figure, flat, indication, interval, key, lick*, mark, natural, pitch, representation, scale, sharp, sign, step, token, tone; SEE CONCEPTS 262,284

note [n3] *attention, heed*
cognizance, mark, mind, notice, observance, observation, regard, remark; SEE CONCEPT 529

note [v] *observe, perceive*
catch, clock, denote, descry, designate, dig, discern, discover, distinguish, document, enter, get a load of*, get an eyeful*, heed, indicate, jot down, mark, mention, notice, pick up on*, put down, record, register, remark, see, set down,

no-
no-

spot, take in*, transcribe, view, write, write down; SEE CONCEPTS **34,626**

notebook [*n*] *writing tablet*
binder, blotter, daybook, diary, exercise book, journal, log, loose-leaf notebook, memo book, pad, scratch pad, spiral notebook, workbook; SEE CONCEPT **271**

noted [*adj*] *famous, eminent*
acclaimed, celeb, celebrated, conspicuous, distinguished, esteemed, illustrious, leading, name, notable, notorious, of note, popular, prominent, recognized, redoubted, renowned, somebody, star, well-known; SEE CONCEPT **568**

note/notes [*n*] *written communication*
agenda, annotation, calendar, comment, commentary, datum, definition, diary, dispatch, entry, epistle, gloss, inscription, jotting, journal, letter, line, marginalia, mark, memo, memorandum, message, minute, missive, obiter dictum, observation, record, remark, reminder, scratch, scrawl, scribble, summary, thank-you, word; SEE CONCEPT **271**

notes [*n*] *outline*
annotation, draft, impressions, jottings, marginalia, record, report, rough draft, summary, synopsis; SEE CONCEPT **268**

noteworthy [*adj*] *important*
boss*, conspicuous, cool*, evident, exceptional, extraordinary, heavy*, high-profile*, hot*, major-league*, manifest, meaningful, memorable, mind-blowing*, murder, nameable, notable, noticeable, observable, outstanding, patent, prominent, red-letter*, remarkable, serious, significant, something else*, splash*, stand-out*, super, terrific, the end*, underlined*, unique, unusual, utmost; SEE CONCEPTS **567,568**

nothingness [*n2*] *insignificance*
pettiness, smallness, unimportance, worthlessness; SEE CONCEPT **668**

nothing/nothingness [*n*] *emptiness, nonexistence*
annihilation, aught, blank, cipher, extinction, fly speck*, insignificancy, naught, nihility, nobody, nonbeing, nonentity, not anything, nought, nullity, obliteration, oblivion, shutout*, trifle, void, wind*, zero*, zilch*; zip; SEE CONCEPTS **407,707**

nothing to it [*adj*] *effortless*
a breeze*, child's play*, duck soup*, easy, easy as ABC*, easy as pie*, no problem*, no sweat*, painless, piece of cake*, simple, snap*, uncomplicated; SEE CONCEPT **565**

notice [*n1*] *observation*
apprehension, attention, care, cognizance, concern, consideration, ear, grasp, heed, mark, mind, note, observance, regard, remark, respect, thought, understanding; SEE CONCEPTS **34,532**

notice [*n2*] *announcement, information*
admonition, advertisement, advice, caution, caveat, circular, clue, comment, comments, communication, criticism, critique, cue, declaration, directive, enlightenment, goods*, handbill, info*, instruction, intelligence, intimation, know*, lowdown*, manifesto, memo, memorandum, news, note, notification, order, picture, poster, proclamation, remark, review, score, sign, squib*, story, tip, warning, whole story*, write-up; SEE CONCEPTS **271,274,278**

notice [*v*] *observe, perceive*
acknowledge, advert, allude, catch, clock, descry, detect, dig*, discern, distinguish, espy, flash on*, get a load of*, heed, look at, make

out*, mark, mind, note, pick up on, recognize, refer, regard, remark, see, spot, take in; SEE CONCEPTS **34,626**

noticeable [*adj*] *conspicuous, evident*
apparent, appreciable, arresting, arrestive, big as life*, can't miss it*, clear, distinct, eye-catching, manifest, marked, notable, noteworthy, observable, obvious, open and shut*, outstanding, palpable, patent, perceptible, plain, pointed, prominent, remarkable, salient, sensational*, signal, spectacular, striking, under one's nose*, unmistakable; SEE CONCEPTS **529,537,567**

notification [*n*] *announcement*
advertisement, advisory, alert, bulletin, communication, communique, declaration, information, message, news, notice, proclamation, release, report, statement, warning; SEE CONCEPTS **49,274**

notify [*v*] *inform*
acquaint, advise, air, alert, announce, apprise, assert, blazon, brief, broadcast, cable, caution, circulate, clue in, convey, cue, debrief, declare, disclose, disseminate, divulge, enlighten, express, fill in, give, herald, hint, let in on, let know, make known, mention, pass out, post, proclaim, promulgate, publish, radio, report, reveal, send word, speak, spread, state, suggest, talk, teach, telephone, tell, tip off, vent, warn, wire, wise up*, write; SEE CONCEPTS **60,79**

notion [*n1*] *belief, idea*
angle, apprehension, approach, assumption, awareness, clue, comprehension, conceit, concept, conception, consciousness, consideration, cue, discernment, flash, hint, image, imagination, impression, inclination, indication, inkling, insight, intellection, intimation, intuition, judgment, knowledge, opinion, penetration, perception, sentiment, slant, spark*, suggestion, telltale, thought, twist, understanding, view, wind, wrinkle; SEE CONCEPTS **529,532,689**

notion [*n2*] *whim, desire*
caprice, conceit, fancy, humor, imagination, impulse, inclination, wish; SEE CONCEPT **20**

notoriety [*n*] *reputation*
ballyhoo*, celebrity, center stage*, dishonor, disrepute, éclat*, fame, flak*, infamy, ink*, name*, obloquy, opprobrium, renown, rep*, scandal, splash*, spotlight*, wise*; SEE CONCEPTS **388,411**

notorious [*adj*] *known for a trait, often an unadmirable one*
belled, blatant, crying, dishonorable, disreputable, flagrant, glaring, ill-famed, infamous, leading, noted, obvious, open, opprobrious, overt, patent, popular, prominent, questionable, scandalous, shady, shameful, undisputed, wanted, well-known, wicked; SEE CONCEPT **404**

notwithstanding [*adv/prep*] *although, however*
after all, against, at any rate, but, despite, for all that, howbeit, in any case, in any event, in spite of, nevertheless, nonetheless, on the other hand, regardless of, though, to the contrary, withal, yet; SEE CONCEPT **544**

nourish [*v*] *feed, care for*
attend, cherish, comfort, cultivate, encourage, foster, furnish, maintain, nurse, nurture, promote, provide, supply, support, sustain, tend; SEE CONCEPTS **140,295**

nourishing [*adj*] *healthful*
alimentative, beneficial, health-giving, healthy,

nutrient, nutrimental, nutritious, nutritive, wholesome; SEE CONCEPTS *462,537*

nourishment [*n*] *food*
aliment, diet, feed, foodstuff, home cooking*, maintenance, nutriment, nutrition, pabulum, pap*, provender, support, sustenance, viands, victuals, vittles*; SEE CONCEPT *457*

nouveau riche [*n*] *new rich*
DINK*, parvenu, social climber, upstart, vulgarian, yuppie*; SEE CONCEPT *423*

novel [*adj*] *new, original*
at cutting edge*, atypical, avant-garde, breaking new ground*, contemporary, different, far cry*, fresh, funky*, innovative, just out*, modernistic, neoteric, newfangled, new-fashioned, now*, odd, offbeat, peculiar, rare, recent, singular, strange, uncommon, unfamiliar, unique, unusual; SEE CONCEPTS *564,578,797*

novel [*n*] *fictional book*
best-seller, cliff-hanger, fiction, narrative, novelette, novella, paperback, potboiler*, prose, romance, story, tale, yarn*; SEE CONCEPT *280*

novelty [*n1*] *newness, originality*
change, crazy*, creation, dernier cri*, freshness, innovation, last word*, modernity, mutation, newfangled contraption, oddball, oddity, original, origination, permutation, recentness, sport*, strangeness, surprise, unfamiliarity, uniqueness, vicissitude, weird*; SEE CONCEPTS *665,697,715*

novelty [*n2*] *trinket, gadget*
bagatelle*, bauble, bibelot*, conversation piece, curio, curiosity, gewgaw*, gimcrack*, gimmick, item, knick-knack, memento, objet d'art*, oddity, souvenir, trifle, whatnot*; SEE CONCEPTS *260,446*

novice [*n*] *person just learning something*
amateur, apprentice, beginner, colt*, convert*, cub*, first of May*, fledgling, greenhorn, gremlin, know from nothing*, learner, mark*, neophyte, newcomer, new kid on the block*, novitiate, plebe, postulant, prentice, probationer, proselyte, punk*, pupil, recruit, rookie, starter, student, tenderfoot*, trainee; SEE CONCEPTS *348,350,423*

now [*adv*] *presently*
any more, at once, at the moment, at this moment, at this time, away, directly, first off, forthwith, here and now, immediately, in a minute, in a moment, in nothing flat, instanter, instantly, just now, like now*, momentarily, nowadays, on the double*, PDQ*, promptly, pronto*, right away, right now, soon, straightaway, these days, this day, today; SEE CONCEPTS *812,820*

now and then [*adv*] *once in a while*
at intervals, at times, every now and then, every once in a while, every so often, from time to time, hardly, infrequently, intermittently, irregularly, now and again, occasionally, off and on, once in a blue moon*, on occasion, periodically, sometimes, sporadically; SEE CONCEPTS *530,541*

noxious [*adj*] *deadly, injurious*
baneful, corrupting, dangerous, deleterious, destructive, detrimental, fetid, foul, harmful, hurtful, insalubrious, insalutary, noisome, pernicious, pestiferous, pestilent, pestilential, poisonous, putrid, sickly, spoiled, stinking, toxic, unhealthful, unhealthy, unwholesome, venomous, virulent; SEE CONCEPTS *485,537*

nozzle [*n*] *spout*
cock, faucet, spigot, tap; SEE CONCEPTS *445,464,499*

nuance [*n*] *slight difference; shading*
dash, degree, distinction, gradation, hint, implication, nicety, refinement, shade, shadow, soupçon, subtlety, suggestion, suspicion, tinge, touch, trace; SEE CONCEPT *665*

nub [*n1*] *core, gist*
basic, bottom line*, crux, essence, heart*, kernel, meat*, meat and potatoes*, nitty-gritty*, nubbin, nucleus, pith, point, short, substance, upshot; SEE CONCEPTS *661,682,826*

nub [*n2*] *bump, knot*
bulge, knob, lump, node, protuberance, swelling; SEE CONCEPT *471*

nuclear energy [*n*] *nuclear power*
atomic energy, atomic power, nuclear fission power, nuclear fusion power, thermonuclear power; SEE CONCEPT *520*

nuclear reactor [*n*] *atomic reactor*
atomic pile, atomic power plant, breeder reactor, core reactor, nuclear power plant, thermonuclear reactor; SEE CONCEPT *520*

nuclear weapon [*n*] *explosive driven by nuclear energy*
A-bomb, atomic bomb, atomic weapon, doomsday machine*, H-bomb, hydrogen bomb, mininuke*, mirv*, MX*, neutron bomb, nuke*; SEE CONCEPT *500*

nucleus [*n*] *core; basis for something's beginning*
bud, center, crux, embryo, focus, foundation, germ, heart, hub, kernel, matter, nub, pivot, premise, principle, seed, spark; SEE CONCEPTS *393,826,828*

nude [*adj*] *without clothes, covering*
au naturel*, bald, bare, bare-skinned, buck naked*, dishabille*, disrobed, exposed, garmentless, in birthday suit, in one's skin*, in the altogether*, naked, peeled*, raw, skin, stark, stark-naked*, stripped, unattired, unclad, unclothed, uncovered, undraped, undressed, wearing only a smile*, without a stitch*; SEE CONCEPT *485*

nudge [*n/v*] *bump, elbow*
dig, jab, jog, poke, prod, punch, push, shove, tap, touch; SEE CONCEPTS *208,612*

nudity [*n*] *nakedness*
bareness, birthday suit*, natural state, naturism, nudism, the buff*, the nude, the raw*, undress; SEE CONCEPT *453*

nugget [*n*] *lump, solid piece; often of metal ore*
asset, bullion, chunk, clod, clump, gold, hunk, ingot, mass, plum, rock, treasure, wad*; SEE CONCEPT *471*

nuisance [*n*] *annoyance; annoying person*
besetment, blister, bore, bother, botheration, botherment, bum*, creep, drag*, drip*, exasperation, frump, gadfly, headache*, inconvenience, infliction, insect*, irritant, irritation, louse, nag*, nudge*, offense, pain, pain in the neck*, pest, pester, pesterer, pill*, plague, poor excuse*, problem, terror, trouble, vexation; SEE CONCEPTS *412,674*

nuke [*n*] *nuclear weapon*
A-bomb, atomic bomb, atomic weapon, doomsday machine*, H-bomb, hydrogen bomb, neutron bomb; SEE CONCEPT *500*

no
nu

nuke [v1] *attack with nuclear weapons*
annihilate, bomb, destroy, eliminate, incinerate, kill, obliterate, wipe out; SEE CONCEPTS *86,252*

nuke [v2] *cook*
bake, brown, heat, microwave, warm up, zap; SEE CONCEPT *170*

null [adj] *ineffectual, valueless*
absent, bad, barren, characterless, imaginary, ineffective, inefficacious, inoperative, invalid, negative, nonexistent, nothing, null and void*, powerless, unavailing, unreal, unsanctioned, useless, vain, void, worthless; SEE CONCEPTS *560,570*

nullify [v] *cancel, revoke*
abate, abolish, abrogate, annihilate, annul, ax, blue pencil*, bring to naught*, call all bets off*, compensate, confine, counteract, counterbalance, countervail, disannul, forget it*, invalidate, kill*, limit, negate, neutralize, nig*, offset, quash*, render null and void*, renege, renig*, repeal, rescind, restrict, scratch*, scrub*, squash*, stamp out*, take out*, torpedo*, trash*, undo, veto, vitiate, void, wash out*, wipe out*, zap*; SEE CONCEPTS *50,88,121,234*

numb [adj] *deadened, insensitive*
aloof, anesthetized, apathetic, asleep, benumbed, callous, casual, comatose, dazed, dead, detached, disinterested, frozen, immobilized, incurious, indifferent, insensate, insensible, insentient, lethargic, listless, numbed, paralyzed, phlegmatic, remote, senseless, stupefied, stuporous, torpid, unconcerned, unconscious, uncurious, unfeeling, uninterested; SEE CONCEPTS *403,609*

numb [v] *deaden*
anesthetize, benumb, blunt, chill, desensitize, dull, freeze, frost, immobilize, obtund, paralyze, stun, stupefy; SEE CONCEPTS *250,255*

number [n1] *unit of the mathematical system*
cardinal, character, chiffer, cipher, count, decimal, denominator, digit, emblem, figure, folio, fraction, googol, integer, numeral, numerator, ordinal, prime, representation, sign, statistic, sum, symbol, total, whole number; SEE CONCEPTS *765,784*

number [n2] *aggregate, bunch*
abundance, amount, caboodle*, collection, company, conglomeration, crowd, estimate, flock, horde, jillion*, lot, manifoldness, many, multitude, plenitude, plenty, product, quantity, slew*, sum, throng, total, totality, umpteen*, volume, whole, zillion*; SEE CONCEPTS *432,787*

number [v] *count, calculate*
account, add, add up, aggregate, amount, come, computer, count heads*, count noses*, count off, enumerate, estimate, figure in, figure out, include, keep tabs, numerate, reckon, run, run down, run into, run to, sum, take account of, tale, tally, tell, tick off*, total, tote*, tote up*; SEE CONCEPT *764*

numbered [adj] *limited in number*
categorized, checked, contained, counted, designated, doomed, enumerated, fated, fixed, included, indicated, marked, specified, told, totalled; SEE CONCEPT *554*

numberless [adj] *infinite*
countless, endless, heaps*, incalculable, innumerable, jillion, many, multitudinous, myriad, no end of*, no end to*, numerous, umpteen*, uncountable, uncounted, unnumbered, untold, zillion*; SEE CONCEPTS *482,762,781*

numbskull [n] *idiot*
blockhead, bonehead*, buffoon, cretin, dimwit, dolt, dork, dumbbell, dummy, dunce, fathead*, fool, halfwit, ignoramus, imbecile, jerk, moron, nincompoop, ninny*, nitwit, pinhead*, simpleton, stupid person; SEE CONCEPT *412*

numeral [n] *symbol of mathematical system*
character, chiffer, cipher, digit, figure, integer, number; SEE CONCEPTS *284,784*

numeric/numerical [adj] *concerning mathematics*
algebraic, algorithmic, arithmetic, arithmetical, binary, differential, digital, exponent, exponential, fraction, fractional, integral, logarithm, logarithmic, mathematical, numeral, numerary, statistical; SEE CONCEPT *762*

numerous [adj] *many, abundant*
big, copious, diverse, great, infinite, large, legion, lousy with*, multifarious, multitudinal, multitudinous, plentiful, populous, profuse, rife, scads*, several, sundry, thick, umpteen*, various, voluminous, zillion*; SEE CONCEPTS *762,781*

nun [n] *woman in religious order*
abbess, anchorite, canoness, mother superior, postulant, prioress, religious woman, sister, vestal; SEE CONCEPT *361*

nunnery [n] *convent*
abbey, cloister, monastery, priory, religious community, retreat; SEE CONCEPTS *368,516*

nuptial [adj] *concerning marriage*
bridal, conjugal, connubial, espousal, marital, married, matrimonial, spousal, wedded, wedding; SEE CONCEPT *555*

nuptials [n] *marriage ceremony*
bridal, espousal, marriage, matrimony, spousal, wedding; SEE CONCEPT *297*

nurse [n] *person who tends to sick, cares for someone*
assistant, attendant, baby sitter, caretaker, foster parent, medic, minder, nurse practitioner, practical nurse, registered nurse, RN, sitter, therapist, wet nurse; SEE CONCEPTS *357,414*

nurse [v1] *care for, tend*
advance, aid, attend, baby-sit, cherish, cradle, cultivate, encourage, father, feed, forward, foster, further, harbor, humor, immunize, indulge, inoculate, irradiate, keep alive, keep an eye on*, keep tabs on*, look after, medicate, minister to, mother, nourish, nurture, pamper, preserve, promote, see to, serve, sit, succor, support, take care of, take charge of, treat, vaccinate, wait on, watch out for, watch over; SEE CONCEPTS *110,140*

nurse [v2] *give milk, usually from breast*
bottle-feed, breast-feed, cradle, dry-nurse, feed, give suck, lactate, nourish, nurture, suck, suckle, wet-nurse; SEE CONCEPTS *140,295*

nursemaid [n] *nanny*
au pair, baby-sitter, governess, nurserymaid, wet nurse; SEE CONCEPT *295*

nursing home [n] *convalescent home*
convalescent hospital, old folks home*, old people's home, rest home, retirement home; SEE CONCEPTS *312,439,449*

nurture [n] *development, nourishment*
breeding, care, diet, discipline, edibles, education, feed, food, instruction, nutriment, provender, provisions, rearing, subsistence, sustenance,

training, upbringing, viands, victuals; SEE CONCEPTS *457,712*

nurture [v] *feed, care for*

back, bolster, bring up, cherish, cultivate, develop, discipline, educate, foster, instruct, nourish, nurse, nursle, provide, raise, rear, school, support, sustain, tend, train, uphold; SEE CONCEPTS *110,140,295*

nut [n1] *seed of fruit, vegetable*

achene, caryopsis, kernel, stone, utricle; SEE CONCEPT *428*

nut [n2] *crazy, overenthusiastic person*

bedlamite, bigot, crackpot, crank, dement, eccentric, fanatic, fiend, freak, harebrain*, loony*, lunatic, maniac, non compos mentis, screwball*, zealot; SEE CONCEPTS *412,423*

nut house [n] *mental health facility*

bughouse*, funny farm*, insane asylum, loony bin, madhouse*, mental hospital, mental institution, psychiatric hospital, psychiatric ward, sanatorium; SEE CONCEPTS *312,439,516*

nutrient [n] *source of nourishment*

fiber, food, health food, mineral, nutriment, supplements, vitamin; SEE CONCEPT *457*

nutrition [n] *food*

diet, menu, nourishment, nutriment, subsistence, sustenance, victuals; SEE CONCEPT *457*

nutritious [adj] *healthy*

alimental, alimentative, balanced, beneficial, good, healthful, health-giving, invigorating, nourishing, nutrient, nutrimental, nutritive, salubrious, salutary, strengthening, wholesome; SEE CONCEPT *462*

nuts/nutty [adj] *mentally deranged*

absurd, batty*, bedlamite, cracked*, crazy, daffy, daft, demented, eccentric, enthusiastic, foolish, gung ho*, harebrained*, insane, irrational, keen, kooky, loony, lunatic, mad, out of one's mind*, ridiculous, touched, unusual, wacky*, warm, zealous; SEE CONCEPT *403*

nuzzle [v] *cuddle*

bundle, burrow, caress, fondle, nestle, nudge, pet, snug, snuggle; SEE CONCEPTS *190,612*

nylons [n] *stockings*

hose, hosiery, panty hose, tights; SEE CONCEPT *451*

nymph [n] *female nature spirit*

dryad, fairy, goddess, mermaid, naiad, nymphet, spirit, sprite, sylph; SEE CONCEPTS *415,424*

O

oaf [n] *person who is clumsy, stupid*

beast, blunderer, bruiser, brute, chump*, clod, clown, dolt, dumb ox*, dunce, fool, goon*, idiot, imbecile, klutz*, loser, lout*, moron, nincompoop*, ox*, sap*, simpleton; SEE CONCEPT *412*

oafish [adj] *clumsy, stupid*

all thumbs*, blundering, blunderous, bumbling, bungling, butterfingered*, dumb, gawkish, gawky, graceless, half-witted*, heavy-handed, idiotic, ignorant, inelegant, inept, klutzy*, lubberly, lumbering, lumpish, moronic, simple, simpleminded, slow, stumbling, uncoordinated,

undexterous, ungainly, unintelligent; SEE CONCEPTS *401,402,548,584*

oasis [n1] *spring*

fountain, watering hole, well, wellspring; SEE CONCEPT *514*

oasis [n2] *refuge*

asylum, cover, escape, harbor, haven, hideaway, resting place, retreat, safe place, sanctuary, sanctum, shelter; SEE CONCEPTS *198,515*

oath [n1] *promise*

adjuration, affidavit, affirmation, avowal, bond, contract, deposition, pledge, profession, sworn declaration, sworn statement, testimony, vow, word, word of honor; SEE CONCEPTS *71,278*

oath [n2] *curse*

blasphemy, cuss*, cuss word*, dirty name*, dirty word*, expletive, four-letter word*, imprecation, malediction, no-no*, profanity, strong language, swearword; SEE CONCEPTS *54,278*

obdurate [adj] *pigheaded, stubborn*

adamant, bullhead*, callous, cold fish*, dogged, firm, fixed, hanging tough*, hard, hard-boiled*, hard-hearted*, hard-nosed*, harsh, heartless, immovable, implacable, indurate, inexorable, inflexible, iron*, mean, mulish*, obstinate, perverse, relentless, rigid, set in stone*, stiff-necked*, thick-skinned*, tough, tough nut to crack*, unbending, uncompassionate, uncompromising, uncooperative, unemotional, unfeeling, unimpressible, unrelenting, unshakable, unsympathetic, unyielding; SEE CONCEPTS *401,542*

obedience [n] *good behavior; submissiveness*

accordance, acquiescence, agreement, compliance, conformability, conformity, deference, docility, duteousness, dutifulness, duty, manageability, meekness, observance, orderliness, quietness, respect, reverence, servility, submission, subservience, tameness, tractability, willingness; SEE CONCEPTS *411,633*

obedient [adj] *well-behaved; submissive*

acquiescent, amenable, at one's beck and call*, attentive, biddable, complaisant, compliant, controllable, deferential, devoted, docile, docious, duteous, dutiful, faithful, governable, honoring, in one's clutches*, in one's pocket*, in one's power*, law-abiding, loyal, obeisant, obliging, observant, on a string*, pliant, regardful, resigned, respectful, reverential, sheeplike*, subservient, tame, tractable, under control, venerating, well-trained, willing, wrapped around finger*, yielding; SEE CONCEPTS *401,404*

obeisance [n] *salutation*

allegiance, bending of the knee*, bow, curtsy, deference, fealty, genuflection, homage, honor, kowtow*, loyalty, praise, respect, reverence, salaam*; SEE CONCEPTS *154,384*

obeisant [adj] *showing respect*

courtly, deferential, dutiful, regarding, respectful, respecting, reverent, reverential, servile, standing; SEE CONCEPT *401*

obese [adj] *very overweight*

adipose, avoirdupois, corpulent, fat, fleshy*, gross*, heavy, outsize, paunchy, plump, porcine, portly, pudgy, rotund, stout; SEE CONCEPT *491*

obesity [n] *corpulence*

bulk, chubbiness, chunkiness, fatness, overweight, paunchiness, plumpness, portliness, rotundness, stoutness; SEE CONCEPT *734*

nu
ob

obey [*v*] *conform, give in*
abide by, accede, accept, accord, acquiesce, act upon, adhere to, agree, answer, assent, be loyal to, be ruled by, bow to*, carry out, comply, concur, discharge, do as one says, do one's bidding, do one's duty, do what is expected, do what one is told, embrace, execute, follow, fulfill, get in line*, give way*, heed, hold fast*, keep, knuckle under*, live by, mind, observe, perform, play second fiddle*, respond, serve, submit, surrender, take orders, toe the line*; SEE CONCEPTS *91,136*

obfuscate [*v*] *confuse*
baffle, becloud, befuddle, bewilder, cloud, complicate, conceal, confound, darken, fog, fuddle, muddle, obscure, perplex, puzzle, rattle; SEE CONCEPT *16*

obituary [*n*] *notice of person's death*
announcement, death notice, eulogy, mortuary tribute, necrology, obit, register; SEE CONCEPTS *268,270*

object [*n1*] *thing able to be seen/felt/perceived*
article, body, bulk, commodity, doodad*, doohickey*, entity, fact, gadget, gizmo*, item, mass, matter, phenomenon, reality, something, substance, thingamajig*, volume, whatchamacallit*, widget*; SEE CONCEPT *433*

object [*n2*] *purpose, use*
aim, design, duty, end, end in view, end purpose, function, goal, idea, intent, intention, mark, mission, motive, objective, point, reason, target, view, wish; SEE CONCEPT *659*

object [*n3*] *aim, recipient*
butt*, focus, ground zero*, receiver, target, victim, zero*; SEE CONCEPTS *124,532*

object [*v*] *disagree, argue against*
balk, be displeased, challenge, complain, crab*, criticize, cross, demur, deprecate, disapprove, disavow, discommend, discountenance, disesteem, dispute, dissent, except, expostulate, frown, go-one-on-one*, gripe, grouse, inveigh, kick*, make a stink*, mix it up with*, oppose, protest, rail, raise objection, rant, rave, remonstrate, sound off*, spurn, squawk*, storm, take exception, take on, tangle*; SEE CONCEPTS *12,21,46*

objection [*n*] *argument, disagreement*
cavil, censure, challenge, counter-argument, criticism, declination, demur, demurral, demurring, difficulty, disapprobation, disapproval, discontent, disesteem, disinclination, dislike, displeasure, dissatisfaction, doubt, exception, grievance, gripe, hesitation, kick, niggle*, odium, opposition, protest, protestation, question, rejection, reluctance, remonstrance, remonstration, repugnancy, revelment, scruple, shrinking, squawk*, stink*, unwillingness; SEE CONCEPTS *21,46,410,689*

objectionable [*adj*] *not nice; unpleasant*
abhorrent, censurable, deplorable, disagreeable, dislikable, displeasing, distasteful, exceptionable, ill-favored, inadmissible, indecorous, inexpedient, insufferable, intolerable, invidious, loathsome, lousy, murder, noxious, obnoxious, offensive, opprobrious, poison, regrettable, repellent, reprehensible, repugnant, repulsive, revolting, unacceptable, undesirable, unfit, unpalatable, unsatisfactory, unseemly, unsuit-

able, unwanted, unwelcome; SEE CONCEPTS *548,558,570*

objective [*adj*] *fair, impartial*
cold, cool, detached, disinterested, dispassionate, equitable, evenhanded, impersonal, judicial, just, like it is*, nondiscriminatory, nonpartisan, open-minded*, straight, strictly business*, unbiased, uncolored, unemotional, uninvolved, unprejudiced, unprepossessed; SEE CONCEPTS *403,542*

objective [*n*] *aim, goal*
ambition, aspiration, design, end, end in view*, ground zero*, intention, mark, mission, object, purpose, target, zero*; SEE CONCEPT *659*

objectively [*adv*] *impartially*
considerately, detachedly, disinterestedly, dispassionately, equitably, evenhandedly, indifferently, justly, neutrally, on the up and up*, open-mindedly*, soberly, squarely, with an open mind*, with impartiality, with objectivity, without favor, without prejudice; SEE CONCEPTS *542,544*

objectivity [*n*] *impartiality*
detachment, disinterest, disinterestedness, dispassion, equality, equitableness, indifference, neutrality, open-mindedness; SEE CONCEPTS *403,542*

objet d'art [*n*] *work of art*
bibelot, bric-a-brac, collector's item, collector's piece, curio, knickknack; SEE CONCEPT *446*

objurgate [*v*] *berate*
bawl out, castigate, censure, chastise, chew out*, chide, give one hell*, jump all over*, rake over the coals*, rebuke, reprimand, reproach, scold, upbraid; SEE CONCEPT *52*

obligate [*v*] *require*
astrict, bind, constrain, force, indebt, make indebted, oblige, restrain, restrict; SEE CONCEPTS *53,130,646*

obligated [*adj*] *bound*
bounden, called by duty, committed, compelled, contracted, duty-bound, enslaved, forced, indebted, indentured, obliged, pledged, required, tied, under obligation, urged; SEE CONCEPT *554*

obligation [*n*] *responsibility*
accountability, accountableness, agreement, bond, burden, business, call, cause, charge, chit*, commitment, committal, compulsion, conscience, constraint, contract, debit, debt, devoir, due bill, dues, duty, engagement, IOU*, liability, must, necessity, need, occasion, onus, ought, part, place, promise, requirement, restraint, right, trust, understanding; SEE CONCEPTS *329,335,388,645*

obligatory [*adj*] *essential, required*
binding, coercive, compulsatory, compulsory, de rigueur, enforced, imperative, imperious, mandatory, necessary, requisite, unavoidable; SEE CONCEPT *546*

oblige [*v1*] *require*
bind, coerce, command, compel, constrain, force, impel, make, necessitate, obligate, shotgun*; SEE CONCEPTS *14,242,646*

oblige [*v2*] *do a favor or kindness*
accommodate, aid, assist, avail, bend over backward*, benefit, come around, contribute, convenience, don't make waves*, favor, fill the bill*, fit in, go fifty-fifty*, gratify, grin and bear it*, help, indulge, make a deal*, make room*, meet halfway*, please, profit, put oneself out*, roll

with it*, serve, swim with the tide*, take it*, toe the mark*; SEE CONCEPTS *110,136,384*

obliged [*adj*] *bound*
bounden, called by duty, committed, compelled, contracted, duty-bound, enslaved, forced, indebted, indentured, obligated, pledged, required, tied, under obligation, urged; SEE CONCEPT *554*

obliging [*adj*] *friendly, helpful*
accommodating, agreeable, amiable, cheerful, civil, complaisant, considerate, cooperative, courteous, eager to please, easy, easygoing, good-humored, good-natured, hospitable, kind, lenient, mild, polite, willing; SEE CONCEPTS *401,404*

oblique [*adj1*] *slanting; at an angle*
angled, askance, askew, aslant, asymmetrical, awry, bent, cater-cornered, crooked, diagonal, distorted, diverging, inclined, inclining, leaning, on the bias, pitched, pitching, sideways, skew, slanted, sloped, sloping, strained, tilted, tilting, tipped, tipping, turned, twisted; SEE CONCEPTS *485,490*

oblique [*adj2*] *indirect, evasive*
backhanded, circuitous, circular, circumlocutory, collateral, devious, implied, obliquitous, obscure, roundabout, sidelong, vague; SEE CONCEPT *267*

obliterate [*v*] *destroy*
annihilate, ax*, black out*, blot out*, blue pencil*, bog, cancel, cover, cut, defeat, delete, do in*, efface, eliminate, eradicate, erase, expunge, exterminate, extirpate, finish, finish off*, kill, knock off*, knock out*, KO*, level*, liquidate, mark out, nix*, obscure, off, ravage, root out*, rub off*, rub out*, scratch, scrub, shoot down, sink, smash, squash, take apart, take out*, torpedo*, total*, trash*, wash out*, waste, wipe off face of earth*, wipe out*, X-out*, zap*; SEE CONCEPT *252*

oblivion [*n1*] *mental blankness*
abeyance, amnesia, carelessness, disregard, forgetfulness, inadvertence, indifference, insensibility, insensibleness, Lethe*, neglect, nirvana*, obliviousness, unawareness, unconcern, unconsciousness, unmindfulness; SEE CONCEPTS *410,633*

oblivion [*n2*] *nothingness, obscurity*
blackness, darkness, eclipse, emptiness, extinction, limbo, nihility, nirvana*, nonexistence, nothing, nowhere*, nullity, out there*, void; SEE CONCEPTS *407,672,679*

oblivious [*adj*] *unaware, ignorant*
absent, absentminded, absorbed, abstracted, amnesic, blind*, blundering, careless, deaf*, disregardful, distracted, dreamy, forgetful, forgetting, gone, heedless, inattentive, incognizant, inconversant, insensible, neglectful, negligent, not all there*, out to lunch*, overlooking, preoccupied, regardless, spacey*, strung out*, unacquainted, unconcerned, unconscious, undiscerning, unfamiliar, uninformed, uninstructed, unknowing, unmindful, unnoticing, unobservant, unrecognizing, unwitting, zonked*; SEE CONCEPTS *402,403,542*

oblong [*adj*] *elongated and rounded*
egg-shaped, ellipsoidal, elliptical, elongate, long, oval, ovaliform, ovaloid, ovate, ovated, ovoid, rectangular; SEE CONCEPT *486*

obloquy [*n*] *calumny*
abuse, animadversion, aspersion, bad press, censure, criticism, defamation, disgrace, humiliation, ignominy, insult, invective, reproach, slander, vituperation; SEE CONCEPTS *271,277,278*

obnoxious [*adj*] *offensive, repulsive*
abhorrent, abominable, annoying, awful, beastly*, big mouth*, detestable, disagreeable, disgusting, dislikable, displeasing, foul, gross*, hateable, hateful, heel, horrid, insufferable, invidious, loathsome, mean, nasty, nauseating, objectionable, odious, off-color*, ornery, pain in the neck*, pesky*, pestiferous, pill*, repellent, reprehensible, repugnant, revolting, rotten, sickening, stinking, unpleasant; SEE CONCEPTS *267,401,542*

obscene [*adj*] *indecent, offensive, immoral*
atrocious, barnyard*, bawdy, blue*, coarse, crude, dirty*, disgusting, evil, filthy, foul, gross, heinous, hideous, horrible, immodest, improper, impure, lascivious, lewd, licentious, loathsome, loose*, lustful, nasty, noisome, outrageous, porno*, pornographic, profane, prurient, rank*, raunchy*, raw, repellent, repugnant, ribald, salacious, scabrous, scatological, scurrilous, shameless, shocking, sickening, smutty*, suggestive, unchaste, unclean, unwholesome, vile, wanton, wicked, X-rated*; SEE CONCEPTS *267,372,545*

obscenity [*n*] *indecency, immorality; vulgarism*
abomination, affront, atrocity, bawdiness, blight, blueness*, coarseness, curse, dirtiness, dirty name*, dirty word*, evil, filthiness, foulness, four-letter word*, immodesty, impropriety, impurity, indecency, indelicacy, lewdness, licentiousness, lubricity, offense, outrage, porn*, pornography, profanity, prurience, salacity, scatology, scurrility, sleaze*, smut*, smuttiness, suggestiveness, swearword, vileness, vulgarity, wrong, X-rating*; SEE CONCEPTS *278,645*

obscure [*adj1*] *not easily understood*
abstruse, ambiguous, arcane, clear as mud*, complicated, concealed, confusing, cryptic, dark, deep, dim, doubtful, enigmatic, enigmatical, esoteric, far-out, hazy, hidden, illegible, illogical, impenetrable, incomprehensible, inconceivable, incredible, indecisive, indefinite, indeterminate, indistinct, inexplicable, inscrutable, insoluble, intricate, involved, mysterious, occult, opaque, recondite, unaccountable, unbelievable, unclear, undefined, unfathomable, unintelligible, vague; SEE CONCEPT *529*

obscure [*adj2*] *cloudy, shadowy*
blurred, caliginous, clouded, dark, dense, dim, dusk, dusky, faint, fuliginous, gloomy, indistinct, lightless, murky, obfuscated, shady, somber, tenebrous, umbrageous, unilluminated, unlit, veiled; SEE CONCEPT *617*

obscure [*adj3*] *out-of-the-way, little-known*
abstruse, arcane, blind, cabalistic, close, covered, cryptic, dark, deep, devious, distant, enigmatic, esoteric, far, far-off, hidden, humble, inaccessible, inconspicuous, inglorious, invisible, irrelevant, lonesome, lowly, minor, mysterious, nameless, odd, oracular, orphic, rare, recondite, remote, removed, reticent, retired, secluded, secret, secretive, seldom seen, sequestered, solitary, undisclosed, undistinguished, unheard-of, unhonored, unimportant, unknown, unnoted, unseen, unsung; SEE CONCEPT *576*

obscure [*v*] *conceal, hide*
adumbrate, becloud, bedim, befog, belie, blear, blind, block, block out, blur, camouflage, cloak,

cloud, cloud the issue*, con, confuse, cover, cover up, darken, dim, disguise, double-talk*, eclipse, equivocate, falsify, fog, fuzz, gloom, gray, haze, mask, misrepresent, mist, muddy, muddy the waters*, murk, obfuscate, overcast, overcloud, overshadow, pettifog*, screen, shade, shadow, shroud, stonewall*, throw up smoke screen*, veil, wrap; SEE CONCEPTS 16,63,172,188

obsequious [*adj*] *groveling, submissive*
abject, beggarly, brownnosing*, complacent, compliable, compliant, cringing, crouching, deferential, enslaved, fawning, flattering, ingratiating, kowtowing*, menial, obeisant, oily*, parasitic, parasitical, prostrate, respectful, servile, slavish, sneaking, sniveling, spineless*, stipendiary, subject, submissive, subordinate, subservient, sycophantic, toadying*, unctuous; SEE CONCEPTS 401,404

obsequy [*n*] *funeral ceremony*
eulogy, funeral rite, funeral service; SEE CONCEPTS 69,278

observable [*adj*] *apparent*
appreciable, clear, detectable, discernible, discoverable, evident, noticeable, obvious, open, palpable, patent, perceivable, perceptible, recognizable, sensible, tangible, visible; SEE CONCEPTS 529,576

observance [*n1*] *attention to, knowledge of something*
acknowledgment, acquittal, acquittance, adherence, awareness, carrying out, celebration, cognizance, compliance, discharge, fidelity, fulfillment, heed, heeding, honoring, keeping, mark, mind, note, notice, obedience, observation, performance, regard, remark, satisfaction; SEE CONCEPTS 409,410,633

observance [*n2*] *ceremony, rite*
celebration, ceremonial, custom, fashion, form, formality, liturgy, performance, practice, ritual, rule, service, tradition; SEE CONCEPTS 377,384,688

observant [*adj*] *alert, watchful*
advertent, alive, attentive, bright, clear-sighted*, comprehending, considering, contemplating, correct, deducing, detecting, discerning, discovering, discriminating, eager, eagle-eyed*, heedful, intelligent, intentive, interested, keen, mindful, not missing a trick*, obedient, observative, on one's toes*, on the ball*, penetrating, perceptive, questioning, quick, regardful, searching, sensitive, sharp, sharp-eyed*, surveying, understanding, vigilant, wide-awake*; SEE CONCEPTS 402,403

observation [*n1*] *attention, scrutiny*
ascertainment, check, cognition, cognizance, conclusion, consideration, detection, estimation, examination, experience, heedfulness, information, inspection, investigation, knowledge, mark, measurement, mind, monitoring, note, notice, noticing, once-over*, overlook, perception, probe, recognizing, regard, remark, research, review, search, study, supervision, surveillance, view, watching; SEE CONCEPTS 409,410

observation [*n2*] *comment on something scrutinized*
annotation, catch phrase, comeback, commentary, crack*, finding, mention, mouthful*, note, obiter dictum, opinion, pronouncement, reflection, remark, saying, say so*, thought, utterance, wisecrack; SEE CONCEPTS 51,278

observe [*v1*] *see, notice*
beam, behold, catch, contemplate, detect, dig, discern, discover, distinguish, eagle-eye*, espy, examine, eyeball*, flash*, get a load of*, get an eyeful of*, inspect, keep one's eye on*, lamp*, look at, make out*, mark, mind, monitor, note, pay attention to, perceive, pick up on*, read, recognize, regard, scrutinize, spot, spy, study, survey, take in*, view, watch, witness; SEE CONCEPTS 24,34,103,265,626

observe [*v2*] *comment, remark*
animadvert, commentate, declare, mention, mouth off*, note, opine, say, state, wisecrack; SEE CONCEPT 51

observe [*v3*] *celebrate, commemorate*
dedicate, hold, honor, keep, remember, respect, revere, reverence, solemnize, venerate; SEE CONCEPT 377

observe [*v4*] *abide by, obey*
adhere, adopt, comply, comply with, conform, follow, fulfill, heed, honor, keep, mind, perform, respect; SEE CONCEPTS 91,384

observer [*n*] *spectator*
beholder, bystander, eyewitness, gaper, gazer, looker, looker-on, onlooker, viewer, watcher, witness; SEE CONCEPTS 366,423

obsess [*v*] *preoccupy*
beset, consume, dominate, engross, grip, harass, haunt, hold, infatuate, possess, torment; SEE CONCEPT 403

obsessed [*adj*] *consumed, driven about belief, desire*
bedeviled, beset, bewitched, captivated, controlled, dogged*, dominated, eat sleep and breathe*, engrossed, fiendish, fixated, gripped, harassed, haunted, have on the brain*, held, hooked, hung up on*, immersed in, infatuated, into*, overpowered, plagued*, possessed, preoccupied, prepossessed, really into*, seized, taken over, tied up*, tormented, troubled, turned on, up to here in*, wound up with*, wrapped up in*; SEE CONCEPTS 403,404

obsession [*n*] *fixation; consumption with belief, desire*
attraction, ax to grind*, bug in ear*, case*, complex, compulsion, concrete idea, craze*, crush, delusion, enthusiasm, fancy, fascination, fetish, hang-up*, idée fixe, infatuation, mania, monkey*, must, neurosis, one-track mind*, passion, phantom, phobia, preoccupation, something on the brain*, thing*, tiger by the tail*; SEE CONCEPTS 20,410,529,689,690

obsolete [*adj*] *no longer in use, in vogue*
anachronistic, ancient, antediluvian, antiquated, antique, archaic, bygone, dated, dead, dead and gone*, dinosaur*, discarded, disused, done for*, dusty, extinct, fossil, gone, had it*, has-been*, horse and buggy*, kaput*, moldy*, moth-eaten*, old, old-fashioned, old-hat, old-school, out*, outmoded, out-of-date, out-of-fashion, outworn, passé, stale, superannuated, superseded, timeworn, unfashionable; SEE CONCEPTS 539,560,589

obstacle [*n*] *impediment, barrier*
bar, block, booby trap*, bump*, catch, Catch-22*, check, clog*, crimp*, difficulty, disincentive, encumbrance, hamper, handicap, hang-up*, hardship, hindrance, hitch*, hurdle, interference, interruption, joker*, monkey wrench*, mountain, obstruction, restriction, rub*, snag, stumbling

block*, traverse, vicissitude; SEE CONCEPTS 470,532,666,674

obstinate [*adj*] *stubborn, determined*
adamant, cantankerous, contradictory, contrary, contumacious, convinced, dead set on*, dogged, dogmatic, firm, hard, hardened, headstrong, heady, immovable, indomitable, inflexible, intractable, intransigent, locked in*, mulish*, obdurate, opinionated, opinionative, persistent, pertinacious, perverse, pigheaded*, recalcitrant, refractory, relentless, resolved, restive, self-willed, steadfast, strong-minded, tenacious, unalterable, unflinching, unmanageable, unyielding, willful; SEE CONCEPTS 401,542

obstreperous [*adj*] *noisy*
blusterous, boisterous, booming, clamorous, disorderly, loud, out of hand, piercing, raising Cain*, raising the roof*, rambunctious, riotous, rowdy, screaming, strepitous, tumultuous, unmanageable, unruly, uproarious, vociferous, wild; SEE CONCEPTS 592,594

obstruct [*v*] *prevent, restrict*
arrest, bar, barricade, block, check, choke, clog, close, congest, crab, curb, cut off, drag one's feet*, fill, foul up, frustrate, get in the way*, hamper, hamstring*, hang up*, hide, hinder, hold up, impede, inhibit, interfere, interrupt, mask, monkey with*, obscure, occlude, plug, restrain, retard, sandbag*, shield, shut off, slow down, stall, stonewall*, stop, stopper, stymie*, terminate, throttle, thwart, trammel, weigh down; SEE CONCEPTS 5,121,130

obstruction [*n*] *obstacle, impediment*
bar, barricade, barrier, block, blockage, blocking, booby trap*, check, checkmate*, circumvention, difficulty, gridlock*, hamper, hindrance, hurdle, interference, jam*, lock, monkey wrench*, mountain*, restraint, roadblock*, snag, stop, stoppage, stumbling block*, trammel, trouble, wall; SEE CONCEPTS 470,532,666,674

obtain [*v*] *get, acquire*
access, accomplish, achieve, annex, attain, beg borrow or steal*, capture, chalk up*, collect, come by, compass, cop*, corral, drum up*, earn, effect, fetch, gain, gather, get at, get hold of*, get one's hands on*, glean, gobble up*, grab, have, hoard, inherit, invade, lay up, make use of, nab*, occupy, pick up, pocket*, procure, purchase, reach, realize, reap, receive, recover, retrieve, salvage, save, score, scrape together, scrape up, secure, seize, snag, take, wangle, win; SEE CONCEPT 120

obtainable [*adj*] *achievable, available*
at hand*, attainable, derivable, duck soup*, gettable, in stock, no problem*, no sweat*, on deck*, on offer*, on tap*, piece of cake*, procurable, purchasable, pushover, ready, realizable, securable, there for the taking*, to be had*; SEE CONCEPTS 528,576

obtrusive [*adj*] *pushy, obvious*
bulging, busy, forward, impertinent, importunate, interfering, intrusive, jutting, meddlesome, meddling, nosy, noticeable, officious, presumptuous, projecting, prominent, protruding, protuberant, prying, sticking out; SEE CONCEPTS 401,542

obtuse [*adj1*] *slow to understand*
dense, dopey*, dull*, dumb, imperceptive, insensitive, opaque, slow on uptake*, stolid, thick, uncomprehending, unintelligent; SEE CONCEPT 402

obtuse [*adj2*] *blunt, not sharp*
round, rounded; SEE CONCEPTS 485,486

obviate [*v*] *make unnecessary*
anticipate, avert, block, counter, counteract, deter, do away with, forestall, forfend, hinder, interfere, interpose, intervene, preclude, prevent, remove, restrain, rule out, stave off, ward; SEE CONCEPT 121

obvious [*adj*] *apparent, understandable*
accessible, barefaced, bright, clear, clear as a bell*, conclusive, conspicuous, discernible, distinct, distinguishable, evident, explicit, exposed, glaring, indisputable, in evidence, lucid, manifest, noticeable, observable, open, overt, palpable, patent, perceivable, perceptible, plain, precise, prominent, pronounced, public, recognizable, self-evident, self-explanatory, standing out, straightforward, transparent, unconcealed, undeniable, undisguised, unmistakable, unsubtle, visible; SEE CONCEPTS 485,529

obviously [*adv*] *unmistakable*
apparently, certainly, clearly, definitely, distinctly, evidently, incontestably, noticeably, of course, openly, plainly, seemingly, surely, undeniably, undoubtedly, unquestionably, visibly, without doubt; SEE CONCEPTS 535,552

occasion [*n1*] *chance*
break*, convenience, demand, excuse, incident, instant, moment, need, occurrence, opening, opportunity, possibility, season, shot*, show, time, use; SEE CONCEPT 693

occasion [*n2*] *reason, cause*
antecedent, basis, call, circumstance, determinant, excuse, foundation, ground, grounds, incident, inducement, influence, justification, motivation, motive, necessity, obligation, prompting, provocation, purpose, right, warrant; SEE CONCEPT 661

occasion [*n3*] *event, happening*
affair, celebration, circumstance, episode, experience, go*, goings-on*, happening, incident, instant, milepost*, milestone, moment, occurrence, scene, thing*, time, while; SEE CONCEPTS 2,386

occasion [*v*] *make happen, bring about*
breed, cause, create, do, effect, elicit, engender, evoke, generate, give rise to, hatch, induce, influence, inspire, lead to, move, muster, originate, persuade, produce, prompt, provoke, work up; SEE CONCEPTS 68,242

occasional [*adj*] *irregular, sporadic*
casual, desultory, especial, exceptional, exclusive, few, incidental, infrequent, intermittent, not habitual, odd, off and on*, particular, random, rare, scarce, seldom, semioccasional, special, specific, uncommon, unfrequent, unusual; SEE CONCEPTS 530,541

occasionally [*adv*] *every now and then*
at intervals, at random, at times, every so often, from time to time, hardly, infrequently, irregularly, now and again, once in a blue moon*, once in a while, once or twice*, on occasion, periodically, seldom, sometimes, sporadically, uncommonly; SEE CONCEPTS 530,541

occlude [*v*] *block, prevent*
choke, clog, close, close out, congest, curb, fill, hinder, impede, leave out, lock out, obstruct, plug, seal, shut, stopper, stop up, throttle; SEE CONCEPTS 121,201

occlusion [*n*] *obstruction*
barricade, barrier, block, blockage, blocking,

ob
oc

closure, stoppage; SEE CONCEPTS *470,532,666, 674*

occult [*adj*] *mysterious, secret; supernatural*
abstruse, acromatic, arcane, cabalistic, concealed, deep, eerie, esoteric, hermetic, hidden, invisible, magic, magical, mystic, mystical, obscure, orphic, preternatural, profound, psychic, recondite, transmundane, unearthly, unknown, unrevealed, veiled, weird; SEE CONCEPTS *576,582*

occupancy [*n*] *residence of place*
control, deed, habitation, holding, inhabitance, inhabitancy, occupation, ownership, possession, retention, settlement, tenancy, tenure, term, title, use; SEE CONCEPTS *518,710*

occupant [*n*] *person who resides in a place*
addressee, denizen, dweller, holder, householder, incumbent, indweller, inhabitant, lessee, occupier, possessor, renter, resident, resider, tenant, user; SEE CONCEPT *414*

occupation [*nl*] *profession, business*
activity, affair, calling, chosen work, craft, daily grind*, day gig*, do, dodge*, employment, game*, grindstone*, hang*, job, lick*, line, line of work, métier, moonlight*, nine-to-five*, play*, post, pursuit, racket*, rat race*, slot*, thing*, trade, vocation, walk of life*, what one is into*, work; SEE CONCEPTS *349,351,360*

occupation [*n2*] *control, possession*
habitation, holding, inhabitancy, inhabitation, occupancy, ownership, residence, settlement, tenancy, tenure, title, use; SEE CONCEPTS *518,710*

occupation [*n3*] *seizure, takeover*
attack, capture, conquest, entering, foreign rule, invasion, subjugation; SEE CONCEPTS *86,90,320*

occupied [*adj1*] *busy*
active, clocked up*, employed, engaged, engrossed, head over heels*, tied up*, too much on plate*, working; SEE CONCEPT *542*

occupied [*adj2*] *inhabited; in use*
busy, engaged, full, leased, lived-in*, peopled*, populated, populous, rented, settled, taken, unavailable, utilized; SEE CONCEPT *560*

occupy [*vl*] *be busy with*
absorb, amuse, attend, be active with, be concerned with, busy, divert, employ, engage, engross, entertain, fill, hold attention, immerse, interest, involve, keep busy, monopolize, preoccupy, soak, take up, tie up, utilize; SEE CONCEPTS *7,17,19,22*

occupy [*v2*] *reside; use*
be established, be in command, be in residence, cover, dwell, ensconce, establish, fill, hold, inhabit, involve, keep, live in, maintain, own, people, permeate, pervade, populate, possess, remain, sit, stay, take up, tenant, utilize; SEE CONCEPTS *225,226*

occupy [*v3*] *seize, take over*
capture, conquer, garrison, hold, invade, keep, obtain, overrun, take possession; SEE CONCEPTS *86,90,320*

occur [*vl*] *take place, happen*
action, appear, arise, befall, be found, be present, betide, chance, come about, come off*, come to pass, cook*, crop up, develop, ensue, eventualize, eventuate, exist, follow, go, jell*, manifest, materialize, obtain, present itself, result, shake*, show, smoke*, take place, transpire, turn out, turn up; SEE CONCEPTS *4,242*

occur [*v2*] *come to mind*
come to one*, cross one's mind*, dawn on*, expose, flash*, go through one's head*, hit, offer itself, present itself, reveal, spring to mind*, strike, suggest itself; SEE CONCEPTS *34,43*

occurrence [*n*] *happening, development*
accident, adventure, affair, appearance, circumstance, condition, contingency, emergency, episode, event, exigency, existence, incidence, incident, instance, juncture, manifestation, materialization, occasion, pass, piece, proceeding, routine, scene, situation, state, thing*, transaction, transpiration; SEE CONCEPTS *3,4,230,696*

ocean [*n*] *very large body of water*
blue*, bounding main*, brine, briny*, briny deep*, Davy Jones's locker*, deep, drink*, high seas*, main, pond, puddle, salt water, sea, seaway, Seven Seas, sink, tide; SEE CONCEPT *514*

oceanic [*adj*] *marine*
aquatic, coastal, maritime, nautical, naval, oceangoing, oceanographic, of the sea, pelagic, seafaring, seagoing; SEE CONCEPT *536*

odd/oddball [*adj1*] *unusual, abnormal*
atypical, avant-garde, bizarre, character, crazy, curious, deviant, different, eccentric, erratic, exceptional, extraordinary, fantastic, flaky*, freak*, freakish*, freaky*, funny, idiosyncratic, irregular, kinky*, kooky*, offbeat, off-the-wall*, outlandish, out of the ordinary, peculiar, quaint, queer, rare, remarkable, singular, spacey*, strange, uncanny, uncommon, unconventional, unique, way out*, weird, weirdo*, whimsical; SEE CONCEPTS *404,542,564*

odd [*adj2*] *miscellaneous, various*
accidental, casual, chance, contingent, different, fluky*, fortuitous, fragmentary, incidental, irregular, occasional, odd-lot*, periodic, random, seasonal, sundry, varied; SEE CONCEPT *552*

odd [*adj3*] *single, unmatched; uneven*
additional, alone, exceeding, individual, irregular, left, leftover, lone, lonely, over, over and above, remaining, singular, sole, solitary, spare, surplus, unconsumed, unitary, unpaired; SEE CONCEPTS *480,577*

oddity [*n1*] *abnormality*
anomaly, bizarreness, characteristic, conversation piece, curiosity, eccentricity, extraordinariness, freak, freakishness, idiosyncrasy, incongruity, irregularity, kink, oddness, outlandishness, peculiarity, phenomenon, queerness, quirk, rarity, singularity, strangeness, unconventionality, unnaturalness; SEE CONCEPTS *260,411,665*

oddity/oddball [*n2*] *person who is very different*
case*, character, duck*, eccentric, fish out of water*, maverick, misfit, odd bird*, original*, rara avis, screwball*, weirdo*; SEE CONCEPT *423*

odds [*n1*] *advantage*
allowance, benefit, bulge, difference, disparity, dissimilarity, distinction, draw, edge, handicap, head start, lead, overlay, start, superiority, vantage; SEE CONCEPT *693*

odds [*n2*] *probability*
balance, chances, favor, likelihood, superiority, toss-up; SEE CONCEPT *650*

odds and ends [*n*] *miscellaneous paraphernalia*
assortment, bits, bits and pieces*, debris, etcetera*, hodgepodge, jumble, leavings, litter, medley, mélange, melee, miscellany, motley, oddments, olio, particles, potpourri, remnants,

rest, rubbish, rummage, scraps, sundry items, this and that*; SEE CONCEPTS 260,432,446

odds-on-favorite [*n*] *front-runner*
best bet, contender, favorite, first choice, top seed; SEE CONCEPTS 423,446

ode [*n*] *poem*
ballad, composition, epode, limerick, lyric, poesy, rhyme, song, sonnet, verse; SEE CONCEPTS 268,282

odious [*adj*] *hateful, horrible*
abhorrent, abominable, creepy*, detestable, disgusting, execrable, foul, hateable, horrid, loathsome, mean, obnoxious, offensive, ornery, pain in the neck*, repellent, repugnant, repulsive, revolting, unpleasant, vile; SEE CONCEPTS 401,404

odium [*n*] *shame, dishonor*
abhorrence, antipathy, aversion, bar sinister*, black eye*, blame, blot, blur, brand, censure, condemnation, detestation, disapproval, discredit, disesteem, disfavor, disgrace, dislike, disprobation, disrepute, enmity, execration, hate, hatred, ignominy, infamy, malice, obloquy, onus, opprobrium, rebuke, reprobation, resentment, slur, spot, stain, stigma; SEE CONCEPTS 29,388

odor [*n*] *scent*
air, aroma, bouquet, effluvium, efflux, emanation, essence, exhalation, flavor, fragrance, musk, perfume, pungence, pungency, redolence, smell, snuff, stench, stink, tang, tincture, trail, whiff; SEE CONCEPT 599

odorless [*adj*] *without fragrance*
deodorant, deodorizing, flat, inodorous, odorfree, unaromatic, unfragrant, unperfumed, unscented, unsmelling; SEE CONCEPT 598

odorous [*adj*] *having fragrance*
aromatic, balmy, dank, effluvious, fetid, flavorsome, flowery, foul, fragrant, heady, honeyed, loud, malodorous, mephitic, miasmic, moldy, musty, nauseous, odoriferant, odoriferous, offensive, olfactive, olfactory, perfumatory, perfumed, perfumy, pungent, putrid, redolent, reeking, rotten, savorous, savory, scented, scentful, scentladen, skunky*, smelly, spicy, stagnant, stale, stinking, strong, sweet, sweet-scented, sweetsmelling, tumaceous, unsavory, whiffy*; SEE CONCEPT 598

odyssey [*n*] *journey*
adventure, excursion, expedition, exploration, pilgrimage, quest, sojourn, tour, travels, trek, trip, voyage, wanderings; SEE CONCEPT 224

of course [*adv*] *as expected*
by all means, certainly, definitely, indeed, indubitably, naturally, obviously, surely, undoubtedly, without a doubt; SEE CONCEPT 544

off [*adj1*] *gone; remote*
absent, canceled, finished, inoperative, negligible, not employed, not on duty, on vacation, outside, postponed, slender, slight, slim, small, unavailable; SEE CONCEPT 552

off [*adj2*] *inferior; spoiled*
bad, decomposed, disappointing, disheartening, displeasing, low-quality, mortifying, not up to par*, not up to snuff*, poor, putrid, quiet, rancid, rotten, slack, sour, substandard, turned, unrewarding, unsatisfactory; SEE CONCEPT 570

off [*adv*] *apart, away*
above, absent, afar, ahead, aside, away from, behind, below, beneath, beside, disappearing, divergent, elsewhere, far, farther away, gone away,

in the distance, not here, out, over, removed, to one side, turning aside, up front, vanishing; SEE CONCEPTS 583,778

off and on [*adv*] *intermittently*
alternately, at intervals, at times, every once in a while, every so often, fluctuating, from time to time, irregularly, now and then, occasionally, once in a while, on occasion, sometimes, sporadically, vacillating, variably; SEE CONCEPTS 530,541

offbeat [*adj*] *strange, very different*
bizarre, bohemian*, eccentric, far-out, freaky, fresh, idiosyncratic, novel, oddball, outré, uncommon, unconventional, unique, unorthodox, unusual, way-out*, weird; SEE CONCEPT 564

off-center [*adj*] *wide*
adrift, askew, astray, far-off, inaccurate, off-course, off-target, off the mark, stray; SEE CONCEPTS 581,583

off-color [*adj*] *risqué*
blue*, indelicate, purple*, racy*, salty*, shady, suggestive, vulgar, wicked; SEE CONCEPT 545

off-course [*adj*] *strayed*
astray, confused, disoriented, lost, lost one's bearing, off-track, roaming, roving; SEE CONCEPTS 576,583

offend [*v*] *displease, insult*
affront, aggrieve, anger, annoy, antagonize, be disagreeable, disgruntle, disgust, disoblige, distress, disturb, exasperate, fret, gall, horrify, hurt, irritate, jar, miff, nauseate, nettle, outrage, pain, pique, provoke, repel, repulse, rile, shock, sicken, sin, slight, slur, snub, sting, transgress, trespass, turn one off*, upset, vex, wound, zing*; SEE CONCEPTS 7,14,19

offender [*n*] *perpetrator*
con*, convict, criminal, crook, culprit, delinquent, felon, guilty party, guilty person, jailbird*, lawbreaker, malefactor, sinner, suspect, transgressor, wrongdoer; SEE CONCEPT 91

offense [*n1*] *violation, trespass*
breach, crime, delinquency, fault, infraction, lapse, malfeasance, misdeed, misdemeanor, peccadillo, sin, transgression, wrong, wrongdoing; SEE CONCEPTS 192,691

offense [*n2*] *insult, displeasure*
affront, aggression, assailment, assault, attack, battery, black eye*, blitz*, blitzkrieg*, dig*, dirty dig*, harm, hit*, hurt, indignation, indignity, injury, injustice, left-handed compliment*, mugging, offensive, onset, onslaught, outrage, push*, put-down*, slam*, slap in the face*, slight, snub, zinger*; SEE CONCEPTS 52,278

offense [*n3*] *anger, hard feelings*
annoyance, conniption*, displeasure, explosion, fit, flare-up*, huff, indignation, ire, miff, needle*, outburst, pique, resentment, scene, tantrum, tizzy*, umbrage, wounded feelings, wrath; SEE CONCEPT 410

offensive [*adj1*] *disrespectful, insulting; displeasing*
abhorrent, abusive, annoying, biting, cutting, detestable, disagreeable, discourteous, distasteful, dreadful, embarrassing, evil, foul, ghastly, grisly, gross, hideous, horrible, horrid, impertinent, insolent, invidious, irritating, nauseating, objectionable, obnoxious, odious, off-color*, offending, opprobrious, outrageous, repellent, reprehensible, repugnant, repulsive, revolting,

rotten, rude, shocking, stinking*, terrible, uncivil, unmannerly; SEE CONCEPTS 267,529,537

offensive [*adj2*] *attacking*
aggressive, assailing, assaulting, belligerent, invading; SEE CONCEPT 548

offensive [*n*] *attack*
aggression, assailment, assault, drive, invasion,
onset, onslaught, push; SEE CONCEPTS 86,320

offer [*n*] *proposal, suggestion*
action, attempt, bid, endeavor, essay, feeler*,
hit*, overture, pass*, pitch*, presentation, proposition, propoundment, rendition, submission, tender; SEE CONCEPTS 66,67,278

offer [*v1*] *present, propose for acceptance*
accord, advance, afford, allow, award, be at service, bid, come forward, display, donate, exhibit,
extend, furnish, give, grant, hold out, lay at one's
feet*, make available, move, place at disposal*,
ply, pose, press, proffer, propound, provide, put
forth, put forward, put on the market, put up, put
up for sale, sacrifice, show, submit, suggest, tender, volunteer; SEE CONCEPT 67

offer [*v2*] *propose*
adduce, advance, advise, allege, cite, make a motion, make a pitch*, present, proposition, submit,
suggest; SEE CONCEPT 66

offer [*v3*] *try*
assay, attempt, endeavor, essay, seek, strive,
struggle, undertake; SEE CONCEPT 87

offering [*n*] *donation*
alms, atonement, benefaction, beneficence, charity, contribution, expiation, gift, oblation, present, sacrifice, subscription; SEE CONCEPTS
337,340

off-guard [*adj*] *unprepared*
asleep, asleep on the job*, daydreaming, flat-
footed*, inattentive, napping, spaced out*,
unalert, unready, unsuspecting, unvigilant, unwatchful, zoned out*; SEE CONCEPTS 403,542

offhand [*adj*] *abrupt, careless*
aloof, breezy, brusque, casual, cavalier, cool*,
curt, easygoing, folksy, glib, informal, laid-back,
mellow, perfunctory, unceremonious, unconcerned, uninterested; SEE CONCEPTS 267,401,542

offhand [*adj2/adv*] *ad-lib, extemporaneous*
extemporary, extempore, impromptu, improvised, informal, off the cuff*, off the hip*, off
the top of head*, spontaneous, spur-of-the-moment*, throwaway*, unpremeditated, unprepared, unrehearsed, unstudied, without
preparation; SEE CONCEPT 267

office [*n1*] *business, responsibility*
appointment, berth, billet, capacity, charge, commission, connection, duty, employment, function, job, obligation, occupation, performance,
place, post, province, responsibility, role, service, situation, spot, station, trust, work; SEE
CONCEPTS 351,362,376

office [*n2*] *place of business*
agency, building, bureau, cave*, center, départ-
ment, facility, factory, foundry, room, salt
mines*, setup, shop, store, suite, warehouse,
workstation; SEE CONCEPTS 312,439,441,448,449

officer [*n1*] *person who has high position in organization*
administrator, agent, appointee, bureaucrat,
chief, civil servant, deputy, dignitary, director,
executive, functionary, head, leader, magistrate,
manager, officeholder, official, president, public
servant, representative; SEE CONCEPT 347

officer [*n2*] *person in law enforcement*
arm*, badge*, black and white*, captain, cop*,
deputy, detective, flatfoot*, mounty, police, police officer, sergeant, sheriff; SEE CONCEPTS
354,355,358

official [*adj*] *authorized, legitimate*
accredited, approved, authentic, authenticated,
authoritative, bona fide, canonical, cathedral,
ceremonious, certified, cleared, conclusive, correct, customary, decided, decisive, definite, endorsed, established, ex cathedra, ex officio,
fitting, formal, legitimate, licensed, okay*, ordered, orthodox, positive, precise, proper, real,
recognized, rightful, sanctioned, suitable, true,
valid; SEE CONCEPT 535

official [*n*] *person representing organization*
administrator, agent, big shot*, boss, brains*,
brass*, bureaucrat, CEO*, chancellor, civil servant, commissioner, comptroller, dignitary, director, exec*, executive, front office*,
functionary, governor, head person, higher-up*,
incumbent, leader, magistrate, manager, marshal,
mayor, minister, officeholder, officer, panjan-
drum, premier, president, representative, secretary, top*, top brass*, top dog*, top drawer*,
treasurer; SEE CONCEPTS 347,354

officiate [*v*] *oversee, manage*
act, boss, chair, command, conduct, direct, do
the honors*, emcee, function, govern, handle,
preside, run, serve, superintend, umpire; SEE
CONCEPT 117

officious [*adj*] *self-important, dictatorial*
busy, forward, impertinent, inquisitive, interfering, intrusive, meddlesome, meddling, obtrusive,
opinionated, overzealous, pragmatic, pushy,
rude; SEE CONCEPT 404

off-key [*adj*] *not harmonious*
abnormal, anomalous, clinker*, deviant, discordant, dissonant, divergent, inharmonious, irregular, jarring, out of keeping*, out of tune*, sour*,
sour note*, unnatural; SEE CONCEPT 594

off-limits [*adj*] *prohibited*
against the law, banned, barred, forbidden, illegal, illicit, no-no*, not allowed, outlawed, out of
bounds*, restricted, taboo, unlawful, verboten;
SEE CONCEPTS 554,576

offset [*v*] *counterbalance, compensate*
account, allow for, atone for, balance, be equivalent, cancel out, charge, counteract, counterpoise, counterpose, countervail, equal, equalize,
equipoise, make amends, make up for, negate,
neutralize, outweigh, recompense, redeem, requite, set off; SEE CONCEPTS 126,232

offshoot [*n*] *development, product*
adjunct, appendage, branch, by-product, derivative, descendant, limb, outgrowth, spin-off,
sprout; SEE CONCEPTS 260,824

offspring [*n*] *child, children*
baby, bambino*, brood, chip off old block*, cub,
descendant, family, generation, heir, heredity,
issue, kid*, lineage, offshoot, posterity, produce,
progenitor, progeny, pup*, scion, seed, spawn,
succession, successor, young; SEE CONCEPTS
296,414

off the cuff [*adj*] *impromptu*
ad-lib, extemporaneous, improv*, improvised,
improviso, off-hand, played by ear*, shot from
the hip*, spontaneous, spur-of-the-moment, unpremeditated, unprepared, unrehearsed, un-

scripted, whipped up*, winged*; SEE CONCEPT
267

off the record [*adj*] *confidential*
arcane, backdoor, classified, hushed, hush-hush*,
in private, inside, not for publication, not public,
on the QT, private, privy, secret, unofficial; SEE
CONCEPTS 267,576

often [*adv*] *frequently*
again and again, a number of times, generally,
many a time, much, oftentimes, ofttimes, over
and over, recurrently, regularly, repeatedly, time
after time, time and again, usually; SEE CONCEPT
541

ogle [*v*] *stare*
eagle eye*, eye, eyeball*, fix, focus, gape at,
gawk, gaze, glare, goggle*, lay eyes on*, leer,
look, look fixedly, make eyes at, peer, rivet, rubberneck*, watch; SEE CONCEPT 623

ogre [*n*] *nasty person*
demon, devil, fiend, giant, monster, monstrosity,
specter, troll; SEE CONCEPT 412

oil [*v*] *lubricate*
anoint, coat, grease, lard, lube, pomade, slick,
smear; SEE CONCEPTS 172,256

oily [*adj1*] *fatty, greasy*
adipose, buttery, creamy, lardy, lubricant, lu-
bricative, lubricous, lustrous, oiled, oil-soaked,
oleaginous, polished, rich, saponaceous, sleek,
slippery, smeary, smooth, soapy, soothing,
swimming, unctuous, waxy; SEE CONCEPTS
603,606

oily [*adj2*] *flattering*
bland*, cajoling, coaxing, compliant, fulsome,
glib, gushing*, hypocritical, ingratiating, insinuating, obsequious, plausible, servile, slick,
smarmy, smooth, smooth-tongued*, suave, supple, unctuous; SEE CONCEPTS 267,401

ointment [*n*] *cream for treatment*
balm, cerate, demulcent, dressing, embrocation,
emollient, lenitive, liniment, lotion, medicine,
salve, unguent; SEE CONCEPTS 311,466

okay [*adj*] *acceptable, satisfactory*
accurate, adequate, all right, approved, convenient, correct, fair, fine, good, in order, middling,
not bad, passable, permitted, so-so*, surely, tolerable; SEE CONCEPT 558

okay [*n*] *agreement*
acceptance, affirmation, approbation, approval,
assent, authorization, benediction, blessing, consent, endorsement, favor, go-ahead*, green
light*, permission, sanction, say-so*, seal of approval*, yes; SEE CONCEPT 684

okay [*v*] *agree to*
accept, accredit, approve, authorize, certify, condone, confirm, consent to, endorse, give one's
consent, give the go-ahead*, give the green
light*, notarize, pass, rubber-stamp*, sanction,
say yes to; SEE CONCEPTS 10,50,88

old [*adj1*] *advanced in age*
aged, aging, advanced in years, ancient, broken down*,
debilitated, decrepit, elderly, enfeebled, exhausted, experienced, fossil*, geriatric, getting
on*, gray, gray-haired*, grizzled*, hoary*, impaired, inactive, infirm, mature, matured, not
young, olden, oldish, over the hill*, past one's
prime*, seasoned, senile, senior, skilled, superannuated, tired, venerable, versed, veteran,
wasted*; SEE CONCEPTS 578,797

old [*adj2*] *obsolete, outdated*
aboriginal, age-old, antediluvian, antiquated, an-

tique, archaic, bygone, cast-off, crumbling,
dated, decayed, demode, done, early, erstwhile,
former, hackneyed*, immemorial, late, moth-
eaten*, of old, of yore, olden, oldfangled, old-
fashioned, old-time, once, onetime, original,
outmoded, out-of-date, passé, past, primeval,
primitive, primordial, pristine, quondam, relic,
remote, rusty, sometime, stale, superannuated,
time-worn, traditional, unfashionable, unoriginal, venerable, worn-out; SEE CONCEPTS
558,560,799

old [*adj3*] *traditional, long-established*
age-old, constant, continuing, enduring, established, experienced, familiar, firm, hardened, inveterate, lifelong, long-lasting, long-lived, of
long standing, perennial, perpetual, practiced,
skilled, solid, staying, steady, time-honored,
versed, veteran, vintage; SEE CONCEPTS
482,530,798

old age [*n*] *latter part of animate life*
advancing years*, age, agedness, autumn of
life*, caducity, debility, declining years*, decrepitude, dotage, elderliness, evening of life*,
feebleness, golden age*, golden years*, infirmity, second childhood*, senectitude, senescence, senility, years; SEE CONCEPTS 715,817

old country [*n*] *native land*
fatherland, homeland, mother country, motherland, the old country*; SEE CONCEPT 516

older [*adj*] *most senior*
earlier, elder, eldest, first, first-born, former,
lower, of a former period, of an earlier time, preceding, prior, senior; SEE CONCEPTS 578,585,797

old-fashioned [*adj*] *outmoded, obsolete*
ancient, antiquated, antique, archaic, behind the
times*, bygone, corny*, dated, dead*, demode,
demoded, disapproved, dowdy*, extinct, grown
old, moldy*, musty, neglected, not current, not
modern, not with it*, obsolescent, odd*, of old,
of olden days*, of the old school*, olden, old-
fangled*, old-hat*, old-time, out*, outdated, out-
of-date, out of it*, out-of-style, outworn, passé,
past, primitive, rococo*, superannuated, unfashionable, unstylish, vintage; SEE CONCEPTS
578,589,797,799

old hand [*n*] *person experienced in something*
expert, longtimer, old guard*, old school*, old-
timer*, pro*, vet*, veteran; SEE CONCEPT 423

old school [*adj*] *traditional*
acceptable, accustomed, classic, classical, conservative, conventional, customary, habitual,
long-established, old, old line, popular, regular,
rooted, time-honored; SEE CONCEPTS 530,533

old-timer [*n*] *elderly person*
fossil*, geezer*, golden-ager, gramps*, mossback, old dog*, old hand, old soldier, senior, veteran, war-horse; SEE CONCEPT 424

old wives' tale [*n*] *superstition*
fairy story, fallacy, false belief, folklore, folk
tale, legend, lore, myth, notion, tall story, tall
tale; SEE CONCEPTS 278,689

oligarchic [*adj*] *governed by small group*
cabalistic, cliquey*, elite, exclusive, select; SEE
CONCEPTS 554,568

omen [*n*] *sign of something to come*
augury, auspice, bodement, boding, foreboding,
foretoken, harbinger, indication, portent, premonition, presage, prognostic, prognostication,
prophecy, straw, warning, writing on the wall*;
SEE CONCEPTS 74,278,689

of
om

ominous [*adj*] *menacing, foreboding*
apocalyptic, augural, baleful, baneful, clouded, dangerous, dark, dire, direful, dismal, doomed, doomful, fateful, fearful, forbidding, gloomy, grim, haunting, hostile, ill-boding, ill-fated, impending, inauspicious, inhospitable, lowering, malefic, malificent, malign, minatory, perilous, portentous, precursive, premonitory, presaging, prescient, prophetic, sinister, suggestive, threatening, unfriendly, unlucky, unpromising, unpropitious; SEE CONCEPT *548*

omission [*n*] *something forgotten or excluded*
blank, breach, break, cancellation, carelessness, chasm, cutting out, default, disregard, disregardance, elimination, elision, excluding, exclusion, failing, failure, forgetfulness, gap, hiatus, ignoring, inadvertence, inadvertency, lack, lacuna, lapse, leaving out, missing, neglect, noninclusion, overlook, overlooking, oversight, passing over, preclusion, preterition, pretermission, prohibition, repudiation, skip, slighting, slip, withholding; SEE CONCEPTS *25,116,699*

omit [*v*] *exclude, forget*
bar, blink at*, bypass, cancel, cast aside, count out, cut, cut out, delete, discard, dismiss, disregard, drop, edit, eliminate, evade, except, fail, ignore, knock off, leave out, leave undone, let go, let slide*, miss, miss out, neglect, overlook, overpass, pass by, pass over, preclude, prohibit, reject, repudiate, skip, slight, snip, trim, void, withhold, X-out*; SEE CONCEPTS *25,121,211*

omitted [*adj*] *excluded*
absent, deleted, erased, expunged, forgotten, left out, missing, neglected, overlooked, precluded; SEE CONCEPTS *121,211*

omnipotent [*adj*] *all-powerful*
almighty, divine, godlike, mighty, supreme, unlimited, unrestricted; SEE CONCEPT *574*

omnipresent [*adj*] *all-present*
everywhere, infinite, pervading, pervasive, ubiquitary, ubiquitous, universal; SEE CONCEPT *583*

omniscient [*adj*] *all-knowing*
all-seeing, almighty, infinite, knowledgeable, pansophical, preeminent, wise; SEE CONCEPT *402*

on [*adv*] *in contact; ahead of*
about, above, adjacent, against, approaching, at, beside, close to, covering, forth, forward, held, leaning on, near, next, on top of, onward, over, resting on, situated on, supported, touching, toward, upon, with; SEE CONCEPTS *585,586,750*

on and off [*adv*] *intermittently*
at intervals, at times, discontinuously, every now and then, every once in a while, every so often, from time to time, hardly, infrequently, intermittently, irregularly, now and again, now and then, occasionally, off and on, once in a blue moon*, once in a while, on occasion, periodically, sometimes, sporadically; SEE CONCEPTS *530,541*

on and on [*adv*] *continuously*
ad nauseam, constantly, forever, never-ending, perpetually, relentlessly, repeatedly, steadily, unceasingly, unremittingly; SEE CONCEPTS *534,798*

on call [*adj*] *standing by*
accessible, at hand, at one's fingertip, night call, on alert, on the spot, prepared, within reach; SEE CONCEPT *576*

once [*adj/adv*] *in the past; occurred one time only*
already, a single time, at one time, away back, back, back when, before, but once, bygone, earlier, erstwhile, formerly, heretofore, in the old days, in the olden days, in times gone by, in times past, late, long ago, old, once only, once upon a time, one, one time before, one time previously, only one time, on one occasion, previously, quondam, sometime, this time, time was, whilom; SEE CONCEPTS *799,820*

once and for all [*adv*] *finally*
after all, at last, at long last*, at the end, conclusively, in conclusion, in the end, it's about time*, sooner or later*; SEE CONCEPT *799*

once in a while [*adv*] *occasionally*
at intervals, at times, every now and then, every so often, from time to time, hardly, infrequently, irregularly, now and again, once in a blue moon*, on occasion, periodically, rarely, seldom, sometimes, sporadically; SEE CONCEPTS *530,541*

oncoming [*adj*] *impending*
advancing, approaching, coming, expected, forthcoming, imminent, looming, nearing, onrushing, upcoming; SEE CONCEPTS *548,799*

on duty [*adj*] *working*
busy, clocked in*, engaged, in a job, in gear, laboring, obliged, on the job, punched in*; SEE CONCEPTS *538,560*

one [*adj*] *individual*
alone, definite, different, lone, odd, one and only, only, particular, precise, precise, separate, single, singular, sole, solitary, special, specific, uncommon, unique; SEE CONCEPTS *577,762,789*

one by one [*adv*] *in succession*
gradually, individually, little by little, one at a time, singly, step by step; SEE CONCEPTS *544,588,799*

on edge [*adj*] *tense*
agitated, anxious, apprehensive, beside oneself*, bundle of nerves*, edgy, excited, fidgety, high-strung*, hyper*, impatient, in a tizzy*, jittery, jumpy, keyed up*, nerve-racking, nervous, nervous wreck*, overanxious, restless, stressful, unnerved, uptight, wired*, worried, wound up*; SEE CONCEPTS *401,403,548*

onerous [*adj*] *difficult; requiring hard labor*
arduous, austere, backbreaking, burdensome, crushing, cumbersome, demanding, difficult, distressing, embittering, exacting, excessive, exhausting, exigent, fatiguing, formidable, galling, grave, grinding, grueling, hard*, harsh, headache, heavy*, intolerable, irksome, laborious, merciless, oppressive, overpowering, overtaxing, painful, plodding, ponderous, pressing, responsible, rigorous, serious, severe, strenuous, taxing, tiresome, tiring, toilsome, troublesome, vexatious, weighty; SEE CONCEPTS *538,565*

one-sided [*adj*] *biased*
colored, discriminatory, favorably, inclined, influenced, partisan, predisposed, prejudiced, unequal, unfair, unjust; SEE CONCEPTS *403,542*

one-track mind [*n*] *obsession*
attraction, compulsion, fascination, fixation, hang-up*, infatuation, passion, preoccupation, tunnel vision; SEE CONCEPTS *20,410,529,689,690*

ongoing [*adj*] *continuous*
advancing, continuing, current, developing, evolving, extant, growing, heading, in process, in progress, marching, open-ended, progressing, successful, unfinished, unfolding; SEE CONCEPTS *482,798*

on guard [*adj*] *defensive*
alert, averting, cautious, checking, defending, expectant, guarding, preservative, preventive, protecting, safeguarding, vigilant, warding off, watchful, withstanding; SEE CONCEPTS *401,550*

on-line [*adj*] *electronically connected*
accessible by computer, installed, linked, networked, on stream*, operative, plugged in, ready for use, wired; SEE CONCEPT *274*

onlooker [*n*] *person observing an event*
beholder, bystander, eyewitness, looker-on, observer, sightseer, spectator, viewer, watcher, witness; SEE CONCEPT *423*

only [*adj*] *singular*
alone, apart, by oneself, exclusive, individual, isolated, lone, matchless, once in a lifetime, one, one and only, one shot, onliest, particular, peerless, single, sole, solitary, solo, unaccompanied, unequaled, unique, unparalleled, unrivaled; SEE CONCEPT *577*

only [*adv*] *barely; exclusively*
alone, at most, but, entirely, hardly, just, merely, nothing but, particularly, plainly, purely, simply, solely, totally, uniquely, utterly, wholly; SEE CONCEPTS *535,772*

on paper [*adv*] *in theory*
abstractly, conceivably, hypothetically, theoretically; SEE CONCEPT *529*

on purpose [*adv*] *deliberately*
after consideration, by design, calculatingly, consciously, designed, freely, in cold blood, intentionally, knowingly, premeditatively, purposely, purposively, voluntarily, willfully, with eyes wide open*, wittingly; SEE CONCEPTS *401,542*

onrush [*n*] *rush*
attack, avalanche, blitz, charge, dash, deluge, flood, flow, flux, haste, hastiness, hurriedness, hurry, onslaught, push, race, scramble, stampede, storm, stream, surge, swiftness; SEE CONCEPTS *145,748,818*

onset [*n*] *beginning; attack*
access, aggression, assailment, assault, birth, charge, commencement, dawn, dawning, encounter, inception, incipience, kickoff*, offense, offensive, onfall, onrush, onslaught, opening, origin, outbreak, outset, outstart, rush, seizure, start; SEE CONCEPTS *86,221,832*

onslaught [*n*] *attack*
aggression, assailment, assault, blitz, charge, incursion, invasion, offense, offensive, onfall, onrush, onset; SEE CONCEPT *86*

on the ball [*adj*] *alert*
active, all ears*, attentive, bright, cagey*, careful, clever, good hands*, heads up*, intelligent, lively, observant, on guard*, on one's toes*, on the job*, on the lookout*, on the stick*, perceptive, quick, ready, sharp, spirited, vigilant, watchful, wise, with it*; SEE CONCEPTS *402,403*

on the blink [*adj*] *broken*
busted, defective, disabled, down, fallen apart, faulty, gone to pieces*, haywire, in disrepair, in need of repair, inoperable, in the shop*, kaput*, not functioning, not working, on the fritz*, on the shelf*, out, out of commission*, out of kilter*, out of order, out of whack*, run-down, shot, spent, wrecked; SEE CONCEPTS *485,560*

on the double [*adv*] *quickly*
chop-chop*, expeditiously, fast, flat-out*, fleetly, full tilt*, hastily, hurriedly, in a flash*, in haste, lickety-split*, like a shot*, like greased lightning*, like wildfire*, promptly, pronto, quick, rapidly, swift, swiftly; SEE CONCEPTS *588,799*

on the fence [*adj*] *undecided*
ambivalent, betwixt and between*, blowing hot and cold*, borderline, debatable, divided, hemming and hawing*, hesitant, iffy*, impartial, indecisive, in the middle*, irresolute, neutral, not definite, not sure, of two minds*, open, running hot and cold*, tentative, torn, uncertain, unclear, uncommitted, undetermined, unsure, up in the air*, waffling, wavering, wishy-washy*; SEE CONCEPTS *403,529*

on the house [*adj*] *free*
chargeless, complimentary, compliments of the house, costless, for nothing, for the asking, freebie*, free of cost, free ride*, gratis, gratuitous, no charge, on the cuff*; SEE CONCEPT *334*

on the level [*adj*] *legitimate*
aboveboard, accepted, accredited, authentic, authorized, for real*, honest, lawful, official, on the up and up, proper, sanctioned, straight, true, valid, verifiable; SEE CONCEPTS *319,558,582*

on the wagon [*adj*] *sober*
abstaining, abstemious, abstinent, cold sober*, dry, drying out, nonindulgent, not drinking, not drunk, not partaking of alcohol, restrained, took the pledge*; SEE CONCEPT *401*

onus [*n*] *burden*
bar sinister*, black eye*, blame, blot, blur, brand, charge, culpability, deadweight*, duty, encumbrance, fault, guilt, incubus, liability, load, millstone*, obligation, odium, oppression, responsibility, slur, spot, stain, stigma, task, tax, weight; SEE CONCEPTS *388,674*

onward/onwards [*adv*] *ahead, beyond*
alee, along, forth, forward, in front, in front of, moving, on, on ahead; SEE CONCEPTS *585,778*

oodles [*n*] *a lot*
abundance, billions, gobs*, heaps*, large number, loads, lots, many, masses, millions, piles*, plenty, scads*, thousands, tons, zillions; SEE CONCEPTS *432,786*

oomph [*n*] *energy*
animation, ardor, birr, dash, drive, effectiveness, endurance, exertion, fire, force, forcefulness, fortitude, get-up-and-go*, go, hardihood, initiative, intensity, juice, life, liveliness, might, moxie*, muscle, pep, pizzazz, pluck, potency, power, punch, spirit, stamina, steam, strength, vigor, vim, virility, vitality, zeal, zest, zing, zip; SEE CONCEPT *411*

ooze [*n*] *liquid emitted*
alluvium, fluid, glop*, goo*, gook*, gunk*, mire, muck*, mud, silt, slime*, sludge; SEE CONCEPTS *466,467*

ooze [*v*] *emit liquid*
bleed, discharge, drain, dribble, drip, drop, escape, exude, filter, flow, issue, leach, leak, overflow, percolate, perspire, seep, spurt, strain, sweat, swelter, trickle, weep, well; SEE CONCEPT *179*

opaque [*adj*] *clouded, muddy*
blurred, cloudy, dark, darkened, dim, dirty, dull, dusky, filmy, foggy, frosty, fuliginous, gloomy, hazy, impenetrable, lusterless, misty, muddied, murky, nontranslucent, nontransparent, nubilous, obfuscated, shady, smoky, sooty, thick, turbid; SEE CONCEPTS *606,617,618*

opaque [*adj2*] *hard to understand*
abstruse, amphibological, arcane, baffling, concealed, cryptic, difficult, enigmatic, equivocal, imperceptive, incomprehensible, nubilous, obscure, obtuse, perplexing, purblind, tenebrous, uncertain, unclear, unfathomable, unintelligible, vague; SEE CONCEPT *529*

open [*adj1*] *unfastened, unclosed*
accessible, agape, airy, ajar, bare, clear, cleared, dehiscent, disclosed, emptied, expanded, expansive, exposed, extended, extensive, free, gaping, made passable, naked, navigable, passable, patent, patulous, peeled, removed, rent, revealed, ringent, rolling, spacious, spread out, stripped, susceptible, unbarred, unblocked, unbolted, unburdened, uncluttered, uncovered, unfolded, unfurled, unimpeded, unlocked, unobstructed, unplugged, unsealed, unshut, unstopped, vacated, wide, yawning; SEE CONCEPTS *485,576*

open [*adj2*] *accessible; not forbidden*
admissible, agreeable, allowable, approachable, appropriate, attainable, available, employable, fit, free, general, getable*, nondiscriminatory, not posted, obtainable, on deck*, on tap*, open-door*, operative, permitted, practicable, proper, public, reachable, securable, suitable, to be had*, unconditional, unoccupied, unqualified, unrestricted, usable, vacant, welcoming, within reach; SEE CONCEPTS *560,576*

open [*adj3*] *clear, obvious*
apparent, avowed, barefaced, blatant, conspicuous, downright, evident, flagrant, frank, manifest, noticeable, overt, plain, unconcealed, undisguised, visible, well-known; SEE CONCEPTS *267,535*

open [*adj4*] *undecided*
ambiguous, arguable, controversial, debatable, doubtful, dubious, dubitable, equivocal, indecisive, in question, moot, problematic, questionable, uncertain, unresolved, unsettled, up for discussion*, up in the air*, yet to be decided*; SEE CONCEPTS *267,529*

open [*adj5*] *honest, objective*
artless, candid, disinterested, fair, frank, free, guileless, impartial, ingenuous, innocent, lay it on the line*, mellow, natural, objective, on the level*, open-and-shut*, openhearted*, plain, receptive, sincere, straightforward, talking turkey*, transparent, unbiased, uncommitted, unconcealed, undisguised, undissembled, unprejudiced, unreserved, up-front*; SEE CONCEPTS *267,542*

open [*vl*] *begin*
begin business, bow, commence, convene, embark, get things rolling*, inaugurate, initiate, jump, kick off, launch, meet, raise the curtain*, ring in*, set in motion, set up shop*, sit, start, start the ball rolling*; SEE CONCEPT *221*

open [*v2*] *clear, expose; spread*
bare, break in, break out, broach, burst, bust in, come apart, crack, disclose, display, disrupt, expand, fissure, free, gap, gape, hole, jimmy, kick in, lacerate, lance, penetrate, perforate, pierce, pop, puncture, release, reveal, rupture, separate, sever, slit, slot, split, tap, throw wide, unbar, unblock, unbolt, unclose, unclothe, uncork, uncover, undo, unfasten, unfold, unfurl, unlatch, unlock, unroll, unseal, unshut, unstop, untie, unwrap, vent, ventilate, yawn, yawp; SEE CONCEPTS *135,250,469*

open-and-shut [*adj*] *obvious*
apparent, cinched, clear, clear as a bell*, conclusive, cut and dried, distinguishable, easy, evident, explicit, glaring, indisputable, ordinary, plain, routine, self-evident, self-explanatory, simple, straightforward, undeniable, undisguised, unmistakable; SEE CONCEPTS *485,529*

openhanded [*adj*] *generous*
altruistic, benevolent, big, big-hearted, bountiful, charitable, considerate, giving, helpful, hospitable, kind, kindhearted, kindly, liberal, magnanimous, philanthropic, thoughtful, unselfish; SEE CONCEPTS *404,542*

openhearted [*adjl*] *frank*
aboveboard, bare-faced*, blunt, candid, direct, downright, forthright, from the hip*, honest, lay it on the line*, like it is*, matter-of-fact, open, plain, plainspoken, saying what one thinks*, sincere, straight, straightforward, truthful, up front*; SEE CONCEPTS *267,582*

openhearted [*adj2*] *kindly*
benevolent, compassionate, friendly, generous, good, good-hearted, gracious, humane, kind, kindhearted, neighborly, sympathetic, thoughtful; SEE CONCEPTS *404,542*

opening [*nl*] *gap, hole*
aperture, breach, break, cavity, chink, cleft, crack, cranny, crevice, cut, discontinuity, door, fissure, hatch, interstice, mouth, orifice, outlet, perforation, recess, rent, rift, rupture, scuttle, slit, slot, space, split, spout, tear, vent, window; SEE CONCEPT *513*

opening [*n2*] *chance*
availability, big break*, connection, cut*, fling*, go*, go-at*, in the running*, iron in the fire*, look-in*, occasion, opportunity, place, possibility, run, scope, shot*, show, squeak*, time, vacancy, whack*; SEE CONCEPT *693*

opening [*n3*] *beginning*
birth, coming out, commencement, curtain-raiser*, dawn, inauguration, inception, initiation, kickoff, launch, launching, onset, opener, outset, start; SEE CONCEPT *832*

openly [*adv*] *honestly*
aboveboard, artlessly, blatantly, brazenly, candidly, face to face, flagrantly, forthrightly, frankly, fully, honestly, in broad daylight, in full view, ingenuously, in public, in the open, naively, naturally, plainly, publicly, readily, shamelessly, simply, straight, unabashedly, unashamedly, under one's nose*, unhesitatingly, unreservedly, wantonly, warts and all*, willingly, without pretense, without reserve; SEE CONCEPTS *267,544*

open-minded [*adj*] *receptive*
acceptant, acceptive, approachable, broad-minded, impartial, interested, observant, open to suggestions, perceptive, persuadable, swayable, tolerant, unbiased, understanding; SEE CONCEPT *404*

operable [*adj*] *possible*
achievable, conceivable, doable, feasible, obtainable, practicable, realizable, serviceable, viable, workable; SEE CONCEPTS *528,552,576*

operate [*vl*] *perform, function*
accomplish, achieve, act, act on, advance, behave, be in action, bend, benefit, bring about, burn, carry on, click*, compel, complete, concern, conduct, contact, contrive, convey, cook*, determine, direct, do, enforce, engage, exert, fin-

ish, fulfill, get results, go, hit*, hum, influence, keep, lift, move, ordain, percolate, proceed, produce, produce a result, progress, promote, react, revolve, roll, run, serve, spin, take, tick, transport, turn, work; SEE CONCEPTS 91,680,706

operate [v2] *manage, use*
administer, be in charge, be in driver's seat*, be in saddle*, call the play*, call the shots*, call the signals*, carry on, command, conduct, drive, handle, hold the reins*, keep, make go*, maneuver, manipulate, ordain, pilot, play, ply, pull the strings*, pull the wires*, run, run the show*, run things*, sit on top of*, steer, wield, work; SEE CONCEPTS 94,117,148

operate [v3] *perform surgery*
amputate, carve up, cut, excise, explore, open up, remove, set, transplant, treat; SEE CONCEPT 310

operation [n1] *movement, working*
act, action, activity, affair, agency, application, ballgame*, bit, carrying on, conveyance, course, deal, deed, doing, effect, effort, employment, engagement, enterprise, exercise, exercising, exertion, exploitation, force, handiwork, happening, influence, instrumentality, labor, manipulation, motion, movement, performance, play, procedure, proceeding, process, progress, progression, scene, service, transaction, transference, trip, undertaking, use, work, workmanship; SEE CONCEPTS 658,680

operation [n2] *business concern*
affair, deal, enterprise, proceeding, transaction, undertaking; SEE CONCEPTS 324,325

operation [n3] *surgical procedure*
biopsy, excision, surgery; SEE CONCEPT 310

operational [adj] *functional*
fit, in service, in working order, operative, practicable, practical, prepared, ready, serviceable, usable, useful, viable, workable, working; SEE CONCEPT 560

operative [adj] *active, functioning; influential*
accessible, alive, crucial, current, dynamic, effective, efficient, employable, functional, important, indicative, in force, in operation, key, live, open, operational, practicable, relevant, running, serviceable, significant, standing, usable, workable, working; SEE CONCEPTS 560,567

opine [v] *think*
believe, conceive, conclude, declare, express an opinion, feel, guess, imagine, judge, presume, say, suggest, suppose, surmise, venture; SEE CONCEPTS 12,26

opinion [n] *belief*
assessment, assumption, attitude, conception, conclusion, conjecture, estimate, estimation, eye*, fancy, feeling, guess, hypothesis, idea, imagining, impression, inclination, inference, judgment, mind, notion, persuasion, point of view, postulate, presumption, presupposition, reaction, say-so*, sentiment, slant, speculation, supposition, surmise, suspicion, take*, theorem, theory, thesis, think*, thought, view, viewpoint; SEE CONCEPT 689

opinionated [adj] *believing very strongly and conveying it*
adamant, arbitrary, assertive, biased, bigoted, bossy, bullheaded*, cocksure*, cocky*, conceited, dictatorial, doctrinaire, dogmatic, hardline*, high-handed, inflexible, intransigent, locked in*, obdurate, obstinate, one-sided, oracular, overbearing, pigheaded*, positive, prag-

matic, pragmatical, prejudiced, self-assertive, set in stone*, set-on, single-minded, stubborn, tilted, uncompromising, unyielding, weighted; SEE CONCEPTS 267,404

opium [n] *narcotic*
brown stuff*, codeine, dope, drug, heroin, hypnotic, morphine, opiate, papaverine, poppy, sleep-inducer, soporific, tar; SEE CONCEPT 307

opponent [n] *person with whom one competes*
adversary, antagonist, anti*, aspirant, assailant, bandit*, bidder, candidate, challenger, competitor, con, contestant, counteragent, dark horse*, disputant, dissentient, enemy, entrant, foe, litigant, match, opposer, opposition, oppugnant, player, rival; SEE CONCEPT 366

opportune [adj] *advantageous, lucky*
appropriate, apt, auspicious, convenient, favorable, felicitous, fit, fitting, fortuitous, fortunate, happy, helpful, pat, proper, propitious, seasonable, suitable, timely, timeous, well-timed; SEE CONCEPTS 548,572

opportunity [n] *lucky chance; favorable circumstances*
befalling, break*, connection, contingency, convenience, cut*, event, excuse, fair shake*, fighting chance*, fitness, fling*, fortuity, freedom, go*, good fortune, good luck, happening, hope, hour, iron in the fire*, juncture, leisure, liberty, moment, occasion, one's move*, one's say*, one's turn*, opening, pass, prayer*, probability, relief, room, run, scope, shot*, show, space, spell, squeak, stab, the hunt*, the running*, time, turn, whack*; SEE CONCEPT 693

oppose [v1] *fight, obstruct*
argue, assail, assault, attack, bar, battle, bombard, call in question, check, combat, confront, contradict, controvert, counter, counterattack, cross, debate, defy, deny, disagree, disapprove, dispute, encounter, expose, face, face down*, fight, fly in the face of*, frown at, gainsay, hinder, neutralize, not countenance, prevent, protest, resist, reverse, run counter to, search out, speak against, stand up to, take a stand, take issue, take on, taunt, thwart, turn the tables*, withstand; SEE CONCEPTS 21,54,106

oppose [v2] *compare, play off*
array, confront, contrast, counter, counterbalance, face, match, pit, set against, vie; SEE CONCEPTS 73,363

opposed/opposing [adj] *antagonistic, against*
against the grain*, allergic, anti*, antipathetic, antithetical, antonymous, at cross-purposes, at odds, averse, battling, clashing, combating, conflicting, confronting, contrary, controverting, counter, crossing, defending, defensive, denying, disagreeing, disputed, disputing, dissentient, enemy, exposing, facing, gainsaying, hostile, incompatible, inimical, in opposition, irreconcilable, objecting, obstructive, opposite, protesting, repelling, restrictive, rival, up against, warring; SEE CONCEPTS 403,542,564

opposite [adj] *unlike, conflicting; completely different*
adverse, antagonistic, antipodal, antipodean, antithetical, contradictory, contrapositive, contrary, contrasted, corresponding, counter, crosswise, diametric, diametrically opposed, different, differing, dissimilar, diverse, facing, flip-side*, fronting, hostile, inconsistent, independent, inimical, inverse, irreconcilable, obverse, opposed,

ornery*, paradoxical, polar, repugnant, retrograde, reverse, reversed, separate, unalike, unconnected, unrelated, unsimilar, violative, vis-à-vis; SEE CONCEPT *564*

opposite [*n*] *something completely unlike another*
adverse, antilogy, antipode, antipole, antithesis, antonym, contra*, contradiction, contrary, contrast, converse, counterpart, foil, inverse, obverse, opposition, other extreme*, other side*, other side of coin*, paradox, reverse, vice versa; SEE CONCEPT *665*

opposition [*n1*] *obstruction, antagonism*
action, antinomy, antithesis, aversion, brush, civil disobedience, clash, combat, competition, con, conflict, confronting, contention, contest, contradistinction, contraposition, contrariety, counteraction, counterattack, defense, defiance, disapproval, duel, encounter, engagement, fray, grapple, hostility, negativism, obstructiveness, opposure, oppugnancy, prevention, repugnance, repulsion, resistance, rivalry, skirmish, strife, struggle, unfriendliness, violation, war, warfare; SEE CONCEPTS *29,92,106,665*

opposition [*n2*] *person, people competing*
adversary, antagonist, disputant, enemy, foe, iconoclast, opponent, other side, rebel, rival; SEE CONCEPTS *348,366*

oppress [*v*] *depress, subdue*
abuse, afflict, aggrieve, annoy, beat down*, burden, crush, despotize, dishearten, dispirit, distress, encumber, force, handicap, harass, harry, hound*, keep down, maltreat, outrage, overcome, overload, overpower, overthrow, overwhelm, persecute, pick on, plague, press, prey on, put down, put screws to*, put the squeeze on*, put upon, ride, rule, sadden, saddle*, smother, strain, subjugate, suppress, tax, torment, torture, trample, trouble, tyrannize, vex, weigh heavy upon, worry, wrong; SEE CONCEPTS *7,14,19,133*

oppressed [*adj*] *downtrodden*
abject, abused, a slave to*, at one's feet*, at one's mercy*, burdened, destitute, distressed, enslaved, exploited, have-not, helpless, maltreated, mistreated, persecuted, subservient, suppressed, tormented, tyrannized, underfoot*, under one's thumb*; SEE CONCEPT *542*

oppression [*n*] *misery, hardship*
abuse, abusiveness, autocracy, brutality, calamity, coercion, compulsion, conquering, control, cruelty, despotism, dictatorship, domination, fascism, force, forcibleness, hardness, harshness, injury, injustice, iron hand*, maltreatment, martial law, overthrowing, persecution, severity, subduing, subjection, suffering, torment, tyranny; SEE CONCEPTS *14,320,674*

oppressive [*adj1*] *overwhelming, repressive*
backbreaking*, bleak, brutal, burdensome, confining, cruel, demanding, depressing, depressive, despotic, dictatorial, discouraging, disheartening, dismal, dispiriting, exacting, exigent, gloomy, grievous, grinding, harsh, headache*, heavy, heavy-handed*, hefty, inhuman, ironhanded*, mean, onerous, overbearing, rough going*, severe, somber, superincumbent, taxing, tough, troublesome, tyrannical, unjust, weighty; SEE CONCEPTS *537,548*

oppressive [*adj2*] *hot and humid*
airless, close, heavy, muggy, overpowering, steam bath*, steamy, sticky, stifling, stuffy, suffocating, sultry, sweat box*, torrid; SEE CONCEPT *525*

oppressor [*n*] *tyrant*
absolute ruler, authoritarian, autocrat, bully, despot, dictator, martinet, persecutor, slave driver, taskmaster; SEE CONCEPTS *354,412*

opprobrious [*adj*] *abusive, hateful*
abasing, calumniatory, contemptuous, contumelious, damaging, debasing, defamatory, defaming, denigrating, depreciative, derogative, despicable, despiteful, detractive, disgracing, dishonoring, disparaging, humiliating, hurting, injuring, injurious, insolent, insulting, invective, libeling, malevolent, malign, malignant, maligning, notorious, offending, offensive, pejorative, reproaching, reviling, scandalous, scurrilous, shaming, spiteful, truculent, vile, vitriolic, vituperative, vulgar; SEE CONCEPTS *267,404,542*

opprobrium [*n*] *disgrace*
black eye*, blemish, debasement, debasing, degradation, discredit, dishonor, disrepute, disrespect, humiliation, ignominy, ill repute, infamy, loss of honor, obloquy, shame, stain, stigma, tarnish; SEE CONCEPT *388*

oppugn [*v*] *oppose*
argue, attack, call into question, contradict, controvert, criticize, debate, shoot down, take issue; SEE CONCEPTS *21,54,106*

opt [*v*] *choose*
cull, decide, elect, exercise choice, go for*, make a selection, mark, pick, prefer, select, single out*, take; SEE CONCEPT *41*

optimal [*adj*] *optimum*
A1*, ace, best, capital, 24-carat*, choice, choicest, excellent, flawless, gilt-edge*, greatest, highest, ideal, matchless, maximum, most advantageous, most favorable, peak, peerless, perfect, select, solid gold*, superlative, top, world class*; SEE CONCEPT *574*

optimism [*n*] *state of having positive beliefs*
anticipation, assurance, brightness, buoyancy, calmness, certainty, cheer, cheerfulness, confidence, easiness, elation, encouragement, enthusiasm, exhilaration, expectation, good cheer, happiness, hopefulness, idealism, looking on bright side*, positivism, rose-colored glasses*, sanguineness, sureness, trust; SEE CONCEPTS *410,689*

optimist [*n*] *positive thinker*
dreamer, hoper, idealist, Pollyanna; SEE CONCEPT *529*

optimistic [*adj*] *believing positively*
assured, bright, buoyant, cheerful, cheering, confident, encouraged, expectant, happy, high, hopeful, hoping, idealistic, keeping the faith, merry on cloud nine*, on top of world*, positive, promising, ray of sunshine*, rose-colored*, rosy, sanguine, sunny*, trusting, upbeat, Utopian; SEE CONCEPTS *404,542*

optimum [*adj*] *best*
A1*, ace, capital, -carat*, choice, choicest, excellent, flawless, gilt-edge*, greatest, highest, ideal, matchless, maximum, most advantageous, most favorable, optimal, peak, peerless, perfect, select, solid gold*, superlative, world class*; SEE CONCEPT *574*

option [*n*] *alternative*
advantage, benefit, choice, claim, dibs*, dilemma, discretion, druthers, election, flipside*, franchise, free will*, grant, license, opportunity

other side of coin*, pickup, preference, prerogative, privilege, right, selection, take it or leave it*; SEE CONCEPTS 376,712

optional [adj] *possible; available as choice*
alternative, arbitrary, discretional, discretionary, elective, extra, facultative, free, noncompulsory, nonobligatory, no strings attached*, not required, open, unforced, unrestricted, up to the individual, volitional, voluntary; SEE CONCEPTS 552,576

opulence [n] *wealth*
abundance, affluence, belongings, excess, fortune, goods, lap of luxury, lavishness, luxury, means, money, plenitude, possessions, property, prosperity, prosperousness, riches, stocks and bonds, substance, substantiality; SEE CONCEPTS 340,710

opulent [adj] *rich, luxurious, profuse*
abundant, affluent, copious, deluxe, extravagant, exuberant, frilly*, lavish, luscious, luxuriant, moneyed, ostentatious, palatial, plentiful, plush, pretentious, prodigal, profusive, prolific, prosperous, rich, riotous, showy, sumptuous, swank, upholstered*, velvet*, wealthy, well-heeled*, well-off*, well-to-do*; SEE CONCEPTS 334,589,781

opus [n] *great work of writing or music*
composition, creation, magnum opus, music, oeuvre, piece, product, production; SEE CONCEPTS 263,271

oracle [n] *prophecy*
answer, apocalypse, augury, canon, commandment, divination, edict, fortune, law, prediction, prognostication, revelation, vision; SEE CONCEPTS 70,278,689

oracular [adj] *prophetic*
ambiguous, anticipating, apocalyptic, arcane, auguring, auspicious, authoritative, cabalistic, clairvoyant, cryptic, Delphian, discovering, divining, divulging, dogmatic, fatidic, foreboding, forecasting, foretelling, imperious, interpretive, mantic, mysterious, mystical, obscure, occult, ominous, peremptory, portending, portentous, positive, predicting, presaging, prescient, proclaiming, prognosticating, prophesying, sage, secret, sibylline, significant, soothsaying, vague, vatic, venerable, wise; SEE CONCEPT 267

oral [adj] *spoken*
articulate, ejaculatory, lingual, narrated, phonated, phonetic, phonic, recounted, related, said, sonant, sounded, told, unwritten, uttered, verbal, viva voce, vocal, voiced, word-of-mouth; SEE CONCEPT 267

orange [n/adj] *combination of red and yellow*
apricot, bittersweet, cantaloupe, carrot, coral, peach, red-yellow, salmon, tangerine, titian; SEE CONCEPTS 618,622

orate [v] *speak*
address, expound, grandstand, lecture, moralize, pontificate, preach, sermonize, talk, vociferate; SEE CONCEPTS 60,285

oration [n] *speech*
address, chalk talk*, declamation, discourse, harangue, homily, lecture, pep talk*, pitch*, sermon, soapbox*, spiel*; SEE CONCEPTS 266,278

orator [n] *speaker*
declaimer, lector, lecturer, pontificator, preacher, public speaker, reciter, rhetorician, sermonizer; SEE CONCEPTS 60,285

oratory [n] *public speaking*
articulation, declamation, diction, elocution, eloquence, grandiloquence, rhetoric, speaking, speech, speechifying, speechmaking; SEE CONCEPTS 60,285

orb [n] *globe*
ball, circle, eye*, lamp, ring, rondure, round, sphere; SEE CONCEPT 436

orbit [n1] *circuit, revolution*
apogee, circle, circumgyration, course, curve, cycle, ellipse, lap, locus, path, pattern, perigee, rotation, round, track, trajectory; SEE CONCEPTS 436,738

orbit [n2] *influence, domain*
ambit, area, arena, boundary, bounds, career, circle, circumference, compass, course, department, dominion, extension, extent, field, jurisdiction, limit, pilgrimage, precinct, province, purview, radius, range, reach, realm, scope, sphere, sweep; SEE CONCEPTS 349,673,687

orchard [n] *fruit farm*
fruit garden, garden, grove, plantation, vineyard; SEE CONCEPTS 449,509,517

orchestra [n] *symphony*
band, ensemble, group, sinfonietta; SEE CONCEPT 294

orchestrate [v] *organize; cause to happen*
arrange, blend, compose, concert, coordinate, harmonize, integrate, manage, present, put together, score, set up, symphonize, synthesize, unify; SEE CONCEPTS 117,242

ordain [v] *establish, install*
anoint, appoint, bless, call, commission, consecrate, constitute, deal, deal with, decree, delegate, destine, dictate, elect, enact, enjoin, fix, frock, impose, institute, invest, lay down the law*, legislate, nominate, order, prescribe, pronounce, put foot down*, rule, set, walk heavy*, will; SEE CONCEPTS 18,50,88,317

ordeal [n] *trouble, suffering*
affliction, agony, anguish, calamity, calvary, cross, crucible, difficulty, distress, nightmare, test, torment, torture, trial, tribulation, visitation; SEE CONCEPTS 674,728

order [n1] *arrangement, organization*
adjustment, aligning, array, assortment, cast, categorization, classification, codification, composition, computation, disposal, disposition, distribution, establishment, form, grouping, harmony, layout, line, lineup, management, method, neatness, ordering, orderliness, pattern, placement, plan, procedure, procession, progression, propriety, regularity, regulation, rule, scale, scheme, sequence, series, setup, standardization, structure, succession, symmetry, system, tidiness, uniformity; SEE CONCEPT 727

order [n2] *lawfulness*
calm, control, decorousness, decorum, discipline, goodness, integrity, law, law and order, niceness, orderliness, peace, peacefulness, probity, properness, propriety, quiet, rectitude, rightness, seemliness, suitability, tranquility, uprightness; SEE CONCEPTS 633,691

order [n3] *class, status*
bracket, branch, breed, cast, caste, degree, description, estate, family, feather, genre, genus, grade, hierarchy, ilk, kidney, kind, line, nature, pecking order*, pigeonhole*, place, position, rank, set, slot, sort, species, station, stripe, subclass, taxonomic group, type; SEE CONCEPT 378

order [n4] *command*
authorization, behest, bidding, charge, com-

op
or

mandment, decree, dictate, direction, directive,
injunction, instruction, law, mandate, ordinance,
permission, precept, regulation, rule, say-so*,
stipulation, ukase, word*; SEE CONCEPTS
53,278,685

order [n5] *request; purchase agreement*
amount, application, booking, bulk, commission,
engagement, goods, materials, purchase, quantity, requisition, reservation, reserve, shipment,
stipulation; SEE CONCEPTS 332,338,684

order [n6] *organization*
association, brotherhood, club, community, company, fraternity, guild, league, lodge, sect, sisterhood, society, sodality, sorority, union; SEE
CONCEPT 387

order [v1] *command, authorize*
adjure, apply for, bid, book, buy, call for, call the
shots*, call the signals*, charge, contract for, decree, dictate, direct, enact, engage, enjoin, hire,
instruct, obtain, ordain, prescribe, pull strings*,
request, require, reserve, rule the roost*, secure,
send away for, tell, warn; SEE CONCEPTS
50,53,88,327

order [v2] *arrange, organize*
adapt, adjust, align, alphabetize, array, assign,
catalogue, class, classify, codify, conduct, control, dispose, distribute, establish, file, fix, formalize, furnish, group, index, lay out, line, line
up, locate, manage, marshal, methodize, neaten,
normalize, pattern, place, plan, put away, put to
rights*, range, regiment, regularize, regulate,
right, routine, set guidelines, set in order, settle,
sort out, space, standardize, streamline, systematize, tabulate, tidy; SEE CONCEPTS 84,158

order about [v] *dominate*
boss, bully, call the shots*, command, control,
dictate, direct, influence, keep under one's
thumb*, manage, master, run the show*; SEE
CONCEPTS 94,117,298

ordered [adj] *orderly*
all together, arranged, businesslike, controlled,
disciplined, in good shape, in order, law-abiding,
methodical, neat, organized, peaceable, precise,
shipshape*, systematic, systematized, tidy, well-
behaved, well-organized; SEE CONCEPTS
326,485,585,589

orderly [adj1] *methodical, organized*
alike, all together, arranged, businesslike, careful, clean, conventional, correct, exact, fixed, formal, framed, in apple-pie order*, in good shape,
in order, in shape, methodic, neat, neat as button*, neat as pin*, precise, regular, regulated,
scientific, set-up, shipshape*, slick, spick-and-
span*, systematic, systematized, thorough, tidy,
together, to rights*, trim, uncluttered, uniform;
SEE CONCEPTS 326,485,585,589

orderly [adj2] *well-behaved*
at peace, calm, controlled, decorous, disciplined,
docile, law-abiding, manageable, nonviolent,
obedient, peaceable, quiet, restrained, submissive, tranquil, well-mannered; SEE CONCEPT 401

ordinance [n] *law, rule*
authorization, canon, code, command, decree,
dictum, direction, edict, enactment, fiat, mandate, order, precept, prescript, reg, regulation,
ruling, statute, ukase; SEE CONCEPT 318

ordinarily [adv] *usually*
as a rule, commonly, customarily, frequently,
generally, habitually, in general, normally, regularly; SEE CONCEPT 530

ordinary [adj1] *common, regular*
accustomed, customary, established, everyday,
familiar, frequent, general, habitual, humdrum*,
natural, normal, popular, prevailing, public, quotidian, routine, run-of-the-mill*, settled, standard, stock, traditional, typical, usual, wonted;
SEE CONCEPTS 533,547

ordinary [adj2] *average; not distinctive*
characterless, common, commonplace, conventional, dull, fair, familiar, garden*, garden variety*, generic, habitual, homespun, household,
humble, indifferent, inferior, mean, mediocre,
modest, no great shakes*, normal, pedestrian,
plain, plastic, prosaic, quotidian, routine,
runof-the-mill*, second-rate, simple, so-so*,
stereotyped, undistinguished, uneventful, unexceptional, uninspired, unmemorable, unnoteworthy, unpretentious, unremarkable, usual,
vanilla*, white-bread*, workaday; SEE CONCEPT
530,575

ordnance [n] *artillery*
arms, big guns*, bombs, heavy stuff*, missiles,
munitions, weapons; SEE CONCEPTS 322,500

organ [n] *means, tool*
agency, agent, channel, device, element, forum,
implement, instrument, journal, magazine,
medium, member, ministry, mouthpiece, newspaper, paper, part, periodical, process, publication, review, structure, unit, vehicle, voice, way;
SEE CONCEPTS 280,499,712

organic [adj] *basic, natural*
amoebic, anatomical, animate, basal, biological,
biotic, cellular, constitutional, elemental, essential, fundamental, inherent, innate, integral, live,
living, necessary, nuclear, original, plasmic, primary, prime, primitive, principal, structural,
vital; SEE CONCEPT 549

organism [n] *living thing*
animal, being, body, creature, entity, morphon,
person, plant, structure; SEE CONCEPTS 389,429

organization [n1] *arrangement, arranging*
alignment, assembling, assembly, chemistry,
composition, configuration, conformation, constitution, construction, coordination, design, disposal, format, formation, forming, formulation,
framework, grouping, harmony, institution,
make-up, making, management, method,
methodology, organism, organizing, pattern,
plan, planning, regulation, running, situation,
standard, standardization, structure, structuring,
symmetry, system, unity, whole; SEE CONCEPT
84,117,727

organization [n2] *group bound by interest/work/
goal*
affiliation, aggregation, alliance, association,
band, body, business, cartel, circle, clique, club,
coalition, combination, combine, company, concern, concord, confederation, consortium, cooperative, corporation, coterie, crew, establishment,
federation, fraternity, guild, house, industry, institute, institution, league, lodge, machine, monopoly, order, outfit, party, profession, set,
society, sodality, sorority, squad, syndicate,
team, trade, troupe, trust, union; SEE CONCEPT
381

organize [v] *arrange, systematize*
adapt, adjust, be responsible for, catalogue, classify, codify, combine, compose, constitute, construct, coordinate, correlate, create, dispose,
establish, fashion, fit, form, formulate, frame, get

going*, get together, group, harmonize, lick into shape*, line up, look after, marshal, methodize, mold, pigeonhole*, put in order, put together, range, regulate, run, see to, settle, set up, shape, standardize, straighten, straighten out, tabulate, tailor, take care of, whip into shape*; SEE CONCEPTS 36,84,158

organized [adj] *arranged, systematized*
catalogued, classified, coordinated, correlated, formed, formulated, grouped, methodized, standardized, straightened out, tabulated; SEE CONCEPTS 84,94

organized crime [n] *the underworld*
Cosa Nostra, gangland, Mafia, mob, organized crime family, the syndicate; SEE CONCEPTS 412,645

organizer [n] *planner*
arranger, coordinator, designer, developer, facilitator, promoter; SEE CONCEPT 347

orgasm [n] *climax*
ejaculation, frenzy, peak, spasm; SEE CONCEPTS 706,836

orgy [n] *celebration devoted to sensual enjoyment*
bacchanal, bacchanalia, bender*, binge*, blowout*, bout*, carousal, circus*, debauch, dissipation, excess, feast, fling*, indulgence, jag*, merrymaking, overindulgence, party, rampage*, revel, revelry, saturnalia, splurge, spree, surfeit, tear*; SEE CONCEPTS 377,383

orient [v] *familiarize*
acclimatize, adapt, adjust, align, conform, determine, direct, get one's bearings*, locate, orientate, turn; SEE CONCEPTS 35,202

orientation [n] *introduction, adjustment*
acclimatization, adaptation, assimilation, bearings, breaking in*, coordination, direction, familiarization, fix*, lay of the land*, location, position, sense of direction, settling in*; SEE CONCEPTS 31,832

orifice [n] *opening*
aperture, cavity, crack, hole, mouth, outlet, slit, spout, vent, window; SEE CONCEPT 513

origin [n1] *cause, basis*
agent, ancestor, ancestry, antecedent, author, base, causality, causation, connection, creator, derivation, determinant, egg*, element, embryo, fountain, generator, germ, horse's mouth*, impulse, inception, inducement, influence, inspiration, mainspring, motive, nucleus, occasion, parent, parentage, principle, producer, progenitor, provenance, provenience, root, roots, seed, source, spring, stock, well, wellspring; SEE CONCEPTS 229,648,661

origin [n2] *beginning, inception*
alpha, birth, blast off, commencement, creation, dawn, dawning, day one*, early stage, embarkation, emergence, entrance, entry, forging, foundation, genesis, git go*, inauguration, ingress, initiation, introduction, launch, nativity, opener, origination, outbreak, outset, rise, square one*, start, starting point*; SEE CONCEPT 832

origin [n3] *family, heritage*
ancestry, beginnings, birth, blood, descent, extraction, lineage, maternity, parentage, paternity, pedigree, stock; SEE CONCEPT 296

original [adj1] *earliest*
aboriginal, archetypal, authentic, autochthonous, beginning, commencing, early, elementary, embryonic, first, first-hand, genuine, inceptive, infant, initial, introductory, opening, pioneer, primary, prime, primeval, primitive, primordial, pristine, prototypal, rudimental, rudimentary, starting, underivative, underived; SEE CONCEPTS 549,585

original [adj2] *fresh, new*
avant garde, breaking new ground*, causal, causative, conceiving, creative, demiurgic, devising, envisioning, fertile, formative, generative, imaginative, ingenious, innovational, innovative, innovatory, inspiring, inventive, novel, originative, productive, quick, ready, resourceful, seminal, sensitive, unconventional, unprecedented, untried, unusual; SEE CONCEPTS 578,589,797

original [n1] *standard, prototype*
archetype, coinage, creation, exemplar, forerunner, invention, model, novelty, paradigm, pattern, precedent, precursor, type; SEE CONCEPTS 260,686

original [n2] *person who is eccentric*
anomaly, card*, case*, character, eccentric, nonconformist, oddball, oddity, queer, weirdo*; SEE CONCEPT 423

originality [n] *creativeness*
boldness, brilliance, cleverness, creative spirit, creativity, daring, freshness, imagination, imaginativeness, individuality, ingeniousness, ingenuity, innovation, innovativeness, invention, inventiveness, modernity, new idea, newness, nonconformity, novelty, resourcefulness, spirit, unconventionality, unorthodoxy; SEE CONCEPTS 409,410

originally [adv] *initially*
at first, at the outset, at the start, basically, by birth, by origin, first, formerly, incipiently, in the beginning, in the first place, primarily, primitively, to begin with; SEE CONCEPTS 578,585,797,799

originate [v1] *begin; spring*
arise, be born, birth, come, come from, come into existence, commence, dawn, derive, emanate, emerge, flow, hail from, issue, proceed, result, rise, start, stem; SEE CONCEPTS 105,221

originate [v2] *create, introduce*
break the ice*, bring about, cause, coin, come up with, compose, conceive, develop, discover, evolve, form, formulate, found, generate, give birth to, hatch, inaugurate, initiate, innovate, institute, invent, launch, make, open up, parent, pioneer, procreate, produce, set in motion, set up, spark, spawn, start, think up, usher in; SEE CONCEPTS 43,173,251

origination [n] *origin*
beginning, birth, commencement, conception, creation, dawn, dawning, discovery, genesis, innovation, introduction, launch, source, start, starting point*; SEE CONCEPT 832

originator [n] *creator*
architect, author, begetter, designer, discoverer, father, founder, initiator, innovator, inventor, maker, mastermind, mother, pioneer, producer; SEE CONCEPTS 348,352,361

ornament [n] *decoration*
accessory, adornment, art, bauble, beautification, design, doodad*, embellishment, embroidery, flower, frill, frou frou*, garnish, gewgaw*, gimcrack*, gingerbread*, honor, jewel, knickknack*, pride, treasure, trimming, trinket; SEE CONCEPTS 259,476

or
or

ornament [v] *decorate*
adorn, array, beautify, bedeck, bedizen, brighten, deck, dress, dress up*, embellish, embroider, enrich, festoon, fix up*, garnish, gild, grace, ornamentalize, polish, prank, prettify, primp, prink, smarten*, spruce up*, trim; SEE CONCEPTS 162,167,177

ornamental [adj] *decorative*
accessory, adorning, attractive, beautiful, beautifying, decking, decorating, delicate, dressy, elaborate, embellishing, enhancing, exquisite, fancy, festooned, florid, for show*, furbishing, garnishing, heightening, luxurious, ornate, setting off*, showy; SEE CONCEPTS 579,589

ornate [adj] *fancily decorated*
adorned, aureate, baroque, beautiful, bedecked, bright, brilliant, busy, colored, convoluted, dazzling, elaborate, elegant, embroidered, fancy, fine, flamboyant, flashy, flaunting, florid, flowery, fussy, gaudy, gilded, glamorous, glitzy, glossy, high-wrought, jeweled, lavish, luscious, magnificent, meretricious, opulent, ornamented, ostentatious, overdone, overelaborate, pretentious, resplendent, rich, rococo, showy, sparkling, splashy, sumptuous, superficial, tawdry, variegated; SEE CONCEPTS 579,589

ornery [adj] *mean*
cantankerous, contemptible, crabby, cranky, crusty*, difficult, disagreeable, grouchy*, grumpy*, hard-nosed*, ignoble, ill-tempered, irritable, nasty, obstinate, quarrelsome, rotten, sour, surly, testy, unfriendly, vicious; SEE CONCEPTS 267,401,542

orphan [n] *child without parents*
foundling, ragamuffin*, stray, waif; SEE CONCEPT 414

orthodox [adj] *accepted, traditional*
according to the book*, acknowledged, admitted, approved, authoritative, buttoned-down*, by the numbers*, canonical, conformist, conservative, conventional, correct, customary, devout, diehard, doctrinal, established, in line*, legitimate, official, old-line*, pious, proper, punctilious, reactionary, received, recognized, religious, right, rightful, sanctioned, sound, square, standard, straight, straight arrow, traditional, traditionalistic, true, well-established; SEE CONCEPTS 533,558

oscillate [v] *change back and forth*
be unsteady, dangle, fishtail, flicker, fluctuate, librate, lurch, palpitate, pendulate, pitch, pivot, reel, ripple, rock, roll, seesaw, stagger, sway, swing, switch, swivel, teeter, teeter-totter*, thrash, toss, totter, undulate, vacillate, vary, vibrate, waddle, wag, waggle, waltz, wave, waver, whirl, wiggle, wobble; SEE CONCEPTS 13,147,697

ossified [adj] *bony*
fossilized, hard, hardened, petrified, rigid; SEE CONCEPTS 404,542

ossify [v] *become hard from aging*
congeal, fossilize, freeze, harden, indurate, petrify, solidify, stiffen, thicken, turn to bone; SEE CONCEPT 469

ossuary [n] *urn*
container, receptacle, vault, vessel; SEE CONCEPT 494

ostensible [adj] *alleged, supposed*
apparent, avowed, colorable, demonstrative, exhibited, illusive, illusory, likely, manifest, notable, outward, plausible, pretended, professed, purported, quasi, seeming, semblant, so-called*, specious, superficial; SEE CONCEPTS 552,582

ostensibly [adv] *apparently*
at first blush*, evidently, externally, for all intents and purposes*, for show*, officially, on the face*, on the surface*, outwardly, professedly, seemingly, sensibly, superficially, supposedly, to the eye*; SEE CONCEPT 582

ostentation [n] *exhibitionism, flashiness*
affectation, array, boast, boasting, brag, braggadocio*, bragging, bravado, demonstration, display, exhibition, false front*, flamboyance, flash*, flaunting, flourish, fuss, garishness, grandstand play*, magnificence, pageant, pageantry, parade, parading, pomp, pomposity, pompousness, pretending, pretension, pretentiousness, put-on, shine*, show, showiness, showing off*, showoff*, spectacle, splendor, splurge, swagger*, swaggering, swank*, vainglory, vaunt*, vaunting*, window-dressing; SEE CONCEPTS 633,655

ostentatious [adj] *flashy, showy*
boastful, chichi*, classy, conspicuous, crass*, dashing, egotistic, exhibitionistic, extravagant, flamboyant, flatulent, flaunted, fussy, garish, gaudy, gay, glittery, grandiose, highfaluting*, jaunty, loud, obtrusive, peacocky, pompous, pretentious, spectacular, splashy, splurgy, sporty, swank, swanky*, theatrical, tinsel*, tony*, uptown*, vain, vulgar; SEE CONCEPTS 401,589

ostracism [n] *banishment*
avoidance, blackballing, boycott, cold-shouldering, exclusion, excommunication, exile, expulsion, isolation, rejection, shunning; SEE CONCEPTS 25,130

ostracize [v] *exile, banish*
avoid, blackball*, blacklist*, boycott, cast out, cold-shoulder*, cut, deport, displace, drop, exclude, excommunicate, expatriate, expel, expulse, leave in the cold, oust, reject, shun, shut out, snub, throw out; SEE CONCEPTS 25,384

other [adj 1] *additional, added*
alternative, another, auxiliary, else, extra, farther, fresh, further, more, new, spare, supplementary; SEE CONCEPT 771

other [adj 2] *different*
contrasting, disparate, dissimilar, distant, distinct, divergent, diverse, opposite, otherwise, remaining, separate, unalike, unequal, unlike, unrelated, variant; SEE CONCEPT 564

otherwise [adv] *in another way; alternatively*
any other way, contrarily, differently, diversely, elseways, if not, in different circumstances, on the other hand, or else, or then, under other conditions, variously; SEE CONCEPT 544

otherworldly [adj] *extraterrestrial; psychic*
alien, ethereal, heavenly, magical, mystical, out of this world, spiritual, supernatural, transcendental, uncanny, unearthly, unworldly, visionary; SEE CONCEPTS 529,549,582

ounce [n] *one-sixteenth of a pound/28.35 grams of weight*
avoirdupois, troy, uncia; SEE CONCEPT 795

oust [v] *expel, get rid of*
banish, bereave, boot out*, bounce*, bundle off*, cast out, chase, depose, deprive, dethrone, discharge, disinherit, dislodge, displace, dispossess, divest, drive out, eject, evict, expulse, fire, force out, give the 1-2-3*, kick out, lay off, let go, lose, ostracize, pack off, pink slip*, relegate,

remove, rob, sack, send packing*, show the door*, throw out, topple, transport, turn out, unseat; SEE CONCEPTS 25,211,351

ouster [*n*] *ejection*
banishment, disbarment, discharge, dismissal, eviction, expulsion, loss of right, overthrow, removal, sack, the heave-ho*; SEE CONCEPTS 179,222

out [*adj*] *not possible; gone*
absent, antiquated, at an end, away, behind the times*, cold, dated, dead, demode, doused, ended, exhausted, expired, extinguished, finished, impossible, not allowed, not on, old-fashioned, old-hat*, outmoded, outside, passé, ruled out, unacceptable, unfashionable, used up; SEE CONCEPTS 539,552,576

out [*adv*] *outside, outdoors*
out of doors, outward, without; SEE CONCEPT 583

out-and-out [*adj*] *complete*
absolute, arrant, consummate, downright, full, outright, perfect, thorough, thoroughgoing, through-and-through, total, uncompromising, undiminished, unmitigated, unqualified, utter, whole; SEE CONCEPT 531

outbreak [*n*] *sudden happening*
beginning, blowup, brawl, break, breaking, burst, bursting, commencement, commotion, convulsion, crack, crash, dawn, detonation, discharge, disorder, disruption, ebullition, effervescence, epidemic, eruption, explosion, fit, flare-up, flash, fury, gush, gushing, insurrection, irruption, mutiny, onset, outburst, outpouring, paroxysm, plague, rebellion, rending, revolution, roar, sally, sortie, spasm, spurt, storm, sundering, surge, thunder, tumult, uprising, volley; SEE CONCEPTS 2,86,179,832

outburst [*n*] *fit of temper*
access, attack, blow, burst, conniption*, discharge, eruption, explosion, flare, flare-up, frenzy, gush, gust, outbreak, outpouring, paroxysm, rapture, scene, spasm, storm, surge, tantrum, transport, upheaval; SEE CONCEPT 633

outcast [*n*] *person who is unwanted, not accepted*
bum*, castaway, deportee, derelict, displaced person, exile, expatriate, fugitive, gypsy, hobo*, persona non grata*, rascal, refugee, reprobate, tramp, untouchable, vagabond, vagrant, wretch; SEE CONCEPT 423

outclass [*v*] *surpass*
beat, best, better, cap, dominate, eclipse, exceed, excel, go beyond, go one better*, improve upon, outdistance, outdo, outhussle, outmatch, outpace, outperform, outplay, outrank, outrival, outrun, outshine, outstrip, pass, put to shame*, rise above, surmount, top, tower, win the race; SEE CONCEPT 141

out cold [*adj*] *unconscious*
benumbed, blacked out*, comatose, dead to the world*, down for the count*, drowsy, feeling no pain*, flattened*, in a trance, numb, on the canvas*, out, out like a light*, passed out*, put away*, senseless, zonked*; SEE CONCEPTS 314,539

outcome [*n*] *consequence, effect*
aftereffect, aftermath, blowoff, causatum, chain reaction*, conclusion, end, end result*, event, fallout, issue, payback*, payoff*, reaction, result, score, sequel, upshot*; SEE CONCEPT 230

outcry [*n*] *scream, exclamation*
clamor, commotion, complaint, convulsion, cry,

ferment, flak*, hoo-ha*, howl, hubba-hubba*, hullabaloo*, noise, objection, outburst, protest, screech, tumult, uproar, upturn, yell; SEE CONCEPTS 77,278

outdated/out-of-date [*adj*] *old-fashioned*
anachronous, antiquated, antique, archaic, back number*, behind the times*, dated, démodé, dusty, has-been*, moth-eaten*, musty, not with it*, obsolete, old, old-hat*, out, outmoded, out-of-style*, passé, square, tired, unfashionable, vintage; SEE CONCEPTS 578,589,797

outdistance [*v*] *outrun*
beat, best, better, exceed, go beyond, go one better*, leave behind, outclass, outdo, outhussle, outpace, outperform, outplay, overtake, pass, surpass, top, win the race; SEE CONCEPT 141

outdo [*v*] *better, overcome*
beat, best, blow out of water*, bulldoze*, bury*, cook*, cream*, defeat, do in*, down*, eclipse, exceed, excel, fake out*, go one better*, leave behind*, lick*, outclass, outdistance, outfox, outgun, outjockey, outmaneuver, outrival, outshine, outsmart, outstrip, pull a fast one*, shake off*, shoot ahead*, snow*, surpass, top, transcend, trash*; SEE CONCEPTS 95,141

outdoor [*adj/adv*] *in the open air*
alfresco, casual, free, garden, healthful, hilltop, informal, in the open, invigorating, mountain, natural, nature-loving, out-of-doors, out of the house, outside, patio, picnic, rustic, unrestricted, woods, yard; SEE CONCEPT 583

outdoors [*n*] *open air; nature*
bucolic surroundings, country, countryside, environment, fresh air, garden, green earth*, hill, mountain, open, out-of-doors, patio, without, woods, yard; SEE CONCEPT 198

outer [*adj*] *external, exposed*
alien, beyond, exoteric, exterior, extraneous, extrinsic, outermost, outlying, outmost, outside, outward, over, peripheral, remote, superficial, surface, without; SEE CONCEPTS 484,583

outermost [*adj*] *outer*
beyond, distant, fringe, furthermost, outlying, outmost, outward, peripheral, remote; SEE CONCEPTS 484,583

outfit [*n1*] *set of clothes or equipment*
accoutrements, apparatus, appliances, clothing, costume, ensemble, garb, gear, get-up*, guise, kit, machinery, materiel, outlay, paraphernalia, provisions, rig, rigging, suit, supplies, tackle, togs, trappings*, wardrobe; SEE CONCEPTS 451,496

outfit [*n2*] *large group; business*
band, clique, company, concern, corps, coterie, crew, enterprise, establishment, firm, house, organization, party, set, squad, team, troop, troupe, unit; SEE CONCEPTS 325,417

outfit [*v*] *clothe, equip*
accoutre, appoint, arm, deck out*, drape, fit out*, furnish, gear, prepare, provide, provision, rig up*, stock, suit, supply, tog*, turn out*; SEE CONCEPTS 167,182

outflank [*v*] *outmaneuver*
beat, best, better, defeat, excel, outclass, outdo, outfox, outperform, outplay, outsmart, outwit, outwit, surpass, top; SEE CONCEPT 141

outflow [*n*] *efflux*
discharge, drainage, effluence, effluent, effluvium, effusion, emergence, gush, gushing out-

pouring, rush, spout, stream, streaming; SEE
CONCEPTS *179,748*

outfox [*v*] *outsmart*
best, defeat, excel, outclass, outdo, outperform,
outplay, outwit, surpass, top; SEE CONCEPT *141*

outgoing [*adj*] *demonstrative, extroverted*
approachable, civil, communicative, cordial,
easy, expansive, extrovert, friendly, genial, gregarious, informal, kind, open, sociable, sympathetic, unconstrained, unreserved, unrestrained,
warm; SEE CONCEPT *404*

outgoing [*adj2*] *leaving*
departing, ex-*, former, last, migratory, out-
bound, outward-bound, past, retiring, withdrawing; SEE CONCEPTS *581,584*

outgrowth [*n1*] *projection*
bulge, enlargement, excrescence, jut, node, offshoot, outcrop, process, prolongation, prominence, protuberance, shoot, sprout, swelling; SEE
CONCEPTS *471,824*

outgrowth [*n2*] *product, consequence*
aftereffect, branch, by-product*, derivative, descendant, development, effect, emergence, end,
end result*, issue, member, offshoot, offspring,
outcome, result, spin-off*, yield; SEE CONCEPTS
230,260

outhouse [*n*] *toilet*
bathroom, latrine, lavatory, outbuilding, privy,
washroom, water closet, WC; SEE CONCEPT *448*

outing [*n*] *short trip*
airing, drive, excursion, expedition, jaunt, junket,
long weekend, picnic, pleasure trip, roundabout,
spin*, vacation, weekend; SEE CONCEPTS
224,386

outing [*n2*] *politically motivated exposure of another's secrets*
announcement, declaration, demystification, disclosure, proclamation, revealing, tossing, unclos-
eting, unmasking; SEE CONCEPT *60*

outlandish [*adj*] *bizarre, strange*
alien, awkward, barbaric, barbarous, boorish,
clumsy, curious, droll, eccentric, erratic, exotic,
extravagant, fantastic, far-out*, foreign, freakish,
gauche, graceless, grotesque, kinky*, odd, outrageous, outré, peculiar, preposterous, quaint,
queer, ridiculous, rude, singular, tasteless, ultra,
unconventional, uncouth, unheard-of*, unorthodox, unusual, weird, whimsical, wild; SEE CON-
CEPTS *401,548*

outlast [*v*] *endure beyond another*
hang on, outlive, outstay, outwear, remain, survive; SEE CONCEPT *407*

outlaw [*n*] *person who is running from the law*
bandit, brigand, con, criminal, crook, desperado,
drifter, ex-con, fugitive, gangster, gunslinger*,
hood*, hoodlum, hooligan*, jailbird, marauder,
mobster, mug*, outcast, pariah, racketeer, robber, wrong number*; SEE CONCEPT *412*

outlaw [*v*] *prohibit; make illegal*
ban, banish, bar, condemn, damn, disallow, embargo, enjoin, exclude, forbid, illegalize, inhibit,
interdict, prevent, proscribe, stop, taboo; SEE
CONCEPTS *121,317*

outlay [*n*] *expenses*
bite*, bottom line*, charge, cost, damage, disbursement, expenditure, expense, highway robbery*, investment, price tag, score*, setback*,
spending, tab*, throw*, tune*; SEE CONCEPT *344*

outlet [*n1*] *place or means of escape, release*
aperture, avenue, break, channel, crack, duct,

egress, escape, exit, hole, nozzle, opening, orifice, porthole, release, safety valve, spout, tear,
vent, way out; SEE CONCEPTS *513,693*

outlet [*n2*] *store that sells discounted items*
factory store, market, mill store, seconds store,
shop, showroom; SEE CONCEPTS *439,448,449*

outline [*n1*] *plan, sketch*
bare facts*, blueprint, diagram, draft, drawing,
floor plan, frame, framework, ground plan, layout, main features, recapitulation, résumé, rough
draft, rough idea, rundown, skeleton, summary,
synopsis, thumbnail sketch*, tracing; SEE CON-
CEPT *268*

outline [*n2*] *form, tracing of an object*
configuration, conformation, contour, delineation, figuration, figure, profile, shape, silhouette; SEE CONCEPTS *436,625*

outline [*v*] *sketch; plan*
adumbrate, block out, characterize, chart, delineate, describe, draft, lay out, paint, plot, recapitulate, rough out, skeleton, skeletonize,
summarize, tell about, trace; SEE CONCEPTS
36,55,174

outlive [*v*] *outlast*
continue, endure, hang on, outstay, prevail, remain, survive; SEE CONCEPT *407*

outlook [*n1*] *point of view*
angle*, attitude, direction, frame of mind*, head-
set*, mind-set*, perspective, routine, scope, side,
size of it*, slant*, standpoint, viewpoint, views,
vision; SEE CONCEPTS *410,689*

outlook [*n2*] *probable future*
appearances, chance, expectation, forecast, law
of averages*, likelihood, normal course, opening, opportunity, possibility, probability*,
prospect, prospects, risk; SEE CONCEPT *679*

outlook [*n3*] *scene, view*
aspect, lookout, panorama, perspective, prospect,
scape, sight, vista; SEE CONCEPTS *509,628*

outlying [*adj*] *in rural area; remote*
afar, backwoods, distant, external, faraway, far-
flung*, far-off, off-lying, outer, out-of-the-way*,
peripheral, provincial, removed; SEE CONCEPT
583

outmoded [*adj*] *obsolete, old-fashioned*
anachronistic, antediluvian, antiquated, antique,
archaic, behind the times*, bent, bygone, dated,
dead, démodé, dinosaur*, disused, extinct, fossilized, has-been*, horse and buggy*, moldy*,
moth-eaten*, musty*, obsolescent, obsolete,
olden, old-hat*, old-time, out, out-of-date, out-
of-style, outworn, passé*, superannuated, superseded, tired, unfashionable, unstylish, unusable,
vintage; SEE CONCEPTS *560,578,589,797*

out of the closet [*adj*] *open*
brought to light, candid, disclosed, divulged, exposed, open and aboveboard, open to view, out
in the open, revealed, unveiled; SEE CONCEPT *60*

output [*n*] *something produced*
achievement, amount, crop, gain, harvest, making, manufacture, manufacturing, producing,
product, production, productivity, profit, take,
turnout, yield; SEE CONCEPTS *205,260*

outrage [*n1*] *atrocity, evil*
abuse, affront, barbarism, damage, desecration,
enormity, evildoing, harm, hurt, indignity, inhumanity, injury, insult, mischief, misdoing, offense, profanation, rape, rapine, ravishing, ruin,
shock, violation, violence, wrongdoing; SEE
CONCEPTS *192,645,674*

outrage [*n2*] *anger*

blowup, flare-up*, fury, huff*, hurt, indignation, resentment, ruckus*, shock*, stew*, storm*, wrath; SEE CONCEPT *29*

outrage [*v*] *wrong, offend, abuse*

affront, aggrieve, boil over*, burn up*, defile, deflower, desecrate, do violence to, fire up*, force, ill-treat, incense, infuriate, injure, insult, jar*, kick up a row*, madden, make hit the ceiling*, maltreat, mistreat, misuse, oppress, persecute, raise Cain*, rape, ravage, ravish, reach boiling point*, scandalize, shock, spoil, violate, whip up*; SEE CONCEPTS *7,19,29,246*

outrageous [*adj1*] *very bad*

abominable, atrocious, barbaric, beastly, brazen, contemptible, contumelious, corrupt, criminal, debasing, debauching, degenerate, depraving, disgraceful, disgracing, egregious, flagitious, flagrant, gross, heinous, horrendous, horrible, ignoble, infamous, inhuman, iniquitous, malevolent, monstrous, nefarious, notorious, odious, opprobrious, scandalous, scurrilous, shameless, shaming, shocking, sinful, unbearable, ungodly, unspeakable, villainous, violent, wanton, wicked; SEE CONCEPT *571*

outrageous [*adj2*] *beyond reasonable limits*

barbarous, crazy*, excessive, exorbitant, extortionate, extravagant, immoderate, inordinate, last straw*, offensive, out of bounds*, preposterous, scandalous, shocking, steep*, too much*, uncivilized, unconscionable, unreasonable; SEE CONCEPTS *569,771*

outright [*adj*] *complete, unconditional*

absolute, all, arrant, consummate, definite, direct, downright, entire, flat, gross, out-and-out*, perfect, positive, pure, straightforward, thorough, thoroughgoing, total, undeniable, unequivocal, unmitigated, unqualified, utter, whole, wholesale; SEE CONCEPTS *531,535*

outside [*adj1*] *external*

alfresco, alien, apart from, away from, exterior, extramural, extraneous, extreme, farther, farthest, foreign, furthest, open-air, out, outdoor, outer, outermost, outward, over, surface; SEE CONCEPTS *484,583*

outside [*adj2*] *slight, slim*

distant, faint, far, marginal, negligible, off, remote, slender, small, unlikely; SEE CONCEPTS *552,789*

outside [*n*] *exterior; out-of-doors*

appearance, covering, facade, face, front, integument, open, open air, outdoors, seeming, sheath, skin, surface, topside, without; SEE CONCEPTS *198,484*

outsider [*n*] *person who is foreign to something*

alien, floater*, foreigner, incomer*, interloper, intruder, newcomer, odd one out*, outlander, refugee, stranger; SEE CONCEPTS *413,423*

outskirts [*n*] *edge of a geographic area*

bedroom community*, border, boundary, edge, environs, limit, outpost, periphery, purlieu, purlieus, sticks*, suburb, suburbia, vicinity; SEE CONCEPTS *508,513*

outspoken [*adj*] *explicit, unreserved*

abrupt, artless, blunt, calling spade a spade*, candid, direct, forthright, frank, free, laying it on the line*, open, plain, plain-spoken, pointblank*, round, square, straightforward, strident, talking turkey*, unceremonious, unequivocal,

unreticent, up front*, vocal; SEE CONCEPTS *267,404*

outstanding [*adj1*] *superior, excellent*

A-1*, ace*, A-number-1*, bad*, boss*, capital*, celebrated, chief, cool*, crack*, distinguished, dominant, eminent, eventful, exceptional, famous, far-out*, great, greatest, hundred-proof*, important, impressive, magnificent, main, major, meritorious, momentous, mostest, number one*, out-of-sight*, out-of-this-world*, phenomenal, predominant, preeminent, primo*, principal, special, standout, star, steller, super, superior, superlative, tops*, well-known, world-class; SEE CONCEPTS *568,574*

outstanding [*adj2*] *noticeable, striking*

arresting, arrestive, conspicuous, distinguished, eye-catching, important, leading, marked, memorable, notable, noteworthy, prominent, pronounced, remarkable, salient, signal; SEE CONCEPTS *485,537*

outstanding [*adj3*] *referring to an unpaid debt*

due, mature, ongoing, open, overdue, owing, payable, pending, remaining, uncollected, unresolved, unsettled; SEE CONCEPT *334*

outward [*adj*] *visible; for appearances*

apparent, evident, exterior, external, from within, noticeable, observable, obvious, on the surface, open, ostensible, out, outer, outside, over, perceptible, superficial, surface, to the eye, toward the edge; SEE CONCEPTS *576,581,583*

outwardly [*adv*] *to all appearances*

apparently, as far as one can see, evidently, externally, for all intents and purposes*, in appearance, officially, on the face of it, on the surface, ostensibly, professedly, seemingly, superficially, to the eye; SEE CONCEPTS *544,576*

outweigh [*v*] *override, dominate*

atone for, balance, cancel out, compensate, counterbalance, counterpoise, countervail, eclipse, exceed, excel, make up for, offset, outbalance, outrival, outrun, overcome, overshadow, predominate, preponderate, prevail, set off, surpass, take precedence, tip the scales; SEE CONCEPT *141*

outwit/outsmart [*v*] *get the better of; figure out before another*

baffle, bamboozle*, beat*, bewilder, cap, cheat, circumvent, con, confuse, deceive, defeat, defraud, dupe, end-run*, fake out*, finagle*, fox*, goose*, gull*, have*, hoax, hoodwink, lead astray*, make a fool of*, make a monkey of*, mislead, outdo, outfox, outgeneral, outguess, outjockey, outmaneuver, outthink, overreach, pull a fast one on*, put one over on*, run circles around*, swindle, take in*, top*, trick, worst*; SEE CONCEPTS *15,59*

oval [*adj*] *long and rounded in shape*

egg-shaped, ellipsoidal, elliptic, elliptical, oblong, ooid, ovaloid, ovate, oviform, ovoid; SEE CONCEPT *486*

ovation [*n*] *clapping and cheers*

acclaim, acclamation, applause, big hand*, bravos, cheering, hand, laudation, plaudits, praise, salvo, testimonial, tribute; SEE CONCEPTS *69,264*

over [*adj*] *accomplished*

ancient history, at an end, by, bygone, closed, completed, concluded, done, done with, ended, finished, gone, past, settled, up; SEE CONCEPTS *531,548*

ou
ov

over [*adj2/adv1*] *in addition*

additionally, beyond, ever, excessively, extra, extremely, immensely, in excess, inordinately, left over, more, over and above, overly, overmuch, remaining, superfluous, surplus, too, unduly, unused; SEE CONCEPTS *544,771*

over [*adv2*] *above*

aloft, beyond, covering, farther up, higher than, in heaven, in the sky, off, on high, on top of, overhead, overtop, straight up, traversely, upstairs; SEE CONCEPTS *583,793*

overabundance [*n*] *excess*

embarrassment of riches*, glut, nimiety, overflow, overkill, overmuch, oversupply, plethora, profusion, superabundance, superfluity, surfeit, surplus, surplusage, too much*; SEE CONCEPTS *767,787*

overall [*adj*] *complete, general*

all-embracing, blanket, comprehensive, global, inclusive, long-range, long-term, sweeping, thorough, total, umbrella; SEE CONCEPT *772*

overall [*adv*] *in general*

all over, chiefly, everyplace, everywhere, generally speaking, in the long run, largely, mainly, mostly, on the whole, predominantly, primarily, principally, throughout; SEE CONCEPTS *548,772*

overbearing [*adj*] *arrogant, domineering*

ascendant, autocratic, bossy, cavalier, cocky*, despotic, dictatorial, disdainful, dogmatic, egotistic, haughty, high-and-mighty*, high-handed*, imperative, imperial, imperious, insolent, magisterial, officious, oppressive, overweening, paramount, peremptory, predominant, preponderant, prevalent, proud, regnant, sniffy*, snotty*, sovereign, stuffy, supercilious, superior, tyrannical, uppity*; SEE CONCEPTS *401,404*

overblown [*adj*] *excessive, too much*

aureate, bombastic, disproportionate, euphuistic, flowery, fulsome, grandiloquent, hyped up*, immoderate, inflated, magniloquent, oratorical, overdone, pompous, pretentious, profuse, rhetorical, sonorous, superfluous, turgid, undue, verbose, windy; SEE CONCEPTS *267,548*

overcast [*adj*] *cloudy, darkened*

clouded, clouded over, dark, dismal, dreary, dull, gray, hazy, leaden, lowering, murky, nebulous, not clear, not fair, oppressive, somber, sunless, threatening; SEE CONCEPT *525*

overcome [*adj*] *overwhelmed; visibly moved*

affected, at a loss for words, beaten, blown-away*, bowled-over*, buried*, conquered, defeated, overthrown, run-over*, speechless, swamped, swept off one's feet*, taken*, unable to continue; SEE CONCEPT *403*

overcome [*v*] *beat, defeat*

best*, be victorious, come out on top*, conquer, crush, down*, drown, get around*, get the better of*, hurdle, knock over*, knock socks off*, lick*, master, outlive, overpower, overthrow, overwhelm, prevail, prostrate, reduce, render, rise above*, shock, stun, subdue, subjugate, surmount, survive, throw*, triumph over, vanquish, weather*, whelm*, win, worst*; SEE CONCEPT *95*

overconfident [*adj*] *overly sure of oneself*

brash, careless, cocksure*, cocky*, foolhardy, heading for a fall*, heedless, hubristic, impudent, overweening, presuming, presumptuous, pushy*, rash, reckless, self-assertive; SEE CONCEPTS *401,542*

overdo [*v*] *go to extremes; carry too far*

amplify, be intemperate, belabor, bite off too much*, do to death, drive oneself, exaggerate, fatigue, go overboard*, go too far*, hype, lay it on*, magnify, make federal case*, not know when to stop*, overburden, overestimate, overindulge, overload, overplay, overrate, overreach, overstate, overtax, overtire, overuse, overvalue, overwork, pile on*, pressure, puff*, run into the ground*, run riot*, strain oneself, stretch, talk big*, wear down*, wear oneself out*; SEE CONCEPTS *87,112,156*

overdue [*adj*] *late, behind schedule*

behindhand, behind time, belated, delinquent, due, held up*, hung up*, jammed*, long delayed, mature, not punctual, outstanding, owing, payable, tardy, unpaid, unpunctual, unsettled; SEE CONCEPTS *334,548,799*

overflow [*n*] *flood, inundation*

advance, cataclysm, cataract, congestion, deluge, discharge, encroachment, enforcement, engorgement, excess, exuberance, flash flood, flooding, infringement, niagara, overabundance, overcrowding, overkill, overmuch, overproduction, plethora, pour, propulsion, push, redundancy, spate, spill, spillover, submergence, submersion, superfluity, surfeit, surplus, torrent; SEE CONCEPT *740*

overflow [*v*] *pour out, flood*

brim, bubble over, cascade, cover, deluge, discharge, drain, drown, engulf, fall over, gush, inundate, irrupt, issue, jet, leak, overbrim, overrun, overtop, pour, run over, rush, shed, shower, slop, slosh, soak, spill, spill over, spout, spray, spurt, squirt, submerge, surge, swamp, water, wave, well, well over, wet, whelm; SEE CONCEPTS *179,256,740*

overhang [*v*] *bulge, hang over*

beetle, be imminent, be suspended, cast a shadow, command, dangle over, droop over, endanger, extend, flap over, impend, jut, loom, menace, overtop, poke, portend, pouch, project, protrude, rise above, stand out, stick out, swing over, threaten, tower above; SEE CONCEPT *752*

overhaul [*v*] *redo, restore*

check, debug, doctor*, do up*, examine, fiddle with*, fix, give facelift*, improve, inspect, mend, modernize, patch, rebuild, recondition, reconstruct, reexamine, renew, repair, retread, revamp, service, survey; SEE CONCEPTS *126,202,212*

overhead [*adj/adv*] *up above*

above, aerial, aloft, atop, hanging, in the sky, on high, over, overhanging, roof, skyward, upper, upward; SEE CONCEPT *586*

overhead [*n*] *general, continuing costs of operation*

budget, burden, cost, depreciation, expense, expenses, insurance, outlay, rent, upkeep, utilities; SEE CONCEPTS *329,332*

overjoyed [*adj*] *extremely happy*

charmed, delighted, deliriously happy, elated, euphoric, happy as a clam*, happy as a lark*, joyful, jubilant, on cloud nine*, only too happy*, over the moon*, rapturous, ravished, thrilled, tickled pink*, transported; SEE CONCEPT *403*

overlap [*v*] *lie over something else*

extend along, flap, fold over, go beyond, imbricate, lap over, overhang, overlay, overlie, overrun, project, protrude, ride, run over, shingle; SEE CONCEPT *759*

overlook [v1] *disregard, neglect*
discount, disdain, fail to notice, forget, ignore, leave out, leave undone, let fall between the cracks*, let go, let slide*, make light of*, miss, omit, overpass, pass, pass by, pay no attention, slight, slip up*; SEE CONCEPTS *30,101,699*

overlook [v2] *make allowances for*
bear with*, blink at*, condone, disregard, excuse, forgive, go along with, grin and bear it*, handle, ignore, let bygones be bygones*, let go, let pass*, live with*, look the other way, pay no mind*, play past*, put up with*, roll with punches*, stand for, stomach, swim with the tide*, take, tune out*, turn blind eye to*, white-wash*, wink at*, wipe slate clean*; SEE CONCEPTS *10,83*

overlook [v3] *have a view of something*
afford a view, command, command a view, dominate, front on, give on, give upon, have a prospect of, inspect, look down, look out, look out on, look over, mount, oversee, overtop, soar above, surmount, survey, top, tower over, view, watch over; SEE CONCEPT *752*

overlook [v4] *supervise*
boss, chaperon, control, oversee, quarterback*, superintend, survey; SEE CONCEPTS *94,117*

overly [adv] *excessively*
ever, exceedingly, extremely, immensely, immoderately, inordinately, over, overfull, overmuch, too, too much, too-too*, unduly, very much; SEE CONCEPT *544*

overplay [v] *be dramatic*
accent, accentuate, blow out of proportion*, dramatize, exaggerate, get carried away*, ham it up*, hyperbolize, labor at, lay it on thick*, magnify, maximize, mug*, overact, overdo, overdraw, overemphasize, overstate, overstress, overuse, overwork, point up*, show off*, stretch; SEE CONCEPTS *59,87,292*

overpower [v] *beat; get the upper hand*
bear down, beat down, blank, blow away*, bulldoze*, bury, clobber, conquer, cream*, crush, defeat, drown, drub*, immobilize, knock out*, lay one out*, murder*, overcome, overthrow, overwhelm, prostrate, put away*, quell, reduce, roll over*, rout, shellack*, shut off*, smash*, subdue, subjugate, swamp*, take care of*, take out*, torpedo*, total*, trash*, trounce, vanquish, waste*, wax*, whelm*; SEE CONCEPTS *95,191*

overrate [v] *assign too much value, importance*
assess too highly, build up, exaggerate, exceed, expect too much of, magnify, make too much of*, overassess, overesteem, overestimate, overpraise, overprize, overreckon, oversell, overvalue, rate too highly, think too highly of*, think too much of*; SEE CONCEPTS *12,49*

overrated [adj] *overvalued*
exaggerated, hyped-up, overestimated, overpaid, overpriced, overpromoted, puffed up, pumped up*; SEE CONCEPTS *267,542,562*

override/overrule [v] *cancel, reverse a decision*
alter, annul, bend to one's will*, control, countermand, direct, disallow, disregard, dominate, govern, ignore, influence, invalidate, make null and void*, make void, not heed, nullify, outvote, outweigh, overturn, prevail over, quash, recall, repeal, rescind, revoke, ride roughshod*, rule against, set aside, supersede, sway, take no account of, thwart, trample, upset, vanquish, veto; SEE CONCEPTS *50,88,121,298,317*

overriding [adj] *central, most important*
cardinal, compelling, determining, dominant, final, main, major, number one*, overruling, paramount, pivotal, predominant, prevailing, primary, prime, principal, ruling, supreme, ultimate; SEE CONCEPT *568*

overrule [v] *repeal*
abrogate, annul, cancel, disallow, invalidate, negate, nullify, override, overturn, quash, rescind, reverse, revoke, strike down, veto, void; SEE CONCEPTS *50,88,121,234*

overrun [v1] *defeat, invade*
beat, clobber, drub*, foray, inroad, lambaste, lick*, massacre, occupy, overwhelm, put to flight, raid, rout, swamp*, thrash, trim, whip*; SEE CONCEPTS *86,95*

overrun [v2] *infest, spread over; exceed*
beset, choke, deluge, go beyond, inundate, invade, overflow, overgrow, overshoot, overspread, overstep, overwhelm, permeate, ravage, run on, run over, spill, spread like wildfire*, surge, surpass, swarm, well over; SEE CONCEPTS *172,179,651*

overseas [adj] *across an ocean*
abroad, across, away, foreign, in foreign land, transatlantic, transoceanic, transpacific; SEE CONCEPT *583*

oversee [v] *manage, supervise*
baby-sit*, be in driver's seat*, boss, call the shots*, captain, chaperon, command, eye*, herd, inspect, keep one's eye on*, look after, overlook, quarterback*, ride herd on*, run the show*, shepherd, sit on top of*, skipper, superintend, survey, watch; SEE CONCEPT *117*

overseer [n] *person who supervises others' work*
executive, head, head honcho*, manager, pit boss*, straw boss*, superintendent, supervisor; SEE CONCEPT *347*

overshadow [v] *make obscure, dim, vague*
adumbrate, becloud, bedim, cloud, command, darken, dim, dominate, dwarf, eclipse, excel, govern, haze, leave in the shade*, obfuscate, outshine, outweigh, overcast, overcloud, overweigh, preponderate, rise above*, rule, shadow, steal spotlight*, surpass, take precedence, tower above*, veil; SEE CONCEPTS *620,668*

oversight [n1] *failure, omission*
blank*, blunder, carelessness, chasm, default, delinquency, dereliction, disregard, error, fault, inattention, lapse, laxity, miscue, mistake, neglect, overlook, overlooking, preterition, pretermission, skip, slip, slipup*; SEE CONCEPT *101*

oversight [n2] *care, supervision*
administration, aegis, charge, check, control, custody, direction, guard, guardianship, handling, inspection, intendance, keep, keeping, maintenance, management, superintendence, surveillance, tutelage; SEE CONCEPT *117*

overstate [v] *exaggerate*
amplify, blow out of proportion*, boast, boost, brag, build up, embellish, embroider, emphasize, enlarge, exalt, expand, fabricate, fudge*, heighten, hike, inflate, lay it on thick*, lie, magnify, misquote, misreport, misrepresent, overdo, overemphasize, overestimate, pad*, play up, puff; SEE CONCEPT *63*

overt [adj] *obvious, unconcealed*
apparent, clear, definite, manifest, observable, open, patent, plain, public, undisguised, visible; SEE CONCEPT *535*

OV
OV

overtake [v] *catch; pass*
beat, befall, better, catch up with, come upon, engulf, gain on, get past, get to, happen, hit, leave behind, outdistance, outdo, outstrip, overhaul, overwhelm, reach, strike, take by surprise; SEE CONCEPTS 95,141

overthrow [v] *defeat, destroy*
abolish, beat, bring down, bring to ruin, conquer, crush, demolish, depose, dethrone, do away with, eradicate, exterminate, knock down, knock out, level, liquidate, oust, overcome, overpower, overrun, overturn, overwhelm, purge, put an end to, raze, ruin, subdue, subjugate, subvert, terminate, tip, topple, tumble, unseat, upend, upset, vanquish; SEE CONCEPTS 95,252,320

overtone [n] *implication, hint*
association, connotation, flavor, inference, innuendo, intimation, meaning, nuance, sense, suggestion, tone, undercurrent, undertone; SEE CONCEPT 278

overture [n] *introduction, approach*
advance, bid, conciliatory move, exordium, foreword, invitation, offer, opening, preamble, preface, prelude, prelusion, presentation, proem, prologue, proposal, proposition, signal, suggestion, tender; SEE CONCEPTS 278,384,828,832

overturn [v] *flip over*
annul, bring down, capsize, countermand, down, invalidate, invert, keel over, knock down, knock over, nullify, overbalance, prostrate, repeal, rescind, reverse, roll, set aside, spill, tip over, topple, tumble, turn over, turn upside down, upend, upset, upturn, void; SEE CONCEPTS 147,232

overview [n] *survey*
analysis, apercu, audit, capsulization, critique, examination, inquiry, inspection, outline, pandect, precis, review, scrutiny, sketch, study, syllabus, synopsis, thumbnail, view; SEE CONCEPTS 37,103,197,271,291

overweight [adj] *heavier than average*
ample, bulky, corpulent, fat, fleshy, gross, heavy, hefty, huge, massive, obese, outsize, overfed, overstuffed, plump, portly, pudgy, rotund, stout, upholstered*, weighty; SEE CONCEPT 491

overwhelm [v1] *flood, beat physically*
bury, conquer, crush, defeat, deluge, destroy, drown, drub*, engulf, inundate, massacre, overcome, overflow, overpower, overrun, overthrow, rout, smother, submerge, swamp, thrash, total*, whip*, win*; SEE CONCEPTS 86,95

overwhelm [v2] *astonish, devastate*
bewilder, blow out of the water*, bowl over*, confound, confuse, demoralize, destroy, disturb, do in*, downgrade*, drown, dumbfound, floor*, kill*, overcome, overpower, prostrate, puzzle, render speechless*, run circles around, shatter, shock, stagger, steamroller*, stun, subordinate, surprise, swamp, upset, wreck; SEE CONCEPTS 16,42

overwhelming [adj] *overpowering*
amazing, astounding, breathtaking, crushing, devastating, exciting, eye-opening, mind-boggling, overcoming, paralyzing, shattering, staggering, stunning, vast; SEE CONCEPT 42

overwrought [adj] *exhausted and excited*
affected, agitated, all shook up*, beside oneself*, crazy, distracted, emotional, excitable, fired-up*, flipped out*, frantic, freaked-out*, high*, hot-and-bothered*, hot under collar*, hyper*, in a state*, keyed-up*, nervous, neurotic, on edge*,

overexcited, overstrung, overworked, spent, steamed up*, stirred*, strung-out*, tense, tired, uneasy, unstrung*, uptight*, weary, wired, worked-up*, worn, wound-up; SEE CONCEPTS 401,403,542

owe [v] *have an obligation*
be beholden, be bound, be contracted, behind, be in arrears, be in debt, be indebted, be into one for, be obligated, be under obligation, feel bound, get on credit, have borrowed, incur, in hock*, lost, on the tab*, ought to, run up a bill*; SEE CONCEPT 335

owing [adj] *unpaid*
attributable, comeuppance, due, in debt, mature, matured, outstanding, overdue, owed, payable, unsettled; SEE CONCEPT 334

own [adj] *belonging to individual*
endemic, hers, his, individual, inherent, intrinsic, its, mine, owned, particular, peculiar, personal, private, resident, theirs, very own, yours; SEE CONCEPT 710

own [v1] *possess; be responsible for*
be in possession of, be possessed of, boast, control, dominate, enjoy, fall heir to, have, have in hand, have rights, have title, hold, inherit, keep, occupy, reserve, retain; SEE CONCEPT 710

own [v2] *acknowledge, admit*
allow, assent to, avow, come clean*, concede, confess, declare, disclose, grant, let on*, make clean breast of*, own up, recognize, tell the truth; SEE CONCEPT 57

owner [n] *person who has possession of something*
buyer, governor, heir, heir-apparent, heiress, heritor, holder, keeper, landowner, legatee, partner, possessor, proprietor, purchaser, sharer, squire, titleholder; SEE CONCEPTS 343,347,414

ownership [n] *possession of property*
buying, claim, control, cut, deed, dominion, end, hand, having, holding, occupancy, partnership, piece, possessorship, property, proprietary rights, proprietorship, purchase, purchasing, residence, slice, takeover, tenancy, tenure, title, use; SEE CONCEPT 710

P

pace [n1] *steps in walking*
clip, footstep, gait, getalong, lick*, measure, step, stride, tread, walk; SEE CONCEPT 149

pace [n2] *speed, tempo of motion*
beat, bounce, celerity, clip, downbeat, lick*, momentum, motion, movement, progress, quickness, rapidity, rapidness, rate, swiftness, time, velocity; SEE CONCEPTS 755,818

pace [v1] *walk back and forth*
ambulate, canter, foot it*, gallop, hoof*, march, patrol, pound*, step, stride, traipse, tread, troop, trot, walk up and down; SEE CONCEPT 149

pace [v2] *measure by footsteps*
count, determine, mark out, step, step off*; SEE CONCEPTS 291,764

pacesetter [n] *pacemaker*
bellwether, forerunner, leader, pacer, pioneer; SEE CONCEPTS 347,354

pacific [*adj*] *appeasing, peaceful*
amicable, at peace, calm, conciliatory, diplomatic, friendly, gentle, neutral, peaceable, peace-loving, peacemaking, placatory, placid, quiet, serene, tranquil, untroubled; SEE CONCEPTS 485,542

pacifist [*n*] *peace-lover*
antiwar demonstrator, conscientious objector, dove, passive resister, peacemaker, peacemonger, peacenik; SEE CONCEPTS 354,416

pacify [*v*] *make peaceful; appease*
allay, ameliorate, assuage, bury the hatchet*, butter up*, calm, chasten, compose, con, conciliate, cool, dulcify, fix up, grease*, kiss and make up*, lay back, lull, make peace, mitigate, moderate, mollify, pacificate, placate, propitiate, put the lid on*, qualify, quell, quiet, relieve, repress, silence, smooth over, soften, soft-pedal*, soothe, square, still, stroke, subdue, sweeten*, take the edge off*, tame, temper, tranquilize; SEE CONCEPTS 7,22,250

pack [*n1*] *kit, package*
backpack, baggage, bale, bundle, burden, equipment, haversack, knapsack, load, luggage, outfit, parcel, rucksack, truss; SEE CONCEPTS 260,446,496

pack [*n2*] *group, bunch*
assemblage, band, barrel, bundle, circle, collection, company, crew, crowd, deck, drove, flock, gang, great deal, heap, herd, horde, lot, lump, mess, mob, mush, multiplicity, number, pack, pile, press, set, swarm, throng, troop; SEE CONCEPTS 397,417,432

pack [*v1*] *make ready for transport*
batch, bind, brace, bunch, bundle, burden, collect, dispose, fasten, gather, get ready, load, package, put in order, store, stow, tie, warehouse; SEE CONCEPTS 202

pack [*v2*] *fill, compact*
arrange, bind, charge, chock, choke, compress, condense, contract, cram, crowd, drive in, heap, insert, jam, jam-pack*, lade, load, mob, pile, press, push, put away, ram, ram in*, sardine*, squeeze, stuff, tamp, throng, thrust in, top off, wedge; SEE CONCEPT 209

pack [*v3*] *transport, carry*
bear, buck, convey, ferry, freight, gun, haul, heel, hump, jag, journey, lug, piggyback*, ride, shlep*, shoulder, tote, trek, truck; SEE CONCEPTS 148,217

package [*n*] *bundle; whole*
amalgamation, assortment, bag, baggage, bale, batch, biddle, bottle, box, bunch, burden, can, carton, combination, container, crate, entity, kit, load, lot, luggage, pack, packet, parcel, pile, sack, sheaf, stack, suitcase, tin, trunk, unit; SEE CONCEPTS 432,494

packed [*adj*] *full*
arranged, awash, brimful, brimming, bundled, chock, chock-full*, compact, compressed, congested, consigned, crammed, crowded, filled, full to the gills*, jammed, jam-packed*, loaded, mobbed, overflowing, overloaded, packed like sardines*, seething, serried, stuffed, swarming, to the roof*, tumid, up to the hilt*, up to the rafters*, wall-to-wall*, wrapped; SEE CONCEPTS 481,483,740,774

packet [*n*] *small, often flat, bundle*
bag, carton, container, envelope, file, folder,

package, parcel, wrapper, wrapping; SEE CONCEPT 494

pact [*n*] *agreement*
alliance, arrangement, bargain, bond, compact, concord, concordat, contract, convention, covenant, deal, league, paper, piece of paper, protocol, settlement, transaction, treaty, understanding; SEE CONCEPTS 271,684

pad/padding [*n1*] *protection*
buffer, cushion, filling, packing, stuffing, wad, wadding, waste; SEE CONCEPTS 473,475

pad [*n2*] *tablet of paper*
block, jotter, memorandum, notebook, notepad, paper, parchment, quire, ream, scratch, scratch pad, slips; SEE CONCEPTS 260,475

pad [*n3*] *dwelling, room*
abode, coop*, crib*, digs*, hangout*, hideout*, hive*, house, layout*, lodging, quarters, residence, residency, setup*; SEE CONCEPT 516

pad [*v1*] *protect with cushioning*
cushion, fill, fill out, line, pack, protect, shape, stuff; SEE CONCEPTS 134,202

pad [*v2*] *elaborate, amplify*
augment, bulk, embellish, embroider, enlarge, exaggerate, expand, fill out, flesh out*, fudge*, increase, lengthen, magnify, overdraw, overstate, protract, spin, stretch; SEE CONCEPTS 63,244

pad [*v3*] *walk quietly; walk ploddingly*
creep, go barefoot, hike, march, patter*, pitter-patter*, plod, pussyfoot*, sneak, steal, traipse, tramp, trek, trudge; SEE CONCEPT 149

paddle [*n*] *item used for propelling object*
oar, paddlewheel, pole, propeller, pull, scull, sweep; SEE CONCEPTS 479,499

paddle [*v*] *propel with arms or tool*
boat, cruise, cut water*, drift, drive, navigate, oar, pull, row, run rapids*, scull, sky an oar*, slop, splash, stir, sweep, thrash, wade; SEE CONCEPT 147

pagan [*adj*] *irreligious*
agnostic, atheistic, heathen, idolatrous, impious, infidel, polytheistic, profane; SEE CONCEPT 542

pagan [*n*] *person who does not believe in an orthodox religion*
agnostic, atheist, doubter, freethinker, heathen, heretic, iconoclast, idolater, idolist, infidel, paganist, pantheist, polytheist, scoffer, skeptic, unbeliever; SEE CONCEPTS 361,423

page [*n1*] *sheet of paper*
folio, leaf, recto, side, signature, surface, verso; SEE CONCEPT 475

page [*n2*] *person who serves others*
attendant, bellhop, equerry, errand runner, servant, youth; SEE CONCEPTS 348,354

page [*v1*] *call for over communications system*
announce, beep, call, call out, call the name of, hunt for, preconize, seek, send for, summon; SEE CONCEPTS 74,78

page [*v2*] *mark sheets of document*
check, count, foliate, number, paginate; SEE CONCEPTS 79,764

pageant [*n*] *spectacle or contest*
celebration, charade, display, exhibition, exposition, extravaganza, fair, make-believe, motorcade, parade, pomp, procession, ritual, show, tableau; SEE CONCEPTS 292,377

pageantry [*n*] *flashy display*
affectation, array, ceremonial, ceremony, extravagance, fanfare, flourish, formality, glitter,

grandeur, grandiosity, magnificence, ostentation, pageant, panoply, parade, pomp, pomposity, show, spectacle, splash, splendor; SEE CONCEPTS 335,377,655

pain [*n1*] *physical suffering*
ache, affliction, agony, burn, catch, convulsion, cramp, crick, discomfort, distress, fever, gripe, hurt, illness, injury, irritation, laceration, malady, misery, pang, paroxysm, prick, sickness, smarting, soreness, spasm, sting, stitch, strain, tenderness, throb, throe, tingle, torment, torture, trouble, twinge, wound; SEE CONCEPTS 316,728

pain [*n2*] *mental suffering*
affliction, agony, anguish, anxiety, bitterness, despondency, distress, grief, heartache, hurt, malaise, martyrdom, misery, rack, sadness, shock, suffering, torment, torture, travail, tribulation, woe, worry, wretchedness; SEE CONCEPTS 410,728

pain [*n3*] *problem*
aggravation, annoyance, bore, bother, drag, effort, exertion, irritation, nuisance, pest, trouble, vexation; SEE CONCEPT 532

pain [*v*] *bother, trouble*
ache, afflict, aggrieve, agonize, ail, anguish, annoy, bite, chafe, chasten, constrain, convulse, cut to the quick*, discomfort, disquiet, distress, exasperate, excruciate, gall, grieve, gripe, harass, harm, harrow, hit where one lives*, hurt, inflame, injure, irk, irritate, nick, prick, punish, rack, rile, sadden, smart, sting, strain, stress, suffer, throb, tingle, torment, torture, upset, vex, worry, wound; SEE CONCEPTS 7,19,246

painful [*adj*] *physically or mentally agonizing*
aching, afflictive, agonizing, arduous, awful, biting, burning, caustic, difficult, dire, disagreeable, distasteful, distressing, dreadful, excruciating, extreme, extremely bad, grievous, hard, harrowing, hurtful, hurting, inflamed, irritated, laborious, piercing, raw, saddening, sensitive, severe, sharp, smarting, sore, stinging, tedious, tender, terrible, throbbing, tormenting, troublesome, trying, uncomfortable, unpleasant, vexatious; SEE CONCEPTS 529,537

painkiller [*n*] *anesthetic*
alleviating, analgesic, anodyne, aspirin, dope*, drug, medicine, morphine, ointment, opiate, pain reliever, sedative, tranquilizer; SEE CONCEPT 307

painstaking [*adj*] *meticulous, thorough*
assiduous, by the book*, by the numbers*, careful, conscientious, consciable, diligent, earnest, exact, exacting, finicky, fussbudget*, fussy, hard-working, heedful, industrious, particular, persevering, persnickety*, picky, punctilious, punctual, scrupulous, sedulous, stickler*, strenuous, thoroughgoing; SEE CONCEPTS 326,538

paint [*n*] *tinted covering*
acrylic, chroma, color, coloring, cosmetic, dye, emulsion, enamel, flat, gloss, greasepaint, latex, makeup, oil, overlay, pigment, rouge, stain, tempera, varnish, veneer, wax; SEE CONCEPTS 467,475

paint [*v*] *apply colored tint, often to make design*
brush, catch a likeness, coat, color, compose, cover, cover up, daub, decorate, delineate, depict, design, draft, draw, dye, figure, fresco, gloss over, limn, ornament, outline, picture, portray, put on coats*, represent, shade, sketch, slap on*,

slather, stipple, swab, tint, touch up, wash; SEE CONCEPTS 172,174

pair [*n*] *two of something*
brace, combination, combine, combo, couple, deuce, doublet, duality, duo, dyad, match, mates, span, team, twins, two, two of a kind, twosome, yoke; SEE CONCEPTS 432,784

pair [*v*] *make, become a twosome*
balance, bracket, combine, couple, join, marry, match, match up, mate, pair off, put together, team, twin, unite, wed, yoke; SEE CONCEPT 113

pajamas [*n*] *sleeping clothes*
jamas*, jammies*, jams*, loungewear, lounging robe, nightdress, nightie*, nightshirt, nightwear, PJ's*, sleeper, sleeping suit; SEE CONCEPT 451

pal [*n*] *person's friend*
amiga, amigo, associate, boon companion*, bosom buddy*, bro*, brother, buddy, chum, companion, comrade, connate, crony, cuz, good buddy*, homeboy, homegirl, mate, sidekick, sis*, sister; SEE CONCEPT 423

palace [*n*] *royal or enormous home*
alcazar, castle, chateau, dwelling, hall, manor, mansion, official residence, royal residence; SEE CONCEPT 516

palatable [*adj*] *delicious, agreeable*
acceptable, A-OK*, aperitive, appetizing, attractive, cool, copacetic, delectable, delightful, divine, enjoyable, fair, flavorsome, good-tasting, heavenly, home-cooking*, luscious, mellow, mouthwatering, peachy, pleasant, relishing, sapid, saporific, saporous, satisfactory, savory, scrumptious, sugar-coated*, sweetened, tasteful, tasty, tempting, toothsome, toothy*, yummy*; SEE CONCEPTS 529,613

palatial [*adj*] *grand, opulent*
deluxe, grandiose, illustrious, imposing, impressive, lush, luxuriant, luxurious, magnificent, majestic, monumental, noble, plush, regal, rich, silken, spacious, splendid, stately, sumptuous, upholstered; SEE CONCEPTS 334,485,589

pale [*adj*] *light in color or effect*
anemic, ashen, ashy, blanched, bleached, bloodless, cadaverous, colorless, deathlike, dim, doughy, dull, faded, faint, feeble, ghastly, gray, haggard, inadequate, ineffective, ineffectual, insubstantial, livid, lurid, pallid, pasty, poor, sallow, sick, sickly, spectral, thin, unsubstantial, wan, washed-out, waxen, waxlike, weak, white, whitish; SEE CONCEPTS 537,618

pale [*v*] *become, make lighter or weakened*
blanch, decrease, dim, diminish, dull, fade, faint, go white, grow dull, lessen, lose color, lose luster, muddy, tarnish, whiten; SEE CONCEPTS 240,250

pall [*n*] *cloud, gloom*
cloak, cloth, covering, damp, damper, dismay, mantle, melancholy, shadow, shroud, veil; SEE CONCEPTS 620,674

pall [*v*] *bore, tire*
become dull, become tedious, cloy, disgust, fill, glut, gorge, jade, sate, satiate, sicken, surfeit, weary; SEE CONCEPTS 7,19

palliate [*v*] *gloss over; cover up*
abate, allay, alleviate, apologize for, assuage, camouflage, cloak, conceal, condone, cover, diminish, disguise, dissemble, ease, exculpate, excuse, extenuate, glaze, hide, hush up*, justify, lessen, lighten, make light of*, mask, minimize, mitigate, moderate, mollify, prettify, put on a

Band-Aid*, qualify, quick fix*, relieve, screen, soften, soothe, sugarcoat*, temper, varnish, veil, veneer, vindicate, white, whiten, whitewash*; SEE CONCEPTS 57,59,172,188

pallid [*adj*] *pale*
anemic, ashen, ashy, blanched, bloodless, colorless, dull, faded, feeble, ghastly, gray, lackluster, lifeless, pasty, sallow, sickly, spiritless, uninspired, wan, weak, whitish; SEE CONCEPTS 537,618

pallor [*n*] *paleness*
achromatic, bloodlessness, cadaverousness, colorlessness, etiolation, pallidity, pastiness, sallowness, wanness, whiteness; SEE CONCEPTS 537,618

palpable [*adj1*] *clear, obvious*
apparent, appreciable, arresting, believable, blatant, certain, colorable, conspicuous, credible, detectable, discernible, distinct, evident, manifest, noticeable, observable, open, ostensible, patent, perceivable, perceptible, plain, plausible, positive, remarkable, seeming, sensible, straightforward, striking, sure, tangible, unequivocal, unmistakable, visible; SEE CONCEPTS 529,535

palpable [*adj2*] *concrete, real*
material, sensible, solid, substantial, tactile, tangible, touchable; SEE CONCEPTS 485,582

palpitate [*v*] *beat at a rapid pace, like a heart*
flutter, pitpat*, pitter-patter*, pound, pulsate, pulse, quiver, shiver, throb, tremble, vibrate; SEE CONCEPTS 152,308

palsied [*adj*] *crippled*
arthritic, atonic, debilitated, disabled, diseased, helpless, neurasthenic, paralytic, paralyzed, rheumatic, sclerotic, shaking, shaky, sick, spastic, trembling, tremorous, weak; SEE CONCEPTS 314,485

palsy-walsy [*adj*] *very friendly*
affectionate, buddy-buddy*, chummy*, close, clubby, confiding, fond, intimate, kissy-huggy*, lovey-dovey*, neighborly, pally, thick; SEE CONCEPT 555

paltry [*adj*] *poor; worthless*
base, beggarly, cheap, common, contemptible, derisory, despicable, inconsiderable, ineffectual, insignificant, limited, low, low-down*, meager, mean, measly, minor, miserable, narrow, petty, picayune, piddling, pitiful, puny, set, shabby, shoddy, sleazy*, slight, small, sorry*, trashy, trifling, trivial, unconsequential, unimportant, vile, wretched; SEE CONCEPTS 334,485

pamper [*v*] *serve one's every need, whim*
baby, caress, cater to, coddle, cosset, dandle*, fondle, gratify, humor, indulge, mollycoddle*, overindulge, pet, please, regale, satisfy, spare the rod*, spoil, spoil rotten*, tickle, yield; SEE CONCEPTS 136,295

pamphlet [*n*] *booklet*
announcement, broadside, brochure, bulletin, circular, compilation, flyer*, folder, handout, leaflet, throwaway*, tract, tractate; SEE CONCEPTS 271,280

pan [*n*] *container for cooking food*
bucket, casserole, double boiler, frying pan, kettle, pail, pannikin, pot, roaster, saucepan, sheet, skillet, vessel; SEE CONCEPTS 493,494

pan [*v1*] *look, search for over a wide area*
follow, move, scan, separate, sift, sweep, swing, track, traverse, wash; SEE CONCEPT 216

pan [*v2*] *criticize strongly*
blame, censure, condemn, cut up, denounce, de-

nunciate, disparage, flay, hammer, jeer at, knock, rap, reprehend, review unfavorably, roast, slam; SEE CONCEPT 52

panacea [*n*] *cure-all*
catholicon, cure, elixir, nostrum, patent medicine, relief, remedy; SEE CONCEPTS 307,311

panache [*n*] *person's flamboyant spirit*
brio, charisma, dash, élan, flair, flamboyance, flourish, style, swagger, verve, vigor; SEE CONCEPT 411

pancake [*n*] *flat, round breakfast cake*
batter cake, blanket*, cake, crepe, flapjack, griddlecake, hot cake, johnnycake, jonnycake, sourdough, waffle, wheat*, wheat cake; SEE CONCEPTS 457,461

pandemonium [*n*] *craziness, commotion*
anarchy, babel, bedlam, bluster, brouhaha*, chaos, clamor, clatter, confusion, din, hassle, hubbub*, hue and cry*, hullabaloo*, jangle, noise, racket, riot, ruckus*, rumpus, tumult, turbulence, turmoil, uproar; SEE CONCEPTS 388,674

pander [*v*] *cater to, indulge*
brownnose*, cajole, fall all over*, gratify, lay it on*, massage, play the game*, play up to*, please, politic, satisfy, snow*, soap*, soften up, stroke, suck up to*; SEE CONCEPTS 59,136,384

panel [*n*] *committee*
board, bureau, cabinet, commission, consultants, council, forum, group, jury, representatives, task force, tribunal; SEE CONCEPT 381

pang [*n*] *ache, twinge*
agony, anguish, bite, discomfort, distress, gripe, misery, pain, prick, spasm, stab, sting, stitch, throb, throe, wrench; SEE CONCEPT 728

panhandle [*v*] *beg*
ask alms, bum*, cadge*, freeload*, hit up*, hold out one's hand*, hustle, live hand to mouth*, mooch*, pass the hat*, scrounge, solicit charity, sponge*; SEE CONCEPT 53

panic [*n1*] *extreme fright*
agitation, alarm, cold feet*, confusion, consternation, crush, dismay, dread, fear, frenzy, horror, hysteria, jam, rush, scare, stampede, terror, trepidation; SEE CONCEPTS 27,410,690

panic [*n2*] *sudden drop in value in financial markets*
Black Monday*, bust, crash, depression, rainy day*, slump; SEE CONCEPT 335

panic [*v*] *become, make afraid or distressed*
alarm, become hysterical, be terror-stricken, chicken out*, clutch, come apart, freeze up*, go to pieces*, have a fit*, lose it*, lose nerve*, overreact, push panic button*, run scared*, scare, shake in boots*, stampede, startle, terrify, unnerve; SEE CONCEPTS 14,27

panorama [*n*] *scene, horizon*
bird's-eye view*, compass, dimension, diorama, extent, orbit, overview, perspective, picture, prospect, purview, radius, range, reach, scenery, scenic view, scope, spectacle, survey, sweep, view, vista; SEE CONCEPTS 529,628,651

panoramic [*adj*] *sweeping*
all-around, all-embracing, all-encompassing, all-inclusive, bird's-eye*, blanket, broad, complete, comprehensive, far-reaching, full, panned, scenic, wide-ranging; SEE CONCEPTS 531,772

pan out [*v*] *come to pass; succeed*
click*, come out*, culminate, eventuate, go, go over*, happen, net*, prove out, result, turn out, work out, yield; SEE CONCEPT 706

pa
pa

pant [*v1*] *gasp for air*
be out of breath, blow, breathe, chuff, gulp, heave, huff, palpitate, puff, snort, throb, wheeze, whiff, wind; SEE CONCEPT *163*

pant [*v2*] *long for*
ache, aim, aspire, covet, crave, desire, hunger, lust, pine, sigh, thirst, want, wish, yearn; SEE CONCEPT *20*

panties [*n*] *women's underwear*
bikini, briefs, intimate things, lingerie, underclothes, undergarment, underpants, undies; SEE CONCEPT *451*

pantry [*n*] *kitchen storage room*
buttery, cellar, chamber, closet, cupboard, larder, store room; SEE CONCEPT *448*

pants [*n*] *clothing for legs, lower half of body*
Bermudas*, bloomers, blue jeans, boxer shorts, breeches, briefs, britches*, chaps*, chinos, clam diggers*, cords*, corduroys, denims, drawers, dungarees, jeans, jodhpurs, knickers, overalls, pantaloons*, panties*, pedal pushers*, shorts, slacks, trousers, underpants; SEE CONCEPT *451*

pantywaist [*n*] *sissy*
baby*, chicken*, coward, cry-baby, fraidy-cat*, milksop, momma's boy*, namby-pamby, pansy, scaredy cat*, weakling, wimp*, wuss*, wussy*; SEE CONCEPT *423*

paparazzi [*n*] *photographers*
cameraperson, celebrity photographer, freelance photographer, paparazzo, shutterbug; SEE CONCEPT *352*

paper [*adj*] *thin, flimsy*
cardboard, disposable, insubstantial, paper-thin, papery, wafer-thin; SEE CONCEPT *606*

paper [*n2*] *newspaper*
daily, gazette, journal, news, organ, rag*, weekly; SEE CONCEPT *280*

paper [*n3*] *thesis, article*
analysis, assignment, composition, critique, dissertation, essay, examination, monograph, report, script, study, theme, treatise; SEE CONCEPTS *271,280*

paper [*n4*] *material upon which one writes*
card, filing card, letterhead, newsprint, note, note card, note pad, onion skin, pad, papyrus, parchment, poster, rag, sheet, stationery, tissue, vellum; SEE CONCEPTS *260,475*

paper [*v*] *line with material*
cover, hang, paste up, plaster, wallpaper; SEE CONCEPTS *172,177*

paper/papers [*n*] *legal document*
affidavit, archive, bill, certificate, certification, citation, contract, credentials, data, deed, diaries, diploma, documentation; dossier, file, grant, ID*, identification papers, indictment, instrument, letter, letters, order, passport, plea, record, subpoena, summons, testimony, token, visa, voucher, warrant, will, writ, writings; SEE CONCEPTS *271,318*

par [*n*] *average, equilibrium*
adequation, balance, coequality, criterion, equal footing, equality, equatability, equivalence, equivalency, level, mean, median, model, norm, parity, sameness, standard, usual; SEE CONCEPTS *636,667*

parable [*n*] *moral story*
allegory, fable, legend, lesson, tale, teaching; SEE CONCEPT *282*

parade [*n*] *pageant, display*
array, autocade, cavalcade, ceremony, column,

demonstration, exhibition, fanfare, flaunting, line, march, ostentation, panoply, pomp, procession, review, ritual, shine, show, spectacle, train, vaunting; SEE CONCEPTS *377,386*

parade [*v*] *show off; march*
advertise, air, boast, brag, brandish, declare, demonstrate, disclose, display, disport, divulge, exhibit, expose, flash, flaunt, march in review, prance, proclaim, publish, reveal, sport, strut, swagger, trot out*, vaunt; SEE CONCEPT *261*

paradigm [*n*] *example*
archetype, beau ideal*, chart, criterion, ensample, exemplar, ideal, mirror, model, original, pattern, prototype, sample, standard; SEE CONCEPT *686*

paradise [*n*] *land, feeling of great pleasure; absence of evil*
Arcadia*, ballpark, bliss, cloud nine*, delight, divine abode*, Eden*, felicity, happy hunting ground*, heaven, heavenly kingdom, kingdom come*, next world*, pearly gates*, promised land, Shangri-la*, Utopia*, wonderland, Zion*; SEE CONCEPTS *370,410,515*

paradox [*n*] *contradiction, puzzle*
absurdity, ambiguity, anomaly, catch, Catch-22*, enigma, error, inconsistency, mistake, mystery, nonsense, oddity, opposite, reverse; SEE CONCEPT *532*

paragon [*n*] *outstanding example*
apotheosis, archetype, beau ideal*, beauty, best, champ, champion, crackerjack*, cream*, criterion, cynosure, epitome, essence, exemplar, gem, ideal, jewel*, love, lovely, model, nonesuch, nonpareil, original, paradigm, pattern, peach*, perfection, pick, prototype, quintessence, standard, sublimation, tops*, trump*, ultimate; SEE CONCEPTS *671,686*

parallel [*adj1*] *aligned, side-by-side*
alongside, coextending, coextensive, coordinate, equidistant, extending equally, in the same direction, lateral, laterally, never meeting, running alongside; SEE CONCEPTS *581,586*

parallel [*adj2*] *akin, similar*
agnate, alike, analogous, comparable, complementary, conforming, consonant, correspondent, corresponding, equal, identical, like, matching, resembling, uniform; SEE CONCEPTS *487,573*

parallel [*n*] *complement, correlation*
analogue, analogy, comparison, corollary, correlate, correspondence, correspondent, counterpart, countertype, double, duplicate, duplication, equal, equivalent, homologue, kin*, likeness, match, parallelism, resemblance, similarity, twin; SEE CONCEPTS *667,670*

parallel [*v*] *be alike*
agree, assimilate, collimate, collocate, compare, complement, conform, copy, correlate, correspond, equal, equate, imitate, keep pace, liken, match, paragon, parallelize; SEE CONCEPTS *111,171,667*

paralytic [*adj*] *impaired in movement*
diplegic, disabled, immobile, immobilized, inactive, incapacitated, insensible, lame, numb, palsied, palsified, paralyzed, paraplegic, powerless, quadriplegic; SEE CONCEPTS *314,485*

paralyze [*v*] *immobilize*
anesthetize, appall, arrest, astound, bemuse, benumb, bring to grinding halt*, close, daunt, daze, deaden, debilitate, demolish, destroy, disable, disarm, enfeeble, freeze, halt, incapacitate,

knock out, lame, make inert, make nerveless, nonplus, numb, palsy, petrify, prostrate, shut down*, stop dead*, stun, stupefy, transfix, weaken; SEE CONCEPTS *14,121,246,252*

paramedic [*n*] *emergency medical technician*
ambulance attendant, EMT, medical assistant, nurse; SEE CONCEPTS *357,414*

parameter [*n*] *limit*
constant, criterion, framework, guideline, limitation, restriction, specification; SEE CONCEPT *688*

paramount [*adj*] *principal, superior*
ascendant, capital, cardinal, chief, commanding, controlling, crowning, dominant, eminent, first, foremost, headmost, leading, main, outstanding, overbearing, predominant, predominate, preeminent, premier, preponderant, prevalent, primary, prime, regnant, sovereign, supreme; SEE CONCEPTS *568,574*

paramour [*n*] *lover*
admirer, beau, boyfriend, concubine, courter, courtesan, doxy, escort, fiancé, fiancée, girlfriend, inamorata, inamorato, kept woman, mistress, steady, sweetheart; SEE CONCEPTS *415,423*

paranormal [*adj*] *supernatural*
abnormal, celestial, ghostly, metaphysical, mysterious, mystic, occult, phenomenal, preternatural, psychic, spectral, transcendental, uncomprehensible, unearthly; SEE CONCEPT *582*

parapet [*n*] *bulwark*
barricade, barrier, bastion, buffet, buttress, defense, embankment, fortification, partition, protection, protective wall, rampart, safeguard; SEE CONCEPTS *96,729*

paraphernalia [*n*] *equipment, belongings*
accoutrements, apparatus, appurtenances, baggage, effects, equipage, gear, habiliments, impedimenta, impediments, machinery, material, materiel, outfit, regalia, stuff, tackle, things, trappings; SEE CONCEPTS *446,496*

paraphrase [*n*] *translation, interpretation*
digest, explanation, rehash, rendering, rendition, rephrasing, restatement, rewording, summary, version; SEE CONCEPTS *55,57,268*

paraphrase [*v*] *interpret, translate*
express in other words, express in own words, recapitulate, rehash, render, rephrase, restate, reword, summarize, transcribe; SEE CONCEPTS *55,57*

parasite [*n*] *something that exists by taking from or depending on another*
barnacle, bloodsucker*, bootlicker*, deadbeat*, dependent, flunky, freeloader*, groupie*, hanger-on*, idler, leech, scrounger, sponge*, stooge*, sucker*, sycophant, taker*; SEE CONCEPTS *394,412*

parcel [*n1*] *container prepared to be sent*
bindle, bundle, carton, load, pack, package, packet; SEE CONCEPT *494*

parcel [*n2*] *group, bunch*
array, band, batch, body, clot, clump, cluster, clutch, collection, company, crew, crowd, gang, lot, pack; SEE CONCEPT *432*

parcel [*n3*] *piece of land*
acreage, plat, plot, property, tract; SEE CONCEPTS *509,513*

parcel [*n4*] *part, piece*
bite, chunk, cut, division, lion's share*, member, moiety, piece of the action*, portion, rake-off*, section, segment, slice; SEE CONCEPTS *829,835*

parch [*v*] *dry, burn*
blister, brown, dehydrate, desiccate, dry up, evaporate, exsiccate, make thirsty, scorch, sear, shrivel, stale, wither; SEE CONCEPTS *249,255*

parched [*adj*] *dry*
arid, burned, cotton-mouth*, dehydrated, dried out, dried up*, dry as dust*, scorched, shriveled, thirsty, waterless, withered; SEE CONCEPT *603*

pardon [*n*] *forgiveness*
absolution, acquittal, allowance, amnesty, anchor, clemency, commute, conciliation, condonation, discharge, exculpation, excuse, exoneration, forbearance, freeing, grace, indemnification, indemnity, indulgence, justification, kindness, lifeboat*, lifesaver*, mercy, release, remission, reprieve, vindication; SEE CONCEPTS *10,318,685*

pardon [*v*] *forgive*
absolve, accept, acquit, amnesty, blink at*, bury the hatchet*, clear, condone, discharge, exculpate, excuse, exonerate, free, give absolution, grant amnesty, justify, let off*, let off easy*, liberate, lifeboat*, overlook, release, remit, reprieve, rescue, spring*, suspend charges, tolerate, wink at*, wipe slate clean*, write off*; SEE CONCEPTS *10,50,88,317*

pare [*v*] *peel, trim*
carve, clip, crop, cut, cut back, cut down, decorticate, decrease, dock, flay, knock off, lop, lower, mark down, prune, reduce, scalp, scrape, shave, shear, skin, skive, slash, strip, thin, uncover; SEE CONCEPTS *176,202,236,247*

parent [*n*] *person, source of product*
ancestor, architect, author, begetter, cause, center, creator, father, folks, forerunner, fountainhead, guardian, mother, origin, originator, procreator, progenitor, prototype, root, source, wellspring; SEE CONCEPTS *414,648*

parental [*adj*] *having the quality or nature of a parent*
affectionate, benevolent, benign, caring, comforting, devoted, fatherly, fond, forbearing, gentle, indulgent, kind, loving, maternal, matriarchal, motherly, paternal, patriarchal, protective, sheltering, supportive, tender, warm, watchful; SEE CONCEPTS *401,542*

parenthetical [*adj*] *incidental*
bracketed, by the way, episodic, explanatory, extraneous, extrinsic, incidental, in parenthesis, inserted, intermediate, interposed, qualifying, related, subordinate; SEE CONCEPTS *544,577*

pariah [*n*] *social outcast*
bum*, castaway, deportee, derelict, displaced person, exile, expatriate, fugitive, hobo*, leper, outsider, persona non grata*, rascal, refugee, tramp, undesirable, vagabond, vagrant, waif; SEE CONCEPT *423*

parish [*n*] *congregation of a church*
archdiocese, bethel, church, churchgoers, community, flock*, fold*, parishioners, territory; SEE CONCEPT *369*

parity [*n*] *equality, balance*
adequation, affinity, agreement, analogy, approximation, closeness, coequality, conformity, congruity, consistency, correspondence, equal terms, equivalence, equivalency, likeness, nearness, par, parallelism, paraphernalia, resemblance, sameness, similarity, similitude, uniformity, unity; SEE CONCEPTS *667,670*

pa
pa

park [*n*] *land that is reserved for pleasure, recreation*
esplanade, estate, forest, garden, grass, green, grounds, lawn, lot, meadow, parkland, place, playground, plaza, pleasure garden, recreation area, square, tract, village green, woodland; SEE CONCEPTS 509,513

park [*v*] *place vehicle in a position*
deposit, leave, line up, maneuver, order, position, put, seat, stand, station, store; SEE CONCEPTS 148,201

parlance [*n*] *idiom*
argot, colloquialism, dialect, diction, expression, idiosyncrasy, jargon, language, lingo*, localism, locution, patois, phrase, provincialism, set phrase, speech, street talk*, talk, tongue, vernacular; SEE CONCEPT 275

parlay [*v*] *bet; maneuver*
engineer, gamble, jockey, lay down, manage, move, plan, play, risk, speculate, venture, wager; SEE CONCEPTS 36,59,292,330

parlor [*n*] *sitting room*
drawing room, front room, guest room, living room, lounge, reception, salon, waiting room; SEE CONCEPT 448

parochial [*adj*] *narrow-minded, restricted*
biased, bigoted, conservative, conventional, insular, inward-looking, limited, local, narrow, petty, prejudiced, provincial, regional, sectarian, sectional, shallow, small-minded, small-town; SEE CONCEPT 542

parody [*n*] *imitation, spoof*
apology, burlesque, caricature, cartoon,, copy, derision, farce, irony, jest, joke, lampoon, mime, mimicry, misrepresentation, mockery, mockheroic*, pastiche, play-on*, raillery, rib*, ridicule, roast*, satire, send-up*, skit, takeoff*, travesty; SEE CONCEPTS 59,273,292

parody [*v*] *imitate, spoof*
ape, burlesque, caricature, copy, deride, disparage, distort, do a takeoff of*, exaggerate, impersonate, jeer, jest, joke, lampoon, laugh at, mime, mimic, mock, poke fun at, put on*, ridicule, roast, satirize, send up, sheik*, take off*, travesty; SEE CONCEPTS 59,111,273

paroxysm [*n*] *seizure, spasm*
agitation, anger, attack, convulsion, eruption, excitement, explosion, fit, flare-up*, frenzy, frothing, fuming, furor, fury, hysterics, outbreak, outburst, passion, rage, violence; SEE CONCEPTS 308,316,410

parrot [*v*] *repeat*
ape, chant, copy, copycat, echo, imitate, mime, mimic, quote, recite, reiterate; SEE CONCEPTS 47,77,171

parry [*v*] *ward off, circumvent*
anticipate, avoid, block, bypass, deflect, dodge, duck*, elude, evade, fence*, fend off, forestall, hold at bay*, preclude, prevent, rebuff, rebuke, repel, repulse, resist, shirk, shun, sidestep, stave off; SEE CONCEPTS 25,30,121

parsimonious [*adj*] *penny-pinching*
avaricious, chintzy*, close, frugal, greedy, illiberal, mean, miserly, penurious, prudent, saving, scrimpy, selfish, skinflint*, sparing, stingy*, tight*, tightfisted*, tightwad*; SEE CONCEPTS 334,401

parson [*n*] *cleric*
chaplain, churchman/woman, clergyman/woman,

ecclesiastic, minister, padre, pastor, preacher, priest, rector, reverend, vicar; SEE CONCEPT 361

part [*n1*] *piece, portion of something*
allotment, any, apportionment, articulation, atom, bit, bite, branch, chip, chunk, component, constituent, cut, department, detail, division, element, extra, factor, fraction, fragment, helping, hunk, ingredient, installment, item, limb, lot, lump, measure, meed, member, module, moiety, molecule, organ, parcel, particle, partition, piece, quantum, quota, ration, scrap, section, sector, segment, share, side, slab, slice, sliver, splinter, subdivision, unit; SEE CONCEPT 834

part [*n2*] *person or group's interest, concern*
behalf, bit, business, capacity, cause, charge, duty, faction, function, involvement, office, party, place, responsibility, role, say, share, side, task, work; SEE CONCEPTS 362,532

part [*n3*] *theatrical role*
antagonist, bit, bit part, cameo, character, dialogue, hero, lead, leading role, lines, minor role, piece, principal character, protagonist, romantic lead, silent bit, stock character, straight part, supporting role, title role, villain, walk-on; SEE CONCEPT 263

part [*v1*] *break, disconnect*
articulate, break up, cleave, come apart, detach, dichotomize, disjoin, dismantle, dissever, disunite, divide, factor, itemize, particularize, partition, portion, rend, section, segment, separate, sever, slice, split, strip, subdivide, sunder, tear; SEE CONCEPTS 98,135

part [*v2*] *leave, go away from someone*
break, break off, break up, clear out*, cut and run*, dedomicile, depart, ease out, go, go separate ways*, hit the road*, leave flat*, part company, pull out*, push off, quit, quit the scene*, say goodbye, separate, ship out*, shove off*, split, split up*, take a hike*, take leave, take off, walk out on, withdraw; SEE CONCEPTS 195,297,384

partake [*v*] *eat, share*
be a party to, be in on, be into, consume, devour, divide, engage, enter into, feed, get in the act, have a finger in, ingest, participate, receive, sample, savor, sip, sit in, sit in on, take, take part, tune in; SEE CONCEPTS 169,225

partial [*adj1*] *incomplete*
fractional, fragmentary, half done, halfway, imperfect, limited, part, sectional, uncompleted, unfinished, unperformed; SEE CONCEPT 531

partial [*adj2*] *biased, prejudiced*
colored, discriminatory, disposed, favorably inclined, influenced, interested, jaundiced, minded, one-sided, partisan, predisposed, prepossessed, tendentious, unfair, unindifferent, unjust, warped; SEE CONCEPTS 403,542

partiality [*n*] *favoritism, fondness*
affinity, bias, cup of tea*, dish, druthers*, flash, inclination, inclining, leaning, liking, love, partisanship, penchant, predilection, predisposition, preference, prejudice, proclivity, propensity, taste, tendency, thing*, type, weakness; SEE CONCEPTS 32,709

partially [*adv*] *incompletely*
by degrees, by installments, fractionally, halfway, in part, in some measure, little by little, moderately, not wholly, partly, piece by piece, piecemeal, somewhat, to a certain degree, to a certain extent; SEE CONCEPTS 531,544

participant [*n*] *person who takes part in activity*
actor, aide, a party to, assistant, associate, attendant, colleague, contributor, helper, in, member, partaker, participator, partner, party, player, shareholder, sharer; SEE CONCEPTS 352,366,423

participate [*v*] *take part in activity*
aid, associate with, be a participant, be a party to, be into*, chip in*, come in, compete, concur, cooperate, engage, engage in, enter into, get in on*, get in on the act*, go into, have a hand in*, have to do with, join in, latch on*, lend a hand, partake, perform, play, share, sit in*, sit in on*, strive, take an interest in, tune in*; SEE CONCEPT 100

particle [*n*] *atom, piece*
bit, crumb, dot, dribble, drop, fleck, fragment, grain, hoot*, iota, jot, minim, mite, modicum, molecule, morsel, mote, ounce, ray, scrap, scruple, seed, shred, smidgen, smithereen, speck, spot, stitch, whit; SEE CONCEPT 831

particular [*adj1*] *exact, specific*
accurate, appropriate, blow-by-blow*, circumstantial, clocklike, detailed, distinct, especial, express, full, individual, intrinsic, itemized, limited, local, meticulous, minute, painstaking, particularized, peculiar, precise, scrupulous, selective, singular, special, thorough, topical; SEE CONCEPT 557

particular [*adj2*] *notable, uncommon*
especial, exceptional, exclusive, lone, marked, noteworthy, odd, one, only, peculiar, personal, remarkable, respective, separate, single, singular, sole, solitary, unique, unusual; SEE CONCEPT 564

particular [*adj3*] *finicky, demanding*
careful, choicy, choosy, critical, dainty, discriminating, exacting, fastidious, finical, fussbudget*, fussy, hard to please, meticulous, nice, nit-picking*, persnickety*, picky*, rough, stickler*, tough; SEE CONCEPTS 404,542

particular [*n*] *detail*
ABC's*, article, bottom line*, brass tacks*, case, chapter and verse*, circumstance, clue, cue, element, fact, facts of life, feature, gospel, item, know*, lowdown*, nitty-gritty*, nuts and bolts*, picture, point, rundown*, scoop*, score*, speciality, specific, specification, story, thing*, what's what*, whole story*; SEE CONCEPTS 274,532,832

particularly [*adv*] *specifically*
decidedly, distinctly, especially, exceptionally, explicitly, expressly, individually, in particular, markedly, notably, outstandingly, peculiarly, principally, singularly, specially, surprisingly, uncommonly, unusually; SEE CONCEPT 557

parting [*adj*] *farewell*
departing, final, goodbye, last, valedictory; SEE CONCEPT 267

parting [*n*] *goodbye, separation*
adieu, bisection, break, breaking, breakup, crossroads*, departure, detachment, divergence, division, farewell, going, leave-taking, on the rocks*, partition, rift, rupture, severance, split, split-up, valediction; SEE CONCEPTS 195,297,384

partisan [*adj*] *interested, factional*
accessory, adhering, biased, bigoted, blind, cliquish, colored, conspiratorial, denominational, devoted, diehard*, exclusive, fanatic, jaundiced, one-sided, overzealous, partial, prejudiced, prepossessed, sectarian, sympathetic, tendentious,

unjust, unreasoning, warped, zealous; SEE CONCEPTS 401,542,548

partisan [*n*] *person devoted to another or cause*
accessory, adherent, backer, champion, cohort, defender, devotee, disciple, follower, satellite, stalwart, supporter, sycophant, sympathizer, upholder, votary, zealot; SEE CONCEPTS 359,423

partition [*n*] *divider, division*
allotment, apportionment, barrier, detachment, disconnection, dissolution, distribution, disunion, dividing, hindrance, obstruction, parting, portion, rationing, rupture, screen, segregation, separation, severance, share, splitting, wall; SEE CONCEPTS 98,440,443,470

partition [*v*] *divide, separate*
apportion, cut, cut in, cut into, cut up, deal, disburse, dispense, disperse, distribute, divvy up*, dole out*, fence off*, measure out, parcel out, portion, screen, section, segment, separate, share, size into, slice, split, split up, subdivide, wall off*; SEE CONCEPTS 98,135

partly [*adv*] *not completely*
at best, at least, at most, at worst, bit by bit, by degrees, carelessly, halfway, inadequately, in a general way, in bits and pieces*, incompletely, in part, in some measure, in some ways, insufficiently, little by little, measurably, notably, not entirely, not fully, noticeably, not strictly speaking, not wholly, partially, piece by piece, piecemeal, relatively, slightly, so far as possible, somewhat, to a certain degree, to a certain extent, up to a certain point, within limits*; SEE CONCEPT 531

partner [*n*] *person who takes part with another*
accomplice, ally, assistant, associate, buddy, chum*, cohort, collaborator, colleague, companion, comrade, confederate, consort, coworker, crony*, date, friend, helper, husband, mate, pal*, participant, playmate, sidekick*, spouse, teammate, wife; SEE CONCEPTS 348,414,423

partnership [*n*] *alliance; participation*
affiliation, assistance, association, band, body, brotherhood, business, cahoots*, cartel, chumminess, clique, club, combination, combine, community, companionship, company, conglomerate, conjunction, connection, consociation, cooperation, cooperative, corporation, coterie, crew, faction, firm, fraternity, friendship, gang, help, hookup, house, interest, joining, lodge, mob, organization, ownership, party, ring, sharing, sisterhood, society, sorority, tie-up, togetherness, union; SEE CONCEPTS 325,381,388

party [*n1*] *social gathering*
affair, amusement, at-home*, ball, banquet, barbecue, bash*, blowout*, carousal, carousing*, celebration, cocktails, coffee klatch, coming-out, dinner, diversion*, do*, entertainment, feast, festive occasion, festivity, fete, fun, function, gala, get-together, luncheon, movable feast*, orgy*, prom, reception, riot, shindig*, social, soiree, splurge*, spree*, tea; SEE CONCEPT 383

party [*n2*] *gang, group*
assembly, band, bevy, body, bunch, cluster, company, corps, covey, crew, crowd, detachment, force, gathering, mob, multitude, outfit, squad, team, troop, troupe, unit; SEE CONCEPTS 417,432

party [*n3*] *group supporting certain beliefs*
alliance, association, bloc, body, cabal, clique,

pa
pa

coalition, combination, combine, confederacy, coterie, electorate, faction, grouping, junta, league, ring, sect, set, side, union; SEE CONCEPTS *301,381*

party [n4] *individual*
being, body, character, creature, human, man, mortal, part, person, personage, somebody, someone, woman; SEE CONCEPT *417*

party [n5] *person(s) involved in legal action*
actor, agent, cojuror, compurgator, confederate, contractor, defendant, litigant, partaker, participant, participator, plaintiff, plotter, sharer; SEE CONCEPT *355*

pass [n1] *opening through solid*
canyon, cut, gap, gorge, passage, passageway, path, ravine; SEE CONCEPTS *509,513*

pass [n2] *authorization, permission*
admission, chit*, comp, free ride*, furlough, identification, license, order, paper, passport, permit, safe-conduct*, ticket, visa, warrant; SEE CONCEPTS *271,685*

pass [n3] *sexual proposition*
advance, approach, overture, play, suggestion; SEE CONCEPTS *375,384*

pass [n4] *predicament*
condition, contingency, crisis, crossroads*, emergency, exigency, juncture, pinch, plight, situation, stage, state, strait, turning point*, zero hour*; SEE CONCEPT *674*

pass [v1] *go by, elapse; move onward*
befall, blow past, catch, come off, come to pass, come up, crawl, cross, cruise, depart, develop, drag, fall out, fare, flow, fly, fly by, get ahead, give, glide, glide by, go, go past, happen, hie, journey, lapse, leave, linger, move, occur, pass away, pass by, proceed, progress, push on, reach, repair, rise, roll, run, run by, run out, slip away, take place, transpire, travel, wend; SEE CONCEPTS *2,149,242*

pass [v2] *surpass, beat*
exceed, excel, go beyond, go by, leave behind, outdistance, outdo, outgo, outrace, outshine, outstrip, shoot ahead of, surmount, top, transcend; SEE CONCEPT *141*

pass [v3] *succeed, graduate*
answer, do, get through, matriculate, pass muster, qualify, suffice, suit; SEE CONCEPT *706*

pass [v4] *give, transfer*
buck, convey, deliver, exchange, hand, hand over, kick, let have, reach, relinquish, send, shoot, throw, transmit; SEE CONCEPTS *108,217*

pass [v5] *cease*
blow over*, cash in*, close, decease, demise, depart, die, disappear, discontinue, dissolve, drop, dwindle, ebb, end, evaporate, expire, fade, go, melt away, pass away, perish, peter out*, stop, succumb, terminate, vanish, wane; SEE CONCEPTS *105,119*

pass [v6] *enact, legislate*
accept, adopt, approve, authorize, become law, become ratified, become valid, be established, be ordained, be sanctioned, carry, decree, engage, establish, ordain, pledge, promise, ratify, sanction, undertake, validate, vote in; SEE CONCEPTS *298,317*

pass [v7] *express formally*
claim, declare, deliver, pronounce, state, utter; SEE CONCEPTS *49,60*

pass [v8] *decide not to do*
decline, discount, disregard, fail, forget, ignore,

miss, neglect, not heed, omit, overlook, pass on, pass up, refuse, skip, slight; SEE CONCEPTS *25,30*

pass [v9] *rid of waste*
defecate, discharge, eliminate, emit, empty, evacuate, excrete, expel, exude, give off, send forth, void; SEE CONCEPT *179*

passable [adj1] *acceptable, admissible*
adequate, allowable, all right, average, common, fair, fair enough, mediocre, middling, moderate, not too bad*, ordinary, presentable, respectable, so-so*, tolerable, unexceptional; SEE CONCEPT *558*

passable [adj2] *clear and able to be traveled*
accessible, attainable, beaten, broad, crossable, easy, fair, graded, motorable, navigable, open, penetrable, reachable, travelable, traveled, traversable, unblocked, unobstructed; SEE CONCEPTS *559,576*

passage/passageway [n1] *path for travel*
access, alley, alleyway, avenue, channel, corridor, course, doorway, entrance, entrance hall, exit, gap, hall, hallway, lane, line, lobby, opening, pathway, road, route, shaft, subway, thoroughfare, tunnel, vestibule, way; SEE CONCEPTS *440,501*

passage [n2] *excerpt from document*
clause, extract, paragraph, piece, portion, quotation, reading, section, sentence, text, transition, verse; SEE CONCEPT *270*

passage [n3] *travel*
advance, change, conversion, crossing, flow, journey, motion, movement, passing, progress, progression, tour, traject, transfer, transference, transit, transition, transmission, transmittal, transmittance, traverse, traversing, trek, trip, voyage; SEE CONCEPTS *145,217,224,704*

passage [n4] *authorization; enactment*
acceptance, allowance, establishment, freedom, legalization, legislation, passing, passport, permission, ratification, right, safe-conduct, visa, warrant; SEE CONCEPTS *318,685*

passageway [n] *corridor*
aisle, alley, couloir, entrance hall, entranceway, hall, hallway, ingress, lobby, passage, path, walkway; SEE CONCEPT *440*

pass away [v] *die*
decease, demise, depart, drop, expire, pass on, perish, succumb; SEE CONCEPT *304*

pass by [v] *neglect, forget*
abandon, disregard, fail, ignore, leave, miss, not choose, omit, overlook, overpass, pass over; SEE CONCEPTS *25,30*

passé [adj] *old-fashioned*
antiquated, belated, dated, dead, démodé, disused, extinct, has-been*, obsolete, outdated, outmoded, out-of-date, outworn, superseded, unfashionable, yesterday; SEE CONCEPTS *578,589,797*

passenger [n] *person who rides in vehicle conducted by another*
commuter, customer, excursionist, fare*, hitchhiker, patron, pilgrim, rider, tourist, traveler, voyager, wanderer, wayfarer; SEE CONCEPT *423*

passing [adj] *brief, casual*
cursory, ephemeral, evanescent, fleeting, fugacious, fugitive, glancing, hasty, impermanent, momentary, quick, shallow, short, short-lived, slight, superficial, temporary, transient, transitory; SEE CONCEPTS *551,798*

passing [n] *death*
decease, defunction, demise, dissolution, end, finish, loss, silence, sleep, termination; SEE CONCEPT *304*

passion [n1] *strong emotion*
affection, affectivity, agony, anger, animation, ardor, dedication, devotion, distress, dolor, eagerness, ecstasy, excitement, feeling, fervor, fire, fit, flare-up, frenzy, fury, heat, hurrah, indignation, intensity, ire, joy, misery, outbreak, outburst, paroxysm, rage, rapture, resentment, sentiment, spirit, storm, suffering, temper, transport, vehemence, warmth, wrath, zeal, zest; SEE CONCEPT *410*

passion [n2] *adoration, love*
affection, amorousness, amour, appetite, ardor, attachment, concupiscence, craving, crush*, desire, emoting, eroticism, excitement, fondness, infatuation, keenness, lust, prurience, urge, weakness, yen; SEE CONCEPTS *32,372*

passion [n3] *strong interest*
craving, craze, drive, enthusiasm, fad*, fancy, fascination, idol, infatuation, jazz*, mania, obsession; SEE CONCEPTS *349,532,690*

passionate [adj1] *sensual, desirous*
amorous, ardent, aroused, concupiscent, desirous, erotic, heavy*, hot*, lascivious, libidinous, loving, lustful, prurient, romantic, sexy, steamy*, stimulated, sultry, turned-on*, wanton, wistful; SEE CONCEPT *372*

passionate [adj2] *excited; enthusiastic*
affecting, animated, ardent, blazing, burning, deep, dramatic, eager, eloquent, emotional, expressive, fervent, fervid, fierce, fiery, flaming, forceful, frenzied, glowing, headlong, heartfelt, heated, high-powered, high-pressure, hot*, hot-blooded*, impassioned, impetuous, impulsive, inspiring, intense, melodramatic, moving, poignant, precipitate, quickened, spirited, steamed up*, stimulated, stirring, strong, thrilling, vehement, violent, warm, wild, zealous; SEE CONCEPTS *401,542*

passionate [adj3] *angry*
all shook up*, choleric, enraged, fiery, frantic, furious, hotheaded*, hottempered*, inflamed, irascible, irritable, mean, peppery, quick-tempered, shaken, steamed-up*, stormy, tempestuous, testy, touchy*, vehement, violent; SEE CONCEPTS *401,542*

passive [adj] *lifeless, inactive*
acquiescent, apathetic, asleep, bearing, compliant, cool, docile, enduring, flat, forbearing, going through motions*, hands off*, idle, indifferent, inert, laid-back*, latent, long-suffering, moony, motionless, nonresistant, nonviolent, patient, phlegmatic, poker-faced*, quiescent, quiet, receptive, resigned, sleepy, static, stolid, submissive, tractable, unassertive, unflappable, uninvolved, unresisting, walking through it*, yielding; SEE CONCEPTS *542,584*

pass off [v] *give because one does not want it*
eject, send foist, make a pretense of*, palm, palm off*, send forth, work off; SEE CONCEPT *108*

pass out [v] *become unconscious, usually from abusing a substance*
black out*, drop, faint, keel over*, lose consciousness, swoon; SEE CONCEPT *308*

pass over [v] *ignore, disregard*
dismiss, fail, forget, miss, neglect, not dwell on, omit, overlook, overpass, pass, pass by, skip, take no notice of*; SEE CONCEPTS *25,30*

passport [n] *identification of origin, country*
authorization, credentials, key, license, pass, permit, safe-conduct*, ticket, travel permit, visa, warrant; SEE CONCEPTS *271,685*

password [n] *secret word given for entry*
countersign, identification, key, key word, open sesame*, parole, phrase, signal, ticket, watchword, word; SEE CONCEPT *278*

past [adj] *preceding, done*
accomplished, ago, antecedent, anterior, completed, elapsed, ended, extinct, finished, foregoing, forgotten, former, gone, gone by, over, over and done, precedent, previous, prior, spent; SEE CONCEPTS *531,585*

past [adj2] *olden, former*
ages ago*, ancient, ancient history*, back when*, behind one*, bygone, bypast, down memory lane*, earlier, early, erstwhile, ex-*, foregoing, gone-by*, good old days*, late, latter, latter-day, long-ago, old, olden days*, once, one-time, over, preceding, previous, prior, quondam, recent, retired, sometime, time was*, way back*, way back when*; SEE CONCEPT *820*

past [nl] *time gone by*
antiquity, days gone by*, former times, good old days*, history, long ago, olden days*, old lang syne, old times*, time immemorial*, times past*, years ago*, yesterday, yesteryear, yore; SEE CONCEPTS *807,811,816,818*

paste [n/v] *glue, adhesive*
cement, fasten, fix, gum, mucilage, patch, plaster, spit, stick, stickum*; SEE CONCEPTS *85,160,466*

pastel [adj] *muted in color*
delicate, light, pale, soft-hued, toned; SEE CONCEPT *618*

pastiche [n] *work of art formed from disparate sources*
assortment, collage, collection, compilation, copy, hodgepodge, imitation, mishmosh*, paste-up, patchwork, potpourri, reappropriation, reproduction, synthesis; SEE CONCEPT *260*

pastime [n] *leisure activity*
amusement, distraction, diversion, entertainment, fun, fun and games*, game, hobby, play, recreation, relaxation, sport; SEE CONCEPT *363*

pastor [n] *person who conducts church services*
cleric, divine, ecclesiastic, minister, parson, preacher, priest, rector, reverend, shepherd, vicar; SEE CONCEPT *361*

pastoral [adj] *peaceful, especially referring to the countryside*
agrarian, agrestic, Arcadian, bucolic, countrified, country, idyllic, outland, provincial, rural, rustic, simple, sylvan; SEE CONCEPT *583*

pastry [n] *baked product made with flour*
bread, cake, croissant, dainty, Danish, delicacy, doughnut, éclair, panettone, patisserie, phyllo, pie, strudel, sweet roll, tart, turnover; SEE CONCEPTS *457,461*

pasty [adj1] *sticky*
adhesive, doughy, gelatinous, gluelike, gluey, glutinous, gooey, mucilaginous, starchy; SEE CONCEPT *606*

pasty [adj2] *pale*
anemic, ashen, bloodless, dull, pallid, sallow, sickly, unhealthy, wan, waxen; SEE CONCEPT *618*

pat [*adj*] *relevant, suitable*
apposite, apropos, apt, auspicious, felicitous, fitting, happy, neat, opportune, pertinent, propitious, rehearsed, timely, to the point; SEE CONCEPT 558

pat [*adv*] *exactly, fittingly*
aptly, faultlessly, flawlessly, just right, opportunely, perfectly, plumb, precisely, relevantly, seasonably; SEE CONCEPTS 535,557

pat [*n1/v*] *tap, touch*
beat, caress, dab, fondle, form, hit, massage, mold, pet, punch, rub, slap, stroke, tip, whittle; SEE CONCEPTS 184,189,612

pat [*n2*] *small slice or slab*
cake, dab, lump, piece, portion; SEE CONCEPTS 458,835

patch [*n1*] *piece, spot, area*
bit, blob, chunk, fix, ground, hunk, land, lot, plat, plot, scrap, shred, stretch, strip, tract; SEE CONCEPTS 452,471,513

patch [*n2*] *piece applied to cover a gap or lack*
application, appliqué, Band-Aid*, mend, reinforcement; SEE CONCEPTS 452,831

patch [*v*] *fix, mend*
cobble, cover, darn, do up, fiddle with, overhaul, rebuild, recondition, reconstruct, reinforce, repair, retread, revamp, sew; SEE CONCEPTS 212,218

patch up [*v*] *settle differences*
adjust, appease, bury the hatchet*, compensate, conciliate, make friends*, mediate, negotiate, placate, restore, settle*, smooth; SEE CONCEPT 384

patchwork [*n*] *mixture, hodgepodge*
check, confusion, disorder, hash*, jumble, medley, miscellany, mishmash, muddle, olio, pastiche, plaid, salad*, salmagundi, stew*, tartan; SEE CONCEPTS 260,432,475

patchy [*adj*] *spotty, not consistent*
erratic, fitful, irregular, random, sketchy, uneven, variable, varying; SEE CONCEPT 482

patent [*adj*] *unconcealed, conspicuous*
apparent, barefaced*, blatant, clear, clear-cut, controlled, crystal clear*, distinct, downright, evident, exclusive, flagrant, glaring, gross*, indisputable, limited, manifest, obvious, open, open and shut*, palpable, plain, prominent, rank, straightforward, transparent, unequivocal, unmistakable; SEE CONCEPT 576

patent [*n*] *copyright on an invention*
charter, concession, control, franchise, license, limitation, privilege, protection; SEE CONCEPTS 271,318,685

path [*n*] *course, way*
aisle, artery, avenue, beat, beaten path, boulevard, byway, crosscut, direction, drag, footpath, groove, highway, lane, line, pass, passage, pathway, procedure, rail, road, roadway, route, rut, shortcut, street, stroll, terrace, thoroughfare, track, trail, walk, walkway; SEE CONCEPTS 6,501

pathetic [*adj*] *sad, affecting*
commiserable, deplorable, distressing, feeble, heartbreaking, heartrending*, inadequate, lamentable, meager, melting, miserable, moving, paltry, petty, piteous, pitiable, pitiful, plaintive, poignant, poor, puny, rueful, sorry*, tender, touching, useless, woeful, worthless, wretched; SEE CONCEPTS 485,529

pathos [*n*] *deep sadness*
desolation, emotion, feeling, passion, pitiableness, pitifulness, plaintiveness, poignance, poignancy, sentiment; SEE CONCEPT 410

patience [*n*] *capacity, willingness to endure*
backbone*, bearing, calmness, composure, constancy, cool*, diligence, endurance, equanimity, even temper, forbearance, fortitude, grit*, guts*, gutsiness, heart, humility, imperturbability, intestinal fortitude*, legs*, leniency, longanimity, long-suffering, moderation, moxie*, nonresistance, passiveness, passivity, perseverance, persistence, poise, resignation, restraint, self-control, serenity, starch*, staying power*, stoicism, submission, sufferance, tolerance, toleration, yielding; SEE CONCEPTS 411,657

patient [*adj*] *capable, willing to endure*
accommodating, calm, composed, easy-going, enduring, even-tempered, forbearing, forgiving, gentle, imperturbable, indulgent, lenient, long-suffering, meek, mild, mild-tempered, persevering, persistent, philosophic, philosophical, quiet, resigned, self-possessed, serene, stoical, submissive, tolerant, tranquil, uncomplaining, understanding, unruffled, untiring; SEE CONCEPTS 404,542

patient [*n*] *person being treated for medical problem*
case, convalescent, emergency, inmate, invalid, outpatient, shut-in, sick person, subject, sufferer, victim; SEE CONCEPT 357

patio [*n*] *porch*
balcony, courtyard, deck, veranda; SEE CONCEPTS 509,513

patrician [*adj*] *upper-class*
aristocratic, blue-blooded*, gentle, grand, highborn, high-class, noble, royal, well-born; SEE CONCEPTS 334,549

patrician [*n*] *person born to upper-class*
aristocrat, blue blood*, gentleperson, noble, nobleperson, peer, silk stocking*, upper cruster*; SEE CONCEPT 423

patriot [*n*] *person who loves his or her country*
flag-waver*, good citizen, jingoist*, loyalist, nationalist, partisan, patrioteer, statesperson, ultranationalist, volunteer; SEE CONCEPT 413

patriotism [*n*] *love of one's country*
allegiance, chauvinism, flag-waving, loyalty, nationalism, public spirit; SEE CONCEPT 689

patrol [*n*] *guarding; guard*
convoying, defending, escorting, garrison, lookout, patroler, policing, protecting, protection, rounds, safeguarding, scouting, sentinel, spy, vigilance, watch, watching, watchperson; SEE CONCEPTS 134,354,358

patrol [*v*] *guard, protect*
cruise, inspect, keep guard, keep watch, make the rounds*, mount, police, pound, range, ride shotgun, safeguard, shotgun, walk the beat*, watch; SEE CONCEPTS 134,623

patron [*n1*] *person who supports a cause*
advocate, angel*, backer, benefactor, booster, champion, defender, encourager, fairy godparent*, fan, financer, friend, front*, guarantor, guardian, guide, head, helper, leader, partisan, patron saint*, philanthropist, protector, sponsor, supporter, surety, sympathizer, well-wisher; SEE CONCEPTS 348,359,423

patron [*n2*] *person who does business at establishment*
buyer, client, customer, frequenter, habitué, purchaser, shopper; SEE CONCEPT 348

patronage [*n1*] *support of a cause*
advocacy, aegis, aid, assistance, auspices, backing, benefaction, championship, encouragement, financing, grant, guardianship, help, promotion, protection, recommendation, sponsorship, subsidy, support; SEE CONCEPTS *110,332,341*

patronage [*n2*] *business done at an establishment*
buying, clientage, clientele, commerce, custom, shopping, trade, trading, traffic; SEE CONCEPTS *323,324*

patronage [*n3*] *condescension*
civility, cronyism, deference, deigning, disdain, insolence, patronization, patronizing, stooping, sufferance, toleration; SEE CONCEPTS *83,300*

patronize [*v1*] *condescend*
be gracious to, be lofty, be overbearing, deign, favor, indulge, look down on*, pat on the back*, snub, stoop, talk down to*, toss a few crumbs*, treat as inferior, treat badly, treat like a child*; SEE CONCEPT *384*

patronize [*v2*] *support a cause*
assist, back, befriend, foster, fund, help, maintain, promote, sponsor, subscribe to; SEE CONCEPTS *110,341*

patronize [*v3*] *do business at an establishment*
be a client, be a customer, buy, buy from, deal with, frequent, give business to, habituate, purchase from, shop at, shop with, trade with; SEE CONCEPTS *324,327*

patsy [*n*] *fall guy*
boob*, chump, doormat*, dupe, easy mark*, fool, goat*, gull*, pigeon*, pushover*, sap*, scapegoat, schmuck*, sitting duck*, stooge, sucker, victim, weakling; SEE CONCEPT *412*

patter [*n1/v1*] *light walk; soft beat*
chatter, pad, pat, pelt, pitapat*, pitter-patter*, rat-a-tat*, rattle, scurry, scuttle, skip, tap, tiptoe, trip; SEE CONCEPTS *65,149*

patter [*n2*] *casual talk*
argot, cant, chatter, dialect, jabber*, jargon, jive*, line*, lingo, monologue, patois, pitch*, prattle*, slant*, spiel*, vernacular; SEE CONCEPTS *276,278*

patter [*v2*] *gab, chatter*
babble, blab*, clack*, hold forth*, jabber, jaw*, prate, prattle, rattle, spiel*, spout, tattle, yak*, yakety-yak*; SEE CONCEPT *266*

pattern [*n1*] *design, motif*
arrangement, decoration, device, diagram, figure, guide, impression, instruction, markings, mold, motive, original, ornament, patterning, plan, stencil, template, trim; SEE CONCEPTS *259,625*

pattern [*n2*] *arrangement, order*
constellation, kind, method, orderliness, plan, sequence, shape, sort, style, system, type, variety; SEE CONCEPTS *6,727,770*

pattern [*n3*] *model, example*
archetype, beau ideal*, copy, criterion, cynosure, ensample, exemplar, guide, mirror, norm, original, paradigm, paragon, prototype, sample, specimen, standard; SEE CONCEPT *686*

pattern [*v*] *copy, imitate; decorate*
design, emulate, follow, form, model, mold, order, shape, style, trim; SEE CONCEPTS *111,171*

paucity [*n*] *lack, scarcity*
absence, dearth, deficiency, famine, fewness, insufficiency, insufficiency, meagerness, paltriness, poverty, rarity, scantiness, scarceness,

shortage, slenderness, slightness, smallness, sparseness, sparsity; SEE CONCEPTS *335,646,767*

paunch [*n*] *large stomach*
abdomen, belly, bulge, epigastrium, fat, gut, potbelly*, spare tire*, tummy*; SEE CONCEPT *399*

pauper [*n*] *person who is poor*
almsperson, bankrupt, beggar, bum, dependent, destitute, down-and-out*, have-not*, homeless person, indigent, insolvent, in the gutter*, lazarus*, mendicant, poor person, supplicant; SEE CONCEPT *423*

pause [*n*] *wait, delay*
abeyance, break, break-off*, breathing space*, breathing spell*, caesura, cessation, coffee break*, comma*, cutoff, deadlock, discontinuance, downtime*, freeze*, gap, gridlock*, halt, happy hour*, hesitancy, hesitation, hiatus, hitch*, hush*, interim, interlude, intermission, interregnum, interruption, interval, lacuna, lapse, layoff, letup*, lull, pausation, recess, respite, rest, rest period, stand, standstill, stay, stillness, stopover, stoppage, suspension, time out*; SEE CONCEPT *807*

pause [*v*] *wait, delay*
break it up*, call time*, catch one's breath*, cease, come to standstill*, deliberate, desist, discontinue, drop, halt, hesitate, hold back, interrupt, put on hold, reflect, rest, shake, sideline, stop briefly, suspend, take a break*, take a breather*, take five*, take ten*, think twice*, waver; SEE CONCEPTS *119,121,234*

pave [*v*] *cover with asphalt, concrete*
brick, cobblestone, flagstone, gravel, lay asphalt, lay concrete, macadamize, surface, tar, tile; SEE CONCEPTS *168,172*

pavement [*n*] *blacktop*
asphalt, concrete, flagstone, road, sidewalk, tar; SEE CONCEPT *604*

pavilion [*n*] *domed building or tent*
awning, canopy, cover, covering, dome, structure; SEE CONCEPT *439*

paw [*v*] *touch roughly*
clap, claw, clutch, dig, feel, finger, fondle, grab, grate, grope, handle, hit, maul, molest, palpate, pat, rake, rasp, rub, scratch, search, slap, smite, stroke; SEE CONCEPTS *375,612*

pawn [*n1*] *security for a loan*
assurance, bond, collateral, earnest, forfeit, gage, gambit, guarantee, guaranty, pledge, security, token, warrant; SEE CONCEPT *332*

pawn [*n2*] *person who is a fool*
creature, dupe*, instrument, mark*, patsy*, pigeon*, puppet, stooge*, sucker*, tool, toy, victim; SEE CONCEPT *412*

pawn [*v*] *give as security for a loan*
deposit, give in earnest, hazard, hock*, hook*, mortgage, pledge; SEE CONCEPTS *115,330*

pay [*n*] *earnings from employment*
allowance, bacon*, bread*, commission, compensation, consideration, defrayment, emoluments, fee, hire*, honorarium, income, indemnity, meed, payment, perquisite, pittance, proceeds, profit, reckoning, recompensation, recompense, redress, reimbursement, remuneration, reparation, requital, return, reward, salary, satisfaction, scale, settlement, stipend, stipendium, take-home*, takings*, wage, wages; SEE CONCEPTS *329,332,340,344*

pay [*v1*] *give money for goods, services*
adjust, bear the cost, bear the expense, bequeath,

bestow, chip in*, clear, come through, compensate, confer, cough up*, defray, dig up*, disburse, discharge, extend, foot*, foot the bill*, grant, handle, hand over*, honor, kick in*, liquidate, make payment, meet, offer, plunk down*, prepay, present, proffer, put up*, recompense, recoup, refund, reimburse, remit, remunerate, render, repay, requite, reward, satisfy, settle, stake, take care of*; SEE CONCEPTS *327,341,351*

pay [v2] *be advantageous*

benefit, be worthwhile, repay, serve; SEE CONCEPT *700*

pay [v3] *make amends*

answer, atone, be punished, compensate, get just desserts*, suffer, suffer consequences; SEE CONCEPT *23*

pay [v4] *profit, yield*

be profitable, be remunerative, bring in, kick back*, make a return, make money, pay dividends, pay off*, pay out*, produce, provide a living, return, show gain, show profit, sweeten*, yield profit; SEE CONCEPT *330*

pay [v5] *get revenge*

avenge oneself, get even, make up for, pay back*, pay one's dues*, punish, reciprocate, recompense, repay, requite, retaliate, settle a score*, square, square things*; SEE CONCEPT *122*

payable [adj] *to be paid*

due, mature, maturing, obligatory, outstanding, overdue, owed, owing, receivable, unpaid, unsettled; SEE CONCEPT *334*

payback [n] *return*

accrual, accruement, compensation, gain, gate, income, interest, proceeds, profit, reciprocation, recompense, reimbursement, reparation, repayment, reward, take, yield; SEE CONCEPTS *340,710*

pay dirt [n] *profit*

accumulation, benefit, bottom line*, cleanup, earnings, gate*, goods*, gravy*, harvest, killing*, net, payoff, proceeds, revenue, score*, split*, surplus, take*, winnings; SEE CONCEPTS *332,344,693*

payment [n] *fee; installment of fee*

acquittal, advance, alimony, amends, amortization, amount, annuity, award, bounty, cash, defrayal, defrayment, deposit, disbursement, discharge, down, fee, hire, indemnification, outlay, part, paying, pay-off, pension, portion, premium, quittance, reckoning, recompense, redress, refund, reimbursement, remittance, remuneration, reparation, repayment, requital, restitution, retaliation, return, reward, salary, settlement, subsidy, sum, support, wage; SEE CONCEPT *344*

payoff [n] *conclusion, climax*

adjustment, clincher*, consequence, culmination, day of reckoning*, finale, final reckoning*, judgment, moment of truth*, outcome, pay, payment, punch line*, result, retribution, reward, settlement, upshot*; SEE CONCEPTS *230,679*

peace [n1] *harmony, agreement*

accord, amity, armistice, cessation, conciliation, concord, friendship, love, neutrality, order, pacification, pacifism, reconciliation, treaty, truce, unanimity, union, unity; SEE CONCEPTS *388,691*

peace [n2] *calm, serenity*

amity, calmness, composure, concord, congeniality, contentment, equanimity, harmony, hush, lull, peacefulness, placidity, quiet, quietude, relaxation, repose, reserve, rest, silence, stillness, sympathy, tranquility; SEE CONCEPTS *410,705, 720*

peaceable [adj] *friendly, serene*

amiable, amicable, calm, complacent, conciliatory, gentle, irenic, mild, neighborly, nonviolent, pacific, pacificatory, pacifist, peaceful, peace-loving, placid, quiet, restful, still, tranquil; SEE CONCEPT *548*

peaceful [adj] *friendly, serene*

all quiet, amicable, at peace, bloodless, calm, collected, composed, constant, easeful, equable, free from strife*, gentle, halcyon, harmonious, irenic, level, mellow, neutral, neutralist, nonbelligerent, nonviolent, on friendly terms*, on good terms*, pacifistic, peaceable, peace-loving, placatory, placid, quiet, restful, smooth, sociable, steady, still, tranquil, undisturbed, unruffled, untroubled, without hostility; SEE CONCEPTS *485,542*

peacemaker [n] *person who settles problem*

appeaser, arbitrator, conciliator, diplomat, makepeace, mediator, negotiator, pacificator, pacifier, pacifist, peacekeeper, peacemonger*, placater, statesperson; SEE CONCEPTS *354,416*

peak [n1] *top of something*

aiguille, alp, apex, brow, bump, cope, crest, crown, hill, mount, mountain, pinnacle, point, roof, spike, summit, tip, vertex; SEE CONCEPTS *509,836*

peak [n2] *maximum, zenith*

acme, apex, apogee, capstone, climax, crown, culmination, greatest, height, high point, meridian, ne plus ultra, pinnacle, summit, tip, top; SEE CONCEPTS *668,766,767,832*

peak [v] *reach highest point*

be at height, climax, come to a head*, crest, culminate, reach the top, reach the zenith, top out*; SEE CONCEPTS *763,780*

peaked [adj] *pale, sick*

ailing, bilious, emaciated, ill, in bad shape*, peaky, poorly, sickly, under the weather*, wan; SEE CONCEPTS *314,618*

peal [n] *chime, clang*

blast, carillon, clamor, clap, crash, resounding, reverberation, ring, ringing, roar, rumble, sound, thunder, tintinnabulation*; SEE CONCEPT *595*

peal [v] *chime, clang*

bell, bong, crack, crash, knell, resonate, resound, reverberate, ring, ring out, roar, roll, rumble, sound, strike, thunder, tintinnabulate*, toll; SEE CONCEPT *65*

pearly [adj] *opalescent*

fair, frosted, iridescent, ivory, milky, nacreous, off-white, opaline, pearl, silver; SEE CONCEPT *618*

peasant [n] *farmer*

boor, bumpkin, countryman/woman, cropper, farmhand, hayseed*, hick*, hired hand, laborer, peon, planter, provincial, rube, rustic, serf, sharecropper, villein; SEE CONCEPTS *347,348,423*

peccadillo [n] *small fault*

bad habit, faux pas, impropriety, indiscretion, minor fault, minor infraction, minor sin, misdemeanor, petty offense, slight transgression, small infraction, small sin, venial sin, vice; SEE CONCEPTS *372,645*

peck [n/v] *bite*

beak, dig, hit, jab, kiss, mark, nibble, pick, pinch, poke, prick, rap, strike, tap; SEE CONCEPTS *169,189*

pecking order [*n*] *hierarchy*
chain of command*, corporate ladder, due order, echelons, grouping, order, placing, position, ranking, scale; SEE CONCEPT 727

peculiar [*adj*] *characteristic, distinguishing*
appropriate, diacritic, diagnostic, distinct, distinctive, endemic, exclusive, idiosyncratic, individual, intrinsic, local, particular, personal, private, proper, restricted, special, specific, typical, unique; SEE CONCEPTS 404,557

peculiar [*adj2*] *bizarre, odd*
abnormal, bent*, creepy*, curious, eccentric, exceptional, extraordinary, flaky*, freakish, freaky, funny, idiosyncratic, kinky*, kooky*, oddball, offbeat, off-the-wall*, outlandish, quaint, queer, singular, strange, uncommon, unconventional, uncustomary, unusual, wacky*, way-out*, weird, wonderful; SEE CONCEPTS 404,564

peculiarity [*n*] *characteristic; oddity*
abnormality, affectation, attribute, bizarreness, character, distinctiveness, eccentricity, feature, foible, freakishness, gimmick, idiosyncrasy, kink*, mannerism, mark, odd trait, particularity, property, quality, queerness, quirk, savor, schtick*, singularity, slant*, specialty, trait, twist*, unusualness; SEE CONCEPTS 411,665

pecuniary [*adj*] *financial*
banking, budgeting, business, economic, fiscal, monetary; SEE CONCEPT 334

pedagogic [*adj*] *educational*
academic, dogmatic, instructive, learned, professorial, profound, scholastic, teaching; SEE CONCEPTS 529,536

pedantic [*adj*] *bookish, precise*
abstruse, academic, arid, didactic, doctrinaire, donnish, dry, dull, egotistic, erudite, formal, fussy, hairsplitting*, learned, nit-picking, ostentatious, overnice, particular, pedagogic, pompous, priggish*, punctilious, scholastic, schoolish, sententious, stilted; SEE CONCEPTS 401,529

peddle [*v*] *sell door to door*
canvas*, hawk*, huckster*, market, monger*, push, shove, solicit, trade, vend; SEE CONCEPT 345

peddler [*n*] *hawker*
huckster, salesperson, street vendor, vendor; SEE CONCEPT 348

pedestrian [*adj*] *everyday, dull*
banal, banausic, blah*, boring, commonplace, dim, dreary, flat, humdrum*, inane, jejune, mediocre, monotone, monotonous, mundane, ordinary, platitudinous, plodding, prosaic, run-of-the-mill*, stodgy, truistic, unimaginative, uninspired, uninteresting, wishy-washy*; SEE CONCEPTS 530,547

pedestrian [*n*] *person traveling on foot*
ambler, hiker, jaywalker*, passerby, stroller, walker; SEE CONCEPT 366

pedigree [*adj*] *purebred*
full-blooded, pedigreed, pure-blood, thoroughbred; SEE CONCEPT 549

pedigree [*n*] *ancestry, heritage*
blood, breed, clan, derivation, descent, extraction, family, family tree, genealogy, heredity, line, lineage, origin, race, stirps, stock; SEE CONCEPT 296

peek/peep [*n*] *sneaked look*
blink, gander*, glance, glimpse, look-see, sight; SEE CONCEPT 623

peek/peep [*v*] *sneak a look*
blink, glance, glimpse, have a gander*, look, peer, snatch, snoop, spy, squint, stare, take a look; SEE CONCEPT 623

peel [*n*] *skin, covering*
bark, cover, epicarp, exocarp, husk, peeling, pellicle, rind, shell, shuck; SEE CONCEPTS 428,484

peel [*v*] *take off outer covering*
decorticate, delaminate, desquamate, excorticate, exfoliate, flake, flay, pare, pull off, scale, shave, skin, strip, tear off, uncover; SEE CONCEPTS 142,176,211

peep [*n1/v1*] *chirp*
chatter, cheep, chirrup, chuck, churr, coo, cry, hoot, pipe, squeak, tweet, twitter; SEE CONCEPT 64

peep/peer [*v2*] *appear briefly*
become visible, crop up, emerge, open to view, peep out, peer out, show partially; SEE CONCEPT 261

peer [*n*] *person who is another's equal*
associate, coequal, companion, compeer, like, match, rival; SEE CONCEPT 423

peer [*v1*] *scan, scrutinize*
bore, eagle eye*, eye*, eyeball*, focus, gape, gawk, gaze, get a load of, glare, glim, gloat, inspect, look, peep, pin*, pry, rubberneck*, snoop, spy, squint, stare; SEE CONCEPTS 103,623

peerless [*adj*] *having no equal; superior*
aces*, all-time, alone, best, beyond compare, champion, excellent, faultless, gilt-edge*, greatest, incomparable, matchless, most, nonpareil*, only, outstanding, perfect, second to none*, solid-gold*, super, superlative, supreme, tops*, unequaled, unexampled, unique, unmatched, unparagoned, unparalleled, unrivaled, unsurpassed, world class*; SEE CONCEPT 574

peeve [*n*] *something strongly disliked*
annoyance, bother, gripe, nuisance, pest, sore point*, vexation; SEE CONCEPTS 532,690

peeve [*v*] *bother, annoy*
aggravate, anger, bug*, bum*, burn*, disturb, drive up the wall*, exasperate, gall, get, get one's goat*, hack*, irk, irritate, miff*, nettle, pique, provoke, put out, rile, roil, rub the wrong way*, steam*, T-off*, vex; SEE CONCEPTS 7,19

peevish [*adj*] *irritable, testy*
acrimonious, angry, bad-tempered, cantankerous, captious, carping, caviling, childish, churlish, complaining, crabbed*, cranky, critical, cross, crotchety*, crusty*, cussed, fault-finding, fractious, fretful, fretting, grouchy, grousing, growling, grumpy, huffy, ill-natured, mean, morose, obstinate, ogre, ornery, out-of-sorts*, pertinacious, petulant, querulous, short-tempered, snappy, splenetic, sulky, sullen, surly, tetchy, touchy, ugly, waspish, waspy, whining; SEE CONCEPTS 401,542

peg [*v*] *attach*
clinch, fasten, fix, join, make fast, pin, secure, tighten; SEE CONCEPTS 85,160

pejorative [*adj*] *negative, belittling*
debasing, deprecatory, depreciatory, derisive, derogatory, detracting, detractive, detractory, disadvantageous, disparaging, irreverent, rude, slighting, uncomplimentary, unpleasant; SEE CONCEPT 267

pell-mell [*adj*] *disordered*
chaotic, confused, disarrayed, disorganized, hap-

pa
pe

hazard, muddled, tumultous/tumultuous; SEE
CONCEPTS 562,585

pell-mell [adv] *hurriedly and carelessly*
foolishly, full tilt*, hastily, headlong, heedlessly,
helter-skelter, impetuously, incontinently, indiscreetly, posthaste, precipitiously, rashly, recklessly, thoughtlessly; SEE CONCEPTS 544,799

pell-mell [n] *disorder*
anarchy, ataxia, chaos, clutter, confusion, disarray, ferment, helter-skelter, huddle, muddle, pandemonium, snarl, tumult, turmoil, upheaval; SEE
CONCEPT 674

pelt [n] *animal fur*
coat, epidermis, fell, hair, hide, jacket, skin,
slough, wool; SEE CONCEPT 399

pelt [v] *beat; throw hard*
assail, batter, belabor, belt, bombard, career,
cast, charge, dash, hammer, hurl, knock, lapidate, pepper, pound, pour, pummel, rain, rush,
shoot, shower, sling, speed, stone, strike, swat,
tear, thrash, wallop; SEE CONCEPTS 189,222

pen [n1] *enclosure*
cage, coop, corral, fence, fold, hedge, hutch, jail,
penitentiary, prison, sty, wall*; SEE CONCEPTS
439,443

pen [n2] *writing instrument*
ball point, felt-tip, fountain pen, marker, nib,
quill, reed, stick, stylograph; SEE CONCEPTS
277,499

pen [v1] *enclose*
box, cage, case, close in, confine, coop, corral,
fence in, hedge, hem in, mew*, shut in; SEE CON-
CEPTS 191,758

pen [v2] *write*
autograph, commit to paper, compose, draft,
draw up, engross, indict, jot down; SEE CONCEPT
79

penal [adj] *disciplinary*
chastening, corrective, penalizing, punishing,
punitive, punitory, reformatory, retributive; SEE
CONCEPTS 548,583

penalize [v] *punish*
amerce, castigate, chasten, chastise, condemn,
correct, discipline, dock*, fine, handicap, hit
with*, impose penalty, inflict handicap, judge,
mulct, put at disadvantage, scold, slap with*,
throw the book at*; SEE CONCEPT 122

penalty [n] *punishment*
amends, amercement, cost, damages, disadvantage, discipline, dues, fall, fine, forfeit, forfeiture,
handicap, mortification, mulct, price, rap*, retribution; SEE CONCEPTS 344,679

penance [n] *reparation for wrong*
absolution, atonement, attrition, compensation,
compunction, confession, contrition, expiation,
forgiveness, hair shirt*, mortification, penalty,
penitence, punishment, purgation, remorse, remorsefulness, repentance, retribution, rue, ruth,
sackcloth and ashes*, self-flagellation*, shrift,
sorrow, suffering; SEE CONCEPTS
126,367,384,410

penchant [n] *fondness, inclination*
affection, affinity, attachment, bias, disposition,
druthers*, inclining, itch*, leaning, liking, partiality, predilection, predisposition, proclivity,
proneness, propensity, taste, tendency, tilt*,
turn*, weakness, yen; SEE CONCEPTS
20,32,411,709

pending [adj] *about to happen*
awaiting, continuing, dependent, forthcoming,

hanging, imminent, impending, indeterminate, in
line*, in the balance*, in the offing*, in the
works*, ominous, on board*, on line*, pensile,
undecided, undetermined, unsettled, up in the
air*; SEE CONCEPT 548

pendulous/pendent [adj] *hanging*
dangling, dependent, drooping, pending, pendu-
lant, pensile, suspended, swinging; SEE CON-
CEPTS 485,584

penetrate [v1] *pierce; get through physically*
access, barge in, bayonet, blow in, bore, break in,
breeze in, bust in, charge, come, crack, diffuse,
drill, drive, eat through, encroach, enter, filter in,
force, get in, gore, go through, impale, infiltrate,
ingress, insert, insinuate, introduce, invade, jab,
knife, make a hole, make an entrance, pass
through, percolate, perforate, permeate, pervade,
pop in, prick, probe, puncture, ream, run into,
saturate, seep, sink into, spear, stab, stick into,
suffuse, thrust, trespass; SEE CONCEPTS
159,179,220

penetrate [v2] *understand or be understood*
affect, become clear, come across*, comprehend,
decipher, discern, fathom, figure out, get across*,
get over*, get through*, get to the bottom*,
grasp, impress, perceive, put over*, see
through*, sink in*, soak in*, touch, unravel,
work out; SEE CONCEPT 15

penetrating [adj] *stinging, harsh*
biting, carrying, clear-cut, crisp, cutting, edged,
entering, forcing, going through, infiltrating, ingoing, intrusive, passing through, penetrant, permeating, pervasive, piercing, pointed,
puncturing, pungent, sharp, shrill, strong, trenchant; SEE CONCEPTS 267,537

penetrating [adj2] *intelligent*
acute, astute, critical, discerning, discriminating,
incisive, keen, penetrative, perceptive, perspicacious, profound, quick, quick-witted, sagacious,
searching, sharp, sharp-witted, shrewd; SEE CON-
CEPT 402

penitence [n] *shame, sorrow*
anguish, attrition, compunction, contriteness,
contrition, debasement, degradation, distress,
grief, humbling, humiliation, penance, qualm, regret, remorse, remorsefulness, repentance, rue,
ruefulness, ruth, sadness, scruple, self-castiga-
tion, self-condemnation, self-flagellation, self-
punishment, self-reproach; SEE CONCEPT 410

penitent [adj] *shamed, sorrowful*
abject, apologetic, atoning, attritional, compunctious, conscience-stricken, contrite, penitential,
regretful, remorseful, repentant, rueful, sorry;
SEE CONCEPTS 403,542

penitentiary [n] *jail*
big house*, campus, can*, college, cooler*, correctional institution, inside*, joint*, lockup*,
pen*, penal institution, prison, reformatory,
slammer*, stockade; SEE CONCEPTS 439,449,516

pen name [n] *pseudonym*
AKA*, alias, anonym, assumed name, nickname,
nom de guerre, nom de plume, professional
name, pseudonym; SEE CONCEPTS 268,683

pennant [n] *flag, banner*
banderole, bunting, burgee, color, decoration,
emblem, ensign, jack, pennon, screamer, standard, streamer; SEE CONCEPTS 260,473

penniless [adj] *without any money*
bankrupt, broke*, clean*, cleaned out*, dead
broke*, destitute, dirt poor*, down to last

penny*, flat*, flat broke*, impecunious, impoverished, indigent, in the gutter*, lacking, moneyless, necessitous, needy, on last leg*, over a barrel*, penurious, poor, poverty-stricken, ruined, strapped*, tapped out*, without a dime*; SEE CONCEPT *334*

pension [*n*] *benefits paid after retirement*
allowance, annuity, gift, grant, IRA*, payment, premium, retirement account, reward, social security, subsidy, subvention, superannuation, support; SEE CONCEPTS *332,344*

pensive [*adj*] *meditative, solemn*
absorbed, abstracted, attentive, cogitative, contemplative, dreamy, grave, musing, pondering, preoccupied, reflecting, reflective, ruminating, ruminative, serious, sober, speculative, thinking, thoughtful, wistful, withdrawn; SEE CONCEPT *403*

pent-up [*adj*] *held within*
bottled-up, bridled, checked, constrained, curbed, held-back, held in check, inhibited, repressed, restrained, restricted, smothered, stifled, suppressed; SEE CONCEPTS *401,403*

penurious [*adj*] *stingy*
avaricious, cheap, chintzy*, close-fisted, costive, curmudgeonly, economical, frugal, greedy, hoarding, miserly, parsimonious, penny-pinching, pennywise*, pinchpenny*, saving, scrimping, sparing, thrifty, tightfisted, uncharitable, ungenerous, ungiving; SEE CONCEPTS *326,334,401*

peon [*n*] *menial worker*
drudge, farmhand, farm worker, gopher, laborer, peasant, serf, servant, slave, unskilled laborer; SEE CONCEPT *348*

people [*n*] *human beings*
bodies, body politic*, bourgeois, cats*, citizens, clan, commonality, common people, community, crowd, family, folk, folks, general public, heads*, herd, hoi polloi*, horde, humanity, humankind, human race, humans, inhabitants, John/Jane Q. Public*, kin, masses, mob, mortals, multitude, nation, nationality, person in the street*, persons, plebeians, populace, population, proletariat, public, rabble, race, rank and file*, riffraff*, society, tribe; SEE CONCEPTS *296,379,380,417*

pep [*n*] *vim, vigor*
animation, bang, birr, energy, get-up-and-go*, go, gusto, hardihood, high spirits, life, liveliness, moxie*, potency, punch*, push, snap*, spirit, starch*, tuck*, verve, vitality, vivacity, zip*; SEE CONCEPTS *411,633*

peppery [*adj1*] *highly seasoned*
fiery, hot, piquant, poignant, pungent, racy, snappy, spicy, zestful, zesty; SEE CONCEPT *613*

peppery [*adj2*] *irritable; sarcastic*
acute, angry, astringent, biting, caustic, choleric, cranky, cross, fiery, hot-tempered, incisive, irascible, keen, lively, passionate, quick-tempered, sharp, sharp-tempered, snappish, spirited, spunky, stinging, testy, touchy, trenchant, waspish; SEE CONCEPTS *267,401,542*

peppy [*adj*] *lively, vigorous*
active, alert, animate, animated, bright, gay, keen, perky, sparkling, spirited, sprightly, vivacious; SEE CONCEPTS *401,404*

pep up [*v*] *invigorate, inspire*
animate, enliven, exhilarate, jazz up*, quicken, stimulate, vitalize, vivify; SEE CONCEPTS *7,22*

perceive [*v1*] *notice, see*
apperceive, apprehend, be aware of, behold, descry, discern, discover, distinguish, divine, espy, feel, grasp, identify, look, make out, mark, mind, note, observe, realize, recognize, regard, remark, seize, sense, spot, spy, take; SEE CONCEPTS *38,626*

perceive [*v2*] *understand*
appreciate, apprehend, comprehend, conclude, copy, deduce, distinguish, feature, feel, flash*, gather, get, get the message*, get the picture*, grasp, know, learn, pin*, read, realize, recognize, see, sense, track; SEE CONCEPT *15*

percentage [*n*] *portion, allotment*
allowance, bite, bonus, chunk, commission, corner*, cut, discount, division, duty, fee, holdout, interest, juice*, payoff, percent, piece, piece of the action*, points*, proportion, quota, rate, ratio, section, slice*, split*, taste*, winnings; SEE CONCEPTS *766,784,835*

perceptible [*adj*] *noticeable, obvious*
apparent, appreciable, audible, clear, cognizable, conspicuous, detectable, discernible, distinct, distinguishable, evident, lucid, observable, palpable, perceivable, perspicuous, recognizable, sensible, signal, tangible, understandable, visible; SEE CONCEPTS *529,576*

perception [*n*] *understanding, idea*
acumen, apprehending, apprehension, approach, attention, attitude, awareness, big idea*, brainchild*, brain wave*, conceit, concept, conception, consciousness, discernment, feeling, flash*, grasp, image, impression, insight, intellection, judgment, knowledge, light, notion, observation, opinion, perspicacity, picture, plan, realizing, recognition, sagacity, sensation, sense, study, taste, thought, viewpoint; SEE CONCEPTS *409,410,689*

perceptive [*adj*] *alert, sensitive*
acute, astute, awake, aware, brainy*, conscious, discerning, discreet, ear to the ground*, gnostic, incisive, insighted, insightful, intuitive, judicious, keen, knowing, knowledgeable, knows what's what*, observant, penetrating, penetrative, percipient, perspicacious, quick, rational, responsive, sagacious, sage, savvy*, sharp, sophic, tuned in*, wise, wise to*; SEE CONCEPTS *402,542*

perch [*n*] *object placed high for sitting on*
branch, landing place, lounge, pole, post, resting place, roost, seat; SEE CONCEPTS *443,479*

perch [*v*] *sit atop of*
alight, balance, land, light, rest, roost, set down, settle, sit on, squat, touch down; SEE CONCEPT *154*

percolate [*v*] *seep, drip (liquid)*
bleed, bubble, charge, drain, exude, filter, filtrate, impregnate, leach, ooze, pass through, penetrate, perk, permeate, pervade, saturate, strain, sweat, transfuse, transude, weep; SEE CONCEPTS *179,181*

perdition [*n*] *hell*
Abaddon*, abyss, affliction, bottomless pit*, condemnation, damnation, everlasting fire*, fire and brimstone*, Gehenna*, Hades, infernal regions, inferno, loss of the soul, lower world, nether world, pit, place of torment, punishment, purgatory, ruin, suffering, underworld; SEE CONCEPTS *370,435,674*

pe
pe

peremptory [*adj*] *overbearing, authoritative*
absolute, arbitrary, assertive, autocratic, binding, bossy, categorical, certain, commanding, compelling, decided, decisive, dictatorial, dogmatic, domineering, final, finished, firm, fixed, high-handed, imperative, imperial, imperious, incontrovertible, intolerant, irrefutable, magisterial, obligatory, obstinate, positive, rigorous, severe, stringent, tyrannical, uncompromising, undeniable; SEE CONCEPTS 535,537,542

perennial [*adj*] *enduring, perpetual*
abiding, annual, ceaseless, chronic, constant, continual, continuing, deathless, durable, eternal, everlasting, immortal, imperishable, incessant, inveterate, lasting, lifelong, long-lasting, long-lived, longstanding, never-ending, old, perdurable, permanent, persistent, recurrent, seasonal, sustained, unceasing, unchanging, undying, unfailing, uninterrupted, yearlong, yearly; SEE CONCEPTS 539,798

perfect [*adj1*] *flawless, superlative*
absolute, accomplished, aces*, adept, A-OK*, beyond compare, blameless, classical, consummate, crowning, culminating, defectless, excellent, excelling, experienced, expert, faultless, finished, foolproof, ideal, immaculate, impeccable, indefectible, matchless, out-of-this-world*, paradisiac, paradisiacal, peerless, pure, skilled, skillful, sound, splendid, spotless, stainless, sublime, superb, supreme, ten*, unblemished, unequaled, unmarred, untainted, untarnished, utopian; SEE CONCEPT 574

perfect [*adj2*] *whole, intact*
absolute, choate, complete, completed, consummate, downright, entire, finished, flawless, full, gross, integral, out-and-out*, outright, positive, rank, sheer, simple, sound, unadulterated, unalloyed, unblemished, unbroken, undamaged, unimpaired, unmitigated, unmixed, unqualified, utter; SEE CONCEPTS 482,485

perfect [*adj3*] *accurate, correct*
appropriate, bull's-eye*, certain, close, dead-on*, definite, distinct, exact, express, faithful, fit, ideal, model, needed, on target*, on the button*, on the money*, precise, proper, required, requisite, right, sharp, strict, suitable, textbook, to a T*, to a turn*, true, unerring, very; SEE CONCEPTS 535,557,558

perfect [*v*] *polish; achieve*
accomplish, ameliorate, carry out, complete, consummate, crown, cultivate, develop, effect, elaborate, finish, fulfill, hone, idealize, improve, perform, put finishing touch on, realize, refine, round, slick, smooth; SEE CONCEPTS 91,244,706

perfection [*n*] *achievement, completeness*
accomplishment, achieving, acme, arete, completion, consummation, crown, ending, entireness, evolution, exactness, excellence, excellency, exquisiteness, faultlessness, finish, finishing, fulfillment, ideal, idealism, impeccability, integrity, maturity, merit, paragon, perfectness, phoenix, precision, purity, quality, realization, ripeness, sublimity, superiority, supremacy, transcendence, virtue, wholeness; SEE CONCEPTS 671,706

perfectionist [*n*] *stickler*
formalist, fussbudget, fusspot, idealist, nitpicker, purist, quibbler; SEE CONCEPTS 359,416,423

perfectly [*adv1*] *absolutely*
altogether, completely, consummately, entirely, fully, quite, thoroughly, totally, utterly, well, wholly; SEE CONCEPTS 531,544

perfectly [*adv2*] *without flaw*
admirably, correctly, excellently, exquisitely, faultlessly, fitly, flawlessly, ideally, impeccably, superbly, superlatively, supremely, to perfection, wonderfully; SEE CONCEPT 574

perfidious [*adj*] *treacherous*
betraying, deceitful, deceptive, double-crossing*, double-dealing*, faithless, false, insidious, misleading, recreant, shifty*, slick*, snake in the grass*, traitorous, two-faced*, two-timing*, undependable, unfaithful, unloyal, unreliable, untrustworthy; SEE CONCEPTS 401,404

perforate [*v*] *make a hole in*
bore, drill, drive, hole, honeycomb*, penetrate, permeate, pierce, pit, poke full of holes*, probe, punch, puncture, shoot full of holes*, slit, stab; SEE CONCEPT 220

perform [*v1*] *carry out, accomplish*
achieve, act, be engaged in, behave, bring about, bring off, carry through, carry to completion, complete, comply, deliver the goods*, discharge, dispose of, do, do justice to*, do a turn*, effect, end, enforce, execute, finish, fulfill, function, go that route*, implement, meet, move, observe, operate, percolate, perk, pull off*, put through, react, realize, run with the ball*, satisfy, take, take care of business*, tick, transact, wind up, work; SEE CONCEPTS 91,199

perform [*v2*] *act, depict as entertainment*
act out, appear as, be on, bring down the house*, discourse, display, do a number*, do a turn*, dramatize, emote, enact, execute, exhibit, give, go on, ham*, ham it up*, impersonate, offer, personate, play, playact, present, produce, put on, render, represent, show, stage, tread the boards*; SEE CONCEPT 292

performance [*n1*] *accomplishment*
achievement, act, administration, attainment, carrying out, completion, conduct, consummation, discharge, doing, enforcement, execution, exploit, feat, fruition, fulfillment, pursuance, realization, work; SEE CONCEPT 706

performance [*n2*] *acting, depiction*
act, appearance, ballet, behavior, burlesque, business, ceremony, concert, custom, dance, display, drama, exhibition, gig*, interpretation, matinee, offering, opera, pageant, play, portrayal, presentation, production, recital, rehearsal, representation, review, revue, rigmarole, rite, set, show, special, spectacle, stage show, stunt, to-do*; SEE CONCEPT 263

performance [*n3*] *efficiency*
action, conduct, effectiveness, efficacy, exercise, functioning, operation, practice, pursuit, running, working; SEE CONCEPT 630

perfume [*n*] *scent, often manufactured and packaged for personal use*
aroma, attar, balm, balminess, bouquet, cologne, eau de cologne, essence, fragrance, incense, odor, oil, redolence, sachet, smell, spice, sweetness; SEE CONCEPTS 599,600

perfunctory [*adj*] *automatic, unthinking*
apathetic, careless, cool, cursory, disinterested, going through the motions*, heedless, impersonal, inattentive, indifferent, involuntary, lackadaisical, laid-back*, mechanical, negligent,

offhand, phoning it in*, routine, sketchy, slipshod*, slovenly, standard, stereotyped, stock, superficial, unaware, unconcerned, uninterested, usual, walking through it*, wooden*; SEE CONCEPTS 542,544

perhaps [adv] *possibly*
as it may be, as the case may be, conceivably, feasibly, for all one knows, imaginably, it may be, maybe, perchance, reasonably; SEE CONCEPT 552

peril [n] *danger, risk*
cause for alarm*, double trouble*, endangerment, exposure, hazard, insecurity, jeopardy, liability, menace, openness, pitfall, risky business*, uncertainty, vulnerability; SEE CONCEPT 675

perilous [adj] *dangerous*
chancy, delicate, dicey*, dynamite, exposed, hairy*, hazardous, insecure, loaded*, on thin ice*, playing with fire*, precarious, risky, rugged, Russian roulette*, shaky, threatening, ticklish, touch and go*, touchy, treacherous, uncertain, unhealthy, unsafe, unsound, unstable, unsteady, unsure, vulnerable, wicked*; SEE CONCEPTS 548,587

perimeter [n] *circumference, border*
ambit, borderline, boundary, bounds, brim, brink, circuit, compass, confines, edge, fringe, hem, limit, margin, outline, periphery, skirt, verge; SEE CONCEPTS 484,745,792

period [n1] *extent of time*
aeon, age, course, cycle, date, days, duration, epoch, era, generation, interval, measure, season, space, span, spell, stage, stretch, term, time, while, years; SEE CONCEPTS 807,822

period [n2] *ending*
cessation, close, closing, closure, conclusion, discontinuance, end, limit, stop, termination; SEE CONCEPT 832

periodic [adj] *at fixed intervals*
alternate, annual, at various times, centennial, cyclic, cyclical, daily, epochal, every once in a while, every so often, fluctuating, hourly, infrequent, intermittent, isochronal, isochronous, monthly, occasional, on-again-off-again*, on certain occasions, orbital, perennial, periodical, recurrent, recurring, regular, repeated, rhythmic, routine, seasonal, serial, spasmodic, sporadic, weekly, yearly; SEE CONCEPTS 541,799

periodical [n] *regular publication*
journal, mag*, magazine, monthly, newspaper, number, paper, quarterly, rag*, review, serial, sheet*, slick*, throwaway*, weekly; SEE CONCEPT 280

peripatetic [adj] *constantly traveling*
ambulant, itinerant, itinerate, migrant, mobile, nomadic, perambulant, roaming, roving, vagabond, vagrant, wandering, wayfaring; SEE CONCEPTS 401,584

peripheral [adj] *minor, outside*
beside the point, borderline, exterior, external, incidental, inessential, irrelevant, minor, outer, outermost, perimetric, secondary, superficial, surface, tangential, unimportant; SEE CONCEPTS 575,583,831

periphery [n] *outskirts, outer edge*
ambit, border, boundary, brim, brink, circuit, circumference, compass, covering, edge, fringe, hem, margin, outside, perimeter, rim, skirt, verge; SEE CONCEPTS 484,745

perish [v] *die, decline, decay*
be destroyed, be killed, be lost, bite the dust*, break down, buy the farm*, cease, check out*, collapse, corrupt, croak, crumble, decease, decompose, demise, depart, disappear, disintegrate, end, expire, fall, give up the ghost*, go, go under, kick the bucket*, lose life, OD*, pass, pass away, pass on, rot, succumb, vanish, waste*, wither; SEE CONCEPTS 13,105,304

perishable [adj] *liable to spoil, rot*
decaying, decomposable, destructible, easily spoiled, short-lived, unstable; SEE CONCEPTS 462,485

perjure [v] *give false testimony*
bear false witness*, commit perjury, deceive, delude, equivocate, falsify, forswear, lie, lie under oath, mislead, prevaricate, swear falsely, trick; SEE CONCEPTS 63,317

perjury [n] *lying while under oath*
deceitfulness, deception, dishonesty, falsehood, false oath, false swearing, false testimony, falsification, untruth, untruthfulness; SEE CONCEPTS 63,278

perk [n] *benefit*
advantage, bonus, dividend, extra, fringe benefit, gratuity, gravy*, lagniappe, largess, perquisite, plus, tip; SEE CONCEPT 344

perk up [v] *cheer*
ameliorate, be refreshed, brighten, buck up*, cheer up, convalesce, gain, improve, invigorate, liven up, look up, mend, pep up, rally, recover, recuperate, refresh, renew, revive, shake, take heart*; SEE CONCEPTS 7,22,244,308

perky [adj] *animated, happy*
active, alert, aware, bouncy, bright, bright-eyed and bushy-tailed*, brisk, bubbly, buoyant, cheerful, cheery, gay, in fine fettle*, jaunty, lively, spirited, sprightly, sunny, vivacious; SEE CONCEPTS 401,404

permanent [adj] *constant, lasting*
abiding, changeless, continual, diurnal, durable, enduring, everlasting, fixed, forever, forever and a day*, for keeps*, immutable, imperishable, indestructible, in for the long haul*, invariable, long-lasting, perdurable, perduring, perennial, perpetual, persistent, set, set in concrete*, set in stone*, stable, steadfast, unchanging, unfading; SEE CONCEPTS 551,649,798

permeable [adj] *absorbent, penetrable*
absorptive, accessible, enterable, passable, pervious, porose, porous, spongelike, spongy; SEE CONCEPTS 576,604,606

permeate [v] *filter, spread throughout*
charge, diffuse, drench, fill, go through, imbue, impregnate, infiltrate, infuse, ingrain, interfuse, invade, pass through, penetrate, percolate, pervade, pierce, saturate, seep, soak, stab, stalk, steep, suffuse, transfuse; SEE CONCEPTS 159,179,256

permissible [adj] *allowable, legal*
acceptable, admissible, all right, approved, authorized, bearable, endorsed, kosher*, lawful, legalized, legit*, legitimate, licit, okay*, on the up and up*, permitted, proper, sanctioned, tolerable, tolerated, unforbidden, unprohibited; SEE CONCEPTS 319,548,554

permission [n] *authorization, consent*
acceptance, acknowledgment, acquiescence, admission, agreement, allowance, approbation, approval, assent, avowal, canonization, carte

blanche*, concession, concurrence, condonance, condonation, dispensation, empowerment, endorsement, freedom, imprimatur, indulgence, leave, letting, liberty, license, okay, permit, privilege, promise, recognition, rubber stamp*, sanctification, sanction, stamp of approval*, sufferance, tolerance, toleration, verification, warrant; SEE CONCEPTS 50,83,88,376,685

permissive [*adj*] *lenient*
acquiescent, agreeable, allowing, approving, easy-going, forbearing, free, indulgent, latitudinarian, lax, liberal, open-minded, permitting, susceptible, tolerant; SEE CONCEPT 401

permit [*n*] *authorization*
admittance, allowance, charter, concession, consent, empowering, favor, franchise, go-ahead*, grant, green light*, indulgence, leave, legalization, liberty, license, pass, passport, patent, permission, privilege, safe-conduct, sanction, sufferance, toleration, visa, warrant; SEE CONCEPTS 271,376,685

permit [*v*] *allow participation*
abet, accede, accept, acquiesce, admit, agree, authorize, bless, blink at*, boost, buy, charter, concede, concur, condone, consent, empower, enable, endorse, endure, franchise, give leave, give permission, go for, grant, have, humor, indulge, leave, let, let pass, license, okay, pass, privilege, sanctify, sanction, say yes, shake on*, sign, sign off on*, suffer, take kindly to*, thumbs up*, tolerate, warrant, wink at*; SEE CONCEPTS 50,83,88

pernicious [*adj*] *bad, hurtful*
baleful, damaging, dangerous, deadly, deleterious, destructive, detrimental, devastating, evil, fatal, harmful, iniquitous, injurious, killing, lethal, maleficent, malevolent, malicious, malign, malignant, miasmatic, miasmic, mortal, nefarious, noisome, noxious, offensive, pestiferous, pestilent, pestilential, poisonous, prejudicial, ruinous, sinister, toxic, venomous, virulent, wicked; SEE CONCEPTS 537,548,571

perpendicular [*adj*] *at right angles to*
erect, horizontal, on end, plumb, sheer, standing, stand-up, steep, straight, straight-up, upright, vertical; SEE CONCEPTS 581,583

perpetrate [*v*] *be responsible for*
act, bring about, carry out, commit, do, effect, enact, execute, inflict, perform, pull, up and do*, wreak; SEE CONCEPT 91

perpetual [*adj*] *continual, lasting*
abiding, ceaseless, constant, continued, continuous, endless, enduring, eternal, everlasting, going on, immortal, imperishable, incessant, infinite, interminable, intermittent, never-ceasing, never-ending, perdurable, perennial, permanent, persistent, recurrent, recurring, reoccurring, repeated, repeating, repetitious, returning, sempiternal, unceasing, unchanging, undying, unending, unfailing, uninterrupted, unremitting, without end; SEE CONCEPTS 551,649,798,799

perpetuate [*v*] *keep going*
bolster, conserve, continue, eternalize, eternize, immortalize, keep, keep alive, keep in existence, keep up, maintain, preserve, secure, support, sustain; SEE CONCEPT 239

perplex [*v*] *confuse, mix up*
astonish, astound, baffle, balk, befuddle, beset, bewilder, buffalo*, complicate, confound, discombobulate*, discompose, dumbfound, encum-

ber, entangle, fog, get to*, involve, jumble, muck, muddle, muddy the waters*, mystify, nonplus, perturb, pose, puzzle, rattle, ravel, snarl up, stumble, stump, surprise, tangle, thicken, thwart; SEE CONCEPTS 16,84

perquisite [*n*] *fringe benefit*
advantage, bonus, dividend, extra, gratuity, gravy*, lagniappe, largess, perk*, plus, reward, tip; SEE CONCEPT 344

per se [*adv*] *essentially*
alone, as such, by and of itself, by definition, by itself, by its very nature, fundamentally, independently, in essence, in itself, intrinsically, of itself, singularly, solely, virtually; SEE CONCEPTS 544,577

persecute [*v*] *wrong, torment*
afflict, aggrieve, annoy, badger, bait, beat, be on one's case*, bother, crucify, distress, dog*, dragoon, drive up the wall*, exile, expel, harass, hector, hound*, hunt, ill-treat, injure, maltreat, martyr, molest, oppress, outrage, pester, pick on, plague, pursue, tease, torture, tyrannize, vex, victimize, worry; SEE CONCEPTS 7,19,44,246

perseverance [*n*] *diligence, hard work*
backbone*, constancy, continuance, cool, dedication, determination, doggedness, drive, endurance, grit*, guts*, immovability, indefatigability, moxie*, persistence, pertinacity, pluck*, prolonging, purposefulness, pursuance, resolution, sedulity, spunk, stamina, steadfastness, stick-to-itiveness*, tenacity; SEE CONCEPTS 411,633

persevere [*v*] *keep at; work hard*
be determined, be resolved, be stubborn, carry on, continue, endure, go for broke*, go for it*, go on, hang in*, hang tough*, hold fast*, hold on, keep driving*, keep going, keep on, leave no stone unturned*, maintain, persist, plug away*, press on, proceed, pursue, remain, see it through*, stand firm*, stay the course*, stick with it*; SEE CONCEPTS 87,239

persist [*v*] *carry on, carry through*
abide, be resolute, be stubborn, continue, endure, follow through*, follow up*, go all the way*, go on, go the limit*, grind, hold on, insist, keep up*, last, leave no stone unturned*, linger, obtain, perdure, persevere, prevail, pursue, recur, remain, repeat, see through, stick it out*, stick to guns*, strive, tough it out*; SEE CONCEPTS 23,87,91,239

persistent [*adj*] *determined; continuous*
assiduous, bound, bound and determined*, bulldogged*, constant, continual, dogged, endless, enduring, firm, fixed, immovable, incessant, indefatigable, in for long haul*, insistent, interminable, like bad penny*, never-ending, obdurate, obstinate, perpetual, perseverant, persevering, persisting, pertinacious, relentless, repeated, resolute, steadfast, steady, sticky*, stubborn, tenacious, tireless, unflagging, unrelenting, unremitting, unshakable; SEE CONCEPTS 326,401,404,538

persnickety [*adj*] *fussy, particular*
careful, choosy, fastidious, finicky, nice, picky; SEE CONCEPT 404

person [*n*] *human being*
being, body, character, creature, customer, gal, guy, human, identity, individual, individuality, joker*, life, living soul, man, mortal, party, per-

sonage, personality, self, somebody, soul, specimen, spirit, unit*, woman; SEE CONCEPT *417*

personable [*adj*] *friendly, sociable*
aces*, affable, agreeable, all heart*, all right*, amiable, attractive, charming, easygoing, good egg*, gregarious, likable, nice, okay, pleasant, pleasing, presentable, sweetheart*, white-hat*, winning; SEE CONCEPT *404*

personage/personality [*n1n2*] *celebrity, notable*
big shot*, bigwig*, brass*, celeb*, chief, cynosure, dignitary, distinguished person, eminence, face*, hot shot*, individual, luminary, monster*, name*, public figure, somebody, star, superstar, top dog*, VIP*, worthy; SEE CONCEPTS *352,354,423*

personal [*adj*] *private, individual*
claimed, exclusive, intimate, own, particular, peculiar, privy, retired, secluded, secret, special; SEE CONCEPT *536*

personal computer [*n*] *computer*
clone, desktop computer, home computer, IBM PC, laptop*, MAC, Macintosh, microcomputer, minicomputer, PC; SEE CONCEPTS *269,463*

personality [*n1*] *person's character, traits*
charisma, charm, complexion, disposition, dynamism, emotions, identity, individuality, likableness, magnetism, makeup, nature, psyche, self, selfdom, selfhood, singularity, temper, temperament; SEE CONCEPT *411*

personally [*adv*] *independently*
alone, by oneself, directly, for oneself, for one's part, individualistically, individually, in one's own view, in person, in the flesh, narrowly, on one's own, privately, solely, specially, subjectively; SEE CONCEPTS *544,577*

personify [*v*] *represent some other being, character*
act out, body forth, contain, copy, emblematize, embody, epitomize, exemplify, express, exteriorize, externalize, hominify, humanize, illustrate, image, imitate, impersonate, incarnate, live as, make human, manifest, materialize, mirror, objectify, personize, substantiate, symbolize, typify; SEE CONCEPTS *261,716*

personnel [*n*] *employees of business or other enterprise*
cadre, corps, crew, faculty, group, helpers, human resources, members, men and women, office, organization, people, shop, staff, troop, troops, workers, work force; SEE CONCEPTS *325,417*

perspective [*n*] *view, outlook*
angle, aspect, attitude, broad view, context, frame of reference*, headset*, landscape, mindset*, objectivity, overview, panorama, proportion, prospect, relation, relative importance, relativity, scene, size of it*, viewpoint, vista, way of looking; SEE CONCEPTS *410,629,689*

perspicacious [*adj*] *observant, perceptive*
acute, alert, astute, aware, clear-sighted, clever, discerning, heady*, judicious, keen, penetrating, percipient, sagacious, savvy*, sharp, sharp-witted, shrewd; SEE CONCEPT *402*

perspicuous [*adj*] *clear, obvious*
apparent, clear-cut, comprehensible, crystal*, crystal-clear*, distinct, easily understood, explicit, intelligible, limpid, lucent, lucid, luminous, pellucid, plain, self-evident, straightforward, transparent, unambiguous, unblurred, understandable; SEE CONCEPT *529*

perspire [*v*] *become wet with sweat*
be damp, be wet, break a sweat*, drip, exude, get in a lather*, glow, lather, pour, secrete, swelter; SEE CONCEPTS *185,469*

persuade [*v*] *cause to believe; convince to do*
actuate, advise, affect, allure, argue into, assure, blandish, brainwash*, bring around, bring to senses, cajole, coax, convert, counsel, draw, enlist, entice, exhort, gain confidence of, get, impel, impress, incite, incline, induce, influence, inveigle, lead, lead to believe, lead to do, move, prevail upon, prompt, propagandize, proselyte, proselytize, reason, satisfy, seduce, sell, stroke, sway, talk into, touch, turn on to, urge, wear down*, wheedle, win argument, win over, woo, work over; SEE CONCEPT *68*

persuasion [*n1*] *influencing to do, believe*
alignment, alluring, arm-twist*, blandishment, brainwashing*, cajolery, cogency, con*, conversion, enticement, exhortation, force, goose*, hard sell*, hook*, inducement, inveiglement, persuasiveness, potency, power, promote, pull*, seduction, sell*, snow job*, soft soap*, squeeze*, sweet talk*, wheedling, winning over, working over; SEE CONCEPTS *68,687*

persuasion [*n2*] *belief, religion*
bias, camp, certitude, church, communion, connection, conviction, credo, creed, cult, denomination, eye, faction, faith, feeling, mind*, opinion, partiality, party, predilection, prejudice, school, school of thought*; sect, sentiment, side, tenet, view; SEE CONCEPT *689*

persuasive [*adj*] *effective, influential*
actuating, alluring, cogent, compelling, conclusive, convictive, convincing, credible, effectual, efficacious, efficient, eloquent, energetic, enticing, forceful, forcible, impelling, impressive, inducing, inspiring, inveigling, logical, luring, moving, plausible, pointed, potent, powerful, seductive, slick, smooth, sound, stimulating, stringent, strong, swaying, telling, touching, unctuous, valid, weighty, wheedling, winning; SEE CONCEPTS *267,537,542*

pert [*adj*] *lively, bold*
animated, audacious, brash, brazen, breezy, bright, brisk, cheeky*, dapper, daring, dashing, disrespectful, flip*, flippant, forward, fresh, gay, impertinent, impudent, insolent, jaunty, keen, nervy, perky, presumptuous, sassy*, saucy*, smart, smart-alecky*, spirited, sprightly, vivacious, wise; SEE CONCEPTS *401,404*

pertain [*v*] *be relevant to*
affect, appertain, apply, associate, be appropriate, bear on, befit, belong, be part of, be pertinent, combine, concern, connect, inhere with, join, refer, regard, relate, touch, vest; SEE CONCEPT *532*

pertinent [*adj*] *relevant, suitable*
admissible, ad rem, applicable, apposite, appropriate, apropos, apt, connected, fit, fitting, germane, kosher*, legit*, material, on target*, on the button*, on the nose*, opportune, pat*, pertaining, proper, related, right on, to the point, to the purpose; SEE CONCEPT *558*

perturb [*v*] *upset, unsettle*
agitate, alarm, annoy, bewilder, bother, bug*, confound, confuse, disarrange, discompose, disconcert, discountenance, dismay, disorder, disquiet, disturb, flurry, fluster, irritate, make a scene*, make waves*, muddle, needle, perplex,

pester, ruffle, stir up*, trouble, vex, worry; SEE CONCEPTS 7,16,19

peruse [v] *check out; examine*
analyze, browse, glance over, inspect, look through, pore over, read, scan, scrutinize, skim, study; SEE CONCEPTS 72,103

pervade [v] *affect strongly; spread through*
charge, diffuse, extend, fill, imbue, impregnate, infuse, overspread, penetrate, percolate, permeate, suffuse, transfuse; SEE CONCEPTS 172,179

pervasive [adj] *extensive*
all over the place*, can't get away from*, common, general, inescapable, omnipresent, permeating, pervading, prevalent, rife, ubiquitous, universal, wall-to-wall*, widespread; SEE CONCEPT 772

perverse [adj] *mean, ornery; troublesome*
abnormal, bad-tempered, cantankerous, capricious, contradictory, contrary, contumacious, corrupt, crabby*, cross, degenerate, delinquent, depraved, deviant, disobedient, dogged*, erring, fractious, hard-nosed*, headstrong, intractable, intransigent, irritable, miscreant, mulish*, nefarious, obdurate, obstinate, petulant, pigheaded*, rebellious, refractory, rotten*, self-willed, spiteful, stubborn, unhealthy, unmanageable, unreasonable, unyielding, villainous, wayward, wicked, willful; SEE CONCEPTS 401,542,571

perversion [n] *sexual abnormality*
aberration, anomaly, corruption, debauchery, deviance, fetish, immorality, kink*, kinkiness, sexual deviation; SEE CONCEPT 545

pervert [n] *person who lacks morals*
debauchee, degenerate, deviant, deviate, freak, weirdo*; SEE CONCEPT 412

pervert [v] *twist, turn away from what is acceptable or correct*
abuse, adulterate, alloy, animalize, brainwash, color, corrupt, cut*, debase, debauch, demoralize, deprave, desecrate, distort, divert, doctor, doctor up*, fake, falsify, fudge*, garble, misconstrue, misinterpret, misrepresent, misstate, mistreat, misuse, phony up*, prostitute, ruin, salt*, seduce, spike, vitiate, warp, water*; SEE CONCEPTS 14,63,156,252

perverted [adj] *immoral, evil*
abandoned, aberrant, abnormal, abused, contorted, corrupt, corrupted, debased, debauched, defiled, depraved, deviant, deviating, distorted, foreign, grotesque, impaired, kinky*, misguided, misused, monstrous, outraged, polluted, queer, sick, tainted, twisted, unhealthy, unnatural, vicious, vitiate, vitiated, warped, wicked; SEE CONCEPTS 485,545

pesky [adj] *bothersome*
annoying, disturbing, irksome, mean, nettlesome, peeving, provoking, troublesome, ugly, vexatious, vexing, wicked; SEE CONCEPTS 529,537

pessimism [n] *belief in bad outcome*
cynicism, dark side*, dejection, depression, despair, despondency, dim view*, distrust, dyspepsia, expectation of worst, gloom, gloominess, gloomy outlook, glumness, grief, hopelessness, low spirits, melancholy, sadness, unhappiness; SEE CONCEPTS 410,689

pessimist [n] *person who expects bad outcome*
complainer, crepehanger*, cynic, defeatist, depreciator, downer, gloomy, killjoy*, misanthrope, party pooper*, prophet of doom*,

sourpuss*, wet blanket*, worrier, worrywart*; SEE CONCEPTS 412,423

pessimistic [adj] *expecting bad outcome*
bleak, cynical, dark, dejected, depressed, despairing, despondent, discouraged, distrustful, downhearted, fatalistic, foreboding, gloomy, glum, hopeless, melancholy, misanthropic, morbid, morose, resigned, sad, sullen, troubled, worried; SEE CONCEPTS 403,548

pest [n] *person or thing that presents problem*
annoyance, badgerer, bane, besetment, blight, blister, bore, bother, botheration, bug*, contagion, crashing bore*, creep, curse, drag, drip, epidemic, exasperation, headache*, infection, irritant, irritation, nag, nudge, nuisance, pain*, pain in the neck*, pesterer, pestilence, pill*, plague*, scourge*, tease*, thorn in side*, tormentor, trial*, trouble, vexation, virus*; SEE CONCEPTS 306,398,412,674

pester [v] *bother, harass*
annoy, badger, be at, bedevil, beleaguer, bug*, disturb, dog*, drive crazy, drive up the wall*, fret, get at*, get in one's hair*, get on one's nerves*, get to*, harry, hassle, hector, hound, importune, insist, irk, mess with*, nag, nudge, pick at*, plague, provoke, remind, ride*, tantalize, tease, torment, work on*, worry; SEE CONCEPTS 7,19,48

pestilence [n] *epidemic*
contagion, disease, endemic, infection, outbreak, plague, rash, scourge, sickness, virus; SEE CONCEPTS 306,316

pestilent/pestilential [adj] *dangerous, harmful*
baneful, contagious, contaminating, corrupting, deadly, deleterious, destructive, detrimental, diseased, evil, fatal, infectious, injurious, lethal, mortal, noxious, pernicious, pestiferous, ruinous, tainting, troublesome, vicious; SEE CONCEPTS 314,537

pet [adj] *favorite*
affectionate, cherished, darling, dear, dearest, endearing, favored, loved, precious, preferred, special; SEE CONCEPTS 568,574

pet [n] *favorite thing, person*
apple of eye*, beloved, cat, darling, dear, dog, evergreen*, idol, jewel*, love, lover, persona grata*, treasure*; SEE CONCEPTS 394,416

pet [v] *stroke, kiss*
baby, caress, coddle, cosset, cuddle, dandle, embrace, fondle, grab, hug, love, make love, neck*, pamper, pat, smooch*, spoil, spoon*, touch; SEE CONCEPTS 375,612

peter out [v] *dwindle, decrease*
abate, come to nothing*, die out*, diminish, drain, ebb, evaporate, fade, fail, give out, lessen, pall, rebate, recede, run dry, run out, stop, taper off, wane; SEE CONCEPTS 105,698

petite [adj] *small*
baby, bantam, dainty, delicate, diminutive, elfin, little, miniature, minikin*, slight, smallish, tiny, wee*; SEE CONCEPTS 773,779,789

petition [n] *appeal, plea*
address, application, entreaty, imploration, imprecation, invocation, memorial, prayer, request, round robin, solicitation, suit, supplication; SEE CONCEPTS 271,662

petition [v] *plead, appeal for*
adjure, ask, beg, beseech, call upon, entreat, impetrate, implore, pray, press, put in for, request,

seek, solicit, sue, supplicate, urge; SEE CONCEPTS *48,53*

petrified [*adj1*] *hardened*
calcified, fossilized, frozen, ossified, solidified; SEE CONCEPTS *483,604*

petrified [*adj2*] *terrified*
afraid, alarmed, anxious, dazed, fearful, frightened, frozen, have cold feet*, immobilized, in a cold sweat*, in a panic*, numb, panicky, pushing the panic button*, scared, scared stiff*, shocked, speechless, spooked, startled, stunned, terrorized, terror-stricken, unnerved; SEE CONCEPTS *403,690*

petrify [*v1*] *make hard*
calcify, clarify, fossilize, harden, lapidify, mineralize, set, solidify, turn to stone; SEE CONCEPT *250*

petrify [*v2*] *frighten*
alarm, amaze, appall, astonish, astound, benumb, chill, confound, daze, dismay, dumbfound, horrify, immobilize, numb, paralyze, put chill on*, scare, scare silly*, scare stiff*, spook*, startle, stun, stupefy, terrify, transfix; SEE CONCEPTS *7,14,19,42*

petroleum [*n*] *oil*
crude oil, fossil fuel, fuel, gas, gasoline, kerosene, naphtha, natural gas, petrol; SEE CONCEPTS *467,520,523,661*

petty [*adj*] *trivial, insignificant*
base, casual, cheap, contemptible, frivolous, inconsequent, inconsiderable, inessential, inferior, irrelevant, junior, lesser, light, little, lower, measly, minor, narrow-minded, negligible, nickel-and-dime*, niggling*, paltry, peanut*, penny-ante*, pettifogging*, picayune, piddling*, scratch, secondary, shabby, shallow, shoestring*, slight, small, small-minded, subordinate, trifling, two-bit*, unimportant; SEE CONCEPTS *403,575*

petulant [*adj*] *crabby, moody*
bad-tempered, captious, caviling, complaining, cranky*, cross, crybaby*, displeased, fault-finding, fractious, fretful, grouchy, grumbling, huffy, ill-humored, impatient, irritable, mean, peevish, perverse, pouting, querulous, snappish, sour, sulky, sullen, testy, touchy, ungracious, uptight*, waspish, whining, whiny; SEE CONCEPTS *401,542*

phantom [*n*] *ghost; figment of the imagination*
apparition, chimera, daydream, delusion, dream, eidolon, figment, hallucination, haunt, ignis fatuus, illusion, mirage, nightmare, phantasm, revenant, shade, shadow, specter, spirit, spook, vision, wraith; SEE CONCEPTS *370,529*

pharmacist [*n*] *druggist*
apothecary, pharmacologist; SEE CONCEPT *357*

phase [*n*] *period in life of something*
appearance, aspect, chapter, condition, development, facet, juncture, point, position, posture, stage, state, step, time; SEE CONCEPTS *816,834*

phenomenal [*adj*] *astounding, exceptional*
extraordinary, fantastic, marvelous, miraculous, outstanding, preternatural, prodigious, rare, remarkable, sensational, singular, substantial, uncommon, unique, unparalleled, unusual, unwonted, wondrous; SEE CONCEPTS *564,574*

phenomenology [*n*] *study of subject and objects of a person's experience*
intentionality, life-world, lived experience, meaning-making; SEE CONCEPTS *282,349*

phenomenon [*n*] *rare occurrence; wonder*
abnormality, actuality, anomaly, appearance, aspect, circumstance, curiosity, episode, event, exception, experience, fact, happening, incident, marvel, miracle, nonpareil, one for the books*, paradox, peculiarity, portent, prodigy, rara avis*, rarity, reality, sensation, sight, something else*, spectacle, stunner*, uniqueness; SEE CONCEPTS *230,529,678*

philanderer [*n*] *person who has many love affairs*
adulterer, chaser, cruiser, dallier, debaucher, flirt, gallant, lover, operator*, swinger; SEE CONCEPT *423*

philanthropic [*adj*] *charitable, giving*
altruistic, beneficent, benevolent, benignant, big-hearted, bountiful, contributing, donating, eleemosynary, generous, good, gracious, helpful, humane, humanitarian, kind, kindhearted, liberal, magnanimous, munificent, openhanded, patriotic, public-spirited; SEE CONCEPTS *404,542*

philanthropist [*n*] *humanitarian*
altruist, benefactor, bleeding heart*, contributor, do-gooder*, donor, Good Samaritan*, good scout*, helper, patron; SEE CONCEPTS *416,423*

philanthropy [*n*] *humanitarianism*
alms, alms-giving, altruism, assistance, benefaction, beneficence, charity, contribution, dole, donation, endowment, fund, generosity, gifting, good works, helping hand*, relief; SEE CONCEPTS *337,657*

philosopher [*n*] *deep thinker*
logician, sage, savant, sophist, theorist, wise person; SEE CONCEPTS *349,687,689*

philosophical/philosophic [*adj1*] *thinking deeply, rationally*
abstract, cogitative, deep, erudite, judicious, learned, logical, pensive, profound, rational, reflective, sagacious, sapient, theoretical, thoughtful, wise; SEE CONCEPT *402*

philosophical/philosophic [*adj2*] *calm, serene*
collected, commonsensical, composed, cool*, cool as cucumber*, enduring, impassive, imperturbable, patient, resigned, stoical, tranquil, unagitated, unflappable, unmoved, unruffled; SEE CONCEPT *401*

philosophy [*n*] *principles, knowledge*
aesthetics, attitude, axiom, beliefs, conception, convictions, doctrine, idea, ideology, logic, metaphysics, ontology, outlook, rationalism, reason, reasoning, system, tenet, theory, thinking, thought, truth, values, view, viewpoint, wisdom; SEE CONCEPTS *349,688,689*

phlegmatic [*adj*] *unemotional*
along for the ride*, apathetic, blah*, cold, cool, deadpan, desensitized, disinterested, dispassionate, dull, emotionless, flat, frigid, groggy, indifferent, lethargic, lifeless, listless, passionless, passive, sluggish, uncompassionate, undemonstrative, unexcitable, unfeeling, uninvolved, unresponsive; SEE CONCEPTS *401,403*

phobia [*n*] *fear*
anxiety, aversion, avoidance, awe, detestation, disgust, dislike, distaste, dread, fear, hang-up*, hatred, horror, irrationality, loathing, neurosis, obsession, repulsion, resentment, revulsion, terror, thing*, thing about*; SEE CONCEPTS *27,29,529*

phobic [*adj*] *fearful*
afraid, anxious, apprehensive, discomposed, disquieted, disturbed, frightened, have cold feet*, irrational, jittery, jumpy, nervous, neurotic, pan-

pe
ph

icky, scared, shy, skittish, tense, worried; SEE
CONCEPT 401

phony [adj] fake, false
affected, artificial, assumed, bogus, counterfeit,
forged, imitation, pseudo, put-on*, sham*, spurious, trick; SEE CONCEPT 582

photocopy [n/v] mechanical image produced
from a copier; making the image
copy, duplicate, reproduce, stat, velox, Xerox;
SEE CONCEPT 269

photograph [n] a still picture taken with a camera
blowup, close-up, image, Kodachrome*,
Kodak*, likeness, microfilm, mug*, negative,
photo, photostat, pic*, picture, pinup*, pix*, Polaroid*, portrait, positive, print, shot*, slide,
snap, snapshot, transparency; SEE CONCEPT 265

photograph [v] take a picture with a camera
capture*, capture on film*, cinematize, close-
up*, copy, film, get, get a likeness*, get a shot*,
illustrate, lens*, make a picture*, microfilm,
mug*, photo, photoengrave, photostat, picture,
print, record, reproduce, roll, shoot, snap*, snapshot, take*, turn*, X-ray*; SEE CONCEPT 174

photographer [n] cameraperson
freelance photographer, paparazzo, photojour-
nalist, shutterbug; SEE CONCEPT 352

photographic [adj] exact, retentive in detail
accurate, cinematic, detailed, faithful, filmic,
graphic, lifelike, minute, natural, pictorial, picturesque, precise, realistic, true-to-life*, visual,
vivid; SEE CONCEPT 557

phrase [n] group of words; way of speaking
byword, catchphrase, catchword, diction, expression, idiom, locution, maxim, motto, parlance,
phraseology, phrasing, remark, saying, shibboleth, slogan, styling, tag, terminology, utterance,
verbalism, verbiage, watchword, wordage, wording; SEE CONCEPTS 275,278

phrase [v] express in words carefully
couch, formulate, frame, present, put, put into
words, say, term, utter, voice, word; SEE CON-
CEPT 55

physical [adj1] tangible, material
concrete, corporeal, environmental, gross, materialistic, natural, objective, palpable, phenomenal, ponderable, real, sensible, solid, somatic,
substantial, visible; SEE CONCEPT 582

physical [adj2] concerning the body
bodily, brute, carnal, corporal, corporeal, earthly,
fleshly, incarnate, mortal, personal, somatic, unspiritual, visceral; SEE CONCEPT 485

physician [n] person trained in medical science
bones*, doc*, doctor, general practitioner,
healer, intern, MD*, medic, medical practitioner,
quack*, sawbones*, specialist, surgeon; SEE
CONCEPT 357

physique [n] build of human body
anatomy, body, built, character, configuration,
constitution, corpus, figure, form, frame, habit,
habitus, makeup, muscles, nature, shape, structure, type; SEE CONCEPTS 405,757

picayune [adj] trivial
diminutive, everyday, frivolous, immaterial, incidental, inconsequential, inconsiderable, insignificant, irrelevant, little, meager, mean,
meaningless, minor, minute, negligible,
nonessential, no account*, paltry, petty, piddling*, puny, slight, small, superficial, trifling,
trite, unimportant; SEE CONCEPT 575

pick [n] a chosen option, usually the choicest
aces, bag, best, choice, choosing, cream*, crème
de la crème*, cup of tea*, decision, druthers*,
elect, elite, flower*, preference, pride, prime,
prize, select, selection, top, tops; SEE CONCEPTS
529,671

pick [v1] choose, select
cull, decide upon, elect, finger*, fix upon, go
down the line*, hand-pick, mark, name, optate,
opt for, pick and choose, pick out, prefer, say so,
separate, settle on, sift out*, single out, slot, sort
out, tab, tag, take, take it or leave it*, tap, winnow; SEE CONCEPT 41

pick [v2] gather, harvest
accumulate, choose, collect, cull, cut, draw,
pluck, pull; SEE CONCEPTS 41,109,206

pick [v3] break into something closed, locked
break open, crack, dent, force, hit, indent, jimmy,
open, pry, strike; SEE CONCEPT 192

pick at/pick on [v] nag, provoke
badger, bait, blame, bully, carp, cavil, criticize,
find fault, foment, get at*, get to*, goad, hector,
incite, instigate, quibble, start, tease, torment;
SEE CONCEPTS 7,19,52

picket [n1] post of structure
pale, paling, palisade, panel, peg, pillar, rail,
stake, stanchion, upright; SEE CONCEPTS 445,479

picket [n2] person who demonstrates for cause
demonstrator, picketer, protester, striker; SEE
CONCEPTS 348,359

picket [n3] person acting as guard
guard, lookout, patrol, scout, sentinel, sentry,
spotter, vedette, ward, watch, watchperson; SEE
CONCEPT 348

picket [v] protest against, for cause
blockade, boycott, demonstrate, hit the bricks*,
strike, walk out; SEE CONCEPTS 300,351

pickle [n] sticky situation
bind, box*, corner*, difficulty, dilemma, disorder, fix, hole*, hot water*, jam*, predicament,
quandary, scrape, spot*, tight spot*; SEE CON-
CEPT 674

pickle [v] preserve fruit or vegetable
can, cure, keep, marinade, salt, souse, steep; SEE
CONCEPT 170

pick-me-up [n] stimulant
analeptic, catalyst, drug, energizer, incentive,
motivation, motive, restorative, reviver, shot in
the arm*, spark pulg*, spur, stimulus, tonic,
upper; SEE CONCEPTS 240,307,661

pick up [v1] lift, raise
elevate, gather, grasp, hoist, rear, take up, uphold, uplift, upraise, uprear; SEE CONCEPT 196

pick up [v2] obtain, find
acquire, annex, buy, chalk up*, come across,
compass, cull, extract, gain, garner, gather, get,
get the hang of*, glean, happen upon*, have,
learn, procure, purchase, score, secure, take; SEE
CONCEPTS 31,120,183

pick up [v3] improve
continue, gain, gain ground*, get better, get well,
increase, make a comeback*, mend, perk up*,
rally, recommence, recover, renew, reopen,
restart, resume, swell, take up; SEE CONCEPTS
234,700

pick up [v4] call for socially
accompany, collect, drop in for*, get*, give a
lift*, go for*, go to get*, invite, offer, proposition, stop for*; SEE CONCEPTS 224,384

pick up [*v5*] *arrest for crime*
apprehend, book*, bust*, collar*, detain, nab, pinch*, pull in*, run in*, take into custody; SEE CONCEPT *317*

picky [*adj*] *choosy, finicky*
captious, critical, dainty, fastidious, fault-finding, fussy, nice, particular, persnickety; SEE CONCEPT *404*

picnic [*n1*] *outdoor meal*
barbecue, clambake, cookout, dining alfresco, excursion, fish fry, outing, weiner roast; SEE CONCEPTS *386,459*

picnic [*n2*] *easy undertaking*
breeze*, child's play*, cinch, duck soup*, kid stuff*, lark*, light work, no trouble, piece of cake*, pushover*, setup*, smooth sailing*, snap, sure thing, walkover*; SEE CONCEPTS *362,693*

picture [*n1*] *illustration, likeness of something*
account, art, blueprint, canvas, cartoon, copy, delineation, depiction, description, doodle, double, draft, drawing, duplicate, effigy, engraving, figure, icon, image, impression, lookalike, outline, painting, panorama, photo, photograph, piece, portrait, portrayal, presentment, print, re-creation, replica, report, representation, ringer*, similitude, simulacrum, sketch, spectacle, spitting image*, statue, tableau, twin; SEE CONCEPTS *259,625*

picture [*n2*] *perfect example*
archetype, embodiment, epitome, essence, idea, personification; SEE CONCEPT *686*

picture [*n3*] *entertainment film*
cartoon, cinema, flick*, motion picture, movie, moving picture, photoplay, picture show, show; SEE CONCEPT *293*

picture [*v1*] *depict, describe*
delineate, draw, illustrate, image, interpret, limn, paint, photograph, portray, render, represent, show, sketch; SEE CONCEPTS *79,174*

picture [*v2*] *form vision in one's mind*
conceive of, create, daydream, dream, envision, fancy, fantasize, imagine, portray, see, see in the mind's eye*, visualize; SEE CONCEPTS *17,43*

picturesque [*adj*] *attractive, referring to scenery*
arresting, artistic, beautiful, charming, colorful, graphic, photographic, pictorial, pleasant, pretty, quaint, scenic, striking, vivid; SEE CONCEPTS *579,589*

piddling [*adj*] *insignificant*
derisory, little, measly*, niggling*, paltry, peanut*, pettifogging*, petty, picayune, puny, trifling, trivial, unimportant, useless, worthless; SEE CONCEPTS *575,789*

piddly [*adj*] *meager, trivial*
barren, deficient, diddly*, flimsy, inconsiderable, insubstantial, insufficient, little, measly*, mere, microscopic, minute, negligible, paltry, petty, puny, rinky-dink*, scant, scrimpy, short, skimpy, slight, small, sparse, superficial, too little too late*, two-bit*, unproductive, worthless; SEE CONCEPTS *546,789*

piece [*n1*] *part*
allotment, bit, bite, chunk, cut, division, dole, end, example, fraction, fragment, gob, half, hunk, instance, interest, iota, item, length, lot, lump, member, moiety, morsel, parcel, percentage, portion, quantity, quota, sample, scrap, section, segment, share, shred, slice, smithereen*, specimen; SEE CONCEPTS *834,835*

piece [*n2*] *work of art, music, writing*
arrangement, article, bit, composition, creation, discourse, dissertation, engraving, exposition, icon, item, lines, painting, paper, part, photograph, print, production, sketch, song, statue, study, theme, thesis, treatise, treatment, vignette, work; SEE CONCEPTS *259,262,263,271*

piece [*v*] *put together*
assemble, combine, compose, create, fix, join, make, mend, patch, repair, restore, unite; SEE CONCEPTS *113,173,193,251*

piece de resistance [*n1*] *outstanding accomplishment*
achievement, chef d'oeuvre, feat, great performance, jewel, magnum opus, masterpiece, master work, prize, showpiece, tour de force*; SEE CONCEPT *259*

piecemeal [*adj/adv*] *bit by bit*
at intervals, by degrees, by fits and starts*, fitfully, fragmentary, gradual, gradually, intermittent, intermittently, interrupted, little by little*, partial, partially, patchy, spotty, step by step*; SEE CONCEPTS *531,544*

pier [*n*] *support; place for boats*
berth, buttress, column, dam, dock, jetty, landing, levee, mole, pierage, pilaster, pile, piling, pillar, post, promenade, quay, slip, upright, wharf; SEE CONCEPTS *439,443,479*

pierce [*v*] *cut, penetrate*
bore, break, break in, break through, cleave, crack, crack open, drill, enter, gash, incise, intrude, pass through, perforate, plow, prick, probe, puncture, run through, slash, slice, slit, spike, stab, stick into, transfix; SEE CONCEPTS *137,159,176,220*

piercing [*adj*] *intense to the senses*
acute, agonizing, arctic, biting, bitter, blaring, cold, deafening, earsplitting, excruciating, exquisite, fierce, freezing, frosty, high, high-pitched, keen, knifelike, loud, numbing, painful, penetrating, powerful, racking, raw, roaring, severe, sharp, shattering, shooting, shrill, stabbing, stentorian, stentorious, thin, treble, wintry; SEE CONCEPTS *406,537,592,594*

piety [*n*] *devotion, religiousness*
allegiance, application, ardor, belief, devoutness, docility, dutifulness, duty, faith, fealty, fervor, fidelity, godliness, grace, holiness, loyalty, obedience, passion, religion, religiosity, reverence, sanctity, veneration, zeal; SEE CONCEPTS *633,689*

piffle [*n*] *nonsense*
balderdash*, baloney*, bull*, bunk*, drivel, empty talk, foolishness, futile talk, gibberish, hogwash*, hooey*, hot air*, jive*, palaver, poppycock*, prattle, rubbish, silliness, trash*, useless words; SEE CONCEPTS *230,388,633*

pig [*n*] *animal of swine family*
boar, cob roller*, hog, piggy*, piglet, porker*, porky, shoat, sow, swine; SEE CONCEPTS *394,400*

pigeonhole [*n*] *compartment*
box, carrel, chamber, corner, cranny, cubbyhole, cubicle, hole, niche, nook, place, pocket, recess, section, slot, stall; SEE CONCEPT *434*

pigeonhole [*v*] *categorize; shelve*
assort, class, classify, defer, delay, dismiss, file, group, hold, hold off, hold up, label, lay aside, peg*, postpone, put aside, put down as, put off, put on hold, put on ice*, put on the bank burner*, rank, sideline, sort, tab, table, type cast; SEE CONCEPTS *39,121*

pigheaded [*adj*] *stubborn*
bullheaded, contrary, dense*, forward, headstrong, inflexible, insistent, intractable, mulish*, obstinate, perverse, recalcitrant, self-willed, stiffnecked, stupid*, unyielding, willful; SEE CONCEPTS 404,542

pigment [*n*] *color, shade*
colorant, coloring, coloring matter, dye, dyestuff, oil, paint, stain, tincture, tint; SEE CONCEPTS 259,622

pig out [*v*] *overeat*
binge, blimp out*, devour, dive in*, eat like a horse*, eat to excess, feed, gluttonize, gobble, gorge, gormandize, gulp, guzzle, hoover*, overindulge, pork out*, scarf out*, shovel it in*, stuff oneself, wolf*; SEE CONCEPT 169

pile [*n1*] *heap, collection*
accumulation, aggregate, aggregation, amassment, assemblage, assortment, bank, barrel, buildup, chunk, conglomeration, drift, gob, great deal, hill, hoard, hunk, jumble, lump, mass, mound, mountain, much, ocean, oodles*, pack, peck, pyramid, quantity, shock, stack, stockpile; SEE CONCEPTS 432,787

pile [*n2*] *wealth*
affluence, boodle*, bundle*, dough*, fortune, mint*, money, pot*, riches, wad*; SEE CONCEPTS 335,340

pile [*v*] *gather, pack; put on top of another*
accumulate, amass, assemble, bank, bunch, collect, crowd, crush, fill, flock, heap, hill, hoard, jam, load, mass, mound, rush, stack, store; SEE CONCEPTS 84,109,201,750

pilfer [*v*] *steal, embezzle*
annex, appropriate, borrow, cop*, crib*, filch*, liberate*, lift*, moonlight*, palm*, pinch*, pluck*, purloin, requisition, rip off*, rob, scrounge, snare, snatch, swipe, take, thieve, walk off with*; SEE CONCEPTS 139,142,192

pilgrimage [*n*] *long journey*
crusade, excursion, expedition, mission, tour, travel, trip, wayfaring; SEE CONCEPT 224

pill [*n1*] *capsule of medicine*
bolus, dose, lozenge, medicine, pellet, pilule, tablet, troche; SEE CONCEPTS 307,470

pill [*n2*] *person who is annoying*
bore, drag*, nuisance, pain*, pain in the neck*, pest, trial*; SEE CONCEPTS 412,423

pillage [*v*] *plunder, destroy*
appropriate, arrogate, confiscate, depredate, desecrate, desolate, despoil, devastate, devour, gut, invade, lay waste*, loot, maraud, nab*, pilfer, pinch*, purloin, raid, ransack, ravage, rifle*, rob, ruin, sack, spoil, spoliate, steal, strip, thieve, trespass, waste; SEE CONCEPTS 86,139,252

pillar [*n1*] *column of building, or freestanding column*
colonnade, mast, obelisk, pedestal, pier, pilaster, piling, post, prop, shaft, stanchion, support, tower, upright; SEE CONCEPT 440

pillar [*n2*] *mainstay; source of strength*
backbone*, guider, leader, light*, rock*, sinew, supporter, tower of strength*, upholder, worthy; SEE CONCEPTS 423,712

pilot [*n*] *person who guides aircraft, ship, or other vehicle*
ace*, aerialist, aeronaut, aviator, bellwether*, captain, conductor, coxswain, dean, director, doyen/doyenne, eagle*, flier*, flyer, guide, helmsperson, jockey*, lead, leader, navigator,

one at the controls, one at the wheel, scout*, steerer, steersperson, wheelperson; SEE CONCEPT 348

pimple [*n*] *small swelling on the skin*
abscess, acne, beauty spot, blackhead, blemish, blister, boil, bump, carbuncle, caruncle, excrescence, furuncle, hickey*, inflammation, lump, papula, papule, pustule, spot, whitehead, zit*; SEE CONCEPT 306

pin [*v*] *attach, hold in place*
affix, bind, clasp, close, fasten, fix, hold down, hold fast, immobilize, join, pinion, press, restrain, secure; SEE CONCEPTS 85,160,190

pinch [*n1*] *tight pressing*
compression, confinement, contraction, cramp, grasp, grasping, hurt, limitation, nip, nipping, pressure, squeeze, torment, tweak, twinge; SEE CONCEPT 728

pinch [*n2*] *small amount*
bit, dash, drop, jot, mite, small quantity, soupçon, speck, splash, splatter, taste; SEE CONCEPT 831

pinch [*n3*] *predicament*
box*, clutch, contingency, crisis, crunch*, difficulty, emergency, exigency, hardship, juncture, necessity, oppression, pass, plight, pressure, strait, stress, tight spot*, tight squeeze*, turning point*, zero hour*; SEE CONCEPT 674

pinch [*v1*] *press tightly*
chafe, compress, confine, cramp, crush, grasp, hurt, nip, pain, squeeze, tweak, twinge, wrench, wrest, wring; SEE CONCEPTS 219,313

pinch [*v2*] *be stingy*
afflict, distress, economize, oppress, pinch pennies*, press, scrape, scrimp, skimp, spare, stint; SEE CONCEPT 330

pinch [*v3*] *steal*
cop*, crib*, filch*, knock off*, lift*, nab*, pilfer, purloin, rob, snatch, swipe, take; SEE CONCEPT 139

pinch [*v4*] *arrest*
apprehend, bust*, collar*, detain, hold, nab*, pick up*, pull in*, run in*, take into custody; SEE CONCEPTS 90,317

pine [*v*] *long for*
ache, agonize, brood, carry a torch*, covet, crave, desire, dream, fret, grieve, hanker, languish for, lust after, mope*, mourn, sigh, spoil for*, thirst for, want, wish, yearn, yen for; SEE CONCEPT 20

pink [*n1/adj*] *rose color*
blush, coral, flush, fuchsia, rose, roseate, salmon; SEE CONCEPT 622

pink [*n2*] *best condition*
acme*, best, bloom*, fitness, good health, height*, peak, perfection, prime, summit, trim*, verdure; SEE CONCEPTS 316,388

pink [*v*] *cut in zigzag*
incise, notch, perforate, prick, punch, scallop, score; SEE CONCEPT 176

pinnacle [*n*] *top, crest*
acme, apex, apogee, climax, cone, crown, culmination, greatest, height, max*, most*, needle*, obelisk, peak, pyramid, spire, steeple, summit, tops, tower, vertex, zenith; SEE CONCEPTS 706,836

pinpoint [*v*] *define, locate*
determinate, diagnose, distinguish, finger*, get a fix on*, home in on*, identify, place, recognize, spot; SEE CONCEPTS 38,183

pioneer [*adj*] *early, first*
avant-garde, brave, experimental, head, inaugural, initial, lead, original, primary, prime; SEE CONCEPT 585

pioneer [*n*] *person who finds a new place, founds something*
colonist, colonizer, create, develop, explorer, founder, frontier settler, guide, homesteader, immigrant, innovator, leader, pathfinder, pilgrim, scout, settler, squatter, trailblazer; SEE CONCEPTS 348,413

pioneer [*v*] *invent; lay the groundwork*
begin, colonize, create, develop, discover, establish, explore, found, go out in front*, initiate, instigate, institute, launch, map out, open up, originate, prepare, show the way, spearhead*, start, take the lead, trailblaze*; SEE CONCEPTS 173,221,324

pious [*adj*] *dedicated, religious*
born-again*, clerical, devoted, devout, divine, ecclesiastical, godly, goody-goody*, orthodox, prayerful, priestly, reverent, righteous, sacred, saintly, sanctimonious, spiritual; SEE CONCEPT 401

pipe [*n*] *passage, tube*
aqueduct, canal, channel, conduit, conveyer, duct, hose, line, main, pipeline, sewer, spout, trough, vent, vessel; SEE CONCEPTS 475,499

pipe [*v1*] *conduct through tube, passage*
bring in, carry, channel, convey, funnel, siphon, supply, traject, transmit; SEE CONCEPT 217

pipe [*v2*] *make a sound; peep*
blubber*, boohoo*, cheep*, cry, play, say, shout, sing, sob, sound, speak, talk, toot*, trill, tweet, twitter, wail, warble, weep, whistle; SEE CONCEPTS 47,65,77

pipe dream [*n*] *fantasy*
air castle, airy hope, castle in the sky*, chimera, daydream, fantastic notion, fool's paradise*, unreal hope, wishful thinking; SEE CONCEPTS 20,529,689

pipsqueak [*n*] *nonentity*
nobody, runt, shrimp, squirt, twerp, whippersnapper; SEE CONCEPT 424

piquant [*adj*] *flavorful, biting*
highly-seasoned, interesting, lively, peppery, poignant, provocative, pungent, racy, savory, sharp, snappy, sparkling, spicy, spirited, stimulating, stinging, tangy, tart, well-flavored, with a kick*, zestful, zesty; SEE CONCEPTS 529,613

pique [*n*] *anger, irritation*
annoyance, blowup*, conniption*, dander*, displeasure, flare-up, grudge, huff, hurt, irk, miff*, offense, peeve, pet*, provocation, resentment, rise, ruckus*, slow burn*, snit, sore*, stew*, storm*, tiff*, umbrage, vexation; SEE CONCEPTS 29,410

pique [*v*] *offend, provoke*
absorb, affront, annoy, arouse, bother, bug*, displease, egg on*, exasperate, excite, fire up*, gall, galvanize, get*, get a rise out of*, get under skin*, give a hard time*, give the business*, goad, goose*, grab, ignite, incense, irk, irritate, kindle, make waves*, miff*, mortify, motivate, move, nettle, offend, peeve, prick, put out*, quicken, rile, rouse, spur, stimulate, sting*, stir, vex, whet, work up*, wound; SEE CONCEPTS 7,14,19,22

piracy [*n*] *robbery*
bootlegging, buccaneering, commandeering, copying, freebooting, hijacking, infringement, marauding, pirating, plagiarism, rapine, stealing, swashbuckling, theft; SEE CONCEPTS 139,192

pirate [*n*] *buccaneer*
corsair, filibuster, freebooter, marauder, picaroon, privateer, raider, rover, sea rover; SEE CONCEPT 412

pissed off [*adj*] *angry*
affronted, annoyed, bent out of shape*, boiling*, cross, displeased, enraged, fighting mad*, fit to be tied*, fuming, furious, hopping mad*, hot, huffy*, in a tizzy*, incensed, inflamed, infuriated, irate, irritated, livid, mad, maddened, offended, outraged, peed*, peeved off*, provoked, raging, riled, sore, steamed, steamed up, steaming, storming, t'd off*, tee'd off*, ticked off*; SEE CONCEPT 403

pistol [*n*] *revolver*
firearm, forty-five*, gun, handgun, piece*, rod*, Saturday night special*, six-shooter, thirty-eight*; SEE CONCEPT 500

pit [*n*] *hole, cavity*
abyss, chasm, crater, dent, depression, dimple, excavation, grave, gulf, hell, hollow, indentation, mine, perforation, pockmark, pothole, puncture, shaft, tomb, trench, well; SEE CONCEPTS 509,513

pit [*v*] *oppose, play off*
contend, counter, match, put in opposition, set against, vie; SEE CONCEPTS 92,363

pitch [*n1*] *tilt*
angle, cant, degree, dip, gradient, height, incline, level, point, slant, slope, steepness; SEE CONCEPTS 692,738

pitch [*n2*] *tone of sound*
frequency, harmonic, modulation, rate, sound, timbre; SEE CONCEPT 65

pitch [*n3*] *talk to convince*
patter*, persuasion, sales talk, song and dance*, spiel*; SEE CONCEPTS 68,278

pitch [*v1*] *throw, hurl*
bung, cast, chuck*, fire, fling, gun, heave, launch, lob, peg, sling, toss, unseat; SEE CONCEPT 222

pitch [*v2*] *put up, erect*
fix, locate, place, plant, raise, settle, set up, station; SEE CONCEPT 168

pitch [*v3*] *dive, roll*
ascend, bend, bicker, careen, descend, dip, drive, drop, fall, flounder, go down, heave, lean, lunge, lurch, plunge, rise, rock, seesaw, slope, slump, stagger, tilt, topple, toss, tumble, vault, wallow, welter, yaw; SEE CONCEPTS 147,181,201

pitcher [*n1*] *jug*
amphora, bottle, canteen, carafe, container, crock, cruet, decanter, ewer, flagon, flask, jar, vase, vessel; SEE CONCEPT 494

pitcher [*n2*] *baseball pitcher*
ace*, baseball player, closer, hurler, knuckleballer, middle reliever, reliever; SEE CONCEPT 366

pitch in [*v*] *help; get busy*
aid, attack, begin, buckle down*, chip in*, come through, commence, contribute, cooperate, do, do one's bit*, fall to*, get cracking*, get going, go to it*, hop to it*, join in, jump in*, launch, lend a hand*, participate, plunge into*, set about, set to, subscribe, tackle, tee off*, volunteer, wade in; SEE CONCEPTS 100,110

piteous [*adj*] *miserable, pathetic*
beseeching, commiserable, deplorable, distressing, doleful, dolorous, entreating, grievous,

heartbreaking, heart-rending, imploring, lamentable, melancholy, mournful, moving, pitiable, pitiful, plaintive, poignant, poor, rueful, ruined, sad, sorrowful, supplicating, woeful, wretched; SEE CONCEPTS *485,529*

pitfall [*n*] *hazard, trap*
booby trap*, catch*, danger, deadfall*, difficulty, downfall, drawback, entanglement, hook*, mesh*, mousetrap*, peril, pit*, quicksand*, risk, setup*, snag*, snare, swindle*, toil, web; SEE CONCEPTS *674,679*

pithy [*adj*] *brief, to the point*
cogent, compact, concise, crisp, curt, down to brass tacks*, effective, epigrammatic, expressive, honed, laconic, meaningful, meaty*, pointed, short, short-and-sweet*, significant, succinct, terse, trenchant; SEE CONCEPT *267*

pitiful [*adj*] *in bad shape; poor*
abject, affecting, afflicted, arousing, base, beggarly, cheap, cheerless, comfortless, commiserative, compassionate, contemptible, deplorable, despicable, dismal, distressed, distressing, grievous, heartbreaking, heartrending, inadequate, insignificant, joyless, lamentable, low, mean, miserable, mournful, moving, paltry, pathetic, piteous, pitiable, sad, scurvy, shabby, sorrowful, sorry, stirring, suffering, tearful, touching, vile, woeful, worthless, wretched; SEE CONCEPTS *485,529*

pitiless [*adj*] *without mercy or care*
austere, barbarous, brutal, callous, cold*, coldblooded*, coldhearted*, cruel, cutthroat*, dog-eat-dog*, frigid, hardhearted*, harsh, hatchetjob*, heartless, implacable, indifferent, inexorable, inhuman, inhumane, insensible, killer instinct*, mean, merciless, obdurate, relentless, remorseless, ruthless, satanic, savage, soulless*, stony*; SEE CONCEPT *401*

pittance [*n*] *small amount*
allowance, bit, chicken feed*, dribble*, drop*, drop in the bucket*, inadequacy, insufficiency, mite, modicum, peanuts*, pension, portion, ration, scrap*, slave wages*, smidgen, trace, trifle; SEE CONCEPTS *344,787*

pity [*n1*] *feeling of mercy toward another*
benevolence, charity, clemency, comfort, commiseration, compassion, compunction, condolement, condolence, dejection, distress, empathy, favor, forbearance, goodness, grace, humanity, kindliness, kindness, lenity, melancholy, mercy, philanthropy, quarter, rue, ruth, sadness, solace, sorrow, sympathy, tenderness, understanding, warmth; SEE CONCEPTS *410,657*

pity [*n2*] *sad situation*
bad luck, catastrophe, crime, crisis, crying shame*, disaster, mischance, misfortune, mishap, regret, shame, sin; SEE CONCEPT *674*

pity [*v*] *feel sorry for; spare*
ache*, be sorry for, be sympathetic, bleed for*, comfort, commiserate, condole, console, feel for, feel with, forgive, give quarter*, grant amnesty, grieve with, have compassion, have mercy on, identify with, lament with, pardon, put out of one's misery*, relent, reprieve, show forgiveness*, show sympathy*, solace, soothe, sympathize, take pity on*, understand, weep for*; SEE CONCEPTS *10,34,83*

pivot [*n*] *center point about which something revolves*
axis, axle, center, focal point, fulcrum, heart,

hinge, hub, kingpin, shaft, spindle, swivel, turning point; SEE CONCEPTS *445,464,498,830*

pivot [*v*] *revolve around center point*
be contingent, depend, hang, hinge, rely, rotate, sheer, spin, swivel, turn, twirl, veer, volte-face, wheel, whip, whirl; SEE CONCEPTS *147,532*

pivotal [*adj*] *important*
cardinal, central, climactic, critical, crucial, decisive, determining, essential, focal, middle, momentous, overriding, overruling, principal, ruling, vital; SEE CONCEPT *568*

pixie [*n*] *fairy*
bogie, brownie, elf, fay, gnome, goblin, gremlin, hob, imp, leprechaun, nisse, puck, spirit, sprite; SEE CONCEPT *370*

pizzazz [*n*] *energy; flamboyance*
ability, animation, aptitude, bounce, dash, drive, effectiveness, elan, fire, force, forcefulness, get-up-and-go*, gift, hustle, intensity, juice, knack, life, liveliness, moxie*, muscle, oomph*, panache, pep, pluck, potency, power, presence, punch, push, shine*, spirit, splash*, spunk, stamina, vim, virility, vitality, vivacity, zeal, zest, zing, zip*; SEE CONCEPTS *411,630,706*

placard [*n*] *sign, notice*
advertisement, announcement, banner, bill, billboard, handbill, marquee, poster, public notice, signboard; SEE CONCEPTS *271,284*

placate [*v*] *soothe, pacify*
appease, assuage, calm, cheer, comfort, conciliate, humor, make peace*, make up*, mollify, pacify, play up to*, pour oil on*, propitiate, reconcile, satisfy, soft-pedal*, soothe, stroke*, sweeten, tranquilize, win over*; SEE CONCEPTS *7,22,126*

place [*n1*] *location with purpose, function*
abode, accommodation, apartment, area, berth, city, community, compass, corner, country, distance, district, domicile, dwelling, field, habitat, hamlet, hangout, hole*, home, house, joint, latitude, lay, locale, locality, locus, longitude, neighborhood, niche, nook, pad*, part, plant, point, position, property, quarter, region, reservation, residence, room, seat, section, site, situation, spot, station, stead, suburb, town, venue, vicinity, village, volume, whereabouts, zone; SEE CONCEPTS *435,515*

place [*n2*] *position, rank*
capacity, character, footing, grade, pecking order*, slot, standing, state, station, status; SEE CONCEPT *388*

place [*n3*] *job, employment*
appointment, berth, connection, occupation, office, position, post, profession, situation, spot, trade; SEE CONCEPT *360*

place [*n4*] *duty, role*
affair, charge, concern, function, prerogative, responsibility, right; SEE CONCEPT *532*

place [*v1*] *locate, situate*
allocate, allot, assign, deposit, distribute, establish, finger, fix, install, lay, lodge, nail, park, peg, plant, position, put, quarter, repose, rest, set, settle, spot, stand, station, stick, store, stow; SEE CONCEPT *201*

place [*v2*] *order, sort*
allocate, appoint, approximate, arrange, assign, call, charge, class, classify, commission, constitute, delegate, deputize, designate, entrust, estimate, fix, give, grade, group, judge, name,

nominate, ordain, put, rank, reckon; SEE CON-
CEPTS 50,84,88,98

place [*v3*] *identify, recognize*
associate, compose, determine, diagnose, distinguish, figure out*, finger*, indicate, know,
nail*, peg*, pinpoint, put one's finger on*, remember, set in context, spot, tell; SEE CONCEPT
38

placebo [*n*] *fake pill*
inactive drug, inactive medicine, inactive substance, sugar pill, test substance; SEE CONCEPTS
260,412

placid [*adj*] *calm, mild*
collected, composed, cool*, cool as a cucumber*, detached, easygoing, equable, even, even-
tempered, gentle, halcyon, hushed,
imperturbable, irenic, peaceful, poised, quiet,
restful, self-possessed, serene, still, tranquil; SEE
CONCEPTS 401,485

plagiarism [*n*] *copying of another's written work*
appropriation, borrowing, counterfeiting, crib-
bing, falsification, fraud, infringement, lifting,
literary theft, piracy, stealing, theft; SEE CON-
CEPTS 139,192

plague [*n1*] *disease that is widespread*
affliction, contagion, curse, epidemic, hydra, infection, infestation, influenza, invasion, outbreak, pandemic, pestilence, rash, ravage,
scourge; SEE CONCEPT 306

plague [*n2*] *annoyance, curse*
affliction, aggravation, bane, besetment, blast,
blight, bother, botheration, calamity, cancer, evil,
exasperation, hydra, irritant, nuisance, pain, pest,
problem, scourge, thorn in side, torment, trial,
vexation; SEE CONCEPTS 674,679

plague [*v*] *annoy, disturb*
afflict, badger, bedevil, beleaguer, bother, chafe,
fret, gall, gnaw, harass, harry, hassle, haunt, hector, hound, infest, irk, molest, pain, persecute,
pester, pursue, ride, tease, torment, torture, trouble, vex, worry; SEE CONCEPTS 7,14,19

plaid [*adj*] *checkered*
checked, tartan, variegated; SEE CONCEPTS
259,625

plain [*adj1*] *clear, obvious*
apparent, audible, big as life*, broad, comprehensible, definite, distinct, evident, legible, lucid,
manifest, open, open-and-shut*, palpable, patent,
talking turkey*, transparent, understandable, visible; SEE CONCEPTS 529,535,576

plain [*adj2*] *straightforward in speech*
abrupt, artless, blunt, candid, direct, forthright,
frank, guileless, honest, impolite, ingenuous,
open, outspoken, rude, sincere; SEE CONCEPT 267

plain [*adj3*] *normal, everyday*
average, common, commonplace, conventional,
dull, homely, lowly, modest, ordinary, quotidian,
routine, simple, traditional, usual, vanilla*,
white-bread*, workaday; SEE CONCEPT 547

plain [*adj4*] *unembellished, basic*
austere, bare, bare bones*, clean, discreet, dry,
modest, muted, pure, restrained, severe, simple,
spartan, stark, stripped down, unvarnished,
vanilla*; SEE CONCEPTS 485,589

plain [*adj5*] *ugly*
deformed, hard on the eyes*, homely, not beautiful, ordinary, plain-featured; SEE CONCEPT 579

plain [*n*] *level land*
champaign, expanse, field, flat, flatland, grassland, heath, level, meadow, moor, moorland,

open country, plateau, prairie, steppe, tundra;
SEE CONCEPT 509

plaintive [*adj*] *pathetic, woebegone*
beefing*, bellyaching*, cantankerous, crabby*,
cranky*, disconsolate, doleful, grief-stricken,
grievous, grousing, grumpy*, heartrending,
lamenting, lugubrious, melancholy, mournful,
out of sorts*, pathetic, piteous, pitiful, rueful,
sad, saddening, sorrowful, wailing, wistful, woeful; SEE CONCEPTS 401,529

plan [*n1*] *scheme, design, way of doing things*
aim, angle, animus, arrangement, big picture*,
contrivance, course of action, deal, device, disposition, expedient, game plan, gimmick, ground
plan, idea, intent, intention, layout, machination,
meaning, means, method, orderliness, outline,
pattern, picture, platform, plot, policy, procedure, program, project, projection, proposal,
proposition, purpose, scenario, stratagem, strategy, suggestion, system, tactics, treatment, trick,
undertaking; SEE CONCEPT 660

plan [*n2*] *written description; diagram*
agenda, agendum, blueprint, chart, delineation,
draft, drawing, form, illustration, layout, map,
projection, prospectus, representation, road map,
rough draft, scale drawing, sketch, time line,
view; SEE CONCEPTS 268,271,625

plan [*v1*] *think out; prepare in advance*
arrange, bargain for, block out, blueprint, brainstorm*, calculate, concoct, conspire, contemplate, contrive, cook up*, craft, design, devise,
draft, engineer, figure on, figure out, fix to, form,
formulate, frame, hatch*, intrigue, invent, lay in
provisions, line up*, make arrangements, map,
meditate, organize, outline, plot, project, quarterback*, ready, reckon on, represent, rough in*,
scheme, set out, shape, sketch, steer, trace, work
out; SEE CONCEPT 36

plan [*v2*] *intend, mean*
aim, bargain for*, contemplate, count on, design,
envisage, foresee, have every intention*, mind,
propose, purpose, reckon on*; SEE CONCEPTS
26,35

plane [*adj*] *level, horizontal*
even, flat, flush, plain, planate, regular, smooth,
uniform; SEE CONCEPTS 490,581

plane [*n1*] *flat surface; level*
condition, degree, extension, face, facet, footing,
grade, horizontal, obverse, position, sphere, stratum; SEE CONCEPTS 744,757

plane [*n2*] *aircraft*
airbus, airplane, airship, bird*, craft, crate, jet,
ship, twin-engine; SEE CONCEPT 504

planet [*n*] *celestial body orbiting a star*
apple*, asteroid, earth, globe, heavenly body, luminous body, marble, orb*, planetoid, sphere,
terrene, wandering star*, world; SEE CONCEPT
511

plant [*n1*] *organism belonging to the vegetable
kingdom*
annual, biennial, bush, creeper*, cutting*,
flower, grass, greenery, herb, perennial, seedling,
shoot, shrub, slip, sprout, tree, vine, weed; SEE
CONCEPT 429

plant [*n2*] *factory and its buildings, equipment*
apparatus, forge, foundry, gear, machinery, manufactory, mill, shop, works, yard; SEE CONCEPTS
439,449,463,496

plant [*v1*] *put in the ground for growing*
bury, cover, farm, grow, implant, pitch, pot,

pi
pl

raise, scatter, seed, seed down, set out, sow, start, stock, transplant; SEE CONCEPTS *178,253*

plant [*v2*] *establish, set*
deposit, fix, found, imbed, insert, install, institute, lodge, park, plank, plank down, plop, plunk, root, settle, station; SEE CONCEPTS *18,201,221*

plantation [*n*] *large farm*
estate, farmstead, hacienda, homestead, orchard, ranch, vineyard; SEE CONCEPTS *258,449,509,517*

plaster [*n*] *thick, gooey material that hardens*
adhesive, binding, cement, coat, dressing, glue, gum, gypsum, lime, mortar, mucilage, paste, plaster of Paris, stucco; SEE CONCEPTS *466,475*

plaster [*v*] *spread, smear*
adhere, bedaub, besmear, bind, cement, coat, cover, daub, glue, gum, overlay, paste, smudge; SEE CONCEPT *202*

plastered [*adj*] *drunk*
bashed, blitzed*, bombed*, boozed up*, buzzed*, crocked*, dead drunk*, dead to the world*, drinking, drunk as a skunk*, drunken, feeling good*, feeling no pain*, flushed*, flying*, fried*, gone*, groggy, half-crocked*, half in the bag*, high*, hooched up*, inebriated, juiced*, liquored up*, lit*, loaded*, pissed*, polluted*, potted*, sauced*, schnockered*, seeing double*, sloshed*, stewed*, stoned*, tanked*, three sheets to the wind*, tipsy, totaled*, under the influence, under the table*, wasted*, woozy*, zonked*; SEE CONCEPTS *314,545*

plastic [*adj1*] *flexible, soft; made of manufactured, treated compounds*
bending, ductile, elastic, fictile, formable, moldable, molded, pliable, pliant, resilient, shapeable, supple, workable; SEE CONCEPT *604*

plastic [*adj2*] *easily influenced*
amenable, bending, compliant, docile, ductile, flexible, giving, impressionable, influenceable, malleable, manageable, moldable, pliable, pliant, receptive, responsive, suggestible, supple, susceptible, tractable, yielding; SEE CONCEPT *542*

plastic [*adj3*] *artificial; made of manufactured compounds*
cast, chemical, ersatz, false, manufactured, phony, pseudo*, substitute, synthetic, unnatural; SEE CONCEPT *582*

plastic surgery [*n*] *cosmetic surgery*
blepharoplasty, breast implant, breast reduction, collagen injections, dermabrasion, dermatoplasty, eyelift, face-lift, face-lifting, liposuction, mammaplasty, mammoplasty, nose job, reconstructive surgery, rhinoplasty, skin grafting, suction lipectomy, tummy tuck; SEE CONCEPT *310*

plate [*n1*] *dish or meal served*
bowl, casserole, course, helping, platter, portion, service, serving, trencher; SEE CONCEPTS *459,493*

plate [*n2*] *sheet, panel*
coat, disc, flake, foil, lamella, lamina, layer, leaf, plane, print, scale, slab, slice, spangle, stratum; SEE CONCEPT *475*

plate [*v*] *coat with metallic material*
anodize, bronze, chrome, cover, electroplate, enamel, encrust, face, flake, foil, gild, laminate, layer, nickel, overlay, platinize, scale, silver, stratify; SEE CONCEPTS *172,202*

plateau [*n*] *level; flat, often high, land*
elevation, highland, mesa, plain, stage, table, tableland, upland; SEE CONCEPTS *509,744*

platform [*n1*] *stand or stage*
belvedere, dais, floor, podium, pulpit, rostrum, scaffold, scaffolding, staging, terrace; SEE CONCEPTS *440,443*

platform [*n2*] *political stance, promises*
manifesto, objectives, party line*, plank, policy, principle, program, soapbox*, stump*, tenets; SEE CONCEPTS *278,689*

platitude [*n*] *dull, overused saying*
banality, boiler plate*, bromide*, buzzword, chestnut*, cliché, commonplace, corn*, evenness, familiar tune*, flatness, hackneyed saying, high camp*, hokum*, inanity, insipidity, monotony, motto, old chestnut*, old story*, potboiler*, prosaicism, proverb, saw*, shibboleth, stereotype, tag*, triteness, trite remark, triviality, truism, vapidity, verbiage; SEE CONCEPTS *278,388*

platonic [*adj*] *expressing nonphysical love*
ideal, idealistic, intellectual, quixotic, spiritual, transcendent, Utopian, visionary; SEE CONCEPTS *403,555*

platoon [*n*] *group of military people*
army, array, batch, battery, bunch, clump, cluster, company, detachment, lot, outfit, parcel, patrol, set, squad, squadron, team, troop, unit; SEE CONCEPTS *322,417*

plaudits [*n*] *applause*
acclaim, acclamation, accolade, big hand, cheering, cheers, clapping, commendation, hand, hurrahs, kudos, laudation, ovation, praise, raves, rooting, stamping, standing ovation; SEE CONCEPTS *69,189*

plausible [*adj*] *reasonable, believable*
conceivable, credible, creditable, like enough*, likely, logical, persuasive, possible, presumable, probable, smooth, sound, supposable, tenable, valid, very likely; SEE CONCEPT *552*

play [*n1*] *theater piece*
comedy, curtain-raiser*, drama, entertainment, farce, flop*, hit*, mask*, musical, one-act*, opera, performance, potboiler*, show, smash*, smash hit*, stage show, theatrical, tragedy, turkey*; SEE CONCEPT *263*

play [*n2*] *amusement, entertainment*
caper, dalliance, delight, disport, diversion, foolery, frisk, frolic, fun, gambol, game, gaming, happiness, humor, jest, joking, lark, match, pastime, pleasure, prank, recreation, relaxation, romp, sport, sportiveness, teasing; SEE CONCEPTS *292,363*

play [*n3*] *latitude, range*
action, activity, elbowroom*, exercise, give, leeway, margin, motion, movement, operation, room, scope, space, sweep, swing, working*; SEE CONCEPTS *651,745*

play [*v1*] *have fun*
amuse oneself, be life of party*, caper, carouse, carry on, cavort, clown, cut capers, cut up*, dally, dance, disport, divert, entertain oneself, fool around, frisk, frolic, gambol, go on a spree*, horse around*, idle away, joke, jump, kibitz*, kick up heels*, let go*, let loose*, let one's hair down*, make merry, mess around*, rejoice, revel, romp, show off, skip, sport, toy, trifle; SEE CONCEPTS *292,384*

play [*v2*] *compete in sport*
be on a team, challenge, contend, contest, disport, engage in, participate, recreate, rival, sport, take on, take part, vie; SEE CONCEPTS *92,363*

play [*v3*] *act; take the part of*
act the part of, discourse, do*, enact, execute,

ham*, ham it up*, impersonate, lay an egg*, perform, personate, playact, play a gig*, portray, present, read a part, represent, take the role of, tread the boards*; SEE CONCEPT 292

play [v4] *gamble, risk*
bet, chance, exploit, finesse, game, hazard, jockey*, lay money on*, maneuver, manipulate, put, set, speculate, stake, take, wager; SEE CONCEPTS 341,363

play [v5] *produce music*
blow, bow, drum, execute, fiddle, fidget, finger, operate, pedal, perform, render, tickle, work; SEE CONCEPT 65

play ball [v] *cooperate*
agree, be in cahoots, collaborate, comply with, conspire, go along with, join forces, join in, participate, play the game*, pull together, stick together, work together; SEE CONCEPTS 110,112

play dirty [v] *cheat*
bamboozle*, beguile, bend the rules*, bilk, burn, caboodle, chisel, con, deceive, defraud, do a number on*, double-cross, double-deal, dupe, finagle, fleece, flimflam, fudge*, hit below the belt*, hoodwink, hose, mislead, pull something funny*, rip off*, rook*, sandbag, scam, screw, shaft, stack the cards*, stretch the rules*, sucker, swindle, trick, victimize; SEE CONCEPTS 59,139,192

play down [v] *pretend as if something were unimportant*
belittle, deemphasize, gloss over*, hold back*, make light of*, make little of*, minimize, mute, restrain, soften, soft-pedal*, underplay, underrate; SEE CONCEPTS 49,59,63

player [n1] *person participating in sport*
amateur, athlete, champ, competitor, contestant, jock*, member, opponent, participant, pro, professional, rookie, sportsperson, superjock*, sweat*, team player; SEE CONCEPT 366

player [n2] *person who acts in performance*
actor, bit player, entertainer, extra, ham*, hambone*, impersonator, lead, mime, mimic, performer, playactor, scene stealer*, stand-in, star, thespian, trouper, understudy, walk-on; SEE CONCEPT 352

player [n3] *person who produces music*
artist, instrumentalist, musician, music maker, performer, rocker, soloist, virtuoso; SEE CONCEPT 352

playful [adj] *funny, fun-loving*
antic, blithe, cheerful, coltish*, comical, elvish*, feeling one's oats*, flirtatious, frisky, frolicsome, full of pep*, gamesome, gay, good-natured, impish, jaunty, jesting, jocund, joking, joyous, lighthearted, lively, merry, mirthful, mischievous, prankish, puckish, rollicking, snappy, spirited, sportive, sprightly, teasing, tongue-in-cheek*, vivacious, waggish, whimsical, zippy*; SEE CONCEPTS 401,542

playground [n] *recreation area*
jungle gym, park, playing field; SEE CONCEPTS 509,513

play it safe [v] *be cautious*
avoid risk, be on the safe side, hedge one's bets*, take no chances, take precautions; SEE CONCEPTS 401,403

plaything [n] *toy*
amusement, bauble, doll, gadget, game, gimcrack, pastime, trifle, trinket; SEE CONCEPT 446

play up [v] *emphasize*
accentuate, bring to the fore*, call attention to, feature, highlight, italicize*, magnify, make a production of*, point up, stress, turn spotlight on*, underline, underscore; SEE CONCEPT 49

playwright [n] *person who writes for the theater*
author, dramatist, dramaturge, dramaturgist, librettist, scenarist, scripter, tragedian, writer; SEE CONCEPT 348

plaza [n] *central location, spot*
common, court, green, park, square, village green; SEE CONCEPTS 509,513

plea [n1] *begging request*
appeal, application, entreaty, imploration, imprecation, intercession, orison, overture, petition, prayer, round robin*, solicitation, suit, supplication; SEE CONCEPT 662

plea [n2] *excuse, defense*
action, alibi, allegation, apology, argument, cause, claim, cop-out*, explanation, extenuation, fish tale*, justification, mitigation, out, palliation, pleading, pretext, rationalization, right, song and dance*, story, vindication, whitewash*; SEE CONCEPTS 57,278,318

plead [v1] *beg, request*
appeal, ask, beseech, cop a plea*, crave, crawl, entreat, entreaty, implore, importune, make up for, petition, pray, solicit, square things*, supplicate; SEE CONCEPT 48

plead [v2] *present a defense*
adduce, advocate, allege, answer charges, argue, assert, avouch, cite, cop a plea*, declare, give evidence, maintain, plea bargain, present, put forward, respond, use as excuse, vouch; SEE CONCEPTS 49,317

pleasant [adj] *acceptable; friendly*
affable, agreeable, amiable, amusing, bland, charming, cheerful, civil, civilized, congenial, convivial, cool*, copacetic, cordial, delectable, delightful, diplomatic, enchanting, engaging, enjoyable, fine, fine and dandy*, fun, genial, goodhumored, gracious, gratifying, homey, jolly, jovial, kindly, likable, lovely, mild, mild-mannered, nice, obliging, pleasing, pleasurable, polite, refreshing, satisfying, social, soft, sweet, sympathetic, urbane, welcome; SEE CONCEPTS 542,548,572

pleasantry [n] *nice remark*
badinage, banter, bon mot*, humor, jest, joke, joking, levity, merriment, quip, quirk, repartee, sally*, squib*, wit, witticism; SEE CONCEPTS 273,278

please [v1] *delight, make happy*
amuse, charm, cheer, content, enchant, entertain, fill the bill*, gladden, go over big*, grab, gratify, hit the spot*, humor, indulge, kill*, make the grade*, overjoy, satisfy, score, suit, sweep off feet*, tickle*, tickle pink*, titillate, turn on*, wow*; SEE CONCEPTS 7,22

please [v2] *will, elect to do*
be inclined, choose, command, demand, desire, like, opt, prefer, see fit, want, wish; SEE CONCEPT 20

pleasing/pleasurable [adj] *welcome, nice*
agreeable, amiable, amusing, charming, congenial, delightful, enchanting, engaging, enjoyable, entertaining, favorable, good, grateful, gratifying, likable, luscious, musical, palatable, pleasant, polite, satisfactory, satisfying, savory, suitable, sweet, winning; SEE CONCEPTS 537,572

pleasure [n1] *delight, happiness*
amusement, bliss, buzz*, comfort, contentment, delectation, diversion, ease, enjoyment, entertainment, felicity, flash*, fruition, game, gladness, gluttony, gratification, gusto, hobby, indulgence, joie de vivre, joy, joyride*, kick*, kicks*, luxury, primrose path*, recreation, relish, revelry, satisfaction, seasoning, self-indulgence, solace, spice, thrill, titillation, turn-on*, velvet*, zest; SEE CONCEPTS **388,410**

pleasure [n2] *will, inclination*
choice, command, desire, fancy, liking, mind, option, preference, purpose, velleity, want, wish; SEE CONCEPTS **20,659**

plebeian [adj] *base, lower-class*
banal, coarse, common, conventional, humble, ignoble, low, lowborn, lowly, mean, ordinary, pedestrian, popular, proletarian, traditional, uncultivated, unrefined, unsophisticated, unwashed*, vulgar, working-class; SEE CONCEPT **549**

plebeian [n] *person of lower class*
commonalty, commoner, common people, peasant, person in the street*, pleb*, plebe*, proletarian, rank and file*; SEE CONCEPTS **413,423**

pledge [n1] *word of honor*
agreement, assurance, covenant, guarantee, health, oath, promise, toast, undertaking, vow, warrant, word; SEE CONCEPTS **71,278**

pledge [n2] *sign of good faith*
bail, bond, collateral, deposit, earnest, gage, guarantee, guaranty, pawn, security, surety, token, warrant, warranty; SEE CONCEPTS **318,332,446**

pledge [v] *guarantee; give word of honor*
contract, covenant, engage, give word*, hock*, hook*, mortgage, pawn, plight, promise, sign for, soak*, swear, undertake, vouch, vow; SEE CONCEPT **71**

plenary [adj] *entire, whole*
absolute, complete, full, general, inclusive, open, sweeping, thorough; SEE CONCEPT **531**

plentiful/plenty [adj] *abundant, productive*
abounding, ample, bounteous, bountiful, bumper*, chock-full*, complete, copious, enough, excessive, extravagant, exuberant, fertile, flowing, flush*, fruitful, full, fulsome, generous, improvident, infinite, large, lavish, liberal, lousy with*, lush, luxuriant, overflowing, plenteous, prodigal, profuse, prolific, replete, rife, sufficient, superabundant, superfluous, swarming, swimming, teeming; SEE CONCEPTS **762,781**

plenty [n] *much, abundance*
affluence, avalanche*, capacity, copiousness, cornucopia, deluge*, enough, flood*, fruitfulness, full house*, fund, good deal*, great deal*, heaps*, loads*, lots, luxury, mass, masses*, mine*, mountains*, oodles*, opulence, peck*, piles*, plethora, profusion, prosperity, quantity, stacks*, store, sufficiency, torrent*, volume, wealth; SEE CONCEPTS **767,787**

plethora [n] *excess*
deluge, flood, glut, many, much, overabundance, overflow, overkill, overmuch, plenty, profusion, superabundance, superfluity, surfeit, surplus; SEE CONCEPTS **767,787**

pliable [adj] *bendable, adaptable*
compliant, docile, ductile, easily led, easy, flexible, impressionable, limber, lithe, malleable, manageable, manipulable, moldable, obedient, plastic, pliant, putty*, receptive, responsive, rolling with the punches*, spongy, submissive, supple, susceptible, tractable, yielding; SEE CONCEPTS **404,488**

plight [n] *dilemma, difficulty; situation*
bad news*, circumstances, condition, corner*, double trouble*, extremity, fix*, hole*, impasse, jam, perplexity, pickle*, pinch*, predicament, quandary, scrape*, spot*, state*, straits, tight situation, trouble; SEE CONCEPTS **666,674**

plod [v1] *walk heavily*
clump*, drag, flounder, hike, lumber*, plug, schlepp*, slog*, stamp, stomp, toil, tramp, trample, tread, tromp, trudge, wallow; SEE CONCEPT **151**

plod [v2] *work slowly and under duress*
bear down*, buckle down*, drudge, grind, knuckle down*, labor, persevere, plough through*, plug away*, scratch*, slave, sweat*, toil; SEE CONCEPTS **87,677**

plot [n1] *plan, scheme*
artifice, booby trap*, cabal, collusion, complicity, connivance, conniving, conspiracy, contrivance, covin, design, device, fix, frame, frame-up*, game, intrigue, little game*, machination, maneuver, practice, ruse, scam, setup, stratagem, trick; SEE CONCEPT **660**

plot [n2] *story line*
action, design, development, enactment, events, incidents, movement, narrative, outline, picture, progress, scenario, scene, scheme, story, structure, subject, suspense, theme, thread, unfolding; SEE CONCEPTS **264,282**

plot [n3] *tract of land*
acreage, allotment, area, division, ground, land, lot, parcel, patch, piece, plat, spread; SEE CONCEPTS **509,513**

plot [v1] *plan, scheme*
angle, brew*, cabal, cogitate, collude, conceive, concoct, connive, conspire, contrive, cook up*, design, devise, draft, finagle, frame, hatch*, imagine, intrigue, lay*, machinate, maneuver, operate, outline, project, promote, rough out*, set up, sketch, wangle; SEE CONCEPT **36**

plot [v2] *map out; draw*
calculate, chart, compute, draft, lay out, locate, mark, outline, put forward; SEE CONCEPTS **36,79,174**

plow [v] *dig up ground for cultivation*
break, break ground, bulldoze, cultivate, farm, furrow, harrow, harvest, list, push, rake, reap, ridge, rush, shove, smash, till, trench, turn, turn over; SEE CONCEPT **178**

ploy [n] *game, trick*
artifice, contrivance, device, dodge, feint, gambit, maneuver, move, play, ruse, scheme, stratagem, subterfuge, tactic, wile; SEE CONCEPT **59**

pluck [n] *person's resolution, courage*
backbone*, boldness, bravery, dauntlessness, determination, grit, guts*, hardihood, heart*, intestinal fortitude*, intrepidity, mettle, moxie*, nerve, resolution, spirit, spunk; SEE CONCEPT **411**

pluck [v] *grab, pull out; pick at*
catch, clutch, collect, cull, draw, finger, gather, harvest, jerk, plunk, pull at, snatch, strum, tug, tweak, yank; SEE CONCEPT **206**

plucky [adj] *brave*
adventurous, bold, confident, courageous, daring, determined, fearless, game, gritty, gutsy, heroic, lionhearted, nervy, persevering, spirited,

sporting, spunky, stalwart, tenacious, unafraid, undaunted, unfearful, valiant; SEE CONCEPT *401*

plug [*n1*] *stopper*
bung, connection, cork, filling, fitting, occlusion, river, spigot, stopple, tampon, wedge; SEE CONCEPTS *471,836*

plug [*n2*] *publicity*
advertisement, blurb*, good word*, hype*, mention, push*, write-up; SEE CONCEPT *274*

plug [*v1*] *stop up*
block, bung, choke, clog, close, congest, cork, cover, drive in, fill, obstruct, occlude, pack, ram, seal, secure, stop, stopper, stopple, stuff; SEE CONCEPT *209*

plug [*v2*] *publicize*
advertise, boost*, build up*, hype*, mention, promote, push*, write up*; SEE CONCEPTS *49,60*

plum [*n*] *reward, prize*
asset, bonus, carrot*, catch*, cream*, dividend, find, meed, nugget*, pick, premium, treasure; SEE CONCEPTS *337,712*

plumb [*adj*] *vertical*
erect, perpendicular, sheer, straight, straight up, up and down, upright; SEE CONCEPT *581*

plumb [*v*] *probe, go into*
delve, explore, fathom, gauge, get to the bottom of*, measure, penetrate, search, sound, take soundings, unravel; SEE CONCEPTS *181,216,291*

plummet [*v*] *fall hard and fast*
collapse, crash, decline, decrease, descend, dip, dive, downturn, drop, drop down, dump, fall, nose-dive, plunge, precipitate, sink, skid, stoop, swoop, tumble; SEE CONCEPTS *181,698,763*

plump [*adj*] *chubby, fat*
beefy*, burly, buxom, chunky*, corpulent, filled, fleshy, full, obese, portly, pudgy*, rotund, round, stout, tubby*; SEE CONCEPT *491*

plunder [*n*] *something stolen*
booty, goods*, graft, hot goods*, loot, make*, pickings*, pillage, plunderage, prey, prize, quarry, rapine, raven, spoil, stuff*, take*, trappings*, winnings*; SEE CONCEPT *710*

plunder [*v*] *ravage, steal*
appropriate, burn, depredate, despoil, devastate, fleece, forage, foray, grab, gut, kip, knock off*, knock over*, lay waste, liberate, lift, loft, loot, maraud, moonlight requisition*, pillage, prey, prowl, raid, ransack, relieve, requisition, rifle, rip off*, rob, sack, salvage, smash and grab*, snatch, spoil, stick up*, strip; SEE CONCEPTS *86,139,252*

plunge [*n*] *quick drop; enthusiastic attempt*
belly flop*, descent, dive, duck, dunk, fall, high dive, immersion, investment, jump, nose-dive, spree, submergence, submersion, swoop, venture; SEE CONCEPTS *100,150,152,181,194*

plunge [*v*] *dive or fall fast*
belly-flop*, career, cast, charge, dash, descend, dip, drive, drop, duck, fling, go down, go the limit, go whole hog*, hurtle, immerge, immerse, jump, keel, lunge, lurch, nose-dive, pitch, plummet, plunk, propel, rush, shoot the works*, sink, sound, submerge, submerse, swoop, take a flyer*, take a header*, tear, throw, throw oneself, thrust, topple, tumble; SEE CONCEPTS *100,150,152,181,194*

plunk [*v*] *throw down*
drop, dump, plonk, plop, plump, unload; SEE CONCEPTS *181,200*

plural [*adj*] *more than one*
dual, many, multiple, not alone, not singular, numerous; SEE CONCEPTS *564,762,772*

plurality [*n*] *large part of a group*
advantage, bulk, greater part, lead, majority, mass, most, multiplicity, nearly all, numerousness, preponderance, profusion, variety; SEE CONCEPTS *382,829*

plus [*adj*] *added, extra*
additional, augmented, boosted, enlarged, expanded, increased, positive, supplementary, surplus; SEE CONCEPTS *762,771*

plus [*n*] *asset; something added*
advantage, benefit, bonus, extra, gain, good point, overage, overstock, oversupply, perk, surplus; SEE CONCEPT *693*

plush [*adj*] *luxurious, rich*
costly, deluxe, elegant, lavish, luscious, lush, luxury, opulent, palatial, ritzy, silken, sumptuous; SEE CONCEPTS *334,589*

ply [*v*] *use, work at*
carry on, dispense, employ, exercise, exert, follow, function, handle, maneuver, manipulate, practice, pursue, put out, swing, throw, utilize, wield; SEE CONCEPTS *100,225*

poach [*v*] *infringe upon; trespass*
appropriate, encroach, filch, fish illegally, hunt illegally, intrude, pilfer, plunder, rob, smuggle, steal; SEE CONCEPTS *139,192*

pocket [*adj*] *small, portable*
abridged, canned, capsule, compact, concise, condensed, diminutive, epitomized, itsy-bitsy*, little, midget, miniature, minute, peewee*, pint-sized*, potted, tiny, wee; SEE CONCEPT *773*

pocket [*n*] *cavity, pouch*
bag, chamber, compartment, hole, hollow, opening, receptacle, sack, socket; SEE CONCEPTS *452,513*

pocket [*v*] *help oneself to something*
abstract, appropriate, conceal, enclose, filch, hide, lift, nab, pilfer, pinch, purloin, shoplift, steal, swipe, take; SEE CONCEPTS *139,142*

pocketbook [*n*] *accessory for carrying personal items*
bag, clutch, frame, handbag, hide, leather, pouch, purse, reticule, suitcase, wallet; SEE CONCEPTS *446,450*

pockmark [*n*] *pitlike scare*
blemish, cavity, crater, dent, dimple, pimple, welt, zit; SEE CONCEPT *580*

pod [*n/v*] *encasement of vegetable seeds*
capsule, case, covering, hull, husk, sheath, sheathing, shell, shuck, skin, vessel; SEE CONCEPTS *428,484*

podium [*n*] *structure from which speakers orate*
dais, platform, pulpit, rostrum, soapbox*, stage, stump*; SEE CONCEPT *443*

poem [*n*] *highly expressive, rhythmical literary piece*
ballad, beat, blank verse, composition, creation, epic, free verse, haiku, limerick, lines, lyric, ode, poesy, poetry, quatrain, rhyme, rime, rune, sestina, song, sonnet, verse, villanelle, words, writing; SEE CONCEPTS *268,282*

poet [*n*] *person who writes expressive, rhythmic verse*
artist, author, balladist, bard, dilettante, dramatist, librettist, lyricist, lyrist, maker, metrist, odist, parodist, poetaster, rhapsodist, rhymer,

pl
po

rimer, sonnetist, versifier, writer; SEE CONCEPTS 348,423

poetic [*adj*] *with rhythm and beauty; related to poetic composition*
anapestic, dactylic, dramatic, elegiac, epic, epical, epodic, iambic, idyllic, imaginative, lyric, lyrical, melodious, metrical, odic, rhythmical, romantic, songlike, tuneful; SEE CONCEPT 267

poetry [*n*] *expressive, rhythmic literary work*
balladry, doggerel, metrical composition, paean, poems, poesy, rhyme, rhyming, rime, rune, song, stanza, verse, versification; SEE CONCEPTS 268,282,349

poignant [*adj1*] *affecting, painful*
agitating, agonizing, bitter, distressing, disturbing, emotional, heartbreaking, heartrending, impressive, intense, moving, passionate, pathetic, perturbing, piteous, pitiful, sad, sentimental, sorrowful, touching, upsetting; SEE CONCEPTS 529,548

poignant [*adj2*] *sharp, bitter*
acrid, acute, biting, caustic, keen, penetrating, peppery, piercing, piquant, pointed, pungent, racy, sarcastic, severe, snappy, spicy, stinging, tangy, zesty; SEE CONCEPTS 267,613

point [*n1*] *speck*
bit, count, dot, fleck, flyspeck, full stop, iota, mark, minim, mite, mote, notch, particle, period, scrap, stop, tittle, trace; SEE CONCEPTS 79,831

point [*n2*] *specific location*
locality, locus, place, position, site, situation, spot, stage, station, where; SEE CONCEPT 198

point [*n3*] *sharp end, top, end of extension*
apex, awn, barb, beak, bill, cape, claw, cusp, dagger, foreland, head, headland, jag, nib, pin point, prick, prickler, promontory, prong, snag, spike, spine, spire, spur, sticker, stiletto, summit, sword, thorn, tine, tip, tooth; SEE CONCEPTS 827,836

point [*n4*] *circumstance, stage; limited time*
brink, condition, date, degree, duration, edge, extent, instant, juncture, limit, moment, period, point in time, position, threshold, time, verge, very minute; SEE CONCEPTS 696,815

point [*n5*] *goal, aim*
appeal, attraction, bottom line*, charm, cogency, design, effectiveness, end, fascination, intent, intention, interest, motive, name of the game*, nitty-gritty*, nub, nuts and bolts*, object, objective, punch*, purpose, reason, significance, use, usefulness, utility, validity, validness; SEE CONCEPT 659

point [*n6*] *meaning, essence*
argument, bottom line*, burden, core, crux, drift, force, gist, head, heart, idea, import, kicker*, main idea, marrow, matter, meat*, motif, motive, name of the game*, nitty-gritty*, nub, nuts and bolts*, pith, pointer, proposition, punch line*, question, score, stuff, subject, subject matter, text, theme, thrust, tip, tip-off*, topic; SEE CONCEPTS 274,682

point [*n7*] *aspect, characteristic*
attribute, case, circumstance, circumstantial, constituent, detail, element, facet, feature, instance, item, material, nicety, part, particular, peculiarity, property, quality, respect, side, thing*, trait; SEE CONCEPTS 274,411,654

point [*n8*] *scoring unit of sport competition*
count, mark, notch, score, tally; SEE CONCEPTS 364,784

point [*v1*] *show as probable; call attention*
bespeak, button down*, denote, designate, direct, finger*, hint, imply, indicate, lead, make*, name, offer, peg*, pin down*, put down for*, put finger on*, signify, suggest, tab*, tag*; SEE CONCEPTS 118,138

point [*v2*] *direct, lead*
aim, beam*, bring to bear, cast, face, guide, head, influence, lay, level, look, slant, steer, tend, train, turn, zero in*; SEE CONCEPTS 187,201,623

pointed [*adj1*] *having a sharp end or part*
acicular, aciculate, acuminate, acuminous, acute, barbed, cornered, cuspidate, edged, fine, keen, mucronate, peaked, piked, pointy, pronged, sharp, sharp-cornered, spiked; SEE CONCEPTS 490,606

pointed [*adj2*] *penetrating, biting*
accurate, acid, acute, barbed, boiled down, calling a spade a spade*, cutting, in a nutshell*, incisive, insinuating, keen, laid on the line*, legit, meaty*, on the button*, on the nose*, pertinent, pregnant, right-on*, right to it*, sarcastic, sharp, short-and-sweet*, tart, telling, trenchant; SEE CONCEPT 267

pointer [*n1*] *indicator*
arrow, dial, director, gauge, guide, hand, index, mark, needle, register, rod, signal; SEE CONCEPTS 464,498

pointer [*n2*] *hint, suggestion*
advice, caution, clue, information, recommendation, steer, tip, tip-off, warning; SEE CONCEPTS 75,274

pointless [*adj*] *ridiculous, senseless*
absurd, aimless, around in circles*, fruitless, futile, going nowhere*, impotent, inane, inconsequential, ineffective, ineffectual, insignificant, in vicious circle*, irrelevant, meaningless, needle in haystack*, nongermane, nonsensical, not pertinent, on treadmill*, powerless, purportless, remote, silly, stupid, trivial, unavailing, uninteresting, unnecessary, unproductive, unprofitable, useless, vague, vain, worthless; SEE CONCEPTS 529,548

point out [*v*] *call attention to*
advert, allude, bring up, denote, designate, identify, indicate, mention, refer, remind, reveal, show, specify; SEE CONCEPTS 49,73,261

poise [*n*] *self-composure, dignity*
address, aplomb, assurance, balance, bearing, calmness, confidence, cool, coolness, delicatesse, diplomacy, elegance, equability, equanimity, equilibrium, grace, gravity, polish, presence, presence of mind, sangfroid, savoir-faire, self-assurance, self-possession, serenity, stasis, tact, tactfulness, tranquility; SEE CONCEPTS 633,717

poise [*v*] *balance, suspend*
ballast, be ready, brood, float, hang, hold, hover, position, stabilize, stand, steady, support, wait; SEE CONCEPT 154

poison [*n*] *substance that causes harm, death*
adulteration, bacteria, bane, blight, cancer, contagion, contamination, corruption, germ, infection, malignancy, miasma, toxicant, toxin, toxoid, venin, venom, virus; SEE CONCEPTS 307,475,674,675

poison [*v*] *contaminate, pollute*
adulterate, corrupt, debase, defile, deprave, destroy, envenom, fester, harm, infect, injure, kill, make ill, murder, pervert, stain, subvert, taint,

undermine, vitiate, warp; SEE CONCEPTS **14,246,252**

poison/poisonous [*adj*] *harmful*
bad, baleful, baneful, corrupt, corruptive, dangerous, deadly, deleterious, destructive, detrimental, evil, fatal, hurtful, infective, lethal, malicious, malignant, mephitic, miasmatic, morbid, mortal, nocuous, noisome, noxious, peccant, pernicious, pestiferous, pestilential, septic, toxic, toxicant, toxiferous, venomous, vicious, viperous, virulent; SEE CONCEPT **537**

poke [*n*] *push, thrust*
blow, boost, bunt, butt, dig, hit, jab, nudge, prod, punch, shove, stab; SEE CONCEPTS **189,208**

poke [*v1*] *push at; thrust*
arouse, awaken, bulge, butt*, crowd, dig, elbow*, goose*, hit, jab, jostle, jut, nudge*, overhang, prod, project, protrude, provoke, punch, ram, rouse, shoulder*, shove, stab, stand out, stick, stick out, stimulate, stir; SEE CONCEPTS **189,208,723**

poke [*v2*] *interfere, snoop*
busybody*, butt in*, intrude, meddle, nose*, peek, pry, tamper; SEE CONCEPT **384**

poke [*v3*] *move along slowly*
dally, dawdle, delay, drag, get no place fast*, idle, lag, loiter, mosey*, procrastinate, put off*, shlep along*, tarry, toddle*, trail; SEE CONCEPT **151**

poker [*n*] *card game*
blind poker, draw poker, five-card stud poker, seven-card stud poker, straight poker, strip poker, stud poker; SEE CONCEPTS **260,271**

polar [*adj1*] *cold*
arctic, extreme, farthest, freezing, frigid, frozen, glacial, icy, north, south, terminal; SEE CONCEPTS **583,605**

polar [*adj2*] *opposite, opposed*
antagonistic, antipodal, antipodean, antithetical, contradictory, contrary, converse, counter, diametric, reverse; SEE CONCEPT **564**

pole [*n*] *bar, post*
beam, extremity, flagpole, flagstaff, leg, mast, pile, plank, rod, shaft, spar, staff, stake, standard, stave, stick, stilt, stud, terminus; SEE CONCEPTS **440,470,475,479**

police/police officer [*n*] *person, people hired to uphold the laws*
arm of the law*, badge*, bear*, beat cop, black and white*, blue*, bluecoat*, bobby, constable, constabulary, cop*, copper*, corps*, detective, fed*, flatfoot*, force, gendarme, heat*, law, law enforcement, narc*, patrol; SEE CONCEPTS **299,354**

policy [*n*] *procedure, tactics*
action, administration, approach, arrangement, behavior, channels, code, course, custom, design, guideline, line, management, method, order, organization, plan, polity, practice, program, protocol, red tape*, rule, scheme, stratagem, strategy, tenet, the book*, the numbers*, theory; SEE CONCEPTS **6,271,660,688**

polish [*n1*] *shine, brightness*
brilliance, burnish, finish, glaze, glint, gloss, luster, sheen, smoothness, sparkle, varnish, veneer, wax; SEE CONCEPTS **492,611,620**

polish [*n2*] *cultivated look, performance*
breeding, class, cultivation, culture, elegance, finesse, finish, grace, politesse, refinement, style, suavity, urbanity; SEE CONCEPTS **388,633,655**

polish [*v1*] *shine, buff*
brighten, burnish, clean, finish, furbish, glaze, gloss, rub, scour, scrub, sleek, slick, smooth, wax; SEE CONCEPTS **202,215**

polish [*v2*] *improve performance, look*
amend, better, brush up, correct, cultivate, emend, enhance, finish, furbish, make improvement, mature, mend, perfect, refine, round, sleek, slick, smooth, touch up; SEE CONCEPT **244**

polish off [*v*] *finish using*
consume, devour, dispatch, dispose of, do away with*, down*, eat, eat up, eliminate, get rid of*, liquidate, put away*, swill*, use up, wolf*; SEE CONCEPTS **169,225**

polite [*adj*] *mannerly, civilized*
affable, amenable, amiable, attentive, bland, civil, complaisant, concerned, conciliatory, condescending, considerate, cordial, courteous, courtly, cultured, deferential, diplomatic, elegant, friendly, genteel, gentle, good-natured, gracious, mild, neighborly, nice, obliging, obsequious, pleasant, polished, politic, punctilious, refined, respectful, smooth, sociable, solicitous, sympathetic, thoughtful, urbane, well-behaved, well-bred, well-mannered; SEE CONCEPT **401**

politic [*adj*] *wise, tactful*
adroit, advisable, canny*, cool, delicate, diplomatic, discreet, expedient, in one's best interests*, judicious, on the lookout*, perspicacious, prudent, sagacious, sensible, sharp, shrewd, smooth, tactical, tuned in*, urbane; SEE CONCEPT **401**

political [*adj*] *governmental*
bureaucratic, civic, constitutional, economical, legislative, official; SEE CONCEPT **535**

politically correct [*adj*] *sensitive to other political views*
bias-free, considerate, diplomatic, gender-free, inclusive, inoffensive, liberal, multicultural, nondiscriminatory, nonracist, nonsexist, PC*, respectful, sensitive; SEE CONCEPTS **529,542**

politician [*n*] *person pursuing or occupying elective office*
baby-kisser*, boss, chieftain, congressperson, democrat, grandstander*, handshaker*, lawmaker, leader, legislator, member of Congress, member of parliament, officeholder, office seeker, orator, partisan, party member, president, public servant, republican, senator, speaker, statesperson, whistle-stopper*; SEE CONCEPT **359**

politics [*n*] *art and science of administration of government*
affairs of state, backroom*, campaigning, civics, domestic affairs, electioneering, foreign affairs, government, government policy, hat in the ring*, internal affairs, jungle*, legislature, matters of state, political science, polity, smoke-filled room*, statecraft, stateship, zoo*; SEE CONCEPTS **300,301**

poll [*n*] *census; tally of answers to questions of opinion*
ballot, canvass, count, figures, opinion, returns, sampling, survey, vote, voting; SEE CONCEPTS **48,300**

poll [*v*] *take census; question*
ballot, canvass, enroll, examine, interview, list, register, sample, send up a balloon*, survey, tally, test the waters*, vote; SEE CONCEPTS **48,300**

po
po

pollster [*n*] *polltaker*
canvasser, market researcher, public opinion gatherer, sampler, survey taker; SEE CONCEPTS 37,103,197,291

pollutant [*n*] *contaminant*
hazardous waste, poison, pollution, toxic waste, toxin; SEE CONCEPT 720

pollute [*v*] *make dirty; corrupt*
adulterate, alloy, befoul, besmirch, contaminate, debase, debauch, defile, deprave, desecrate, dirty, dishonor, foul, infect, make filthy, mar, poison, profane, soil, spoil, stain, sully, taint, violate; SEE CONCEPTS 246,254

pollution [*n*] *dirtiness, contamination*
abuse, adulteration, besmearing, besmirching, blight, corruption, decomposition, defilement, desecration, deterioration, dirtying, fouling, foulness, impairment, impurity, infection, misuse, polluting, profanation, rottenness, soiling, spoliation, taint, tainting, uncleanness, vitiation; SEE CONCEPT 720

Pollyanna [*n*] *optimist*
dreamer, hoper, idealist, positive thinker; SEE CONCEPTS 410,689

poltergeist [*n*] *ghost*
apparition, appearance, banshee, demon, doppelganger, haunter, kelpie, phantasm, phantom, revenant, specter, spirit, spook, vision, visitor; SEE CONCEPT 370

polygamy [*n*] *plural marriage*
bigamy, polyandry, polygyny; SEE CONCEPTS 297,388

pomp [*n*] *pageantry, display*
affectation, array, ceremonial, ceremony, fanfare, flourish, formality, grandeur, grandiosity, magnificence, ostentation, pageant, panoply, parade, pomposity, ritual, shine, show, solemnity, splendor, state, vainglory; SEE CONCEPTS 335,377,655

pompous [*adj*] *arrogant, egotistic*
affected, bloated, boastful, bombastic, conceited, flatulent, flaunting, flowery, fustian, grandiloquent, grandiose, high and mighty*, highfaluting*, high-flown*, imperious, important, inflated, magisterial, magniloquent, narcissistic, orotund, ostentatious, overbearing, overblown, pontifical, portentous, presumptuous, pretentious, puffed up*, puffy*, rhetorical, self-centered, self-important, selfish, showy, sonorous, stuck-up*, supercilious, turgid, uppity*, vain, vainglorious, windy*; SEE CONCEPTS 267,401,542

poncho [*n*] *cloak*
cape, capote, coat, manteau, mantle, raincoat, shawl, wrap; SEE CONCEPTS 451,475,680

pond [*n*] *small body of water*
basin, dew, duck pond, lagoon, lily pond, millpond, pool, puddle, small lake, splash; SEE CONCEPT 514

ponder [*v*] *think about seriously*
appraise, brood, build castles in air*, cerebrate, cogitate, consider, contemplate, daydream, debate, deliberate, dwell, evaluate, examine, excogitate, figure, give thought to, meditate, mind, moon*, mull, mull over, muse, noodle around*, perpend, pipe dream*, put on thinking cap*, puzzle over, reason, reflect, revolve, ruminate, speculate, study, think out, think over, turn over, weigh, woolgather*; SEE CONCEPTS 17,24

ponderous [*adj*] *heavy, cumbersome*
awkward, bulky, burdensome, clumsy, cumbrous, dull, elephantine, graceless, hefty, huge, laborious, lifeless, lumbering, massive, onerous, oppressive, substantial, troublesome, unhandy, unwieldy, weighty; SEE CONCEPTS 491,565

ponderous [*adj*] *dreary, tedious*
arid, barren, cardboard*, dry, dull, heavy, humdrum*, labored, lifeless, long-winded*, monotonous, pedantic, pedestrian, plodding, prolix, stiff*, stilted, stodgy, stuffy*, vapid, verbose, wooden*; SEE CONCEPTS 267,529,542

pontificate [*v*] *sermonize*
address, admonish, dogmatize, evangelize, get on a soapbox*, give sermon, harangue, lecture, minister, moralize, preach, pulpiteer, teach; SEE CONCEPTS 51,75,285,367

pool [*n1*] *collection of liquid*
basin, bath, lagoon, lake, mere, millpond, mud puddle, natatorium, pond, puddle, splash, swimming pool, tank, tarn; SEE CONCEPTS 364,514

pool [*n2*] *supply of money, goods*
bank, combine, conglomerate, equipment, funds, group, jackpot, kitty*, pot, provisions, stakes; SEE CONCEPTS 340,432

pool [*v*] *combine*
amalgamate, blend, join forces, league, merge, put together, share; SEE CONCEPTS 113,193

pooped [*adj*] *tired*
beat*, burned out*, bushed*, collapsing, dead on one's feet*, dog-tired*, done for*, done in*, drained, drooping, drowsy, enervated, exhausted, fatigued, fried*, out of gas*, overworked, played out*, run-down, run ragged, shot*, sleepy, spent, tuckered out, wasted, weary, worn out; SEE CONCEPTS 314,403,406

poor [*adj1*] *lacking sufficient money*
bad off*, bankrupt, beggared, beggarly, behind eight ball*, broke*, destitute, dirt poor*, downand-out*, empty-handed*, flat*, flat broke*, fortuneless, hard up*, impecunious, impoverished, indigent, in need, insolvent, in want, low, meager, moneyless, necessitous, needy, penniless, penurious, pinched*, poverty-stricken, reduced*, scanty*, stone broke*, strapped*, suffering, truly needy, underprivileged, unprosperous; SEE CONCEPT 334

poor [*adj2*] *deficient, inadequate*
base, below par, common, contemptible, crude, diminutive, dwarfed, exiguous, faulty, feeble, humble, imperfect, incomplete, inferior, insignificant, insufficient, lacking, low-grade, lowly, meager, mean, mediocre, miserable, modest, niggardly*, ordinary, paltry, pitiable, pitiful, plain, reduced, rotten, scanty, second-rate*, shabby, shoddy, skimpy, slight, sorry*, sparse, subnormal, subpar, substandard, trifling, trivial, unsatisfactory, valueless, weak, worthless; SEE CONCEPTS 570,574

poor [*adj3*] *weak, unfertile*
bare, barren, depleted, exhausted, feeble, fruitless, impaired, imperfect, impoverished, indisposed, infertile, infirm, puny, sick, sterile, unfruitful, unproductive, worthless; SEE CONCEPT 314

poor [*adj4*] *unfortunate, unhappy*
commiserable, hapless, ill-fated, luckless, miserable, pathetic, piteous, pitiable, pitiful, rueful, unlucky, wretched; SEE CONCEPTS 542,548

poorly [*adj*] *not well*
ailing, below par, failing, ill, indisposed, low,

mean, out of sorts*, rotten*, sick, sickly, under the weather*, unwell; SEE CONCEPT *314*

poorly [*adv*] *unsatisfactorily*
badly, crudely, defectively, inadequately, incompetently, inexpertly, inferiorly, insufficiently, meanly, shabbily, unsuccessfully; SEE CONCEPTS *544,571,574*

pop [*n*] *bang*
burst, crack, explosion, jump, leap, report, snap, strike, thrust, whack; SEE CONCEPT *595*

pop [*v*] *jump, burst*
appear, bang, blow, crack, dart, explode, go, go off, hit, insert, leap, protrude, push, put, report, rise, shove, snap, sock, stick, strike, thrust, whack; SEE CONCEPT *145*

poppycock [*n*] *nonsense*
babble, balderdash*, baloney*, bull*, bunk*, drivel, empty talk, foolery, foolishness, gibberish, hogwash*, hooey*, hot air*, jive*, malarkey, mumbo jumbo*, palaver, prattle, rubbish, silliness, trash*; SEE CONCEPTS *230,388,633*

popular [*adj*] *well-known, favorite*
accepted, approved, attractive, beloved, caught on*, celebrated, crowd-pleasing*, faddish*, famous, fashionable, favored, in*, in demand, in favor, in the mainstream*, in vogue, leading, likable, liked, lovable, noted, notorious, now*, okay*, pleasing, praised, preferred, prevailing, prominent, promoted, right stuff*, run-after*, selling, social, societal, sought, sought-after, stylish, suitable, the rage*, thing*, trendy, well-liked, well-received; SEE CONCEPTS *555,589*

popular [*adj2*] *common, standard*
accepted, accessible, adopted, approved, conventional, current, demanded, embraced, familiar, general, in demand, in use, ordinary, prevailing, prevalent, proletarian, public, rampant, regnant, rife, ruling, stock, ubiquitous, universal, widespread; SEE CONCEPT *530*

popularity [*n*] *recognition, celebrity*
acceptance, acclaim, adoration, approval, currency, demand, esteem, fame, fashion, fashionableness, favor, following, heyday, idolization, lionization, prevalence, regard, renown, reputation, repute, universality, vogue; SEE CONCEPTS *388,655*

popularize [*v*] *make widely popular, accessible*
catch on, disseminate, familiarize, generalize, give currency, make available, promote, restore, resurrect, revive, simplify, spread, universalize; SEE CONCEPTS *324,384*

population [*n*] *inhabitants of a place*
citizenry, community, culture, denizens, dwellers, folk, natives, people, populace, public, residents, society, state; SEE CONCEPT *379*

populous [*adj*] *packed with inhabitants*
crawling, crowded, dense, heavily populated, jammed, legion, many, multifarious, multitudinal, multitudinous, numerous, occupied, overpopulated, peopled, populated, settled, several, swarming, teeming, thick, thronged, various, voluminous; SEE CONCEPT *583*

porch [*n*] *patio*
balcony, deck, portico, steps, stoop, veranda; SEE CONCEPTS *509,513*

pore [*n*] *small aperture in skin*
foramen, opening, orifice, outlet, stoma, sweat gland, vesicle; SEE CONCEPT *418*

pore [*v*] *go over carefully*
brood, contemplate, dwell on, examine, look over, muse, peruse, ponder, read, regard, scan, scrutinize, study; SEE CONCEPTS *24,72,103*

pornographic [*adj*] *obscene*
adult, immoral, indecent, lewd, off-color, offensive, porn*, porno*, prurient, purple*, raunchy*, rough, salacious, sexy, smutty*, steamy*, X-rated*; SEE CONCEPTS *267,372,545*

pornography [*n*] *obscenity*
adult material, adult movie, bawdiness, dirt, dirty movie, erotica, filth, girlie magazine, hard-core pornography, indecency, obscene materials, porn, porno, porno film, sexploitation, sexually explicit material, skin flick, smut, soft-core pornography, stag film, X-rated material, X-rated movie; SEE CONCEPTS *372,545*

porous [*adj*] *having holes; absorbent*
absorptive, penetrable, permeable, pervious, spongelike, spongy; SEE CONCEPT *606*

port [*n*] *place for boat docking, traffic, and storage*
anchorage, boatyard, dockage, docks, dockyard, gate, harbor, harborage, haven, landing, piers, refuge, retreat, roads, roadstead, sanctuary, seaport, shelter, wharf; SEE CONCEPTS *449,509*

portable [*adj*] *easily transported*
carriageable, cartable, compact, convenient, conveyable, easily carried, handy, haulable, light, lightweight, manageable, movable, portative, transportable, wieldy; SEE CONCEPTS *491,584,773*

portal [*n*] *hole or door in vessel*
doorway, entrance, entry, entryway, gate, gateway, ingress, opening, way in; SEE CONCEPT *502*

portend [*v*] *foreshadow, indicate*
adumbrate, augur, be in the cards*, bespeak, betoken, bode, call*, crystal-ball*, forebode, forecast, foreshow, foretell, foretoken, forewarn, harbinger, have a hunch, herald, hint, omen, point to, predict, premonish, presage, prognosticate, promise, prophesy, read, see coming*, threaten, warn of; SEE CONCEPTS *71,78,261*

portent [*n1*] *indication, forewarning*
augury, bodement, boding, caution, clue, foreboding, foreshadowing, foretoken, funny feeling*, handwriting on the wall*, harbinger, hunch, omen, premonition, presage, presentiment, prognostic, prognostication, sign, sinking feeling*, threat, vibes*, warning; SEE CONCEPT *278*

portent [*n2*] *miracle*
marvel, phenomenon, prodigy, sensation, stunner, wonder; SEE CONCEPTS *230,529*

portentous [*adj*] *exciting; foreboding*
alarming, amazing, apocalyptic, astounding, augural, destined, doomed, exhilarating, extraordinary, fated, fateful, haunting, ill-boding, ill-fated, impending, important, inauspicious, inspiring, intriguing, ominous, phenomenal, premonitory, prophetic, remarkable, suggestive, threatening, thrilling; SEE CONCEPTS *529,542,548*

porter [*n*] *person who serves as attendant, caretaker*
baggage carrier, bearer, bellhop, carrier, concierge, doorkeeper, doorperson, gatekeeper, janitor, red cap*, sky cap*, transporter; SEE CONCEPT *348*

portfolio [*n*] *flat case for transporting papers*
attaché case, bag, brief bag, briefcase, case, container, envelope, folder, notebook, valise; SEE CONCEPT *494*

po
po

portion [n1] *share, cut, ration*
allocation, allotment, allowance, apportionment, bang, bit, chunk, division, divvy*, drag*, dram, excerpt, extract, fix, fraction, fragment, gob, helping, hit, hunk, lagniappe, lion's share*, lot, lump, measure, meed, member, moiety, morsel, parcel, part, piece, piece of action*, plum, quantity, quantum, quota, scrap, section, segment, serving, shot*, slug*, smithereen*, taste; SEE CONCEPT **835**

portion [n2] *fate, destiny*
circumstance, cup*, doom, fortune, kismet*, lot*, luck; SEE CONCEPT **679**

portion [v] *divide into pieces*
administer, allocate, allot, apportion, assign, deal, dispense, distribute, divvy up*, dole out*, mete out*, parcel, part, partition, piece, prorate, quota, ration, section, share, shift; SEE CONCEPTS **98,140**

portly [adj] *bulky, fat*
ample, avoirdupois, beefy*, broad, burly, corpulent, fleshy, heavy, hefty, husky, large, obese, overweight, plump, rotund, stout; SEE CONCEPT **491**

portrait [n] *drawn representation; description*
account, characterization, depiction, figure, image, likeness, model, painting, photograph, picture, portraiture, portrayal, profile, silhouette, simulacrum, sketch, snapshot, spitting image*, vignette; SEE CONCEPTS **259,268,625**

portray [v] *represent, imitate*
act like, characterize, copy, delineate, depict, describe, draw, duplicate, figure, illustrate, image, impersonate, interpret, limn, mimic, paint, parody, photograph, picture, render, reproduce, simulate, sketch; SEE CONCEPTS **55,174,265**

pose [n] *artificial position*
act, affectation, air, attitude, attitudinizing, bearing, carriage, facade, fake, false show, front, guise, mannerism, masquerade, mien, posture, posturing, pretense, pretension, role, stance, stand; SEE CONCEPTS **633,716**

pose [v1] *sit, stand in place*
arrange, model, peacock, poise, position, posture, sit for, strike a pose, strut; SEE CONCEPTS **154,174**

pose [v2] *pretend, fake*
act, affect, attitudinize, feign, grandstand*, impersonate, make believe, make out like*, masquerade, pass off*, peacock*, playact, posture, profess, purport, put on airs*, put up a front*, sham*, show off*, strike an attitude*, take off as*; SEE CONCEPTS **59,63,633**

pose [v3] *offer, put forward idea*
advance, ask, extend, give, hold out, posit, prefer, present, proffer, propose, proposition, propound, put, query, question, set, state, submit, suggest, tender; SEE CONCEPTS **66,67,75**

posh [adj] *luxurious, upper-class*
chic, classy, deluxe, elegant, exclusive, fashionable, grand, high-class, la-di-da*, luxury, modish*, opulent, rich, ritzy*, smart, swank, swanky*, swish*, trendy; SEE CONCEPTS **334,589**

position [n1] *physical place*
area, bearings, district, environment, fix, geography, ground, locale, locality, location, locus, point, post, reference, region, scene, seat, setting, site, situation, space, spot, stand, station, surroundings, topography, tract, whereabouts*; SEE CONCEPT **198**

position [n2] *posture, stance*
arrangement, attitude, ballgame*, bearing, carriage, circumstances, condition, deportment, disposition, form, habit, how things stack up*, like it is*, manner, mien, pass, plight, port, pose, predicament, situation, spot, stand, state, status, strait, the size of it*; SEE CONCEPT **696**

position [n3] *belief, point of view*
angle, attitude, color, judgment, opinion, outlook, slant, stance, stand, standpoint, view, viewpoint; SEE CONCEPT **689**

position [n4] *class, stature*
cachet, capacity, caste, character, consequence, dignity, footing, importance, place, prestige, rank, reputation, situation, sphere, standing, station, status; SEE CONCEPTS **378,388**

position [n5] *responsibility in business or other enterprise*
berth, billet, capacity, connection, do*, duty, employment, function, job, nine-to-five*, occupation, office, place, post, profession, role, situation, slot*, spot*, trade; SEE CONCEPTS **324,349,360**

position [v] *place physically in location*
arrange, array, dispose, fix, lay out, locate, put, set, settle, stand, stick; SEE CONCEPTS **158,201**

positive [adj1] *definite, certain*
absolute, actual, affirmative, assured, categorical, clear, clear-cut, cocksure*, cold*, complete, conclusive, concrete, confident, consummate, convinced, decided, decisive, direct, downright, explicit, express, factual, firm, forceful, forcible, genuine, hard, inarguable, incontestable, incontrovertible, indisputable, indubitable, irrefutable, out-and-out*, outright, perfect, rank, real, specific, sure, thorough, thoroughgoing, unambiguous, undeniable, unequivocal, unmistakable, unmitigated; SEE CONCEPTS **535,582**

positive [adj2] *beneficial, helpful*
affirmative, constructive, effective, efficacious, forward-looking, good, practical, productive, progressive, reasonable, sound, useful; SEE CONCEPT **572**

positively [adv] *absolutely, definitely*
amen*, assuredly, categorically, certainly, doubtless, doubtlessly, easily, emphatically, firmly, flat*, flat out*, for a fact*, indubitably, no catch*, no holds barred*, no ifs ands or buts*, no kicker*, no strings attached*, on the money*, on the nose*, really truly*, right on*, sure, surely, the ticket*, to a tee*, undeniably, undoubtedly, unequivocally, unmistakably, unquestionably, with certainty, without qualification; SEE CONCEPTS **535,544,582**

possess [v] *have or obtain*
acquire, bear, be blessed with, be born with, be endowed with, carry, control, corner*, corner the market*, dominate, enjoy, get hands on*, get hold of*, grab, have to name*, hog*, hold, latch on to, lock up, maintain, occupy, own, retain, seize, sit on, take over, take possession; SEE CONCEPTS **120,710**

possessed [adj] *bewitched; under a spell*
bedeviled, berserk*, consumed, crazed*, cursed, demented, enchanted, enthralled, fiendish, frenetic, frenzied, gone*, haunted, hooked*, insane, into*, mad*, obsessed, raving*, taken over*, violent; SEE CONCEPT **401**

possession [n1] *control, ownership*
custody, dominion, hold, occupancy, occupation,

possessorship, proprietary, proprietary rights, proprietorship, retention, tenancy, tenure, title; SEE CONCEPTS 343,710

possession [n2] *something owned; property*
accessories, appointments, appurtenances, assets, baggage, belongings, chattels, effects, equipment, estate, fixtures, furnishings, furniture, goods, impedimenta, paraphernalia, province, real estate, settlement, tangibles, territory, things, trappings, tricks, wealth; SEE CONCEPTS 446,710

possessive [adj] *greedy*
acquisitive, avaricious, controlling, craving, desirous, dominating, grabby, grasping, hoggish*, selfish; SEE CONCEPTS 326,403,542

possibilities [n] *potential*
capabilities, potentiality, promise, prospects, talent; SEE CONCEPTS 411,650

possibility [n] *feasibility, likelihood; chance*
achievability, action, attainableness, break, circumstance, contingency, fair shake*, fifty-fifty*, fling*, fluke*, fortuity, happening, hazard, hope, incident, instance, liability, likeliness, occasion, occurrence, odds*, opportunity, outside chance*, plausibility, play*, potentiality, practicability, prayer*, probability, prospect, risk*, shot*, stab*, toss-up*, workableness; SEE CONCEPTS 650,693

possible [adj] *likely, attainable*
accessible, achievable, adventitious, advisable, available, breeze*, can do*, cinch, conceivable, credible, dependent, desirable, doable, dormant, duck soup*, easy as pie*, expedient, feasible, fortuitous, hopeful, hypothetical, imaginable, indeterminate, latent, no sweat*, obtainable, piece of cake*, potential, practicable, probable, promising, pushover*, realizable, setup, simple as ABC*, snap, thinkable, uncertain, viable, welcome, within reach, workable; SEE CONCEPTS 528,552,576

possibly [adv] *by chance; in some way*
at all, by any chance, by any means, conceivably, could be, God willing*, if possible, in any way, likely, maybe, not impossibly, peradventure, perchance, perhaps, probably, within realm of possibility; SEE CONCEPTS 544,552

post [n1] *upright support*
column, doorpost, leg, mast, newel, pale, palisade, panel, pedestal, picket, pile, pillar, pole, prop, rail, shaft, stake, standard, stilt, stock, stud; SEE CONCEPTS 440,445,470,479

post [n2] *job, employment*
appointment, assignment, berth, billet, office, place, position, situation; SEE CONCEPTS 351,362

post [n3] *lookout, station*
beat, locus, place, position, whereabouts; SEE CONCEPTS 198,321,439

post [n4] *mail service*
collection, delivery, mail, PO*, postal service, post office; SEE CONCEPTS 299,770

post [v1] *situate, position*
assign, establish, locate, place, put, set, station; SEE CONCEPT 201

post [v2] *advise, inform*
acquaint, apprive, brief, clue, fill in, notify, put wise to, report, tell, warn, wise up; SEE CONCEPT 60

poster [n] *large paper advertisement*
affiche, announcement, banner, bill, billboard, broadside, handbill, notice, placard, public no-

tice, sheet, sign, signboard, sticker; SEE CONCEPT 271

posterior [adj1] *rear*
after, back, behind, dorsal, hind, hinder, hindmost, in back of, last, retral; SEE CONCEPTS 583,827

posterior [adj2] *subsequent*
after, coming after, ensuing, following, later, latter, next, postliminary, subsequential, succeeding; SEE CONCEPTS 585,799

posterior [n] *behind of animate being*
back, backside, bottom, butt*, buttocks, can*, cheeks*, derriere, duff*, fanny*, hind part, keester*, moon*, rear, rear end, rump, seat, tail, tail end, tuchis*, tush*; SEE CONCEPT 392

posterity [n] *future generations*
breed, brood, children, descendants, family, heirs, issue, lineage, next generation, offspring, progeniture, progeny, scions, seed, stock, succeeding generations, successors, unborn; SEE CONCEPT 296

posthaste [adj/adv] *fast*
at once, breakneck*, directly, double-quick*, expeditious, flat-out*, fleet, fleetly, full tilt*, hastily, hasty, headlong, lickety-split*, pell-mell*, promptly, pronto, quick, quickly, rapid, rapidly, speedily, speedy, straightaway, swift, swiftly; SEE CONCEPTS 544,588,799

postmortem [adj] *following death*
future, later, posthumous, postmundane, post-obit, post-obituary; SEE CONCEPT 799

postmortem [n] *analysis after death*
autopsy, coroner's report, dissection, examination, necropsy, post*; SEE CONCEPTS 103,310

postpone [v] *put off till later time*
adjourn, cool it*, defer, delay, give a rain check*, hang fire*, hold off, hold over, hold up, lay over, pigeonhole*, prorogue, put back, put on back burner*, put on hold, shelve, suspend, table; SEE CONCEPT 130

postulate [v] *suppose, figure*
advance, affirm, assert, assume, aver, estimate, guess, hypothesize, posit, predicate, premise, presuppose, propose, put forward, speculate, suppose, take for granted, theorize; SEE CONCEPTS 12,26

posture [n1] *stance, circumstance*
aspect, attitude, bearing, brace, carriage, condition, demeanor, deportment, disposition, mien, mode, phase, port, pose, position, posture, presence, set, situation, state; SEE CONCEPTS 657,723

posture [n2] *beliefs*
attitude, disposition, feeling, frame of mind, inclination, mood, outlook, point of view, sentiment, stance, standpoint; SEE CONCEPT 410

posture [v] *display an attitude*
affect, attitudinize, display, do a bit*, do for effect*, fake, fake it, make a show*, masquerade, pass for, pass off, playact, pose, put on airs*, put up a front*, show off*; SEE CONCEPTS 59,261

pot [n1] *container, cauldron*
basin, bowl, bucket, can, canister, crock, crucible, cup, jar, jug, kettle, mug, pan, pitcher, receptacle, saucepan, tankard, urn, vessel; SEE CONCEPT 494

pot [n2] *marijuana*
cannabis, grass*, hashish, maryjane*, weed*; SEE CONCEPT 307

potable [adj] *drinkable*
edible, palatable, safe to drink; SEE CONCEPT 169

potable [*n*] *beverage*
alcoholic beverage, cooler, draft, drink, libation, liquor; SEE CONCEPT *454*

potency [*n*] *effectiveness*
authority, birr, capability, capacity, command, control, dominion, efficacy, efficiency, energy, force, go*, hardihood, influence, juice*, kick*, might, moxie*, muscle*, pep, potential, power, puissance, punch, sinew*, snap, sock*, steam*, strength, sway, vigor, virtue, what it takes*, zap*, zing*, zip*; SEE CONCEPTS *260,432*

potent [*adj*] *effective, powerful, forceful*
almighty, authoritative, ball of fire*, cogent, commanding, compelling, convincing, dominant, dynamic, efficacious, forcible, full-bodied, go-getter*, great, gutsy*, impressive, influential, lusty, mighty, persuasive, powerhouse, puissant, punchy, robust, spanking, stiff, strong, sturdy, telling, trenchant, useful, vigorous; SEE CONCEPTS *372,489,540*

potentate [*n*] *monarch*
autocrat, chief, chieftain, crowned head, despot, dictator, emperor, empress, head of state, king, leader, majesty, prince, princess, queen, royalty, ruler, sovereign; SEE CONCEPTS *354,422*

potential [*adj*] *promising*
abeyant, budding, conceivable, dormant, embryonic, future, hidden, imaginable, implied, inherent, latent, likely, lurking, plausible, possible, prepatent, probable, quiescent, thinkable, undeveloped, unrealized, within realm of possibility; SEE CONCEPTS *528,552*

potential [*n*] *possibility for achievement*
ability, aptitude, capability, capacity, potentiality, power, the makings*, what it takes*, wherewithal; SEE CONCEPTS *650,706*

pothole [*n*] *chuckhole*
cavity, crater, depression, dip, fracture, gap, hole, pit, pocket, rut, split; SEE CONCEPT *513*

potion [*n*] *concoction prepared for mental or physical effect*
aromatic, brew, cordial, cup, dose, draft, dram, draught, drink, elixir, libation, liquid, liquor, medicine, mixture, nip, philter, remedy, restorative, spirits, stimulant, tonic; SEE CONCEPTS *307,467*

potpourri [*n*] *miscellany*
assortment, blend, collection, combination, combo, gallimaufry, goulash, hash, hodgepodge, medley, mélange, mishmash, mixed bag, mixture, motley, olio*, pastiche*, patchwork, salmagundi*, soup, stew; SEE CONCEPTS *260,432*

pottery [*n*] *containers made from clay; clay art*
ceramics, crockery, earthenware, firing, glazing, porcelain, porcelainware, stoneware, terra cotta; SEE CONCEPTS *174,259,494*

pouch [*n*] *soft container, often made of cloth or skin*
bag, pocket, poke, purse, receptacle, sac, sack; SEE CONCEPTS *446,450,494*

pounce [*n/v*] *leap at; take by surprise*
ambush, attack, bound, dart, dash, dive, drop, fall upon, jump, snatch, spring, strike, surge, swoop, take unawares; SEE CONCEPTS *86,159,194*

pound [*n*] *sixteen ounces/.454 kilograms of weight*
avoirdupois, pint, troy; SEE CONCEPT *795*

pound [*v1*] *crush; beat rhythmically*
batter, belabor, bruise, buffet, clobber, comminute, drub, hammer, hit, malleate, palpitate,

pelt, pestle, powder, pulsate, pulse, pulverize, pummel, stomp, strike, thrash, throb, thump, tramp, triturate, wallop; SEE CONCEPTS *150,186,189*

pound [*v2*] *impress; make someone listen*
din, drive, drub, drum, grave, hammer, stamp; SEE CONCEPTS *14,49*

pour [*v*] *be or make flowing*
cascade, cataract, course, crowd, decant, deluge, discharge, drain, drench, emit, flood, flow, give off, gush, inundate, issue, jet, let flow, proceed, rain, rill, roll, run, rush, sheet, shower, sluice, spew, spill, splash, spout, spring, stream, surge, swarm, teem, throng; SEE CONCEPTS *146,179,209*

pout [*n*] *sad face*
frown, glower, long face, moue, sullen look; SEE CONCEPT *716*

pout [*v*] *make a sad face; be sad*
be cross, be in bad mood*, be moody, be petulant, be sullen, frown, grouch, grump*, make a long face*, make a moue, mope, stick one's lip out*; sulk; SEE CONCEPTS *261,410*

poverty [*n*] *want; extreme need, often financial*
abjection, aridity, bankruptcy, barrenness, beggary, dearth, debt, deficiency, deficit, depletion, destitution, difficulty, distress, emptiness, exiguity, famine, hardship, impecuniousness, impoverishment, inadequacy, indigence, insolvency, insufficiency, lack, meagerness, necessitousness, necessity, pass, paucity, pauperism, penuriousness, penury, pinch, poorness, privation, reduction, scarcity, shortage, starvation, straits, underdevelopment, vacancy; SEE CONCEPTS *335,709*

poverty-stricken [*adj*] *in great need; financially poor*
bad off*, bankrupt, beggared, beggarly, broke*, destitute, dirt poor*, distressed, down-and-out*, hard up*, impecunious, impoverished, indigent, in dire circumstances, in want, moneyless, necessitous, needful, needy, penniless, penurious, short*, stone broke*, stranded*, strapped*, unmoneyed, wanting; SEE CONCEPT *334*

powder [*n*] *fine, loose grains made by crushing a solid*
crumb, dust, film, grain, grit, meal, particle, pounce, pulverulence, seed, talc; SEE CONCEPTS *471,831*

powder [*v*] *crush into fine grains; sprinkle fine grains*
abrade, bray, comminute, cover, crumble, crunch, dredge, dust, file, flour, granulate, grate, grind, pestle, pound, pulverize, rasp, reduce, scatter, scrape, smash, strew, triturate; SEE CONCEPTS *186,222*

powdery [*adj*] *consisting of fine, loose grains*
arenaceous, arenose, bran ny, chalky, crumbling, crumbly, dry, dusty, fine, floury, friable, grainy, granular, gravelly, gritty, impalpable, loose, mealy, pulverized, pulverulent, sandy; SEE CONCEPT *606*

power [*n1*] *ability, competence*
aptitude, bent, capability, capacity, competency, dynamism, effectiveness, efficacy, endowment, faculty, function, gift, influence, potential, potentiality, qualification, skill, talent, turn, virtue; SEE CONCEPT *630*

power [*n2*] *physical ability, capacity*
applied force, arm*, brawn, dynamism, energy, force, forcefulness, horsepower, intensity, me-

chanical energy, might, muscle*, omnipotence, potency, potential, puissance, sinew*, strength, vigor, vim, virtue, voltage, weight; SEE CONCEPTS 520,641,732

power [n3] *control, dominance*
ascendancy, authority, authorization, birthright, clout, command, connection, diadem, direction, domination, dominion, hegemony, imperium, influence, inside track*, jurisdiction, law, leadership, license, management, might, moxie*, omnipotence, paramountcy, predominance, prerogative, prestige, privilege, regency, right, rule, say-so*, sovereignty, steam, strength, strings*, superiority, supremacy, sway, warrant, weight*, wire*; SEE CONCEPTS 376,671

powerful [adj] *strong, effective*
able, all-powerful, almighty, authoritarian, authoritative, capable, cogent, commanding, compelling, competent, controlling, convincing, dominant, dynamic, effectual, efficacious, energetic, forceful, forcible, impressive, in control, influential, in the saddle*, mighty, omnipotent, overruling, paramount, persuasive, potent, preeminent, prevailing, puissant, robust, ruling, sovereign, stalwart, strapping*, strengthy, sturdy, supreme, telling, upper hand*, vigorous, weighty, wicked*, wieldy; SEE CONCEPTS 489,527,540,574

powerfully [adv] *with energy, authority*
effectively, energetically, forcefully, forcibly, hard, intensely, mightily, severely, strongly, vigorously, with might and main; SEE CONCEPTS 540,544,569

powerless [adj] *weak; unable*
blank, chicken*, debilitated, defenseless, dependent, disabled, disenfranchised, etiolated, feeble, frail, gutless, helpless, impotent, incapable, incapacitated, ineffective, ineffectual, inert, infirm, out of gas*, paralyzed, passive, prostrate, subject, supine, tied, unarmed, unfit, vulnerable, wimp*, wishy-washy*; SEE CONCEPTS 489,527

powwow [n] *discussion*
confab*, confabulation, conference, consultation, council, get-together, huddle, meeting, palaver, parley, talk; SEE CONCEPTS 56,324,384

powwow [v] *discuss*
advise, confab*, confabulate, confer, consult, get together, go into a huddle*, huddle, meet, palaver, parley, talk, treat; SEE CONCEPT 56

practicable [adj] *within the realm of possibility*
accessible, achievable, applicable, attainable, doable, employable, feasible, functional, handy, open, operative, performable, possible, practical, serviceable, usable, useful, utile, utilizable, viable, workable; SEE CONCEPT 560

practical [adj1] *realistic, useful*
applied, both feet on the ground*, businesslike, commonsensical, constructive, doable, down-to-earth, efficient, empirical, experimental, factual, feasible, functional, handy, hard-boiled*, implicit, in action, in operation, matter-of-fact*, nuts and bolts*, operative, orderly, possible, practicable, pragmatic, rational, reasonable, sane, sensible, serviceable, sober, solid, sound, systematic, unidealistic, unromantic, usable, utile, utilitarian, virtual, workable, workaday, working; SEE CONCEPTS 533,542,560

practical [adj2] *experienced, proficient*
accomplished, cosmopolitan, effective, efficient, qualified, seasoned, skilled, sophisticated,

trained, versed, vet*, veteran, working, worldly, worldly-wise; SEE CONCEPTS 326,527,528,678

practically [adj] *almost; nearly*
about, all but, approximately, as good as, as much as, basically, close to, essentially, for all intents and purposes*, fundamentally, in effect, in essence, morally, most, much, nearly, nigh, virtually, well-nigh; SEE CONCEPTS 531,772

practice [n1] *routine, usual procedure*
convenance, convention, custom, fashion, form, habit, habitude, manner, method, mode, praxis, proceeding, process, rule, system, tradition, trick, usage, use, usefulness, utility, way, wont; SEE CONCEPT 688

practice [n2] *exercise, application*
action, assignment, background, discipline, drill, drilling, effect, experience, homework, iteration, operation, preparation, prepping, recitation, recounting, rehearsal, relating, repetition, seasoning, study, training, tune-up, use, work-out; SEE CONCEPTS 87,100,658

practice [n3] *business; clientele of business*
career, clients, patients, profession, vocation, work; SEE CONCEPTS 325,417

practice [v1] *repeat action to improve*
become seasoned, build up, discipline, do again, dress, dress rehearse*, drill, dry run*, exercise, go over, habituate, hone, iterate, polish, prepare, recite, rehearse, run through, shake-down*, sharpen, study, train, try out, tune up, walk through, warm up, work, work out; SEE CONCEPTS 87,100

practice [v2] *carry out; undertake*
apply, carry on, do, engage in, execute, follow, fulfill, function, live up to, observe, perform, ply, pursue, put into effect, specialize in, work at; SEE CONCEPTS 91,310,317,324

practitioner [n] *expert*
doctor, master, pro, professional, specialist; SEE CONCEPTS 348,350,416

pragmatic [adj] *sensible*
businesslike, commonsensical, down-to-earth, efficient, hard, hard-boiled*, hardheaded*, logical, matter-of-fact, practical, realistic, sober, unidealistic, utilitarian; SEE CONCEPTS 401,542

prairie [n] *grassland*
grassy field, meadow, pasturage, pasture, plain, savanna, steppe, veldt; SEE CONCEPT 509

praise [n] *congratulations; adoration*
acclaim, acclamation, accolade, applause, appreciation, approbation, approval, big hand*, boost, bravo, celebration, cheer, cheering, citation, commendation, compliment, cry, devotion, encomium, esteem, eulogy, exaltation, extolment, flattery, glorification, glory, good word*, homage, hurrah, hymn, kudos*, laudation, obeisance, ovation, panegyric, pat on the back*, plaudit, puff*, rave, recognition, recommendation, regard, sycophancy, thanks, tribute, worship; SEE CONCEPTS 69,278

praise [v] *congratulate; adore*
acclaim, admire, adulate, advocate, aggrandize, applaud, appreciate, approve, bless, boost, bow down*, build up*, cajole, celebrate, cheer, cite, clap, commend, compliment, cry up*, dignify, distinguish, elevate, ennoble, eulogize, exalt, extol, flatter, give thanks, glorify, hail, honor, laud, make much of*, panegyrize, pay homage, pay tribute, proclaim, puff*, rave over, recommend, resound, reverence, root*, sanction,

po
pr

sing the praises*, smile on*, stroke*, tout, worship; SEE CONCEPT 69

praiseworthy [*adj*] *deserving congratulations, adoration*
admirable, commendable, creditable, estimable, excellent, exemplary, fine, gnarly, gone, honorable, keen, laudable, meritable, meritorious, pillar, salt of earth*, select, slick, stellar, swell, thankworthy, tough, worthy; SEE CONCEPTS 568,574

prance [*v*] *cavort; show off*
bound, caper, dance, flounce, foot it*, frisk, gambol, hoof it*, jump, leap, mince, parade, romp, sashay, skip, spring, stalk, step, strut, swagger, sweep, tread; SEE CONCEPTS 150,292,384

prank [*n*] *practical joke; frivolity*
antic, caper, caprice, escapade, fancy, fooling, frolic, gag, gambol, high jinks*, horseplay*, hotfoot*, lark, levity, lightness, monkeyshines*, play, put-on, rib*, rollick, roughhouse*, roughhousing*, rowdiness, shenanigans, shine*, skylarking*, spoof, sport, tomfoolery, trick, whim; SEE CONCEPTS 59,384

prattle [*n*] *babble*
blubbering, burble, chatter, chit-chat, drivel, gab, gabble, gibberish, gossip, hot air*, idle talk, jabber, jabbering, jargon, murmur, ranting, small talk, tattling, trivial talk, twaddle; SEE CONCEPTS 266,278

pray [*v*] *plead; call upon for help, answer*
adjure, appeal, ask, beseech, brace, commune with, crave, cry for, entreat, implore, importune, invocate, invoke, petition, recite, request, say, solicit, sue, supplicate, urge; SEE CONCEPTS 48,367

prayer [*n*] *pleading, especially with a deity; request for help, answer*
adoration, appeal, application, begging, benediction, beseeching, communion, devotion, entreaty, grace, imploration, imploring, imprecation, invocation, litany, orison, petition, plea, pleading, request, rogation, service, suit, supplication, worship; SEE CONCEPTS 48,367,662

preach [*v1*] *speak publicly about beliefs*
address, deliver, deliver sermon, evangelize, exhort, give sermon, homilize, inform, minister, mission, missionary, orate, prophesy, pulpiteer, sermonize, talk, teach; SEE CONCEPTS 51,285,367

preach [*v2*] *lecture, moralize*
admonish, advocate, blow, exhort, get on a soapbox*, harangue, pile it on*, preachify, sermonize, talk big*, urge; SEE CONCEPTS 51,75

preacher [*n*] *person who gives religious instruction*
clergy, cleric, clerical, divine, ecclesiastic, evangelist, evangelizer, minister, missionary, parson, pulpiter, reverend, revivalist, sermonizer; SEE CONCEPT 361

precarious [*adj*] *tricky, doubtful*
ambiguous, borderline, chancy, contingent, dangerous, delicate, dicey*, dubious, dynamite, equivocal, hairy*, hanging by a thread*, hazardous, iffy*, impugnable, indecisive, insecure, loaded, on thin ice*, open, out on a limb*, perilous, problematic, risky, rocky, rugged*, sensitive, shaky, slippery, ticklish, touch and go*, touchy, uncertain, unhealthy, unreliable, unsafe, unsettled, unstable, unsteady, unsure; SEE CONCEPTS 535,587

precaution [*n*] *carefulness; preventative measure*
anticipation, canniness, care, caution, circumspection, discreetness, discretion, foresight, forethought, insurance, protection, providence, provision, prudence, regard, safeguard, safety measure, wariness; SEE CONCEPTS 410,633,729

precede [*v*] *go ahead of*
antecede, antedate, anticipate, be ahead of, come first, forerun, foreshadow, go before, go in advance, guide, harbinger, have a head start*, head, head up, herald, in space, introduce, lead, light the way*, order announce, outrank, pace, pave the way*, pioneer, predate, pre-exist, preface, presage, rank, ring in*, run ahead, scout, take precedence, time, usher; SEE CONCEPTS 727,747,813,818

precedence [*n*] *highest in rank; first in order*
antecedence, anteposition, earliness, lead, precedency, precession, preeminence, preexistence, preference, prevenience, previousness, primary, priority, rank, seniority, superiority, supremacy; SEE CONCEPTS 671,727,747,818

precedent [*n*] *authoritative example*
antecedent, authority, criterion, exemplar, instance, model, paradigm; SEE CONCEPT 686

preceding [*adj*] *earlier, above*
above-mentioned, above-named, aforeknown, aforementioned, aforesaid, ahead of, antecedent, anterior, before, erstwhile, foregoing, forerunning, former, forward, front, head, heretofore, introductory, lead, leading, one time, other, past, pioneer, pioneering, precedent, precursive, precursory, preexistent, prefatory, preliminary, preparatory, prevenient, previous, prior, supra; SEE CONCEPTS 585,586,799,811,818

precept [*n*] *law, rule of behavior, action*
axiom, behest, bidding, byword, canon, command, commandment, decree, decretum, direction, doctrine, dogma, edict, formula, fundamental, guideline, injunction, instruction, law, mandate, maxim, motto, order, ordinance, prescript, principle, regulation, rule, saying, statute, tenet; SEE CONCEPTS 318,688

precinct [*n*] *subdivision*
area, community, department, development, district, division, neighborhood, provence, quarter, section, tract, ward, zone; SEE CONCEPTS 513,835

precious [*adj*] *favorite, valued*
adored, beloved, cherished, darling, dear, dearest, idolized, inestimable, loved, pet, prized, treasured; SEE CONCEPTS 529,567

precious [*adj2*] *expensive; rare*
choice, costly, dear, exquisite, fine, high-priced, inestimable, invaluable, priceless, prizable, prized, recherché, rich, treasurable, valuable, worth a king's ransom*, worth eyeteeth*, worth one's weight in gold*; SEE CONCEPT 334

precious [*adj3*] *extremely sophisticated and picky*
affected, alembicated, artful, artificial, chichi*, choosy, dainty, delicate, fastidious, finicky, fragile, fussy, la-di-da*, nice, ostentatious, overnice, overrefined, particular, persnickety*, precieux, pretentious, refined, showy, stagy, studied; SEE CONCEPT 401

precipice [*n*] *face or brink of a rock, mountain*
bluff, cliff, crag, height, sheer drop, steep; SEE CONCEPTS 509,513

precipitate [*v*] *hurry, speed*
accelerate, advance, bring on, cast, discharge, dispatch, expedite, fling, further, hasten, hurl, launch, let fly, press, push forward, quicken, send forth, speed up, throw, trigger; SEE CONCEPTS 152,242,704

precipitation [*n*] *moisture in air or falling from sky*
cloudburst, condensation, drizzle, hail, hailstorm, heavy dew, precip*, rain, rainfall, rainstorm, sleet, snow, storm, wetness; SEE CONCEPTS 467,524,526

precipitous [*adj*] *steep, falling sharply*
abrupt, arduous, craggy, dizzy, dizzying, high, perpendicular, precipitate, sharp, sheer; SEE CONCEPTS 490,583,779

precipitous/precipitate [*adj1*] *fast, sudden; impulsive; initial*
abrupt, breakneck*, brief, frantic, gone off half-cocked*, harum-scarum*, hasty, headlong, heedless, hurried, ill-advised, impatient, impetuous, indiscreet, jump the gun*, madcap, off the hip*, off the top of head*, plunging, precipitant, quick, rapid, rash, reckless, refractory, rushing, subitaneous, swift, unanticipated, uncontrolled, unexpected, unforeseen, violent, willful, without warning; SEE CONCEPTS 229,401,542,588,799

precis [*n*] *abridgment*
abstract, aperçu, compendium, condensation, digest, outline, pandect, résumé, rundown, sketch, summary, survey, syllabus, synopsis; SEE CONCEPT 283

precise [*adj1*] *exact, accurate*
absolute, actual, categorical, circumscribed, clear-cut, correct, decisive, definite, determinate, explicit, express, fixed, individual, limited, literal, narrow, nice, on the button*, on the money*, on the nose*, particular, proper, restricted, right, rigid, rigorous, specific, strict, stringent, unequivocal, very, well-defined; SEE CONCEPTS 535,557,653

precise [*adj2*] *meticulous, fastidious*
careful, ceremonious, choosy, exact, finicky, formal, fussy, genteel, inflexible, nice, particular, persnickety*, picky, priggish, prim, prissy, punctilious, rigid, scrupulous, stickling, stiff*, strict, stuffy, uncompromising; SEE CONCEPTS 401,542

precisely [*adv*] *exactly, just*
absolutely, accurately, as well, correctly, definitely, even, expressly, for a fact, for sure, just so, literally, no ifs ands or buts*, no mistake*, on the button*, on the money*, on the nose*, plumb, right, sharp, smack*, smack-dab*, specifically, square, squarely, strictly, sure, sure thing*, the ticket*, the very thing*, to a tee*, yes; SEE CONCEPTS 535,557

precision [*n*] *accuracy*
attention, care, carefulness, correctness, definiteness, definitiveness, definitude, exactitude, exactness, fidelity, heed, meticulousness, nicety, particularity, preciseness, rigor, sureness; SEE CONCEPTS 638,654

preclude [*v*] *inhibit; make impossible*
avert, cease, check, debar, deter, discontinue, exclude, forestall, forfend, hinder, impede, interrupt, make impracticable, obviate, prevent, prohibit, put a stop to, quit, restrain, rule out, stave off, stop, ward; SEE CONCEPTS 121,234

precocious [*adj*] *exceptionally smart, ahead of age in understanding*
advanced, aggressive, ahead of time*, beforehand, bold, brassy*, bright, cheeky*, cocky*, developed, early, flip*, flippant, forward, fresh, intelligent, mature, nervy, premature, presumptuous, pushy, quick, sassy*, smart-alecky*; SEE CONCEPT 402

precognition [*n*] *clairvoyance*
acumen, discernment, ESP, extra sensory perception, feeling, foreknowledge, foresight, fortunetelling, insight, intuition, omen, penetration, perception, prediction, premonition, prophecy, psyche, second sight, sixth sense*, telepathy; SEE CONCEPTS 409,410

preconception [*n*] *idea formed before event occurs or facts are received*
assumption, bias, delusion, illusion, inclination, notion, preconceived idea, predisposition, prejudgment, prejudice, prepossession, presumption, presuppositition; SEE CONCEPT 689

precursor [*n1*] *something that indicates outcome or event beforehand*
forerunner, harbinger, herald, messenger, outrider, usher, vanguard; SEE CONCEPTS 70,278

precursor [*n2*] *something that precedes another*
ancestor, antecedent, antecessor, forebear, foregoer, forerunner, original, originator, parent, pioneer, predecessor, prototype; SEE CONCEPTS 648,727,828

predator [*n*] *hunter, killer*
animal of prey, beast of prey, carnivore, meat-eater; SEE CONCEPT 252

predatory [*adj*] *eating, destroying for sustenance or without conscience*
bloodthirsty, carnivorous, depredatory, despoiling, greedy, hungry, hunting, marauding, pillaging, plundering, predacious, predative, preying, rapacious, raptorial, ravaging, ravening, thieving, voracious, vulturine, vulturous, wolfish; SEE CONCEPTS 401,406

predecessor [*n*] *something, someone that comes before*
ancestor, antecedent, antecessor, forebear, foregoer, forerunner, former, precursor, previous, prior, prototype; SEE CONCEPTS 414,828

predestination [*n*] *destiny*
course of events, divine decree, fate, foreordination, fortune, God's will, inevitability, karma, kismet*, ordinance, portion, predetermination, way the ball bounces*, way the cookie crumbles*, what is written*; SEE CONCEPT 679

predetermined [*adj*] *decided in advance*
agreed, arranged, calculated, cut and dried*, deliberate, destined, determined, doomed, fated, fixed, foredestined, foreordained, forethought, planned, prearranged, precogitated, predestined, premeditated, preordained, preplanned, proposed, set, settled, set up; SEE CONCEPT 548

predicament [*n*] *difficult situation*
asperity, bad news*, bind*, Catch-22*, circumstance, clutch, condition, corner*, crisis, deadlock, deep water*, dilemma, drag*, emergency, exigency, fix*, hang-up*, hardship, hole, hot water*, imbroglio, impasse, jam*, juncture, large order*, lot, mess*, muddle, pass, perplexity, pickle*, pinch, plight, position, posture, puzzle, quagmire, quandary, rigor, rough go*, scrape*, soup*, spot*, state*, strait, tall order* ticklish

pr
pr

spot* tight situation* trouble, vicissitude; SEE CONCEPTS 388,674

predict [v] *express an outcome in advance*
adumbrate, anticipate, augur, be afraid, call, call it, conclude, conjecture, croak, crystal-ball* divine, envision, figure, figure out, forebode, forecast, foresee, forespeak, foretell, gather, guess, have a hunch*, hazard a guess*, infer, judge, make book*, omen, portend, presage, presume, prognosticate, prophesy, psych out*, read, see coming*, see handwriting on wall*, size up*, soothsay, suppose, surmise, telegraph*, think, vaticinate; SEE CONCEPT 70

predictable [adj] *easy to foretell*
anticipated, calculable, certain, expected, foreseeable, foreseen, likely, prepared, sure, sure-fire*; SEE CONCEPTS 404,542,548

prediction [n] *declaration made in advance of event*
anticipation, augury, cast, conjecture, crystal gazing*, divination, dope, forecast, forecasting, foresight, foretelling, fortune-telling, guess, horoscope, hunch*, indicator, omen, palmistry, presage, prevision, prognosis, prognostication, prophecy, soothsaying, surmising, tip, vaticination, zodiac; SEE CONCEPTS 70,278,689

predilection [n] *inclination, preference toward something*
bent*, bias, cup of tea*, dish*, druthers*, fancy, flash, fondness, groove, inclining, leaning, liking, love, mindset*, partiality, penchant, predisposition, proclivity, proneness, propensity, taste*, tendency, thing*, type, weakness; SEE CONCEPTS 20,32,709

predispose [v] *influence to believe something*
activate, affect, animate, bend*, bias, cultivate, dispose, govern, impress, incline, indoctrinate, induce, inspire, lead, make expectant, make of a mind to*, prejudice, prepare, prime, prompt, stimulate, strike, sway, teach, urge; SEE CONCEPTS 12,14,26,68

predisposed [adj] *willing, inclined*
agreeable, amenable, biased, eager, enthusiastic, fain, given to, liable, likely, minded, partial, prone, ready, subject, susceptible; SEE CONCEPT 403

predisposition [n] *willingness, inclination*
bent*, bias, choice, cup of tea*, dish*, disposition, druthers*, flash, groove, leaning, likelihood, liking, option, partiality, penchant, potentiality, predilection, preference, proclivity, proneness, propensity, susceptibility, tendency, thing*, type, weakness; SEE CONCEPTS 20,32,410,709

predominant [adj] *ruling; most important*
absolute, all-powerful, almighty, arbitrary, ascendant, authoritative, capital, chief, controlling, directing, dominant, dominating, effective, efficacious, governing, holding the reins*, imperious, influential, leading, main, mighty, official, omnipotent, overbearing, overpowering, paramount, potent, predominate, preponderant, prevailing, prevalent, primary, prime, principal, prominent, reigning, sovereign, superior, superlative, supervisory, supreme, surpassing, transcendent, weighty; SEE CONCEPTS 568,574

predominate [v] *be the most important, noticeable*
carry weight*, command, dominate, domineer, get the upper hand*, govern, hold sway*, manage, outweigh, overrule, overshadow, preponder-ate, prevail, reign, rule, tell; SEE CONCEPTS 94,117,141

preeminent [adj] *most important; superior*
capital, chief, consummate, distinguished, dominant, excellent, foremost, incomparable, main, major, matchless, number one*, outstanding, paramount, peerless, predominant, principal, renowned, stellar, supreme, surpassing, towering, transcendent, ultimate, unequalled, unmatchable, unrivalled, unsurpassable, unsurpassed; SEE CONCEPTS 568,574

preempt [v] *take over in place of another*
accroach, acquire, annex, anticipate, appropriate, arrogate, assume, bump, commandeer, confiscate, expropriate, obtain, seize, sequester, take, usurp; SEE CONCEPTS 121,142,234

preface [n] *introduction*
beginning, exordium, explanation, foreword, overture, preamble, preliminary, prelude, prelusion, proem, prolegomenon, prologue; SEE CONCEPT 270

preface [v] *introduce*
begin, commence, launch, lead, lead up to, open, precede, prefix, usher; SEE CONCEPTS 57,221

prefer [v] *favor; single out*
adopt, advance, aggrandize, be partial to, be turned on to, choose, cull, desire, elect, elevate, fancy, finger, fix upon, go for, incline, like better, mark, optate, opt for, pick, place, pose, present, promote, propone, proposition, propound, put, put forward, raise, select, suggest, tag, take, tap, upgrade, wish, would rather*, would sooner*; SEE CONCEPTS 20,41

preference [n1] *first choice*
alternative, choice, cup of tea*, desire, druthers*, election, favorite, flash*, groove, inclination, option, partiality, pick, predilection, prepossession, propensity, say, say so*, selection, top, weakness; SEE CONCEPTS 20,529,709

preference [n2] *favorable treatment*
advancement, advantage, elevation, favoritism, first place, precedence, preferment, prelation, pride of place, priority, promotion, upgrading; SEE CONCEPT 693

preferred [adj] *favorite, chosen*
adopted, approved, culled, decided upon, elected, endorsed, fancied, favored, handpicked, liked, named, picked, popular, sanctioned, selected, set apart, settled upon, singled out, taken, well-liked; SEE CONCEPTS 555,574

pregnancy [n] *gestation*
child-bearing, fertilization, germination, gravidity, gravidness, impregnation, parturiency, propagation; SEE CONCEPT 427

pregnant [adj1] *carrying developing offspring within the body*
abundant, anticipating, carrying a child, enceinte, expectant, expecting*, fecund, fertile, fraught, fruitful, gestating, gravid, heavy, hopeful, in family way*, parous, parturient, preggers*, productive, prolific, replete, teeming, with child*; SEE CONCEPTS 406,485

pregnant [adj2] *significant, meaningful*
charged, cogent, consequential, creative, eloquent, expressive, fecund, imaginative, important, inventive, loaded, momentous, original, pointed, redolent, rich, seminal, sententious, suggestive, telling, weighty; SEE CONCEPTS 267,567

prehistoric [adj] *before recorded history*
ancient, antediluvian, antiquated, archaic, earli-

est, early, old, olden, primeval, primitive, primordial; SEE CONCEPTS *558,560,799*

prejudice [*n*] *belief without basis, information; intolerance*
ageism, animosity, antipathy, apartheid, aversion, bad opinion, bias, bigotry, chauvinism, contemptuousness, detriment, discrimination, disgust, dislike, displeasure, disrelish, enmity, foregone conclusion, illiberality, injustice, jaundiced eye, mindset*, misjudgment, narrow-mindedness, one-sidedness, partiality, pique, preconceived notion, preconception, prejudgment, prepossession, racism, repugnance, revulsion, sexism, slant, spleen, tilt, twist, umbrage, unfairness, warp, xenophobia; SEE CONCEPT *689*

prejudice [*v*] *influence another's beliefs without basis, information*
angle*, bend*, bias, blemish*, color*, damage, dispose, distort, harm, hinder, hurt, impair, incline, indoctrinate, injure, jaundice, mar, poison*, predispose, prejudge, prepossess, skew*, slant*, spoil, sway*, twist*, undermine, vitiate, warp*; SEE CONCEPTS *7,14,19*

prejudicial [*adj*] *harmful, undermining*
bad, biased, bigoted, counterproductive, damaging, deleterious, detrimental, differential, disadvantageous, discriminatory, evil, hurtful, inimical, injurious, mischievous, nocuous, unfavorable, unjust; SEE CONCEPTS *537,545,570*

preliminary [*adj*] *introductory, initial*
basic, elemental, elementary, exploratory, first, fundamental, inductive, initiatory, opening, pilot, preceding, precursory, prefatory, preparing, primal, primary, prior, qualifying, reading, test, trial; SEE CONCEPTS *549,585,799*

preliminary [*n*] *introductory event; beginning*
first round, foundation, groundwork, initiation, introduction, opening, preamble, preface, prelims*, prelude, preparation, start; SEE CONCEPTS *828,832*

prelude [*n*] *beginning of event*
commencement, curtain-raiser*, exordium, foreword, intro*, introduction, overture, preamble, preface, preliminary, prelusion, preparation, proem, prolegomenon, prologue, start; SEE CONCEPTS *264,832*

premature [*adj1*] *earlier in occurrence than anticipated*
a bit previous, abortive, early on, embryonic, forward, green*, immature, incomplete, inopportune, overearly, oversoon, precipitate, predeveloped, previous, raw*, soon, unanticipated, undeveloped, unfledged, unripe, untimely; SEE CONCEPTS *485,594*

premature [*adj2*] *rash, impulsive*
half-baked*, half-cocked*, hasty, ill-considered, inopportune, jumping the gun*, overhasty, precipitate, previous, too soon, untimely; SEE CONCEPTS *401,542*

premeditated [*adj*] *planned, intended*
advised, aforethought, calculated, conscious, considered, contrived, deliberate, designed, fixed, framed up, intentional, laid-out*, prepense, purposed, rigged*, set-up*, sewn-up*, stacked deck*, studied, thought-out, willful; SEE CONCEPTS *542,548*

premier [*adj*] *leading; original*
arch, beginning, champion, chief, earliest, first, foremost, head, highest, inaugural, initial, main, opening, primary, prime, principal; SEE CONCEPTS *568,585*

premiere [*n*] *original production*
beginning, debut, first night, first performance, first showing, opening, opening night; SEE CONCEPTS *263,832*

premise [*n*] *hypothesis, argument*
apriorism, assertion, assumption, basis, evidence, ground, posit, postulate, postulation, presumption, presupposition, proof, proposition, supposition, thesis; SEE CONCEPTS *529,689*

premise [*v*] *hypothesize*
announce, assume, begin, commence, introduce, posit, postulate, predicate, presume, presuppose, start, state, suppose; SEE CONCEPTS *18,37*

premises [*n*] *grounds and buildings*
bounds, campus, digs, establishment, fix, flat, hangout*, home, house, joint*, land, lay, layout, limits, neck of the woods*, office, pad, place, plant, property, real estate*, roof, scene, site, spot, terrace, turf, zone; SEE CONCEPTS *198,515*

premium [*adj*] *excellent*
choice, exceptional, prime, select, selected, superior; SEE CONCEPT *574*

premium [*n*] *bonus, prize*
appreciation, boon, bounty, carrot*, dividend, extra, fee*, gravy*, guerdon, meed, percentage, perk*, perquisite, plum*, recompense, regard, remuneration, reward, spiff*, stock, store, value; SEE CONCEPTS *337,344*

premonition [*n*] *feeling that an event is about to occur*
apprehension, apprehensiveness, feeling, feeling in bones*, foreboding, forewarning, funny feeling, handwriting on wall*, hunch, idea, intuition, misgiving, omen, portent, prenotion, presage, presentiment, sign, sinking feeling, suspicion, vibes, vibrations, warning, wind change*, winds*, winds of change*, worriment; SEE CONCEPTS *410,529,689,690*

preoccupied [*adj*] *busy; mentally caught up in something*
absent, absent-minded, absorbed, abstracted, airheaded*, asleep*, bemused, bugged*, daydreaming, deep*, distracted, distrait, engaged, engrossed, faraway, fascinated, forgetful, have on the brain*, heedless, hung up*, immersed, inconscient, intent, lost, lost in thought*, mooning*, moony*, oblivious, obsessed, rapt, removed, spellbound, spread out*, taken up, unaware, woolgathering*, wrapped-up*; SEE CONCEPT *403*

preparation [*n1*] *development, readiness*
alertness, anticipation, arrangement, background, base, basis, build-up*, construction, dry run*, education, establishment, evolution, expectation, fitting, foresight, formation, foundation, gestation, getting ready, groundwork, homework, incubation, lead time*, making ready, manufacture, measure, plan, precaution, preparedness, preparing, provision, putting in order, qualification, readying, rehearsal, rundown, safeguard, schoolwork, study, substructure, training, tryout, workout; SEE CONCEPTS *35,202,285*

preparation [*n2*] *something concocted, put together*
arrangement, blend, brew, composition, compound, concoction, confection, decoction, medicine, mixture, product, tincture; SEE CONCEPT *260*

pr
pr

preparatory [*adj*] *introductory, basic*
before, elementary, in advance of, in anticipation of, inductive, opening, precautionary, prefatory, preliminary, prelusive, prep*, preparative, previous, primary, prior to; SEE CONCEPTS *546,585*

prepare [*v*] *make or get ready*
adapt, adjust, anticipate, appoint, arrange, assemble, brace, build up, coach, concoct, construct, contrive, cook, develop, dispose, draw up, endow, equip, fabricate, fashion, fill in, fit, fit out, fix, form, formulate, fortify, furnish, gird, groom, lay the groundwork, make, make provision, make up, outfit, perfect, plan, practice, prime, produce, provide, put in order, put together, qualify, ready, settle, smooth the way*, steel*, strengthen, supply, train, turn out, warm up; SEE CONCEPTS *35,202*

prepared [*adj*] *ready in body or mind*
able, adapted, adjusted, all bases covered*, all set*, all systems go*, arranged, available, disposed, fit, fixed, framed, gaffed, groomed, handy, inclined, in order, in readiness, minded, of a mind, on guard*, planned, predisposed, prepped, primed, processed, psyched-up*, put up, qualified, rehearsed, rigged*, set, set-up, sewed-up, stacked, up*, up on*, willing, wired; SEE CONCEPTS *403,485,560*

preponderance [*n*] *great numbers; supremacy*
advantage, ascendancy, bigger half*, bulk, command, dominance, domination, dominion, extensiveness, greater part, lion's share*, mass, max*, mostest, power, predominance, prevalence, superiority, sway, weight; SEE CONCEPTS *671,687,767*

prepossessed [*adj*] *made partial by initial impression*
biased, colored, inclined, jaundiced, one-sided, opinionated, partisan, predisposed, prejudiced, tendentious, unindifferent, warped; SEE CONCEPTS *403,542*

prepossessing [*adj*] *attractive, handsome*
alluring, amiable, appealing, attracting, beautiful, bewitching, captivating, charming, drawing, enchanting, engaging, fair, fascinating, fetching, good-looking, inviting, likable, lovable, magnetic, pleasant, pleasing, striking, taking, winning; SEE CONCEPTS *404,537*

preposterous [*adj*] *ridiculous, bizarre*
absurd, asinine, crazy, excessive, exorbitant, extravagant, extreme, fantastic, far-out*, foolish, harebrained*, impossible, incredible, insane, irrational, laughable, ludicrous, monstrous, nonsensical, out of the question*, outrageous, senseless, shocking, silly, stupid, taking the cake*, thick*, too much*, unbelievable, unreasonable, unthinkable, unusual, wacky*, wild; SEE CONCEPTS *529,548,552*

prerequisite [*adj*] *necessary*
called for, essential, expedient, imperative, important, indispensable, mandatory, necessitous, needful, obligatory, of the essence, required, requisite, vital; SEE CONCEPT *546*

prerequisite [*n*] *condition, necessity*
essential, imperative, must, need, postulate, precondition, qualification, requirement, requisite, sine qua non; SEE CONCEPTS *646,709*

prerogative [*n*] *right, privilege*
advantage, appanage, authority, birthright, choice, claim, droit, due, exemption, immunity, liberty, perquisite, sanction, title; SEE CONCEPT *376*

presage [*n*] *prediction, indication*
apprehension, apprehensiveness, augury, auspice, bodement, boding, forecast, foretoken, forewarning, harbinger, intimation, misgiving, omen, portent, premonition, prenotion, presentiment, prognostic, prognostication, prophecy, sign, warning; SEE CONCEPTS *410,529,689*

presage [*v*] *predict or have a feeling*
adumbrate, announce, augur, betoken, bode, divine, feel, forebode, forecast, forerun, foresee, foreshadow, foreshow, foretell, foretoken, forewarn, harbinger, herald, intuit, omen, point to, portend, preindicate, prognosticate, promise, prophesy, sense, signify, soothsay, vaticinate, warn; SEE CONCEPTS *34,70,118*

preschool [*n*] *nursery school*
day care center, kindergarten, playgroup, pre-K; SEE CONCEPTS *287,289*

prescribe [*v*] *stipulate action to be taken*
appoint, assign, choose, command, decide, decree, define, designate, determine, dictate, direct, enjoin, establish, fix, guide, impose, lay down, ordain, order, pick out, require, rule, select, set, settle, specify, write prescription; SEE CONCEPTS *50,60,61,88*

prescription [*n*] *formula, medicine*
decree, direction, drug, edict, instruction, law, mixture, ordinance, preparation, prescript, recipe, regulation, remedy, rule; SEE CONCEPTS *274,307,311,318*

presence [*n1*] *occupancy, attendance*
being, companionship, company, existence, habitation, inhabitance, latency, occupation, omnipresence, potentiality, residence, subsistence, ubiety, ubiquity, whereabouts; SEE CONCEPTS *407,518,710*

presence [*n2*] *appearance, demeanor*
address, air, aspect, aura, bearing, behavior, carriage, comportment, deportment, ease, look, mien, personality, poise, port, seeming, self-assurance, set; SEE CONCEPTS *411,673,716*

presence [*n3*] *closeness, vicinity*
immediate circle, nearness, neighborhood, propinquity, proximity; SEE CONCEPT *747*

presence [*n4*] *ghost*
apparition, manifestation, shade, specter, spirit, supernatural being, wraith; SEE CONCEPT *370*

presence [*n5*] *composure of mind*
acumen, alertness, aplomb, calmness, cool, coolness, imperturbability, levelheadedness, quickness, sangfroid, self-assurance, self-command, self-composure, self-possession, sensibility, sobriety, watchfulness, wits; SEE CONCEPTS *410,657*

presence of mind [*n*] *coolheadedness*
calm, clearheadedness, coolness, patience; SEE CONCEPTS *388,411,720*

present [*adj1*] *existing; at this time*
ad hoc, already, at this moment, begun, being, coeval, commenced, contemporaneous, contemporary, current, even now, existent, extant, for the time being, going on, immediate, in duration, in process, instant, just now, modern, nowadays, present-day, prompt, started, today, topical, under consideration, up-to-date; SEE CONCEPT *820*

present [*adj2*] *nearby, here*
accounted for, at hand, attendant, available, existent, in attendance, in view, made the scene*, near, on board, on deck, on hand, on-the-spot,

ready, show up, there, there with bells on*, within reach; SEE CONCEPTS *539,583*

present [n1] *existing time*
here and now, instant, nonce, now, present moment, the time being, this day, this time, today; SEE CONCEPTS *802,807,815*

present [n2] *gift*
benefaction, benevolence, boon, bounty, compliment, donation, endowment, favor, gifting, giveaway, goodie*, grant, gratuity, handout, largess, lump, offering, stake, write-off; SEE CONCEPT *337*

present [v1] *introduce; demonstrate*
acquaint, adduce, advance, allege, cite, declare, display, do, do the honors, exhibit, expose, expound, extend, fix up, get together, give, give an introduction, hold out, imply, infer, intimate, lay, make a pitch*, make known, manifest, mount, offer, open to view, perform, pitch, pose, produce, proffer, proposition, put forward, put on, raise, recount, relate, roll out, show, stage, state, submit, suggest, tender, trot out; SEE CONCEPTS *66,261*

present [v2] *give, hand over*
award, bestow, come up with, confer, devote, donate, entrust, furnish, gift, give away, grant, hand out, kick in*, lay on*, offer, proffer, put at disposal, put forth; SEE CONCEPTS *67,108*

presentable [adj] *respectable; fit to be seen*
acceptable, attractive, becoming, decent, fit, good enough*, not bad*, okay*, passable, prepared, proper, satisfactory, suitable, tolerable; SEE CONCEPTS *558,579*

presentation [n] *performance; something given, displayed*
act, appearance, arrangement, award, bestowal, coming out, conferral, debut, delivering, delivery, demonstration, display, dog and pony show*, donation, exhibition, exposition, giving, introduction, investiture, knockdown*, launch, launching, offering, overture, pitch, present, production, proposal, proposition, reception, remembrance, rendition, representation, sales pitch*, show, staging, submission; SEE CONCEPTS *261,263,337*

presentiment [n] *anticipation, expectation*
apprehension, apprehensiveness, discomposure, disquietude, disturbance, fear, feeling, feeling in bones*, foreboding, forecast, forethought, funny feeling*, handwriting on wall*, hunch, intuition, misgiving, perturbation, premonition, prenotion, presage, sinking feeling, vibes*, worriment; SEE CONCEPTS *410,532,689*

presently [adv] *in a short while*
anon, before long, before you know it, by and by, directly, down the line*; down the pike*, down the road*; immediately, in a minute, in a moment, in a short time, now, nowadays, pretty soon, shortly, soon, today, without delay; SEE CONCEPT *820*

preservation [n] *maintenance, protection*
canning, care, conservancy, conservation, curing, defense, evaporation, freezing, guard, guardianship, keeping, perpetuation, pickling, preserval, refrigeration, safeguard, safeguarding, safekeeping, safety, salvation, saving, security, shield, storage, support, sustentation, tanning, upholding, ward; SEE CONCEPTS *134,170,202,257*

preserve [v] *care for, maintain; continue*
bottle, can, conserve, cure, defend, evaporate,

freeze, guard, keep, keep up, mothball*, mummify, perpetuate, pickle, process, protect, put up, refrigerate, retain, safeguard, save, season, secure, shelter, shield, store, sustain, uphold; SEE CONCEPTS *134,170,202*

preserves [n] *thickened fruit prepared for storage and use as a condiment*
confection, confiture, conserve, extract, gelatin, jam, jell, jelly, marmalade, pectin, spread, sweet; SEE CONCEPTS *457,461*

preside [v] *be in authority*
administer, advise, be at the head of*, be in driver's seat*, call the signals*, carry on, chair, conduct, control, direct, do the honors, govern, handle, head, head up, keep, lead, manage, officiate, operate, ordain, oversee, pull the strings*, run, run the show*, sit on top of*, supervise; SEE CONCEPTS *94,177*

president [n] *chief executive*
boss, CEO, chief executive officer, chief of state, commander-in-chief, head of state, leader, person in charge, premier, prime minister; SEE CONCEPT *347*

press [n1] *people or person working in communications*
columnist, correspondent, editor, fourth estate*, interviewer, journalism, journalist, magazine, media, newspaper, newsperson, paper, periodical, photographer, publicist, publisher, reporter, writer; SEE CONCEPTS *280,349,356*

press [n2] *horde, large group*
bunch, crowd, crush, drove, flock, herd, host, mob, multitude, pack, push, swarm, throng; SEE CONCEPT *432*

press [n3] *strain, pressure*
bustle, confusion, demand, hassle, haste, hurry, rush, stress, urgency; SEE CONCEPTS *230,674*

press [v1] *push on with force*
bear down, bear heavily, bulldoze*, clasp, compress, condense, constrain, crowd, crush, cumber, depress, embrace, enfold, express, finish, flatten, force down, hold, hug, impel, iron, jam, level, mangle, mash, mass, move, pack, pile, pin down, ram, reduce, scrunch, shove, smooth, squash, squeeze, squish, steam, stuff, thrust, unwrinkle, weigh; SEE CONCEPTS *191,208*

press [v2] *pressure, trouble*
afflict, assail, beg, beset, besiege, buttonhole*, come at, compel, constrain, demand, depress, disquiet, enjoin, entreat, exhort, force, harass, implore, importune, insist on, lean on, oppress, petition, plague, plead, pressurize, push, railroad*, sadden, sell, squeeze, sue, supplicate, torment, urge, vex, weigh down, work on, worry; SEE CONCEPT *14*

pressing [adj] *important; urgent*
acute, burning, claiming, clamant, clamorous, compelling, constraining, critical, crucial, crying, demanding, dire, distressing, exacting, exigent, forcing, heat-on*, high-priority, hurry-up*, immediate, imperative, importunate, insistent, instant, life-and-death*, obliging, requiring, serious, vital; SEE CONCEPTS *548,568*

pressure [n1] *physical force, weight*
burden, compressing, compression, crushing, encumbrance, heaviness, load, mass, shear, squeeze, squeezing, strain, strength, stress, tension, thrust; SEE CONCEPTS *641,734*

pressure [n2] *demand, difficulty*
adversity, affliction, albatross*, burden, choke,

pr
pr

clout, coercion, compulsion, confinement, constraint, crunch, discipline, distress, drag, duress, exigency, force, full court press*, hardship, hassle, heat, hurry, influence, inside track*, load, misfortune, necessity, obligation, persuasion, power, press, pressure cooker*, pull, requirement, strain, stress, sway, tension, trouble, unnaturalness, urgency, weight; SEE CONCEPTS *14,666,674,687*

pressure [v] *bother, urge*
come at, compel, constrain, drive, impel, insist, lean on*, politick, press, push, push around*, rush, sell, squeeze, twist arm*, work over*; SEE CONCEPTS *7,14,19,22*

prestige [n] *fame, influence*
authority, cachet, celebrity, consequence, control, credit, dignity, distinction, éclat*, eminence, esteem, fame, illustriousness, importance, kudos*, position, power, preeminence, prominence, prominency, rank, regard, renown, reputation, repute, standing, state, stature, status, sway, weight; SEE CONCEPTS *388,668*

prestigious [adj] *famous, influential*
celebrated, distinguished, eminent, esteemed, exalted, famed, great, illustrious, important, imposing, impressive, notable, prominent, renowned, reputable, respected; SEE CONCEPTS *555,568*

presumably [adv] *likely, reasonably*
apparently, assumably, credible, doubtless, doubtlessly, hypothetically, in all likelihood, in all probability, indubitably, it would seem, most likely, on the face of it, presumptively, probably, seemingly, supposedly, surely, theoretically, unquestionably; SEE CONCEPTS *544,552*

presume [v1] *make assumption; believe*
assume, bank on*, be afraid, conclude, conjecture, consider, count on, depend, figure, gather, guess, infer, jump the gun*, posit, postulate, predicate, premise, presuppose, pretend, rely, speculate, suppose, surmise, take for granted, take it, think, trust; SEE CONCEPTS *12,26,28*

presume [v2] *dare; take the liberty*
go so far, have the audacity, impose, infringe, intrude, make bold, undertake, venture; SEE CONCEPT *87*

presumption [n1] *belief, hypothesis*
anticipation, apriorism, assumption, basis, chance, conjecture, grounds, guess, likelihood, opinion, plausibility, posit, postulate, postulation, premise, presupposition, probability, reason, shot, shot in the dark*, sneaking suspicion*, stab, supposition, surmise, suspicion, thesis; SEE CONCEPT *689*

presumption [n2] *forwardness, daring*
arrogance, assurance, audacity, boldness, brashness, brass, cheek*, chutzpah*, confidence, contumely, effrontery, gall, impudence, insolence, nerve, presumptuousness, rudeness, temerity; SEE CONCEPT *633*

presumptuous [adj] *self-confident*
arrogant, audacious, bold, cheeky*, conceited, confident, contumelious, egotistic, foolhardy, forward, fresh, insolent, overconfident, overfamiliar, overweening, pompous, presuming, pretentious, pushy, rash, rude, self-assertive, self-assured, self-satisfied, smug, supercilious, uppity*; SEE CONCEPTS *401,542*

pretend [v1] *fake, falsify*
act, affect, allege, assume, be deceitful, beguile, be hypocritical, bluff, cheat, claim, claim falsely, counterfeit, cozen, deceive, delude, dissemble, dissimulate, dupe, fake out*, feign, fish*, fool, fudge*, hoodwink*, impersonate, jazz*, jive*, lay claim*, let on*, make out*, malinger, masquerade, mislead, pass off*, pass oneself off as*, profess, purport, put on*, put up a front*, sham*, shuck and jive*, simulate, stonewall*, sucker*, whitewash*; SEE CONCEPTS *59,63*

pretend [v2] *play the part of*
act, assume the role, imagine, imitate, impersonate, make as if, make believe, make out like, make up, masquerade, mimic, play, playact, portray, pose, purport, put on a front*, put on airs*, put on an act*, represent, reproduce, suppose; SEE CONCEPTS *111,171,292,384*

pretended [adj] *alleged; imaginary*
affected, artificial, assumed, avowed, bluffing, bogus, charlatan, cheating, concealed, counterfeit, covered, dissimulated, factitious, fake, false, falsified, feigned, fictitious, impostrous, imposturous, lying, make-believe, masked, mock, ostensible, phony, pretend, professed, pseudo*, purported, put-on*, quack*, sham*, shammed*, simulated, so-called, spurious, supposed; SEE CONCEPTS *545,582*

pretense [n] *falsehood, affected show; cover*
act, acting, affectation, appearance, artifice, charade, claim, cloak, deceit, deception, display, dissimulation, double-dealing*, dumb act*, evasion, excuse, fabrication, facade, fakery, faking, falsification, feigning, gag, guise, insincerity, invention, make-believe, mask, masquerade, misrepresentation, misstatement, ostentation, posing, posturing, pretentiousness, pretext, routine, ruse, schtick*, semblance, sham*, shuffling, simulation, stall, stunt, subterfuge, trickery, veil, veneer, wile; SEE CONCEPTS *59,63,633,716*

pretension [n1] *airs, snobbishness*
affectation, big talk*, charade, conceit, disguise, fake*, false front*, front, hypocrisy, ostentation, phony, pomposity, pretentiousness, put-on*, self-importance, show, showboat*, showiness, showoff, snobbery, splash*, vainglory, vanity; SEE CONCEPT *633*

pretension [n2] *false claim, assertion of importance*
allegation, ambition, ambitiousness, aspiration, assumption, charade, declaration, demand, disguise, maintenance, make-believe, pageant, pretense, pretext, profession, title; SEE CONCEPTS *278,657*

pretentious [adj] *snobbish, conceited*
affected, arty, assuming, aureate, big*, bombastic, chichi*, conspicuous, euphuistic, exaggerated, extravagant, feigned, flamboyant, flashy, flaunting, flowery, gaudy, grandiloquent, grandiose, highfaluting*, high-flown*, high-sounding*, hollow, imposing, inflated, jazzy*, la-di-da*, lofty, magniloquent, mincing, ornate, ostentatious, overambitious, overblown, pompous, puffed up*, put-on*, rhetorical, showy, specious, splashy, stilted, swank, too-too*, tumid, turgid, utopian, vainglorious; SEE CONCEPTS *401,542,589*

preternatural [adj] *unusual, abnormal*
aberrant, anomalous, atypical, deviant, deviative, extraordinary, ghostly, inexplicable, irregular, marvelous, miraculous, mysterious, odd, peculiar, strange, superhuman, superior, supermundane, supernatural, unaccountable, unearthly,

unnatural, unrepresentative, untypical; SEE CONCEPT *564*

pretext [*n*] *disguise; alleged reason*
affectation, alibi, appearance, bluff, cleanup, cloak, color*, coloring*, copout*, cover, cover story*, cover-up*, device, excuse, face, feint, fig leaf*, front, guise, mask, masquerade, plea, ploy, pretense, red herring*, routine, ruse, semblance, show, simulation, song and dance*, stall, stratagem, subterfuge, veil*; SEE CONCEPTS *59,661,716*

pretty [*adj*] *attractive*
appealing, beauteous, beautiful, boss*, charming, cheerful, cher*, comely, cute, dainty, darling, delicate, delightful, dishy*, dreamboat*, elegant, eyeful*, fair, fine, foxy*, good-looking, graceful, handsome, looker, lovely, neat, nice, picture, pleasant, pleasing, pulchritudinous, tasteful; SEE CONCEPT *579*

pretty [*adv*] *considerable; somewhat*
a little, ample, fairly, kind of, large, moderately, more or less, much, notable, pretty much, quite, rather, reasonably, sizable, some, something, sort of, tolerably; SEE CONCEPTS *531,569*

prevail [*v*] *dominate, control*
abound, beat, be common, be current, be prevalent, best, be usual, be victorious, be widespread, carry, come out on top*, command, conquer, domineer, exist generally, gain, get there, go great guns*, go places*, hit pay dirt*, luck out*, make it, make out, master, move out, obtain, overcome, overrule, predominate, preponderate, prove, reign, succeed, take off, triumph, win; SEE CONCEPTS *94,95,141*

prevailing [*adj*] *general, dominant*
all-embracing, by the numbers*, catholic, common, comprehensive, current, customary, ecumenical, established, familiar, fashionable, influential, in style, in vogue, main, operative, ordinary, popular, predominant, predominating, preponderating, prevalent, principal, rampant, regnant, regular, rife, ruling, set, steady, sweeping, universal, usual, widespread, worldwide; SEE CONCEPT *530*

prevail upon/prevail on [*v*] *persuade, influence*
affect, argue into, bring around, convince, crack, dispose, draw, get, get around, impress, incline, induce, promote, prompt, put across, ram down throat*, sell*, suck in*, sway, talk into, win over; SEE CONCEPT *68*

prevalent [*adj1*] *accepted, widespread*
accustomed, common, commonplace, current, customary, established, everyday, extensive, faddy, frequent, general, habitual, in use, latest*, latest word*, leading edge*, natural, new, normal, now*, ongoing, popular, prevailing, rampant, regnant, regular, rife, run-of-the-mill*, state-of-the-art*, stylish, swinging, trendy, typic, typical, ubiquitous, universal, up-to-date, usual, with it*, wonted; SEE CONCEPTS *530,547,589*

prevalent [*adj2*] *governing, superior*
ascendant, compelling, dominant, overbearing, paramount, powerful, predominant, predominate, preponderant, prevailing, regnant, ruling, sovereign, successful; SEE CONCEPTS *536,574*

prevaricate [*v*] *deceive; stretch the truth*
beat around the bush*, beg the question*, belie, cavil, con, distort, dodge, equivocate, evade, exaggerate, fabricate, falsify, fib, garble, hedge, invent, jive*, lie*, misrepresent, misspeak, palter,

phony up*, put on*, quibble, shift, shuffle, tergiversate; SEE CONCEPT *63*

prevent [*v*] *keep from happening or continuing*
anticipate, arrest, avert, avoid, baffle, balk, bar, block, check, chill*, cool, cork, counter, counteract, dam, debar, defend against, foil, forbid, forestall, forfend, frustrate, halt, hamper, head off, hinder, hold back, hold off, impede, inhibit, intercept, interdict, interrupt, keep lid on*, limit, nip in the bud*, obstruct, obviate, preclude, prohibit, put an end to, put a stop to, repress, restrain, restrict, retard, rule out, shut out, stave off, stop, thwart, turn aside, ward off; SEE CONCEPT *121*

prevention [*n*] *stop*
avoidance, blockage, deterence, determent, forestalling, halt, hindrance, impediment, inhibitor, interception, interruption, obstacle, obstruction, prohibition, stoppage, thwarting; SEE CONCEPTS *240,832*

preview [*n*] *preliminary showing*
examination, preliminary study, research, show, sneak, sneak peek*, survey, viewing; SEE CONCEPTS *263,292,832*

previous [*adj1*] *former, prior*
antecedent, anterior, earlier, erstwhile, ex, foregoing, one-time, past, precedent, preceding, quondam, sometime; SEE CONCEPTS *585,811,818,820*

previous [*adj2*] *premature*
ahead, early, inopportune, overearly, oversoon, precipitate, soon, too early, too soon, unfounded, untimely, unwarranted; SEE CONCEPTS *558,799*

previously [*adv*] *earlier*
ahead, already, ante, antecedently, at one time, away back, a while ago, back, back when, before, beforehand, erstwhile, fore, formerly, forward, heretofore, hitherto, in advance, in anticipation, in days gone by, in the past, long ago, once, one-shot, precedently, then, time was, until now; SEE CONCEPT *820*

prey [*n*] *target of attack*
casualty, chased*, dupe*, game, kill, loot, mark, martyr, mug*, pillage, quarry, quest, raven, spoil, sufferer, underdog, victim; SEE CONCEPTS *394,423*

prey on [*v*] *attack, terrorize*
blackmail, bleed, bully, burden, consume, depredate, devour, distress, eat, exploit, feed on, fleece, haunt, hunt, intimidate, live off, load, oppress, plunder, raid, seize, take advantage of, tax, trouble, victimize, weigh, worry; SEE CONCEPTS *14,86,169*

price [*n1*] *financial value*
amount, appraisal, appraisement, asking price, assessment, barter, bill, bounty, ceiling, charge, compensation, consideration, cost, damage, demand, disbursement, discount, dues, estimate, exaction, expenditure, expense, face value, fare, fee, figure, hire, outlay, output, pay, payment, premium, prize, quotation, ransom, rate, reckoning, retail, return, reward, score, sticker*, tab, tariff, ticket, toll, tune*, valuation, wages, wholesale, worth; SEE CONCEPT *329*

price [*n2*] *consequences of action*
cost, expense, penalty, sacrifice, toll; SEE CONCEPT *230*

price [*v*] *assess financial value*
appraise, cost, estimate, evaluate, fix, mark

down, mark up, put a price on, rate, reduce, sticker, value; SEE CONCEPT *330*

priceless [*adj1*] *precious, irreplaceable*
beyond price, cherished, collectible, costly, dear, expensive, incalculable, incomparable, inestimable, invaluable, out-of-bounds*, out-of-sight*, prized, rare, rich, treasured, valuable, valued, without price, worth a king's ransom*, worth its weight in gold*; SEE CONCEPTS *334,568*

priceless [*adj2*] *extremely funny*
absurd, amusing, comic, droll, hilarious, humorous, killing, rib-tickling*, ridiculous, riotous, scream, sidesplitting; SEE CONCEPT *267*

prick [*n*] *small hole made by stab*
cut, gash, jab, jag, perforation, pinhole, prickle, puncture, stab, wound; SEE CONCEPT *309*

prick [*v*] *stab, perforate*
bore, cut, drill, enter, hurt, jab, lance, pierce, pink, punch, puncture, slash, slit, smart, spur, sting; SEE CONCEPT *220*

prickly [*adj1*] *thorny or difficult*
annoying, barbed, bothersome, brambly, briery, bristly, complicated, echinated, intricate, involved, knotty, nettlesome, pointed, sharp, spiny, stimulating, ticklish, tricky, troublesome, trying; SEE CONCEPTS *485,565*

prickly [*adj2*] *irritable, bad-tempered*
cantankerous, edgy, fractious, fretful, grumpy, irritable, peevish, petulant, snappish, touchy, waspish; SEE CONCEPT *401*

pride [*n1*] *self-esteem*
amour-propre, delight, dignity, ego, egoism, egotism, ego trip, face, gratification, happiness, honor, joy, pleasure, pridefulness, repletion, satisfaction, self-admiration, self-confidence, self-glorification, self-love, self-regard, self-respect, self-satisfaction, self-sufficiency, self-trust, self-worth, sufficiency; SEE CONCEPT *411*

pride [*n2*] *arrogance, self-importance*
airs, assumption, big-headedness*, cockiness*, conceit, condescension, contumely, disdain, disdainfulness, egoism, egotism, haughtiness, hauteur, hubris, huff, immodesty, insolence, loftiness, narcissism, overconfidence, patronage, pragmatism, presumption, pretension, pretentiousness, proud flesh*, self-exaltation, self-love, smugness, snobbery, superbity, superciliousness, swagger, swelled head*, vainglory, vanity; SEE CONCEPT *633*

pride [*n3*] *treasure; best*
boast, choice, cream, elite, fat, flower*, gem*, glory, jewel*, pick, pride and joy*, prime, prize, top*; SEE CONCEPTS *446,668,689*

pride [*v*] *take pleasure in accomplishment*
be proud, boast, brag, congratulate, crow, exult, felicitate, flatter oneself, gasconade, glory in, hold head high, overbear, pique*, plume*, prance, preen, presume, puff up*, revel in, strut, swagger, swell, vaunt; SEE CONCEPTS *10,633*

priest [*n*] *man who is minister in Roman or Orthodox Catholic church*
clergyperson, cleric, curate, divine, ecclesiastic, elder, father, father confessor, friar, holy man, lama, man of God, man of the cloth*, monk, padre, pontiff, preacher, rector, vicar; SEE CONCEPT *361*

priesthood [*n*] *clergy*
canonicate, canonry, cardinalate, deaconry, diaconate, ecclesiastics, ministry, pastorate, rabbinate, the cloth, the pulpit; SEE CONCEPT *369*

prim [*adj*] *particular, fussy*
blue-nose*, ceremonial, ceremonious, choosy, cleanly, conventional, correct, dapper*, decorous, demure, fastidious, formal, genteel, good, goody-goody*, nice, nit-picking*, orderly, overmodest, polite, precise, priggish, prissy, proper, prudish, puritanical, rigid, shipshape*, spic-and-span*, spruce, stickling, stiff, straight, strait-laced, stuffy*, tidy, uncluttered, upright, Victorian, well-groomed, wooden*; SEE CONCEPTS *401,404*

prima donna [*n1*] *star*
diva, first lady, headliner, leading lady, lead vocalist, opera singer, singer, soloist, superstar, topliner*; SEE CONCEPTS *352,366*

prima donna [*n2*] *temperamental person*
conceited person, crybaby, egotist, narcissist, princess, self-centered person, spoiled brat, vain person; SEE CONCEPT *411*

primal [*adj*] *primeval; primary*
aboriginal, ancient, central, chief, earliest, early, first, fundamental, highest, old, original, paramount, past, prehistoric, primitive, primordial, principal, pristine; SEE CONCEPT *799*

primarily [*adv1*] *generally; for the most part*
above all, basically, chiefly, especially, essentially, fundamentally, generally, largely, mainly, mostly, on the whole, overall, predominantly, principally; SEE CONCEPTS *531,544,772*

primarily [*adv2*] *in the beginning*
at first, at the start, first and foremost, from the start, initially, in the first place, originally, primitively; SEE CONCEPTS *548,799*

primary/prime [*adj1*] *best, principal*
capital, cardinal, chief, crackerjack*, dominant, excellent, fab*, first, first-class*, greatest, heavy, highest, hot*, leading, main, number one*, paramount, primo*, state-of-the-art*, stellar, top, top-of-the-line*, tough*, world-class*; SEE CONCEPTS *567,574*

primary/prime [*adj2*] *earliest*
aboriginal, beginning, direct, first, firsthand, immediate, initial, original, pioneer, primal, primeval, primitive, primordial, pristine; SEE CONCEPTS *585,799*

primary/prime [*adj3*] *basic, fundamental*
basal, beginning, bottom, central, elemental, elementary, essential, first, foundational, introductory, meat-and-potatoes*, original, primitive, principal, radical, rudimentary, simple, three R's*, ultimate, underivative, underived, underlying; SEE CONCEPTS *549,585*

prime [*n1*] *best part of existence*
best, best days*, bloom, choice, cream*, elite, fat*, flower*, flowering*, height, heyday, maturity, peak, perfection, pink*, prize, spring, springtime, top, verdure, vitality, zenith; SEE CONCEPT *816*

prime [*n2*] *beginning; spring*
adolescence, aurora, dawn, daybreak, dew, greenness*, juvenility, morn*, morning, opening, puberty, pubescence, springtime, start, sunrise, sunup, tender years*, vitality, youth, youthfulness; SEE CONCEPTS *817,832*

prime [*v*] *get ready; prepare*
break in, brief, clue*, coach, cram, excite, fill in, fit, galvanize, groom, inform, innervate, make ready, motivate, move, notify, prep*, provoke, rehearse, stimulate, tell, train; SEE CONCEPTS *7,19,22,35,202*

prime minister [*n*] *premier*
chancellor, chief executive, chief of state, commander-in-chief, head of state, leader, person in charge, president; SEE CONCEPTS *347,354*

primeval [*adj*] *ancient*
earliest, early, first, old, original, prehistoric, primal, primary, primitive, primordial, pristine; SEE CONCEPT *799*

primitive [*adj1*] *ancient, original*
archaic, basic, earliest, early, elementary, essential, first, fundamental, old, primal, primary, primeval, primordial, pristine, substratal, underivative, underived, underlying, undeveloped, unevolved; SEE CONCEPT *799*

primitive [*adj2*] *barbaric, crude*
animal, atavistic, austere, barbarian, barbarous, brutish, childlike, fierce, ignorant, naive, natural, nonliterate, preliterate, raw, rough, rude, rudimentary, savage, simple, uncivilized, uncultivated, uncultured, underdeveloped, undeveloped, undomesticated, unlearned, unrefined, unsophisticated, untamed, untaught, untrained, untutored, vestigial, wild; SEE CONCEPTS *406,485*

primordial [*adj*] *earliest*
basic, early, elemental, first, fundamental, original, prehistoric, primal, primary, prime, primeval, primitive, pristine, radical; SEE CONCEPT *799*

primp [*v*] *beautify and dress nicely*
deck out*, dress up, fix up, get dressed up, groom, gussy up*, preen, prepare, slick*, smarten, spiff, spruce, titivate; SEE CONCEPTS *162,167,202*

principal [*adj*] *most important*
arch, basic, cardinal, champion, chief, controlling, crowning, dominant, essential, first, foremost, greatest, head, highest, incomparable, key, leading, main, mainline, major, matchless, maximum, outstanding, paramount, peerless, predominant, preeminent, premier, prevailing, primary, prime, prominent, second-to-none, sovereign, star, stellar, strongest, supereminent, superior, supreme, transcendent, unapproachable, unequaled, unparalleled, unrivaled; SEE CONCEPTS *568,574*

principal [*n1*] *person in charge of organization, often an educational one*
administrator, boss, chief, dean, director, exec*, head, key player*, lead, leader, preceptor, protagonist, rector, ruler, star, superintendent; SEE CONCEPTS *347,350*

principal [*n2*] *original amount of property either owned or owed*
assets, capital, capital funds, money; SEE CONCEPT *332*

principally [*adv*] *mainly*
above all, basically, before anything else, cardinally, chiefly, dominantly, eminently, especially, essentially, first and foremost, first of all, for the most part, fundamentally, generally, importantly, in the first place, in the main, largely, materially, mostly, notably, particularly, peculiarly, predominantly, preeminently, prevailingly, prevalently, primarily, substantially, superlatively, supremely, to a great degree, universally, vitally; SEE CONCEPTS *531,544,772*

principle [*n1*] *law, standard*
assumption, axiom, basis, canon, convention, criterion, dictum, doctrine, dogma, ethic, form, formula, foundation, fundamental, golden rule*, ground, maxim, origin, postulate, precept, prescript, principium, proposition, regulation, rule, source, theorem, truth, usage, verity; SEE CONCEPTS *318,688*

principle/principles [*n2*] *belief, morality; morals*
attitude, character, code, conduct, conscience, credo, ethic, ethics, faith, ideals, integrity, opinion, policy, probity, rectitude, scruples, sense of duty, sense of honor, system, teaching, tenet, uprightness; SEE CONCEPTS *645,689*

print [*n*] *publication; something impressed*
black-and-white*, book, characters, composition, copy, edition, engraving, face, font, impress, impression, imprint, indentation, issue, lettering, letters, lithograph, magazine, newspaper, newsprint, periodical, photograph, printed matter, stamp, type, typeface, typescript, typesetting, writing; SEE CONCEPTS *259,265,280*

print [*v*] *produce writing, impression; reproduce publication*
calligraph, compose, disseminate, engrave, go to press, impress, imprint, issue, let roll, letter, mark, offset, publish, put to bed*, reissue, reprint, run off, set, set type, stamp, strike off; SEE CONCEPTS *174,203,205*

printer [*n1*] *typesetter*
compositor, pressperson, publisher, typographer; SEE CONCEPTS *174,203,205*

printer [*n2*] *computer peripheral device*
ball printer, character printer, color printer, daisy-wheel printer, dot-matrix printer, graphics printer, ink-jet printer, laser printer, LCD printer, LED printer, line printer, thermal printer; SEE CONCEPT *463*

prior [*adj*] *earlier*
above-mentioned, aforementioned, ahead, antecedent, anterior, before, foregoing, former, forward, past, precedent, preceding, preexistent, preexisting, previous; SEE CONCEPTS *811,812,818,820*

priority [*n*] *first concern*
antecedence, arrangement, crash project*, greatest importance, lead, order, precedence, preeminence, preference, prerogative, previousness, rank, right of way*, seniority, superiority, supremacy, transcendence; SEE CONCEPTS *532,668,727*

prison [*n*] *residence for incarcerating criminals*
bastille, can*, clink*, confinement, cooler*, dungeon, G*, guardhouse, jail, keep, lockup, pen*, penal institution, penitentiary, reformatory, slammer*, statesville*, stockade, up the river*; SEE CONCEPTS *439,449,516*

prisoner [*n*] *person jailed for crime; person kept against their will*
captive, chain gang member, con, convict, culprit, detainee, hostage, internee, jailbird*, lag*, lifer*, loser*, tough*, yardbird*; SEE CONCEPT *412*

prissy [*adj*] *particular and fussy*
epicene, fastidious, finicky, genteel, goody-goody*, goody-two-shoes*, overnice, pansified, persnickety, picky, precious, prim, prim and proper*, prudish, puritanical, sissified, sissy, squeamish, stickling, strait-laced, stuffy*, tight-laced*, Victorian; SEE CONCEPTS *401,404*

pristine [*adj*] *clean, pure; primeval*
earliest, early, first, immaculate, intact, natural, original, primal, purified, refined, sanitary, snowy, spotless, stainless, sterile, sterilized,

pr
pr

taintless, unadulterated, uncorrupted, undebased, unpolluted, unsoiled, unspotted, unstained, unsullied, untainted, untarnished, untouched, virginal, wholesome; SEE CONCEPTS 621,799

privacy [n] *solitude, secrecy*
aloofness, clandestineness, concealment, confidentiality, isolation, one's space, penetralia, privateness, quiet, retirement, retreat, seclusion, separateness, separation, sequestration, solitude; SEE CONCEPTS 388,631,714

private [adj] *personal, intimate*
behind the scenes*, clandestine, closet*, close to one's chest*, confidential, discreet, exclusive, hushed, hush-hush*, independent, individual, inside, nonpublic, not open, off the record*, own, particular, privy*, reserved, secret, separate, special, under one's hat*, unofficial; SEE CONCEPTS 267,406

private [adj2] *hidden, isolated*
concealed, discreet, quiet, removed, retired, secluded, secret, separate, sequestered, solitary, withdrawn; SEE CONCEPTS 576,583

private [n] *lowest rank of person enlisted in armed service*
enlisted person, first-class*, GI, infantry, private soldier, sailor, second-class*, soldier; SEE CONCEPT 358

private eye [n] *private detective*
agent, bird dog*, bloodhound*, cop, dick*, peeper*, P.I.*, private investigator, sleuth, snoop*, tail*; SEE CONCEPT 348

privation [n] *deprivation*
destitution, disadvantage, hardship, indigence, lack, necessity, need, neediness, poverty, want; SEE CONCEPTS 121,142,709

privilege [n] *right, due*
advantage, allowance, appanage, appurtenance, authority, authorization, benefit, birthright, boon, chance, charter, claim, concession, entitlement, event, exemption, favor, franchise, freedom, grant, immunity, liberty, license, opportunity, perquisite, prerogative, right, sanction; SEE CONCEPT 376

privileged [adj1] *favored, elite*
advantaged, entitled, honored, indulged, powerful, ruling, special; SEE CONCEPTS 334,574

privileged [adj2] *allowed, exempt*
authorized, chartered, eligible, empowered, entitled, excused, franchised, free, furnished, granted, immune, kosher*, legit*, licensed, okay*, okayed*, palatine, qualified, sanctioned, special, vested; SEE CONCEPT 548

privileged [adj3] *confidential, secret*
exceptional, for eyes only*, inside, not for publication, off the record*, on the QT*, privy, special, top secret, under one's hat*; SEE CONCEPT 267

privy [adj1] *secret*
buried, concealed, confidential, covert, hidden, hush-hush*, obscured, off the record*, personal, private, separate, shrouded, ulterior; SEE CONCEPTS 267,576

privy [adj2] *aware*
acquainted, apprised, cognizant, conscious, informed, in on*, in the know*, private, privileged, wise; SEE CONCEPT 402

prize [adj] *best*
award-winning, champion, choice, cream*, elite, fat*, first-class*, first-rate*, outstanding, pick, prime, top, topnotch, winning; SEE CONCEPT 574

prize [n1] *award, winnings*
accolade, acquirement, acquisition, advantage, blue ribbon*, bonus, bounty, cake*, capture, carrot*, championship, citation, crown, decoration, dividend, feather in cap*, first place*, gold*, gold star*, gravy*, guerdon, haul, honor, inducement, jackpot, laurel, loot*, medal, meed, payoff*, pickings*, pillage, plum*, plunder*, possession, premium, privilege, purse, recompense, requital, reward, scholarship, spoil, spoils, stakes, strokes*, swag*, title, trophy, windfall; SEE CONCEPTS 337,344,693,710

prize [n2] *goal; best*
aim, ambition, choice, conquest, cream*, desire, elite, fat, flower*, gain, gold*, hope, pick, pride, prime, top*; SEE CONCEPTS 659,709

prize [v] *value highly*
appreciate, apprize, cherish, count, enshrine, esteem, guard, hold dear, rate, regard highly, set store by*, treasure; SEE CONCEPTS 10,32

probability [n] *likelihood of something happening*
anticipation, chance, chances, conceivability, contingency, credibility, expectation, feasibility, hazard, liability, likeliness, odds, outside chance*, plausibility, possibility, practicability, prayer, presumption, promise, prospect, reasonableness, shot, snowball's chance*, toss-up*; SEE CONCEPT 650

probable [adj] *likely to happen*
apparent, believable, credible, earthly, feasible, illusory, in the cards*, mortal, most likely, odds on*, ostensible, plausible, possible, presumable, presumed, rational, reasonable, seeming; SEE CONCEPT 552

probably [adv] *likely to happen*
apparently, as likely as not, assumably, as the case may be, believably, dollars to doughnuts*, doubtless, expediently, feasibly, imaginably, in all likelihood, in all probability, like enough, maybe, most likely, no doubt, one can assume, perchance, perhaps, plausibly, possibly, practicably, presumably, presumptively, reasonably, seemingly, to all appearances; SEE CONCEPT 552

probation [n] *trial period*
apprenticeship, noviciate, test period, trial; SEE CONCEPTS 87,290,291

probe [n] *investigation*
delving, detection, examination, exploration, fishing expedition*, inquest, inquiry, inquisition, legwork*, probing, quest, research, scrutiny, study, third degree*; SEE CONCEPTS 31,103,216,290

probe [v] *explore, investigate*
ask, catechize, check, check out, check over, check up, delve into, dig, examine, eye, feel around, feel out, go into, inquire, interrogate, look into, look-see, penetrate, pierce, poke, prod, prospect, put out a feeler*, query, quiz, scrutinize, search, sift, sound, sound out, study, test the waters*, verify; SEE CONCEPT 31,103,216

probity [n] *fairness, honesty*
equity, fidelity, goodness, honor, integrity, justice, morality, rectitude, righteousness, rightness, sincerity, trustworthiness, truthfulness, uprightness, virtue, worth; SEE CONCEPTS 411,645

problem [n1] *difficulty; bad situation*
botheration, box*, can of worms*, complication, count*, crunch*, dilemma, disagreement, dispute, disputed point, doubt, headache*, hitch,

hot water*, issue, mess*, obstacle, pickle*, point at issue*, predicament, quandary, question, scrape*, squeeze*, trouble, worriment; SEE CONCEPTS 666,674

problem [n2] *puzzle, question*
brainteaser*, bugaboo*, cliff-hanger*, conundrum, enigma, example, grabber*, illustration, intricacy, mind-boggler*, mystery, poser*, puzzler, query, riddle, sixty-four thousand dollar question*, stickler, stumper, teaser, twister; SEE CONCEPTS 529,532

problematic [adj] *open to doubt*
ambiguous, arguable, chancy, debatable, disputable, doubtful, dubious, dubitable, enigmatic, iffy*, indecisive, moot, open, precarious, problematical, puzzling, questionable, suspect, tricky, uncertain, unsettled, up for grabs*; SEE CONCEPT 529

procedure [n] *process, system for accomplishing something*
action, agenda, agendum, channels, conduct, course, custom, daily grind*, fashion, form, formula, game plan*, gimmick, grind, idea, layout, line, maneuver, measure, method, mode, modus operandi, move, nuts and bolts*, operation, performance, plan, policy, polity, practice, proceeding, program, red tape*, routine, scheme, setup, step, strategy, style, the book*, the numbers*, transaction; SEE CONCEPT 6

proceed [v1] *physically or mentally carry on, carry out*
advance, continue, fare, get, get going, get on with, get under way*, go ahead, go on, hie, journey, make a start, march, move on, move out, pass, press on, progress, push on, repair, set in motion, travel, wend; SEE CONCEPTS 43,91

proceed [v2] *flow from; originate*
arise, come, derive, emanate, ensue, extend, follow, head, issue, pass, result, rise, spring, stem; SEE CONCEPTS 179,230,676

proceeding [n] *undertaking, course of action*
act, action, adventure, casualty, circumstance, come off, deed, exercise, experiment, go-down*, goings-on*, happening, incident, maneuver, measure, move, movement, occurrence, operation, performance, procedure, process, step, transaction, venture; SEE CONCEPTS 2,3

proceedings [n] *account, report of event*
affairs, annals, archives, business, dealings, documents, doings*, matters, minutes, records, transactions; SEE CONCEPT 271

proceeds [n] *earnings from business*
gain, gate, handle, income, interest, lucre, produce, product, profit, receipts, result, returns, revenue, reward, split, take, takings, till, yield; SEE CONCEPT 344

process [n] *method; series of actions to achieve result*
action, advance, case, channels*, course, course of action*, development, evolution, fashion, formation, growth, manner, means, measure, mechanism, mode, modus operandi, movement, operation, outgrowth, performance, practice, procedure, proceeding, progress, prolog, red tape*, routine, rule, stage, step, suit, system, technique, transaction, trial, unfolding, way, wise, working; SEE CONCEPT 6

process [v] *subject to series of actions to achieve result*
alter, concoct, convert, deal with, dispose of, ful-

fill, handle, make ready, prepare, refine, take care of, transform, treat; SEE CONCEPT 204

procession [n] *parade, sequence*
advance, autocade, cavalcade, column, consecution, cortege, course, cycle, file, march, motorcade, movement, order, process, run, series, string, succession, train; SEE CONCEPTS 155,727

proclaim [v] *advertise, make known*
affirm, announce, annunciate, blast, blaze, blazon, broadcast, call, circulate, declare, demonstrate, disseminate, enunciate, evidence, evince, exhibit, expound, get on a soapbox*, give out, herald, illustrate, indicate, manifest, mark, ostend, pass the word*, profess, promulgate, publish, shoot off mouth*, shout out, show, sound off, spiel*, spout, spread it around*, stump*, trumpet*, utter, vent, ventilate, voice; SEE CONCEPTS 49,60

proclamation [n] *advertisement, announcement*
broadcast, declaration, decree, edict, manifesto, notice, notification, promulgation, pronouncement, pronunciamento*, publication; SEE CONCEPTS 271,278

proclivity [n] *inclination, tendency*
bent*, bias, cup of tea*, disposition, druthers, facility, flash*, groove*, inclining, leaning, liableness, penchant, predilection, predisposition, proneness, propensity, thing for*, type, weakness; SEE CONCEPTS 20,32,411

procrastinate [v] *delay, put off doing*
adjourn, be dilatory, cool*, dally, dawdle, defer, drag, drag one's feet*, give the run around*, goldbrick*, hang fire*, hesitate, hold off, lag*, let slide, linger, loiter, pause, play a waiting game*, play for time*, poke*, postpone, prolong, protract, retard, shilly-shally*, stall, stay, suspend, tarry, temporize, wait; SEE CONCEPTS 121,237,681

procreate [v] *reproduce*
beget, breed, conceive, create, engender, father, generate, get, give birth to, hatch, impregnate, make, mother, multiply, originate, parent, produce, progenerate, proliferate, propagate, sire, spawn; SEE CONCEPTS 173,251,374

procure [v] *acquire, obtain*
annex, appropriate, bring around, buy, buy out, buy up, come by, compass, cop*, corral, draw, earn, effect, find, gain, get, get hold of, grab, have, induce, land*, latch on to, lay hands on, make a haul*, manage to get*, persuade, pick up, prevail upon, promote, purchase, score, secure, solicit, wangle, win; SEE CONCEPTS 68,120,327

prod [v1] *poke at*
crowd, dig, drive, elbow, goose, jab, jog, nudge, press, prick, punch, push, shove; SEE CONCEPT 208

prod [v2] *urge, incite*
crowd*, egg on*, excite, exhort, goad, goose*, impel, instigate, jog memory, motivate, move, pique, prick, prompt, propel, provoke, push, remind, rouse, sic*, sound, spark, spur, stimulate, stir up, trigger, turn on; SEE CONCEPTS 7,19,22,242

prodigal [adj1] *wasteful*
dissipated, excessive, extravagant, immoderate, improvident, intemperate, lavish, profligate, reckless, spendthrift, squandering, wanton; SEE CONCEPTS 401,560

prodigal [adj2] *luxurious, profuse*
abundant, bounteous, bountiful, copious, exuber-

ant, lavish, lush, luxuriant, moneyed, munificent, opulent, riotous, sumptuous, superabundant, teeming; SEE CONCEPTS 334,781

prodigal [n] *person who spends a lot*
big spender*, compulsive shopper*, deep pockets*, dissipator, high roller*, profligate, spender, spendthrift, sport, squanderer, waster, wastrel*; SEE CONCEPTS 348,412

prodigious [adj1] *huge, enormous*
big, colossal*, fantastic, giant, gigantic, gross, Herculean*, immeasurable, immense, inordinate, jumbo*, king-size*, large, mammoth, massive, mighty, monstrous, monumental, mortal, stupendous, towering, tremendous, vast; SEE CONCEPTS 773,781

prodigious [adj2] *extraordinary, fabulous*
abnormal, amazing, astonishing, astounding, bad, exceptional, fab*, fantastic, heavy, impressive, marvelous, miraculous, out-of-this-world*, phenomenal, preternatural, remarkable, spectacular, staggering, startling, state-of-the-art*, striking, stupendous, surprising, unreal, unusual, utmost, wonderful; SEE CONCEPTS 567,572,574

prodigy [n] *person or thing that is extraordinary*
brain*, child genius, curiosity, enormity, freak*, genius, intellect, marvel, mastermind, miracle, monster, natural, one in a million*, phenomenon, portent, rare bird*, rarity, sensation, spectacle, stunner, talent, whiz*, whiz kid*, wizard, wonder, wonder child, wunderkind; SEE CONCEPTS 416,671,706

produce [n] *fruit and vegetables*
crop, fruitage, goods, greengrocery, harvest, outcome, outgrowth, outturn, production, yield; SEE CONCEPTS 426,429,431,457,461

produce [v1] *generate, create*
afford, assemble, author, bear, beget, blossom, breed, bring forth, bring out, build, come through, compose, conceive, construct, contribute, cultivate, deliver, design, develop, devise, effectuate, engender, erect, fabricate, fetch, flower, form, frame, furnish, give, give birth, give forth, imagine, invent, make, manufacture, multiply, offer, originate, parent, present, procreate, propagate, provide, put together, render, reproduce, return, show fruit, supply, turn out, write, yield; SEE CONCEPTS 173,205,251,374

produce [v2] *cause, effect*
beget, breed, bring about, draw on, engender, generate, get up, give rise to, hatch, induce, make, make for*, muster, occasion, provoke, result in, secure, set off, work up; SEE CONCEPT 242

produce [v3] *demonstrate, show*
advance, bring forward, bring to light, display, exhibit, offer, present, put forward, set forth, unfold; SEE CONCEPT 261

produce [v4] *put on a public performance*
act, come through, direct, do, exhibit, make, mount, percolate, perform, perk, play, present, pull off*, show, stage; SEE CONCEPTS 292,324

product [n] *result or goods created*
aftermath, amount, artifact, blend, brand, brew, by-product, commodity, compound, concoction, confection, consequence, contrivance, creation, crop, decoction, device, effect, emolument, fabrication, fruit, gain, handiwork, invention, issue, legacy, line, manufacture, merchandise, offshoot, outcome, outgrowth, output, preparation, produce, production, profit, realization, result, returns, spinoff, stock, synthetic, upshot, work, yield; SEE CONCEPTS 230,338

production [n] *creating of goods, result*
assembly, authoring, bearing, blossoming, construction, creation, direction, elongation, engendering, extention, fabrication, formulation, fructification, generation, giving, lengthening, making, management, manufacture, manufacturing, origination, preparation, presentation, producing, prolongation, protraction, provision, rendering, reproduction, return, staging, yielding; SEE CONCEPT 205

productive [adj] *fruitful, creative*
advantageous, beneficial, constructive, dynamic, effective, energetic, fecund, fertile, gainful, generative, gratifying, inventive, plentiful, producing, profitable, prolific, rewarding, rich, teeming, useful, valuable, vigorous, worthwhile; SEE CONCEPTS 537,542,560

productivity [n] *output, work rate*
abundance, capacity, fecundity, fertility, mass production, potency, production, productiveness, richness, yield; SEE CONCEPT 630

profane [adj] *immoral, crude, disrespectful of religion*
abusive, atheistic, blasphemous, coarse, dirty*, filthy*, foul, godless, heathen, idolatrous, impious, impure, indecent, infidel, irreligious, irreverent, irreverential, mundane, nasty, obscene, pagan, profanatory, raunchy, sacrilegious, sinful, smutty*, temporal, transient, transitory, unconsecrated, ungodly, unhallowed, unholy, unsanctified, vulgar, wicked, worldly; SEE CONCEPTS 267,401,545

profane [v] *defile, desecrate*
abuse, be evil, befoul, blaspheme, commit sacrilege, commit sin, contaminate, curse, cuss, damn, darn, debase, despoil, do wrong, flame, hoodoo*, misuse, mock, mudsling*, pervert, pollute, prostitute, put double whammy on*, revile, scorn, swear, talk dirty*, tar, trash, vice, violate, vitiate, voodoo*; SEE CONCEPTS 44,52,58,63

profanity [n] *foul language*
abuse, blasphemy, curse, cursing, cuss, cuss word, dirty language*, dirty name*, dirty word*, execration, four-letter word*, impiety, imprecation, irreverence, malediction, no-no*, obscenity, profaneness, sacrilege, swearing, swearword, taboo; SEE CONCEPTS 278,645

profess [v] *declare, assert*
acknowledge, act as if, admit, affirm, allege, announce, asseverate, aver, avouch, avow, blow hot air*, certify, claim, come out*, confess, confirm, constate, croon, cross heart*, depose, dissemble, fake, feign, get off chest*, get on soapbox*, maintain, make out, open up*, own own up*, predicate, pretend, proclaim, purport, say so*, sing*, soapbox*, spiel*, spout*, state, stump*, swear on bible*, swear up and down*, talk big*, vouch; SEE CONCEPTS 49,63

profession [n1] *line of work requiring academic or practical preparation*
art, avocation, berth, billet, biz*, business, calling, career, chosen work, concern, craft, dodge*, employment, engagement, field, game*, handicraft, lifework, line*, line of work*, métier, occupation, office, position, post, pursuit, rat race*, role, service, situation, slot*, specialty, sphere, thing*, trade, undertaking, vocation, walk of life*; SEE CONCEPT 360

profession [n2] *declaration*
acknowledgment, affirmation, assertion, attestation, avowal, claim, confession, pretense, statement, testimony, vow; SEE CONCEPT 278

professional [adj] *skilled, trained*
able, ace, acknowledged, adept, competent, crackerjack*, efficient, experienced, expert, finished, knowing one's stuff*, known, learned, licensed, on the ball*, polished, practiced, proficient, qualified, sharp, skillful, slick*, there*, up to speed*, well-qualified; SEE CONCEPTS 326,402,527,528

professional [n] *person prepared for work by extended study or practice*
adept, artist, artiste, authority, brain*, egghead*, expert, hotshot*, old hand*, old pro*, old warhorse*, phenom*, powerhouse, pro, proficient, pundit, shark, specialist, star, superstar, virtuoso, whiz*, whiz kid*, wizard; SEE CONCEPTS 347,348

professor [n] *person who teaches college courses*
assistant, brain*, educator, egghead*, faculty member, fellow, instructor, lecturer, pedagogue, principal, prof*, pundit, quant*, rocket scientist*, sage, savant, teacher, tutor; SEE CONCEPT 350

proffer [v] *suggest, offer*
extend, gift, give, hand, hit on, hold out, make a pitch*, pose, present, propose, proposition, propound, submit, tender, volunteer; SEE CONCEPTS 66,67,75

proficiency [n] *ability, skillfulness*
accomplishment, advance, advancement, aptitude, chops, competence, dexterity, efficiency, expertise, expertness, facility, formula, green thumb*, headway*, knack*, know-how*, knowledge, learning, makings, mastery, moxie*, oil*, progress, right stuff*, savvy*, skill, stuff, talent, what it takes*; SEE CONCEPTS 409,630,706

proficient [adj] *able, skilled*
accomplished, adept, apt, capable, clever, competent, consummate, conversant, crack*, crackerjack*, drilled, effective, effectual, efficient, exercised, experienced, expert, finished, gifted, on the beam*, phenom*, pro, qualified, savvy*, sharp, skillful, slick*, talented, trained, up to speed*, versed, whiz*, with it*; SEE CONCEPTS 402,527,528

profile [n1] *drawing of outline*
contour, delineation, figuration, figure, form, likeness, line, lineament, lineation, portrait, shadow, shape, side view, silhouette, sketch; SEE CONCEPTS 259,625

profile [n2] *description, characterization*
analysis, biography, character sketch, chart, diagram, review, sketch, study, survey, thumbnail sketch, vignette, vita; SEE CONCEPTS 268,283

profit [n] *gain*
accumulation, acquisition, advancement, advantage, aggrandizement, augmentation, avail, benefit, bottom line*, cleanup, earnings, emoluments, gate*, goods*, gravy*, gross, harvest, income, interest, killing, lucre, net, output, outturn, percentage, proceeds, product, production, receipt, receipts, remuneration, return, revenue, saving, skim*, split*, surplus, take*, takings*, turnout, use, value, velvet*, winnings, yield; SEE CONCEPTS 332,344,693

profit [v] *gain; get or give an advantage*
aid, avail, benefit, be of advantage, better, capitalize on, cash in on, clean up, clear, contribute, earn, exploit, help, improve, learn from, make a haul*, make a killing*, make capital, make good use of*, make it big*, make money, make the most of*, pay, pay off, promote, prosper, put to good use*, realize, reap the benefit*, recover, score, serve*, stand in good stead*, take advantage of, thrive, turn to advantage, use, utilize, work for; SEE CONCEPTS 110,124,330,693

profitable [adj] *advantageous; money-making*
assisting, beneficial, commercial, conducive, contributive, cost-effective, effective, effectual, favorable, fruitful, gainful, going*, good, instrumental, in the black*, lucrative, paid off, paying, paying well, practical, pragmatic, productive, remunerative, rewarding, self-sustaining, serviceable, successful, sustaining, sweet*, useful, valuable, well-paying, worthwhile; SEE CONCEPTS 334,537,572

profligate [adj1] *immoral, corrupt*
abandoned, debauched, degenerate, depraved, dissipated, dissolute, iniquitous, lax, lewd, libertine, licentious, loose, promiscuous, reprobate, shameless, unprincipled, vicious, vitiated, wanton, wicked, wild; SEE CONCEPT 545

profligate [adj2] *wasteful*
extravagant, immoderate, improvident, lavish, prodigal, reckless, spendthrift, squandering; SEE CONCEPTS 334,401

profligate [n] *person who is immoral*
debauchee, degenerate, dissipater, good-for-nothing*, lecher, libertine, nighthawk*, no-good*, old goat*, operator*, prodigal, rake, reprobate, roué, swinger, waster, wastrel; SEE CONCEPT 412

profound [adj1] *intellectual, thoughtful*
abstruse, acroamatic, deep, difficult, discerning, enlightened, erudite, esoteric, heavy*, hermetic, informed, intellectual, intelligent, knowing, knowledgeable, learned, mysterious, occult, Orphic, penetrating, philosophical, recondite, reflective, sagacious, sage, scholarly, secret, serious, shrewd, skilled, subtle, thorough, weighty, wise; SEE CONCEPTS 402,529

profound [adj2] *bottomless*
abysmal, buried, cavernous, deep, fathomless, subterranean, yawning; SEE CONCEPT 777

profound [adj3] *intense; emotional*
abject, absolute, acute, consummate, deep, deeply felt, deep-seated, exhaustive, extensive, extreme, far-reaching, great, hard, heartfelt, heartrending, hearty, keen, out-and-out*, pronounced, sincere, thorough, total, utter; SEE CONCEPTS 403,531,569

profuse [adj] *abundant, excessive*
abounding, alive with*, ample, aplenty, bounteous, bountiful, copious, crawling with*, dime a dozen*, extravagant, extreme, exuberant, fulsome, galore, generous, immoderate, lavish, liberal, lush, luxuriant, no end*, openhanded, opulent, overflowing, plentiful, plenty, prodigal, profusive, prolific, riotous, sumptuous, superfluous, swarming, teeming, thick with*, unstinting; SEE CONCEPTS 762,781

profusion [n] *abundance*
ampleness, copiousness, excess, extravagance, flood, glut, great quantity, opulence, outpouring, overflow, plenitude, plenty, prosperity, prosperousness, surplus, wealth; SEE CONCEPTS 710,767

progeny [n] *offspring*
begats, breed, children, descendants, family, get*, issue, kids*, lineage, posterity, progeniture, race, scions, seed, stock, young; SEE CONCEPTS *296,414*

prognosis [n] *forecast*
cast, diagnosis, expectation, foretelling, guess, prediction, prevision, prognostication, projection, prophecy, speculation, surmise; SEE CONCEPTS *274,689*

prognosticate [v] *predict, foretell*
adumbrate, augur, betoken, call it*, crystal-ball*, divine, forebode, forecast, foreshadow, harbinger, have a hunch*, herald, make book*, point to, portend, presage, prophesy, read, see coming*, soothsay, vaticinate; SEE CONCEPT *70*

prognosticator [n] *forecaster*
augur, channeller, diviner, fortune-teller, medium, oracle, prophet, seer, soothsayer, telepathist, visionary; SEE CONCEPT *423*

program [nl] *agenda, list*
affairs, appointments, arrangements, bill, bulletin, business, calendar, card, catalog, chores, curriculum, details, docket, happenings, index, lineup, listing, meetings, memoranda, necessary acts*, order of business*, order of events*, order of the day*, plan, plans, preparations, record, schedule, series of events, slate, syllabus, things to do*, timetable; SEE CONCEPTS *281,283*

program [n2] *scheme, plan*
course, design, instructions, line, order, plan of action, policy, polity, procedure, project, sequence; SEE CONCEPTS *274,660*

program [n3] *performance in medium*
broadcast, presentation, production, show; SEE CONCEPT *263*

program [v] *plan out; supply instructions*
arrange, bill, book, budget, calculate, compile, compute, design, draft, edit, engage, enter, estimate, feed, figure, formulate, get on line*, itemize, lay on, lay out, line up, list, map out, pencil in*, poll, prearrange, prioritize, process, register, schedule, set, set up, slate, work out; SEE CONCEPTS *36,60,84,384*

progress [n] *advancement, gain*
advance, amelioration, anabasis, betterment, boost, break, breakthrough, buildup, course, dash, development, evolution, evolvement, expedition, flowering, growth, headway, hike, impetus, improvement, increase, journey, lunge, march, momentum, motion, movement, ongoing, pace, passage, process, procession, proficiency, progression, promotion, rate, rise, step forward, stride, tour, unfolding, voyage, way; SEE CONCEPTS *704,706*

progress [vl] *move forward*
advance, continue, cover ground*, dash, edge, forge ahead, gain ground, get along, get on, go forward, keep going, lunge, make headway*, make strides*, move on, proceed, shoot, speed, travel; SEE CONCEPTS *149,159*

progress [v2] *improve, advance*
ameliorate, become better, better, blossom, boost, develop, gain, grow, increase, make first rate, mature, shape up, straighten up, truck, turn over new leaf*, upgrade; SEE CONCEPT *700*

progression [n] *progress*
advance, advancement, amelioration, betterment, boost, break, breakthrough, development, evolution, evolvement, forward march, furtherance,

getting ahead, giant strides, going forward, growth, headway, improvement, promotion, step forward; SEE CONCEPTS *704,706*

progressive [adj] *liberal; growing*
accelerating, advanced, advancing, avant-garde*, bleeding-heart*, broad, broad-minded, continuing, continuous, developing, dynamic, enlightened, enterprising, escalating, forward-looking, go-ahead*, gradual, graduated, increasing, intensifying, left*, left of center*, lenient, modern, ongoing, onward, open-minded, radical, reformist, revolutionary, tolerant, up-and-coming*, up-to-date, wide; SEE CONCEPTS *542,544*

prohibit [v] *make impossible; stop*
ban, block, bottle up*, box in*, bring to screeching halt*, constrain, cool*, cork*, debar, disallow, enjoin, forbid, forfend, freeze*, gridlock, halt, hamper, hang up*, hinder, hold up, impede, inhibit, interdict, jam up*, keep lid on*, kill, lock up, nix, obstruct, outlaw, pass on*, preclude, prevent, proscribe, put a lock on*, put a stopper in*, put chill on*, put down, put half nelson on*, restrain, restrict, rule out, shut out, spike*, stymie*, taboo*, throw cold water on*, tie up*, veto, zing*; SEE CONCEPTS *50,88,121,130,317*

prohibited [adj] *forbidden*
banned, barred, closed down, contraband, crooked*, illegal, illicit, no-no*, not allowed, not approved, off limits*, out of bounds*, out of line*, proscribed, refused, restricted, shady*, taboo, verboten, vetoed, wildcat*; SEE CONCEPTS *554,576*

prohibition [n] *ban, forbiddance*
bar, constraint, disallowance, don't*, embargo, exclusion, injunction, interdict, interdiction, negation, no-no*, obstruction, off limits*, out of bounds*, prevention, proscription, refusal, repudiation, restriction, taboo, temperance, veto; SEE CONCEPTS *121,130,652,691*

prohibitive [adj] *restrictive; beyond one's financial means*
conditional, excessive, exorbitant, expensive, extortionate, forbidding, high-priced, limiting, preposterous, preventing, prohibiting, proscriptive, repressive, restraining, sky-high*, steep*, suppressive; SEE CONCEPTS *334,554*

project [n] *undertaking, work*
activity, adventure, affair, aim, assignment, baby*, blueprint*, business, concern, deal, design, enterprise, exploit, feat, game plan, intention, job, matter, occupation, outline, pet*, plan, program, proposal, proposition, scheme, setup, strategy, task, thing*, venture; SEE CONCEPTS *324,349,362*

project [vl] *plan*
arrange, blueprint, calculate, cast, chart, conceive, contemplate, contrive, delineate, design, devise, diagram, draft, envisage, envision, estimate, extrapolate, feature, forecast, frame, gauge, image, imagine, intend, map out, outline, predetermine, predict, propose, purpose, reckon, scheme, see, think, vision, visualize; SEE CONCEPTS *28,36,37,70*

project [v2] *bulge, hang out*
be conspicuous, beetle, be prominent, extend, hang over, jut, lengthen, overhang, poke, pop out, pout, prolong, protrude, protuberate, push out, stand out, stick out, stretch out, thrust out; SEE CONCEPT *747*

project [v3] *throw, discharge*
cast, fling, heave, hurl, launch, pitch, propel, shoot, transmit; SEE CONCEPTS *179,222*

projection [n1] *bulge, overhang*
bump, bunch, eaves, extension, hook, jut, knob, ledge, outthrust, point, prolongation, prominence, protrusion, protuberance, ridge, rim, shelf, sill, spine, spur, step, swelling; SEE CONCEPTS *471,509,513*

projection [n2] *prediction*
calculation, computation, estimate, estimation, extrapolation, forecast, guess, prognostication, reckoning; SEE CONCEPTS *28,278*

proletariat [n1] *working class*
blue-collar workers, bourgeoisie, commoners, common people, hoi polloi, lower class, peasant, plebians, proletarian, rank and file, working stiff; SEE CONCEPTS *413,423*

proliferate [v] *increase quickly*
breed, burgeon, engender, escalate, expand, generate, grow rapidly, multiply, mushroom*, procreate, propagate, reproduce, run riot*, snowball*; SEE CONCEPT *780*

prolific [adj] *fruitful, productive*
abounding, abundant, bountiful, breeding, copious, creative, fecund, fertile, generating, generative, luxuriant, profuse, proliferant, rank, reproducing, reproductive, rich, spawning, swarming, teeming, yielding; SEE CONCEPTS *485,542*

prologue [n] *preface*
beginning, exordium, explanation, foreword, introduction, opening, overture, preamble, prelude, proem, prolegomenon; SEE CONCEPT *270*

prolong [v] *extend, draw out*
carry on, continue, delay, drag one's feet*, drag out*, hold, hold up, increase, lengthen, let it ride*, make longer, pad*, perpetuate, protract, spin out*, stall, stretch, stretch out; SEE CONCEPTS *239,250*

prominence [n1] *something that sticks out*
bulge, bump, cliff, conspicuousness, crag, crest, elevation, eminence, headland, height, high point, jutting, markedness, mound, pinnacle, projection, promontory, protrusion, protuberance, rise, spur, swelling, tor; SEE CONCEPTS *513,836*

prominence [n2] *distinction, outstandingness*
celebrity, eminence, fame, greatness, illustriousness, importance, influence, kudos*, name, notability, precedence, preeminence, prestige, rank, renown, reputation, salience, specialness, standing, top billing*, weight; SEE CONCEPT *668*

prominent [adj1] *sticking out; conspicuous*
arresting, beetling, bulging, easily seen, embossed, extended, extrusive, eye-catching, flashy, hanging out, hilly, in the foreground, jutting, marked, noticeable, obtrusive, obvious, outstanding, projecting, pronounced, protruding, protrusive, protuberant, raised, relieved, remarkable, rough, rugged, salient, shooting out, signal, standing out, striking, to the fore, unmistakable; SEE CONCEPTS *485,583,619*

prominent [adj2] *important; famous*
big-league*, big-name*, big-shot*, celebrated, chief, distinguished, eminent, famed, foremost, great, high-profile*, leading, main, notable, noted, notorious, outstanding, popular, preeminent, renowned, respected, top, underlined, VIP*, well-known, well-thought-of, world-class*; SEE CONCEPT *568*

promiscuous [adj] *indiscriminately sexually active*
abandoned, debauched, dissipated, dissolute, easy*, fast*, immoral, indiscriminate, lax, libertine, licentious, loose*, of easy virtue, oversexed, profligate, pushover, unbridled, unchaste, undiscriminating, unrestricted, wanton, wild; SEE CONCEPTS *372,545*

promise [n1] *one's word that something will be done*
affiance, affirmation, agreement, asseveration, assurance, avowal, betrothal, bond, commitment, compact, consent, contract, covenant, earnest, engagement, espousal, guarantee, insurance, marriage, oath, obligation, pact, parole, pawn, pledge, plight, profession, promissory note, sacred word, security, stipulation, swear, swearing, token, troth, undertaking, vow, warrant, warranty, word, word of honor; SEE CONCEPTS *71,278*

promise [n2] *hope, possibility*
ability, aptitude, capability, capacity, encouragement, flair, good omen, outlook, potential, talent; SEE CONCEPTS *630,650*

promise [v1] *give word that something will be done*
accede, affiance, affirm, agree, answer for, assent, asseverate, assure, bargain, betroth, bind, commit, compact, consent, contract, covenant, cross heart*, declare, engage, ensure, espouse, guarantee, hock*, insure, live up to*, mortgage, obligate, pass, pawn*, pledge, plight, profess, say so*, secure, stipulate, string along*, subscribe, swear, swear on bible*, swear up and down*, take an oath, undertake, underwrite, vouch, vow, warrant; SEE CONCEPT *71*

promise [v2] *bring hope, possibility*
augur, bespeak, betoken, bode, denote, encourage, forebode, foreshadow, foretoken, give hope, hint, hold out hope*, hold probability, indicate, lead to expect, like, look, omen, portend, presage, seem likely, show signs of*, suggest; SEE CONCEPTS *118,650*

promising [adj] *hopeful*
able, assuring, auspicious, bright, encouraging, favorable, gifted, happy, likely, lucky, propitious, reassuring, rising, roseate, rosy, talented, up-and-coming; SEE CONCEPTS *406,548*

promontory [n] *headland*
bluff, cape, cheronese, foreland, jetty, jutty, peninsula, point, ridge; SEE CONCEPTS *509,514*

promote [v1] *help, advance*
advertise, advocate, aid, assist, avail, back, befriend, benefit, bolster, boost, build up*, call attention to, champion, contribute, cooperate, cry*, develop, encourage, endorse, espouse, forward, foster, further, get behind, hype*, improve, nourish, nurture, patronize, plug*, popularize, propagandize, publicize, puff*, push, push for, recommend, sell, serve, speak for, speed, sponsor, stimulate, subsidize, succor, support, uphold, urge, work for; SEE CONCEPTS *49,110,324*

promote [v2] *give a higher position in organization*
advance, aggrandize, ascend, better, dignify, elevate, ennoble, exalt, favor, graduate, honor, increase, kick upstairs*, magnify, move up, prefer, raise, skip, up*, upgrade; SEE CONCEPT *351*

promoter [n] *supporter*
advertiser, advocate, ally, backer, booster, en-

dorser, follower, organizer, publicist, sponsor; SEE CONCEPT 423

promotion [n1] *higher position in organization*
advance, advancement, advocacy, aggrandizement, backing, betterment, boost, break, breakthrough, buildup, bump, elevation, encouragement, ennoblement, exaltation, favoring, furtherance, go-ahead*, hike, honor, improvement, jump, jump up, lift, move up, preference, preferment, prelation, progress, raise, rise, step up, support, upgrade, upgrading; SEE CONCEPT 351

promotion [n2] *publicity*
advertising, advertising campaign, ballyhoo*, blurb*, buildup*, hard sell*, hoopla*, hype*, notice, pitch, pizzazz*, plug*, PR*, press*, press-agentry, promo*, propaganda, publicity, public relations, puff*, puffery*, pushing, squib*; SEE CONCEPTS 49,110,271,324

prompt [adj] *early, responsive*
alert, apt, brisk, eager, efficient, expeditious, immediate, instant, instantaneous, on the ball*, on the button*, on the dot*, on the nose*, on time, precise, punctual, quick, rapid, ready, smart, speedy, swift, timely, unhesitating, vigilant, watchful, wide-awake, willing; SEE CONCEPTS 401,799

prompt [n] *hint*
cue, help, jog, jolt, mnemonic, prod, reminder, spur, stimulus, twit; SEE CONCEPT 274

prompt [v] *incite, cue*
advise, aid, arouse, assist, bring up, call forth, cause, convince, draw, egg on*, elicit, evoke, exhort, get, give rise to, goad, help, help out, hint, impel, imply, indicate, induce, inspire, instigate, jog, mention, motivate, move, occasion, persuade, prick*, prod, propel, propose, provoke, refresh, remind, sic*, spur, stimulate, suggest, talk into, urge, win over; SEE CONCEPTS 68,242

promptly [adv] *immediately*
at once, directly, expeditiously, fast, flat-out*, fleetly, hastily, in nothing flat*, instantly, lickety-split*, like a shot*, now, on the dot*, on the double*, on time, PDQ*, posthaste, pronto, punctually, quickly, rapidly, right away, sharp, speedily, straightaway, swiftly, unhesitatingly; SEE CONCEPTS 544,799

promulgate [v] *make known*
advertise, announce, annunciate, broadcast, call, circulate, communicate, declare, decree, disseminate, drum, issue, make public, notify, pass the word*, proclaim, promote, publish, sound, spread, toot, trumpet; SEE CONCEPT 60

prone [adj1] *lying down*
decumbent, face down, flat, horizontal, level, procumbent, prostrate, reclining, recumbent, resupine, supine; SEE CONCEPT 583

prone [adj2] *liable, likely*
apt, bent, devoted, disposed, exposed, fain, given, inclined, minded, open, predisposed, ready, sensitive, subject, susceptible, tending, willing; SEE CONCEPTS 542,552

pronounce [v1] *produce words vocally*
accent, articulate, enunciate, phonate, say, sound, speak, stress, utter, verbalize, vocalize, voice; SEE CONCEPT 47

pronounce [v2] *announce, declare*
affirm, assert, blast, call, decree, deliver, drum, judge, mouth, proclaim, say, sound off, spread around, trumpet, verbalize; SEE CONCEPT 49

pronounced [adj] *distinct, evident*
arresting, assured, broad, clear, clear-cut, conspicuous, decided, definite, marked, notable, noticeable, obvious, outstanding, striking, strong, unmistakable; SEE CONCEPTS 535,576,619

pronouncement [n] *declaration, statement*
advertisement, announcement, broadcast, decree, dictum, edict, judgment, manifesto, notification, proclamation, promulgation, pronunciamiento*, publication, report, ukase; SEE CONCEPTS 271,274,278

proof [n1] *evidence, authentication*
affidavit, argument, attestation, averment, case, certification, chapter and verse*, clincher*, clue, confirmation, corroboration, credentials, criterion, cue*, data, demonstration, deposition, documents, establishment, exhibit, facts, goods*, grabber*, grounds, information, lowdown*, nitty-gritty*, paper trail*, picture, reason, reasons, record, scoop*, score*, skinny*, smoking gun*, straight stuff*, substantiation, testament, testimony, trace, validation, verification, warrant, wherefore*, why*, whyfor*, witness; SEE CONCEPT 274

proof [n2] *photographic print*
galley, galley proof, impression, page proof, pass, pull, repro, revise, slip, stereo, trial, trial print, trial proof; SEE CONCEPT 265

proofread [v] *copyedit*
-analyze, blue-pencil*, check, correct, cut, delete, edit, go over, rearrange, refine, remove error, rephrase, revise, strike out; SEE CONCEPTS 79,126,203

prop [n] *support*
aid, assistance, brace, buttress, column, mainstay, post, shore, stanchion, stay, strengthener, strut, truss, underpinning; SEE CONCEPTS 440,475

prop [v] *hold up or lean against*
bear up, bolster, brace, buoy, buttress, carry, maintain, rest, set, shore, stand, stay, strengthen, support, sustain, truss, underprop, uphold; SEE CONCEPTS 190,201

propaganda [n] *information that is designed to mislead or persuade*
advertising, agitprop, announcement, brainwashing*, disinformation, doctrine, evangelism, handout, hogwash*, hype*, implantation, inculcation, indoctrination, newspeak, promotion, promulgation, proselytism, publication, publicity; SEE CONCEPT 278

propagate [v1] *breed, reproduce*
bear, beget, engender, father, fecundate, fertilize, generate, grow, impregnate, increase, inseminate, make pregnant, mother, multiply, originate, procreate, produce, proliferate, raise, sire; SEE CONCEPT 374

propagate [v2] *spread, make known*
broadcast, circulate, develop, diffuse, disperse, disseminate, distribute, proclaim, promulgate, publicize, publish, radiate, scatter, strew, transmit; SEE CONCEPTS 60,222

propel [v] *throw; release into air*
actuate, drive, force, impel, launch, mobilize, move, press, push, send, set going, set in motion, shoot, shove, start, thrust; SEE CONCEPTS 208,221,222

propensity [n] *inclination, weakness*
ability, aptness, bent*, bias, capacity, competence, disposition, flash, inclining, leaning, liability, partiality, penchant, predilection, pro-

disposition, proclivity, proneness, susceptibility, sweet tooth*, talent, tendency, thing*, tilt*, yen; SEE CONCEPTS **20,411,630,709**

roper [*adj1*] *suitable*

able, applicable, appropriate, apt, au fait, becoming, befitting, capable, competent, convenient, decent, desired, felicitous, fit, fitting, good, happy, just, legitimate, meet, qualified, right, suited, true, useful; SEE CONCEPT **558**

roper [*adj2*] *mannerly, decent*

becoming, befitting, by the book*, by the numbers*, comely, comme il faut*, conforming, correct, decorous, demure, de rigueur*, genteel, in line, kosher*, moral, nice, polite, precise, priggish, prim, prissy, prudish, punctilious, puritanical, refined, respectable, right, seemly, solid, square*, stone, straight*, strait-laced*, stuffy*; SEE CONCEPTS **401,404**

roper [*adj3*] *conventional, correct*

absolute, accepted, accurate, arrant, complete, consummate, customary, decorous, established, exact, formal, free of error, on target*, on the button*, on the nose*, on the right track*, orthodox, out-and-out*, precise, right, unmistaken, usual, utter; SEE CONCEPTS **326,533**

roper [*adj4*] *individual, personal*

characteristic, distinctive, idiosyncratic, own, particular, peculiar, private, respective, special, specific; SEE CONCEPTS **549,557**

roperty [*n1*] *possessions, real estate*

acreage, acres, assets, belongings, buildings, capital, chattels, claim, dominion, effects, equity, estate, farm, freehold, goods, holdings, home, house, inheritance, land, means, ownership, plot, possessorship, premises, proprietary, proprietorship, realty, resources, riches, substance, title, tract, wealth, worth; SEE CONCEPTS **446,509,515,710**

roperty [*n2*] *characteristic, feature*

ability, affection, attribute, character, hallmark, idiosyncrasy, mark, peculiarity, quality, trait, virtue; SEE CONCEPTS **411,654**

rophecy [*n*] *prediction*

apocalypse, augury, cast, divination, forecast, foretelling, oracle, presage, prevision, prognosis, prognostication, revelation, second sight, soothsaying, vision; SEE CONCEPTS **70,278,689**

rophesy [*v*] *predict, warn*

adumbrate, augur, call*, call the turn*, crystalball*, divine, forecast, foresee, foretell, forewarn, have a hunch*, make book*, portend, predict, presage, prognosticate, psych it out*, see coming*, soothsay, vaticinate; SEE CONCEPT **70**

rophet [*n*] *person, thing that predicts future*

astrologer, augur, auspex, bard, clairvoyant, diviner, druid, evocator, forecaster, fortuneteller, haruspex, horoscopist, magus, medium, meteorologist, oracle, ovate, palmist, predictor, prognosticator, prophesier, reader, seer, seeress, sibyl, soothsayer, sorcerer, tea-leaf reader, witch, wizard; SEE CONCEPTS **361,423**

rophetic [*adj*] *telling of the future*

apocalyptic, augural, Delphian*, divinatory, fatidic, foreshadowing, mantic, occult, oracular, predictive, presaging, prescient, prognostic, prophetical, pythonic, sibylline, vaticinal, veiled; SEE CONCEPT **267**

ropitious [*adj1*] *full of promise; good, favorable*

advantageous, auspicious, beneficial, benign, brave, bright, dexter, encouraging, favoring, fortunate, happy, hopeful, lucky, opportune, pat*, promising, prosperous, rosy, seasonable, timely, toward, useful, well-timed; SEE CONCEPTS **548,560,572**

propitious [*adj2*] *friendly*

benevolent, benign, favorably inclined, gracious, kind, nice, well-disposed; SEE CONCEPT **401**

proponent [*n*] *person who advocates, supports cause*

advocate, backer, champion, defender, enthusiast, exponent, expounder, friend, partisan, patron, protector, second, seconder, spokesperson, subscriber, supporter, upholder, vindicator; SEE CONCEPTS **355,359,423**

proportion [*n1*] *relative amount, size of part to whole*

admeasurement, amplitude, apportionment, breadth, bulk, capacity, cut, degree, dimension, distribution, division, equation, expanse, extent, fraction, magnitude, measure, measurement, part, percentage, portion, quota, rate, ratio, relationship, scale, scope, segment, share, volume; SEE CONCEPTS **730,783**

proportion [*n2*] *balance between parts of whole*

agreement, congruity, correspondence, harmony, symmetry; SEE CONCEPTS **664,717**

proportionate/proportional [*adj*] *balanced, corresponding*

commensurable, commensurate, comparable, comparative, compatible, consistent, contingent, correlative, correspondent, corresponding, dependent, equal, equitable, equivalent, even, in proportion, just, reciprocal, relative, symmetrical, uniform; SEE CONCEPTS **480,563**

proportions [*n*] *measurements*

amount, area, breadth, compass, depth, diameter, dimensions, expanse, extent, height, length, magnitude, range, scope, size, volume, width; SEE CONCEPTS **730,792**

proposal [*n*] *suggestion, presentation for action*

angle, bid, big idea*, brain child*, design, feeler*, game plan*, idea, layout, motion, offer, outline, overture, pass, picture, pitch, plan, proffer, program, project, proposition, recommendation, scenario, scheme, setup, tender, terms; SEE CONCEPTS **271,324,662**

propose [*v1*] *suggest, present for action*

adduce, advance, advise, affirm, ask, assert, broach, come up with*, contend, counsel, hit on*, hold out, introduce, invite, kibitz*, lay before*, lay on the line*, make a motion, make a pitch*, move for, name, nominate, offer, pose, prefer, press, proffer, propone, proposition, propound, put forward, put to, put up, recommend, request, set forth, solicit, speak one's piece*, spitball*, state, submit, tender, urge, volunteer; SEE CONCEPTS **66,75**

propose [*v2*] *intend; have in mind*

aim, contemplate, design, have every intention, mean, mind, plan, purpose, scheme; SEE CONCEPTS **26,36**

propose [*v3*] *ask for hand in marriage*

ask in marriage, fire the question*, get down on one knee*, make a proposal, offer marriage, pop the question*, press one's suit*; SEE CONCEPTS **48,297**

proposition [*n*] *suggestion; scheme*

hypothesis, invitation, motion, overture, plan, premise, presentation, proffer, program, project, proposal, recommendation; SEE CONCEPTS 384,662

proposition [v] *make suggestion, often improper*
accost, approach, ask, pose, prefer, propose, propound, put, solicit, suggest; SEE CONCEPTS 48,375

proprietor [n] *person who owns something*
freeholder*, front office, holder, land owner, meal ticket*, owner, possessor, proprietary, title-holder; SEE CONCEPTS 343,347

propriety [n1] *suitableness, appropriateness*
accordance, advisability, agreeableness, appositeness, aptness, becomingness, compatibility, concord, congruity, consonance, convenience, correctness, correspondence, decorum, ethicality, expedience, fitness, harmony, justice, legitimacy, meetness, morality, order, pleasantness, properness, recommendability, rectitude, respectability, rightness, seemliness, suitability; SEE CONCEPT 656

propriety [n2] *good manners*
accepted conduct, amenities, breeding, civilities, correctness, courtesy, decency, decorum, delicacy, dignity, etiquette, good behavior, good form, modesty, mores*, niceties, politeness, politesse, protocol, punctilio, rectitude, refinement, respectability, rules of conduct, seemliness, social conventions, social grace, the done thing*; SEE CONCEPTS 633,644

propulsion [n] *force*
drive, effort, energy, full head of steam*, horsepower, impulse, momentum, muscle, power, pressure, punch, push, speed, steam, strength, stress, tension, thrust, velocity; SEE CONCEPTS 641,724

pro rata [adv] *in proportion*
correlatively, proportionately, respectively; SEE CONCEPTS 480,563

prosaic [adj] *unimaginative*
actual, banal, blah*, boring, clean, colorless, common, commonplace, dead*, diddly*, drab, dry, dull, everyday, factual, flat*, garden-variety*, hackneyed, ho-hum*, humdrum*, irksome, lackluster, lifeless, literal, lowly, lusterless, matter-of-fact, monotonous, mundane, nothing, nowhere, ordinary, pabulum*, pedestrian, platitudinous, plebeian, practicable, practical, prose, prosy, routine, square, stale, tame, tedious, trite, uneventful, unexceptional, uninspiring, vanilla*, vapid, workaday, yawn*, zero*; SEE CONCEPTS 267,537,547

proscribe [v] *condemn, exclude*
ban, banish, blackball*, boycott, censure, damn, denounce, deport, doom*, embargo, excommunicate, exile, expatriate, expel, forbid, interdict, ostracize, outlaw, prohibit, reject, sentence; SEE CONCEPTS 25,121,317

prose [n] *written, nonrhythmic literature*
book, composition, essay, exposition, fiction, nonfiction, speech, story, talk, text, tongue*, writing; SEE CONCEPTS 268,271

prosecute [v1] *bring action against in court*
arraign, bring suit, bring to trial, contest, do, haul into court*, indict, involve in litigation, law, litigate, prefer charges, pull up, put away*, put on docket, put on trial, see in court*, seek redress, sue, summon, take to court, try, turn on the heat*; SEE CONCEPT 317

prosecute [v2] *follow through, persevere*
carry on, carry through, conduct, continue, direct, discharge, engage in, execute, follow up, manage, perform, persist, practice, pursue, push through, see through, wage, work at; SEE CONCEPT 91

proselytize [v] *convert, espouse*
accept, adopt, advocate, alter conviction, approve, be born again*, cause to adopt, change belief, convince, defend, embrace, get into*, persuade, stand behind*, sway, uphold; SEE CONCEPTS 10,12,14,35

prospect [n1] *outlook for future*
anticipation, calculation, chance, contemplation, expectancy, expectation, forecast, future, hope, in the cards*, irons in the fire*, likelihood, odds, opening, plan, possibility, presumption, probability, promise, proposal, thought; SEE CONCEPTS 689,693

prospect [n2] *landscape, vista*
aspect, lookout, outlook, overlook, panorama, perspective, scape, scene, sight, spectacle, view, vision; SEE CONCEPTS 509,628

prospect [v] *look for; seek*
delve, dig, explore, go after, go into, inquire, investigate, look, look into, probe, search, sift, survey; SEE CONCEPT 216

prospective [adj] *anticipated, potential*
about to be, approaching, awaited, coming, considered, destined, eventual, expected, forthcoming, future, hoped-for, imminent, impending, intended, likely, looked-for, planned, possible, promised, proposed, soon-to-be, to be*, to come; SEE CONCEPTS 548,552

prospectus [n] *details, outline of event*
announcement, catalogue, conspectus, design, list, plan, program, scheme, syllabus, synopsis; SEE CONCEPT 283

prosper [v] *be fortunate; succeed*
advance, arrive, augment, batten, bear, bear fruit, become rich, become wealthy, be enriched, benefit, bloom, blossom, catch on*, do well, do wonders*, fare well, fatten*, feather nest*, flourish, flower, gain, get on*, get there*, go places*, go to town*, grow rich, hit it big, hit the jackpot*, increase, make a killing*, make good*, make it*, make mark*, make money, make out*, multiply, produce, progress, rise, score*, strike rich*, thrive, turn out well, yield; SEE CONCEPT 706

prosperity [n] *affluence, good fortune*
abundance, accomplishment, advantage, arrival, bed of roses*, benefit, boom, clover, do, ease*, easy street*, exorbitance, expansion, flying colors*, fortune, good, good times, gravy train*, growth, high on the hog*, increase, inflation, interest, life of luxury*, luxury, opulence, plenteousness, plenty, prosperousness, riches, success, successfulness, the good life*, thriving, velvet, victory, wealth, welfare, well-being; SEE CONCEPTS 335,706

prosperous [adj1] *successful, thriving*
affluent, blooming, booming, comfortable, doing well, easy, flourishing, fortunate, halcyon, in clover*, in the money*, lousy rich, lucky, mainline*, moneyed, money to burn*, on top of heap*, opulent, palmy, prospering, rich, roaring, robust, sitting pretty*, snug, substantial, upper class*, uptown, wealthy, well, well-heeled*, well-off, well-to-do; SEE CONCEPTS 334,528

prosperous [adj2] *promising, advantageous*
appropriate, auspicious, bright, convenient, de-

prostitute [*n*] *person who sells own abilities, talent, or name for inferior purpose*
betrayer, cheater, deceiver, gigolo, hustler, seducer; SEE CONCEPT *412*

prostitute [*v*] *to put one's talent to an unworthy use*
abuse, cheapen, corrupt, debase, debauch, degrade, demean, deprave, devalue, misapply, misemploy, misuse, pervert, profane, vitiate; SEE CONCEPTS *156,645*

prostrate [*adj1*] *flat, horizontal*
abject, bowed low, procumbent, prone, reclining, recumbent, supine; SEE CONCEPT *583*

prostrate [*adj2*] *helpless*
beaten, defenseless, disarmed, impotent, open, overcome, overpowered, overwhelmed, paralyzed, powerless, reduced, weak; SEE CONCEPT *542*

prostrate [*adj3*] *tired, worn*
crippled, dejected, depressed, disarmed, drained, drowned, exhausted, fagged*, fallen, frazzled*, immobilized, incapacitated, inconsolable, knocked over*, obedient, overcome, paralyzed, pooped*, spent*, submissive, subservient, tuckered*, wearied, worn out; SEE CONCEPTS *406,485*

prostrate [*v1*] *fall on knees; submit*
abase, bow, bow down, cast before, cringe, fall at feet, give in, grovel, kneel, kowtow*, obey, surrender; SEE CONCEPT *384*

prostrate [*v2*] *overwhelm; wear out*
bring low, cripple, debilitate, defeat, destroy, disable, disarm, drain, drown, exhaust, fatigue, fell, floor, frazzle*, immobilize, impair, incapacitate, knock over, level, mow*, overcome, overpower, overthrow, overtire, overturn, paralyze, reduce, ruin, sap, tire, tucker out*, weary, whelm, wreck; SEE CONCEPTS *95,250,252*

protagonist [*n*] *person who takes the lead; central figure of narrative*
advocate, central character, champion, combatant, exemplar, exponent, hero, idol, lead, lead character, leader, mainstay, prime mover, principal, standard-bearer, warrior; SEE CONCEPTS *352,359,423*

protect [*v*] *take care of; guard from harm*
assure, bulwark, care for, champion, chaperon, conserve, cover, cover all bases*, cover up, cushion, defend, fend, foster, give refuge, give sanctuary*, go to bat for*, harbor, hedge, insulate, keep, keep safe, look after, preserve, ride shotgun for*, safeguard, save, screen, secure, sentinel, shade, shelter, shield, shotgun*, stand guard, stonewall*, support, take under wing*, watch, watch over; SEE CONCEPTS *96,134*

protection [*n*] *care, guardianship*
aegis, armament, armor, assurance, barrier, buffer, bulwark, camouflage, certainty, charge, conservation, cover, custody, defense, fix, guard, guarding, insurance, invulnerability, preservation, protecting, reassurance, refuge, safeguard, safekeeping, safety, salvation, screen, security, self-defense, shelter, shield, stability, strength, surety, tutelage, umbrella*, ward, wardship; SEE CONCEPTS *712,729*

protective [*adj*] *guarding, securing*
careful, conservational, conservative, covering,

custodial, defensive, emergency, guardian, insulating, jealous, possessive, preservative, protecting, safeguarding, sheltering, shielding, vigilant, warm, watchful; SEE CONCEPTS *542,550*

protégé [*n*] *dependant, pupil*
apprentice, charge, discovery, star student, student, ward; SEE CONCEPTS *348,423*

protest [*n*] *complaint, disapproval*
bellyache*, big, stink*, blackball*, challenge, clamor, declaration, demonstration, demur, demurral, difficulty, dissent, flak*, formal complaint, grievance, gripe, grouse*, holler*, howl, kick*, knock*, march, moratorium, nix, objection, outcry, protestation, question, rally, remonstrance, remonstration, revolt, riot, stink*, tumult, turmoil; SEE CONCEPTS *52,54,300*

protest [*v*] *complain, disapprove; argue against*
affirm, assert, asseverate, attest, avouch, avow, back-talk*, be against, be displeased by, blast*, buck, combat, constate, contend, cry out, declare, demonstrate, demur, disagree, except, expostulate, fight, holler, howl, insist, inveigh against, kick*, maintain, make a stink*, object, oppose, predicate, profess, put up a fight*, rebel, remonstrate, resist, revolt, say no*, sound off*, squawk*, take exception*, testify, thumbs down*; SEE CONCEPTS *46,52,54,300*

protocol [*n*] *rules of conduct, behavior in certain situation*
agreement, code, compact, concordat, contract, conventions, courtesy, covenant, custom, decorum, etiquette, formalities, good form, manners, obligation, order, pact, politesse, propriety, p's and q's*, treaty; SEE CONCEPTS *684,688*

prototype [*n*] *original, example*
ancestor, antecedent, antecessor, archetype, criterion, first, forerunner, ideal, mock-up*, model, norm, paradigm, pattern, precedent, precursor, predecessor, standard, type; SEE CONCEPT *686*

protract [*v*] *extend, draw out*
continue, cool*, defer, delay, drag on*, drag out*, draw, elongate, hold off, hold up, keep going, lengthen, pad*, postpone, procrastinate, prolong, prolongate, put off, put on hold, spin out*, stall, stretch, stretch out; SEE CONCEPTS *237,239,250*

protrude [*v*] *stick out*
beetle, bulge, butt out, come through, distend, extend, extrude, jut, jut out, obtrude, overhang, point, poke, pop, pouch, pout, project, shoot out, stand out, start, stick up, swell; SEE CONCEPTS *208,746*

protuberance [*n*] *lump, outgrowth*
bulge, bump, excrescence, jut, jutting, knob, outthrust, process, projection, prominence, protrusion, swelling, tumor; SEE CONCEPTS *471,824*

proud [*adj1*] *pleased, pleasing*
appreciative, august, content, contented, dignified, eminent, fiery, fine, glad, glorious, gorgeous, grand, gratified, gratifying, great, great-hearted, honored, illustrious, imposing, impressive, magnificent, majestic, memorable, noble, red-letter*, rewarding, satisfied, satisfying, self-respecting, spirited, splendid, stately, sublime, superb, valiant, vigorous, well-pleased; SEE CONCEPTS *403,572,574*

proud [*adj2*] *arrogant, self-important*
bloated, boastful, cavalier, cocky*, conceited, contemptuous, cool*, disdainful, dismissive, domineering, egotistic, egotistical, haughty,

pr
pr

high-and-mighty*, high-handed*, huffy*, imperious, insolent, lofty, narcissistic, ostentatious, overbearing, pompous, presumptuous, pretentious, puffed up*, scornful, self-satisfied, sniffy*, snobbish, snooty*, stuck-up*, supercilious, superior, vain, vainglorious; SEE CONCEPTS *401,542*

prove [v] *establish facts; put to a test*
add up, affirm, analyze, ascertain, assay, attest, authenticate, back, bear out, certify, check, confirm, convince, corroborate, declare, demonstrate, determine, document, end up, evidence, evince, examine, experiment, explain, find, fix, have a case*, justify, make evident, manifest, pan out*, result, settle, show, show clearly, show once and for all*, substantiate, sustain, test, testify, trial, try, turn out, uphold, validate, verify, warrant, witness; SEE CONCEPTS *57,118,138*

proverb [n] *saying referring to common fact, knowledge*
adage, aphorism, apophthegm, axiom, byword, catch phrase, daffodil*, dictum, epigram, folk wisdom, gnome, maxim, moral, motto, platitude, precept, repartee, saw*, text, truism, witticism, word; SEE CONCEPTS *275,278*

proverbial [adj] *conventional, traditional*
accepted, acknowledged, archetypal, axiomatic, current, customary, famed, familiar, famous, general, legendary, notorious, self-evident, time-honored, typical, unquestioned, well-known; SEE CONCEPT *530*

provide [v1] *supply, support*
accommodate, add, administer, afford, arrange, bestow, bring, care, cater, contribute, dispense, equip, favor, feather*, feed, fit, fit out, fix up, fix up with, furnish, give, grant, hand over, heel*, impart, implement, indulge, keep, lend, line, look after, maintain, minister, outfit, prepare, present, procure, produce, proffer, provision, ration, ready, render, replenish, serve, stake, stock, stock up*, store, sustain, take care of, transfer, turn out, yield; SEE CONCEPTS *108,110,136,140*

provide [v2] *determine, specify*
condition, lay down, postulate, require, state, stipulate; SEE CONCEPTS *18,646*

provident [adj] *careful, frugal*
canny, cautious, discreet, economical, expedient, far-sighted, foresighted, judicious, penny-pinching*, politic, prepared, prudent, sagacious, saving, shrewd, sparing, thrifty, tight, unwasteful, vigilant, well-prepared, wise; SEE CONCEPTS *334,401*

providing/provided [conj] *as long as; with the understanding*
contingent upon, given, if, if and only if, in case, in the case that, in the event, on condition, on the assumption, on these terms, subject to, supposing, with the proviso; SEE CONCEPTS *544,546*

province [n] *area of rule, responsibility*
arena, bailiwick, business, calling, canton, capacity, champaign, charge, colony, concern, county, demesne, department, dependency, district, division, domain, dominion, duty, employment, field, function, jurisdiction, line, office, orbit, part, post, pursuit, realm, region, role, section, shire, sphere, terrain, territory, tract, walk, work, zone; SEE CONCEPTS *198,349,362,508,532*

provincial [adj] *countrified; limited*
bigoted, bucolic, country, hidebound, home-grown, homespun, insular, inward-looking, local, narrow, narrow-minded, parochial, pas-

toral, petty, rude, rural, rustic, sectarian, small-minded, small-town, uninformed, unpolished, unsophisticated; SEE CONCEPTS *403,549,589*

provision [n1] *supplies, supplying*
accouterment, arrangement, catering, emergency, equipping, fitting out, foundation, furnishing, groundwork, outline, plan, prearrangement, precaution, preparation, procurement, providing, stock, store, supplying; SEE CONCEPTS *140,712*

provisional [adj] *contingent, tentative*
conditional, dependent, ephemeral, experimental, interim, limited, makeshift, passing, pro tem, provisionary, provisory, qualified, rough-and-ready*, stopgap*, temporary, test, transient, transitional; SEE CONCEPTS *546,554,711*

provision/proviso [n2] *stipulation, condition of agreement*
agreement, catch*, Catch-22*, clause, demand, fine print*, joker*, kicker*, limitation, prerequisite, qualification, requirement, reservation, restriction, rider, small print*, specification, stipulation, strings*, term, terms; SEE CONCEPTS *270,684,711*

provocation [n] *incitement, stimulus*
affront, annoyance, bothering, brickbat*, casus belli, cause, challenge, dare, defy, grabber*, grievance, grounds, harassment, incentive, indignity, inducement, injury, instigation, insult, irking, justification, motivation, offense, provoking, reason, taunt, vexation, vexing; SEE CONCEPTS *14,240,532*

provocative [adj] *aggravating*
annoying, challenging, disturbing, exciting, galling, goading, heady, incensing, inciting, influential, inspirational, insulting, intoxicating, offensive, outrageous, provoking, pushing, spurring, stimulant, stimulating; SEE CONCEPT *529*

provocative [adj2] *sexually stimulating*
alluring, arousing, enchanting, erotic, exciting, heady, interesting, intoxicating, intriguing, inviting, seductive, sexy, stimulating, suggestive, tantalizing, tempting; SEE CONCEPTS *372,537*

provoke [v1] *make angry*
abet, abrade, affront, aggravate, anger, annoy, bother, bug*, chafe, enrage, exasperate, exercise, foment, fret, gall*, get*, get on one's nerves*, get under one's skin*, grate, hit where one lives*, incense, incite, inflame, infuriate, insult, irk, irritate, madden, make blood boil*, make waves*, nag, offend, perturb, pique, put out, raise, rile, roil, ruffle, set*, set on*, try one's patience*, upset, vex, whip up*, work into lather*, work up*; SEE CONCEPTS *7,19*

provoke [v2] *start, evoke; stimulate*
animate, arouse, awaken, begin, bestir, bring about, bring down, bring on, bring to one's feet*, build up, call forth, cause, challenge, draw forth, electrify, elicit, enthuse, excite, fire, fire up*, galvanize, generate, give rise to, incite, induce, inflame, innervate, innerve, inspire, instigate, kindle, lead to, make, motivate, move, occasion, pique, precipitate, prime, produce, promote, prompt, quicken, rally, rouse, roust, stir, suscitate, thrill, titillate, titivate, waken, whet; SEE CONCEPTS *7,19,22,221,242*

prowess [n1] *ability, skill*
accomplishment, address, adeptness, adroitness, aptitude, attainment, command, deftness, dexter-

ity, excellence, expertise, expertness, genius, mastery, readiness, sleight, talent; SEE CONCEPT 630

prowess [n2] *bravery*
backbone*, boldness, courage, daring, dauntlessness, fearlessness, gallantry, grit*, guts*, heart*, heroism, intrepidity, mettle, moxie*, nerve, pluck, right stuff*, spunk, starch*, stomach*, stuff*, true grit*, valiance, valiancy, valor, valorousness, what it takes*; SEE CONCEPTS 411,633

prowl [v] *move stealthily*
cruise, hunt, lurk, nose around*, patrol, range, roam, rove, scavenge, skulk, slink, snake, sneak, stalk, steal, stroll, tramp; SEE CONCEPT 151

prowler [n] *thief*
burglar, crook, housebreaker, lurker, pilferer*, robber, sneakthief*; SEE CONCEPT 412

proximity [n] *nearness to something*
adjacency, appropinquity, closeness, concurrence, contiguity, contiguousness, immediacy, juxtaposition, propinquity, togetherness; SEE CONCEPT 747

proxy [n] *agent*
alternate, ambassador, assignee, attorney, backup, broker, delegate, deputy, emissary, envoy, executor, intermediary, lawyer, mediary, negotiator, representative, stand-in, substitute, surrogate; SEE CONCEPT 348

prude [n] *prig*
goody-goody, goody two-shoes*, Mrs. Grundy, old maid, puritan, Victorian; SEE CONCEPT 416

prudent [adj] *wise, sensible in action and thought*
advisable, canny, careful, cautious, circumspect, discerning, discreet, economical, far-sighted, frugal, hedging one's bets*, judgmatic, judicious, leery, playing safe*, politic, provident, reasonable, sagacious, sage, sane, sapient, shrewd, sound, sparing, tactical, thinking twice*, thrifty, vigilant, wary; SEE CONCEPTS 401,542

prudish [adj] *shy and strict in behavior*
affected, artificial, austere, bigoted, conventional, demure, fastidious, finicky*, genteel, illiberal, mincing, narrow, narrow-minded, offish, overexact, overmodest, overnice, precise, pretentious, priggish*, prim, prissy*, proper, puritanical, rigid, rigorous, scrupulous, severe, simpering, square, squeamish*, starchy*, stern, stiff*, stilted, strait-laced, stuffy, uptight*, Victorian*; SEE CONCEPT 401

prune [v] *trim; cut short*
clip, cut back, dock, eliminate, exclude, gut, knock off, lop, pare down, reduce, shape, shave, shear, shorten, skive, snip, thin; SEE CONCEPTS 137,176,236,247

prurient [adj] *lascivious*
bawdy, carnal, crude, desirous, erotic, fleshly, horny, hot*, lecherous, lewd, libertine, libidinous, licentious, lustful, obscene, offensive, orgiastic, pornographic, raunchy*, salacious, sensual, sexual, smutty*, suggestive, unchaste, vulgar; SEE CONCEPTS 372,403

pry [v1] *interfere in someone else's business*
be a busybody*, be all ears*, be curious, be inquisitive, be nosy, bug*, ferret out, gape, gaze, hunt, inquire, intrude, investigate, listen in, meddle, nose, peek, peep, peer, poke, poke nose into*, ransack, reconnoiter, rubberneck*, search, snoop, spy, stare, tap, tune in on*, wiretap; SEE CONCEPTS 216,384,623

pry [v2] *force or break open*
disengage, disjoin, divide, elevate, elicit, extort, extract, heave, hoist, jimmy, lever, lift, move, pick up, press, prize, pull, push, raise, rear, separate, take up, tear, tilt, turn, turn out, twist, uplift, upraise, uprear, wrest, wring; SEE CONCEPTS 196,206,211

psalm [n] *song of praise*
canticle, celebration, chant, chorale, eulogy, hymn, paean, shout, verse; SEE CONCEPT 595

pseudo [adj] *artificial, fake*
bogus, counterfeit, ersatz, false, imitation, mock, not genuine, not kosher*, not legit*, not real, phony, pirate, pretend, pretended, quasi*, sham*, simulated, spurious, wrong; SEE CONCEPT 582

pseudonym [n] *false name*
AKA*, alias, ananym, anonym, assumed name, handle*, incognito*, nickname, nom de guerre, nom de plume, pen name, professional name, stage name, summer name*; SEE CONCEPTS 268,683

psyche [n] *innermost self; personality*
anima, animus, character, ego, élan vital, essential nature, individuality, inner child, inner self, mind, pneuma, self, soul, spirit, spirituality, subconscious, true being; SEE CONCEPTS 410,411

psyched [adj] *excited*
animated, aroused, awakened, beside oneself*, charged, delighted, eager, enthusiastic, feverish, fired up*, high*, inspired, juiced up*, keyed up*, moved, on fire*, passionate, pumped, stimulated, stirred, thrilled, wild, worked up; SEE CONCEPTS 401,403

psychedelic [adj] *affecting the mind so as to produce vivid visions*
consciousness-expanding, crazy*, experimental, freaky*, hallucinatory, hallucinogenic, kaleidoscopic, mind-bending*, mind-blowing*, mind-changing, mind-expanding*, multicolored*, psychoactive, psychotomimetic, psychotropic, trip*; SEE CONCEPTS 529,537

psychiatrist [n] *person who treats mental disorders*
analyst, clinician, doctor, psychoanalyst, psychologist, psychotherapist, shrink*, therapist; SEE CONCEPT 357

psychic [adj] *extrasensory in perception*
analytic, cerebral, clairvoyant, immaterial, impressible, impressionable, intellective, intellectual, mental, metaphysical, mystic, occult, preternatural, psychal, psychical, psychogenic, psychological, responsive, sensible, sensile, sensitive, sentient, spiritual, supernatural, supersensible, supersensitive, supersensory, supersensual, susceptible, susceptive, telekinetic, telepathic, transmundane, unworldly; SEE CONCEPTS 402,403

psychobabble [n] *rhetoric using psychological terms*
argot, buzzword, jargon, patter, pop psych*, psychospeak, self-help; SEE CONCEPT 275

psychological [adj] *concerning the mind*
cerebral, cognitive, emotional, experimental, imaginary, intellective, intellectual, in the mind, mental, psychical, subconscious, subjective, unconscious; SEE CONCEPTS 403,536

psychology [n] *study of the mind; emotional and mental constitution*
attitude, behaviorism, medicine, mental makeup, mental processes, personality study, psych*,

pr
ps

science of the mind, therapy, way of thinking*, where head is at*; SEE CONCEPTS 349,360,410

psychopath [n] *person who is mentally deranged, often prone to hurt others*
antisocial personality, insane person, lunatic, mad person, maniac, mental case*, nutcase*, psycho*, psychotic, schizoid*, sociopath, unstable personality; SEE CONCEPT 412

psychotic [adj] *mentally deranged*
certifiable*, crazy, demented, distracted, flipped-out*, insane, lunatic, mad, manic-depressive, mental, non compos mentis, nuts*, off one's rocker*, over the edge*, psycho*, psychopathic, schizophrenic, sick, unbalanced, unhinged*; SEE CONCEPT 403

pub [n] *business where liquor and food are served*
after-hours joint*, ale house*, bar, barroom, beer joint*, drinkery, drinking establishment, gin mill*, inn, joint*, lounge, public house, roadhouse, saloon, taproom, tavern; SEE CONCEPTS 439,448,449

puberty [n] *young adulthood*
adolescence, awkward stage*, boyhood, girlhood, greenness*, high-school years, juvenescence, juvenility, potency, preadolescence, pubescence, spring*, springtide*, springtime*, teenage years, teens, youth, youthfulness; SEE CONCEPT 817

public [adj1] *community, general*
accessible, city, civic, civil, common, communal, conjoint, conjunct, country, federal, free, free to all, government, governmental, intermutual, metropolitan, municipal, mutual, national, not private, open, open-door, popular, social, state, universal, unrestricted, urban, widespread, without charge; SEE CONCEPTS 536,576

public [adj2] *known, acknowledged*
exposed, general, in circulation, notorious, obvious, open, overt, patent, plain, popular, prevalent, published, recognized, social, societal, usual, vulgar, widespread; SEE CONCEPTS 267,530

public [n] *people of community; people interested in something*
audience, bodies*, buyers, citizens, clientele, commonalty, community, country, electorate, everyone, followers, following, heads, masses, men and women, mob, multitude, nation, patrons, people, populace, population, society, suite, supporters, voters; SEE CONCEPTS 379,417

publication [n1] *printing of written or visual material*
advertisement, airing, announcement, appearance, broadcast, broadcasting, communication, declaration, disclosure, discovery, dissemination, divulgation, issuance, issuing, notification, proclamation, promulgation, pronunciamento, publicity, public relations, publishing, reporting, revelation, statement, ventilation, writing; SEE CONCEPTS 60,274,292

publication [n2] *something printed for reading*
annual, book, booklet, brochure, handbill, information, issue, leaflet, magazine, news, newsletter, newspaper, pamphlet, periodical; SEE CONCEPT 280

publicity [n] *promotion of something, someone*
advertising, announcement, announcing, attention, ballyhoo*, big noise*, billing, blurb*, boost*, broadcasting, build-up*, clout*, commercial, currency, distribution, fame, handout, hoopla*, hype*, ink*, limelight*, noise*, notoriety, pitch, plug*, PR*, press, press-agentry, promo*, promulgation, propaganda, public notice, public relations, puff*, puffery*, pushing, réclame, release, report, scratch*, spotlight*, spread, write-up; SEE CONCEPTS 274,280,293

publicize [v] *make widely known; promote*
advance, advertise, announce, bill, billboard, boost*, broadcast, build up*, cry, drum*, extol, hard sell*, headline, hype*, immortalize, make a pitch for, pitch, play up*, plug*, press-agent, promulgate, propagandize, puff*, push, put on the map*, skywrite*, soft-sell*, splash, spot*, spotlight*, tout, trumpet*, write up; SEE CONCEPTS 60,292,324

publish [v] *have printed, issue*
announce, bring out, broadcast, circulate, communicate, declare, disclose, distribute, divulge, let it be known*, print, proclaim, produce, promulgate, publicize, put in print, put out, report, spotlight; SEE CONCEPTS 60,140,292

pucker [n] *wrinkle*
crease, crinkle, crumple, fold, furrow, plait, ruck, ruckle; SEE CONCEPT 754

pucker [v] *draw together; wrinkle*
cockle, compress, condense, contract, crease, crinkle, crumple, fold, furrow, gather, knit, purse, ruckle, ruck up, ruffle, screw up, squeeze, tighten; SEE CONCEPTS 185,219

pudgy [adj] *slightly fat*
chubby*, hefty, plump, plumpish, rotund, round, stout, thick-bodied, tubby*; SEE CONCEPTS 491,773

puerile [adj] *childish*
babyish, babylike, callow, foolish, green*, immature, inane, inexperienced, infantile, irresponsible, jejune, juvenile, naive, petty, ridiculous, silly, trivial, unfledged, ungrown, weak, young; SEE CONCEPTS 401,578,797

puff [n1] *blast of air*
breath, draft, drag, draught, draw, emanation, flatus, flurry, gust, pull, smoke, waft, whiff, wind, wisp; SEE CONCEPTS 437,524

puff [n2] *advertisement*
advertising, blurb*, boost*, buildup*, commendation, favorable mention, good word, hype*, laudation, plug*, praise, press-agentry, promo*, promotion, publicity, puffery*, push*, sales talk, write-up; SEE CONCEPTS 69,278,324

puff [v1] *inhale or exhale air*
blow, breathe, distend, drag, draw, enlarge, fill, gasp, gulp, heave, huff, huff and puff*, inflate, pant, pull at, pull on, smoke, suck, swell, wheeze, whiff; SEE CONCEPTS 163,185,526

puff [v2] *publicize*
admire, advertise, ballyhoo*, blow up*, build, commend, congratulate, cry*, flatter, hype*, overpraise, plug*, praise, press-agent*, promote, push; SEE CONCEPTS 49,69

puffy [adj] *swollen*
billowy, bloated, blown, bulgy, distended, distent, enlarged, expanded, full, increased, inflamed, inflated, puffed up; SEE CONCEPT 485

pugnacious [adj] *belligerent*
aggressive, antagonistic, argumentative, bellicose, brawling, cantankerous, chip on shoulder*, choleric, combative, contentious, defiant, disputatious, have a bone to pick*, hot-tempered, irascible, irritable, itching to fight*, militant,

petulant, pushing, pushy*, quarrelsome, ready to fight, rebellious, salty*, scrappy*, self-assertive, truculent, warlike; SEE CONCEPTS *401;542*

pulchritude [*n*] *beauty*
adorableness, allure, allurement, attraction, elegance, exquisiteness, glamor, good looks, handsomeness, loveliness, physical attractiveness, prettiness, shapeliness; SEE CONCEPT *718*

pull [*v1*] *drawing something with force*
cull, dislocate, drag, evolve, extract, gather, haul, heave, jerk, lug, paddle, pick, pluck, remove, rend, rip, row, schlepp*, sprain, strain, stretch, take out, tear, tow, trail, truck, tug, twitch, uproot, weed*, wrench, yank; SEE CONCEPT *206*

pull [*v2*] *attract*
draw, entice, get, lure, magnetize, obtain, pick up, secure, win; SEE CONCEPT *11*

pull down [*v*] *destroy; knock over*
annihilate, bulldoze, demolish, destruct, dismantle, let down, lower, raze, remove, ruin, take down, tear down, wreck; SEE CONCEPT *252*

pull in [*v1*] *arrest*
apprehend, bust, collar, detain, nab, nail, pick up, pinch, run in, take into custody; SEE CONCEPTS *90,317*

pull in [*v2*] *attract, obtain*
absorb, bring in, clear, draw, draw in, earn, gain, gross, make, net, pocket, suck, take home*; SEE CONCEPT *120*

pull off [*v*] *accomplish*
achieve, bring off, carry out, manage, score, score a success, secure, succeed, win; SEE CONCEPTS *91,706*

pull out [*v*] *quit*
abandon, depart, evacuate, exit, get off, go, leave, retire, retreat, shove off, stop, stop participating, take off, withdraw; SEE CONCEPTS *119,121,195*

pull through [*v*] *recover*
come through, get better, get over, improve, rally, ride out*, survive, triumph, weather*; SEE CONCEPTS *303,700,706*

pull up [*v*] *stop, halt*
arrive, brake, bring up, come to a halt, come to a stop, draw up, fetch up, get there, haul up, pause, reach a standstill; SEE CONCEPTS *119,121,159*

pulp [*adj*] *cheap, vulgar, especially regarding reading material*
lurid, mushy, rubbish, sensational, trash, trashy; SEE CONCEPT *267*

pulp [*n*] *flesh of plant, animal*
batter, curd, dough, grume, jam, marrow, mash, mush, pap, paste, pomace, poultice, sarcocarp, semisolid, soft part, sponge, triturate; SEE CONCEPTS *399,428*

pulp [*v*] *mash, pulverize*
bruise, coagulate, crush, gelatinate, macerate, squash, triturate; SEE CONCEPTS *208,219*

pulpit [*n*] *structure from which sermon is given*
desk, lectern, platform, podium, rostrum, soapbox*, stage, stump*; SEE CONCEPTS *368,443*

pulsate/pulse [*v*] *quiver, beat*
drum, fluctuate, hammer, oscillate, palpitate, pound, pump, roar, throb, thrum, thud, thump, tick, vibrate; SEE CONCEPTS *147,185*

pulse [*n*] *rhythm, beat*
beating, oscillation, pulsation, stroke, throb, throbbing, vibration; SEE CONCEPTS *147,185*

pulverize [*v1*] *smash by beating, crushing*
abrade, atomize, beat, bray, break up, buck, comminute, contriturate, crumble, crunch, crush, flour, fragment, fragmentalize, fragmentize, granulate, grate, grind, levigate, micronize, mill, mull, pestle, pound, powder, shatter, splinter, triturate; SEE CONCEPTS *186,219*

pulverize [*v2*] *destroy*
annihilate, crush, decimate, defeat, demolish, destruct, dynamite, flatten, rub out*, ruin, shatter, smash, tear down*, vanquish, vaporize, wax, wreck; SEE CONCEPT *252*

pummel [*v*] *beat, pommel*
bash, batter, belt, clout, club, crush, cudgel, flog, hammer, hit, knock, lash, let one have it*, lick, mash, maul, pelt, pound, punch, ram, slug, smack, strike, swat, thrash, trounce, wallop, whale, wham, whip; SEE CONCEPTS *189,246*

pump [*v1*] *draw or push out*
bail out, blow up, dilate, distend, draft, drain, draw, draw off, drive, drive out, elevate, empty, force, force out, inflate, inject, pour, push, send, siphon, supply, swell, tap; SEE CONCEPTS *142,206,208*

pump [*v2*] *question relentlessly*
cross-examine, draw out, give the third degree*, grill, interrogate, probe, query, question, quiz, worm out of*; SEE CONCEPTS *48,53*

pumped [*adj*] *excited*
animated, aroused, awakened, beside oneself*, charged, cranked up, delighted, eager, enthusiastic, feverish, fired up*, geared up, high*, inspired, juiced up*, keyed up*, moved, on fire*, passionate, psyched, rarin' to go*, stimulated, stirred, thrilled, wild, worked up; SEE CONCEPTS *401,403*

pun [*n*] *play on words*
ambiguity, calembour, conceit, double entendre, double meaning, equivoque, joke, paronomasia, quibble, quip, witticism; SEE CONCEPTS *273,278*

punch [*n1/v1*] *hit*
bash, belt, biff, blow, bop, box, buffet, clip, clout, cuff, dig, jab, jog, knock, lollop, nudge, one-two*, plug, plunk*, poke, prod, pummel, rap, shot, slam, slap, slug, smack, smash, sock, strike, stroke, thrust, thump, wallop; SEE CONCEPT *189*

punch [*n2*] *energy, vigor*
bite, cogency, drive, effectiveness, force, forcefulness, impact, point, validity, validness, verve; SEE CONCEPTS *676,682*

punch [*v2*] *perforate, prick*
bore, cut, drill, jab, pierce, poke, puncture, stab, stamp; SEE CONCEPT *220*

punch-drunk [*adj*] *dazed*
agog, baffled, befuddled, confused, dazzled, dizzy, dumbfounded, dumbstruck, flustered, lost, muddled, perplexed, punchy*, puzzled, rattled, slap-happy, unsteady; SEE CONCEPTS *402,403*

punctilio [*n*] *etiquette*
ceremony, civility, code, convention, courtesy, customs, decorum, dignity, form, formalities, formality, mores, nicety, politesse, proper behavior, protocol, p's and q's*, refinement, rules, social graces; SEE CONCEPT *633*

punctilious [*adj*] *careful, finicky*
ceremonious, conscientious, conscionable, conventional, exact, formal, formalistic, fussy, good eye*, heedful, meticulous, nice, observant, overconscientious, overscrupulous, painstaking, par-

**ps
pu**

ticular, persnickety, precise, proper, punctual, right on*, scrupulous, strict; SEE CONCEPTS **401,542,557**

punctual [*adj*] *on time*
accurate, careful, conscientious, conscionable, constant, cyclic, dependable, early, exact, expeditious, fussy, heedful, in good time*, meticulous, on schedule, on the button*, on the dot*, on the nose*, painstaking, particular, periodic, precise, prompt, punctilious, quick, ready, recurrent, regular, reliable, scrupulous, seasonable, steady, strict, timely, under the wire*; SEE CONCEPTS **544,550,799**

punctuate [*v*] *lay stress on*
accent, accentuate, break, divide, emphasize, interject, interrupt, intersect, intersperse, mark, pepper*, point, point up*, separate, sprinkle, stress, underline; SEE CONCEPTS **49,79,98,266**

puncture [*n*] *hole, rupture*
break, cut, damage, flat, flat tire*, jab, leak, nick, opening, perforation, prick, slit, stab; SEE CONCEPTS **309,513,674**

puncture [*vl*] *poke hole in*
bore, cut, cut through, deflate, drill, go down, go flat, knife, lacerate, lance, nick, open, penetrate, perforate, pierce, prick, punch, riddle, rupture; SEE CONCEPTS **137,220**

puncture [*v2*] *deflate someone's idea, feelings*
blow sky high*, discourage, discredit, disillusion, disprove, explode, flatten*, humble, knock bottom out*, knock props from under*, poke full of holes*, shoot full of holes*, take down a peg*, take wind out of sails*; SEE CONCEPTS **7,19,54**

pundit [*n*] *person who is authority*
auger, bookworm, brain*, buff, cereb*, cognoscenti, egghead*, expert, intellectual, learned one, philosopher, professor, savant, scholar, solon, teacher, thinker; SEE CONCEPTS **416,423**

pungent [*adj1*] *highly flavored*
acid, acrid, aromatic, bitter, effluvious, hot, nosey*, odoriferous, peppery, piquant, poignant, racy, rich, salty, seasoned, sharp, snappy, sour, spicy, stinking*, strong, tangy, tart, whiffy*, zesty; SEE CONCEPT **613**

pungent [*adj2*] *sharp, stinging in speech*
acrimonious, acute, barbed, biting, bitter, caustic, cutting, exciting, hot, incisive, keen, mordant, penetrating, peppery, piercing, poignant, pointed, provocative, racy, salt, salty, sarcastic, scathing, snappy, spicy, stimulating, stringent, telling, trenchant, zesty; SEE CONCEPT **267**

punish [*v*] *penalize for wrongdoing*
abuse, attend to, batter, beat, beat up, blacklist, castigate, chasten, chastise, correct, crack down on*, cuff, debar, defrock, discipline, dismiss, do in, execute, exile, expel, fine, flog, give a going over*, give the works*, harm, hurt, immure, incarcerate, injure, knock about, lash, lecture, maltreat, misuse, oppress, paddle, rap knuckles*, reprove, rough up, scourge, sentence, slap wrist, spank, switch, teach a lesson, throw the book at*, train, whip; SEE CONCEPT **122**

punishment [*n*] *penalty*
abuse, amercement, beating, castigation, chastening, chastisement, comeuppance, confiscation, correction, deprivation, disciplinary action, discipline, forfeit, forfeiture, gallows, hard work, infliction, just desserts*, lumps, maltreatment, mortification, mulct, ostracism, pain, penance,

proof, punitive measures, purgatory, reparation, retribution, rod, rough treatment, sanction, sequestration, short shrift*, slave labor*, suffering, torture, trial, unhappiness, victimization, what for*; SEE CONCEPT **123**

punitive [*adj*] *concerning punishment*
castigating, correctional, disciplinary, in reprisal, in retaliation, penal, punishing, punitory, retaliative, retaliatory, revengeful, vindictive; SEE CONCEPT **319**

punk [*n*] *hoodlum*
bully, criminal, delinquent, gangster, goon*, hood, hooligan, mobster, rioter, rowdy, ruffian, thug, troublemaker; SEE CONCEPT **412**

puny [*adj*] *small, insignificant*
diminutive, feeble, fragile, frail, half-pint*, inconsequential, inferior, infirm, little, measly*, minor, niggling*, nothing, paltry, peanut*, peewee*, petty, picayune, piddling*, pint-sized*, puny and simple, real, simple, straight, total, runt, shrimp*, small-fry*, small time*, stunted, tiny, trifling, trivial, two-bit*, unconsequential, underfed, undersized, undeveloped, unsound, unsubstantial, weak, weakly, wee*, worthless, zero*, zilch*; SEE CONCEPTS **489,575,773**

pupil [*n*] *person who is learning something*
adherent, attendant, beginner, bookworm*, brain*, catechumen, disciple, first-year student, follower, graduate student, junior, learner, neophyte, novice, satellite, scholar, schoolboy/girl, senior, sophomore, student, tenderfoot*, undergraduate; SEE CONCEPT **350**

puppet [*n*] *person or toy manipulated by another*
creature, doll, dupe*, figurehead, figurine, instrument, jerk*, manikin, marionette, moppet, mouthpiece*, patsy*, pawn, pushover, schlemiel*, servant, soft touch*, stooge*, tool*, victim; SEE CONCEPTS **423,446**

purchase [*n*] *possession obtained with money*
acquirement, acquisition, asset, bargain, booty*, buy, gain, investment, property, steal; SEE CONCEPTS **446,710**

purchase [*v*] *buy, obtain*
achieve, acquire, attain, come by, cop*, deal in, earn, gain, get hold of, go shopping, invest, make a buy, make a purchase, market, patronize, pay for, pick up, procure, realize, redeem, secure, shop, shop for, take, take up, truck*, win; SEE CONCEPT **327**

pure [*adj1*] *unmixed, genuine*
authentic, bright, classic, clear, complete, fair, flawless, kosher*, limpid, lucid, natural, neat, out-and-out*, pellucid, perfect, plain, plenary, pure and simple, real, simple, straight, total, transparent, true, twenty-four carat*, unadulterated, unalloyed, unclouded, undiluted, unmingled; SEE CONCEPT **485**

pure [*adj2*] *clean, uncontaminated*
disinfected, germ-free, immaculate, intemerate, pasteurized, pristine, purified, refined, sanitary, snowy, spotless, stainless, sterile, sterilized, taintless, unadulterated, unblemished, undebased, unpolluted, unsoiled, unspotted, unstained, unsullied, untainted, untarnished, wholesome; SEE CONCEPT **621**

pure [*adj3*] *virginal, chaste*
babe in woods*, blameless, celibate, clean, continent, decent, exemplary, fresh, good, guileless, honest, immaculate, inculpable, innocent, inviolate, irreproachable, kid, lily white*, maidenly, modest, pure as driven snow*, righteous, sinless,

spotless, stainless, true, unblemished, unblighted, uncorrupted, undefiled, unprofaned, unspotted, unstained, unsullied, upright, virgin, virtuous, wet behind ears*, wide-eyed; SEE CONCEPT 372

pure [*adj4*] *absolute, utter*
blasted*, blessed*, complete, confounded, infernal*, mere, out-and-out, sheer, thorough, unmitigated, unqualified; SEE CONCEPTS 531,535

pure [*adj5*] *theoretical*
abstract, academic, philosophical, speculative, tentative, unproved; SEE CONCEPT 529

purely [*adv*] *simply, absolutely*
all, all in all, altogether, barely, completely, entirely, essentially, exactly, exclusively, in toto*, just, merely, only, plainly, quite, solely, totally, utterly, wholly; SEE CONCEPTS 531,544

purgatory [*n*] *hell*
Abaddon*, abyss, bottomless pit*, everlasting fire*, fire and brimstone*, Gehenna, Hades, infernal regions, limbo, lower world, nether world, perdition, pit, place of torment, suffering, underworld; SEE CONCEPTS 370,435,674

purge [*n*] *elimination, removal*
abolition, abstersion, catharsis, clarification, cleaning, cleanup, coup, crushing, disposal, disposition, ejection, eradication, evacuation, excretion, expulsion, expurgation, extermination, extirpation, liquidation, murder, purification, reign of terror*, suppression, witch hunt; SEE CONCEPTS 165,211,252

purge [*v*] *rid of; clean out*
abolish, absolve, clarify, cleanse, clear, depurate, disabuse, dismiss, dispose of, do away with*, eject, eradicate, erase, excrete, exonerate, expel, expiate, expunge, exterminate, forgive, kill, liquidate, oust, pardon, prevent, purify, remove, rout out, shake out*, sweep out, unload, wash, wipe off map*, wipe out; SEE CONCEPTS 165,211,252

purification [*n*] *freeing, cleansing*
ablution, absolution, atonement, baptism, bathing, catharsis, depuration, disinfection, distillation, expiation, expurgation, forgiveness, grace, lavation, laving, lustration, purgation, purge, purifying, rarefaction, rebirth, redemption, refinement, regeneration, salvation, sanctification, washing; SEE CONCEPTS 165,367

purify [*v*] *free; make clean*
absolve, aerate, aerify, atone, chasten, clarify, clean, cleanse, clear, decontaminate, deodorize, depurate, deterge, disinfect, edulcorate, elutriate, exculpate, exonerate, expiate, filter, fumigate, lustrate, oxygenate, purge, rarify, redeem, refine, remit, sanctify, sanitize, shrive, sublimate, wash; SEE CONCEPTS 165,367

puritanical [*adj*] *proper, straitlaced*
abstinent, austere, conforming, moral, priggish, prim, prissy, prudish, rigid, stern, strict, stuffy; SEE CONCEPTS 401,404

purloin [*v*] *steal*
appropriate, burglarize, cheat, defraud, embezzle, filch, heist, lift*, make off with*, misappropriate, pilfer, pillage, pinch*, plunder, poach, rip off*, shoplift, snitch, swindle, take, thieve; SEE CONCEPT 139

purple [*n/adj*] *blue and red colors mixed together*
amaranthine, amethyst, bluish red, color, heliotrope, lavender, lilac, magenta, mauve, mulberry, orchid, perse, plum, pomegranate, reddish blue, violaceous, violet, wine; SEE CONCEPTS 618,622

purport [*n*] *meaning, implication*
acceptation, aim, bearing, burden, connotation, core, design, drift, gist, heart, idea, import, intendment, intent, intention, matter, meat, message, nub, object, objective, pith, plan, point, purpose, score, sense, significance, significancy, signification, spirit, stuff, substance, tendency, tenor, thrust, understanding, upshot; SEE CONCEPTS 20,659,660,689

purport [*v*] *assert, mean*
allege, betoken, claim, convey, declare, denote, express, imply, import, indicate, intend, maintain, point to, pose as, pretend, proclaim, profess, signify, suggest; SEE CONCEPTS 49,682

purpose [*n1*] *intention, meaning, aim*
ambition, animus, aspiration, big idea*, bourn, calculation, design, desire, destination, determination, direction, dream, drift, end, expectation, function, goal, hope, idea, intendment, intent, mecca, mission, object, objective, plan, point, premeditation, principle, project, proposal, proposition, prospect, reason, resolve, scheme, scope, target, ulterior motive, view, whatfor*, where one's headed*, whole idea*, why and wherefore*, whyfor*, will, wish; SEE CONCEPTS 20,659,660,689

purpose [*n2*] *persistence, resolve*
confidence, constancy, determination, faith, firmness, resolution, single-mindedness, steadfastness, tenacity, will; SEE CONCEPTS 633,644

purpose [*n3*] *use*
advantage, avail, benefit, duty, effect, function, gain, goal, good, mark, mission, object, objective, outcome, profit, result, return, target, utility; SEE CONCEPTS 658,694

purpose [*v*] *intend, set sights on*
aim, aspire, bid for, commit, conclude, consider, contemplate, decide, design, determine, have a mind to*, have in view, intend, make up one's mind*, mean, meditate, mind, plan, ponder, propose, pursue, resolve, think to, work for, work toward; SEE CONCEPTS 18,36,87

purposeful [*adj*] *resolved to do something*
bent, be out for blood*, bound, calculated, dead set on*, decided, deliberate, determined, firm, fixed, intense, intent, mean business*, obstinate, persistent, playing hard ball*, positive, purposive, resolute, settled, single-minded, stalwart, staunch, steadfast, steady, strong-willed, stubborn, telelogical, tenacious, undeviating, unfaltering, unwavering; SEE CONCEPTS 326,403,542

purposeless [*adj*] *useless, insignificant*
aimless, designless, desultory, drifting, empty, feckless, floundering, fustian, goalless, good-for-nothing*, haphazard, hit-or-miss*, indiscriminate, irregular, meaningless, motiveless, needless, nonsensical, pointless, purportless, random, senseless, uncalled for, undirected, unhelpful, unnecessary, unplanned, unprofitable, unpurposed, vacuous, wanton, worthless; SEE CONCEPTS 544,560

purposely [*adv*] *intentionally*
advisedly, by design, calculatedly, consciously, deliberately, designedly, explicitly, expressly, knowingly, on purpose, prepensely, purposedly, willfully, with intent; SEE CONCEPTS 529,544

pu
pu

purse [*n1*] *tote for carrying personal items*
bag, billfold, bursa, carryall, clutch, frame, handbag, hide, leather, lizard, moneybag, pocket, pocketbook, poke, pouch, receptacle, reticule, sack, wallet; SEE CONCEPTS *339,446,450,494*

purse [*n2*] *award; winnings*
coffers, exchequer, funds, gift, means, money, present, prize, resources, reward, stake, treasury, wealth, wherewithal; SEE CONCEPTS *337,344*

purse [*v*] *press together*
close, cockle, contract, crease, knit, pucker, ruffle, tighten, wrinkle; SEE CONCEPTS *185,208*

pursue [*v1*] *chase, follow*
accompany, attend, badger, bait, bird-dog*, bug, camp on the doorstep of*, chivy, dog*, fish*, give chase, go after, harass, harry, haunt, hound, hunt, hunt down, move behind, nose around*, oppress, persevere, persist, plague, play catch up*, poke around, prowl after, ride, run after, run down, scout out, search for, search high heaven*, search out, seek, shadow, stalk, tag, tail*, take out after*, trace, track, track down, trail; SEE CONCEPT *207*

pursue [*v2*] *have as one's goal*
aim for, aspire to, attempt, desire, go in for, go out for, have a go at, purpose, seek, strive for, try for, work for, work toward; SEE CONCEPTS *20,36*

pursue [*v3*] *persist, persevere*
adhere, apply oneself, carry on, conduct, continue, cultivate, engage in, hold to, keep on, maintain, perform, ply, practice, proceed, prosecute, see through, tackle, wage, work at; SEE CONCEPTS *87,100,239*

pursue [*v4*] *seek social alliance with*
address, call, chase, chase after, court, date, go after, go for, gun, infatuate, pay court*, play up to, rush*, spark, sue, sweetheart*, woo; SEE CONCEPT *384*

pursuit [*n1*] *chase, search*
following, going all out, hunt, hunting, inquiry, pursual, pursuance, pursuing, quest, reaching, seeking, stalk, tracking, trail, trailing; SEE CONCEPT *207*

pursuit [*n2*] *occupation, interest of person*
accomplishing, accomplishment, activity, biz*, business, calling, career, do*, employment, game*, go*, hang*, hobby, job, line*, occupation, pastime, pleasure, racket, thing*, undertaking, venture, vocation, work; SEE CONCEPT *349*

push [*n1*] *physical force*
advance, assault, attack, bearing, blow, butt, charge, drive, driving, effort, energy, exerting, exertion, forcing, impact, jolt, lean, mass, nudge, offensive, onset, poke, prod, propulsion, shove, shoving, straining, thrust, thrusting, weight; SEE CONCEPTS *200,208,641,724*

push [*n2*] *mental determination*
ambition, drive, dynamism, energy, enterprise, get-up-and-go*, go*, gumption*, guts*, initiative, pep, punch, snap, spunk, starch, vigor, vitality; SEE CONCEPTS *410,411*

push [*v1*] *thrust, press with force*
accelerate, bear down, budge, bulldoze*, bump, butt, crowd, crush against, depress, dig, drive, elbow, exert, force, gore, high pressure*, hustle, impel, jam, jostle, launch, lie on, make one's way*, move, muscle, nudge, poke, pour it on*, pressure, propel, push the arm on*, railroad*, ram*, rest on, shift, shoulder, shove, squash,

squeeze, squish, steamroll*, stir, strain, strong-arm*; SEE CONCEPTS *200,208,243*

push [*v2*] *incite, urge*
bear down, browbeat, bulldoze*, coerce, constrain, dragoon, egg on*, encourage, exert influence, expedite, fire up*, goad, goose*, go to town on*, hurry, impel, influence, inspire, jolly, key up*, kid, lean on*, motivate, oblige, overpress, persuade, pour it on*, press, pressure, prod, push around, put the screws to*, put up to*, railroad*, sell on*, speed, speed up, spur, squeeze, steamroll*, strong-arm*, turn on*; SEE CONCEPTS *14,68,243*

push [*v3*] *advertise, promote*
advance, boost, cry up*, hype*, make known, plug*, propagandize, publicize, puff*; SEE CONCEPTS *49,324*

push off/push on [*v*] *leave; go to another place*
beat it*, continue, depart, exit, fare, get away, get lost*, go, go away, hie, hit the road*, journey, keep going, launch, light out, make oneself scarce*, make progress, pass, proceed, process, pull out, quit, repair, shove off, start, take off, travel, wend, withdraw; SEE CONCEPTS *195,704*

pushover [*n*] *something or someone easily influenced*
breeze, child's play*, chump*, cinch, duck soup*, easy game*, easy mark*, easy pickings*, fool, kid stuff*, picnic*, piece of cake*, setup, snap, soft touch*, stooge*, sucker, victim, walkover; SEE CONCEPTS *423,693*

pushy [*adj*] *aggressive, offensive*
ambitious, assertive, bold, brash, bumptious, forceful, loud, militant, obnoxious, obtrusive, officious, presumptuous, pushful, pushing, self-assertive; SEE CONCEPTS *401,404*

pussyfoot [*v*] *be cautious*
avoid, beat around the bush*, be noncommittal, creep, dodge, duck the issues, equivocate, evade, glide, hedge, hem and haw*, lurk, play it close to the vest*, prevaricate, prowl, shuffle, sidestep, sit on the fence*, skirt*, skulk, slide, slink, slip, sneak, steal, tergiversate, tergiverse, tiptoe, tread warily, watch one's step*, weasel*; SEE CONCEPTS *151,410*

put [*v1*] *position*
bring, concenter, concentrate, deposit, embed, establish, fasten, fix, fixate, focus, insert, install, invest, lay, nail, park, peg, place, plank, plank down, plant, plop, plunk, plunk down, quarter, repose, rest, rivet, seat, set, settle, situate, stick; SEE CONCEPT *201*

put [*v2*] *propose; express in words*
advance, air, bring forward, couch, express, formulate, forward, give, offer, phrase, pose, posit, prefer, present, propone, proposition, propound, render, set, set before, state, submit, suggest, tender, translate, transpose, turn, utter, vent, ventilate, word; SEE CONCEPTS *47,66,67*

put [*v3*] *commit, assign*
condemn, consign, constrain, doom, employ, enjoin, force, impose, induce, inflict, levy, make, oblige, require, set, subject, subject to; SEE CONCEPTS *14,242*

putative [*adj*] *commonly believed*
accepted, alleged, assumed, conjectural, hypothetical, imputed, presumed, presumptive, reported, reputed, supposed, suppositional, supposititious; SEE CONCEPT *529*

put away [*v2*] *incarcerate*
certify, commit, confine, institutionalize, jail, lock up; SEE CONCEPT *317*

put away [*v3*] *consume*
devour, eat up, gobble*, gulp down, polish off*, punish, put down, shift, swill, wolf down*; SEE CONCEPT *169*

put away [*v4*] *kill*
assassinate, bury, cool*, cut off, destroy, dispatch, do away with, do in*, dust off*, execute, finish, inter, knock off*, liquidate, murder, plant, put down*, put out of its misery*, put to sleep*, slay, tomb; SEE CONCEPT *252*

put away/put aside/put by [*v1/v*] *keep in reserve*
cache, deposit, keep, lay aside, lay away, lay by, lay in, put by, put out of the way, salt away*, save, set aside, squirrel away*, stockpile, store, store away*, stow away; SEE CONCEPTS *129,134*

put-down [*n*] *nasty commentary*
cut*, dig*, disparagement, gibe*, humiliation, indignity, insult, jibe*, knock*, pan*, rebuff, sarcasm, slight, sneer*, snub, suppression; SEE CONCEPTS *54,278*

put down [*v1*] *write into record*
enter, inscribe, jot down, log, record, set down, take down, transcribe, write down; SEE CONCEPT *79*

put down [*v2*] *subdue*
annihilate, crush, defeat, dismiss, extinguish, quash*, quell, reject, repress, silence, squash*, stamp out*, suppress; SEE CONCEPTS *95,252*

put down [*v3*] *comment negatively*
belittle, condemn, crush, decry, deflate, derogate, discount, dismiss, disparage, downcry, humiliate, minimize, mortify, opprobriate, reject, run down, shame, slight, snub, write off; SEE CONCEPT *54*

put off [*v*] *defer, delay*
adjourn, dally, dawdle, dillydally*, drag one's feet*, hold off, hold over, lag*, lay over, linger, loiter, poke*, postpone, prorogue, put back, reschedule, retard, shelve, stay, suspend, tarry, trail; SEE CONCEPTS *121,234*

put on [*v1*] *pretend*
act, affect, assume, bluff, confound, confuse, counterfeit, deceive, don, fake, feign, make believe, masquerade, playact, pose, pull, put on a front, put on an act, sham, simulate, strike, take on, trick; SEE CONCEPT *59*

put on [*v2*] *stage a performance*
do, mount, present, produce, show; SEE CONCEPT *292*

put out [*v1*] *upset, irritate; inconvenience*
aggravate, anger, annoy, bother, burn, confound, discomfit, discommode, discompose, disconcert, discountenance, disoblige, displease, dissatisfy, disturb, embarrass, exasperate, gall, get*, grate, harass, impose upon, incommode, inflame, irk, nettle, perturb, provoke, put on the spot*, rile, roil, trouble, vex; SEE CONCEPTS *7,14,19*

put out [*v2*] *extinguish fire*
blow out, douse, out, quench, smother, snuff out, stamp out; SEE CONCEPT *252*

putrefy [*v*] *rot*
break down, corrupt, crumble, decay, decompose, deteriorate, disintegrate, go bad*, molder, putresce, spoil, stink, taint, turn; SEE CONCEPT *469*

putrid [*adj*] *rotten, stinking*
bad, contaminated, corrupt, decayed, decom-

posed, fetid, foul, high, malodorous, moldered, nidorous, noisome, off, putrefied, rancid, rank, reeking, rotting, smelly, spoiled, strong, tainted, whiffy*; SEE CONCEPTS *485,598*

putter [*v*] *dawdle*
doodle, fiddle, fritter, goof around*, loiter, mess, mess around*, niggle, poke*, potter*, puddle*, shuffle around, tinker*; SEE CONCEPTS *87,210*

put up [*v1*] *accommodate guest*
bestow, billet, board, bunk, domicile, entertain, give lodging, harbor, house, lodge, make welcome, provide, quarter, take in; SEE CONCEPTS *324,384*

put up [*v2*] *build, erect*
construct, fabricate, forge, make, put together, raise, rear, shape, uprear; SEE CONCEPT *168*

puzzle [*v1*] *baffle, confuse*
addle, amaze, bamboozle*, beat, befog, befuddle, bemuse, bewilder, buffalo*, complicate, confound, discombobulate*, disconcert, distract, disturb, dumbfound, flabbergast, floor*, flummox, foil, frustrate, get to*, mystify, nonplus, obscure, perplex, pose, profundicate, psych out*, put off, rattle, snow*, stir, stumble, stump, throw; SEE CONCEPT *16*

puzzle [*v2*] *wonder about*
ask oneself, brood, cudgel, marvel, mull over, muse*, ponder, rack one's brains*, study, think about, think hard; SEE CONCEPT *17*

puzzled [*adj*] *confused*
at a loss*, at sea*, baffled, bewildered, bollixed, clueless, come apart, come unzipped*, discombobulated*, dopey*, doubtful, floored*, foggy, fouled up*, hung up*, in a fog*, lost, loused up*, messed up*, mind-blown*, mixed up*, mucked up*, mystified, nonplussed, perplexed, rattled, screwed up*, shook, shook up, spaced out*, stuck, stumped, thrown, unglued*, without a clue; SEE CONCEPTS *403,690*

puzzling [*adj*] *confusing*
abstruse, ambiguous, baffling, bewildering, beyond one, difficult, enigmatic, hard, incomprehensible, inexplicable, involved, knotty, labyrinthine, misleading, mystifying, obscure, perplexing, surprising, unaccountable, unclear, unfathomable; SEE CONCEPT *529*

pyramid [*n*] *monument*
cairn, cenotaph, edifice, mastaba, memorial, monolith, obelisk, shrine, tomb, tribute; SEE CONCEPTS *259,271,305,470*

Q

quack [*adj*] *counterfeit*
bum*, dishonest, dissembling, fake, false, fraudulent, phony, pretended, pretentious, pseudo*, sham*, simulated, unprincipled; SEE CONCEPT *582*

quack [*n*] *person who pretends to be an expert*
actor, bum*, bunco artist, charlatan, cheat, con artist, counterfeit, counterfeiter, fake, faker, flimflammer*, four-flusher*, fraud, hoser*, humbug, impostor, mountebank, phony, playactor, pretender, pseudo*, put-on*, quacksalver*, sham,

shammer*, shark*, sharp*, simulator, slicker*, whip*; SEE CONCEPT *412*

quaff [*v*] *drink down*

down, gulp, guzzle, imbibe, ingurgitate, partake, sip, sup, swallow, swig, swill, toss; SEE CONCEPT *169*

quagmire [*n1*] *bad situation*

box*, corner*, difficulty, dilemma, entanglement, fix, hole*, imbroglio, impasse, involvement, jam, mire, morass, muddle, pass, perplexity, pickle*, pinch*, plight, predicament, quandary, scrape, trouble; SEE CONCEPTS *666,674*

quagmire [*n2*] *bog*

fen, marsh, marshland, mire, morass, moss, quag, quicksand, slough, swamp; SEE CONCEPT *509*

quail [*v*] *cower, shrink*

blanch, blench, cringe, droop, faint, falter, flinch, have cold feet*, quake, recoil, shake, shudder, start, tremble, wince; SEE CONCEPTS *35,149,195*

quaint [*adj*] *strange, odd*

bizarre, curious, droll, eccentric, erratic, fanciful, fantastic, freakish, freaky*, funny, idiosyncratic, laughable, oddball, offbeat, off the beaten track*, original, outlandish, peculiar, queer, singular, special, unusual, weird*, whimsical; SEE CONCEPTS *564,589*

quaint [*adj2*] *old-fashioned; nostalgically attractive*

affected, ancient, antiquated, antique, archaic, artful, baroque, captivating, charming, colonial, curious, cute, enchanting, fanciful, Gothic*, ingenious, old-world, picturesque, pleasing, Victorian*, whimsical; SEE CONCEPTS *578,589,797*

quake [*n*] *earthquake*

aftershock, convulsion, quaker, seism, shake, shock, temblor, tremblor, tremor; SEE CONCEPT *526*

quake [*v*] *shake, vibrate*

convulse, cower, fluctuate, jar, jitter, move, pulsate, quail, quiver, rock, shiver, shrink, shudder, throb, totter, tremble, twitter, waver, wobble; SEE CONCEPT *152*

qualification [*n1*] *ability, aptitude*

accomplishment, adequacy, attainment, attribute, capability, capacity, competence, eligibility, endowment, experience, fitness, goods, makings, might, qualifiedness, quality, skill, stuff, suitability, suitableness, what it takes*; SEE CONCEPT *630*

qualification [*n2*] *requirement, restriction*

allowance, caveat, condition, contingency, criterion, essential, exception, exemption, limitation, modification, need, objection, postulate, prerequisite, provision, proviso, requisite, reservation, stipulation; SEE CONCEPTS *646,652*

qualified [*adj*] *able, skillful*

accomplished, adept, adequate, all around, au fait, capable, catechized, certified, competent, disciplined, efficient, equipped, examined, experienced, expert, fit, fitted, good, instructed, knowledgeable, licensed, practiced, pro*, proficient, proper, proved, quizzed, talented, tested, trained, tried, up to snuff*, up to speed*, vet*, veteran, war-horse*, wicked; SEE CONCEPT *527*

qualified [*adj2*] *limited, restricted*

bounded, circumscribed, conditional, confined, contingent, definite, determined, equivocal,

fixed, guarded, modified, partial, provisional, reserved; SEE CONCEPT *554*

qualify [*v1*] *make or become ready, prepared*

authorize, capacitate, certify, check out, come up to snuff*, commission, condition, cut it*, earn one's wings*, empower, enable, endow, entitle, equip, fill the bill*, fit, get by*, ground, hack it*, make it*, make the cut*, make the grade*, measure up, meet, pass, pass muster*, permit, ready, sanction, score, suffice, suit, train; SEE CONCEPTS *99,630*

qualify [*v2*] *lessen, restrict*

abate, adapt, alter, assuage, change, circumscribe, diminish, ease, limit, mitigate, moderate, modify, modulate, reduce, regulate, restrain, soften, temper, vary, weaken; SEE CONCEPTS *240,698*

qualify [*v3*] *characterize, distinguish*

ascribe, assign, attribute, describe, designate, impute, individualize, individuate, mark, name, predicate, signalize, singularize; SEE CONCEPT *411*

quality [*n1*] *characteristic, feature*

affection, affirmation, aspect, attribute, character, condition, constitution, description, element, endowment, essence, factor, genius, individuality, kind, make, mark, name of tune*, nature, nature of beast*, parameter, peculiarity, predication, property, savor, sort, trait, virtue, way of it*; SEE CONCEPT *543*

quality [*n2*] *value, status*

arete, caliber, capacity, character, class, condition, distinction, excellence, excellency, footing, grade, group, kind, merit, perfection, place, position, preeminence, rank, repute, standing, state, station, stature, step, superbness, superiority, variety, virtue, worth; SEE CONCEPTS *346,378,668*

qualm [*n*] *nagging doubt*

agitation, anxiety, apprehension, compunction, conscience, demur, disquiet, foreboding, hesitation, indecision, insecurity, misdoubt, misgiving, mistrust, nervousness, objection, pang, perturbation, presentiment, regret, reluctance, remonstrance, remorse, scruple, suspicion, twinge, uncertainty, unease, uneasiness; SEE CONCEPTS *410,532*

quandary [*n*] *delicate situation*

bewilderment, bind, Catch-22*, clutch, corner*, difficulty, dilemma, double trouble*, doubt, embarrassment, hang-up*, impasse, mire, perplexity, pickle*, plight, predicament, puzzle, spot*, strait, uncertainty, up a tree*; SEE CONCEPTS *532,674,690*

quantify [*v*] *measure*

appraise, assess, calibrate, check, compute, count, determine, estimate, evaluate, figure, gauge, look over, rank, rate, size, specify, value, weigh; SEE CONCEPTS *103,197,764*

quantity [*n*] *number or amount*

abundance, aggregate, allotment, amplitude, batch, body, budget, bulk, capacity, deal, expanse, extent, figure, greatness, length, load, lot, magnitude, mass, measure, multitude, part, pile, portion, profusion, quota, size, sum, total, variety, volume; SEE CONCEPT *787*

quantum leap [*n*] *abrupt change*

advance, breakthrough, giant strides, jump, leaps and bounds, radical change; SEE CONCEPTS *230,260,701*

quarantine [*n*] *isolation*
detention, lazaretto, seclusion, segregation, separation, sequestration; SEE CONCEPTS *135,188, 388,631*

quarantine [*v*] *isolate*
block off, close off, confine, cordon, detach, insulate, keep apart, remove, restrict, seal off, seclude, segregate, separate, sequester; SEE CONCEPTS *188,201*

quarrel [*n*] *disagreement*
affray, altercation, argument, battle royal*, beef*, bickering*, brannigan*, brawl, breach, broil*, catfight*, combat, commotion, complaint, contention, controversy, difference, difference of opinion, dispute, dissension, dissidence, disturbance, dust*, falling-out*, feud, fight, fisticuffs*, fracas, fray, fuss, hassle, misunderstanding, objection, rhubarb*, row, ruckus*, run-in, scrap, set-to*, spat, squabble, strife, struggle, tiff, tumult, vendetta, wrangle; SEE CONCEPTS *46,106*

quarrel [*v*] *disagree*
altercate, argue, battle, be at loggerheads*, bicker, brawl, break with, bump, carp, caterwaul, cavil, charge, clash, collide, complain, contend, contest, cross swords*, differ, disapprove, dispute, dissent, divide, embroil, fall out*, feud, fight, find fault, get tough with*, hassle, have it out*, have words*, lock horns*, mix it up*, object to, row, scrap, set to, spar, spat, squabble, strive, struggle, take exception, take on, tangle, vary, war, wrangle; SEE CONCEPTS *46,106*

quarrelsome [*adj*] *being disagreeable*
argumentative, bad-tempered, bellicose, belligerent, brawling, cantankerous, cat-and-dog*, choleric, churlish, clash, combative, contentious, crabby*, cross, disputatious, dissentious, excitable, fiery, fractious, gladiatorial, hasty, have chip on shoulder*, hotheaded*, huffy, impassioned*, irascible, irritable, litigious, ornery, passionate, peevish, pettish, petulant, pugnacious, querulous, ructious, snappy, tempestuous, thin-skinned*, touchy, truculent, turbulent, unruly, violent, war; SEE CONCEPTS *401,542*

quarry [*n*] *goal*
aim, chase, game, objective, prey, prize, quest, raven, victim; SEE CONCEPT *659*

quarter [*n1*] *one of four equal parts*
division, farthing, fourth, one-fourth, part, portion, quad, quadrant, quartern, section, semester, span, term, two bits*; SEE CONCEPT *835*

quarter [*n2*] *area, neighborhood*
barrio, bearing, direction, district, division, domain, ghetto, inner city, locality, location, neck of the woods*, old town, part, place, point, position, precinct, province, region, section, sector, side, skid row, slum, spot, station, stomping ground*, territory, turf, zone, zoo*; SEE CONCEPTS *508,512*

quarter [*n3*] *forgiveness*
clemency, compassion, favor, grace, leniency, lenity, mercy, pity; SEE CONCEPTS *410,633*

quarter [*v1*] *divide into four equal parts*
cleave, cut, cut up, dismember, fourth; SEE CONCEPT *98*

quarter [*v2*] *provide lodging*
accommodate, billet, board, bunk, canton, domicile, domiciliate, entertain, establish, harbor, house, install, lodge, place, post, put up, settle, shelter, station; SEE CONCEPT *140*

quarters [*n*] *place to live or sleep*
abode, accommodation, apartment, barracks, billet, cabin, cantonment, chambers, condo, cottage, digs*, domicile, dorm, dwelling, flat, fraternity, habitat, habitation, home, house, lodge, lodging, place, post, ranch, residence, room, roost*, shelter, sorority, station, tent; SEE CONCEPT *516*

quash [*v1*] *destroy, defeat*
annihilate, beat, crush, extinguish, extirpate, overcome, overthrow, put down, quell, quench, repress, scrunch*, snow under*, squash*, squish*, subdue, suppress, trash; SEE CONCEPTS *95,252*

quash [*v2*] *nullify, cancel*
abrogate, annul, black out*, bottle up*, clamp down on, cork up*, crack down on*, declare null and void*, discharge, dissolve, hush up*, invalidate, kill, negate, overrule, overthrow, put damper on*, put the lid on*, repeal, rescind, reverse, revoke, set aside, shut down, squelch, undo, vacate, veto, vitiate, void, watergate*; SEE CONCEPTS *121,234,266*

quasi [*adj*] *almost; to a certain extent*
apparent, apparently, fake, mock, near, nominal, partly, pretended, pseudo-*, seeming, seemingly, semi-, sham*, so-called, supposedly, synthetic, virtual, would-be*; SEE CONCEPT *582*

queasy [*adj*] *not feeling well; not comfortable*
anxious, bilious, concerned, fidgety, green around gills*, groggy, ill, ill at ease, indisposed, nauseated, pukish, qualmish, queer, restless, rocky*, sick, sick as a dog*, sickly, squeamish, troubled, uncertain, uncomfortable, under the weather*, uneasy, unwell, upset, worried; SEE CONCEPTS *314,403*

queer [*adj1*] *odd; abnormal*
anomalous, atypical, bizarre, crazy, curious, demented, disquieting, doubtful, droll, dubious, eccentric, eerie, erratic, extraordinary, fishy*, flaky*, fly ball*, freaky*, funny, idiosyncratic, irrational, irregular, kinky*, kooky*, mad, mysterious, oddball, off the wall*, outlandish, outré, peculiar, puzzling, quaint, questionable, remarkable, shady, singular, strange, suspicious, touched, unbalanced, uncanny, uncommon, unconventional, unhinged, unnatural, unorthodox, unusual, wacky*, weird; SEE CONCEPTS *404,548,564*

queer [*adj2*] *not feeling well*
dizzy, faint, giddy, green*, ill, lightheaded, pukish*, qualmish, qualmy*, queasy*, reeling, sick, squeamish*, uneasy; SEE CONCEPT *314*

quell [*v1*] *defeat, suppress*
annihilate, conquer, crush, extinguish, hush up*, kill, overcome, overpower, put down, put the lid on*, queer, quench, shut down, silence, sit on, stamp out*, stifle, stop, subdue, subjugate, vanquish; SEE CONCEPTS *95,121,234*

quell [*v2*] *alleviate, calm*
allay, appease, assuage, check, compose, deaden, dull, ease, mitigate, moderate, mollify, pacify, quiet, reduce, silence, soothe, still; SEE CONCEPTS *7,22,110*

quench [*v1*] *destroy, extinguish*
annihilate, check, choke, crush, dampen, decimate, demolish, destruct, dismantle, douse, end, kill, knock down, moisten, put down, quash*, quell, raze, ruin, shatter, smother, snuff out*, stifle, suppress, wreck; SEE CONCEPTS *234,252*

quench [v2] *satisfy, especially thirst*
allay, alleviate, appease, assuage, content, cool*, glut, gorge, gratify, lighten, mitigate, moisten, relieve, sate, satiate, slake; SEE CONCEPTS 136,244

querulous [adj] *grouchy, hard to please*
bearish, bemoaning, cantankerous, captious, carping, censorious, complaining, critical, cross, crying, deploring, discontented, dissatisfied, edgy, fault-finding, fretful, grousing, grumbling, grumbly, huffy* irascible, irritable, lamenting, out of sorts* peevish, petulant, plaintive, scrappy, snappy, sour, testy, thin-skinned* touchy, uptight, wailing, waspish, waspy, whimpering, whining, whiny; SEE CONCEPTS 401,542

query [n] *demand for answers*
concern, doubt, dubiety, inquiry, interrogation, interrogatory, mistrust, objection, problem, question, questioning, reservation, skepticism, suspicion, uncertainty; SEE CONCEPTS 21,48,53,662

query [v] *ask*
catechize, challenge, disbelieve, dispute, distrust, doubt, enquire, examine, hit up, impeach, impugn, inquire, interrogate, knock, mistrust, put out a feeler* question, quiz, suspect, test the waters*; SEE CONCEPTS 21,48,53

quest [n] *search, exploration*
adventure, chase, crusade, delving, enterprise, examination, expedition, hunt, inquest, inquiry, inquisition, investigation, journey, mission, pilgrimmage, prey, probe, probing, pursual, pursuit, quarry, research, seeking, voyage; SEE CONCEPTS 48,103,216

question [n1] *asking for answer*
catechism, examination, inquest, inquiring, inquiry, inquisition, interrogation, interrogatory, investigation, poll, Q and A*, query, questioning, third degree*, wringer*; SEE CONCEPTS 48,53

question [n2] *controversy, doubt*
argument, challenge, confusion, contention, debate, demur, demurral, difficulty, dispute, dubiety, enigma, misgiving, mystery, objection, problem, protest, puzzle, query, remonstrance, remonstration, uncertainty; SEE CONCEPTS 666,674

question [n3] *issue, point at issue*
discussion, motion, point, problem, proposal, proposition, subject, theme, topic; SEE CONCEPTS 532,690

question [v1] *ask for answer*
ask about, catechize, challenge, cross-examine, enquire, examine, give the third degree*, go over, grill, hit*, hit up*, hold out for, inquire, interrogate, interview, investigate, knock*, make inquiry, petition, pick one's brains*, probe, pry, pump, put through the wringer*, put to the question*, query, quest, quiz, raise question, roast*, search, seek, show curiosity, solicit, sound out*, sweat it out of*, work over*; SEE CONCEPTS 48,53

question [v2] *doubt*
call into question, cast doubt upon, challenge, controvert, disbelieve, dispute, distrust, hesitate, impeach, impugn, mistrust, oppose, puzzle over, query, suspect, suspicion, wonder about; SEE CONCEPT 21

questionable [adj] *doubtful, uncertain*
ambiguous, apocryphal, arguable, contingent,

controversial, controvertible, cryptic, debatable, disputable, dubious, dubitable, enigmatic, equivocal, fishy*, hard to believe, hypothetical, iffy*, indecisive, indefinite, indeterminate, moot, mysterious, obscure, occult, open to doubt, open to question, oracular, paradoxical, problematic, problematical, provisional, shady, suspect, suspicious, unconfirmed, undefined, under advisement, under examination, unproven, unreliable, unsettled, vague; SEE CONCEPTS 529,535

queue [n] *sequence*
chain, concatenation, echelon, file, line, order, progression, rank, row, series, string, succession, tail, tier, train; SEE CONCEPTS 432,727

quibble [n] *objection, complaint*
artifice, cavil, criticism, dodge, duplicity, equivocation, evasion, hair-splitter*, nicety, niggle*, nit-picker*, pretense, prevarication, protest, quiddity, quirk, shift, sophism, subterfuge, subtlety; SEE CONCEPTS 46,52

quibble [v] *disagree over minor issues*
altercate, argue over, argufy, avoid, bicker, blow hot and cold*, carp, catch at straws*, cavil, chicane, criticize, dispute, equivocate, evade, fence*, flip-flop*, hassle, have at it*, hem and haw*, hypercriticize*, make a big thing about*, nit-pick*, paralogize, pettifog*, pretend, prevaricate, put up an argument, set to, shift, spar, split hairs*, squabble, talk back, waffle, wrangle; SEE CONCEPTS 46,52

quick [adj1] *fast, speedy*
abrupt, accelerated, active, agile, alert, a move on*, animated, ASAP*, breakneck*, brief, brisk, cursory, curt, double time*, energetic, expeditious, expeditive, express, fleet, flying, going, harefooted*, hasty, headlong, hurried, immediate, impatient, impetuous, instantaneous, keen, lively, mercurial, move it, nimble, on the double*, perfunctory, posthaste, prompt, pronto*, rapid, snappy, spirited, sprightly, spry, sudden, swift, the lead out*, winged*; SEE CONCEPTS 544,588

quick [adj2] *smart*
able, active, acute, adept, adroit, all there, apt, astute, bright, canny, capable, clever, competent, deft, dexterous, discerning, effective, effectual, intelligent, keen, nimble-witted, on the ball*, perceptive, perspicacious, prompt, quick on the draw, quick on the trigger*, quick on the uptake*, quick-witted, ready, receptive, savvy*, sharp, sharp as a tack*, shrewd, skillful, slick, smart as a whip*, vigorous, whiz*, wired*, wise; SEE CONCEPT 402

quicken [v] *make faster; invigorate*
accelerate, activate, actuate, animate, arouse, awaken, dispatch, energize, excite, expedite, galvanize, goad, grow, hasten, hurry, impel, incite, increase, innervate, innerve, inspire, kindle, liven, make haste, motivate, move, pique, precipitate, promote, refresh, revitalize, revive, rouse, shake up, speed, spring, spur, step up, stimulate, stir, strengthen, urge, vitalize, vivificate, vivify; SEE CONCEPTS 7,19,22,250

quickly [adv] *fast*
apace, briskly, chop-chop*, expeditiously, flat-out*, fleetly, full tilt*, hastily, hurriedly, immediately, in a flash*, in haste, in nothing flat*, in short order*, instantaneously, instantly, lickety-split*, like a bat out of hell*, like a flash*, like a

shot*, promptly, pronto, quick, rapidly, speedily, swift, swiftly; SEE CONCEPTS *588,799*

quick-tempered [*adj*] *easily upset, angered*
choleric, cranky, cross, excitable, fiery, hot-tempered, impatient, impulsive, inflammable, irascible, irritable, passionate, peppery, petulant, quarrelsome, ratty, sensitive, short-tempered, shrewish, splenetic, temperamental, testy, waspish; SEE CONCEPTS *401,404*

quick-witted [*adj*] *smart*
acute, agile, alert, apt, astute, brainy, bright, brilliant, canny, clever, facetious, humorous, intelligent, keen, knowing, nimble-witted, on the ball*, penetrating, penetrative, perceptive, prompt, quick, quick on the draw*, quick on the uptake*, ready, savvy*, sharp, sharp as a tack*, sharp-sighted, sharp-witted, shrewd, slick*, whiz*, wired*, wise, witty; SEE CONCEPTS *267,402*

quiet [*adj*] *without or with little sound*
buttoned up*, clammed up*, close, close-mouthed, could hear a pin drop*, dumb, hushed, hushful, inaudible, low, low-pitched, muffled, mute, muted, noiseless, not saying boo*, peaceful, quiescent, quieted, reserved, reticent, secretive, silent, soft, soundless, speechless, still, stilled, taciturn, tight-lipped*, uncommunicative, unexpressed, unspeaking, unuttered, whist; SEE CONCEPTS *592,594*

quiet [*adj2*] *calm, peaceful*
collected, contented, docile, fixed, gentle, halcyon, hushed, inactive, isolated, level, meek, mild, motionless, pacific, placid, private, remote, reserved, restful, retired, secluded, secret, sedate, sequestered, serene, shy, smooth, stable, stagnant, still, tranquil, unanxious, undisturbed, unexcited, unfrequented, unruffled, untroubled; SEE CONCEPTS *401,583,584,705*

quiet [*adj3*] *simple, unobtrusive*
conservative, homely, inobtrusive, modest, plain, restrained, sober, subdued, tasteful, unassuming, unpretentious; SEE CONCEPT *589*

quiet [*n*] *calmness, silence*
calm, cessation, dead air*, ease, hush, lull, noiselessness, peace, quietness, quietude, relaxation, repose, rest, serenity, soundlessness, speechlessness, still, stillness, stop, termination, tranquility; SEE CONCEPTS *65,315,592,673,705*

quiet [*v*] *make silent, calm*
allay, ameliorate, appease, assuage, becalm, button one's lip*, calm down, can it, choke, clam up*, compose, console, cool it*, cool out*, dummy up*, fix up, gag, gratify, hold it down, hush, ice*, inactivate, lull, moderate, mollify, muffle, muzzle, pacify, palliate, patch things up*, please, quieten, reconcile, relax, satisfy, settle, shush, shut up, silence, slack, smooth, soften, soft-pedal*, soothe, square, squash, squelch, still, stroke, subdue, take the bite out of*, tranquilize; SEE CONCEPTS *6,315,592,673,705*

quilt [*n*] *thick bedcovering made of patches*
batt, bedspread, blanket, comforter, counterpane, cover, coverlet, down, duvet, eiderdown, pad, patchwork, pouf, puff; SEE CONCEPTS *445,451,473*

quintessence [*n*] *essence, core*
apotheosis, bottom, distillation, epitome, essentiality, extract, gist, heart, kernel, last word, lifeblood, marrow, pith, quiddity, soul, spirit, stuff, substance, ultimate, virtuality; SEE CONCEPTS *682,826*

quip [*n*] *witty communication, often verbal*
badinage, banter, bon mot, crack, drollery, gag, gibe, insult, jeer, jest, joke, mockery, offense, pleasantry, pun, repartee, retort, riposte, sally, satire, spoof, wisecrack, witticism; SEE CONCEPTS *273,278*

quirk [*n*] *oddity of personality, way of doing something*
aberration, caprice, characteristic, conceit, crotchet, eccentricity, equivocation, fancy, fetish, foible, habit, humor, idée fixe, idiosyncrasy, irregularity, kink, knack, mannerism, peculiarity, quibble, singularity, subterfuge, trait, turn, twist, vagary, whim, whimsy; SEE CONCEPTS *411,644*

quit [*v1*] *abandon, leave*
abdicate, blow*, book*, bow out, check out, cut out*, decamp, depart, desert, drop, drop out, evacuate, exit, forsake, get off, give up, go, go away from, hang it up*, leave flat*, leave hanging*, pull out, push off*, relinquish, renounce, resign, retire, run out on, surrender, take a walk*, take off, throw over*, vacate, walk out on, withdraw, yield; SEE CONCEPT *195*

quit [*v2*] *stop doing something*
abandon, break off, call it a day*, call it quits*, cease, conclude, cut it out*, desist, discontinue, drop, end, get on the wagon*, give notice, give over*, give up, halt, hang it up*, kick over*, kick the habit*, knock off*, leave, leave off*, pack in*, quit cold, resign, retire, secede, sew up*, surcease, suspend, take the cure*, terminate, wind up*, withdraw, wrap up*; SEE CONCEPTS *119,234*

quite [*adv1*] *completely*
absolutely, actually, all, all in all, all told, altogether, considerably, entirely, fully, in all respects, in fact, in reality, in toto, in truth, just, largely, perfectly, positively, precisely, purely, really, thoroughly, totally, truly, utterly, well, wholly, without reservation; SEE CONCEPTS *531,582*

quite [*adv2*] *to a certain extent*
considerably, fairly, far, moderately, more or less, pretty, rather, reasonably, relatively, significantly, somewhat, to some degree, very; SEE CONCEPTS *569,772*

quiver [*n*] *shaking, vibration*
convulsion, flash, glimmer, glitter, oscillation, palpitation, pulsation, shake, shimmer, shiver, shudder, sparkle, spasm, throb, tic, tremble, tremor, twinkle; SEE CONCEPT *152*

quiver [*v*] *shake, vibrate*
agitate, beat, convulse, dither, jitter, oscillate, palpitate, pulsate, pulse, quake, quaver, shiver, shudder, thrill, throb, tremble, tremor, twitter; SEE CONCEPT *152*

quixotic [*adj*] *idealistic*
chimerical, chivalrous, dreaming, dreamy, foolish, impetuous, impractical, impulsive, romantic, starry-eyed, unrealistic, utopian, visionary; SEE CONCEPTS *529,560,582*

quiz [*n*] *questioning, often in an organized academic setting*
blue book*, check, exam, examination, investigation, query, shotgun*; test; SEE CONCEPT *290*

quiz [*v*] *question*
ask, catechize, check, cross-examine, examine, give the third degree*, grill*, inquire, interrogate, investigate, pick one's brains*, pump*, query, test; SEE CONCEPT *48*

qu
qu

quizzical [*adj*] *appearing confused or curious*
amusing, aporetic, arch, bantering, derisive, disbelieving, eccentric, incredulous, inquiring, inquisitive, mocking, odd, probing, quaint, queer, questioning, sardonic, searching, show-me*, skeptical, supercilious, suspicious, teasing, unbelieving, unusual; SEE CONCEPTS 267,485

quota [*n*] *portion allotted to something*
allocation, allotment, allowance, apportionment, assignment, bite, chunk, cut, division, divvy*, end, lot, measure, meed, part, partage, percentage, piece, piece of action*, proportion, quantum, ration, share, slice, split; SEE CONCEPTS 768,835

quotation/quote [*n1*] *repetition of something spoken or written by someone*
citation, citing, cutting, excerpt, extract, passage, quote, recitation, reference, saying, selection; SEE CONCEPTS 274,278

quotation/quote [*n2*] *financial estimate*
bid, bid price, charge, cost, current price, figure, market price, price, price named, published price, quote, rate, stated price, tender; SEE CONCEPTS 274,332,784

quote [*v*] *repeat something spoken, written by another*
adduce, attest, cite, detail, excerpt, extract, instance, name, paraphrase, parrot, proclaim, recall, recite, recollect, reference, refer to, retell; SEE CONCEPTS 79,171

R

rabble [*n*] *mob*
commonality, commoners, crowd, drove, flock, gang, gathering, herd, hoi polloi, horde, lower class, mass, masses, multitude, pack, proletariat, rank and file, riffraff, ring, riot, scum, throng; SEE CONCEPTS 378,417,432

rabid [*adj*] *very angry; maniacal*
berserk, bigoted, bitten, corybantic, crazed*, crazy, delirious, deranged, enthusiastic, extreme, extremist, fanatical, fervent, flipped*, foaming at the mouth*, frantic, freaked out*, frenetic, frenzied, furious, hot*, infuriated, insane, intemperate, intolerant, irrational, keen, mad, mad-dog*, narrow-minded, nutty*, obsessed, overboard, poisoned, radical, raging, revolutionary, sick*, sizzling, smoking*, steamed up*, ultra, ultraist, violent, virulent, wild, zealous; SEE CONCEPT 403

race [*n1*] *pursuit; running; speeding*
chase, clash, clip, competition, contention, contest, course, dash, engagement, event, go, marathon, match, meet, relay, rivalry, run, rush, scurry, sprint, spurt; SEE CONCEPT 363

race [*n2*] *ethnic group*
blood, breed, clan, color, cultural group, culture, family, folk, house, issue, kin, kind, kindred, line, lineage, nation, nationality, offspring, people, progeny, seed, species, stock, strain, tribe, type, variety; SEE CONCEPT 380

race [*n3*] *stream, river*
branch, brook, creek, duct, gill, raceway, rill, rindle, rivulet, run, runnel, sluice, tide; SEE CONCEPT 514

race [*v*] *run, speed in competition*
boil, bolt, bustle, career, chase, compete, contest, course, dart, dash, fling, fly, gallop, haste, hasten, hie, hurry, hustle, lash, outstrip, plunge ahead, post, pursue, rush, scamper, scramble, scud, scuttle, shoot, skim, sprint, spurt, swoop, tear, whisk, wing; SEE CONCEPTS 150,363

racial [*adj*] *ethnic*
ancestral, ethnological, folk, genealogical, genetic, hereditary, lineal, national, phyletic, phylogenetic, tribal; SEE CONCEPT 549

racism [*n*] *prejudice against an ethnic group*
apartheid, bias, bigotry, discrimination, illiberality, one-sidedness, partiality, racialism, sectarianism, segregation, unfairness; SEE CONCEPT 689

racist [*adj*] *bigoted*
anti-Semitic, biased, illiberal, intolerant, narrow-minded, opinionated, partial, prejudiced, sectarian, small-minded, xenophobic; SEE CONCEPTS 403,555

racist [*n*] *bigot*
anti-Semite, black supremacist, chauvinist, diehard, doctrinaire, fanatic, klansperson, opinionated person, prejudiced person, sectarian, segregationist, sexist person, white supremacist, xenophobe; SEE CONCEPTS 359,423

rack [*n*] *frame, framework*
arbor, bed, box, bracket, counter, furniture, holder, ledge, perch, receptacle, shelf, stand, structure, trestle; SEE CONCEPTS 443,479

rack [*v*] *torture; strain*
afflict, agonize, crucify, distress, excruciate, force, harass, harrow, martyr, oppress, pain, persecute, pull, shake, stress, stretch, tear, torment, try, wrench, wring; SEE CONCEPTS 7,19,246

racket [*n1*] *commotion; fight*
agitation, babel, battle, blare, brawl, clamor, clangor, clash, clatter, din, disturbance, fracas, free-for-all*, fuss, hoo-ha*, hubbub*, jangle, noise, outcry, pandemonium, riot, roar, row, ruction, rumpus*, shouting, shuffle, squabble, squall, stir, to-do*, tumult, turbulence, turmoil, uproar, vociferation, wrangle; SEE CONCEPTS 65,106,230

racket [*n2*] *criminal activity*
cheating, confidence game, con game, conspiracy, corruption, crime, dirty pool*, dishonesty, dodge, extortion, fraud, game, graft, illegality, illicit scheme, intrigue, lawlessness, lay, plot, push, scheme, shakedown, squeeze*, swindle, swindling, theft, trick, underworld; SEE CONCEPT 192

rack up [*v*] *achieve, gain*
accomplish, acquire, actualize, attain, carry out, do, earn, get done, obtain, produce, reach, realize, score, wind up; SEE CONCEPT 706

racy [*adj1*] *energetic; zestful*
animated, bright, buoyant, clever, distinctive, entertaining, exciting, exhilarating, fiery, forceful, forcible, gingery, heady, keen, lively, mettlesome, peppery, piquant, playful, poignant, pungent, rich, salty, saucy*, sharp, snappy, sparkling, spicy, spirited, sportive, sprightly, stimulating, strong, tangy, tart, tasty, vigorous, vivacious, witty, zesty; SEE CONCEPTS 401,613

racy [*adj2*] *risqué, vulgar*
bawdy, blue*, broad, erotic, immodest, indecent, indelicate, lewd, lurid, naughty, off-color*, purple*, shady*, smutty*, spicy*, suggestive, wicked; SEE CONCEPTS 267,545

radar [*n*] *radio detecting and ranging*
direction finding, scanning system, sonar, tracking system; SEE CONCEPT 279

radiance [*n1*] *brightness, luminescence*
brilliance, effulgence, glare, gleam, glitter, glow, incandescence, light, luminosity, luster, resplendence, shine; SEE CONCEPT 620

radiance [*n2*] *happiness*
delight, gaiety, joy, pleasure, rapture, warmth; SEE CONCEPT 633

radiant [*adj1*] *bright, luminous*
beaming, brilliant, effulgent, gleaming, glittering, glorious, glowing, incandescent, lambent, lucent, lustrous, radiating, refulgent, resplendent, shining, sparkling, sunny; SEE CONCEPT 617

radiant [*adj2*] *happy in appearance*
beaming, beatific, blissful, bright, cheerful, cheery, delighted, ecstatic, gay, glad, glowing, joyful, joyous, rapturous; SEE CONCEPT 401

radiate [*v*] *give off; scatter*
afford, beam, branch out, broadcast, circulate, diffuse, disseminate, distribute, diverge, emanate, emit, expand, give out, gleam, glitter, illumine, irradiate, issue, light up, pour, proliferate, propagate, ramble, ramify, send out, shed, shine, shoot out, spread, spread out, sprinkle, strew, throw out, transmit, yield; SEE CONCEPTS 118,217,620,716

radical [*adj1*] *fundamental, basic*
basal, bottom, cardinal, constitutional, deep-seated, essential, foundational, inherent, innate, intrinsic, meat-and-potatoes*, native, natural, organic, original, primal, primary, primitive, profound, thoroughgoing, underlying, vital; SEE CONCEPTS 546,549

radical [*adj2*] *deviating by extremes*
advanced, anarchistic, complete, entire, excessive, extremist, fanatical, far-out*, freethinking, iconoclastic, immoderate, insubordinate, insurgent, insurrectionary, intransigent, lawless, leftist, militant, mutinous, nihilistic, progressive, rabid, rebellious, recalcitrant, recusant, refractory, restive, revolutionary, riotous, seditious, severe, sweeping, thorough, ultra, ultraist, uncompromising, violent, way out*; SEE CONCEPTS 403,529,542

radical [*n*] *person who advocates significant, often extreme change*
agitator, anarchist, avant-garde, extremist, fanatic, firebrand, freethinker, iconoclast, insurgent, insurrectionist, leftist, left-winger, militant, mutineer, nihilist, nonconformist, objector, pacifist, progressive, rebel, reformer, renegade, revolter, revolutionary, rioter, secessionist, subversive, ultraist; SEE CONCEPT 359

radio [*n*] *communication by electronic air waves*
AM-FM, CB, Marconi, radionics, radiotelegraph, radiotelegraphy, radiotelephone, radiotelephonics, receiver, shortwave, telegraphy, telephony, transmission, Walkman, wireless; SEE CONCEPT 279

radius [*n*] *range, sweep*
ambit, boundary, compass, expanse, extension, extent, interval, limit, orbit, purview, reach, semidiameter, space, span, spoke; SEE CONCEPT 651

raffish [*adj*] *unmindful of social conventions*
bohemian*, careless, casual, coarse, dashing, devil-may-care*, disreputable, fast*, gay, jaunty, rakish, sporty, tasteless, tawdry, unconventional, uncouth, vulgar, wild; SEE CONCEPT 401

raffle [*n*] *lottery for a prize*
bet, betting, disposition, draw, drawing, flier*, gambling, game of chance, gaming, long odds*, lots*, numbers*, numbers game*, pool, random shot, speculation, stake, sweep, sweepstake, tossup*, wager, wagering; SEE CONCEPTS 363,364

ragamuffin [*n*] *person who is poor, tattered*
beggar, bum*, gamin, guttersnipe*, hobo, loafer, orphan, scarecrow, street person, tatterdemalion*, tramp, urchin, vagabond, vagrant, waif, wastrel; SEE CONCEPTS 412,423

rage [*n1*] *extreme anger*
acerbity, acrimony, agitation, animosity, apoplexy, asperity, bitterness, blowup*, bluster, choler, convulsion, dander, eruption, exasperation, excitement, explosion, ferment, ferocity, fireworks, frenzy, furor, fury, gall, heat*, hemorrhage, huff*, hysterics, indignation, ire, irritation, madness, mania, obsession, outburst, paroxysm, passion, rampage, raving, resentment, spasm, spleen, squall, storm, tantrum, temper, umbrage, uproar, upset, vehemence, violence, winging*; SEE CONCEPTS 410,657

rage [*n2*] *something in vogue; popular notion*
caprice, chic, conceit, craze, crotchet, cry, dernier cri, enthusiasm, fad, fancy, fashion, freak, furor, happening, hot spot*, in*, in-spot*, in-thing*, last word*, latest*, latest thing*, latest wrinkle*, mania, mode, newest wrinkle*, now*, passion, style, thing*, up to the minute*, vagary, whim; SEE CONCEPTS 388,655

rage [*v*] *be angry*
be beside oneself*, be furious, be uncontrollable, blow a fuse*, blow one's top*, blow up*, boil over*, bristle, chafe, champ at bit*, erupt, fly off the handle*, foam at the mouth*, fret, fulminate, fume, go berserk, have a fit, have a tantrum, let off steam*, look daggers*, make a fuss over, overflow, rail at, rampage, rant, rant and rave*, rave, roar, scold, scream, seethe, snap at, splutter, steam, storm, surge, tear, throw a fit*, work oneself into sweat*; yell; SEE CONCEPTS 29,410

ragged [*adj*] *worn-out; in shreds*
badly dressed, badly worn, battered, broken, contemptible, crude, desultory, dilapidated, dingy, disorganized, down at the heel*, fragmented, frayed, frazzled, full of holes*, in holes*, in rags, in tatters*, irregular, jagged, mean, moth-eaten, notched, patched, poor, poorly made, rent, rough, rugged, scraggy, seedy, serrated, shabby, shaggy, shoddy, shredded, tacky*, tattered, tatty*, threadbare, torn, uneven, unfinished, unkempt, unpressed, worse for wear*; SEE CONCEPT 485

raging [*adj*] *violent; mad*
angry, at boiling point*, bent*, bent out of shape*, beside oneself*, blowing a gasket*, blowing one's top*, blustering, blustery, boiling mad*, boiling over*, enraged, fit to be tied*, frenzied, fuming, furious, going ape*, incensed, infuriated, irate, mad as a hornet*, on the warpath*, rabid*, ranting and raving*, raving, raving mad*, rough, seeing red*, seething, stormy, tempestuous, throwing a fit, turbulent, wild; SEE CONCEPTS 403,542

raid [*n*] *attack, seizure*
arrest, assault, break-in, bust, capture, descent,

qu
ra

foray, forced entrance, hit-and-run*, incursion, inroad, invasion, irruption, onset, onslaught, pull, reconnaissance, roundup, sally*, shootup*, sortie*, surprise attack, sweep, tipover*; SEE CONCEPTS 86,317

raid [v] *attack, pillage*

assail, assault, blockade, bomb, bombard, breach, break in, charge, descend on, despoil, devastate, fall upon, fire on, forage, foray, harass, harry, heat, inroad, invade, knock off*, knock over*, lean against, lean on, loot, maraud, march on, overrun, pirate, plunder, rake, ransack, rifle, rob, sack, sally, sally forth, shell, slough, spoliate, storm, strafe, strike, sweep, swoop, tip over*, torpedo, waste; SEE CONCEPT 86

rail [v] *criticize harshly*

abuse, attack, bawl out*, berate, blast, castigate, censure, chew out*, complain, fulminate, fume, inveigh, jaw, objurate, rant, rate, revile, scold, thunder, tongue-lash*, upbraid, vituperate, vociferate, whip; SEE CONCEPT 52

rail/railing [n] *post, pole along an edge*

balustrade, banister, bar, barrier, fence, paling, rails, rest, siding; SEE CONCEPTS 443,479

railroad [n] *train line*

elevated railway, line, metro, monorail, rail line, railway, streetcar line, subway, tracks, trolley line, tube, underground railway; SEE CONCEPTS 155,503

rain [n] *downpour of water or other substance*

cat-and-dog weather*, cloudburst, condensation, deluge, drencher, drizzle, fall, flood, flurry, hail, heavy dew, liquid sunshine*, mist, monsoon, pour, pouring, precip*, precipitation, raindrops, rainfall, rainstorm, sheets, shower, showers, sleet, spate, spit, sprinkle, sprinkling, stream, sun shower*, torrent, volley*, wet stuff*, window washer*; SEE CONCEPT 526

rain [v] *drop water or other substance*

bestow, bucket, come down in buckets*, deposit, drizzle, fall, hail, lavish, mist, patter, pour, shower, sleet, sprinkle, storm; SEE CONCEPT 526

rainbow [n] *color spectrum*

arc, band of color, bow, crescent, curve, prism, variegation; SEE CONCEPT 436

raise [n] *increase in salary or position*

accession, accretion, addition, advance, augmentation, boost, bump, hike, hold-up*, increment, jump, jump-up*, leg*, leg-up*, move-up*, promotion, raising, rise, step-up*; SEE CONCEPTS 344,351,763

raise [v1] *lift; build from the ground*

boost, bring up, construct, elevate, erect, establish, exalt, heave, hoist, hold up, lever, lift, lift up, mount, move up, place up, promote, pry, pull up, put on its end, put up, rear, run up, set up, set upright, shove, stand up, take up, throw up, upcast, upheave, uplift, upraise, uprear; SEE CONCEPTS 168,196

raise [v2] *increase, augment*

advance, aggravate, amplify, assemble, boost, build up, collect, congregate, congress, dignify, enhance, enlarge, escalate, exaggerate, exalt, fetch up, forgather, form, gather, get, goose*, goose up*, heighten, hike, hike up*, honor, inflate, intensify, jack up, jump, jump up, levy, look up, magnify, mass, mobilize, mushroom*, muster, obtain, perk up, pick up, promote, put up, pyramid, rally, recruit, reinforce, rendezvous,

run up*, send through the roof*, shoot up, snowball*, strengthen, up; SEE CONCEPTS 236,244,245

raise [v3] *start up, motivate; introduce*

abet, activate, advance, arouse, awaken, bring up, broach, cause, evoke, excite, foment, foster, incite, instigate, kindle, moot, motivate, provoke, put forward, resurrect, set, set on, stir up, suggest, whip up; SEE CONCEPTS 75,221

raise [v4] *nurture, care for*

breed, bring up, cultivate, develop, drag up, fetch up, foster, group, grow, nourish, nurse, plant, produce, propagate, provide, rear, sow, suckle, support, train, wean; SEE CONCEPTS 253,257,295

raison d'etre [n] *reason for being*

basis, justification for existing, rationale, reason for existing, reason why; SEE CONCEPT 661

rake [v] *scrape up, hoe*

break up, clean up, clear, clear up, collect, comb, enfilade, examine, finecomb, fine-tooth-comb*, gather, grade, graze, grub, harrow, hunt, ransack, rasp, remove, rummage, scan, scour, scrape, scratch, scrutinize, search, smooth, sweep, weed; SEE CONCEPTS 109,165,178,216

rakish [adj] *charming and immoral*

abandoned, chic, dashing, debauched, depraved, devil-may-care*, dissipated, dissolute, fashionable, fast*, flashy, gay, jaunty, lecherous, licentious, loose*, natty, prodigal, profligate, raffish, saucy, sinful, smart, sporty, wanton, wild; SEE CONCEPTS 401,545

rally [n1] *celebratory meeting*

assemblage, assembly, celebration, clambake*, convention, convocation, get-together, mass meeting, meet, pep rally, pow-wow*, session; SEE CONCEPTS 377,386

rally [n2] *turn for the better*

comeback, improvement, recovery, recuperation, renewal, resurgence, revival, turning point; SEE CONCEPT 700

rally [v1] *reorganize, unite*

arouse, assemble, awaken, bestir, bond together, bring together, bring to order, call to arms*, challenge, charge, collect, come about, come together, come to order, convene, counterattack, encourage, fire, gather, get together, inspirit, kindle, marshal, mobilize, muster, organize, reassemble, redouble, reform, refresh, regroup, rejuvenate, renew, restore, resurrect, resuscitate, revive, round up, rouse, summon, surge, urge, wake, waken, whet, wreak havoc*; SEE CONCEPTS 7,22,117,320

rally [v2] *revive; take a turn for the better*

bounce back, brace up, come along, come around, come from behind, enliven, get act together*, get back in shape*, get better, get second wind*, grow stronger, improve, invigorate, make a comeback, perk up, pick up, pull through, recover, recuperate, refresh, regain strength, shape up, snap out of it, surge, turn around, turn things around*; SEE CONCEPT 700

ram [v] *bang into; pack forcibly*

beat, butt, collide with, cram, crash, crowd, dash, dig, drive, drum, force, hammer, hit, hook, impact, jack, jam-pack, pack, plunge, poke, pound, run, run into, sink, slam, smash, stab, stick, strike, strike head-on, stuff, tamp, thrust, wedge; SEE CONCEPTS 189,208,209

ramble [n] *aimless walk*

constitutional, excursion, hike, perambulation,

peregrination, roaming, roving, saunter, stroll, tour, traipse, trip, turn; SEE CONCEPTS 151,224

ramble [v1] *wander about; travel aimlessly*
amble, bat around*, be all over the map*, branch off, clamber, climb, cruise, depart, digress, divagate, diverge, drift, excurse, extend, fork, gad, gallivant, get sidetracked*, knock about*, knock around*, meander, perambulate, percolate, peregrinate, promenade, range, roam, rove, saunter, scramble, snake, sprangle, sprawl, spread, spread-eagle, straddle, straggle, stray, stroll, trail, traipse, turn, twist, walk, wind, zigzag; SEE CONCEPTS 151,154,581,692

ramble [v2] *talk aimlessly, endlessly*
amplify, babble, beat around bush*, be diffuse, blather, chatter, depart, descant, digress, divagate, diverge, drift, drivel, dwell on, enlarge, excurse, expatiate, 'get off the subject*, go astray, go off on tangent*, go on and on*, gossip, harp on, lose the thread*, maunder, meander, prose, protract, rant and rave*, rattle on*, stray, talk nonsense, talk off top of head*, talk randomly, wander; SEE CONCEPT 51

rambling [adj1] *disconnected, wordy*
circuitous, confused, desultory, diffuse, digressive, discursive, disjointed, incoherent, incongruous, irregular, long-winded, periphrastic, prolix; SEE CONCEPT 267

rambling [adj2] *sprawling, spread out*
at length, covering, gangling, here and there, irregular, random, scattered, spreading, straggling, strewn, trailing, unplanned; SEE CONCEPTS 485,772

rambunctious [adj] *loud, energetic*
boisterous, noisy, raucous, rough, rowdy, rude, termagant, tumultous/tumultuous, turbulent, unruly; SEE CONCEPT 542

ramification [n] *consequence, development*
bifurcation, branch, branching, breaking, complication, consequence, divarication, division, excrescence, extension, forking, offshoot, outgrowth, partition, radiation, result, sequel, subdividing, subdivision, upshot; SEE CONCEPTS 98,230,824

ramp [n] *incline*
access, adit, grade, gradient, hill, inclination, inclined plane, rise, slope; SEE CONCEPTS 443,757

rampage [n] *storm, violence*
binge, blowup, boiling point*, destruction, disturbance, ferment, fling, frenzy, fury, mad*, more heat than light*, orgy, rage, ruckus, splurge, spree, tear, tempest, tumult, turmoil, uproar, wingding; SEE CONCEPT 86

rampage [v] *go crazy; storm*
go berserk, rage, run amuck, run riot, run wild, tear; SEE CONCEPTS 86,384

rampant [adj] *uncontrolled, out of hand*
aggressive, blustering, boisterous, clamorous, dominant, epidemic, exceeding bounds, excessive, extravagant, exuberant, fanatical, flagrant, furious, growing, impetuous, impulsive, luxuriant, on the rampage, out of control, outrageous, pandemic, predominant, prevalent, profuse, raging, rampaging, rank, rife, riotous, spreading, tumultous/tumultuous, turbulent, unbridled, unchecked, uncontrollable, ungovernable, unrestrained, unruly, vehement, violent, wanton, widespread, wild; SEE CONCEPTS 544,554,772

rampart [n] *fortification, stronghold*
barricade, barrier, bastion, breastwork, bulwark,

defense, earthwork, elevation, embankment, fence, fort, guard, hill, mound, parapet, protection, ridge, security, support, vallation, wall; SEE CONCEPTS 321,439,509

ramshackle [adj] *falling apart; in poor condition*
broken-down, crumbling, decrepit, derelict, dilapidated, flimsy, jerry-built*, rickety, shabby, shaky, tottering, tumble-down, unfirm, unsafe, unsteady; SEE CONCEPTS 485,488

ranch [n] *farm*
acreage, cattle farm, dairy farm, estate, farmstead, hacienda, homestead, land, plantation; SEE CONCEPTS 258,449,517

rancid [adj] *rotten, strong-smelling*
bad, carious, contaminated, curdled, decomposing, disagreeable, disgusting, evil-smelling, feculent, fetid, foul, frowzy, fusty, gamy, high, impure, loathsome, malodorous, moldy, musty, nasty, nidorous, noisome, noxious, off, offensive, olid, polluted, putrefactive, putrefied, putrescent, putrid, rank, reeky, repulsive, sharp, smelly, sour, soured, stale, stinking, strong, tainted, turned, unhealthy, whiffy; SEE CONCEPTS 462,570,598,613

rancor [n] *bitterness, hatefulness*
acerbity, acrimony, animosity, animus, antagonism, antipathy, aversion, bad blood*, bile*, dudgeon, enmity, grudge, hardness of heart*, harshness, hate, hatred, hostility, ill feeling, ill will, malevolence, malice, malignity, mordacity, pique, resentfulness, resentment, retaliation, revengefulness, ruthlessness, spite, spitefulness, spleen, umbrage, uncharitableness, unfriendliness, variance, vengeance, vengefulness, venom, vindictiveness, virulence; SEE CONCEPTS 29,410, 633

random [adj] *haphazard, chance*
accidental, adventitious, aimless, arbitrary, casual, contingent, designless, desultory, driftless, fluky, fortuitous, hit-or-miss*, incidental, indiscriminate, irregular, objectless, odd, promiscuous, purposeless, slapdash*, spot, stray, unaimed, unconsidered, unplanned, unpremeditated; SEE CONCEPTS 535,548,557

range [n1] *sphere, distance, extent*
ambit, amplitude, area, bounds, circle, compass, confines, diapason, dimension, dimensions, domain, earshot*, elbowroom*, expanse, extension, extensity, field, gamut, hearing, ken, latitude, leeway, length, limits, magnitude, matter, neighborhood, orbit, order, panorama, parameters, play, province, purview, radius, reach, realm, run, run of, scope, space, span, spectrum, sphere, spread, stretch, sweep, swing, territory, tune, vicinity, width; SEE CONCEPTS 651,743,745, 756,761,788

range [n2] *order, series*
assortment, chain, class, collection, file, gamut, kind, line, lot, rank, row, selection, sequence, sort, string, tier, variety; SEE CONCEPTS 727,769

range [v1] *order, categorize*
align, allineate, arrange, array, assort, bias, bracket, catalogue, categorize, class, classify, dispose, draw up, file, grade, group, incline, line, line up, pigeonhole*, predispose, rank; SEE CONCEPTS 84,158

range [v2] *wander, roam*
circumambulate, cover, cross, cruise, drift, encompass, explore, float, follow one's nose*, gallivant, globe-trot*, hit the road*, hit the trail*,

make circuit, meander, pass over, ply, prowl, ramble, reach, reconnoiter, rove, scour, search, spread, straggle, stray, stroll, sweep, traipse, tramp, travel, traverse, trek; SEE CONCEPTS 151,224

range [v3] extend; change within limits
differ, diverge from, fluctuate, go, reach, run, stretch, vary, vary between; SEE CONCEPT 697

rangy [adj] long and lean
gangling, gangly, lanky, leggy, long-legged, long-limbed, ready, skinny, spindling, spindly, thin, weedy; SEE CONCEPTS 491,779

rank [adj1] stinking, foul
bad, dank, disagreeable, disgusting, evil-smelling, feculent, fetid, funky*, fusty*, gamy*, graveolent, gross*, high, humid, loathsome, mephitic, moldy, musty, nasty, nauseating, noisome, noxious, obnoxious, off, offensive, olid, pungent, putrescent, putrid, rancid, reeking, repulsive, revolting, smelly, sour, stale, strong, strong-smelling, tainted, turned; SEE CONCEPT 598

rank [adj2] abundant, luxurious
coarse, dense, excessive, extreme, exuberant, fertile, flourishing, fructiferous, grown, high-growing, junglelike, lavish, lush, luxuriant, over-abundant, overgrown, productive, profuse, prolific, rampant, rich, semitropical, tropical, vigorous, wild; SEE CONCEPT 485

rank [adj3] utter, absolute
arrant, blatant, capital, complete, conspicuous, consummate, downright, egregious, excessive, extravagant, flagrant, glaring, gross, noticeable, outright, outstanding, perfect, positive, rampant, sheer, thorough, total, undisguised, unmitigated; SEE CONCEPTS 531,535

rank [adj4] obscene, vulgar
abusive, atrocious, coarse, crass, dirty, filthy, foul, gross, indecent, nasty, outrageous, raunchy, scurrilous, shocking, smutty, wicked; SEE CONCEPT 545

rank [n1] standing in a system, often a social one
ancestry, authority, birth, blood, cachet, capacity, caste, circumstance, class, classification, condition, consequence, degree, dignity, distinction, division, echelon, estate, esteem, family, footing, grade, hierarchy, level, nobility, note, order, paramountcy, parentage, pecking order, pedigree, place, position, primacy, privilege, quality, reputation, seniority, situation, slot, sort, sovereignty, sphere, state, station, stature, status, stock, stratum, supremacy, type; SEE CONCEPTS 296,378,388,744

rank [n2] column, tier of individuals
echelon, file, formation, group, hierarchy, line, queue, range, row, series, string; SEE CONCEPT 727

rank [v1] line up; classify in system
align, arrange, array, assign, assort, button down*, class, dispose, establish, estimate, evaluate, fix*, give precedence, grade, include, judge, list, locate, marshal, order, peg, pigeonhole*, place, place in formation, position, put, put away, put down as, put down for, put in line, range, rate, regard, settle, size up, sort, tab, typecast, valuate, value; SEE CONCEPTS 37,84,158

rank [v2] be worthwhile; have supremacy
antecede, be classed, belong, be worth, come first, count among, forerun, go ahead of, go be-

fore, have the advantage, outrank, precede, stand, take the lead; SEE CONCEPTS 388,671

rankle [v] annoy, irritate
aggravate, anger, bother, chafe, embitter, exasperate, fester, fret, gall, get one's goat*, harass, hurt, inflame, irk, irritate, mortify, nettle, obsess, pain, pester, plague, rile, torment, vex; SEE CONCEPTS 7,14,19

ransack [v] turn inside out in search; ravage
appropriate, comb, despoil, explore, ferret, filch, go over with a fine-tooth comb*, go through, gut*, hunt, investigate, lay waste, leave no stone unturned*, lift, look all over for*, look high and low*, look into, loot, make off with*, maraud, overhaul, peer, pilfer, pillage, pinch, plunder, poach, probe, pry, purloin, raid, rake, rape, ravish, rifle, rob, rummage, rustle, sack, scan, scour, scrutinize, search, seek, seize, shake down*, sound, spoil, spy, steal, strip, take away, thieve; SEE CONCEPTS 103,139,142,216

ransom [n] blackmail money paid for return of possession or person
bribe, compensation, deliverance, expiation, liberation money, payment, payoff, price, redemption, release, rescue; SEE CONCEPT 344

ransom [v] pay blackmail money for return of possession or person
buy freedom of, buy out, deliver, emancipate, extricate, free, liberate, manumit, obtain release of, pay for release of, recover, redeem, regain, release, reprise, repurchase, rescue, save, set free, unchain, unfetter; SEE CONCEPTS 127,131,341

rant [n] yelling, raving
bluster, bombast, diatribe, fustian, harangue, oration, philippic, rhapsody, rhetoric, rodomontade, tirade, vociferation; SEE CONCEPTS 44,49,52

rant [v] yell, rave
bellow, bloviate, blow one's top*, bluster, carry on, clamor, cry, declaim, fume, harangue, mouth, objurgate, orate, perorate, rage, rail, roar, scold, shout, sizzle*, soapbox*, sound off*, spiel*, spout*, storm*, stump*, take on*, vociferate; SEE CONCEPTS 44,49,52

rap [n1/v1] hit quickly and lightly
beat, blow, conk, crack, knock, lick, pat, strike, swat, swipe, tap, whack; SEE CONCEPT 189

rap [n2] conversation
causerie, chat, chin*, colloquy, confabulation, conference, deliberation, dialogue, discourse, discussion, prose, talk, ventilation, yarn; SEE CONCEPTS 56,266

rap [n3] blame; criticism
admonishment, admonition, censure, chiding, flak, knock, pan*, punishment, rebuke, reprimand, reproach, reproof, responsibility, sentence, swipe; SEE CONCEPTS 52,123,317

rap [v2] talk casually; speak abruptly
babble, bark, chat, chatter, chitchat, confabulate, converse, discourse, jabber, palaver, run off at the mouth*, spit, talk; SEE CONCEPTS 56,266

rap [v3] criticize
blame, castigate, censure, condemn, denounce, denunciate, knock*, pan*, reprehend, reprimand, reprobate, scold, skin, tick off*; SEE CONCEPT 52

rapacious [adj] plundering
avaricious, ferocious, furious, greedy, marauding, murderous, predatory, preying, ravening, ravenous, savage, voracious; SEE CONCEPTS 326,403,406,542

rape [*n*] *defilement; a forced sexual assault*
abduction, abuse, criminal attack, depredation, despoilment, despoliation, forcible violation, maltreatment, molestation, pillage, plunder, plundering, rapine, spoliation, statutory offense, violation; SEE CONCEPTS *192,375*

rape [*v*] *sexual assault by force; act of plunder*
abuse, attack, betray, compromise, corrupt, deceive, despoil, force, loot, molest, pillage, plunder, ransack, ruin, sack, seize, spoliate, violate; SEE CONCEPTS *192,375*

rapid [*adj*] *very quick*
accelerated, active, agile, breakneck, brisk, double time, expeditious, expeditive, express, fast, fleet, fleet of foot*, flying, hasty, hurried, in nothing flat*, light-footed*, like a house on fire*, lively, mercurial, nimble, on the double*, precipitate, prompt, quick as a wink*, quickened, ready, really rolling*, screaming*, speedy, spry, swift, winged; SEE CONCEPTS *541,588,799*

rapidity [*n*] *quickness*
acceleration, alacrity, bat, briskness, celerity, dispatch, expedition, fleetness, gait, haste, hurry, pace, precipitateness, promptitude, promptness, rapidness, rush, speed, speediness, swiftness, velocity; SEE CONCEPTS *755,805*

rapidly [*adv*] *very quickly*
at speed, briskly, expeditiously, fast, flat out*, full tilt*, hastily, hurriedly, immediately, in a hurry, in a rush, in haste, lickety-split*, like a shot*, posthaste, precipitately, promptly, speedily, swiftly, with dispatch; SEE CONCEPTS *544,588,799*

rapport [*n*] *understanding between people*
affinity, agreement, bond, compatibility, concord, cotton, empathy, good vibes*, good vibrations, groove, harmony, hitting it off*, interrelationship, link, relationship, same wavelength*, simpatico*, soul, sympathy, the groove*, togetherness, unity; SEE CONCEPTS *388*

rapprochement [*n*] *restoration of harmony*
agreement, cordiality, detente, friendliness, friendship, harmonization, harmony, reconcilement, reconciliation, reunion, softening; SEE CONCEPTS *384,388*

rapt [*adj*] *absorbed, fascinated*
absent, absent-minded, abstracted, beguiled, bewitched, blissful, busy, captivated, carried away*, caught up in*, charmed, daydreaming, deep*, delighted, dreaming, ecstatic, employed, enamored, engaged, engrossed, enraptured, enthralled, entranced, gripped, happy, held, hung up*, hypnotized, immersed, inattentive, intent, involved, lost, oblivious, occupied, overwhelmed, preoccupied, rapturous, ravished, spellbound, taken*, transported, unconscious, wrapped*, wrapped up*; SEE CONCEPT *403*

rapture [*n*] *extreme happiness and delight in something*
at-oneness*, beatitude, bliss, buoyancy, cheer, cloud nine*, communion, contentment, cool*, delectation, ecstasy, elation, elysium, enchantment, enjoyment, enthusiasm, euphoria, exaltation, exhilaration, felicity, gaiety, gladness, glory, good spirits, gratification, heaven, inspiration, joy, jubilation, nirvana, paradise, passion, pleasure, ravishment, rhapsody, satisfaction, seventh heaven*, spell, transport, well-being; SEE CONCEPTS *32,410*

rare [*adj1*] *exceptional, infrequent*
attenuate, attenuated, deficient, extraordinary, few, few and far between*, flimsy, inconceivable, isolated, light, limited, occasional, out of the ordinary, rarefied, recherché, scanty, scarce, scattered, seldom, semioccasional, short, singular, sparse, sporadic, strange, subtile, subtle, tenuous, thin, uncommon, unfrequent, unheard of, unimaginable, unique, unlikely, unthinkable, unusual, unwonted; SEE CONCEPTS *530,576*

rare [*adj2*] *precious, excellent*
admirable, choice, dainty, delicate, elegant, exquisite, extreme, fine, great, incomparable, invaluable, matchless, peerless, priceless, recherché, rich, select, superb, superlative, unique; SEE CONCEPT *574*

rare [*adj3*] *not fully cooked*
bloody, half-cooked, half-raw, moderately done, nearly raw, not done, rarely done, red, undercooked, underdone; SEE CONCEPT *462*

rarely [*adv*] *not often; exceptionally*
almost never, barely, extra, extraordinarily, extremely, finely, hardly, hardly ever, infrequently, little, notably, now and then, once in a while, once in blue moon*, on rare occasions, remarkably, scarcely ever, seldom, singularly, uncommon, uncommonly, unfrequently, unoften, unusually; SEE CONCEPTS *530,541*

rascal [*n*] *person who is unprincipled, does not work hard*
beggar, blackguard, black sheep*, bully, bum, cad, cardsharp*, charlatan, cheat, delinquent, devil, disgrace, felon, fraud, good-for-nothing*, grafter, hooligan*, hypocrite, idler, imp, liar, loafer, mischief-maker, miscreant, opportunist, pretender, prodigal, profligate, recreant, reprobate, robber, rowdy, ruffian, scamp, scoundrel, sinner, skunk*, sneak*, swindler, tough*, tramp, trickster, varmint*, villain, wastrel, wretch; SEE CONCEPT *412*

rash [*adj*] *careless, impulsive*
adventurous, audacious, bold, brash, daring, determined, devil-may-care*, fiery, foolhardy, frenzied, furious, harebrained, hasty, headlong, headstrong, heedless, hotheaded, ill-advised, ill-considered, immature, impetuous, imprudent, incautious, indiscreet, injudicious, insuppressible, irrational, jumping to conclusions*, madcap, overhasty, passionate, precipitant, precipitate, premature, reckless, thoughtless, unguarded, unthinking, unwary, venturesome, venturous, wild; SEE CONCEPT *401*

rash [*n*] *outbreak of disease or condition*
breakout, epidemic, eruption, flood, hives, pandemic, plague, series, spate, succession, wave; SEE CONCEPTS *230,306*

rasp [*v*] *grind, rub*
abrade, bray, excoriate, file, grate, irk, irritate, jar, pound, raze, rub, sand, scour, scrape, scratch, vex, wear; SEE CONCEPTS *7,19,186,215*

raspy [*adj*] *rough*
cracked, croaky, dry, grating, gravelly, gruff, harsh, hoarse, husky, scratchy, thick, throaty; SEE CONCEPT *594*

rat [*n*] *informer*
backstabber, betrayer, blabbermouth*, canary*, deep throat*, double-crosser, fink, informant, sneak, snitch, source, squealer, stoolie, stool pigeon*, tattler, tattletale, turncoat, whistleblower; SEE CONCEPTS *348,354,423*

ra
ra

rate [*n1*] *ratio, proportion*
amount, comparison, degree, estimate, percentage, progression, quota, relation, relationship, relative, scale, standard, weight; SEE CONCEPT *768*

rate [*n2*] *fee charged for service, privilege, goods*
allowance, charge, cost, dues, duty, estimate, figure, hire, price, price tag, quotation, tab, tariff, tax, toll, valuation; SEE CONCEPTS *329,766*

rate [*n3*] *speed, pace*
clip, dash, flow, gait, gallop, hop, measure, motion, movement, pace, spurt, tempo, time, tread, velocity; SEE CONCEPT *755*

rate [*v1*] *judge, classify*
adjudge, admire, appraise, apprise, assay, assess, button down*, calculate, class, consider, count, deem, determine, esteem, estimate, evaluate, fix, grade, guess at, measure, peg, pigeonhole*, price, put away, put down as*, put down for*, rank, reckon, redline*, regard, relate to standard, respect, score, set at, size up*, stand in with, survey, tab*, tag, take one's measure, think highly of, typecast*, valuate, value, weigh; SEE CONCEPTS *12,37*

rate [*v2*] *be entitled to*
be accepted, be favorite, be welcome, be worthy, deserve, earn, merit, prosper, succeed, triumph; SEE CONCEPTS *129,376,388*

rather [*adv1*] *moderately*
a bit, a little, averagely, comparatively, enough, fairly, in a certain degree, kind of, more or less, passably, pretty, quite, ratherish, reasonably, relatively, slightly, some, something, somewhat, sort of, so-so*, tolerably, to some degree, to some extent; SEE CONCEPTS *544,548*

rather [*adv2*] *significantly*
a good bit, considerably, noticeably, quite, somewhat, very, well; SEE CONCEPTS *544,772*

rather [*adv3*] *preferably; instead*
alternately, alternatively, as a matter of choice, by choice, by preference, first, in lieu of, in preference, just as soon, more readily, more willingly, much sooner, sooner, willingly; SEE CONCEPT *529*

ratify [*v*] *affirm, authorize*
accredit, approve, authenticate, bear out, bind, bless, certify, commission, confirm, consent, corroborate, endorse, establish, give stamp of approval*, go for*, license, okay*, rubber stamp*, sanction, sign, substantiate, uphold, validate; SEE CONCEPTS *50,88*

rating [*n*] *grade*
appraisal, assessment, category, class, classification, degree, judgment, level, mark, order, rank, score, standard, tier, valuation; SEE CONCEPTS *286,378,665,727,744*

ratio [*n*] *percentage, relation of part to whole*
arrangement, correlation, correspondence, equation, fraction, proportion, proportionality, quota, quotient, rate, relationship, scale; SEE CONCEPT *768*

ration [*n*] *allotment of limited supply*
allowance, apportionment, assignment, bit, consignment, cut, distribution, division, dole, drag, food, helping, measure, meed, part, piece of action*, portion, provender, provision, quantum, quota, share, store, supply; SEE CONCEPTS *457,835*

ration [*v*] *divide something into portions*
allocate, allot, apportion, assign, budget, conserve, control, deal, distribute, divvy*, divvy up*, dole, give out, issue, limit, measure out, mete, mete out, parcel, parcel out, proportion, prorate, quota, restrict, save, share; SEE CONCEPTS *98,140*

rational [*adj*] *realistic; of sound mind*
all there*, analytical, balanced, calm, cerebral, circumspect, cognitive, collected, cool*, deductive, deliberate, discerning, discriminating, enlightened, far-sighted, impartial, intellectual, intelligent, judicious, knowing, levelheaded, logical, lucid, normal, objective, perspicacious, philosophic, prudent, ratiocinative, reasonable, reasoning, reflective, sagacious, sane, sensible, sober, sound, stable, synthetic, thinking, thoughtful, together, well-advised, wise; SEE CONCEPT *402*

rationale [*n*] *logic for belief, action*
account, excuse, explanation, exposition, grounds, hypothesis, justification, motivation, motive, philosophy, principle, raison d'être, rationalization, reason, reasons, song and dance*, sour grapes*, story*, the big idea*, theory, the whole idea*, whatfor*, why and wherefore*, whyfor*; SEE CONCEPT *661*

rationalize [*v*] *make excuse; justify*
account for, apply logic, cop a plea*, cop out*, deliberate, elucidate, excise, excuse, explain away, extenuate, give alibi*, intellectualize, justify, make allowance, reason, reason out, reconcile, resolve, think, think through, vindicate; SEE CONCEPT *57*

rattle [*v1*] *bang, jiggle*
bicker, bounce, clack, clatter, drum, jangle, jar, jolt, jounce, knock, shake, shatter, sound, vibrate; SEE CONCEPTS *65,152*

rattle [*v2*] *talk aimlessly, endlessly*
babble, cackle, chat, chatter, clack, gab, gabble, gush, jabber, jaw, list, prate, prattle, reel off, run on, run through, yak; SEE CONCEPT *51*

rattle [*v3*] *disconcert, upset someone*
abash, addle, bewilder, bother, confound, confuse, discombobulate, discomfit, discompose, discountenance, distract, disturb, embarrass, faze, flummox, frighten, get to*, muddle, nonplus, perplex, perturb, psych out*, put off, put out, put out of countenance, rattle one's cage*, scare, shake, throw, unnerve; SEE CONCEPT *16*

raucous [*adj1*] *noisy, rough*
absonant, acute, atonal, blaring, blatant, braying, brusque, cacophonous, discordant, dissonant, dry, ear-piercing, grating, grinding, gruff, harsh, hoarse, husky, inharmonious, jarring, loud, piercing, rasping, sharp, squawking, stertorous, strident, thick, unharmonious, unmusical; SEE CONCEPTS *592,594*

raucous [*adj2*] *rowdy*
boisterous, disorderly, intemperate, rambunctious, tumultuous/tumultuous, turbulent, unruly; SEE CONCEPT *401*

raunchy [*adj*] *lewd, obscene*
bawdy, dirty, erotic, filthy*, foul-mouthed, gross*, hard-core*, improper, in bad taste, lascivious, lecherous, lustful, naughty, off-color*, pornographic, racy*, risqué, sexually explicit, smutty, suggestive, taboo, vulgar, wicked, X-rated*; SEE CONCEPTS *372,542,545*

ravage [*v*] *destroy, ransack*
annihilate, break up, capture, consume, cream*, crush, damage, demolish, desecrate, desolate, despoil, devastate, dismantle, disorganize, disrupt, exterminate, extinguish, forage, foray, gut, harry, impair, lay waste, leave in ruins, loot, overrun, overthrow, overwhelm, pillage, pirate, plunder, prey, prostrate, pull down, raid, rape, raze, rob, ruin, sack, seize, shatter, sink, smash, spoil, spoliate, stamp out, strip, sweep away, total*, trample, trash, waste, wreak havoc, wreck, wrest; SEE CONCEPTS *86,252*

rave [*v1*] *talk endlessly*
babble, be delirious, bloviate, blow one's top*, carry on*, come unglued*, declaim, flip one's lid*, freak out*, fume, gabble, go ape*, go bananas*, go crazy, go mad, harangue, jabber, make a to-do*, mouth, orate, perorate, prate, prattle, rage, rail, rant, rattle on, roar, run amuck*, splutter, storm, talk wildly, thunder, wander; SEE CONCEPTS *51,54*

rave [*v2*] *be very enthusiastic*
be delighted, be excited, be mad about, be wild about, bubble*, carry on about*, cry up*, effervesce, enthuse, fall all over*, go on about*, gush, make a to-do*, praise, rhapsodize; SEE CONCEPTS *49,410*

ravel [*v*] *come apart; unwind*
disentangle, free, loosen, make plain, smooth out, unbraid, unravel, unsnarl, untangle, untwine, untwist, unweave, unwind, weave out; SEE CONCEPTS *250,469*

ravenous [*adj*] *very hungry; desirous*
avaricious, could eat a horse*, covetous, devouring, edacious, empty, famished, ferocious, gluttonous, grasping, greedy, insatiable, insatiate, omnivorous, predatory, rapacious, ravening, starved, starved to death*, starving, voracious, wolfish; SEE CONCEPT *406*

ravine [*n*] *gap in earth's surface*
abyss, arroyo, break, canyon, chasm, clove, coulee, crevasse, crevice, cut, defile, ditch, fissure, flume, gorge, gulch, gulf, gully, notch, pass, valley, wash; SEE CONCEPTS *509,513*

ravish [*v1*] *enchant*
allure, attract, bewitch, captivate, charm, delight, draw, enrapture, enthrall, entrance, fascinate, hold, hypnotize, magnetize, mesmerize, overjoy, please, spellbind, trance, transport; SEE CONCEPT *11*

ravish [*v2*] *sexually assault*
abduct, abuse, force, rape, violate; SEE CONCEPTS *192,375*

ravishing [*adj*] *attractive*
adorable, alluring, appealing, beautiful, bewitching, captivating, charming, dazzling, enchanting, enticing, glamorous, good-looking, gorgeous, handsome, inviting, lovely, luring, pleasing, pretty, radiant, seductive, stunning, tantalizing; SEE CONCEPTS *529,579*

raw [*adj1*] *not cooked, prepared*
basic, bloody, callow, coarse, crude, fibrous, fresh, green, hard, immature, impure, native, natural, organic, rough, roughhewn, rude, unbaked, uncooked, undercooked, underdone, undressed, unfashioned, unformed, unfried, ungraded, unpasteurized, unprepared, unprocessed, unrefined, unripe, unsorted, unstained, untreated; SEE CONCEPTS *462,485*

raw [*adj2*] *exposed, tender, referring to skin*
abraded, au naturel, blistered, bruised, chafed, cut, dressed, galled, grazed, naked, nude, open, pared, peeled, scraped, scratched, sensitive, skinned, sore, unclad, unclothed, uncovered, wounded; SEE CONCEPTS *406,485*

raw [*adj3*] *inexperienced*
callow, fresh, green, ignorant, immature, inexperienced, new, unconversant, undisciplined, unpracticed, unseasoned, unskilled, untaught, untrained, untried, unversed, young; SEE CONCEPT *527*

raw [*adj4*] *vulgar, nasty*
coarse, crass, crude, dirty, filthy, foul, gross, indecent, inelegant, low, mean, obscene, pornographic, rank, rough, rude, smutty, uncouth, unrefined, unscrupulous; SEE CONCEPTS *372,545*

raw [*adj5*] *harsh, unpleasant, referring to weather*
biting, bitter, bleak, breezy, chill, chilly, cold, damp, freezing, piercing, wet, wind-swept, windy; SEE CONCEPT *525*

ray [*n*] *beam; indication*
bar, blaze, blink, emanation, flash, flicker, gleam, glimmer, glint, glitter, hint, incandescence, irradiation, light, moonbeam, patch, pencil, radiance, radiation, scintilla, shaft, shine, spark, sparkle, streak, stream, sunbeam, trace, wave; SEE CONCEPTS *624,628*

raze [*v*] *flatten, knock down; wipe out*
batter, blow down, bomb, break down, bulldoze, capsize, cast down, crash, decimate, delete, demolish, destroy, dynamite, efface, erase, expunge, extinguish, extirpate, fell, level, mow down, obliterate, overthrow, overturn, pull down, reduce, remove, rub out*, ruin, scatter, scratch out, smash, spill, strike out, subvert, tear down, tear up, throw down, topple, total, unbuild, undo, unmake, upset, wipe out, wrack, wreck, zap*; SEE CONCEPT *252*

reach [*n*] *extent, range; stretch*
ability, ambit, capacity, command, compass, distance, extension, gamut, grasp, horizon, influence, jurisdiction, ken, latitude, magnitude, mastery, orbit, play, power, purview, radius, scope, spread, sweep, swing; SEE CONCEPTS *651,756*

reach [*v1*] *arrive at*
arrive, attain, catch up to, check in, clock in*, come, come to, enter, gain on*, get as far as, get in, get to, hit, hit town*, land, make, make it, make the scene*, overtake, ring in*, roll in, show, show up, sign in, turn up, wind up at; SEE CONCEPT *159*

reach [*v2*] *stretch to; touch*
approach, attain, buck, carry to, come at, come up to, contact, continue to, encompass, end, equal, extend to, feel for, get a hold of, get hold of, get to, go, go as far as, go on, go to, grasp, hand, hold out, join, lead, lunge, make, make contact with, overtake, pass, pass along, put out, roll on, seize, shake hands, shoot, span, spread, stand, strain, strike; SEE CONCEPTS *108,612,756*

reach [*v3*] *attain; rise*
accomplish, achieve, amount to, arrive at, climb to, come to, drop, fall, gain, move, rack up*, realize, score, sink, win; SEE CONCEPTS *706,763,780*

reach [*v4*] *communicate with*
affect, approach, contact, get, get in touch, get

ra
re

through, get to, influence, keep in contact, keep in touch, maintain, move, sway, touch; SEE CONCEPTS 7,19,22,266

react [v] *respond; conduct oneself*
acknowledge, act, answer, answer back, backfire, be affected, behave, boomerang*, bounce back*, counter, echo, feel, function, get back at, give a snappy comeback*, give back, have a funny feeling*, have vibes*, operate, perform, proceed, rebound, reciprocate, recoil, recur, reply, return, revert, take, talk back, turn back, work; SEE CONCEPTS 45,633

reaction [n1] *response*
acknowledgment, answer, attitude, backfire, backlash, back talk*, boomerang*, comeback, compensation, counteraction, counterbalance, counterpoise, double-take*, echo, feedback, feeling, hit, kick, knee-jerk*, lip*, opinion, reagency, rebound, reception, receptivity, reciprocation, recoil, reflection, reflex, rejoinder, repercussion, reply, retort, return, reverberation, revulsion, sass*, snappy comeback*, take*, vibes*, wisecrack; SEE CONCEPTS 45,633

reaction [n2] *political conservatism*
backlash, backsliding, counterrevolution, obscurantism, regression, relapse, retreat, retrenchment, retrogression, right, right wing, status quo, Toryism, withdrawal; SEE CONCEPTS 300,689

reactionary [adj] *conservative*
counterrevolutionary, die-hard*, obscurantist, old-line*, orthodox, regressive, retrogressive, right, rightist*, rigid, standpat*, tory*, traditional, traditionalistic; SEE CONCEPTS 529,542

reactionary [n] *person who is politically conservative*
bitter-ender*, counterrevolutionary, diehard*, hard hat*, intransigent, obscurantist, reactionist, rightist*, right-winger, royalist, standpatter*, Tory*, traditionalist, ultraconservative; SEE CONCEPT 359

read [v1] *look at and understand written word*
apprehend, bury oneself in*, comprehend, construe, decipher, dip into*, discover, flip through*, gather, glance, go over, go through, interpret, know, leaf through*, learn, make out*, perceive, peruse, pore over*, refer to, scan, scratch the surface*, see, skim, study, translate, unravel, view; SEE CONCEPT 72

read [v2] *express, state*
affirm, announce, assert, declaim, deliver, display, explain, expound, hold, indicate, mark, paraphrase, pronounce, recite, record, register, render, restate, say, show, speak, utter; SEE CONCEPT 266

readable [adj1] *understandable, legible*
clear, coherent, comprehensible, decipherable, distinct, explicit, flowing, fluent, graphic, intelligible, lucid, orderly, plain, precise, regular, simple, smooth, straightforward, tidy, unequivocal, unmistakable; SEE CONCEPTS 272,529

readable [adj2] *pleasurable to peruse*
absorbing, amusing, appealing, brilliant, clever, easy, eloquent, engaging, engrossing, enjoyable, entertaining, enthralling, exciting, fascinating, gratifying, gripping, ingenious, interesting, inviting, pleasant, pleasing, relaxing, rewarding, satisfying, smooth, stimulating, well-written, worthwhile; SEE CONCEPT 272

readily [adv] *quickly; effortlessly*
at once, at the drop of a hat*, cheerfully, eagerly,

easily, facilely, freely, gladly, hands down*, immediately, in a jiffy*, in no time*, lightly, no sweat*, nothing to it*, piece of cake*, promptly, quick as a wink*, right away, slick as whistle*, smoothly, speedily, straight away, swimmingly, unhesitatingly, well, willingly, without delay, without demur, without difficulty, without hesitation; SEE CONCEPTS 544,820

readiness [n] *skill; eagerness*
address, adroitness, alacrity, aptness, deftness, dexterity, dispatch, ease, eloquence, expedience, expedition, facility, fitness, fluency, good will, handiness, inclination, keenness, maturity, preparation, preparedness, promptitude, promptness, prowess, quickness, rapidity, ripeness, sleight, volubility, willingness; SEE CONCEPTS 630,633,678

reading [n] *interpretation of written word*
account, book-learning, commentary, conception, construction, edification, education, erudition, examination, grasp, impression, inspection, knowledge, learning, lesson, paraphrase, perusal, rendering, rendition, review, scholarship, scrutiny, study, translation, treatment, understanding, version; SEE CONCEPTS 72,271,274

ready [adj1] *prepared; available*
accessible, adjusted, all set, all systems go*, anticipating, apt, arranged, at beck and call*, at fingertips*, at hand, at the ready, champing at bit*, close to hand, completed, convenient, covered, equal to, equipped, expectant, fit, fixed for, handy, in line, in order, in place, in position, in readiness, in the saddle*, near, on call, on hand, on tap*, on the brink*, open to, organized, primed, qualified, ripe, set, waiting, wired*; SEE CONCEPTS 560,576,799

ready [adj2] *willing, inclined*
agreeable, apt, ardent, disposed, eager, enthusiastic, fain, game, game for, glad, happy, keen, minded, predisposed, prompt, prone, psyched up*, wired*, zealous; SEE CONCEPTS 401,542

ready [adj3] *skillful, intelligent*
active, acute, adept, adroit, alert, apt, astute, bright, brilliant, clever, deft, dexterous, dynamic, expert, handy, keen, live, masterly, perceptive, proficient, prompt, quick, quick-witted, rapid, resourceful, sharp, skilled, smart; SEE CONCEPTS 402,527

ready [v] *prepare*
arrange, brace, brief, clear the decks*, equip, fill in, fit, fit out, fix, fortify, gear up*, get, get ready, get set, gird, keep posted*, let in on*, make, make ready, make up, order, organize, pave the way*, post, prep, provide, psych up*, put on to*, set, strengthen, warm up, wise up*; SEE CONCEPTS 35,60,202

real [adj] *genuine in existence*
absolute, actual, authentic, bodily, bona fide, certain, concrete, corporal, corporeal, de facto, embodied, essential, evident, existent, existing, factual, firm, heartfelt, honest, incarnate, indubitable, in the flesh*, intrinsic, irrefutable, legitimate, live, material, original, palpable, perceptible, physical, positive, present, right, rightful, sensible, sincere, solid, sound, stable, substantial, substantive, tangible, true, unaffected, undeniable, undoubted, unfeigned, valid, veritable; SEE CONCEPT 582

realistic [adj1] *sensible, matter-of-fact*
astute, businesslike, commonsense, down-to-

earth, earthy, hard, hard-boiled*, levelheaded, practical, pragmatic, pragmatical, prudent, rational, real, reasonable, sane, sensible, shrewd, sober, sound, unfantastic, unidealistic, unromantic, unsentimental, utilitarian; SEE CONCEPTS 403,542,548

realistic [adj2] *genuine*
authentic, faithful, graphic, lifelike, natural, original, representational, representative, true, true to life, truthful; SEE CONCEPT 582

reality [n] *facts of existence*
absoluteness, actuality, authenticity, being, bottom line*, brass tacks*, certainty, concreteness, corporeality, deed, entity, existence, genuineness, how things are*, like it is*, materiality, matter, name of the game*, nuts and bolts*, object, palpability, perceptibility, phenomenon, presence, realism, realness, real world*, sensibility, solidity, substance, substantiality, substantive, tangibility, truth, validity, verisimilitude, verity, way of it*, what's what*; SEE CONCEPTS 689,725

realize [v1] *appreciate, become aware of*
apprehend, be cognizant of, become conscious of, catch, catch on*, comprehend, conceive, discern, envisage, envision, fancy*, feature*, get, get it*, get the idea*, get the picture*, get through one's head*, grasp, image, imagine, know, think, pick up*, recognize, see daylight*, take in*, understand, vision, visualize; SEE CONCEPT 15

realize [v2] *accomplish*
actualize, bring about, bring off*, bring to fruition, carry out, carry through, complete, consummate, corporealize, do, effect, effectuate, fulfill, make concrete, make good*, make happen, materialize, perfect, perform, reify; SEE CONCEPT 91

realize [v3] *gain, earn*
accomplish, achieve, acquire, attain, bring in, clear, get, go for*, make, make a profit, net, obtain, produce, rack up*, reach, receive, score*, sell for, take in, win; SEE CONCEPTS 120,124,330

really [adv] *without a doubt*
absolutely, actually, admittedly, as a matter of fact, assuredly, authentically, beyond doubt, categorically, certainly, de facto, easily, for real*, genuinely, honestly, in actuality, indeed, indubitably, in effect, in fact, in point of fact, in reality, legitimately, literally, no ifs ands or buts*, nothing else but, of course, positively, precisely, surely, truly, undoubtedly, unmistakably, unquestionably, verily, well; SEE CONCEPTS 535,582

realm [n] *area of responsibility or rule*
branch, compass, country, department, dimension, domain, dominion, empire, expanse, extent, field, ground, kingdom, land, monarchy, neck of the woods*, neighborhood, orbit, place, principality, province, purview, radius, range, reach, region, scope, sphere, state, stomping grounds*, sweep, territory, turf*, world, zone; SEE CONCEPTS 349,362,512,651

reap [v] *collect, harvest*
acquire, bring in, come to have, crop, cull, cut, derive, draw, gain, garner, gather, get, get as a result, glean, ingather, mow, obtain, pick, pick up, pluck, procure, produce, profit, realize, receive, recover, retrieve, secure, strip, take in, win; SEE CONCEPTS 109,120,124,257

rear [adj] *back, end*
aft, after, astern, backward, behind, dorsal, following, hind, hinder, hindermost, hindmost, last, mizzen, posterior, postern, rearmost, rearward, retral, reverse, stern, tail; SEE CONCEPT 583

rear [n] *back or end part*
afterpart, back, back door*, back end, back seat*, backside, behind, bottom, butt, buttocks, end, heel, hind, hind part, hindquarters, posterior, postern, rear end, rear guard, rearward, reverse, rump, seat, stern, tail, tail end, tailpiece, tush*; SEE CONCEPTS 825,827

rear [v1] *raise young*
breed, bring up, care for, cultivate, educate, foster, grow, nurse, nurture, propagate, train; SEE CONCEPT 295

rear [v2] *lift, rise*
bring up, elevate, hoist, hold up, jump, leap, loom, pick up, raise, set upright, soar, spring up, support, take up, tower, turn up, uphold, uplift, upraise; SEE CONCEPTS 194,196,741

rear [v3] *build*
construct, erect, fabricate, put up, raise, set up, uprear; SEE CONCEPT 168

reason [n1] *mental analysis*
acumen, apprehension, argumentation, bounds, brain*, brains*, comprehension, deduction, dialectics, discernment, generalization, induction, inference, intellect, intellection, judgment, limits, logic, lucidity, marbles*, mentality, mind, moderation, propriety, ratiocination, rationalism, rationality, rationalization, reasonableness, reasoning, saneness, sanity, sense, senses*, sensibleness, sound mind, soundness, speculation, understanding, wisdom, wit; SEE CONCEPTS 37,409

reason [n2] *intention, aim*
antecedent, argument, basis, cause, consideration, design, determinant, end, goal, grounds, idea, impetus, incentive, inducement, motivation, motive, object, occasion, proof, purpose, rationale, root, spring, target, ulterior motive, warrant, wherefore*, why, why and wherefore*, whyfor*; SEE CONCEPT 659

reason [n3] *explanation for an action*
account, apologia, apology, argument, case, cover, defense, excuse, exposition, ground, idea, justification, notion, proof, rationale, rationalization, song and dance*, sour grapes*, the whole idea*, vindication, whatfor*, wherefore*, why*, why and wherefore*, whyfor*; SEE CONCEPT 661

reason [v1] *mentally analyze*
adduce, cerebrate, cogitate, conclude, contemplate, decide, deduce, deduct, deliberate, draw conclusion, draw from, examine, figure out, gather, generalize, infer, make out, philosophize, ratiocinate, rationalize, reflect, resolve, solve, speculate, study, suppose, syllogize, think, think through, thresh out, work out; SEE CONCEPT 37

reason [v2] *argue, persuade*
bring around, contend, debate, demonstrate, discourse, discuss, dispute, dissuade, establish, expostulate, justify, move, point out, prevail upon, prove, remonstrate, show error of ways*, talk into, talk out of, urge, win over; SEE CONCEPTS 46,56,68

reasonable [adj1] *moderate, tolerable*
acceptable, analytical, average, cheap, circumspect, conservative, controlled, discreet, equitable, fair, feasible, fit, honest, humane,

re
re

impartial, inexpensive, judicious, just, justifiable, knowing, legit, legitimate, low-cost, low-priced, making sense, modest, objective, okay, plausible, politic, proper, prudent, rational, reflective, restrained, right, sane, sapient, sensible, sound, standing to reason*, temperate, understandable, unexcessive, unextreme, valid, within reason; SEE CONCEPTS **547,558**

reasonable [*adj2*] *intelligent, practical*
advisable, all there*, arguable, believeable, cerebral, clear-cut, cognitive, commonsensical, conscious, consequent, consistent, cool*, credible, in one's right mind*, judicious, justifiable, level-headed, logical, perceiving, percipient, plausible, ratiocinative, rational, reasoned, reasoning, reflective, sane, sensible, sober, sound, tenable, thoughtful, thought-out, together*, tolerant, unbiased, unprejudiced, well-advised, wise; SEE CONCEPT **402**

reasoning [*n*] *logic, interpretation*
acumen, analysis, apriority, argument, case, cogitation, concluding, corollary, deduction, dialectics, exposition, generalization, hypothesis, illation, induction, inference, interpretation, logistics, premise, proof, proposition, ratiocination, rationale, rationalizing, reason, syllogism, syllogization, thinking, thought, train of thought; SEE CONCEPTS **37,529**

reassure [*v*] *restore confidence to*
assure, bolster, brace, buoy, cheer, comfort, console, convince, encourage, give a lift*, give confidence, guarantee, hearten, inspire, inspirit, perk up, pick up*, put one's mind to rest*, relieve, snap one out of it*; SEE CONCEPTS **7,22**

rebate [*n*] *refund given to purchaser*
abatement, allowance, bonus, deduction, discount, kickback, payback, reduction, reimbursement, remission, repayment, subtraction; SEE CONCEPT **344**

rebel [*adj*] *not obeying*
insubordinate, insurgent, insurrectionary, mutinous, rebellious, revolutionary; SEE CONCEPT **401**

rebel [*n*] *person who does not obey*
agitator, anarchist, antagonist, apostate, demagogue, deserter, dissectarian, dissenter, experientialist, experimenter, frondeur, guerrilla, heretic, iconoclast, independent, individualist, innovator, insurgent, insurrectionist, malcontent, mutineer, nihilist, nonconformist, opponent, overthrower, recreant, renegade, resistance, revolter, revolutionary, revolutionist, rioter, schismatic, secessionist, seditionist, separatist, subverter, traitor, turncoat; SEE CONCEPTS **359,412,423**

rebel [*v*] *refuse to obey*
be insubordinate, boycott, break with*, censure, combat, come out against*, criticize, defy, denounce, disobey, dissent, drop out*, fight, get out of line*, insurrect, make waves*, mutiny, oppose, opt out*, overthrow, overturn, remonstrate, renounce, resist, revolt, riot, rise up*, rock the boat*, run amok*, secede, strike, take up arms, turn against, upset; SEE CONCEPTS **106,633**

rebellion [*n*] *disobedience; revolt*
apostasy, defiance, disobedience, dissent, heresy, insubordination, insurgence, insurgency, insurrection, nonconformity, revolution, rising, schism, uprising; SEE CONCEPTS **106,300,320,633**

rebellious [*adj*] *disobedient, unmanageable*
alienated, anarchic, attacking, bellicose, contumacious, defiant, difficult, disaffected, disloyal,

disobedient, disorderly, dissident, factious, fractious, iconoclastic, incorrigible, individualistic, insurgent, insurrectionary, intractable, mutinous, obstinate, pugnacious, quarrelsome, radical, rebel, recalcitrant, refractory, resistant, restless, revolutionary, rioting, riotous, sabotaging, seditious, threatening, treasonable, turbulent, ungovernable, unruly, warring; SEE CONCEPTS **401,529,542**

rebound [*v*] *bounce back; ricochet*
backfire, boomerang, convalesce, get back on one's feet*, get better, get in shape, get well, heal, kick back, make a comeback*, mend, overcome, pick up, pull through, rally, recoil, recuperate, regain one's health, rejuvenate, return, return to form, revive, snap back*, spring back, start anew; SEE CONCEPTS **150,194,195,303,700**

rebuff [*n*] *turning away; ignoring*
brushoff*, check, cold shoulder*, cut, defeat, denial, discouragement, go-by*, hard time*, insult, kick in the teeth*, nix*, nothing doing*, opposition, rebuke, refusal, rejection, reprimand, repulse, slight, snub, thumbs down*, turndown; SEE CONCEPTS **30,278**

rebuff [*v*] *turn away; give the cold shoulder*
beat off, brush off, check, chide, cross, cut, decline, deny, disallow, discourage, dismiss, disregard, fend off, hold off, ignore, keep at a distance*, keep at arm's length*, keep at bay, lash out at, neglect, not hear of, oppose, pass up, push back, put in one's place*, put off, rebuke, refuse, reject, repel, reprove, repudiate, repulse, resist, send away, slight, snub, spurn, stave off, tell off*, turn down, ward off; SEE CONCEPTS **30,54**

rebuke [*n*] *reprimand; harsh criticism*
admonishment, admonition, affliction, bawling-out*, berating, blame, castigation, censure, chewing-out*, chiding, comeuppance, condemnation, correction, disapproval, dressing-down*, earful*, expostulation, going-over*, hard time*, kick in the teeth*, lecture, lesson, objurgation, ostracism, punishment, put-down, rap*, rating, rebuff, refusal, remonstrance, reprehension, reproach, reproof, reproval, repulse, row, scolding, slap in the face*, snub, talking-to*, telling-off*, tongue-lashing*, upbraiding; SEE CONCEPTS **44,52,278**

rebuke [*v*] *reprimand; criticize harshly*
admonish, bawl out*, berate, blame, call on the carpet*, carp on, castigate, censure, chew out*, chide, climb all over*, dress down*, fry*, go after*, jawbone*, jump down one's throat*, jump on*, lay into*, lean on*, lecture, lesson, monish, oppose, pay, rake, read*, reprehend, reprimand, reproach, reprove, rip*, scold, sit on*, sound off*, take to task*, tear apart*, tell off*, tick off*, upbraid, zap*; SEE CONCEPTS **44,52**

rebut [*v*] *argue against; prove wrong*
break, come back at, confound, confute, controvert, cross, defeat, deny, disconfirm, disprove, evert, fend off, get back at, hold off, invalidate, keep off, negate, negative, overturn, prove false, quash, refute, repel, repulse, stave off, take on, top, ward off; SEE CONCEPTS **46,54**

rebuttal [*n*] *counterstatement*
answer, confutation, counteraccusation, counter-argument, countercharge, counterclaim, defense, rejoinder, reply; SEE CONCEPTS **274,278**

recalcitrant [*adj*] *disobedient, uncontrollable*
contrary, contumacious, defiant, fractious, indomitable, insubmissive, insubordinate, intractable, obstinate, opposing, radical, rebellious, refractory, resistant, resisting, stubborn, undisciplinable, undisciplined, ungovernable, unmanageable, unruly, untoward, unwilling, wayward, wild, willful, withstanding; SEE CONCEPT *401*

recall [*n1*] *remembrance*
anamnesis, memory, recollection, reminiscence; SEE CONCEPT *529*

recall [*n2*] *request for return*
annulment, cancellation, nullification, recision, repeal, rescindment, rescission, retraction, revocation, withdrawal; SEE CONCEPTS *662,685*

recall [*v1*] *remember*
arouse, awaken, bethink, bring to mind, call to mind, call up, cite, come to one, educe, elicit, evoke, extract, flash, flash on*, look back, mind, nail it down*, recollect, reestablish, reinstate, reintroduce, remind, reminisce, renew, retain, retrospect, revive, ring a bell*, rouse, stir, strike a note*, summon, think back*, think of, waken; SEE CONCEPT *40*

recall [*v2*] *ask for return of offending thing*
abjure, annul, call back, call in, cancel, countermand, discharge, dismantle, dismiss, disqualify, forswear, lift, nullify, palinode, recant, repeal, rescind, retract, reverse, revoke, suspend, take back, unsay, withdraw; SEE CONCEPTS *50,88,131,143*

recant [*v*] *take back something said*
abjure, abnegate, abrogate, annul, apostatize, back down, back off, back out, backtrack*, call back, cancel, contradict, countermand, deny, dial back*, disavow, disclaim, disown, eat one's words*, forswear, go back on one's word*, nullify, recall, renege, renounce, repeal, repudiate, rescind, retract, revoke, take back, unsay, void, weasel out*, welsh*, withdraw, worm out of*; SEE CONCEPTS *25,266*

recapitulate [*v*] *go over something again*
epitomize, go over same ground*, go the same round*, outline, paraphrase, recap*, recount, rehash, reiterate, repeat, rephrase, replay, restate, review, reword, run over*, run through again*, summarize, sum up; SEE CONCEPT *266*

recede [*v*] *withdraw; diminish*
abate, back, close, decline, decrease, depart, die off, diminish, drain away, draw back, drop, dwindle, ebb, fade, fall back, flow back, go away, go back, lessen, reduce, regress, retire, retract, retreat, retrocede, retrograde, retrogress, return, shrink, sink, subside, taper, wane; SEE CONCEPTS *195,698,776*

receipt [*n1*] *acknowledgment of delivery*
cancellation, certificate, chit, counterfoil, declaration, discharge, letter, notice, proof of purchase, quittance, release, sales slip, slip, stub, voucher; SEE CONCEPTS *271,332*

receipt [*n2*] *delivery of goods*
acceptance, accession, acquiring, acquisition, admission, admitting, arrival, getting, intaking, receiving, reception, recipience, taking; SEE CONCEPT *124*

receipts [*n*] *money earned in business venture*
bottom line*, cash flow, comings in*, earnings, gain, gate, get*, gross, handle*, income, net, proceeds, profit, return, revenue, revenue stream, royalty, take*, take-in*, taking*; SEE CONCEPT *344*

receive [*v1*] *accept delivery of something*
accept, acquire, admit, apprehend, appropriate, arrogate, assume, be given, be informed, be in receipt of, be told, catch, collect, come by, come into, cop*, corral*, derive, draw, earn, gain, gather, get, get from, get hands on*, get hold of*, grab, hear, hold, inherit, latch on to*, make, obtain, perceive, pick up, pocket*, procure, pull, pull down*, reap, redeem, secure, seize, snag*, take, take in, take possession, win; SEE CONCEPT *124*

receive [*v2*] *endure, sustain*
bear, be subjected to, encounter, experience, go through, meet with, suffer, undergo; SEE CONCEPT *23*

receive [*v3*] *take in guest or member*
accept, accommodate, admit, allow entrance, bring in, entertain, greet, host, induct, initiate, install, introduce, invite, let in, let through, make comfortable, make welcome, meet, permit, roll out red carpet*, shake hands*, show in, take in, usher in, welcome; SEE CONCEPTS *50,83,88,140*

recent [*adj*] *current*
contempo*, contemporary, fresh, hot off the fire*, hot off the press*, just out*, late, latter, latter-day, modern, modernistic, neoteric, new, newborn, newfangled, novel, present-day, the latest*, today, up-to-date, young; SEE CONCEPTS *578,797,820*

recently [*adv*] *currently*
afresh, anew, freshly, in recent past, in recent times, just a while ago, just now, lately, latterly, new, newly, not long ago, of late, short while ago, the other day; SEE CONCEPT *820*

receptacle [*n*] *container for disposal, storage*
bowl, box, holder, hopper, repository, vessel, wastebasket; SEE CONCEPT *494*

reception [*n1*] *acceptance; acknowledgment*
accession, acquisition, admission, disposition, encounter, gathering, greeting, induction, introduction, meeting, reaction, receipt, receiving, recipience, recognition, response, salutation, treatment, welcome; SEE CONCEPTS *83,124,384*

reception [*n2*] *celebratory party*
buffet, dinner, do*, entertainment, function, gathering, levee, matinee, soiree, supper, tea; SEE CONCEPT *383*

receptive [*adj*] *open to new ideas*
acceptant, acceptive, accessible, alert, amenable, approachable, bright, favorable, friendly, hospitable, influenceable, interested, observant, open, open-minded, open to suggestions, perceptive, persuadable, pushover*, quick on the uptake*, ready, recipient, responsive, sensitive, suggestible, susceptible, swayable, sympathetic, welcoming, well-disposed; SEE CONCEPT *404*

recess [*n1*] *niche, corner*
alcove, ambush, angle, apse, bay, break, carrel, cavity, cell, closet, cove, cranny, crutch, crypt, cubicle, dent, depression, depths, embrasure, fork, heart, hiding place, hole, hollow, indentation, mouth, nook, opening, oriel, penetralia, reaches, retreat, secret place, slot, socket; SEE CONCEPTS *440,513*

recess [*n2*] *break, interval in action*
break-off, breather*, breathing spell*, cessation, closure, coffee break*, cutoff, downtime*, halt,

happy hour*, hiatus, holiday, interlude, intermission, interregnum, layoff, letup, lull, pause, respite, rest, stop, suspension, ten*, time-out, vacation; SEE CONCEPT *807*

recess [*v*] *stop action*
adjourn, break off*, break up*, call time*, dissolve, drop, drop it, pigeonhole*, prorogate, prorogue, put on hold, rise, shake, sideline*, take a break, take a breather*, take five*, take ten*, terminate; SEE CONCEPTS *119,121*

recession [*n*] *reversal of action; reduction of business activity*
bad times*, bankruptcy, big trouble*, bottomout*, bust, collapse, decline, deflation, depression, downturn, hard times*, inflation, rainy days*, shakeout*, slide, slump, stagnation, unemployment; SEE CONCEPT *335*

recharge [*v*] *revitalize*
bounce back*, breathe new life into*, bring back to life*, come to life, energize, invigorate, reenergize, refresh, regenerate, rejuvenate, renew, restore, resuscitate, revitalize, revive; SEE CONCEPTS *13,221,469,697*

recipe [*n*] *directions, formula*
compound, ingredients, instructions, method, modus operandi, prescription, procedure, process, program, receipt, technique; SEE CONCEPT *274*

reciprocal [*adj*] *exchanged, alternate*
changeable, companion, complementary, convertible, coordinate, correlative, corresponding, dependent, double, duplicate, equivalent, exchangeable, fellow, give-and-take*, interchangeable, interdependent, matching, mutual, reciprocative, reciprocatory, twin; SEE CONCEPTS *566,570*

reciprocate [*v*] *exchange, alternate; equal*
barter, be equivalent, correspond, equal, feel in return, interchange, make up for*, match, pay one's dues*, recompense, render, repay, reply, requite, respond, retaliate, retort, return, return the compliment*, scratch one's back*, serve out, share, square, swap, swing, tit for tat*, trade, vacillate; SEE CONCEPTS *45,104,384*

recital [*n*] *narrative, rendering*
account, concert, description, detailing, enumeration, fable, musical, musicale, narration, narrative, performance, portrayal, presentation, reading, recapitulation, recitation, recountal, recounting, rehearsal, relation, repetition, report, statement, story, tale, telling; SEE CONCEPTS *263,264*

recitation [*n*] *reading to audience*
address, appeal, declaiming, delivery, discourse, discoursing, discussion, exercise, holding forth, lecture, monologue, narrating, narration, oration, passage, performance, piece, playing, proclamation, recital, recounting, rehearsal, rendering, report, selection, soliloquizing, speaking, talk, telling; SEE CONCEPTS *72,263,266*

recite [*v*] *read out loud; narrate*
account for, address, answer, chant, communicate, convey, declaim, delineate, deliver, describe, detail, discourse, dramatize, enact, enlarge, enumerate, expatiate, explain, give an account, give a report, give verbal account, hold forth, impart, interpret, itemize, mention, narrate, parrot*, perform, picture, portray, quote, recapitulate, recount, reel off*, rehearse, relate, render,

repeat, reply, report, retell, soliloquize, speak, state, tell, utter; SEE CONCEPTS *55,57,72,266*

reckless [*adj*] *irresponsible in thought, deed*
adventuresome, adventurous, any which way*, audacious, brash, breakneck, carefree, careless, daredevil, daring, desperate, devil-may-care*, fast and loose*, feckless, foolhardy, harebrained, hasty, headlong, heedless, helter-skelter, hopeless, hotheaded*, ill-advised, imprudent, inattentive, incautious, inconsiderate, indiscreet, kooky*, madcap, mindless, negligent, overventuresome, playing with fire*, precipitate, rash, regardless, temerarious, thoughtless, uncareful, venturesome, venturous, wild; SEE CONCEPTS *401,542*

reckon [*v1*] *add up; evaluate*
account, appraise, approximate, calculate, call, cast, cipher, compute, conjecture, consider, count, count heads*, count noses*, deem, enumerate, esteem, estimate, figure, figure out, foot, gauge, guess, hold, judge, keep tabs*, look upon, number, place, put, rate, regard, run down, square, sum, surmise, take account of, tally, think of, tick off*, tot, total, tote*, tote up*, tote up, view; SEE CONCEPTS *37,764*

reckon [*v2*] *suppose, imagine*
assume, bank on, bargain for, believe, be of the opinion, build on, conjecture, count on, depend on, expect, fancy, gather, guess, plan on, rely on, surmise, suspect, take, think, trust in, understand; SEE CONCEPTS *12,26*

reckoning [*n*] *computation, account*
adding, addition, arithmetic, bad news*, bill, calculation, charge, check, ciphering, cost, count, counting, debt, due, estimate, estimation, fee, figuring, grunt*, invoice, IOU*, score, settlement, statement, summation, tab, working; SEE CONCEPT *331*

recline [*v*] *lie down*
be recumbent, cant, heel, lay down, lean, lie, list, loll, lounge, repose, rest, slant, slope, sprawl, stretch, stretch out, tilt, tip; SEE CONCEPTS *154,201*

recluse [*n*] *person who does not want social contact*
anchorite, ascetic, cenobite, eremite, hermit, monk, nun, solitaire, solitary, troglodyte; SEE CONCEPT *423*

recluse/reclusive [*adj*] *hermitlike, unsociable*
antisocial, ascetic, cloistered, eremetic, hermetic, isolated, misanthropic, monastic, reserved, retiring, secluded, secluse, seclusive, sequestered, solitary, standoffish, withdrawn; SEE CONCEPTS *404,555*

recognition [*n1*] *identification, acknowledgment*
acceptance, acknowledging, admission, allowance, apperception, appreciation, apprehending, assimilation, avowal, awareness, cognizance, concession, confession, consciousness, detection, discovery, double take*, high sign*, identifying, memory, notice, noticing, perceiving, perception, realization, recall, recalling, recognizance, recollection, recurrence, remembering, remembrance, respect, salute, sensibility, tumble*, understanding, verifying; SEE CONCEPT *38*

recognition [*n2*] *appreciation given*
acceptance, acknowledgment, approval, attention, credit, esteem, gratitude, greeting, honor, notice, pat on back*, pat on head*, plum*, puff*,

puffing up*, pumping up*, rave, regard, renown, salute, strokes*; SEE CONCEPTS *10,337,689*

recognize [*v1*] *identify*
admit, be familiar, button down*, descry, determinate, diagnose, diagnosticate, distinguish, espy, finger*, flash on*, know, know again, make*, make out, nail*, note, notice, observe, peg*, perceive, pinpoint, place, recall, recollect, remark, remember, ring a bell*, see, sight, spot, tab, tag, verify; SEE CONCEPT *38*

recognize [*v2*] *acknowledge, understand; approve*
accept, admit, agree, allow, appreciate, assent, avow, be aware of, comprehend, concede, confess, grant, greet, honor, make, own, perceive, realize, respect, salute, sanction, see; SEE CONCEPT *15*

recoil [*v*] *shrink away*
backfire, balk, blanch, blench, blink, carom, cringe, demur, dodge, draw back, duck, falter, flinch, hesitate, jerk, kick, pull back, quail, quake, react, rebound, reel, resile, shake, shirk, shrink, shudder, shy away, spring, start, step back, stick, stickle, swerve, tremble, turn away, waver, wince, withdraw; SEE CONCEPTS *150,194,195*

recollect [*v*] *remember*
arouse, awaken, bethink, bring to mind, call to mind, cite, come to one, flash, flash on*, look back on, mind, place, recall, recognize, remind, reminisce, retain, retrospect, revive, rouse, stir, summon, waken; SEE CONCEPT *40*

recommend [*v*] *advise, approve*
acclaim, advance, advocate, applaud, back, be all for*, be satisfied with, celebrate, commend, compliment, confirm, counsel, endorse, enjoin, esteem, eulogize, exalt, exhort, extol, favor, front for*, glorify, go on record for*, hold up, justify, laud, magnify, plug*, praise, prescribe, prize, propose, put forward, put in a good word*, put on to*, sanction, second, speak highly of, speak well of, stand by, steer, suggest, think highly of, uphold, urge, value, vouch for; SEE CONCEPTS *10,75*

recommendation [*n*] *advice, approval*
advocacy, approbation, blessing, certificate, character reference, charge, commendation, counsel, direction, endorsement, esteem, eulogy, favorable mention, good word*, guidance, injunction, instruction, judgment, letter of support, order, pass, plug*, praise, proposal, proposition, reference, sanction, steer*, suggestion, support, testimonial, tip, tribute, two cents' worth*, urging; SEE CONCEPTS *274,278*

recompense [*n*] *something returned, paid back*
amends, atonement, bus fare*, compensation, cue, damages, emolument, expiation, gravy*, indemnification, indemnity, overcompensation, pay, payment, propitiation, quittance, recoupment, recovery, redemption, redress, remuneration, reparation, repayment, requital, restitution, retrieval, retrievement, return, reward, salvo, satisfaction, solatium, sweetener*, tip, wages; SEE CONCEPTS *340,344*

recompense [*v*] *pay back, make restitution*
ante up*, atone, atone for, balance, comp*, compensate, cough up*, counterbalance, counterpoise, countervail, do business*, equalize, expiate, fix, give satisfaction, grease*, indemnify, make amends, make good*, make up for,

offset, overcompensate, pay, pay for, propitiate, put out*, reciprocate, recoup, recover, redress, reimburse, remunerate, repay, requite, retaliate, retrieve, return, reward, satisfy, spring for, square*, sweeten the pot*, swing for*, take care of; SEE CONCEPTS *126,341*

reconcile [*v1*] *make peace; adjust*
accommodate, accord, accustom, appease, arbitrate, arrange, assuage, attune, bring together, bring to terms, bury the hatchet*, come together, compose, conciliate, conform, cool*, coordinate, fit, fix up, get together on, harmonize, integrate, intercede, kiss and make up*, make matters up, make up, mediate, mitigate, pacify, patch things up*, patch up*, placate, propitiate, proportion, reconciliate, rectify, re-establish, regulate, resolve, restore harmony, reunite, settle, suit, tune, win over; SEE CONCEPTS *384,697*

reconcile [*v2*] *resign oneself to something*
accept, accommodate, get used to*, make the best of*, put up with*, resign, submit, yield; SEE CONCEPT *23*

recondite [*adj*] *mysterious, obscure*
abstruse, academic, acroamatic, arcane, cabalistic, concealed, cryptic, dark, deep, difficult, esoteric, hard, heavy*, hermetic, hidden, involved, little-known, mystic, mystical, occult, orphic, pedantic, profound, scholarly, secret; SEE CONCEPTS *529,576*

reconnaissance [*n*] *inspection*
exploration, investigation, maneuvers, probe, recon, reconnoiter, review, scan, scrutiny, search, surveillance, survey; SEE CONCEPTS *103,290*

reconsider [*v*] *think about again*
amend, change one's mind, consider again, correct, emend, go over, have second thoughts*, polish, rearrange, reassess, recheck, reevaluate, reexamine, rehash, replan, rethink, retrace, review, revise, reweigh, rework, run through, see in a new light*, sleep on, take another look, think better of*, think over, think twice*, work over; SEE CONCEPT *17*

reconstruct [*v*] *reorganize, build up*
copy, deduce, doctor*, do up*, fix, fix up, make over, modernize, overhaul, patch, piece together, reassemble, rebuild, recast, recondition, reconstitute, recreate, reestablish, refashion, reform, regenerate, rehabilitate, rejuvenate, remake, remodel, remold, renovate, reorient, repair, replace, reproduce, reshuffle, restore, retool, revamp, rework; SEE CONCEPTS *84,168,171*

record [*n1*] *account of event or proceedings*
almanac, annals, archive, archives, chronicle, comic book*, diary, directory, document, documentation, entry, evidence, file, history, inscription, jacket, journal, legend, log, manuscript, memo, memoir, memorandum, memorial, minutes, monument, note, paper trail*, register, registry, remembrance, report, script, scroll, story, swindle sheet*, testimony, trace, track record*, transcript, transcription, witness, writing, written material; SEE CONCEPTS *271,281*

record [*n2*] *background, experience*
accomplishment, administration, career, case history, conduct, curriculum vitae, history, past behavior, performance, reign, studies, track record*, way of life*, work; SEE CONCEPT *678*

record [*n3*] *achievement*
ceiling, maximum; SEE CONCEPT *706*

re
re

record [*vl*] *write down; store information*
book, can*, catalog, chalk up*, chronicle, copy, cut, cut a track*, document, dub*, enroll, enter, enumerate, file, indite, inscribe, insert, jot down, keep account, lay down, list, log, make a recording, mark, mark down, matriculate, note, post, preserve, put down, put in writing, put on file*, put on paper*, put on tape*, register, report, set down, tabulate, take down, tape, tape-record, transcribe, video*, videotape, wax*, write in; SEE CONCEPT *125*

record [*v2*] *give evidence of*
contain, designate, explain, indicate, mark, point out, point to, read, register, say, show; SEE CONCEPT *261*

recount [*v*] *tell a story*
break a story*, convey, delineate, depict, describe, detail, echo, enumerate, give an account of, itemize, narrate, picture, play back, portray, recap*, recapitulate, recite, rehash, rehearse, relate, repeat, report, run by again*, run down*, run through*, say again, state, tell, track, unload, verbalize; SEE CONCEPTS *55,266*

recoup [*v*] *recover, make up for*
compensate, get back, get out from under*, get well, make good, make redress for, make well, redeem, refund, regain, reimburse, remunerate, repay, repossess, requite, retrieve, satisfy, win back; SEE CONCEPTS *124,126,342,700*

recourse [*n*] *alternative*
aid, appeal, choice, expediency, expedient, help, makeshift, option, refuge, remedy, resort, resource, shift, stand-by, stopgap, substitute, support, way out; SEE CONCEPTS *693,712*

recover [*vl*] *find again*
balance, bring back, catch up, compensate, get back, make good, obtain again, offset, reacquire, recapture, reclaim, recoup, recruit, redeem, rediscover, regain, reoccupy, repair, replevin, replevy, repossess, rescue, restore, resume, retake, retrieve, salvage, take back, win back; SEE CONCEPTS *120,183*

recover [*v2*] *improve in health*
be out of woods*, better, bounce back*, come around, convalesce, feel oneself again*, forge ahead, gain, get back on feet*, get better, get in shape, get out from under*, get over, get well, grow, heal, increase, make a comeback*, mend, overcome, perk up*, pick up, pull through, rally, rebound, recuperate, refresh, regain one's health, regain one's strength, rejuvenate, renew, restore, return to form, revive, snap back*, sober up*, start anew, take turn for better; SEE CONCEPTS *303,700*

recreation [*n*] *sports, games, special interests*
amusement, avocation, ball*, disport, dissipation, distraction, diversion, divertissement, ease, enjoyment, entertainment, exercise, festivity, field day*, frolic, fun, fun and games*, game, hilarity, hobby, holiday, jollity, laughs*, leisure activity, mirth, pastime, picnic, play, playtime, pleasure, R and R*, rec, refreshment, relaxation, relief, repose, rollick, sport, vacation; SEE CONCEPTS *363,364*

recruit [*n*] *person beginning service*
apprentice, beginner, convert, draftee, enlisted person, fledgling, GI*, greenhorn*, helper, initiate, learner, neophyte, newcomer, new person, novice, novitiate, plebe*, proselyte, rookie, sailor, selectee, serviceperson, soldier, tenderfoot*, trainee, volunteer; SEE CONCEPTS *348,358*

recruit [*v*] *gather resources*
augment, better, build up, call to arms, call up, deliver, draft, engage, enlist, enroll, fill up, find human resources, gain, impress, improve, induct, levy, mobilize, muster, obtain, procure, proselytize, raise, reanimate, recoup, recover, recuperate, refresh, regain, reinforce, renew, repair, replenish, repossess, restore, retrieve, revive, round up, select, sign on, sign up, store up, strengthen, supply, take in, take on, win over; SEE CONCEPTS *41,109,120,320*

rectify [*v*] *correct a situation; make something right*
adjust, amend, clean up, clean up act*, debug, dial back*, doctor, emend, fix, fix up, go over, improve, launder, make good*, make up for*, mend, pay one's dues*, pick up, put right, recalibrate, redress, reform, remedy, repair, revise, right, scrub, shape up, square, straighten out, straighten up, turn things around*; SEE CONCEPT *126*

recumbent [*adj*] *lying down*
decumbent, flat, horizontal, level, procumbent, prostrate, reclining, resupine, sprawling, supine; SEE CONCEPT *583*

recuperate [*v*] *improve in health*
ameliorate, be on the mend*, be out of the woods*, bounce back*, convalesce, gain, get back on one's feet*, get better, get well, heal, look up, make a comeback*, mend, perk up*, pick up, pull out of it*, pull through, rally, recover, regain health, snap out of it*, turn the corner*; SEE CONCEPTS *303,700*

recur [*v*] *happen again; repeat in one's mind*
be remembered, be repeated, come again, come and go, come back, crop up again*, haunt thoughts*, iterate, persist, reappear, recrudesce, reiterate, repeat, return, return to mind, revert, run through one's mind*, turn back; SEE CONCEPTS *3,242*

recurrent [*adj*] *repeating*
alternate, chain, continued, cyclical, frequent, habitual, intermittent, isochronal, isochronous, periodic, periodical, recurring, regular, reoccurring, repeated, repetitive, rolling; SEE CONCEPTS *541,544*

red [*n/adj*] *color of blood; shade resembling such a color*
bittersweet, bloodshot, blooming, blush, brick, burgundy, cardinal, carmine, cerise, cherry, chestnut, claret, copper, coral, crimson, dahlia, flaming, florid, flushed, fuchsia, garnet, geranium, glowing, healthy, inflamed, infrared, magenta, maroon, pink, puce, rose, roseate, rosy, rubicund, ruby, ruddy, rufescent, russet, rust, salmon, sanguine, scarlet, titian, vermilion, wine; SEE CONCEPTS *618,622*

redden [*v*] *blush, make rosy*
bloody, color, crimson, dye, encarmine, encarnadine, flush, glow, go red, mantle, paint, pink, pinken, rose, rouge, rubify, rubric, rubricate, ruby, ruddle, ruddy, rust, suffuse, tint, turn red; SEE CONCEPTS *250,469*

redeem [*vl*] *recover possession*
buy back, buy off, call in, cash, cash in, change, cover, defray, discharge, exchange, get back, make good, pay off, purchase, ransom, recapture, reclaim, recoup, regain, reinstate, repay, re-

plevin, replevy, repossess, repurchase, restore, retrieve, settle, take in, trade in, win back; SEE CONCEPTS *104,131,327*

redeem [*v2*] *free; buy the freedom of*
deliver, disenthrall, disimprison, emancipate, extricate, liberate, loose, manumit, pay ransom, ransom, release, rescue, save, set free, unbind, unchain, unfetter; SEE CONCEPTS *127,327*

redeem [*v3*] *atone for; compensate*
abide by, absolve, acquit, adhere to, balance, carry out, compensate, counterbalance, counterpoise, countervail, defray, discharge, fulfill, hold to, keep, keep the faith*, make amends, make good, make up for, meet, offset, outweigh, perform, redress, rehabilitate, reinstate, restore, satisfy, save, set off; SEE CONCEPTS *91,126*

red herring [*n*] *distraction*
attention-grabber, bait, commotion, deviation, disturbance, diversion, gimmick, interruption, maneuver, ploy, smoke screen, wild-goose chase*; SEE CONCEPTS *293,410,532,690*

redneck [*n*] *hick*
backwoodsman/woman, boor, bumpkin, clodhopper, cornfed*, country boy/girl, country cousin*, countryman/woman, farmer, good old boy*, hayseed*, hillbilly, local yokel*, rube, rural, rustic, yokel*; SEE CONCEPT *413*

redolent [*adj*] *aromatic; suggestive*
ambrosial, balmy, evocative, fragrant, odoriferous, perfumed, pungent, reminiscent, reminiscent, scented, sweet-smelling; SEE CONCEPTS *267,529, 598*

redress [*n*] *help, compensation*
aid, amendment, amends, assistance, atonement, balancing, change, conciliation, correction, cure, ease, indemnity, justice, offsetting, payment, quittance, recompense, rectification, reestablishment, reformation, rehabilitation, relief, remedy, remission, remodeling, renewal, repair, reparation, reprisal, requital, restitution, retribution, return, revision, reward, reworking, satisfaction, vengeance; SEE CONCEPTS *344,712*

redress [*v*] *change, rectify*
adjust, amend, annul, balance, cancel, compensate, correct, counteract, countercheck, dial back*, ease, even out, frustrate, make amends, make reparation, make restitution, make up for, mend, negate, negative, neutralize, pay for, pay one's dues*, put right*, recalibrate, recompense, reform, regulate, relieve, remedy, repair, restore, revise, square, turn around, turn over new leaf*, turn things around*, vindicate; SEE CONCEPTS *126,697*

red tape [*n*] *bureaucracy*
authority, city hall*, government, management, officialdom, officialism, powers that be*, proper channels, regulatory commission, the Establishment*, the system*; SEE CONCEPTS *325,770*

reduce [*v1*] *make less; decrease*
abate, abridge, bankrupt, bant, break, cheapen, chop, clip, contract, curtail, cut, cut back, cut down, debase, deflate, depreciate, depress, diet, dilute, diminish, discount, drain, dwindle, go on a diet*, impair, impoverish, lessen, lose weight, lower, mark down, moderate, nutshell, pare, pauperize, rebate, recede, roll back, ruin, scale down, shave, shorten, slash, slim, slow down, step down, take off weight, taper, taper off, tone down, trim, truncate, turn down, weaken, wind down; SEE CONCEPTS *137,236,240,247,698*

reduce [*v2*] *defeat*
bear down, beat down, break, bring, conquer, cripple, crush, disable, drive, enfeeble, force, master, overcome, overpower, ruin, subdue, subjugate, undermine, vanquish, weaken; SEE CONCEPT *95*

reduce [*v3*] *humble, humiliate*
abase, break, bring low, bump*, bust*, declass, degrade, demerit, demote, disgrade, disrate, downgrade, lower, take down a peg*; SEE CONCEPTS *7,19,384*

redundant [*adj*] *excessive; repetitious*
bombastic, de trop*, diffuse, extra, extravagant, inessential, inordinate, iterating, long-winded*, loquacious, oratorical, padded*, palaverous, periphrastic, pleonastic, prolix, reiterating, spare, supererogatory, superfluous, supernumerary, surplus, tautological, unnecessary, unwanted, verbose, wordy; SEE CONCEPTS *553,781*

reef [*n*] *underwater or partially submerged ledge*
atoll, bank, bar, beach, cay, coral reef, ridge, rock, rock barrier, sand bar, shoal, skerry; SEE CONCEPT *509*

reek [*n*] *strong odor*
effluvium, fetor, mephitis, smell, stench, stink; SEE CONCEPT *600*

reek [*v*] *smell of; be characterized by*
be permeated by, be redolent of, emit, fume, give off odor, have an odor, smell, smoke, steam, stench, stink; SEE CONCEPT *600*

reel [*v*] *wobble; spin around*
bob, careen, falter, feel giddy, go around, lurch, pitch, revolve, rock, roll, shake, stagger, stumble, sway, swim, swing, swirl, teeter, titubate, totter, turn, twirl, waver, weave, wheel, whirl; SEE CONCEPTS *151,153*

refer [*v1*] *mention*
accredit, adduce, advert, allude, ascribe, assign, associate, attribute, bring up, charge, cite, credit, designate, direct attention, excerpt, exemplify, extract, give as example, glance, hint, impute, indicate, insert, instance, interpolate, introduce, invoke, lay, make allusion, make mention of, make reference, name, notice, point, point out, put down to, quote, speak about, speak of, specify, touch on; SEE CONCEPT *73*

refer [*v2*] *direct, guide*
commit, consign, deliver, hand in, hand over, introduce, pass on, point, put in touch, recommend, relegate, send, submit, transfer, turn over; SEE CONCEPTS *143,187*

refer [*v3*] *concern, apply*
answer, appertain, be about, be a matter of, bear upon, be directed to, belong, be relevant, connect, correspond with, cover, deal with, encompass, have a bearing on, have reference, have relation, have to do with, hold, include, incorporate, involve, pertain, point, regard, relate, take in, touch; SEE CONCEPT *532*

refer [*v4*] *seek information*
advise, apply, commune, confer, consult, go, have recourse, look up, recur, repair, resort, run, turn, turn to; SEE CONCEPTS *72,216*

referee [*n*] *person who mediates; judges*
adjudicator, arbiter, arbitrator, conciliator, judge, ref*, umpire; SEE CONCEPTS *348,366*

referee [*v*] *judge, mediate*
adjudge, adjudicate, arbitrate, umpire; SEE CONCEPT *18*

re
re

reference [*n1*] *remark, citation*
advertence, allusion, associating, attributing, bringing up, connecting, hint, implication, indicating, innuendo, insinuation, mention, mentioning, note, plug*, pointing out, quotation, relating, resource, source, stating; SEE CONCEPT *278*

reference [*n2*] *testimonial of good character*
certificate, certification, character, credentials, endorsement, good word, recommendation, tribute; SEE CONCEPTS *69,274*

reference [*n3*] *printed matter with information*
archives, cyclopedia, dictionary, encyclopedia, evidence, source, thesaurus, writing; SEE CONCEPTS *271,280*

refine [*v1*] *purify*
clarify, cleanse, distill, filter, process, rarefy, strain; SEE CONCEPT *165*

refine [*v2*] *perfect, polish*
better, civilize, clarify, cultivate, elevate, explain, hone, improve, make clear, round, sleek, slick, smooth, temper; SEE CONCEPT *244*

refined [*adj1*] *cultured, civilized*
aesthetic, civil, classy*, courteous, courtly, cultivated, delicate, discerning, discriminating, elegant, enlightened, exact, fastidious, fine, finespun, genteel, gracious, high-brow*, high-minded, nice, plush, polished, polite, posh, precise, punctilious, restrained, ritzy*, sensitive, snazzy*, sophisticated, spiffy*, suave, sublime, subtle, swanky*, tasteful, urbane, well-bred, well-mannered; SEE CONCEPTS *401,555,589*

refined [*adj2*] *cleaned of impurities*
aerated, boiled down, clarified, clean, cleansed, distilled, drained, expurgated, filtered, processed, pure, purified, rarefied, strained, washed; SEE CONCEPT *621*

refinement [*n1*] *cleansing*
clarification, cleaning, depuration, detersion, distillation, draining, filtering, processing, purification, rarefaction, rectification; SEE CONCEPT *165*

refinement [*n2*] *cultivation, civilization*
affability, civility, courtesy, courtliness, delicacy, dignity, discrimination, elegance, enlightenment, erudition, fastidiousness, fineness, fine point*, finesse, fine tuning*, finish, gentility, gentleness, good breeding, good manners, grace, graciousness, knowledge, lore, nicety, nuance, polish, politeness, politesse, precision, sophistication, style, suavity, subtlety, tact, taste, urbanity; SEE CONCEPTS *388,633,655*

reflect [*v1*] *give back*
cast, catch, copy, echo, emulate, flash, follow, give forth, imitate, match, mirror, rebound, repeat, repercuss, reply, reproduce, resonate, resound, return, reverberate, reverse, revert, shine, take after, throw back; SEE CONCEPTS *65,171,624*

reflect [*v2*] *think about*
cerebrate, chew*, cogitate, consider, contemplate, deliberate, meditate, mull over, muse, ponder, reason, ruminate, speculate, stew*, study, think, weigh, wonder; SEE CONCEPTS *17,24*

reflect [*v3*] *demonstrate, indicate*
bear out, bespeak, communicate, display, evince, exhibit, express, indicate, manifest, reveal, show; SEE CONCEPT *261*

reflection [*n1*] *thought, thinking*
absorption, brainwork, cerebration, cogitation, consideration, contemplation, deliberation, idea, imagination, impression, meditation, musing, observation, opinion, pensiveness, pondering, rumination, speculation, study, view; SEE CONCEPTS *17,24*

reflection [*n2*] *mirror image*
appearance, counterpart, duplicate, echo, idea, image, impression, light, likeness, picture, representation, reproduction, shadow; SEE CONCEPT *628*

reflection [*n3*] *criticism*
animadversion, aspersion, blame, censure, derogation, discredit, disesteem, imputation, obloquy, reproach, slam, slur, stricture; SEE CONCEPT *52*

reflective [*adj*] *thoughtful*
cogitating, contemplative, deliberate, meditative, pensive, pondering, reasoning, ruminative, speculative, studious; SEE CONCEPT *403*

reform [*v*] *correct, rectify*
ameliorate, amend, better, bring up to code*, change one's ways*, clean up, clean up one's act*, convert, correct, cure, emend, go straight*, improve, make amends, make over, mend, rearrange, rebuild, reclaim, reconstitute, reconstruct, redeem, refashion, regenerate, rehabilitate, remake, remedy, remodel, renew, renovate, reorganize, repair, resolve, restore, revise, revolutionize, rework, shape up, standardize, swear off, transform, turn over a new leaf*, uplift; SEE CONCEPTS *35,110,126,202*

reformatory [*n*] *reform school*
boot camp*, cooler*, correctional facility, correctional institution, jail, penal institution, penitentiary, prison, training school; SEE CONCEPTS *439,449,516*

refrain [*n*] *chorus of musical piece*
burden, melody, music, song, strain, theme, tune, undersong; SEE CONCEPTS *264,595*

refrain [*v*] *do without; keep from doing*
abstain, arrest, avoid, be temperate, cease, check, curb, desist, eschew, forbear, forgo, give up, go on the wagon*, halt, inhibit, interrupt, keep, leave off, not do, pass, pass up, quit, renounce, resist, restrain, sit out*, stop, take the cure*, take the pledge*, withhold; SEE CONCEPTS *121,681*

refresh [*v*] *make like new; give new life*
brace, breathe new life into, bring around, brush up, cheer, cool, enliven, exhilarate, freshen, inspirit, jog, modernize, prod, prompt, quicken, reanimate, recreate, regain, reinvigorate, rejuvenate, renovate, repair, replenish, restore, resuscitate, revitalize, revive, revivify, stimulate, update, vivify; SEE CONCEPTS *35,202,697*

refreshing [*adj*] *new; rejuvenating*
bracing, cooling, different, energizing, exhilarating, fresh, invigorating, novel, original, rejuvenating, restorative, restoring, revitalizing, revivifying, stimulating, thirst-quenching, unique; SEE CONCEPTS *564,578,797*

refreshment [*n*] *small amount of food or drink*
bite, pick-me-up*, snack, spread, tidbit; SEE CONCEPT *457*

refrigerate [*v*] *chill, usually in storage*
air-condition, air-cool, cool, freeze, ice, keep cold, make cold; SEE CONCEPTS *202,255*

refuge [*n*] *place to hide, have privacy*
ambush, anchorage, asylum, cover, covert, den, escape, exit, expedient, fortress, harbor, harborage, haven, hideaway, hideout, hiding place, hole, home, immunity, ivory tower*, makeshift, opening, outlet, port, preserve, protection, recourse, resort, resource, retreat, safe place, sanc-

tuary, security, shelter, shield, stopgap*, stronghold, way out*; SEE CONCEPTS *198,515*

refugee [n] *person running from something, often oppression*

alien, boat person*, castaway, defector, derelict, deserter, displaced person, DP*, emigrant, émigré, escapee, evacuee, exile, expatriate, expellee, foreigner, foundling, fugitive, homeless person, leper, maroon, outcast, outlaw, prodigal, renegade, runaway, stateless person; SEE CONCEPTS *359,413*

refund [n] *returned money*

acquittance, allowance, compensation, consolation, discharge, discount, give-back*, give-up*, kickback, money back, payment, rebate, reimbursement, remuneration, repayment, restitution, retribution, return, satisfaction, settlement; SEE CONCEPTS *340,344*

refund [v] *return money; rebate*

adjust, balance, compensate, give back, honor a claim, indemnify, make amends, make good*, make repayment, make up for, pay back, recompense, recoup, redeem, redress, reimburse, relinquish, remit, remunerate, repay, restore, reward, settle; SEE CONCEPT *341*

refurbish [v] *spruce up*

clean up, do up*, fix up, gussy up*, mend, modernize, overhaul, recondition, redo, reequip, refit, refresh, rehab, rehabilitate, rejuvenate, remodel, renew, renovate, repair, restore, retread, revamp, set to rights, spruce, update; SEE CONCEPTS *177,202*

refusal [n] *denial of responsibility; unwillingness*

abnegation, ban, choice, cold shoulder*, declension, declination, defiance, disallowance, disapproval, disavowal, disclaimer, discountenancing, disfavor, dissent, enjoinment, exclusion, forbidding, interdiction, knockback*, negation, nix*, no, nonacceptance, noncompliance, nonconsent, option, pass*, prohibition, proscription, rebuff, refutation, regrets, rejection, renouncement, renunciation, repudiation, repulse, repulsion, reversal, thumbs down*, turndown, veto, withholding, writ; SEE CONCEPTS *278,633*

refuse [n] *garbage*

debris, dregs, dross, dump, dust, hogwash*, junk, leavings, litter, muck, offal, rejectamenta*, remains, residue, rubbish, scraps, scum*, sediment, slop*, sweepings, swill, trash, waste, waste matter; SEE CONCEPT *260*

refuse [v] *deny; say no*

beg off, brush off*, decline, demur, desist, disaccord, disallow, disapprove, dispense with, dissent, dodge, evade, give thumbs down to*, hold back, hold off, hold out, ignore, make excuses, nix*, not budge, not budget, not buy*, not care to*, pass up, protest, rebuff, refuse to receive, regret, reject, repel, reprobate, repudiate, send off*, send regrets*, set aside*, shun, spurn, turn away, turn deaf ear to*, turn down, turn from, turn one's back on*, withdraw, withhold; SEE CONCEPTS *30,49,266*

refute [v] *prove false; discredit*

abnegate, argue against, blow sky high*, break, burn, burn down, cancel, cancel out, confute, contend, contradict, contravene, convict, counter, crush, debate, demolish, disclaim, disconfirm, dispose of, disprove, dispute, evert, explode, expose, gainsay, give the lie to*, give thumbs down to*, invalidate, negate, oppose, overthrow, parry,

quash, rebut, reply to, repudiate, shoot down, shoot full of holes*, show up, silence, squelch, take a stand against, tear down*, top*; SEE CONCEPT *54*

regain [v] *get back, get back to*

achieve, attain, compass, gain, get out from under, get well, make well, reach, reach again, reacquire, reattain, recapture, reclaim, recoup, recover, recruit, redeem, repossess, retake, retrieve, return to, save, take back, win back; SEE CONCEPTS *120,124,131*

regal [adj] *fit for royalty*

august, glorious, imposing, kingly, magnificent, majestic, monarchal, monarchical, noble, proud, queenly, resplendent, royal, sovereign, splendid, stately, sublime; SEE CONCEPT *589*

regale [v] *throw a party; have fun*

amuse, delight, divert, entertain, feast, fracture, give a party, grab, gratify, have a get-together, laugh it up, nurture, party, please, ply, refresh, satisfy, serve, toss a party; SEE CONCEPTS *292,384*

regard [n1] *attention, look*

care, carefulness, cognizance, concern, consciousness, curiosity, gaze, glance, heed, interest, interestedness, mark, mind, note, notice, observance, observation, once-over*, remark, scrutiny, stare, view; SEE CONCEPTS *596,623,626, 690*

regard [n2] *affection, good opinion*

account, appreciation, approbation, approval, attachment, care, cherishing, concern, consideration, curiosity, deference, devotion, esteem, estimation, favor, fondness, homage, honor, interest, interestedness, liking, love, note, opinion, prizing, reputation, repute, respect, reverence, satisfaction, store, sympathy, thought, value, valuing, veneration, worship; SEE CONCEPTS *10,532,689*

regard [n3] *feature, detail*

aspect, bearing, concern, connection, item, matter, particular, point, reference, relation, relevance, respect; SEE CONCEPTS *532,644*

regard [v1] *look at; listen to*

advertise, attend, beam, behold, contemplate, eye, eyeball*, flash, gaze, get a load of*, give attention, heed, look on, mark, mind, note, notice, observe, overlook, pay attention, pipe*, pore over*, read, remark, respect, scan, scrutinize, see, spy, stare at, take into consideration, take notice of, view, watch, witness; SEE CONCEPTS *596,623,626*

regard [v2] *believe, judge*

account, adjudge, admire, assay, assess, consider, deem, esteem, estimate, look upon, rate, reckon, respect, revere, see, suppose, surmise, think, treat, value, view; SEE CONCEPTS *10,12*

regard [v3] *have something to do with*

apply to, bear upon, be relevant to, concern, have a bearing on, have to do with*, interest, pertain to, refer to, relate to; SEE CONCEPT *532*

regardful [adj] *attentive, observant*

advertent, arrect, aware, careful, considerate, deferential, duteous, dutiful, heedful, intentive, mindful, observative, observing, respectful, thoughtful, watchful; SEE CONCEPT *401*

regardless [adj] *indifferent, unconcerned*

behindhand, blind, careless, coarse, crude, deaf, delinquent, derelict, disregarding, heedless, inadvertent, inattentive, inconsiderate, insensitive,

re
re

lax, listless, mindless, neglectful, negligent, nonobservant, rash, reckless, remiss, rude, slack, unfeeling, unheeding, uninterested, unmindful; SEE CONCEPT *401*

regardless [*adv*] *despite everything*
against, although, anyway, aside from, at any cost, but, come what may, despite, distinct from, for all that, in any case, in spite of everything, leaving aside, nevertheless, no matter what, nonetheless, notwithstanding, without considering, without regard to; SEE CONCEPTS *544,548*

regards [*n*] *best wishes*
commendations, compliments, deference, devoirs, good wishes, greeting, love, love and kisses*, remembrances, respects, salutation, salutations; SEE CONCEPT *278*

regenerate [*v*] *breathe new life into*
change, exhilarate, inspirit, invigorate, produce, raise from the dead*, reanimate, reawaken, reconstruct, recreate, reestablish, refresh, reinvigorate, rejuvenate, renew, renovate, reproduce, restore, revive, revivify, uplift; SEE CONCEPTS *7,22,173,202,251*

regime [*n*] *leadership of organization*
administration, dynasty, establishment, government, incumbency, management, pecking order*, reign, rule, system, tenure; SEE CONCEPTS *299,325*

region [*n*] *area, domain; scope*
arena, bailiwick, belt, block, clearing, country, demesne, district, division, domain, dominion, environs, expanse, field, ghetto, ground, inner city, jungle, land, locale, locality, neck of woods*, neighborhood, part, place, precinct, province, quarter, range, realm, scene, section, sector, shire, sphere, stomping ground*, suburb, terrain, territory, tract, turf*, vicinity, walk, ward, world, zone; SEE CONCEPTS *198,508,512*

register [*n*] *list, record*
annals, archives, book, catalog, catalogue, chronicle, diary, entry, file, ledger, log, memorandum, registry, roll, roll call, roster, schedule, scroll; SEE CONCEPT *281*

register [*v1*] *enter in list, record*
catalogue, check in, chronicle, enlist, enroll, file, inscribe, join, list, note, record, schedule, set down, sign on, sign up, sign up for, subscribe, take down, weigh in; SEE CONCEPTS *79,114,125*

register [*v2*] *indicate, reveal*
be shown, bespeak, betray, disclose, display, exhibit, express, manifest, mark, point out, point to, read, record, reflect, say, show; SEE CONCEPT *261*

register [*v3*] *make an impression*
come home to, dawn on, get through to, have an effect on, impress, sink in, tell; SEE CONCEPTS *7,19,22*

regress [*v*] *return to earlier way of doing things*
backslide, degenerate, deteriorate, ebb, fall away, fall back, fall off, go back, lapse, lose ground, recede, relapse, retreat, retrogress, revert, roll back, sink, throw back, turn back; SEE CONCEPTS *633,698*

regret [*n*] *upset over past action*
affliction, anguish, annoyance, apologies, apology, bitterness, care, compunction, concern, conscience, contrition, demur, disappointment, discomfort, dissatisfaction, dole, grief, heartache, heartbreak, lamentation, misgiving, nostalgia, pang, penitence, qualm, regretfulness, remorse, repentance, ruefulness, scruple, self-accusation, self-condemnation, self-disgust, self-reproach, sorrow, uneasiness, woe, worry; SEE CONCEPTS *21,410*

regret [*v*] *be upset about*
apologize, be disturbed, bemoan, be sorry for, bewail, cry over*, cry over spilled milk*, deplore, deprecate, disapprove, feel remorse, feel sorry, feel uneasy, grieve, have compunctions*, have qualms*, kick oneself*, lament, look back, miss, moan, mourn, repent, repine, rue, weep, weep over; SEE CONCEPTS *21,410*

regretful [*adj*] *sad, sorry*
apologetic, ashamed, attritional, compunctious, contrite, disappointed, mournful, penitent, remorseful, repentant, rueful, sorrowful; SEE CONCEPT *403*

regrettable [*adj*] *unfortunate, wrong*
afflictive, calamitous, deplorable, dire, disappointing, distressing, dreadful, grievous, heartbreaking, ill-advised, lamentable, pitiable, pitiful, sad, shameful, unfavorable, unhappy, woeful; SEE CONCEPTS *548,571*

regular [*adj*] *normal, common*
approved, bona fide, classic, commonplace, correct, customary, daily, established, everyday, formal, general, habitual, lawful, legitimate, natural, normal, official, ordinary, orthodox, prevailing, prevalent, proper, routine, run-of-the-mill*, sanctioned, standard, time-honored, traditional, typic, typical, unexceptional, unvarying, usual; SEE CONCEPTS *530,533,547*

regular [*adj2*] *orderly, consistent, balanced*
accordant, alternating, arranged, automatic, classified, congruous, consonant, constant, cyclic, dependable, efficient, established, even, exact, expected, fixed, flat, formal, harmonious, in order, invariable, level, measured, mechanical, methodical, momentary, ordered, organized, patterned, periodic, precise, probable, punctual, rational, recurrent, regulated, rhythmic, routine, serial, set, smooth, standardized, stated, steady, straight, successive, symmetrical, systematic, uniform; SEE CONCEPTS *326,544,566,585*

regulate [*v*] *manage, organize*
adapt, adjust, administer, allocate, arrange, balance, classify, conduct, control, coordinate, correct, determine, direct, dispose, fit, fix, govern, guide, handle, improve, legislate, measure, methodize, moderate, modulate, monitor, order, oversee, pull things together*, put in order, readjust, reconcile, rectify, rule, run, set, settle, shape up*, square, standardize, straighten up, superintend, supervise, systematize, temper, time, true, tune, tune up*; SEE CONCEPTS *94,117*

regulation [*n1*] *managing, organizing*
adjustment, administration, arrangement, classification, codification, control, coordination, direction, governance, governing, government, guidance, handling, management, moderation, modulation, reconciliation, regimentation, reorganization, settlement, standardization, superintendence, supervision, systematization, tuning; SEE CONCEPTS *94,117*

regulation [*n2*] *rule, requirement*
bible, book, canon, charge and verse*, code, commandment, decree, decretum, dictate, direction, edict, law, no-nos*, numbers, order, ordinance, precept, prescript, principle, procedure, reg*, standing order, statute; SEE CONCEPTS *318,688*

regurgitate [v] *vomit*
be seasick*, be sick, boff*, drive the bus*, dry heave*, eject, emit, expel, gag*, heave*, hurl*, lose one's lunch*, pray to the porcelain god*, puke*, ralph*, retch, spew, spit up, throw up, toss one's cookies*, upchuck*, urp*; SEE CONCEPTS *179,185,308*

rehabilitate [v] *renovate, adjust*
change, clear, convert, fix up, furbish, improve, make good*, mend, rebuild, reclaim, recondition, reconstitute, reconstruct, recover, redeem, reestablish, reform, refurbish, rehab*, reinstate, reintegrate, reinvigorate, rejuvenate, renew, restitute, restore, save; SEE CONCEPTS *35,126,134,202*

rehash [v] *talk over again*
change, discuss, reiterate, repeat, rephrase, restate, reuse, rework, rewrite, say again, state differently; SEE CONCEPT *56*

rehearsal [n] *preparation for performance*
call, description, drill, dry run*, experiment, going-over, practice, practice session, prep*, reading, readying, recital, recitation, recounting, rehearsing, relation, retelling, run-through, shakedown*, test flight*, trial balloon*, trial performance, tryout, workout; SEE CONCEPTS *264,292,363*

rehearse [v] *prepare for performance*
act, depict, describe, do over, drill, dry run*, experiment, go over, go through, hold a reading*, hone, iterate, learn one's part, narrate, practice, ready, recapitulate, recite, recount, reenact, reiterate, relate, repeat, review, run lines, run through, study, take from the top*, tell, test, train, try out, tune up, walk through*, warm up, work out; SEE CONCEPTS *266,292,363*

reign [n] *rule, dominion*
administration, ascendancy, command, control, dynasty, empire, hegemony, incumbency, influence, monarchy, power, regime, sovereignty, supremacy, sway, tenure; SEE CONCEPTS *198,376*

reign [v] *have power over; prevail*
administer, be in power, be in the driver's seat*, be supreme, boss, command, dominate, domineer, govern, head up, helm, hold power, hold sway*, influence, manage, obtain, occupy, overrule, predominate, preponderate, rule, rule the roost*, run the show*, run things*, sit, superabound, wear the crown*; SEE CONCEPTS *117,298*

reimburse [v] *pay back something owed*
balance, compensate, indemnify, make reparations, make up for, offset, pay, recompense, recover, refund, remunerate, repay, requite, restore, return, square, square up; SEE CONCEPT *341*

rein [n] *restraint, control*
bit, brake, bridle, check, curb, deterrent, governor, halter, harness, hold, line, restriction, strap; SEE CONCEPT *499*

rein [v] *restrain, control*
bridle, check, collect, compose, cool, curb, halt, hold, hold back, limit, repress, restrict, simmer down, slow down, smother, suppress; SEE CONCEPT *130*

reinforce [v] *strengthen, augment*
add fuel to fire*, add to, back up, beef up*, bolster, boost, build up, buttress, carry, emphasize, energize, enlarge, fortify, harden, heat up, hype, increase, lend a hand, multiply, pick up, pillar,

prop, prop up, punch up, shore up, soup up*, stand up for, stiffen, stress, stroke, supplement, support, sustain, toughen, underline; SEE CONCEPTS *5,236,245,250*

reinstate [v] *give back responsibility*
bring back, put back, put in power again, recall, redeem, reelect, reestablish, rehabilitate, rehire, reintroduce, reinvest, renew, replace, restore, return, revive; SEE CONCEPTS *351,384*

reiterate [v] *say or do again*
come again, ditto*, double-check, echo, go over again, ingeminate, iterate, play back, recap*, recapitulate, recheck, rehash, renew, repeat, reprise, resay, restate, retell, rewarn, say again; SEE CONCEPTS *100,171,266*

reject [v] *say no to*
burn*, cashier*, cast aside, cast off, cast out, chuck, decline, deny, despise, disallow, disbelieve, discard, discount, discredit, disdain, dismiss, eliminate, exclude*, give thumbs down to*, jettison, jilt, kill*, nix*, not buy*, pass by, pass on, pass up, put down, rebuff, refuse, renounce, repel, reprobate, repudiate, repulse, scoff, scorn, scout, scrap, second, shed, shoot down*, shun, slough, spurn, throw away, throw out, turn down, veto; SEE CONCEPTS *21,30,180*

rejection [n] *denial, refusal*
bounce, brushoff*, cold shoulder*, disallowance, dismissal, elimination, exclusion, hard time*, kick in teeth*, nix*, no dice*, no go*, nothing doing*, no way*, pass*, rebuff, renunciation, repudiation, slap in the face*, thumbs down*, turndown, veto; SEE CONCEPTS *21,30,180*

rejoice [v] *be very happy about something*
be glad, be overjoyed, celebrate, delight, enjoy, exult, feel happy, glory, joy, jump for joy, make merry, revel, triumph; SEE CONCEPT *410*

rejoinder [n] *answer, reply*
comeback, confutation, counteraccusation, counterargument, countercharge, counterclaim, counterstatement, defense, rebuttal, repartee, response, retort, return, wisecrack; SEE CONCEPTS *274,278*

rejuvenate [v] *make new again*
breathe new life into*, do, do up*, exhilarate, give face lift to*, give new life to, make young again, modernize, reanimate, reclaim, recondition, reconstruct, recover, refresh, refurbish, regenerate, rehab, reinvigorate, renew, renovate, restitute, restore, retread, revitalize, revivify, spruce, spruce up*, update; SEE CONCEPTS *35,202*

relapse [n] *deterioration, weakening*
backsliding, fall, fall from grace*, lapse, loss, recidivism, recurrence, regression, repetition, retrogression, return, reversion, setback, turn for the worse*, worsening; SEE CONCEPT *698*

relapse [v] *deteriorate, weaken*
backslide, be overcome, be overtaken, degenerate, fade, fail, fall, fall back, lapse, recidivate, regress, retrogress, revert, sicken, sink, slide back, slip back, suffer, turn back, worsen; SEE CONCEPT *698*

relate [v1] *give an account of*
break a story*, chronicle, clue one in*, depict, describe, detail, disclose, divulge, express, get off one's chest*, give the word*, impart, itemize, lay it on the line*, let one's hair down*, narrate, particularize, picture, present, recite, recount, rehearse, report, retell, reveal, run down, run

through, set forth, shoot the breeze*, sling*, spill, spill the beans*, spin a yarn*, state, tell, track, verbalize; SEE CONCEPT 55

relate [v2] *correlate, pertain*
affect, ally, appertain, apply, ascribe, assign, associate, bear upon, be joined with, be relevant to, bracket, combine, compare, concern, conjoin, connect, consociate, coordinate, correspond to, couple, credit, have reference to, have to do with, identify with, impute, interconnect, interdepend, interrelate, join, link, orient, orientate, pertain, refer, tie in with, touch, unite, yoke; SEE CONCEPT 532

related [adj] *connected, accompanying*
affiliated, agnate, akin, alike, allied, analogous, associated, cognate, complementary, concomitant, connate, connatural, consanguine, convertible, correlated, correspondent, dependent, enmeshed, fraternal, germane, incident, interchangeable, interconnected, interdependent, interrelated, intertwined, interwoven, in the same category, in touch with, joint, knit together*, like, linked, mutual, of that ilk, parallel, pertinent, reciprocal, relevant, similar, tied up; SEE CONCEPTS 487,573,577

relation [n] *connection, family connection*
affiliation, affinity, alliance, association, consanguinity, kin, kindred, kinship, kinsperson, liaison, propinquity, relationship, relative, sibling, similarity; SEE CONCEPTS 296,414,421,714

relationship [n] *connection; friendship*
accord, affair, affiliation, affinity, alliance, analogy, appositeness, association, bond, communication, conjunction, consanguinity, consociation, contact, contingency, correlation, dependence, dependency, exchange, homogeneity, hookup, interconnection, interrelation, interrelationship, kinship, liaison, likeness, link, marriage, nearness, network, parallel, pertinence, pertinency, proportion, rapport, ratio, relation, relativity, relevance, similarity, tie, tie-in, tie-up; SEE CONCEPTS 388,714

relative [adj1] *comparative, respective*
about, allied, analogous, approximate, associated, concerning, conditional, connected, contingent, corresponding, dependent, in regard to, near, parallel, proportionate, reciprocal, referring, related, relating to, reliant, with respect to; SEE CONCEPT 563

relative [adj2] *pertinent, applicable*
apposite, appropriate, appurtenant, apropos, contingent, dependent, germane, pertaining, referring, related, relevant; SEE CONCEPT 558

relative [n] *member of a family*
agnate, aunt, blood, brother-in-law, clansperson, cognate, connection, cousin, father, father-in-law, folk, folks, grandparents, great-grandparents, in-laws, kinsperson, mother, mother-in-law, nephew, niece, relation, sib*, sibling, sister-in-law, stepbrother, stepparent, stepsister, uncle; SEE CONCEPT 414

relatively [adv] *in or by comparison*
almost, approximately, comparably, comparatively, nearly, proportionately, rather, somewhat, to some extent; SEE CONCEPTS 544,772

relax [v1] *be or feel at ease*
breathe easy*, calm, calm down*, collect oneself, compose oneself, cool off*, ease off, feel at home, hang loose*, knock off*, laze, let oneself go*, lie down, loosen up, make oneself at home*, put one's feet up*, recline, repose, rest, settle back, simmer down*, sit around, sit back, soften, stop work, take a break*, take a breather*, take it easy*, take one's time*, take ten*, take time out*, tranquilize, unbend, unlax*, unwind; SEE CONCEPT 210

relax [v2] *diminish, lessen*
abate, ease, ease off, ebb, lax, let up, loose, loosen, lose speed, lower, mitigate, moderate, modify, modulate, reduce, relieve, remit, slack, slacken, slow, slow down, untighten, weaken; SEE CONCEPTS 240,698

relaxation [n] *entertainment; resting or recovering*
alleviation, amusement, assuagement, diversion, enjoyment, fun, leisure, loosening, mitigation, pleasure, reclining, recreation, refreshment, relief, repose, requiescence, rest; SEE CONCEPTS 210,292,363

relay [v] *pass on, transmit*
broadcast, carry, communicate, deliver, hand down, hand on, hand over, send, send forth, spread, transfer, turn over; SEE CONCEPT 143

release [n1] *delivery; dispensation*
absolution, acquittal, acquittance, charge, clemency, commute, deliverance, discharge, dispensation, emancipation, exemption, exoneration, floater, freedom, freeing, let-off*, liberation, liberty, lifeboat, lifesaver, manumission, relief, spring, turnout, walkout; SEE CONCEPTS 127,685

release [n2] *publication*
announcement, flash*, handout, issue, leak, news, notice, offering, proclamation, propaganda, publicity, story; SEE CONCEPTS 271,280

release [v] *let go, let out*
absolve, acquit, bail out, cast loose, clear, commute, deliver, discharge, disengage, dispense, drop, emancipate, exculpate, excuse, exempt, exonerate, extricate, free, give off, give out, go easy on, issue, leak, let off, let off steam*, let up on*, liberate, loose, loosen, manumit, open up, set at large, set free, set loose, spring, surrender, take out, turn loose, turn out, unbind, unchain, undo, unfasten, unfetter, unleash, unloose, unshackle, untie, vent, wipe slate clean*, yield; SEE CONCEPTS 50,60,88,127,143

relegate [v1] *assign, transfer*
accredit, charge, commend, commit, confide, consign, credit, delegate, entrust, hand over, pass on, refer, turn over; SEE CONCEPTS 41,143

relegate [v2] *banish, downgrade*
demote, deport, dismiss, displace, eject, exile, expatriate, expel, expulse, lag, ostracize, remove, throw out, transport; SEE CONCEPTS 30,121,211

relent [v] *die down; let up*
acquiesce, be merciful, capitulate, cave in*, change one's mind, come around, comply, cool it*, cry uncle*, die away, drop, ease, ease off, ease up on*, ebb, fall, fold, forbear, give in, give quarter*, give some slack*, give up, give way, go along with, go easy on*, have mercy, have pity, lay back, let go, let it happen*, lighten up*, mellow out*, melt, moderate, quit, relax, say uncle*, show mercy, slacken, slow, soften, subside, wane, weaken, yield; SEE CONCEPTS 35,698,776

relentless [adj1] *cruel, merciless*
adamant, bound, bound and determined, dead set on*, determined, dogged, ferocious, fierce, go

for broke*, grim, hang in*, hang-tough*, hard, harsh, implacable, inexorable, inflexible, inhuman, mortal, obdurate, pitiless, remorseless, rigid, rigorous, ruthless, single-minded, stiff, stop at nothing, strict, stringent, unappeasable, unbending, uncompromising, undeviating, unflinching, unforgiving, unrelenting, unstoppable, unyielding, vindictive; SEE CONCEPT *401*

relentless [*adj2*] *continuous, neverending*
incessant, nonstop, persistent, pertinacious, punishing, sustained, tenacious, unabated, unbroken, unfaltering, unflagging, unrelenting, unrelieved, unremitting, unstoppable; SEE CONCEPTS *326, 534,798*

relevant [*adj*] *appropriate; to the purpose*
accordant, admissible, ad rem, allowable, applicable, applicatory, apposite, appurtenant, apt, becoming, cognate, compatible, concerning, conformant, conforming, congruent, congruous, consistent, consonant, correlated, correspondent, fit, fitting, germane, harmonious, having direct bearing on, having to do with, important, material, on the button*, on the nose*, pat*, pertaining to, pertinent, pointful, proper, referring, related, relative, significant, suitable, suited to, to the point, weighty; SEE CONCEPT *558*

reliable [*adj*] *trustworthy*
candid, careful, certain, conscientious, constant, decent, decisive, definite, dependable, determined, devoted, faithful, firm, good, high-principled, honest, honorable, impeccable, incorrupt, loyal, okay, positive, predictable, proved, reputable, respectable, responsible, righteous, safe, sincere, solid, sound, stable, staunch, steadfast, steady, sterling, strong, sure, there, tried, tried-and-true*, true, true-blue*, true-hearted, trusty, unequivocal, unfailing, unimpeachable, upright, veracious; SEE CONCEPTS *535,542,544*

reliance [*n*] *confidence*
assurance, belief, credence, credit, dependence, faith, hope, interdependence, interdependency, stock, trust; SEE CONCEPT *689*

relic [*n*] *something saved from the past*
antique, antiquity, archaism, artifact, curio, curiosity, evidence, fragment, heirloom, keepsake, memento, memorial, monument, remains, remembrance, remembrancer, reminder, remnant, residue, ruins, scrap, souvenir, survival, testimonial, token, trace, trophy, vestige; SEE CONCEPT *446*

relief [*n*] *remedy, aid; relaxation*
abatement, allayment, alleviation, amelioration, appeasement, assistance, assuagement, balm, break, breather, cheer, comfort, comforting, consolation, contentment, cure, deliverance, diversion, ease, easement, extrication, fix, hand, happiness, help, let-up, lift, lightening, load off one's mind*, maintenance, mitigation, mollification, palliative, quick fix*, refreshment, release, remedy, remission, reprieve, respite, rest, restfulness, satisfaction, softening, solace, succor, support, sustenance; SEE CONCEPTS *681,712*

relieve [*v1*] *make less painful; let up on*
abate, allay, alleviate, appease, assuage, break, brighten, calm, comfort, console, cure, decrease, diminish, divert, dull, ease, free, interrupt, lighten, mitigate, moderate, mollify, palliate, quiet, relax, salve, slacken, soften, solace, soothe, subdue, take load off one's chest*,

take load off one's mind*, temper, vary; SEE CONCEPTS *244,700*

relieve [*v2*] *help; give assistance*
aid, assist, bring aid, give a break*, give a hand*, give a rest, spell, stand in for, substitute for, succor, support, sustain, take over from, take the place of; SEE CONCEPT *110*

relieve [*v3*] *remove blame, responsibility*
absolve, deliver, discharge, disembarrass, disencumber, dismiss, dispense, excuse, exempt, force to resign, free, let off, privilege, pull, release, spare, throw out, unburden, yank*; SEE CONCEPTS *50,88,351*

religion [*n*] *belief in divinity; system of beliefs*
church, communion, creed, cult, denomination, devotion, doctrine, higher power, morality, myth, mythology, observance, orthodoxy, pietism, piety, prayer, preference, religiosity, rites, ritual, sacrifice, sanctification, sect, spirituality, spiritual-mindedness, standards, superstition, theology, veneration; SEE CONCEPTS *368,689*

religious [*adj1*] *concerning belief in divinity*
believing, born-again*, canonical, churchgoing, churchly, clerical, deistic, devotional, devout, divine, doctrinal, ecclesiastical, god-fearing, godly, holy, ministerial, moral, orthodox, pietistic, pious, pontifical, prayerful, priestly, pure, reverent, righteous, sacerdotal, sacred, sacrosanct, saintlike, saintly, scriptural, sectarian, spiritual, supernatural, theistic, theological; SEE CONCEPTS *536,545*

religious [*adj2*] *conscientious, scrupulous*
exact, faithful, fastidious, meticulous, punctilious, rigid, rigorous, steadfast, unerring, unswerving; SEE CONCEPT *538*

relinquish [*v*] *give up, let go*
abandon, abdicate, abnegate, back down, cast, cast off, cede, cut loose*, desert, discard, ditch*, drop, drop like hot potato*, drop out, dump*, forbear, forgo, forsake, forswear, hand over, kick, kiss good-bye*, lay aside, leave, opt out, quit, quit cold turkey*, release, renounce, repudiate, resign, retire from, sacrifice, shed, stand down, surrender, swear off*, take the oath*, take the pledge*, vacate, waive, withdraw, yield; SEE CONCEPTS *119,127,234*

relish [*n*] *great appreciation of something*
appetite, bias, delectation, diversion, enjoying, enjoyment, fancy, flair, flavor, fondness, gusto, heart, leaning, liking, love, loving, palate, partiality, penchant, pleasure, predilection, prejudice, propensity, sapidity, sapor, savor, smack, stomach, tang, taste, zest; SEE CONCEPTS *20,32*

relish [*v*] *look forward to; appreciate*
admire, be fond of, cherish, delight in, dig*, enjoy, fancy, go, go for*, like, luxuriate in, mind, prefer, revel in, savor, taste; SEE CONCEPT *32*

reluctant [*adj*] *unenthusiastic, unwilling*
afraid, averse, backward, calculating, cautious, chary, circumspect, demurring, diffident, discouraged, disheartened, disinclined, grudging, hanging back, hesitant, hesitating, indisposed, involuntary, laggard, loath, opposed, queasy, recalcitrant, remiss, shy, slack, slow, squeamish, tardy, uncertain, uneager, wary; SEE CONCEPT *401*

rely [*v*] *have confidence in*
await, be confident of, believe in, be sure of, bet, bet bottom dollar on*, build, calculate,

re
re

commit, confide, count, depend, entrust, expect, gamble on, have faith in, hope, lay money on*, lean, look, reckon, ride on coattails*, swear by*, trust; SEE CONCEPTS 12,26

remain [v] *stay, wait*
abide, be left, bide, bivouac, bunk*, cling, continue, delay, dwell, endure, freeze, go on, halt, hang, hang out, hold over, hold the fort*, hover, inhabit, keep on, last, linger, live, lodge, make camp, nest, outlast, outlive, pause, perch, persist, prevail, put on hold, remain standing, reside, rest, roost, sit out, sit through, sit tight*, sojourn, squat, stand, stay behind, stay in, stay over, stay put, stick around, stop, survive, tarry, visit, wait; SEE CONCEPTS 23,239,681,804

remainder [n] *balance, residue*
bottom of barrel*, butt, carry-over, detritus, dregs, excess, fragment, garbage, hangover*, heel, junk, leavings, leftover, obverse, oddment, odds and ends*, overplus, refuse, relic, remains, remnant, residuum, rest, ruins, salvage, scrap, stump, surplus, trace, vestige, waste, wreck, wreckage; SEE CONCEPTS 260,835

remark [n] *comment, observation*
acknowledgment, annotation, assertion, attention, back talk, bon mot*, cognizance, comeback, commentary, conclusion, consideration, crack*, declaration, elucidation, exegesis, explanation, explication, exposition, expression, gloss, heed, illustration, interpretation, mention, mind, note, notice, obiter dictum, observance, observation, opinion, point, recognition, reflection, regard, saying, statement, talk, thought, two cents' worth*, utterance, wisecrack, witticism, word; SEE CONCEPTS 51,278

remark [v] *notice and comment*
animadvert, behold, catch, commentate, crack*, declare, descry, espy, heed, make out, mark, mention, mouth off*, note, observe, pass comment, perceive, pick up on, reflect, regard, say, see, speak, spot, state, take note, take notice, utter, wisecrack; SEE CONCEPTS 38,51,626

remarkable [adj] *extraordinary, unusual*
arresting, arrestive, conspicuous, curious, distinguished, exceptional, famous, gilt-edged*, greatest, important, impressive, marked, miraculous, momentous, notable, noteworthy, noticeable, odd, outstanding, peculiar, phenomenal, preeminent, primo*, prominent, rare, salient, signal, significant, singular, smashing, solid, splashy*, strange, striking, super, surprising, uncommon, uncustomary, unique, unordinary, unwonted, weighty, wicked*, wonderful, world class*, zero cool*; SEE CONCEPT 574

remedial [adj] *healing, restorative*
alleviative, antidotal, antiseptic, corrective, curative, curing, healthful, health-giving, invigorating, medicating, medicinal, purifying, recuperative, reformative, remedying, repairing, restitutive, restorative, sanative, sanatory, solving, soothing, therapeutic, tonic, treating, vulnerary, wholesome; SEE CONCEPT 537

remedy [n] *cure, solution*
antidote, assistance, biologic, corrective, counteractant, counteraction, counteractive, counteragent, countermeasure, counterstep, cure-all*, drug, elixir, fix, improvement, medicament, medicant, medicine, panacea, pharmaceutical, pharmacon, physic, pill, quick fix*, redress, relief, restorative, support, therapy, treatment; SEE CONCEPTS 307,311,693,712

remedy [v] *fix, cure*
aid, alleviate, ameliorate, amend, assuage, attend, change, clean up, clean up one's act*, control, correct, debug*, doctor, ease, fiddle with, fix up, go over, heal, help, launder, make up for, mitigate, palliate, pick up, put right, recalibrate, rectify, redress, reform, relieve, renew, repair, restore, revise, right, scrub, set right, set to rights*, shape up, solve, soothe, square*, square up*, straighten out, treat, upgrade; SEE CONCEPTS 126,212,310

remember [v] *keep in mind; summon into mind*
bear in mind, bethink, brood over, call to mind, call up, cite, commemorate, conjure up, dig into the past*, dwell upon, educe, elicit, enshrine, extract, fix in the mind, flash on*, get, go back, have memories, hold dear*, keep forever, know by heart*, learn, look back, memorialize, memorize, mind, nail down*, recall, recognize, recollect, refresh memory, relive, remind, reminisce, retain, retrospect, revive, revoke, ring a bell*, strike a note*, summon up, think back, treasure; SEE CONCEPT 40

remembrance [n1] *memory, recollection*
afterthought, anamnesis, flash*, flashback*, hindsight*, mental image, mind, recall, recognition, reconstruction, regard, reminiscence, retrospect, thought; SEE CONCEPTS 40,529

remembrance [n2] *gift, testimonial*
commemoration, favor, keepsake, memento, memorial, monument, present, relic, remembrancer, reminder, reward, souvenir, token, trophy; SEE CONCEPT 337

remind [v] *awaken memories of something*
admonish, advise, bethink, bring back to, bring to mind, call attention, call to mind, call up, caution, cite, emphasize, give a cue*, hint, imply, intimate, jog one's memory*, make one remember, make one think, mention, note, point out, prod, prompt, put in mind, recall, recollect, refresh memory, remember, reminisce, retain, retrospect, revive, stir up, stress, suggest, warn; SEE CONCEPTS 7,19,22,40,78

reminder [n] *warning, notice; keepsake*
admonition, expression, gesture, hint, indication, intimation, memento, memo, memorandum, memorial, note, notice, relic, remembrance, remembrancer, sign, souvenir, suggestion, token, trinket, trophy; SEE CONCEPTS 271,278,529

reminisce [v] *go over in one's memory*
bethink, call up, cite, hark back, live in the past, look back, mind, muse over, recall, recollect, remember, remind, retain, retrospect, review, revive, think back; SEE CONCEPTS 17,40

reminiscent [adj] *suggestive of something in the past*
bringing to mind, evocative, implicative, mnemonic, nostalgic, recollective, redolent, remindful, similar; SEE CONCEPT 529

remiss [adj] *careless, thoughtless*
any old way*, any which way*, asleep at switch*, asleep on job*, behindhand, culpable, daydreaming, defaultant, delinquent, derelict, dilatory, disregardful, fainéant, forgetful, heedless, inattentive, indifferent, indolent, lackadaisical, lax, lazy, neglectful, negligent, regardless, slack, slapdash, slipshod, sloppy, slothful, slow,

tardy, uninterested, unmindful, woolgathering*; SEE CONCEPT 401

remission [n1] *acquittal, pardon*
absolution, amnesty, discharge, excuse, exemption, exoneration, forgiveness, indulgence, mercy, pardon, release, reprieve; SEE CONCEPT 685

remission [n2] *pause; lessening*
abatement, abeyance, alleviation, amelioration, break, decrease, delay, diminution, ebb, interruption, let-up, lull, moderation, reduction, relaxation, release, respite, suspension; SEE CONCEPTS 303,698,807

remit [v1] *send, transfer*
address, consign, dispatch, forward, mail, make payment, pay, post, route, settle, ship, square, transmit; SEE CONCEPTS 217,341

remit [v2] *stop, postpone*
abate, absolve, alleviate, amnesty, cancel, condone, decrease, defer, delay, desist, diminish, dwindle, ease up, excuse, exonerate, fall away, forbear, forgive, halt, hold off, hold up, intermit, mitigate, moderate, modify, modulate, pardon, prorogue, put off, reduce, relax, release, repeal, reprieve, rescind, respite, shelve, sink, slack, slacken, soften, stay, suspend, wane, weaken; SEE CONCEPTS 234,698

remnant [n] *leftover part*
balance, bit, dregs, dross, end, end piece, excess, fragment, hangover*, heel, leavings, lees, leftovers, odds and ends*, orts, part, particle, piece, portion, remainder, remains, residual, residue, residuum, rest, rump, scrap, shred, strip, surplus, survival, vestige; SEE CONCEPTS 260,835

remodel [v] *reconstruct*
do up*, fix, fix up, make over, modernize, overhaul, reassemble, rebuild, recast, recondition, recreate, redesign, refurbish, rehabilitate, rejuvenate, remake, renovate, repair, restore, revamp, upgrade; SEE CONCEPTS 84,168,171

remonstrate [v] *argue against anim*
advert, blame, censure, challenge, combat, complain, criticize, decry, demur, deprecate, disapprove, disparage, dispute, dissent, except, expostulate, fight, find fault, frown upon, inveigh, kick*, nag, object, oppose, pick at, protest, rain, recriminate, resist, scold, sound off*, take exception, take issue, withstand; SEE CONCEPTS 46,52,54

remorse [n] *guilty or bad conscience*
anguish, attrition, compassion, compunction, contriteness, contrition, grief, guilt, pangs of conscience*, penance, penitence, penitency, pity, regret, remorsefulness, repentance, rue, ruefulness, self-reproach, shame, sorrow; SEE CONCEPTS 410,728

remorseful [adj] *guilty, ashamed*
apologetic, attritional, chastened, compunctious, conscience-stricken, contrite, guilt-ridden, mournful, penitent, penitential, regretful, repentant, rueful, sad, self-reproachful, sorrowful, sorry; SEE CONCEPT 401

remorseless [adj] *without guilt in spite of wrongdoing*
avaricious, barbarous, bloody, callous, cruel, fierce, forbidding, greedy, grim, hard, hard-bitten, hardened, hard-hearted, harsh, impenitent, implacable, inexorable, inhuman, inhumane, insensitive, intolerant, merciless, murderous, obdurate, pitiless, relentless, rigorous, ruthless,

sanguinary, savage, shameless, sour, tough, tyrannical, uncompassionate, uncontrite, unforgiving, unmerciful, unregenerate, unrelenting, unremitting, unrepenting, unyielding, vindictive; SEE CONCEPT 401

remote [adj1] *out-of-the-way; in the distance*
alien, back, backwoods, beyond, boondocks*, devious, distant, far, faraway, far-flung, far-off, foreign, frontier, godforsaken*, god-knows-where*, in a backwater*, inaccessible, isolated, lonely, lonesome, middle of nowhere*, obscure, off-lying, off the beaten path*, outlandish, outlying, private, removed, retired, secluded, secret, undiscovered, unknown, unsettled, wild; SEE CONCEPT 583

remote [adj2] *irrelevant, unrelated*
abstracted, alien, alone, apart, detached, exclusive, extraneous, extrinsic, farfetched, foreign, immaterial, inappropriate, indirect, nongermane, obscure, outside, pointless, removed, strange, unconnected; SEE CONCEPTS 564,575

remote [adj3] *unlikely, improbable*
doubtful, dubious, faint, implausible, inconsiderable, meager, negligible, off, outside, poor, slender, slight, slim, small; SEE CONCEPT 552

remote [adj4] *cold, detached; unapproachable*
abstracted, aloof, casual, cool*, disinterested, distant, faraway, icy, incurious, indifferent, introspective, introverted, laid-back*, offish, putting on airs, removed, reserved, standoffish, stuck up, uncommunicative, unconcerned, uninterested, uninvolved, uppity, withdrawn; SEE CONCEPTS 401,404

remove [v1] *lift or move object; take off, away*
abolish, abstract, amputate, carry away, carry off, cart off, clear away, cut out, delete, depose, detach, dethrone, dig out, discard, discharge, dislodge, dismiss, displace, disturb, do away with, doff, efface, eject, eliminate, erase, evacuate, expel, expunge, extract, get rid of, junk*, oust, pull out, purge, raise, relegate, rip out, separate, shed, ship, skim, strike out, take down, take out, tear out, throw out, transfer, transport, unload, unseat, uproot, wipe out*, withdraw; SEE CONCEPT 211

remove [v2] *do away with; kill*
assassinate, blot out*, clear away, dispose of, do away with, do in*, drag, drag down, efface, eliminate, eradicate, erase, exclude, execute, expunge, exterminate, extirpate, get rid of, liquidate, murder, obliterate, purge, scratch, sterilize, take down, take out, waste*, wipe out*; SEE CONCEPTS 121,252

remunerate [v] *compensate, reward*
accord, ante up*, award, dish out*, do business*, grant, guerdon, indemnify, pay, pay off, pay up, post, recompense, redress, reimburse, repay, requite, shell out*, spring for*, vouchsafe; SEE CONCEPT 341

renaissance [n] *rebirth*
awakening, invigoration, new dawn, reawakening, regeneration, rejuvenation, renascence, renewal, resurgence, revitalization, revival; SEE CONCEPTS 119,221

render [v1] *contribute*
cede, deliver, distribute, exchange, furnish, give, give back, give up, hand over, impart, make available, make restitution, minister, part with, pay, pay back, present, provide, relinquish, repay, restore, return, show, submit, supply, sur-

render, swap, tender, trade, turn over, yield; SEE CONCEPTS *108,140*

render [*v2*] *show; execute*
act, administer, administrate, carry out, delineate, depict, display, do, evince, exhibit, give, govern, image, interpret, limn, manifest, perform, picture, play, portray, present, represent; SEE CONCEPTS *91,261*

render [*v3*] *translate, explain*
construe, deliver, interpret, paraphrase, pass, put, reproduce, restate, reword, state, transcribe, transliterate, transpose, turn; SEE CONCEPTS *57,266*

rendezvous [*n1*] *get-together*
affair, appointment, assignation, blind date, date, double date, engagement, heavy date*, matinee, meet, meeting, one night stand*, tête-à-tête, tryst; SEE CONCEPT *384*

rendezvous [*n2*] *place for get-together*
gathering point, hangout*, haunt, love nest*, meeting place, purlieu, resort, spot, stomping ground*, venue, watering hole*; SEE CONCEPT *198*

rendezvous [*v*] *meet, often secretly*
assemble, be closeted, be reunited, collect, come together, congregate, congress, converge, forgather, gather, get-together, join up, meet behind closed doors*, meet privately, muster, raise, rally; SEE CONCEPT *384*

rendition [*n*] *explanation; interpretation*
arrangement, construction, delivery, depiction, execution, interpretation, performance, portrayal, presentation, reading, rendering, transcription, translation, version; SEE CONCEPTS *263,278*

renegade [*adj*] *rebellious*
apostate, backsliding, disloyal, dissident, heterodox, mutinous, outlaw, radical, reactionary, rebel, recreant, revolutionary, runaway, schismatic, traitorous, unfaithful, untraditional; SEE CONCEPTS *401,542*

renegade [*n*] *person who is rebellious*
abandoner, apostate, backslider, betrayer, defector, deserter, dissident, double-crosser*, escapee, exile, forsaker, fugitive, heretic, iconoclast, insurgent, mutineer, outlaw, rebel, recreant, refugee, runaway, schismatic, snake*, snake in the grass*, tergiversator, traitor, turnabout, turncoat; SEE CONCEPTS *359,412*

renege [*v*] *go back on one's word*
break one's promise, cop out*, default, reverse, weasel out*, welsh; SEE CONCEPTS *59,63,330*

renew [*v*] *start over; refurbish*
begin again, brace, breathe new life into*, bring up to date*, continue, exhilarate, extend, fix up, freshen, gentrify, go over, mend, modernize, overhaul, prolong, reaffirm, reawaken, recommence, recondition, recreate, reestablish, refit, refresh, regenerate, rehabilitate, reinvigorate, rejuvenate, remodel, renovate, reopen, repair, repeat, replace, replenish, restate, restock, restore, resume, resuscitate, retread, revitalize, revive, spruce, stimulate, transform; SEE CONCEPTS *35,202,221*

renounce [*v*] *abandon, reject*
abdicate, abjure, abnegate, abstain from, apostacize, arrogate, cast off, decline, defect, demit, deny, desert, disavow, discard, disclaim, disown, divorce oneself from*, drop out, dump*, eschew, forgo, forsake, forswear, give up, leave flat*, leave off, opt out, quit, rat*, recant, reject, relin-

quish, repudiate, resign, sell out*, spurn, swear off, take the pledge*, tergiversate, tergiverse, throw off, throw over, toss over, turn, waive, walk out on, wash hands of*; SEE CONCEPTS *30,54,195*

renovate [*v*] *fix up, modernize*
clean, cleanse, do*, do up*, face-lift*, gussy up*, make over, overhaul, reactivate, recondition, reconstitute, recreate, refit, reform, refresh, refurbish, rehabilitate, rekindle, remake, remodel, renew, repair, restore, resurrect, resuscitate, retread, retrieve, revamp, revitalize, revive, revivify, spruce, spruce up*, update; SEE CONCEPTS *168,177,202*

renown [*adj*] *fame*
acclaim, celebrity, distinction, éclat, eminence, glory, honor, illustriousness, kudos, luster, mark, note, notoriety, preeminence, prestige, prominence, prominency, rep*, reputation, repute, stardom; SEE CONCEPT *668*

renowned [*adj*] *famous*
acclaimed, celebrated, celebrious, distinguished, eminent, esteemed, extolled, famed, great, illustrious, in the limelight*, lauded, monster*, name*, notable, noted, of note, outstanding, praised, prominent, redoubted, signal, splashy, star, superstar, well-known; SEE CONCEPTS *568,574*

rent [*n1*] *fee paid for use, service, or privilege*
hire, lease, payment, rental, tariff; SEE CONCEPT *329*

rent [*n2*] *opening, split*
breach, break, chink, cleavage, crack, discord, dissension, division, faction, fissure, flaw, fracture, gash, hole, perforation, rift, rip, rupture, schism, slash, slit, tatter, tear; SEE CONCEPTS *513,665*

rent [*v*] *pay or charge fee for use, service, or privilege*
allow the use of, borrow, charter, contract, engage, hire, lease, lend, let, loan, make available, put on loan, sublet, take it; SEE CONCEPTS *89,115*

renunciation [*n*] *abandonment, rejection*
abdication, abjuration, abnegation, abstention, cancellation, denial, disavowal, disclaimer, eschewal, eschewing, forbearing, forswearing, giving up, rebuff, refusal, relinquishment, remission, renouncement, repeal, repudiation, resignation, sacrifice, self-abnegation, self-denial, self-sacrifice, spurning, surrender, veto, waiver, yielding; SEE CONCEPTS *30,54,195*

repair [*n*] *restoration, fixing*
adjustment, darn, improvement, mend, new part, overhaul, patch, reconstruction, reformation, rehabilitation, replacement, substitution; SEE CONCEPTS *513,700,824*

repair [*v1*] *fix, restore*
compensate for, correct, darn, debug*, doctor*, do up*, emend, fiddle with, give a face-lift*, heal, improve, make good, make up for, mend, overhaul, patch, patch up, put back together, put in order, put right, rebuild, recondition, recover, rectify, redress, reform, refresh, refurbish, rejuvenate, remedy, renew, renovate, restore, retread, retrieve, revamp, revive, right, settle, sew, square*, touch up; SEE CONCEPT *212*

repair [*v2*] *leave; retire*
apply, betake oneself, fare, go, head for, hie, journey, move, pass, proceed, process, push on,

recur, refer, remove, resort, run, set off for; travel, turn, wend, withdraw; SEE CONCEPT *195*

reparation [*n*] *compensation, amends*
adjustment, apology, atonement, damages, dues, emolument, expiation, indemnification, indemnity, making good, payment, penance, propitiation; quittance, recompense, redemption, redress, remuneration, renewal, repair, repayment, reprisal, requital, restitution, retribution, reward, satisfaction, settlement, squaring things*; SEE CONCEPTS *337,344,712*

repartee [*n*] *pleasant conversation*
answer, badinage, banter, bon mot*, comeback, humor, irony, persiflage, pleasantry, quip, raillery, rejoinder, reply, response, retort, riposte, sally, sarcasm, satire, wit, witticism, wittiness, wordplay; SEE CONCEPTS *45,56,266*

repast [*n*] *meal*
banquet, chow*, eats*, fare, feast, feed, food, grub*, mess, refection, refreshment, snack, spread, victuals; SEE CONCEPT *459*

repay [*v1*] *give back money or possession*
accord, award, balance, compensate, indemnify, make amends, make restitution, make up for, offset, pay back, pay dues, rebate, recompense, refund, reimburse, remunerate, requite, restore, return, reward, settle up, square*; SEE CONCEPTS *131,341*

repay [*v2*] *get even; obtain restitution for past injustice*
avenge, even the score, get back at, get revenge, make reprisal, pay back, reciprocate, requite, retaliate, return, return the compliment*, revenge, settle the score*, square accounts*; SEE CONCEPTS *7,19,246,384*

repeal [*n*] *cancellation*
abolition, abrogation, annulment, invalidation, nullification, rescinding, rescindment, rescission, revocation, withdrawal; SEE CONCEPTS *121,318,685*

repeal [*v*] *declare null and void*
abolish, abrogate, annul, back out, backpedal*, blow, call off*, cancel, countermand, dismantle, invalidate, kill*, KO*, lift, nix*, nullify, opt out, recall, renig, rescind, reverse, revoke, scrub, set aside, shoot down, stand down, throw over, vacate, void, wash out, weasel out*, wipe out, withdraw, worm out*, X-out*, zap*; SEE CONCEPTS *50,88,121,317*

repeat [*n*] *something done over; duplicate*
echo, recapitulation, reiteration, repetition, replay, reproduction, rerun, reshowing; SEE CONCEPT *695*

repeat [*v*] *duplicate, do again*
chime, come again, din, ditto*, drum into*, duplicate, echo, go over again, hold over, imitate, ingeminate, iterate, make like*, occur again, play back, play over, quote, read back, reappear, recapitulate, recast, reciprocate, recite, reconstruct, recrudesce, recur, redo, refashion, reform, rehash*, rehearse, reissue, reiterate, relate, remake, renew, reoccur, replay, reprise, reproduce, rerun, resay, reshow, restate, retell, return, revert, revolve, rework*, run over, sing same old song*; SEE CONCEPTS *91,111,171*

repeatedly [*adv*] *over and over again*
again, again and again, frequently, many a time, many times, much, oft, often, oftentimes, ofttimes, regularly, time after time, time and again; SEE CONCEPT *553*

repel [*v1*] *push away; repulse*
beat back, beat off, brush off, buck, cast aside, chase away, check, confront, cool*, cut, decline, dismiss, disown, dispute, drive away, drive back, drive off, duel, fend off, fight, force back, force off, give cold shoulder to*, hold back, hold off, keep at arm's length*, keep at bay*, keep off, kick, knock down, oppose, parry, push back, put down, put to flight, rebuff, rebut, refuse, reject, resist, stand up against, stave off, traverse, turn down, ward off, withstand; SEE CONCEPTS *30,208*

repel [*v2*] *induce aversion*
disgust, give a pain in neck*, make sick*, offend, put off*, reluct, repulse, revolt, sicken, turn off*, turn one's stomach*; SEE CONCEPTS *7,19,303*

repent [*v*] *ask forgiveness*
apologize, atone, be ashamed, be contrite, be sorry, bewail, deplore, feel remorse, have qualms, lament, reform, regret, relent, reproach oneself, rue, see error of ways*, show penitence, sorrow; SEE CONCEPTS *48,410*

repentance [*n*] *feeling bad for past action*
attrition, compunction, conscience, contriteness, contrition, grief, guilt, penitence, penitency, regret, remorse, rue, ruth, self-reproach, sorriness, sorrow; SEE CONCEPTS *410,728*

repercussion [*n*] *consequence*
backlash, chain reaction, echo, effect, fallout, feedback, flak*, follow-through*, follow-up, impact, imprint, influence, kickback*, mark, reaction, rebound, recoil, re-echo, result, reverberation, side effect, spinoff*, waves*; SEE CONCEPT *230*

repertory [*n*] *collection*
bit, cache, depot, list, range, rep*, repertoire, repository, routine, schtick*, stock, stockroom, store, storehouse, stunt*, supply; SEE CONCEPTS *263,432,712*

repetition [*n*] *duplication; doing again*
alliteration, broken record*, chant, chorus, copy, echo, encore, ingemination, iteracy, iterance, iteration, litany, paraphrase, periodicity, perseveration, practice, reappearance, recapitulation, recital, recurrence, redundancy, rehearsal, reiteration, relation, renewal, reoccurrence, repeat, repetitiousness, replication, report, reproduction, restatement, return, rhythm, rote, tautology; SEE CONCEPT *695*

repetitious [*adj*] *wordy, tedious*
alliterative, boring, dull, echoic, iterant, iterative, long-winded, plangent, pleonastic, prolix, recapitulatory, redundant, reiterative, repeating, repetitive, resonant, tautological, verbose, windy; SEE CONCEPT *553*

replace [*v*] *take the place of; put in place of*
alter, back up, change, compensate, displace, fill in, follow, front for*, give back, mend, oust, outplace, patch, pinch hit for*, put back, reconstitute, recoup, recover, redeem, redress, reestablish, refund, regain, reimburse, reinstate, repay, restitute, restore, retrieve, ring, ring in, shift, sit in, stand in, stand in lieu of, step into shoes of*, sub*, substitute, succeed, supersede, supplant, supply, swap places, take out, take over, take over from; SEE CONCEPTS *104,128, 211,697*

replenish [*v*] *fill, stock*
furnish, make up, provide, provision, refill, refresh, reload, renew, replace, restock, restore, stock, top; SEE CONCEPTS *140,209*

re
re

replete [*adj*] *full, well-stocked*
abounding, abundant, alive, awash, brimful, brimming, charged, chock-full*, complete, crammed, crowded, filled, full up*, glutted, gorged, jammed, jam-packed, lavish, loaded, luxurious, overfed, overflowing, packed, plenteous, rife, sated, satiated, stuffed, swarming, teeming, thronged, well-provided; SEE CONCEPTS *483,740*

replica [*n*] *duplicate*
carbon, carbon copy, chip off old block*, clone, copy, ditto*, dupe*, facsimile, flimsy*, imitation, likeness, lookalike, mimeo, mimic, miniature, model, photocopy, reduplication, repeat, replication, repro, reproduction, stat, Xerox*; SEE CONCEPTS *260,670,686*

reply [*n*] *answer*
acknowledgment, antiphon, back talk*, comeback, counter, echo, feedback, knee-jerk reaction*, lip*, reaction, reciprocation, rejoinder, respond, response, retaliation, retort, return, riposte, sass*, snappy comeback*, vibes*, wisecrack; SEE CONCEPT *278*

reply [*v*] *answer*
acknowledge, be in touch*, come back*, counter, echo, feedback, field the question*, get back to, react, reciprocate, rejoin, respond, retaliate, retort, return, riposte, shoot back*, squelch*, top*, write back; SEE CONCEPT *278*

report [*n1*] *account, story*
address, announcement, article, blow by blow*, brief, broadcast, cable, chronicle, communication, communique, declaration, description, detail, digest, dispatch, handout, history, hot wire*, information, message, narration, narrative, news, note, opinion, outline, paper, picture, piece, precis, proclamation, pronouncement, recital, record, relation, release, résumé, rundown, scoop*, statement, summary, tale, telegram, tidings, version, wire, word*, write-up; SEE CONCEPTS *274,282,283*

report [*n2*] *gossip, talk*
advice, blow by blow*, buzz*, canard, chat, chatter, chitchat, comment, conversation, cry*, dirt*, earful, grapevine*, hash*, hearsay, intelligence, murmur, news, prating, rumble*, rumor, scandal, scuttlebutt*, small talk*, speech, tattle, the latest*, tidings, whispering, word*; SEE CONCEPTS *51,278*

report [*n3*] *loud noise*
bang, blast, boom, crack, crash, detonation, discharge, explosion, reverberation, sound; SEE CONCEPT *595*

report [*n4*] *reputation*
character, esteem, fame, name, regard, rep*, repute; SEE CONCEPT *388*

report [*v1*] *communicate information, knowledge*
account for, advise, air, announce, bring word, broadcast, cable, circulate, cover, declare, describe, detail, disclose, document, enunciate, give an account of, give the facts, impart, inform, inscribe, itemize, list, make known, make public, mention, narrate, note, notify, pass on, present, proclaim, promulgate, provide details, publish, recite, record, recount, rehearse, relate, relay, retail, reveal, set forth, spread, state, summarize, telephone, tell, trumpet, wire, write up; SEE CONCEPT *60*

report [*v2*] *present oneself*
appear, arrive, be at hand, be present, clock in*, come, get to, reach, show, show up, turn up*; SEE CONCEPT *159*

reporter [*n*] *person who informs*
anchor, anchorperson, announcer, columnist, correspondent, cub*, editor, ink slinger*, interviewer, journalist, legperson*, newscaster, newshound*, newsperson, newswriter, press person, scribe, scrivener, stringer, writer; SEE CONCEPTS *348,356*

repose [*n*] *restfulness; calm*
ease, inaction, inactivity, leisure, peace, quiet, quietness, quietude, refreshment, relaxation, relaxing, renewal, requiescence, respite, rest, restoration, sleep, slumber, stillness, tranquillity; SEE CONCEPTS *410,681,720*

repose [*v*] *relax; recline*
deposit, lay down, lie, lie down, loaf, loll, lounge, place, rest, settle, settle down, slant, sleep, slumber, stretch, stretch out, take it easy, tilt; SEE CONCEPTS *154,210*

repository [*n*] *warehouse*
archive, depository, depot, magazine, safe, stockroom, storage place, storehouse, store room, vault; SEE CONCEPTS *435,439,449*

repossess [*v*] *take back*
get back, obtain again, reacquire, recapture, reclaim, recover, retake, retrieve; SEE CONCEPTS *120,183*

reprehensible [*adj*] *very bad; shameful*
amiss, blamable, blameworthy, censurable, condemnable, culpable, delinquent, demeritorious, discreditable, disgraceful, errant, erring, guilty, ignoble, objectionable, opprobrious, remiss, sinful, unholy, unworthy, wicked; SEE CONCEPT *571*

represent [*v1*] *present image of; symbolize*
act as, act as broker, act for, act in place of, appear as, assume the role of, be, be agent for, be attorney for, be proxy for, betoken, body, buy for, copy, correspond to, do business for, emblematize, embody, enact, epitomize, equal, equate, exemplify, exhibit, express, factor, hold office, imitate, impersonate, mean, perform, personify, play the part, produce, put on, reproduce, sell for, serve, serve as, show, speak for, stage, stand for, steward, substitute, symbolize, typify; SEE CONCEPTS *87,317,682,716*

represent [*v2*] *depict, show*
body forth, delineate, denote, describe, design, designate, display, draft, enact, evoke, exhibit, express, hint, illustrate, interpret, limn, mirror, narrate, outline, picture, portray, realize, relate, render, reproduce, run down, run through, sketch, suggest, track; SEE CONCEPTS *138,261*

representative [*adj*] *characteristic, typical*
adumbrative, archetypal, classic, classical, delineative, depictive, emblematic, evocative, exemplary, ideal, illustrative, model, presentational, prototypal, prototypical, quintessential, rep*, symbolic, symbolical; SEE CONCEPTS *487,573*

representative [*n1*] *person who acts in the stead of another*
agent, assemblyperson, attorney, commissioner, congressperson, councilor, councilperson, counselor, delegate, deputy, lawyer, legislator, member, messenger, proxy, rep*, salesperson, senator, spokesperson; SEE CONCEPTS *348,354*

representative [*n2*] *typical example*
archetype, case, case history, embodiment, epitome, exemplar, illustration, instance, personifi-

cation, sample, sampling, specimen, type; SEE CONCEPT 686

repress [v] *keep back, hold in*
black out*, bottle, chasten, check, collect, compose, control, cool*, cork*, crush, curb, gridlock*, hinder, hold back, inhibit, jam up, keep in, keep in check, keep under wraps*, kill*, lock, master, muffle, overcome, overpower, quash, quelch, quell, rein, restrain, shush, silence, simmer down*, smother, squelch, stifle, subdue, subjugate, suppress, swallow, throw cold water on*, tie up*; SEE CONCEPTS 121,130

reprieve [n] *relief of blame, responsibility*
abatement, abeyance, absolution, acquittal, alleviation, amnesty, anchor*, clearance, clemency, commute, deferment, freeing, let-up*, lifeboat*, lifesaver*, mitigation, palliation, pardon, postponement, release, remission, respite, spring*, stay, suspension, truce; SEE CONCEPTS 318,685

reprieve [v] *relieve of blame, responsibility*
abate, absolve, allay, alleviate, amnesty, excuse, forgive, grant a stay, let go, let off, let off the hook*, let off this time*, let up on*, mitigate, palliate, pardon, postpone, remit, respite; SEE CONCEPTS 50,88,317

reprimand [n] *oral punishment*
admonishment, admonition, bawling out*, blame, calling down*, castigation, censure, chiding, comeuppance, dressing-down*, going over*, grooming, hard time*, lecture, piece of one's mind*, ragging*, rap*, rebuke, reprehension, reproof, scolding, slap on wrist*, talking-to, telling-off*, tongue-lashing, what for*; SEE CONCEPTS 123,278

reprimand [v] *blame, scold*
admonish, call on the carpet*, castigate, censure, check, chew out*, chide, come down on*, criticize, denounce, dress down*, give piece of one's mind*, give the dickens*, lecture, lesson, light into*, lower the boom*, monish, rap, rebuke, reprehend, reproach, reprove, take to task*, tell off, tick off*, upbraid; SEE CONCEPTS 44,52

reprisal [n] *revenge*
avengement, avenging, counterblow, counterstroke, eye for an eye*, paying back, requital, retaliation, retribution, vengeance; SEE CONCEPT 384

reproach [n] *strong criticism; dishonor*
abuse, admonishment, admonition, blame, blemish, censure, chiding, condemnation, contempt, disapproval, discredit, disgrace, disrepute, ignominy, indignity, obloquy, odium, opprobrium, rap*, rebuke, reprehension, reprimand, reproof, scorn, shame, slight, slur, stain, stigma; SEE CONCEPTS 44,52,123,388

reproach [v] *find fault with*
abuse, admonish, blame, call down, call to task*, cavil, censure, chide, condemn, criticize, defame, discredit, disparage, give comeuppance*, give the devil*, jawbone*, lay on*, lesson, rake, ream, rebuke, reprehend, reprimand, reprove, scold, sit on*, take to task, trim, upbraid; SEE CONCEPTS 44,52

reprobate [adj] *shameless*
bad, corrupt, degenerate, foul, immoral, improper, incorrigible, lewd, rude, sinful, unprincipled, vile, wanton, wicked; SEE CONCEPTS 401,545

reproduce [v1] *make more copies of*
carbon*, clone, copy, do again, dupe*, duplicate,

echo, emulate, engross, follow, imitate, knock off, manifold, match, mimeo*, mimeograph, mirror, parallel, photocopy, photograph, photostat, pirate, portray, print, reawaken, recount, recreate, redo, reduplicate, reenact, reflect, relive, remake, repeat, replicate, represent, reprint, restamp, revive, stereotype, transcribe, type, Xerox*; SEE CONCEPTS 111,171

reproduce [v2] *make something new; give birth*
bear, beget, breed, engender, father, fecundate, generate, hatch, impregnate, multiply, procreate, produce young, progenerate, proliferate, propagate, repopulate, sire, spawn; SEE CONCEPTS 173,251,374

reproduction [n] *something duplicated; duplication*
breeding, carbon*, carbon copy, chip off old block*, clone, copy, ditto*, dupe*, facsimile, fake, flimsy, generation, imitation, increase, look-alike, mimeo*, mimeograph, mirror image*, multiplication, offprint, photocopy, photograph, Photostat, pic*, picture, portrayal, print, procreation, proliferation, propagation, recreation, reduplication, reenactment, renewal, replica, replication, reprinting, repro*, revival, stat, transcription, twin, Xerox*, X-ray*; SEE CONCEPTS 173,625,670,716

reprove [v] *rebuke*
admonish, bawl out*, berate, castigate, censure, chew out*, chide, condemn, jump down one's throat*, lambaste, lay into*, lecture, read the riot act*, reprimand, reproach, scold, take to task*, upbraid; SEE CONCEPTS 44,52

repudiate [v] *reject; turn one's back on*
abandon, abjure, apostatize, banish, be against, break with, cast, cast off, cut off, decline, default, defect, demur, deny, desert, disacknowledge, disapprove, disavow, discard, disclaim, dishonor, disinherit, dismiss, disown, dump, flush*, fly in the face of*, forsake, nix*, oust, rat*, recant, refuse, renounce, repeal, reprobate, rescind, retract, reverse, revoke, spurn, tergiversate, tergiverse, turn, turn down, wash one's hands of*; SEE CONCEPTS 13,21,30

repugnant [adj] *bad, obnoxious; hostile*
abhorrent, abominable, adverse, against, alien, antagonistic, antipathetic, averse, conflicting, contradictory, counter, creepy*, different, disagreeable, disgusting, distasteful, extraneous, extrinsic, foreign, foul, hateful, horrid, incompatible, inconsistent, inconsonant, inimical, in opposition, invidious, loathsome, nasty, nauseating, noisome, objectionable, odious, offensive, opposed, opposite, repellent, revolting, revulsive, sickening, unconformable, unfitted, unfriendly, vile; SEE CONCEPTS 401,564,571

repulse [n] *snub; rejection*
brush-off*, check, cold shoulder*, defeat, disappointment, failure, nix*, nothing doing*, rebuff, refusal, reverse, slap in the face*, spurning, thumbs down*, turndown; SEE CONCEPTS 388,674

repulse [v1] *push away*
beat off, brush off*, check, defeat, drive back, fend off, fight off, heave-ho*, hold off, keep off, kick in the teeth*, nix*, overthrow, push back, put down, rebuff, rebut, reject, repel, resist, set back, stave off, throw back, ward off; SEE CONCEPTS 96,208

re
re

repulse [v2] *make sick*
disdain, disgust, disregard, give a pain*, rebuff, refuse, reject, reluct, repel, revolt, sicken, snub, spurn, turn down, turn off; SEE CONCEPTS 21,410

repulsion [n] *hatred, disgust*
abhorrence, abomination, antipathy, aversion, denial, detestation, disrelish, distaste, hate, horror, loathing, malice, rebuff, refusal, repugnance, repugnancy, resentment, revolt, revulsion, snub; SEE CONCEPT 29

repulsive [adj] *very disgusting, offensive*
abhorrent, abominable, animal*, creepy*, disagreeable, distasteful, forbidding, foul, gross, hateful, hideous, horrid, loathsome, nasty, nauseating, noisome, objectionable, obnoxious, odious, off-putting, pugnacious, repellent, revolting, sickening, sleazy*, ugly, undesirable, unpleasant, unsightly, vile; SEE CONCEPTS 529,571,579

reputable [adj] *worthy of respect*
acclaimed, celebrated, conscientious, constant, creditable, dependable, distinguished, eminent, esteemed, estimable, excellent, · fair, faithful, famed, famous, favored, good, high-principled, high-ranking, honest, honorable, honored, illustrious, in high favor, just, legitimate, notable, of good repute, popular, prominent, redoubted, reliable, renowned, respectable, righteous, salt of the earth*, sincere, straightforward, trustworthy, truthful, upright, well-known, well-thought-of; SEE CONCEPTS 545,567,574

reputation [n] *commonly held opinion of person's character*
acceptability, account, approval, authority, character, credit, dependability, distinction, éclat, eminence, esteem, estimation, fame, favor, honor, influence, mark*, name*, notoriety, opinion, position, prestige, privilege, prominence, rank, regard, reliability, renown, rep*, report, repute, respectability, standing, stature, trustworthiness, weight; SEE CONCEPTS 388,411,689

reputed [adj] *believed*
accounted, alleged, assumed, conjectural, considered, deemed, estimated, gossiped, held, hypothetical, ostensible, putative, reckoned, regarded, reported, rumored, said, seeming, supposed, suppositional, suppositious, supposititious, suppositive, suppository, thought; SEE CONCEPT 529

request [n] *question or petition*
appeal, application, asking, begging, call, commercial, demand, desire, entreaty, inquiry, invitation, offer, prayer, recourse, requisition, solicitation, suit, supplication; SEE CONCEPT 662

request [v] *ask for*
appeal, apply, beg, beseech, bespeak, call for, demand, desire, entreat, hit, hit up for*, hold out for*, hustle*, inquire, petition, pray, promote, put in for*, requisition, seek, solicit, sponge*, sue, supplicate, touch; SEE CONCEPT 53

requiem [n] *hymn, mass*
canticle, ceremony, chant, death song, dirge, elegy, eulogy, funeral hymn, liturgy, memorial service, monody, psalm, religious song, ritual, sermon, threnody, worship; SEE CONCEPTS 262,368,595

require [v1] *need, want*
crave, depend upon, desire, feel necessity for, have need, hurting for, lack, miss, stand in need, wish; SEE CONCEPTS 20,646

require [v2] *ask, demand; necessitate*
assert oneself, beg, beseech, bid, call for, call upon, cause, challenge, claim, command, compel, constrain, crave, demand, direct, enjoin, entail, exact, expect, insist upon, instruct, involve, look for, obligate, oblige, order, postulate, push for, request, requisition, solicit, take; SEE CONCEPTS 53,646

required/requisite [adj] *necessary*
appropriate, called for, compulsatory, compulsory, condign, demanded, deserved, due, enforced, essential, imperative, imperious, indispensable, just, mandatory, needed, needful, obligatory, prerequisite, prescribed, recommended, right, rightful, set, suitable, unavoidable, vital; SEE CONCEPT 546

requirement/requisite [n] *necessity, want*
claim, compulsion, concern, condition, demand, desideratum, element, engrossment, essential, exaction, exigency, extremity, fulfillment, fundamental, imperative, lack, must, need, obligation, obsession, pinch, precondition, preliminary, preoccupation, prepossession, prerequisite, prescription, provision, proviso, qualification, sine qua non, specification, stipulation, terms, urgency, vital part; SEE CONCEPTS 646,709

requisition [n] *demand; application for need*
appropriation, call, commandeering, demand, occupation, request, seizure, summons, takeover; SEE CONCEPT 662

requisition [v] *ask for; apply for something needed*
buy, call for, challenge, claim, demand, exact, order, postulate, put dibs on*, put in for, request, require, solicit; SEE CONCEPTS 48,53

requite [v] *compensate, give in return*
indemnify, make, make amends, make good, pay, pay off, quit, reciprocate, recompense, redeem, redress, reimburse, remunerate, repay, respond, restitution, retaliate, return, revenge, reward, satisfy, settle; SEE CONCEPTS 126,131,341,384

rescind [v] *declare null and void*
abolish, abrogate, annul, back out of, backpedal*, backwater*, call off, cancel, countermand, crawl out of*, dismantle, forget, invalidate, lift, nix*, overturn, pull the plug*, quash, recall, remove, renege, repeal, retract, reverse, revoke, scrub*, set aside, void, wangle out*, weasel out*, X-out*; SEE CONCEPTS 121,234,317

rescue [n] *saving from danger*
deliverance, delivery, disembarrassment, disentanglement, emancipation, exploit, extrication, feat, heroics, heroism, liberation, performance, ransom, reclaiming, reclamation, recovering, recovery, redemption, release, relief, salvage, salvation, saving; SEE CONCEPT 134

rescue [v] *save from danger*
bail one out*, conserve, deliver, disembarrass, disentangle, emancipate, extricate, free, get off the hook*, get out, get out of hock*, give a break, hold over, keep, liberate, manumit, preserve, protect, pull out of the fire*, ransom, recapture, recover, redeem, regain, release, retain, retrieve, safeguard, salvage, save life of, set free, spring*, unleash, unloose; SEE CONCEPT 134

research [n] *examination, study*
analysis, delving, experimentation, exploration, fact-finding, fishing expedition*, groundwork, inquest, inquiry, inquisition, investigation, leg-

work*, probe, probing, quest, R and D*, scrutiny; SEE CONCEPTS 349,362

research [v] *examine, study*
analyze, consult, do tests, experiment, explore, inquire, investigate, look into, look up, play around with*, probe, read up on, scrutinize; SEE CONCEPTS 31,103

researcher [n] *research worker*
analyst, analyzer, clinician, experimenter, investigator, scientist, tester; SEE CONCEPTS 348,357

resemblance [n] *correspondence, similarity*
affinity, alikeness, analogy, birds of a feather*, carbon*, carbon copy, clone, closeness, coincidence, comparability, comparison, conformity, counterpart, double, facsimile, image, kinship, likeness, like of, look-alike, parallel, parity, peas in a pod*, ringer*, sameness, semblance, simile, similitude, spitting image*, two of a kind*, Xerox*; SEE CONCEPTS 664,670,716

resemble [v] *look or be like*
appear like, approximate, bear resemblance to, be similar to, be the very picture of*, bring to mind, coincide, come close to, come near, correspond to, double, duplicate, echo, favor, feature, follow, have earmarks of*, have signs of, match, mirror, parallel, pass for, relate, remind one of, seem like, simulate, smack of*, sound like, take after; SEE CONCEPTS 664,670,716

resent [v] *be angry about*
bear a grudge, begrudge, be in a huff*, be insulted, be offended by, be put off by*, be rubbed wrong way*, be vexed, dislike, feel bitter, feel sore*, frown at, get nose out of joint*, grudge, harbor a grudge*, have hard feelings*, object to, take amiss, take as an insult, take exception, take offense, take umbrage; SEE CONCEPTS 29,410

resentment [n] *hate, anger*
acerbity, acrimony, animosity, animus, annoyance, antagonism, bad feeling, bitterness, choler, cynicism, displeasure, dudgeon, exacerbation, exasperation, fog, fury, grudge, huff, hurt, ill feeling, ill will, indignation, ire, irritation, malice, malignity, miff, offense, outrage, passion, perturbation, pique, rage, rancor, rise, spite, umbrage, vehemence, vexation, wrath; SEE CONCEPTS 29,410

reservation [n1] *condition, stipulation*
catch, circumscription, demur, doubt, fine print*, grain of salt*, hesitancy, kicker*, provision, proviso, qualification, restriction, scruple, skepticism, string*, strings*, terms; SEE CONCEPTS 646,711

reservation [n2] *the act of holding something, or thing held for future use*
bespeaking, booking, exclusive possession, place, restriction, retaining, retainment, setting aside, withholding; SEE CONCEPT 710

reservation [n3] *habitat for large group*
enclave, homeland, preserve, reserve, sanctuary, territory, tract; SEE CONCEPTS 512,516

reserve [n1] *supply*
ace in hole*, assets, backlog, cache, capital, drop, emergency fund*, fund, hoard, insurance, inventory, nest egg*, plant, provisions, rainy day fund*, reservoir, resources, savings, stash*, stock, stockpile, store, wealth; SEE CONCEPTS 340,710,712

reserve [n2] *coolness of manner*
aloofness, backwardness, calmness, caution, coldness, constraint, coyness, demureness, diffi-

dence, formality, inhibition, modesty, quietness, reluctance, repression, reservation, restraint, reticence, secretiveness, self-restraint, shyness, silence, suppression, taciturnity, uncommunicativeness, unresponsiveness; SEE CONCEPT 633

reserve [v1] *keep, hold back*
conserve, defer, delay, duck*, have, hoard, hold, keep back, keep out, lay up, maintain, plant, possess, postpone, preserve, put away, put by, put off, retain, save, set aside, squirrel*, squirrel away*, stash, stockpile, store, store up, stow away, withhold; SEE CONCEPT 129

reserve [v2] *hold for future use*
bespeak, book, contract, engage, prearrange, preengage, retain, schedule, secure; SEE CONCEPT 53

reserved [adj1] *silent, unsociable; constrained*
aloof, backward, bashful, cautious, ceremonious, close, close-mouthed, cold*, collected, composed, conventional, cool, demure, diffident, distant, eremitic, formal, frigid, gentle, icy*, mild, misanthropic, modest, noncommittal, offish, peaceful, placid, prim, quiet, reclusive, restrained, reticent, retiring, secretive, sedate, self-contained, serene, shy, soft-spoken, solitary, standoffish, taciturn, unapproachable, uncommunicative, uncompanionable, undemonstrative, unresponsive, withdrawn; SEE CONCEPTS 401,404

reserved [adj2] *held for future use*
appropriated, arrogated, booked, claimed, engaged, kept, laid away, limited, preempted, private, qualified, restricted, retained, roped off, set apart, set aside, spoken for, taken; SEE CONCEPTS 576,710

reservoir [n] *accumulation, repository*
backlog, basin, cistern, container, fund, holder, lake, nest egg*, pond, pool, receptacle, reserve, source, spring, stock, stockpile, storage, store, supply, tank, tarn; SEE CONCEPTS 514,712

reside [v] *live or exist in*
abide, be intrinsic to, be vested, bide, consist, continue, crash*, dig*, dwell, endure, hang one's hat*, inhabit, inhere, lie, locate, lodge, nest, occupy, park*, people, perch, populate, remain, rest with, roost, settle, sojourn, squat, stay, take up residence, tenant; SEE CONCEPTS 226,407

residence [n] *place for living*
abode, address, apartment, condo, co-op, domicile, dwelling, habitation, hall, headquarters, hole, home, homeplace*, house, household, inhabitancy, inhabitation, living quarters, lodging, manor, mansion, occupancy, occupation, palace, rack*, roof*, roost*, seat, settlement, villa; SEE CONCEPT 516

resident [n] *person living in a particular place*
citizen, denizen, dweller, habitant, householder, indweller, inhabitant, inmate, liver, local, lodger, native, occupant, resider, squatter, suburbanite, tenant, urbanite; SEE CONCEPT 413

residual [adj] *leftover*
balance, continuing, enduring, extra, lingering, net, remaining, surplus, unconsumed, unused, vestigial; SEE CONCEPTS 560,771

residue [n] *leftover part*
balance, debris, dregs, dross, excess, extra, garbage, heel, junk, leavings, leftovers, orts, parings, remainder, remains, remnant, residual, residuum, rest, scourings, scraps, scum, sewage,

re
re

shavings, silt, slag, surplus, trash; SEE CONCEPTS 260,432

resign [v] *give up responsibility*
abandon, abdicate, bail out, bow out, capitulate, cease work, cede, demit, divorce oneself from, drop, drop out, end service, fold, forgo, forsake, give notice, give up the ship*, hand in resignation, hand over, hang it up*, leave, quit, relinquish, renounce, retire, secede, separate oneself from, sign off, stand aside, stand down, step down, surrender, terminate, throw in the towel*, turn over, vacate, waive, walk out, wash hands of*, yield; SEE CONCEPTS *119,195,351*

resignation [n1] *relinquishment of responsibility*
abandonment, abdication, departure, giving up, leaving, notice, quitting, renunciation, retirement, surrender, tendering, termination, vacating, withdrawal; SEE CONCEPTS *119,195,351*

resignation [n2] *endurance, passivity*
acceptance, acquiescence, compliance, conformity, deference, docility, forbearing, fortitude, humbleness, humility, longanimity, lowliness, meekness, modesty, nonresistance, patience, patientness, resignedness, submission, submissiveness, sufferance; SEE CONCEPTS *410,657*

resigned [adj] *enduring, passive*
accommodated, acquiescent, adapted, adjusted, agreeable, amenable, biddable, calm, compliant, cordial, deferential, docile, genial, gentle, long-suffering, manageable, nonresisting, obedient, patient, peaceable, philosophical, pliant, quiescent, quiet, ready, reconciled, relinquishing, renouncing, satisfied, stoical, subdued, submissive, subservient, tame, tolerant, tractable, unassertive, unprotesting, unresisting, well-disposed, willing, yielding; SEE CONCEPTS *401,542*

resilient [adj] *bouncy, flexible*
airy, buoyant, effervescent, elastic, expansive, hardy, irrepressible, plastic, pliable, quick to recover, rebounding, rolling with punches*, rubbery, snapping back, springy, stretchy, strong, supple, tough, volatile; SEE CONCEPTS *488,489*

resist [v] *withstand, oppose*
abide, abstain from, antagonize, assail, assault, battle, bear, brook, buck, check, combat, confront, contend, continue, counteract, countervail, curb, defy, die hard, dispute, duel, endure, fight back, forbear, forgo, hinder, hold, hold off, hold out against, keep from, leave alone, maintain, persevere, persist, prevent, put up a fight, refrain, refuse, remain, remain firm, repel, stand up to, stay, stonewall*, struggle against, suffer, thwart, traverse, turn down, weather, withstand; SEE CONCEPTS *23,35,96,106*

resistance [n] *fighting, opposition*
battle, blocking, check, combat, contention, counteraction, cover, defiance, detention, fight, friction, halting, hindrance, holding, impedance, impediment, impeding, intransigence, obstruction, parrying, protecting, protection, rebuff, refusal, retardation, safeguard, screen, shield, stand, striking back, struggle, support, warding off, watch, withstanding; SEE CONCEPTS *23,96,106,410*

resolute [adj] *determined, strong-willed*
adamant, bold, constant, courageous, dead set on*, decided, dogged, faithful, firm, fixed, immutable, inflexible, intent upon, intrepid, loyal, meaning business*, obstinate, persevering, persistent, persisting, purposeful, relentless, resolved, serious, set, settled, staunch, steadfast, steady, strong, stubborn, tenacious, true, unbending, unchanging, uncompromising, undaunted, unfaltering, unflagging, unflinching, unshakable, unshaken, unwavering, unyielding, valiant; SEE CONCEPTS *403,542*

resolution [n1] *determination, strong will*
aim, boldness, constancy, courage, dauntlessness, decidedness, decision, declaration, dedication, determination, doggedness, earnestness, energy, firmness, fixed purpose, fortitude, guts*, heart*, immovability, intent, intention, judgment, mettle, moxie*, obstinacy, perseverance, pluck, purpose, purposefulness, purposiveness, relentlessness, resoluteness, resolve, settlement, sincerity, spirit, spunk, staunchness, staying power, steadfastness, stubbornness, tenacity, verdict, willpower; SEE CONCEPTS *410,657*

resolution [n2] *answer, judgment*
analysis, assertion, breakdown, call, conclusion, decision, declaration, determination, dissection, elucidation, end, exposition, finding, interpretation, motion, nod, outcome, pay dirt*, presentation, proposal, proposition, quick fix*, recitation, recommendation, resolve, settlement, solution, solving, sorting out, ticket*, unravelling, upshot, verdict, working out; SEE CONCEPTS *18,230,274*

resolve [n] *decision, determination*
boldness, conclusion, courage, decidedness, design, earnestness, firmness, fixed purpose, intention, objective, project, purpose, purposefulness, purposiveness, resoluteness, resolution, steadfastness, undertaking, will, willpower; SEE CONCEPTS *410,659,689*

resolve [v] *make up one's mind; find solution*
agree, analyze, anatomize, answer, break, break down, choose, clear up, clinch*, conclude, deal with, decide, decipher, decree, design, determine, dissect, dissolve, elect, elucidate, fathom, figure, fix, intend, iron out*, lick, make a point of, pan out*, pass upon, propose, purpose, puzzle out, remain firm, rule, settle, solve, take a stand, undertake, unfold, unravel, untangle, unzip*, will, work, work out, work through; SEE CONCEPTS *15,18,24*

resonant [adj] *vibrant in sound*
beating, booming, clangorous, consonant, deep, deep-toned, earsplitting, echoing, electrifying, enhanced, full, heightened, intensified, loud, mellow, noisy, orotund, plangent, powerful, profound, pulsating, pulsing, resounding, reverberant, reverberating, rich, ringing, roaring, round, sonorant, sonorous, stentorian, strident, thrilling, throbbing, thundering, thunderous; SEE CONCEPT *594*

resonate [v] *resound*
echo, oscillate, reproduce, reverberate, ring, sound, vibrate; SEE CONCEPT *65,91,171*

resort [n1] *vacation place*
camp, fat farm*, hangout, harbor, haunt, haven, hideaway, hideout, holiday spot, hotel, hot spring*, inn, lodge, mineral spring, motel, nest, park, purlieu, refuge, rendezvous, retreat, spa, spot, spring, stomping ground*, tourist center, tourist trap*; SEE CONCEPTS *198,516*

resort [n2] *alternative, recourse*
chance, course, device, expediency, expedient, hope, makeshift, opportunity, possibility, reference, refuge, relief, resource, shift, stopgap, substitute, surrogate; SEE CONCEPTS *693,712*

resort [*v*] *have recourse to; make use of*
address, affect, apply, avail oneself of, benefit by, bring into play, devote, direct, employ, exercise, fall back on, frequent, go, go to, haunt, head for, look to, make use of, put to use, recur, recur to, refer to, repair, run, take up, try, turn, turn to, use, utilize, visit; SEE CONCEPT 225

resound [*v*] *resonate*
boom, bounce back, echo, reproduce, reverberate, ring, sound, vibrate; SEE CONCEPTS 65,91,171

resource [*n*] *supply drawn upon, either material or nonmaterial*
ability, appliance, artifice, assets, capability, capital, cleverness, contraption, contrivance, course, creation, device, expedient, fortune, hoard, ingenuity, initiative, inventiveness, makeshift, means, measure, method, mode, nest egg*, property, quick-witness, recourse, refuge, relief, reserve, resourcefulness, riches, shift, source, step, stock, stockpile, store, stratagem, substance, substitute, support, surrogate, system, talent, way, wealth, worth; SEE CONCEPTS 340,523,658,710,712

resourceful [*adj*] *imaginative*
able, active, adventurous, aggressive, bright, capable, clever, creative, enterprising, ingenious, intelligent, inventive, original, quick-witted, sharp, talented, venturesome; SEE CONCEPT 402

resources [*n*] *money, possessions, natural resources*
ace in hole*, assets, backing, bankroll, basics, belongings, budget, capital, collateral, effects, funds, holdings, income, kitty*, material goods, means, nest egg*, nut*, property, reserves, revenue, riches, savings, sock*, stuff, supplies, the goods*, ways and means*, wealth, wherewithal*; SEE CONCEPTS 340,446,523,710,712

respect [*n1*] *admiration given by others*
account, adoration, appreciation, approbation, awe, consideration, courtesy, deference, dignity, esteem, estimation, favor, fear, homage, honor, obeisance, ovation, recognition, regard, repute, reverence, testimonial, tribute, veneration, worship; SEE CONCEPT 689

respect [*n2*] *way, sense*
aspect, bearing, character, connection, detail, facet, feature, matter, particular, point, reference, regard, relation; SEE CONCEPT 682

respect [*v*] *admire; obey*
abide by, adhere to, adore, appreciate, attend, be awed by, be kind to, comply with, defer to, esteem, follow, have good opinion of, have high opinion, heed, honor, look up to, note, notice, observe of, pay attention, recognize, regard, revere, reverence, set store by, show consideration, show courtesy, spare, take into account, think highly of, uphold, value, venerate; SEE CONCEPTS 10,32

respectable [*adj1*] *good, honest*
admirable, appropriate, august, becoming, befitting, comely, conforming, correct, creditable, decent, decorous, dignified, done, estimable, fair, honorable, mediocre, moderate, modest, nice, ordinary, passable, presentable, proper, redoubtable, redoubted, reputable, reputed, respected, satisfactory, seemly, sublime, suitable, tolerable, upright, venerable, virtuous, well-thought-of, worthy; SEE CONCEPT 572

respectable [*adj2*] *substantial, ample*
appreciable, considerable, decent, fair, fairly good, good, goodly, presentable, reasonable, sensible, sizable, tidy, tolerable; SEE CONCEPT 771

respectful [*adj*] *courteous, mannerly*
admiring, appreciative, civil, considerate, courtly, deferential, duteous, dutiful, gracious, humble, obedient, obeisant, polite, recognizing, regardful, regarding, reverent, reverential, self-effacing, submissive, upholding, venerating, well-mannered; SEE CONCEPT 401

respective [*adj*] *particular, specific*
corresponding, each, individual, own, personal, relevant, separate, several, singular, various; SEE CONCEPT 556

respects [*n*] *good wishes*
best wishes, compliments, courtesies, deference, devoirs, greetings, kind wishes, regards, salaam*, salutations; SEE CONCEPT 278

respite [*n*] *pause, suspension in activity*
acquittal, adjournment, break, breath*, breather*, breathing space*, cessation, coffee break*, deadlock, deferment, delay, deliverance, discharge, downtime*, ease, exculpation, five*, forgiveness, halt, hiatus, immunity, intermission, interregnum, interruption, interval, layoff, leisure, letup*, lull, moratorium, pardon, postponement, protraction, recess, relaxation, release, relief, reprieve, rest, stay, stop, ten*, time, time out*, truce; SEE CONCEPTS 121,681,807

resplendent [*adj*] *bright, radiant*
beaming, blazing, brilliant, dazzling, effulgent, flaming, gleaming, glittering, glorious, glossy, glowing, gorgeous, irradiant, luminous, lustrous, magnificent, proud, refulgent, shining, shiny, splendid, splendiferous, splendorous, sublime, superb; SEE CONCEPTS 579,589,617

respond [*v*] *act in answer to something*
acknowledge, act in response, answer, answer back, behave, be in touch with, come back, come back at, come in, counter, feedback, feel for, field the question*, get back to*, get in touch, react, reciprocate, rejoin, reply, retort, return, talk back; SEE CONCEPTS 45,384

response [*n*] *answer, reaction*
acknowledgment, antiphon, back talk*, comeback, counter, double-take*, echo, feedback, hit, kickback*, knee-jerk reaction*, lip*, rejoinder, reply, respond, retort, return, reverberation, riposte, sass*, snappy comeback*, vibes*, wisecrack; SEE CONCEPT 278

responsibility [*n1*] *accountability, blame*
albatross*, amenability, answerability, authority, boundness, burden, care, charge, constraint, contract, culpability, duty, encumbrance, engagement, fault, guilt, holding the bag*, importance, incubus, incumbency, liability, obligation, obligatoriness, onus, pledge, power, rap, restraint, subjection, trust; SEE CONCEPT 645

responsibility [*n2*] *maturity, trustworthiness*
ability, capableness, capacity, competency, conscientiousness, dependability, dependableness, efficiency, faithfulness, firmness, honesty, level-headedness, loyalty, rationality, reliability, sensibleness, soberness, stability, steadfastness, trustiness, uprightness; SEE CONCEPTS 411,633

responsible [*adj*] *accountable, in charge*
answerable, at fault, at the helm, authoritative, bonded, bound, bound to, carrying the load, cen-

surable, chargeable, compelled, constrained, contracted, culpable, decision-making, devolving on, duty-bound, engaged, executive, exposed, fettered, guilty, hampered, held, high, important, in authority, in control, incumbent, liable, minding the store*, obligated, obliged, on the hook*, open, pledged, subject, susceptive, sworn to, tied, to blame, under contract, under obligation; SEE CONCEPT 545

responsible [*adj*2] *trustworthy, mature*
able, adult, capable, competent, conscientious, dependable, dutiful; effective, efficient, faithful, firm, levelheaded, loyal, qualified, rational, reliable, self-reliant, sensible, sober, sound, stable, steadfast, steady, tried, trusty, upright; SEE CONCEPTS 401,404

responsive [*adj*] *quick to react*
acknowledging, active, alive, answering, awake, aware, compassionate, conscious, forthcoming, impressionable, influenceable, kindhearted, open, passionate, perceptive, persuadable, reactive, receptive, replying, respondent, sensible, sensile, sensitive, sentient, sharp, softhearted, susceptible, susceptive, sympathetic, tender, warm, warmhearted; SEE CONCEPTS 401,542

rest [*n1*] *inactivity*
break, breather*, breathing space*, calm, calmness, cessation, coffee break*, comfort, composure, cutoff, downtime*, doze, dreaminess, ease, forty winks*, halt, holiday, hush, idleness, interlude, intermission, interval, leisure, letup*, lull, motionlessness, nap, pause, peace, quiescence, quiet, quietude, recess, recreation, refreshment, relaxation, relief, repose, respite, siesta, silence, sleep, slumber, somnolence, standstill, stay, stillness, stop, time off, tranquillity, vacation; SEE CONCEPTS 315,681,807

rest [*n2*] *remainder of something*
balance, bottom of barrel*, dregs, dross, excess, heel, leavings, leftovers, odds and ends*, orts, others, overplus, remains, remnant, residual, residue, residuum, rump, superfluity, surplus; SEE CONCEPTS 260,835

rest [*n3*] *base, foundation*
basis, bed, bottom, footing, ground, groundwork, holder, pedestal, pediment, pillar, prop, seat, seating, shelf, stand, stay, support, trestle; SEE CONCEPTS 442,825

rest [*v1*] *be calm; sleep*
be at ease, be comfortable, breathe, compose oneself, doze, dream, drowse, ease off, ease up, idle, laze, lean, let down, let up, lie by, lie down, lie still, loaf, loll, lounge, nap, nod, put feet up*, recline, refresh oneself, relax, repose, sit down, slack, slacken, slack off, sleep, slumber, snooze, spell, stretch out, take a break, take a nap, take five*, take it easy*, take life easy*, take ten*, take time out, unbend, unlax*, unwind, wind down; SEE CONCEPTS 210,315,681

rest [*v2*] *lie, recline*
be quiet, be supported, lay, lean, lie still, loll, lounge, pause, prop, repose, roost, settle, sit, stand, stand still, stretch out; SEE CONCEPTS 154,681

rest [*v3*] *depend, hinge*
base, be based, be contingent, be dependent, be founded, be seated on, be supported, be upheld, bottom, count, establish, found, ground, hang, lie, predicate, rely, reside, stay, turn; SEE CONCEPT 711

restaurant [*n*] *business establishment serving food and drink*
bar, café, cafeteria, canteen, chophouse*, coffee shop, diner, dining room, dive*, doughtnut shop, drive-in, eatery, eating house, eating place, fast-food place, greasy spoon*, grill, hamburger stand, hashery*, hideaway*, hotdog stand, inn, joint*, luncheonette, lunchroom, night club, outlet*, pizzeria, saloon, soda fountain, watering hole*; SEE CONCEPTS 439,448,449

restful [*adj*] *quiet*
calm, comfortable, contented, hushed, inactive, motionless, pacific, peaceful, placid, relaxed, relaxing, retired, sedate, serene, soothing, still, tranquil, unanxious, unexcited, untroubled; SEE CONCEPTS 401,583,705

restitution [*n*] *compensation, repayment*
amends, dues, indemnification, indemnity, payment, quittance, rebate, recompense, redress, refund, reimbursement, remuneration, reparation, reprisal, requital, restoration, return, satisfaction, squaring things*; SEE CONCEPT 344

restive [*adj*] *impatient, nervous*
agitated, balky, contrary, edgy, fidgety, fractious, fretful, froward, ill at ease, jittery, jumpy, nervy, obstinate, on edge, ornery*, perverse, recalcitrant, refractory, restless, stubborn, tense, uneasy, unruly, unyielding, uptight; SEE CONCEPTS 401,542

restless [*adj*] *not content; moving about*
active, agitated, antsy*, anxious, bundle of nerves*, bustling, changeable, disturbed, edgy, fidgeting, fidgety, fitful, footloose*, fretful, hurried, ill at ease, inconstant, intermittent, irresolute, itchy*, jumpy, nervous, nomadic, on edge, perturbed, restive, roving, sleepless, spasmodic, strung out*, tossing and turning*, transient, troubled, turbulent, uneasy, unpeaceful, unquiet, unrestful, unruly, unsettled, unstable, unsteady, wandering, worried; SEE CONCEPTS 403,542,584

restlessness [*n*] *constant motion; discontent*
activity, agitation, ailment, ants*, antsiness*, anxiety, bustle, disquiet, disquietude, disturbance, edginess, excitability, ferment, fitfulness, fretfulness, hurry, inconstancy, inquietude, insomnia, instability, jitters, jumpiness, movement, nervousness, restiveness, transience, turbulence, turmoil, uneasiness, unrest, unsettledness, worriedness; SEE CONCEPTS 410,657,748

restore [*v1*] *fix, make new*
bring back, build up, cure, heal, improve, make healthy, make restitution, mend, modernize, reanimate, rebuild, recall, recondition, reconstitute, reconstruct, recover, redeem, reenforce, reerect, re-establish, refresh, refurbish, rehabilitate, reimpose, reinstate, reintroduce, rejuvenate, renew, renovate, repair, replace, rescue, retouch, revitalize, revive, revivify, set to rights, strengthen, touch up, update, win back; SEE CONCEPTS 126,212,244

restore [*v2*] *give back*
hand back, put back, replace, return, send back; SEE CONCEPTS 131,232

restrain [*v*] *keep under control; hold back*
arrest, bind, bottle up, box up, bridle, chain, check, choke back, circumscribe, confine, constrain, contain, control, cool*, cork*, crack down*, curb, curtail, debar, delimit, detain, deter, direct, fetter, gag, govern, guide, hamper, handicap, harness, hem in, hinder, hogtie*, hold,

impound, imprison, inhibit, jail, keep, keep down, keep in line*, kill*, limit, lock up, manacle, muzzle, pinion, prevent, proscribe, pull back, repress, restrict, sit on, stay, subdue, suppress, tie down, tie up; SEE CONCEPTS 121,130,191

restrained [*adj*] *calm, quiet*
bottled up, calm and collected, chilled, conservative, controlled, cool, corked up, discreet, in charge, in check, inobtrusive, laid-back*, mild, moderate, muted, on a leash*, plain, reasonable, reticent, retiring, self-controlled, shrinking, soft, steady, subdued, tasteful, temperate, unaffable, undemonstrative, under control, under wraps*, unexcessive, unexpansive, unextreme, unobtrusive, uptight, withdrawn; SEE CONCEPTS 401,542

restraint [*n1*] *self-control*
abstemiousness, abstinence, caution, coercion, command, compulsion, confines, constraint, control, coolness, curtailment, economy, forbearance, grip, hindrance, hold, inhibition, limitation, moderation, prevention, repression, reserve, restriction, secretiveness, self-denial, self-discipline, self-government, self-possession, self-restraint, silence, suppression, unnaturalness, withholding; SEE CONCEPT 633

restraint [*n2*] *limitation; something that holds*
abridgment, arrest, ban, bar, barrier, bondage, bridle, captivity, chains, check, command, confinement, constraint, cramp, curb, decrease, deprivation, detention, determent, deterrence, embargo, fetters, hindrance, impediment, imprisonment, instruction, interdict, limit, manacles, obstacle, obstruction, order, pinions, prohibition, reduction, rein, repression, restriction, rope, stop, stoppage, straitjacket, string*, taboo, weight; SEE CONCEPTS 5,666,674

restrict [*v*] *confine, limit situation or ability to participate*
bind, bottle up, bound, chain, check, circumscribe, come down on, constrict, contain, contract, cool down, cramp, curb, decrease, define, delimit, delimitate, demarcate, demark, diminish, encircle, enclose, hamper, handicap, hang up, hem in, hold back, hold down, impede, inclose, inhibit, keep within bounds, keep within limits, moderate, modify, narrow, pin down, prelimit, put away, put on ice*, qualify, reduce, regulate, restrain, send up, shorten, shrink, shut in, surround, temper, tether, tie; SEE CONCEPT 130

restriction [*n*] *limit*
ball and chain*, bounds, brake, catch, check, circumscription, condition, confinement, constraint, containment, contraction, control, cramp, curb, custody, demarcation, excess baggage*, fine print*, glitch*, grain of salt*, handicap, hang-up*, inhibition, limitation, limits, lock*, no-no*, qualification, regulation, reservation, restraint, rule, small difficulty, stint, stipulation, stricture, string*, stumbling block*; SEE CONCEPTS 666,674

result [*n*] *effect brought about by something*
aftereffect, aftermath, arrangement, backwash*, by-product, close, completion, conclusion, consequence, consummation, corollary, creature, crop, decision, denouement, determination, development, emanation, end, ensual, event, eventuality, execution, finish, fruit*, fruition, harvest, issue, offshoot*, outcome, outcropping, outgrowth, payoff, proceeds, product, production,

reaction, repercussion, returns, sequel, sequence, settlement, termination, upshot; SEE CONCEPT 230

result [*v*] *happen, develop*
accrue, appear, arise, attend, become of, be due to, come about, come forth, come from, come of, come out, conclude, culminate, derive, effect, emanate, emerge, end, ensue, eventualize, eventuate, finish, flow, follow, fruit, germinate, grow, happen, issue, occur, originate, pan out, proceed, produce, rise, spring, stem, terminate, turn out, wind up, work out; SEE CONCEPTS 4,119,242

résumé [*n*] *outline of experience*
abstract, bio*, biography, curriculum vitae, CV*, digest, epitome, precis, recapitulation, review, rundown, sum, summary, summation, summing-up, synopsis, vita, work history; SEE CONCEPTS 271,283

resume [*v*] *begin again*
assume again, carry on, come back, continue, go on, go on with, keep on, keep up, occupy again, pick up, proceed, reassume, recapitulate, recommence, recoup, regain, reinstitute, reoccupy, reopen, repossess, restart, retake, return to, take back, take up; SEE CONCEPTS 221,239

resurgence [*n*] *revival*
comeback, reawakening, rebirth, rebound, recovery, rejuvenation, renaissance, renascence, renewal, restoration, resurrection, return, revitalization, triumph; SEE CONCEPTS 119,221,706

resurrection [*n*] *awakening from the dead*
reappearance, reawakening, rebirth, restoration, resurgence, return to life, revival; SEE CONCEPTS 119,221

resuscitate [*v*] *revive*
arouse, awaken, breathe new life into*, bring back to life, bring to*, come to life, energize, enkindle, enliven, give mouth-to-mouth resuscitation, invigorate, perform CPR, rejuvenate, renovate, restore, resurrect, revitalize, save, wake up; SEE CONCEPTS 13,221,469,697

retain [*v1*] *hold on to physically or mentally*
absorb, bear in mind, cling to, clutch, contain, detain, enjoy, grasp, hand onto, have, hold, hold fast, husband, keep, keep in mind, keep possession, maintain, memorize, mind, own, possess, preserve, put away, recall, recognize, recollect, remember, reminisce, reserve, restrain, retrospect, save, withhold; SEE CONCEPTS 40,190,710

retain [*v2*] *hire*
commission, contract, employ, engage, maintain, pay, reserve; SEE CONCEPT 351

retaliate [*v*] *get even with someone*
even the score*, exact retribution, get, get back at, give and take*, make reprisal, pay, pay back, reciprocate, recompense, repay, requite, retrospect, return, return the compliment, revenge, revive, settle, square accounts*, strike back, take an eye for an eye*, take revenge, turn the tables on*, turn upon, wreak vengeance; SEE CONCEPTS 126,384

retard [*v*] *hinder, obstruct*
arrest, back off, baffle, balk, bog, bog down, brake, bring to screeching halt*, check, choke, choke off, clog, close off, crimp, dawdle, decelerate, decrease, defer, delay, detain, down, encumber, falter, fetter, flag, hamper, handicap, hang up, hesitate, hold back, hold up, impede, lessen, let up, loaf, loiter, mire, poke, postpone,

reduce, retardate, set back, shut down, shut off, slacken, slow down, slow up, stall, take down; SEE CONCEPTS 121,130,190,240

reticent [adj] *secretive, quiet*
bashful, clammed up*, close, close-mouthed, dried up*, dummied up*, hesitant, mum, reserved, restrained, shy, silent, taciturn, tight-lipped, uncommunicative, unforthcoming, unspeaking, uptight*; SEE CONCEPTS 267,401

retire [v] *leave a place or responsibility*
absent oneself, decamp, deny oneself, depart, draw back, ebb, exit, fall back, get away, get off, give ground, give up work, give way, go, go away, go to bed, go to one's room*, go to sleep, hand over, hit the sack*, leave service, make vacant, part, pull back, pull out, recede, regress, relinquish, remove, repeal, rescind, resign, retreat, revoke, run along, rusticate, secede, seclude oneself, separate, sever connections, stop working, surrender, take off, turn in, withdraw; SEE CONCEPTS 195,234,351

retiring [adj] *shy, undemonstrative*
backward, bashful, coy, demure, diffident, humble, meek, modest, nongregarious, not forward, quiet, rabbity, recessive, reclusive, reserved, restrained, reticent, self-effacing, shrinking, timid, timorous, unaffable, unassertive, unassuming, unexpansive, unsociable, withdrawing, withdrawn; SEE CONCEPT 401

retort [n] *snappy answer*
antiphon, back answer, back talk, comeback, cooler, counter, crack*, gag*, jape, jest, joke, lip*, parting shot*, quip, rejoinder, repartee, reply, reprisal, respond, response, retaliation, return, revenge, riposte, sally, snappy comeback*, topper*, wisecrack, witticism; SEE CONCEPT 278

retort [v] *answer*
answer back, come back at*, counter, crack*, rebut, rejoin, repay, reply, requite, respond, retaliate, return, riposte, sass*, shoot back*, snap back*, squelch*, talk back, top*; SEE CONCEPT 45

retract [v] *take back; renege on*
abjure, back, back down, back off, back out of, call off, cancel, change one's mind, countermand, deny, disavow, disclaim, disown, draw in, eat one's words*, eliminate, exclude, fall back, forget it, forswear, go back on, have change of heart*, nig*, pull back, pull in, recall, recant, recede, reel in*, renege, renounce, repeal, repudiate, rescind, retreat, retrocede, retrograde, reverse, revoke, rule out, sheathe, suspend, take back, take in, unsay, welsh*, withdraw; SEE CONCEPTS 25,49,119,697

retreat [n] *departure*
ebb, evacuation, flight, retirement, withdrawal; SEE CONCEPTS 30,195

retreat [n2] *place one goes for peace*
adytum, ark, asylum, cell, cloister, convent, cover, covert, defense, den, habitat, harbor, haunt, haven, hermitage, hideaway, hiding place, ivory tower*, port, privacy, refuge, resort, retirement, safe house, safe place, sanctuary, seclusion, security, shelter, solitude; SEE CONCEPT 516

retreat [v] *pull back, go away*
abandon, avoid, back, back away, back down, back off, back out, backtrack, beat it, cave in, decamp, depart, disengage, draw back, ebb, elude, escape, evacuate, evade, fall back, fold, give ground, go, go along with, go back, hand over,

hide, keep aloof, keep apart, lay down, leave, move back, opt out*, pull out, quail, quit, recede, recoil, reel, regress, relinquish, resign, retire, retrocede, retrograde, reverse, run, seclude oneself, sequester, shrink, start back, turn tail*, vacate, withdraw; SEE CONCEPTS 30,195

retribution [n] *payback for another's action*
avengement, avenging, comeuppance, compensation, counterblow, eye for an eye*, just desserts*, justice, punishment, reckoning, recompense, redress, repayment, reprisal, requital, retaliation, revanche, revenge, reward, satisfaction, vengeance, what for*; SEE CONCEPTS 123,126,384

retrieve [v] *get back*
bring back, fetch, get back, reacquire, recall, recapture, reclaim, recoup, recover, recruit, redeem, regain, repair, repossess, rescue, restore, salvage, save, win back; SEE CONCEPTS 120,124,131

retrospect [n] *afterthought*
hindsight, recollection, reconsideration, reexamination, remembering, remembrance, reminiscence, retrospection, review, revision, survey; SEE CONCEPTS 17,40,410

return [n1] *coming again*
acknowledgment, answer, appearance, arrival, coming, entrance, entry, homecoming, occurrence, reaction, reappearance, rebound, recoil, recoiling, recompense, recompensing, recovery, recrudescence, recurrence, reestablishment, reinstatement, rejoinder, reoccurrence, replacement, repossession, restitution, restoration, restoring, retreat, reversion, revisitation; SEE CONCEPTS 4,695

return [n2] *earnings, benefit*
accrual, accruement, advantage, avail, compensation, gain, gate, income, interest, lucre, proceeds, profit, reciprocation, recompense, reimbursement, reparation, repayment, requital, results, retaliation, revenue, reward, take*, takings, yield; SEE CONCEPTS 340,710

return [n3] *answer*
antiphon, comeback, rejoinder, reply, respond, response, retort, riposte; SEE CONCEPT 278

return [n4] *summary*
account, form, list, record, report, statement, tabulation; SEE CONCEPTS 283,331

return [v1] *go back, turn back*
back up, bounce back, circle back, come again, come back, double back, go again, hark back to, move back, react, reappear, rebound, recoil, reconsider, recrudesce, recur, reel back, reenter, reexamine, reoccur, repair, repeat, retire, retrace steps, retreat, revert, revisit, revolve, rotate, turn, turn back; SEE CONCEPTS 159,242

return [v2] *give back, send back*
bestow, carry back, convey, give, hand back, make restitution, pay back, put back, react, rebate, reciprocate, recompense, reestablish, refund, reimburse, reinsert, reinstate, remit, render, repay, replace, requite, reseat, restitute, restore, retaliate, roll back, send, take back, thrust back, toss back, transmit; SEE CONCEPTS 108,131,217

return [v3] *earn*
bring in, cash in on*, clean up*, clear*, make, make a killing*, net, pay, pay dividend, pay off, repay, score, show profit, yield; SEE CONCEPT 330

return [*v4*] *answer*
announce, arrive at, bring in, come back, come in, come to, communicate, declare, deliver, pass, rejoin, render, reply, report, respond, retort, state, submit; SEE CONCEPT 45

reunion [*n*] *social gathering*
assembly, get-together, homecoming, making up*, reconciliation, reuniting; SEE CONCEPTS 109,113

revamp [*v*] *renovate*
clean, do up*, face-lift*, make over, overhaul, recondition, refresh, refurbish, rehabilitate, remake, remodel, renew, repair, restore, resurrect, retread, revitalize, revive, spruce up*; update; SEE CONCEPTS 168,177,202

reveal [*v1*] *disclose, tell*
acknowledge, admit, affirm, announce, avow, betray, break the news*, bring out into open*, bring to light*, broadcast, come out with, communicate, concede, confess, declare, divulge, explain, expose, get out of system*, give away, give out, give the low-down*, impart, inform, leak, let cat out of the bag*, let fall, let on, let out, let slip*, make known, make plain, make public, notify, proclaim, publish, put cards on table*, report, talk, tell, unfold, utter; SEE CONCEPT 60

reveal [*v2*] *show, uncover*
bare, disclose, display, exhibit, expose, flash, lay bare, manifest, open, unclothe, unearth, unmask, unveil; SEE CONCEPT 138

revel [*n*] *celebration, merrymaking*
bacchanal, carousal, carouse, debauch, festivity, frolic, gaiety, gala, high jinks*, jollification, jollity, merriment, party, reveling, revelment, saturnalia, skylarking*, spree, wassail, whoopee*; SEE CONCEPTS 292,377

revel [*v*] *take pleasure; celebrate*
bask, blow off steam*, carouse, carry on, crow, cut loose*, delight, enjoy, fool around*, frolic, gloat, go on a spree*, indulge, kick up heels*, kid around*, lap up*, lark, let go*, let loose*, live it up*, luxuriate, make merry, paint the town*, rejoice, relish, riot, roister, roll, rollick, run around, savor, step out, thrive, wallow, whoop it up*; SEE CONCEPTS 292,377,384

revelation [*n*] *disclosure, telling*
adumbration, announcement, apocalypse, betrayal, blow by blow*, break, broadcasting, clue, communication, cue, discovery, display, divination, divulgement, earful, exhibition, expose, exposition, exposure, eye-opener*, flash, foreshadowing, inspiration, leak, lightning bolt*, manifestation, news, oracle, proclamation, prophecy, publication, scoop*, showing, sign, the latest*, tip, uncovering, unearthing, unveiling, vision; SEE CONCEPTS 60,274

revelry [*n*] *merrymaking*
carousal, carouse, celebration, debauch, debauchery, entertainment, festival, festivity, fun, gaiety, high jinks*, jollification, jollity, party, reveling, revelment, saturnalia, spree, whoop-de-do*, whoopla*; SEE CONCEPTS 377,384

revenge [*n*] *retaliation for wrong, grievance*
animus, attack, avenging, avengment, counterblow, counterinsurgency, counterplay, eye for an eye*, fight, getting even*, ill will, implacability, malevolence, measure for measure, rancor, repayment, reprisal, requital, retribution, return, ruthlessness, satisfaction, sortie, spitefulness, tit for tat*, vengeance, vengefulness, vindictiveness; SEE CONCEPTS 86,122,384

revenge [*v*] *retaliate for wrong, grievance*
avenge, be out for blood*, defend, even the score*, fight back, fix, fix one's wagon*, get, get back at, get even, give comeuppance, give just desserts*, hit back, justify, kick back, make reprisal, match, pay back, pay back in spades*, pay off, punish, reciprocate, redress, repay, requite, retort, return, return the compliment*, score, settle up, settle with, square, stick it to, take an eye for an eye*, turn the tables on*, venge, vindicate; SEE CONCEPTS 86,122,384

revenue [*n*] *income, profit*
acquirement, annuity, bottom line*, cash flow, credit, dividend, earnings, emolument, fruits*, fund, gain, gate*, get*, gravy*, handle*, interest, means, net, pay, payoff, perquisite, proceeds, receipt, resources, return, reward, salary, split*, stock, strength, take*, takings*, wages, wealth, yield; SEE CONCEPTS 329,332,344

reverberate [*v*] *vibrate in sound*
echo, react, rebound, recoil, redound, re-echo, resound, ring; SEE CONCEPT 65

reverence [*n*] *high opinion of something*
admiration, adoration, apotheosis, approbation, approval, awe, bow, deference, deification, devotion, devoutness, esteem, fealty, fear, genuflection, high esteem, homage, honor, love, loyalty, obeisance, obsequiousness, piety, praise, prostration, religiousness, respect, veneration, worship; SEE CONCEPTS 10,32

reverent [*adj*] *respectful*
admiring, appreciative, deferential, devout, dutiful, gracious, humble, obedient, obeisant, pious, polite, regardful, reverential, solemn, upholding, worshipping; SEE CONCEPT 401

revere/reverence [*v*] *have a high opinion of*
admire, adore, apotheosize, appreciate, be in awe of, cherish, defer to, deify, enjoy, esteem, exalt, hold in awe, honor, look up to*, love, magnify, pay homage, prize, put on pedestal*, regard, respect, think highly of, treasure, value, venerate, worship; SEE CONCEPTS 10,32

reverie [*n*] *daydream*
absent-mindedness, absorption, abstraction, castle-building*, castles in the air*, contemplation, detachment, dreaminess, dreaming, fantasy, fool's paradise*, head trip*, inattention, meditation, mind trip*, muse, musing, pensiveness, phantasy, pipe dream*, preoccupation, study, thought, trance, trip*, woolgathering*; SEE CONCEPTS 529,532

reversal [*n*] *about-face*
annulment, backpedaling, cancellation, change in direction, doubleback, repeal, rescinding, retraction, switch, turnabout, turnaround, U-turn, volte-face; SEE CONCEPT 697

reverse [*n1*] *opposite*
about-face, antipode, antipole, antithesis, back, bottom, change of mind, contra, contradiction, contradictory, contrary, converse, counter, counterpole, flip-flop*, flip side*, inverse, other side, overturning, rear, regression, retrogression, retroversion, reversal, reversement, reversion, switch, turn, turnabout, turn around, turning, underside, verso, volte-face, wrong side; SEE CONCEPTS 665,697,738

reverse [*n2*] *bad luck; failure*
adversity, affliction, bath, blow, catastrophe,

re
re

check, conquering, defeat, disappointment, hardship, misadventure, misfortune, mishap, repulse, reversal, setback, trial, turnabout, vanquishment, vicissitude; SEE CONCEPTS 674,679

reverse [v1] *turn upside down or backwards*
about-face*, back, backpedal*, backtrack, back up, capsize, double back*, evaginate, evert, exchange, flip-flop*, go back, go backwards, interchange, inverse, invert, move backwards, overturn, rearrange, retreat, revert, shift, switch, transfer, transplace, transpose, turn around, turn back, turn over, upend, upset; SEE CONCEPTS 158,213,697

reverse [v2] *cancel, change*
alter, annul, backpedal*, backtrack, convert, countermand, declare null and void*, dismantle, double back*, flip-flop*, invalidate, lift, modify, negate, nullify, overrule, overset, overthrow, overturn, quash, recall, renege, repeal, rescind, retract, revoke, set aside, turn around, turn the tables*, undo, upset; SEE CONCEPTS 13,234,697

revert [v] *return to an earlier, less-developed condition*
about-face*, backslide, change, come back, decline, degenerate, deteriorate, fall off the wagon*, flip-flop*, go back, hark back, inverse, invert, lapse, react, recrudesce, recur, regress, relapse, resume, retrograde, retrogress, return, take up where left off*, throw back, transpose, turn, turn back; SEE CONCEPTS 13,385,698

review [n1] *examination, study*
analysis, another look*, audit, check, checkup, drill, file, fresh look*, inspection, march past*, once-over*, parade, procession, reassessment, recapitulation, reconsideration, reflection, report, rethink, retrospect, revision, scan, scrutiny, second look, second thought, survey, view; SEE CONCEPTS 24,103

review [n2] *critique; summary*
abstract, analysis, appraisal, article, assessment, blurb, book review, canvass, column, comment, commentary, criticism, discourse, discussion, dissertation, essay, evaluation, exposition, inspection, investigation, journal, judgment, magazine, mention, monograph, notice, organ, outline, pan*, periodical, recapitulation, redraft, reviewal, revision, study, synopsis, theme, thesis, treatise, write-up; SEE CONCEPTS 280,283

review [v1] *go over again*
analyze, brush up*, call to mind, check out, check thoroughly, debrief, go over, hash over*, look at again, look back on, polish up, reassess, recall, recap*, recapitulate, recollect, reconsider, reevaluate, reexamine, reflect on, rehash*, remember, rethink, revise, revisit, run over, run through, run up flagpole*, summon up, take another look, think over; SEE CONCEPT 103

review [v2] *criticize, scrutinize*
assess, bad-mouth*, correct, discuss, evaluate, examine, give one's opinion, inspect, judge, knock*, pan*, put down*, rave, read through, re-edit, revise, rip, skin alive*, slam*, study, swipe at*, take down*, trash*, weigh, write a critique, zap*; SEE CONCEPTS 49,52

reviewer [n] *critic*
analyst, appraiser, commentator, connoisseur, evaluator, expert, interpreter, judge, reporter; SEE CONCEPT 348

revile [v] *scold*
abuse, admonish, berate, blame, castigate, cen-

sure, chide, criticize, denigrate, denounce, disparage, give a talking to*, lambaste, lay down the law*, lecture, rake over the coals*, ream, reprimand, reproach, reprobate, reprove, scorn, tongue-lash, vilify, vituperate; SEE CONCEPTS 44,52,54

revise [v] *correct, edit*
alter, amend, blue pencil*, change, clean up, compare, cut, debug, develop, emend, go over, improve, launder, look over, modify, overhaul, perfect, polish, recalibrate, recast, reconsider, redo, redraft, redraw, reexamine, rehash, reorganize, restyle, revamp, review, rework, rewrite, run through, scan, scrub, scrutinize, study, tighten, update, upgrade; SEE CONCEPTS 79,126,244

revision [n] *change; rewriting*
afterlight, alteration, amendment, correction, editing, emendation, homework, improvement, modification, overhauling, polish, recension, reconsideration, rectification, rectifying, redaction, redraft, reediting, reexamination, rescript, restyling, retrospect, retrospection, review, revisal, revise, updating; SEE CONCEPTS 79,126,244,700

revival [n] *rebirth, reawakening*
awakening, cheering, consolation, enkindling, freshening, invigoration, quickening, reanimation, recovery, recrudescence, regeneration, rejuvenation, renaissance, renascence, renewal, restoration, resurgence, resurrection, resuscitation, revitalization, revivification, risorgimento; SEE CONCEPTS 119,221

revive [v] *start again; bring back to life*
animate, arouse, awaken, bounce back*, breathe new life into*, brighten, bring around*, bring to*, cheer, come around*, come to life, comfort, console, encourage, energize, enkindle, enliven, exhilarate, gladden, inspirit, invigorate, make whole*, overcome, please, quicken, rally, reanimate, recondition, recover, refresh, rejuvenate, rekindle, relieve, renew, renovate, repair, restore, resurrect, resuscitate, revitalize, rouse, snap out of it*, solace, spring up*, strengthen, touch up*, wake up; SEE CONCEPTS 13,221,469,697

revoke [v] *take back; cancel*
abjure, abolish, abrogate, annul, back out of, backpedal*, call back, call off, countermand, counterorder, declare null and void*, deny, disclaim, dismantle, dismiss, disown, erase, expunge, forswear, invalidate, lift, negate, nix*, nullify, obliterate, quash*, recall, recant, remove, renounce, repeal, repudiate, rescind, retract, reverse, rub out*, scrub*, set aside, vacate, void, wipe out*, withdraw; SEE CONCEPTS 50,88,121,234

revolt [n] *uprising*
defection, displeasure, insurgency, insurrection, mutiny, rebellion, revolution, rising, sedition; SEE CONCEPTS 106,300,320

revolt [v1] *rebel, rise up against*
arise, boycott, break, defect, defy, drop out, get out of line*, insurrect, make waves*, mutiny, oppose, opt out, overthrow, overturn, rebel, renounce, resist, riot, rock the boat*, strike, take up arms, turn against; SEE CONCEPTS 106,300,320

revolt [v2] *disgust, nauseate*
crawl*, gross out*, make flesh crawl*, make sick, offend, pain, reluct, repel, repulse, shock,

sicken, turn off*, turn stomach*; SEE CONCEPTS 7,19

revolting [*adj*] *disgusting, nauseating*
abhorrent, abominable, appalling, awful, distasteful, foul, gross, horrible, horrid, loathsome, nasty, nauseous, noisome, obnoxious, offensive, repellent, repugnant, repulsive, rotten, shocking, sickening, sleazy*; vile; SEE CONCEPT 529

revolution [*n1*] *drastic action or change, often in politics*
anarchy, bloodshed, cabal, coup, coup d'état, crime, debacle, destruction, disorder, foment, golpe, guerrilla activity, innovation, insubordination, insurgency, metamorphosis, mutiny, outbreak, overthrow, overturn, plot, radical change, rebellion, reformation, reversal, revolt, rising, row, shake-up, shift, strife, strike, subversion, transformation, tumult, turbulence, turmoil, turnover, underground activity, unrest, upheaval, uprising, uproar, upset, violence; SEE CONCEPTS 106,300,320,697

revolution [*n2*] *circuit around something*
circle, circumvolution, cycle, gyration, gyre, lap, orbit, pirouette, reel, revolve, revolving, roll, rotation, round, spin, swirl, turn, turning, twirl, wheel, whirl; SEE CONCEPTS 436,484,738,792

revolutionary [*adj*] *rebellious*
anarchistic, defiant, disobedient, disorderly, factious, insubordinate, insurgent, mutinous, radical, rebel, rioting, riotous, subversive, warring; SEE CONCEPTS 401,529,542

revolutionary [*adj2*] *new, progressive*
advanced, advancing, avant-garde*, contemporary, cutting edge*, developing, forward-looking, innovative, just out*, latest, left, modern, novel, open-minded, radical, state-of-the-art*, up-and-coming*; SEE CONCEPTS 542,544,564, 578,797

revolve [*v1*] *turn, circle*
circumduct, go around, gyrate, gyre, orbit, roll, rotate, spin, turn around, twist, wheel, whirl; SEE CONCEPTS 147,738

revolve [*v2*] *think about*
consider, deliberate, meditate, mull over, muse, ponder, reflect, roll, ruminate, study, think over, turn over in mind; SEE CONCEPT 17

revulsion [*n*] *disgust, hatred*
abhorrence, abomination, aversion, detestation, dislike, distaste, hate, horror, loathing, recoil, repugnance, repulsion; SEE CONCEPT 29

reward [*n*] *payment, prize*
accolade, award, benefit, bonus, bounty, carrot*, comeuppance, compensation, crown*, cue, dividend, feather in cap*, fringe benefit, garland, goodies*, gravy*, grease*, guerdon, honor, just deserts*, meed, merit, perks*, plum*, premium, profit, punishment, recompense, remuneration, repayment, requital, retribution, return, salve, strokes*, sweetener*, tip, wages; SEE CONCEPTS 337,344

reward [*v*] *pay; give prize*
compensate, honor, recompense, remunerate, repay, requite, stroke*, sugarcoat*, take care of*, tip; SEE CONCEPTS 108,132,341

rewarding [*adj*] *beneficial, pleasing*
advantageous, edifying, fruitful, fulfilling, gainful, gratifying, productive, profitable, remunerative, satisfying, sweet, tasty; SEE CONCEPTS 548,572

rhetoric [*n*] *wordiness; long speech*
address, balderdash*, big talk*, bombast, composition, discourse, elocution, eloquence, flowery language, fustian, grandiloquence, hot air*, hyperbole, magniloquence, oration, oratory, pomposity, rant, verbosity; SEE CONCEPTS 51,277,278

rhetorical [*adj*] *wordy; flowery in speech*
articulate, aureate, bombastic, declamatory, eloquent, embellished, euphuistic, exaggerated, flamboyant, flashy*, florid, fluent, glib*, grand, grandiloquent, grandiose, high-flown, hyperbolic, imposing, inflated, magniloquent, mouthy, oratorical, ornate, ostentatious, overblown, overdone, overwrought, pompous, pretentious, showy, silver-tongued, sonorous, stilted, swollen, tumescent, tumid, turgid, verbose, vocal, voluble, windy*; SEE CONCEPT 267

rhyme [*n*] *poetry in which lines end with like sounds*
alliteration, beat, cadence, couplet, doggerel, half-rhyme, harmony, iambic pentameter, measure, meter, nursery rhyme, ode, poem, poesy, poetry, rhythm, rune, slant rhyme, song, tune, verse, vowel-chime; SEE CONCEPTS 278,595

rhythm [*n*] *beat, accent of sound, music*
bounce, cadence, cadency, downbeat, flow, lilt, measure, meter, metre, movement, pattern, periodicity, pulse, regularity, rhyme, rise and fall, swing, tempo, time, uniformity; SEE CONCEPT 595

ribald [*adj*] *vulgar, obscene*
base, bawdy, blue*, coarse, devilish, earthy, fast*, filthy*, foul-mouthed, gross*, indecent, indecorous, juicy, lascivious, lewd, licentious, low-down and dirty, naughty, off-color, out of line*, purple*, racy, rascally, raunchy, raw*, risqué*, rogue, rough, rude, salacious, salty, scabrous, scurrilous, sly, smutty, spicy*, unbecoming; SEE CONCEPTS 267,401

rich [*adj1*] *having a lot of money*
affluent, bloated, comfortable, easy, fat, filthy rich*, flush, gilded, in clover*, independent, in the money*, loaded*, made of money*, moneyed, opulent, plush, propertied, prosperous, rolling in it*, swimming, upscale, uptown, wealthy, well-heeled*, well-off*, well provided for*, well-to-do*, worth a million*; SEE CONCEPT 334

rich [*adj2*] *abundant, well-supplied*
abounding, ample, chic, classy, copious, costly, deluxe, elaborate, elegant, embellished, expensive, exquisite, extravagant, exuberant, fancy, fecund, fertile, fine, fruitful, full, gorgeous, grand, high-class, lavish, lush, luxurious, magnificent, ornate, palatial, plenteous, plentiful, plush, posh, precious, priceless, productive, prolific, resplendent, ritzy*, smart, snazzy*, spiffy, splendid, stylish, sumptuous, superb, swank*, swanky*, swell*, valuable, well-endowed; SEE CONCEPTS 334,589,771

rich [*adj3*] *flavorful*
creamy, delicious, fatty, full-bodied, heavy, highly flavored, juicy, luscious, nourishing, nutritious, oily, satisfying, savory, spicy, succulent, sustaining, sweet, tasty; SEE CONCEPT 613

rich [*adj4*] *full in color or sound*
bright, canorous, deep, dulcet, eloquent, expressive, intense, mellifluous, mellow, resonant, ro-

re
ri

tund, significant, silvery, sonorous, strong, vibrant, vivid, warm; SEE CONCEPTS 406,594,618

rich [adj5] *very funny*
absurd, amusing, comical, diverting, droll, entertaining, farcical, foolish, hilarious, humorous, incongruous, laughable, ludicrous, odd, preposterous, queer, ridiculous, risible, side-splitting*, slaying*, splitting*, strange; SEE CONCEPTS 267,529

rich [n] *wealthy people or institutions*
bountiful, haves*, landed, monied, nouveau riche, old money, upper class, upper crust*, well-to-do*; SEE CONCEPT 423

riches [n] *money and possessions*
abundance, affluence, assets, clover, fortune, gold, lap of luxury*, means, opulence, plenty, property, resources, richness, substance, treasure, wealth, worth; SEE CONCEPTS 335,340,446,710

rickety [adj] *unsound, broken-down*
broken, decrepit, derelict, dilapidated, feeble, flimsy, fragile, frail, imperfect, infirm, insecure, jerry-built*, precarious, ramshackle, rattletrap*, rocky, shaky, tottering, tottery*, tumble-down, unsteady, wavering, weak, wobbly; SEE CONCEPT 488

ricochet [v] *rebound*
backfire, boomerang, bounce back, deflect, kick back, recoil, return, snap back*, spring back; SEE CONCEPTS 150,194,195,303,700

rid [v] *do away with; free*
abolish, clear, deliver, disabuse, disburden, disembarrass, disencumber, dump*, eject, eliminate, eradicate, expel, exterminate, extinguish, extirpate, fire, give the brush*, heave-ho*, junk*, kiss goodbye*, liberate, make free, purge, release, relieve, remove, roust, scrap, send packing*, shake off, shed, throw away, throw out, toss out, unburden, unload, uproot; SEE CONCEPTS 180,211

riddle [n] *brain-teaser*
bewilderment, brain-twister*, charade, closed book*, complexity, complication, confusion, conundrum, cryptogram, dilemma, distraction, doubt, embarrassment, enigma, entanglement, intricacy, knotty question*, labyrinth, maze, mind-boggler*, mystery, mystification, perplexity, plight, poser, predicament, problem, puzzle, puzzlement, quandary, question, rebus, sixty-four dollar question*, stickler*, strait, stumper*, teaser, tough nut to crack*, tough proposition, twister*; SEE CONCEPT 532

riddle [v] *perforate, permeate*
bore, corrupt, damage, honeycomb*, impair, infest, mar, pepper, pervade, pierce, pit, puncture, spoil; SEE CONCEPTS 156,220

ride [n] *journey, trip in vehicle*
airing, commute, drive, excursion, expedition, hitch, jaunt, joyride*, lift, outing, pick up*, run, spin, Sunday drive, tour, transportation, turn, whirl; SEE CONCEPT 224

ride [v1] *carry or be carried*
be supported, control, cruise, curb, direct, drift, drive, float, go, go with, guide, handle, hitch a ride*, hitchhike, journey, manage, motor, move, post, progress, restrain, roll, sit, sit on, thumb a ride*, tool around*, tour, travel; SEE CONCEPTS 94,148,224

ride [v2] *dominate, oppress*
afflict, annoy, badger, bait, be arbitrary, be autocratic, berate, disparage, domineer, enslave, grip,

harass, harry, haunt, hector, hound, override, persecute, rate, reproach, revile, scold, torment, torture, tyrannize, upbraid; SEE CONCEPTS 7,14,19

rider [n1] *equestrian; commuter*
cowboy, driver, gaucho, horseback rider, horseman/woman, passenger, straphanger*, suburbanite, traveler; SEE CONCEPT 348

rider [n2] *amendment, clause*
addendum, addition, adjunct, alteration, attachment, clarification, codicil, measure, modification, revision, supplement; SEE CONCEPT 270

ridge [n] *raised part of solid*
backbone, chine, corrugation, crease, crinkle, elevation, esker, fold, furrow, hill, hogback, moraine, parapet, plica, pole, range, rib, rim, rimple, rivel, ruck, seam, spine, upland, wrinkle; SEE CONCEPTS 471,509,513

ridicule [n] *contemptuous laughter at someone or something*
badinage, banter, buffoonery, burlesque, caricature, chaff, comeback, contempt, derision, dig*, disdain, disparagement, farce, foolery, gibe, irony, jab*, jeer, laughter, leer, mockery, mordancy, needling, parody, parting shot*, persiflage, putdown*, put-on*, raillery, rally, razz*, rib*, roast*, sarcasm, sardonicism, satire, scorn, slam*, sneer*, swipe*, taunt, taunting, travesty; SEE CONCEPTS 54,59

ridicule [v] *make contemptuous fun of something or someone*
banter, caricature, cartoon, chaff, deflate, deride, expose, fleer, gibe, haze, humiliate, jape, jeer, jive, jolly, josh*, kid, lampoon, laugh at, make a fool of*, make a game of*, make a laughingstock*, make fun of, mimic, mock, needle, pan*, parody, poke fun at*, pooh-pooh*, pull one's leg*, put down*, quiz, rag, rail at, rally, razz*, rib*, ride*, roast*, run down*, satirize, scoff, scorn, send up*, show up, sneer, takeoff, taunt, travesty, twit, unmask; SEE CONCEPTS 54,59

ridiculous [adj] *stupid, funny*
absurd, antic, bizarre, comic, comical, contemptible, daffy*, derisory, droll, fantastic, farcical, foolheaded*, foolish, gelastic, goofy*, grotesque, harebrained*, hilarious, impossible, incredible, jerky*, laughable, ludicrous, nonsensical, nutty*, outrageous, preposterous, risible, sappy*, silly, slaphappy*, unbelievable, wacky*; SEE CONCEPTS 529,548,552

rife [adj] *overflowing*
abounding, abundant, alive, common, current, epidemic, extensive, frequent, general, many, multitudinous, numerous, pandemic, plentiful, popular, prevailing, prevalent, profuse, raging, rampant, regnant, replete, ruling, swarming, teeming, thronged, ubiquitous, universal, widespread; SEE CONCEPTS 771,772

riffraff [n] *rabble*
commonality, commoners, dregs of society*, gang, gathering, hoi polloi, lower class, mob, one-percenters, outcast, rank and file, ring, scum*, trash, undesirables, vermin; SEE CONCEPTS 378,417,432

rifle [v] *ransack*
burglarize, burgle, despoil, go through, grab, gut, loot, pillage, plunder, rip, rip off*, rob, rummage, sack, smash and grab*, strip, take, tip over*, trash*, waste*; SEE CONCEPT 139

rift [*n1*] *break, crack*
breach, chink, cleavage, cleft, cranny, crevice, fault, fissure, flaw, fracture, gap, hiatus, interruption, interval, opening, parting, rent, rima, rime, space, split; SEE CONCEPT 513

rift [*n2*] *difference of opinion*
alienation, breach, break, clash, disagreement, division, estrangement, falling out*, misunderstanding, quarrel, rupture, schism, separation, split; SEE CONCEPTS 46,106,388

rig [*n*] *equipment*
accouterments, apparatus, equipage, fittings, fixtures, gear, machinery, outfit, paraphernalia, tackle; SEE CONCEPT 496

rig [*v1*] *outfit, supply*
accouter, appoint, arm, array, attire, clothe, costume, dress, equip, fit out, furnish, gear, kit, provision, set up, turn out; SEE CONCEPTS 140,167, 182

rig [*v2*] *arrange for certain outcome*
doctor, engineer, fake, falsify, fiddle with*, fix, gerrymander*, juggle, manipulate, tamper with, trump up*; SEE CONCEPTS 202,697

right [*adj1*] *fair, just*
appropriate, condign, conscientious, deserved, due, equitable, ethical, fitting, good, honest, honorable, justifiable, lawful, legal, legitimate, merited, moral, proper, requisite, righteous, rightful, scrupulous, stand-up*, suitable, true, upright, virtuous; SEE CONCEPT 545

right [*adj2*] *accurate, precise*
absolute, admissible, amen, authentic, bona fide, complete, correct, exact, factual, faithful, free of error, genuine, immaculate, indubitable, inerrant, infallible, just, nice, on the money*, on the nose*, out-and-out*, perfect, proper, punctilious, real, right as rain*, righteous, right on*, rigorous, satisfactory, solemn, sound, strict, sure, thoroughgoing, true, undistorted, undoubted, unerring, unmistaken, utter, valid, veracious, veridical, veritable, watertight*; SEE CONCEPTS 535,557,582

right [*adj3*] *appropriate, fitting*
acceptable, adequate, advantageous, all right, becoming, befitting, comely, comme il faut, common, condign, convenient, correct, decent, decorous, deserved, desirable, done*, due, favorable, felicitous, fit, good, happy, ideal, merited, nice, opportune, proper, propitious, requisite, rightful, satisfactory, seemly, sufficient, suitable, tolerable; SEE CONCEPTS 558,572

right [*adj4*] *sane, healthy*
all there, balanced, circumspect, compos mentis, discerning, discreet, enlightened, far-sighted, fine, fit, hale, in good health*, in the pink*, judicious, lucid, normal, penetrating, rational, reasonable, sound, unimpaired, up to par*, well, wise; SEE CONCEPTS 314,403

right [*adj5*] *conservative politically*
die-hard*, old-line*, orthodox, reactionary, right wing, traditionalistic; SEE CONCEPTS 529,689

right [*adj6*] *opposite of left*
clockwise, dexter, dextral, right-handed; SEE CONCEPT 581

right [*adv1*] *accurately, precisely*
absolutely, all the way, altogether, bang*, clear, completely, correctly, entirely, exactly, factually, fully, genuinely, just, perfectly, precisely, quite, sharp, slap, smack-dab*, square, squarely, thoroughly, totally, truly, utterly, well, wholly; SEE CONCEPTS 531,557,582

right [*adv2*] *appropriately, suitably*
acceptably, adequately, amply, aptly, becomingly, befittingly, fittingly, properly, satisfactorily, well; SEE CONCEPTS 558,572

right [*adv3*] *fairly, justly*
conscientiously, decently, dispassionately, equitably, ethically, evenly, honestly, honorably, impartially, lawfully, legitimately, morally, objectively, properly, reliably, righteously, sincerely, squarely, virtuously, without bias, without prejudice; SEE CONCEPT 545

right [*adv4*] *beneficially*
advantageously, exceedingly, extremely, favorably, for the better, fortunately, highly, notably, perfectly, remarkably, to advantage, very, well; SEE CONCEPTS 537,572

right [*adv5*] *directly, without delay*
at once, away, direct, due, first off, forthwith, immediately, instanter, instantly, now, promptly, quickly, right away, straight, straight away, straightly, undeviatingly; SEE CONCEPT 799

right [*n1*] *privilege*
advantage, appanage, authority, benefit, birthright, business, claim, comeuppance, desert, deserving, due, exemption, favor, franchise, freedom, immunity, interest, liberty, license, merit, permission, perquisite, power, preference, prerogative, priority, title; SEE CONCEPT 376

right [*n2*] *justice, morality*
correctness, emancipation, enfranchisement, equity, freedom, good, goodness, honor, independence, integrity, lawfulness, legality, liberty, morality, properness, propriety, reason, rectitude, righteousness, rightness, straight, truth, uprightness, virtue; SEE CONCEPT 645

right [*v*] *fix, correct*
adjust, amend, balance, clean up, compensate for, debug*, dial back*, doctor*, do justice, emend, fiddle with*, fix up, go straight, launder, make up for, mend, overhaul, patch, pick up, put in place, put right, recalibrate, recompense, recondition, reconstruct, rectify, redress, repair, restore, reward, scrub, set straight, settle, set upright, shape up, sort out, square, straighten, straighten out, turn around, vindicate; SEE CONCEPTS 126,212

righteous [*adj*] *good, honest*
angelic, blameless, charitable, commendable, conscientious, creditable, deserving, devoted, devout, dutiful, equitable, ethical, exemplary, fair, faithful, godlike, guiltless, holy, honorable, impartial, innocent, irreproachable, just, laudable, law-abiding, matchless, meritorious, moral, noble, peerless, philanthropic, philanthropical, praiseworthy, punctilious, pure, reverent, right-minded, saintly, scrupulous, sinless, spiritual, sterling, trustworthy, upright, virtuous, worthy; SEE CONCEPT 545

rightful [*adj*] *legitimate*
applicable, appropriate, apt, authorized, befitting, bona fide, canonical, card-carrying*, condign, deserved, due, ethical, fair, fit, fitting, holding water, honest, just, kosher*, lawful, legal, legit*, merited, moral, moralistic, noble, official, on the level*, on the up and up*, orthodox, permitted, principled, proper, real, requisite, right, right-minded, suitable, true, twenty-four carat*, valid, virtuous; SEE CONCEPTS 545,558

ri
ri

right stuff [*n*] *essential qualities*
abilities, bravery, courage, credentials, dependability, drive, experience, guts, knowledge, power, self-confidence, skills, talent, what it takes; SEE CONCEPT *630*

rigid [*adj*] *stiff, strict, severe*
adamant, adamantine, austere, bullheaded, changeless, chiseled*, dead set*, definite, determined, exact, firm, fixed, hard, hard-line*, harsh, incompliant, inelastic, inexorable, inflexible, intransigent, invariable, locked in*, obdurate, rigorous, set, set in stone*, single-minded, solid, static, stern, strait-laced*, stringent, tough nut to crack*, unalterable, unbending, unbreakable, unchanging, uncompromising, undeviating, unmoving, unpermissive, unrelenting, unyielding; SEE CONCEPTS *403,534,535*

rigmarole [*n*] *nonsense*
babble, balderdash*, baloney, blather, bull, bunk*, drivel, foolishness, gibberish, gobbledygook*, hogwash*, hot air*, jargon, jive*, madness, mumbo jumbo*, palaver, poppycock*, prattle, rubbish, senselessness, silliness, trash*; SEE CONCEPTS *230,388,633*

rigor [*n*] *strictness, exactness*
accuracy, affliction, asperity, austerity, conscientiousness, conventionalism, difficulty, exactitude, firmness, hardness, hardship, harshness, inclemency, inflexibility, intolerance, meticulousness, obduracy, ordeal, preciseness, precision, privation, punctiliousness, rigidity, roughness, severity, sternness, stiffness, stringency, suffering, tenacity, thoroughness, traditionalism, trial, tribulation, vicissitude, visitation; SEE CONCEPTS *638,654,666*

rigorous [*adj*] *severe; exact*
accurate, ascetic, austere, bitter, brutal, burdensome, correct, definite, dogmatic, exact, exacting, hard, harsh, inclement, inflexible, intemperate, ironhanded, meticulous, nice, onerous, oppressive, precise, proper, punctilious, right, rigid, rugged, scrupulous, stern, stiff, strict, stringent, uncompromising, unpermissive; SEE CONCEPTS *535,557,565*

rile [*v*] *anger, upset*
acerbate, aggravate, annoy, bother, bug*, disturb, exasperate, gall, get one's goat*, get under skin*, grate, inflame, irk, irritate, nettle, peeve, pique, provoke, put out*, roil, rub one the wrong way*, try one's patience*, vex; SEE CONCEPTS *7,19*

rim [*n*] *border; top edge*
band, brim, brink, brow, circumference, confine, curb, end, fringe, hem, ledge, limit, line, lip, margin, outline, perimeter, periphery, ring, skirt, strip, terminus, top, verge; SEE CONCEPTS *484,836*

ring [*n1*] *circle; circular object*
arena, band, brim, circlet, circuit, circus, enclosure, eye, girdle, halo, hoop, loop, ringlet, rink, round; SEE CONCEPTS *436,446*

ring [*n2*] *group participating together*
association, band, bloc, bunch, cabal, camp, cartel, cell, circle, clan, clique, coalition, combination, combine, corner, coterie, crew, crowd, faction, gang, in-group, junta, junto, knot, Mafia, mob, monopoly, organization, outfit, party, pool, push, racket, syndicate, troop, troupe, trust; SEE CONCEPTS *325,381*

ring [*n3*] *chime, bell-like noise*
buzz, call, clangor, clank, jangle, jingle, knell, peal, reverberation, tinkle, toll, vibration; SEE CONCEPT *595*

ring [*v1*] *encircle*
begird, belt, circle, circumscribe, compass, confine, enclose, encompass, gird, girdle, hem in, inclose, loop, move around, rim, round, seal off, surround; SEE CONCEPT *758*

ring [*v2*] *chime; make bell-like noise*
bang, beat, bong, buzz, clang, clap, jangle, jingle, knell, peal, play, pull, punch, resonate, resound, reverberate, sound, strike, tinkle, tintinnabulate, toll, vibrate; SEE CONCEPT *65*

ringleader [*n*] *leader*
agitator, boss, brains*, captain, chief, chieftain, commander, general, head, head honcho*, inciter, instigator, mastermind, orchestrator, president, ruler, skipper, spokesperson, troublemaker; SEE CONCEPTS *347,354*

rinse [*v*] *wash off, out*
bathe, clean, cleanse, dip, flush, soak, splash, wash, water, wet; SEE CONCEPTS *165,256*

riot [*n1*] *uprising, disorder*
anarchism, anarchy, branigan*, brawl, burst, commotion, confusion, distemper, disturbance, flap, fray, free-for-all*, fuss, hassle, lawlessness, misrule, mix-up, mob violence, protest, quarrel, racket, row, ruckus, ruction, rumble, rumpus, run-in, scene, shivaree, shower, snarl, stir, storm, street fighting, strife, to-do*, trouble, tumult, turbulence, turmoil, uproar, winging*; SEE CONCEPTS *106,300*

riot [*n2*] *very funny happening*
boisterousness, carousal, confusion, excess, extravaganza, festivity, flourish, frolic, high jinks*, howl*, jollification, lark, merrymaking, panic*, revelry, romp, scream*, sensation, show, sidesplitter*, skylark*, smash*, splash*, tumult, uproar, wow*; SEE CONCEPTS *384,386*

riot [*v*] *protest; cause an uproar*
arise, debauch, dissipate, fight, go on rampage, racket, rampage, rebel, revolt, rise, run riot*, stir up trouble*, take to the streets*; SEE CONCEPTS *106,300*

riotous [*adj*] *chaotic, wild*
anarchic, deranged, disordered, disorderly, disorganized, helter-skelter*, insurrectionary, lawless, mutinous, out of control, rampageous, rebellious, rowdy, tumultuous, turbid, turbulent, uncontrolled, unruly, violent; SEE CONCEPT *548*

rip [*n*] *tear, cut*
cleavage, gash, hole, laceration, rent, slash, slit, split; SEE CONCEPTS *309,513*

rip [*v*] *tear, cut*
burst, claw, cleave, fray, frazzle, gash, hack, lacerate, rend, rive, score, shred, slash, slit, split; SEE CONCEPT *214*

ripe [*adj1*] *fully developed; experienced*
accomplished, adult, aged, completed, conditioned, consummate, enlightened, enriched, filled out, finished, fit, full, full-blown, full-fledged, fully grown, grown, grown-up, increased, informed, in readiness, judicious, learned, mature, matured, mellow, overdue, perfected, plump, prepared, prime, ready, ripened, sagacious, seasoned, skilled, skillful, sound, timely, usable, versed, well-timed, wise; SEE CONCEPTS *462,560,578,797*

ripe [*adj2*] *favorable, ideal*
auspicious, opportune, right, suitable, timely; SEE CONCEPT *558*

rip-off [n] *trick; robbery*
cheat, con*, exploitation, fraud, gyp*, larceny, lift*, pinch*, purloining, racket*, steal, stealing, swindle, theft, thievery, thieving; SEE CONCEPTS *139,192*

rip off [v] *rob; trick*
abuse, appropriate, bleed*, cheat, con*, cop*, defraud, dupe, exploit, filch*, fleece*, heist, impose on*, lift*, nab*, pilfer, pinch, plunder, ransack, relieve, rifle, skin*, soak*, stick*, swindle, swipe, thieve, use; SEE CONCEPTS *139,192*

ripple [n] *wave; wrinkle*
billow, breaker, crest, curl, fold, furrow, line, rippling, rush, surge, swell, tide, undulation, whitecap; SEE CONCEPTS *147,436,514*

ripple [v] *wave*
coil, curl, flow, fluctuate, flutter, motion, oscillate, palpitate, pulsate, quiver, splash, stir, surge, sway, swell, swish, undulate, vacillate, vibrate; SEE CONCEPTS *74,147,149*

rise [n1] *increase, improvement*
acceleration, accession, accretion, addition, advance, advancement, aggrandizement, ascent, augmentation, boost, breakthrough, climb, distention, doubling, enlargement, growth, heightening, hike, increment, inflation, intensification, intensifying, multiplication, piling up, progress, promotion, raise, stacking up, step-up, surge, swell, upgrade, upsurge, upswing, upturn, waxing; SEE CONCEPTS *700,780*

rise [n2] *movement upward; upward slope*
acclivity, ascension, ascent, climb, elevation, eminence, highland, hillock, incline, lift, mount, rising, rising ground, soaring, surge, towering, upland, upsurge; SEE CONCEPTS *166,738,752*

rise [v1] *get up; ascend*
arise, arouse, aspire, awake, be erect, be located, be situated, blast off*, bob up*, climb, come up, get out of bed, get steeper, get to one's feet*, go uphill, grow, have foundation, levitate, lift, mount, move up, pile out*, push up, reach up, rise and shine*, rise up, rocket, roll out*, rouse, scale, sit up, slope upwards, soar, sprout, stand up, straighten up, surface, surge, surmount, sweep upward, tower, turn out, up*, upspring; SEE CONCEPTS *154,166,738*

rise [v2] *increase, grow*
accelerate, add to, advance, aggravate, arise, ascend, augment, billow, build, bulge, climb, deepen, distend, double, enhance, enlarge, expand, go through the roof*, go up, heighten, improve, inflate, intensate, intensify, levitate, lift, magnify, mount, move up, multiply, perk up, pick up, pile up, raise, redouble, rouse, soar, speed up, spread, stack up, swell, take off, upsurge, wax; SEE CONCEPTS *700,780*

rise [v3] *progress in business*
advance, be elevated, be promoted, better oneself, climb the ladder*, flourish, get on, get somewhere*, go places*, progress, prosper, succeed, thrive, work one's way up*; SEE CONCEPTS *351,704*

rise [v4] *become apparent*
appear, arise, befall, begin, betide, chance, come, crop up, dawn, derive, develop, emanate, emerge, eventuate, fall out*, flare up, flow, go, happen, head, issue, loom, occur, originate, proceed, spring, stem, surface, transpire, turn up*; SEE CONCEPTS *4,716*

rise [v5] *rebel*
insurrect, mount, mutiny, resist, revolt, riot, take up arms; SEE CONCEPT *106*

risk [n] *chance taken*
accident, contingency, danger, exposedness, exposure, flyer*, fortuity, fortune, gamble, hazard, header, jeopardy, liability, liableness, luck, openness, opportunity, peril, plunge, possibility, prospect, shot in the dark*, speculation, stab*, uncertainty, venture, wager; SEE CONCEPTS *675,693*

risk [v] *take a chance*
adventure, beard, be caught short*, brave, chance, compromise, confront, dare, defy, defy danger, encounter, endanger, expose to danger, face, gamble, go out of one's depth*, hang by a thread*, hazard, imperil, jeopardize, jeopardy, leap before looking*, leave to luck*, meet, menace, peril, play with fire*, plunge, put in jeopardy, run the chance, run the risk, skate on thin ice*, speculate, tackle, take a flyer*, take a header*, take a plunge*, take on*, take the liberty*, venture, wager; SEE CONCEPTS *87,100*

risky [adj] *dangerous*
chancy, delicate, dicey*, endangered, fraught with danger*, going for broke*, hairy*, hanging by a thread*, hazardous, iffy*, insecure, jeopardous, long shot*, not a prayer*, off the deep end*, on slippery ground*, on the spot*, on thin ice*, out on a limb*, perilous, playing with fire*, precarious, rocky*, sensitive, speculative, ticklish, touch-and-go*, touchy, treacherous, tricky, uncertain, unhealthy, unsafe, unsound, venturesome, wicked, wide-open; SEE CONCEPT *548*

risqué [adj] *improper, referring to sex*
amoral, bawdy*, blue*, breezy, crude, daring, dirty, earthy, erotic, filthy*, foul, gross*, hot*, immodest, immoral, indecent, indecorous, indelicate, indiscreet, inelegant, lewd, lurid, naughty, obscene, off-base*, off-color, offensive, out-of-line, provocative, purple*, racy, raw, ribald, salacious, salty, shady, sizzling, smart, smutty, spicy*, suggestive, unrefined, vulgar, wanton, warm, wicked, X-rated*; SEE CONCEPTS *267,545,548*

rite [n] *ceremony, tradition*
act, celebration, ceremonial, communion, custom, form, formality, liturgy, observance, occasion, ordinance, practice, procedure, ritual, sacrament, service, solemnity; SEE CONCEPTS *377,386*

ritual [n] *ceremony, tradition*
act, ceremonial, communion, convention, custom, form, formality, habit, liturgy, observance, ordinance, practice, prescription, procedure, protocol, red tape*, rite, routine, sacrament, service, solemnity, stereotype, usage; SEE CONCEPTS *386,634,688*

ritzy [adj] *elegant, luxurious*
aristocratic, chic, choice, classy, cultivated, dignified, elaborate, expensive, exquisite, fancy, fine, grand, grandiose, handsome, lavish, lush, opulent, ornamented, ornate, ostentatious, overdone, plush, posh, refined, rich, snazzy, stately, stuffy, sumptuous, swank; SEE CONCEPTS *544,574,579,589*

rival [adj] *opposing*
battling, combatant, combating, competing, competitive, conflicting, contending, contesting, cut-

ri
ri

throat, disputing, emulating, emulous, equal, opposed, striving, vying; SEE CONCEPTS 542,564

rival [n] *person who opposes in competition*
adversary, antagonist, bandit, buddy, challenger, competition, competitor, contender, contestant, emulator, entrant, equal, equivalent, match, opponent, opposite number, peer; SEE CONCEPTS 348,366,423

rival [v] *oppose; be a match for*
amount, approach, approximate, bear comparison with*, come near to*, come up to*, compare with, compete, contend, contest, correspond, emulate, equal, go after, go for, jockey for position*, match, measure up to, meet, near, partake, resemble, rivalize, scramble for, seek to displace, tie, touch, vie with; SEE CONCEPTS 92,667

rivalry [n] *competition*
antagonism, athletic event, bout, candidacy, clash, conflict, contest, duel, emulation, encounter, engagement, event, fight, game, jealousy, match, matchup, one on one*, opposition, race, sport, strife, struggle, tournament, tug-of-war; SEE CONCEPTS 92,363

river [n] *waterway*
beck, branch, brook, course, creek, estuary, rill, rivulet, run, runnel, stream, tributary, watercourse; SEE CONCEPT 514

riveting [adj] *fascinating, gripping*
absorbing, alluring, appealing, bewitching, captivating, compelling, enchanting, engaging, engrossing, enthralling, enticing, hypnotic, intriguing, irresistible, magnetic, mesmerizing, seducing, seductive, spellbinding; SEE CONCEPT 529

road [n] *path upon which travel occurs*
alley, artery, asphalt, avenue, back street, boulevard, byway, cobblestone, concrete, course, crossroad, direction, drag*, dragway, drive, expressway, highway, lane, line, main drag*, parking lot*, parkway, passage, pathway, pavement, pike, roadway, route, street, subway, terrace, thoroughfare, throughway, thruway, track, trail, turnpike, viaduct, way; SEE CONCEPT 501

roam [v] *wander about*
bum*, bum around*, drift, gad, gallivant, hike, hit the road*, knock around*, meander, peregrinate, prowl, ramble, range, rove, saunter, straggle, stray, stroll, struggle along, traipse, tramp, travel, traverse, trek, vagabond, walk; SEE CONCEPTS 151,224

roar [n1] *growl, howl*
barrage, bawl, bay, bellow, blast, bluster, boom, clamor, clash, crash, cry, detonation, din, drum, explosion, holler, outcry, reverberation, rumble, shout, thunder, uproar, yell; SEE CONCEPTS 77,595

roar [n2/v2] *laugh loudly*
belly laugh, guffaw, hoot, howl, scream; SEE CONCEPT 77

roar [v1] *growl, howl*
bark, bawl, bay, bellow, blast, bluster, boom, brawl, bray, clamor, crash, cry, detonate, din, drum, explode, holler, rebound, reecho, repercuss, resound, reverberate, roll, rout, rumble, shout, sound, thunder, trumpet, vociferate, yell; SEE CONCEPTS 64,77

rob [v] *steal, deprive*
abscond, appropriate, bereave, break into, burglarize, burgle, cheat, con, cop*, defalcate, defraud, despoil, disinherit, dispossess, divest, do

out of*, embezzle, filch*, heist, hijack, hold up*, hustle, liberate, lift*, loot, lose, mug, oust, peculate, pilfer, pillage, pinch, plunder, promote, purloin, raid, ransack, relieve, requisition, rifle, rip off*, roll*, sack*, scrounge, snitch*, stick up, strip, strong-arm*, swindle, swipe, take, thieve, withhold; SEE CONCEPTS 139,142,192

robber [n] *person who steals*
bandit, brigand, buccaneer, burglar, cardsharper*, cat burglar, cattle thief*, cheat*, chiseler*, con artist, corsair, crook, desperado, despoiler, fence, forager, fraud, grafter, hijacker, holdup artist*, housebreaker, looter, marauder, mugger, operator, pickpocket, pilferer, pillager, pirate, plunderer, prowler, punk*, raider, rustler, safe-cracker, sandbagger*, second-story operator*, shoplifter, stealer, stickup, swindler, thief, thug; SEE CONCEPT 412

robbery [n] *stealing*
break-in, burglary, caper, embezzlement, felony, heist*, hit, holdup*, job, larceny, looting, mortal sin, mugging, purse-snatching, stickup*, theft, thievery, unlawful act, wrongdoing; SEE CONCEPT 192

robe [n] *gown, often for wearing at home*
bathrobe, cape, costume, covering, dress, dressing gown, frock, garment, habit, housecoat, kimono, mantle, muumuu, negligee, outfit, peignoir, vestment, wrapper; SEE CONCEPT 451

robot [n] *android, machine*
automation, bionic person, cyborg, mechanical person; SEE CONCEPT 463

robust [adj] *healthy, strong*
able-bodied, athletic, boisterous, booming, brawny, built, concentrated, fit, fit as fiddle*, flourishing, full-bodied, hale, hardy, hearty, hefty, husky, in fine fettle*, in good health, in good shape, in the pink*, live, lusty, muscular, peppy, potent, powerful, powerhouse, prospering, prosperous, roaring, rough, rugged, sinewy, snappy, sound, stout, strapping, sturdy, thriving, tiger*, tough, vigorous, well, wicked*, zappy*, zippy*; SEE CONCEPTS 314,489,613

rock [n1] *stone*
bedrock, boulder, cobblestone, crag, crust, earth, gravel, lava, lodge, mass, metal, mineral, ore, pebble, promontory, quarry, reef, rubble, shelf, slab, slag; SEE CONCEPTS 470,474,477,478,509, 523

rock [n2] *foundation*
anchor, bulwark, cornerstone, defense, mainstay, protection, Rock of Gibraltar*, strength, support; SEE CONCEPTS 442,712

rock [v] *move back and forth*
agitate, billow, careen, concuss, convulse, falter, heave, jiggle, jog, jolt, jounce, lurch, move, oscillate, pitch, push and pull, quake, quaver, quiver, reel, roll, roll about, shake, shock, stagger, sway, swing, toss, totter, tremble, undulate, vibrate, wobble; SEE CONCEPTS 147,149

rocket [n] *projectile*
booster, firework, guided missile, ICBM, intercontinental ballistic missile, missile, spacecraft, spaceship, torpedo, weapon; SEE CONCEPT 500

rocket [v] *shoot up*
ascend, climb, escalate, go through the ceiling, grow, lift, rise, sail, skyrocket, soar, take off*, tower, zoom; SEE CONCEPTS 148,150

rock the boat [v] *cause trouble*
complain, disagree, disturb, make a stink*, make

waves*, not conform*, object, protest, stir things up*, upset the apple cart*; SEE CONCEPTS 46,52,54,300

rocky [*adj 1*] *rugged, stony*
bouldered, craggy, flinty, hard, inflexible, jagged, lapidarian, lithic, pebbly, petrified, petrous, rockbound, rock-ribbed, rough, solid, stonelike; SEE CONCEPTS 485,604

rocky [*adj 2*] *unyielding, inflexible*
adamant, bloodless, firm, flinty, hard, impassible, insensate, insensible, insensitive, obdurate, pitiless, rocklike, rough, rugged, solid, steady, tough; SEE CONCEPT 401

rocky [*adj 3*] *doubtful, undependable*
dizzy, ill, rickety, shaky, sick, sickly, staggering, ticklish, tottering, tricky, uncertain, unreliable, unstable, unsteady, unwell, weak, wobbly; SEE CONCEPTS 314,488,489

rod [*n*] *bar, pole*
baton, billet, birch, cane, cylinder, dowel, ingot, mace, pin, rodule, scepter, sceptre, shaft, slab, spike, staff, stave, stick, strip, switch, wand; SEE CONCEPTS 436,470,479

rogue [*n*] *person who deceives, swindles*
bad egg*, bad news*, blackguard*, black sheep*, charlatan, cheat, cheater, con artist, criminal, crook, defrauder, devil, fraud, heel*, hooligan*, lowlife*, mischief, miscreant, monstrosity, ne'er-do-well*, outlaw, problem*, rapscallion, rascal, reprobate, scalawag, scamp, scoundrel, swindler, trickster, villain; SEE CONCEPT 412

roguish [*adj*] *deceitful; mischievous*
beguiling, crafty, crooked, cunning, deceiving, deceptive, devilish, dishonest, fraudulent, impish, knavish, lying, naughty, playful, puckish, rascally, shifty, slick, sly, sneaky, tricky, underhand, underhanded, unprincipled, untruthful; SEE CONCEPTS 401,545

role [*n 1*] *impersonation of a character*
act, acting, appearance, aspect, bit, character, clothing, execution, extra, guise, hero, ingenue, lead, look, part, performance, personification, piece, player, portrayal, presentation, representation, seeming, semblance, show, star, stint, super, title, walk-on; SEE CONCEPTS 263,716

role [*n 2*] *duty, function*
act, bit, business, capacity, execution, game*, guise, job, office, part, piece, pose, position, post, posture, province, stint, task, what one is into*; SEE CONCEPTS 362,694

roll [*n 1*] *revolving, turning*
cycle, gyration, reel, revolution, rotation, run, spin, trundling, turn, twirl, undulation, whirl; SEE CONCEPTS 147,201

roll [*n 2*] *cylindrical object*
ball, barrel, bobbin, cartouche, coil, cone, convolution, cornucopia, cylinder, fold, reel, rundle, scroll, shell, spiral, spool, trundle, volute, wheel, whorl; SEE CONCEPT 436

roll [*n 3*] *list, roster*
annals, catalog, census, chronicle, directory, head count, index, muster, nose count*, register, roll call, schedule, scroll, table; SEE CONCEPT 281

roll [*n 4*] *growl, reverberation*
barrage, boom, booming, clangor, drone, drumbeat, drumming, echoing, grumble, quaver, racket, rat-a-tat*, resonance, roar, rumble, rumbling, thunder; SEE CONCEPT 595

roll [*v 1*] *revolve, turn; proceed smoothly*
alternate, be in sequence, bowl, circle, circumduct, coil, curve, drape, drive, eddy, elapse, enfold, entwine, envelop, flow, fold, follow, furl, go around, go past, gyrate, gyre, impel, pass, pirouette, pivot, propel, reel, rock, rotate, run, spin, spiral, succeed, swaddle, swathe, swing around, swirl, swivel, trundle, twirl, twist, undulate, wheel, whirl, wind, wrap; SEE CONCEPTS 147,201

roll [*v 2*] *spread out*
even, flatten, grind, level, press, pulverize, smooth; SEE CONCEPTS 137,208,250

roll [*v 3*] *thunder, reverberate*
bombinate, boom, cannonade, drum, echo, growl, grumble, hum, pattern, quaver, rattle, re-echo, resound, roar, ruffle, rumble, rustle, sound, trill, whirr; SEE CONCEPT 65

roll [*v 4*] *rock, sway*
billow, drift, flow, glide, heave, incline, jibe, lean, lumber, lurch, pitch, ramble, range, reel, roam, rove, run, stagger, stray, surge, swagger, swing, toss, tumble, undulate, waddle, wallow, wave, welter, yaw; SEE CONCEPTS 147,149

rollicking [*adj*] *fun-loving, lively*
antic, boisterous, carefree, cavorting, cheerful, devil-may-care*, exuberant, frisky, frolicsome, glad, happy, hearty, jaunty, jovial, joyful, joyous, lighthearted, merry, playful, rip-roaring*, romping, spirited, sportive, sprightly; SEE CONCEPTS 401,548

roly-poly [*adj*] *pudgy*
buxom, chubby*, dumpy, fat, hefty, obese, overweight, plump, plumpish, rotund, round, stout, thick-bodied, tubby*; SEE CONCEPTS 491,773

romance [*n 1*] *love affair*
affair, affair of the heart*, amour, attachment, courtship, enchantment, fascination, fling, flirtation, intrigue, liaison, love, love story, passion, relationship; SEE CONCEPTS 375,384

romance [*n 2*] *fanciful story or narrative*
ballad, fairy tale, fantasy, fiction, idealization, idyll, legend, love story, lyric, melodrama, novel, story, tale, tear-jerker*; SEE CONCEPT 280

romance [*n 3*] *adventure, flight of fancy*
charm, color, excitement, exoticness, fairy tale, fancy, fantasy, fascination, glamour, hazard, idealization, idyll, mystery, nostalgia, risk, sentiment, venture; SEE CONCEPT 673

romantic [*adj*] *sentimental, idealistic*
adventurous, amorous, bathetic, charming, chimerical, chivalrous, colorful, corny*, daring, dreamy, enchanting, erotic, exciting, exotic, extravagant, fairy-tale, fanciful, fantastic, fascinating, fond, glamorous, idyllic, impractical, lovey-dovey*, loving, maudlin, mushy*, mysterious, nostalgic, passionate, picturesque, poetic, quixotic, sloppy*, soppy*, starry-eyed, syrupy, tear-jerking*, tender, unrealistic, utopian, visionary, whimsical, wild; SEE CONCEPTS 403,542,548

romp [*n*] *fun; caper*
antic, cakewalk*, cavort, dance, escapade, frisk, frolic, gambol, hop, lark, leap, play, rollick, rout, skip, sport; SEE CONCEPTS 292,384

romp [*v*] *have fun, enjoy oneself*
caper, cavort, celebrate, cut capers*, cut up*, fool around*, frisk, frolic, gambol, go on the town*, kid around*, lark, let loose*, make merry,

ri
ro

play, prance, revel, roister, rollic, skip, skylark, sport, whoop it up*; SEE CONCEPTS *292,384*

rookie [*n*] *novice*
amateur, apprentice, beginner, colt*, cub*, fledgling, freshman/woman, greenhorn, neophyte, newcomer, new kid on the block*, tenderfoot*, trainee; SEE CONCEPTS *348,350,423*

room [*n1*] *space, range*
allowance, area, capacity, chance, clearance, compass, elbowroom, expanse, extent, latitude, leeway, license, margin, occasion, opening, opportunity, place, play, range, reach, rein, rope, scope, sway, sweep, territory, vastness, volume; SEE CONCEPTS *651,756*

room [*n2*] *enclosed section of building designed for specific purpose*
accommodation, alcove, apartment, cabin, cave*, chamber, cubbyhole, cubicle, den, flat, flop*, joint*, lodging, niche, office, setup*, suite, turf, vault; SEE CONCEPT *448*

roomy [*adj*] *having ample space*
ample, broad, capacious, commodious, extensive, generous, large, sizable, spacious, wide; SEE CONCEPT *583*

root [*n*] *base, core*
basis, bedrock, beginnings, bottom, cause, center, crux, derivation, essence, essentiality, footing, foundation, fountain, fountainhead, fundamental, germ, ground, groundwork, heart, inception, infrastructure, mainspring, marrow, motive, nub, nucleus, occasion, origin, pith, provenance, provenience, quick, quintessence, radicle, radix, reason, rhizome, rock bottom*, seat, seed, soul, source, starting point, stem, stuff, substance, substratum, tuber, underpinning, well; SEE CONCEPTS *442,648,661,826,829*

root [*v*] *dig and search*
burrow, delve, embed, ferret, forage, grub, grub up, hunt, ingrain, lodge, nose, place, poke, pry, rummage; SEE CONCEPT *178*

rootin'-tootin [*adj*] *rowdy*
boisterous, disorderly, loud, loudmouthed, mischievous, noisy, rambunctious, raucous, unruly, uproarious, vigorous, wild; SEE CONCEPT *401*

roots [*n*] *ancestry*
background, birthplace, blood, breed, descent, family history, family tree, genealogy, heritage, kindred, line, lineage, origin, parentage, pedigree, race; SEE CONCEPTS *414,648*

rope [*n*] *cord, line*
braiding, cable, cordage, hawser, lace, lanyard, lariat, lasso, strand, string, tape, thread, twine; SEE CONCEPT *475*

roster [*n*] *list of items, names*
agenda, catalog, head count, index, inventory, listing, muster, nose count*, program, record, register, roll, roll call, rota, schedule, scroll, table; SEE CONCEPTS *281,283*

rosy [*adj1*] *pink, reddish in color*
aflush, blooming, blushing, colored, coral, deep pink, fresh, glowing, healthy-looking, high-colored, incarnadine, pale red, peach, red, red-complexioned, red-faced, roseate, rose-colored, rubicund, ruddy; SEE CONCEPT *618*

rosy [*adj2*] *cheerful, hopeful*
alluring, auspicious, bright, encouraging, favorable, glowing, likely, optimistic, pleasing, promising, reassuring, roseate, rose-colored, sunny; SEE CONCEPTS *529,548*

rot [*n1*] *corrosion, disintegration*
blight, canker, corrosion, decay, decomposition, deterioration, mold, putrefaction, putrescence; SEE CONCEPTS *469,698*

rot [*n2*] *garbage, nonsense*
balderdash, bilge, bunk, claptrap, drivel, foolishness, guff, hogwash, hooey*, moonshine*, poppycock, rubbish, silliness, stuff and nonsense*, tommyrot; SEE CONCEPTS *278,529*

rot [*v*] *corrode, deteriorate*
break down, corrupt, crumble, debase, debauch, decay, decline, decompose, degenerate, demoralize, deprave, descend, disimprove, disintegrate, fester, go bad*, go downhill*, go to pot*, languish, molder, perish, pervert, putrefy, retrograde, sink, spoil, stain, taint, turn, warp, waste away, wither, worsen; SEE CONCEPTS *240,469,698*

rotary [*adj*] *turning*
encircling, gyral, gyratory, revolving, rotating, rotational, rotatory, spinning, vertiginous, vorticular, whirligig, whirling; SEE CONCEPTS *581,584*

rotate [*v1*] *go around in circle*
circle, circumduct, circumvolve, gyrate, gyre, move, pirouette, pivot, reel, revolve, roll, spin, swivel, troll, trundle, turn, twirl, twist, waltz, wheel, whirl, whirligig, whirr; SEE CONCEPTS *147,738*

rotate [*v2*] *alternate*
bandy, ensue, exchange, follow, follow in sequence, interchange, relieve, spell, succeed, switch, take turns; SEE CONCEPTS *104,697*

rotten [*adj1*] *decayed, decaying*
bad, bad-smelling, corroded, corrupt, crumbled, crumbling, decomposed, decomposing, disgusting, disintegrated, disintegrating, fecal, feculent, festering, fetid, foul, gross, infected, loathsome, loud, mephitic, moldering, moldy, noisome, noxious, offensive, overripe, perished, polluted, purulent, pustular, putrescent, putrid, putrified, rancid, rank, rotting, smelling, sour, spoiled, stale, stinking, strong, tainted, touched, unsound; SEE CONCEPTS *462,485*

rotten [*adj2*] *dishonest, immoral*
bent, bribable, contaminated, corrupt, crooked, debauched, deceitful, defiled, degenerate, depraved, dirtied, dishonorable, disloyal, faithless, filthy, flagitious, impure, mercenary, nefarious, perfidious, perverse, polluted, soiled, sullied, tainted, treacherous, unclean, untrustworthy, venal, vicious, villainous, vitiated; SEE CONCEPTS *404,545*

rotten [*adj3*] *despicable, inferior, bad*
amiss, base, below par*, bruised, bum*, contemptible, crummy*, defective, deplorable, dirty, disagreeable, disappointing, diseased, displeasing, dissatisfactory, filthy, impaired, inadequate, injured, lousy*, low-grade, mean, nasty, poor, punk*, regrettable, rough, scurrilous, shaky, sorry, sour, substandard, unacceptable, unfortunate, unhappy, unlucky, unpleasant, unsatisfactory, unsound, vile, wasted, wicked, withering, wrong; SEE CONCEPTS *570,571,574*

rotund [*adj1*] *fat*
beefy*, big, broad, burly, chunky*, dumpy, elephantine, fleshy, heavy, heavyset, hefty, husky, obese, overweight, plump, plumpish, portly, pudgy*, roly-poly*, round, solid, stout, tubby*, weighty; SEE CONCEPT *491*

otund [*adj2*] *sonorous*
booming, loud, resonant, resounding; SEE CONCEPTS *592,594*

ough [*adj1*] *uneven, irregular*
asperous, bearded, brambly, bristly, broken, bumpy, bushy, chapped, choppy, coarse, cragged, craggy, cross-grained, disheveled, fuzzy, hairy, harsh, jagged, knobby, knotty, nappy, nodular, not smooth, ridged, rocky, ruffled, rugged, scabrous, scraggy, shaggy, sharp, stony, tangled, tousled, tufted, unequal, uneven, unfinished, unlevel, unshaven, unshorn, woolly, wrinkled, wrinkly; SEE CONCEPTS *485,606*

ough [*adj2*] *stormy; not quiet*
agitated, blustering, blustery, boisterous, buffeting, cacophonous, choppy, coarse, discordant, dry, furious, grating, gruff, harsh, hoarse, husky, inclement, inharmonious, jarring, raging, rasping, raucous, rugged, squally, stridulent, tempestuous, tumultuous/tumultuous, turbulent, unmusical, wild; SEE CONCEPTS *525,592,594*

ough [*adj3*] *rude, impolite*
bearish, bluff, blunt, boisterous, boorish, brief, brusque, churlish, coarse, crass, crude, cruel, crusty, curt, discourteous, drastic, extreme, gross*, hairy*, hard, harsh, ill-mannered, improper, inconsiderate, indecorous, indelicate, inelegant, loud, loutish, mean, nasty, raw, rowdy, severe, sharp, short, tough, unceremonious, uncivil, uncouth, uncultivated, uncultured, unfeeling, ungracious, unjust, unmannerly, unpleasant, unpolished, unrefined, untutored, violent, vulgar; SEE CONCEPTS *267,401*

ough [*adj4*] *basic, incomplete*
austere, crude, cursory, formless, hard, imperfect, raw, rough-and-ready*, roughhewn, rudimentary, shapeless, sketchy, spartan, uncompleted, uncut, undressed, unfashioned, unfinished, unformed, unhewn, unpolished, unprocessed, unrefined, unwrought; SEE CONCEPT *531*

ough [*adj5*] *approximate*
amorphous, estimated, foggy, general, hazy, imprecise, inexact, proximate, rude, sketchy, uncertain, unprecise, vague; SEE CONCEPT *557*

oughly [*adv*] *about*
approximately, around, in the ball park*, in the neighborhood, more or less, practically, pretty near, somewhere around; SEE CONCEPT *583*

ough out [*v*] *do preliminary design*
adumbrate, block out, chalk, characterize, delineate, draft, outline, plan, skeleton, sketch, suggest; SEE CONCEPTS *36,79,174*

ough up [*v*] *beat up*
bash, batter, hit, knock about, knock around, maltreat, mishandle, mistreat, roughhouse, slap around, thrash; SEE CONCEPTS *189,246*

ound [*adj1*] *ball-shaped; semicircular area*
annular, arced, arched, arciform, bent, bowed, bulbous, circular, coiled, curled, curved, curvilinear, cylindrical, discoid, disk-shaped, domical, egg-shaped, elliptical, globose, globular, looped, orbed, orbicular, orbiculate, oval, ringed, rotund, rounded, spherical, spheroid, spiral; SEE CONCEPT *486*

ound [*adj2*] *complete*
accomplished, done, entire, finished, full, rounded, solid, unbroken, undivided, whole; SEE CONCEPT *531*

round [*adj3*] *full-bodied, ample in size*
chubby, expansive, fleshy, generous, large, plump, plumpish, pudgy*, roly-poly*, rotund, rounded, tubby; SEE CONCEPTS *491,773*

round [*adj4*] *resonant, rich in sound*
consonant, full, mellifluous, orotund, plangent, resounding, ringing, rotund, sonorous, vibrant; SEE CONCEPT *594*

round [*adj5*] *honest, direct*
blunt, candid, frank, free, outspoken, plain, straightforward, unmodified, vocal; SEE CONCEPT *267*

round [*adv*] *approximate*
about, all but, almost, around, as good as, close to, in the neighborhood of, just about, most, near, nearly, practically, roughly; SEE CONCEPT *762*

round [*n1*] *globe, ball; semicircular area*
arc, arch, band, bend, bow, circle, circlet, curvation, curvature, curve, disc, disk, equator, eye, gyre, hoop, loop, orb, orbit, ring, ringlet, sphere, wheel; SEE CONCEPT *436*

round [*n2*] *cycle, stage*
ambit, beat, bout, circuit, circulation, circumvolution, compass, course, division, gyration, lap, level, performance, period, revolution, rotation, round trip, routine, schedule, sequence, series, session, succession, tour, turn, wheel, whirl; SEE CONCEPTS *364,727,807*

round [*n3*] *unit of ammunition*
bullet, cartridge, charge, discharge, load, shell, shot; SEE CONCEPTS *498,500*

round [*v1*] *turn; encircle*
begird, bypass, circle, circulate, circumnavigate, compass, encompass, flank, gird, girdle, go around, gyrate, hem, pivot, revolve, ring, roll, rotate, skirt, spin, surround, wheel, whirl; SEE CONCEPTS *147,149,187*

round [*v2*] *make curved; remove angles*
arch, bend, bow, coil, convolute, crook, curl, curve, form, loop, mold, perfect, polish, recurve, refine, shape, sleek, slick, smooth, whorl; SEE CONCEPTS *184,202*

roundabout [*adj*] *indirect*
ambiguous, circuitous, circular, circumlocutory, collateral, deviating, devious, discursive, evasive, meandering, oblique, obliquitous, periphrastic, taking the long way*, tortuous; SEE CONCEPTS *559,581,584*

round off [*v*] *finish*
bring to a close, cap, climax, close, complete, conclude, crown, culminate, finish off, settle, top off; SEE CONCEPT *234*

roundup [*n*] *collection, collation*
assembly, branding, gathering, herding, marshalling, muster, rally, summary, survey; SEE CONCEPTS *257,397*

round up [*v*] *collect, gather*
assemble, bring in, bring together, cluster, drive, group, herd, marshal, muster, rally; SEE CONCEPTS *109,257*

rouse [*v1*] *wake*
arouse, awake, awaken, call, get up, raise, rise, stir, wake up; SEE CONCEPT *250*

rouse [*v2*] *stimulate, excite*
aggravate, agitate, anger, animate, arouse, ask for it*, awaken, bestir, bug*, challenge, craze, deepen, disturb, enhance, enliven, exhilarate, fire up*, foment, galvanize, get going, heighten, incite, inflame, innervate, innerve, instigate, intensate, intensify, key up*, kindle, magnify, make

waves*, mount, move, needle, pep up*, pique, provoke, quicken, rally, redouble, rile, rise, startle, steam up*, stir, trigger, urge, vivify, wake, waken, wake up, whet, whip up*, work up; SEE CONCEPTS 7,22,244

rousing [*adj*] *stirring*
active, alert, animated, astir, bouncy, bright, brisk, buoyant, bustling, busy, buzzing, chirpy, dashing, energetic, enthusiastic, frisky, full of pep*, hyper*, industrious, jumping, lively, peppy*, perky, refreshing, snappy, spirited, spry, stimulating, vigorous, zippy*; SEE CONCEPTS 401,542,548

rout [*n*] *overwhelming defeat*
beating, clobbering*, comedown, confusion, debacle, disaster, drubbing*, embarrassment, flight, hiding, overthrow, retreat, romp, ruin, shambles, shutout, thrashing, trashing*, upset, vanquishment, walkover*, washout*, waxing*, whipping; SEE CONCEPTS 95,119,363

rout [*v*] *defeat overwhelmingly*
bash, beat, blow out of water*, bulldoze*, bury*, chase, clean up on*, clobber, conquer, cream*, crush, cut to pieces*, destroy, discomfit, dispel, drive off, expel, finish*, hunt, kill*, lambaste*, larrup*, murder*, outmaneuver, overpower, overthrow, put to flight*, repulse, scatter, scuttle, shut out*, skunk*, subdue, subjugate, swamp*, torpedo*, total*, trounce, vanquish, wallop, wax*, whip, wipe off map*, wipe out*, worst, zap*; SEE CONCEPT 95

route [*n*] *path over which someone or something travels*
avenue, beat, beeline, byway, circuit, course, detour, digression, direction, divergence, itinerary, journey, line, meandering, passage, pavement, pike, plot, program, rambling, range, road, round, rounds, run, short cut, tack, track, trail, wandering, way; SEE CONCEPTS 501,660

route [*v*] *send along a path*
address, conduct, consign, convey, direct, dispatch, escort, forward, guide, lead, pilot, remit, see, shepherd, ship, show, steer, transmit; SEE CONCEPTS 187,217

routine [*adj*] *habitual*
accepted, accustomed, chronic, conventional, customary, everyday, familiar, general, methodical, normal, ordinary, periodic, plain, quotidian, regular, seasonal, standard, typical, unremarkable, usual, wonted, workaday; SEE CONCEPTS 530,547,548

routine [*n*] *habitual activity*
act, beaten path*, bit, channels, custom, cycle, daily grind*, drill, formula, grind*, groove*, habit, line, method, order, pace, pattern, piece, practice, procedure, program, rat race*, rote, round, rut, schtick*, spiel*, system, tack, technique, treadmill, usage, way, wont; SEE CONCEPTS 6,362,770

row [*n1*] *sequence, series*
bank, chain, column, consecution, echelon, file, line, order, progression, queue, range, rank, string, succession, tier, train; SEE CONCEPTS 432,727,744

row [*n2*] *fight, ruckus*
affray, altercation, bickering, brawl, castigation, commotion, controversy, dispute, disturbance, falling-out*, fracas, fray, fuss, knock-down-drag-out*, lecture, melee, noise, quarrel, racket, reprimand, reproof, riot, rumpus, run-in*, scrap*,

set-to*, shouting match*, squabble, talking-to*, telling-off*, tiff, tongue-lashing*, trouble, tumult, uproar, words*, wrangle; SEE CONCEPTS 46,52,106

row [*v1*] *move boat with paddle*
drag, oar, paddle, pull, punt, sail, scud, scull, sky an oar, swim*; SEE CONCEPT 187

row [*v2*] *argue, fight*
bawl out, berate, bicker, brawl, call on the carpet*, dispute, jaw, quarrel, ream, scold, scrap, spat, squabble, tiff, tongue-lash*, wrangle; SEE CONCEPTS 46,106

rowdy [*adj*] *boisterous, noisy*
disorderly, lawless, loud, loudmouthed, loutish, mischievous, obstreperous, rambunctious, raucous, rebellious, rough, roughhouse, rude, turbulent, unruly, uproarious, wild; SEE CONCEPT 401

rowdy [*n*] *person who is boisterous, noisy*
brawler, bully, hellion, hooligan, lout, punk, roughneck, ruffian, terror*, troublemaker; SEE CONCEPT 412

royal [*adj*] *monarchical, grand*
aristocratic, august, authoritative, baronial, commanding, dignified, elevated, eminent, grandiose, high, high-born, honorable, illustrious, imperial, imposing, impressive, kingly, lofty, magnificent, majestic, noble, queenly, regal, regnant, reigning, renowned, resplendent, ruling, sovereign, splendid, stately, superb, superior, supreme, worthy; SEE CONCEPTS 549,574

rub [*n1*] *stroke, massage*
abrasion, attrition, brushing, caress, friction, grinding, kneading, pat, polish, rasping, scouring, scraping, shine, smear, smoothing, stroking, swab, swipe, wear, wipe; SEE CONCEPT 215

rub [*n2*] *difficulty, problem*
bar, catch, crimp, dilemma, drawback, hamper, hindrance, hitch, hurdle, impediment, obstacle, predicament, snag, stumbling block*, traverse, trouble; SEE CONCEPTS 666,674

rub [*v*] *stroke, massage*
abrade, anoint, apply, bark, brush, buff, burnish, caress, chafe, clean, coat, cover, curry, daub, erase, erode, excoriate, file, fray, fret, furbish, glance, glaze, gloss, grate, graze, grind, knead, mop, paint, pat, plaster, polish, put, rasp, scour, scrape, scrub, shine, slather, smear, smooth, spread, swab, triturate, wear, wear down, wipe; SEE CONCEPT 215

rubberneck [*v*] *stare*
eagle eye*, eye, eyeball*, focus, gawk, gaze, glare, goggle*, lay eyes on*, look, ogle, peer, rivet; SEE CONCEPT 623

rubbish [*n1*] *garbage*
debris, dregs, dross, junk, litter, lumber, offal, refuse, rubble, rummage, scrap, sweepings, trash, waste; SEE CONCEPT 260

rubbish [*n2*] *nonsense*
balderdash, bilge*, bunkum, drivel, gibberish, hogwash, hooey*, poppycock, rot*, stuff and nonsense*, tommyrot; SEE CONCEPTS 230,278

rubdown [*n*] *massage*
back rub, chirapsia, kneading, manipulation, stroking; SEE CONCEPTS 308,310

rub the wrong way [*v*] *irritate*
aggravate, anger, annoy, bother, bug*, disturb, drive up the wall*, enrage, get on one's nerves*, get to, get under one's skin*, infuriate, irk, needle*, pester, rattle, ruffle one's feathers*; SEE CONCEPTS 7,19

ruckus [n] *disturbance*

big scene*, big stink*, bother, brawl, brouhaha*, commotion, disorder, disruption, distraction, explosion, fisticuffs, fracas, fray, fuss, hubbub*, hullabaloo*, interruption, quarrel, racket, rampage, riot, rumble, rumpus, stink*, stir, turmoil, upheaval, uprising, uproar; SEE CONCEPTS 388,410,674,720

ruddy [adj] *pinkish, blushing*

blooming, blowsy, bronzed, crimson, florid, flush, flushed, fresh, full-blooded, glowing, healthy, pink, red, red-complexioned, reddish, roseate, rosy, rubicund, ruby, sanguine, scarlet; SEE CONCEPT 618

rude [adj1] *disrespectful, rough*

abrupt, abusive, bad-mannered, barbarian, barbaric, barbarous, blunt, boorish, brusque, brutish, cheeky, churlish, coarse, crabbed, crude, curt, discourteous, graceless, gross, gruff, ignorant, illiterate, impertinent, impolite, impudent, inconsiderate, insolent, insulting, intrusive, loutish, low, obscene, offhand, peremptory, raw, savage, scurrilous, short, surly, uncivil, uncivilized, uncouth, uncultured, uneducated, ungracious, unmannerly, unpolished, unrefined, vulgar, wild; SEE CONCEPTS 267,401

rude [adj2] *crude, primitive*

angular, artless, barbarous, callow, coarse, formless, fresh, green, ignorant, inartistic, inelegant, inexperienced, inexpert, makeshift, primal, raw, rough, roughhewn, roughly made, rudimental, rudimentary, shapeless, simple, uncivilized, unconversant, uncultivated, unfashioned, unfinished, unformed, unhewn, unpolished, unprocessed, unrefined, wild; SEE CONCEPTS 490, 531

rude [adj3] *sudden; approximate*

abrupt, guessed, harsh, imperfect, imprecise, inexact, in the ballpark*, proximate, rough, sharp, startling, stormy, surmised, turbulent, unpleasant, unprecise, violent; SEE CONCEPTS 557,799

rudimentary [adj] *basic, fundamental*

abecedarian, basal, beginning, early, elemental, elementary, embryonic, immature, initial, introductory, larval, nuts-and-bolts*, primary, primitive, simple, simplest, uncompleted, undeveloped, vestigial; SEE CONCEPTS 546,549

rudiments [n] *fundamentals*

ABCs*, basics, beginnings, elements, essentials, first principles, foundation, guts*, heart, nittygritty, principles; SEE CONCEPTS 668,687,826, 829

rue [v] *regret*

apologize, be sorry for, cry over*, deplore, feel remorse, feel sorry, grieve, kick oneself*, lament, mourn, weep over*; SEE CONCEPTS 21,410

rueful [adj] *regretful*

apologetic, ashamed, deplorable, lamentable, mournful, remorseful, repentant, sad, sorrowful, sorry; SEE CONCEPT 403

ruffian [n] *hoodlum*

brute, bully, criminal, delinquent, gangster, goon*, hood, hooligan, mobster, punk, rioter, rowdy, thug, tough guy*, troublemaker; SEE CONCEPT 412

ruffle [v] *mess up*

cockle, confuse, crease, crinkle, crumple, crush, derange, disarrange, discompose, dishevel, disor-

der, pucker, purse, rifle, rumple, tangle, tousle, wrinkle; SEE CONCEPT 158

ruffle [v2] *upset, irritate*

abrade, agitate, anger, annoy, bluster, bother, browbeat, bully, chafe, confuse, cow*, disconcert, disquiet, disturb, excite, floor*, flummox, flurry, fluster, fret, fuddle, gall, get to*, harass, intimidate, irk, nettle, peeve, perturb, provoke, put off, put out, rattle, rattle one's cage*, shake up*, stir, stump, throw into tizzy*, torment, trouble, vex, wear, worry; SEE CONCEPTS 7,14,19

rug [n1] *carpet*

carpeting, floor covering, mat, matting, runner, shag*, tapestry, throw rug, wall-to-wall carpeting; SEE CONCEPT 473

rug [n2] *hairpiece*

false hair, hair extension, hair implant, hair weaving, toupee, wig; SEE CONCEPT 392

rugged [adj1] *bumpy, weathered*

asperous, broken, coarse, craggy, difficult, furrowed, harsh, hilly, irregular, jagged, leathery, lumpy, mountainous, ragged, rocky, rough, roughhewn, scabrous, scraggy, stark, uneven, unlevel, unpolished, unrefined, unsmooth, weather-beaten, worn, wrinkled; SEE CONCEPTS 490,606

rugged [adj2] *severe, violent*

bitter, brutal, difficult, hard, harsh, inclement, intemperate, rigorous, rough, stormy, tempestuous, turbulent; SEE CONCEPTS 525,537

rugged [adj3] *uncouth, mean*

barbarous, blunt, boorish, churlish, graceless, illbred, loutish, rude, uncultured, unpolished, unrefined; SEE CONCEPT 401

rugged [adj4] *difficult, rigorous*

arduous, demanding, exacting, formidable, hairy*, hard, harsh, heavy*, heavy sledding*, knotty*, laborious, large order*, mean, murder*, no picnic*, operose, rough, stern, strenuous, taxing, tough, trying, uncompromising, uphill*; SEE CONCEPTS 538,565

rugged [adj5] *big, strong*

able-bodied, athletic, brawny, energetic, forceful, hale, hardy, healthy, husky, indefatigable, lusty, muscular, robust, sturdy, tough, unflagging, vigorous, well-built; SEE CONCEPTS 314,489

ruin [n] *situation of devastation*

atrophy, bane, bankruptcy, bath, breakdown, collapse, confusion, crackup, crash, crumbling, damage, decay, defeat, degeneracy, degeneration, demolition, destitution, destruction, deterioration, dilapidation, disintegration, disrepair, dissolution, downfall, downgrade, extinction, failure, fall, havoc, insolvency, loss, nemesis, overthrow, ruination, skids*, subversion, the end*, undoing, waste, waterloo, wreck, wreckage; SEE CONCEPT 674

ruin [v] *devastate, destroy*

bankrupt, beggar, botch, break, bring down, bring to ruin, bust, clean out, crush, decimate, deface, defeat, defile, demolish, deplete, deplore, depredate, desecrate, despoil, devour, dilapidate, disfigure, do in*, drain, exhaust, fleece, impoverish, injure, lay waste, maim, make a mess of, mangle, mar, mutilate, overthrow, overturn, overwhelm, pauperize, pillage, rape, ravish, raze, reduce, sack, shatter, smash, spoil, spoilate, total, use up, wipe out*, wrack, wreak havoc on, wreck; SEE CONCEPTS 234,246,252

ro
ru

ruinous [*adj*] *disastrous, devastating*
annihilative, baleful, baneful, calamitous, cataclysmic, catastrophic, crippling, damaging, deadly, deleterious, depleting, dire, disastrous, draining, exhausting, extravagant, fatal, fateful, harmful, hurtful, immoderate, impoverishing, injurious, murderous, noxious, pernicious, shattering, suicidal, unfortunate, wasteful, withering, wrackful; SEE CONCEPTS *537,548,570*

ruins [*n*] *buildings that are dilapidated*
ashes, debris, destruction, detritus, foundation, relics, remains, remnants, residue, rubble, traces, vestiges, wreck, wreckage; SEE CONCEPTS *439,733*

rule [*n1*] *standard, principle of behavior*
aphorism, apothegm, assize, axiom, basis, brocard, canon, chapter and verse*, command, commandment, criterion, decorum, decree, decretion, dictum, direction, edict, etiquette, formula, fundamental, gnome, guide, guideline, keynote, keystone, law, maxim, model, moral, no-no's*, order, ordinance, precedent, precept, prescription, propriety, regimen, regulation, ruling, statute, tenet, test, the book*, the numbers*, truism; SEE CONCEPT *688*

rule [*n2*] *leadership of organization*
administration, ascendancy, authority, command, control, direction, domination, dominion, empire, government, influence, jurisdiction, power, regime, regnancy, reign, sovereignty, supremacy, sway; SEE CONCEPTS *299,376*

rule [*n3*] *method, way*
course, custom, formula, habit, normalcy, normality, order of things, policy, practice, procedure, routine; SEE CONCEPTS *6,647*

rule [*v1*] *govern, manage*
administer, be in authority, be in driver's seat*, be in power, bridle, command, conduct, control, crack the whip*, curb, decree, dictate, direct, dominate, domineer, guide, hold sway*, hold the reins*, keep under one's thumb*, lay down the law*, lead, order, overrule, predominate, preponderate, preside, prevail, regulate, reign, restrain, rule the roost*, run, run the show*, sit on top of*, sway, take over; SEE CONCEPTS *117,133,298*

rule [*v2*] *judge, decide*
adjudge, adjudicate, conclude, decree, deduce, determine, establish, figure, find, fix, gather, hold, infer, lay down, pass upon, postulate, prescribe, pronounce, resolve, settle; theorize; SEE CONCEPTS *18,81*

rule out [*v*] *exclude, reject*
abolish, avert, ban, bate, cancel, count out, debar, deter, dismiss, eliminate, except, forbid, forestall, forfend, leave out, not consider, obviate, preclude, prevent, prohibit, proscribe, recant, revoke, stave off, suspend, ward off; SEE CONCEPTS *25,121*

ruler [*n*] *historically, person who ruled an area*
baron, baroness, caesar, caliph, contessa, count, countess, crowned head, czar, czarina, dame, duchess, duke, dynast, emperor, empress, gerent, imperator, kaiser, khan, king, lady, lord, magnate, maharajah, maharani, majesty, mikado, mogul, monarch, oligarch, overlord, pasha, potentate, prince, princess, queen, rajah, rani, rex, royal, shah, sovereign, sultan, sultana, tycoon; SEE CONCEPT *422*

ruler [*n2*] *tool for measuring or calculatin___*
length
folding rule, measure, measuring stick, rul___
slide rule, straightedge, T-square, yardstick; s___
CONCEPT *499*

ruling [*adj1*] *dominant, governing*
cardinal, central, commanding, controlling, lea___
ing, overriding, overruling, pivotal, regnar___
reigning, sovereign, supreme, upper; SEE CO___
CEPT *574*

ruling [*adj2*] *prevailing, main*
chief, current, dominant, pivotal, popular, pr___
dominant, preeminent, preponderant, prevaler___
principal, rampant, rife, widespread; SEE CO___
CEPT *568*

ruling [*n*] *judgment, decree*
adjudication, decision, directive, edict, findin___
judgment, law, order, precept, pronouncemer___
resolution, rule, ukase, verdict; SEE CONCEPT *3___*

rumble [*v*] *growl, thunder*
boom, grumble, resound, roar, roll; SEE CONCE___
65

ruminate [*v*] *think about seriously*
brainstorm*, brood, chew over, cogitate, co___
sider, contemplate, deliberate, excogitate, figur___
meditate, mull over, muse, ponder, rack one___
brains*, reflect, revolve, stew about*, think, tur___
over, use one's head*, weigh; SEE CONCEPT *24*

rummage [*v*] *ransack, search*
beat the bushes*, comb, delve, dig out, di___
arrange, disarray, disorder, disorganize, disrup___
disturb, examine, explore, ferret out, fish, forag___
grub, hunt, jumble, leave no stone unturned___
look high and low*, mess up, mix up, poke, rak___
root, scour, search high heaven*, seek, shak___
shake down, spy, toss, turn inside out*, turn u___
side down*; SEE CONCEPTS *158,216*

rumor [*n*] *talk about supposed truth*
back-fence talk*, breeze*, bruit, canard, cor___
ment, cry, dispatch, earful*, fabrication, false___
hood, fame, fiction, gossip, grapevine*, hearsa___
hoax, innuendo, intelligence, invention, li___
news, notoriety, report, repute, rumble, scanda___
scuttlebutt*, story, suggestion, supposition, tal___
tattle, tidings, whisper, wire*; word; SEE CO___
CEPTS *274,277,278*

rumor [*v*] *tell a supposed truth*
bruit, buzz*, circulate, gossip, noise about*, pa___
around, publish, report, say, talk, tattle, whispe___
SEE CONCEPTS *49,54*

rump [*n*] *bottom, posterior of animal or human*
back, backside, beam, behind, breech, bum___
butt, butt end, buttocks, can*, croup, derriè___
duff*, fanny*, haunches, hind end, hindquarter___
keister*, moon*, prat, rear, rear end, sacrur___
seat, tail*, tail end, tush*; SEE CONCEPTS *392,82___*

rumple [*v*] *crush, wrinkle*
bedraggle, cockle, crease, crimp, crinkle, crum___
ple, derange, dishevel, disorder, fold, mess u___
muss up, pucker, ruck up, ruffle, screw u___
scrunch, seam, tousle, wreathe; SEE CONCEPT___
137,219,250

rumpus [*n*] *clamor*
brouhaha*, commotion, discord, disturbanc___
donnybrook, fracas, fuss, hassle, hubba-hubba___
hubbub, hullabaloo*, noise, outcry, pandem___
nium, racket, rhubarb, ruckus, tumult, turmo___
upheaval, uproar; SEE CONCEPTS *386,595,674*

run [*n1*] *fast moving on foot*
amble, bound, break, canter, dart, dash, drop, e___

cape, fall, flight, gallop, jog, lope, pace, race, rush, scamper, scuttle, spring, spurt, tear, trot, whisk; SEE CONCEPTS *150,195*

run [n2] *journey*
drive, excursion, jaunt, joy ride*, lift, outing, ride, round, spin, tour, travel, trip; SEE CONCEPT *224*

run [n3] *sequence, course*
bearing, chain, continuance, continuation, continuity, current, cycle, drift, duration, endurance, field, flow, line, motion, movement, passage, path, period, persistence, progress, prolongation, round, ply, route, season, series, spell, streak, stream, stretch, string, succession, swing, tendency, tenor, tide, trend, way; SEE CONCEPTS *721,727,738*

run [v1] *move fast on foot*
abscond, amble, barrel, beat it*, bolt, bound, bustle, canter, career, clear out, course, cut and run*, dart, dash, decamp, depart, dog it*, escape, flee, flit, fly, gallop, go like lightning*, hasten, hie, hotfoot*, hurry, hustle, jog, leg it*, light out*, lope, make a break*, make off, make tracks*, pace, race, rush, scamper, scoot, scorch, scramble, scud, scurry, shag, shoot, skedaddle*, skip, skitter, smoke*, speed, spring, sprint, spurt, take flight, take off, tear, tear out, travel, trot, whisk; SEE CONCEPTS *150,195*

run [v2] *move rapidly, flowingly*
bleed, cascade, course, deliquesce, diffuse, discharge, dissolve, drop, fall, flow, flux, fuse, glide, go, go soft, gush, issue, leak, leap, liquefy, melt, pass, pour, proceed, roll, sail, scud, skim, slide, spill, spin, spout, spread, stream, thaw, tumble, turn to liquid, whirl, whiz; SEE CONCEPT *146*

run [v3] *operate, drive*
act, bear, carry, command, control, convey, go, govern, handle, manage, maneuver, move, perform, ply, propel, tick, transport, use, work; SEE CONCEPTS *225,680*

run [v4] *manage, supervise*
administer, be in charge, be in driver's seat*, be in saddle*, boss, carry on, conduct, control, coordinate, direct, head, head up*, helm*, keep, lead, look after, operate, ordain, oversee, own, pull the strings*, regulate, ride herd on*, superintend, take care of*; SEE CONCEPT *117*

run [v5] *continue, range*
be current, circulate, cover, encompass, extend, go, go around, go on, last, lie, move past, persevere, proceed, reach, spread, stretch, trail, vary; SEE CONCEPTS *651,721*

run [v6] *attempt to be elected to public office*
be a candidate, challenge, compete, contend, contest, hit the campaign trail*, kiss babies*, oppose, politick, race, ring doorbells*, shake hands*, stand, stump, whistlestop*; SEE CONCEPT *300*

run-around [n] *avoidance*
come-off, delay, detour, difficulty, diversion, elusion, escape, escaping, eschewal, evasion, inertia, postponement, roundabout, shunning; SEE CONCEPTS *30,121*

runaway [adj] *out of control*
delinquent, disorderly, escaped, fleeing, fugitive, loose, out of hand*, running, uncontrolled, wild; SEE CONCEPT *401*

runaway [n] *person who is trying to escape*
absconder, delinquent, deserter, escapee, es-

caper, fugitive, lawbreaker, maroon, offender, truant, wanted person; SEE CONCEPT *412*

run-down [adj] *shabby, in bad shape*
abandoned, beat-up, below par, broken-down, crumbling, debilitated, decrepit, derelict, deserted, desolate, dilapidated, dingy, dog-eared*, down-at-the-heel*, drained, enervated, exhausted, fatigued, forsaken, frowzy*, in a bad way*, neglected, old, out of condition, peaked, ramshackle, ratty*, rickety, seedy, shabby, tacky, tattered, tired, tumble-down, uncared-for, under the weather*, unhealthy, untended, used up, weak, weary, worn-out; SEE CONCEPTS *314,485,570*

rundown [n] *summary*
briefing, outline, precis, recap*, recapitulation, report, résumé, review, run-through, sketch, synopsis; SEE CONCEPT *283*

run down [v] *ridicule*
belittle, criticize, decry, defame, denigrate, depreciate, derogate, detract, diminish, disparage, dispraise, downcry, knock*, make fun of, opprobriate, revile, speak ill of, vilify; SEE CONCEPTS *52,54*

rung [n] *notch, step*
bar, board, crossbar, crosspiece, degree, grade, level, rod, round, rundle, stage, tread; SEE CONCEPTS *471,744*

run-in [n] *argument*
altercation, bickering, brush, confrontation, contretemps, dispute, encounter, falling-out*, fight, hassle, quarrel, row, set-to*, skirmish, tussle; SEE CONCEPTS *46,106*

run in [v] *arrest*
apprehend, bust, collar, cop*, detain, handcuff, jail, nab, pick up, pinch*, pull in, put the cuffs on*, take into custody, throw in jail*; SEE CONCEPTS *298,317*

running [adj] *continuous, flowing, operating*
active, alive, constant, cursive, dynamic, easy, effortless, executing, fluent, functioning, going, in action, incessant, in operation, in succession, live, moving, operative, perpetual, proceeding, producing, smooth, together, unbroken, unceasing, uninterrupted, working; SEE CONCEPTS *538,560,584*

running [adv] *continually*
consecutively, continuously, night and day*, successively, together, unintermittedly, uninterruptedly; SEE CONCEPTS *482,798*

running [n] *management of organization*
administration, care, charge, conduct, control, coordination, direction, functioning, handling, intendance, leadership, maintenance, operation, organization, oversight, performance, regulation, superintendency, supervision, working; SEE CONCEPT *117*

run-of-the-mill [adj] *average*
common, commonplace, customary, dime a dozen, everyday, fair, fair to middling*, garden-variety*, humdrum, intermediate, mainstream, mediocre, medium, middle of the road*, middling, ordinary, regular, routine, so-so*, undistinguished, unexceptional, usual; SEE CONCEPT *547*

run out [v] *fail, be exhausted*
be cleaned out*, be out of, cease, close, come to a close, depart, dissipate, dry up, end, exhaust, expire, finish, give out, go, have no more, have none left, lose, peter out*, stop, terminate, tire,

waste, waste away, weaken, wear out; SEE CONCEPTS *105,699*

runt [*n*] *very small person*
half-pint*, homunculus, Lilliputian, midget, peewee*, punk*, shrimp*; SEE CONCEPT *424*

run through [*v*] *use up; waste*
blow, consume, dissipate, exhaust, expend, finish, fritter away, lose, spend, squander, throw away, wash up; SEE CONCEPT *156*

rupture [*n1*] *break, split*
breach, burst, cleavage, cleft, crack, division, fissure, fracture, hernia, herniation, parting, rent, schism, tear; SEE CONCEPTS *309,513*

rupture [*n2*] *disagreement, dissolution*
altercation, breach, break, break-up, bustup*, clash, contention, detachment, disruption, disunion, division, divorce, divorcement, estrangement, falling-out, feud, hostility, misunderstanding, parting, partition, quarrel, rift, schism, separation, split, split-up*; SEE CONCEPTS *46,388*

rupture [*v1*] *break open*
breach, burst, cleave, crack, disrupt, divide, erupt, fracture, hold, open, part, puncture, rend, rive, separate, sever, shatter, split, sunder, tear; SEE CONCEPTS *98,246,308*

rupture [*v2*] *disagree; dissolve union*
break off, break up, come between, disjoin, disrupt, dissect, dissever, disunite, divide, divorce, part, separate, split, split up, sunder; SEE CONCEPTS *297,384*

rural [*adj*] *country, not urban*
agrarian, agricultural, agronomic, Arcadian, backwoods, bucolic, countrified, farm, georgic, idyllic, natural, outland, pastoral, provincial, ranch, rustic, rustical, simple, sylvan, unsophisticated; SEE CONCEPT *583*

ruse [*n*] *trick, deception*
angle, artifice, blind, booby trap*, curveball*, deceit, device, dodge, feint, gambit, game, game plan*, gimmick, hoax, imposture, jig*, maneuver, ploy, scenario, sham, shenanigans*, shift, stratagem, stunt, subterfuge, switch*, twist*, wile; SEE CONCEPTS *59,674*

rush [*n1*] *hurry, speed*
blitz, charge, dash, dispatch, expedition, flood, flow, flux, haste, hastiness, hurriedness, precipitance, precipitancy, precipitation, race, scramble, stream, surge, swiftness, urgency; SEE CONCEPTS *145,748,818*

rush [*n2*] *attack*
assault, blitz, charge, onslaught, push, storm, surge, violence; SEE CONCEPT *86*

rush [*v1*] *hurry, speed*
accelerate, barrel, bolt, break, career, charge, chase, course, dart, dash, dispatch, expedite, fire up*, fleet, fling, flit, fly, get cracking*, get the lead out*, go like lightning*, haste, hasten, hotfoot*, hurry up, hustle, lose no time*, make haste, make short work of*, press, push, quicken, race, roll, run, scramble, scud, scurry, shake a leg*, shoot, speed up, sprint, step on gas*, streak, surge, tear, whiz*, zip*, zoom*; SEE CONCEPTS *91,150,152*

rush [*v2*] *charge, attack*
capture, overcome, storm, surge, take by storm*; SEE CONCEPT *86*

rust [*n*] *corrosion*
blight, corruption, decay, decomposition, dilapi-

dation, mold, oxidation, rot, wear; SEE CONCEPTS *309,720*

rust [*v*] *corrode*
decay, decline, degenerate, deteriorate, oxidize, stale, tarnish, wither; SEE CONCEPT *469*

rustic [*adj1*] *country, rural*
agrarian, agricultural, Arcadian, artless, austere, bucolic, countrified, homely, homespun, homey, honest, natural, outland, pastoral, picturesque, plain, primitive, provincial, simple, sylvan, unaffected, unpolished, unrefined, unsophisticated, verdant; SEE CONCEPTS *583,589*

rustic [*adj2*] *crude, uncouth*
awkward, boorish, churlish, clodhopping, clownish, coarse, countrified, dull, foolish, graceless, ignorant, inelegant, loutish, maladroit, rough, rude, stupid, uncultured, uneducated, ungainly, unmannerly, unpolished, unsophisticated; SEE CONCEPT *401*

rustic [*n*] *person from the country, with little experience*
backwoodsperson, boor, country cousin*, countryperson, farmer, hayseed*, hick*, hillbilly, mountaineer, peasant, provincial, redneck*, rural, yokel*; SEE CONCEPT *413*

rustle [*n*] *whisper, swish*
crackle, crepitation, crinkling, friction, noise, patter, ripple, rustling, sound, stir; SEE CONCEPT *595*

rustle [*v*] *swish, whisper*
crackle, crepitate, crinkle, hum, murmur, patter, sigh, stir, tap, whir, whish, whoosh; SEE CONCEPT *65*

rustle up [*v*] *provide*
accommodate, arrange, assemble, bring, cater, cook, furnish, get ready, give, hand over, indulge, make, prepare, present, produce, put together, ready, render, scrape up, serve, supply, take care of, turn out; SEE CONCEPTS *35,108,110, 136,140,202*

rusty [*adj1*] *corroded*
decayed, oxidized, rust-covered, rusted; SEE CONCEPT *485*

rusty [*adj2*] *out of practice; inexperienced*
deficient, impaired, neglected, not what it was*, sluggish, soft, stale, unpracticed, unqualified, weak; SEE CONCEPT *527*

rut [*n1*] *groove, indentation*
furrow, gouge, hollow, pothole, rabbet, score, track, trench, trough; SEE CONCEPT *513*

rut [*n2*] *routine of daily life*
circle, circuit, course, custom, daily grind*, dead end*, grind*, groove, habit, humdrum*, pace, pattern, performance, practice, procedure, rote, round, system, treadmill, usage, wont; SEE CONCEPTS *6,647*

ruthless [*adj*] *mean, heartless*
adamant, barbarous, brutal, callous, cold, cold-blooded, cruel, cutthroat, dog-eat-dog*, feral, ferocious, fierce, grim, hard, hard-hearted, harsh, implacable, inexorable, inhuman, ironfisted, killer, malevolent, merciless, mortal, obdurate, pitiless, rancorous, relentless, remorseless, revengeful, sadistic, savage, severe, stern, stony, surly, unappeasable, unfeeling, unforgiving, unmerciful, unrelenting, unsympathetic, unyielding, vicious, vindictive, without pity; SEE CONCEPTS *401,404*

S

sabbatical [n] *leave*
break, furlough, holiday, leave of absence, liberty, recess, time off, vacation; SEE CONCEPTS 802,807

sable [adj] *very dark in color*
black, dark, dusky, dusty, ebon, ebony, gloomy, inky, jet, jetty, murky, pitch-black, pitch-dark, raven, somber; SEE CONCEPT 618

sabotage [n] *damage*
demolition, destruction, disruption, impairment, injury, mischief, overthrow, subversion, subversiveness, treachery, treason, undermining, vandalism, wreckage, wrecking; SEE CONCEPTS 86,246,252

sabotage [v] *incapacitate, damage*
attack, block, bollix, break up, cripple, deep six*, destroy, disable, disrupt, do*, do in*, foul up*, frustrate, hamper, hinder, louse up*, mess up*, obstruct, put out of action, put out of commission*, screw up*, subvert, take out*, throw a monkey wrench into*, torpedo*, undermine, vandalize, wreck; SEE CONCEPTS 86,246,252

sack [v1] *remove from position of responsibility*
ax*, bounce*, can*, cashier, discharge, dismiss, drop, expel, fire, give a pink slip*, give marching orders*, give the boot*, kick out, send packing*, ship, terminate; SEE CONCEPT 351

sack [v2] *raid, plunder*
demolish, depredate, desecrate, desolate, despoil, destroy, devastate, devour, fleece, gut, lay waste, loot, maraud, pillage, ravage, rifle, rob, ruin, spoil, spoliate, strip, waste; SEE CONCEPTS 139,252

sacrament [n] *rite*
baptism, celebration, ceremony, communion, confession, confirmation, custom, holy orders, liturgy, marriage, matrimony, oath, observance, practice, ritual, service, vow; SEE CONCEPTS 377,386

sacred [adj1] *holy, blessed*
angelic, cherished, consecrated, divine, enshrined, godly, hallowed, numinous, pious, pure, religious, revered, sacramental, saintly, sanctified, solemn, spiritual, unprofane, venerable; SEE CONCEPT 574

sacred [adj2] *protected*
dedicated, defended, guarded, immune, inviolable, inviolate, invulnerable, sacrosanct, secure, shielded, untouchable; SEE CONCEPT 587

sacrifice [v] *give up, let go*
cede, drop, endure, eschew, forfeit, forgo, immolate, kiss goodbye*, lose, offer, offer up, part with, renounce, resign oneself to, spare, suffer, surrender, waive, yield; SEE CONCEPTS 108,116

sacrilege [n] *irreverence*
blasphemy, crime, curse, desecration, heresy, impiety, mockery, offense, profanation, profaneness, profanity, sin, violation; SEE CONCEPT 645

sacrilegious [adj] *profane*
atheistic, blasphemous, desecrating, dirty*, filthy*, foul, godless, heathen, impious, indecent, infidel, irreligious, irreverent, irreverential, obscene, pagan, sinful, ungodly, unhallowed, unholy, violating; SEE CONCEPTS 267,401,545

sacrosanct [adj] *sacred*
blessed, consecrated, divine, godly, hallowed, holy, pious, pure, religious, revered, sacramental, saintly, sanctified, spiritual, unprofane, venerated; SEE CONCEPT 574

sad [adj1] *unhappy, depressed*
bereaved, bitter, blue*, cheerless, dejected, despairing, despondent, disconsolate, dismal, distressed, doleful, down, downcast, down in dumps*, down in mouth*, forlorn, gloomy, glum, grief-stricken, grieved, heartbroken, heartsick, heavyhearted, hurting, in doldrums*, in grief, in the dumps*, languishing, low, low-spirited, lugubrious, melancholy, morbid, morose, mournful, out of sorts*, pensive, pessimistic, sick at heart*, somber, sorrowful, sorry, troubled, weeping, wistful, woebegone; SEE CONCEPT 403

sad [adj2] *unfortunate, distressing*
bad, calamitous, dark, dejecting, deplorable, depressing, disastrous, discomposing, discouraging, disheartening, dismal, dispiriting, dreary, funereal, grave, grievous, hapless, heart-rending, joyless, lachrymose, lamentable, lugubrious, melancholic, miserable, moving, oppressive, pathetic, pitiable, pitiful, poignant, regrettable, saddening, serious, shabby, sorry, tearful, tear-jerking*, tragic, unhappy, unsatisfactory, upsetting, wretched; SEE CONCEPTS 529,548

sadden [v] *upset, depress*
break one's heart*, bring one down*, bum out*, cast down, dampen spirits, dash, deject, deplore, desolate, discourage, dishearten, dispirit, distress, down, drag down*, grieve, make blue*, oppress, press, put a damper on*, put into a funk*, throw cold water on*, turn one into a funk*, weigh down*; SEE CONCEPTS 7,19

sadistic [adj] *cruel, perverted*
barbarous, brutal, fiendish, perverse, ruthless, vicious; SEE CONCEPTS 542,545

sadness [n] *unhappiness, depression*
anguish, blahs*, bleakness, blue devils*, blue funk*, broken heart*, bummer, cheerlessness, dejection, despondency, disconsolateness, dismals*, dispiritedness, distress, dolefulness, dolor, downcastness, downer*, dysphoria, forlornness, funk, gloominess, grief, grieving, heartache, heartbreak, heavy heart*, hopelessness, letdown, listlessness, melancholy, misery, moodiness, mopes*, mournfulness, mourning, poignancy, sorrow, sorrowfulness, the blues*, the dumps*, tribulation, woe; SEE CONCEPT 410

safari [n] *hunting expedition*
hunt, journey, quest, trek, trip; SEE CONCEPT 224

safe [adj1] *free from harm*
buttoned up*, cherished, free from danger, guarded, home-free*, impervious, impregnable, in safety, intact, inviolable, invulnerable, maintained, okay*, out of danger, out of harm's way*, preserved, protected, safe and sound*, safeguarded, secure, sheltered, shielded, sitting pretty*, snug, tended, unassailable, undamaged, under lock and key*, under one's wing*, unharmed, unhurt, uninjured, unmolested, unscathed, unthreatened, vindicated, watched; SEE CONCEPT 587

safe [adj2] *not dangerous*
certain, checked, clear, competent, decontaminated, dependable, harmless, healthy, innocent, innocuous, innoxious, inoffensive, neutralized, nonpoisonous, nontoxic, pure, reliable, risk-free, riskless, secure, sound, tame, trustworthy, unin-

jurious, unpolluted, wholesome; SEE CONCEPTS
314,537,548

safe [adj3] *cautious, conservative*
calculating, careful, chary, circumspect, competent, considerate, dependable, discreet, gingerly,
guarded, on safe side*, prudent, realistic, reliable, sure, tried and true*, trustworthy, unadven-
turous, wary; SEE CONCEPTS 401,542

safeguard [n] *protection*
aegis, armament, armor, buffer, bulwark, convoy, defense, escort, guard, screen, security,
shield, surety, ward; SEE CONCEPT 712

safeguard [v] *protect*
assure, bulwark, conserve, cover, defend, ensure,
fend, guard, insure, look after, preserve, ride
shotgun*, save, screen, secure, shield, watch
over; SEE CONCEPT 96

safekeeping [n] *protection*
aegis, assurance, care, certainty, cover, custody,
guardianship, guarding, insurance, preservation,
protecting, reassurance, refuge, safeguard, security, shelter, supervision, trust; SEE CONCEPTS
712,729

safety [n] *protection from harm*
assurance, asylum, cover, defense, freedom, immunity, impregnability, inviolability, invulnerability, refuge, safeness, sanctuary, security,
shelter; SEE CONCEPT 729

safety net [n] *level of economic security guaranteed by government*
benefits, buffer, government aid, insurance, precaution, protective umbrella, safeguard, subsidy;
SEE CONCEPT 344

sag [n] *drop, decline*
basin, cant, concavity, depression, dip, distortion, downslide*, downswing*, downtrend,
downturn, droop, fall, fall-off, hollow, list, settling, sink, sinkage, sinkhole, sinking, slant, slip,
slump, tilt; SEE CONCEPTS 181,698,776

sag [v] *droop*
bag, bend, bow, bulge, cave in, curve, dangle,
decline, dip, droop, drop off, fail, fall, fall away,
fall off, flag, flap, flop, give way, hang, hang
down, languish, lean, settle, sink, slide, slip,
slump, swag, wilt; SEE CONCEPTS 181,698,776

saga [n] *story, often long*
adventure, chronicle, epic, legend, narrative,
soap opera*, tale, yarn; SEE CONCEPT 282

sagacious [adj] *smart, judicious*
acute, apt, astucious, astute, cagey, canny, clear-
sighted, clever, cool*, discerning, discriminating, far-sighted, foxy*, gnostic, heady, hip*,
insightful, intelligent, keen, knowing, knowledgeable, perceptive, perspicacious, prudent, rational, sage, sapient, savvy*, sensible, sharp,
shrewd, smooth, sophic, wise, witty; SEE CON-
CEPT 402

sagacity [n] *wisdom*
acumen, astuteness, brains*, clear thinking,
common sense, comprehension, discernment,
discrimination, enlightenment, experience,
foresight, good judgment, insight, intelligence,
judgment, knowledge, level-headedness, perceptiveness, perspicacity, practicality, prudence,
sageness, sapience, sense, shrewdness, understanding; SEE CONCEPT 409

sage [adj] *wise*
astute, aware, careful, clever, contemplative,
cunning, discerning, educated, enlightened, experienced, foresighted, informed, insightful, in-

telligent, intuitive, judicious, knowing, knowledgeable, learned, perceptive, reflective, sagacious, sapient, scholarly, sensible, sharp, shrewd,
smart, sound, thoughtful, understanding; SEE
CONCEPT 402

sage [n] *wise person*
guide, guru, intellect, intellectual, learned person, mahatma, master, mentor, philosopher, pundit, savant, teacher, thinker, wise man/woman;
SEE CONCEPTS 350,409,416

sail [v] *travel through water, air; glide*
boat, captain, cast anchor, cast off, cross, cruise,
dart, drift, embark, flit, float, fly, get under way*,
leave, make headway, motor, move, navigate,
pilot, put to sea*, reach, run, scud, set sail, shoot,
skim, skipper, skirr, soar, steer, sweep, tack, voyage, weigh anchor, wing; SEE CONCEPT 224

sailboat [n] *a boat propelled with wind by sailcloth*
bark, brig, brigantine, catamaran, clipper, craft,
cutter, dory, gaff-rigged sailboat, galleon, galley,
jack, ketch, pinnace, ragboat*, schooner, ship,
skiff, sloop, Sunfish, tall ship, vessel, windjammer, wooden boat, yacht, yawl; SEE CONCEPT
506

sailor [n] *person who travels by sea*
able-bodied sailor, bluejacket*, boater, cadet,
circumnavigator, deck hand, diver, hearty*,
jack*, lascar*, marine, mariner, mate, middy,
midshipman/woman, navigator, old salt*, pilot,
pirate, salt*, sea dog*, seafarer, sea person, shellback*, shipmate, swab, swabber*, swabbie*,
tar*, tarpaulin*, water dog*, windjammer*,
yachter; SEE CONCEPTS 348,358,366

saint [n] *holy person*
angel, glorified soul, good person, holy being,
loved one, martyr, pietist; SEE CONCEPTS 361,370

saintly [adj] *good, righteous*
angelic, beatific, blameless, blessed, devout, divine, god-fearing, godly, holy, pious, pure, religious, sainted, saintlike, seraph, sinless, upright,
upstanding, virtuous, worthy; SEE CONCEPT 404

sake [n1] *benefit, gain*
account, advantage, behalf, consideration, good,
interest, profit, regard, respect, welfare, well-
being; SEE CONCEPT 693

sake [n2] *reason, objective*
aim, cause, consequence, end, final cause, motive, principle, purpose, score; SEE CONCEPTS
659,661

salacious [adj] *lascivious*
bawdy, carnal, erotic, fast*, horny, hot*, indecent, lecherous, lewd, libertine, libidinous, licentious, lubricious, lustful, nasty, obscene,
orgiastic, prurient, raunchy, sensual, smutty*,
steamy, suggestive, voluptuous, wanton; SEE
CONCEPTS 372,403

salad [n] *dish of vegetables*
coleslaw, fruit salad, greens, mixed greens,
potato salad, tossed salad, Waldorf salad; SEE
CONCEPT 431

salary [n] *money paid for work done*
bacon*, bread*, earnings, emolument, fee, hire,
income, pay, payroll, recompense, remuneration,
scale, stipend, take, take-home*, wage, wages;
SEE CONCEPT 344

sale [n] *exchange of object for money*
auction, barter, business, buying, clearance,
closeout, commerce, consuming, deal, demand,
disposal, dumping, enterprise, marketing, negoti-

ation, purchase, purchasing, reduction, selling, trade, transaction, unloading, vending, vendition; SEE CONCEPTS 324,345

salesperson [n] salesman/woman
businessperson, clerk, dealer, peddler, rep, sales assistant, salesclerk, salesgirl, saleslady, sales rep, sales representative, seller, store clerk, traveling salesperson, vendor; SEE CONCEPT 348

salient [adj] noticeable, important
arresting, arrestive, conspicuous, famous, impressive, intrusive, jutting, marked, moving, notable, obtrusive, obvious, outstanding, pertinent, projecting, prominent, pronounced, protruding, remarkable, signal, significant, striking, weighty; SEE CONCEPT 567

saliva [n] spit
dribble, drool, froth, slaver, slobber, spittle, sputum; SEE CONCEPT 467

sallow [adj] pale, unhealthy
anemic, ashen, ashy, bilious, colorless, dull, greenish-yellow, jaundiced, muddy, pallid, pasty, wan, waxy, yellowish; SEE CONCEPT 618

saloon [n] business establishment that primarily serves liquor
alehouse, bar, barroom, beer joint*, cocktail lounge, dive*, drinkery, gin mill*, hangout*, joint*, night club, pub, public house, speakeasy, taproom, tavern, watering hole*; SEE CONCEPTS 439,448,449

salt away [v] save, store up
accumulate, amass, bank, cache, hide, hoard, invest, lay aside, lay away, put away, put by, put in the bank, save, save for rainy day*, set aside, spare, stash, stockpile; SEE CONCEPT 330

salty [adj1] flavored with sodium chloride
acrid, alkaline, brackish, briny, highly flavored, oversalted, pungent, saliferous, saline, salt, salted, saltish, sour; SEE CONCEPTS 462,613

salty [adj2] spicy, colorful
humorous, lively, piquant, pungent, racy, sharp, snappy, tangy, tart, witty, zestful; SEE CONCEPTS 401,589

salubrious [adj] health-giving
beneficial, good, healthful, healthy, hygienic, invigorating, salutary, sanitary, wholesome; SEE CONCEPTS 560,572

salutary [adj] healthy
aiding, beneficial, fit, good, healing, healthful, nourishing, nutritious, restorative, salubrious, sound, tonic, well, wholesome; SEE CONCEPTS 314,462,537545

salute [v] greet; honor
accost, acknowledge, address, bow, call to, congratulate, hail, pay homage, pay respects, pay tribute, present arms, receive, recognize, snap to attention*, speak, take hat off to*, welcome; SEE CONCEPTS 38,69,320

salute/salutation [n] greeting, recognition
address, bow, howdy*, kiss, obeisance, tribute, welcome; SEE CONCEPT 38

salvage [v] save, rescue
deliver, get back, glean, ransom, reclaim, recover, redeem, regain, restore, retrieve, salve; SEE CONCEPT 134

salvation [n] rescue, saving
conservancy, conservation, deliverance, emancipation, escape, exemption, extrication, keeping, liberation, lifeline, pardon, preserval, preservation, redemption, release, reprieve, restoration, safekeeping, sustentation; SEE CONCEPT 134

salve [n] ointment for relief of pain or illness
aid, balm, cerate, counterirritant, cream, cure, dressing, emolient, help, liniment, lotion, lubricant, medication, medicine, remedy, unction, unguent; SEE CONCEPTS 311,466

salve [v] soothe
alleviate, ally, assuage, balm, becalm, calm, calm down, cool off*, ease, heal, mollify, pacify, pour oil on*, quiet, relieve, settle, smooth down, soften, still, take the edge off*, take the sting out of*, unburden, untrouble; SEE CONCEPTS 7,22,110,384

same [adj1] alike, identical
aforementioned, aforesaid, carbon*, carbon-copy*, clone, coequal, comparable, compatible, corresponding, ditto*, double, dupe*, duplicate, equal, equivalent, indistinguishable, interchangeable, in the same manner, like, likewise, look-alike, related, same difference, selfsame, similar, similarly, synonymous, tantamount, twin, very, Xerox*; SEE CONCEPTS 487,566,573

same [adj2] unchanging
changeless, consistent, constant, invariable, perpetual, unaltered, unchanged, unfailing, uniform, unvarying; SEE CONCEPT 534

sameness [n] likeness, similarity
adequation, alikeness, analogy, equality, equivalency, identicalness, identity, indistinguishability, monotony, no difference, oneness, par, parity, predictability, repetition, resemblance, selfsameness, standardization, tedium, uniformity, unison, unity, unvariedness; SEE CONCEPTS 667,670

sample [n] example, model
bit, bite, case, case history, constituent, cross section, element, exemplification, fragment, illustration, indication, individual, instance, morsel, part, pattern, pièce, portion, representative, sampling, segment, sign, specimen, typification, unit; SEE CONCEPTS 686,835

sample [v] taste, try
examine, experience, experiment, inspect, partake, savor, sip, test; SEE CONCEPTS 103,616

sanctify [v] hold in highest esteem
absolve, anoint, bless, cleanse, consecrate, dedicate, deify, enshrine, glorify, hallow, purify, set apart, worship; SEE CONCEPTS 10,12

sanctimonious [adj] self-righteous
bigoted, canting, deceiving, false, goody-goody*, holier-than-thou*, hypocritical, insincere, pharisaical, .pietistic, pious, preachy, self-satisfied, smug, stuffy, unctuous; SEE CONCEPTS 401,404

sanction [n1] authorization
acquiescence, allowance, approbation, approval, assent, authority, backing, confirmation, consent, countenance, encouragement, endorsement, fiat, go-ahead*, green light*, leave, nod, okay*, permission, permit, ratification, recommendation, seal of approval*, stamp of approval*, sufferance, support, word; SEE CONCEPT 685

sanction [n2] embargo, punishment
ban, boycott, coercive measure, command, decree, injunction, penalty, punitive measure, sentence, writ; SEE CONCEPT 123

sanction [v] authorize, confirm
accredit, allow, approve, back, bless, certify, commission, countenance, empower, endorse, get behind*, give the go-ahead*, give the green light*, give the nod*, go for*, license, okay*,

sa
sa

permit, ratify, support, vouch for, warrant; SEE
CONCEPTS 50,88

sanctioned [adj] authorized
accepted, accredited, allowed, approved, confirmed, empowered, licensed, okayed, permitted,
warranted; SEE CONCEPTS 542,798

sanctity [n] holiness
asceticism, blessedness, consecration, devotion,
devoutness, divineness, divinity, faith, godliness,
goodness, grace, hallowedness, inviolability,
mercy, piety, purity, religiousness, reverence,
righteousness, sacredness, saintliness, solemnity,
spirituality, venerableness; SEE CONCEPTS
368,645

sanctuary [n1] church; holiest room or area in
religious building
altar, chancel, holy place, sanctorium, sanctum,
shrine, temple; SEE CONCEPTS 368,439,448

sanctuary [n2] place to hide, be safe
asylum, church, convent, cover, covert, defense,
den, harbor, harborage, haven, hideaway, hideout, hole, hole-up*, ivory tower*, oasis, port,
protection, refuge, resort, retreat, safe house,
screen, shelter, shield; SEE CONCEPTS 515,516

sanctuary [n3] safe place for wildlife
asylum, conservation area, game refuge, harborage, national park, nature preserve, park, preserve, refuge, reserve, retreat, shelter; SEE
CONCEPT 517

sandwich [n] grinder
BLT, club sandwich, Dagwood*, hero*, hoagie,
open-faced sandwich, Reuben, sub, submarine
sandwich; SEE CONCEPTS 457,460,461

sane [adj] mentally sound; reasonable
all there*, balanced, both oars in water*, commonsensical, compos mentis, discerning, fair-
minded, fit, having all marbles*, healthy, in
one's right mind*, intelligent, judicious, levelheaded, logical, lucid, moderate, normal, of
sound mind, oriented, playing with full deck*,
prudent, rational, right, right-minded, sagacious,
sage, sapient, self-possessed, sensible, sober,
sound, steady, together*, well, wise; SEE CON-
CEPTS 314,402,403

sanguine [adj1] happy; optimistic
animated, assured, buoyant, cheerful, confident,
enthusiastic, expectant, hopeful, lively, positive,
secure, self-assured, self-confident, spirited, undoubtful, upbeat; SEE CONCEPTS 403,542

sanguine [adj2] reddish; flushed
bloody, florid, flush, glowing, red, rubicund,
ruddy, scarlet; SEE CONCEPT 618

sanitary [adj] clean, germ-free
healthful, healthy, hygienic, prophylactic, purified, salubrious, sanative, sterile, uncontaminated, uninfected, unpolluted, unsullied,
wholesome; SEE CONCEPT 621

sanitize [v] sterilize
antisepticize, asceptize, aseptify, clean, decontaminate, disinfect, freshen, fumigate, make sanitary, purify; SEE CONCEPTS 231,250

sanity [n] mental health; soundness of judgment
acumen, balance, clear mind, common sense,
comprehension, good judgment, healthy mind,
intelligence, judiciousness, levelheadedness, lucidity, lucidness, marbles*, normality, prudence,
rationality, reason, reasonableness, right mind*,
sagacity, saneness, sense, sound mind, soundness, stability, understanding, wit; SEE CONCEPTS
409,410

sap [n] stupid person
chump, dolt, dupe, fool, idiot, jerk, nitwit,
patsy*, pigeon*, simpleton, sucker*, weakling*;
SEE CONCEPT 412

sap [v] squeeze out; weaken
attenuate, bleed, blunt, cripple, debilitate, deplete, destroy, devitalize, disable, drain, enervate, enfeeble, erode, exhaust, impair, prostrate,
rob, ruin, subvert, undermine, vitiate, wear
down, wreck; SEE CONCEPTS 142,156,240,246

sapient [adj] sagacious
acute, astucious, astute, cagey*, canny, clear-
sighted, clever, contemplative, discerning, discriminating, educated, enlightened, experienced,
far-sighted, foxy*, informed, insightful, intelligent, judicious, keen, knowing, knowledgeable,
perceptive, reflective, sage, scholarly, sensible,
sharp, shrewd, smart, thoughtful, wise; SEE CON-
CEPT 402

sappy [adj] foolish, sentimental
absurd, balmy, bathetic, crazy*, drippy*, idiotic,
illogical, insane, loony*, maudlin, mushy*, preposterous, silly, slushy*, soppy*, sticky*, stupid;
SEE CONCEPTS 403,542

sarcasm [n] mocking remark
acrimony, aspersion, banter, bitterness, burlesque, causticness, censure, comeback, contempt, corrosiveness, criticism, cut*, cynicism,
derision, dig*, disparagement, flouting, invective, irony, lampooning, mockery, mordancy,
put-down*, raillery, rancor, ridicule, satire,
scoffing, scorn, sharpness, sneering, superciliousness, wisecrack; SEE CONCEPTS 52,54,277,
278

sarcastic [adj] nasty, mocking in speech
acerb, acerbic, acid, acrimonious, arrogant, austere, backhanded, biting, bitter, brusque, captious, carping, caustic, chaffing, contemptuous,
contumelious, corrosive, cussed*, cutting, cynical, derisive, disillusioned, disparaging, disrespectful, evil, hostile, irascible, ironical, mean,
mordant, needling, offensive, ornery*, salty, sardonic, satirical, saucy*, scorching, scornful,
scurrilous, severe, sharp, smart-alecky*,
snarling, sneering, taunting, trenchant, twitting,
weisenheiming*; SEE CONCEPT 267

sardonic [adj] sarcastic
acerbic, arrogant, biting, bitter, carping, caustic,
cynical, derisive, disrespectful, evil, irascible,
mean, mocking, mordant, nasty, offensive,
salty*, satirical, scorching, scornful, sharp,
smart-alecky*, sneering, taunting, wise*; SEE
CONCEPT 267

sass [n] back talk
answer, cheek, guff, lip, mouth, nasty reply, retort, sauce; SEE CONCEPTS 46,278

sass [v] talk back
answer back, give lip*, mouth off*, wise off*;
SEE CONCEPT 401

sassy [adj] impudent
arrant, audacious, bold, brassy, brazen, cheeky*,
discourteous, disrespectful, flip*, flippant, fresh,
insolent, mouthy*, overbold, rude, saucy*,
smart-alecky*, smart-mouthed, wise; SEE CON-
CEPT 401

Satan [n] the Devil
Angel of Darkness, Antichrist, Apollyon, archfiend, Beelzebub, demon, Diabolus, King of
Hell, Lucifer, Mephistopheles, Prince of Darkness, the Evil Spirit; SEE CONCEPTS 370,412

satanic [*adj*] *demonic*
crazed, cruel, devilish, diabolic, diabolical, evil, fiendish, frenetic, hellish, infernal, mad, maniacal, possessed, unhallowed, vicious, wicked; SEE CONCEPTS *404,545*

satchel [*n*] *small bag*
attache, backpack, briefcase, carryall, carry-on, duffel bag, garment bag, handbag, haversack, knapsack, overnight bag, pack, pouch, rucksack, saddlebag, suitcase, tote, travel bag; SEE CONCEPTS *339,450,494*

satiate [*v*] *stuff, satisfy completely or excessively*
cloy, content, feed to gills*, fill, glut, gorge, gratify, indulge, jade, nauseate, overdose, overfill, pall, sate, saturate, slake, surfeit; SEE CONCEPTS *169,740*

satire [*n*] *ridicule intended to expose truth*
banter, burlesque, caricature, causticity, chaffing, irony, lampoon, lampoonery, mockery, parody, pasquinade, persiflage, play-on, put-on*, raillery, sarcasm, send-up*, skit, spoof, squib*, takeoff*, travesty, wit, witticism; SEE CONCEPTS *263,271,280*

satirical/satiric [*adj*] *mocking*
abusive, bantering, biting, bitter, burlesque, caustic, censorious, chaffing, cutting, cynical, farcical, incisive, ironical, lampooning, mordant, paradoxical, parodying, pungent, ridiculing, sarcastic, sardonic, spoofing, taunting; SEE CONCEPT *267*

satirize [*v*] *ridicule*
banter, burlesque, caricature, caricaturize, cartoon, deride, haze, humiliate, jape, jeer, jive, josh, kid, lampoon, laugh at, make a fool of*, make fun of*, mimic, mock, needle, pan*, parody, poke fun at*, pull one's leg, razz*, rib*, ride*, roast*, spoof; SEE CONCEPTS *54,59*

satisfaction [*n*] *giving or enjoying a state of comfort, content*
achievement, amends, amusement, atonement, bliss, cheerfulness, comfort, compensation, complacency, conciliation, contentedness, contentment, delight, ease, enjoyment, fulfillment, gladness, good fortune, gratification, happiness, indemnification, indulgence, joy, justice, peace of mind, pleasure, pride, propitiation, recompense, redress, refreshment, reimbursement, relief, reparation, repletion, resolution, reward, satiety, serenity, settlement, vindication, wellbeing; SEE CONCEPTS *344,410,520*

satisfactory [*adj*] *acceptable, sufficient*
adequate, all right, ample, A-OK*, appeasing, assuaging, assuasive, average, cogent, comfortable, competent, cool*, decent,* delighting, enough, fair, fulfilling, good, good enough, gratifying, groovy*, passable, peachy*, pleasing, satisfying, solid, sound, sufficing, suitable, tolerable, unexceptional, up to snuff*, valid; SEE CONCEPTS *529,558,560*

satisfy [*v1*] *please, content*
amuse, animate, appease, assuage, befriend, brighten up, captivate, capture, cheer, cloy, comfort, conciliate, content, delight, do the trick*, elate, enliven, entertain, enthrall, exhilarate, fascinate, fill, fill the bill*, flatter, get by, gladden, glut, gorge, gratify, hit the spot*, humor, indulge, make merry, make the grade*, mollify, pacify, placate, propitiate, quench, rejoice, sate, satiate, score, sell, sell on, slake, suit, surfeit; SEE CONCEPTS *7,22*

satisfy [*v2*] *answer, persuade*
accomplish, appease, assuage, assure, avail, be adequate, be enough, be sufficient, come up to, complete, comply with, conform to, convince, dispel doubt, do, equip, fill, fulfill, furnish, get by, induce, inveigle, keep promise, make good, make the grade*, meet, observe, pass muster*, perform, provide, put mind at ease*, qualify, quiet, reassure, score, sell, serve, serve the purpose*, suffice, tide over*, win over; SEE CONCEPTS *108,140,656*

satisfy [*v3*] *pay, compensate*
answer, atone, clear up, disburse, discharge, indemnify, liquidate, make good*, make reparation, meet, pay off, quit, recompense, remunerate, repay, requite, reward, settle, square*; SEE CONCEPTS *126,341*

satisfying [*adj*] *fulfilling*
delightful, enjoyable, favorable, gratifying, hitting the spot, pleasant, pleasing, pleasurable, refreshing, rewarding, satiating, satisfactory, savory, sweet; SEE CONCEPTS *537,572*

saturate [*v*] *drench, wet through*
bathe, douche, douse, imbue, immerse, impregnate, infuse, overfill, penetrate, percolate, permeate, pervade, sate, satiate, soak, sop, souse, steep, suffuse, surfeit, transfuse, wash, waterlog; SEE CONCEPT *256*

saturnine [*adj*] *gloomy*
blue*, cheerless, dejected, depressed, desolate, despondent, dispirited, dour, down, down in the dumps*, forlorn, glum, grave, hopeless, in low spirits*, in the dumps*, low, melancholy, miserable, moping, morose, sad, solemn, sorrowful, sulky, sullen, unhappy, woebegone, woeful; SEE CONCEPT *403*

saucy [*adj*] *disrespectful*
arch, audacious, bold, brash, brazen, cheeky*, combative, contumelious, flip*, flippant, forward, fresh, impertinent, impudent, insolent, intrusive, meddlesome, nervy, obtrusive, pert, presumptuous, rude, sassy, smart, smart-alecky*, smug, snippy*, volatile, weisenheiming*, wise; SEE CONCEPTS *267,401*

saunter [*n*] *stroll*
airing, amble, constitutional, promenade, ramble, turn, walk; SEE CONCEPT *151*

saunter [*v*] *stroll along*
amble, ankle, dally, drift, linger, loiter, meander, mope*, mosey*, ooze*, percolate, promenade, ramble, roam, rove, sashay, stump, tarry, toddle, traipse, trill, wander; SEE CONCEPT *151*

savage [*adj1*] *wild, untamed*
aboriginal, ancient, archaic, barbarian, barbaric, bestial, brutal, brute, crude, earliest, feral, ferocious, fierce, first, fundamental, harsh, in a state of nature, lupine, native, natural, nonliterate, original, primary, primeval, primitive, primordial, pristine, rough, rude, rugged, rustic, simple, turbulent, unbroken, uncivilized, uncultivated, uncultured, undomesticated, unmodified, unrestrained, unspoiled, vicious; SEE CONCEPTS *401,485*

savage [*adj2*] *cruel, vicious*
atrocious, barbarous, beastly, bestial, bloodthirsty, bloody, brutal, brutish, cold-blooded, crazed, demoniac, destructive, devilish, diabolical, fell, feral, ferine, ferocious, fierce, frantic, furious, grim, harsh, heartless, hellish, infernal, inhuman, inhumane, malevolent, malicious, mer-

ciless, murderous, pitiless, rabid, raging, rapacious, ravening, relentless, remorseless, ruthless, sadistic, truculent, unrelenting, violent, wolfish; SEE CONCEPTS *401,540,542*

savanna/savannah [*n*] *grassland*
grassy field, llano, meadow, pasturage, pasture, plain, prairie, steppe, veldt; SEE CONCEPT *509*

savant [*n*] *scholar*
academic, bookworm, brain*, egghead*, expert, intellect, intellectual, learned person, learner, master, philosopher, pundit, sage, wise person; SEE CONCEPT *350*

save [*v1*] *rescue*
bail out, come to rescue, defend, deliver, emancipate, extricate, free, get off the hook*, get out of hock*, give a break, liberate, pull out of fire*, ransom, recover, redeem, salvage, save one's neck*, set free, spring, unchain, unshackle; SEE CONCEPTS *127,134*

save [*v2*] *economize; set money aside for later use*
amass, be frugal, be thrifty, cache, collect, conserve, cut corners*, deposit, economize, feather nest*, gather, hide away, hoard, hold, keep, lay aside, lay away, maintain, make ends meet*, manage, pile up, pinch pennies*, put by, reserve, retrench, roll back*, salt away*, save for rainy day*, scrimp, skimp, sock away*, spare, squirrel*, stash, stockpile, store, stow away, tighten belt*, treasure; SEE CONCEPTS *120,129,330*

save [*v3*] *guard, protect*
conserve, defend, keep safe, keep up, look after, maintain, preserve, safeguard, screen, shield, sustain, take care of; SEE CONCEPTS *96,117*

savings [*n*] *provision for future*
accumulation, ace in hole*, cache, fund, funds, gleanings, harvest, hoard, investment, kitty*, mattress full*, means, money in the bank, nest egg*, property, provision, provisions, rainy day fund*, reserve, reserves, resources, riches, sock, stake, stockpile, store; SEE CONCEPTS *335,340, 446,710*

savior [*n*] *person who redeems, aids in time of difficulty*
conservator, defender, deliverer, friend in need*, Good Samaritan*, guardian, guardian angel, hero, liberator, preserver, protector, rescuer, salvager, salvation; SEE CONCEPTS *370,416*

savor [*n1*] *taste, flavor*
odor, piquancy, relish, salt, sapidity, sapor, scent, smack, smell, spice, tang, tincture, zest; SEE CONCEPT *614*

savor [*n2*] *distinctive quality*
affection, attribute, character, characteristic, excitement, feature, flavor, interest, mark, property, salt, spice, trait, virtue, zest; SEE CONCEPTS *411,543*

savor [*v*] *delight in, enjoy*
appreciate, experience, feel, gloat, know, like, luxuriate in, partake, relish, revel in, sample, sip, smack, smell, taste; SEE CONCEPTS *32,616*

savory [*adj*] *pleasing, delicious in flavor*
agreeable, ambrosial, aperitive, appetizing, aromatic, dainty, decent, delectable, exquisite, fragrant, full-flavored, good, luscious, mellow, mouthwatering, palatable, perfumed, piquant, pungent, redolent, relishing, respectable, rich, sapid, savorous, scrumptious, spicy, sweet, tangy, tasty, tempting, toothsome, wholesome; SEE CONCEPT *613*

savvy [*adj*] *shrewd*
acute, astute, brainy*, cagey*, calculating, canny, clever, crafty, cunning, discerning, experienced, far-sighted, foxy*, heady*, ingenious, intelligent, in the know*, judicious, keen, knowing, on the ball*, perceptive, sagacious, sensible, sharp, slick*, sly, smart, smooth, streetwise, wise; SEE CONCEPTS *401,402*

savvy [*n*] *shrewdness*
acumen, awareness, comprehension, discernment, experience, grasp, grip, insight, intellect, intelligence, judgment, know-how, knowing, knowledge, mastery, perception, perceptiveness, sense, sharpness, smarts*, understanding; SEE CONCEPT *409*

say [*v*] *make declaration*
add, affirm, allege, announce, answer, assert, break silence*, claim, come out with, communicate, conjecture, convey, declare, deliver, disclose, divulge, do, estimate, express, flap*, gab*, give voice*, guess, imagine, imply, jaw, judge, lip*, maintain, make known, mention, opine, orate, perform, pronounce, put forth, put into words, rap*, read, recite, rehearse, relate, remark, render, repeat, reply, report, respond, reveal, rumor, speak, spiel*, state, suggest, tell, utter, verbalize, voice, yak*; SEE CONCEPTS *51,266*

saying [*n*] *maxim, proverb*
adage, aphorism, apophthegm, axiom, byword, dictum, epigram, motto, precept, saw, statement, truism; SEE CONCEPT *278*

scads [*n*] *large quantity*
bags*, barrels*, bunches, bundles*, gobs*, heaps*, jillion*, large number, loads, lots, many and then some*, oodles*, piles, plenty, scores, stacks, tons, zillions; SEE CONCEPTS *432,787*

scale [*n1*] *graduated system*
calibration, computation, degrees, extent, gamut, gradation, hierarchy, ladder, order, pecking order*, progression, proportion, range, ranking, rate, ratio, reach, register, rule, scope, sequence, series, spectrum, spread, steps, system, way; SEE CONCEPTS *651,744,770,788*

scale [*n2*] *thin covering, skin*
film, flake, incrustation, lamina, layer, plate, scurf; SEE CONCEPTS *399,484*

scale [*v1*] *ascend, climb*
clamber, escalade, escalate, go up, mount, surmount; SEE CONCEPT *166*

scale [*v2*] *measure*
adjust, balance, calibrate, compare, compute, estimate, gauge, graduate, proportion, prorate, regulate, size; SEE CONCEPT *764*

scam [*n*] *swindle*
blackmail, cheating, con, con game, crooked deal*, deceit, deception, dirty pool*, doublecross*, double-dealing*, extortion, fast one*, flimflam*, fraud, hoax, hosing*, hustle, racket*, rip-off*, shady deal*, shakedown, sham, shell game*, snow job*, sting, sucker game*; SEE CONCEPTS *59,139,192*

scamp [*n*] *rascal*
cheat, cheater, delinquent, fraud, hooligan*, liar, mischief-maker, prankster, rapscallion, reprobate, rogue, rowdy, ruffian, scalawag, scallywag, scoundrel, shyster, sneak, swindler, trickster, troublemaker, villain, whippersnapper; SEE CONCEPT *412*

scamper [*v*] *run, dash*

bolt, dart, flee, fly, hasten, hie, hurry, light out, make off, race, romp, rush off, scoot, scurry, scuttle, shoot, skedaddle*, skip, speed, speed away, sprint, tear, trot, whip, zip*; SEE CONCEPT *150*

scan [*v*] *look over, scrutinize lightly*

browse, check, consider, contemplate, dip into*, examine, flash*, flip through, give the once-over*, glance at, glance over, have a look-see*, inquire, investigate, leaf through*, look, look through, look up and down*, overlook, regard, riff, riffle, rumble, run over, run through, scour, search, size up, skim, study, survey, sweep, take a gander*, take stock of*, thumb through*; SEE CONCEPTS *103,623*

scandal [*n*] *public embarrassment*

aspersion, backbiting, backstabbing, belittlement, calumny, crime, defamation, depreciation, detraction, dirty linen*, discredit, disgrace, dishonor, disparagement, disrepute, dynamite, eavesdropping, gossip, hearsay, idle rumor, ignominy, infamy, mud, obloquy, opprobrium, reproach, rumor, scorcher, shame, sin, skeleton in closet*, slander, tale, talk, turpitude, wrongdoing; SEE CONCEPTS *278,645,674*

scandalous [*adj*] *disreputable*

atrocious, backbiting, calumnious, crying, defamatory, desperate, detracting, detractive, disgraceful, gossiping, heinous, ignominious, infamous, libelous, maligning, monstrous, odious, opprobrious, outrageous, red hot*, scurrilous, shameful, shocking, slanderous, traducing, unseemly, untrue, vilifying; SEE CONCEPT *545*

scant/scanty [*adj*] *inadequate*

bare, barely sufficient, close, deficient, exiguous, failing, insufficient, limited, little, meager, minimal, narrow, poor, rare, restricted, scrimpy, short, shy, skimpy, slender, spare, sparing, sparse, stingy, thin, tight, wanting; SEE CONCEPTS *766,767,789*

scapegoat [*n*] *person who takes blame for another's action*

boob*, chump, doormat*, dupe, easy mark*, fall guy*, fool, goat*, gull*, mark*, patsy, pigeon*, pushover*, sacrifice, sap*, schmuck*, sitting duck*, stooge, sucker, victim, weakling*; SEE CONCEPT *412*

scar [*n*] *blemish from previous injury or illness*

blister, cacatrice, cicatrix, crater, defect, discoloration, disfigurement, flaw, hurt, mark, pockmark, scab, track, wound; SEE CONCEPT *580*

scar [*v*] *mark, hurt*

beat, blemish, brand, cut, damage, deface, disfigure, flaw, injure, maim, mar, pinch, score, scratch, slash, stab, traumatize; SEE CONCEPTS *7,19,137,176,246*

scarce [*adj*] *insufficient, infrequent*

at a premium, deficient, failing, few, few and far between*, in short supply, limited, occasional, rare, scant, scanty, seldom, seldom met with, semioccasional, short, shortened, shy, sparse, sporadic, truncated, uncommon, unusual, wanting; SEE CONCEPTS *541,789*

scarcely [*adv*] *barely*

hardly, imperceptibly, infrequently, just, just barely, only just, rarely, scantily, seldom, slightly; SEE CONCEPTS *541,789*

scare [*n*] *frightened state*

alarm, alert, fright, panic, shock, start, terror; SEE CONCEPTS *230,410*

scare [*v*] *frighten someone*

affright, alarm, awe, chill, daunt, dismay, freeze, give a fright, give a turn*, intimidate, panic, paralyze, petrify, scare silly*, scare stiff*, scare the pants off*, shake up*, shock, spook, startle, strike terror in, terrify, terrorize; SEE CONCEPTS *7,19,42*

scared [*adj*] *frightened*

afraid, aghast, anxious, fearful, having cold feet*, panicked, panicky, panic-stricken, petrified, shaken, startled, terrified, terror-stricken; SEE CONCEPT *403*

scarf [*n*] *muffler*

ascot, bandanna, boa, kerchief, neckwear, shawl, stole, wrapping; SEE CONCEPT *451*

scary [*adj*] *frightening, terrifying*

alarming, bloodcurdling, chilling, creepy, eerie, hair-raising, hairy*, horrendous, horrifying, intimidating, shocking, spine-chilling, spooky, unnerving; SEE CONCEPTS *529,548*

scathing [*adj*] *nasty, critical in remarks*

belittling, biting, brutal, burning, caustic, cruel, cutting, harsh, mordacious, mordant, salty, sarcastic, scorching, scornful, searing, severe, sulphurous, trenchant, withering; SEE CONCEPT *267*

scatter [*v*] *strew, disperse*

besprinkle, broadcast, cast, derange, diffuse, disband, discard, disject, dispel, disseminate, dissipate, distribute, disunite, diverge, divide, expend, fling, intersperse, litter, migrate, part, pour, put to flight*, run away, scramble, separate, set, set asunder, sever, shatter, shed, shower, sow, spend, split up, spray, spread, sprinkle, sunder, take off in all directions*, throw around, throw out; SEE CONCEPTS *179,217,222*

scatterbrained [*adj*] *not thinking clearly*

birdbrained*, careless, dizzy, empty-headed*, featherbrained*, flighty, forgetful, frivolous, giddy, harebrained*, illogical, inattentive, irrational, irresponsible, madcap, silly, slaphappy*, stupid, thoughtless; SEE CONCEPT *402*

scenario [*n*] *master plan; sequence of events*

book, outline, pages, plot, résumé, rundown, scheme, sides, sketch, story line, summary, synopsis; SEE CONCEPTS *282,283,660*

scene [*n1*] *setting of a performance or event*

arena, backdrop, background, blackout, display, exhibition, flat, flats, landscape, locale, locality, location, mise en scène, outlook, pageant, picture, place, representation, scenery, seascape, set, setting, show, sight, site, spectacle, spot, stage, tableau, theater, view; SEE CONCEPTS *263,625, 628*

scene [*n2*] *part of a dramatic performance*

act, bit, episode, incident, part, piece, routine, schtick, spot; SEE CONCEPT *264*

scene [*n3*] *display of emotion*

carrying-on*, commotion, confrontation, exhibition, fit, fuss, performance, row, tantrum, temper tantrum, to-do*, upset; SEE CONCEPT *633*

scene [*n4*] *field of interest*

arena, business, compass, culture, environment, field, milieu, setting, sphere, world; SEE CONCEPT *349*

scenery [*n*] *surroundings*

backdrop, decor, flat, flats, furnishings, furniture, landscape, mise en scène, neighborhood, proper-

sa
sc

ties, props, prospect, set, setting, spectacle, sphere, stage set, stage setting, terrain, view, vista; SEE CONCEPTS 263,628

scenic [adj] *beautiful, picturesque*
breathtaking, dramatic, grand, impressive, panoramic, spectacular, striking; SEE CONCEPTS 485,579

scent [n] *smell, aroma*
aura, balm, bouquet, essence, fragrance, incense, odor, perfume, redolence, spice, tang, track, trail, whiff; SEE CONCEPT 599

scent [v] *detect, smell*
be on the track of*, be on the trail of*, discern, get wind of*, nose, nose out*, recognize, sense, sniff; SEE CONCEPTS 601,602

scented [adj] *fragrant*
ambrosial, aromal, aromatic, balmy, delectable, odoriferous, odorous, perfumed, perfumy, redolent, smelling, spicy, sweet-smelling; SEE CONCEPT 598

schedule [n] *plan for one's time*
agenda, appointments, calendar, catalog, chart, diagram, docket, inventory, itinerary, lineup*, list, order of business, program, record, registry, roll, roster, sked*, table, timetable; SEE CONCEPTS 271,283,660

schedule [v] *plan one's time*
appoint, arrange, be due, book, card, catalog, engage, get on line*, line up*, list, note, organize, pencil in*, program, record, register, reserve, set, set up, sew up*, slate, time, write in one's book*; SEE CONCEPTS 36,125

scheme [n1] *course of action*
arrangement, blueprint, chart, codification, contrivance, design, device, diagram, disposition, draft, expedient, game plan, layout, order, ordering, outline, pattern, plan, presentation, program, project, proposal, proposition, purpose, schedule, schema, strategy, suggestion, system, tactics, theory; SEE CONCEPTS 271,625,660

scheme [n2] *plot, maneuver to get result*
action, angle*, brainchild*, cabal, conspiracy, covin, dodge*, frame-up*, game, game plan*, gimmick, hookup*, hustle, hype*, intrigue, layout, machination, picture*, pitch, ploy, practice, proposition, put-up job*, ruse, scenario, scene, setup*, shift*, story, stratagem, subterfuge, tactics, trick*, twist*; SEE CONCEPTS 59,645,660

scheming [adj] *deceitful, sly*
artful, calculating, conniving, crafty, cunning, designing, duplicitous, foxy, slippery, tricky, underhand, wily; SEE CONCEPT 542

schism [n] *separation*
alienation, break, breakup, difference, disagreement, discord, dissension, disunion, division, divorce, faction, fissure, fracture, gap, parting, rift, rupture, secession, splinter group, split; SEE CONCEPTS 135,195,297,388

schlemiel [n] *dolt*
blockhead*, boob*, bungler, dimwit*, dope, dork*, dumbbell*, dunce, fool, goof*, goon*, idiot, ignoramus, jerk, lunkhead*, meathead*, nincompoop*, ninny*, nitwit*, sap*, schmuck, simpleton, stooge*, stupid; SEE CONCEPTS 412,423

schlep [v] *lug*
carry, drag, haul, heave, lift, lurch, pull, tote, tow, tug, yank; SEE CONCEPT 206

scholar [n] *person who is very involved in education and learning*
academic, augur, bookish person, bookworm*, brain*, critic, disciple, doctor, egghead*, gnome*, grind*, intellectual, learned person, learner, litterateur, person of letters, philosopher, professor, pupil, sage, savant, schoolchild, scientist, student, teacher, tool, wise person; SEE CONCEPT 350

scholarly [adj] *academic*
bookish, cultured, educated, erudite, intellectual, learned, lettered, literate, longhair*, scholastic, schooled, studious, taught, trained, well-read; SEE CONCEPT 402

scholarship [n1] *knowledge*
ability, awareness, cognition, comprehension, discernment, education, erudition, expertise, grasp, insight, instruction, intelligence, know-how*, learnedness, learning, lore, philosophy, schooling, wisdom; SEE CONCEPTS 274,409,529

scholarship [n2] *grant*
assistance, award, bursary, charity, donation, fellowship, financial aid, reward; SEE CONCEPTS 337,344

school [n1] *place, system for educating*
academy, alma mater, blackboard*, college, department, discipline, establishment, faculty, hall, halls of ivy*, institute, institution, jail*, schoolhouse, seminary, university; SEE CONCEPTS 287,289

school [n2] *persons receiving education*
academy, adherents, circle, class, clique, denomination, devotees, disciples, faction, followers, following, group, party, pupils, sect, set; SEE CONCEPTS 288,350

school [n3] *body of philosophy on subject*
belief, creed, faith, outlook, persuasion, school of thought, stamp*, way, way of life; SEE CONCEPTS 349,689

school [v] *teach*
advance, coach, control, cultivate, direct, discipline, drill, educate, guide, indoctrinate, inform, instruct, lead, manage, prepare, prime, show, train, tutor, verse; SEE CONCEPT 285

science [n] *methodical study of part of material world*
art, body of knowledge, branch, discipline, education, erudition, information, learning, lore, scholarship, skill, system, technique, wisdom; SEE CONCEPTS 274,349,360

scientific [adj] *systematic; discovered through experimentation*
accurate, clear, controlled, deductive, exact, experimental, logical, mathematical, methodical, objective, precise, sound; SEE CONCEPT 535

scientist [n] *researcher*
analyst, chemist, examiner, expert, lab technician, physicist, prober, tester; SEE CONCEPTS 349,362

scintilla [n] *small bit, trace*
atom, crumb, dab, dash, drop, flash, hint, iota, particle, pinch, ray, shade, shred, small quantity, smidgen, soupcon, sparkle, speck, spot, whiff, whisper; SEE CONCEPTS 529,831

scintillating [adj] *bright, stimulating*
animated, brilliant, clever, dazzling, ebullient, exciting, flashing, gleaming, glimmering, glinting, glittering, lively, shining, smart, sparkling, sprightly, twinkling, witty; SEE CONCEPTS 401,529,617

scion [*n*] *offshoot, descendant*
begotten, branch, brood, child, chip off old block*, graft, heir, heiress, issue, junior, offspring, progeny, seed, shoot, slip, sprout, successor, twig; SEE CONCEPTS 414,428

scoff [*v*] *make fun of; despise*
belittle, boo*, contemn, deride, dig at*, disbelieve, discount, discredit, disdain, flout, gibe, jeer, knock*, laugh at, make light of*, mock, pan*, poke fun at, pooh-pooh*, rag*, rally, reject, revile, ride, ridicule, scorn, show contempt, sneer, tease; SEE CONCEPT 54

scold [*v*] *find fault with*
abuse, admonish, asperse, berate, blame, castigate, cavil, censure, chasten, chide, criticize, denounce, disparage, dress down*, expostulate, give a talking-to*, jump on*, keep aft*, lay down the law*, lecture, light into*, nag, objurate, preach, put down, rail, rake over the coals*, rate, ream, rebuke, recriminate, reprimand, reproach, reprobate, reprove, revile, take to task*, taunt, tell off*, upbraid, vilify, vituperate; SEE CONCEPTS 44,52,54

scoop [*n1*] *utensil, tool for shovelling*
bail, dipper, ladle, shovel, spade, spoon, trowel; SEE CONCEPTS 493,499

scoop [*n2*] *previously secret information that is suddenly public*
beat, exclusive, exposé, inside story*, news, revelation, sensation; SEE CONCEPT 274

scoop [*v*] *dig up; shovel*
bail, clear away, dig, dig out, dip, empty, excavate, gather, gouge, grub, hollow, ladle, ladle, lift, pick up, remove, scrape, spade, sweep away, sweep up, take up; SEE CONCEPT 178

scoot [*v*] *hurry*
accelerate, beeline*, be quick, bolt, clear out, dart, dash, expedite, fly, get a move on*, go like lightning, hasten, hurry up, hustle, make haste, make time*, make tracks*, move, move fast, race, run, rush, scamper, scurry, shake a leg*, skedaddle, speed, split, spur, step on it*, vamoose, whiz, zip; SEE CONCEPTS 150,234

scope [*n*] *extent or range of something*
ambit, amplitude, area, breadth, capacity, compass, comprehensiveness, confines, elbow room*, extension, field, field of reference, freedom, fullness, latitude, leeway, liberty, margin, opportunity, orbit, outlook, play, purview, radius, reach, room, run, space, span, sphere, wideness; SEE CONCEPTS 651,739,788

scorch [*v*] *burn*
bake, blacken, blister, broil, char, cook, melt, parch, roast, scald, sear, seethe, shrivel, simmer, singe, stale, stew, swelter, wither; SEE CONCEPTS 249,255

score [*n1*] *total, points*
account, addition, aggregate, amount, average, count, final count, grade, mark, number, outcome, rate, reckoning, record, result, stock, sum, summary, summation, tab, tally; SEE CONCEPTS 364,784

score/scores [*n2*] *large group; a great number*
army, cloud, crowd, drove, flock, host, hundred, legion, lot, mass, million, multitude, myriad, rout, swarm, throng, very many; SEE CONCEPT 432

score [*n3*] *musical arrangement*
charts, composition, music, orchestration, transcript; SEE CONCEPT 262

score [*n4*] *obligation; account payable*
account, amount due, bill, charge, debt, grievance, grudge, injury, injustice, invoice, reckoning, statement, tab, tally, total; SEE CONCEPTS 332,645

score [*v1*] *keep count*
add, calculate, chalk up, count, enumerate, keep tally, rack up*, reckon, record, register, tally, total; SEE CONCEPTS 125,764

score [*v2*] *achieve, succeed*
accomplish, amass, arrive, attain, chalk up*, connect, flourish, gain, gain advantage, get*, hit pay dirt*, impress, luck out*, make a killing*, make an impression*, make the grade*, notch, procure, prosper, pull off*, put over*, rack up*, reach, realize, secure, take the cake*, thrive, triumph, win; SEE CONCEPTS 704,706

score [*v3*] *cut, nick*
cleave, crosshatch, deface, furrow, gash, gouge, graze, groove, indent, line, mark, mill, notch, scrape, scratch, serrate, slash, slit; SEE CONCEPTS 137,176

score [*v4*] *write a musical arrangement*
adapt, arrange, compose, orchestrate, set; SEE CONCEPTS 79,292

scorn [*n*] *contempt toward something*
contemptuousness, contumely, derision, despisal, despisement, despite, disdain, disparagement, disregard, jeering, mockery, ridicule, sarcasm, scoffing, scornfulness, slight, sneer, sport, taunting, teasing; SEE CONCEPTS 29,54

scorn [*v*] *hold in contempt; look down on*
abhor, avoid, be above, confute, consider beneath one*, contemn, defy, deride, despise, disdain, disregard, flout, gibe, hate, ignore, make fun of, mock, put down, refuse, refute, reject, renounce, repudiate, ridicule, run down*, scoff at, shun, slight, sneer, spurn, taunt, trash*, turn back on*, turn nose up at*; SEE CONCEPTS 21,30,52,54

scoundrel [*n*] *person who is deceptive and uncaring of others*
bad egg*, bad news*, blackguard*, black sheep*, caitiff, cheat, creep, crook, dastard, good-for-nothing*, heel, imp, incorrigible, lowlife*, maggot*, mischiefmaker, miscreant, ne'er-do-well*, rascal, reprobate, scalawag, scamp, thief, vagabond, villain, wretch; SEE CONCEPT 412

scour [*v1*] *clean, polish thoroughly*
abrade, brush, buff, burnish, cleanse, flush, furbish, mop, pumice, purge, rub, sand, scrub, wash, whiten; SEE CONCEPT 165

scour [*v2*] *search thoroughly*
beat, comb, ferret out, find, forage, go over with a fine-tooth comb*, grub, hunt, inquire, leave no stone unturned*, look for, look high and low*, look up and down*, rake, ransack, rout, rummage, seek, track down, turn inside out*, turn upside-down*; SEE CONCEPT 216

scourge [*n*] *plague, torment*
affliction, bane, correction, curse, infliction, misfortune, penalty, pest, pestilence, punishment, terror, visitation; SEE CONCEPTS 674,675

scourge [*v*] *beat, punish, often physically*
afflict, belt, cane*, castigate, chastise, curse, discipline, excoriate, flail, flog, harass, hit, horsewhip*, lambaste*, lash, penalize, plague, scathe, scorch*, tan*, terrorize, thrash, torment, trounce, wallop*, whale*, whip; SEE CONCEPTS 14,52, 122,189

SC
SC

scout [*n*] *person who is searching, investigating*
advance, adventurer, detective, escort, explorer, guard, lookout, outpost, outrider, patrol, picket, pioneer, precursor, reconnoiterer, recruiter, runner, sleuth, spotter, spy, vanguard; SEE CONCEPTS *348,358*

scout [*v*] *investigate, check out*
case, examine, explore, ferret, have a look-see*, hunt, inspect, look for, observe, probe, reconnoiter, run reconnaissance, rustle up*, search, seek, set eyes on*, spot, spy, stake out, survey, take in, track down, watch; SEE CONCEPTS *103,216,623*

scowl [*n*] *frown*
black look*, dirty look*, evil eye*, glower, grimace; SEE CONCEPTS *185,716*

scowl [*v*] *frown*
disapprove, glare, gloom, glower, grimace, look daggers at*, lour, lower, make a face*; SEE CONCEPT *185*

scraggly [*adj*] *ragged*
badly dressed, badly worn, bedraggled, dilapidated, dingy, dirty, disheveled, frayed, frazzled, full of holes*, grubby*, grungy*, in tatters*, messy, moth-eaten, scruffy, shabby, sloppy, tacky*, tattered, threadbare, torn, unclean, uncombed, ungroomed, unkempt, worse for wear*; SEE CONCEPTS *485,621*

scram [*v*] *leave quickly*
beat it*, clear out*, decamp, depart, disappear, get lost*, go away, hightail*, make oneself scarce*, make tracks*, scoot*, skedaddle*, take off, vamoose*; SEE CONCEPT *195*

scramble [*n*] *mix-up, confusion*
clutter, commotion, competition, conglomeration, free-for-all*, hash*, hassle, hustle, jumble, jungle, litter, melee, mishmash, muddle, race, rat race*, rush, shuffle, struggle, tumble, tussle; SEE CONCEPTS *230,388,432*

scramble [*v*] *race; get into position clumsily*
clamber, climb, contend, crawl, hasten, jockey for position*, jostle, look alive*, make haste, move, push, run, rush, scrabble, scurry, scuttle, strive, struggle, swarm, trek, vie; SEE CONCEPTS *87,150*

scrap [*n1*] *tiny bit of something*
atom, bite, bits and pieces*, butt, castoff, chip, chunk, crumb, cutting, discard, end, fragment, glob, gob, grain, hunk, iota, jot, junk, leaving, leftover*, lump, mite, modicum, morsel, mouthful, odds and ends*, orts, part, particle, piece, portion, remains, shred, slice, sliver, smithereen*, snatch, snippet, speck, stump, trace, waste; SEE CONCEPTS *831,835*

scrap [*n2*] *argument, fight*
affray, battle, brawl, broil*, disagreement, dispute, fracas, fray, quarrel, row, scuffle, set-to*, squabble, tiff*, wrangle; SEE CONCEPTS *46,106*

scrap [*v1*] *abandon; throw away*
abandon, break up, cast, chuck, consign to scrap heap*, demolish, discard, dismiss, dispense with, ditch, do away with*, drop, forsake, get rid of, jettison, junk, put out to pasture*, reject, retire, shed, slough, throw out, toss out, write off; SEE CONCEPTS *121,180*

scrap [*v2*] *fight, argue*
battle, bicker, caterwaul, come to blows*, fall out, have shouting match*, have words*, quarrel, row, spat, squabble, tiff, wrangle; SEE CONCEPTS *46,106*

scrape [*n*] *bad or embarrassing situation*
awkward situation, corner*, difficulty, dilemma, discomfiture, distress, embarrassment, fix*, hole*, jam*, mess*, pickle*, plight, predicament, tight spot*, trouble; SEE CONCEPT *674*

scrape [*v1*] *scratch, remove outer layer*
abrade, bark, bray, chafe, clean, erase, file, grate, graze, grind, irritate, pare, peel, rasp, rub, scour, scuff, shave, skin, squeak, thin, triturate; SEE CONCEPTS *165,186,215*

scrape [*v2*] *be very frugal*
cut it close*, get along, get by, pinch, save, scrimp, shave, skimp, stint, struggle; SEE CONCEPT *330*

scratch [*n*] *small cut or mark*
blemish, claw mark, gash, graze, hurt, laceration, score, scrape; SEE CONCEPTS *309,513*

scratch [*v1*] *cut; make a mark on*
claw, damage, etch, grate, graze, incise, lacerate, mark, prick, rasp, rub, scarify, score, scrape, scrawl, scribble; SEE CONCEPTS *79,176*

scratch [*v2*] *cancel*
annul, delete, eliminate, erase, pull, pull out, strike, withdraw; SEE CONCEPT *121*

scrawl [*v*] *write erratically*
doodle, inscribe, scrabble, scratch, scribble, squiggle; SEE CONCEPT *79*

scrawny [*adj*] *unhealthily thin*
angular, bony, gaunt, lank, lanky, lean, rawboned, scraggy, skeletal, skin-and-bones*, skinny, spare, undernourished, underweight; SEE CONCEPTS *490,491,773*

scream [*n1*] *outcry*
cry, high-pitched shout, holler*, howl, screech, shriek, wail, yell, yelp; SEE CONCEPT *595*

scream [*n2*] *person or thing that is very funny*
card*, character*, comedian, comedienne, comic, entertainer, guffaw*, hoot*, howl*, joker, laugh, panic*, riot, sensation, sidesplitter*, wit; SEE CONCEPTS *423,529*

scream [*v*] *cry out*
bawl, bellow, blare, caterwaul, holler*, howl, jar, roar, screak, screech, shout, shriek, shrill, sing out, squeal, voice, wail, yell, yip, yowl; SEE CONCEPT *77*

screen [*n*] *protection used in or as furniture, motion picture display*
awning, canopy, cloak, concealment, cover, covering, curtain, divider, envelope, guard, hedge, mantle, mask, net, partition, security, shade, shelter, shield, shroud, veil; SEE CONCEPTS *277,440,443,445,473*

screen [*v1*] *hide, protect*
adumbrate, blind, block out, bulwark, bury, cache, camouflage, cloak, close, conceal, cover, cover up, defend, disguise, ensconce, fend, guard, mask, obscure, obstruct, safeguard, seclude, secrete, secure, separate, shade, shadow, shelter, shield, shroud, shut off, shut out, shutter, stash, umbrage, veil, wall off; SEE CONCEPTS *96,188*

screen [*v2*] *examine and choose*
cull, eliminate, evaluate, extract, filter, gauge, grade, pick out, process, riddle, scan, select, separate, sieve, sift, sort, winnow; SEE CONCEPT *41*

screw [*v1*] *twist in*
spiral, tighten, turn, twine, wind, work; SEE CONCEPTS *85,160*

screw [*v2*] *twist, contort*
contract, crimp, crinkle, crumple, distort, pucker,

rimple, ruck up, rumple, scrunch, wrinkle; SEE CONCEPT 219

screw [v3] *pressure*
bilk, bleed, cheat, chisel, coerce, constrain, defraud, do*, exact, extort, extract, force, hold a knife to*, oppress, pinch*, pressurize, put screws to*, ream*, shake down*, squeeze, wrench, wrest, wring; SEE CONCEPTS 14,192

screw up [v] *make a mess of*
blow, bobble, bollix*, botch, bungle, confuse, flub*, foul up, goof*, goof up*, louse, make hash of*, mess, mess up, mishandle, mismanage, muck up*, muddle, muff, queer, snafu*, spoil; SEE CONCEPT 101

screwy [adj] *eccentric*
abnormal, batty, bizarre, crazy, daft, dotty, far out*, flaky, funky*, irregular, kooky, mad, nutty, odd, oddball, offbeat, off-center, off the wall*, out in left field*, outlandish, peculiar, queer, quirky, strange, uncommon, unconventional, weird; SEE CONCEPTS 547,564

scribble [v] *write illegibly*
doodle, jot, scratch, scrawl, squiggle, write badly, write erratically; SEE CONCEPT 79

scrimp [v] *economize*
be cheap, be economical, be frugal, be prudent, be sparing, conserve, curtail, cut back, cut corners*, make ends meet*, pinch pennies*, run a tight ship*, save, skimp, stretch a dollar*, tighten one's belt*; SEE CONCEPT 330

script [n1] *handwriting*
calligraphy, characters, chirography, fist, hand, letters, longhand, penmanship, writing; SEE CONCEPTS 79,284

script [n2] *story for a performance*
article, book, copy, dialogue, libretto, lines, manuscript, playbook, scenario, text, typescript, words; SEE CONCEPTS 263,271

Scrooge [n] *skinflint*
cheapskate, meanie, misanthrope, misanthropist, miser, moneygrubber, niggard, penny-pincher, tightwad; SEE CONCEPT 412

scrounge [v] *beg, forage for*
bum, freeload, hunt, sponge, wheedle; SEE CONCEPTS 48,216

scrub [v1] *clean with force*
abrade, brush, buff, cleanse, mop, polish, rub, scour, wash; SEE CONCEPT 165

scrub [v2] *cancel*
abandon, abolish, abort, call off, delete, discontinue, do away with, drop, forget about, give up; SEE CONCEPTS 121,234

scruffy [adj] *rough, bedraggled*
badly groomed, frowzy*, mangy*, messy, ragged, run-down, seedy, shabby, slovenly, tacky*, tattered, threadbare, ungroomed, unkempt, untidy; SEE CONCEPTS 485,589

scrumptious [adj] *delicious*
ambrosial, appetizing, delectable, delightful, exquisite, heavenly, inviting, luscious, lush, magnificent, mouthwatering, rich, succulent, tasty, yummy; SEE CONCEPTS 529,613

scruple [n] *misgiving, doubt*
anxiety, caution, censor, compunction, conscience, demur, difficulty, faltering, hesitancy, hesitation, pause, perplexity, qualm, reconsideration, reluctance, reluctancy, second thought*, squeamishness, superego, twinge, uneasiness; SEE CONCEPTS 532,690

scruple [v] *balk, have misgivings*
be loath, be reluctant, be unwilling, boggle, demur, doubt, falter, fret, gag, have qualms, hesitate, question, shy, stick, stickle, stumble, think twice about*, vacillate, waver, worry; SEE CONCEPT 21

scrupulous [adj] *extremely careful*
conscientious, conscionable, critical, exact, fastidious, fussy, heedful, honest, honorable, just, meticulous, minute, moral, nice, painstaking, particular, precise, principled, punctilious, punctual, right, rigorous, strict, thinking twice*, true, upright; SEE CONCEPTS 401,538,542

scrutinize [v] *examine closely*
analyze, burn up, candle, canvass, case, check, check out, check over, comb*, consider, contemplate, dig, dissect, explore, eyeball*, get a load of*, go over with a fine-tooth comb*, inquire into, inspect, investigate, look over, overlook, peg*, penetrate, perlustrate, peruse, pierce, pore over, probe, put under a microscope*, scan, scope, scrutinate, search, sift, smoke*, stare, study, survey, take the measure of, view, watch, weigh; SEE CONCEPTS 24,103,623

scrutiny [n] *close examination*
analysis, audit, close-up, eagle eye*, exploration, inquiry, inspection, investigation, long hard look*, perlustration, perusal, review, scan, search, sifting, study, surveillance, survey, tab*, the eye*, view; SEE CONCEPTS 24,103,623

scuffle [n] *fight*
affray, brawl, broil, commotion, disturbance, fracas, fray, fuss*, go*, jump, mix-up, row, ruckus, ruction, rumpus, scrap, set-to*, shuffle, strife, tussle, wrangle; SEE CONCEPT 106

scuffle [v] *fight*
clash, come to blows, contend, cuff, grapple, jostle, skirmish, struggle, tussle, wrestle; SEE CONCEPT 106

sculpture [v] *form a three-dimensional art object*
carve, cast, chisel, cut, engrave, fashion, hew, model, mold, sculp, sculpt, shape; SEE CONCEPTS 137,174,184

scum [n1] *superficial impurities, dirt*
algae, crust, dross, film, froth, residue, scruff, spume, waste; SEE CONCEPT 260

scum [n2] *people who are bad, despicable*
curs*, dregs, lowest, mass, mob, proletariat, rabble, riffraff, rubbish*, scum of the earth*, trash*, unwashed, vermin; SEE CONCEPT 412

scurrilous [adj] *foul-mouthed, vulgar*
abusive, coarse, contumelious, defamatory, dirty, filthy, foul, gross, indecent, infamous, insulting, invective, lewd, low, nasty, obscene, offending, offensive, opprobrious, outrageous, raunchy, ribald, salacious, scabrous, scandalous, shameless, slanderous, smutty*, truculent, vituperative, vituperatory, vituperous; SEE CONCEPTS 267,542,545

scurry [v] *move along swiftly*
barrel, bustle, dart, dash, dust, fly, hasten, hop along, hurry, race, rip, run, rush, scamper, scoot, scud, scutter, scuttle, shoot, skim, sprint, step along, tear, whirl, whisk, zip*; SEE CONCEPT 150

scuttlebutt [n] *gossip*
babble, back-fence talk*, blather, chatter, chitchat, dirty laundry*, grapevine*, hearsay, meddling, prattle, rumor, talk; SEE CONCEPTS 274,278

sea [n] *large body of water; large mass*
abundance, blue*, bounding main*, brine,

SC
SE

briny*, briny deep*, Davy Jones's locker*, deep, drink*, expanse, lake, main, multitude, number, ocean, plethora, pond, profusion, sheet, splash*, surf, swell, waves; SEE CONCEPT 514

seafarer [n] sailor
bluejacket, boater, boatman/woman, deck hand, mariner, mate, middy, midshipman/woman, old salt*, pirate, sailorman/woman, sea dog*, seaman/woman, swabbie*, yachtsman/woman; SEE CONCEPTS 348,358,366

seal [n] authentication; stamp
allowance, assurance, attestation, authorization, cachet, confirmation, imprimatur, insignia, notification, permission, permit, ratification, signet, sticker, tape, tie; SEE CONCEPTS 284,685

seal [v] make airtight
close, cork, enclose, fasten, gum, isolate, paste, plaster, plug, quarantine, secure, segregate, shut, stop, stopper, stop up, waterproof; SEE CONCEPTS 85,160

seal [v2] ensure, finalize
assure, attest, authenticate, clinch, conclude, confirm, consummate, establish, ratify, settle, shake hands on*, stamp, validate; SEE CONCEPTS 234,324

seam [n] line where two objects are connected
bond, closure, connection, coupling, gore, gusset, hem, joint, junction, juncture, pleat, stitching, suture, tuck, union; SEE CONCEPTS 452,471

seaman/woman [n] sailor
bluejacket, boater, boatman/woman, deck hand, mariner, mate, middy, midshipman/woman, old salt*, pirate, sailorman/woman, sea dog*, seafarer, swabbie*, yachtsman/woman; SEE CONCEPTS 348,358,366

seamy [adj] corrupt, unwholesome
bad, dark, degraded, disagreeable, disappointing, disreputable, disturbing, low, nasty, rough, sordid, squalid, unpleasant; SEE CONCEPT 545

sear [v] dry, burn
blight, brand, brown, burn up, cauterize, cook, dehydrate, desiccate, dry out, dry up, exsiccate, harden, parch, scorch, seal, shrivel, sizzle, tan, toast, wilt, wither; SEE CONCEPTS 170,249

search [n] seeking to find something
chase, examination, exploration, fishing expedition*, frisking*, going-over*, hunt, inquest, inquiry, inspection, investigation, legwork*, perquisition, pursual, pursuance, pursuing, pursuit, quest, research, rummage, scrutiny, shakedown*, wild-goose chase*, witch hunt*; SEE CONCEPT 216

search [v] seek to find something
beat, beat about, cast about, chase after, check, comb, examine, explore, ferret, forage, frisk, go in quest of, go over with a fine-tooth comb*, go through, grope, grub, gun for*, hunt, hunt for, inquire, inspect, investigate, leave no stone unturned*, look, look for, look high and low*, look over, poke into, probe, prospect, pry, quest, rake, ransack, rifle through, root, rummage, run down, scan, scour, scout, scrutinize, seek, shake down, sift, smell around, study, track down, turn inside out*, turn upside down*; SEE CONCEPT 216

searching [adj] probing
curious, experimental, exploratory, fact-finding, inquiring, inquisitive, penetrating, seeking, sharp, studious; SEE CONCEPT 402

seashore [n] beach
bank, coast, littoral, oceanfront, seaboard,

seafront, seaside, shingle, shore, strand, waterfront; SEE CONCEPTS 509,514

season [n] time of year governed by annual equinoxes
autumn, division, fall, interval, juncture, occasion, opportunity, period, spell, spring, summer, term, time, while, winter; SEE CONCEPT 814

season [v1] flavor food
color, enliven, lace, leaven, pep, pepper, salt, spice; SEE CONCEPT 170

season [v2] acclimatize, prepare
acclimate, accustom, anneal, climatize, discipline, fit, habituate, harden, inure, mature, qualify, school, steel, temper, toughen, train; SEE CONCEPTS 35,202

seasonable [adj] timely, appropriate
apropos, apt, auspicious, convenient, favorable, fit, opportune, pertinent, propitious, prosperous, providential, relevant, seasonal, suitable, timeous, towardly, welcome, well-timed; SEE CONCEPT 558

seasoned [adj] experienced
accomplished, adept, battle-scarred, been around*, been there*, competent, expert, familiar, hardened, instructed, knowledgeable, matured, old hand*, practiced, prepared, pro, professional, qualified, skillful, tested, toughened, trained, tried, vet, veteran, weathered, wise, worldly, worldly wise*; SEE CONCEPTS 402,527

seasoning [n] flavoring for food
condiment, dressing, gravy, herb, pepper, pungency, relish, salt, sauce, spice, zest; SEE CONCEPTS 457,461

seat [n1] furniture for sitting, reclining
bench, chair, chaise lounge, chesterfield, couch, davenport, lounge, loveseat, pew, recliner, settee, settle, stall, stool, wing chair; SEE CONCEPT 443

seat [n2] central location of organization
abode, axis, capital, center, cradle, focal point, fulcrum, headquarters, heart, house, hub, location, mansion, nerve center, place, polestar, post, residence, site, situation, source, spot, station; SEE CONCEPT 198

seat [n3] base, foundation
basement, basis, bed, bottom, cause, fitting, footing, ground, groundwork, rest, seating, support; SEE CONCEPT 442

seat [n4] rear end of animate being
backside, behind, bottom, breech, derrière, duff*, fanny*, fundament*, keister*, posterior, rear, rear end, rump, tush*; SEE CONCEPTS 392,825, 827

seat [v] place in furniture, position
accommodate, deposit, establish, fix, hold, install, locate, lounge, nestle, perch, plant, put, roost, set, settle, sit, squat, take; SEE CONCEPTS 154,201,384

secede [v] pull away; split from
abdicate, apostatize, break with, disaffiliate, leave, quit, resign, retire, retract, retreat, separate, withdraw; SEE CONCEPTS 119,298,384

secession [n] withdrawal
breakaway, breakup, defection, disaffiliation, dissension, disunion, division, exiting, parting, rift, rupture, schism, separation, splinter group, split; SEE CONCEPTS 135,195,211,297,388,685

seclude [v] isolate, hide
blockade, boycott, cloister, closet, conceal, confine, cover, embargo, enclose, evict, immure, os-

tracize, quarantine, retire, screen, segregate, separate, sequester, shut off, withdraw; SEE CONCEPTS **121,135,188**

secluded [*adj*] *isolated, sheltered*
abandoned, alone, aloof, beleaguered, blockaded, cloistered, close, closet, confidential, covert, cut off, deserted, hermetic, hidden, incommunicado, insular, isolate, lonely, lonesome, off the beaten track*, out-of-the-way*, personal, private, quarantined, quiet, reclusive, remote, removed, reserved, retired, screened, secluse, seclusive, secret, segregated, sequestered, shut off, shy, singular, solitary, tucked away*, unapproachable, unfrequented, uninhabited, unsociable, withdrawn; SEE CONCEPTS **401,576,583**

seclusion [*n*] *isolation*
aloneness, aloofness, beleaguerment, blockade, concealment, desolation, detachment, hiding, privacy, privateness, quarantine, reclusion, reclusiveness, remoteness, retirement, retreat, seclusiveness, separateness, separation, sequestration, shelter, solitude, withdrawal; SEE CONCEPTS **135,188,388,631**

second [*adj*] *next; subordinate*
additional, alternative, another, double, duplicate, extra, following, further, inferior, lesser, lower, next, next in order, other, place, repeated, reproduction, runner-up, secondary, subsequent, succeeding, supporting, twin, unimportant; SEE CONCEPTS **575,585**

second [*n1*] *shortest interval of time*
bat of an eye*, flash, instant, jiffy*, moment, nothing flat*, sec*, shake*, split second, twinkling*, wink; SEE CONCEPTS **803,821**

second [*n2*] *support; duplicate*
assistant, backer, double, exponent, helper, placer, proponent, reproduction, runner-up, supporter, twin; SEE CONCEPTS **423,670**

second [*v*] *support, advance a suggestion*
aid, approve, assist, back, back up, encourage, endorse, forward, further, give moral support, go along with, promote, stand by, uphold; SEE CONCEPTS **298,324,384**

secondary [*adj1*] *subordinate; less important*
accessory, alternate, auxiliary, backup, bush-league*, collateral, consequential, contingent, dependent, dinky*, extra, inconsiderable, inferior, insignificant, lesser, lower, minor, minor-league*, petty, relief, reserve, second, second-rate, small, small-fry*, small-time*, subject, subservient, subsidiary, substract, supporting, tributary, trivial, under, unimportant; SEE CONCEPTS **574,575**

secondary [*adj2*] *derivative*
auxiliary, borrowed, consequent, dependent, derivate, derivational, derived, developed, eventual, indirect, proximate, resultant, resulting, second-hand, subordinate, subsequent, subsidiary, vicarious; SEE CONCEPT **549**

secondhand [*adj*] *used*
handed down, hand-me-down, not new, old, pre-owned, previously owned, unnew; SEE CONCEPTS **578,797**

second-rate/second-class [*adj*] *inferior, cheap*
cheap and dirty*, common, commonplace, déclassé, hack*, low-grade, low-quality, mean, mediocre, poor, shoddy*, substandard, tacky*, tawdry*; SEE CONCEPTS **334,567,574**

secrecy [*n*] *concealment*
clandestineness, confidence, confidentiality,

covertness, dark, darkness, furtiveness, hiding, hush, isolation, mystery, privacy, reticence, retirement, seclusion, secretiveness, secretness, silence, solitude, stealth, suppression, surreptitiousness; SEE CONCEPT **631**

secret [*adj1*] *hidden, unrevealed*
abstruse, ambiguous, arcane, backdoor, camouflaged, classified, cloak-and-dagger*, close, closet, clouded, conspiratorial, covered, covert, cryptic, dark, deep, disguised, enigmatical, esoteric, furtive, hush-hush*, mysterious, mystic, mystical, obscure, occult, on the QT*, out-of-the-way*, private, recondite, reticent, retired, secluded, shrouded, strange, undercover, underground, under wraps*, undisclosed, unenlightened, unfrequented, unintelligible, unknown, unpublished, unseen, veiled; SEE CONCEPTS **529,576**

secret [*adj2*] *underhand, clandestine*
backdoor, backstairs, camouflaged, classified, close, confidential, covert, cryptic, discreet, disguised, dissembled, dissimulated, furtive, hush-hush*, in ambush, incognito, inside, restricted, secretive, sly, sneak, sneaky, stealthy, sub-rosa, surreptitious, top secret, unacknowledged, under false pretense*, underhanded, under-the-table*; SEE CONCEPTS **545,576**

secret [*n*] *something kept hidden, unrevealed*
cipher, classified information, code, confidence, confidential information, enigma, formula, key, magic number*, mystery, occult, oracle, password, privileged information, puzzle, skeleton in cupboard*, unknown; SEE CONCEPTS **274,631**

secretary [*n1*] *office worker*
assistant, clerk, executive secretary, receptionist, typist, word processor; SEE CONCEPT **348**

secretary [*n2*] *desk*
bureau, davenport, escritoire, secretaire, writing desk, writing table; SEE CONCEPT **443**

secrete [*v1*] *hide*
bury, cache, conceal, cover, cover up, deposit, disguise, ditch, ensconce, finesse, harbor, hide out, keep quiet, keep secret, keep to oneself, keep under wraps*, palm*, paper, plant, screen, seclude, secure, shroud, squirrel*, stash, stash away, stonewall*, stow, sweep under rug*, veil, whitewash*, withhold; SEE CONCEPTS **188,266**

secrete [*v2*] *give off, emit*
discharge, emanate, excrete, extravasate, extrude, exude, perspire, produce, sweat; SEE CONCEPTS **146,179**

secretive [*adj*] *uncommunicative*
backstairs*, buttoned up*, cagey, clammed up*, close, close-mouthed*, covert, cryptic, enigmatic, feline, furtive, hushed, in chambers*, in privacy*, in private, in the background*, in the dark*, on the QT*, reserved, reticent, silent, taciturn, tight-lipped*, undercover, unforthcoming, withdrawn, zipped*; SEE CONCEPTS **267,548**

secretly [*adv*] *in hidden manner*
behind closed doors*, behind someone's back*, by stealth, clandestinely, confidentially, covertly, furtively, hush-hush*, in camera*, in confidence, in holes and corners*, in secret, insidiously, in strict confidence*, intimately, obscurely, on the QT*, on the quiet*, on the sly*, personally, privately, privily, quietly, slyly, stealthily, sub rosa, surreptitiously, underhandedly, under the table*, unobserved; SEE CONCEPTS **267,548**

se
se

sect [*n*] *school of thought*
camp, church, communion, connection, creed, crew, cult, denomination, division, faction, faith, following, group, order, party, persuasion, religion, school, splinter group, team, wing; SEE CONCEPTS 381,382

sectarian [*adj*] *narrow-minded, exclusive*
bigoted, clannish, cliquish, dissident, doctrinaire, dogmatic, factional, fanatic, fanatical, hidebound, insular, limited, local, nonconforming, nonconformist, parochial, partisan, provincial, rigid, schismatic, skeptical, small-town*, splinter; SEE CONCEPT 403

sectarian [*n*] *person who is narrow-minded*
adherent, bigot, cohort, disciple, dissenter, dissident, dogmatist, extremist, fanatic, heretic, maverick, misbeliever, nonconformist, partisan, radical, rebel, revolutionary, satellite, schismatic, separatist, supporter, true believer, zealot; SEE CONCEPTS 359,423

section [*n*] *division, portion*
area, belt, bite, branch, category, chunk, classification, component, cross section, cut, department, district, drag, end, field, fraction, fragment, hunk, installment, locality, lump, member, moiety, parcel, part, passage, piece, precinct, quarter, region, sample, sector, segment, share, slice, slot, sphere, split, subdivision, territory, tier, tract, vicinity, zone; SEE CONCEPT 835

sectional [*adj*] *localized, divided*
exclusive, factional, local, narrow, partial, regional, selfish, separate, separatist; SEE CONCEPTS 557,785

sector [*n*] *area, subdivision*
category, district, division, part, precinct, quarter, region, stratum, zone; SEE CONCEPTS 508,835

secular [*adj*] *not spiritual or religious*
civil, earthly, laic, laical, lay, material, materialistic, nonclerical, nonreligious, of this world*, profane, temporal, unsacred, worldly; SEE CONCEPTS 529,549

secure [*adj1*] *safe*
defended, guarded, immune, impregnable, out of harm's way, protected, riskless, safe, sheltered, shielded, unassailable, undamaged, unharmed; SEE CONCEPT 587

secure [*adj2*] *fastened, stable*
adjusted, anchored, bound, buttoned down*, fast, firm, fixed, fortified, immovable, iron, locked, nailed, safe and sound*, set, solid, solid as a rock*, sound, staunch, steady, strong, sure, tenacious, tight; SEE CONCEPT 488

secure [*adj3*] *certain, definite*
able, absolute, assured, at ease, balanced, carefree, cinch, conclusive, confident, determined, easy, established, firm, hopeful, in the bag*, locked on*, nailed down*, on ice*, reassured, reliable, resolute, sanguine, self-assured, self-confident, settled, shoo-in*, solid, sound, stable, steadfast, steady, strong, sure, sure thing*, tried and true*, unanxious, undoubtful, well-founded; SEE CONCEPTS 403,535

secure [*v1*] *obtain*
access, achieve, acquire, annex, assure, bag*, buy, capture, catch, chalk up*, cinch, come by, ensure, gain, get, get hold of, grasp, guarantee, have, hook, insure, land, lock, lock up, make sure, pick up, procure, rack up*, take, win; SEE CONCEPT 120

secure [*v2*] *attach, tie up*
adjust, anchor, batten down, bind, bolt, button, button down, catch, cement, chain, clamp, clinch, close, fasten, fix, hitch, hook on, lash, lock, lock up, make fast, moor, nail, padlock, pinion, rivet, settle, tack, tie, tie down, tighten; SEE CONCEPTS 85,160

secure [*v3*] *protect, make safe*
assure, bulwark, cover, defend, ensure, fend, guarantee, guard, *insure, safeguard, screen, shield; SEE CONCEPT 96

security [*n1*] *safety, protection*
aegis, agreement, armament, armor, asylum, bail, bond, care, collateral, compact, contract, covenant, cover, custody, defense, earnest, freedom, guarantee, guard, immunity, insurance, pact, pawn, pledge, precaution, preservation, promise, protection, redemption, refuge, retreat, safeguard, safekeeping, safeness, safety measure, salvation, sanctuary, shelter, shield, surety, surveillance, token, ward, warrant; SEE CONCEPTS 712,729

security [*n2*] *peace of mind*
assurance, calm, certainty, confidence, conviction, ease, freedom, positiveness, reliance, soundness, sureness, surety; SEE CONCEPT 410

sedate [*adj*] *calm, collected*
cold sober*, composed, cool, cool as cucumber*, decorous, deliberate, demure, dignified, dispassionate, earnest, grave, imperturbable, laidback*, no-nonsense, placid, proper, quiet, seemly, serene, serious, sober, solemn, somber, staid, steady, tranquil, unflappable, unruffled; SEE CONCEPTS 404,542

sedative [*adj*] *soothing*
allaying, anodyne, calmative, calming, lenitive, relaxing, sleep-inducing, soporific, tranquillizing; SEE CONCEPT 537

sedative [*n*] *soothing agent, medicine*
analgesic, anodyne, barbiturate, calmant, calmative, depressant, dope*, downer, drug, hypnotic, knockout pill, medication, narcotic, nerve medicine, opiate, pacifier, pain-killer, pain pill*, quietive, sleeping pill, tranquillizer; SEE CONCEPT 307

sedentary [*adj*] *motionless, lazy*
desk, desk-bound, idle, inactive, seated, settled, sitting, sluggish, stationary, torpid; SEE CONCEPTS 542,584

sediment [*n*] *solid residue from liquid solution*
debris, deposit, dregs, dross, gook*, grounds, gunk*, lees, matter, powder, precipitate, precipitation, residuum, settling, silt, slag, solids, trash, waste; SEE CONCEPT 260

sedition [*n*] *rebellion*
agitation, defiance, disobedience, dissent, insubordination, insurgence, insurgency, insurrection, mutiny, revolt, revolution, treason, uprising; SEE CONCEPTS 106,300,320,633

seditious [*adj*] *rebellious*
anarchistic, bellicose, defiant, disloyal, disobedient, disorderly, dissident, factious, iconoclastic, insurgent, insurrectionary, mutinous, radical, rebel, resistant, revolutionary, riotous, subversive, treasonable, warring; SEE CONCEPTS 401,529,542

seduce [*v1*] *tempt, ensnare*
bait, beguile, betray, bribe, coax, deceive, decoy, delude, draw, entice, entrap, hook, induce, inveigle, invite, lead astray*, lead on*, lure, mislead,

mousetrap*, persuade, pull, rope in, steer, string along*, sucker*, wheedle; SEE CONCEPT *11*

seduce [*v2*] *entice sexually*
allure, attract, beguile, captivate, charm, come on to*, enamour, entrance, sweep off one's feet*, tempt; SEE CONCEPT *375*

seduction [*n*] *enticement*
allurement, attraction, cajolery, come-on*, inducement, lure, persuasion, tantalizing, temptation; SEE CONCEPTS *7,19,22,68*

seductive [*adj*] *alluring, sexy*
attracting, attractive, beguiling, bewitching, captivating, charming, come-hither*, desirable, drawing, enchanting, enticing, fascinating, flirtatious, inviting, irresistible, magnetic, provocative, ravishing, siren, specious, tempting; SEE CONCEPTS *372,579*

sedulous [*adj*] *assiduous*
active, busy, determined, diligent, hard-working, industrious, laborious, persevering, plugging, tireless; SEE CONCEPTS *538,542*

see [*v1*] *perceive with eyes*
beam, be apprised of, behold, catch a glimpse of, catch sight of, clock*, contemplate, descry, detect, discern, distinguish, espy, examine, eye, flash, gape, gawk, gaze, get a load of*, glare, glimpse, heed, identify, inspect, lay eyes on*, look, look at, make out, mark, mind, note, notice, observe, pay attention to, peek, peep, peer, peg*, penetrate, pierce, recognize, regard, remark, scan, scope, scrutinize, sight, spot, spy, stare, survey, take notice, view, watch, witness; SEE CONCEPTS *590,626*

see [*v2*] *appreciate, comprehend*
appraise, ascertain, behold, catch, catch on, conceive, descry, determine, discern, discover, distinguish, envisage, envision, espy, experience, fancy, fathom, feature, feel, find out, follow, get, get the drift*, get the hang of*, grasp, have, hear, imagine, investigate, know, learn, make out, mark, mind, note, notice, observe, perceive, ponder, realize, recognize, remark, study, suffer, sustain, take in, think, tumble, undergo, understand, unearth, view, visualize, weigh; SEE CONCEPTS *15,31,43*

see [*v3*] *accompany, guide*
associate with, attend, bear company, call, come by, come over, conduct, consort with, date, direct, drop by, drop in, encounter, escort, go out with, go with, keep company with, lead, look up, meet, pilot, pop in, receive, route, run into, shepherd, show, speak to, steer, stop by, stop in, take out, usher, visit, walk; SEE CONCEPTS *187,227,384*

see [*v4*] *visualize*
anticipate, conceive, divine, envisage, envision, fancy, feature, foresee, foretell, imagine, picture, realize, think, vision; SEE CONCEPT *12*

seed [*n1*] *beginning, source*
berry, bud, cell, conceit, concept, conception, core, corn, ear, egg, embryo, germ, grain, image, impression, inkling, kernel, notion, nucleus, nut, ovule, ovum, particle, rudiment*, semen, spark, sperm, spore, start, suspicion; SEE CONCEPTS *393,428,648*

seed [*n2*] *children*
brood, descendants, heirs, issue, offspring, posterity, progeniture, progeny, race, scions, spawn, successors; SEE CONCEPT *414*

seedy [*adj*] *run-down, dilapidated*
ailing, beat up, bedraggled, crummy*, decaying, decrepit, dingy, dog-eared*, down-at-the-heel*, drooping, droopy, faded, flagging, frowzy, gone to seed*, grubby, in a bad way*, mangy, messy, neglected, old, overgrown, poor, poorly, ragged, ratty, sagging, scruffy, shabby, sickly, sleazy*, slovenly, squalid, tacky, tattered, threadbare, tired, torn, unkempt, untidy, unwell, used up, wilted, wilting, worn; SEE CONCEPTS *485,570*

seek [*v1*] *look for*
be after, beat the bushes*, bird-dog*, bob for, cast about, chase, comb, delve, delve for, dig for, dragnet, explore, fan, ferret out, fish, fish for*, follow, go after, gun for*, hunt, inquire, investigate, leave no stone unturned*, look about, look around, look high and low*, mouse*, nose*, prowl, pursue, quest, ransack, root, run after, scout, scratch, search for, search out, sniff out*, track down; SEE CONCEPT *216*

seek [*v2*] *try, attempt*
aim, aspire to, assay, endeavor, essay, have a go at*, offer, pursue, strive, struggle, undertake; SEE CONCEPT *87*

seek [*v3*] *ask, inquire*
beg, entreat, find out, invite, petition, query, request, solicit; SEE CONCEPT *48*

seem [*v*] *appear; give the impression*
assume, be suggestive of, convey the impression, create the impression, give the feeling of*, give the idea of*, have the appearance of, have the aspects of, have the earmarks of*, have the features of, have the qualities of, hint, imply, insinuate, intimate, look, look as if, look like, look to be, make a show of, pretend, resemble, show, show every sign of, sound, sound like, strike one as being, suggest; SEE CONCEPT *543*

seeming [*adj*] *apparent*
appearing, illusive, illusory, ostensible, outward, professed, quasi-, semblant, specious, surface; SEE CONCEPTS *487,573*

seemly [*adj*] *appropriate, suitable*
becoming, befitting, comme il faut, compatible, conforming, congenial, congruous, consistent, consonant, correct, decent, decorous, fit, fitting, in good taste, meet, nice, pleasing, proper, suited, timely; SEE CONCEPT *558*

seep [*v*] *leak*
bleed, drain, drip, exude, flow, ooze, percolate, permeate, soak, sweat, transude, trickle, weep, well; SEE CONCEPTS *146,179*

seer [*n*] *clairvoyant*
augur, channeller, crystal ball gazer, diviner, forecaster, fortune-teller, medium, oracle, palm reader, prophet, psychic, soothsayer; SEE CONCEPT *423*

seethe [*v*] *be very angry*
be furious, be incensed, be livid, be mad, be on the warpath*, blow one's stack*, blow up*, boil, breathe fire*, bristle, burn, ferment, flare, flip, foam, foam at mouth*, froth, fume, hit the ceiling*, rage, see red*, simmer, smolder, spark, stew*, storm; SEE CONCEPTS *29,34*

segment [*n*] *part of something*
articulation, bit, compartment, cut, division, member, moiety, parcel, piece, portion, section, sector, slice, subdivision, wedge; SEE CONCEPT *835*

segregate [*v*] *discriminate and separate*
choose, close off, cut off, disconnect, dissociate,

se
se

divide, insulate, island, isolate, quarantine, select, sequester, set apart, sever, single out, split up; SEE CONCEPTS *21,135,645*

segregation [*n*] *separation*
apartheid, discrimination, dissociation, disunion, division, exlusion, isolation, partition, seclusion, splitting up; SEE CONCEPTS *135,195,297,388*

seize [*v1*] *grab, take*
appropriate, catch, catch hold of, clasp, clench, clinch, clutch, compass, embrace, enclose, enfold, envelope, fasten, grapple, grasp, grip, hang onto, hold fast, lay hands on*, lay hold of*, pinch, pluck, snag, snatch, squeeze, take hold of; SEE CONCEPTS *142,164,190*

seize [*v2*] *abduct; take by force*
ambush, annex, apprehend, appropriate, arrest, arrogate, bag, bust, capture, carry off, catch, claw, clutch, commandeer, confiscate, conquer, exact, force, gain, get, grab, grasp, hijack, hook, impound, incorporate, kidnap, lift, nab, nail*, occupy, overcome, overpower, overrun, overwhelm, pick up, pounce, secure, snag, snare, spirit away*, subdue, take, take by storm*, take captive, take over, take possession of, throttle, trap, usurp, wrench; SEE CONCEPT *90*

seizure [*n1*] *convulsive attack*
access, breakdown, convulsion, fit, illness, paroxysm, spasm, spell, stroke, throe, turn; SEE CONCEPT *308*

seizure [*n2*] *capture, taking*
abduction, annexation, apprehension, arrest, bust*, collar*, commandeering, confiscation, drop, grab, grabbing, hook*, pinch*, seizing, snatch; SEE CONCEPT *90*

seldom [*adv*] *infrequently*
a few times, every now and then, from time to time, hardly, hardly ever, in a few cases, inhabitually, irregularly, little, not often, not very often, occasionally, on and off, once in a blue moon*, once in a while, rarely, scarcely, scarcely ever, semioccasionally, sometimes, sporadically, uncommonly, unoften, unusually, whimsically; SEE CONCEPT *541*

select [*adj*] *excellent, elite, preferable*
best, blue-chip*, boss*, choice, chosen, cool*, cream*, culled, delicate, discriminating, eclectic, elect, elegant, exclusive, exquisite, favored, first-class*, first-rate*, handpicked, limited, number one*, pick, picked, posh, preferred, prime, privileged, rare, recherché, screened, selected, selective, special, superior, top, topnotch, tops*, weeded*, winner, winnowed, world-class*; SEE CONCEPTS *574,653*

select [*v*] *pick out, prefer from among choices*
choose, cull, decide, elect, make, make a choice, make a selection, mark, name, opt, optate, opt for, peg*, pick, pin down, say so*, single out, slot*, sort out, tab*, tag*, take, tap*, winnow; SEE CONCEPT *41*

selection [*n*] *preference from among choices*
alternative, choice, choosing, collection, culling, draft, druthers*, election, excerpt, option, pick, picking; SEE CONCEPT *529*

selective [*adj*] *discriminating*
careful, choicy, choosy, discerning, discriminatory, eclectic, fussy, judicious, particular, persnickety*, picky, scrupulous, select; SEE CONCEPTS *404,542*

self-assured [*adj*] *confident*
assured, believing, bold, brave, cocksure*,

cocky, courageous, expectant, expecting, fearless, overconfident, positive, puffed up*, secure, sure, unafraid; SEE CONCEPTS *403,404*

self-centered [*adj*] *absorbed with oneself*
egocentric, egoistic, egomaniacal, egotistical, grandstanding, having a swelled head*, independent, inward-looking, know-it-all*, narcissistic, on an ego trip*, self-absorbed, self-indulgent, self-interested, self-involved, selfish, self-seeking, self-serving, self-sufficient, stuck on oneself*, wrapped up with oneself*; SEE CONCEPT *404*

self-confident [*adj*] *secure with oneself*
assured, fearless, hotdog*, hotshot*, know-it-all*, poised, sanguine, self-assured, self-reliant, sure of oneself, undoubtful; SEE CONCEPT *404*

self-conscious [*adj*] *insecure with oneself*
affected, anxious, artificial, awkward, bashful, diffident, discomfited, embarrassed, ill-at-ease, mannered, nervous, out of countenance, shamefaced, sheepish, shy, stiff, stilted, uncertain, uncomfortable, uneasy, unsure; SEE CONCEPTS *401,404*

self-control [*n*] *willpower over one's actions*
abstemiousness, aplomb, balance, constraint, dignity, discipline, discretion, poise, repression, reserve, restraint, reticence, self-constraint, self-discipline, self-government, sobriety, stability, stoicism, strength of character; SEE CONCEPT *633*

self-evident/self-explanatory [*adj*] *obvious*
apparent, axiomatic, clear, comprehensible, incontrovertible, inescapable, manifest, patently true, plain, prima facie, undeniable, understandable, unmistakable, unquestionable, visible; SEE CONCEPTS *529,548*

self-important [*adj*] *conceited*
arrogant, bigheaded*, cocky, egotistical, full of hot air*, immodest, know-it-all, overbearing, pompous, puffed up*, smug, stuck up*, swollen-headed*, vain, vainglorious; SEE CONCEPT *404*

selfish [*adj*] *thinking only of oneself*
egocentric, egoistic, egoistical, egomaniacal, egotistic, egotistical, greedy*, hoggish*, mean, mercenary, miserly, narcissistic, narrow, narrow-minded, out for number one*, parsimonious, prejudiced, self-centered, self-indulgent, self-interested, self-seeking, stingy, ungenerous, wrapped up in oneself*; SEE CONCEPTS *404,542*

self-reliant [*adj*] *independent*
autonomous, on one's own, self-contained, self-governing, self-sufficient, self-supporting, self-sustaining, unaided, unallied; SEE CONCEPT *554*

self-respect/self-esteem [*n*] *pride in oneself*
amour-propre, conceit, confidence, dignity, egotism, faith in oneself, morale, narcissism, self-assurance, self-content, self-regard, self-satisfaction, vanity, worth; SEE CONCEPTS *411,689*

self-righteous [*adj*] *smug*
affected, canting, complacent, egotistical, goody-goody*, holier-than-thou*, hypocritical, noble, pharisaic, pietistic, pious, preachy, sanctimonious, self-satisfied, superior; SEE CONCEPTS *401,542*

self-satisfaction [*n*] *pride, contentment*
complacency, conceit, glow, peace of mind, self-approbation, self-approval, self-pleasure, smugness; SEE CONCEPTS *410,689*

self-satisfied [*adj*] *proud, content*
complacent, conceited, egotistic, flushed,

pleased, puffed up*, self-congratulatory, smug, vain; SEE CONCEPTS 404,542

self-sufficient [adj] able to take care of oneself
arrogant, closed, competent, conceited, confident, doing one's own thing*, efficient, egotistic, haughty, independent, individual, on one's own, out for number one*, self-confident, self-dependent, self-sufficing, self-supported, self-supporting, self-sustained, self-sustaining, smug, unit; SEE CONCEPTS 334,404

sell [v1] exchange an object for money
advertise, auction, bargain, barter, be in business*, boost, clinch the deal, close, close the deal, contract, deal in, dispose, drum, dump, exchange, handle, hawk, hustle, market, merchandise, move, peddle, persuade, pitch, plug, puff*, push, put across, put up for sale, retail, retain, snow, soft sell*, soft soap*, spiel*, stock, sweet talk*, trade, traffic, unload, vend, wholesale; SEE CONCEPT 345

seller [n] person who gives object in exchange for money
agent, auctioneer, businessperson, dealer, marketer, merchant, peddler, representative, retailer, sales help, salesperson, shopkeeper, storekeeper, trader, tradesperson, vendor; SEE CONCEPTS 347,348

sell/sell out [v2] betray
beguile, break faith, bunk, cross, deceive, deliver up, delude, disappoint, double-cross*, fail, four-flush*, give away, give up, mislead, play false, rat on*, sell down the river*, stab in the back*, surrender, take in, violate; SEE CONCEPTS 14,63

semblance [n] aura, appearance
affinity, air, alikeness, analogy, aspect, bearing, comparison, facade, face, false front*, feel, feeling, figure, form, front, guise, image, likeness, mask, mien, mood, pose, pretense, resemblance, seeming, show, showing, similarity, simile, similitude, simulacrum, veil, veneer; SEE CONCEPTS 673,716

semester [n] term
course, period, quarter, session; SEE CONCEPTS 807,822

seminar [n] conference
convention, discussion, forum, group discussion, meeting, open discussion, palaver, powwow*, rap session, round table, symposium, workshop; SEE CONCEPTS 56,324,386

semiotics [n] study of signs as elements of communication
langue, parole, pragmatics, semantics, sign systems, symbolism, syntactics; SEE CONCEPT 349

send [v1] transmit, transfer through a system
accelerate, address, advance, assign, broadcast, cast, circulate, commission, commit, communicate, consign, convey, delegate, deliver, detail, direct, dispatch, drop, emit, expedite, express, fire, fling, forward, freight, get under way, give off, grant, hasten, hurl, hurry off, impart, issue, let fly, mail, post, propel, put out, radiate, relay, remit, route, rush off, ship, shoot, televise, troll, wire; SEE CONCEPTS 217,223

send [v2] please
charm, delight, electrify, enrapture, enthrall, enthuse, excite, intoxicate, move, please, ravish, stir, thrill, titillate, turn on; SEE CONCEPTS 7,11,22

senile [adj] failing in physical and mental capabilities due to old age
aged, ancient, anile, decrepit, doddering, doting, enfeebled, feeble, imbecile, infirm, in second childhood*, old, senescent, shattered, sick, weak; SEE CONCEPTS 314,402,403

senior [adj] older or of higher rank
chief, elder, higher, leading, major, more advanced, next higher, superior; SEE CONCEPTS 574,578,585,797

senior [n] older person
ancient, doyen, doyenne, elder, elderly person, first-born, golden-ager*, grandfather, grandmother, head, matriarch, old folk*, oldster*, old-timer*, patriarch, pensioner, retired person, senior citizen; SEE CONCEPTS 414,424

seniority [n] rank in organization due to length of service
advantage, antiquity, eldership, precedence, preference, priority, rank, ranking, standing, station, superiority; SEE CONCEPTS 671,727

sensation [n1] feeling, perception
awareness, consciousness, emotion, gut reaction*, impression, passion, response, sense, sensibility, sensitiveness, sensitivity, sentiment, susceptibility, thought, tingle, vibes*; SEE CONCEPTS 34,410,529

sensation [n2] something wonderful or awe-inspiring
agitation, bomb*, bombshell*, commotion, excitement, flash, furor, hit, marvel, miracle, phenomenon, portent, prodigy, scandal, stir, stunner, surprise, thrill, wonder, wow*; SEE CONCEPTS 293,529

sensational [adj1] startling, exaggerated
amazing, arresting, astounding, breathtaking, coarse, colored, conspicuous, dramatic, electrifying, emotional, excessive, exciting, extravagant, hair-raising, horrifying, juicy*, livid, lurid, marked, melodramatic, noticeable, outstanding, piquant, pointed, prominent, pungent, remarkable, revealing, rough, salient, scandalous, sensationalistic, shocking, signal, spectacular, staggering, stimulating, sultry, tabloid*, thrilling, vulgar, X-rated*; SEE CONCEPTS 267,537,545

sensational [adj2] excellent, superb
agitating, astonishing, breathtaking, cool*, dandy*, divine, dramatic, eloquent, exceptional, exciting, fabulous, first-class*, glorious, impressive, incredible, keen, marvelous, mind-blowing, most*, moving, out of this world*, smashing, spectacular, stirring, surprising, thrilling, zero cool*; SEE CONCEPT 574

sensationalism [n] exaggeration
aggrandizement, boasting, excess, fabrication, fish story*, hype, hyperbole, overemphasis, puffery, tabloid journalism, tall story*, whopper*, yellow journalism*; SEE CONCEPTS 63,278,663

sense [n1] feeling of animate being
faculty, feel, function, hearing, impression, kinesthesia, sensation, sensibility, sensitivity, sight, smell, taste, touch; SEE CONCEPT 405

sense [n2] awareness, perception
ability, appreciation, atmosphere, aura, brains, capacity, clear-headedness, cleverness, cognizance, common sense, consciousness, discernment, discrimination, feel, feeling, gumption*, imagination, impression, insight, intellect, intelligence, intuition, judgment, knowledge, mental-

se
se

ity, mind, premonition, presentiment, prudence, quickness, reason, reasoning, recognition, sagacity, sanity, sentiment, sharpness, smarts*, soul, spirit, tact, thought, understanding, wisdom, wit; SEE CONCEPTS 33,409

sense [n3] *point, meaning*
acceptation, advantage, bottom line*, burden, core, definition, denotatiton, drift, gist, good, heart, implication, import, intendment, interpretation, logic, matter, meat*, meat and potatoes*, message, name of the game*, nature of the beast*, nitty-gritty*, nuance, nub, nuts and bolts*, punch line*, purport, purpose, reason, short, significance, significancy, signification, stuff, substance, thrust, understanding, upshot, use, value, worth; SEE CONCEPTS 668,682

sense [v] *become aware of*
anticipate, apperceive, appreciate, apprehend, believe, be with it, catch, catch on, catch the drift*, consider, credit, deem, dig*, discern, divine, feel, feel in bones*, feel in gut*, get the drift*, get the idea*, get the impression*, get the picture*, get vibes*, grasp, have a feeling*, have a hunch*, hold, know, notice, observe, perceive, pick up, read, realize, savvy*, suspect, take in, think, understand; SEE CONCEPT 34

senseless [adj] *silly, meaningless*
absurd, asinine, batty, crazy, daft, doublespeak*, double talk*, fatuous, flaky, foolish, idiotic, illogical, imbecilic, inane, incongruous, inconsistent, insignificant, irrational, ludicrous, mad, mindless, moronic, nonsensical, nutty, pointless, purportless, purposeless, ridiculous, simple, stupid, trivial, unimportant, unintelligent, unmeaning, unreasonable, unsound, unwise, wacky*, without rhyme or reason*; SEE CONCEPTS 548,558

sensibility [n] *responsiveness; ability to feel*
affection, appreciation, awareness, discernment, emotion, feeling, gut reaction*, heart*, insight, intuition, judgment, keenness, perceptiveness, rationale, sensation, sense, sensitiveness, sensitivity, sentiment, susceptibility, taste, vibes*; SEE CONCEPTS 409,410

sensible [adj] *realistic, reasonable*
all there*, astute, attentive, au courant, aware, canny, cognizant, commonsensical, conscious, consequent, conversant, cool*, discerning, discreet, discriminating, down-to-earth, far-sighted, having all one's marbles*, informed, in right mind, intelligent, judicious, knowing, logical, matter-of-fact, practical, prudent, rational, sagacious, sage, sane, sentient, shrewd, sober, sound, together, well-reasoned, well-thought-out, wise, witting; SEE CONCEPTS 402,542

sensitive [adj1] *impressionable*
acute, cognizant, conscious, delicate, easily affected, emotionable, emotional, feeling, fine, high-strung, hung up*, hypersensitive, impressible, irritable, keen, knowing, nervous, oversensitive, perceiving, perceptive, precarious, precise, psychic, reactive, receptive, responsive, seeing, sensatory, sensile, sensorial, sensory, sentient, supersensitive, susceptible, tense, ticklish, touchy, touchy feely*, tricky, tuned in*, turned on to*, umbrageous, understanding, unstable, wired*; SEE CONCEPT 403

sensitive [adj2] *easily hurt*
delicate, easily harmed, painful, sore, tender; SEE CONCEPT 406

sensitivity [n] *responsiveness to stimuli*
acuteness, affectibility, awareness, consciousness, delicacy, feeling, impressionability, nervousness, reactiveness, reactivity, receptiveness, sensation, sense, sensitiveness, subtlety, susceptibility, sympathy; SEE CONCEPTS 405,410.

sensory [adj] *affecting animate nerve organs*
acoustic, afferent, audible, audiovisual, auditory, aural, auricular, clear, discernible, distinct, gustative, gustatory, hearable, lingual, neural, neurological, ocular, olfactive, olfactory, ophthalmic, optic, perceptible, phonic, plain, receptive, sensational, sensatory, sensible, sensual, sonic, tactile, visual; SEE CONCEPT 406

sensual [adj] *physical, erotic*
animal, animalistic, arousing, bodily, carnal, debauched, delightful, epicurean, exciting, fleshly, heavy*, hedonic, hot*, lascivious, lecherous, lewd, libidinous, licentious, lustful, moving, pleasing, rough, sensuous, sexual, sexy, sharpened, steamy, stimulating, stirring, tactile, unchaste, unspiritual, voluptuous, X-rated*; SEE CONCEPTS 372,401

sensuous [adj] *gratifying to senses*
carnal, epicurean, exciting, fleshly, fleshy, hedonistic, luscious, lush, luxurious, passionate, physical, pleasurable, pleasure-loving, pleasure-seeking, primrose, rich, self-indulgent, sensory, sensual, sensualistic, sumptuous, sybaritic, voluptuous; SEE CONCEPTS 372,537

sentence [n] *punishing decree*
book, censure, clock, condemnation, considered opinion, decision, determination, dictum, doom, edict, fall, getup*, hitch, jolt, judgment, knock, order, penalty, pronouncement, punishment, rap*, ruling, sending up the river*, sleep, stretch, term, time, trick, vacation, verdict; SEE CONCEPT 318

sentence [v] *decide punishment*
adjudge, adjudicate, blame, condemn, confine, convict, damn, denounce, devote, doom, impound, imprison, incarcerate, jail, judge, mete out, ordain, pass judgment, penalize, proscribe, punish, put away*, put on ice*, railroad*, rule, send to prison, send up the river*, settle, take the fall*, throw the book at*; SEE CONCEPTS 122,317

sentient [adj] *conscious*
able to recognize, alert, apperceptive, attentive, awake, aware, cognizant, feeling, informed, in on*, in the right mind, knowing, noticing, observing, perceiving, receptive, recognizing, responsive, seeing, sensitive to, understanding, watchful; SEE CONCEPTS 402,539

sentiment [n] *emotion, belief*
affect, affectivity, attitude, bias, conception, conviction, disposition, emotionalism, eye, feeling, hearts and flowers*, idea, inclination, inclining, judgment, leaning, mind, opinion, overemotionalism, partiality, passion, penchant, persuasion, position, posture, predilection, propensity, romanticism, sensibility, sentimentality, slant, softheartedness, tendency, tender feeling, tenderness, thought, view, way of thinking; SEE CONCEPTS 32,410,689 -

sentimental [adj] *emotional, romantic*
affected, affectionate, corny*, demonstrative, dewy-eyed, dreamy, effusive, gushing, gushy, idealistic, impressionable, inane, insipid, jejune, languishing, lovey-dovey*, loving, maudlin, moonstruck*, mushy*, nostalgic, overacted,

overemotional, passionate, pathetic, rosewater*, saccharine*, sappy*, schmaltzy*, silly, simpering, sloppy*, slushy*, soapy*, soft, softhearted*, sugary*, sweet, syrupy*, tearful, tear-jerking*, tender, touching, vapid, visionary, weepy; SEE CONCEPTS 267,401,542

sentinel [n] *sentry*
guard, keeper, lookout, picket, protector, watchman/woman, watchperson; SEE CONCEPT 348

separate [adj1] *disconnected*
abstracted, apart, apportioned, asunder, cut apart, cut in two, detached, disassociated, discrete, disembodied, disjointed, distant, distributed, disunited, divergent, divided, divorced, far between, free, independent, in halves, isolated, loose, marked, parted, partitioned, put asunder, removed, scattered, set apart, set asunder, severed, sovereign, sundered, unattached, unconnected; SEE CONCEPT 577

separate [adj2] *alone, individual*
apart, autonomous, detached, different, discrete, distinct, distinctive, diverse, free, independent, lone, one, only, particular, peculiar, several, single, sole, solitary, unique, various; SEE CONCEPTS 557,564

separate [v1] *remove something from group; keep or set apart*
break, break off, cleave, come apart, come away, come between, detach, dichotomize, disconnect, disentangle, disjoin, disjoint, dissect, dissever, distribute, divide, divorce, intersect, part, rupture, sever, split, split up, sunder, uncombine, uncouple, undo; SEE CONCEPT 135

separate [v2] *isolate, segregate*
assign, break up, classify, close off, comb, compartment, compartmentalize, cut off, discriminate, distribute, draw apart, group, insulate, interval, intervene, island, order, put on one side, rope off, seclude, sequester, sift, single out, sort, space, split up, stand between, winnow; SEE CONCEPTS 158,201

separate [v3] *part company in a romantic relationship or marriage*
alienate, bifurcate, break it off*, break off, break up, dedomicile, depart, discontinue, disunify, disunite, diverge, divorce, drop, estrange, go away, go different ways*, go separate ways*, leave, part, pull out, split up, take leave, uncouple, unlink, untie the knot*; SEE CONCEPTS 297,384

separately [adv] *alone, individually*
apart, clearly, definitely, disjointly, distinctly, independently, one at a time, one by one, personally, severally, singly, solely; SEE CONCEPTS 544,577

separation [n] *being apart; break-up*
break, break-up, dedomiciling, departure, detachment, disconnection, disengagement, disjunction, disrelation, dissociation, dissolution, disunion, division, divorce, divorcement, embarkation, estrangement, farewell, gap, leavetaking*, parting, parting of the ways*, partition, pffft*, rift, rupture, segregation, severance, split, split-up*; SEE CONCEPTS 135,195,297,388

sepulchral [adj] *gloomy*
black, bleak, cheerless, dark, deathly, dismal, dreary, forlorn, funereal, grave, hollow, morbid, mournful, obscure, somber; SEE CONCEPTS 525,617,618

sequel [n] *follow-up*
aftereffect, aftermath, alternation, causatum, chain, close, closing, conclusion, consecution, consequence, continuation, development, effect, end, ending, epilogue, eventuality, finish, finishing, issue, order, outcome, part two*, payoff, progression, result, row, sequence, sequent, series, spin-off*, termination, train, upshot; SEE CONCEPTS 271,293,824,832

sequence [n] *series, order*
arrangement, array, catenation, chain, classification, concatenation, consecution, consecutiveness, continuance, continuity, continuousness, course, cycle, disposition, distribution, flow, graduation, grouping, ordering, pecking order*, perpetuity, placement, procession, progression, row, run, sequel, skein, streak, string, subsequence, succession, successiveness, track, train; SEE CONCEPTS 721,727

sequential [adj] *occurring in an order*
consecutive, constant, continuous, following, incessant, later, next, persistent, regular, sequent, serial, steady, subsequent, subsequential, succedent, succeeding, successive; SEE CONCEPTS 482,548,585

sequester [v] *isolate, seclude*
cloister, close off, cut off, draw back, enisle, hide, insulate, island, secrete, segregate, separate, set apart, set off, withdraw; SEE CONCEPTS 90,188

serendipity [n] *accidental discovery*
blessing, break*, dumb luck*, fluke*, good luck, happenstance, happy chance, luck, lucky break*, stumbling upon, tripping over; SEE CONCEPT 693

serene [adj] *calm, undisturbed*
at peace, clear, collected, comfortable, composed, content, cool*, cool as a cucumber*, dispassionate, easy, easygoing, fair, halcyon, imperturbable, laid-back*, limpid, patient, peaceful, pellucid, phlegmatic, placid, poised, quiescent, quiet, reconciled, resting, satisfied, sedate, self-possessed, smooth, still, stoical, tranquil, undisturbed, unflappable, unruffled, untroubled; SEE CONCEPTS 401,485

serenity [n] *calm, peacefulness*
calmness, composure, cool, patience, peace, peace of mind, placidity, quietness, quietude, stillness, tranquillity; SEE CONCEPTS 633,673

serf [n] *slave*
bondservant, bondsman/woman, chattel, laborer, peon, servant, vassal, villain, villein; SEE CONCEPT 348

serial [adj] *in continuing order*
consecutive, continual, continued, continuing, ensuing, following, going on, sequent, sequential, succedent, succeeding, successional, successive; SEE CONCEPTS 482,585

series [n] *order, succession*
alternation, arrangement, array, category, chain, classification, column, consecution, continuity, course, file, gradation, group, line, list, procession, progression, range, row, run, scale, sequel, sequence, set, skein, streak, string, suit, suite, tier, train; SEE CONCEPTS 721,727,769

serious [adj] *somber, humorless*
austere, bound, bound and determined*, businesslike, cold sober*, contemplative, deadpan*, deliberate, determined, downbeat*, earnest, funereal, genuine, go for broke*, grave, grim, honest, intent, long-faced*, meditative,

se
se

no-nonsense*, pensive, pokerfaced*, reflective, resolute, resolved, sedate, set, severe, sincere, sober, solemn, staid, steady, stern, thoughtful, unhumorous, unsmiling, weighty; SEE CONCEPTS 403,542

serious [*adj 2*] *crucial, weighty*
arduous, dangerous, deep, difficult, far-reaching, fateful, fell, formidable, grave, grievous, grim, hard, heavy, important, laborious, major, meaning business*, meaningful, menacing, momentous, no joke*, no laughing matter*, of consequence, operose, out for blood*, playing hard ball*, pressing, severe, significant, smoking*, sobering, strenuous, strictly business*, threatening, tough, ugly, unamusing, unhumorous, urgent, worrying; SEE CONCEPTS 538,565, 568

seriously [*adv 1*] *not humorously*
actively, all joking aside*, cool it*, cut the comedy*, determinedly, down, earnestly, fervently, for real*, gravely, in all conscience, in all seriousness, in earnest, intently, passionately, purposefully, resolutely, sedately, simmer down*, sincerely, soberly, solemnly, sternly, straighten out, thoughtfully, vigorously, with a straight face*, with forethought, with sobriety, zealously; SEE CONCEPTS 535,542,544

seriously [*adv 2*] *dangerously, critically*
acutely, badly, decidedly, deplorably, distressingly, gravely, grievously, harmfully, intensely, menacingly, perilously, precariously, quite, regrettably, severely, sorely, threateningly, very; SEE CONCEPTS 544,565,568

seriousness [*n 1*] *humorlessness*
calmness, coolness, earnest, earnestness, gravity, intentness, sedateness, serious-mindedness, sincerity, sober-mindedness, sobriety, solemnity, staidness, sternness, thoughtfulness; SEE CONCEPTS 410,657

seriousness [*n 2*] *danger; criticalness*
enormity, gravity, importance, moment, significance, urgency, weight; SEE CONCEPTS 668,675

sermon [*n*] *instructive speech with a moral*
address, advice, discourse, doctrine, exhortation, harangue, homily, lecture, lesson, moralism, pastoral, preach, preaching, preachment, tirade; SEE CONCEPTS 278,368

serpentine [*adj*] *winding; sly*
anfractuous, artful, cagey, circuitous, clever, coiling, convoluted, crafty, cunning, curved, curvy, foxy, indirect, mazy, meandering, meandrous, shrewd, sinuous, slick, slinky, snakelike, snaky*, subtle, supple, twisting, twisting and turning*, wily; SEE CONCEPTS 401,542,581

serrated [*adj*] *jagged*
denticulate, indented, notched, ragged, sawlike, sawtooth, saw-toothed, scored, serrate, serried, serriform, serrulate, toothed; SEE CONCEPT 486

servant [*n*] *person who waits on another*
assistant, attendant, cleaning person, dependent, domestic, drudge, help, helper, hireling, live-in, menial, minion, retainer, serf, server, slave; SEE CONCEPT 348

serve [*v 1*] *aid, help; supply*
arrange, assist, attend to, be of assistance, be of use, care for, deal, deliver, dish up*, distribute, do for, give, handle, hit, minister to, nurse, oblige, play, present, provide, provision, set out, succor, wait on, work for; SEE CONCEPTS 110,136,140

serve [*v 2*] *act, do*
accept, agree, attend, be employed by, carry on, complete, discharge, follow, fulfill, function, go through, hearken, labor, obey, observe, officiate, pass, perform, subserve, toil, work; SEE CONCEPT 91

serve [*v 3*] *suffice; do the work of*
advantage, answer, answer the purpose, apply, avail, be acceptable, be adequate, be good enough, benefit, be of use, be useful, content, do, do duty as, fill the bill*, fit, function, make, profit, satisfy, service, suit, work, work for; SEE CONCEPTS 656,658

service [*n 1*] *aid, help*
account, advantage, applicability, appropriateness, assistance, avail, benefit, business, check, courtesy, dispensation, duty, employ, employment, favor, fitness, indulgence, kindness, labor, maintenance, ministration, office, overhaul, relevance, serviceability, servicing, supply, use, usefulness, utility, value, work; SEE CONCEPTS 110,324,658

service [*n 2*] *rite of a church*
ceremonial, ceremony, formality, function, liturgy, observance, ritual, sermon, worship; SEE CONCEPT 368

service [*n 3*] *time in military operation*
action, active duty, combat, duty, fighting, sting; SEE CONCEPTS 320,321

serviceable [*adj*] *useful, functional*
advantageous, aiding, assistive, beneficial, convenient, dependable, durable, efficient, handy, hard-wearing, helpful, invaluable, operative, practical, profitable, usable, utile, utilitarian, valuable; SEE CONCEPT 560

servile [*adj*] *grovelling, subservient*
abject, base, beggarly, bootlicking, craven, cringing, despicable, eating crow*, eating humble pie*, fawning, humble, ignoble, low, mean, obedient, obeisant, obsequious, passive, slavish, submissive, sycophantic, toadying, unctuous, unresisting; SEE CONCEPTS 401,404

servitude [*n*] *slavery*
bondage, bonds, chains, confinement, enslavement, obedience, peonage, serfdom, serfhood, subjection, subjugation, thrall, thralldom, vassalage, yoke; SEE CONCEPTS 388,410

session [*n*] *meeting, gathering*
affair, assembly, concourse, conference, discussion, get-together, hearing, huddle, jam session*, meet, period, showdown, sitting, term; SEE CONCEPTS 114,324

set [*adj 1*] *decided*
agreed, appointed, arranged, bent, certain, concluded, confirmed, customary, dead set on*, decisive, definite, determined, entrenched, established, firm, fixed, immovable, intent, inveterate, ironclad, locked in*, obstinate, pat, pigheaded*, prearranged, predetermined, prescribed, regular, resolute, resolved, rigid, rooted, scheduled, set in stone*, settled, solid as a rock*, specified, stated, steadfast, still resolute, stipulated, stubborn, unflappable, usual, well-set; SEE CONCEPTS 535,542

set [*adj 2*] *firm, hardened; inflexible*
entrenched, fixed, hard and fast, hidebound, immovable, jelled, located, placed, positioned, rigid, settled, sited, situate, situated, solid, stable, stiff, strict, stubborn, unyielding; SEE CONCEPT 488

set [*n1*] *physical bearing*
address, air, attitude, carriage, comportment, demeanor, deportment, fit, hang, inclination, mien, port, position, posture, presence, turn; SEE CONCEPT 757

set [*n2*] *stage setting*
flats, mise en scène, scene, scenery, setting, stage set; SEE CONCEPT 263

set [*n3*] *group, assortment*
array, assemblage, band, batch, body, bunch, bundle, camp, circle, clan, class, 'clique, clump, cluster, clutch, collection, company, compendium, coterie, crew, crowd, faction, gaggle, gang, kit, lot, mob, organization, outfit, pack, push, rat pack*, sect, series; SEE CONCEPTS 417,432,769

set [*v1*] *position, place*
affix, aim, anchor, apply, arrange, bestow, cast, deposit, direct, embed, ensconce, establish, fasten, fix, head, insert, install, introduce, lay, level, locate, lock, lodge, make fast, make ready, mount, park, plank, plant, plop, plunk, point, post, prepare, put, rest, seat, settle, situate, spread, station, stick, train, turn, wedge, zero in*; SEE CONCEPTS 201,202

set [*v2*] *decide upon*
agree upon, allocate, allot, appoint, arrange, assign, conclude, decree, designate, determine, dictate, direct, establish, estimate, fix, fix price, impose, instruct, lay down, make, name, ordain, prescribe, price, rate, regulate, resolve, schedule, settle, specify, stipulate, value; SEE CONCEPT 18

set [*v3*] *harden*
become firm, cake, clot, coagulate, condense, congeal, crystallize, fix, gel, gelate, gelatinize, jell, jellify, jelly, solidify, stiffen, thicken; SEE CONCEPT 250

set [*v4*] *decline*
descend, dip, disappear, drop, go down, sink, subside, vanish; SEE CONCEPT 181

set [*v5*] *start, incite*
abet, begin, commence, foment, initiate, instigate, provoke, put in motion, raise, set on*, stir up*, whip up*; SEE CONCEPT 221

setback [*n*] *disappointment*
about-face*, backset, bath*, blow, bottom, check, comedown, defeat, delay, difficulty, drawing board*, flip-flop*, hindrance, hitch*, hold-up, impediment, misfortune, obstacle, rebuff, regress, regression, reversal, reversal of fortune, reverse, slowdown, stumbling block*, trouble, upset, whole new ballgame*; SEE CONCEPTS 388,674,679

set back [*v*] *delay, hinder*
bog down*, decelerate, defeat, detain, embog, hang up*, hold up, impede, mire, retard, reverse, slow, slow down, slow up; SEE CONCEPT 130

setting [*n*] *scene, background*
ambience, backdrop, context, distance, environment, frame, framework, horizon, jungle, locale, location, mise en scène, mounting, perspective, set, shade, shadow, site, stage set, stage setting, surroundings; SEE CONCEPTS 198,263

settle [*v1*] *straighten out, resolve*
achieve, adjudicate, adjust, appoint, arrange, call the shots*, choose, cinch, clean up, clear, clear up, clinch, come to a conclusion, come to a decision, come to an agreement, complete, concert, conclude, confirm, decide, determine, discharge, dispose, end, establish, figure, fix, form judg-

ment, judge, make a decision, make certain, mediate, nail down*, negotiate, order, pay, put an end to, put into order, reconcile, regulate, rule, satisfy, seal, set to rights, square, verify, work out; SEE CONCEPTS 18,126,341

settle [*v2*] *calm, relieve*
allay, assure, becalm, compose, lull, pacify, quell, quiet, quieten, reassure, relax, sedate, soothe, still, tranquilize; SEE CONCEPTS 7,22,469

settle [*v3*] *come to rest; fall*
alight, bed down, decline, descend, flop, immerse, land, lay, light, lodge, perch, place, plop, plunge, put, repose, roost, seat, set down, settle down, sink, sit, submerge, submerse, subside, touch down; SEE CONCEPT 181

settle [*v4*] *make one's home*
abide, colonize, dwell, establish, hang up one's hat*, inhabit, keep house, live, locate, lodge, move to, park, put down roots*, reside, set up home, squat, take root*, take up residence; SEE CONCEPT 226

settlement [*n1*] *decision, conclusion*
adjustment, agreement, arrangement, clearance, compact, compensation, completion, conclusion, confirmation, contract, covenant, deal, defrayal, determination, discharge, disposition, establishment, happy medium*, liquidation, pay, payment, payoff, quietus, reimbursement, remuneration, resolution, satisfaction, showdown, termination, trade-off, working out; SEE CONCEPTS 230,684

settlement [*n2*] *community*
colonization, colony, encampment, establishment, foundation, habitation, hamlet, inhabitancy, occupancy, occupation, outpost, plantation, principality, residence; SEE CONCEPTS 512,515

set up [*v*] *start*
arrange, assemble, back, begin, build, build up, compose, constitute, construct, create, elevate, erect, establish, excite, exhilarate, found, inaugurate, initiate, inspire, install, institute, introduce, launch, make provision for, open, organize, originate, prearrange, prepare, put together, put up, raise, rear, stimulate, strengthen, subsidize, usher in; SEE CONCEPT 221

sever [*v1*] *cut apart*
bisect, carve, cleave, cut, cut in two, detach, disconnect, disjoin, dissect, dissever, dissociate, disunite, divide, part, rend, rive, separate, slice, split, sunder; SEE CONCEPTS 98,176

sever [*v2*] *dissociate*
abandon, break off, disjoint, dissolve, divide, divorce, put an end to, separate, terminate; SEE CONCEPTS 297,384

several [*adj*] *assorted, various*
a few, a lot, any, certain, considerable, definite, different, disparate, distinct, divers, diverse, handful, hardly any, indefinite, individual, infrequent, manifold, many, not many, numerous, only a few, particular, personal, plural, proportionate, quite a few, rare, respective, scant, scanty, scarce, scarcely any, separate, single, small number, some, sparse, special, specific, sundry; SEE CONCEPTS 564,762

severe [*adj*] *uncompromising, stern*
astringent, austere, biting, caustic, close, cold, cruel, cutting, disapproving, dour, earnest, firm, flinty, forbidding, grave, grim, hard, hardnosed*, harsh, inconsiderate, inexorable, inflexi-

se
se

ble, iron-handed, obdurate, oppressive, peremptory, pitiless, relentless, resolute, resolved, rigid, satirical, scathing, serious, sober, stern, stiff*, strait-laced*, strict, tight-lipped*, unalterable, unbending, unchanging, unfeeling, unrelenting, unsmiling, unsparing; SEE CONCEPTS 401,534,542

severe [adj2] *difficult, harsh*
acute, arduous, ascetic, austere, bitter, bleak, consequential, critical, dangerous, dear, demanding, despotic, distressing, domineering, drastic, effortful, exacting, extreme, fierce, forbidding, grave, grim, grinding, hard, heavy, hefty, implacable, inclement, intemperate, intense, mordant, oppressive, overbearing, pitiless, punishing, rigorous, rugged, serious, sharp, sore, strenuous, stringent, taxing, toilsome, tough, tyrannical, unpleasant, unrelenting, violent, weighty, wicked; SEE CONCEPTS 565,569

severely [adv] *harshly*
acutely, badly, critically, dangerously, extremely, firmly, gravely, hard, hardly, intensely, markedly, painfully, rigorously, roughly, seriously, sharply, sorely, sternly, strictly, with an iron hand; SEE CONCEPT 569

sew [v] *prepare fabric for clothing, covering*
baste, bind, embroider, fasten, piece, seam, stitch, tack, tailor, work; SEE CONCEPT 218

sewage [n] *waste*
discharge, excess, excrement, garbage, junk, leavings, rubbish, runoff, slop, trash; SEE CONCEPT 260

sex [n1] *male or female gender*
femininity, manhood, manliness, masculinity, sexuality, womanhood, womanliness; SEE CONCEPT 648

sex [n2] *intercourse between animate beings*
birds and the bees*, coition, coitus, copulation, facts of life*, fornication, generation, intimacy, lovemaking, magnetism, procreation, relations, reproduction, sensuality, sexuality; SEE CONCEPT 375

sex appeal [n] *magnetism*
allure, appeal, attraction, attractiveness, charisma, charm, drawing power, enchantment, glamour, it*, lure, pull, seductiveness; SEE CONCEPTS 411,676

sexism [n] *sex discrimination*
bias, bigotry, chauvinism, inequality, inequity, partiality, prejudice; SEE CONCEPTS 29,689

sexual [adj] *concerning reproduction, intercourse*
animal, animalistic, bestial, carnal, erotic, fleshly, generative, genital, genitive, intimate, loving, passionate, procreative, reproductive, sensual, sharing, venereal, voluptuous, wanton; SEE CONCEPT 372

sexual assault [n] *violation*
date rape, grope, molestation, rape, ravishment, sex crime, sexual abuse; SEE CONCEPTS 192,375

sexual harassment [n] *unwanted sexual advances*
inappropriate behavior, sexual abuse, sexual pressure, suggestive comments, unprofessional behavior, victimization; SEE CONCEPT 246

sexually transmitted disease [n] *STD*
acquired immune deficiency syndrome, AIDS, chancroid, chlamydia, crab louse, crabs, genital herpes, genital warts, gonorrhea, herpes, herpes simplex, HIV, scabies, SIDA, social disease, syphilis, tabes dorsalis, VD, venereal disease; SEE CONCEPT 306

sexy [adj] *being erotically attractive to another*
arousing, come-hither*, cuddly, flirtatious, hot*, inviting, kissable, libidinous, mature, provocative, provoking, racy, risqué, seductive, sensual, sensuous, slinky*, spicy*, steamy*, suggestive, titillating, voluptuous; SEE CONCEPT 372

shabby [adj1] *broken-down; in poor shape*
bare, bedraggled, crummy, decayed, decaying, decrepit, degenerated, desolate, deteriorated, deteriorating, dilapidated, dingy, disfigured, disreputable, dog-eared*, faded, frayed, gone to seed*, mangy, meager, mean, miserable, moth-eaten, neglected, pitiful, poor, poverty-stricken, ragged, ramshackle, ratty, rickety, ruined, ruinous, run-down, scrubby, scruffy, seedy, shoddy, sleazy, slipshod, squalid, tacky, tattered, threadbare, tired, worn, worn-out, worse for wear*, wretched; SEE CONCEPT 485

shabby [adj2] *despicable*
beggarly, cheap, contemptible, despisable, dirty, disgraceful, dishonorable, disreputable, ignoble, ignominious, inconsiderate, inglorious, low, low-down, mean, mercenary, miserly, rotten, scummy, selfish, shady, shameful, shoddy, sordid, sorry, stingy, thoughtless, unkind, unworthy; SEE CONCEPTS 401,404

shack [n] *shanty*
cabin, camp, cottage, hut, lean-to, shed, shelter, small house, tiny house; SEE CONCEPT 516

shackle [n] *restraint*
bracelet, chain, cuff, electronic ankle bracelet, fetter, handcuff, irons, leg-iron, manacle, rope, trammel; SEE CONCEPTS 130,191,500

shackle [v] *restrain*
bind, chain, confine, cuff, fetter, handcuff, hog-tie*, hold, hold captive, manacle, put a strait-jacket on*, secure, tie up, trammel; SEE CONCEPTS 130,191

shade [n1] *dimness*
adumbration, blackness, coolness, cover, darkness, dusk, gloominess, obscuration, obscurity, penumbra, screen, semidarkness, shadiness, shadow, shadows, umbra, umbrage; SEE CONCEPT 620

shade [n2] *blind, shield*
awning, canopy, cover, covering, curtain, screen, veil; SEE CONCEPT 445

shade [n3] *color, hue*
brilliance, cast, saturation, stain, tinge, tint, tone; SEE CONCEPTS 620,622

shade [n4] *slight difference*
amount, cast, dash, degree, distinction, gradation, hint, nuance, proposal, semblance, soupçon, spice, streak, suggestion, suspicion, tincture, tinge, trace, variation, variety; SEE CONCEPT 665

shade [n5] *ghost*
apparition, bogey, haunt, manes, phantasm, phantom, revenant, shadow, specter, spirit, umbra, wraith; SEE CONCEPT 370

shade [v] *shut out the light*
adumbrate, be overcast, blacken, cast a shadow, cloud, cloud over, cloud up, conceal, cover, darken, deepen, dim, eclipse, gray, hide, inumbrate, mute, obscure, overshadow, protect, screen, shadow, shelter, shield, shutter, tone down, umbrage, veil; SEE CONCEPTS 250,526

shadow [n1] *darkness*
adumbration, cover, dark, dimness, dusk, gloom,

obscuration, obscurity, penumbra, protection, shade, shelter, umbra, umbrage; SEE CONCEPTS 620,622

shadow [*n2*] *hint, suggestion*
breath, intimation, memento, relic, smack, suspicion, tincture, tinge, touch, trace, vestige; SEE CONCEPT 278

shadow [*v1*] *make dark*
adumbrate, becloud, bedim, cast a shadow, cloud, darken, dim, gray, haze, inumbrate, obscure, overcast, overcloud, overhang, overshadow, screen, shade, shelter, shield, umbrage, veil; SEE CONCEPT 250

shadow [*v2*] *follow secretly*
dog, keep in sight, pursue, spy on, stalk, tag, tail, trail, watch; SEE CONCEPT 207

shady [*adj1*] *dark, covered*
adumbral, bosky, cloudy, cool, dim, dusky, indistinct, leafy, out of the sun*, screened, shaded, shadowed, shadowy, sheltered, umbrageous, umbrous, under a cloud, vague; SEE CONCEPTS 485,617

shady [*adj2*] *disreputable, suspicious*
crooked, disgraceful, dishonest, dishonorable, dubious, fishy, ignominious, infamous, inglorious, notorious, questionable, scandalous, shabby, shameful, shifty, shoddy, slippery, suspect, suspicious, underhanded, unethical, unreputable, unscrupulous, untrustworthy; SEE CONCEPT 545

shaggy [*adj*] *hairy, unkempt*
furry, hirsute, long-haired, ragged, rough, ruffled, rugged, uncombed, unshorn; SEE CONCEPT 485

shake [*v1*] *quiver, tremble*
agitate, brandish, bump, chatter, churn, commove, concuss, convulse, discompose, disquiet, disturb, dither, dodder, flap, flicker, flit, flitter, flourish, fluctuate, flutter, jar, jerk, jog, joggle, jolt, jounce, move, oscillate, palpitate, perturb, quail, quake, quaver, rattle, reel, rock, roil, ruffle, set in motion, shimmer, shimmy, shiver, shudder, stagger, stir up, succuss, sway, swing, totter, tremble, tremor, twitter, upset, vibrate, waggle, water, wave, whip, wobble; SEE CONCEPTS 150,152

shake [*v2*] *upset deeply*
appall, bother, consternate, daunt, discompose, dismay, distress, disturb, frighten, horrify, impair, intimidate, jar, knock props out*, make waves*, move, rattle, throw, throw a curve*, undermine, unnerve, unsettle, unstring, upset, weaken, worry; SEE CONCEPTS 7,19

shake off [*v*] *lose by getting away*
clear, dislodge, drop, elude, get away from, get rid of, give the slip*, leave behind, remove, rid oneself of, throw off, unburden; SEE CONCEPTS 102,195

shake up [*v*] *upset, unsettle*
agitate, break with past*, cause revolution*, churn up*, clean out, clean up, clear out, disturb, liquidate, make a clean sweep*, mix, overturn, purge, remove, reorganize, rid, shock, stir up, turn upside down*; SEE CONCEPTS 14,324

shaky [*adj1*] *trembling*
all aquiver*, aquake, aquiver, ashake, faltering, fluctuant, infirm, insecure, jellylike, jerry-built*, jittery, nervous, not set, precarious, quaking, quivery, rattletrap, rickety, rocky, rootless, shaking, tottering, tottery, trembling, tremorous, tremulous, tumbledown, unfirm, unsettled, un-

sound, unstable, unsteady, unsure, vacillating, wavering, weak, wobbly, yielding; SEE CONCEPT 488

shaky [*adj2*] *doubtful*
dubious, indecisive, not dependable, not reliable, precarious, problematic, questionable, suspect, uncertain, unclear, undependable, unreliable, unsettled, unsound, unsteady, unsupported, unsure; SEE CONCEPT 535

shallow [*adj1*] *not deep*
cursory, depthless, empty, flat, hollow, inconsiderable, sand bar, shelf, shoal, slight, superficial, surface, trifling, trivial, unsound; SEE CONCEPTS 737,777

shallow [*adj2*] *unintelligent, ignorant*
cursory, empty, empty-headed, farcical, featherbrained, flighty, flimsy, foolish, frivolous, frothy, half-baked*, hollow, idle, inane, lightweight, meaningless, paltry, petty, piddling, puerile, simple, sketchy, skin-deep*, slight, superficial, surface, trifling, trivial, uncritical, unthinking, vain, wishy-washy*; SEE CONCEPT 402

sham [*adj*] *artificial, counterfeit*
adulterated, affected, assumed, bogus*, dummy, ersatz*, fake, false, feigned, fictitious, forged, fraudulent, imitation, lying, make-believe, misleading, mock, phony, plaster*, pretend, pretended, pseudo*, simulated, so-called, spurious, substitute, synthetic, untrue; SEE CONCEPT 582

sham [*n*] *hoax, trick*
burlesque, cant, caricature, cheat, counterfeit, cover-up, deceit, deception, facade, fake, fakery, false front, farce, feint, flimflam*, forgery, fraud, hypocrisy, hypocriticalness, imitation, impostor, imposture, jive*, mock, mockery, pharisaism, phoniness, pretend, pretense, pretext, pseudo*, put-on, sell, smoke*, snow job*, spoof, travesty, whitewash; SEE CONCEPTS 59,192

sham [*v*] *trick; pull a hoax*
act, affect, ape, assume, bluff, copy, counterfeit, create, do a number*, fake, fake it, feign, imitate, invent, lie, make like, mislead, mock, play possum*, pretend, put on, put up a front*, shuck and jive*, simulate, sucker*; SEE CONCEPTS 59,111,171

shaman [*n*] *religious specialist*
healer, medicine man, priest, sorcerer, witch doctor; SEE CONCEPT 361

shambles [*n*] *a mess*
anarchy, babel, bedlam, botch, chaos, confusion, disarray, disorder, disorganization, hash, havoc, hodge-podge, madhouse, maelstrom, mess-up, mix-up, muddle; SEE CONCEPTS 230,674

shame [*n*] *disgrace, embarrassment*
abashment, bad conscience*, blot, chagrin, compunction, confusion, contempt, contrition, degradation, derision, discomposure, discredit, disesteem, dishonor, disrepute, guilt, humiliation, ignominy, ill repute, infamy, irritation, loss of face*, mortification, obloquy, odium, opprobrium, pang, pudency, remorse, reproach, scandal, self-disgust, self-reproach, self-reproof, shamefacedness, skeleton in the cupboard*, smear, stigma, stupefaction, treachery; SEE CONCEPTS 388,410

shame [*v*] *disgrace, embarrass*
abash, blot, confound, cut down to size*, debase, defile, degrade, disconcert, discredit, dishonor, give a black eye*, humble, humiliate, mortify, reproach, ridicule, shoot down*, smear, stain,

take down*, take down a peg*; SEE CONCEPTS
7,14,19

shamefaced [adj] *embarrassed*
abashed, chagrined, disgraced, guilty, humble,
humbled, humiliated, mortified, regretful,
shamed, sorry; SEE CONCEPT 550

shameful [adj] *atrocious; disreputable*
base, carnal, contemptible, corrupt, dastardly,
debauched, degrading, diabolical, disgraceful,
dishonorable, drunken, embarrassing, flagrant,
heinous, humiliating, ignominious, immodest,
immoral, impure, indecent, infamous, intemperate, lewd, low, mean, mortifying, notorious, obscene, opprobrious, outrageous, profligate,
reprehensible, reprobate, ribald, scandalous,
shaming, shocking, sinful, unbecoming, unclean,
unworthy, vile, villainous, vulgar, wicked; SEE
CONCEPTS 401,545,571

shameless [adj] *corrupt, indecent*
abandoned, arrant, audacious, barefaced, bold,
brash, brassy, brazen, cheeky*, depraved, dissolute, flagrant, forward, hardened, high-
handed*, immodest, immoral, improper,
impudent, incorrigible, insolent, lewd, outrageous, overbold, presumptuous, profligate,
reprobate, rude, unabashed, unashamed, unblushing, unchaste, unprincipled, wanton; SEE
CONCEPTS 401,545

shanghai [v] *kidnap*
abduct, capture, carry away, carry off, grab, hijack, hold for ransom, pirate, run away with,
seize, skyjack, snatch; SEE CONCEPTS 90,139

Shangri-la [n] *utopia*
Arcadia, bliss, Eden, Elysian Fields*, Erehwon*,
Garden of Eden, heaven, paradise, promised
land*, seventh heaven, Xanadu; SEE CONCEPTS
370,689

shanty [n] *shack*
cabin, camp, cottage, hut, lean-to, shed, shelter,
small house, tiny house; SEE CONCEPT 516

shape [n1] *form, structure*
appearance, architecture, aspect, body, build,
cast, chassis, circumscription, configuration,
conformation, constitution, construction, contour, cut, embodiment, figure, format, frame,
guise, likeness, lineation, lines, look, make,
metamorphosis, model, mold, outline, pattern,
profile, semblance, shadow, silhouette, simulacrum, stamp, symmetry; SEE CONCEPTS
436,754,757

shape [n2] *condition, health*
case, estate, fettle, fitness, kilter, order, repair,
state, trim, whack*; SEE CONCEPTS 316,720

shape [v1] *form, create*
assemble, block out, bring together, build, carve,
cast, chisel, construct, crystallize, cut, embody,
fabricate, fashion, forge, frame, hew, knead,
make, mint, model, mold, pat, pattern, produce,
roughhew, sculpture, sketch, stamp, streamline,
throw together*, trim, whittle; SEE CONCEPTS
137,184

shape [v2] *devise, plan*
accommodate, adapt, become, define, develop,
form, frame, grow, guide, modify, prepare, regulate, remodel, tailor, take form, work up; SEE
CONCEPT 36

shapeless [adj] *formless*
abnormal, amorphic, amorphous, anomalous,
assymetrical, baggy, deformed, disfigured, embryonic, ill-formed, inchoate, indefinite, indeter-

minate, indistinct, invisible, irregular, malformed, misshapen, mutilated, nebulous, undeveloped, unformed, ungraceful, unmade,
unshapely, unstructured, unsymmetrical, vague,
without character, without form; SEE CONCEPTS
486,589

shapely [adj] *well-proportioned*
balanced, beautiful, built, comely, curvaceous,
elegant, full-figured, graceful, neat, pleasing,
proportioned, regular, rounded, sightly, statuesque, sylphlike, symmetrical, trim, well-
formed, well-turned; SEE CONCEPTS 406,490

share [n] *portion, allotment*
allowance, apportionment, bite, chunk, claim,
commission, contribution, cut, cut in, cut up, divide, dividend, division, divvy*, dose, drag*,
due, end, fifty-fifty*, fraction, fragment, halver,
helping, heritage, interest, lagniappe, lot, measure, meed, parcel, part, partage, percentage,
piece, pittance, plum, points, proportion, quantum, quota, quotient, quotum, rake-off*, ration,
segment, serving, slice, split, stake, taste,
whack*; SEE CONCEPTS 710,835

share [v] *use in common with others*
accord, administer, allot, apportion, assign, be a
party to, bestow, cut the pie*, deal, dispense, distribute, divide, divide with, divvy*, divvy up*,
dole out, experience, give and take, give out, go
Dutch*, go fifty-fifty*, go halves*, go in with,
have a hand in, have a portion of, mete out, parcel out, part, partake, participate, partition, pay
half, piece up, prorate, quota, ration, receive,
shift, slice, slice up, split, split up, take a part of,
yield; SEE CONCEPTS 98,100,384

sharp [adj1] *knifelike, cutting*
aciculate, acuate, acuminate, acuminous, acute,
apical, barbed, briery,*cuspate, cuspidate, edged,
fine, ground fine, honed, horned, jagged, keen,
keen-edged, knife-edged, needlelike, needle-
pointed, peaked, pointed, pointy, prickly,
pronged, razor-sharp, salient, serrated, sharp-
edged, sharpened, spiked, spiky, spiny, splintery,
stinging, tapered, tapering, thorny, tined, tipped,
unblunted, whetted; SEE CONCEPT 486

sharp [adj2] *sudden*
abrupt, distinct, extreme, intense, marked; SEE
CONCEPTS 581,799

sharp [adj3] *perceptive, quick-witted*
acute, adroit, alert, apt, astute, brainy, bright,
brilliant, canny, clever, critical, cute, discerning,
discriminating, fast, foxy*, having smarts*, ingenious, intelligent, keen, knowing, nimble, nobody's fool*, not born yesterday*, observant, on
the ball*, original, penetrating, penetrative,
quick, quick on the trigger*, quick on the uptake*, ready, resourceful, savvy*, sensitive,
slick, smart, smart as a tack*, subtle, wise; SEE
CONCEPT 402

sharp [adj4] *dishonest, deceitful*
artful, bent, crafty, cunning, designing, ornery,
salty, shady, shrewd, slick, slippery, sly, smart,
snaky, two-faced*, underhand, unethical, unscrupulous, wily; SEE CONCEPT 545

sharp [adj5] *severe, intense*
acute, agonizing, biting, cutting, distinct, distressing, drilling, excruciating, fierce, keen,
knifelike, painful, paralyzing, penetrating, piercing, shooting, smart, sore, stabbing, stinging, violent; SEE CONCEPTS 537,569

sharp [*adj6*] *distinct, well-defined*
audible, clear, clear-cut, crisp, definite, explicit, obvious, visible; SEE CONCEPT 535

sharp [*adj7*] *stylish*
chic, classy, dashing, distinctive, dressy, excellent, fashionable, fine, first-class*, fly*, in style, smart, snappy*, swank*, tony*, trendy; SEE CONCEPT 589

sharp [*adj8*] *hurtful, bitter in speech*
acrimonious, angry, barbed, biting, caustic, cutting, double-edged, harsh, incisive, inconsiderate, penetrating, peppery, piercing, pointed, pungent, sarcastic, sardonic, scathing, severe, short, stabbing, stinging, tart, thoughtless, trenchant, unceremonious, ungracious, virulent, vitriolic; SEE CONCEPT 267

sharp [*adj9*] *having strong affect on animate senses*
acerbic, acid, acrid, active, astringent, austere, bitter, brisk, burning, harsh, hot, lively, odorous, piquant, pungent, sour, strong-smelling, suffocating, tart, vigorous, vinegary; SEE CONCEPTS 537,598,613

sharp [*adv*] *on time*
abruptly, accurately, bang, exactly, just, on the button*, on the dot*, precisely, promptly, punctually, right, smack-dab*, square, squarely, suddenly; SEE CONCEPT 799

sharpen [*v*] *make knifelike*
acuminate, dress, edge, file, grind, hone, make acute, make sharp, put an edge on, put a point on, sharp, stroke, strop, taper, whet; SEE CONCEPTS 137,250

sharp-tongued [*adj*] *critical*
belittling, biting, carping, censuring, condemning, cursing, cutting, cynical, demeaning, derogatory, harsh, hypercritical, mean, nasty, sarcastic, satirical; SEE CONCEPT 267

shatter [*v1*] *break into small pieces*
blast, blight, burst, crack, crash, crunch, crush, dash, demolish, destroy, disable, exhaust, explode, fracture, fragment, fragmentalize, fragmentize, impair, implode, overturn, pulverize, rend, rive, ruin, scrunch, shiver, smash, smash to smithereens*, smatter, snap, splinter, splinterize*, split, torpedo*, total*, wrack up*, wreck; SEE CONCEPTS 246,252

shatter [*v2*] *hurt someone badly*
break a heart*, crush, destroy, devastate, dumbfound, rattle, ruin, upset; SEE CONCEPTS 7,19

shave [*v*] *cut outer covering off*
barber, brush, clip, crop, cut, cut back, cut down, decorticate, graze, kiss, make bare, pare, peel, plane, prune, shear, shingle, shred, skim, skin, slash, slice thin, sliver, strip, touch, trim; SEE CONCEPTS 137,162,176,202

shear [*v*] *clip, cut*
crop, cut back, fleece, groom, mow, pare, prune, shave, shorten, snip, trim; SEE CONCEPTS 137,176

shed [*v*] *cast off*
afford, beam, cashier, cast, diffuse, disburden, discard, doff, drop, emit, exude, exuviate, give, give forth, jettison, junk, let fall, molt, pour forth, radiate, reject, scatter, scrap, send forth, shower, slip, slough, spill, sprinkle, take off, throw, throw away, throw out, yield; SEE CONCEPTS 179,180,181,211

sheen [*n*] *brightness, shine*
burnish, finish, glaze, gleam, glint, gloss, luster,

patina, polish, shimmer, shininess, wax; SEE CONCEPT 620

sheepish [*adj*] *shy, embarrassed*
abashed, ashamed, chagrined, diffident, docile, foolish, guilty, mortified, retiring, self-conscious, shamefaced, silly, tame, timid, timorous, uncomfortable; SEE CONCEPT 401

sheer [*adj1*] *abrupt, steep*
arduous, erect, headlong, perpendicular, precipitate, precipitous, sideling, upright; SEE CONCEPTS 490,581

sheer [*adj2*] *utter, absolute*
altogether, arrant, blasted, blessed, complete, confounded, downright, gross, infernal, out-and-out*, outright, perfect, pure, quite, rank, simple, single, thoroughgoing, total, unadulterated, unalloyed, undiluted, unmitigated, unmixed, unqualified; SEE CONCEPTS 531,535,544

sheer [*adj3*] *see-through, thin*
airy, chiffon, clear, cobwebby, delicate, diaphanous, filmy, fine, flimsy, fragile, gauzy, gossamer, lacy, limpid, lucid, pellucid, pure, slight, smooth, soft, tiffany, translucent, transparent; SEE CONCEPT 606

sheet [*n*] *coating, covering; page*
area, blanket, coat, expanse, film, foil, folio, lamina, layer, leaf, membrane, overlay, pane, panel, piece, plate, ply, slab, stratum, stretch, surface, sweep, veneer; SEE CONCEPTS 172,270,475,484

shelf [*n*] *jutting, flat area or piece*
bank, bracket, console, counter, cupboard, ledge, mantelpiece, mantle, rack, reef, ridge, rock, shallow, shoal; SEE CONCEPTS 445,509,513

shell [*n*] *structure; covering*
carapace, case, chassis, crust, frame, framework, hull, husk, integument, nut, pericarp, plastron, pod, scale, shard, shuck, skeleton, skin; SEE CONCEPTS 399,428,484

shell out [*v*] *give*
ante up, disburse, expend, fork over*, hand over, lay out, outlay, pay, pay for, pay out, spend; SEE CONCEPT 341

shelter [*n*] *protection, habitat*
apartment, asylum, cave, condo, co-op, cover, covert, crib*, defense, den, digs*, dwelling, guard, guardian, harbor, harborage, haven, hermitage, hide, hideaway, hideout, hole in the wall*, home, homeplate*, house, housing, hut, joint*, lodging, pad*, pen, port, preserve, protector, quarterage, rack, refuge, retirement, retreat, roof, roof over head*, roost*, safety, sanctuary, screen, security, shack, shade, shadow, shed, shield, tent, tower, turf, umbrella; SEE CONCEPTS 515,712

shelter [*v*] *provide safety, cover*
chamber, conceal, cover, cover up, defend, enclose, guard, harbor, haven, hide, house, lodge, preserve, protect, roof, safeguard, screen, secure, shield, surround, take care of, take in, ward, watch over; SEE CONCEPTS 134,188

shelve [*v*] *defer, postpone*
delay, dismiss, drop, freeze*, give up, hang up, hold, hold off, hold over, hold up, lay aside, mothball*, pigeonhole*, prolong, prorogue, put aside, put off, put on back burner*, put on hold, put on ice*, scrub*, sideline, slow up, stay, suspend, table, tie up, waive; SEE CONCEPT 121

shenanigans [*n*] *mischief*
antics, capers, dirty trick*, fooling around, frolicsomeness, funny business*, gag, hanky-

panky*, high jinks*, horseplay, horsing around, misbehavior, mischievousness, monkey business*, naughtiness, nonsense, prank, trouble, vandalism; SEE CONCEPTS 192,633,645

shield [n] protection
absorber, aegis, armament, armor, buckler, buffer, bulwark, bumper, cover, defense, escutcheon, guard, mail, rampart, safeguard, screen, security, shelter, ward; SEE CONCEPTS 712,729

shield [v] protect
bulwark, chamber, conceal, cover, cover all bases*, cover up, defend, fend, give cover, give shelter, go to bat for*, guard, harbor, haven, house, ride shotgun*, roof, safeguard, screen, secure, shelter, shotgun*, stonewall*, take under one's wing*, ward off; SEE CONCEPTS 96,134

shift [n1] switch, fluctuation
about-face*, alteration, bend, change, changeover, conversion, deflection, deviation, displacement, double, fault, modification, move, passage, permutation, rearrangement, removal, shifting, substitution, switch, tack, transfer, transference, transformation, transit, translocation, turn, variation, veering, yaw; SEE CONCEPTS 213,697

shift [n2] trick, stratagem
artifice, contrivance, craft, device, dodge, equivocation, evasion, expediency, expedient, gambit, hoax, makeshift, maneuver, move, ploy, recourse, refuge, resort, resource, ruse, stopgap*, strategy, substitute, subterfuge, wile; SEE CONCEPTS 59,660

shift [n3] time served doing work
bout, go, period, spell, stint, time, tour, trick, turn, working time; SEE CONCEPT 802

shift [v] switch, fluctuate
about-face*, alter, blow hot and cold*, bottom out*, budge, change, change gears, cook*, deviate, dial back*, dislocate, displace, disturb, do up*, drift, exchange, fault, flip-flop*, hem and haw*, move, move around, move over, rearrange, recalibrate, relocate, remove, replace, reposition, ship, shuffle, slip, stir, substitute, swap places, swerve, switch over, tack, transfer, transmogrify, transpose, turn, turn around, turn the corner*, turn the tables*, vacillate, vary, veer, waffle, yo-yo*; SEE CONCEPTS 213,232,697

shiftless [adj] lazy
apathetic, dallying, directionless, good-for-nothing, idle, inattentive, incompetent, indolent, lackadaisical, laggard, lagging, lethargic, lifeless, loafing, procrastinating, slack, slothful, unambitious, unenergetic, unindustrious, unmotivated; SEE CONCEPTS 401,404

shifty [adj] deceitful, untrustworthy
cagey, collusive, conniving, contriving, crafty, crooked, cunning, devious, dishonest, dodging, duplicitous, elusive, equivocating, evasive, fly-by-night*, foxy, fraudulent, furtive, insidious, lying, mendacious, prevaricative, prevaricatory, roguish, scheming, shady, shrewd, shuffling, slick, slimy*, slippery, sly, sneaky, treacherous, tricky, underhand, unhonest, unprincipled, untruthful, wily; SEE CONCEPTS 401,404

shimmer [n] gleam
blinking, coruscation, diffused light, flash, glimmer, glint, glisten, glitter, gloss, glow, incandescence, iridescence, luster, phosphorescence,

scintillation, sheen, spangle, spark, sparkle, twinkle; SEE CONCEPTS 620,624

shimmer [v] glisten
blaze, coruscate, dance, flare, flash, gleam, glint, glow, jiggle, phosphoresce, scintillate, shimmy, shine, sparkle, twinkle; SEE CONCEPT 624

shindig [n] party
affair, ball, banquet, barbecue, bash*, blowout*, celebration, dance, dinner, feast, festivity, function, gala, get-together, reception, shindy, social gathering; SEE CONCEPT 383

shine [n] brightness; polish
flash, glare, glaze, gleam, glint, glitz, gloss, lambency, light, luminosity, luster, patina, polish, radiance, rub, sheen, shimmer, show, sparkle; SEE CONCEPT 620

shine [v1] give off or reflect light
beam, bedazzle, blaze, blink, burn, dazzle, deflect, emit light, flare, flash, flicker, give light, glare, gleam, glimmer, glisten, glitter, glow, illuminate, illumine, incandesce, irradiate, luminesce, mirror, radiate, scintillate, shimmer, sparkle, twinkle; SEE CONCEPT 624

shine [v2] polish, burnish
brush, buff, buff up, finish, furbish, give a sheen, glance, glaze, gloss, make brilliant, put a finish on, put a gloss on, rub, scour, sleek, wax; SEE CONCEPT 202

shiny [adj] bright, glistening
agleam, burnished, clear, gleaming, glossy, lustrous, polished, satiny, sheeny, slick, sparkling, sunny; SEE CONCEPT 617

ship [v] send, transport
address, consign, direct, dispatch, drop, embark, export, forward, freight, go aboard, haul, move, put on board, remit, route, shift, ship out, smuggle, transfer, transmit; SEE CONCEPTS 148,217

shipshape [adj] tidy
businesslike, chipper, clean, in good shape, in tip-top condition, neat, ordered, orderly, spick-and-span*, trim, uncluttered, well-groomed, well-kept; SEE CONCEPTS 485,585,621

shirk [v] avoid, get out of responsibility
bypass, cheat, creep, dodge, dog*, duck, elude, eschew, evade, fence, get around, goldbrick*, lie down on job*, lurk, malinger, parry, pussyfoot*, quit, shuffle off, shun, sidestep, skulk, slack, slink, slip, slough off, snake, sneak, steal; SEE CONCEPTS 30,59,681

shirker [n] slacker
avoider, bum, deadbeat*, goldbrick, good-for-nothing, goof-off*, idler, loafer, quitter, slouch; SEE CONCEPTS 412,423

shiver [v1] shake, tremble
be cold, dither, flutter, freeze, have the quivers, have the shakes, palpitate, quake, quaver, quiver, shudder, tremor, twitter, vibrate, wave; SEE CONCEPTS 152,185

shiver [v2] shatter; break into small pieces
burst, crack, fragment, fragmentalize, pash, rive, smash, smash to smithereens*, smatter, splinter, splinterize*; SEE CONCEPTS 246,252

shock [n] complete surprise; blow
awe, bombshell*, breakdown, bump, clash, collapse, collision, concussion, confusion, consternation, crash, distress, disturbance, double whammy*, earthquake, encounter, excitement, eye-opener*, hysteria, impact, injury, jarring, jolt, percussion, prostration, ram, scare, start, stroke, stupefaction, stupor, trauma, traumatism,

turn, upset, whammy*, wreck; SEE CONCEPTS 33,309,529

shock [v] *completely surprise*
abash, agitate, anger, antagonize, appall, astound, awe, bowl over*, daze, disgust, dismay, displease, disquiet, disturb, electrify, flabbergast, flood, floor*, give a turn*, hit like ton of bricks*, horrify, insult, jar, jolt, knock out*, nauseate, numb, offend, outrage, overcome, overwhelm, paralyze, revolt, rock, scandalize, shake, shake up, sicken, stagger, startle, stun, stupefy, throw a curve*, traumatize, unsettle; SEE CONCEPT 42

shocking [adj] *outrageous; very surprising*
abominable, appalling, atrocious, awful, burning, crying, desperate, detestable, direful, disgraceful, disgusting, disquieting, distressing, dreadful, fearful, formidable, foul, frightful, ghastly, glaring, hateful, heinous, hideous, horrible, horrific, horrifying, loathsome, monstrous, nauseating, odious, offensive, repulsive, revolting, scandalous, shameful, sickening, stupefying, terrible, ugly, unspeakable; SEE CONCEPTS 548,571

shoddy [adj] *in bad shape*
base, broken-down, cheap, cheesy*, common, dilapidated, dingy, discreditable, disgraceful, dishonorable, disreputable, gaudy, ignominious, inferior, inglorious, junky, makeshift, mean, not up to snuff*, paltry, plastic, poor, pretentious, run-down, scruffy*, second-rate*, seedy, shabby, shady, shameful, sleazy*, slipshod, tacky*, tawdry, trashy, unrespectable; SEE CONCEPTS 485,571

shoe [n] *footwear*
basketball shoe, boat shoe, boot, cleat, clog, cowboy boot, flip-flops*, footgear, golf shoe, high heels, hightops*, loafer, moccasin, penny loafer, platform shoe, pump, running shoe, sandals, slipper, sneaker, tennis shoe, wing-tip, work shoe; SEE CONCEPT 451

shoot [v1] *discharge a projectile, often to injure or kill*
bag*, barrage, blast, bombard, bring down, catapult, dispatch, drop the hammer*, emit, execute, expel, explode, fire, fling, gun, hit, hurl, ignite, kill, launch, let fly, let go with, loose, murder, open fire*, open up*, pick off*, plug, pop*, project, propel, pull the trigger, pump*, set off, throw lead*, torpedo, trigger, zap*; SEE CONCEPTS 179,246,252

shoot [v2] *dash*
boil, bolt, charge, chase, dart, flash, fling, fly, gallop, hotfoot*, hurry, hurtle, lash, pass, race, reach, run, rush, scoot, skirr, speed, spring, spurt, streak, tear, whisk, whiz; SEE CONCEPTS 150,152

shoot the breeze [v] *chat, converse*
BS*, chatter, chew the fat*, gab*, palaver, prate, prattle*, run off at the mouth*, schmooze*, shoot the bull*, yack*, yap*; SEE CONCEPT 266

shop [n] *place of retail business*
boutique, chain, deli, department store, emporium, five-and-dime, market, mill, outlet, showroom, stand, store, supermarket; SEE CONCEPTS 439,441,448,449

shop [v] *look for merchandise to buy*
buy, go shopping, hunt for, look for, market, purchase, try to buy; SEE CONCEPTS 327,330

shopkeeper [n] *merchant*
businessperson, dealer, entrepreneur, proprietor, retailer, salesperson, seller, storekeeper, store owner, vendor, wholesaler; SEE CONCEPT 347

shoplift [v] *steal*
burglarize, carry off, defraud, embezzle, heist, hold up, lift*, loot, make off with*, pilfer, pillage, pinch*, rip off*, run off with*, snatch*, stick up*, swipe, take, walk off with*; SEE CONCEPT 139

shopper [n] *customer*
browser, buyer, client, clientele, consumer, patron, prospect, purchaser, window-shopper; SEE CONCEPT 348

shopping [n] *buying*
browsing, e-commerce, electronic commerce, purchasing, spending; SEE CONCEPT 327

shore [n] *waterside*
bank, beach, border, brim, brink, coast, coastland, embankment, lakeshore, lakeside, littoral, margin, river bank, riverside, sand, sands, seaboard, seacoast, seashore, shingle, strand, waterfront; SEE CONCEPT 509

shore [v] *reinforce*
bear up, bolster, brace, bulwark, buttress, carry, hold, prop, strengthen, support, sustain, underpin, upbear, uphold; SEE CONCEPTS 110,190

short [adj1] *abridged*
abbreviate, abbreviated, aphoristic, bare, boiled down, breviloquent, brief, compendiary, compendious, compressed, concise, condensed, curtailed, curtate, cut short, cut to the bone*, decreased, decurtate, diminished, epigrammatic, fleeting, in a nutshell*, laconic, lessened, little, momentary, not protracted, pithy, pointed, precise, sententious, short and sweet*, shortened, short-lived, short-term, succinct, summarized, summary, terse, undersized, unprolonged, unsustained; SEE CONCEPTS 267,272,798

short [adj2] *not tall*
abbreviated, chunky, close to the ground, compact, diminutive, little, low, not long, petite, pint-sized*, pocket, pocket-sized*, runty, sawed-off*, skimpy, slight, small, squat, squatty, stocky, stubby, stunted, thick, thickset, tiny, undersized, wee; SEE CONCEPTS 773,779,782

short [adj3] *insufficient*
deficient, exiguous, failing, inadequate, lacking, limited, low on, meager, needing, niggardly, poor, scant, scanty, scarce, short-handed*, shy, skimpy, slender, slim, sparse, tight, wanting; SEE CONCEPTS 527,560,762

short [adj4] *abrupt, discourteous*
bad-tempered, blunt, breviloquent, brief, brusque, curt, direct, gruff, impolite, inconsiderate, irascible, offhand, rude, sharp, short-spoken, short-tempered, snappy*, snippety*, snippy*, straight, terse, testy, thoughtless, unceremonious, uncivil, ungracious; SEE CONCEPTS 267,401

short [adj5] *crumbly*
brittle, crisp, crunchy, delicate, fragile, friable; SEE CONCEPT 462

short [adv] *abruptly*
aback, by surprise, forthwith, sudden, suddenly, unanticipatedly, unaware, unawares, unexpectedly, without delay, without hesitation, without warning; SEE CONCEPT 799

shortage [n] *deficiency*
curtailment, dearth, defalcation, deficit, failure, inadequacy, insufficiency, lack, lapse, leanness, paucity, pinch, poverty, scantiness, scarcity, shortfall, tightness, underage, want, weakness; SEE CONCEPTS 646,709,767

sh
sh

shortchange [v] *cheat*
bamboozle*, bilk, deceive, defraud, double-deal, dupe, finagle, fleece, flimflam, gyp*, hose, mislead, rip off*, rook*, sandbag, scam, screw, shaft, stiff, swindle, take, trick; SEE CONCEPTS 59,139,192

shortcoming [n] *weak point*
bug*, catch*, defect, deficiency, demerit, drawback, failing, fault, flaw, frailty, imperfection, infirmity, lack, lapse, sin, weakness; SEE CONCEPTS 411,666,674,679

shorten [v] *diminish, decrease*
abbreviate, abridge, blue pencil*, bob, boil down*, chop, clip, compress, condense, contract, curtail, cut, cut back, cut down, cut to the bone*, dock, edit, elide, excerpt, lessen, lop, make a long story short*, minimize, put in a nutshell*, reduce, retrench, shrink, slash, snip, trim; SEE CONCEPTS 137,236,240,247

shortfall [n] *deficit; imperfection*
arrears, default, defectiveness, deficiency, flaw, inadequacy, incompleteness, insufficiency, insufficiency, in the hole*, in the red, lack, loss, red ink*, shortage, shortcoming, underage; SEE CONCEPTS 230,335,646,671,718

short-lived [adj] *temporary*
brief, ephemeral, evanescent, fleeting, fugacious, fugitive, impermanent, momentary, passing, short, short-haul*, short-run, short-term, transient, transitory; SEE CONCEPT 798

shortly [adv] *right away*
anon, any minute now, before long, by and by, in a little while, presently, proximately, quickly, soon; SEE CONCEPT 820

short-sighted [adj] *unmindful of future consequences*
astigmatic, blind, careless, foolish, headlong, ill-advised, ill-considered, imperceptive, impolitic, impractical, improvident, imprudent, injudicious, myopic, near-sighted, rash, stupid, unsagacious, unwary; SEE CONCEPTS 401,542

shot [n 1] *try, chance*
attempt, break, conjecture, effort, endeavor, fling*, go*, guess, occasion, opening, opportunity, pop*, show, slap*, stab*, surmise, time, turn, whack*, whirl*; SEE CONCEPT 693

shot [n 2] *discharge; ammunition*
ball, buckshot, bullet, dart, lead, lob, missile, pellet, projectile, slug, throw; SEE CONCEPT 498

shoulder [v 1] *be responsible for*
accept, assume, bear, carry, take on, take upon oneself; SEE CONCEPT 23

shoulder [v 2] *push, jostle*
bulldoze*, elbow, hustle, nudge, press, push aside, shove, thrust; SEE CONCEPT 208

shout [n] *loud outcry*
bark, bawl, bellow, call, cheer, clamor, cry, howl, hue, roar, salvo, scream, screech, shriek, squall, squawk, tumult, vociferation, whoop*, yammer*, yap*, yawp*, yell; SEE CONCEPTS 77,595

shout [v] *cry out loudly*
bawl, bay, bellow, call out, cheer, clamor, exclaim, holler*, raise voice, roar, scream, screech, shriek, squall, squawk, vociferate, whoop*, yammer*, yap*, yawp*, yell; SEE CONCEPT 77

shove [v] *push without gentleness*
boost, buck, bulldoze*, cram, crowd, dig, drive, elbow, hustle, impel, jab, jam, jostle, nudge, poke, press, prod, propel, shoulder, thrust; SEE CONCEPT 208

shove off [v] *leave quickly*
blow, clear out, depart, exit, get off, go, go away, pull out, push off, quit, run along, start out, take off, vamoose*; SEE CONCEPT 195

show [n 1] *demonstration, exhibition*
appearance, array, display, expo*, exposition, fair, fanfare, fireworks, grandstand, manifestation, occurrence, pageant, pageantry, panoply, parade, pomp, presentation, program, representation, shine*, showboat*, showing, sight, spectacle, splash*, view; SEE CONCEPT 261

show [n 2] *entertainment event*
act, appearance, burlesque, carnival, cinema, comedy, drama, entertainment, film, flick*, motion picture, movie, pageant, picture, play, presentation, production, showing, spectacle; SEE CONCEPTS 263,293

show [n 3] *false front; appearance given*
affectation, air, display, effect, face*, front, grandstand play*, guise, illusion, impression, likeness, make-believe*, ostentation, parade, pose, pretense, pretext, profession, seeming, semblance, sham, shine*, showboat*, showing, simulacrum, splash*; SEE CONCEPTS 633,716

show [v 1] *actively exhibit something*
afford, air, arrive, attend, bare, blazon, brandish, deal in, demonstrate, display, disport, exhibit, expose, flash, flaunt, flourish, lay bare, lay out, mount, offer, parade, present, produce, proffer, put on, reveal, sell, set out, showcase, show off, sport, spread, stage, streak, submit, supply, trot out, unfold, unfurl, unveil, vaunt, wave; SEE CONCEPT 138

show [v 2] *passively exhibit something*
appear, arrive, assert, be visible, blow in, clarify, come, demonstrate, determine, disclose, discover, display, divulge, elucidate, emerge, establish, evidence, evince, explain, get, get in, illustrate, indicate, instruct, lay out, loom, make known, make out, make the scene*, manifest, mark, materialize, note, ostend, point, present, proclaim, project, prove, put in appearance, reach, register, reveal, show one's face*, show up, teach, testify to, turn up, unveil; SEE CONCEPT 261

show [v 3] *grant*
accord, act with, bestow, confer, dispense, give; SEE CONCEPT 108

show [v 4] *accompany*
attend, conduct, direct, escort, guide, lead, pilot, route, see, shepherd, steer; SEE CONCEPTS 187,384

show business [n] *entertainment industry*
Broadway, Hollywood, motion picture industry, movie industry, show biz, the stage, the theater; SEE CONCEPTS 383,384,386,388

showdown [n] *confrontation*
breaking point, clash, climax, crisis, culmination, exposé, moment of truth, unfolding; SEE CONCEPTS 388,674

shower [n] *precipitation*
cloudburst, deluge, downpour, drizzle, flood, hail, rain, rainstorm, sleet, storm, thunderstorm; SEE CONCEPTS 467,524,526

shower [v 1] *rain*
come down in buckets*, downpour, drench, drizzle, fall, hail, mist, patter, pour, sleet, spray, sprinkle, storm; SEE CONCEPT 526

shower [*v2*] *lavish*
be generous, deluge, give, pamper; SEE CONCEPTS *110,327,341*

showoff [*n*] *person who brags about him-or herself*
boaster, braggadocio, braggart, egotist, exhibitionist, swaggerer, vulgarian; SEE CONCEPT *412*

show off [*v*] *flaunt; brag*
advertise, boast, brandish, demonstrate, display, disport, exhibit, expose, flash*, hand a line*, make a spectacle of, parade, spread out, swagger, trot out*; SEE CONCEPTS *49,261*

showpiece [*n*] *exhibit*
display, masterpiece, model, work of art; SEE CONCEPTS *259,261*

show up [*v1*] *arrive, attend*
appear, be conspicuous, be visible, blow in*, come, get, get in, make an appearance, put in appearance, reach, show, stand out, turn up; SEE CONCEPT *159*

show up [*v2*] *expose, embarrass*
belittle, convict, debunk, defeat, discover, discredit, highlight, invalidate, lay bare, let down, mortify, pinpoint, put spotlight on*, put to shame*, reveal, shame, show in bad light*, uncloak, undress, unmask, unshroud, worst; SEE CONCEPTS *54,60*

showy [*adj*] *flamboyant, flashy*
classy, dashing, flash, garish, gaudy, glaring, histrionic, jazzy*, loud, luxurious, meretricious, opulent, ornate, ostentatious, overdone, overwrought, peacocky, pompous, pretentious, resplendent, screaming, sensational, snazzy*, splashy, splendiferous, sumptuous, swank*, tawdry, tinsel*, tony*; SEE CONCEPT *589*

shred [*n*] *tiny piece*
atom, bit, cantlet, crumb, fragment, grain, iota, jot, modicum, ounce, part, particle, rag, ray, ribbon, scintilla, scrap, shadow, sliver, smidgen, snippet, speck, stitch, tatter, trace, whit; SEE CONCEPT *831*

shred [*v*] *cut into ribbons*
cut, fray, frazzle, make ragged, reduce, shave, sliver, strip, tatter, tear; SEE CONCEPT *176*

shrewd [*adj*] *clever, intelligent*
acute, argute, artful, astucious, astute, brainy*, cagey, calculating, canny, crafty, cunning, cutting*, deep*, discerning, discriminating, farsighted, foxy*, heady*, ingenious, inside, in the know*, judicious, keen, knowing, on the inside*, on top of*, penetrating, perceptive, perspicacious, piercing, probing, profound, prudent, quick-witted, sagacious, savvy*, sensible, shark, sharp, slick*, slippery*, sly, smart, smooth, streetwise, tricky, underhand, up on*, wily, wise, wised up*; SEE CONCEPTS *401,402*

shriek [*n/v*] *high-pitched scream*
blare, cry, howl, screech, shout, shrill, squawk, squeal, wail, whoop, yell; SEE CONCEPTS *77,595*

shrill [*adj*] *high-pitched, harsh in sound*
acute, argute, blaring, blatant, cacophonous, clanging, clangorous, deafening, discordant, earpiercing, ear-splitting, high, metallic, noisy, penetrating, piercing, piping, raucous, screeching, sharp, strident, thin, treble; SEE CONCEPTS *592,594*

shrine [*n*] *tribute to a god, idol, or spirit*
altar, chapel, church, enshrinement, grave, hallowed place, holy place, mausoleum, reliquary,

sacred place, sanctorium, sanctuary, sanctum, sepulcher, temple; SEE CONCEPTS *368,439,448*

shrink [*v1*] *become smaller*
compress, concentrate, condense, constrict, contract, decrease, deflate, diminish, drop off, dwindle, fail, fall off, fall short, grow smaller, lessen, narrow, reduce, shorten, shrivel, wane, waste, waste away, weaken, wither, wrinkle; SEE CONCEPTS *137,698,776*

shrink [*v2*] *recoil, shy away*
blench, boggle, contract, cower, cringe, crouch, demur, draw back, flinch, hang back, huddle, quail, recede, refuse, retire, retreat, scruple, shudder, slink, wince, withdraw; SEE CONCEPTS *188,195*

shrivel [*v*] *dehydrate, dry up*
burn, contract, desiccate, dwindle, fossilize, mummify, mummy, parch, scorch, sear, shrink, stale, welter, wilt, wither, wizen, wrinkle; SEE CONCEPTS *137,250,255*

shudder [*v*] *shake, quiver*
convulse, dither, gyrate, jitter, quake, shimmy, shiver, tremble, tremor, twitter, wave; SEE CONCEPTS *34,150,152*

shuffle [*v1*] *move along lazily*
drag, limp, muddle, pad, scrape, scuff, scuffle, shamble, straggle, stumble, trail; SEE CONCEPT *151*

shuffle [*v2*] *rearrange, mix up*
break the deck*, change, change the order, confuse, disarrange, disarray, discompose, dislocate, disorder, disorganize, disrupt, disturb, intermix, jumble, mess up*, shift; SEE CONCEPTS *158,363*

shun [*v*] *avoid, ignore*
bilk, cold-shoulder*, cut, decline, despise, disdain, ditch*, dodge, double, duck, elude, escape, eschew, evade, get around, give a wide berth*, give the runaround*, have no part of*, have nothing to do with*, hide out, keep away from, keep clear of, neglect, palm off*, pass up, refuse, reject, scorn, shake, shake off, shy, snub, stall, stand aloof from, stay shy of, steer clear of*, turn back on*; SEE CONCEPTS *30,384*

shut [*v*] *close*
bar, batten down*, cage, close down, close up, confine, draw, drop the curtain*, enclose, exclude, fasten, fold, fold up, imprison, lock, push, put to, seal, secure, shut down, slam, wall off; SEE CONCEPTS *85,121,160,206,208,324*

shut off/shut out [*v*] *exclude; screen*
bar, beleaguer, blockade, block out, close, conceal, cover, debar, discontinue, evict, fence off, hide, keep out, lock out, mask, obstruct, ostracize, refuse, seclude, shroud, veil; SEE CONCEPTS *25,121,188*

shuttle [*n*] *space shuttle*
airplane, plane, shuttle bus, spacecraft, spaceport, train, transporter; SEE CONCEPT *504*

shuttle [*v*] *travel back and forth*
commute, drive back and forth, go back and forth, transport to and fro, travel; SEE CONCEPT *224*

shut up [*v*] *be or make quiet*
bottle up*, choke, dry up*, dummy up*, fall silent, gag, hold tongue*, hush, keep trap shut*, muzzle, pipe down*, quiet, quieten, quit chattering, shush*, silence, soft-pedal*, still, stop talking; SEE CONCEPT *77*

shy [*adj*] *quiet and self-conscious*
afraid, apprehensive, averse, backward, bashful,

sh

sh

cautious, chary, circumspect, conscious, coy, demure, diffident, disinclined, distrustful, fearful, hesitant, humble, indisposed, introvert, introverted, loath, loner, modest, nervous, recessive, reluctant, reserved, reticent, retiring, self-effacing, shamefaced, sheepish, shrinking, skittish, suspicious, timid, unassertive, unassured, uneager, uneffusive, unresponsive, unsocial, unwilling, wary; SEE CONCEPTS 401,404

shy [adj2] lacking, failing
deficient, inadequate, insufficient, scant, scanty, scarce, short, unsufficient, wanting; SEE CONCEPTS 546,762,789

shyster [n] unscrupulous lawyer; swindler
ambulance chaser, cheater, chiseler, crooked lawyer, mouthpiece*, pettifogger, scammer, trickster, unethical lawyer; SEE CONCEPT 412

sick [adj1] not healthy, not feeling well
ailing, bedridden, broken down, confined, debilitated, declining, defective, delicate, diseased, disordered, down, feeble, feverish, frail, funny*, green*, hospitalized, ill, impaired, imperfect, in a bad way*, incurable, indisposed, infected, infirm, in poor health, invalid, laid-up, lousy, mean, nauseated, not so hot*, peaked, poorly, qualmish, queasy, rickety, rocky, rotten, run down, sick as a dog*, suffering, tottering, under medication, under the weather*, unhealthy, unwell, weak, wobbly; SEE CONCEPT 314

sick [adj2] morbid, gross
black, ghoulish, macabre, morose, sadistic, sickly; SEE CONCEPTS 537,571

sick [adj3] fed up, displeased
blasé, bored, disgusted, jaded, revolted, satiated, tired, up to here with*, weary; SEE CONCEPT 403

sicken [v] revolt, make ill
affect, afflict, derange, disgust, disorder, gross out*, nauseate, offend, reluct, repel, repulse, turn, turn one's stomach*, unhinge, unsettle, upset; SEE CONCEPTS 14,246

sickening [adj] disgusting, awful
diseased, distasteful, foul, gross*, icky*, loathsome, nasty, nauseating, nauseous, noisome, offensive, putrid, repugnant, repulsive, revolting, rotten, stinking, stomach-turning, tainted; SEE CONCEPTS 529,571

sickly [adj1] not healthy
ailing, below par, bilious, cranky, delicate, diseased, down, dragging, faint, feeble, indisposed, infirm, in poor health, lackluster, laid-low, languid, low, mean, off-color*, out of action*, out of shape*, pallid, peaked, peaky, pining, poorly, rocky, run-down, seedy, sickish, unhealthy, wan, weak; SEE CONCEPT 314

sickly [adj2] revolting
bilious, cloying, insalubrious, mawkish, morbid, morose, nauseating, noisome, noxious, sick, unwholesome; SEE CONCEPTS 537,571

sickness [n] ill or abnormal condition
affection, affliction, ailment, bug*, complaint, condition, disease, diseasedness, disorder, ill, ill health, illness, indisposition, infirmity, malady, nausea, queasiness, syndrome, unhealth, unhealthfulness, unwellness; SEE CONCEPT 306

side [adj] minor; flanking
ancillary, incidental, indirect, lateral, lesser, marginal, not the main, oblique, off-center, postern, roundabout, secondary, sidelong, sideward, sideways, sidewise, skirting, subordinate, subsidiary, superficial; SEE CONCEPT 575

side [n1] edge, exteriority of object
aspect, attitude, border, bottom, boundary, direction, disposition, division, elevation, face, facet, flank, front, hand, haunch, jamb, lee, limit, loin, margin, part, perimeter, periphery, posture, quarter, rear, rim, sector, stance, stand, surface, top, verge, view, wing; SEE CONCEPTS 513,835

side [n2] point of view
angle, appearance, aspect, belief, direction, facet, hand, light, opinion, outlook, phase, position, slant, stand, standpoint, viewpoint; SEE CONCEPT 689

side [n3] opposing person or view
behalf, belligerent, camp, cause, combatant, competition, contestant, crew, enemy, faction, foe, interest, part, party, rival, sect, team; SEE CONCEPTS 301,365

sidekick [n] companion
accompaniment, accomplice, aide, ally, amigo, assistant, associate, buddy, chum, cohort, colleague, comrade, consort, coworker, crony, friend, pal, partner, playmate; SEE CONCEPT 423

sidesplitting [adj] extremely funny
amusing, entertaining, farcical, good-humored, hilarious, hysterical, joking, knee-slapper*, silly, slapstick, uproarious, witty; SEE CONCEPTS 267,529,537

sidestep [v] dodge
avoid, bypass, dance around*, ditch, duck, elude, escape, evade, fudge*, get around, get out of, give the slip*, go around, juke, pussyfoot*, put the move on*, shake, shake off*, shirk, skip out on*, skirt, weasel*; SEE CONCEPTS 59,102

sidetrack [v] divert
alter, avert, change, deflect, digress, redirect, swerve, switch, veer; SEE CONCEPTS 187,213

sideways [adv] to the edge, exteriority
alongside, aside, aslant, aslope, athwart, broadside, crabwise, edgeways, indirectly, laterally, obliquely, side by side, sidelong, sidewards, slanting, slantingly, slantwise, sloping, to the side; SEE CONCEPTS 581,583

sift [v] take out residue; remove impurities
analyze, clean, colander, comb, delve into, dig into, drain, evaluate, examine, explore, fathom, filter, go into, go through, grade, inquire, investigate, look into, pan, part, pore over, probe, prospect, purify, riddle, screen, scrutinize, search, separate, sieve, size, sort, strain, winnow; SEE CONCEPTS 103,165

sigh [v1] breathe out heavily
blow, complain, cry, exhale, gasp, grieve, groan, howl, lament, moan, murmur, pant, respire, roar, sob, sorrow, sough, suspire, wheeze, whine, whisper, whistle; SEE CONCEPT 163

sigh [v2] long for
ache, crave, dream, hanker, hunger, languish, lust, mourn, pine, suspire, thirst, yearn; SEE CONCEPT 20

sight [n1] ability to perceive with eyes
afterimage, appearance, apperception, apprehension, eye, eyes, eyeshot, eyesight, field of vision, ken, perception, range of vision, seeing, view, viewing, visibility, vision; SEE CONCEPT 629

sight [n2] spectacle
display, exhibit, exhibition, outlook, pageant, parade, point of interest, scene, show, view, vista; SEE CONCEPTS 261,293

sight [n3] horrifying person or thing
blot, eyesore, fright, mess, monstrosity, ogre,

ogress, scarecrow, slob, spectacle, tramp; SEE
CONCEPTS *412,513*

sight [v] *see*
behold, discern, distinguish, eyeball*, make
out*, observe, perceive, spot, view, witness; SEE
CONCEPT *626*

sign [n1] *indication, evidence*
assurance, augury, auspice, badge, beacon, bell,
caution, clue, divination, flag, flash, foreboding,
foreknowledge, foreshadowing, foretoken, forewarning, gesture, giveaway, handwriting on
wall*, harbinger, herald, high sign*, hint, light,
manifestation, mark, nod, note, omen, portent,
precursor, prediction, premonition, presage, presentiment, prognostic, proof, signal, suggestion,
symbol, symptom, token, trace, vestige, warning,
wave, whistle, wink; SEE CONCEPTS
274,529,673,689

sign [n2] *document with information; symbol*
badge, board, character, cipher, crest, device,
emblem, ensign, guidepost, insignia, logo, mark,
notice, placard, proof, representation, signboard,
signpost, symbolization, token, type, warning;
SEE CONCEPTS *271,284*

sign [v1] *write name*
acknowledge, authorize, autograph, confirm, endorse, initial, ink, inscribe, put John Hancock
on*, put John Henry on*, rubber-stamp*, set
one's hand to*, signature, subscribe, witness; SEE
CONCEPT *79*

sign [v2] *motion to another*
beckon, express, flag, gesticulate, gesture, indicate, motion, signal, signalize, signify, use sign
language, wave; SEE CONCEPT *74*

signal [adj] *extraordinary, outstanding*
arresting, arrestive, characteristic, conspicuous,
distinctive, distinguished, eminent, exceptional,
eye-catching, famous, illustrious, individual,
marked, memorable, momentous, notable, noteworthy, noticeable, peculiar, prominent, pronounced, remarkable, renowned, salient,
significant, striking; SEE CONCEPTS *568,574*

signal [n] *indication; authorization*
alarm, alert, beacon, bleep, blinker, cue, flag,
flare, gesture, go-ahead*, green light*, high
sign*, indicator, mark, Mayday*, movement,
nod, okay*, omen, sign, SOS*, tocsin, token,
wink; SEE CONCEPTS *74,284,529,685*

signal [v] *indicate; give a sign to*
beckon, communicate, flag, flash, gesticulate,
gesture, motion, nod, semaphore, sign, signalize,
warn, wave, wink; SEE CONCEPT *74*

significance [n1] *meaning*
acceptation, bottom line*, connotation, drift,
force, heart, implication, import, intendment,
kicker*, meat*, message, name of the game*, nature of the beast*, nitty-gritty*, nub, nuts and
bolts*, point, punch line*, purport, score, sense,
significancy, signification, stuff, understanding;
SEE CONCEPT *682*

significance [n2] *importance*
authority, consequence, consideration, credit, excellence, gravity, import, impressiveness, influence, magnitude, matter, merit, moment,
momentousness, perfection, pith, prestige, relevance, signification, virtue, weight, weightiness;
SEE CONCEPT *668*

significant [adj1] *telling, meaningful*
cogent, compelling, convincing, denoting, eloquent, expressing, expressive, facund, forceful,

heavy, important, indicative, knowing, meaning,
momentous, powerful, pregnant, representative,
rich, sententious, serious, sound, suggestive,
symbolic, valid, weighty; SEE CONCEPTS *267,567*

significant [adj2] *important, critical*
big, carrying a lot of weight*, consequential,
considerable, heavy, material, meaningful, momentous, notable, noteworthy, serious, substantial, vital, weighty; SEE CONCEPT *568*

signify [v1] *mean, indicate*
add up to, announce, bear, be a sign of, bespeak,
betoken, carry, communicate, connote, convey,
denote, disclose, evidence, evince, exhibit, express, flash, imply, import, insinuate, intend, intimate, manifest, matter, portend, proclaim,
purport, represent, show, sign, spell, stand for,
suggest, symbolize, talk, tell, wink; SEE CON-
CEPTS *55,266,682*

signify [v2] *be of importance*
be of consequence, be of significance, carry
weight, count, import, matter, mean, weigh; SEE
CONCEPT *668*

silence [n] *absence of sound, speech*
blackout, calm, censorship, dead air, death,
dumbness, hush, hush-hush*, inarticulateness,
iron curtain*, laconism, lull, muteness, noiselessness, peace, quiescence, quiet, quietness, quietude, quietus, reserve, reticence, saturninity,
secrecy, sleep, speechlessness, still, stillness,
sulk, sullenness, taciturnity, uncommunicativeness; SEE CONCEPT *65*

silence [v] *make or be quiet*
choke off*, clam, clam up*, close up, cool it*,
cut off, cut short, dampen, deaden, decrease the
volume, dry up*, dull, dumb, dummy up*, extinguish, gag, hold one's tongue*, hush, hush-
hush*, hush one's mouth*, keep it down*, lull,
muffle, mute, muzzle, overawe, pipe down*,
quash, quell, quiet, quiet down, quieten, say
nothing, shush*, shut up, sit on*, soft-pedal*,
squelch, stifle, still, strike dumb*, subdue, suppress, tongue-tie*; SEE CONCEPT *266*

silent [adj1] *quiet; speechless*
bashful, buttoned up*, checked, clammed up*,
close*, closed up, closemouthed, curbed, dumb,
dummied up*, faint, hush, hushed, iced*, inarticulate, incoherent, inconversable, indistinct, inhibited, laconic, mousy, mum, mute, muted,
noiseless, nonvocal, not talkative, reserved, restrained, reticent, shy, silentious, soundless, still,
struck dumb, taciturn, tongue-tied, unclear, uncommunicative, unheard, unsociable, unspeaking, voiceless, wordless, zipped*; SEE CONCEPT
594

silent [adj2] *understood, implied*
aphonic, implicit, indescribable, inexpressible,
nameless, tacit, unexpressed, unpronounced, unspoken, unuttered, unvoiced, wordless; SEE CON-
CEPT *267*

silhouette [n] *outline*
contour, delineation, etching, figuration, form,
likeness, line, lineament, lineation, portrait, profile, shade, shadow, shape; SEE CONCEPTS
259,625

silky [adj] *very smooth; like satin*
cottony, delicate, glossy, like silk, luxurious,
plush, satiny, silk, silken, sleek, soft, tender, velvety; SEE CONCEPT *606*

silly [adj] *absurd, giddy, foolish*
asinine, balmy, brainless, childish, crazy, dippy*,

sh
si

dizzy*, empty, empty-headed*, fatuous, feather-brained*, flighty, foolhardy, frivolous, hare-brained*, idiotic, ignorant, illogical, immature, imprudent, inane, inappropriate, inconsistent, irrational, irresponsible, ludicrous, meaningless, muddle-headed*, nitwitted, nonsensical, pointless, preposterous, puerile, ridiculous, senseless, sheepheaded*, simple, simpleminded, stupid, unintelligent, unreasonable, unwise, vacuous, witless; SEE CONCEPTS *401,403,542*

silver [*adj*] *shiny gray in color*
argent, argentate, bright, lustrous, pale, pearly, plated, resplendent, silvered, silvery, sterling, white; SEE CONCEPT *618*

similar [*adj*] *very much alike*
agnate, akin, allied, analogous, coincident, coincidental, coinciding, collateral, companion, comparable, complementary, congruent, congruous, consonant, consubstantial, correlative, corresponding, homogeneous, identical, in agreement, kin, kindred, like, matching, much the same, parallel, reciprocal, related, resembling, same, twin, uniform; SEE CONCEPTS *487,573*

similarity [*n*] *likeness, correspondence*
affinity, agreement, alikeness, analogy, approximation, association, closeness, coincidence, collation, community, comparability, comparison, concordance, concurrence, conformity, congruence, congruity, connection, correlation, dead ringer*, harmony, homogeneity, identity, interrelation, kinship, likes of, look-alike, parallel, parallelism, parity, peas in a pod*, proportion, reciprocity, relation, relationship, resemblance, sameness, semblance, simile, similitude, synonymity, two of a kind*; SEE CONCEPT *670*

simmer [*v*] *boil, smolder*
be agitated, be angry, be tense, be uptight*, bubble, burn, churn, cook, effervesce, ferment, fizz, fret, fricassee, fume, parboil, rage, seethe, smart, sparkle, stew, stir, warm; SEE CONCEPTS *35,170,410*

simple [*adj1*] *clear, understandable; easy*
child's play*, cinch*, clean, easy as pie*, effortless, elementary, facile, incomplex, intelligible, light, lucid, manageable, mild, no problem*, no sweat*, not difficult, picnic*, piece of cake*, plain, quiet, self-explanatory, simple as ABC*, smooth, snap*, straightforward, transparent, uncomplicated, uninvolved, unmistakable, untroublesome, walkover*; SEE CONCEPTS *529,538*

simple [*adj2*] *uncluttered, natural*
absolute, austere, classic, clean, discreet, elementary, folksy, homely, homey, humble, inelaborate, lowly, mere, modest, not complex, open and shut*, plain, pure, pure and simple*, rustic, sheer, single, Spartan, unadorned, unadulterated, unaffected, unalloyed, unblended, uncombined, uncomplicated, uncompounded, undecorated, unelaborate, unembellished, unfussy, unmitigated, unmixed, unornamented, unostentatious, unpretentious, unqualified, vanilla*; SEE CONCEPTS *562,589*

simple [*adj3*] *childlike, innocent*
amateur, artless, bald, basic, childish, direct, frank, green, guileless, honest, ingenuous, naive, naked, natural, plain, sincere, square, stark, trusting, unaffected, unartificial, undeniable, unexperienced, unpretentious, unschooled, unsophisticated, unstudied, unvarnished; SEE CONCEPTS *267,401,542*

simple [*adj4*] *feeble-minded; not intelligent*
amateur, asinine, backward, brainless, credulous, dense, dimwitted, dull, dumb, fat, feeble, foolish, green*, gullible, half-witted, idiotic, ignorant, illiterate, imbecile, inane, inexperienced, inexpert, insensate, mindless, moronic, nitwitted, obtuse, senseless, shallow, silly, simple-minded, slow, soft, soft-headed*, stupid, thick, uneducated, unintelligent, witless; SEE CONCEPT *402*

simpleminded [*adj*] *unsophisticated*
brainless, childlike, clueless, crude, dumb, feeble-minded, idiotic, ignorant, moronic, naïve, slow, stupid, uncomplicated, unschooled, unstudied, untutored, unworldly; SEE CONCEPTS *401,548,562*

simpleton [*n*] *fool*
birdbrain*, blockhead*, bonehead*, boob*, buffoon, clod*, clown, dimwit*, dolt*, dope*, dunce, dunderhead*, fathead*, idiot, ignoramus, imbecile, jerk*, lamebrain*, lunkhead*, moron, nitwit, numskull*, oaf, stooge*; SEE CONCEPTS *412,423*

simplicity [*n*] *absence of complication, sophistication*
artlessness, candor, chastity, clarity, classicality, clean lines, clearness, directness, ease, easiness, elementariness, guilelessness, homogeneity, ingenuousness, innocence, integrity, lack of adornment, modesty, monotony, naïveté, naivety, naturalness, obviousness, openness, plainness, primitiveness, purity, restraint, severity, singleness, straightforwardness, uniformity, unity; SEE CONCEPTS *633,655,663*

simplify [*v*] *make easy, intelligible*
abridge, analyze, boil down, break down, break it down, chasten, clarify, clean it up*, clean up, clear up, cut down, cut the frills*, decipher, disentangle, disinvolve, draw a picture*, elucidate, explain, facilitate, get down to basics*, get to the meat*, hit the high spots*, interpret, lay out, let daylight in*, let sunlight in*, make clear, make perfectly clear, make plain, order, put in a nutshell*, put one straight*, reduce, shorten, spell out, streamline, unscramble; SEE CONCEPTS *57,110,261*

simply [*adv1*] *plainly, clearly*
artlessly, candidly, commonly, directly, easily, frankly, guilelessly, honestly, ingenuously, intelligibly, matter-of-factly, modestly, naturally, openly, ordinarily, quietly, sincerely, straightforwardly, unaffectedly, unpretentiously, without any elaboration; SEE CONCEPTS *544,562*

simply [*adv2*] *merely*
barely, but, just, only, purely, solely, utterly; SEE CONCEPTS *544,557*

simply [*adv3*] *absolutely, completely*
in fact, ltogether, really, totally, unreservedly, utterly, wholly; SEE CONCEPTS *531,535*

simulate [*v*] *pretend, imitate*
act, act like, affect, ape, assume, bluff, borrow, cheat, concoct, copy, counterfeit, crib*, deceive, disguise, dissemble, do, do a take-off*, do alike*, equivocate, exaggerate, fabricate, fake, favor, feature, feign, fence, gloss over, invent, knock off*, lie, lift, make believe, mimic, mirror, misrepresent, phony, pirate, play, playact, pose, prevaricate, put on*, put on an act*, replicate, reproduce, resemble, steal; SEE CONCEPTS *59,63,111,171*

simulation [*n*] *imitation*
carbon copy, clone, copy, counterfeit, duplicate, duplication, facsimile, fake, image, likeness, match, mirroring, paralleling, reflection, replica, reproduction, sham; SEE CONCEPTS 171,260,716

simultaneous [*adj*] *happening at about the same time*
accompanying, agreeing, at the same time, coetaneous, coeval, coexistent, coexisting, coincident, coinciding, concurrent, concurring, contemporaneous, contemporary, dead heat*, in sync*, synchronal, synchronic, synchronous, with the beat*; SEE CONCEPTS 548,799

sin [*n*] *illegal or immoral action*
anger, covetousness, crime, damnation, debt, deficiency, demerit, disobedience, envy, error, evil, evil-doing, fault, gluttony, guilt, immorality, imperfection, iniquity, lust, misdeed, offense, peccability, peccadillo, peccancy, pride, shortcoming, sinfulness, sloth, tort, transgression, trespass, ungodliness, unrighteousness, veniality, vice, violation, wickedness, wrong, wrongdoing, wrongness; SEE CONCEPTS 101,645

sin [*v*] *commit illegal or immoral action*
backslide*, break commandment, break law, cheat, commit crime, deviate, do wrong, err, fall, fall from grace*, go astray*, lapse, live in sin, misbehave, misconduct, offend, sow wild oats*, stray, take the primrose path*, transgress, trespass, wallow in the mire*, wander; SEE CONCEPTS 101,375,645

sincere [*adj*] *straightforward, honest*
aboveboard, actual, artless, bona fide, candid, dead-level*, dear, devout, earnest, faithful, forthright, frank, genuine, guileless, heartfelt, honest to God*, like it is*, meant, natural, no fooling*, no-nonsense*, on the level*, on the line*, on up and up*, open, outspoken, plain, pretensionless, real, regular, righteous, saintly, serious, square*, sure enough, true, true-blue*, trustworthy, twenty-four carat*, unaffected, undesigning, undissembled, unfeigned, unpretentious, upfront*, wholehearted; SEE CONCEPTS 267,401, 542

sincerely [*adv*] *seriously, honestly*
aboveboard, candidly, deeply, earnestly, frankly, from bottom of heart, genuinely, in all conscience, in all sincerity, ingenuously, in good faith, naturally, profoundly, really, truly, truthfully, wholeheartedly, without equivocation; SEE CONCEPTS 267,582

sincerity [*n*] *straightforwardness, honesty*
artlessness, bona fides, candor, earnestness, frankness, genuineness, good faith, goodwill, guilelessness, heart, honor, impartiality, innocence, justice, openness, probity, reliability, seriousness, sincereness, singleness, trustworthiness, truth, truthfulness, veracity, wholeheartedness; SEE CONCEPTS 633,657

sinewy [*adj*] *stringy, tough*
athletic, brawny, fibrous, firm, hard, leathery, muscular, powerful, strong, sturdy, vigorous; SEE CONCEPTS 314,485,489,490

sinful [*adj*] *immoral, criminal*
amiss, bad, base, blamable, blameful, blameworthy, censurable, corrupt, culpable, damnable, demeritorious, depraved, disgraceful, erring, evil, guilty, iniquitous, irreligious, low, morally wrong, reprehensible, reprobate, shameful, ungodly, unholy, unregenerate, unrighteous, vicious, vile, wicked, wrong; SEE CONCEPTS 545,548

sing [*v*] *carry a tune with one's voice*
belt out*, burst into song*, buzz*, canary*, cantillate, carol, chant, chirp, choir, croon, descant, duet, groan*, harmonize, hum, hymn, intone, lift up a voice*, line out*, lullaby, make melody*, mouth, pipe, purr*, resound, roar, serenade, shout, singsong, solo, trill, troll, tune, vocalize, wait, warble, whine, whistle, yodel; SEE CONCEPTS 47,77,292

sing [*v2*] *tattle on someone*
betray, blow the whistle*, fink*, inform, peach*, rat*, snitch*, spill the beans*, talk, turn in; SEE CONCEPTS 60,317

singe [*v*] *burn*
blacken, blaze, brand, brown, cauterize, char, cook, flame, ignite, incinerate, parch, scald, scorch, sear, toast, torch; SEE CONCEPT 249

singer [*n*] *person who can carry a tune*
accompanist, artist, artiste, chanter, chanteuse, choralist, chorister, crooner, diva, intoner, melodist, minstrel, musician, nightingale, serenader, soloist, songbird, songster, troubadour, vocalist, voice, warbler, yodeler; SEE CONCEPT 352

single [*adj*] *alone, distinct*
distinct, distinguished, especial, exceptional, exclusive, individual, indivisible, isolated, lone, loner, not general, not public, odd, one, only, original, particular, peerless, personal, private, rare, restricted, secluded, separate, separated, simple, singled-out, singular, sole, solitary, special, specific, strange, unalloyed, unblended, uncommon, uncompounded, undivided, unique, unitary, unmixed, unrivaled, unshared, unusual, without equal; SEE CONCEPTS 564,577,762

single [*adj2*] *not married*
bachelor, companionless, divorced, eligible, free, living alone, loner, separated, sole, solo, spouseless, unattached, unfettered, unmarried, unwed; SEE CONCEPT 555

single-handed [*adj*] *unassisted*
alone, by oneself, independent, on one's own, solitary, solo, unaided; SEE CONCEPTS 577,583

singles bar [*n*] *dating bar*
bar, club, cocktail lounge, lounge, meat market*, nightclub, pickup joint*, pub; SEE CONCEPTS 325,439

singly [*adv*] *individually*
apart, independently, one at a time, one by one, particularly, respectively, separately, severally; SEE CONCEPT 577

singular [*adj*] *unique, odd*
atypical, avant-garde, bizarre, breaking new ground*, conspicuous, cool*, curious, eccentric, eminent, exceptional, extraordinary, loner, noteworthy, original, outlandish, out-of-the-way, outstanding, peculiar, prodigious, puzzling, queer, rare, remarkable, special, strange, uncommon, unimaginable, unordinary, unparalleled, unprecedented, unthinkable, unusual, unwonted, weird; SEE CONCEPT 564

singular [*adj2*] *alone, separate*
certain, definite, discrete, exclusive, individual, one, only, particular, respective, single, sole, solitary, solo, unique, unrepeatable; SEE CONCEPT 577

sinister [*adj*] *nasty, menacing*
adverse, apocalyptic, bad, baleful, baneful,

si
si

blackhearted, corrupt, deleterious, dire, disastrous, dishonest, disquieting, doomful, evil, foreboding, harmful, hurtful, ill-boding, inauspicious, injurious, lowering, malefic, malevolent, malign, malignant, menacing, mischievous, obnoxious, ominous, pernicious, perverse, poisonous, portentous, threatening, unfavorable, unfortunate, unlucky, unpropitious, woeful; SEE CONCEPTS 401,548,571

sink [v1] *fall in, go under*
bore, bring down, capsize, cast down, cave in, couch, decline, demit, depress, descend, dig, dip, disappear, drill, drive, droop, drop, drown, ebb, engulf, excavate, fall, flounder, force down, founder, go down, go to the bottom, immerse, lay, let down, lower, overturn, overwhelm, plummet, plunge, put down, ram, regress, run, sag, scuttle, set, settle, shipwreck, slope, slump, stab, stick, stoop, submerge, subside, swamp, thrust, tip over, touch bottom, wreck; SEE CONCEPTS 181,213

sink [v2] *fall, decrease*
abate, collapse, diminish, drop, lapse, lessen, relapse, retrogress, slip, slump, subside, wane; SEE CONCEPTS 698,776

sink [v3] *deteriorate*
decay, decline, decrease, degenerate, depreciate, descend, deteriorate, die, diminish, disimprove, disintegrate, dwindle, fade, fail, flag, go downhill*, lessen, retrograde, rot, spoil, waste, weaken, worsen; SEE CONCEPTS 469,698

sink [v4] *be humble or humbled*
abase, bemean, be reduced to, cast down, debase, degrade, demean, humiliate, lower, stoop, succumb; SEE CONCEPTS 7,19,35

sinuous [adj] *winding, twisting*
anfractuous, circuitous, coiling, convoluted, crooked, curved, curvy, deviative, devious, flexuous, indirect, meandering, meandrous, serpentine, snaky*, supple, tortuous, twisting and turning*, undulating, vagrant; SEE CONCEPT 581

sip [v] *drink slowly*
drink in, extract, imbibe, partake, quaff, sample, savor, sup, swallow, taste, toss; SEE CONCEPT 169

sissy [n] *weakling*
baby, chicken*, coward, cream puff*, crybaby, daisy*, jellyfish*, milksop, momma's boy*, namby-pamby, pansy, pantywaist*, pushover, wimp*, wuss*, yellow belly*; SEE CONCEPTS 412,423

sister [n] *female sibling*
blood sister, kin, kinsperson, relation, relative, twin; SEE CONCEPTS 414,415

sit [v1] *rest on one's behind*
bear on, be seated, cover, ensconce, give feet a rest*, grab a chair*, have a place, have a seat, hunker*, install, lie, park*, perch*, plop down*, pose, posture, put it there*, relax, remain, rest, seat, seat oneself, settle, squat, take a load off*, take a place, take a seat; SEE CONCEPTS 154,201

sit [v2] *hold a meeting*
assemble, be in session, come together, convene, deliberate, hold an assembly, meet, officiate, open, preside; SEE CONCEPTS 324,384

site [n] *place of activity*
fix, ground, habitat, hangout, haunt, home, lay, layout, locale, locality, location, locus, mise en scène, plot, point, position, post, range, scene,

section, situation, slot, spot, station, wherever, X marks the spot*; SEE CONCEPT 198

sit-in [n] *protest*
complaint, demonstration, fast, grievance, love-in*, march, peace march, rally, revolt, riot, strike, walkout; SEE CONCEPTS 52,54,261,300

sit tight [v] *be patient, wait*
anticipate, bide one's time*, cool it*, fill time, hang around*, hang out, hold on, hold the phone*, keep your shirt on*, lie in wait*, lie low*, linger, mark time*, put on hold*, stall, stand by, stay put*, stick around*; SEE CONCEPTS 210,681

situate [v] *locate*
establish, fix, park, place, position, put, put in place, set, settle, stand; SEE CONCEPT 226

situated [adj] *located*
established, fixed, occupying, parked, placed, planted, positioned, set, settled, stationed; SEE CONCEPT 488

situation [n1] *place of activity*
bearings, direction, footing, latitude, locale, locality, location, locus, longitude, position, post, seat, setting, site, spot, stage, station, where, whereabouts; SEE CONCEPT 198

situation [n2] *circumstances, status*
ballgame*, bargain, capacity, case, character, condition, footing*, how things stack up*, like it is*, mode, picture, place, plight, position, posture, rank, scene, size of it*, sphere, stage, standing, standpoint, state, state of affairs, station, status quo*; SEE CONCEPTS 388,696

situation [n3] *employment status*
appointment, berth, billet, capacity, connection, employment, engagement, hire, job, office, place, placement, position, post, profession, spot, trade; SEE CONCEPTS 351,360,668

sixth sense [n] *intuition*
clairvoyance, divination, ESP*, extrasensory perception, feeling, foreknowledge, gut feeling*, instinct, perception, premonition, second sight*, vibes; SEE CONCEPTS 409,689

sizable [adj] *considerable, large*
ample, big, burly, capacious, comprehensive, decent, decent-sized, extensive, good, goodly, great, gross, hefty, husky, jumbo*, largish, major, massive, ponderous, respectable, sensible, spacious, strapping, substantial, tidy, voluminous, whopping*; SEE CONCEPT 781

size [n] *extent or bulk of some dimension*
admeasurement, amount, amplitude, area, bigness, body, breadth, caliber, capaciousness, capacity, content, diameter, dimensions, enormity, extension, extent, greatness, height, highness, hugeness, immensity, intensity, largeness, length, magnitude, mass, measurement, proportion, proportions, range, scope, spread, stature, stretch, substance, substantiality, tonnage, vastness, volume, voluminosity, width; SEE CONCEPTS 730,792

sizzle [v] *hiss, fry*
broil, brown, buzz, cook, crackle, fizz, fizzle, frizzle, grill, roast, sear, sibilate, spit, sputter, swish, wheeze, whisper, whiz; SEE CONCEPTS 65,170

skate [v] *slide*
coast, flow, glide, glissade, ice skate, roller skate, sail along, skim; SEE CONCEPTS 150,152

skedaddle [v] *flee*
blow*, bolt, clear out, dart, dash, decamp, expe-

dite, fly, fly the coop*, get a move on*, go like lightning, hasten, hightail it*, hurry, hurry up, hustle, leave, make haste, make oneself scarce*, make time*, make tracks*, move, move fast, race, run, rush, scamper, scat, scoot, scurry, shake a leg*, speed, split, spur, step on it*, take off, vamoose, whiz, zip; SEE CONCEPTS 102,150,195,234

skeleton [n] *structure of bones in animate being or supports in an object*
bones, bony structure, cage, design, draft, frame, framework, osteology, outline, scaffolding, sketch, support; SEE CONCEPTS 393,733

skeptic [n] *person who is leery, unbelieving*
agnostic, apostate, atheist, cynic, disbeliever, dissenter, doubter, doubting Thomas*, freethinker, heathen, heretic, infidel, materialist, misanthrope, misbeliever, nihilist, pagan, pessimist, profaner, questioner, rationalist, scoffer, unbeliever; SEE CONCEPTS 361,423

skeptical [adj] *disbelieving, leery*
agnostic, aporetic, cynical, dissenting, doubtful, doubting, dubious, freethinking, hesitating, incredulous, mistrustful, questioning, quizzical, scoffing, show-me*, suspicious, unbelieving, unconvinced; SEE CONCEPT 403

skepticism [n] *doubt*
agnosticism, apprehension, disbelief, distrust, dubiety, dubiousness, faithlessness, hesitation, indecision, lack of confidence, leeriness, questioning, reluctance, suspicion, uncertainty; SEE CONCEPTS 21,410,689,692

sketch [n] *drawing, outline*
account, adumbration, aperçu, blueprint, cartoon, chart, compendium, configuration, copy, delineation, depiction, description, design, diagram, digest, depiction, doodle, draft, figuration, figure, form, illustration, likeness, monograph, painting, picture, piece, plan, portrayal, precis, report, representation, rough, shape, skeleton, summary, survey, syllabus, version, vignette; SEE CONCEPTS 268,283,625

sketch [v] *draw, outline*
adumbrate, block out*, blueprint*, chalk, characterize, chart, delineate, depict, describe, design, detail, develop, diagram, doodle, draft, lay out*, line, map out, paint, plan, plot, portray, represent, rough out*, skeleton, skeletonize, trace; SEE CONCEPTS 36,174

sketchy [adj] *rough, incomplete*
coarse, crude, cursory, defective, depthless, faulty, imperfect, inadequate, insufficient, introductory, perfunctory, preliminary, rough, scrappy, shallow, skimpy, slight, superficial, uncritical, unfinished, vague; SEE CONCEPT 531

skew [v] *distort*
alter, bend, bias, change, color, contort, curve, doctor*, fake, falsify, fudge*, misrepresent, misshape, slant, throw off balance, twist, warp; SEE CONCEPTS 63,137,232,250

skid [v] *slide against will*
drift, glide, go into skid, move, sheer, skew, slip, slue, swerve, veer; SEE CONCEPT 152

skill [n] *ability, talent to do something*
accomplishment, address, adroitness, aptitude, art, artistry, cleverness, clout, command, competence, craft, cunning, deftness, dexterity, dodge*, ease, experience, expertise, expertism, expertness, facility, finesse, goods*, handiness, ingenuity, intelligence, job, knack*, know-how*, line,

makings, moxie*, one's thing*, profession, proficiency, prowess, quickness, readiness, right stuff*, savvy*, skillfulness, sleight, smarts*, stuff*, technique, trade, what it takes*; SEE CONCEPTS 409,630

skillful [adj] *able, talented*
accomplished, adept, adroit, a hand at*, apt, brainy, clever, competent, cool*, crack*, crackerjack*, dexterous, experienced, expert, good, handy, into*, learned, old*, on the ball*, practical, practiced, prepared, pretty, primed, pro*, professional, proficient, quick, ready, really into*, savvy*, seasoned, sharp, skilled, smart, smooth, there*, trained, tuned in*, versant, versed, vet*, veteran, well-versed, whiz, wicked*, wised up*; SEE CONCEPTS 402,527

skim [v1] *remove the top part*
brush, cream, dip, get the cream, glance, graze, ladle, ream, scoop, separate, shave, top; SEE CONCEPT 211

skim [v2] *glide over quickly, lightly*
brush, carom, coast, dart, float, fly, graze, kiss, ricochet, sail, scud, shoot, skate, skip, skirr, skitter, smooth along, soar, trip; SEE CONCEPTS 150,152

skim [v3] *look through cursorily*
browse, brush over, dip, examine, flip through, get the cream, give the once-over*, glance, glance over, go once over lightly*, hit the high spots*, leaf through*, read, read swiftly, riff, riffle, run eye over*, scan, skip, thumb through*, turn the pages*; SEE CONCEPTS 72,103,623

skimp [v] *be cheap or frugal about*
be mean with, be sparing, cut corners*, make ends meet*, pinch, pinch pennies*, roll back, save, scamp, scant, scrape, screw, scrimp, slight, spare, stint, tighten one's belt*, withhold; SEE CONCEPT 330

skimpy [adj] *sparse, inadequate*
deficient, exiguous, failing, insufficient, meager, miserly, niggardly, poor, scant, scanty, scrimp, scrimpy, short, shy, sparse, stingy, thin, tight, unsufficient, wanting; SEE CONCEPTS 334,762,789

skin [n] *outer covering, especially of animate being*
bark, carapace, case, casing, coating, crust, cutis, derma, dermis, epidermis, fell, film, fur, hide, hull, husk, integument, jacket, membrane, outside, parchment, peel, pelt, rind, sheath, sheathing, shell, shuck, slough, surface, tegument, vellum; SEE CONCEPTS 392,428,484

skin [v] *remove outer covering*
abrade, bare, bark, cast, cut off, decorticate, excoriate, exuviate, flay, gall, graze, hull, husk, lay bare, pare, peel, pull off, remove, rind, scale, scalp, scrape, shave, shed, shuck, slough, strip, trim; SEE CONCEPTS 176,211

skin-deep [adj] *superficial*
apparent, casual, cursory, empty, flimsy, meaningless, one-dimensional, on the surface, shallow, trivial; SEE CONCEPTS 557,777

skinflint [n] *cheapskate*
hoarder, miser, moneygrubber*, penny-pincher*, pinchfist*, pinchpenny*, Scrooge*, tightwad; SEE CONCEPTS 348,412,423

skinny [adj] *very thin*
angular, bony, emaciated, gaunt, lank, lanky, lean, like a rail*, malnourished, rawboned, scraggy, scrawny, skeletal, skin-and-bone*, slen-

skip [v1] *bounce or jump over*
bob, bolt, bound, buck, canter, caper, carom, cavort, dance, flee, flit, fly, frisk, gambol, glance, graze, hippety-hop*, hop, leap, lope, make off, prance, ricochet, run, scamper, scoot, skedaddle*, skim, skirr, skitter, spring, step, tiptoe, trip; SEE CONCEPTS *150,194*

skip [v2] *avoid, miss*
cut, desert, disregard, escape, eschew, flee, leave out, miss out, neglect, omit, pass over, pass up, play hooky*, run away, skim over, split; SEE CONCEPTS *30,681*

skirmish [n] *fight*
altercation, argument, battle, bout, brawl, brush, clash, combat, conflict, confrontation, disagreement, dispute, encounter, engagement, feud, fisticuffs*, fracas, fray, melee, quarrel, row, ruckus, rumble, run-in*, scrap*, scuffle, strife, tiff, tussle, war; SEE CONCEPT *106*

skirmish [v] *fight*
altercate, argue, battle, bicker, brawl, clash, combat, conflict, cross swords, dispute, do battle, engage, feud, go to war, grapple, mix it up*, quarrel, scrap, scuffle, spar, struggle, tussle, wage war, war, wrangle, wrestle; SEE CONCEPT *106*

skirt [n1] *border, edge*
brim, brink, fringe, hem, margin, outskirts, perimeter, periphery, purlieus, rim, skirting, verge; SEE CONCEPTS *484,825*

skirt [n2] *ladies' garment that hangs from waist*
culottes, dirndl, dress, hoop, kilt, midi, mini, pannier, petticoat, sarong, tutu; SEE CONCEPT *451*

skirt [v1] *border; be on the edge*
bound, define, edge, flank, fringe, hem, lie along, lie alongside, margin, rim, surround, verge; SEE CONCEPT *751*

skirt [v2] *avoid; get around*
burke, bypass, circumnavigate, circumvent, detour, dodge, duck, elude, equivocate, escape, evade, hedge, ignore, sidestep, skip, steer clear of; SEE CONCEPTS *30,102,147*

skit [n] *sketch*
act, parody, performance, play, satire, spoof, takeoff; SEE CONCEPT *263*

skittish [adj] *very nervous*
agitable, alarmable, capricious, changeable, combustible, dizzy*, edgy, excitable, excited, fearful, fickle, fidgety, flighty, frivolous, giddy, harebrained, high-strung*, irresponsible, jumpy, lightheaded, lively, peppy, playful, restive, scatterbrained*, sensitive, spirited, undependable, unreliable, volatile, whimsical, zippy*; SEE CONCEPT *401*

skulk [v] *lurk; shirk*
avoid, bypass, conceal oneself, creep, crouch, dodge, elude, evade, hide, lie in wait, prowl, pussyfoot*, sidestep, slack, slink, snake, sneak, snoop, steal; SEE CONCEPTS *30,59,151,188,681*

sky [n] *Earth's atmosphere*
azure, celestial sphere, empyrean, firmament, heavens, lid*, the blue*, upper atmosphere, vault, vault of heaven*, welkin, wild blue yonder*; SEE CONCEPT *437*

skyrocket [v] *soar*
arise, ascend, catapult, escalate, go through the ceiling*, go through the roof*, lift, rise, rocket,

shoot, shoot up, take off, tower, vault up, zoom; SEE CONCEPTS *148,150*

skyscraper [n] *tall building*
high-rise, high-rise building, superstructure, tower; SEE CONCEPTS *439,441*

slab [n] *chunk of solid object*
bar, billet, bit, board, boulder, chip, cut, cutting, hunk, ingot, lump, muck, piece, plate, portion, rod, slice, stave, stick, stone, strip, wedge; SEE CONCEPTS *471,835*

slack [adj1] *loose, baggy; inactive*
dull, easy, feeble, flabby, flaccid, flexible, flimsy, inert, infirm, laggard, lax, leisurely, limp, not taut, passive, quaggy, quiet, relaxed, sloppy, slow, slow-moving, sluggish, soft, supine, unsteady, weak; SEE CONCEPTS *485,584,589*

slack [adj2] *lazy, negligent*
asleep on the job*, behindhand, careless, delinquent, derelict, dilatory, disregardful, dormant, dull, easy-going, faineant, idle, inactive, inattentive, indolent, inert, lackadaisical, lax, lethargic, neglectful, not busy, permissive, quiescent, quiet, regardless, remiss, slothful, slow, slow-moving, sluggish, stagnant, tardy; SEE CONCEPT *538*

slack [n] *looseness, excess*
give, leeway, play, room, slackening, slowdown, slow-up; SEE CONCEPTS *513,807*

slacker [n] *shirker*
avoider, bum, deadbeat*, goldbrick, good-for-nothing, goof-off*, idler, loafer, quitter, slouch; SEE CONCEPTS *412,423*

slack/slacken [v] *do little or nothing; loosen*
abate, decrease, diminish, dodge, drop off, dwindle, ease, ease off, featherbed*, flag, goldbrick*, goof off*, idle, lax, lay back, lessen, let up, lie down on job*, loose, moderate, neglect, reduce, relax, release, shirk, slack off, slow down, taper, tire, untighten, wane; SEE CONCEPTS *210,681,698*

slam [n1] *loud noise from impact*
bang, blast, blow, boom, burst, clap, crack, crash, ding, pound, smack, smash, whack, wham; SEE CONCEPTS *189,595*

slam [n2] *harsh criticism*
animadversion, aspersion, jab, obloquy, potshot*, slap*, slur*, stricture, swipe*; SEE CONCEPTS *52,278*

slam [v1] *throw or push very hard*
bang, bat, batter, beat, belt, blast, clobber, close, crash, cudgel, dash, fling, hammer, hit, hurl, knock, pound, shut, slap, slug, smash, strike, swat, thump, thwack, wallop; SEE CONCEPTS *189,208,222*

slam [v2] *criticize very harshly*
attack, castigate, damn, excoriate, flay, lambaste*, lash into*, pan, scathe, scourge, shoot down, slap, slash, vilify; SEE CONCEPTS *52,54*

slander [n] *scandalous remark*
aspersion, backbiting*, backstabbing*, belittlement, black eye*, calumny, defamation, depreciation, detraction, dirt*, dirty linen*, disparagement, hit*, libel, lie, misrepresentation, muckraking, mud*, mud-slinging*, obloquy, rap*, scandal, slam*, slime*, smear*, tale; SEE CONCEPTS *54,192,278*

slander [v] *make a scandalous remark*
asperse, assail, attack, backbite*, bad-mouth*, belie, belittle, besmirch, blacken name*, blaspheme, blister, blot, calumniate, cast a slur on, curse, damage, decry, defame, defile, denigrate,

depreciate, derogate, detract, dishonor, disparage, give a bad name*, hit*, hurt, injure, libel, malign, muckrake, pan*, plaster, revile, roast*, run smear campaign*, scandalize, scorch, slam*, sling mud*, slur, smear, smirch, sneer, strumpet, sully, tarnish, tear down, traduce, vilify; SEE CONCEPTS *54,192*

slang [*n*] *casual dialect*
argot, cant, colloquialism, informal speech, jargon, lingo, neologism, patois, patter, pidgin, shoptalk, slanguage* street talk, vernacular, vulgarism, vulgarity; SEE CONCEPT *276*

slant [*n*] *angle, slope*
camber, cant, declination, diagonal, grade, gradient, inclination, incline, lean, leaning, pitch, rake, ramp, tilt; SEE CONCEPT *738*

slant [*n2*] *particular opinion*
angle, attitude, bias, direction, emphasis, judgment, leaning, one-sidedness, outlook, point of view, predilection, predisposition, prejudice, prepossession, sentiment, side, standpoint, view, viewpoint; SEE CONCEPT *689*

slant [*v1*] *angle off, slope*
aim, bank, beam, bend, bevel, cant, decline, descend, deviate, direct, diverge, grade, heel, incline, lean, level, lie obliquely, list, point, skew, splay, swerve, tilt, tip, train, veer; SEE CONCEPTS *201,738*

slant [*v2*] *change to suit; distort*
aim, angle, bias, color, concentrate, direct, focus, influence, orient, point, prejudice, train, twist, warp, weight; SEE CONCEPTS *63,266*

slap [*n/v*] *hard hit, often with hand*
bang, bash, blip, blow, box, buffet, bust, chop, clap, clout, crack, cuff, pat, percuss, poke, potch, punch, slam, smack, sock, spank, strike, swat, wallop, whack, wham; SEE CONCEPT *189*

slapdash [*adj*] *careless*
clumsy, haphazard, hasty, heedless, improvident, irresponsible, lackadaisical, lax, messy, negligent, nonchalant, reckless, slipshod, sloppy; SEE CONCEPT *542*

slaphappy [*adj*] *dazed*
befuddled, bewildered, dazzled, gaga*, giddy, groggy*, hazy, punch-drunk*, punchy*, puzzled, senile, silly, staggered, staggering, tipsy, unsteady, weak in the knees*, weak-kneed*, wobbly, woozy; SEE CONCEPTS *314,480*

slash [*v1*] *cut*
carve, chop, gash, hack, incise, injure, lacerate, open up, pierce, rend, rip, score, sever, slice, slit, wound; SEE CONCEPTS *137,176*

slash [*v2*] *reduce greatly*
abbreviate, abridge, clip, curtail, cut, cut back, cut down, drop, hack, lower, mark down, pare, retrench, shave, shorten; SEE CONCEPTS *236,240,247*

slaughter [*n*] *killing*
annihilation, bloodbath, bloodshed, butchery, carnage, destruction, extermination, liquidation, massacre, murder, slaying; SEE CONCEPT *252*

slaughter [*v*] *kill*
butcher, crush, decimate, defeat, destroy, do in* exterminate, finish, liquidate, maim, mangle, massacre, murder, mutilate, overwhelm, rout, slay, stick, thrash, torture, total* trounce, vanquish, waste, wipe out*; SEE CONCEPT *252*

slave [*n*] *person who serves, often under duress*
bondservant, captive, chattel, drudge, help, laborer, menial, peon, retainer, serf, servant, skivvy, subservient, thrall, toiler, vassal, victim, worker, workhorse; SEE CONCEPT *348*

slave [*v*] *work very hard*
be servile, drudge, grind, grovel, grub, muck, plod, skivvy, slog, toil, work fingers to bone*; SEE CONCEPT *87*

slavery [*n*] *state of working under duress or without freedom*
bondage, bullwork, captivity, chains* constraint, drudge, drudgery, enslavement, enthrallment, feudalism, grind, helotry, indenture, labor, menial labor, moil, peonage, restraint, serfdom, serfhood, servitude, subjection, subjugation, thrall, thralldom, toil, vassalage, work; SEE CONCEPTS *324,388*

slay [*v*] *kill*
annihilate, assassinate, butcher, cut off, destroy, dispatch, do*, do away with, do in*, down*, eliminate, erase, execute, exterminate, finish, hit, knock off*, liquidate, massacre, murder, neutralize, put away*, rub out*, slaughter, snuff*, waste*; SEE CONCEPT *252*

sleazebag [*n*] *creep*
crud*, degenerate, deviant, dip*, dirtbag*, dirtball*, pervert, pig*, scum*, scumbag*, scuzzbag*, sleaze*, sleazeball*, slimebag*, slimeball*, slimebucket*, slob*, weirdo*; SEE CONCEPT *412*

sleazy [*adj*] *disreputable*
base, broken-down, cheap, common, dilapidated, flimsy, limp, low, mean, paltry, poor, run-down, seedy, shabby, shoddy, sordid, squalid, tacky*, trashy, unsubstantial; SEE CONCEPTS *334,485,589*

sled [*n*] *sleigh*
bobsled, dog sled, horse sleigh, luge, sledge, toboggan; SEE CONCEPTS *187,217*

sleek [*adj*] *smooth, glossy*
glassy, glistening, lustrous, polished, satin, shiny, silken, silky; SEE CONCEPT *606*

sleep [*n*] *suspension of consciousness*
bedtime, catnap, coma, dormancy, doze, dream, dullness, few z's*, forty winks*, hibernation, lethargy, nap, nod, repose, rest, sack time*, sandman*, shuteye*, siesta, slumber, slumberland*, snooze, torpidity, torpor, trance; SEE CONCEPT *315*

sleep [*v*] *suspend consciousness*
bed down*, bunk*, catch a wink*, catch forty winks*, catnap, conk out*, cop some z's*, crash*, doze, dream, drop off*, drowse, fall asleep, fall out*, flop*, hibernate, hit the hay*, hit the sack*, languish, nap, nod, nod off, oversleep, relax, repose, rest, retire, sack out*, saw wood*, slumber, snooze, snore, take a nap, turn in*, yawn, zonk out*, zzz*; SEE CONCEPT *315*

sleepless [*adj*] *insomniac, restless*
active, alert, antsy*, anxious, bustling, edgy, fidgeting, fidgety, jumpy, nervous, on edge, strung out*, tossing and turning*, troubled, unsettled, wakeful, wide-awake, wired*, worried; SEE CONCEPTS *403,542,584*

sleepy [*adj*] *tired, dull*
asleep, blah*, comatose, dopey*, dozy, draggy, drowsy, heavy, hypnotic, inactive, lethargic, listless, out*, out of it*, quiet, sleeping, sleepyhead*, slow, sluggish, slumberous, slumbersome, snoozy*, somnolent, soporific, torpid, yawning; SEE CONCEPTS *315,539*

sk
sl

sleigh [*n*] *sled*
bobsled, dog sled, horse sleigh, luge, sledge, toboggan; SEE CONCEPTS *187,217*

slender/slim [*adj1*] *thin, not heavy*
attenuate, beanpole*, beanstalk*, fine, insubstantial, lean, lithe, narrow, reedy, skeleton, skinny, slight, spare, stalky, stick, svelte, sylphlike, tenuous, threadlike, trim, twiggy, willowy; SEE CONCEPTS *490,491*

slender/slim [*adj2*] *inadequate, flimsy*
bare, deficient, faint, feeble, fragile, inconsiderable, insufficient, little, meager, poor, remote, scant, scanty, scarce, short, shy, slight, small, spare, tenuous, thin, wanting, weak; SEE CONCEPTS *552,771*

sleuth [*n*] *detective*
agent, bloodhound*, cop, dick*, eavesdropper, flatfoot*, gumshoe*, investigator, P.I.*, police officer, private detective, private eye, private investigator, sleuthhound, spy, tail*, tracker; SEE CONCEPT *348*

slice [*n*] *piece; share*
allotment, allowance, bite, chop, cut, helping, lot, part, piece of pie*, portion, quota, segment, sliver, thin piece, triangle, wedge; SEE CONCEPT *835*

slice [*v*] *cut into portions, shares*
carve, chiv, cleave, dissect, dissever, divide, gash, hack, incise, pierce, segment, sever, shave, shred, slash, slit, split, strip, subdivide, sunder; SEE CONCEPTS *98,137,176*

slick [*adj1*] *smooth, polished*
glossy, greasy, icy, lubricious, oily, oleaginous, shiny, sleek, sleeky, slippery, slithery, soapy; SEE CONCEPT *606*

slick [*adj2*] *smart, clever*
adroit, cagey, canny, deft, dextrous, foxy, glib, knowing, meretricious, plausible, professional, quick, sharp, shrewd, skillful, sly, smooth, smooth-spoken, sophisticated, specious, streetwise*, unctuous, urbane, wise; SEE CONCEPTS *401,402*

slide [*v*] *move smoothly; move down*
accelerate, coast, drift, drive, drop, fall, fall off, flow, glide, glissade, launch, move, move along, move over, propel, sag, scooch*, shift, shove, skate, skid, skim, slip, slither, slump, smooth along, spill, stream, thrust, toboggan, tumble, veer; SEE CONCEPTS *150,152*

slight [*adj1*] *insignificant, small*
fat, feeble, inconsiderable, insubstantial, meager, minor, modest, negligible, off, outside, paltry, petty, piddling, remote, scanty, slender, slim, sparse, superficial, trifling, trivial, unessential, unimportant, weak; SEE CONCEPTS *575,762,789*

slight [*adj2*] *thin, small in build*
attenuate, broomstick*, dainty, delicate, feeble, flimsy, fragile, frail, light, reedy, shadow, skeleton, skinny, slender, slim, spare, stick, twiggy; SEE CONCEPTS *490,491*

slight [*n*] *insult, disrespect*
affront, brush-off, call-down, cold shoulder*, contempt, cut, discourtesy, disdain, disregard, inattention, indifference, kick, neglect, putdown*, rebuff, rejection, slap in the face*, snub; SEE CONCEPTS *30,384,529*

slight [*v*] *offend, insult*
affront, blink at, brush off, chill, contemn, cool*, cut*, despise, discount, disdain, disparage, disregard, fail, flout, forget, give the brush*, give the

cold shoulder to*, ignore, make light of, neglect, not give time of day*, omit, overlook, poohpooh*, reject, scoff, scorn, show disrespect, shrug off, skip, slur, sneeze at*, snub, treat with contempt, turn deaf ear to*, upstage; SEE CONCEPTS *7,19,30,384*

slightly [*adv*] *a little*
hardly, hardly at all, hardly noticeable, imperceptibly, inappreciably, inconsiderably, insignificantly, kind of, lightly, marginally, more or less, on a small scale, pretty, scarcely any, somewhat, to some degree, to some extent; SEE CONCEPTS *544,772*

slim [*v*] *lose weight*
diet, reduce, slenderize; SEE CONCEPT *202*

slime [*n*] *muck, gelled waste*
fungus, glop*, goo*, gunk*, mire, mucus, mud, ooze, scum, sludge; SEE CONCEPT *260*

slimy [*adj*] *oozy, gooey*
clammy, glutinous, miry, mucky, mucous, muculent, muddy, scummy, viscous, yukky*; SEE CONCEPTS *485,621*

sling [*v*] *throw or hang over*
bung, cast, catapult, chuck, dangle, fire, fling, heave, hoist, hurl, launch, lob, peg, pitch, raise, send, shoot, suspend, swing, toss, weight; SEE CONCEPTS *181,222*

slink/slither [*v*] *creep by*
coast, cower, glide, glissade, go stealthily, gumshoe*, lurk, meander, pass quietly, prowl, pussyfoot*, shirk, sidle, skitter, skulk, slick, slide, slip, snake, sneak, steal, undulate; SEE CONCEPT *151*

slip [*n1*] *error, goof*
blooper*, blunder, bungle, failure, fault, flub*, fluff*, foul-up*, gaff, howler*, imprudence, indiscretion, lapse, misdeed, misstep, mistake, muff*, omission, oversight, screw-up*, slip of the tongue*, slip-up*, trip; SEE CONCEPT *101*

slip [*n2*] *piece of paper*
label, leaf, page, sheet, sliver, strip, tag, ticket; SEE CONCEPTS *270,475*

slip [*v1*] *fall; glide*
drop, glissade, lose balance, lose footing, lurch, move, shift, skate, skid, slick, slide, slither, smooth along, totter, trip; SEE CONCEPTS *150,152*

slip [*v2*] *err*
blunder, drop the ball*, flub*, fluff*, goof*, go wrong, make a mistake, miscalculate, misjudge, mistake, muff*, put foot in mouth*, slip up, stumble, trip; SEE CONCEPT *101*

slippery [*adj1*] *smooth, slick*
glace, glassy, glazed, glistening, greasy, icy, like a skating rink*, lubricious, lustrous, perilous, polished, satiny, silky, sleek, slimy, soapy, unctuous, unsafe, unstable, unsteady, waxy, wet; SEE CONCEPT *606*

slippery [*adj2*] *uncertain, unreliable*
cagey, changeable, crafty, cunning, devious, dishonest, duplicitous, elusive, evasive, false, flyby-night*, foxy, inconstant, insecure, mutable, shifty, slick, slithery, smooth, sneaky, treacherous, tricky, two-faced*, unpredictable, unsafe, unstable, unsteady, untrustworthy, variable; SEE CONCEPTS *401,534,535*

slipshod [*adj*] *careless; not well done*
bedraggled, botched*, disheveled, faulty, fly-by-night*, fouled-up*, haphazard, imperfect, inaccurate, inexact, junky*, loose, messed-up, messy, neglected, negligent, raunchy, screwed-up*,

scrubby*, scruffy*, shabby*, shoddy*, slapdash*, sloppy, slovenly, tacky*, tattered, threadbare, unkempt, unmeticulous, unsystematic, unthorough, untidy; SEE CONCEPTS 485,570,589

slipup [n] *error*
blooper, blunder, boner*, boo-boo*, bungle, faux pas, flaw, glitch, goof*, lapse, miscalculation, miscue, misjudgment, misstep, mistake, misunderstanding, oversight, screwup, slight, stumble, transgression; SEE CONCEPTS 101,230,674,699

slit [n] *small opening, cut*
aperture, breach, cleavage, cleft, crack, crevice, fissure, gap, hole, incision, rent, split, tear; SEE CONCEPT 513

slit [v] *cut open*
gash, incise, knife, lance, pierce, rip, sever, slash, slice, slot, split open, tear; SEE CONCEPT 176

slither [v] *slide*
coast, crawl, glide, glissade, move, skate, skid, slink, slip, snake*, sneak, wriggle; SEE CONCEPTS 150,152

sliver [n] *tiny piece, usually of wood or metal*
bit, flake, fragment, paring, shaving, shred, slice, slip, snip, snippet, splinter, thorn; SEE CONCEPTS 471,831

slobber [v] *drool*
dribble, drip, drivel, froth, salivate, slabber, slaver, water at the mouth; SEE CONCEPT 185

slog [v] *plod*
bear down*, buckle down*, drag, drudge, flounder, grind, labor, lumber*, plough through*, plug, schlepp*, slave, stomp, sweat*, toil, tramp, trample, trudge; SEE CONCEPTS 87,151,677

slogan [n] *motto*
byword, catchphrase, catchword, expression, idiom, jingle, phrase, proverb, rallying cry*, saying, shibboleth*, trademark*, war cry*, watchword; SEE CONCEPT 278

slop [v] *splash; make a mess*
dash, drip, flounder, let run out, let run over, overflow, slosh, smear, smudge, spatter, spill, splatter, spray, wallow; SEE CONCEPT 250

slope [n] *slant, tilt*
abruptness, bank, bend, bevel, bias, cant, declination, declivity, deflection, descent, deviation, diagonal, downgrade, gradient, hill, inclination, incline, lean, leaning, obliqueness, obliquity, pitch, ramp, rise, rising ground, shelf, skew, steepness, swag, sway, tip; SEE CONCEPTS 738,757

slope [v] *slant, tilt*
angle, ascend, bank, bevel, cant, descend, dip, drop, drop away, fall, heel, incline, lean, list, pitch, rake, recline, rise, shelve, skew, splay, tip; SEE CONCEPTS 201,738

sloppy [adj] *messy*
awkward, bedraggled, botched, careless, clumsy, dingy, dirty, disheveled, inattentive, mediocre, muddy, not clean, poor, slapdash, slipshod, slovenly, sludgy*, slushy*, splashy*, tacky*, unkempt, unthorough, untidy, watery, wet; SEE CONCEPTS 531,603,621

slot [n] *opening, place*
aperture, channel, cut, groove, hole, niche, position, recess, slit, socket, space, time, vacancy; SEE CONCEPT 513

sloth [n] *laziness*
do-nothingness, idleness, inactivity, indolence, inertia, lackadaisicalness, languidness, laxness, lethargy, listlessness, slackness, slothfulness,

slowness, sluggishness, supineness; SEE CONCEPTS 411,633

slothful [adj] *lazy*
comatose, dallying, dull, idle, inactive, inattentive, indolent, inert, lackadaisical, laggard, lagging, languid, lethargic, lifeless, listless, loafing, passive, procrastinating, slack, slow, sluggish, snoozy*, supine, tired, unenergetic; SEE CONCEPTS 401,404

slouch [v] *slump over*
be lazy, bend, bow, crouch, droop, lean, loaf, loll, lounge, sag, stoop, wilt; SEE CONCEPTS 154,201

slovenly [adj] *dirty, disordered*
bedraggled, botched, careless, dingy, disheveled, disorderly, dowdy, down-at-the-heel*, frowzy*, frumpy*, grody*, grubby, grungy*, heedless, icky*, loose, messed up*, messy, mussy, negligent, pigpen*, raunchy, seedy, slack, slapdash, sleazy*, slipshod, sloppy, tacky, topsy-turvy, unfastidious, unkempt, unthorough, untidy; SEE CONCEPTS 485,621

slow [adj1] *unhurried, lazy*
apathetic, crawling, creeping, dawdling, delaying, deliberate, dilatory, disinclined, dreamy, drowsy, easy, gradual, heavy, idle, imperceptible, inactive, indolent, inert, lackadaisical, laggard, lagging, leaden, leisurely, lethargic, listless, loitering, measured, moderate, negligent, passive, phlegmatic, plodding, ponderous, postponing, procrastinating, quiet, reluctant, remiss, slack, sleepy, slothful, slow-moving, sluggish, snaillike, stagnant, supine, tardy, torpid, tortoiselike; SEE CONCEPTS 538,584,588

slow [adj2] *behind, late*
backward, behindhand, belated, conservative, dead, delayed, detained, dilatory, down, draggy*, dull, gradual, hindered, impeded, inactive, lingering, long-delayed, long-drawn-out*, low, moderate, off, overdue, prolonged, protracted, reduced, slack, sleepy, sluggish, stagnant, stiff, tame, tardy, tedious, time-consuming, uneventful, unproductive, unprogressive, unpunctual; SEE CONCEPTS 529,537,548

slow [adj3] *unintelligent*
backward, dense, dim, dimwitted, dull, dumb, dunce, imbecile, limited, moronic, obtuse, simple, slow on the uptake*, stupid, thick, unresponsive; SEE CONCEPT 402

slow [v] *delay, restrict*
abate, anchor it, back-water*, bog down, brake, check, choke, curb, curtail, cut back, cut down, decelerate, decrease, detain, diminish, ease off, ease up, encumber, handicap, hinder, hit the brakes*, hold back, hold up, impede, keep waiting, lag, lessen, let down flaps*, loiter, lose speed, lose steam*, mire, moderate, postpone, procrastinate, qualify, quiet, reduce, reduce speed, reef, regulate, rein in, relax, retard, retardate, set back, slacken, stall, stunt, temper, wind down; SEE CONCEPTS 130,234,250

slowdown [n] *slacking off; gradual decrease*
arrest, deceleration, decline, delay, downtrend, downturn, drop, drop-off, falloff, freeze, inactivity, retardation, slack, slackening, slow-up, stagnation, stoppage, strike; SEE CONCEPTS 121,130

slowpoke [n] *laggard*
dawdler, dilly-dallyer, idler, plodder, procrastinator, slug, sluggard, snail, straggler; SEE CONCEPTS 121,237,681

sl
sl

sludge [*n*] *mud*

glop*, goo*, goop*, grease, gunk*, mire, muck, oil, ooze, scum, sediment, silt, slime, slop; SEE CONCEPT *260*

slug [*v*] *hit*

bang, bash, bat, batter, beat, belt, box*, bump, clobber, clock*, clout, club, crack, flail, flog, hammer*, jab, knock, KO*, lambaste, let have it*, nail*, pelt, pop, pound, punch, slam, slap, smack, sock, swat, thrash, thwack, wallop, whack*, whale; SEE CONCEPTS *189,200*

slugfest [*n*] *fight*

altercation, argument, battle, battle royal*, bout, brawl, clash, conflict, dispute, dogfight, donny-brook, engagement, feud, fisticuffs*, fracas, fray, free-for-all*, melee, riot, ruckus, rumble, strug-gle, tussle, war; SEE CONCEPT *106*

sluggish [*adj*] *dull, slow-moving*

apathetic, blah*, comatose, dopey*, down, drag-ging, draggy*, drippy*, heavy, hebetudinous, in-active, indolent, inert, laid-back*, languid, languorous, leaden, lethargic, lifeless, listless, lumpish, mooney*, off, phlegmatic, pokey*, slack, sleepyheaded*, slothful, slow, sluggard, slumberous, stagnant, stiff, sullen, torpid, unre-sponsive; SEE CONCEPTS *401,584*

slum [*n*] *ghetto*

blighted area, public squalor, run-down neigh-borhood, shanty town, skid row, tenement hous-ing; SEE CONCEPTS *335,709*

slumber [*n*] *sleep*

coma, dormancy, doze, drowse, forty winks*, in-activity, languor, lethargy, nap, repose, rest, sack time*, shut-eye*, snooze, stupor, torpor; SEE CONCEPT *315*

slump [*n*] *decline, failure*

bad period, bad times, blight, blue devils*, blue funk*, bottom, bust, collapse, crash, deprecia-tion, depression, descent, dip, downer*, downslide*, downswing*, downtrend, downturn, drop, dumps*, fall, falling-off*, funk, hard times*, letdown*, low, rainy days*, recession, reverse, rut, sag, slide, slip, stagnation, the skids*, trough; SEE CONCEPTS *335,410,674*

slump [*v*] *decline, sink*

bend, blight, cave in, collapse, crash, decay, de-teriorate, droop, drop, fall, fall off*, go down, go downhill*, go to ruin*, hunch, keel over, loll, pitch, plummet, plunge, reach new low*, sag, slide, slip, slouch, topple, tumble; SEE CONCEPTS *181,698,699,763*

slur [*n*] *insult*

accusation, affront, animadversion, aspersion, bar sinister*, black eye*, blemish, blot, blur, brand, brickbat*, calumny, dirty dig*, discredit, disgrace, dump, expose, hit, innuendo, insinua-tion, knock, obloquy, odium, onus, put-down*, rap*, reflection, reproach, slam, smear, stain, stigma, stricture, zinger*; SEE CONCEPTS *44,54,278*

slur [*v1*] *insult*

blacken, blemish, blister, blot, blow off*, brand, calumniate, cap, chop*, cut to the quick*, cut up*, defame, denigrate, detract, discredit, dis-grace, dump on*, give a black eye*, hit where one lives*, insinuate, kick in the teeth*, libel, malign, miff, offend, push, put down*, reproach, roast*, scorch*, skin alive*, slander, slap in the face*, slight, smear*, snub, spatter, stain, tear

down, traduce, vilify, zing*; SEE CONCEPTS *7,19,44,54*

slur [*v2*] *mumble words*

garble, mispronounce, miss, skip, stutter; SEE CONCEPT *47*

sly [*adj*] *clever, devious*

arch, artful, astute, bluffing, cagey, calculating, canny, captious, conniving, covert, crafty, crooked, cunning, deceitful, deceptive, delusive, designing, dishonest, dishonorable, dissembling, double-dealing, elusive, foxy, furtive, guileful, illusory, impish, ingenious, insidious, intriguing, mean, mischievous, plotting, roguish, scheming, secret, sharp, shifty, shrewd, slick, smart, smooth, sneaking, stealthy, subtle, traitorous, treacherous, tricky, underhand, unscrupulous, wily; SEE CONCEPTS *401,542*

smack [*adv*] *directly, exactly*

accurately, bang*, clearly, just, plumb, point-blank*, precisely, right, sharp, square, squarely, straight; SEE CONCEPT *557*

smack [*n/v*] *strike, often with hand*

bang, blip, blow, box, buffet, chop, clap, clout, crack, cuff, hit, pat, punch, slap, snap, sock, spank, tap; SEE CONCEPT *189*

small [*adj1*] *tiny in size, quantity*

baby, bantam, bitty*, cramped, diminutive, hum-ble, immature, inadequate, inconsequential, in-considerable, insufficient, limited, little, meager, microscopic, mini*, miniature, minuscule, minute, modest, narrow, paltry, petite, petty, picayune, piddling*, pint-sized*, pitiful, pocket-sized*, poor, puny*, runty*, scanty, scrubby, short, shrimp*, slight, small-scale, stunted, teensy*, teeny, toy, trifling, trivial, undersized, unpretentious, wee*, young; SEE CONCEPTS *773,789*

small [*adj2*] *unimportant*

bush-league*, inadequate, inconsiderable, inef-fectual, inferior, insignificant, lesser, light, lim-ited, lower, mean, minor, minor-league*, minute, narrow, negligible, paltry, petty, secondary, set, small-fry*, small-time*, trifling, trivial, unessen-tial; SEE CONCEPT *575*

small [*adj3*] *narrow-minded, nasty*

base, grudging, ignoble, illiberal, limited, little, mean, narrow, petty, rude, selfish, set, vulgar; SEE CONCEPT *401*

small-minded [*adj*] *narrow-minded*

biased, bigoted, conservative, illiberal, intoler-ant, opinionated, petty, prejudiced, selfish, short-sighted; SEE CONCEPTS *403,542*

small talk [*n*] *casual conversation*

babble, blab*, blather, chatter, chitchat*, gossip, idle chatter, idle talk, jabber*, prattle, yakking*; SEE CONCEPTS *274,278*

small-time [*adj*] *minor*

bush-league*, dinky*, inconsequential, inconsid-erable, insignificant, low, petty, piddling*, sec-ondary, second-string*, trivial, two-bit*, unimportant; SEE CONCEPTS *575,773,789*

smart [*adj1*] *intelligent*

acute, adept, agile, alert, apt, astute, bold, brainy*, bright, brilliant, brisk, canny, clever, crafty, effective, eggheaded*, fresh, genius, good, impertinent, ingenious, keen, knowing, long-haired*, nervy, nimble, on the ball*, pert, pointed, quick, quick-witted, ready, resourceful, sassy, sharp, shrewd, skull, slick*, whiz*, wise; SEE CONCEPT *402*

smart [*adj2*] *stylish, fashionable*
chic, dapper, dashing, dressed to kill*, elegant, exclusive, fine, fly*, in fashion, last word*, latest thing*, modish, natty, neat, snappy, spruce, swank, trendy, trim, well turned-out, with it*; SEE CONCEPT 589

smart [*adj3*] *brisk, lively*
active, bold, brazen, cracking, energetic, forward, good, jaunty, nervy, pert, quick, saucy, scintillating, spanking, spirited, sprightly, vigorous; SEE CONCEPTS 401,542

smart [*v*] *hurt, pain*
ache, be painful, bite, burn, prick, prickle, sting, suffer, throb, tingle; SEE CONCEPTS 246,728

smart-aleck [*n*] *wise guy*
bigmouth*, know-it-all*, smart ass*, smarty-pants*, wiseacre, wiseass, wisenheimer; SEE CONCEPT 412

smarts [*n*] *intelligence*
acuity, acumen, alertness, aptitude, brainpower, brains*, brightness, brilliance, cleverness, competence, comprehension, gray matter*, intellect, IQ*, judgment, know-how, mind, perception, perspicacity, precocity, reason, savvy, sense, the right stuff*, understanding, what it takes*; SEE CONCEPT 409

smash [*n1*] *collision; defeat*
accident, bang, bash, blast, blow, boom, breakdown, breaking, breakup, burst, clap, collapse, crack, crack-up, crash, debacle, destruction, disaster, downfall, failure, pile-up, ruin, shattering, slam, smash-up, sock, wallop, welt, whack, wham, wreck; SEE CONCEPTS 674,675

smash [*n2*] *great success*
hit, knockout, sensation, wow*; SEE CONCEPT 706

smash [*v1*] *break into pieces*
bang, belt, blast, break to smithereens*, burst, clobber, collide, crack, crash, crush, demolish, disintegrate, fracture, fragment, hit, make mincemeat of*, pound, powder, pulverize, rive, scrunch, shatter, shiver, slam, slug,* splinter, squash, squish, trash, wallop; SEE CONCEPTS 246,252

smash [*v2*] *defeat, destroy*
annihilate, break up, decimate, demolish, destruct, disrupt, lay in ruins*, lay waste*, overthrow, overturn, put out of action*, put out of commission*, raze, ruin, shatter, tear down, topple, trash, tumble, wreck; SEE CONCEPTS 95,252

smashup [*n*] *wreck*
accident, collision, crack-up*, crash, fender bender, impact, jolt, mess, pile-up*, rear-ender*, sideswipe, total, wreckage; SEE CONCEPTS 189,260,674

smear [*v1*] *rub on, spread over*
apply, bedaub, besmirch, blur, coat, cover, dab, daub, defile, dirty, discolor, overlay, overspread, patch, plaster, slop, smudge, soil, spatter, spray, sprinkle, stain, sully, taint, tar, tarnish; SEE CONCEPTS 172,202,215

smear [*v2*] *tarnish a reputation*
asperse, bad-mouth*, befoul, besmirch, blacken, blackguard*, blister, calumniate, defame, defile, denigrate, discolor, drag through mud*, give a black eye*, hit*, libel, malign, pan*, poormouth*, rap*, rip up*, scorch*, slam*, slander, sling mud*, slur, sully, taint, traduce, vilify; SEE CONCEPTS 54,63

smear campaign [*n*] *mudslinging*
character assassination, defamation of character, dragging one's name through the mud*, slander, whispering campaign; SEE CONCEPTS 54,192,278

smell [*n*] *odor*
aroma, bouquet, emanation, essence, flavor, fragrance, incense, perfume, redolence, savor, scent, spice, stench, stink, tang, trace, trail, whiff; SEE CONCEPTS 590,599

smell [*v1*] *perceive with the nose*
breathe, detect, discover, find, get a whiff*, identify, inhale, nose, scent, sniff, snuff; SEE CONCEPTS 590,601,602

smell [*v2*] *have an odor*
be malodorous, funk*, reek, smell to high heaven*, stench, stink, whiff; SEE CONCEPT 600

smelly [*adj*] *having a bad odor*
evil-smelling, fetid, foul, foul-smelling, funky*, high, malodorous, mephitic, noisome, olid, putrid, rancid, rank, reeking, stinking, strong, strong-smelling, whiffy*; SEE CONCEPT 598

smidgen [*n*] *tiny amount*
atom, chicken feed*, crumb, dab, dash, drop, fraction, fragment, grain, iota, little bit, mite, morsel, particle, pinch, scintilla, scrap, shard, shaving, shred, sliver, small amount, small bit, small quantity, speck, tad, taste, trace, wee bit*, whiff, whisper; SEE CONCEPTS 529,831,835

smile [*v*] *put on a happy expression*
beam, be gracious, express friendliness, express tenderness, grin, laugh, look amused, look delighted, look happy, look pleased, simper, smirk; SEE CONCEPT 185

smirk [*n*] *sly smile*
beam, grin, leer, simper, smug look, sneer; SEE CONCEPT 185

smog [*n*] *air pollution*
acid rain, carbon dioxide, fog, haze, smoke, soot; SEE CONCEPT 720

smoke [*n*] *fume; cigarette*
butt*, cig*, exhaust, fog, gas, mist, pollution, smog, soot, vapor; SEE CONCEPT 720

smoke detector [*n*] *smoke alarm*
danger signal, emergency alarm, fire alarm, fire bell, heat sensor, siren; SEE CONCEPTS 269,463

smoky [*adj*] *hazy, sooty*
begrimed, black, burning, caliginous, dingy, fumy, gray, grimy, messy, murky, reeking, silvery, smoke-colored, smoldering, thick, vaporous; SEE CONCEPTS 485,618

smolder [*v*] *burn, simmer*
boil, bubble, churn, consume, erupt, explode, ferment, fester, fulminate, fume, seethe, smoke, steam, stir; SEE CONCEPT 35,249

smooch [*v*] *kiss*
butterfly*, French*, greet, lip*, make out*, mush*, neck*, park*, peck, pucker up*, smack; SEE CONCEPTS 185,375

smooth [*adj1*] *level, unwrinkled; flowing*
bland, continuous, creamy, easy, effortless, equable, even, flat, fluent, fluid, flush, frictionless, gentle, glassy, glossy, hairless, horizontal, invariable, lustrous, mild, mirrorlike, monotonous, peaceful, plain, planate, plane, polished, quiet, regular, rhythmic, rippleless, serene, shaven, shiny, silky, sleek, soft, soothing, stable, steady, still, tranquil, unbroken, undeviating, undisturbed, uneventful, uniform, uninterrupted, unruffled, untroubled, unvarying, velvety; SEE CONCEPTS 406,480,606

sl

sm

smooth [*adj2*] *suave in behavior*
agreeable, bland, civilized, courteous, courtly, facile, genial, glib, ingratiating, mellow, mild, persuasive, pleasant, polite, slick, smarmy*, unctuous, urbane; SEE CONCEPT *401*

smooth [*v1*] *make level*
burnish, clear, even, flatten, flush, glaze, gloss, grade, iron, lay, level, make uniform, perfect, plane, polish, press, refine, round, sand, sleek, slick, varnish; SEE CONCEPTS *137,250*

smooth [*v2*] *make peace*
allay, alleviate, appease, assuage, calm, comfort, cool*, ease, extenuate, facilitate, iron out, mellow, mitigate, mollify, palliate, pat, pave the way*, soften, stroke, take the edge off*, take the sting out*; SEE CONCEPTS *7,22*

smother [*v*] *extinguish; cover, hide*
asphyxiate, choke, collect, compose, conceal, control, cool, cork, douse, envelop, heap, hush up*, inundate, keep back, kill, muffle, overwhelm, quash, quell, quench, rein, repress, restrain, shower, shroud, simmer down, snuff, squelch, stamp out, stifle, strangle, suffocate, suppress, surround, throttle; SEE CONCEPTS *130,172,188,234*

smudge [*n*] *dirt smear*
blemish, blot, blur, macule, smut, smutch, soiled spot, spot; SEE CONCEPT *723*

smudge [*v*] *smear, dirty*
begrime, blacken, blotch, blur, daub, defile, foul, grime, mark, plaster, slop, smirch, soil, spatter, sully, taint, tarnish; SEE CONCEPT *254*

smug [*adj*] *pleased with oneself*
complacent, conceited, egoistic, egotistical, holier-than-thou*, hotshot*, pompous, priggish, puffed-up*, self-contented, self-righteous, self-satisfied, snobbish, stuck on oneself*, stuck-up*, stuffy, superior, vainglorious; SEE CONCEPTS *404,542*

smuggle [*v*] *transfer illegal goods*
bootleg, deal, export, hide, moonshine*, pirate, push, run, run contraband*, run rum*, snake in*; SEE CONCEPT *192*

smut [*n*] *pornography*
adult material, adult movie, bawdiness, dirt, dirty movie, erotica, filth, girlie magazine, hard-core pornography, indecency, indecent material, obscene materials, obscenity, porn, porno, porno film, sexploitation, sexually explicit material, skin flick, smut, soft-core pornography, stag film, X-rated material, X-rated movie; SEE CONCEPTS *267,372,545*

smutty [*adj*] *obscene, vulgar*
bawdy, blue*, coarse, crude, dirty, filthy, foul, immoral, improper, indecent, indelicate, lewd, nasty, off-color, pornographic, prurient, racy, raunchy, raw, risqué, rough, salacious, salty, scatological, suggestive, X-rated*; SEE CONCEPTS *267,372,545*

snack [*n*] *tiny meal*
bite, bite to eat*, break, eats*, goodies*, grub*, light meal, lunch, luncheon, midnight snack, morsel, munch*, nibble, nosh*, pickings, piece, refreshment, tea, tidbit; SEE CONCEPTS *457,459*

snafu [*n*] *mistake*
blooper*, blunder, bungle, confusion, error, false step, faux pas, flub*, foul-up, goof-up, mess, miscalculation, misjudgment, misunderstanding, mix-up, oversight, screw-up*, slip, slipup*; SEE CONCEPTS *101,230,410*

snag [*n*] *complication in situation*
bar, barrier, blockade, brake, bug*, catch, Catch-22, clog, crimp, cropper, crunch, curb, difficulty, disadvantage, drag*, drawback, fix*, glitch, hamper, hitch, hold-up*, hole*, hurdle, impediment, inconvenience, knot, obstacle, obstruction, pickle*, problem, puzzler, scrape, spot, stumbling block, the rub*, tight spot*; SEE CONCEPTS *666,674*

snag [*v*] *catch on something*
hole, nail, rip, run into, tear; SEE CONCEPT *214*

snaky [*adj1*] *winding*
anfractuous, convoluted, entwined, flexuous, indirect, meandering, meandrous, serpentine, sinuous, tortuous, twisted, twisting, writhing, zigzag; SEE CONCEPT *581*

snaky [*adj2*] *devious, sly*
crafty, insidious, lurking, perfidious, slinking, sneaky, subtle, treacherous, venomous, vipery, virulent; SEE CONCEPT *401*

snap [*n*] *easy thing to accomplish*
breeze*, child's play*, cinch, duck soup*, ease, easy as pie*, kid stuff*, no problem, picnic*, pie*, smooth sailing*, soft touch*, walkover*; SEE CONCEPT *693*

snap [*v1*] *separate, break*
click, come apart, crack, crackle, fracture, give way, pop; SEE CONCEPTS *98,246*

snap [*v2*] *bite, seize*
bite at, catch, clutch, grab, grasp, grip, jerk, lurch, nip, snatch, twitch, yank; SEE CONCEPTS *90,191*

snap [*v3*] *speak sharply*
bark, flare, flash, fly off the handle*, get angry, growl, grumble, grunt, jump down throat*, lash out, retort, roar, snarl, snort, take it out on*, vent, yell; SEE CONCEPTS *54,77*

snappy [*adj1*] *nasty, irritable*
cross, disagreeable, edgy, fractious, hasty, huffy, petulant, quick-tempered, snappish, tart, testy, touchy, waspish; SEE CONCEPTS *267,401*

snappy [*adj2*] *fashionable*
chic, classy, dapper, dashing, fly*, in good taste, modish, natty, sharp, smart, stylish, swank*, tony*, trendy, up-to-the-minute, with style; SEE CONCEPT *589*

snappy [*adj3*] *fast*
abrupt, breakneck, expeditious, fleet, harefooted, hasty, immediate, instant, on-the-spot, quick, rapid, speedy, sudden, swift, unpremeditated; SEE CONCEPTS *588,799*

snare [*n*] *trap*
allurement, bait, booby trap*, catch, come-on*, deception, decoy, enticement, entrapment, inveiglement, lure, net, noose, pitfall, quicksand, seducement, temptation, trick, wire*; SEE CONCEPTS *529,674*

snare [*v*] *catch, trap*
arrest, bag*, corral*, decoy, enmesh, entangle, entrap, get hands on*, involve, land, lure, net, pull in, round up, seduce, seize, tempt, wire*; SEE CONCEPTS *11,90*

snarl [*n*] *complication, mess*
chaos, clutter, complexity, confusion, disarray, disorder, entanglement, intricacy, intricateness, jam, jungle, knot, labyrinth, maze, mishmash, morass, muddle, muss, skein, swarm, tangle, web; SEE CONCEPTS *663,666,674*

snarl [*v1*] *grumble*
abuse, bark, bluster, bully, complain, fulminate,

gnarl, gnash teeth, growl, mumble, murmur, mutter, quarrel, show teeth, snap, threaten, thunder, yelp; SEE CONCEPT 77

snarl [v2] *complicate, mess up*
confuse, embroil, enmesh, ensnarl, entangle, entwine, involve, muck, muddle, perplex, ravel, tangle; SEE CONCEPTS 16,158

snatch [n] *small part*
bit, fragment, piece, smattering, snippet, spell; SEE CONCEPTS 264,832

snatch [v] *grab away*
abduct, catch, clap hands on, clutch, collar*, gain, get fingers on*, grapple, grasp, grip, jerk, jump, kidnap, make off with, nab, nail*, pluck, pull, rescue, seize, snag, spirit away, steal, take, win, wrench, wrest, yank; SEE CONCEPTS 90,191

snazzy [adj] *stylish*
attractive, beautiful, chic, chichi*, classy, dapper, dashing, dressed to kill*, dressy, fashionable, flashy, in vogue, jazzy, nifty, now*, ritzy, sharp, slick*, smart, snappy, sophisticated, swank*, trendy, upscale, uptown, voguish; SEE CONCEPTS 579,589

sneak [n] *person who is very dishonest*
cheater, con artist, coward, cur, dastard, heel*, informer, louse, rascal, reptile, scoundrel, skunk*, slink*, snake*, snake in grass*, toad*, weasel*, wretch; SEE CONCEPT 412

sneak [v] *move stealthily*
ambush, case, cheat, cower, crawl, creep, deceive, delude, evade, glide, gumshoe*, hide, lurk, mooch, move secretly, ooze, pad, pass, prowl, pussyfoot*, secrete, shirk, sidle, skulk, slide, slink, slip, slither, sly, smuggle, snake, snook, spirit, steal, worm; SEE CONCEPTS 151,188

sneaker [n] *running shoe*
basketball shoe, cleat, footgear, footwear, gym shoe, hightop*, rubber-soled shoe, shoe, sneak, tennis shoe; SEE CONCEPT 451

sneaky [adj] *underhanded, dishonest*
base, contemptible, cowardly, deceitful, devious, disingenuous, double-dealing*, duplicitous, furtive, guileful, indirect, low, malicious, mean, nasty, recreant, secretive, shifty, slippery, sly, sneaking, snide, stealthy, surreptitious, tricky, underhand, unreliable, unscrupulous, untrustworthy, yellow*; SEE CONCEPTS 267,401,542

sneer [v] *mock, condemn*
affront, belittle, burlesque, caricature, crack, curl one's lip at*, decry, deride, detract, disdain, disparage, dump, fleer, flout, gibe, gird, give Bronx cheer, grin, hold in contempt*, hold up to ridicule*, insult, jeer, jest, lampoon, laugh at, leer, look down on, put down, quip at, rally, rank out, ridicule, satirize, scoff, scorn, slam, slight, smile, sneeze at*, sniff at*, snigger, swipe, taunt, travesty, turn up one's nose*, twit, underrate; SEE CONCEPTS 30,52,54

sneeze at [v] *disregard*
blink at*, brush aside, brush away, brush off, discount, have no use for*, laugh off*, let pass*, look the other way*, overlook, pass over, pay no attention to, pay no heed to, pay no mind*, shut eyes to*, slight, snub, take lightly, take no notice of, turn a blind eye*, turn a deaf ear*; SEE CONCEPT 30

snicker/snigger/sniggle [v] *laugh at mockingly*
chortle, chuckle, giggle, guffaw, hee-haw, smirk, sneer, teehee, titter; SEE CONCEPT 77

snide [adj] *hateful, nasty*
base, cynical, disparaging, hurtful, insinuating, malicious, mean, sarcastic, scornful, sneering, spiteful, unkind; SEE CONCEPT 401

sniff [v] *breathe in*
detect, inhale, inspire, nose, scent, smell, snift, snuff, snuffle; SEE CONCEPTS 601,602

snippy [adj] *curt*
abrupt, blunt, brief, brusque, churlish, gruff, impertinent, rude, sharp, sharp-tongued, snappish, snippety; SEE CONCEPT 267

snitch [n] *informer*
betrayer, blabbermouth*, canary*, deep throat*, double-crosser, fink*, informant, narc*, nark*, rat*, sneak, snitcher, source, squealer*, stoolie*, stool pigeon*, tattler, tattletale, tipster*, turncoat, weasel*, whistle-blower; SEE CONCEPTS 348,354,423

snitch [v1] *steal*
burglarize, carry off, defraud, embezzle, heist, hold up, keep, lift*, loot, make off with*, pickpocket, pilfer, pillage, pinch*, plunder, poach, remove, rip off*, shoplift, swipe, take, walk off with*; SEE CONCEPT 139

snitch [v2] *inform*
betray, blab*, confess, give away, leak, rat on*, squeal, tattle, tell, tell on, tip, turn in; SEE CONCEPT 60

snob [n] *person who looks down on others*
braggart, highbrow, name-dropper, parvenu, pretender, smarty pants*, stiff neck*, upstart; SEE CONCEPT 423

snobbish [adj] *stuck-up, conceited*
aloof, arrogant, condescending, egotistic, haughty, high-and-mighty*, high-flown*, high-hat*, ostentatious, overbearing, patronizing, persnickety*, pompous, pretentious, putting on airs*, remote, sniffy*, snippy*, snooty*, snotty*, supercilious, superior, swanky, tony*, uppish, uppity*; SEE CONCEPT 401

snoop [n] *person who noses around*
busybody, butt-in*, detective, eavesdropper, ferret, gumshoe*, meddler, peeping Tom*, pragmatist, pry, pryer, quidnunc, rubberneck*, scout, sleuth, snooper; SEE CONCEPTS 348,423

snoop [v] *nose around*
busybody*, interfere, intrude, meddle, mess with, mouse*, nose, peek, peep, peer, poke, poke nose in*, snook, spy, stare; SEE CONCEPTS 216,384,623

snooty [adj] *haughty*
arrogant, cavalier*, conceited, condescending, egotistic, egotistical, high and mighty*, hoity-toity, la-di-da*, lofty, on a high horse*, pompous, pretentious, snobbish, snotty*, stuck-up*, superior, uppity*; SEE CONCEPT 401

snooze [n] *light sleep*
catnap, doze, forty winks*, nap, siesta, slumber; SEE CONCEPT 315

snooze [v] *sleep lightly*
catnap, doze, drop off, drowse, nap, nod off*, siesta, slumber, take forty winks*; SEE CONCEPTS 210,315

snore [v] *make sounds when sleeping*
breathe heavily, saw logs*, saw wood*, sleep, snort, snuffle, wheeze; SEE CONCEPTS 77,315

snotty [adj] *arrogant*
cheeky, cocky, conceited, fresh, haughty, high and mighty*, highfalutin'*, impertinent, know-it-all*, la-de-da*, pompous, pretentious, puffed

sm
sn

up*, sassy, self-important, smart-alecky, smug, snippy*, snobby, snooty, stuck-up*, uppity; SEE CONCEPTS *401,404*

snub [v] *give someone the cold shoulder*
act cool*, boycott, brush off*, burr, censure, chill, cool, cut, cut dead*, disdain, disregard, duck, give the brush*, humble, humiliate, ice*, ice out*, ignore, look coldly upon, look right through*, mortify, neglect, not give time of day*, offend, ostracize, pass up, put down, put the chill on*, rebuff, scold, scorn, scratch, shame, shun, slight, slur, snob, swank, upstage; SEE CONCEPTS *30,54,384*

snug [adj] *cozy, warm*
close, comfortable, comfy, compact, convenient, cushy, easeful, easy, homelike, homely, intimate, neat, restful, sheltered, snug as a bug in a rug*, soft, substantial, tight, trim, well-off; SEE CONCEPT *485*

snuggle [v] *cuddle*
bundle, burrow, curl up, grasp, huddle, hug, nestle, nuzzle, snug, spoon; SEE CONCEPTS *190,201*

soak [v] *drench, wet*
absorb, assimilate, bathe, damp, dip, drink, drown, dunk, flood, imbrue, immerge, immerse, impregnate, infiltrate, infuse, macerate, marinate, merge, moisten, penetrate, percolate, permeate, pour into, pour on, saturate, seethe, soften, sop, souse, steep, submerge, take in, wash, water, waterlog; SEE CONCEPT *256*

soaked [adj] *saturated*
dank, drenched, dripping, drowned, soaking, sodden, soggy, sopping, soppy, soused, waterlogged, wet, wringing-wet; SEE CONCEPT *603*

soar [v] *climb, fly*
arise, ascend, aspire, escalate, glide, lift, mount, rise, rocket, sail, shoot, shoot up, skyrocket, top, tower, up, uprear, wing; SEE CONCEPTS *148,150*

soaring [adj] *high*
aerial, ascending, climbing, elevated, flying, going through the ceiling*, going through the roof*, high-reaching, lofty, sky-high, steep, towering; SEE CONCEPTS *779,782*

sob [v] *cry hard*
bawl, blub, blubber, boohoo*, break down, cry a river*, cry convulsively, cry eyes out*, howl, lament, shed tears, snivel, turn on waterworks*, wail, weep, whimper; SEE CONCEPTS *185,410*

sober [adj1] *not partaking of alcohol*
abstaining, abstemious, abstinent, ascetic, calm, clear-headed, cold sober*, continent, controlled, dry, moderate, nonindulgent, not drunk, on the wagon*, restrained, sedate, self-possessed, serious, steady, temperate, took the pledge*; SEE CONCEPT *401*

sober [adj2] *calm, peaceful; dull*
abnegating, abstaining, calm, clear-headed, cold, collected, composed, constrained, cool, dark, disciplined, dispassionate, down-to-earth*, drab, earnest, eschewing, forgoing, grave, hard-boiled*, imperturbable, inhibited, levelheaded, low-key, lucid, no-nonsense, pacific, peaceful, plain, practical, quiet, rational, realistic, reasonable, reserved, restrained, sedate, serene, serious, severe, soft, solemn, somber, sound, staid, steady, subdued, toned down, unexcited, unimpassioned, unruffled; SEE CONCEPTS *401,542*

sobriety [n] *abstinence*
abstaining, abstemiousness, continence, moderation, refraining, self-restraint, soberness, teetotalism, temperance; SEE CONCEPT *633*

sobriquet [n] *nickname*
AKA*, alias, anonym, appellation, assumed name, byname, handle*, label, moniker, nom de guerre, nom de plume, nomenclature, pen name, pet name*, professional name, pseudonym, tag*; SEE CONCEPTS *268,683*

so-called [adj] *supposed*
alleged, allegedly, commonly named, formal, nominal, ostensible, pretended, professed, purported, self-named, self-styled, soi-disant, supposed, titular, wrongly named; SEE CONCEPT *552*

sociable [adj] *friendly, outgoing*
accessible, affable, approachable, close, clubby*, companionable, conversable, convivial, cordial, familiar, genial, good-natured, gregarious, intimate, neighborly, regular, social, warm; SEE CONCEPTS *401,555*

social [adj] *public, friendly*
amusing, civil, collective, common, communal, communicative, community, companionable, convivial, cordial, diverting, entertaining, familiar, general, gracious, gregarious, group, hospitable, informative, mannerly, neighborly, nice, organized, pleasant, pleasurable, polished, polite, popular, public, sociable, societal; SEE CONCEPTS *536,555*

socialism [n] *socialist government*
Bolshevism, collective ownership, collectivism, communism, Fabianism, Leninism, Maoism, Marxism, state ownerhsip; SEE CONCEPT *301*

socialite [n] *aristocrat*
blueblood, Brahmin, deb*, debutante, gentleperson, lace curtain*, member of the upper class, noble, patrician, silk stocking, upper cruster; SEE CONCEPT *423*

socialize [v] *be friendly at gatherings*
associate, chum with*, club*, consort, entertain, fraternize, get about, get around, get together, go out, hang around with*, hang out, hobnob, join, keep company, league, make advances, make the rounds*, mingle, mix, pal around*, run with*, tie up with*; SEE CONCEPT *384*

society [n1] *humankind, people*
association, camaraderie, civilization, commonality, commonwealth, community, companionship, company, comradeship, culture, friendship, general public, humanity, jungle*, nation, population, public, rat race*, social order, world, zoo*; SEE CONCEPTS *379,417*

society [n2] *organization, institution*
alliance, association, circle, clan, clique, club, companionship, comradeship, corporation, coterie, gang, group, guild, hookup, institute, league, network, order, outfit, ring, sodality, syndicate, tie-in*, tie-up*, union; SEE CONCEPTS *381,387*

society [n3] *upper class of people*
aristocracy, beau monde*, beautiful people*, country set*, elite, flower*, gentry, glitterati*, haut monde, high society, jet set*, main line, patriciate, polite society, quality, smart set*, top drawer*, upper crust*, who's who*; SEE CONCEPTS *387,388,417*

sociopath [n] *psychopath*
antisocial personality, crazy person, deranged person, insane person, lunatic, mad person, maniac, psycho*, psychotic, schizoid*; SEE CONCEPT *412*

sock [n/v] *hit hard*
beat, belt, bop, buffet, chop, clout, cuff, ding, nail, paste, punch, slap, smack, smash, soak, whack; SEE CONCEPT *189*

sofa [n] *couch*
chaise longue, chesterfield, convertible couch, davenport, daybed, divan, futon, love seat, ottoman, settee, sofa bed, window seat; SEE CONCEPT *443*

soft [adj1] *cushioned, squishy*
bendable, comfortable, comfy, cottony, cozy, creamy, cushiony, cushy, delicate, doughy, downy, ductile, easeful, easy, elastic, feathery, fine, flabby, fleecy, fleshy, flexible, flimsy, flocculent, flowing, fluffy, fluid, formless, furry, gelatinous, impressible, limp, malleable, moldable, mushy, pappy, pithy, plastic, pliable, pulpy, quaggy, rounded, satiny, silken, silky, smooth, snug, spongy, squashy, supple, thin, velvety, yielding; SEE CONCEPTS *488,606*

soft [adj2] *faint, temperate*
ashen, balmy, bland, caressing, comfortable, cool, cushy, delicate, diffuse, dim, dimmed, dulcet, dull, dusky, faint, gentle, hazy, lenient, light, low, low-key, mellifluous, mellow, melodious, mild, misty, murmured, muted, pale, pallid, pastel, pleasing, quiet, restful, shaded, smooth, sober, soothing, subdued, sweet, tinted, toned down, twilight, understated, wan, whispered; SEE CONCEPTS *525,537,592,618*

soft [adj3] *compassionate*
affectionate, amiable, benign, courteous, easy, easy-going, effortless, gentle, gracious, indulgent, kind, kindly, lax, lenient, liberal, manageable, overindulgent, permissive, pitying, sensitive, sentimental, simple, spineless, sympathetic, tender, tender-hearted, undemanding, weak; SEE CONCEPT *401*

soft [adj4] *out of condition*
doughy, fat, flabby, flaccid, fleshy, formless, gone to seed*, limp, out of shape*, overindulged, pampered, untrained, weak; SEE CONCEPTS *314,485*

soft [adj5] *stupid*
daft, fatuous, feeble-minded, foolish, silly, simple, witless; SEE CONCEPT *402*

soften [v] *calm, soothe*
abate, allay, alleviate, appease, assuage, become tender, bend, cushion, diminish, disintegrate, dissolve, ease, enfeeble, give, knead, lessen, lighten, lower, mash, mellow, melt, mitigate, moderate, modify, moisten, mollify, palliate, qualify, quell, relax, relent, still, subdue, temper, tenderize, thaw, tone down, turn down, weaken, yield; SEE CONCEPT *250*

softhearted [adj] *tender*
all heart*, benevolent, big-hearted, bleedingheart*, caring, charitable, compassionate, considerate, emotional, forgiving, generous, gentle, kind, lenient, merciful, moving, sensitive, sentimental, soft, sympathetic, tenderhearted, warm, warmhearted; SEE CONCEPTS *401,542*

softly [adv] *lightly*
agilely, airily, breezily, carelessly, daintily, delicately, faintly, gently, gingerly, gradually, nimbly, quietly, smoothly, tenderly; SEE CONCEPTS *538,544,584*

soft-spoken [adj] *quiet*
close-mouthed, gentle, hushed, hushful, low, low-keyed, low-pitched, mild, muffled, peaceful, reserved, silent, soft, still; SEE CONCEPTS *592,594*

software [n] *computer program*
application software, bundled software, courseware, file management system, freeware, groupware, operating system, presentation software, productivity software, program, shareware, spreadsheet, systems software, vaporware; SEE CONCEPTS *269,463*

soggy [adj] *damp or soaking*
clammy, dank, dripping, heavy, humid, moist, mucky, muggy, mushy, pasty, pulpy, saturated, soaked, sodden, soft, sopping, spongy, sticky, sultry, waterlogged; SEE CONCEPT *603*

soil [n1] *earth, dirt*
clay, dry land, dust, grime, ground, land, loam, soot, terra firma; SEE CONCEPT *509*

soil [n2] *land where one lives*
country, home, homeland, homestead, region, spread, terra firma; SEE CONCEPTS *198,510,511*

soil [v] *make dirty*
bedraggle, befoul, begrime, besmirch, contaminate, crumb, debase, defile, degrade, dirty, discolor, disgrace, foul, grime, maculate, mess, mess up, muck*, muck up*, muddy, muss*, muss up*, pollute, shame, smear, smudge, spatter, spoil, spot, stain, sully, taint, tar, tarnish; SEE CONCEPT *254*

sojourn [n] *brief travel; visit*
layover, residence, rest, stay, stop, stopover, tarriance, vacation; SEE CONCEPTS *224,226,227*

sojourn [v] *travel briefly; visit*
abide, dwell, inhabit, linger, lodge, nest, perch, reside, rest, roost, squat, stay, stay over, stop, tarry, vacation; SEE CONCEPTS *224,226,227*

solace [n] *comfort, peace*
alleviation, assuagement, condolement, condolence, consolation, pity, relief; SEE CONCEPTS *7,22,410*

solace [v] *give comfort, peace*
allay, alleviate, buck up, cheer, comfort, condole with, console, mitigate, soften, soothe, upraise; SEE CONCEPTS *7,22*

soldier [n] *person serving in military*
airforce member, cadet, cavalryperson, commando, conscript, draftee, enlisted person, fighter, GI*, Green Beret, guard, guerrilla, gunner, infantry, infantryperson, marine, mercenary, military person, musketeer, officer, paratrooper, pilot, private, rank, recruit, scout, selectee, serviceperson, soldier, soldier-at-arms, trooper, veteran, volunteer, warmonger, warrior; SEE CONCEPT *358*

sole [adj] *alone, singular*
ace, exclusive, individual, lone, one, one and only, onliest, only, only one, particular, remaining, separate, single, solitary, solo, unique, unshared; SEE CONCEPTS *555,564,577*

solely [adv] *only, alone*
barely, but, completely, entirely, exclusively, individually, merely, onliest, purely, simply, single-handedly, singly, singularly, totally, undividedly, wholly; SEE CONCEPTS *544,577*

solemn [adj1] *quiet, serious*
austere, brooding, cold sober*, deliberate, dignified, downbeat, earnest, funereal, glum, grave, heavy, intense, matter of life and death*, moody, no fooling*, no-nonsense*, pensive, portentous, reflective, sedate, sober, somber, staid, stern, thoughtful, weighty; SEE CONCEPTS *403,542*

sn
so

solemn [*adj2*] *impressive, sacred*
august, awe-inspiring, ceremonial, ceremonious, conventional, devotional, dignified, divine, formal, full, grand, grave, hallowed, holy, imposing, impressive, magnificent, majestic, momentous, ostentatious, overwhelming, plenary, religious, reverential, ritual, sanctified, stately, venerable; SEE CONCEPT *574*

solicit [*v*] *plead for; try to sell*
accost, apply, approach, ask, beg, beseech, bespeak, bum, cadge, call, canvass, challenge, claim, come on to*, crave, demand, desire, drum*, drum up*, entreat, exact, go, hawk, hit on*, hit up*, hustle, implore, importune, inquire, mooch, panhandle, pass the hat*, peddle, petition, postulate, pray, promote, proposition, query, question, refer, request, require, requisition, resort, seduce, seek, sponge, steer, sue for, supplicate, touch, tout, turn, whistle for*; SEE CONCEPTS *53,345*

solicitous [*adj*] *worried*
anxious, appetent, apprehensive, ardent, athirst, attentive, avid, beside oneself, careful, caring, concerned, devoted, eager, earnest, heedful, impatient, keen, loving, mindful, raring, regardful, tender, thirsty, troubled, uneasy, worried sick*, worried stiff*, zealous; SEE CONCEPT *403*

solicitude [*n*] *worry, anxiety*
attention, attentiveness, care, compunction, concern, concernment, consideration, consideration, disquiet, disquietude, heed, presentiment, qualm, regard, scruple, tender loving care*, TLC*, unease, uneasiness, watchfulness; SEE CONCEPT *410*

solid [*adj1*] *hard, dimensional*
brick wall*, close, compact, compacted, concentrated, concrete, consolidated, dense, firm, fixed, heavy, hefty, hulk, hunk, husky, massed, material, physical, rock, rocklike, rooted, secure, set, sound, stable, strong, sturdy, substantial, thick, tight, unshakable; SEE CONCEPTS *483,604*

solid [*adj2*] *continuous, complete*
agreed, brick wall*, consecutive, consentient, continued, firm, like a rock, regular, set in stone*, stable, steady, unalloyed, unanimous, unbroken, undivided, uninterrupted, united, unmixed; SEE CONCEPTS *482,488,531*

solid [*adj3*] *dependable, reliable*
cogent, constant, decent, estimable, genuine, good, law-abiding, levelheaded, pure, real, satisfactory, satisfying, sensible, serious, sober, sound, stalwart, steadfast, trustworthy, trusty, upright, upstanding, valid, worthy; SEE CONCEPTS *401,534*

solidarity [*n*] *unity*
accord, agreement, alliance, comradeship, confederation, consensus, federation, fellowship, harmony, indivisibility, oneness, sameness, support, teamwork, unanimity, undividedness, unification, uniformity, union; SEE CONCEPTS *664, 714,837*

solidify [*v*] *harden*
amalgamate, anneal, bake, cake, cement, clot, coagulate, cohere, congeal, crystallize, densify, dry, firm, freeze, jell, petrify, set, stiffen, strengthen, thicken; SEE CONCEPTS *250,469*

solitary [*adj*] *alone, single; unsociable*
aloof, antisocial, cloistered, companionless, deserted, desolate, distant, eremetic, forsaken, friendless, hermitical, hidden, individual, introverted, isolated, lone, lonely, lonesome, lorn, misanthropic, offish, only, out-of-the-way*, particular, reclusive, remote, reserved, retired, secluded, separate, sequestered, singular, sole, solo, stag, standoffish, unaccompanied, unapproachable, unattended, uncompanionable, unfrequented, unique, unsocial, withdrawn; SEE CONCEPTS *555,577,583*

solitude [*n*] *aloneness*
confinement, desert, detachment, emptiness, isolation, loneliness, loneness, lonesomeness, peace and quiet*, privacy, quarantine, reclusiveness, retirement, seclusion, separateness, silence, solitariness, waste, wasteland, wilderness, withdrawal; SEE CONCEPTS *388,673,714*

solo [*adj*] *alone*
by oneself, companionless, friendless, individual, in solitary*, me and my shadow*, me and I*, on one's own, single, solitary, stag, unaccompanied, unaided, unassisted, unescorted, unmarried; SEE CONCEPTS *577,583*

solution [*n1*] *answer, resolution*
Band-Aid*, clarification, elucidation, explanation, explication, key, pay dirt*, quick fix*, result, solving, the ticket*, unfolding, unraveling, unravelment; SEE CONCEPTS *230,661,712*

solution [*n2*] *mixture of liquid and another substance*
blend, compound, dissolvent, elixir, emulsion, extract, fluid, juice, mix, sap, solvent, suspension; SEE CONCEPTS *260,467*

solve [*v*] *answer, resolve*
break*, clarify, clear up, construe, crack*, deal with, decide, decipher, decode, determine, disentangle, divine, do, elucidate, enlighten, explain, expound, fathom, figure out, find out, fix, get, get right, get to the bottom*, have, hit, hit upon*, illuminate, interpret, iron out*, lick*, make a dent*, make out*, pan out*, put two and two together*, puzzle, reason, settle, think out, unfold, unlock, unravel, unriddle, untangle, work, work out; SEE CONCEPTS *15,18,37*

solvent [*adj*] *financially sound*
able to pay, financially stable, firm, fit, in the pink*, out of the red*, solid, stable; SEE CONCEPTS *314,488*

somber [*adj*] *sad, depressing*
black, bleak, blue*, caliginous, cloudy, dark, depressive, dim, dingy, dire, dismal, dispiriting, doleful, down, drab, dragged, dreary, dull, dusky, earnest, funereal, gloomy, grave, grim, hurting, joyless, lugubrious, melancholy, mournful, murky, no-nonsense, obscure, sad, sedate, sepulchral, serious, shadowy, shady, sober, solemn, sourpuss, staid, tenebrous, weighty; SEE CONCEPTS *403,485,529*

somebody [*n*] *person of fame, importance*
celebrity, dignitary, heavyweight*, household name*, luminary, name*, notable, one, personage, person of note, public figure, so-and-so*, someone*, some person*, star, superstar, VIP*, whoever*; SEE CONCEPT *423*

someday [*adv*] *eventually*
after a while, anytime, at a future time, finally, in a time to come, on a day, one day, one fine day*, one of these days, one time, one time or another, sometime, sooner or later, subsequently, ultimately, yet; SEE CONCEPTS *548,820*

somehow [*adv*] *by some means*
after a fashion, anyhow, anyway, anywise, by

hook or crook*, come what may*, in one way or another, in some such way, in some way, one way or another, somehow or another, somehow or other; SEE CONCEPT 544

something [*n*] *entity*
article, being, commodity, existence, existent, individual, object, substance, thing; SEE CONCEPT 433

sometimes [*adv*] *every now and then*
at intervals, at times, consistently, constantly, ever and again, every so often, frequently, from time to time, here and there, intermittently, now and again, now and then, occasionally, off and on, once in a blue moon*, once in a while, on occasion, periodically, recurrently; SEE CONCEPT 805

somewhat [*adv*] *to some extent*
adequately, a little, bearably, considerably, fairly, far, incompletely, in part, insignificantly, kind of, moderately, more or less, not much, partially, pretty, quite, rather, ratherish, significantly, slightly, some, something, sort of, to a degree, tolerably, well; SEE CONCEPTS 548,569,772

somewhere [*adv*] *in, or at some place*
about, any old place, around, around somewhere, elsewhere, here and there, in one place or another, kicking around*, parts unknown*, scattered, someplace, someplace or another, someplace or other, somewheres; SEE CONCEPT 583

somnolent [*adj*] *sleepy*
asleep, dozy, drowsy, listless, nodding off, out of it*, sleeping, snoozy*, soporific, tired; SEE CONCEPTS 315,539

song [*n*] *melody sung or played with musical instrument*
air, anthem, aria, ballad, canticle, carol, chant, chorale, chorus, ditty, expression, golden oldie*, hymn, lay, lullaby, lyric, melody, number, oldie*, opera, piece, poem, psalm, refrain, rock, rock and roll, round, shanty, strain, tune, verse, vocal; SEE CONCEPTS 262,293,595

sonorous [*adj*] *resonant*
booming, full-voiced, loud, loud-voiced, powerful, resounding, reverberating, rich, ringing, rotund, thundering; SEE CONCEPTS 592,594

soon [*adv*] *in the near future*
anon, any minute now, before long, betimes, by and by, coming down the pike*, directly, early, ere long, expeditiously, fast, fleetly, forthwith, hastily, in a little while, in a minute, in a second, in a short time, in due time, in short order, instantly, in time, lickety-split*, on time, posthaste, presently, promptly, pronto, quick, quickly, rapidly, short, shortly, speedily; SEE CONCEPTS 548,798,820

soothe [*v*] *calm, ease*
allay, alleviate, appease, assuage, balm, becalm, butter up*, calm down, cheer, compose, console, cool, cool off*, dulcify, help, hush, lighten, lull, make nice*, make up, mitigate, mollify, pacify, patch things up*, play up to*, pour oil on*, quiet, quieten, relieve, settle, smooth down, soften, square, still, stroke, subdue, take the edge off*, take the sting out*, tranquilize, unburden, untrouble; SEE CONCEPTS 7,22,110,384

soothing [*adj*] *comforting*
alleviating, calming, consolatory, consoling, easing, mollifying, pacifying, palliative, reassuring, relaxing, relieving, remedying, softening, tranquilizing, warming; SEE CONCEPT 529

soothsayer [*n*] *seer*
augur, channeller, clairvoyant, crystal ball gazer, diviner, forecaster, fortune-teller, medium, oracle, palm reader, prophet, psychic, soothsayer; SEE CONCEPT 423

sophisticated [*adj*] *cosmopolitan, cultured*
adult, artificial, been around, blasé, bored, citified, cool*, couth, cultivated, cynical, disenchanted, disillusioned, experienced, in, in the know*, into*, jaded, jet-set*, knowing, laid-back*, mature, mondaine, on to*, practical, practiced, refined, schooled, seasoned, sharp, skeptical, smooth, stagy*, streetwise, studied, suave, svelte, switched on*, uptown*, urbane, well-bred, wised up*, wise to*, with it*, worldly, worldly wise, world-weary; SEE CONCEPTS 401,404,589

sophisticated [*adj2*] *complex, advanced*
complicated, delicate, elaborate, highly developed, intricate, involved, knotty, labyrinthine, modern, multifaceted, refined, subtle; SEE CONCEPT 562

sophistication [*n*] *culture, style*
composure, elegance, finesse, poise, refinement, savoir faire, savoir vivre, social grace, tact, urbanity, worldliness, worldly wisdom; SEE CONCEPTS 388,633,655

sophomoric [*adj*] *inexperienced*
brash, foolish, naive, reckless, young; SEE CONCEPT 401

soporific [*adj*] *sleepy; sleep-inducing*
anesthetic, balmy, calming, deadening, dozy*, drowsy, dull, hypnotic, mesmerizing, narcotic, nodding, numbing, opiate, quietening, sedative, slumberous, snoozy*, somniferous, somnolent, soothing, tranquilizing; SEE CONCEPTS 537,539

sopping [*adj*] *wet*
dank, drenched, dripping, drowned, saturated, soaked, soaking, sodden, soggy, soppy, soused, water-logged, wringing-wet; SEE CONCEPT 603

sorcerer [*n*] *wizard*
alchemist, augurer, charmer, clairvoyant, conjurer, diviner, enchanter, fortune-teller, magician, medium, necromancer, occultist, seer, shaman, soothsayer, sorceress, thaumaturge, warlock, witch; SEE CONCEPT 361

sorcery [*n*] *black magic, witchcraft*
abracadabra*, alchemy, bewitchment, black art, charm, conjuring, devilry, divination, enchantment, evil eye, hocus-pocus*, hoodoo*, incantation, jinx, magic, mumbo-jumbo*, necromancy, spell, thaumaturgy, voodoo, witchery, witching, wizardry; SEE CONCEPTS 370,689

sordid [*adj*] *dirty, bad, low*
abject, avaricious, base, black, calculated, corrupt, covetous, debauched, degenerate, degraded, despicable, disreputable, dowdy, filthy, foul, grasping, grubby, ignoble, impure, low-down, mean, mercenary, miserable, miserly, nasty, poor, scurvy, seedy, selfish, self-seeking, servile, shabby, shameful, sleazy, slovenly, slum, slummy, small, small-minded, squalid, unclean, uncleanly, ungenerous, venal, vicious, vile, wretched; SEE CONCEPTS 334,545,571

sore [*adj*] *hurt physically*
abscessed, aching, acute, afflicted, annoying, bruised, burned, burning, chafed, critical, distressing, extreme, hurtful, hurting, inflamed, irri-

SO
SO

tated, pained, painful, raw, reddened, sensitive, severe, sharp, smarting, tender, ulcerated, uncomfortable, unpleasant, vexatious; SEE CONCEPT 314

sore [adj2] *angry; hurt mentally*
afflicted, aggrieved, annoyed, annoying, critical, distressing, grieved, grieving, indignant, irked, irritated, pained, peeved, pressing, resentful, sensitive, smarting, stung, troubled, upset, urgent, vexed, weighty; SEE CONCEPT 403

sorrow [n] *extreme upset, grief*
affliction, agony, anguish, bad news*, big trouble*, blow, blues*, care, catastrophe, dejection, depression, distress, dolor, grieving, hardship, heartache, heartbreak, lamenting, melancholy, misery, misfortune, mourning, pain, rain*, regret, remorse, repentence, rue, sadness, suffering, trial, tribulation, trouble, unhappiness, weeping, woe, worry, wretchedness; SEE CONCEPT 410

sorrow [v] *be very upset, grieved*
agonize, bemoan, be sad, bewail, carry on, cry a river*, deplore, eat heart out*, grieve, groan, hang crepe*, lament, moan, mourn, regret, sing the blues*, sob, take on*; weep; SEE CONCEPTS 34,410

sorrowful [adj] *very upset; grieving*
affecting, afflicted, dejected, depressed, disconsolate, distressing, doleful, dolent, full of sorrow, grievous, heartbroken, heartrending, heavy-hearted, hurting, in mourning, in pain, in sorrow, lamentable, lugubrious, melancholy, miserable, mournful, painful, piteous, plaintive, rueful, ruthful, sad, sick at heart, singing the blues*, sorry, tearful, tear-jerking*, unhappy, woebegone, woeful, wretched; SEE CONCEPT 403

sorry [adj1] *remorseful, regretful*
apologetic, attritional, compunctious, conscience-stricken, contrite, guilt-ridden, melted, penitent, penitential, repentant, self-accusing, self-condemnatory, self-reproachful, shamefaced, softened, touched; SEE CONCEPTS 403,545

sorry [adj2] *sad, heartbroken*
bad, disconsolate, distressed, grieved, heavy-hearted, melancholy, mournful, pitiful, rueful, saddened, sorrowful, unhappy; SEE CONCEPT 403

sorry [adj3] *despicable, pathetic*
abject, base, beggarly, cheap, contemptible, deplorable, despisable, disgraceful, dismal, distressing, inadequate, insignificant, mean, miserable, paltry, piteous, pitiable, pitiful, poor, sad, scruffy*, scummy*, scurvy, shabby, shoddy, small, trifling, trivial, unimportant, vile, worthless, wretched; SEE CONCEPTS 485,529

sort [n] *type, variety*
array, batch, battery, body, brand, breed, category, character, class, clutch, denomination, description, family, genus, group, ilk, kind, likes, likes of*, lot, make, nature, number, order, parcel, quality, race, set, species, stamp, stripe, style, suite; SEE CONCEPT 378

sort [v] *place in order*
arrange, assort, button down*, catalogue, categorize, choose, class, classify, comb, cull, distribute, divide, file, grade, group, order, peg, pick, pigeonhole*, put down as, put down for, put in order, put in shape, put to rights*, rank, riddle, screen, select, separate, sift, size up, systematize, tab, typecast, winnow; SEE CONCEPTS 84,158

sortie [n] *armed attack*
assault, charge, invasion, mission, offense, raid, rush, sally*, strike; SEE CONCEPTS 86,317

so-so [adj] *adequate, passable*
average, enough, fair, fairish, fair to middling*, indifferent, mediocre, medium, middling*, moderate, not bad*, okay*, ordinary, respectable, run-of-the-mill*, tolerable, undistinguished; SEE CONCEPTS 533,575

soul [n1] *psyche, inspiration, energy*
anima, animating principle, animation, animus, ardor, bosom, bottom, breast, breath of life, cause, conscience, courage, disposition, ego, elan vital, essence, feeling, fervor, force, genius, heart, individuality, intellect, intelligence, life, marrow, mind, nobility, noumenon, personality, pith, pneuma, principle, quintessence, reason, recesses of heart*, secret self*, spirit, spiritual being, stuff, substance, thought, vital force, vitality, vivacity; SEE CONCEPTS 409,410,411

soul [n2] *being*
body, character, creature, ghost, human being, individual, living soul*, man, mortal, person, personage, phantom, shadow, spirit, umbra, woman; SEE CONCEPT 389

soulful [adj] *emotional*
ardent, deep, expressive, feeling, fervent, fervid, fiery, impassioned, meaningful, moving, passionate, stirred, stirring, tender, touching; SEE CONCEPTS 403,542

soul-searching [n] *introspection*
contemplation, deep thought, heart-searching, meditation, reflection, rumination, self-analysis, self-examination, self-questioning; SEE CONCEPTS 24,410

sound [adj1] *complete, healthy*
alive and kicking*, effectual, entire, firm, fit, flawless, hale, hearty, intact, in the pink*, perfect, right, right as rain*, robust, safe, sane, solid, stable, sturdy, substantial, thorough, total, unblemished, undamaged, undecayed, unhurt, unimpaired, uninjured, up to snuff*, vibrant, vigorous, vital, well, well-constructed, whole, wholesome, wrapped tight*; SEE CONCEPTS 314,488

sound [adj2] *logical, reasonable*
accurate, advisable, all there*, cogent, commonsensical, consequent, convincing, cool*, correct, deep, exact, fair, faultless, flawless, got it together*, impeccable, intellectual, judicious, just, levelheaded, orthodox, precise, profound, proper, prudent, rational, reliable, responsible, right, right-minded, right-thinking, satisfactory, satisfying, sensible, sober, solid, telling, thoughtful, together*, true, trustworthy, valid, well-advised, well-founded, well-grounded, wise; SEE CONCEPTS 403,529,558

sound [adj3] *accepted, established*
all there*, authoritative, canonical, dependable, fair, faithful, fly*, go*, hanging together*, holding together*, holding up*, holding up in wash*, holding water*, kosher*, legal, legit*, loyal, orthodox, proper, proven, received, recognized, reliable, reputable, safe, sanctioned, secure, significant, solid, solvent, stable, standing up*, tried-and-true*, true, valid, washing; SEE CONCEPTS 535,552,582

sound [n] *something heard or audible*
accent, din, harmony, intonation, loudness, melody, modulation, music, noise, note, pitch,

sound [*vl*] *produce noise*
babble, bang, bark, blare, blow, boom, burst, buzz, cackle, chatter, clack, clang, clank, clap, clatter, clink, crash, creak, detonate, echo, emit, explode, hum, jabber, jangle, jar, moan, murmur, patter, play, rattle, reflect, resonate, resound, reverberate, ring, roar, rumble, shout, shriek, shrill, sing, slam, smash, snort, squawk, thud, thump, thunder, toot, trumpet, vibrate, whine, whisper; SEE CONCEPT 65

sound [*v2*] *give the impression*
appear, appear to be, look, seem, strike as being; SEE CONCEPTS 543,716

sound bite [*n*] *very brief broadcast statement*
blurb*, buzzword, clip, excerpt, fifteen minutes of fame*, newsbreak, news item, notation, note, one-liner, outtake, passage, photo opportunity, piece, quotation, quote, saying, selection, slogan, snippet, spot news; SEE CONCEPT 277

soundproof [*adj*] *silent*
hushed, insulated, noiseless, quiet, soundless; SEE CONCEPT 594

soupçon [*n*] *small amount*
atom, crumb, dab, dash, drop, flash, hint, iota, particle, pinch, ray, scintilla, shade, shred, small bit, small quantity, smidgen, sparkle, speck, spot, suggestion, tinge, trace, whiff, whisper; SEE CONCEPTS 529,831

sour [*adj1*] *bad-tasting; gone bad*
acerb, acetic, acetose, acetous, acid, acidic, acidulated, acrid, astringent, bad, biting, bitter, briny, caustic, curdled, cutting, dry, fermented, green, keen, musty, peppery, pungent, pungent, rancid, salty, sharp, soured, sourish, stinging, tart, turned, unpleasant, unripe, unsavory, unwholesome, vinegary, with a kick*; SEE CONCEPTS 462,613

sour [*adj2*] *in a bad mood*
acid, acrid, acrimonious, bitter, churlish, crabby, cynical, disagreeable, discontented, displeasing, embittered, grouchy, grudging, ill-natured, ill-tempered, irritable, jaundiced, on edge*, peevish, rotten, tart, ungenerous, unhappy, unpleasant, waspish; SEE CONCEPTS 403,542

sour [*v*] *alienate*
acidify, curdle, disenchant, embitter, envenom, exacerbate, exasperate, make sour, spoil, turn, turn off; SEE CONCEPTS 14,250

source [*n*] *beginning; point of supply*
antecedent, author, authority, authorship, begetter, birthplace, cause, commencement, connection, dawn, dawning, derivation, determinant, expert, father, fount, fountain*, fountainhead, horse's mouth*, inception, informant, maternity, mother, onset, opening, origin, origination, originator, parent, paternity, provenance, provenience, rise, rising, root, specialist, spring, start, starting point, wellspring; SEE CONCEPT 648

sourpuss [*n*] *grouch*
bellyacher*, crab, crank, crosspatch, curmudgeon, faultfinder, griper, growler, grumbler, grump*, killjoy, moaner, sorehead*, sulker, whiner; SEE CONCEPTS 412,423

souse [*v*] *make very wet*
brine, deluge, dip, douse, drench, drown, duck, dunk, immerse, impregnate, marinate, pickle,

---

sound [*n*]
racket, report, resonance, reverberation, ringing, softness, sonance, sonancy, sonority, sonorousness, static, tenor, tonality, tone, vibration, voice; SEE CONCEPT 595

preserve, seethe, soak, sop, steep, submerge, submerse, waterlog, wet; SEE CONCEPT 256

soused [*adj*] *drunk*
bashed, boozed up*, buzzed*, crocked*, feeling no pain*, flushed*, flying*, groggy, high*, inebriated, intoxicated, juiced*, laced*, liquored up*, lit*, plastered*, potted*, seeing double*, sloshed*, smashed*, stewed*, stoned*, tanked*, three sheets to the wind*, tipsy, totaled*, under the influence, under the table*, wasted*; SEE CONCEPTS 314,545

souvenir [*n*] *keepsake from event*
gift, memento, memorial, relic, remembrance, remembrancer, reminder, token, trophy; SEE CONCEPTS 337,446

sovereign [*adj*] *dominant, effective*
absolute, ascendant, autonomous, chief, commanding, directing, effectual, efficacious, excellent, guiding, highest, imperial, independent, lofty, majestic, monarchal, monarchial, overbearing, paramount, predominant, predominate, preponderant, prevalent, principal, regal, regnant, reigning, royal, ruling, self-governed, supreme, unlimited; SEE CONCEPTS 536,568

sovereign [*n*] *supreme ruler*
autocrat, chief, czar, emperor, empress, king, leader, majesty, monarch, potentate, prince, princess, queen, ruler; SEE CONCEPT 354

sovereignty [*n*] *domination*
ascendancy, ascendant, dominance, dominion, jurisdiction, preeminence, prepotence, prepotency, primacy, supremacy, supreme power, sway; SEE CONCEPT 299

sow [*v*] *plant*
broadcast, disject, disseminate, drill, fling, grow, implant, inseminate, lodge, pitch, propagate, put in, raise, scatter, seed, strew, toss; SEE CONCEPTS 253,257

spa [*n*] *resort*
day spa, fat farm*, health club, health facility, holiday spot, hotel, hot spring*, lodge, mineral spring resort, sanitarium, sauna, whirlpool; SEE CONCEPTS 198,516

space [*n1*] *room, scope*
amplitude, area, arena, blank, breadth, capacity, compass, distance, elbowroom, expanse, expansion, extension, extent, field, gap, headroom, headway, infinity, interval, lacuna, leeway, location, margin, omission, play, range, reach, slot, spaciousness, sphere, spot, spread, stretch, territory, tract, turf, volume, zone; SEE CONCEPTS 739,746,756

space [*n2*] *time interval*
bit, duration, period, season, span, spell, stretch, term, time, while; SEE CONCEPT 807

spacecraft [*n*] *spaceship*
flying saucer, rocket, rocket ship, satellite, shuttle, space capsule, space probe, space shuttle, UFO, unidentified flying object; SEE CONCEPT 504

spacey/spacy [*adj*] *eccentric*
beat*, bizarre, crazy, dizzy, erratic, far out*, flaky, flighty, freakish, kooky, nutty, odd, oddball, offbeat, off-center, off the wall*, out in left field, out to lunch*, peculiar, quirky, spaced out*, strange, way out*, weird; SEE CONCEPTS 547,564

spacious [*adj*] *extensive, expansive*
ample, big, boundless, broad, capacious, cavernous, comfortable, commodious, endless, enor-

so
sp

mous, extended, generous, great, huge, immense, infinite, large, limitless, roomy, sizable, uncrowded, vast, voluminous, wide, widespread; SEE CONCEPTS 481,482,774

span [n] *distance, duration*
amount, compass, extent, interval, length, measure, period, reach, space, spell, spread, stretch, term, time; SEE CONCEPTS 756,807,822

span [v] *stretch over*
arch, bridge, connect, cover, cross, extend, ford, go across, link, pass over, range, reach, traverse, vault; SEE CONCEPT 756

spank [v] *slap, usually on bottom*
belt, blip, box, buffet, cane, chastise, clobber, clout, cuff, flax, flog, hide, larrup*, lash, lather*, leather*, lick, paddle, punch, punish, put over one's knee*, smack, sock, tan*, tan one's hide*, thrash, trim, wallop, welt, whip, whup*; SEE CONCEPT 189

spare [adj1] *extra, reserve*
additional, backup, de trop, emergency, free, in excess, in reserve, in store, lagniappe, leftover, more than enough*, odd, option, over, supererogatory, superfluous, supernumerary, surplus, unoccupied, unused, unwanted; SEE CONCEPTS 771,824

spare [adj2] *thin; sparse*
angular, bony, economical, exiguous, frugal, gaunt, lank, lanky, lean, meager, modest, poor, rangy, rawboned, scant, scanty, scraggy, scrawny, shadow, skimpy, skinny, slender, slight, slim, sparing, sparse, stick, stilt, stingy, wiry; SEE CONCEPTS 490,491,771

spare [v1] *do or manage without*
afford, allow, bestow, dispense with, give, grant, part with, pinch, provide, put by, relinquish, salt away*, save, scrape, scrimp, short, skimp, stint, supply; SEE CONCEPT 129

spare [v2] *forgive; have mercy upon*
absolve, bail out, be lenient, be merciful, discharge, dispense, excuse, exonerate, forbear, get off the hook*, get out of hock*, give a break*, give quarter to, go easy on*, leave, let go, let off*, pardon, pity, privilege from, pull out of the fire*, refrain from, release, relent, relieve from, save bacon*, save from, save neck*, spring; SEE CONCEPTS 50,88,134

sparing [adj] *careful, economical*
avaricious, canny, chary, close, cost-conscious, frugal, humane, mean, money-conscious, parsimonious, provident, prudent, saving, stewardly, stingy, thrifty, tight, tight-fisted, tolerant, ungiving, unwasteful, wary; SEE CONCEPTS 334,401

spark [n] *flash, trace*
atom, beam, fire, flare, flicker, gleam, glint, glitter, glow, hint, jot, nucleus, ray, scintilla, scintillation, scrap, sparkle, spit, vestige; SEE CONCEPTS 519,624,828,831

spark [n] *start, inspire*
animate, excite, kindle, precipitate, provoke, set in motion, set off, stimulate, stir, touch off, trigger; SEE CONCEPT 221

sparkle [n] *glitter, shine*
animation, brilliance, coruscation, dash, dazzle, élan, flash, flicker, gaiety, gleam, glimmer, glint, glitz, glow, life, panache, radiance, scintillation, shimmer, show, spark, spirit, twinkle, vim, vitality, vivacity, zap*, zip*; SEE CONCEPTS 411,624,628

sparkle [v] *glitter, shine*
beam, bubble, coruscate, dance, effervesce, fizz, fizzle, flash, flicker, gleam, glimmer, glint, glisten, glow, scintillate, shimmer, spark, twinkle, wink; SEE CONCEPT 624

sparse [adj] *very few and scattered*
dispersed, exiguous, few and far between, inadequate, infrequent, meager, occasional, poor, rare, scant, scanty, scarce, scrimpy, skimpy, spare, sporadic, thin, uncommon; SEE CONCEPTS 762,789

spasm [n] *twitch, fit*
access, attack, burst, contraction, convulsion, eruption, frenzy, jerk, outburst, pain, paroxysm, seizure, throe, yank; SEE CONCEPTS 185,728

spasmodic [adj] *twitching, erratic*
bits and pieces*, changeable, choppy, convulsive, desultory, fitful, fits and starts*, intermittent, irregular, jerky, on-again-off-again*, periodic, shaky, spastic, sporadic, spotty, spurtive, uncertain; SEE CONCEPTS 482,530,541

spat [n] *dispute, quarrel*
altercation, argument, beef*, bickering, brouhaha, conflict, difference of opinion, disagreement, discord, dissension, embroilment, falling-out, feud, flare-up, fracas, friction, fuss, hubbub, miff*, misunderstanding, row, rumpus*, run-in*, squabble, strife, tiff, words; SEE CONCEPTS 46,106,278

spatter [v] *splash, sprinkle*
bespatter, bestrew, broadcast, dash, daub, dirty, discharge, disperse, dot, douse, dribble, mottle, polka-dot, scatter, shower, slop, smudge, soil, spangle, speck, speckle, splutter, spot, spray, sputter, stipple, strew, swash, wet; SEE CONCEPTS 172,179,256

spawn [v] *produce*
bring forth, create, father, generate, give rise to, hatch, issue, make, mother, originate, parent, procreate, reproduce, sire; SEE CONCEPTS 173,251,374

speak [v1] *talk*
allege, articulate, assert, aver, blab*, break silence, chat, chew*, communicate, converse, convey, declare, deliver, descant, discourse, drawl, enunciate, expatiate, express, gab*, gas*, go*, jaw*, lip*, make known, make public, modulate, mouth, mumble, murmur, mutter, open one's mouth, perorate, pop off*, pronounce, put into words, rap*, say, shout, sound, speak one's piece*, spiel*, spill, state, tell, utter, verbalize, vocalize, voice, whisper, yak*, yakkety-yak*, yammer; SEE CONCEPTS 47,266

speak [v2] *address; give a lecture*
argue, declaim, descant, discourse, get across, harangue, hold forth, orate, pitch, plead, prelect, recite, sermonize, spiel*, spout*, stump, talk; SEE CONCEPTS 60,285

speaker [n] *talker*
after-dinner speaker, announcer, elocutionist, keynoter, lecturer, mouthpiece, orator, public speaker, rhetorician, speechmaker, spokesperson; SEE CONCEPT 348

speak out/speak up [v] *make one's position known*
assert, come out with, declare, have one's say*, insist, let voice be heard*, make oneself heard, make plain, say loud and clear*, sound off*, speak loudly, speak one's mind*, stand up for; SEE CONCEPTS 49,57

spearhead [v] *lead, start*
bring, bring on, cause, direct, get the jump on*, go out in front*, guide, head, helm, influence, initiate, introduce, launch, motivate, move, originate, persuade, pioneer, produce, prompt, quarterback*, run things*, shepherd, spur, trailblaze*; SEE CONCEPTS 68,117,221

special [adj] *distinguished, distinctive; important in own way*
appropriate, best, certain, characteristic, chief, choice, defined, definite, designated, determinate, different, earmarked, especial, exceptional, exclusive, express, extraordinary, festive, first, gala, individual, limited, main, major, marked, memorable, momentous, out of the ordinary, particular, peculiar, personal, primary, proper, rare, red-letter*, reserved, restricted, select, set, significant, smashing*, sole, specialized, specific, uncommon, unique, unreal*, unusual; SEE CONCEPTS 557,564,567

specialist [n] *person who is an expert in a field*
ace, adept, authority, connoisseur, consultant, devotee, doctor, guru*, old hand*, old pro*, pro*, professional, pundit, sage, savant, scholar, technician, veteran, virtuoso; SEE CONCEPTS 347,357

specialize [v] *concentrate on specific area*
be into, develop oneself in, do one's thing*, go in for, have a weakness for*, limit oneself to, practice, practice exclusively, pursue, study intensively, train, work in; SEE CONCEPTS 91,213

specially [adv] *particularly*
distinctively, especially, expressly, in specie, specifically, uniquely; SEE CONCEPT 557

specialty [n] *distinctive feature; concentration*
career, claim to fame, cup of tea*, distinguishing feature, field of concentration, forte, game*, hobby, job, long suit*, magnum opus, major, masterpiece, minor, number, object of attention, object of study, occupation, pièce de résistance*, practice, profession, pursuit, racket*, special, speciality, special project, thing*, vocation, weakness, work; SEE CONCEPT 349

species [n] *class, variety*
breed, category, collection, description, division, group, kind, likes*, lot, nature, number, order, sort, stripe*, type; SEE CONCEPT 378

specific [adj] *particular, distinguishing*
bull's eye*, categorical, characteristic, clean-cut, clear-cut, cut fine*, dead on*, definite, definitive, different, distinct, downright, drawn fine, especial, exact, explicit, express, flat out*, hit nail on head*, individual, limited, on target, outright, peculiar, precise, reserved, restricted, right on, set, sole, special, specialized, straight-out, unambiguous, unequivocal, unique; SEE CONCEPTS 535,557,564

specifically [adv] *expressly, particularly*
accurately, categorically, characteristically, clearly, concretely, correctly, definitely, distinctively, especially, exactly, explicitly, in detail, indicatively, individually, in specie, minutely, peculiarly, pointedly, precisely, respectively, specially; SEE CONCEPTS 557,564

specification [n] *requirement, qualification*
blueprint, condition, designation, detail, item, particular, particularization, spec*, stipulation, term; SEE CONCEPTS 270,646

specify [v] *designate; decide definitely*
be specific, blueprint*, button down*, cite, come to the point, condition, define, detail, determine, draw a picture*, enumerate, establish, finger*, fix, get down to brass tacks*, get to the point*, go into detail, indicate, individualize, instance, inventory, itemize, lay out, limit, list, make, mention, name, particularize, peg, pin down, point out, precise, put down, put finger on*, set, settle, show clearly, slot, specialize, specificate, specificize, spell out, stipulate, tab, tag, tick off; SEE CONCEPTS 18,57

specimen [n] *example, sample*
case, case history, copy, cross section, embodiment, exemplar, exemplification, exhibit, illustration, individual, instance, model, part, pattern, proof, representation, representative, sampling, sort, species, type, unit, variety; SEE CONCEPTS 686,831

specious [adj] *misleading*
apparent, apparently right, beguiling, captious, casuistic, colorable, credible, deceptive, delusive, empty, erroneous, fallacious, false, flattering, hollow, idle, illogical, inaccurate, incorrect, likely, nugatory, ostensible, ostentatious, plausible, presumable, presumptive, pretentious, probable, seeming, sophistic, sophistical, sophisticated, spurious, unsound, untrue, vain, wrong; SEE CONCEPTS 552,582

speck [n] *tiny bit*
atom, blemish, blot, crumb, defect, dot, fault, flaw, fleck, flyspeck, grain, iota, jot, mark, mite, modicum, molecule, mote, particle, point, shred, smidgen, speckle, splotch, spot, stain, trace, whit; SEE CONCEPT 831

speckled [adj] *dotted*
brindled, dappled, flaked, flecked, freckled, mosaic, motley, mottled, particolored, patchy, peppered, punctate, spotted, spotty, sprinkled, stippled, studded, variegated; SEE CONCEPTS 485,618

spectacle [n] *something showy; exhibition*
comedy, curiosity, demonstration, display, drama, event, exposition, extravaganza, marvel, movie, pageant, parade, performance, phenomenon, play, production, representation, scene, show, sight, spectacular, tableau, view, wonder; SEE CONCEPTS 261,529

spectacles [n] *eyeglasses*
bifocals, blinkers*, contact lenses, contacts, glasses, goggles, lorgnette, monocle, pair of glasses, pince-nez, reading glasses, shades*, specs*, sunglasses, trifocals; SEE CONCEPT 446

spectacular [adj] *wonderful, impressive*
amazing, astonishing, astounding, breathtaking, daring, dazzling, dramatic, eye-catching, fabulous, fantastic, grand, histrionic, magnificent, marked, marvelous, miraculous, prodigious, razzle-dazzle*, remarkable, sensational, splendid, staggering, striking, stunning, stupendous, theatrical, thrilling, wondrous; SEE CONCEPTS 529,537,574

spectator [n] *person who watches event*
beholder, bystander, clapper, eyewitness, fan, gaper*, gazer, kibitzer*, looker, looker-on, moviegoer, observer, onlooker, perceiver, playgoer, seer, showgoer, sports fan, standee, stander-by, theatergoer, viewer, watcher, witness; SEE CONCEPTS 366,423

specter [n] *ghost*
apparition, appearance, demon, doppelganger,

sp
sp

phantasm, phantom, poltergeist, presence, shadow, spirit, spook, vision; SEE CONCEPT *370*

spectral [*adj*] *ghostly*
apparitional, eerie, haunted, illusory, phantasmal, phantom, scary, shadowy, spiritual, spooky, supernatural; SEE CONCEPTS *485,537*

speculate [*v1*] *think about deeply and theorize*
beat one's brains*, brainstorm*, build castles in air*, call it, call the turn, cerebrate, chew over*, cogitate, conjecture, consider, contemplate, deliberate, dope*, dope out*, excogitate, figure, figure out*, guess, guesstimate*, have a hunch*, hazard a guess, head trip*, hypothesize, kick around*, meditate, muse, pipe-dream*, psych out*, read, read between lines*, reason, reflect, review, ruminate, run it up flagpole*, scheme, size up, study, suppose, surmise, suspect, weigh, wonder; SEE CONCEPTS *17,24,28,37*

speculate [*v2*] *gamble, risk*
dare, hazard, make book*, margin up*, play, play the market*, plunge, pour money into*, spec*, stick neck out*, take a chance, take a flier*, take a fling*, venture, wildcat; SEE CONCEPTS *28,330,363*

speculation [*n1*] *theory, guess*
belief, brainwork*, cerebration, cogitation, conjecture, consideration, contemplation, deliberation, excogitation, guesstimate*, guesswork, hunch, hypothesis, meditation, opinion, reflection, review, shot, shot in the dark*, sneaking suspicion*; stab, stab in the dark*, studying, supposition, surmise, thinking, thought, weighing; SEE CONCEPTS *24,28,529,689*

speculation [*n2*] *risk, gamble*
backing, flier*, flutter, gambling, hazard, hunch, piece, plunge, right money*, risky business*, risky venture, shot, shot in the dark*, smart money*, spec*, speculative enterprise, stab*, venture, wager; SEE CONCEPTS *192,330,363*

speculative [*adj*] *theoretical*
abstract, analytical, assumed, conceptive, dangerous, dicey, experimental, formularized, hairy, hazardous, hypothetical, ideal, idealized, ideological, iffy, intellectual, in theory, logical, notional, philosophical, presumed, risky, uncertain, unproved, unproven, unsubstantiated; SEE CONCEPT *529*

speech [*n1*] *talk*
accent, articulation, communication, conversation, dialect, dialogue, diction, discussion, doublespeak*, double talk*, elocution, enunciation, expressing, expression, idiom, intercourse, jargon, language, lingo, locution, mother tongue, native tongue, oral communication, palaver, parlance, prattle, pronunciation, prose, speaking, spiel, tone, tongue, utterance, verbalization, vernacular, vocal expression, vocalization, vocalizing, voice, voicing; SEE CONCEPTS *47,266,276*

speech [*n2*] *formal talk to audience*
address, allocution, appeal, bombast, chalk talk*, commentary, debate, declamation, diatribe, discourse, disquisition, dissertation, eulogy, exhortation, harangue, homily, invocation, keynote, lecture, opus, oration, oratory, panegyric, paper, parlance, parley, pep talk*, pitch, prelection, recitation, rhetoric, salutation, sermon, spiel*, stump*, tirade, valedictory; SEE CONCEPTS *60,285*

speechless [*adj*] *without ability to talk*
aghast, amazed, aphonic, astounded, buttoned up*, clammed up*, close-mouthed, cool*, cool as cucumber*, dazed, dumb, dumbfounded, dumbstruck, inarticulate, mum, mute, not saying boo*, reserved, shocked, silent, taciturn, thunderstruck*, tight-lipped*, tongue-tied*, uncommunicative, unflappable, voiceless, wordless; SEE CONCEPT *267*

speed [*n*] *rate of motion, often a high rate*
acceleration, activity, agility, alacrity, breeze, briskness, celerity, clip, dispatch, eagerness, expedition, fleetness, gait, haste, headway, hurry, hustle, legerity, lick, liveliness, momentum, pace, precipitancy, precipitation, promptitude, promptness, quickness, rapidity, rapidness, readiness, rush, rustle, snap, steam, swiftness, urgency, velocity; SEE CONCEPT *755*

speed [*v*] *move along quickly*
advance, aid, assist, barrel, belt, bomb, boost, bowl over, career, cover ground*, cut along, dispatch, expedite, facilitate, flash, fly, further, gallop, gather momentum, gear up*, get a move on*, get moving, get under way, go all out*, go fast, go like the wind*, hasten, help, hightail*, hurry, impel, lose no time*, make haste, open up throttle*, press on, promote, quicken, race, ride, run, rush, sail, spring, step on it*, tear, urge, whiz, zoom; SEE CONCEPTS *110,150,152*

speedy [*adj*] *fast, quick*
accelerated, agile, alacritous, breakneck, brisk, expeditious, express, fleet, harefooted, hasty, headlong, hurried, immediate, lissome, lively, nimble,. precipitate, prompt, quick-fire, rapid, rapid-fire, ready, snappy, summary, supersonic, swift, ultrasonic, winged; SEE CONCEPTS *548,584,588*

spell [*n1*] *interval, period*
bit, bout, course, go, hitch, interlude, intermission, patch, relay, season, shift, space, stint, streak, stretch, term, time, tour, tour of duty, trick, turn, while; SEE CONCEPTS *807,817,822*

spell [*n2*] *magical aura over an entity*
abracadabra*, allure, amulet, bewitching, bewitchment, charm, conjuration, enchanting, enchantment, exorcism, fascination, glamour, hex, hexing, hocus-pocus*, incantation, jinx, magic, mumbo-jumbo*, rune, sorcery, talisman, trance, voodoo*, whack*, whammy*, witchery; SEE CONCEPTS *370,673,689*

spell [*n3*] *seizure*
access, attack, fit, illness, jag, paroxysm, spasm, stroke, throe, turn; SEE CONCEPTS *306,308*

spell [*v1*] *mean, imply*
add up to, amount to, augur, connote, denote, express, herald, import, indicate, intend, point to, portend, presage, promise, signify, suggest; SEE CONCEPTS *55,74,75*

spell [*v2*] *give rest, relief*
allow, breathe, free, lay off, lie by, release, relieve, stand in for, take over, take the place of; SEE CONCEPTS *83,110*

spellbound [*adj*] *enchanted, fascinated*
agape, amazed, bemused, bewildered, bewitched, breathless, captivated, caught up, charmed, enthralled, gripped, held, hooked, mesmerized, open-mouthed, petrified, possessed, rapt, transfixed, transported, under a spell; SEE CONCEPT *403*

spell out [*v*] *clarify, explain*
break down, brief, clear up, clue in, decipher, decode, define, describe, diagram, draw a map*,

expound, fill someone in*, get across*, go into detail, illustrate, interpret, justify, make plain*, point out, put across, put in plain English*, teach, tell, throw light upon*, translate, unfold, unravel, untangle; SEE CONCEPT 57

spend [v1] *give, pay out*
absorb, allocate, ante up*, apply, bestow, blow*, cast away, come across, come through, concentrate, confer, consume, contribute, cough up*, defray, deplete, disburse, dispense, dissipate, donate, drain, drop, employ, empty, evote, exhaust, expend, foot the bill*, fritter, give, hand out, invest, lavish, lay out, liquidate, misspend, outlay, pay down, pay up, put in, run through, settle, shell out*, spring for*, squander, throw away, use, use up, waste; SEE CONCEPTS 156,169,225, 341

spend [v2] *use time; occupy*
consume, devote, drift, employ, fill, fool around*, fritter, go, idle, kill, laze, let pass, misuse, pass, put in, squander, waste, while away*; SEE CONCEPT 100

spendthrift [n] *person careless with money*
big spender*, dissipater, high-roller*, improvident, imprudent, prodigal, profligate, spender, sport, squanderer, waster, wastrel; SEE CONCEPTS 348,353,423

spent [adj] *used up, gone; tired out*
all in*, bleary, blown, burnt-out*, bushed, consumed, dead*, debilitated, depleted, disbursed, dissipated, dog-tired*, done-in*, down the drain*, drained, effete, enervated, exhausted, expended, fagged, far-gone*, finished, had it*, limp, lost, played-out*, prostrate, ready to drop*, shattered, shot, thrown away, used, washed-up*, wasted, weakened, wearied, weary, worn out; SEE CONCEPTS 314,560,771

spew [v] *spit out*
belch, bring up, cascade, disgorge, eject, eruct, erupt, expel, flood, gush, heave, irrupt, puke*, regurgitate, scatter, spit, spit up, spread, spritz, throw up, urp*, vomit; SEE CONCEPTS 179,308

sphere [n1] *globular object*
apple*, ball, big blue marble*, circle, Earth, globe, globule, orb, pellet, pill, planet, rondure, round; SEE CONCEPTS 436,511

sphere [n2] *domain of influence*
bailiwick, capacity, champaign, circle, class, compass, demesne, department, dominion, employment, field, function, ground, jungle, jurisdiction, level, neck of the woods*, orbit, pale, position, precinct, province, range, rank, realm, scope, station, stomping ground*, stratum, terrain, territory, turf*, walk of life, zone; SEE CONCEPTS 349,388,687

spice [n] *flavor; zest*
aroma, color, excitement, fragrance, gusto, guts*, kick, pep, piquancy, pungency, relish, salt, savor, scent, seasoning, tang, zap*, zip*; SEE CONCEPTS 614,673

spick-and-span [adj] *spotless*
clean, fresh, gleaming, hygienic, immaculate, neat, polished, pure, sanitary, shining, shipshape, tidy, unsoiled, unstained, untarnished, very clean; SEE CONCEPTS 404,621

spicy [adj] *pungent, flavorful*
ambrosial, appetizing, aromal, aromatic, distinctive, fiery, flavorsome, fragrant, fresh, herbaceous, highly seasoned, hot, keen, odoriferous, peppery, perfumed, piquant, poignant, racy,

redolent, savory, scented, seasoned, snappy, spirited, sweet, tangy, tasty, zesty, zippy*; SEE CONCEPT 613

spicy [adj2] *off-color, vulgar*
breezy, broad, erotic, hot*, indelicate, racy, red hot*, ribald, risqué, salty*, scandalous, sensational, sophisticated, suggestive, titillating, unseemly, wicked, X-rated*; SEE CONCEPTS 267,372,545

spiel [n] *patter, sales pitch*
chatter, empty talk, jabber*, jive*, line*, pitch*, sales talk, song and dance*; SEE CONCEPTS 276,278

spiffy [adj] *stylish*
a la mode*, beautiful, chic, chichi*, classy, dandy, dapper, dashing, dressed to kill*, fashionable, high-class*, in fashion, in vogue, jazzy*, mod*, now*, ritzy, sharp, showy, sleek, slick*, smart, snappy*, snazzy*, stunning, swank*, upscale, uptown, voguish; SEE CONCEPTS 579,589

spike [v] *pierce*
fasten, impale, lance, make fast, nail, pin, prick, skewer, spear, spit, stick, transfix; SEE CONCEPT 220

spill [v1] *slop, drop*
discharge, disgorge, dribble, drip, empty, flow, lose, overfill, overflow, overrun, overturn, pour, run, run out, run over, scatter, shed, spill over, splash, splatter, spray, sprinkle, spurt, squirt, stream, throw off, upset, well over; SEE CONCEPTS 179,181

spill [v2] *reveal*
betray, blab, blow, disclose, divulge, give away, inform, let the cat out of the bag*, mouth, squeal, tattle, tell; SEE CONCEPT 60

spin [n] *circular motion*
circuit, gyration, revolution, roll, rotation, spiral, turn, twist, whirl; SEE CONCEPT 748

spin [v] *go around, make go around*
gyrate, gyre, oscillate, pendulate, pirouette, purl, reel, revolve, rotate, spiral, swim, turn, twirl, twist, wheel, whirl; SEE CONCEPTS 150,152,218

spine [n] *backbone*
back, bone, chine, rachis, ridge, spinal column, vertebrae, vertebral column; SEE CONCEPTS 393,420

spineless [adj] *cowardly*
amoebalike*, faint-hearted, fearful, feeble, forceless, frightened, gutless*, impotent, inadequate, ineffective, ineffectual, invertebrate, irresolute, lily-livered*, nerveless, pithless, soft, spiritless, squeamish, submissive, timid, vacillating, weak, weak-kneed, weak-willed, yellow*, yellow-bellied*; SEE CONCEPTS 401,542

spin-off [n] *offshoot*
adjunct, branch, by-product, derivative, descendant, division, offspring, outgrowth, sequel; SEE CONCEPTS 260,824

spiral [adj] *curling, winding*
circling, circular, circumvoluted, cochlear, coiled, corkscrew, curled, helical, helicoid, radial, rolled, screw-shaped, scrolled, tendrillar, tortile, voluted, whorled, wound; SEE CONCEPT 486

spiral [n] *curled shape*
coil, corkscrew, curlicue, flourish, gyration, gyre, helix, quirk, screw, volute, whorl; SEE CONCEPT 436

spirit [n1] *soul, attitude*
air, animation, ardor, backbone*, boldness,

breath, character, complexion, courage, dauntlessness, disposition, earnestness, energy, enterprise, enthusiasm, essence, fire, force, frame of mind, gameness, grit*, guts*, heart, humor, jazz*, life, life force, liveliness, mettle, mood, morale, motivation, nerve, oomph*, outlook, psyche, quality, resolution, resolve, sparkle, spunk*, stouteartedness, substance, temper, temperament, tenor, vigor, vitality, vital spark, warmth, will, willpower, zest; SEE CONCEPTS 407,411

spirit [n2] *atmosphere, essence*
feeling, genius, gist, humor, intent, intention, meaning, purport, purpose, quality, sense, substance, temper, tenor, timbre, tone; SEE CONCEPTS 673,682

spirit [n3] *ghost*
apparition, eidolon, phantasm, phantom, poltergeist, shade, shadow, soul, specter, spook, sprite, supernatural being, umbra, vision, wraith; SEE CONCEPT 370

spirited [adj] *lively, vivacious*
active, alert, animate, animated, ardent, audacious, avid, bold, bouncy, brave, bright, burning, chirpy, courageous, dauntless, eager, effervescent, energetic, enthusiastic, fearless, fiery, full of life, game, gingery*, gritty, gutsy*, high-spirited, hot, hyper*, intrepid, jumping, keen, mettlesome, nervy, passionate, peppery, peppy, plucky, resolute, rocking, sharp, snappy, sparkling, sprightly, spunky, vigorous, zappy*, zealous, zesty, zingy*, zippy*; SEE CONCEPTS 404,542

spiritless [adj] *depressed*
apathetic, blah*, blue*, broken, cast down, dejected, despondent, disconsolate, dispirited, dopey*, down, downcast, downhearted, down in the dumps*, down in the mouth*, draggy, drippy, droopy, dull, enervated, flat*, flat tire*, inanimate, indifferent, lackadaisical, lackluster, languid, languishing, languorous, lifeless, limp, listless, low, melancholic, melancholy, mopy, slothful, subdued, submissive, tame, torpid, unconcerned, unenthusiastic, unmoved, zero*; SEE CONCEPTS 403,542

spiritual [adj] *religious, otherworldly*
airy, asomatous, devotional, discarnate, disembodied, divine, ethereal, extramundane, ghostly, holy, immaterial, incorporeal, intangible, metaphysical, nonmaterial, nonphysical, platonic, pure, rarefied, refined, sacred, supernal, unfleshly, unphysical; SEE CONCEPTS 536,582

spit [n1] *saliva*
discharge, dribble, drool, slaver, spittle, sputum, water; SEE CONCEPT 467

spit [v] *eject saliva or substance*
discharge, drool, expectorate, hawk, hiss, sibilate, sizz, slobber, spatter, spew, splutter, spritz, sputter, throw out; SEE CONCEPTS 179,185

spite [n] *hateful feeling*
animosity, antipathy, bad blood*, contempt, despite, enmity, gall, grudge, harsh feeling, hate, hatred, ill will, malevolence, malice, maliciousness, malignity, peeve, pique, rancor, resentment, revenge, spitefulness, spleen, umbrage, vengeance, vengefulness, venom, vindictiveness; SEE CONCEPT 29

spite [v] *offend, hurt*
annoy, begrudge, beset, crab*, cramp style*, discomfit, gall, get even*, grudge, hang up*, harass, harm, injure, louse up*, needle, nettle, persecute,

pique, provoke, put out*, upset the apple cart*, vex; SEE CONCEPTS 7,19,121

spiteful [adj] *hurtful, nasty*
accidentally on purpose*, angry, barbed, catty*, cruel, cussed*, despiteful, dirty, evil, hateful, illdisposed, ill-natured, malevolent, malicious, malign, malignant, mean, ornery*, rancorous, snide, spleenful, splenetic, venomous, vicious, vindictive, waspish, wicked; SEE CONCEPTS 401,542

spitting image [n] *look-alike*
carbon copy, clone, double, duplicate, exact likeness, likeness, match, replica, ringer*, twin, very image; SEE CONCEPTS 414,664,670

splash [n] *spattering, impact*
burst, dash, display, effect, patch, sensation, splurge, stir, touch; SEE CONCEPT 676

splash [v] *throw liquid*
bathe, bespatter, broadcast, dabble, dash, douse, drench, drown, get wet, moisten, paddle, plash, plunge, shower, slop, slosh, soak, sop, spatter, splatter, spray, spread, sprinkle, squirt, strew, throw, wade, wallow, wet; SEE CONCEPTS 222,256

splatter [v] *splash*
bespatter, douse, drench, drown, get wet, moisten, plunge, shower, slosh, soak, sop, spatter, spray, sprinkle, squirt, wet; SEE CONCEPTS 222,256

splendid [adj] *luxurious, expensive*
baroque, beaming, beautiful, bright, brilliant, costly, dazzling, elegant, fab*, fat*, flamboyant, glittering, glowing, gorgeous, grand, grandiose, imposing, impressive, lavish, lustrous, mad*, magnificent, magnifico, marvelous, ornate, plush, posh, radiant, refulgent, resplendent, rich, solid gold*, splashy, splendiferous, splendrous, sumptuous, superb, swanky*; SEE CONCEPTS 334,485,589

splendid [adj2] *excellent, illustrious*
admirable, brilliant, celebrated, distinguished, divine, eminent, exceptional, exquisite, fantastic, fine, first-class, glorious, gorgeous, grand, great, heroic, impressive, magnificent, marvelous, matchless, outstanding, peerless, premium, proud, rare, remarkable, renowned, resplendent, royal, splendiferous, splendorous, sterling, sublime, superb, superlative, supreme, transcendent, unparalleled, unsurpassed, very good, wonderful; SEE CONCEPTS 568,574

splendor [n] *radiance, glory*
brightness, brilliance, ceremony, dazzle, display, effulgence, gorgeousness, grandeur, luster, magnificence, majesty, pageant, pomp, refulgence, renown, resplendence, richness, show, solemnity, spectacle, stateliness, sumptuousness; SEE CONCEPTS 620,655,673

splice [v] *join, interweave*
braid, entwine, graft, hitch, interlace, intertwine, intertwist, knit, marry, mate, mesh, plait, tie, unite, weave, wed, yoke; SEE CONCEPT 193

splinter [n] *thin piece of solid*
bit, chip, flake, fragment, needle, paring, shaving, sliver, wood; SEE CONCEPTS 471,479,831

splinter [v] *break into thin, small pieces*
break to smithereens*, burst, disintegrate, fracture, fragment, pash, rive, shatter, shiver, smash, split; SEE CONCEPT 246

split [n1] *opening*
breach, chasm, chink, cleavage, cleft, crack, damage, division, fissure, gap, rent, rift, rima, ri-

mation, rime, rip, rupture, separation, slash, slit, tear; SEE CONCEPT 513

split [*n2*] *difference, disunion*
alienation, breach, break, break-up, discord, disruption, dissension, divergence, division, estrangement, fissure, fracture, partition, rent, rift, rupture, schism; SEE CONCEPTS 297,388

split [*v1*] *break up, pull apart*
bifurcate, branch, break, burst, cleave, come apart, come undone, crack, dichotomize, disband, disjoin, dissever, disunite, diverge, divide, divorce, fork, gape, give way, go separate ways, hack, isolate, open, part, part company, put asunder, rend, rip, rive, separate, sever, slash, slit, snap, splinter, sunder, tear, whack; SEE CONCEPTS 135,176,297

split [*v2*] *divide into parts*
allocate, allot, apportion, carve up, distribute, divide, divvy*, divvy up*, dole, go even-steven*, go fifty-fifty*, halve, mete out, parcel out, partition, share, slice, slice the pie*, slice up; SEE CONCEPT 98

split up [*v*] *keep apart; segregate; separate*
break off, break up, come apart, detach, disband, disconnect, divide, divorce, go separate ways, group, part, part company, rope off, seclude, sever, sort, stand between, undo; SEE CONCEPTS 135,158,201,297,384

splurge [*v*] *spend lavishly*
be extravagant, binge, celebrate, fling, give a party*, rampage, spread; SEE CONCEPTS 327,377

spoil [*v1*] *ruin, hurt*
blemish, damage, debase, deface, defile, demolish, depredate, desecrate, desolate, despoil, destroy, devastate, disfigure, disgrace, harm, impair, injure, make useless, mar, mess up*, muck up*, pillage, plunder, prejudice, ravage, sack, smash, spoliate, squash, take apart, tarnish, trash*, undo, upset, vitiate, waste, wreck; SEE CONCEPTS 14,136

spoil [*v2*] *baby, indulge*
accommodate, cater to, coddle, cosset, favor, humor, kill with kindness*, mollycoddle*, oblige, overindulge, pamper, spoon-feed*; SEE CONCEPTS 14,136

spoil [*v3*] *decay, turn bad*
addle, become tainted, become useless, break down, crumble, curdle, decompose, deteriorate, disintegrate, go bad, go off, mildew, molder, putrefy, rot, taint, turn; SEE CONCEPTS 456,469

spoils [*n*] *possessions stolen or gained*
booty*, cut*, gain, goods, graft, hot goods*, loot, make*, pickings, pillage, plunder, prey, prize, squeeze, swag, take; SEE CONCEPTS 337,710

spoken [*adj*] *by word of mouth*
announced, articulate, communicated, expressed, lingual, mentioned, oral, phonetic, phonic, put into words, said, sonant, told, traditional, unwritten, uttered, verbal, viva voce, voiced; SEE CONCEPT 267

spokesperson [*n*] *person who communicates for another*
agent, champion, delegate, deputy, mediator, mouth, mouthpiece*, prolocutor, prophet, protagonist, representative, speaker, stand-in, substitute, talker; SEE CONCEPTS 348,354,359

sponge [*n*] *moocher*
bum*, cadger, deadbeat*, freeloader*, hanger-on, leech*, panhandler, parasite, scrounger; SEE CONCEPTS 412,423

sponge [*v*] *mooch*
beg, bum*, cadge, chisel*, freeload*, hit up*, hustle, live off of, panhandle, scrounge; SEE CONCEPT 53

spongy [*adj*] *cushioned, absorbent*
absorptive, cushiony, elastic, light, mushy, pappy, porous, pulpous, pulpy, resilient, rubbery, soft, springy, squishy, yielding; SEE CONCEPT 606

sponsor [*n*] *person who helps, promotes another*
adherent, advocate, angel*, backer, benefactor, godparent, grubstaker, guarantor, mainstay, patron, promoter, supporter, surety, sustainer, underwriter; SEE CONCEPTS 348,423

sponsor [*v*] *help, promote*
answer for, back, bankroll, be responsible for, finance, fund, grubstake, guarantee, patronize, put up money, stake, subsidize, vouch for; SEE CONCEPTS 110,341

spontaneous [*adj*] *impulsive, willing*
ad-lib*, automatic, break loose, casual, down, extemporaneous, extempore, free, free spirited, from the hip*, impetuous, impromptu, improvised, inevitable, instinctive, involuntary, irresistible, natural, offhand, off the cuff*, off top of head*, simple, unartful, unavoidable, unbidden, uncompelled, unconscious, unconstrained, uncontrived, uncontrolled, unforced, unintentional, unplanned, unpremediated, unprepared, unsophisticated, unstudied, up front, voluntary; SEE CONCEPTS 401,542,548

spoof [*n*] *trick, mockery*
bluff, bon mot, burlesque, caricature, cheat, deceit, deception, fake, flim-flam*, game, hoax, imposture, jest, joke, lampoon, parody, phony, prank, put-on, quip, satire, sell, send-up*, sham, take-off, travesty, trickery, wisecrack; SEE CONCEPTS 59,273

spook [*v*] *frighten, scare*
alarm, curdle the blood*, discomfort, horrify, make one's blood run cold*, make one's teeth chatter*, panic, petrify, scare away, scare stiff*, scare the pants off of*, scare to death*, startle, strike terror into*, terrify, unnerve; SEE CONCEPTS 7,14,19,42

spooky [*adj*] *frightening*
chilling, creepy, eerie, ghostly, mysterious, ominous, scary, spine-chilling, supernatural, uncanny, unearthly, weird; SEE CONCEPTS 529,537

spoon-feed [*v*] *pamper*
baby, cater to, coddle, give in, indulge, mollycoddle*, overindulge, spoil, spoil rotten*; SEE CONCEPTS 136,295

sporadic [*adj*] *on and off*
bits and pieces*, desultory, few, fitful, fits and starts*, hit-or-miss*, infrequent, intermittent, irregular, isolated, occasional, on-again-off-again*, random, rare, scarce, scattered, seldom, semioccasional, spasmodic, spotty, uncommon, unfrequent; SEE CONCEPT 541

sport [*n1*] *recreational activity; entertainment*
action, amusement, athletics, ball, disport, diversion, exercise, frolic, fun, fun and games*, gaiety, game, games, pastime, physical activity, picnic, play, pleasure, recreation; SEE CONCEPT 363

sport [*n2*] *fun, joking*
badinage, banter, derision, drollery, escapade, frolic, horseplay, jest, jesting, joke, jollification,

sp
sp

jollity, kidding, laughter, merriment, mirth, mockery, mummery, nonsense, pleasantry, practical joke, raillery, scorn, teasing, tomfoolery, trifling; SEE CONCEPTS *59,273*

sport [*n3*] *person who takes kidding*
buffoon, butt, jestee, joke, laughingstock, mock, mockery, object of derision, object of ridicule, plaything, target; SEE CONCEPT *423*

sport [*v*] *display, wear*
be dressed in, don, exhibit, have on, model, show off; SEE CONCEPTS *167,261*

sporting/sportive [*adj*] *playful and fair*
antic, coltish, considerate, devil-may-care*, frisky, frolicsome, full of fun*, game, gamesome, gay, generous, impish, jaunty, joyous, larkish, lively, merry, mischievous, reasonable, roguish, rollicking, sportspersonlike, sprightly, square, wild; SEE CONCEPT *401*

sportsmanship [*n*] *integrity*
fairness, forthrightness, gamemanship, goodness, honesty, honor, honorableness, principle, righteousness, sincerity, virtue; SEE CONCEPT *411*

sporty [*adj*] *casual; flashy*
brazen, flamboyant, flaunting, gaudy, glittering, glittery, glitzy, informal, jazzy*, loud, natty, ornate, showy, snazzy; SEE CONCEPTS *401,542,589*

spot [*n1*] *mark, stain*
atom, blemish, blot, blotch, daub, discoloration, dollop, dram, drop, flaw, iota, jot, little bit, mite, molecule, mote, nip, particle, pimple, pinch, shot, smidgen, smudge, snort, speck, taint, whit; SEE CONCEPTS *284,831*

spot [*n2*] *location*
hangout*, hole*, joint*, layout, locality, locus, office, pad, place, plant, point, position, post, roof, scene, seat, section, sector, site, situation, slot, station, wherever*, X*, X marks the spot*; SEE CONCEPT *198*

spot [*n3*] *bad situation*
box*, corner*, difficulty, dilemma, fix, hole*, jam, mess, pickle*, plight, predicament, quandary, scrape, trouble; SEE CONCEPTS *666,674*

spot [*n4*] *position in organization*
appointment, berth, billet, connection, job, office, place, post, responsibility, situation, station, work; SEE CONCEPTS *351,362*

spot [*v1*] *mark, stain*
besmirch, bespatter, blot, blotch, dapple, dirty, dot, fleck, maculate, marble, mottle, pepper, pimple, soil, spatter, speck, speckle, splash, splotch, stipple, streak, stripe, stud, sully, taint, tarnish; SEE CONCEPTS *79,179*

spot [*v2*] *see, recognize*
catch, catch sight of, descry, detect, determinate, diagnose, discern, discover, distinguish, encounter, espy, ferret out, find, identify, locate, make out, meet with, observe, pick out, pinpoint, place, point out, sight, trace, track, turn up; SEE CONCEPTS *38,183,626*

spotless [*adj*] *very clean; innocent*
above reproach, blameless, chaste, clean, decent, faultless, flawless, gleaming, hygienic, immaculate, irreproachable, modest, pure, sanitary, shining, snowy, stainless, unblemished, undefiled, unimpeachable, unsoiled, unstained, unsullied, untarnished; SEE CONCEPTS *404,621*

spotlight [*n*] *attention; bright beam of light*
center stage, fame, flashlight, floodlight, interest,

light, limelight, notoriety, public attention, public eye, publicity; SEE CONCEPTS *388,624,668*

spotlight [*v*] *focus attention on*
accentuate, draw attention, feature, floodlight*, give prominence, highlight, illuminate, limelight*, point up, publicize, put on center stage*; SEE CONCEPTS *261,292*

spotted [*adj*] *speckled*
blotched, dappled, dotted, flaked, flecked, freckled, mosaic, motley, patchy, pied, spotty, sprinkled; SEE CONCEPTS *485,618*

spotty [*adj*] *blotchy, irregular*
desultory, erratic, flickering, fluctuating, not uniform, on-again-off-again*, patchy, pimply, spasmodic, sporadic, unequal, uneven; SEE CONCEPT *534*

spouse [*n*] *one of a married couple*
better half*, bride, companion, groom, helpmate, husband, man, mate, partner, roommate, wife, woman; SEE CONCEPT *414*

spout [*v1*] *spurt, emit*
cascade, discharge, eject, erupt, expel, exude, gush, jet, pour, roll, shoot, spill, spray, squirt, stream, surge; SEE CONCEPT *179*

spout [*v2*] *talk forcefully*
boast, brag, chatter, declaim, expatiate, go on, gush, harangue, hold forth, orate, pontificate, ramble, rant, sermonize, shoot off one's mouth*, speechify, spellbind, spiel, vapor, yell; SEE CONCEPTS *49,51*

sprawl [*v*] *sit or lie spread out*
drape, extend, flop, lie, lie spread-eagle*, loll, lounge, ramble, recline, sit, slouch, slump, spread, straddle, straggle, stretch, trail; SEE CONCEPT *201*

spray [*n*] *fine mist*
aerosol, atomizer, drizzle, droplets, duster, fog, froth, moisture, spindrift, splash, sprayer, sprinkler, vaporizer; SEE CONCEPTS *514,680*

spray [*v*] *sprinkle, diffuse*
atomize, drizzle, dust, scatter, shoot, shower, smear, spatter, splash, spritz, squirt, throw around; SEE CONCEPTS *179,256*

spread [*n1*] *expansion, development; extent*
advance, advancement, compass, diffusion, dispersion, dissemination, enlargement, escalation, expanse, extension, increase, period, profusion, proliferation, radiation, ramification, range, reach, scope, span, spreading, stretch, suffusion, sweep, term, transfusion, transmission; SEE CONCEPTS *651,704,721,788*

spread [*n2*] *outlay of food, meal*
array, banquet, blowout, dinner, feast, lunch, regale, repast; SEE CONCEPT *459*

spread [*v1*] *open or fan out*
arrange, array, be displayed, be distributed, bloat, branch off, broaden, cast, circulate, coat, cover, daub, develop, diffuse, dilate, disperse, diverge, enlarge, escalate, even out, expand, extend, flatten, flow, gloss, increase, lay, lengthen, level, lie, multiply, mushroom, open, outstretch, overlay, paint, pervade, prepare, proliferate, radiate, reach, roll out, set, settle, smear, sprawl, spray, stretch, strew, suffuse, swell, uncoil, unfold, unfurl, unroll, untwist, unwind, widen; SEE CONCEPTS *158,172,201*

spread [*v2*] *publicize*
advertise, blazon, broadcast, cast, circulate, declare, diffuse, disseminate, distribute, make known, make public, proclaim, promulgate,

propagate, publish, radiate, scatter, shed, sow, strew, transmit; SEE CONCEPT *60*

spree [*n*] *wild activity*
bacchanalia, ball, bash, binge, caper, carousal, carouse, carousing, celebration, field day*, fling, frolic, high jinks*, high time*, jag, jamboree, junket, lark, merry-go-round*, orgy, party, rampage, revel, rip*, spending expedition, splurge, tear*; SEE CONCEPTS *327,377,384*

sprightly [*adj*] *fun, vivacious*
active, agile, airy, alert, animate, animated, blithe, bouncy, breezy, bright, brisk, cheerful, cheery, chipper, chirpy, clever, dapper, dashing, energetic, fairylike, frolicsome, gay, good, grooving, hyper, jaunty, jolly, joyous, jumping, keen, keen-witted, light, lively, nimble, peppy, perky, playful, quick, quick-witted, saucy, scintillating, smart, snappy, spirited, sportive, spry, swinging, zappy*, zingy*, zippy*; SEE CONCEPTS *401,404,542*

spring [*n1*] *jump, skip*
bounce, bounciness, bound, buck, buoyancy, elasticity, flexibility, give, hop, leap, recoil, resilience, saltation, springiness, vault; SEE CONCEPTS *194,731*

spring [*n2*] *season following winter*
blackberry winter*, budding, budtime, flowering, prime, seedtime, springtide, springtime, vernal equinox, vernal season; SEE CONCEPT *814*

spring [*n3*] *origin*
beginning, cause, consideration, fount, fountain, fountainhead, impetus, motive, root, source, stimulus, well, wellspring, whence; SEE CONCEPTS *648,661*

spring [*n4*] *body of rushing waters*
artesian well, baths, fountain, geyser, hot spring, hydrolysate, spa, thermal spring, watering place, wells; SEE CONCEPT *514*

spring [*v1*] *jump, skip*
bolt, bounce, bound, hippety hop*, hop, hurdle, leap, lop, lope, rebound, recoil, skitter, start, startle, trip, vault; SEE CONCEPT *194*

spring [*v2*] *originate, emerge*
appear, arise, arrive, be derived, be descended, begin, birth, burgeon, come, come into being, come into existence, come out, commence, derive, descend, develop, emanate, flow, grow, hatch, head, issue, loom, mushroom, proceed, rise, shoot up, start, stem, upspring; SEE CONCEPTS *105,302,373*

springy [*adj*] *elastic*
adaptable, bouncy, flexible, limber, malleable, pliable, pliant, resilient, rubberlike, rubbery, stretchable, stretchy; SEE CONCEPTS *490,606*

sprinkle [*v*] *scatter, disseminate*
baptize, christen, dampen, dot, dredge, dust, freckle, mist, moisten, pepper, powder, rain, shake, shower, smear, speck, speckle, spit, spot, spray, spritz, squirt, strew, stud; SEE CONCEPTS *179,222,256*

sprinkling [*n*] *hint, dash*
admixture, dust, dusting, few, handful, lick, mixture, powdering, scattering, several, smattering, sprinkle, strain, taste, tinge, touch, trace; SEE CONCEPT *831*

sprint [*v*] *run very fast*
dart, dash, go at top speed, hotfoot*, race, rush, scamper, scoot, scurry, shoot, tear, whiz*; SEE CONCEPT *150*

sprout [*v*] *develop*
bud, burgeon, germinate, grow, push, shoot, shoot up, spring, take root, vegetate; SEE CONCEPT *257*

spruce [*adj*] *stylish, neat*
classy, clean, dainty, dapper, elegant, prim, smart, tidy, trim, well-groomed; SEE CONCEPT *589*

spruce up [*v*] *make neat, well-groomed*
brush, deck out*, dress up, fix up, groom, prim, primp, sleek, slick, smarten, tidy, titivate, wash; SEE CONCEPTS *162,167,202*

spry [*adj*] *active, vivacious*
agile, alert, brisk, energetic, fleet, full of pep, healthy, in full swing*, lithe, nimble, on the go*, prompt, quick, quick on the draw*, ready, robust, rocking, sound, spirited, sprightly, supple, vigorous; SEE CONCEPT *401*

spunk [*n*] *courage, nerve*
backbone, determination, doggedness, fortitude, gameness, grit*, gumption*, guts*, intestinal fortitude*, mettle, moxie*, pluck, resolution, spirit, toughness, true grit*; SEE CONCEPTS *411,633*

spunky [*adj*] *spirited*
active, alert, animated, bold, bouncy, brave, chirpy, courageous, eager, energetic, enthusiastic, fearless, fiery, full of life, full of spirit, game, gritty, gutsy*, high-spirited, peppy, plucky, snappy, sprightly, tough, vigorous, zesty, zippy*; SEE CONCEPTS *404,542*

spur [*n*] *incitement, stimulus*
activation, actuation, catalyst, excitant, goad, goose*, impetus, impulse, incentive, incitation, inducement, motivation, motive, needle*, prick, stimulant, trigger, turn-on*, urge; SEE CONCEPT *661*

spur [*v*] *incite, prompt*
animate, arouse, awaken, countenance, drive, egg on*, exhort, favor, fire up*, goad, goose*, impel, instigate, key up, press, prick, prod, propel, push, put up to, rally, rouse, sic*, spark, stimulate, stir, trigger, turn on, urge, work up; SEE CONCEPTS *14,68*

spurious [*adj*] *counterfeit, fake*
affected, apocryphal, artificial, assumed, bastard*, bent, bogus, bum, contrived, deceitful, deceptive, dummy*, ersatz, faked, false, feigned, forged, framed, illegitimate, imitation, make-believe, mock, phony, pirate, pretend, pretended, pseudo*, put-on*, sham*, simulated, specious, substitute, unauthentic, ungenuine, unreal; SEE CONCEPT *582*

spurn [*v*] *turn away; ignore*
air, contemn, cut, decline, despise, disapprove, disdain, dismiss, disregard, drop, dump, flout, flush*, give the cold shoulder*, hold in contempt, look down on*, nix*, not hear of*, pass by, rebuff, refuse, reject, reprobate, repudiate, repulse, scoff, scorn, slight, sneer, sneeze at*, snub, steer clear*, turn down, turn nose up at*; SEE CONCEPTS *21,30,384*

spurt [*n*] *burst of activity*
access, commotion, discharge, eruption, explosion, fit, jet, outburst, rush, spate, spritz, squirt, stream, surge; SEE CONCEPTS *1,119,179*

spurt [*v*] *erupt*
burst, emerge, flow, flow out, gush, issue, jet, ooze, pour out, shoot, spew, spout, spritz, squirt, stream, surge, well; SEE CONCEPT *179*

sp
sp

spy [*n*] *person who secretly finds out about another's business*
agent, detective, double agent, emissary, espionage agent, foreign agent, informer, inside agent, intelligencer, investigator, lookout, mole*, observer, operative, patrol, picket, plant*, scout, secret agent, secret service, sleeper, sleuth, snoop, spook, spotter, undercover agent, watcher; SEE CONCEPTS 348,412

spy [*v*] *secretly follow, watch another's actions*
case, catch sight of, discover, examine, eyeball*, fish out*, get a load of*, glimpse, keep under surveillance, look for, meddle, notice, observe, peep, pry, recon*, reconnoiter, scout, scrutinize, search, set eyes on, shadow, sleuth, snoop, spot, stag, stake out, tail, take in, take note, trail, view, watch; SEE CONCEPTS 103,623

squabble [*n*] *argument*
altercation, bickering, controversy, difference, difference of opinion, disagreement, dispute, feud, fight, flap*, fuss*, hassle, quarrel, row*, scene*, scrap*, set-to*, spat*, tiff*, words*, wrangle; SEE CONCEPT 46

squabble [*v*] *argue*
argufy, bicker, brawl, clash, disagree, dispute, encounter, fall out*, fight, hassle, have words*, quarrel, quibble, row, scrap, spat, tiff*, wrangle; SEE CONCEPT 46

squad [*n*] *team, crew*
band, battalion, company, division, force, gang, group, regiment, squadron, troop; SEE CONCEPTS 322,365,417

squalid [*adj*] *poor, run-down*
abominable, base, broken-down, decayed, despicable, dingy, dirty, disgusting, disheveled, fetid, filthy, foul, grimy, gruesome, horrible, horrid, ignoble, impure, low, mean, miry, moldy, muddy, musty, nasty, odorous, offensive, poverty-stricken, ramshackle, reeking, repellent, repulsive, scurvy, seedy, shabby, shoddy, sloppy, slovenly, soiled, sordid, ugly, unclean, unkempt, vile, wretched; SEE CONCEPTS 334,485,570

squalor [*n*] *filth, poverty*
decay, destitution, dirtiness, foulness, grunginess, impoverishment, indigence, poorness, seediness, starvation, wretchedness; SEE CONCEPTS 335,709

squander [*v*] *fritter away, use up*
be prodigal with, be wasteful, blow*, cash out*, consume, dissipate, expend, frivol, frivol away, go through, lavish, misspend, misuse, prodigalize, put out*, run through, scatter, spend, spend like water*, spring for*, throw away, throw money around*, trifle, waste; SEE CONCEPTS 156,225,327

square [*adj1*] *honest, genuine*
aboveboard, decent, equal, equitable, ethical, even, fair, fair-and-square, impartial, impersonal, just, nonpartisan, objective, on-the-level, sporting, sportspersonlike, straight, straightforward, unbiased, unprejudiced, upright; SEE CONCEPTS 267,542

square [*adj2*] *four-sided*
boxlike, boxy, equal-sided, equilateral, four-square, orthogonal, quadrate, quadratic, quadratical, rectangular, rectilinear, right-angled, squared, squarish; SEE CONCEPT 486

square [*adj3*] *old-fashioned, conventional*
behind the times, bourgeois, button-down*, conservative, dated, orthodox, out-of-date, straight*, strait-laced*, stuffy*; SEE CONCEPTS 401,404

square [*n1*] *person who is old-fashioned, conventional*
antediluvian, conservative, diehard*, fuddy-duddy*, reactionary, stick-in-the-mud*, traditionalist; SEE CONCEPT 423

square [*n2*] *municipal park*
area, center, circle, common, green, plaza, space, village green; SEE CONCEPT 509

square [*v1*] *correspond, agree*
accord, balance, check out, coincide, conform, dovetail*, fit, fit in, gee, harmonize, jibe, match, reconcile, tally; SEE CONCEPT 664

square [*v2*] *pay off, satisfy*
balance, bribe, buy, buy off, clear, clear off, clear up, corrupt, discharge, fix, have, liquidate, make even, pay, pay up, quit, rig, settle, tamper with; SEE CONCEPT 341

square [*v3*] *adapt, regulate*
accommodate, adjust, align, conform, even up, fit, level, quadrate, reconcile, suit, tailor, tailor-make*, true; SEE CONCEPTS 126,202

squash [*v*] *compress*
annihilate, bear, bruise, crowd, crush, distort, extinguish, flatten, jam, kill, macerate, mash, pound, press, pulp, push, put down, quash, quell, scrunch, shut down, sit on, smash, squeeze, squish, stamp on, suppress, trample, triturate; SEE CONCEPTS 121,208,219

squat [*adj*] *short and stocky*
broad, chunky, dumpy*, fat, heavy, heavyset, splay, thick, thick-bodied, thickset; SEE CONCEPTS 491,773,779

squat [*v*] *lower body by bending knees*
bow, cower, crouch, hunch, hunker down, perch, roost, settle, sit, stoop; SEE CONCEPT 201

squawk [*v1*] *make high-pitched, animal-like sound*
cackle, caw, crow, cry, hoot, screech, yap, yawp, yelp; SEE CONCEPTS 64,77

squawk [*v2*] *gripe*
bellyache*, complain, kick up a fuss*, protest, raise Cain*, squeal, yammer; SEE CONCEPTS 52,54

squeak [*v*] *make sharp, high-pitched sound*
cheep, creak, cry, grate, peep, pipe, scream, screech, scritch, shrill, sing, sound, squeal, talk, whine, yelp; SEE CONCEPTS 64,65

squeal [*n/v1*] *yell in a loud and high-pitched manner*
bleat, cheep, creak, grate, howl, peep, rasp, scream, scream bloody murder*, screech, shout, shriek, shrill, squawk, wail, yelp, yip, yowl; SEE CONCEPTS 64,77

squeal [*v2*] *inform on*
betray, blab*, complain, protest, rat on*, sell down the river*, sing*, snitch*, squawk*, talk, tattle, tattletale*, tell; SEE CONCEPTS 54,60

squeamish [*adj*] *nauseated; finicky*
annoyed, captious, delicate, disgusted, dizzy, exacting, fastidious, fussy, hypercritical, mincing, particular, prim, prudish, puritanical, qualmish, queasy, queer, scrupulous, shaky, sick, sickly, sick to one's stomach*, strait-laced, unsettled, upset, vertiginous; SEE CONCEPTS 314,401,404

squeeze [*n*] *pressure, crushing*
clasp, clutch, congestion, crowd, crunch, crush, embrace, force, handclasp, hold, hug, influence,

am, press, restraint, squash; SEE CONCEPTS
219,674,687

queeze [v1] *exert pressure on sides, parts of
something*
bear, choke, clasp, clip, clutch, compress, contract, cram, crowd, crush, cuddle, embrace, enfold, force, grip, hold tight, hug, jam, jostle, nip,
pack, pinch, press, quash, ram, scrunch, squash,
squish, strangle, stuff, throttle, thrust, wedge,
wring; SEE CONCEPT 219

queeze [v2] *try to get money out of*
bleed*, bring pressure to bear, eke out, extort,
extract, lean on*, milk*, oppress, pinch*, pressure, pressurize*, put screws to*, shake down*,
wrench, wring; SEE CONCEPTS 53,192,342

quelch [v] *suppress, restrain*
black out, censure, crush, extinguish, kill, muffle, oppress, quelch, quench, repress, settle,
shush, sit on, smother, squash, stifle, strangle,
thwart; SEE CONCEPT 130

quint [v] *scrunch up eyes when viewing*
cock the eye, look, look askance, look cross-
eyed, peek, peep, screw up eyes, squinch*; SEE
CONCEPTS 185,623

quire [v] *accompany*
assist, attend, chaperon, companion, date, escort,
serve; SEE CONCEPTS 384,714

quirm [v] *wiggle, fidget*
agonize, flounder, shift, skew, squiggle, toss,
twist, wind, worm, wriggle, writhe; SEE CONCEPT
213

quirt [v] *squeeze out liquid*
eject, emit, flow, jet, pour, spatter, spit, splash,
splur, spray, sprinkle, spritz, spurt, stream, surge;
SEE CONCEPTS 179,256

quish [v] *squash*
crush, flatten, jam, mash, pound, press, scrunch,
sit on, smash, squeeze, stamp on, trample; SEE
CONCEPTS 121,208,219

ab [n1] *piercing cut*
ache, blow, gash, hurt, incision, jab, jag, pang,
piercing, prick, puncture, rent, stick, thrust,
transfixion, twinge, wound; SEE CONCEPT 309

ab [n2] *attempt*
attempt, crack*, endeavor, essay, fling*, go*,
one's best*, shot*, try, venture, whack*, whirl*;
SEE CONCEPT 87

ab [v] *puncture, pierce with sharp, pointed object*
bayonet, brand, carve, chop, cleave, clip, cut,
drive, gore, hit, hurt, injure, jab, jag, knife, open
up, penetrate, pierce, plow, plunge, prick, prong,
punch, ram, run through, saber, shank, sink,
slice, spear, stick, thrust, transfix, wound; SEE
CONCEPT 220

ability [n] *resistance of some degree*
adherence, aplomb, assurance, backbone, balance, cohesion, constancy, dependability, determination, durability, endurance, establishment,
firmness, immobility, immovability, maturity,
permanence, perseverance, resoluteness, security, solidity, solidness, soundness, stableness,
steadfastness, steadiness, strength, substantiality,
support, toughness; SEE CONCEPTS 411,731

abilize [v] *make or keep in steady state; make
resistant to change*
balance, ballast, bolt, brace, buttress, counterbalance, counterpoise, equalize, fasten, firm, firm
up*, fix, freeze*, maintain, ossify, poise, preserve, prop, secure, set, settle, stabilitate, steady,

stiffen, support, sustain, uphold; SEE CONCEPTS
110,250

stab in the back [v] *betray*
abandon, be disloyal, be unfaithful, break
promise, commit treason, cross, deceive, double-
cross, finger*, go back on, inform on, play
Judas*, sell down the river*, sell out, trick, turn
in, turn informer, turn traitor; SEE CONCEPT 384

stable [adj] *constant, fixed; resistant*
abiding, anchored, balanced, brick-wall*, calm,
deep-rooted, durable, enduring, equable, established, even, fast, firm, immutable, invariable,
lasting, nailed, perdurable, permanent, poised,
reliable, resolute, safe, secure, set, set in stone*,
solid, solid as a rock*, sound, stabile, stalwart,
stationary, staunch, staying put, steadfast, steady,
stout, strong, sturdy, substantial, sure, together,
tough, unalterable, unchangeable, unfluctuating,
uniform, unvarying, unwavering, well-built,
well-founded; SEE CONCEPTS 404,488

stack [n] *pile*
assemblage, bank, bundle, cock, drift, heap, hill,
hoard, load, mass, mound, mountain, pack, pyramid, sheaf; SEE CONCEPTS 432,440,509

stack [v] *pile up*
accumulate, amass, bank up, cock, drift, heap,
hill, load, mound, pile, rick, stockpile; SEE CON-
CEPTS 109,158

stadium [n] *arena for recreation or spectating*
amphitheater, athletic field, bowl, coliseum, diamond, field, garden, gridiron, gymnasium, pit,
ring, stade, strand; SEE CONCEPT 438

staff [n1] *employees of organization*
agents, assistants, cadre, cast, crew, deputies,
faculty, force, help, officers, operatives, organization, personnel, servants, shop, teachers, team,
workers, work force; SEE CONCEPT 325

staff [n2] *stick, usually for walking*
cane, club, pikestaff, pole, prop, rod, stave, walking stick, wand; SEE CONCEPTS 311,479

stage [n1] *level, period within structure or system*
date, degree, division, footing, grade, juncture,
lap, leg, length, moment, node, notch, phase,
plane, point, point in time, rung, standing, status,
step; SEE CONCEPTS 727,744,816

stage [n2] *theater platform; theater layer*
arena, boards*, Broadway, dais, drama, footlights, frame, legit*, limelight*, mise-en-scène,
off-Broadway, play, scaffold, scaffolding, scene,
scenery, set, setting, show biz*, show business,
spotlight, stage set, staging, theater; SEE CON-
CEPTS 263,349,438,439,448

stage [v] *arrange, produce*
bring out, do, engineer, execute, give, mount,
open, orchestrate, organize, perform, play, present, put on, show; SEE CONCEPTS 94,292

stagger [v1] *walk falteringly*
alternate, careen, dither, falter, halt, hesitate,
lurch, overlap, pitch, reel, shake, stammer, step,
sway, swing, teeter, titubate, topple, totter, vacillate, waver, wheel, whiffle, wobble, zigzag; SEE
CONCEPT 151

stagger [v2] *astound, shock*
amaze, astonish, boggle, bowl over*, confound,
consternate, devastate, dumbfound, flabbergast,
floor*, give a shock, nonplus, overpower, overwhelm, paralyze, perplex, puzzle, shake, shatter,
startle, strike dumb*, stump, stun, stupefy, surprise, take aback, take breath away*, throw off
balance*; SEE CONCEPTS 7,19,42

sp
st

staggering [*adj*] *overwhelming*
amazing, astonishing, astounding, distressing, mind-blowing, mind-boggling, shocking, stunning; SEE CONCEPTS 548,571

stagnant [*adj*] *motionless, dirty*
brackish, dead, dormant, filthy, foul, idle, immobile, inactive, inert, lifeless, listless, passive, putrid, quiet, sluggish, stale, standing, static, stationary, still, unmoving; SEE CONCEPTS 584,621

stagnate [*v*] *deteriorate by lack of action*
constipate, decay, decline, fester, go to seed*, hibernate, idle, languish, lie fallow, not move, putrefy, rot, rust, stall, stand, stand still, stifle, stultify, trammel, vegetate; SEE CONCEPTS 698,748

staid [*adj*] *restrained, set*
calm, cold sober*, collected, composed, cool, decorous, demure, dignified, earnest, formal, grave, no-nonsense*, quiet, sedate, self-restrained, serious, settled, sober, solemn, somber, starchy, steady, stuffy, weighty; SEE CONCEPTS 401,404

stain [*n*] *spot of dirt, blot bar*
black eye*, blemish, blot, blotch, blur, brand, color, discoloration, disgrace, dishonor, drip, dye, infamy, ink spot, mottle, odium, onus, reproach, shame, sinister*, slur, smirch, smudge, spatter, speck, splotch, spot, stigma, tint; SEE CONCEPTS 230,622

stain [*v*] *dirty, taint*
animalize, bastardize, besmirch, bestialize, blacken, blemish, blot, brutalize, color, contaminate, corrupt, daub, debase, debauch, defile, demoralize, deprave, discolor, disgrace, drag through the mud*, dye, mark, pervert, smear, smudge, soil, spot, sully, tar, tarnish, tinge, tint; SEE CONCEPTS 54,250,254

stake [*n1*] *pole*
pale, paling, picket, post, rod, spike, stave, stick; SEE CONCEPTS 471,479

stake [*n2*] *bet, wager*
ante, chance, hazard, peril, pledge, pot, risk, venture; SEE CONCEPTS 329,363

stake [*n3*] *share, investment*
award, claim, concern, interest, involvement, prize, purse; SEE CONCEPTS 344,710,835

stake [*v*] *bet, wager*
back, bankroll*, capitalize, chance, finance, gamble, game, grubstake*, hazard, imperil, jeopardize, lay, play, pledge, put, put on, risk, set, stake down, venture; SEE CONCEPTS 330,363

stale [*adj*] *old, decayed*
dried, dry, faded, fetid, flat, fusty, hard, insipid, malodorous, musty, noisome, parched, rank, reeking, smelly, sour, spoiled, stagnant, stenchy, stinking, tasteless, watery, weak, zestless; SEE CONCEPTS 462,485,598

stale [*adj2*] *overused, out-of-date*
antiquated, banal, bent, cliché, clichéd, cliché-ridden, common, commonplace, corny*, dead, drab, dull, dusty, effete, flat, fusty, hackneyed, insipid, like a dinosaur*, mawkish, moth-eaten*, out*, passé, past, platitudinous, repetitious, shopworn, stereotyped, threadbare, timeworn, tired, trite, unoriginal, well-worn, worn-out, yesterday's*, zestless; SEE CONCEPTS 267,578,589,797

stalemate [*n*] *deadlock*
arrest, Catch-22*, check, delay, draw, gridlock,

impasse, pause, standoff, standstill, tie; SEE CONCEPTS 230,807,832

stalk [*n*] *stem of plant*
axis, bent, helm, pedicel, pedicle, reed, shaft, spike, spire, support, trunk, twig, upright; SEE CONCEPT 428

stalk [*v*] *follow, creep up on*
ambush, approach, chase, drive, flush out, haunt, hunt, pace, pursue, shadow, striddle, stride, tail, track, trail, walk up to; SEE CONCEPTS 149,159,749

stall [*v*] *delay for own purposes*
arrest, avoid the issue*, beat around the bush*, brake, check, die, drag one's feet*, equivocate, fence, filibuster, halt, hamper, hedge, hinder, hold off, interrupt, not move, play for time*, postpone, prevaricate, put off, quibble, shut down, slow, slow down, stand, stand off, stand still, stay, still, stonewall*, stop, suspend, take one's time*, tarry, temporize; SEE CONCEPTS 121,234

stalwart [*adj*] *strong, valiant*
athletic, bold, bound, bound and determined*, brave, brawny, brick-wall*, courageous, daring, dauntless, dead set on*, dependable, fearless, forceful, gutsy*, hanging tough*, hefty, husky, indomitable, intrepid, lusty, muscular, nervy* powerhouse*, redoubtable, robust, rugged, sinewy, solid, spunky*, staunch, steamroller*, stout, stouthearted, strapping, sturdy, substantial, tenacious, tough, unafraid, undaunted, valorous, vigorous; SEE CONCEPTS 404,489

stamina [*n*] *strength, vigor*
backbone*, endurance, energy, force, fortitude, grit*, guts*, gutsiness, heart, indefatigability, intestinal fortitude*, legs*, lustiness, moxie*, power, power of endurance, resilience, resistance, starch*, staying power, tolerance, toleration, vim, vitality, zip*; SEE CONCEPTS 411,732

stammer [*v*] *stutter in speech*
falter, halt, hammer, hem and haw*, hesitate, jabber, lurch, pause, repeat, splutter, sputter, stop, stumble, wobble; SEE CONCEPTS 47,266

stamp [*n1*] *impression, symbol, seal*
brand, cast, earmark, emblem, hallmark, impress, imprint, indentation, mark, mold, print, signature, sticker; SEE CONCEPTS 259,284

stamp [*n2*] *character*
breed, cast, cut, description, fashion, form, ilk, kind, lot, mold, sort, stripe, type; SEE CONCEPT 411

stamp [*v1*] *step on hard*
beat, clomp, clump, crush, stomp, stump, tramp, trample, tromp; SEE CONCEPT 149

stamp [*v2*] *imprint; press mark on*
brand, cast, drive, engrave, etch, fix, grave, hammer, impress, infix, inscribe, letter, mark, mold, offset, pound, print; SEE CONCEPTS 79,174

stampede [*n*] *rush of animals*
charge, chase, crash, dash, flight, fling, hurry, panic, rout, run, scattering, shoot, smash, tear; SEE CONCEPT 152

stamp out [*v*] *extinguish*
abolish, blot out*, crush, destroy, eliminate, end, eradicate, expunge, exterminate, kill, put down, quell, snuff out, suppress, wipe out*; SEE CONCEPTS 95,252

stance [*n*] *position, posture*
attitude, bearing, carriage, color, deportment

posture, say-so*, slant, stand, standpoint, viewpoint; SEE CONCEPTS *689,757*

tand [*n1*] *position, opinion*
angle, attitude, belief, carriage, determination, notion, poise, pose, sentiment, slant, sound, stance, standpoint, twist, two cents' worth*, view; SEE CONCEPT *689*

tand [*n2*] *base, stage*
board, booth, bracket, counter, dais, frame, gantry, grandstand, place, platform, rack, rank, staging, stall, station, support, table; SEE CONCEPTS *442,443*

tand [*v1*] *be or get upright*
be erect, be on feet, be vertical, cock, dispose, erect, jump up, locate, mount, place, poise, position, put, rank, rise, set, settle; SEE CONCEPT *201*

tand [*v3*] *be in force, exist*
be located, belong, be situated, be valid, continue, endure, fill, halt, hold, last, obtain, occupy, pause, prevail, remain, rest, stay, stop, take up; SEE CONCEPT *407*

tandard [*adj*] *regular, approved*
accepted, authoritative, average, basic, boilerplate*, canonical, classic, common, customary, definitive, established, everyday, garden variety*, general, normal, official, orthodox, popular, prevailing, recognized, regulation, run-of-the-mill*, set, staple, stock, typical, usual, vanilla*; SEE CONCEPT *533*

tandard [*n1*] *guideline, principle*
archetype, average, axiom, barometer, beau ideal, belief, benchmark, canon, code, criterion, ethics, example, exemplar, fundamental, gauge, grade, guide, guideline, ideal, ideals, law, mean, measure, median, mirror, model, morals, norm, par, paradigm, pattern, principle, requirement, rule, rule of thumb*, sample, specification, test, touchstone, type, yardstick; SEE CONCEPT *688*

tandard [*n2*] *flag*
banderole, banner, bannerol, color, colors, emblem, ensign, figure, insignia, jack, pennant, streamer, symbol; SEE CONCEPT *475*

tandardize [*v*] *make regular, similar*
assimilate, bring into line, homogenize, institute, institutionalize, mass produce, normalize, order, regiment, stereotype, systematize; SEE CONCEPT *126*

tandby [*n*] *substitute*
assistant, backup, deputy, double, fill-in, pinch-hitter*, relief, replacement, reserve, stalwart, stand-in, sub*, successor, temp*, temporary, understudy; SEE CONCEPTS *423,712*

tand for [*v*] *signify, mean*
answer for, appear for, betoken, denote, exemplify, imply, indicate, represent, signify, suggest, symbol, symbolize; SEE CONCEPT *682*

tanding [*adj*] *permanent*
continuing, existing, fixed, perpetual, regular, repeated; SEE CONCEPT *551*

tanding [*n*] *position, rank*
cachet, capacity, character, condition, consequence, credit, dignity, eminence, estimation, footing, place, prestige, reputation, repute, scene, situation, slot, state, station, stature, status, term; SEE CONCEPTS *388,727*

tandoff [*n*] *draw, tie*
dead heat*, deadlock, drawn battle*, even game, impasse, level, Mexican standoff*, stalemate, toss-up, wash; SEE CONCEPTS *364,667*

standoffish [*adj*] *cold, distant*
aloof, antisocial, cool, distant, eremitic, haughty, indifferent, misanthropic, reclusive, remote, reserved, solitary, unapproachable, uncompanionable, unsociable, withdrawn; SEE CONCEPTS *401,404*

stand out [*v*] *be conspicuous, prominent*
attract attention, be distinct, beetle, be highlighted, be striking, bulge, bulk, catch the eye, emerge, jut, loom, overhang, poke, pouch, project, protrude, stick out; SEE CONCEPT *716*

standpoint [*n*] *belief, position*
angle, attitude, judgment, opinion, outlook, point of view, stance, stand, view, viewpoint; SEE CONCEPT *689*

stand/stand for [*v2*] *endure, bear*
abide, allow, bear with, brook, cope, countenance, experience, handle, hang on, hold, last, live with, put up with, resign oneself to, stay the course*, stomach*, submit, suffer, support, sustain, swallow, take, tolerate, undergo, wear, weather, withstand; SEE CONCEPT *23*

standstill [*n*] *stop*
arrest, cessation, check, checkmate, corner*, dead end*, deadlock, dead stop*, delay, gridlock, halt, hole, impasse, inaction, pause, stalemate, standoff, wait; SEE CONCEPTS *119,832*

staple [*adj*] *necessary, basic*
chief, essential, fundamental, important, in demand, key, main, popular, predominant, primary, principal, standard; SEE CONCEPT *546*

star [*adj*] *famous, illustrious*
brilliant, capital, celebrated, chief, dominant, leading, main, major, outstanding, paramount, predominant, preeminent, principal, prominent, talented, well-known; SEE CONCEPT *568*

star [*n*] *person who is famous*
celebrity, draw*, favorite, headliner, hero, idol, lead, leading role, luminary, name, starlet, superstar, topliner*; SEE CONCEPTS *352,366*

starchy [*adj*] *formal, stiff*
ceremonious, conventional, inflexible, mannered, prim, reserved, rigid, starched*, stilted, strait-laced, strict, stuffy*; SEE CONCEPT *401*

star-crossed [*adj*] *doomed*
catastrophic, cursed, damned, disastrous, ill-fated, ill-omened, ill-starred, jinxed, luckless, misfortunate, unfortunate, unlucky; SEE CONCEPTS *537,548*

stardom [*n*] *fame*
acclaim, celebrity, distinction, éclat, eminence, esteem, glory, greatness, honor, illustriousness, immortality, nobility, notoriety, popularity, preeminence, prestige, prominence, public esteem, recognition, renown, standing; SEE CONCEPTS *388,668*

stare [*v*] *gape, watch*
beam*, bore*, eagle eye*, eye, eyeball*, fix, focus, gawk, gaze, glare, glim*, goggle*, lay eyes on*, look, look fixedly, ogle, peer, rivet, rubberneck*, take in; SEE CONCEPT *623*

stark [*adj1*] *utter, absolute*
abrupt, arrant, bald, bare, blasted, blessed, blunt, complete, confounded, consummate, downright, entire, firm, flagrant, gross, infernal, out-and-out*, outright, palpable, patent, pure, rank, severe, sheer, simple, stiff, unalloyed, unmitigated; SEE CONCEPTS *531,569*

stark [*adj2*] *bare, unadorned*
au naturel, austere, bald, barren, bleak, chaste,

st
st

clear, cold, depressing, desolate, dreary, empty, forsaken, grim, harsh, naked, nude, plain, raw, severe, solitary, stripped, unclad, unclothed, uncovered, undraped, vacant, vacuous, void; SEE CONCEPT 485

starry-eyed [*adj*] *unrealistic*
dreaming, half-baked*, hoping, impossible, improbable, ivory-tower*, nonrealistic, not sensible, on cloud nine*, optimistic, romantic, silly; SEE CONCEPTS 552,560

start [*n1*] *beginning*
alpha*, birth, bow, commencement, countdown, dawn, dawning, day one*, derivation, embarkation, exit, first step, flying start*, foundation, inauguration, inception, initiation, jump-off, kickoff*, leaving, onset, opening, origin, outset, running start, setting out, source, spring, square one*, start-off, takeoff; SEE CONCEPTS 648,832

start [*n2*] *advantage*
allowance, backing, break, bulge, chance, draw, edge, handicap, head start, helping hand, introduction, lead, odds, opening, opportunity, sponsorship, vantage; SEE CONCEPT 693

start [*n3*] *flinch*
convulsion, jar, jump, scare, shock, spasm, turn, twitch; SEE CONCEPTS 150,194

start [*v1*] *begin; come into existence*
activate, appear, arise, arouse, come into being, commence, create, depart, embark, engender, enter upon, establish, found, get going, get under way*, go ahead, hit the road*, inaugurate, incite, initiate, instigate, institute, introduce, issue, launch, lay foundation, leave, light, make a beginning, open, originate, pioneer, rise, rouse, sally forth, see light, set in motion, set out, set up, spring, take first step*, take the plunge*, turn on; SEE CONCEPTS 221,241

start [*v2*] *flinch*
blanch, blench, bolt, bounce, bound, buck, dart, draw back, jerk, jump, jump the gun*, leap, quail, recoil, shrink, shy, spring, squinch, startle, twitch, wince; SEE CONCEPTS 150,194

startle [*v*] *frighten, surprise*
affright, agitate, alarm, amaze, astonish, astound, awe, bolt, consternate, floor, fright, give a turn*, jump, make jump, rock, scare, scare to death*, shake up, shock, spook, spring, spring something on*, stagger, start, stun, take aback, terrify, terrorize; SEE CONCEPTS 7,19,42

starving/starved [*adj*] *deprived of food*
could eat a horse*, craving, dehydrated, drawn, dying, emaciated, empty, faint, famished, haggard, hungering, hungry, malnourished, peaked, peckish, perishing, pinched, ravenous, skinny, thin, underfed, undernourished, weakened; SEE CONCEPTS 406,546

state [*n1*] *condition or mode of being*
accompaniment, attitude, capacity, case, category, chances, character, circumstance, circumstances, contingency, element, environment, essential, estate, event, eventuality, fix, footing, form, frame of mind, humor, imperative, juncture, limitation, mood, nature, occasion, occurrence, outlook, pass, phase, plight, position, posture, predicament, prerequisite, proviso, reputation, requirement, shape, situation, spirits, stand, standing, state of affairs, station, status, stipulation, time, welfare; SEE CONCEPTS 410,639,696,701,720

state [*n2*] *dignity, grandeur*
cachet, ceremony, consequence, display, glory, majesty, pomp, position, prestige, rank, splendor, standing, stature, status, style; SEE CONCEPT 388

state [*n3*] *government, country*
body politic, commonwealth, community, federation, land, nation, republic, sovereignty, territory, union; SEE CONCEPTS 508,510

state [*v*] *declare, assert*
affirm, air, articulate, asseverate, aver, bring out, chime in*, come out with, deliver, describe, elucidate, enounce, enumerate, enunciate, explain, expound, express, give, give blow-by-blow*, give rundown*, interpret, narrate, pitch, present, pronounce, propound, put, recite, recount, rehearse, relate, report, say, set forth, speak, specify, spiel*, tell, throw out*, utter, vent, ventilate, voice; SEE CONCEPTS 49,51,55

stately [*adj*] *dignified, impressive*
august, ceremonial, ceremonious, conventional, courtly, deliberate, elegant, elevated, formal, gallant, gracious, grand, grandiose, haughty, high highfaluting*, high-minded*, imperial, imperious, imposing, kingly, large, lofty, luxurious, magnificent, majestic, massive, measured, monumental, noble, opulent, palatial, pompous, portly, proud, queenly, regal, royal, solemn, stiff, sumptuous, superb, towering; SEE CONCEPTS 401,574,589

statement [*n1*] *declaration, assertion*
ABCs*, account, acknowledgment, affidavit, affirmation, allegation, announcement, articulation, aside, asseveration, assurance, averment avowal, blow-by-blow*, charge, comment, communication, communiqué, description, dictum ejaculation, explanation, make*, manifesto, mention, narrative, observation, picture, presentation presentment, proclamation, profession, protestation, recital, recitation, relation, remark, report rundown, testimony, utterance, ventilation, verbalization, vocalization, voice, word; SEE CONCEPTS 271,274,278

statement [*n2*] *account of finances*
affidavit, audit, bill, budget, charge, invoice reckoning, record, report, score, tab; SEE CONCEPT 331

state-of-the-art [*adj*] *up-to-date*
advanced, all the rage*, au courant, avant-garde brand-new, contemporary, cutting edge*, fashionable, in, in-thing*, leading edge, modernistic new, newest, newfangled, red-hot*, stylish trendsetting, trendy, ultramodern, up-to-the-minute; SEE CONCEPTS 578,589,797,799

static [*adj*] *motionless, changeless*
at a standstill, constant, deadlocked, fixed, format, gridlocked, immobile, immovable, inactive inert, latent, passive, rigid, stabile, stable, stagnant, stalled, standing still, stationary, sticky still, stopped, stuck, unchanging, unfluctuating unmoving, unvarying; SEE CONCEPTS 534,584

station [*n1*] *headquarters, base*
base of operations, depot, home office, house, location, locus, main office, place, position, post seat, site, situation, spot, stop, terminal, whereabouts; SEE CONCEPT 198

station [*n2*] *social or occupational status*
appointment, business, calling, capacity, caste character, class, duty, employment, estate, footing, grade, level, occupation, order, place, position, post, rank, service, situation, sphere

standing, state, stratum; SEE CONCEPTS 349,376,388

ation [*v*] *place at a location*
allot, appoint, assign, base, commission, establish, fix, garrison, install, lodge, park, plant, post, put, set; SEE CONCEPTS 50,88,201,320,351

ationary [*adj*] *not moving; fixed*
anchored, at a standstill, immobile, inert, moored, motionless, nailed*, nailed down*, parked*, pat*, permanent, stable, stagnant, standing, static, stock-still, unmoving; SEE CONCEPTS 488,551

ationery [*n*] *writing materials*
envelopes, letterhead, office supplies, pen and paper, writing paper; SEE CONCEPTS 260,475

atue [*n*] *trophy or memorial*
bronze, bust, cast, effigy, figure, icon, image, ivory, likeness, marble, piece, representation, sculpture, simulacrum, statuary, statuette, torso; SEE CONCEPT 259

atuesque [*adj*] *tall and dignifed*
beautiful, graceful, grand, imposing, majestic, regal, shapely, stately, trim, well-proportioned; SEE CONCEPTS 579,589,779

ature [*n*] *importance*
ability, cachet, caliber, capacity, competence, consequence, development, dignity, elevation, eminence, growth, merit, position, prestige, prominence, qualification, quality, rank, size, standing, state, station, status, tallness, value, virtue, worth; SEE CONCEPTS 668,741

atus [*n*] *rank*
cachet, caliber, capacity, character, condition, consequence, degree, dignity, distinction, eminence, footing, grade, merit, mode, place, position, prestige, prominence, quality, rating, renown, situation, stage, standing, state, station, stature, worth; SEE CONCEPTS 388,668

atus quo [*n*] *existing conditions*
circumstances, how things stand, no change, state, state of affairs; SEE CONCEPTS 410,639,696, 701,720

atute [*n*] *rule, law*
act, assize, bill, canon, decree, decretum, edict, enactment, measure, ordinance, precept, regulation; SEE CONCEPT 318

taunch [*adj*] *resolute, dependable*
allegiant, ardent, constant, faithful, fast, firm, inflexible, liege, loyal, reliable, secure, sound, stable, stalwart, steadfast, stiff, stout, strong, sure, tough, tried-and-true, true, true-blue, trustworthy, trusty; SEE CONCEPTS 401,534,542

tay [*n1*] *visit*
break, halt, holiday, sojourn, stop, stopover, vacation; SEE CONCEPT 227

tay [*n2*] *hold, delay*
deferment, halt, pause, postponement, remission, reprieve, standstill, stop, stopping, suspension; SEE CONCEPTS 121,832

tay [*n3*] *support, underpinning*
brace, buttress, column, hold, prop, reinforcement, shore, shoring, stanchion, truss, underpropping; SEE CONCEPTS 440,445

tay [*v1*] *wait*
abide, bide, bunk, continue, dally, delay, endure, establish oneself, halt, hang, hang about, hang around, hang in, hang out, hold the fort*, hover, lag, last, linger, loiter, nest, outstay, pause, perch, procrastinate, put down roots*, remain, reprieve, reside, respite, roost*, settle, sit tight*,

sojourn, squat, stand, stay out, stay put, stick around*, stop, sweat*, sweat it out*, tarry; SEE CONCEPTS 210,681

stay [*v2*] *visit*
be accommodated, bide, dwell, live, lodge, put up, sojourn, stop, stop over, tarry; SEE CONCEPTS 226,227

stay [*v3*] *hold in abeyance*
adjourn, arrest, check, curb, defer, delay, detain, discontinue, halt, hinder, hold, hold over, impede, intermit, interrupt, obstruct, postpone, prevent, prorogue, put off, shelve, stall, stop, suspend, ward off; SEE CONCEPT 121

staying power [*n*] *stamina*
backbone*, endurance, fortitude, grit*, guts*, gutsiness, heart, intestinal fortitude*, legs*, power of endurance, resilience, tolerance, vitality; SEE CONCEPTS 411,732

steadfast [*adj*] *loyal, steady*
abiding, adamant, allegiant, ardent, bound, changeless, constant, dedicated, dependable, enduring, established, faithful, fast, firm, fixed, immobile, immovable, inexorable, inflexible, intense, intent, liege, never-failing, obdurate, persevering, relentless, reliable, resolute, rigid, single-minded, stable, staunch, stubborn, sure, tried-and-true*, true, true-blue*, unbending, unfaltering, unflinching, unmovable, unqualified, unquestioning, unswerving, unwavering, unyielding, wholehearted; SEE CONCEPTS 401,534, 542

steady [*adj1*] *stable, fixed*
abiding, brick-wall*, certain, changeless, constant, durable, enduring, equable, even, firm, immovable, never-failing, patterned, regular, reliable, safe, set, set in stone*, solid, solid as a rock*, stabile, steadfast, steady-going, substantial, sure, unchangeable, unchanging, unfaltering, unfluctuating, uniform, unqualified, unquestioning, unshaken, unvarying, unwavering; SEE CONCEPTS 488,534

steady [*adj2*] *continuing*
ceaseless, confirmed, consistent, constant, continuous, equable, eternal, even, faithful, habitual, incessant, never-ending, nonstop, persistent, regular, rhythmic, stabile, stable, steady-going, unbroken, unfaltering, unfluctuating, uniform, uninterrupted, unremitting, unvarying, unwavering; SEE CONCEPT 798

steady [*adj3*] *balanced, faithful in mind*
allegiant, ardent, calm, constant, cool, dependable, equable, fast, imperturbable, intense, level-headed, liege, loyal, poised, reliable, reserved, resolute, sedate, self-possessed, sensible, serene, serious-minded, settled, single-minded, sober, staid, staunch, steadfast, unswerving, unwavering, wholehearted; SEE CONCEPTS 403,542

steal [*v1*] *take something without permission*
abduct, appropriate, blackmail, burglarize, carry off, cheat, cozen, defraud, despoil, divert, embezzle, heist, hold for ransom, hold up, housebreak*, keep, kidnap, lift*, loot, make off with*, misappropriate, peculate, pilfer, pillage, pinch*, pirate, plagiarize, plunder, poach, purloin, ransack, remove, rifle, rip off*, run off with*, sack*, shoplift, snitch*, stick up*, strip, swindle, swipe, take, take possession of*, thieve, walk off with*, withdraw; SEE CONCEPT 139

steal [*v2*] *sneak around*
creep, flit, glide, go stealthily, insinuate, lurk,

st
st

pass quietly, skulk, slide, slink, slip, snake, tiptoe; SEE CONCEPTS 151,207

stealthy [*adj*] *quiet and secretive*
catlike, catty*, clandestine, covert, crafty, cunning, enigmatic, feline, furtive, hush-hush*,
noiseless, private, secret, shifty, silent, skulking,
slinking, sly, sneak, sneaking, sneaky, sub-rosa*,
surreptitious, undercover, underhand, under
wraps*, wily; SEE CONCEPTS 401,576

steam [*n*] *energy*
beef, force, might, muscle, potency, power, puissance, sinew, strength, vigor, vim; SEE CONCEPT
633

steel [*v*] *prepare oneself*
animate, brace, buck up*, cheer, embolden, encourage, fortify, gird, grit teeth*, harden,
hearten, inspirit, make up one's mind*, prepare,
rally, ready, reinforce, strengthen; SEE CONCEPT
35

steep [*adj1*] *extreme in direction, course*
abrupt, arduous, breakneck, declivitous, elevated, erect, headlong, high, hilly, lifted, lofty,
perpendicular, precipitate, precipitous, prerupt,
raised, sharp, sheer, straight-up; SEE CONCEPT
581

steep [*adj2*] *very expensive*
dizzying, excessive, exorbitant, extortionate, extreme, high, immoderate, inordinate, overpriced,
stiff, towering, uncalled-for, undue, unmeasurable, unreasonable; SEE CONCEPTS 334,762

steep [*v*] *let soak*
bathe, damp, drench, fill, imbue, immerse, impregnate, infuse, ingrain, invest, macerate, marinate, moisten, permeate, pervade, saturate, soak,
sodden, sop, souse, submerge, suffuse, waterlog;
SEE CONCEPT 256

steer [*v*] *guide, direct on a course*
beacon, be in the driver's seat*, captain, conduct,
control, drive, escort, govern, head for, helm,
herd, lead, pilot, point, route, run, run things, see,
shepherd, show, skipper*, take over, take the
helm, take the reins; SEE CONCEPTS 94,187

stem [*n*] *stalk of plant*
axis, branch, pedicel, pedicle, peduncle, petiole,
shoot, stock, trunk; SEE CONCEPT 428

stem [*v.l*] *come from*
arise, be bred, be brought about, be caused, be
generated, derive, develop, emanate, flow, head,
issue, originate, proceed, rise, spring; SEE CON-
CEPT 648

stem [*v2*] *prevent, stop*
arrest, bring to a standstill, check, contain, control, curb, dam, hinder, hold back, oppose, resist,
restrain, stay, withstand; SEE CONCEPT 121

stench [*n*] *foul odor*
fetor, funk*, malodor, mephitis, noisomeness,
redolence, smell, stink*; SEE CONCEPTS 599,600

step [*n1*] *pace of feet in walking*
footfall, footprint, footstep, gait, impression,
mark, print, spoor, stepping, stride, trace, track,
trail, tread, vestige, walk; SEE CONCEPT 149

step [*n2*] *action, move*
act, advance, advancement, deed, degree, expedient, gradation, grade, level, maneuver, means,
measure, motion, notch, phase, point, procedure,
proceeding, process, progression, rank, remove,
rung, stage, start; SEE CONCEPTS 1,832

step [*n3*] *one level of stairs*
doorstep, gradation, notch, rest, round, run, rung,
stair, tread; SEE CONCEPTS 440,445

step [*v*] *move foot to walk*
advance, ambulate, ascend, dance, descend, go
backward, go down, go forward, go up, hoof,
mince, move backward, move forward, pace,
prance, skip, stride, tiptoe, traipse, tread, trip,
troop, walk; SEE CONCEPT 149

step down [*v*] *resign*
abandon, abdicate, bow out, cease work, drop
out, give notice, hand in resignation, hang it up*,
leave, quit, retire, sign off, terminate, throw in
the towel*, walk out; SEE CONCEPTS 119,195,351

step in [*v*] *become involved*
arrive, be invited, chip in*, come, enter, intercede, interfere, intermediate, interpose, intervene, lend a hand*, mediate, negotiate, take
action; SEE CONCEPTS 100,324,384

step up [*v*] *accelerate*
augment, boost, escalate, hasten, hurry, improve,
increase, intensify, lift, quicken, raise, shake up,
speed, speed up, up; SEE CONCEPTS 236,244,245

stereotype [*n*] *idea held as standard, example*
average, boilerplate*, convention, custom, fashion, formula, institution, mold, pattern, received
idea; SEE CONCEPT 686

stereotype [*v*] *categorize as being example, standard*
catalogue, conventionalize, define, dub, institutionalize, methodize, normalize, pigeonhole*,
regulate, standardize, systematize, take to be,
typecast*; SEE CONCEPTS 38,49

stereotyped [*adj*] *standard, conventional*
banal, clichéd, cliché-ridden, commonplace,
corny*, dull, hackneyed, mass-produced, ordinary, overused, platitudinous, played out*, stale,
standardized, stock, threadbare*, tired*, trite, unoriginal, well-worn, worn-out, worn thin; SEE
CONCEPT 530

sterile [*adj*] *unproductive, clean*
antiseptic, arid, aseptic, bare, barren, bleak, dead,
decontaminated, desert, desolate, disinfected,
dry, effete, empty, fallow, fruitless, futile, gaunt,
germ-free, hygienic, impotent, infecund, infertile, pasteurized, sanitary, septic, sterilized, unfruitful, uninfected, unprofitable, unprolific,
vain, waste, without issue; SEE CONCEPTS
485,621

sterilize [*v*] *make clean or unproductive*
alter, antisepticize, asceptize, aseptify, autoclave,
castrate, change, clean, decontaminate, desexualize, disinfect, emasculate, fix, fumigate, incapacitate, make sterile, neuter, pasteurize, purify,
sanitize, spay; SEE CONCEPTS 231,250

sterling [*adj*] *high-quality*
admirable, choice, excellent, exquisite, fine, first-
rate, grand, magnificent, marvelous, outstanding,
pure, splendid, stunning, superior, the best, very
best; SEE CONCEPT 574

stern [*adj*] *serious, authoritarian*
ascetic, astringent, austere, bitter, bullheaded, by
the book*, cruel, disciplinary, dyed-in-the-
wool*, flinty, forbidding, frowning, grim, hang-
tough*, hard, hard-boiled*, hard-core*,
hardheaded*, hard-line*, hard-nosed*, hard-
shell*, harsh, implacable, inexorable, inflexible,
mortified, mulish, relentless, rigid, rigorous,
rough, severe, steely, stiff-necked*, strict, stubborn, tough, unrelenting, unsparing, unyielding;
SEE CONCEPTS 401,542

stew [*n1*] *mixture, miscellany*
brew, goulash*, hash, jumble, medley, mélange,

mishmash, mulligan*, olio*, pasticcio*, pie*, potpourri, salmagundi*, soup; SEE CONCEPTS *432,457,460,461*

stew [*n2*] *commotion; mental upset*
agitation, confusion, dither, flap, fretting, fuming, fuss, lather, pother, snit, sweat, tizzy, tumult, turbulence, turmoil, worry; SEE CONCEPT *410*

stew [*v*] *worry; steam*
boil, chafe, cook, fret, fume, fuss, pother, seethe, simmer; SEE CONCEPT *35*

stick [*n*] *pole, often wooden*
bar, bat, baton, billet, birch, bludgeon, board, branch, cane, club, cudgel, drumstick, ferrule, ingot, mast, rod, rule, ruler, shoot, slab, slat, staff, stake, stalk, stave, stem, strip, switch, timber, twig, wand, wedge; SEE CONCEPTS *470,479*

stick [*v1*] *adhere, affix*
attach, be bogged down, become embedded, become immobilized, bind, bond, braze, catch, cement, clasp, cleave, cling, cling like ivy*, clog, cohere, fasten, fix, freeze to, fuse, glue, hold, hold fast, hold on, hug, jam, join, linger, lodge, paste, persist, remain, snag, solder, stay, stay put, stick like barnacle*, stick together, unite, weld; SEE CONCEPTS *85,160*

stick [*v2*] *poke with pointed object*
dig, drive, gore, impale, insert, jab, penetrate, pierce, pin, plunge, prod, puncture, ram, run, sink, spear, stab, thrust, transfix; SEE CONCEPT *220*

stick [*v3*] *position, lay*
deposit, drop, establish, fix, install, place, plant, plonk, plunk, put, set, settle, store, stuff; SEE CONCEPT *201*

stick [*v4*] *endure*
abide, bear, bear up under, brook, get on with, go, grin and bear it*, last, persist, put up with, see through, stand, stay, stomach*, suffer, support, take, take it, tolerate, weather; SEE CONCEPT *23*

stick-in-the-mud [*n*] *person set in ways*
antediluvian, conservative, diehard*, fossil*, mossback*, old fogy*, reactionary; SEE CONCEPT *423*

stick out [*v*] *bulge*
beetle, come through, extend, extrude, jut, obtrude, outthrust, overhang, poke, pouch, pout, project, pretend, protrude, push, show, stand out; SEE CONCEPT *751*

stickup [*n*] *holdup*
armed robbery, burglary, crime, mugging, robbery, stealing, theft; SEE CONCEPT *192*

sticky [*adj1*] *gummy, adhesive*
agglutinative, clinging, gluey, glutinous, ropy, syrupy, tacky, tenacious, viscid, viscous; SEE CONCEPT *606*

sticky [*adj2*] *humid and hot*
clammy, close, dank, mucky, muggy, oppressive, soggy, sultry, sweltering; SEE CONCEPT *525*

sticky [*adj3*] *difficult, embarrassing*
awkward, delicate, discomforting, formidable, hairy*, hard, heavy*, knotty, laborious, nasty, operose, painful, rough, rugged, strenuous, thorny, tricky, unpleasant; SEE CONCEPT *565*

stiff [*adj1*] *hard, inflexible*
annealed, arthritic, benumbed, brittle, buckram, cemented, chilled, congealed, contracted, creaky, firm, fixed, frozen, graceless, hardened, immalleable, impliable, incompliant, indurate, inelastic, jelled, mechanical, numbed, ossified,

petrified, refractory, resistant, rheumatic, rigid, set, solid, solidified, starched, starchy, stark, steely, stiff as a board*, stony, taut, tense, thick, thickened, tight, unbending, unflexible, ungraceful, unsupple, unyielding, wooden; SEE CONCEPT *604*

stiff [*adj2*] *formal, standoffish*
angular, artificial, austere, ceremonious, , cold, constrained, forced, hardheaded, headstrong, inflexible, intractable, labored, mannered, obstinate, pertinacious, pompous, priggish, prim, punctilious, relentless, starchy, stilted, strong, stubborn, uneasy, ungainly, ungraceful, unnatural, unrelaxed, unrelenting, wooden; SEE CONCEPT *401*

stiff [*adj3*] *difficult*
arduous, exacting, fatiguing, formidable, hard, laborious, tough, trying, uphill; SEE CONCEPT *565*

stiff [*adj4*] *extreme, severe*
austere, brisk, cruel, drastic, exact, excessive, exorbitant, extravagant, great, hard, harsh, heavy, immoderate, inexorable, inordinate, oppressive, pitiless, potent, powerful, rigorous, sharp, steep, strict, stringent, strong, towering, unconscionable, undue, vigorous; SEE CONCEPTS *540,569*

stiffen [*v*] *make or become harder*
anneal, benumb, brace, cake, candy, cement, chill, clot, coagulate, condense, congeal, crystallize, curdle, firm, fix, freeze, gel, harden, inflate, inspissate, jell, jelly, ossify, petrify, precipitate, prop, reinforce, set, solidify, stabilize, starch, steady, strengthen, tauten, tense, thicken; SEE CONCEPTS *137,250,469*

stifle [*v*] *prevent, restrain*
asphyxiate, black out, bring to screeching halt*, burke, check, choke, choke back, clamp down*, clam up*, constipate, cork, cover up, crack down*, curb, dry up*, extinguish, gag, hold it down, hush, hush up, kill*, muffle, muzzle, prevent, put the lid on*, repress, restrain, shut up, silence, sit on*, smother, spike, squash, squelch, stagnate, stop, strangle, stultify, suffocate, suppress, torpedo*, trammel; SEE CONCEPTS *121,130,191*

stigma [*n*] *shame*
bar sinister*, besmirchment, black mark*, blame, blemish, blot, brand, disfigurement, disgrace, dishonor, imputation, lost face*, mark, odium, onus, reproach, scar, slur, spot, stain, taint; SEE CONCEPTS *230,388,689*

stigmatize [*v*] *brand, label*
characterize, class, classify, defame, denounce, designate, disgrace, mark, stamp, tag; SEE CONCEPTS *62,79*

still [*adj*] *calm, motionless, quiet*
at rest, buttoned up*, clammed up*, closed, close-mouthed, deathlike, deathly, deathly quiet, deathly still, fixed, halcyon, hushed, hushful, inert, lifeless, noiseless, pacific, peaceful, placid, restful, sealed, serene, silent, smooth, soundless, stable, stagnant, static, stationary, stock-still, tranquil, undisturbed, unruffled, unstirring, untroubled, whist; SEE CONCEPTS *584,594*

still [*conj*] *however*
after all, besides, but, even, for all that, furthermore, howbeit, nevertheless, nonetheless, notwithstanding, still and all, though, withal, yet; SEE CONCEPT *544*

st
st

still [*n*] *quiet*
hush, noiselessness, peace, quietness, quietude, silence, soundlessness, still, stillness, tranquility; SEE CONCEPTS *65,748*

still [*v*] *make quiet, motionless, calm*
allay, alleviate, appease, arrest, balm, becalm, calm, choke, compose, decrease volume, fix, gag, hush, lull, muffle, muzzle, pacify, quiet, quieten, settle, shush*, shut down, shut up, silence, slack, smooth, smooth over, soothe, squash, squelch, stall, stop, subdue, tranquilize; SEE CONCEPTS *7,22,65,121*

stillness [*n*] *silence*
calm, calmness, hush, inaction, inactivity, lull, noiselessness, peace, placidity, quiet, quietness, quietude, serenity, still, tranquility; SEE CONCEPTS *65,388,411,720*

stilted [*adj*] *artificial, pretentious*
affected, angular, aureate, bombastic, constrained, decorous, egotistic, euphuistic, flowery, forced, formal, genteel, grandiloquent, high-flown, high-sounding, inflated, labored, magniloquent, mincing, overblown, pedantic, pompous, prim, rhetorical, sonorous, stiff, unnatural, wooden; SEE CONCEPTS *267,401*

stimulant [*n*] *substance that invigorates*
analeptic, bracer, catalyst, drug, energizer, excitant, goad, impetus, impulse, incentive, incitation, incitement, motivation, motive, pick-me-up*, restorative, reviver, shot in the arm*, spark plug*, spur, stimulus, tonic, upper; SEE CONCEPTS *240,307,661*

stimulate [*v*] *excite, provoke*
activate, animate, arouse, build a fire under*, commove, dynamize, elate, encourage, energize, enliven, exhilarate, fan, fire, fire up*, foment, foster, galvanize, get one going*, get one started*, goad, grab, hook, impel, incite, inflame, innervate, innerve, inspire, instigate, jazz*, juice*, key up*, motivate, move, perk, pique, prod, prompt, quicken, rouse, send, set up, spark, spirit, spur, steam up*, stir up*, support, trigger, turn on*, urge, vitalize, vivify, wake up*, whet, work up*; SEE CONCEPTS *14,242*

stimulating [*adj*] *exciting*
adrenalizing, appealing, arousing, bracing, breathtaking, challenging, electrifying, energizing, exhilarating, gripping, hair-raising*, hectic, inspiring, interesting, invigorating, lively, moving, provocative, rousing, spine-tingling*, stirring, thought-provoking, thrilling, titillating; SEE CONCEPTS *529,542,548*

stimulus [*n*] *provocation*
bang*, boost, catalyst, cause, charge, encouragement, eye-opener*, fillip, fireworks*, flash*, goad, impetus, impulse, incentive, incitation, incitement, inducement, instigation, invitation, kick*, motivation, motive, piquing, propellant, provocation, push, shot in the arm*, spur, stimulant, stimulation, sting*, turn-on*, urging; SEE CONCEPTS *240,307,661*

sting [*v*] *prick, pain*
bite, burn, electrify, hurt, injure, inspire, needle, pique, poke, prickle, smart, tingle, wound; SEE CONCEPTS *220,246,313,728*

stingy [*adj*] *penny-pinching, averse to spending money*
acquisitive, avaricious, chary, cheap, chintzy*, churlish, close, close-fisted, costive, covetous, curmudgeonly, economical, extortionate, frugal, grasping, greedy, grudging, ignoble, illiberal, ironfisted, mean, miserly, narrow, near, parsimonious, pennywise*, penurious, petty, pinchpenny*, rapacious, saving, scrimping, scurvy, selfish, skimping, sordid, sparing, thrifty, tight-fisted, uncharitable, ungenerous, ungiving; SEE CONCEPTS *326,334,401*

stink [*n*] *bad smell*
fetor, foulness, foul odor, malodor, noisomeness, offensive smell, stench; SEE CONCEPTS *599,600*

stink [*v*] *smell badly*
be offensive, be rotten, funk*, have an odor, offend, reek*, smell up, stink to high heaven*; SEE CONCEPT *600*

stink [*v2*] *be lousy, bad*
be abhorrent, be detestable, be held in disrepute, be no good, be offensive, be rotten, have a bad name*, smell; SEE CONCEPTS *230,388*

stinking [*adj*] *smelly*
fetid, foul, foul-smelling, funky*, malodorous, mephitic, noisome, odiferous, offensive, putrid, rancid, rank, reeking, stenchy, stinking, strong-smelling; SEE CONCEPT *598*

stint [*n*] *period of responsibility*
assignment, bit, chore, consignment, duty, job, participation, quota, share, shift, spell, stretch, task, term, time, tour, turn, work; SEE CONCEPTS *362,807,822*

stint [*v*] *economize; hold back*
be frugal, begrudge, be parsimonious, be sparing, be stingy, confine, cut corners*, define, go easy on, grudge, limit, make ends meet*, penny-pinch*, pinch, restrain, roll back*, save, save for rainy day*, scrape, scrimp, skimp on*, sock away*, spare, squirrel*, stash, tighten belt*, withhold; SEE CONCEPT *330*

stipend [*n*] *payment for services*
allowance, award, consideration, emolument, fee, gratuity, hire, pay, pension, salary, take, wage; SEE CONCEPT *344*

stipulate [*v*] *decide on conditions*
agree, arrange, bargain, condition, contract, covenant, designate, detail, engage, guarantee, impose, insist upon, lay down, lay finger on, make, make a point, name, particularize, pin down, pledge, postulate, promise, provide, put down for, require, settle, slot, specificalize, specificize, specify, spell out, state; SEE CONCEPTS *8,18,60*

stipulation [*n*] *condition of agreement*
agreement, arrangement, circumscription, clause, contract, designation, engagement, fine print*, limit, obligation, precondition, prerequisite, provision, proviso, qualification, requirement, reservation, restriction, settlement, sine qua non, small print*, specification, string attached*, term, terms; SEE CONCEPTS *270,318,684*

stir [*n*] *commotion, excitement*
activity, ado, agitation, backwash*, bustle, din, disorder, disquiet, disturbance, ferment, flap*, flurry, furor, fuss, movement, pandemonium, pother, racket, row, scene, to-do*, tumult, turmoil, uproar, whirl, whirlwind; SEE CONCEPTS *230,388*

stir [*v1*] *mix up, agitate*
beat, blend, disturb, flutter, mix, move, move about, quiver, rustle, shake, toss, tremble, whip, whisk; SEE CONCEPTS *158,170*

stir [*v2*] *incite, stimulate*
abet, actuate, add fuel to fire*, adjy*, affect, agi-

tate, animate, arouse, awaken, bestir, challenge, craze, drive, electrify, energize, excite, feed the fire*, foment, galvanize, impel, inflame, inspire, kindle, make waves*, motivate, move, prompt, provoke, psych*, quicken, raise, rally, rile, rouse, roust, rout, set, spark, spook*, spur, stimulate, stir embers*, stir up, switch on, thrill, touch, trigger, urge, vitalize, wake, waken, whet, whip up*, work up*; SEE CONCEPTS *14,221*

'tir [v3] *get up and going*
awake, awaken, bestir, be up and about, budge, exert, get a move on*, get moving, hasten, look alive, make an effort, mill about, move, rouse, shake a leg*, wake, waken; SEE CONCEPT *149*

'tirring [adj] *moving, rousing*
arousing, awakening, dynamic, electrifying, emotional, exhilarating, gripping, heartbreaking, heartrending, inspirational, inspiring, motivating, provoking, stimulating, touching; SEE CONCEPTS *529,537* .

'ock [adj] *commonplace*
banal, basic, common, conventional, customary, dull, established, formal, hackneyed, normal, ordinary, overused, regular, routine, run-of-the-mill*, set, standard, staple, stereotyped, traditional, trite, typical, usual, worn-out; SEE CONCEPTS *530,547*

'ock [n1] *merchandise*
accumulation, array, articles, assets, assortment, backlog, cache, choice, commodities, fund, goods, hoard, inventory, nest egg*, produce, range, reserve, reservoir, selection, stockpile, store, supply, variety, wares; SEE CONCEPT *338*

'ock [n2] *animals raised on a farm*
animals, beasts, cattle, cows, domestic, farm animals, flock, fowl, herd, hogs, horses, livestock, pigs, sheep, swine; SEE CONCEPTS *394,397*

'ock [n3] *ancestry*
background, breed, clan, descent, extraction, family, folk, forebears, house, kin, kindred, line, lineage, line of descent, parentage, pedigree, race, species, strain, tribe, type, variety; SEE CONCEPTS *296,378*

'ock [n4] *investment in company*
assets, blue chips, bonds, capital, convertible, funds, over-the-counter*, paper, property, share; SEE CONCEPT *332*

'ock [n5] *estimation, faith*
appraisal, appraisement, assessment, confidence, count, dependence, estimate, evaluation, figure, hope, inventory, judgment, reliance, review, trust; SEE CONCEPTS *37,689,764*

'ock [v] *supply with merchandise*
accumulate, amass, carry, deal in, equip, fill, furnish, gather, handle, have, hoard, keep, keep on hand, lay in, provide, provision, put away, reserve, save, sell, stockpile, store, stow away, trade in; SEE CONCEPTS *140,182,324*

'ockade [n] *enclosure; jail*
barrier, cage, camp, can*, cell, clink*, cooler*, coop, corral, detention camp, dungeon, fence, jailhouse, joint*, pen, penal institution, penitentiary, pound, prison, protection, slammer*, sty; SEE CONCEPTS *439,448,449,513,516*

'ock market [n] *stock exchange*
American Stock Exchange, AMEX, Big Board, Chicago Board of Trade, commodities exchange, Dow Jones, futures exchange, NASDAQ, National Association of Securities Dealers Auto-

mated Quotations, New York Stock Exchange, Wall Street; SEE CONCEPTS *323,333,449*

stockpile [n] *supply*
accumulation, buildup, cache, hoard, inventory, nest egg, reserve, source, stash, stock, store, surplus; SEE CONCEPT *712*

stockpile [v] *stock*
accumulate, amass, build up, gather, hoard, keep on hand, put away, reserve, save, squirrel away, stash, stock up, store, stow away; SEE CONCEPTS *140,182,324*

stocky [adj] *short and overweight; short and muscular*
chunky, corpulent, fat, heavyset, plump, solid, squat, stout, stubby, sturdy, thick, thickset; SEE CONCEPTS *491,773*

stodgy [adj] *dull, stuffy*
banausic, boring, dim, dreary, formal, heavy, labored, monotonous, pedantic, pedestrian, plodding, ponderous, staid, tedious, turgid, unexciting, unimaginative, uninspired, uninteresting, weighty; SEE CONCEPTS *401,404*

stoic/stoical [adj] *philosophic, calm*
aloof, apathetic, cool, cool as cucumber*, detached, dispassionate, dry, enduring, impassive, imperturbable, indifferent, indomitable, long-suffering, matter-of-fact, patient, phlegmatic, resigned, rolling with punches*, self-controlled, sober, stolid, unconcerned, unemotional, unflappable, unmoved; SEE CONCEPTS *401,404*

stolid [adj] *apathetic, stupid*
blunt, bovine, dense, doltish, dry, dull, dumb, heavy, impassive, inactive, indifferent, inert, lumpish, matter-of-fact, obtuse, passive, phlegmatic, slow, stoic, supine, unemotional, unexcitable, wooden; SEE CONCEPTS *401,402*

stomach [n1] *digestive organ of animate being; exterior*
abdominal region abdomen, belly, below the belt*, breadbasket*, gut, inside, insides, maw*, paunch, pot*, potbelly*, solar plexus, spare tire*, tummy*; SEE CONCEPTS *393,420*

stomach [n2] *appetite*
appetence, desire, inclination, mind, relish, taste, tooth; SEE CONCEPT *20*

stomach [v] *endure, tolerate*
abide, bear, bear with, bite the bullet*, brook, digest, grin and bear it*, live with*, put up with, reconcile oneself, resign oneself, stand, submit to, suffer, swallow, sweat, take, tolerate; SEE CONCEPT *23*

stone [n] *hard piece of earth's surface*
boulder, crag, crystal, gem, grain, gravel, jewel, metal, mineral, ore, pebble, rock; SEE CONCEPTS *474,477*

stoned [adj] *high on alcohol or drugs*
baked*, bombed*, boozed up*, buzzed*, doped, drugged, drunk, feeling no pain*, flying*, fried, inebriated, intoxicated, loaded, on a trip*, plastered, ripped*, sloshed*, smashed*, spaced out*, stewed*, strung out*, tanked*, tipsy, totaled*, tripping*, wasted*; SEE CONCEPT *314*

stony [adj] *hard, icy in appearance, response*
adamant, blank, callous, chilly, cold, cold-blooded, coldhearted, cruel, expressionless, firm, frigid, hard-boiled*, hardened, heartless, hostile, indifferent, inexorable, inflexible, merciless, obdurate, pitiless, rough, tough, uncompassionate, unfeeling, unforgiving, unrelenting, unresponsive, unsympathetic; SEE CONCEPTS *401,485*

st
st

stooge [*n*] *dupe*
chump*, easy mark*, fall guy, flunky, fool, lackey, patsy*, pawn, pigeon*, puppet, pushover*, sap*, sucker, victim; SEE CONCEPT *423*

stool pigeon [*n*] *informer*
betrayer, blabbermouth*, canary*, decoy, deep throat*, double-crosser, fink*, informant, narc*, nark*, rat*, sneak, snitch, snitcher, source, squealer*, stoolie*, tattler, tattletale, tipster*, turncoat, weasel*, whistle-blower; SEE CONCEPTS *348,354,423*

stoop [*n*] *slouched posture*
droop, round shoulders, sag, slouch, slump; SEE CONCEPT *757*

stoop [*v1*] *bow down*
be bowed, bend, be servile, bow, cringe, crouch, descend, dip, duck, hunch, incline, kneel, lean, relax, sink, slant, squat; SEE CONCEPTS *181,201*

stoop [*v2*] *condescend; lower oneself to another*
accommodate, act beneath oneself, concede, debase oneself, deign, demean oneself, descend, favor, oblige, patronize, relax, resort, sink, thaw, unbend, vouchsafe; SEE CONCEPTS *35,384*

stop [*n1*] *end, halt; impediment*
bar, barricade, blank wall*, block, blockade, break, break off, brick wall*, cease, cessation, check, close, closing, conclusion, control, cutoff, desistance, discontinuation, ending, fence, finish, freeze*, grinding halt*, hindrance, layoff, letup, lull, pause, plug, roadblock*, screeching halt*, standstill, stay, stoppage, termination, wall; SEE CONCEPTS *240,832*

stop [*n2*] *visit; place of rest*
break, depot, destination, halt, rest, sojourn, stage, station, stay, stopover, termination, terminus; SEE CONCEPTS *198,227*

stop [*v1*] *bring or come to a halt or end*
be over, blow off*, break, break off, call it a day*, cease, close, cold turkey*, come to a standstill*, conclude, cool it*, cut out*, cut short, desist, discontinue, draw up, drop, end, finish, halt, hang it up*, hold, kill, pause, pull up, put an end to, quit, quit cold*, refrain, run its course*, scrub*, shut down, sign off*, stall, stand, stay, tarry, terminate, wind up*, wrap up*; SEE CONCEPTS *119,234,237*

stop [*v2*] *prevent, hold back*
arrest, avoid, bar, block, bottle, break, check, choke, choke off, clog, close, congest, cut off, disrupt, fill, fix, forestall, frustrate, gag, hinder, hush, impede, intercept, interrupt, muzzle, obstruct, occlude, plug, put a stop to, rein in, repress, restrain, seal, shut down, shut off, shut out, silence, stall, staunch, stay, stem, still, stopper, suspend, throw over, turn off, ward off; SEE CONCEPT *121*

stopgap [*adj*] *temporarily helping*
Band-Aid*, emergency, expedient, impromptu, improvised, makeshift, practical, provisional, rough-and-ready*, rough-and-tumble*, substitute, temp, temporary, throwaway*; SEE CONCEPTS *551,560*

stopgap [*n*] *temporary help*
Band-Aid*, expediency, expedient, improvisation, makeshift, pis aller*, recourse, refuge, resort, resource, shift, substitute, temporary expedient; SEE CONCEPT *712*

stoppage [*n*] *halt, curtailment*
abeyance, arrest, blockage, check, close, closure, cutoff, deduction, discontinuance, down, downtime*, hindrance, interruption, layoff, lockout, obstruction, occlusion, shutdown, sit-down, standstill, stopping, walkout; SEE CONCEPT *832*

store [*n1*] *collection, supply*
abundance, accumulation, backlog, cache, fount, fountain, fund, hoard, inventory, lode, lot, mine, nest egg*, plenty, plethora, provision, quantity, reserve, reservoir, savings, spring, stock, stockpile, treasure, wares, wealth, well; SEE CONCEPTS *432,710*

store [*n2*] *place for keeping supply*
arsenal, bank, barn, box, cache, conservatory, depository, depot, magazine, pantry, repository, reservoir, stable, storehouse, storeroom, tank, treasury, vault, warehouse; SEE CONCEPTS *439,441,448,494*

store [*n3*] *business establishment that sells goods*
boutique, chain store, convenience store, deli, department store, discount house, discount store, drugstore, emporium, five-and-dime*, five-and-ten*, grocery store, market, mart, outlet, repository, shop, shopping center, showroom, specialty shop, stand, storehouse, super*, superette*, supermarket; SEE CONCEPTS *325,439,448,449*

store [*v*] *collect and put aside*
accumulate, amass, bank, bin, bottle, bury, cache, can, cumulate, deposit, freeze, garner, hide, hive, hoard, hutch, keep, keep in reserve, lay away, lay up*, lock away, lock up, mothball*, pack, pack away, park, plant, put, put away, put by, put in storage, reserve, roll up, salt away*, save, save for rainy day*, sock away*, squirrel*, stash, stock, stockpile, treasure, victual, warehouse; SEE CONCEPTS *109,129*

storekeeper [*n*] *shopkeeper*
businessperson, dealer, entrepreneur, grocer, merchant, proprietor, retailer, salesperson, seller, storekeeper, store owner, vendor, wholesaler; SEE CONCEPT *347*

storeroom [*n*] *repository*
archive, arsenal, cellar, depository, depot, granary, magazine, safe, silo, stockroom, storage place, storehouse, vault, warehouse; SEE CONCEPTS *435,439,449*

storm [*n1*] *strong weather*
blast, blizzard, blow, cloudburst, cyclone; disturbance, downpour, gale, gust, hurricane, monsoon, precip*, precipitation, raining cats and dogs*, snowstorm, squall, tempest, tornado, twister, whirlwind, windstorm; SEE CONCEPT *526*

storm [*n2*] *commotion, turmoil*
agitation, anger, annoyance, assault, attack, barrage, blitz, blitzkrieg, bluster, bomb, bombardment, broadside, burst, bustle, cannonade, clamor, clatter, convulsion, disturbance, drumfire, furor, fury, fusillade, hail, hassle, hysteria, offensive, onset, onslaught, outbreak, outburst, outcry, passion, perturbation, pother, rabidity, racket, rage, rampancy, roar, row, ruction, rumpus, rush, salvo, squall, stir, strife, temper, tumult, upheaval, violence, volley; SEE CONCEPTS *86,230,674*

storm [*v*] *attack, rush*
aggress, assail, assault, beset, blow violently, bluster, breathe fire*, burn up, carry on*, charge, come at*, complain, drizzle, drop, fly, fume, go on, howl, pour, rage, rain, rant, rave, rip, roar, scold, set in, sizzle, sound off, spit, squall, stalk,

steam up*, stomp, strike, take by storm*, take on*, tear, thunder*; SEE CONCEPTS *52,86,150,526*

stormy [*adj*] *rough (referring to weather)*
bitter, blowy, blustering, blustery, boisterous, cold, coming down*, damp, dirty, foul, frigid, furious, gusty, howling, menacing, murky, pouring, raging, raining cats and dogs*, rainy, riproaring*, roaring, savage, squally, stormful, storming, tempestuous, threatening, torrid, turbulent, violent, wet, wild, windy; SEE CONCEPT *525*

story [*n1*] *account, news*
adventure, allegory, anecdote, apologue, article, autobiography, beat, biography, book, chronicle, cliffhanger*, comedy, conte, description, drama, epic, fable, fairy tale, fantasy, feature, fiction, folktale, gag, history, information, legend, long and short of it*, memoir, myth, narration, narrative, news item, nonfiction, novel, old saw*, parable, potboiler*, recital, record, relation, report, romance, saga, scoop*, sequel, serial, spiel*, tale, tragedy, version, yarn*; SEE CONCEPTS *270,274,282*

story [*n2*] *lie*
canard, cock-and-bull story*, fabrication, falsehood, falsity, fib, fiction, misrepresentation, prevarication, tale, untruism, untruth, white lie*; SEE CONCEPTS *278,282*

stout [*adj*] *overweight*
big, bulky, burly, corpulent, fat, fleshy, heavy, obese, plenitudinous, plump, porcine, portly, rotund, substantial, thick-bodied, tubby, upholstered, weighty, zaftig*; SEE CONCEPTS *491,773*

stout [*adj2*] *strong, brawny*
able-bodied, athletic, hard, hardy, hulking, husky, indomitable, invincible, lusty, muscular, robust, stable, stalwart, staunch, strapping, sturdy, substantial, tenacious, tough, vigorous; SEE CONCEPTS *489,490*

stout [*adj3*] *courageous*
bold, brave, dauntless, fearless, gallant, heroic, intrepid, lionhearted, plucky, resolute, stalwart, undaunted, valiant, valorous; SEE CONCEPTS *403,542*

stouthearted [*adj*] *brave, courageous*
adventurous, bold, daring, dashing, fearless, gallant, game, gritty, gutsy, hardy, heroic, lionhearted, plucky, spunky, stalwart, unafraid, undaunted, unfearful, valiant; SEE CONCEPT *401*

stove [*n*] *range; furnace*
boiler, convection oven, cooker, electric stove, heater, kiln, microwave, oven, toaster oven, warmer, wood stove; SEE CONCEPT *463*

stow [*v*] *reserve, store*
bundle, deposit, load, pack, pack like sardines*, put away, secrete, stash, stuff, top off, tuck, warehouse*; SEE CONCEPT *209*

straggle [*v*] *wander, stray*
be late, dawdle, drift, lag, loiter, maunder, meander, poke, poke around, ramble, range, roam, rove, scramble, spread, straddle, string out, tail, trail; SEE CONCEPT *151*

straight [*adj1*] *aligned; not curved*
beeline*, collinear, consecutive, continuous, direct, erect, even, horizontal, in a line, in a row, inflexible, in line, invariable, level, like an arrow*, lineal, linear, near, nonstop, perpendicular, plumb, precipitous, rectilineal, rectilinear, right, running, sheer, short, smooth, solid, square, straightforward, successive, through, true, unbent, unbroken, uncurled, undeviating,

undistorted, uninterrupted, unrelieved, unswerving, upright, vertical; SEE CONCEPTS *482,486,581*

straight [*adj2*] *honest, fair*
aboveboard, accurate, authentic, bald, blunt, candid, categorical, decent, equitable, fair and square*, forthright, frank, good, honorable, just, law-abiding, moral, outright, plain, point-blank*, reliable, respectable, straightforward, summary, trustworthy, unqualified, upright; SEE CONCEPTS *267,542*

straight [*adj3*] *orderly*
arranged, correct, exact, in order, neat, organized, put to rights, right, shipshape*, sorted, tidy; SEE CONCEPTS *535,585*

straight [*adj4*] *unmixed*
concentrated, neat, out-and-out*, plain, pure, strong, thoroughgoing, unadulterated, undiluted, unmodified, unqualified; SEE CONCEPTS *462,621*

straight [*adj5*] *conventional, square*
bourgeois, buttoned-down*, conservative, orthodox, traditional; SEE CONCEPT *404*

straight [*adv1*] *immediately, directly*
as the crow flies*, at once, away, dead*, direct, due, exactly, first off, forthwith, in direct line, instanter, instantly, lineally, now, point-blank*, right, right away, straightaway, straightforwardly, straightly, undeviatingly; SEE CONCEPTS *581,820*

straight [*adv2*] *honestly*
candidly, frankly, in plain English*, no holds barred*, no punches*, point-blank*; SEE CONCEPTS *267,544*

straighten [*v*] *put in neat or aligned order*
align, arrange, compose, correct, even, level, make plumb, make straight, neaten, order, put in order, put perpendicular, put straight, put to rights, put upright, put vertical, rectify, set to rights, smarten up*, spruce up*, tidy, unbend, uncoil, uncurl, unfold, unravel, unsnarl, untwist; SEE CONCEPTS *158,202,231*

straightforward [*adj1*] *honest*
aboveboard, barefaced*, candid, direct, forthright, frank, genuine, guileless, honorable, just, laid on the line*, level, like it is*, methodical, open, outspoken, plain, plain-dealing*, pretenseless, right-on*, sincere, square-shooting*, straight, straight-arrow*, talking turkey*, truthful, unconcealed, undisguised, undissembled, undissembling, unequivocal, unvarnished, up front*, upright, upstanding, veracious; SEE CONCEPT *267*

straightforward [*adj2*] *simple, easy*
apparent, clear, clear-cut, direct, distinct, elementary, evident, manifest, palpable, patent, plain, routine, straight, through, unambiguous, uncomplicated, undemanding, unequivocal, uninterrupted; SEE CONCEPTS *535,538*

strain [*n1*] *pain, due to exertion*
ache, anxiety, bruise, brunt, burden, constriction, effort, endeavor, exertion, force, injury, jerk, pressure, pull, sprain, stress, stretch, struggle, tautness, tension, tensity, twist, wrench; SEE CONCEPT *728*

strain [*n2*] *ancestry*
blood, breed, descent, extraction, family, lineage, pedigree, race, species, stock; SEE CONCEPTS *296,380*

strain [*n3*] *suggestion, hint*
humor, manner, mind, shade, soupçon, spirit, streak, style, suspicion, temper, tendency, tinge,

tone, touch, trace, trait, vein, way; SEE CONCEPTS *410,529,682*

strain [*n4*] *melody*
air, descant, diapason, lay, measure, song, tune, warble; SEE CONCEPTS *262,595*

strain [*v1*] *stretch, often to limit*
constrict, distend, distort, draw tight, drive, exert, extend, fatigue, injure, overexert, overtax, overwork, pull, push, push to the limit, rack, sprain, task, tauten, tax, tear, tighten, tire, twist, weaken, wrench; SEE CONCEPTS *156,206,208,313*

strain [*v2*] *work very hard*
bear down, endeavor, exert, go all out*, go for broke*, grind, hammer, hustle, labor, moil, peg away*, plug, push, strive, struggle, sweat, toil, try; SEE CONCEPT *87*

strain [*v3*] *filter*
exude, percolate, purify, refine, riddle, screen, seep, separate, sieve, sift; SEE CONCEPTS *135,202*

strain [*v4*] *cause mental stress*
distress, harass, hassle, irk, pain, pick at, push, stress, trouble, try; SEE CONCEPTS *7,19*

strained [*adj*] *forced, pretended*
artificial, at end of rope*, awkward, choked, constrained, difficult, embarrassed, false, farfetched, hard put*, in a state*, labored, nervous wreck*, put, self-conscious, stiff, strung out*, taut, tense, tight, uncomfortable, uneasy, unglued, unnatural, unrelaxed, uptight, wired*, wreck*; SEE CONCEPTS *267,401*

strait [*n1*] *crisis, difficulty*
bewilderment, bind, bottleneck*, choke point*, contingency, crossroad, dilemma, distress, embarrassment, emergency, exigency, extremity, hardship, hole*, mess*, mystification, pass, perplexity, pinch*, plight, predicament, rigor, squeeze*, turning point*, vicissitude, zero hour*; SEE CONCEPT *674*

strait [*n2*] *water channel*
inlet, narrows, sound; SEE CONCEPT *514*

strait-laced [*adj*] *prudish*
old-maidish, priggish*, prim, prissy*, proper, puritanical, rigid, square, starchy, stiff*, strict, stuffy, uptight, Victorian*; SEE CONCEPT *401*

strand [*n*] *fine thread*
fiber, filament, length, lock, rope, string, tress; SEE CONCEPTS *392,452,475*

stranded [*adj*] *marooned, abandoned*
aground, ashore, beached, cast away, godforsaken*, grounded, helpless, high and dry*, homeless, left at the altar*, left in the lurch*, on the rocks*, out in left field*, passed up, penniless, run aground, shipwrecked, sidelined, sidetracked*, wrecked; SEE CONCEPT *577*

strange [*adj1*] *deviating, unfamiliar*
aberrant, abnormal, astonishing, astounding, atypical, bizarre, curious, different, eccentric, erratic, exceptional, extraordinary, fantastic, farout*, funny, idiosyncratic, ignorant, inexperienced, irregular, marvelous, mystifying, new, newfangled*, odd, oddball*, off, offbeat*, outlandish, out-of-the-way*, peculiar, perplexing, quaint, queer, rare, remarkable, singular, unaccountable, unaccustomed, uncanny, uncommon, unheard of, unseasoned, unusual, weird, wonderful; SEE CONCEPT *564*

strange [*adj2*] *exotic, foreign*
alien, apart, awkward, detached, external, faraway, irrelevant, isolated, lost, new, novel, out of place, outside, remote, romanesque, romantic,

unexplored, unfamiliar, unknown, unrelated, untried; SEE CONCEPTS *549,576*

stranger [*n*] *person who is unfamiliar*
alien, drifter, foreign body, foreigner, guest, immigrant, incomer, interloper, intruder, itinerant person, migrant, migratory worker, new arrival, newcomer, outcomer, outlander, out-of-stater*, outsider, party crasher*, perfect stranger*, squatter*, transient, uninvited person, unknown, unknown person, visitor, wanderer; SEE CONCEPTS *413,423*

strangle [*v*] *choke, stifle*
asphyxiate, gag, garrote/garrotte, inhibit, kill, muffle, quelch, repress, restrain, shush, smother, squelch, strangulate, subdue, suffocate, suppress, throttle; SEE CONCEPTS *130,191,252*

strap [*n*] *long piece of material*
band, belt, harness, leash, strop, switch, thong, tie, whip; SEE CONCEPTS *471,475*

strapped [*adj*] *destitute*
beggared, broke*, dirt poor*, flat*, fortuneless, impoverished, out of money, penniless, penurious, poor, stone-broke*; SEE CONCEPT *334*

strapping [*adj*] *big and strong*
brawny, burly, hefty, hulk, hulking, hunk, husky, ox, powerful, powerhouse, robust, stalwart, stout, sturdy, tall, vigorous, well-built; SEE CONCEPTS *489,773*

strategem [*n*] *trick*
action, angle, artifice, bit*, booby trap*, brainchild*, con, deception, device, dodge, feint, gambit, game, game plan*, gimmick, grift, intrigue, layout, maneuver, method, pitch, plan, play, plot, ploy, pretext, proposition, racket, ruse, scenario, scene, scheme, setup, shift, slant, stall, story, subterfuge, switch, twist, wile; SEE CONCEPTS *59,660*

strategic [*adj1*] *crucial*
cardinal, critical, decisive, imperative, important, key, necessary, vital; SEE CONCEPTS *546,567*

strategic [*adj2*] *clever, calculated*
cunning, deliberate, diplomatic, dishonest, planned, politic, tricky; SEE CONCEPT *544*

strategy [*n*] *plan of action*
action, angle, approach, artifice, blueprint*, brainchild*, craft, cunning, design, game, game plan*, gimmick, grand design, layout, maneuvering, method, plan, planning, policy, procedure, program, project, proposition, racket*, scenario, scene, scheme, setup, slant, story, subtlety, system, tactics; SEE CONCEPT *660*

stray [*adj*] *abandoned, wandering*
devious, erratic, homeless, lost, roaming, roving, vagrant; SEE CONCEPT *583*

stray [*v1*] *deviate, err*
circumlocute, depart, digress, divagate, diverge, do wrong, excurse, get off the subject*, get off the track*, get sidetracked*, go off on a tangent*, ramble, sin, wander; SEE CONCEPTS *101,266*

stray [*v2*] *wander; get lost*
be abandoned, be lost, deviate, drift, err, gad*, gallivant, go all over the map*, go amiss, go astray, lose one's way, meander, ramble, range, roam, rove, straggle, swerve, traipse, turn, wander away, wander off; SEE CONCEPT *149*

streak [*n*] *vein, line; small part*
band, bar, beam, dash, element, hint, intimation, layer, ray, ridge, rule, shade, slash, smear, strain, stream, strip, stripe, stroke, suggestion, suspi-

cion, touch, trace; SEE CONCEPTS *436,628,657,727*

streak [*v*] *make a line on*

band, dapple, daub, fleck, marble, slash, smear, spot, strake, striate, stripe, variegate, vein; SEE CONCEPT *250*

stream [*n*] *small river*

beck, branch, brook, burn, course, creek, current, drift, flood, flow, freshet, race, rill, rindle, rivulet, run, runnel, rush, spate, spritz, surge, tide, torrent, tributary, watercourse; SEE CONCEPT *514*

stream [*v*] *flow from*

cascade, continue, course, emerge, emit, flood, glide, gush, issue, move past, pour, roll, run, shed, sluice, spill, spout, spritz, spurt, surge; SEE CONCEPTS *146,179*

street [*n*] *path upon which travel occurs*

artery, avenue, back alley*, boulevard, byway, court, dead end*, drag*, drive, highway, lane, parkway, passage, pavement, place, road, roadway, route, row, stroll, terrace, thoroughfare, track, trail, turf*, way; SEE CONCEPT *501*

street person [*n*] *homeless person*

bag lady, beggar, bum, derelict, drifter, hobo, vagabond, vagrant, wino; SEE CONCEPT *539*

street smart [*adj*] *shrewd*

artful, astute, cagey, calculating, canny, clever, crafty, cunning, experienced, foxy*, ingenious, intelligent, perceptive, quick-witted, savvy*, seasoned, sharp, slick*, sly, smart, smooth, streetwise, wily, wise; SEE CONCEPTS *401,402*

strength [*n1*] *stamina, mental or physical*

backbone, body, brawn, brawniness, brute force*, clout, courage, durability, energy, firmness, force, fortitude, hardiness, health, healthiness, lustiness, might, muscle, nerve, physique, pith, potency, pow*, power, powerhouse*, robustness, security, sinew, sock*, soundness, stability, stableness, stalwartness, steadiness, steamroller, stoutness, strong arm*, sturdiness, substance, tenacity, toughness, verdure, vigor, vim, vitality, zip*; SEE CONCEPTS *410,732*

strength [*n2*] *intensity*

clout, cogency, concentration, depth, effectiveness, efficacy, energy, extremity, fervor, force, juice*, kick*, potency, power, resolution, spirit, vehemence, vigor, virtue; SEE CONCEPT *669*

strength [*n3*] *advantage, substance*

anchor, asset, body, burden, connection, core, gist, guts, in, internal fortitude, license, mainstay, meat, pith, purport, security, sense, strong point, succor, upper hand, weight, wire; SEE CONCEPTS *682,693*

strengthen [*v1*] *make more forceful, powerful*

add, add fuel to fire*, anneal, ascend, bolster, brace, build up, buttress, confirm, corroborate, empower, enhance, enlarge, establish, extend, fortify, harden, heighten, increase, intensify, invigorate, justify, make firm, mount, multiply, regenerate, reinforce, rejuvenate, renew, restore, rise, set up, sinew*, steel, step up, substantiate, support, sustain, temper, tone, tone up, toughen, wax*; SEE CONCEPTS *244,250*

strengthen [*v2*] *encourage, hearten*

animate, back, back up, bear out, bloom, brace, brace up, burgeon, carry weight, cheer, consolidate, embolden, enhearten, enliven, flourish, flower, fortify, gather resources, gird, give weight, harden, inspirit, invigorate, nerve, nour-

ish, prepare, prosper, rally, ready, refresh, rejuvenate, restore, steel, substantiate, temper, thrive, toughen, uphold; SEE CONCEPTS *7,22,35*

strenuous [*adj1*] *difficult; requiring hard work*

arduous, demanding, effortful, energy-consuming, exhausting, hard, Herculean, laborious, mean, operose, taxing, toilful, toilsome, tough, tough going*, uphill*, wicked; SEE CONCEPT *538*

strenuous [*adj2*] *energetic, zealous*

active, aggressive, ardent, bold, determined, dynamic, eager, earnest, lusty, persistent, red-blooded, resolute, spirited, strong, tireless, vigorous, vital; SEE CONCEPTS *401,542*

stress [*n1*] *emphasis*

accent, accentuation, beat, force, import, importance, significance, urgency, weight; SEE CONCEPTS *65,668*

stress [*n2*] *physical or mental pressure*

affliction, agony, alarm, albatross*, anxiety, apprehensiveness, burden, clutch, crunch, disquiet, disquietude, distention, draw, dread, expectancy, extension, fear, fearfulness, ferment, flutter, force, hardship, hassle, heat, impatience, intensity, misgiving, mistrust, nervousness, nervous tension, oppression, overextension, passion, protraction, pull, restlessness, spring, strain, stretch, tautness, tenseness, tension, tensity, tightness, traction, trauma, trepidation, trial, urgency, worry; SEE CONCEPTS *410,720,728*

stress [*v1*] *accentuate, emphasize*

accent, belabor, dwell on, feature, harp on*, headline*, italicize*, lay emphasis on, make emphatic, play up, point up, repeat, rub in*, spot, spotlight*, underline*, underscore*; SEE CONCEPTS *49,68*

stress [*v2*] *put under physical or mental pressure*

afflict, burden, crunch, distend, force, fret, hassle, overdo, overextend, pull, put in traction*, put on trial*, spring, strain, stretch, tense, tense up*, traumatize, worry; SEE CONCEPTS *7,19,246,313*

stretch [*n1*] *expanse*

amplitude, area, branch, breadth, bridge, compass, dimension, distance, expansion, extension, extent, gamut, length, orbit, proliferation, purview, radius, range, reach, region, scope, space, span, spread, sweep, tract, wing; SEE CONCEPTS *651,721,746*

stretch [*n2*] *period of time*

bit, continuance, duration, extent, length, run, space, span, spell, stint, term, time, while; SEE CONCEPTS *807,822*

stretch [*v*] *extend, elongate*

amplify, branch out, bridge, burst forth, cover, crane, develop, distend, drag out, draw, draw out, expand, fill, go, grow, inflate, lengthen, lie out, magnify, make, make taut, make tense, open, overlap, pad, prolong, prolongate, protract, pull, pull out, pyramid, rack, range, reach, recline, repose, run, shoot up, span, spin out, spread, spread out, spring up, strain, string out, swell, tauten, tighten, unfold, unroll, widen; SEE CONCEPTS *137,250*

strict [*adj1*] *authoritarian*

austere, dead set*, disciplinary, dour, draconian*, exacting, firm, forbidding, grim, hard, hard-boiled*, harsh, iron-fisted*, no-nonsense*, oppressive, picky, prudish, punctilious, puritanical, rigid, rigorous, scrupulous, set, severe, square, stern, stickling, straight, strait-laced*,

st
st

stringent, stuffy*, tough, unpermissive, unsparing, uptight*; SEE CONCEPTS 401,542

strict [adj2] *accurate, absolute*
close, complete, exact, faithful, just, meticulous, particular, perfect, precise, religious, right, scrupulous, total, true, undistorted, utter, veracious, veridical; SEE CONCEPTS 535,557

stride [v] *walk purposefully*
clump, drill, march, pace, parade, pound, stalk, stamp, stomp, striddle, stump, traipse, tramp, tromp; SEE CONCEPT 149

strident [adj] *harsh, shrill*
blatant, boisterous, clamorous, clashing, discordant, grating, hoarse, jangling, jarring, loud, noisy, obstreperous, rasping, raucous, screeching, squawky, squeaky, stentorian, stertorous, stridulant, stridulous, unmusical, vociferant, vociferous; SEE CONCEPTS 592,594

strife [n] *struggle, battle*
affray, altercation, animosity, argument, bickering, blowup, brawl, clash, combat, competition, conflict, contention, contest, controversy, difference, disagreement, discord, dispute, dissension, dissent, dissidence, disunity, emulation, faction, factionalism, fighting, friction, fuss, hassle, quarrel, rivalry, spat, squabble, squabbling, static, striving, tug of war*, variance, warfare, words*, wrangle, wrangling; SEE CONCEPTS 46,106,674

strike [v1] *hit hard*
bang, bash, beat, boff, bonk, box, buffet, bump into, chastise, clash, clobber, clout, collide, conk*, crash, cuff*, drive, force, hammer, impel, knock, percuss, plant*, pop*, pound, pummel, punch, rap, run into, slap, slug, smack, smash into, sock, swat, thrust, thump, touch, wallop, whop*; SEE CONCEPT 189

strike [v2] *make an impact*
affect, be plausible, carry, come to mind*, dawn on*, get*, have semblance, hit*, impress, influence, inspire, look, move, occur to, reach, register*, seem, sway, touch; SEE CONCEPTS 7,19,22,716

strike [v3] *find, discover*
achieve, arrive at, attain, catch, chance upon*, come across, come upon, dig up*, effect, encounter, happen upon*, hit upon*, lay bare*, light upon, open up, reach, seize, stumble across*, take, turn up*, uncover, unearth; SEE CONCEPTS 120,183

strike [v4] *devastate, affect*
afflict, aggress, assail, assault, attack, beset, deal a blow, excruciate, fall upon, harrow, hit, invade, martyr, rack, set upon, smite, storm, torment, torture, try, wring; SEE CONCEPTS 7,19

strike [v5] *walk out of job in protest*
arbitrate, be on strike, boycott, go on strike, hit the bricks*, hold out, mediate, mutiny, negotiate, picket, quit, refuse to work, resist, revolt, sit down*, sit in*, slow down, stick out, stop, tie up; SEE CONCEPT 351

strike out [v] *leave to begin new venture*
bear, begin, get under way*, head, initiate, light out*, make, set out, start, start out, take off*; SEE CONCEPT 195

striking [adj] *extraordinary; beautiful*
arresting, arrestive, astonishing, attractive, bizarre, charming, cogent, commanding, compelling, confounding, conspicuous, dazzling, distinguished, dynamite, electrifying, eye-catching, fascinating, forceful, forcible, handsome, impressive, jazzy*, lofty, marked, memorable, noteworthy, noticeable, out of the ordinary*, outstanding, powerful, prominent, remarkable, salient, showy, signal, singular, staggering, startling, stunning, surprising, telling, unusual, wonderful, wondrous; SEE CONCEPTS 574,579

string [n1] *long fiber*
cord, rope, strand, twine, twist; SEE CONCEPT 475

string [n2] *succession, series*
chain, consecution, echelon, file, line, order, procession, queue, rank, row, sequel, sequence, strand, tier, train; SEE CONCEPTS 727,769

string along [v] *play with; keep dangling*
bluff, coquet, dally, deceive, dupe, flirt, fool, hoax, lead on*, put one over on*, take for a ride*, toy, trifle, wanton; SEE CONCEPT 59

stringent [adj] *rigid, tight*
acrimonious, binding, brick-wall*, by the book*, by the numbers*, compelling, confining, convincing, dead set on*, demanding, draconian, drawing, dyed-in-the-wool*, exacting, forceful, hard, hard-nosed*, harsh, inflexible, ironclad, iron-fisted, picky, poignant, powerful, rigorous, rough, set, severe, stiff, strict, tough, unpermissive, valid; SEE CONCEPTS 401,535,569

stringy [adj] *long, thin*
fibrous, gangling, gristly, lank, lanky, muscular, reedy, ropy, sinewy, spindling, spindly, threadlike, tough, wiry; SEE CONCEPT 490

strip [n] *thin piece of material*
band, banding, bar, belt, billet, bit, fillet, ingot, layer, ribbon, rod, section, segment, shred, slab, slip, stick, stripe, swathe, tape, tongue; SEE CONCEPTS 471,834

strip [v] *bare, uncover*
decorticate, denude, deprive, despoil, dismantle, displace, disrobe, divest, empty, excorticate, expose, gut, hull, husk, lay bare, lift, peel, pillage, plunder, ransack, ravage*, remove, rob, scale, shave, shed, shuck, skin, slip out of, spoil, take off, tear, unclothe, undress, withdraw; SEE CONCEPT 211

stripe [n] *line, strip*
band, banding, bar, border, decoration, division, fillet, layer, ribbon, rule, streak, striation, stroke; SEE CONCEPTS 284,622

strive [v] *try for, exert oneself*
aim, assay, attempt, bear down, bend over backward*, break one's neck*, compete, contend, do one's best*, do one's utmost*, drive, endeavor, essay, fight, go after, go all out*, go for broke*, go for the jugular*, go the limit*, hassle, jockey*, knock oneself out*, labor, leave no stone unturned*, make every effort, moil, offer, push, scramble, seek, shoot for*, strain, struggle, sweat, tackle, take on, toil, try hard, tug*, work; SEE CONCEPT 87

stroke [n1] *accomplishment*
achievement, blow*, feat, flourish, hit*, move, movement; SEE CONCEPT 706

stroke [n2] *seizure*
apoplexy, attack, collapse, convulsion, fit, shock; SEE CONCEPTS 33,308

stroke [v] *pat lengthwise*
brush, caress, chuck, comfort, fondle, pet, rub, smooth, soothe, tickle; SEE CONCEPT 612

stroll [n] *lazy walk*
airing, breath of fresh air*, constitutional, cruise, excursion, promenade, ramble, saunter, turn; SEE CONCEPT 151

stroll [v] *walk along lazily*
amble, cruise, drift, gallivant, linger, make one's way*, mope*, mosey*, promenade, ramble, roam, rove, sashay*, saunter, toddle, traipse, tramp, wander; SEE CONCEPT 151

strong [adj1] *healthy, powerful*
able, able-bodied, active, athletic, big, capable, durable, enduring, energetic, firm, fixed, forceful, forcible, hale, hard as nails*, hardy, hearty, heavy, heavy-duty*, in fine feather*, mighty, muscular, reinforced, robust, rugged, secure, sinewy, solid, sound, stable, stalwart, stark, staunch, steady, stout, strapping, sturdy, substantial, tenacious, tough, unyielding, vigorous, well-built, well-founded, well-made; SEE CONCEPTS 314,489,540

strong [adj2] *determined, resolute*
aggressive, brave, clear, cogent, courageous, dedicated, deep, eager, fervent, fervid, fierce, firm, forceful, gutsy*, handful*, hard-nosed*, independent, intelligent, intense, iron-willed, keen, mean, perceptive, plucky, potent, pushy, resilient, resourceful, sagacious, self-assertive, severe, staunch, steadfast, take charge*, tenacious, tough, unbending, uncompromising, unyielding, vehement, violent, wicked*, zealous; SEE CONCEPTS 403,542

strong [adj3] *distinct, unmistakable*
clear, clear-cut, cogent, compelling, convincing, effective, fast, firm, forceful, formidable, great, hard, influential, marked, mighty, overpowering, persuasive, potent, powerful, redoubtable, secure, sharp, sound, stiff, stimulating, telling, trenchant, urgent, weighty, well-established, well-founded; SEE CONCEPTS 535,537

strong [adj4] *extreme*
acute, draconian, drastic, forceful, intense, keen, severe, sharp, strict; SEE CONCEPT 569

strong [adj5] *forceful on the senses*
biting, bold, bright, brilliant, concentrated, dazzling, effective, fetid, full-bodied, glaring, hard, heady, high, highly flavored, highly seasoned, hot, inebriating, intoxicating, loud, malodorous, noisome, piquant, potent, powerful, pungent, pure, rancid, rank, rich, robust, sharp, spicy, stark, stimulating, stinking, straight, strong-flavored, undiluted, unmixed; SEE CONCEPTS 462,598,618

stronghold [n] *refuge*
bastion, bulwark, castle, citadel, fastness, fort, fortification, fortress, garrison, keep, presidio, redoubt; SEE CONCEPTS 439,712

structure [n1] *makeup, form*
anatomy, architecture, arrangement, build, complex, configuration, conformation, construction, design, fabric, fabrication, format, formation, frame, framework, interrelation, make, morphology, network, order, organization, skeleton, system, texture; SEE CONCEPT 733

structure [n2] *building*
cage, construction, edifice, erection, fabric, house, pile, pile of bricks*, rockpile, skyscraper; SEE CONCEPT 439

struggle [n] *hard try; fight to win*
attempt, battle, brush, clash, combat, conflict, contest, effort, encounter, endeavor, essay, exertion, free-for-all*, grind, hassle, jam, jump, labor, long haul*, pains*, roughhouse*, row, scramble, set-to*, skirmish, strife, striving, toil,

trial, tussle, undertaking, work, wrangle; SEE CONCEPTS 87,106,674

struggle [v1] *labor, work*
assay, attempt, bend over backwards*, break one's back*, break one's neck*, cope, dig, endeavor, exert oneself, give it one's best shot*, give the old college try*, go all out*, grind, hassle, have one's nose to grindstone*, hustle, make every effort*, offer, plug, plug away*, scratch, seek, slave, strain, strive, sweat, tackle, take a crack*, take a stab*, take on, toil, try, try one's hardest*, undertake, work like a dog*; SEE CONCEPT 87

struggle [v2] *fight, wrestle*
battle, brawl, buck, bump heads*, compete, contend, contest, cross swords*, go up against*, grapple, hassle, lock horns*, put up a fight*, romp, rough-house*, row, scrap, scuffle, shuffle, slug, smack, tangle; SEE CONCEPT 106

strumpet [n] *prostitute*
call girl*, harlot, hooker, hussy, lady of the evening*, slut, streetwalker, whore, woman of the street*; SEE CONCEPT 412

strut [v] *walk pompously*
flaunt, flounce, grandstand*, mince, parade, peacock*, play to audience, prance, put on airs*, sashay*, show off, stalk, stride, swagger, swank, sweep; SEE CONCEPTS 149,261

stub [n] *stumpy end*
butt, counterfoil, dock, remainder, remnant, root, short end*, snag, stump, tag, tail, tail end*; SEE CONCEPTS 825,827

stubborn [adj] *obstinate, unyielding*
adamant, balky, bullheaded, cantankerous, contumacious, cussed*, determined, dogged, firm, fixed, hardheaded, headstrong, inexorable, inflexible, insubordinate, intractable, mulish, obdurate, opinionated, ornery*, persevering, persistent, pertinacious, perverse, pigheaded*, rebellious, recalcitrant, refractory, relentless, rigid, self-willed, set in one's ways*, single-minded, steadfast, stiff-necked*, tenacious, tough, unbending, unmanageable, unreasonable, unshakable, untoward, willful; SEE CONCEPTS 401,404

stubby [adj] *short and thick*
fat, heavyset, squat, stocky, stout, stumpy, thick-bodied, thickset; SEE CONCEPTS 491,773,779

stuck-up [adj] *snobbish*
arrogant, big-headed, cocky, conceited, condescending, egotistic, haughty, high-and-mighty*, hoity-toity, nose in the air*, ostentatious, patronizing, pompous, pretentious, puffed up, snippy*, snooty*, snotty*, too big for one's britches*, uppity*, vain; SEE CONCEPT 401

student [n] *person actively learning*
apprentice, disciple, docent, first-year student, grad, graduate, junior, learner, novice, observer, pupil, registrant, scholar, schoolchild, skill, sophomore, undergrad*, undergraduate; SEE CONCEPT 350

studied [adj] *intentional*
advised, affected, aforethought, calculated, conscious, considered, deliberate, designed, examined, gone into, investigated, planned, plotted, premeditated, prepared, prepense, purposeful, reviewed, studious, thought-about, thoughtful, thought-out, thought-through, voluntary, well-considered, willful, willing; SEE CONCEPTS 538,548

studious [*adj*] *scholarly, attentive*
academic, assiduous, bookish*, bookworm*, busy, careful, contemplative, diligent, eager, earnest, grubbing, hard-working, industrious, intellectual, learned, lettered, meditative, reflective, sedulous, serious, thoughtful, well-informed, well-read; SEE CONCEPTS *402,538*

study [*n*] *learning, analysis*
abstraction, academic work, analyzing, application, attention, class, cogitation, comparison, concentration, consideration, contemplation, course, cramming, debate, deliberation, examination, exercise, inquiry, inspection, investigation, lesson, meditation, memorizing, muse, musing, pondering, questioning, reading, reasoning, reflection, research, reverie, review, rumination, schoolwork, scrutiny, subject, survey, thought, trance, weighing; SEE CONCEPTS *31,103*

study [*v1*] *contemplate, learn*
apply oneself, bone up*, brood over, burn midnight oil*, bury oneself in*, coach, cogitate, consider, crack the books*, cram, dig*, dive into*, examine, excogitate, go into, go over, grind*, hit the books*, inquire, learn, learn the ropes*, lucubrate, meditate, mind, mull over, perpend, peruse, plug*, plunge, polish up*, ponder, pore over*, read, read up, refresh, think, think out, think over, tutor, weigh; SEE CONCEPT *31*

study [*v2*] *examine, analyze*
brainstorm*, canvass, case, check out, check over, check up, compare, deliberate, do research, figure, give the eagle eye*, inspect, investigate, keep tabs*, look into, peruse, read, research, scope, scrutinize, sort out, survey, view; SEE CONCEPT *103*

stuff [*n1*] *personal belongings*
being, effects, equipment, gear, goods, impedimenta, individual, junk*, kit, luggage, objects, paraphernalia, possessions, substance, tackle, things, trappings; SEE CONCEPTS *432,446*

stuff [*n2*] *essence, substance*
bottom, bottom line*, essentiality, heart, marrow*, matter, meat*, nitty-gritty*, nuts and bolts*, pith, principle, quintessence, soul, staple, virtuality; SEE CONCEPTS *668,682*

stuff [*n3*] *fabric*
cloth, material, raw material, textile, woven material; SEE CONCEPT *167*

stuff [*v*] *load with*
choke up, clog up, compress, congest, cram, crowd, fill, fill to overflowing, fill to the brim, force, glut, gobble, gorge, gormandize, guzzle, jam, jam-pack*, overfill, overindulge, overstuff, pack, pad, push, ram, sate, satiate, shove, squeeze, stow, wad, wedge; SEE CONCEPTS *169,209*

stuffed [*adj*] *crammed*
bursting, crowded, filled, full, glutted, gorged, jammed, jam-packed*, loaded, overflowing, packed, packed like sardines*, running over, satisfied, saturated, tight; SEE CONCEPTS *481,483,773,774,786*

stuffy [*adj1*] *close, oppressive*
airless, breathless, confined, fetid, heavy, humid, muggy, stagnant, stale, stifling, suffocating, sultry, thick, unventilated; SEE CONCEPT *525*

stuffy [*adj2*] *old-fashioned, prim*
arrogant, bloated, conventional, dreary, dull, fusty, genteel, humorless, important, magisterial, musty, narrow-minded, pompous, priggish, prim

and proper*, prissy, prudish, puffy, puritanical, self-important, staid, stilted, stodgy, straitlaced*, uninteresting, Victorian*; SEE CONCEPTS *401,404*

stumble [*v1*] *slip, stagger*
blunder, bumble, careen, err, fall, fall down, falter, flounder, hesitate, limp, lose balance, lumber, lurch, muddle, pitch, reel, shuffle, stammer, swing, tilt, topple, totter, trip, wallow, waver, wobble; SEE CONCEPTS *101,181*

stumble [*v2*] *happen upon*
blunder upon*, bump, chance, chance upon*, come across, come up against, discover, encounter, fall upon, find, happen upon*, hit, light, light upon*, luck*, meet, run across, stub toe on*, tumble, turn up; SEE CONCEPTS *183,693*

stumbling block [*n*] *impediment*
barricade, barrier, blockage, catch*, Catch-22*, clog, delay, difficulty, drag*, drawback, handicap, hindrance, holdup, hurdle, obstacle, obstruction, road block*, setback, snag; SEE CONCEPT *666*

stump [*n*] *end piece*
butt, end, projection, stub, tail end, tip; SEE CONCEPTS *825,827*

stump [*v1*] *confuse, bewilder*
baffle, bring up short, confound, dumbfound, foil, mystify, nonplus, outwit, perplex, puzzle, stagger, stick, stop, stymie; SEE CONCEPT *16*

stump [*v2*] *walk with deliberation*
barge, clomp, clump, galumph, lumber, plod, stamp, stomp, stumble, trudge; SEE CONCEPT *149*

stunned [*adj*] *dazed*
aghast, amazed, astonished, astounded, bewildered, blown away*, bowled over*, breathless, confounded, confused, dismayed, dumbfounded, flabbergasted, floored, frozen, numb, overcome, overwhelmed, shocked, speechless, startled, stumped, stupefied, surprised, taken aback; SEE CONCEPT *403*

stunning [*adj*] *beautiful, marvelous*
beauteous, bonny, brilliant, comely, dazzling, devastating, excellent, fair, famous, fine, first-class*, first-rate*, gorgeous, great, handsome, heavenly, impressive, lovely, number one*, out of this world*, pretty, ravishing, remarkable, royal, sensational, smashing, spectacular, striking, superior, top, wonderful; SEE CONCEPTS *574,579*

stun/stupefy [*v*] *amaze, shock*
astonish, astound, bemuse, bewilder, blow away*, bowl over*, confound, confuse, daze, dumbfound, flabbergast, floor*, fog*, give a turn*, hit like ton of bricks*, knock out*, knock over*, knock unconscious, muddle, overcome, overpower, overwhelm, paralyze, petrify, rock*, shake up*, stagger, strike dumb*, surprise, take breath away*, throw a curve*; SEE CONCEPT *42*

stunt [*n*] *deed, trick*
achievement, act, antic, caper, exploit, feat, feature, performance, sketch, skit, tour de force; SEE CONCEPTS *264,384*

stunted [*adj*] *kept from growing*
bantam, diminutive, dwarf, dwarfed, dwarfish, half-pint*, little, measly, mite, peanut*, peewee*, pint-sized*, runted, runtish, runty, scrub, short, shot, shrimp*, small, small fry*, tiny, undergrown, undersized, wee*, yea big*, yea high*; SEE CONCEPTS *773,779*

stupefied [*adj*] *dazed*
amazed, astonished, astounded, bewildered,

blown away*, bowled over*, breathless, confounded, confused, dismayed, dumbfounded, flabbergasted, floored, frozen, numb, overcome, overwhelmed, puzzled, shocked, speechless, startled, stumped, stunned, surprised, taken aback; SEE CONCEPT *403*

stupendous [*adj*] *wonderful, amazing*
astonishing, astounding, breathtaking, colossal, dynamite, enormous, fab*, fabulous, fantastic, fat*, gigantic, great, huge, marvelous, mind-blowing*, mind-boggling*, miraculous, monster, monumental, overwhelming, phenomenal, prodigious, radical*, smashing, spectacular, staggering, stunning, super, superb, surprising, terrific, titanic, too much*, tremendous, unreal*, utmost*, vast, wonderful, wondrous; SEE CONCEPTS *574,781*

stupid [*adj*] *not intelligent; irresponsible*
brainless, dazed, deficient, dense, dim, doltish, dopey*, dull, dumb, foolish, footish, futile, gullible, half-baked*, half-witted*, idiotic, ill-advised, imbecilic, inane, indiscreet, insensate, irrelevant, irresponsible, laughable, loser*, ludicrous, meaningless, mindless, moronic, naive, nonsensical, obtuse, out to lunch*, pointless, puerile, rash, senseless, shortsighted, simple, simpleminded, slow, sluggish, stolid, stupefied, thick, thick-headed*, trivial, unintelligent, unthinking, witless; SEE CONCEPTS *402,548*

stupor [*n*] *daze, unconsciousness*
amazement, anaesthesia, apathy, asphyxia, bewilderment, coma, dullness, fainting, hebetude, hypnosis, inertia, inertness, insensibility, languor, lassitude, lethargy, narcosis, numbness, petrifaction, sleep, slumber, somnolence, stupefaction, suspended animation, swoon, swooning, torpor, trance; SEE CONCEPTS *315,316*

sturdy [*adj*] *solid, durable*
athletic, built to last*, bulky, determined, durable, firm, flourishing, hardy, hearty, hefty, hulking, husky, lusty, muscular, powerful, powerhouse*, resolute, robust, rugged, secure, solid, sound, stalwart, staunch, steadfast, stiff, stout, stouthearted, strapping, strong, strong-arm*, substantial, tenacious, tough, unyielding, vigorous, well-built, well-made; SEE CONCEPTS *314,488, 489*

stutter [*v*] *speak haltingly*
dribble, falter, hesitate, splutter, sputter, stammer, stumble; SEE CONCEPT *77*

style [*n1*] *fashion, manner*
appearance, approach, bearing, behavior, carriage, characteristic, cup of tea*, custom, cut*, description, design, druthers*, flash*, form, genre, groove*, habit, hand, idiosyncrasy, kind, method, mode, number, pattern, peculiarity, rage*, sort, spirit, strain, technique, tenor, thing*, tone, trait, trend, type, variety, vein, vogue, way; SEE CONCEPTS *411,655*

style [*n2*] *fashionableness*
chichi*, comfort, cosmopolitanism, craze, dash, delicacy, dernier cri, dressiness, ease, élan, elegance, fad, flair, grace, grandeur, luxury, mode, panache, polish, rage, refinement, savoir-faire, smartness, sophistication, stylishness, taste, thing*, urbanity, vogue; SEE CONCEPTS *655,668*

style [*n3*] *way of speaking, writing, expressing oneself*
diction, expression, mode of expression, phraseology, phrasing, treatment, turn of phrase*, vein, wording; SEE CONCEPT *276*

style [*v*] *name, title*
address, baptize, call, christen, denominate, designate, dub, entitle, label, name, term; SEE CONCEPT *62*

stylish [*adj*] *fashionable*
à la mode*, beautiful, chic, chichi*, classy, dap, dapper, dashing, dressed to kill*, dressed to the teeth*, dressy, fly*, groovy*, high-class*, in, in fashion, in the mainstream*, in vogue, jazzy*, latest, mod*, modernistic, new, nifty, now*, ostentatious, polished, pretentious, rakish, ritzy, sassy*, sharp, showy, sleek, slick*, smart, snappy*, snazzy*, swank*, swell, tony*, trendy, upscale, up-to-date, uptown, urbane, voguish; SEE CONCEPTS *579,589*

stymie [*v*] *frustrate, hinder*
balk, block, choke off, confound, corner, crab*, cramp, cramp one's style*, crimp, cut off, dead-end*, defeat, foil, give the run around*, hang fire*, hang up*, hold off, hold up, impede, mystify, nonplus, obstruct, pigeonhole*, prevent, put on back burner*, put on hold, puzzle, shelve, snooker*, stall, stonewall*, stump, throw a monkey wrench into*, thwart; SEE CONCEPTS *121,130*

suave [*adj*] *charming, smooth*
affable, agreeable, bland, civilized, cordial, courteous, courtly, cultivated, cultured, diplomatic, distingué, fulsome, genial, glib, gracious, ingratiating, obliging, oily*, pleasant, pleasing, polished, polite, politic, refined, smooth-tongued*, sociable, soft*, soft-spoken, sophisticated, unctuous, urbane, well-bred, worldly; SEE CONCEPTS *401,404*

subconscious [*adj*] *innermost in thought*
hidden, inmost, inner, intuitive, latent, mental, repressed, subliminal, suppressed, unconscious; SEE CONCEPT *529*

subconscious [*n*] *inner thoughts*
essence, mind, psyche, soul, subconsciousness, subliminal, subliminal self, submerged mind, underconsciousness, undersense; SEE CONCEPT *410*

subdivision [*n*] *smaller entity of whole*
class, community, development, group, lower group, minor group, subclass, subsidiary, tract; SEE CONCEPTS *513,835*

subdue [*v*] *keep under control; moderate*
bear down, beat down, break, break in, check, conquer, control, crush, defeat, discipline, dominate, drop, extinguish, gentle, get the better of*, get the upper hand*, get under control, humble, mellow, overcome, overpower, overrun, put down, quash, quell, quench, quiet, quieten, reduce, repress, restrain, shut down, soften, squelch, subjugate, suppress, tame, temper, tone down, trample, triumph over, vanquish; SEE CONCEPTS *121,130,252*

subdued [*adj*] *quiet, controlled*
chastened, crestfallen, dejected, dim, domestic, domesticated, downcast, down in the mouth*, grave, hushed, inobtrusive, low-key*, mellow*, moderated, muted, neutral, out of spirits*, repentant, repressed, restrained, sad, serious, shaded, sober, soft, softened, solemn, submissive, subtle, tasteful, tempered, toned down, unobtrusive; SEE CONCEPTS *401,403,594*

subject [*adj*] *at the mercy of; answerable*
accountable, apt, at one's feet*, bound by, captive, collateral, conditional, contingent, con-

st
su

trolled, dependent, directed, disposed, enslaved, exposed, governed, in danger of, inferior, liable, likely, obedient, open, prone, provisional, ruled, satellite, secondary, sensitive, servile, slavish, sub*, subaltern, subjugated, submissive, subordinate, subservient, substract, susceptible, tentative, tributary, under, vulnerable; SEE CONCEPTS 552,575

subject [n1] *issue, matter*
affair, argument, business, case, chapter, class, core, course, discussion, field of reference, gist, head, idea, item, material, matter at hand, meat*, motif, motion, motive, object, point, principal object, problem, proposal, question, resolution, study, subject matter, substance, text, theme, theorem, thesis, thought, topic; SEE CONCEPTS 529,532,689

subject [n2] *one under authority of another*
case, client, customer, dependent, guinea pig*, liege, national, patient, serf, subordinate, vassal; SEE CONCEPTS 413,423

subjective [adj] *emotional; based on inner experience rather than fact*
abstract, biased, fanciful, idiosyncratic, illusory, individual, instinctive, introspective, introverted, intuitive, nonobjective, nonrepresentative, personal, prejudiced, unobjective; SEE CONCEPTS 529,542

subjugate [v] *overpower, defeat*
bear down, beat down, bring to heel*, bring to knees*, coerce, compel, conquer, crush, enslave, enthrall, force, hold sway, keep under thumb*, kick around*, overcome, overthrow, put down, quell, reduce, reel back in*, rule, rule over, subdue, suppress, tame, triumph, vanquish; SEE CONCEPTS 95,117,133

sublime [adj] *great, magnificent*
abstract, august, divine, dynamite, elevated, eminent, exalted, glorious, gorgeous, grand, heavenly, high, holy, ideal, imposing, lofty, majestic, noble, outrageous, proud, resplendent, sacred, spiritual, splendiferous, splendorous, stately, super, superb, the most*, too much*, transcendent, transcendental; SEE CONCEPT 574

submarine [n1] *sub*
nuclear submarine, submersible, U-boat, underwater craft, underwater robot; SEE CONCEPT 506

submarine [n2] *sandwich*
grinder, hero, hoagie, sub*, torpedo; SEE CONCEPTS 457,460,461

submerge [v] *dunk in liquid*
deluge, descend, dip, douse, drench, drown, duck, engulf, flood, go down, go under, immerse, impregnate, inundate, overflow, overwhelm, plunge, sink, sound, souse, submerse, subside, swamp, whelm; SEE CONCEPTS 181,256

submission [n] *compliance*
acquiescence, appeasement, assent, backing down, bowing, capitulation, cringing, defeatism, deference, docility, giving in, humbleness, humility, malleability, meekness, nonresistance, obedience, passivism, passivity, pliability, prostration, recreancy, resignation, servility, subjection, submissiveness, submitting, surrender, tractability, unassertiveness, yielding; SEE CONCEPT 633

submissive [adj] *compliant*
abject, accommodating, acquiescent, amenable, bowing down, comformable, complying, deferential, docile, domesticated, dutiful, giving-in*,

humble, ingratiating, lowly, malleable, meek, menial, nonresistant, nonresisting, obedient, obeisant, obeying, obsequious, passive, patient, pliable, pliant, resigned, servile, slavish, subdued, tame, tractable, uncomplaining, unresisting, yes*, yielding; SEE CONCEPT 401

submit [v1] *comply, endure*
abide, accede, acknowledge, acquiesce, agree, appease, bend, be submissive, bow, buckle, capitulate, cave, cede, concede, defer, eat crow*, fold, give away, give ground, give in, give way, go with the flow*, grin and bear it*, humor, indulge, knuckle, knuckle under*, kowtow*, lay down arms, obey, put up with, quit, relent, relinquish, resign oneself, say uncle*, stoop, succumb, surrender, throw in the towel*, toe the line*, tolerate, truckle, withstand, yield; SEE CONCEPT 23

submit [v2] *present, offer; argue for*
advance, advise, affirm, argue, assert, claim, commit, contend, hand in, make a pitch*, move, proffer, propose, proposition, propound, put, put forward, refer, state, suggest, table, tender, theorize, urge, volunteer; SEE CONCEPT 66

subordinate [adj] *lesser, supplementary*
accessory, adjuvant, ancillary, auxiliary, baser, below par, collateral, contributory, dependent, inferior, insignificant, junior, low, lower, minor, paltry, satellite, secondary, second-fiddle*, second-string*, smaller, sub, subaltern, subalternate, subject, submissive, subnormal, subservient, subsidiary, substract, tributary, under, underaverage, unequal; SEE CONCEPT 575

subordinate [n] *person that serves another*
aide, assistant, attendant, dependent, deputy, flunky*, gofer*, helper, inferior, junior, peon, poor relation*, scrub*, second, second fiddle*, second string*, serf, servant, slave, subaltern, third string*, underling; SEE CONCEPTS 348,423

subpoena [n] *writ*
command, court order, decree, mandate, summons, warrant, written order; SEE CONCEPT 318

subpoena [v] *issue a writ*
cite, order to testify, serve a court order, serve notice, summon; SEE CONCEPT 318

subscribe [v1] *pay for use; contribute*
advocate, ante up*, buy, chip in*, come through*, consent, donate, do one's part*, endorse, enroll, give, grant, ink*, make a deal*, offer, pitch in*, pledge, promise, put up*, register, second, set, sign, signature, sign up*, support; SEE CONCEPTS 129,341

subscribe [v2] *agree*
accede, acquiesce, advocate, approve, assent, autograph*, back, bless, boost, consent, cosign, countenance, ditto*, endorse, favor, get behind*, give stamp of approval* give the go-ahead*, go along with*, hold with*, ink*, obey, okay*, put John Hancock on*, rubber-stamp*, sanction, sign, signature, support, take, undersign, underwrite, yes*; SEE CONCEPTS 10,50,88

subsequent [adj] *after*
consecutive, consequent, consequential, ensuing, following, later, next, posterior, postliminary, proximate, resultant, resulting, sequent, sequential, serial, subsequential, succeeding, successional, successive; SEE CONCEPTS 585,820

subsequently [adv] *afterward*
after, afterwards, afterwhile, at a later date, behind, by and by, consequently, finally, infra, in

the aftermath, in the end, later, latterly, next; SEE CONCEPTS *585,820*

subservient [*adj1*] *extremely compliant*
abject, acquiescent, a slave to*, at one's beck and call*, at one's mercy*, bootlicking, cowering, cringing, dancing, deferential, docile, fawning, ignoble, inferior, in one's clutches*, in one's pocket*, in one's power*, mean, menial, obeisant, obsequious, resigned, servile, slavish, subject, submissive, sycophantic, under one's thumb*; SEE CONCEPTS *401,404*

subservient [*adj2*] *secondary, useful*
accessory, adjuvant, ancillary, appurtenant, auxiliary, bush-league*, collateral, conducive, contributory, flunky, helpful, inferior, instrumental, minor, serviceable, subordinate, subsidiary, supplemental, supplementary; SEE CONCEPTS *560,575*

subside [*v*] *die down; decrease*
abate, cave in, collapse, decline, de-escalate, descend, die away, diminish, drop, dwindle, ease, ease off, ebb, fall, let up, level off, lower, lull, melt, moderate, peter out*, quieten, recede, settle, sink, slacken, taper, wane; SEE CONCEPTS *181,698,776*

subsidiary [*adj*] *secondary, helpful*
accessory, adjuvant, aiding, ancillary, appurtenant, assistant, assisting, auxiliary, backup, branch, collateral, contributory, cooperative, lesser, minor, serviceable, subject, subordinate, subservient, supplemental, supplementary, tributory, useful; SEE CONCEPTS *560,575*

subsidize [*v*] *give money to get started*
angel*, back, bankroll*, contribute, endow, finance, fund, grubstake*, help, juice*, pick up the check*, pick up the tab*, prime the pump*, promote, put up the money for, sponsor, stake, support, underwrite; SEE CONCEPTS *110,341*

subsidy [*n*] *money given to help another*
aid, alimony, allowance, appropriation, assistance, bequest, bonus, bounty, contribution, endowment, fellowship, financial aid, gift, grant, gratuity, help, honorarium, indemnity, payment, pension, premium, reward, scholarship, subsidization, subvention, support, tribute; SEE CONCEPTS *337,344*

subsist [*v*] *keep going, living*
barely exist*, be, breathe, continue, eke out a living*, eke out an existence*, endure, exist, get along*, get by*, hang in*, hang on*, hang tough*, just make it*, last, live, make ends meet*, make it*, manage, move, remain, remain alive, ride out*, scrape by*, stay alive, stick it out*, stick with it*, survive, sustain; SEE CONCEPTS *23,330,407*

subsistence [*n*] *provisions for survival*
affluence, aliment, alimentation, bread*, bread and butter*, capital, circumstances, competence, earnings, existence, food, fortune, gratuity, income, independence, keep, legacy, livelihood, living, maintenance, means, money, necessities, nurture, pension, property, provision, ration, resources, riches, salary, salt*, substance, support, sustenance, upkeep, victuals, wages, wealth, wherewithal; SEE CONCEPTS *446,457,646,710*

substance [*n1*] *entity, element*
actuality, animal, being, body, bulk, concreteness, core, corpus, fabric, force, hunk, individual, item, mass, material, matter, object, person, phenomenon, reality, something, staple, stuff, texture, thing; SEE CONCEPTS *433,478,523*

substance [*n2*] *essence, meaning*
ABCs*, amount, basis, body, bottom, bottom line*, brass tacks*, burden, center, core, corpus, crux, drift, effect, essentiality, focus, general meaning, gist, gravamen, guts*, heart, import, innards, kernel, marrow, mass, matter, meat*, name of the game*, nitty-gritty*, nub, nuts and bolts*, pith, point, purport, quintessence, sense, significance, soul, staple, strength, stuff, subject, sum total*, tenor, theme, thrust, upshot, virtuality, way of it*; SEE CONCEPTS *682,689*

substance [*n3*] *wealth*
affluence, assets, estate, fortune, means, property, resources, riches, worth; SEE CONCEPT *335*

substance abuse [*n*] *chemical abuse*
addiction, alcoholic addiction, alcoholism, drug abuse, drug dependence, habit; SEE CONCEPTS *20,316,709*

substandard [*adj*] *inferior*
bad, base, below average, below par, below standard, cheap, inadequate, junk*, lemon*, lousy, low-grade, poor, second-rate, shoddy, subpar, unacceptable; SEE CONCEPT *574*

substantial [*adj1*] *important, ample*
abundant, big, big-deal*, bulky, consequential, considerable, durable, extraordinary, firm, generous, goodly, heavy, heavyweight, hefty, key, large, major-league*, massive, material, meaningful, momentous, plentiful, principal, serious, significant, sizable, solid, sound, stable, steady, stout, strong, sturdy, superabundant, tidy, valuable, vast, weighty, well-built, worthwhile; SEE CONCEPTS *568,773,781*

substantial [*adj2*] *material, real*
actual, card-carrying*, concrete, corporeal, existent, for real*, honest-to-god*, legit*, objective, phenomenal, physical, positive, righteous, sensible, solid, sure enough*, tangible, true, twenty-four-carat*, valid, visible, weighty; SEE CONCEPT *582*

substantial [*adj3*] *rich*
affluent, comfortable, easy, opulent, prosperous, snug, solid, solvent, wealthy, well, well-heeled, well-off, well-to-do; SEE CONCEPT *334*

substantially [*adv*] *to a large extent*
considerably, essentially, extensively, heavily, in essence, in fact, in reality, in substance, in the main, largely, mainly, materially, much, really; SEE CONCEPTS *569,772*

substantiate [*v*] *back up a statement, idea*
actualize, affirm, approve, attest to, authenticate, bear out, check out, check up, complete, confirm, corroborate, debunk, demonstrate, establish, incarnate, justify, manifest, materialize, objectify, personify, prove, ratify, realize, reify, support, test, try, try on, try out, validate, verify; SEE CONCEPTS *49,138,317*

substitute [*adj*] *alternative*
acting, additional, alternate, another, artificial, backup, counterfeit, dummy, ersatz*, experimental, false, imitation, makeshift, mock, near, other, provisional, proxy, pseudo*, replacement, representative, reserve, second, sham, simulated, spurious, stopgap*, substitutive, supplemental, supplementary, suppositious, surrogate, symbolic, temporary, tentative, vicarial, vicarious; SEE CONCEPTS *560,575*

SU
SU

substitute [n] *someone or something that takes the place of another*

agent, alternate, assistant, auxiliary, backup, changeling, delegate, deputy, dernier ressort*, double, dummy, equivalent, expediency, expedient, fill-in, ghost, ghost writer, locum, locum tenens, makeshift, pinch-hitter*, procurator, proxy, recourse, refuge, relay, relief, replacement, representative, reserve, resort, resource, stand-by, stand-in, stopgap*, sub*, succedaneum, successor, supplanter, supply, surrogate, symbol, temp*, temporary, temporary expedient, understudy, vicar; SEE CONCEPTS *423,712*

substitute [v] *interchange, exchange*

act for, alternate, answer for, back up, be in place of, change, commute, cover for, deputize, displace, do the work of, double for, fill in for, fill one's position, go as, proxy, relieve, replace, serve in one's stead, spell, stand for, stand in for, sub*, supersede, supplant, swap, swap places with*, switch, take another's place, take over; SEE CONCEPTS *87,104*

subterranean [adj] *hidden, underground*

below ground, buried, covered, covert, hush-hush*, on the QT*, private, secret, subterrestrial, subversive, sunken, underfoot, under wraps*; SEE CONCEPT *583*

subtle [adj1] *nice, quiet, delicate*

attenuate, attenuated, deep, discriminating, ethereal, exquisite, faint, fine, finespun, hairline, hairsplitting, illusive, implied, inconspicuous, indirect, indistinct, inferred, ingenious, insinuated, mental, penetrating, profound, refined, slight, sophisticated, suggestive, tenuous, thin, understated; SEE CONCEPTS *537,544*

subtle [adj2] *clever, cunning*

analytic, analytical, artful, astute, complex, crafty, deep, designing, detailed, devious, dexterous, exacting, foxy, guileful, insidious, intriguing, keen, penetrating, perceptive, precise, ratiocinative, scheming, shrewd, skillful, sly, wily; SEE CONCEPT *402*

subtract [v] *take away*

decrease, deduct, detract, diminish, discount, draw back, knock off, remove, take, take from, take off, take out, withdraw, withhold; SEE CONCEPTS *211,764*

suburb [n] *neighborhood outside of but reliant on nearby large city*

bedroom community*, burb*, country, countryside, environs, fringe, hamlet, hinterland, outlying area, outpost, outskirts, precinct, purlieu, residential area, slub, suburbia, village; SEE CONCEPTS *508,512*

subversive [adj] *rebellious, destructive*

incendiary, inflammatory, insurgent, insurrectionary, overthrowing, perversive, riotous, ruinous, seditious, treasonous, underground, undermining; SEE CONCEPT *401*

subvert [v] *rebel, destroy*

capsize, contaminate, corrupt, debase, defeat, demolish, deprave, depress, extinguish, invalidate, invert, level, overthrow, overturn, pervert, poison, pull down, raze, reverse, ruin, sabotage, supersede, supplant, suppress, topple, tumble, undermine, upset, vitiate, wreck; SEE CONCEPTS *86,95,252*

succeed [v1] *attain good outcome*

accomplish, achieve, acquire, arrive, avail, benefit, be successful, carry off*, come off*, conquer, distance, do all right*, do the trick*, earn, flourish, fulfill, gain, get, get to the top*, grow famous, hit*, make a fortune*, make good*, make it*, make out*, obtain, outdistance, outwit, overcome, possess, prevail, profit, prosper, pull off*, realize, reap, receive, recover, retrieve, score, secure, surmount, thrive, triumph, turn out*, vanquish, win, work, worst; SEE CONCEPTS *141,706*

succeed [v2] *come after; take the place of*

accede, assume, be subsequent, come into, come into possession, come next, displace, ensue, enter upon, follow, follow after, follow in order, go next, inherit, postdate, replace, result, supersede, supervene, supplant, take over; SEE CONCEPTS *727,749,813*

succeeding/successive [adj] *following*

alternating, consecutive, ensuing, following after, in a row, in line, next, next in line for, next in order, next off, next up, rotating, sequent, sequential, serial, seriate, subsequent, subsequential, succedent, successional; SEE CONCEPTS *585,811,812,818,820*

success [n] *favorable outcome*

accomplishment, achievement, advance, arrival, ascendancy, attainment, bed of roses*, benefit, big hit*, boom*, clover*, consummation, do well, Easy Street*, éclat, eminence, fame, flying colors*, fortune, fruition, gain, good luck*, good times*, grand slam*, gravy train*, happiness, happy days*, hit, killing, lap of luxury*, laugher*, maturation, profit, progress, prosperity, realization, reward, savvy, sensation, snap, strike, successfulness, triumph, victory, walkaway*, walkover*, win; SEE CONCEPTS *693,706*

successful [adj] *favorable, profitable*

acknowledged, advantageous, ahead of the game*, at the top*, at top of ladder*, auspicious, bestselling, blooming, blossoming, booming, champion, crowned, efficacious, extraordinary, flourishing, fortuitous, fortunate, fruitful, happy, lucky, lucrative, moneymaking, notable, noteworthy, on track*, out in front*, outstanding, paying, prosperous, rewarding, rolling, strong, thriving, top, triumphant, unbeaten, undefeated, victorious, wealthy; SEE CONCEPT *528*

successor [n] *heir*

beneficiary, descendant, follower, heritor, inheritor, next in line, replacement, scion; SEE CONCEPTS *355,414*

succinct [adj] *brief, to the point*

blunt, boiled down*, breviloquent, brusque, compact, compendiary, compendious, concise, condensed, curt, cut to the bone*, in a nutshell*, in few words*, laconic, pithy, short, summary, terse; SEE CONCEPT *267*

succulent [adj] *juicy, delicious*

divine, heavenly, luscious, lush, mellow, moist, mouthwatering, pulpy, rich, sappy, tasty, yummy*; SEE CONCEPTS *462,613*

succumb [v] *die or surrender*

accede, bow, break down, buckle, capitulate, cave, cave in*, cease, collapse, croak, decease, defer, demise, depart, drop, eat crow*, expire, fall, fall victim to, flake out*, fold, give in, give into, give out, give up the ghost*, give way, go, go down, go under, knuckle, knuckle under*, meet waterloo*, pack it in*, pass, pass away, perish, quit, show white flag*, submit, take the

count*, throw in the towel*, wilt, yield; SEE CON-
CEPTS 35,105,385

such [adj/conj] aforementioned, specific
aforesaid, akin, alike, analogous, comparable,
corresponding, equivalent, like, parallel, said,
similar, such a one, such a person, such a thing,
suchlike, that, the like, this; SEE CONCEPT 557

sudden [adj] unexpected; happening quickly
abrupt, accelerated, acute, expeditious, fast,
flash, fleet, hasty, headlong, hurried, immediate,
impetuous, impromptu, impulsive, out of the
blue*, precipitant, precipitate, precipitous, quick,
quickened, rapid, rash, rushing, spasmodic,
speeded, subito, swift, unforeseen, unusual; SEE
CONCEPT 799

suddenly [adv] unexpectedly
aback, abruptly, all at once, all of a sudden, asud-
den, forthwith, on spur of moment*, quickly,
short, sudden, swiftly, unanticipatedly, unaware,
unawares, without warning; SEE CONCEPT 799

sue [v] bring legal charges against
accuse, appeal, beg, beseech, bring an action,
charge, claim, claim damages, contest, demand,
drag into court, enter a plea, entreat, file, file a
claim, file suit, follow up, haul into court, have
the law on, have up, indict, institute legal proceedings, litigate, petition, plead, prefer charges
against, prosecute, pull up, put away, see in
court, solicit, summon, supplicate, take out after,
take to court; SEE CONCEPT 317

suffer [v1] be in pain
ache, agonize, ail, be affected, be at disadvantage, be convulsed, be handicapped, be impaired,
be racked, be wounded, brave, complain of, deteriorate, droop, endure, experience, fall off, feel
wretched, flag, get, go through, grieve, have a
bad time*, hurt, languish, pain, sicken, smart,
undergo, writhe; SEE CONCEPTS 308,313

suffer [v2] endure, permit
abide, accept, acquiesce, admit, allow, bear, bear
with, bleed, bow, brave, brook, carry the torch*,
concede, countenance, encounter, experience,
feel, go through, have, hurt, indulge, know, let,
license, live with, put up with, receive, sanction,
see, sit and take it, stand, stomach*, submit, support, sustain, swallow*, sweat*, take*, take it*,
tolerate, undergo, wait out, yield; SEE CONCEPTS
23,83

suffering [n] pain, agony
adversity, affliction, anguish, difficulty, discomfort, distress, dolor, hardship, martyrdom, misery, misfortune, ordeal, passion, torment, torture;
SEE CONCEPT 728

suffice [v] be adequate, enough
answer, avail, be good enough, be sufficient, be
the ticket*, content, do, do the trick*, fill the
bill*, get by, go over big*, hack it*, hit the spot*,
make a hit*, make the grade*, meet, meet requirement, satisfy, serve, suit; SEE CONCEPT 713

sufficient [adj] enough, adequate
acceptable, agreeable, all right*, ample, aplenty,
appreciate, comfortable, commensurable, commensurate, common, competent, copious, decent, due, galore, pleasing, plenteous, plentiful,
plenty, proportionate, satisfactory, sufficing, tolerable, unexceptionable, unexceptional, unobjectionable; SEE CONCEPTS 558,560,771

suffocate [v] choke
asphyxiate, drown, smother, stifle, strangle; SEE
CONCEPTS 163,246

sugarcoat [v] sweeten
add sugar, add sweetening, alleviate, candy-coat,
make more appealing, make sweet, mollify,
pacify, soften up, soothe; SEE CONCEPTS 7,22,170

suggest [v1] convey advice, plan, desire
advance, advise, advocate, broach, commend,
conjecture, exhort, give a tip*, move, offer,
plug*, pose, prefer, propone, propose, proposition, propound, put, put forward, put in two
cents*, put on to something*, recommend, steer,
submit, theorize, tip, tip off*, tout; SEE CONCEPT
75

suggest [v2] imply; bring to mind
adumbrate, advert, allude, be a sign of, connote,
cross the mind, denote, evoke, hint, indicate,
infer, insinuate, intimate, lead to believe, occur,
point, point in direction of, promise, put in mind
of, refer, represent, shadow, signify, symbolize,
typify; SEE CONCEPTS 74,682

suggestion [n1] advice, plan
advancement, angle, approach, bid, big idea*,
bit*, brainchild*, charge, commendation, exhortation, game plan*, gimmick, hot lead*, idea, injunction, instruction, invitation, lead, motion,
opinion, outline, pitch, presentation, proffer, proposal, proposition, recommendation, reminder,
resolution, scheme, setup, sneaking suspicion*,
steer*, submission, telltale, tender, testimonial,
thesis, tip, tip-off*; SEE CONCEPTS 278,689

suggestion [n2] hint, implication
allusion, association, autosuggestion, breath,
clue, connotation, cue, indication, inkling, innuendo, insinuation, intimation, notion, overtone,
reminder, self-suggestion, shade, signification,
smack, soupçon, strain, suspicion, symbol, symbolism, symbolization, symbology, telltale,
thought, tinge, trace, undertone, vein, whisper,
wind; SEE CONCEPT 529

suggestive [adj1] signifying
evocative, evocatory, expressive, giving an
inkling*, indicative, intriguing, pregnant, redolent, remindful, reminiscent, significative, symbolic, symptomatic; SEE CONCEPTS 267,529

suggestive [adj2] dirty, vulgar
bawdy, blue*, broad, erotic, immodest, improper, indecent, indelicate, obscene, off-color*,
provocative, prurient, racy, ribald, risqué, rude,
seductive, sexy, shady, tempting, titillating, unseemly, wicked; SEE CONCEPTS 372,545

suit [n1] matching top and bottom clothing
clothing, costume, dress, ensemble, getup*, gray
flannel*, habit, livery, outfit, threads*, tuxedo,
uniform, wardrobe; SEE CONCEPT 451

suit [n2] legal action
case, cause, lawsuit, litigation, proceeding, prosecution, trial; SEE CONCEPT 318

suit [n3] appeal, request
address, application, asking, attention, court,
courtship, entreaty, imploration, imprecation, invocation, petition, plea, prayer, requesting, solicitation, soliciting, supplication, wooing; SEE
CONCEPT 662

suit [v1] be acceptable, appropriate
accord, agree, answer, answer a need, become,
befit, benefit, be proper for, beseem, be seemly,
check, check out, conform, correspond, cut the
mustard*, do, enhance, fill the bill*, fit, fit in,
flatter, fulfill, get by, go, go together, go with,
gratify, harmonize, make the grade*, match, pass

su
su

muster*, please, satisfy, serve, square, suffice, tally; SEE CONCEPT 656

suit [v2] *adapt, tailor*
accommodate, adjust, amuse, change, conform, entertain, fashion, fill, fit, fit in, gratify, modify, please, proportion, quadrate, readjust, reconcile, revise, satisfy, tailor-make*, toe the mark*; SEE CONCEPTS 126,697

suitable [adj] *appropriate, acceptable*
advisable, applicable, apposite, apt, becoming, befitting, commodious, condign, convenient, copacetic, correct, cut out for*, deserved, due, expedient, felicitous, fit, fitting, good, good enough*, handy, happy, in character, in keeping*, just, kosher*, legit*, meet, merited, nice, okay*, opportune, peachy, pertinent, politic, presentable, proper, reasonable, relevant, requisite, right, righteous, rightful, satisfactory, seemly, sufficient, suited, swell, up to snuff*, useful, user friendly; SEE CONCEPT 558

suite [n1] *set of rooms or furniture*
apartment, array, batch, body, chambers, collection, flat, group, lodging, lot, parcel, rental, series, set, tenement; SEE CONCEPTS 441,516

suite [n2] *entourage of people*
array, attendants, batch, body, clutch, cortege, court, escort, faculty, followers, group, lot, retainers, retinue, servants, set, staff, train; SEE CONCEPT 417

suite [n3] *series*
chain, concatenation, consecution, line, order, progression, row, scale, sequel, sequence, string, succession, train; SEE CONCEPT 727

suitor [n] *person who desires another*
admirer, beau, boyfriend, cavalier*, courter, date, follower, girlfriend, lover, man, paramour, supplicant, swain, woman, wooer; SEE CONCEPT 423

sulk [v] *pout*
be down in the mouth*, be in a huff*, be morose, be out of sorts*, be silent, brood, frown, gloom, glower, gripe, grouse, grump*, look sullen, lower, moon*, mope*, scowl, take on; SEE CONCEPTS 35,52

sulky [adj] *sullen*
brooding, cheerless, crabby*, depressed, dismal, dour, fretful, frowning, gloomy, glum, gruff, grumpy*, ill-humored, irritable, mean, moody, moping, morose, obstinate, ornery*, pouting, pouty, sour, sourpussed*, sulking, withdrawn; SEE CONCEPT 403

sullen [adj] *brooding, upset*
bad-tempered, cheerless, churlish, crabbed*, crabby*, cross, cynical, dismal, dour, dull, fretful, frowning, gloomy, glowering, glum, gruff, grumpy*, heavy, hostile, ill-humored, inert, irritable, malevolent, malicious, malign, mean, moody, morose, obstinate, ornery*, out of sorts*, peevish, perverse, pessimistic, petulant, pouting, pouty, querulous, saturnine, silent, somber, sour, sourpussed*, stubborn, sulking, sulky, surly, tenebrific, tenebrous, ugly, unsociable, uptight*; SEE CONCEPT 403

sully [v] *soil, stain*
besmirch, blacken, blot, contaminate, corrupt, debase, debauch, defile, dirty, discolor, disgrace, dishonor, drag through the mud*, make unclean, mark, smear, smudge, spot, taint, tar, tarnish; SEE CONCEPTS 54,250,254

sultry [adj1] *hot and humid*
baking, broiling, burning, close, hot, mucky, muggy, oppressive, red-hot*, scorching, sizzling, smothering, soggy, sticky, stifling, stuffy, suffocating, sweltering, sweltry, torrid, wet; SEE CONCEPTS 525,605

sultry [adj2] *sensuous*
desirable, erotic, heavy*, hot*, lurid, passionate, provocative, seductive, sexy, steamy*, voluptuous, X-rated*; SEE CONCEPT 372

sum [n] *total*
aggregate, all, amount, body, bulk, entirety, entity, epitome, gross, integral, mass, quantity, reckoning, résumé, score, structure, summary, summation, sum total*, synopsis, system, tally, totality, value, whole, works*, worth; SEE CONCEPTS 432,784,787

summarily [adv] *without delay*
arbitrarily, at short notice, expeditiously, forthwith, immediately, on the spot, peremptorily, promptly, readily, speedily, swiftly, without waste; SEE CONCEPTS 544,799

summarize [v] *give a rundown*
abridge, abstract, boil down*, cipher, compile, condense, cut, cut back, cut down, digest, encapsulate, epitomize, get to meat*, give main points, inventory, outline, pare, precis, prune*, put in a nutshell*, recap*, recapitulate, rehash*, retrograde, review, run down*, run through*, shorten, skim, snip, sum, summate, sum up, synopsize, trim; SEE CONCEPTS 55,236,247

summary [adj] *concise, to the point*
arbitrary, boiled down*, breviloquent, brief, compact, compacted, compendiary, compendious, condensed, cursory, curt, hasty, in a nutshell*, laconic, perfunctory, pithy*, recapped, rehashed, run-down, run-through, short, short and sweet*, succinct, terse; SEE CONCEPTS 267,272

summary [n] *short statement of main points*
abbreviation, abridgment, abstract, analysis, apercu, brief, capitulation, case, compendium, condensation, conspectus, core, digest, epitome, essence, extract, inventory, long and short of it*, nutshell*, outline, pandect, precis, prospectus, recap*, recapitulation, reduction, rehash*, report, résumé, review, roundup, rundown, run-through, sense, skeleton*, sketch, sum and substance*, summing-up*, survey, syllabus, synopsis, version, wrap-up*; SEE CONCEPT 283

summer [n] *hot season of the year*
daylight savings time*, dog days*, heat, midsummer, picnic days*, riot time*, summer solstice, summertide, summertime, sunny season, vacation; SEE CONCEPT 814

summit [n] *top, crowning point*
acme, apex, apogee, climax, crest, crown, culmination, head, height, max, meridian, most, peak, pinnacle, roof, vertex, zenith; SEE CONCEPT 836

summon [v] *call to a place*
arouse, ask, assemble, beckon, beep, bid, call, call back, call for, call forth, call in, call into action, call together, call upon, charge, cite, command, conjure, convene, convoke, direct, draft, draw on, enjoin, gather, hail, invite, invoke, mobilize, motion, muster, order, petition, rally, recall, request, ring, rouse, send for, sign, signal, subpoena, toll; SEE CONCEPT 53

sumptuous [*adj*] *luxurious, splendid*
awe-inspiring, beautiful, costly, dear, deluxe, elegant, expensive, extravagant, gorgeous, grand, grandiose, imposing, impressive, lavish, luscious, luxuriant, magnificent, opulent, out of this world, palatial, plush, pompous, posh, prodigal, profuse, rich, ritzy*, splendiferous, superb, swank*, ultra*, upholstered; SEE CONCEPTS **334,485,574**

sum up [*v*] *form an opinion of; summarize*
close, conclude, condense, digest, epitomize, estimate, examine, get the measure of, inventory, put in a nutshell*, recapitulate, review, size up, sum, synopsize, total; SEE CONCEPT **55**

sunder [*v*] *separate, sever*
break, break apart, break off, come apart, cut in two, detach, disconnect, disjoin, divide, part, rend, slice, split, split up, uncouple, undo, wedge apart; SEE CONCEPT **135**

sundry [*adj*] *miscellaneous*
assorted, different, divers, manifold, many, quite a few, several, some, varied, various; SEE CONCEPTS **564,772**

sunken [*adj*] *depressed, hollowed; submerged*
buried, caved-in, concave, fallen-in, immersed, indented, recessed; SEE CONCEPT **490**

sunny [*adj*] *bright, clear (referring to weather)*
brilliant, clarion, cloudless, fine, light, luminous, pleasant, radiant, rainless, shining, shiny, summery, sunlit, sunshiny, unclouded, undarkened; SEE CONCEPTS **525,617**

sunny [*adj2*] *happy*
beaming, blithe, buoyant, cheerful, cheery, chirpy, genial, joyful, lighthearted, lightsome, optimistic, pleasant, smiling, sunbeamy; SEE CONCEPTS **401,542**

sunrise [*n*] *rise of sun above horizon*
aurora, break of day*, bright, cockcrow*, dawn, dawning, daybreak, daylight, early bright*, light, morn, morning, sunup; SEE CONCEPT **810**

sunscreen [*n*] *sunblock*
skin protection, sunblocker, sun cream, suntan lotion; SEE CONCEPTS **466,467,468**

sunset [*n*] *fall of sun below horizon*
close of day, crepuscular light, dusk, eve, evening, eventide, gloaming, nightfall, sundown, twilight; SEE CONCEPT **810**

super [*adj*] *excellent*
cool*, divine, glorious, great, groovy*, hot*, incomparable, keen, magnificent, marvelous, matchless, neat, outstanding, peerless, sensational, smashing*, superb, terrific, topnotch, wonderful; SEE CONCEPT **574**

superabundance [*n*] *overabundance*
excess, glut, great quantity, more than enough, overflow, overmuch, oversupply, plenty, plethora, superfluity, surfeit, surplus, too much*; SEE CONCEPTS **767,787**

superb [*adj*] *excellent, first-rate*
admirable, august, best, breathtaking, choice, elegant, elevated, exalted, exquisite, fine, glorious, gorgeous, grand, great, lofty, magnificent, majestic, marvelous, matchless, noble, optimal, optimum, outstanding, peerless, prime, proud, resplendent, solid, splendid, splendiferous, splendorous, standout, state-of-the-art*, stunning, sublime, super, superior, superlative, unrivaled, very best; SEE CONCEPT **574**

supercilious [*adj*] *arrogant, stuck-up*
bossy, cavalier, cocky*, condescending, contemptuous, disdainful, egotistic, haughty, high-and-mighty*, imperious, insolent, lofty, nervy*, overbearing, patronizing, proud, putting on airs*, scornful, snobby, superior, uppity*, vainglorious; SEE CONCEPT **401**

superficial [*adj*] *without depth, detail*
apparent, casual, cosmetic, cursory, depthless, desultory, empty, evident, exterior, external, flash, flimsy, frivolous, general, glib, half-baked*, hasty, hurried, ignorant, inattentive, lightweight, nodding, one-dimensional*, on the surface*, ostensible, outward, partial, passing, perfunctory, peripheral, quick-fix*, seeming, shallow, shoal, silly, sketchy, skin-deep*, slapdash*, slight, smattery, summary, surface, tip of the iceberg*, trivial, uncritical, warped; SEE CONCEPTS **557,777**

superficially [*adv*] *lightly; without care*
apparently, at first glance, carelessly, casually, externally, extraneously, flimsily, frivolously, hastily, ignorantly, not profoundly, not thoroughly, once over lightly*, on the surface*, ostensibly, outwardly, partially, skim, to the casual eye*; SEE CONCEPTS **531,544**

superfluous [*adj*] *extra, unnecessary*
abounding, de trop, dispensable, excess, excessive, exorbitant, expendable, extravagant, extreme, gratuitous, inessential, in excess, inordinate, lavish, leftover, needless, nonessential, overflowing, overmuch, pleonastic, profuse, redundant, remaining, residuary, spare, superabundant, supererogatory, superfluent, supernumerary, surplus, unasked, uncalled-for, unneeded, unrequired, unwanted, useless; SEE CONCEPTS **546,560,824**

superintendent [*n*] *person who oversees organization*
administrator, boss, caretaker, chief, conductor, controller, curator, custodian, director, foreperson, governor, head, head person, inspector, manager, overseer, sitter, slave driver*, straw boss*, super*, supervisor, zookeeper*; SEE CONCEPT **347**

superior [*adj1*] *better, greater, higher; excellent*
above, a cut above*, admirable, capital, choice, dandy, deluxe, distinguished, exceeding, excellent, exceptional, exclusive, expert, famous, fine, finer, first-class, first-rate, first-string*, five-star*, good, good quality, grander, high-caliber, high-class, major, more advanced, more skillful, noteworthy, of higher rank, over, overlying, paramount, predominant, preferable, preferred, premium, prevailing, primary, remarkable, senior, superhuman, superincumbent, surpassing, unrivaled; SEE CONCEPT **574**

superior [*adj2*] *arrogant, haughty*
airy, bossy, cavalier, cocky*, condescending, cool, disdainful, high-and-mighty*, high-hat*, insolent, lofty, overbearing, patronizing, pretentious, proud, snobbish, stuck-up*, supercilious, uppity*, upstage*, wiseguy*; SEE CONCEPT **401**

superior [*n*] *person higher or highest in rank*
boss, brass*, CEO*, chief, chieftain, director, elder, exec*, executive, head, head honcho*, heavyweight*, higher-up*, key player*, leader, manager, principal, ruler, senior, supervisor, VIP*; SEE CONCEPT **347**

superiority [*n*] *advantage, predominance*
ahead, ascendancy, authority, better, bulge, dominance, edge, eminence, excellence, influence,

lead, meliority, nobility, perfection, position, power, predomination, preeminence, preponderance, prestige, prevalence, pull, rank, spark, supremacy, top, transcendence, upper hand*, vantage, victory, whip hand*; SEE CONCEPT 671

superlative [adj] *excellent, first-class*
A-1*, accomplished, all-time*, best, capital, consummate, crack, effusive, exaggerated, excessive, extreme, finished, gilt-edge*, greatest, highest, hundred-proof*, inflated, magnificent, matchless, of highest order*, optimum, outstanding, peerless, standout*, superb, supreme, surpassing, tops*, transcendent, unexcelled, unparalleled, unrivaled, unsurpassed, winning, world-class*; SEE CONCEPT 574

supernal [adj] *celestial*
angelic, astral, elevated, empyreal, empyrean, ethereal, heavenly, lofty, otherworldly, seraphic, uplifted; SEE CONCEPTS 536,673

supernatural [adj] *mysterious, not of this world*
abnormal, celestial, concealed, dark, fabulous, fairy, ghostly, heavenly, hidden, impenetrable, invisible, legendary, metaphysical, miraculous, mystic, mythical, mythological, numinous, obscure, occult, paranormal, phantom, phenomenal, preternatural, psychic, rare, secret, spectral, superhuman, superior, supermundane, superordinary, supranatural, transcendental, uncanny, uncomprehensible, unearthly, unfathomable, unintelligible, unknowable, unknown, unnatural, unrevealed, unusual; SEE CONCEPT 582

supersede [v] *take the place of; override*
abandon, annul, desert, discard, displace, forsake, oust, outmode, outplace, overrule, reject, remove, replace, repudiate, set aside, succeed, supplant, supplement, suspend, take over, usurp; SEE CONCEPTS 128,141

superstition [n] *belief in sign of things to come*
false belief, fear, irrationality, notion, shibboleth*, unfounded fear; SEE CONCEPT 689

supervise [v] *manage people, project*
administer, be in charge*, be in driver's seat*, be in the saddle, be on duty, be responsible for, boss, call the play*, call the shots*, chaperon, conduct, control, crack the whip*, deal with, direct, handle, inspect, keep an eye on*, look after, overlook, oversee, preside over, quarterback*, ride herd on*, run, run the show*, run things*, sit on top of*, superintend, survey, take care of; SEE CONCEPT 117

supervision [n] *management of people, project*
administration, auspices, care, charge, conduct, control, direction, guidance, handling, instruction, intendance, oversight, running, superintendence, superintendency, surveillance; SEE CONCEPT 117

supervisor [n] *person who manages people, project*
administrator, boss, brass hat*, caretaker, chief, curator, custodian, director, executive, foreperson, head, inspector, manager, overseer, slave driver*, straw boss*, super*, superintendent, zookeeper*; SEE CONCEPT 347

supine [adj 1] *lying down*
decumbent, flat, flat on one's back, horizontal, level, procumbent, prone, prostrate, reclining, recumbent, stretched out; SEE CONCEPT 583

supine [adj2] *inactive*
do-nothing*, dormant, dull, idle, indolent, inert, lackadaisical, lax, lazy, lethargic, listless, motionless, passive, quiet, sedentary, slack, sleepy, slothful, sluggish, unoccupied, unresponsive; SEE CONCEPTS 401,560,584

supplant [v] *displace, replace*
back up, bounce, cast out, crowd, cut out, eject, expel, fill in, force, force out, front for, oust, outplace, overthrow, remove, ring, ring in, sit in, stand in, substitute, succeed, supersede, swap places with, take out, take over, take the place of, transfer, undermine, unseat, usurp; SEE CONCEPT 128

supple [adj] *bendable*
adaptable, agile, bending, ductile, elastic, flexible, graceful, limber, lissome, lithe, lithesome, malleable, moldable, plastic, pliable, pliant, resilient, rubber, springy, stretch, stretchy, svelte, willowy, wiry, yielding; SEE CONCEPTS 488,604

supplement [n] *something added*
added feature*, addendum, addition, additive, appendix, bell*, bells and whistles*, codicil, complement, continuation, extra, insert, option, postscript, pullout, rider, sequel, spin-off*, subsidiary; SEE CONCEPTS 270,824

supplement [v] *add to*
add fuel to fire*, augment, beef up*, build up, buttress, complement, complete, enhance, enrich, extend, fill out, fill up, fortify, heat up*, improve, increase, jazz up*, pad*, punch up*, reinforce, step up, strengthen, subsidize, supply, top; SEE CONCEPTS 236,244,245

supplementary [adj] *additional*
accompanying, added, ancillary, appended, augmenting, auxiliary, extra, increased, more; SEE CONCEPT 771

supplicate [v] *ask for, pray for*
appeal, beg, beseech, desire, petition, pray, put in for*, seek, solicit; SEE CONCEPT 53

supplies [n] *equipment, provisions*
food, foodstuffs, items, material, materials, necessities, provender, rations, raw materials, replenishments, stock, store, stores; SEE CONCEPTS 446,451,457

supply [n] *reserve of goods*
accumulation, amount, backlog, cache, fund, hoard, inventory, number, quantity, reservoir, source, stock, stockpile, store, surplus; SEE CONCEPT 712

supply [v] *furnish, provide, give a resource*
afford, cater, cater to, come across with*, come through*, come up with, contribute, deliver, dispense, drop, endow, equip, feed, fill, find, fix up, fulfill, give with, grant, hand, hand over, heel*, kick in*, minister, outfit, pony up*, produce, provide, provision, purvey, put out, put up, replenish, satisfy, stake, stock, store, transfer, turn over, victual, yield; SEE CONCEPTS 107,140

support [n1] *something that holds up structure*
abutment, agency, back, backing, base, bed, bedding, block, brace, buttress, collar, column, cornerstone, device, flotation, foothold, footing, foundation, fulcrum, groundwork, guide, hold, lining, means, medium, pillar, platform, pole, post, prop, rampart, reinforcement, rest, rib, rod, shore, stake, stanchion, stave, stay, stiffener, stilt, substratum, substructure, sustentation, timber, underpinning; SEE CONCEPTS 440,442,445, 471

support [n2] *help, approval*
aid, assist, assistance, backing, blessing, championship, comfort, encouragement, friendship, fur-

therance, hand, lift, loyalty, moral support, patronage, protection, relief, succor, sustenance; SEE CONCEPTS 10,110,388,712

support [n3] *food, money, possessions for staying alive*
alimentation, alimony, allowance, care, keep, livelihood, living, maintenance, necessities, nutriment, payment, provision, relief, responsibility, stock, stores, subsidy, subsistence, sustenance, upkeep, victuals; SEE CONCEPTS 340,446,457,712

support/supporter [n4] *person who helps another*
adherent, advocate, ally, angel*, apologist, backbone, backer, benefactor, champion, cohort, comforter, confederate, coworker, defender, disciple, endorser, espouser, exponent, expounder, fan, follower, friend, helper, mainstay, maintainer, partisan, patron, pillar, preserver, prop, proponent, satellite*, second, sponsor, stalwart, stay, subscriber, supporter, sustainer, tower of strength*, upholder, well-wisher*; SEE CONCEPT 423

support [v1] *hold up*
base, be a foundation for, bear, bed, bolster, bottom, brace, buttress, carry, cradle, crutch, embed, found, ground, hold, keep from falling, keep up, mainstay, poise, prop, reinforce, shore, shore up, shoulder, stand, stay, strut, sustain, undergird, upbear, uphold; SEE CONCEPT 190

support [v2] *take care of, provide for*
angel*, attend to, back, bankroll*, be a source of strength*, bring up, buoy up, care for, chaperon, cherish, earn one's keep, encourage, feed, finance, fortify, foster, fund, give a leg up*, guard, keep, keep an eye on*, look after, maintain, make a living, nourish, nurse, pay expenses of, pay for, pick up the check*, prop, put up money for*, raise, set up, sponsor, stake, stiffen, strengthen, stroke, subsidize, succor, sustain, underwrite, uphold; SEE CONCEPTS 7,19,22,140, 295,341

support [v3] *defend, advocate belief*
abet, advance, agree with, aid, approve, assist, back, bear out, bolster, boost, boost morale, carry, champion, cheer, comfort, countenance, endorse, establish, forward, get behind*, go along with, go to bat for*, help, hold, justify, keep up, maintain, plead for, promote, pull for, put forward, rally round, second, side with, stand behind, stand up for, stay, stick by*, stick up for*, substantiate, sustain, take one's side*, take the part of*, throw in one's lot with*, throw in with*, uphold, verify; SEE CONCEPTS 10,49,110

support [v4] *endure*
abide, bear, bear with, brook, carry on, continue, countenance, go, go through, handle, keep up, live with*, maintain, put up with*, stand, stand for*, stay the course*, stick it out*, stomach*, submit, suffer, swallow*, sweat out*, tolerate, undergo, wait out; SEE CONCEPT 23

suppose [v1] *assume, guess*
accept, admit, brainstorm, calculate, conjecture, cook up*, dare-say*, deem, divine, dream, estimate, expect, figure, go out on a limb*, grant, guess, guesstimate*, hazard a guess*, hypothesize, imagine, infer, judge, opine, posit, predicate, presume, presuppose, pretend, spark, speculate, surmise, suspect, take, take for

granted, theorize, think, understand; SEE CONCEPT 28

suppose [v2] *believe*
assume, be afraid, conceive, conclude, conjecture, consider, deem, dream, expect, fancy, feel, gather, have a hunch*, have sneaking suspicion*, hypothesize, imagine, judge, postulate, pretend, reckon, regard, suspect, swear by, take, take as gospel truth*, take stock in*, think, understand, view; SEE CONCEPT 12

supposition [n] *guess, belief*
apriorism, assumption, condition, conjecture, doubt, guessing, guesstimate*, guesswork, hunch, hypothesis, idea, likelihood, notion, opinion, posit, postulate, postulation, premise, presumption, presupposition, rough guess*, shot in the dark*, sneaking suspicion*, speculation, stab in the dark*, suppose, surmise, suspicion, theory, thesis, view; SEE CONCEPT 689

suppress [v] *restrain, hold in check*
abolish, annihilate, beat down, bottle, bring to naught, burke, censor, check, clamp, conceal, conquer, contain, cover up, crack down on, crush, curb, cut off, extinguish, hold back, hold down, hold in, interrupt, keep in, keep secret, muffle, muzzle, overcome, overpower, overthrow, put an end to, put down, put kibosh on*, put lid on*, quash, quell, quench, repress, shush*, silence, sit on*, smother, snuff out*, spike, squash*, stamp out*, stifle, stop, subdue, trample, withhold; SEE CONCEPTS 121,130,252

supremacy [n] *total domination*
absolute rule, ascendancy, authority, command, control, dominance, dominion, driver's seat*, paramountcy, power, predominance, preeminence, preponderance, prepotence, primacy, principality, sovereignty, superiority, supreme authority, sway, transcendence; SEE CONCEPTS 133,376

supreme [adj] *greatest, principal*
absolute, best, cardinal, chief, closing, crowning, culminating, excellent, extreme, final, first, foremost, head, highest, incomparable, last, leading, marvelous, matchless, maximum, paramount, peerless, perfect, predominant, preeminent, prevailing, prime, sovereign, superb, superlative, surpassing, terminal, top, top-drawer*, towering, transcendent, ultimate, unequaled, unmatched, unparalleled, unsurpassable, unsurpassed, utmost; SEE CONCEPTS 568,574

surcharge [n] *fee*
additional charge, cost, expense, extra, overcharge, overload, payment, price, surtax, tax; SEE CONCEPTS 329,344

sure [adj1] *certain, definite*
abiding, assured, changeless, clear, confident, constant, convinced, convincing, decided, doubtless, enduring, firm, fixed, for a fact, free from doubt*, genuine, incontestable, incontrovertible, indisputable, indubitable, never-failing, persuaded, positive, real, satisfied, set, steadfast, steady, telling, unchangeable, unchanging, uncompromising, undeniable, unequivocal, unfailing, unfaltering, unqualified, unquestionable, unquestioning, unshakable, unshaken, unvarying, unwavering, valid; SEE CONCEPT 535

sure [adj2] *physically stable*
fast, firm, fixed, safe, secure, solid, staunch, steady, strong; SEE CONCEPT 488

SU
SU

sure [*adj3*] *inevitable*
assured, bound, certain, guaranteed, indisputable, ineluctable, inerrant, inescapable, infallible, irrevocable, surefire, unavoidable, unerring, unfailing; SEE CONCEPT *548*

sure [*adj4*] *self-confident*
arrogant, assured, certain, composed, confident, decided, decisive, positive, self-assured, self-possessed; SEE CONCEPT *401*

surely [*adv*] *without doubt*
absolutely, admittedly, assuredly, beyond doubt, beyond shadow of doubt*, certainly, clearly, come what may*, conclusively, decidedly, definitely, distinctly, doubtlessly, evidently, explicitly, fixedly, for certain, for real, indeed, indubitably, inevitably, inexorably, infallibly, irrefutably, manifestly, nothing else but, plainly, positively, rain or shine*, to be sure, undoubtedly, unequivocally, unerringly, unfailingly, unmistakably, unquestionably, unshakably, with certainty, without fail; SEE CONCEPT *535*

sure thing [*n*] *certainty*
all sewn up*, belief, cinch, definiteness, foregone conclusion, lock*, open and shut case*, positiveness, rain or shine*, safe bet, shoo-in*, small risk, sure bet*, surefire*, surety; SEE CONCEPTS *638,725*

surface [*adj*] *external*
apparent, covering, depthless, exterior, facial, outer, outside, outward, shallow, shoal, superficial, top; SEE CONCEPTS *485,583*

surface [*n*] *external part of something*
area, cover, covering, expanse, exterior, exteriority, externality, facade, face, facet, level, obverse, outside, peel, periphery, plane, rind, side, skin, stretch, superficiality, superficies, top, veneer; SEE CONCEPT *484*

surface [*v*] *come to the top of*
appear, arise, come to light, come up, crop up, emerge, flare up, materialize, rise, transpire; SEE CONCEPTS *166,716*

surfeit [*n*] *excess*
bellyful*, excess, glut*, overabundance, overflow, overfullness, overindulgence, overkill, overmuch, overplus, plenitude, plethora, profusion, remainder, repletion, satiety, satisfaction, saturation, superabundance, superfluity, surplus, up to here*; SEE CONCEPT *740*

surfeit [*v*] *overfill*
cloy, cram, eat, fill, glut, gorge, jade, overfeed, overindulge, pall, sate, satiate, satisfy, stuff; SEE CONCEPTS *209,740*

surge [*n*] *rush, usually of liquid*
billow, breaker, deluge, efflux, flood, flow, growth, gush, intensification, outpouring, rise, roll, surf, swell, upsurge, wave; SEE CONCEPTS *432,467,787*

surge [*v*] *rush, usually in liquid form*
arise, billow, climb, deluge, eddy, flow, grow, gush, heave, mount, pour, ripple, rise, roll, sluice, stream, swell, swirl, tower, undulate, well forth; SEE CONCEPTS *146,179*

surly [*adj*] *gruff, bearish*
boorish, brusque, churlish, cross, crusty, curmudgeonly, discourteous, dour, fractious, glum, grouchy, ill-mannered, ill-natured, irritable, morose, perverse, rude, saturnine, sulky, sullen, testy, ugly, uncivil, ungracious; SEE CONCEPT *401*

surmise [*n*] *guess, conclusion*
assumption, attempt, conjecture, deduction, guesstimate*, guesswork, hunch, hypothesis, idea, inference, notion, opinion, possibility, presumption, sneaking suspicion*, speculation, supposition, suspicion, theory, thought; SEE CONCEPTS *529,689*

surmise [*v*] *come to a conclusion*
assume, conclude, conjecture, consider, deduce, fancy, guess, guesstimate*, hazard a guess*, hypothesize, imagine, infer, opine, presume, pretend, regard, risk assuming, speculate, suppose, suspect, take a shot*, take a stab*, theorize, think, venture a guess; SEE CONCEPTS *18,28*

surmount [*v*] *overcome, triumph over*
best, better, cap, clear, conquer, crest, crown, defeat, down, exceed, hurdle, leap, lick*, negotiate, outdo, outstrip, over, overpower, overtop, pass, prevail over, rise above, subdue, surpass, throw*, top*, vanquish, vault; SEE CONCEPTS *95,141*

surname [*n*] *family name*
cognomen, last name, matronymic, metronymic, patronymic; SEE CONCEPTS *268,683*

surpass [*v*] *outdo something or someone*
beat, best, better, cap, eclipse, exceed, excel, go beyond, go one better*, improve upon, outdistance, outgo, outmatch, outpace, outperform, outrank, outrival, outrun, outshine, outstep, outstrip, outweigh, override, overshadow, overstep, pass, put to shame*, rank*, surmount, top, tower, tower above*, transcend, trump*; SEE CONCEPT *141*

surplus [*adj*] *extra*
de trop, excess, in excess, leftover, odd*, over, remaining, spare, superfluent, superfluous, supernumerary, too much, unused; SEE CONCEPTS *560,781,824*

surplus [*n*] *extra material*
balance, excess, overage, overflow, overkill, overmuch, overrun, overstock, oversupply, plethora, plus, remainder, residue, something extra, superabundance, superfluity, surfeit, surplusage, the limit, too much; SEE CONCEPTS *260,658,824*

surprise [*n*] *something amazing; state of amazement*
abruptness, amazement, astonishment, astoundment, attack, awe, bewilderment, bombshell*, consternation, curiosity, curveball*, disappointment, disillusion, eye-opener*, fortune, godsend*, incredulity, jolt*, kick*, marvel, miracle, miscalculation, phenomenon, portent, precipitance, precipitation, precipitousness, prodigy, rarity, revelation, shock, start, stupefaction, suddenness, thunderbolt*, unexpected, unforeseen, whammy*, wonder, wonderment; SEE CONCEPTS *410,529*

surprise [*v1*] *astonish; cause amazement*
amaze, astound, awe, bewilder, blow away*, bowl over*, cause wonder, confound, confuse, consternate, daze, dazzle, discomfit, disconcert, dismay, dumbfound, electrify, flabbergast, floor, jar, jolt, leave aghast, leave open-mouthed, nonplus, overwhelm, perplex, petrify, rattle, shake up, shock, spring something on, stagger, startle, strike dumb*, strike with awe, stun, stupefy, take aback, take one's breath away*, throw a curve*, unsettle; SEE CONCEPT *42*

surprise [*v2*] *sneak up on; catch*
ambush, burst in on, bushwhack*, capture, catch

in the act*, catch off-balance*, catch off-guard*, catch red-handed*, catch unawares*, come down on, discover, drop in on, grab, grasp, lay for, lie in wait*, nab, seize, spring on, startle, take, take by surprise, waylay; SEE CONCEPTS *42,86*

surprising [*adj*] *unexpected*
accidental, amazing, astonishing, chance, electrifying, extraordinary, fortuitous, from left field*, impulsive, out of the blue*, remarkable, shocking, startling, stunning, sudden, unanticipated, unforeseen, unpredictable, unpredicted, without warning, wonderful; SEE CONCEPTS *544,548*

surrender [*n*] *giving up; resignation*
abandonment, abdication, acquiescence, appeasement, capitulation, cessation, dedition, delivery, giving way, relenting, relinquishment, renunciation, submission, succumbing, white flag*, yielding; SEE CONCEPTS *67,108,119,320*

surrender [*v*] *give up; resign*
abandon, buckle under*, capitulate, cave in*, cede, commit, concede, consign, cry uncle*, deliver up, eat crow*, eat humble pie*, entrust, fall, fold, forego, give in, go along with, go down, go under, hand over, knuckle, knuckle under*, leave, let go, pack it in*, part with, play dead*, put up white flag*, quit, relinquish, renounce, roll over*, submit, succumb, throw in the towel*, toss it in*, waive, yield; SEE CONCEPTS *67,108,119,320*

surreptitious [*adj*] *sneaky, secret*
clandestine, covert, fraudulent, furtive, hidden, hole-and-corner*, hush-hush*, on the QT*, on the sly*, private, skulking, slinking, sly, sneaking, stealthy, stub-rosa, unauthorized, undercover, underhand, under-the-table*, under wraps*, veiled; SEE CONCEPT *548*

surrogate [*n*] *person or thing that acts as substitute*
agent, alternate, backup, delegate, deputy, expediency, expedient, fill-in, makeshift, pinch hitter*, proxy, recourse, refuge, replacement, representative, resort, resource, stand-in, stopgap*, sub*; SEE CONCEPTS *348,414,423*

surround [*v*] *enclose, encircle something*
beleaguer, beset, besiege, blockade, border, bound, box in, circle, circumscribe, circumvent, close around, close in, close in on, compass, confine, edge, enclose, encompass, envelop, environ, fence in, fringe, gird, girdle, go around, hem in, inundate, invest, lay siege to, limit, loop, margin, outline, rim, ring, round, shut in, skirt, verge; SEE CONCEPT *758*

surroundings [*n*] *environment*
ambience, atmosphere, background, climate, community, environs, home, location, medium, milieu, neighborhood, setting, vicinity; SEE CONCEPTS *198,673*

surveillance [*n*] *close observation, following*
body mike*, bug*, bugging*, care, control, direction, eagle eye*, examination, eye, inspection, lookout, peeled eye*, scrutiny, spying, stakeout, superintendence, supervision, surveyance, tab*, tail*, tap*, track*, vigil, vigilance, watch, wiretap; SEE CONCEPTS *103,298,749*

survey [*n*] *scrutiny, examination*
analysis, aperçu, audit, check, compendium, critique, digest, inquiry, inspection, outline, overview, pandect, perlustration, perusal, precis, review, sample, scan, sketch, study, syllabus, view; SEE CONCEPTS *37,103,197,271,291*

survey [*v*] *scrutinize, take stock of*
appraise, assay, assess, canvass, case, check, check out, check over, check up, contemplate, estimate, evaluate, examine, give the once over*, inspect, look over, look upon, measure, observe, overlook, oversee, plan, plot, prospect, rate, read, reconnoiter, research, review, scan, scope, scrutinize, set at, size, size up, stake out, study, summarize, superintend, supervise, take stock of*, test the waters*, valuate, value, view; SEE CONCEPTS *37,48,103,197,291*

survive [*v*] *continue to live*
bear, be extant, be left, carry on, carry through, come through, cut it, endure, exist, get on, get through, go all the way*, go the limit*, handle, hold out, keep, keep afloat, last, live, live down, live on, live out, live through, make a comeback*, make the cut*, outlast, outlive, outwear, persevere, persist, pull out of it*, pull through, recover, remain, remain alive, revive, ride out*, see through, stand up, subsist, suffer, sustain, tough it out*, weather, withstand; SEE CONCEPTS *23,239,407*

susceptible [*adj*] *exposed, naive*
affected, aroused, be taken in, disposed, easily moved, easy, fall for, given, gullible, impressed, impressible, impressionable, inclined, influenced, liable, mark, movable, nonresistant, obnoxious, open, out on a limb*, persuadable, predisposed, prone, pushover, ready, receptive, responsive, roused, sensible, sensile, sensitive, sentient, sitting duck*, soft, stirred, subject, sucker*, suggestible, susceptive, swallow, swayed, tender, touched, tumble for*, vulnerable, wide open; SEE CONCEPTS *403,542*

suspect [*adj*] *doubtful*
doubtable, dubious, fishy*, incredible, open, problematic, pseudo*, questionable, ridiculous, shaky*, suspected, suspicious, thick*, thin*, unbelievable, uncertain, unclear, unlikely, unsure; SEE CONCEPTS *529,582*

suspect [*v*] *distrust; guess*
assume, be afraid, believe, conceive, conclude, conjecture, consider, disbelieve, doubt, expect, feel, gather, harbor suspicion*, have a hunch*, have doubt, have sneaking suspicion*, hazard a guess*, hold, imagine, mistrust, presume, reckon, smell a rat*, speculate, suppose, surmise, think, think probable, understand, wonder; SEE CONCEPTS *21,28*

suspend [*v1*] *hang from above*
append, attach, be pendent, dangle, depend, hang down, hang up, hook up, sling, swing, wave; SEE CONCEPTS *181,190*

suspend [*v2*] *delay, hold off*
adjourn, arrest, bar, break up, can, cease, check, count out, cut short, debar, defer, discontinue, eject, eliminate, exclude, file, halt, hang, hang fire*, hang up, hold up, inactivate, intermit, interrupt, lay aside, lay off, lay on the table*, lay over, omit, pigeonhole*, pink-slip*, postpone, procrastinate, prorogue, protract, put an end to, put a stop to, put off, put on back burner*, put on hold, put on ice*, put on the shelf*, reject, retard, rule out, shelve, stave off, stay, waive, withhold; SEE CONCEPTS *119,121,130,351*

suspense [*n*] *anticipation*
anxiety, apprehension, chiller*, cliff-hanger*, cloak and dagger*, confusion, dilemma, doubt, eagerness, expectancy, expectation, grabber*,

hesitancy, hesitation, impatience, indecision, indecisiveness, insecurity, irresolution, page-turner*, perplexity, potboiler*, tension, thriller*, uncertainty, wavering; SEE CONCEPTS 410,679

suspension [n] *delay*
abeyance, abeyancy, adjournment, break, breather*, breathing spell*, cessation, coffee break*, concluding, conclusion, cutoff, deferment, disbarment, discontinuation, discontinuing, doldrums, dormancy, downtime*, end, ending, finish, five*, freeze, halt, heave-ho*, intermission, interruption, latency, layoff, letup, moratorium, pause, period, postponement, quiescence, quiescency, remission, respite, stay, stoppage, suspense, ten*, termination, time-out*; SEE CONCEPTS 119,807,832

suspicion [n1] *doubt*
bad vibes*, chariness, conjecture, cynicism, distrust, dubiety, dubiosity, funny feeling*, guess, guesswork, gut feeling*, hunch, idea, impression, incertitude, incredulity, jealousy, lack of confidence, misgiving, mistrust, nonbelief, notion, qualm, skepticism, sneaking suspicion*, supposition, surmise, uncertainty, wariness, wonder; SEE CONCEPTS 532,689,690

suspicion [n2] *hint, trace*
cast, glimmer, intimation, shade, shadow, smell, soupçon, strain, streak, suggestion, tinge, touch, whiff; SEE CONCEPTS 529,831

suspicious [adj1] *distrustful*
apprehensive, cagey, careful, cautious, doubtful, green-eyed*, incredulous, in doubt, jealous, leery, mistrustful, not born yesterday* on the lookout*, questioning, quizzical, skeptical, suspect, suspecting, unbelieving, uptight*, wary, watchful, without belief, without faith, wondering; SEE CONCEPTS 403,542

suspicious [adj2] *doubtful, fishy*
borderline, debatable, different, disputable, doubtable, dubious, equivocal, farfetched, funny*, irregular, not kosher*, open, open to doubt, open to question, out of line*, overt, peculiar, phony, problematic, queer, questionable, reaching, rings untrue*, shady, shaky*, suspect, too much*, uncertain, uncommon, unsure, unusual, won't wash*; SEE CONCEPTS 529,564

sustain [v1] *keep up, maintain*
aid, approve, assist, back, bankroll, bear, befriend, bolster, brace, buoy, buttress, carry, comfort, confirm, continue, convey, defend, endorse, favor, feed, foster, go for, help, keep alive, keep from falling, keep going, lend a hand*, lug, nourish, nurse, nurture, pack, preserve, prolong, prop, protract, provide for, ratify, relieve, save, shore up, stand by, stick up for, supply, support, tote, transfer, transport, uphold, validate, verify; SEE CONCEPTS 110,140,190

sustain [v2] *endure, experience*
abide, bear, bear up under, bear with, brook, digest, encounter, feel, go, hang in, have, know, live with*, put up with*, see, stand*, stand up to, stomach*, suffer, take it, tolerate, undergo, withstand; SEE CONCEPTS 23,678

sustenance [n] *necessities for existence*
aid, aliment, bacon*, bread*, bread and butter*, comestible, daily bread*, eatables, edibles, food, keep, livelihood, maintenance, nourishment, nutrition, pap*, provender, provision, ration, refreshment, salt*, subsistence, support, victual, wherewithal; SEE CONCEPTS 340,446,457,709

svelte [adj] *thin and well-built*
graceful, lean, lissom, lithe, slender, slinky, smooth, sylphlike, willowy; SEE CONCEPTS 490,491

swagger [v] *show off; walk pompously*
bluster, boast, brag, brandish, bully, cock, flourish, gasconade, gloat, grandstand*, hector, look big*, lord, parade, parade one's wares*, peacock*, play to the crowd*, pontificate, prance, put on, put on airs*, sashay*, saunter, strut, swank*, swashbuckle*, sway, sweep, swell; SEE CONCEPTS 49,149,716

swallow [v1] *consume*
absorb, belt*, bolt*, chugalug*, devour, dispatch, dispose, down, drink, drop, eat, gobble, gulp, imbibe, ingest, ingurgitate, inhale, put away, quaff, sip, slurp, swig, swill, take, toss, wash down*, wolf; SEE CONCEPT 169

swallow [v2] *believe without much thought*
accept, be naive, buy, fall for; SEE CONCEPT 12

swami [n] *religious teacher*
guiding light*, guru, master, mentor, mystic, sage, teacher, yogi; SEE CONCEPT 350

swamp [n] *wet land covered with vegetation*
bog, bottoms, everglade, fen, glade, holm, marsh, marshland, mire, moor, morass, mud, muskeg, peat bog, polder, quag, quagmire, slough, swale, swampland; SEE CONCEPT 509

swamp [v] *overwhelm, flood*
beset, besiege, crowd, drench, drown, engulf, inundate, overcrowd, overflow, overload, satiate, saturate, sink, snow*, submerge, submerse, surfeit, swallow up, upset, wash, waterlog, whelm; SEE CONCEPTS 146,179,641

swank/swanky [adj] *plush, stylish*
chichi*, classy, deluxe, exclusive, expensive, fancy, fashionable, flamboyant, flashy, glamorous, grand, lavish, luxurious, ostentatious, peacocky, plushy*, posh, pretentious, rich, ritzy*, sharp, showy, smart, snappy, splashy, sumptuous, tony*, trendy, with-it*; SEE CONCEPT 589

swan song [n] *final appearance or performance*
adieu, climax, closer*, conclusion, crowning achievement, crowning glory*, culmination, end piece, finis, goodbye, last act, last hurrah, peroration, windup*; SEE CONCEPT 832

swap/swop [v] *exchange*
bandy, bargain, barter, change, interchange, substitute, switch, trade, traffic, truck; SEE CONCEPT 104

swarm [n] *large, moving group*
army, bevy, blowout, concourse, covey, crowd, crush, drove, flock, herd, horde, host, jam, mass, mob, multitude, myriad, pack, press, push, school, shoal, throng, troop, turnout; SEE CONCEPTS 397,417,432

swarm [v] *move forward as a group*
abound, be alive, be numerous, cluster, congregate, crawl, crowd, flock, flow, gather, gather like bees*, jam, mass, mob, move in a crowd, overrun, pullulate, rush together, stream, teem, throng; SEE CONCEPTS 113,114,159

swarthy [adj] *dark-complexioned*
black, brown, brunet, dark, dark-hued, darkish, dark-skinned, dusky, swart, tan, tawny; SEE CONCEPT 618

swat [v] *hit*
beat, belt, biff, box, buffet, clobber, clout, cuff,

ding, knock, slap, slug, smack, smash, sock, strike, wallop, whack; SEE CONCEPT *189*

sway [*n*] *strong influence*
amplitude, authority, clout, command, control, dominion, empire, expanse, government, jurisdiction, mastery, might, power, predominance, range, reach, regime, reign, rule, run, scope, sovereignty, spread, stretch, sweep; SEE CONCEPTS *376,687*

sway [*v1*] *move back and forth*
bend, blow hot and cold*, careen, fluctuate, hem and haw*, incline, lean, lurch, oscillate, pendulate, pulsate, rock, roll, stagger, swagger, swing, undulate, vibrate, wave, waver, weave, wobble, yo-yo*; SEE CONCEPTS *13,145,151*

sway [*v2*] *influence, affect*
bias, brainwash, carry, conduct, control, crack*, direct, dispose, dominate, get*, govern, guide, hold sway over, hook, impact on, impress, incline, induce, inspire, lead by the nose*, manage, move, overrule, persuade, predispose, prevail on, put across, reign, rule, rule over, sell*, soften up*, strike, suck in*, touch, turn one's head*, twist one's arm*, whitewash*, win over, work on; SEE CONCEPTS *14,68,117*

swear [*v1*] *declare under oath*
affirm, assert, attest, avow, covenant, cross one's heart*, depend on, depose, give one's word*, give witness, have confidence in, maintain, make an affidavit, pledge oneself, plight, promise, rely on, say so*, state, state under oath, swear by, swear to God*, swear up and down*, take an oath, testify, trust, vouch, vow, warrant; SEE CONCEPT *49*

swear [*v2*] *speak profanely; be vulgar*
bedamn, be foul-mouthed, blaspheme, curse, cuss*, execrate, flame*, imprecate, take name in vain*, talk dirty*, use bad language*, utter profanity; SEE CONCEPTS *52,54*

swear by [*v*] *be certain, recommend*
advocate, back, bank on, believe in, be satisfied with, compliment, depend on it, endorse, go on the record for*, have faith in, plug*, praise, put in a good word*, speak highly of, speak well of, stand by, suggest, think highly of, vouch for; SEE CONCEPTS *10,75*

swearing [*n*] *foul language*
bad language*, blasphemy, cursing, cuss*, cussing*, dirty language*, dirty name*, dirty talk*, dirty word*, execration, expletives, four-letter word*, imprecation, malediction, no-no*, profanity, swearword; SEE CONCEPTS *54,276,278*

sweat [*n1*] *body's perspiring*
diaphoresis, excretion, exudation, perspiration, steam, transudation; SEE CONCEPTS *185,467*

sweat [*n2*] *hard work*
backbreaker*, chore, drudgery, effort, grind, labor, moil, slavery, task, toil, travail, work; SEE CONCEPTS *362,677*

sweat [*v1*] *perspire*
break out in a sweat, drip, eject, exude, glow, ooze, secrete, seep, spout, swelter, transude, wilt; SEE CONCEPT *185*

sweat [*v2*] *worry about; bear*
abide, agonize, be on pins and needles*, be on tenterhooks*, brook, chafe, endure, exert, fret, go, labor, lose sleep over*, stand, stay the course*, stick it out*, stomach*, suffer, take, toil, tolerate, torture, work hard; SEE CONCEPTS *23,35*

sweaty [*adj*] *damp with perspiration*
bathed, clammy, covered with sweat, drenched, dripping, drippy, glowing, hot, moist, perspiring, perspiry, soaked, sticky, stinky, sweating, wet; SEE CONCEPT *406*

sweep [*n1*] *range, extent*
ambit, breadth, compass, extension, latitude, length, orbit, purview, radius, reach, region, scope, span, stretch, vista; SEE CONCEPTS *651,756,788*

sweep [*n2*] *movement*
arc, bend, course, curve, gesture, move, play, progress, stroke, swing; SEE CONCEPTS *145,748*

sweep [*v1*] *brush off, away*
broom, brush, brush up, clean, clear, clear up, mop, ready, remove, scrub, tidy, vacuum; SEE CONCEPT *165*

sweep [*v2*] *fly, glide*
career, fleet, flit, flounce, glance, hurtle, pass, sail, scud, skim, tear, wing, zoom; SEE CONCEPTS *150,152*

sweeping [*adj*] *wide-ranging*
across-the-board, all-around, all-embracing, all-encompassing, all-inclusive, all-out, bird's-eye*, blanket, broad, complete, comprehensive, exaggerated, exhaustive, extensive, full, general, global, inclusive, indiscriminate, out-and-out*, overall, overdrawn, overstated, radical, thorough, thorough-going, unqualified, vast, wall-to-wall*, whole-hog*, wholesale*, wide; SEE CONCEPTS *531,772*

sweet [*adj1*] *sugary*
candied, candy-coated, cloying, delicious, honeyed, like candy, like honey, luscious, nectarous, saccharine, sugar-coated, sugared, sweetened, syrupy, toothsome; SEE CONCEPTS *462,613*

sweet [*adj2*] *friendly, kind*
affectionate, agreeable, amiable, angelic, appealing, attractive, beautiful, beloved, charming, cherished, companionable, considerate, darling, dear, dearest, delectable, delicious, delightful, dulcet, engaging, fair, generous, gentle, good-humored, good-natured, heavenly, lovable, loving, luscious, mild, mushy, patient, pet, pleasant, pleasing, precious, reasonable, saccharine, sweet-tempered, sympathetic, taking, tender, thoughtful, treasured, unselfish, winning, winsome; SEE CONCEPTS *401,404,542*

sweet [*adj3*] *nice-smelling*
ambrosial, aromal, aromatic, balmy, clean, fragrant, fresh, new, perfumed, perfumy, pure, redolent, savory, scented, spicy, sweet-smelling, wholesome; SEE CONCEPT *598*

sweet [*adj4*] *nice-sounding*
dulcet, euphonic, euphonious, harmonious, mellifluous, mellow, melodic, melodious, musical, orotund, rich, rotund, silver-tongued, silvery, smooth, soft, sonorous, soothing, sweet-sounding, tuneful; SEE CONCEPT *594*

sweet [*n*] *sugary food*
bonbon, candy, chocolate, confection, confectionery, confiture, delight, dessert, enjoyment, final course, gratification, joy, pleasure, pudding, snack, sugarplum, sweetmeat; SEE CONCEPTS *457,461*

sweeten [*v1*] *add sugar*
add sweetening, candy, candy-coat, honey, make sweet, make toothsome, mull, sugar, sugar-coat; SEE CONCEPT *170*

SU
SW

sweeten [v2] *make happy; appease*
alleviate, assuage, conciliate, mollify, pacify, placate, propitiate, soften up, soothe; SEE CONCEPTS 7,22

sweetheart [n] *person whom another loves*
admirer, beau, beloved, boyfriend, companion, darling, dear, dear one, flame, girlfriend, heart-throb, honey*, inamorata, inamorato, love, love-bird*, lover, one and only*, paramour, pet, significant other, steady*, suitor, swain, sweet treasure*, truelove, valentine;. SEE CONCEPTS 414,423

swell [adj] *wonderful*
awesome, cool*, dandy*, deluxe, desirable, excellent, exclusive, fashionable, fine, fly*, grand, groovy*, keen, marvelous, neat, nifty, plush, posh, ritzy*, smart, stylish, super, terrific; SEE CONCEPTS 548,574

swell [n] *large increase, flow*
billow, crescendo, growth, ripple, rise, seat, surf, surge, undulation, uprise, wave; SEE CONCEPT 780

swell [v] *become larger*
accumulate, add to, aggravate, amplify, augment, balloon, become bloated, become distended, become swollen, be inflated, belly, billow, blister, bloat, bulge, dilate, distend, enhance, enlarge, expand, extend, fatten, fill out, grow, grow larger, heighten, increase, intensity, mount, plump, pouch, pout, protrude, puff, puff up, rise, round out, surge, tumefy, uprise, well up; SEE CONCEPTS 236,245,780

swelling [n] *physical growth; lump*
abscess, blister, boil, bruise, bulge, bump, bunion, carbuncle, contusion, corn, dilation, distention, enlargement, hump, increase, inflammation, injury, knob, knurl, node, nodule, pimple, pock, protuberance, puff, puffiness, pustule, ridge, sore, tumescence, tumor, wale, wart, weal, welt; SEE CONCEPTS 306,309

sweltering [adj] *very hot*
airless, baking, broiling, burning, close, fiery, humid, oppressive, perspiring, scorching, sizzling, stewing, sticky, stifling, stuffy, sultry, sweaty, sweltry, torrid; SEE CONCEPT 605

swerve [v] *turn aside, often to avoid collision*
bend, deflect, depart, depart from, deviate, dip, diverge, err, get off course, go off course, incline, lurch, move, sheer, sheer off, shift, sideslip, sidestep, skew, skid, slue, stray, swing, tack, train off, turn, veer, wander, waver, wind; SEE CONCEPTS 150,195,201

swift [adj] *very fast*
abrupt, alacritous, barrelling, breakneck, cracking*, double-quick*, expeditious, express, fleet, fleet-footed*, flying, hasty, headlong, hurried, in nothing flat*, like crazy*, like mad*, nimble, on the double*, precipitate, prompt, pronto, quick, rapid, ready, screaming, shaking a leg*, short, short-lived, snappy*, spanking*, speedball*, speedy, sudden, supersonic, unexpected, winged; SEE CONCEPTS 588,799

swiftly/swift [adv] *very fast*
apace, double-quick*, expeditiously, flat-out*, fleetly, full tilt*, hastily, hurriedly, in no time*, posthaste, promptly, quick, quickly, rapidly, speedily, without losing time*, without warning*; SEE CONCEPTS 588,799

swim [v] *make way through water using arms, legs*
bathe, breast-stroke, crawl, dive, dog paddle, float, freestyle, glide, go for a swim, go swimming, go wading, high-dive, move, paddle, practice, race, skinny-dip*, slip, stroke, submerge, take a dip, wade; SEE CONCEPT 363

swimmingly [adv] *very well*
as planned, cosily, easily, effectively, effortlessly, favorably, fortunately, happily, like a dream*, like clockwork*, prosperously, quickly, satisfyingly, smoothly, successfully, well, with flying colors*, with no trouble, without a hitch*; SEE CONCEPTS 528,544

swimsuit [n] *bathing suit*
bathing costume, beach costume, beachwear, bikini, jams, maillot, one-piece, swimwear, thong, trunks, two-piece; SEE CONCEPT 451

swindle [n] *cheating, stealing*
blackmail, cheat, con, crooked deal*, deceit, deception, dirty pool*, double-cross*, double-dealing*, extortion, fake, fast one*, fast shuffle*, frame-up, fraud, hoax, hustle, imposition, imposture, knavery, racket*, rip-off*, scam, sell, shady deal*, shakedown, sham, sharp practice*, shell game*, sting, trick, trickery; SEE CONCEPTS 59,139,192

swindle [v] *cheat, steal*
bamboozle, beat*, bilk, clip*, con*, cozen, deceive, defraud, diddle*, do*, dupe, extort, fleece*, flimflam*, fool, frame*, fudge*, gouge*, gull*, hoodwink, overcharge, pluck, pull a fast one*, put one over on*, rip off*, rook, run a game on*, sandbag, scam, sell a bill of goods*, set up, shaft, stiff*, sting*, sucker, take for a ride*, take to the cleaners*, trick, trim*, victimize; SEE CONCEPTS 59,139,192

swindler [n] *person who cheats another*
absconder, charlatan, cheat, cheater, chiseler, clip, con artist, confidence artist, counterfeiter, crook, deceiver, defrauder, dodger, double-dealer, falsifier, forger, four-flusher*, fraud, gouger, grifter, impostor, mechanic, mountebank, operator, rascal, rook, scammer, scoundrel, shark, sharp, sharper, slicker, thief, trickster; SEE CONCEPT 412

swing [n] *moving back and forth*
beat, cadence, cadency, fluctuation, lilt, measure, meter, motion, oscillation, rhythm, stroke, sway, swaying, tempo, undulation, vibration; SEE CONCEPTS 65,748

swing [v] *move back and forth; be suspended*
avert, away, be pendent, curve, dangle, deflect, divert, flap, fluctuate, hang, lurch, oscillate, palpitate, pendulate, pitch, pivot, reel, revolve, rock, roll, rotate, sheer, shunt, suspend, sway, swerve, swivel, turn, turn about, turn on an axis, twirl, undulate, vary, veer, vibrate, volte-face, wag, waggle, wave, wheel, whirl, wiggle, wobble; SEE CONCEPT 145

swipe [n/v] *hit*
bash, blow, clip, clout, clump, cuff, knock, lash out, lick, rap, slap, smack, sock, strike, swat, wallop, wipe; SEE CONCEPT 189

swipe [v2] *steal*
appropriate, cop, filch, heist, hook, lift, make off with, nab, nick, pilfer, pinch, purloin, sneak, snitch; SEE CONCEPT 139

swirl [v] *spin around*
agitate, boil, churn, coil, crimp, crisp, curl, eddy,

purl, roil, roll, snake, surge, swoosh*, twirl, whirl, whirlpool, whorl, wriggle; SEE CONCEPTS 145,738

swish [*adj*] *fashionable, elegant*
classy, deluxe, exclusive, grand, in, plush, posh, ritzy*, smart, stylish, sumptuous, swank, swell, tony*, trendy, with-it*; SEE CONCEPT 589

switch [*n*] *change; exchange*
about-face, alteration, change of direction, reversal, shift, substitution, swap, transformation; SEE CONCEPT 697

switch [*v*] *change, exchange*
change course, convert, deflect, deviate, divert, interchange, rearrange, replace, shift, shunt, sidetrack, substitute, swap, trade, turn, turnabout, turn aside, veer; SEE CONCEPTS 104,232,697

swivel [*v*] *spin around axis*
hinge, pirouette, pivot, revolve, rotate, swing around, turn, whirl; SEE CONCEPT 145

swollen [*adj*] *enlarged*
bloated, bulgy, distended, distent, inflamed, inflated, puffed, puffy, tumescent, tumid; SEE CONCEPT 485

swoon [*v*] *faint*
become unconscious, be overcome, black out, collapse, drop, feel giddy, feel lightheaded, go out like a light*, keel over, lose consciousness, pass out, weaken; SEE CONCEPTS 303,308

swoop [*v*] *descend quickly*
dive, fall, plummet, plunge, pounce, rush, slide, stoop, sweep; SEE CONCEPTS 150,181

sycophant [*n*] *person who caters to another*
adulator, backscratcher*, backslapper*, bootlicker*, brownnoser*, doormat*, fan, fawner, flatterer, flunky*, groupie*, groveler, handshaker*, hanger-on*, lackey, minion, parasite, politician, puppet, slave; SEE CONCEPT 423

syllabus [*n*] *summary*
apercu, capitulation, conspectus, curriculum, outline, program, review, rundown, schedule, sketch, synopsis; SEE CONCEPT 283

symbol [*n*] *letter, character, sign of written communication*
attribute, badge, denotation, design, device, emblem, figure, image, indication, logo, mark, motif, note, numeral, pattern, regalia, representation, stamp, token, type; SEE CONCEPT 284

symbolic [*adj*] *representative*
allegorical, characteristic, denotative, emblematic, figurative, indicative, indicatory, significant, suggestive, symptomatic, token, typical; SEE CONCEPT 267

symbolize [*v*] *represent; stand for*
betoken, body forth, connote, denote, emblematize, embody, epitomize, exemplify, express, illustrate, indicate, mean, mirror, personify, show, signify, suggest, symbol, typify; SEE CONCEPTS 74,138,682

symmetrical [*adj*] *well-proportioned*
balanced, commensurable, commensurate, equal, in proportion, proportional, regular, shapely, well-formed; SEE CONCEPTS 480,485,579

symmetry [*n*] *proportion*
agreement, arrangement, balance, centrality, conformity, correspondence, equality, equilibrium, equipoise, equivalence, evenness, finish, form, harmony, order, proportionality, regularity, rhythm, shapeliness, similarity; SEE CONCEPTS 716,717

sympathetic [*adj*] *concerned, feeling*
affectionate, all heart*, appreciating, benign, benignant, caring, commiserating, compassionate, comprehending, condoling, considerate, having heart in right place*, interested, kind, kindhearted, kindly, loving, pitying, responsive, sensitive, soft, softhearted, supportive, sympathizing, tender, thoughtful, understanding, vicarious, warm, warmhearted; SEE CONCEPT 542

sympathetic [*adj2*] *agreeable, friendly*
amenable, appreciative, approving, companionable, compatible, congenial, congruous, consistent, consonant, cool, down, encouraging, favorably disposed, having a heart*, in sympathy with, like-minded, on same wavelength*, open, open-minded, pro*, receptive, responsive, simpatico, tuned in*, vicarious, well-disposed, well-intentioned; SEE CONCEPTS 401,542,563

sympathize [*v*] *feel for, be compassionate*
ache, agree, appreciate, be in accord, be in sympathy, be kind to, be there for*, be understanding, bleed for*, comfort, commiserate, compassionate, comprehend, condole, empathize, feel heart go out to*, go along with, grieve with, have compassion, identify with, love, offer consolation, pick up on, pity, relate to*, share another's sorrow, show kindliness, show mercy, show tenderness, side with*, tune in*, understand; SEE CONCEPTS 34,110

sympathy [*n1*] *shared feeling*
accord, affinity, agreement, alliance, attraction, benignancy, close relation, commiseration, compassion, concord, congeniality, connection, correspondence, empathy, feelings, fellow feeling, harmony, heart, kindliness, kindness, mutual attraction, mutual fondness, rapport, responsiveness, sensitivity, tenderness, understanding, union, unity, warmheartedness, warmth; SEE CONCEPTS 388,410,664

sympathy [*n2*] *pity*
aid, cheer, comfort, commiseration, compassion, condolence, consolation, empathy, encouragement, reassurance, rue, ruth, solace, tenderness, thoughtfulness, understanding; SEE CONCEPTS 410,633

symposium [*n*] *conference*
colloquium, convention, discussion, discussion group, forum, gabfest*, huddle, meeting, panel discussion, parley, powwow, rap session, round table, seminar, talk; SEE CONCEPTS 56,324,386

symptom [*n*] *sign of illness or problem*
evidence, expression, index, indication, indicia, manifestation, mark, note, significant, syndrome, token, warning; SEE CONCEPTS 306,316

symptomatic [*adj*] *indicative*
associated, characteristic, demonstrative, denotative, denotive, designative, emblematic, evidential, indicating, pointing to, significant, suggestive, symbolic; SEE CONCEPT 267

synagogue [*n*] *church*
abbey, cathedral, chapel, house of God, house of prayer, house of worship, mosque, parish, shrine, shul, tabernacle, temple; SEE CONCEPTS 368,449

synchronize [*v*] *coordinate*
adjust, agree, atune, attune, harmonize, integrate, keep time with, match, mesh, organize, pool proportion, pull together, put in sync*, set; SEE CONCEPTS 36,84,158

sw
sy

syndicate [*n*] *group of business entities*
association, board, bunch, cabinet, cartel, chain, chamber, combine, committee, company, conglomerate, council, crew, gang, group, megacorp*, mob, multinational*, organization, outfit, partnership, pool, ring, trust, union; SEE CONCEPTS 323,325

syndrome [*n*] *disease, condition*
affection, ailment, complaint, complex, diagnostics, disorder, infirmity, malady, problem, prognostics, sickness, sign, symptoms; SEE CONCEPTS 306,316,674

synergy [*n*] *collaboration, cooperation*
alliance, coaction, combined effort, harmony, symbiosis, synergism, team effort, teaming, teamwork, union, unity, working together; SEE CONCEPTS 110,112,388,677

synonymous [*adj*] *equivalent*
alike, apposite, coincident, compatible, convertible, correspondent, corresponding, equal, identical, identified, interchangeable, like, one and the same, same, similar, synonymic, tantamount; SEE CONCEPTS 487,573

synopsis [*n*] *digest, summary*
abridgment, abstract, aperçu, breviary, brief, capsule, compendium, condensation, conspectus, epitome, outline, précis, résumé, review, rundown, run-through, sketch; SEE CONCEPT 283

synthesis [*n*] *combining; combination*
amalgam, amalgamation, blend, building a whole, coalescence, composite, compound, constructing, construction, entirety, forming, fusion, integrating, integration, making one, organism, organization, structure, unification, union, unit, welding, whole; SEE CONCEPTS 113,837

synthesize [*v*] *combine; make whole*
amalgamate, arrange, blend, harmonize, incorporate, integrate, manufacture, orchestrate, symphonize, unify; SEE CONCEPTS 113;205

synthetic [*adj*] *artificial*
constructed, counterfeit, ersatz*, fabricated, factitious, fake, false, hokey*, made, makeshift, manufactured, mock, phony, plastic, unnatural; SEE CONCEPTS 485,582

system [*n1*] *order, whole*
arrangement, classification, combination, complex, conformity, coordination, entity, fixed order, frame of reference, ideology, integral, integrate, logical order, orderliness, organization, philosophy, red tape*, regularity, rule, scheme, setup, structure, sum, theory, totality; SEE CONCEPTS 770,837

system [*n2*] *method, plan*
arrangement, artifice, course of action, custom, definite plan, fashion, logical process, manner, methodicalness, methodology, mode, modus, modus operandi, operation, orderliness, orderly process, pattern, policy, practice, procedure, proceeding, process, regularity, routine, scheme, strategy, structure, systematic process, systematization, tactics, technique, theory, usage, way, wise; SEE CONCEPT 6

systematic [*adj*] *orderly*
analytical, arranged, businesslike, complete, efficient, logical, methodic, methodical, ordered, organized, out-and-out*, precise, regular, standardized, systematized, thoroughgoing, well-ordered; SEE CONCEPTS 557,585

systematize [*v*] *put in order*
arrange, array, contrive, design, devise, dispose, establish, frame, get act together, institute, make uniform, marshal, methodize, order, organize, plan, project, pull together, rationalize, regulate, schematize, shape up, standardize, straighten up, systemize, tighten up; SEE CONCEPTS 84,94

T

tab [*n1*] *ticket, label*
bookmark, clip, flag, flap, holder, logo, loop, marker, slip, sticker, stop, strip, tag; SEE CONCEPTS 270,475

tab [*n2*] *bill for service*
account, charge, check, cost, invoice, price, price tag, rate, reckoning, score, statement, tariff; SEE CONCEPT 329

table [*n1*] *furniture upon which to work, eat*
bar, bench, board, buffet, bureau, console, counter, desk, dining table, dinner table, dresser, lectern, pulpit, sideboard, sink, slab, stand, wagon; SEE CONCEPT 443

table [*n2*] *meal*
bill of fare, board, cuisine, diet, fare, food, meat and drink, menu, spread, victuals; SEE CONCEPT 459

table [*n3*] *flatland*
flat, mesa, plain, plateau, tableland, upland; SEE CONCEPT 509

table [*n4*] *diagram with columns of information*
agenda, appendix, canon, catalogue, chart, compendium, digest, graph, illustration, index, inventory, list, plan, record, register, roll, schedule, statistics, summary, synopsis, table of contents, tabulation; SEE CONCEPTS 283,625

table [*v*] *postpone a proposition*
cool*, defer, delay, enter, hang*, hold off, hold up, move, pigeonhole*, propose, put aside, put forward, put off, put on back burner*, put on hold*, put on ice*, put on the shelf*, shelve, submit, suggest; SEE CONCEPTS 121,324

tableau [*n*] *scene, often painted*
illustration, picture, representation, spectacle, view; SEE CONCEPTS 625,716

tablet [*n1*] *sheaf of papers that are connected*
book, folder, memo pad, notebook, pad, quire, ream, scratch, scratch pad, sheets; SEE CONCEPT 475

tablet [*n2*] *encapsulated medicine*
cake, capsule, dose, lozenge, medicine, pellet, pill, square, troche; SEE CONCEPT 307

tableware [*n*] *flatware*
dishes, forks, glasses, glassware, knives, silverware, spoons, utensils; SEE CONCEPTS 433,499

tabloid [*n*] *newspaper*
paper, rag*, scandal sheet*, sheet; SEE CONCEPTS 279,280

taboo [*adj*] *not allowed, permitted*
anathema, banned, beyond the pale*, disapproved, forbidden, frowned on*, illegal, off limits*, outlawed, out of bounds*, prohibited, proscribed, reserved, restricted, ruled out, unacceptable, unmentionable, unthinkable; SEE CONCEPT 548

taboo [*n*] *something not allowed, permitted*
anathema, ban, disapproval, don't*, forbiddance,

inhibition, interdict, law, limitation, no-no*, prohibition, proscription, regulation, religious convention, reservation, restraint, restriction, sanction, social convention, stricture, superstition, thou-shalt-not*; SEE CONCEPTS 532,688

tabulate [v] *figure, classify*
alphabetize, arrange, catalogue, categorize, chart, codify, digest, enumerate, formulate, grade, index, list, methodize, order, range, register, systematize, tabularize; SEE CONCEPTS 84,764

tacit [adj] *taken for granted; not said aloud*
alluded to, allusive, assumed, hinted at, implicit, implied, inarticulate, indirect, inferred, intimated, silent, suggested, undeclared, understood, unexpressed, unsaid, unspoken, unstated, unvoiced, wordless; SEE CONCEPTS 529,548

taciturn [adj] *uncommunicative*
aloof, antisocial, brooding, clammed up*, close, close-mouthed*, cold, curt, distant, dour, dried-up*, dumb, laconic, mum, mute, quiet, reserved, reticent, sententious, silent, sparing, speechless, tight-lipped*, unexpressive, unforthcoming, withdrawn; SEE CONCEPTS 267,401

tack [n] *course of movement*
aim, alteration, approach, bearing, bend, deflection, deviation, digression, direction, double, echelon, heading, line, method, oblique course, path, plan, point of sail, procedure, set, shift, siding, sidling, sweep, swerve, switch, tactic, tangent, turn, variation, way, yaw, zigzag; SEE CONCEPTS 692,738

tack [n2] *short pin for attaching*
brad, nail, point, pushpin, staple, thumbtack; SEE CONCEPT 475

tack [v] *attach*
add, affix, annex, append, baste, fasten, fix, hem, mount, nail, paste, pin, sew, staple, stitch, tag, tie; SEE CONCEPTS 85,160,218

tackle [n] *equipment for activity*
accoutrement, apparatus, appliance, gear, goods, habiliments, hook, impedimenta, implements, line, machinery, materiel, outfit, paraphernalia, rig, rigging, tools, trappings; SEE CONCEPT 496

tackle [v1] *make an effort*
accept, apply oneself, attack, attempt, bang away at*, begin, come to grips with*, deal with, devote oneself to, embark upon, engage in, essay, give a try*, give a whirl*, go for it*, launch, make a run at*, pitch into, set about, square off*, start the ball rolling*, take a shot at*, take in hand*, take on, take up, try, try on for size*, turn one's hand to*, turn to, undertake, work on; SEE CONCEPTS 87,100

tackle [v2] *jump on and grab*
attack, block, bring down, bring to the ground*, catch, challenge, clutch, confront, down, grapple, grasp, halt, intercept, nail, put the freeze on*, sack, seize, smear, stop, take, take hold of, throw, throw down, upset; SEE CONCEPTS 90,164,191

tacky [adj] *cheap, tasteless*
broken-down, crude, dilapidated, dingy, dowdy, down-at-heel*, faded, frumpy*, gaudy, inelegant, mangy*, messy, nasty*, outmoded, out-of-date, poky*, ratty, run-down, seedy, shabby, shoddy, sleazy*, sloppy*, slovenly, stodgy, threadbare, unbecoming, unkempt, unstylish, unsuitable, untidy, vulgar; SEE CONCEPTS 485,589

tact [n] *finesse, thoughtfulness*
acumen, acuteness, address, adroitness, amenity, aptness, care, common sense, consideration, control, courtesy, delicacy, delicatesse, diplomacy, discernment, discretion, discrimination, gallantry, good taste, head, horse sense*, intelligence, judgment, penetration, perception, perspicacity, poise, policy, politicness, presence, prudence, refinement, repose, savoir-faire, sensitivity, skill, smoothness, suavity, subtlety, tactfulness, understanding, urbanity; SEE CONCEPT 633

tactful [adj] *thoughtful, careful*
adroit, aware, cautious, civil, considerate, courteous, deft, delicate, diplomatic, discreet, gentle, judicious, observant, perceptive, poised, polished, polite, politic, prudent, sensitive, skilled, skillful, suave, subtle, sympathetic, tactical, understanding, urbane, wise; SEE CONCEPT 401

tactical [adj] *strategic*
calculated, clever, cunning, deliberate, diplomatic, planned, politic, prudent, skillful, smart, well-planned; SEE CONCEPT 544

tactics [n] *strategy*
approach, campaign, channels, course, defense, device, disposition, generalship, line, maneuver, maneuvering, means, method, move, plan, plan of attack, ploy, policy, procedure, red tape*, scheme, stratagem, system, tack, technique, trick, way; SEE CONCEPT 660

tactile [adj] *touchable*
material, palpable, physical, solid, tactual, tangible; SEE CONCEPTS 529,582

tactless [adj] *unthinking, careless*
awkward, blundering, boorish, brash, bungling, clumsy, crude, discourteous, gauche, gruff, harsh, hasty, impolite, impolitic, imprudent, inconsiderate, indelicate, indiscreet, inept, injudicious, insensitive, maladroit, misunderstanding, rash, rough, rude, sharp, stupid, thoughtless, uncivil, unconsiderate, undiplomatic, unfeeling, unkind, unperceptive, unpolished, unsubtle, unsympathetic, untactful, vulgar; SEE CONCEPT 401

tag [n] *label, ticket*
badge, button, card, check, chip, docket, emblem, flap, ID*, identification, inscription, insignia, logo, mark, marker, motto, note, pin, slip, stamp, sticker, stub, tab, tally, trademark, voucher; SEE CONCEPTS 270,284,475

tag [v1] *label; attach label*
add, adjoin, affix, annex, append, call, check, christen, designate, docket, dub, earmark, fasten, hold, identify, mark, name, nickname, style, tack, tally, tap, term, ticket, title, touch; SEE CONCEPTS 62,85,160

tag [v2] *follow*
accompany, attend, bedog, chase, dog, heel, hunt, pursue, shadow, tail, trace, track, track down, trail; SEE CONCEPT 207

tail [n] *end piece, part*
appendage, behind, butt*, buttocks, caudal appendage, conclusion, empennage, end, extremity, fag end*, hind end, hindmost part, hind part, last part, posterior, rear, rear end, reverse, rudder, rump*, stub, tag, tag end, tailpiece, train, tush*, wagger*; SEE CONCEPTS 392,825,827

tail [v] *follow*
bedog, dog, eye*, hound, keep an eye on, pursue, shadow, stalk, tag, track, trail; SEE CONCEPT 207

tailor [n] *person who sews clothing*
clothier, costumier, couturier, dressmaker, gar-

sy
ta

ment maker, needle worker*, outfitter, suit maker; SEE CONCEPT 348

tailor [*v*] *make to fit; adjust*
accommodate, adapt, alter, conform, convert, custom-make, cut, cut to fit, dovetail*, fashion, fit, make to order, modify, mold, quadrate, reconcile, shape, shape up, square, style, suit, tailor-make*; SEE CONCEPTS 126,202,218

tailor-made [*adj*] *custom-made*
comfortable, custom-built, custom-fit, fitted, made-to-measure, made to order, perfect, snug, suitable, suited, tailored; SEE CONCEPT 558

taint [*n*] *contamination, corruption*
black mark, blemish, blot, contagion, defect, disgrace, dishonor, fault, flaw, infection, pollution, shame, smear, spot, stain, stigma; SEE CONCEPTS 230,388

taint [*v*] *dirty, contaminate; ruin*
adulterate, besmirch, blacken, blemish, blight, blot, blur, brand, break down, cast a slur, cloud, cook, corrupt, crud up*, crumble, cut, damage, debase, decay, decompose, defile, deprave, discolor, discredit, disgrace, dishonor, disintegrate, doctor, foul, give a bad name*, harm, hurt, infect, muddy, poison, pollute, putrefy, rot, shame, smear, soil, spike, spoil, stain, stigmatize, sully, tar, tarnish, trash*, turn, water, water down; SEE CONCEPTS 246,254,384

take [*n*] *profit*
booty*, catch, catching, cut, gate, haul*, holding, part, proceeds, receipts, return, returns, revenue, share, takings; yield; SEE CONCEPT 344

take [*v1*] *get; help oneself to*
abduct, accept, acquire, arrest, attain, capture, carry off, carve out, catch, clasp, clutch, collar*, collect, earn, ensnare, entrap, gain possession, gather up, get hold of, grab, grasp, grip, handle, haul in, have, hold, lay hold of, obtain, overtake, pick up, prehend, pull in, reach, reap, receive, secure, seize, snag, snatch, strike, take hold of, take in, win; SEE CONCEPTS 120,142

take [*v2*] *steal*
abduct, abstract, accroach, annex, appropriate, arrogate, borrow, carry off, commandeer, confiscate, expropriate, filch*, haul in, liberate, lift*, misappropriate, nab*, nail*, nip*, pick up, pinch*, pluck, pocket*, preempt, pull in, purloin, rip off*, run off with*, salvage, seize, sequester, snag, snare, snatch*, snitch*, swipe*, take in; SEE CONCEPT 139

take [*v3*] *buy; reserve*
book, borrow, charter, choose, cull, decide on, derive draw, elect, engage, gain, get, hire, lease, mark, obtain, optate, opt for, pay for, pick, prefer, procure, purchase, rent, select, single out; SEE CONCEPTS 41,327

take [*v4*] *endure*
abide, accept, accommodate, bear, bear with, brave, brook, contain, give access, go, go through, grin and bear it*, hack*, hang in*, hang on*, hang tough*, hold, let in, live with, put up with, receive, ride out*, stand, stand for, stick it out*, stomach, submit to, suffer, swallow, take it, take it lying down*, take it on the chin*, tolerate, undergo, weather, welcome, withstand; SEE CONCEPT 23

take [*v5*] *consume*
devour, down, drink, eat, feed, feed on, imbibe,

ingest, inhale, meal, partake of, swallow; SEE CONCEPT 169

take [*v6*] *accept, adopt; use*
accommodate, admit, appropriate, assume, be aware of, behave, bring, deal with, delight in, do, effect, enjoy, enter upon, execute, exercise, exert, experience, function, give access, have, include, let in, like, luxuriate in, make, observe, operate, perform, play, practice, put in practice, react, receive, relish, sense, serve, take in, treat, undertake, utilize, welcome, work; SEE CONCEPTS 100,124,225

take [*v7*] *understand*
accept, apprehend, assume, be aware of, believe, catch, compass, comprehend, consider, deem, expect, experience, feel, follow, gather, grasp, hold, imagine, interpret as, know, look upon, observe, perceive, presume, receive, reckon*, regard, see, see as, sense, suppose, suspect, take in, think, think of as; SEE CONCEPT 15

take [*v8*] *win; be successful*
beat, be efficacious, do the trick, have effect, operate, prevail, succeed, triumph, work; SEE CONCEPT 706

take [*v9*] *carry, transport; accompany*
attend, back, bear, bring, buck, cart, conduct, convey, convoy, drive, escort, ferry, fetch, go with, guide, gun, haul, heel, jag, journey, lead, lug, move, pack, piggyback*, pilot, ride, schlepp*, shoulder, steer, tote, tour, trek, truck, usher; SEE CONCEPTS 114,187,217

take [*v10*] *captivate, enchant*
allure, attract, become popular, bewitch, charm, delight, draw, entertain, fascinate, magnetize, overwhelm, please, wile, win favor; SEE CONCEPT 11

take [*v11*] *require*
ask, call for, crave, demand, necessitate, need; SEE CONCEPT 646

take [*v12*] *subtract*
deduct, discount, draw back, eliminate, knock off, remove, subtract, take away, take off, take out; SEE CONCEPTS 211,236,247

take [*v13*] *cheat, deceive*
bamboozle*, beat*, bilk, con, cozen, defraud, do*, dupe, fiddle, flimflam*, gull, hoodwink, pull a fast one*, swindle, take for a ride*, trick; SEE CONCEPTS 59,192

take [*v14*] *contract, catch*
be seized, come down with*, derive, draw, get, sicken with, take sick with; SEE CONCEPT 308

take a crack at [*v*] *try*
attempt, do one's best*, drive for, give a go*, give a whirl*, go after, go all out*, go for, have a crack*, have a go*, have a rip*, have a shot*, have a stab*, have a whack*, make an attempt, make an effort, make a pass at*, make a stab*, risk, shoot for*, tackle, undertake, vie for; SEE CONCEPT 87

take after [*v*] *emulate*
act like, be like, copy, ditto*, do like*, follow, follow in the footsteps of*, follow suit*, follow the example of*, imitate, inherit, look like, make like*, mimic, mirror, pattern after*, rival; SEE CONCEPTS 87,171

take back [*v*] *retract*
abjure, back down, backpedal, call off, cancel, change one's mind, eat one's words*, forget it, go back on, have change of heart*, recall, recant,

reclaim, renege, repeal, repossess, repudiate, rescind, revoke, withdraw; SEE CONCEPTS 25,49,119,697

take down [*v1*] *write down*
inscribe, jot down, make a note of, minute, note, note down, put on record, record, set down, transcribe; SEE CONCEPT 125

take down [*v2*] *humble*
deflate, humiliate, let down, lower, mortify, pull down, put down, take apart; SEE CONCEPTS 7,19,52

take in [*v1*] *deceive, fool*
beguile, betray, bilk, bluff, cheat, con, defraud, delude, do*, double-cross*, dupe, flimflam*, four-flush*, gull, hoodwink, lie, mislead, pull wool over eyes*, swindle, trick; SEE CONCEPT 59

take in [*v2*] *understand*
absorb, assimilate, comprehend, digest, get, grasp, perceive, receive, savvy, see, soak up, take; SEE CONCEPT 15

take it [*v*] *accept, endure*
acknowledge, agree, bear with, bite the bullet, capitulate, don't make waves*, don't rock the boat*, face the music*, go along with, grin and bear it*, hang tough, live with, play the game*, put up with, sit still for*, stand for, stick it out, stomach, submit to, suffer, swallow, take, take one's lumps*, take one's medicine*, tolerate; SEE CONCEPT 23

takeoff [*n1*] *leaving*
ascent, climb, departure, hop, jump, launch, liftoff, rise, upward flight; SEE CONCEPTS 148,195,224

takeoff [*n2*] *mockery, satire*
burlesque, caricature, cartoon, comedy, imitation, lampoon, mocking, parody, ridicule, send-up, spoof, travesty; SEE CONCEPTS 111,263,292

take off [*v1*] *leave; leave the ground*
ascend, bear, beat it, become airborne, begone, blast off, blow*, clear out*, decamp, depart, disappear, exit, get off, get out, go, go away, head, hightail*, hit the road*, hit the trail*, lift off, light out*, make*, pull out, quit, scram*, set out*, shove off*, soar, split, take to the air*, vamoose*, withdraw; SEE CONCEPTS 148,195,224

take off [*v2*] *mock, satirize*
ape, burlesque, caricature, imitate, lampoon, mimic, parody, ridicule, send up*, spoof, travesty; SEE CONCEPTS 111,273,292

take on [*v1*] *assume, accept*
acquire, add, address oneself to, adopt, agree to do, annex, append, attempt, become, begin, come to have, commence, develop, embrace, employ, endeavor, engage, enlist, enroll, espouse, handle, have a go at*, hire, launch, put on, retain, set about, tackle, take in hand*, take up, take upon oneself*, try, turn, undertake, venture; SEE CONCEPTS 87,221

take on [*v2*] *compete*
attack, battle, contend, contest, encounter, engage, face, fight, match, meet, oppose, pit, vie; SEE CONCEPT 92

take on [*v3*] *challenge, oppose*
brave, buck*, call out, confront, dare, defy, denounce, dispute, face off, go eyeball to eyeball with*, go one on one with*, go toe to toe with*, go up against, hang in*, insist upon, investigate, invite competition, make a stand, object to, question, stand up to, throw down the gauntlet*; SEE CONCEPT 53

take up [*v*] *begin or start again*
adopt, assume, become involved in, carry on, commence, continue, embrace, engage in, enter, espouse, follow through, get off, go on, initiate, kick off, open, pick up, proceed, recommence, renew, reopen, restart, resume, set to, start, tackle, take on, tee off, undertake; SEE CONCEPTS 221,239

tale [*n1*] *story*
account, anecdote, fable, fairy tale, fiction, folk tale, legend, myth, narration, narrative, novel, relation, report, romance, saga, short story, yarn; SEE CONCEPT 282

tale [*n2*] *made-up story*
canard, chestnut*, clothesline*, cock-and-bull story*, defamation, detraction, exaggeration, fabrication, falsehood, falsity, fib, fiction, lie, misrepresentation, prevarication, rigmarole*, rumor, scandal, slander, spiel*, tall story*, untruism, untruth, yarn*; SEE CONCEPTS 278,282

talent [*n*] *ability*
aptitude, aptness, art, a way with*, bent*, capability, capacity, craft, endowment, expertise, facility, faculty, flair, forte, genius, gift, green thumb*, head*, inventiveness, knack*, knowhow*, nose*, power, savvy*, set, skill, smarts*, the formula*, the goods*, the right stuff*, thing*, turn*, what it takes*; SEE CONCEPT 630

talented [*adj*] *gifted*
able, accomplished, adept, adroit, artistic, brilliant, capable, clever, cut out for, endowed, expert, having a knack*, ingenious, intelligent, masterly, proficient, shining at*, skilled, smart; SEE CONCEPTS 402,527,528

talisman [*n*] *charm*
fetish, good-luck piece, juju, lucky piece, phylactery, rabbit's foot; SEE CONCEPTS 260,284,446

talk [*n1*] *speech, address to group*
allocution, chalk talk*, declamation, descant, discourse, disquisition, dissertation, epilogue, exhortation, expatiation, harangue, homily, lecture, monologue, oration, peroration, prelection, recitation, screed, sermon, spiel*; SEE CONCEPTS 60,285

talk [*n2*] *gossip*
allusion, badinage, banter, blather*, bombast, bunk*, buzz*, cant, chat, chatter, chitchat, conversation, cry, gab, grapevine*, hearsay, hint, hot air*, idle talk, innuendo, insinuation, jaw*, jive*, lip*, noise, nonsense*, palaver, persiflage, prose, racket*, raillery, report, rot*, rubbish*, rumble*, rumor, scuttlebutt*, small talk, tête-à-tête, trash*, yarn*; SEE CONCEPTS 51,278

talk [*n3*] *discussion*
argument, colloquy, conclave, confabulation, conference, consultation, conversation, deliberation, dialogue, earful, encounter, eyeball-to-eyeball*, huddle*, interlocution, interview, meeting, negotiation, palaver, parlance, parley, powwow*, seminar, spiel*, straight talk, symposium, ventilation, visit; SEE CONCEPT 56

talk [*n4*] *communication with language*
argot, chatter, dialect, discourse, jargon, lingo, locution, parlance, patois, slang, speaking, speech, utterance, verbalization, vocalization, words; SEE CONCEPTS 47,65

talk [*v1*] *produce words; inform*
articulate, babble, broach, chant, chat, chatter, comment on, communicate, confess, converse, describe, divulge, drawl, drone, express, flap

one's tongue*, gab, gabble*, give voice to, gossip, influence, intone, notify, palaver, parley, patter, persuade, prate, prattle, pronounce, reveal, rhapsodize, run on*, say, sing*, soliloquize, speak, spill the beans*, spout, squeak*, squeal*, talk one's leg off*, tell, tell all*, use, utter, ventriloquize, verbalize, voice, yak*; SEE CONCEPTS 60,266

talk [*v2*] *discuss with another*
argue, be in contact, canvass, carry on conversation, chew*, collogue, commune, confabulate, confer, confide, consult, contact, deliberate, dialogue, engage in conversation, exchange, go into a huddle*, groupthink*, have a meet*, hold discussion, huddle*, interact, interface, interview, join in conversation, keep in touch*, negotiate, network*, palaver, parley, reach out, reason, relate, thrash out*, touch*, touch base*, vent, visit; SEE CONCEPT 56

talk [*v3*] *address group*
accost, deliver a speech, discourse, give a talk, give speech, harangue, hold forth, induce, influence, lecture, orate, persuade, pitch, prelect, sermonize, speak, spiel*, spout*, stump*, sway*; SEE CONCEPTS 60,285

talkative [*adj*] *excessively communicative*
articulate, big-mouthed*, chattering, chatty*, effusive, eloquent, fluent, full of hot air*, gabby*, garrulous, glib, gossipy, long-winded*, loose-lipped*, loquacious, loudmouthed*, mouthy*, multiloquent, prolix, rattling, slick*, smooth*, talky, verbal, verbose, vocal, voluble, windy*, wordy; SEE CONCEPT 267

tall [*adj1*] *high in stature, length*
alpine, altitudinous, beanstalk*, big, elevated, giant, great, high-reaching, lank, lanky, lofty, rangy, sizable, sky-high, skyscraping, soaring, statuesque, towering; SEE CONCEPTS 779,782

tall [*adj2*] *exaggerated, unreasonable*
absurd, demanding, difficult, embellished, exorbitant, farfetched, hard, implausible, impossible, outlandish, *overblown*, posterous, steep, unbelievable; SEE CONCEPTS 529,565

tally [*n*] *count, record*
account, mark, poll, reckoning, running total, score, summation, tab, total; SEE CONCEPTS 283,787

tally [*v*] *add up; count, record*
catalog, compute, enumerate, inventory, itemize, keep score, mark, mark down, number, numerate, reckon, register, sum, tale, tell, total, write down; SEE CONCEPTS 125,764

tame [*adj1*] *domesticated, compliant*
acclimatized, amenable, biddable, bridled, broken, busted, civilized, cultivated, disciplined, docile, domestic, fearless, gentle, gentle as a lamb*, habituated, harmless, harnessed, housebroken, kindly, manageable, meek, mild, muzzled, obedient, overcome, pliable, pliant, subdued, submissive, tractable, trained, unafraid, unresisting, yoked*; SEE CONCEPT 401

tame [*adj2*] *dull, uninteresting*
bland, bloodless, boiled down*, boring, conventional, diluted, feeble, flat*, halfhearted, humdrum*, insipid, lifeless, limp, mild, monotonous, prosaic, routine, spiritless, tedious, unexciting, uninspiring, vapid, weak, wearisome, whitebread*, without punch*; SEE CONCEPTS 529,542,548

tame [*v*] *domesticate, make compliant*
break, break in, break the spirit*, bridle, bring to heel*, bust, check, conquer, curb, discipline, domesticize, domiciliate, enslave, gentle, housebreak, house-train, humble, mitigate, mute, pacify, repress, restrain, soften, subdue, subjugate, suppress, temper, tone down, train, vanquish, water down*; SEE CONCEPTS 14,250

tamper [*v1*] *interfere, alter*
busybody*, butt in*, change, cook, cut, damage, destroy, diversify, doctor, fiddle with*, fool, horn in*, interfere, interlope, interpose, intrude, irrigate, manipulate, meddle, mess around with*, monkey around*, muck about*, phony up*, plant*, poke nose into*, spike*, tinker, vary, water*; SEE CONCEPT 232

tamper [*v2*] *bribe*
buy, buy off, corrupt, fix, get to, have, influence, lubricate, manipulate, reach, rig, square*; SEE CONCEPT 192

tan [*n/adj*] *light brown*
beige, biscuit, bronze, brown, brownish, buff, cream, drab, ecru, gold, khaki, leather-colored, natural, olive, olive-brown, saddle, sand, suntan, tawny, umber, yellowish; SEE CONCEPTS 618,622

tan [*v*] *flog, whip*
baste, beat, belt, cane, dust someone's britches*, flay, hide, hit, lambaste, lash, leather, paddle, paddlewhack, punish, spank, strap, strike, switch, tan one's hide*, thrash, warm someone's seat*, wax, whack, whale*, whomp*; SEE CONCEPT 189

tang [*n*] *biting taste or odor*
aroma, bite, flavor, guts*, kick*, nip, piquancy, pungency, reek, relish, sapidity, sapor, savor, scent, smack*, smell, spiciness, tanginess, thrill, twang, zest, zip*; SEE CONCEPTS 599,600,614

tangible [*adj*] *real, concrete*
actual, appreciable, corporeal, definite, detectable, discernible, distinct, embodied, evident, factual, gross, incarnated, manifest, material, objective, observable, obvious, palpable, patent, perceivable, perceptible, phenomenal, physical, plain, positive, sensible, solid, stable, substantial, tactile, touchable, verifiable, visible, well-grounded; SEE CONCEPTS 529,582

tangle [*n*] *knot, confusion*
coil, complication, entanglement, jam, jungle, labyrinth, mass, mat, maze, mesh, mess, mix-up, morass, muddle, rummage, skein, snag, snarl, twist, web; SEE CONCEPTS 230,674,720

tangle [*v*] *knot, complicate*
catch, coil, confuse, derange, discompose, disorganize, drag into, embroil, enmesh, ensnare, entangle, entrap, foul up*, hamper, implicate, interlace, interlock, intertwist, interweave, involve, jam, kink, make a party to*, mat, mesh, mess up*, mix up*, muck up*, obstruct, perplex, ravel, snarl, tie up, trap, twist, unbalance, upset; SEE CONCEPTS 112,190

tangy [*adj*] *sharp, spicy*
appetizing, aromatic, biting, bitter, fiery, flavorful, flavorsome, harsh, highly seasoned, hot, peppery, piquant, pungent, salty, seasoned, sweet, tart, tasty, vinegary, zesty, zippy*; SEE CONCEPTS 537,598,613

tantalize [*v*] *provoke, tease*
annoy, badger, baffle, bait, bedevil, beleaguer, charm, entice, fascinate, frustrate, gnaw, harass,

harry, keep hanging*, lead on, make mouth water*, pester, plague, taunt, thwart, titillate, torment, torture, worry; SEE CONCEPTS 7,11,19,22

tantamount [*adj*] *same*
alike, as good as, commensurate, duplicate, equal, equivalent, identical, indistinguishable, like, parallel, same as, selfsame, synonymous, uniform, very; SEE CONCEPTS 487,573

tantrum [*n*] *fit*
anger, animosity, conniption, dander*, flare-up, hemorrhage*, huff*, hysterics, outburst, storm*, temper, temper tantrum, wax; SEE CONCEPTS 306,384

tap [*n*] *faucet*
bibcock, cock, egress, hydrant, nozzle, petcock, spigot, spout, stopcock, valve; SEE CONCEPTS 445,464

tap [*v1*] *hit lightly*
beat, bob, dab, drum, knock, palpate, pat, percuss, rap, strike, tag, thud, thump, tip, touch; SEE CONCEPT 189

tap [*v2*] *pierce to drain*
bleed, bore, broach, draft, drain, draw, draw forth, draw off, draw out, drill, empty, lance, milk, mine, open, penetrate, perforate, pump, riddle, siphon, spear, spike, stab, unplug, unstopper, use, utilize; SEE CONCEPTS 142,220

tape [*n*] *ribbon of material*
band, braid, edging, line, rope, strip; SEE CONCEPT 475

tape [*v1*] *stick together with material*
bandage, bind, bond, fasten, hold together, rope, seal, secure, support, swathe, tie, tie up, truss, wire, wrap; SEE CONCEPTS 85,160

tape [*v2*] *record sounds, sights*
audiotape, make a tape, register, tape-record, video, videotape; SEE CONCEPTS 125,292

taper/taper off [*v*] *decrease to a point*
abate, bate, close, come to a point, die away, die out, diminish, drain, dwindle, fade, lessen, narrow, recede, reduce, rescind, subside, thin, thin out, wane, weaken, wind down; SEE CONCEPTS 137,698,776

tardy [*adj*] *late*
backward, behindhand, belated, dawdling, delayed, delinquent, detained, dilatory, held up, hung up*, in a bind, jammed, laggard, loitering, not arrived, not done, overdue, procrastinating, retarded, slack, slow, sluggish, strapped for time*, too late, unpunctual; SEE CONCEPTS 542,548,799

target [*n1*] *aim, goal*
ambition, bull's-eye*, destination, duty, end, function, ground zero*, intention, mark, object, objective, point, purpose, spot, use; SEE CONCEPT 659

target [*n2*] *person as object of ridicule*
butt*, byword, game, mark*, pigeon*, prey, quarry, scapegoat*, scorn, sitting duck*, sport, victim; SEE CONCEPT 423

tariff [*n*] *tax or fee*
assessment, charge, cost, duty, excise, impost, levy, price, price tag, rate, tab, tax, toll; SEE CONCEPT 329

tarnish [*v*] *dirty, corrupt*
befoul, begrime, blacken, blemish, blot, contaminate, damage, darken, defame, defile, dim, discolor, disgrace, dull, embarrass, grime, harm, hurt, impair, injure, lose luster, lose shine, mar, muddy, pale, pollute, rust, slander, smear,

smudge, soil, spoil, spot, stain, sully, taint, tar, vitiate; SEE CONCEPTS 246,254,469

tarry [*v*] *dawdle, delay*
abide, bide, dally, drag, drag one's feet*, dwell, filibuster, get no place fast*, goof around*, hang around*, hold the phone*, lag, linger, lodge, loiter, lose time, pause, poke, procrastinate, put off, remain, rest, sojourn, stall, stay, stick around, stop, stop over, tail, take one's time*, temporize, tool*, trail, visit, wait, warm a chair*; SEE CONCEPTS 35,151,210

tart [*adj*] *bitter, sour in taste or effect*
acerb, acerbic, acetose, acid, acidulous, acrimonious, astringent, barbed, biting, caustic, cutting, dry, harsh, nasty, piquant, pungent, scathing, sharp, short, snappish, snappy, snippy, tangy, testy, trenchant, vinegary, wounding; SEE CONCEPTS 267,613

tart [*n*] *pastry*
bun, Danish, eclair, fruit tart, pie, popover, roll, turnover; SEE CONCEPT 457

task [*n*] *job or chore, often assigned*
assignment, bother, burden, business, calling, charge, daily grind*, deadweight*, duty, effort, employment, enterprise, errand, exercise, fun and games*, function, gig*, grind*, grindstone*, headache*, job, labor, load, long row to hoe*, millstone*, mission, nuisance, occupation, office, onus, pain, project, province, responsibility, stint, strain, tax, toil, trouble, undertaking, vocation, work; SEE CONCEPTS 362,666

task [*v*] *assign, burden*
charge, encumber, entrust, exhaust, lade, load, oppress, overload, push, saddle, strain, tax, test, weary, weigh, weight; SEE CONCEPTS 14,112,666

taskmaster [*n*] *slave driver*
boss, director, disciplinarian, dominator, employer, foreperson, head honcho*, manager, overseer, owner, person in charge, supervisor, taskperson, tyrant; SEE CONCEPT 347

taste [*n1*] *flavor of some quality*
aftertaste, aroma, bang*, bitter, drive, ginger, jolt, kick*, oomph*, palatableness, piquancy, punch*, relish, salt, sapidity, savor, savor, savoriness, smack, sour, sting*, suggestion, sweet, tang*, wallop, zest, zing*, zip*; SEE CONCEPT 614

taste [*n2*] *tiny sample*
appetizer, bit, bite, canapé, chaw, dash, delicacy, drop, fragment, hint, hors d'oeuvre, morsel, mouthful, nip, sampling, sip, soupçon, spoonful, sprinkling, suggestion, swallow, tidbit, tincture, tinge, titbit, touch, trifle, whiff*, wink*; SEE CONCEPTS 458,835

taste [*n3*] *inclination, preference*
affection, appetence, appetite, attachment, bent*, comprehension, cup of tea*, desire, disposition, druthers*, fancy, fondness, gusto, heart, leaning, liking, palate, partiality, penchant, predilection, predisposition, prepossession, relish, soft spot*, stomach*, tendency, thing*, type, understanding, weakness, zest; SEE CONCEPTS 20,32,529,659

taste [*n4*] *capacity to sense flavor*
appetence, appetite, gout, gustation, palate, stomach, taste buds, tongue; SEE CONCEPTS 590,615

taste [*n5*] *judgment, propriety*
acumen, acuteness, aestheticism, appreciation, correctness, cultivation, culture, decorum, delicacy, discernment, discretion, discrimination,

ta
ta

distinction, elegance, feeling, finesse, good taste, grace, nicety, penetration, perception, polish, politeness, refinement, restraint, style, susceptibility, tact, tactfulness, tastefulness; SEE CONCEPTS *388,411,655,689*

taste [*v1*] *judge, try*
assay, bite, chew, criticize, differentiate, discern, distinguish, eat, enjoy, lick, nibble, partake, perceive, relish, sample, savor, sense, sip, test, touch, try, try the flavor of; SEE CONCEPTS *169,616*

taste [*v2*] *experience*
appreciate, be exposed to, come up against, encounter, feel, have knowledge of, know, meet with, partake of, perceive, run up against, savor, undergo; SEE CONCEPT *678*

tasteful [*adj*] *nice, refined*
aesthetically pleasing, artistic, beautiful, charming, chaste, classical, classy, cultivated, cultured, delectable, delicate, discriminating, elegant, esthetic, exquisite, fastidious, fine, graceful, gratifying, handsome, harmonious, in good taste, pleasing, plush, polished, posh, precise, pure, quiet, restrained, rich, savory, smart, snazzy*, spiffy*, splendiferous, stylish, subdued, swank*, tasty, unaffected, unobtrusive, uptown*; SEE CONCEPTS *529,574,589*

tasteless [*adj1*] *without flavor*
big zero*, blah*, bland, boring, distasteful, dull, flat, flavorless, insipid, mild, nowhere*, pabulum*, plain, plain vanilla*, savorless, stale, tame, thin, unappetizing, uninspired, uninteresting, unpalatable, unpleasurable, unsavory, unseasoned, vanilla*, vapid, watered-down, watery, weak, without spice, zero*; SEE CONCEPT *613*

tasteless [*adj2*] *cheap, vulgar*
artificial, barbaric, barbarous, coarse, crass, crude, flashy, foolish, garish, gaudy, graceless, hideous, impolite, improper, indecorous, indelicate, indiscreet, inelegant, loud, low, low-down, low-down-and-dirty*, makeshift*, off-color*, ornate, ostentatious, outlandish, pretentious, raunchy*, rough, rude, showy, stupid, tacky, tactless, tawdry, trivial, uncouth, unlovely, unpolished, unrefined, unseemly, unsightly, useless, wild; SEE CONCEPTS *401,570,589*

tasty [*adj*] *delicious*
appetizing, delectable, delish*, divine, flavorful, flavorsome, full-flavored, full-flavor, good-tasting, heavenly, luscious, mellow, palatable, piquant, pungent, sapid, savory, scrumptious, spicy, sugar-coated, sweetened, tasteful, toothsome, toothy, yummy, zestful; SEE CONCEPT *613*

tattered [*adj*] *shredded*
badly dressed, badly worn, battered, broken, dilapidated, frayed, frazzled, full of holes*, in rags, in shreds, in tatters*, moth-eaten, poorly made, ripped, rugged, scraggy, seedy, shabby, shaggy, shoddy, threadbare, torn, torn to pieces, unkempt; SEE CONCEPT *485*

tattle [*v*] *gossip; tell rumor*
babble, blab*, chat, chatter, give away, give the show away*, gossip, have a big mouth*, jabber, leak, noise, prate, prattle*, rumor, snitch, spill, spill the beans*, spread rumor*, squeal, talk, talk idly, tell on, tell tale*, yak*; SEE CONCEPTS *54,60*

tattletale/tattler [*n*] *person who gossips, tells rumors*
bigmouth*, blabberer, blabbermouth*, busybody, canary*, fat mouth*, fink*, gossip, informer, rat*, rumormonger, scandalmonger, snitch*, squealer*, stool pigeon*, talebearer, taleteller, telltale*, tipster, troublemaker, whistleblower, windbag*; SEE CONCEPTS *412,423*

taunt [*n*] *provocation; teasing*
backhanded compliment*, barb, brickbat*, censure, comeback, crack, cut, derision, dig, dirty dig*, dump, gibe, insult, jab, jeer, mockery, outrage, parting shot*, put-down*, reproach, ridicule, sarcasm, slam*, slap*, snappy comeback*, swipe*; SEE CONCEPTS *7,19,266*

taunt [*v*] *provoke, reproach; tease*
affront, bother, deride, dig*, disdain, dump on*, flout, insult, jab*, jeer, lout, mock, offend, outrage, put down, quiz, rally, revile, ridicule, scoff at, scorn, scout, slam*, slap*, sneer, swipe at, tantalize, torment, twitter, upbraid; SEE CONCEPTS *7,19,54*

taut [*adj*] *rigid, tight*
close, firm, flexed, snug, stiff, strained, stressed, stretched, tense, tightly drawn, trim, unyielding; SEE CONCEPTS *488,604*

tavern [*n*] *business establishment for serving drink, food*
alehouse, bar, barroom, beer joint*, dive*, drinkery, gin mill*, grog shop*, honky tonk*, hostelry, hotel, inn, joint*, lodge, lounge, night spot, nineteenth hole*, pub, public house, roadhouse, saloon, speakeasy*, suds*, taphouse*, taproom, watering hole*; SEE CONCEPTS *439,448,449*

tawdry [*adj*] *cheap, tasteless*
blatant, brazen, chintzy*, common, crude, dirty, flaring, flashy, flaunting, garish, gaudy, gimcrack, glaring, glittering, glitzy, jazzy, junky*, loud, meretricious, obtrusive, offensive, plastic, poor, raffish, screaming, showy, sleazy*, sporty, tacky*, tinsel, vulgar; SEE CONCEPTS *334,589*

tax [*n1*] *charge levied by government on property, income*
assessment, bite*, brokerage, capitation, contribution, cost, custom, dues, duty, excise, expense, fine, giveaway*, imposition, impost, levy, obligation, pork barrel*, price, rate, salvage, tariff, tithe, toll, towage, tribute; SEE CONCEPT *329*

tax [*n2*] *burden*
albatross*, charge, deadweight*, demand, difficulty, drain, duty, imposition, load, millstone*, onus, pressure, strain, task, weight; SEE CONCEPTS *362,666*

tax [*v1*] *levy charge on property, income*
assess, charge, charge duty, demand, demand toll, enact, exact, exact tribute, extract, impose, lay an impost, rate, require contribution, tithe; SEE CONCEPT *298*

tax [*v2*] *burden*
charge, cumber, drain, encumber, enervate, exhaust, lade, load, make demands on, oppress, overburden, overtax, overuse, overwork, press hard on, pressure, prey on, push, put pressure on, saddle, sap, strain, stress, stretch, task, tire, try, weaken, wear out, weary, weigh, weigh down, weigh heavily on, weight; SEE CONCEPTS *14,208,240*

tax [*v3*] *accuse*
arraign, blame, censure, charge, criminate, impeach, impugn, impute, incriminate, inculpate, indict, reproach, reprove; SEE CONCEPT *44*

taxing [*adj*] *burdensome*
demanding, difficult, disturbing, enervating, exacting, exigent, grievous, heavy, onerous, oppressive, punishing, sapping, stressful, tedious, tiring, tough, troublesome, trying, wearing, wearisome, weighty; SEE CONCEPT 565

teach [*v*] *educate; instill knowledge*
advise, brainwash*, break in*, brief, catechize, coach, communicate, cram, demonstrate, develop, direct, discipline, drill, edify, enlighten, exercise, explain, expound, fit, form, give instruction, give lessons, give the facts, ground, guide, illustrate, imbue, impart, implant, improve mind, inculcate, indoctrinate, inform, initiate, instruct, interpret, lecture, nurture, open eyes*, polish up*, pound into*, prepare, profess, rear, school, sharpen, show, show the ropes*, train, tutor; SEE CONCEPT 285

teacher [*n*] *person who educates*
abecedary, adviser, assistant, coach, disciplinarian, educator, faculty member, guide, instructor, lecturer, mentor, pedagogue, preceptor, professor, pundit, scholar, schoolteacher, supervisor, teach*, trainer, tutor; SEE CONCEPT 350

teaching [*n*] *education*
apprenticeship, book learning*, coaching, cultivation, culture, discipline, drilling, enlightenment, guidance, instruction, learning, reading, schooling, training, tutelage, tutoring; SEE CONCEPTS 285,287,409

team [*n*] *group, crew*
aggregation, band, body, bunch, club, company, contingent, duo, faction, foursome, gang, lineup, organization, outfit, pair, partners, party, rig, sect, set, side, span, squad, stable, string, tandem, trio, troop, troupe, unit, workers, yoke; SEE CONCEPTS 365,397,417

teamwork [*n*] *collaboration, cooperation*
alliance, assistance, coalition, combined effort, confederacy, confederation, doing business with, esprit de corps, federation, harmony, help, joint effort, partisanship, partnership, pulling together, symbiosis, synergism, synergy, team effort, teaming, union, unity, working together; SEE CONCEPTS 110,112,388,677

tear [*n1*] *rip, cut*
breach, break, crack, damage, fissure, gash, hole, imperfection, laceration, mutilation, rent, run, rupture, scratch, split, tatter; SEE CONCEPT 513

tear/tears [*n2*] *droplets from eyes, often caused by emotion*
blubbering, crying, discharge, distress, drops, grieving, lachryma, lamentation, lamenting, moisture, mourning, pain, regret, sadness, sob, sob act*, sobbing, sorrow, teardrop, wailing, water, waterworks*, weep, weeping, weeps*, whimpering, woe; SEE CONCEPTS 185,467

tear [*n3*] *wild action*
bender, binge, bust, carousal, carouse, drunk, spree, wassail; SEE CONCEPTS 383,384

tear [*v1*] *cut, rip an object*
break, claw, cleave, crack, damage, divide, evulse, extract, fray, frazzle, gash, grab, impair, incise, injure, lacerate, mangle, mutilate, pluck, pull, pull apart, rend, ribbon, rift, rive, run, rupture, scratch, seize, separate, sever, shred, slash, slit, snatch, split, sunder, wrench, wrest, yank; SEE CONCEPTS 206,214

tear [*v2*] *move very fast*
boil, bolt, career, charge, chase, course, dart,
dash, fling, fly, gallop, hurry, lash, race, run, rush, shoot, speed, spring, zoom; SEE CONCEPTS 150,152

tear down [*v*] *demolish, raze*
annihilate, bulldoze, crush, decimate, devastate, devour, dilapidate, disassemble, dismantle, flatten, knock down, level, obliterate, pulverize, ruin, smash, take apart, total*, trash*, wipe off the map*, wreck; SEE CONCEPTS 169,252

tearful [*adj*] *crying, very upset*
bawling*, blubbering*, blubbery*, distressed, dolorous, in tears, lachrymose, lamentable, lamenting, moist, mournful, pathetic, pitiable, pitiful, poignant, sad, sniveling*, sobbing, sorrowful, teary, watery, weeping, weepy, wet, whimpering, woeful; SEE CONCEPTS 401,403

tease [*v*] *aggravate, provoke*
annoy, badger, bait, banter, be at, bedevil, beleaguer, bother, chaff, devil, disturb, dog*, gibe, give a hard time*, gnaw, goad, harass, harry, hector, importune, jive*, josh, lead on*, mock, needle*, nudge, pester, pick on*, plague, put down*, rag*, rally, razz*, rib*, ride, ridicule, roast*, send up* slam, snap, sound, spoof, swipe at, tantalize, taunt, torment, vex, worry; SEE CONCEPTS 7,11,19,22

technical [*adj*] *concerning details, mechanics*
abstruse, high-tech*, industrial, mechanical, methodological, occupational, professional, restricted, scholarly, scientific, special, specialized, technological, vocational; SEE CONCEPT 536

technicality [*n*] *loophole; minor detail*
escape clause, formality, minor point, nothing to speak of, nothing to write home about; SEE CONCEPT 633

technique [*n*] *method*
address, approach, art, artistry, capability, capacity, course, craft, delivery, execution, facility, fashion, knack*, know-how*, manner, means, mode, modus, modus operandi, performance, procedure, proficiency, routine, skill, style, system, tactics, technic, touch, usage, way, wise; SEE CONCEPTS 6,630

technology [*n*] *electronics, science*
applied science, automation, computers, electronic components, high tech*, hi tech*, industrial science, machinery, mechanics, mechanization, robotics, scientific know-how, scientific knowledge, technical knowledge, telecommunications; SEE CONCEPTS 463,499

tedious [*adj*] *dull, monotonous*
annoying, arid, banal, boring, bromidic, drab, dragging, draggy*, dreary, drudging, dry, dull as dishwater*, dusty*, endless, enervating, exhausting, fatiguing, ho-hum*, humdrum, insipid, irksome, laborious, lifeless, long-drawn-out*, mortal, pabulum*, poky*, prosaic, prosy, slow, snooze*, soporific, tiresome, tiring, unexciting, uninteresting, vapid, wearful, wearisome; SEE CONCEPTS 529,548

tedium [*n*] *dullness, monotony*
banality, boredom, deadness*, doldrums, drabness, dreariness, ennui, irksomeness, lack of interest, lifelessness, routine, sameness, tediousness, tiresomeness, wearisomeness, yawn*; SEE CONCEPTS 388,410,668

teem [*v*] *be abundant, full*
abound, bear, be crawling with, be full of, be numerous, be plentiful, be prolific, brim, bristle,

ta
te

burst, burst at seams*, bustle, crawl, crowd, flow, grow, jam, overflow, overrun, pack, pour, pour out, produce, prosper, pullulate, rain, roll in, shower, superabound, swarm, swell, swim in, wallow in; SEE CONCEPTS *146,179,740*

teeming [*adj*] *abundant, full*
alive, brimful, brimming, bristling, bursting, chock-full, crammed, crawling, filled, fruitful, multitudinous, numerous, overflowing, packed, plentiful, populous, pregnant, replete, rife, swarming, thick, thronged; SEE CONCEPTS *481,483,774*

teenager [*n*] *adolescent*
juvenile, minor, stripling, sweet sixteen*, teen, teenybopper*, youngster, youth; SEE CONCEPT *424*

teeny/teensy [*adj*] *very small*
diminutive, Lilliputian, microscopic, miniature, minuscule, minute, teensy-weensy*, teeny-weeny*, tiny, wee, weeny*; SEE CONCEPTS *773,789*

teeter [*v*] *wobble back and forth*
balance, dangle, falter, flutter, lurch, pivot, quiver, reel, rock, seesaw, stagger, stammer, stumble, sway, teeter-totter*, topple, totter, tremble, tremble precariously, waver, weave, wiggle; SEE CONCEPT *145*

telecast [*n*] *broadcast*
air time, newscast, program, show, simulcast, transmission; SEE CONCEPTS *274,293*

telegram [*n*] *message sent by coded radio signals*
buzzer, cable, cablegram, call, coded message, flash, radiogram, report, signal, summons, telegraph, telegraphic message, teletype, telex, wire; SEE CONCEPTS *269,271*

telepathy [*n*] *ability to know another's thoughts*
clairvoyance, ESP*, extrasensory perception, insight, mind-reading, parapsychology, premonition, presentiment, second sight*, sixth sense*, spiritualism, telepathic transmission, telesthesia, thought transference; SEE CONCEPTS *410,630*

telephone [*v*] *communicate through telephone system*
buzz*, call, call up, contact, dial, get back to*, get on the horn*, get on the line*, give a call, give a jingle*, give a ring*, make a call, phone, pick up*, put a call through*, ring, ring up, touch base with*; SEE CONCEPTS *225,266,269*

televise [*v*] *broadcast*
air, announce, beam, be on the air, communicate, go on the air, go on the airwaves, put on television, put on the air, show, simulcast, transmit; SEE CONCEPTS *60,292*

television [*n*] *visual and audio entertainment transmitted via radio waves*
audio, baby-sitter*, boob tube*, box*, eye*, idiot box*, receiver, small screen, station, telly*, tube, TV, TV set, vid*, video; SEE CONCEPTS *277,279,293,463*

tell [*v1*] *communicate*
acquaint, advise, announce, apprise, authorize, bid, break the news*, call upon, clue in*, command, confess, declare, direct, disclose, divulge, enjoin, explain, express, fill in*, give facts, give out, impart, inform, instruct, keep posted*, lay open*, leak, leave word, let in on*, let know, let slip*, level, make known, mention, notify, open up, order, proclaim, put before, recite, reel off*,

report, represent, require, reveal, say, speak, spit it out*, state, summon, utter; SEE CONCEPT *266*

tell [*v2*] *narrate, describe*
chronicle, depict, express, give an account of, portray, recount, rehearse, relate, report, set forth, speak, state; SEE CONCEPT *55*

tell [*v3*] *understand, discern*
ascertain, be sure, clinch, comprehend, deduce, determine, differentiate, discover, discriminate, distinguish, divine, find out, identify, know, know for certain, learn, make out, perceive, recognize, see; SEE CONCEPT *15*

tell [*v4*] *carry weight*
count, have effect, have force, make presence felt, make presence known, militate, register, take effect, take its toll*, weigh; SEE CONCEPT *676*

tell [*v5*] *calculate*
compute, count, count one by one, enumerate, number, numerate, reckon, tale, tally; SEE CONCEPT *764*

telling [*adj*] *effective, significant*
cogent, considerable, conspicuous, convincing, crucial, decisive, devastating, effectual, forceful, forcible, important, impressive, influential, marked, operative, potent, powerful, satisfactory, satisfying, solid, sound, striking, trenchant, valid, weighty; SEE CONCEPTS *537,567*

tell off [*v*] *reprimand; criticize harshly*
berate, censure, chide, give piece of one's mind*, give tongue-lashing*, lecture, rail, rake over the coals*, rebuke, reproach, reprove, revile, scold, take to task*, tick off*, upbraid, vituperate; SEE CONCEPTS *44,52*

telltale [*adj*] *revealing*
disclosing, evidential, giveaway, indicatory, informative, meaningful, pointing to, prognostic, significant, significatory, suggestive; SEE CONCEPT *267*

temerity [*n*] *nerve, audacity*
assurance, boldness, brass*, carelessness, daring, effrontery, foolhardiness, forwardness, gall, hardihood, hastiness, heedlessness, impertinence, impetuosity, imprudence, impudence, impulsiveness, indiscretion, intrepidity, intrusiveness, nerve, overconfidence, pluck, precipitacy, precipitateness, precipitation, presumption, rashness, recklessness, rudeness, thoughtlessness, venturesomeness; SEE CONCEPTS *411,633*

temper [*n1*] *state of mind*
atmosphere, attitude, attribute, aura, character, climate, complexion, condition, constitution, disposition, drift, frame of mind, humor, individualism, individuality, leaning, makeup, mind, mood, nature, orientation, outlook, peculiarity, personality, posture, property, quality, scene, soul, spirit, state, strain, style, temperament, tendency, tenor, thing*, timbre, tone, trend, type, vein, way; SEE CONCEPTS *410,411*

temper [*n2*] *angriness; bad mood*
acerbity, anger, annoyance, bad-humor, cantankerousness, crossness, dander*, excitability, fit, fretfulness, furor, fury, grouchiness, heat*, hotheadedness, huffiness, ill-humor, impatience, irascibility, ire, irritability, irritation, miff, outburst, passion, peevishness, petulance, pugnacity, rage, resentment, sensitivity, short fuse*, slow burn*, snit, sourness, stew*, sullenness,

surliness, tantrum, tartness, tear*, tiff, tizzy*, touchiness, wax; SEE CONCEPTS **29,410**

temper [n3] *calmness*
calm, composure, cool, coolness, equanimity, good humor, moderation, poise, self-control, tranquility; SEE CONCEPTS **32,410**

temper [vl] *calm, moderate*
abate, adjust, admix, allay, alleviate, assuage, chill out*, cool, cool out*, curb, dilute, ease, fine tune, lessen, make reasonable, mitigate, modulate, mollify, monkey around with*, pacify, palliate, relieve, restrain, revamp, soften, soft-pedal*, soothe, switch, take the bite out of*, take the edge off*, take the sting out of*, tone down, transmogrify, weaken; SEE CONCEPTS **7,22,110,126**

temper [v2] *harden*
anneal, bake, braze, cement, chill, congeal, dry, indurate, mold, petrify, set, solidify, starch, steel, stiffen, strengthen, toughen, toughen up; SEE CONCEPTS **250,726**

temperament [n] *disposition, personality*
attitude, bent, capacity, cast, character, complexion, constitution, distinctiveness, ego, emotions, frame of mind, humor, idiosyncrasy, inclination, individualism, individuality, inner nature, intellect, kind, makeup, mentality, mettle, mood, nature, outlook, peculiarity, quality, soul, spirit, stamp, structure, susceptibility, temperament, tendency, turn, type, way; SEE CONCEPTS **410,411**

temperamental [adj] *angry most of the time; moody*
capricious, changeable, cussed*, easily upset, emotional, erratic, excitable, explosive, fickle, fiery, froward, headstrong, high-strung*, hot-headed*, hyper*, hypersensitive, impatient, in bad mood, inconsistent, irritable, mean, mercurial, neurotic, ornery, passionate, petulant, sensitive, thin-skinned*, ticklish, touchy, uncertain, undependable, unpredictable, unreliable, unstable, variable, volatile, willful; SEE CONCEPT **403**

temperance [n] *self-restraint; abstinence*
abnegation, abstemiousness, asceticism, astringency, austerity, conservatism, constraint, continence, control, discretion, eschewal, forbearance, forgoing, frugality, golden mean*, happy medium*, measure, moderateness, moderation, moderatism, mortification, prohibition, prudence, reasonableness, refrainment, restraint, sacrifice, self-control, self-denial, self-deprivation, self-discipline, soberness, sobriety, stoicism, teetotalism, uninebriation, unintoxication; SEE CONCEPTS **410,633**

temperate [adj1] *calm, moderate*
agreeable, balmy, checked, clement, collected, composed, conservative, constant, cool, curbed, discreet, dispassionate, equable, even, even-tempered, fair, gentle, levelheaded, medium, mild, modest, pleasant, reasonable, regulated, restrained, self-controlled, self-restrained, sensible, sober, soft, stable, steady, unexcessive, unextreme, unimpassioned, warm; SEE CONCEPTS **525,542,547**

temperate [adj2] *controlled, sober*
abstemious, abstentious, abstinent, continent, moderate, restrained, self-restraining; SEE CONCEPT **401**

temperature [n] *hotness, coldness of some degree*
body heat, calefaction, climate, cold, condition, degrees, febricity, feverishness, heat, incalescence, pyrexia, thermal reading, warmth; SEE CONCEPT **610**

tempest [n] *wild storm; commotion*
blizzard, bluster, chaos, convulsion, cyclone, disturbance, ferment, furor, gale, hurricane, squall, tornado, tumult, typhoon, upheaval, uproar, wildness, windstorm; SEE CONCEPTS **230,526**

tempestuous [adj] *wild, stormy*
agitated, blustering, blustery, boisterous, breezy, coarse, emotional, excited, feverish, furious, gusty, heated, hysterical, impassioned, intense, passionate, raging, rough, rugged, squally, storming, tumultous/tumultuous, turbulent, unbridled, uncontrolled, unrestrained, violent, windy; SEE CONCEPTS **401,525,542**

temple [n] *house of worship*
cathedral, chapel, church, holy place, house, house of God*, house of prayer*, mosque, pagoda, pantheon, place of worship, sanctuary, shrine, synagogue, tabernacle; SEE CONCEPTS **368,439**

tempo [n] *beat, rhythm*
bounce, cadence, downbeat, measure, meter, momentum, pace, pulse, rate, speed, time, velocity; SEE CONCEPT **65**

temporal [adj1] *material, worldly*
banausic, carnal, civil, earthly, earthy, fleshly, lay, materialistic, mortal, mundane, nonsacred, nonspiritual, physical, profane, secular, sensual, subcelestial, sublunary, terrestrial, unhallowed, unsacred, unsanctified, unspiritual; SEE CONCEPT **582**

temporal [adj2] *momentary*
chronological, ephemeral, evanescent, fleeting, fugacious, fugitive, impermanent, momentary, of time, passing, short-lived, temporary, transient, transitory; SEE CONCEPT **799**

temporary [adj] *lasting only a short while*
acting, ad hoc, ad interim, alternate, Band-Aid*, brief, changeable, ephemeral, evanescent, fleeting, for the time being*, fugacious, fugitive, impermanent, interim, limited, make-do*, makeshift*, momentary, mortal, overnight, passing, perishable, pro tem, pro tempore, provisional, provisory, shifting, short, short-lived, slapdash*, stopgap*, substitute, summary, supply, temp*, transient, transitory, unfixed, unstable, volatile; SEE CONCEPTS **551,798**

tempt [v] *lure, entice*
allure, appeal to, attract, bait, butter up*, captivate, charm, coax, court, dare, decoy, draw, draw out, entrap, fascinate, honey*, hook*, incite, induce, influence, instigate, intrigue, inveigle, invite, lead on, make mouth water*, motivate, mousetrap*, move, oil, persuade, play up to, promote, provoke, risk, rouse, seduce, solicit, stimulate, tantalize, test, train, try, turn one's head*, wheedle, whet, woo*; SEE CONCEPTS **11,68**

temptation [n] *lure, attraction*
allurement, appeal, attractiveness, bait, blandishment, coaxing, come-on*, decoy, draw, enticement, fancy, fascination, hankering, inducement, inveiglement, invitation, provocation, pull, seducement, seduction, snare, tantalization, trap*, yen; SEE CONCEPTS **20,529,532,690,709**

te
te

tempting [*adj*] *alluring, inviting*
appetizing, attractive, charming, divine, enticing, fascinating, fetching, heavenly, intriguing, luring, magnetic, mouth-watering*, provoking, rousing, scrumptious, seductive, tantalizing, yummy*; SEE CONCEPTS *462,529*

tenable [*adj*] *reasonable*
arguable, believable, condonable, credible, defendable, defensible, excusable, impregnable, justifiable, maintainable, plausible, rational, reliable, secure, sound, strong, trustworthy, viable, vindicable, warrantable; SEE CONCEPTS *552,558*

tenacious [*adj1*] *strong, unyielding*
adamant, bound, clinging, coherent, cohesive, determined, dogged, fast, firm, forceful, inflexible, intransigent, iron, meaning business*, mulish, obdurate, obstinate, persevering, persistent, persisting, pertinacious, possessive, purposeful, relentless, resolute, retentive, set, solid, spunky, stalwart, staunch, steadfast, stout, strong-willed, stubborn, sturdy, sure, tight, tough, true, unforgetful, unshakable, unswerving; SEE CONCEPTS *326,401,489,542*

tenacious [*adj2*] *sticky*
adhesive, clinging, clingy, fast, firm, fixed, glutinous, gummy, inseparable, mucilaginous, resisting, retentive, secure, set, tacky, tight, viscid, viscose, viscous, waxy; SEE CONCEPTS *488,606*

tenacity [*n*] *diligence, stubbornness*
application, backbone, chutzpah*, clock*, courage, determination, doggedness, firmness, grit, guts*, gutsiness*, guttiness*, heart*, inflexibility, intestinal fortitude*, intransigence, moxie*, nerve, obduracy, obstinacy, perseverance, persistence, pertinacity, resoluteness, resolution, resolve, spunk, starch*, staunchness, steadfastness, stick-to-itiveness*, stomach*, strength of purpose, true grit*, what it takes*, willfulness; SEE CONCEPTS *411,657*

tenant [*n*] *person who leases a place*
addressee, boarder, dweller, holder, householder, indweller, inhabitant, leaseholder, lessee, lodger, occupant, occupier, possessor, renter, rent payer, resident, roomer; SEE CONCEPTS *348,423*

tend [*v1*] *be apt, likely*
aim, bear, be biased, be conducive, be disposed, be inclined, be in the habit of, be liable, bend, be predisposed, be prejudiced, conduce, contribute, dispose, drift, favor, go, gravitate, have an inclination, have a tendency, head, impel, incline, influence, lead, lean, look, make for, move, move toward, point, redound, result in, serve to, trend, turn, verge on; SEE CONCEPTS *411,650*

tend [*v2*] *care for*
accomplish, administer, attend, baby-sit, cater to, cherish, control, corral, cultivate, defend, direct, do, do for, feed, foster, guard, handle, keep, keep an eye on*, keep tabs on*, look after, maintain, manage, mind, minister to, nurse, nurture, oversee, perform, protect, ride herd on*, safeguard, see after, see to, serve, shepherd, shield, sit, superintend, supervise, take care of, take under wing*, wait on, watch, watch out for, watch over; SEE CONCEPTS *136,257,295*

tendency [*n1*] *inclination to think or do in a certain way*
addiction, affection, bent*, bias, current, custom, disposition, drift, habit, impulse, inclining, leaning, liability, mind, mindset*, partiality, penchant, predilection, predisposition, proclivity, proneness, propensity, readiness, run, set, shift, slant, susceptibility, temperament, thing*, trend, turn, type, usage, way*, weakness; SEE CONCEPT *657*

tendency [*n2*] *direction of movement*
aim, bearing, bent, bias, course, current, curve, drift, drive, heading, inclination, leaning, movement, purport, run, shift, tenor, trend, turn, turning, way; SEE CONCEPTS *692,738*

tender [*adj1*] *fragile, soft*
breakable, dainty, delicate, effete, feeble, frail, supple, weak; SEE CONCEPTS *604,606*

tender [*adj2*] *young, inexperienced*
callow, childish, childlike, green*, immature, impressionable, new, raw*, rookie*, sensitive, unripe, vernal, vulnerable, wet behind the ears*, youthful; SEE CONCEPTS *578,797*

tender [*adj3*] *affectionate, loving*
all heart*, amorous, benevolent, bleeding-heart*, caring, charitable, commiserative, compassionate, considerate, demonstrative, emotional, evocative, fond, forgiving, gentle, humane, kind, lenient, lovey-dovey*, merciful, mild, moving, mushy*, poignant, responsive, romantic, sensitive, sentimental, soft, softhearted, solicitous, sympathetic, tenderhearted, thoughtful, ticklish, tolerant, touching, touchy, warm, warmhearted, yielding; SEE CONCEPTS *401,542*

tender [*adj4*] *painful, sore*
aching, acute, bruised, delicate, hypersensitive, inflamed, irritated, oversensitive, raw, sensitive, smarting, thin-skinned, ticklish, touchy; SEE CONCEPTS *314,403,548*

tenderfoot [*n*] *newcomer*
amateur, beginner, colt*, greenhorn*, Johnny-come-lately*, neophyte, new kid on the block*, novice, novitiate, rookie, tyro; SEE CONCEPTS *413,423*

tenderhearted [*adj*] *tender*
affectionate, all heart*, benevolent, bleeding heart*, caring, charitable, compassionate, considerate, emotional, forgiving, gentle, humane, kind, kindhearted, lenient, loving, merciful, mushy*, sensitive, sentimental, soft, softhearted, sweet, sympathetic, thoughtful, understanding, warm, warmhearted; SEE CONCEPTS *401,542*

tenebrous [*adj*] *dark, ominous*
ambiguous, amphibological, caliginous, dim, dingy, dusk, dusky, equivocal, gloomy, lightless, murky, obscure, shadowy, shady, somber, sunless, uncertain, unclear, unexplicit, unilluminated, unintelligible, unlit, vague; SEE CONCEPTS *535,617*

tenement [*n*] *apartment house*
apartment complex, boarding house, coop, cooperative, den*, digs*, dump*, flat, high-rise, high-rise apartment building, living quarters, pad*, project housing, rental, slum; SEE CONCEPTS *448,516*

tenet [*n*] *belief, principle*
article of faith, assumption, canon, conception, conviction, credo, creed, doctrine, dogma, faith, impression, maxim, opinion, persuasion, position, precept, presumption, profession, rule, self-conviction, system, teaching, thesis, trust, view; SEE CONCEPTS *688,689*

tenor [*n1*] *meaning, intent*
aim, body, burden, core, course, course of thought, current, direction, drift, evolution, gist, inclination, meat, mood, path, pith, purport, pur-

pose, run, sense, stuff, substance, tendency, theme, tone, trend, way; SEE CONCEPTS *529,682*

tenor [*n2*] *high male voice*
alto, countertenor, falsetto; SEE CONCEPT *65*

tense [*adj1*] *tight, stretched*
close, firm, rigid, stiff, strained, taut; SEE CONCEPTS *485,604*

tense [*adj2*] *under stress, pressure*
agitated, anxious, apprehensive, beside oneself*, bundle of nerves*, choked, clutched, concerned, edgy, excited, fidgety, fluttery, high-strung*, hung up*, hyper*, in a tizzy*, jittery, jumpy, keyed up*, moved, moving, nerve-racking, nervous, nervous wreck*, on edge, overanxious, overwrought, queasy, restive, restless, shaky, shot*, shot to pieces*, strained, stressful, strung out*, uneasy, unnerved, unquiet, up the wall*, uptight*, white knuckled*, wired*, worried, worrying, wound up*, wreck*; SEE CONCEPTS *401,403,548*

tension [*n1*] *tightness*
astriction, balance, constriction, force, pressure, rigidity, stiffness, strain, straining, stress, stretching, tautness, tenseness, tensity; SEE CONCEPTS *723,726*

tension [*n2*] *mental stress*
agitation, antsiness*, ants in pants*, anxiety, apprehension, bad feeling*, brunt, concern, discomfort, disquiet, edginess*, hostility, jitters*, jumps*, nail-biting*, nerves, nervousness, pins and needles*, pressure, restlessness, shakes*, strain, suspense, unease, uneasiness, worriment, worry; SEE CONCEPT *410*

tent [*n*] *portable canvas shelter*
big top*, canvas, pavilion, tabernacle, tepee, tupik, wigwam, yurt; SEE CONCEPTS *515,712*

tentative [*adj1*] *conditional, experimental*
acting, ad interim, conjectural, contingent, dependent, iffy*, indefinite, makeshift, not final, not settled, on trial, open for consideration, probationary, provisional, provisionary, provisory, speculative, subject to change, temporary, test, trial, unconfirmed, undecided, unsettled; SEE CONCEPTS *551,552*

tentative [*adj2*] *indefinite, uncertain*
backward, cautious, diffident, disinclined, doubtful, faltering, halting, hesitant, irresolute, reluctant, timid, undecided, unsure, vacillating, vacillatory, wobbly; SEE CONCEPTS *534,535,542*

tenuous [*adj*] *weak, thin*
aerial, airy, attenuate, attenuated, delicate, doubtful, dubious, ethereal, fine, flimsy, gossamer, insignificant, insubstantial, light, narrow, nebulous, questionable, rare, rarefied, reedy, shaky, sketchy, slender, slight, slim, subtle, twiggy; SEE CONCEPTS *489,491,575*

tenure [*n*] *time in position of responsibility*
administration, clamp, clasp, clench, clinch, clutch, dynasty, grasp, grip, hold, holding, incumbency, occupancy, occupation*, ownership, possession, proprietorship, regime, reign, residence, security, tenancy, term; SEE CONCEPTS *287,816*

tepid [*adj*] *lukewarm*
apathetic, cool, disinterested, dull, halfhearted, indifferent, languid, lifeless, mild, milk-warm, moderate, slightly warm, spiritless, temperate, unenthusiastic, unlively, warm, warmish; SEE CONCEPTS *542,605*

term [*n1*] *description of a concept*
appellation, article, caption, denomination, designation, expression, head, indication, language, locution, moniker*, name, nomenclature, phrase, style, terminology, title, vocable, word; SEE CONCEPTS *275,683*

term [*n2*] *time period*
course, cycle, duration, go*, hitch*, interval, phase, quarter, season, semester, session, space, span, spell, standing, stretch, time, tour, turn, while; SEE CONCEPTS *807,822*

term [*n3*] *limit*
bound, boundary, close, conclusion, confine, confines, culmination, end, finish, fruition, limitation, terminus; SEE CONCEPTS *745,832*

term [*v*] *name something*
baptize, call, christen, denominate, describe, designate, dub, entitle, label, style, subtitle, tag, title; SEE CONCEPT *62*

terminal [*adj*] *final, deadly*
bounding, check out*, closing, concluding, eventual, extreme, fatal, hindmost, incurable, killing, lag, last, latest, latter, lethal, limiting, mortal, on way out*, period, ultimate, utmost; SEE CONCEPTS *314,548*

terminal [*n1*] *end of road; limit*
boundary, depot, end, end of the line, extremity, station, termination, terminus; SEE CONCEPTS *198,745*

terminal [*n2*] *computer screen, computer input/output device*
cathode ray tube, CRT*, display, input device, monitor, screen, VDT*, video display; SEE CONCEPT *463*

terminate [*v*] *stop, finish*
abolish, abort, achieve, adjourn, annul, bounce, bound, bring to an end, cancel, cease, close, come to an end, complete, conclude, confine, cut off, define, desist, determine, discharge, discontinue, dismiss, dissolve, drop, eliminate, end, expire, extinguish, fire, halt, issue, lapse, limit, perfect, prorogate, prorogue, put an end to, recess, restrict, result, run out, sack, scratch, scrub*, tether, ultimate, wind down, wind up*, wrap*, wrap up*; SEE CONCEPTS *119,121,234*

termination [*n*] *end*
abortion, ballgame*, cease, cessation, close, completion, conclusion, consequence, curtains*, cut-off*, desistance, discontinuation, effect, ending, end of the line*, expiry, finale, finis, finish, issue, kiss-off*, outcome, payoff*, period, result, stop, terminus, windup*, wrap-up*; SEE CONCEPTS *119,832*

terminology [*n*] *wording*
choice of words, diction, jargon, language, lingo, locution, nomenclature, onomastics, phraseology, phrasing, turn of phrase, vocabulary, wordage, words; SEE CONCEPTS *278,682*

terms [*n1*] *conditions, agreement*
charge, circumstances, conclusion, condition, details, fee, fine print*, items, nitty-gritty*, particulars, payment, points, premise, premises, price, provision, provisions, proviso, provisos, qualifications, rate, reservation, size of it*, small print*, specifications, stipulation, stipulations, strings*, treaty, understanding, what it is*; SEE CONCEPTS *270,318,684*

terms [*n2*] *status of relationship*
balance, equality, equivalence, footing, par, par-

ity, position, relations, relationship, standing; SEE CONCEPT 388

terrain [n] *landscape*
area, bailiwick, contour, country, domain, dominion, field, form, ground, land, profile, province, region, shape, soil, sphere, territory, topography, turf; SEE CONCEPTS 508,509

terrestrial [adj] *earthly*
earthbound, earthlike, earthy, global, mundane, physical, profane, prosaic, secular, sublunary, subsolar, telluric, temporal, terrene, uncelestial, unspiritual, worldly; SEE CONCEPT 536

terrible [adj] *bad, horrible*
abhorrent, appalling, atrocious, awe-inspiring, awesome, awful, beastly, dangerous, desperate, dire, disastrous, disturbing, dread, dreaded, dreadful, extreme, fearful, frightful, ghastly, gruesome, harrowing, hateful, hideous, horrendous, horrible, horrid, horrifying, inconvenient, loathsome, monstrous, obnoxious, odious, offensive, petrifying, poor, repulsive, revolting, rotten, serious, severe, shocking, unfortunate, unnerving, unpleasant, unwelcome, vile; SEE CONCEPT 571

terribly [adv] *very*
awfully, badly, decidedly, desperately, discouragingly, disturbingly, drastically, dreadfully, exceedingly, extremely, fearfully, frightfully, gravely, greatly, highly, horribly, intensely, markedly, mightily, much, notoriously, remarkably, seriously, staggeringly, thoroughly, unbelievably, unfortunately, unhappily; SEE CONCEPTS 569,570

terrific [adj1] *intense*
agitating, appalling, awesome, awful, deafening, disquieting, dreadful, enormous, excessive, extreme, fearful, fierce, formidable, frightful, gigantic, great, harsh, horrible, horrific, huge, immense, large, monstrous, severe, shocking, terrible, terrorizing, thunderous, tremendous, upsetting; SEE CONCEPT 569

terrific [adj2] *wonderful*
ace*, amazing, breathtaking, divine, excellent, fabulous, fantastic, fine, glorious, great, groovy*, hot*, keen*, magnificent, marvelous, outstanding, sensational, smashing*, stupendous, super, superb, swell, very good; SEE CONCEPT 572

terrify [v] *scare*
alarm, appall, awe, chill, dismay, freeze, fright, frighten, horrify, intimidate, paralyze, petrify, scare stiff*, scare the pants off of*, scare to death*, shock, spook, startle, strike fear into*, stun, stupefy, terrorize; SEE CONCEPTS 7,19,42

territory [n] *domain, region*
area, belt, block, boundary, colony, commonwealth, country, district, dominion, empire, enclave, exclave, expanse, extent, field, land, mandate, nation, neck of the woods*, neighborhood, province, quarter, section, sector, sphere, state, stomping grounds*, street, terrain, terrene, township, tract, turf*, walk, zone; SEE CONCEPTS 198,349,508

terror [n] *intense fear*
alarm, anxiety, awe, consternation, dismay, dread, fearfulness, fright, horror, intimidation, panic, shock, trepidation, trepidity; SEE CONCEPTS 27,690

terrorize [v] *upset, threaten*
alarm, appall, awe, bludgeon, browbeat, bulldoze*, bully, coerce, cow, dismay, dragoon,

fright, frighten, hector, horrify, intimidate, menace, oppress, petrify, scare, scare to death*, shock, spook, startle, strike terror into*, strongarm*, terrify; SEE CONCEPTS 7,14,19

terse [adj] *brief, short*
abrupt, aphoristic, boiled down*, breviloquent, brusque, clear-cut, clipped, close, compact, compendiary, compendious, concise, condensed, crisp, cryptic, curt, cut to the bone*, elliptical, epigrammatic, exact, gnomic, in a nutshell*, incisive, laconic, lean, neat, pithy, pointed, precise, sententious, short and sweet*, snappy, succinct, summary, taut, to the point, trenchant; SEE CONCEPTS 267,272

test [n] *examination, quiz*
analysis, approval, assessment, attempt, blue book*, catechism, check, comp*, confirmation, corroboration, countdown, criterion, dry run*, elimination, essay, evaluation, exam, experiment, final, fling*, go*, inquest, inquiry, inspection, investigation, lick*, oral*, ordeal, pop quiz, preliminary, probation, probing, proof, questionnaire, scrutiny, search, shibboleth, standard, substantiation, touchstone*, trial, trial and error*, trial run, try, tryout, verification, yardstick*; SEE CONCEPTS 5,290

test [v] *examine, quiz*
analyze, assay, assess, check, confirm, demonstrate, experiment, experimentalize, give a tryout, inquire, investigate, look into, make a trial run, match up, prove, prove out, put to the test*, question, run idea by someone*, run it up a flagpole*, see how it flies*, see how wind blows*, send up a balloon*, shake down*, stack up, substantiate, try, try on, try on for size*, try out, validate, verify; SEE CONCEPTS 5,103,291

testament [n] *tribute; last wishes*
attestation, colloquy, confirmation, covenant, demonstration, earnest, evidence, exemplification, instrument, proof, testimonial, testimony, will, witness; SEE CONCEPT 318

tested [adj] *proven*
approved, certified, creditworthy, dependable, loyal, proved, reliable, safe, tried-and-true*, trustworthy, trusty; SEE CONCEPT 535

testify [v] *vouch for; give testimony*
affirm, announce, argue, assert, attest, bear witness, bespeak, betoken, certify, corroborate, cross one's heart*, declare, demonstrate, depone, depose, evince, give evidence, give facts, give one's word*, indicate, make evident, mount, point to, prove, say so*, show, sing*, stand up for, state, swear, swear to, swear up and down*, token, warrant, witness; SEE CONCEPTS 49,317

testimonial [n] *tribute*
affidavit, appreciation, attestation, certificate, character, commemoration, commendation, confirmation, credential, degree, endorsement, evidence, homage, honor, indication, manifestation, memorial, memorialization, monument*, ovation, plug*, proof, recommendation, reference, remembrance, salute, salvo, say-so*, show, sign, symbol, testament, testimony, token, voucher, witness; SEE CONCEPTS 49,278,318

testimony [n] *declaration about truth; proof*
affidavit, affirmation, attestation, avowal, confirmation, corroboration, data, demonstration, deposition, documentation, evidence, facts, grounds, illustration, indication, information, manifestation, profession, statement, submission,

substantiation, support, testament, verification, witness; SEE CONCEPTS **49,278,318**

testy [*adj*] *irritable, touchy*
annoyed, bad-tempered, cantankerous, captious, choleric, crabbed, cranky*, cross, crotchety, edgy, exasperated, fretful, grouchy, grumpy*, impatient, irascible, mean, ornery*, out of sorts, peevish, peppery, petulant, quarrelsome, quick-tempered, short-tempered, snappy*, splenetic, sullen, thin-skinned*, uptight*, waspish; SEE CONCEPTS **401,403,542**

tete-a-tete [*n*] *conversation*
chat, colloquy, confabulation, confidential discussion, consultation, cozy chat, dialogue, discussion, exchange, face-to-face talk, fireside chat, friendly chat, heart-to-heart talk, intimate discussion, one-on-one talk, pillow talk*, pow-wow*, talk; SEE CONCEPT **266**

tether [*n*] *fastening*
binding, bond, chain, cord, fetter, halter, harness, lead, leash, picket, restraint, rope, shackle; SEE CONCEPT **475**

tether [*v*] *fasten*
batten, bind, chain, fetter, leash, manacle, moor, picket, restrain, rope, secure, shackle, tie; SEE CONCEPTS **85,160**

text [*n1*] *subject matter of document*
argument, body, consideration, content, contents, context, document, extract, fundamentals, head, idea, issue, line, lines, main body, matter, motify, motive, paragraph, passage, point, quotation, sentence, stanza, subject, theme, thesis, topic, verse, vocabulary, wording, words; SEE CONCEPTS **270,682**

text [*n2*] *book used in education*
assignment, class book, course book, handbook, manual, reader, reference, reference book, required reading, schoolbook, source, syllabus, textbook, workbook; SEE CONCEPTS **280,287**

textbook [*n*] *text*
assigned text, class book, course book, primer, reader, required reading, schoolbook, workbook; SEE CONCEPTS **280,287**

texture [*n*] *characteristics of a surface*
arrangement, balance, being, character, coarseness, composition, consistency, constitution, disposition, essence, essentiality, fabric, feel, feeling, fiber, fineness, flexibility, form, framework, grain, intermixture, make, makeup, nap, nature, organization, pattern, quality, roughness, scheme, sense, smoothness, stiffness, strategy, structure, surface, taste, tissue, touch, warp, weave, web, woof; SEE CONCEPTS **611,673,682**

thank [*v*] *express gratitude*
acknowledge, be grateful, be indebted, be obligated, be obliged, bless, bow down*, give thanks, kiss*, praise, say thank you, show appreciation, show courtesy, show gratitude, smile on*; SEE CONCEPTS **60,69,76**

thankful [*adj*] *appreciative*
beholden, content, contented, grateful, gratified, indebted, much obliged, obliged, overwhelmed, pleased, relieved, satisfied; SEE CONCEPTS **401,403**

thankless [*adj1*] *unappreciated*
barren, disagreeable, distasteful, fruitless, futile, miserable, not worth it*, ungrateful, unpleasant, unprofitable, unrecognized, unrequited, unreturned, unrewarding, useless, vain, wretched; SEE CONCEPTS **538,548**

thankless [*adj2*] *unappreciative, inconsiderate (in behavior)*
careless, cruel, heedless, inappreciative, rude, self-centered, thoughtless, ungracious, ungrateful, unmindful, unthankful; SEE CONCEPT **401**

thanks [*n*] *spoken or written appreciation*
acknowledgment, benediction, blessing, credit, grace, gramercy, gratefulness, gratitude, praise, recognition, thankfulness, thanksgiving, thank you note; SEE CONCEPTS **60,69,278**

thaw [*v*] *unfreeze, warm*
become liquid, become soft, defrost, deliquesce, dissolve, flow, flux, fuse, liquefy, loosen, melt, mollify, open up, relax, relent, run, soften, unbend, warm up; SEE CONCEPTS **13,255,469**

theater/theatre [*n*] *stage, building for performance*
amphitheater, arena, assembly hall, auditorium, barn, boards*, cinema, coliseum, concert hall, deck, drama, drive-in, footlights, hall, hippodrome, house, locale, movie, movie house, oak*, odeum, opera house, playhouse, room, scene, show hall, site; SEE CONCEPTS **263,293,439,448**

theatrical [*adj*] *dramatic*
affected, amateur, artificial, campy*, ceremonious, comic, dramaturgic, exaggerated, ham*, hammy*, histrionic, legitimate, mannered, melodramatic, meretricious, operatic, ostentatious, pompous, schmaltzy*, show, showy, staged, stilted, superficial, theatric, thespian, tragic, unnatural, unreal, vaudeville; SEE CONCEPTS **401,536**

theft [*n*] *stealing*
annexation, appropriation, break-in, burglary, caper, cheating, crime, defrauding, deprivation, embezzlement, extortion, filch, fleece*, fraud, grab*, heist, holdup, hustle*, job*, larceny, lift*, looting, mugging, peculation, pilferage, pilfering, pillage, pinch*, piracy, plunder, purloining, racket*, rapacity, rip-off*, robbery, robbing, score*, shoplifting, snatch*, snitch*, steal, stickup, swindle, swindling, swiping*, thievery, thieving, touch*, vandalism; SEE CONCEPTS **139,192**

theme [*n1*] *idea, subject matter*
affair, argument, burden, business, case, head, keynote, leitmotif, line, matter, matter in hand, motif, motive, point, point at issue, problem, proposition, question, stuff, subject, text, thesis, thought, topic; SEE CONCEPTS **278,682,689**

theme [*n2*] *written composition*
article, description, dissertation, essay, exercise, exposition, manuscript, paper, report, statement, thesis; SEE CONCEPT **271**

then [*adv1*] *before; at another time*
again, all at once, anon, at that instant, at that moment, at that point, at that time, before long, formerly, later, next, on that occasion, soon after, suddenly, thereupon, when, years ago; SEE CONCEPT **799**

then [*adv2*] *therefore*
accordingly, consequently, ergo, from that time, from then on, from there on, hence, so, thence, thenceforth, thereupon, thus, whence; SEE CONCEPT **548**

theological [*adj*] *religious, concerning a god-centered philosophy*
apostolic, canonical, churchly, deistic, divine, doctrinal, ecclesiastical, metaphysical, scriptural, theistic; SEE CONCEPT **536**

te
th

theorem [*n*] *explanation based on hypothesis and experiments*
assumption, axiom, belief, deduction, dictum, doctrine, formula, fundamental, law, postulate, principium, principle, proposition, rule, statement, theory, thesis; SEE CONCEPTS *529,688,689*

theoretical [*adj*] *hypothetical*
abstract, academic, analytical, as a premise, assumed, codified, conjectural, contingent, formalistic, formularized, general, ideal, idealized, ideational, ideological, imaginative, impractical, instanced, intellectual, in the abstract, in theory, logical, metaphysical, notional, on paper*, pedantic, philosophical, postulated, presumed, problematical, pure, quixotic, speculative, suppositional, tentative, transcendent, transcendental, unearthly, unproved, unsubstantiated, vague; SEE CONCEPT *529*

theorize [*v*] *hypothesize*
conjecture, formulate, guess, project, propound, speculate, submit, suggest, suppose, think; SEE CONCEPT *43*

theory [*n*] *hypothesis, belief*
approach, argument, assumption, base, basis, belief, code, codification, concept, conditions, conjecture, doctrine, dogma, feeling, formularization, foundation, grounds, guess, guesswork, hunch, idea, ideology, impression, method, outlook, philosophy, plan, position, postulate, premise, presentiment, presumption, proposal, provision, rationale, scheme, shot*, speculation, stab*, supposal, suppose, supposition, surmise, suspicion, system, systemization, theorem, thesis, understanding; SEE CONCEPTS *529,689*

therapeutic [*adj*] *healing*
ameliorative, analeptic, beneficial, corrective, curative, good, remedial, restorative, salubrious, salutary, sanative; SEE CONCEPT *537*

therapist [*n*] *counselor*
adviser, analyst, clinician, doctor, physician, psychiatrist, psychoanalyst, psychologist, psychotherapist, shrink*; SEE CONCEPT *357*

therapy [*n*] *healing treatment*
analysis, cure, healing, medicine, remedial treatment, remedy, therapeutics; SEE CONCEPT *310*

thereabout [*adv*] *about there*
almost, approximately, around, close at hand, in the neighborhood, in the vicinity, just about, near, nearby, nearly, roughly; SEE CONCEPTS *581,586*

thereafter [*adv*] *from that time forward*
after that, consequently, following, forever after, from that day forward, from that day on, from there on, hereafter, thenceforth, thenceforward; SEE CONCEPT *799*

therefore [*adv*] *as a result; for that reason*
accordingly, and so, consequently, ergo, for, forasmuch as, for this reason, hence, inasmuch as, in consequence, in that event, on account of, on the grounds, since, so, then, thence, therefrom, thereupon, thus, to that end, whence, wherefore; SEE CONCEPTS *230,676*

thermal [*adj*] *warm*
heated, hot, lukewarm, melting, roasting, scorching, sizzling, snug, summery, sweltering, thermic, toasty; SEE CONCEPT *605*

thesaurus [*n*] *dictionary of synonyms and antonyms*
glossary, language reference book, lexicon, onomasticon, reference book, sourcebook, storehouse of words, terminology, treasury of words, vocabulary, word list; SEE CONCEPT *280*

thesis [*n1*] *belief, assumption to be tested*
apriorism, contention, contestation, hypothesis, idea, line, opinion, point, posit, position, postulate, postulation, premise, presumption, presupposition, principle, proposal, proposition, sentiment, statement, supposition, surmise, theory, view; SEE CONCEPTS *529,689*

thesis [*n2*] *written dissertation*
argument, argumentation, composition, discourse, disquisition, essay, exposition, memoir, monograph, monography, paper, research, theme, tractate, treatise; SEE CONCEPTS *271,287*

thespian [*n*] *actor, actress*
artist, bit player, character, entertainer, extra, ham*, headliner, idol, lead, performer, player, actor, player, star, straight person, thesp*, understudy; SEE CONCEPT *352*

thick [*adj1*] *deep, bulky*
blubbery, broad, bulky, burly, chunky, compact, concrete, consolidated, fat, firm, hard, heavy, high, husky, massive, obese, pudgy, solid, squat, stocky, stubby, stumpy, substantial, thickset, wide; SEE CONCEPTS *491,773*

thick [*adj2*] *concentrated, dense*
caked, clabbered, close, clotted, coagulated, compact, compressed, concrete, condensed, congealed, consolidated, crowded, curdled, deep, firm, fixed, gelatinous, gloppy*, gooey, gummous, gummy, gunky*, heavy, impenetrable, impervious, jelled, jellied, opaque, ossified, ropy, set, sloppy, solid, solidified, stiff, syrupy, thickened, turbid, viscid, viscous, vitrified; SEE CONCEPTS *483,606*

thick [*adj3*] *crowded, packed*
abundant, brimming, bristling, bursting, chockfull*, close, compact, compressed, concentrated, condensed, considerable, covered, crammed, crawling with*, dense, frequent, full, great, heaped, impenetrable, impervious, inspissated, like sardines*, localized, multitudinous, numerous, populated, populous, profuse, rank, replete, several, solid, swarming, teeming, tight; SEE CONCEPT *771*

thick [*adj4*] *stupid*
blockheaded, boneheaded, brainless, dense, dimwitted, doltish, dopey*, dull, dumb, ignorant, insensitive, moronic, numbskulled, obtuse, slow, slow-witted, thickheaded; SEE CONCEPT *402*

thick [*adj5*] *dense (referring to weather)*
cloudy, dull, foggy, heavy, impenetrable, indistinct, muddy, obscure, soupy*, turbid; SEE CONCEPT *525*

thick [*adj6*] *friendly*
chummy*, close, confidential, cordial, devoted, familiar, hand in glove*, inseparable, intimate, on good terms; SEE CONCEPT *555*

thick [*adj7*] *unreasonable*
excessive, flimsy*, implausible, improbable, inconceivable, incredible, thin*, too much*, unbelievable, unconvincing, unfair, unjust, unsubstantial; SEE CONCEPTS *529,548*

thicken [*v*] *set; make more dense*
add, buttress, cake, clabber, clot, coagulate, condense, congeal, curdle, deepen, enlarge, expand, freeze, gel, grow thick, harden, inspissate, jell, jelly, ossify, petrify, reinforce, solidify, stiffen, swell, widen; SEE CONCEPTS *137,250,469*

thick-skinned [*adj*] *hardened*
benumbed, callous, coldhearted*, hard-as-nails*, hardhearted*, insensitive, seasoned, tough, toughened, unbending, unfeeling; SEE CONCEPTS *404,542*

thief [*n*] *person who steals*
bandit, burglar, cat burglar, cheat, clip*, criminal, crook, defalcator, embezzler, heister*, highway robber, hijacker, holdup artist, housebreaker, kleptomaniac, larcener, larcenist, lifter*, moonlighter*, mugger, owl*, pickpocket, pilferer, pirate, plunderer, porch climber*, prowler, punk*, purloiner, robber, scrounger, shoplifter, sniper, spider*, stealer, stickup artist*, swindler; SEE CONCEPT *412*

thieving/thievish [*adj*] *criminal*
crooked, cunning, dishonest, fraudulent, furtive, kleptomaniacal*, larcenous, light-fingered*, oilfering, piratic*, plunderous, predatory, rapacious, secretive, sly, spoliative, stealthy, sticky-fingered*; SEE CONCEPT *401*

thin [*adj1*] *fine, light, slender*
attenuate, attenuated, beanpole*, beanstalk*, bony*, cadaverous, delicate, emaciated, ethereal, featherweight, fragile, gangling, gangly, gaunt, haggard, lank, lanky, lean, lightweight, meager, narrow, peaked, pinched, pole*, puny*, rangy, rarefied, rawboned, reedy, rickety, scraggy*, scrawny, shadow, shriveled, skeletal, skinny, slight, slim, slinky, small, spare, spindly, stalky*, starved, stick*, stilt*, subtle, threadlike, twiggy*, twiglike, undernourished, underweight, wan, wasted, wizened; SEE CONCEPTS *491,773*

thin [*adj2*] *transparent, fine*
attenuate, attenuated, delicate, diaphanous, filmy, flimsy, gossamer, paper-thin, permeable, rare, rarefied, refined, see-through, sheer, slight, slim, subtile, subtle, tenuous, translucent, unsubstantial, wafer-thin, wispy; SEE CONCEPT *606*

thin [*adj3*] *deficient, weak*
diluted, feeble*, flat*, flimsy*, implausible, improbable, inadequate, inconceivable, incredible, insubstantial, insufficient, lame, meager, poor, questionable, scant, scanty, scarce, scattered, shallow, sketchy, skimpy*, slight, sparse, stretched, superficial, thick*, transparent, unbelievable, unconvincing, unpersuasive, unsubstantial, untenable, vapid, weak-kneed*; SEE CONCEPT *771*

thin [*adj4*] *diluted*
diffuse, dilute, dispersed, fine, light, rarefied, refined, runny, subtle, watery, weak, wishy-washy*; SEE CONCEPT *485*

thin [*v*] *make diluted or less dense*
attenuate, cook, cut, cut back, decrease, delete, diminish, disperse, doctor, edit, emaciate, expand, extenuate, irrigate, lace*, needle*, prune, rarefy, reduce, refine, shave, spike, trim, water, water down, weaken, weed out; SEE CONCEPTS *137,250*

thing [*n1*] *something felt, seen, perceived*
affair, anything, apparatus, article, being, body, business, circumstance, commodity, concept, concern, configuration, contrivance, corporeality, creature, device, element, entity, everything, existence, existent, fact, figure, form, gadget, goods, implement, individual, information, instrument, item, machine, material, materiality, matter, means, mechanism, object, part, person, phenomenon, piece, point, portion, shape, situation, stuff, subject, substance, tool, word; SEE CONCEPT *433*

thing [*n2*] *act*
accomplishment, action, circumstance, deed, doing, duty, episode, event, eventuality, exploit, feat, happening, incident, job, movement, obligation, occasion, occurrence, phenomenon, proceeding, stunt, task, work; SEE CONCEPT *3*

thing [*n3*] *aspect, characteristic*
article, attribute, detail, element, facet, factor, feature, item, particular, point, property, quality, statement, thought, trait; SEE CONCEPTS *411,657,834*

thing [*n5*] *idea, obsession*
attitude, bee in bonnet*, craze, fad, fetish, fixation, hang-up*, idée fixe, impression, mania, notion, opinion, phobia, preoccupation, quirk, style, thought; SEE CONCEPT *529*

thing/things [*n4*] *personal possessions*
apparel, attire, baggage, belongings, chattels, clothes, clothing, duds*, effects, equipment, gear, goods, habiliments, impedimenta, luggage, odds and ends*, paraphernalia, personal effects, personals*, property, raiment, stuff, trappings, tricks; SEE CONCEPTS *446,451*

think [*v1*] *believe; anticipate*
assume, be convinced, comprehend, conceive, conclude, consider, credit, deem, determine, envisage, envision, esteem, estimate, expect, fancy, feature, feel, foresee, gather, guess, hold, image, imagine, judge, plan for, presume, project, realize, reckon, regard, see, sense, suppose, surmise, suspect, take, understand, vision, visualize; SEE CONCEPTS *12,26*

think [*v2*] *contemplate*
analyze, appraise, appreciate, brood, cerebrate, cogitate, comprehend, conceive, consider, deduce, deliberate, estimate, evaluate, examine, figure out, have in mind, ideate, imagine, infer, intellectualize, judge, logicalize, meditate, mull, mull over, muse, ponder, rack one's brains*, rationalize, reason, reflect, resolve, revolve, ruminate, sort out, speculate, stew*, stop to consider, study, take under consideration, turn over, use one's head*; weigh; SEE CONCEPTS *17,33,43*

think [*v3*] *remember*
call to mind, recall, recollect, reminisce; SEE CONCEPT *40*

thinkable [*adj*] *believable, feasible*
cogitable, comprehendible, comprehensible, conceivable, convincing, imaginable, likely, possible, practicable, practical, presumable, reasonable, supposable, within realm of possibility*, within the limits; SEE CONCEPT *529*

thin-skinned [*adj*] *sensitive*
delicate, easily hurt, hypersensitive, oversensitive, soft, touchy, vulnerable; SEE CONCEPT *406*

third world [*n*] *underdeveloped countries*
developing countries, developing nations, economically developing countries, economically developing nations, emergent nations, underdeveloped nations; SEE CONCEPTS *378,391*

thirst [*n*] *craving (especially for liquid)*
appetite, aridity, desire, drought, dryness, eagerness, hankering, hunger, keenness, longing, lust, passion, thirstiness, yearning, yen; SEE CONCEPTS *20,709*

thirsty [*adj*] *dry, desirous (especially for liquid)*
agog*, anxious, appetent, ardent, arid, athirst, avid, bone-dry*, breathless, burning, cotton-

mouthed*, craving, crazy for*, dehydrated, droughty, dry as dust*, dying for*, eager, greedy, hankering, hungry, impatient, inclined, itching for*, juiceless, keen, longing, lusting, parched, partial to, sapless, thirsting, waterless, wild for*, yearning; SEE CONCEPTS 403,603

thorny [adj1] *sharp, pointed*
barbed, briery, bristling, bristly, prickly, spiked, spiky, spinous, spiny, stinging, thistly; SEE CON-CEPT 485

thorny [adj2] *difficult, problematic*
awkward, baffling, bothersome, formidable, ha-rassing, hard, irksome, nettlesome, perplexing, prickly, severe, sticky, ticklish, tough, tricky, troublesome, trying, unpleasant, upsetting, vexa-tious, worrying; SEE CONCEPT 565

thoroughbred [adj] *pure, unmixed*
blood, full-blooded, graded, papered, pedigree, pedigreed, pure-blooded, purebred; SEE CONCEPT 549

thoroughly [adv1] *exhaustively*
all, assiduously, carefully, completely, compre-hensively, conscientiously, earnestly, efficiently, exceedingly, exceptionally, extremely, flat out*, from A to Z*, from top to bottom*, fully, hard, highly, hugely, in and out*, in detail, inside out*, intensely, intensively, meticulously, notably, painstakingly, remarkably, scrupulously, strik-ingly, sweepingly, through and through*, throughout, unremittingly, up and down*, very, whole hog*, wholly; SEE CONCEPTS 531,538

thoroughly [adv2] *utterly*
absolutely, altogether, completely, downright, entirely, fully, perfectly, plumb, quite, totally, to the full, well, wholly, without reservation; SEE CONCEPTS 531,535,557

thorough/thoroughgoing [adj1] *exhaustive*
absolute, all-embracing, all-inclusive, all-out*, all the way*, assiduous, blow-by-blow*, careful, circumstantial, clocklike, complete, comprehen-sive, conscientious, detailed, efficient, exact, from A to Z*, full, full-dress*, in-depth, inten-sive, itemized, meticulous, minute, painstaking, particular, particularized, plenty, royal, scrupu-lous, slam bang*, soup to nuts*, sweeping, tough, whole-hog*; SEE CONCEPTS 531,538

thorough/thoroughgoing [adj2] *absolute, utter*
arrant, complete, consummate, downright, entire, out-and-out*, outright, perfect, pure, rank, sheer, straight-out*, total, unmitigated, unqualified; SEE CONCEPTS 531,535,557

though [adv] *however*
after all, all the same, for all that, howbeit, never-theless, nonetheless, notwithstanding, still, still and all, withal, yet; SEE CONCEPT 544

though [conj] *while*
albeit, allowing, although, but, despite, despite the fact, even if, even supposing, even though, granted, howbeit, if, much as, notwithstanding, when, whereas; SEE CONCEPT 544

thought [n1] *formation of mental objects*
anticipation, apprehending, attention, brainwork, cerebration, cogitation, cognition, concluding, consideration, considering, contemplation, de-ducing, deduction, deliberation, deriving, dis-cerning, heed, hope, ideation, inducing, inferring, introspection, intuition, judging, know-ing, logic, meditation, musing, perceiving, ratio-nalization, rationalizing, realizing, reasoning, reflection, regard, rumination, scrutiny, seeing,

speculation, study, theorization, thinking, under-standing; SEE CONCEPTS 17,43,409,410

thought [n2] *idea, concept*
aim, anxiety, appreciation, aspiration, assess-ment, assumption, attentiveness, belief, brain-child*, brainstorm*, caring, compassion, conception, concern, conclusion, conjecture, conviction, design, dream, drift, estimation, ex-pectation, fancy, feeling, guess, hope, hypothe-sis, image, inference, intention, intuition, judgment, kindness, knowledge, notion, object, opinion, plan, premise, prospect, purpose, re-gard, reverie, solicitude, supposition, sympathy, theory, thinking, understanding, view, worry; SEE CONCEPT 529

thoughtful [adj1] *caring, mindful*
anxious, astute, attentive, aware, benign, canny, careful, cautious, charitable, chivalrous, circum-spect, civil, concerned, considerate, cooperative, courteous, deliberate, diplomatic, discreet, friendly, gallant, gracious, heedful, helpful, in-dulgent, kind, kindly, mindful, neighborly, oblig-ing, observant, observative, observing, polite, prudent, regardful, responsive, sensitive, social, solicitous, tactful, unselfish, wary, well-bred, well thought-out; SEE CONCEPTS 401,555

thoughtful [adj2] *contemplative, introspective*
absorbed, analytical, attentive, brainy*, calculat-ing, cerebral, cogitative, deep, deliberative, dis-cerning, earnest, engrossed, farsighted, grave, intellectual, intent, keen, levelheaded, logical, lost in thought*, meditative, melancholy, muse-ful, musing, pensive, philosophic, pondering, preoccupied, rapt, rational, reasonable, reason-ing, reflecting, reflective, retrospective, rumina-tive, serious, sober, studious, subjective, thinking, wise, wistful; SEE CONCEPTS 402,403, 542

thoughtless [adj1] *inconsiderate*
antisocial, apathetic, asocial, blind, boorish, brash, deaf, discourteous, egocentric, hasty, heedless, hot-headed, impolite, inattentive, in-cautious, indelicate, indifferent, indiscreet, in-sensitive, listless, madcap, neglectful, negligent, primitive, rash, reckless, rude, self-centered, selfish, sharp, short, tactless, uncaring, uncere-monious, unconcerned, undiplomatic, ungra-cious, unheeding, unkind, unmindful, unrefined; SEE CONCEPTS 401,555

thoughtless [adj2] *absent-minded, unobservant*
bovine, careless, confused, doltish, dull, empty-headed, flighty, foolish, heedless, ill-advised, ill-considered, imprudent, inadvertent, inane, inattentive, incomprehensible, inept, injudicious, irrational, irreflective, lamebrained*, loony*, mindless, neglectful, negligent, obtuse, puerile, rash, reckless, regardless, remiss, senseless, silly, stupid, undiscerning, unheeding, unmindful, un-reasonable, unreasoning, unreflective, unthink-ing, vacuous, witless; SEE CONCEPTS 402,403,542

thought-provoking [adj] *stimulating*
absorbing, captivating, exciting, fascinating, gripping, inspirational, interesting, intriguing, inviting, provocative, refreshing, riveting, stir-ring; SEE CONCEPTS 372,529,537,572

thrash [v] *flail about; beat*
batter, beat up, belabor, belt, birch, buffet, bury, cane, chasten, chastise, clobber, crush, defeat, flagellate, flog, jerk, kill, lambaste*, lick, maul, murder, overwhelm, paste, pelt, pitch, pound,

pummel, punish, rout, rush, scourge, seesaw, slaughter, spank, stir, strike, surge, tan, tan one's hide*, thresh, toss, toss and turn*, trash, trim, trounce, wallop, wax*, whip, work over*, writhe; SEE CONCEPTS 95,189

threadbare [adj1] worn, frayed
beat up*, damaged, dilapidated, dingy, dog-eared, down-at-the-heel*, faded, frowzy*, impaired, injured, old, ragged, ratty*, run-down, scruffy, seedy, shabby, shopworn, tacky, tattered, timeworn, used, used-up, worn-out, worse for wear*; SEE CONCEPTS 485,606

threadbare [adj2] trite, corny
banal, bathetic, cliché, clichéd, cliché-ridden, common, commonplace, conventional, dull, everyday, familiar, hackneyed, imitative, moth-eaten*, musty, overused, poor, set, stale, stereotyped, stock, tedious, tired, uncreative, well-worn, worn-out; SEE CONCEPT 267

threads [n] clothes, clothing
accouterment, apparel, attire, civvies*, costume, dress, duds*, finery, garb, garments, gear, habiliment, outfit, personal attire, rags*, raiment, Sunday best*, wardrobe, weeds*; SEE CONCEPT 451

threat [n] warning; danger
blackmail, bluff, commination, fix, foreboding, foreshadowing, fulmination, hazard, impendence, intimidation, menace, omen, peril, portent, presage, risk, thunder, writing on the wall*; SEE CONCEPTS 278,675

threaten [v1] warn, pressure
abuse, admonish, augur, blackmail, bluster, browbeat, bully, caution, comminate, cow, enforce, flex muscles*, forebode, forewarn, fulminate, growl, intimidate, look daggers*, make threat, menace, portend, presage, pressurize, push around*, scare, scowl, shake fist at*, snarl, spook, terrorize, torment, walk heavy*; SEE CONCEPTS 7,19,78

threaten [v2] endanger
advance, approach, be dangerous, be gathering, be imminent, be in the air*, be in the offing*, be on the horizon*, brewing, come on, forebode, foreshadow, frighten, hang over*, impend, imperil, jeopardize, loom, overhang, portend, presage, put at risk, put in jeopardy, warn; SEE CONCEPTS 231,407

threatening [adj] menacing, ominous
aggressive, alarming, apocalyptic, at hand, baleful, baneful, black, bullying, cautionary, close, comminatory, dangerous, dire, fateful, forthcoming, grim, ill-boding, imminent, impendent, impending, inauspicious, intimidatory, looming, loury, lowering, lowery, minacious, minatory, near, overhanging, portending, portentous, scowling, sinister, terrorizing, ugly, unlucky, unpropitious, unsafe, upcoming, warning; SEE CONCEPTS 525,548,570

threshold [n] opening; beginning
brink, dawn, door, doorstep, doorway, edge, entrance, gate, inception, origin, outset, point, point of departure, sill, start, starting point, verge, vestibule; SEE CONCEPTS 440,513,648,832

thrift [n] economy
austerity, carefulness, economizing, frugality, parsimony, providence, prudence, saving, stinginess, thriftiness; SEE CONCEPT 335

thrifty [adj] economical
canny, careful, chary, cheap, chintzy*, close*, close-fisted, conserving, frugal, mean, parsimonious, penny-pinching, preserving, provident, prudent, saving, scrimpy*, sparing, steal, stingy*, tight*, unwasteful; SEE CONCEPTS 334,401

thrill [n] sudden excitement
adventure, bang*, blast, charge*, circus, fireworks, flash*, flush*, fun, good feeling, inspiration, kicks*, lift*, pleasure, refreshment, response, sensation, stimulation, tingle*, titillation, turn-on*, twitter*, upper*, wallop*; SEE CONCEPTS 32,529

thrill [v] excite, stimulate
animate, arouse, blow away*, delight, electrify, enchant, enthuse, fire up*, flush, flutter, galvanize, glow, go over big*, grab*, inspire, juice*, key up*, knock one's socks off*, move, palpitate, quicken, quiver, race one's motor*, rally, rouse, score, send, stir, stir up, tickle*, tingle*, titillate, tremble, turn on*, wow*; SEE CONCEPTS 7,22

thrilling [adj] exciting
blood-tingling*, boss*, breathtaking, electrifying, enchanting, exquisite, fab*, fabulous, frantic, gripping, hair-raising*, large, mad, magnificent, mind-bending*, mind-blowing*, miraculous, overwhelming, rip-roaring*, riveting, rousing, sensational, shivering, stimulating, stirring, swinging, trembling, wild, wondrous, zero cool*; SEE CONCEPTS 548,572

thrive [v] do well
advance, arrive, batten, bear fruit, bloom, blossom, boom, burgeon, develop, flourish, get ahead*, get fat*, get on*, get places*, get there*, grow, grow rich, increase, make a go*, mushroom*, progress, prosper, radiate, rise, score*, shine, shoot up, succeed, turn out well, wax; SEE CONCEPTS 704,706

thriving [adj] successful
advancing, arrived, blooming, booming, burgeoning, cooking*, developing, doing well, flourishing, going strong*, growing, have it made*, have the wherewithal*, healthy, home free*, on top of heap*, progressing, prolific, prospering, prosperous, rich, roaring, robust, rolling*, sitting pretty*, wealthy; SEE CONCEPTS 334,528

throb [v] pulsate, beat
flutter, palpitate, pitpat, pound, pulse, resonate, thrill, thump, tingle, tremble, twitter, vibrate; SEE CONCEPTS 152,185

throng [n] large crowd
assemblage, assembly, bunch, collection, concourse, congregation, crush, drove, everybody, flock, gathering, horde, host, jam, mass, mob, multitude, pack, press, push, sellout, swarm; SEE CONCEPTS 417,432

throttle [v] choke
burke, control, gag, inhibit, silence, smother, stifle, strangle, strangulate, suppress; SEE CONCEPT 191

through [adj1] done
buttoned up*, complete, completed, concluded, ended, finis*, finished, in the bag*, over, terminated, wound up*, wrapped up*; SEE CONCEPTS 531,548

through [adj2] direct
constant, free, nonstop, one-way, opened, rapid, regular, straight, straightforward, unbroken, unhindered, uninterrupted; SEE CONCEPTS 482,581

th
th

through [*prep1*] *by way of*
as a consequence, as a result, at the hand of, because of, by, by dint of, by means of, by reason, by the agency of, by virtue of, for, in consequence of, in virtue of, per, through the medium of, using, via, with, with the help of; SEE CONCEPT *544*

through [*prep2*] *between, during*
about, by, clear, for the period, from beginning to end, in, in and out, in the middle, into, past, round, straight, throughout, within; SEE CONCEPTS *583,798*

throughout [*adj*] *during the whole of*
all over, all the time, all through, around, at full length, completely, during, every bit, everyplace, everywhere, far and near, far and wide, for the duration, from beginning to end, from end to end, from one end to the other, from start to finish, from the start, from the word go*, high and low, in all respects, in every place, in everything, inside and out, on all accounts*, over, overall, right through, round, the whole time, through the whole of, to the end, up and down; SEE CONCEPTS *482,531,798*

throw [*v1*] *propel something through the air*
bandy, barrage, bombard, buck, bunt, butt, cant, cast, catapult, chuck, dash, deliver, discharge, dislodge, drive, fell, fire, flick, fling, fling off, flip, floor, force, heave, hurl, impel, lapidate, launch, let fly*, let go, lift, lob, overturn, overwhelm, peg, pellet, pelt, pepper, pitch, precipitate, project, push, put, scatter, send, shove, shower, shy, sling, splatter, spray, sprinkle, start, stone, strew, thrust, toss, tumble, unhorse, unseat, upset, volley, waft; SEE CONCEPT *222*

throw [*v2*] *confuse*
addle, astonish, baffle, befuddle, bewilder, confound, disconcert, distract, disturb, dizzy, dumbfound, fluster, mix up*, throw off*, unsettle, upset; SEE CONCEPT *16*

throw away [*v1*] *dispose of*
abandon, cast, cast off, chase, clear, discard, dismiss, dispense with, ditch*, drop*, dump*, eject, eliminate, evict, extrude, free oneself of, get rid of, jettison, junk*, lose, refuse, reject, rid oneself of, scrap*, shake off*, shed, shuck, slip, throw off, throw out, turn down, unburden; SEE CONCEPT *180*

throw away [*v2*] *waste*
be wasteful, blow, consume, dissipate, fail to exploit, fritter, lose, refuse, reject, squander, trifle, turn down; SEE CONCEPT *156*

throw off [*v*] *elude, escape*
abuse, deceive, evade, get away from, give the slip*, leave behind, lose, outdistance, outrun, shake off, trick; SEE CONCEPT *102*

throw out [*v*] *comment*
bring forward, bring to light*, bring up, chime in*, come out with, declare, deliver, produce, reveal, say, state, suggest, tell, utter; SEE CONCEPT *51*

throw over [*v*] *abandon, leave*
break up with, break with, desert, discard, drop, eighty-six*, finish with, forsake, jilt*, quit, renounce, split up with, walk out on*; SEE CONCEPTS *195,384*

throw up [*v1*] *vomit, be nauseous*
be sick, bring up, disgorge, heave, puke*, regurgitate, retch, spew, spit up, upchuck*; SEE CONCEPTS *179,308*

throw up [*v2*] *build quickly*
build overnight*, jerrybuild*, knock together*, patch, put together, roughcast, roughhew, run up*, slap together*, throw together*; SEE CONCEPT *168*

thrust [*n1*] *point of communication*
burden, core, effect, gist, meaning, meat*, pith*, purport, sense, short, substance, upshot; SEE CONCEPT *682*

thrust [*n2*] *forward movement*
advance, blitz, boost, drive, impetus, impulsion, jump, lunge, momentum, onset, onslaught, poke, pressure, prod, propulsion, punch, push, shove, stab, whack, wham; SEE CONCEPTS *208,222*

thrust [*v*] *push hard*
advance, assail, assault, attack, bear down, boost, buck, butt, chuck, chunk, clip, clout, crowd, cut, dig, drive, elbow*, embed, fire, force, heave, hump, impale, impel, interject, jab, jam, jostle, lob, lunge, nick, nudge, peg, pierce, pitch, plunge, poke, pour it on*, press, prod, propel, punch, push forward, put, railroad*, ram, run, shove, sink, sling, smack, stab*, stick, toss, transfix, urge, wham*; SEE CONCEPTS *208,222*

thud/thump [*n/v*] *dull crash; dull sound*
bang, beat, blow, clonk, clout, clump, clunk, fall, flutter, hammer, hit, knock, plop, poke, pound, pounding, pulse, rap, slap, smack, strike, throb, thunk*, thwack*, wallop*, whack*; SEE CONCEPTS *65,181,189*

thug [*n*] *hoodlum*
assassin, bandit, bully, criminal, delinquent, gang member, gangster, goon*, gorilla*, gunman, hired killer, hood, hooligan, killer, mobster, murderer, professional killer, punk, rioter, rowdy, ruffian, troublemaker; SEE CONCEPT *412*

thunder [*n*] *crashing sound*
barrage, blast, boom, booming, cannonade, clap, cracking, crash, crashing, detonation, discharge, drumfire, explosion, fulmination, outburst, peal, pealing, roar, rumble, rumbling, thunderbolt, thundercrack, uproar; SEE CONCEPTS *524,595*

thunder [*v1*] *boom, crash*
blast, clamor, clap, crack, deafen, detonate, drum, explode, peal, resound, reverberate, roar, rumble, storm; SEE CONCEPTS *65,521,526*

thunder [*v2*] *yell at*
bark, bellow, curse, declaim, denounce, fulminate, gnarl, growl, rail, roar, shout, snarl, threaten, utter threat; SEE CONCEPTS *52,54*

thunderstruck [*adj*] *amazed, astonished*
agape, aghast, astounded, awestruck, bowled over*, confounded, dazed, dismayed, dumbfounded, flabbergasted, floored, overwhelmed, petrified, shocked, staggered, startled, stunned; SEE CONCEPTS *403,690*

thus [*adv1*] *in this manner*
along these lines, as follows, hence, in kind, in such a way, in this fashion, in this way, just like that, like so, like this, so, thus and so, thus and thus, thusly, to such a degree; SEE CONCEPT *544*

thus [*adv2*] *accordingly*
consequently, ergo, for this reason, hence, on that account, so, then, therefore, thereupon; SEE CONCEPT *544*

thwart [*v*] *stop, hinder*
baffle, balk, beat, bilk, check, circumvent, confuse, counter, crab*, cramp, crimp, cross, curb, dash, defeat, disappoint, ditch, dodge, double-cross*, duck, foil, foul up*, frustrate, give the

slip*, hold up, impede, louse up*, match, obstruct, oppose, outwit, pit, play off, prevent, queer*, restrain, ruin, scotch*, skin, snafu*, stymie, take down, take wind out of*, trammel, upset, upset one's apple cart*; SEE CONCEPTS 121,130

tiara [n] *crown*

chaplet, circlet, coronal, coronet, crown jewels, diadem, garland, headband, headdress, miter, royal crown, wreath; SEE CONCEPT 452

tic [n] *spasm*

contraction, fit, jerk, twitch; SEE CONCEPT 308

tick [n1] *clicking sound; one beat*

beat, blow, clack, click, clicking, flash, instant, metallic sound, minute, moment, pulsation, pulse, rap, second, shake, tap, tapping, throb, ticktock, twinkling, wink; SEE CONCEPTS 595,808,810

tick [n2] *checkmark*

check, cross, dash, flick, indication, line, mark, stroke, X*; SEE CONCEPT 284

tick [v] *click*

beat, clack, pulsate, tap, thump, ticktock; SEE CONCEPTS 65,189

ticket [n] *authorization on paper*

admission, badge, board, card, certificate, check, chit, coupon, credential, docket, document, invite, key, label, license, marker, note, notice, open sesame, paper, pass, passage, passport, password, permit, raincheck, receipt, record, slip, sticker, stub, tab, tag, token, voucher; SEE CONCEPTS 271,685

tickle [v] *make laugh*

amuse, brush, caress, convulse, delight, divert, enchant, entertain, excite, gratify, itch, pat, pet, please, stimulate, stroke, thrill, tingle, titillate, touch, vellicate; SEE CONCEPTS 7,22,612

ticklish [adj] *difficult, tricky*

awkward, capricious, chancy, changeable, critical, dangerous, delicate, fickle, inconstant, mercurial, nice, precarious, risky, rocky, sensitive, temperamental, thorny, touchy, trying, uncertain, unstable, unsteady, variable, volatile; SEE CONCEPTS 548,565

tidbit [n] *tiny portion*

bit, bite, delicacy, goody*, morsel, mouthful, snack, soupçon, titbit, treat; SEE CONCEPTS 458,835

tide [n] *flow, current*

course, direction, drag, drift, ebb, eddy, flood, flow, flux, movement, race, run, rush, sluice, spate, stream, tendency, torrent, trend, undercurrent, undertow, vortex, wave, whirlpool; SEE CONCEPT 514

tide over [v] *help along*

aid, assist, bridge the gap*, keep head above water*, keep one going, see through; SEE CONCEPT 110

tidings [n] *greetings, news*

advice, bulletin, communication, dirt, information, intelligence, message, report, word; SEE CONCEPT 274

tidy [adj1] *clean, neat*

apple-pie order*, businesslike, chipper*, cleanly, in good shape, methodical, neat as a pin*, ordered, orderly, shipshape*, sleek, snug, spick-and-span*, spruce, systematic, to rights*, trim, uncluttered, well-groomed, well-kept, well-ordered; SEE CONCEPTS 485,585,621

tidy [adj2] *considerable*

ample, fair, generous, good, goodly, handsome, healthy, large, largish, respectable, sizable, substantial, vast; SEE CONCEPTS 762,781

tidy [v] *make neat and orderly*

clean, clear the decks*, fix up, frame*, get act together*, groom, neaten, order, police, pull together, put in good shape, put in order, put in shape, put to rights*, shape up, spruce, spruce up*, straighten, straighten up, tauten, whip into shape*; SEE CONCEPT 250

tie [n1] *fastening*

attachment, band, bandage, bond, brace, connection, cord, fastener, gag, hookup, joint, knot, ligament, ligature, link, network, nexus, outfit, rope, strap, string, tackle, tie-in, tie-up, yoke, zipper; SEE CONCEPT 680

tie [n2] *deadlock*

dead heat*, draw, drawn battle*, equivalence, even game, level, photo finish*, push, stalemate, standoff; SEE CONCEPTS 364,667

tie [n3] *relationship*

affiliation, allegiance, association, bond, commitment, connection, duty, hookup, kinship, liaison, network, obligation, outfit, tie-in; SEE CONCEPT 388

tie [v1] *connect, interlace*

anchor, attach, band, bind, cinch, clinch, do up, fasten, gird, join, knot, lash, link, make a bow, make a hitch, make a knot, make fast, marry, moor, rivet, rope, secure, splice, tether, tie up, tighten, truss, unite, wed; SEE CONCEPTS 85,160,193

tie [v3] *equal*

balance, be even, be neck and neck*, be on a par, break even*, deadlock*, draw, even up, keep up with, match, measure up, meet, parallel, rival, touch; SEE CONCEPTS 92,667

tier [n] *level*

bank, category, class, course, echelon, file, grade, group, grouping, layer, league, line, order, pigeonhole*, queue, range, rank, row, series, story, stratum, string; SEE CONCEPTS 378,727,744

tie/tie up [v2] *hamper, hinder*

bind, clog, confine, curb, delay, entrammel, fetter, hog-tie*, hold, leash, limit, lock up, obstruct, restrain, restrict, shackle, stop, tie one's hands*, trammel; SEE CONCEPT 130

tiff [n] *argument*

altercation, bad mood, bickering, difference, disagreement, dispute, falling-out*, fit, huff*, miff*, pet, quarrel, row*, run-in*, scrap, spat, squabble, sulk, tantrum, temper, words*, wrangle; SEE CONCEPTS 46,674

tight [adj1] *close, snug*

bound, clasped, close-fitting, compact, constricted, contracted, cramped, crowded, dense, drawn, enduring, established, fast, firm, fixed, hidebound, inflexible, invulnerable, narrow, quick, rigid, secure, set, skintight, solid, stable, steady, stiff, strained, stretched, strong, sturdy, taut, tenacious, tense, thick, tightened, unbending, unyielding; SEE CONCEPTS 483,485

tight [adj2] *sealed*

airtight, blind, blocked, bolted, choking, clumped, cramping, crushing, cutting, fast, fastened, firm, fixed, hermetic, hermetically sealed, impenetrable, impermeable, impervious, locked, nailed, obstructed, padlocked, pinching, plugged, proof, sealed, secure, short, shrunken, shut,

skintight, slammed, smothering, snapped, sound, stopped up, tied, tied up, uncomfortable, watertight; SEE CONCEPTS *489,576*

tight [*adj3*] *stingy*
cheap, close, grasping, mean, miserly, parsimonious, penny-pinching*, penurious, sparing, tightfisted; SEE CONCEPTS *334,401*

tight [*adj4*] *difficult, troublesome*
arduous, close, critical, dangerous, distressing, disturbing, exacting, hazardous, near, perilous, precarious, punishing, rough, sticky, tense, ticklish, tough, tricky, trying, upsetting, worrisome; SEE CONCEPTS *548,565*

tight [*adj5*] *intoxicated*
boozy*, buzzed*, drunk, drunken, high*, inebriated, loaded*, pickled*, plastered*, smashed*, stewed*, stoned*, tipsy, under the influence; SEE CONCEPTS *401,406*

tighten [*v*] *constrict*
bind, clench, close, compress, condense, congeal, contract, cramp, crush, fasten, fix, grip, harden, narrow, pinch, pressure, rigidify, screw, secure, squeeze, stiffen, strain, strangle, stretch, tauten, tense, toughen; SEE CONCEPTS *250,469,697*

tightfisted [*adj*] *cheap*
chintzy*, close-fisted, economical, frugal, greedy, mean, mingy, miserly, money-conscious, parsimonious, penny-pinching, pennywise*, penurious, pinchpenny*, saving, scrimping, stingy, thrifty, tight*, tight-wad*, ungenerous; SEE CONCEPTS *326,332,334,401*

tight-lipped [*adj*] *silent*
buttoned up*, clammed up*, closemouthed, dumb, hushed, mum, mute, muted, not talkative, quiet, reserved, restrained, reticent, secretive, taciturn, tongue-tied, zipped; SEE CONCEPT *594*

tightwad [*n*] *miser*
cheapskate*, churl, hoarder, moneygrubber*, penny-pincher*, pinchfist*, pinchpenny*, Scrooge*, skinflint, stiff; SEE CONCEPTS *348,412, 423*

till [*n*] *cash box*
box, cash drawer, cash register, kitty*, money box, safe, tray, treasury, vault; SEE CONCEPT *339*

till [*v*] *cultivate land*
dig, dress, farm, grow, harrow, hoe, labor, mulch, plant, plough, plow, prepare, raise crops, sow, tend, turn, turn over, work; SEE CONCEPTS *253,257*

tilt [*n1*] *lean, slope*
angle, cant, dip, drop, fall, grade, gradient, inclination, incline, leaning, list, pitch, rake, slant, slide; SEE CONCEPT *738*

tilt [*n2*] *fight*
attack, bout, clash, collision, combat, conflict, contest, duel, encounter, fracas, joust, meet, scrimmage, scuffle, set-to, skirmish, struggle, tournament, tourney, tussle; SEE CONCEPT *106*

tilt [*v1*] *lean, slant*
bend, cant, careen, dip, heel, incline, list, lurch, pitch, rake, recline, seesaw, set at an angle, shift, slope, slouch, swag, sway, tip, turn, yaw; SEE CONCEPTS *147,149*

tilt [*v2*] *attack, fight*
break, charge, clash, combat, contend, cross swords*, duel, encounter, joust, overthrow, spar, thrust; SEE CONCEPT *106*

timber [*n*] *trees, wood*
balk, beam, board, boom, club, forest, frame, girder, grove, hardwood, log, mast, plank, pole, rafter, rib, stake, timberland, weald, woodland, wood lot, woods; SEE CONCEPTS *430,479*

time [*n1*] *temporal length of event or entity's existence, period*
age, allotment, bit, bout, chronology, clock, continuance, date, day, duration, epoch, era, eternity, extent, future, generation, go*, hour, infinity, instance, instant, interval, juncture, lastingness, life, life span, lifetime, many a moon*, moment, month, occasion, pace, past, point, present, season, second, shift, space, span, spell, stage, stint, stretch, tempo, term, tide, tour, turn, week, while, year; SEE CONCEPTS *801,806,809,819,823*

time [*n2*] *opportunity*
break, chance, heyday, look-in*, occasion, opening, peak, shot, show, squeak*; SEE CONCEPT *693*

time-honored [*adj*] *traditional*
accustomed, ancestral, classic, classical, conventional, customary, fixed, folk, historic, long-established, old, popular, regular, rooted, standard, taken for granted, universal, usual, vintage, widespread; SEE CONCEPTS *530,533,547*

timeless [*adj*] *eternal*
abiding, ageless, always, amaranthine, constant, continual, continued, dateless, deathless, endless, enduring, everlasting, forever, illimitable, immemorial, immortal, indefinite, infinite, lasting, never-ending, perennial, permanent, perpetual, persistent, undying, unending, without end; SEE CONCEPTS *482,798*

timely [*adj*] *at the right time*
appropriate, auspicious, convenient, favorable, fit, fitting, in good time*, in the nick of time*, judicious, likely, meet, modern, now, opportune, pat, promising, prompt, propitious, prosperous, punctual, seasonable, suitable, timeous, towardly, up-to-date, up-to-the-minute, well-timed, with it*; SEE CONCEPTS *558,799*

timetable [*n*] *schedule*
agenda, appointments, calendar, chart, chronology, docket, itinerary, list, order of business, plan, program, record; SEE CONCEPTS *271,283, 660*

timid [*adj*] *shy*
afraid, ambivalent, apprehensive, badgered, bashful, browbeaten, bullied, capricious, cowardly, cowed, cowering, coy, daunted, demure, diffident, fainthearted, fearful, feeble, frightened, gentle, having cold feet*, humble, intimidated, irresolute, milquetoast, modest, mousy, nervous, pusillanimous, retiring, shaky, shrinking, shy, soft, spineless, spiritless, submissive, timid, timorous, trembling, unassertive, unassured, unnerved, vacillating, wavering, weak, yellow*; SEE CONCEPT *401*

tinge [*n1*] *color*
cast, colorant, coloration, coloring, dye, dyestuff, hue, nib, pigment, shade, stain, tincture, tint, tone, wash; SEE CONCEPT *622*

tinge [*n2*] *hint*
bit, dash, drop, intimation, nib, pinch, shade, smack, smattering, soupçon, sprinkling, strain, streak, suggestion, tincture, touch, trace; SEE CONCEPTS *529,831*

tinge [*v*] *color*
complexion, dye, imbue, impregnate, infiltrate, saturate, shade, stain, streak, suffuse, tincture, tint; SEE CONCEPT *250*

tingle [v] *feel tickled, itchy*
creep, get excited, have goose bumps*, itch, prickle, shiver, sting, thrill, throb, tickle, twitter; SEE CONCEPT 612

tinker [v] *fiddle with*
dabble, doodle*, fix, mess*, mess with*, monkey*, muck about*, niggle*, play, play with, puddle, putter, repair, take apart, toy, trifle with; SEE CONCEPTS 87,212

tinkle [v] *jingle, ring*
chime, chink, chinkle, clink, ding, jangle, make bell sound, plink, sound, ting, tingle, tintinnabulate; SEE CONCEPT 65

tint [n] *shade of color*
cast, chroma, color, coloration, complexion, dash, dye, flush, glow, hint, hue, luminosity, pigmentation, rinse, stain, suggestion, taint, tinct, tincture, tinge, tone, touch, trace, wash; SEE CONCEPT 622

tint [v] *color with a certain shade*
affect, complexion, dye, influence, rinse, shade, stain, taint, tincture, tinge, touch, wash; SEE CONCEPT 250

tiny [adj] *very small*
bitsy*, bitty, diminutive, infinitesimal, insignificant, itsy-bitsy*, itty-bitty*, Lilliputian, little, microscopic, midget, mini*, miniature, minikin, minimum, minuscule, minuscule, minute, negligible, pee-wee*, petite, pint-sized*, pocket, pocket-size*, puny, slight, teensy*, teensy-weensy*, teeny, trifling, wee, yea big*; SEE CONCEPTS 762,773,789

tip/tipoff [n] *inside information*
bang*, bug*, buzz*, clue, cue, dope*, forecast, hint, in*, information, inkling, inside wire, knowledge, news, point, pointer, prediction, prompt, secret information, steer*, suggestion, two cents' worth*, warning, whisper, word, word of advice, word to the wise*; SEE CONCEPT 274

tip [n2] *very top*
apex, cap, crown, cusp, edge, end, extremity, head, nip, peak, point, stub, summit, tiptop, vertex; SEE CONCEPT 836

tip [n3] *gratuity paid*
compensation, cue, fee, gift, handout, lagniappe, money, one-way*, perk, perquisite, pourboire, reward, small change, something*, sweetener; SEE CONCEPT 344

tip [v1] *knock over; cause to lean*
bend, cant, capsize, careen, dump, empty, heel, incline, lean, list, overset, overturn, pour, recline, shift, slant, slope, spill, tilt, topple, topple over, turn over, unload, upend, upset, upturn; SEE CONCEPTS 189,201,208

tip [v2] *give eye inside information*
advise, caution, clue, cue, forewarn, give a clue, give a hint, give the low-down*, hint, prompt, steer, suggest, tip off, warn; SEE CONCEPT 60

tipsy [adj] *inebriated*
addled, dazed, drunk, drunken, fuddled, happy, high*, intoxicated, irrigated*, lit*, loaded*, mellow, merry, stewed*, tight, unsteady, woozy; SEE CONCEPTS 401,406

tirade [n] *abuse, outburst*
anger, berating, censure, condemnation, denunciation, diatribe, dispute, fulmination, harangue, invective, jeremiad*, lecture, malediction, philippic*, ranting, revilement, screed, sermon,

tongue-lashing*, vituperation; SEE CONCEPTS 44,54,278

tire [v] *exhaust, weary*
annoy, bore, burn out*, bush*, collapse, crawl, debilitate, deject, depress, disgust, dishearten, dispirit, displease, distress, drain, droop, drop, enervate, ennui, exasperate, fag, fail, faint, fatigue, flag, fold, give out, go stale, grow weary, harass, irk, irritate, jade, nauseate, overburden, overstrain, overtax, overwork, pain, pall, peter out*, poop out*, prostrate, put to sleep, sap, sicken, sink, strain, tax, vex, weaken, wear, wear down, wear out, weary, wilt, worry, yawn*; SEE CONCEPTS 13,14,469

tired [adj] *exhausted, weary*
all in*, annoyed, asleep, beat*, bored, broken-down, burned out*, collapsing, consumed, dead on one's feet*, distressed, dog-tired*, done for*, done in*, drained, drooping, droopy, drowsy, empty, enervated, exasperated, fagged, faint, fatigued, fed up*, finished, flagging, haggard, irked, irritated, jaded, narcoleptic, overtaxed, overworked, petered out*, played out*, pooped*, prostrated, run-down, sick of, sleepy, spent, stale, tuckered out*, wasted, weary, worn out; SEE CONCEPTS 314,403,406

tireless [adj] *determined*
active, ball of fire*, eager, energetic, enthusiastic, grind, hard-working*, hyper*, incessant, indefatigable, industrious, jumping, on the go*, perky, persevering, resolute, steadfast, strenuous, unflagging, untiring, unwearied, unwearying, vigorous; SEE CONCEPTS 538,542

tiresome [adj] *irritating, exasperating*
a bit much*, annoying, arduous, boresome, boring, burdensome, demanding, difficult, drag, dragging, drudging, dull, enervative, exacting, exhausting, fatiguing, flat, hard, heavy, hefty, ho-hum*, humdrum, irksome, jading, laborious, monotonous, nowhere, onerous, oppressive, strenuous, tedious, tired, tiring, too much*, tough, trying, uncool*, uninteresting, unrelieved, vexatious, wearing, wearisome, wearying, yawn*; SEE CONCEPTS 529,537,538

titanic [adj] *gigantic, very large*
Brobdingnagian*, colossal, elephantine, enormous, epic, gargantuan, giant, Herculean*, huge, immense, jumbo*, larger-than-life, mammoth, massive, monstrous, monumental, titan, towering, tremendous, vast; SEE CONCEPTS 491,773, 779,781

titillate [v] *excite, stimulate*
amuse, arouse, entertain, grab, grapple, hook, interest, palpate, provoke, switch on, tantalize, tease, thrill, tickle, tickle pink*, turn on; SEE CONCEPTS 7,11,22

title [n1] *heading, label*
appellation, banner, caption, close, description, head, headline, inscription, legend, name, rubric, salutation, sign, streamer, style, subtitle; SEE CONCEPT 283

title [n2] *name*
appellation, appellative, brand, cognomen, denomination, designation, epithet, handle*, honorific, label, moniker*, nom de plume, nomen, pseudonym, sobriquet, style, tab*, tag*, term; SEE CONCEPT 683

title [n3] *possession, laurel*
authority, championship, claim, commission, crest, crown, decoration, deed, degree, desert,

dibs*, due, entitlement, holding, justification, license, medal, merit, ownership, power, prerogative, pretense, pretension, privilege, proof, ribbon, right; SEE CONCEPTS *376,710*

title [v] *name*
baptize, call, christen, denominate, designate, dub, entitle, label, style, term; SEE CONCEPT *62*

toady [n] *sycophant*
adulator, apple polisher, ass-kisser*, backscratcher*, backslapper*, bootlicker*, brownnoser*, doormat, doter, fan, fawner, flatterer, flunky, groupie*, hanger-on*, kiss-up*, lackey, minion, teacher's pet, yes-person*; SEE CONCEPT *423*

toady [v] *fawn*
apple-polish*, be servile, bootlick*, brownnose*, butter up*, cajole, fall all over, fall on one's knees*, flatter, honey up*, kiss one's feet*, kiss-up*, kowtow*, lay it on*, lick boots*, massage*, oil*, pay court*, play up to*, scratch one's back*, stroke*, suck up to*, truckle, woo*; SEE CONCEPTS *110,384*

toast [n] *salutation when drinking alcohol*
acknowledgment, celebration, ceremony, commemoration, compliment, down, drink, health, honor, pledge, proposal, salute, sentiment, shingle, thanksgiving, tribute; SEE CONCEPT *278*

toast [v] *brown with heat*
cook, crisp, dry, grill, heat, parch, roast, warm; SEE CONCEPT *170*

toddler [n] *baby*
child, infant, kid, little one*, preschooler, rug rat*, tot, youngster; SEE CONCEPTS *414,424*

to-do [n] *commotion, excitement*
agitation, bother, brouhaha*, bustle, clamor, disorder, disturbance, flap*, furor, fuss, hassle, hooha*, hoopla*, hubbub*, hurly-burly*, hurrah, performance, pother, quarrel, racket, ruction, rumpus, stir, tumult, turmoil, unrest, uproar, whirl; SEE CONCEPTS *230,674*

together [adj] *composed*
calm, cool*, in sync*, stable, well-adjusted, well-balanced, well-organized; SEE CONCEPT *542*

together [adv1] *as a group; all at once*
all together, as one, at one fell swoop*, closely, coincidentally, collectively, combined, commonly, concertedly, concomitantly, concurrently, conjointly, contemporaneously, en masse, hand in glove*, hand in hand*, in a body, in concert, in cooperation, in one breath*, in sync*, in unison, jointly, mutually, on the beat*, side by side, simultaneously, synchronically, unanimously, unitedly, with one accord, with one voice, with the beat; SEE CONCEPTS *538,544,548*

together [adv2] *in a row*
consecutively, continually, continuously, in succession, night and day, one after the other, on end, running, successively, unintermittedly, without a break, without interruption; SEE CONCEPTS *482,585*

toil [n] *hard work*
application, drudgery, effort, exertion, industry, labor, moil, nine-to-five*, occupation, pains*, sweat, travail; SEE CONCEPTS *100,362,677*

toil [v] *work hard*
drive, drudge, grind, knock oneself out*, labor, moil, peg away*, plod, plug, push oneself, slave, strain, strive, struggle, sweat, tug, work, work like a dog*; SEE CONCEPTS *100,677*

toilsome [adj] *laborious*
arduous, backbreaking, burdensome, demanding, difficult, exhausting, hard, labored, onerous, operose, rough, strenuous, taxing, tiresome, uphill*; SEE CONCEPT *538*

token [n] *indication, remembrance*
badge, clue, demonstration, earnest, evidence, expression, favor, gift, index, indicia, keepsake, manifestation, mark, memento, memorial, note, omen, pawn, pledge, presage, proof, relic, reminder, representation, sample, security, sign, significant, souvenir, symbol, symptom, trophy, warning, warrant; SEE CONCEPTS *284,337,529*

tolerable [adj] *acceptable, good enough*
adequate, allowable, all right, average, bearable, better than nothing*, common, decent, endurable, fair, fairly good, fair to middling*, goodish*, indifferent, livable, mediocre, middling*, not bad*, okay*, ordinary, passable, presentable, respectable, run-of-the-mill*, satisfactory, so-so*, sufferable, sufficient, supportable, sustainable, tidy, unexceptionable, unexceptional, unimpeachable; SEE CONCEPTS *529,548*

tolerance [n1] *open-mindedness*
altruism, benevolence, broad-mindedness, charity, clemency, compassion, concession, endurance, forbearance, freedom, good will, grace, humanity, indulgence, kindness, lenience, leniency, lenity, liberalism, liberality, liberalness, license, magnanimity, mercifulness, mercy, patience, permission, permissiveness, sensitivity, sufferance, sympathy, toleration, understanding; SEE CONCEPTS *410,657*

tolerance [n2] *fortitude, grit*
endurance, guts*, hardiness, hardness, opposition, patience, resilience, resistance, stamina, staying power*, steadfastness, steadiness, strength, sufferance, toughness, vigor; SEE CONCEPT *732*

tolerant [adj] *open-minded, easygoing*
advanced, benevolent, big, broad, broad-minded, catholic, charitable, clement, complaisant, condoning, easy on, easy with, excusing, fair, forbearing, forgiving, free and easy*, humane, indulgent, kindhearted*, lax, lenient, liberal, long-suffering*, magnanimous, merciful, patient, permissive, progressive, radical, receptive, soft, sophisticated, sympathetic, understanding, unprejudiced, wide; SEE CONCEPTS *403,542*

tolerate [v] *allow, indulge*
abide, accept, admit, authorize, bear, bear with, blink at*, brook, condone, consent to, countenance, endure, go, go along with, have, hear, humor, live with, permit, pocket, put up with, receive, sanction, sit and take it*, sit still for*, stand, stand for, stay the course*, stomach*, string along, submit to, suffer, sustain, swallow*, take, tough out*, undergo, wink at*; SEE CONCEPTS *23,83*

toll [n1] *fee*
assessment, charge, cost, customs, demand, duty, exaction, expense, impost, levy, payment, price, rate, tariff, tax, tribute; SEE CONCEPT *329*

toll [n2] *damage, deaths*
casualties, cost, expense, inroad, loss, losses, penalty, price; SEE CONCEPT *230*

toll [v] *ring out*
announce, bell, bong, call, chime, clang, knell, peal, signal, sound, strike, summon, warn; SEE CONCEPT *65*

tomb [*n*] *burial place*
box, burial, burial chamber, catacomb, coffin, crypt, grave, mausoleum, monument, pit, sepulcher, trough, vault; SEE CONCEPT *305*

tome [*n*] *large, scholarly book*
classic, great work, magnum opus, novel, opus, publication, reference book, schoolbook, textbook, title, tradebook, volume, work, writing; SEE CONCEPT *280*

tomfoolery [*n*] *nonsense*
absurdity, antics, bunk, carrying-on*, clowning, craziness, folly, foolery, fooling around, foolishness, fun, funny business, giddiness, high jinks, horseplay, insanity, irresponsibility, joking, kidding around, ludicrousness, lunacy, madness, ridiculousness, senselessness, shenanigans*, silliness; SEE CONCEPTS *230,388,633*

tone [*n1*] *pitch, volume*
accent, emphasis, force, inflection, intonation, modulation, resonance, strength, stress, timbre, tonality; SEE CONCEPT *65*

tone [*n2*] *attitude, spirit*
air, approach, aspect, character, condition, current, drift, effect, expression, fashion, feel, frame, grain, habit, humor, manner, mind, mode, mood, movement, nature, note, quality, state of things, strain, style, temper, tenor, trend, vein; SEE CONCEPTS *655,673,682*

tone [*n3*] *color*
blend, cast, coloration, hue, shade, tinge, tint, value; SEE CONCEPT *622*

tone [*n4*] *condition of the body*
elasticity, health, healthiness, resiliency, strength, tonicity, tonus, vigor; SEE CONCEPT *316*

tone down [*v*] *moderate*
chill out*, cloud, dampen, darken, deepen, dim, mitigate, modulate, play down, reduce, restrain, shade, sober, soften, soft-pedal*, subdue, temper; SEE CONCEPT *240*

tongue [*n*] *language*
argot, articulation, dialect, discourse, expression, idiom, language, lingo, parlance, patois, speech, talk, utterance, vernacular, voice; SEE CONCEPT *276*

tongue-in-cheek [*adj*] *facetious*
amusing, blithe, clever, comic, comical, dry, farcical, flip*, flippant, funny, humorous, in fun, in jest, ironic, ironical, irreverent, jesting, jocular, joking, joshing, laughable, not serious, playful, pulling one's leg*, putting one on*, sarcastic, satirical, smart, whimsical, wisecracking, witty; SEE CONCEPT *267*

tongue-tied [*adj*] *speechless*
aghast, amazed, astounded, at a loss for words, bashful, choked up, dazed, dumbfounded, dumbstruck, inarticulate, mum, mute, shocked, shy, silent, stammering, uncommunicative, voiceless; SEE CONCEPT *267*

tonic [*n*] *restorative drink, medicine*
analeptic, boost, bracer, conditioner, cordial, drug, fillip, invigorator, livener, pick-me-up*, pickup, refresher, restorative, roborant, shot in the arm*, stimulant, strengthener; SEE CONCEPT *307*

too [*adv1*] *also*
additionally, along, as well, besides, further, furthermore, in addition, into the bargain, likewise, more, moreover, to boot, withal; SEE CONCEPTS *544,771*

too [*adv2*] *excessively*
awfully, beyond, ever, exceptionally, exorbitantly, extremely, greatly, highly, immensely, immoderately, in excess, inordinately, notably, over, over and above, overly, overmuch, remarkably, strikingly, unconscionably, unduly, unreasonably, very; SEE CONCEPTS *569,772*

tool [*n1*] *instrument used to shape, form, finish*
apparatus, appliance, contraption, contrivance, device, engine, gadget, gizmo*, implement, job, machine, means, mechanism, utensil, weapon, whatchamacallit*; SEE CONCEPT *499*

tool [*n2*] *person who allows himself to be used*
accessory, accomplice, agent, auxiliary, chump*, creature, dupe, easy mark*, figurehead, flunky*, go-between, greenhorn*, hireling, idiot, intermediary, jackal, lackey, mark*, medium, messenger, minion, patsy*, pawn, peon, puppet, stooge, stool pigeon*, sucker*; SEE CONCEPTS *348,412,423*

toothsome [*adj*] *delicious*
adorable, ambrosial, appetizing, delectable, delightful, divine, flavorful, good, heavenly, luscious, lush, mouthwatering, nectarous, nice, palatable, pleasant, pleasing, rich, savory, scrumptious, sweet, tasteful, tasty, titillating, yummy*; SEE CONCEPTS *572,613*

top [*adj*] *best, most important; highest*
apical, capital, chief, crack, crowning, culminating, dominant, elite, excellent, fine, finest, first, first-class, first-rate, five-star*, foremost, greatest, head, lead, leading, loftiest, maximal, maximum, outside, paramount, preeminent, primary, prime, principal, ruling, sovereign, superior, supreme, tiptop*, top-drawer*, topmost, topnotch, upper, uppermost; SEE CONCEPTS *567,574,583*

top [*n1*] *highest point*
acme, apex, apogee, cap, capital, ceiling, climax, cork, cover, crest, crown, culmination, cusp, face, fastigium, finial, head, height, high point, lid, limit, maximum, meridian, peak, pinnacle, point, roof, spire, stopper, summit, superficies, surface, tip, utmost, vertex, zenith; SEE CONCEPT *836*

top [*n2*] *highest rank*
best, captain, chief, choice, cream, elite, first place, flower, head, lead, leader, pick, pride, prime, prize, utmost; SEE CONCEPT *668*

top [*v1*] *place on or reach highest part*
ascend, cap, climb, cloak, clothe, cover, crest, crown, face, finish, garnish, piggyback*, protect, reinforce, roof, scale, spread over, superimpose, surmount, tip; SEE CONCEPTS *172,201,750*

top [*v2*] *surpass*
bash, beat, be first, best, better, blow away*, clobber*, eclipse, exceed, excel, fake out*, finagle*, fox*, go beyond, goose*, outdo, outfox, outshine, outstrip, overrun, run circles around*, shut out*, total*, transcend; SEE CONCEPTS *95,141*

top [*v3*] *remove the upper part*
amputate, cream, crop, curtail, cut off, decapitate, detruncate, dock, file off, lop off, pare, pollard, prune, ream, scrape off, shave off, shear, shorten, skim, trim, truncate; SEE CONCEPT *211*

topic [*n*] *subject matter*
affair, argument, business, case, division, field, head, issue, material, matter, matter in hand, moot point, motif, motion, motive, point, point in

ti
to

question, problem, proposition, question, resolution, subject, text, theme, theorem, thesis; SEE CONCEPT 532

topical [*adj1*] *current*
contemporary, modern, newsworthy, nominal, popular, subjective, thematic, up-to-date; SEE CONCEPT 820

topical [*adj2*] *restricted, local*
confined, insular, limited, parochial, particular, regional, sectional; SEE CONCEPTS 557,583

top-level [*adj*] *high-ranking, important*
aristocratic, distinguished, esteemed, famous, first-class*, foremost, four-star*, front-page*, grand, high-level, high-profile, high-up, honored, illustrious, leading, majestic, major-league*, noble, notable, noted, noteworthy, powerful, preeminent, prominent, top-drawer*, top-notch*, upper-class, VIP*, well-known; SEE CONCEPTS 555,574

top-notch [*adj*] *first-rate*
A-1, ace, blue-chip*, choice, excellent, fine, first-class, first-string*, five-star, highest quality, in a class all by itself*, prime*, sound, superior, supreme, tiptop*, top-level, uppermost, very best, very good; SEE CONCEPT 574

topple [*v*] *fall or knock over; overthrow*
bring down, capsize, collapse, do a pratfall*, fall, falter, founder, go belly up*, go down, hit the dirt*, keel over, knock down, land, lose it*, lurch, nose-dive, oust, overbalance, overturn, pitch, plunge, slump, stagger, stumble, take a header*, teeter, tip over, totter, tumble, turn over, unhorse, unseat, upset; SEE CONCEPTS 95,147,181,208

topsy-turvy [*adj*] *mixed-up*
chaotic, cluttered, cockeyed, confused, disarranged, disheveled, disjointed, dislocated, disordered, disorderly, disorganized, downside-up*, inside-out, inverted, jumbled, littered, messy, muddled, overturned, pell-mell*, riotous, tangled, tumultuous/tumultuous, unhinged, untidy, upended, upside-down, upturned; SEE CONCEPTS 485,548,585

torment [*n*] *severe mental distress*
affliction, agony, anguish, annoyance, bane, bother, excruciation, harassment, hell, irritation, misery, nag, nagging, nuisance, pain, pain in the neck*, persecution, pest, plague, provocation, rack, scourge, suffering, torture, trouble, vexation, worry; SEE CONCEPTS 410,728

torment [*v*] *be or make very upset*
abuse, afflict, agonize, annoy, bait, bedevil, bone, bother, break, crucify, devil, distress, drive bananas*, drive up the wall*, excruciate, give a hard time*, harass, harrow, harry, heckle, hound, hurt, irritate, mistreat, molest, nag, pain, persecute, pester, plague, play cat and mouse*, provoke, punish, put through wringer*, rack, rub salt in wound*, smite, tease, torture, trouble, try, vex, worry, wring; SEE CONCEPTS 7,19,313

torn [*adj1*] *cut open*
broken, burst, cleaved, cracked, damaged, divided, fractured, gashed, impaired, lacerated, mangled, ragged, rent, ripped, ruptured, severed, shabby, slashed, sliced, slit, snapped, split, wrenched; SEE CONCEPT 485

torn [*adj2*] *undecided*
divided, irresolute, of two minds*, split, uncertain, unsure, vacillating, wavering; SEE CONCEPTS 403,542

torpid [*adj*] *lazy, slow*
apathetic, benumbed, comatose, dopey*, dormant, drowsy, dull, faineant, heavy, hebetudinous, idle, inactive, indifferent, indolent, inert, lackadaisical, languid, languorous, latent, leaden, lethargic, listless, lymphatic, motionless, numb, paralyzed, passive, slothful, slow-moving, sluggish, slumberous, sodden, somnolent, stagnant, static, stupid, stuporous; SEE CONCEPTS 401,538

torpor [*n*] *lethargy*
apathy, disinterest, dormancy, drowsiness, dullness, idleness, impassivity, inaction, inactivity, languor, laziness, lifelessness, listlessness, passiveness, sleepiness, sloth, slowness, sluggishness, slumber, stupor, torpidity; SEE CONCEPTS 315,410,633,748

torrent [*n*] *heavy flow*
cascade, cataclysm, cataract, cloudburst, deluge, downpour, effusion, flood, flooding, flux, gush, inundation, niagara, outburst, overflow, pour, rush, shower, spate, stream, tide, waterfall; SEE CONCEPTS 146,179,526

torrid [*adj1*] *very hot*
arid, austral, blazing, blistering, boiling, broiling, burning, dried, dry, fiery, heated, parched, parching, red-hot*, scalding, scorched, scorching, sizzling, stifling, sultry, sweltering, tropic, tropical; SEE CONCEPT 605

torrid [*adj2*] *sensuous*
ardent, blazing, burning, erotic, fervent, flaming, hot*, hot-blooded*, impassioned, intense, passionate, red-hot*, sexy, steamy*, sultry, whitehot*; SEE CONCEPT 372

tortuous [*adj1*] *very twisted*
anfractuous, bent, circuitous, convoluted, crooked, curved, flexuous, indirect, involute, labyrinthine, mazy, meandering, meandrous, roundabout, serpentine, sinuous, snaky, twisting, vermiculate, winding, zigzag; SEE CONCEPT 581

tortuous [*adj2*] *complicated*
ambiguous, convoluted, cunning, deceptive, devious, indirect, involute, involved, misleading, perverse, roundabout, tricky; SEE CONCEPT 562

torture [*n*] *severe mental or physical pain*
ache, affliction, agony, anguish, cruciation, crucifixion, distress, dolor, excruciation, impalement, laceration, martyrdom, misery, pang, persecution, rack, suffering, third degree*, torment, tribulation, twinge; SEE CONCEPTS 410,728

torture [*v*] *upset or hurt severely*
abuse, afflict, agonize, annoy, beat, bother, crucify, distress, disturb, excruciate, grill, harrow, impale, injure, irritate, lacerate, maim, mangle, martyr, martyrize, mistreat, mutilate, oppress, pain, persecute, rack, smite, torment, try, whip, wound, wring, wrong; SEE CONCEPTS 7,19,246,313

toss [*n/v1*] *throw*
bung, cast, chuck, chunk, fire, fling, flip, heave, hurl, launch, lob, peg, pitch, project, propel, sling, twirl, wing; SEE CONCEPT 222

toss [*v2*] *move back and forth*
agitate, agonize, bob, buffet, disturb, flounder, heave, jiggle, joggle, jolt, labor, lurch, move restlessly, oscillate, pitch, rise and fall, rock, roll, seesaw, shake, squirm, stir, sway, swing, thrash, tumble, undulate, wallow, wave, wobble, wriggle, writhe; SEE CONCEPT 147

total [*adj*] *complete, thorough*
absolute, all-out, comprehensive, consummate,

downright, entire, every, full, full-blown, full-scale, gross, inclusive, integral, out-and-out, outright, overall, perfect, plenary, positive, sheer, sweeping, thoroughgoing, totalitarian, unconditional, undisputed, undivided, unlimited, unmitigated, unqualified, unreserved, unrestricted, utter, whole; SEE CONCEPTS *531,762*

total [*n*] *whole*
aggregate, all, amount, body, budget, bulk, entirety, flat out*, full amount, gross, jackpot*, mass, quantity, quantum, result, sum, sum total*, tale, the works*, totality; SEE CONCEPTS *787,837*

total [*v*] *add up*
add, aggregate, amount to, calculate, cast, come, come to, comprise, consist of, equal, figure, foot, mount up to, number, pile up, reach, reckon, result in, ring up*, run into, run to, stack up, summate, sum up, totalize, tote*, yield; SEE CONCEPT *764*

totalitarian [*adj*] *dictatorial*
absolute, authoritarian, autocratic, communist*, despotic, fascistic, monolithic, Nazi*, one-party, oppressive, total, totalistic, tyrannical, undemocratic; SEE CONCEPT *536*

totally [*adv*] *completely*
absolutely, all, all in all, altogether, comprehensively, consummately, entirely, exactly, exclusively, flat out*, full blast*, fully, in toto*, just, perfectly, quite, thoroughly, top to bottom*, unconditionally, unmitigatedly, utterly, wholeheartedly, wholly; SEE CONCEPT *531*

totter [*v*] *move falteringly*
blunder, careen, dodder, falter, flounder, hesitate, lurch, quake, quiver, reel, rock, roll, seesaw, shake, shimmy, slide, slip, stagger, stammer, stumble, sway, teeter, topple, tremble, trip, walk unsteadily, waver, weave, wheel, wobble, zigzag; SEE CONCEPT *151*

touch [*n1*] *physical contact*
blow, brush, caress, collision, communication, contact, contingence, crash, cuddling, embrace, feel, feeling, fondling, graze, grope, handling, hit, hug, impact, junction, kiss, lick, manipulation, nudge, palpation, pat, peck, perception, percussion, petting, push, rub, rubbing, scratch, shock, stroke, stroking, tactility, taction, tap, taste, touching; SEE CONCEPTS *590,608,612*

touch [*n2*] *tiny amount*
bit, dash, detail, drop, hint, inkling, intimation, jot, pinch, scent, shade, smack, small amount, smattering, soupçon, speck, spot, streak, suggestion, suspicion, taste, tincture, tinge, trace, whiff; SEE CONCEPTS *529,831,832*

touch [*n3*] *manner, method*
ability, acquaintance, adeptness, adroitness, approach, art, artistry, awareness, characteristic, command, communication, contact, deftness, direction, effect, facility, faculty, familiarity, finish, flair, hand, handiwork, influence, knack, mastery, skill, style, talent, technique, trademark, understanding, virtuosity, way; SEE CONCEPTS *6,630,655*

touch [*v1*] *make physical contact*
abut, adjoin, be in contact, border, brush, butt on, caress, come together, communicate, contact, converge, dab, examine, feel, feel up*, finger, fondle, frisk, glance, graze, grope, handle, hit, impinge upon, inspect, join, kiss, lay a finger on*, lick, line, manipulate, march, massage, meet, neighbor, osculate, palm, palpate, partake,

pat, paw, percuss, pet, probe, push, reach, rub, scrutinize, sip, smooth, strike, stroke, suck, sweep, tag, tap, taste, thumb, tickle, tip, toy, verge; SEE CONCEPT *612*

touch [*v2*] *have an effect on*
affect, arouse, carry, disturb, excite, feel out, get through to*, get to*, grab, impress, influence, inspire, make an impression*, mark, melt, move, quicken, soften, stimulate, stir, strike, strike a chord*, stroke, sway, tug at the heart*, upset; SEE CONCEPTS *7,19,22*

touch [*v3*] *have to do with; regard*
affect, be a party to, bear on, bear upon, be associated with, belong to, center upon, concern, concern oneself with, consume, deal with, drink, eat, get involved in, handle, have to do with, interest, involve, partake of, pertain to, refer to, use, utilize; SEE CONCEPT *532*

touch [*v4*] *make mention*
allude to, bring in, cover, deal with, discuss, go over, mention, note, refer to, speak of, treat; SEE CONCEPT *51*

touch [*v5*] *compare with; correspond to*
amount, approach, be a match for*, be in the same league*, come to a par*, come near, come to, come up to, equal, hold a candle to*, match, measure up, meet, parallel, partake of, rival, tie, verge on; SEE CONCEPT *561*

touched [*adj1*] *deeply moved emotionally*
affected, disturbed, grabbed*, impressed, melted*, softened, stirred, swayed, turned on by*, turned on to*, upset; SEE CONCEPTS *403,542*

touched [*adj2*] *crazy*
batty*, bizarre, bonkers*, cuckoo*, daft, eccentric, fanatic, flighty, insane, neurotic, not all there*, not right*, nuts*, nutty*, obsessed, out of one's mind*, peculiar, pixilated, queer, unhinged; SEE CONCEPTS *402,403*

touching [*adj*] *affecting, moving emotionally*
compassionate, emotive, heartbreaking, heart-rending, impressive, melting, mind-blowing*, pathetic, piteous, pitiable, pitiful, poignant, responsive, sad, stirring, stunning, sympathetic, tear-jerking, tender, wistful; SEE CONCEPTS *529,537*

touch up [*v*] *fix up; improve*
amend, brush up, do up, enhance, finish off, give a face-lift*, gloss, make improvements, modify, patch up, perfect, polish, put finishing touches on*, remodel, renew, renovate, repair, retouch, revamp, rework, round off, tease*; SEE CONCEPTS *212,244*

touchy [*adj*] *easily offended*
bad-tempered, bundle of nerves*, cantankerous, captious, choleric, crabbed, cranky, cross, delicate, dicey*, grouchy, grumpy, hazardous, hypersensitive, irascible, irritable, jumpy*, mean, ornery*, oversensitive, peevish, perturbable, pettish, petulant, precarious, querulous, quick-tempered, risky, sensitive, splenetic, surly, temperamental, testy, thin-skinned*, ticklish*, tricky, unpredictable, unsafe, uptight*, volatile, wired up*, wound up*; SEE CONCEPTS *401,542,548*

tough [*adj1*] *sturdy, strong*
brawny, cohesive, conditioned, dense, durable, fibrous, fit, flinty, hard, hard as nails*, hard-bitten*, hardened, hardy, healthy, indigestible, inflexible, leathery, lusty, mighty, molded, resilient, resistant, rigid, robust, rugged, seasoned,

to
to

sinewy, solid, stalwart, steeled, stiff, stout, strapping, tenacious, tight, tough as nails*, unbreakable, unyielding, vigorous, withstanding; SEE CONCEPTS 314,489

tough [adj2] obstinate, rough
adamant, arbitrary, callous, confirmed, cruel, desperate, drastic, exacting, ferocious, fierce, firm, fixed, hard, hard-bitten*, hard-boiled*, hard-line*, hard-nosed*, hard-shelled*, harsh, headstrong, immutable, inflexible, intractable, merciless, narrow, obdurate, pugnacious, refractory, resolute, ruffianly, ruthless, savage, severe, stern, stiff, strict, stubborn, taut, terrible, unalterable, unbending, uncompromising, uncontrollable, unforgiving, unmanageable, unyielding, vicious, violent; SEE CONCEPTS 403,542

tough [adj3] difficult, laborious
arduous, backbreaking*, baffling, burdensome, demanding, effortful, exacting, exhausting, exigent, grievous, hairy*, handful*, hard, heavy, intractable, intricate, irksome, knotty*, labored, mean, no piece of cake*, onerous, oppressive, perplexing, puzzling, resisting, severe, stiff, strenuous, taxing, thorny, toilsome, troublesome, trying, unyielding, uphill*, weighty*, wicked; SEE CONCEPTS 538,565

tough [n] person who is rowdy, mean
bruiser, brute, bully, criminal, gangster, goon*, hood*, hoodlum, hooligan, punk*, rough*, roughneck, rowdy, ruffian, thug, villain; SEE CONCEPT 412

toughen [v] harden
acclimate, acclimatize, anneal, brutalize, climatize, develop, inure, make difficult, season, strengthen, temper; SEE CONCEPTS 202,250

toupee [n] wig
false hair, hair extension, hair implant, hairpiece, hair weaving, periwig, peruke, postiche, rug*; SEE CONCEPT 392

tour [n] journey; stint
bout*, circle tour*, circuit, course, cruise, excursion, expedition, getaway*, go*, hitch*, hop*, jaunt*, junket, outing, overnight*, peregrination, progress, road, round*, roundabout*, round trip, run, shift, spell, stretch, stump*, swing*, time, travel, trek, trick*, trip, turn, voyage, weekend, whistle-stop*; SEE CONCEPTS 81,224,807

tour [v] visit, journey
barnstorm*, cruise, explore, globe-trot*, go on the road*, holiday*, hop*, jaunt, jet, junket, peregrinate, sightsee, stump*, swing*, take a trip, travel, vacation, voyage; SEE CONCEPTS 224,227

tour de force [n] great achievement
accomplishment, attainment, conquest, deed, exploit, masterpiece, performance, stroke of genius, success, triumph, victory; SEE CONCEPTS 1,706

tourist [n] person who visits a place
day-tripper, excursionist, globetrotter, jet-setter, journeyer, rubberneck*, sightseer, stranger, traveler, tripper*, vacationist, visitor, voyager, wayfarer; SEE CONCEPT 423

tournament [n] sporting competition
clash, contest, duel, event, fight, games, joust, match, meet, meeting, series, sport, test, tilt, tourney; SEE CONCEPT 363

tousled [adj] disarrayed
beat-up*, dirty, disarranged, disheveled, disordered, grubby*, messed-up*, messy, mussed-up*, ruffled, rumpled, sloppy, tangled, uncombed, unkempt; SEE CONCEPTS 485,589

tout [v] brag about, show off
acclaim, ballyhoo*, boost, give a boost*, herald, laud, plug*, praise, proclaim, promote, publicize, push, steer, tip, tip off*, trumpet; SEE CONCEPTS 69,138

tow [v] pull along
drag, draw, ferry, haul, lug, propel, push, trail, trawl, tug, yank; SEE CONCEPT 206

toward/towards [prep1] on the way to; near
against, almost, approaching, close to, coming up, contra, en route, facing, for, fronting, headed for, in relation to, in the direction of, in the vicinity, just before, moving, nearing, nearly, not quite, on the road to, over against, pointing to, proceeding, shortly before, to, via, vis-a'-vis; SEE CONCEPT 586

toward/towards [prep2] concerning
about, against, anent, apropos, as for, as to, for, in re, re, regarding, with regard to, with respect to; SEE CONCEPT 532

tower [n] very high building or building part
belfry, castle, citadel, cloud buster*, column, fort, fortification, fortress, high rise*, keep, lookout, mast, minaret, monolith, obelisk, pillar, refuge, skyscraper, spire, steeple, stronghold, turret; SEE CONCEPTS 439,440

tower [v] rise above
ascend, be above, dominate, exceed, extend above, look down, look over, loom, mount, overlook, overtop, rear, soar, surmount, surpass, top, transcend; SEE CONCEPTS 141,752

towering [adj] huge, excessive
aerial, airy, colossal, elevated, extraordinary, extravagant, extreme, fantastic, gigantic, great, high, immoderate, imperial, imposing, impressive, inordinate, intense, lofty, magnificent, massive, mighty, monumental, outstanding, paramount, preeminent, prodigious, skyscraping, soaring, spiring, stately, stupendous, sublime, superior, supreme, surpassing, tall, towery, transcendent, tremendous, ultimate, undue, unmatchable, unmeasurable; SEE CONCEPTS 567,779

town [n] incorporated community
apple*, boondocks, borough, burg*, city, hamlet, metropolis, municipality, seat, sticks*, township, whistle-stop*; SEE CONCEPTS 507,508

toxic [adj] poisonous
baneful, deadly, harmful, lethal, mephitic, noxious, pernicious, pestilential, poison, septic, toxicant, venomous, virulent; SEE CONCEPT 537

toxin [n] poison
blight, cancer, contagion, contamination, germ, infection, noxious substance, poisonous substance, toxicant, toxoid, venom, virus; SEE CONCEPTS 307,475,674,675

toy [n] entertainment article
bauble, curio, doll, game, knickknack, novelty, plaything, trifle, trinket; SEE CONCEPT 446

toy [v] play with
amuse oneself, coquet, cosset, dally, dandle, fiddle, flirt, fool, fool around*, jest, lead on, mess around*, pet, play, play around, play games, sport, string along*, tease, trifle, wanton; SEE CONCEPT 384

trace [n] evidence; small bit
breath, crumb, dab, dash, drop, element, footmark, footprint, fragment, hint, indication, inti-

mation, iota, jot, mark, memento, minimum, nib, nuance, particle, pinch, proof, record, relic, remains, remnant, scintilla, shade, shadow, shred, sign, slot, smell, smidgen, snippet, soupçon, speck, spoor, spot, sprinkling, strain, streak, suggestion, survival, suspicion, taste, tincture, tinge, tittle, token, touch, track, trail, tread, trifle, vestige, whiff, whisper; SEE CONCEPTS 529,831

trace [v1] *seek, follow*
ascertain, detect, determine, discern, discover, ferret out, find, hunt, perceive, pursue, run down, search for, shadow, smell out, spoor, spot, stalk, track, trail, unearth; SEE CONCEPTS 207,216

trace [v2] *draw around*
chart, copy, delineate, depict, duplicate, map, mark out, outline, record, reproduce, show, sketch; SEE CONCEPTS 79,174

track [n1] *mark, print made by something*
clue, footmark, footprint, footstep, groove, impress, impression, imprint, indication, memorial, monument, path, print, record, remains, remnant, rut, scent, sign, slot, spoor, step, symbol, token, trace, track, trail, tread, vestige, wake; SEE CONCEPTS 513,628

track [n2] *path, way*
alley, artery, avenue, beaten path*, boulevard, clearing, course, cut*, drag*, footpath, highway, lane, line, orbit, passage, pathway, rail, rails, road, roadway, route, street, thoroughfare, track, trackway, trail, trajectory, walk; SEE CONCEPT 501

track/track down [v] *follow, pursue*
apprehend, beat the bushes*, be hot on the trail*, bird-dog*, bring to light*, capture, catch, chase, cover, dig up, discover, do, dog*, dog footsteps of*, draw an inference, expose, ferret out, find, go after, hunt, piece together, put together, run down, scout, shadow, smell out*, sniff out*, stalk, stick to, tail, trace, trail, travel, traverse, unearth; SEE CONCEPTS 183,207,216

tract [n] *area, lot*
amplitude, belt, district, estate, expanse, extent, field, parcel, part, piece, plat, plot, portion, quarter, region, section, sector, spread, stretch, zone; SEE CONCEPTS 508,513

tractable [adj] *manageable*
acquiescent, amenable, biddable, complaisant, compliant, controllable, docile, ductile, facile, flexible, game, going along with*, governable, hanging loose*, malleable, meek, obedient, persuadable, plastic, pliable, pliant, putty in hands*, rolling with punches*, subdued, submissive, tame, tractile, willing, workable, yielding; SEE CONCEPTS 401,488,542

traction [n] *physical resistance, friction*
absorption, adherence, adhesion, constriction, contraction, drag, draught, drawing, grip, haulage, pull, pulling, purchase, resorption, strain, stress, stretch, suck, suction, towage; SEE CONCEPTS 731,748

trade [n1] *buying and selling*
barter, business, clientele, commerce, contract, custom, customers, deal, dealing, enterprise, exchange, industry, interchange, market, merchantry, patronage, public, sales, swap, traffic, transaction, truck; SEE CONCEPTS 324,327,330, 345

trade [n2] *profession, work*
art, avocation, business, calling, craft, employment, game, handicraft, job, line, line of work,

métier, nine-to-five*, occupation, position, pursuit, skill, thing*, vocation; SEE CONCEPTS 349,360

trademark [n] *logo, symbol*
brand, brand name, identification, initials, label, logo, logotype, mark, stamp, tag; SEE CONCEPTS 259,284

tradition [n] *established practice*
attitude, belief, birthright, conclusion, convention, culture, custom, customs, ethic, ethics, fable, folklore, form, habit, heritage, idea, inheritance, institution, law, legend, lore, mores, myth, mythology, mythos, opinion, practice, praxis, ritual, unwritten law, usage, wisdom; SEE CONCEPT 688

traditional [adj] *usual, established*
acceptable, accustomed, acknowledged, ancestral, classic, classical, common, conventional, customary, doctrinal, fixed, folk, habitual, historic, immemorial, long-established, old, oral, popular, prescribed, regular, rooted, sanctioned, taken for granted, time-honored, transmitted, universal, unwritten, widely used, widespread; SEE CONCEPTS 530,533

traffic [n1] *coming and going*
cartage, flux, freight, gridlock, influx, jam, movement, parking lot*, passage, passengers, rush hour, service, shipment, transfer, transit, transport, transportation, travel, truckage, vehicles; SEE CONCEPTS 224,505,770

traffic [n2] *buying and selling*
barter, business, closeness, commerce, communication, communion, connection, custom, dealing, dealings*, doings*, exchange, familiarity, industry, interchange, intercourse, intimacy, merchantry, patronage, peddling, relations, relationship, soliciting, trade, transactions, truck*; SEE CONCEPTS 330,335

traffic [v] *buy and sell; do business*
bargain, barter, black-market*, bootleg*, connect with, contact, deal, deal in*, dicker, exchange, fence, handle, have dealings, have transaction, horse trade*, interact, interface, make a deal, market, moonshine*, negotiate, network, peddle, push, reach out, relate, shove, swap, touch, touch base*, trade, truck*, work out; SEE CONCEPTS 324,327,330,345

tragedy [n] *disaster*
adversity, affliction, bad fortune, bad luck, blight, blow, calamity, cataclysm, catastrophe, contretemps, curse, curtains*, dole, dolor, doom, downer*, failure, hard knocks*, hardship, humiliation, lot, misadventure, mischance, misfortune, mishap, reverse, shock, struggle, the worst*, unluckiness, waterloo*, woe, wreck; SEE CONCEPTS 674,675

tragic [adj] *catastrophic, very bad*
adverse, anguished, appalling, awful, calamitous, cataclysmic, crushing, deadly, deathly, deplorable, desolate, destructive, dire, disastrous, doleful, dreadful, fatal, fateful, forlorn, grievous, grim, hapless, harrowing, heartbreaking, heartrending, ill-fated, ill-starred, lamentable, miserable, mournful, painful, pathetic, pitiable, pitiful, ruinous, sad, shocking, sorrowful, terrible, unfortunate, unhappy, woeful, wretched; SEE CONCEPTS 548,571

trail [n] *path, track*
aisle, beaten track*, byway, footpath, footprints, footsteps, groove*, mark, marks, pathway, road,

to
tr

route, rut, scent, spoor, stream, stroll, tail, trace, train, wake, way; SEE CONCEPT *501*

trail [*v*] *lag behind, follow*
bedog, bring up the rear*, chase, dally, dangle, dawdle, delay, dog*, drag, draggle, draw, droop, drop back, extend, fall back, fall behind, falter, flag, follow a scent*, halt, hang, hang back, hang down, haul, hunt, lag, linger, loiter, nose out*, plod, poke, poke along*, procrastinate, pull, pursue, shadow, shag, spook*, spoor, stalk, straggle, stream, string along*, tag along*, tail, take out after, tarry, tow, trace, track, traipse, trudge; SEE CONCEPTS *207,727,753*

train [*n*] *series*
alternation, appendage, caravan, chain, column, concatenation, consecution, convoy, cortege, course, court, entourage, file, following, gradation, line, order, procession, progression, retinue, row, run, scale, sequel, sequence, set, string, succession, suite, tail, thread, tier, track, trail, wake; SEE CONCEPTS *432,727*

train [*vl*] *prepare*
accustom, brainwash*, break in, care for, coach, cultivate, develop, discipline, drill, drum into, dry run*, educate, enlighten, equip, exercise, get a workout, get in shape, ground, grow strong, guide, habituate, harden, hone, improve, instruct, inure, make ready, mold, prime, qualify, rear, rehearse, run through, school, season, shape, sharpen, show the ropes*, study, tame, teach, tutor, update, warm up*, whip into shape*, wise up*, work out; SEE CONCEPTS *35,202,285*

train [*v2*] *aim at*
beam, bring to bear, cast, cock, direct, draw a bead*, focus, get in one's sights*, head, incline, lay, level, line up, point, slant, turn, zero in*; SEE CONCEPT *201*

trainee [*n*] *beginner*
abecedarian, amateur, apprentice, buckwheater*, cadet, colt*, greenhorn, learner, neophyte, newcomer, new kid on the block*, novice, novitiate, pupil, recruit, rookie, starter, student, tenderfoot*, tyro; SEE CONCEPTS *423,424*

trainer [*n*] *instructor, teacher*
adviser, breeder, coach, demonstrator, drill sergeant, guide, handler, lecturer, mentor, professor, tutor; SEE CONCEPT *350*

training [*n*] *preparation*
background, basics, buildup, chalk talk*, coaching, cultivation, discipline, domestication, drill, education, exercise, foundation, grounding, groundwork, guidance, indoctrination, instruction, practice, preliminaries, preparation, principles, readying, schooling, seasoning, sharpening, teaching, tuition, tune-up*, tutelage, upbringing, warm-up*, workout*; SEE CONCEPTS *202,285,678*

traipse [*v*] *walk*
amble, ambulate, gad, go on foot*, hike, knock about*, lumber, march, meander, pace, parade, plod, prance, promenade, roam, rove, shuffle, step, stride, stroll, strut, take a walk, tour, travel on foot, traverse, trek, troop, trudge, wander; SEE CONCEPT *149*

trait [*n*] *characteristic*
affection, attribute, birthmark, cast, character, custom, denominator, feature, habit, idiosyncrasy, lineament, manner, mannerism, mark, nature of the beast*, oddity, peculiarity, point, property, quality, quirk, savor, thing*, trick, virtue; SEE CONCEPTS *411,644,834*

traitor [*n*] *person who is disloyal*
apostate, backslider*, back-stabber*, Benedict Arnold*, betrayer, conspirator, deceiver, defector, deserter, double-crosser*, fink*, hypocrite, impostor, informer, intriguer, Judas*, miscreant, quisling, rebel, renegade, snake*, sneak*, snitch*, snitcher*, spy, squealer*, stool pigeon*, tattletale, traducer, treasonist, turncoat, two-timer*, whistle-blower*, wolf*; SEE CONCEPT *412*

traitorous [*adj*] *disloyal*
apostate, betraying, double-crossing, faithless, perfidious, recreant, subversive, treacherous, treasonable, treasonous, two-faced*, two-timing, undutiful, unfaithful, unpatriotic, untrue, wormlike; SEE CONCEPT *401*

trajectory [*n*] *course*
curve, direction, flight, flow, line, movement, orbit, path, range, route, track, trail; SEE CONCEPTS *501,514*

tramp [*nl*] *person who is poor, desperate*
beggar, bum, derelict, down-and-out*, drifter, floater, hitchhiker, hobo, homeless person, loafer, outcast, panhandler, vagabond, vagrant, wanderer; SEE CONCEPT *412*

tramp [*n2*] *heavy walk*
cruise, excursion, expedition, footfall, footstep, hike, jaunt, march, ramble, saunter, slog, stomp, stroll, tour, traipse, tread, trek, turn, walking trip; SEE CONCEPTS *151,224*

tramp [*v*] *walk heavily*
crush, footslog, gallop, hike, hop, march, navigate, plod, pound, ramble, range, roam, rove, slog, stamp, stodge, stomp, stroll, stump, thud, toil, tour, traipse, trample, tread, trek, trip, tromp, trudge, walk over; SEE CONCEPTS *151,224*

trample [*v*] *walk forcibly over*
bruise, crush, encroach, flatten, grind, hurt, infringe, injure, override, overwhelm, pound, ride roughshod over*, run over, squash, stamp, step on, stomp, tramp, tread, tromp, violate; SEE CONCEPTS *137,208,246*

trance [*n*] *hypnotic state*
abstraction, coma, daze, dream, ecstasy, glaze, insensibility, muse, petrifaction, rapture, reverie, spell, study, stupor, transfixion, transfixture, unconsciousness; SEE CONCEPT *410*

tranquil [*adj*] *quiet, peaceful*
agreeable, amicable, at ease, at peace, balmy, calm, collected, comforting, composed, cool, easy, easygoing, even, even-tempered, gentle, halcyon, hushed, lenient, low, measured, mild, moderate, murmuring, pacific, paradisiacal, pastoral, patient, placid, pleasing, poised, possessed, quiet, reasonable, restful, sedate, sedative, serene, smooth, sober, soft, soothing, stable, still, tame, temperate, undisturbed, unexcitable, unexcited, unperturbed, unruffled, untroubled, whispering; SEE CONCEPTS *525,542,594*

tranquility [*n*] *peace, quiet*
ataraxia, calm, calmness, composure, coolness, equanimity, hush, imperturbability, imperturbation, law and order, order, peacefulness, placidity, quietness, quietude, repose, rest, restfulness, sedateness, serenity, stillness; SEE CONCEPTS *65,673*

tranquilize [*v*] *make calm, quiet*
balm, calm, calm down, compose, hush, lull,

pacify, put at rest, quell, quiet, quieten, relax, sedate, settle one's nerves*, soothe, still, subdue, unruffle; SEE CONCEPTS 7,22,310

transact [v] *do business, carry out*
accomplish, button down*, button up*, buy, carry on, clinch, close, conclude, conduct, discharge, do*, effectuate, enact, execute, finish, handle, jell, manage, move, negotiate, operate, perform, prosecute, pull off, run with the ball*, see to, sell, settle, sew up*, take care of, TCB*, work out a deal*, wrap up*; SEE CONCEPTS 91,223,324,330,706

transaction [n] *business dealing; undertaking*
act, action, activity, affair, agreement, bargain, bond, business, buying, compact, contract, convention, coup, covenant, deal, deed, disposal, doings*, enterprise, event, execution, goings-on*, happening, intercourse, matter, negotiation, occurrence, pact, performance, play, proceeding, purchase, purchasing, sale, selling, step; SEE CONCEPTS 223,324,330,684

transcend [v] *go beyond; surpass*
beat, best, be superior, better, eclipse, exceed, excel, go above, leave behind, leave in the dust*, outdo, outrival, outshine, outstrip, outvie, overstep, overtop, rise above, top, transform; SEE CONCEPT 141

transcendent/transcendental [adj] *extraordinary, superior*
absolute, abstract, accomplished, beyond grasp, boundless, consummate, entire, eternal, exceeding, fantastic, finished, hypothetical, ideal, incomparable, infinite, innate, intact, intellectual, intuitive, matchless, obscure, original, otherworldly, peerless, perfect, preeminent, primordial, second to none*, sublime, supernatural, supreme, surpassing, theoretical, towering, transcending, transmundane, ultimate, unequalable, unequalled, unique, unparalleled, unrivalled, whole; SEE CONCEPT 574

transcribe [v] *transfer to another medium*
copy out, decipher, duplicate, engross, interpret, note, record, render, reprint, reproduce, rewrite, set out, take down, tape, tape-record, transfer, translate, transliterate, write out; SEE CONCEPTS 79,125,171

transcript [n] *copy*
carbon copy*, ditto*, duplicate, facsimile, hard copy, imprint, manuscript, mimeograph, minutes, notes, print, record, recorded material, recording, reprint, reproduction, transcription; translation; SEE CONCEPTS 269,667,716

transfer [n] *change of possession*
alteration, assignment, conduction, convection, deportation, displacement, move, relegation, relocation, removal, shift, substitution, transference, translation, transmission, transmittal, transposition, variation; SEE CONCEPTS 108,143,217,223

transfer [v] *pass possession to*
assign, bear, bring, carry, cart, cede, change, consign, convert, convey, deed, delegate, deliver, dislocate, dispatch, dispense, displace, disturb, express, feed, ferry, find, forward, give, hand, hand over, haul, lug, mail, make over, metamorphose, move, pass on, pass the buck*, post, provide, relegate, relocate, remove, sell, send, shift, ship, shoulder, sign over, supply, taxi, tote, transfigure, translate, transmit, transmogrify, transmute, transplant, transport, transpose, turn over; SEE CONCEPTS 108,143,217,223,243

transfix [v1] *hold one's attention*
bewitch, captivate, enchant, engross, fascinate, hold, hypnotize, mesmerize, palsy, paralyze, petrify, rivet, root, spellbind, stop in one's tracks*, stop one dead*, stun; SEE CONCEPTS 11,14

transfix [v2] *pierce*
fix, impale, lance, nail down, penetrate, pin down, puncture, run through, skewer, skiver, spear, spike, spit, stick, transpierce; SEE CONCEPT 220

transform [v] *change completely*
alter, commute, convert, cook, denature, doctor, make over, metamorphose, mold, mutate, reconstruct, remodel, renew, revamp, revolutionize, shift gears*, sing different tune*, switch, switch over, transfer, transfigure, translate, transmogrify, transmute, transpose, turn around, turn over new leaf*, turn the corner*, turn the tables*; SEE CONCEPTS 232,697

transformation [n] *complete change*
about-face*, alteration, changeover, conversion, flip-flop*, metamorphosis, radical change, renewal, revolution, shift, switch, transfiguration, transmogrification, transmutation; SEE CONCEPT 697

transgression [n] *violation, misbehavior*
breach, breaking of the law, contravention, crime, defiance, disobedience, encroachment, erring, error, fault, infraction, infringement, iniquity, lapse, misdeed, misdemeanor, offense, overstepping, sin, slip, trespass, vice, wrong, wrongdoing; SEE CONCEPTS 101,192,645

transient/transitory [adj] *temporary, brief*
changeable, deciduous, emigrating, ephemeral, evanescent, flash, fleeting, flitting, fly-by-night*, flying, fugacious, fugitive, going by, impermanent, insubstantial, migrating, momentary, moving, passing, provisional, short, short-lived, short-term, temporal, transmigratory, unstable, vacating, volatile; SEE CONCEPT 798

transit [n] *transportation*
alteration, carriage, carrying, conveyance, crossing, infiltration, motion, movement, osmosis, passage, penetration, permeation, portage, shift, shipment, transfer, transference, transport, transporting, travel, traverse; SEE CONCEPTS 155,224

transition [n] *change, often major*
alteration, changeover, conversion, development, evolution, flux, growth, metamorphosis, metastasis, passage, passing, progress, progression, realignment, shift, transformation, transit, transmutation, turn, turning point, upheaval; SEE CONCEPT 697

translate [v1] *interpret, explain*
construe, convert, decipher, decode, do into, elucidate, explicate, gloss, make clear, metaphrase, paraphrase, put, render, reword, simplify, spell out, transcribe, transliterate, transpose, turn; SEE CONCEPTS 55,57

translate [v2]
alter, commute, convert, metamorphose, transfigure, transform, transmogrify, transmute, transpose, turn; SEE CONCEPT 232

translation [n] *rewording; interpretation*
adaptation, construction, crib*, decoding, elucidation, explanation, gloss, key, metaphrase, paraphrase, reading, rendering, rendition,

tr
tr

rephrasing, restatement, simplification, transcription, transliteration, version; SEE CONCEPTS 268,277,278

translator [*n*] *interpreter*
adapter, cryptographer, cryptologist, decoder, dragoman, explainer, glossator, linguist, polyglot; SEE CONCEPTS 57,292

translucent [*adj*] *clear*
clear-cut, crystal, crystalline, diaphanous, glassy, limpid, lucent, lucid, luminous, pellucid, see-through, semiopaque, semitransparent, translucid, unblurred; SEE CONCEPT 618

transmit [*v*] *communicate, send*
address, bear, bequeath, break, broadcast, carry, channel, conduct, consign, convey, diffuse, dispatch, disseminate, drop a line*, drop a note*, forward, funnel, give a call*, give a ring*, hand down, hand on, impart, instill, issue, mail, pass on, pipe, put on the air*, radio, relay, remit, route, send, send out, ship, siphon, spread, take, traject, transfer, transfuse, translate, transport; SEE CONCEPTS 217,266,292

transparent [*adj*] *see-through*
cellophane, clear, crystal-clear, crystalline, diaphanous, filmy, gauzy, glassy, gossamer, hyaline, limpid, lucent, lucid, pellucid, permeable, plain, sheer, thin, tiffany, translucent, transpicuous, vitreous; SEE CONCEPTS 606,618

transparent [*adj2*] *obvious, understandable*
apparent, articulate, artless, candid, clear-cut, direct, distinct, distinguishable, easily seen, easy, evident, explicit, forthright, frank, guileless, honest, ingenuous, manifest, open, patent, perspicuous, plain, plain-spoken, recognizable, self-explanatory, sincere, straight, straightforward, unambiguous, undisguised, unequivocal, unmistakable, unsophisticated, visible; SEE CONCEPT 267

transpire [*v1*] *occur, happen*
arise, befall, betide, chance, come about, come to pass, develop, ensue, eventuate, fall out*, gel, go, occur, result, shake, take place, turn up; SEE CONCEPT 3

transpire [*v2*] *become known*
be disclosed, be discovered, be made public, break, come out, come to light, emerge, get out, leak; SEE CONCEPTS 261,266

transplant [*v*] *relocate*
displace, emigrate, graft, immigrate, move, readapt, recondition, remove, reorient, reset, resettle, revamp, shift, transfer, transpose, uproot; SEE CONCEPTS 213,310

transport [*n1*] *move, transfer*
carriage, carrier, carrying, carting, conveyance, conveying, conveyor, freightage, hauling, lift, movement, mover, moving, passage, removal, shipment, shipping, transference, transferring, transit, transportation, transporting, transshipment, truckage, vehicle; SEE CONCEPTS 155,503

transport [*n2*] *delight*
ardor, bliss, cloud nine*, ecstasy, enchantment, enthusiasm, euphoria, fervor, happiness, heaven, passion, rapture, ravishment, rhapsody, seventh heaven*; SEE CONCEPT 32,410

transport [*v1*] *move, transfer*
back, bear, bring, carry, conduct, convey, ferry, fetch, haul, heel*, jag, lug, pack, piggyback*, remove, ride, run, schlepp*, ship, shoulder, take, tote, truck; SEE CONCEPTS 147,187,217

transport [*v2*] *exile*
banish, cast out, deport, displace, expel, expulse oust, relegate, sentence; SEE CONCEPTS 211,317

transport [*v3*] *captivate, delight*
agitate, carry away, electrify, elevate, enchant enrapture, entrance, excite, inflame, move, provoke, quicken, ravish, send, slay, spellbind, stimulate, stir, thrill, trance, uplight, wow; SEE CONCEPTS 7,22

transpose [*v*] *swap, switch*
alter, backtrack*, change, commute, convert double back, exchange, flip-flop*, interchange inverse, invert, metamorphose, move, put, rearrange, relocate, render, reorder, reverse, revert shift, substitute, transfer, transfigure, transform translate, transmogrify, transmute, turn, turn the tables*; SEE CONCEPTS 104,232,697

trap [*n*] *snare, trick*
allurement, ambuscade, ambush, artifice, bait booby trap*, come-on*, conspiracy, deception decoy, device, dragnet, enticement, feint, gambit hook*, intrigue, inveiglement, lasso*, lure machination, maneuver, net, noose, pitfall, plot ploy, prank, quagmire, quicksand, ruse, seducement, snag*, stratagem, subterfuge, temptation wile; SEE CONCEPT 674

trap [*v*] *catch, snare; trick*
ambuscade, ambush, beguile, box in*, circumvent, collar*, corner*, corral*, deceive, decoy dupe, enmesh, ensnare, entangle, entrap, fool grab, hook, inveigle, land*, mousetrap*, nab nail*, net, overtake, rope in*, seduce, snag, suck in*, surprise, take, tangle, trammel, trip up*; SEE CONCEPTS 59,90

trappings [*n*] *paraphernalia, equipment*
accouterment, adornment, apparel, appointment decoration, dress, embellishment, finery, fitting fixture, furnishing, gear, livery, ornament panoply, personal effects, raiment, rigging things, trimming; SEE CONCEPTS 446,451,496

trash [*n1*] *garbage*
debris, dregs, droppings, dross, excess, filth fragments, junk, leavings, litter, oddments, odds and ends*, offal, pieces, refuse, residue, rubbish rubble, rummage, scourings, scrap, scraps scum*, sediment, shavings, sweepings, waste SEE CONCEPTS 260,834

trash [*n3*] *ridiculous communication*
balderdash, bilge*, drivel, foolish talk, hogwash inanity, malarkey*, nonsense, rot, rubbish, tripe twaddle; SEE CONCEPT 278

trashy [*adj*] *worthless*
abandoned, barren, bogus, cheap, cheesy crappy*, cruddy*, crummy*, despicable, empty flimsy, garbage, good-for-nothing*, grungy, inferior, junky, lousy, low in quality, no-good* ratty, raunchy, shabby, shoddy, sleazy, tawdry useless, valueless; SEE CONCEPTS 560,570,575 589

trauma [*n*] *severe mental or physical pain*
agony, anguish, blow, collapse, confusion, damage, derangement, disturbance, hurt, injury, jolt ordeal, outburst, shock, strain, stress, suffering torture, traumatization, upheaval, upset, wound SEE CONCEPT 728

travel [*n*] *journey*
biking, commutation, cruising, drive, driving excursion, expedition, flying, globe-trotting* hop*, junket, movement, navigation, overnight passage, peregrination, ramble, ride, riding, sail

ing, seafaring, sightseeing, swing, tour, touring, transit, trek, trekking, trip, voyage, voyaging, walk, wandering, wanderlust, wayfaring, weekend; SEE CONCEPTS 224

travel [v] *journey on a trip or tour*
adventure, carry, cover, cover ground, cross, cruise, drive, explore, fly, get through, go, go abroad, go camping, go into orbit*, go riding, hop*, jaunt, jet*, junket*, knock around, make a journey, make one's way, migrate, motor, move, overnight*, proceed, progress, ramble, roam, rove, sail, scour, set forth, set out, sightsee, take a boat, take a plane, take a train, take a trip, tour, transmit, traverse, trek, vacation, visit, voyage, walk, wander, weekend*, wend; SEE CONCEPT 224

traveler [n] *person who journeys*
adventurer, barnstormer*, bum*, commuter, displaced person, drifter, excursionist, expeditionist, explorer, floater, gadabout*, globetrotter, gypsy, haj, hiker, hobo, itinerant, jet-setter, journeyer, junketer, migrant, navigator, nomad, passenger, peddler, pilgrim, rambler, roamer, rover, sailor, seafarer, sightseer, tourist, tramp, transmigrant, trekker, tripper, trouper, truant, vagabond, vagrant, voyager, wanderer, wayfarer; SEE CONCEPTS 348,423

traverse [v1] *cross over; travel*
bisect, bridge, cover, crisscross, cross, cut across, decussate, do, go across, go over, intersect, move over, negotiate, pace, pass over, pass through, perambulate, peregrinate, ply, quarter, range, roam, span, track, transverse, travel over, tread, walk, wander; SEE CONCEPTS 147,201,692,750

traverse [v2] *resist, contradict*
balk, buck, check, combat, contest, contravene, counter, counteract, cross, deny, disaffirm, dispute, duel, fight, frustrate, gainsay, go against, hinder, impede, impugn, negate, negative, obstruct, oppose, repel, thwart, withstand; SEE CONCEPTS 54,121

travesty [n] *spoof, ridicule*
burlesque, caricature, distortion, exaggeration, farce, lampoon, lampoonery, mimicry, mock, mockery, parody, perversion, play, put-on*, roast*, satire, send-up*, sham*, takeoff*; SEE CONCEPTS 273,292

travesty [v] *ridicule, spoof*
ape, burlesque, caricature, deride, distort, imitate, lampoon, make a mockery of, make fun of, mimic, mock, parody, pervert, play on*, put on*, satirize, send up*, sham*, take off*; SEE CONCEPTS 273,292

treacherous [adj1] *dishonest, disloyal*
betraying, catchy, deceitful, deceptive, double-crossing*, double-dealing*, duplicitous, faithless, false, false-hearted, fly-by-night*, insidious, misleading, perfidious, recreant, shifty*, slick*, slippery*, snake in the grass*, traitorous, treasonable, tricky, two-faced*, two-timing*, undependable, unfaithful, unloyal, unreliable, untrue, untrustworthy; SEE CONCEPTS 401,404

treacherous [adj2] *dangerous*
alarming, chancy, deceptive, difficult, dissembled, faulty, hairy*, hazardous, icy*, insecure, jeopardous, menacing, misleading, ominous, perilous, precarious, risky, shaky, slippery, ticklish, tricky, undependable, unhealthy, unreliable, un-

safe, unsound, unstable, wicked; SEE CONCEPTS 565,587

treachery [n] *disloyalty, dishonesty*
betrayal, bunco, corruption, dirty dealing*, dirty pool*, dirty trick*, dirty work*, disaffection, dodge, double-cross*, double-dealing*, duplicity, faithlessness, fake, falseness, fast shuffle*, flimflam*, grift, gyp*, infidelity, perfidiousness, perfidy, put-on*, racket*, recreancy, scam*, sellout, shell game*, skin game*, spoof, stab in the back*, sweet talk*, treacherousness, treason, two-timing*, whitewash*; SEE CONCEPTS 633,645

tread [n] *walk*
footstep, footsteps, gait, march, pace, step, stride, trace, track, tramp; SEE CONCEPTS 149,284

tread [v] *walk; bear down*
ambulate, crush, foot, hike, hoof, march, oppress, pace, plod, quell, repress, squash, stamp, stamp on, step, step on, stride, subdue, subjugate, suppress, traipse, tramp, trample, troop, trudge; SEE CONCEPT 149

treason [n] *disloyalty*
breach of faith, crime, deceit, deceitfulness, deception, disaffection, dishonesty, duplicity, faithlessness, le 'se majesté, mutiny, perfidy, revolt, revolutionary, sedition, seditious act, seditiousness, subversion, traitorousness, treachery; SEE CONCEPTS 192,645

treasonous [adj] *disloyal*
apostate, betraying, double-crossing, faithless, insubordinate, mutinous, perfidious, recreant, subversive, traitorous, treacherous, treasonable, two-faced, two-timing, undutiful, unfaithful, unpatriotic, untrue, wormlike; SEE CONCEPT 401

treasure [n] *prized possession or entity*
abundance, apple of one's eye*, cache, capital, cash, catch*, darling, find, fortune, funds, gem, gold, hoard, jewel, money, nest egg*, nonpareil, paragon, pearl*, pile*, plum*, pride and joy*, prize, reserve, riches, richness, store, treasure trove, valuable, wealth; SEE CONCEPTS 332,337,446,710

treasure [v] *hold dear*
adore, appreciate, apprize, cherish, conserve, dote on, esteem, guard, idolize, love, preserve, prize, revere, reverence, save, value, venerate, worship; SEE CONCEPT 32

treasury [n] *place where money, valuables are kept*
archive, bank, bursar, bursary, cache, chest, coffer, damper, depository, exchange, exchequer, Fort Knox*, gallery, hoard, museum, register, repository, safe, storage, store, storehouse, strongbox, treasure house, vault; SEE CONCEPTS 339,439,449

treat [n] *pleasing entity or occurrence*
amusement, banquet, celebration, dainty, delicacy, delight, enjoyment, entertainment, feast, fun, gift, goody*, gratification, joy, party, pleasure, refreshment, satisfaction, surprise, sweet, thrill, tidbit; SEE CONCEPTS 457,529,693

treat [v1] *act, behave towards*
account, act with regard to, appraise, conduct, conduct oneself toward, consider, deal with*, employ, estimate, evaluate, handle, have business with*, have recourse to*, have to do with*, hold, look upon, manage, negotiate, play, rate, react toward, regard, respect, serve, take, use, value, wield; SEE CONCEPT 633

tr
tr

treat [v2] *doctor, medicate*
administer, apply treatment, attend, care for, cure, dose, dress, heal, medicament, minister to, nurse, operate, prescribe; SEE CONCEPT *310*

treat [v3] *pay the bill for someone else*
amuse, blow, buy for, divert, entertain, escort, feast, foot the bill*, give, indulge, pay for, pick up the check*, pick up the tab*, play host*, provide, regale, satisfy, set up, spring for*, stake, stand*, take out, wine and dine*; SEE CONCEPTS *327,384*

treat [v4] *be concerned with; discuss*
advise, approach, arrange, comment, confabulate, confer, consider, consult, contain, criticize, deal with, deliberate, discourse on, discuss, enlarge upon, explain, go into, interpret, manipulate, reason, review, speak about, study, tackle, talk about, think, touch upon, weigh, write about; SEE CONCEPTS *17,56*

treatise [n] *written study of a subject*
argument, book, commentary, composition, discourse, discussion, disquisition, dissertation, essay, exposition, memoir, monograph, pamphlet, paper, review, script, thesis, tract, tractate, work, writing; SEE CONCEPTS *271,280*

treatment [n1] *medical care*
analysis, cure, diet, doctoring, healing, hospitalization, medication, medicine, operation, prescription, regimen, remedy, surgery, therapeutics, therapy; SEE CONCEPT *310*

treatment [n2] *handling of entity, situation*
action towards, angle, approach, behavior towards, conduct, custom, dealing, employment, execution, habit, line, management, manipulation, manner, method, mode, modus operandi, practice, procedure, proceeding, processing, reception, strategy, usage, way; SEE CONCEPTS *117,633*

treaty [n] *agreement, contract*
accord, alliance, arrangement, bargain, bond, cartel, charter, compact, concord, concordat, convention, covenant, deal, entente, league, negotiation, pact, reconciliation, sanction, settlement, understanding; SEE CONCEPTS *684,685*

tree [n] *large plant enclosed in bark and shedding leaves*
forest, hardwood, pulp, sapling, seedling, shrub, softwood, stock, timber, wood, woods; SEE CONCEPT *430*

trek [n] *long journey*
expedition, footslog, hegira, hike, long haul, march, odyssey, peregrination, slog, tramp, travel, trip; SEE CONCEPT *224*

trek [v] *journey*
be on the move*, be on the trail*, foot, hike, hit the road*, march, migrate, plod, range, roam, rove, slog, traipse, tramp, travel, trudge, walk; SEE CONCEPT *224*

tremble [v] *shake, vibrate*
flutter, have the shakes*, jar, jitter, oscillate, palpitate, quake, quaver, quiver, rock, shiver, shudder, teeter, throb, totter, tremor, wobble; SEE CONCEPT *152*

tremendous [adj] *huge, overwhelming*
amazing, appalling, astounding, awesome, awful, blimp, colossal, cracking, deafening, dreadful, enormous, excellent, exceptional, extraordinary, fabulous, fantastic, fearful, formidable, frightful, gargantuan, gigantic, great, great big*, huge, humongous, immense, incredible,

jumbo*, large, mammoth, marvelous, massive, mondo*, monstrous, monumental, prodigious, stupendous, super, terrible, terrific, titanic, towering, vast, whale*, whopper, whopping, wonderful; SEE CONCEPTS *574,773,781*

tremor [n] *shaking, shock*
agitation, earthquake, flutter, quake, quaking, quaver, quiver, quivering, ripple, shake, shiver, shivering, tremble, trembling, trepidation, upheaval, vibration, wobble; SEE CONCEPTS *145,526*

trench [n] *ditch, channel dug in earth*
arroyo, canal, cut, depression, dike, drain, drill, dugout, earthwork, entrenchment, excavation, fosse, foxhole, furrow, gorge, gulch, gully, gutter, hollow, main, moat, pit, rut, sink, trough, tube, waterway; SEE CONCEPTS *509,513*

trenchant [adj] *sarcastic, scathing*
acerbic, acid, acidulous, acute, astringent, biting, caustic, clear, clear-cut, crisp, critical, crushing, cutting, distinct, driving, dynamic, effective, effectual, emphatic, energetic, explicit, forceful, forcible, graphic, hurtful, impressive, incisive, intense, keen, mordant, penetrating, piquant, pointed, potent, powerful, pungent, razor-sharp*, salient, salty*, sardonic, sententious, severe, sharp, significant, strong, tart, to the point, unequivocal, unsparing, vigorous, weighty, well-defined; SEE CONCEPTS *267,537*

trend [n1] *flow, current*
aim, bearing, bent, bias, course, direction, drift, inclination, leaning, movement, orientation, progression, run, swing, tendency, tenor, wind; SEE CONCEPTS *230,657,738*

trend [n2] *style, fashion that is in favor*
craze, cry, fad, furor, in-thing*, latest thing*, look, mode, newest wrinkle*, rage, thing*, vogue; SEE CONCEPT *655*

trendy [adj] *in fashion, style*
a' la mode*, contemporary, fashionable, fly*, in, in vogue, latest, modish*, now*, popular, stylish, swank*, tony*, up-to-the-minute, voguish, with-it*; SEE CONCEPT *589*

trepidation [n] *anxiety, worry*
agitation, alarm, apprehension, blue funk*, butterflies*, cold feet*, cold sweat*, consternation, creeps*, dismay, disquiet, disturbance, dread, emotion, excitement, fear, fright, goose bumps*, horror, jitters, nervousness, palpitation, panic, perturbation, shock, terror, trepidity, uneasiness, worriment; SEE CONCEPT *27*

trespass [n] *invasion, offense*
breach, contravention, crime, delinquency, encroachment, entrenchment, error, evildoing, fault, infraction, infringement, iniquity, injury, intrusion, misbehavior, misconduct, misdeed, misdemeanor, obtrusion, poaching, sin, transgression, unlawful entry, violation, wrongdoing, wrongful entry; SEE CONCEPTS *101,192,645,691*

trespass [v] *infringe, offend*
butt in*, chisel in*, crash, crash the gates*, deviate, displease, do wrong by, encroach, entrench, err, horn in*, interlope, intrude, invade, kibitz*, lapse, meddle, misbehave, mix in, muscle in*, nose in*, obtrude, overstep, penetrate, poach, poke, sin, stick nose in*, transgress, violate, wrong; SEE CONCEPTS *101,159,192,384*

trial [adj] *experimental*
balloon, exploratory, pilot, preliminary, proba-

tionary, provisional, tentative, test, testing; SEE CONCEPTS *548,560*

trial [*n1*] *test*
analysis, assay, attempt, audition, check, crack*, dry run*, effort, endeavor, essay, examination, experience, experiment, experimentation, fling*, go*, hassle*, investigation, lick*, probation, proof, R and D*, research and development, shakedown*, shot*, showcase*, stab*, striving, struggle, testing, test run, trial and error*, trial run, try, try on*, tryout, undertaking, venture, whack*, workout; SEE CONCEPTS *87,290,291*

trial [*n2*] *legal proceeding*
action, arraignment, case, citation, claim, contest, counterclaim, court action, court martial, cross-examination, habeas corpus, hearing, impeachment, indictment, lawsuit, litigation, prosecution, rap*, seizure, suit, tribunal; SEE CONCEPTS *317,691*

trial [*n3*] *trouble, big problem*
adversity, affliction, albatross*, anguish, annoyance, bane, blow, bother, burden, calvary, care, complication, cross to bear*, crucible*, difficulty, distress, drag*, grief, hardship, hard time*, hassle*, heartbreak, inconvenience, irritation, load, misery, misfortune, nightmare, nuisance, ordeal, pain, pain in the neck*, pest, plague, rigor, severe test, sorrow, suffering, thorn, tribulation, trying time*, unhappiness, vexation, vicissitude, visitation, woe, wretchedness; SEE CONCEPTS *674,728*

tribe [*n*] *ethnic group; family*
association, blood, caste, clan, class, division, dynasty, horde, house, ilk, kin, kind, kindred, lineage, people, race, seed, society, sort, stock, type; SEE CONCEPTS *296,380,421*

tribulation [*n*] *pain, unhappiness*
adversity, affliction, albatross*, bad luck*, blow*, bummer*, burden, care, cross to bear*, crucible*, curse, difficulty, distress, double whammy*, downer*, drag*, grief, hard knock*, hard time*, headache*, heartache*, misery, misfortune, oppression, ordeal, persecution, rainy day*, reverse, sorrow, suffering, trial, trouble, vexation, visitation, woe, worry, wretchedness, wronging; SEE CONCEPTS *666,728*

tribunal [*n*] *court*
bar, bench, board, committee, council, court of justice, forum, judge, judiciary, justice, law court, magistrate, seat of judgment; SEE CONCEPTS *299,318*

tributary [*adj*] *secondary; branch*
accessory, dependent, feeding, minor, satellite, shoot, side, sub, subject, subordinate, under; SEE CONCEPT *560*

tribute [*n*] *testimonial, praise*
accolade, acknowledgment, applause, appreciation, citation, commendation, compliment, encomium, esteem, eulogy, gift, gratitude, honor, laudation, memorial, offering, panegyric, recognition, recommendation, respect, salutation, salvo; SEE CONCEPTS *69,278*

tick [*n1*] *deceit*
ambush, artifice, blind, bluff, casuistry, cheat, chicanery, circumvention, con*, concealment, conspiracy, conundrum, cover, deception, decoy, delusion, device, disguise, distortion, dodge*, double-dealing, duplicity, equivocation, evasion, fabrication, fake, falsehood, feint, forgery, fraud, game, gimmick, hoax, illusion, imposition, im-

posture, intrigue, invention, machination, maneuver, perjury, plot, ploy, pretense, ruse, snare, stratagem, subterfuge, swindle, trap, treachery, wile; SEE CONCEPTS *59,645*

trick [*n2*] *prank, joke*
accomplishment, antic, caper, catch, device, escapade, feat, frolic, funny business, gag*, gambol, jape, jest, lark, monkeyshine*, practical joke, put-on*, shenanigan*, sleight of hand, sport, stunt, tomfoolery; SEE CONCEPTS *59,273,384*

trick [*n3*] *expertise, know-how*
ability, art, command, craft, device, facility, gift, hang, knack, method, secret, skill, swing, technique; SEE CONCEPT *630*

trick [*n4*] *characteristic, habit*
crotchet, custom, foible, habitude, idiosyncrasy, manner, mannerism, peculiarity, practice, praxis, quirk, trait, usage, use, way, wont; SEE CONCEPTS *411,657*

trick [*n5*] *time working at something*
bout, go*, hitch, shift, spell, stint, tour, turn; SEE CONCEPT *807*

trick [*v*] *fool; play joke on*
bamboozle, catch*, cheat, con, deceive, defraud, delude, disinform, double deal*, dupe, fake, flimflam, fool, gull, hoax, hocus-pocus*, hoodwink, impose upon, jive*, mislead, outwit, play for a fool*, pull wool over*, put one over on*, rook*, screw*, set up*, swindle, take for a ride*, take in*, throw, trap, victimize; SEE CONCEPT *59*

trickery [*n*] *deception, joke*
bait and switch*, cheat, cheating, chicane, chicanery, con, deceit, dishonesty, dodge, double-cross*, double-dealing*, dupery, fast shuffle*, flimflam*, fourberie, fraud, funny business*, guile, hoax, imposture, pretense, quackery, razzle-dazzle*, scam, sharp practice, shell game*, shenanigans*, snow job*, sting*, stunt, swindling, underhandedness; SEE CONCEPTS *59,645*

trickle [*v*] *run out*
crawl, creep, distill, dribble, drip, drop, exude, flow, issue, leak, ooze, percolate, seep, stream, trill, weep; SEE CONCEPTS *146,179*

tricky [*adj*] *complicated, difficult*
catchy, complex, critical, delicate, intricate, involved, knotty*, perplexing, precarious, problematic, quirky, risky, rocky, sensitive, sticky, thorny, ticklish, touch-and-go*, touchy, undependable, unstable; SEE CONCEPT *562*

tricky [*adj2*] *deceptive, sly*
artful, astute, cagey, catchy, clever, crafty, cunning, deceitful, deep, delusive, delusory, devious, dishonest, foxy, greasy*, guileful, insidious, intelligent, keen, misleading, scheming, shady, sharp, shifty, shrewd, slick*, slippery*, smooth, streetwise*, subtle, treacherous, wily, witted, wry; SEE CONCEPT *401*

tried [*adj*] *reliable*
approved, certified, constant, demonstrated, dependable, faithful, proved, secure, staunch, steadfast, tested, tried-and-true*, true-blue*, trustworthy, trusty, used; SEE CONCEPT *535*

tried-and-true [*adj*] *tested*
approved, certified, creditworthy, dependable, loyal, proved, proven, reliable, safe, tried, trustworthy, trusty; SEE CONCEPT *535*

trifle [*n1*] *novelty item*
bagatelle, bauble, bibelot, curio, gewgaw*, knickknack, nothing*, novelty, objet d'art, play-

tr
tr

thing, toy, trinket, triviality, whatnot*; SEE CONCEPT 446

trifle [n2] *very small amout*

bit, dash, diddly*, drop, eyelash*, fly speck*, fraction, hint, jot, little, no big deal*, particle, picayune*, piece, pinch, shade, smack, soupçon*, speck, spice, spot, squat, suggestion, suspicion, touch, trace; SEE CONCEPTS 668,831

trifle [v] *toy with; mess around*

amuse oneself, be insincere, coquet, dabble, dally, dawdle, dilly-dally*, doodle, fidget, flirt, fool, fool around*, fool with*, fribble*, fritter, futz around*, horse around*, idle, indulge in, lead on, loiter, lollygag*, lounge, mess with*, misuse, monkey, monkey with*, palter, philander, play, play games with*, play with, potter, putter, squander, string along*, toy, twiddle, use up, wanton, waste, waste time, wink at*; SEE CONCEPTS 210,292,363

trifling [adj] *insignificant, worthless*

banal, dinky*, empty, forget it*, frivolous, hollow, idle, idling, inane, inconsequential, inconsiderable, insipid, jejune, loitering, measly, minuscule, negligible, niggling*, no big deal*, no big thing*, nugatory, paltry, petty, picayune, piddling, puny, shallow, silly, slight, small, tiny, trivial, unimportant, vain, valueless, vapid; SEE CONCEPTS 575,789

trigger [v] *cause to happen*

activate, bring about, cause, elicit, generate, give rise to, produce, prompt, provoke, set in motion, set off, spark, start; SEE CONCEPT 242

trim [adj1] *neat, orderly*

apple-pie order*, clean, clean-cut, compact, dapper, fit, in good shape, neat as a pin*, nice, shipshape*, slick, smart, snug, spick-and-span*, spruce, streamlined, symmetrical, tidy, to rights*, uncluttered, well-groomed; SEE CONCEPTS 485,621

trim [adj2] *shapely*

beautiful, clean, comely, fit, graceful, in fine fettle*, in good shape, sleek, slender, slick, slim, statuesque, streamlined, svelte, well-balanced, well-proportioned, willowy; SEE CONCEPTS 314,490,491

trim [n1] *decoration*

adornment, border, edging, embellishment, frill, fringe, garnish, gingerbread*, ornamentation, piping, trimming; SEE CONCEPTS 475,824

trim [n2] *condition, health*

commission, fettle*, fitness, form, kilter*, order, repair, shape, situation, state, whack*; SEE CONCEPT 316

trim [v1] *cut shorter*

abbreviate, barber, blue pencil*, bob, boil down*, clip, crop, curtail, cut, cut back, cut down, dock, edit, even up, lop, mow, pare, pare down, plane, prune, put in a nutshell*, shave, shear, shorten, slice off, snip, tidy, truncate, whittle down*; SEE CONCEPTS 176,236,247

trim [v2] *decorate*

adorn, array, beautify, bedeck, beribbon, deck, dress, dress up, embellish, emblazon, embroider, garnish, ornament, prank, pretty up*, print*, spangle, spruce up*; SEE CONCEPTS 162,177

trim [v3] *beat, defeat*

clobber, drub, lambaste, lick, smother, thrash, trounce, wax*, whip; SEE CONCEPT 95

trimmings [n] *accessories, extras*

accent, accompaniments, additions, clippings,

decorations, fixings, frills, garnish, ornaments, supplements, trappings; SEE CONCEPT 834

trinket [n] *knickknack*

bagatelle, bauble, bead, bibelot, curio, doodad*, gadget, gewgaw*, gimcrack*, glass*, hardware, jewel, jewelry, junk, nothing*, novelty, objet d'art, ornament, plaything, rock*, sparkler*, stone, toy, trifle, whatnot*; SEE CONCEPTS 446

trio/triple [n] *three of something*

leash, set of three, ternion, threesome, trey, triad, triangle, trilogy, trine, trinity, triplet, triplicate, triptych, triumvirate, triune, troika; SEE CONCEPTS 784,787

trip [n1] *journey, excursion*

cruise, errand, expedition, foray, hop*, jaunt, junket, outing, overnight, peregrination, ramble*, run, swing*, tour, travel, trek, voyage, weekend; SEE CONCEPT 224

trip [n2] *error, blunder*

bungle, fall, false move, false step, faux pas*, indiscretion, lapse, misstep, mistake, slip, stumble; SEE CONCEPTS 101,230

trip [v] *fall, err*

buck, canter, confuse, disconcert, fall, fall over, founder, frolic, go headlong*, go wrong, hop, lapse, lope, lose balance, lose footing, lurch, make a faux pas*, miscalculate, misstep, pitch, play, plunge, skip, slide, slip, slip on, slip up, sprawl, spring, stumble, throw off, topple, tumble, unsettle; SEE CONCEPTS 101,149

tripe [n] *nonsense, rubbish*

balderdash, baloney*, bilge, bosh, BS*, bull*, bunk*, drivel, garbage, gibberish, hogwash, hooey*, hot air*, poppycock, trash; SEE CONCEPTS 230,278

trite [adj] *silly, commonplace*

banal, bathetic, bromidic, chain, cliché, clichéd, common, cornball*, corny*, drained, dull, exhausted, familiar tune*, flat, hackneyed, hokey*, jejune, mildewed*, moth-eaten*, musty*, old hat*, ordinary, pedestrian, platitudinous, prosaic, ready-made, routine, run-of-the-mill*, set, shopworn, stale, stereotyped, stock, threadbare, timeworn, tired, uninspired, unoriginal, used-up, vapid, warmed-over*, well-worn, worn, wornout; SEE CONCEPTS 267,530

triumph [n1] *extreme happiness*

celebration, elation, exultance, exultation, festivity, joy, jubilance, jubilation, jubilee, merriment, pride, rejoicing, reveling; SEE CONCEPT 410

triumph [n2] *victory, achievement*

accomplishment, ascendancy, attainment, big hit*, big win*, cinch, clean sweep*, conquest, coup, feat, feather in cap*, gain, grand slam*, hit, hole in one*, homer*, pushover*, riot, score, sell, sensation, shoo-in*, smash-hit*, splash, success, sure bet*, sure thing*, surmounting, takeover, the gold*, tour de force*, vanquishing, vanquishment, walkover*, win; SEE CONCEPT 706

triumph [v1] *be very happy*

celebrate, crow, delight, exult, gloat, glory, jubilate, rejoice, revel, swagger; SEE CONCEPT 32

triumph [v2] *achieve, succeed*

beat the game*, beat the system*, best, blow away*, carry the day*, come out on top*, conquer, dominate, flourish, get last laugh*, overcome, overwhelm, prevail, prosper, sink, strike it big*, subdue, sweep, take it all*, take the cake*, thrive, trounce, vanquish, win, win hands down*, win out*; SEE CONCEPTS 95,141,706

riumphant [adj] *successful*
boastful, celebratory, champion, conquering, dominant, elated, exultant, glorious, happy, in the lead*, jubilant, looking good, lucky, on top, out front*, prizewinning, proud, rejoicing, swaggering, triumphal, unbeaten, undefeated, victorious, winning; SEE CONCEPT 528

rivia [n] *details*
fine points, memorabilia, minutiae, trifles, trivialities; SEE CONCEPTS 274,543

rivial [adj] *not important*
atomic, beside the point*, commonplace, diminutive, evanescent, everyday, flimsy, frivolous, immaterial, inappreciable, incidental, inconsequential, inconsiderable, insignificant, irrelevant, little, meager, mean, meaningless, microscopic, minor, minute, momentary, negligible, nonessential, nugatory, of no account, paltry, petty, piddling*, puny, scanty, skin-deep*, slight, small, superficial, trifling, trite, unimportant, useless, vanishing, worthless; SEE CONCEPT 575

roll [n] *elf*
demon, dwarf, giant, gnome, goblin, hobgoblin, kobold, leprechaun, monster, mythical creature, ogre; SEE CONCEPT 412

roop/troops [n] *group, often military*
armed forces, army, assemblage, assembly, band, body, bunch, collection, combatants, company, contingent, corps, crew, crowd, delegation, drove, fighting forces, flock, forces, gang, gathering, herd, horde, host, legion, military, multitude, number, outfit, pack, party, personnel, service personnel, soldiers, soldiery, squad, swarm, team, throng, troopers, troupe, unit; SEE CONCEPTS 322,417

rophy [n] *physical award*
blue ribbon*, booty, citation, crown, cup, decoration, gold*, gold star*, guerdon, keepsake, laurels, medal, memento, memorial, palm, prize, reminder, ribbon, souvenir, spoils*, token; SEE CONCEPT 337

ropical [adj] *warm and humid*
close, equatorial, hot, lush, steamy, sticky, stifling, sultry, sweaty, sweltering, torrid, tropic; SEE CONCEPTS 525,605

rot [v] *move along briskly*
amble, canter, go, hurry, jog, lope, pad, rack, ride, run, scamper, step lively; SEE CONCEPT 150

rot out [v] *bring forward*
brandish, bring up, come out with, display, disport, drag up, exhibit, expose, flash, flaunt, parade, recite, rehearse, reiterate, relate, repeat, represent, show, show off; SEE CONCEPT 138

roubadour [n] *singer*
accompanist, artist, balladeer, bard, crooner, jongleur, minnesinger, minstrel, musician, poet, serenader, songster, songwriter, trouveer, vocalist; SEE CONCEPT 352

rouble [n1] *annoyance, worry*
agitation, anxiety, bad news*, bind, bother, commotion, concern, danger, difficulty, dilemma, dire straits, discontent, discord, disorder, disquiet, dissatisfaction, distress, disturbance, grief, hang-up*, heartache, hindrance, hot water*, inconvenience, irritation, mess, misfortune, nuisance, pain, pest, pickle*, predicament, problem, puzzle, row, scrape, sorrow, spot, strain, stress, strife, struggle, suffering, task, torment, tribula-

tion, tumult, unrest, vexation, woe; SEE CONCEPTS 532,674,675,690,728

trouble [n2] *something requiring great effort*
ado, attention, bother, bustle, care, concern, difficulty, effort, exertion, flurry, fuss, hardship, inconvenience, labor, pains, pother, rigor, strain, stress, struggle, thought, trial, while, work, worry; SEE CONCEPTS 666,677

trouble [n3] *bad health*
affliction, ailment, complaint, curse, defect, disability, disease, disorder, failure, illness, malady, malfunction, upset; SEE CONCEPT 316

trouble [v1] *bother, worry*
afflict, agitate, ail, annoy, bug*, burden, burn up*, concern, discommode, discompose, disconcert, disoblige, disquiet, distress, disturb, drive up the wall*, flip out*, fret, get to, give a bad time*, give a hard time*, grieve, harass, harry, impose on, inconvenience, irk, irritate, make a fuss*, make a scene*, make waves*, pain, perplex, perturb, pester, plague, psych*, put out*, sadden, spook*, stir up, strain, stress, torment, try, upset, vex; SEE CONCEPTS 7,19

trouble [v2] *make an effort*
be concerned with, exert, go to the effort of, take pains*, take the time*; SEE CONCEPT 100

troublemaker [n] *person who causes a problem*
agent provocateur, agitator, bad actor*, firebrand*, gremlin*, heel*, hellion, incendiary, inciter, inflamer, instigator, loose cannon*, meddler, mischief-maker, nuisance, phony*, punk*, rabble-rouser*, rascal, recreant, smart aleck*, snake*, stormy petrel*, weasel*; SEE CONCEPT 412

troubleshooter [n] *fixer, repair person*
maintenance person, mender, Mr. Fixit*, service person, technician; SEE CONCEPTS 126,212

troublesome [adj] *bothersome, worrisome*
alarming, annoying, arduous, burdensome, damaging, dangerous, demanding, difficult, disquieting, harassing, hard, heavy, importunate, inconvenient, infestive, intractable, irksome, irritating, laborious, mean, messy, murder, oppressive, painful, pesky, pestiferous, pestilential, problematic, refractory, repressive, rough, taxing, tiresome, tough, tricky, troublous, trying, ugly, ungovernable, unruly, uphill, upsetting, vexatious, vexing, wearisome, wicked, worrying; SEE CONCEPTS 529,565

trough [n] *gutter, depression*
canal, channel, crib, cup, dike, dip, ditch, duct, flume, furrow, gully, hollow, manger, moat, trench, watercourse; SEE CONCEPTS 509,513

trounce [v] *defeat overwhelmingly*
bash, beat, blank, bury, bust*, cap, clobber, conquer, cook one's goose*, crush, drub, dust*, fix one's wagon*, flog, hammer*, lambaste*, lather*, lick*, make mincemeat of*, murder, overcome, overwhelm, paste*, pommel*, put away*, rout, swamp, thrash*, total*, trash*, walk over*, wallop*, waste*, wax*, whip, win, wipe off the mat*; SEE CONCEPT 95

troupe [n] *company*
acting company, actors, association, band, cast, crew, ensemble, gang*, group, party, performers, repertory company, stock company, team, troop; SEE CONCEPT 417

trousers [n] *pants*
bloomers, blue jeans, breeches, britches*, chaps*, chinos, cords*, corduroys, denims, dun-

tr
tr

garees, jeans, knickers, overalls, pantaloons, rompers, slacks; SEE CONCEPT 451

truant [*adj*] *absent*
absent without leave, astray, away, AWOL*, cutting class*, gone, hooky*, missing, no-show*, not present, playing hooky*, skipping school*; SEE CONCEPT 583

truant [*n*] *absentee*
delinquent, deserter, draft dodger, hooky player, malingerer, no-show*, runaway, shirker; SEE CONCEPTS 358,412,423

truce [*n*] *peaceful solution*
accord, agreement, amnesty, armistice, break, breather*, cease-fire, cessation, de-escalation, detente, halt, intermission, interval, letup, lull, moratorium, olive branch*, pause, peace, reconciliation, reprieve, respite, rest, stay, suspension, temporary peace, terms, treaty, white flag*, wind-down*; SEE CONCEPTS 230,298,684

truck [*n1*] *commerce, merchandise*
barter, business, buying and selling, commercial goods, commodities, communication, communion, connection, contact, dealings, exchange, goods*, intercourse, relations, stock, stuff*, trade, traffic, wares*; SEE CONCEPTS 324,330,338

truck [*n2*] *wheeled vehicle for hauling*
buggy*, car, carryall, crate*, dump, eighteen-wheeler*, four by eight*, four by four*, four-wheel drive*, freighter, jeep, lorry, pickup, rig*, semi*, van, wagon, wheels*; SEE CONCEPT 505

truck [*v*] *buy and sell*
bargain, barter, deal, deal in*, do business, exchange, handle, have dealings, negotiate, peddle, retail, swap, trade, traffic, transact, wholesale*; SEE CONCEPTS 324,327,345

truckle [*v*] *fawn*
apple-polish*, be servile, bootlick*, brownnose*, butter up*, cajole, fall all over, fall on one's knees*, flatter, grovel, honey up*, kiss one's feet*, kiss-up*, kowtow*, lay it on*, lick boots*, massage*, oil*, pay court*, play up to*, scratch one's back*, stroke*, suck up to*, toady, truckle, woo*; SEE CONCEPTS 110,384

truculent [*adj*] *belligerent, hateful*
abusive, aggressive, antagonistic, bad-tempered, barbarous, bellicose, browbeating, brutal, bullying, caustic, combative, contentious, contumelious, cowing, cross, defiant, ferocious, fierce, frightening, harsh, hostile, inhuman, inhumane, intimidating, invective, mean, militant, mordacious, mordant, obstreperous, opprobrious, ornery*, pugnacious, quarrelsome, rude, savage, scathing, scrappy, scurrilous, sharp, sullen, terrifying, terrorizing, trenchant, violent, vituperative, vituperous; SEE CONCEPTS 267,401

trudge [*v*] *walk heavily*
clump, drag oneself*, footslog, hike, lumber, march, plod, plug along*, schlepp*, slog, step, stumble, stump, traipse, tramp, tread, trek, wade; SEE CONCEPT 151

true [*adj1*] *real, valid; concordant with facts*
accurate, actual, appropriate, authentic, authoritative, bona fide, correct, dependable, direct, exact, factual, fitting, genuine, honest, indubitable, kosher*, lawful, legal, legitimate, natural, normal, on target*, perfect, precise, proper, pure, regular, right, rightful, sincere, straight, sure-enough*, trustworthy, truthful, typical, undeniable, undesigning, undoubted, unerring, unfaked, unfeigned, unquestionable, veracious,

veridical, veritable, very, wash*; SEE CONCEPTS 267,535,582

true [*adj2*] *loyal*
allegiant, ardent, confirmed, conscientious, constant, creditable, dedicated, dependable, devoted, dutiful, estimable, faithful, fast, firm, high-principled, honest, honorable, just, liege, no lie*, on the up and up*, pure, reliable, resolute, right, right-minded, scrupulous, sincere, square, staunch, steadfast, steady, straight, strict, sure, true-blue*, truehearted, trustworthy, trusty, unaffected, undistorted, unfeigned, unswerving, up front*, upright, veracious, veridical, wholehearted, worthy; SEE CONCEPTS 267,401,542

true [*adv*] *honestly, accurately*
correctly, on target, perfectly, precisely, properly, rightly, truthfully, unerringly, veraciously, veritably; SEE CONCEPTS 267,535,544

true-blue [*adj*] *faithful, loyal*
allegiant, ardent, behind one, dedicated, dependable, devoted, die-hard, dutiful, firm, genuine, hard-core*, honorable, patriotic, staunch, steadfast, sure, tried, tried-and-true*, trustworthy, truthful, upright; SEE CONCEPTS 401,545

truly [*adv*] *really, doubtlessly*
absolutely, accurately, actually, authentically, beyond doubt, beyond question, confirmedly, constantly, correctly, de facto, definitely, devotedly, exactly, factually, faithfully, firmly, genuinely, honestly, honorably, in actuality, in fact in reality, in truth, legitimately, loyally, positively, precisely, reliably, righteously, rightly, sincerely, staunchly, steadily, surely, truthfully, unequivocally, veraciously, veritably, very, with all one's heart*, with devotion, without a doubt; SEE CONCEPTS 267,535,582

trumped up [*adj*] *false*
bogus, concocted, cooked-up*, deceitful, dishonest, fabricated, fake, falsified, fictitious, fishy, framed, fraudulent, imaginary, incorrect, invalid, invented, lying, made up, misleading, phony, sham, unfounded, unsound, untrue; SEE CONCEPTS 267,570,582

truncate [*v*] *shorten*
abbreviate, abridge, clip, crop, curtail, cut, cut off, cut short, lop, pare, prune, shear, top, trim; SEE CONCEPTS 137,236,247

trunk [*n1*] *body, core*
block, bole, butt, column, log, soma, stalk, stem, stock, thorax, torso; SEE CONCEPTS 392,428,826

trunk [*n2*] *long nose of animal*
beak, proboscis, prow, snoot*, snout; SEE CONCEPT 399

trunk [*n3*] *container, box*
bag, baggage, bin, case, chest, coffer, coffin, crate, foot locker, locker, luggage, portmanteau, suitcase, wardrobe; SEE CONCEPTS 494,502

trust [*n1*] *belief in something as true, trustworth*
assurance, certainty, certitude, confidence, conviction, credence, credit, dependence, entrustment, expectation, faith, gospel truth*, hope, positiveness, reliance, stock, store, sureness; SEE CONCEPT 689

trust [*n2*] *responsibility, custody*
account, care, charge, duty, guard, guardianship, keeping, liability, moment, obligation, protection, safekeeping, trusteeship, ward; SEE CONCEPTS 376,645

trust [*n3*] *large company*
bunch, business, cartel, chain, combine, con

glomerate, corporation, crew, crowd, gang, group, institution, megacorp*, mob, monopoly, multinational organization, outfit, pool, ring, syndicate; SEE CONCEPTS *323,325*

rust [*vI*] *believe, place confidence in*
accredit, assume, bank on, be convinced, bet bottom dollar on*, bet on, build on, calculate on, confide in, count on, depend on, expect, gamble on, have faith in, hope, imagine, lay money on*, lean on, look to, place confidence in, place trust in, presume, reckon on, rely upon, suppose, surmise, swear by, take, take at face value*, think likely; SEE CONCEPT *12*

rust [*v2*] *give to for safekeeping*
advance, aid, assign, command, commission, commit, confer, confide, consign, delegate, entrust, give over, grant, lend, let, let out, loan, make trustee, patronize, put into hands of, sign over, store, transfer, turn over; SEE CONCEPT *115*

rustee [*n*] *administrator*
agent, custodian, executor, executrix, fiduciary, guardian, keeper, warden; SEE CONCEPTS *414,423*

rusting [*adj*] *trustful*
believing, confiding, credulous, gullible, innocent, naïve, undoubting, unquestioning, unsuspecting, unsuspicious; SEE CONCEPTS *401,542, 678*

rustworthy/trusty [*adj*] *reliable, believable*
accurate, always there*, authentic, authoritative, convincjng, credible, dependable, ethical, exact, honest, honorable, kosher*, levelheaded, mature, on the level*, on up and up*, open, plausible, principled, realistic, responsible, righteous, rock solid*, saintly, secure, sensible, solid, square, steadfast, straight, there*, to be trusted, tried, tried-and-true*, true, true-blue*, trustable, truthful, unfailing, up-front*, upright, valid, veracious; SEE CONCEPTS *267,404,535*

-uth [*n1*] *reality, validity*
accuracy, actuality, authenticity, axiom, case, certainty, correctness, dope*, exactitude, exactness, fact, facts, factualism, factuality, factualness, genuineness, gospel*, gospel truth*, honest truth*, infallibility, inside track*, legitimacy, maxim, naked truth*, nitty-gritty*, perfection, picture, plain talk, precision, principle, rectitude, rightness, scoop, score, trueness, truism, truthfulness, unvarnished truth, veracity, verisimilitude, verity, whole story*; SEE CONCEPTS *278,638,725*

-uth [*n2*] *honesty, loyalty*
authenticity, candor, constancy, dedication, devotion, dutifulness, faith, faithfulness, fidelity, frankness, integrity, openness, realism, revelation, sincerity, uprightness, veridicality, verity; SEE CONCEPT *657*

-uthful [*adj*] *accurate, honest*
believable, candid, correct, exact, factual, faithful, forthright, frank, guileless, ingenuous, just, kosher*, legit*, like it is*, literal, on the level*, on the up and up*, open, outspoken, plainspoken, precise, real, realistic, reliable, righteous, scrupulous, sincere, square, straight, straightforward, true, true-blue*, trustworthy, truth-telling, unfeigned, unreserved, veracious, veritable; SEE CONCEPTS *267,542*

-y [*n*] *attempt*
all one's got*, best shot*, bid, crack*, dab, effort, endeavor, essay, fling*, go*, jab*, pop*,

shot*, slap*, stab*, striving, struggle, trial, undertaking, whack*, whirl*; SEE CONCEPTS *87,677*

try [*vI*] *attempt*
aim, aspire, attack, bear down, chip away at*, compete, contend, contest, do one's best*, drive for, endeavor, essay, exert oneself, go after, go all out*, go for, have a crack*, have a go*, have a shot*, have a stab*, have a whack*, knock oneself out*, labor, lift a finger*, make a bid, make an attempt, make an effort, make a pass at*, propose, put oneself out*, risk, seek, shoot for*, speculate, strive, struggle, tackle, undertake, venture, vie for, work, wrangle; SEE CONCEPT *87*

try [*v2*] *experiment, test*
appraise, assay, check, check out, evaluate, examine, inspect, investigate, judge, prove, put to the proof*, put to the test*, sample, scrutinize, taste, try out, weigh; SEE CONCEPTS *103,291*

try [*v3*] *bother, afflict*
agonize, annoy, crucify, distress, excruciate, harass, inconvenience, irk, irritate, martyr, pain, plague, rack, strain, stress, tax, tire, torment, torture, trouble, upset, vex, weary, wring; SEE CONCEPTS *7,19*

try [*v4*] *bring before a judge*
adjudge, adjudicate, arbitrate, decide, examine, give a hearing, hear, judge, referee, sit in judgment; SEE CONCEPT *317*

trying [*adj*] *difficult, bothersome*
aggravating, annoying, arduous, demanding, exacting, exasperating, exigent, fatiguing, hard, irksome, irritating, onerous, oppressive, pestilent, provocative, rough, severe, sticky, strenuous, stressful, taxing, tight, tiresome, tough, tricky, troublesome, upsetting, vexing, wearisome, weighty; SEE CONCEPTS *548,565*

try on/try out [*v*] *evaluate, test*
appraise, audition, check out, demonstrate, experiment, fit, give a try, have a dry run*, have a fitting*, inspect, practice, probe, prove, put into practice, put to the test, sample, scrutinize, taste, try for size, wear; SEE CONCEPTS *103,167,291, 453*

tryst [*n*] *meeting during a love affair*
appointment, assignation, date, engagement, meet, meeting, rendezvous, union; SEE CONCEPTS *375,384*

tubby [*adj*] *fat*
beefy*, big, brawny, broad, bulging, bulky, burly, chubby*, chunky*, dumpy, elephantine, fleshy, gargantuan, gross, heavy, heavyset*, hefty, husky, large, obese, oversize, overweight, plump, portly, potbellied, pudgy*, roly-poly*, stout, weighty; SEE CONCEPT *491*

tuck [*v*] *fold together*
constrict, contract, draw together, enfold, gather, hem, insert, make snug, pinch, plait, pleat, push, put in, seam, squeeze in, swaddle, wrap; SEE CONCEPTS *193,218*

tuckered out [*adj*] *tired*
asleep, beat*, burned out*, collapsing, dead on one's feet*, dog-tired*, done for*, done in*, drained, drooping, droopy, drowsy, enervated, exasperated, exhausted, fatigued, finished, overworked, played out*, pooped*, run-down, sleepy, spent, wasted, weary, worn out; SEE CONCEPTS *314,403,406*

tuft [*n*] *clump of strands of something*
bunch, cluster, collection, cowlick, feathers,

tr
tu

group, knot, plumage, ruff, shock, topknot, tussock; SEE CONCEPTS *392,432,471*

tug [*n/v*] *quick pull*
drag, draw, haul, heave, jerk, lug, strain, toil, tow, traction, wrench, yank; SEE CONCEPT *206*

tuition [*n*] *education; education costs*
charge, expenditure, fee, instruction, lessons, price, schooling, teaching, training, tutelage, tutoring; SEE CONCEPT *287*

tumble [*v*] *fall or make fall awkwardly*
bowl down, bring down, descend, dip, disarrange, disarray, disorder, disturb, do a pratfall, down, drop, fall headlong*, flatten, floor, flop, go belly up*, go down, hit the dirt*, jumble, keel, keel over, knock down, knock over, level, lose footing, lose it*, mess up, nose-dive, pitch, plummet, plunge, roll, sag, skid, slip, slump, spill, stumble, take a header*, tip over, topple, toss, trip, unsettle, upset; SEE CONCEPTS *147,149,181*

tumescent [*adj*] *swollen*
bloated, bulging, bulgy, bursting, distended, distent, enlarged, expanding, inflated, puffed, puffy, tumid; SEE CONCEPT *485*

tummy [*n*] *stomach*
abdomen, belly, below the belt*, breadbasket*, gut, insides, paunch, pot*, solar plexus, spare tire*; SEE CONCEPTS *393,420*

tumor [*n*] *abnormal growth in animate being*
bump, cancer, carcinoma, cyst, lump, neoplasm, sarcoma, swelling, tumefaction; SEE CONCEPT *316*

tumult [*n*] *uproar, confusion*
ado, affray, agitation, altercation, babel, bedlam, brawl, clamor, commotion, convulsion, din, disorder, disturbance, dither, excitement, ferment, fight, fracas, fuss, hassle*, jangle, lather*, maelstrom, noise, outbreak, outcry, pandemonium, paroxysm, pother, quarrel, racket, riot, row, ruction, seething, stir, strife, turbulence, turmoil, unrest, unsettlement, upheaval, upturn, wildness; SEE CONCEPTS *230,674*

tumultuous/tumultuous [*adj*] *confused; in an uproar*
agitated, boisterous, clamorous, disorderly, disturbed, excited, fierce, hectic, irregular, lawless, noisy, obstreperous, passionate, raging, rambunctious, raucous, restless, riotous, rowdy, rowdydowdy, rumbunctious, stormy, termagant, turbulent, unrestrained, unruly, uproarious, violent, vociferous, wild; SEE CONCEPT *548*

tundra [*n*] *plain*
expanse, field, flat, flatland, open country, plateau, prairie, steppe, wasteland; SEE CONCEPT *509*

tune [*n*] *melody, harmony*
air, aria, carol, chorus, composition, concert, consonance, descant, diapason, ditty*, harmony, jingle, lay, measure, melodia, motif, number, piece, song, strain, theme, warble; SEE CONCEPTS *264,595*

tune [*n2*] *agreement*
accord, chime, chorus, concert, concord, concordance, consonance, euphony, harmony, pitch, sympathy, unison; SEE CONCEPTS *670,714*

tuneful [*adj*] *melodic, melodious*
canorous, catchy*, dulcet, euphonic, euphonious, harmonic, harmonious, in tune, musical, pleasing, pleasing to the ear, resonant, songful, sonorous, sweet-sounding, symphonic, symphonious, tuned, well-tuned; SEE CONCEPT *594*

tune/tune up [*v*] *bring into harmony*
accommodate, adapt, adjust, attune, conform, coordinate, dial, fix, harmonize, integrate, modulate, pitch, proportion, reconcile, regulate, set, string, tighten; SEE CONCEPTS *65,126*

tunnel [*n*] *covered passageway*
adit, burrow, channel, crawl space, crawlway, crosscut, drift, hole, hole in the wall*, mine, passage, pit, shaft, subway, tube, underpass; SEE CONCEPTS *509,513*

tunnel [*v*] *dig a passage through*
burrow, excavate, mine, penetrate, sap, scoop out, undermine; SEE CONCEPT *178*

turbulent [*adj1*] *unsettled, raging (referring to weather)*
agitated, bitter, blustering, blustery, boiling, bumpy, choppy, coarse, confused, destructive, disordered, disturbed, fierce, foaming, furious, howling, inclement, moiling, noisy, restless, riotous, roaring, rough, ruffled, rugged, stirred up, stormful, storming, stormy, swirling, tempestuous, thunderous, tremulous, tumultuous/tumultuous, unstable, violent, wild; SEE CONCEPT *525*

turbulent [*adj2*] *rebellious, unmanageable*
agitated, anarchic, angry, bitter, boisterous, chaotic, demonstrative, destructive, disorderly, excited, fierce, fiery, foaming, insubordinate, lawless, mutinous, obstreperous, passionate, perturbed, quarrelsome, rabid, rambunctious, rampant, raucous, refractory, riotous, rough, roughhouse*, rowdy, rude, seditious, shaking, stern, storming, termagant, tumultuous/tumultuous, unbridled, uncontrolled, undisciplined, ungovernable, unruly, untamed, uproarious, vehement, violent, vociferous, wild; SEE CONCEPT *401*

turmoil [*n*] *chaos*
agitation, ailment, anxiety, anxiousness, bedlam, bustle, commotion, confusion, disorder, disquiet, disquietude, distress, disturbance, dither, ferment, flap*, flurry, free-for-all*, fuss, hassle*, hectic, hubbub*, lather*, mix-up, noise, pandemonium, pother, restiveness, restlessness, riot, row, ruckus, stir, strife, to-do*, topsy-turvy, trouble, tumult, turbulence, unrest, uproar, violence, whirl; SEE CONCEPTS *230,674*

turn [*n1*] *revolution, curving*
about-face, angle, bend, bias, bow, branch, change, changeabout, circle, circuit, circulation, circumvolution, corner, curve, cycle, departure, detour, deviation, direction, drift, flection, flexure, fork, gyration, gyre, heading, hook, pirouette, pivot, quirk, retroversion, reversal, reverse, reversion, right-about, roll, rotation, round, shift, spin, spiral, swing, tack, tendency, trend, turnabout, turning, twist, twisting, wheel, whirl, wind, winding, yaw; SEE CONCEPTS *198,738,754*

turn [*n2*] *sudden change*
alteration, bend, branch, crotch, deflection, departure, detour, deviation, digression, distortion, divarication, double, fork, modification, mutation, shift, tack, twist, variation, warp, yaw; SEE CONCEPT *697*

turn [*n3*] *chance, opportunity*
accomplishment, act, action, bit, bout, crack*, deed, favor, fling*, gesture, go*, go around*, move, period, round, routine, say*, service, shift,

shot*, spell, stint, succession, time, tour, trick, try; SEE CONCEPT *693*

turn [*n4*] *walk, outing*
airing, circuit, constitutional, drive, excursion, jaunt, promenade, ramble, ride, saunter, spin, stroll; SEE CONCEPTS *147,224,363*

turn [*n5*] *aptitude, knack*
affinity, aptness, bent, bias, bump, disposition, faculty, flair, genius, gift, head, inclination, leaning, predisposition, propensity, talent; SEE CONCEPTS *411,630*

turn [*n6*] *scare*
attack, blow, fit, fright, jolt, seizure, shock, spell, start, surprise; SEE CONCEPTS *230,410*

turn [*v1*] *revolve, curve*
arc, bend, circle, circulate, circumduct, come around, corner, cut, eddy, go around, go round, ground, gyrate, gyre, hang a left*, hang a right*, incline, loop, make a left, make a right, move in a circle, negotiate, orbit, oscillate, pass, pass around, pirouette, pivot, revolve, roll, rotate, round, spin, sway, swing, swivel, take a bend*, twirl, twist, vibrate, weave, wheel, whirl, wind, yaw; SEE CONCEPTS *147,201,738,748*

turn [*v2*] *reverse; change course*
about-face, aim, alter, alternate, backslide, call off, capsize, change, change position, convert, curve, depart, detour, detract, deviate, digress, direct, diverge, double back, face about, go back, incline, inverse, invert, loop, move, pivot, rechannel, recoil, redirect, regress, relapse, retrace, return, revert, sheer, shift, shunt, shy away, sidetrack, subvert, sway, swerve, swing, swirl, switch, tack, transform, twist, upset, vary, veer, volte-face, wheel, whip, whirl, zigzag; SEE CONCEPTS *195,198,213*

turn [*v3*] *adapt, fit*
alter, become, change, change into, come, convert, divert, fashion, form, get, go, grow into, metamorphose, modify, mold, mutate, pass into, put, refashion, remake, remodel, render, run, shape, transfigure, transform, translate, transmute, transpose, vary, wax; SEE CONCEPTS *232,697*

turn [*v4*] *become sour or tainted*
acidify, become rancid, break down, crumble, curdle, decay, decompose, disintegrate, dull, ferment, go bad, molder, putrefy, rot, sour, spoil, taint; SEE CONCEPTS *456,469*

turn [*v5*] *use; resort to*
address, appeal, apply, approach, bend, be predisposed to, devote, direct, employ, favor, give, go, have recourse, incline, lend, look, prefer, recur, repair, run, tend, throw, turn one's energies to*, turn one's hand to*, undertake, utilize; SEE CONCEPTS *100,225*

turn [*v6*] *sicken*
derange, discompose, disgust, disorder, make one sick*, nauseate, revolt, unbalance, undo, unhinge*, unsettle, upset; SEE CONCEPTS *7,19,250*

turn [*v7*] *change one's mind; defect*
apostatize, bring round, change sides, desert, go over, influence, persuade, prejudice, prevail upon, rat*, renege, renounce, repudiate, retract, talk into, tergiversate, tergiverse; SEE CONCEPTS *21,41,54*

turn [*v8*] *twist a body part*
bruise, crick, dislocate, hurt, sprain, strain, wrench; SEE CONCEPT *246*

turnabout [*n*] *about-face*
changeabout, change of direction, doubleback, flip-flop, reversal, reverse, shift, turnaround, U-turn, volte-face; SEE CONCEPT *697*

turncoat [*n*] *traitor*
apostate, back-stabber*, Benedict Arnold*, betrayer, conspirator, deceiver, defector, deserter, double-crosser*, fink*, informer, Judas*, quisling, rat*, rebel, renegade, snake*, sneak*, snitch*, spy, squealer*, stool pigeon*, tattletale, tergiversator, treasonist, two-timer*, whistle-blower*; SEE CONCEPT *412*

turn down [*v*] *reject*
decline, disapprove, dismiss, rebuff, refuse, reprobate, repudiate, say no, scorn, spurn, throw out; SEE CONCEPTS *18,54*

turn in [*v*] *go to bed*
bed, catch some z's*, flop*, go to sleep, hit the hay*, hit the sack*, lie down, nap, pile in, rest, retire, roll in; SEE CONCEPT *210*

turning point [*n*] *crucial occurrence*
axis, change, climacteric, climax, contingency, crisis, critical moment, critical period, crossing, crossroads, crux, culmination, decisive moment, development, emergency, exigency, hinge, juncture, moment of truth*, pass, peak, pinch, pivot, shift, strait, transition, twist, zero hour*; SEE CONCEPTS *679,832*

turn off [*v1*] *disgust*
alienate, bore, disenchant, disinterest, displease, irritate, lose one's interest, make one sick*, nauseate, offend, put off, repel, sicken; SEE CONCEPTS *7,19*

turn off [*v2*] *stop from operating*
close, cut, cut out, douse, extinguish, halt, hit the switch*, kill*, log off, put out, shut, shut down, shut off, switch off, turn out, unplug; SEE CONCEPTS *121,234*

turn on [*v1*] *excite, please*
arouse, attract, captivate, enchant, get started, initiate, introduce, show, stimulate, stir up, thrill, titillate, work up; SEE CONCEPT *11*

turn on [*v2*] *start the operation of*
activate, begin, energize, get started, ignite, initiate, introduce, log on, put in gear, put on, set in motion, start up, switch on; SEE CONCEPT *221*

turnout [*n1*] *group assembling for event*
assemblage, assembly, attendance, audience, congregation, crowd, gate, gathering, number, throng; SEE CONCEPT *417*

turnout [*n2*] *amount produced*
aggregate, output, outturn, product, production, productivity, quota, turnover, volume, yield; SEE CONCEPTS *338,787*

turn out [*v1*] *equip; produce*
accouter, appoint, arm, bear, bring out, build, clothe, dress, fabricate, finish, fit, fit out*, furnish, make, manufacture, outfit, process, put out, rig*, rig out*, yield; SEE CONCEPTS *167,205,234*

turn out [*v2*] *get out of bed*
appear, arise, come, emerge, get up, pile out*, rise, rise and shine*, roll out*, show up, uprise, wake, wake up; SEE CONCEPT *159*

turn over [*v1*] *give, transfer*
assign, come across with, commend, commit, confer, confide, consign, convey, delegate, deliver, entrust, feed, find, furnish, give over, give up, hand over, hand, pass on, provide, relegate, relinquish, render, supply, surrender, yield; SEE CONCEPTS *108,143*

tu
tu

turn over [v2] *think about seriously*
consider, contemplate, deliberate, give thought
to, meditate, mull over, muse, ponder, reflect on,
revolve, roll, ruminate, think over, wonder
about; SEE CONCEPTS *17,24*

turnpike [n] *highway*
expressway, four-lane*, freeway, interstate,
parkway, pike*, roadway, state highway, superhighway, toll road; SEE CONCEPT *501*

turn up [v1] *come, arrive*
appear, attend, blow in*, come, come in, enter,
get, get in, make an appearance*, materialize,
pop in*, punch in*, put in an appearance*, reach,
roll in*, show, show up*, weigh in*; SEE CON-
CEPT *159*

turn up [v2] *discover or be discovered*
become known, be found, bring to light*, catch,
come across, come to light*, come to pass, crop
up, descry, detect, dig up*, disclose, encounter,
espy, expose, find, hit upon*, learn, meet, meet
with*, pop up*, reveal, see, spot, track, track
down*, transpire, uncover, unearth; SEE CON-
CEPTS *31,183*

turpitude [n] *depravity*
baseness, corruption, criminality, debasement,
debauchery, degradation, evil, immorality, improbity, lewdness, licentiousness, perversion,
sinfulness, vice, viciousness, vileness, wickedness; SEE CONCEPT *645*

tussle [n] *struggle*
battle, brawl, brush, clash, combat, conflict, contest, donnybrook, encounter, fight, fray, free-for-
all*, grind, hassle, jam, roughhouse, row,
rumble*, scramble, scrap*, scuffle, skirmish,
strife, undertaking; SEE CONCEPTS *87,106,674*

tussle [v] *struggle*
battle, box, brawl, bump heads*, conflict, contest, fight, go up against*, grapple, hassle, lock
horns*, put up a fight*, romp, rough-house*,
row, scrap, scuffle, tangle, wrestle; SEE CONCEPT
106

tutelage [n] *guardianship; teaching*
apprenticeship, care, coaching, custody, drilling,
education, guidance, instruction, lesson, preparation, protection, schooling, supervision, training,
tutoring; SEE CONCEPTS *274,285*

tutor [n] *person who teaches another privately*
coach, educator, governor, grind, guardian,
guide, instructor, lecturer, mentor, preceptor, private teacher, prof*, teach*, teacher; SEE CONCEPT
350

tutor [v] *teach someone privately*
clue, coach, direct, discipline, drill, drum into*,
edify, educate, guide, instruct, lay it out for*,
lecture, let in on*, ready, school, train, update;
SEE CONCEPT *285*

twaddle [n] *nonsense*
babble, balderdash*, baloney*, BS*, bull, bunk*,
chatter, crap*, drivel, foolishness, gibberish,
hogwash*, hooey*, hot air*, idle talk, jive*,
mumbo jumbo*, palaver, poppycock*, prattle,
rubbish, silliness, trash*, tripe; SEE CONCEPTS
230,388,633

twilight [n] *onset of darkness at end of day*
afterglow, afterlight, crepuscular light, decline,
dimness, dusk, early evening, ebb, end, evening,
eventide, gloaming, half-light, last phase*, late-
afternoon, night, nightfall, sundown, sunset; SEE
CONCEPTS *810,832*

twin [adj] *duplicate, similar*
accompanying, bifold, binary, copied, corresponding, coupled, double, dual, duplicating,
geminate, identical, joint, like, matched, matching, paired, parallel, same, second, selfsame,
twofold, very same; SEE CONCEPTS *487,563,573*

twin [n] *something exactly like another*
clone, companion, coordinate, corollary, counterpart, doppelgänger, double, duplicate, fraternal twin, identical twin, likeness, lookalike,
match, mate, reciprocal, ringer*, Siamese twin;
SEE CONCEPTS *414,664,670*

twine [n] *rope, cord*
braid, coil, convolution, cordage, knot, snarl,
string, tangle, thread, twist, whorl, yarn; SEE
CONCEPT *475*

twine [v] *coil, twist together*
bend, braid, corkscrew, curl, encircle, enmesh,
entangle, entwine, interlace, interweave, knit,
loop, meander, plait, spiral, splice, surround, tangle, twist, undulate, weave, wind, wrap, wreathe;
SEE CONCEPTS *147,201,742*

twinge [n] *sharp pain*
ache, bite, gripe, lancination, misery, pang,
pinch, prick, shiver, smart, spasm, stab, stitch,
throb, throe, tic, tweak, twist, twitch; SEE CON-
CEPT *728*

twinkle [v] *glimmer, shine*
blink, coruscate, flash, flicker, gleam, glint, glisten, glitter, glow, illuminate, light, light up, scintillate, shimmer, sparkle, wink; SEE CONCEPT *624*

twirl [v] *turn around circularly*
gyrate, gyre, pirouette, pivot, purl, revolve, rotate, spin, turn, twist, wheel, whirl, whirligig,
wind; SEE CONCEPTS *150,152*

twist [n1] *curl, spin*
arc, bend, braid, coil, convolution, curlicue,
curve, flourish, hank, helix, jerk, meander, plug,
ply, pull, roll, spiral, swivel, torsion, turn, twine,
undulation, warp, wind, wrench, yank, zigzag;
SEE CONCEPTS *738,754*

twist [n2] *sudden development; oddity*
aberration, bent, change, characteristic, confusion, crotchet, eccentricity, entanglement, foible,
idiosyncrasy, kink, knot, mess, mix-up, peculiarity, proclivity, quirk, revelation, screw up*,
slant, snarl, surprise, tangle, trait, turn, variation;
SEE CONCEPTS *411,832*

twist [v1] *curl, spin*
coil, contort, corkscrew, encircle, entwine, intertwine, rick, screw, spiral, sprain, squirm, swivel,
turn, turn around, twine, twirl, warp, weave, wiggle, wind, wrap, wrap around, wreathe, wrench,
wriggle, wring, writhe, zigzag; SEE CONCEPTS
80,147,184,201,206,738

twist [v2] *misrepresent*
alter, belie, change, color, contort, distort, falsify, garble, misquote, misstate, pervert, warp;
SEE CONCEPT *63*

twitch [v] *have a spasm*
beat, blink, clasp, clutch, flutter, grab, grasp,
grip, jerk, jiggle, jump, kick, lug, lurch, nip,
pain, palpitate, pluck, pull, seize, shiver, shudder, snap, snatch, squirm, tic, tremble, tug,
twinge, vellicate, yank; SEE CONCEPTS *185,206*

two-bit [adj] *cheap, worth very little*
base, catchpenny, cheesy, crappy*, cruddy,
garbage, gaudy, inferior, junky*, lousy, no good,
piddling, poor, ratty, rinky-dink*, second-rate,

shoddy, sleazy, small-time*, tatty, trashy, value-less, worthless; SEE CONCEPT 589

two-faced [*adj*] *deceitful*
artful, backstabbing, beguiling, crafty, cunning, deceiving, deceptive, dishonest, double-dealing, foxy, fraudulent, guileful, hypocritical, insincere, knavish, lying, misleading, shifty, sly, sneaky, tricky, underhanded, untruthful; SEE CONCEPT 401

two-time [*v*] *deceive*
backstab, be dishonest, be disloyal, betray, be unfaithful, burn, cheat, con, defraud, double-cross, dupe, mislead, take advantage of, trick, victimize; SEE CONCEPTS 7,19,59

tycoon [*n*] *person who has a lot of money, power*
administrator, big shot*, boss, business person, capitalist, captain of industry*, director, entrepreneur, executive, fat cat*, financier, industrialist, investor, magnate, mogul, wealthy person; SEE CONCEPT 347

type [*n1*] *class, kind*
blazon, brand, breed, cast, category, character, classification, cut, description, feather, form, genre, group, ilk, likes, lot, mold, nature, number, order, persuasion, rubric, sample, sort, species, specimen, stamp, standard, strain, subdivision, variety, way; SEE CONCEPTS 378,411

type [*n2*] *example, model*
archetype, epitome, essence, exemplar, original, paradigm, pattern, personification, prototype, quintessence, representative, sample, specimen, standard; SEE CONCEPT 686

type [*n3*] *printed characters*
case, emblem, face, figure, font, point size, print, printing, sign, symbol; SEE CONCEPTS 79,284

type [*v1*] *classify*
arrange, button down*, categorize, class, peg, pigeonhole*, put away, put down as, sort, standardize, stereotype, tab*, typecast; SEE CONCEPTS 18,84

type [*v2*] *hit keys on machine to print document*
copy, dash off*, enter data, hunt-and-peck*, teletype, touch, touch-type, transcribe, typewrite, write; SEE CONCEPTS 79,199,203

typical [*adj*] *usual, conventional*
archetypal, archetypical, average, characteristic, classic, classical, common, commonplace, emblematic, essential, everyday, exemplary, expected, general, habitual, ideal, illustrative, in character*, indicative, in keeping, matter-of-course*, model, natural, normal, old hat*, ordinary, orthodox, paradigmatic, patterned, prevalent, prototypal, prototypical, quintessential, regular, representative, standard, standardized, stock, suggestive, symbolic, typic, unexceptional; SEE CONCEPTS 530,533,547

typify [*v*] *represent, characterize*
body forth, characterize, describe, emblematize, embody, epitomize, exemplify, feature, illustrate, incarnate, mean, mirror, model, personify, stand for, sum up, symbolize; SEE CONCEPTS 55,261,682

tyrannical [*adj*] *despotic, oppressive*
authoritarian, autocratic, brutal, cruel, demanding, dictatorial, domineering, harsh, heavy-handed*, ironhanded*, mean, overbearing, repressive, ruthless, totalitarian, tough, unjust; SEE CONCEPTS 537,548

tyranny [*n*] *dictatorship*
absolutism, authoritarianism, autocracy, coer-cion, cruelty, despotism, domination, fascism, high-handedness, imperiousness, monocracy, oligarchy, oppression, peremptoriness, reign of terror*, severity, terrorism, totalitarianism, totality, unreasonableness; SEE CONCEPTS 299,301

tyrant [*n*] *person who dictates, oppresses*
absolute ruler, absolutist, authoritarian, autocrat, bully, despot, dictator, Hitler*, inquisitor, martinet, oppressor, slave driver*, Stalin*; SEE CONCEPTS 354,412

tyro [*n*] *beginner*
abecedarian, amateur, apprentice, buckwheater*, cadet, colt*, greenhorn, learner, neophyte, newcomer, new kid on the block*, novice, novitiate, pupil, recruit, rookie, starter, student, tenderfoot*, trainee; SEE CONCEPTS 423,424

U

ubiquitous [*adj*] *ever-present*
all-over, everywhere, omnipresent, pervasive, ubiquity, universal, wall-to-wall*; SEE CONCEPT 530

UFO [*n*] *unidentified flying object*
extraterrestrial spacecraft, flying saucer, rocket, rocketship, spaceship; SEE CONCEPT 504

ugly [*adj1*] *unattractive*
animal, appalling, awful, bad-looking, beastly, deformed, disfigured, foul, frightful, grisly, gross, grotesque, hard-featured, hideous, homely, horrid, ill-favored, loathsome, misshapen, monstrous, not much to look at*, plain, repelling, repugnant, repulsive, revolting, unbeautiful, uncomely, uninviting, unlovely, unprepossessing, unseemly, unsightly; SEE CONCEPT 579

ugly [*adj2*] *unpleasant, disagreeable*
base, despicable, dirty, disgusting, distasteful, filthy, foul, frightful, hideous, horrid, ignoble, low, low-down, mean, messy, monstrous, nasty, nauseous, noisome, objectionable, odious, offensive, pesky, repellent, repugnant, repulsive, revolting, scandalous, servile, shocking, sickening, sordid, sorry, terrible, troublesome, troublous, vexatious, vile, wicked, wretched; SEE CONCEPTS 403,571

ugly [*adj3*] *dangerous, threatening*
angry, bellicose, black, cantankerous, crabbed, crabby, dark, disagreeable, dour, evil, fell, forbidding, formidable, gloomy, glum, grave, grievous, major, malevolent, menacing, morose, nasty, obnoxious, ominous, pugnacious, quarrelsome, rough, saturnine, scowling, serious, sinister, spiteful, sullen, surly, treacherous, truculent, vicious, violent, wicked; SEE CONCEPTS 401,548

ulterior [*adj*] *secret; pertaining to a hidden goal*
ambiguous, buried, concealed, covert, cryptic, dark, enigmatic, equivocal, guarded, hidden, implied, obscure, obscured, personal, privy, remote, secondary, selfish, shrouded, under cover, under wraps*, undisclosed, undivulged, unexpressed, unsaid; SEE CONCEPTS 544,576

ultimate [*adj1*] *last, final*
capping, chips down*, closing, concluding, conclusive, decisive, end, eventual, extreme, far out*, farthermost, farthest, final curtain*, further-

tu
ul

most, furthest, hindmost, latest, latter, lattermost, most distant, terminal; SEE CONCEPTS 799,820

ultimate [*adj2*] *best, greatest*
extreme, highest, incomparable, max*, maxi*, maximum, most, paramount, preeminent, significant, superlative, supreme, surpassing, the most, topmost, towering, transcendent, unequalable, unmatchable, unsurpassable, utmost; SEE CONCEPTS 568,574

ultimate [*adj3*] *fundamental*
absolute, basic, categorical, elemental, empyreal, empyrean, primary, radical, sublime, transcendental; SEE CONCEPTS 535,546

ultimately [*adv*] *eventually*
after all, after a while, as a conclusion, at last, at long last, at the close, basically, by and by, climactically, conclusively, finally, fundamentally, hereafter, in conclusion, in consummation, in due time, in future, in the end, in the sequel, presently, sequentially, someday, sometime, somewhere, sooner or later, yet; SEE CONCEPT 820

ultimatum [*n*] *final offer*
conditions, demand, final notice, final proposal, final terms, final warning, final word, last chance, last offer, last word, sticking point, warning; SEE CONCEPT 662

ultra [*adj*] *extreme*
all out*, drastic, excessive, extremist, fanatical, far-out*, gone*, immoderate, outlandish, out of bounds*, outré, rabid*, radical, revolutionary, too much*; SEE CONCEPTS 562,569

ultramodern [*adj*] *up-to-date*
advanced, ahead of its time, avant-garde, contemporary, current, cutting-edge*, fresh, futuristic, latest, leading-edge*, modernistic, modish, new, new-fashioned, nontraditional, now, present-day, revolutionary, state-of-the-art*, stylish, today, twenty-first century*, up-to-the-minute; SEE CONCEPTS 168,177,202

umbrage [*n*] *personal displeasure*
anger, annoyance, chagrin, exasperation, fury, grudge, high dudgeon*, huff, indignation, injury, ire, irking, irritation, miff*, nettling*, offense, pique, provoking, rage, resentment, sense of injury, vexation, wrath; SEE CONCEPTS 29,410

umpire [*n*] *person who settles dispute*
adjudicator, arbiter, arbitrator, assessor, compromiser, inspector, judge, justice, mediator, moderator, negotiator, peacemaker, proprietor, ref*, referee, settler, ump*; SEE CONCEPTS 348,366,423

unable [*adj*] *not having talent, skill*
can't cut it*, can't hack it*, can't make the grade*, clumsy, helpless, hog-tied*, impotent, impuissant, inadequate, incapable, incapacitated, incompetent, ineffectual, inefficacious, inefficient, inept, inoperative, no can do*, no good*, not able, not cut out for*, not equal to*, not up to*, out of commission*, powerless, sidelined*, unfit, unfitted, unqualified, unskilled, weak; SEE CONCEPT 527

unabridged [*adj*] *not shortened*
complete, entire, full-length, intact, total, unabbreviated, uncondensed, uncut, unexpurgated, unshortened, whole; SEE CONCEPTS 267,531

unacceptable [*adj*] *not suitable or satisfactory*
below par*, damaged, disagreeable, displeasing, distasteful, exceptionable, half-baked*, ill-favored, improper, inadmissible, insupportable,

lousy*, not up to snuff*, objectionable, obnoxious, offensive, reject, repugnant, unappealing, undesirable, uninviting, unpleasant, unsatisfactory, unwanted, unwelcome, won't do*; SEE CONCEPTS 529,558

unaccompanied [*adj*] *alone*
abandoned, a cappella*, apart, by oneself, deserted, detached, hermit, individual, isolate, isolated, lone, loner, odd, on one's own, removed, single, solitary, solo, stag, traveling light*, unattended, unescorted; SEE CONCEPTS 555,577

unaccountable [*adj*] *not explainable; mysterious*
arcane, astonishing, baffling, extraordinary, impenetrable, incomprehensible, inexplicable, inscrutable, mystic, odd, peculiar, puzzling, strange, uncommon, unexplainable, unfathomable, unheard-of, unintelligible, unknowable, unusual, unwonted; SEE CONCEPTS 529,564

unaccustomed [*adj1*] *not prepared, ready; new*
ignorant, incompetent, inexperienced, newcome, not given to*, not used to, novice, to green*, unacquainted, unfamiliar with, uninformed, uninstructed, unpracticed, unseasoned, unskilled, untaught, untrained, unused to, unversed in; SEE CONCEPTS 527,678

unaccustomed [*adj2*] *new, strange*
alien, altered, bizarre, different, eccentric, exceptional, exotic, foreign, imported, novel, outlandish, out of the ordinary, quaint, remarkable, singular, special, surprising, uncommon, unconventional, uncustomary, unexpected, unfamiliar, unknown, unorthodox, unprecedented, unusual, unwonted, variant; SEE CONCEPTS 547,564

unadorned [*adj*] *plain, simple*
austere, bare, basic, modest, stark, stripped down, undecorated, unembellished; SEE CONCEPTS 485,589

unadulterated [*adj*] *clean, pure; unmixed*
immaculate, purified, refined, sanitary, spotless, stainless, sterile, sterilized, unblemished, uncontaminated, uncorrupted, undebased, undefiled, undiluted, unpolluted, unsoiled, unstained, unsullied, untainted, untarnished, untouched, wholesome; SEE CONCEPT 621

unadvised [*adj*] *not smart; careless*
brash, hasty, heedless, hot-headed, ignorant, ill-advised, imprudent, inadvisable, incautious, inconsiderate, indiscreet, injudicious, in the dark*, rash, reckless, thoughtless, unaware, unconsidered, uninformed, unknowing, unsuspecting, unwarned, unwary, unwise; SEE CONCEPTS 403,548

unaffected [*adj1*] *honest, unsophisticated*
artless, candid, direct, folksy*, forthright, frank, genuine, guileless, homey*, ingenuous, modest, naive, natural, plain, simple, sincere, single, spontaneous, straightforward, true, unartificial, unassuming, unpretentious, unschooled, unspoilt, unstudied, up front*; SEE CONCEPTS 401,404

unaffected [*adj2*] *unchanged, unmoved*
aloof, callous, calm, casual, cold fish*, cool, easy-going, hard-boiled*, hard-hearted*, impassive, impervious, laid-back*, not influenced, proof, steady, thick-skinned*, unaltered, unconcerned, unexcited, unimpressed, uninfluenced, unresponsive, unruffled, unstirred, untouched; SEE CONCEPTS 542,548

unafraid [*adj*] *fearless*
assured, ballsy*, bold, brassy, brave, cheeky*, cocky, confident, courageous, daring, dashing,

dauntless, gallant, game, gritty, gutsy, having nerves of steel*, heroic, nervy, plucky, spunky, sure, undaunted, unfearing, unfrightened, unscared, unshakable, valiant; SEE CONCEPT *401*

unanimous [*adj*] *in agreement; uncontested*
accepted, accordant, agreed, agreeing, as one, assenting, collective, combined, common, communal, concerted, concordant, concurrent, consensual, consentient, consistent, consonant, harmonious, homogeneous, in complete accord, like-minded, of one mind, popular, public, shared, single, solid, undisputed, undivided, unified, united, universal, unquestioned, with one voice*; SEE CONCEPTS *8,267,563*

unappetizing [*adj*] *distasteful*
flat, flavorless, grody*, gross, icky*, insipid, savorless, stinky, tasteless, unappealing, unattractive, uninteresting, uninviting, unpalatable, unpleasant, unsavory, vapid, yucky*; SEE CONCEPTS *462,529*

unapproachable [*adj*] *unfriendly*
aloof, chilly*, cold, cool, distant, frigid, hesitant, inaccessible, remote, reserved, standoffish, uncommunicative, unsociable, withdrawn; SEE CONCEPTS *404,555*

unapproachable [*adj2*] *difficult to get to*
inaccessible, out of reach, out-of-the-way, remote, unattainable, unobtainable, unreachable; SEE CONCEPT *576*

unarmed [*adj*] *disarmed*
exposed, hands tied*, helpless, indefensible, like a sitting duck*, naked*, open, powerless, unguarded, unprotected, unshielded, vulnerable, weaponless, wide open*; SEE CONCEPTS *555,576*

unasked [*adj*] *voluntary*
arrogant, gratuitous, impudent, not asked, of one's own accord, overbearing, presumptuous, spontaneous, supererogatory, unbidden, uncalled-for, undemanded, undesired, uninvited, unprompted, unrequested, unsought, unwanted, unwelcome, voluntarily, willing, without prompting; SEE CONCEPTS *401,558*

unassuming [*adj*] *shy*
backward, bashful, diffident, humble, lowly, meek, modest, mousy*, plain, prim, quiet, reserved, retiring, self-effacing, simple, unambitious, unassertive, unobtrusive, unostentatious, unpretending, unpretentious; SEE CONCEPTS *401,404*

unattached [*adj*] *disconnected, free*
apart, at liberty, autonomous, available, detached, fancy-free*, footloose*, independent, off the hook*, on one's own*, separate, single, unaffiliated, uncommitted, unconnected, uninvolved, unmarried; SEE CONCEPTS *267,401,482,542*

unattractive [*adj*] *ugly*
bad-looking, beastly, deformed, disfigured, disgusting, frightful, gross, grotesque, hideous, homely, horrid, monstrous, not much to look at*, plain, repelling, repugnant, repulsive, revolting, unalluring, unappealing, unsightly; SEE CONCEPT *579*

unauthorized [*adj*] *not sanctioned, permitted*
crooked*, dirty*, illegal, illegitimate, no-no*, off base*, out of bounds*, out of line*, over the line*, pirated, shady*, unapproved, unconstitutional, under the table*, unjustified, unlawful, unofficial, unsanctioned, unwarranted, wildcat*, wrongful; SEE CONCEPTS *319,548*

unavailing [*adj*] *futile*
barren, empty, exhausted, fruitless, idle, impractical, ineffective, ineffectual, in vain, on a treadmill*, save one's breath*, to no avail*, to no effect*, to no purpose*, trifling, trivial, unavailing, unproductive, unprofitable, unsuccessful, useless, vain, valueless, worthless; SEE CONCEPTS *528,548,560*

unavoidable [*adj*] *bound to happen*
certain, compulsory, fated, impending, ineluctable, ineludible, inescapable, inevasible, inevitable, inexorable, locked up*, necessary, obligatory, open and shut*, set, sure, unescapable; SEE CONCEPT *535*

unaware [*adj*] *ignorant*
blind, careless, caught napping*, daydreaming, deaf, deaf to*, doped*, forgetful, heedless, ignorant, in a daze*, inattentive, incognizant, inconversant, insensible, mooning, negligent, nescient, not all there*, not cognizant, oblivious, out cold*, out of it*, out to lunch*, spacey*, unacquainted, unconcerned, unconscious, unenlightened, unfamiliar, uninformed, uninstructed, unknowing, unmindful, unsuspecting, unwitting; SEE CONCEPT *402*

unawares [*adv*] *without warning; suddenly*
aback, abruptly, accidentally, by accident, by mistake, by surprise, carelessly, ignorantly, inadvertently, mistakenly, off guard, short, sudden, surprisingly, unconsciously, unexpectedly, unintentionally, unknowingly, unprepared, unready, unwittingly, without warning; SEE CONCEPTS *544,548,799*

unbalanced [*adj1*] *not even, stable*
asymmetric, asymmetrical, disproportionate, irregular, lopsided, not balanced, off-balance, shaky, top-heavy, treacherous, unequal, uneven, unstable, unsteady, unsymmetrical, wobbly; SEE CONCEPT *480*

unbalanced [*adj2*] *crazy; mentally disturbed*
batty*, daft, demented, deranged, eccentric, erratic, flaky*, freaky*, insane, irrational, kinky*, kooky*, lunatic, mad, nobody home*, non compos mentis*, not all there*, nutty*, out to lunch*, psychotic, touched, troubled, unglued*, unhinged*, unscrewed*, unsound, unstable; SEE CONCEPT *403*

unbearable [*adj*] *very bad; too much*
a bit much*, enough, heavy-handed*, inadmissible, insufferable, insupportable, intolerable, last straw*, oppressive, unacceptable, unendurable, unsurpassable; SEE CONCEPTS *537,571*

unbecoming [*adj*] *improper, unsuitable*
awkward, clumsy, discreditable, gauche, ill-suited, inappropriate, inapt, incongruous, indecent, indecorous, indelicate, inept, maladroit, malapropos, offensive, rough, salacious, tacky*, tasteless, unattractive, unbefitting, uncomely, undue, unfair, unfit, unfitting, unflattering, ungodly, unhandsome, unlovely, unseasonable, unseemly, unsightly, unsuited, untimely, untoward, unworthy; SEE CONCEPTS *558,579,589*

unbelievable [*adj*] *beyond the imagination*
astonishing, beyond belief, cockamamie*, cock-eyed*, doubtful, dubious, far-fetched, fishy*, flaky*, flimsy*, for the birds*, full of holes*, harebrained*, implausible, impossible, improbable, incogitable, inconceivable, incredible, kooky*, lamebrained*, open to doubt, outlandish, past belief, phony, preposterous, ques-

ul
un

tionable, reaching, scatterbrained*, screwy*, staggering, suspect, thick*, thin*, too much*, unconvincing, unimaginable, unsubstantial, unthinkable, weak, won't hold water*, won't wash*; SEE CONCEPTS 529,548

unbelieving [adj] *skeptical*
agnostic, cynical, disbelieving, distrustful, doubtful, doubting, dubious, freethinking, leery, mistrustful, nonbelieving, not born yesterday*, questioning, show-me*, suspicious, unconvinced; SEE CONCEPT 403

unbending [adj] *rigid, tough*
aloof, crisp, distant, do or die*, dug in*, firm, formal, hard as nails*, hard-line*, hold one's ground*, hold the fort*, hold the line*, incompliant, inelastic, inexorable, inflexible, intractable, locked in*, obdurate, obstinate, relentless, reserved, resolute, set in stone*, severe, single-minded, standing one's ground*, standing pat*, sticking to one's guns*, stiff, strict, stubborn, uncompromising, unflexible, unrelenting, unswayable, unyielding, uptight; SEE CONCEPTS 401,534,604

unbiased [adj] *not prejudiced*
aloof, cold, disinterested, dispassionate, equal, equitable, even-handed, fair, honest, impartial, just, neutral, nondiscriminatory, nonpartisan, objective, on the fence*, open-minded, straight, unbigoted, uncolored, uninterested, unprejudiced; SEE CONCEPT 542

unblemished [adj] *not flawed*
chaste, clean, decent, faultless, flawless, immaculate, intact, modest, perfect, pure, sound, spotless, stainless, undamaged, undefiled, unflawed, unhurt, unimpaired, uninjured, unmarked, unmarred, unspotted, unstained, unsullied, untarnished, whole; SEE CONCEPTS 485,621

unbreakable [adj] *strong, tough*
adamantine, armored, brass-bound, durable, everlasting, firm, incorruptible, indestructible, infrangible, invulnerable, lasting, nonbreakable, perdurable, resistant, rugged, shatterproof, solid, tight, toughened, unshakable, unyielding; SEE CONCEPTS 488,489,798

unbridled [adj] *unrestrained*
berserk, chaotic, crazed, crazy, enthusiastic, hysterical, madcap, noisy, rabid, riotous, turbulent, unchecked, unconstrained, uncontrolled, uncurbed, undisciplined, ungovernable, unmanageable, violent, wild; SEE CONCEPT 401

unbroken [v] *continuous, whole*
ceaseless, constant, deep, endless, entire, even, fast, incessant, intact, perfect, perpetual, profound, progressive, regular, solid, sound, successive, total, undisturbed, unimpaired, uninterrupted, unremitting, unruffled, untroubled; SEE CONCEPTS 482,485,798

unburden [adj] *get rid of*
clear, confess, confide, disburden, discharge, disclose, disencumber, dispose of, divulge, dump, ease, empty, get off one's chest*, lay bare*, let hair down*, lighten, lose, out with it*, own, relieve, relinquish, reveal, shake, shake off*, tell all*, throw off, unbosom, unload; SEE CONCEPTS 60,211,244

uncalled-for [adj] *unnecessary*
accidental, avoidable, fortuitous, futile, inappropriate, inessential, needless, nonessential, not required, optional, unessential, uninvited, un-

needed, unrequired, unwanted, unwarranted, unwelcome, useless; SEE CONCEPT 546

uncanny [adj] *very strange, unusual*
astonishing, astounding, creepy, devilish, eerie, exceptional, extraordinary, fantastic, ghostly, ghoulish, incredible, inexplainable, inspired, magical, miraculous, mysterious, mystifying, preternatural, prodigious, queer, remarkable, scary, secret, singular, spooky, superhuman, supernatural, supernormal, supranormal, unearthly, unheard-of, unnatural, weird; SEE CONCEPTS 537,564

uncaring [adj] *indifferent*
aloof, blasé, callous, cold, cool, detached, disinterested, dispassionate, heartless, impervious, listless, nonchalant, passionless, unaroused, unconcerned, unemotional, uninvolved, unmoved, unsympathetic; SEE CONCEPTS 403,542

unceasing [adj] *incessant*
ceaseless, constant, continual, continuous, day-and-night*, endless, eternal, everlasting, lasting, never-ending, nonstop, permanent, perpetual, persistent, relentless, round-the-clock*, steady, unending, uninterrupted, unyielding; SEE CONCEPTS 534,798

uncertain [adj] *doubtful, changeable*
ambiguous, ambivalent, chancy, conjectural, dubious, erratic, fitful, hanging by a thread*, hazy, hesitant, iffy*, incalculable, inconstant, indefinite, indeterminate, indistinct, insecure, irregular, irresolute, on thin ice*, precarious, questionable, risky, speculative, touch and go*, unclear, unconfirmed, undecided, undetermined, unfixed, unforeseeable, unpredictable, unreliable, unresolved, unsettled, unsure, up for grabs*, up in the air*, vacillating, vague, variable, wavering; SEE CONCEPTS 529,534,535

uncertainty [n] *doubt, changeableness*
ambiguity, ambivalence, anxiety, bewilderment, concern, confusion, conjecture, contingency, dilemma, disquiet, distrust, doubtfulness, dubiety, guesswork, hesitancy, hesitation, incertitude, inconclusiveness, indecision, irresolution, lack of confidence, misgiving, mistrust, mystification, oscillation, perplexity, puzzle, puzzlement, qualm, quandary, query, questionableness, reserve, scruple, skepticism, suspicion, trouble, uneasiness, unpredictability, vagueness, wonder, worry; SEE CONCEPTS 388,410,696

unchangeable [adj] *constant, steadfast*
changeless, continuing, firm, fixed, immovable, immutable, inalterable, inevitable, inflexible, invariable, irreversible, permanent, resolute, stable, strong, unalterable, unmodifiable, unmovable; SEE CONCEPT 534

unchanging [adj] *constant, permanent*
abiding, changeless, consistent, continuing, enduring, equable, eternal, even, fixed, immutable, imperishable, invariable, lasting, perpetual, rigid, same, stabile, static, unchanged, unfading, unfailing, unfluctuating, uniform, unvarying; SEE CONCEPTS 534,551,649

uncharted [adj] *unknown*
alien, concealed, distant, exotic, faraway, far-off, foreign, hidden, little known, remote, undiscovered, unexplored, unheard-of, unidentified, unmapped, unnamed; SEE CONCEPT 576

uncivil [adj] *rude*
abrupt, bad-mannered, barbaric, blunt, boorish, coarse, curt, discourteous, gross, gruff, ill-man-

nered, impolite, inconsiderate, insulting, mannerless, uncivilized, uncouth, uncultured, unfriendly, ungentlemanly, unmannerly, unpolished, unrefined, vulgar; SEE CONCEPTS 267,401

uncivilized [*adj*] *wild, uncultured*
barbarian, barbaric, barbarous, boorish, brutish, churlish, coarse, crass, crude, discourteous, disrespectful, gross, ill-bred, impertinent, impolite, loutish, mannerless, outrageous, philistine, primitive, rude, rugged, savage, unconscionable, uncontrolled, uncouth, uncultivated, · uneducated, ungodly, unholy, unmannered, unpolished, unrefined, unsophisticated, vulgar, wicked; SEE CONCEPT 401

unclean [*adj*] *dirty*
bedraggled, befouled, besmirched, black, blurred, common, contaminated, corrupt, decayed, defiled, desecrated, dusty, evil, feculent, fetid, filthy, foul, grimy, impure, messy, muddy, nasty, polluted, profaned, putrescent, putrid, rancid, rank, rotten, sloppy, slovenly, smeared, smudged, soiled, sooty, sordid, spotted, squalid, stable, stained, stall, stinking, sullied, tainted, tarnished, unhealthful, vile; SEE CONCEPT 621

uncomfortable [*adj*] *painful, rough*
afflictive, agonizing, annoying, awkward, bitter, cramped, difficult, disagreeable, distressing, dolorous, excruciating, galling, grievous, hard, harsh, ill-fitting, incommodious, irritating, thorny, torturing, troublesome, vexatious, wearisome; SEE CONCEPTS 529,537,583

uncomfortable [*adj2*] *distressed, upset*
aching, angry, anguished, annoyed, awkward, chafed, cheerless, comfortless, confused, discomfited, discomposed, disquieted, disturbed, embarrassed, exhausted, fatigued, galled, harsh, hurt, ill at ease, in pain, miserable, nervous, pained, restless, self-conscious, smarting, sore, stiff, strained, suffering, tired, troubled, uneasy, vexed, weary, worn, wracked, wretched; SEE CONCEPTS 403,485

uncommitted [*adj*] *free; not involved*
cut loose*, don't care*, fence-sitting*, floating, free-spirited, laid-back*, middle ground*, middle of the road*, neutral, nonaligned, nonpartisan, on the fence*, restrained, unaffiliated, unattached, uninvolved, unpledged; SEE CONCEPTS 403,542

uncommon [*adj1*] *very different*
aberrant, abnormal, anomalous, arcane, bizarre, curious, eccentric, egregious, exceptional, exotic, extraordinary, extreme, fantastic, few, freakish, infrequent, irregular, nondescript, noteworthy, novel, odd, original, out of the ordinary, out of the way*, outré, peculiar, prodigious, queer, rare, remarkable, scarce, seldom, singular, sporadic, startling, strange, surprising, unaccustomed, unconventional, uncustomary, unfamiliar, unheard of, unique, unorthodox, unusual, weird; SEE CONCEPT 564

uncommon [*adj2*] *wonderful, exceptional*
distinctive, extraordinary, incomparable, inimitable, notable, noteworthy, outstanding, rare, remarkable, singular, special, superior, unimaginable, unique, unparalleled, unprecedented, unthinkable, unwonted; SEE CONCEPT 574

uncommonly [*adv*] *infrequently*
exceptionally, extra, extremely, hardly ever, in few instances, irregularly, not often, now and then, occasionally, oddly, on occasion, particu-

larly, peculiarly, rarely, remarkably, scarcely ever, seldom, sporadically, strangely, unusually, very; SEE CONCEPT 541

uncommunicative [*adj*] *shy, silent*
aloof, buttoned up*, clammed up*, close, closemouthed*, curt, distant, dried up*, evasive, guarded, hush-hush*, offish*, on the QT*, quiet, reserved, reticent, retiring, secretive, short, standoffish, taciturn, tight-lipped*, unapproachable, unresponsive, unsociable; SEE CONCEPT 267

uncomplicated [*adj*] *easy*
apparent, basic, child's play*, cinch, clear, easily done, effortless, elementary, evident, manageable, no bother*, no problem*, no sweat*, not burdensome, not difficult, nothing to it*, no trouble, obvious, painless, piece of cake*, simple, simple as ABC*, snap, straightforward, uninvolved; SEE CONCEPT 565

uncompromising [*adj*] *stubborn*
brick-wall*, decided, determined, firm, hardcore*, hard-line*, inexorable, inflexible, intransigent, locked, obdurate, obstinate, pigheaded*, relentless, resolute, rigid, set in stone*, single-minded, steadfast, stiff-necked*, strict, strong, tough, unbending; SEE CONCEPTS 401,542

unconcerned [*adj*] *carefree; apathetic*
aloof, blind, blithe, callous, careless, cold, cool, deaf, detached, dispassionate, distant, easy, feckless, forgetful, hardened, hard-hearted, heedless, impassive, inattentive, incurious, indifferent, insensible, insensitive, insouciant, lackadaisical, lukewarm, negligent, neutral, nonchalant, oblivious, phlegmatic, relaxed, reserved, self-centered, serene, stony, supine, unbothered, uninterested, uninvolved, unmoved, unperturbed, unruffled, unsympathetic, untroubled, unworried; SEE CONCEPTS 403,542

unconditional [*adj*] *absolute, total*
actual, all out, assured, categorical, certain, clear, complete, decisive, definite, determinate, downright, entire, explicit, final, flat out, full, genuine, indubitable, no catch*, no fine print*, no holds barred*, no ifs ands or buts*, no kicker*, no strings*, open, out-and-out*, outright, plenary, positive, straight out, thorough, thoroughgoing, unconstrained, unequivocal, unlimited, unmistakable, unmitigated, unqualified, unquestionable, unreserved, unrestricted, utter, whole, wide; SEE CONCEPTS 531,535,544

unconscionable [*adj*] *immoral, immoderate*
amoral, barbarous, conscienceless, criminal, dishonest, excessive, exorbitant, extravagant, extreme, inordinate, knavish, outrageous, preposterous, sneaky, too much*, uncivilized, undue, unethical, unfair, ungodly, unholy, unjust, unprincipled, unreasonable, unscrupulous, wanton, wicked; SEE CONCEPTS 545,569

unconscious [*adj1*] *not awake; out cold*
benumbed, blacked out*, bombed*, cold*, comatose, dead to the world*, drowsy, entranced, feeling no pain*, flattened*, inanimate, in a trance, inert, insensate, insensible, knocked*, lethargic, numb, on the canvas*, out, out like a light*, palsied, paralyzed, passed out*, put away*, raving, senseless, stunned, stupefied, swooning, torpid, tranced, zonked*; SEE CONCEPTS 314,539

unconscious [*adj2*] *ignorant; automatic*
accidental, gut*, ignorant, inadvertent, inattentive, inherent, innate, instinctive, involuntary, la-

tent, lost, reflex, repressed, subconscious, subliminal, suppressed, unaware, uncalculated, undeliberate, unheeding, unintended, unintentional, unmindful, unpremeditated, unrealized, unwitting; SEE CONCEPTS 542,544

unconstitutional [*adj*] *illegal*
against the law, banned, criminal, felonious, forbidden, illegitimate, illicit, lawless, not legal, outlawed, prohibited, prosecutable, unauthorized, unlawful, violating, wrongful; SEE CONCEPTS 319,545

uncontrollable [*adj*] *wild; carried away*
beside oneself, disorderly, excited, fractious, frantic, freaked, furious, headstrong, indocile, indomitable, insuppressible, insurgent, intractable, irrepressible, irresistible, lawless, like a loose cannon*, mad, obdurate, obstinate, recalcitrant, strong, stubborn, uncontainable, undisciplinable, undisciplined, ungovernable, unmanageable, unrestrainable, unruly, violent; SEE CONCEPT 401

unconventional [*adj*] *very different; odd*
anarchistic, atypical, avant-garde, beat, bizarre, crazy, eccentric, far-out*, freakish, freaky, free and easy*, idiosyncratic, individual, individualistic, informal, irregular, kinky*, kooky*, nonconformist, oddball*, offbeat, off the beaten track*, off the wall*, original, out in left field*, out of the ordinary, unceremonious, uncommon, uncustomary, unique, unorthodox, unusual, wayout*, weirdo*; SEE CONCEPT 564

uncoordinated [*adj*] *awkward, clumsy*
all thumbs*, bumbling, bungling, butterfingered*, gawkish, gawky, graceless, heavyhanded, klutzy*, like a bull in a china shop*, lumbering, not agile, stumbling, unadept, ungainly, ungraceful, unhandy, unskillful; SEE CONCEPTS 401,402,584

uncouth [*adj*] *clumsy, uncultivated*
awkward, barbaric, boorish, cheap, clownish, clumsy, coarse, crass, crude, discourteous, disgracious, gawky, graceless, gross, heavy-handed, ill-bred, ill-mannered, impertinent, impolite, inelegant, loud, loud-mouthed, loutish, oafish, raunchy, raw, rough, rude, rustic, strange, tacky*, uncalled-for*, uncivil, uncivilized, uncultivated, ungainly, ungenteel, ungentlemanly, unpolished, unrefined, unseemly, vulgar; SEE CONCEPT 401

uncover [*v*] *reveal, disclose*
bare, betray, break, bring to light*, crack, denude, dig up*, disclose, discover, display, divulge, expose, give away, hit upon, lay bare, lay open, leak, make known, open, open up, reveal, show, strike, strip, stumble on, subject, tap, tell, tip one's hand*, unclothe, unearth, unmask, unveil, unwrap; SEE CONCEPTS 60,183,261

uncovered [*adj*] *exposed*
bare, brought to light*, caught, disclosed, discovered, divulged, dug up*, found out, laid bare*, made public, naked, nude, on display, on view, revealed, shown, solved, stripped, unconcealed, unmasked, unprotected, unveiled, visible, vulnerable, weakened; SEE CONCEPT 576

uncritical [*adj*] *casual, unfussy*
careless, cursory, easily pleased, imperceptive, imprecise, imprudent, inaccurate, indiscriminate, offhand, perfunctory, shallow, slipshod, superficial, undiscerning, undiscriminating, unexacting, uninformed, unperceptive, unselective, unthinking; SEE CONCEPT 542

undaunted [*adj*] *brave, bold*
audacious, coming on strong*, courageous, dauntless, fearless, fire-eating*, gallant, icy*, indomitable, intrepid, not discouraged, not put off*, resolute, spunky, steadfast, unafraid, unalarmed, unapprehensive, undeterred, undiscouraged, undismayed, unfaltering, unflinching, unshrinking, valiant, valorous; SEE CONCEPT 401

undecided [*adj*] *not sure, not definite*
ambivalent, betwixt and between*, blowing hot and cold*, borderline, debatable, dithering*, doubtful, dubious, equivocal, hemming and hawing*, hesitant, iffy*, indecisive, indefinite, in the middle*, irresolute, moot, of two minds*, on the fence*, open, pendent, pending, running hot and cold*, tentative, torn, uncertain, unclear, uncommitted, undetermined, unfinished, unsettled, unsure, up in the air*, vague, waffling, wavering, wishy-washy*; SEE CONCEPTS 403,529

undeniable [*adj*] *definite, proven*
actual, beyond doubt, beyond question, binding, certain, clear, compulsory, evident, for sure*, inarguable, incontestable, incontrovertible, indisputable, indubitable, irrefutable, manifest, necessary, no ifs and or buts*, obligatory, obvious, open and shut*, patent, positive, real, sound, sure, sure thing*, true, unanswerable, unassailable, undoubted, unquestionable; SEE CONCEPT 535

undependable [*adj*] *irresponsible*
bum, capricious, careless, changeable, dubious, erratic, fickle, fly-by-night*, inconsistent, inconstant, indefinite, indeterminate, loose*, no bargain*, no-good*, treacherous, trick, tricky, trustless, unassured, uncertain, unpredictable, unreliable, unsafe, unsound, unstable, unsure, untrustworthy, variable; SEE CONCEPTS 401,535

under [*adv1/prep1*] *below*
beneath, bottom, concealed by, covered by, down, downward, held down, inferior, lower, nether, on the bottom, on the nether side, on the underside, pinned, pressed down, supporting, to the bottom, underneath; SEE CONCEPTS 586,735,793

under [*adv2/prep2*] *secondary*
amenable, belonging, collateral, consequent, corollary, dependent, directed, following, governed, included, inferior, in the power of, junior, lesser, low, lower, obedient, obeying, reporting, sub, subject, subjugated, subordinate, subsequent, subservient, subsidiary, substract, subsumed; SEE CONCEPTS 560,575,577

undercover [*adj*] *secret, spy*
clandestine, concealed, confidential, covert, creep, furtive, hidden, hole-and-corner*, hushhush*, incognito*, intelligence, on the QT*, private, stealth, stealthy, sub-rosa*, surreptitious, underground, underhand, underneath, under wraps*; SEE CONCEPTS 544,576

undercurrent [*n*] *drift, pull*
atmosphere, aura, crosscurrent, direction, eddy, feeling, flavor, hint, inclination, indication, insinuation, intimation, murmur, overtone, propensity, riptide, sense, suggestion, tendency, tenor, tinge, trace, trend, underflow, undertone, undertow, vibes*, vibrations; SEE CONCEPTS 673,738

underdog [*n*] *unlikely winner in a contest or struggle*
bottom dog, dark horse, longshot, out-of-towner; SEE CONCEPTS 366,423

underestimate [v] *minimize; rate too low*
belittle, deprecate, depreciate, disesteem, disparage, make light of*, miscalculate, miscarry, not do justice*, put down*, sell short*, slight, think too little of*, underrate, undervalue; SEE CONCEPTS *12,54,764*

undergo [v] *be subjected to*
abide, bear, bear up, bow, defer, encounter, endure, experience, feel, go through, have, know, meet with, put up with, see, share, stand, submit to, suffer, support, sustain, tolerate, weather, withstand, yield; SEE CONCEPT *23*

underground [adj1] *below the surface*
below ground, buried, covered, in the recesses, subterranean, subterrestrial, sunken, underfoot; SEE CONCEPT *583*

underground [adj2] *secret, subversive*
alternative, avant-garde, clandestine, concealed, covert, experimental, hidden, hush-hush*, on the QT*, on the sly*, private, radical, resistant, resistive, revolutionary, surreptitious, unbowed, unconventional, undercover, under wraps*, unusual; SEE CONCEPTS *564,576*

underhand [adj] *deceitful*
clandestine, concealed, crafty, crooked, cunning, deceptive, devious, dirty-dealing*, dishonest, dishonorable*, double-crossing*, duplicitous, fraudulent, furtive, guileful, hush-hush*, indirect, insidious, oblique, on the QT*, on the quiet*, secret, secretive, shady, shifty, slippery*, sly*, sneaking, sneaky, stealthy, sub-rosa*, surreptitious, treacherous, tricky, two-faced*, two-timing*, undercover, underhanded, under wraps*, unethical, unfair, unjust, unscrupulous, wily; SEE CONCEPTS *401,544*

underline [v] *emphasize; mark*
accentuate, bracket, call attention to, caption, check off, draw attention to, feature, give emphasis, highlight, indicate, interlineate, italicize, play up, point to, point up, rule, stress, underscore; SEE CONCEPTS *49,79*

underling [n] *subordinate*
aide, assistant, attendant, deputy, flunky*, gofer*, helper, inferior, lackey*, minion, peon, scrub*, second, second fiddle*, second stringer*, serf, servant, slave; SEE CONCEPTS *348,423*

underlying [adj] *fundamental, latent*
basal, basic, bottom, bottom-line*, cardinal, concealed, critical, crucial, elemental, elementary, essential, hidden, indispensable, intrinsic, lurking, necessary, needful, nitty-gritty*, nub, primary, prime, primitive, radical, root, substratal, veiled, vital; SEE CONCEPTS *546,549*

undermine [v] *weaken*
attenuate, blunt, clip one's wings*, corrode, cripple, debilitate, dig, dig out*, disable, eat away*, enfeeble, erode, excavate, foil, frustrate, hollow out, hurt, impair, knock the bottom out of*, mine, poke full of holes*, ruin, sabotage, sandbag*, sap, soften, subvert, threaten, thwart, torpedo*, tunnel, undercut, wear, whittle away, wreck; SEE CONCEPTS *14,240*

underneath [adv/prep] *below*
beneath, bottom, covered, lower, neath, nether, under; SEE CONCEPTS *586,735*

underprivileged [adj] *poor*
badly off*, depressed, deprived, destitute, disadvantaged, down and out*, handicapped, hapless,

hard up*, have-not*, ill-fated, ill-starred, impoverished, indigent, in dire straits, in need, in want, needy, unfortunate, unlucky; SEE CONCEPT *334*

underscore [v] *underline, emphasize*
accent, accentuate, call attention to, caption, draw attention to, feature, give emphasis, highlight, indicate, italicize, mark, point to, stress; SEE CONCEPTS *49,79*

understand [v1] *appreciate, comprehend*
accept, apprehend, be aware, be conscious of, be with it*, catch, catch on, conceive, deduce, discern, distinguish, explain, fathom, figure out, find out, follow, get*, get the hang of*, get the idea*, get the picture*, get the point*, grasp, have knowledge of, identify with, infer, interpret, ken*, know, learn, make out*, make sense of, master, note, penetrate, perceive, possess, read, realize, recognize, register, savvy*, see, seize, sense, sympathize, take in*, take meaning, tolerate; SEE CONCEPT *15*

understand [v2] *think, believe*
accept, assume, be informed, concede, conceive, conclude, conjecture, consider, count on, deduce, expect, fancy, feel for, gather, guess, hear, imagine, infer, learn, presume, reckon, suppose, surmise, suspect, take for granted, take it, think; SEE CONCEPT *12*

understanding [adj] *accepting, tolerant*
compassionate, considerate, discerning, empathetic, forbearing, forgiving, generous, kind, kindly, patient, perceptive, responsive, sensitive, sympathetic; SEE CONCEPTS *401,542*

understanding [n1] *comprehension, appreciation*
acumen, apperception, apprehension, assimilation, awareness, decipherment, discernment, discrimination, grasp, grip, insight, intellect, intelligence, intuition, judgment, ken, knowing, knowledge, mastery, penetration, perception, perceptiveness, perceptivity, percipience, perspicacity, prehension, realization, reason, recognition, savvy, sense, sharpness, wit; SEE CONCEPT *409*

understanding [n2] *belief*
acceptation, conception, conclusion, estimation, idea, import, impression, inkling, intendment, interpretation, judgment, knowledge, meaning, message, notion, opinion, perception, purport, sense, significance, significancy, signification, sympathy, view, viewpoint; SEE CONCEPTS *682,689*

understanding [n3] *informal agreement*
accord, common view, concord, deal, handshake*, harmony, meeting of minds*, pact; SEE CONCEPT *684*

understood [adj] *assumed, implicit*
accepted, appreciated, axiomatic, down pat*, implied, inferential, inferred, known, on to*, pat, presumed, roger*, tacit, taken for granted, undeclared, unexpressed, unsaid, unspoken, unstated, wise to, wordless; SEE CONCEPT *529*

understudy [n] *substitute*
alternate, backup, double, fill-in, pinch-hitter*, replacement, reserve, stand-by, stand-in, sub*, successor; SEE CONCEPTS *423,712*

undertake [v] *attempt, engage in*
address oneself, agree, answer for, bargain, begin, commence, commit, commit oneself, con-

un
un

tract, covenant, devote, embark, endeavor, enter upon, fall into, go about, go for, go in for, go into, guarantee, have a hand in*, have a try, hazard, initiate, launch, make a run at*, move, offer, pitch in, pledge, promise, set about, set in motion, set out, shoulder, stake, stipulate, tackle, take on, take the plunge*, take upon oneself, try, try out, venture, volunteer; SEE CONCEPTS 87,100

undertaker [n] *funeral director*
embalmer, grave digger, mortician; SEE CONCEPT 304

undertaking [n] *endeavor, attempt*
adventure, affair, business, deal, effort, engagement, enterprise, essay, experiment, game, happening, hassle, hazard, job, move, operation, outfit, play, project, proposition, pursuit, shop, striving, struggle, task, thing*, trial, try, venture, what one is into*, work; SEE CONCEPTS 87,324,349,362

undertone [n] *suggestion, whisper*
association, atmosphere, buzz, connotation, feeling, flavor, hint, hum, implication, low tone, mumble, murmur, mutter, overtone, rumor, tinge, touch, trace, undercurrent; SEE CONCEPTS 65,682

underwear [n] *clothing worn under outerwear*
bikini, boxers*, boxer shorts, bra, briefs, BVDs*, corset, drawers*, intimate things, jockeys, jockey shorts, lingerie, long johns, panties, shorts, skivvies*, smallclothes, underclothes, underclothing, undergarment, underpants, undershirt, underthings, undies; SEE CONCEPT 451

underweight [adj] *thin*
angular, anorectic, bony, gangly, malnourished, puny, scrawny, shadow, skeleton*, skin and bones*, skinny, starved, stringbean*, undernourished, undersized; SEE CONCEPT 491

underworld [n] *criminal activity, element*
abyss, Cosa Nostra, criminals, felonry, gangland, gangsters, Mafia, mob*, organized crime, racket*, riffraff*, syndicate; SEE CONCEPTS 412,645

underwrite [v] *endorse, insure*
accede, agree to, angel*, approve, back, bankroll*, collateral, consent, countersign, endow, finance, float, fund, guarantee, help, initial, okay*, pay, provide, provide financing, sanction, seal, secure, sign, sponsor, stake; subscribe, subsidize, support; SEE CONCEPTS 50,88,110,341

undesirable [adj] *offensive, unacceptable*
abominable, annoying, bothersome, defective, disagreeable, disliked, displeasing, distasteful, dreaded, icky, inadmissible, incommodious, inconvenient, inexpedient, insufferable, loathed, loathsome, objectionable, obnoxious, offensive, outcast, out of place, rejected, repellent, repugnant, scorned, shunned, to be avoided, troublesome, unacceptable, unattractive, unlikable, unpleasing, unpopular, unsatisfactory, unsavory, unsought, unsuitable, unwanted, unwelcome, unwished for, useless; SEE CONCEPTS 529,570

undeveloped [adj] *immature*
abortive, backward, behindhand, embryonic, half-baked, ignored, inchoate, incipient, inexperienced, latent, potential, primitive, primordial, unactualized, underdeveloped, unevolved, unprogressive, untaught, untrained; SEE CONCEPTS 485,578,797

undisciplined [adj] *uncontrolled*
defiant, disorderly, headstrong, inconsistent, insubordinate, lacking self controll, mischievous, naughty, noncompliant, ungoverned, unrestrained, unruly, untrained, wayward; SEE CONCEPT 401

undisputed/undisputable [adj] *positive, accepted*
acknowledged, admitted, arbitrary, assured, authoritative, beyond question, certain, conclusive, decided, dogmatic, final, incontestable, incontrovertible, indisputable, indubitable, irrefutable, not disputed, positive, recognized, sure, tyrannous, unchallenged, uncontested, undeniable, undoubted, unequivocal, unerring, unquestioned; SEE CONCEPT 535

undistinguished [adj] *ordinary*
average, characterless, common, commonplace, dull, everyday, fair, garden-variety*, generic, mean, mediocre, modest, no great shakes*, normal, nothing special, nothing to write home about*, pedestrian, plain, prosaic, routine, run-of-the-mill*, second-rate, so-so*, typical, uneventful, unexceptional, unexciting, uninspired, unmemorable, unnoteworthy, unremarkable, usual; SEE CONCEPTS 530,575

undivided [adj] *whole*
absorbed, circumspect, collective, combined, complete, concentrated, concerted, continued, deliberate, detailed, diligent, engrossed, entire, exclusive, fast, fixed, full, intense, intent, joined, lock stock and barrel*, minute, rigid, scrupulous, single, solid, steady, thorough, unanimous, unbroken, uncut, undistracted, unflagging, united, unswerving, vigilant, wholehearted; SEE CONCEPTS 482,531

undo [v1] *open*
disengage, distangle, free, loose, loosen, release, unbind, unblock, unbutton, unclose, unfasten, unfix, unlock, unloose, unloosen, unravel, unshut, unstop, untie, unwrap; SEE CONCEPT 135

undo [v2] *nullify, invalidate*
abate, abolish, abrogate, annihilate, annul, break, bring down, bring to naught*, cancel, cramp*, craze, crimp*, decimate, defeat, demolish, destroy, have*, impoverish, injure, make waves*, mar, negate, neutralize, offset, outfox, outmaneuver, outsmart, overreach, overthrow, overturn, quash, queer*, raze, reverse, ruin, screw up*, shatter, skin*, smash, spoil, stymie*, subvert, unbuild, undermine, unsettle, upset, vitiate, wipe out*, wrack, wreck; SEE CONCEPTS 7,19,121,252

undoing [n] *destruction, misfortune*
accident, adversity, affliction, bad luck, bad omen, bane, blight, blow, blunder, calamity, casualty, catastrophe, collapse, curse, defeat, destroyer, difficulty, disgrace, doom, downfall, error, failure, fault, faux pas, flaw, fumble, grief, humiliation, last straw*, misadventure, miscalculation, mischance, mishap, misstep, omission, overthrow, overturn, reversal, reverse, ruin, rumination, shame, slip, smash, stumble, subversion, trial, trip, trouble, visitation, weakness, wreck; SEE CONCEPTS 230,674,679

undoubtedly [adv] *certainly*
assuredly, beyond question, beyond shadow of a doubt*, definitely, doubtless, easily, indeed, of course, really, surely, truly, undeniably, unmis-

takably, unquestionably, well, without doubt; SEE CONCEPT *535*

undress [*v*] *take off clothes*
denude, disarray, dismantle, disrobe, divest oneself, doff, get off, get out of, husk, peel, shed, shock, slip off, slip out of, strip, unattire, uncloak, unclothe, unmask; SEE CONCEPTS *211,453*

undue [*adj*] *excessive, unnecessary*
disproportionate, exceeding, exorbitant, extravagant, extreme, forbidden, illegal, ill-timed, immoderate, improper, inappropriate, inapt, indecorous, inept, inordinate, intemperate, needless, overmuch, sinister, too great, too much, unapt, uncalled-for, unconscionable, underhanded, undeserved, unfair, unfitting, unjust, unjustifiable, unjustified, unmeasurable, unreasonable, unseasonable, unseemly, unsuitable, untimely, unwarrantable, unwarranted; SEE CONCEPTS *546,558,569*

unduly [*adv*] *excessively*
disproportionately, ever, extravagantly, extremely, illegally, immensely, immoderately, improperly, indecorously, inordinately, out of proportion, over, overfull, overly, overmuch, too, underhandedly, unfairly, unjustifiably, unjustly, unnecessarily, unreasonably; SEE CONCEPTS *544,546,569*

undying [*adj*] *never-ending*
constant, continuing, deathless, eternal, everlasting, immortal, imperishable, indestructible, inextinguishable, infinite, interminable, perennial, permanent, perpetual, persistent, unceasing, undiminished, unended, unending, unfading; SEE CONCEPT *798*

unearned [*adj*] *undeserved*
not deserved, not earned, not merited, not warranted, unmerited, unwarranted; SEE CONCEPTS *545,548,558*

unearth [*v*] *dig up*
ascertain, bring to light*, catch on*, delve, determine, discover, disinter, dredge up, excavate, exhibit, exhume, expose, ferret, find, find out, hear, hit upon, learn, reveal, root, see, see the light, show, spark, spotlight*, strike, stumble on, turn up, unbury, uncover, uproot; SEE CONCEPTS *178,183*

unearthly [*adj*] *supernatural; very strange*
abnormal, absurd, appalling, demoniac, devilish, eerie, ethereal, extraordinary, fiendish, frightening, funereal, ghastly, ghostly, ghoulish, hair-raising, haunted, heavenly, hyperphysical, miraculous, nightmarish, not of this world, phantom, preternatural, ridiculous, scary, sepulchral, spectral, spooky*, sublime, superhuman, uncanny, ungodly, unholy, unreasonable, weird; SEE CONCEPTS *536,564,582*

uneasy [*adj*] *awkward, uncomfortable*
afraid, agitated, alarmed, all nerves*, anguished, anxious, apprehensive, bothered, constrained, discomposed, dismayed, disquieted, disturbed, edgy, fearful, fidgety, fretful, harassed, ill at ease, impatient, insecure, in turmoil, irascible, irritable, jittery, jumpy, nervous, on edge, on the qui vive, palpitant, peevish, perplexed, perturbed, precarious, restive, restless, shaken, shaky, strained, suspicious, tense, tormented, troubled, unquiet, unsettled, unstable, upset, vexed, worried, wrung; SEE CONCEPTS *403,548,690*

uneducated [*adj*] *lacking knowledge*
benighted, empty-headed, ignoramus, ignorant, illiterate, inerudite, know-nothing*, lowbrow*, uncultivated, uncultured, uninstructed, unlearned, unlettered, unread, unrefined, unschooled, untaught, untutored; SEE CONCEPT *402*

unemotional [*adj*] *not responsive*
along for the ride*, apathetic, blah*, callous, chill*, cold, coldhearted*, cool, deadpan, dispassionate, emotionless, flat, frigid, glacial, going with the flow*, hard-boiled*, hard-hearted*, heartless, impassive, indifferent, insensitive, laid-back*, listless, marble*, obdurate, passionless, phlegmatic, quiet, reserved, reticent, rolling with the punches*, thick-skinned*, uncompassionate, undemonstrative, unexcitable, unfeeling, unimpressionable, unresponsive, unsympathetic; SEE CONCEPTS *401,403*

unemployed [*adj*] *without a job*
at liberty*, between jobs*, closed down*, disengaged, down, fired, free, idle, inactive, jobless, laid off, leisured, loafing*, on layoff, on the bench*, on the dole*, on the shelf*, out of action*, out of a job, out of work, resting, unapplied, underemployed, unengaged, unexercised, unoccupied, unused, without gainful employment, workless; SEE CONCEPT *538*

unending [*adj*] *continuing*
amaranthine, ceaseless, constant, continual, continuous, endless, eternal, everlasting, immortal, incessant, infinite, interminable, never-ending, perpetual, steady, unceasing, uninterrupted, unremitting; SEE CONCEPTS *482,798*

unequal [*adj1*] *different*
differing, disparate, dissimilar, distant, divergent, diverse, incommensurate, like night and day*, mismatched, not uniform, odd, poles apart*, unalike, unequivalent, uneven, unlike, unmatched, unsimilar, variable, various, varying, weird*; SEE CONCEPT *564*

unequal [*adj2*] *not balanced; lopsided*
asymmetrical, disproportionate, ill-matched, inequitable, irregular, nonsymmetrical, off-balance, one-sided, overbalanced, unbalanced, uneven, unproportionate, unsymmetrical; SEE CONCEPT *480*

unequaled [*adj*] *supreme, pre-eminent*
alone, beyond compare, incomparable, inimitable, matchless, nonpareil, only, paramount, peerless, second to none*, surpassing, towering, transcendent, ultimate, unique, unmatched, unparagoned, unparalleled, unrivaled, unsurpassed, without equal; SEE CONCEPT *574*

unequivocal [*adj*] *definite, positive*
absolute, apparent, categorical, certain, clear, clear-cut, decided, decisive, direct, distinct, downright, evident, explicit, flat out*, incontestable, incontrovertible, indisputable, indubitable, manifest, no catch*, no fine print*, no holds barred*, no ifs and or buts*, no strings attached*, obvious, open and shut*, palpable, patent, plain, straight, straightforward, straight out, unambiguous, uncontestable, undeniable, undisputable, univocal, unmistakable, unquestionable; SEE CONCEPT *535*

unerring [*adj*] *accurate*
certain, errorless, exact, faultless, impeccable, inerrable, inerrant, infallible, invariable, just, perfect, reliable, sure, true, trustworthy, unfailing; SEE CONCEPTS *535,574*

un
un

unessential [adj] unnecessary

avoidable, beside the point*, dispensable, expendable, futile, inessential, irrelevant, needless, nonessential, optional, uncalled-for, unimportant, unneeded, unrequired, useless, worthless; SEE CONCEPT 546

unethical [adj] dishonest, immoral

cheating, corrupt, crooked, dirty*, dirty-dealing*, dishonorable, disreputable, double-crossing*, fake, fishy*, flimflam*, fly-by-night*, illegal, improper, mercenary, scam*, shady*, sharp*, slick*, slippery*, sneaky*, two-faced*, two-timing*, underhand, unfair, unprincipled, unprofessional, unscrupulous, wrong; SEE CONCEPT 545

uneven [adj] not smooth or balanced

asperous, asymmetrical, broken, bumpy, changeable, craggy, differing, discrepant, disparate, disproportionate, fitful, fluctuating, harsh, ill-matched, intermittent, irregular, jagged, jerky, leftover, lopsided, nonsymmetrical, notched, not flat, not level, not parallel, odd, off-balance, one-sided, overbalanced, patchy, remaining, rough, rugged, scabrous, scraggy, serrate, spasmodic, spotty, unbalanced, unequal, unfair, unlevel, unsmooth, unsteady, unsymmetrical, variable; SEE CONCEPTS 480,566,606

uneventful [adj] monotonous, dull

boring, common, commonplace, humdrum, inconclusive, indecisive, ordinary, prosaic, quiet, routine, tedious, unexceptional, unexciting, unfateful, uninteresting, unmemorable, unnoteworthy, unremarkable, unvaried; SEE CONCEPT 548

unexceptional [adj] ordinary

average, characterless, common, commonplace, conventional, dull, everyday, fair, garden-variety*, insignificant, mediocre, modest, no great shakes*, normal, nothing special, nothing to write home about*, pedestrian, plain, prosaic, routine, run-of-the-mill*, second-rate, so-so*, typical, undistinguished, uneventful, unexciting, unimpressive, uninspired, unmemorable, unnoteworthy, unremarkable, usual; SEE CONCEPTS 530,575

unexciting [adj] dull

big yawn*, blah, boring, common, dead, dreary, familiar, ho hum*, humdrum*, long-winded, monotonous, ordinary, plain, prosaic, routine, run-of-the-mill*, uneventful, unimaginative, uninspiring, uninteresting, usual, usual thing; SEE CONCEPTS 529,530

unexpected [adj] surprising

abrupt, accidental, amazing, astonishing, chance, electrifying, eye-opening*, fortuitous, from left field*, impetuous, impulsive, instantaneous, not bargained for*, not in the cards*, out of the blue*, payback, prodigious, staggering, startling, stunning, sudden, swift, unanticipated, unforeseen, unheralded, unlooked-for, unpredictable, unpredicted, wonderful; SEE CONCEPTS 544,548

unfailing [adj] certain, unchanging

absolute, assiduous, bottomless, boundless, ceaseless, come-through*, consistent, constant, continual, continuing, continuous, counted on, delivering, dependable, diligent, dyed-in-the-wool*, endless, eternal, faithful, inexhaustible, infallible, invariable, loyal, never-failing, persistent, reliable, rock solid*, same, solid, staunch, steadfast, straight, sure, surefire, there*, tried-and-true*, true, trustworthy, unflagging, unlimited, unrelenting; SEE CONCEPTS 534,535,538

unfair [adj] prejudiced, wrongful

arbitrary, bad, base, biased, bigoted, blameworthy, cheating, criminal, crooked, cruel, culpable, discreditable, discriminatory, dishonest, dishonorable, foul, grievous, illegal, immoral, improper, inequitable, inexcusable, iniquitous, injurious, low, mean, one-sided, partial, partisan, petty, shameful, shameless, uncalled-for, undue, unethical, unjust, unjustifiable, unlawful, unprincipled, unreasonable, unrightful, unscrupulous, unsporting, unwarranted, vicious, vile, wicked, wrong; SEE CONCEPTS 544,545,548

unfaithful [adj] disloyal, adulterous

adulterine, cheating, deceitful, double-crossing*, faithless, false, false-hearted, fickle, foresworn, inconstant, incontinent, moonlighting*, not true to, of bad faith, perfidious, philandering, recreant, shifty*, snaky*, sneaking, traitorous, treacherous, treasonable, two-faced*, two-timing*, unchaste, unreliable, untrue, untrustworthy, wicked; SEE CONCEPT 545

unfaltering [adj] steadfast

abiding, bent on, bound, bound and determined*, dead set on*, enduring, firm, going all the way*, indefatigable, meaning business*, mulish*, never-failing, persevering, pigheaded, resolute, set, steady, stiff-necked*, stubborn, sure, tireless, unfailing, unflagging, unflappable, unflinching, unqualified, unquestioning, unswerving, untiring, unwavering, wholehearted; SEE CONCEPTS 403,535,538

unfamiliar [adj1] different, strange

alien, anomalous, bizarre, curious, exotic, extraordinary, fantastic, foreign, little known, new, novel, obscure, original, outlandish, out-of-the-way*, peculiar, recondite, remarkable, remote, unaccustomed, uncommon, unexpected, unexplored, uninvestigated, unknown, unusual; SEE CONCEPT 564

unfamiliar [adj2] inexperienced; not knowing about

ignorant, incognizant, inconversant, not associated, not versed in, oblivious, out of contact, unaccustomed, unacquainted, unaware, unconversant, uninformed, uninitiated, uninstructed, unknowing, unknown, unpracticed, unskilled, unversed, unwitting; SEE CONCEPTS 402,678

unfathomable [adj1] bottomless

abysmal, boundless, deep, eternal, immeasurable, infinite, soundless, unending, unmeasured, unplumbed; SEE CONCEPTS 482,777

unfathomable [adj2] hard to believe; difficult to understand

abstruse, baffling, clear as mud*, deep, enigmatic, esoteric, heavy, impenetrable, incognizable, incomprehensible, indecipherable, inexplicable, obscure, profound, too deep*, uncomprehensible, ungraspable, unintelligible, unknowable; SEE CONCEPT 529

unfavorable [adj] very bad

adverse, antagonistic, calamitous, contrary, damaging, destructive, disadvantageous, discommodious, hostile, ill-advised, improper, inadvisable, inauspicious, inconvenient, inexpedient, infelicitous, inimical, inopportune, late, low, malapropos, negative, objectionable, ominous, opposed, poor, regrettable, tardy, threatening, troublesome, unfit, unfortunate, unfriendly, unlucky, unpromising, unpropitious, unseasonable, unseemly, unsuited, untimely, untoward, wrong; SEE CONCEPT 529,571

unfeeling [adj] *hard-hearted, numb*
anesthetized, apathetic, asleep, benumbed, brutal, callous, cantankerous, churlish, cold, cold-blooded, cold fish*, cold-hearted, crotchety, cruel, deadened, exacting, feelingless, hard, hardened, heartless, icy, inanimate, inhuman, insensate, insensible, insensitive, iron-hearted, merciless, obdurate, pitiless, ruthless, sensationless, senseless, severe, stony, surly, thick-skinned*, tough, unamiable, uncaring, uncompassionate, uncordial, unemotional, unkind, unsympathetic; SEE CONCEPTS 314,403,542

unfinished [adj] *not completed*
amateurish, bare, crude, cut short, dabbling, defective, deficient, dilettante, faulty, formless, found wanting, fragmentary, half-baked*, half-done*, immature, imperfect, incomplete, in the making, in the rough*, lacking, natural, not done, plain, raw, rough, roughhewn, shapeless, sketchy, tentative, unaccomplished, unadorned, unassembled, uncompleted, unconcluded, under construction, undeveloped, undone, unexecuted, unfashioned, unfulfilled, unperfected, unpolished, unrefined, wanting; SEE CONCEPTS 485,531

unfit [adj1] *not appropriate or suited*
below par*, can't make the grade*, debilitated, decrepit, discordant, down, dragging, feeble, flimsy, ill-adapted, ill-equipped, ill-suited, improper, inadequate, inapplicable, inappropriate, incompatible, incongruous, incorrect, ineffective, inexpedient, infelicitous, inharmonious, laid low*, mistaken, not fit, out of element*, out of place, out of shape, poorly, rocky*, unbecoming, uncongenial, uncool, unhealthy, unlikely, unmeet, unpromising, unsuitable, unsuited, useless, valueless; SEE CONCEPT 558

unfit [adj2] *not ready*
amateur, awkward, blundering, bungling, bush league's*, butter-fingered*, clumsy, debilitated, disqualified, feeble, heavy-handed, ill-equipped, impotent, inadequate, incapable, incapacitated, incompetent, ineffective, inefficient, ineligible, inept, inexperienced, inexpert, maladjusted, maladroit, no good*, not cut out for*, not equal to, not up to*, unable, unapt, unfitted, unhandy, unpracticed, unprepared, unproficient, unqualified, unskilled, unskillful, untrained, useless, weak; SEE CONCEPT 527

unflagging [adj] *persistent*
active, assiduous, constant, diligent, dynamic, energetic, fixed, indefatigable, inexhaustible, persevering, staunch, steady, tireless, unceasing, undeviating, unfailing, unfaltering, unrelenting, unremitting, unretiring, untiring, unwearied; SEE CONCEPTS 538,798

unflappable [adj] *cool and calm*
collected, composed, deliberate, disimpassioned, easy, impassive, imperturbable, level-headed, nonchalant, relaxed, self-possessed, unruffled; SEE CONCEPTS 401,542

unfold [v1] *spread out*
disentangle, display, expand, extend, fan, fan out, flatten, loosen, open, outspread, outstretch, reel out, release, shake out, spread, straighten,

stretch out, unbend, uncoil, uncrease, uncurl, undo, unfurl, unravel, unroll, untwist, unwind, unwrap; SEE CONCEPT 201

unfold [v2] *make known*
announce, clarify, clear up, decipher, describe, disclose, discover, display, divulge, dope out, elucidate, explain, explicate, expose, figure out, illustrate, present, publish, resolve, reveal, show, solve, uncover, unravel; SEE CONCEPTS 55,261

unfold [v3] *develop*
bear fruit, demonstrate, elaborate, evidence, evince, evolve, expand, grow, manifest, mature; SEE CONCEPT 704

unforeseeable [adj] *unpredictable*
capricious, chance, chancy, changeable, fluky*, from left field*, incalculable, random, uncertain, unexpected, unknowable; SEE CONCEPT 534

unforeseen [adj] *surprising*
abrupt, accidental, from left field*, not bargained for*, out of the blue*, startling, sudden, surprise, unanticipated, uncalculated, unexpected, unlooked-for; SEE CONCEPTS 544,548

unforgettable [adj] *memorable*
catchy, distinguished, enduring, eventful, exceptional, extraordinary, famous, great, historic, illustrious, important, lasting, meaningful, monumental, notable, noteworthy, not to be forgotten, remarkable, rememberable, remembered, significant, super; SEE CONCEPTS 529,548

unforgivable [adj] *inexcusable*
blameworthy, contemptible, deplorable, disgraceful, indefensible, inexpiable, not forgivable, outrageous, reprehensible, shameful, unallowable, unconscionable, unjustifiable, unpardonable, unpermissible, untenable, wrong; SEE CONCEPTS 545,570

unfortunate [adj] *unlucky, bad*
adverse, afflicted, broken, burdened, calamitous, cursed, damaging, deplorable, desperate, destitute, disastrous, doomed, forsaken, hapless, hopeless, ill-fated, ill-starred, in a bad way*, inappropriate, infelicitous, inopportune, jinxed, lamentable, luckless, out of luck*, pained, poor, regrettable, ruined, ruinous, shattered, star-crossed*, stricken, troubled, unbecoming, unfavorable, unhappy, unpropitious, unprosperous, unsuccessful, unsuitable, untoward, wretched; SEE CONCEPTS 334,548,570

unfounded [adj] *not based on fact*
baseless, bottomless, deceptive, fabricated, fallacious, false, foundationless, gratuitous, groundless, idle, illogical, mendacious, misleading, off-base, spurious, trumped up*, uncalled-for, unjustified, unproven, unreal, unsubstantiated, untrue, untruthful, unwarranted, vain, without basis, without foundation; SEE CONCEPTS 267,582

unfriendly [adj] *nasty, hostile*
acrimonious, against, alien, aloof, antagonistic, antisocial, censorious, chilly, cold, combative, competitive, conflicting, contrary, disaffected, disagreeable, distant, estranged, grouchy, grudging, gruff, hateful, ill-disposed, inauspicious, inhospitable, inimical, malicious, malignant, misanthropic, not on speaking terms*, opposed, opposite, quarrelsome, sour, spiteful, surly, uncharitable, uncongenial, unfavorable, unneighborly, unpropitious, unsociable, vengeful, warlike; SEE CONCEPTS 401,548

un
un

ungodly [adj1] *not accepting a religious doctrine; impious*
atheistic, blasphemous, corrupt, depraved, godless, improper, indecent, indecorous, indelicate, irreligious, malevolent, profane, rough, sinful, undecorous, unhallowed, unholy, unseemly, vile, wicked; SEE CONCEPTS 542,545

ungodly [adj2] *outrageous*
atrocious, barbarous, dreadful, horrendous, horrid, intolerable, nasty, shocking, unbelievable, uncivilized, unconscionable, unearthly, unreasonable, unseemly; SEE CONCEPTS 529,548,570

ungrateful [adj] *not appreciative*
careless, demanding, dissatisfied, faultfinding, forgetful, grasping, grumbling, heedless, ingrate, insensible, oblivious, self-centered, selfish, thankless, unappreciative, unmindful, unnatural, unthankful; SEE CONCEPT 401

unguarded [adj] *thoughtless; unwary*
accessible, artless, candid, careless, casual, direct, foolhardy, frank, headlong, heedless, honest, ill-considered, impolitic, imprudent, impulsive, incautious, indiscreet, ingenuous, naive, offhand, rash, spontaneous, straightforward, unalert, uncircumspect, unconscious, undiplomatic, unpremeditated, unreflective, unthinking, unvigilant, unwatchful, unwise, vulnerable, weak; SEE CONCEPT 401

unhappy [adj1] *sad*
bleak, bleeding*, blue*, bummed out*, cheerless, crestfallen, depressed, despondent, destroyed, disconsolate, dismal, dispirited, down*, down and out*, downbeat, downcast, down in the mouth*, dragged, dreary, gloomy, grim, heavy-hearted, hurting, in a blue funk*, in pain, in the dumps*, let-down*, long-faced, low, melancholy, mirthless, miserable, mournful, oppressive, put away*, ripped*, sad, saddened, sorrowful, sorry, teary, troubled; SEE CONCEPT 403

unhappy [adj2] *unfortunate, unlucky*
afflicted, cursed, hapless, ill-fated, ill-starred, luckless, misfortunate, troubled, untoward, wretched; SEE CONCEPT 548

unharmed [adj] *unhurt*
all right, free from danger, in one piece*, intact, not hurt, okay*, out of danger, out of harm's way*, protected, safe, safe and sound*, sound, undamaged, uninjured, unscarred, unscathed, unscratched, untouched; SEE CONCEPTS 314,587

unhealthy [adj1] *sick*
ailing, below par, debilitated, delicate, diseased, down, dragging, feeble, frail, ill, in a decline, infirm, in ill health, in poor health, invalid, laid low*, out of action*, out of shape, peaked, poorly, run-down, shaky, sickly, unsound, unwell, weak; SEE CONCEPT 314

unhealthy [adj2] *very bad in effect on well-being*
baneful, chancy, corrupt, corrupting, dangerous, degenerate, degrading, deleterious, demoralizing, detrimental, harmful, hazardous, insalubrious, jeopardous, morbid, nefarious, negative, noisome, noxious, perilous, poisonous, risky, rotten, treacherous, undesirable, unhealthful, unsanitary, unsound, unwholesome, villainous, virulent, wicked; SEE CONCEPTS 537,571

unheard-of [adj] *unique, obscure*
exceptional, inconceivable, little-known, nameless, new, novel, outlandish, preposterous, rare, shocking, singular, unbelievable, undiscovered, unfamiliar, unknown, unlikely, unprecedented,

unrenowned, unsung, unusual; SEE CONCEPTS 564,576

unholy [adj1] *sacreligious*
base, blameful, corrupt, culpable, depraved, dishonest, evil, godless, guilty, heinous, immoral, impious, iniquitous, irreligious, irreverent, irreverential, profane, sinful, truly, ungodly, unhallowed, unsanctified, vile, wicked; SEE CONCEPTS 542,548

unholy [adj2] *outrageous*
appalling, awful, barbarous, dreadful, horrendous, shocking, uncivilized, unearthly, ungodly, unnatural, unreasonable; SEE CONCEPT 537

unidentified [adj] *secret*
anonymous, mysterious, nameless, not known, pseudonymous, unclassified, unfamiliar, unknown, unmarked, unnamed, unrecognized, unrevealed; SEE CONCEPT 576

unification [n] *joining together*
affinity, alliance, amalgamation, coalescence, coalition, combination, concurrence, confederation, connection, consolidation, coupling, federation, fusion, hookup, interlocking, linkage, melding, merger, merging, union, uniting; SEE CONCEPTS 230,388

unified [adj] *united*
affiliated, allied, banded, collective, combined, consolidated, cooperative, one, incorporated, joined up, leagued, linked, one, pooled, tied in, together, undivided; SEE CONCEPTS 563,577

uniform [adj1] *consistent*
compatible, consonant, constant, equable, even, fated, fateful, fixed, habitual, homogeneous, immutable, incorrigible, inflexible, invariable, irreversible, level, methodical, monolithic, normal, of a piece*, ordered, orderly, ossified, plumb, regular, reliable, rigid, smooth, stable, static, steady, straight, symmetrical, systematic, true, unalterable, unbroken, unchanging, undeviating, undiversified, unfluctuating, unmodifiable, unvarying, well-balanced, well-proportioned; SEE CONCEPT 534

uniform [adj2] *alike*
agnate, akin, analogous, comparable, consistent, consonant, correspondent, ditto*, double, equal, identical, like, mated, monotonous, parallel, same, same difference*, self-same, similar, treadmill*, undifferentiated, unvaried; SEE CONCEPTS 487,573

uniform [n] *coordinated outfit*
attire, costume, dress, garb, gown, habit, khaki*, livery, monkey suit*, OD*, olive drab*, regalia, regimentals, robe, stripes*, suit; SEE CONCEPT 451

unify [v] *unite*
affiliate, ally, associate, band, become one, bring together, combine, connect, consolidate, cooperate, couple, gather together, hook up with, join, join forces, link, marry, merge, pool, pull together, stick together, wed; SEE CONCEPTS 113,193

unimaginable [adj] *mind-boggling*
beyond wildest dreams*, doubtful, exceptional, extraordinary, fantastic, impossible, improbable, inapprehensible, incogitable, incomprehensible, inconceivable, incredible, indescribable, ineffable, not understandable, rare, singular, unbelievable, uncommon, unheard-of, unique, unknowable, unordinary, unthinkable; SEE CONCEPTS 529,548

unimaginative [adj] *dull, predictable*
banal, barren, bromidic, common, commonplace, derivative, dime a dozen*, dry, dull as dishwater*, flat, hackneyed, ho hum*, lifeless, matter-of-fact, ordinary, pabulum, pedestrian, prosaic, routine, square*, tame, tedious, trite, uncreative, uninspired, unoriginal, unromantic, usual, vanilla*, well-worn, zero*; SEE CONCEPTS 542,547,548

unimportant [adj] *of no real worth, value*
beside the point*, casual, frivolous, frothy, immaterial, inconsequential, inconsiderable, indifferent, insignificant, irrelevant, little, low-ranking, meaningless, minor, minute, negligible, nonessential, nothing*, nugatory, null, of no account, of no consequence, paltry, petty, picayune, second-rate*, shoestring*, slight, trifling, trivial, unnecessary, useless, worthless, zero*, zilch*, zip*; SEE CONCEPT 575

uninformed [adj] *unaware*
blind, caught napping*, daydreaming, deaf, ignorant, inattentive, in the dark*, negligent, not informed, not told, oblivious, out of it*, out to lunch*, unbriefed, unconscious, uneducated, unenlightened, uninstructed, unknowing, unschooled; SEE CONCEPT 402

uninhibited [adj] *free and easy; without restraint*
audacious, candid, cut loose*, expansive, fancy-free*, footloose*, frank, free, hanging out*, informal, instinctive, liberated, natural, no holds barred*, off the cuff*, open, relaxed, spontaneous, unbridled, unchecked, unconstrained, uncontrolled, uncurbed, ungoverned, unhampered, unrepressed, unreserved, unrestrained, unrestricted, unself-conscious, unsuppressed; SEE CONCEPTS 267,401

uninspired [adj] *dull, unoriginal*
bromidic, commonplace, corny*, everyday, heavy-handed, humdrum, indifferent, old hat*, ordinary, phoned in*, ponderous, prosaic, stale, sterile, stock, uncreative, unexciting, unimaginative, unimpressed, uninspiring, uninteresting, uninventive, unmoved, yawn*; SEE CONCEPTS 542,547,548

unintelligent [adj] *stupid*
brainless, deficient, dense, doltish, dumb, empty-headed*, foolish, half-witted*, idiotic, imbecilic, inane, meaningless, mentally deficient, mentally handicapped, mindless, moronic, not intelligent, pointless, senseless, simple, simpleminded, slow, thick-headed*, unthinking, witless; SEE CONCEPTS 402,548

unintelligible [adj] *not understandable*
ambiguous, equivocal, fathomless, Greek*, illegible, impenetrable, inarticulate, incognizable, incoherent, incomprehensible, indecipherable, indistinct, inexplicit, jumbled, meaningless, muddled, obscure, opaque, tenebrous, uncertain, unclear, unexplicit, unfathomable, ungraspable, unknowable, unreadable, vague; SEE CONCEPT 267

unintentional/unintended [adj] *not planned*
accidental, aimless, casual, chance, erratic, extemporaneous, fortuitous, haphazard, inadvertent, involuntary, purposeless, random, unconscious, undesigned, undevised, unexpected, unforeseen, unintended, unplanned, unpremeditated, unthinking, unthought, unwitting; SEE CONCEPTS 401,548

uninterested [adj] *oblivious to*
aloof, apathetic, blasé, bored, bored stiff*, casual, could care less*, detached, disinterested, distant, going through motions*, hard-hearted*, impassive, incurious, indifferent, listless, remote, thick-skinned*, turned off*, unconcerned, uncurious, uninvolved, unresponsive, weary, withdrawn; SEE CONCEPTS 401,403

uninteresting [adj] *boring, uneventful*
arid, banal, big yawn*, bromidic, common, commonplace, depressing, dismal, drab, dreary, dry, dull, dusty*, fatiguing, flat, ho hum*, humdrum, insipid, irksome, jejune, monotonous, nothing*, nowhere*, pedestrian, prosaic, prosy, soporific, stale, stupid, tedious, tired, tiresome, trite, unenjoyable, unentertaining, unexciting, uninspiring, wearisome; SEE CONCEPTS 529,548

uninterrupted [adj] *continuing; unbroken*
ceaseless, consecutive, constant, continual, continuous, direct, endless, interminable, nonstop, peaceful, perpetual, steady, straight, straightforward, sustained, through, unceasing, undisturbed, unending, unremitting; SEE CONCEPTS 482,798

uninvited [adj] *unwanted*
blackballed*, excluded, inadmissible, left out in the cold*, not in the picture*, not wanted, rejected, shut out, unasked, undesired, unpopular, unsolicited, unwelcome; SEE CONCEPTS 529,555, 570

uninviting [adj] *disagreeable, not pleasant*
awful, bad, disgusting, displeasing, distasteful, nasty, nauseating, offensive, repulsive, rotten, sickening, sour, unappealing, unappetizing, unpalatable, unpleasant; SEE CONCEPTS 537,548

union [n1] *merger, joining*
abutment, accord, agglutination, agreement, amalgam, amalgamation, blend, centralization, coadunation, combination, coming together, commixture, compound, concatenation, conciliation, concord, concurrence, confluence, congregation, conjunction, consolidation, correlation, coupling, fusion, harmony, hookup, incorporation, intercourse, joint, junction, juncture, meeting, melding, merging, mixture, seam, symbiosis, synthesis, tie-in, tie-up, unanimity, unification, unison, uniting, unity; SEE CONCEPTS 113,664,714

union [n2] *group with shared interest, cause*
alliance, association, brotherhood, club, coalition, confederacy, confederation, congress, employees, federation, guild, labor union, league, local, order, sisterhood, society, sodality, syndicate, trade union; SEE CONCEPTS 325,381

unique [adj1] *alone, singular*
different, exclusive, individual, lone, one, one and only*, onliest*, only, particular, rare, separate, single, solitary, solo, sui generis, uncommon, unexampled; SEE CONCEPTS 564,577

unique [adj2] *one-of-a-kind; without equal*
anomalous, best, exceptional, extraordinary, far-out*, incomparable, inimitable, matchless, most, nonpareil, novel, only, peerless, primo*, rare, singular, something else*, special, standout, strange, uncommon, unequaled, unexampled, unimaginable, unmatched, unparagoned, unparalleled, unprecedented, unreal, unrivaled, utmost, weird*; SEE CONCEPTS 564,574

unison [n] *harmony*
accord, accordance, agreement, alliance, com-

un
un

unit [*n1*] *whole*
assemblage, assembly, bunch, complement, crew, crowd, detachment, entirety, entity, gang, group, mob, one, outfit, ring, section, system, total, totality; SEE CONCEPTS *432,837*

unit [*n2*] *part*
arm, block, component, constituent, detachment, detail, digit, element, factor, feature, fraction, ingredient, integer, item, joint, layer, length, link, member, module, piece, portion, section, segment, square, wing; SEE CONCEPT *834*

unite [*v*] *combine; join together*
affiliate, ally, amalgamate, associate, band, band together, become one, blend, close ranks*, coadjute, coalesce, commingle, concur, confederate, conjoin, connect, consolidate, cooperate, couple, embody, fuse, gather together, hang together*, harden, hook up with, incorporate, intertwine, join, join forces, keep together, league, link, marry, meet, merge, mix, pool, pull together, relate, solidify, stay together, stick together, strengthen, throw in with*, unify, wed; SEE CONCEPTS *113,193*

united [*adj*] *combined; in agreement*
affiliated, agreed, allied, amalgamated, assembled, associated, banded, coadunate, cognate, collective, concerted, concordant, confederated, congruent, conjoint, conjugate, conjunctive, consolidated, cooperative, corporate, federal, homogeneous, hooked up*, in accord, in cahoots*, incorporated, integrated, joined up, leagued, likeminded*, lined up*, linked, of one mind, of the same opinion, one, plugged in*, pooled, tied in, unanimous, undivided, unified, unitary; SEE CONCEPTS *563,577*

unity [*n*] *wholeness*
accord, agreement, alliance, coadunation, combination, concord, concurrence, confederation, consensus, consent, consonance, entity, federation, harmony, homogeneity, homogeneousness, identity, individuality, indivisibility, integral, integrality, integrity, interconnection, oneness, peace, rapport, sameness, singleness, singularity, soleness, solidarity, synthesis, totality, unanimity, undividedness, unification, uniformity, union, unison; SEE CONCEPTS *664,714,837*

universal [*adj*] *worldwide, entire*
accepted, all, all-embracing, all-inclusive, allover, astronomical, broad, catholic, celestial, common, comprehensive, cosmic, cosmopolitan, customary, diffuse, ecumenical, empyrean, extensive, general, generic, global, multinational, mundane, omnipresent, planetary, prevalent, regular, stellar, sweeping, terrestrial, total, ubiquitous, undisputed, unlimited, unrestricted, usual, whole, widespread, worldly; SEE CONCEPTS *536,772*

universe [*n*] *everything in creation*
cosmos, everything, macrocosm, natural world, nature, world; SEE CONCEPTS *370,511*

unjust [*adj*] *not fair*
below the belt*, biased, fixed*, inequitable, influenced, low-down*, one-sided, partial, partisan, prejudiced, shabby*, underhand, undeserved, unfair, unforgivable, unjustified,

unmerited, unrighteous, wrong, wrongful; SEE CONCEPT *545*

unjustifiable [*adj*] *unwarranted*
baseless, foundationless, groundless, indefensible, inexcusable, uncalled-for, unconscionable, unforgivable, unfounded, ungrounded, unjust, unjustified, unmerited, unpardonable, wrong; SEE CONCEPTS *545,548,558*

unkempt [*adj*] *shabby, sloppy*
bedraggled, coarse, crude, dilapidated, dirty, disarranged, disarrayed, disheveled, disordered, grubby*, grungy*, messed up, messy, mussed up*, neglected, rough, rumpled, scruffy, shaggy, slipshod, slovenly, tousled, unclean, uncombed, unfastidious, ungroomed, unimproved, unneat, unpolished, untidy, vulgar; SEE CONCEPTS *485,621*

unkind [*adj*] *not nice*
barbarous, brutal, cold-blooded, coldhearted, cruel, hard-hearted, harsh, hateful, heartless, inconsiderate, inhuman, inhumane, insensitive, malevolent, malicious, malignant, mean, nasty, sadistic, savage, spiteful, thoughtless, uncaring, uncharitable, unfeeling, unfriendly, unsympathetic; SEE CONCEPT *401*

unknowing [*adj*] *unaware*
blank, blind, caught napping*, daydreaming, deaf, ignorant, inattentive, in the dark*, negligent, not informed, not knowing, not told, oblivious, out of it*, out to lunch*, unbriefed, unconscious, uneducated, unenlightened, uninformed, uninstructed, unschooled; SEE CONCEPT *402*

unknown [*adj*] *obscure, mysterious*
alien, anonymous, concealed, dark, desolate, distant, exotic, far, faraway, far-off, foreign, hidden, humble, incog*, incognito, little known, nameless, new, remote, secret, so-and-so*, strange, such-and-such*, unapprehended, unascertained, uncelebrated, uncharted, undiscovered, undistinguished, unexplained, unexplored, unfamiliar, unheard-of, unidentified, unnamed, unnoted, unperceived, unrecognized, unrenowned, unrevealed, unsung, untold, X*; SEE CONCEPT *576*

unlawful [*adj*] *against the law*
actionable, banned, bootleg*, criminal, flagitious, forbidden, illegal, illegitimate, illicit, improper, iniquitous, lawless, nefarious, outlawed, prohibited, taboo, unauthorized, under-the-counter*, unlicensed, wrongful; SEE CONCEPT *319*

unlike [*adj*] *different*
apples and oranges*, clashing, conflicting, contradictory, contrary, contrasted, discordant, disharmonious, disparate, dissimilar, dissonant, distant, distinct, divergent, diverse, far cry from*, heterogeneous, hostile, incompatible, incongruous, inconsistent, mismatched, not alike, offbeat, opposed, opposite, poles apart*, separate, unalike, unequal, unrelated, variant, various, weird; SEE CONCEPT *564*

unlikely [*adj*] *not probable*
absurd, contrary, doubtful, dubious, faint, implausible, improbable, inconceivable, incredible, not likely, out of the ordinary, outside chance, questionable, rare, remote, slight, strange, unbelievable, unconvincing, unheard-of, unimaginable, untoward; SEE CONCEPT *552*

unlimited [*adj*] *extensive, complete*
absolute, all-encompassing, all-out*, boundless,

countless, endless, full, full-blown*, full-out*, full-scale, great, illimitable, immeasurable, immense, incalculable, incomprehensible, indefinite, infinite, interminable, limitless, measureless, no end of*, no end to*, no strings*, numberless, total, totalitarian, unbounded, unconditional, unconfined, unconstrained, unfathomed, unfettered, universal, unqualified, unrestrained, unrestricted, untold, vast, wide open; SEE CONCEPT 772

unload [v] *take off; empty*
break bulk, cast, clear out, disburden, discharge, discommode, disencumber, disgorge, dump, get rid of, jettison, lighten, off-load, relieve, remove, rid, slough, take a load off, unburden, unlade, unpack, void; SEE CONCEPTS 180,211

unlock [v] *open; solve*
break in, crack, decipher, free, jimmy, liberate, open the door*, pop, release, set free, solve, unbolt, unbutton, uncork, undo, unfasten, unhook, unlatch, unravel, unseal, unshut; SEE CONCEPTS 135,250,469

unlucky [adj] *unfortunate, doomed*
afflicted, bad break*, behind eight ball*, black, calamitous, cataclysmic, catastrophic, cursed, dire, disastrous, down on luck*, hapless, hard luck, ill-fated, ill-starred, inauspicious, luckless, miserable, ominous, out of luck, star-crossed*, tough luck, tragic, unfavorable, unhappy, unsuccessful, untimely, untoward; SEE CONCEPTS 529,548

unmanageable [adj] *unruly, wild*
awkward, berserk, chaotic, crazy, disobedient, disorderly, hysterical, lawless, madcap, nuts, out of control, outrageous, riotous, rowdy, turbulent, unbridled, uncontrollable, uncontrolled, undisciplined, ungovernable, unrestrained, violent; SEE CONCEPT 401

unmarried [adj] *not presently wed*
bachelor, eligible, husbandless, single, sole, spouseless, unattached, uncoupled, unwed, unwedded, widowed, wifeless; SEE CONCEPT 555

unmask [v] *reveal*
acknowledge, admit, announce, bare, bring out into the open*, bring to light*, come out with, confess, disclose, display, divulge, exhibit, expose, leak, let cat out of the bag*, make known, make public, show, tell, unclothe, uncover, unearth, unveil; SEE CONCEPTS 60,138

unmerciful [adj] *cruel*
bestial, bloodthirsty, brutal, coldhearted, hard, heartless, hurtful, implacable, inhumane, merciless, monstrous, pitiless, relentless, remorseless, ruthless, tyrannous, uncaring, unfeeling, unpitying, unrelenting, unsparing, vengeful, vindictive; SEE CONCEPT 401

unmistakable [adj] *certain, definite*
apparent, clear, conspicuous, decided, distinct, evident, explicit, for certain, glaring, indisputable, manifest, no ifs ands or buts*, obvious, open and shut*, palpable, patent, plain, positive, pronounced, self-explanatory, straightforward, sure, transparent, unambiguous, unequivocal, univocal; SEE CONCEPT 535

unmitigated [adj] *absolute, pure*
arrant, austere, clear-cut, complete, consummate, damned, downright, gross, intense, oppressive, out-and-out*, outright, perfect, persistent, rank, relentless, rigid, severe, sheer, simple, straightout*, thorough, thoroughgoing, unabated,

unabridged, unadulterated, unalleviated, unbending, unbroken, undiluted, unmixed, unqualified, unrelieved, utter; SEE CONCEPTS 531,535,569

unmotivated [adj] *uninspired*
apathetic, dull, everyday, humdrum, indifferent, lazy, old hat*, ordinary, prosaic, stale, unambitious, uncreative, unexciting, unimaginative, uninspiring, uninteresting, unmoved; SEE CONCEPTS 542,547,548

unnatural [adj] *not regular; artificial*
aberrant, abnormal, affected, anomalous, assumed, bizarre, concocted, contrary, contrived, ersatz*, extraordinary, fabricated, factitious, false, feigned, forced, freakish, freaky, imitation, incredible, insincere, irregular, labored, made-up*, make-believe*, odd, outlandish, outrageous, perverse, perverted, phony, preposterous, pseudo*, put-on*, queer, staged, stiff, stilted*, strained, strange, studied, supernatural, synthetic, theatrical, unaccountable, uncanny, unconforming, unorthodox, unusual; SEE CONCEPTS 564,582

unnecessary [adj] *not required*
accidental, additional, avoidable, beside the point*, casual, causeless, chance, dispensable, excess, exorbitant, expendable, extraneous, extrinsic, fortuitous, futile, gratuitous, haphazard, inessential, irrelevant, lavish, needless, noncompulsory, nonessential, optional, prodigal, profuse, random, redundant, supererogatory, superfluous, surplus, uncalled-for, uncritical, undesirable, unessential, unneeded, unrequired, useless, wanton, worthless; SEE CONCEPT 546

unnerve [v] *upset, intimidate*
agitate, bewilder, bowl over*, buffalo*, chill*, confound, daunt, demoralize, disarm, discombobulate, disconcert, discourage, dishearten, dismay, dispirit, distract, enervate, enfeeble, floor*, fluster, frighten, get to*, give a turn*, intimidate, needle*, perturb, psych out*, rattle, ride, sap*, shake, spook, throw, throw off*, uncalm, undermine, unhinge, unsettle, weaken; SEE CONCEPTS 7,14,19

unnoticed [adj] *ignored*
disregarded, glossed over, hidden, inconspicuous, neglected, overlooked, passed by, pushed aside, secret, unconsidered, undiscovered, unheeded, unobserved, unobtrusive, unperceived, unrecognized, unremarked, unremembered, unrespected, unseen, winked at*; SEE CONCEPT 529

unobtrusive [adj] *keeping a low profile*
humble, inconspicuous, low-key, low-profile, meek, modest, quiet, reserved, restrained, retiring, self-effacing, soft-pedaled*, subdued, tasteful, unassuming, unnoticeable, unostentatious, unpretentious; SEE CONCEPTS 401,548

unorganized [adj] *disorderly, disorganized*
all over the place*, chaotic, cluttered, confused, dislocated, disordered, jumbled, messed up, messy, mixed up, scattered, scrambled, sloppy, unarranged, unkempt, unsystematic, untidy; SEE CONCEPTS 485,535

unorthodox [adj] *abnormal; other than accepted*
beatnik*, crazy*, different, dissident, eccentric, far-out, flaky*, heretical, heterodox, irregular, kinky*, nonconformist, off the beaten path*, schismatic, sectarian, unconventional, uncustomary, unusual, unwonted, way-out*, weird*; SEE CONCEPT 564

unpaid [adj] *free, voluntary*
contributed, donated, due, freewilled, gratuitous,

honorary, unindemnified, unrewarded, un-salaried, volunteer; SEE CONCEPT 538

unpaid [*adj2*] *not settled; taken without remuneration*

delinquent, due, in arrears, mature, not discharged, outstanding, overdue, owing, past due, payable, undefrayed, unliquidated, unsettled; SEE CONCEPT 334

unparalleled [*adj*] *superlative*

all-time*, alone, beyond compare, champ*, champion, consummate, exceptional, greatest, incomparable, matchless, most, nonpareil, only, peerless, rare, single, singular, solid gold*, ten*, tops*, unequaled, unique, unmatched, unprecedented, unrivaled, unsurpassed, winner, without equal, world-class*; SEE CONCEPT 574

unpleasant [*adj*] *bad*

abhorrent, bad news*, bad scene*, disagreeable, displeasing, distasteful, fierce, grody*, gross, hard-time*, icky*, irksome, lousy, nasty, objectionable, obnoxious, poisonous, repulsive, rotten, sour, troublesome, unacceptable, unattractive, uncool*, undesirable, unhappy, unlikable, unlovely, unpalatable, yucky*; SEE CONCEPTS 529,570

unpopular [*adj*] *not liked or sought after*

abhorred, avoided, creepy*, despised, detested, disesteemed, disfavored, disliked, drip*, dumpy*, execrated, gross*, loathed, loser*, lousy, nerdy*, obnoxious, ostracized, out, out of favor, rejected, scorned, shunned, unaccepted, unattractive, uncared for, undesirable, unloved, unvalued, unwanted, unwelcome, weird, wimpy*; SEE CONCEPTS 529,555

unprecedented [*adj*] *exceptional, original*

aberrant, abnormal, anomalous, bizarre, eccentric, exotic, extraordinary, fantastic, freakish, idiosyncratic, marvelous, miraculous, modern, new, newfangled, novel, odd, outlandish, out-of-the-way*, outré, preternatural, prodigious, remarkable, signal, singular, sui generis, uncommon, unexampled, unheard-of, unique, unparalleled, unrivaled, unusual; SEE CONCEPTS 549,564,574

unpredictable [*adj*] *changeable*

capricious, chance, chancy, dicey*, doubtful, erratic, fickle, fluctuating, fluky*, from left field*, hanging by a thread*, iffy*, incalculable, inconstant, random, touch and go*, touchy, uncertain, unforeseeable, unreliable, unstable, up for grabs*, variable, whimsical; SEE CONCEPT 534

unprejudiced [*adj*] *fair*

balanced, dispassionate, equal, equitable, even-handed, fair-minded, impartial, just, liberal, nondiscriminatory, nonpartisan, objective, open-minded, straight, unbiased, unbigoted, uncolored, uninfluenced; SEE CONCEPTS 319,401,542

unprepared [*adj*] *not ready*

ad-lib*, caught off guard*, ill-considered, impromptu, improvised, napping, not prepared, off-hand, off the cuff*, off the top of one's head*, played by ear*, spontaneous, surprised, taken off guard*, unaware, unexpected, unplanned, unready, unrehearsed, unschooled, unskilled, untrained, vulnerable, winged*; SEE CONCEPT 267

unpretentious [*adj*] *simple, honest*

discreet, down, down home*, easy-going, folksy*, free-spirited, homey*, humble, inelaborate, laid-back*, lowly, modest, plain, prosaic, straightforward, unaffected, unambitious, unas-suming, unbeautified, uncomplex, unembellished, unimposing, unobtrusive, unostentatious, unpresumptuous, unspoiled, up front; SEE CONCEPTS 401,404

unprincipled [*adj*] *corrupt*

abandoned, amoral, bent*, cheating, conscienceless, crooked, deceitful, devious, dirty-dealing*, dishonest, dissolute, double-crossing*, double-dealing*, immoral, licentious, mercenary, praetorian, profligate, reprobate, shady, sly, stop-at-nothing*, tricky, two-faced*, two-timing*, unconscionable, underhand, unethical, unprofessional, unscrupulous, venal, wanton; SEE CONCEPT 545

unproductive [*adj*] *idle, nonproductive*

barren, empty, fruitless, futile, ineffective, infertile, pointless, sterile, trivial, unprofitable, useless, worthless; SEE CONCEPTS 267,560

unprofessional [*adj*] *not done well or skillfully*

amateur, amateurish, ignorant, improper, inadequate, incompetent, inefficient, inexperienced, inexpert, lax, negligent, nonexpert, unethical, unfitting, unsuitable, untrained, unworthy; SEE CONCEPTS 527,538

unprotected [*adj*] *defenseless*

caught, endangered, exposed, helpless, indefensible, in the line of fire*, like a sitting duck*, naked*, open, out on a limb*, powerless, pregnable, unarmed, unguarded, unsafe, vulnerable, weak, wide open*; SEE CONCEPTS 555,576

unqualified [*adj1*] *not prepared, incompetent*

amateur, bush, bush-league*, disqualified, ill-equipped, inadequate, incapable, incompetent, ineligible, inexperienced, not equal to, not up to*, unequipped, unfit, unfitted, unprepared, unskilled; SEE CONCEPT 527

unqualified [*adj2*] *outright, absolute*

abiding, blasted, blessed, categorical, certain, clear, complete, confounded, consummate, downright, enduring, entire, explicit, express, firm, flat out*, infernal, never-failing, no catch*, no ifs ands or buts*, out-and-out*, perfect, positive, rank, sheer, simple, steadfast, steady, sure, thorough, thoroughgoing, total, unadulterated, unalloyed, unconditional, unfaltering, unlimited, unmitigated, unreserved, unrestrained, unrestricted, utter, wholehearted, without reservation; SEE CONCEPTS 531,535

unquestionable [*adj*] *definite; beyond doubt*

absolute, accurate, authentic, bona fide*, certain, clear, cold, conclusive, dependable, down pat*, downright, established, faultless, flat*, flawless, for certain, genuine, incontestable, incontrovertible, indisputable, indubitable, irrefutable, manifest, no ifs ands or buts*, obvious, pat, patent, perfect, positive, real, reliable, self-evident, superior, sure, sure-enough, true, undeniable, undisputable, undoubted, unequivocal, unimpeachable, unmistakable, veritable, well-founded, well-grounded; SEE CONCEPTS 529,535

unreadable [*adj*] *illegible*

cacographic, crabbed, difficult to read, hard to make out*, incomprehensible, indecipherable, scrawled, scribbled, unclear, undecipherable; SEE CONCEPTS 535,576

unreal [*adj*] *fake, make-believe; hypothetical*

aerial, artificial, chimerical, delusive, dreamlike, fabled, fabulous, false, fanciful, fictitious, fictive, figmental, hallucinatory, ideal, illusory, imaginary, imagined, immaterial, impalpable, insincere, insubstantial, intangible, invented, legendary, misleading, mock, mythical, nebulous, nonexistent, notional, ostensible, phantasmagoric*, pretended, reachy, romantic, seeming, sham*, storybook*, supposititious, suppositititious, theoretical, unbelievable, unsubstantial, visionary; SEE CONCEPT *582*

unrealistic [*adj*] *not believable or practical*
blue sky*, floating, gone*, half-baked*, impossible, impracticable, impractical, improbable, ivory-tower*, nonrealistic, nonsensical, not applicable, on cloud nine*, quixotic, reachy, romantic, silly, starry-eyed, theoretical, unreal, unworkable; SEE CONCEPTS *552,560*

unreasonable [*adj1*] *not logical or sensible*
absurd, all wet*, arbitrary, biased, capricious, contradictory, erratic, fallacious, far-fetched, foolish, full of hot air*, headstrong, illogical, incoherent, incongruous, inconsequential, inconsistent, invalid, irrational, loose, mad, nonsensical, off the wall*, opinionated, preposterous, quirky, reasonless, senseless, silly, stupid, thoughtless, unreasoned, vacant, wrong; SEE CONCEPTS *401,548*

unreasonable [*adj2*] *extravagant; beyond normal limits*
absonant, arbitrary, costing an arm and a leg*, dear, excessive, exorbitant, extortionate, extreme, far-out*, illegitimate, immoderate, improper, inordinate, intemperate, out of bounds*, overkill*, overmuch, peremptory, posh, pricey*, senseless, steep*, stiff*, too great, too much, too-too*, uncalled-for*, unconscionable, undue, unfair, unjust, unjustifiable, unlawful, unrightful, unwarrantable, unwarranted, up to here*, way out*, wrongful; SEE CONCEPTS *334,762,771*

unrehearsed [*adj*] *spontaneous*
ad-lib*, extemporaneous, from the hip*, impromptu, improvised, impulsive, not rehearsed, off the cuff*, off the top of one's head*, spur of the moment, unpracticed, unprepared; SEE CONCEPTS *401,542,548*

unrelated [*adj*] *independent; different*
beside the point*, dissimilar, extraneous, inapplicable, inappropriate, irrelative, irrelevant, mismatched, nongermane, not germane, not kin, not kindred, not related, separate, unassociated, unattached, unconnected, unlike; SEE CONCEPTS *563,564*

unrelenting [*adj*] *merciless*
bound, bound and determined, brick-wall*, ceaseless, constant, continual, continuous, cruel, dead set on*, endless, grim, hanging tough*, hard-headed*, implacable, incessant, inexorable, intransigent, iron-fisted, mortal, perpetual, persistent, pitiless, relentless, remorseless, rigid, ruthless, set, steady, stern, stiff, stiff-necked*, tenacious, tough, unabated, unbending, unbroken, unflinching, unremitting, unsparing, unwavering, unyielding; SEE CONCEPTS *401,548,798*

unreliable [*adj*] *not trustworthy, not true*
capricious, deceitful, deceptive, delusive, disreputable, dubious, erroneous, fake, fallible, false, fickle, fly-by-night*, furtive, hallucinatory, hollow, implausible, inaccurate, inconstant, irresponsible, makeshift, meretricious, mistaken, pretended, pseudo*, questionable, sham, shifty, specious, treacherous, tricky, uncertain, unconvincing, undependable, underhand, underhanded, unfaithful, unsound, unstable, unsure, untrue, un-

trustworthy, vacillating, wavering, weak; SEE CONCEPTS *542,552,587*

unresolved [*adj*] *uncertain; not settled*
betwixt and between*, changing, doubtful, faltering, hesitant, hesitating, hot and cold*, incomplete, indecisive, irresolute, moot, open to question*, pending, problematical, pussyfooting*, unanswered, unconcluded, undecided, undetermined, unfinished, unsettled, unsolved, up in the air*, vacillating, vague, waffling; SEE CONCEPTS *529,534*

unrest [*n*] *state of agitation; disturbance*
altercation, anarchy, annoyance, anxiety, bickering, bother, chagrin, change, confusion, contention, controversy, crisis, debate, disaffection, discontent, discord, disease, disquiet, dissatisfaction, dissension, distress, dither*, ennui, grief, insurrection, irritation, malaise, moodiness, mortification, perplexity, perturbation, protest, quarrel, rebellion, restlessness, sedition, sorrow, strife, tension, tizzy*, trouble, tumult, turmoil, unease, uneasiness, uproar, upset, vexation, worry; SEE CONCEPTS *410,674*

unrestricted [*adj*] *free*
able, allowed, at liberty, free-spirited, independent, lax, liberal, liberated, on one's own*, open, relaxed, unbounded, uncommitted, unconditional, unconstrained, unlimited, unregulated; SEE CONCEPTS *401,542*

unrivaled [*adj*] *peerless*
best, beyond compare, champion, excellent, faultless, greatest, incomparable, matchless, outstanding, perfect, second to none*, super, superior, supreme, tops*, unequaled, unmatched, unparalleled, unsurpassed, without equal; SEE CONCEPT *574*

unruly [*adj*] *disobedient*
assertive, bawdy, disorderly, drunken, forward, fractious, headstrong, heedless, impervious, impetuous, imprudent, impulsive, incorrigible, inexorable, insubordinate, intemperate, intractable, lawless, mean, mutinous, obstreperous, opinionated, ornery, out of control, out of line*, perverse, quarrelsome, rash, rebellious, recalcitrant, reckless, refractory, restive, riotous, rowdy, turbulent, uncontrollable, ungovernable, unmanageable, unyielding, violent, wayward, wild, willful; SEE CONCEPT *401*

unsafe [*adj*] *dangerous*
alarming, chancy, erratic, explosive, fearsome, hanging by a thread*, hazardous, insecure, on a limb*, on thin ice*, perilous, precarious, risky, shaky, slippery, threatening, ticklish*, touch and go*, touchy*, treacherous, uncertain, independable, unreliable, unsound, unstable, untrustworthy; SEE CONCEPT *587*

unsaid [*adj*] *not expressed or partially expressed*
implicit, implied, inferred, left to the imagination*, silenced, tacit, undeclared, understood, unexpressed, unspoken, unstated, unuttered, unvoiced, wordless; SEE CONCEPT *267*

unsanitary [*adj*] *dirty, unclean*
contaminated, dusty, filthy, foul, grimy, messy, muddy, polluted, rancid, rank, rotten, sloppy, soiled, stained, stinking, sullied, tarnished, unhealthful, unhealthy, unhygienic; SEE CONCEPT *621*

unsatisfactory [*adj*] *insufficient, inadequate*
amiss, bad, damaged, deficient, disappointing, disconcerting, displeasing, disquieting, distress-

un
un

ing, disturbing, for the birds*, junky*, lame, mediocre, no good, not good enough, not up to par*, offensive, poor, regrettable, rotten, schlocky*, second, thin, unacceptable, undesirable, unsuitable, unwelcome, unworthy, upsetting, vexing, weak, wrong; SEE CONCEPTS 529,558,570

unsavory [adj] *revolting, sickening*
acid, bitter, bland, disagreeable, distasteful, dull, flavorless, gross*, icky*, insipid, lousy, nasty, nauseating, no good*, objectionable, obnoxious, offensive, rancid, rank, raunchy*, repellent, repugnant, repulsive, rough, sad, shady, sharp, shifty, sour, stinking, tart, tasteless, tough, unappetizing, unpalatable, unpleasant, wrong; SEE CONCEPTS 462,571,613

unscathed [adj] *not hurt*
in one piece*, safe, sound, unharmed, unhurt, uninjured, unmarked, unscarred, unscratched, untouched, whole; SEE CONCEPT 314

unscrupulous [adj] *immoral*
arrant, base, casuistic, conscienceless, corrupt, crafty, crooked, deceitful, degraded, degrading, disgraceful, dishonest, dishonorable, exploitative, illegal, improper, low-down*, mercenary, perfidious, petty, questionable, recreant, ruthless, scandalous, scheming, selfish, self-seeking, shady, shameless, shifty, sinister, slippery, sly, two-faced*, unconscientious, unconscionable, underhand, underhanded, unethical, unfair, unprincipled, unworthy, venal, wicked, wrongful; SEE CONCEPTS 401,545

unseemly [adj] *improper; in bad taste*
cheap, coarse, crude, discreditable, disreputable, inappropriate, inapt, incorrect, indecent, indecorous, indelicate, inelegant, inept, in poor taste, malapropos, malodorous, out of keeping, out of place, poor, raffish, rough, rowdy, rude, ruffian, tawdry, unapt, unbecoming, unbefitting, undignified, ungodly, unrefined, unsuitable, untoward, vulgar, wrong; SEE CONCEPTS 401,558

unseen [adj] *hidden*
concealed, curtained, dark, imaginary, imagined, impalpable, impenetrable, imperceptible, inconspicuous, invisible, lurking, not in sight, obscure, occult, out of sight, shrouded, undetected, undiscovered, unnoticed, unobserved, unobtrusive, unperceived, unsuspected, veiled; SEE CONCEPT 576

unselfish [adj] *kind, giving*
altruistic, benevolent, charitable, chivalrous, denying, devoted, disinterested, extroverted, generous, helpful, humanitarian, incorruptible, indulgent, liberal, loving, magnanimous, noble, open-handed, self-effacing, self-forgetting, selfless, self-sacrificing; SEE CONCEPTS 401,404

unsettle [v] *bother, upset*
agitate, confuse, dement, derange, disarrange, disarray, discommode, discompose, disconcert, disorder, disorganize, displace, disquiet, disrupt, disturb, down, flurry, fluster, fuddle, get to*, jumble, needle, perturb, psych out*, put off, rattle, ruffle, rummage, sicken, spook, throw, throw off*, trouble, turn, unbalance, unhinge*, unnerve; SEE CONCEPTS 7,19,242

unsettled [adj1] *bothered, upset*
active, agitated, antsy*, anxious, busy, changeable, changeful, changing, complex, complicated, confused, disorderly, disturbed, explosive, fidgety, fluid, flustered, inconstant, insecure, ki-

netic, mobile, mutable, on edge*, perilous, perturbed, precarious, rattled, restive, restless, shaken, shaky, shifting, shook up*, tense, thrown, ticklish, troubled, unbalanced, uncertain, uneasy, unnerved, unpeaceful, unpredictable, unquiet, unrestful, unstable, unsteady, variable, wavering, wobbling; SEE CONCEPTS 401,403

unsettled [adj2] *not decided, taken care of*
betwixt and between*, clouded*, debatable, doubtful, dubious, dubitable, due, immature, in arrears, moot, open, outstanding, overdue, owing, payable, pendent, pending, problematic, uncertain, unclear, undecided, undetermined, unfixed, unpaid, unresolved, up for grabs*, waffling; SEE CONCEPTS 334,535

unsightly [adj] *not pretty*
deformed, disagreeable, drab, dull, hideous, homely, horrid, lackluster, repulsive, revolting, ugly, unattractive, unpleasant, unprepossessing, unshapely; SEE CONCEPT 579

unskilled [adj] *untrained*
awkward, green*, inadequate, incompetent, inept, inexperienced, inexpert, inproficient, not up to*, raw*, unable, undeveloped, uneducated, unequipped, unhandy, unqualified, unschooled, untalented; SEE CONCEPT 527

unsociable [adj] *unfriendly*
aloof, antagonistic, brooding, cold, cool, distant, easy-going, hostile, inaccessible, inhospitable, introverted, laid-back*, nongregarious, recessive, reclusive, reserved, retiring, secretive, sensitive, shy, standoffish*, stuck-up*, timid, unapproachable, unbending, uncommunicative, uncongenial, unforthcoming, unneighborly, unsocial, uppity*, withdrawn; SEE CONCEPTS 401,555

unsolicited [adj] *unasked for*
free, freewilled, gratis*, gratuitous, offered, spontaneous, uncalled-for*, undesirable, undesired, unforced, uninvited, unrequested, unsought, unwelcome, voluntary, volunteered; SEE CONCEPT 538

unsophisticated [adj] *natural, simple*
artless, authentic, bush-league*, callow, childlike, clean, cornball*, corny*, crude, folksy, genuine, green*, guileless, homey*, inexperienced, ingenuous, innocent, kid*, naive, plain, pure, raw, rookie, straightforward, unadulterated, unaffected, unartificial, uncomplicated, uninvolved, unrefined, unschooled, unstudied, untutored, unworldly, wide-eyed*; SEE CONCEPTS 401,548,562

unsound [adj] *not well; flimsy*
ailing, crazed, dangerous, decrepit, defective, delicate, demented, deranged, diseased, erroneous, fallacious, false, faulty, flawed, fragile, frail, ill, illogical, inaccurate, incongruous, incorrect, infirm, in poor health, insane, insecure, insubstantial, invalid, lunatic, mad, not solid, rickety, shaky, specious, tottering, unbacked, unbalanced, unhealthy, unhinged, unreliable, unsafe, unstable, unsteady, unsubstantial, unwell, weak, wobbly; SEE CONCEPTS 314,403,587

unspeakable [adj] *very bad; beyond description*
abominable, alarming, appalling, atrocious, awful, beastly, beyond words, calamitous, detestable, dire, disgusting, dreadful, evil, execrable, fearful, frightening, frightful, heinous, horrible, horrid, incommunicable, inconceivable, indefinable, indescribable, ineffable, inexpressible, inhuman, loathsome, monstrous, nameless,

obnoxious, odious, offensive, outrageous, overwhelming, preternatural, repellent, repugnant, repulsive, revolting, shocking, unbelievable, unimaginable, unutterable; SEE CONCEPTS 548,571

unspoiled [*adj*] *fresh*
clean, clear, crisp, just out*, latest, natural, new, original, pristine, pure, recent, refreshing, sparkling, uncontaminated, unpolluted, unprocessed, untainted, untouched, whole, young; SEE CONCEPTS 537,578,797

unstable/unsteady [*adj*] *doubtful, weak*
ambiguous, borderline, capricious, changeable, dizzy, dubious, erratic, fickle, fitful, fluctuating, giddy, inconsistent, inconstant, insecure, irrational, lubricious, mercurial, mobile, movable, moving, mutable, not fixed, precarious, rickety, risky, rocky, sensitive, shaky, shifty, slippery, suspect, teetering, temperamental, ticklish, tricky, uncertain, unpredictable, unsettled, unsteady, untrustworthy, vacillating, variable, volatile, wavering, weaving, wiggly, wobbly; SEE CONCEPTS 488,534,542

unsubstantiated [*adj*] *questionable, unproven*
arguable, controversial, debatable, disputable, doubtful, dubious, dubitable, fishy*, hard to believe, iffy*, indefinite, open to doubt, open to question, suspect, suspicious, uncertain, unconfirmed, uncorroborated, unsupported; SEE CONCEPTS 529,535

unsuccessful [*adj*] *failing*
abortive, defeated, disastrous, doomed, failed, foiled, fruitless, futile, ill-fated, ineffective, ineffectual, losing, thwarted, unlucky, useless, vain; SEE CONCEPTS 485,489

unsuitable [*adj*] *not proper, inappropriate*
clashing, disagreeable, discordant, discrepant, disparate, disproportionate, dissident, dissonant, ill-suited, improper, inadequate, inadmissible, inapposite, inappropriate, inapt, incompatible, incongruous, inconsistent, ineligible, infelicitous, inharmonious, interfering, irrelevant, jarring, malapropos, out of character*, out of keeping, out of place, senseless, unacceptable, unbecoming, unbefitting, uncalled-for, undue, unfit, unfitting, unmatched, unseasonable, unseemly, unsuited; SEE CONCEPT 558

unsung [*adj*] *uncelebrated*
anonymous, disregarded, forgotten, nameless, neglected, overlooked, unacclaimed, unacknowledged, undistinguished, unfamed, unglorified, unhailed, unhonored, unknown, unnamed, unrecognized, unrenowned; SEE CONCEPTS 267,576

unsure [*adj*] *doubtful, insecure*
betwixt and between*, borderline, distrustful, dubious, fluctuant, fly-by-night*, hesitant, iffy*, in a quandary, indecisive, indeterminate, irresolute, lacking, mistrustful, open, problematic, rootless, shaky, skeptical, suspicious, touch and go*, unassured, uncertain, unclear, unconfident, unconvinced, undecided, undependable, unreliable, unstable, untrustworthy, untrusty, up for grabs*, vacillating, wavering, weak, wimpy*, wobbly; SEE CONCEPT 535

unsurpassed [*adj*] *supreme*
absolute, best, culminating, excellent, final, first, foremost, greatest, highest, incomparable, leading, matchless, paramount, peerless, perfect, prevailing, superior, top, ultimate, unequaled,

unmatched, unparalleled, unrivaled; SEE CONCEPTS 568,574

unsuspecting [*adj*] *gullible*
confiding, credulous, easy, inexperienced, ingenuous, innocent, naive, off guard*, simple, swallowing, taken in*, trustful, trusting, unconscious, undoubting, unsuspicious, unwarned, unwary; SEE CONCEPTS 401,404

unsympathetic [*adj*] *without agreement in feeling*
aloof, antipathetic, apathetic, aversive, callous, cold, cold-blooded, cool, cruel, disinterested, frigid, halfhearted, hard, harsh, heartless, icy, indifferent, insensitive, lukewarm*, mean, nasty, obdurate, repellent, repugnant, stony, tough, uncompassionate, unconcerned, uncongenial, unemotional, unfeeling, unkind, unmoved, unpitying, unpleasant, unresponsive; SEE CONCEPTS 401,542

untamed [*adj*] *wild*
barbarian, barbaric, barbarous, feral, ferocious, fierce, native, overgrown, overrun, rampant, savage, uncivilized, uncontrollable, uncultivated, undomesticated, uninhabited, unmanageable, vicious; SEE CONCEPTS 406,583

untangle [*v*] *straighten out*
clear up, disembroil, disencumber, disentangle, explain, extricate, put in order, solve, unravel, unscramble, unsnarl, untwist, unweave; SEE CONCEPT 126

unthinkable [*adj*] *incredible, unusual*
absurd, beyond belief, beyond possibility, exceptional, extraordinary, illogical, implausible, impossible, improbable, incogitable, inconceivable, insupportable, outlandish, out of the question*, preposterous, rare, singular, unbelievable, uncommon, unimaginable, unique, unlikely, unordinary, unreasonable; SEE CONCEPTS 564,582

unthinking [*adj*] *careless*
blundering, brutish, feckless, foolish, heedless, impulsive, inadvertent, inconsiderate, indelicate, insensitive, instinctive, mechanical, napping, negligent, oblivious, outrageous, rash, rude, selfish, senseless, tactless, thoughtless, uncaring, unconscious, undiplomatic, unheeding, unintended, unmeant, unmindful, unpremeditated, unreasoning, untactful, unwise, vacant, witless; SEE CONCEPT 401

untidy [*adj*] *dirty, disorderly*
bedraggled, careless, chaotic, cluttered, disarranged, disarrayed, disheveled, dowdy*, frowzy*, in disorder, jumbled, littered, mess, messy, mixed up*, muddled, rumpled, slapdash*, slipshod*, sloppy, slovenly, snarled, tacky*, tangled, topsy-turvy, tousled, uncombed, unfastidious, unkempt, unneat, unorderly, unsettled, upset; SEE CONCEPTS 589,621

until [*prep*] *just before*
as far as, before, before the coming, continuously, down to, in advance of, in expectation, prior to, till, to, up till, up to; SEE CONCEPT 820

untimely [*adj*] *inappropriate*
a bit previous*, abortive, anachronistic, awkward, badly timed, bright and early*, disagreeable, early, early bird*, early on, ill-timed, improper, inappropriate, inauspicious, inconvenient, inexpedient, inopportune, intrusive, malapropos, mistimed, out-of-date, previous, soon, too early, too late, undue, unfavorable, unfit, unfortunate,

un
un

unlucky, unpropitious, unseasonable, unseemly, unsuitable, unsuited, wrong; SEE CONCEPTS 548,799

untiring [*adj*] *determined, persevering*
constant, continued, continuing, dedicated, devoted, dogged, eager beaver*, fireball*, firm, go-go*, grind*, hyper*, incessant, indefatigable, indomitable, inexhaustible, jumping, patient, perky, persistent, pertinacious, plodding, plugging, resolute, staunch, steady, strong, tenacious, tireless, unceasing, undeterred, unfailing, unfaltering, unflagging, unflinching, unremitting, unstinted, unswerving, unwavering, unwearied; SEE CONCEPT 538

untold [*adj*] *very many; enormous*
beyond measure, countless, gigantic, hidden, huge, immense, incalculable, indescribable, inexpressible, innumerable, innumerous, mammoth, manifold, many, measureless, mighty, monstrous, multiple, multitudinous, myriad, numberless, private, prodigious, staggering, suppressed, titanic, uncountable, uncounted, undreamed of, unexpressed, unimaginable, unknown, unnumberable, unnumbered, unspeakable, unthinkable, vast; SEE CONCEPTS 529,762,781

untouched [*adj*] *whole; not spoiled*
clear, entire, flawless, fresh, good, immaculate, incorrupt, indifferent, in good condition, intact, out of danger, perfect, pure, safe and sound*, sanitary, secure, shipshape, sound, spotless, unaffected, unblemished, unbroken, unconcerned, undamaged, unharmed, unhurt, unimpressed, uninjured, unmarred, unmoved, unscathed, unstained, unstirred, untried, virgin, virginal, without a scratch; SEE CONCEPTS 403,485,621

untoward [*adj*] *troublesome*
adverse, annoying, awkward, contrary, disastrous, disturbing, fractious, hapless, ill-starred, inauspicious, inconvenient, indocile, inimical, inopportune, intractable, irritating, luckless, misfortunate, perverse, recalcitrant, refractory, star-crossed, undisciplined, unfavorable, unfortunate, ungovernable, unhappy, unlucky, unmanageable, unpliable, unpropitious, unruly, untimely, unyielding, vexatious, wild; SEE CONCEPTS 542,548,570

untoward [*adj2*] *improper; not suitable*
improprietous, inappropriate, indecent, indecorous, indelicate, malodorous, out of place*, rough*, unbecoming, uncouth, unfitting, ungodly*, unseemly; SEE CONCEPTS 401,558

untroubled [*adj*] *calm, peaceful*
composed, cool, halcyon, hushed, placid, quiet, serene, steady, still, tranquil, unagitated, unconcerned, undisturbed, unflappable, unflustered, unperturbed, unruffled, unstirred, unworried; SEE CONCEPTS 403,548,594

untrue [*adj*] *dishonest*
apocryphal, cheating, counterfactual, deceitful, deceptive, delusive, deviant, disloyal, dissembling, distorted, erroneous, faithless, fallacious, false, fictitious, forsworn, hollow, imprecise, inaccurate, inconstant, incorrect, inexact, lying, meretricious, misleading, mistaken, off*, out of line*, perfidious, perjured, prevaricating, recreant, sham*, specious, spurious, traitorous, treacherous, two-faced*, unfaithful, unloyal, unsound, untrustworthy, untruthful, wide, wrong; SEE CONCEPTS 267,545,582

untrustworthy [*adj*] *not dependable, unfaithful*
capricious, conniving, crooked, deceitful, devious, dishonest, disloyal, dubious, fair-weather*, faithless, false, fickle, fink*, fly-by-night*, guileful, irresponsible, questionable, shady, sharp, shifty*, slippery, sneaky, treacherous, tricky, trustless, two-faced*, two-timing*, unassured, undependable, unfaithful, unreliable, unsafe, unsure, untrue, untrusty; SEE CONCEPTS 401,542,545

untruthful [*adj*] *dishonest*
bluffing, cheating, corrupt, crooked, deceitful, deceiving, deceptive, disreputable, double-crossing, double-dealing, false, fraudulent, lying, misleading, shady, shifty, sneaking, sneaky, tricky, two-faced*, two-timing*, underhanded, untrustworthy; SEE CONCEPT 267

unusual [*adj*] *different*
abnormal, amazing, astonishing, atypical, awe-inspiring, awesome, bizarre, conspicuous, curious, different, distinguished, eminent, exceptional, extraordinary, far-out*, inconceivable, incredible, memorable, noteworthy, odd, out of the ordinary*, outstanding, phenomenal, prodigious, prominent, queer, rare, refreshing, remarkable, significant, singular, something else*, special, strange, surprising, uncommon, unconventional, unexpected, unfamiliar, unique, unparalleled, unwonted, weird*; SEE CONCEPT 564

unusually [*adv*] *extremely*
almighty*, awful*, awfully, curiously, especially, extra, extraordinarily, mighty, oddly, peculiarly, plenty, powerful, rarely, real, really, remarkably, right, so, so much, strangely, surprisingly, terribly, terrifically, too much, uncommon, uncommonly, very; SEE CONCEPTS 544,569

unvarnished [*adj*] *plain, honest*
bare, candid, clean, folksy*, for real*, frank, genuine, homey*, naked, open, open and shut*, pure, pure and simple*, simple, sincere, stark, straight, straightforward, unadorned, unconcealed, undisguised, undissembled, unembellished, vanilla*; SEE CONCEPTS 267,582

unveil [*v*] *reveal*
bare, betray, bring to light*, come out, disclose, discover, display, divulge, expose, give away, lay bare*, lay open*, let it all hang out*, make known, make public, open, open up, show, spring, tell, tip one's hand*, unbosom, uncover; SEE CONCEPTS 60,138

unwarranted [*adj*] *not reasonable or right*
baseless, bottomless, foundationless, gratuitous, groundless, indefensible, inexcusable, uncalled-for, unconscionable, undue, unfair, unfounded, ungrounded, unjust, unjustifiable, unjustified, unprovoked, unreasonable, unwarrantable, wrong; SEE CONCEPTS 545,548,558

unwary [*adj*] *thoughtless, heedless*
brash, careless, credulous, hasty, ignorant, ill-advised, impetuous, imprudent, incautious, inconsiderate, indiscreet, negligent, rash, reckless, unadvised, unalert, uncircumspect, unguarded, unprepared, unsuspecting, unsuspicious, unvigilant, unwatchful; SEE CONCEPTS 401,403

unwavering [*adj*] *consistent, unchanging*
abiding, brick-wall*, dead set on*, dedicated, determined, enduring, firm, fixed, intense, never-failing, pat, regular, resolute, set, set in stone*, single-minded, solid, staunch, steadfast, steady,

sure, undeviating, unfaltering, unflagging, unflappable, unqualified, unshakable, unshaken, unswerving, untiring; SEE CONCEPTS 488,535,542

unwelcome [*adj*] *not wanted, desired*
blackballed*, disagreeable, displeasing, distasteful, exceptionable, excess baggage*, excluded, ill-favored, inadmissible, left out in cold*, lousy, not in the picture*, objectionable, obnoxious, rejected, repellent, shut out, thankless, unacceptable, unasked, undesirable, uninvited, unpleasant, unpopular, unsought, unwanted, unwished-for; SEE CONCEPTS 529,555,570

unwell [*adj*] *sick*
ailing, bedridden, broken down, debilitated, diseased, feeble, feverish, frail, hospitalized, ill, impaired, incurable, infected, infirm, in poor health, invalid, laid-up, nauseated, not feeling well, run down, sick as a dog*, sickly, suffering, under medication, under the weather*, unhealthy, weak; SEE CONCEPT 314

unwieldy [*adj*] *awkward, bulky*
burdensome, bedridden, cumbersome, cumbrous, encumbering, gross, hefty, inconvenient, lumbering, massive, onerous, ponderous, uncontrollable, ungainly, unhandy, unmanageable, weighty; SEE CONCEPTS 562,781

unwilling [*adj*] *not in the mood*
afraid, against, against the grain*, averse, backward, begrudging, compelled, contrary, demurring, disinclined, disobliging, evasive, forced, grudging, hesitating, indisposed, indocile, involuntary, laggard, loath, malcontent, opposed, recalcitrant, refractory, reluctant, remiss, resistant, shrinking, shy, slack, slow, unaccommodating, uncheerful, uncooperative, uneager, unenthusiastic, uninclined, unobliging, unready, unwishful, wayward; SEE CONCEPTS 401,542

unwind [*v1*] *undo, untangle*
disentangle, free, loose, loosen, ravel, separate, slacken, unbend, uncoil, unfurl, unravel, unreel, unroll, untwine, untwist, unwrap; SEE CONCEPT 158

unwind [*v2*] *relax*
calm down*, ease off*, loosen up*, quiet down*, quieten, recline, rest, sit back*, slow down*, take a break*, take it easy*, wind down*; SEE CONCEPT 210

unwise [*adj*] *stupid, irresponsible*
childish, foolhardy, foolish, ill-advised, ill-considered, immature, impolitic, improvident, imprudent, inadvisable, inane, inappropriate, indiscreet, inept, injudicious, misguided, naive, rash, reckless, senseless, short-sighted, silly, thoughtless, undesirable, unfortunate, unintelligent, unsound, witless; SEE CONCEPTS 401,402,548

unwitting [*adj*] *without fully realizing*
accidental, aimless, chance, comatose, forgetful, haphazard, ignorant, inadvertent, incognizant, inconversant, innocent, involuntary, numb, oblivious, senseless, unacquainted, unaware, unconscious, undesigned, unfamiliar, uninformed, uninstructed, unintended, unintentional, unknowing, unmeant, unmindful, unplanned, unsuspecting, unthinking; SEE CONCEPTS 401,544,548

unworldly [*adj1*] *spiritual*
abstract, astral, celestial, daydreaming, daydreamy, dreamy, ethereal, extraterrestrial, fantas-

tic, incorporeal, metaphysical, nonmaterialistic, otherworldly, religious, supersensory, transcendental, unearthly, unreal, visionary; SEE CONCEPTS 536,582

unworldly [*adj2*] *not sophisticated; inexperienced*
artless, babe in woods*, clean, corn-fed*, country, folksy*, green*, idealistic, ingenuous, innocent, naive, natural, raw*, simple, trusting, unaffected, unartificial, uncool, unschooled, unsophisticated, unstudied, unripe, wide-eyed*; SEE CONCEPTS 401,555,589

unworthy [*adj*] *not of value*
base, beneath, blamable, contemptible, degrading, disgraceful, dishonorable, disreputable, good-for-nothing, ignoble, improper, inappropriate, ineligible, inexcusable, no-account*, no-good*, not deserving, not fit, not good enough, nothing, not worth, offensive, out of place*, recreant, reprehensible, shameful, unbecoming, unbefitting, undeserving, unfit, unmerited, unseemly, unsuitable, valueless, vile, wretched, wrong; SEE CONCEPTS 404,558,571

unwritten [*adj*] *understood*
accepted, conventional, customary, oral, spoken, tacit, traditional, unformulated, unrecorded, unsaid, verbal, vocal, word-of-mouth; SEE CONCEPTS 267,533

unyielding [*adj*] *steadfast, resolute*
adamant, dead set on*, determined, firm, fixed, hard, hard-core*, hardheaded, hard-line*, hard-nosed*, headstrong*, immalleable, immovable, implacable, impliable, inexorable, inflexible, intractable, locked in, merciless, mulish, obdurate, obstinate, pertinacious, pigheaded*, refractory, relentless, resolute, rigid, ruthless, single-minded, solid, staunch, stiff, stiff-necked, stubborn, tough, unbending, uncompliant, uncompromising, unmovable, unrelenting, unswayable, unwavering; SEE CONCEPTS 401,542

up-and-coming [*adj*] *rising*
ambitious, climbing, coming on strong*, determined, eager, enterprising, get up and go*, go-getter*, high-reaching, hungry, promising, soaring, striving, succeeding; SEE CONCEPTS 326,542

upbeat [*adj*] *cheerful*
buoyant, cheery, encouraging, favorable, fond, happy, heartening, hopeful, optimistic, positive, promising, rosy, sanguine; SEE CONCEPTS 403,572

upbraid [*v*] *scold*
admonish, berate, blame, castigate, censure, chasten, chastise, chew out*, chide, criticize, give a talking-to*, jump on*, lay down the law*, lecture, light into*, put down, rake over the coals*, ream, reprimand, reproach, take to task*, tell off*; SEE CONCEPTS 44,52,54

update [*v*] *bring up to date*
amend, modernize, refresh, refurbish, rejuvenate, renew, renovate, restore, revise; SEE CONCEPT 244

upgrade [*v*] *improve*
advance, better, boost, elevate, enhance, increase, lift, make better, make strides, move up, progress, promote, raise; SEE CONCEPTS 244,700

upheaval [*n*] *major change*
about-face*, alteration, cataclysm, catastrophe, clamor, commotion, convulsion, disaster, disorder, disruption, disturbance, eruption, explosion,

un
up

ferment, flip-flop*, new ball-game*, new deal*, outbreak, outburst, outcry, overthrow, revolution, shakeout*, stirring, switch, temblor, tremor, tumult, turmoil, turnaround, upturn; SEE CONCEPT 230

uphill [adj1] going up
acclivous, ascending, climbing, mounting, rising, skyward, sloping upward, toward summit, up, uprising; SEE CONCEPT 581

uphill [adj2] difficult, laborious
arduous, effortful, exhausting, grueling, hard, labored, operose, punishing, rugged, strenuous, taxing, toilsome, tough, wearisome; SEE CONCEPTS 538,565

uphold [v] maintain, support
advocate, aid, assist, back, back up, bolster, boost, brace, buoy up, buttress, carry, champion, confirm, countenance, defend, elevate, encourage, endorse, help, hoist, hold to, hold up one's end*, justify, pick up, promote, prop, raise, rear, second, shore up, side with, stand by, stick by, stick up for*, sustain, take up, upbear, uplift, upraise, uprear, vindicate; SEE CONCEPT 110

upkeep [n] maintenance
budget, conservation, costs, expenditure, expenses, keep, outlay, overhead, preservation, price, repair, running, subsistence, support, sustenance, sustentation; SEE CONCEPTS 117,344

uplift [v] elevate, inspire
boost, brighten, bring up, cheer, elate, excite, exhilarate, improve, lift up*, perk up*, raise spirits; SEE CONCEPTS 7,22

upper [adj1] above
high, higher, loftier, more elevated, overhead, top, topmost, uppermost, upward; SEE CONCEPT 583

upper [adj2] superior
beautiful, elevated, elite, eminent, greater, important, more important; SEE CONCEPTS 555,567

upper hand [n] advantage
benefit, break, control, dominance, edge, favor, gain, help, improvement, leverage, rule, superiority, supremacy; SEE CONCEPT 574

uppermost [adj1] top
apical, culminating, highest, loftiest, most elevated, topmost, upmost; SEE CONCEPT 583

uppermost [adj2] most important; chief
best, big, boss, dominant, executive, foremost, greatest, high-up*, leading, main, paramount, predominant, preeminent, primary, principal, supreme, the most*, tops*, winner, world-class*; SEE CONCEPTS 568,632

uppity [adj] arrogant
audacious, bossy, bragging, cavalier, cheeky, cocky, conceited, egotistic, haughty, high and mighty*, high falutin*, know-it-all*, overbearing, pompous, presumptuous, pretentious, puffed up*, self-important, smug, snobbish, snooty*, snotty*, stuck up*, superior, vain; SEE CONCEPTS 401,404

upright [adj1] straight-up
cocked, end on, end up, erect, on end, perpendicular, plumb, raised, sheer, standing, stand-up, steep, straight, upended, upstanding, upward, vertical; SEE CONCEPTS 581,583

upright [adj2] honorable, honest
aboveboard, blameless, circumspect, conscientious, correct, equitable, ethical, exemplary, fair, faithful, good, high-minded, impartial, incorruptible, just, kosher*, legit*, moral, noble, principled, punctilious, pure, right, righteous, square, straight, straightforward, true, true-blue*, trustworthy, unimpeachable, up front*, virtuous; SEE CONCEPTS 404,545

uprising [n] disturbance
insurgence, insurrection, mutiny, outbreak, rebellion, revolt, revolution, riot, upheaval; SEE CONCEPTS 106,674

uproar [n] commotion, pandemonium
ado, babble, babel, bedlam, bickering, big scene*, brawl, broil*, bustle, chaos, clamor, clangor, clatter, confusion, din, disorder, flap*, fracas*, free-for-all*, furor, fuss, hassle, jangle, mayhem, melee, noise, outcry, racket, riot, roughhouse*, row, ruction, shivaree*, stink*, stir, strife, to-do*, turbulence, turmoil, violence; SEE CONCEPTS 46,65,106,674

uproot [v] destroy; rip out of a place
abate, abolish, annihilate, blot out, demolish, deracinate, dig up, displace, do away with*, eliminate, eradicate, excavate, exile, exterminate, extirpate, extract, move, overthrow, overturn, pull up, remove, root out, tear up, weed, weed out, wipe out; SEE CONCEPTS 147,178,211,252

upset [adj] disturbed, bothered
agitated, all torn up*, amazed, antsy*, apprehensive, blue*, broken up*, bummed out*, capsized, chaotic, come apart*, confused, disconcerted, dismayed, disordered, disquieted, distressed, disturbed, dragged*, frantic, grieved, hurt, ill, in disarray, jittery, jumpy, low, muddled, overturned, overwrought, psyched out*, rattled, ruffled*, shocked, shook up*, sick, spilled, thrown, tipped over, toppled, troubled, tumbled, unglued*, unsettled, unzipped*, upside-down, worried; SEE CONCEPTS 403,485,570

upset [n] problem
agitation, bother, complaint, defeat, destruction, disorder, disquiet, distress, disturbance, free-for-all*, goulash*, hassle, illness, malady, overthrow, queasiness, reverse, reversion, screw-up*, shake-up*, shock, sickness, stew*, subversion, surprise, tizzy*, trouble, turmoil, worry; SEE CONCEPT 674

upset [v1] disorder; knock over
capsize, change, derange, disarray, disorganize, disturb, invert, jumble, keel over, mess up*, mix up, muddle, overset, overturn, pitch, put out of order, reverse, rummage, spill, spoil, subvert, tilt, tip over, topple, tumble, turn, turn inside-out*, turn topsy-turvy*, turn upside-down*, unsettle, upend, upturn; SEE CONCEPTS 147,208,213

upset [v2] bother, trouble
adjy*, afflict, agitate, ail, bewilder, bug*, confound, cramp, craze, debilitate, derange, discombobulate*, discompose, disconcert, dismay, disquiet, distract, distress, disturb, egg on*, fire up*, flip*, flip out*, floor*, flurry, fluster, get to*, give a hard time*, grieve, incapacitate, indispose, key up*, lay up, make a scene*, make waves*, perturb, pick on*, pother, psych*, rattle, rock the boat*, ruffle, sicken, spook, stir up, throw off balance*, turn, turn on, unhinge*, unnerve, unsettle; SEE CONCEPTS 7,19

upset [v3] defeat
beat, be victorious, conquer, get the better of*, outplay, overcome, overpower, overthrow, overturn, topple, triumph over, win; SEE CONCEPT 95

upshot [n] end result
aftereffect, aftermath, burden, climax, completion, conclusion, consequence, core, culmina-

tion, denouement, development, effect, end, ending, event, eventuality, finale, finish, gist, issue, meaning, meat*, outcome, payoff, pith*, purport, result, sense, sequel, substance, termination, thrust; SEE CONCEPTS 230,682

upside-down [adj] *overturned, inverted*
backward, bottom-side up, bottom up, confused, disordered, downside-up*, haywire*, helter-skelter*, in chaos, in disarray, jumbled, mixed-up, on head, reversed, tangled, topsy-turvy*, upended, wrong-side-up, wrong way; SEE CONCEPT 583

upstanding [adj] *honorable*
ethical, good, honest, incorruptible, moral, principled, straightforward, true, trustworthy, upright; SEE CONCEPT 545

upstart [n] *newly rich*
name-dropper, nouveau riche, parvenue, social climber, status seeker; SEE CONCEPT 347

uptight [adj] *nervous*
anxious, apprehensive, cautious, concerned, conventional, edgy, nervy, old-fashioned, on edge*, on the defensive*, restive, strict, tense, troubled, uneasy, withdrawn, worried; SEE CONCEPT 401

up-to-date [adj] *current, modern*
abreast, advanced, a' la mode*, all the rage*, au courant, avant-garde, brand-new, contemporary, cutting edge*, dashing, expedient, faddish*, fashionable, fitting, hot*, in, in fashion, in-thing*, in vogue, modernistic, modish, neoteric, new, newest, newfangled, now*, opportune, popular, red-hot*, state-of-the-art*, stylish, suitable, timely, today*, trendy, up*, up-to-the-minute, with it*; SEE CONCEPTS 578,589,797,799

urban [adj] *city*
burghal, central, citified, civic, civil, downtown, inner-city, metropolitan, municipal, nonrural, oppidan, popular, public, town, village; SEE CONCEPT 536

urbane [adj] *civilized*
affable, balanced, bland, civil, cosmopolitan, courteous, cultivated, cultured, debonair, elegant, genteel, gracious, mannerly, metropolitan, obliging, poised, polished, polite, refined, smooth, sophisticated, suave, well-bred, well-mannered; SEE CONCEPT 401

urchin [n] *mischievous youngster*
brat*, cub, dickens*, gamin, imp, juvenile delinquent, punk*, pup*, ragamuffin, waif; SEE CONCEPT 423

urge [n] *very strong desire*
appetite, appetition, compulsion, craving, drive, druthers, fancy, fire in belly*, goad, impetus, impulse, incentive, itch*, longing, lust, motive, passion, pressure, stimulant, stimulus, sweet tooth*, weakness, wish, yearning, yen; SEE CONCEPTS 20,532

urge [v] *beg, push for, encourage*
adjure, advance, advise, advocate, appeal to, ask, attract, beseech, champion, charge, commend, compel, conjure, counsel, countenance, drive, egg on*, endorse, entreat, exhort, favor, fire up*, force, further, goad, hasten, impel, implore, incite, induce, influence, insist on, inspire, instigate, maneuver, move, plead, press, promote, prompt, propel, propose, push, put up to*, rationalize, recommend, request, sanction, solicit, speak for, spur, stimulate, support, tempt, wheedle; SEE CONCEPTS 68,75

urgent [adj] *needing immediate attention*
burning*, called-for, capital, chief, clamant,

clamorous, compelling, critical, crucial, crying*, demanded, demanding, driving, essential, exigent, foremost, heavy*, hurry-up, immediate, impelling, imperative, important, importunate, indispensable, insistent, instant, leading, life and death*, momentous, necessary, paramount, persuasive, pressing, primary, principal, required, salient, serious, top-priority, touch and go*, touchy*, vital, wanted, weighty*; SEE CONCEPTS 548,568

usable [adj] *available, working*
accessible, adaptable, advantageous, applicable, at disposal, at hand, beneficial, consumable, convenient, current, employable, exhaustible, expendable, exploitable, fit, functional, good, helpful, in order, instrumental, open, operative, practicable, practical, profitable, ready, running, serviceable, subservient, unused, useful, utile, utilizable, valid, valuable, wieldy; SEE CONCEPTS 560,576

usage [n] *habit, custom*
acceptance, control, convention, currency, form, formula, habitude, handling, management, matter of course, method, mode, operation, practice, praxis, procedure, regime, regulation, rote, routine, rule, running, tradition, treatment, trick, use, way, wont; SEE CONCEPTS 6,658

use [n] *application; employment*
account, adoption, advantage, appliance, applicability, appropriateness, avail, benefit, call, capitalization, cause, convenience, custom, end, exercise, exercising, exertion, fitness, good, habit, handling, help, helpfulness, mileage, mobilization, necessity, need, object, occasion, operation, point, practice, profit, purpose, reason, relevance, service, serviceability, treatment, usability, usage, usefulness, utility, value, way, wear and tear*, wont, worth; SEE CONCEPTS 225,658,709

use [v] *work with; consume*
accept, adopt, apply, avail oneself of, bestow, bring into play*, bring to bear*, capitalize, control, do with, draw on, employ, exercise, exert, exhaust, expend, exploit, find a use, govern, handle, make do with*, make the most of*, make use, manage, manipulate, operate, play on, ply, practice, press into service*, put forth*, put into action, put to use, put to work, regulate, relate, run, run through, set in motion, spend, take advantage of*, turn to account, utilize, waste, wield, work; SEE CONCEPTS 169,225

used [adj] *secondhand*
hand-me-down, nearly new, not new, passed down, pre-owned, recycled, worn; SEE CONCEPTS 334,567,574

used to [adj] *familiar with*
acclimated, accustomed, at home with*, common, commonplace, customary, everyday, knowing, known, old hat*, ordinary, plain, recognizable, routine, well-known; SEE CONCEPTS 530,547

useful [adj] *beneficial, valuable*
advantageous, all-purpose, applied, appropriate, brave, commodious, convenient, effective, favorable, fit, fruitful, functional, good, handy, helpful, instrumental, meet, of assistance, of service, of use, practicable, practical, pragmatic, profitable, proper, propitious, purposive, salutary, serviceable, subsidiary, suitable, suited, toward, utile, utilitarian, workaday, worthwhile; SEE CONCEPT 560

up
us

useless [*adj*] *not working; not valuable*
abortive, bootless, counterproductive, disadvantageous, dysfunctional, expendable, feckless, fruitless, futile, good-for-nothing*, hopeless, idle, impracticable, impractical, incompetent, ineffective, ineffectual, inept, inoperative, inutile, meaningless, no good, nonfunctional, of no use, pointless, profitless, purposeless, scrap, stupid*, unavailable, unavailing, unfunctional, unproductive, unprofitable, unpurposed, unusuable, unworkable, vain, valueless, waste, weak, worthless; SEE CONCEPT *560*

user-friendly [*adj*] *easily operated*
accessible, adaptable, convenient, easy to use, feasible, foolproof, handy, manageable, practical, simple, straightforward, uncomplicated, useful, wieldy; SEE CONCEPTS *560,576*

usher [*n*] *person who guides others to place*
attendant, conductor, doorkeeper, doorperson, escort, guide, herald, lead, leader, page, pilot, precursor; SEE CONCEPT *352*

usher [*v*] *guide*
bring in, conduct, direct, escort, herald, inaugurate, initiate, institute, introduce, launch, lead, marshal, open the door, originate, pave the way*, pilot, precede, preface, receive, set up, show around, show in, show out, steer; SEE CONCEPTS *187,221*

usual [*adj*] *common, typical*
accepted, accustomed, average, chronic, commonplace, constant, conventional, current, customary, cut-and-dried*, everyday, expected, familiar, fixed, frequent, garden variety*, general, grind, habitual, mainstream, matter-of-course, natural, normal, ordinary, plain, plastic, prevailing, prevalent, quotidian, regular, rife, routine, run-of-the-mill*, so-so*, standard, stock, typic, unremarkable, vanilla*, white-bread*, wonted, workaday; SEE CONCEPTS *530,547*

usually [*adv*] *for the most part*
as a rule, as is the custom, as is usual, as usual, by and large, commonly, consistently, customarily, frequently, generally, habitually, in the main, mainly, more often than not, mostly, most often, normally, now and again, now and then, occasionally, once and again, on the whole, ordinarily, regularly, routinely, sometimes; SEE CONCEPTS *530,541*

usurp [*v*] *take over*
accroach, annex, appropriate, arrogate, assume, barge in*, butt in*, clap hands on*, commandeer, cut out, displace, elbow in*, get hands on*, grab, grab hold of, highjack*, infringe upon, lay hold of, muscle in*, preempt, seize, squeeze in, supplant, swipe, take, work in, worm in*, wrest; SEE CONCEPTS *142,384*

utensil [*n*] *tool, usually for eating*
apparatus, appliance, contrivance, convenience, device, equipment, fork, gadget, implement, instrument, knife, silverware, spoon, tableware, ware; SEE CONCEPTS *493,499*

utilitarian [*adj*] *practical*
commonsensical, down-to-earth, effective, efficient, functional, hard, hardheaded, matter-of-fact, nuts and bolts*, pragmatic, pragmatical, realistic, sensible, serviceable, unidealistic, unromantic, useful; SEE CONCEPT *560*

utility [*n*] *serviceableness*
account, adequacy, advantage, advantageousness, applicability, appropriateness, avail, benefit, convenience, efficacy, efficiency, expediency, favor, fitness, function, point, practicality, productiveness, profit, relevance, service, serviceability, use, usefulness; SEE CONCEPT *658*

utilize [*v*] *make use of*
advance, apply, appropriate, avail oneself of, bestow, employ, exercise, exploit, forward, further, handle, have recourse to, profit by, promote, put to use, resort to, take advantage of, turn to account, use; SEE CONCEPT *225*

utmost [*adj*] *extreme, maximum*
absolute, all-out*, chief, complete, entire, exhaustive, farthest, final, full, furthermost, greatest, highest, last, last straw*, maximal, most, most distant, outermost, out of bounds*, outside, paramount, plenary, preeminent, remotest, sheer, supreme, thorough, thoroughgoing, too much*, too-too*, top, topmost, total, ultimate, ultra*, unconditional, undiminished, unlimited, unmitigated, unqualified, unreserved, uttermost, whole, worst case*; SEE CONCEPTS *531,574,772*

utopia [*n*] *ideal place and life*
Arcadia, bliss, dreamland, dreamworld, Eden, Elysian Fields*, Erewhon*, fairyland, Garden of Eden, heaven, land of milk and honey*, never-never land*, paradise, perfection, pie in the sky*, promised land*, seventh heaven*, Shangri-La*, wonderland; SEE CONCEPTS *370,689*

utopian [*adj*] *imaginary, ideal*
abstract, airy, ambitious, arcadian, chimerical, dream, fanciful, fantasy, grandiose, hopeful, idealist, idealistic, ideological, illusory, impossible, impractical, lofty, otherworldly, perfect, pie-in-the-sky*, pretentious, quixotic, romantic, transcendental, unfeasible, visionary; SEE CONCEPTS *572,574,582*

utter [*adj*] *outright, absolute*
all-fired*, arrant, blasted*, blessed*, blooming*, complete, confounded, consummate, downright, entire, flat-out*, infernal, out-and-out*, perfect, pure, sheer, stark, straight-out*, thorough, thoroughgoing, total, unmitigated, unqualified; SEE CONCEPTS *531,535*

utter [*v*] *say, reveal*
affirm, air, announce, articulate, assert, asseverate, blurt, bring out, chime, chin*, come out with*, declaim, declare, deliver, disclose, divulge, ejaculate, enunciate, exclaim, express, give words to*, go, jaw*, lip*, make known, modulate, mouth*, mutter, proclaim, promulgate, pronounce, publish, put into words, recite, say, shout, speak, spiel*, state, talk, throw out, verbalize, vocalize, voice, whisper; SEE CONCEPTS *47,55*

utterance [*n*] *revelation*
announcement, articulation, assertion, asseveration, declaration, delivery, discourse, ejaculation, expression, opinion, oration, peroration, pronouncement, rant, recitation, remark, reply, response, saying, sentence, speaking, speech, spiel, statement, talk, vent, verbalization, vocalization, vociferation, voice, word, words; SEE CONCEPTS *47,278*

utterly [*adv*] *completely*
absolutely, all, all in all, altogether, entirely, exactly, extremely, fully, in toto, just, perfectly, plumb*, purely, quite, thoroughly, totally, to the core*, to the nth degree*, well, wholly; SEE CONCEPT *531*

uttermost [*adj*] *extreme*
farthest, final, furthermost, furthest, last, outermost, outmost, remotest, utmost; SEE CONCEPTS *585,778*

V

vacancy [*n*] *opening*
abstraction, blankness, desertedness, emptiness, gap, job, lack, opportunity, position, post, room, situation, space, vacuity, vacuousness, vacuum, void, voidness; SEE CONCEPTS *513,516,693*

vacant [*adj1*] *empty; unoccupied*
abandoned, available, bare, clear, deserted, devoid, disengaged, free, idle, not in use, stark, tenantless, to let, unemployed, unengaged, unfilled, uninhabited, unlived in, untaken, untenanted, unused, void, without contents; SEE CONCEPTS *481,560,740,774*

vacant [*adj2*] *absent-minded; expressionless*
abstracted, blank, daydreaming, deadpan, dreaming, dreamy, empty-headed*, foolish, idle, inane, incurious, inexpressive, silly, stupid, thoughtless, unexpressive, unintelligent, unthinking, vacuous, vapid, witless; SEE CONCEPT *402*

vacate [*v*] *leave empty*
abandon, abrogate, annul, clear, depart, discharge, dissolve, empty, evacuate, give up, go away, leave, move out, move out of, part with, quash, quit, relinquish, renounce, rescind, retract, reverse, revoke, void, withdraw; SEE CONCEPTS *195,234*

vacation [*n*] *planned time spent not working*
break, breathing space*, day of rest, few days off*, fiesta, furlough, holiday, intermission, layoff, leave, leave of absence, liberty, long weekend*, R and R*, recess, recreation, respite, rest, sabbatical, spell, time off, two weeks with pay*; SEE CONCEPTS *363,807*

vaccinate [*v*] *give a shot to treat or prevent disease*
immunize, inject, inoculate, mitigate, prevent, protect, treat, variolate; SEE CONCEPT *310*

vaccination [*n*] *immunization*
inoculation, shot*; SEE CONCEPT *307*

vacillate [*v*] *go back and forth*
alternate, be indecisive, be irresolute, change, change mind, dither, fence-straddle*, fluctuate, hedge, hem and haw*, hesitate, hover, oscillate, pause, pussyfoot around*, reel, rock, run hot and cold*, seesaw, shilly-shally*, stagger, straddle, sway, swing, waffle, waver, whiffle*, yo-yo*; SEE CONCEPT *13*

vacuous [*adj*] *empty; unintelligent*
airheaded*, birdbrained*, blank, drained, dull, dumb, emptied, foolish, half-baked*, inane, lamebrained*, minus*, shallow, silly*, stupid, superficial, uncomprehending, unreasoning, vacant, void; SEE CONCEPT *402*

vacuum [*n*] *emptiness*
exhaustion, free space, gap, nothingness, rarefaction, space, vacuity, void; SEE CONCEPTS *513,740*

vagabond [*adj*] *unsettled; vagrant*
aimless, destitute, down-and-out*, drifting, errant, fancy-free*, fly-by-night*, footloose*, idle, itinerant, itinerate, journeying, mendicant, migratory, moving, nomadic, perambulant, perambulatory, peripatetic, prodigal, rambling, roaming, rootless, roving, sauntering, shifting, shiftless, straggling, stray, strolling, transient, travelling, unsettled, wandering, wayfaring, wayward; SEE CONCEPT *539*

vagabond [*n*] *person who leads an unsettled life; traveler*
explorer, gypsy, haji, pathfinder, pilgrim, pioneer, rambler, rover, tourist, trailblazer, trekker, wanderer, wayfarer; SEE CONCEPT *423*

vagary [*n*] *caprice*
crotchet, fancy, fool notion*, humor, idea, impulse, inconsistency, inconstancy, notion, quirk, whim, whimsy; SEE CONCEPTS *13,410*

vagrant [*n*] *person with no permanent home and often with no means of support*
drifter, floater, homeless person, itinerant, rolling stone*, street person, transient, wanderer; SEE CONCEPT *423*

vague [*adj*] *not definite or clear*
ambiguous, amorphous, amphibological, bewildering, bleary, blurred, cloudy, dark, dim, doubtful, dreamlike, dubious, enigmatic, equivocal, faint, fuzzy, generalized, hazy, ill-defined, impalpable, imprecise, indefinite, indeterminate, indistinct, inexplicable, lax, loose, misunderstood, muddy, nebulous, obscure, perplexing, problematic, puzzling, questionable, shadowy, superficial, tenebrous, uncertain, unclear, undetermined, unexplicit, unintelligible, unknown, unsettled, unspecified, unsure; SEE CONCEPTS *267,485,529*

vain [*adj1*] *egotistical*
arrogant, big-headed*, boastful, cocky*, conceited, egocentric, egoistic, haughty, high-and-mighty*, inflated, narcissistic, ostentatious, overweening, pleased with oneself*, proud, puffed up*, self-important, stuck-up*, swaggering*, swollen-headed*, vainglorious; SEE CONCEPTS *401,404*

vain [*adj2*] *futile, useless*
abortive, barren, bootless, delusive, delusory, empty, frivolous, fruitless, going nowhere*, hollow, idle, inefficacious, insignificant, in vicious circle*, misleading, not a prayer*, no-win*, nugatory, on a treadmill*, otiose, paltry, petty, pointless, profitless, puny, senseless, shuck, slight, sterile, time-wasting, trifling, trivial, unavailing, unimportant, unnotable, unproductive, unprofitable, valueless, void, worthless; SEE CONCEPTS *552,575*

vainglorious [*adj*] *boastful, proud*
arrogant, blowing one's own horn*, boasting, bragging, cavalier, cocky*, conceited, egotistic, egotistical, haughty, high-and-mighty*, high-handed*, huffy*, overbearing, pompous, presumptuous, pretentious, puffed up*, self-important, snobbish, snooty*, strutting, stuck-up*, swaggering, vain; SEE CONCEPTS *401,542*

vainglory [*n*] *pride*
arrogance, big-headedness*, boastfulness, bragging, cockiness*, conceit, condescension, egoism, egotism, haughtiness, huff, overconfidence, patronage, presumption, pretension, self-importance, smugness, snobbery, strutting, swagger, swelled head*, vanity; SEE CONCEPT *633*

valedictory [*adj*] *farewell*
departing, final, goodbye, last, parting, terminal; SEE CONCEPT 267

valiant [*adj*] *brave*
adventurous, assertive, audacious, bold, brave, chivalrous, courageous, dauntless, fearless, fire-eating*, gallant, game, grand, great, gritty*, gutsy*, gutty*, heroic, high-spirited, indomitable, intrepid, lion-hearted, magnanimous, nervy*, noble, plucky*, powerful, puissant, redoubtable, self-reliant, spunky*, stalwart, steadfast, stout, stouthearted, strong-willed, unafraid, undaunted, undismayed, valorous, venturesome, venturous, vigorous, worthy; SEE CONCEPTS 401,404,538

valid [*adj*] *right, genuine*
accurate, attested, authentic, authoritative, binding, bona fide, cogent, compelling, conclusive, confirmed, convincing, credible, determinative, efficacious, efficient, good, in force, irrefutable, just, kosher*, lawful, legal, legit*, legitimate, logical, official, original, persuasive, potent, powerful, proven, pure, solid, sound, stringent, strong, substantial, telling, tested, true, trustworthy, ultimate, unadulterated, unanswerable, uncorrupted, weighty, well-founded, well-grounded; SEE CONCEPTS 319,545,582

validate [*v*] *ascertain the truth, authenticity of something*
approve, authenticate, authorize, bear out, certify, confirm, constitute, corroborate, endorse, give stamp of approval*, give the go-ahead*, give the green light*, give the nod*, John Hancock*, justify, legalize, legitimize, make binding*, make legal*, make stick*, okay*, ratify, rubber-stamp*, sanction, set seal on*, sign of on*, substantiate, verify; SEE CONCEPTS 50,88,317

validity [*n*] *genuineness, lawfulness*
authority, cogency, effectiveness, efficacy, force, foundation, gravity, grounds, legality, legitimacy, persuasiveness, point, potency, power, punch, right, soundness, strength, substance, validness, weight; SEE CONCEPTS 645,691,725

valley [*n*] *hollow in the land*
basin, bottom, canyon, channel, coulee, dale, dell, depression, dingle, glen, gorge, lowland, notch, plain, swale, trough, vale; SEE CONCEPTS 509,513

valor [*n*] *bravery*
backbone*, boldness, courage, dash*, defiance, derring-do*, determination, fearlessness, fight, firmness, fortitude, gallantry, grit*, guts*, hardihood, heart, heroism, indomitableness, intestinal fortitude*, intrepidity, invincibility, mettle, moxie*, nerve, pluck, prowess, resolution, sand*, spirit, spunk, starch*, stomach*, tenacity, valiance, valiancy; SEE CONCEPTS 411,633

valorous [*adj*] *courageous*
adventuresome, adventurous, bold, brave, chivalrous, daredevil, daring, dauntless, fearless, gallant, game, gritty*, gutsy*, heroic, lionhearted, nervy, plucky*, Spartan, stalwart, stouthearted, strong, tough, unafraid, undaunted, valiant, venturous; SEE CONCEPTS 401,404

valuable [*adj*] *very important; priceless*
admired, appreciated, beneficial, cherished, collectible, costly, dear, esteemed, estimable, expensive, heirloom, held dear, helpful, high-priced, hot*, hot property*, important, in demand, inestimable, invaluable, of value, precious, prized, profitable, relevant, respected, scarce, serviceable, treasured, useful, valued, worthwhile, worthy; SEE CONCEPTS 334,560,568

valuable [*n*] *prized possession*
advantage, antique, asset, benefit, collectible, commodity, heirloom, nugget*, plum*, treasure; SEE CONCEPT 446

value [*n1*] *financial worth*
amount, appraisal, assessment, charge, cost, equivalent, expense, market price, monetary worth, price, profit, rate; SEE CONCEPTS 335,336

value [*n2*] *advantage, worth*
account, bearing, benefit, caliber, condition, connotation, consequence, content, denotation, desirability, distinction, drift, eminence, esteem, estimation, excellence, finish, force, goodness, grade, help, implication, import, importance, interpretation, mark, marketability, meaning, merit, power, preference, profit, purpose, quality, regard, repute, sense, serviceableness, significance, state, stature, substance, superiority, use, usefulness, utility, valuation; SEE CONCEPTS 346,658,668,682

valued [*adj*] *costly; treasured*
admired, appreciated, beloved, cherished, dear, esteemed, expensive, fancy, highly regarded, high-priced, loved, precious, priceless, prized, respected, valuable; SEE CONCEPTS 334,555,567

values [*n*] *principles*
attitude, beliefs, character, code, conduct, conscience, ethics, ideals, integrity, morals, mores, scruples, sense of duty, sense of honor, standards; SEE CONCEPTS 645,689

valve [*n*] *on-and-off device*
cock, faucet, flap, gate, hydrant, lid, pipe, plug, shutoff, spigot, stopper, tap; SEE CONCEPTS 445,464,499

vandal [*n*] *person who defiles property*
defacer, despoiler, destroyer, hoodlum, looter, mischief-maker, pillager, pirate, plunderer, ravager, thief; SEE CONCEPT 412

vandalism [*n*] *destruction*
defacing, graffiti, mischief, ravaging, ruin, sacking, smashing, trashing, wreckage, wrecking; SEE CONCEPTS 230,252

vandalize [*v*] *destroy*
annihilate, damage, deface, demolish, despoil, disfigure, impair, mar, ravage, ravish, raze, ruin, smash, spray paint, trash*, wreck; SEE CONCEPTS 246,252

vanilla [*adj*] *simple, unadorned*
austere, clean, elementary, folksy, homely, humble, inelaborate, modest, plain, pure and simple*, rustic, uncluttered, uncomplicated, undecorated, unelaborate, unembellished, unornamented, unostentatious, unpretentious, your basic; SEE CONCEPTS 562,589

vanish [*v*] *disappear*
become invisible, be lost, clear, dematerialize, die, die out, dissolve, evanesce, evaporate, exit, fade, fade away, go away, melt; SEE CONCEPT 105

vanity [*n*] *conceit, egotism*
affectation, airs, arrogance, big-headedness*, conceitedness, display, ego trip*, narcissism, ostentation, pretension, pride, self-admiration, self-love, self-worship, show*, showing off*, smugness, vainglory; SEE CONCEPT 410

vanquish [v] *defeat soundly*
bear down, beat, conquer, crush, humble, overcome, overpower, overturn, overwhelm, put down, quell, reduce, repress, rout, subdue, subjugate, subvert, surmount, trample, triumph over; SEE CONCEPT 95

vapid [adj] *flat, dull*
bland, boring, colorless, dead*, driveling, flat, flat tire*, flavorless, inane, innocuous, insipid, jejune, least, lifeless, limp, milk-and-water*, milquetoast*, nothing, nowhere, stale, tame, tasteless, tedious, tiresome, unimaginative, uninspiring, uninteresting, unpalatable, vacant, vacuous, watery, weak, wishy-washy*, zero*; SEE CONCEPTS 529,537,575

vapor [n] *fumes, mist*
breath, condensation, dampness, dew, effluvium, exhalation, fog, gas, haze, miasma, moisture, reek, smog, smoke, steam; SEE CONCEPTS 437,524

variable [adj] *changing, changeable*
capricious, changeful, fickle, fitful, flexible, fluctuating, fluid, iffy*, inconstant, irregular, mercurial, mobile, mutable, protean, shifting, shifty, slippery*, spasmodic, temperamental, ticklish, uncertain, unequal, unsettled, unstable, unsteady, vacillating, volatile, waffling, wavering, yo-yo*; SEE CONCEPT 534

variance [n] *difference*
about-face*, argument, change, conflict, contention, deviation, difference of opinion, different strokes*, disaccord, disagreement, discord, discrepancy, dissension, dissent, dissidence, disunity, divergence, diversity, division, flip-flop*, fluctuation, incongruity, inconsistency, midcourse correction*, mutation, separation, severing, strife, sundering, switch, transmogrification, unharmoniousness, variation, variety; SEE CONCEPTS 388,665,697

variant [adj] *different*
alternative, derived, differing, divergent, exceptional, modified, various, varying; SEE CONCEPT 564

variant [n] *derived form*
alternative, branch, development, exception, irregularity, modification, result, spinoff, variation, version; SEE CONCEPT 665

variation [n] *difference; alternative*
aberration, abnormality, adaptation, alteration, bend, break, change, contradistinction, contrast, curve, deflection, departure, departure from the norm*, deviation, digression, discrepancy, disparity, displacement, dissimilarity, dissimilitude, distinction, divergence, diversification, diversity, exception, fluctuation, inequality, innovation, modification, mutation, novelty, shift, swerve, turn, unconformity, variety; SEE CONCEPTS 665,697

varied [adj] *different*
assorted, conglomerate, discrete, diverse, heterogeneous, indiscriminate, miscellaneous, mixed, motley, multifarious, separate, sundry, various; SEE CONCEPT 564

variegated [adj] *diversified; varicolored*
assorted, changeable, checkered, diverse, kaleidoscopic, mixed, motley, mottled, multicolor, multicolored, particolored, patched, spotted, streaked, striped, varied, versicolor; SEE CONCEPTS 564,618,772

variety [n1] *difference*
array, assortment, change, collection, combo*, conglomeration, cross section, departure, discrepancy, disparateness, divergency, diversification, diversity, fluctuation, heterogeneity, incongruity, intermixture, many-sidedness, medley, mélange, miscellany, mishmash, mixed bag*, mixture, modification, multifariousness, multiplicity, potpourri, range, shift, soup, stew, variance, variation; SEE CONCEPTS 432,665

variety [n2] *type, sort*
assortment, brand, breed, category, character, class, classification, description, division, family, genus, grade, ilk, kidney, kind, make, nature, order, quality, race, rank, species, strain, stripe, tribe; SEE CONCEPT 378

various [adj] *miscellaneous, differing*
all manner of*, assorted, changeable, changing, different, discrete, disparate, distinct, distinctive, diverse, diversified, heterogeneous, individual, legion, manifold, many, many-sided, multifarious, multitudinous, numerous, omnifarious, peculiar, populous, separate, several, sundry, unalike, unequal, unlike, variant, varied, variegated; SEE CONCEPTS 564,771

varnish [v] *add a layer to; embellish*
adorn, coat, cover, decorate, enamel, finish, gild, glaze, gloss, japan, lacquer, luster, paint, polish, shellac, surface, veneer, wash, wax; SEE CONCEPTS 172,177

vary [v] *change*
alter, alternate, assort, be unlike, blow hot and cold*, convert, depart, deviate, differ, digress, disagree, displace, dissent, divaricate, diverge, diversify, divide, fluctuate, hem and haw*, inflect, interchange, modify, mutate, part, permutate, range, separate, shilly-shally*, swerve, take turns, transform, turn, variegate, yo-yo*; SEE CONCEPT 697

varying [adj] *variable*
alternating, changeable, changing, deviating, differing, flexible, fluctuating, inconstant, irregular, shifting, uncertain, unstable, unsteady, vacillating, volatile, waffling, wavering; SEE CONCEPT 534

vast [adj] *very large; wide in range*
all-inclusive, ample, astronomical, big, boundless, broad, capacious, colossal, comprehensive, detailed, endless, enormous, eternal, expanded, extensive, far-flung, far-reaching, forever, giant, gigantic, great, huge, illimitable, immeasurable, immense, infinite, limitless, mammoth, massive, measureless, monstrous, monumental, neverending, prodigious, prolonged, spacious, spreadout, stretched-out, sweeping, titanic, tremendous, unbounded, unlimited, voluminous, widespread; SEE CONCEPTS 772,773,781

vault [n] *depository*
basement, box, can, catacomb, cavern, cellar, crib*, crypt, dungeon, grave, mausoleum, pit, repository, safe, safe-deposit box, sepulcher, strong room, tomb; SEE CONCEPT 494

vault [v] *jump over; span*
arch, ascend, bend, bounce, bound, bow, clear, curve, hop, hurdle, leap, mount, negotiate, over, overleap, rise, soar, spring, surmount; SEE CONCEPTS 194,752

veer [v] *change direction*
angle off, avert, bear, be deflected, bend, change, change course, curve, cut, deflect, depart, devi-

va
ve

ate, digress, dip, divagate, diverge, divert, drift, get around, make a left*, make a right*, pivot, sheer, shift, skew, skid, swerve, swing, swivel, tack, train off, turn, twist, volte-face*, wheel, whip, whirl; SEE CONCEPTS 148,150,213

vegetable [n] *edible part of plant*
edible, green, greens, herb, herbaceous plant, legume, produce, root, salad, truck, yellow; SEE CONCEPT 431

vegetate [v1] *be very passive*
be inert, decay, deteriorate, exist, go to pot*, go to seed*, hibernate, idle, languish, loaf*, pass time, stagnate, weaken; SEE CONCEPTS 210,698

vegetate [v2] *grow, sprout*
bloom, blossom, bud, burgeon, germinate, shoot, spring, swell; SEE CONCEPTS 253,257

vehement [adj] *passionate, opinionated*
angry, ardent, concentrated, delirious, desperate, eager, earnest, emphatic, enthusiastic, exquisite, fervent, fervid, fierce, fiery, forceful, forcible, frantic, furious, hearty, heated, hopped up*, hot*, hyper*, impassioned, impetuous, inflamed, intense, lively, on the make*, potent, powerful, pronounced, rabid, strong, terrible, vicious, violent, wild, zealous; SEE CONCEPTS 401,542

vehicle [n1] *machine used for transportation*
agent, automobile, bicycle, boat, buggy, bus, cab, car, carrier, chariot, conveyance, crate*, jalopy*, jeep, mechanism, motorcycle, taxi, transport, truck, van, vector, wagon, wheels; SEE CONCEPT 503

vehicle [n2] *means of attaining end*
agency, agent, apparatus, channel, expedient, implement, instrument, instrumentality, intermediary, means of expression, mechanism, medium, ministry, organ, tool, vector, way, ways and means*; SEE CONCEPTS 6,277,278,694,712

veil [n] *disguise*
blind, cloak, coloring, cover, curtain, facade, false front, film, front, guise, mantilla, mask, screen, shade, shroud, veiling; SEE CONCEPTS 451,673

veil [v] *hide*
beard*, blanket, camouflage, cloak, conceal, cover, cover up, curtain*, dim, disguise, drape, enclose, enfold, enshroud, envelop, finesse, invest, launder, mantle, mask, obscure, put up a front*, screen, secrete, shield, shroud, stonewall*, whitewash*, wrap; SEE CONCEPT 172

veiled [adj] *disguised*
camouflaged, cloaked, concealed, covered, hidden, hooded, invisible, masked, screened, secret, shielded, shrouded, undercover, unexposed, unrecognizable, unrevealed; SEE CONCEPTS 547,576,619

vein [n1] *mood, tone*
attitude, bent, character, characteristic, complexion, dash, disposition, faculty, fashion, fettle, hint, humor, line, manner, mind, mode, nature, note, spice, spirit, strain, streak, style, suggestion, suspicion, tang, temper, temperament, tenor, tinge, touch, trace, turn, wave, way; SEE CONCEPTS 411,673,682

vein [n2] *blood vessel*
capillary, course, current, duct, follicle, hair, lode, nerve, seam, stratum, streak, stripe, thread, venation; SEE CONCEPTS 393,420

velocity [n] *speed*
acceleration, celerity, dispatch, expedition, fleetness, gait, haste, headway, hurry, impetus, mo-

mentum, pace, quickness, rapidity, rapidness, rate, swiftness, tempo; SEE CONCEPTS 755,792

venal [adj] *bribable, corruptible*
amoral, bent*, buyable, conscienceless, corrupt, crooked, dishonest, double-dealing, immoral, mercenary, on the take*, padded*, purchasable, unethical, unprincipled, unprofessional, unscrupulous; SEE CONCEPT 545

vendetta [n] *feud*
argument, bad blood*, bickering, conflict, disagreement, discord, dispute, dissension, falling out*, family feud, fight, fracas, grudge, hostility, quarrel, revenge, rivalry, row, squabble, strife; SEE CONCEPTS 46,106,388

vendor [n] *person who sells wares*
businessperson, dealer, hawker, huckster*, merchant, outcrier, peddler, pitcher, traveler, traveling salesperson; SEE CONCEPT 348

veneer [n] *pretense, front*
appearance, coating, cover, covering, disguise, exterior, facade, face, finish, gloss, guise, layer, leaf, mask, overlay, semblance, show, surface, window dressing*; SEE CONCEPTS 633,673,716

veneer [v] *cover, overlay*
blanch, coat, extenuate, face, finish, gloss, palliate, plate, shellac, sugarcoat, surface, varnish, whiten, whitewash; SEE CONCEPT 172

venerable [adj] *respected*
admirable, aged, august, dignified, esteemed, estimable, experienced, grand, grave, honorable, honored, imposing, matriarchal, noble, patriarchal, philosophical, revered, reverenced, reverend, sacred, sage, sedate, serious, stately, venerated, wise, worshipful, worshipped; SEE CONCEPT 574

venerate [v] *revere*
admire, adore, apotheosize, appreciate, be in awe of, cherish, deify, esteem, exalt, hallow, hold in awe, honor, idolize, look up to*, love, put on a pedestal*, regard, respect, reverence, think highly of, treasure, value, worship; SEE CONCEPTS 10,32

vengeance [n] *retaliation for another's act*
avengement, avenging, counterblow, evening of score*, eye for an eye*, getting even*, repayment, reprisal, requital, retribution, return, revenge, settling of score*, tit for tat*, vengefulness, wrath; SEE CONCEPTS 29,384

vengeful [adj] *retaliating; hating*
antagonistic, avenging, hostile, implacable, inimical, punitive, rancorous, relentless, retaliatory, revengeful, spiteful, unforgiving, vindictive; SEE CONCEPTS 401,542

venial [adj] *pardonable*
allowable, all right, defensible, excusable, explainable, forgivable, justifiable, minor, not serious*, not too bad*, okay, permissible, slight, tolerable, trivial, understandable; SEE CONCEPT 558

venom [n] *poison; hating*
acidity, acrimony, anger, bane, bitterness, contagion, gall, grudge, hate, hatred, ill will, infection, malevolence, malice, maliciousness, malignity, rancor, spite, spitefulness, spleen, taint, toxin, virulence, virus; SEE CONCEPTS 29,399

venomous [adj] *poisonous; hateful*
accidentally on purpose*, antagonistic, baleful, baneful, catty*, cussed*, deadly, destructive, dirty, evil, hostile, lethal, malefic, malevolent, malicious, malign, malignant, mean, mephitic,

noxious, ornery*, poisonous, rancorous, savage, spiteful, toxic, toxicant, vicious, vindictive, viperish, viperous, virulent, waspish; SEE CONCEPTS 537,542,544

vent [*n*] *outlet*
aperture, avenue, chimney, drain, duct, exit, flue, hole, opening, orifice, pipe, split, spout, ventilator; SEE CONCEPTS 440,464

vent [*v*] *let out; express*
air, assert, come out with, declare, discharge, drive out, emit, empty, express, give, give off, give out, issue, loose, pour out, provide escape, put, release, state, take out on*, throw off*, unleash, utter, ventilate, verbalize, voice; SEE CONCEPTS 49,51,179

ventilate [*v*] *air out; make known*
advertise, air, bring into the open, bring up, broach, broadcast, circulate, debate, deliberate, discourse, discuss, examine, express, free, give, go into, introduce, moot, publish, put, scrutinize, sift, state, take up, talk about, talk of, talk over, thresh out, vent, verbalize; SEE CONCEPTS 51,60

venture [*n*] *gamble, attempt*
adventure, baby*, chance, deal, endeavor, enterprise, essay, experiment, exploit, feat*, hazard, header, investment, jeopardy, peril, pet project*, project, proposition, pursuit, risk, setup*, shot*, spec*, speculation, stab*, stake, test, thing*, trial, undertaking, wager; SEE CONCEPTS 87,675

venture [*v*] *take a chance*
advance, assay, attempt, bet, brave, challenge, chance, dare, dare say*, defy, endanger, essay, experiment, expose, feel, front*, gamble, get down*, go out on a limb*, grope, have a fling at*, hazard, imperil, jeopardize, lay open, make a stab at*, make bold, operate, play for, play the market*, presume, put in jeopardy*, put up*, risk, speculate, stake, stick one's neck out*, take a crack at*, take a flyer*, take a plunge*, try, try out, volunteer, wager; SEE CONCEPTS 87,330,363

venturesome [*adj*] *courageous*
adventurous, aggressive, audacious, bold, brave, daredevil, daring, enterprising, fearless, foolhardy, gutsy, intrepid, overbold, plucky, pushy, rash, reckless, resourceful, risky, spirited, spunky, stalwart, stout, sturdy, temerarious, venturous; SEE CONCEPTS 401,548

veracious [*adj*] *true*
accurate, credible, dependable, direct, ethical, factual, faithful, frank, genuine, high-principled, honest, just, kosher*, legit*, like it is*, on the level*, on the line*, on the up and up*, open, reliable, right, righteous, straight-arrow*, straightforward, strict, true-blue*, trustworthy, truthful, undeceptive, up front*, valid, veridical; SEE CONCEPTS 267,545,582

veracity [*n*] *truth*
accuracy, actuality, authenticity, candor, correctness, credibility, exactitude, exactness, fact, fairness, fidelity, frankness, genuineness, gospel*, honest-to-god truth*, honesty, honor, impartiality, integrity, like it is*, openness, precision, probity, reality, real McCoy*, rectitude, rightness, sincerity, straight stuff*, trueness, truism, trustworthiness, truthfulness, uprightness, verisimilitude, verity, word*; SEE CONCEPTS 278,645

verbal [*adj*] *spoken*
exact, expressed, lingual, literal, oral, rhetorical, said, stated, told, unwritten, verbatim, word-for-word*, word-of-mouth*; SEE CONCEPT 267

verbalize [*v*] *speak*
articulate, blab*, break silence, chat, communicate, converse, enunciate, express, gab*, make known, mouth, mumble, open one's mouth, pronounce, put into words, rap*, say, shout, sound, state, talk, tell, utter, vocalize, voice, whisper, yak*, yammer; SEE CONCEPTS 47,266

verbatim [*adj*] *exactly*
accurately, direct, directly, literally, literatim, precisely, sic, to the letter*, word-for-word*; SEE CONCEPTS 267,535

verbiage [*n*] *repetition, wordiness*
circumlocution, expansiveness, floridity, longwindedness, loquacity, periphrase, periphrasis, pleonasm, prolixity, redundancy, tautology, verbosity; SEE CONCEPTS 278,695

verbose [*adj*] *wordy, long-winded*
bombastic, circumlocutory, diffuse, flowery, full of air*, fustian, gabby*, garrulous, grandiloquent, involved, loquacious, magniloquent, palaverous, periphrastic, pleonastic, prolix, redundant, repeating, repetitious, repetitive, rhetorical, talkative, talky*, tautological, tautologous, tedious, tortuous, windy*, yacking*; SEE CONCEPT 267

verbosity [*n*] *wordiness*
garrulous, logorrhea, long-windedness, loquaciousness, loquacity, prolixity, talkativeness, verbiage, verboseness; SEE CONCEPT 267

verdant [*adj*] *green, blooming*
flourishing, fresh, grassy, leafy, lush, verdurous; SEE CONCEPTS 485,618

verdict [*n*] *law judgment*
adjudication, answer, arbitrament, award, conclusion, decision, decree, deduction, determination, finding, opinion, ruling, sentence; SEE CONCEPT 318

verge [*n*] *extremity, limit*
border, borderline, boundary, brim, brink, edge, extreme, fringe, hem, lip, margin, point, rim, selvage, skirt, terminus, threshold; SEE CONCEPT 484

verge [*v*] *come near*
abut, adjoin, approach, be on the edge*, border, bound, brink on, butt on*, communicate, edge, end, fringe, gravitate toward, hem, incline, join, lean, line, march, margin, neighbor, outline, rim, skirt, surround, tend, touch, trench, trend; SEE CONCEPTS 657,749

verification [*n*] *proof*
affidavit, attestation, authentication, averment, certification, confirmation, credentials, deposition, documents, authentication, evidence, facts, information, record, scoop*, seal, signature, stamp, substantiation, testament, testimony; SEE CONCEPT 274

verify [*v*] *confirm, validate*
add up*, attest, authenticate, bear out, certify, check, check out, check up, check up on*, confirm, corroborate, debunk, demonstrate, document, double-check, establish, eye*, eyeball*, find out, hold up, justify, make certain, make sure, pan out*, peg*, prove, settle, size*, size up*, stand up*, substantiate, support, test, try; SEE CONCEPTS 291,317

verisimilitude [*n*] *authenticity*
color, credibility, genuineness, likeliness, likeness, plausibility, realism, resemblance, semblance, show, similarity, virtual reality; SEE CONCEPT 725

ve
ve

veritable [*adj*] *authentic*
actual, bona fide, factual, for real*, genuine, indubitable, kosher*, legit*, real, true, undoubted, unquestionable, very; SEE CONCEPT *582*

vernacular [*adj*] *native, colloquial*
common, dialectal, domesticated, idiomatic, indigenous, informal, ingrained, inherent, local, natural, ordinary, plebian, popular, vulgar; SEE CONCEPTS *267,549*

vernacular [*n*] *native language*
argot, cant, dialect, idiom, jargon, jive talk*, language, lingo*, lingua franca, native tongue, parlance, patois, patter, phraseology, slang, speech, street talk*, tongue; SEE CONCEPT *276*

versatile [*adj*] *adjustable, flexible*
able, accomplished, adaptable, adroit, all-around, all-purpose, ambidextrous, conversant, dexterous, elastic, facile, functional, gifted, handy, ingenuous, many-sided, mobile, multifaceted, plastic, pliable, protean, puttylike*, ready, resourceful, skilled, skillful, talented, variable, varied; SEE CONCEPTS *527,542*

verse [*n*] *written composition*
ballad, epic, jingle, lay, lyric, ode, poem, poesy, poetry, rhyme, rune, song, sonnet, stanza; SEE CONCEPT *282*

versed [*adj*] *experienced, informed*
abreast, accomplished, acquainted, au courant*, au fait*, competent, conversant, familiar, in the know*, knowledgeable, learned, practical, practiced, proficient, qualified, savvy, seasoned, skilled, trained, tuned in*, up*, up on*, versant, veteran, well-informed; SEE CONCEPTS *402,403, 527*

version [*n*] *account of a happening*
adaptation, chronicle, clarification, condensation, construction, exercise, form, history, interpretation, narrative, paraphrase, portrayal, reading, redaction, rendering, rendition, report, restatement, rewording, side, simplification, sketch, statement, story, tale, transcription, translation, variant; SEE CONCEPT *282*

vertex [*n*] *top*
acme, apex, apogee, cap, cope, crest, crown, culmination, extremity, fastigium, height, peak, pinnacle, roof, summit, tip, upper extremity, zenith; SEE CONCEPT *836*

vertical [*adj*] *upright*
bolt upright, cocked, erect, on end, perpendicular, plumb, sheer, steep, straight-up, up-and-down, upward; SEE CONCEPTS *581,583*

vertigo [*n*] *dizziness*
disequilibrium, giddiness, lightheadedness, loss of balance, loss of equilibrium, shakiness, spinning head, unsteadiness, wobbliness, wooziness; SEE CONCEPTS *314,480*

verve [*n*] *energy, enthusiasm*
activity, ardor, dash, drive, elan, endurance, fire, force, forcefulness, get-up-and-go*, go, gumption, gusto, hardihood, intensity, juice, liveliness, moxie*, passion, pep, pizzazz, pluck, power, punch, sparkle, spirit, spunk, stamina, steam, strength, toughness, vigor, vim, virility, vitality, zeal, zest, zing, zip*; SEE CONCEPT *411*

very [*adj*] *real, exact*
actual, appropriate, authentic, bare, bona fide, correct, especial, express, genuine, ideal, identical, indubitable, mere, model, perfect, plain, precise, pure, right, same, selfsame, sheer, simple, special, sure-enough, true, undoubted, unquali-

fied, unquestionable, veritable, very same; SEE CONCEPTS *535,557*

very [*adv*] *much, really; to a high degree*
absolutely, acutely, amply, astonishingly, awfully, certainly, considerably, dearly, decidedly, deeply, eminently, emphatically, exaggeratedly, exceedingly, excessively, extensively, extraordinarily, extremely, greatly, highly, incredibly, indispensably, largely, notably, noticeably, particularly, positively, powerfully, pressingly, pretty, prodigiously, profoundly, remarkably, substantially, superlatively, surpassingly, surprisingly, terribly, truly, uncommonly, unusually, vastly, wonderfully; SEE CONCEPTS *544,569,772*

vessel [*n1*] *ship*
barge, bark, bateau, boat, bottom, bucket*, can*, craft, liner, ocean liner, steamer, tanker, tub*; SEE CONCEPT *506*

vessel [*n2*] *container, bowl*
basin, kettle, pitcher, pot, receptacle, urn, utensil; SEE CONCEPT *494*

vest [*v*] *authorize, entrust*
belong, bestow, confer, consign, empower, endow, furnish, invest, lodge, pertain, place, put in the hands of*, settle; SEE CONCEPTS *50,88*

vestibule [*n*] *small room for arrivals*
antechamber, anteroom, doorway, entrance, entrance hall, entry, entryway, foyer, gateway, hall, hallway, lobby, narthex, porch, portal, portico; SEE CONCEPT *448*

vestige [*n*] *sign, indication*
evidence, glimmer, hint, memento, print, relic, remainder, remains, remnant, residue, scrap, shadow, suspicion, token, trace, track; SEE CONCEPTS *260,284,673*

veteran [*adj*] *experienced, seasoned*
adept, battle-scarred*, been around*, disciplined, exercised, expert, from way back*, hardened, inured, knows one's stuff*, long-serving, longtime, not born yesterday*, of the old school*, old, old-time, practical, practiced, pro*, proficient, skilled, sophisticated, steady, trained, up to speed*, versed, vet*, weathered, wise, wise to ways*, worldly; SEE CONCEPTS *402,527,678*

veteran [*n*] *person with much experience; particularly in war*
expert, GI*, old guard*, old hand*, old pro*, old salt*, old soldier*, old-timer*, pro, shellback*, sourdough*, trouper, vet*, warhorse*; SEE CONCEPTS *358,423*

veto [*n*] *refusal of permission*
ban, blackball*, declination, denial, embargo, interdict, interdiction, negative, nonconsent, prohibition; SEE CONCEPTS *81,121,298,685*

veto [*v*] *refuse permission*
ban, blackball*, burn, cut, decline, defeat, deny, disallow, disapprove, discountenance, forbid, give thumbs down*, interdict, kill, negate, negative, nix*, not go for*, pass, pass by, pass on, prohibit, put down, refuse, reject, rule out*, shoot down*, throw away*, throw out*, thumbs down*, turn down; SEE CONCEPTS *50,81,88,121, 298*

vex [*v*] *distress, bother*
abrade, afflict, aggravate, agitate, anger, annoy, be at, chafe, depress, displease, disquiet, disturb, eat*, embarrass, exasperate, fret, gall*, get in one's hair*, get under one's skin*, give a bad time*, give a hard time*, grate on*, harass,

harry, hassle, infuriate, irk, irritate, molest, needle, nettle, offend, peeve, perplex, pester, pique, plague, provoke, put out*, rasp, ride, rile, tease, tick off*, torment, trouble, turn off*, upset, worry; SEE CONCEPTS 7,19

vexatious [*adj*] *distressing, bothersome*
afflicting, aggravating, annoying, burdensome, disagreeable, disappointing, disturbing, exasperating, irksome, irritating, mean, nagging, pesky*, provoking, teasing, tormenting, troublesome, troublous, trying, ugly, unpleasant, upsetting, wicked, worrisome, worrying; SEE CONCEPTS 529,537

via [*prep*] *by way of*
along, as a means, by, by dint of, by means of, by this route, by virtue of, on the way, over, per, through, through the medium of, through this medium, with; SEE CONCEPT 544

viable [*adj*] *reasonable, practicable*
applicable, doable, feasible, operable, possible, usable, within possibility, workable; SEE CONCEPTS 552,560

vibrant [*adj1*] *alive, colorful*
active, animated, dynamic, electrifying, energetic, lively, peppy, responsive, sensitive, sound, sparkling, spirited, vigorous, virile, vital, vivacious, vivid, zesty*, zippy*; SEE CONCEPTS 401,618

vibrant [*adj2*] *throbbing*
aquiver, consonant, oscillating, palpitating, pulsating, pulsing, quaking, quivering, resonant, resounding, reverberant, ringing, sonorant, sonorous, trembling; SEE CONCEPT 584

vibrate [*v*] *shake, quiver*
beat, echo, fluctuate, flutter, jar, oscillate, palpitate, pulsate, pulse, quake, resonate, resound, reverberate, ripple, shiver, sway, swing, throb, tremble, tremor, undulate, wave, waver; SEE CONCEPTS 152,748

vibration [*n*] *shaking, quivering*
beating, fluctuation, judder, oscillation, pulsation, pulse, quake, quiver, resonance, reverberation, shake, shimmy, throb, throbbing, trembling, tremor, vacillation, wave, wavering; SEE CONCEPTS 152,748

vicarious [*adj*] *done or felt for, or on behalf of, another*
by proxy, commissioned, delegated, deputed, empathetic, eventual, imagined, indirect, pretended, secondary, substituted, substitutional, surrogate, sympathetic; SEE CONCEPTS 401,538

vice [*n1*] *bad habit; sin*
carnality, corruption, debasement, debauchery, decay, degeneracy, depravity, evil, evildoing, ill, immorality, indecency, iniquity, lechery, lewdness, libidinousness, licentiousness, looseness, lubricity, lust, maleficence, malignance, offense, perversion, profligacy, rot, sensuality, squalor, transgression, trespass, venality, wickedness, wrong; SEE CONCEPTS 372,645

vice [*n2*] *weakness*
blemish, defect, demerit, failing, fault, flaw, foible, frailty, imperfection, mar, shortcoming, weak point; SEE CONCEPTS 411,657,666

vice versa [*adv*] *contrary, oppositely*
about-face*, again, contra, contrariwise*, conversely, far from it*, in reverse, on the contrary, the other way around*, turn about; SEE CONCEPTS 544,564

vicinity [*n*] *local area*
around*, ballpark*, district, environment, environs, hood, locality, nearness, neck of the woods*, neighborhood, precinct, pretty near*, propinquity, proximity, purlieus, range, region, surroundings, territory, turf*, vicinage; SEE CONCEPTS 198,747

vicious [*adj1*] *corrupt, wrong*
abandoned, abhorrent, atrocious, bad, barbarous, base, contaminated, cruel, dangerous, debased, degenerate, degraded, demoralized, depraved, diabolical, faulty, ferocious, fiendish, flagitious, foul, heinous, immoral, impious, impure, indecent, infamous, iniquitous, insubordinate, lewd, libidinous, licentious, miscreant, monstrous, nefarious, perverse, profligate, putrid, reprehensible, reprobate, rotten, savage, sinful, unprincipled, untamed, vile, villainous, violent, wicked, wild, worthless; SEE CONCEPTS 401,545,571

vicious [*adj2*] *nasty, hateful*
backbiting*, beastly, bloodthirsty, brutal, cruel, cussed*, defamatory, despiteful, dirty*, evil, fierce, frightful, furious, horrid, intense, lousy*, malevolent, malicious, malign, mean, murderous, ornery*, poisonous, rancorous, rough, savage, slanderous, spiteful, tough, vehement, venomous, vindictive, violent, wicked; SEE CONCEPTS 267,401,542

vicissitude [*n*] *change*
about-face*, alteration, alternation, diversity, flip-flop*, fluctuation, innovation, mid-course correction*, mutability, mutation, novelty, permutation, progression, reversal, revolution, shift, sport, switch, switchover, transposition, turnaround, uncertainty, ups and downs*, variation, variety; SEE CONCEPT 697

victim [*n*] *someone or something sacrificed, preyed upon*
babe in woods*, butt, casualty, clown, dupe, easy make*, easy mark*, fatality, fool, gambit, gopher*, gudgeon*, gull, hireling, hunted, immolation, injured party, innocent, mark, martyr, patsy, pawn, pigeon*, prey, pushover*, quarry, sacrifice, scapegoat, sitting duck*, sitting target*, soft touch*, stooge*, sucker*, sufferer, underdog, wretch; SEE CONCEPTS 423,659

victimize [*v*] *cheat, fool*
bamboozle*, burn*, chisel*, clip*, con, cozen, deceive, defraud, discriminate against, dupe, exploit, fleece, flimflam*, gull, have it in for*, hoax, hoodwink, immolate, persecute, pick on, pigeon*, prey on, rope in*, screw*, set up*, snow*, stack the deck*, stiff*, sting*, sucker*, swindle, take advantage of, trick, use; SEE CONCEPTS 14,59,192

victor [*n*] *person who wins*
champ, champion, conquering hero*, conqueror, defeater, first*, gold medalist, greatest, hero, king, medalist, prizewinner, queen, subjugator, title holder, top*, top dog*, vanquisher, winner; SEE CONCEPTS 366,416

Victorian [*adj*] *prudish*
conservative, conventional, demure, genteel, priggish*, prim, prissy*, proper, puritanical, respectable, rigid, smug, square*, starchy*, stiff*, strait-laced, stuffy, uptight*; SEE CONCEPT 401

victorious [*adj*] *successful, winning*
arrived, champion, conquering, on top, prizewinning, triumphant, vanquishing; SEE CONCEPT 528

ve
vi

victory [*n*] *win, success*
achievement, advantage, ascendancy, bull's-eye*, clean sweep*, conquest, control, defeat, defeating, destruction, dominion, feather in cap*, gain, grand slam*, hit, hole in one*, killing*, laurels, mission accomplished*, overthrow, prize, subjugation, superiority, supremacy, sweep, the gold*, triumph, upper hand*, upset, winning; SEE CONCEPTS 95,671,706,832

victuals [*n*] *food supplies*
aliment, bread, chow*, comestibles, eatables, eats, edibles, fare, feed, foodstuff, goodies*, groceries*, grub, larder, meal, nourishment, provender, provisions, rations, refreshments, snack, supplies, viands, vittles; SEE CONCEPTS 457,460,461

video [*n/adj*] *related to the televised image*
broadcast, canned*, music video, prerecorded, program, promotional film, recorded, taped, telegenic, television, TV; SEE CONCEPTS 277,293.

videocassette [*n*] *magnetic tape on which video image is recorded*
cartridge, flick*, movie, recording, rental, vid*, videotape; SEE CONCEPTS 277,293,464.

vie [*v*] *compete*
be rivals, buck, challenge, contend, contest, counter, go for*, go for broke*, go for the gold*, go for the jugular*, jockey for position*, match, oppose, pit, play, play off, push, rival, scramble for, strive, struggle, sweat; SEE CONCEPTS 92,363

view [*n1*] *something that is seen*
appearance, aspect, composition, contour, design, field of vision, glimpse, illustration, landscape, look, opening, outline, outlook, panorama, perspective, picture, prospect, range of vision, representation, scene, seascape, show, sight, spectacle, stretch, tableau, vision, vista, way; SEE CONCEPT 628

view [*n2*] *examination*
analysis, audit, check, contemplation, display, eyeball*, flash*, gander*, inspection, lamp*, look, look-see, perlustration, review, scan, scrutiny, sight, slant, squint*, survey, viewing; SEE CONCEPTS 24,103

view [*n3*] *belief*
attitude, belief, close-up, concept, conception, consideration, conviction, deduction, eye*, feeling, impression, inference, judgment, judgment call*, mind, notion, opinion, persuasion, point of view, say-so*, sentiment, slant*, thought, twist, two cents' worth*, value judgment*, way of thinking; SEE CONCEPT 689

view [*v1*] *look at*
beam, behold, canvass, check out*, check over, consider, contemplate, descry, dig*, discern, distinguish, eagle eye*, espy, examine, explore, eye*, feast eyes on*, flash*, gaze, get a load of*, inspect, lay eyes on, mark, notice, observe, perceive, pipe*, read, regard, rubberneck*, scan, scope, scrutinize, see, set eyes on, spot, spy, stare, survey, take in*, watch, witness; SEE CONCEPTS 623,626

view [*v2*] *believe*
account, consider, deem, judge, look on, reckon, regard, think about; SEE CONCEPT 12

viewpoint [*n*] *way of thinking*
angle, aspect, attitude, direction, estimation, eye*, frame of reference, ground, light, long view, outlook, perspective, point of observation, point of view, position, posture, respect, side,

slant, stance, stand, standpoint, twist, two cents' worth*, vantage point, view; SEE CONCEPT 689

vigil [*n*] *watch*
attention, awareness, duty, eagle eye*, guard, lookout, monitoring, nightwatch, notice, observance, observation, patrol, stake-out, surveillance, vigilance, watchfulness; SEE CONCEPTS 134,623

vigilance [*n*] *carefulness*
acuity, alertness, attention, attentiveness, caution, circumspection, diligence, lookout, observance, surveillance, vigil, watch, watchfulness; SEE CONCEPTS 644,657

vigilant [*adj*] *careful, watchful*
acute, agog, alert, anxious, attentive, aware, cautious, circumspect, guarded, keen, looking for, looking to, observant, on alert, on guard, on the ball*, on the job*, on the lookout, on the qui vive, on toes*, open-eyed*, sharp, sleepless, unsleeping, waiting on, wakeful, wary, wide-awake, with eyes peeled*, with weather eye open*; SEE CONCEPTS 401,542,576

vigor [*n*] *power, energy*
ability, action, activity, agility, alertness, bang*, birr, bounce, capability, capacity, dash, drive, dynamism, endurance, enterprise, exercise, fire, force, get-up-and-go*, go*, hardiness, healthiness, intensity, juice*, kick*, liveliness, lustiness, might, motion, moxie*, muscle*, nimbleness, pep*, pith, potency, puissance, punch*, push, quickness, snap*, sock, soundness, starch*, steam*, strength, tuck*, urgency, vehemence, vim, vitality, well-being, zing*, zip*; SEE CONCEPTS 316,411,732

vigorous [*adj*] *energetic, powerful*
active, athletic, ball of fire*, bouncing, brisk, dashing, driving, dynamic, effective, efficient, enterprising, exuberant, flourishing, forceful, forcible, hale, hard-driving, hardy, healthy, hearty, intense, lively, lusty, mettlesome, peppy, persuasive, potent, red-blooded*, robust, rugged, snappy, sound, spanking, spirited, steamroller*, strapping, strenuous, strong, strong as an ox*, sturdy, take-charge*, take-over*, tough, vital, zealous, zippy*; SEE CONCEPTS 314,404,489

vile [*adj*] *offensive, horrible*
abandoned, abject, appalling, bad, base, coarse, contemptible, corrupt, debased, degenerate, depraved, despicable, dirty, disgraceful, disgusting, evil, filthy, foul, horrid, humiliating, ignoble, immoral, impure, iniquitous, loathsome, low, mean, miserable, nasty, nauseating, nefarious, noxious, perverted, repellent, repugnant, repulsive, revolting, shocking, sickening, sinful, sleazy*, stinking*, ugly, vicious, vulgar, wicked, worthless, wretched; SEE CONCEPTS 529,545,571

vilify [*v*] *criticize very harshly*
abuse, asperse, assail, attack, bad-mouth*, berate, blister, call down*, calumniate, censure, curse, cuss*, damn, debase, decry, defame, denigrate, denounce, dig*, disparage, dress down*, dump on*, give a black eye*, jinx, knock*, libel, malign, mistreat, mudsling*, pan*, put a whammy on*, put down*, rag on*, rap*, revile, rip up*, roast*, run down, scorch, skin alive*, slam*, slander, slur, smear*, speak ill of, tear down*, tear into*, traduce, vituperate, voodoo*; SEE CONCEPTS 44,52

villa [*n*] *country estate*
chateau, country house, large house, manor,

mansion, summer house, vacation home; SEE CONCEPTS *439,516*

village [*n*] *small town*
center, crossroads, hamlet, suburb; SEE CONCEPT *507*

villain [*n*] *evil person*
antihero, blackguard*, brute, caitiff, creep*, criminal, devil, enfant terrible*, evildoer, heel, libertine, lowlife*, malefactor, mischief-maker*, miscreant, offender, profligate, rapscallion, rascal, reprobate, scoundrel, sinner, wretch; SEE CONCEPT *412*

villainous [*adj*] *criminal*
atrocious, bad, corrupt, crooked, cruel, culpable, deplorable, depraved, diabolical, dirty, evil, felonious, hateful, ignoble, illegal, illicit, immoral, iniquitous, knavish, lawless, low, mean, nefarious, peccant, reprehensible, scandalous, shady*, sinful, unlawful, vile, wicked; SEE CONCEPT *545*

vindicate [*v*] *prove one's innocence*
absolve, acquit, advocate, argue, assert, bear out, claim, clear, confute, contend, corroborate, defend, disculpate, disprove, do justice to, establish, exculpate, excuse, exonerate, extenuate, free, free from blame, guard, justify, maintain, plead for, protect, prove, rationalize, refute, rehabilitate, second, shield, substantiate, support, uphold, warrant, whitewash*; SEE CONCEPTS *49,57,317*

vindictive [*adj*] *hateful, revengeful*
avenging, cruel, grim, grudging, implacable, malicious, malignant, merciless, rancorous, relentless, resentful, retaliatory, ruthless, spiteful, unforgiving, unrelenting, vengeful, venomous, wreakful; SEE CONCEPTS *401,542*

vintage [*adj*] *superior*
best, choice, classic, classical, excellent, mature, old, prime, rare, ripe, select, selected, venerable; SEE CONCEPTS *574,578,797*

vintage [*n*] *crop, especially of wine*
collection, epoch, era, generation, grapes, harvest, origin, wine, year; SEE CONCEPT *429*

violate [*v1*] *break a law, agreement*
breach, contaminate, contravene, defy, disobey, disregard, disrupt, encroach, err, infract, infringe, meddle, offend, oppose, outrage, profane, resist, sacrilege, sin, tamper with, trample on, transgress, trespass, withstand; SEE CONCEPTS *101,192*

violate [*v2*] *rape, defile*
abuse, assault, befoul, debauch, defile, desecrate, force, invade, outrage, pollute, profane, ravish, spoil; SEE CONCEPTS *246,375*

violation [*n1*] *breach; breaking of the law*
abuse, break, breaking, contravention, encroachment, illegality, infraction, infringement, misbehavior, misdemeanor, negligence, nonobservance, offense, rupture, transgressing, transgression, trespass, trespassing, violating, wrong; SEE CONCEPTS *101,192*

violation [*n2*] *rape, defilement*
assault, blasphemy, debasement, defacement, defacing, degradation, desecration, destruction, devastation, dishonor, invasion, mistreatment, outrage, pollution, profanation, rapine, ravishment, ruin, sacrilege, spoliation; SEE CONCEPTS *246,252,375*

violence [*n*] *extreme force, intensity*
abandon, acuteness, assault, attack, bestiality, bloodshed, blowup, brutality, brute force, clash, coercion, compulsion, confusion, constraint, cruelty, destructiveness, disorder, disturbance, duress, ferocity, fervor, fierceness, fighting, flap, foul play, frenzy, fury, fuss, harshness, murderousness, onslaught, passion, power, raging, rampage, roughness, ruckus, rumble, savagery, severity, sharpness, storm, storminess, struggle, terrorism, tumult, turbulence, uproar, vehemence, wildness; SEE CONCEPTS *29,641,669,675*

violent [*adj1*] *destructive*
agitated, aroused, berserk, bloodthirsty, brutal, coercive, crazy, cruel, demoniac, desperate, distraught, disturbed, enraged, fierce, fiery, forceful, forcible, frantic, fuming, furious, great, headstrong, homicidal, hotheaded*, hysterical, impassioned, impetuous, inflamed, intemperate, mad, maddened, maniacal, mighty, murderous, passionate, potent, powerful, raging, riotous, rough, savage, strong, uncontrollable, ungovernable, unrestrained, urgent, vehement, vicious, wild; SEE CONCEPTS *401,540,544*

violent [*adj2*] *severe, extreme*
acute, agonizing, biting, blustery, coercive, concentrated, devastating, excruciating, exquisite, forceful, forcible, gale force*, great, harsh, immoderate, intense, mighty, outrageous, painful, potent, powerful, raging, rough, ruinous, sharp, strong, tempestuous, terrible, tumultous/tumultuous, turbulent, wild; SEE CONCEPTS *525,569*

viperous [*adj*] *malicious, venomous*
bad-natured, baleful, bitter, evil, evil-minded, green-eyed*, jealous, malevolent, mean, nasty, ornery, poisonous, rancorous, resentful, spiteful, vengeful, vicious, vindictive, wicked; SEE CONCEPTS *267,401,542*

virginity [*n*] *celibacy, chastity*
abstinence, chasteness, cleanness, continence, honor, immaculacy, innocence, integrity, maidenhood, purity, restraint, sinlessness, spotlessness, virtue; SEE CONCEPT *633*

virgin/virginal [*adj*] *brand-new, unused*
first, fresh, idle, immaculate, initial, innocent, intact, modest, natural, new, original, primeval, pristine, pure, spotless, uncorrupted, undefiled, undisturbed, unmarred, unspoiled, unsullied, untapped, untested, untouched, untried, vestal; SEE CONCEPTS *372,560,578,797*

virile [*adj*] *potent, powerful*
driving, energetic, forceful, generative, lusty, macho*, procreative, red-blooded*, reproductive, robust, sound, strong, vibrant, vigorous, vital; SEE CONCEPTS *372,401,404*

virility [*n*] *masculinity*
forceful, machismo, macho*, maleness, manhood, manliness, muscularity, potency, power, ruggedness, strength, vigor; SEE CONCEPTS *371,372,408,648*

virtual [*adj*] *in essence*
basic, constructive, essential, fundamental, implicit, implied, in all but name*, in conduct, indirect, in effect, in practice, potential, practical, pragmatic, tacit, unacknowledged; SEE CONCEPTS *487,537,544,573*

virtually [*adv*] *for all practical purposes*
around, as good as, basically, effectually, essentially, for all intents and purposes*, fundamentally, give or take a little*, guesstimate*, implicitly, in all but name*, in effect, in essence, in substance, in the ballpark*, in the neighbor-

vi
vi

hood*, morally, nearly, not absolutely, not actually, practically, something like*, upwards of*; SEE CONCEPTS 487,544,573

virtue [*n*] *honor, integrity*
advantage, asset, character, charity, chastity, consideration, credit, ethic, ethicality, ethicalness, excellence, faith, faithfulness, fineness, fortitude, generosity, goodness, good point*, high-mindedness, hope, ideal, incorruptibility, innocence, justice, kindness, love, merit, morality, plus*, probity, prudence, purity, quality, rectitude, respectability, righteousness, temper, temperance, trustworthiness, uprightness, value, worth, worthiness; SEE CONCEPTS 411,645

virtuoso [*n*] *person who is an expert*
ace, adept, artist, artiste, authority, big league*, brain*, celebrity, champ*, champion, crackerjack*, dillettante, egghead, genius, hotshot*, hot stuff*, intelligent, magician, musician, natural*, no slouch*, old hand*, old pro*, performer, pro*, prodigy, professional, pundit, sharp*, star, superstar, whiz*, wizard; SEE CONCEPTS 348,352,416

virtuous [*adj*] *good, ethical; innocent*
blameless, celibate, chaste, clean-living, effective, effectual, efficient, excellent, exemplary, faithful, guiltless, high-principled, honest, honorable, incorruptible, inculpable, in the clear*, irreprehensible, kosher*, legit*, moral, moralistic, noble, on the level*, on the up and up*, praiseworthy, principled, pure, regular, righteous, right-minded, spotless, straight, true-blue*, unsullied, untainted, untarnished, up front*, upright, wholesome, without reproach, worthy; SEE CONCEPTS 401,545

virulent [*adj1*] *poisonous, lethal*
baneful, deadly, destructive, fatal, harmful, infective, injurious, malign, malignant, mephitic, pernicious, poison, septic, toxic, toxicant, unhealthy, unwholesome, venomous; SEE CONCEPTS 537,571

virulent [*adj2*] *hostile*
acrimonious, antagonistic, bitter, cutting, hateful, malevolent, malicious, rancorous, resentful, scathing, sharp, spiteful, splenetic, stabbing, unfriendly, venomous, vicious, vindictive, vitriolic; SEE CONCEPTS 267,542

virus [*n*] *bacterium, bug*
ailment, bacillus, disease, germ, illness, infection, microbe, microorganism, pathogen, sickness; SEE CONCEPT 306

visceral [*adj*] *instinctive*
accustomed, automatic, congenital, habitual, inborn, ingrained, inherent, innate, instinctual, intrinsic, intuitional, intuitive, knee-jerk*, natural, reflex, rooted, second-nature*; SEE CONCEPT 544

viscous [*adj*] *sticky, gummy*
adhesive, clammy, gelatinous, gluey*, glutinous, gooey*, mucilaginous, ropy, slimy, stiff, syrupy, tenacious, thick, tough, viscid; SEE CONCEPT 606

visible [*adj*] *apparent, seeable*
arresting, big as life*, bold, clear, conspicuous, detectable, discernible, discoverable, distinguishable, evident, inescapable, in sight, in view, macroscopic, manifest, marked, not hidden, noticeable, observable, obtrusive, obvious, ocular, open, out in the open*, outstanding, palpable, patent, perceivable, perceptible, plain, pointed, pronounced, revealed, salient, seen, signal, striking, to be seen, unconcealed, under one's nose*,

unhidden, unmistakable, viewable, visual; SEE CONCEPTS 529,576,619

vision [*n1*] *ability to perceive with eyes*
eyes*, eyesight, faculty, optics, perceiving, perception, range of view, seeing, sight, view; SEE CONCEPT 629

vision [*n2*] *mental image, concept*
angle, aspect, astuteness, breadth of view, castles in the air*, conception, daydream, discernment, divination, dream, facet, fancy, fantasy, farsightedness, foreknowledge, foresight, head trip*, idea, ideal, ideality, imagination, insight, intuition, keenness, mental picture, muse, nightmare, outlook, penetration, perspective, phantasm, pie in the sky*, pipe dream*, point of view, prescience, retrospect, slant, standpoint, trip, understanding, view; SEE CONCEPTS 529,532,689

vision [*n3*] *apparition*
apocalypse, chimera, delusion, ecstasy, fantasy, ghost, hallucination, haunt, illusion, mirage, nightmare, oracle, phantasm, phantom, phenomenon, presence, prophecy, revelation, specter, spirit, spook, trance, warlock, wraith; SEE CONCEPTS 370,529

vision [*n4*] *very beautiful thing or person*
angel*, dazzler, dream, eyeful*, feast for the eyes*, perfect picture*, picture, sight, sight for sore eyes*, spectacle, stunner*; SEE CONCEPTS 424,529

visionary [*adj*] *idealized, romantic*
abstracted, ambitious, astral, chimerical, daydreaming, delusory, dreaming, dreamy, exalted, fanciful, fantastic, grandiose, ideal, idealist, idealistic, illusory, imaginary, impractical, in the clouds*, introspective, lofty, musing, noble, otherworldly, pretentious, prophetic, quixotic, radical, speculative, starry-eyed*, unreal, unrealistic, unworkable, unworldly, utopian; SEE CONCEPTS 529,560,582

visionary [*n*] *person who dreams, is idealistic*
castle-builder*, daydreamer, Don Quixote*, dreamer, enthusiast, idealist, mystic, prophet, romancer, romantic, seer, stargazer, theorist, utopian, zealot; SEE CONCEPTS 361,416

visit [*n*] *social call upon another*
appointment, call, evening, holiday, interview, sojourn, stay, stop, stopover, talk, tarriance, vacation, visitation, weekend; SEE CONCEPTS 226,227

visit [*v1*] *be a guest of*
call, call on, chat, come around, come by, converse, crash, drop by, drop in, drop over, dwell, frequent, go over to*, go to see*, hit, inspect, look around, look in on, look up, pay a call*, pay a visit to, play, pop in*, reside, see, sojourn, stay at, stay with, step in, stop by*, stop off*, swing by*, take in, talk, tarry, tour; SEE CONCEPTS 226,227

visit [*v2*] *bother, haunt*
afflict, assail, attack, avenge, befall, bring down on, descend upon, force upon, impose, inflict, pain, punish, smite, trouble, wreak, wreck; SEE CONCEPTS 7,14,19

visitor [*n*] *person temporarily in a foreign location*
caller, company, foreigner, guest, habitué, inspector, invitee, out-of-towner, transient, visitant; SEE CONCEPT 423

vista [*n*] *view*
field of vision, glimpse, landscape, look, outline,

panorama, perspective, scene, scenery, seascape, sight, vision; SEE CONCEPT *628*

visual [*adj*] *able to be seen with eyes*
beheld, discernible, imaged, observable, observed, ocular, optic, optical, perceptible, seeable, seen, viewable, viewed, visible, visional; SEE CONCEPTS *485,576,619*

visualize [*v*] *make a picture of in the mind*
anticipate, apprehend, bring to mind, call to mind, call up, conceive of, conjure up, create, divine, dream up, envisage, envision, fancy, feature, foresee, get the picture*, image, imagine, object, picture, reflect, see, see in the mind's eye*, think, view, vision; SEE CONCEPTS *17,34*

vital [*adj1*] *essential*
basic, bottom-line*, cardinal, coal-and-ice*, constitutive, critical, crucial, decisive, fundamental, heavy*, imperative, important, indispensable, integral, key, life-or-death*, meaningful, meat-and-potatoes*, name, name-of-the-game*, necessary, needed, nitty-gritty*, prerequisite, required, requisite, significant, underlined, urgent; SEE CONCEPTS *546,567*

vital [*adj2*] *lively*
animated, dynamic, energetic, forceful, lusty, red-blooded, spirited, strenuous, vibrant, vigorous, vivacious, zestful; SEE CONCEPT *401*

vital [*adj3*] *alive*
animate, animated, breathing, generative, invigorative, life-giving, live, living, quickening; SEE CONCEPT *539*

vitality [*n*] *energy, spirit*
animation, ardor, audacity, bang, being, bloom, bounce, clout, continuity, drive, endurance, existence, exuberance, fervor, force, get-up-and-go*, go, guts*, intensity, life, liveliness, lustiness, pep, pizzazz*, power, pulse, punch, robustness, snap, sparkle, spunk*, stamina, starch*, steam, strength, stuff*, venturesomeness, verve, vigor, vim, vivaciousness, vivacity, zest, zing*, zip*; SEE CONCEPTS *407,411,633*

vitiate [*v1*] *cancel*
abate, abolish, abrogate, annul, delete, deny, invalidate, negate, nullify, quash, recant, revoke, undermine, undo; SEE CONCEPTS *121,317*

vitiate [*v2*] *hurt, corrupt*
blemish, blight, brutalize, contaminate, damage, debase, debauch, defile, deprave, deteriorate, devalue, harm, impair, injure, mar, pervert, pollute, prejudice, spoil, sully, taint, tarnish, violate, warp, water down, weaken; SEE CONCEPTS *246,250*

vitriol [*n*] *bitterness*
acrimoniousness, contempt, disdain, hatefulness, hostility, malevolence, maliciousness, nastiness, sarcasm, venom, virulence; SEE CONCEPTS *410,633*

vittles [*n*] *food*
chow*, comestibles, eatables, eats, edibles, fare, foodstuff, goodies*, groceries*, grub, larder, meal, nourishment, provender, provisions, refreshments, snack, viands, victuals; SEE CONCEPTS *457,460,461*

vituperate [*v*] *criticize harshly*
abuse, accuse, asperse, bark at*, bawl out*, berate, blame, calumniate, castigate, censure, chew out*, condemn, curse, denounce, find fault, growl, insult, lambaste*, lash, malign, rail, rate, reproach, revile, rip into*, run down*, scold,

smear, tear into*, tongue-lash*, traduce, upbraid, vilify, yell at*; SEE CONCEPTS *44,52,54*

vituperation [*n*] *verbal attack*
bad-mouthing*, berating, blame, castigation, censure, criticism, defamation, insults, libel, obloquy, reprimand, reproach, scolding, slander, tirade, upbraiding, verbal abuse; SEE CONCEPT *54*

vivacious [*adj*] *lively, spirited*
active, alert, animate, animated, bouncy, brash, breezy, bubbling, cheerful, ebullient, effervescent, exuberant, frolicsome, full of life*, gay, happy, high-spirited, jolly, jumping, keen, lighthearted, merry, playful, rocking, scintillating, sparkling, sportive, sprightly, swinging, upbeat, vibrant, vital, zesty; SEE CONCEPTS *401,404*

vivid [*adj*] *intense, powerful*
active, animated, bright, brilliant, clear, colorful, definite, distinct, dramatic, dynamic, eloquent, energetic, expressive, flamboyant, gay, glowing, graphic, highly colored, lifelike, lively, lucid, meaningful, memorable, picturesque, realistic, resplendent, rich, sharp, shining, spirited, stirring, striking, strong, telling, theatrical, true-to-life, vigorous; SEE CONCEPTS *537,569,618*

vocabulary [*n*] *language of a person or people*
cant, dictionary, glossary, jargon, lexicon, palaver, phraseology, terminology, thesaurus, wordbook, word-hoard*, words, word-stock*; SEE CONCEPTS *276,280*

vocal [*adj1*] *spoken*
articulate, articulated, choral, expressed, intonated, lyric, modulated, operatic, oral, phonetic, phonic, pronounced, put into words*, said, singing, sonant, sung, uttered, verbal, viva voce, vocalic, vocalized, voiced, vowel; SEE CONCEPTS *267,594*

vocal [*adj2*] *extroverted about opinion*
articulate, blunt, clamorous, eloquent, expressive, facile, fluent, forthright, frank, free, free-spoken, glib, noisy, outspoken, plain-spoken, round, smooth-spoken, stentorian, strident, venting, vociferous; SEE CONCEPTS *267,404*

vocalize [*v*] *put into words or song*
belt out*, canary*, chant, chirp, communicate, convey, croon, emit, enunciate, express, give out*, groan, impart, let out*, moan, pronounce, say, shout, sing, sound, speak, talk, utter, vent, verbalize, voice, warble, yodel; SEE CONCEPT *77*

vocation [*n*] *life's work*
art, business, calling, career, craft, do*, dodge*, duty, employment, field, game, handicraft, job, lifework, line*, line of business*, métier, mission, nine-to-five*, occupation, office, post, profession, pursuit, racket*, role, thing*, trade, undertaking; SEE CONCEPTS *349,360*

vociferous [*adj*] *loud, insistent*
boisterous, clamant, clamorous, distracting, loud-mouthed, noisy, obstreperous, ranting, shouting, shrill, strident, uproarious, vehement, vociferant; SEE CONCEPTS *267,592,594*

vogue [*adj*] *fashionable*
faddy*, in*, latest, mod*, modish, now, popular, prevalent, rage*, state-of-the-art*, trendy, up-to-the-minute*, with it*; SEE CONCEPT *589*

vogue [*n*] *fashion; current practice*
chic, craze*, currency, custom, dernier cri, fad*, fashionableness, favor, in thing*, last word*, latest, mode, popularity, practice, prevalence, rage*, style, stylishness, thing*, trend, usage, use, way; SEE CONCEPT *655*

voice [*n1*] *expression, language*
articulation, call, cry, delivery, exclamation, inflection, intonation, modulation, murmur, mutter, roar, shout, song, sound, speech, statement, tone, tongue, utterance, vent, vocalization, vociferation, words, yell; SEE CONCEPTS 77,276

voice [*n2*] *opinion*
approval, choice, decision, expression, option, part, participation, preference, representation, right of free speech, say, say-so*, suffrage, vent, view, vote, vox populi, will, wish; SEE CONCEPTS 278,376

voice [*v*] *express opinion; put into words*
air, announce, articulate, assert, come out with*, cry, declare, deliver, divulge, emphasize, enunciate, give expression, give utterance, inflect, intonate, modulate, present, proclaim, pronounce, put, recount, say, sound, speak, talk, tell, utter, vent, verbalize, vocalize; SEE CONCEPTS 49,51

void [*adj1*] *empty*
abandoned, bare, barren, bereft, clear, deprived, destitute, devoid, drained, emptied, free, lacking, scant, short, shy, tenantless, unfilled, unoccupied, vacant, vacuous, without; SEE CONCEPTS 481,583,740,774

void [*adj2*] *nullified, meaningless*
avoided, bad, dead, forceless, fruitless, ineffective, ineffectual, inoperative, invalid, negated, not viable, nugatory, null, null and void, set aside, sterile, unconfirmed, unenforceable, unfruitful, unratified, unsanctioned, unsuccessful, useless, vain, voided, worthless; SEE CONCEPT 560

void [*n*] *emptiness, want*
blank, blankness, cavity, gap, hole, hollow, lack, nihility, nothingness, nullity, opening, space, vacuity, vacuum; SEE CONCEPTS 513,646,709

void [*v1*] *get rid of; empty*
clear, deplete, discharge, dispose, drain, dump, eject, eliminate, emit, evacuate, flow, give off, go, pour, relieve, remove, throw out, vacate; SEE CONCEPTS 179,180

void [*v2*] *nullify, cancel*
abnegate, abrogate, annul, black out*, bleep*, blue pencil*, clean up, cut, declare null and void*, discharge, dissolve, drop*, gut*, invalidate, launder, rescind, sanitize, sterilize, take out, trim, vacate; SEE CONCEPTS 50,88,121,211

volatile [*adj*] *explosive, changeable*
airy, buoyant, capricious, effervescent, elastic, elusive, ephemeral, erratic, expansive, fickle, fleeting, flighty, flippant, frivolous, fugacious, fugitive, gaseous, gay, giddy, impermanent, imponderable, inconsistent, inconstant, light, lively, lubricious, mercurial, momentary, playful, resilient, short-lived, sprightly, subtle, temperamental, ticklish, transient, transitory, unsettled, unstable, unsteady, up-anddown, vaporous, variable, whimsical; SEE CONCEPTS 401,534

volition [*n*] *free will*
accord, choice, choosing, conation, desire, determination, discretion, election, option, preference, purpose, resolution, selection, will, willingness, wish; SEE CONCEPTS 20,41

volley [*n*] *barrage*
battery, bombardment, burst, cannonade, crossfire, enfilade, firing, fussilade, gunfire, hail, round, salvo, shelling, shower, storm; SEE CONCEPT 320

voluble [*adj*] *talkative*
articulate, bigmouthed*, chattering, chatty*, fluent, full of hot air*, gabby, garrulous, long-winded*, loquacious, mouthy*, multiloquent, prolix, rambling, running on*, slick*, smooth*, talky, verbal, windy*, wordy; SEE CONCEPT 267

volume [*n1*] *capacity, measure of capacity*
aggregate, amount, body, bulk, compass, content, contents, cubic measure, dimensions, extent, figure, mass, number, object, quantity, size, total; SEE CONCEPTS 719,740,794

volume [*n2*] *loudness of a sound*
amplification, degree, intensity, power, sonority, strength; SEE CONCEPTS 65,792

volume [*n3*] *book*
album, edition, publication, tome, treatise, version; SEE CONCEPT 280

voluminous [*adj*] *big, vast*
abundant, ample, billowing, bulky, capacious, cavernous, comprehensive, convoluted, copious, covering, expansive, extensive, full, great, large, legion, many, massive, multifarious, multitudinous, numerous, prolific, roomy, several, simple, spacious, sundry, swelling, various; SEE CONCEPTS 773,781

voluntarily [*adv*] *of one's own free will*
at one's discretion, by choice, by preference, deliberately, freely, intentionally, of one's own accord*, on one's own, on one's own initiative*, optionally, spontaneously, willingly, with all one's heart*, without being asked, without prompting; SEE CONCEPTS 538,544

voluntary [*adj*] *willing*
autonomous, chosen, deliberate, designful, discretional, elected, free, freely, free-willed, gratuitous, honorary, independent, intended, intentional, opted, optional, spontaneous, unasked, unbidden, uncompelled, unconstrained, unforced, unpaid, unprescribed, volitional, volunteer, willed, willful, wished, witting; SEE CONCEPTS 538,544

volunteer [*v*] *offer to do something*
advance, bring forward, chip in*, come forward, do on one's own volition*, enlist, go in*, let oneself in for*, offer services, present, proffer, propose, put at one's disposal*, put forward, sign up, speak up, stand up, step forward, submit oneself, suggest, take bull by the horns*, take initiative*, take the plunge*, take upon oneself*, tender; SEE CONCEPTS 66,67

voluptuous [*adj*] *given to sensual pleasure; pleasurable to the senses*
appealing, attractive, delightful, desirable, enticing, erotic, fleshly, hedonist, hedonistic, indulgent, lubricious, luxurious, pleasing, salacious, self-indulgent, sensuous, sexy, sybaritic, wanton; SEE CONCEPTS 372,485

vomit [*v*] *disgorge*
be seasick*, be sick, bring up*, dry heave*, eject, emit, expel, gag*, heave*, hurl*, puke*, regurgitate, retch, ruminate, spew, spit up, throw up, upchuck*; SEE CONCEPTS 179,185,308

voodoo [*n*] *black magic*
abracadabra*, alchemy, black art, charm, conjuring, devilry, divination, enchantment, evil eye, hocus-pocus*, hoodoo, jinx, mumbo-jumbo*, necromancy, obeah, obi, sorcery, spell, witchcraft, witchery, wizardry; SEE CONCEPTS 370,689

voracious [*adj*] *very hungry, greedy*
avid, covetous, devouring, dog-hungry*, eda-

cious, empty, gluttonous, gorging, grasping, gross, insatiable, omnivorous, piggy*, prodigious, rapacious, ravening, ravenous, sating, starved, starved to death*, starving, uncontrolled, unquenchable; SEE CONCEPTS 20,401

vote [n] *decision or right to decide representation*
aye*, ballot, choice, franchise, majority, nay*, plebiscite, poll, referendum, secret ballot, show of hands*, suffrage, tally, ticket, will, wish, yea*, yes or no*; SEE CONCEPTS 300,376

vote [v] *decide on representation*
ballot, cast ballot, cast vote, choose, confer, declare, determine, effect, elect, enact, enfranchise, establish, go to the polls*, grant, judge, opt, pronounce, propose, put in office*, recommend, return, second, suggest; SEE CONCEPTS 41,300

vouch [v] *give assurance*
act as a witness, affirm, answer for, assert, asseverate, assure, attest to, avert, avow, back, bear testimony, be responsible for, certify, confirm, contend, corroborate, cosign, declare, get behind*, give an affidavit, guarantee, maintain, okay*, predicate, profess, prove, put forth, rubber-stamp*, say so*, sign for, sponsor, stand up for*, substantiate, support, swear to, swear up and down*, testify, uphold, verify, vow, warrant, witness; SEE CONCEPTS 49,71,317

voucher [n] *receipt*
certificate, check, chit, coupon, credential, debenture, IOU*, note, notice, proof of purchase, release, sales slip, slip, stub, ticket, token; SEE CONCEPTS 271,332

vow [n] *promise*
affiance, assertion, asseveration, oath, pledge, profession, troth, word of honor; SEE CONCEPTS 278,689

vow [v] *make a solemn promise*
affirm, assure, consecrate, covenant, cross one's heart*, declare, dedicate, devote, give word of honor*, pledge, plight, promise, swear, swear up and down*, testify, undertake solemnly*, vouch, warrant; SEE CONCEPTS 71,297

voyage [n] *journey, often by water*
boating, crossing, cruise, excursion, hop, jaunt, junket, overnight, passage, sail, swing, tour, travel, travels, trek, trip, weekend; SEE CONCEPTS 155,224

vulgar [adj1] *rude, offensive*
base, blue*, boorish, cheap, coarse, common, contemptible, crude, dirty, disgusting, dishonorable, filthy, fractious, gross*, hard-core*, ignoble, impolite, improper, indecent, indecorous, indelicate, inferior, low, malicious, nasty, naughty, obscene, odious, off-color, profane, raw, repulsive, ribald, risqué, rough, rude, scatological, slippery, smutty, sneaking, soft-core*, sordid, suggestive, tasteless, tawdry, uncouth, unmannerly, unrefined, unworthy, villainous, X-rated*; SEE CONCEPTS 267,372,545

vulgar [adj2] *common, general*
colloquial, conversational, dime a dozen*, everyday, familiar, garden variety*, low, native, ordinary, plastic, plebeian, popular, public, run-of-the-mill*, unrefined, vernacular; SEE CONCEPT 530

vulnerable [adj] *open to attack*
accessible, assailable, defenseless, exposed, liable, naked, on the line*, on the spot*, out on a limb*, ready, sensitive, sitting duck*, sucker*,

susceptible, tender, thin-skinned*, unguarded, unprotected, unsafe, weak, wide open*; SEE CONCEPTS 403,587

W

wacky [adj] *acting crazy*
absurd, balmy, crazed, crazy, daft, demented, deranged, eccentric, erratic, foolish, hare-brained, insane, irrational, loony*, lunatic, mad, nuts*, nutty*, odd, preposterous, screwy*, silly, unpredictable, wild, zany*; SEE CONCEPTS 401,403

wad [n] *ball of something*
back, block, boodle, bunch, bundle, chunk, clump, cushion, fortune, gathering, heap, hunk, lining, lump, mass, mint, nugget, packet, pad, pile, plug, pot, ream, roll, slew, stuff, tuft, wadding; SEE CONCEPTS 432,436

waddle [v] *walk like a duck*
rock, shuffle, sway, toddle, totter, wiggle, wobble; SEE CONCEPT 151

wade [v] *plod, often through water*
attack, attempt, bathe, drudge, fall to, ford, get feet wet*, get stuck in*, go for, initiate, jump in, labor, launch, light into, paddle, pitch in, set about, set to, splash, start, stumble, tackle, tear into*, toil, trek, walk, work through; SEE CONCEPTS 87,151

waft [v] *carry*
bear, be carried, blow, carry, convey, drift, float, ride, transmit, transport; SEE CONCEPTS 147,217

wag [n] *person who is very funny*
a million laughs*, card*, clown, comedian, comic, cutup*, droll*, farceur*, funny person, funster*, humorist, jester*, joker, jokester, kibitzer*, kidder, life of the party*, madcap*, prankster, punster, quipster, show-off*, trickster, wisecracker, wit, zany; SEE CONCEPTS 416,423

wag [v] *wiggle back and forth*
beat, bob, fish-tail*, flutter, lash, move side to side, nod, oscillate, quiver, rock, shake, shimmy, stir, sway, swing, switch, twitch, vibrate, waggle, wave; SEE CONCEPTS 150,152

wage [v] *carry on*
carry out, conduct, do, engage in, fulfill, make, practice, proceed with, prosecute, pursue, undertake; SEE CONCEPTS 91,100

wager [n] *money or something gambled*
action, ante*, bet, challenge, chunk, fifty-fifty*, fighting chance*, flyer*, gamble, handle, hazard, hedge, hunch, long shot*, odds on*, outside chance*, parlay, play, pledge, plunge, pot*, risk, stake, toss-up, venture; SEE CONCEPTS 329,363,364

wager [v] *bet money or something else in a gamble*
adventure, chance, gamble, game, hazard, hedge, hustle, lay, lay a wager, parlay, play, play the market*, pledge, plunge, put on*, put on the line*, put up, risk, set*, shoot*, shoot the works*, spec*, speculate, stake, take action, venture; SEE CONCEPTS 28,363

wage/wages [n] *earnings for work*
allowance, bacon*, bacon and eggs*, bread*, compensation, cut, emolument, fee, hire, pay,

payment, price, receipts, recompense, remuneration, return, returns, reward, salary, share, stipend, sugar*, take*, take-home*; SEE CONCEPT 344

waggish [*adj*] *playful*
amusing, blithe, bubbly, cheerful, clowning, comical, frolicsome, funny, gamesome, gay, humorous, jaunty, jesting, jocular, jocund, joking, jolly, joyous, kittenish, lighthearted, lively, merry, mirthful, snappy, spirited, teasing, whimsical, witty; SEE CONCEPTS 401,542

waif [*n*] *lost or unclaimed person or thing*
castaway, dogie, drop*, fetch*, flotsam, foundling, homeless one, jetsam, orphan, ragamuffin, stray, urchin; SEE CONCEPT 423

wail [*v*] *cry loudly*
bawl, bay, bemoan, bewail, carry on*, complain, cry the blues*, deplore, fuss, grieve, howl, jowl, keen, kick, lament, moan, mourn, repine, sob, squall, ululate, weep, whimper, whine; SEE CONCEPTS 77,185

wait [*n*] *pause, delay*
down, downtime*, halt, hold*, hold-up, interim, interval, on hold*, rest, stay, time wasted*; SEE CONCEPT 807

wait [*v*] *pause, rest*
abide, anticipate, await, bide, bide one's time*, cool it*, dally, delay, expect, fill time, foresee, hang*, hang around*, hang onto your hat*, hang out, hold back, hold everything*, hold on, hold the phone*, hole up*, keep shirt on*, lie in wait*, lie low*, linger, look for, look forward to, mark time*, put on hold*, remain, save it*, sit tight*, sit up for*, stall, stand by, stay, stay up for, stick around*, sweat it*, tarry, watch; SEE CONCEPTS 210,681

wait on [*v*] *serve*
arrange, attend, care for, deal, deliver, help, minister, nurse, portion, ready, set, tend; SEE CONCEPTS 136,324

waive [*v*] *give up; let go*
abandon, allow, cede, defer, delay, disclaim, disown, dispense with, forgo, grant, hand over, hold off, hold up, leave, neglect, postpone, prorogue, put off, refrain from, reject, relinquish, remit, remove, renege, renounce, reserve, resign, set aside, shelve, stay, surrender, suspend, table, turn over, yield; SEE CONCEPTS 121,234,317

waiver [*n*] *giving up; letting go*
abandonment, abdication, disclaimer, foregoing, postponement, refusal, rejection, relinquishment, remission, renunciation, reservation, resignation, setting aside, surrender, tabling; SEE CONCEPTS 121,318,685

wake [*n1*] *formal observance of a body before funeral*
deathwatch, funeral service, last rites, obsequies, rites, vigil, watch; SEE CONCEPTS 367,377

wake [*n2*] *trail behind something*
aftermath, backwash, furrow, path, track, train, wash, wave; SEE CONCEPTS 753,824

wakeful [*adj*] *alert, restless*
alive, astir, attentive, careful, heedful, insomniac, insomnious, observant, on guard, on the alert, on the lookout, on the qui vive, sleepless, unsleeping, vigilant, waking, wary, watchful, wideawake; SEE CONCEPTS 539,542

wake/waken [*v1*] *stop sleeping*
arise, awake, awaken, be roused, bestir, bring to life*, call, come to, get out of bed*, get up,

nudge, open one's eyes*, prod, rise, rise and shine*, roll out, rouse, shake, stir, stretch, tumble out*, turn out, wake up; SEE CONCEPT 105

wake/waken [*v2*] *excite, stimulate*
activate, animate, arouse, awaken, challenge, enliven, fire, fire up*, freshen, galvanize, grasp, jazz up*, key up*, kindle, notice, pep up*, provoke, quicken, rally, renew, rouse, see, steam up*, stir up, switch on*, understand, whet, zip up*; SEE CONCEPTS 7,14,22

walk [*n1*] *brief travel on foot*
airing, carriage, circuit, constitutional, gait, hike, jaunt, march, pace, parade, perambulation, peregrination, promenade, ramble, saunter, schlepp*, step, stretch, stride, stroll, tour, traipse, tramp, tread, turn; SEE CONCEPTS 149,224

walk [*n2*] *pathway*
aisle, alley, avenue, boardwalk, boulevard, bricks, bypath, byway, catwalk, cloister, course, court, crossing, esplanade, footpath, gangway, lane, mall, passage, path, pavement, pier, platform, promenade, road, sidewalk, street, track, trail; SEE CONCEPT 501

walk [*n3*] *discipline*
area, arena, bailiwick, calling, career, course, domain, dominion, field, line, metier, profession, province, sphere, terrain, territory, trade, vocation; SEE CONCEPTS 349,360

walk [*v*] *move along on foot*
advance, amble, ambulate, canter, escort, exercise, file, foot, go, go on foot*, hike, hit the road*, hoof it, knock about*, lead, leg*, locomote, lumber, march, meander, pace, pad, parade, patrol, perambulate, plod, prance, promenade, race, roam, rove, run, saunter, scuff, shamble, shuffle, slog, stalk, step, stride, stroll, strut, stump, take a walk, toddle, tour, traipse, tramp, travel on foot, traverse, tread, trek, troop, trudge, wander, wend one's way*; SEE CONCEPT 149

wall [*n*] *obstruction, divider*
bank, bar, barricade, barrier, block, blockade, bulwark, curb, dam, embankment, enclosure, facade, fence, fortification, hindrance, hurdle, impediment, levee, limitation, palisade, panel, paneling, parapet, partition, rampart, restriction, retainer, roadblock, screen, side, stockade, stop, surface; SEE CONCEPTS 440,666

wallop [*n*] *strong hit*
bash, belt, blow, bop, bump, clash, collision, crash, haymaker*, impact, jar, jolt, kick, percussion, punch, shock, slam, slug, smack, smash, thump, thwack*, whack; SEE CONCEPT 189

wallop [*v1*] *beat, hit*
bam, bash, batter, belt, blast, boff, bop, buffet, bushwhack*, clobber*, drub*, hide, lambaste*, paste, pelt, plant one*, pound, pummel, punch, slam, slog, slug, smack, smash, sock, strike, swat, take out, tan*, thrash, thump, whack, wham, whomp, zap*; SEE CONCEPT 189

wallop [*v2*] *defeat soundly*
beat, best, clobber*, crush*, drub*, lambaste*, lick*, rout, shellac*, thrash*, trim*, trounce, vanquish, whip*; SEE CONCEPT 95

wallow [*v1*] *slosh around in*
bathe in, be immersed, blunder, flounder, get stuck, immerse, lie, loll, lurch, move around in, reel, roll, roll about, roll around in, splash around, sprawl, stagger, stumble, sway, toss, totter, tumble, wade, welter; SEE CONCEPTS 149,201

wallow [*v2*] *become very involved in*
bask, delight, enjoy, glory, grovel, humor, indulge oneself, luxuriate, pamper, relish, revel, roll, rollick, spoil, take pleasure; SEE CONCEPT *384*

wan [*adj*] *colorless, weak*
anemic, ashen, ashy, bilious, blanched, bleached, bloodless, cadaverous, dim, discolored, faint, feeble, forceless, ghastly, haggard, ineffective, ineffectual, livid, pale, pallid, pasty, peaked, sickly, washed-out, waxen, white, worn; SEE CONCEPTS *314,618*

wand [*n*] *rod*
baton, caduceus, scepter, sprig, staff, stick, twig; SEE CONCEPTS *470,499*

wander [*v1*] *move about aimlessly*
aberrate, amble, circumambulate, circumlocute, circumnutate, cruise, deviate, divagate, diverge, drift, float, follow one's nose*, gad*, gallivant*, globe-trot, hike, hopscotch*, jaunt, maunder, meander, peregrinate, ramble, range, roam, roll, rove, saunter, straggle, stray, stroll, take to the road*, trail, traipse, tramp, trek, vagabond, walk the tracks*; SEE CONCEPTS *151,224*

wander [*v2*] *digress; get lost*
babble, depart, deviate, divagate, diverge, err, get off the track*, get sidetracked*, go astray*, go off on a tangent*, lose one's way, lose train of thought*, ramble, rave, shift, stray, swerve, talk nonsense*, veer; SEE CONCEPTS *101,266,665*

wanderer [*n*] *person who travels aimlessly*
adventurer, beachcomber, bum, drifter, explorer, floater, gad*, gadabout, gallivanter, globe-trotter, gypsy, itinerant, meanderer, nomad, pilgrim, rambler, ranger, roamer, rolling stone*, rover, straggler, stray, stroller, traveler, vagabond, vagrant, voyager; SEE CONCEPT *423*

wane [*v*] *diminish, lessen*
abate, atrophy, decline, decrease, die away, die down, die out, dim, draw to a close*, drop, dwindle, ease off, ebb, fade, fade away, fail, fall, fall short, let up, moderate, peter out*, relent, shrink, sink, slacken, slack off, subside, taper off, waste away, weaken, wind down*, wither; SEE CONCEPTS *698,776*

want [*n1*] *desire*
appetite, craving, demand, fancy, hankering, hunger, longing, necessity, need, requirement, thirst, wish, yearning, yen; SEE CONCEPT *20*

want [*n2*] *lack, need*
absence, dearth, default, defect, deficiency, destitution, exigency, exiguousness, famine, impecuniousness, impoverishment, inadequacy, indigence, insufficiency, meagerness, neediness, paucity, pauperism, penury, poorness, poverty, privation, scantiness, scarcity, shortage, skimpiness; SEE CONCEPTS *646,709*

want [*v1*] *desire*
ache, aspire, be greedy, choose, could do with*, covet, crave, desiderate, fancy, feel a need, hanker*, have ambition, have an urge for*, have a passion for*, have a yen for*, have eyes for*, hunger, incline toward*, itch for*, long, lust, need, pine, prefer, require, spoil for*, thirst, wish, yearn; SEE CONCEPT *20*

want [*v2*] *lack, need*
be deficient, be deprived of, be found wanting, be insufficient, be poor, be short of, be without, call for, demand, fall short in, have need of,
miss, require, stand in need of, starve; SEE CONCEPT *646*

wanting [*adj*] *lacking, inadequate*
absent, away, bankrupt, bereft, burned out*, cooked*, cut off, defective, deficient, deprived, destitute, devoid, disappointing, empty, failing, faulty, gone, half-baked*, imperfect, incomplete, in default, inferior, less, minus, missing, needed, not good enough, not up to par*, omitted, out of gas*, patchy, poor, scant, scanty, scarce, short, shy, sketchy, substandard, too little too late*, unfulfilled, unsound; SEE CONCEPTS *531,546,560*

wanton [*adj1*] *extravagant, lustful*
abandoned, fast*, lax, lewd, libertine, libidinous, licentious, outrageous, profligate, promiscuous, shameless, speedy*, unprincipled, unscrupulous, wayward, X-rated*; SEE CONCEPTS *372,401,545*

wanton [*adj2*] *cruel, malicious*
accidentally on purpose*, arbitrary, contrary, double-crossing*, evil, gratuitous, groundless, inconsiderate, malevolent, malicious, mean, merciless, motiveless, needless, ornery, perverse, senseless, spiteful, unasked, uncalled-for*, unfair, unjust, unjustifiable, unjustified, unprovoked, vicious, wayward, wicked, willful; SEE CONCEPT *401*

wanton [*adj3*] *careless*
capricious, changeable, devil-may-care*, extravagant, fanciful, fickle, fitful, fluctuating, free, frivolous, heedless, hot and cold*, immoderate, inconstant, intemperate, lavish, outrageous, prodigal, profuse, rash, reckless, spendthrift, spoiled, thriftless, unfettered, unreserved, unrestrained, up and down*, variable, volatile, wasteful, whimsical, wild; SEE CONCEPTS *534,542*

wanton [*n*] *profligate person*
debauchee, libertine, rake; SEE CONCEPTS *412,415,419*

war [*n*] *armed conflict*
battle, bloodshed, cold war, combat, conflict, contention, contest, enmity, fighting, hostilities, hostility, police action, strife, strike, struggle, warfare; SEE CONCEPT *320*

war [*v*] *fight, battle*
attack, attempt, bombard, campaign against, challenge, clash, combat, contend, contest, differ, disagree, endeavor, engage in combat, go to war, kill, make war, march against, meet, murder, oppugn, shell, shoot, strive, struggle, take on, take the field against, take up arms, tug, wage war; SEE CONCEPTS *106,320*

ward [*n1*] *district*
area, canton, department, diocese, division, parish, precinct, quarter, territory, zone; SEE CONCEPTS *508,513*

ward [*n2*] *custody; person in one's custody*
adopted child, care, charge, child, client, dependent, foster child, godchild, guardianship, keeping, minor, orphan, pensioner, protection, protégé, protégée, pupil, safekeeping, trust; SEE CONCEPTS *414,691*

warden [*n*] *person who guards and manages*
administrator, bodyguard, caretaker, curator, custodian, deacon, dogcatcher, gamekeeper, governor, guard, guardian, jailer/jailor, janitor, keeper, officer, overseer, prison head, ranger, skipper, superintendent, watchdog, watchkeeper; SEE CONCEPT *347*

wa
wa

wardrobe [n] *clothes or furniture for storing clothes*

apparel, attire, buffet, bureau, chest, chiffonier, closet, clothing, commode, costumes, cupboard, drapes*, dresser, dry goods, duds*, ensembles, garments, locker, outfits, rags*, suits, threads*, toggery, togs, trousseau, trunk, vestments, weeds*; SEE CONCEPTS 443,451

ward/ward off [v] *defend, guard*

avert, avoid, beat off, block, check, deflect, deter, divert, fend, foil, forestall, frustrate, halt, hold off, interrupt, keep at arm's length*, keep at bay*, keep off, obviate, parry, preclude, prevent, rebuff, rebut, repel, repulse, rule out, stave off, stop, stymie*, thwart, turn, turn aside, turn away; SEE CONCEPTS 96,134

warehouse [n] *storage place*

barn, bin, depository, depot, distribution center, establishment, repository, shed, stash house, stockpile, stockroom, store, storehouse; SEE CONCEPTS 439,449

wares [n] *merchandise for sale*

articles, commodities, goods, line, lines, manufactures, material, produce, product, products, range, seconds, stock, stuff, vendibles; SEE CONCEPT 338

warfare [n] *armed conflict*

armed struggle, arms, battle, blows, campaigning, clash, combat, competition, contest, counterinsurgency, discord, emulation, fighting, hostilities, military operation, passage of arms, rivalry, strategy, strife, striving, struggle, tug-of-war*, war; SEE CONCEPT 320

wariness [n] *caution*

alertness, attention, care, carefulness, deliberation, discretion, guardedness, heed, heedfulness, prudence, vigilance, watchfulness; SEE CONCEPT 410

warlike [adj] *hostile, battling*

aggressive, attacking, bellicose, belligerent, bloodthirsty, combative, contending, contentious, contrary, fighting, gladiatorial, hawkish, inimical, martial, militant, militaristic, military, offensive, pugnacious, quarrelsome, ructious, soldierly, truculent, unfriendly, warmongering, warring; SEE CONCEPTS 401,548

warlock [n] *sorcerer, wizard*

astrologer, augurer, clairvoyant, conjurer, diviner, enchanter, fortune-teller, magician, medium, necromancer, occultist, seer, soothsayer, thaumaturge, witch; SEE CONCEPT 361

warm [adj1] *moderately hot*

balmy, broiling, clement, close, flushed, glowing, heated, hot, lukewarm, melting, mild, perspiring, pleasant, roasting, scorching, sizzling, snug, summery, sunny, sweating, sweaty, sweltering, temperate, tepid, thermal, toasty, warmish; SEE CONCEPT 605

warm [adj2] *friendly, kind*

affable, affectionate, amiable, amorous, ardent, cheerful, compassionate, cordial, empathetic, fervent, genial, gracious, happy, heartfelt, hearty, hospitable, kindhearted, kindly, loving, pleasant, responsive, sincere, softhearted, sympathetic, tender, warmhearted, wholehearted; SEE CONCEPTS 267,401,404

warm [adj3] *enthusiastic*

amorous, angry, animated, ardent, earnest, effusive, emotional, excitable, excited, fervent, fervid, glowing, gung-ho*, heated, hot*, intense, irascible, keen, lively, nutty*, passionate, spirited, stormy, vehement, vigorous, violent, zealous; SEE CONCEPTS 401,542

warm [v] *heat up*

bake, chafe, cook, fix, heat, melt, microwave, prepare, put on the fire, thaw, toast, warm over, warm up; SEE CONCEPTS 170,255

warmhearted [adj] *compassionate, kindly*

all heart, benevolent, charitable, cordial, friendly, generous, genial, gentle, good-hearted, good-natured, gracious, hearty, kind, kindhearted, merciful, neighborly, pleasant, polite, softhearted, sympathetic, tenderhearted, thoughtful, warm; SEE CONCEPTS 401,403,404,542

warmonger [n] *militarist*

combatant, fighter, hawk*, jingoist, militant; SEE CONCEPTS 358,359

warn [v] *give notice of possible occurrence*

acquaint, address, admonish, advise, advocate, alert, apprise, caution, clue, clue in*, counsel, cry wolf*, deprecate, direct, dissuade, enjoin, exhort, fill in, forbid, forearm, forewarn, give fair warning, give the high sign*, guide, hint, inform, instruct, lay it out*, make aware, notify, order, post, predict, prepare, prescribe, prompt, put on guard, recommend, remind, remonstrate, reprove, signal, suggest, summon, tell, threaten, tip, tip off*, urge, wise up*; SEE CONCEPT 78

warning [adj] *cautionary*

admonishing, admonitory, cautioning, exemplary, exhortatory, monitorial, monitory, ominous, premonitory, threatening; SEE CONCEPT 267

warning [n] *notice of possible occurrence*

admonition, advice, alarm, alert, augury, caution, caveat, distress signal, example, exhortation, fore, foretoken, forewarning, guidance, handwriting on wall*, heads up*, hint, indication, information, injunction, intimation, lesson, look out*, Mayday*, notification, omen, portent, prediction, premonition, presage, recommendation, sign, signal, SOS*, suggestion, threat, tip, tip-off*, token, watch-it*, wink, word, word to the wise*; SEE CONCEPTS 78,274

warp [v] *bend, distort*

bastardize*, brutalize, color, contort, corrupt, crook, curve, debase, debauch, deform, deprave, deviate, misrepresent, misshape, pervert, swerve, torture, turn, twist, vitiate, wind; SEE CONCEPTS 63,137,213,250

warrant [n] *authorization*

accreditation, assurance, authentication, authority, basis, carte blanche, certificate, commission, credential, credentials, ducat, earnest, foundation, go-ahead*, green light*, guarantee, license, official document, okay*, pass, passport, pawn, permission, permit, pledge, right, sanction, security, shingle*, sticker, subpoena, summons, tag, testimonial, ticket, token, verification, warranty, word; SEE CONCEPTS 376,685

warrant [v] *guarantee, justify, authorize*

affirm, answer for, approve, argue, assert, assure, attest, avouch, back, bear out, call for, certify, claim, commission, contend, declare, defend, delegate, demand, empower, endorse, ensure, entitle, excuse, explain, give grounds for, guarantee, guaranty, insure, license, maintain, necessitate, permit, pledge, privilege, promise, require, sanction, secure, sponsor, stand behind, state, stipulate, swear, take an oath*, undertake, underwrite, uphold, vindicate, vouch for, vow; SEE CONCEPTS 50,57,71,88

warranty [n] *promise*
assurance, bail, bond, certificate, contract, covenant, guarantee, guaranty, pledge, security, surety, written promise; SEE CONCEPTS 684,685

warrior [n] *person who fights in combat*
battler, champion, combatant, conscript, enlisted person, fighter, fighting person, GI*, hero, serviceperson, soldier, trooper; SEE CONCEPT 358

wary [adj] *careful, cautious*
alert, attentive, cagey, calculating, canny, chary, circumspect, considerate, discreet, distrustful, doubting, frugal, gingerly, guarded, handling with kid gloves*, heedful, keeping on one's toes*, leery, on guard, on the lookout*, on the qui vive, provident, prudent, safe, saving, sly, sparing, suspicious, thinking twice*, thrifty, unwasteful, vigilant, walking on eggs*, watchful, watching one's step*, watching out, wide-awake; SEE CONCEPTS 401,403

wash [n1] *laundry, bath*
ablution, bathe, cleaning, cleansing, dirty clothes, laundering, rinse, scrub, shampoo, shower, washing; SEE CONCEPTS 451,514

wash [n2] *wave; water movement*
ebb and flow, eddy, flow, gush, heave, lapping, murmur, roll, rush, spurt, surge, surging, sweep, swell, swirl, swishing, undulation; SEE CONCEPT 748

wash [n3] *coloring*
coat, coating, film, layer, overlay, rinse, stain, suffusion, swab; SEE CONCEPT 475

wash [v1] *bathe, clean*
bath, brush up, bubble, cleanse, clean up, dip, do the dishes*, do the laundry*, douse, drench, float, freshen up*, fresh up*, hose, imbue, immerse, lap, launder, lave, moisten, rinse, scour, scrub, shampoo, shine, shower, slosh, soak, soap, sponge, starch, swab, take a bath*, take a shower*, tub, wash up*, wet, wipe; SEE CONCEPT 165

wash [v2] *be convincing*
be acceptable, bear scrutiny, be plausible, be reasonable, carry weight, convince, endure, hold up, hold water*, stand up*, stick*; SEE CONCEPT 676

washed-out [adj] *faded*
bleached, colorless, discolored, drained, drawn, dull, etiolated, fatigued, lusterless, not shiny, pale, pallid, run-down, shopworn, tattered, threadbare, tired, worn; SEE CONCEPTS 560,617, 618

washed-up [adj] *finished*
broken down, come to an end, concluded, done, done for, done with, ended, over and done*, over the hill*, shot*, through, useless; SEE CONCEPTS 528,531

wassail [n] *celebration*
bash*, blast*, blowout*, carousal, ceremony, festival, festivity, frolic, gala, hoopla, hullabaloo*, joviality, jubilee, merriment, merrymaking, party, revelry, shindig*, spree, wingding*; SEE CONCEPT 377

wassail [v] *celebrate, toast*
applaud, carouse, clink glasses, drink to, extol, feast, get drunk, honor, jubilate, let loose*, live it up*, make merry, party, pledge, raise one's glass to*, revel, salute; SEE CONCEPT 377

waste [n1] *spending, use without thought*
decay, desolation, destruction, devastation, dilapidation, dissipation, disuse, exhaustion, expenditure, extravagance, fritter*, havoc, improvidence, lavishness, loss, lost opportunity*, misapplication, misuse, overdoing, prodigality, ravage, ruin, squander, squandering, unthriftiness, wastage, wastefulness; SEE CONCEPTS 156,252

waste [n2] *land that is uncultivated*
badlands, barren, bog, brush, brushland, bush, desert, dust bowl, fen, jungle, marsh, marshland, moor, quagmire, solitude, swamp, tundra, void, wasteland, wild, wilderness, wilds; SEE CONCEPT 509

waste [n3] *garbage, refuse*
debris, dreck, dregs, dross, excess, hogwash*, junk, leavings, leftovers, litter, offal, offscourings, rubbish, rubble, ruins, rummage, scrap, slop, sweepings, swill, trash; SEE CONCEPT 260

waste [v1] *spend or use without thought; dwindle*
atrophy, be of no avail*, blow, burn up, consume, corrode, crumble, debilitate, decay, decline, decrease, deplete, disable, disappear, dissipate, divert, drain, droop, eat away, ebb, emaciate, empty, enfeeble, exhaust, fade, fritter away*, frivol away*, gamble away, gnaw, go to waste, lavish, lose, misapply, misemploy, misuse, perish, pour down the drain*, run dry, run through*, sap, sink, splurge, squander, thin, throw away, trifle away, undermine, wane, wear, wear out, wilt, wither; SEE CONCEPT 156

waste [v2] *ruin, destroy*
depredate, desecrate, desolate, despoil, devastate, devour, lay waste, pillage, rape, ravage, raze, reduce, sack, spoil, spoliate, wreak havoc; SEE CONCEPT 252

wasted [adj1] *emaciated*
anorexic, atrophied, attenuated, bony, famished, gaunt, haggard, lank, lean, scrawny, shrivelled, skeletal, skin-and-bones*, skinny, starved, thin, underfed, undernourished, withered; SEE CONCEPTS 490,491

wasted [adj2] *high on drugs*
baked*, bombed*, buzzed*, doped, drugged, drunk, feeling no pain*, flying*, fried, inebriated, intoxicated, loaded, on a trip*, plastered, ripped*, sloshed*, smashed*, spaced out*, stewed*, stoned*, strung out*, tanked*, tipsy, totaled*, tripping*; SEE CONCEPT 314

wasteful [adj] *not economical*
careless, cavalier, destructive, dissipative, extravagant, immoderate, improvident, incontinent, lavish, liberal, overdone, overgenerous, poundfoolish*, prodigal, profligate, profuse, reckless, ruinous, spendthrift, squandering, thriftless, uneconomical, unthrifty, wanton, wild; SEE CONCEPT 401

watch [n1] *clock worn on body*
analog watch, chronometer, digital watch, pocket watch, stopwatch, ticker*, timepiece, timer, wristwatch; SEE CONCEPT 463

watch [n2] *lookout*
alertness, attention, awareness, duty, eagle eye*, eye*, gander, guard, hawk, heed, inspection, notice, observance, observation, patrol, picket, scrutiny, sentinel, sentry, supervision, surveillance, tab, tout, vigil, vigilance, watchfulness, weather eye*; SEE CONCEPTS 134,623

wa
wa

watch [v1] *look at*

attend, case, check out, concentrate, contemplate, eagle-eye*, examine, eye*, eyeball*, focus, follow, gaze, get a load of*, give the once over*, have a look-see*, inspect, keep an eye on*, keep tabs on*, listen, look, mark, mind, note, observe, pay attention, peer, pipe*, regard, rubberneck*, scan, scope, scrutinize, see, spy, stare, take in, take notice, view, wait; SEE CONCEPT 623

watch [v2] *guard, protect*

attend, be on alert*, be on the lookout*, be vigilant*, be wary, be watchful, care for, keep, keep eyes open*, keep eyes peeled*, keep watch over, look after, look out, mind, oversee, patrol, pick up on, police, ride shotgun for*, superintend, take care of, take heed*, tend, wait; SEE CONCEPTS 134,623

watchful [adj] *on the lookout*

alert, all ears*, attentive, careful, cautious, chary, circumspect, glued*, guarded, heedful, hooked*, keen, not missing a trick*, observant, on guard, on one's toes*, on the ball*, on the job*, on the qui vive, on the watch, open-eyed, prepared, ready, see after, see to, suspicious, unsleeping, vigilant, wakeful, wary, wide-awake, with eyes peeled*; SEE CONCEPT 401

watchkeeper [n] *person who guards, is on lookout*

caretaker, curator, custodian, detective, flagger, guard, keeper, lookout, observer, patrol, picket, police officer, ranger, scout, security guard, security officer, sentinel, sentry, signaller, spotter, spy, ward, warden, watch, watcher; SEE CONCEPT 348

water [n] *pure liquid hydrogen and oxygen*

Adam's ale*, aqua, aqua pura*, drink, H_2O, rain, rainwater, saliva, tears; SEE CONCEPT 467

water [v] *dampen; put water in*

baptize, bathe, damp, dilute, doctor, douse, drench, drool, flood, hose, imbue, inundate, irrigate, moisten, saturate, soak, sodden, souse, spatter, spray, sprinkle, steep, thin, wash, weaken, wet; SEE CONCEPT 256

waterfall [n] *cascade*

cataract, chute, fall, rapids, shoot, weir; SEE CONCEPTS 514,787

waterlogged [adj] *saturated*

dank, drenched, dripping, drowned, soaked, soaking, sodden, soggy, sopping, soppy, soused, wet, wringing-wet; SEE CONCEPT 603

waterloo [n] *final defeat, total defeat*

annihilation, beating, collapse, conquest, crushing defeat, drubbing*, failure, fall, licking, massacre, overthrow, rout, shellacking*, slaughter, thrashing, trashing, trouncing, vanquishment, waxing, whipping, whitewashing; SEE CONCEPT 95

watery [adj] *liquid, diluted*

adulterated, anemic, aqueous, bloodless, colorless, damp, dilute, doused, flavorless, fluid, humid, insipid, marshy, moist, pale, runny, serous, sodden, soggy, tasteless, thin, washed, watered-down, waterlike, water-logged, weak, wet; SEE CONCEPTS 485,603,618

wave [n] *sea surf, current*

bending, billow, breaker, coil, comber, convolution, corkscrew, crest, crush, curl, curlicue, drift, flood, foam, ground swell, gush, heave, influx, loop, movement, outbreak, rash, ridge, ripple, rippling, rocking, roll, roller, rush, scroll, sign, signal, stream, surge, sweep, swell, tendency, tide, tube, twirl, twist, undulation, unevenness, uprising, upsurge, whitecap, winding; SEE CONCEPTS 147,436,514

wave [v] *move back and forth; gesture*

beckon, billow, brandish, coil, curl, direct, falter, flap, flourish, flow, fluctuate, flutter, fly, gesticulate, indicate, motion, move to and fro, oscillate, palpitate, pulsate, pulse, quaver, quiver, reel, ripple, seesaw, shake, sign, signal, stir, stream, surge, sway, swell, swing, swirl, swish, switch, tremble, twirl, twist, undulate, vacillate, vibrate, wag, waggle, waver, whirl, wield, wigwag*, wobble; SEE CONCEPTS 74,147,149

waver [v] *shift back and forth; be indecisive*

be irresolute, be unable to decide*, blow hot and cold*, change, deliberate, dilly-dally*, dither, falter, flicker, fluctuate, halt, hedge, hem and haw*, hesitate, oscillate, palter, pause, pussyfoot around*, quiver, reel, run hot and cold*, seesaw*, shake, stagger, sway, teeter, totter, tremble, trim, undulate, vacillate, vary, waffle, wave, weave, whiffle, wobble, yo-yo*; SEE CONCEPTS 18,147,410

wax [v] *become large, fuller*

augment, become, build, come, develop, dilate, enlarge, expand, fill out, get bigger, get to, grow, grow full, heighten, increase, magnify, mount, multiply, rise, run, swell, turn, upsurge; SEE CONCEPTS 704,780

way [n1] *method, technique*

action, approach, contrivance, course, course of action, custom, design, expedient, fashion, form, groove*, habit, habitude, hang-up*, hook*, idea, instrument, kick, manner, means, measure, mode, modus, move, outline, plan, plot, policy, practice, procedure, process, scheme, shot, step, stroke, style, system, tack, thing*, usage, use, vehicle, wise, wont; SEE CONCEPT 6

way [n2] *direction, route*

access, admission, admittance, advance, alternative, approach, artery, avenue, bearing, boulevard, byway, channel, course, distance, door, drag*, elbowroom, entrance, entrée, entry, extent, forward motion, gate, gateway, headway, highway, ingress, journey, lane, length, line, march, movement, opening, orbit, passage, path, pathway, progress, progression, ride, road, room, row, space, stone's throw*, street, stretch, tendency, thataway*, thoroughfare, track, trail, trend, walk; SEE CONCEPTS 501,738,739

way [n3] *characteristic, habit*

aspect, behavior, circumstance, condition, conduct, consuetude, custom, detail, fashion, feature, fettle, form, gait, groove, guise, habit, hook, idiosyncrasy, kick*, manner, nature, particular, personality, point, practice, praxis, respect, sense, shape, shot, situation, state, status, style, thing*, tone, trait, trick, usage, use, wont; SEE CONCEPT 411

wayfarer [n] *traveler*

adventurer, barnstormer*, bum*, drifter, excursionist, explorer, gadabout*, globetrotter, gypsy, hiker, hitchhiker, hobo, itinerant, journeyer, nomad, peddler, pilgrim, rambler, roamer, rover, trekker, vagabond, vagrant, walker, wanderer; SEE CONCEPTS 348,423

wayfaring [adj] *traveling*

drifting, gadabout, globe-trotting, itinerant, itin-

erate, jet-setting*, journeying, nomadic, perambulant, perambulatory, peripatetic, rambling,
roving, rubbernecking*, vagabond, vagrant, voyaging, walking, wandering; SEE CONCEPT *401*

waylay [v] *intercept, ambush*
accost, ambuscade, assail, attack, box*, bushwhack*, catch, hold up, intercept, jump, lay for*,
lie in wait, lurk, pounce on, prowl, set upon,
skulk, slink, surprise, swoop down on*; SEE CON-
CEPTS *86,121*

wayward [adj] *contrary, unmanageable*
aberrant, arbitrary, balky, capricious, changeable, contumacious, cross-grained, delinquent,
disobedient, disorderly, errant, erratic, fickle,
flighty, fractious, froward, headstrong, immoral,
inconstant, incorrigible, insubordinate, intractable, mulish, obdurate, obstinate, ornery*,
perverse, rebellious, recalcitrant, refractory,
restive, self-indulgent, self-willed, stubborn, uncompliant, undependable, ungovernable, unpredictable, unruly, unstable, variable, whimsical,
willful; SEE CONCEPT *401*

weak [adj] *not strong*
anemic, debilitated, decrepit, delicate, effete, enervated, exhausted, faint, feeble, flaccid, flimsy,
forceless, fragile, frail, hesitant, impuissant, infirm, insubstantial, irresolute, lackadaisical*, languid, languorous, limp, makeshift, out of gas*,
powerless, prostrate, puny, rickety, rocky*, rotten, senile, shaky, sickly, sluggish, spent,
spindly, supine, tender, torpid, uncertain, undependable, unsound, unsteady, unsubstantial,
wasted, wavering, weakened, weakly, wobbly;
SEE CONCEPTS *314,488,489*

weak [adj2] *cowardly*
faint-hearted, fluctuant, frightened, hesitant, impotent, indecisive, ineffectual, infirm, insecure,
irresolute, laid-back*, nerveless, nervous,
palsied, powerless, shaky, soft, spineless, tender,
timorous, uncertain, undependable, unreliable,
unstable, unsure, vacillating, wavering, weak-
kneed*, wimpy*, wishy-washy*, wobbly, zero*;
SEE CONCEPTS *402,403,542*

weak [adj3] *faint, soft*
bated, dim, distant, dull, feeble, gentle, imperceptible, inaudible, indistinct, low, muffled, pale,
poor, quiet, reedy, slight, small, stifled, thin, un-
accented, unstressed, whispered; SEE CONCEPT
594

weak [adj4] *deficient, feeble*
faulty, flabby, flimsy, forceless, green*, handicapped, hollow, immature, implausible, impotent, improbable, inadequate, incompetent,
incomplete, inconceivable, inconclusive, incredible, ineffective, ineffectual, inept, invalid, lacking, lame, limited, pathetic, poor, raw, shaky,
shallow, slight, slim, small, spineless, substandard, thick, thin, unbelievable, unconvincing,
unprepared, unqualified, unsatisfactory, unsubstantial, unsure, untrained, wanting; SEE CON-
CEPTS *537,558,570*

weak [adj5] *exposed, vulnerable*
accessible, assailable, defenseless, helpless, indefensible, unguarded, unprotected, unsafe, untenable, wide-open*, woundable; SEE CONCEPTS
576,587

weak [adj6] *watered-down*
dilute, diluted, insipid, milk-and-water*, runny,
tasteless, thin, washy, waterish, watery, wishy-
washy*; SEE CONCEPTS *462,485*

weaken [v] *reduce the strength of*
abate, adulterate, break up, cripple, crumble, cut,
debase, debilitate, decline, decrease, depress, devitalize, dilute, diminish, droop, dwindle, ease
up, enervate, exhaust, fade, fail, faint, flag, give
way, halt, impair, impoverish, invalidate, languish, lessen, limp, lose, lose spirit, lower, minimize, mitigate, moderate, reduce, relapse, relax,
sap, slow down, soften, temper, thin, thin out,
tire, totter, tremble, undermine, vitiate, wane,
water down, wilt; SEE CONCEPTS *240,698*

weakling [n] *person who has no strength*
baby, chicken*, chicken heart*, coward, cream
puff*, crybaby, dotard, invertebrate, jellyfish*,
misfit, pushover, wimp*, yellow belly*; SEE
CONCEPTS *412,423*

weak-minded [adj] *indecisive*
astraddle, changeable, hemming and hawing*,
hesitant, hesitating, indeterminate, irresolute,
on the fence*, spineless, tentative, uncertain,
undecided, undetermined, waffling, wavering,
weak-kneed*, wishy-washy*, without guts*,
yellow-bellied*; SEE CONCEPTS *534,535*

weakness [n] *defect, proneness*
Achilles heel*, appetite*, blemish, chink in
armor*, debility, decrepitude, deficiency, delicacy, enervation, failing, faintness, fault, feebleness, flaw, fondness, fragility, frailty, gap,
impairment, imperfection, impotence, inclination, inconstancy, indecision, infirmity, instability, invalidity, irresolution, lack, languor, lapse,
liking, passion, penchant, powerlessness,
predilection, proclivity, prostration, senility,
shortcoming, soft spot*, sore point*, taste*, vice,
vitiation, vulnerability; SEE CONCEPTS *411,674,*
732

wealth [n] *money, resources*
abundance, affluence, assets, belongings, bounty,
cache, capital, cash, clover*, commodities, copiousness, cornucopia, dough*, estate, fortune,
funds, gold, goods, hoard, holdings, lap of luxury*, long green*, lucre, luxuriance, luxury,
means, opulence, pelf, plenitude, plenty, possessions, profusion, property, prosperity, prosperousness, revenue, riches, richness, security,
stocks and bonds, store, substance, substantiality,
treasure, velvet*, worth; SEE CONCEPTS *340,710*

wealthy [adj] *rich; having a lot of money*
affluent, booming, comfortable, having it made*,
independent, in the money*, loaded, made of
money*, moneyed, of independent means,
opulent, pecunious, prosperous, rolling in it*,
substantial, upscale, well-heeled*, well-off*,
well-to-do*; SEE CONCEPT *334*

weapon [n] *arm, armament*
ammunition, anlace, arbalest, archery, arrow, as-
segai, atlatl, ax, axe, backsword, ballista, bander-
illa, barong, bat, baton, battle-ax, bayonet,
bazooka, billy club, blackjack, blade, blowgun,
bludgeon, bomb, boomerang, bow and arrow,
bowie knife, brass knuckles, cannon, catapult,
cleaver, club, crossbow, cudgel, cutlass, dagger,
dart, dirk, firearm, flamethrower, gun, harpoon,
hatchet, howitzer, hunting knife, knife, lance,
machete, machine gun, missile, musket, nerve
gas, nuclear bomb, nunchaku, pistol, revolver,
rifle, saber, scythe, shotgun, slingshot, spear,
spike, stiletto, switchblade, sword, tear gas; SEE
CONCEPT *500*

wa
we

wear [*n*] *use, corrosion*
abrasion, attrition, damage, depreciation, deterioration, dilapidation, diminution, disappearance, employment, erosion, friction, impairment, inroads, loss, mileage, service, usefulness, utility, waste, wear and tear; SEE CONCEPTS *658,698*

wear [*v1*] *be clothed in*
array, attire, bear, be dressed in, carry, clothe oneself, cover, display, don, draw on, dress in, effect, exhibit, fit out, get into, get on, harness, have on, put on, show, slip on, sport, suit up*, turn out*, wrap; SEE CONCEPTS *167,453*

wear [*v2*] *corrode, use*
abrade, become threadbare, become worn, be worthless, chafe, consume, crumble, cut down, decay, decline, decrease, deteriorate, diminish, drain, dwindle, erode, exhaust, fade, fatigue, fray, gall, go to seed*, graze, grind, impair, jade, overuse, overwork, rub, scrape, scrape off, scuff, shrink, tax, tire, use up, wash away, waste, wear out, wear thin, weary, weather; SEE CONCEPTS *156,225,240,698*

wear [*v3*] *bother, undermine*
annoy, drain, enervate, exasperate, exhaust, fatigue, get the better of, harass, irk, pester, reduce, tax, vex, weaken, wear down, weary; SEE CONCEPTS *7,19*

wear [*v4*] *endure*
bear up, be durable, hold up, last, remain, stand, stand up yet; SEE CONCEPT *23*

weary [*adj*] *tired*
all in*, beat*, bone-tired*, bored, burned out*, bushed, dead*, dead tired*, discontented, disgusted, dog-tired*, done in*, drained, drooping, drowsy, enervated, exhausted, fagged, fatigued, fed up, flagging, had it*, impatient, indifferent, jaded, knocked out, out of gas*, overworked, pooped*, punchy*, ready to drop*, sick, sick and tired*, sleepy, spent*, taxed, wearied, wearing, wiped out*, worn out, zonked*; SEE CONCEPTS *314,403,485*

weary [*v*] *make tired*
annoy, bore, burden, cause ennui, cloy, debilitate, depress, disgust, dishearten, distress, drain, droop, drowse, enervate, enfeeble, exasperate, exhaust, fade, fag, fail, fall off, fatigue, flag, glut, grow tired, harass, have had enough*, irk, jade, leave one cold*, lose interest, make discontented, nauseate, oppress, overwork, pain, plague, sap, sicken, sink, strain, take it out of*, tax, tire, tire out, try the patience of*, tucker out*, vex, weaken, wear down, wear out, weigh; SEE CONCEPTS *13,250,303*

weasel [*n*] *sneak*
betrayer, blabbermouth*, canary*, deceiver, deep throat*, double-crosser, fink*, informant, informer, narc*, nark*, rat*, sneak, snitch, snitcher, source, squealer*, stoolie*, stool pigeon*, tattler, tattletale, tipster*, turncoat, weasel*, whistle-blower; SEE CONCEPTS *348,354,423*

weasel [*v*] *avoid, evade*
balk, beat around the bush*, circumvent, cop out, dance around an issue*, dodge, duck, elude, equivocate, eschew, flee, get around, give the runaround*, hedge, hem and haw*, lay low*, pussyfoot, put off, renege, shirk, shuck, sidestep, slip out, sneak away*, tap dance*, waffle*, welsh, worm one's way out of*; SEE CONCEPTS *30,102*

weather [*n*] *atmospheric conditions*
climate, clime, elements; SEE CONCEPTS *522,524*

weather [*v*] *endure*
acclimate, bear the brunt of*, bear up against*, become toughened, brave, come through, expose, get through, grow hardened, grow strong, harden, make it, overcome, pull through, resist, ride out*, rise above*, season, stand, stick it out*, suffer, surmount, survive, toughen, withstand; SEE CONCEPTS *23,35,202*

weatherperson [*n*] *meteorologist*
climatologist, storm chaser, weathercaster, weather-forecaster, weatherman/woman; SEE CONCEPTS *60,292*

weave [*v*] *blend, unite; contrive*
braid, build, careen, complect, complicate, compose, construct, create, criss-cross, crochet, cue, entwine, fabricate, fold, fuse, incorporate, interfold, interlace, interlink, intermingle, intertwine, introduce, knit, knot, loop, lurch, make, make up, manufacture, mat, merge, mesh, move in and out, net, piece together, plait, ply, put together, reticulate, sew, snake, spin, splice, twine, twist, twist and turn, whip through, wind, wreathe, writhe, zigzag; SEE CONCEPTS *147,158*

web [*n*] *netting*
cobweb, complexity, entanglement, fabric, fiber, filigree, gossamer, interconnection, interlacing, involvement, labyrinth, lacework, lattice, mat, matting, maze, mesh, meshwork, morass, net, network, plait, reticulation, screen, skein, snarl, tangle, texture, tissue, toil, trellis, warp, weave, webbing, weft, wicker, woof; SEE CONCEPTS *260,473*

wed [*v1*] *marry*
become husband and wife, be married, couple, espouse, get hitched*, get married, join, lead to the altar, make one*, receive in marriage, say I do*, take in marriage, tie*, tie the knot*, unite; SEE CONCEPT *297*

wed [*v2*] *join, unite*
ally, associate, blend, coalesce, cojoin, combine, commingle, connect, couple, dedicate, fuse, interweave, link, marry, merge, relate, unify, yoke; SEE CONCEPTS *113,193*

wedding [*n*] *marriage rite*
bells*, bridal, espousal, hook, marriage, marriage ceremony, matrimony, nuptial rite, nuptials, spousal, union, wedlock; SEE CONCEPT *297*

wedge [*n*] *solid piece, often triangular*
block, chock, chunk, cleat, cotter, cusp, keystone, lump, prong, quoin, shim, spire, taper; SEE CONCEPTS *471,499*

wedlock [*n*] *marriage*
alliance, association, conjugality, connubiality, coupling, espousal, holy matrimony, mating, matrimony, nuptials, spousal, union, wedded bliss*, wedding; SEE CONCEPTS *297,388*

wee [*adj*] *very small, tiny*
bitsy*, bitty, diminutive, infinitesimal, insignificant, itsy-bitsy*, itty-bitty*, Lilliputian, little, microscopic, miniature, minuscular, minuscule, minute, negligible, pee-wee*, petite, pint-sized*, pocket-size*, puny, slight, teensy*, teensy-weensy*, teeny*; SEE CONCEPTS *762,773,789*

weep [*v*] *cry*
bawl, bemoan, bewail, blubber*, boohoo*, break down*, burst into tears*, complain, deplore, drip, grieve, howl, keen, lament, let go*, let it out*, mewl, moan, mourn, shed tears, snivel, sob,

squall, ululate, wail, whimper, yowl; SEE CONCEPTS *49,185*

weigh [*v1*] *measure heaviness*
counterbalance, have a weight of, heft, measure, put in the balance, put on the scale, scale, tip the scales at; SEE CONCEPT *103*

weigh [*v2*] *consider, contemplate*
analyze, appraise, balance, brainstorm*, deliberate, estimate, evaluate, examine, excogitate, give thought to, hash over*, meditate, mind, mull over, perpend, ponder, rate, reflect upon, rehash, sort out, study, sweat*, think about, think out, think over, track; SEE CONCEPT *24*

weigh [*v3*] *have influence*
be heavy, be important, be influential, be something, burden, carry weight, charge, count, cumber, cut, cut some ice, import, impress, lade, matter, mean, militate, press, pull, register, saddle, show, signify, stack up against*, tax, tell; SEE CONCEPTS *7,19,22,237,682*

weigh down [*v*] *depress*
bear down, burden, cumber, get down, hold down, oppress, overburden, overload, press, press down, prey on, pull down, sadden, task, trouble, weight, weigh upon, worry; SEE CONCEPTS *7,19*

weight [*n1*] *heaviness*
adiposity, avoirdupois, ballast, burden, density, G-factor*, gravity, gross, heft, heftiness, load, mass, measurement, net, ponderosity, ponderousness, poundage, pressure, substance, tonnage; SEE CONCEPT *795*

weight [*n2*] *something used to measure heaviness*
anchor, ballast, bob, counterbalance, counterpoise, counterweight, mass, pendulum, plumb, plumb bob, poundage, pressure, rock, sandbag, sinker, stone; SEE CONCEPTS *290,470*

weight [*n3*] *importance*
access, authority, clout, connection, consequence, consideration, credit, effectiveness, efficacy, emphasis, forcefulness, forcibleness, impact, import, influence, magnitude, moment, momentousness, persuasiveness, pith, potency, power, powerfulness, prestige, pull, significance, signification, substance, sway, value, weightiness; SEE CONCEPTS *668,682*

weight [*n4*] *burden*
albatross*, ball and chain*, charge, cumber, cumbrance, deadweight*, duty, encumbrance, excess baggage*, load, millstone*, onus, oppression, pressure, responsibility, strain, task, tax; SEE CONCEPTS *532,674,679,690*

weighty [*adj1*] *heavy*
burdensome, cumbersome, cumbrous, dense, fat, fleshy, hefty, massive, obese, overweight, ponderous, porcine, portly, stout; SEE CONCEPT *491*

weighty [*adj2*] *serious, important*
big, big deal*, consequential, considerable, critical, crucial, earnest, forcible, grave, heavy*, heavyweight, life and death*, material, meaningful, momentous, no-nonsense*, portentous, sedate, severe, significant, sober, solemn, somber, staid, substantial, underlined; SEE CONCEPTS *548,568*

weighty [*adj3*] *troublesome, difficult*
backbreaking, burdensome, crushing, demanding, exacting, exigent, grievous, onerous, oppressive, superincumbent, taxing, tough, worrisome, worrying; SEE CONCEPTS *538,565*

weird [*adj*] *odd, bizarre*
awe-inspiring, awful, creepy*, curious, dreadful, eccentric, eerie*, far-out*, fearful, flaky*, freaky*, funky*, ghastly, ghostly, grotesque, haunting, horrific, inscrutable, kinky*, kooky*, magical, mysterious, occult, oddball*, ominous, outlandish, peculiar, preternatural, queer, secret, singular, spooky*, strange, supernal, supernatural, uncanny, uncouth, unearthly, unnatural; SEE CONCEPTS *564,570*

weirdo [*n*] *freak, oddball*
case*, character, crackpot*, eccentric, flake*, fruitcake*, geek*, misfit, nutcase, odd bird*, screwball*, strange bird*; SEE CONCEPT *423*

welcome [*adj*] *gladly received*
acceptable, accepted, agreeable, appreciated, cherished, congenial, contenting, cordial, delightful, desirable, desired, esteemed, favorable, genial, good, grateful, gratifying, honored, invited, nice, pleasant, pleasing, pleasurable, refreshing, satisfying, sympathetic, wanted; SEE CONCEPTS *555,572*

welcome [*n*] *greeting*
acceptance, entertainment, entrée, friendliness, handshake, hello, hospitality, howdy*, key to the city*, ovation, reception, red carpet*, rumble*, salutation, salute, tumble*; SEE CONCEPT *278*

welcome [*v*] *receive gladly*
accept, accept gladly, accost, admit, bid welcome, embrace, entertain, flag*, greet, hail, hug, meet, offer hospitality, receive, roll out red carpet*, salute, show in, take in, tumble*, usher in; SEE CONCEPTS *266,384*

weld [*v*] *bind, connect*
bond, braze, cement, combine, fix, fuse, join, link, solder, unite; SEE CONCEPT *193*

welfare/well-being [*n*] *health and prosperity*
abundance, advantage, benefit, contentment, ease, easy street*, euphoria, felicity, good, good fortune, happiness, interest, luck, profit, progress, satisfaction, success, thriving; SEE CONCEPTS *316,693,706*

well [*adj1*] *healthy*
able-bodied, alive and kicking*, blooming, bright-eyed*, bushy-tailed*, chipper*, fine, fit, flourishing, fresh, great, hale, hardy, hearty, husky, in good health, in the pink*, right, right as rain*, robust, sane, solid as a rock*, sound, strong, strong as an ox*, together, trim, up to par*, vigorous, whole, wholesome, wrapped tight*; SEE CONCEPT *314*

well [*adj2*] *lucky, fortunate*
advisable, agreeable, bright, comfortable, fine, fitting, flourishing, good, happy, pleasing, profitable, proper, prosperous, providential, prudent, right, satisfactory, thriving, useful; SEE CONCEPTS *548,572*

well [*adv1*] *happily, pleasantly; capably*
ably, accurately, adeptly, adequately, admirably, agreeably, attentively, capitally, carefully, closely, commendably, competently, completely, conscientiously, correctly, effectively, efficiently, excellently, expertly, famously, favorably, fully, in a satisfactory manner, irreproachably, nicely, proficiently, profoundly, properly, rightly, satisfactorily, skillfully, smoothly, soundly, splendidly, strongly, successfully, suitably, thoroughly, with skill; SEE CONCEPTS *527,528,544*

we
we

well [*adv2*] *sufficiently*
abundantly, adequately, amply, appropriately, becomingly, by a wide margin, completely, considerably, easily, effortlessly, entirely, extremely, far, fittingly, freely, fully, greatly, heartily, highly, luxuriantly, plentifully, properly, quite, rather, readily, right, satisfactorily, smoothly, somewhat, substantially, suitably, thoroughly, very much, wholly; SEE CONCEPTS *558,772*

well [*n*] *water hole*
abyss, bore, chasm, depression, derivation, fount, fountain, fountainhead, geyser, hole, inception, mine, mouth, origin, pit, pool, repository, reservoir, root, shaft, source, spa, spout, spring, springs, watering place, wellspring; SEE CONCEPTS *509,513,514*

well-balanced [*adj*] *sensible; equal*
all there*, astute, aware, cognizant, discriminating, graceful, having all one's marbles*, informed, intelligent, knowing, level-headed, logical, mentally stable, practical, proportional, prudent, rational, reasonable, sane, sound, symmetrical, together, well-thought-out, wise; SEE CONCEPTS *402,542*

well-bred [*adj*] *mannerly*
aristocratic, blue-blooded*, civil, considerate, courteous, courtly, cultivated, cultured, gallant, genteel, gentle, noble, patrician, polished, polite, refined, taught, trained, upper-crust*, urbane, well-behaved, well-mannered; SEE CONCEPTS *334,401*

well-defined [*adj*] *clear*
apparent, audible, clear-cut, comprehensible, distinct, explicit, graspable, intelligible, legible, lucent, lucid, obvious, plain, precise, sharp, spelled out*, straightforward, transparent, unambiguous, unblurred, understandable, well-marked; SEE CONCEPTS *402,562*

well-known [*adj*] *familiar, famous*
acclaimed, big, big name*, celeb*, celebrated, common, conspicuous, eminent, illustrious, important, infamous, in the limelight*, in the public eye*, known, large, leading, name, notable, noted, notorious, outstanding, popular, prominent, public, recognized, renowned, reputable, somebody, splashy, star, superstar, VIP*, widely known, WK*; SEE CONCEPT *568*

well-off [*adj*] *successful, wealthy*
affluent, comfortable, easy, flourishing, flush, fortunate, loaded, lucky, moneyed, prosperous, rich, snug, substantial, thriving, well, well-to-do; SEE CONCEPT *334*

well-preserved [*adj*] *well-kept*
boyish, childish, fresh, girlish, gull of life, tender, unspoiled, young; SEE CONCEPTS *542,578, 797*

well-to-do [*adj*] *well-off*
affluent, comfortable, flourishing, loaded, money-eyed, prosperous, rich, rolling in it*, set for life*, snug, successful, wealthy; SEE CONCEPT *334*

welsh [*v*] *renege, swindle*
bamboozle, beat around the bush*, bilk, cheat, con, cop out, deceive, defraud, dodge, duck, dupe, fleece*, flimflam, fool, gull*, hoodwink, pull a fast one*, rip off*, sandbag, scam, shaft, slip out, sting*, take for a ride*, take to the cleaners*, trick, weasel*, worm one's way out of*; SEE CONCEPTS *59,139,192*

welt [*n*] *red mark*
bruise, contusion, injury, mouse, ridge, scar, streak, stripe, wale, weal, wheal, wound; SEE CONCEPT *309*

wet [*adj*] *damp, moist*
aqueous, clammy, dank, dewy, drenched, dripping, drizzling, foggy, humid, misty, moistened, muggy, pouring, raining, rainy, saturate, saturated, showery, slimy, slippery, slushy, snowy, soaked, soaking, sodden, soggy, sopping, soppy, soused, stormy, teary, teeming, water-logged, watery, wringing-wet; SEE CONCEPT *603*

wet [*n*] *dampness, moisture*
clamminess, condensation, damp, drizzle, humidity, liquid, rain, rains, water, wetness; SEE CONCEPT *607*

wet [*v*] *cause to become damp, moist*
bathe, damp, dampen, deluge, dip, douse, drench, drown, hose, humidity, imbue, irrigate, moisten, rinse, saturate, soak, sop, souse, splash, spray, sprinkle, steep, wash, water; SEE CONCEPTS *161,256*

whack [*n1/v*] *hit*
bang, bash, bat, beat, belt, biff, box, buffet, clobber, clout, crack, cuff, ding*, lambaste*, nail, rap, slap, slug, smack, smash, sock, strike, thrash, thump, thwack*, wallop, wham*; SEE CONCEPT *189*

whack [*n2*] *try, attempt*
bash, crack, fling, go, pop, shot, slap, stab, turn, whirl; SEE CONCEPT *87*

whammy [*n*] *spell*
abracadabra*, charm, conjuration, curse, double whammy*, evil eye, hex, hexing, hocus-pocus*, jinx, magic, mumbo-jumbo*, triple whammy*, voodoo; SEE CONCEPTS *370,673,689*

wharf [*n*] *boat storage*
berth, breakwater, dock, jetty, landing, landing stage, levee, pier, quay, slip; SEE CONCEPT *439*

wheedle [*v*] *talk into*
banter, blandish, butter up*, cajole, charm, coax, con, court, draw, entice, finagle, flatter, inveigle, kowtow*, lay it on*, oil*, persuade, seduce, snow*, soap*, soften up*, soft-soap*, spread it on*, sweeten up*, sweet-talk*, work on*, worm*; SEE CONCEPT *68*

wheel [*n*] *circle, revolution*
caster, circuit, circulation, circumvolution, cycle, disk, drum, gyration, gyre, hoop, pivot, pulley, ratchet, ring, roll, roller, rotation, round, spin, trolley, turn, twirl, whirl; SEE CONCEPTS *436,464,502*

wheel [*v*] *turn, rotate*
circle, gyrate, orbit, pirouette, pivot, reel, revolve, roll, spin, swing, swivel, trundle, twirl, whirl; SEE CONCEPT *147*

wheeze [*v*] *breathe roughly, heavily*
buzz, catch one's breath, cough, gasp, hiss, murmur, pant, puff, rasp, sibilate, snore, whisper, whistle; SEE CONCEPTS *163,308*

when [*conj*] *though*
albeit, although, at, at the same time, during, howbeit, immediately upon, just after, just as, meanwhile, much as, whereas, while; SEE CONCEPT *799*

where [*n*] *place*
location, locus, point, position, site, situation, spot, station; SEE CONCEPT *198*

where/wherever [*adv*] *at which point*
anywhere, everywhere, in whatever place, in

which, to what end, to which, whereabouts, whither; SEE CONCEPT *583*

whet [*v1*] *make sharp*
edge, file, finish, grind, hone, sharpen, strop; SEE CONCEPTS *137,250*

whet [*v2*] *arouse, excite*
animate, awaken, challenge, enhance, incite, increase, kindle, pique, provoke, quicken, rally, rouse, stimulate, stir, wake, wake; SEE CONCEPTS *7,11,22*

whiff [*n*] *smell of an odor*
aroma, blast, breath, dash, draught, flatus, fume, gust, hint, inhalation, odor, puff, scent, shade, smack, sniff, snuff, soupçon, trace, trifle, waft; SEE CONCEPTS *599,601,602*

while [*conj1*] *as long as*
although, at, at the same time, during, during the time, in the time, throughout the time, whilst; SEE CONCEPT *799*

while [*conj2*] *even though*
albeit, although, howbeit, much as, though, when, whereas; SEE CONCEPT *544*

while [*n*] *time interval*
bit, instant, interim, meantime, moment, occasion, period, space, spell, stretch, time; SEE CONCEPTS *807,822*

whim [*n*] *sudden idea*
caprice, conceit, craze, desire, disposition, dream, fad, fancy, fantasy, freak, humor, impulse, inclination, notion, passing thought, quirk, sport, thought, urge, vagary, vision, whimsy; SEE CONCEPTS *529,661*

whimper [*v*] *cry softly*
bleat, blubber, complain, fuss, mewl, moan, object, pule, snivel, sob, weep, whine; SEE CONCEPTS *77,185*

whimsical [*adj*] *playful, fanciful*
amusing, arbitrary, capricious, chancy, chimerical, comical, curious, dicey, droll, eccentric, erratic, fantastic, flaky*, freakish, funny, kinky*, mischievous, odd, peculiar, quaint, queer*, quizzical, singular, uncertain, unpredictable, unusual, waggish, wayward, weird*; SEE CONCEPTS *401,548*

whine [*n*] *complaint, cry*
gripe, grouse, grumble, moan, plaintive cry, sob, wail, whimper; SEE CONCEPTS *54,77*

whine [*v*] *complain, cry*
bellyache, carp, drone, fuss, gripe, grouse, grumble, howl, kick, mewl, moan, murmur, pule, repine, snivel, sob, wail, whimper, yowl; SEE CONCEPTS *54,77*

whip [*n*] *length of material for hitting*
bat, belt, birch, bullwhip, cane, cat-o'-nine-tails, crop, goad, horsewhip, knout, lash, prod, push, rawhide, rod, ruler, scourge, strap, switch, thong; SEE CONCEPT *499*

whip [*v1*] *hit repeatedly*
bash, beat, birch, bludgeon, cane, castigate, chastise, cudgel, drub, ferule, flagellate, flog, hide, larrup*, lash, lather*, punish, scourge, spank, strap, strike, switch, tan, thrash, trash, wallop, whale, whomp*; SEE CONCEPT *189*

whip [*v2*] *defeat soundly*
beat, best, blast, clobber, conquer, drub, hammer*, kill*, lambaste, lick*, mop up*, outdo, overcome, overpower, overrun, overwhelm, put away*, rout, run circles around*, settle, steamroller*, subdue, take apart*, thrash, top, trim*,

trounce, vanquish, wallop, wax*, whomp*, worst*; SEE CONCEPT *95*

whip [*v3*] *dash, dart*
avert, deflect, dive, divert, flash, flit, fly, jerk, pivot, pull, rush, seize, sheer, shoot, snatch, surge, tear, turn, veer, wheel, whirl, whisk; SEE CONCEPTS *150,152*

whip [*v4*] *agitate, stir up*
beat, blend, mix, whisk, work up; SEE CONCEPTS *152,170*

whipping [*n*] *beating*
caning, flogging, licking, pasting, pounding, pummeling, punishment, spanking, tanning, thrashing, trouncing, whalloping; SEE CONCEPT *123*

whipping boy [*n*] *scapegoat*
dupe, fall guy*, goat*, mark*, patsy*, sacrifice, sucker, target, victim; SEE CONCEPT *412*

whip up [*v*] *incite, excite*
abet, agitate, arouse, compel, disturb, drive, foment, goad, hound, inflame, instigate, kindle, prick, prod, provoke, push, raise, set, set on, spur, start, stir, stir up, urge, work up; SEE CONCEPTS *14,221*

whirl [*n1*] *spin, revolution*
circle, circuit, circulation, circumvolution, flurry, gyration, gyre, pirouette, reel, roll, rotation, round, spin, surge, swirl, turn, twirl, twist, wheel, whir, whirlpool; SEE CONCEPTS *152,738*

whirl [*n2*] *commotion, confusion*
ado*, agitation, bustle, clatter, daze, dither, ferment, flurry, fluster, flutter, furor, fuss, hubbub*, hurly-burly*, hurry, merry-go-round*, moil, pother, round, ruction, rush, series, spin, stir, storm, succession, tempest, tumult, turbulence, uproar, whirlwind; SEE CONCEPTS *230,388*

whirl [*n3*] *attempt*
bash, crack, fling, go, pop, shot, slap, stab, try, whack*; SEE CONCEPT *87*

whirl [*v*] *spin around*
circle, eddy, gyrate, gyre, pirouette, pivot, purl, reel, revolve, roll, rotate, swirl, swoosh, turn, turn around, twirl, twist, wheel, whir; SEE CONCEPT *152*

whirlpool [*n*] *spinning water*
eddy, maelstrom, stir, undercurrent, undertow, vortex, whirl; SEE CONCEPT *514*

whirlwind [*adj*] *very fast*
cyclonic, hasty, headlong, hurricane, impetuous, impulsive, lightning, quick, rapid, rash, short, speedy, swift, tornado; SEE CONCEPTS *588,798*

whisk [*v*] *brush quickly; hasten*
barrel, bullet, dart, dash, flick, flit, flutter, fly, hurry, race, rush, shoot, speed, sweep, tear, whip, whiz, wipe, zip; SEE CONCEPT *152*

whisper [*n1*] *rumor; information expressed in soft voice*
buzz*, confidence, disclosure, divulgence, gossip, hint, hum, hushed tone, innuendo, insinuation, low voice, mumble, murmur, mutter, report, secret, secret message, sigh, sighing, susurration, undertone, word; SEE CONCEPTS *274,278*

whisper [*n2*] *trace, suggestion*
breath, dash, fraction, hint, shade, shadow, soupçon, suspicion, tinge, touch, whiff; SEE CONCEPTS *529,673,831*

whisper [*v*] *speak softly*
breathe, buzz*, confide, gossip, hint, hiss, insinuate, intimate, mumble, murmur, mutter, say softly, say under one's breath*, sibilate, sigh,

we
wh

speak confidentially, spread rumor, susurrate, talk into someone's ear*, talk low, tell, tell a secret; SEE CONCEPTS 60,266

whistle [v] *make sharp, shrill sound*
blare, blast, fife, flute, hiss, pipe, shriek, signal, skirl, sound, toot, tootle, trill, warble, wheeze, whine, whiz*; SEE CONCEPTS 65,77

whit [n] *very tiny bit*
atom, crumb, dash, drop, fragment, grain, hoot*, iota, jot, little, mite, modicum, particle, piece, pinch, scrap, shred, speck, trace; SEE CONCEPTS 831,835

white [adj] *extremely pale; lacking color*
achromatic, achromic, alabaster, ashen, blanched, bleached, bloodless, chalky, clear, fair, frosted, ghastly, hoary, immaculate, ivory, light, milky, neutral, pallid, pasty, pearly, silver, silvery, snowy, transparent, wan, waxen; SEE CONCEPT 618

whiten [v] *make or become extremely pale*
blanch, bleach, blench, chalk, decolor, decolorize, dull, etiolate, fade, frost, grizzle, lighten, pale, silver, turn pale, white, whitewash; SEE CONCEPT 250

whitewash [v] *cover up the truth*
blanch, camouflage, conceal, exonerate, extenuate, gloss over, launder*, liberate, make light of*, paint, palliate, sugarcoat*, suppress, varnish, veneer, vindicate, white, whiten; SEE CONCEPTS 49,63

whittle [v] *cut away at; reduce*
carve, chip, consume, decrease, diminish, eat away, erode, fashion, form, hew, lessen, model, mold, pare, sculpt, shape, shave, trim, undermine, wear away; SEE CONCEPTS 176,184,236, 247

whiz [n] *very intelligent person*
adept, expert, genius, gifted person, marvel, pro*, prodigy, professional, star, virtuoso, wonder; SEE CONCEPT 416

whiz [v] *move quickly by*
bullet, buzz, dart, flit, fly, hiss, hum, hurry, hurtle, race, speed, swish, whir, whirl, whisk, whoosh*, zip; SEE CONCEPT 150

whole [adj1] *entire, complete*
accomplished, aggregate, all, choate, completed, concentrated, conclusive, consummate, every, exclusive, exhaustive, fixed, fulfilled, full, full-length, gross, inclusive, in one piece, integral, outright, perfect, plenary, rounded, total, unabbreviated, unabridged, uncut, undivided, unexpurgated, unqualified, utter; SEE CONCEPT 531

whole [adj2] *unbroken, perfect*
complete, completed, developed, faultless, flawless, good, in good order*, in one piece*, intact, inviolate, mature, mint, plenary, preserved, replete, safe, ship-shape, solid, sound, thorough, together, undamaged, unharmed, unhurt, unimpaired, uninjured, unmarred, unmutilated, unscathed, untouched, without a scratch; SEE CONCEPTS 485,574

whole [adj3] *healthy*
able-bodied, better, cured, fit, hale, healed, hearty, in fine fettle, in good health, recovered, right, robust, sane, sound, strong, well, wholesome; SEE CONCEPT 314

whole [n] *total made up of parts*
aggregate, aggregation, all, amount, assemblage, assembly, being, big picture, body, bulk, coherence, collectivity, combination, complex, ensemble, entirety, entity, everything, fullness, gross, hook line and sinker*, integral, jackpot*, linkage, lock stock and barrel*, lot, lump, oneness, organism, organization, piece, quantity, quantum, result, sum, summation, sum total*, supply, system, the works*, totality, unit, unity, whole ball of wax*, whole enchilada*, whole nine yards*, whole shebang*; SEE CONCEPTS 432,635,837

wholehearted/whole-hearted [adj] *enthusiastic, sincere*
abiding, ardent, authentic, bona fide, candid, committed, complete, dedicated, determined, devoted, earnest, emphatic, enduring, fervent, frank, genuine, heartfelt, hearty, impassioned, never-failing, passionate, real, serious, steadfast, steady, sure, true, unfaltering, unfeigned, unqualified, unquestioning, unreserved, unstinting, unwavering, warm, zealous; SEE CONCEPTS 542,548,582

wholesale [adj] *all-inclusive*
broad, bulk, complete, comprehensive, extensive, far-reaching, general, in bulk, indiscriminate, in quantity, in the mass, large-scale, mass, overall, quantitative, sweeping, total, wide-ranging, widespread; SEE CONCEPTS 771,772

wholesome [adj] *healthy, decent*
all there, beneficial, clean, edifying, ethical, exemplary, fit, good, hale, healthful, health-giving, helpful, honorable, hygienic, in fine feather*, innocent, in the pink*, invigorating, moral, nice, normal, nourishing, nutritious, nutritive, pure, respectable, restorative, right, righteous, safe, salubrious, salutary, sane, sanitary, sound, strengthening, together, virtuous, well, worthy; SEE CONCEPTS 314,462,537,545

wholly [adv1] *completely, entirely*
all, all in all*, all the way*, altogether, comprehensively, from A to Z*, fully, heart and soul*, in every respect*, in toto, one hundred percent*, outright, perfectly, quite, roundly, thoroughly, top to bottom*, totally, utterly, well; SEE CONCEPTS 531,772

wholly [adv2] *exclusively*
individually, just, only, purely, solely, specifically, without exception; SEE CONCEPT 557

whoop [n/v] *hurrah*
bellow, boo, cheer, cry, cry out, holler, hoot, howl, jeer, scream, shout, shriek, squawk, yell; SEE CONCEPT 77

whopping [adj] *enormous*
big, colossal, extraordinary, gargantuan, giant, gigantic, great, huge, immense, large, mammoth, massive, mighty, monstrous, mountainous, prodigious, tremendous; SEE CONCEPTS 773,781

whore [n] *prostitute*
call girl, escort, fallen woman, harlot, hooker*, hustler, lady of the evening*, pro*, slut, street-walker, strumpet, tramp, working girl*; SEE CONCEPT 412

whorehouse [n] *brothel*
bagnio, bawdy house*, bordello, call house*, cathouse*, den of iniquity*, house of assignation, house of ill fame*, house of ill repute, house of prostitution, house with red doors*, massage parlor, red-light district; SEE CONCEPT 449

whorl [n] *spiral*
coil, corkscrew, curl, eddy, helix, swirl, twirl, twist, vortex, whirlpool; SEE CONCEPT 436

wicked [*adj1*] *corrupt, bad*
abandoned, abominable, amoral, arch, atrocious, bad news*, base, contemptible, debased, degenerate, depraved, devilish, dissolute, egregious, evil, fiendish, flagitious, foul, gross, guilty, heartless, heinous, immoral, impious, impish, incorrigible, indecent, iniquitous, irreligious, lowdown, mean, mischievous, nasty, naughty, nefarious, profane, reprobate, rotten, scandalous, shameful, shameless, sinful, unethical, unprincipled, unrighteous, vicious, vile, villainous, wayward, worthless; SEE CONCEPTS *401,545*

wicked [*adj2*] *destructive, troublesome*
acute, agonizing, awful, barbarous, bothersome, chancy, crashing, dangerous, difficult, distressing, dreadful, fearful, fierce, galling, harmful, hazardous, injurious, intense, mean, mighty, offensive, outrageous, painful, perilous, pesky, risky, severe, terrible, treacherous, troublous, trying, ugly, uncivilized, unconscionable, ungodly, unhealthy, unholy, unpleasant, unsound, vexatious; SEE CONCEPTS *537,565,571*

wicked [*adj3*] *expert*
able, adept, adroit, au fait, capable, clever, competent, deft, good, masterly, mighty, outstanding, powerful, pretty, qualified, skillful, strong; SEE CONCEPT *527*

wide [*adj1*] *expansive, roomy*
advanced, all-inclusive, ample, baggy, broad, capacious, catholic, commodious, comprehensive, deep, dilated, distended, encyclopedic, expanded, extensive, far-ranging, far-reaching, full, general, immense, inclusive, large, large-scale, liberal, loose, open, outspread, outstretched, progressive, radical, scopic, spacious, splay, squat, sweeping, tolerant, universal, vast, voluminous; SEE CONCEPTS *772,773,796*

wide [*adj2*] *off-course*
astray, away, distant, far, far-off, inaccurate, off, off-target, off the mark, remote; SEE CONCEPTS *581,583*

wide-awake [*adj*] *alert*
active, all ears*, attentive, bright, bright-eyed and bushy-tailed*, fast on the draw*, heads up*, intelligent, lively, on guard*, on one's toes*, on the ball*, on the job*, on the lookout*, psyched up*, quick, ready, sharp, spirited, vigilant, watchful, wired*; SEE CONCEPTS *402,403*

widen [*v*] *open up*
add to, augment, broaden, dilate, distend, enlarge, expand, extend, grow, grow larger, increase, multiply, open, open out, open wide, ream, spread, spread out, stretch, swell, unfold; SEE CONCEPTS *236,245,780*

widespread [*adj*] *extensive*
across the board*, all over the place*, boundless, broad, common, comprehensive, current, diffuse, epidemic, far-flung, far-reaching, general, on a large scale, outspread, overall, pandemic, pervasive, popular, prevailing, prevalent, public, rampant, regnant, rife, ruling, sweeping, universal, unlimited, unrestricted, wall-to-wall*, wholesale; SEE CONCEPTS *530,536,772*

widget [*n*] *gadget*
apparatus, appliance, contraption, contrivance, device, doodad*, doohickey*, gizmo*, invention, object, thing*, thingamabob*, thingamajig*, tool, whatchamacallit*; SEE CONCEPTS *463,499*

width [*n*] *breadth, wideness of some amount*
amplitude, area, broadness, compass, cross measure, diameter, distance across, expanse, extent, girth, measure, range, reach, scope, span, squatness, stretch, thickness; SEE CONCEPTS *760,788,792*

wield [*v*] *control, use*
apply, brandish, command, conduct, employ, exercise, exert, flourish, handle, have, have at one's disposal, hold, maintain, make use of, manage, maneuver, manipulate, operate, ply, possess, put to use, shake, swing, throw, utilize, wave, work; SEE CONCEPTS *94,147,225*

wife [*n*] *married woman*
bride, companion, consort, helpmate, mate, monogamist, other half*, partner, roommate, spouse; SEE CONCEPTS *414,415*

wig [*n*] *hairpiece*
false hair, hair extension, hair implant, hairpiece, hair weaving, periwig, peruke, postiche, rug*, toupee; SEE CONCEPT *392*

wiggle [*n/v*] *shake back and forth*
jerk, jiggle, shimmy, squirm, twist, twitch, wag, waggle, wave, worm, wriggle, writhe, zigzag; SEE CONCEPTS *80,150,152*

wild [*adj1*] *untamed*
agrarian, barbarian, barbaric, barbarous, dense, desert, deserted, desolate, escaped, feral, ferocious, fierce, free, indigenous, lush, luxuriant, native, natural, neglected, overgrown, overrun, primitive, rampant, rude, savage, unbroken, uncivilized, uncultivated, undomesticated, uninhabited, untouched, vicious, waste; SEE CONCEPTS *406,583*

wild [*adj2*] *disorderly, rowdy*
avid, berserk, boisterous, chaotic, crazed, crazy, eager, enthusiastic, extravagant, flighty, foolhardy, foolish, giddy, hysterical, impetuous, impracticable, imprudent, incautious, irrational, lawless, licentious, mad, madcap, noisy, nuts, outrageous, preposterous, profligate, rabid, rash, raving, reckless, riotous, rough, self-willed, turbulent, unbridled, uncontrolled, undisciplined, unfettered, ungovernable, unmanageable, unrestrained, unruly, uproarious, violent, wayward; SEE CONCEPT *401*

wild [*adj3*] *intense, stormy*
blustering, blustery, choppy, disturbed, furious, howling, inclement, raging, rough, storming, tempestuous, turbulent, violent; SEE CONCEPTS *525,569*

wilderness/wilds [*n*] *uninhabited area*
back country, back of beyond*, badland, barrens, boondocks, bush, desert, forest, hinterland, jungle, middle of nowhere*, outback, primeval forest, sticks*, waste, wasteland, wild; SEE CONCEPT *517*

wile [*n*] *cunning*
angle, artfulness, artifice, cheating, chicane, chicanery, con*, contrivance, craft, craftiness, deceit, deception, device, dishonesty, dissimulation, dodge, feint, flimflam*, fraud, gambit, game, gimmick, guile, hoax, horseplay, imposition, little game*, lure, maneuver, monkey business*, monkeyshines*, plot, ploy, racket*, ruse, scam*, scheming, setup*, shenanigans*, skullduggery*, slant, slyness, stratagem, stunt, subterfuge, switch, trick, trickery, twist; SEE CONCEPTS *59,63*

wh
wi

will [*n1*] *personal choice*
aim, appetite, attitude, character, conviction, craving, decision, decisiveness, decree, design, desire, determination, discipline, discretion, disposition, fancy, feeling, hankering, heart's desire*, inclination, intention, liking, longing, mind, option, passion, pining, pleasure, power, preference, prerogative, purpose, resolution, resolve, self-control, self-discipline, self-restraint, temperament, urge, velleity, volition, willfulness, willpower, wish, wishes, yearning; SEE CONCEPTS *20,411,659*

will [*n2*] *last wishes; command*
bequest, bestowal, declaration, decree, device, directions, dispensation, disposition, estate, heritage, inheritance, insistence, instructions, legacy, order, property, testament; SEE CONCEPT *318*

will [*vl*] *cause*
authorize, bid, bring about, command, decide on, decree, demand, determine, direct, effect, enjoin, exert, insist, intend, ordain, order, request, resolve; SEE CONCEPT *242*

will [*v2*] *choose*
be inclined, crave, desire, elect, have a mind to*, incline, like, opt, please, prefer, see fit*, want, wish; SEE CONCEPT *20*

will [*v3*] *give, bequeath to another*
bequest, confer, cut off, devise, disherit, disinherit, leave, legate, pass on, probate, transfer; SEE CONCEPTS *108,317*

willful [*adj1*] *stubborn, obstinate*
adamant, bullheaded, contumacious, determined, dogged, fractious, froward, headstrong, inflexible, intractable, intransigent, mulish, obdurate, persistent, pertinacious, perverse, pigheaded, refractory, resolved, self-willed, stiffnecked, uncompromising, unyielding; SEE CONCEPTS *401,542*

willful [*adj2*] *voluntary*
conscious, contemplated, deliberate, designed, intended, intentional, planned, premeditated, purposeful, studied, unforced, volitional, willed, willing, witting; SEE CONCEPTS *401,535*

willing [*adj*] *agreeable, ready*
accommodating, active, amenable, cheerful, compliant, consenting, content, deliberate, desirous, disposed, eager, energetic, enthusiastic, fair, favorable, feeling, forward, game, go along with, happy, in accord with, inclined, in favor, intentional, in the mood, like-minded, obedient, one, pleased, predisposed, prepared, prompt, prone, reliable, responsible, tractable, unasked, unbidden, unforced, voluntary, well-disposed, willful, witting, zealous; SEE CONCEPTS *401,403,576*

willowy [*adj*] *graceful, slender*
adroit, agile, dainty, delicate, elastic, elegant, flowing, limber, lithe, lithesome, nimble, pliant, shapely, skinny, springy, svelte, thin, trim; SEE CONCEPTS *579,584,589*

willpower [*n*] *personal determination*
discipline, drive, firmness, fixity, force, grit, resolution, resolve, self-control, self-discipline, self-government, self-restraint, single-mindedness, strength, will; SEE CONCEPT *411*

wilt [*v*] *sag, fail*
become limp, break down, cave in, collapse, diminish, droop, drop, dry up, dwindle, ebb, fade, faint, flag, give out, languish, melt, mummify, shrivel, sink, succumb, wane, waste, waste away, weaken, wither, wizen; SEE CONCEPTS *181,427,469,699*

wily [*adj*] *crafty, clever*
arch, artful, astute, cagey, crazy like a fox*, crooked, cunning, deceitful, deceptive, deep, designing, foxy, greasy*, guileful, insidious, intriguing, knowing, sagacious, scheming, sharp, shifty, shrewd, slick*, slippery*, sly, smooth, sneaky, streetwise, tricky, underhanded; SEE CONCEPTS *401,545*

wimp [*n*] *weakling*
baby, caitiff, chicken*, chicken heart*, chicken liver*, coward, cream puff*, crybaby, daisy*, featherweight*, fraidy-cat*, jellyfish*, lily liver, loser, milksop, momma's boy*, namby-pamby, pansy, pantywaist*, puppy*, pushover, scaredy cat*, schlemiel*, sissy, wuss*, wussy*, yellow belly*; SEE CONCEPTS *412,423*

win [*n*] *victory*
accomplishment, achievement, conquest, gain, gold*, gold star*, kill*, killing*, pay dirt*, score, slam, success, sweep, triumph; SEE CONCEPTS *95,141,832*

win [*vl*] *finish first; succeed*
achieve, beat, be first, be victorious, carry the day*, come in first, conquer, edge, finish in front*, finish off, gain, gain victory, overcome, overwhelm, prevail, run circles around*, shut out*, sink*, take the prize, triumph, upset, walk away with*, walk off with*; SEE CONCEPTS *95,141,363*

win [*v2*] *achieve, obtain*
accomplish, acquire, annex, approach, attain, bag*, bring in, catch, collect, come away with*, derive, earn, effect, gain, get, harvest, have, make, net, pick up, procure, rack up*, reach, realize, receive, score, secure; SEE CONCEPTS *120,706*

win/win over [*v3*] *influence, persuade*
allure, argue into, attract, bring around, carry, charm, convert, convince, disarm, draw, get, induce, overcome, prevail upon, prompt, sway, talk into, wow*; SEE CONCEPTS *11,68*

wince [*v*] *draw back*
back off, blanch, blench, cower, cringe, dodge, duck, flinch, grimace, jib, make a face*, quail, recoil, shrink, shy, start, swerve, turn; SEE CONCEPTS *154,185*

wind [*n1*] *air currents*
air, blast, blow, breath, breeze, chinook, cyclone, draft, draught, flurry, flutter, gale, gust, mistral, puff, tempest, typhoon, wafting, whiff, whirlwind, whisk, zephyr; SEE CONCEPT *524*

wind [*n2*] *warning, report*
babble, clue, cue, gossip, hint, hot air*, idle talk, inkling, intimation, notice, rumor, suggestion, talk, tidings, whisper; SEE CONCEPT *278*

wind [*v*] *bend, turn*
coil, convolute, corkscrew, cover, crook, curl, curve, deviate, distort, encircle, enclose, envelop, fold, furl, loop, meander, ramble, reel, roll, screw, slither, snake, spiral, swerve, twine, twist, weave, wrap, wreathe, wriggle, zigzag; SEE CONCEPTS *201,738*

windbag [*n*] *bigmouth, chatterer*
bag of wind*, big talker*, blabberer, blowhard*, boaster, braggart, bragger, gasbag*, gascon*, jabberer, know-it-all, motor-mouth*; SEE CONCEPTS *412,423*

windfall [n] *jackpot, profit*
bonanza, bonus, find, fortune, gift from the gods*, godsend, gravy*, lucky find, money from heaven*, pennies from heaven*, stroke of luck; SEE CONCEPTS 337,679

winding [adj] *bending, turning*
ambiguous, anfractuous, circuitous, convoluted, crooked, curving, devious, flexuous, gyrating, indirect, intricate, involved, labyrinthine, mazy, meandering, roundabout, serpentine, sinuous, snaky, spiraling, tortuous, twisting, wriggly, zigzag; SEE CONCEPTS 581,584

wind up [v] *finish*
be through with, bring to a close, clean up*, close, close down, come to the end, complete, conclude, determine, do, end, end up*, finalize, finish up, halt, liquidate, settle, terminate, tie up loose ends*, wrap up*; SEE CONCEPT 234

windy [adj1] *breezy*
airy, blowing, blowy, blustering, blustery, boisterous, brisk, drafty, fresh, gusty, raw, squally, stormy, tempestuous, wild, windswept; SEE CONCEPT 525

windy [adj2] *talkative; boastful*
bombastic, diffuse, empty, garrulous, inflated, lengthy, long-winded, loquacious, meandering, palaverous, pompous, prolix, rambling, redundant, turgid, verbose, wordy; SEE CONCEPT 267

wing [n1] *organ, device of flight*
aileron, airfoil, appendage, feather, pennon, pinion; SEE CONCEPTS 399,502

wing [n2] *section; extension*
addition, adjunct, annex, arm, block, branch, bulge, circle, clique, coterie, detachment, division, ell, expansion, faction, group, part, projection, prolongation, protrusion, protuberance, section, segment, set, side, unit; SEE CONCEPTS 440,441,824,835

wing it [v] *improvise*
ad-lib, concoct, devise, do offhand, do off the top of your head*, fake it, improv*, invent, make do*, make up, play it by ear*, speak off the cuff*, throw together*; SEE CONCEPTS 173,266

wink [n1/v] *flutter, flick*
bat, blink, flash, gleam, glimmer, glitter, nictate, nictitate, sparkle, squinch, squint, twinkle; SEE CONCEPTS 185,624

wink [n2] *moment*
flash*, instant, jiffy*, minute, second, shake*, split second*, twinkle*, twinkling*; SEE CONCEPTS 808,821

winner [n] *someone or something that succeeds*
champ, champion, conquering hero, conqueror, first, hero, medalist, medalwinner, number one*, prizewinner, title-holder, top dog*, vanquisher, victor; SEE CONCEPTS 366,416

winning/winsome [adj1] *attractive, charming*
acceptable, adorable, agreeable, alluring, amiable, bewitching, captivating, cute, delectable, delightful, disarming, enchanting, endearing, engaging, fascinating, fetching, gratifying, lovable, lovely, pleasing, prepossessing, sweet, taking; SEE CONCEPTS 401,404

winning [adj2] *triumphant*
champion, conquering, leading, successful, victorious; SEE CONCEPTS 528,632

wino [n] *drunk*
alcoholic, boozer*, bum*, carouser*, dipsomaniac, drinker, drunkard, guzzler*, hobo, inebriate, lush*, sot*, sponge*; SEE CONCEPT 423

winsome [adj] *charming*
absorbing, alluring, appealing, attractive, captivating, charismatic, cute, dainty, delicate, delightful, desirable, elegant, enamoring, engaging, enthralling, eye-catching, fascinating, glamorous, inviting, irresistible, lovable, pleasant, pleasing, pretty, rapturous, ravishing, seducing, seductive, sweet, tantalizing, titillating, winning; SEE CONCEPT 404

winter [n] *cold season of the year*
chill, cold, frost, Jack Frost*, wintertide, wintertime; SEE CONCEPT 814

wintry [adj] *cold, snowy*
biting, bleak, brumal, chilly, cutting, desolate, dismal, freezing, frigid, frosty, frozen, harsh, hibernal, hiemal, icebox*, icy, raw, snappy, three-dog night*; SEE CONCEPTS 525,605

wipe [v] *brush, swab*
clean, clean off, clear, dry, dust, erase, mop, obliterate, remove, rub, sponge, take away, towel, wash; SEE CONCEPT 165

wipeout [n] *fall*
collapse, crash, destruction, dive, downfall, drop, spill, tumble, yard sale*; SEE CONCEPTS 116,230, 674,699

wipe out [v] *destroy; get rid of*
abate, abolish, annihilate, black out, blot out, cancel, decimate, delete, efface, eliminate, eradicate, erase, expunge, exterminate, extinguish, extirpate, kill, massacre, obliterate, remove, root out, slaughter, slay, uproot, X-out*; SEE CONCEPT 252

wiry [adj] *thin and strong*
agile, athletic, bristly, fibrous, lean, light, limber, muscular, ropy, sinewy, stiff, strapping, stringy, supple, tough; SEE CONCEPTS 490,491

wisdom [n] *insight, common sense*
acumen, astuteness, balance, brains*, caution, circumspection, clear thinking, comprehension, discernment, discrimination, enlightenment, erudition, experience, foresight, good judgment, gumption*, horse sense*, information, intelligence, judgment, judiciousness, knowledge, learning, pansophy, penetration, perspicacity, poise, practicality, prudence, reason, sagacity, sageness, sanity, sapience, savoir faire, savvy*, shrewdness, solidity, sophistication, stability, understanding; SEE CONCEPT 409

wise [adj] *intelligent, reasonable*
astute, aware, calculating, careful, clever, cogitative, contemplative, crafty, cunning, discerning, discreet, educated, enlightened, erudite, experienced, foresighted, grasping, informed, insightful, intuitive, judicious, keen, knowing, knowledgeable, perceptive, perspicacious, politic, prudent, rational, reflective, sagacious, sage, sane, sapient, scholarly, sensible, sensing, sharp, shrewd, smart, sophic, sound, tactful, taught, thoughtful, understanding, wary, well-informed, witty; SEE CONCEPT 402

wisecrack [n] *joke*
antic, caper, clowning, dig, escapade, farce, frolic, gag, lark, laugh, mischief, monkeyshine*, one-liner*, parody, prank, put-on, quip, remark, retort, rib, shenanigan*, smart crack*, stunt, trick, witticism, yarn, zinger*; SEE CONCEPT 273

wise guy [n] *smart-aleck; gangster*
bigmouth*, criminal, crook, hood, hoodlum, know-it-all*, Mafioso*, member of the family,

wi
wi

mobster, smart ass*, smarty-pants*, wiseacre, wiseass, wisenheimer; SEE CONCEPT *412*

wish [*n*] *desire*
ambition, aspiration, choice, disposition, hankering, hope, hunger, inclination, intention, invocation, itch, liking, longing, pleasure, prayer, preference, request, thirst, urge, want, whim, will, yearning, yen; SEE CONCEPTS *20,709*

wish [*v*] *desire*
aspire, beg, choose, command, covet, crave, desiderate, elect, entreat, envy, expect, fancy, hanker*, hope, hunger, invoke, itch, like, long, look forward to*, need, order, please, pray for, prefer, request, set one's heart on*, sigh for, solicit, spoil for*, thirst, want, will, yearn, yen; SEE CONCEPT *20*

wishful [*adj*] *desirous*
acquisitive, ambitious, aspiring, craving, daydreaming, desiring, greedy, hankering, hopeful, itchy*, keen, longful, longing, lustful, wishing, yearning; SEE CONCEPTS *403,529*

wishy-washy [*adj*] *bland, dull*
banal, characterless, cowardly, enervated, feeble, flat, flavorless, indecisive, ineffective, ineffectual, insipid, irresolute, jejune, languid, listless, mediocre, namby-pamby*, sapless, spiritless, tasteless, thin, vacillating, vapid, watered-down, watery, wavering, weak, weak-kneed*; SEE CONCEPT *404*

wisp [*n*] *strand*
bit, lock, piece, shock, shred, snippet, string, thread, tuft, twist; SEE CONCEPTS *392,831*

wistful [*adj*] *daydreaming, longing*
contemplative, desirous, disconsolate, dreaming, dreamy, forlorn, hopeless, meditative, melancholy, mournful, musing, nostalgic, pensive, plaintive, reflective, sad, thoughtful, wishful, yearning; SEE CONCEPT *403*

wit [*n1*] *humor*
aphorism, badinage, banter, bon mot, burlesque, drollery, facetiousness, fun, gag, jest, jocularity, joke, lark, levity, pleasantry, practical joke, prank, pun, quip, raillery, repartee, sally, satire, trick, whimsicality, wisecrack, wittiness, wordplay; SEE CONCEPTS *59,273,411*

wit [*n2*] *person who is very funny*
a million laughs*, banterer, card, comedian, comic, cutup*, epigrammatist, farceur, funster, gag person, humorist, jester, joker, jokesmith, jokester, life of the party*, madcap, punster, quipster, trickster, wag, wisecracker; SEE CONCEPTS *352,416*

witch [*n*] *person who casts spells over others*
conjurer, enchanter, magician, necromancer, occultist, sorcerer; SEE CONCEPTS *361,412,415*

witchcraft [*n*] *spell-casting, magic*
abracadabra*, bewitchment, black art, black magic, charisma, conjuring, divination, enchantment, hocus-pocus*, hoodoo*, incantation, jinx, magnetism, mumbo-jumbo*, necromancy, occult, occultism, sorcery, spell, thaumaturgy, voodoo, voodooism, whammy*, witchery, witching, wizardry; SEE CONCEPTS *367,370,689*

witch doctor [*n*] *shaman*
healer, medicine man, priest, sorcerer, wizard; SEE CONCEPT *361*

withdraw [*v1*] *remove something or someone from situation*
abjure, absent oneself, back out, bail out, blow, book, bow out, check out, depart, detach, disen-

gage, draw away, draw back, drop out, ease out, eliminate, exfiltrate, exit, extract, fall back, get away, get lost, get off, give ground, give way, go, keep aloof, keep apart, leave, make oneself scarce*, phase out, pull back, pull out, quail, quit, recede, recoil, retire, retreat, run along, secede, seclude oneself, shrink, switch, take a hike*, take away, take leave, take off, take out, vacate; SEE CONCEPTS *195,211*

withdraw [*v2*] *retract; declare void*
abjure, abolish, abrogate, annul, ban, bar, call off, disavow, disclaim, dissolve, forswear, invalidate, nullify, quash, recall, recant, renege, renig, repress, repudiate, rescind, retire, reverse, revoke, stamp out, suppress, take back, unsay; SEE CONCEPTS *50,88,121,697*

withdrawal [*n*] *removal; retraction*
abandonment, abdication, abjuration, alienation, departure, disavowal, disclaimer, disengagement, egress, egression, exit, exiting, exodus, extraction, marooning, palinode, recall, recantation, relinquishment, repudiation, rescission, resignation, retirement, retreat, revocation, revulsion, secession; SEE CONCEPTS *195,211,685*

withdrawn [*adj1*] *unsociable*
aloof, aseptic, casual, cool, detached, disinterested, distant, incurious, indifferent, introverted, nongregarious, offish, quiet, recluse, reclusive, remote, reserved, restrained, retired, retiring, retreated, shrinking, shy, silent, solitary, standoffish, taciturn, timorous, uncommunicative, uncompanionable, unconcerned, uncurious, undemonstrative, unforthcoming, uninterested; SEE CONCEPT *401*

withdrawn [*adj2*] *hidden, remote*
cloistered, departed, isolated, out-of-the-way, private, recluse, removed, retreated, secluded, solitary, taken out; SEE CONCEPT *583*

wither [*v*] *droop, decline*
atrophy, become stale, blast, blight, collapse, constrict, contract, decay, deflate, desiccate, deteriorate, die, disintegrate, dry, dry up, fade, fold, languish, perish, shrink, shrivel, wane, waste, waste away, wilt, wizen; SEE CONCEPTS *427,698*

withhold [*v*] *keep back*
abstain, bridle, check, clam up*, conceal, constrain, curb, deduct, deny, detain, disallow, dummy up*, hide, hold, hold back, hold down, hold out, hold out on, inhibit, keep, keep secret, keep to oneself*, keep under one's hat*, keep under wraps*, kill, refrain, refuse, repress, reserve, resist, restrain, retain, sit on, spike, stop oneself, suppress; SEE CONCEPTS *35,121,188*

within [*adv*] *inside*
in, in a period, indoors, inner, in reach, interior, inward, not beyond, not outside, not over; SEE CONCEPTS *586,772*

with it [*adj*] *cognizant; stylish*
alive, apprehensive, au courant, awake, aware, chic, conscious, cool*, familiar, groovy*, hep to*, hip to*, in, in fashion, informed, in, in the know, in vogue, knowing, knowledgeable, latest, mod*, now*, observant, on to*, perceptive, plugged in, savvy, switched on*, trendy, tuned in*, turned on*, up on*, versed, wise to*; SEE CONCEPTS *402,579,589*

without [*adv*] *outside*
after, beyond, externally, left out, on the outside, out, outdoors, out-of-doors, outwardly, past; SEE CONCEPTS *586,772*

withstand [*v*] *endure, bear*
brace, brave, buck, combat, confront, contest, cope, cross, defy, dispute, duel, face, fight, fly in the face of*, grapple with, hang on*, hang tough*, hold off*, hold one's ground*, hold out*, oppose, prevail against, put up struggle*, put up with*, remain firm, repel, resist, ride out*, sit and take it*, stand, stand fast*, stand firm*, stand one's ground*, stand up against*, stand up to*, stick*, stick fast*, suffer, take, take it*, take on, thwart, tolerate, traverse, violate, weather, win out; SEE CONCEPTS *23,96*

witless [*adj*] *foolish*
absurd, asinine, birdbrained*, brainless, cockamamy*, crazy, daffy*, doltish*, dotty*, dumb, feebleminded*, half-baked*, half-witted*, harebrained*, idiotic, ill-advised, irrational, jerky*, kooky*, loony*, ludicrous, lunatic, mad, mindless, moronic, nonsensical, nutty*, ridiculous, senseless, silly, stupid, unintelligent, unwise, wacky*, zany*; SEE CONCEPTS *401,542,544*

witness [*n*] *person who observes an event*
attestant, attestor, beholder, bystander, corroborator, deponent, eyewitness, gawker, looker-on, observer, onlooker, proof, rubbernecker*, signatory, spectator, testifier, testimony, viewer, watcher; SEE CONCEPTS *355,423*

witness [*v1*] *observe*
attend, be a witness, behold, be on hand*, be on the scene*, be present, eyeball*, flash on*, get a load of*, look on, mark, note, notice, perceive, pick up on, pipe*, read, see, sight, spot, spy, take in view, watch; SEE CONCEPT *626*

witness [*v2*] *testify; authenticate*
affirm, announce, argue, attest, bear out, bear witness, be a witness, bespeak, betoken, certify, confirm, corroborate, countersign, depone, depose, endorse, give evidence, give testimony, indicate, say under oath, sign, stand for, subscribe, vouch for; SEE CONCEPTS *49,50,88,317*

witty [*adj*] *funny and clever*
amusing, bright, brilliant, campy*, crazy*, diverting, droll, entertaining, epigrammatic, facetious, fanciful, gay, humorous, ingenious, intelligent, jocose, jocular, joshing, keen, lively, original, penetrating, piercing, piquant, quickwitted, ridiculous, scintillating, screaming*, slapstick, sparkling, waggish, whimsical; SEE CONCEPTS *267,542*

wit/wits [*n3*] *judgment, intelligence*
acumen, acuteness, astucity, astuteness, awareness, balance, brainpower, brains*, cleverness, common sense, comprehension, depth of perception, discernment, discrimination, esprit, grasp, ingenuity, insight, keenness, lucidity, marbles*, mentality, mind, perception, perspicacity, practicality, prudence, rationality, reason, sagaciousness, sagacity, sageness, saneness, sanity, sapience, sense, shrewdness, soundness, understanding, wisdom; SEE CONCEPT *409*

wizard [*n1*] *person who can perform magic*
astrologer, augurer, clairvoyant, conjurer, diviner, enchanter, fortuneteller, hypnotist, magician, magus, medium, necromancer, occultist, palmist, seer, shaman, soothsayer, sorcerer, thaumaturge, warlock, witch; SEE CONCEPT *361*

wizard [*n2*] *person who is highly skilled*
ace*, adept, artist, authority, crackerjack*, expert, genius, hot shot*, pro*, prodigy, professional, proficient, shark*, star, virtuoso, whiz*, whiz kid*, wiz*; SEE CONCEPTS *348,423*

wizened [*adj*] *dried, shriveled up*
diminished, gnarled, lean, macerated, mummified, old, reduced, shrunk, shrunken, wilted, withered, worn, wrinkled; SEE CONCEPTS *485,603*

wobble [*v*] *stagger, quake*
be unsteady, careen, falter, flounder, lurch, oscillate, quiver, reel, rock, roll, seesaw, shake, shimmy, stumble, sway, swing, teeter, totter, tremble, vacillate, vibrate, waver, weave, wiggle; SEE CONCEPTS *150,152*

wobbly [*adj*] *shaky*
fluctuant, insecure, precarious, rattletrap, rickety, rocky, teetering, tottering, unbalanced, uneven, unsafe, unstable, unsteady, unsure, vacillating, wavering, wavy, weak, wiggling; SEE CONCEPT *488*

woe [*n*] *suffering*
adversity, affliction, agony, anguish, bemoaning, blues*, burden, calamity, care, cataclysm, catastrophe, curse, dejection, deploring, depression, disaster, distress, dole, drag, gloom, grief, grieving, hardship, headache*, heartache*, heartbreak, lamentation, melancholy, misadventure, misery, misfortune, pain, rain*, regret, rue, sadness, sorrow, tragedy, trial, tribulation, trouble, unhappiness, wretchedness; SEE CONCEPTS *410,532,690, 728*

woebegone [*adj*] *depressed, troubled*
black, bleak, blue*, bummed out*, chapfallen, cheerless, crestfallen, dejected, despondent, disconsolate, dismal, dispirited, doleful, down, downcast, downhearted, down-in-the-mouth*, dreary, forlorn, gloomy, grief-stricken, grim, hangdog*, hurting, in pain*, long-faced*, low, lugubrious, melancholy, miserable, mournful, sad, shot down*, sorrowful, unhappy, woeful, wretched; SEE CONCEPT *403*

woeful [*adj*] *terrible, sad*
afflicted, agonized, anguished, appalling, awful, bad, calamitous, catastrophic, cruel, deplorable, disappointing, disastrous, disconsolate, disgraceful, distressing, doleful, dreadful, feeble, gloomy, grieving, grievous, grim, heartbreaking, heartrending, heartsick, hopeless, inadequate, lamentable, lousy*, mean, miserable, mournful, paltry, pathetic, piteous, pitiable, pitiful, plaintive, poor, racked, rotten, shocking, sorrowful, sorry, tortured, tragic, unfortunate, unhappy, wretched; SEE CONCEPTS *548,571*

wolf [*v*] *consume sloppily and fast*
bolt, cram, devour, gobble, gorge, gulp, guzzle, ingurgitate, pack, slop, slosh, stuff, swallow; SEE CONCEPT *169*

woman [*n*] *female human*
aunt, daughter, gentlewoman, girl, girlfriend, grandmother, matron, mother, Ms./Miss/Mrs., niece, she, spouse, wife; SEE CONCEPTS *414,415*

womanizer [*n*] *philanderer*
Casanova, Don Juan, gigolo, heartbreaker, ladies' man, lady-killer, lecher, libertine, lothario, lover, lover-boy*, rake, Romeo, seducer, skirt chaser, stud*, wolf*; SEE CONCEPT *423*

womanly [*adj*] *feminine*
female, girlish, ladylike, maidenly, matronly, motherly, womanish; SEE CONCEPTS *371,372, 408,648*

wi
wo

wonder [n1] *amazement*
admiration, astonishment, awe, bewilderment, concern, confusion, consternation, curiosity, doubt, fascination, fear, incredulity, jar, jolt, marveling, perplexity, perturbation, puzzlement, reverence, shock, skepticism, start, stupefaction, stupor, surprise, suspicion, uncertainty, wondering, wonderment; SEE CONCEPTS 410,532,690

wonder [n2] *something that is amazing*
act of God*, curiosity, cynosure, freak, marvel, miracle, nonpareil, oddity, phenomenon, portent, prodigy, rara avis, rarity, sensation, sight, spectacle, stunner*, wonderment; SEE CONCEPTS 529,687

wonder [v1] *doubt; ponder*
ask oneself, be curious, be inquisitive, conjecture, disbelieve, inquire, meditate, puzzle, query, question, speculate, think; SEE CONCEPTS 17,21

wonder [v2] *be amazed*
admire, be astonished, be awestruck, be confounded, be dumbstruck, be fascinated, be flabbergasted, be startled, be taken aback, boggle, gape, gawk, look aghast, marvel, stare; SEE CONCEPT 34

wonderful [adj] *great, extraordinary*
admirable, amazing, astonishing, astounding, awe-inspiring, awesome, brilliant, cool*, divine*, dynamite*, enjoyable, excellent, fabulous, fantastic, fine, groovy*, incredible, magnificent, marvelous, miraculous, outstanding, peachy*, phenomenal, pleasant, pleasing, prime, remarkable, sensational, something else*, staggering, startling, strange, stupendous, super, superb, surprising, swell, terrific, too much*, tremendous, unheard-of, wondrous; SEE CONCEPTS 529,574

wonderment [n] *astonishment*
amazement, astoundment, awe, bewilderment, curiosity, fascination, marvel, shock, stunner, surprise, wonder; SEE CONCEPTS 230,410

wonk [n] *excessive studier*
bookworm, brain*, dweeb*, geek*, greasy grind*, grind*, grub*, nerd, poindexter, swotter*; SEE CONCEPT 350

woo [v] *seek romantic partner*
address, aim for, beg, bill and coo*, butter up*, caress, charm, chase, court, cultivate, curry favor*, date, entreat, go steady, importune, keep company, make advances, make love, press one's suit with*, propose, pursue, run after, rush, seek in marriage*, seek the hand of*, set one's cap for*, solicit, spark*, spoon*; SEE CONCEPTS 297,375,384

wooden [adj1] *made of timber*
board, clapboard, frame, ligneous, log, peg, plant, slab, timber, timbered, woody; SEE CONCEPT 485

wooden [adj2] *stiff, inflexible*
awkward, bumbling, clumsy, gauche, gawky, graceless, heavy, heavy-handed, inelegant, inept, maladroit, obstinate, ponderous, rigid, stilted, unbending, ungainly, ungraceful, unhandy, unyielding, weighty; SEE CONCEPTS 488,542

wood/woods [n] *forest*
copse, grove, lumber, thicket, timber, timberland, trees, weald, woodland; SEE CONCEPTS 430,509,517

woozy [adj] *dizzy*
befuddled, bemused, bewildered, confused, dazed, dazzled, dumbfounded, faint, gaga*, giddy, groggy*, hazy, light-headed, muddled, off

balance*, punch-drunk*, punchy*, puzzled, queasy, reeling, seeing stars*, shaky, slaphappy*, staggered, staggering, tipsy, unsteady, weak in the knees*, weak-kneed*, wobbly; SEE CONCEPTS 314,480

word [n1] *discussion*
chat, chitchat*, colloquy, confab*, confabulation, consultation, conversation, discussion, talk, tête-à-tête; SEE CONCEPT 56

word [n2] *statement*
account, adage, advice, announcement, bulletin, byword, comment, communication, communiqué, declaration, directive, discourse, dispatch, expression, gossip, hearsay, information, intelligence, intimation, introduction, message, news, notice, pronouncement, proverb, remark, report, rumble, rumor, saw, saying, scuttlebutt, speech, talk, tidings, utterance; SEE CONCEPTS 274,278

word [n3] *unit of language*
concept, designation, expression, idiom, lexeme, locution, morpheme, name, phrase, sound, term, usage, utterance, vocable; SEE CONCEPT 275

word [n4] *command*
behest, bidding, charge, commandment, decree, dictate, edict, go-ahead*, green light*, injunction, mandate, order, signal, ukase, will; SEE CONCEPT 685

word [n5] *promise*
affirmation, assertion, assurance, commitment, declaration, engagement, guarantee, oath, parole, pledge, plight, solemn oath*, solemn word*, vow, warrant, word of honor; SEE CONCEPTS 71,278,689

word [n6] *password*
countersign, slogan, watchword; SEE CONCEPTS 684,685

wording [n] *way of expressing a thought*
choice of words, diction, language, locution, manner, mode, parlance, phraseology, phrasing, style, terminology, turn of phrase, wordage, words; SEE CONCEPTS 278,682

wordy [adj] *talkative*
bombastic, chatty*, diffuse, discursive, flatulent, gabby*, garrulous, inflated, lengthy, longwinded, loquacious, palaverous, pleonastic, prolix, rambling, redundant, rhetorical, tedious, turgid, verbose, voluble, windy*; SEE CONCEPT 267

work [n1] *labor, chore*
assignment, attempt, commission, daily grind*, drudge, drudgery, effort, elbow grease*, endeavor, exertion, functioning, grind, grindstone*, industry, job, moil, muscle, obligation, pains*, performance, production, push, salt mines*, servitude, slogging, stint, stress, striving, struggle, sweat*, task, toil, travail, trial, trouble, undertaking; SEE CONCEPTS 87,362,677

work [n2] *business, occupation*
activity, art, calling, commitment, contract, craft, do*, duty, employment, endeavor, gig*, grind*, industry, job, line, line of business, livelihood, métier, nine-to-five*, obligation, office, practice, profession, pursuit, racket*, responsibility, skill, slot*, specialization, stint, swindle, task, thing*, trade, vocation, walk; SEE CONCEPTS 349,351,360

work [n3] *achievement*
act, application, article, composition, creation, deed, end product, function, handicraft, handi-

work, oeuvre, opus, output, performance, piece, product, production; SEE CONCEPTS 260,706

work [v1] *be employed; exert oneself*
apply oneself, be gainfully employed, buckle down*, carry on, dig, do a job, do business, drive, drudge, earn a living*, freelance, have a job, hold a job, hustle*, knuckle down*, labor, manage, manufacture, moil, moonlight*, nine-to-five it*, peg away*, plug away*, ply, punch a clock*, pursue, report, scratch, slave, slog*, specialize, strain, strive, sweat*, take on, toil, try; SEE CONCEPTS 100,351

work [v2] *manipulate, operate*
accomplish, achieve, act, behave, bring about, carry out, cause, contrive, control, create, direct, drive, effect, execute, force, function, go, handle, implement, manage, maneuver, move, perform, ply, progress, react, run, serve, take, tick, use, wield; SEE CONCEPTS 94,117,199,204

work [v3] *cultivate, form*
care for, dig, dress, farm, fashion, handle, knead, labor, make, manipulate, mold, process, shape, tend, till; SEE CONCEPTS 173,184,257

workable [adj] *feasible*
applicable, breeze*, cinch*, doable, duck soup*, easy, easy as pie*, exploitable, functional, no sweat*, piece of cake*, possible, practicable, practical, simple as ABC*, snap, usable, useful, viable, working; SEE CONCEPTS 538,552,560

worker [n] *person who is employed*
artisan, blue collar*, breadwinner, company person, craftsperson, employee, hand, help, laborer, nine-to-fiver*, operative, peasant, proletarian, serf, slave, stiff, toiler, trader, tradesperson, wage earner, white collar*, working person, working stiff*; SEE CONCEPT 348

working [adj] *active, occupied*
alive, busy, dynamic, effective, employed, engaged, functioning, going, hot*, in a job, in force, in full swing, in gear, in process, laboring, live, moving, on fire*, on the job, on track*, operative, practical, running, useful, viable; SEE CONCEPTS 538,560

workmanship [n] *craftsmanship*
artisanship, artistry, artwork, craft, design, expertise, handicraft, handiwork, know-how*, skill, skillfulness, technique; SEE CONCEPTS 259,409,630

workout [n] *exercise, practice*
conditioning, constitutional, drill, rehearsal, routine, session, test; training, tryout, warm-up, work; SEE CONCEPTS 290,363

work out [v] *solve; satisfy*
accomplish, achieve, arrange, attain, be effective, bring off, clear, come out, come to terms*, complete, compromise, construct, contrive, develop, devise, elaborate, evolve, figure out, find out, finish, fix, form, formulate, get something done*, go, go well, handle, happen, manipulate, pan out*, plan, prosper, pull off*, put together, reach agreement, resolve, result, succeed, swing*, turn out, up, win; SEE CONCEPTS 706,713

work up [v] *stimulate*
agitate, animate, arouse, breed, cause, develop, engender, excite, generate, get up, hatch, improve, incite, induce, inflame, instigate, move, muster up, occasion, produce, rouse, spur, stir up; SEE CONCEPTS 14,242

world [n1] *planet, globe*
cosmos, creation, earth, heavenly body, macro-

cosm, microcosm, nature, sphere, star, terrene, universe; SEE CONCEPTS 511,770

world [n2] *class of existing beings*
class, division, everybody, everyone, group, humanity, humankind, human race, race, realm; SEE CONCEPTS 378,391

world [n3] *person's environment, experience*
ambience, area, atmosphere, business, domain, field, life, matters, memory, province, pursuits, realm, sphere, system; SEE CONCEPT 678

worldly [adj] *material, nonreligious*
carnal, earthly, earthy, fleshly, human, lay, materialistic, mundane, natural, physical, practical, profane, secular, sublunary, telluric, temporal, terrene, terrestrial, ungodly; SEE CONCEPTS 536,582

worldly [adj2] *sophisticated, materialistic*
avaricious, been around, blasé, callous, cool*, cosmopolitan, covetous, disenchanted, grasping, greedy, hardened, knowing, opportunistic, power-loving, practical, self-centered, selfish, unprincipled, uptown*, urbane, worldly wise; SEE CONCEPT 401

worldwide [adj] *general*
catholic, common, comprehensive, cosmic, ecumenical, extensive, global, international, multinational, omnipresent, pandemic, planetary, ubiquitous, universal; SEE CONCEPT 536

worn/worn-out [adj] *used, tired*
beat, burned out*, bushed*, busted*, clichéd, consumed, depleted, destroyed, deteriorated, drained, drawn, effete, exhausted, fatigued, frayed, gone, hackneyed, had it*, haggard, jaded, kaput*, knocked out*, old, out of gas*, overused, overworked, pinched, played out*, pooped*, ragged, ruined, shabby, shot, spent, stale, tattered, the worse for wear*, threadbare, timeworn, tired out, totaled*, used up, useless, wearied, weary, well-worn, wiped out, worn down, wrung out*; SEE CONCEPTS 485,560

worried [adj] *anxious, troubled*
afraid, apprehensive, beside oneself, bothered, clutched, concerned, distracted, distraught, distressed, disturbed, fearful, fretful, frightened, hung up*, ill-at-ease, nervous, on edge*, on pins and needles*, overwrought, perturbed, solicitous, tense, tormented, uneasy, upset, uptight, worried stiff*; SEE CONCEPT 403

worrisome [adj] *troublesome*
agonizing, alarming, annoying, anxious, apprehensive, bothersome, burdensome, disquieting, disturbing, inconvenient, irksome, irritating, nervous, taxing, tiresome, trying, uneasy, unnerving, upsetting, vexing, wearisome, worrying; SEE CONCEPTS 529,565

worry [n] *anxiety, trouble*
anguish, annoyance, apprehension, bad news*, care, concern, disquiet, distress, disturbance, doubt, fear, headache*, heartache*, irritation, misery, misgiving, nag*, pain*, perplexity, pest, plague, presentiment, problem, torment, torture, trial, uncertainty, uneasiness, vexation, woe, worriment; SEE CONCEPTS 532,690

worry [v] *be or make anxious, troubled*
afflict, aggrieve, agonize, ail, annoy, attack, bedevil, beleaguer, beset, bite one's nails*, bother, brood, bug*, chafe, concern oneself, depress, despair, disquiet, distress, dun, feel uneasy, fret, gnaw at, goad, go for*, harass, harry, hassle, have qualms, hector, importune, irritate, needle,

oppress, persecute, perturb, pester, plague, stew*, sweat out*, take on, tantalize, tear, tease, test, torment, torture, trouble, try, unsettle, upset, vex, wince, writhe, wrong; SEE CONCEPTS 7,14,19,410

worsen [*v*] *diminish, decay*
aggravate, corrode, damage, decline, degenerate, depress, descend, deteriorate, disintegrate, exacerbate, fall off, get worse, go downhill*, impair, lower, retrograde, retrogress, rot, sink; SEE CONCEPTS 240,698

worship [*n*] *honoring, glorification*
adoration, adulation, awe, beatification, benediction, chapel, church service, deification, devotion, exaltation, genuflection, glory, homage, honor, idolatry, idolization, invocation, laudation, love, offering, praise, prayer, prostration, regard, respect, reverence, rite, ritual, service, supplication, veneration, vespers; SEE CONCEPTS 69,367

worship [*v*] *honor, glorify*
admire, adore, adulate, bow down to, canonize, celebrate, chant, deify, dote on, esteem, exalt, extol, idolize, laud, love, magnify, offer prayers to, pay homage to, praise, pray to, put on a pedestal*, respect, revere, reverence, sanctify, sing, sing praises to*, venerate; SEE CONCEPTS 69,367

worth [*n*] *value, estimation associated with something*
account, aid, assistance, avail, benefit, caliber, class, consequence, cost, credit, desirability, dignity, equivalence, excellence, goodness, help, importance, mark, meaningfulness, merit, moment, note, perfection, price, quality, rate, significance, stature, use, usefulness, utility, valuation, virtue, weight, worthiness; SEE CONCEPTS 335,346

worthless [*adj*] *of no use; without value*
abandoned, abject, barren, base, bogus, cheap, contemptible, counterproductive, despicable, empty, futile, good-for-nothing*, ignoble, inconsequential, ineffective, ineffectual, inferior, insignificant, inutile, meaningless, mediocre, miserable, no-account*, no-good*, nothing, nugatory, paltry, pointless, poor, profitless, sterile, trashy, trifling, trivial, unavailing, unessential, unimportant, unproductive, unprofitable, unusable, useless, valueless, waste, wretched; SEE CONCEPTS 560,570,575

worthwhile [*adj*] *helpful*
advantageous, beneficial, constructive, estimable, excellent, gainful, good, important, invaluable, justifiable, lucrative, meritorious, money-making, paying, priceless, productive, profitable, remunerative, rewarding, serviceable, useful, valuable, worthy; SEE CONCEPTS 560,567,572

worthy [*adj*] *honorable, respectable*
A-1*, aces*, admirable, best, blameless, choice, commendable, creditable, decent, dependable, deserving, desirable, divine, estimable, ethical, excellent, exemplary, first-class*, first-rate*, good, honest, incorrupt, invaluable, laudable, meritorious, model, moral, noble, pleasing, praiseworthy, precious, priceless, pure, reliable, reputable, righteous, right-minded, salt of the earth*, satisfying, sterling, top-drawer*, topnotch*, true, trustworthy, upright, valuable, vir-

tuous, winning, worthwhile; SEE CONCEPTS 545,567,572

wound [*n*] *injury*
anguish, bruise, cut, damage, distress, gash, grief, harm, heartbreak, hurt, insult, laceration, lesion, pain, pang, shock, slash, torment, torture, trauma; SEE CONCEPT 309

wound [*v1*] *cause bodily damage*
bruise, carve, clip*, contuse, cut, damage, ding*, gash, harm, hit, hurt, injure, irritate, lacerate, nick, open up, ouch*, pierce, rough up*, scrape, scratch, slash, slice, stick, total*; SEE CONCEPTS 137,246,313

wound [*v2*] *cause mental hurt*
bother, cut to the quick*, distress, disturb, do in*, dump on*, get*, grieve, hurt, hurt one's feelings, mortify, offend, outrage, pain, put down*, shake up*, sting, traumatize, trouble, upset; SEE CONCEPTS 7,14,19

wow [*v*] *amuse, delight*
bowl over*, break one up*, charm, cheer, crack up*, entertain, go over big*, kill*, knock dead*, knock someone's socks off*, make laugh, make roll in the aisles*, slay*, tickle, tickle pink*, tickle to death*; SEE CONCEPTS 7,9,22,292,384

wrangle [*n*] *fight, argument*
altercation, battle royal*, bickering, blow-off*, blowup*, branigan*, brawl, brouhaha*, clash, contest, controversy, disagreement, dispute, exchange, falling-out*, flap*, fracas, hassle, knockdown drag-out*, quarrel, row, ruckus*, ruction, rumble, rumpus, scene, set-to*, squabble, tiff; SEE CONCEPTS 46,106

wrangle [*v*] *fight, argue*
altercate, bicker, brawl, bump heads*, contend, cross swords*, disagree, dispute, fall out*, hassle, have at it*, have words*, lock horns*, pick a bone*, put up a fight, quarrel, quibble, row, scrap, spat, squabble, take on, tangle, tiff; SEE CONCEPTS 46,106

wrap [*n*] *clothing that is worn over for warmth*
blanket, cape, cloak, coat, cover, fur, jacket, mantle, shawl, stole; SEE CONCEPT 451

wrap [*v*] *surround with a covering*
absorb, bandage, bind, bundle, bundle up, camouflage, cloak, clothe, cover, drape, encase, encircle, enclose, enfold, envelop, fold, gift-wrap*, hide, immerse, invest, mask, muffle, pack, package, protect, roll up, sheathe, shelter, shroud, swaddle, swathe, twine, veil, wind; SEE CONCEPT 172

wrap up [*v*] *finish*
bring to a close, close, complete, conclude, determine, end, halt, polish off, terminate, wind up; SEE CONCEPT 234

wrath [*n*] *extreme anger*
acrimony, asperity, boiling point*, conniption*, dander, displeasure, exasperation, flare-up, fury, hate, hatefulness, huff, indignation, ire, irritation, mad, madness, offense, passion, rage, resentment, rise, stew*, storm, temper, vengeance; SEE CONCEPTS 29,410

wrathful [*adj*] *very angry*
beside oneself, displeased, enraged, furious, heated, incensed, indignant, infuriated, irate, ireful, mad, on the warpath*, raging, storming; SEE CONCEPT 403

wreak [*v*] *force, cause*
bring about, carry out, create, effect, execute, ex-

ercise, force upon, inflict, unleash, vent, visit, work, wreck; SEE CONCEPT 242

wreath [n] *circular decoration*
band, bay, bouquet, chaplet, circlet, coronal, coronet, crown, festoon, garland, laurel, lei, loop, ring, ringlet; SEE CONCEPTS 259,260,429

wreck [n] *severe damage or severely damaged goods*
collapse, crash, crate, debacle, debris, derelict, destruction, devastation, disruption, fender bender*, heap*, hulk*, jalopy*, junk*, junker*, litter, mess, pile-up*, rear-ender*, relic, ruin, ruins, shipwreck, smashup*, total*, waste, wreckage; SEE CONCEPTS 260,674

wreck [v] *ruin, destroy*
bash, batter, beach, break, capsize, crack up*, crash, cripple, dash, decimate, demolish, devastate, dilapidate, disable, do in*, efface, founder, impair, injure, mangle, mar, mess up*, pile up*, put out of commission*, ravage, raze, run aground, sabotage, scuttle, shatter, shipwreck, sink, smash, smash up, spoil, strand, subvert, take apart, take out, tear up, torpedo*, total*, trash*, undermine, vandalize, wrack*, wrack up*; SEE CONCEPT 252

wrench [v] *jerk, force violently*
bend, coerce, compel, contort, dislocate, dislodge, distort, drag, exact, extract, pervert, pinch, pull, rend, rip, screw, sprain, squeeze, strain, tear, tug, tweak, twist, wrest, wring, yank; SEE CONCEPTS 80,206

wrestle [v] *struggle physically or mentally with something*
battle, combat, contend, endeavor, essay, exert, fight, grapple, grunt, scuffle, strain, strive, tangle, tussle, work; SEE CONCEPTS 17,191,208

wretched [adj] *terrible, very bad*
abject, afflicted, base, bummed, calamitous, cheap, contemptible, dejected, deplorable, depressed, despicable, disconsolate, distressed, dolorous, down, down-and-out*, downcast, faulty, flimsy, forlorn, gloomy, hapless, hopeless, hurting, inferior, in the pits*, low, low-down*, mean, melancholy, miserable, paltry, pathetic, pitiable, pitiful, poor, shabby, shameful, sordid, sorrowful, sorry, spiritless, tragic, unfortunate, unhappy, vile, weak, woebegone, woeful, worthless; SEE CONCEPTS 403,571

wriggle [v] *maneuver out of; wiggle*
convulse, crawl, dodge, extricate oneself, glide, jerk, jiggle, ooze, skew, slink, slip, snake, sneak, squirm, turn, twist, twitch, wag, waggle, worm, writhe, zigzag; SEE CONCEPTS 30,149

wring [v] *twist, contort*
choke, coerce, compress, draw out, exact, extort, extract, force, gouge, hurt, pain, pinch, pry, push, screw, shake down, squeeze, strain, strangle, throttle, turn, wrench, wrest; SEE CONCEPTS 142,206,208

wrinkle [n] *crinkle, fold*
contraction, corrugation, crease, crow's-foot*, crumple, depression, furrow, gather, line, pleat, plica, pucker, ridge, rimple, rumple, tuck; SEE CONCEPTS 418,513

wrinkle [v] *crinkle, fold*
compress, corrugate, crease, crimp, crisp, crumple, furrow, gather, line, prune up, pucker, purse, rimple, ruck, rumple, screw up, scrunch, seam, shrivel, twist; SEE CONCEPTS 185,201

writ [n] *court order*
command, decree, document, habeas corpus, mandate, paper, prescript, process, replevin, subpoena, summons, warrant; SEE CONCEPT 318

write [v] *put language down on paper*
address, author, autograph, bang out*, chalk*, commit, communicate, comp*, compose, copy, correspond, create, dash off*, draft, draw up*, drop a line*, drop a note*, engross, formulate, ghost, indite, ink, inscribe, jot down, knock off*, knock out*, letter, note, note down*, pen, pencil, print, push a pencil*, put in writing, record, reproduce, rewrite, scrawl, scribble, scribe, scriven, set down, set forth, sign, take down, tell, transcribe, turn out, typewrite, write down, write up; SEE CONCEPTS 79,203

write off [v] *devalue; forget about*
cancel, cross out, decry, depreciate, disregard, downgrade, give up, lower, mark down, shelve, take a loss on, underrate, undervalue; SEE CONCEPT 54

writer [n] *person who composes with language*
author, biographer, columnist, contributor, correspondent, critic, dramatist, editor, essayist, freelancer, ghostwriter, journalist, newspaper person, novelist, person of letters, poet, reporter, screenwriter, scribbler, scribe, scripter, stenographer, stringer, wordsmith; SEE CONCEPTS 348,356

writhe [v] *contort; toss back and forth*
agonize, bend, distort, jerk, recoil, squirm, struggle, suffer, thrash, thresh, twist, wiggle, wince, worm, wriggle; SEE CONCEPTS 80,150

writing [n1] *printing on paper*
autograph, calligraphy, chirography, cuneiform, hand, handwriting, hieroglyphics, longhand, manuscription, print, scrawl, scribble, script, shorthand; SEE CONCEPTS 79,284

writing [n2] *printed composition*
article, belles-lettres, book, discourse, dissertation, document, editorial, essay, letter, literature, manuscript, novel, ode, opus, pamphlet, paper, piece, play, poem, prose, publication, record, review, signature, theme, thesis, tract, treatise, work; SEE CONCEPT 271

wrong [adj1] *incorrect*
amiss, askew, astray, at fault, awry, bad, counterfactual, defective, erratic, erring, erroneous, fallacious, false, faulty, fluffed, goofed*, inaccurate, in error, inexact, miscalculated, misconstrued, misfigured, misguided, mishandled, mistaken, not precise, not right, not working, off-target*, on the wrong track*, out, out of commission*, out of line*, out of order*, perverse, rotten*, sophistical, specious, spurious, ungrounded, unsatisfactory, unsound, unsubstantial, untrue, wide; SEE CONCEPTS 571,582

wrong [adj2] *immoral, dishonest*
amoral, bad, base, blamable, blameworthy, blasphemous, censurable, corrupt, criminal, crooked, debauched, depraved, dishonorable, dissipated, dissolute, evil, felonious, illegal, illicit, indecent, iniquitous, naughty, profane, profligate, reprehensible, reprobate, risqué, sacrilegious, salacious, shady, sinful, smutty, unethical, unfair, ungodly, unholy, unjust, unlawful, unrighteous, vicious, wanton, wicked, wrongful; SEE CONCEPT 545

wrong [adj3] *inappropriate, not suitable*
amiss, awkward, bad, disproportionate, funny, gauche, ill-advised, improper, inapt, incongru-

ous, incorrect, indecorous, infelicitous, malapropos, misplaced, not done*, off-balance, rotten*, unacceptable, unbecoming, unconventional, undesirable, unfit, unfitted, unfitting, unhappy, unsatisfactory, unseemly, unsuitable; SEE CONCEPT 558

wrong [adj4] *reverse, opposite*
back, inside, inverse, obverse; SEE CONCEPT 586

wrong [adv] *astray*
afield, amiss, askew, badly, erroneously, inaccurately, incorrectly, mistakenly, unfavorably, wrongly; SEE CONCEPTS 544,548

wrong [n] *offense, sin*
abuse, bad deed, bias, blunder, crime, cruelty, damage, delinquency, discourtesy, error, evil, faux pas, favor, foul play, grievance, harm, hurt, immorality, imposition, indecency, inequity, inhumanity, iniquity, injury, injustice, insult, libel, malevolence, miscarriage, misdeed, misdemeanor, misdoing, mistake, oppression, persecution, prejudice, sinfulness, slander, slight, spite, tort, transgression, trespass, turpitude, unfairness, vice, villainy, violation, wickedness, wrongdoing; SEE CONCEPT 645

wrong [v] *hurt, mistreat another*
abuse, aggrieve, cheat, damage, defame, discredit, dishonor, harm, hurt, ill-treat, impose upon, injure, malign, maltreat, misrepresent, mistreat, offend, oppress, outrage, persecute, take advantage of; SEE CONCEPTS 7,19,246,313

wrongful [adj] *evil, illegal*
blameworthy, criminal, dishonest, dishonorable, felonious, illegitimate, illicit, immoral, improper, lawless, reprehensible, unethical, unfair, unjust, unlawful, wicked; SEE CONCEPTS 319,545

wry [adj] *sarcastic, distorted*
askew, aslant, awry, contorted, crooked, cynical, deformed, droll, dry, ironic, mocking, sardonic, twisted, uneven, warped; SEE CONCEPTS 267,581

X

Xanadu [n] *utopia*
Arcadia, dreamland, dreamworld, Eden, heaven, land of milk and honey*, never-never land*, paradise, promised land*, Shangri-La*, wonderland; SEE CONCEPTS 370,689

xerophagy [n] *fasting*
hunger strike, keeping fast, Lenten fast, strict fast, without food, xerophagia; SEE CONCEPT 169

Xerox [v] *copy*
carbon, clone, counterfeit, ditto, duplicate, forge, mimeograph, photocopy, photostat, replicate, reprint, reproduce, trace; SEE CONCEPT 171

X-rated [adj] *pornographic*
adult, bawdy, dirty, erotic, fleshy, hard-core, immoral, indecent, lascivious, lewd, obscene, off-color, offensive, porn*, porno*, raunchy, sensual, sexual, sexy, smutty*, steamy*; SEE CONCEPTS 267,372,545

x-ray [n] *picture of inside a body*
actinism, cathode rays, encephalogram, fluoroscope, radioactivity, radiograph, refractometry, Roentgen rays, ultraviolet rays; SEE CONCEPT 311

Y

yacht [n] *pleasure boat*
cabin cruiser, cruiser, ketch, racer, sailboat, sailing boat, sloop, yawl; SEE CONCEPT 506

yak/yap [n/v] *talk a lot*
babble, blather, chat, chatter, clack, confabulate, gab, gossip, jabber, jaw*, prate, prattle, run on*, tattle, yammer; SEE CONCEPTS 51,266

yammer [v] *whine*
bellyache, carp, complain, fuss, gripe, grumble, howl, moan, repine, wail, whimper, yowl; SEE CONCEPTS 54,77

yank [v] *pull hard and fast*
draw, evulse, extract, hitch, jerk, lug, snap, snatch, tear, tug, twitch, vellicate, wrench; SEE CONCEPT 206

yard [n] *grassy area around a structure*
backyard, barnyard, clearing, close, corral, court, courtyard, enclosure, fold, garden, grass, lawn, lot, patch, patio, playground, quadrangle, terrace; SEE CONCEPT 509

yardstick [n] *gauge*
barometer, basis, benchmark, criterion, example, guide, guideline, indicator, mark, measure, meter, model, norm, rule, sample, scale, standard, tape measure, test; SEE CONCEPTS 647,680,688,792

yarn [n1] *fiber for knitting*
cotton fiber, flaxen thread, fleece, spun wool, thread, twist, wool; SEE CONCEPT 473

yarn [n2] *story, often long and made-up*
adventure, alibi, anecdote, fable, fabrication, fairy tale, lie, line, narrative, potboiler*, prose, sea story*, song*, song and dance*, string*, tale, tall story*, tall tale; SEE CONCEPT 282

yawn [v] *open mouth wide, usually sign of fatigue*
catch flies*, divide, doze, drowse, expand, gap, gape, give, nap, part, sleep, snooze, spread, yaw, yawp*; SEE CONCEPTS 163,185

yearly [adj] *every twelve months*
annual, annually, once a year, per annum, perennial, regularly, year by year, yearlong; SEE CONCEPTS 541,823

yearn [v] *desire strongly*
ache, be desirous of, be eager for, be passionate, chafe, covet, crave, dream, hanker, have a crush on*, have a yen for, hunger, itch, languish, long, lust, pine, set one's heart on*, thirst, want, wish for; SEE CONCEPT 20

yearning [n] *desire*
ache, ambition, appetite, aspiration, craving, craze, eagerness, fancy, fascination, hankering*, hunger, infatuation, liking, longing, love, need, passion, thirst, urge, want; SEE CONCEPTS 20,709

years [n] *age; old age*
age, agedness, caducity, dotage, elderliness, generation, lifespan, lifetime, oldness, senescence, senility; SEE CONCEPT 715

yell [n/v] *loud communication*
bawl, bellow, call, cheer, complain, cry, holler*, hoot, howl, lament, roar, scream, screech, shout, shriek, shrill, squawk, squeal, ululate, vociferate, wail, weep, whoop, yap, yelp, yip; SEE CONCEPTS 47,595

yellow [adj2] *cowardly*
chicken*, craven, deceitful, gutless, lily-livered*

low, offensive, pusillanimous, sneaking, treacherous, tricky, unethical, unprincipled; SEE CONCEPTS *267,401*

yellow [*n/adj*] *sunny color*
amber, bisque, blond, buff, chrome, cream, gold, ivory, lemon, saffron, sand, tawny; SEE CONCEPTS *618,622*

yelp [*n/v*] *short, high cry*
bark, hoot, howl, screech, yap, yip, yowl; SEE CONCEPT *64*

yen [*n*] *strong want*
craving, desire, hankering, hunger, itch, longing, lust, passion, thirst, urge, yearning; SEE CONCEPTS *20,709*

yes [*adv*] *agreed*
affirmative, all right*, amen, aye*, beyond a doubt, by all means, certainly, definitely, even so, exactly, fine, gladly, good, good enough, granted, indubitably, just so, most assuredly, naturally, of course, okay*, positively, precisely, surely, sure thing*, true, undoubtedly, unquestionably, very well, willingly, without fail, yea*, yep*; SEE CONCEPTS *535,572*

yes-person [*n*] *sycophant*
apple polisher*, backscratcher*, backslapper*, bootlicker*, brownnoser*, doormat*, fan, fawner, flatterer, flunky*, groupie*, hanger-on*, lackey, minion, puppet, toady; SEE CONCEPT *423*

yesterday [*n*] *the day before today*
bygone, foretime, lang syne*, last day, not long ago, past, recently, the other day*; SEE CONCEPT *815*

yet [*adv1*] *up until now*
as yet, earlier, hitherto, prior to, so far, still, thus far, till, until now, up to now; SEE CONCEPT *820*

yet [*adv2*] *in spite of*
after all, although, at any rate, but, despite, even though, howbeit, however, nevertheless, nonetheless, notwithstanding, on the other hand, still, still and all, though, withal; SEE CONCEPT *544*

yet [*adv3*] *in addition*
additionally, along, also, as well, besides, further, furthermore, likewise, more, moreover, over and above*, still, still further, to boot*, too; SEE CONCEPT *548*

yet [*adv4*] *in the future*
after a while, at some future time, beyond this, even, eventually, finally, in due course, in the course of time, someday, sometime, sooner or later, still, ultimately; SEE CONCEPT *799*

yield [*n*] *production of labor*
crop, earnings, harvest, income, output, outturn, produce, profit, return, revenue, takings, turnout; SEE CONCEPTS *260,338*

yield [*v1*] *produce*
accrue, admit, afford, allow, beam, bear, blossom, bring forth, bring in, discharge, earn, furnish, generate, give, give off, hold out, net, offer, pay, proffer, provide, return, sell for, supply, tender, turn out; SEE CONCEPT *205*

yield [*v2*] *give in, surrender*
abandon, abdicate, admit defeat, back down, bend, bow, break, buy, call it quits*, capitulate, cave in, cede, collapse, come to terms*, crumple, defer, fold, fold up, give oneself over, give up, give way*, go, hand over, knuckle, knuckle under*, lay down arms*, leave, let go*, part with, relax, relent, relinquish, resign, sag, submit, succumb, suffer defeat, surrender, throw in the towel*; SEE CONCEPTS *14,18,35*

yield [*v3*] *grant, allow*
accede, accept, acknowledge, acquiesce, admit, agree, assent, bow, break, comply, concede, concur, consent, defer, fail, fit in, go along with*, go with the flow*, permit, play the game*, surrender, toe the line*, toe the mark*, waive; SEE CONCEPT *8*

yielding [*adj1*] *accommodating*
acquiescent, biddable, compliant, docile, easy, flexible, humble, nonresistant, obedient, passive, pliable, pliant, putty in one's hands, resigned, submissive, tractable; SEE CONCEPTS *401,404*

yielding [*adj2*] *soft, flexible*
elastic, malleable, mushy, pappy, plastic, pliable, pulpy, quaggy, resilient, spongy, springy, squishy, supple, tractable, tractile, unresisting; SEE CONCEPTS *488,606*

yoke [*n*] *bondage, bond*
burden, chain, coupling, enslavement, helotry, knot, ligament, ligature, link, nexus, oppression, peonage, serfdom, service, servility, servitude, slavery, tie; SEE CONCEPTS *513,677*

yoke [*v*] *bond together; join*
associate, attach, bracket, buckle, combine, conjoin, conjugate, connect, couple, fasten, fix, harness, hitch, link, secure, splice, strap, tack, tie, unite, wed; SEE CONCEPTS *85,160,193*

yokel [*n*] *person who is mired in local custom*
backwoods person, boor*, country cousin*, country person, hayseed*, peasant, rustic; SEE CONCEPT *413*

yonder [*adv*] *faraway*
away, beyond, distant, farther, further, remote, yon; SEE CONCEPTS *586,778*

young [*adj*] *immature*
adolescent, blooming, blossoming, boyish, boy-like, budding, burgeoning, callow, childish, childlike, crude, developing, early, fledgling, fresh, girlish, girllike, green*, growing, half-grown, ignorant, inexperienced, infant, inferior, junior, juvenile, little, modern, new, newborn, newish, not aged, pubescent, puerile, punk, raw, recent, tender, tenderfoot*, undeveloped, undisciplined, unfinished, unfledged, unlearned, unpracticed, unripe, unseasoned, untried, unversed, vernal, youthful; SEE CONCEPTS *578,678,715,797*

young [*n*] *animate beings that are not mature*
babies, baby, brood, family, infants, issue, litter, little ones*, offspring, progeny; SEE CONCEPTS *394,414,424*

youngster/youth [*n*] *person before the age of maturity*
boy, chick*, cub*, fledgling, girl, junior, juvenile, juvenile delinquent*, kid*, lad, lass, pup, pupil, student, teenager, young person; SEE CONCEPTS *414,424*

youth [*n*] *early period in life of animate being*
adolescence, awkward age, bloom, boyhood, childhood, girlhood, greenness, ignorance, immaturity, inexperience, innocence, juvenescence, minority, prime, puberty, salad days*, springtide, springtime of life, teens, tender age*, youthfulness; SEE CONCEPT *817*

youthful [*adj*] *new, immature*
active, adolescent, boyish, budding, buoyant, callow, childish, childlike, enthusiastic, fresh, full of life, girlish, green*, inexperienced, infant, juvenile, keen, pubescent, puerile, tender, under-

wr
yo

age, vernal, vigorous, young; SEE CONCEPTS 542,578,797

yowl [n/v] *long, loud animate sound*
bawl, bay, caterwaul, cry, holler*, howl, mewl, scream, screech, squall, squeal, ululate, wail, whine, yell, yelp, yip; SEE CONCEPT 77

yucky [adj] *disgusting*
abominable, awful, beastly, crappy*, creepy, cruddy*, crummy*, detestable, distasteful, foul, funky*, grody*, gross, gruesome, hideous, icky*, loathsome, lousy, nasty, nauseating, odious, offensive, raunchy, repugnant, repulsive, revolting, rotten, scuzzy*, sickening, skanky*, sleazy*, stinking, vile, vulgar, yecchy*; SEE CONCEPTS 485,548

yummy [adj] *delicious*
ambrosial, appetizing, choice, delectable, delightful, divine, enticing, fit for a king*, good, heavenly, juicy, luscious, mouthwatering, nectarous, out of this world*, palatable, piquant, pleasant, rich, sapid, savory, scrumptious, spicy, succulent, super, sweet, tasteful, tasty, tempting, toothsome; SEE CONCEPTS 572,423

yuppie [n/adj] *young upwardly mobile professional*
button-down, clone, conspicuous consumer, suit, three-piecer, urban professional, white-collar worker; SEE CONCEPT 348

Z

zany [adj] *crazy, funny*
camp*, campy*, clownish, comical, dumb, eccentric, fool, foolish, goofy, hare-brained*, humorous, joshing, kooky*, loony*, madcap*, nutty*, sappy*, wacky*, witty; SEE CONCEPTS 267,401

zany [n] *person who is wildly funny*
buffoon, card*, clown, comedian, comic, cutup*, farceur, funny person, gag person, humorist, idiot, jester, joker, madcap*, moron, nut*, practical joker, prankster, screwball*, show-off, simpleton*, wag*, wisecracker*; SEE CONCEPTS 352,423

zeal [n] *enthusiasm*
alacrity, ardor, bustle, determination, devotion, diligence, dispatch, drive, eagerness, earnestness, enterprise, fanaticism, fervor, fierceness, fire, gusto, hustle, inclination, initiative, intensity, intentness, keenness, mania, passion, perseverance, push, readiness, sincerity, spirit, stick-to-itiveness*, urgency, vehemence, verve, warmth, what-it-takes*, yen, zest; SEE CONCEPTS 32,410,411

zealous [adj] *enthusiastic*
afire, antsy*, ardent, avid, burning, coming on strong*, dedicated, devoted, eager, earnest, fanatic, fanatical, fervent, fervid, fireball*, fired, frenetic, gung-ho*, hot*, impassioned, itchy*, keen, obsessed, passionate, possessed, pushy*, rabid, ripe, self-starting, spirited, wild-eyed*; SEE CONCEPTS 326,401,404

zenith [n] *top*
acme, altitude, apex, apogee, cap, capper, capstone, climax, crest, crown, culmination, eleva-

tion, eminence, height, high noon*, high point, meridian, payoff*, peak, pinnacle, roof, summit, tiptop*, topper*, vertex; SEE CONCEPTS 706,832,836

zero [n] *nothing*
aught, blank, bottom, cipher, insignificancy, love*, lowest point, nada*, nadir, naught, nil*, nix*, nobody*, nonentity, nought, nullity, oblivion, ought, rock bottom*, scratch, shutout, void, zilch*, zip*, zot*; SEE CONCEPTS 407,784

zero hour [n] *vital moment*
appointed hour*, climax, contingency, countdown, crisis, crossroad, D-day*, emergency, exigency, jumping-off point*, juncture, moment of truth*, pinch, strait, target, the time*, turning point*; SEE CONCEPTS 668,815,832

zest [n1] *taste, flavor*
bite, body, charm, flavoring, ginger, guts*, interest, kick*, nip, piquancy, punch*, pungency, relish, salt, savor, seasoning, smack*, snap*, spice, tang, zap*, zip*; SEE CONCEPT 614

zest [n2] *energy, gusto*
appetite, ardor, bliss, bounce, cheer, delectation, delight, eagerness, ecstasy, elation, enjoyment, enthusiasm, fervor, guts*, happiness, keenness, moxie*, passion, pep*, pleasure, relish*, satisfaction, zeal, zing*; SEE CONCEPTS 410,411

zigzag [adj] *moving side to side*
askew, awry, bent, crinkled, crooked, devious, diagonal, erratic, fluctuating, inclined, indirect, irregular, jagged, meandering, oblique, oscillating, rambling, serrated, sinuous, sloping, snaking, tortuous, transverse, twisted, twisting, undulating, waggling, winding; SEE CONCEPT 581

zilch [n] *nothing*
blank, diddly-squat*, goose egg*, hill of beans*, insignificancy, nada*, naught, not anything, nothingness, nought, void, zero, zip, zippo*; SEE CONCEPTS 407,707

zing [n] *liveliness*
brio, dash, drive, elan, energy, enthusiasm, getup-and-go*, go, gusto, life, oomph*, pep, pizazz, punch, sparkle, spirit, verve, vigor, vim, vitality, zest, zip; SEE CONCEPTS 411,633

zip [n] *enthusiasm, energy*
brio, drive, get-up-and-go*, go*, gusto, life, liveliness, oomph*, pep, pizazz*, punch, sparkle, spirit, verve, vigor, vim, vitality, zest, zing*; SEE CONCEPTS 411,633

zip [v] *move about quickly*
bustle, dash, flash, fly, hasten, hurry, run, rush, shoot, speed, tear, waltz, whisk, whiz, zoom; SEE CONCEPT 150

zippy [adj] *energetic*
active, animated, ball of fire*, brisk, chipper, dashing, dynamic, enterprising, full of energy, full of life, full of pep, high-powered, kinetic, lively, peppy, potent, powerful, snappy, speedy, spirited, sprightly, spry, strong, tireless, untiring, vigorous, vital, vivacious, zestful, zingy*; SEE CONCEPTS 404,542

zit [n] *pimple*
abscess, acne, blackhead, blemish, bump, carbuncle, excrescence, goober*, goophead*, papula, papule, putsule, whitehead; SEE CONCEPT 306

zone [n] *district*
area, band, belt, circuit, ground, realm, region,

section, sector, segment, sphere, territory, tract; SEE CONCEPTS *508,513*

zonked [*adj*] *drunk, intoxicated; stunned*
amazed, astonished, bashed, boozed up*, buzzed*, crocked*, dazed, dumbfounded, feeling no pain*, flying*, groggy, high*, inebriated, juiced*, laced*, liquored up*, lit*, plastered*, seeing double*, sloshed*, stewed*, stoned*, tanked*, three sheets to the wind*, thunderstruck, tipsy, totaled*, under the influence, under the table*, wasted*; SEE CONCEPTS *314,545*

zoom [*v*] *move very quickly*
buzz, dart, dash, dive, flash, fly, hum, hurtle, outstrip, rip, rocket, rush, shoot, shoot up, skyrocket, speed, streak, surge, tear, whirl, whiz, zip*; SEE CONCEPT *150*

ROGET'S 21st CENTURY CONCEPT INDEX

HOW TO USE THE CONCEPT INDEX

Simply put, a thesaurus is a collection of words grouped according to idea. Appearing in the A to Z listings of *Roget's 21st Century Thesaurus, Second Edition* are about 20,000 words and 500,000 synonyms to choose from. This selection alone would seem generous enough to satisfy the lexicographer's expectation of what a thesaurus should contain. But a wealth of new alternatives is created when we begin to think about the higher connections that can be made between words and ideas in the language. This is the purpose of *Roget's 21st Century's* Concept Index.

The Concept Index not only helps writers and thinkers to *organize* their ideas but leads them from those very ideas to the words that can best express them. It is a semantic hierarchy of the most common concepts we use in American English as it is spoken and written today.

There are 837 concepts classified according to their subject and usage, and grouped under ten general categories of interest: Actions, Causes, Fields of Human Activity, Life Forms, Objects, the Planet, Qualities, Senses, States, and Weights and Measures.

All of *Roget's 21st Century Thesaurus's* 20,000 main entries are cross-referenced to related concepts. For example, when you look up the entry for "knowledgeable" in the A to Z listing, it is referenced to concept #402. Turning in the index to concept #402, "attribute of intelligence," you will see over 100 other main entries that are also related to this concept:

MAIN ENTRY

with synonym list as it appears in the A to Z listing

> **knowledgeable** [*adj*] *aware, educated*
> abreast, acquainted, alert, appreciative, apprised, au courant, au fait, brainy*, bright, brilliant, clever, cognizant, conscious, conversant, discerning, erudite, experienced, familiar; informed, insightful, intelligent, in the know, knowing, learned, lettered, omniscient, perceptive, plugged in*, posted, prescient, privy, quick-witted, sagacious, sage, savvy, scholarly, sensible, sharp, smart, sophic, sophisticated, tuned-in*, understanding, versed, well-informed, well-rounded, wise, with-it; SEE CONCEPT *402*

CONCEPT

with collection of main entry words referenced to it in the index

> **402 attribute of intelligence:** able, abreast, abstruse, academic, accident-prone, acquainted, acute, adept, alert, amenable, analytic/analytical, appreciative, apt, asinine, astute, awake, aware, backward, bewildered, blank, blind, bright, brilliant, calculable, canny, catatonic, cerebral, childish, clairvoyant, clear, clever, clumsy, cognizant, coherent, common-sense, complex, comprehensible, conscious, considered, contemplative, conversant, creative, cunning, dark, deducible, deep, delirious, dense, designedly, dexterous, dim, discerning, dizzy, dopey, down-to-earth, dull, dumb, eagle-eyed, educated, efficient, elevated, empty, empty-headed, enlightened, erudite, experienced, expert, familiar, far-sighted,

fatuous, feebleminded, forgotten, frivolous, gifted, gullible, harebrained, hazy, highbrow, idiotic, ignorant, illiterate, imbecile, impressionable, incisive, incomprehensible, inefficient, ineligible, inept, inexperienced, informed, ingenious, inquiring, inquisitive, insightful, insipid, intellectual, intelligent, intuitive, inventive, irrational, judicious, keen, knowing, knowledgeable, learned, literate, logical, lowbrowed, lucid, mental, mindful, mistaken, moronic, nimble, not born yesterday, oblivious, observant, obtuse, omniscient, on the ball, penetrating, perceptive, perspicacious, philosophical/philosophic, precocious, privy, professional, proficient, profound, psychic, quick, quick-witted, rational, ready, reasonable, resourceful, sagacious, sage, sane, sapient, savvy, scatterbrained, scholarly, searching, seasoned, senile, sensible, sentient, shallow, sharp, shrewd, simple, skillful, slick, slow, smart, soft, stolid, studious, stupid, subtle, talented, thick, thoughtful, thoughtless, touched, unaware, uncoordinated, uneducated, unfamiliar, uninformed, unintelligent, unknowing, unwise, vacant, vacuous, versed, veteran, weak, well-balanced, well-defined, wideawake, wise, with it

Any of these main entry words appearing together as attributes of intelligence in the Concept Index—from "able" to "ingenious" to "perspicacious" to "wise"—may be the perfect word you are looking for. Or, intrigued by the associations the word "veteran" brings to mind, you could return to the A to Z listing to explore its synonyms:

veteran [*adj*] *experienced, seasoned*
adept, battle-scarred*, been around*, disciplined, exercised, expert, from way back*, hardened, inured, knows one's stuff*, long-serving, longtime, not born yesterday*, of the old school*, old, old-time, practical, practiced, pro*, proficient, skilled, sophisticated, steady, trained, up to speed*, versed, vet*, weathered, wise, wise to ways*, worldly; SEE CONCEPTS *402,527,678*

Even further possibilities exist, when you realize that "veteran" is referenced to two additional concepts: #527, the quality of "ability" and #678, the state of "experience." Many main entries are referenced to as many as three or four different concepts.

Simple to use, the Concept Index becomes invaluable in the effort to turn an idea into a specific word. By linking together the main entries that share similar concepts, but may not be direct synonyms, the index makes possible creative semantic connections between words in our language, stimulating thought and broadening vocabulary.

Whether you begin by browsing through the Concept Index for ideas, or in the A to Z listing with a particular word in mind, you will find that *Roget's 21st Century Thesaurus, Second Edition* goes beyond traditional thesauri and synonymfinders to offer thousands of word choices through access to its unique Concept Index.

QUICK REFERENCE GUIDE TO CONCEPTS

Actions

CLASS OF

1 **action:** act, action, activity, behave, doings, feat, spurt, step, tour de force
2 **event:** affair, anything, be, event, eventuate, experience, fact, incident, locomotion, milestone, move, movement, occasion, outbreak, pass, proceeding
3 **occurrence:** development, episode, occurrence, proceeding, recur, thing, transpire
4 **occurrence with one participant:** act, befall, behave, break, chance, coincidence, come, come off, deed, episode, fall out, fluke, go, happen, happening, intervene, occur, occurrence, result, return, rise
5 **occurrence with two participants:** boundary, guideline, limit, measure, obstruct, reinforce, restraint, test
6 **series of related actions:** channel, commit, disposition, elapse, esplanade, form, instrument, maneuver, manner, means, mechanism, method, methodology, mode, modus operandi, path, pattern, policy, procedure, process, routine, rule, rut, system, technique, touch, usage, vehicle, way

COGNITIVE

7 **affect:** abandon, abase, acerbate; affect, afflict, affront, aggravate, agitate, agonize, alarm, alienate, allay, alleviate, allure, anger, annoy, antagonize, appall/appal, appeal, appease, appeasement, arouse, arrest, assuage, attract, awaken, awe, baffle, bait, beckon, bedazzle, befuddle, beguile, beleaguer, bemuse, beset, besiege, bewitch, bias, bombard, bore, bother, brighten, bring down, bring on, bug, buoy (up), burden, captivate, chafe, chagrin, charm, cheer, chill, clear, cloud, comfort, complicate, compose, concern, console, content, cow, craze, cross, crucify, crush, dampen, dash, daunt, debase, deceive, deception, defame, deflate, defuse, degrade, delight, demean, demoralize, deprecate, depreciate, depress, depressant, disaffect, disappoint, disarm, discomfit, discomfort, discommode, discompose, disconcert, discountenance, disgust, dishearten, dismay, disoblige, disparage, displease, disquiet, distress, disturb, divert, double-cross, downgrade, draw, dwarf, electrify, elevate, embarrass, embitter, embolden, embroil, enamor, enchant, encourage, encouragement, encroach, endear, energize, enliven, enrage, enrapture, enthrall, entice, enticement, entrance, estrange, exacerbate, exasperate, excite, exercise, exhilarate, fail, fascinate, faze, ferment, flurry, fluster, fortify, freak, fret, frustrate, fulfill, gall, galling, galvanize, get, gladden, govern, grate, gratify, grieve, grip, gripe, harass, harm, harry, hearten, henpeck, hoodwink, horrify, hound, hurt, impress, inflame, ingratiate, inspire, instigate, interest, intimidate, intrigue, invigorate, irk, irritate, jar, kid around, kindle, let down, lighten, lower, lull, madden, matter, menace, miff, mock, molest, mollify, mortify, move, nag, needle, nerve, nettle, nonaggression, occupy, offend, oppress, outrage, pacify, pain, pall, peeve, pep up, perk up, persecute, perturb, pester, petrify, pick at/pick on, pique, placate, plague, please, prejudice, pressure, prime, prod, provoke, puncture, put out, quell, quicken, rack, rally, rankle, rasp, reach, reassure, reduce, regenerate, register, remind, repay, repel, revolt, ride, rile, rouse, rub the wrong way, ruffle, sadden, salve, satisfy, scar, scare, seduction, send, settle, shake, shame, shatter, sink, slight, slur, smooth, solace, soothe, spite, spook, stagger, startle, still, strain, strengthen, stress, strike, sugarcoat, support, sweeten, take down, tantalize, taunt, tease, temper, terrify, terrorize, threaten, thrill, tickle, titillate, torment, torture, touch, tranquilize, transport, trouble, try, turn, turn off, two-time, undo, unnerve, unsettle, uplift, upset, vex, visit, wake/waken, wear, weigh, weigh down, whet, worry, wound, wow, wrong

8 **agree:** accede, accept, acceptance, accession, accord, acknowledge, acknowledgment, acquiesce, acquiescence, agree, align, assent, avowal, back, bear, cleave, cohere, comply, compromise, concur, consent, conspire, contract, covenant, draft, enlist, follow, give in/give up, go, go along/go along with, go by, grant, league, negotiate, stipulate, unanimous, yield

9 **amuse:** amuse, bait, divert, entertain, humor, wow

10 **approve:** acquiesce, acquiescence, advocate, agree, applaud, appreciate, approbation, approval, approve, authorize, blessing, champion, concur, condone, countenance, defend, deference, endorse, envy, espouse, exalt, exculpate, excuse, exonerate, favor, go for, go to bat for, honor, idolize, league, nod, okay, overlook, pardon, pity, pride, prize, proselytize, recognition, recommend, regard, respect, revere/reverence, reverence, sanctify, subscribe, support, sway by, venerate

11 **attract:** attract, fascinate, grip, interest, intrigue, inveigle, kid around, lure, mesmerize, pull, ravish, seduce, send, snare, take, tantalize, tease, tempt, titillate, transfix, turn on, whet, win/win over

12 **believe:** accept, acceptance, acknowledge, appreciate, appreciation, assume, authenticate, bank on, bear, believe, bleed, consider, convert, count on/count upon, credit, deem, disagree, eat up, embrace, esteem, expect, extrapolate, feel, forgive, glorify, glory, hold, imagine, infer, lean, make believe, misjudge, object, opine, overrate, postulate, predispose, presume, proselytize, rate, reckon, regard, rely, sanctify, see, suppose, swallow, think, trust, underestimate, understand, view

13 **change conception:** ache, alternate, awakening, caprice, catharsis, concession, conform, conformity, crack, crack up, fit, flare, flip out, fluctuate, give, go back, go back on, go crazy, oscillate, perish, recharge, repudiate,

resuscitate, reverse, revert, revive, sway, thaw, tire, vacillate, vagary, weary

14 compel: abet, ail, alarm, attraction, badger, bait, bewilder, bewilderment, bind, boss around, brainwash, browbeat, brutality, bulldoze, bully, burden, butt in, coerce, coercion, come between, compel, confusion, conjure, constrain, constraint, convert, corrupt, dare, debauch, defeat, demoralize, deprave, discourage, disgrace, dispel, distract, domineer, duress, embitter, engross, enrage, enslave, entrance, excite, fan, fire, foist, foment, force, freeze, frighten, galvanize, get back at, goad, grate, grind, harass, harassment, hassle, haunt, horrify, humble, humiliate, hurt, impel, impinge, imposition, incense, incite, inconvenience, inculcate, indoctrinate, induce, infest, inflame, infuriate, instill, interject, intimidate, intrude, inveigle, invigorate, jinx, jog, kindle, load, lumber, make, manipulate, meddle, mesmerize, mistreat, molest, motivate, nauseate, nerve, nettle, nonplus, oblige, offend, oppress, oppression, panic, paralyze, pervert, petrify, pique, plague, poison, pound, predispose, prejudice, press, pressure, prey on, provocation, push, put, put out, rankle, ride, ruffle, scourge, screw, sell/sell out, shake up, shame, sicken, sour, spoil, spook, spur, stimulate, stir, sway, tame, task, tax, terrorize, tire, transfix, undermine, unnerve, victimize, visit, wake/waken, whip up, work up, worry, wound, yield

15 comprehend: appreciate, appreciation, apprehend, assimilate, catch, comprehend, conceive, decipher, decode, deduce, deduction, derive, determine, differentiate, dig, digest, discern, discriminate, distinguish, do, draw, embrace, extrapolate, familiarize, fathom, feel, figure, follow, gather, get, grasp, have someone's number, hear, identify with, infer, inure, know, make, make out, misapprehend, misconstrue, mistake, misunderstand, outwit/outsmart, penetrate, perceive, realize, recognize, resolve, see, solve, take, take in, tell, understand

16 confuse: confound, confuse, daze, dazzle, decoy, derange, disconcert, disrupt, distract, dumbfound, floor, fluster, foul up, get, hassle, humble, jumble, mix up, muddle, mystify, nonplus, obfuscate, obscure, overwhelm, perplex, perturb, puzzle, rattle, snarl, stump, throw

17 consider: absorb, ache, balance, begrudge, bleed, brood, buckle down, cogitate, commune, concentrate, consider, consult, contemplate, cook up, cram, daydream, deliberate, deliberation, devote, dream, dream up, dwell on/dwell upon, engross, entertain, envisage/envision, excogitate, eye, fancy, fantasize, fixate, focus, gnaw, grieve, harbor, heed, hide, hindsight, immerse, marvel, meditation, meditate, mull, muse, occupy, picture, ponder, puzzle, reconsider, reflect, reflection, reminisce, retrospect, revolve, speculate, think, thought, treat, turn over, visualize, wonder, wrestle

18 decide: abnegation, adjudicate, adopt, adoption, appraisal, appraise, call off, cancel, circumscribe, classification, classify, conclude, convict, count, credit, date, decide, dedicate,

define, derive, destine, determine, disapprove, disavow, dispose of, distinguish, evaluate, falter, figure, fix, go along/go along with, go by, ground, group, have someone's number, hedge, impose, influence, intend, judge, make out, misjudge, moderate, ordain, plant, premise, provide, purpose, referee, resolution, resolve, rule, set, settle, solve, specify, stipulate, surmise, turn down, type, waver, yield

19 depress: abandon, abase, acerbate, affect, afflict, affront, aggravate, agitate, agonize, alarm, alienate, anger, annoy, antagonize, appall/appal, appeal, arouse, arrest, awaken, awe, baffle, bait, befuddle, beguile, beleaguer, bemuse, beset, besiege, bias, bombard, bore, bother, bring down, bring on, bug, burden, chafe, chagrin, chill, cloud, complicate, concern, cow, crass, cross, crucify, crush, dampen, dash, daunt, debase, deceive, deception, defame, deflate, degrade, demean, demoralize, deprecate, depreciate, depress, disaffect, disappoint, disarm, discomfit, discomfort, discommode, discompose, disconcert, discountenance, disgust, dishearten, dismay, disoblige, disparage, displease, disquiet, distress, disturb, divert, double-cross, downgrade, draw, dwarf, embarrass, embitter, embroil, encroach, enrage, enthrall, entice, enticement, estrange, exacerbate, exasperate, excite, exercise, fail, faze, ferment, flurry, fluster, freak, fret, frustrate, gall, galling, get, govern, grate, grieve, gripe, harass, harm, harry, henpeck, hoodwink, horrify, hound, hurt, impress, inflame, instigate, intimidate, irk, irritate, jar, let down, lower, madden, matter, menace, miff, mock, molest, mortify, move, nag, needle, nettle, occupy, offend, oppress, outrage, pain, pall, peeve, persecute, perturb, pester, petrify, pick at/pick on, pique, plague, prejudice, pressure, prime, prod, provoke, puncture, put out, quicken, rack, rankle, rasp, reach, reduce, register, remind, repay, repel, revolt, ride, rile, rub the wrong way, ruffle, sadden, scar, scare, seduction, shake, shame, shatter, sink, slight, slur, spite, stagger, startle, strain, stress, strike, support, take down, tantalize, taunt, tease, terrify, terrorize, threaten, torment, torture, touch, trouble, try, turn, turn off, two-time, undo, unnerve, unsettle, upset, vex, visit, wear, weigh, weigh down, worry, wound, wrong

20 desire: addiction, advance(s), affinity, aim, alcoholism, ambition, angle for, appetite, aspiration, aspire, avid, behest, burn, care, covet, crave, craving, crush, cupidity, curiosity, dependence/dependency, desire, drool, eagerness, envy, eroticism, expect, famished, fancy, fantasy, fascination, fish for, free will, gluttonous, goad, greed, hanker after/hanker for, hankering, hope, hunger, hungry, impulse, inclination, indulge, insatiable, interest, itch, lack, languish, lean, leaning, lechery, libido, like, liking, long, longing, lust, malnutrition, mania, mind, miss, moon, mope, motivation, motive, need, nostalgia, notion, obsession, one-track mind, pant, penchant, pine, pipe dream, please, pleasure, predilection, predisposition, prefer, preference, proclivity, propensity, purport, purpose, pursue, relish, require, sigh, stomach, substance abuse, taste, temptation, thirst, urge, volition, voracious, want, will, wish, yearn, yearning, yen

21 doubt: begrudge, break with, controvert, deplore, despair, disallow, disapprove, disbelief, disbelieve, discount, discountenance, discredit, dissent, distrust, doubt, frown, fume, grudge, hesitate, hesitation, lovelorn, lovesick, mind, misgiving, mistrust, object, objection, oppose, oppugn, query, question, regret, reject, rejection, repudiate, repulse, rue, scorn, scruple, segregate, skepticism, spurn, suspect, turn, wonder

22 elated: affect, allay, alleviate, appeal, appease, appeasement, arouse, arrest, assuage, attract, awaken, awe, beckon, bedazzle, beguile, bemuse, bewitch, brighten, buoy (up), captivate, charm, cheer, clear, comfort, compose, concern, console, content, defuse, delight, depressant, disarm, divert, draw, elated, electrify, elevate, embolden, enamor, enchant, encourage, encouragement, endear, energize, enliven, enrapture, enthrall, entice, enticement, entrance, excite, exhilarate, fascinate, ferment, fortify, fulfill, galvanize, get, gladden, govern, gratify, grip, hearten, impress, inflame, ingratiate, inspire, instigate, interest, intrigue, invigorate, kindle, lighten, lull, matter, mollify, move, nerve, nonaggression, occupy, pacify, pep up, perk up, pique, placate, please, pressure, prime, prod, provoke, quell, quicken, rally, reach, reassure, regenerate, register, remind, rouse, salve, satisfy, send, settle, smooth, solace, soothe, still, strengthen, strike, support, sugarcoat, sweeten, tantalize, tease, temper, thrill, tickle, titillate, touch, tranquilize, transport, uplift, wake/waken, weigh, whet

23 endure: abide, accept, accommodate, acquiesce, bear up, bear with, bite the bullet, bow, brave, brook, come in for, come through, condone, cope, descend, digest, do without, endure, face, face the music, go, go through, hang on, hang tough, have, keep at, keep up, linger, lump, make out, manage, mind, mourn, pay, persist, receive, reconcile, remain, resist, resistance, shoulder, stand/stand for, stick, stomach, submit, subsist, suffer, support, survive, sustain, sweat, take, take it, tolerate, undergo, wear, weather, withstand

24 examine: analysis, analyze, assay, assess, assessment, bury, canvass, check, chew, cogitate, compare, comparison, consider, consideration, debate, decompose, deduce, deduction, deliberate, deliberation, dissect, dissection, enquire, enquiry, evaluate, evaluation, examine, excogitate, experiment, go into, go over, inquire, inquiry, introspection, meditation, observe, ponder, pore, reflect, reflection, resolve, review, ruminate, scrutinize, scrutiny, soul-searching, speculate, speculation, turn over, view, weigh

25 exclude: abnegation, abstain, blackball, blacklist, boycott, count out, deactivate, decommission, disallow, disavow, disinherit, except, exception, exclude, exclusion, jump, omission, omit, ostracism, ostracize, oust,

parry, pass, pass by, pass over, proscribe, recant, retract, rule out, shut/shut out, take back

26 expect: anticipate, anticipation, assume, await, bargain for, calculate, count, count on/count upon, demand, depend, expect, foresee, imagine, lean, look, mean, opine, plan, postulate, predispose, presume, propose, reckon, rely, think

27 fear: apprehension, blanch, cold feet, cowardice, dismay, dread, fear, funk, horror, mistrust, panic, phobia, terror, trepidation

28 guess: accounting, believe, bet, calculation, call, conjecture, deem, divine, estimate, estimation, forecast, gamble, guess, hazard, implication, lottery, presume, project, projection, speculate, speculation, suppose, surmise, suspect, wager

29 hate: abhor, abominable, abominate, abomination, aggression, anarchy, anger, animosity, antagonism, antipathy, atrocity, aversion, bad blood, bad manners, blow up, boil, burn, contempt, deplore, despise, detest, discrimination, disdain, disfavor, disinclination, dislike, disrespect, dissatisfaction, dissent, distaste, enmity, exasperation, execrate, execration, frown, fume, fury, grudge, hate, hatred, horror, ill will, incivility, indignation, inhumanity, lament/lamentation, loath, loathe, loathing,, look down on, malice, mind, odium, opposition, outrage, phobia, pique, rage, rancor, repulsion, resent, resentment, revulsion, scorn, seethe, sexism, spite, temper, umbrage, vengeance, venom, violence, wrath

30 ignore: abjure, abnegate, blink, break with, brush aside/brush off, bypass, cold shoulder, disallow, discount, disdain, disobey, dispense with, disregard, drop, eliminate, elude, eschew, evade, except, exception, exclude, exclusion, fence, forget, forsake, get off someone's back, give the cold shoulder, goof off, hedge, ignore, leave, lose, lovelorn, lovesick, neglect, negligence, overlook, parry, pass, pass by, pass over, rebuff, refuse, reject, rejection, relegate, renounce, renunciation, repel, repudiate, retreat, run-around, scorn, shirk, shun, skip, skirt, skulk, slight, sneer, sneeze at, snub, spurn, weasel, wriggle

31 learn: absorb, acquaint, ascertain, catch, decipher, decode, determine, dig, discover, discovery, edification, find out, get, glean, hear, learn, master, orientation, pick up, probe, research, see, study, turn up

32 love: acceptance, activity, admiration, admire, adoration, adore, adulation, affair, affection, affinity, amour, appetite, appreciate, appreciation, approval, attachment, attention, bag, bask, bathos, bewitched, bliss, canonize, care, charity, cherish, consideration, consolation, constancy, court, delight in, devotion, dig, discriminate, discrimination, dote on/dote upon, empathy, enamored, endear, enjoy, enjoyment, esteem, exaltation, exult, exultation, fall for, fancy, fascinated, fascination, favor, fidelity, flame, flirtation, fond, fondness, get a kick out of, go for, gratitude, homage, idolize, infatuated, leaning, liaison, like, liking, love, lure, mad, mania, mercy, partiality, passion, penchant, predilection, predisposition, prize, proclivity, rapture, relish, respect, revere/reverence, reverence, savor, sentiment, taste, temper, thrill, transport, treasure, triumph, venerate, zeal

33 **mental event:** learn, sense, shock, stroke, think

34 **mental perception:** ascertain, attend, behold, beware, burn, come at, empathize, feel, gnaw, gravitate, grope, hallucinate, learn, mind, note, notice, observe, occur, pity, presage, seethe, sensation, sense, shudder, sorrow, sympathize, visualize, wonder

35 **mental preparation:** abide, accustom, adjust, bottle up, brainstorm, capitulate, center, centralize, comply, concede, conceive, condition, convert, cope, crawl, dare, deign, descend, design, determine, dismiss, dispel, face, forbear, get over, go straight, habituate, harden, look out, manufacture, melt, orient, plan, preparation, prepare, prime, quail, ready, reform, refresh, rehabilitate, rejuvenate, relent, renew, resist, rustle up, season, simmer, sink, smolder, steel, stew, stoop, strengthen, succumb, sulk, sweat, tarry, train, weather, withhold, yield

36 **plan:** arrange, assure, base, block out, book, brew, budget, calculate, chart, coin, concoct, connive, conspire, contemplate, contrive, cook up, coordinate, daydream, delineate, design, devise, draft, dream up, engineer, fabricate, finagle, finesse, fix, formulate, frame, hatch, intend, intrigue, invent, lay, lay out, machinate, maneuver, manufacture, mean, organize, outline, parlay, plan, plot, program, project, propose, purpose, pursue, rough out, schedule, shape, sketch, synchronize

37 **reason:** analyze, cipher, clear up, conclude, construe, crack, criticize, date, decipher, dialectic, do, educe, equate, estimate, figure, forecast, gauge, generalize, induction, infer, judgment, logic, make, mapmaker, overview, pollster, premise, project, rank, rate, reason, reasoning, reckon, solve, speculate, stock, survey

38 **recognize:** acknowledge, ascertain, come across, come upon, conjure up, crack, cut, detect, detection, diagnose, differentiate, discern, discriminate, distinguish, elude, encounter, familiarize, fathom, feel, identify, inure, know, mark, perceive, pinpoint, place, recognition, recognize, remark, salute/salutation, salute, spot, stereotype

39 **relate:** ascribe, associate, association, categorize, class, classification, classify, codify, compare, comparison, contrast, correlate, equate, identify with, implication, liken, pigeonhole

40 **remember:** block out, déjà vu, flashback, forget, hindsight, memorize, mind, recall, recollect, remember, remembrance, remind, reminisce, retain, retrospect, think

41 **select:** aim, allocate, allot, allow, appoint, appointment, assign, assignment, cast, choice, choose, cull, designate, designation, elect, election, excerpt, favoritism, finger, like, name, nepotism, nominate, nomination, opt, pick, prefer, recruit, relegate, screen, select, take, turn, volition, vote

42 **surprise:** alarm, amaze, appall/appal, aston-

ish, astound, awe, backfire, baffle, bedazzle, befuddle, bewilder, bowl over, confound, daze, dazzle, deluge, dumbfound, dumbstruck, electrify, flabbergast, frighten, jolt, overwhelm, overwhelming, petrify, scare, shock, stagger, startle, stun/stupefy, surprise, terrify

43 **think:** count, design, devise, envisage/envision, fancy, imagine, mint, occur, originate, picture, proceed, see, theorize, think, thought

COMMUNICATIVE

44 **accuse:** accuse, admonition, affront, arraign, bastardize, betray, betrayal, blame, blow up, catcall, charge, condemn, condemnation, decry, denounce, discredit, forswear, gripe, groan, grumble, heckle, hoot, humble, humiliate, impeach, implicate, impute, incriminate, indict, indictment, invective, inveigh, malign, mouth off, persecute, profane, rant, rebuke, reprimand, reproach, reprove, revile, scold, slur, tax, tell off, tirade, upbraid, vilify, vituperate

45 **answer:** acknowledge, agree, answer, counter, decline, denial, disclaimer, fill in, give in/give up, react, reaction, reciprocate, repartee, reply, respond, retort, return

46 **argue:** ado, agitate, altercation, argue, argument, back talk, battle, beard, bicker, brawl, cause celebre, clash, conflict, confront, confrontation, confute, contend, contention, contest, contradict, contradiction, contravene, controversy, controvert, demur, deny, dicker, differ, difference, difficulty, disagree, disagreement, dispute, dissension, dissent, diverge, divide, donnybrook, double standard, encounter, expostulate, fall out, falling out, feud, fight, fracas, friction, fuss, haggle, hassle, hue and cry, hullabaloo, imbroglio, maintain, misunderstanding, negate, object, objection, protest, quarrel, quibble, reason, rebut, remonstrate, rift, rock the boat, row, run-in, rupture, sass, scrap, squabble, strife, tiff, uproar, vendetta, wrangle

47 **articulate:** articulate, call, catcall, cry, delivery, diction, elocution, enunciate, exclaim, expression, hail, heckle, holler, hoot, mumble, parrot, pipe, pronounce, put, sing, slur, speak, speech, stammer, talk, utter, utterance, verbalize, yell

48 **ask:** accost, apologize, apology, appeal, application, apply, approach, ask, beg, beseech, canvass, catechize, charter, conjure, consult, consultation, crave, crawl, cross-examine, debrief, desire, enquire, enquiry, entreat, examine, FAQ, grill, hearing, implore, inquest, inquire, inquiry, interrogate, interview, investigate, investigation, invitation, invite, invocation, invoke, pester, petition, plead, poll, pray, prayer, propose, proposition, pump, query, quest, question, quiz, repent, requisition, scrounge, seek, survey

49 **assert:** accredit, acknowledge, adduce, advance, advocate, affirm, affirmation, allegation, allege, announce, announcement, ascribe, assert, assertion, attest, avow, bemoan, blow up, bluster, boast, brag, bravado, bring out, color, come clean, corroborate,

crow, debunk, declaim, declaration, declare, defend, deny, dramatize, drum into, embellish, emphasize, establish, exclaim, exclamation, exult, generalize, gloat, glory, gloss, go to bat for, gush, impress, impute, insinuate, insist, intimate, justify, lay, level, magnify, maintain, mock, mockery, notification, overrate, pass, play down, play up, plead, plug, point out, pound, proclaim, profess, promote, promotion, pronounce, puff, punctuate, purport, push, rant, rave, refuse, retract, review, rumor, show off, speak out/speak up, spout, state, stereotype, stress, substantiate, support, swagger, swear, take back, testify, testimonial, testimony, underline, underscore, vent, vindicate, voice, vouch, weep, whitewash, witness

50 **authorize:** accede, accord, accredit, acknowledge, acknowledgment, acquit, affirm, aggrandize, appoint, appointment, approve, arm, assign, authorize, back, ban, bar, bear out, bless, blessing, certify, charter, chicken out, commission, concession, consent, constitute, contract, countenance, countermand, crown, decree, dedicate, delegate, delegation, detail, disown, empower, enable, enact, endorse, enforce, enjoin, entitle, entrust, establish, exempt, fire, forgive, grant, induct, inflict, invest, invoke, lay, let, let off, license, make, name, negate, nod, nominate, nomination, notarize, nullify, okay, ordain, order, override, overrule, pardon, permission, permit, place, prescribe, prohibit, ratify, recall, receive, release, relieve, repeal, reprieve, revoke, sanction, spare, station, subscribe, underwrite, validate, vest, veto, void, warrant, withdraw, witness

51 **comment:** accost, acknowledge, add, air, annotate, aside, babble, badger, bemoan, brag, bravado, bring up, broach, circumlocution, comment, commentary, congratulate, conjecture, couch, critique, declaim, decline, deliver, discourse, editorial, enunciate, express, extemporize, fumigate, greet, greeting, harangue, hearsay, interject, interrupt, jabber, jaw, moralize, observation, observe, pontificate, preach, ramble, rattle, rave, remark, report, rhetoric, say, spout, state, talk, throw out, touch, vent, ventilate, voice, yak/yap

52 **criticize:** abuse, admonish, admonition, air, aspersion, assail, assault, attack, bad-mouth, barb, baste, beat up, beef, belittle, berate, blast, browbeat, carp, castigate, censure, chasten, chastise, chew out, chide, come down on, complain, complaint, condemn, condemnation, confront, correct, cow, criticism, criticize, critique, crucify, cut, cut up, damn, darn, debase, decry, denigrate, denounce, denunciation, deny, deprecate, depreciate, deride, derision, detract, detraction, diatribe, disapprove, disparage, disparagement, dress down, excoriate, flak, flame, fulminate, fulmination, gainsay, gibe, gird, grievance, gripe, groan, grouch, grumble, hiss, humble, humiliate, impeach, impugn, insult, invective, inveigh, jaw, kick, knock, lambaste, lament, lash, lay into, lecture, malign, moan, mortify, mouth off, mug, mutter, nag, objurgate, offense, pan, pick at/pick on, profane, protest, quibble, rail, rant, rap, re-

buke, reflection, remonstrate, reprimand, reproach, reprove, review, revile, rock the boat, row, run down, sarcasm, scold, scorn, scourge, sit-in, slam, sneer, squawk, storm, sulk, swear, take down, tell off, thunder, upbraid, vilify, vituperate

53 **demand:** adjure, ask, beckon, beg, behest, bid, bidding, bribe, call, challenge, charge, claim, command, countermand, crave, cross-examine, dare, debrief, decree, demand, dictate, direct, duel, enjoin, entreat, exact, extort, extortion, FAQ, grease, grill, importune, impose, inflict, insist, instruct, interrogate, necessitate, obligate, order, panhandle, petition, pump, query, question, request, require, requisition, reserve, solicit, sponge, squeeze, summon, supplicate, take on

54 **deny:** abjure, abnegate, abuse, accusation, affront, aspersion, attack, backbiting, backstab, bad-mouth, barb, belie, belittle, blacken, blame, blemish, casuistry, confront, contradict, curse, damn, darn, debase, defamation, defame, defile, demean, demur, denial, denigrate, deride, detract, detraction, dig, diminish, disclaim, disclaimer, discountenance, discredit, disgrace, dishonor, disown, disparage, disparagement, downgrade, downplay, embarrass, explode, flame, flout, forswear, fulminate, fulmination, gainsay, gibe, gird, insult, invective, inveigh, jeer, lambaste, lament, laugh at, lecture, lip, malign, mimic, minimize, mortify, mouth, mudslinging, needle, oath, oppose, oppugn, protest, puncture, put down, put-down, rave, rebuff, rebut, refute, revile, remonstrate, renounce, renunciation, ridicule, run down, sarcasm, satirize, scoff, scold, scorn, show up, sit-in, slam, slander, slur, smear, smear campaign, snap, sneer, snub, squawk, squeal, stain, sully, swear, swearing, tattle, taunt, thunder, tirade, traverse, turn, turn down, underestimate, vituperate, vituperation, whine, write off, yammer

55 **describe:** articulate, articulation, blab, define, delineate, denote, describe, detail, mean, narrate, narration, outline, paraphrase, phrase, portray, recite, recount, relate, signify, spell, state, summarize, sum up, tell, translate, typify, unfold, utter

56 **discuss:** argue, bargain, belabor, canvass, communicate, confer, conference, consult, debate, deliberate, deliberation, dialogue/dialog, discourse, discuss, discussion, gossip, huddle, intercede, interchange, jabber, jaw, negotiate, negotiation, powwow, rap, reason, rehash, repartee, seminar, symposium, talk, treat, word

57 **explain:** account for, admission, admit, annotate, apprise, bring out, cite, clarification, clarify, clear up, come clean, comment, concede, confide, confirm, construe, corroborate, declare, defense, define, demonstrate, detail, dilate, elaborate, elucidate, emphasize, enlighten, enumerate, evidence, excuse, expand, explain, explicate, expound, gloss, illuminate, illustrate, interpret, itemize, justify, let on, own, palliate, paraphrase, plea, preface, prove, rationalize, recite, render, simplify, speak out/speak up, specify, spell out, translate, translator, vindicate, warrant

58 fabricate: aspersion, backbiting, belie, bluff, disprove, embroider, fabricate, impugn, profane

59 fool: adulate, affect, artifice, assume, bamboozle, banter, beguile, bilk, blow up, bluff, brownnose, burn, cajole, charade, cheat, chicanery, circumvent, color, con, copy, corner, counterfeit, cross, deceit, deceive, deception, decoy, default, defraud, delude, dirty tricks, disguise, dishonesty, dissemble, dissimulate, do, dodge, do out of, double-cross, double-dealing, dramatize, dupe, duplicity, elude, enmesh, ensnare, entangle, entrap, evasion, excuse, extort, fake, feign, fence, finagle, finesse, flatter, flatterer, flattery, fleece, flimflam, fool, fooling, forge, forgery, fraud, frolic, fudge, gag, game, garble, gimmick, goof off, grift, gyp, hanky-panky, have, hoax, hocus-pocus, humbug, impersonate, imposition, imposture, inveigle, invent, juggle, kid, legerdemain, make believe, maneuver, masquerade, mimic, mince, mislead, mock, outwit/outsmart, overplay, palliate, pander, parlay, parody, play dirty, play down, ploy, pose, posture, prank, pretend, pretense, pretext, put on, renege, ridicule, ruse, satirize, scam, scheme, sham, shift, shirk, shortchange, sidestep, simulate, skulk, spoof, sport, strategem, string along, swindle, take, take in, trap, trick, trickery, victimize, welsh, wile, wit

60 inform: acknowledge, acquaint, address, advance, advertise, advise, allow, allude, allusion, announce, apprise, avow, bare, betray, betrayal, bill, blab, break, breathe, brief, briefing, bring out, broadcast, buzz, chronicle, circulate, clue, come out, come out with, confess, confession, convene, convey, cover, debunk, declare, define, deliver, detail, develop, dictate, disclose, divulge, enlighten, expose, exposure, feature, fumigate, furnish, get across, give, give away, gossip, herald, hint, impart, inform, instruct, intimate, introduce, issue, leak, lecture, let on, newscaster, notify, pass, plug, post, prescribe, proclaim, program, promulgate, propagate, publication, publicize, publish, ready, release, report, reveal, revelation, show up, sing, speak, speech, spill, spread, squeal, stipulate, talk, tattle, tip, unburden, uncover, unmask, unveil, ventilate, weatherperson, whisper

61 instruct: bar, direct, educate, instruct, prescribe

62 label: attach, brand, call, christen, define, designate, dub, entitle, identify, label, name, stigmatize, style, tag, term, title

63 lie: backbiting, belie, bunk, cant, casuistry, color, default, detraction, distort, distortion, duplicity, embroider, equivocate, equivocation, evasion, exaggerate, exaggeration, fabricate, fabrication, falsehood, falsify, feign, fib, fiction, fudge, garble, gloss, hoax, humbug, hypocrisy, invent, invention, juggle, libel, lie, malign, misinform, mislead, misrepresent/misquote, misrepresentation, misstatement, mock, obscure, overstate, pad, perjure, perjury, pervert, play down, pose, pretend, pretense, prevaricate, profane, profess, renege, sell/sell out, sensationalism,

simulate, skew, slant, smear, twist, warp, whitewash, wile

64 noise, animal: bark, bay, call, cheep, chirp, howl, peep, roar, squawk, squeak, squeal, yelp

65 noise-making: bang, blare, blast, blow, boom, buzz, cadence, chant, chime, clank, clash, clatter, click, clink, clump, cough, crash, creak, crinkle, drone, drum, grumble, gurgle, harmony, honk, hue and cry, hullabaloo, hum, hush, inflection, intonation, jangle, jar, jingle, measure, meter, muffle, murmur, mute, patter, peal, pipe, pitch, play, quiet, racket, rattle, reflect, resonate, resound, reverberate, ring, roll, rumble, rustle, silence, sizzle, sound, squeak, still, stillness, stress, swing, talk, tempo, tenor, thud/thump, thunder, tick, tinkle, toll, tone, tranquility, tune/tune up, undertone, uproar, volume, whistle

66 offer: allude, extend, lay, offer, pose, present, proffer, propose, put, submit, volunteer

67 offer to give: amends, apologize, apology, bid, bidding, come forward, concession, expiate, extend, furnish, offer, pose, present, proffer, put, surrender, volunteer

68 persuade: advance, argue, argument, assure, bend, bring around, budge, cajole, carry, coax, coerce, coercion, convince, disarm, discourage, dissuade, draw, drive, drum up, egg on, elicit, eloquence, entice, enticement, forward, get, goad, hammer away/hammer into, impel, induce, inducement, influence, ingratiate, invite, lead, lobby, maintain, motivate, negotiate, negotiation, occasion, persuade, persuasion, pitch, predispose, prevail upon/prevail on, procure, prompt, push, reason, spearhead, spur, stress, sway, tempt, urge, wheedle, win/win over

69 praise: accent, acclaim, acclamation, accolade, accredit, adulate, adulation, aggrandize, apotheosis, applaud, applause, approbation, benediction, blarney, bless, brownnose, champion, cheer, citation, commemorate, commend, commendation, compliment, congratulate, congratulations, consecrate, credit, crown, dedicate, dedication, deify, distinguish, elevate, elevation, endorse, enshrine, eulogize, eulogy, exalt, exaltation, extol, felicitate, flatter, flatterer, flattery, further, glorify, hail, homage, kudos, laud, laurels, lionize, magnify, obsequy, ovation, plaudits, praise, puff, reference, salute, thank, thanks, tout, tribute, worship

70 predict: announce, anticipate, astrology, augur, augury, call, divination, forebode, forecast, foreordain, foresee, foreshadow, foretell, horoscope, oracle, precursor, predict, prediction, presage, prognosticate, project, prophecy, prophesy

71 promise: assurance, assure, avow, bear witness, commitment, covenant, ensure, escrow, go back/go back on, guarantee, oath, pledge, portend, promise, vouch, vow, warrant, word

72 read: leaf, look up, narrate, narration, peruse, pore, read, reading, recitation, recite, refer, skim

73 refer: attach, attribute, drive at, instance, intend, mean, mention, oppose, point out, refer

74 signal: beckon, beep, call, doorbell, flag,

gesture, gesture/gesticulate, hail, harbinger, hint, indicate, indication, nod, omen, page, ripple, sign, signal, spell, suggest, symbolize, wave

75 suggest: advice, advise, advocate, approach, ask, cajole, come up with, commend, connote, counsel, drum into, enlighten, exhort, exhortation, fish for, foreshadow, get at, guidance, guide, hint, imply, innuendo, insinuate, intimate, moralize, motion, move, nominate, nomination, pointer, pontificate, pose, preach, proffer, propose, raise, recommend, spell, suggest, swear by, urge

76 thank: appreciate, gratitude, thank

77 vocalize: accent, air, bark, bawl, bellow, blare, cackle, caterwaul, chant, cheer, chortle, chuckle, clamor, croak, cry, drawl, drone, exclamation, giggle, groan, growl, grumble, guffaw, hail, harmonize, hiss, howl, hum, laugh/laughter, laugh, locution, moan, mumble, murmur, mutter, outcry, parrot, pipe, roar, scream, shout, shriek, shut up, sing, snap, snarl, snicker/snigger/sniggle, snore, squawk, squeal, stutter, vocalize, voice, wail, whimper, whine, whistle, whoop, yammer, yowl

78 warn: admonish, admonition, alert, bluster, caution, cautionary tale, caveat, charge, defy, dissuade, enjoin, exhort, exhortation, forebode, foreboding, forecast, foretell, forewarn, page, portend, remind, threaten, warn, warning

79 write: abstract, address, annotate, autograph, brand, chronicle, compile, compose, correspond, correspondence, cover, depict, dot, draft, draw, draw up, edit, emboss, endorse, engrave, engraving, enroll, extract, fill in, fleck, font, graffiti, hand, inscribe, label, line, list, mark, notify, page, pen, picture, plot, point, proofread, punctuate, put down, quote, register, revise, revision, rough out, score, scratch, scrawl, scribble, script, sign, spot, stamp, stigmatize, trace, transcribe, type, underline, underscore, write, writing

GENERAL

80 act abstractly: freak, jerk, lurch, twist, wiggle, wrench, writhe

81 act over an area: decree, rule, tour, veto

82 admit: accede, accept, acquiesce, admit, allow, concede, concur, grant

83 allow: absolve, accord, acquit, admission, admit, allow, approve, authorize, capitulate, capitulation, contribute, defer, enable, entitle, excuse, exempt, get off someone's back, grant, have, leave, let, let off, liberate, license, overlook, patronage, permission, permit, pity, receive, reception, spell, suffer, tolerate

84 arrange: adjust, alphabetize, antedate, arrange, arrangement, array, center, centralize, codify, collate, collocate, compile, concentrate, configuration, coordinate, derange, dispose, disrupt, distribute, disturb, divide, file, graduate, group, index, jumble, line, marshal, muddle, order, organization, organize, organized, perplex, pile, place, pro-

gram, range, rank, reconstruct, remodel, sort, synchronize, systematize, tabulate, type

85 attach: adhere, adhesion, adjoin, affix, anchor, annex, append, attach, batten, bind, bond, cement, chain, clamp, clasp, cling, cohere, connect, engage, fasten, fix, gasket, hitch, juxtapose, knot, latch, lock, moor, nail, paste, peg, pin, screw, seal, secure, shut, stick, tack, tag, tape, tether, tie, yoke

86 attack: aggression, ambush, assail, assault, attack, bashing, beat up, besiege, blast, blindside, blitz, bomb, bombard, brutality, burst, charge, combat, come at, coup d'état, descent, embroil, encounter, encroach, engage, fire, fix, foray, fray, go for, incursion, infest, inroad, insurrection, invade, invasion, lambaste, lay into, maraud, mug, nuke, occupation, occupy, offensive, onset, onslaught, outbreak, overrun, overwhelm, pillage, plunder, pounce, prey on, raid, rampage, ravage, revenge, rush, sabotage, sortie, storm, subvert, surprise, waylay

87 attempt: acid test, adhere, angle for, answer, apply, assume, attempt, bid, bother, buckle down, campaign, chance, commit, counteract, counterbalance, crack, dabble, dare, defy, delve, dip into, direct, drill, drive, drudge, effort, elbow grease, electioneering, emulate, endeavor, engage, enterprise, essay, exercise, exert, exertion, experiment, fiddle, function, further, go, go for it, hammer away/hammer into, hazard, hunt, imitate, keep at, keep up, labor, mess around, monkey, offer, overdo, overplay, persevere, persist, plod, practice, presume, probation, purpose, pursue, putter, represent, risk, scramble, seek, slave, slog, stab, strain, strive, struggle, substitute, tackle, take after, take a crack at, take on, tinker, trial, try, tussle, undertake, undertaking, venture, wade, whack, whirl, work

88 authorize: accede, accord, accredit, acknowledge, acknowledgment, acquit, affirm, aggrandize, appoint, appointment, approve, arm, assign, authorize, avowal, back, ban, bar, bear out, bless, blessing, certify, charter, chicken out, commission, concession, consent, constitute, contract, countenance, countermand, crown, decree, dedicate, delegate, delegation, detail, disown, empower, enable, enact, endorse, enforce, enjoin, entitle, entrust, establish, exempt, fire, forgive, grant, induct, inflict, invest, invoke, lay, let, let off, license, make, name, negate, nod, nominate, nomination, notarize, nullify, okay, ordain, order, override, overrule, pardon, permission, permit, place, prescribe, prohibit, ratify, recall, receive, release, relieve, repeal, reprieve, revoke, sanction, spare, station, subscribe, underwrite, validate, vest, veto, void, warrant, withdraw, witness

89 borrow: borrow, charter, lease, let, mooch, rent

90 capture: abducted, abduction, apprehend, apprehension, arrest, bag, besiege, capture, catch, collar, commandeer, confinement, conquer, corner, coup d'état, custody, enslave, ensnare, entangle, entrap, expropriate, fetch, foray, get, grab, grasp, hijack, hijacker, hog, imprison, incarcerate, kidnap, nab, nail, net, occupation, occupy, pinch, pull in, seize, seizure, sequester, shanghai, snap, snare, snatch, tackle, trap

91 carry out: accomplish, action, actualize, application, assure, avail, clone, complement, complete, comply, conclude, contrive, discharge, do, duplicate, echo, effect, enact, execute, execution, fill, finalize, finish, follow, follow through, fulfill, get the lead out, hammer out, handle, hustle, implement, make, make out, manage, meet, mind, obey, observe, offender, operate, perfect, perform, perpetrate, persist, practice, proceed, prosecute, pull off, realize, redeem, render, repeat, resonate, resound, rush, serve, specialize, transact, wage

92 compete: bout, boxing, compete, competition, contend, contention, contest, opposition, pit, play, rival, rivalry, take on, tie, vie

93 contract: catch, come down with, contract, get, incur, waterloo

94 control: aegis, auspices, contain, contrive, deal/deal with, determine, deregulate, direct, discipline, dominate, domineer, harness, manage, moderate, monopolize, operate, order about, organized, overlook, predominate, preside, prevail, regulate, regulation, ride, stage, steer, systematize, wield, work

95 defeat: beat, best, confute, conquer, conquest, coup de grâce, crush, defeat, discomfit, drub, edge, extinguish, finish, floor, landslide, lick, outdo, overcome, overpower, overrun, overtake, overthrow, overwhelm, prevail, prostrate, put down, quash, quell, reduce, rout, smash, stamp out, subjugate, subvert, surmount, thrash, top, topple, trim, triumph, trounce, upset, vanquish, victory, wallop, whip, win

96 defend: beard, bite the bullet, bulwark, convoy, counteract, counterbalance, cover, defend, ensure, fend, fend off, fight back/fight off, guard, parapet, protect, repulse, resist, resistance, safeguard, save, screen, secure, shield, ward/ward off, withstand

97 demonstrate: advertising, bear out, demonstrate, establish, evidence, exemplify, give, illustrate, imply

98 divide: allocate, apportion, bestow, bisect, cleave, dichotomy, disconnect, dismember, disrupt, dissect, distribute, distribution, divide, division, divvy up, fork, fragment, halve, mete, part, partition, place, portion, punctuate, quarter, ramification, ration, rupture, sever, share, slice, snap, split

99 enable: allow, enable, implement, qualify

100 engage in: address, anticipate, apply, collaborate, dig in, drudge, elbow grease, embark on, exist, fall to, fare, fend for, fight, give, go about, go for it, go into, go on, grub, immerse, labor, make, participate, pitch in, plunge, ply, practice, pursue, reiterate, risk, share, spend, step in, tackle, take, toil, trouble, turn, undertake, wage, work

101 err: Achilles' heel, blunder, boo boo, boner, botch, bungle, butcher, compromise, err, error, fault, faux pas, flounder, fluff, frailty, fumble, gaffe, glitch, goof, guilt, impropriety, inaccuracy, indiscretion, lapse, malpractice, miscalculate, mishandle/mismanage, misjudge, miss, misstep, mistake, muff, ne-

glect, overlook, oversight, screw up, sin, slip, slip up, snafu, stray, stumble, transgression, trespass, trip, violate, violation, wander

102 escape: abscond, avoid, avoidance, bail out, break, break out, bypass, circumvent, close call, decamp, disappear, disappearance, dodge, duck, elude, equivocate, escape, eschew, evade, evasion, extricate, flee, flight, flinch, fly, getaway, get out, loophole, lose, make off, pussy foot, shake off, sidestep, skedaddle, skirt, throw off, weasel

103 examine: adjudication, analysis, analyze, assay, audit, authenticate, autopsy, case, check, compare, confirm, criticize, decompose, delve, dig, evaluate, evaluation, examination, examine, experiment, explore, follow up, go into, go over, go through, grade, graduate, hearing, inspect, inspection, investigate, investigation, judgment, look into, mapmaker, measure, nose, observe, overview, peer, peruse, pollster, pore, postmortem, probe, quantify, quest, ransack, reconnaissance, research, review, sample, scan, scout, scrutinize, scrutiny, sift, skim, spy, study, surveillance, survey, test, try, try on/try out, view, weigh

104 exchange: alternate, amends, barter, commute, exchange, interchange, reciprocate, redeem, replace, rotate, substitute, swap/swop, switch, transpose

105 existential change: age, arise, awaken, awakening, begin, come from, date, demise, disappear, disappearance, dissipate, dissolution, dissolve, emerge, fade, form, go, go out, languish, materialize, originate, pass, perish, peter out, run out, spring, succumb, vanish, wake/waken

106 fight: act up, ado, altercation, battle, bout, box, brawl, brush, clamor, clash, combat, conflict, confrontation, contend, contention, contest, contravene, dispute, donnybrook, encounter, engage, engagement, faction, ferment, feud, fight, fight back/fight off, fighting, fracas, fray, free-for-all, friction, fuss, grapple, hassle, imbroglio, mayhem, melee, misunderstanding, oppose, opposition, quarrel, racket, rebel, rebellion, resist, resistance, revolt, revolution, rift, riot, rise, row, run-in, scrap, scuffle, sedition, skirmish, slugfest, spat, strife, struggle, tilt, tussle, uprising, uproar, vendetta, war, wrangle

107 fuel: charge, feed, fill, fuel, supply

108 give: administer, afford, allocate, allot, allow, apportion, atone, bear, bequeath, bestow, cast, cede, commend, commit, compensate, confide, consign, consignment, contribute, deal, defray, deliver, delivery, descend, devote, disburse, disseminate, dole out, donate, drop off, emit, endow, entrust, finance, furnish, give, give away, hand out, hand over, impart, kick in, leave, mete, pass, pass off, present, provide, reach, render, return, reward, rustle up, sacrifice, satisfy, show, surrender, transfer, turn over, will

109 group: aggregate, alloy, amass, bank, blend, bunch, cluster, collect, collection, commingle, compilation, compile, compound, concentrate, confluence, congregate, consolidate, consolidation, cull, distribution, flock, garner, gather, get together, group, heap, herd,

muster, pick, pile, rake, reap, recruit, reunion, round up, stack, store

110 help: abet, aid, alleviate, assist, assistance,
attend, baby, backing, bail out, befriend,
benefit, bolster, boost, break, care, chip in,
coddle, commiserate, contribute, convoy,
cooperate, cooperation, cover, cultivate, cultivation, cure, defend, dispense, doctor, do
for, ease, empathize, encourage, encouragement, facilitate, favor, fawn, forward, foster,
free, further, furtherance, go straight, guarantee, guide, hand, help, hold, indulge, intercede, intervene, invigorate, keep, kindness,
lavish, liberate, lift, lighten, mind, minister,
nurse, nurture, oblige, patronage, patronize,
pitch in, play ball, profit, promote, promotion, provide, quell, reform, relieve, serve,
service, shore, shower, simplify, soothe,
speed, spell, sponsor, stabilize, synchronize,
subsidize, support, sustain, sympathize,
teamwork, temper, tide over, toady, truckle,
underwrite, uphold

111 imitate: ape, imitate, mimic, mirror, mock,
mockery, parallel, parody, pattern, pretend,
repeat, reproduce, sham, simulate, takeoff,
take off

112 involve: attack, coalesce, confuse, contain,
cooperate, cooperation, count, devote, embody, embrace, encapsulate, enclose, encompass, enmesh, entangle, entrap, figure in,
implicate, include, incorporate, interpolate,
introduce, involve, mire, overdo, play ball,
synchronize, tangle, task, teamwork

113 join: accompany, add, adhere, adjoin, affiliate, affix, alloy, amalgamate, annex, annexation, append, articulate, articulation,
assemble, assembly, attach, band, bridge,
butt, cleave, close, coalesce, cohere, combine, compound, connect, converge, couple,
desegregate, dovetail, embody, engage, fasten, fix, fuse, fusion, get together, graft,
hitch, incorporate, integrate, intermingle, intersect, intertwine/interweave, introduce,
join, juxtapose, knit, knot, lace, link, meeting, meld, merge, mesh, mix, pair, piece,
pool, reunion, swarm, synthesis, synthesize,
unify, union, unite, wed

114 join socially: affiliate, align, assemble, associate, attach, attend, band, belong, bump into,
cahoots, call, cavort, chaperon, collect, collusion, confluence, congregate, consort, consultation, convene, convention, converge,
convocation, couple, dalliance, dally/dally
with, date, desegregate, enroll, enter, escort,
fraternize, gather, group, hang about/hang
around/hang out, horse around, huddle, integrate, intermingle, intertwine/interweave,
join, league, link, matriculate, meet, mix,
register, session, swarm, take

115 lend: defray, finance, fund, hock, invest,
lease, lend, let, loan, pawn, rent, trust

116 lose: deliver, fall, forfeit, forget, leak, lose,
misplace, omission, sacrifice, wipeout

117 manage: adjust, administer, administration,
boss, carry on, charge, compose, conduct,
control, custody, deal/deal with, deregulate,
direct, dispense, dispose, dominate, drill,
economy, face, fare, farm, farming, fend for,
get along, get by, get on, guide, handle, handling, head, lead, manage, management, mar-

shal, monitor, officiate, operate, orchestrate,
order about, organization, overlook, oversee,
oversight, predominate, preside, rally, regulate, regulation, reign, rule, run, running,
save, spearhead, subjugate, supervise, supervision, sway, treatment, upkeep, work

118 manifest: agree, comprehend, connote, embodiment, embody, emerge, evince, exemplify, exude, give, indicate, loom, manifest,
mirror, point, presage, promise, prove, radiate

119 modify an event: abide, abrogation, advent,
balk, birth, cancellation, cessation, close, closure, come on, come out, come up, coming,
commence, complement, completion, conception, conclude, conclusion, culminate,
dawn, desist, develop, discontinuance, disposal, embargo, end, ending, end up, ensue,
entrance, expiration, expire, fall, finish, genesis, give in/give up, graduation, halt, knock
off, lapse, lay off, matriculate, moratorium,
pass, pause, pull out, pull up, quit, recess, relinquish, renaissance, resign, resignation, result, resurgence, resurrection, retract, revival,
rout, secede, spurt, standstill, step down,
stop, surrender, suspend, suspension, terminate, termination

120 obtain: acquire, acquisition, amass, attain,
capitalize, earn, gain, get, get at, get back,
land, lay up/lay by, make, obtain, pick up,
possess, procure, pull in, realize, reap, recover, recruit, regain, repossess, retrieve,
save, secure, strike, take win

121 prevent: abolish, abolition, abort, abrogate,
abstain, adjourn, adjournment, anticipate, arrest, asphyxiate, avert, avoid, avoidance, baffle, balk, ban, banish, bar, birth control,
block, bog down, brake, break, bridle, censor, cheat, check, choke, circumvent, clog,
close, confine, constrain, constraint, contravene, cop out, counter, cripple, cross, curb,
cut short, dash, deactivate, decommission,
defeat, defer, deferment/deferral, delay, deprivation, deprive, deter, discharge, discontinue, discourage, dispossess, disqualify,
dissolve, drop, drop out, encumber, exclude,
exclusion, foil, forbear, forbid, forgo, freeze,
frustrate, gag, halt, hesitate, hesitation, hinder, hold back/hold off, hold up, impede, impound, incapacitate, inhibit, intercept,
interfere, interference, interrupt, invalidate,
jam, keep, keep one's cool, kill, localize,
mire, muffle, muzzle, negate, negation, neutralize, nip, nullify, obstruct, obviate, occlude, omit, outlaw, override/overrule,
paralyze, parry, pause, pigeonhole, preclude,
preempt, prevent, privation, procrastinate,
prohibit, prohibition, proscribe, pull out, pull
up, pussyfoot, put off, quash, quell, recess,
refrain, relegate, remove, repeal, repress, rescind, respite, restrain, retard, revoke, rule
out, run-around, scrap, scratch, scrub, seclude, shelve, shut, shut off/shut out, slowdown, slowpoke, spite, squash, squish, stall,
stay, stem, stifle, still, stop, stymie, subdue,
suppress, suspend, table, terminate, thwart,
traverse, turn off, undo, veto, vitiate, void,
waive, waiver, waylay, withdraw, withhold

122 punish: avenge, chasten, chastise, correct,
correction, discipline, evict, exile, expel,

fine, pay, penalize, punish, revenge, scourge, sentence

123 punishment: blackmail, damage(s), discipline, dressing-down, eviction, fine, forfeit, lesson, punishment, rap, reprimand, reproach, retribution, sanction, whipping

124 receive: accept, acceptance, acquire, acquisition, bring in, come by, come in for, fetch, find, gain, have, inherit, make, object, profit, realize, reap, receipt, receive, reception, recoup, regain, retrieve, take

125 record: enroll, enter, enumerate, itemize, list, record, register, schedule, score, take down, tally, tape, transcribe

126 rectify: accommodate, amend, appease, appeasement, arbitrate, arbitration, atone, atonement, avenge, break even, compensate, conclude, correct, correction, counteract, counterbalance, cover, cure, debug, do up, edit, emend, equalize, expiate, fix, get even, iron out, make up, mediate, mediation, mend, offset, overhaul, penance, placate, proofread, quiet, recompense, recoup, rectify, redeem, redress, reform, rehabilitate, remedy, requite, restore, retaliate, retribution, revise, revision, right, satisfy, settle, square, standardize, suit, tailor, temper, tune/tune up, troubleshooter, untangle

127 release: acquittal, cede, clear, deliver, delivery, discharge, disentangle, dismiss, dismissal, emancipate, exculpate, exempt, exonerate, extricate, free, loose/loosen, ransom, redeem, release, relinquish, save

128 replace: change, fill in, follow, needlework, replace, supersede, supplant

129 reserve: allocate, assign, assignment, assumption, claim, clear, come by, deserts, deserve, designate, earmark, earn, engage, enroll, entitle, gain, intend, merit, put away/put aside/put by, rate, reserve, save, spare, store, subscribe

130 restrict: bar, barricade, bind, block, bound, boycott, brake, check, circumscribe, clog, cocoon, confine, constrain, constraint, constrict, constriction, control, cramp, curb, curtail, dam, deaden, defer, deferment/deferral, delay, desensitize, disable, embargo, encumber, enjoin, enslave, expatriate, expel, expulsion, fetter, fetters, foil, forbear, forgo, gag, govern, grind, ground, hamper, hamstring, handicap, harness, hem/hem in, hinder, hobble, hold back/hold off, hold up, impair, impede, imposition, impound, inhibit, keep one's cool, limit, localize, matter, moderate, narrow, obligate, obstruct, ostracism, postpone, prohibit, prohibition, rein, repress, restrain, restrict, retard, set back, shackle, slow, slowdown, smother, squelch, stifle, strangle, stymie, subdue, suppress, suspend, thwart, tie/tie up

131 return: deliver, fetch, hand over, ransom, recall, redeem, regain, repay, requite, restore, retrieve, return

132 reward: award, commend, confer, decorate, reward

133 rule: abdicate, accession, command, depose, deposition, dictatorship, displace, enforce, enforcement, govern, impose, oppress, rule, subjugate, supremacy

134 save: cocoon, conservation, conserve, deliverance, deposit, ecology, guard, harbor, lay up/lay by, maintain, maintenance, pad, patrol, preservation, preserve, protect, put away/put aside/put by, rehabilitate, rescue, salvage, salvation, save, shelter, shield, spare, vigil, ward/ward off, watch

135 separate: abstract, analyze, appropriate, appropriation, assign, class, classification, classify, dedicate, detach, dichotomy, disaffect, disconnect, disengage, disentangle, dislocate, dismantle, dismember, disperse, disrupt, dissociate, divide, division, filter, fragment, gape, garner, glean, hoard, isolation, loneliness, open, part, partition, quarantine, schism, secession, seclude, seclusion, segregate, segregation, separate, separation, split, split up, strain, sunder, undo, unlock

136 serve: accommodate, administer, board, bondage, cater, mollycoddle, obey, oblige, pamper, pander, provide, quench, serve, spoil, spoon-feed, tend, wait on

137 shape change: beat, bevel, bruise, carve, chip, chisel, cleave, clip, compact, crimp, crinkle, cut, depreciation, desiccate, disfigure, disguise, distort, disturb, divide, do in, edge, elongate, enlarge, fatigue, file, flatten, fragment, gash, hack, hone, lacerate, lance, mow, mutilated, nick, notch, pierce, prune, puncture, reduce, roll, rumple, scar, score, sculpture, shape, sharpen, shave, shear, shorten, shrink, shrivel, skew, slash, slice, smooth, stiffen, stretch, taper/taper off, thicken, thin, trample, truncate, warp, whet, wound

138 show: advertising, bare, circulate, model, point, prove, represent, reveal, show, substantiate, symbolize, tout, trot out, unveil

139 steal: abduct, abducted, abduction, appropriate, appropriation, assume, bilk, break in, burglary, cheat, confiscate, copy, divest, do out of, embezzle, embezzlement, extort, extortion, filch, fleece, flimflam, grift, heist, hijack, hijacker, hold up, kidnap, knock off, larceny, lift, loot, maraud, milk, misappropriate, pilfer, pillage, pinch, piracy, plagiarism, play dirty, plunder, poach, pocket, purloin, ransack, rifle, rip off, rip-off, rob, sack, shanghai, shoplift, shortchange, snitch, steal, swindle, swipe, take, theft, unmask, welsh

140 supply: appoint, contribute, deal, deluge, dish out, dispensation, dispense, disseminate, distribute, distribution, divide, divvy up, dole out, equip, feed, foster, fuel, furnish, give, hand out, infuse, issue, keep, kick in, larder, lend, maintain, make out, nourish, nurse, nurture, portion, provide, provision, publish, quarter, ration, receive, render, replenish, rig, satisfy, serve, stock, stockpile, supply, support, sustain

141 surpass: abound, beat, better, break, cap, conquer, eclipse, exceed, excel, flourish, get ahead, go by, hack it, lead, lick, outclass, outdistance, outdo, outflank, outfox, outweigh, overtake, pass, predominate, prevail, succeed, supersede, surmount, surpass, top, tower, transcend, triumph, win

142 take: acquire, acquisition, arrogate, assume, assumption, broach, burn, commandeer, compass, confiscate, cull, deplete, deprivation, deprive, disarm, disarmament, dispossess, divest, drain, draw, educe, elicit, exact, excerpt, exfoliate, expropriate, extract, filch, harvest, have, leach, milk, molt, nip, peel, pilfer, pocket, preempt, privation, pump, ransack, rob, sap, seize, take, tap, usurp, wring

143 **transfer abstractly:** afford, bear, bring, commit, consign, consignment, conveyance, delegate, delegation, infect, recall, refer, relay, release, relegate, transfer, turn over

MOTION

144 **be moved:** earthquake, elapse, flop, hang, lap

145 **change of place:** flicker, locomotion, motion, movement, onrush, passage, pop, rush, sway, sweep, swing, swirl, swivel, teeter, tremor

146 **flow:** flow, pour, run, secrete, seep, stream, surge, swamp, teem, torrent, trickle

147 **move:** bob, budge, careen, churn, circulate, circulation, contort, cruise, curl, curve, dandle, deflect, descend, descent, dislocate, dislodge, displace, dive, drift, drive, entwine, falter, fidget, flex, flourish, gyrate, haul, lean, loop, move, oscillate, overturn, paddle, pitch, pivot, pulsate/pulse, pulse, revolve, ripple, rock, roll, rotate, round, skirt, tilt, topple, toss, transport, traverse, tumble, turn, twine, twist, uproot, upset, waft, wave, waver, weave, wheel, wield

148 **move mechanically:** aviation, bank, carriage, carry, cart, drive, fly, haul, mobilize, navigate, operate, pack, park, ride, rocket, ship, skyrocket, soar, takeoff, take off, veer

149 **move oneself:** ascend, ascension, bend, constitutional, flap, flex, flounce, gad, gait, gallivant, gambol, go ahead, go for, gyrate, hike, jerk, lope, motion, mount, mountaineer, mountaineering, move, negotiate, pace, pad, pass, patter, progress, quail, ripple, rock, roll, round, stalk, stamp, step, stir, stray, stride, strut, stump, swagger, tilt, traipse, tread, trip, tumble, walk, wallow, wave, wriggle

150 **move oneself quickly:** barge in/barge into, beat, bolt, bounce, bustle, capsize, coast, course, dart, dash, decamp, dodder, flash, flee, flinch, flit, flutter, fly, gallop, get the lead out, glide, hasten, hurry, hurtle, hustle, jerk, jiggle, lurch, make off, march, plunge, pound, prance, race, rebound, recoil, ricochet, rocket, run, rush, scamper, scoot, scramble, scurry, shake, shoot, shudder, skate, skedaddle, skim, skip, skyrocket, slide, slip, slither, soar, speed, spin, sprint, start, storm, sweep, swerve, swoop, tear, trot, twirl, veer, wag, whip, whiz, wiggle, wobble, writhe, zip, zoom

151 **move oneself slowly:** amble, crawl, creep, cruise, dalliance, dally, decline, dilly-dally, drag, hobble, jog, knock about/knock around, lag, laggard, limp, linger, loiter, lumber, lurk, meander, mosey, plod, poke, prowl, pussyfoot, ramble, range, reel, roam, saunter, shuffle, slink/slither, slog, sneak, stagger, steal, straggle, stroll, sway, tarry, totter, tramp, trudge, waddle, wade, wander

152 **move quickly:** advance, advancement, agitate, bear down, capsize, convulsion, course, discharge, dispatch, dodder, ejaculate, fall, flicker, flourish, flutter, hasten, jerk, jiggle, jostle, keel over, lurch, palpitate, plunge, precipitate, quake, quiver, rattle, rush, shake, shiver, shoot, shudder, skate, skid, skim, slide, slip, slither, speed, spin, stampede, sweep, tear, throb, tremble, twirl, vibrate, vibration, wag, whip, whirl, whisk, wiggle, wobble

153 **move slowly:** dangle, float, lag, reel

154 **position oneself:** arise, bow, cant, duck, get down, get off, get up, hover, huddle, hunch, kneel, lie, list, loll, lounge, mount, nestle, obeisance, perch, poise, pose, ramble, recline, repose, rest, rise, seat, sit, slouch, wince

155 **travelling:** lift, navigation, procession, railroad, transit, transport, voyage

PHYSICAL

156 **abuse:** abuse, charge, consumption, cop out, corrode, defile, dissipate, dope, enervate, exploit, exploitation, force, frazzle, fritter, impinge, lose, malpractice, milk, misappropriate, mishandle/mismanage, mistreat, misuse, overdo, pervert, prostitute, riddle, run through, sap, spend, squander, strain, throw away, waste, wear

157 **anatomical change:** distend, flake, neuter

158 **arrange:** agitation, align, arrange, bundle, collate, coordinate, crease, deploy, dispose, file, group, indent, lay, lay out, located, mess up, mix up, muss, order, organize, position, range, rank, reverse, ruffle, rummage, separate, shuffle, snarl, sort, split up, spread, stack, stir, straighten, unwind, weave

159 **arrive:** admission, advent, alight, appear, appearance, approach, arrival, arrive, billow, board, butt in, come, come in, coming, cross, cruise, disembark, dock, embark, encroach, enter, entrance, foray, get, get back, get in, get on, go, go ahead, gravitate, immigrate, infiltrate, influx, insinuate, intrude, invade, invasion, jaunt, lance, land, light, loom, lunge, make, penetrate, permeate, pierce, pounce, progress, pull up, reach, report, return, show up, stalk, swarm, trespass, turn out, turn up

160 **attach:** adhere, adhesion, adjoin, affix, anchor, annex, append, attach, batten, bind, bond, cement, chain, clamp, clasp, cling, cohere, connect, engage, fasten, fix, gasket, hitch, knot, latch, lock, moor, nail, paste, peg, pin, screw, seal, secure, shut, stick, tack, tag, tape, tether, tie, yoke

161 **bathe:** ablution, bath, bathe, clean, decontaminate, wet

162 **beautify:** accessorize, adorn, adornment, bask, beautify, comb, decorate, decoration, doll up, embellish, enhance, facelift, festoon, fix up, flatter, furbish, groom, ornament, primp, shave, spruce up, trim

163 **breathe:** breath, breathe, draw, exhale, expire, gasp, heave, huff, inhale, pant, puff, sigh, suffocate, wheeze, yawn

164 **catch:** catch, field, intercept, seize, tackle

165 **clean:** ablution, abrade, bath, bathe, brush, catharsis, clarify, clean, cleanse, clear, decontaminate, disinfect, distill, distillation, do up, exorcism, expurgate, filter, flush, furbish, gut, housework, lather, launder, mop, purge, purification, purify, rake, refine, refinement, rinse, scour, scrape, scrub, sift, sweep, wash, wipe

166 **climb:** arise, ascend, ascension, ascent, climb, get on, mount, rise, scale, surface

167 **clothe:** array, attire, clothe, deck, disrobe, doll up, dress, dress up, garb, get on, ornament, outfit, primp, rig, sport, spruce up, stuff, try on/try out, turn out, wear

168 **construct:** build, compose, construct, construction, dismantle, erect, establish, fashion, forge, form, found, frame, make, modernize, pave, pitch, put up, raise, rear, reconstruct, remodel, renovate, revamp, throw up, ultramodern

169 **consume:** absorption, bolt, chew, chug, consume, consumption, contract, corrode, crunch, demolish, deplete, devour, diet, digest, dig in, dine, dispatch, dissipate, draft, drink, eat, engulf, exhaust, fast, feast, feed on, finish, gargle, glut, gnaw, gobble, gorge, gormandize, go through, graze, gulp, guzzle, imbibe, ingest, munch, nibble, nip, nosh, partake, peck, pig out, polish off, potable, prey on, put away, quaff, satiate, sip, spend, stuff, swallow, take, taste, tear down, use, wolf, xerophagy

170 **cook:** agitation, bake, barbecue, baste, beat, boil, brew, broil, butcher, can, churn, coddle, cook, cure, distill, fix, flavor, foam, fry, grill, honeyed, housework, knead, mash, microwave, nuke, pickle, preservation, preserve, sear, season, simmer, sizzle, stir, sweeten, toast, warm, whip

171 **copy:** ape, clone, copy, counterfeit, duplicate, echo, emulate, follow, forge, forgery, imitate, imitation, mimic, mirror, multiply, parallel, parrot, pattern, pretend, quote, reconstruct, reflect, reiterate, repeat, reproduce, sham, simulate, simulation, take after, transcribe, xerox

172 **cover:** blanket, bury, camouflage, coat, cover, daub, disguise, dissimulate, drape, dress, dust, engulf, enshroud, envelop, face, finish, funeral, gild, glaze, insulate, inter, inundate, laminate, lap, line, mask, masquerade, morgue, muzzle, obscure, oil, overrun, paint, palliate, paper, pave, pervade, plate, sheet, smear, smother, spatter, spread, top, varnish, veil, veneer, wrap

173 **create:** bear, beget, brainstorm, breed, coin, come up with, compose, conceive, concoct, constitute, construct, contrive, create, creation, design, draft, engineer, establish, establishment, fabricate, fashion, father, film, forge, form, formation, formulate, frame, generate, generation, hatch, improvise, institute, invent, make, make up, materialize, mint, mold, originate, piece, pioneer, procreate, produce, regenerate, reproduce, reproduction, spawn, wing it, work

174 **create art:** chart, compose, depict, dot, draw, engrave, engraving, etch, illustrate, impress, imprint, lay out, mount, outline, paint, photograph, picture, plot, portray, pose, pottery, print, printer, rough out, sculpture, sketch, stamp, trace

175 **create with effort:** beat, forge, mold

176 **cut:** amputate, ax/axe, behead, bisect, carve, chisel, chop, cleave, clip, crop, cut, cut up, decapitate, dent, dismember, dissect, dissection, engrave, engraving, etch, exfoliate, fell, gash, hack, knife, lacerate, lop, mangle, mince, molt, mow, mutilate, nick, notch, pare, peel, pierce, pink, prune, scar, score, scratch, sever, shave, shear, shred, skin, slash, slice, slit, split, trim, whittle

177 **decorate:** accessorize, adorn, adornment, decorate, decoration, embellish, embellishment, emblazon, embroider, enhance, enrich, festoon, furnish, gild, modernize, ornament, paper, refurbish, renovate, revamp, trim, ultramodern, varnish

178 **dig:** bore, burrow, claw, dig, dredge, embed, excavate, excavation, exhume, grub, hollow, inter, mine, plant, plow, rake, root, scoop, tunnel, unearth, uproot

179 **discharge:** blast, blowout, blow up, bubble, burst, cascade, come from, deliver, detonate, detonation, discharge, disgorge, drain, dribble, drop, effusion, ejaculate, eject, ejection, emanate, emanation, emission, emit, erupt, eruption, evacuate, excrete, exorcise, expel, explode, explosion, express, exude, fire, flare, flood, flow, flush, gag, give off/give out, go off, gush, heave, impregnate, infest, infiltrate, inflow, infuse, inject, inundate, issue, jet, launch, leak, liftoff, mushroom, ooze, ouster, outbreak, outflow, overflow, overrun, pass, penetrate, percolate, permeate, pervade, pour, proceed, project, regurgitate, scatter, secrete, seep, shed, shoot, spatter, spew, spill, spit, spot, spout, spray, sprinkle, spurt, squirt, stream, surge, swamp, teem, throw up, torrent, trickle, vent, void, vomit

180 **dispose:** boot, buck, chuck, discard, discharge, dispose, dispose of, ditch, do away with, dump, elimination, jettison, kick out, reject, rejection, rid, scrap, shed, throw away, unload, void

181 **drop:** alight, clatter, crash, crumble, decline, descend, descent, dip, dive, drip, droop, drop, duck, dump, fall, fell, flop, founder, fumble, go down, go under, ground, keel over, land, light, lower, percolate, pitch, plumb, plummet, plunge, plunk, sag, set, settle, shed, sink, sling, slump, spill, stoop, stumble, submerge, subside, suspend, swoop, thud/thump, topple, tumble, wilt

182 **equip:** arm, armed, do up, equip, fit, furnish, gear, outfit, rig, stock, stockpile

183 **find:** come across, detect, detection, discover, discovery, ferret out, find, find out, learn, locate, meet, pick up, pinpoint, recover, repossess, spot, strike, stumble, track/track down, turn up, uncover, unearth

184 **form:** arch, bend, bloat, braid, carve, chisel, constitute, contort, crumple, curl, curve, fold, form, materialize, model, mold, pat, round, sculpture, shape, twist, whittle, work

185 **gesture:** bawl, beam, beat, belch, bite, bleed, blink, blow, chew, clap, disgorge, drag, dribble, drivel, drool, excrete, expire, frown, ges-

ture, gnaw, grimace, grin, guffaw, gulp, hemorrhage, itch, kink, kiss, laugh/laughter, laugh, lick, munch, necking, nod, perspire, pucker, puff, pulsate/pulse, pulse, purse, regurgitate, scowl, shiver, slobber, smile, smirk, smooch, sob, spasm, spit, squint, sweat, tear/tears, throb, twitch, vomit, wail, weep, whimper, wince, wink, wrinkle, yawn

186 grind: abrade, abrasion, corrode, creak, crunch, file, frazzle, gnash, granulate, grate, grind, mash, mill, pound, powder, pulverize, rasp, scrape

187 guide: aviation, channel, conduct, convey, direct, divert, drive, ease, ferry, funnel, guide, infuse, inject, jockey, lay, lead, level, maneuver, marshal, mobilize, navigate, navigation, point, refer, round, route, row, see, show, sidetrack, sled, sleigh, steer, take, transport, usher

188 hide: ambush, balk, bury, cache, camouflage, cloak, conceal, concealment, cover, coverup, cower, cringe, cut, disguise, dissemble, dissimulate, eavesdrop, embed, encode, ensconce, enshroud, envelop, harbor, hide, isolate, isolation, loneliness, lurk, mask, masquerade, obscure, palliate, quarantine, screen, seclude, seclusion, secrete, sequester, shelter, shrink, shut off/shut out, smother, sneak, withhold

189 hit: applaud, applause, bang, bash, baste, bat, batter, battery, beat, belt, blind-side, blow, boot, box, buffet, bump, bunt, butt, chip, clap, clash, clatter, clip, clobber, clout, club, collide, collision, concussion, crack, crash, crown, cuff, dash, deflect, dent, drive, drum, flail, flog, glance, hail, hammer, hand, hit, impact, jab, jar, jostle, kick, knock, lash, lick, maul, nail, pat, peck, pelt, plaudits, poke, pound, pummel, punch, ram, rap, rough up, scourge, slam, slap, slug, smack, smashup, sock, spank, strike, swat, swipe, tan, tap, thrash, thud/thump, tick, tip, wallop, whack, whip

190 hold: anchor, cling, clog, clutch, cradle, cuddle, dangle, embrace, fondle, grab, hog, hold, hook, hug, nip, nuzzle, pin, prop, retain, retard, seize, shore, snuggle, support, suspend, sustain, tangle

191 hold forcefully: apprehend, brace, cage, captivity, clasp, clench, clinch, clutch, confinement, constrict, constriction, contain, cramp, dam, detain, detention, embrace, enfold, enslave, fetter, fetters, grapple, grasp, grip, gripe, harness, hold, imprison, incarcerate, leash, overpower, pen, press, restrain, shackle, snap, snatch, stifle, strangle, tackle, throttle, wrestle

192 illegal behavior: backstab, blackmail, bleed, breach, break, break in, bribe, bug, buy, cheat, conspire, contraband, contravene, crime, delinquency, depredation, disobey, entrench, extortion, fault, felony, fix, foul, fraud, graft, grease, hara-kiri, have, holdup, hold up, imposture, infraction, infringe, injustice, intrigue, jinx, kickback, knock off, larceny, libel, loot, mischief, misconduct, misdeed/misdemeanor, murder, offense, outrage, pick, pilfer, piracy, plagiarism, poach, racket, rape, ravish, rip off, rip-off, rob, robbery, screw, sexual assault, sham, shenani-

gans, slander, smear campaign, smuggle, speculation, squeeze, stick up, swindle, take, tamper, theft, transgression, treason, trespass, victimize, violate, violation

193 join physically: link, meld, merge, mesh, mingle, mix, piece, pool, splice, tie, tuck, unify, unite, wed, weld, yoke

194 jump: bounce, bound, clear, deflect, dive, flip, gallop, gambol, hop, hurdle, jump, leap, lunge, lurch, plunge, pounce, rear, rebound, recoil, ricochet, skip, spring, start, vault

195 leave: abandon, abscond, back, beat it, blow, board, bolt, brain drain, break, break away, break out, clear out, cringe, curtains, dart, defection, depart, departure, desert, desertion, deviate, diaspora, digress, disappear, disappearance, dismount, distance, diverge, draw back, drop, ebb, egress, embark, evacuate, exit, exodus, fall back, farewell, flee, flight, fly, forsake, get along, get off, get out, go, goodbye, go off, go out, jaunt, jilt, leave, light out, make off, maroon, part, parting, pull out, push off/push on, quail, quit, recede, recoil, renounce, renunciation, repair, resign, resignation, retire, retreat, run, schism, scram, secession, segregation, separation, shake off, shove off, shrink, step down, strike out, swerve, takeoff, take off, threads, throw over, trousers, turn, vacate, withdraw, withdrawal

196 lift: boost, dip, elevate, elevator, heave, hoist, lift, pick up, pry, raise, rear

197 measure: balance, figure, measure, quantify, survey

198 move living quarters: anyplace, anywhere, approach, arena, battlefield, camp, colonization, cover, defect, defection, deport, deportation, destination, dominion, element, emigrate, empire, encampment, evict, eviction, exile, expatriate, expel, hideout, jurisdiction, landmark, locale/locality, location, lookout, migrate, move, nest, neighborhood, oasis, outdoors, outside, point, position, post, premises, province, refuge, region, reign, rendezvous, resort, seat, setting, site, situation, soil, spa, spot, station, stop, surroundings, terminal, territory, turn, vicinity, where

199 perform: fan, hit, perform, type, work

200 physical action: application, apply, bash, clout, drop, hit, hold, lift, plunk, push, slug

201 position: aim, barricade, bow, button, cant, close, cock, coil, deposit, dial, dip, direct, disseminate, ensconce, entwine, fix, hang, indent, insert, install, installation, interpolate, intersperse, isolate, jut, lap, lay, lean, lie, list, located, lodge, loop, misplace, occlude, park, pile, pitch, place, plant, point, position, post, prop, put, quarantine, recline, roll, seat, separate, set, sit, slant, slope, slouch, snuggle, sprawl, spread, squat, stand, station, stick, stoop, swerve, tip, top, train, traverse, turn, twine, twist, unfold, wallow, wind, wrinkle

202 prepare physically: acclimate, acculturation, accustom, adjust, braid, brush, brush up, buff, bundle, burnish, coat, condition, disguise, doll up, domesticate, do up, dress, embalm, embattle, face, fine-tune, finish, fix up, formulate, fortify, freezer, gear, get, gild, glaze, gloss, grace, grease, groom, habituate, housework, knit, lubricate, make up, modernize, modulate, orient, overhaul, pack, pad, pare, plaster, plate, polish, preparation, prepare, preservation, preserve, prime, primp, ready, reform, refresh, refrigerate, refurbish, regenerate, rehabilitate, rejuvenate, renew, renovate, rig, round, season, set, shave, shine, slim, smear, spruce up, square, straighten, strain, tailor, toughen, train, training, weather

203 print: edit, print, printer, type, write

204 process: gnash, grind, process, work

205 produce: agriculture, fabricate, fabrication, film, forge, form, generate, generation, horticulture, lay, make, manufacture, mint, output, print, produce, production, synthesize, turn out, yield

206 pull: drag, draw, extract, gut, lug, pick, pluck, pry, pull, pump, schlep, shut, strain, tear, tow, tug, twist, twitch, wrench, wring, yank

207 pursue: chase, dog, dragnet, follow, hound, hunt, pursue, pursuit, shadow, steal, tag, tail, trace, track/track down, trail

208 push: advance, advancement, back, balloon, barge in/barge into, bear down, billow, bloat, blow up, boost, bulge, bulldoze, burst, compact, compress, cram, crowd, crumple, crush, dent, depress, dig, drive, elbow, extrude, fan, force, hit, indent, inject, insinuate, intrude, jam, jog, jolt, jostle, knead, level, mash, massage, mob, nick, notch, nudge, poke, press, prod, propel, protrude, pulp, pump, purse, push, ram, repel, repulse, roll, shoulder, shove, shut, slam, squash, squish, strain, tax, thrust, tip, topple, trample, upset, wrestle, wring

209 put in container: box, encapsulate, enclose, fill, flood, fold, glut, imbue, inject, insert, interpolate, introduce, load, pack, plug, pour, ram, replenish, stow, stuff, surfeit

210 relax: asleep, bask, dalliance, dally, dawdle, dilly-dally, drop off, kick back, loaf, loiter, loll, lounge, lull, nap, nod, putter, relax, relaxation, repose, rest, sit tight, slack/slacken, snooze, stay, tarry, trifle, turn in, unwind, vegetate, wait

211 remove: abstract, amputate, blot, bounce, break off, call off, cancel, cashier, clear, clear out, cut out, delete, denude, deport, deportation, disarm, disarmament, discharge, distill, divest, doff, download, drain, efface, eliminate, empty, eradicate, erase, evict, eviction, except, exception, excerpt, excise, excoriate, expatriate, expulsion, expunge, extirpate, extract, extraction, free, gut, hollow, leach, omit, oust, peel, pry, purge, relegate, remove, replace, rid, shed, skim, skin, strip, subtract, take, top, transport, unburden, undress, unload, uproot, void, withdraw, withdrawal

212 repair: adjust, compensate, debug, fine-tune, fix, overhaul, patch, remedy, repair, restore, right, tinker, touch up, troubleshooter

213 reposition: bank, bow, bump, crimp, crinkle, crook, crouch, curl, curve, deploy, descend, descent, dislocate, dislodge, displace, divert, drag, draw back, invert, jump, reverse, shift, sidetrack, sink, squirm, transplant, turn, upset, veer, warp

214 rip: claw, fray, lacerate, rip, snag, tear

215 rub: bite, buff, burnish, chafe, creak, efface, erase, excoriate, file, fret, friction, gall, glaze, gloss, grate, grind, polish, rasp, rub, scrape, smear

216 search: comb, delve, dig, exploration, explore, ferret out, forage, frisk, grope, grub, hunt, investigate, investigation, look up, nose, pan, plumb, probe, prospect, pry, quest, rake, ransack, refer, rummage, scour, scout, scrounge, search, seek, snoop, trace, track/track down

217 send: banish, carriage, carry, cart, channel, commit, consign, consignment, convey, deliver, delivery, deport, deportation, direct, dismiss, dismissal, dispatch, disperse, distribute, distribution, download, export, extradite, ferry, forward, funnel, mail, pack, pass, passage, pipe, radiate, remit, return, route, scatter, send, ship, sled, sleigh, take, transfer, transmit, transport, waft

218 sew: baste, embroider, embroidery, knit, line, patch, sew, spin, tack, tailor, tuck

219 squeeze: choke, clasp, clinch, constrict, constriction, crease, crush, distill, enfold, gripe, pinch, pucker, pulp, pulverize, rumple, screw, squash, squeeze

220 stab: claw, drill, gore, gouge, impale, knife, lacerate, penetrate, perforate, pierce, prick, punch, puncture, riddle, spike, stab, stick, sting, tap, transfix

221 start: actuate, boot, emanate, emanation, embark on, engage, engender, erect, establish, establishment, fall to, foment, found, go back to square one, impel, implement, inaugurate, incite, initiate, initiation, inspire, install, installation, instigate, instill, institute, introduce, invent, kindle, launch, lead, make, mobilize, onset, open, originate, pioneer, plant, preface, propel, provoke, raise, recharge, renaissance, renew, resume, resurgence, resurrection, resuscitate, revival, revive, set, set up, spark, start, stir, take on, take up, turn on, usher, whip up

222 throw: buck, cast, chuck, dart, dash, deliver, disseminate, dust, eject, erupt, extrude, fire, fling, flip, heave, hurl, intersperse, jettison, launch, liftoff, lob, ouster, pelt, pitch, powder, project, propagate, propel, scatter, slam, sling, splash, splatter, sprinkle, throw, thrust, toss

223 transfer of an object: download, give, send, transact, transaction, transfer

224 travel: accompany, commute, cover, cross, cruise, do, double back, drive, embark, excursion, expedition, exploration, explore, field trip, flight, fly, gad, gallivant, hike, jaunt, journey, knock about/knock around, make, migrate, mountaineer, mountaineering, navigate, navigation, negotiate, odyssey, outing, passage, pick up, pilgrimage, ramble, range, ride, roam, run, safari, sail, shuttle, sojourn, takeoff, take off, tour, traffic, tramp, transit, travel, trek, trip, turn, voyage, walk, wander

225 use: apply, avail, bolt, borrow, broach, consume, consumption, deplete, devour, dip, drain, draw on, eat, employ, employment, enervate, exercise, exert, exhaust, expend, exploit, exploitation, fatigue, finish, gormandize, jockey, maneuver, manipulate, milk, occupy, partake, ply, polish off, resort, run, spend, squander, take, telephone, turn, use, utilize, wear, wield

226 **use living quarters:** abide, accommodate, cohabit, dwell, exist, hang about/hang around/hang out, inhabit, live, locate, lodge, occupy, reside, settle, situate, sojourn, stay, visit

227 **visit:** call, come by, drop in, frequent, see, sojourn, stay, stop, tour, visit

Causes

ABSTRACT

228 **affect:** affect, cause, change, evoke

229 **event that causes another:** account, beginning, cause, origin, precipitous/precipitate

230 **state of causation:** abortion, Achilles' heel, adaptation, aftermath, amazement, anticlimax, armistice, astonishment, awe, backlash, backwash, bang, bedlam, bereavement, bind, blessing, bliss, blot, blunder, boo boo, boner, boom, bottom line, break, buildup, by-product, catharsis, cease-fire, certainty, change, chaos, check, clincher, coincidence, collapse, collision, comfort, complication, compromise, congestion, consequence, consternation, contamination, corollary, culmination, decay, deception, decomposition, decoy, degeneracy, degradation, descent, destruction, deterioration, disadvantage, disappointment, disarray, disaster area, disorder, disposal, disrepair, dissipation, dissolution, effect, end, ending, entropy, error, event, eventuality, fall, flap, fluff, flurry, frailty, frenzy, fruit, fulfillment, furor, gaffe, give and take, glitch, goof, gridlock, headway, hubbub, huddle, humbug, impact, imperfection, implode, impression, improvement, impurity, inaccuracy, infection, irony, issue, jinx, jitters, lapse, lather, maelstrom, malarky, mess, miscarriage, mistake, mix-up, morass, muddle, muss, nonsense, occurrence, outcome, outgrowth, payoff, phenomenon, piffle, poppycock, portent, press, price, proceed, product, quantum leap, racket, ramification, rash, repercussion, resolution, result, rigmarole, rubbish, scare, scramble, settlement, shambles, shortfall, slipup, snafu, solution, stain, stalemate, stigma, stink, stir, storm, taint, tangle, tempest, therefore, to-do, toll, tomfoolery, trend, trip, tripe, truce, tumult, turmoil, turn, twaddle, undoing, unification, upheaval, upshot, vandalism, whirl, wipeout, wonderment

231 **to be:** alienate, animate, antagonize, awake, awaken, awakening, calm, cause, compound, endangered, energize, even, materialize, sanitize, sterilize, straighten, threaten

232 **to change:** adapt, adjust, alter, alternate, assimilate, attune, break even, cancel, change, commute, conversion, convert, co-opt, differentiate, distort, diversify, double back, equalize, expurgate, fashion, fit, fix, invert, modify, neutralize, offset, overturn, restore, shift, switch, tamper, transform, translate, transpose, turn

233 **to change abstractly:** demote, heighten, intensify, mitigate

234 **to change an event:** abbreviate, accelerate, acceleration, activate, actuate, adjourn, approach, arrest, bed, begin, break off, break up, build, cancel, cease, close, commence, complement, conclude, consummate, continue, crown, cut in, cut off, cut short, desist, determine, disband, discontinue, dispatch, dispose of, disrupt, dissolve, end, enter, finish, floor it, foul up, graduate, halt, hurry, intervene, invalidate, kick, knock off, lay off, leave, leave off, lift, manipulate, nip, nullify, pause, pick up, preclude, preempt, put off, quash, quell, quench, quit, relinquish, remit, rescind, retire, reverse, revoke, round off, ruin, scoot, scrub, seal, slow, smother, stall, stop, terminate, turn off, turn out, vacate, waive, wind up, wrap up

235 **to change cognitively:** agree, change, concede, harden, lay

236 **to change number or quantity:** abbreviate, abridge, abstract, accumulate, add, addition, advance, aggrandize, alleviate, amplification, amplify, augment, blow up, boost, build, build up, bump, commute, compress, condense, contract, curtail, cut, cut back, deduct, deepen, deflate, detract, digest, dilate, discount, double, downsize, draw out, encapsulate, enlarge, epitomize, escalate, evolve, expand, extend, extension, fatten, hike, imbue, increase, inflate, jump, lengthen, lift, lop, lower, magnify, modify, narrow, pare, prune, raise, reduce, reinforce, shorten, slash, step up, summarize, supplement, swell, take, trim, truncate, whittle, widen

237 **to change or affect an event:** delay, procrastinate, protract, slowpoke, stop, weigh

238 **to change state of being:** dispatch, do for

239 **to continue:** abide, bear, broaden, carry on, come, come back, continue, create, drag on/drag out, draw, drawl, draw out, dwell on/dwell upon, eke out, elongate, endure, extend, fated, go, go on, hammer away/hammer into, hang on, hold, kill, lengthen, linger, perpetuate, persevere, persist, prolong, protract, pursue, remain, resume, scam, survive, take up

240 **to diminish:** abate, adulterate, aggravate, aggravation, alloy, attenuate, blot, blunt, break, canker, cheapen, compound, compromise, cool, corrupt, crackdown, cut, deaden, debase, debauch, debilitate, decay, decline, decrease, degrade, depress, desensitize, disarrange, disorder, doctor, downgrade, downplay, downsize, emasculate, enfeeble, fatigue, geld, impair, imperil, let up, lower, minimize, mitigate, moderate, modify, muffle, mute, pale, pick-me-up, prevention, provocation, qualify, reduce, relax, retard, rot, sap, shorten, slash, stimulant, stimulus, stop, tax, tone down, undermine, weaken, wear, worsen

241 to function: animate, begin, cause, go back to square one, start

242 to happen: accelerate, boomerang, breathe, bring, copy, engender, ensue, entail, eventuate, evoke, expedite, expedition, facilitate, floor it, follow, impel, incite, inconvenience, induce, inflict, influence, inspire, instigate, institute, intervene, make, motivate, move, muddle, necessitate, oblige, occasion, occur, orchestrate, pass, precipitate, prod, produce, prompt, provoke, put, recur, result, return, stimulate, trigger, unsettle, will, work up, wreak

243 to have: accent, download, give, push, transfer

244 to improve: advance, allay, ameliorate, amend, assuage, augment, augmentation, become, benefit, better, betterment, boost, brighten, bring about, brush up, civilize, confirm, contribute, cultivate, cure, dignify, enhance, enrich, freshen, garnish, help, improve, lift, lighten, magnify, mend, mollify, pad, perfect, perk up, polish, quench, quiet, raise, refine, relieve, restore, revise, revision, rouse, step up, strengthen, supplement, touch up, unburden, update, upgrade

245 to increase quantity: accumulate, add, addition, advance, aggrandize, amplification, amplify, augment, augmentation, blow up, boost, build, build up, bump, deepen, dilate, double, draw out, enlarge, escalate, evolve, expand, extend, extension, fatten, hike, imbue, increase, inflate, jump, lengthen, lift, magnify, raise, reinforce, step up, supplement, swell, widen

246 to injure: abuse, afflict, ail, asphyxiate, batter, battery, beat, blemish, bruise, chip, cost, cripple, crush, damage, debilitate, decay, deface, defile, deform, dent, desecrate, desecration, devastate, disable, disagree, discomfort, disfigure, endanger, expose, flail, fragment, get back at, gripe, hamstring, handicap, harm, hurt, impair, incapacitate, infect, injure, irritate, jeopardize, knife, lacerate, lay up, maim, mangle, mar, maul, mistreat, molest, mutilate, mutilated, outrage, pain, paralyze, persecute, poison, pollute, pummel, rack, repay, rough up, ruin, rupture, sabotage, sap, scar, sexual harassment, shatter, shiver, shoot, sicken, smart, smash, snap, splinter, spoil, sting, stress, suffocate, taint, tarnish, torture, trample, turn, vandalize, violate, violation, vitiate, wound, wrong

247 to reduce quantity: abbreviate, abridge, abstract, alleviate, commute, compress, condense, contract, curtail, cut, cut back, deduct, deflate, detract, digest, discount, downsize, encapsulate, epitomize, extenuate, lessen, lower, minimize, modify, narrow, pare, prune, reduce, shorten, slash, summarize, take, trim, truncate, whittle

PHYSICAL

248 to break: collide, crack, crash, crumble, dash

249 to burn: arson, blaze, burn, char, conflagration, fire, flame, flare, glow, ignite, incinerate, inflame, kindle, lick, light, parch, scorch, sear, singe, smolder

250 to change physically: awake, bite, blacken, black out, bleach, blush, brighten, bruise, buttress, chip, color, compact, confirm, congeal, consolidate, corrode, crimp, crinkle, cross, darken, daub, debase, deepen, deform, dehydrate, desiccate, dilute, dim, disarrange, discolor, disfigure, disorder, disorganize, distort, disturb, do in, douse, dry, dye, eclipse, edge, elongate, emasculate, enervate, exhaust, fade, fatigue, fatten, ferment, file, flatten, flush, fog, foul, geld, gird, harden, heighten, hone, hypnotize, intensify, jell, lay, level, light, lighten, liquefy, loose/loosen, mark, melt, muzzle, neaten, neuter, numb, open, pacify, pale, petrify, prolong, prostrate, protract, quicken, ravel, redden, reinforce, roll, rouse, rumple, sanitize, set, shade, shadow, sharpen, shrivel, slop, slow, smooth, soften, solidify, sour, stabilize, stain, sterilize, stiffen, streak, strengthen, stretch, sully, tame, temper, thicken, thin, tidy, tighten, tinge, tint, toughen, turn, unlock, vitiate, warp, weary, whet, whiten

251 to create: bear, beget, breed, conceive, concoct, constitute, construct, create, engineer, establish, fabricate, forge, form, generate, hatch, materialize, mint, mold, originate, piece, procreate, produce, regenerate, reproduce, spawn

252 to destroy: ablate, abolish, abolition, annihilate, annul, assassinate, batter, blight, bomb, break, bring down, bulldoze, burst, bust, butcher, carnage, clobber, collapse, come unglued, consume, consumption, contaminate, coup de grâce, crucify, crumple, crush, cut down, damage, decimate, deface, deforestation, demolish, demolition, depredation, desecrate, desecration, desolate, despoil, destroy, destruction, devastate, disintegrate, dismantle, disorganize, dispatch, dissolve, do away with, do for, do in, drown, end, endanger, enfeeble, eradicate, erode, erosion, euthanasia, execute, execution, expunge, exterminate, extinction, extinguish, extirpate, finish, hang, genocide, gore, hara-kiri, holocaust, homicide, hunt, jeopardize, kaput, kill, killing, knock off, level, liquidate, lynching, mangle, manslaughter, massacre, mess up, murder, nuke, obliterate, overthrow, paralyze, pervert, pillage, plunder, poison, predator, prostrate, pull down, pulverize, purge, put away, put down, put out, quash, quench, ravage, raze, remove, ruin, sabotage, sack, shatter, shiver, shoot, slaughter, slay, smash, spoil, stamp out, strangle, subdue, subvert, suppress, tear down, undo, uproot, vandalism, vandalize, violation, waste, wipe out, wreck

253 to grow: cultivate, develop, farm, farming, flower, plant, raise, sow, till, vegetate

254 to make dirty: adulterate, blur, clutter, contaminate, dirty, litter, mess up, pollute, smudge, soil, stain, taint, tarnish

255 to make hot or cold: air, boil, chill, cool, freeze, freezer, heat, liquefy, melt, molten, numb, parch, refrigerate, scorch, shrivel, thaw, warm

256 to make wet: absorb, absorption, dampen,

deluge, dip, douse, drench, drivel, drool, drown, dunk, engulf, extinguish, immerse, marinate, moisten, oil, overflow, permeate, rinse, saturate, soak, souse, spatter, splash, splatter, spray, sprinkle, squirt, steep, submerge, water, wet

Fields of human activity

AGRICULTURE

257 action: agriculture, bed, bury, conservation, cross, cultivate, cultivation, culture, deforestation, ecology, erosion, fertilize, gather, graft, harvest, horticulture, preservation, raise, reap, roundup, round up, sow, sprout, tend, till, vegetate, work

258 organization: cowboy, farm, grange, plantation, ranch

THE ARTS

259 art object: antique, antiquity, canvas, classic, coat, collage, composition, creation, decal, decoration, depiction, design, dye, emblem, embroidery, enamel, etching, exhibit, figure, flourish, glaze, handicraft, illustration, image, insignia, knickknack, landscape, lattice, logo, masterpiece, medium, model, monument, ornament, pattern, picture, piece, piece de resistance, pigment, plaid, portrait, pottery, print, profile, pyramid, showpiece, silhouette, stamp, statue, trademark, workmanship, wreath

260 created object: alloy, amulet, apparatus, ash(es), badge, brew, by-product, camouflage, capsule, card, change, charlatan, cinder, composite, composition, compound, concoction, contrivance, creation, curiosity, debris, decoration, derivative, detritus, dip, discovery, dregs, droppings, dung, embers, enamel, essence, excrement, fabrication, fake, fence, fertilizer, filth, flotsam, foam, folder, formation, froth, fusion, fuzz, garbage, garland, gimmick, glass, grime, grit, grounds, half-breed, hash, hodgepodge, hook, huddle, hybrid, imitation, innovation, invention, jalopy, junk, knickknack, lather, leftover, litter, manure, mess, mishmash, mix/mixture, novelty, oddity, odds and ends, offshoot, original, outgrowth, output, pack, pad, paper, pastiche, patchwork, pennant, placebo, poker, potpourri, preparation, quantum leap, refuse, remainder, remnant, replica, residue, rest, rubbish, scum, sediment, sewage, simulation, slime, sludge, smashup, solution, spin-off, stationery, surplus, talisman, trash, vestige, waste, web, work, wreath, wreck, yield

261 exhibition: appear, appearance, boast, brandish, declassify, demonstrate, demonstration, develop, display, evince, exhibit, exhibition, exhibitionism, expose, exposure, flash, flaunt, foreshadow, glitz, grandstand, impress, look, loom, manifest, mark, mount, parade, peep/peer, personify, point out, portend, posture, pout, present, presentation, produce, record, reflect, register, render, represent, show, show off, showpiece, sight, simplify, spectacle, sport, spotlight, strut, transpire, typify, uncover, unfold

262 musical instrument: accompaniment, arrangement, baton, bugle, compact disc, elegy, harmony, hymn, measure, medley, melody, meter, note, piece, requiem, score, song, strain

263 performance: anthem, aria, ballet, broadcasting, burlesque, carol, chant, character, comedy, composition, concert, drama, dramatization, enactment, event, extravaganza, farce, impression, lampoon, manuscript, medium, motion picture, movie, music, music hall, opus, part, performance, piece, play, premiere, presentation, preview, program, recital, recitation, rendition, repertory, role, satire, scene, scenery, script, set, setting, show, skit, stage, takeoff, theater/theatre

264 performance part: act, chorus, encore, epilogue, ovation, plot, prelude, recital, refrain, rehearsal, scene, snatch, stunt, tune

265 photograph: observe, photograph, portray, print, proof

COMMUNICATIONS

266 communication: address, ad-lib, answer, arrogate, audience, babble, back down, beam, bewail, bid, build up, call, carry, censor, chat, chatter, circumlocution, colloquy, commune, communicate, communication, contact, conversation, converse, correspond, debrief, digress, discourse, divide, drivel, effusion, E-mail, emit, exult, falter, gab, get, give, hush up, improvise, indicate, interact, intercourse, interplay, intervene, intrude, lecture, magnify, mince, monologue, oration, patter, prattle, punctuate, quash, quiet, rap, reach, read, recant, recapitulate, recitation, recite, recount, refuse, rehearse, reiterate, render, repartee, say, secrete, shoot the breeze, signify, silence, slant, speak, speech, stammer, stray, talk, taunt, telephone, tell, tête-a-tête, transmit, transpire, verbalize, wander, welcome, whisper, wing it, yak/yap

267 communicative quality: abusive, acerbity, acid, acidulous, acrid, acrimonious, ad-lib, ambiguous, amusing, apologetic, articulate, artless, behind one's back, biting, bitter, bluff, blunt, boastful, bombastic, brazen, brief, broken, brusque, candid, captious, caustic, censorious, chatty, classified, close, closemouthed, colloquial, communicative, complimentary, confidential, confidentially, convincing, courteous, crisp, critical, crude, cryptic, curt, cutting, cynical, debatable, defamatory, degrading, demonstrative, derisive, derogatory, descriptive, destructive, diffuse, direct, directly, dirty, disconnected, discursive, dishonest, disjointed, disrespectful, doctrinaire, dogmatic, droll, dry, effusive, eloquent, embittered, emphatic, encyclopedic, erroneous, et cetera, evasive, even, exaggerated, expansive, explanatory, explicit, expository, expressive, extemporaneous/extempory, facetious, fallacious, false, falsely, farcical, fault-finding, feeble, fictitious, figurative, filthy, firm, firsthand, flaming, flatulent, flimsy, florid, flowery, fluent, forceful, forcible, foreign, forensic, forthright, foul, fractious, frank, frankly, fresh, fulsome, funny, fustian, gabby, garrulous, genuine, glib, glowing, grandiloquent, graphic, gross, grouchy, groundless, gruff, guileless, hackneyed, hard-line, harsh, hateful, heartfelt, heated, highfalutin, hollow, honest, honorable, humorous, hypercritical, hypocritical, idle, illogical, illustrative, imperative, imperious, implicit, implied, importunate, impromptu, improvised, imprudent, inarticulate, incisive, incoherent, indescribable, indicative, ineffable, inelegant, inexplicable, inflated, informative, ingenuous, inoffensive, insincere, insistent, insolent, instructive, insulting, ironic/ironical, jerrybuilt, jocular/jocose/jocund, jolly, keen, laconic, laudatory, laughable, legendary, legible, lengthy, libelous, lip service, literal, literally, literary, long-winded, loose, loquacious, lurid, lying, malicious, malign, matter-of-fact, mean, meaningful, meaty, mendacious, metaphorical, misleading, mordant, mouthy, mushy, musty, mythical/mythological, naked, nameless, narrative, natural, negative, noncommittal, oblique, obnoxious, obscene, offensive, offhand, off the cuff, off the record, oily, open, openhearted, openly, opinionated, opprobrious, oracular, oral, ornery, outspoken, overblown, overrated, parting, pejorative, penetrating, peppery, persuasive, pithy, plain, poetic, poignant, pointed, pompous, ponderous, pornographic, pregnant, priceless, private, privileged, privy, profane, prophetic, prosaic, public, pulp, pungent, quick-witted, quizzical, racy, rambling, redolent, reticent, rhetorical, ribald, rich, risqué, rough, round, rude, sacrilegious, sarcastic, satirical/satiric, saucy, scathing, scurrilous, secretive, secretly, sensational, sentimental, sharp, sharp-tongued, short, sidesplitting, significant, silent, simple, sincere, sincerely, smut, smutty, snappy, sneaky, snippy, speechless, spicy, spoken, square, stale, stilted, straight, straightforward, strained, succinct, suggestive, summary, symbolic, symptomatic, taciturn, talkative, tart, telltale, terse, threadbare, tongue-in-cheek, tongue-tied, transparent, trenchant, trite, truculent, true, truly, trumped up, trustworthy/trusty, truthful, unabridged, unanimous, unattached, uncivil, uncommunicative, unfounded, uninhibited, unintelligible, unsaid, untrue, untruthful, unvarnished, unwritten, vague, valedictory, veracious, verbal, verbatim, verbose, verbosity, vernacular, vicious, viperous, virulent, vocal, vociferous, voluble, vulgar, warm, warning, windy, witty, wordy, wry, X-rated, yellow, zany

268 description: appellation, deconstructionist, denotation, depiction, description, design,

exposition, expression, formula, gloss, hermeneutical, history, hyperbole, identification, illustration, kudos, label, legend, moniker, name, news, nickname, nom de plume, notation, notes, obituary, ode, outline, paraphrase, pen name, plan, poem, poetry, portrait, profile, prose, pseudonym, sketch, sobriquet, surname, translation

269 devices used for: alarm, artificial intelligence, calculator, computer, copy, data processor, distress signal, downlink, fax, fire alarm, foghorn, personal computer, photocopy, smoke detector, software, telegram, telephone, transcript

270 document, part: addendum, advertisement, amendment, appendix, article, banner, body, chapter, clause, codicil, condition, entry, epilogue, excerpt, extract, feature, foreword, introduction, item, label, leaf, legend, margin, obituary, passage, preface, prologue, provision/proviso, rider, sheet, slip, sound bite, specification, stipulation, story, supplement, tab, tag, terms, text

271 document, physical object: act, affidavit, agreement, album, analysis, annal(s), Annie Oakley, annual, archive, article, balance sheet, bill, blueprint, book, bulletin, card, caricature, catalog/catalogue, certificate, chronicle, circular, commitment, compact, composition, concord, constitution, contract, convention, corpus, credentials, criticism, critique, declaration, deed, deposition, digest, diploma, direction(s), directive, dispatch, dissertation, docket, document, documentary, dossier, draft, drama, enclosure, entente, epistle, escrow, essay, explanation, exposition, facsimile, fiction, file, form, green card, guarantee, guideline, history, identification, injunction, journal, ledger, letter, life, line, log, mail, manifesto, manuscript, material, memoir, memorandum/memo, message, missive, monument, narrative, note/notes, notebook, notice, obloquy, opus, pact, pamphlet, paper/papers, paper, pass, passport, patent, permit, petition, piece, placard, plan, poker, policy, poster, proceedings, proclamation, promotion, pronouncement, proposal, prose, pyramid, reading, receipt, record, reference, release, reminder, résumé, satire, schedule, scheme, script, sequel, sign, statement, survey, telegram, theme, thesis, ticket, timetable, treatise, voucher, writing

272 document quality: readable, short, summary, terse

273 humorous tale: banter, chaff, crack, jest, joke, kid, lampoon, levity, parody, pleasantry, pun, quip, spoof, sport, take off, travesty, trick, wisecrack, wit

274 information: ace in the hole, admonition, advice, allusion, analysis, annotation, announcement, answer, back door, bit, broadcast, bulletin, buzz, byte, calendar, caution, cautionary tale, caveat, charge, clarification, clue, command, commitment, communication, confession, conjecture, construction, counsel, cybernetics, data, data bank, declaration, definition, dictate, digital library, direction(s), directive, dirt, disclosure, dope, evidence, excerpt, exhortation, explanation, exposé, fact, facts, freeware, gossip, grounds, groundwork, guidance, guide, guideline, herald, hint, hypermedia, illumination, indicator, information, instruction, intelligence, intimation, key, knowledge, lead, learning, lesson, light, lore, manifesto, material, message, minutiae, multimedia, news, notice, notification, on-line, particular, plug, point, pointer, prescription, prognosis, program, prompt, pronouncement, proof, publication, publicity, quotation/quote, reading, rebuttal, recipe, recommendation, reference, rejoinder, report, resolution, revelation, rumor, scholarship, science, scoop, scuttlebutt, secret, sign, small talk, sound bite, statement, story, telecast, tidings, tip/tipoff, trivia, tutelage, verification, warning, whisper, word

275 integral language parts: adjective, adverb, antonym, aphorism, bad form, banality, barbarism, buzzword, byword, cant, catchword, clause, cliché, computerese, euphemism, expletive, figure of speech, gobbledygook, grammar, idiom, jargon, metaphor, neologism, nomenclature, parlance, phrase, proverb, psychobabble, term, word

276 language: adage, adieu, alphabet, argot, code, computerese, dialect, diction, expression, gobbledygook, grammar, jargon, language, lexicon, lingo, nomenclature, patter, slang, speech, style, swearing, tongue, vernacular, vocabulary, voice

277 media: advertisement, banner, correspondence, criticism, desktop publishing, dispatch, infomercial, memorandum/memo, obloquy, pen, perjury, prattle, rebuttal, rejoinder, rhetoric, rumor, sarcasm, sass, screen, scuttlebutt, sensationalism, small talk, sound bite, spiel, television, terminology, translation, tripe, vehicle, video, videocassette

278 object used in: address, advertisement, alert, analogy, anathema, answer, aphorism, approach, assertion, assurance, axiom, babble, back talk, banner, banter, breath, bunk, call, cant, catchword, cause celebre, chat, chatter, claim, cliché, comeback, comment, commentary, commonplace, compliment, congratulations, contact, contention, contradiction, controversy, correspondence, criticism, cry, cue, curse, decision, declaration, defense, definition, derision, dialogue/dialog, dibs, dictum, digression, dirt, disapproval, dispatch, disputation, dispute, dissension, dissidence, dissonance, divination, double entendre, double standard, double-talk, dressing-down, drivel, edict, editorial, eloquence, embellishment, epigram, epilogue, epitaph, equivocation, eulogy, euphemism, exaggeration, exaltation, fabrication, falsehood, falsity, farewell, feedback, fib, figure of speech, flak, fulmination, gab, gibberish, gibe, goodbye, gossip, grace, gratitude, grievance, gripe, groan, guidance, harangue, hearsay, hiss, hocus-pocus, hogwash, honor, implication, impropriety, indication, indignity, innuendo, instruction, insult, invective, invention, invocation, irony, issue, knock, lament/lamentation, laurels, lecture, legerdemain, letter, lie, line, lip, litany, malediction, maxim, meaning, memorandum/memo, mention, missive,

mockery, monologue, moral, motif, motion, motto, mouth, negation, negative, notice, oath, obscenity, obsequy, observation, offense, offer, omen, oracle, oration, order, outcry, overtone, overture, password, patter, phrase, pitch, platform, platitude, plea, pleasantry, pledge, portent, praise, precursor, prediction, pretension, proclamation, profanity, profession, projection, promise, pronouncement, propaganda, prophecy, proverb, puff, pun, put-down, quip, quotation/quote, rebuff, rebuke, recommendation, reference, refusal, regards, remark, reminder, rendition, reply, report, reprimand, respects, response, retort, return, rhetoric, rhyme, rot, rubbish, rumor, sarcasm, saying, scandal, sermon, shadow, slam, slander, slogan, slur, statement, story, suggestion, swearing, tale, talk, testimonial, testimony, thanks, theme, threat, tirade, toast, translation, trash, tribute, truth, utterance, vehicle, veracity, verbiage, voice, vow, welcome, whisper, wind, word, wording

279 organization: bandwidth, ghetto box, media, newsletter, newspaper, radar, radio, tabloid, television

280 publication: advertisement, almanac, anthology, article, authority, autobiography, bible, bill, biography, book, brochure, canon, cartoon, catalog/catalogue, daybook, dictionary, directory, edition, erotica, fiction, glossary, guidebook, handbook, issue, journal, journalism, ledger, lexicon, literature, magazine, manual, memoir, newsletter, newspaper, novel, organ, pamphlet, paper, periodical, press, print, publication, publicity, reference, release, review, romance, satire, tabloid, text, textbook, thesaurus, tome, treatise, vocabulary, volume

281 record: annal(s), archive, calendar, dossier, itinerary, list, program, record, register, roll, roster

282 story: account, allegory, anecdote, biography, chronicle, documentary, epic, fable, fib, fiction, folklore, legend, lore, memoir, mystery, myth, mythology, narration, narrative, ode, old wives' tale, parable, phenomenology, plot, poem, poetry, report, saga, scenario, story, tale, verse, version, yarn

283 summary: abbreviation, abridgement, abstract, agenda, annotation, bill, breakdown, brief, caption, census, citation, compendium, condensation, daybook, diagnosis, diary, directory, epitome, heading, inscription, inventory, menu, moral, precis, profile, program, prospectus, report, résumé, return, review, roster, rundown, scenario, schedule, sketch, summary, syllabus, synopsis, table, tally, timetable, title

284 symbol: arms, augury, autograph, badge, beep, brand, capital, character, charm, check, code, crest, cue, decal, device, dot, emblem, emoticon, ensign, exponent, flag, fleck, flourish, font, graffiti, hallmark, handwriting, harbinger, herald, impression, imprint, index, indication, insignia, John Hancock, label, landmark, lead, letter, line, logo, mark, notation, note, numeral, placard, script, seal, sign, signal, spot, stamp, stripe, symbol, tag, talisman, tick, token, trademark, tread, type, vestige, writing

EDUCATION

285 educate: address, break in, breed, care, catechize, coach, domesticate, drill, educate, education, form, groom, ground, illuminate, inculcate, indoctrinate, initiate, instill, instruct, instruction, lesson, orate, orator, oratory, preach, preparation, school, speak, speech, talk, teach, teaching, train, training, tutelage, tutor

286 education level: class, grade, level, rating

287 objects used in: academia, class, college, course, dissertation, edification, education, erudition, lesson, lore, preschool, school, teaching, tenure, text, textbook, thesis, tuition

288 organization: academia, academy, alma mater, class, college, enrollment, faculty, institute/institution, school

289 place of: academy, alma mater, class, college, preschool, school

290 test: acid test, assay, audition, criterion, dissection, drill, examination, exercise, experiment, guinea pig, index, inquest, inquiry, inspection, investigation, probation, probe, quiz, reconnaissance, test, trial, weight, workout

291 testing: fiddle, grade, pace, plumb, survey, test, trial, try, try on/try out, verify

ENTERTAINMENT

292 action: act, acting, amuse, amusement, antic, appear, arrange, bet, bill, broadcast, cruise, dance, diversion, dramatize, emote, enact, enactment, entertain, featuring, feign, game, host, hype, impersonate, interpret, issue, overplay, pageant, parody, perform, play, prance, pretend, preview, produce, publication, publicize, put on, regale, rehearsal, rehearse, relaxation, revel, romp, score, sing, spotlight, stage, takeoff, take off, tape, televise, translator, transmit, travesty, trifle, weatherperson

293 object: absent-mindedness, auditorium, balloon, bet, broadcast, broadcasting, butt, cinema, circus, comedy, disco, distraction, drama, dramatization, elegy, extravaganza, farce, film, firecracker, fireworks, humor, lounge, medium, motion picture, movie, movie hall, news, nightclub, picture, publicity, red herring, sensation, sequel, show, sight, song, telecast, television, theater/theatre, video, videocassette

294 organization: band, cast, chorus, corps, ensemble, following, gallery, orchestra

FAMILY

295 child raising: au pair, baby, baby-sit, breed, bring up, care, coddle, cradle, cultivate, daycare, form, foster, mind, mollycoddle, nanny, nourish, nurse, nursemaid, nurture, pamper, raise, rear, spoon-feed, support, tend

296 family: aristocracy, birth, blood, bride, bridegroom, brood, clan, class, consanguinity, court, descendant, descent, doll, extraction, family, family tree, folk, folks, genealogy, heritage, house, household, issue, kin, kindred, kinship, line, lineage, mate, offspring, origin, pedigree, people, posterity, progeny, rank, relation, stock, strain, tribe

297 marriage: annul, annulment, betroth, betrothal, couple, desert, desertion, divorce, elope, engage, engagement, espouse, estrange, estrangement, jilt, marriage, marry, match, mate, matrimony, nuptials, part, parting, polygamy, propose, rupture, separate, separation, sever, split, vow, wed, wedding, wedlock, woo

GOVERNMENT AND POLITICS

298 government action: abdicate, abolish, abolition, accession, administer, administration, amnesty, bust, cease-fire, colonization, command, decriminalize, depose, deposition, dethrone, displace, dominate, enact, enforce, enforcement, exile, expulsion, filibuster, legalize, override/overrule, pass, reign, rule, run in, secede, second, surveillance, tax, truce, veto

299 government organization: administration, ally, cabinet, capitalism, capitol, chamber, confederacy, congress, cop, council, court, delegation, democracy, deregulation, dictatorship, direction, empire, fascism, government, house, jury, legislature, police/police officer, post, regime, rule, sovereignty, tribunal, tyranny

300 political action: amnesty, arbitrate, arbitration, ballot, campaign, canvass, crusade, demonstrate, demonstration, displace, drive, drum up, elect, election, endorse, lobby, mutiny, nominate, nomination, patronage, picket, politics, poll, protest, reaction, rebellion, revolt, revolution, riot, run, sedition, vote

301 political organization: alliance, ballot, caucus, commonwealth, communism, confederacy, delegation, faction, fascism, machine, party, politics, side, socialism, tyranny

HEALTH

302 birth: bear, birth, breed, childbirth, conception, delivery, spring

303 change in: ache, black out, come down with, faint, fit, look up, mend, pull through, recover, recuperate, remission, repel, swoon, weary

304 death: abort, abortion, curtains, death, decease, demise, die, dissolution, end, expiration, expire, fatality, mortician, mortuary, pass away, passing, perish, undertaker

305 deathplace: boneyard, cemetery, crypt, grave, graveyard, mausoleum, monument, necropolis, tomb

306 disease: abscess, affliction, AIDS, ailment, bacteria, blight, bug, cancer, canker, carpal tunnel syndrome, complaint, condition, contagion, contamination, cyst, diarrhea, disease, disorder, epidemic, germ, growth, illness, impurity, indigestion, infection, infirmity, inflammation, malady, microbe, microorganism, pest, pestilence, pimple, plague, rash, sexually transmitted disease, sickness, spell, swelling, symptom, syndrome, tantrum, virus, zit

307 drug: acid, amphetamine, analgesic, anesthetic/anaesthetic, angel dust, antibiotic, antidote, antiseptic, antitoxin, balm, capsule, cocaine, condom, contraceptive, cure, dope, dose, drug, elixir, hashish, herbicide, heroin, laxative, LSD, marijuana, medicine/medication, narcotic, nostrum, opium, painkiller, panacea, pick-me-up, pill, poison, pot, potion, prescription, remedy, sedative, stimulant, stimulus, tablet, tonic, toxin, vaccination

308 event: abort, abortion, ache, attack, cardiac arrest, catch, contract, convulsion, cough, cramp, crick, faint, gag, gargle, heal, heart attack, massage, nauseate, palpitate, paroxysm, pass out, perk up, rubdown, rupture, seizure, spell, spew, stroke, suffer, swoon, take, throw up, tic, vomit, wheeze

309 injury: abrasion, abscess, affliction, bite, blister, boil, boo boo, bruise, concussion, contusion, corrosion, cut, damage, defect, detriment, disability, disadvantage, disservice, fracture, gash, harm, incision, inflammation, injury, laceration, lesion, prick, puncture, rip, rupture, rust, scratch, shock, stab, swelling, welt, wound

310 medical action: alter, analyze, autopsy, bandage, castrate, cure, diagnose, dissection, doctor, dope, dress, drug, ease, examination, heal, inject, inoculation, malpractice, massage, operate, operation, plastic surgery, postmortem, practice, remedy, rubdown, therapy, tranquilize, transplant, treat, treatment, vaccinate

311 medical instruments: bandage, cure, elixir, emollient, injection, liniment, lotion, matter, moisturizer, nostrum, ointment, panacea, prescription, remedy, salve, staff, x-ray

312 medical organization: asylum, clinic, delivery room, emergency room, headquarters, hospital, laboratory, loony bin, madhouse, mental hospital, nursing home, nut house, office

313 pain: ache, afflict, anesthesia/anaesthesia, discomfort, distress, gripe, harassment, harm, hurt, itch, pinch, sting, strain, stress, suffer, torment, torture, wound, wrong

314 quality of: able-bodied, adaptive, ailing, anemic, bad, bedridden, benign, better, burning, catching, clean, communicable, congenital, contagious, convalescent, crippled, curable, curative, delicate, disabled, diseased, ditsy, dizzy, doddering, done in, drugged, drunk, dysfunctional, epidemic, excruciating, faint, febrile, fit, full-blooded, game, genetic, giddy, gory, green around the gills, groggy, haggard, hale, hardy, healthy, hearty, high, hurt, ill, immune, incapacitated, indisposed, inebriated, infectious, infirm, insane, invalid, irreparable, lame, light-headed, low, lusty, malignant, mental, morbid, nauseating, nauseous, neurotic, normal, out cold, palsied, paralytic, peaked, pestilent/pestilential, plastered, pooped, poor, poorly, queasy,

queer, right, robust, rocky, rugged, run-down, safe, salutary, sane, senile, sick, sickly, sinewy, slaphappy, soft, solvent, sore, sound, soused, spent, squeamish, stoned, strong, sturdy, tender, terminal, tired, tough, trim, tuckered out, unconscious, unfeeling, unharmed, unhealthy, unscathed, unsound, unwell, vertigo, vigorous, wan, wasted, weak, weary, well, whole, wholesome, woozy, zoned

315 sleep: anesthesia/anaesthesia, asleep, awake, coma, doze, drop off, hibernate, insomnia, languor, lassitude, lethargy, nap, nightmare, nod, quiet, rest, sleep, sleepy, slumber, snooze, snore, somnolent, stupor

316 state of: ache, addiction, ailment, apoplexy, beat, collapse, complaint, condition, cough, debility, dementia, disability, dislocation, eating disorder, epidemic, faint, fatigue, fitness, form, gestation, hangover, headache, health, hurt, hygiene, ill, immunity, implode, insanity, lapse, madness, neurosis, pain, paroxysm, pestilence, pink, shape, stupor, substance abuse, symptom, syndrome, tone, trim, trouble, tumor, vigor, welfare/wellbeing

LEGAL

317 legal action: absolve, acquit, acquittal, action, adjudicate, adopt, adoption, annul, annulment, apprehend, apprehension, arraign, arrest, bear witness, bequeath, book, bring, bust, charge, cite, collar, commute, condemn, condemnation, convict, conviction, counsel, covenant, cross-examine, cut off, decree, decriminalize, detain, detention, disinherit, enact, enforce, enforcement, evidence, excommunicate, exculpate, exonerate, extradite, hearing, impeach, imprison, incarcerate, indict, indictment, inherit, insure, jail, judge, leave, legalize, let off, lift, litigate, moderate, nab, nail, ordain, outlaw, override/overrule, pardon, pass, perjure, pick up, pinch, plead, practice, prohibit, proscribe, prosecute, pull in, put away, raid, rap, repeal, represent, reprieve, rescind, run in, sentence, sing, sortie, substantiate, sue, testify, transport, trial, try, validate, verify, vindicate, vitiate, vouch, waive, will, witness

318 objects used in legal practice: acquittal, act, affidavit, article, bail, bar, bench, bequest, bill, bond, brief, canon, case, claim, code, constitution, court, debenture, decree, deed, deposition, dibs, dictate, easement, enactment, entreaty, evidence, indictment, injunction, inquest, institute, insurance, jury, law, lawsuit, legislation, libel, litigation, mandate, measure, ordinance, paper/papers, pardon, passage, patent, plea, pledge, precept, prescription, principle, regulation, repeal, reprieve, ruling, sentence, statute, stipulation, subpoena, suit, terms, testament, testimonial, testimony, tribunal, verdict, waiver, will, writ

319 quality of law: administrative, authoritarian, authoritative, autocratic, canonical, clear, constitutional, contraband, democratic, effectual, egalitarian, exempt, forensic, free, high-handed, illegal, illegitimate, illicit, inadmissible, judicial, just, kosher, lawful, lawless, legal, legislative, legitimate, misbegotten, on the level, permissible, punitive, unauthorized, unconstitutional, unlawful, unprejudiced, valid, wrongful

MILITARY

320 military action: action, aggression, barrage, blitz, blow up, campaign, conflict, contest, coup d'état, defeat, deploy, depose, deposition, descent, dethrone, detonation, disarm, disarmament, draft, electioneering, engage, engagement, enlist, explode, explosion, fire, incursion, induct, induction, insurrection, invade, invasion, maneuver, mobilize, occupation, occupy, offensive, oppression, overthrow, rally, rebellion, recruit, revolt, revolution, salute, service, station, surrender, volley, war, warfare

321 object used by military: armory, barracks, battery, battlefield, citadel, defense, draft, fort/fortress, garrison, magazine, post, rampart, service

322 organization: ally, army, artillery, battalion, brigade, cavalry, corps, defense, detachment, detail, enemy, fleet, flotilla, force, legion, military, navy, ordnance, platoon, squad, troop/troops

MONETARY AND FINANCIAL AFFAIRS

323 association: association, black market, board, cartel, conglomerate, establishment, federation, firm, grocery store, industry, mall, market/mart, merger, patronage, stock market, syndicate, trust

324 business action: advertise, advertising, annexation, appear, appointment, auction, aviation, cashier, commercialize, commission, conclave, conference, consultation, convene, convention, cry, cut a deal, deal, dealings, deficit spending, depression, dictate, discharge, dismiss, drudge, enterprise, exchange, export, farm, farming, fold, gathering, hold, hype, incorporate, intercourse, malpractice, management, manufacture/manufacturing, market, mediate, mediation, meet, meeting, merge, merger, monopolize, operation, patronage, patronize, pioneer, popularize, position, powwow, practice, produce, project, promote, promotion, proposal, publicize, puff, push, put up, sale, seal, second, seminar, service, session, shake up, shut, sit, slavery, specialize, step in, stock, symposium, table, trade, traffic, transact, transaction, truck, undertaking, wait on

325 business organization: agency, airport, association, bakery, bar, branch, bureau, bureaucracy, business, cartel, clientele, commerce, company, concern, conglomerate, corporation, council, department store, direction, dispensation, enterprise, establishment, exchange, field, firm, house, industry, labor, mall, management, operation, outfit, partner-

ship, personnel, practice, red tape, regime, ring, singles bar, staff, store, syndicate, trust, union

326 business quality: accomplished, ambitious, businesslike, busy, careful, concentrated, diligent, discipline, eager, earnest, enterprising, grasping, greedy, methodical/methodic, miserly, ordered, orderly, painstaking, penurious, persistent, possessive, practical, professional, proper, purposeful, rapacious, regular, relentless, stingy, tenacious, tightfisted, up-and-coming, zealous

327 buying: buy, charge, lavish, lay out, order, patronize, pay, procure, purchase, redeem, shop, shortchange, shower, splurge, spree, squander, take, trade, traffic, treat, truck

328 cost: appraisal, cost, expense

329 fee: amount, bet, bill, bribe, charge, commission, damage(s), debt, duty, excise, expense, fare, fee, invoice, levy, obligation, overhead, pay, price, rate, rent, revenue, stake, surcharge, tab, tariff, tax, toll, wager

330 financial action: assess, audit, bank, bargain, bet, bid, bidding, bill, bring, bring in, budget, bust, cash, charge, deduct, default, deficit spending, deposit, depress, depression, devalue, dicker, discount, earn, economize, economy, endorse, fail, frugality, gross, hock, insure, invest, investment, levy, liquidate, mutual fund, net, pawn, pay, pinch, price, profit, realize, reckon, salt away, save, scrape, scrimp, shop, skimp, speculate, speculation, stake, stint, subsist, trade, traffic, transact, transaction, truck, venture

331 financial document: account, agreement, book, coupon, entente, reckoning, return, statement

332 financial object: account, adjustment, arrears, assessment, asset(s), backing, bail, balance, balance sheet, bargain, bill, bonanza, budget, capital, cheap, draft, equity, fund, insurance, interest, investment, invoice, liability, loan, lucre, means, mortgage, mutual fund, order, overhead, patronage, pawn, pay, pay dirt, pension, pledge, principal, profit, quotation/quote, receipt, revenue, score, stock, tightfisted, treasure, voucher

333 financial organization: bank, board, grocery store, mall, market/mart, stock market

334 financial quality: affluent, balanced, bankrupt, behind, broke, bush league, charitable, cheap, close, comfortable, commercial, complimentary, costly, cushy, dear, depressed, destitute, disadvantaged, disadvantageous, down-and-out, due, economic, economical, exorbitant, expensive, extravagant, fat, financial, finished, fiscal, flush, free, frugal, gainful, generous, ghetto, gold mine, good, grasping, gratis, gratuitous, high, humble, impecunious, impoverished, improvident, indebted, indigent, inexpensive, insolvent, invaluable, lavish, liberal, liquid, low, lucrative, marketable, mean, miserly, modest, monetary, moneyed, moneymaking, munificent, narrow, needy, net, nominal, on the house, opulent, outstanding, overdue, owing, palatial, paltry, parsimonious, patrician, payable, pecuniary, penniless, penurious, plush, poor, posh, poverty-stricken, precious, priceless, privileged, prodigal, profitable, profligate, prohibitive, prosperous, provident, rich, second-rate/second-class, self-sufficient, skimpy, sleazy, sordid, sparing, splendid, squalid, steep, stingy, strapped, substantial, sumptuous, tawdry, thrifty, thriving, tight, underprivileged, unfortunate, unpaid, unreasonable, unsettled, used, valuable, valued, wealthy, well-bred, well-off, well-to-do

335 **financial state:** afford, arrears, avarice, bankruptcy, boom, bring, circumstances, credit, cutback, default, deficit, depression, devalue, discount, economy, extravagance, fail, fortune, frugality, hyperinflation, inadequacy, individual retirement account, inflation, IRA, living, misery, need, obligation, owe, pageantry, panic, paucity, pile, pomp, poverty, prosperity, recession, riches, savings, shortfall, slum, slump, squalor, substance, thrift, traffic, value, worth

336 **financial value state:** cost, decline, downturn, expense, value

337 **gift:** acquisition, allowance, alms, arrival, atonement, award, balm, benefit, bequest, bonanza, bonus, boon, booty, bounty, charity, citation, comfort, commendation, compensation, contribution, courtesy, decoration, diploma, dispensation, dividend, dole, donation, due, endowment, extravagance, find, freebie, fruit, fundraiser, gain, gem, gift, godsend, good, grant, gratuity, haul, heirloom, honor, indulgence, inheritance, laurels, legacy, loot, luxury, medal, memento, memorabilia, memorial, offering, philanthropy, plum, premium, present, presentation, prize, purse, recognition, remembrance, reparation, reward, scholarship, souvenir, spoils, subsidy, token, treasure, trophy, windfall

338 **merchandise:** bargain, cargo, commodity, consignment, contraband, fabrication, freight, goods, hardware, harvest, haul, inventory, line, load, merchandise, order, product, stock, truck, turnout, wares, yield

339 **monetary container:** bag, bank, purse, satchel, till, treasury

340 **money:** ace in the hole, advance, affluence, allowance, appropriation, asset(s), bill, bread, cash, change, chicken feed, chips, coin, contribution, currency, deposit, dollar, donation, dough, endowment, estate, finances, financing, fund, funds, income, individual retirement account, investment, IRA, loot, lucre, maintenance, means, mint, money, offering, opulence, pay, payback, pile, pool, recompense, refund, reserve, resource, resources, return, riches, savings, support, sustenance, wealth

341 **money giving:** advance, blow, buy, compensate, disburse, discharge, endow, expend, finance, fritter, fund, invest, lavish, lay out, misappropriate, patronage, patronize, pay, play, ransom, recompense, refund, reimburse, remit, remunerate, repay, requite, reward, satisfy, settle, shell out, spend, sponsor, square, subscribe, subsidize, support, underwrite

342 **money taking:** bill, blackmail, bleed, clear, collect, extort, extortion, fine, fleece, recoup, squeeze

343 **ownership part:** hold, owner, possession, proprietor

344 **payment:** advance, alimony, bounty, collateral, commission, compensation, consideration, cut, deal, debt, deficit spending, deposit, disbursement, discharge, dividend, dole, draft, dues, earnings, equity, expenditure, expense, fee, financing, gain, graft, grant, gratuity, gross, income, installment, interest, kickback, outlay, pay, pay dirt, payment, penalty, pension, perk, perquisite, pittance, premium, prize, proceeds, profit, purse, raise, ransom, rebate, receipts, recompense, redress, refund, reparation, restitution, revenue, reward, safety net, salary, satisfaction, scholarship, stake, stipend, subsidy, surcharge, take, tip, upkeep, wage/wages

345 **selling:** auction, bazaar, charge, handle, market, merchandise, peddle, sale, sell, solicit, trade, traffic, truck

346 **value state:** appreciation, benefit, decline, downturn, import, importance, mark, quality, value, worth

PROFESSIONS

347 **business manager:** administrator, banker, best shot, boss, bureaucrat, businessperson, capitalist, captain, chief, commander, conductor, dealer, director, distributor, emir, emperor, employer, empress, entrepreneur, establishment, executive, farmer, financier, flagship, founder, front runner, hawker, head, huckster, impresario, investor, landlord, leader, magnate, manager, master, merchant, mogul, mover and shaker, notable, officer, official, overseer, owner, pacesetter, peasant, president, prime minister, principal, professional, proprietor, ringleader, seller, shopkeeper, specialist, storekeeper, superintendent, superior, supervisor, taskmaster, tycoon, upstart, warden

348 **businessperson:** abettor, accountant, adjutant, adviser/advisor, agent, aid/aide, analyst, announcer, applicant, apprentice, arbitrator, archaeologist, architect, assistant, associate, astronaut, attendant, auditor, author, authority, aviator, baker, banker, barber, bean counter, bearer, body guard, broker, builder, businessperson, butcher, buyer, caregiver, caretaker, carpenter, cartoonist, cashier, chair, chairperson, chef, clerk, client, collaborator, colleague, commuter, computer geek, connection, conservator, consultant, consumer, cook, correspondent, courier, court, craftsperson, creator, critic, curator, custodian, customer, cyberpunk, dabbler, deputy, desk jockey, detective, developer, devil's advocate, disc jockey, drudge, emissary, employee, engineer, envoy, epicure, espionage, expert, explorer, farmer, fellow, financier, flier, floozy, flyer, fortune-teller, fountainhead, freshman, friend, gatekeeper, go-between, gofer, gourmet, groom, guard, guide, guru, hack, hacker, hairdresser, hand, harlot, hawker, help, helper, henchman, hooker, housekeeper, huckster, hussy, inferior, informant/informer, innovator, inspector, intermediary, interviewer, inventor, investigator,

jailer, janitor, journalist, labor, laborer, liaison, lobbyist, machine, mariner, maverick, mediator, messenger, middle person, miser, model, moderator, mole, monitor, narrator, navigator, negotiator, newsman/woman, novice, opposition, originator, page, partner, patron, peasant, peddler, peon, picket, pilot, pioneer, playwright, poet, porter, practitioner, private eye, prodigal, professional, protégé, proxy, rat, recruit, referee, reporter, representative, researcher, reviewer, rider, rival, rookie, sailor, salesperson, scout, seafarer, seaman/woman, secretary, seller, sentinel, serf, servant, shopper, skinflint, slave, sleuth, snitch, snoop, speaker, spendthrift, spokesperson, sponsor, spy, stool pigeon, subordinate, surrogate, tailor, tenant, tightwad, tool, traveler, umpire, underling, vendor, virtuoso, watchkeeper, wayfarer, weasel, wizard, worker, writer, yuppie

349 **discipline:** affair, anatomy, anthropology, appointment, archaeology, architecture, arithmetic, art, astronomy, board, botany, browser, bulletin board, career, chat room, cinema, communications, cybernetics, cyberspace, demography, department, discipline, domain, employment, ergonomics, field, geography, hermeneutics, journalism, lifework, line, livelihood, logic, mathematics, matter, metier, occupation, orbit, passion, phenomenology, philosopher, philosophy, poetry, position, press, project, province, psychology, pursuit, realm, research, scene, school, science, scientist, semiotics, specialty, sphere, stage, station, territory, trade, undertaking, vocation, walk, work

350 **educator:** academic, adviser/advisor, alumnus/alumna, brain, coach, college student, conductor, consultant, cretin, dean, disciplinarian, educator, egghead, expert, faculty, fountainhead, freshman, genius, graduate, guru, half-wit, instructor, intellectual, inventor, learner, maharishi, martinet, master, mastermind, mentor, monitor, novice, practitioner, principal, professor, pupil, rookie, sage, savant, scholar, school, student, swami, teacher, trainer, tutor, wonk

351 **employment:** ax/axe, bounce, can, collaborate, commission, demote, discharge, dismiss, dismissal, earn, elevate, elevation, employ, employment, engage, fire, gross, headhunting, hire, interview, job, kick out, labor, layoff, lay off, live, livelihood, living, make, metier, occupation, office, oust, pay, picket, post, promote, promotion, raise, reinstate, relieve, resign, resignation, retain, retire, rise, sack, situation, spot, station, strike, suspend, work

352 **entertainer:** acrobat, actor, actress, adherent, aficionado, artist, ballet dancer, buff, character, comedian, comic, connoisseur, creator, dancer, director, diva, fan, fanatic, fledgling, follower, freak, geek, groupie, hero/heroine, host, humorist, idol, inventor, joker, luminary, lyricist, magician, mimic, minion, musician, name, notable, originator, paparazzi, participant, personage/personality, photographer, player, prima donna, protagonist, singer, star, thespian, troubadour, usher, virtuoso, wit, zany

353 **financier:** accountant, banker, bean counter, bearer, broker, financier, investor, spendthrift

354 **government officer:** administrator, ally, ambassador, arbiter, authoritarian, authority, autocracy, autocrat, bureaucrat, conqueror, consul, cop, delegate, deputy, despot, dictator, diplomat, disciplinarian, emir, emperor, empress, envoy, establishment, executive, exile, expatriate, fascist, figure, figurehead, flagship, front runner, governor, informant/informer, inhabitant, intermediary, justice, leader, legislator, liaison, lobbyist, magistrate, martinet, master, minister, mogul, monarch, mouthpiece, negotiator, officer, official, oppressor, pacesetter, pacifist, page, patrol, peacemaker, personage/personality, police/police officer, potentate, prime minister, rat, representative, ringleader, snitch, sovereign, spokesperson, stool pigeon, tyrant, weasel

355 **legal practitioner:** attorney, bench, beneficiary, consul, counsel, counselor, heir, investigator, judge, jurist, lawyer, notary, officer, party, proponent, successor, witness

356 **media person:** commentator, interviewer, journalist, narrator, newsman/woman, press, reporter, writer

357 **medical practitioner:** analyst, doctor, druggist, healer, nurse, paramedic, patient, pharmacist, physician, psychiatrist, researcher, specialist, therapist

358 **military person:** combatant, commander, conqueror, deserter, fighter, GI, gladiator, guerrilla, lookout, mercenary, militant, officer, patrol, private, recruit, sailor, scout, seafarer, seaman/woman, soldier, truant, veteran, warmonger, warrior

359 **politician:** advocate, ally, anarchist, apostate, apostle, applicant, arbitrator, backer, bigot, candidate, conservative, demagogue, diehard, diplomat, dissident, donor, extremist, fanatic, firebrand, free spirit, hostage, iconoclast, idealist, insurgent, militant, misfit, mouthpiece, nominee, nonconformist, partisan, patron, perfectionist, picket, politician, proponent, protagonist, racist, radical, reactionary, rebel, refugee, renegade, sectarian, spokesperson, warmonger

360 **profession:** business, calling, career, craft, employment, finance, hacker, job, labor, lifework, line, livelihood, mission, occupation, place, position, profession, psychology, science, situation, trade, vocation, walk, work

361 **religious person:** acolyte, agnostic, angel, apostle, atheist, believer, chaplain, clergyperson, conformist, convert, creator, cynic, deacon, disciple, doubter, doubting Thomas, dreamer, enchantress, evangelism, evangelist, father, femme fatale, genie, hermit, inventor, layperson, loner, magician, minister, missionary, monk, nun, pagan, parson, pastor, preacher, priest, prophet, saint, shaman, skeptic, sorcerer, visionary, warlock, witch, witch doctor, wizard

362 **task:** affair, assignment, bee, berth, chore, commission, concern, drudgery, duty, effort, enterprise, errand, exercise, exertion, function, grind, groove, job, labor, mission, office, part, picnic, post, project, province,

realm, research, role, routine, scientist, spot, stint, sweat, task, tax, toil, undertaking, work

RECREATION

363 **action:** acrobatics, aerobics/aerobic, angle, athletics, basketball, boating, bowl, boxing, bunt, championship, chance, coach, competition, contest, cruise, dance, deal, defeat, dissipation, diversion, engage, event, exercise, fish, fishing, gamble, gambol, game, gymnastics, hike, hobby, hunt, keep up, lay, leisure, lottery, marathon, match, meet, meeting, mess around, oppose, pastime, pit, play, race, raffle, recreation, rehearsal, rehearse, relaxation, rivalry, rout, shuffle, speculate, speculation, sport, stake, swim, tournament, trifle, turn, vacation, venture, vie, wager, win, workout

364 **objects used in:** amusement, avocation, bicycle, club, equipment, field, game, gymnasium, hobby, holiday, lap, motorcycle, point, pool, raffle, recreation, round, score, standoff, tie, wager

365 **organization:** conference, field, league, side, squad, team

366 **participants:** abolitionist, adherent, aficionado, amateur, aspirant, athlete, aviator, champion, coach, competitor, contestant, dabbler, dark horse, doozy, entrant, entry, fan, fanatic, fighter, fledgling, follower, freak, geek, gladiator, groupie, hacker, jock, mariner, master, minion, moderator, name, observer, opponent, opposition, participant, pedestrian, pitcher, player, prima donna, referee, rival, sailor, spectator, star, umpire, underdog, victor, winner

RELIGIOUS

367 **action:** anoint, apotheosis, baptism, baptize, bless, blessing, burial, bury, canonize, christen, communion, consecrate, dedicate, dedication, defect, defection, deify, distillation, enshrine, entomb, excommunicate, exorcism, inter, interment, penance, pray, prayer, preach, purification, purify, wake, witchcraft, worship

368 **objects used in:** abbey, beads, bible, boneyard, casket, cathedral, cemetery, church, cloister, coffin, convent, deity, denomination, divinity, faith, grace, holiness, invocation, litany, liturgy, monastery, mosque, necropolis, nunnery, pulpit, religion, requiem, sanctity, sanctuary, sermon, service, shrine, synagogue, temple

369 **organization:** church, clergy, congregation, cult, Jewish, parish, priesthood

370 **supernatural:** abracadabra, alchemy, angel, apparition, black magic, bottomless, deep space, deity, demon, devil, divinity, Eden, elf, eternity, fairy, fat city, galaxy, ghost, ghoul, goblin, god, heaven, hell, hereafter, hex, hobgoblin, incantation, incubus, inferno, leprechaun, Lucifer, magic, monster, necromancy, paradise, perdition, phantom, pixie, poltergeist, presence, purgatory, saint, Satan, savior, shade, Shangri-la, sorcery, specter,

spell, spirit, universe, utopia, vision, voodoo, whammy, witchcraft, Xanadu

SEX AND REPRODUCTION

371 **attribute of gender:** female, femininity/feminine, he-man, machismo, macho, male, masculinity/masculine, virility, womanly

372 **attribute of sexuality:** AC-DC, adulterous, amatory, amorous, androgynous, aphrodisiac, bisexual, carnal, celibate, chaste, close, desirable, erotic, femininity/feminine, fertile, fertility, fleshly, gay, homosexual, horny, hot, kinky, lascivious, lecherous, lewd, libidinous, licentious, loose, lothario, loving, masculinity/masculine, nasty, naughty, obscene, passion, passionate, peccadillo, pornographic, pornography, potent, promiscuous, provocative, prurient, pure, raunchy, raw, salicious, seductive, sensual, sensuous, sexual, sexy, smut, smutty, spicy, suggestive, sultry, thought-provoking, torrid, vice, virgin/virginal, virile, virility, voluptuous, vulgar, wanton, womanly, X-rated

373 **birth:** bear, birth, breed, childbirth, conception, delivery, spring

374 **child bearing:** beget, deliver, delivery, fertilize, generate, generation, get, have, labor, multiply, procreate, produce, propagate, reproduce, spawn

375 **sex act:** affair, alter, assignation, birth control, caress, climax, cohabit, conception, copulate, coquet, couple, cuddle, dalliance, dally/dally with, debauch, deflower, enamor, fertilize, flirt, flirtation, fondle, foreplay, fornicate, fornication, hug, impregnate, intercourse, kiss, love, love affair, lovemaking, mate, molest, necking, pass, paw, pet, proposition, rape, ravish, romance, seduce, sex, sexual assault, sin, smooch, tryst, violate, violation, woo

SOCIAL INTERACTIONS

376 **authority:** aegis, agency, agent, ascendancy/ascendency, auspices, authority, blabbermouth, carte blanche, censorship, chair, chairperson, chief, choice, civil rights, claim, clearance, cogency, command, connoisseur, control, curb, custody, dominance, domination, dominion, duty, ease, empire, franchise, green card, immunity, impunity, independence, jurisdiction, justice, leadership, leave, office, option, permission, permit, power, prerogative, privilege, rate, reign, right, rule, station, supremacy, sway, title, trust, voice, vote, warrant

377 **celebration:** acclamation, affair, banquet, baptism, carnival, celebrate, celebration, commemorate, commemoration, commencement, entertain, fair, fanfare, feast, festival, festivity, fete, fiesta, gaiety, gala, have a ball, jamboree, keep, observance, observe, orgy, pageant, pageantry, parade, pomp, rally, revel, revelry, rite, sacrament, splurge, spree, wake, wassail

378 class: branch, brand, breed, caste, category, class, classification, cut, denomination, description, division, echelon, estate, family, folks, form, genre/genus, gradation, grade, ilk, kind, manner, mob, model, mold, nature, nobility, order, position, quality, rabble, rank, rating, riffraff, sort, species, stock, third world, tier, type, variety, world

379 community: colony, commune, community, constituency, country, folk, hoi polloi, neighborhood, people, population, public, society

380 ethnic group: nationality, people, race, strain, tribe

381 organization: affiliate, affiliation, agency, apparatus, assembly, bar, brigade, coalition, combination, commission, committee, council, crew, crowd, department, federation, foundation, fraternity, guild, institute/institution, Internet, league, membership, movement, network, organization, panel, partnership, party, ring, sect, society, union

382 part of a group: chapter, division, plurality, sect

383 party: affair, bash, blowout, dance, entertainment, festivity, gala, masquerade, orgy, party, reception, shindig, show business, tear

384 social action: abuse, accept, advance(s), adventure, amends, amuse, appeal, appointment, associate, befriend, betray, bite, blackball, blooper, booking, bounce, break the ice, caper, carouse, cavort, cohabit, collaborate, come upon, commemorate, compel, conclave, conduct, consort, cool, coquet, court, cower, cultivate, cut up, disaffect, discriminate, disgrace, disobey, disorganize, dissociate, encounter, endanger, engagement, enjoy, entertain, entertainment, escapade, escort, estrange, excursion, faux pas, fawn, fete, fight, flirt, flirtation, flock, fornicate, fornication, forsake, fraternize, frequent, frisk, frolic, get a kick out of, get even, go together/go with, grovel, hanky-panky, haunt, hold, horse around, host, hubbub, induct, induction, infringe, insinuate, interfere, interference, interrupt, introduce, invitation, invite, jilt, kick out, know, kowtow, lose, love, make up, maroon, mask, meddle, mediate, mediation, meet, meeting, mingle, mishandle/mismanage, mutiny, network, obeisance, oblige, observance, observe, ostracize, overture, pander, part, parting, pass, patch up, patronize, penance, pick up, play, poke, popularize, powwow, prance, prank, pretend, program, proposition, prostrate, pry, pursue, put up, rampage, rapprochement, reception, reciprocate, reconcile, reduce, regale, reinstate, rendezvous, repay, reprisal, requite, respond, retaliate, retribution, revel, revelry, revenge, riot, romance, romp, rupture, seat, secede, second, see, separate, sever, share, show, show business, shun, sit, slight, snoop, snub, socialize, soothe, spree, spurn, squire, stab in the back, step in, stoop, stunt, taint, tantrum, tear, throw over, toady, toy, treat, trespass, trick, truckle, tryst, usurp, vengeance, wallow, welcome, woo

385 social change: breakup, civilize, give in/give up, revert, succumb

386 social event: adventure, assignation, ball,

bee, bells and whistles, benefit, binge, blast, bustle, caper, caricature, carnival, ceremony, clamor, clown, come between, conference, date, debut, display, dissipation, diversion, entertainment, escapade, exhibition, exhibitionism, exposition, fair, feature, field trip, fiesta, fling, frolic, fun, function, funeral, gathering, horseplay, inauguration, initiation, memorial, merriment/merrymaking, morgue, occasion, outing, parade, picnic, rally, riot, rite, ritual, rumpus, sacrament

387 social organization: association, band, brotherhood, circle, clan, class, clique, club, congregation, congress, crowd, cult, fraternity, elite, entourage, faction, fellowship, following, gang, guild, high society, jet set, league, legion, order, society

388 social state: abasement, admittance, affirmative action, amity, association, attendance, awkwardness, bad luck, behind, belong, belonging, bigotry, bond, brand, breach, break, breeding, brotherhood, calm, camaraderie, care, caste, celebrity, celibacy, censorship, ceremony, circumstances, civilization, class, clutches, coherence, commotion, companionship, compatibility, complicity, concert, concord, conflict, conjunction, connection, consanguinity, consequence, contact, contempt, cooperation, correlation, courtesy, courtship, credit, crunch, culture, dalliance, degree, detachment, détente, difference, dignitary, dignity, diplomacy, disaffection, disagreement, discord, disfavor, disgrace, disharmony, dishonor, disorder, dissociation, dissolution, distinction, disturbance, division, duty, ease, echelon, elite, eminence, enrollment, entertainment, entrée, entry, equality, estate, estrangement, excitement, face, falling-out, fame, familiarity, favoritism, fellowship, feud, fidelity, footing, foreplay, friendliness, friendship, frivolity, fun, furor, fuss, gaiety, genre/genus, gentility, get along, get on, glory, harmony, height, high society, hit it off, hoopla, hospitality, housing, hubbub, humbug, humiliation, immortality, immunity, importance, infidelity, intimacy, intrigue, jet set, juncture, kick, laissez-faire, lapse, lather, league, level, liaison, liberty, love affair, luxury, malarky, marriage, match, men's movement, mirth, mortification, mourning, mutiny, name, nepotism, network, nobility, nonsense, nonviolence, notch, notoriety, obligation, odium, onus, opprobrium, pandemonium, partnership, peace, piffle, pink, place, platitude, pleasure, polish, polygamy, poppycock, popularity, position, predicament, presence of mind, prestige, privacy, rage, rank, rapport, rapprochement, rate, refinement, relationship, report, reproach, repulse, reputation, rift, ruckus, rupture, scramble, seclusion, separation, servitude, setback, shame, showdown, situation, slavery, society, solitude, sophistication, sphere, split, spotlight, standing, stardom, state, station, status, stigma, stillness, stimulating, stink, stir, support, sympathy, taint, taste, tedium, terms, tie, tomfoolery, twaddle, uncertainty, unification, variance, wedlock, whirl

Life forms

BEINGS

389 beings: being, body, cell, creation, creature, cur, egg, form, individual, life, organism, soul

390 former beings: body, cadaver, carcass/carcase, corpse

391 group of beings: band, flock, group, third world, world

392 limb or appendage of: ankle, arm, back, backside, beak, behind, branch, bust, butt/buttocks, calf, chest, claw, derriere, digit, duff, egg, extremity, eye, fanny, fiber, finger, flank, flesh, foot, freckle, germ, hair, hand, head, jaw, leg, limb, lip, member, microorganism, mop, mouth, nose, posterior, rug, rump, seat, skin, strand, tail, toupee, trunk, tuft, wig, wisp

393 organ: abdomen, abdominal, bacteria, belly, blood, bone, bowels, brain, dentures, entrails, false teeth, gut, heart, joint, mind, molecule, muscle, nucleus, seed, skeleton, spine, stomach, tummy, vein

BEINGS, ANIMAL

394 animal: adult, animal, beast, brute, buck, calf, cat, cattle, chicken, clam, cock, colt, cur, dad, father, fawn, frog, game, goat, half-breed, hog, horse, hound, hybrid, leech, litter, mom, mongrel, monkey, monster, mother, parasite, pet, pig, prey, stock, young

395 bird: bird, chicken

396 fish: aquarium, aquatic

397 group of animals: drove, family, herd, horde, insect, litter, pack, roundup, stock, swarm, team

398 insect: bee, bug, grub, pest

399 limb or appendage of: bill, chin, coat, crest, feather, fertilizer, fur, hot dog, manure, meat, mop, paunch, pelt, pulp, scale, shell, trunk, venom, wing

400 mammal: cat, dad, dog, donkey, father, fawn, goat, hog, hound, mom, mother, pig

GENERAL CHARACTERISTICS

401 attribute of behavior: abstemious, accident-prone, acerbity, acid, acrid, acrimonious, active, adamant, adolescent, affable, affected, affectionate, agog, agreeable, agreeably, aimless, alive, aloof, amiable, amuck, animate, animated, antsy, anxious, apathetic, arbitrary, arch, ardent, argumentative, arrogant, artificial, ascetic, assured, attentive, audacious, austere, authoritarian, avid, babyish, backhanded, backward, bad, balky, barbarian, barbaric, barbarous, barefaced, beaming, beastly, belligerent, benevolent, big, bland, blindly, bloodthirsty, boisterous, bold, bossy, brash, brassy, brave, brazen, brittle, brusque, brutal, cagey, calculating, calm, cantanker-

ous, capricious, carnivorous, casual, cautious, cavalier, chary, cheeky, childish, chill, chivalrous, chummy, civil, clumsy, coarse, cocky/cocksure, collected, combative, comic/comical, common, compassionate, complacent, complaisant, composed, compulsive, concerned, conciliatory, condescending, considerate, constructive, contemptuous, contentious, contrary, contumacious, convivial, cool, cordial, correct, corrupt, country, courageous, courteous, courtly, covetous, cowardly, coy, crabby/crabbed, crafty, cranky, crass, craven, cross, crotchety, crude, cruel, crusty, cunning, cutthroat, daring, dark, dauntless, deaf, debonair, deceitful, decent, deceptive, decided, decorous, defensive, deferential, defiant, deliberate, deliberately, delicate, delightful, delinquent, delirious, demonstrative, demure, desperate, detached, devious, diffident, diplomatic, disagreeable, disarming, discourteous, discreet, disdainful, disgruntled, disingenuous, disinterested, disloyal, disobedient, disobliging, disorderly, dispassionate, disputatious, disrespectful, disruptive, dissipated, dissolute, distant, distraught, ditsy, divisive, docile, doctrinaire, dogged, dolorous, domineering, doting, double-dealing, dour, draconian, duplicitous, eager, earnest, easy, ebullient, edgy, effeminate, effervescent, elfin, emotionless, enthusiastic, envious, epicurean, equable, equal, evasive, even, even-tempered, exacting, excitable, excited, exuberant, fainthearted, faithful, faithless, fake, fallow, false, falsely, fanatical, favorable, favorably, fawning, fearful, fearless, feigned, feral, ferocious, ferocity, fervent/fervid, feverish, fickle, fidgety, fiery, fighting, finicky, flagrant, flamboyant, flexible, flighty, flippant, flirtatious, flushed, foolhardy, foolish, foolishly, footloose, forceful, formal, forward, foxy, fractious, free, freely, fresh, fretful, frisky, frivolous, fulsome, fussy, fustian, gamely, genial, genteel, giddy, glacial, glowing, gluttonous, good, goody-goody, goofy, graceless, gracious, grandiose, grave, gritty, grouchy, gruff, grumpy, gung ho, halcyon, halfhearted, hard, hardhearted, haram-scarum, haughty, headstrong, heartless, hearty, heedless, helpless, heroic, high and mighty, high-handed, high-strung, holier-than-thou, hostile, hot, hotheaded, huffy, humane, humble, hyperactive, hypocritical, icy, idle, ill at ease, ill-mannered, ill-natured, ill-tempered, immodest, impatient, impersonal, impertinent, impish, impolite, impolitic, importunate, impossible, impudent, impulsive, inactive, inclement, inconsiderate, inexorable, ingratiating, inhospitable, inhuman/inhumane, inimical, innocuous, insensitive, insidious, insolent, insubordinate, insurgent, intractable/intransigent, intrepid, introverted, intrusive, invidious, irascible, irreconcilable, irrepressible, irreverent, irritable, jaded, jaundiced, jaunty, jazzed-up, jittery, jovial, jubilant, jumpy, juvenile, keen, kind, kittenish, kosher, lax, lazy, lecherous, lenient, lethargic, level, liberal, licentious, lifeless, light, light-headed, listless, litigious, lively, lofty, loose, loquacious, lothario, loud, loud-mouthed, loving, lunatic, Machiavellian maladroit, malevolent, malicious, manageable, mannered, mannerly, martial, mawkish, mean, meat-eating, meek, menacing, mercenary, merciful, merciless, mercurial, mild, militant, mincing, mischievous, miscreant, miserly, modest, mousy, mulish, munificent, mutinous, naive, narcissistic, nasty, natural, naughty, nefarious, neglectful, negligent, neighborly, nerveless, nervy, noble, nomadic, nonchalant, noncompliant, nonconformist, nonviolent, nosy, obdurate, obedient, obeisant, obliging, obnoxious, obsequious, obstinate, obtrusive, odious, offhand, oily, on edge, on guard, on purpose, on the wagon, orderly, ornery, ostentatious, outlandish, overbearing, overconfident, overwrought, parental, parsimonious, partisan, passionate, pedantic, peevish, pent-up, peppery, peppy, perfidious, peripatetic, perky, permissive, persistent, pert, perverse, petulant, philosophical/philosophic, phlegmatic, phobic, pious, pitiless, placid, plaintive, playful, play it safe, plucky, polite, politic, politically correct, pompous, possessed, pragmatic, precious, precipitous/precipitate, precise, predatory, premature, presumptuous, pretentious, prickly, prim, prissy, prodigal, profane, profligate, prompt, proper, propitious, proud, provident, prudent, prudish, psyched, puerile, pugnacious, pumped, punctilious, puritanical, pushy, quarrelsome, querulous, quick-tempered, quiet, racy, radiant, raffish, rakish, rash, raucous, ready, rebel, rebellious, recalcitrant, reckless, refined, regardful, regardless, relentless, reluctant, remiss, remorseful, remorseless, remote, renegade, reprobate, repugnant, reserved, resigned, respectful, responsible, responsive, restful, restive, restrained, reticent, retiring, reverent, revolutionary, ribald, rocky, roguish, rollicking, rootin'-tootin', rough, rousing, rowdy, rude, rugged, runaway, rustic, ruthless, sacrilegious, safe, salty, sanctimonious, sass, sassy, saucy, savage, savvy, scintillating, scrupulous, secluded, seditious, self-conscious, self-righteous, sensual, sentimental, serene, serpentine, servile, severe, shabby, shameful, shameless, sheepish, shiftless, shifty, short, short-sighted, shrewd, shy, silly, simple, simpleminded, sincere, sinister, skittish, slick, slippery, slothful, sluggish, sly, small, smart, smooth, snaky, snappy, sneaky, snide, snobbish, snooty, snotty, sober, sociable, soft, softhearted, solid, sophisticated, sophomoric, sparing, spineless, spiteful, spontaneous, sporting/sportive, sporty, sprightly, spry, square, squeamish, staid, standoffish, starchy, stately, staunch, steadfast, stealthy, stern, stiff, stilted, stingy, stodgy, stoic/stoical, stolid, stony, stouthearted, strained, strait-laced, street smart, strenuous, strict, stringent, stubborn, stuck-up, stuffy, suave, subdued, submissive, subservient, subversive, sunny, supercilious, superior, supine, sure, surly, sweet, sympa-

thetic, taciturn, tactful, tactless, tame, tasteless, tearful, temperate, tempestuous, tenacious, tender, tenderhearted, tense, testy, thankful, thankless, theatrical, thieving/ thievish, thoughtful, thoughtless, thrifty, tight, timid, tipsy, torpid, touchy, tractable, traitorous, treacherous, treasonous, tricky, truculent, true, true-blue, trusting, turbulent, two-faced, ugly, unaffected, unafraid, unasked, unassuming, unattached, unbending, unbridled, uncivil, uncivilized, uncompromising, uncontrollable, uncoordinated, uncouth, undaunted, undependable, undisciplined, underhand, understanding, unemotional, unflappable, unfriendly, ungrateful, unguarded, uninhibited, unintentional/unintended, uninterested, unkind, unmanageable, unmerciful, unobtrusive, unprejudiced, unpretentious, unreasonable, unrehearsed, unrelenting, unrestricted, unruly, unscrupulous, unseemly, unselfish, unsettled, unsociable, unsophisticated, unsuspecting, unsympathetic, unthinking, untoward, untrustworthy, unwary, unwilling, unwise, unwitting, unworldly, unyielding, uppity, uptight, urbane, vain, vainglorious, valiant, valorous, vehement, vengeful, venturesome, vibrant, vicarious, vicious, Victorian, vigilant, vindictive, violent, viperous, virile, virtuous, vital, vivacious, volatile, voracious, wacky, waggish, wanton, warlike, warm, warmhearted, wary, wasteful, watchful, wayfaring, wayward, well-bred, whimsical, wicked, wild, willful, willing, wily, winning/winsome, withdrawn, witless, worldly, yellow, yielding, zany, zealous

402 **attribute of intelligence:** able, abreast, abstruse, academic, accident-prone, acquainted, acute, adept, alert, amenable, analytic/analytical, appreciative, apt, asinine, astute, awake, aware, backward, bewildered, blank, blind, bright, brilliant, calculable, canny, catatonic, cerebral, childish, clairvoyant, clear, clever, clumsy, cognizant, coherent, common-sense, complex, comprehensible, conscious, considered, contemplative, conversant, creative, cunning, dark, deducible, deep, delirious, dense, designedly, dexterous, dim, discerning, dizzy, dopey, down-to-earth, dull, dumb, eagle-eyed, educated, efficient, elevated, empty, empty-headed, enlightened, erudite, experienced, expert, familiar, far-sighted, fatuous, feebleminded, forgotten, frivolous, gifted, gullible, harebrained, hazy, highbrow, idiotic, ignorant, illiterate, imbecile, impressionable, incisive, incomprehensible, inefficient, ineligible, inept, inexperienced, informed, ingenious, inquiring, inquisitive, insightful, insipid, intellectual, intelligent, intuitive, inventive, irrational, judicious, keen, knowing, knowledgeable, learned, literate, logical, lowbrowed, lucid, mental, mindful, mistaken, moronic, nimble, not born yesterday, oblivious, observant, obtuse, omniscient, on the ball, penetrating, perceptive, perspicacious, philosophical/philosophic, precocious, privy, professional, proficient, profound, psychic, quick, quick-witted, rational, ready, reasonable, resourceful, sagacious, sage, sane, sapient, savvy, scatterbrained, scholarly, searching, seasoned, senile, sensible, sentient, shallow, sharp, shrewd, simple, skillful, slick, slow, smart, soft, stolid, studious, stupid, subtle, talented, thick, thoughtful, thoughtless, touched, unaware, uncoordinated, uneducated, unfamiliar, uninformed, unintelligent, unknowing, unwise, vacant, vacuous, versed, veteran, weak, well-balanced, well-defined, wide-awake, wise, with it

403 attribute of mentality: aback, abashed, abscondere, absentee, absent-minded, absorbed, absorbing, abstracted, accustomed, addled, affected, affectionate, afraid, aggrieved, aghast, agonizing, alert, allergic, amatory, amorous, angry, anxious, apathetic, appreciative, apprehensive, aspiring, assumed, attention deficit disorder, attentive, automatic, averse, avid, bad, balmy, beaten, beholden, believable, bent, berserk, beside oneself, bewildered, bewitched, bigoted, black, bleak, blissful, blue, boiling, breathless, broad, broad-minded, broken, broken-hearted, buoyant, burning, calculating, captive, carnal, cautious, certain, cheerful, cheerless, chipper, circumspect, clairvoyant, clear, compassionate, complacent, concerned, confident, confused, conscious, contemplative, content, contented, contrite, crabby/crabbed, cranky, crazy, crestfallen, cross, crotchety, curious, cynical, daffy, daft, dearly, decided, dejected, delighted, delirious, demented, depressed, deranged, desolate, despairing, desperately, despondent, disaffected, disappointed, disbelieving, disconcerted, disconsolate, discontented/discontent, discouraged, discouraging, disenchanted, disgruntled, disgusted, disillusioned, disinclined, disinterested, disoriented, dispirited, dissatisfied, dissident, distraught, distressed, distrustful, doleful, dolorous, dotty, doubtful, down, downbeat, downcast, downhearted, dumbfounded, ecstatic, elated, elegiac, emotional, emotionless, enamored, engrossed, enraged, envious, excited, expectant, exultant, fascinated, fed up, festive, firm, flaming, flushed, foggy, forgetful, forgotten, forlorn, frantic, frenetic, fretful, frightened, frustrated, fulfilled, funereal, furious, gay, glad, gladly, gleeful, gloomy, glum, goofy, grateful, greedy, grief-stricken, grumpy, gut, half-baked, hangdog, happily, happy, hard, hard-boiled, hardline, harried, haywire, headstrong, healthy, heartsick, heavy, high, homesick, hopeful, hot, huffy, hurt, hysterical, ill at ease, ill-tempered, impartial, impassioned, impressionable, inattentive, incensed, inconsolable, incredulous, indifferent, indignant, indiscriminate, infatuated, insane, insatiable, insecure, insular, intent, intently, interested, intolerant, intoxicated, invidious, irate, irrational, irresolute, irritable, jaundiced, jealous, jovial, joyful/joyous, joyless, jubilant, judicious, keen, lackadaisical, languid, lascivious, lethargic, levelheaded, livid, lonely, lonesome, longing, loony, lost, low, lucid, lukewarm, lunatic, mad, malcontent, malleable, manic/maniacal, melancholy, mental, merry, mindful, mindless, mirthful, miser-

able, mixed-up, moody, morbid, morose, mournful, narrow, narrow-minded, negative, nerveless, nervous, neurotic, neutral, new age, noncommittal, normal, nostalgic, numb, nuts/nutty, objective, objectivity, oblivious, observant, obsess, obsessed, off-guard, on edge, one-sided, on the ball, on the fence, opposed/opposing, overcome, overjoyed, overwrought, partial, penitent, pensive, pent-up, pessimistic, petrified, petty, phlegmatic, pissed off, platonic, play it safe, pooped, possessive, predisposed, preoccupied, prepared, prepossessed, profound, proud, provincial, prurient, psyched, psychic, psychological, psychotic, pumped, punch-drunk, purposeful, puzzled, queasy, rabid, racist, radical, raging, rapacious, rapt, realistic, reflective, regretful, resolute, restless, right, rigid, romantic, rueful, sad, salacious, sane, sanguine, sappy, saturnine, scared, sectarian, secure, self-assured, senile, sensitive, serious, sick, silly, skeptical, sleepless, small-minded, solemn, solicitous, somber, sore, sorrowful, sorry, soulful, sound, sour, spellbound, spiritless, steady, stout, strong, stunned, stupefied, subdued, sulky, sullen, susceptible, suspicious, tearful, temperamental, tender, tense, testy, thankful, thirsty, thoughtful, thoughtless, thunderstruck, tired, tolerant, torn, touched, tough, tuckered out, ugly, unadvised, unbalanced, unbelieving, uncaring, uncomfortable, uncommitted, unconcerned, undecided, uneasy, unemotional, unfaltering, unfeeling, unhappy, uninterested, unsettled, unsound, untouched, untroubled, unwary, upbeat, upset, versed, vulnerable, wacky, warm-hearted, wary, weak, weary, wide-awake, willing, wishful, wistful, woebegone, worried, wrathful, wretched

404 attribute of personality: aboveboard, abrasive, adventurous, aggressive, airy, altruistic, amenable, amorphous, approachable, ardent, arrogant, artful, assertive, assuming, assured, audacious, august, avaricious, bashful, belligerent, belonging to, big, big-hearted, bitter, blasé, blessed, blithe, bloodless, boastful, bold, boorish, bossy, brash, bright, buoyant, busy, callous, calm, captious, carefree, catty, charitable, charming, chaste, cheeky, cheerful, childlike, chill, chilly, choosy, churlish, clean, clear, clement, clinical, close, cocky/cocksure, co-dependent, cold, colorful, colorless, combative, conceited, confident, convivial, cool, courageous, coy, credulous, culpable, cursed, cute, cutthroat, dainty, dashing, dastardly, decent, dedicated, deep, delicate, delightful, demonic/demoniac/demoniacal, demure, dependent, deserving, despicable, detached, determined, devious, dewy-eyed, die-hard, difficult, dignified, discriminating, dispassionate, disreputable, distant, docile, dynamic, easy, easygoing, effeminate, egocentric, egotistic/egoistic, elastic, embittered, enchanting, endearing, energetic, engaging, enterprising, even-tempered, exacting, exalted, excitable, exemplary, extroverted, feckless, feisty, finicky, finished, flatulent, flirtatious, forbearing, fortunate, forward, foxy, free, fresh, frigid, fussy, gallant, game, garrulous, gauche, generous, genial, genteel, gentle, glacial, glib, good, good-humored, good-natured, green, gregarious, gritty, gutless, gutsy, halcyon, happy-go-lucky, hardened, hardhearted, hard-nosed/hardheaded, hateful, hell-bent, heroic, high and mighty, highstrung, humble, hyperactive, hypercritical, icy, ill-natured, immaculate, immovable, impassive, imperturbable, impetuous, individual, indomitable, indulgent, inexperienced, infamous, inflexible, inherent, inhibited, innocent, insipid, insouciant, intolerant, intrinsic, introverted, inveterate, inviting, irresponsible, jaunty, jazzed-up, kind, kindhearted, kindly, kosher, laid-back, largesse, latent, lazy, liberal, lighthearted, likable, little, loutish, lovable, low, lowly, loyal, magnanimous, magnetic, manageable, matronly, mercurial, meritorious, mild, mincing, misanthropic, miserly, modest, mulish, narcissistic, native, natural, nice, noble, nonchalant, notorious, obedient, obliging, obsequious, obsessed, odd/oddball, odious, officious, openhanded, openhearted, open-minded, opinionated, opprobrious, optimistic, ossified, outgoing, outspoken, overbearing, particular, patient, peculiar, peppy, perfidious, perky, persistent, persnickety, personable, pert, philanthropic, picky, pigheaded, pliable, predictable, prepossessing, prim, prissy, proper, puritanical, pushy, queer, quick-tempered, receptive, recluse/reclusive, remote, reserved, responsible, rotten, ruthless, saintly, sanctimonious, Satanic, sedate, selective, self-assured, self-centered, self-confident, self-conscious, selfish, self-satisfied, self-sufficient, servile, shabby, shiftless, shifty, shy, slothful, smug, snotty, sophisticated, spick-and-span, spirited, spotless, sprightly, spunky, square, squeamish, stable, staid, stalwart, standoffish, stodgy, stoic/stoical, straight, stubborn, stuffy, suave, subservient, sweet, thick-skinned, treacherous, trustworthy/trusty, unaffected, unapproachable, unassuming, unpretentious, unselfish, unsuspecting, unworthy, uppity, upright, vain, valiant, valorous, vigorous, virile, vivacious, vocal, warm, winning, winsome, wishy-washy, yielding, zealous, zippy

405 essential property of life forms: allergy, awkwardness, body, complexion, dotage, fatigue, hygiene, physique, sense, sensitivity

406 essential quality of life forms: adult, alimentary, animal, athletic, awake, awkward, barefoot, bearded, blank, bodily, breathless, brunette/brunet, bushy, buxom, cadaverous, corpulent, curly, curvaceous, dark, deadpan, decrepit, drowsy, empty, exhausted, expectant, expecting, expressionless, fair, famished, fleshy, florid, full, gaunt, glassy, haggard, hairless, hairy, high, human, hungry, imperceptible, inborn/inbred, infertile, innate, insensitive, intestinal/intestine, intoxicated, intrinsic, jaded, light, limber, lumbering, piercing, predatory, pregnant, primitive, private, promising, prostrate, ravenous, raw, rich, sensitive, sensory, shapely, smooth, starving/starved, sweaty, thin-skinned, tight, tipsy, tired, untamed, wild

407 existential state: be, being, casualty, coexistence, endangered, endure, exist, existence, fettle, flesh, gone, live, loss, manage, matter, mortality, nature, none, nothing/nothingness, oblivion, outlast, outlive, presence, reside, spirit, stand, subsist, survive, threaten, vitality, zero, zilch

408 gender: female, femininity/feminine, gender, he-man, machismo, macho, male, masculinity/masculine

409 intelligence: acquaintance, acumen, anticipation, appreciation, apprehension, aptitude, attention, awareness, bent, brain, capacity, clairvoyance, clarity, cleverness, cognizance/cognition, common sense, comprehension, conception, consciousness, craft, creativity, dark, darkness, delusion, depth, dexterity, education, efficiency, empathy, enlightenment, erudition, experience, expertise/expertness, extrasensory perception, familiarity, fancy, feeling, finesse, foresight, forte, genius, gift, grasp, grip, head, idiocy, ignorance, illumination, imagination, ingenuity, innocence, insight, intellect, intelligence, interpretation, intuition, invention, judgment, ken, knack, know-how, knowledge, learning, light, literacy, memory, mentality, mind, misconception, misunderstanding, nirvana, observance, observation, originality, perception, precognition, proficiency, reason, sagacity, sage, sanity, savvy, scholarship, sense, sensibility, sixth sense, skill, smarts, soul, thought, understanding, wisdom, wit/wits, workmanship

410 mentality: abhorrence, absent-mindedness, absorption, abstraction, accession, ache, afterlife, aggravation, agility, agonize, agony, alarm, alienation, allergy, alter ego, amazement, anger, angst, anguish, anticipation, anxiety, apathy, application, assurance, astonishment, attention, attitude, attrition, avarice, awe, bad time, bathos, beatitude, behalf, belief, belonging, bigotry, bitterness, blues, boast, boredom, bosom, breakdown, breast, bristle, buoyancy/buoyance, cabin fever, capitulation, caprice, care, caution, censure, chagrin, cheer, clairvoyance, clemency, cliffhanger, cogitation, collapse, comfort, compassion, complex, composure, compulsion, compunction, conception, concern, confusion, conquest, consideration, consolation, constancy, contemplation, content, contentment, contrition, conviction, corollary, creativity, credit, cult, curiosity, dark, darkness, daze, decision, defeat, deference, degradation, delight, delight in, delirium, delusion, dementia, dependence/dependency, depression, design, desolation, despair, desperation, difficulty, disability, disaffection, disappointment, discipline, discomfiture, discomfort, discontent, discouragement, discrimination, disgust, disinclination, dismay, disorder, displeasure, disquiet, dissatisfaction, distraction, distress, disturbance, doldrums, dolor, doubt, dumps, ease, ecstasy, Eden, elation, embarrassment, emotion, encouragement, enjoyment, ennui, envy, equanimity, esprit de corps, euphoria, exaltation, exasperation, excitement, exhaustion, exhilaration, expectancy, expectation, extrasensory perception, exultation, fallacy, fat city, feeling, felicity, fever, firmness, fluster, fog, folly, forbearance, force, foresight, forethought, forgetfulness, fortitude, frame of mind, frazzle, free will, frenzy, fret, fright, frustration, fume, funk, furor, fury, gladness, glee, gloom, gratification, gratitude, grief, grieve, happiness, health, heart, heartache, heartbreak, heat, heaven, hesitation, hoopla, hope, huff, humbug, humanity, humiliation, humor, hysteria, idiocy, imagination, impulse, indifference, indignity, insanity, insight, instability, introspection, ire, jealousy, jitters, joy, ken, kick, lament/lamentation, languor, letdown, lethargy, levity, lunacy, madness, malaise, mania, martyrdom, melancholy, mental illness, merriment/merrymaking, mindset, mirth, mistake, monotony, mood, mope, morale, mortification, mourn, mourning, muddle, nausea, negative attitude, neglect, nerves, nervous breakdown, nervousness, neurosis, nostalgia, objection, oblivion, observance, observation, obsession, offense, optimism, originality, outlook, pain, panic, paradise, paroxysm, passion, pathos, peace, penance, penitence, perception, perspective, pessimism, pique, pity, pleasure, Pollyanna, posture, pout, precaution, precognition, predisposition, premonition, presage, presence, presentiment, psyche, psychology, push, pussyfoot, qualm, quarter, rage, rancor, rapture, rave, red herring, regret, rejoice, remorse, repent, repentance, repose, repulse, resent, resentment, resignation, resistance, resolution, resolve, restlessness, retrospect, ruckus, rue, sadness, sanity, satisfaction, scare, security, self-satisfaction, sensation, sensibility, sensitivity, sentiment, seriousness, servitude, shame, simmer, skepticism, slump, sob, solace, solicitude, sorrow, soul, soul-searching, state, status quo, stew, strain, strength, stress, subconscious, surprise, suspense, sympathy, tedium, telepathy, temper, temperament, temperance, tension, thought, tolerance, torment, torpor, torture, trance, transport, triumph, turn, umbrage, uncertainty, unrest, vagary, vanity, wariness, waver, woe, wonder, wonderment, worry, wrath, zeal, zest

411 personality: aggression, ardor, arrogance, art, artifice, assumption, atrocity, attribute, audacity, backbone, bearing, being, best, bounce, bravery, buoyancy/buoyance, caliber, calm, candor, character, characteristic, charisma, charity, charm, complexion, compliance, conceit, confidence, constraint, courage, cultivation, dash, decision, dedication, demeanor, determination, dignity, disposition, disrepute, distinction, drive, effrontery, ego, egoism/egotism, élan, empathy, endowment, endurance, energy, enterprise, entity, esprit de corps, essence, eye, failing, fettle, fiber, fight, fire, foible, forte, fortitude, frailty, gall, gallantry, generosity, geniality, gentility, glint, go, goodness, good will/goodwill, greatness, grit, gumption, gusto, guts, hauteur, heart, heroism, honor, hubris, humor, identity, idiosyncrasy, ilk, inclination, individuality, infamy, inhibition, initiative, innocence, integrity, kind, kink, laziness, life, longevity, loyalty, magnetism,

makeup, manner, mark, martyrdom, mentality, mettle, mien, might, mold, monstrosity, mood, morale, morals, motivation, moxie, mystique, nature, nerve, notoriety, obedience, oddity, oomph, panache, patience, peculiarity, penchant, pep, perseverance, personality, pizzazz, pluck, point, possibilities, potency, presence, presence of mind, pride, prima donna, probity, proclivity, propensity, property, prowess, psyche, push, qualify, quirk, reputation, responsibility, savor, self-respect/self-esteem, sex appeal, shortcoming, sloth, soul, sparkle, spirit, sportsmanship, spunk, stability, stamina, stamp, staying power, style, taste, temerity, temper, temperament, tenacity, tend, thing, trait, trick, turn, twist, type, valor, vein, verve, vice, vigor, virtue, vitality, way, weakness, will, willpower, wit, zeal, zest, zing, zip

HUMANS

412 bad person: accessory, accomplice, accurser, addict, adversary, agent provocateur, aggressor, agitator, alarmist, anarchist, antagonist, apostate, ass, assailant, assassin, attacker, authoritarian, bandit, barbarian, beggar, bigmouth, blabbermouth, bottom feeder, braggart, bum, bungler, burglar, butterfingers, cad, cannibal, captive, character, charlatan, cheat, clod, clown, cold fish, confederate, conspirator, convict, criminal, critic, crook, crybaby, culprit, cur, deadbeat, defendant, delinquent, demagogue, demon, demonstrator, derelict, deserter, desperado, despot, devil, dimwit, dirty old man, ditz, dolt, do-nothing, doomsayer, dope, drag queen, dregs, drifter, drone, dullard, dumbbell, dummy, dunce, enchantress, enemy, escapee, espionage, evildoer, exile, expatriate, failure, fake, fall guy, felon, femme fatale, fiend, fighter, fink, firebrand, foe, fool, fraud, fugitive, gadfly, gangster, ghoul, glutton, good-for-nothing, goon, gossip, grouch, grump, harlot, hellion, hit man, hobo, hog, hot dog, hussy, hypocrite, idiot, imbecile, imp, impostor, incendiary, incubus, instigator, insurgent, interloper, intruder, joke, Judas, juvenile delinquent, killer, killjoy, klutz, know-it-all, kook, lawbreaker, leech, lemon, liar, loafer, looter, loser, Lucifer, lummox, lunatic, mad person, malingerer, maniac, marauder, menace, mercenary, misanthrope, miscreant, miser, mobster, mole, monster, mountebank, murderer, naysayer, ne'-er-do-well, nitwit, nuisance, numbskull, nut, oaf, ogre, oppressor, organized crime, outlaw, parasite, patsy, pawn, pervert, pessimist, pest, pill, pirate, placebo, prisoner, prodigal, profligate, prostitute, prowler, psychopath, punk, quack, ragamuffin, rascal, rebel, renegade, robber, rogue, rowdy, ruffian, runaway, sap, Satan, scamp, scapegoat, schlemiel, scoundrel, Scrooge, scum, shirked, showoff, shyster, sight, simpleton, sissy, skinflint, slacker, sleazebag, smart aleck, sneak, sociopath, sourpuss, sponge, spy, strumpet, swindler, tattletale/tattler, thief, thug, tightwad, tool, tough, traitor, tramp, troll, troublemaker, truant, turncoat, tyrant, underworld, vandal, villain, wanton, weakling, whipping boy, whore, wimp, wise guy, witch

413 community group member: aborigine, citizen, denizen, emigrant, émigré, explorer, foreigner, hayseed, hick, hillbilly, immigrant, inhabitant, innovator, local, migrant, native, newcomer, nomad, outsider, patriot, pioneer, plebeian, proletariat, redneck, refugee, resident, rustic, stranger, subject, tenderfoot, yokel

414 family member: ancestor, ancestry, antecedent(s), babe, baby, broad, brother, child, conservationist, damsel, descendant, domestic partner, father, fetus, fiancé/fiancée, forebearer, forefather, forerunner, guardian, guy, heir, he-man, husband, hybrid, infant, issue, keeper, kid, kin, kindred, kinship, man, mother, newborn, nurse, occupant, offspring, orphan, owner, paramedic, parent, partner, predecessor, progeny, relation, relative, roots, scion, seed, senior, sister, spitting image, spouse, successor, surrogate, sweetheart, toddler, trustee, twin, ward, woman, young, youngster/youth

415 female: bachelor, bride, broad, damsel, dated, debutante, dish, doll, female, girl, girlfriend, housekeeper, Jezebel, minx, nymph, paramour, sister, wanton, wife, woman

416 good person: ace, angel, benefactor, do-gooder, doozy, dreamer, egghead, expert, genius, hero/heroine, humanitarian, idealist, intellect, intellectual, intimate, missionary, pacifist, peacemaker, perfectionist, pet, philanthropist, prodigy, prude, pundit, savior, victor, virtuoso, visionary, wag, whiz, winner, wit

417 group of people: anybody, anyone, army, assemblage, attendance, audience, band, beanpole, board, body, cadre, caucus, circle, civilization, class, clientele, clique, cloud, company, congregation, contingent, convention, corps, corpse, crew, crowd, crush, earthling, elite, enrollment, entourage, everybody/everyone, expedition, federation, field, flesh, following, force, gallery, gathering, hoi polloi, horde, host, huddle, human, humanity, humankind, legion, masses, member, membership, mob, mortal, mortality, multitude, muster, outfit, pack, party, people, person, personnel, platoon, practice, public, rabble, riffraff, set, society, squad, suite, swarm, team, throng, troop/troops, troupe, turnout

418 limb or appendage: ankle, beard, bosom, bottom, braid, breast, bristle, brow, can, cheek, coiffure, curl, elbow, features, pore, wrinkle

419 male: bachelor, boy, boyfriend, bridegroom, brother, escort, father, floozy, groom, guy, he-man, hooker, husband, Jezebel, lad, male, man, wanton

420 organ: backbone, blood, bone, brain, heart, muscle, spine, stomach, tummy, vein

421 racial group member: kin, kindred, relation, tribe

422 royalty: crown, monarch, noble, potentate

423 social group member: accurser, acquaintance, addict, admirer, adventurer, advocate, alarmist, alcoholic, alien, alliance, alter ego, another, apprentice, aristocracy, aristocrat, arrival, aspirant, assistant, associate, atheist, augur, auxiliary, bachelor, beatnik, beau, beggar, beginner, believer, beloved, benefactor, beneficiary, best-seller, bigmouth, bigot, big shot, birds of a feather, blabbermouth, black sheep, bohemian, boor, bore, boyfriend, braggart, brownnose, brute, buddy, buff, buffoon, bully, bum, bungler, busybody, butt, butterfingers, bystander, captive, casualty, celebrity, chaperon, character, chicken, chum, churl, civilian, clairvoyant, clod, clown, cohort, collaborator, colleague, comedian, comic, companion, company, competitor, comrade, confidant, conformist, connection, conquest, conservationist, consort, convoy, correspondent, couch potato, coward, craven, cretin, crony, cynic, darling, daredevil, dark horse, date, deadbeat, dear, derelict, deserter, devil's advocate, devotee, diehard, dilettante, disciple, disciplinarian, dissident, ditz, do-gooder, doll, dolt, Don Juan, donor, do-nothing, doomsayer, dope, doubter, doubting Thomas, drifter, driver, drunk/drunkard, dude, dullard, dumbbell, dummy, dunce, dupe, eccentric, elitist, emigrant, emissary, enthusiast, entrant, epicure, epicurean, equal, escort, exception, exile, expatriate, exponent, extraterrestrial, extremist, extrovert, eyewitness, failure, fan, father, favorite, fellow, fiancé/fiancée, fiend, figure, figurehead, fink, fisherman, flame, flirt, follower, fool, fop, forerunner, fortune-teller, founder, freak, friend, fuddy-duddy, gentleperson, gigolo, girlfriend, go-between, goon, gourmet, greenhorn, grouch, grump, guardian, guest, guide, half-wit, hanger-on, hedonist, helper, henchman, herald, hermit, hippie, hobo, homeboy, hostage, humanitarian, humorist, iconoclast, idealist, idol, inferior, informant/informer, interloper, intimate, introvert, intruder, jerk, jester, joke, joker, keeper, killjoy, know-it-all, kook, layperson, lemon, liaison, local, loner, loser, lout, love, lover, luminary, machine, mad person, marionette, master, mate, maverick, mediator, milksop, mind reader, miser, misfit, moron, mother, namby-pamby, name-dropper, naysayer, negotiator, neighbor, neophyte, newcomer, noble, nobody/nonentity, nonconformist, notable, notary, nouveau riche, novice, nut, observer, oddity/oddball, odds-on-favorite, old hand, onlooker, original, outcast, outsider, pagan, pal, pantywaist, paramour, pariah, participant, partisan, partner, passenger, patrician, patron, pauper, peer, personage/personality, pessimist, philanderer, philanthropist, pill, pillar, plebeian, poet, prey, prognosticator, proletariat, promoter, prophet, proponent, protagonist, protégé, pundit, puppet, pushover, racist, ragamuffin, rebel, recluse, rich, rival, scream, second, sectarian, seer, shirked, sidekick, simpleton, sissy, skeptic, slacker, snob, snoop, socialite, somebody, soothsayer, sourpuss, spectator, spendthrift, sponge, sponsor, sport, square, standby, stick-in-the-mud, stooge, stranger, subject, subordinate, substitute, suitor, support/supporter, surrogate, sweetheart, sycophant, target, tattletale/tattler, tenderfoot, tenant, toady, tool, tourist, trainee, traveler, trustee, tyro, umpire, underdog, underling, understudy, urchin, vagabond, vagrant, veteran, victim, visitor, wag, waif, wanderer, wayfarer, weakling, weirdo, wimp, windbag, wino, witness, wizard, womanizer, yes-person, zany

424 traits: adolescent, adult, babe, baby, beauty, beginner, boy, brat, child, childish, colossus, daughter, debutante, dish, doll, dwarf, elder, eyeful, fetus, fledgling, freak, giant, girl, gnome, grown-up, infant, invalid, juvenile, kid, lad, midget, minor, mossback, mutant, neophyte, newborn, nymph, old-timer, pipsqueak, runt, senior, teenager, toddler, trainee, tyro, vision, young, youngster/youth

Objects

ment, dome, door, egress, entrance, entry, exit, fireplace, floor, flue, foyer, gallery, gate, gazebo, gutter, hall, lectern, locker, niche, nook, partition, passage/passageway, pillar, platform, pole, post, prop, recess, screen, stack, stay, step, support, threshold, tower, vent, wall, wing

441 business place: agency, annex, boutique, building, bureau, factory, foyer, hall, lobby, office, shop, skyscraper, store, suite, wing

442 foundation: backbone, base, basis, bed, bottom, core, cornerstone, easel, foot, footing, foundation, frame, groundwork, infrastructure, kiosk, nadir, nitty-gritty, rest, rock, root, seat, stand, support

443 furniture: altar, antique, banister, bed, bench, bleachers, booth, buffet, bunk, bureau, cabinet, can, chair, cot, couch, cradle, crib, cupboard, davenport, desk, dresser, fireplace, furnishings, furniture, futon, gazebo, jetty, kiosk, lectern, mirror, partition, pen, perch, pier, platform, podium, pulpit, rack, rail/railing, ramp, screen, seat, secretary, sofa, stand, table, wardrobe

444 furniture accessory: bedding, bedspread, candlestick, canopy, chandelier, curtain, cushion

445 furniture part: button, faucet, gate, handle, knob, latch, ledge, nozzle, picket, pivot, post, quilt, screen, shade, shelf, stay, step, support, tap, valve

446 personal item: adornment, album, amulet, backpack, beads, belongings, best-seller, bracelet, briefcase, brooch, cache, camera, cargo, chain, charm, condom, contraceptive, curio, disguise, doll, effects, emollient, equipment, eyeglasses, favorite, fetish, gem, gimcrack, glasses, goods, handbag, jewel, jewelry, keepsake, knickknack, lotion, luggage, makeup, marionette, memento, memorabilia, moisturizer, necklace, nest egg, novelty, object d'art, odds and ends, odds-on-favorite, pack, paraphernalia, plaything, pledge, pocketbook, possession, pouch, pride, property, puppet, purchase, purse, relic, resources, riches, ring, savings, souvenir, spectacles, stuff, subsistence, supplies, support, sustenance, thing/things, toy, trappings, treasure, trifle, trinket, valuable

447 recreation area: cabaret, casino, hangout, landmark

448 room: alcove, apartment, attic, auditorium, bath, bathroom, bedroom, bistro, boutique, cell, cellar, chamber, den, dormitory, enclosure, food court, foyer, gallery, gin mill, greasy spoon, hall, kitchen, lavatory, loft, office, outhouse, outlet, parlor, pub, restaurant, room, saloon, sanctuary, shop, shrine, stage, stockade, store, tavern, tenement, theater/theatre, vestibule

449 workplace: bakery, base, bazaar, bistro, brothel, bureau, business, cabaret, café, cafeteria, canteen, capitol, church, clinic, conservatory, consulate, dairy, delicatessen, depot, diner, dive, dump, dungeon, embassy, emporium, establishment, exchange, factory, farm, field, flophouse, food court, gallery, garage, hangout, hospital, hotel, inn, jail, joint, landfill, lounge, madhouse, mall, market/mart,

mill, mine, motel, museum, nightclub, office, orchard, outlet, penitentiary, plant, plantation, port, prison, pub, ranch, reformatory, restaurant, saloon, shop, store, synagogue, tavern, treasury, warehouse, whorehouse

CLOTHING

450 accessory: bag, bandanna, belt, boot, buckle, cap, collar, mask, pocketbook, pouch, purse, satchel

451 clothing: apparel, armor, array, attire, bathing suit, blouse, cape, cloak, clothes/clothing, coat, costume, disguise, dress, duds, dungarees, ensemble, falsies, finery, frock, garb, garment, gear, girdle, glove, gown, habit, hat, helmet, jacket, masquerade, negligee, nightgown, nylons, outfit, pajamas, panties, pants, poncho, quilt, robe, scarf, shoe, skirt, sneaker, suit, supplies, swimsuit, thing/things, threads, trappings, trousers, underwear, uniform, veil, wardrobe, wash, wrap

452 part: collar, crease, crown, patch, pocket, seam, strand, tiara

453 state of dress: bareness, doff, nudity, try on/try out, undress, wear

FOOD AND DRINK

454 beverage: alcohol, ale, beverage, brew, coffee, draft, drink, moonshine, potable

455 beverage, alcoholic: beer, liquer, liquor

456 change in: curdle, spoil, turn

457 food: appetizer, batter, bite, bread, brew, broth, bun, candy, casserole, comfort food, condiment, confection, cracker, delicacy, diet, dish, doughnut, fare, feed, fodder, food, frankfurter, frosting, game, grub, hamburger, helping, hero, hors d'oeuvre, hot dog, leftover, loaf, macaroni, maintenance, meat, morsel, nosh, nourishment, nurture, nutrient, nutrition, pancake, pastry, preserves, produce, ration, refreshment, sandwich, seasoning, snack, smoke, submarine, subsistence, supplies, support, sustenance, sweet, tart, treat, victuals, vittles

458 food part: morsel, nibble, nip, pat, taste, tidbit

459 meal: banquet, barbecue, bite, board, buffet, cuisine, diet, dinner, fare, feast, meal, nosh, picnic, plate, repast, snack, spread, table

460 produced from animal: comfort food, dish, feed, fodder, food, frankfurter, frosting, game, grub, hamburger, hero, loaf, macaroni, meat, sandwich, stew, submarine, victuals, vittles

461 produced from plant: condiment, dish, doughnut, food, loaf, pancake, pastry, preserves, produce, seasoning, stew, sweet

462 quality of: acerbity, alcoholic, baked, crusty, done, eatable, edible, effervescent, mellow, natural, nourishing, nutritious, perishable, rancid, rare, raw, ripe, rotten, salty, salutary, short, sour, stale, straight, strong, succulent, sweet, tempting, unappetizing, unsavory, weak, wholesome

MACHINES

463 machine: accordion, alarm, apparatus, appliance, artificial intelligence, boom box, brake, calculator, camera, catapult, clock, computer, contraption, contrivance, dashboard, data processor, device, distress signal, doodad, doohickey, droid, electronics, engine, fan, fire alarm, fixture, foghorn, furnace, gadget, gadgetry, gizmo, incinerator, installation, instrument, jet, machine, machinery, mechanism, model, motor, personal computer, plant, printer, robot, smoke detector, software, stove, technology, television, terminal, watch, widget

464 machine part: anchor, antenna, axle, bank, cog, cushion, engine, faucet, gear, helm, motor, nozzle, pivot, pointer, tap, valve, vent, videocassette, wheel

MATTER, CONDITIONS OF

465 gas: fart, gas, jet, miasma

466 gel: balm, batter, clot, cream, dip, gum, liniment, lotion, ointment, ooze, paste, plaster, salve, sunscreen

467 liquid: alcohol, broth, cream, dew, drool, drop, enamel, eruption, essence, flow, fluid, froth, fuel, gasoline, gush, jet, juice, liquid, matter, milk, moisture, moonshine, ooze, paint, petroleum, potion, precipitation, saliva, shower, solution, spit, sunscreen, surge, sweat, tear/tears, water

468 liquid part: cream, drop, froth

469 physical change: ablate, attrition, bubble, clot, cloud, coagulate, coagulation, collapse, color, come unglued, congeal, consolidation, contraction, crack, crumble, cry, darken, decay, decompose, degeneracy, degenerate, dehydrate, die, discolor, disintegrate, dissipate, dissolution, dissolve, distend, dry, eat, erode, evaporate, evaporation, exhaust, fade, fester, fizz, flake, flare, flatten, fluctuate, flush, foam, foul, fragment, give, glow, go out, grow, growth, harden, heat, jell, languish, metamorphose, metamorphosis, open, ossify, perspire, putrefy, ravel, redden, revive, rot, rust, settle, sink, solidify, spoil, stiffen, tarnish, thaw, thicken, tighten, tire, turn, wilt

470 solid: band, bar, barricade, barrier, baton, block, blockade, bolt, brace, bulge, cake, cast, clot, club, clump, cord, dam, deposit, fossil, glass, glob, hedge, hunk, hurdle, ice, jump, lump, matter, mirror, monument, night stick, obstacle, obstruction, occlusion, partition, pill, pole, post, prop, rock, rod, stick, wand, weight

471 solid part: arm, attachment, back, bar, beam, block, bolt, branch, button, chunk, chute, closure, corner, deposit, flap, girder, hinge, hump, hunk, knob, knot, leg, ligature, link, lump, node/nodule, nub, nugget, outgrowth, patch, plug, powder, projection, protuberance, ridge, rung, seam, slab, sliver, splinter, stake, strap, strip, support, tuft, wedge

MATTER, DIVISIONS OF

472 chemical: alkali, alkaline, ammonia, antiseptic

473 fabric: apparel, awning, bedding, blanket, canvas, carpet, cloth, ensign, fabric, filigree, flag, lace, mesh, nap, napkin, net, pad/padding, pennant, quilt, rug, screen, web, yarn

474 gem: gem, jewel, rock, stone

475 material: appointment, binding, blanket, brace, cast, cement, cloak, coat, coating, glaze, glue, herbicide, lace, lacquer, lasso, leash, line, material, pad/padding, pad, page, paint, paper, patchwork, pipe, plaster, plate, poison, pole, poncho, rope, sheet, slip, standard, strand, stationery, strap, string, tab, tablet, tack, tag, tape, tether, toxin, trim, twine, wash

476 metallic: alloy, armor, badge, can, chain, fence, iron, medal, metal, ornament

477 mineral: rock, stone

478 natural element: allergen, blaze, bonfire, carbohydrate, cell, conflagration, embers, ferment, film, fire, flame, jewel, rock, substance

479 wood: beam, board, cane, coffin, fence, framework, girder, log, paddle, perch, picket, pier, pole, post, rack, rail/railing, rod, splinter, staff, stake, stick, timber

MATTER, QUALITIES OF

480 balance: asymmetrical, awkward, dizzy, even, inequitable, lopsided, odd, proportionate/proportional, pro rata, slaphappy, smooth, symmetrical, unbalanced, unequal, uneven, vertigo, woozy

481 capacity: brimming/brimful, capacious, capacity, close, compact, congested, crowded, empty, full, packed, spacious, stuffed, teeming, vacant, void

482 continuity: broken, connected, continuous, direct, disconnected, discontinuous, disjointed, dragging, durable, elongated, endless, entire, episodic, eternal, fitful, flowing, indelible, intermittent, lengthy, long, never-ending, nonstop, numberless, old, ongoing, patchy, perfect, running, sequential, serial, solid, spacious, spasmodic, straight, through, throughout, timeless, together, unbroken, undivided, unending, unfathomable, uninterrupted

483 density: airtight, anemic, close, compact, concentrated, congested, cramped, crowded, dense, devoid, fraught, full, hollow, impenetrable, impermeable, packed, petrified, replete, solid, stuffed, teeming, thick, tight

484 exteriority: adjunct, adornment, annex, border, bound/bounds, boundary, brink, buffer, casing, circuit, circumference, compass, confines, corner, cover, crust, cushion, edge, exterior, extreme, extremity, face, fringe, hem, horizon, hull, husk, jacket, lip, margin, membrane, mug, outer, outermost, outside, peel, perimeter, periphery, pod, revolution, rim, scale, sheet, shell, skin, skirt, surface, verge

485 physical: abhorrent, ablaze, acid, acute,

adulterated, aesthetic/esthetic, agile, alimentary, antiseptic, atomic, austere, bad, bald, bare, barren, bearded, beautiful, bedridden, bland, blank, bloody, blunt, brawny, broken, bumpy, burning, caustic, chintzy, clean, combustible, comfortable, corrugated, corrupt, cozy, crippled, crumbly, cuddly, curable, damaged, decayed, decrepit, deformed, deserted, desolate, devoid, dilapidated, diluted/dilute, dingy, dirty, disgusting, disheveled, disordered, disorderly, disorganized, disrepair, distended, done in, drained, drawn, droopy, ducky, dusty, effervescent, enervated, erect, exhausted, expectant, expecting, exposed, failing, faint, fallow, fat, fatigued, fatty, featureless, fertile, filthy, fireproof, fit, flaccid, flaming, flammable, flexible, foamy, forked, formless, foul, fragile, frail, free, fresh, frothy, game, gaping, ghastly, ghetto, ghostly, gnarled, godforsaken, good, green, grimy, grubby, gruesome, grungy, hardy, haywire, immature, impaired, impalpable, impervious, impotent, inchoate, inconspicuous, incorruptible, incurable, indistinct, infirm, inflammable, insubstantial, intact, invisible, irreparable, knurled, laden, leafy, lean, lifeless, liquid, livable, loathsome, loose, lusty, magnificent, malleable, mangy, marked, material, mature, mean, messy, mild, miserable, misshapen, mixed, moth-eaten, muddy, muscular, naked, nasty, natural, neat, neutral, noxious, nude, oblique, obtuse, obvious, on-the-blink, open, open-and-shut, ordered, orderly, outstanding, pacific, palatial, palpable, palsied, paltry, paralytic, pathetic, peaceful, pendulous/pendent, perfect, perishable, perverted, physical, piteous, pitiful, placid, plain, pregnant, premature, prepared, prickly, primitive, prolific, prominent, prostrate, puffy, pure, putrid, quizzical, ragged, rambling, ramshackle, rank, raw, rocky, rotten, rough, run-down, rusty, savage, scenic, scraggly, scruffy, seedy, serene, shabby, shady, shaggy, shipshape, shoddy, sinewy, slack, sleazy, slimy, slipshod, slovenly, smoky, snug, soft, somber, sorry, speckled, spectral, splendid, spotty, squalid, stale, stark, sterile, stony, sumptuous, surface, swollen, symmetrical, synthetic, tacky, tattered, tense, thin, thorny, threadbare, tidy, tight, topsy-turvy, torn, tousled, trim, tumescent, unadorned, unblemished, unbroken, uncomfortable, undeveloped, unfinished, unkempt, unorganized, unsuccessful, untouched, upset, vague, verdant, visual, voluptuous, watery, weak, weary, whole, wizened, wooden, worn/worn-out

486 shape: angular, baggy, beaten, billowy, blunt, checkered, circular, concave, conical/conic, convex, crescent, crooked, curly, curved, deformed, dull, elliptical, flabby, flat, flush, gnarled, grotesque, kinky, malformed, misshapen, oblong, obtuse, oval, round, serrated, shapeless, sharp, spiral, square, straight

487 similarity: akin, alike, analogous, approximate, closely, cognate, comparable, comparative, conformable, different, equal, equivalent, faithful, homogenous, identical, interchangeable, like, like-minded, parallel, related, representative, same, seeming, similar, synonymous, tantamount, twin, uniform, virtual, virtually

488 stability: adhesive, adrift, brittle, carved in stone, choppy, doddering, ductile, durable, fast, firm, firmly, fixed, flexible, hard, immobile, immovable, insecure, limber, lissom, lithe, motionless, movable, moving, pliable, ramshackle, resilient, rickety, rocky, secure, set, shaky, situated, soft, solid, solvent, sound, stable, stationary, steady, sturdy, supple, sure, taut, tenacious, tractable, unbreakable, unstable/unsteady, unwavering, weak, wobbly, wooden, yielding

489 strength: able-bodied, adaptive, athletic, brawny, breakable, brute, durable, failing, feeble, firmly, flimsy, fragile, frail, full-blooded, full-bodied, hale, hardy, Herculean, impregnable, indestructible, indomitable, infirm, invincible, lame, leathery, lusty, mighty, muscular, potent, powerful, powerless, puny, resilient, robust, rocky, rugged, stalwart, stout, strapping, strong, sturdy, tenacious, tenuous, tight, tough, unbreakable, unsuccessful, vigorous, weak

490 structure: airtight, airy, amorphous, anorexic, baggy, bare, beaten, bleak, blind, budding, cavernous, clean-cut, clear, cleft, composite, conglomerate, craggy, crooked, curvaceous, curved, dainty, delicate, depressed, detached, diaphanous, ductile, elastic, emaciated, even, flabby, flat, flush, gangling, gaping, gaunt, hollow, incarnate, irregular, jagged, level, limp, oblique, plane, pointed, precipitous, rude, rugged, scrawny, shapely, sheer, skinny, slender/slim, slight, spare, springy, stout, stringy, sunken, svelte, trim, wasted, wiry

491 weight: anorexic, bantam, beaten, buoyant, cadaverous, chubby, chunky, corpulent, dainty, dumpy, emaciated, ethereal, fat, fine, fleshy, gangling, gargantuan, gaunt, giant, gigantic, haggard, heavy, hefty, lanky, lean, light, lightweight, lithe, meager, obese, overweight, plump, ponderous, portable, portly, pudgy, rangy, roly-poly, rotund, round, scrawny, skinny, slender/slim, slight, spare, squat, stocky, stout, stubby, svelte, tenuous, thick, thin, titanic, trim, tubby, underweight, wasted, weighty, wiry

TOOLS

492 cleaner: antiseptic, cleanser, deodorant, detergent, polish

493 cooking: barbecue, bowl, china, frying pan, pan, plate, scoop, utensil

494 container: bag, baggage, barrel, basin, basket, bottle, bowl, box, briefcase, bucket, cabinet, cage, can, canteen, carton, case, cask, casket, cell, chamber, chest, coffer, coffin, container, crate, cup, decanter, dish, envelope, flask, frying pan, glass, hamper, jar, jug, keg, kettle, kit, luggage, main, mug, ossuary, package, packet, pan, parcel, pitcher, portfolio, pot, pottery, pouch, purse, receptacle, store, trunk, vault, vessel

495 cutting: blade, chisel, dagger, knife
496 equipment: equipment, gear, harness, installation, kit, outfit, pack, paraphernalia, plant, rig, tackle, trappings
497 grasping: bond, bridle, catch, clasp, curb, manacle
498 part: ammunition, hinge, hook, munitions, pivot, pointer, round, shot
499 tool: accordion, apparatus, ax/axe, blade, brace, broom, brush, cart, chain, chisel, clamp, club, conduit, connection, contraption, contrivance, dagger, dashboard, device, dolly, doodad, doohickey, drill, electronics, fastener, gadget, gadgetry, gizmo, hardware, implement, instrument, key, knife, latch, lock, mop, night stick, organ, paddle, pen, pipe, rein, ruler, scoop, tableware, technology, tool, utensil, valve, wand, wedge, whip, widget
500 weapon: A-bomb, ammunition, armament(s), arms, arrow, artillery, atom bomb, baton, battery, bomb, bullet, cannon, catapult, cudgel, defense, dynamite, explosive, fetters, firearm, fission, gun, magazine, missile, munitions, nuclear weapon, nuke, ordnance, pistol, rocket, round, weapon

TRANSPORTATION

501 object used for: access, alley, approach, arcade, artery, avenue, boulevard, bridge, career, channel, circuit, concourse, conduit, conveyance, course, crossing, detour, diversion, drain, duct, esplanade, expressway, flume, freeway, heading, highway, intersection, lane, line, mall, passage/passageway, path, road, route, street, track, trail, trajectory, turnpike, walk, way
502 part, vehicle: anchor, bow, fender, handle, portal, trunk, wheel, wing
503 vehicle: camper, caravan, conveyance, jet, motorcade, railroad, transport, vehicle
504 vehicle, air: aircraft, airplane, armada, balloon, blimp, craft, dirigible, flying saucer, helicopter, plane, shuttle, spacecraft, UFO
505 vehicle, land: ambulance, automobile, bicycle, cab, car, cart, cherry-picker, coach, dolly, earthmover, excavator, hack, model, motorcycle, traffic, truck
506 vehicle, water: armada, barge, boat, canoe, craft, ferry, fleet, flying saucer, sailboat, vessel, yacht

The Planet

GEOGRAPHY

507 city: capital, center, city, hamlet, metropolis, municipality, town, village
508 geographic division: area, country, county, department, desert, district, dynasty, grounds, kingdom, land, outskirts, province, quarter, region, sector, state, suburb, terrain, territory, town, tract, ward, zone
509 land: abyss, acreage, avalanche, backwoods, bank, basin, bay, beach, bed, black hole, bluff, bog, campus, canyon, cape, cave, cavern, clay, cliff, coast, compost, court, cove, crevice/crevasse, culvert, dirt, ditch, downgrade, drop, dune, earth, elevation, eminence, estuary, excavation, expanse, farm, field, forest, fossil, frontier, garden, geography, glacier, glen, gorge, grassland, green, grotto, ground, gulch, gulf, gully, harbor, hill, hillock, horizon, inlet, island, knoll, land, landscape, landslide, lawn, levee, lot, marsh, marshy, meadow, menagerie, mesa, mine, mire, moat, morass, mound, mountain, mountainous, mud, nature, orchard, outlook, parcel, park, pass, patio, peak, pit, plain, plateau, playground, plaza, plot, porch, port, prairie, precipice, projection, promontory, property, prospect, quagmire, rampart, ravine, reef, ridge, rock, savanna, seashore, shelf, shore, soil, square, stack, swamp, table, terrain, trench, trough, tundra, tunnel, valley, waste, well, wood/woods, yard
510 nation: country, fatherland, home, kingdom, land, nation, nationality, native land, soil, state
511 planet: cosmos, deep space, Earth, environment, galaxy, globe, moon, nature, planet, soil, sphere, universe, world
512 region: capital, colony, commonwealth, community, quarter, realm, region, reservation, settlement, suburb
513 section: acreage, across-the-board, aisle, alcove, backyard, barrier, beat, bed, belt, berth, blank, border, breach, brink, canyon, cavity, cell, chasm, chink, clearance, clearing, cleavage, cleft, corner, country, county, court, crack, cranny, crevice/crevasse, crossing, deadline, den, depression, dip, ditch, edge, enclosure, excavation, expanse, footprint, fracture, frontier, furrow, gap, green, groove, gulch, gulf, gully, gutter, hem, hinterland, hole, hump, interstice, lawn, leak, ledge, limit, lip, margin, marginal, menagerie, moat, mouth, niche, nook, notch, opening, orifice, outlet, outskirts, parcel, park, pass, patch, patio, pit, playground, plaza, plot, pocket, porch, pothole, precinct, precipice, projection, prominence, puncture, ravine, recess, rent, repair, ridge, rift, rip, rupture, rut, scratch, shelf, side, sight, slack, slit, slot, split, subdivision, tear, threshold, track, tract, trench, trough, tunnel, vacancy, vacuum, valley, void, ward, well, wrinkle, yoke, zone
514 water: abyss, aquarium, aqueduct, arm, basin, bay, beach, billow, blackball, brine, brook, canal, cape, cascade, channel, coast, condensation, course, creek, current, deep, eddy, estuary, flume, fountain, geyser, gulf, harbor, heading, ice, inlet, lagoon, lake, maelstrom, oasis, ocean, pond, pool, promontory, race, reservoir, rise, sea, seashore, spray, spring, strait, stream, tide, trajectory, wash, waterfall, wave, well, whirlpool

HABITATS

515 habitat: abode, asylum, ecosystem, environment, environmentalist, fatherland, habitat/habitation, hideout, harbor, haven, home, lair, land, native land, nest, oasis, paradise, place, premises, property, refuge, sanctuary, settlement, shelter, tent

516 habitat, human: accommodations, address, apartment, asylum, barracks, berth, cabin, camp, castle, cloister, condominium, convent, cottage, domesticity, domicile, dungeon, dwelling, element, embassy, encampment, environs, estate, flat, grange, grounds, hacienda, haunt, home, hotel, house, household, housing, hovel, hut, inn, jail, lodge, lodging, loony bin, madhouse, mansion, monastery, motel, neighborhood, nunnery, old country, pad, palace, penitentiary, prison, quarters, reservation, residence, resort, retreat, sanctuary, shack, shanty, spa, suite, tenement, vacancy, villa

517 habitat, rural: barn, belt, burrow, cobweb, conservatory, dairy, desert, desolation, farm, field, forest, garden, grange, grove, jungle, lawn, sanctuary, wilderness/wilds, wood/woods

518 state of: domain, eco-rich, entrench, occupancy, occupation, presence

NATURAL RESOURCES

519 electricity: beam, current, spark
520 energy: electricity, energy, fuel, gasoline, nuclear energy, nuclear reactor, petroleum, power

521 expression of energy: blast, blaze, bonfire, boom, chill, combustion, concussion, crash, discharge, explosion, fire, flame, flash, freeze, noise, thunder

522 natural event: eclipse, effervescence, meteorology, weather

523 resources: fuel, material, resource, resources, rock, substance

WEATHER

524 object connected with: avalanche, blast, breeze, chill, climate, cloud, cold, deluge, dew, drift, film, flood, flurry, fog, frost, gale, gust, hail, haze, humidity, hurricane, landslide, meteorology, mist, moisture, precipitation, puff, shower, thunder, vapor, weather, wind

525 quality of: breezy, bright, clear, clement, close, cloudy, crisp, dirty, dismal, dreary, fair, fierce, fiercely, filmy, fine, foggy, furious, gentle, gloomy, gusty, hazy, heavy, humid, inclement, intimidating, mild, misty, muggy, oppressive, overcast, raw, rough, rugged, sepulchral, soft, sticky, stormy, stuffy, sultry, sunny, temperate, tempestuous, thick, threatening, tranquil, tropical, turbulent, violent, wild, windy, wintry

526 type of: blizzard, blow, cloud, downpour, drizzle, earthquake, fog, gale, hail, hurricane, mist, precipitation, puff, quake, rain, shade, shower, storm, tempest, thunder, torrent, tremor

Qualities

ABSTRACT

527 ability: able, ably, accountable, adept, adroit, agile, all-around, amateurish, artistic, awkward, barren, capable, commendable, competent, deft, dexterous, dilettante, disabled, easy as pie, effete, efficient, eligible, executive, experienced, expert, facile, feeble, gifted, good, great, handy, Herculean, inapt, incapable, incapacitated, incompetent, inefficient, inept, inexperienced, master, masterful, neat, nimble, not born yesterday, powerful, powerless, practical, professional, proficient, qualified, raw, ready, rusty, seasoned, short, skillful, talented, unable, unaccustomed, unfit, unprofessional, unqualified, unskilled, versatile, versed, veteran, well, wicked

528 achievement: able, abortive, achievable, accomplished, ace, artful, attainable, banner, complete, consummate, crack, defensible, done, effectual, efficacious, feasible, fine, finished, flourishing, forward, fruitful, fruitless, futile, gifted, great, obtainable, operable, possible, potential, practical, professional, proficient, prosperous, successful, swimmingly, thriving, triumphant, unavailing, victorious, washed-up, well, winning

529 cognitive: academic, ad nauseum, affective, afraid, afterthought, alluring, alternative, amicable, anathema, appalling, attractive, axiomatic, bad, bag, balm, bane, bearable, belief, beta, black, boring, bothersome, breast, breathtaking, burdensome, charismatic, cheering, chimera, comforting, comic/comical, comparison, complex, comprehensible, conceivable, considered, considering, corollary, crazy, daydream, deducible, deep, déjà vu, demonstrable, deplorable, depressing, derivable, desirous, detestable, dialectic, difficult, discouraging, disputable, disquieting, dissatisfactory, distasteful, doleful, doubtful, dream, dry, dull, dullsville, elusive, enchanting, engrossing, enigmatic/enigmatical, enjoyable, entertaining, equivocal, esoteric, evident, exalted, exciting, exhilarating, explicit, eye-catching, fabulous, fanciful, fantasy, far-fetched, fascinating, favored, favorite, fearful, fetish, figment, flashback, flat, fleshly, forerunner, forgotten, foul, frightful/frightening, frightful, funny, ghastly, ghoulish, glad, golden, good, grating, groundbreaking, hair-raising, half-baked, hallucination, harbinger, hard, harebrained, harrowing, haunting, hazy, heady, heartbreaking, heartrending, heinous, hellish, heretical, hilarious, homesick, hopeless, horizon, horrible/horrendous/horrid, humorous, hypnotic, hypothetical, idea, ideal, idealistic, idyllic, illogical, illusory/illusive, image, imaginable, imaginary, imaginative, impalpable, impenetrable, impression, inadvisable, incomprehensible, inconceivable, incredible, incredulous, indelible, indicator, inexplicable, inner, innovation, innovative, inscrutable, inside, insoluble, inspiration, instinct, insufferable, intelligible, interesting, intimate, intolerable, intriguing, inviting, inward, irksome, irrational, irrefutable, irresistible, itch, jocular/jocose/jocund, joy, knotty, knowledge, known, lamentable, leery, left, left-wing, liberal, liking, limit, loathsome, logical, loose, lucid, luminous, lure, mad, maddening, make-believe, mania, manifest, marvel, marvelous, matter, maudlin, maze, measurable, memorable, memory, metaphysical, miraculous, mirage, mistaken, mode, monotonous, moving, mutinous, mysterious, mystic/mystical, naked, nauseating, nauseous, nemesis, nettlesome, new age, nightmarish, nondescript, nostalgic, note, noticeable, notion, obscure, observable, obsession, obvious, offensive, on paper, on the fence, opaque, open, open-and-shut, optimist, otherworldly, painful, palatable, palpable, panorama, pathetic, pedagogic, pedantic, perceptible, perspicuous, pesky, phantom, phenomenon, phobia, pick, pipe dream, piquant, piteous, pitiful, plain, plaintive, poignant, pointless, politically correct, ponderous, portent, portentous, precious, preference, premise, premonition, preposterous, presage, problem, problematic, profound, provocative, psychedelic, pure, purposely, putative, puzzling, questionable, quixotic, radical, rather, ravishing, reactionary, readable, reasoning, rebellious, recall, recondite, redolent, remembrance, reminder, reminiscent, repulsive, reputed, reverie, revolting, revolutionary, rich, ridiculous, right, riveting, rosy, rot, sad, satisfactory, scary, scintilla, scintillating, scream, scrumptious, secret, secular, seditious, selection, self-evident/self-explanatory, sensation, shock, sickening, sidesplitting, sign, signal, simple, slight, slow, smidgen, snare, somber, soothing, sorry, sound, soupçon, spectacle, spectacular, speculation, speculative, spooky, stimulating, stirring, strain, subconscious, subject, subjective, suggestion, suggestive, surmise, surprise, suspect, suspicion, suspicious, tacit, tactile, tall, tame, tangible, taste, tasteful, tedious, temptation, tempting, tenor, theorem, theoretical, theory, thesis, thick, thing, thinkable, thought, thought-provoking, thrill, tinge, tiresome, token, tolerable, touch, touching, trace, treat, troublesome, unacceptable, unaccountable, unappetizing, unbelievable, uncertain, uncomfortable, undecided, understood, undesirable, unexciting, unfathomable, unfavorable, unforgettable, ungodly, unimaginable, uninteresting, uninvited, unlucky, unnoticed, unpleasant, unpopular, unquestionable, unresolved, unsatisfactory, untold, unwelcome, vague, vapid, vexatious, vile, visible, vision, visionary, whim, whisper, wishful, wonder, wonderful, worrisome

530 **commonality:** accidental, addictive, antiquated, antique, au courant, automatic, banal, bourgeois, common, commonly, commonplace, conventional, current, customarily, customary, diffuse, dogmatic, dull, everyday, fair, familiar, frequent, frequently, general, generally, generic, habitual, hackneyed, infrequent, lay, less, little, mainly, mainstream, much, musty, natural, now and then, occasional, occasionally, off and on, old, old school, on and off, once in a while, ordinarily, ordinary, pedestrian, popular, prevailing, prevalent, proverbial, public, rare, rarely, regular, routine, spasmodic, stereotyped, stock, time-honored, traditional, trite, typical, ubiquitous, undistinguished, unexceptional, unexciting, used to, usual, usually, vulgar, widespread

531 **completeness:** absolutely, all-out, almost, altogether, blank, bodily, capsule, clean, complete, completely, comprehensive, conscientious, crowning, dead, deeply, deficient, definitive, demonstrative, done, downright, entire, entirely, every, exhaustive, fatal, final, finished, fulfilled, full, full-scale, fully, halfway, holistic, incomplete, inseparable, intact, integral, intensive, out-and-out, outright, over, panoramic, partial, partially, partly, past, perfectly, piecemeal, plenary, practically, pretty, primarily, principally, profound, pure, purely, quite, rank, right, rough, round, rude, sheer, simply, sketchy, sloppy, solid, stark, superficially, sweeping, thorough/thoroughgoing, thoroughly, through, throughout, total, totally, unabridged, unconditional, undivided, unfinished, unmitigated, unqualified, utmost, utter, utterly, wanting, washed-up, whole, wholly

532 **concerned with:** about, albatross, angst, anxiety, appertain, apply, apropos, bad news, barrier, bear on/bear upon, beat, behalf, behind, belong, bother, bug, burden, business, can of worms, care, catch-22, challenge, charge, compulsion, concept, concern, consideration, conundrum, craze, debate, difficulty, discovery, disputation, disquiet, distraction, distress, duel, ear, encumbrance, enigma, fancy, fascination, feeling, fixation, focus, forbidden fruit, guilt, hallucination, hang-up, heed, horror, include, interest, issue, keynote/keystone, matter, millstone, mystery, notice, notion, object, obstacle, obstruction, occlusion, pain, paradox, part, particular, passion, peeve, pertain, pivot, place, presentiment, priority, problem, province, provocation, qualm, quandary, question, refer, regard, relate, reverie, riddle, scruple, subject, suspicion, taboo, temptation, topic, touch, toward/towards, trouble, urge, vision, weight, woe, wonder, worry

533 **conformity:** acceptable, adequate, admissible, befitting, classic, decent, formal, ideal, mediocre, medium, middle-of-the-road, moderate, old school, ordinary, orthodox, practical, proper, regular, so-so, standard, time-honored, traditional, typical, unwritten

534 **constancy:** adjustable, ambivalent, arbitrary, borderline, changeable, chronic, consistent, constant, continual, fickle, firmly, fitful, fluid, forever, formative, frozen, grim, halt-

ing, hesitant, immovable, immutable, impervious, incessant, inconsistent, inconstant, indecisive, indestructible, indomitable, inexorable, insistent, intermittent, intractable/intransigent, invariable, inveterate, iron, irregular, irrevocable, monotonous, on and on, relentless, rigid, same, severe, slippery, solid, spotty, static, staunch, steadfast, steady, tentative, unbending, unceasing, uncertain, unchangeable, unchanging, unfailing, unforeseeable, uniform, unpredictable, unresolved, unstable/unsteady, variable, varying, volatile, wanton, weak-minded

535 definiteness: absolute, absolutely, accurate, accurately, ad hoc, aimless, airtight, ambiguous, apparent, apparently, assured, automatic, canonical, categorical, certain, certainly, clean, clean-cut, clear-cut, clearly, close, complete, conclusive, concrete, conscious, controversial, dead-on, debatable, decided, decidedly, decisive, deep-seated, definite, definitely, definitive, demonstrable, designedly, desultory, dicey, discernible, disordered, disorderly, disputable, distinct, doubtful, doubtless, dubious, easily, elective, emphatic, entirely, equivocal, erratic, especial, especially, evident, evidently, exact, exactly, experimental, explicit, express, expressly, factual, fail-safe, final, finally, finite, fixed, flat, foolproof, formless, for sure, graphic, gross, guaranteed, haphazard, hard, hard-core, hesitant, hit-or-miss, illegible, impeccable, implicit, implied, inalienable, incalculable, incontrovertible, indecisive, indeed, indefinite, indeterminate, indisputable, indistinct, indubitably, inevitable, infallible, ingrained, intangible, in the bag, ironclad, irrefutable, irresolute, just, legible, limpid, main, marked, markedly, mere, moot, nebulous, necessarily, necessary, obviously, official, only, open, outright, overt, palpable, pat, peremptory, perfect, plain, political, positive, positively, precarious, precise, precisely, pronounced, pure, questionable, random, rank, really, reliable, right, rigid, rigorous, scientific, secure, seriously, set, shaky, sharp, sheer, simply, slippery, sound, specific, straight, straightforward, strict, stringent, strong, sure, surely, tenebrous, tentative, tested, thorough/thoroughgoing, thoroughly, tried, tried-and-true, true, truly, trustworthy/trusty, ultimate, unavoidable, uncertain, unconditional, undeniable, undependable, unequivocal/undisputable, undoubtedly, unequivocal, unerring, unfailing, unfaltering, unmistakable, unmitigated, unorganized, unqualified, unquestionable, unreadable, unsettled, unsubstantiated, unsure, unwavering, utter, verbatim, very, weak-minded, willful, yes

536 domain: absolute, academic, administrative, agrarian, agricultural, aquatic, athletic, authoritative, autocratic, blessed, bridal, bucolic, captive, celestial, chemical, city, civic, civil, classical, clerical, commanding, commercial, communal, confederate, constituent, country, democratic, dismal, domestic, drab, earthly, ecclesiastical, economic, educational, egalitarian, endemic, fleshly, foreign, free, global, God-fearing, home, homegrown,

homemade, homespun, household, industrial, infernal, internal, international, itinerant, literary, local, marine/maritime, metropolitan, military, multinational, municipal, national, native, nautical/naval, nomadic, oceanic, pedagogic, personal, prevalent, psychological, public, religious, social, sovereign, spiritual, supernal, technical, terrestrial, theatrical, theological, totalitarian, unearthly, universal, unworldly, urban, widespread, worldly, worldwide

537 effects: advantageous, advisory, aphrodisiac, awesome, awry, bad, baleful, baneful, beastly, benign, bitter, bleak, bracing, bright, burning, calamitous, charismatic, cogent, combustible, coming, consequent, convincing, corrective, corrosive, costly, cultural, curative, damaging, deadly, deathly, deep, defamatory, deleterious, demonstrative, desperate, destined, destructive, detrimental, dire, direful, disadvantageous, disagreeable, disastrous, disruptive, divisive, done for, doomed, dramatic, drastic, dread, dreadful, eclectic, ecumenical, eerie, effective, effectual, efficacious, embarrassing, emergent, entertaining, epidemic, exigent, expressive, extenuating, faint, fatal, fateful, favorable, favorably, fearful, fecund, fetching, fierce, fiercely, flat, food poisoning, fooled, forbidding, forcible, foreign, for kicks, formidable, fortunately, foul, fresh, frightful/frightening, fruitful, fruitless, fun, funereal, funny, furious, general, gentle, ghastly, ghostly, gloomy, gold mine, good, gory, grateful, grave, greatly, grievous, grisly, gross, grotesque, harmful, harmless, harsh, haunting, healthful/healthy, heartbreaking, heartrending, heavenly, helpful, hideous, highly, histrionic, horrible/horrendous/horrid, hurtful, hypnotic, ill, ill-fated/ill-starred, imperceptible, imposing, incendiary, inconclusive, inconvenient, ineffective/ineffectual, inflammatory, influential, inimical, injurious, insipid, insufferable, insulting, intoxicating, invigorating, inviting, jazzy, juicy, lamentable, lethal, lovely, lucky, lurid, macabre, madly, magic/magical, magnetic, malign, memorial, menacing, mighty, mild, monstrous, morbid, mortal, moving, narcotic, nasty, nettlesome, neutral, nightmarish, noisome, nondescript, noticeable, nourishing, noxious, offensive, oppressive, outstanding, painful, pale, pallid, pallor, penetrating, peremptory, pernicious, persuasive, pesky, pestilent/pestilential, piercing, pleasing/pleasurable, poison/poisonous, prejudicial, prepossessing, productive, profitable, prosaic, provocative, psychedelic, remedial, right, rugged, ruinous, safe, satisfying, sedative, sensational, sensuous, sharp, sick, sickly, slow, soft, soporific, spectacular, spooky, star-crossed, stirring, strong, subtle, tangy, telling, therapeutic, tiresome, touching, toxic, trenchant, tyrannical, unbearable, uncanny, uncomfortable, unhealthy, unholy, uninviting, unspoiled, vapid, venomous, vexatious, virtual, virulent, vivid, weak, wholesome, wicked

538 efforts: amateurish, ambitious, applied, assiduous, automated, automatic, backbreaking, concerted, conscientious, cooperative, difficult, diligent, employed, gladly, go-ahead, hard, heavy, homicidal, idle, indolent, industrious, inexhaustible, jobless, labored, laborious, laden, light, lightly, mechanize, mindless, murderous, on duty, onerous, painstaking, persistent, religious, rugged, running, scrupulous, sedulous, serious, simple, slack, slow, softly, straightforward, strenuous, studied, studious, thankless, thorough/thoroughgoing, thoroughly, tireless, tiresome, together, toilsome, torpid, tough, unemployed, unfailing, unfaltering, unflagging, unpaid, unprofessional, unsolicited, untiring, uphill, valiant, vicarious, voluntarily, voluntary, weighty, workable, working

539 existential: alive, almighty, animate, comatose, conscious, consist, dead, deadly, deceased, defunct, departed, dormant, drowsy, dying, extant, extinct, fallen, fatal, immaterial, immortal, inanimate, incarnate, late, lifeless, live, living, lost, luxuriate, missing, moribund, nil, nonexistent, obsolete, out, out cold, perennial, present, sentient, sleepy, somnolent, soporific, street person, unconscious, vagabond, vital, wakeful

540 forcefulness: almighty, bang, blatant, bloody, brute, cumulative, desperate, driving, dynamic, effective, electric/electrical, fierce, fiercely, hard, high-powered, impregnable, insistent, invincible, invulnerable, madly, mightily, mighty, potent, powerful, powerfully, savage, stiff, strong, violent

541 frequency: annual, annually, casual, commonly, daily, hardly, nightly, now and then, occasional, occasionally, off and on, often, on and off, once in a while, periodic, rapid, rarely, recurrent, scarce, scarcely, seldom, spasmodic, sporadic, uncommonly, usually, yearly

542 inclination: abrupt, accommodating, acquisitive, active, addicted, adrift, adventurous, affirmative, aggressive, agog, agreeable, alive, all-around, allergic, aloof, ambitious, amicable, antithetical, anxious, apt, arbitrary, arid, assiduous, attention deficit disorder, avaricious, base, beastly, benign, big-hearted, blindly, brisk, busy, careful, carefully, careless, casual, characteristic, charitable, cheap, co-dependent, cold-blooded, competitive, conducive, confirmed, conflicting, conservative, conspicuous, constant, contentious, contradictory, corporal, corporeal, correct, cost-effective, crack, creditable, curious, decent, dedicated, deep, deliberate, deliberately, delicate, delicately, demanding, dependable, derelict, designing, determined, detestable, devoted, devout, dewy-eyed, dictatorial, die-hard, difficult, dilatory, diligent, dim, diplomatic, dirty, discriminating, disinclined, disingenuous, disposed, disputatious, distrustful, dog-eat-dog, dogged, dogmatic, domestic, doubtful, dour, downtrodden, dull, dutiful, dynamic, eager, eagle-eyed, earnest, earthy, easy, economical, effervescent, effusive, elusive, emotional, emotionless, energetic, engaged, engrossed, enterprising, enthusiastic, equable, equal, equitable, errant, erratic, evasive, even, even-handed, exact, exaggerated, exciting, execrable, exi-

gent, exotic, expeditious, explosive, factious, fail-safe, fair, fairly, fallible, farcical, fast, fastidious, feckless, feisty, feral, ferocious, ferocity, fervent/fervid, fiery, firm, firmly, flexible, fluid, fly-by-night, fond, foolish, foolishly, footloose, forbearing, forced, fortunate, frantic, free, frenzied, fresh, frisky, frolicsome, funeral, gaily, gallant, gay, generous, gentle, genuine, gingerly, given to, gladly, go-ahead, godless, godly, good, gracious, grandiose, grasping, gratuitous, greedy, gross, guarded, guileless, gullible, gung ho, gutless, gutsy, hair-raising, half-hearted, happily, happy-go-lucky, hard, hard-boiled, hard-core, hardened, hard-nosed/hardheaded, harsh, harum-scarum, hasty, headlong, heartless, heartwarming, hearty, hell-bent, helpless, hesitant, highfalutin, hooked, hospitable, hostile, hotheaded, humane, humanitarian, hurtful, hypocritical, hysterical, idle, ignoble, ignorant, imaginative, immersed, impartial, impassive, impatient, impersonal, impetuous, implacable, improper, improvident, imprudent, impulsive, inadvertent, inane, inattentive, incautious, inclined, indefatigable, indifferent, indignant, indiscreet, indiscriminate, indisposed, indolent, indulgent, inelegant, inert, inexhaustible, infant/infantile, inflammatory, ingenuous, inhibited, innocent, inoffensive, inquiring, insecure, insidious, insightful, insincere, insouciant, intent, intolerant, intractable/intransigent, intrusive, inventive, involved, irate, jaundiced, jealous, jolly, joyful/joyous, joyless, judicious, kind, kindhearted, kindly, kinky, lackadaisical, lackluster, languid, largesse, lax, left-wing, lenient, levelheaded, lewd, liable, liberal, lifeless, light, lighthearted, lip service, litigious, live, lively, livid, loath, loud, loving, low, low-key, lukewarm, magnanimous, malevolent, malicious, malign, materialistic, maudlin, mawkish, mean, melodramatic, merciful, merciless, meretricious, methodical/methodic, meticulous, mindful, mushy, naive, narrow, narrow-minded, neat, neglectful, negligent, nerveless, nervous, neutral, nice, nonchalant, noncommittal, noncompliant, nonconformist, nonpartisan, obdurate, objective, objectively, objectivity, oblivious, obnoxious, obstinate, obtrusive, occupied, odd/oddball, off-guard, offhand, one-sided, on purpose, open, openhanded, openhearted, opposed/opposing, oppressed, opprobrious, optimistic, ossified, overconfident, overrated, overwrought, pacific, pagan, parental, parochial, partial, particular, partisan, passionate, passive, patient, peaceful, peevish, penitent, peppery, perceptive, peremptory, perfunctory, persuasive, perverse, petulant, philanthropic, pigheaded, plastic, playful, pleasant, politically correct, pompous, ponderous, poor, portentous, practical, pragmatic, precipitous/precipitate, precise, predictable, premature, premeditated, prepossessed, presumptuous, pretentious, productive, progressive, prolific, prone, prostrate, protective, proud, prudent, pugnacious, punctilious, purposeful, quarrelsome, querulous, radical, raging, rambunctious, raunchy, reactionary, ready, realistic, rebellious, reckless, reliable, renegade, resigned, resolute, responsive, restive, restless, restrained, revolutionary, rival, romantic, rousing, sadistic, safe, sanctioned, sanguine, sappy, savage, scheming, scrupulous, scurrilous, sedate, sedentary, sedulous, selective, selfish, self-righteous, self-satisfied, sensible, sentimental, serious, seriously, serpentine, set, severe, short-sighted, silly, simple, sincere, slapdash, sleepless, sly, small-minded, smart, smug, sneaky, sober, softhearted, solemn, soulful, sour, spineless, spirited, spiritless, spiteful, spontaneous, sporty, sprightly, spunky, square, staunch, steadfast, steady, stern, stimulating, stout, straight, strenuous, strict, strong, subjective, sunny, susceptible, suspicious, sweet, sympathetic, tame, tardy, temperate, tempestuous, tenacious, tender, tenderhearted, tentative, tepid, testy, thick-skinned, thoughtful, thoughtless, tireless, together, tolerant, torn, touched, touchy, tough, tractable, tranquil, true, trusting, truthful, unaffected, unbiased, uncaring, uncommitted, uncompromising, unconcerned, unconscious, uncritical, understanding, unfeeling, unflappable, ungodly, unholy, unimaginative, uninspired, unprejudiced, unrehearsed, unreliable, unrestricted, unstable/unsteady, unsympathetic, untoward, untrustworthy, unwavering, unwilling, unyielding, up-and-coming, vainglorious, vehement, vengeful, venomous, versatile, vicious, vigilant, vindictive, virulent, voucher, wakeful, wanton, warm, weak, well-balanced, well-preserved, wholehearted/whole-hearted, willful, witless, witty, wooden, youthful, zippy

543 is an attribute of: appear, appearance, belong, minutiae, quality, savor, seem, sound, trivia

544 manner: abominable, absurd, advisedly, aimless, although, anyhow, anyway, as, backhanded, beautifully, blah, blind, breezy, broken, brutal, brutally, busily, businesslike, busy, by, by hand, calm, camp, casual, catchy, circuitous, circumspect, counter, covert, covertly, cumbersome, delicately, deluxe, despite, dreary, easy, eat high on the hog, equable, ergo, even, foolish, foolishly, for, forcibly, forthwith, fortunately, freely, frenzied, frequently, gradual, gradually, grievous, grim, grisly, hastily, helter-skelter, how, however, ill-advised, immediately, immoderate, impersonal, impolitic, inadvertent, incautious, incidentally, indelicate, indirect, individually, inequitable, instant, instantly, instinctive, intentional, intently, involuntary, irregularly, irresponsible, just, justly, kindly, lackadaisical, largely, leisurely, less, lightly, little, long, low-key, luckily, luxuriate, luxurious, madly, mainly, manual, markedly, mechanical, methodical/methodic, meticulous, mightily, misguided, misspent, moderately, monotonous, more, moreover, mortally, most, mostly, motorized, much, mutually, narrowly, naturally, necessarily, nevertheless, notwithstanding, objectively, of course, one by one, openly, otherwise, outwardly, over, overly, parenthetical, partially, pell-

mell, perfectly, perfunctory, per se, personally, piecemeal, poorly, positively, possibly, posthaste, powerfully, presumably, primarily, principally, progressive, promptly, providing/provided, punctual, purely, purposeless, purposely, quick, rampant, rapidly, rather, readily, recurrent, regardless, regular, relatively, reliable, revolutionary, ritzy, separately, seriously, sheer, simply, slightly, softly, solely, somehow, still, straight, strategic, subtle, summarily, superficially, surprising, swimmingly, tactical, though, through, thus, together, too, true, ulterior, unawares, unconditional, unconscious, undercover, underhand, unduly, unexpected, unfair, unforeseen, unusually, unwitting, venomous, very, via, vice versa, violent, virtual, virtually, visceral, voluntarily, voluntary, well, while, wrong, yet

545 morality: abandoned, above suspicion, answerable, arrant, astray, atrocious, bad, badly, bawdy, black, blasphemous, blue, broad, cagey, coarse, common, conscientious, contraband, corrupt, criminal, crooked, culpable, cunning, damnable, damned, dark, dastardly, debauched, decadent, degenerate, demonic/demoniac/demoniacal, depraved, devilish, diabolic, dirty, disorderly, dissipated, dissolute, drunk, egregious, elevated, elfin, equitable, erotic, errant, ethical, evil, faithful, faithless, fast, faultless, felonious, fickle, fiendish, filthy, flagrant, fleshly, fraudulent, frightful, God-fearing, good, gross, guileless, guiltless, guilty, heathen, heretical, high-minded, holy, honest, honorable, hood, hoodlum, hooligan, ignoble, ill, illegal, illicit, immaculate, immodest, immoral, impious, improper, impure, incorruptible, indecent, indefensible, indelicate, inexcusable, infamous, infernal, inhuman/inhumane, innocent, irreligious, insidious, insincere, involved, irreproachable, just, justifiable, justly, lawful, lawless, lewd, liable, libidinous, licentious, loose, loyal, Machiavellian, mischievous, miscreant, moral, nasty, naughty, nefarious, obscene, off-color, perversion, perverted, plastered, pornographic, pornography, prejudicial, pretended, profane, profligate, promiscuous, racy, rakish, rank, raw, religious, reprobate, reputable, responsible, right, righteous, rightful, risqué, roguish, rotten, sadistic, satanic, scandalous, scurrilous, seamy, secret, sensational, shady, shameful, shameless, sharp, sinful, smutty, sordid, sorry, soused, spicy, suggestive, true-blue, unconscionable, unconstitutional, unearned, unethical, unfair, unfaithful, unforgivable, ungodly, unjust, unjustified, unprincipled, unscrupulous, untrue, untrustworthy, unwarranted, upright, upstanding, valid, venal, veracious, vicious, villainous, vile, virtuous, vulgar, wanton, wholesome, wicked, wily, worthy, wrong, wrongful, zonked

546 necessity: absent, applied, auxiliary, backup, bereft, binding, capital, chosen, collateral, component, compulsory, controversial, deciding, dependent, dire, discretionary, dispensable, elementary, enough, essential, expendable, extra, extraneous, famished, fresh, fundamental, gratuitous, imperative, inadequate, inapplicable, indebted, indispensable, insatiable, insufficient, integral, intrinsic, introductory, lacking, main, mandatory, marketable, meager, necessary, needless, nonessential, obligatory, piddle, preparatory, prerequisite, providing/provided, provisional, radical, r2quired/requisite, rudimentary, shy, staple, starving/ starved, strategic, superfluous, ultimate, uncalled for, underlying, undue, unduly, unessential, unnecessary, vital, wanting

547 normality: aberrant, abnormal, accepted, accustomed, addictive, all right, amazing, anomalous, astonishing, atypical, average, bizarre, characteristic, classic, common, conventional, curious, customarily, customary, disguised, eccentric, everyday, exorbitant, extreme, familiar, flaky, formal, general, generally, gonzo, habitual, incidental, incongruous, irregular, lowly, macabre, maladjusted, mean, mediocre, medium, middle, middling, mind-blowing, mind-boggling, moderate, modest, mundane, natural, nondescript, normal, normally, ordinary, pedestrian, plain, prevalent, prosaic, reasonable, regular, routine, run-of-the-mill, screwy, spacey/spacy, stock, temperate, typical, unaccustomed, unimaginative, uninspired, unmotivated, used to, usual, veiled

548 occurrence: abhorrent, accidentally, accursed, amusing, asinine, astounding, atrocious, behind one's back, ceremonial, ceremonious, chaotic, chronological, closed, coincident, coincidental, consequent, covert, covertly, crowning, cumulative, cursed, dangerous, dangerously, dark, desperate, desultory, didactic, dire, disagreeable, disastrous, disgusting, dismal, downbeat, dramatic, droll, ducky, dull, dullsville, egregious, embarrassing, empirical/empiric, endurable, enjoyable, ensuing, eventful, exciting, excruciating, exhilarating, exigent, exposed, express, fated, feebleminded, festive, forbidden, forced, forcibly, forthcoming, fortuitous, foul, furious, furtive, futile, gala, ghoulish, gloomy, grateful, grave, grievous, gruesome, hairy, half-baked, hapless, happily, harrowing, hazardous, heartwarming, heavy, hectic, heinous, historic, historical, histrionic, hit-or-miss, homicidal, hopeful, hopeless, humdrum, hurried, ill-advised, ill-fated/ill-starred, ill-timed, imminent, impending, inane, inauspicious, incidental, inconclusive, inconvenient, incurable, indefensible, informal, insane, ironic/ironical, irregularly, intimidating, jolly, joyful/joyous, joyless, juicy, lackluster, lass, late, limit, lively, low-key, ludicrous, madcap, magic/magical, maiden, memorable, menacing, meritorious, merry, meteoric, miraculous, mirthful, misguided, misleading, moronic, mostly, much, murderous, nasty, nearing, necessary, nefarious, nerve-racking, nice, oafish, objectionable, offensive, ominous, oncoming, opportune, oppressive, outlandish, over, overall, overblown, overdue, partisan, peaceable, penal, pending, perilous, permissible, pernicious, pessimistic, pleasant, poignant, pointless, poor, predetermined,

predictable, premeditated, preposterous, pressing, primarily, privileged, promising, propitious, prospective, prosperous, queer, random, rather, realistic, regardless, regrettable, rewarding, ridiculous, riotous, risky, risqué, rollicking, romantic, rosy, routine, ruinous, sad, safe, scary, secretive, secretly, self-evident/self-explanatory, senseless, sequential, shocking, simpleminded, simultaneous, sinful, sinister, slow, someday, somewhat, soon, speedy, spontaneous, staggering, star-crossed, studied, stupid, sure, surprising, surreptitious, swell, taboo, tacit, tame, tardy, tedious, tender, tense, terminal, thankless, then, thick, threatening, thrilling, through, ticklish, tight, together, tolerable, topsy-turvy, touchy, tragic, trial, trying, tumultuous/tumultuous, tyrannical, ugly, unadvised, unaffected, unauthorized, unavailing, unawares, unbelievable, unearned, uneasy, uneventful, unexpected, unfair, unforeseen, unforgettable, unfortunate, unfriendly, ungodly, unhappy, unholy, unimaginable, unimaginative, uninspired, unintelligent, unintentional/unintended, uninteresting, uninviting, unjustifiable, unlucky, unobtrusive, unreasonable, unrelenting, unsophisticated, unspeakable, untimely, untoward, untroubled, unwarranted, unwise, unwitting, urgent, venturesome, warlike, weighty, well, whimsical, wholehearted/whole-hearted, woeful, wrong, yet

549 original: aboriginal, ancestral, automated, automatic, bastard, belonging to, born, built-in, classical, colonial, congenital, constitutional, counterfeit, deep-seated, derivative, domestic, essential, ethereal, ethnic, exotic, extraneous, extrinsic, foreign, from, genetic, hereditary, human, humble, ignoble, illegitimate, implicit, imported, inborn/inbred, indigenous, ingrained, inherent, inherited, innate, intimate, low, lowly, mechanize, medieval, misbegotten, mortal, mystic/mystical, native, noble, organic, original, otherworldly, patrician, pedigree, plebeian, preliminary, premature, primary/prime, proper, provincial, racial, radical, royal, rudimentary, secondary, secular, strange, thoroughbred, underlying, unprecedented, vernacular

550 peculiarity: ablaze, adaptable, aggressive, airy, ashamed, austere, authoritative, babyish, born, characteristic, clement, closed, contemptible, continent, conventional, corny, craven, cultured, dead, defensive, dreadful, fastidious, forbidding, forceful, forgetful, gawky, gingerly, halting, hokey, laborious, laughable, leisurely, on guard, protective, punctual, shamefaced

551 permanency: abiding, always, carved in stone, chronic, endless, evanescent, fixed, fleeting, fly-by-night, forever, fugitive, invincible, invulnerable, irrevocable, lasting, long-standing, makeshift, passing, permanent, perpetual, standing, stationary, stopgap, temporary, tentative, unchanging

552 probability: absurd, accidental, accidentally, achievable, alleged, apparent, apparently, attainable, chance, chancy, clearly, conceivable, contingent, convincing, credible, definitely, dicey, disposed, doubtless, dubious, earthly, easily, eventual, eventually, far-fetched, fat chance, feasible, fishy, fluky, for sure, fortuitous, funny, groundless, hardly, hypothetical, ideal, iffy, illusory/illusive, imaginable, immune, implausible, impossible, impractical/impracticable, improbable, inclined, inconceivable, incredible, inevitable, insurmountable, intended, invalid, legendary, liable, likely, logical, marvelous, maybe, negligible, obviously, odd, off, operable, optional, ostensible, out, outside, perhaps, plausible, possible, possibly, potential, preposterous, presumably, probable, probably, prone, prospective, remote, ridiculous, slender/slim, so-called, sound, specious, starry-eyed, subject, tenable, tentative, unlikely, unrealistic, unreliable, vain, viable, workable

553 **repetition:** again, alternate, away, redundant, repeatedly, repetitious

554 **restrictiveness:** absolute, all, autonomous, beyond, binding, bound, bounded, boundless, captive, cloistered, concentrated, conditional, confined, dye-in-the-wool, exclusive, exclusively, exclusive of, exempt, finite, fixed, freelance, independent, independently, ironclad, limited, narrow, nonconforming, numbered, obligated, obliged, off-limits, oligarchic, permissible, prohibited, prohibitive, provisional, qualified, rampant, self-reliant

555 **social:** accommodating, allied, amorous, antisocial, aristocratic, awkward, bigoted, blameless, brotherly, burlesque, busy, chummy, civilian, clandestine, clannish, close, commemorative, companionable, compatible, congenial, conjugal, connubial, cooperative, cultural, dear, defenseless, degrading, depressed, difficult, dignified, disadvantageous, disaffected, disgraceful, dishonorable, elite, eminent, engaged, fallen, familiar, forsaken, friendless, friendly, frisky, gentle, homeless, hospitable, hot, important, inelegant, inglorious, intimate, lonely, lonesome, marital, matrimonial, matronly, meddlesome, near, noble, nuptial, palsy-walsy, platonic, popular, preferred, prestigious, racist, recluse/reclusive, refined, single, sociable, social, sole, solitary, thick, thoughtful, thoughtless, top-level, unaccompanied, unapproachable, unarmed, uninvited, unmarried, unpopular, unprotected, unsociable, unwelcome, unworldly, upper, valued, welcome

556 **specialization:** alone, circumstantial, express, expressly, finicky, respective

557 **specificity:** accurate, accurately, ad hoc, all right, approximate, careless, catholic, certain, closely, correct, definite, descriptive, detailed, exact, exactly, extra, fine, general, just, lax, limited, literal, literally, meticulous, minute, namely, nice, particular, particularly, pat, peculiar, perfect, photographic, precise, precisely, proper, punctilious, random, right, rigorous, rough, rude, sectional, separate, simply, skin-deep, smack, special, specially, specific, specifically, strict, such, superficial, systematic, thorough/thoroughgoing, thoroughly, topical, very, wholly

558 **suitability:** absurd, acceptable, accepted, accordant, accordingly, adequate, adequately, advantageous, agreeable, all right, ample, amply, applicable, appropriate, apropos, apt, awkward, becoming, befitting, best, conformable, congruous, correct, correctly, cut out for, decent, decorous, de rigueur, discordant, dissatisfactory, done, down-to-earth, due, duly, eligible, enough, excusable, exorbitant, expedient, extreme, favorable, favorably, feasible, felicitous, felicity, fit, fitted, fitting, full-grown/full-fledged, fully, germane, good, granted, happy, ill-suited, improper, inadmissible, inadvisable, inapplicable, inappropriate, inapt, incongruous, incorrect, ineligible, inept, inopportune, just, justifiable, kosher, lame, legitimate, livable, meet, nice, objectionable, okay, old, on the level, orthodox, passable, pat, perfect, pertinent, prehistoric, presentable, previous, proper, reasonable, relative, relevant, right, rightful, ripe, satisfactory, seasonable, seemly, senseless, sound, sufficient, suitable, tailor-made, tenable, timely, unacceptable, unasked, unbecoming, undue, unfit, unsatisfactory, unseemly, unsuitable, untoward, unwarranted, unworthy, venial, weak, well, wrong

559 **transmission:** infectious, passable, roundabout

560 **usefulness:** acting, adequately, barren, broken, convenient, damaged, dead, defective, defunct, dependable, derelict, desert, desirable, desolate, dilapidated, dissipated, drained, effective, effete, efficient, employed, enervated, excessive, exhausted, expedient, extravagant, faded, fallow, faulty, finished, fitted, fixed, fruitful, fruitless, functional, futile, futility, godforsaken, good, handy, helpful, hollow, idle, idealistic, impaired, impoverished, inactive, ineffective/ineffectual, inefficient, infallible, infertile, instead, instrumental, interim, invalid, irrelevant, leftover, live, living, "lost, makeshift, misspent, neither here nor there, null, obsolete, occupied, old, on duty, on the blink, open, operational, operative, outmoded, practicable, practical, prehistoric, prepared, prodigal, productive, propitious, purposeless, quixotic, ready, residual, ripe, running, salubrious, satisfactory, serviceable, short, spent, starry-eyed, stopgap, subservient, subsidiary, substitute, sufficient, superfluous, supine, surplus, trashy, trial, tributary, under, unproductive, unrealistic, usable, useful, useless, user-friendly, utilitarian, vacant, valuable, viable, virgin/virginal, visionary, void, wanting, washed-out, workable, working, worn/worn-out, worthless, worthwhile

COMPARATIVE

561 **compared with:** contrast, mark, touch

562 **complexity:** abstruse, artless, backward, bare, baroque, bilateral, blank, civilized, clarion, clear, complex, complicated, crude, cursory, elaborate, elementary, exaggerated, fancy, folksy, graphic, high-flown, intricate, involved, modest, pell-mell, simple, simply,

sophisticated, tortuous, tricky, ultra, unsophisticated, unwieldy, vanilla, well-defined

563 correspondence: accordant, akin, allied, applicable, close, commensurate, concerning, concurrent, conformable, congruent, congruous, consistent, consonant, corporate, duplicate, euphonious, harmonious, kindred, likewise, moderate, mutual, proportionate/proportional, pro rata, relative, sympathetic, truant, twin, unanimous, unified, united, unrelated

564 difference: against, alien, altered, alternative, ambivalent, another, assorted, atypical, avant-garde, averse, bizarre, contrived, converse, curious, deviant, diametric/diametrical, different, differently, discordant, discrepant, discrete, disparate, disproportionate, dissimilar, dissonant, distinct, distinctive, divergent, diverse, eccentric, especial, especially, exceptional, extraordinary, fantastic, flaky, freakish, funny, gonzo, heterogeneous, incompatible, inconsistent, individual, inverse, irreconcilable, manifold, miscellaneous, mixed, monstrous, motley, multiple/multifarious, nerd, new, novel, odd/oddball, offbeat, opposed/opposing, opposite, other, particular, peculiar, phenomenal, plural, polar, preternatural, quaint, queer, refreshing, remote, repugnant, rival, screwy, separate, several, single, singular, sole, spacey/spacy, special, specific, specifically, strange, sundry, suspicious, unaccountable, unaccustomed, uncanny, uncommon, unconventional, underground, unearthly, unequal, unfamiliar, unheard-of, unique, unlike, unnatural, unorthodox, unprecedented, unrelated, unthinkable, unusual, variant, varied, variegated, various, vice versa, weird

565 difficulty: agonizing, arduous, awkward, complicated, defective, deficient, delicate, demanding, easily, easy, easy as pie, effortless, facile, formidable, grueling, hard, heavy, inaccurate, insurmountable, knotty, laborious, maddening, mortally, murderous, nerve-racking, nothing to it, onerous, ponderous, prickly, rigorous, rugged, serious, seriously, severe, sticky, stiff, tall, taxing, thorny, ticklish, tight, tough, treacherous, troublesome, trying, uncomplicated, uphill, weighty, wicked, worrisome

566 equivalence: alike, alternate, approximately, asymmetrical, balanced, commensurate, comparable, comparative, coordinate, corresponding, disproportionate, duplicate, equal, equivalent, even, identical, indistinguishable, level, matching, mock, model, more or less, nearly, reciprocal, regular, same, uneven

567 importance: above, august, below, beneath, beneficial, big league, bush-league, central, chiefly, chosen, climactic/climacteric, collateral, component, conspicuous, costly, dear, dogmatic, elevated, essential, estimable, exclusive, front, fundamental, grave, high, holy, immediate, important, inferior, known, life-and-death, main, majestic, material, meaningful, newsworthy, noteworthy, noticeable, operative, precious, pregnant, primary/prime, prodigious, reputable, salient, second-rate/second-class, significant, special,

strategic, telling, top, towering, upper, used, vital, worthwhile, worthy

568 importance, extreme: acclaimed, acute, basic, basically, beloved, best, better, big, big league, blessed, bright, brilliant, burning, capital, cardinal, celebrated, chief, consequential, considerable, critical, crucial, deciding, dire, divine, dominant, earnest, eminent, exigent, fabled, famous, fatal, fateful, favored, favorite, first, foremost, glorious, grand, great, hallowed, head, high-class, historic, illustrious, immortal, influential, invaluable, key, larger than life, legendary, major, master, momentous, monumental, necessary, notable, noted, noteworthy, oligarchic, outstanding, overriding, paramount, pet, pivotal, praiseworthy, predominant, pre-eminent, premier, pressing, prestigious, priceless, principal, prominent, renowned, ruling, serious, seriously, signal, significant, sovereign, splendid, star, substantial, supreme, ultimate, unsurpassed, uppermost, urgent, valuable, weighty, well-known

569 intensity: acute, almighty, awfully, bad, badly, biting, blatant, bloody, concentrated, considerably, desperate, desperately, drastic, exceedingly, exquisite, extra, extreme, extremely, greatly, harsh, heavy, high, highly, immoderate, insanely, intense, mightily, most, notably, outrageous, powerfully, pretty, profound, quite, severe, severely, sharp, somewhat, stark, stiff, stringent, strong, substantially, terribly, terrific, too, ultra, unconscionable, undue, unduly, unmitigated, unusually, very, violent, vivid, wild

570 negative: adverse, affected, amiss, apocryphal, awful, awfully, bad, baleful, baneful, base, beside oneself, black, conflicting, creepy, cruel, damnable, damned, defiled, degenerate, deleterious, delinquent, deplorable, derogatory, despicable, detrimental, dire, direful, done for, egregious, empty, erroneous, evil, fallacious, false, faulty, fearful, filthy, grim, grisly, heinous, hellish, icky, ill, imperfect, inadequate, inauspicious, incendiary, incorrect, incorrigible, inexcusable, infamous, injurious, inordinate, insecure, lame, loathsome, miserable, misguided, misspent, negative, nerd, null, objectionable, off, poor, prejudicial, rancid, rotten, ruinous, rundown, seedy, slipshod, squalid, tasteless, terribly, threatening, trashy, trumped up, undesirable, unforgivable, unfortunate, ungodly, unpleasant, unsatisfactory, untoward, unwelcome, upset, weak, weird, worthless

571 negative, extreme: abject, abominable, accursed, ad nauseum, astounding, atrocious, awful, awfully, bad, badly, crappy, crummy, cursed, lousy, nasty, noisome, outrageous, pernicious, perverse, poorly, regrettable, reprehensible, repugnant, repulsive, rotten, shameful, shocking, shoddy, sick, sickening, sickly, sinister, sordid, staggering, terrible, tragic, ugly, unbearable, unfavorable, unhealthy, unsavory, unspeakable, unworthy, vicious, vile, virulent, wicked, woeful, wretched, wrong

572 positive: admirable, affirmative, agreeable, agreeably, all right, amazing, angelic, astonishing, auspicious, awesome, beloved, beneficial, benign, best, better, boss, comfort, comfortable, commendable, consummate, cool, decent, delicious, desirable, estimable, exceptional, exemplary, extraordinary, fabulous, fanciful, fantastic, far-out, faultless, favorable, favorably, for kicks, fortunate, fortunately, fun, good, grateful, groovy, heavenly, high-class, homey, idyllic, incredible, innocuous, interesting, intriguing, luckily, lucky, magnificent, majestic, meritorious, merry, mind-blowing, mind-boggling, miraculous, nice, nifty, noble, opportune, pleasant, pleasing/pleasurable, positive, prodigious, profitable, propitious, prosperous, proud, respectable, rewarding, right, salubrious, satisfying, terrific, thrilling, toothsome, upbeat, utopian, welcome, well, worthwhile, worthy, yes, yummy

573 **similarity:** akin, alike, analogous, approximate, closely, cognate, comparable, comparative, conformable, different, equal, equivalent, faithful, homogenous, identical, interchangeable, like, like-minded, parallel, related, representative, same, seeming, similar, synonymous, tantamount, twin, uniform, virtual, virtually

574 **superiority:** absolute, acclaimed, admirable, advanced, advantage, advisable, all right, all-time, arch, below par, capital, cardinal, champion, chief, choice, chosen, classic/classical, coarse, commanding, correct, crack, dandy, definitive, delectable, delicate, deluxe, dependent, deplorable, dignified, distinctive, distinguished, divine, dominant, elegant, elite, eminently, enviable, especial, especially, excellent, exceptional, exemplary, exquisite, fantastic, fine, first-class/first-rate, flat-out, flawless, glorious, gnarly, golden, grand, great, head, high-powered, holy, ideal, impeccable, imperative, imperfect, imperious, important, imposing, impressive, incomparable, ineffable, infallible, inferior, inimitable, irreproachable, irresistible, junior, laudable, leading, less, lofty, low, luscious, lush, luxuriant, luxurious, magic, major, marvelous, matchless, maximum, menial, mint, model, omnipotent, optimal, optimum, outstanding, paramount, peerless, perfect, perfectly, pet, phenomenal, poor, poorly, powerful, praiseworthy, predominant, preeminent, preferred, premium, prevalent, primary/prime, principal, privileged, prize, prodigious, proud, rare, remarkable, renowned, reputable, ritzy, rotten, royal, ruling, sacred, sacrosanct, secondary, secondrate/second-class, select, senior, sensational, signal, solemn, spectacular, splendid, stately, sterling, striking, stunning, stupendous, sublime, substandard, sumptuous, super, superb, superior, superlative, supreme, swell, tasteful, top, top-level, top-notch, transcendent/transcendental, tremendous, ultimate, uncommon, unequaled, unerring, unique, unparalleled, unprecedented, unrivaled, unsurpassed, upper hand, utmost, utopian, venerable, vintage, whole, wonderful

575 **unimportance:** beside the point, empty, expendable, frivolous, hand-me-down, immaterial, inconsequential/inconsiderable, insignificant, irrelevant, lesser, lightweight, little, meaningless, menial, middle-of-the-road, minor, minute, moderate, needless, negligible, neither here nor there, nominal, nonessential, ordinary, peripheral, petty, picayune, piddling, puny, remote, second, secondary, side, slight, small, small-time, so-so, subject, subordinate, subservient, subsidiary, substitute, tenuous, trifling, trivial, under, undistinguished, unexceptional, unimportant, vain, vapid, worthless

PHYSICAL

576 **accessibility:** accessible, adaptable, approachable, arcane, arrant, available, beset, blind, broad, clandestine, classified, close, closed, concealed, confidential, confidentially, cryptic, dark, defenseless, depleted, discernible, dissipated, distant, dubious, engaged, enigmatic/enigmatical, esoteric, exposed, far-flung, flagrant, furtive, glaring, graphic, hidden, hush-hush, illegible, impenetrable, inaccessible, incognito, inconspicuous, inner, inscrutable, inside, insoluble, known, latent, legible, lost, manifest, missing, mobile, mysterious, nameless, obscure, observable, obtainable, occult, off-course, off-limits, off the record, on call, open, optional, out, outward, outwardly, passable, patent, perceptible, permeable, plain, possible, private, privy, prohibited, pronounced, public, rare, ready, recondite, reserved, secluded, secret, stealthy, strange, tight, ulterior, unapproachable, unarmed, uncharted, uncovered, undercover, underground, unheard-of, unidentified, unknown, unprotected, unreadable, unseen, unsung, usable, user-friendly, veiled, vigilant, visible, visual, weak, willing

577 **accompaniment:** abandoned, again, alone, along, also, and, attendant, complementary, concomitant, connected, corporate, deserted, each, en masse, en route, ensemble, et cetera, except, furthermore, incidental, including, isolated, joint, jointly, left, lone, mutually, odd, one, only, parenthetical, per se, personally, reciprocal, related, separate, separately, single, single-handed, singly, singular, sole, solely, solitary, solo, stranded, unaccompanied, under, unified, unique, united

578 **age:** adolescent, advanced, afresh, aged, ancient, antediluvian, antiquarian, antiquated, antique, archaic, big, callow, childish, contemporary, crude, dated, doddering, elder, elderly, embryonic, fresh, full-grown/full-fledged, futuristic, green, groundbreaking, hoary, immature, immemorial, inchoate, infant/infantile, innovative, junior, juvenile, late, mature, medieval, mellow, mint, modern, modish, musty, new, newfangled, novel, old, older, old-fashioned, original, originally, outdated/out-of-date, outmoded, passé, puerile, quaint, recent, refreshing, ripe, secondhand, senior, stale, state-of-the-art, tender, undeveloped, unspoiled, up-to-date, vintage, well-preserved, young, youthful

579 **appearance:** adorable, aesthetic/esthetic, alluring, artistic, attractive, beautiful, becom-

ing, comely, cosmetic, crisp, cute, dapper, deathly, decorative, delectable, desirable, disheveled, dressy, elegant, exquisite, eye-catching, fair, fancy, fashionable, fetching, fine, flawless, glamorous, glorious, good-looking, gorgeous, graceful, grotesque, grungy, handsome, hideous, hip, homely, imperfect, irresistible, lovely, natty, ornamental, ornate, picturesque, plain, presentable, pretty, ravishing, refreshing, repulsive, resplendent, scenic, seductive, snazzy, spiffy, statuesque, striking, stunning, stylish, symmetrical, ugly, unattractive, unbecoming, unsightly, willowy, with it

580 deformity: acne, birth defect, birthmark, blemish, blot, blotch, bug, chip, contortion, defect, deformity, dent, distortion, fault, flaw, frailty, freak, hip, malformation, misrepresentation, misstatement, mole, mutant, pockmark, scar

581 direction: about, across, adrift, along, around, askance, astern, astray, at, away, awry, backward, below, centrifugal, circuitous, counter, crooked, crosswise/crossways, devious, diagonal, diagonally, direct, directly, due, erect, errant, erratic, forked, forth, forward, haphazard, horizontal, indirect, inward, lateral, left, north, off-center, outgoing, outward, parallel, perpendicular, plane, plumb, ramble, right, rotary, roundabout, sharp, sheer, sideways, sinuous, snaky, steep, straight, thereabout, through, tortuous, uphill, upright, vertical, wide, winding, wry, zigzag

582 genuineness: abstract, actual, actually, airy, alias, allegorical, apocryphal, apparent, apparently, artificial, arty, assumed, authentic, authoritative, baseless, believable, beta, bogus, bona fide, certain, circumstantial, colored, concrete, conjectural, contrived, counterfeit, credible, dark, deceptive, de facto, delusive, dogmatic, dreamy, duplicitous, ecclesiastical, effective, empirical/empiric, enigmatic/enigmatical, erroneous, ersatz, esoteric, ethereal, extant, factual, fake, fallacious, false, fantastic, far-fetched, feigned, fictitious, figurative, foolproof, frank, fraudulent, genuine, good, groundless, hard, heartfelt, historical, honest-to-God, hypothetical, illusory/illusive, imaginary, imitative, inaccurate, indisputable, intangible, invisible, irrefutable, just, legitimate, lifelike, made-up, magic/magical, make-believe, matter-of-fact, metaphorical, metaphysical, mock, monstrous, mystic/mystical, mythical/mythological, nominal, nonexistent, occult, openhearted, ostensible, ostensibly, palpable, paranormal, phony, physical, plastic, positive, positively, pretended, pseudo, quack, quasi, quite, real, realistic, really, right, sham, sincerely, sound, specious, spiritual, spurious, substantial, supernatural, suspect, synthetic, tactile, tangible, temporal, true, truly, unearthly, unfounded, unnatural, unreal, unthinkable, untrue, unvarnished, unworldly, utopian, valid, veracious, veritable, visionary, wholehearted/whole-hearted, worldly, wrong

583 location: aboard, about, abroad, absconder, absent, absentee, advance, aerial, agricul-

tural, aground, airy, alone, ashore, askance, astride, at, beached, bucolic, center, central, civic, civil, cloistered, coastal, diffuse, down, everywhere, exterior, external, fixed, forward, from, front, here, horizontal, inside, insular, interior, isolated, lateral, leafy, left, lonely, low, middle, north, off, off-center, off-course, omnipresent, out, outdoor, outer, outermost, outlying, outside, outward, over, overseas, pastoral, penal, peripheral, perpendicular, polar, populous, posterior, precipitous, present, private, prominent, prone, prostrate, quiet, rear, recumbent, remote, restful, roomy, roughly, rural, rustic, secluded, sideways, single-handed, solitary, solo, somewhere, stray, subterranean, surface, supernal, through, top, topical, truant, uncomfortable, underground, untamed, upper, uppermost, upright, upside-down, vertical, void, where/wherever, wide, wild, withdrawn

584 movement: ambulatory, billowy, brisk, centrifugal, clumsy, destined, fleet, flowing, fluent, flying, frozen, fugitive, gawky, graceful, graceless, heavy, immobile, inactive, indolent, inert, itinerant, languid, leisurely, lethargic, lifeless, lightly, liquid, listless, lithe, lumbering, maladroit, migrant/migratory, mobile, motionless, movable, moving, nimble, nomadic, nonstop, oafish, outgoing, passive, pendulous/pendent, peripatetic, portable, quiet, restless, rotary, roundabout, running, sedentary, slack, slow, sluggish, speedy, stagnant, static, still, vibrant, willowy, winding

585 order: advance, advanced, alphabetical, avant-garde, bottom, center, chronological, collective, confused, consecutive, direct, disjointed, disorganized, first, following, fore, foregoing, foremost, former, formerly, forward, from scratch, front, hand-me-down, immediate, incipient, indiscriminate, initial, intermediate, internal, introductory, jumbled, lass, last, lastly, latter, leading, least, maiden, mean, median, methodical/methodic, muddled, neatly, next, older, on, onward/onwards, orderly, original, originally, past, pell-mell, pioneer, posterior, preceding, preliminary, premier, preparatory, previous, primary/prime, regular, second, senior, sequential, serial, shipshape, straight, subsequent, subsequently, succeeding/successive, systematic, tidy, together, topsy-turvy, uttermost

586 relative placement: abaft, about, abreast, adjacent, adjoining, after, ahead, ajar, almost, along, alongside, amid/amidst, among, apart, approximate, around, aside, askew, behind, below, beneath, beside, between, bottom, by, close, cockeyed, contiguous, convenient, direct, down, downhill, elsewhere, en route, far, faraway, farther, farthest, furthest, gone, halfway, handy, hard, immediate, lower, near, nearby, next, on, overhead, parallel, preceding, thereabout, toward/towards, under, underneath, within, without, wrong, yonder

587 safety: chancy, chary, perilous, precarious, sacred, safe, secure, treacherous, unharmed, unreliable, unsafe, unsound, vulnerable, weak

588 speed: agile, cursory, expeditious, express, fast, fleet, gradual, gradually, hastily, hasty, headlong, hurried, instant, instantly, one by one, on the double, posthaste, precipitous/precipitate, quick, quickly, rapid, rapidly, slow, snappy, speedy, swift, swiftly/swift, whirlwind

589 style: adorable, bald, baroque, beautiful, becoming, bedraggled, black, bland, bold, bourgeois, brassy, casual, cheap, chic, class, classical, classy, conglomerate, contemporary, cosmopolitan, country, crude, cultural, cursory, dashing, distasteful, dowdy, dressy, eat high on the hog, elegant, exquisite, fashionable, featureless, fitted, flamboyant, flashy, floral, florid, flowery, folksy, formless, frumpy, futuristic, gaily, garish, gaudy, gay, generous, glamorous, glaring, gorgeous,

graceful, grand, grandiose, graphic, homely, hot, humble, improvised, incognito, informal, ingenuous, innovative, jazzy, kinky, lavish, loud, lovely, lush, luxuriate, luxurious, marked, mean, mere, meretricious, modern, modish, naked, neat, neatly, new, newfangled, obsolete, old-fashioned, opulent, orderly, original, ornamental, ornate, ostentatious, outdated/out-of-date, outmoded, palatial, passé, picturesque, plain, plush, popular, posh, pretentious, prevalent, provincial, quaint, quiet, refined, regal, resplendent, rich, rustic, salty, scruffy, shapeless, sharp, showy, simple, slack, sleazy, slipshod, smart, snappy, snazzy, sophisticated, spiffy, splendid, spruce, stale, stately, state-of-the-art, statuesque, stylish, swank/swanky, swish, tacky, tasteful, tasteless, tawdry, tousled, trendy, two-bit, unadorned, unbecoming, untidy, unworldly, up-to-date, vanilla, vogue

Senses

ASPECTS OF PERCEPTION

590 physical: burn, caress, hear, see, smell, taste, touch

AUDITORY

591 attribute of hearing: acoustic, audible, deaf, distinct

592 attribute of noise: blatant, brassy, cacophonous, clarion, deafening, discordant, dissonant, earsplitting, grating, loud, noisy, obstreperous, piercing, quiet, raucous, rough, shrill, soft, soft-spoken, sonorous, strident, vociferous

593 attribute of noise-making: dumb, mute

594 attribute of sound: acoustic, aloud, audible, blatant, brassy, cacophonous, clarion, deafening, deep, discordant, dissonant, dulcet, dull, earsplitting, faint, full, gentle, grating, gruff, guttural, high, hoarse, hollow, husky, inaudible, loud, low, lyric, lyrical, mellifluous, mellow, melodious/melodic, muffled, mum, musical, noiseless, noiseproof, noisy, obstreperous, off-key, piercing, quiet, raspy, raucous, resonant, rich, rough, round, shrill, silent, still, soft-spoken, sonorous, soundproof, strident, subdued, sweet, tight-lipped, tranquil, tuneful, untroubled, vocal, vociferous, weak

595 audible object: acknowledgment, acoustics, air, alert, anthem, aria, arrangement, ballad, bang, bell, blast, boom, buzz, carillon, carol, chant, clamor, clank, clap, clatter, click, clink, clump, crack, crash, delivery, din, dirge, discord, dissonance, ditty, drone, echo, gasp, groan, growl, gurgle, harmony, hiss, holler, howl, hymn, inflection, intonation, jangle, jazz, melody, murmur, music, noise, peal, pop, psalm, refrain, report, rhyme, rhythm, ring, roar, roll, rumpus, rustle,

scream, shout, shriek, slam, song, sound, strain, thunder, tick, tune, yell

596 hearing: attend, bug, commiserate, eavesdrop, hear, listen, mind, monitor, regard

597 sound perception: hearing

OLFACTORY

598 attribute of odor: aromatic, astringent, fetid, fragrant, gamy, high, malodorous, musty, noisome, odorless, odorous, putrid, rancid, rank, scented, sharp, smelly, stale, stinking, strong, sweet, tangy

599 object that can be smelled: aroma, bouquet, breath, cologne, incense, odor, perfume, scent, smell, stench, stink, tang, whiff

600 odor: cologne, fragrance, fumes, incense, perfume, reek, smell, stench, stink, tang

601 olfactory perception: breathe, inhale, nose, scent, smell, sniff, whiff

602 smelling: scent, smell, sniff, whiff

TACTILE

603 attribute of dryness: absorbent, arid, balmy, clammy, damp, dank, dry, filmy, fluid, humid, juicy, liquid, misty, moist, moldy, muggy, musty, oily, parched, sloppy, soaked, soggy, sopping, thirsty, waterlogged, watery, wet, wizened

604 attribute of hardness: adamant, concrete, downy, erect, firm, firmly, flaccid, flinty, hard, impenetrable, impermeable, impervious, inflexible, iron, limp, lissome, mushy, pavement, permeable, petrified, plastic, rocky, solid, stiff, supple, taut, tender, tense, unbending

605 attribute of temperature: ablaze, arctic, balmy, benign, biting, bland, boiling, bracing, brisk, broiling, burning, chill, chilly, close, cold, cool, cozy, crisp, febrile, feverish, fiery, freezing, frigid, frosty, frozen, glacial, heated, hot, icy, lukewarm, polar, sultry, sweltering, tepid, thermal, torrid, tropical, warm, wintry

606 **attribute of texture:** abrasive, adhesive, beaten, bias, breakable, brittle, bumpy, bushy, coarse, corrugated, cozy, craggy, creamy, crisp, crumbly, crunchy, crusty, dainty, delicate, diaphanous, diluted/dilute, downy, elastic, ethereal, fibrous, filmy, fine, firm, fleecy, flimsy, fluff, fluffy, fuzzy, gauzy, gelatinous, glassy, glossy, gooey, gossamer, greasy, gritty, icy, irregular, jagged, knurled, lacy, leathery, lubricant, lucid, matted, mottled, muddy, mushy, nappy, oily, opaque, paper, pasty, permeable, pointed, porous, powdery, rough, rugged, sheer, silky, sleek, slick, slippery, smooth, soft, spongy, springy, sticky, tenacious, tender, thick, thin, threadbare, transparent, uneven, viscous, yielding

607 **dryness:** drought, evaporation, humidity, wet

608 **tactile perception:** feeling, itch, touch

609 **tactile quality:** excruciating, numb

610 **temperature:** cold, fever, frost, glow, heat, temperature

611 **texture:** consistency, delicacy, feel, fiber, finish, gloss, grain, mesh, nap, polish, texture

612 **touching:** brush, caress, dab, feel, finger, flick, graze, grope, handle, itch, lick, manipulate, meet, monkey, nestle, nudge, nuzzle, pat, paw, pet, reach, stroke, tickle, tingle, toothsome, touch, yummy

TASTING

613 **attribute of taste:** acerbic, acerbity, acid, acidulous, acrid, appetizing, astringent, bad, bitter, bland, corrupt, delectable, delicious, distasteful, done, eatable, edible, full-bodied, hot, insipid, luscious, mouth-watering, palatable, peppery, piquant, poignant, pungent, racy, rancid, rich, robust, salty, savory, scrumptious, sharp, sour, spicy, succulent, sweet, tart, tasteless, tasty, unsavory, yummy

614 **taste:** acidity, bite, bitterness, flavor, savor, spice, tang, taste, zest

615 **taste perception:** taste

616 **tasting:** bite, gargle, sample, savor, taste

VISUAL

617 **attribute of brightness:** ablaze, beaming, bold, bright, brilliant, clear, colorful, crystal, dark, dazzling, dim, dingy, drab, dull, dusky, effulgent, faded, faint, glaring, gloomy, glossy, glowing, incandescent, lackluster, light, lucid, luminescent, luminous, lustrous, misty, murky, nebulous, obscure, opaque, radiant, resplendent, scintillating, sepulchral, shady, shiny, sunny, tenebrous, washed-out

618 **attribute of color:** amber, anemic, ashen, beige, black, blond/blonde, bloodless, blue, bold, bright, bronze, brown, brunette/brunet, buff, cadaverous, cherry, clear, colored, colorful, colorless, crystal, dappled, dark, deathly, deep, drab, dusky, faded, fair, florid, flushed, gaudy, gay, gloomy, glowing,

gold/golden, gray/grey, green, hoary, iridescent, jet, light, livid, mauve, milky, motley, mottled, mousy, muddy, multicolored, murky, neutral, opaque, orange, pale, pallid, pallor, pastel, pasty, peaked, pearly, purple, red, rich, rosy, ruddy, sable, sallow, sanguine, silver, smoky, soft, speckled, strong, swarthy, tan, translucent, transparent, variegated, verdant, vibrant, vivid, wan, watery, white, yellow

619 **attribute of vision:** appreciable, blind, clear, concealed, conspicuous, discernible, disguised, distinct, fuzzy, glaring, glassy, graphic, impalpable, invisible, lucid, myopic, nearsighted, prominent, pronounced, visible, visual

620 **brightness:** dark, darkness, gleam, glitter, gloom, gloss, glow, illumination, lamp, lantern, light, luster, murk, night, overshadow, pall, polish, radiance, radiate, shade, shadow, sheen, shimmer, shine, splendor

621 **clean:** grimy, grubby, hygienic, immaculate, impeccable, impure, mangy, messy, neat, pristine, pure, refined, sanitary, scraggly, slimy, sloppy, slovenly, spick-and-span, spotless, stagnant, sterile, straight, tidy, trim, unadulterated, unblemished, unclean, unkempt, unsanitary, untidy, untouched

622 **color:** auburn, beige, blush, cast, color, complexion, decor, fade, flush, gloom, glow, hue, orange, pigment, pink, purple, red, shade, shadow, stain, stripe, tan, tinge, tint, tone, yellow

623 **looking:** attend, avert, bear in mind, browse, contemplate, contemplation, dip into, eye, face, fix, fixate, focus, gape, gawk, gaze, glance, glare, glimpse, glower, heed, inspect, leaf, leer, look, lookout, look out, mind, monitor, ogle, patrol, peek/peep, peer, point, pry, regard, rubberneck, scan, scout, scrutinize, scrutiny, skim, snoop, spy, squint, stare, view, vigil, watch

624 **occurrence of light:** beam, blink, bolt, cast, eclipse, flash, flicker, glance, glare, gleam, glimmer, glint, glisten, glitter, glow, halo, illuminate, illumination, lamp, lantern, light, lighten, ray, reflect, shimmer, shine, spark, sparkle, spotlight, twinkle, wink

625 **picture:** arms, blueprint, caricature, cartoon, chart, design, diagram, drawing, emblem, engraving, facsimile, figure, flowchart, format, graphics, handwriting, impression, imprint, layout, map, model, outline, pattern, picture, plaid, plan, portrait, profile, reproduction, scene, scheme, silhouette, sketch, table, tableau

626 **seeing:** behold, distinguish, eye, gaze, make out, mark, meet, note, notice, observe, perceive, regard, remark, see, sight, spot, view, witness

627 **visibility change:** blur, clear, dim, fog

628 **visible object:** acknowledgment, alert, aspect, beacon, beam, blaze, buoy, cue, footprint, glance, glare, hallmark, halo, handwriting, light, mirage, model, outlook, panorama, prospect, ray, reflection, scene, scenery, sparkle, streak, track, view, vista

629 **visual perception:** blindness, eyesight, perspective, sight, vision

States

ABSTRACT

630 **ability:** ability, agility, artifice, artistry, awkwardness, bent, can, capability, capacity, competence, dexterity, disqualification, ease, efficiency, eloquence, endowment, expertise/expertness, facility, faculty, feebleness, flair, gift, hand, handicraft, head, inability, inclination, knack, know-how, league, literacy, master, mastery, mind, modus operandi, niche, performance, pizzazz, power, productivity, proficiency, promise, propensity, prowess, qualification, qualify, readiness, right stuff, skill, talent, technique, telepathy, touch, trick, turn

631 **accessibility:** access, back door, circulation, concealment, cover-up, privacy, seclusion, secrecy, secret

632 **be ahead:** ahead, first, front, uppermost, winning

633 **behavior:** abandon, abstention, abstinence, acquit, acrimony, act, act up, adultery, affectation, airs, alacrity, altruism, amenity, antithesis, apathy, arrogance, asperity, audacity, austerity, bad form, bad manners, balance, barbarism, barbarity, bearing, behave, behavior, benevolence, betrayal, bitterness, bluster, brass, bravery, carriage, carry on, chastity, cheek, chivalry, chutzpah, coarseness, cold shoulder, compassion, complaisance, condescend, condescension, condolence, conduct, continence, cordiality, correctness, corruption, countenance, courage, courtesy, cruelty, culture, custom, cut, debauchery, deceit, decency, decorum, deference, defiance, demeanor, deportment, desperation, detachment, diffidence, diplomacy, dirty tricks, dishonesty, disloyalty, disobedience, disregard, disrespect, dissidence, dissipation, distance, do, eagerness, earnestness, ebullience, effervescence, effrontery, endurance, enthusiasm, equanimity, equilibrium, etiquette, excess, excitement, exuberance, face, faithfulness, faithlessness, falderal, flare-up, fanaticism, feint, fervor, firmness, flightiness, flippancy, folly, foolishness, forbearance, formality, freedom, frivolity, fusillade, fuss, gall, geniality, grace, grit, grovel, haughtiness, hauteur, heroism, honesty, honor, hostility, hubris, humanity, humility, hypocrisy, impatience, impertinence, incivility, indecency, indiscretion, insolence, insubordination, irreverence, kindness, laziness, lethargy, license, lifestyle, longevity, lunacy, manhood/womanhood, manner, manners, mercy, misbehave, misbehavior, mischief, misconduct, misdeed/misdemeanor, moderation, , modesty, monkey business, moxie, mutiny, naïveté, negligence, nonconformity, nonsense, obedience, oblivion, observance, order, ostentation, outburst, pep, perseverance, piety, poise, polish, pose, precaution, presumption, pretense, pretension, pride, propriety, prowess, punctilio, purpose, quarter, radiance, rancor, react, reaction, readiness, rebel, rebellion, refinement, refusal, regress, reserve, responsibility, restraint, rigmarole, scene, self-control, serenity, shenanigans, show, simplicity, sincerity, sloth, sobriety, sophistication, spunk, steam, submission, sympathy, tact, technicality, temerity, temperance, treachery, treat, treatment, vainglory, valor, veneer, virginity, vitality, vitriol, zing, zip

634 **commonality:** diffusion, frequency, ritual

635 **completeness:** bulk, clincher, complement, culmination, deficiency, entirety, finality, fullness, integrity, whole

636 **conformity:** adequacy, adhere, archetype, cohere, fidelity, par

637 **constancy:** consistency, constancy, continuance, instability, monotony

638 **definiteness:** accuracy, ambiguity, certainty, clarity, correctness, exactness, finality, precision, rigor, sure thing, truth

639 **exist in a condition:** blame, condition, existence, state, status quo

640 **extension:** addition, continuation

641 **forcefulness:** clasp, clutches, dictatorship, efficacy, force, gravity, impact, impetus, impulse, intensity, kick, might, momentum, muscle, power, pressure, propulsion, push, swamp, violence

642 **made of:** compose, have, inclusion, manifestation

643 **make up:** accompany, comprise, consist of, cover, form, include, make up

644 **mannerism:** air, attention(s), austerity, characterize, clemency, courtesy, custom, earmark, entity, epitomize, fashion, foible, forgetfulness, habit, idiosyncrasy, manner, mannerism, mark, methodology, mien, mode, mores, propriety, purpose, quirk, regard, trait, vigilance

645 **morality:** abandon, accountability, affirmative action, atrocity, blasphemy, coarseness, conscience, corruption, craft, debauchery, decadence, degeneracy, delinquency, depravity, dirt, disservice, enormity, environment, equality, equity, ethics/ethic, evil, excess, fairness, faithfulness, faithlessness, falsity, foul play, favoritism, fraud, good, goodness, good will/goodwill, greatness, guile, guilt, guise, holiness, honesty, honor, ideals, imposition, imposture, indecency, infamy, infidelity, infraction, inhumanity, iniquity, injustice, innocence, justice, liability, license, loyalty, misbehave, misbehavior, mischief, misconduct, misdeed/misdemeanor, morality, morals, obligation, obscenity, organized crime, outrage, peccadillo, principle/principles, probity, profanity, prostitute, responsibility, right, sacrilege, sanctity, scandal, scheme, score, segregate, sin, transgression, treachery, treason, trespass, trick, trickery, trust, turpitude, underworld, validity, values, veracity, vice, virtue, wrong

646 **necessity:** absence, behoove, call for, dearth, defect, deficit, demand, do, do without, drought, enough, entail, essential, exigency/exigence, frill, go without, have, lack, mainstay, must, necessitate, necessity, need, obligate, oblige, paucity, prerequisite, provide,

qualification, require, requirement/requisite, reservation, shortage, specification, subsistence, take, void, want

647 normality: aberration, abnormality, anomaly, average, eccentricity, gauge, norm, rule, rut, yardstick

648 origin: ancestry, birth, bottom, counterfeit, cradle, DNA, derivation, derive from, emanate, emanation, extraction, femininity/feminine, font, fountain, funny money, germ, geyser, hail, head, heredity, heritage, home, inception, issue, masculinity/masculine, matrix, mortality, origin, parent, precursor, root(s), seed, sex, source, spring, start, stem, threshold

649 permanency: constant, fixed, forever, permanent, perpetual, unchanging

650 probability: absurdity, chance, contingency, credibility, eventuality, liability, likelihood, must, odds, possibilities, possibility, potential, probability, promise, tend

651 range: area, breadth, circulation, compass, continuation, country mile, degree, diffusion, dissemination, dissipation, distance, diversity, expanse, extent, gamut, go, jurisdiction, latitude, length, matter, overrun, panorama, play, radius, range, reach, realm, room, run, scale, scope, spread, stretch, sweep

652 restrictiveness: abbreviation, abridgement, autonomy, bar, block, blockade, bondage, captivity, constraint, curb, exemption, flexibility, prohibition, qualification

653 specialization: alone, circumstantial, express, precise, select

654 specificity: accuracy, correctness, exactness, model, point, precision, property, rigor

655 style: appeal, approach, artistry, behavior, clash, classic, classicism, cultivation, cut, dash, dernier cri, discrimination, elegance, fad, fashion, finish, frill, frippery, genre/genus, glamour, glitter, grace, look, mode, ostentation, polish, pomp, popularity, rage, refinement, simplicity, sophistication, splendor, style, taste, tone, touch, trend, vogue

656 suitability: absurdity, adequacy, agree, awkwardness, blend, consistency, correctness, do, expediency/expedience, fitness, propriety, satisfy, serve, suit

657 tendency: acrimony, alacrity, alms, animation, aptitude, atrocity, cabin fever, care, charity, cultivation, dedication, defiance, determination, devotion, diligence, direction, discretion, dishonesty, disinclination, eagerness, earnestness, effervescence, enterprise, enthusiasm, equity, face, fairness, fashion, fervor, finesse, fundraiser, gallantry, generosity, grace, guile, gusto, guts, heat, hospitality, hostility, humility, hurry, hypocrisy, idleness, impatience, incline, indifference, indignation, indulgence, inertia, inhibition, initiative, kindness, liability, mind, moderation, monstrosity, naïveté, neglect, nervousness, nonconformity, patience, philanthropy, pity, posture, presence, pretension, rage, resignation, resolution, restlessness, seriousness, sincerity, streak, tenacity, tendency, thing, tolerance, trend, trick, truth, verge, vice, vigilance

658 usefulness: abend, agency, agent, convenience, efficiency, employment, expediency/expedience, good, help, makeshift, malfunction, medium, operation, practice, purpose, resource, serve, service, surplus, usage, use, utility, value, wear

COGNITIVE

659 goal: aim, ambition, aspiration, destination, dream, end, function, goal, intent/intention, mark, meaning, mission, object, objective, pleasure, point, prize, purport, purpose, quarry, reason, resolve, sake, target, taste, victim, will

660 plan: angle, approach, architecture, cahoots, calculation, channel, chart, chicanery, collusion, complicity, concoction, conspiracy, contrivance, craft, deceit, design, device, diagram, diet, dispensation, disposition, dodge, draft, expediency/expedience, expedient, feint, flowchart, form, format, freeware, gambit, game, gimmick, groundwork, idea, innovation, intrigue, invention, itinerary, layout, logistics, machination, maneuver, manner, method, move, plan, plot, policy, program, purport, purpose, route, scenario, schedule, scheme, shift, strategem, strategy, tactics

661 reason: alibi, angle, asset, ax to grind, basis, benefit, blame, boon, cause, confirmation, essence, essential, excuse, explanation, footing, fuel, goad, grounds, groundwork, hypothesis, idea, impetus, incentive, inducement, inspiration, justification, keynote/keystone, lesson, meaning, message, motive, nub, occasion, origin, pretext, raison d'être, rationale, reason, root, sake, solution, spring, spur, stimulant, stimulus, whim

662 request: command, demand, desire, directive, edict, entreaty, petition, plea, prayer, proposal, proposition, query, recall, request, requisition, suit, ultimatum

COMPARATIVE

663 complexity: complexity, exaggeration, labyrinth, simplicity, snarl

664 correspondence: accord, answer, approximate, balance, clash, clone, community, conform, conformity, connection, consonance, consort, correspond, correspondence, double, dovetail, duplicate, fit, flatter, go, go together/go with, harmonize, harmony, identity, jibe, likeness, look-alike, make, match, mate, proportion, resemblance, resemble, solidarity, spitting image, square, sympathy, twin, union, unison, unity

665 difference: aberration, antithesis, assortment, backslide, contradict, contradiction, contrast, controversy, converse, depart, departure, deviate, deviation, differ, difference, digression, disagree, disagreement, discrepancy, disharmony, disparity, disproportion, dissension, dissent, dissimilarity, dissonance, distinction, diverge, divergence, diversity, eccentricity, exception, flip side, foil, gap, gradation, grade, inequality, innovation, miscellany, mismatch, mixed bag, multiculturalism, mutation, novelty, nuance, oddity, opposite, opposition, peculiarity, rent, reverse, shade, variance, variant, variation, variety, wander

666 difficulty: abomination, awkwardness, bottleneck, conundrum, deficiency, delay, disadvantage(s), downside, drawback, enormity, entanglement, facility, handicap, hindrance, hitch, impediment, labyrinth, limitation, matter, misery, muddle, obstacle, obstruction, plight, pressure, problem, quagmire, question, restraint, restriction, rigor, rub, shortcoming, snag, snarl, spot, stumbling block, task, tax, tribulation, trouble, vice, wall

667 equivalence: alternate, amount, balance, border on, cancel, clone, cohere, coincide, coincidence, come up to, copy, correlation, counterpart, disproportion, ditto, duplicate, equal, equality, equate, equivalence, equivalent, fax, image, make, match, model, par, parallel, parity, rival, sameness, standoff, tie, transcript

668 importance: accent, aspect, bearing, beauty, berth, best, celebrity, character, cipher, consequence, core, count, cream, crux, cutting edge, dignitary, dignity, dominance, element, elevation, eminence, emphasis, essence, flower, forefront/foreground, fundamental, glory, grandeur, gravity, greatness, height, honor, honorary, humdinger, immortality, import, importance, kernel, key, lead, magnitude, mark, matter, moment, name, nobility, nothingness, overshadow, peak, prestige, pride, priority, prominence, quality, renown, rudiments, sense, seriousness, significance, signify, situation, spotlight, stardom, stature, status, stress, stuff, style, tedium, top, trifle, value, weight, zero hour

669 intensity: intensity, strength, violence

670 similarity: affinity, agree, analogy, community, consistency, equivalence, equivalent, identity, likeness, parallel, parity, replica, reproduction, resemblance, resemble, sameness, second, similarity, tune, twin

671 superiority: ascendancy/ascendency, distinction, elegance, eminence, excel, excellence, hairsplitting, ideal, imperfection, importance, jewel, landslide, marvel, miracle, paragon, perfection, pick, power, precedence, preponderance, prodigy, rank, seniority, superiority, victory

OF BEING

672 abstraction: manifestation, oblivion

673 aura: abracadabra, air, allure, ambience, appeal, appearance, aspect, atmosphere, attribute, aura, background, being, blaze, celestial, charm, chorus, climate, cultivation, dash, dump, ease, environment, environmentalist, feel, feeling, flavor, glory, glow, hex, kind, look, medium, milieu, monotony, mood, orbit, presence, quiet, romance, semblance, serenity, sign, solitude, spell, spice, spirit, splendor, supernal, surroundings, texture, tone, tranquility, undercurrent, veil, vein, veneer, vestige, whammy, whisper

674 bad situation: abend, abortion, accident, act of God, adversity, affliction, anarchy, anticli-

max, apocalypse, atrophy, backwash, bad luck, bad scene, bad trip, bane, beaten, bedlam, bereavement, bind, blight, blooper, blow, bottleneck, brunt, bug, bum wrap, bummer, calamity, can of worms, casualty, cataclysm, catastrophe, catch, chagrin, chaos, clamor, clog, clutter, cobweb, collapse, collision, comedown, commotion, complication, conflict, contamination, contempt, corner, crisis, critical mass, crunch, curse, damage, dead end, deadlock, dearth, debacle, decay, decline, decomposition, deficiency, descent, detriment, devastation, difficulty, dilemma, disadvantage(s), disappointment, disaster, disaster area, discomfiture, discouragement, disorganization, disrepair, disservice, distress, disturbance, downer, downfall, downside, drag, drama, drawback, dud, duress, embarrassment, emergency, entanglement, error, exigency/exigence, eyesore, failing, fall, famine, ferment, fiasco, filth, fix, flap, flash point, flaw, flip-flop, flop, flotsam, frenzy, friction, frustration, gadfly, handicap, hang-up, hardship, harm, hassle, havoc, headache, hell, hindrance, histrionics, hitch, holdup, hole, hurdle, ill, impasse, imposture, impropriety, inadequacy, inconvenience, indiscretion, infirmity, injustice, jalopy, jam, jump, kink, lapse, liability, limitation, load, lose, loss, madhouse, maelstrom, malfunction, matter, maze, mess, mire, misadventure, misery, misfortune/mishap, misstep, mix-up, muss, neglect, nemesis, nightmare, nuisance, obstacle, obstruction, onus, oppression, ordeal, outrage, pall, pandemonium, pass, pellmell, pest, pickle, pinch, pitfall, pity, plague, plight, poison, predicament, press, pressure, problem, puncture, quagmire, quandary, question, repulse, restraint, restriction, reverse, rub, ruin, ruse, scandal, scourge, scrape, setback, shambles, shortcoming, showdown, slump, smash, snag, snare, snarl, spot, squeeze, storm, strait, strife, struggle, syndrome, tangle, tiff, to-do, tragedy, trap, trial, trouble, tumult, turmoil, tussle, undoing, unrest, uprising, uproar, upset, weakness, weight, wreck

675 danger: act of God, bad scene, bad trip, bête noire, calamity, carcinogen, cataclysm, corner, crapshoot, crunch, curse, danger, dilemma, disaster, emergency, fatality, hardship, hazard, ill, jeopardy, mayhem, menace, peril, poison, risk, scourge, seriousness, smash, threat, tragedy, trouble, venture, violence

676 effect: amount, attraction, because, cogency, combustion, cost, culmination, effectiveness, efficacy, feebleness, magnetism, potency, proceed, punch, sex appeal, splash, tell, therefore, wash

677 effort: concentration, cooperation, difficulty, diligence, direct, effort, exertion, force, go, groove, headache, idleness, industry, plod, sweat, toil, trouble, try, work, yoke

678 experience: background, callow, career, culture, heritage, history, ignorance, lead (a life), life, live, maturity, mellow, memory, naive, naiveté, phenomenon, practical, readiness, record, sustain, taste, training, unaccustomed, unfamiliar, veteran, world, young

679 fate: accident, blessing, break, bum rap, bummer, catch, chaff, chance, contingency, cost, damnation, demise, destiny, disadvantage, doom, downer, downfall, dues, duty, fate, flip-flop, fluke, fortune, freak, future, godsend, good, jinx, judgment, kismet, limbo, long shot, lot, luck, misfortune/ mishap, oblivion, outlook, payoff, penalty, pitfall, plague, portion, predestination, reverse, setback, shortcoming, suspense, turning point, úndoing, weight, windfall

680 function: application, avail, bar, begin, bolt, cloak, closure, cord, cushion, decoy, deterrent, disguise, dump, gauge, operate, operation, run, spray, tie, yardstick

681 inaction: abeyance, abide, asleep, bide, dalliance, dally, dawdle, doze, drag, fool around, forbear, forgo, hang, hesitate, hesitation, idleness, inertia, leisure, linger, loaf, loiter, lounge, neglect, nod, procrastinate, refrain, relief, remain, repose, respite, rest, shirk, sit tight, skip, slack/slacken, stay, wait

682 meaning: ambiguity, connotation, content, context, cryptic, denotation, denote, double entendre, drift, drive at, emphasis, express, fiber, gist, imply, import, importance, light, matter, mean, meaning, meat, message, motif, nature, nub, point, punch, purport, quintessence, represent, respect, sense, significance, signify, spirit, stand for, strain, strength, stuff, substance, suggest, symbolize, tenor, terminology, text, texture, theme, thrust, tone, typify, understanding, undertone, upshot, value, vein, weigh, weight, wording

683 name: alias, anonymous, appellation, denomination, designation, epithet, handle, moniker, name, nickname, nom de plume, nomenclature, pen name, pseudonym, sobriquet, surname, term, title

684 of agreement: accord, agreement, alliance, armistice, arrangement, assent, bargain, bond, charter, chorus, coherence, coincidence, communion, compact, compliance, compromise, concert, concord, consensus, consent, contract, convention, covenant, deal, debenture, faction, give-and-take, meeting, negotiation, okay, order, pact, protocol, provision/proviso, settlement, stipulation, terms, transaction, treaty, truce, understanding, warranty, word

685 of authorization: absolution, admittance, Annie Oakley, approval, authority, certificate, charter, confirmation, consent, credentials, decree, delegation, determination, dispensation, fiat, finding, forgiveness, go-ahead, grace, guarantee, induction, leave, license, mandate, negation, nod, order, pardon, pass, passage, passport, patent, permission, permit, recall, release, remission, repeal, reprieve, sanction, seal, signal, ticket, treaty, veto, waiver, warrant, warranty, withdraw l, word

686 of being an example: archetype, case, classic, clout, embodiment, epitome, example, exemplar, exponent, guide, ideal, illustration, instance, lesson, light, measure, model, norm, original, paradigm, paragon, pattern, picture, precedent, prototype, replica, representative, sample, specimen, stereotype, type

687 of being an influence: bolt, contact, effect, effectiveness, fetish, forbidden fruit, gush, influence, instrument, leadership, leverage, mores, muscle, orbit, persuasion, philosopher, preponderance, pressure, rudiments, sphere, squeeze, sway, wonder

688 of being a rule: authority, axiom, ban, basis, benchmark, canon, code, condition, convention, creed, criterion, custom, democracy, dictate, doctrine, dogma, edict, essence, ethics/ethic, fact, form, formality, formula, fundamental, gauge, generality, ideology, institute, keynote/keystone, law, line, measure, model, morals, norm, observance, parameter, philosophy, policy, practice, precept, principle, protocol, regulation, ritual, rule, standard, taboo, tenet, theorem, tradition

689 of belief: absolution, activism, adjudication, advocacy, ageism, alchemy, allegiance, anticipation, apartheid, aphorism, apparition, archetype, assumed, assumption, atheism, attitude, attrition, axiom, ax to grind, basis, belief, bias, black magic, capitalism, case, cause, chauvinism, church, commonplace, complaint, concept, conception, conclusion, confidence, conformity, conjecture, connotation, conscience, consensus, contention, conviction, credence, creed, cult, culture, decision, deduction, definition, delusion, democracy, denomination, dependence/dependency, derision, determination, diagnosis, dictum, disapproval, disbelief, discrimination, dissent, dissidence, dissonance, distrust, divinity, doctrine, dogma, doubt, estimate, ethics/ethic, evaluation, expectancy, expectation, eye, fait accompli, faith, faithfulness, fallacy, fanaticism, fantasy, fascism, fatalism, favor, feeling, fetish, foreboding, forgiveness, frame of mind, generality, gospel, grievance, guess, heresy, honor, honorary, hunch, hypothesis, idea, ideals, ideology, illusion, image, impression, incantation, induction, inkling, instinct, intimation, intuition, judgment, leaning, line, logic, magic, make-believe, maxim, millstone, mind, mindset, miracle, misconception, misgiving, misogynist, motivation, motive, multiculturalism, necromancy, negative attitude, nihilism, nonconformity, notion, objection, obsession, old wives' tale, omen, opinion, optimism, oracle, outlook, patriotism, perception, perspective, persuasion, pessimism, philosophy, piety, platform, Pollyanna, position, preconception, prediction, prejudice, premise, premonition, presage, presentiment, presumption, pride, principle/principles, prognosis, prophecy, prospect, purport, purpose, racism, reaction, reality, recognition, regard, reliance, religion, reputation, resolve, respect, right, school, self-respect/self-esteem, self-satisfaction, sentiment, sexism, Shangri-la, side, sign, sixth sense, slant, sorcery, speculation, spell, stance, stand, standpoint, stigma, stock, subject, substance, suggestion, superstition, supposition, surmise, suspicion, taste, tenet, theme, theorem, theory, thesis, trust, understanding, utopia, values, view, viewpoint, vision, voodoo, vow, witchcraft, word, Xanadu

690 of concern: afraid, aghast, alarm, albatross, anxiety, anxious, apprehension, burden, concern, conundrum, craze, difficulty, dismay, disquiet, distraction, distraught, distress, doubt, encumbrance, fascination, feeling, fixation, foreboding, frightened, guilt, hallucination, hang-up, harried, horror, interest, jitters, jittery, jumpy, millstone, misgiving, mistrust, obsession, one-track mind, panic, passion, peeve, petrified, premonition, puzzled, quandary, question, scruple, suspicion, temptation, terror, thunderstruck, trouble, uneasy, weight, woe, wonder, worry

691 of law: abomination, annulment, autocracy, custody, détente, emancipation, exemption, foul, freedom, independence, justice, laissez-faire, liberation, liberty, nonviolence, offense, order, peace, prohibition, trespass, trial, validity, ward

692 on a course: career, pitch, ramble, tack, tendency, traverse

693 opportunity: big win, cinch, contingency, crapshoot, duck soup, facility, fluke, freedom, handicap, hazard, hearing, interest, juncture, lead, leverage, luck, merit, miracle, occasion, odds, opening, opportunity, outlet, picnic, plus, possibility, preference, prize, profit, prospect, pushover, recourse, remedy, resort, risk, sake, serendipity, shot, snap, start, strength, stumble, success, time, treat, turn, vacancy, welfare/well-being

694 purpose: application, employment, help, purpose, role, vehicle

695 repetition: boomerang, echo, repeat, repetition, return, verbiage

696 situation: case, circumstance, condition, context, ecosystem, environment, experience, instance, landmark, matter, medium, mystery, occurrence, point, position, situation, state, uncertainty

OF CHANGE

697 abstract: about-face, accommodation, adapt, adaptation, adjust, adjustment, back down, back out, backslide, balance, deepen, depart, departure, deviate, deviation, digress, digression, dip, diversify, fluctuate, flux, get, interchange, metamorphose, metamorphosis, movement, mutation, novelty, oscillate, range, reconcile, redress, refresh, replace, retract, reversal, reverse, revive, revolution, rig, rotate, shift, suit, switch, tighten, transform, transformation, transition, transpose, turn, turnabout, variance, variation, vary, vicissitude, withdraw

698 diminish: abate, atrophy, come down, cut, cutback, decline, decrease, degenerate, depreciate, deteriorate, deterioration, die, diminish, diminution, drain, drop, drop off, dwarf, dwindle, ebb, entropy, erosion, evaporate, evaporation, extenuate, fade, fester, flag, go, go down, lapse, lessen, let up, lull, mollify, peter out, plummet, qualify, recede, reduce, regress, relapse, relax, relent, remission, remit, revert, rot, sag, shrink, sink, slack/slacken, slump, stagnate, subside,

taper/taper off, vegetate, wane, weaken, wear, wither, worsen

699 fail: abortion, blow, blow over, bomb, comedown, crash, decline, default, disappoint, disqualify, downfall, droop, error, fail, failure, fall, fault, fizzle, flag, flop, flounder, fold, founder, go, go down, go under, miscarriage, misfire, miss, misstep, neglect, omission, overlook, run out, slump, wilt

700 improve: accession, advance, advancement, amendment, boom, boost, clear up, come along, correction, develop, development, dignify, edification, elevate, embellish, embellishment, energize, expansion, furbish, grace, improve, improvement, lift, look up, mend, pay, pick up, progress, pull through, rally, recoup, recover, recuperate, relieve, repair, revision, rise, upgrade

701 of state: acclimate, acculturation, aging, alteration, alternate, approach, assimilate, backfire, become, break out, change, come, come about, conversion, convert, co-opt, metamorphose, metamorphosis, state

702 of structure: buckle, collapse, degenerate, dissolve, flatten

703 organizational: adjournment, dissolution, expansionism, growth, merger

704 progress: advance, advancement, batten, boom, breakthrough, breeze, bring off, buildup, click, climax, coast, come on, consummate, course, develop, development, evolution, evolve, expansion, expansionism, fare, flourish, flower, form, fruition, furtherance, gestation, get along, get on, go, go ahead, go far, grow, growth, headway, inroad, jump, mature, mellow, mount, mushroom, natural selection, passage, precipitate, progress, progression, push off/push on, rise, score, spread, thrive, unfold, wax

705 unchanged: abeyance, calm, limbo, peace, quiet

OF NEED OR ACHIEVEMENT

706 achievement: ability, accomplish, accomplishment, achieve, achievement, acme, action, apex, arrive, art, attain, attainment, background, big win, bloom, blossom, bring about, bring off, carry, carry out, climax, clinch, come at, comeback, come through, compass, completion, conquer, conquest, consummate, consummation, coup, craft, crash, crown, deed, degree, discharge, distinction, doer, doing, draw, drive, dynamo, eager beaver, effect, efficacy, excel, execute, execution, exercise, exploit, extreme, extremity, failure, feat, find, finish, flair, flourish, fruition, fulfill, fulfillment, gain, get, get ahead, gift, gig, go far, go over, graduation, hack it, hairsplitting, hammer out, hit, land, manage, maximum, milestone, operate, orgasm, pan out, pass, perfect, perfection, performance, pinnacle, potential, prodigy, proficiency, progress, progression, prosper, prosperity, pull off, pull through, rack up, reach, record, score, smash, stroke, succeed, success, take, thrive, tour de force, transact, triumph,. victory, welfare/well-being, win, work, work out, zenith

707 **lack:** lack, loss, nothing/nothingness, zilch

708 **mutual possession:** communal, joint, mutual

709 **need:** addiction, affinity, alcoholism, bait, call, charge, claim, craving, cupidity, dearth, default, dependence/dependency, deprivation, desire, eroticism, exigency/exigence, famine, hankering, hope, hunger, inadequacy, lack, lechery, libido, longing, lust, malnutrition, must, necessity, need, partiality, penchant, poverty, predilection, predisposition, preference, prerequisite, prize, propensity, requirement/requisite, shortage, slum, squalor, sustenance, temptation, thirst, use, void, want, wish, yearning, yen

710 **possession:** abundance, acquisition, asset(s), belongings, boast, booty, buy, cache, capital, cash, clutches, commodity, custody, deserts, desolation, division, domain, dominion, due, dynasty, effects, enjoy, enjoyment, entrench, estate, exuberance, finances, fortune, fund, funds, gain, get, grasp, have, hoard, hold, keep, legacy, lot, monopolize, monopoly, nest egg, occupancy, occupation, opulence, own, ownership, payback, plunder, possess, possession, presence, prize, profusion, property, purchase, reservation, reserve, reserved, resource, resources, retain, return, riches, savings, share, spoils, stake, store, subsistence, title, treasure, wealth

711 **requirement:** depend, hinge, larder, provision/proviso, provisional, reservation, rest, safekeeping, standby, stockpile, tent, understudy

712 **resource:** amenity, ballast, bastion, catalyst, comfort, convenience, edge, expediency/expedience, expedient, facility, find, guard, hoard, indulgence, luxury, mainstay, maintenance, makeshift, medium, mine, momentum, nurture, option, organ, pillar, plum, protection, provision, recourse, redress, relief, remedy, reparation, repertory, reserve, reservoir, resort, resource, resources, rock, safeguard, safekeeping, security, shelter, shield, solution, stockpile, stopgap, stronghold, substitute, supply, support, vehicle

713 **satisfaction:** afford, suffice, work out

PHYSICAL

714 **accompaniment:** attend, both, chaperon, coincide, coincidence, conjunction, escort, friendship, go, privacy, relation, relationship, solidarity, solitude, squire, tune, union, unity

715 **age:** antiquity, dotage, freshness, majority, manhood/womanhood, maturity, novelty, old age, years, young

716 **appearance:** appear, appearance, beard, blind, braid, cast, color, copy, countenance, decay, dissemble, ditto, double, dummy, duplicate, echo, expression, eyesore, facade, face, facsimile, favor, fax, forgery, front, glare, grimace, grin, guise, illusion, image, imitation, likeness, look, look-alike, mark, mask, match, mug, personify, pose, pout, presence, pretense, pretext, radiate, represent, reproduction, resemblance, resemble, rise, role, scowl, semblance, show, sound,

stand out, strike, surface, swagger, symmetry, tableau, veneer

717 **balance:** awkwardness, poise, proportion, symmetry

718 **beauty:** Afro, beauty, coiffure, countenance, elegance, embellishment, fright, glamour, glory, grace, hairstyle, imperfection, pulchritude

719 **capacity:** content, fill, hold, volume

720 **condition:** abhorrence, allure, apoplexy, beat, calm, carriage, comfort, connection, corrosion, disability, disgust, dislocation, dissipation, distress, disturbance, emptiness, exhaustion, form, frazzle, health, maturity, peace, pollutant, pollution, repose, rust, satisfaction, shape, smog, smoke, state, stress, tangle

721 **continuity:** alignment, bridge, concatenation, continuity, durability, halt, length, run, sequence, series, spread, stretch

722 **density:** consistency, density, firmness

723 **essential:** austerity, brawn, corruption, decor, fat, fertility, fitness, grease, love handles, poke, posture, smudge, tension

724 **force:** combustion, effort, force, propulsion, push

725 **genuineness:** actuality, appear, certainty, counterfeit, credibility, fact, fait accompli, fallacy, falsity, feint, funny money, make-believe, reality, sure thing, truth, validity, verisimilitude

726 **hardness:** firmness, temper, tension

727 **order:** alignment, arrangement, chain, column, concatenation, configuration, confusion, cosmos, course, disarray, dislocation, disorganization, distribution, file, form, gradation, grade, head, hierarchy, introduction, line, mean, median, method, order, organization, pattern, pecking order, precede, precedence, precursor, priority, procession, queue, range, rank, round, row, run, seniority, sequence, series, stage, standing, streak, string, succeed, suite, tier, trail, train

728 **pain:** ache, affliction, agony, anesthesia/anaesthesia, bad news, bad time, bête noire, boo boo, cramp, crick, discomfort, distress, grief, harm, headache, heartbreak, hurt, injury, itch, kink, letdown, misery, ordeal, pain, pang, pinch, remorse, repentance, smart, spasm, sting, strain, stress, suffering, torment, torture, trauma, trial, tribulation, trouble, twinge, woe

729 **safety:** buffer, bulwark, fortification, parapet, precaution, protection, safekeeping, safety, security, shield

730 **size:** brevity, bulk, caliber, condensation, dimensions/dimension, enormity, extent, fullness, greatness, infinity, magnitude, measurement, miniature, proportion(s), size

731 **stability:** anchor, durability, equilibrium, firmness, flexibility, instability, spring, stability, traction

732 **strength:** brawn, durability, feebleness, firmness, infirmity, kick, might, potency, power, stamina, staying power, strength, tolerance, vigor, weakness

733 **structure:** anatomy, architecture, composition, delicacy, easel, emptiness, fabric, figure, frame, framework, mesh, ruins, skeleton, structure

734 **weight:** buoyancy/buoyance, fat, fatness, grease, love handles, obesity, pressure

735 **below:** below, bottom, down, downhill, under, underneath

736 **containment:** capacity, contain, fill

737 **depth:** deep, depth, shallow

738 **direction:** ascent, circulation, crook, cross, current, curve, decline, descent, deviation, dip, direction, diverge, divergence, diversion, downgrade, fork, grade, gradient, inclination, incline, intersect, lean, level, line, list, meander, orbit, pitch, reverse, revolution, revolve, rise, rotate, run, slant, slope, swirl, tack, tendency, tilt, trend, turn, twist, undercurrent, way, whirl, wind

739 **distance:** altitude, bearing/bearings, country mile, distance, latitude, leeway, scope, space, way

740 **fill:** brim, charge, cloy, content, cram, crowd, flood, glut, hollow, overflow, packed, replete, satiate, surfeit, teem, vacant, vacuum, void, volume

741 **height:** dominate, dwarf, elevation, eminence, height, rear, stature

742 **inside:** contain, have, hold, interior, twine

743 **length:** extent, height, length, range

744 **level:** gradation, grade, layer, level, line, mesa, notch, plane, plateau, rank, row, rung, scale, stage, tier

745 **limits, physical:** abutment, boundary, confines, curb, decline, demarcation, end, extent, extreme, extremity, frontier, hinterland, limit, perimeter, periphery, play, range, term, terminal

746 **location:** absence, absenteeism, bearing/bearings, dissemination, front, hang, junc-

tion/juncture, lie, look, median, middle, protrude, space, stretch

747 **location, relative:** adjoin, border, butt, contact, cross, detachment, face, join, near miss, precede, precedence, presence, project, proximity, vicinity

748 **motion:** activity, agility, convulsion, discharge, ejection, hurry, lassitude, lethargy, onrush, outflow, restlessness, rush, spin, stagnate, still, sweep, swing, traction, turn, vibrate, vibration, wash

749 **nearness:** abut, border on, intersect, stalk, succeed, surveillance, verge

750 **on:** casing, cover, on, pile, top, traverse

751 **outside:** band, edge, skirt, stick out

752 **over:** above, altitude, dominate, overhang, overlook, rise, tower, vault

753 **sequential:** line, trail, wake

754 **shape:** bag, conformation, curvature, cut, entwine, figure, fold, form, hollow, loop, pucker, shape, turn, twist

755 **speed:** celerity, dispatch, expedition, haste, hurry, pace, rapidity, rate, speed, velocity

756 **spread:** balloon, branch off/branch out, breadth, bridge, go, latitude, range, reach, room, space, span, sweep

757 **structure:** aperture, ascent, attitude, bag, beef, break, build, composition, condition, conformation, constitution, construction, crease, curvature, even, fabric, figure, fluid, form, frame, grade, gradient, makeup, physique, plane, ramp, set, shape, slope, stance, stoop

758 **surrounding:** circle, coil, compass, define, edge, encircle, enclose, encompass, fence, frame, gird, hedge, hem/hem in, mob, pen, ring, surround

759 **touching:** meet, neighbor, overlap

760 **width:** breadth, diameter, width

761 **within a group:** middle, range

Weights and measures

762 **attribute of a number:** abounding, any, apiece, average, calculable, countless, dual, flat-out, immeasurable, infinite, innumerable, just about, legion, less, light, limitless, manifold, many, mathematical, maximum, minimal, minimum, more, multiple/multifarious, multitudinous, myriad, nil, numberless, numeric/numerical, numerous, one, plentiful/plenty, plural, plus, profuse, round, several, short, shy, single, skimpy, slight, sparse, steep, tidy, tiny, total, unreasonable, untold, wee

763 **change in number:** accrue, appreciate, appreciation, deduction, discount, increase, increment, inflation, jump, peak, plummet, raise, reach, slump

764 **mathematic reasoning:** accounting, add, addition, appraise, arithmetic, average, balance, calculate, calculation, cast, computation, compute, count, enumerate, estimate, figure, gauge, mathematics, measure, number, pace, page, reckon, scale, score, stock, subtract, tabulate, tally, tell, total, underestimate

765 **numeric symbol:** digit, fraction, number

766 **numeric value:** appraisal, count, couple, majority, maximum, peak, percentage, rate, scant/scanty

767 **quantity:** abundance, copiousness, enough, exuberance, greatness, overabundance, paucity, peak, plenty, plethora, preponderance, profusion, scant/scanty, shortage, superabundance

768 **ratio:** quota, rate, ratio

769 **series:** array, chain, range, series, set, string

770 **system:** apparatus, automation, board, browser, bulletin board, bureaucracy, business, capitalism, channel, chat room, circuit, commerce, communications, complex, cosmos, cyberspace, dispensation, file, finance, grammar, Internet, machinery, mail, mesh, method, net, network, pattern, post, red tape, routine, scale, system, traffic, world

771 **attribute of quantity:** about, additional, affluent, all, altogether, amply, below, best,

better, big, bountiful, brimming/brimful, copious, depleted, disproportionate, double, dual, elephantine, enough, excessive, exhausted, exiguous, extra, extravagant, extreme, extremely, few, flush, fraught, further, good, hardly, huge, inadequate, insufficient, just about, lacking, leftover, liberal, limited, limitless, lush, luxuriant, many, more, most, much, new, nil, other, outrageous, over, plus, residual, respectable, rich, rife, slender/slim, spare, spent, sufficient, supplementary, thick, thin, too, unreasonable, various, wholesale

772 attribute of range: abysmal, across-the-board, all, all-out, barely, besides, beyond, blanket, bodily, bounded, boundless, broad, capacious, catholic, chiefly, comprehensive, cosmic, dead, dearly, deeply, different, diffuse, diverse, eclectic, ecumenical, encyclopedic, exhaustive, expansive, extended, extensive, far, far-reaching, full-scale, fully, general, generally, global, greatly, inclusive, increasingly, indiscriminate, inexhaustible, international, largely, lower, mainly, mixed, moderately, more, moreover, most, mostly, motley, much, multinational, multiple/multifarious, only, overall, panoramic, pervasive, practically, primarily, principally, quite, rambling, rampant, rather, relatively, rife, slightly, somewhat, substantially, sundry, sweeping, too, universal, unlimited, utmost, vast, very, well, wholesale, wholly, wide, widespread, within, without

773 attribute of size: angular, atomic, baby, bantam, better, big, brief, broad, burly, capacious, capsule, cavernous, chubby, chunky, commodious, compact, compendious, concise, corpulent, cramped, cumbersome, dwarf, elephantine, enormous, extensive, fleshy, full, gargantuan, giant, gigantic, grand, great, gross, hearty, hefty, huge, hulking, husky, immeasurable, immense, imposing, impressive, incalculable, infinitesimal, inflated, laconic, large, little, major, mammoth, massive, microscopic, midget, mighty, miniature, minimal, miniscule/minuscule, minor, minute, monolithic, monstrous, monumental, narrow, petite, pocket, portable, prodigious, pudgy, puny, roly-poly, round, scrawny, short, small, small-time, squat, stocky, stout, strapping, stubby, stunted, substantial, teeny/teensy, thick, thin, tiny, titanic, tremendous, vast, voluminous, wee, whopping, wide

774 capacity: brimming/brimful, capacious, capacity, close, compact, congested, crowded, empty, full, packed, spacious, teeming, vacant, void

775 change of quantity: accession, allowance, develop, development, grow, growth

776 decreasing: attrition, contraction, cut, cutback, deduction, deflate, depreciate, diminish, diminution, drop, drop off, dwindle, fall, lessen, recede, relent, sag, shrink, sink, subside, taper/taper off, wane

777 depth: abysmal, deep, profound, shallow, skin-deep, superficial, unfathomable

778 distance: about, afar, away, beyond, contiguous, directly, distant, extreme, far, far-away, far-flung, farther, farthest, furthest,

immediate, last, near, nearby, off, onward/onwards, uttermost, yonder

779 height: alpine, elevated, elongated, giant, gigantic, high, lanky, lofty, long, low, midget, petite, precipitous, rangy, short, soaring, squat, statuesque, stubby, stunted, tall, towering

780 increasing: accretion, accrual, accrue, accumulation, amplification, boost, bulge, distend, enlarge, enlargement, expansion, gather, increase, increment, inflate, inflation, leap, mount, peak, proliferate, reach, rise, swell, wax, widen

781 large: abounding, abundant, aggregate, ample, appreciable, bulky, colossal, commodious, considerable, countless, excessive, extreme, extremely, exuberant, fantastic, far, generous, giant, gigantic, good, great, gross, handsome, handsomely, hulking, immeasurable, incalculable, infinite, inordinate, jumbo, large, lavish, legion, manifold, massive, maximum, mighty, monolithic, monstrous, much, multitudinous, myriad, numberless, numerous, opulent, plentiful/plenty, prodigal, prodigious, profuse, redundant, sizable, stupendous, substantial, surplus, tidy, tremendous, untold, unwieldy, vast, voluminous, whopping

782 length: extended, high, lengthy, low, short, soaring, tall

783 measurement: degree, extent, mark, proportion

784 number: amount, digit, estimate, figure, number, numeral, pair, percentage, point, quotation/quote, score, sum, trio/triple, zero

785 portion: among, apart, asunder, fractional, fragmentary, gross, half, sectional

786 quantity: agglomeration, all, amount, array, avalanche, average, backlog, barrage, batch, buildup, bundle, calculation, cascade, census, cipher, deal, deluge, dollop, duo, excess, extravagance, few, figure, flood, flow, glut, gust, heap, lot, many, mass, measure, minimum, mint, myriad, number, oodles, overabundance, pile, pittance, plenty, plethora, quantity, sum, surge, tally, total, trio/triple, turnout

787 range: bound/bounds, breadth, compass, confines, expanse, extent, gamut, latitude, length, range, scads, scale, scope, spread, superabundance, sweep, waterfall, width

788 relative: cumulative, empty, fairly, full, influx

789 small: compendious, diminutive, dinky, exiguous, few, handful, infinitesimal, least, less, light, little, low, marginal, meager, measly, microscopic, miniature, minimal, minimum, miniscule/minuscule, minor, minute, negligible, nominal, one, outside, petite, piddling, piddly, scant/scanty, scarce, scarcely, shy, skimpy, slight, small, sparse, teeny/teensy, tiny, trifling

790 unit of distance measure: depth, distance, foot, inch, mile

791 unit of height measure: altitude, foot, height, inch, mile

792 unit of measure: acre, area, degree, dimensions/dimension, gauge, mass, measure, measurement, perimeter, proportions, revolution, size, velocity, volume, width

793 unit of scalar measure: above, abysmal, lesser, low, over, under

794 unit of volume measure: capacity, fill, volume

795 unit of weight measure: ounce, pound, weight

796 width: broad, cavernous, wide

TIME

797 attribute of age: adolescent, advanced, afresh, aged, ancient, antediluvian, antiquarian, antiquated, antique, archaic, behind the times, big, callow, childish, contemporary, crude, dated, doddering, elder, elderly, embryonic, fresh, full-grown/full-fledged, hoary, green, immature, immemorial, inchoate, infant/infantile, innovative, junior, juvenile, late, mature, medieval, mellow, mint, modern, modish, moldy, musty, new, newfangled, novel, old, older, old-fashioned, original, originally, outdated/out-of-date, outmoded, passé, puerile, quaint, recent, ripe, secondhand, senior, stale, tender, undeveloped, up-to-date, vintage, young, youthful

798 attribute of duration: ad infinitum, all-time, always, annual, awhile, brief, ceaseless, chronic, compact, concise, confirmed, constant, continual, continuous, dragging, endless, ephemeral, eternal, eternally, evanescent, ever, everlasting, extended, fleeting, forever, for keeps, fugitive, immortal, incessant, indefinitely, infinite, interminable, inveterate, laconic, lasting, lifelong, limitless, long, long-standing, meteoric, momentary, never-ending, nonstop, old, on and on, ongoing, passing, perennial, permanent, perpetual, relentless, running, sanctioned, short, short-lived, soon, steady, temporary, through, throughout, timeless, transient/transitory, unbreakable, unbroken, unceasing, undying, unending, unflagging, uninterrupted, unrelenting, whirlwind

799 attribute of time: actual, advance, afterward/afterwards, again, almost, already, antediluvian, anterior, at, behind, behind the times, bottom, colonial, coming, concurrent, consecutive, dilatory, dire, due, duly, early, effective, ever, extemporaneous/extemporary, fast, felicitous, finally, foremost, forever, for keeps, forthcoming, forward, frequently, from scratch, gradual, gradually, hasty, hence, hereafter, hurried, immemorial, initial, instant, instantly, intermittent, irregular, irregularly, just about, last, lastly, late, later, latter, leisurely, meantime, meanwhile, meteoric, narrowly, never, next, nightly, nocturnal, old, old-fashioned, once, once and for all, oncoming, on the double, originally, overdue, pell-mell, periodic, perpetual, posterior, posthaste, postmortem, preceding, precipitous/precipitate, preliminary, previous, primal, primarily, primary/prime, primeval, primitive, primordial, pristine, prompt, promptly, punctual, quickly, rapid, rapidly, ready, right, rude, sharp, short, simultaneous, snappy, sudden, suddenly, summarily, swift, swiftly/swift, tardy, temporal,

then, thereafter, timely, ultimate, unawares, untimely, up-to-date, when, while, yet

800 date: anniversary, date

801 day: afternoon, almanac, anniversary, daily, date, day, ephemeral, evening, journal, midnight, morning, night, nightly, nocturnal, noon, time

802 definite period: date, day, furlough, holiday, instant, leave, midnight, morning, noon, present, sabbatical, shift

803 division of: day, minute, second

804 duration: brevity, continuance, continuation, course, duration, endurance, endure, eternity, extent, go, halt, length, remain

805 frequency: rapidity, sometimes

806 hour: afternoon, evening, morning, night, noon, time

807 indefinite period: age, antiquity, anytime, bit, bout, break, breath, continuance, convenience, downtime, eon, epoch, era, furlough, future, generation, hiatus, history, infinity, interim, interlude, intermission, interruption, interval, lapse, leave, leisure, letup, lull, meantime, millenium, minute, moment, moratorium, past, pause, period, present, recess, remission, respite, rest, round, sabbatical, semester, stint, slack, space, span, spell, stalemate, stint, stretch, suspension, term, tour, trick, vacation, wait, while

808 minute: flash, instant, jiffy, moment, tick, wink

809 month: almanac, calendar, gestation, lunatic, moon, time

810 part of a day: afternoon, dark, dawn, day, daybreak, daylight, dusk, evening, gloom, light, morning, night, nightfall, sunrise, sunset, tick, twilight

811 past or future: following, future, past, preceding, previous, prior, succeeding/successive

812 proximity: immediate, near, now, prior, succeeding/successive

813 relative order: follow, precede, succeed

814 season: autumn, season, spring, summer, winter

815 specific: anniversary, beginning, date, dawn, daybreak, for openers, instance, juncture, point, present, yesterday, zero hour

816 stage of existence: administration, age, childhood, cycle, day, era, generation, life, millenium, past, phase, prime, stage, tenure

817 stage of life form: adolescence, age, babyhood, childhood, cradle, cycle, landmark, life, lifetime, majority, maternity, old age, prime, puberty, spell, youth

818 temporal association: anachronism, clockwork, dispatch, elapse, eternity, fly, following, future, haste, pace, past, precede, precedence, preceding, previous, prior, rush, succeeding/successive

819 temporal object: anytime, clock, time

820 time relative to present: abaft, after, after, ago, ahead, amid/amidst, anew, antecedent, au courant, back, before, beforehand, behind, belated, between, bygone, circa, coincident, contemporary, current, deferred, destined, directly, during, early, ensuing, erstwhile, eventual, eventually, fated, final, first, following, fore, foregoing, former, formerly, forthwith, future, historical, immediate, immediately, imminent, impending, infant/infantile, instantaneous, just, lately, momentarily, near, nearing, new, newly, now, once, past, present, presently, previous, previously, prior, readily, recent, recently, shortly, someday, soon, straight, subsequent, subsequently, succeeding/successive, topical, ultimate, ultimately, until, yet

821 **unit of time measure:** day, flash, minute, second, wink

822 **within a time period:** epoch, interim, interval, period, semester, span, spell, stint, stretch, term, while

823 **year:** almanac, anniversary, annual, annually, time, yearly

WHOLENESS OR DIVISION

824 **added part:** arm, attachment, auxiliary, backup, complement, complementary, excess, extension, extra, fitting, flap, fresh, frill, frippery, furthermore, garnish, new, offshoot, outgrowth, protuberance, ramification, repair, sequel, spare, spin-off, superfluous, supplement, surplus, trim, wake, wing

825 **bottom part:** fringe, rear, rest, rump, seat, skirt, stub, stump, tail

826 **core part:** base, bosom, bottom, constituent, core, cornerstone, crux, element, essential, filling/filler, focus, foundation, fundamental, germ, heart, hub, infrastructure, inner, interior, internal, kernel, marrow, meat, nerve center, nub, nucleus, quintessence, root, trunk

827 **end part:** abutment, addendum, back, border, butt, end, point, posterior, rear, seat, stub, stump, tail

828 **first part:** appetizer, early, hors d'oeuvre, initial, introduction, lead, nucleus, overture, precursor, predecessor, preliminary, spark

829 **main part:** bells and whistle, body, bulk, capital, chief, element, feature, flower, focus, fundamental, hulk, hull, main, majority, nerve center, parcel, plurality, root

830 **middle part:** aisle, axis, axle, bowels, center, central, filling/filler, inner, inside, interior, intermediate, internal, joint, junction/juncture, mean, median, middle, midst, pivot

831 **minor part:** atom, bit, breath, cereal, chip, collateral, component, crumb, dandruff, dash, detail, dot, drop, drop in the bucket, factor, feature, fiber, flake, fleck, flicker, glimmer, grain, grit, handle, iota, item, joint, lick, ligature, minimum, modicum, molecule, morsel, mote, nibble, nip, node/nodule, particle, patch, peripheral, pinch, point, powder, scintilla, scrap, shred, sliver, smidgen, soupçon, spark, specimen, speck, splinter, spot, sprinkling, suspicion, tinge, touch, trace, trifle, whisper, whit, wisp

832 **of an event:** chapter, close, conclusion, crackdown, dawn, denouement, end, ending, finale, finality, finish, genesis, germ, head, height, highlight, inception, installation, interruption, last, leg, limit, meridian, onset, opening, orientation, origin, origination, outbreak, overture, particular, peak, period, preliminary, prelude, premiere, prevention, preview, prime, sequel, snatch, stalemate, standstill, start, stay, step, stop, stoppage, suspension, swan song, term, termination, threshold, touch, turning point, twilight, twist, victory, win, zenith, zero hour

833 **of an order:** back, beginning, end, for openers, front, middle

834 **part:** accessory, accompaniment, attribute, component, constituent, counterpart, feature, member, part, phase, piece, strip, thing, trait, trash, trimmings, unit

835 **portion:** accompaniment, addition, adjunct, allocation, allotment, ancillary, appendage, arm, bit, bite, branch, constituent, contents, dab, deal, division, dollop, dose, drop, end, excerpt, excess, extract, facet, factor, feature, fraction, fragment, front, half, ingredient, installment, interest, item, layer, link, little, lot, majority, mass, measure, member, morsel, parcel, pat, percentage, piece, portion, precinct, quarter, quota, ration, remainder, remnant, rest, sample, scrap, section, sector, segment, share, side, slab, slice, stake, subdivision, taste, tidbit, whit, wing

836 **top part:** acme, alpine, apex, barb, brim, ceiling, citadel, climax, crescendo, crest, crown, extreme, extremity, face, front, head, height, lid, maximum, meridian, orgasm, peak, pinnacle, plug, point, prominence, rim, summit, tip, top, vertex, zenith

837 **whole:** all, amount, entirety, everything, gross, synthesis, system, total, unit, unity, whole